THIS GENERATION

Revised Edition

A SELECTION OF BRITISH AND AMERICAN LITERATURE

FROM 1914 TO THE PRESENT

WITH HISTORICAL AND CRITICAL ESSAYS

This generation

REVISED EDITION

GEORGE K. ANDERSON   *Brown University*

EDA LOU WALTON   *New York University*

SCOTT, FORESMAN AND COMPANY

Chicago

Atlanta   Dallas   Palo Alto

Fair Lawn, N.J.

PREFACE

THIS GENERATION attempts—by means of selected texts, introductory essays, biographical sketches which contain critical material, headnotes, and footnotes—to show the dominant moods, manner, and content of British and American literature from about 1914 to the present. In order to point up these dominant trends, the editors have organized the material into a fourfold division—"Carrying On the Tradition," "The War and the Waste Landers," "Chorus for Survival," and "The Age of Anxiety."

For the present edition of *This Generation* as well as the original edition (1939), the selection of authors and writers was extremely difficult. The period has been enormously prolific; and even with a double-column text running to more than a thousand pages, rigid standards for what might and what might not go in had to be set up and sternly adhered to. Writers whose chief work was done in the period between 1914 and 1948 were admitted on the basis of their achievements—either notable in themselves or typical of the age. Using this standard, the editors believe that most of the important writers of the period are included. The works of older writers not really representative of "this generation"—for example Kipling, Barrie, and Masefield—are omitted. Such authors, although they lived on into the period between 1914 and 1948, were of the nineteenth century in mood and manner. But older writers whose work seemed to be in the mood of the twentieth century are included. Even for the first section, "Carrying On the Tradition," the editors have felt that the authors should possess some trait (for example the pronouncedly liberal social sympathies of Galsworthy) which looked forward to the changes in form or content characteristic of the twentieth century.

The editors are pleased to point out that three writers notably missing in the first edition (because of reprint restrictions) are now here in a considerable representation—William Butler Yeats, T. S. Eliot (as poet), and Vachel Lindsay. Perhaps the only eligible "giant" not in these pages is the elusive (at least as far as anthologies are concerned) George Bernard Shaw, who can be seen in the movies and inexpensive reprints; and it is hoped that the book has at last become a truly comprehensive and representative collection of the literature of the twentieth century.

One important difference between the present edition and the original is the greater attention to the novelists of the time. Of course, the inclusion of whole novels was out of the question. Consequently, where possible, a writer of fiction is represented by short stories. But for some authors—Thomas Wolfe, Virginia Woolf, and Sinclair Lewis, for example—short stories are manifestly not enough. A few excerpts from their novels, therefore, have been included, not so much to illustrate the particular novel as to illustrate the method and temper of the individual author concerned.

It must be conceded that it is always impossible to complete a book on contemporary literature since the publication of books is a continuous performance. New authors of significance can spring up almost overnight; new works of importance may come from the press at any time; earth-shaking world events may take place at any moment of the day or night. For example, on the very day when the original edition of this book came from the press (September 1, 1939), Europe had committed itself to a second great twentieth-century war. Fully aware that the monoliths of the present day may be only the pebbles of tomorrow, the editors have tried to bring this work as up to date as possible by adding a new section on the literature following the Second World War. In our efforts to understand our contemporary literature and times, we must have as clear a look as possible at this literature and the present-day trends.

This Generation should lend itself to a variety of programs and uses, but will perhaps make its greatest contribution in more or less full-dress courses on "recent" British and American literature. A world-shaping as well as world-shaking era has been rounded out; we stand at the middle of the twentieth century; all in all we seem indeed at the point where the college curriculum should feature something later than the Victorian age. We have tried to develop *This Generation* so that it will enrich and implement—but not limit—a close and penetrating study of contemporary literature, wherever it may fall in the curriculum.

To indicate the individual work of the editors, the critical essays have been initialed and the editors are individually responsible for the biographies, texts, and notes as follows:

E.L.W. (Eda Lou Walton): Edwin Arlington Robinson, Robert Frost, William Butler Yeats, Walter de la Mare, Edna St. Vincent Millay, Elinor Wylie, Louise Bogan, Léonie Adams, Wilfred Owen, Siegfried Sassoon, Edith Sitwell, T. S. Eliot, Marianne Moore, Ezra Pound, Robinson Jeffers, E. E. Cummings, Wallace Stevens, John Crowe Ransom, Joseph Wood Krutch, Katherine Mansfield, Gertrude Stein, Carl Sandburg, Vachel Lindsay, Hart Crane, Horace Gregory, William Carlos Williams, Sterling Brown, Kenneth Fearing, W. H. Auden, Stephen Spender, Hugh MacDiarmid, Robert Lowell, George Barker, Roy Campbell, Karl Shapiro, Dylan Thomas, James Agee, Ben Belitt, Elizabeth Bishop, Randall Jarrell, Stanley Kunitz, Louis MacNeice, David Schubert, John Betjeman.

G.K.A. (George K. Anderson): Van Wyck Brooks, H. L. Mencken, John Galsworthy, Lytton Strachey, Philip Guedalla, Woodrow Wilson, Theodore Dreiser, Sherwood Anderson, Willa Cather, Katherine Anne Porter, Sinclair Lewis, F. Scott Fitzgerald, Ernest Hemingway, Ring Lardner, Eugene O'Neill, D. H. Lawrence, Somerset Maugham, Aldous Huxley, Noel Coward, James Joyce, Virginia Woolf, Randolph Bourne, Frederick L. Allen, Bertrand Russell, John Dos Passos, Wilbur Daniel Steele, Thomas Wolfe, William Faulkner, James T. Farrell, John Steinbeck, Paul Green, E. B. White, Thomas Owen Beachcroft, John Strachey, A. P. Herbert, Kenneth Burke, Franklin Delano Roosevelt, Winston Churchill, Arnold J. Toynbee, John Hersey, William Sansom, Irwin Shaw, and Stephen Vincent Benét.

The editors wish to express their appreciation to Hugh Edwards, the Assistant Curator of the Department of Prints and Drawings, Art Institute of Chicago. Mr. Edwards not only selected the reproductions which appear throughout the text as a kind of pictorial backdrop but also wrote "A Note on the Reproductions," pages vi–vii, and the explanatory captions.

George K. Anderson
Eda Lou Walton

v

A NOTE ON THE REPRODUCTIONS

THE PRINTS and drawings reproduced in this volume were not selected as illustrations for the text. Nor are they, for the most part, the work of British and American artists. They have been included to give some indication of work in the graphic arts (that broad term which implies all pictorial arts) paralleling, chronologically at least, the writing of which this book is a summary. Their appearance here may seem a little unusual to the reader at first encounter; but their relationship to the motives which impelled the representative writers of our time will, it is hoped, establish itself and become more obvious with familiarity.

The quality of being contemporary, which is one of the great marks of relationship among all the arts in any period, may be readily seen in each of these pictures, and perhaps the purpose they serve here, which is to accompany the text but not to illustrate it, will actually heighten the individual character of each print and drawing.

As T. S. Eliot has said in "Tradition and the Individual Talent" (p. 229), "art never improves, but . . . the material of art is never quite the same." The greatest practitioners of any art—graphic, plastic, or literary—are those who use the materials of their time to present to us life, nature, or an idea with freshness, meaning, and intensity. The ever-lengthening tradition of man's arts serves as their background and they become in turn a part of that background, but perhaps their greatest importance is to their own time, and it lies in the contemporaneity of their interpretation.

However, during these past fifty years when so many apparently drastic changes in method and technique have been made, the graphic arts have not, in their most worthy examples, betrayed tradition. The really valuable contributions of the art of our time continue to be related to man's tradition and man's life; they are infused with nature, though of course they are not intended simply as imitations of nature. In the case of the examples shown here, this fact should become increasingly evident as the prints and drawings grow familiar.

Drawings and prints have been chosen because these media are closer to the everyday artistic currency than the other graphic techniques. The drawing, which Matisse has called the spiritual element in any graphic work, has gained in importance during recent years and has attained such popularity that it is now prized for itself and no longer regarded merely as the hasty notation of an idea to be worked out and "finished." Its brevity, its intensity, its presentation of artistic form in the guises of apparent spontaneity, have made it greatly liked in an age which has produced the Hemingway short story and the lyrics of Jarrell and Shapiro. The drawing is a kind of emotional cipher which—although it does not convey ideas in the literary sense—is able to produce emotions in us without actually expressing emotions in itself.

Etchings, engravings, woodcuts, lithographs, all the various media in which prints are made, have their origin in a popular, social need for more and more pictures. The skill and preparation involved in their production belie the appearance of spontaneity which characterizes them. But at their best they convey to us —from the early woodcuts of the fifteenth century to those you will find in these pages—the feeling of vivid, almost palpable life in its most powerful and its most fleeting moments.

Certainly, in this time when illustrators have been so active and so much attention has been given the illustrated book, it may be asked why the selections for *This Generation* were not made from illustrated literary works, even from editions of some of the books included here. But painting, sculpture, drawings, prints, are not literature, nor can they successfully demonstrate the meaning of literature. Literature alone, as Jean-Paul Sartre has pointed out in "What Is Literature?" touches the ordinary life of contemporary man, and perhaps literature alone can directly influence his ideas and actions. Paintings, drawings, prints, are self-contained; they are more objects than means of communication; born in contemplation, they demand contemplation of anyone who approaches them.

We have tried to point to sources more than to derivations and have attempted to choose examples which are particularly notable for their individual and courageous expression. The selection was not intended to offer a history of the art of the period. Modern art has been restless and untiring in its search for new techniques and craftsmanship. However, as never before, artists have made use of the most fundamental and simple media for their most immediate statement. Some of these specimens— those by Miró (p. 863), Cocteau (p. 850), and Maillol (p. 6), for example—are technically as simple as handwriting; others, like those of Pechstein (p. 29), Grosz (p. 541), Mendez (p. 11), and Vallotton (p. 23), employ technical elaboration when necessary for emphasis, strength, or simple richness. None was made by artists who wished merely to experiment with a technique; each is the embodiment of an idea. Many of the artists represented are better known for their attainments in other media and in other schools, but the works reproduced here display their artistic maturity if not their final positions. Because of the difficulty of reproduction in this book, the elaborate examples of Georges Rouault and Paul Klee, and the complex products of Salvador Dali, among others, have been regretfully omitted. Two or three artists here included may seem a little "early" for the period covered by this book, but they were almost clairvoyant in their day in foreseeing the future, so they are not outside the spirit of the time.

All the prints and drawings, excepting Joan Miró's "Lithograph XXXII," which is from "The Prints of Joan Miró," published by Curt Valentin, New York (1947), and several which are on anonymous loan to the Art Institute of Chicago, are in the collection of the Department of Prints and Drawings of the Art Institute of Chicago.

(H. E.)

Part Three

"CHORUS FOR SURVIVAL" *Critical Essay* 540

Part Four

"THE AGE OF ANXIETY" *Critical Essay*. 844

"Peace in Our Time"

The Religious Revival

A Search for the Inner Self

Poets of the Present

Juan Gris
3. 21

Juan Gris: Head of a Boy
Gris, after Picasso the outstanding exponent
of Cubism, has been said to sum up the Cubist movement;
but here he uses a pure, simple manner
which is the reverse of his extremely ordered
and elaborate Cubist style of composition.

Passing in review

THE "WAR to end all war" suspended hostilities on November 11, 1918. A little less than twenty-one years later a second and greater world war burst upon unwilling humanity. There is every reason to regard the First and Second World Wars as one mighty conflict—a twentieth-century Thirty Years' War in which the ultimate issue was the rights of the common man.

Indeed, the armistice of November 1918 was not even a protracted armistice. In the years following, warfare raged in Russia, in Poland, in northern Africa, in Siberia, in South America, in Ethiopia, in China, in Asia Minor, and in Spain. Conflicting theories of the state, engendered in the nineteenth century and brought to maturity either during the First World War or shortly thereafter, came into constant, often extremely dangerous opposition. In addition to the wars actually fought on the battlefield, there were innumerable antagonisms between varying conceptions of government, morality, religion, art, and science. Although peace conferences and other movements intended to reconcile the warring elements in contemporary civilization gave some hope of brighter days to come, the world was at last face to face with the fact that hostilities had begun anew. And so, even before a boy born in November 1918 had attained his majority, the plague and desolation of war once more descended to afflict mankind, and this time on an unprecedented scale, with newer, more effective, and more terrifying weapons.

The Treaty of Versailles, which concluded the outward manifestations of the First World

1

War, gave to Great Britain and France the bulk of the victor's spoils. Italy, which had eventually come over to the side of the Allies late in 1914, was virtually ignored; and in truth it is clear now that she had been more a liability than an asset to the Allied cause. Ignored also was Japan, whose presence among the Allies had been scarcely more than nominal. Germany had been vanquished, saddled with an enormous indemnity, and left to her own devices, although her industrial potential had been left intact. Russia had dropped out of the First World War, a loser, early in 1918 and had emerged (minus Finland, Latvia, Esthonia, Lithuania, and Russian Poland) geared to a new and disturbing machinery of government —communism—which she proceeded to put into operation while all the other nations of the Western world expressed their aversion. Small nations, however—with the exception of Bulgaria and Turkey, which had fought on the side of Germany and Austria—were given promise of increased independence and prestige through the plan of the League of Nations, a plan which had come to fruition largely through the efforts of Woodrow Wilson at the Peace Conference (1919). For the greater part, the world soon came to be divided in the political sense into nations that "had" (those who had profited somehow from the First World War) and those who "had not." But these terms, while assiduously cultivated and even welcomed by the "have-nots," can be used here only for the sake of convenience. Many of those that supposedly "had not" actually had a great deal, yet it suited their purposes to appear as indigent relatives at the family feast of nations. At any rate, it is obvious that the so-called "have-nots" were the troublemakers between 1918 and 1939.

In Russia, as has been said, the communistic government established itself and has been maintained, despite various alarums and rumblings and the fiery test of a foreign invasion of the homeland, to the present time, under the able dictatorships first of Lenin, who died in 1924, and then of Stalin. Although communism envisages state control of all agencies of production and at least some degree of equal distribution among the people, the contemporary regime in Russia cannot be called fairly a rule either of or for the people. It is a totalitarian government; that is, it demands and enforces absolute obedience to the policies, plans, and prestige of the state. Totalitarian also, though in somewhat different ways, were the governments of Germany, Italy, and Japan until the close of the Second World War. All three of these nations exacted the same absolute obedience to the state as Russia does now; and all three assumed for their chief ideal an almost religious concept of the nation itself. In the politics and society of these countries there was liberated an extreme nationalistic emotion concentrated upon the figure of the ruler. This nationalism bound together all aspects of life in the state.

In Germany, Adolf Hitler was the supreme leader of the "National Socialist" party—hence the special name of Nazism for his brand of fascism. It created a fictitious identity of nation and race; it assailed all foreigners in general and all Jews in particular; it even established a cult of state-religion founded upon primitive Germanic myths. In Italy, the first nation to adopt fascism after 1918, Benito Mussolini transcended in power and prestige the uninspiring figure of King Victor Emmanuel. Mussolini's attitude was much less fanatical than that of Hitler; but his ideals for Italy were not unlike those of Hitler for Germany, except that Mussolini was much less daring and became, willy-nilly, in view of Germany's far greater strength, the jackal to Hitler's tiger. In Japan the sacred symbol of the Mikado typified the spiritual national bonds; but the nation had long been under the control of a jingoistic military party whose belief that might made right was as unshakable as that of the most confirmed Prussian militarist. All three of these nations, the most powerful of the "have-nots," banded together in the famous Berlin-Rome-Tokyo Axis against the most powerful of the "haves"—Great Britain, France, and the United States, all of which can in one sense or another be called democracies. Over against these two inimical trios, and hostile to both, stood Russia, whose vast population and resources are even yet imponderables still viewed by most outsiders with doubt and suspicion.

It is not practicable to undertake here any explanation of the process by which the "have-nots" became what they were. The democracies, rich and successful, could at first afford to be conciliatory and even passive. Democratic processes, functioning according to due courses of parliamentary procedure, which must reflect the will of the people as a whole, are necessarily slow and unwieldy in an emergency. In addition, democracy seems loath to believe the worst of others. It is furthermore peculiarly distrustful of the military tradition as a solution to anything. It often leans toward an attitude of isolation which can no longer be practical. The impression left in the minds of those who do not understand democracy is that democratic nations are both visionary and materially selfish, that they are interested solely —each man for himself—in the piling up of riches, and that they are cowardly and weak, so soft as to be unwilling to stand up against a virile totalitarian nation.

The Axis powers, working on these fallacious assumptions, took advantage of what they conceived to be the impotence of democratic policies; and, having carefully built up their military strength, they boldly took what they could get; theirs was at all times an aggressive and truculent attitude. Italy seized Ethiopia (1935–36) and Albania (1939). Germany marched into the Rhineland (1936) and annexed Austria (March 1938), the outlying German districts of Czechoslovakia (September 1938), and soon the remainder of that country (March 1939). When, on September 1, 1939, Germany invaded Poland, she brought upon herself the Second World War; for Britain and France realized that they must fight to save themselves, and declared war on Hitler two days later.

In the meantime Japan, on two separate occasions—in 1931 and again in 1937—invaded and occupied Chinese territory. The first "incident" produced the puppet kingdom of Manchukuo in the north; the second resolved itself for four years into one of the greatest of modern dual wars. Yet the end was not in sight, for the empire of the Rising Sun, ambitious to put into effect its Asiatic "co-prosperity sphere" (which meant the conquest of all eastern Asia and its outlying islands), took the opportunity offered by the Second World War and the temporary embarrassments of the democracies to attack all American and European possessions in the Far East (December 1941).

We scarcely need a chronicle of the horrible years between 1939 and 1945; the losses suffered in men and resources, the broken homes, and the dislocations of economic, social, and political life—these are all still too fresh in mind. But the events of these years and, even more, their disastrous implications, must be always before us if we are to have any understanding of contemporary thought. The democracies were in desperate plight for half of those six years. France was overrun in 1940; England, absorbing a terrible battering from the air for a full year, barely managed to avoid an invasion which would almost certainly have succeeded. The tide turned as the contributions in armaments from the United States made themselves felt during 1941, when, in June, Germany suddenly attacked Russia, and when Japan, six months later, forced the United States into open warfare and thereby made an active participant of a nation whose technical and natural resources, harnessed to a war economy, were unparalleled. After Pearl Harbor it was largely a matter of time before the greatly superior war potentials of Britain, the United States, and Russia overcame the Axis, which was hemmed in both by sea and in the air.

The final articles of capitulation were signed on the American battleship *Missouri* in Tokyo Bay (September 1, 1945), six years to the day after Germany invaded Poland.

Ignoring all the causative factors of power politics, the struggles for world markets, for "the place in the sun"—all of which contributed greatly to the outbreak of the Second World War, as indeed of most wars—we can see that this particular war was fought primarily between the democratic and the totalitarian philosophies of statehood, although the presence of Russia on the side of the Allies is symbolic of the confused logic of the whole picture. Among the smaller nations of the world there have been repercussions of the fundamental battle, as well as premonitory symptoms. The civil war in Spain (1936–39) is a fearful example. In some countries, such as Spain and Argentina, fascism has remained triumphant at the expense of democracy, to breed infection in the future; in many of the small European countries, on the other hand, there has been some inclination toward democracy and away from fascism. Except in Russia and China, and in small countries within the Russian "sphere of influence," communism has made but little headway. But that statement points up the most difficult and dangerous problem in the world of 1949.

During the war, Russia fought efficiently and valiantly and played an extremely important part in the defeat of fascistic totalitarianism. But once the fighting on the battlefield had stopped, the Soviet government demonstrated an uncoöperativeness in the United Nations and a self-assertiveness in its dealings with the democracies which could only be interpreted as inimical to the interests of world peace. Increasing distrust and suspicion led eventually to the so-called "cold war" of diplomatic maneuvers and minor overt acts. As Russian influence extended to the several small countries where communism had been established, their governments seemed also to be aligning themselves against the democracies in the continuing search for world harmony. Russian apologists claimed that the USSR was of necessity first directing its attention to economic and social democracy before political democracy, and remaining militarily strong and expansionistic out of fear of "capitalistic encirclement"; but to most Americans and British—with their firm traditions of individual liberty—the reports of ruthless suppression and regimentation of life and thought within Russia, the truculence of Russian officials at conferences, the coups as in the case of Czechoslovakia were profoundly and increasingly disillusioning and disturbing. Whether some mellowing of the Russian government could or would yet be brought about by the Russian people on the one hand and such factors as the Marshall plan on the other remained to be seen. It is obvious that on the relationship of the two great blocs,

perhaps politically irreconcilable but still, it is to be hoped, humanly sympathetic, the immediate future of the civilized world depends.

Apart from the paths of politics and statecraft, the years since Armistice Day 1918 have seen great progress in technical science—an amazing acceleration in transportation and communication, thanks to the radio and radar, the automobile, and the airplane, with a consequent breaking down of isolating geographical barriers such as the nineteenth century knew. It is clear, however, that these freer contacts between members of the human race, such as have been made possible by this shrinking of the frontiers of space and thought, have not as yet made for a greater understanding among nations; and the dream of a harmonious federation of nations in which the lion can lie down with the lamb is still far away, in spite of the sincere efforts of the United Nations Council.

Man has recently exhibited, in the mass, a disturbing tendency to throw overboard much that is good as well as bad of traditional thought and procedure and to substitute for it a selfish opportunism. How this tendency has worked upon the literature of the era will be discussed later. And yet, it may be maintained, this literature demonstrates that man as an individual can still believe that

> *Each age is a dream that is dying*
> *Or one that is coming to birth.*

It remains to be seen how the English-speaking peoples have reacted in general to the effects of the Thirty Years' War (new style), to the hope of a new world, and to the crushing impact of what has justly been termed a world revolution, wrapped up in a war.

THE UNITED STATES SINCE 1918

❧ "IT IS *a fearful thing to lead this great peaceful people into war, into the most terrible and disastrous of all wars, civilization itself seeming to be in the balance. But the right is more precious than peace, and we shall fight for the things which we have always carried nearest our hearts . . . for a universal dominion of right by such a concert of free peoples* as shall bring peace and safety to all nations and make the world itself at last free."

In the light of what has happened since Woodrow Wilson spoke these words on that mild, rainy night of April 2, 1917, there is a poignant and chastening irony in the very memory of his idealism. Yet his were undoubtedly the ideals of most Americans at the time the United States entered the First World War. In a mood of exaltation the country bent itself to the winning of the conflict. It raised an army of two million men and transported them successfully to France, where they were of inestimable value not only in elevating French and British morale but more materially in helping to check the final desperate German offensives of July 1918; and it offered unlimited financial and industrial support with great intensity and vitality. This mood of high purpose was sustained steadily through the frenzied outbursts of November 11, 1918, when Wilson announced that "everything for which America fought has been accomplished."

But revulsion against this idealism set in almost immediately. President Wilson departed for Paris and the peace negotiations. There, in association with two hard-headed realists—the opportunist Lloyd George and the single-tracked, vindictive Clemenceau—he was forced into concessions and compromises; and his glowing dream of the "self-determination of peoples" died a lingering death, although its ghost still uneasily haunts the future of Europe. The Treaty of Versailles, signed in 1919 by delegates of all the warring nations, contained the framework, or Covenant, of the League of Nations. But political enemies of Wilson in the United States—enemies whom he did nothing to placate—the traditional tendency of the United States toward isolationism, and the undoubted general popular reaction against the President's personality and idealism conspired to defeat the treaty in the Senate and to kill America's participation in the League. Not until 1921 did Congress pass a resolution declaring the war between Germany and the United States to be at an end.

The United States in 1919 was sick of the war, bitterly disillusioned and ready to withdraw in upon itself. It desired once more its "splendid isolation," or, as Warren Harding, the Republican presidential candidate in 1920, put it in his campaign, "a return to normalcy." The nation wanted comfortable realities again; it felt it had sacrificed enough in the war (although but an infinitesimal fraction of what Britain, France, Germany, and Russia had sacrificed); it longed for a return of material prosperity and the "full dinner pail" objectives of

pre-war Republicans. It had just witnessed blood and degradation—however holy the purposes thereof—and strange inimical philosophies of the state such as had overtaken Russia, and it would have none of them.

The years in America since Armistice Day 1918 seem to fall naturally into four well-defined stages. There is, first, the stage of recovery from the immediate effects of the war—a period of numbing disillusionment, nervousness, instability both political and social, moral recklessness, and pessimism—the trying time of economic readjustment. This period ended about five years after the war—between 1922 and 1924. Next come a half-dozen years of remarkable material prosperity—the "Gilded Twenties," when fortunes in Wall Street piled up overnight, when rock-ribbed conservative policies in government contrasted amazingly with lawlessness, contempt for traditionalism, and crazy inconsistency in popular tastes and habits. The crash of the stock market late in 1929 rounds out this second stage and incidentally the first hectic decade following the war. These two periods, in literature as well as in art, are known as the Jazz Age, or the Age of the Lost Generation. The great depression marks the third stage; there are evident a strong tendency toward the left in politics, a willingness to experiment, and a reluctant, often tacit, acknowledgment of the greater importance of the group than of the individual. Withal it is a gropingly constructive era. The fourth stage is, of course, the period of the Second World War, beginning even before the actual entry of the United States. Whether this fourth stage has really come to an end and has merged into some later stage is not yet clear.

Readjustment in America: 1918–23

Viewed as a whole, the years from 1918 to 1923 do not shine in American history. There were, to be sure, a few bright spots. Suffrage for all women twenty-one and over became an accepted fact; the Nineteenth Amendment was passed by Congress in 1919 and ratified in August 1920. The presidential election of 1920 was the first in which women voted. That same election saw the first prominent use of the radio broadcast, "a marvelous new invention." The first transatlantic flight of an airplane was

5

Aristide Maillol: Shepherd Playing on His Pipe
This woodcut is a good example of the great sculptor's ability to create the effect of mass and volume in a small linear composition.

made in June 1919 by the Englishmen Alcock and Brown. Banting, in Canada, introduced insulin for the treatment of diabetes, a great human scourge (1921)—this headed a long series of remarkable discoveries in the field of medicine. There was a promising amount of mechanical and scientific progress toward the comfort and well-being of mankind. There was a rush on the part of young people toward higher education, whether or not they were fitted for it. Theaters, bookstores, concert halls, art galleries prospered. There was, in short, an external manifestation of the desire for intellectual, possibly spiritual, betterment.

On the other hand, these years from 1918 to 1923 presented in somber hues the discouraging spectacle of political self-seeking, corruption in high office, bigotry, and intolerance in the social scene, and a strange restlessness and irritability in modes of living. The immediate problem raised by the conclusion of the war—the terms of the peace treaty—brought on a violent political controversy and served as the chief issue in the presidential campaign of 1920. Woodrow Wilson's fight to persuade the American people that the Covenant of the League of Nations should be included in the Treaty of Versailles caused his own physical collapse in September 1919; thenceforth for a year and a half the executive branch of the government was crippled and virtually not

functioning. The Republicans, chiefly under the leadership of Henry Cabot Lodge, made the most of the chaotic conditions by combating the idea of the League and the principles of Wilson and by proclaiming loudly the virtues of isolation as a national policy. The result was an overwhelming victory in 1920 for the Republicans, with their "dark-horse" candidate, Warren Harding, a handsome, likable, weak, "front-porch" nonentity. The tragedy of the dissipation of America's wartime idealism is symbolized in the picture of the statuesque Harding riding to his inauguration beside the broken Wilson—a tragedy because the successor proved to be of such poor stuff, and the character of his administration so sinister.

The National Prohibition Amendment (the Eighteenth Amendment) was set into operation January 16, 1920. That the amendment was neither popular nor effective was obvious from the astonishing degree to which the law was flouted from the first: it was finally repealed in 1933. The importance of prohibition in the social scheme of the United States during the 1920's can hardly be overestimated.

The prohibition experiment was one example of the reformer's attempts to make man act as he supposedly should. There were many who tried to make man think as he supposedly should—from the point of view of the reformer, of course. The revulsion against idealistic internationalism, as evinced by the opposition to the concept of a League of Nations, has already been pointed out, but not the neurotic defense of the American Constitution which attended the revulsion.

There had been some anarchistic manifestations in the United States before the First World War—the activities of the I.W.W. in American labor, especially in the West; the consequent bombing of the Los Angeles *Times* (1910); the Preparedness Day bombing in San Francisco (July 22, 1916), out of which grew the notorious Mooney and Billings case; the figures of Big Bill Haywood, Emma Goldman, and others. During America's actual participation in the war these figures faded into the background, but the fear of their subversive teachings remained.

To the average American, whose knowledge of foreign matters had never hitherto been remarkable, anarchism and bolshevism were one;

there was no distinction between a violent, bomb-throwing preacher of world revolution and a sober, logical communist. Therefore the victory of the Bolsheviks in Russia, followed by the close of the war, raised the fever of apprehension to the danger point and prompted action on the part of American state and federal officials which was often obstructive of true justice. The famous "Red Scare" was on. Radicals, particularly aliens, were hounded, mauled, deprived of their civil rights, imprisoned, and deported on general suspicion of their radicalness.

A good example—the most famous of the period—was the Sacco-Vanzetti case. In April 1920 there was a payroll robbery in South Braintree, Massachusetts, in which a gang of bandits killed two men. The murder, then as now, bore every sign of being a crime by professional bandits. Two radicals, Nicola Sacco and Bartolomeo Vanzetti, were arrested on flimsy evidence, indicted on dubious testimony, and convicted in an atmosphere of tense hostility. Subsequently discovered evidence fixed the probabilities of the crime on a well-known gang of professionals; but the two unfortunate nobodies were eventually executed (August 1927), not before a world-wide storm of protest, which elevated the leading characters in the pathetic muddle to the rank of martyrs.

Yet in all this there was fire as well as smoke. Attempts were made early in 1919 to assassinate Attorney-General Palmer and other officials by sending them bombs through the mails. There can be no doubt that the Wall Street explosion of September 16, 1920, which killed scores of people, wounded many more, and caused great property damage in the financial center of the nation, was the work of an anarchist or anarchists unknown.

The Red Scare was fed, in the minds of the general public, by an almost continuous series of labor disputes and strikes all through the years 1919 and 1920. The failure of war prices, boosted during the war years by the demand for labor and materials and the usual amount of profiteering, to return to a level more nearly normal meant financial hardship to millions and contributed to the general economic and social unrest. The steel strike of September 1919 marks the peak of the trouble in the field of labor; the strike of the Boston police in the same month, which led to rioting and anarchy, showed what could happen when public servants failed to carry out their duties.

Yet the most ominous manifestations of this nationalistic bigotry against the nonconformist in politics or economic views and the foreigner in nationality or race did not show themselves openly until late in 1920. On October 30 there was a parade in Jacksonville, Florida, of white-gowned individuals; these represented the twentieth-century reincarnation of the Ku Klux Klan of the days following the Civil War. But whereas the old Klan was directed against the Negro, the present organization extended the scope of its attack to include Negroes, Catholics, Jews, and any persons of non-American origins whom the Klan might consider a menace to national integrity. There were shocking race riots in Chicago, East St. Louis, and Washington. The political powers of the Klan were for a time considerable; but its public appearances became fewer after the ridicule heaped upon it following the national conclaves in Washington in 1925 and 1926. A similar revival, on a smaller scale, was noticed in the South after World War II. Laughable or tragic, however, the Klan typified an unyielding and ignorant kind of fundamentalism in American thought which, as one looks back upon the years that revived it, seems entirely appropriate to the period and the environment.

Unfortunately, this triumphant braying of loyalty to the good old days of "normalcy" resounded too often to its own confusion. There may have been national administrations more corrupt than that of Warren Harding, but none was more pitilessly exposed. The great scandal here was the Teapot Dome affair, an astounding story of political graft and selfishness, far too complex for any but the most sketchy treatment in these pages. Albert B. Fall, Secretary of the Interior, took from the Navy Department—through the ineptness of the then Secretary of the Navy—the administration of certain oil reserves. One of these, near the picturesquely named Teapot Dome Mountain in Wyoming, he leased to Harry Sinclair, an oil operator; another, at Elk Hills, in California, to Edward L. Doheny, another operator—both, it was said, for considerations. The case was opened in October 1922, and dragged on for years. The eventual outcome was the conviction and imprisonment of Fall for accepting a bribe; but in the course of the investigations dozens of reputations had been smirched; the executive branch of the government lost prestige; and the faith of the American people in the dignity of their traditions was so shaken that the next few years brought a soulless kind of interlude which, in retrospect, appears to be faintly incredible.

The Gilded Twenties: 1923–29

In the course of a tour through the Far West, President Harding died suddenly at San Francisco (August 2, 1923); he was succeeded by Calvin Coolidge. The death of the incumbent naturally made more commotion than an ordinary sudden death—ugly rumors began to spring up that it was not altogether natural, though these remained rumors and nothing more. One still hears occasional echoes of such reports. The most charitable thing to be said is that, in view of later developments, Harding's death was most opportune for himself. In the next few months the Teapot Dome scandal was shocking the people of the country, and more than a few drops of oil landed on Harding's doorstep. No doubt the ghost of Woodrow Wilson, who died in February 1924, must have been ironically amused at the plight of those whom he, in his last public address (November 10, 1923), had charged bitterly with selfish and sullen isolationism.

Coolidge filled out Harding's unexpired term and was triumphantly elected to the presidency in 1924. His administration was virtually devoid of real achievement; it marks the plateau of the fabulous 1920's, when life was hectic and prodigal for the American people, and the economic whirlwind was being sown.

In this atmosphere of growing recklessness and heightening tension, it is the gaudy, the lurid, the neurotic, and the cynical in the age which fascinate the thoughtful student. The picture of the years 1923–29 is of the crazy-quilt variety. The rise of the gangster from local hoodlum to political and social menace, sardonic, ruthless, powerful, and utterly intolerant of opposition, is the most disturbing part of the picture. The gangster's strength lay in his organization. He was not necessarily a bootlegger, that unholy spawn of prohibition,

although most of the gangsters got their start in that occupation. Essentially it was the age of rackets—the beer racket, the clothing racket, the cleaning and dyeing racket, the white-slave racket—the list is too long to quote in full. Yet such was the complaisance of the American public that these rackets were permitted to flourish in Hydra-headed luxuriance for nearly a score of years.

The American of this decade did not always seem to see the beam in his own eye. He was, however, exceedingly prone to see the mote in his brother's. Fundamentalism coursed throughout the era, now broadening, now narrowing. The restriction of immigration (1924) to annual quotas had been coming for a long time; but its actual arrival seemed to be beautifully timed. It was now "America for the Americans." Oaths of allegiance to the Constitution began to spring up in one state after another, particularly special oaths for teachers, who were supposed to be disseminators of wisdom and upbringers of the young. These oaths, obviously directed against subversive teachings, represented embattled fundamentalism continuing its fight against communism. The Catholic Church and the American Legion defended the oaths uncompromisingly. That someone might take the oath with tongue in cheek seems never to have occurred to the naïve proponents of the oath-bills.

The same fundamentalist attitude appeared in laws passed by certain states, particularly in the South, against the teaching of the theory of evolution. The test case in Tennessee resulted in the famous Scopes trial of 1925. Young Scopes, a high-school teacher of science, was defended by the brilliant showman and rabble-shocker, Clarence Darrow; William Jennings Bryan was the prosecutor. The trial was attended by all the noise and garishness of a county fair. Although Scopes was found guilty and fined, the appeal of the verdict to the Tennessee Supreme Court led to his acquittal on a technicality and an official closing of the case; but the reputation of America for maintaining a high standard of education and a progressive civilization was sadly beclouded.

And always there was the craving for riches and possessions, turning sooner or later to a sad end. In 1924 began the tremendous Florida land boom, which was aimed to develop a new paradise in that delightful wintering place. Real estate values rocketed almost overnight, and there was a great exodus from all other parts of the country of those eager to partake of the benefits of paradise. The population of Miami, for instance, increased almost tenfold over what it had been at the turn of the century. But two appalling hurricanes in September 1926 pricked this new financial bubble. Many were ruined; and the frenzied vociferation of the promoters took on a hollow, tinny sound as the boom collapsed. In a way, this Florida fiasco served as a kind of dress rehearsal for the far more cosmic crash of 1929.

But if the hurricanes of 1926 were in any way a foreboding of what was to come, the American people took no notice of the omen, as any reading of the stock-market reports from 1926 to 1929 will show. Investment on margin became the vogue; so did dealing on credit with inadequate security or collateral. Speculation, in short, is the history of American business during these years.

In keeping with this thoroughly specious kind of transaction, the social history of the age developed the same unstable patterns. The news stories of the day—the Hall-Mills murder trial (1926), with its lurid melodrama; the sordid love life of silly old Daddy Browning and his Peaches (1926); the rock-bottom seaminess of the Snyder murder (1927)—all these regaled the American reading public. The older generation was more than shocked by the behavior of girls and grown women who smoked, drank, in spite of prohibition, and wore too scanty garments. Experts agreed that morality was at a lower level even than in 1922, if such were possible. The whole tone of living seemed to be crass and ignoble, if one were to believe only what one read. The hysterical outbursts which greeted Gertrude Ederle when she returned from swimming the English Channel in 1926 and the far wilder reception of Lindbergh after he had flown the Atlantic in May 1927 are not, therefore, surprising. These individuals had broken through the fetid cloud of animalism that seemed to be everywhere. And yet the fact that the subsequent lives of these two popular heroes of the day were anticlimactic, to put it mildly, is somehow quite characteristic of the period.

The presidential campaign of 1928 was re-markable in many ways. On the Republican side was Herbert Hoover, who had earned a great reputation as Food Administrator during the First World War and as Secretary of Commerce under Harding and Coolidge. On the Democratic side was Alfred E. Smith, colorful and popular; an Irish Catholic, a former consorter with Tammany Hall but an extremely successful governor of New York, he had barely missed the Democratic presidential nomination in 1924. The Republicans were riding the wave of prosperity; in any plans for change, the burden of proof was still on the Democrats. Smith was decisively defeated in electoral votes, but there were many signs which the Republicans should have read differently. Smith lost in the South and West because he was a Catholic and a former Tammanyite, not because his liberal, anti-Prohibition platform was too much for the American voter to accept. As it was, he achieved a larger popular vote than any losing candidate had ever previously received.

Hoover had little opportunity to enjoy his victory. The peak of the stock market was reached in 1928; and the collapse which came late in 1929 seemed unbelievable. Yet on October 24, 1929, "Black Thursday," more than sixteen million shares turned over in Wall Street as the market plunged downward. The rout was on; thenceforth the mounting waves of private bankruptcy, annihilation of values, unemployment, and the sorry spectacle of bread lines and flophouses became the chief concern of American society. The Hoover administration proved to be one of the most unfortunate reigns of a well-intentioned misfit in recent history. The only actual civil clash came when the President dispersed the "Bonus Army," a nondescript group of war veterans who had marched upon Washington to demand a veterans' bonus, which, in spite of Congress, had been vetoed and pigeonholed. The camp of these marchers, who were there more because they were unemployed than because they were war veterans, was destroyed by a mechanized Army unit in July 1932. If Hoover had ever had a chance for reëlection, this lamentable blunder ruined it. The climax came as Hoover was leaving the White House at the end of his term; on that day (March 4, 1933) virtually every bank in the United States was closed.

Depression Years: 1929–39

The election of Franklin Roosevelt in 1932 was not merely the result of a reaction against a party too long in power; Roosevelt received millions of votes from people nominally Republican who were striving desperately for a remedy. Not that the Hoover administration had made no moves at all to relieve the growing tendency toward unemployment and poverty which was showing itself beneath the glitter of stock-market pyrotechnics. But the theory of the Republican administration was that which assumed the condition of the country to be "fundamentally sound," with "prosperity around the corner." Now it was clear that the disease from which the United States and all the nations of Europe were suffering was in part a monetary disorder; and this the Hoover administration either did not realize or was too slow to cope with.

For example, the First World War had brought about a tremendous expansion of credit granted by the United States to its allies; the ensuing debts, staggering in size, must be paid in either gold or goods. In the former case, the foreign nations could continue to pay only so long as their gold supply was adequate or so long as the United States would continue to extend credit. The United States was a creditor nation. The European nations were low in gold. This country, on the other hand, had a superfluity of the precious metal. A concentration of gold here was therefore unavoidable so long as nations were on the gold standard. But —and this is probably the most important single cause of the world depression—the United States, along with the other nations, had given way to the promptings of economic nationalism; it had set up high protective tariffs and so had contributed to the collapse of the world market. Such was the delicate balance of world trade that this country could not fully prosper so long as other nations were floundering.

Unfortunately, this economic nationalism was about the last thing the Republicans would ever have abandoned. Add to this situation the crazy speculation indulged in throughout the 1920's, the tremendous industrial and agricultural overproduction, to say nothing of the inequable distribution—clearly a state of economic chaos could not be far away.

It would be impossible to give here all the steps by which the first Roosevelt administration tried to correct the situation. The fact remains that the first administration was confronted not by theories but by a critical series of facts, and strove to act as best it could to meet and defeat these facts. It attempted to improve world trade through judicious economic treaties, to secure somehow a greater financial return to labor, which, it believed, had been sadly neglected for almost a century; to bring about economic recovery by borrowing instead of taxing; and to speed a general recuperation of business by the process of "priming the pump." The desire for a greater return to labor and better living and working conditions gave rise to the NRA, or National Recovery Administration, which attempted to fix "codes of fair competition" upon all business. The NRA lasted but a little over a year (1933–34). Its effects were probably transient, yet it showed a definite tendency on the part of the government toward the planning of the nation's industrial life, a tendency which has won, for better or for worse, the appellation of "the New Deal." In short, the days of the "rugged individualism" of earlier American history had gone, whether forever or not no one knew.

Further to help the unemployed and to give the worker a chance to work for his wages rather than submit to the giving out of money in the form of a dole, and at the same time to bring about needed constructive work of all kinds, there were organized the Public Works Administration (PWA), the Works Progress Administration (WPA), and a most interesting experiment in the planned conservation of natural beauty and resources, the Civilian Conservation Corps (CCC). The policy of borrowing instead of taxing to raise the economic level underlay some of the organizations just mentioned. The Agricultural Adjustment Act and the Agricultural Adjustment Administration (AAA) tried to control crop acreage of vital commodities and livestock, in order to avoid overproduction. But such an organization did little to recover lost foreign markets; and the ultimate value of the principle, while theoretically plausible, was not convincingly proved by later practical results. The need for conservation and planning, however, remained great. The dust storms in the Plains states during the

1930's did grave injury to American agriculture; and when it was realized that these disasters were largely due to generations of careless treatment of valuable soil, the administration's efforts were far better appreciated. The same was true of the movements toward flood control, for the valleys of the Mississippi and Ohio rivers, as well as of the rivers in the northeastern states, were subjected during the 1920's and 1930's to much punishment which might well have been avoided.

There was no question of the desire of the first two Roosevelt administrations to ameliorate conditions. In addition to the acts just cited, the administration pressed immediately (1933) for the repeal of prohibition, which was accomplished in April 1934. It undertook the development of the Tennessee River Valley (TVA), long a region where immense natural resources for power had been neglected. It attempted to facilitate the ownership of homes (HOLC). Through the WPA it rebuilt schools and public buildings, encouraged the growth of arterial highways, and gave its blessing to certain projects for the cultural betterment of the people, such as the building of programs for theatrical arts, music, and general creative work. But again, the net results of all this activity are still to be appraised, although it may be conceded that the repeal of prohibition and the establishment of the TVA (later of great value in atomic research) have been beneficial.

As we look back from the vantage point of the next decade, one thing seems fairly evident. Here in the United States, although to a lesser extent than in Europe, the 1930's saw a growing tendency for people to join together in some sort of union for security. At least society had come to a stronger sense of its responsibility to its members. The Social Security Act (1935) provided, in coöperation with the states, for various kinds of assistance to the aged, the blind, and dependent children. As Roosevelt termed it, it was "a cornerstone in a structure which is being built but which is by no means complete." In the meantime, by February 1936, two thirds of the states had themselves passed some kind of old-age pension legislation.

So effectively had the various plans for reform seized hold upon the imagination of the people that the presidential election of 1936

was no contest at all. Only two states, Maine and Vermont, were carried by the luckless Republican candidate, Alfred E. Landon. The old Republican guard seemed to have been completely discredited, though it proved to be rather that they had only been driven underground. The congressional elections of 1938 indicated a slight swing back toward the older order, and it is a matter for nice speculation whether this swing would have been accentuated in 1940 had it not been for the Second World War. At any rate, there were signs of a more even distribution of party power in

Leopoldo Mendez: Wall Street
This wood engraving is a graphic recollection of a trip to the United States in the 1930's. Like that of most Mexican artists, the work of Mendez is strong in social content.

the future, although whether the names, Republican and Democrat, would preserve much of their old significance was uncertain. There was some indication that the alignment of the dim future would be between conservatives and liberals, and would cut across existing party divisions.

During the 1930's there were, of course, spectacular news events which may or may not have had social significance. The gangster activities of the underworld assumed a particularly unsavory form; kidnapings became appallingly common. The most notorious of these, the Lindbergh case (1932), spun an amazing story of crime that would baffle any fictionmonger; and the subsequent trial of Hauptmann (1934) challenged favorable consideration, along with the Hall-Mills and Snyder-Gray cases, as the most vulgar exhibition of American bad taste yet to be advertised. One consequence of the Lindbergh case and of others of its kind was the building up of the Federal Bureau of Investigation (FBI) to a high point of efficiency among the police organizations of the world.

The War Resumes: 1939–45

It was Roosevelt himself who took the lead in warning the American people of what lay ahead. As early as 1937 he had suggested a "quarantine" of the offending aggressor nations; and when the crises of 1938 and 1939 broke upon a world reluctant to face them, Roosevelt personally intervened to try to stave off the inevitable. His efforts were brusquely rejected, contemptuously so by Hitler. All through the years from 1938 to 1941 the policy of the administration was shaped more and more by the events across the Atlantic, until the American people began to complain that their domestic affairs were being forgotten.

Enough Americans, however, were glad to have in the White House a man with Roosevelt's grasp of the situation, and enough were willing to go along with the political astuteness of one of the most knowing and able politicians in American history, to elect Roosevelt twice more to the presidency. In 1940 he was opposed by Wendell Willkie, a brilliant, popular, but rather unorthodox candidate without previous political experience, an able man with

vision, whose internationalism came to him too late, however, to do him any good in the election, although he made a far better showing than either Hoover or Landon. Shortly before the Democratic convention of 1940 the debacle on the western front in Europe had begun to unfold itself and France had fallen soon thereafter. The country, while reluctant and resentful, seemed willing to admit tacitly that America needed the fifty thousand planes which Roosevelt had called for in June 1940 and the most unwelcome conscription of young men which began some three weeks before the presidential election of 1940. Willkie fought valiantly, but Roosevelt was too magnetic and experienced a leader to be turned out at such a time. The very efforts of Germany to interfere in the election (through the agitation of American fascist groups like the German Bund and the America First Party) and thus to assure the defeat of Roosevelt, abortive as they may have been, were nevertheless significant.

In 1944, although he was in failing health, Roosevelt ran again as candidate for President. But for the war, it seems clear now that he would never have been nominated, much less reëlected. His opponent, Thomas Dewey, a young and vigorous governor of New York, made the best fight against Roosevelt of any of his four unsuccessful antagonists. But in 1944 the tide had turned in military affairs with a vengeance; and Roosevelt, with his wide understanding of international affairs and his prestige in foreign countries—a prestige which the American people has not realized to this day— was considered an indispensable party to the forthcoming peace conference, which would take place, it seemed virtually certain, before the expiration of the fourth term. Yet only three months after his fourth inauguration, Roosevelt died (April 12, 1945); the passing of this man, extravagantly hated, worshiped, viewed with contempt, and loved, marks the end of an important era in the twentieth century, and the presidency devolved upon Harry Truman, an earnest, hard-working, but utterly prosaic former senator.

Until the presidential year of 1948, Truman was beset by all the manifold problems of a crepuscular period, half-war and half-peace, with its inevitable social unrest, economic problems, and political anxieties. The ineluctable reaction against the rigors of a wartime economy (particularly in this Second World War, when America was subject to the rationing of food and commodities on an unprecedented scale) caused the Truman administration woe multiplied. Congress, representing the people as a whole, became rebellious and removed such things as rationing and price controls. The natural consequence was inflation, and a meteoric rise in the cost of living. Dissatisfaction with more than a dozen years of "New Deal" government in one form or another was reflected in the elections of 1946, when the people returned a Congress that was dominated by the Republicans. This Eightieth Congress enacted certain legislation of a reactionary nature, particularly designed to curb the power of labor and the tendency of certain union leaders toward the reckless use of the strike. Also in evidence was a strong Congressional leaning toward the investigation of all people in governmental positions with real or alleged affiliations with Communism.

Against a background of spiraling prices, a deficiency in the production of many hitherto staple commodities, the threat of the cold war and the struggle over possession of the souls of the cold and hungry in depleted Europe, a bewilderment and smoldering resentment on the part of labor against both the administration and Congress, the presidential campaign of 1948 got under way. The Republicans once more nominated Thomas Dewey; the Democrats Truman—in spite of two serious defections within the party—one by those who felt that Truman should have appeased Russia (the Progressive Action Party, headed by former Vice-President Wallace), and another by certain Southern Democrats who resented Truman's insistence upon the equality of privilege between whites and Negroes in civil rights (the so-called Dixiecrats, headed by Governor Thurmond of South Carolina). In the early stages of the campaign, the Republicans were looked upon as sure winners. But they relied upon glittering generalities, whereas Truman, with great personal energy and fight, attacked the record of the Eightieth Congress, raking it fore and aft. Labor and the independent vote tended to fall in behind him, so that he achieved the presidency in spite of the fact that he failed to carry New York, Pennsylvania, and no less than four states in the South—a remarkable performance that put to shame all the prophecies of polls and periodicals.

As one reads the chronicle of post-war events in America since September 1, 1945, and compares it with the chronicle of post-war events in America after November 11, 1918, the appalling similarity of patterns is grimly evident. The thinking person may well ponder whether we are following the same path as formerly—following it over a broader, concrete highway instead of over the dirt road of 1918–38.

GREAT BRITAIN SINCE 1918

❦ BESIDE THE febrile course of events on this side of the Atlantic, the history of Great Britain during the past thirty years is much more placid, more orderly, and far less interesting to the spectator until we get near the end of the period. For two centuries and a half England has been

A land of settled government,
A land of just and old renown,
Where Freedom slowly broadens down
From precedent to precedent.

And although the past thirty years have brought conditions which Tennyson with all his poetic vision would scarcely have dreamed of, it is still true that the fundamental conservatism of the English people accounts in great measure for the relatively sober time that England had of it in the years immediately following 1918. Yet the pattern of her history parallels roughly that of American history. She has had her scandals, her sensational crimes, her Jazz Age controversies; but they have never been so blatantly proclaimed to the world in general and do not seem to have left so deep a wound upon the body politic.

There were a few years of immediate readjustment after the First World War. But there was at no time in England a "Coolidge prosperity" during the 1920's. England was never so badly off as Germany or even France, but her economic condition was troubled all through the decade. The financial collapse of 1929 affected her as it did the United States; but again, she did not slide so far down the economic ladder, and righted herself after the depression more quickly than the United States. Nor was she obliged to introduce so many social innovations as the Roosevelt administration saw fit to bring to the United States; some of them, such as unemployment insurance, old age pensions, and housing acts, she had already established. Others did not interest her, either because she was too shortsighted to see any permanent good in them or because she was so far-sighted as to see their futility. She has been aptly likened to an old model of an automobile that is nevertheless serviceable and easy to turn around in heavy traffic.

Yet when the Second World War came, Britain took more physical punishment than ever before in her history, and the trend toward the obliteration of social classes, still one of the curses of British insular civilization, already a talking point in 1936, was definitely accelerated. As usual, however, the picture is clouded.

A Period of Readjustment: 1918–23

Britain came out of the negotiations which led to the Treaty of Versailles with satisfactory gains. True, she was obliged to join the new League of Nations; and many of her more practical statesmen foresaw trouble in that quarter. The nation, of course, had suffered terribly in the loss of men and material assets for more than four years. It was sadly depleted financially; but it was resolved to be "a land fit for heroes to live in." It anticipated unemployment for returned soldiers and arranged for a dole of twenty-five shillings a week to jobless veterans. The government at this time was a coalition ministry of Conservatives and Liberals handled by the fiery timeserver, David Lloyd George. Its policy was by helping labor to help the nation get on its feet. New housing acts were devised; national economy was stressed. But the dislocation of wartime prices by peace conditions brought financial hardship to labor, in spite of the provisions of the government,

and a series of strikes broke out in 1919—the same year that saw many American strikes. As in the United States, too, the climax came with a police strike in Liverpool and other cities. Labor profited from these strikes in England more than in the United States, however, because it had tighter organization. The powerful unions of miners, railroad workers, and transport workers united for a time in the Triple Alliance of labor, forming the basis of a solid political Labour Party which was to grow in importance as the decade advanced.

In spite of these difficulties, the first few years after 1918 brought a moderate degree of prosperity at home which lasted well through the winter of 1921–22. Abroad, on the other hand, Britain was in constant difficulty during this same period. In Ireland, the nationalist Sinn Fein party began to agitate for an Irish Free State (1920). The government first dealt with the problem stupidly and harshly by sending to Ireland a force of Royal Irish Constabulary, known as the "Black and Tans." After a great deal of violence and bloodshed, for which there can be little excuse, the cause of the Irish nationalists attracted respectful attention from the government. In December 1921 the Irish Free State was proclaimed by treaty, with the status of a Dominion of the British Crown—the same status as that of Canada, Australia, New Zealand, South Africa, and (at that time) Newfoundland. The Irish Free State comprised the Catholic counties of Ireland; Ulster, in the north, objected vigorously to the arrangement and remains still an integral part of the United Kingdom. The moderate Cosgrave, as president of the Irish Free State, smoothed the troubled waters; but the uncompromising Eamon de Valera, who succeeded him and who has remained the most powerful single individual in Ireland, strove successfully for nothing less than a completely independent Republic of Ireland. This independence was achieved in December 1948.

India, soon after the close of the First World War, in which she had dismayed the Germans and delighted the British by her loyalty to the cause of the Allies, became the source of great worry to the government because of the suspicion that the Indian millions were being subjected to a systematic subversion at the hands of the communistic Russian government. After some official investigation, the Rowlatt Acts were passed (1919), whereby civil administration could be superseded by the military when and where the need might arise. These acts were bitterly resented by the Indians—Brahmans, Moslems, and Untouchables alike. That most remarkable individual, Mohandas K. Gandhi, the Mahatma, certainly one of the most important personalities to come into prominence in the twentieth century, had already begun his work for Indian independence. His presence in the unimportant town of Amritsar in March 1919 led to a colossal blunder by the British administration in India—the cold-blooded shooting of two thousand Indians in what was virtually a massacre, an indefensible attempt to make an object lesson of all political dissenters. Gandhi then led movements, first for dominion status for India, then for complete independence (*swaraj*) of the Indian federation of states. His methods were, to the Occidental mind, both novel and incomprehensible; they were based upon the principles of civil disobedience and passive resistance. The astonishing events that followed—his imprisonment and subsequent release; the boycotting of British goods in India; the veneration and worship accorded Gandhi; the "march to the sea," when he and his followers filled their buckets with salt water and by boiling away the water produced their own salt, thus breaking a British monopoly—these forced Britain to make concessions. First came an all-Indian legislature (1920), then round-table conferences in London (1929–30). Although these conferences broke down because of the essential religious and social disunities of India, which not even a Gandhi could reconcile, there could be no question of the vast menace to British colonial life and the British Empire posed by the Indian agitation for independence. The groundwork laid down by Gandhi in these his most active years was thus instrumental in the emergence of the sovereign nations of Hindustan and Pakistan; and although Gandhi was killed by an assassin in 1948, he could die with the realization that his significant work had been accomplished.

Of less significance in their impact upon world opinion were the similar nationalistic urges in Egypt, which had been left as an English protectorate after the First World War. The Egyptians demanded autonomy; there was some rioting and many uncomfortable moments for foreigners living in that country. These demands were met in 1922, although England reserved her military interest in the Suez Canal and the frontiers of the Sudan. At the same time a cloud no bigger than a man's hand appeared over the horizon in Palestine; but it was not until the end of the Second World War that the Jewish impasse in the Holy Land attained serious proportions. Then, however, the Zionist State, gradually built up by refugees from Europe and the United States, was recognized by the United Nations as a sovereign state, the Republic of Israel, and a still inconclusive contest arose between the Jewish and Moslem inhabitants of the Holy Land.

The year 1922 therefore saw the major problems of the post-war decade well established. The foreign situation was bleak. The United States had begun to press for payment in cash of the war debts due her. Germany was showing unmistakable signs of financial collapse. The British coalition ministry vacillated and then fell almost simultaneously with the German mark. A desperate return to the Conservatives under Bonar Law brought a few months of definite governmental stagnation; Bonar Law himself was in poor health, and Stanley Baldwin, the rising hope of the Conservatives, was not yet in a position to make an administration successful. The year 1923 brought a peak of unemployment; and although some historians are prone to see in the Bonar Law government a signpost of the "return to normalcy" of the contemporary Harding administration in the United States, the comparison is not at all apt. Actually, it appears now that 1923 was the preliminary rumble of the world depression of a half-dozen years later, but certain events interposed themselves to stave off the calamity for the moment. In the meantime, the Jazz Age had been launched in England, to the dismay of the Archbishops of Canterbury and York and others of a conservative, sober cast of thought.

The Mediocre Years: 1923–29

The Labour Party, which had been growing in power steadily since the First World War, gained control of the government in January 1924 under Ramsay MacDonald. This achievement has no contemporary American counterpart. The British Labour Party was a composite of socialism and trade-unionism; it was by no means so radical as its name implied to some. Even so, MacDonald, its presiding genius, ultimately abandoned it. The advent of this party to power was not so startling, therefore, as Conservatives had feared or as labor itself had hoped. There were, to be sure, some disquieting signs—several labor organizations struck to advance wages, which had slumped since 1921 and 1922. These strikes were not particularly successful. The government attempted to negotiate a trade treaty with Russia; but the conservative opinion of the country as a whole and some injudicious statements by certain of the Labour Party itself defeated this plan, and the MacDonald ministry collapsed late in 1924, to be replaced by the Conservatives under Stanley Baldwin.

More serious than the Russian treaty matter was the situation now confronting the coal industry. The fact is that the entire coal-mining industry of Britain was trying to get along with antiquated plants and machinery; and there was, under such circumstances, little opportunity to compete successfully with other coal-producing nations. A special commission headed by Sir Herbert Samuel to investigate the industry reported that three fourths of the coal mined in Britain was produced at a loss, and that some kind of governmental subsidy would have to be forthcoming. The details of this proposed government aid, particularly the demand that wages be reduced until a new, definite wage scale could be established, satisfactory to all concerned, were not pleasing to the Trades Union Council. The result, a demonstration of sympathy to the coal miners, was the General Strike of May 1926. For a time nearly all ordinary business activities were at a standstill; but volunteers from all ranks of society rushed into the breach, and the strike collapsed after about ten days' stringency, although the ultimate problem of the wage scale for the miners was not settled for months. The feature of this strike was the coolness of the public in the emergency and the comparatively good-natured way in which both sides viewed the unprecedented proceedings. The strike as a weapon, however, was badly discredited in England for some time by this affair of 1926, and relatively few

serious developments of this sort have since taken place in Britain. Still, the General Strike had come under the ministry of the Conservatives, under Stanley Baldwin, and so the Labour Party could not be blamed officially by those who believed that all misfortunes stem from the political party in power.

Apart from the General Strike, however, the period was quiet enough. To the credit of the Baldwin ministry should be mentioned the Locarno Pact of 1925, whereby the existing boundaries of France, Germany, Belgium, Poland, and Czechoslovakia were to be respected in the future. How much this Pact was worth was grimly demonstrated by the Munich Agreement of 1938. Yet at the time, no doubt, the Locarno Pact represented a sincere effort by all the nations concerned to keep some modicum of peace and stability on the continent of Europe. In 1928 the United States made a hopeful contribution to the theory of world peace with the Kellogg-Briand Pact, which renounced all international aggression leading to war. But again, sincere though the efforts of this treaty undoubtedly were, the attention paid the Pact by governments in power proved to be, unfortunately, a hollow lip service.

In other ways the Baldwin ministry of 1924–29 was not devoid of accomplishment. The vote was eventually given (1928) to all women over twenty-one—it had already been granted for some time to those over thirty. Universal adult suffrage, after a century's struggle, had finally come to Britain. There were further difficulties with Russia, largely because of the industrious anti-British propaganda of the Soviet. There were various studies of unemployment, which persisted tenaciously close to the million mark. Affairs were quiet enough, but the discouraging lag in business activity was all the more apparent when one looked westward over the Atlantic and saw the skyrocketing of the stock market in the days of Coolidge.

Skirting the Crises: 1929–39

The eventual fall of the Baldwin ministry in 1929, prompted by this apathy in business, enabled Ramsay MacDonald and the Labourites to return to power; but the Prime Minister himself had lost touch with the more radical members of his party. The world depression of 1929 followed soon after; in England the nadir of business activity was reached in 1931. It was virtually a matter of national emergency; and, as in the First World War, a coalition of parties was deemed desirable. Accordingly, in August 1931, MacDonald retired as Prime Minister of the Labourite persuasion and returned immediately as the head of a new national government. This new ministry applied itself with devotion to the cause of saving the economy of the nation from bankruptcy. The gold standard was abandoned in this same year, as it was to be abandoned in the United States about a year and a half later; attempts were made to reduce unemployment with the aid of subsidies; the matter of unemployment insurance was simplified and systematized; the farmers of the nation were assisted by the same instrument of subsidy. All in all, the picture of Britain at this time was not unlike that of the United States during the first administration of Roosevelt. But England did not have so far to sink financially; she is by nature a less extravagant nation than the United States; she has the advantage of an electorate more homogeneous, to whom issues are therefore clearer. Still, it is doubtful whether Britain's recovery was any more rapid than that of the United States. Taxes were at this time infinitely higher in Britain—the income tax alone approximated 27 per cent, whereas, in the United States before 1940, it was only 4 per cent for incomes in the lower brackets. It must be admitted, however, that both nations managed even in the 1930's to exact hidden taxes which do not appear in the external tax rates.

One sinister element in this British income tax of the 1930's was the fact that much of it had to go to the building and maintaining of a program of armaments and military conscription. For all that, however, we can see now that Britain did not arm herself in any degree commensurate with her dangerous situation, simply because she refused to see the danger.

Instead, Britain turned to more pleasant matters. The celebration in 1935 of the Silver Jubilee of the reign of George V, a span of twenty-five years since the death of his father, Edward VII, gave the nation an opportunity to appraise itself according to its own self-encouraging standards.

As if feeling that its work in an emergency had been completed, the coalition cabinet of Ramsay MacDonald resigned in November 1935, and the conservative Stanley Baldwin reappeared as head of the new government. But the future had some new tricks in store for Britain. In January 1936—thirty-five years almost to the day after the death of his grandmother, the famous Victoria—King George V died in his palace at Sandringham. His successor, the most popular traveler of the age, the oft-fêted and romantic Prince of Wales, took the royal title of King Edward VIII. He had been schooled since boyhood in the social duties of a king and emperor; he had been sent all over the globe to act as good-will messenger and emissary to the colonial subjects of the British Crown. He evidently had a sincere regard for his people and his country; he was liberal in his tendencies and altogether impatient of the restraints which his office, particularly under a Conservative regime, imposed upon him. At first all went well. Plans were made for a sumptuous coronation in May 1937. British trade was to be boosted and the glory of the royal throne enhanced. The coronation was held on schedule, but another head was the recipient of the crown. The King had become entangled with an American divorcée, Mrs. Wallis Warfield Spencer Simpson of Baltimore; married at the time to an English broker in London, she obtained a divorce in the autumn of 1936. The King horrified the nation by announcing his intention to marry Mrs. Simpson. The issue was now drawn between the British tradition against divorcées and kings' wilfulness—a tradition buttressed by the Archbishop of Canterbury, the Conservative cabinet, and the ruling gentry of England —on one side and on the other the King himself, some rebellious souls in the Church of England, and a fair proportion of the lower classes. Traditionalism won the day; the King, in one of the most tear-inducing radio broadcasts on record, renounced his throne in favor of Mrs. Simpson, "the woman I love," and departed into virtual exile in France, where, under the title of Duke of Windsor, he married the lady.

Incredible as this spectacle appeared to the curious American audience, it actually strengthened Baldwin's hold upon the Government; and when he retired shortly after the corona-

17

tion of the new king, George VI, brother of the erstwhile King Edward VIII—a well-intentioned, good-looking, but colorless sovereign with an attractive family and no desire to rock the parliamentary or ecclesiastical boats—the grip of the Conservatives upon the nation was amply demonstrated. These Conservatives comprised the Established Church of England, the landed gentry and peers of the realm, the capitalists, noble or bourgeois, and all people who preferred the certain immediately safe to the possibly ultimately better. Neville Chamberlain, successor to Baldwin, represented all these groups.

The first crisis which Chamberlain's Government faced was a most serious one. Hitler and Mussolini had banded together to demand from Czechoslovakia, a child of the Allies by the Treaty of Versailles in 1919, those outlying portions of the country that were contiguous to Germany and were strongly German in population (the Sudetenland). In March 1938, as noted above (p. 3), Hitler had devoured Austria with privy paw, and nothing had been said, except by supposedly militaristic firebrands like Winston Churchill. But Czechoslovakia in those anxious days of September 1938 showed fight, calling upon France, Russia, and England to help her, in accordance with the terms of the Locarno Pact. Chamberlain and his group, naturally enough, felt that the safety of Europe was at stake; he himself was a man of peace with little aptitude for dealing with such intractable personalities as Hitler and Mussolini. Besides, he knew that Britain lacked the military power to command respect from the totalitarian dictators. Nor was France, which had been going through a series of disastrous political fumblings throughout the 1930's, in a position to do any better.

The consequence was the fabulous Munich Agreement, by which Britain and France stepped aside and let Germany take what she wanted. She took not only the Sudetenland but a few months thereafter the whole of Czechoslovakia. Chamberlain flew to Germany to be harangued by Hitler; he flew back with the signed statement which he assured the crowd at the Croydon Airport, in the phrase from the Anglican prayer book, would bring "peace in our time."

Chamberlain weathered the storm raised among the English by the Munich Agreement, perhaps because it was realized that he, and the nation as well, had been forced to do what had been done. Still there was a point beyond which even the most confirmed conservative could not go in any manner consistent with national integrity. The policy of "appeasement" could stretch only so far. The most unmilitary voice of Chamberlain announcing over the radio that Britain and France were at war with Germany (September 3, 1939) symbolized the condition in which the nation entered the Second World War.

The terrible experiences of Britain in this war—the dislocation of all normal life, the material damage, the spiritual and moral ordeals—these are all too near us in time to bear repetition. The great leader of the British war effort, an individual ideally suited to the task, was Winston Churchill, who assumed the premiership following the German invasion of Holland and Belgium in May 1940. Churchill was an inspired champion, particularly when the outlook was blackest; a stout-hearted personality and a phrase-maker of the old school— a warrior, indeed, fighting in shining armor first for the survival of Britain and then for the survival of the British Empire. However, he was a throwback to the days of Victorian imperialism into which he had been born; and so it is not surprising that he should have been dropped from power after the war with Germany had been won. The Labour Party under Clement Attlee won a sweeping victory at the polls in the summer of 1945 and proceeded to put into effect a definitely socialistic program which envisaged state control of banking and the heavy industries.

This program, in spite of the misgivings of conservatives in both Britain and America— misgivings which remind one of the alarm which greeted MacDonald's victory in 1924— has been anything but radical. Indeed, to opposing foreign statesmen like Molotov and Stalin of Russia, it would seem that the Labourites were as staunch defenders of the traditional British way as Winston Churchill and his group had been.

Still, if the two world wars, our present-day Thirty Years' War, can be said to have been fought for any purpose whatsoever, it has been for human freedom; and the English electorate evidently believed that a greater degree of freedom for Britain and for the world in general was possible under the Labour Party than under the conservative wartime ministry that ruled from 1940 to 1945. As for the position of Britain as a world power, it is evident that the United Kingdom itself can never hope to have the power and prestige it once held as the center of imperial Britain. It is too vulnerable and too dependent upon the outside world.

On the other hand, the British dominions—the Commonwealth of Nations—possess those resources which command the material respect of all the rest of the world. The conclusion to be reached is that the British Empire, heretofore a hardy plant, will probably survive in transplanted form. Britain has come to an important crossroads; she has chosen a particular way, but there is no signpost to indicate her ultimate destination.

A BACKWARD GLANCE

THERE are scores of events which crowd upon him who looks in retrospect upon the days since the hysterical outburst of the original Armistice Day. To each individual who has lived through that span of years, particular events will naturally appeal in different ways. But in some there are irresistible drama and supreme historical significance—Woodrow Wilson, in the last few minutes of his administration, facing the victorious and contemptuous Republican leader of the Senate, Henry Cabot Lodge, the man who more than anyone else was responsible for the defeat in America of the Treaty of Versailles and of the League of Nations, which went with it; Calvin Coolidge being sworn in as President of the United States by his aged father in a little Vermont farmhouse in the dead of a quiet August night, with nothing but lamplight and a family Bible to serve; the tiny speck of an airplane sighted high over Ireland on May 21, 1927; the broken, passionate eloquence of Bartolomeo Vanzetti as he stood in the courtroom in Dedham to re-

ceive the sentence of death; Gandhi dipping his bucket into the Indian Ocean; Neville Chamberlain stepping from the airplane which had brought him back from Germany and the crucial Munich Conference, waving aloft a piece of paper which, he fondly hoped, would bring us "peace in our time"; the same Chamberlain who lay dying in his country home while German bombs fell all around; the unbelievable scenes of confusion in the Raffles Hotel in falling Singapore in February 1942; the blind girl in New Mexico who "saw" a sudden flash of light when the first atomic bomb was set off at Los Alamos; the blaring from the loud-speakers of "The Star-Spangled Banner" and "God Save the King" in the tenement districts of New York and London on the evening of August 14, 1945, while the voices of President Truman and Prime Minister Attlee proclaimed the end of the Second World War; the impressive theatricals staged on the deck of the *Missouri* on September 1, 1945. These events help form the history of our generation.

INTRODUCING THE LITERATURE OF THE AGE

IT IS FOR us now to examine the course of literature from 1918 to the present. The details will be given later; here it may be observed, however, that the same divisions which applied to the history of the United States and Britain in this period will apply also to the literature of the two countries.

Until about 1923 writers preserved the accepted themes of nineteenth-century literature,

although bowing to the new temper from time to time. There is here the lingering of the romantic—the expression of the love of nature in its sensuous beauties, the triumph of the individual man over the obstacles of reality, a proud emotional statement of the artistic and ethical standards of the past, the creation of an imaginative world which yields beauty and inspiration—but always with an increasing restlessness and disquiet, premonitory of the sharp disillusion soon to fall upon literature and thought. In other words, the traditional in literature remains while the writers are groping about for something else.

Hard-and-fast dates are particularly unreliable in any outline of contemporary literature. But as the preliminary period of readjustment passes away, the neurotic reaction to the First World War and its temporary idealism strikes literature like a mighty wave. There follow a skepticism about, and then a denial of, most of the artistic and moral standards of the preceding generation, which, the writers of the 1920's seem to think, were responsible for the cataclysm of the First World War. In this skepticism and denial are born the pessimistic utterances of those who conceive of the world in which they are living as a waste land, devoid of beauty, faith, and purpose, where blind forces strive for futile mastery, and man, if he has any importance at all, is merely a part of the heartless machine of destiny. The full force of this tide of disillusioned pessimism is experienced about 1923, in the middle of the Jazz Age of which it is the proud progenitor, and continues for many years thereafter. Spiritual values are thrown overboard in favor of the animalistic (or at least behavioristic) interpretation of man; instead of high motives of divine origin to account for man's actions, they are more likely to be explained, let us say, by the functions of the endocrine glands. Traditional standards are in contempt; there grow up a recklessness and a feverish instability that frequently approach the morbid. The writers of this period laid a great deal of emphasis upon sex, as if that peculiar biological plan had never been heard of before. This tendency, strong throughout contemporary literature, reaches its peak about 1928 and again in the 1940's; but between these dates comes the world depression, when hunger and a craving for physical comfort, well-being, and security became fully as important as sex.

Literature after 1929 kept pace with the political programs for economic and social amelioration; it was a socially conscious literature, in which the individual was likely to be submerged in a cause. There was a strong radical trend which was responsible for a good deal of frankly proletarian literature—literature which, in brief, exalts the laborer above the capitalist, the subordinate above the officer. Reaction set in strongly against the belief of the 1920's that man was a mere cog in the machine; man was now determined to control social and political forces wherever it was humanly possible to do so. He was even ready to overthrow by revolutions the conditions that once made him the aforementioned cog in the machine; some of the most vital of contemporary writers are manifestly revolutionary in their message and exceedingly class conscious. To them Marx is of far greater importance as a nineteenth-century figure than Keats or Tennyson or Thackeray, in spite of the fact that Marx was an inferior writer as such. The message—at times sheer propaganda in favor of the workers of the world—is to them more essential than artistic or esthetic considerations, neither of which appears to bulk large in the interest of these writers or in their powers of comprehension. Then came the Second World War, in which for a long time Russia held an equivocal position; and the years following this war, in which the Soviet Union remained to the Western world an irritating paradox. The reaction against communism therefore set in, as it had a quarter of a century before.

The literature of the 1940's became more confused than ever; its aims were generally hopeful, but its sense of reality made it frequently overtense and sometimes completely negative, as with the so-called "existentialist" school. Its writers as a group were less able than those who came after the First World War. One is tempted to think that we may go through another cycle of literary development which will imitate the pattern of the cycle between 1918 and 1938, but that remains to be seen. History is certainly repeating itself; and literary movements generally do the same, though never in exactly the same words, for in a time relationship one can never return to exactly the same spot.

One obvious characteristic of contemporary literature in all its stages has been its willingness to experiment. Its poetry may be in traditional rhyme or meter, or it may be in free verse, or it may actually be written as formal prose. Its prose will often disregard niceties of syntax or of conventional structure. And in altering the accepted forms of literature this freedom knows no apparent restrictions; it is a hardy soul, perhaps a rash one, who will venture upon abstract definition of the structure of the contemporary short story or novel. Even so rigid a mold as that imposed by the drama has been broken to form new molds—broken in such a way that an Aristotle or a John Dryden could neither approve these new molds nor condemn them, because he would probably not even understand them. The language of the literature often has been concentrated, realistic, frequently in bizarre arrangement, with inevitable compression of thought and strangeness of effect. Once again, the reader who has been trained in the appreciation of earlier periods of literature cannot fail to note the way in which contemporary literature scorns well-established esthetic value.

Another characteristic that inevitably impresses the impartial reader is the unappeasable itch of contemporary literature to be new. One of the most deadly comments a contemporary critic can make about a piece of literary work is to say, or even to imply, "That thing has been said *that way* before!" Not that the material can always be new—even the most confirmed modernist will admit that there are too many eternal verities which cannot be removed from the scene. The desire for novelty, however, an almost morbid lust for freshness of approach, coupled with the notable self-consciousness of most modern writers, has led in many instances to the oversubjective and thence to the obscure. There is a surprising lack of calmness about this literature, as if the sober or sedate were somehow in bad taste. Too often, indeed, the contemporary writer is out to shock his reader, or "debunk" him, or turn old values upside down. In America especially there is a liking for cliques, fads, and cults. And an astonishing amount of this literature, impressive in its first reading, proves to be ephemeral when subjected to the test of time, which is the only true test. Yet it pours forth in a never-ending stream, which not even the paper shortage of the war years could dam up effectively.

With all its manifest faults, however, contemporary literature is a vivid literature—reck-

Ernst Barlach: The Foundling
*Barlach, famous also as sculptor,
here exemplifies the translation of
solid sculptural form into
the graphic element*

less, self-flattering, self-conscious, dashing, cynical, bawdy, satirical, tender, sentimental, brutal, and exasperating by turns. Occasionally its disregard for form and its encouragement of eccentricity and obscurantism lead it into the paths of downright worthlessness. Sometimes it is virtually incomprehensible even to the devoted admirers of its author. Frequently it offends those who have lived long enough to have experienced the older traditions in their full flower. Its beauty can be the beauty of the tranquil landscape and the peaceful heart; but it turns with even more delight to the skyscraper, the subway, the horrid metallic clang of the modern city. It does not hesitate to peer into recesses which had always been considered dangerous to explore. But it is still tremendously alive; its excesses can be accounted for by its very sinew. The best that can be said for it is that it knows no illusions, no fears, no limits—and it is all our own.   (G. K. A.)

PART ONE

Felix Vallotton: Procession in Single File
*Vallotton, primarily a designer
and illustrator, demonstrates in this
zincograph how a large, almost mural design
can be reduced to the small area
of a book page without sacrifice of power*

Carrying on the Tradition

IN AN AGE of transition, in a period which has
seen two wars and a depression, literature reflects both the nostalgia for the values that
have been and the urge toward the creation of
new values. Not until the First World War did
English and American writers begin to analyze
the effects of science and industrialism upon
the imaginative sensitivity. Then the older writers turned in homesickness toward the past;
the younger writers grappled with the present.
Both groups realized they were living in two
worlds—both faced the knowledge that the
life of reality contradicted much that the
world of imagination had or could dream toward. Life was no longer whole; everywhere
social and individual confusion reigned. The
artist was no longer at home in his culture. It

LE MONÔME.

seemed to give him little sustenance. Consequently literature in the twentieth century reads like a swelling chorus of complaint. As the century progresses, the artist becomes the exile or the prophet in the wilderness. Since, nevertheless, it is in the long run always the artist who passes judgment upon his culture, since in the residue of art is the record of an age, it may be well for us to attempt to analyze the record our literature gives us of the times in which we live.

First let us trace briefly the main ideas in nineteenth-century literature and such movements of thought as, optimistically advanced at first, had come by the new century to seem to many writers contradictory to the main drives of our culture. The intellectual enthusiasm of the

nineteenth century had sprung from the growth of individualism. Advancements in science and industrialism had been in part due to man's conviction that he could direct his own destiny. Freed from earlier superstitions by the knowledge of the physical sciences, man at first saw no limits to his investigations. The romantic movement in literature was in its early period the optimistic recording of the growth in man's freedom and of man's insistence upon more democratic forms of government. Early romanticism rejected the idea that man must not inquire into the affairs of God or of the ruling class. But with the increasing complexity of the industrial machine, man came to realize that the very scientific world which he had created could ensnare him.

❦ LET US FIRST briefly define the word "romantic" and its opposite, "classical," and outline the growth of the romantic movement from its roots in social necessity and philosophical idealism to its flowering and its fading in anarchistic individualism. Psychologically these two terms represent two processes (or two stages in a single process) of the human mind: the process of newly stimulated emotional awareness leading to an extension of knowledge may be called the romantic process; the process of formulating and ordering thought may be called the classical. In other words literature in romantic periods expresses new stimulations and heightened sensibilities, as likely as not in new forms, whereas in classical periods it expresses in some accepted order values and awarenesses already familiar.

The genius of recent English literature is on the whole more romantic than classical. This may be due to the fact that it has constantly fed upon new ideas from continental sources and that, furthermore, it pictures a fairly rapid growth of social organization. The first half of the nineteenth century was a period of progress in social organization. To begin with, it was the period of man's awakening to a sensuous delight in nature. Jean Jacques Rousseau, the French philosopher of the eighteenth century, had made popular the idea that natural man was good. His "noble savage" was soon to become the symbol of the instinctive goodness of man unthwarted by social restrictions. Rightly seen, Rousseau argued, all men were good and all men were equal. Therefore, all men should be free. The American and French Revolutions, indeed, put such ideas as these into social action. And an insistence on man's instinctive goodness led the writers to stress a sensuous interpretation of nature, completely in agreement with their belief, also stressed, that man had the right to govern himself. The doors were open to an exploration of individualistic self-expression through moods aroused by nature and through a political awareness of the brotherhood of man.

No sooner had the "noble savage" appeared on the horizon, however, than discoveries in the physical sciences weakened the belief that nature was the voice of God. The rapid development of industrialism harnessed physical forces for man's material gain, and awe concerning nature became old-fashioned. Shortly the emphasis shifted from natural man to man as a social being ruled by convention. The Victorian period had begun.

Tennyson becomes the spokesman of morality

Tennyson, the main spokesman of Victorianism, was determined to uphold man's divinity. With the "noble savage" he would have nothing to do, but with man as a highly moral creature living within the conventions and bowing before Mother Grundy he was much impressed. With the physical sciences which had led to the development of machines increasing man's wealth, Tennyson took no issue. But Darwin and his theories of evolution were another matter; here was an attack on man as a moral and spiritual being. Tennyson insisted that whatever might be said of man's body, man's mind was undeniably divine. Spiritual individualism he held to be a progressive force.

Small wonder, then, it is argued, that Tennyson dressed the knights of King Arthur in Victorian clothes, made sure that their ladies were properly chaperoned, and insisted that their brave and solitary searches for the Holy Grail were symbolic of the way in which the English gentleman understood truth. As Tennyson saw it, the fall of England's greatness could be due only to Guinevere's falseness to the king. The future of England appeared to Tennyson as one of uninterrupted progress. But immorality, which might result from any undue stressing of individual passion such as the early nineteenth-century romantics had allowed themselves, was a thought not to be sanctioned. Having to end his legend somehow, Tennyson placed the blame upon the woman. Thus he killed two birds with one stone. He glorified England, and he warned English mothers and daughters. As far as Tennyson was concerned, men were the great spiritual leaders. About the divinity of women's minds he was not greatly concerned. With the rise of women into literary importance, even as domestic novelists, picturing realistically enough English home life, he was a little annoyed. In his poem "The Princess," therefore, he satirized women's attempts to be independent of men. Above all things else, he was upholding the English home.

Tennyson, voicing the virtues of normality, however, could not stem the tide of literature still bent on expressing the rights of the individual, rather than those of a stuffy middle-class society. Even earlier, William Morris had taken the legend of Guinevere out of the closet again and, in his defense of that queen, had the lady argue that King Arthur was a "stuffed shirt" and Launcelot a proper lover. Protesting against industrialism, moreover, Morris proposed a return to handicraft as a method of stimulating man's natural desire to be creative and to live in a beautiful world. The Pre-Raphaelite poets, in the meantime, refusing to treat of ordinary English life, went back to the primitive school of painters preceding the Italian Renaissance as inspiration for a more primitive and less social conception of beauty.

The decline of romanticism

The 1890's saw loosed again the romantic tendencies of the early part of the century but with a difference. Tired of treating of Victorian characters and their manners and morals pleasantly, such writers as Oscar Wilde, Ernest Dowson, and Arthur Symons by this time came to feel themselves creatures quite distinct from the ordinary run of human beings. Their themes became anti-social; some of them, finding no values in society, stressed only personal values and moments of passion. Some poets in particular took to drugs and drink to induce in themselves an emotionalism which was temporary and somewhat morbid. Wine, women, song, and art were their themes. They had nothing else to write about in a conservative and prosperous country, which would brook no criticism. If they were accused of immorality in their individualistic self-expression, they countered with an insistence on the moral-

ity of art as art. Once and for all, most of them stated the separateness of the world of the imagination from the world of fact. They thought the Victorian world as old-fashioned as Queen Victoria's hats. And they spent their energies in shocking the bourgeoisie. The great romantic poets had been individualistic but sincere rebels against what they considered actual wrongs in England, had been martyrs to some extent to their beliefs; and some—like Shelley and Byron—were exiles because they were regarded as dangerous by the conventional minds of England. The poets of the nineties forswore social criticism in any active sense and spent rather less time in ridiculing conventional morality than in admiring their own attitudes. Such is the decline of the romantic movement. Deprived of its passion by a society which could not feed it, romanticism in the nineties shriveled into a kind of lifeless decoration.

Many of the writers of the nineties, having found no substance for inspiration in the English scene, turned to France and took as their masters the French symbolists, whose creed was chiefly that literature should not concern itself with ideas. It might express impressions of an unthinking life of action. It might, even better, stress mood or dream personal to the writer and therefore often exotic. Such writers as followed the French symbolists wrote chiefly of dreams and hallucinations as the only reality. Meanwhile Kipling and Henley stressed the life of action as one escape from thinking. Kipling, indeed, because he upheld English imperialism, was one of the best-known poets of the day. But the larger group of writers known as the esthetes, disliking the world of life, stressed "Art for Art's Sake." They formed their own "Rhymers' Club" and began the publication of the *Yellow Book*, in size and color suggesting a French novel. France had become the literary capital of London. Max Beerbohm gives an amusing picture of the esthetes as led by Oscar Wilde in his essay "1880," which appeared in the *Yellow Book*.

Beauty had existed long before 1880. It was Mr. Oscar Wilde who managed her début. To study the period is to admit that to him was due no small part of the social vogue that Beauty began to enjoy. Fired by his fervid *words, men and women hurled their mahogany into the streets and ransacked the curio-shops for the furniture of Annish days. Dadoes arose upon every wall, sunflowers and the feathers of peacocks curved in every corner, tea grew quite cold while the guests were praising the Willow Pattern of its cup. A few fashionable women even dressed themselves in sinuous draperies and unheard-of greens. Into whatsoever ballroom you went, you would surely find, among the women in tiaras and the fops and the distinguished foreigners, half a score of comely ragamuffins in velveteen, murmuring sonnets, posturing, waving their hands. Beauty was sought in the most unlikely places. Young painters found her mobled in the fogs, and bank clerks, versed in the writings of Mr. Hamerton, were heard to declare, as they sped home from the City, that the Underground Railway was beautiful from London Bridge to Westminster, but not from Sloane Square to Notting Hill Gate.**

The English poets' ideal of Beauty undergoes changes

The ideal of Beauty, always sought by the artist, had indeed existed long before 1880. During the nineteenth century she had first been conjured up as a nature goddess only to be scared out from behind the trees and hedge-rows by the physical sciences, which denied her existence. For a time, then, she had taken up her residence in the form of the virtuous heroine of the early nineteenth-century novelists. Once more science had besieged her. The biological theory of evolution seemed to deny womanhood as well as manhood its worship. Tennyson had put Beauty on a pedestal again by imprisoning her in the noble-minded spirit. Here she led a somewhat unwholesome existence, for little that men or women did or said in practical life exemplified her. She had already become the Lady of Shalott, lost if she turned from her mirror to the real world. To her rescue again came the esthetes of the nineties, to whom beauty was an ideal purely personal. As Yeats said to her at this time,

* From *The Works of Max Beerbohm* (London, John Lane, 1896), pp. 49–50. Reprinted by permission of Dodd, Mead & Company, Inc.

"When my arms wrap you round, I press my heart upon the loveliness that has long faded from the world." From the long-necked, slightly goiterish, red-haired ladies of the Pre-Raphaelite painters down, Beauty has been imaged by artists in the feminine rather than the masculine form. Some poets of the nineties, to be sure, had tried to widen the concept of her to include even fairly realistic barmaids. But in general, she was something passing in a dream. She was the world of the creative imagination, which had no semblance in reality.

William Butler Yeats was the first among the poets of the nineties who had wooed this wan, phantom beauty in female guise to discover how to bring her back to fleshliness. Had he remained in the pale Irish fairyland of imagination typical of his early poems, Yeats would have been merely another poet of the nineties, intent upon expressing romantic individualism as the only glory left to dwell upon. But seven years in political life and work among the humble people of Ireland brought Yeats to a more realistic observation of life about him. He acknowledged that, unlike Shelley, he did not find it necessary to seek poetic inspiration in female shape from afar lest his love become, in Wordsworth's phrase, "A spirit yet a woman too," and refute rather than inspire the poetic imagination. Loving Maud Gonne, an Irish Revolutionist, seeing her grow aged and embittered in a violent struggle of which he did not by any means entirely approve, Yeats kept the image of woman in his imagination by keeping his memory of his love's extraordinary beauty during her youth. In poems about Maud Gonne's loss of loveliness realistically observed, Yeats suddenly recalls her beauty as it remains in his memory. He argues that memory is as true as are the commonplaces of life. All this is psychologically sound and allows Yeats, the last great romanticist, to fuse the realm of imagination and the real scene.

His later poetry, recognized by the modern critics as his greatest, makes use repeatedly of (1) an actual scene, (2) the personal emotions this scene awakens, and (3) the exalted speculations and visionary revelations of life which these emotions suggest. Yeats is one of the most important figures emerging from the nineties. He taught the twentieth-century writers once more that actual life and the intensities of the creative imagination did not cancel each other. Upholding individualism and the furthest reaches of imaginative speculation, he also faced to some extent the facts of poverty, struggle, and the most disillusioning fact of all, that however intense a man may be, he grows old. In his later writing Yeats pictured Beauty both as all she has meant in the past to romantic imaginative thinkers and as something of what she is to become to the more realistic twentieth-century poets. He hugged the poetic intensities to the end. The poetry of his old age is a deliberate study of the contradictions between fact and the heroic illusions to which the artist holds in order to believe in art as the one truth.

ENGLISH NOVELIST, BIOGRAPHER, AND PLAYWRIGHT ADJUST THEMSELVES TO THE NEW INDUSTRIAL SCENE

CERTAIN OTHER WRITERS who came forward from the nineties into the twentieth century made different adjustments as best they could to the fact that the sea of faith could be heard now only in a "melancholy, long, withdrawing roar." Because the novelist and dramatist must usually be concerned rather more closely than the poet with conflict between men and their ideas, fairly obvious criticism of society is to be found first in biography, fiction, and drama. Biographers like Lytton Strachey reconstructed the past to bolster up the Englishman's pride. Certain figures, like Shaw, accepted twentieth-century skepticism. Others, like Galsworthy, clung to the worship of Beauty and fought the forces which would kill idealism.

It was George Bernard Shaw, even into old age a conscientious objector to practically everything popular, who took up for the first time the new discoveries of sociology. Most of the thinking of the nineteenth century had been about political freedom as something quite apart from economic freedom. This may be due, of course, to the fact that throughout the nineteenth century the standards of living were rising and the purchasing power of the average man was increasing. In all the hubbub about political injustice and man's right to freedom little mention was made of the observations of Marx and Hegel. Capitalism was accepted as a consistently progressive force, and there was little denunciation of the slums and the class distinctions which later thinkers claimed capitalism produced. But Shaw became a socialist who lived to expose social wrongs as well as to glorify himself.

Never out of touch with reality, Shaw sought to destroy English conventionality by satirizing it. For him the world of fact and the world of literature were one, and he entered the twentieth century the warrior against prudishness that he had been in the 1890's. He was always completely on the side of science and, unlike many of the writers of the nineties, was totally undisturbed by the seeming overthrow of God by the skeptics. That man could doubt seemed to him to justify the belief that man was made of pretty good stuff. A good psychologist in his best prefaces and in such dramas as *Saint Joan, Man and Superman,* and *Back to Methuselah,* Shaw loved to emphasize the discrepancies between man's actual conduct, frequently pretty silly, and man's pompous conception of himself. He has always glorified the honestly bewildered but earnestly striving man, whatever his field. Even in the present day, he still snipes at English public opinion by expressing some sly interest in Communism.

John Galsworthy was a writer precisely divided between an emotional worship of beauty and an intellectual realization that this worship has in the modern world no utilitarian value. In *The Man of Property* Galsworthy attacks the possessiveness which motivates the wealthy Englishman in his personal as well as his business life. He pictures the ardent individualism which was progressive in the nineteenth century as growing, in the twentieth century, into a reactionary, spiritually sweeping force. His dramas, too, take up early the special problems of contemporary social injustices, concerning which his arguments are humanitarian rather than broadly sociological. But inherently Galsworthy too was a romanticist hungering for the old virtues and values once held undeniable. Irene, throughout the *Forsyte Saga* a woman never fully described, is a symbol of the impingement of beauty upon the material-minded characters among whom she moves. She represents the romantic delight in loveliness seen as a kind of lost and brief dream.

Drama in general, however, was not at all an important form in the late nineteenth century or early twentieth century. The only great dramatist of the late romantic period was a Norwegian. Henrik Ibsen and his problem plays, which stressed the needs of the individual against social conventions, influenced Arthur Wing Pinero, Henry Arthur Jones, and the whimsical James Barrie to be, in various degrees, critical of society. In Ireland the rise of nationalism had interested Yeats, Lady Gregory, and John Millington Synge in the use of the theater as a means of persuading Ireland of her own greatness and of inspiring Irish nationalism. Their romantic plays, particularly those of Yeats, emphasized the legendary and poetic background of Irish thought and feeling. When younger Irish dramatists, however, attempted to portray the homely virtues and vices of their people, their realism was at first seen as a criticism of Ireland, and their patriotic audiences grew angry. Not until after World War I were such realistic studies of the Irish people as Sean O'Casey's praised as fine art. From then on, Irish drama because of its honesty and revolutionary fervor influenced modern drama. It is one type of drama in the English speech which has the vitality of a good deal of European experimental drama and of folk drama combined. The literary inspiration of the romantic age did not meet neatly with theatrical requirements. Although popular playwrights appeared and disappeared, even the early romantic drama such as Shelley's *Cenci* was indeed poetic closet drama more suitable for reading than for stage production. The latter part of the century consequently saw the rise of light, drawing-room drama which, because it catered to the taste of people who did not wish to think too seriously about life, took in large receipts at the box office. And early twentieth-century drama, save for the work of such serious playwrights as we have mentioned, followed the same pattern—it was written primarily to amuse.

In summary

Nursed on nineteenth-century thought, the men of literature in the older generation were not easily weaned. They could not become adults and modify the childhood beliefs in honor, patriotism, love, and friendship which they held. Many of the writers we have discussed remained idealists, and save for such figures as Shaw—figures from birth seemingly full-whiskered and adult—they could not integrate their ideals and the facts. Hence they made literature antithetical to life. That the practical world often denied them proof of individual values they recognized sadly. They were reduced to dreaming, and the worst was yet to come.

Entering the twentieth century, we observe the final slaughter of the innocents. Psychology, as many artists understand it, destroys the last justification for man's thinking of himself as the divinely appointed master of creation. Not content with having analyzed and made useful natural forces, or with tracing man's relationship to simpler forms of life, scientists turned now to dissect the very instrument with which they worked, the human mind. The new science of psychology began to be one of the chief fields for study. Watson's theory of behaviorism presented human action as a result of conditioning. This theory, not fully accepted, nevertheless sketched man as merely a set of conditioned reflexes. Nor was this all. Early in the twentieth century Sigmund Freud began his study of the power of the subconscious. According to his findings, the power of reason might at any moment be overbalanced by emotional compulsions. The view that reason was free, which had been fundamental to nineteenth-century thinking, was thus overthrown. Twentieth-century thought no longer insists that man will embrace truth if he sees it, or form opinions on reasonable grounds. The science of psychology often brings about a skepticism concerning all laws or explanations of conduct.

Max Pechstein: Italian Town
*Instead of being drawn with crayon, as is commonly done, this lithograph
was made directly on the stone with a brush dipped in tusche,
a greasy substance like lithographer's ink*

According to Freud, conduct is merely a process by which we obtain what we want. It is a well-known fact that man will subscribe to laws more willingly if he believes them to be the embodiments of final truths about human nature. But Freud's theory that religion, art, and thought are activities of compensation on the part of the individual, who is not allowed to fulfill his instinctive nature, leads to a general skepticism of all authority. Authority, indeed, in the twentieth century is often described as merely the assertion of an impulse to power on the part of some person or body. Religion, for scientific thinkers, has lost the dogmatic assurance it once had. Character, according to the new psychology, is to some extent something made for us, not by us, and if this theory is accepted, there is therefore no point in expressing regret for our deficiencies or pride in our virtues. Our loves, our friendships, even our patriotism are analyzed by twentieth-century psychologists as being merely momentary reactions of an emotional nature or as pathological states of mind. Soon after 1900 many writers and thinkers began to note that in matters of morals the twentieth-century generation refused to subscribe to the restraints and taboos of the last. Morality in the first twenty-five years of the twentieth century consists of self-expression—which might lead anywhere. Thinking is anti-authoritarian, and so much skepticism concerning man's ability to reason and fatalism with regard to the way he may behave have had an increasingly devitalizing effect upon the very intellectual curiosity which is responsible for the new science of psychology itself.

When man the thinker feels he cannot think, he becomes pathetic. He may wallow in the irrational with some enthusiasm or sit with his head in his hands cursing a world which denies him dignity. He is likely to look back to the past with longing eyes, seeing there an image of himself nobler than he now recognizes himself to be. Mirrored in the twentieth-century glass, man is the ghastly reflection of a sick and bored person. He looks not at all like the complacent portraits of himself that decorated every nineteenth-century home. More than anything else, he had prided himself on being civilized, but Freud, at least temporarily, has convinced him that his civilization has been but a thin crust over the volcano of primitive reaction. He can no longer believe in himself, since all the old truths concerning him are scientifically explained as but the vestments of ignorance which until modern times concealed the puny thing called man.

It is scarcely any wonder that so surrounded on all sides by disillusionment, so beset by cold scientific facts belittling man's importance, the late romantic writers feel homesick for what they regard as the lost age of faith. They know that they cannot recapture this entirely. But,

as we have noticed, such writers as Yeats and Galsworthy seek nevertheless to sound echoes of hope even while they live in the feeling that hope eludes them. Walter de la Mare, for example, clings to the memory of childhood, the period in which he still believed in the beauty of life and the dignity of the individual. He makes use of the Celtic interpretation of nature as peopled by fairies and elves to represent the world of awe and wonder, lost to scientific man. His poetry is a dreamer's poetry, but the dreamer is half awake. He may create the fantasies he would like to believe in, but he hears the voice of his intelligence telling him that these are but an escape from a world he hates. In the years immediately preceding World War I, English poetry, save for some attempts at realism, stressed the fact that the poet was living in an "ivory tower," writing of dreams recalled from childhood.

INFLUENCE OF PURITANISM AND THE FRONTIER UPON AMERICAN LITERATURE

❦ LET US TURN to a closer examination of American literature and particularly of the special elements which distinguish it from English literature. These elements are puritanism and the frontier. Oppression of the English Puritans had sent as settlers to our country the most rigorous of the seventeenth-century religious dissenters. While in England, after the restoration of the monarchy and the end of Cromwell's reign, this sect had been gradually assimilated, in America it persisted in its sternest guise. A God of Wrath was a fairly inevitable deity for a country in which survival was difficult, and this God lived long in the New England hills (though New England was not the only seat of puritanism). That we have in American literature no such sensuous picture of nature as characterized early nineteenth-century English literature is explained in part by the persistence here of the puritan creed. No such symbol of man as the "noble savage" was agreeable to the rather strict and moral New England thinkers of the nineteenth century. They disliked on the whole any emphasis on the sensual and kept their eyes on heaven. They had, moreover, met the American Indian,

and in their eyes he was rather lacking in nobility. A very real "savage" had opposed the early interests of the American settlers, and the American frontiersman continued to meet this savage as he moved west. The American frontiersman was the Yankee's youngest son, the most rebellious youth of New England families, and long after those Yankees who remained in eastern cities had modified their God of Wrath so that he became a God of Love—a deity more suitable to an increasingly prosperous world—the frontiersman, sternly realistic in his attitude toward nature, kept his sense of sin.

As the small towns and villages sprang up behind the frontier, puritanism adapted itself to conditions and became a kind of social ethics. This explains why H. L. Mencken, in his attempt to analyze what he found wrong with American art, blamed puritanism as it finally took practical shape in the rapidly developing country:

The American, save in moments of unconscious and swiftly lamented deviltry, casts up all ponderable values including even the value of Beauty, in terms of right and wrong. He is beyond all things else a judge and a policeman.

Now a judge or a policeman does not usually go about staring at stars or smelling a rose. Relatively few American writers of the nineteenth century had concerned themselves with the rich individualistic self-expression and desire for identification with nature which we find typical of the romantic English writers. Instead, they treated of the special problem of the puritan faith—a faith which denied a fulfilled life.

Romantic naturalism, as we have described its rise and decline in England, clearly had no continuous tradition in America, where for the most part puritanism and the difficult conditions of frontier living restricted self-expression or any abandonment to sensualism. Something of Rousseau's theory of naturalism and of the instinctive goodness in human beings did strengthen Thoreau in his philosophy of individualism, but even Thoreau's retreat to the woodlands and refusal to be regimented was due in part to his hatred of a materialistic world. Insisting that the essence of puritanism lay in the idea that man should not sacrifice his spiritual mission to any economic success but should rather sacrifice the economic to the spiritual, he built his forest retreat in order to have the leisure of which the workaday society deprived him. Thoreau, in other words, made of his naturalism a criticism of American forms of group living. He was an arch-individualist.

The dualism of the American government, indeed, which stressed on the one hand the rights of the individual and on the other hand the rights of property, made in America and thus in America's writers for a more lasting faith in the principles of free choice and individualism than was possible for the older civilizations. Nevertheless, writers and thinkers evaluating American civilization reflected in their works the economic development of the particular section from which they came.

In those sections of the country where a group of well-educated propertied people first grew up, in New England and the South primarily, the artists tended to depict the rights of property and either to accept these or to criticize them as being antithetical to spiritual growth. The South remained agrarian, and its writers continued to stress the values of agrarian culture long after the Civil War. Meanwhile the East became industrialized, and literature concerning genteel people gave way to literature glorifying or criticizing the power of money. Frontier literature had stressed the rights of the average individual as against the rights of a powerful propertied group only during the brief respite before industrialism conquered the West, too. Then writers in the Middle West and later in the Far West turned to studies of the virtues and evils of a materialistic culture. The size of America itself and the different stages of development it represented led to a kind of sectionalism in its literature. Industrialism conquered in fifty years in America, instead of the one hundred and fifty in which it had reached maturity in England. The instability of social conditions in America caused the artist to be conditioned in part, at least, by the special region in which he grew up and of which he therefore treated in his books. We have in America, in other words, no such consistent record of the growth of man's thoughts from the nineteenth into the twentieth century as we have in England.

The world grew smaller as the twentieth century began. Science and industry had conquered. American literature was no longer a replica of the English. But both American and Englishman faced the same general situation. The seeming overthrow of truths which had been considered final in the nineteenth century did not, of course, cause the American writer so much concern as the British, since he was on the whole more of a realist. In America, moreover, the rapid shift from an agrarian to an industrial culture had made for a conflict of ideas not so clearly recorded in the literature of England, where industrialism developed more gradually. In general, however, the outlines of thought in American literature and English became finally in this modern period very much the same. Only a few years separated the same literary developments in both countries. Everywhere, especially after the First World War, were chaos and contradiction, but one fact was certain—that many progressive writers saw something amiss. To them the world as a whole and the researches of science and economics seemed to be proving that the machine age, the complex industrial society, was no longer entirely beneficial. The fight for markets between nations and between individual businessmen often reached violence.

Late romanticism and individualism in twentieth-century America

Puritanism, with its singleness of purpose, was, however, at this time still a dominant characteristic in American thought. Two American poets, Edwin Arlington Robinson and Robert Frost, expounded its meaning. Both these poets received recognition only after they had long struggled against the echoes in American literature of the British Victorians. And Robinson, more than Frost, related his puritanic search for spiritual values to the real scene in industrial America. Robinson closely observed the strong drive of his country toward material success, and he resented America's rejection of the older spiritual and cultural values of the early religious American fathers. In "Cassandra" (see p. 44), he denounces what seemed to him the American flight from true cultural worth:

> Your dollar is your only Word,
> The wrath of it your only fear.

He hated our materialistic complacency, and he prophesied that America would suffer because of it:

> Because a few complacent years
> Have made your peril of your pride,
> Think you that you are to go on
> Forever pampered and untried?

Robinson sided with Henry James in warning of the evils for the artist which lay in a civilization throwing its energies into money making. Unlike James, however, Robinson never turned his eyes to Europe as a refuge for the artist in which puritan moral insight might possibly combine with the graces of an old culture. He felt, as James did not, that a mechanized and competitive culture could sustain neither the dignity of man nor the sensitivity of the artist. If he failed to perceive the contributions of modern science to man's betterment, he felt rather strongly that a society which he saw as worshiping money as the symbol of success could not nourish sensitivity. He could give no allegiance to such a society. Therefore Robinson consistently opposed the typical American success story of his times, that of a man moving from poverty to riches, and insisted that an American, to be a moral

and spiritual success, must go against the main social current. Again and again, his heroes are men who to society are failures: they are the sensitive, the exploited in spirit, the inquiring minds of our time who reject the drive toward power in business or politics. A man who dreams a symphony and can never write it, a man who tries to write a book and fails, a man who writes verse and cannot earn a living: these are Robinson's great men. He shows them as failures, socially and financially. Over and over he asserts that success in spiritual or esthetic inquiry incapacitates a man for money-grubbing.

From short portraits of good and evil in men in our civilization, Robinson turned to long narrative and psychological studies of the evils men do for power or for money. He saw that men were evil either through loving anything possessively or through being blind to the needs and sensitivities of others. He deeply believed that no one had really lived, no matter how powerful or successful he might be (see *Matthias at the Door*), unless he had spent his life in an awareness of man's spiritual and creative possibilities. To Robinson, the actual enemy was materialism: in philosophy, in science, and in practice. And before he died, Robinson wrote *King Jasper*, a long poem prophetic of the second world conflict in which he saw force against force in a world consumed in hatred. This late work was in a sense a sequel to Robinson's treatment of World War I in his retelling of the Arthurian myth. For him, Arthur's kingdom fell not because of a woman's sin, as in Tennyson's story, but because of greed for power.

Robinson interpreted the modern world as a world without moral integrity, where no force can breed anything but an opposing force, where no king has wisdom, where power must ever be separated from integrity and sensitiveness. While Robinson understood fascism and hated it, he did not support the use of force to destroy it. Until man could return to his conscience, until power became spiritual, civilization seemed lost to him. A broadly humanitarian poet given to intense moral and puritan convictions, Robinson denounced his America for its worship of material rather than spiritual values. Save for a lack of money, Robinson was in a way what Santayana defines as the "Last

Puritan"—a man who must deny himself even his puritanism or it becomes to him a mere possession, not a spiritual and motivating force.

Frost, unlike Robinson, emphasizes not the possible vices but rather the sturdy virtues of puritanic individualism. In the New England backwoods there are farms and farmers still quite remote from civilization. And to these scenes and these people goes Robert Frost for his inspiration. Descended from the English pastoral poets in tradition and first accepted as an authentic poet by English critics, Frost returned to America at the opening of World War I and settled down in rural New England, to become a prime interpreter of the survival of puritanism found there. A farmer himself, he writes realistically of a farmer's life, finding in it a kind of austere beauty and bitterness mingled. To his way of thinking, the life of the New England farmer asserts the dignity of individual life in its struggle against nature. He is psychologist enough to understand that the hardships of his characters' lives in their isolation may lead to eccentric behavior and even to madness. Nevertheless, Frost greatly admires Yankee self-sufficiency, which to him is more dignified than any acceptance of American city living or any orthodox religion. But he feels as he grows older that his are a vanishing people and that his country is invaded by hot-dog stands, tourists, factories, and a foreign peasantry. And in his later poems he presents farmers as forced to work in factories; he recognizes that the Yankee, for all his ability to draw in his belt, has not learned to live on scenery. Frost cannot accept chaos and he sees in modern industrialism only chaos and cause for fear. He prefers to live in a world of fixed values.

That he is disillusioned about a mechanistic society is implied by his insistence on the dignity of the solitary and simple life—the only realm in which man's independence may still be declared. As he says in *A Masque of Rea-*

Henri Rousseau: War
This is the only print by the famous modern "primitive" Rousseau.
It bears a strong relationship to the work of the unknown popular artists
who created the French "épinal" woodcuts of the nineteenth century

son, "there's no connection man can reason out between his just deserts and what he gets"; this is the reason for man's sufferings which only God accounts for; for mercy we must also turn to God rather than to man (see *A Masque of Mercy*). Whatever universal contradictions the twentieth century ponders, Frost refuses to ponder; he gives us the old answers by which it may still be possible to live—these and the stark beauty of nature, the stark beauty of man's loneliness.

Romanticism springing from the optimism and youth of our country flourished in America long after it was lost in England. During the early part of the twentieth century, England had come to feel herself an old country settling into a mold. But in America between 1910 and 1917 we were enjoying what has been called "The Dissenters' Golden Age." At this time most American intellectuals professed some form of radicalism. To be a socialist, a syndicalist, an anarchist, or a feminist, to campaign for birth control or for free verse was to be in tune with America's still highly optimistic feeling that our country, given a little push in the right direction, was, unlike England or any of the European countries, the divinely appointed home for freedom. America felt young, and particularly youthful when she looked across the Atlantic. And the intellectual and artistic renaissance, so-called, which took place in America at this time was based on America's belief that she had just come of age and had a radiant future ahead. Despite the expansion of industrialism, many Americans looked upon individualism as still capable of growth. Our country was wealthy, and we had acquired a sense of our own importance. Some artists in this period decided that with puritanism thrown overboard we should allow ourselves a certain abandonment. One of the chief of our "radical" movements at this time was feminism, and consequently a hundred feminine poets decided that it was high time they made a place for themselves in the literary scene. About 1915, encouraged by the publication of *Poetry*, edited by Harriet Monroe in Chicago, American poets became somewhat unduly enthusiastic about their own art as something entirely new.

Indeed, in their rather noisy struggle against puritanism many American artists now suddenly blinded themselves to the more significant struggles against the social injustices which, having no such scapegoat as puritanism and being less politically naïve, the European writers of the same period inveighed against.

"Art for Art's Sake" in America

An "Art for Art's Sake" movement not unlike that of the nineties in England sprang up between 1915 and 1925 and took lodging in Greenwich Village, New York City. Poets willing to starve for art's sake and intent on shocking the middle classes moved into the cheap rooms of that section of the city and lived and wrote of their own lives. Among these was Edna St. Vincent Millay, leader of the feminist parade. That she recorded what was in the wind in the way of heightened excitement over the individual's right to lead his own life there can be little doubt. As a feminist, and one of many who fought rather more strenuously for self-expression than for the vote, Miss Millay stressed the anti-puritan theme of woman's freedom in matters of the heart. Taking a leaf from the poets of the nineties in England, she sang—and not alone—of wine, men, and song. She became the leader of the group later designated by Edmund Wilson (then very markedly of this period himself) as the "god-the-pain girls," because they cried out all their feelings. She was a fine lyrical singer but not startlingly new in subject matter. After a few collections of poetry which freshly pictured her young life, she wrote graceful but rather literary verse deriving inspiration, sometimes even imagery, from Shakespeare, Donne, and other great English poets. Important to her always was the theme that the validity of emotions alone remained unquestionable. She wrote chiefly of love consummated, and love consummated is less viable in poetry than was sometimes assumed by the lady poets of the period. Like many lyric poets of the twenties, she continued to be, far beyond the jazz age, the romantic individualist.

When the new sociological interpretation of man's place in the scheme of things caught up with her, she handled it in light verse (*Con-*

versation at Midnight) and from the point of view of a rather flippant liberal. As for the artist, Miss Millay seems to suggest, he is above the battle of political beliefs. Her more recent volumes show little range of subject matter. During World War II, she published a number of journalistic, somewhat overemotional, but sincere and spirited poems against the inhumanity of war.

All in all, the so-called American Renaissance of the 1920's was in reality one of the last revolts in this country against the growing conviction among artists that man is the victim of society. That it was a rebellion, too, against puritanism is clear. But it was short-lived. More serious matters were soon to concern the poets and novelists intent upon emphasizing the value of individual life.

Conflict between emotion and reason in poetry

Certain transitional poets writing from the early twenties through to the present years emphasize the conflict between emotionalism and intellectual skepticism. These poets attempt to keep the balance between what the heart holds true and what the mind acknowledges as fact. They will not relinquish the values of individual sensitivity, but the youngest among them acknowledge that individual sensitivity is narrowed or widened by sensitivity to a social scheme.

The first of these poets in whom intellectualism checks the emotions, Elinor Wylie, like Edna Millay, wrote chiefly of love. Unlike Miss Millay, she perceived that, however strong this emotion may be, it is only a temporary refuge against the knowledge that human relationships are often unstable and human life brief. Whereas Miss Millay presents the full flesh and sensuous impression, Mrs. Wylie insists on the beauty of the skeleton. Hers is a skeptical and stoical mind. An invalid most of her life and a person unable to adjust easily to other people, she insisted on her own uniqueness, but she took small comfort in it. While her earlier poems were often psychological studies of women and men of the upper classes, she indicated a feeling that aristocratic sensibilities might be decadent. Mrs. Wylie toward the end

of her life identified herself strongly with another person, a man whom she met in England, who was, like herself, overwrought, ill, and soon to die. To him she wrote metaphysical love poems in a spirit of deep humility totally unlike Miss Millay's flaunting personal feminism. That this man symbolized more than love, symbolized indeed a brave way of living in a tortured world, there can be no doubt. These last love songs are really Mrs. Wylie's final and complete acceptance of the beauty and terror of life.

In Louise Bogan's poetry the chief theme is a modern one. The poet analyzes the relationship between the sexes, as this relationship is understood in the light of modern psychological studies. She insists that men never understand women. She is not, however, sentimental about her own sex. If men are the betrayers, women are often the fools. Miss Bogan studies chiefly the conflict between reason and emotion. Possessed of a fine mind, she presents feeling together with an intellectual analysis of feeling. The one authentic delight she recognizes is the delight in a creative imagination, and she never accepts the idea that the artist should be forced to speak against, or for, any political theory. In this belief in the special privilege of the artist to write what he understands best, Miss Bogan is a complete individualist. She is also, however, a poet who takes for granted that none of the old values is to be believed in today. Her skepticism increases as she grows older and as her poetry becomes less personal and more a comment on the separateness of the artist.

The American poet Léonie Adams, too, is one of the better lyric poets of our century. She is one of the literary figures who bridges the gap between literature which stresses sensitivity to nature and the later literature which stresses man's position under industrialism, chiefly because of her acceptance of the conflict between the real scene and an imaginative vision of life. This conflict she resolves by her almost mystical faith in the powers of the imagination to create beauty whatever the real scene may be. Her master was William Butler Yeats, the last great romantic, who brought his vision to bear upon and illuminate his understanding of people and political events. Like

Pierre Bonnard:
Sunday Morning in the
Country
*Bonnard heads a group
of French artists who,
although they reacted
against the Impression-
ists, did much to extend
the possibilities of Im-
pressionism. The free-
dom of his decorative
and unobtrusive style
found a congenial me-
dium in lithography*

Yeats, Miss Adams is aware of the practical limits into which life forces us. Like him, too, she insists that the imagination knows no limits. She is a modern metaphysical poet. Accepting the dualism implicit in our life, she argues that the individual develops greatness through his knowledge of both good and evil, beauty and ugliness. Miss Adams states no belief in an afterworld. For her, heaven is merely a subjective conviction of beauty. This poet presents life as a whole cycle through which she herself lives with faith in the entire mortal pattern.

Disillusionment of Middle-Western novelists

While the lyric singers in America wrote poetry in which the emotional life was given its full value, even as it was checked and counterchecked by intellectual doubt, in the Middle West the prose writers were concerned less with examining themselves than with examining the social scene and the American citizen. Even while the Greenwich Villagers in New York stressed art, Sinclair Lewis began to satirize middle-class America. He made up to the Rotarian, swapped drinks with him, and revealed to us all the unlovely details of the pompous American businessman's life. A realist and a satirist, he had no compunction. Not

even the banker was sacred to him. As Vernon Parrington has argued, the tremendous "discovery" that Lewis made much of is that the United States is peopled by a mighty herd

. . . which like those earlier herds that rumbled about the plains, drives foolishly in whatever direction their noses point—a herd endowed with tremendous blind power, with big bull leaders, but with minds rarely above their bellies and their dams. In the mass and at their own romantic rating, they are distinctly imposing—big-necked, redblooded, lusty, with glossy coats got from rich feeding-grounds, and with a herd power which sweeps majestically onwards in a cloud of dust of its own raising, veritable lords and masters of a continent. But considered more critically, and resolved into individual members, they appear to the realist somewhat stupid, feeble in brain and will, stuffed with conceit of their own excellence, esteeming themselves the great end for which creation has been in travail, the finest handiwork of the Most High who spread the plains for their feeding-grounds; with a vast respect for totems and fetishes; purveyors and victims of the mysterious thing called Bunk, who valiantly horn to death any audacious heretic who may suggest that rumbling about the plains, filling their bellies, bellowing sacred slogans, and cornering the lushest grass

*are scarcely adequate objectives for such immense power: a vast middleman herd that dominates the continent, but cannot reduce it to order or decency . . . "God help the country," said Fenimore Cooper years ago when this herd was small, "that has only commercial towns for its capitals." "Such a country is past helping," retorts Sinclair Lewis . . . a people that worships the great god Bunk shall have its reward! ***

Alas, Lewis seemed to be saying, what has happened to the "Democratic Vistas," those expanses of freedom in which Whitman thought he saw individualism in America fully realized? They have narrowed to "Main Street," where every right-minded citizen seemed to him to look as much like every other citizen as possible. America, Parrington claimed, has become a Babbittry. This is the point to which science and industrialism have led us. Puritanism, Lewis argued, takes up its home at present in clerical fundamentalists and in the religious wives of the self-righteous but unscrupulous businessmen. And, Sinclair Lewis maintained, man is a lonely animal in private, a loud-speaking, club-joining egotist in public.

Lewis is a satirist, and satire does not become a form of literature until a society has sufficiently settled in a mold to afford the artist precise material to make fun of. Disillusioned by material progress, Sinclair Lewis is still an echo, nevertheless, of Rousseau and the golden hope of the French philosophy of enlightenment. Lewis would like to see some sort of practical Utopia in America. In many of his books he evidently felt that if he satirized human nature it would somehow better itself. He looked, for example, to the doctor to rescue science from commercial prostitution and ended by concluding that in America this could not be done unless the doctor became a hermit. He got out a search warrant for an artist true to the spirit of America, and found that artist to be a successful hotel-keeper, a real he-man who made an art of life. As for the "professional" religious men in America, Lewis could not stomach them. His religion was science, about which he was quite sentimental. Somehow, anyhow, Lewis seemed to be saying at this point in his career, we can still find a way to enlighten a people who do not want to be enlightened.

But before Lewis had lived much longer, "radical" thought was leading into channels he did not like. He viewed Germany with alarm, but he also viewed American radical youth with alarm. And in *The Prodigal Parents* we behold the curious spectacle of the critic of Babbitt suddenly becoming the lover of Babbittry. Actually, of course, Lewis had always been very definitely one of his own American Babbitts. He had been the bad boy among them, the joker who loved to poke fun at them. Threatened, however, by "radical youth," Lewis (until the end of the second war clarified anew for him the problems of racial discrimination and inspired him to write *Kingsblood Royal*) fled back to his armchair and his big cigar, and found his Rotary Club a very congenial place in which to reminisce over the general stability of the good old-fashioned American businessman and the virtues of individualism.

IN SUMMARY

❦ BUT DESPITE Sinclair Lewis' belated defense, clearly, in America, as earlier in England, many writers found the day of optimistic individualism over by the end of the 1920's. In actual fact, as our more thoughtful writers had seen, America was already at the crossroads by the time of World War I. Never so conscious politically as the English of what was going on in Europe, Americans had not so soon realized that in their country the growth of large industries, monopolistic business practices, wage and job competition, were leading to some of the same dangers as already threatened Europe. In America the earlier

* From *Main Currents in American Thought* (p. 362) by Vernon Parrington (1930). Reprinted by permission of Harcourt, Brace and Company, Inc.

conceptions of individualism had enjoyed a somewhat longer breathing spell, but already we were, even more than the English, a people herded into huge cities with their penthouses and their slums. Already, as we shall see even more clearly in our next chapter, we had our writers critical of a culture leaning toward the worship of financial success. Some of them stated their conviction that neither our puritanism nor our anti-puritanism, neither our revolutionary heritage nor its several antitheses, could make us deviate vitally from the pattern of the other and older cultures with their stratifications of rich and poor.

This survey of English and American literature has, of course, neglected many of the minor aspects of the literary scene. For reasons of space we have passed over this scene rapidly. Such changes as industrialism wrought had been long in coming and yet had been lit-

tle commented on until the First World War gave us writers whose resentment rose in a chorus. Literature now described man as trapped by his own invention, the machine. A few writers, moreover, saw him as free only when he realized that political freedom could be worthless without economic freedom. But the time had not yet come when most of the writers would urge social change. There was a war to be fought, and in our next essay we turn to examine the Waste Land of doubt and despair which was the First World War's aftermath. If the late romantic writers dreamed of a prolonged sunset, of the golden light of belief still dim on the hills, the writers of the war and of the Waste Land caused thereby walked in darkness, negating all belief in human goodness, clinging to that residue of the past recorded by art for any proof of man's now forgotten greatness. (E. L. W.)

❦ Puritanism and the Frontier

EDWIN ARLINGTON ROBINSON

Edwin Arlington Robinson, born in Head Tide, Maine, December 22, 1869, was the last child of a puritan family of moderate means. He was an intelligent though dreamy child, and his parents seemed to feel that he would work out his own destiny. By the time he was of college age family illness and misfortune made it necessary for him to help support his parents and a sick brother; and it was not until 1891 that he was able to save enough money to enter Harvard. Always alien to commercially successful people, Robinson came to see in his own family—in his delicate mother, his brother whose health and spirit were broken by the strain of his medical practice—that the more intelligent and sensitive often fail in our society.

The Robinson family had moved to Gardiner, Maine, the "Tilbury Town" of later poems; and the young boy sought out for friendship the town misfits, the philosophers and the literary. In the two years at Harvard he came in contact for the first time with young minds like his own, and he developed rapidly, choosing what courses most interested him and finding friends who were interested in his verse writing. But his mother's death and his father's illness compelled him to return to Gardiner, where neither of his elder brothers was able to keep poverty from the door. The devoted family was beginning to disintegrate. Robinson was worried and exhausted, but he had not entirely given up his writing. In 1896 he published privately, since no publisher would accept it, *The Torrent and the Night Before*. The poetry was immediately attacked as viewing the world as a prison house. To this Robinson answered, "The world is not a prison house but a kind of

spiritual kindergarten, where millions of bewildered infants are trying to spell God with the wrong blocks."

In 1897, released from too much family pressure, Robinson came to New York, beginning the long years of living in cheap rooming houses. He was sure of one thing: that come what might, he was a poet and must use the only gift that had been given him. He felt himself to be a failure in the business world; but seeing that many sensitive people were failures, he persisted in his own work. In 1897 he published *Children of the Night*. No shout of acclaim went up. Robinson came to know such recognized literary figures as William Vaughn Moody, Ridgely Torrence, and Percy MacKaye, who helped him as best they could—chiefly by encouragement, for he was not one to seek financial assistance. He was furious when his working as a checker in the New York subway was publicized, for he felt that such advertising, when his talent was still unknown, vulgarized him. Eventually his friends brought his situation to the attention of President Theodore Roosevelt, who had read *Children of the Night;* and the poet was offered economic security in the form of a position in the Customs House which he held from 1905 until 1910, rigorously performing his duties. In 1910 he began to devote all his time to writing; *The Town Down the River* was published, and with this volume and the publicity given him by the President, Robinson's work began to be known. Soon, moreover, he had a place in which to work. Mrs. Edward MacDowell invited him to the MacDowell Colony at Peterborough, New Hampshire, and although he went with a telegram in his pocket recalling him to New York, he soon came so to love this artists' colony as to regard it as his summer home and workshop. In 1916 he published *The Man Against the Sky* and, backed by Harriet Monroe and the dauntless Amy Lowell, was recognized finally as a leading American poet.

Robinson, in his clear Yankee rhythms, summed up in poetry the transcendentalism of the late puritan age. As a puritan he opposed the materialistic philosophy of success. The characters of his short early poems were expanded and elaborated upon in his long later poems, and all of them were the sensitive, earnest individualists who believed that human dignity meant using one's own talents, whatever direction they took, and did not mean the obvious social success of money making. Robinson hated greed and complacency. He saw America following the same downward course into spiritual chaos as had Europe. In this his thinking was ahead of his time, though in his rejection of science because of its materialism he sometimes seemed almost reactionary. He refused to accept the Darwinian theory of man's creation, yet he was ahead of his period in understanding of psychology. He wanted an explanation of life which granted men dignity if they persisted in their struggle against evil. Rejecting the puritan belief in Hell, Robinson held that men were their brothers' keepers. For him art was a kind of moral weapon. In his later books, *Merlin* (1917), *The Three Taverns* and *Lancelot* (1920), *Avon's Harvest* (1921), and *Collected Poems* (1924), Robinson was commenting upon the conditions which had given birth to the First World War. Like Tennyson he used the Arthurian cycle, but unlike Tennyson, who interpreted these tales according to Victorian morality, Robinson treated of them as an allegory of the way in which greed and power destroy a kingdom. All his long inner dramas, *The Man Who Died Twice* (1924), *Cavender's House* (1929), *The Glory of the Nightingales* (1930), and *Matthias at the Door* (1931) have to do with the moral contradictions in our society, and *King Jasper*, published posthumously (1935), foretold another world war as a conflict between two brutal, power-mad, and mechanized societies which would obliterate civiliza-

tion. At the end of the poem only Zoe (life or experience) survives the holocaust. Thus symbolically Robinson asserted his belief that life is unquenchable.

Unlike Frost, Robinson was a cosmopolitan. While Frost explored the backwaters of puritanism, Robinson studied the intellectual, educated, city-dwelling men, the same type of "last puritan" that Santayana examined in his novel. These characters were, of course, aspects of himself, phases of good and evil or of man's conscience. Although he tried, Robinson could not write actual dramas. He could write the drama of psychological and very subjective conflicts.

Robinson used every form of verse but predominantly the sonnet and blank verse, which he made his own and to which he fitted the speech rhythms of the cultivated Yankee. "I don't know whether I'm a great poet or not," he once remarked. "Time alone can tell about that. But I do know that I've never consciously injured anyone, and that at least is something." Such a statement indicates the purposes to which Robinson put his poetry. Always he was psychologically acute and morally concerned about the significance of what he portrayed.

In Peterborough, Robinson became the center of an admiring group of younger writers, but he never sought to make them his disciples. The dignity of the tall, thin, always a little lonely man, whose bushy eyebrows were more expressive than speech, was unforgettable. By 1934 it was obvious that his health was failing; an operation was unsuccessful. Many of those who saw him in his last days realized that he was dying with the same consideration he had shown others during his entire life. He never complained or denied his friends, and one of his last gestures was to give to a typical failure, whom he had long known and who had indeed long been seeking handouts, the five dollars for which he asked.

Robinson died April 6, 1935. *King Jasper* was published that year, with a beautiful introduction by Robert Frost. A final *Collected Poems* appeared in 1937. The book written by his friend Hermann Hagedorn, *Edwin Arlington Robinson, A Biography,* is a touching, if somewhat sentimental, account of Robinson's long struggle to be an artist.

The Man Against the Sky

BETWEEN me and the sunset, like a dome
Against the glory of a world on fire,
Now burned a sudden hill,
Bleak, round and high, by flame-lit height
    made higher,
With nothing on it for the flame to kill   5
Save one who moved and was alone up there
To loom before the chaos and the glare
As if he were the last god going home
Unto his last desire.   9

Dark, marvelous, and inscrutable he moved on
Till down the fiery distance he was gone,
Like one of those eternal, remote things
That range across a man's imaginings
When a sure music fills him and he knows   14
What he may say thereafter to few men—
The touch of ages having wrought
An echo and a glimpse of what he thought
A phantom or a legend until then;
For whether lighted over ways that save,
Or lured from all repose,   20
If he go on too far to find a grave,
Mostly alone he goes.

Even he, who stood where I had found him,
On high with fire all round him,
Who moved along the molten west,   25
And over the round hill's crest
That seemed half ready with him to go down,
Flame-bitten and flame-cleft,
As if there were to be no last thing left
Of a nameless unimaginable town—   30
Even he who climbed and vanished may have
    taken
Down to the perils of a depth not known,
From death defended, though by men for-
    saken,
The bread that every man must eat alone;

"The Man Against the Sky," "Cassandra," "Flammonde," and "Mr. Flood's Party," from *Collected Poems*, by Edwin Arlington Robinson. Copyright, 1921, by The Macmillan Company. Reprinted by permission of The Macmillan Company.
The Man Against the Sky. The poem is Robinson's statement of his late Puritan faith; a faith based largely on the feeling that there must be some reason for living other than that implied by the materialist concept of the universe. Since all men die alone, they die as they have lived, striving to the end for what they believe in, some relying on an easy optimism, others pretending to believe in any one of the iconoclastic attitudes of the modern world. None of these will Robinson accept. He holds that we would not continue to bear children and to project life if all we held true were the mechanistic laws of science. Therefore, he argues, the word of God, although dimly understood, must be that to which we cling.

He may have walked while others hardly
    dared   35
Look on to see him stand where many fell;
And upward out of that, as out of hell,
He may have sung and striven
To mount where more of him shall yet be
    given,
Bereft of all retreat,   40
To sevenfold heat—
As on a day when three in Dura shared
The furnace, and were spared
For glory by that king of Babylon
Who made himself so great that God, who
    heard,   45
Covered him with long feathers, like a bird.

Again, he may have gone down easily,
By comfortable altitudes, and found,
As always, underneath him solid ground
Whereon to be sufficient and to stand   50
Possessed already of the promised land,
Far stretched and fair to see:
A good sight, verily,
And one to make the eyes of her who bore him
Shine glad with hidden tears.   55
Why question of his ease of who before him,
In one place or another where they left
Their names as far behind them as their bones
And yet by dint of slaughter, toil, and theft,
And shrewdly sharpened stones,   60
Carved hard the way for his ascendency
Through deserts of lost years?
Why trouble him now who sees and hears
No more than what his innocence requires,
And therefore to no other height aspires   65
Than one at which he neither quails nor tires?
He may do more by seeing what he sees
Than others eager for iniquities;
He may, by seeing all things for the best,
Incite futurity to do the rest.   70

Or with an even likelihood,
He may have met with atrabilious eyes
The fires of time on equal terms and passed
Indifferently down, until at last
His only kind of grandeur would have been,   75
Apparently, in being seen.
He may have had for evil or for good

42. **three . . . furnace.** Shadrach, Meshach, and Abednego were placed in a furnace by the Babylonian king, but survived the ordeal unscathed. (Cf. Daniel 3.) 46. **long feathers.** Nebuchadnezzar was condemned to go on all fours and to live off grass. In old pictures he is always represented as covered with feathers or fur.

No argument; he may have had no care
For what without himself went anywhere
To failure or to glory, and least of all   80
For such a stale, flamboyant miracle;
He may have been the prophet of an art
Immovable to old idolatries;
He may have been a player without a part,
Annoyed that even the sun should have the
    skies   85
For such a flaming way to advertise;
He may have been a painter sick at heart
With Nature's toiling for a new surprise;
He may have been a cynic, who now, for all
Of anything divine that his effete   90
Negation may have tasted,
Saw truth in his own image, rather small,
Forbore to fever the ephemeral,
Found any barren height a good retreat
From any swarming street,   95
And in the sun saw power superbly wasted:
And when the primitive old-fashioned stars
Came out again to shine on joys and wars
More primitive, and all arrayed for doom,
He may have proved a world a sorry thing   100
In his imagining,
And life a lighted highway to the tomb.

Or, mounting with infirm unsearching tread,
His hopes to chaos led,   104
He may have stumbled up there from the past,
And with an aching strangeness viewed the
    last
Abysmal conflagration of his dreams—
A flame where nothing seems
To burn but flame itself, by nothing fed;
And while it all went out,   110
Not even the faint anodyne of doubt
May then have eased a painful going down
From pictured heights of power and lost re-
    nown,
Revealed at length to his outlived endeavor
Remote and unapproachable forever;   115
And at his heart there may have gnawed
Sick memories of a dead faith foiled and
    flawed
And long dishonored by the living death
Assigned alike by chance
To brutes and hierophants;   120
And anguish fallen on those he loved around
    him

120. **hierophants,** priests.

May once have dealt the last blow to confound
    him,
And so have left him as death leaves a child,
Who sees it all too near;   124
And he who knows no young way to forget
May struggle to the tomb unreconciled.
Whatever suns may rise or set
There may be nothing kinder for him here
Than shafts and agonies;
And under these   130
He may cry out and stay on horribly;
Or, seeing in death too small a thing to fear,
He may go forward like a stoic Roman
Where pangs and terrors in his pathway lie—
Or, seizing the swift logic of a woman,   135
Curse God and die.

Or maybe there, like many another one
Who might have stood aloft and looked ahead,
Black-drawn against wild red,
He may have built, unawed by fiery gules   140
That in him no commotion stirred,
A living reason out of molecules
Why molecules occurred,
And one for smiling when he might have
    sighed
Had he seen far enough   145
And in the same inevitable stuff
Discovered an odd reason too for pride
In being what he must have been by laws
Infrangible and for no kind of cause.
Deterred by no confusion or surprise   150
He may have seen with his mechanic eyes
A world without a meaning, and had room,
Alone amid magnificence and doom,
To build himself an airy monument   154
That should, or fail him in his vague intent,
Outlast an accidental universe—
To call it nothing worse—
Or, by the burrowing guile
Of Time disintegrated and effaced,   159
Like once-remembered mighty trees go down
To ruin, of which by man may now be traced
No part sufficient even to be rotten,
And in the book of things that are forgotten
Is entered as a thing not quite worth while.
He may have been so great   165
That satraps would have shivered at his
    frown,

136. **Curse . . . die.** Job's wife's advice to him during his great tribulations (Job 2:9). 166. **satraps,** governors of a province under the ancient Persian empire.

And all he prized alive may rule a state
No larger than a grave that holds a clown;
He may have been a master of his fate,
And of his atoms—ready as another   170
In his emergence to exonerate
His father and his mother;
He may have been a captain of a host,
Self-eloquent and ripe for prodigies,   174
Doomed here to swell by dangerous degrees,
And then give up the ghost.
Nahum's great grasshoppers were such as
    these,
Sun-scattered and soon lost.

Whatever the dark road he may have taken,
This man who stood on high   180
And faced alone the sky,
Whatever drove or lured or guided him—
A vision answering a faith unshaken,
An easy trust assumed of easy trials,
A sick negation born of weak denials,   185
A crazed abhorrence of an old condition,
A blind attendance on a brief ambition—
Whatever stayed him or derided him,
His way was even as ours;
And we, with all our wounds and all our pow-
    ers,   190
Must each await alone at his own height
Another darkness or another light;
And there, of our poor self dominion reft,
If inference and reason shun
Hell, Heaven, and Oblivion,   195
May thwarted will (perforce precarious,
But for our conservation better thus)
Have no misgiving left
Of doing yet what here we leave undone?
Of if unto the last of these we cleave,   200
Believing or protesting we believe
In such an idle and ephemeral
Florescence of the diabolical—
If, robbed of two fond old enormities,
Our being had no onward auguries,   205
What then were this great love of ours to say
For launching other lives to voyage again
A little farther into time and pain,
A little faster in a futile chase
For a kingdom and a power and a Race   210

177. **Nahum's great grasshoppers,** a reference to the vision of Nahum, prophesying the destruction of Nineveh (Nahum 3:17): "Thy crowned are as the locusts, and thy captains as the great grasshoppers, which camp in the hedges in the cold day, but when the sun ariseth they flee away, and their place is not known where they are."

That would have still in sight
A manifest end of ashes and eternal night?
Is this the music of the toys we shake
So loud—as if there might be no mistake
Somewhere in our indomitable will?   215
Are we no greater than the noise we make
Along one blind atomic pilgrimage
Whereon by crass chance billeted we go
Because our brains and bones and cartilage
Will have it so?   220
If this we say, then let us all be still
About our share in it, and live and die
More quietly thereby.

Where was he going, this man against the sky?
You know not, nor do I.   225
But this we know, if we know anything:
That we may laugh and fight and sing
And of our transience here make offering
To an orient Word that will not be erased,
Or, save in incommunicable gleams   230
Too permanent for dreams,
Be found or known.
No tonic or ambitious irritant
Of increase or of want
Has made an otherwise insensate waste   235
Of ages overthrown
A ruthless, veiled, implacable foretaste
Of other ages that are still to be
Depleted and rewarded variously
Because a few, by fate's economy   240
Shall seem to move the world the way it goes,
No soft evangel of equality,
Safe-cradled in a communal repose
That huddles into death and may at last
Be covered well with equatorial snows—   245
And all for what, the devil only knows—
Will aggregate an inkling to confirm
The credit of a sage or of a worm,
Or tell us why one man in five
Should have a care to stay alive   250
While in his heart he feels no violence
Laid on his humor and intelligence
When infant Science makes a pleasant face
And waves again that hollow toy, the Race;
No planetary trap where souls are wrought
For nothing but the sake of being caught   256
And sent again to nothing will attune
Itself to any key of any reason
Why man should hunger through another sea-
    son

To find out why 'twere better late than soon
To go away and let the sun and moon   261
And all the silly stars illuminate
A place for creeping things,
And those that root and trumpet and have
        wings,
And herd and ruminate,   265
Or dive and flash and poise in rivers and seas,
Or by their loyal tails in lofty trees
Hang screeching lewd victorious derision
Of man's immortal vision.
Shall we, because Eternity records   270
Too vast an answer for the time-born words
We spell, whereof so many are dead that once
In our capricious lexicons
Were so alive and final, hear no more
The Word itself, the living word   275
That none alive has ever heard
Or ever spelt,
And few have ever felt
Without the fears and old surrenderings
And terrors that began   280
When Death let fall a feather from his wings
And humbled the first man?
Because the weight of our humility,
Wherefrom we gain
A little wisdom and much pain,   285
Falls here too sore and there too tedious,
Are we in anguish or complacency,
Not looking far enough ahead
To see by what mad couriers we are led
Along the roads of the ridiculous,   290
To pity ourselves and laugh at faith
And while we curse life bear it?
And if we see the soul's dead end in death,
Are we to fear it?
What folly is here that has not yet a name   295
Unless we say outright that we are liars?
What have we seen beyond our sunset fires
That lights again the way by which we came?
Why pay we such a price, and one we give
So clamoringly, for each racked empty day   300
That leads one more last human hope away,
As quiet fiends would lead past our crazed
        eyes
Our children to an unseen sacrifice?
If after all that we have lived and thought,
All comes to Nought—   305
If there be nothing after Now,
And we be nothing anyhow,
And we know that—why live?

'Twere sure but weaklings' vain distress
To suffer dungeons where so many doors   310
Will open on the cold eternal shores
That look sheer down
To the dark tideless floods of Nothingness
Where all who know may drown.

Cassandra

I HEARD one who said: "Verily,
    What word have I for children here?
Your Dollar is your only Word,
    The wrath of it your only fear.

"You build it altars tall enough   5
    To make you see, but you are blind;
You cannot leave it long enough
    To look before you or behind.

"When Reason beckons you to pause,
    You laugh and say that you know best;   10
But what it is you know, you keep
    As dark as ingots in a chest.

"You laugh and answer, 'We are young;
    O leave us now, and let us grow.'—
Not asking how much more of this   15
    Will Time endure or Fate bestow.

"Because a few complacent years
    Have made your peril of your pride,
Think you that you are to go on
    Forever pampered and untried?   20

"What lost eclipse of history,
    What bivouac of the marching stars,
Has given the sign for you to see
    Millenniums and last great wars?

"What unrecorded overthrow   25
    Of all the world has ever known,
Or ever been, has made itself
    So plain to you, and you alone?

"Your Dollar, Dove and Eagle make
    A Trinity that even you   30

Cassandra, in Greek myth the daughter of Priam and Hecuba, who was gifted with the power of prophecy, but cursed in that no one would believe her. Here Robinson indicates that her prophecy for America has gone unheard.

Rate higher than you rate yourselves;
    It pays, it flatters, and it's new.

"And though your very flesh and blood
    Be what your Eagle eats and drinks,
You'll praise him for the best of birds,   35
    Not knowing what the Eagle thinks.

"The power is yours, but not the sight;
    You see not upon what you tread;
You have the ages for your guide,
    But not the wisdom to be led.   40

"Think you to tread forever down
    The merciless old verities?
And are you never to have eyes
    To see the world for what it is?

"Are you to pay for what you have   45
    With all you are?"—No other word
We caught, but with a laughing crowd
    Moved on. None heeded, and few heard.

Flammonde

THE MAN Flammonde, from God knows
    where,
With firm address and foreign air,
With news of nations in his talk
And something royal in his walk,
With glint of iron in his eyes,   5
But never doubt, nor yet surprise,
Appeared, and stayed, and held his head
As one by kings accredited.

Erect, with his alert repose
About him, and about his clothes,   10
He pictured all tradition hears
Of what we owe to fifty years.
His cleansing heritage of taste
Paraded neither want nor waste;
And what he needed for his fee   15
To live, he borrowed graciously.

He never told us what he was,
Or what mischance, or other cause,
Had banished him from better days
To play the Prince of Castaways.   20

Flammonde. No more a real character than any of the other creations of Robinson's mind. But names with a slight foreign cast are frequently used by this poet when he would analyze the life of a man who is not quite identifiable as the usual citizen of a New England village.

Meanwhile he played surpassing well
A part, for most, unplayable;
In fine, one pauses, half afraid
To say for certain that he played.

For that, one may as well forego   25
Conviction as to yes or no;
Nor can I say just how intense
Would then have been the difference
To several, who, having striven
In vain to get what he was given,   30
Would see the stranger taken on
By friends not easy to be won.

Moreover, many a malcontent
He soothed and found munificent;
His courtesy beguiled and foiled   35
Suspicion that his years were soiled;
His mien distinguished any crowd,
His credit strengthened when he bowed;
And women, young and old, were fond
Of looking at the man Flammonde.   40

There was a woman in our town
On whom the fashion was to frown;
But while our talk renewed the tinge
Of a long-faded scarlet fringe,
The man Flammonde saw none of that,   45
And what he saw we wondered at—
That none of us, in her distress,
Could hide or find our littleness.

There was a boy that all agreed
Had shut within him the rare seed   50
Of learning. We could understand,
But none of us could lift a hand.
The man Flammonde appraised the youth,
And told a few of us the truth;
And thereby, for a little gold,   55
A flowered future was enrolled.

There were two citizens who fought
For years and years, and over nought;
They made life awkward for their friends,
And shortened their own dividends.   60
The man Flammonde said what was wrong
Should be made right; nor was it long
Before they were again in line,
And had each other in to dine.

And these I mention are but four   65
Of many out of many more.
So much for them. But what of him—

So firm in every look and limb?
What small satanic sort of kink
Was in his brain? What broken link   70
Withheld him from the destinies
That came so near to being his?

What was he, when we came to sift
His meaning, and to note the drift
Of incommunicable ways   75
That make us ponder while we praise?
Why was it that his charm revealed
Somehow the surface of a shield?
What was it that we never caught?
What was he, and what was he not?   80

How much it was of him we met
We cannot ever know; nor yet
Shall all he gave us quite atone
For what was his, and his alone;
Nor need we now, since he knew best,   85
Nourish an ethical unrest:
Rarely at once will nature give
The power to be Flammonde and live.

We cannot know how much we learn
From those who never will return,   90
Until a flash of unforeseen
Remembrance falls on what has been.
We've each a darkening hill to climb;
And this is why, from time to time
In Tilbury Town, we looked beyond   95
Horizons for the man Flammonde.

Mr. Flood's Party

OLD EBEN FLOOD, climbing alone one night
Over the hill between the town below
And the forsaken upland hermitage
That held as much as he should ever know
On earth again of home, paused warily.   5
The road was his with not a native near;
And Eben, having leisure, said aloud,
For no man else in Tilbury Town to hear:

'Well, Mr. Flood, we have the harvest moon
Again, and we may not have many more;   10
The bird is on the wing, the poet says,
And you and I have said it here before.
Drink to the bird.' He raised up to the light
The jug that he had gone so far to fill,

And answered huskily: 'Well, Mr. Flood,   15
Since you propose it, I believe I will.'

Alone, as if enduring to the end
A valiant armor of scarred hopes outworn,
He stood there in the middle of the road
Like Roland's ghost winding a silent horn.   20
Below him, in the town among the trees,
Where friends of other days had honored him,
A phantom salutation of the dead
Rang thinly till old Eben's eyes were dim.

Then, as a mother lays her sleeping child   25
Down tenderly, fearing it may awake,
He set the jug down slowly at his feet
With trembling care, knowing that most things
      break;
And only when assured that on firm earth
It stood, as the uncertain lives of men   30
Assuredly did not, he paced away,
And with his hand extended paused again:

'Well, Mr. Flood, we have not met like this
In a long time; and many a change has come
To both of us, I fear, since last it was   35
We had a drop together. Welcome home!'
Convivially returning with himself,
Again he raised the jug up to the light;
And with an acquiescent quaver said:
'Well, Mr. Flood, if you insist, I might.   40

'Only a very little, Mr. Flood—
For auld lang syne. No more, sir; that will do.'
So, for the time, apparently it did,
And Eben evidently thought so too;
For soon amid the silver loneliness   45
Of night he lifted up his voice and sang,
Secure, with only two moons listening,
Until the whole harmonious landscape rang—

'For auld lang syne.' The weary throat gave
      out,   49
The last word wavered, and the song was done.
He raised again the jug regretfully
And shook his head, and was again alone.
There was not much that was ahead of him,
And there was nothing in the town below—
Where strangers would have shut the many
      doors   55
That many friends had opened long ago.

20. **Roland,** the great hero of medieval French legend, who used to summon assistance with his magic horn, Olivant.

Miniver Cheevy

Miniver Cheevy, child of scorn,
Grew lean while he assailed the seasons;
He wept that he was ever born,
And he had reasons.

Miniver loved the days of old   5
When swords were bright and steeds were
    prancing;
The vision of a warrior bold
Would set him dancing.

Miniver sighed for what was not,   9
And dreamed, and rested from his labors;
He dreamed of Thebes and Camelot,
And Priam's neighbors.

Miniver mourned the ripe renown
That made so many a name so fragrant;
He mourned Romance, now on the town,   15
And Art, a vagrant.

Miniver loved the Medici,
Albeit he had never seen one;
He would have sinned incessantly
Could he have been one.   20

Miniver cursed the commonplace
And eyed a khaki suit with loathing;
He missed the mediaeval grace
Of iron clothing.

Miniver scorned the gold he sought,   25
But sore annoyed was he without it;
Miniver thought, and thought, and thought,
And thought about it.

Miniver Cheevy, born too late,   29
Scratched his head and kept on thinking;
Miniver coughed, and called it fate,
And kept on drinking.

How Annandale Went Out

They called it Annandale—and I was there
To flourish, to find words, and to attend:
Liar, physician, hypocrite, and friend,
I watched him; and the sight was not so fair
As one or two that I have seen elsewhere: 5
An apparatus not for me to mend—
A wreck, with hell between him and the end,
Remained of Annandale; and I was there.

"I knew the ruin as I knew the man;
So put the two together, if you can,   10
Remembering the worst you know of me.
Now view yourself as I was, on the spot,
With a slight kind of engine. Do you see?
Like this . . . You wouldn't hang me? I
    thought not."

The Garden of the Nations

When we that are the bitten flower and
    fruit
Of time's achievement are undone between
The blight above, where blight has always
    been,
And the old worm of evil at the root,
We shall not have to crumble destitute   5
Of recompense, or measure our chagrin;
We shall be dead, and so shall not be seen
Amid the salvage of our disrepute.

And when we are all gone, shall mightier seeds
And scions of a warmer spring put forth   10
A bloom and fruitage of a larger worth
Than ours? God save the garden, if by chance,
Or by approved short sight, more numerous
    weeds
And weevils be the next inheritance!

"Miniver Cheevy" and "How Annandale Went Out" reprinted from *The Town Down the River* by Edwin Arlington Robinson; copyright, 1910, by Charles Scribner's Sons, 1938, by Ruth Niveson; used by permission of the Publisher, Charles Scribner's Sons.
Miniver Cheevy. Mr. Robinson's most famous poem on the misfit in the modern age. Here he is the romantic who fools himself. 11. **Thebes,** chief city of Boeotia, Greece; rich in association with Greek legend. **Camelot,** the traditional seat of King Arthur and his court. 12. **Priam,** Trojan king who married Hecuba and had many famous children. 17. **Medici,** the famous Florentine family of the fourteenth to seventeenth centuries.

How Annandale Went Out. This name turns up again in the long poem "The Book of Annandale," another study of a man whose creativeness was frustrated and never allowed to mature fully. The poem is another of Robinson's studies of the hidden contradictions in life. 13. **slight kind of engine,** obviously a hypodermic needle. This type of obscure epithet for a person or an act is a common poetic trick of Robinson's. Usually it is used to avoid bluntness.
"The Garden of the Nations" from E. A. Robinson: *Dionysius in Doubt;* copyright, 1925, by The Macmillan Company and used with their permission.
The Garden of the Nations. Robinson visited England the year (1923) this poem was written.

ROBERT FROST

Returning from England in 1915 because of the war, Robert Frost found himself famous. Behind this fame, however, lay twenty years of hard and until then unrecognized work. This most New England of New England poets was born March 26, 1876, in San Francisco, California, and was named Robert Lee because of his father's copperhead sympathies with the South. When the boy was ten years old his father died, and his Scottish mother brought her children to their paternal grandfather in Lawrence, Massachusetts.

Once through public school Frost spent a few months at Dartmouth, but he left college shortly to teach in country schools and to work on farms and as a bobbin-boy in the mills. It was then that he gained his knowledge of the rural New Englanders whose long winters of loneliness and moments of tragedy are recorded in his poetry. In 1895 he married Elinor White, who in 1897 persuaded him to return to his college studies. This time he went to Harvard, but finding it still impossible to overcome his distaste for academic studies, he left to teach and farm in Derry, New Hampshire.

Unsuccessful in publishing his poetry, and wanting a new perspective on his native land, Frost sold his farm in 1912 and took his family to England, where for the first time he met poets and writers and where, when he was thirty-seven, his first book of poems, *A Boy's Will*, was published. English critics warmly welcomed the new poet, and with the publication in 1914 of *North of Boston*, Frost was recognized as one of America's leading poets.

World War I forced him to return to the United States, and he took up residence near Franconia, New Hampshire. Presented to the American public by that vigorous and strenuous champion of new poetic movements, Amy Lowell, the once spurned poet soon found it easy to publish. Before long the academic world also recognized him by the conferring of honorary degrees.

From 1916 to 1920 Frost was Professor in Residence at Amherst College, holding informal seminars and talking with the college poets. *Mountain Interval,* published in 1916, contains some of his finest lyrics. In 1920 he helped to found the Bread Loaf School of English, where he lectures annually. Between 1921 and 1923 he was Poet in Residence at the University of Michigan. *New Hampshire* (1923) won the Pulitzer Prize. After 1926 he returned to Amherst as an informal adviser to young poets. *West-Running Brook* appeared in 1928, *Selected Poems* in 1923 and 1928, and *Collected Poems* in 1930 and 1939. *Collected Poems* won the Pulitzer Prize in 1930. *A Further Range* (1936) shows that his contacts with youth had forced him to consider some of the problems of modern society. Essentially he argues for the poet as a commentator and not as an actor in the historical struggle. His later books are his *Collected Poems* and *Come In* (1943); his commentary on the Book of Job, entitled *A Masque of Reason* (1945); *Steeple Bush* (1947), and *A Masque of Mercy* (1948). In the poetic drama *A Masque of Reason,* Job, after a thousand years, finds out why God put him through his long test:

I've had you on my mind a thousand years
To thank you someday for the way you helped
   me
Establish once for all the principle
There's no connection man can reason out
Between his just deserts and what he gets.

Most of Frost's poems come to a boil slowly. First he describes a real experience; then he makes us aware of the overtones of the experience. Note how in "After Apple-Picking" the sense of physical weariness is conveyed; then suddenly Frost gives this weariness its larger, universal application:

For I have had too much
Of apple-picking: I am overtired
Of the great harvest I myself desired.

Frost's poetic material is often taken directly from the hard and lonely life of the small New England farmer, the last puritan, whom he knows so well, whose psychology and turns of speech he has so accurately recorded in his verse. In general, Frost's poetry falls into two groups: the dramatic monologues, usually in rough blank verse, and the lyrics, in which the poet speaks for himself. To Frost, imaginative truth, recorded in the mind, springs from the objective world with its smells and sights and sounds.

Acquainted with the Night

I HAVE been one acquainted with the night.
I have walked out in rain—and back in rain.
I have outwalked the furthest city light.

I have looked down the saddest city lane.
I have passed by the watchman on his beat   5
And dropped my eyes, unwilling to explain.

I have stood still and stopped the sound of
     feet
When far away an interrupted cry
Came over houses from another street,

But not to call me back or say good-bye;   10
And further still at an unearthly height,
One luminary clock against the sky

Proclaimed the time was neither wrong nor
     right.
I have been one acquainted with the night.

The Aim Was Song

BEFORE man came to blow it right
     The wind once blew itself untaught,
And did its loudest day and night
     In any rough place where it caught.

"Acquainted with the Night" from *West-Running Brook*; "The Aim Was Song," "Stopping by Woods on a Snowy Evening," "To Earthward," "For Once, Then, Something," "Good-Bye and Keep Cold," "Our Singing Strength," and "A Brook in the City" from *New Hampshire*; "A Lone Striker" and "To a Thinker" from *A Further Range*; "Home Burial," "The Death of the Hired Man," "Mending Wall," and "After Apple-Picking" from *North of Boston*; "Birches" from *Mountain Interval*; and an excerpt from *A Masque of Reason* (copyright, 1945, by Robert Frost), reprinted by permission of Henry Holt and Company.

Man came to tell it what was wrong: 5
     It hadn't found the place to blow;
It blew too hard—the aim was song.
     And listen—how it ought to go!

He took a little in his mouth,
     And held it long enough for north   10
To be converted into south,
     And then by measure blew it forth.

By measure. It was word and note,
     The wind the wind had meant to be—
A little through the lips and throat.   15
     The aim was song—the wind could see.

Stopping by Woods on a Snowy Evening

WHOSE woods these are I think I know.
     His house is in the village though;
He will not see me stopping here
To watch his woods fill up with snow.

My little horse must think it queer   5
To stop without a farmhouse near
Between the woods and frozen lake
The darkest evening of the year.

He gives his harness bells a shake
To ask if there is some mistake.   10
The only other sound's the sweep
Of easy wind and downy flake.

The woods are lovely, dark and deep.
But I have promises to keep,
And miles to go before I sleep,   15
And miles to go before I sleep.

To Earthward

LOVE at the lips was touch
     As sweet as I could bear;
And once that seemed too much;
I lived on air

That crossed me from sweet things,   5
The flow of—was it musk
From hidden grapevine springs
Down hill at dusk?

I had the swirl and ache
From sprays of honeysuckle   10
That when they're gathered shake
Dew on the knuckle.

I craved strong sweets, but those
Seemed strong when I was young;
The petal of the rose   15
It was that stung.

Now no joy but lacks salt
That is not dashed with pain
And weariness and fault;
I crave the stain   20

Of tears, the aftermark
Of almost too much love,
The sweet of bitter bark
And burning clove.

When stiff and sore and scarred   25
I take away my hand
From leaning on it hard
In grass and sand,

The hurt is not enough:
I long for weight and strength   30
To feel the earth as rough
To all my length.

For Once, Then, Something

OTHERS taunt me with having knelt at well-
     curbs
Always wrong to the light, so never seeing
Deeper down in the well than where the water
Gives me back in a shining surface picture
Me myself in the summer heaven godlike   5
Looking out of a wreath of fern and cloud
     puffs.
Once, when trying with chin against a well-
     curb,
I discerned, as I thought, beyond the picture,
Through the picture, a something white, un-
     certain,
Something more of the depths—and then I lost
     it.   10
Water came to rebuke the too clear water.
One drop fell from a fern, and lo, a ripple
Shook whatever it was lay there at bottom,
Blurred it, blotted it out. What was that white-
     ness?
Truth? A pebble of quartz? For once, then,
     something.

For Once, Then, Something. Frost here is answering his critics who have said he was too much a realist without flights into
the visionary or philosophic attitude toward life. He asks which
is really the greater truth, the material fact of the pebble or
abstract truth. He also hints that each man must seek truth
for himself.

Good-bye and Keep Cold

THIS saying good-bye on the edge of the
     dark
And cold to an orchard so young in the bark
Reminds me of all that can happen to harm
An orchard away at the end of the farm
All winter, cut off by a hill from the house.   5
I don't want it girdled by rabbit and mouse,
I don't want it dreamily nibbled for browse
By deer, and I don't want it budded by grouse.
(If certain it wouldn't be idle to call   9
I'd summon grouse, rabbit, and deer to the wall
And warn them away with a stick for a gun.)
I don't want it stirred by the heat of the sun.
(We made it secure against being, I hope,
By setting it out on a northerly slope.)   14
No orchard's the worse for the wintriest storm;
But one thing about it, it mustn't get warm.
"How often already you've had to be told,
Keep cold, young orchard. Good-bye and keep
     cold.
Dread fifty above more than fifty below."
I have to be gone for a season or so.   20
My business awhile is with different trees,
Less carefully nourished, less fruitful than
     these,
And such as is done to their wood with an axe—
Maples and birches and tamaracks.
I wish I could promise to lie in the night   25
And think of an orchard's arboreal plight
When slowly (and nobody comes with a light)
Its heart sinks lower under the sod.
But something has to be left to God.

Home Burial

HE SAW her from the bottom of the stairs
     Before she saw him. She was starting
          down,
Looking back over her shoulder at some fear.
She took a doubtful step and then undid it
To raise herself and look again. He spoke   5
Advancing toward her: "What is it you see
From up there always—for I want to know."
She turned and sank upon her skirts at that,
And her face changed from terrified to dull.
He said to gain time: "What is it you see,"   10
Mounting until she cowered under him.
"I will find out now—you must tell me, dear."

She, in her place refused him any help
With the least stiffening of her neck and si-
    lence.   14
She let him look, sure that he wouldn't see,
Blind creature; and a while he didn't see.
But at last he murmured, "Oh," and again,
    "Oh."

"What is it—what?" she said.
                "Just that I see."

"You don't," she challenged. "Tell me what it
    is."

"The wonder is I didn't see at once.   20
I never noticed it from here before.
I must be wonted to it—that's the reason.
The little graveyard where my people are!
So small the window frames the whole of it.
Not so much larger than a bedroom, is it? 25
There are three stones of slate and one of mar-
    ble,
Broad-shouldered little slabs there in the sun-
    light
On the sidehill. We haven't to mind *those*.
But I understand: it is not the stones, 29
But the child's mound—"

        "Don't, don't, don't, don't," she cried.

She withdrew shrinking from beneath his arm
That rested on the banister, and slid down-
    stairs;
And turned on him with such a daunting look,
He said twice over before he knew himself:
"Can't a man speak of his own child he's
    lost?"   35

"Not you! Oh, where's my hat? Oh, I don't
    need it!
I must get out of here. I must get air.
I don't know rightly whether any man can."

"Amy! Don't go to someone else this time. 39
Listen to me. I won't come down the stairs."
He sat and fixed his chin between his fists.
"There's something I should like to ask you,
    dear."

"You don't know how to ask it."

                "Help me, then."

Her fingers moved the latch for all reply.
"My words are nearly always an offense. 45

I don't know how to speak of anything
So as to please you. But I might be taught
I should suppose. I can't say I see how.
A man must partly give up being a man
With women-folk. We could have some ar-
    rangement   50
By which I'd bind myself to keep hands off
Anything special you're a-mind to name.
Though I don't like such things 'twixt those
    that love.
Two that don't love can't live together without
    them.   54
But two that do can't live together with them."
She moved the latch a little. "Don't—don't go.
Don't carry it to someone else this time.
Tell me about it if it's something human.
Let me into your grief. I'm not so much
Unlike other folks as your standing there   60
Apart would make me out. Give me my chance.
I do think, though, you overdo it a little.
What was it brought you up to think it the
    thing
To take your mother-loss of a first child
So inconsolably—in the face of love.   65
You'd think his memory might be satisfied—"

"There you go sneering now!"

                "I'm not, I'm not!
You make me angry. I'll come down to you.
God, what a woman! And it's come to this,
A man can't speak of his own child that's
    dead."   70

"You can't because you don't know how.
If you had any feeling, you that dug
With your own hand—how could you?—his lit-
    tle grave;
I saw you from that very window there,
Making the gravel leap and leap in air,   75
Leap up, like that, like that, and land so
    lightly
And roll back down the mound beside the hole.
I thought, Who is that man? I didn't know you.
And I crept down the stairs and up the stairs
To look again, and still your spade kept lifting.
Then you came in. I heard your rumbling voice
Out in the kitchen, and I don't know why, 82
But I went near to see with my own eyes.
You could sit there with the stains on your
    shoes

Of the fresh earth from your own baby's grave
And talk about your everyday concerns.   86
You had stood the spade up against the wall
Outside there in the entry, for I saw it."

"I shall laugh the worst laugh I ever laughed.
I'm cursed. God, if I don't believe I'm cursed."

"I can repeat the very words you were saying.
'Three foggy mornings and one rainy day   92
Will rot the best birch fence a man can build.'
Think of it, talk like that at such a time!
What had how long it takes a birch to rot   95
To do with what was in the darkened parlour.
You *couldn't* care! The nearest friends can go
With anyone to death, comes so far short
They might as well not try to go at all.   99
No, from the time when one is sick to death,
One is alone, and he dies more alone.
Friends make pretence of following to the
    grave,
But before one is in it, their minds are turned
And making the best of their way back to life
And living people, and things they understand.
But the world's evil. I won't have grief so   106
If I can change it. Oh, I won't, I won't!"

"There, you have said it all and you feel better.
You won't go now. You're crying. Close the
    door.   109
The heart's gone out of it: why keep it up.
Amy! There's someone coming down the road!"

"*You*—oh, you think the talk is all. I must go—
Somewhere out of this house. How can I make
    you—"

"If—you—do!" She was opening the door wider.
"Where do you mean to go? First tell me
    that.   115
I'll follow and bring you back by force. I
will!—"

Our Singing Strength

IT SNOWED in spring on earth so dry and warm
The flakes could find no landing place to
    form.
Hordes spent themselves to make it wet and
    cold,
And still they failed of any lasting hold.   4
They made no white impression on the black.
They disappeared as if earth sent them back.

Not till from separate flakes they changed at
    night
To almost strips and tapes of ragged white
Did grass and garden ground confess it
    snowed,
And all go back to winter but the road.   10
Next day the scene was piled and puffed and
    dead.
The grass lay flattened under one great tread.
Borne down until the end almost took root,
The rangey bough anticipated fruit   14
With snowballs cupped in every opening bud.
The road alone maintained itself in mud,
Whatever its secret was of greater heat
From inward fires or brush of passing feet.

In spring more mortal singers than belong
To any one place cover us with song.   20
Thrush, bluebird, blackbird, sparrow, and
    robin throng;
Some to go further north to Hudson's Bay,
Some that have come too far north back away,
Really a very few to build and stay.   24
Now was seen how these liked belated snow.
The fields had nowhere left for them to go;
They'd soon exhausted all there was in flying;
The trees they'd had enough of with once try-
    ing
And setting off their heavy powder load.   29
They could find nothing open but the road.
So there they let their lives be narrowed in
By thousands the bad weather made akin.
The road became a channel running flocks
Of glossy birds like ripples over rocks.
I drove them under foot in bits of flight   35
That kept the ground, almost disputing right
Of way with me from apathy of wing,
A talking twitter all they had to sing.
A few I must have driven to despair
Made quick asides, but having done in air   40
A whir among white branches great and small
As in some too much carven marble hall
Where one false wing beat would have brought
    down all,
Came tamely back in front of me, the Drover,
To suffer the same driven nightmare over.   45
One such storm in a lifetime couldn't teach
    them
That back behind pursuit it couldn't reach
    them;
None flew behind me to be left alone.

Well, something for a snowstorm to have
    shown
The country's singing strength thus brought to-
    gether,   50
That though repressed and moody with the
    weather
Was none the less there ready to be freed
And sing the wildflowers up from root and
    seed.

A Lone Striker

THE SWINGING mill bell changed its rate
  To tolling like the count of fate,
And though at that the tardy ran,
One failed to make the closing gate.
There was a law of God or man   5
That on the one who came too late
The gate for half an hour be locked,
His time be lost, his pittance docked.
He stood rebuked and unemployed.
The straining mill began to shake.   10
The mill, though many, many eyed,
Had eyes inscrutably opaque;
So that he couldn't look inside
To see if some forlorn machine
Was standing idle for his sake.   15
(He couldn't hope its heart would break.)

And yet he thought he saw the scene:
The air was full of dust of wool.
A thousand yarns were under pull,
But pull so slow, with such a twist,   20
All day from spool to lesser spool,
It seldom overtaxed their strength;
They safely grew in slender length.
And if one broke by any chance,
The spinner saw it at a glance.   25
The spinner still was there to spin.
That's where the human still came in.
Her deft hand showed with finger rings
Among the harp-like spread of strings.
She caught the pieces end to end   30
And, with a touch that never missed,
Not so much tied as made them blend.
Man's ingenuity was good.
He saw it plainly where he stood,
Yet found it easy to resist.   35

He knew another place, a wood,
And in it, tall as trees, were cliffs;

And if he stood on one of these,
'Twould be among the tops of trees,   39
Their upper branches round him wreathing,
Their breathing mingled with his breathing.
If—if he stood! Enough of ifs!
He knew a path that wanted walking;
He knew a spring that wanted drinking;
A thought that wanted further thinking;   45
A love that wanted re-renewing.
Nor was this just a way of talking
To save him the expense of doing.
With him it boded action, deed.

The factory was very fine;   50
He wished it all the modern speed.
Yet, after all, 'twas not divine,
That is to say, 'twas not a church.
He never would assume that he'd
Be any institution's need.   55
But he said then and still would say
If there should ever come a day
When industry seemed like to die
Because he left it in the lurch,
Or even merely seemed to pine   60
For want of his approval, why
Come get him—they knew where to search.

To a Thinker

THE LAST step taken found your heft
  Decidedly upon the left.
One more would throw you on the right.
Another still—you see your plight.
You call this thinking, but it's walking.   5
Not even that, it's only rocking,
Or weaving like a stabled horse:
From force to matter and back to force,
From form to content and back to form,
From norm to crazy and back to norm,   10
From bound to free and back to bound,
From sound to sense and back to sound.
So back and forth. It almost scares
A man the way things come in pairs.
Just now you're off democracy   15
(With a polite regret to be),
And leaning on dictatorship;
But if you will accept the tip,
In less than no time, tongue and pen,
You'll be a democrat again.   20
A reasoner and good as such,
Don't let it bother you too much

If it makes you look helpless please
And a temptation to the tease.
Suppose you've no direction in you, 25
I don't see but you must continue
To use the gift you do possess,
And sway with reason more or less.
I own I never really warmed
To the reformer or reformed, 30
And yet conversion has its place
Not halfway down the scale of grace.
So if you find you must repent
From side to side in argument,
At least don't use your mind too hard, 35
But trust my instinct—I'm a bard.

The Death of the Hired Man

Mary sat musing on the lamp-flame at the table
Waiting for Warren. When she heard his step,
She ran on tip-toe down the darkened passage
To meet him in the doorway with the news
And put him on his guard. "Silas is back." 5
She pushed him outward with her through the door
And shut it after her. "Be kind," she said.
She took the market things from Warren's arms
And set them on the porch, then drew him down
To sit beside her on the wooden steps. 10
"When was I ever anything but kind to him?
But I'll not have the fellow back," he said.
"I told him so last haying, didn't I?
'If he left then,' I said, 'that ended it.'
What good is he? Who else will harbour him
At his age for the little he can do? 16
What help he is there's no depending on.
Off he goes always when I need him most.
'He thinks he ought to earn a little pay,
Enough at least to buy tobacco with, 20
So he won't have to beg and be beholden.'
'All right,' I say, 'I can't afford to pay
Any fixed wages, though I wish I could.'
'Someone else can.' 'Then someone else will have to.'
I shouldn't mind his bettering himself 25
If that was what it was. You can be certain,
When he begins like that, there's someone at him

Trying to coax him off with pocket-money,—
In haying time, when any help is scarce.
In winter he comes back to us. I'm done." 30

"Sh! not so loud: he'll hear you," Mary said.

"I want him to: he'll have to soon or late."

"He's worn out. He's asleep beside the stove.
When I came up from Rowe's I found him here,
Huddled against the barn-door fast asleep, 35
A miserable sight, and frightening, too—
You needn't smile—I didn't recognise him—

I wasn't looking for him—and he's changed.
Wait till you see."

       "Where did you say he'd been?" 39

"He didn't say. I dragged him to the house,
And gave him tea and tried to make him smoke.
I tried to make him talk about his travels. 41
Nothing would do: he just kept nodding off."

"What did he say? Did he say anything?"

"But little."

       "Anything? Mary, confess 45
He said he'd come to ditch the meadow for me."

"Warren!"

       "But did he? I just want to know."
"Of course he did. What would you have him say?
Surely you wouldn't grudge the poor old man
Some humble way to save his self-respect. 50
He added, if you really care to know,
He meant to clear the upper pasture, too.
That sounds like something you have heard before?
Warren, I wish you could have heard the way
He jumbled everything. I stopped to look 55
Two or three times—he made me feel so queer—
To see if he was talking in his sleep.
He ran on Harold Wilson—you remember—
The boy you had in haying four years since.
He's finished school, and teaching in his college. 60
Silas declares you'll have to get him back.
He says they two will make a team for work:
Between them they will lay this farm as smooth!

The way he mixed that in with other things.
He thinks young Wilson a likely lad, though
    daft   65
On education—you know how they fought
All through July under the blazing sun,
Silas up on the cart to build the load,
Harold along beside to pitch it on."   69

"Yes, I took care to keep well out of earshot."

"Well, those days trouble Silas like a dream.
You wouldn't think they would. How some
    things linger!
Harold's young college boy's assurance piqued
    him.
After so many years he still keeps finding
Good arguments he sees he might have used.
I sympathize. I know just how it feels   76
To think of the right thing to say too late.
Harold's associated in his mind with Latin.
He asked me what I thought of Harold's saying
He studied Latin like the violin   80
Because he liked it—that an argument!
He said he couldn't make the boy believe
He could find water with a hazel prong—
Which showed how much good school had ever
    done him.
He wanted to go over that. But most of all   85
He thinks if he could have another chance
To teach him how to build a load of hay—"

"I know, that's Silas' one accomplishment.
He bundles every forkful in its place,
And tags and numbers it for future reference,
So he can find and easily dislodge it   91
In the unloading. Silas does that well.
He takes it out in bunches like big birds' nests.
You never see him standing on the hay   94
He's trying to lift, straining to lift himself."

"He thinks if he could teach him that, he'd be
Some good perhaps to someone in the world.
He hates to see a boy the fool of books.
Poor Silas, so concerned for other folk,   99
And nothing to look backward to with pride,
And nothing to look forward to with hope,
So now and never any different."

Part of a moon was falling down the west,
Dragging the whole sky with it to the hills.
Its light poured softly in her lap. She saw   105
And spread her apron to it. She put out her
    hand

Among the harp-like morning-glory strings,
Taut with the dew from garden bed to eaves,
As if she played unheard the tenderness   109
That wrought on him beside her in the night.
"Warren," she said, "he has come home to die:
You needn't be afraid he'll leave you this time."

"Home," he mocked gently.

        "Yes, what else but home?
It all depends on what you mean by home.
Of course he's nothing to us, any more   115
Than was the hound that came a stranger to us
Out of the woods, worn out upon the trail."

"Home is the place where, when you have to go
    there,
They have to take you in."

        "I should have called it   119
Something you somehow haven't to deserve."

Warren leaned out and took a step or two,
Picked up a little stick, and brought it back
And broke it in his hand and tossed it by.
"Silas has better claim on us you think
Than on his brother? Thirteen little miles   125
As the road winds would bring him to his
    door.
Silas has walked that far no doubt to-day.
Why didn't he go there? His brother's rich,
A somebody—director in the bank."

"He never told us that."

        "We know it though."   130

"I think his brother ought to help, of course.
I'll see to that if there is need. He ought of
    right
To take him in, and might be willing to—
He may be better than appearances.   134
But have some pity on Silas. Do you think
If he'd had any pride in claiming kin
Or anything he looked for from his brother,
He'd keep so still about him all this time?"

"I wonder what's between them."

        "I can tell you.   139
Silas is what he is—we wouldn't mind him—
But just the kind that kinsfolk can't abide.
He never did a thing so very bad.
He don't know why he isn't quite as good
As anyone. He won't be made ashamed   144
To please his brother, worthless though he is."

"I can't think Si ever hurt anyone."

"No, but he hurt my heart the way he lay
And rolled his old head on that sharp-edged
    chair-back.
He wouldn't let me put him on the lounge.
You must go in and see what you can do.   150
I made the bed up for him there to-night.
You'll be surprised at him—how much he's bro-
    ken.
His working days are done; I'm sure of it."

"I'd not be in a hurry to say that."   154

"I haven't been. Go, look, see for yourself.
But, Warren, please remember how it is:
He's come to help you ditch the meadow.
He has a plan. You mustn't laugh at him.
He may not speak of it, and then he may.
I'll sit and see if that small sailing cloud   160
Will hit or miss the moon."

                It hit the moon.
Then there were three there, making a dim
    row,
The moon, the little silver cloud, and she.

Warren returned—too soon, it seemed to her,
Slipped to her side, caught up her hand and
    waited.   165

"Warren," she questioned.
             "Dead," was all he answered.

Mending Wall

SOMETHING there is that doesn't love a wall,
That sends the frozen-ground-swell under it,
And spills the upper boulders in the sun;
And makes gaps even two can pass abreast.
The work of hunters is another thing: 5
I have come after them and made repair
Where they have left not one stone on a stone,
But they would have the rabbit out of hiding,
To please the yelping dogs. The gaps I mean,
No one has seen them made or heard them
    made,   10
But at spring mending-time we find them there.
I let my neighbour know beyond the hill;

And on a day we meet to walk the line
And set the wall between us once again.
We keep the wall between us as we go.   15
To each the boulders that have fallen to each.
And some are loaves and some so nearly balls
We have to use a spell to make them balance:
"Stay where you are until our backs are
    turned!"
We wear our fingers rough with handling them.
Oh, just another kind of out-door game,   21
One on a side. It comes to little more:
There where it is we do not need the wall:
He is all pine and I am apple orchard.
My apple trees will never get across   25
And eat the cones under his pines, I tell him.
He only says, "Good fences make good neigh-
    bours."
Spring is the mischief in me, and I wonder
If I could put a notion in his head: 29
"*Why* do they make good neighbours? Isn't it
Where there are cows? But here there are no
    cows.
Before I built a wall I'd ask to know
What I was walling in or walling out,
And to whom I was like to give offense.
Something there is that doesn't love a wall,
That wants it down." I could say "Elves" to
    him,   36
But it's not elves exactly, and I'd rather
He said it for himself. I see him there
Bringing a stone grasped firmly by the top
In each hand, like an old-stone savage armed.
He moves in darkness as it seems to me,   41
Not of woods only and the shade of trees.
He will not go behind his father's saying,
And he likes having thought of it so well
He says again, "Good fences make good neigh-
    bours."

After Apple-Picking

MY LONG two-pointed ladder's sticking
    through a tree
Toward heaven still,
And there's a barrel that I didn't fill
Beside it, and there may be two or three
Apples I didn't pick upon some bough.   5
But I am done with apple-picking now.

Essence of winter sleep is on the night,
The scent of apples: I am drowsing off.
I cannot rub the strangeness from my sight
I got from looking through a pane of glass   10
I skimmed this morning from the drinking
          trough
And held against the world of hoary grass.
It melted, and I let it fall and break.
But I was well
Upon my way to sleep before it fell,   15
And I could tell
What form my dreaming was about to take.
Magnified apples appear and disappear,
Stem end and blossom end,
And every fleck of russet showing clear.   20
My instep arch not only keeps the ache,
It keeps the pressure of a ladder-round.
I feel the ladder sway as the boughs bend.
And I keep hearing from the cellar bin
The rumbling sound   25
Of load on load of apples coming in.
For I have had too much
Of apple-picking: I am overtired
Of the great harvest I myself desired.
There were ten thousand thousand fruit to
          touch,   30
Cherish in hand, lift down, and not let fall.
For all
That struck the earth,
No matter if not bruised or spiked with stub-
          ble,
Went surely to the cider-apple heap   35
As of no worth.
One can see what will trouble
This sleep of mine, whatever sleep it is.
Were he not gone,
The woodchuck could say whether it's like his
Long sleep, as I describe its coming on,   41
Or just some human sleep.

A Brook in the City

THE FARM house lingers, though averse to
          square
With the new city street it has to wear
A number in. But what about the brook
That held the house as in an elbow-crook?   4

I ask as one who knew the brook, its strength
And impulse, having dipped a finger length
And made it leap my knuckle, having tossed
A flower to try its currents where they crossed.
The meadow grass could be cemented down
From growing under pavements of a town;   10
The apple trees be sent to hearth-stone flame.
Is water wood to serve a brook the same?
How else dispose of an immortal force
No longer needed? Staunch it at its source
With cinder loads dumped down? The brook
          was thrown   15
Deep in a sewer dungeon under stone
In fetid darkness still to live and run—
And all for nothing it had ever done
Except forget to go in fear perhaps: 19
No one would know except for ancient maps
That such a brook ran water. But I wonder
If from its being kept forever under
The thoughts may not have risen that so keep
This new-built city from both work and sleep.

Birches

WHEN I see birches bend to left and right
          Across the lines of straighter darker
          trees,
I like to think some boy's been swinging them.
But swinging doesn't bend them down to stay.
Ice-storms do that. Often you must have seen
          them   5
Loaded with ice a sunny winter morning
After a rain. They click upon themselves
As the breeze rises, and turn many-colored
As the stir cracks and crazes their enamel.
Soon the sun's warmth makes them shed crys-
          tal shells   10
Shattering and avalanching on the snow-crust—
Such heaps of broken glass to sweep away
You'd think the inner dome of heaven had
          fallen.
They are dragged to the withered bracken by
          the load,
And they seem not to break; though once they
          are bowed   15
So low for long, they never right themselves:
You may see their trunks arching in the woods

Years afterwards, trailing their leaves on the
    ground
Like girls on hands and knees that throw their
    hair   19
Before them over their heads to dry in the sun.
But I was going to say when Truth broke in
With all her matter-of-fact about the ice-storm
(Now am I free to be poetical?)
I should prefer to have some boy bend them
As he went out and in to fetch the cows—   25
Some boy too far from town to learn baseball,
Whose only play was what he found himself,
Summer or winter, and could play alone.
One by one he subdued his father's trees
By riding them down over and over again   30
Until he took the stiffness out of them,
And not one but hung limp, not one was left
For him to conquer. He learned all there
    was
To learn about not launching out too soon
And so not carrying the tree away   35
Clear to the ground. He always kept his
    poise
To the top branches, climbing carefully
With the same pains you use to fill a cup
Up to the brim, and even above the brim.   39
Then he flung outward, feet first, with a
    swish,
Kicking his way down through the air to the
    ground.
So was I once myself a swinger of birches.
And so I dream of going back to be.
It's when I'm weary of considerations,
And life is too much like a pathless wood   45
Where your face burns and tickles with the
    cobwebs
Broken across it, and one eye is weeping
From a twig's having lashed across it open.
I'd like to get away from earth awhile
And then come back to it and begin over.   50
May no fate willfully misunderstand me
And half grant what I wish and snatch me
    away
Not to return. Earth's the right place for
    love:
I don't know where it's likely to go better.
I'd like to go by climbing a birch tree,   55
And climb black branches up a snow-white
    trunk
Toward heaven, till the tree could bear no
    more,

But dipped its top and set me down again.
That would be good both going and coming
    back.
One could do worse than be a swinger of
    birches.

from A Masque of Reason

[God speaks.]

YES, BY AND BY. But first a larger matter.
    I've had you on my mind a thousand years
To thank you someday for the way you helped
    me
Establish once for all the principle
There's no connection man can reason out   5
Between his just deserts and what he gets.
Virtue may fail and wickedness succeed.
'Twas a great demonstration we put on.
I should have spoken sooner had I found   9
The word I wanted. You would have supposed
One who in the beginning *was* the Word
Would be in a position to command it.
I have to wait for words like anyone.
Too long I've owed you this apology
For the apparently unmeaning sorrow   15
You were afflicted with in those old days.
But it was of the essence of the trial
You shouldn't understand it at the time.
It had to seem unmeaning to have meaning.
And it came out all right. I have no doubt   20
You realize by now the part you played
To stultify the Deuteronomist
And change the tenor of religious thought.
My thanks are to you for releasing me
From moral bondage to the human race.   25
The only free will there at first was man's
Who could do good or evil as he chose.
I had no choice but I must follow him
With forfeits and rewards he understood—
Unless I liked to suffer loss of worship.   30
I had to prosper good and punish evil.
You changed all that. You set me free to reign.
You are the Emancipator of your God,
And as such I promote you to a saint.

A Masque of Reason. This section of a long poem states Frost's
ironic theme that man himself has allowed the image of power
to become God. 22. **Deuteronomist,** Moses. Deuteronomy,
the fifth Book of Moses, containing the Ten Commandments,
is a book of fundamental law based on a just and loving God,
who in return for absolute obedience grants prosperity and
communal well-being.

VAN WYCK BROOKS

Van Wyck Brooks, one of the most stimulating of present-day literary critics, was born in Plainfield, New Jersey, on February 16, 1886. After the usual secondary education he went to Harvard, where he graduated in 1907. He first was employed in the publishing house of Doubleday Page (1908–9) and later in the Century Company (1915–18), but he varied his occupation between times by serving as instructor in English at Leland Stanford from 1911 to 1913. After the termination of his stay with Century he devoted himself entirely to writing and lecturing. He is living at present in Westport, Connecticut.

His list of published works, all in the field of criticism, is a distinguished one. He has done translations and editings of foreign writers, often obscure ones; but he is best known for his new interpretations of American writers of the nineteenth and twentieth centuries, particularly for his reactions to New England life and letters. This interest is expressed first in *The Wine of the Puritans* (1909) and *The Malady of the Ideal* (1913) and continues through *The Ordeal of Mark Twain* (1920), a study of the Westerner transplanted to New England, and *The Life of Emerson* (1932). With four excellent studies, *The Flowering of New England* (1936), *New England: Indian Summer* (1940), *The World of Washington Irving* (1944), and *The Times of Melville and Whitman* (1947), he has perhaps reached the climax of such interest. But his range is wide; although his most useful and characteristic work thus far has been the attempt to explain America's "coming of age" in the world of literature, Brooks has a cosmopolitan taste which makes him at home in dealing with such dissimilar figures as Whitman, Dostoevski, John Addington Symonds, H. G. Wells, the Swiss poet and critic Henri Amiel, and Christopher Columbus.

In addition to those works just mentioned, Mr. Brooks' most important achievements are *John Addington Symonds* (1914), *The World of H. G. Wells* (1915), *America's Coming-of-Age* (1915), *Letters and Leadership* (1918), *The Pilgrimage of Henry James* (1925), *Emerson and Others* (1927), *Sketches in Criticism* (1932), *Three Essays on America* (1934), *The Opinions of Oliver Allston* (1941) and *Chilmark Miscellany* (1948).

In 1923 Brooks was awarded the *Dial* Prize for his "new point of view in criticism." What this point of view is can best be revealed by the following passage from an essay in *Letters and Leadership.*

Undoubtedly the gospel of self-expression, makeshift as it is, has revealed a promise in America that we have always taken for granted but hardly reckoned with. Isolated, secretive, bottled up as we have been in the past, how could we ever have guessed what aims and hopes we have in common had they not been brought to light, even in the crudest and most inadequate ways? That they have at least been brought to light I think few will deny; but will they get any further? Only, it seems to me, if we are able to build up . . . a programme for the conservation of our spiritual resources.

. . . That nationalities are the workshops of humanity, that each nationality has a special duty to perform, a special genius to exert, a special gift to contribute to the general stock of civilization, and that each, in consequence, growing by the trust that other nationalities place in it, must be a living, homogeneous entity, with its own faith and consciousness of self—could any idea more perfectly than this express the dream, the necessity of Young America? To live creatively, to live completely, to live in behalf of some great corporate purpose—that is its desire. A national faith we had once, a national dream, the dream of the "great American experiment." But had it not been sadly compromised, would the younger generation find itself adrift as it is today? Too many elements of that old faith of ours were at war with all that was good in it, and it admitted so few of the factors of life; it was betrayed by what was false within; it was unable to embrace the freer impulses of a new time. That is why it contributes so little to the new faith without which America cannot live.

To discover that faith, to formulate that new technique, to build up . . . that programme for the conservation of our spiritual resources is the task of American criticism. Let it first observe the "object" and the conditions of the object. It should then be able to make the "situation."

In more recent years, however, it is apparent that Brooks has become more and more a traditionalist in his reactions to literature and life. He pleads against the exaltation of the faddish or that which constitutes a coterie of art and writing; he abhors the bizarre and the artificial per se. In an age given all too much to cliques and gangs and mob rule in literature, his is a salutary, if somewhat disconcerting, attitude.

from **The Flowering of New England**

Thoreau at Walden

Henry Thoreau had built a hut at Walden. In March, 1845, he had borrowed Alcott's axe,—which he took pains to return with a sharper edge,—and cut down some tall arrowy pines for the timbers, studs and rafters. For the boards he bought a shanty from one of the Irish labourers on the railroad. The hut was ten

"Thoreau at Walden" from *The Flowering of New England* by Van Wyck Brooks, published and copyrighted by E. P. Dutton & Co., Inc., New York.
1. **Thoreau.** Henry David Thoreau (1817–1862), surveyor, pencil-maker, farmer, and writer, was a member of the famous group of American men of letters who made their home in Concord, Massachusetts. He was an intimate friend and helper of Ralph Waldo Emerson (1803–1882); and his other literary acquaintances of importance in his native Concord were the novelist Nathaniel Hawthorne (1804–1864); Bronson Alcott (1799–1888), theorist, mystic, and scholar; William Ellery Channing, the younger (1818–1901), a poet; and George William Curtis, essayist, traveler, and later magazine editor (1824–1892). Many of these are mentioned in the selection here given. Thoreau was one of the greatest of American individualists, a believer in the gospel of the simple, the passive, and the contemplative life. His Walden experiment, described below, was a two years' sojourn in a cabin by the shores of Walden Pond, Concord, undertaken to demonstrate the practical possibility of reducing life to the simplest terms. When Thoreau had become satisfied with his accomplishment, he returned to life in the village. *Walden, or Life in the Woods* (1854) tells the story of the adventure; other characteristic works by Thoreau are *A Week on the Concord and Merrimac Rivers* (1849); *The Maine Woods* (1864); and *Cape Cod* (1865). 7. **Irish labourers.** The decade of the 1840's brought to the United States a large immigration of Irish, who came to furnish cheap and efficient

feet by fifteen, shingled and plastered, with a garret and closet, a trap-door below, a brick fireplace, windows at the sides and a door facing the cove. The cost, all told, was $28.12½,— less than the annual rent of a student's room in Cambridge. There was a bean-field, close by, with a patch of potatoes, corn, peas and turnips. As a quasi-Pythagorean, Thoreau seldom indulged in beans. He exchanged his crop for rice in the village. Rice was the proper diet for one who loved so well the writings of the Oriental sages.

He had long cherished the notion of a forest-life. Ellery Channing had built himself a hut on the prairie in Illinois, and Henry's college class-mate, Stearns Wheeler, who had just died in Leipzig, had also built a rough woodland cabin, over at Flint's Pond, where he had lived for a year to save money, to buy Greek books and pay his way to Germany to study. Henry had spent six weeks in Wheeler's cabin, sharing one of his bunks of straw. There was nothing new in his own adventure, and he could not understand why his friends thought it was so peculiar. Some of them spoke as if he had gone to the woods in order to starve or freeze. Emerson had bought land on both sides of the pond, intending to build a summer-house, and Henry had carried out the project. Alcott, who liked to tinker at rustic architecture, helped him with his saw and hammer, along with the young Brook Farmer, George William Curtis of New York, who was boarding at Edmund Hosmer's in the village and working as a farm-hand. Henry felt at home in his sylvan dwelling. It made him think of some of those mountain-houses he had seen on his inland excursions, high-placed, airy, fragrant, with a fresh, auroral atmosphere about them. It was quiet, clean and cool, fit to entertain a traveling god. For company, birds flitted

labor. They settled in New England and have since become a large element in the population of that section.   15. **As . . . beans.** Pythagoras, the famous Greek philosopher and mathematician (sixth century B.C.), preached abstention from beans.   39. **Brook Farmer.** George Ripley (1802–1880), a Unitarian minister and a member of the philosophical group known as transcendentalists (a term covering mystics, believers in the idealistic teachings of Plato or in the spiritual development preached by Oriental religions and in social experiments based on Utopian principles) founded (1841) a community at Brook Farm (now West Roxbury, Massachusetts), the aim of which was to demonstrate the feasibility of a self-dependent group of contemplative thinkers. Hawthorne was for a time a member of the Brook Farm experiment. The project never recovered from a disastrous fire in 1847.   45. **inland excursions.** Thoreau had taken various trips into the heart of New England, as the titles of his works (see note to 1.1) indicate.

through his chamber, red squirrels raced over the roof, chickadees perched on the armfuls of wood he carried. There were moles living in the cellar. He had occasional visits from a hare. As he sat at his door in the evening, he remembered that he was descended from the Greeks of old. He was a wanderer, too, one of the crew of Ulysses. The shore of the cove was another Ithaca.

There was nothing about his "experiment," as his friends liked to call it, to arouse such curiosity and contempt. It was a commonsensible undertaking, and only a slight departure from Henry's usual mode of living. His average weekly outlay, for necessaries he could not supply himself, was twenty-seven cents. A few days at manual labour, building a boat or a fence, planting, grafting or surveying,—six weeks of work out of the year, when he had grown extravagant and had to have a microscope,—gave him an ample surplus. Why should anyone live by the sweat of his brow and bore his fellow-men by talking about it? Why should not everyone live with an ample margin?—as anyone could do, provided he followed the path of simplification, logically and ruthlessly enough. The mass of men led lives of quiet desperation. Why, if not to maintain a "standard of living" that every law of the universe controverted? Did they not know that the wisest had always lived, with respect to comforts and luxuries, a life more simple and meagre than the poor? Had all the philosophers, Hindu, Greek and Persian, lived and taught in vain? Had anyone measured man's capacities? Was it fair to judge by precedents, when so very little had been attempted? Who could say that if a man advanced, boldly, in the direction of his dreams, endeavouring to live the life he had imagined, he would not meet with a success that he had never expected in common hours? Henry believed, and wished to prove, that the more one simplified one's life the less complex the laws of life would seem. Why all this pother about possessions? He liked to think of the ancient Mexicans, who burned all their goods every fifty years. Hawthorne, in one of his stories, had pictured a similar holocaust; and this

was the kind of reform that Henry thought was worth considering. He meant to have his furniture, actual and symbolic, as simple as an Indian's or an Arab's. There were three bits of limestone on his table. They had to be dusted every day, while the furniture of his mind was still undusted. Out of the window, quick!

If he had had the wealth of Croesus, Henry's mode of living would not have been different. Space, air, time, a few tools, a note-book, a pen, a copy of Homer, what could he wish more than these? A bath in the pond at sunrise, a little Spartan sweeping and cleaning, then a bath for the intellect, perhaps in the Bhagavad-Gita, the pure water of Walden, mingling in his mind with the sacred water of the Ganges. The day was his, for any wild adventure. Sometimes, on a summer morning, he would sit for hours in his sunny doorway, amid the pines and hickories and sumachs, in undisturbed solitude and stillness. The birds flitted noiselessly about him. He could feel himself growing like the corn. He knew what the Orientals meant by contemplation and the forsaking of works. He was a Yogi, too, a forest-seer, who might have composed the Upanishads. His Reality was also Brahma, not the actualities of the world, but its potentialities. What did he care for temporal interests? It was his vocation to discover God. His days were no longer days of the week, bearing the names of pagan deities, nor were they minced into hours or fretted by the ticking of a clock. He felt like a Puri Indian or a Mexican. If you had put a watch in his hand and asked him what the hour was, he might have looked at the dial and said, "Quien sabe?" The sounds of the railway rose and died in his ears like the distant drumming of a partridge.

His life here seemed to flow in its proper channels. It followed its own fresh currents, and he felt himself lurking in crystalline

47. **Hawthorne . . . stories,** in "Earth's Holocaust," from *Mosses from an Old Manse* (1846–1854), a satirical tale describing a huge fire into which various moral reformers throw the institutions of which they particularly disapprove. None of them, however, can destroy the human heart (human nature).

63. **Bhagavad-Gita,** a philosophical poem of ancient India. 73. **Yogi.** In Hindu philosophy, the *yogi* is a practicer of *yoga,* a mental discipline based upon the direction of the attention entirely upon any object, concrete or abstract, with a view to the identification of consciousness with that object. *Yoga* includes various physical disciplines; it has for its aim the control of physical forces and of one's own body, and the attaining of occult powers, chiefly to gain union with the universal spirit, Brahma. 74. **Upanishads,** a collection of ancient East Indian disquisitions on the nature of man, the Supreme Being, the human soul, and immortality. 81. **Puri,** a district in southeast India, containing the world-famous Hindu shrine of Jagganath or Juggernaut. 84. **"Quien sabe?"** "Who knows?"

thought as the trout lurked under the verdurous banks. Not so much as a bubble rose to the surface. At sunset, he jumped into his boat and paddled to the middle of the pond. There he played on his flute, while the charmed perch hovered about the stern, and the moon traveled over the floor of the pond, strewn with the wrecks of the forest. The wildest imagination could not conceive the manner of life he was living, for the Concord nights were as strange as Arabian nights. He struck the side of the boat with his paddle, filling the woods with a circle of sound. What a pleasant mission it would be to go about the country in search of echoes! He knew where to find the prophetic places, the vocal, resounding, sonorous, hollow places, where oracles might be established, sites for oracles, sacred ears of Nature.

What could he say to a man who feared the woods, who shuddered at their solitude and darkness? What salvation was there for such a man? Did he not know that God was mysterious and silent? Henry could never have wearied of the woods, as long as he could visit a nighthawk on her nest. He could hardly believe his eyes when he stood within seven feet of her. There she was, sitting on her eggs, so sphinx-like, so Saturnian, so one with the earth, a relic of the reign of Saturn that Jupiter had failed to destroy, a riddle that might cause a man to go and dash his head against a stone. No living creature, surely, far less a wingéd creature of the air. A figure in stone or bronze, like a gryphon or a phoenix. With its flat, greyish, weather-beaten crown, its eyes were all but closed with stony cunning; and yet all the time this sculptured image, motionless as the earth, was watching with intense anxiety, through those narrow slits in its eyelids. Wonderful creature, sitting on its eggs, on the bare, exposed hill, through pelting storms of rain or hail, as if it were a part of the earth itself, the outside of the globe, with its eyes shut and its wings folded. It was enough to fill a man with awe. Henry thought for a moment that he had strayed into the Caucasus, and that around the hill, on the other slope, he would find Prometheus chained to the rock.

Round and round the pond, Henry followed the foot-path worn by the feet of Indian hunters, old as the race of men in Massachusetts. The critics and poets were always complaining that there were no American antiquities, no ruins to remind one of the past, yet the wind could hardly blow away the surface anywhere, exposing the spotless sand, but one found the fragments of some Indian pot or the little chips of flint left by some aboriginal arrow-maker. When winter came, and the scent of the gale wafted over the naked ground, Henry tramped through the snow a dozen miles to keep an appointment with a beech-tree, or a yellow birch perhaps, or some old acquaintance among the pines. He ranged like a grey moose, winding his way through the shrub-oak patches, bending the twigs aside, guiding himself by the sun, over hills and plains and valleys, resting in the clear grassy spaces. He liked the wholesome colour of the shrub-oak leaves, well-tanned, seasoned by the sun, the colour of the cow and the deer, silvery-downy underneath, over the bleached and russet fields. He loved the shrub-oak, with its scanty raiment, rising above the snow, lowly whispering to him, akin to winter, the covert which the hare and partridge sought. It was one of his own cousins, rigid as iron, clean as the atmosphere, hardy as all virtue, tenacious of its leaves, leaves that did not shrivel but kept their wintry life, firm shields, painted in fast colours. It loved the earth, which it overspread, tough to support the snow, indigenous, robust. The squirrel and the rabbit knew it well, and Henry could understand why the deer-mouse had its hole in the snow by the shrub-oak's stem. Winter was his own chosen season. When, for all variety in his walks he had only a rustling oak-leaf or the faint metallic cheep of a tree-sparrow, his life felt conti-

---

29. **Saturnian.** In classical myth there was once an ideal period of civilization, the Golden Age, in which the ruler of the world was the god Saturn. His reign was ended by the advent of the gods of Olympus under Jupiter, who unseated Saturn, although he did not destroy him. In most accounts Jupiter was the son of Saturn—the conflict, in short, is another example of the conflict between father and son so common in primitive folklore. The adjective *Saturnian* is here used to refer to conditions of the Golden Age—peace, happiness, contentment, and quiet.

47. **Caucasus . . . Prometheus.** In Greek myth Prometheus, a giant and demigod (Titan), befriended man by teaching him the use of fire, an element which Prometheus brought down from heaven. For his presumption in assuming the responsibility for this, he was punished by his master, Zeus (Jupiter), by being chained to a mountain in the Caucasus—a lofty mountain range in present-day Armenia and Turkestan—where he was daily attacked by a huge bird of prey who tore out his side, the same being restored to him during the ensuing night. Finally Jupiter relented and restored him to Olympus. According to some versions Prometheus was the creator of the human race.

nent and sweet as the kernel of a nut. Alone in
the distant woods or fields, in the unpretending
sproutlands or pastures tracked by rabbits, on
a bleak and, to most, a cheerless day, when a
villager would be thinking of his fire, he came
to himself and felt himself grandly related.
Cold and solitude were his dearest friends. Better a single shrub-oak leaf at the end of a wintry glade, rustling a welcome at his approach,
than a ship-load of stars and garters from the
kings of the earth. By poverty, if one chose to
use the word, monotony, simplicity, he felt so-
lidified and crystallized, as water and vapour
are crystallized by cold.

All praise to winter, then, was Henry's feeling. Let others have their sultry luxuries. How
full of creative genius was the air in which
these snow-crystals were generated. He could
hardly have marvelled more if real stars had
fallen and lodged on his coat. What a world to
live in, where myriads of these little discs, so
beautiful to the most prying eye, were whirled
down on every traveller's coat, on the restless
squirrel's fur and on the far-stretching fields
and forests, the wooded dells and mountain-
tops,—these glorious spangles, the sweepings of
heaven's floor. He watched the men cutting the
ice on the pond. Some of this ice, stowed in
the holds of ships, was going over to India; and
many a seeker of Brahma in Calcutta was destined to drink from his own Walden well. If
winter drove one indoors, all the better. It
compelled one to try new fields and resources.
Days of merry snowstorms and cheerful winter
evenings by the fire. Evenings for books of natural history, Audubon, for one. It was pleasant
to read about the Florida Keys, the flowering
magnolia, the warm spice-breezes, while the
wind beat the snow against one's window.
Days to sit at home over one's journal, in one's
own nest, perhaps on a single egg, though it
might prove to be an egg of chalk.

These were the days for writing, days to
speak like a man in a waking moment to others
in their waking moments. For Henry was hard
at work. He was writing articles, which Hor-

ace Greeley placed for him. He had begun
to write a book, and he wished to pay his
tribute to Carlyle, who had liberated the English language, cutting away the fetters imposed
upon it by the pedantic writers of the British
reviews. The frigid *North American* was even
worse, a venerable cobweb that had escaped
the broom. He liked to think of Carlyle, on
his vacations, riding on his horse "Yankee,"
bought from the American sale of his books.
His own book, rewritten from his journal, was
the *Week on the Concord and Merrimac Rivers,* the story of the journey with his brother,
never to be forgotten, when they had doubled
so many capes and run before the wind and
brought back news of far-away men. He did
not propose to crowd his day with work, even
if the book had to be written. A writer, he
thought, should saunter to his task surrounded
by a halo of ease and leisure, and the labour of
his hands should remove from his style all trace
of sentimentality and palaver. One did not
dance idly at one's writing when one had wood
to cut and cord. As the strokes rang cheerily
through the wood, so the stroke of the pen
should ring on the reader's ear. Was the voyage
an old story, eight or nine years old, and only
a week at that? It represented a lifetime's memories. No boy who had grown up on the Mississippi recalled those floating enchantments,
the river-boats, and the fabulous river-men,
with more of a thrill than Henry felt, remembering the canal-boats of his childhood. The
news had spread through Concord that one of
these boats was stealing through the meadows,
silent as a cloud, with its crew of "foreigners"
from New Hampshire, and all the village boys
had flocked to see it. Henry wished to write a
book that would be saturated with his thought
and reading, yet one that would not smell so
much of the study, even the poet's cabin, as of
the fields and woods. He dreamed of an un-
roofed book, lying open under the ether, a
book that could hardly be forced to lie on a
shelf.

He was not by nature a hermit. He might
have frequented the bar-rooms, he thought,
if he had had any business that called him
thither. Almost every day he walked to the vil-

36. **Audubon,** John James Audubon (1785–1851), a great
American naturalist and traveler, especially noted for his careful, scholarly, and painstaking studies and classifications of
the birds of North America. 46. **Horace Greeley.** Horace
Greeley (1811–1872), one of the greatest of American journalists, is always associated with the *New York Tribune,* which
he founded in 1841.

49. **Carlyle,** Thomas Carlyle (1795–1881), a great English
essayist, anti-democrat, anti-materialist, and severe critic of
his generation.

lage, to trade his beans for rice, to get a boot repaired, to collect the news of the family. Sometimes he returned late at night, with a bag of rye or Indian meal, sailing back under the moon to his harbour in the woods. It was only that he was wary of gossip. He did not wish to lumber his mind with the rubbish that most men seemed to rejoice in, the details, for example, of some case in court. One day he was 10 arrested in the village for refusing to pay his poll-tax. He felt as Alcott felt. The government supported slavery, the government was backing the Mexican War; well, he would not support the government. He did not wish to trace the course of his dollar until it bought a man, or bought a gun to shoot a Mexican. He spent the night in jail,—a fruitful night. It inspired his essay on *Civil Disobedience*. He wished to establish a principle, that one man locked up in jail 20 for refusing to countenance slavery would be the end of slavery, or, to express it on a broader basis, "If the alternative is to keep all just men in prison, or give up war and slavery, the State will not hesitate which to choose." A foolish notion, many people thought, but some of them changed their minds, in later years, when one of Henry's Hindu readers, Gandhi, acting on the principle, disturbed the British Empire for several months. The next morning, 30 Henry, released from jail, gathered some of the boys and girls for a huckleberry party, on a hill, whence the State was nowhere to be seen. He never fastened his door at Walden, though sometimes, in his absence, he had unwelcome visitors. How did Mrs. X happen to know that his sheets were not as clean as hers? But nothing was ever stolen, except his copy of Homer. One had to keep one's eye on bookish people.

40 He had other guests, especially in April, when all the world seemed to be on the move. A runaway slave appeared, then Alek Therien, the French-Canadian woodchopper, a true Homeric peasant who had learned a little Greek from his priest in the north, then Hugh Quoil, an Irish soldier, who had fought at the Battle of Waterloo. Old Quoil, with his wife

and his jug, was patiently waiting for death in a hut in the woods. The shanty-Irish folk along the railroad sometimes came to see him. Henry 50 thought them shiftless enough, with their women washing under the trees and the pigs poking about among the tubs. He eyed them with a vague hostility, as the red men had eyed the first settlers, and with as much reason; for were they not the first wave of the sea that was to sweep away so many landmarks? Among the little ragamuffins that swarmed about these cabins, there were some in whom the prophetic eye might have seen the masters of the future, 60 the lords of Greater Boston, mayors, governors, captains of police, even, perhaps, a cardinal. Henry had one good friend among them, little Johnny Riordan, with his quaint "old worthy" face, behind the sober visor of his cap plodding to school through the snow in his next-to-nothing, facing and routing it like a Persian army. A great sight, Johnny, in his rags, beside the well-fed villagers, waddling about in their furs and finery. Emerson also came, of course. 70 Henry read aloud to him some pages from his book, while they sat under an oak beside the pond. Alcott arrived one night, struggling through the snow. Ellery Channing spent a fortnight with him. When the poets and sages came, he was glad his dwelling was so spacious. As the conversation assumed a grander and loftier tone, they shoved their chairs further and further apart, until they touched the walls in opposite corners. This left plenty of 80 neutral ground for their sentences to deploy in martial order.

Once Henry left his house for a fortnight's excursion. He had cousins in Bangor, Maine, one of them in the lumber-trade, a good excuse to visit the northern woods. He wished to study the Indians in their forest wilderness, and he wished to climb Mount Ktaadn. He never travelled without prayer and fasting, for he did not wish to dissipate his mind. With all 90 the industry of a busy life, how could one hope to know, really know, an area more than six miles square? Isaac Hecker had asked him to go to Rome, the two of them together. Hecker to pay the expenses, for Hecker, who had tried

18. *Civil Disobedience.* This pungent essay, the content of which should be obvious from the context, was most influential upon the mind of Mahatma Gandhi, the twentieth-century leader of the East Indians for independence from the British Empire (see p. 14).

64. **"old worthy,"** a wrinkled face, as that of an old man. 67. **Persian army.** The ancient Persians were always easily defeated by the Greeks whenever they fought. 88. **Ktaadn,** Mount Katahdin, the highest mountain in Maine.

Brook Farm and Fruitlands, was boarding with Mrs. Thoreau for a taste of Concord. He hoped to carry Henry over to Rome, in more than one fashion. Later, another friend, an Englishman, invited him for a visit in England. In both cases, Henry said, No. If Europe was much in his mind, and became more and more to him, Concord might become less and less; and what sort of bargain would that be? He did not wish 10 his life to lose its homely savour. If the fields and streams and woods that he loved so well, and the simple occupations of his townsmen, ever ceased to interest and surprise him, what culture or wealth could ever atone for the loss? He did not wish to go to Europe, nor did he wish to go—like the farmers—west. What could he think of this foolish American habit, going east or west to a "better land," without lifting an honest finger to till and redeem one's own 20 New England soil? As for the rush to California, it was a disgrace to humankind,—digging gold, the merest lottery, a kind of toil, if it deserved the name, in no sense beneficial to the world. A startling development, this, of the ethics of trade and all the modes of getting a living. It filled Henry with a cold scorn. For the rest, he had his own western horizon, towards which he was always moving, pitching his tent each day nearer the Golden Gate. But 30 the really fertile soils and luxuriant prairies lay on one's own side of the Alleghenies, wherever a man minded his own business. Were not all the essentials of life to be found in Concord, ten times found if one properly valued them? —which a man could only do if he stood his ground. Henry had something to say to the men in the covered wagons, who were running away from something besides the rocks. If the men in the covered wagons had no ears for 40 Henry, he would be glad to wait for a few generations. The great-great-grandsons of the covered wagons would be ready to listen to him.

Nobody knew the riches of Concord. As for natural history, he had found some of the Arctic phenomena there, red snow and one or two Labrador plants. Still, a little travel now and then was not so bad to give one's mind an airing, especially if it offered him a chance to observe the ways of the Indians. For the Indians 50 had a special charm for Henry; they suggested a simpler mode of life and a greater nearness to the earth. Were there not two eternities, one behind him, which the Indians represented, as well as one before? Wherever he went, he trod in their tracks, yet only a few poets remembered them. Here and there, one saw their lonely wigwams, on the banks of some quiet stream, like the cabins of the muskrats in the meadows,—an old squaw, perhaps, living in her 60 solitary hut, with her dog, her only companion, making baskets and picking berries, insulted by the village boys and girls. Henry dreamed of writing a book about them; for their memory seemed to him to harmonize with the russet hue of autumn that he loved. A race that had exhausted the secrets of nature, a race tanned with age, while the young, fair Anglo-Saxon slip, on whom the sun had shone for so short a time, was only just beginning its career. As 70 sportsmen went in pursuit of ducks, and scholars of rare books, and all men went in pursuit of money, Henry went in search of arrow-heads, when the proper season came round again. He often spent whole afternoons, especially in the spring, when the rains had washed the ground bare, pacing back and forth over a sandy field, looking for these relics. It might have rained arrow-heads. They lay all over the surface of the country, sometimes mingled with arrow- 80 headiferous soil, ash-coloured, left by Indian fires. They were like so many fossil thoughts to Henry, forever recalling the far-away minds that shaped them.

To Maine, then!—where the Indians grew with the moose. A fortnight in the forest, the home of the bear and the caribou, the wolf, the beaver, and the Penobscot redskins, where the wild fir flourished and the spruce-tops, seen from an elevation, were like the odour of cake 90 in a schoolboy's nostrils. Hemlocks and cedars, silver and yellow birches, watery maples, damp and moss-grown rocks, real woods, these, wild and bearded. One caught the whistle of ducks

1. **Fruitlands,** like Brook Farm (p. 60, l. 39 and note) a Utopian community, located near Harvard, Massachusetts, and supervised by Bronson Alcott. It had a very brief life, lasting only a year (1844). 20. **rush to California.** The famous California Gold Rush began shortly after the discovery of gold at Sutter's mill, near Sacramento, in 1848.

63. **Henry . . . them.** Thoreau left eleven manuscript volumes, about 3000 pages, filled with notes about the Indians for the book he had hoped to write. (Author's note.)

on solitary streams, the flicker of the darting chickadee, the loon's desolate laugh. Sometimes, through the moss-clad aisles, one heard a dull, dry, rustling sound, as if smothered under the fungus-covered forest, the falling of a tree, like the shutting of a door in some distant entry of the dark and shaggy wilderness. There one could feel at home, shooting the rapids in one's birch canoe, like a bait bobbing for some river monster, darting from side to side of the stream, then gliding swift and smoothly. This was the place to sing the "Canadian boat-song," or to play one's flute, at night, under the stars, while the wolves howled about, in the darkness of the continent. Henry watched Joe Polis, the Indian guide, glued to the bank on his stomach, talking to the muskrats in their sylvan language. Sometimes, by the fireside, Joe Polis also sang, a mild and simple nasal chant, like the dawn of civilization over the woods. The white man's brow was clear and distinct, but over the brow of the Indian lingered a haze or mist. For the Indian, the white man's noon was four o'clock in the morning.

A journey like this was only a foretaste, too rewarding not to be repeated. Henry was writing about his travels, and one of the magazines was glad to print his essay on Ktaadn. Later, on two occasions, he went to Maine again. He wished to visit Chestuncook, the Allegash and the East Branch. He was in his element in the woods, as Richard Henry Dana on the sea, as an old French-Canadian *coureur de bois*. Was he not a Frenchman as well as a Yankee, who might have run wild with Du Lhut and harried the woods for beavers? In the meantime, he had left his Walden cabin. Why? For as good a reason as he had gone there. He had other lives to live, and he had no more time to spare for this one. He wanted a change, he did not wish to stagnate. About two o'clock in the afternoon, he had felt the world's axle creaking a little, as if it needed greasing, as if the oxen laboured with the wain and could hardly get their load over the ridge of the day. Who

would accept heaven on terms like this?—and a ticket for heaven had to include, for Henry, tickets for hell and purgatory also. Walden was only a bivouac in his campaign. He had other journeys in mind, to Cape Cod, for instance, with Ellery Channing, and later a jaunt to Canada, Quebec and Montreal. (Total expense, two guidebooks included, $12.75.) Ellery was not a man for camping out,—that was an art one had to acquire slowly; but he shared Henry's taste for a simple equipment. And Henry would no more have thought of dressing,—dressing for a journey!—than he would have blacked boots for fishing. Honest travelling was dirty work. A pair of overalls was the proper costume, a grey sack, corduroys perhaps; and as for this blacking of boots, he despised it on all occasions. In this, he was like some of the Harvard professors, who, as Mrs. Story was shocked to note, on one of her visits from Italy, did not have their boots blacked even for Commencement. Henry, who always carried a piece of tallow, in order to keep the water out of the leather, looked like a woodchuck or musquash. This was his desire, at least,—the more like a quadruped the better, tawny, russet, yellow-brown, the colour of the sands. Vermont grey was not so bad; and once he had had the perfect suit, a skilful mixture of browns, with light and dark cleverly proportioned, and a few threads of green. He had looked like a corner of a pasture, with patches of sweet-fern and lechea. He had been able to glide over the fields, as unperceived from the farmer's windows as a painted cruiser through a spyglass. The wild animals thought he was one of them. Ellery, who was not so systematic, shared Henry's feeling in the matter of hats. His own hat was old and weather-beaten and had plenty of holes around the brim. It was as rare and high as a good Stilton cheese. As for the rest of Henry's outfit, a handkerchief served for a bag, or a firm, stout sheet of brown paper, well tied up. What else? An umbrella, of course, a knapsack, with partitions for books and papers, a music-book for pressing flowers, a field-glass, and a measuring-tape. A fish-line, spoon and dipper, a little salt and sugar, tea, Indian meal and a slice of fruitcake. If

---

33. **Richard Henry Dana,** Richard Henry Dana, Jr. (1815–1882), author of *Two Years Before the Mast* (1840), one of the best accounts of a sea-journey in the English language. 34. *coureur de bois,* a woodsman of French Canada, a guide, a trapper. 36. **Du Lhut,** Daniel Greysolon, Sieur du Lhut, a French military officer and explorer of the North Country of central United States and Canada during the seventeenth century. He has left his name to the city of Duluth, Minnesota.

62. **sack,** sack coat. 65. **Mrs. Story,** wife of William Wetmore Story (1819–1895), lawyer in Salem, Massachusetts, poet, and sculptor of note. She was a copious letter-writer.

anyone asked him along the way to do a little tinkering, that was a tribute to his common sense.

So Henry tramped to Provincetown. Having seen the woods, he wished to see the ocean, and Cape Cod was surely the place to see it. There, on the stretches of sand blown clean by the wind, he could forget the towns, where he felt so unspeakably mean and disgraced. He could forget the bar-rooms of Massachusetts, where the full-grown were not weaned from their savage and filthy habits, sucking cigars and guzzling whiskey-punch. On the Cape, one saw wholesome faces, well preserved by the salty air, faces bleached like old sails, hanging cliffs of weather-beaten flesh. The Cape Cod boys leaped from their leading strings into the shrouds; it was only a bound from their mother's laps to the masthead. They boxed the compass in their infant day-dreams. They could hand, reef and steer by the time they flew a kite. This was a country almost as thrilling as Maine. Henry had three books more or less on the stocks: *The Maine Woods,* full of the scents of the forest, *Cape Cod,* redolent of the sea, even *A Yankee in Canada.* The well-known publishers, Time & Co., could be trusted to see that they were safely printed. One of his neighbours wrote about Human Culture. Why should he not write about Cape Cod, another name for the same thing, and hardly a sandier phase of it? Or Canada, for that matter? He wrote an opening paragraph, with both hands clenched: "Read my book if you dare!"

29. **neighbours . . . Culture,** Bronson Alcott, in *The Doctrine and Discipline of Human Culture* (1836).

H. L. MENCKEN

"The Blond Beast of Baltimore," "The Ogre of Hollins Street," "The Bogey-Man of Booboisie" —these uncomplimentary epithets, and many others even more pungent, have been applied at one time or another to Henry Louis Mencken, the most vociferous of the many caustic critics of the generation. He was the most violently hated—and the most fanatically admired—of any American man of letters during the turbulent decades of the post-war period. To some he was a demon with a cloven hoof, to others a boorish mountebank with a dangerous facility of the pen, to still others a prophet of truth and enlightenment crying in a dark and depressing wilderness of ignorance and intolerance. To some he was a man with perilous alien sympathies, in the pay of Kaiser Wilhelm II; to others a fearless castigator of the weaknesses of the American people, who by using the rod would drive out their devils and bring them to see the truth that would make them free.

Opinion was cleanly divided on Mencken during the years of his greatest literary activity; there was apparently no opportunity to take a middle ground. Now that the social, political, literary, and artistic disputes in which he bore a joyful part have begun to recede into the distance, and the Mencken vogue has spent its force, it is possible to reach a calmer state of consideration regarding Mencken's work. That he was a kind of intellectual currycomb strikes even the casual reader today. His personality was stimulating and antiseptic in an irritating way; and he unquestionably did a great service in his valiant combat against hypocrisy and sham and bigotry of the ignorant variety. That he was overprejudiced against the Victorian world and mind is not entirely his fault; he represents well the natural reaction against the tastes, artistic standards, and moral shibboleths of the nineteenth century. His mind was keen and decisive; his irreverence wholesome though crude; his command of language effective and refreshingly impudent. He made famous many a phrase of invective; indeed, he can be regarded as the most successful wielder of satire in a direct frontal attack that twentieth-century America has thus far produced. The fact that he was often brash and ignorant—that he himself had not learned enough and imbibed enough tolerance—can be blamed as much upon the age as upon Mencken. After all, the period following the First World War had all Mencken's vices grossly magnified, but in general it was not so disarmingly frank in exhibiting them.

Actually Mencken is a brilliant example of the professional journalist, and the story of his life has been placid enough to suit any of the "boob" bourgeoisie that he belabored to the satiation point. He was born in Baltimore on September 12, 1880. His family had been tobacco dealers for two generations before him; his grandfather, an immigrant from Germany, had established the business. Mencken, as a boy, had been expected to continue the tradition; but he had always been interested in letters. He read early and late and, somewhat like a great English figure of the eighteenth century, to whom he shows a certain kinship—Alexander Pope—he began to "lisp in numbers" while he was in his teens. But this lust for composition turned to music as well as to poetry. Mencken has always been a competent student of music. He was educated at first privately and then at the Baltimore Polytechnic Institute, which he left in 1896. Thomas Huxley (1825–1895), the great English scientist, seems to have influenced him greatly. There are in Mencken's mind the preciseness of thinking and attempt at objectivity that would be expected of a trained scientist. But the comparative briefness of Mencken's formal schooling should be noted; he has always adopted an attitude of distaste for the academic. Perhaps it would be fairer to say that Mencken has always hated the pedantic; but he seems never to have been able to distinguish between the careful scholar and the fussy, pompous pundit —they are all called "doctors" and "professors," with civil leers sometimes uncivil. This is a characteristic illustration of the weaknesses of Mencken's critical position.

Mencken fell naturally into a career of journalism. He became a reporter on the Baltimore *Morning Herald* in 1899 and by 1903 was city editor of that newspaper and general editor of the evening edition by 1905. His connection with the Baltimore *Sun*—the famous "Sunpapers" on the history of which he collaborated in 1937—began in 1906 and has continued in greater or less degree to the present. In 1908 he became literary critic for the sophisticated

Smart Set, forerunner of the present type of satirical popular magazine best represented by *The New Yorker.* Six years later (1914) he became co-editor of *The Smart Set* with George Jean Nathan, a voluble critic with the same audacity of thought and mannerisms of style as Mencken, but a critic who seems never to have advanced much beyond the sophomoric outlook. *The Smart Set* ceased to appear in 1923; in the meantime Mencken had contributed to other periodicals and had become contributing editor of *The Nation* in 1921.

The discontinuance of *The Smart Set* led Mencken and Nathan to the founding of the famous *American Mercury* in 1924; and Mencken remained the presiding genius of this magazine until his retirement in 1933. The periodical was frankly an organ to give voice to Mencken's points of view; in addition to its leading articles of a grandly "debunking" nature, it was noteworthy for its caustic "Americana" section, in which the editors presented all kinds of news reports and "human stories" which suggested the stupidity or narrowness or bourgeois flatness of the American people, no section of the United States being spared. To the public who read and approved such exposés of provincial America as Sinclair Lewis' *Main Street* (p. 333), the *Mercury* was irresistible. H. L. Mencken became the beaconlight of the young American intelligentsia. Young men, particularly in the colleges, imitated his style and his insolence with lamentable results; many a college woman fancied herself as Mencken's mistress in seraphic attachments à la Plato. It was chiefly the publication of the *American Mercury* that won for Mencken the opprobrious epithets in which he delighted, as well as the stuffy condemnations of windy pulpiteers and static mossbacks in politics and of dignified literary critics like Stuart Sherman and Paul Elmer More (p. 79, note to l. 19). But Mencken continued to ride out the storms and return buffet for buffet with blue-eyed innocence of manner; and when he retired from the management of the *Mercury,* most of the vitality of the magazine departed with him.

Mencken's journalistic endeavors, however, were not all carried on from the editor's chair. In 1916 and 1917 he was a sympathetic war correspondent with the German army, whence the charge that he was in the pay of the Prussian Junkers. National presidential conventions were likely to bring him out in his splendor, and he fairly reveled in the notorious Scopes trial of 1925 (p. 8). His miscellaneous writings were considerable. *Ventures in Verse* (1903), of course, had best be ignored. One phase of his writing represents a characteristic paradox: he has professed himself a hater of the theater; but he actually wrote a play, *The Artist* (1912), and collaborated in another, *Heliogabalus* (1920), and has edited the dramatic works of Henrik Ibsen (1828–1906) and Eugène Brieux (1858–1932), and has written *George Bernard Shaw, His Plays* (1905). He is not, however, to be regarded as a leading American playwright. He took part in the controversy over the works of Friedrich Nietzsche (1844–1900) which was raised during the First World War and later; his *Philosophy of Friedrich Nietzsche* (1908) anticipated the controversy and is favorable to the iconoclastic attitude of that powerful German writer.

It was, however, the salty, half-humorous, half-serious, and wholly stimulating essays which he began in 1916 that will undoubtedly keep Mencken's name alive for some time. These treat of language, literature, music, politics, society in general—and H. L. Mencken. The series begins with *A Book of Burlesques* (1916) and continues with *A Little Book in C Major* (1916); *A Book of Prefaces* (1917, 1924, 1928), one of the most popular of them all; *In Defense of Women* (1918); *Damn—A Book of Calumny* (1917); and his well-known six series of *Prejudices* (1919–27), which show Mencken at his characteristic best. *The American Language* (1919, 1921, 1923, revised in a greatly enlarged edition in 1936) and *Supplements I* (1945) and *II* (1948) represent a serious study of American usage and vocabulary, very industrious and extremely readable although, because they fail to treat pronunciation adequately, they cause the judicious to grieve. It is utterly typical of the author that he should have collected the unflattering opinions of himself held by his enemies and published them in book form—the most amusing *Schimpflexikon,* or dictionary of abuse (1928) —by which those hostile to him could help pay him royalties.

In later years Mencken has turned chiefly to politics, with some animadversions on religion; in such a group of works fall his *Notes on Democracy* (1926), *Making a President* (1932), and *A Treatise on Right and Wrong* (1934). Mencken considers *A Treatise on the Gods* (1930) as his best work; and there is much to be said for this opinion, inasmuch as the book is an honest and powerful attack upon religious institutions which are man-made and which stifle human instinct in the name of "society." Politically, however, Mencken's liberal views are not advanced enough to include Franklin D. Roosevelt's New Deal. For the rest, he is a thoroughgoing skeptic and agnostic who calls down upon himself horrible warnings from churchmen and statesmen but who goes on his way unperturbed. This unruffled air is particularly apparent in his three autobiographical books, *Happy Days* (1940), *Newspaper Days* (1941), and *Heathen Days* (1943).

It is significant in a melancholy way, however, that Mencken's last important literary study, *James Branch Cabell* (1927), considers a writer of meteoric prominence whose vogue has become as dead as the vogue for Mencken is likely to become in the not too distant future. A pleasant personality, an active mind, and a vigorous force is Mencken—but he does not wear well. Still, in his day he was an impressive figure; and he cannot be dismissed as an idle critic at any time, for too much of what he says is true.

Puritanism As a Literary Force

1

"CALVINISM," says Dr. Leon Kellner, in his excellent little history of American literature, "is the natural theology of the disinherited; it never flourished, therefore, anywhere as it did in the barren hills of Scotland and in the wilds of North America." The learned doctor is here speaking of theology in what may

"Puritanism As a Literary Force" reprinted from *A Book of Prefaces* by H. L. Mencken, by permission of and special arrangement with Alfred A. Knopf, Inc., authorized publishers. 2. **history . . . literature,** *American Literature,* translated by Julia Franklin; New York, Doubleday, Page & Co., 1915. (Author's note.) 6. **learned doctor,** a typical Menckenism with the usual suggestion of sarcasm.

be called its narrow technical sense—that is, as a theory of God. Under Calvinism, in the New World as well as in the Old, it became no more than a luxuriant demonology; even God himself was transformed into a superior sort of devil, ever wary and wholly merciless. That primitive demonology still survives in the barbaric doctrines of the Methodists and Baptists, particularly in the South; but it has been ameliorated, even there, by a growing sense of the divine grace, and so the old God of Plymouth Rock, as practically conceived, is now scarcely worse than the average jail warden or Italian padrone. On the ethical side, however, Calvinism is dying a much harder death, and we are still a long way from the enlightenment. Save where Continental influences have measurably corrupted the Puritan idea—e.g., in such cities as New York, San Francisco and New Orleans, —the prevailing American view of the world and its mysteries is still a moral one, and no other human concern gets half the attention that is endlessly lavished upon the problem of conduct, particularly of the other fellow. It needed no official announcement to define the function and office of the republic as that of an international expert in morals, and the mentor and exemplar of the more backward nations. Within, as well as without, the eternal rapping of knuckles and proclaiming of new austerities goes on. The American, save in moments of conscious and swiftly lamented deviltry, casts up all ponderable values, including even the values of beauty, in terms of right and wrong. He is beyond all things else, a judge and a policeman; he believes firmly that there is a mysterious power in law; he supports and embellishes its operation with a fanatical vigilance.

Naturally enough, this moral obsession has given a strong colour to American literature. In truth, it has coloured it so brilliantly that American literature is set off sharply from all other literatures. In none other will you find so wholesale and ecstatic a sacrifice of aesthetic ideas, of all the fine gusto of passion and beauty, to notions of what is meet, proper and nice. From the books of grisly sermons that were the first American contribution to letters down to that amazing literature of "inspiration" which now flowers so prodigiously, with two literary ex-Presidents among its chief virtuosi, one observes no relaxation of the moral pressure. In the history of every other literature there have been periods of what might be called moral innocence—periods in which a naif *joie de vivre* has broken through all concepts of duty and responsibility, and the wonder and glory of the universe have been hymned with unashamed zest. The age of Shakespeare comes to mind at once: the violence of the Puritan reaction offers a measure of the pendulum's wild swing. But in America no such general rising of the blood has ever been seen. The literature of the nation, even the literature of the enlightened minority, has been under harsh Puritan restraints from the beginning, and despite a few stealthy efforts at revolt—usually quite without artistic value or even common honesty, as in the case of the cheap fiction magazines and that of smutty plays on Broadway, and always very shortlived—it shows not the slightest sign of emancipating itself today. The American, try as he will, can never imagine any work of the imagination as wholly devoid of moral content. It must either tend toward the promotion of virtue, or be suspect and abominable.

If any doubt of this is in your mind, turn to the critical articles in the newspapers and literary weeklies; you will encounter enough proofs in a month's explorations to convince you forever. A novel or a play is judged among us, not by its dignity of conception, its artistic honesty, its perfection of workmanship, but almost entirely by its orthodoxy of doctrine, its platitudinousness, its usefulness as a moral tract. A digest of the reviews of such a book as David Graham Phillips' "Susan Lenox" or of

14. **padrone,** literally, an Italian landlord or innkeeper. The word is used, however, for a special type of employment agent found in America among basic Italo-American populations. The *padrone* finds employment for unskilled Italian laborers and assists them in banking and other financial arrangements. The opportunity for exploitation of the laborers has been often very great.

51. **two . . . ex-Presidents,** Ulysses S. Grant, who published his *Memoirs* shortly before his death in 1885; and Theodore Roosevelt, who wrote many books on travel, history, and natural history. No doubt Mencken is thinking as much of *The Strenuous Life* (1900) as of the work generally considered Roosevelt's best, *The Winning of the West* (1889–1896). Calvin Coolidge wrote an autobiography and contributed to a newspaper column in his later years. Woodrow Wilson (p. 213) was a writer of great literary power. 56. *joie de vivre,* joy of living. 88. **"Susan Lenox" . . . "Hedda Gabler."** Both *Susan Lenox: Her Fall and Rise* (1909), a novel by the American David Graham Phillips (1867–1911), and *Hedda Gabler* (1890), a play by the Norwegian Henrik Ibsen (1828–1906), deal with women who fly in the face of convention and end tragically.

such a play as Ibsen's "Hedda Gabler" would make astounding reading for a Continental European. Not only the childish incompetents who write for the daily press, but also most of our critics of experience and reputation, seem quite unable to estimate a piece of writing as a piece of writing, a work of art as a work of art; they almost inevitably drag in irrelevant gabble as to whether this or that personage in it is respectable, or this or that situation in accordance with the national notions of what is edifying and nice. Fully nine-tenths of the reviews of Dreiser's "The Titan," without question the best American novel of its year, were devoted chiefly to indignant denunciations of the morals of Frank Cowperwood, its central character. That the man was superbly imagined and magnificently depicted, that he stood out from the book in all the flashing vigour of life, that his creation was an artistic achievement of a very high and difficult order—these facts seem to have made no impression upon the reviewers whatever. They were Puritans writing for Puritans, and all they could see in Cowperwood was an anti-Puritan, and in his creator another. It will remain for Europeans, I daresay, to discover the true stature of "The Titan," as it remained for Europeans to discover the true stature of "Sister Carrie."

Just how deeply this corrective knife has cut you may find plainly displayed in Dr. Kellner's little book. He sees the throttling influence of an ever alert and bellicose Puritanism, not only in our grand literature, but also in our petit literature, our minor poetry, even in our humour. The Puritan's utter lack of aesthetic sense, his distrust of all romantic emotion, his unnatural intolerance of opposition, his unbreakable belief in his own bleak and narrow views, his savage cruelty of attack, his lust for relentless and barbarous persecution—these things have put an almost unbearable burden upon the exchange of ideas in the United States, and particularly upon that form of it which involves playing with them for the mere game's sake. On the one hand, the writer who would deal seriously and honestly with the larger problems of life, particularly in the rigidly-partitioned ethical field, is restrained by laws that would have kept a Balzac or a Zola in prison from year's end to year's end; and on the other hand the writer who would proceed against the reigning superstitions by mockery has been silenced by taboos that are quite as stringent, and by an indifference that is even worse. For all our professed delight in and capacity for jocosity, we have produced so far but one genuine wit—Ambrose Bierce—and, save to a small circle, he remains unknown today. Our great humourists, including even Mark Twain, have had to take protective colouration, whether willingly or unwillingly, from the prevailing ethical foliage, and so one finds them levelling their darts, not at the stupidities of the Puritan majority, but at the evidences of lessening stupidity in the anti-Puritan minority. In other words, they have done battle, not against, but *for* Philistinism—and Philistinism is no more than another name for Puritanism. Both wage a ceaseless warfare upon beauty in its every form, from painting to religious ritual, and from the drama to the dance—the first because it holds beauty to be a mean and stupid thing, and the second because it holds beauty to be distracting and corrupting.

Mark Twain, without question, was a great artist; there was in him something of that prodigality of imagination, that aloof engrossment in the human comedy, that penetrating cynicism, which one associates with the great artists of the Renaissance. But his nationality hung around his neck like a millstone; he could never throw off his native Philistinism. One ploughs through "The Innocents Abroad" and through parts of "A Tramp Abroad" with in-

---

13. **"The Titan,"** a novel by Theodore Dreiser (p. 289) published in 1914, noted especially for its leading male character, Frank Cowperwood, a ruthless businessman and pursuer of women. 29. **"Sister Carrie,"** another novel by Dreiser, published in 1900, is a powerful realistic story of a woman outside the social law.

51. **Balzac . . . Zola.** Honoré Balzac (1799–1850) and Emile Zola (1840–1902) were two remarkable French novelists: Balzac was known for his monumental series of realistic novels of French middle-class life called *La Comédie Humaine;* Zola, for his many "naturalistic" case-histories of poor Frenchmen and for his quasi-scientific reportorial skill. 59. **Ambrose Bierce,** a distinctive American writer (1842–1913?) who served in the Civil War and later became a free-lance journalist and miscellaneous writer in California. For a time he was a political journalist in Washington. He disappeared into Mexico at the time of Villa's insurrection in that country, and his fate is unknown. As a writer he was a master of the weird, the horribly naturalistic, the cynical mingled with the picturesque, and a Swift-like wit. He earned well the name of "Bitter Bierce." 69. **Philistinism.** The Philistines were in Old Testament times the wealthy, prosperous nation opposed to the Israelites. In the last century the name was applied to all those who were enemies of learning and culture, specifically the prosperous industrial middle class of England and America.

credulous amazement. Is such coarse and ignorant clowning to be accepted as humour, as great humour, as the best humour that the most humorous of peoples has produced? Is it really the mark of a smart fellow to lift a peasant's cackle over "Lohengrin"? Is Titian's chromo of Moses in the bullrushes seriously to be regarded as the noblest picture in Europe? Is there nothing in Latin Christianity, after all, save petty grafting, monastic scandals and the worship of the knuckles and shin-bones of dubious saints? May not a civilized man, disbelieving in it, still find himself profoundly moved by its dazzling history, the lingering remnants of its old magnificence, the charm of its gorgeous and melancholy loveliness? In the presence of all beauty of man's creation—in brief, of what we roughly call art, whatever its form—the voice of Mark Twain was the voice of the Philistine. A literary artist of very high rank himself, with instinctive gifts that lifted him, in "Huckleberry Finn," to kinship with Cervantes and Aristophanes, he was yet so far the victim of his nationality that he seems to have had no capacity for distinguishing between the good and the bad in the work of other men of his own craft. The literary criticism that one occasionally finds in his writings is chiefly trivial and ignorant; his private inclination appears to have been toward such romantic sentimentality as entrances schoolboys; the thing that interested him in Shakespeare was not the man's colossal genius, but the absurd theory that Bacon wrote his plays. Had he been born in France (the country of his chief abomination!) instead of in a Puritan village of the American hinterland, I venture that he would have conquered the world. But try as he would, being what he was, he could not get rid of the Puritan smugness and cocksureness, the Puritan distrust of new ideas, the Puritan incapacity for seeing beauty as a thing in itself, and the full peer of the true and the good.

It is, indeed, precisely in the works of such men as Mark Twain that one finds the best proofs of the Puritan influence in American letters, for it is there that it is least expected and hence most significant. Our native critics, unanimously Puritans themselves, are anaesthetic to the flavour, but to Dr. Kellner, with his half-European, half-Oriental culture, it is always distinctly perceptible. He senses it, not only in the harsh Calvinistic fables of Hawthorne and the pious gurglings of Longfellow, but also in the poetry of Bryant, the tea-party niceness of Howells, the "maiden-like reserve" of James Lane Allen, and even in the work of Joel Chandler Harris. What! A Southern Puritan? Well, why not? What could be more erroneous than the common assumption that Puritanism is exclusively a Northern, a New England, madness? The truth is that it is as thoroughly national as the kindred belief in the devil, and runs almost unobstructed from Portland to Portland and from the Lakes to the Gulf. It is in the South, indeed, and not in the North, that it takes on its most bellicose and extravagant forms. Between the upper tier of New England and the Potomac river there is not a single prohibition state—but thereafter, alas, they come in huge blocks!· And behind that infinitely prosperous Puritanism there is a long and unbroken tradition. Berkeley, the last of the Cavaliers, was kicked out of power in Virginia so long ago as 1650. Lord Baltimore, the Proprietor of Maryland, was brought to terms by the Puritans of the Severn in 1657. The Scotch Covenanter, the most uncompromising and unenlightened of all Puritans, flourished in the Carolinas from the start, and in 1698, or thereabout, he was reinforced from New England. In 1757 a band of Puritans invaded what

74. **Berkeley.** Sir William Berkeley (1610–1677) became governor of Virginia in 1641. Cromwell forced his resignation in 1650. When the Stuarts returned under Charles II (1660), Berkeley was reinstated. His last administration was unsuccessful and tyrannous, culminating in a rebellion headed by Nathaniel Bacon (1676) and crushed violently; Charles II remarked that "that old fool hath taken more lives in that naked country than I have for the murder of my father." 76. **Baltimore.** George Calvert, Lord Baltimore (1580–1632) was given a grant to what is now the state of Maryland (1625). Upon his death the grant was turned over to his brother, Leonard Calvert, who became colonial governor of Maryland (1633). Lord Baltimore's son Cecil has always been regarded as the real founder of Maryland, however, because of his interest in the development of the colony, although he never visited it. The Baltimores were Catholic; the Puritan settlement on the Severn came into conflict with them in 1657 (during the period of the English Commonwealth, an administration by the Puritan Cromwell following upon the Puritans' victory in the Civil War). 79. **Covenanter.** Prior to the outbreak of the English Civil War, King Charles I attempted (1638) to force the Church of England upon the Scottish Presbyterians (who, as Protestant Calvinists, were occasionally referred to loosely as Puritans). The Presbyterians, uniting in defense of their faith, signed a National Covenant resisting Charles' impositions. After the Restoration of the Stuarts (1660) the name Covenanters was applied to the descendants of the original signers of the National Covenant. Many of them fled to the New World, particularly when the Revolution of 1688 failed to reconcile them to the English church. They were instrumental in the founding of both the Carolinas.

is now Georgia—and Georgia has been a Puritan barbarism ever since. Even while the early (and half-mythical) Cavaliers were still in nominal control of all these Southern plantations, they clung to the sea-coast. The population that moved down the chain of the Appalachians during the latter part of the eighteenth century, and then swept over them into the Mississippi valley, was composed almost entirely of Puritans—chiefly intransigeants from New England (where Unitarianism was getting on its legs), kirk-crazy Scotch, and that plupious and beauty-hating folk, the Scotch-Irish. "In the South today," said John Fiske a generation ago, "there is more Puritanism surviving than in New England." In that whole region, an area three times as large as France or Germany, there is not a single orchestra capable of playing Beethoven's C minor symphony, or a single painting worth looking at, or a single public building or monument of any genuine distinction, or a single factory devoted to the making of beautiful things, or a single poet, novelist, historian, musician, painter or sculptor whose reputation extends beyond his own country. Between the Mason and Dixon line and the mouth of the Mississippi there is but one opera-house, and that one was built by a Frenchman, and is now, I believe, closed. The only domestic art this huge and opulent empire knows is in the hands of Mexican greasers; its only native music it owes to the despised Negro; its only genuine poet was permitted to die up an alley like a stray dog.

2

In studying the anatomy and physiology of American Puritanism, and its effects upon the national literature, one quickly discerns two main streams of influence. On the one hand,

1. **Georgia.** The colony had really been founded by James Oglethorpe in 1733 as a refuge to poor debtors and oppressed German Protestants. The grant had been made to Oglethorpe as a private individual; he surrendered it to the Crown in 1753, and Georgia became a royal province. 10. **intransigeants,** irreconcilables; people who refuse to compromise. 12. **plupious,** over-pious. This word will not be found in any standard dictionary. It is a good example of Mencken's freedom with the English language—clearly a term of contempt, it has a soft, squashy, unpleasant sound. 19. **Beethoven's . . . symphony,** more commonly known as Beethoven's Fifth Symphony. 33. **poet . . . dog,** Edgar Allan Poe, who was found on the streets of Baltimore in a drugged condition; he died shortly thereafter (October 7, 1849). Poor health, the death of his wife, and disappointment at his failure to win greater recognition have been advanced as contributing to his physical and moral collapse, but the exact circumstances of his fatal seizure have never been made clear.

there is the influence of the original Puritans—whether of New England or of the South—, who came to the New World with a ready-made philosophy of the utmost clarity, positiveness and inclusiveness of scope, and who attained to such a position of political and intellectual leadership that they were able to force it almost unchanged upon the whole population, and to endow it with such vitality that it successfully resisted alien opposition later on. And on the other hand, one sees a complex of social and economic conditions which worked in countless irresistible ways against the rise of that dionysian spirit, that joyful acquiescence in life, that philosophy of the *Ja-sager,* which offers to Puritanism, today as in times past, its chief and perhaps only effective antagonism. In other words, the American of the days since the Revolution has had Puritanism diligently pressed upon him from without, and at the same time he has led, in the main, a life that has engendered a chronic hospitality to it, or at all events to its salient principles, within.

Dr. Kellner accurately describes the process whereby the aesthetic spirit, and its concomitant spirit of joy, were squeezed out of the original New Englanders, so that no trace of it showed in their literature, or even in their lives, for a century and a half after the first settlements. "Absorption in God," he says, "seems incompatible with the presentation (*i.e.,* aesthetically) of mankind. The God of the Puritans was in this respect a jealous God who brooked no sort of creative rivalry. The inspired moments of the loftiest souls were filled with the thought of God and His designs; spiritual life was wholly dominated by solicitude regarding salvation, the hereafter, grace; how could such petty concerns as personal experience of a lyric nature, the transports or the pangs of love, find utterance? What did a lyric occurrence like the first call of the cuckoo, elsewhere so welcome, or the first sight of the snowdrop, signify compared with the last Sunday's sermon and the new interpretation of the old riddle of evil in the world? And apart from the fact that everything of a personal nature must have appeared so trivial, all the sources of sec-

52. **dionysian.** In classical myth Dionysus, or Bacchus, was the god of wine and fertility; hence the adjective signifies the festive spirit in an unrestrained state. 53. **Ja-sager,** literally, the "Yes-sayer" the optimist, the believer in the joy of living.

ular lyric poetry were offensive and impious to Puritan theology. . . . One thing is an established fact: up to the close of the eighteenth century America had no belletristic literature."

This Puritan bedevilment by the idea of personal sin, this reign of the God-crazy, gave way in later years, as we shall see, to other and somewhat milder forms of pious enthusiasm. At the time of the Revolution, indeed, the importation of French political ideas was accompanied by an importation of French theological ideas, and such men as Franklin and Jefferson dallied with what, in those days at least, was regarded as downright atheism. Even in New England this influence made itself felt; there was a gradual letting down of Calvinism to the softness of Unitarianism, and that change was presently to flower in the vague temporizing of Transcendentalism. But as Puritanism, in the strict sense, declined in virulence and took deceptive new forms, there was a compensating growth of its brother, Philistinism, and by the first quarter of the nineteenth century, the distrust of beauty, and of the joy that is its object, was as firmly established throughout the land as it had ever been in New England. The original Puritans had at least been men of a certain education, and even of a certain austere culture. They were inordinately hostile to beauty in all its forms, but one somehow suspects that much of their hostility was due to a sense of their weakness before it, a realization of its disarming psychical pull. But the American of the new republic was of a different kidney. He was not so much hostile to beauty as devoid of any consciousness of it; he stood as unmoved before its phenomena as a savage before a table of logarithms. What he had set up on this continent, in brief, was a commonwealth of peasants and small traders, a paradise of the third-rate, and its national philosophy, almost wholly unchecked by the more sophisticated and civilized ideas of an aristocracy, was precisely the

philosophy that one finds among peasants and small traders at all times and everywhere. The difference between the United States and any other nation did not lie in any essential difference between American peasants and other peasants, but simply in the fact that here, alone, the voice of the peasant was the single voice of the nation—that here, alone, the only way to eminence and public influence was the way of acquiescence in the opinions and prejudices of the untutored and Philistine mob. Jackson was the *Stammvater* of the new statesmen and philosophers; he carried the mob's distrust of good taste even into the field of conduct; he was the first to put the rewards of conformity above the dictates of common decency; he founded a whole hierarchy of Philistine messiahs, the roaring of which still belabours the ear.

Once established, this culture of the intellectually disinherited tended to defend and perpetuate itself. On the one hand, there was no appearance of a challenge from within, for the exigent problems of existence in a country that was yet but half settled and organized left its people with no energy for questioning what at least satisfied their gross needs, and so met the pragmatic test. And on the other hand, there was no critical pressure from without, for the English culture which alone reached over the sea was itself entering upon its Victorian decline, and the influence of the native aristocracy—the degenerating *Junkers* of the great estates and the boorish magnates of the city *bourgeoisie*—was quite without any cultural direction at all. The chief concern of the American people, even above the bread-and-butter question, was politics. They were incessantly hag-ridden by political difficulties, both internal and external, of an inordinate complexity, and these occupied all the leisure they could steal from the sordid work of everyday. More, their new and troubled political ideas tended to absorb all the rancorous certainty of

17. **Unitarianism,** the religion which believes that God exists only in one person, as opposed to Trinitarianism, which believes that God exists in three persons (the Father, the Son, and the Holy Ghost). It is a philosophical type of religion, "softer" in the sense that it does not envisage a harsh, unforgiving, "jealous" God. 19. **Transcendentalism.** See p. 60, note to l. 39. 39. **What . . . third-rate.** The premises of Mencken's argument here become highly questionable; there is much to show that the early colonizers of America were not all third-rate. But it is characteristic of this author to proceed from his basic prejudice without regard to the other side of his question.

55. **Jackson . . . Stammvater.** Andrew Jackson (1767–1845), seventh President of the United States, was considered the first president to be elected by the masses; in other words, the first president truly representative of the Southern and Western agriculturalist rather than of the Northern and Eastern industrial aristocracy. He is therefore referred to by Mencken as the *Stammvater*, or patriarch, of the new universal democracy. The term just defined is characteristic of Mencken's liberal sprinkling about of German words. 71. **pragmatic,** practical. 76. **Junkers,** originally the name given the conservative Prussian aristocracy but used here to indicate the conservative landed gentry of England during the nineteenth century.

their fading religious ideas, so that devotion to a theory or a candidate became translated into devotion to a revelation, and the game of politics turned itself into a holy war. The custom of connecting purely political doctrines with pietistic concepts of an inflammable nature, then firmly set up by skilful persuaders of the mob, has never quite died out in the United States. There has not been a presidential con-
10 test since Jackson's day without its Armageddons, its marching of Christian soldiers, its crosses of gold, its crowns of thorns. The most successful American politicians, beginning with the anti-slavery agitators, have been those most adept at twisting the ancient gauds and shibboleths of Puritanism to partisan uses. Every campaign that we have seen for eighty years has been, on each side, a pursuit of bugaboos, a denunciation of heresies, a snouting up of
20 immoralities.

But it was during the long contest against slavery, beginning with the appearance of William Lloyd Garrison's *Liberator* in 1831 and ending at Appomattox, that this gigantic supernaturalization of politics reached its most astounding heights. In those days, indeed, politics and religion coalesced in a manner not seen in the world since the Middle Ages, and the combined pull of the two was so powerful
30 that none could quite resist it. All men of any ability and ambition turned to political activity for self-expression. It engaged the press to the exclusion of everything else; it conquered the pulpit: it even laid its hand upon industry and trade. Drawing the best imaginative talent into its service—Jefferson and Lincoln may well stand as examples—it left the cultivation of belles lettres, and of all the other arts no less, to women and admittedly second-rate men.
40 And when, breaking through this taboo, some chance first-rate man gave himself over to purely aesthetic expression, his reward was not

only neglect, but even a sort of ignominy, as if such enterprises were not fitting for males with hair on their chests. I need not point to Poe and Whitman, both disdained as dreamers and wasters, and both proceeded against with the utmost rigours of outraged Philistinism.

In brief, the literature of that whole period, as Algernon Tassin shows in "The Magazine in 50 America," was almost completely disassociated from life as men were then living it. Save one counts in such crude politico-puritan tracts as "Uncle Tom's Cabin," it is difficult to find a single contemporaneous work that interprets the culture of the time, or even accurately represents it. Later on, it found historians and anatomists, and in one work, at least, to wit, "Huckleberry Finn," it was studied and projected with the highest art, but no such im- 60 pulse to make imaginative use of it showed itself contemporaneously, and there was not even the crude sentimentalization of here and now that one finds in the popular novels of to-day. Fenimore Cooper filled his romances, not with the people about him, but with the Indians beyond the skyline, and made them half-fabulous to boot. Irving told fairy tales about the forgotten Knickerbockers; Hawthorne turned backward to the Puritans of Plymouth 70 Rock; Longfellow to the Acadians and the prehistoric Indians; Emerson took flight from earth altogether; even Poe sought refuge in a land of fantasy. It was only the frank second-raters—*e.g.*, Whittier and Lowell—who ventured to turn to the life around them, and the banality of the result is a sufficient indication of the crudeness of the current taste, and the mean position assigned to the art of letters. This was pre-eminently the era of the moral 80 tale, the Sunday-school book. Literature was conceived not as a thing in itself, but merely as a hand-maiden to politics or religion. The great celebrity of Emerson in New England was not the celebrity of a literary artist, but that of a theologian and metaphysician; he was esteemed in much the same way that Jonathan Edwards had been esteemed. Even down

10. **Armageddon,** the place mentioned in Revelation 16:16 as the site of a great battle to be fought "on the great day of God" between the powers of good and evil. 12. **crosses . . . thorns,** an echo of the concluding sentence from the famous "Cross of Gold" oration delivered by William Jennings Bryan (1860–1925) at the Democratic National Convention, held in Chicago in July 1896. The Democratic platform was based on the free-silver movement among the agricultural and mining groups of the Middle West and South; this movement favored the free coinage of silver in the ratio of 16 to 1, regardless of world conditions. Bryan, in defending the movement, concluded his oration: " 'You shall not press down upon the brow of labor this crown of thorns; you shall not crucify mankind upon a cross of gold.' " 36. **Jefferson.** Thomas Jefferson, of course, does not belong in the period following 1831.

50. **"The . . . America,"** New York, Dodd, Mead & Co., 1916. (Author's note.) 87. **Jonathan Edwards,** the uncompromising Calvinist divine (1703–1758); a Puritan mystic and idealist who furnished a most stubborn defense of Puritan dogma. He is generally considered one of the greatest minds which America has produced—certainly he was one of her most intense personalities.

to our own time, indeed, his vague and empty philosophizing has been put above his undeniable capacity for graceful utterance, and it remained for Dr. Kellner to consider him purely as a literary artist, and to give him due praise for his skill.

The Civil War brought that era of sterility to an end. As I shall show later on, the shock of it completely reorganized the American scheme
10 of things, and even made certain important changes in the national Puritanism, or, at all events, in its machinery. Whitman, whose career straddled, so to speak, the four years of the war, was the leader—and for a long while, the only trooper—of a double revolt. On the one hand he offered a courageous challenge to the intolerable prudishness and dirty-mindedness of Puritanism, and on the other hand he boldly sought the themes and even the modes
20 of expression of his poetry in the arduous, contentious and highly melodramatic life that lay all about him. Whitman, however, was clearly before his time. His countrymen could see him only as immoralist; save for a pitiful few of them, they were dead to any understanding of his stature as artist, and even unaware that such a category of men existed. He was put down as an invader of the public decencies, a disturber of the public peace; even his elo-
30 quent war poems, surely the best of all his work, were insufficient to get him a hearing; the sentimental rubbish of "The Blue and the Gray" and the ecstatic supernaturalism of "The Battle Hymn of the Republic" were far more to the public taste. Where Whitman failed, indeed, all subsequent explorers of the same field have failed with him, and the great war has left no more mark upon American letters than if it had never been fought. Nothing remotely
40 approaching the bulk and beam of Tolstoi's "War and Peace," or, to descend to a smaller scale, Zola's "The Attack on the Mill," has come out of it. Its appeal to the national imagination was undoubtedly of the most profound character; it coloured politics for fifty years, and is today a dominating influence in

the thought of whole sections of the American people. But in all that stirring up there was no upheaval of artistic consciousness, for the plain reason that there was no artistic consciousness 50 there to heave up, and all we have in the way of Civil War literature is a few conventional melodramas, a few half-forgotten short stories by Ambrose Bierce and Stephen Crane, and a half dozen idiotic popular songs in the manner of Randall's "Maryland, My Maryland."

In the seventies and eighties, with the appearance of such men as Henry James, William Dean Howells, Mark Twain and Bret Harte, a better day seemed to be dawning. 60 Here, after a full century of infantile romanticizing, were four writers who at least deserved respectful consideration as literary artists, and what is more, three of them turned from the conventionalized themes of the past to the teeming and colourful life that lay under their noses. But this promise of better things was soon found to be no more than a promise. Mark Twain, after "The Gilded Age," slipped back into romanticism tempered by Philistin- 70 ism, and was presently in the era before the Civil War, and finally in the Middle Ages, and even beyond. Harte, a brilliant technician, had displayed his whole stock when he had displayed his technique: his stories were not even superficially true to the life they presumed to depict; one searched them in vain for an interpretation of it; they were simply idle tales. As for Howells and James, both quickly showed that timorousness and reticence which are the 80 distinguishing marks of the Puritan, even in his most intellectual incarnations. The American scene that they depicted with such meticulous care was chiefly peopled with marionettes. They shrunk, characteristically, from those larger, harsher clashes of will and purpose which one finds in all truly first-rate literature. In particular, they shrunk from any interpretation of life which grounded itself upon an acknowledgment of its inexorable and inexplica- 90

32. "The . . . Gray," an extremely popular poem, of considerable banality, it may be added, composed by Francis Miles Finch in 1867. The theme is the dead of the Civil War.
42. "The . . . Mill." Zola has already been mentioned (p. 71, l. 50 and note). *The Attack on the Mill* is a powerful, realistic tale of an incident in the Franco-Prussian War of 1870-71.

54. **Stephen Crane,** one of the most promising of American authors (1871–1900), whose novel *The Red Badge of Courage* (1895) has been hailed as the greatest piece of imaginative writing in American letters and whose poems foreshadowed the modern impressionist school. 72. **finally . . . Ages.** What Mencken does not point out is that one of Mark Twain's works "in the Middle Ages," *The Mysterious Stranger* (1910), is one of the most sustained pieces of plain-spoken pessimism in American literature.

ble tragedy. In the vast combat of instincts and aspirations about them they saw only a feeble jousting of comedians, unserious and insignificant. Of the great questions that have agitated the minds of men in Howells' time one gets no more than a faint and far-away echo in his novels. His investigations, one may say, are carried on *in vacuo;* his discoveries are not expressed in terms of passion, but in terms of giggles.

In the followers of Howells and James one finds little save an empty imitation of their emptiness, a somewhat puerile parodying of their highly artful but essentially personal technique. To wade through the books of such characteristic American fictioneers as Frances Hodgson Burnett, Mary E. Wilkins Freeman, F. Hopkinson Smith, Alice Brown, James Lane Allen, Winston Churchill, Ellen Glasgow, Gertrude Atherton and Sarah Orne Jewett is to undergo an experience that is almost terrible. The flow of words is completely purged of ideas; in place of them one finds no more than a romantic restatement of all the old platitudes and formulae. To call such an emission of graceful poppycock a literature, of course, is to mouth an absurdity, and yet, if the college professors who write treatises on letters are to be believed, it is the best we have to show. Turn, for example, to "A History of American Literature Since 1870," by Prof. Fred Lewis Pattee, one of the latest and undoubtedly one of the least unintelligent of these books. In it the gifted pedagogue gives extended notice to no less than six of the nine writers I have mentioned, and upon all of them his verdicts are flattering. He bestows

high praises, direct and indirect, upon Mrs. Freeman's "grim and austere" manner, her "repression," her entire lack of poetical illumination. He compares Miss Jewett to both Howells and Hawthorne, not to mention Mrs. Gaskell—and Addison! He grows enthusiastic over a hollow piece of fine writing by Miss Brown. And he forgets altogether to mention Dreiser, or Sinclair, or Medill Patterson, or Harry Leon Wilson, or George Ade! . . .

So much for the best. The worst is beyond description. France has her Brieux and her Henry Bordeaux; Germany has her Mühlbach, her stars of the *Gartenlaube;* England contributes Caine, Corelli, Oppenheim and company. But it is in our country alone that banality in letters takes on the proportions of a national movement; it is only here that a work of the imagination is habitually judged by its sheer emptiness of ideas, its fundamental platitudinousness, its correspondence with the imbecility of mob thinking; it is only here that "glad" books run up sales of hundreds of thousands. Richard Harding Davis, with his ideals of a floor-walker; Gene Stratton Porter, with her snuffling sentimentality; Robert W. Chambers, with his "society" romances for shop-girls; Irvin Cobb, with his laboured, *Ayers' Almanac* jocosity; the authors of the *Saturday Evening*

8. *in vacuo,* in a vacuum. 17. **Burnett . . . Jewett,** Frances Eliza Hodgson Burnett (1849–1924), author of *Little Lord Fauntleroy* (1886); Mary E. Wilkins Freeman (1852–1930), a follower of the terse, sharp, realistic French school of the short story; F. Hopkinson Smith (1838–1915), an artist and a leisurely fiction-writer of the genteel variety; Alice Brown (1857–1948), a New Hampshire writer of poetry and fiction; James Lane Allen (1849–1925), a "local color" author whose specialty was old, aristocratic Kentucky and who wrote in a careful, grave style with occasional overtones of keen realism; Winston Churchill (1871–1944), a writer of romantic, historical novels like *The Crisis* (1901) or arraignments in fiction of church and politics like *Coniston* (1906) or *The Inside of the Cup* (1913); Ellen Glasgow (1874–1945), a brilliant and solid delineator of the South, a follower of the realist Thomas Hardy (1840–1928); Gertrude Atherton (1857–1948), a caustic, fearless critic of cosmopolitan aristocratic society; Sarah Orne Jewett (1849–1909), one of the first—and best—of the American "local color" school, whose stories of the Maine coast are still quietly effective. With the exception of Mrs. Burnett, it is difficult to see how Mencken's remarks here are anything but grossly unfair.

46. **Sinclair . . . Ade.** Upton Sinclair (1878–   ) is an effective, modern propagandist in fiction. The rest are insignificant enough writers; George Ade (1866–1944) made a name through his *Fables in Slang.* But the whole passage illustrates Mencken's inability to stand up unharmed in the light of subsequent thought, although his utterances at the time made plenty of noise. 49. **Brieux . . . Bordeaux.** Eugène Brieux (1858–1932) was a French novelist and dramatist with an earnest social outlook, notably in his *Damaged Goods* (1898); Henri Bordeaux (1870–   ) is a second-rate French critic and miscellaneous writer. 50. **Mühlbach . . . Gartenlaube.** Luise Mühlbach (1814–1873), a minor German novelist, was known chiefly for her novel of social criticism, *Aphra Behn* (1849), and her historical novels. The *Gartenlaube* ("Garden Wreath") is a German magazine which was founded in 1853. 52. **Caine . . . Oppenheim.** Hall Caine (1853–1931) was a popular writer of mediocre novels with a Manx setting; Marie Corelli (1864–1924) was a purveyor of melodrama in her many neurotic novels; E. Phillips Oppenheim (1866–1944) specialized in novels of international intrigue and mystery. 61. **Davis . . . Cobb,** Richard Harding Davis (1864–1916), in his day an extremely successful writer of journalism and stories mixing romanticism and realism, with the romanticism on top, particularly *Van Bibber* (1892) and *Soldiers of Fortune* (1897); Gene Stratton Porter (1868–1924), an extremely saccharine worshiper of health and happiness in love; Robert W. Chambers (1865–1933), an inexhaustible dealer in pure romance, combining sex with an often very effective historical flavor; Irvin Cobb (1876–1945), a fairly good short-story writer, but unfortunately a "professional" humorist. May it be asked what the "ideals of a floor-walker" really are? 65. *Ayers' Almanac,* one of the vast number of almanacs issued by dealers in patent medicine, containing miscellanea of historical, geographical, astronomical, agricultural, and medical facts.

Post school, with their heroic drummers and stockbrokers, their ecstatic celebration of the stupid, the sordid, the ignoble—these, after all, are our typical *literati*. The Puritan fear of ideas is the master of them all. Some of them, in truth, most of them, have undeniable talent; in a more favourable environment not a few of them might be doing sound work. But they see how small the ring is, and they make their tricks small to fit it. Not many of them ever venture a leg outside. The lash of the ringmaster is swift, and it stings damnably. . . .

I say not many; I surely do not mean none at all. As a matter of fact, there have been intermittent rebellions against the prevailing pecksniffery and sentimentality ever since the days of Irving and Hawthorne. Poe led one of them—as critic more than as creative artist. His scathing attacks upon the Gerald Stanley Lees, the Hamilton Wright Mabies and the George E. Woodberrys of his time keep a liveliness and appositeness that the years have not staled; his criticism deserves to be better remembered. Poe sensed the Philistine pull of a Puritan civilization as none had before him, and combated it with his whole artillery of rhetoric. Another rebel, of course, was Whitman; how he came to grief is too well known to need recalling. What is less familiar is the fact that both the *Atlantic Monthly* and the *Century* (first called *Scribner's*) were set up by men in revolt against the reign of mush, as *Putnam's* and the *Dial* had been before them. The salutary of the *Dial,* dated 1840, stated the case against the national mugginess clearly. The aim of the magazine, it said, was to oppose "that rigour of our conventions of religion and education which is turning us to stone" and to give expression to "new views and the dreams of youth." Alas, for these brave *ré-*

voltés! Putnam's succumbed to the circumambient rigours and duly turned to stone, and is now no more. The *Atlantic,* once so heretical, has become as respectable as the New York *Evening Post.* As for the *Dial,* it was until lately the very pope of orthodoxy and jealously guarded the college professors who read it from the pollution of ideas. Only the *Century* has kept the faith unbrokenly. It is, indeed, the one first-class American magazine that has always welcomed newcomers, and that maintains an intelligent contact with the literature that is in being, and that consistently tries to make the best terms possible with the dominant Philistinism. It cannot go the whole way without running into danger; let it be said to the credit of its editors that they have more than once braved that danger.

The tale might be lengthened. Mark Twain, in his day, felt the stirrings of revolt, and not all his Philistinism was sufficient to hold him altogether in check. If you want to find out about the struggle that went on within him, read the biography by Albert Bigelow Paine, or, better still, "The Mysterious Stranger" and "What is Man?" Alive, he had his position to consider; dead, he now speaks out. In the preface to "What is Man?" dated 1905, there is a curious confession of his incapacity for defying the taboos which surrounded him. The studies for the book, he says, were begun "twenty-five or twenty-seven years ago"—the period of "A Tramp Abroad" and "The Prince and the Pauper." It was actually written "seven years ago" —that is, just after "Following the Equator" and "Personal Recollections of Joan of Arc." And why did it lie so long in manuscript, and finally go out stealthily, under a private imprint? Simply because, as Mark frankly confesses, he "dreaded (*and could not bear*) the disapproval of the people around" him. He knew how hard his fight for recognition had been; he knew what direful penalties outraged orthodoxy could inflict; he had in him the somewhat pathetic discretion of a respectable family man. But, dead, he is safely beyond reprisal, and so, after a prudent interval, the faithful Paine begins printing books in which, writing knowingly behind six feet of earth, he

16. **pecksniffery,** hypocrisy combined with hollow pretentiousness; the word is derived from Pecksniff, a striking character in Charles Dickens' *Martin Chuzzlewit.* 20. **Lee . . . Woodberry,** Gerald Stanley Lee (1861–   ), professor of English at Smith College for many years and the author of many essays and criticisms of the "inspirational" variety; Hamilton W. Mabie (1845–1916), lawyer and journalist, associated for years with the *Outlook* (*Christian Union*) magazine, author of stories for children and essays of a gentle, serene type; George E. Woodberry (1855–1930), poet and critic, descendant of New England transcendentalism, professor at the University of Nebraska, Columbia, and elsewhere, author of many books on literary figures, particularly Poe, Hawthorne, and Shelley, incisive and rebellious in his earlier years, wistful and out of step with the world in his later days. Obviously he is superior to Lee and Mabie. 40. **révoltés,** rebels.

67. **In the preface . . . imprint.** The first edition for public sale did not appear until June, 1917, and in it the preface was suppressed. (Author's note.)

could set down his true ideas without fear. Some day, perhaps, we shall have his microbe story, and maybe even his picture of the court of Elizabeth.

A sneer in Prof. Pattee's history, before mentioned, recalls the fact that Hamlin Garland was also a rebel in his day and bawled for the Truth with a capital T. That was in 1893. Two years later the guardians of the national rectitude fell afoul of "Rose of Dutchers' Coolly" and Garland began to think it over; today he devotes himself to the safer enterprise of chasing spooks; his name is conspicuously absent from the Dreiser Protest. Nine years before his brief offending John Hay had set off a discreet bomb in "The Bread-Winners"—anonymously because "my standing would be seriously compromised" by an avowal. Six years later Frank Norris shook up the Phelpses and Mores of the time with "McTeague." Since then there have been assaults timorous and assaults head-long —by Bierce, by Dreiser, by Phillips, by Fuller —by Mary MacLanes and by Upton Sinclairs— by ploughboy poets from the Middle West and by jitney geniuses in Greenwich Village—assaults gradually tapering off to a mere sophomoric brashness and deviltry. And all of them like snow-ballings of Verdun. All of them

2. **microbe . . . Elizabeth,** two incredibly flat and vulgar tales of the Rabelaisian streak. 12. **enterprise . . . spooks.** Hamlin Garland's later work, unlike his realistic novels of his early years, is reminiscent, autobiographical, and rather wistfully romantic. 14. **Dreiser Protest.** Many of Dreiser's early novels had caused difficulties with publishers because of the subject matter. In 1917 the author, with the assistance of some friends, organized the idea of an author's aid society to combat the Societies for the Suppression of Vice. The plan fell through. But in March of that year Dreiser brought suit against his publishers in a test case. The case was finally tried in Brooklyn in May 1918; the book chosen for the test case was *The "Genius,"* the novel about Eugene Witla, an artist with weak will and weaker morality. A protest signed by 478 American and 7 English writers was submitted in defense of Dreiser. The judgment was against Dreiser; he did not appeal the decision, and the novel was not reprinted until 1922. 15. **Hay . . . "The Bread-Winners."** John Hay (1838–1905) found time from his governmental and diplomatic work as Secretary of State and Ambassador to Great Britain under President McKinley to edit the letters of Lincoln, to compose folk-poetry like *Pike County Ballads* (1871), and to experiment with a novel of industrial unrest, *The Bread-Winners* (1884). 19. **Phelpses and Mores.** William Lyon Phelps (1865–1944), for a long time Professor of English at Yale, was a voluminous popular critic and littérateur; Paul Elmer More (1864–1937) was a leader of the conservative school of American literary critics and protested in strong academic fashion against the tendencies of modern literature. 22. **Fuller,** Henry Balek Fuller (1857–1929), journalist and able writer of fiction which tried to analyze social progress. 23. **Mary MacLane** (1881–1929), an extremely introspective writer with, however, a considerable amount of critical insight. 28. **Verdun,** scene of the great six months' battle of World War I, in which the French ultimately repulsed the Germans (1916).

petered out and ineffectual. The normal, the typical American book of today is as fully a re-mouthing of old husks as the normal book of Griswold's day. The whole atmosphere of our literature, in William James' phrase, is "mawkish and dishwatery." Books are still judged among us, not by their form and organization as works of art, their accuracy and vividness as representations of life, their validity and perspicacity as interpretations of it, but by their conformity to the national prejudices, their accordance with set standards of niceness and propriety. The thing irrevocably demanded is a "sane" book; the ideal is a "clean," an "inspiring," a "glad" book.

3

All this may be called the Puritan impulse from within. It is, indeed, but a single manifestation of one of the deepest prejudices of a religious and half-cultured people—the prejudice against beauty as a form of debauchery and corruption—the distrust of all ideas that do not fit readily into certain accepted axioms—the belief in the eternal validity of moral concepts— in brief, the whole mental sluggishness of the lower orders of men. But in addition to this internal resistance, there has been laid upon American letters the heavy hand of a Puritan authority from without, and no examination of the history and present condition of our literature could be of any value which did not take it constantly into account, and work out the means of its influence and operation. That authority, as I shall show, transcends both in power and in alertness the natural reactions of the national mind, and is incomparably more potent in combating ideas. It is supported by a body of law that is unmatched in any other country of Christendom, and it is exercised with a fanatical harshness and vigilance that make escape from its operations well nigh impossible. Some of its effects, both direct and

32. **Griswold,** Rufus Griswold (1815–1857), probably the leading authority in American literary criticism of the first half of the nineteenth century. He was noted particularly for his troubled relations with Edgar Allan Poe. 33. **William James,** one of the American pioneers in the study of psychology (1842–1910), professor of philosophy at Harvard, commentator on the temper of his age, and brother of the noted Anglo-American novelist Henry James (1843–1916).

indirect, I shall describe later, but before doing so it may be well to trace its genesis and development.

At bottom, of course, it rests upon the inherent Puritanism of the people; it could not survive a year if they were opposed to the principle visible in it. That deep-seated and uncorrupted Puritanism, that conviction of the pervasiveness of sin, of the supreme importance of moral correctness, of the need of savage and inquisitorial laws, has been a dominating force in American life since the very beginning. There has never been any question before the nation, whether political or economic, religious or military, diplomatic or sociological, which did not resolve itself, soon or late, into a purely moral question. Nor has there ever been any surcease of the spiritual eagerness which lay at the bottom of the original Puritan's moral obsession: the American has been, from the very start, a man genuinely interested in the eternal mysteries, and fearful of missing their correct solution. The frank theocracy of the New England colonies had scarcely succumbed to the libertarianism of a godless Crown before there came the Great Awakening of 1734, with its orgies of homiletics and its restoration of talmudism to the first place among polite sciences. The Revolution, of course, brought a setback: the colonists faced so urgent a need of unity in politics that they declared a sort of *Treuga Dei* in religion, and that truce, armed though it was, left its imprint upon the First Amendment to the Constitution. But immediately the young Republic emerged from the stresses of adolescence, a missionary army took to the field again, and before long the Asbury revival was paling that

of Whitefield, Wesley and Jonathan Edwards, not only in its hortatory violence but also in the length of its lists of slain.

Thereafter, down to the outbreak of the Civil War, the country was rocked again and again by furious attacks upon the devil. On the one hand, this great campaign took a purely theological form, with a hundred new and fantastic creeds as its fruits; on the other hand, it crystallized into the hysterical temperance movement of the 30's and 40's, which penetrated to the very floor of Congress and put "dry" laws upon the statute-books of ten States; and on the third hand, as it were, it established a prudery in speech and thought from which we are yet but half delivered. Such ancient and innocent words as "bitch" and "bastard" disappeared from the American language; Bartlett tells us, indeed, in his "Dictionary of Americanisms," that even "bull" was softened to "male cow." This was the Golden Age of euphemism, as it was of euphuism; the worst inventions of the English mid-Victorians were adopted and improved. The word "woman" became a term of opprobrium, verging close upon downright libel; legs became the inimitable "limbs"; the stomach began to run from the "bosom" to the pelvic arch; pantaloons faded into "unmentionables"; the newspapers spun their parts of speech into such gossamer webs as "a statutory offence," "a house of questionable repute" and "an interesting condition." And meanwhile the Good Templars and Sons of Temperance swarmed in the land like a plague of celestial locusts. There was not a hamlet without its uniformed phalanx, its affecting exhibit of reformed drunkards. The Kentucky Legislature succumbed to a travelling recruiting officer, and two-thirds of the members signed the pledge. The National House of Representatives took recess after recess to hear eminent excoriators of the Rum Demon, and more than a dozen of its members forsook their duties to carry the new gospel to

24. **theocracy,** rule by God. In terms of a state, the ancient Israelites were the most notable examples of a theocracy. But the Puritan colony in Massachusetts Bay was the same; it avowed an allegiance to Almighty God that transcended earthly ties; "governors" like John Winthrop were merely the medium by which God's will could be administered. 26. **godless Crown,** the rule of the Stuarts after the Restoration, during the reign of Charles II in particular. **Great Awakening,** an evangelical movement of fundamentalist nature, by which the conservative Calvinists among the American colonists attempted to retrieve their slipping hold upon the growingly prosperous colonials. Probably the greatest leader in this Great Awakening was Jonathan Edwards. 28. **talmudism.** The *Talmud* is the body of ancient Hebrew civil and ecclesiastical law; talmudism is, therefore, adherence to such a body of law. 32. *Treuga Dei,* Truce of God. 38. **Asbury revival,** under Francis Asbury (1745–1816), first Methodist bishop in America. His ministrations increased the number of Methodist communicants from 316 to 214,000.

39. **Whitefield, Wesley.** John Wesley (1703–1791) was the founder of Methodism. On trips to the American colonies and the Continent he became interested in the Moravian form of Protestantism, which enjoined a strict, "methodical" worship of God and a strongly emotional evangelism. He began holding open-air meetings in 1739, in which he was associated with George Whitefield (1714–1770), prominent as an evangelist. 57. **"Dictionary of Americanisms,"** second edition, Boston, Little, Brown & Co., 1859, xxvi. (Author's note.)

the bucolic heathen—the vanguard, one may note in passing, of the innumerable Chautauquan caravan of later years.

Beneath all this bubbling on the surface, of course, ran the deep and swift undercurrent of anti-slavery feeling—a tide of passion which historians now attempt to account for on economic grounds, but which showed no trace of economic origin while it lasted. Its true quality
10 was moral, devout, ecstatic; it culminated, to change the figure, in a supreme discharge of moral electricity, almost fatal to the nation. The crack of that great spark emptied the jar; the American people forgot all about their pledges and pruderies during the four years of Civil War. The Good Templars, indeed, were never heard of again, and with them into memory went many other singular virtuosi of virtue —for example, the Millerites. But almost before
20 the last smoke of battle cleared away, a renaissance of Puritan ardour began, and by the middle of the 70's it was in full flower. Its high points and flashing lighthouses halt the backward-looking eye; the Moody and Sankey uproar, the triumphal entry of the Salvation Army, the recrudescence of the temperance agitation and its culmination in prohibition, the rise of the Young Men's Christian Association and of the Sunday-school, the almost miracu-
30 lous growth of the Christian Endeavour movement, the beginnings of the vice crusade, the renewed injection of moral conceptions and rages into party politics (the "crime" of 1873!),

the furious preaching of baroque Utopias, the invention of muckraking, the mad, glad war of extermination upon the Mormons, the hysteria over the Breckenridge-Pollard case and other like causes, the enormous multiplication of moral and religious associations, the spread of zoöphilia, the attack upon Mammon, the dawn 40 of the uplift, and last but far from least, comstockery.

In comstockery, if I do not err, the new Puritanism gave a sign of its formal departure from the old, and moral endeavour suffered a general overhauling and tightening of the screws. The difference between the two forms is very well represented by the difference between the program of the half-forgotten Good Templars and the program set forth in the 50 Webb Law of 1913, or by that between the somewhat diffident prudery of the 40's and the astoundingly ferocious and uncompromising vice-crusading of today. In brief, a difference between the *renunciation* and *denunciation*, asceticism and Mohammedanism, the hair shirt and the flaming sword. The distinguishing mark of the elder Puritanism, at least after it had attained to the stature of a national philosophy, was its appeal to the individual con- 60 science, its exclusive concern with the elect, its strong flavour of self-accusing. Even the rage against slavery was, in large measure, an emotion of the mourners' bench. The thing that worried the more ecstatic Abolitionists was their sneaking sense of responsibility, the fear that they themselves were flouting the fire by letting slavery go on. The thirst to punish the concrete slave-owner, as an end in itself, did not appear until opposition had added ex- 70 asperation to fervour. In most of the earlier harangues against his practice, indeed, you will

2. **Chautauquan.** On the shores of Lake Chautauqua, in western New York, was founded in 1874 a Biblical Institute and Sunday School Assembly, the purpose of which was educational and Christian. The plan was to hold assemblies each summer. The idea was extremely successful and was copied all over the country, down into the present generation. The original Chautauqua assembly is still held, but the Chautauqua circuits are rapidly disappearing. 19. **Millerites,** followers of William Miller (d. 1849), who predicted that the world was to come to an end in 1843 or 1844 and enjoined a life of strict virtue in the meantime. 24. **Moody and Sankey.** Dwight L. Moody (1837–1899) and Ira D. Sankey (1840–1908) constituted the most famous evangelical pair produced by the United States. Moody was the preacher; Sankey, the singer, furnished the necessary musical inspiration. The Moody and Sankey gospel hymns were known wherever the English language was spoken. 33. **"crime" of 1873,** possibly referring to the demonetization of silver and the financial panic of 1873; possibly to the Credit Mobilier scandal. The latter involved contracts for the completion of the Union Pacific Railroad; sales of holding-company stock to interested congressmen; and accusations of bribery of numerous high government officials. No other political scandal in American history, with the possible exception of the Teapot Dome affair of the 1920's (cf. p. 7), so shook the fundamental faith of the American people in their government.

34. **baroque,** a style of architecture prevailing from the late Renaissance (c. 1550) through the eighteenth century, and marked especially by curves and distortion. The epithet is not very appropriate here but suggests the bizarre, ill-proportioned, or ill-balanced. 36. **Mormons.** Public opinion forced the Mormons of Utah to disavow polygamy as an essential part of their religion (1890). 37. **Breckenridge-Pollard.** W. Campbell P. Breckenridge (1837–1904), congressman from Kentucky and member of a distinguished Southern family, was defeated for reëlection in 1894 because of the adverse public opinion stirred up by a breach-of-promise suit directed against him by one Madeline Pollard. 40. **zoöphilia,** love of animals. Mencken is here referring to the spread of charitable organizations for the care of animals. 41. **comstockery,** described below (p. 84, note to l. 83). 51. **Webb Law.** The Webb-Kenyon Act prohibited the interstate shipment of alcoholic liquor.

find a perfect willingness to grant that slave-owner's good faith, and even to compensate him for his property. But the new Puritanism —or, perhaps more accurately, considering the shades of prefixes, the neo-Puritanism—is a frank harking back to the primitive spirit. The original Puritan of the bleak New England coast was not content to flay his own wayward carcass: full satisfaction did not sit upon him until he had jailed a Quaker. That is to say, the sinner who excited his highest zeal and passion was not so much himself as his neighbour; to borrow a term from psychopathology, he was less the masochist than the sadist. And it is that very peculiarity which sets off his descendant of today from the ameliorated Puritan of the era between the Revolution and the Civil War. The new Puritanism is not ascetic, but militant. Its aim is not to lift up saints but to knock down sinners. Its supreme manifestation is the vice crusade, an armed pursuit of helpless outcasts by the whole military and naval forces of the Republic. Its supreme hero is Comstock Himself, with his pious boast that the sinners he jailed during his astounding career, if gathered into one penitential party, would have filled a train of sixty-one coaches, allowing sixty to the coach.

So much for the general trend and tenor of the movement. At the bottom of it, it is plain, there lies that insistent presentation of the idea of sin, that enchantment by concepts of carnality, which has engaged a certain type of man, to the exclusion of all other notions, since the dawn of history. The remote ancestors of our Puritan-Philistines of today are to be met with in the Old Testament and the New, and their nearer grandfathers clamoured against the snares of the flesh in all the councils of the Early Church. Not only Western Christianity has had to reckon with them: they have brothers today among the Mohammedan Sufi and in obscure Buddhist sects, and they were the chief preachers of the Russian Raskol, or Reformation. "The Ironsides of Cromwell and the Puritans of New England," says Heard, in his book on the Russian church, "bear a strong re-

semblance to the Old Believers." But here, in the main, we have asceticism more than Puritanism, as it is now visible; here the sinner combated is chiefly the one within. How are we to account for the wholesale transvaluation of values that came after the Civil War, the transfer of ire from the Old Adam to the happy rascal across the street, the sinister rise of a new Inquisition in the midst of a growing luxury that even the Puritans themselves succumbed to? The answer is to be sought, it seems to me, in the direction of the Golden Calf—in the direction of the fat fields of our Midlands, the full nets of our lakes and coasts, the factory smoke of our cities—even in the direction of Wall Street, that devil's chasm. In brief, Puritanism has become bellicose and tyrannical by becoming rich. The will to power has been aroused to a high flame by an increase in the available draught and fuel, as militarism is engendered and nourished by the presence of men and materials. Wealth, discovering its power, has reached out its long arms to grab the distant and innumerable sinner; it has gone down into its deep pockets to pay for his costly pursuit and flaying; it has created the Puritan *entrepreneur,* the daring and imaginative organizer of Puritanism, the baron of moral endeavour, the invincible prophet of new austerities. And, by the same token, it has issued its letters of marque to the Puritan mercenary, the professional hound of heaven, the moral *Junker,* the Comstock, and out of his skill at his trade there has arisen the whole machinery, so complicated and so effective, of the new Holy Office.

Poverty is a soft pedal upon all branches of human activity, not excepting the spiritual, and even the original Puritans, for all their fire, felt its throttling caress. I think it is Bill Nye who has humorously pictured their arduous life: how they had to dig clams all winter that they would have strength enough to plant corn, and how they had to hoe corn all summer that they would have strength enough to dig clams. That low ebb of fortune worked against the full satisfaction of their zeal in two

42. **Sufi,** a mystic organization within the Mohammedan faith. A member of the Sufi possesses nothing and desires nothing. 44. **Raskol,** a rigorous fundamentalistic Russian religious sect, which sprang up during the seventeenth century.

74. *entrepreneur,* one who undertakes; generally used of an employer who assumes responsibility for his business. 87. **Bill Nye,** Edgar Wilson Nye (1850–1896), a Will Rogers type of American writer.

distinct ways. On the one hand, it kept them but ill-prepared for the cost of offensive enterprise: even their occasional missionarying raids upon the Indians took too much productive energy from their business with the corn and the clams. And on the other hand, it kept a certain restraining humility in their hearts, so that for every Quaker they hanged, they let a dozen go. Poverty, of course, is no discredit, but at all events, it is a subtle criticism. The man oppressed by material wants is not in the best of moods for the more ambitious forms of moral adventure. He not only lacks the means; he is also deficient in the self-assurance, the sense of superiority, the secure and lofty point of departure. If he is haunted by notions of the sinfulness of his neighbours, he is apt to see some of its worst manifestations within himself, and that disquieting discovery will tend to take his thoughts from the other fellow. It is by no arbitrary fiat, indeed, that the brothers of all the expiatory orders are vowed to poverty. History teaches us that wealth, whenever it has come to them by chance, has put an end to their soul-searching. The Puritans of the elder generations, with few exceptions, were poor. Nearly all Americans, down to the Civil War, were poor. And being poor, they subscribed to a *Sklavenmoral*. That is to say, they were spiritually humble. Their eyes were fixed, not upon the abyss below them, but upon the long and rocky road ahead of them. Their moral passion spent most of its force in self-accusing, self-denial and self-scourging. They began by howling their sins from the mourners' bench; they came to their end, many of them, in the supreme immolation of battle.

But out of the War came prosperity, and out of prosperity came a new morality, to wit, the *Herrenmoral*. Many great fortunes were made in the War itself; an uncountable number got started during the two decades following. What is more, this material prosperity was generally dispersed through all classes: it affected the common workman and the remote farmer quite as much as the actual merchant and manufacturer. Its first effect, as we all know, was a universal cockiness, a rise in pretensions, a com-

forting feeling that the Republic was a success, and with it, its every citizen. This change made itself quickly obvious, and even odious, in all the secular relations of life. The American became a sort of braggart playboy of the western world, enormously sure of himself and ludicrously contemptuous of all other men. And on the ghostly side there appeared the same accession of confidence, the same sure assumption of authority, though at first less self-evidently and offensively. The religion of the American thus began to lose its inward direction; it became less and less a scheme of personal salvation and more and more a scheme of pious derring-do. The revivals of the 70's had all the bounce and fervour of those of half a century before, but the mourners' bench began to lose its standing as their symbol, and in its place appeared the collection basket. Instead of accusing himself, the convert volunteered to track down and bring in the other fellow. His enthusiasm was not for repentance, but for what he began to call service. In brief, the national sense of energy and fitness gradually superimposed itself upon the national Puritanism, and from that marriage sprung a keen *Wille zur Macht,* a lusty will to power. The American Puritan, by now, was not content with the rescue of his own soul; he felt an irresistible impulse to hand salvation on, to disperse and multiply it, to ram it down reluctant throats, to make it free, universal and compulsory. He had the men, he had the guns and he had the money too. All that was needed was organization. The rescue of the unsaved could be converted into a wholesale business, unsentimentally and economically conducted, and with all the usual aids to efficiency, from skilful sales management to seductive advertising, and from rigorous accounting to the diligent shutting off of competition.

Out of that new will to power came many enterprises more or less futile and harmless, with the "institutional" church at their head. Piety was cunningly disguised as basketball, billiards and squash; the sinner was lured to grace with Turkish baths, lectures on foreign

---

29. *Sklavenmoral,* the psychology of a slave. 40. *Herrenmoral,* the psychology of a master.

71. **In brief . . . power.** Cf. "The Puritan," by Owen Hatteras, *The Smart Set,* July, 1916; and "The Puritan's Will to Power," by Randolph S. Bourne, *The Seven Arts,* April, 1917. (Author's note.)

travel, and free instructions in stenography, rhetoric and double-entry book-keeping. Religion lost all its old contemplative and esoteric character, and became a frankly worldly enterprise, a thing of balance-sheets and ponderable profits, heavily capitalized and astutely manned. There was no longer any room for the spiritual type of leader, with his white choker and his interminable fourthlies. He was dis-
10 placed by a brisk gentleman in a "business suit" who looked, talked and thought like a seller of Mexican mine stock. Scheme after scheme for the swift evangelization of the nation was launched, some of them of truly astonishing sweep and daring. They kept pace, step by step, with the mushroom growth of enterprise in the commercial field. The Y. M. C. A. swelled to the proportions of a Standard Oil Company, a United States Steel Corpora-
20 tion. Its huge buildings began to rise in every city; it developed a swarm of specialists in new and fantastic moral and social sciences; it enlisted the same gargantuan talent which managed the railroads, the big banks and the larger national industries. And beside it rose the Young People's Society of Christian Endeavour, the Sunday-school associations and a score of other such grandiose organizations, each with its seductive baits for recruits and money.
30 Even the enterprises that had come down from an elder and less expansive day were pumped up and put on a Wall Street basis: the American Bible Society, for example, began to give away Bibles by the million instead of by the thousand, and the venerable Tract Society took on the feverish ardour of a daily newspaper, even of a yellow journal. Down into our own day this trustification of pious endeavour has gone on. The Men and Religion Forward
40 Movement proposed to convert the whole country by 12 o'clock noon of such and such a day; the Order of Gideons plans to make every traveller read the Bible (American Revised Version!) whether he will or not; in a score of cities there are committees of opulent devotees who take half-pages in the newspapers, and advertise the Decalogue and the Beatitudes as if they were commodities of trade.
50 Thus the national energy which created the Beef Trust and the Oil Trust achieved equal

marvels in the field of religious organization and by exactly the same methods. One needs be no psychologist to perceive in all this a good deal less actual religious zeal than mere lust for staggering accomplishment, for empty bigness, for the unprecedented and the prodigious. Many of these great religious enterprises, indeed, soon lost all save the faintest flavour of devotion—for example, the Y. M. C. A., which 60 is now no more than a sort of national club system, with its doors open to any one not palpably felonious. (I have drunk cocktails in Y. M. C. A. lamaseries, and helped fallen lamas to bed.) But while the war upon godlessness thus degenerated into a secular sport in one direction, it maintained all its pristine quality, and even took on a new ferocity in another direction. Here it was that the lamp of American Puritanism kept on burning; here, it was, in- 70 deed, that the lamp became converted into a huge bonfire, or rather a blast-furnace, with flames mounting to the very heavens, and sinners stacked like cordwood at the hand of an eager black gang. In brief, the new will to power, working in the true Puritan as in the mere religious sportsman, stimulated him to a campaign of repression and punishment perhaps unequalled in the history of the world, and developed an art of militant morality as 80 complex in technique and as rich in professors as the elder art of iniquity.

If we take the passage of the Comstock Postal Act, on March 3, 1873, as a starting point, the legislative stakes of this new Puritan movement sweep upward in a grand curve to the passage of the Mann and Webb Acts, in 1910 and 1913, the first of which ratifies the Seventh Commandment with a salvo of artillery, and the second of which puts the over- 90 whelming power of the Federal Government behind the enforcement of the prohibition laws in the so-called "dry" States. The mind at once recalls the salient campaigns of this war of a generation: first the attack upon "vicious" literature, begun by Comstock and the New York Society for the Suppression of Vice, but quickly extending to every city in the land; then the

64. **lamaseries.** In the religion of Tibet the *Lama* is a Buddhist priest of faith and saintliness. The *lamasery* is the monastery. 83. **Comstock Postal Act,** prohibiting the sending of "obscene matter" through the United States Mail. 87. **Mann Act,** prohibiting white-slave traffic.

long fight upon the open gambling house, culminating in its practical disappearance; then the recrudescence of prohibition, abandoned at the outbreak of the Civil War, and the attempt to enforce it in a rapidly growing list of States; then the successful onslaught upon the Louisiana lottery, and upon its swarm of rivals and successors; then the gradual stamping-out of horse-racing, until finally but two or three
10 States permitted it, and the consequent attack upon the pool-room; then the rise of a theatre-censorship in most of the large cities, and of a moving picture censorship following it; then the revival of Sabbatarianism, with the Lord's Day Alliance, a Canadian invention, in the van; then the gradual tightening of the laws against sexual irregularity, with the unenforceable New York Adultery Act as a typical product; and lastly, the general ploughing up and
20 emotional discussion of sexual matters, with compulsory instruction in "sex hygiene" as its mildest manifestation and the mediaeval fury of the vice crusade as its worst. Differing widely in their targets, these various Puritan enterprises had one character in common: they were all efforts to combat immorality with the weapons designed for crime. In each of them there was a visible effort to erect the individual's offence against himself into an offence
30 against society. Beneath all of them there was the dubious principle—the very determining principle, indeed, of Puritanism—that it is competent for the community to limit and condition the private acts of its members, and with it the inevitable corollary that there are some members of the community who have a special talent for such legislation, and that their arbitrary fiats are, and of a right ought to be, binding upon all.

4

40   This is the essential fact of the new Puritanism; its recognition of the moral expert, the professional sinhound, the virtuoso of virtue. Under the original Puritan theocracy, as in

Scotland, for example, the chase and punishment of sinners was a purely ecclesiastical function, and during the slow disintegration of the theocracy the only change introduced was the extension of that function to lay helpers, and finally to the whole body of laymen. This change, however, did not materially corrupt 50 the ecclesiastical quality of the enterprise: the leader in the so-called militant field still remained the same man who led in the spiritual field. But with the capitalization of Puritan effort there came a radical overhauling of method. The secular arm, as it were, conquered as it helped. That is to say, the special business of forcing sinners to be good was taken away from the preachers and put into the hands of laymen trained in its technique 60 and mystery, and there it remains. The new Puritanism has created an army of gladiators who are not only distinct from the hierarchy, but who, in many instances, actually command and intimidate the hierarchy. This is conspicuously evident in the case of the Anti-Saloon League, an enormously effective fighting organization, with a large staff of highly accomplished experts in its service. These experts do not wait for ecclesiastical support, nor even ask 70 for it; they force it. The clergyman who presumes to protest against their war upon the saloon, even upon the quite virtuous ground that it is not effective enough, runs a risk of condign and merciless punishment. So plainly is this understood, indeed, that in more than one State the clergy of the Puritan denominations openly take orders from these specialists in excoriation, and court their favour without shame. Here a single moral enterprise, heavily capital- 80 ized and carefully officered, has engulfed the entire Puritan movement, and a part has become more than the whole.

In a dozen other directions this tendency to transform a religious business into a purely secular business, with lay backers and lay officers, is plainly visible. The increasing wealth of Puritanism has not only augmented its scope and its daring, but it has also had the effect of attracting clever men, of no particular spiritual 90

7. **Louisiana lottery.** The state of Louisiana was the last to encourage a public lottery, a device that had been used frequently in the colonies during the eighteenth century for various public enterprises. Agitation against the Louisiana lottery began about the time of the Civil War, but it was not until 1894 that public opinion caused the Louisiana legislature to refrain from renewing the charter of the lottery which had expired.

66. **Anti-Saloon league . . . whole.** An instructive account of the organization and methods of the Anti-Saloon League, a thoroughly typical Puritan engine, is to be found in *Alcohol and Society*, by John Koren, New York, Henry Holt & Co., 1916. (Author's note.)

enthusiasm, to its service. Moral endeavour, in brief, has become a recognized trade, or rather a profession, and there have appeared men who pretend to a special and enormous knowledge of it, and who show enough truth in their pretension to gain the unlimited support of Puritan capitalists. The vice crusade, to mention one example, has produced a large crop of such self-constituted experts, and some of them are in such demand that they are overwhelmed with engagements. The majority of these men have wholly lost the flavour of sacerdotalism. They are not pastors, but detectives, statisticians and mob orators, and not infrequently their secularity becomes distressingly evident. Their aim, as they say, is to do things. Assuming that "moral sentiment" is behind them, they override all criticism and opposition without argument, and proceed to the business of dispersing prostitutes, of browbeating and terrorizing weak officials, and of forcing legislation of their own invention through City Councils and State Legislatures. Their very cocksureness is their chief source of strength. They combat objection with such violence and with such a devastating cynicism that it quickly fades away. The more astute politicians, in the face of so ruthless a fire, commonly profess conversion and join the colours, just as their brethren go over to prohibition in the "dry" States, and the newspapers seldom hold out much longer. The result is that the "investigation" of the social evil becomes an orgy, and that the ensuing "report" of the inevitable "vice commission" is made up of two parts sensational fiction and three parts platitude. Of all the vice commissions that have sat of late in the United States, not one has done its work without the aid of these singularly confident experts, and not one has contributed an original and sagacious idea, nor even an idea of ordinary common sense, to the solution of the problem.

I need not go on piling up examples of this new form of Puritan activity, with its definite departure from a religious foundation and its elaborate development as an everyday business. The impulse behind it I have called a *Wille zur Macht,* a will to power. In terms more homely, it was described by John Fiske as "the disposition to domineer," and in his

usual unerring way, he saw its dependence on the gratuitous assumption of infallibility. But even stronger than the Puritan's belief in his own inspiration is his yearning to make some one jump. In other words, he has an ineradicable liking for cruelty in him: he is a sportsman even before he is a moralist, and very often his blood-lust leads him into lamentable excesses. The various vice crusades afford innumerable cases in point. In one city, if the press dispatches are to be believed, the proscribed women of the Tenderloin were pursued with such ferocity that seven of them were driven to suicide. And in another city, after a campaign of repression so unfortunate in its effects that there were actually protests against it by clergymen elsewhere, a distinguished (and very friendly) connoisseur of such affairs referred to it ingenuously as more fun "than a fleet of aeroplanes." Such disorderly combats with evil, of course, produce no permanent good. It is a commonplace, indeed, that a city is usually in worse condition after it has been "cleaned up" than it was before, and I need not point to New York, Los Angeles and Des Moines for the evidence as to the social evil, and to Savannah, Atlanta and Charleston, South Carolina, for the evidence as to the saloon. But the Puritans who finance such enterprises get their thrills, not out of any possible obliteration of vice, but out of the galloping pursuit of the vicious. The new Puritan gives no more serious thought to the rights and feelings of his quarry than the gunner gives to the rights and feelings of his birds. From the beginning of the prohibition campaign, for example, the principle of compensation has been violently opposed, despite its obvious justice, and a complaisant judiciary has ratified the Puritan position. In England and on the Continent that principle is safeguarded by the fundamental laws, and during the early days of the anti-slavery agitation in this country it was accepted as incontrovertible, but if any statesman of the "dry" States were to propose today that it be applied to the license-holder whose lawful franchise is taken away from him arbitrarily, or to the brewer or distiller whose costly plant is rendered useless and valueless, he would see the days of his statesmanship brought to a quick and violent close.

But does all this argue a total lack of justice in the American character, or even a lack of common decency? I doubt that it would be well to go so far in accusation. What it does argue is a tendency to put moral considerations above all other considerations, and to define morality in the narrow Puritan sense. The American, in other words, thinks that the sinner has no rights that any one is bound to respect, and he is prone to mistake an unsupported charge of sinning, provided it be made violently enough, for actual proof and confession. What is more, he takes an intense joy in the mere chase: he has the true Puritan taste for an *auto da fé* in him. "I am ag'inst capital punishment," said Mr. Dooley, "but we won't get rid av it so long as the people enjie it so much." But though he is thus an eager spectator, and may even be lured into taking part in the pursuit, the average American is not disposed to initiate it, nor to pay for it. The larger Puritan enterprises of today are not popular in the sense of originating in the bleachers, but only in the sense of being applauded from the bleachers. The burdens of the fray, both of toil and of expense, are always upon a relatively small number of men. In a State rocked and racked by a war upon the saloon, it was recently shown, for example, that but five per cent. of the members of the Puritan denominations contributed to the war-chest. And yet the Anti-Saloon League of that State was so sure of support from below that it presumed to stand as the spokesman of the whole Christian community, and even ventured to launch excommunications upon contumacious Christians, both lay and clerical, who objected to its methods. Moreover, the great majority of the persons included in the contributing five per cent, gave no more than a few cents a year. The whole support of the League devolved upon a dozen men, all of them rich and all of them Puritans of purest ray serene. These men

supported a costly organization for their private entertainment and stimulation. It was their means of recreation, their sporting club. They were willing to spend a lot of money to procure good sport for themselves—*i.e.*, to procure the best crusading talent available—and they were so successful in that endeavour that they enchanted the populace too, and so shook the State.

Naturally enough, this organization of Puritanism upon a business and sporting basis has had a tendency to attract and create a type of "expert" crusader, whose determination to give his employers a good show is uncontaminated by any consideration for the public welfare. The result has been a steady increase of scandals, a constant collapse of moral organizations, a frequent unveiling of whited sepulchres. Various observers have sought to direct the public attention to this significant corruption of the new Puritanism. The New York *Sun*, for example, in the course of a protest against the appointment of a vice commission for New York, has denounced the paid agents of private reform organizations as "notoriously corrupt, undependable and dishonest," and the Rev. Dr. W. S. Rainsford, supporting the charge, has borne testimony out of his own wide experience to their lawlessness, their absurd pretensions to special knowledge, their habit of manufacturing evidence, and their devious methods of shutting off criticism. But so far, at all events, no organized war upon them has been undertaken, and they seem to flourish more luxuriantly year after year. The individual whose common rights are invaded by such persons has little chance of getting justice, and less of getting redress. When he attempts to defend himself he finds that he is opposed, not only by a financial power that is ample for all purposes of the combat and that does not shrink at intimidating juries, prosecuting officers and judges, but also by a shrewdness which shapes the laws to its own uses, and takes full advantage of the miserable cowardice of legislatures. The moral gladiators, in brief, know the game. They come before a legislature with a bill ostensibly designed to cure some great and admitted evil, they procure its enactment by scarcely veiled insinuations that all who stand against it must be

15. ***auto da fé***, "act of faith," the formal judgment pronounced by the Inquisition in the days of the Protestant Reformation. After the pronouncement of the judgment the prisoner was turned over to secular authorities for the execution of the punishment prescribed by the ecclesiastical court. The term is now applied to the punishment rather than the judgment; hence, to any kind of punishment of a severe and arbitrary nature. 16. **Mr. Dooley,** an extremely rational and shrewd Irish-American, chief character in the many satirical papers of Finley Peter Dunne (1867–1936), who himself adopted as his pseudonym the name of this favorite character.

apologists for the evil itself, and then they proceed to extend its aims by bold inferences, and to dragoon the courts into ratifying those inferences, and to employ it as a means of persecution, terrorism and blackmail. The history of the Mann Act offers a shining example of this purpose. It was carried through Congress, over the veto of President Taft, who discerned its extravagance, on the plea that it was
10 needed to put down the traffic in prostitutes; it is enforced today against men who are no more engaged in the traffic in prostitutes than you or I. Naturally enough, the effect of this extension of its purposes, against which its author has publicly protested, has been to make it a truly deadly weapon in the hands of professional Puritans and of denouncers of delinquency even less honest. "Blackmailers of both sexes have arisen," says Mr. Justice McKenna,
20 "using the terrors of the construction now sanctioned by the [Supreme] Court as a help—indeed, the means—for their brigandage. The result is grave and should give us pause."

But that is as far as objection has yet gone; the majority of the learned jurist's colleagues swallowed both the statute and its consequences. There is, indeed, no sign as yet of any organized war upon the alliance between the blackmailing Puritan and the pseudo-Puritan
30 blackmailer. It must wait until a sense of reason and justice shows itself in the American people, strong enough to overcome their prejudice in favour of the moralist on the one hand, and their delight in barbarous pursuits and punishments on the other. I see but faint promise of that change today.

6

So beset, it is no wonder that the typical American maker of books becomes a timorous and ineffective fellow, whose work tends in-
40 evitably toward a feeble superficiality. Sucking

18. **"Blackmailers . . . pause,"** in *U. S. Rep.*, Vol. 242, No. 7, p. 502. (Author's note.) 25. **the majority . . . consequences.** The majority opinion, written by Mr. Justice Day, is given in *U. S. Rep.*, Vol. 242, No. 7, pp. 482–496. (Author's note.) 37. Section 5 of this essay has been omitted. It treats at considerable length of the activities of Anthony Comstock (1844–1916), the reformer, of his successful pushing through Congress and State legislatures of laws to regulate the morals of art and literature. It explains that the implementing of these laws has resulted in a one-sided procedure wherein an author can do little to defend himself. It speaks bitingly of the capriciousness and utter unfairness with which the laws are invoked. But the section is long and out of proportion; it is really a bit of special pleading; and it is dull reading as compared with the rest of the essay.

in the Puritan spirit with the very air he breathes, and perhaps burdened inwardly with an inheritance of the actual Puritan stupidity, he is further kept upon the straight path of chemical purity by the very real perils that I have just rehearsed. The result is a literature full of the mawkishness that the late Henry James so often roared against—a literature almost wholly detached from life as men are living it in the world—in George Moore's phrase, 50 a literature still at nurse. It is on the side of sex that the appointed virtuosi of virtue exercise their chief repressions, for it is sex that especially fascinates the lubricious Puritan mind; but the conventional reticence that thus becomes the enforced fashion in one field extends itself to all others. Our fiction, in general, is marked by an artificiality as marked as that of Eighteenth Century poetry or the later Georgian drama. The romance in it runs to set 60 forms and stale situations; the revelation, by such a book as "The Titan," that there may be a glamour as entrancing in the way of a conqueror of men as in the way of a youth with a maid, remains isolated and exotic. We have no first-rate political or religious novel; we have no first-rate war story; despite all our national engrossment in commercial enterprise, we have few second-rate tales of business. Romance, in American fiction, still means only a somewhat 70 childish amorousness and sentimentality—the love affairs of Paul and Virginia, or the pale adulteries of their elders. And on the side of realism there is an almost equal vacuity and lack of veracity. The action of all the novels of the Howells school goes on within four walls of painted canvas; they begin to shock once they describe an attack of asthma or a steak burning below stairs; they never penetrate beneath the flow of social concealments and ur- 80 banities to the passions that actually move men and women to their acts, and the great forces that circumscribe and condition personality. So obvious a piece of reporting as Upton Sinclair's "The Jungle" or Robert Herrick's "Together" makes a sensation; the appearance of a "Jennie Gerhardt" or a "Hagar Revelly"

50. **George Moore,** an eminent Anglo-Irish novelist (1853–1933), a master stylist in prose, with a keen realistic approach; his best-known novel is probably *Esther Waters* (1894). He was also a poet of talent. 72. **Paul and Virginia,** the childlike—and childish—hero and heroine of the idyllic *Paul et Virginie,* a novel (1787) by Bernardin de St. Pierre (1737–1814).

brings forth a growl of astonishment and rage.

In all this dread of free inquiry, this childish skittishness in both writers and public, this dearth of courage and even of curiosity, the influence of comstockery is undoubtedly to be detected. It constitutes a sinister and ever-present menace to all men of ideas; it affrights the publisher and paralyzes the author; no one on the outside can image its burden as a prac-
10 tical concern. I am, in moments borrowed from more palatable business, the editor of an American magazine, and I thus know at first hand what the burden is. That magazine is anything but a popular one, in the current sense. It sells at a relatively high price; it contains no pictures or other baits for the childish; it is frankly addressed to a sophisticated minority. I may thus assume reasonably, I believe, that its readers are not sex-curious and
20 itching adolescents, just as my colleague of the *Atlantic Monthly* may assume reasonably that his readers are not Italian immigrants. Nevertheless, as a practical editor, I find that the Comstocks, near and far, are oftener in my mind's eye than my actual patrons. The thing I always have to decide about a manuscript offered for publication, before ever I give any thought to its artistic merit and suitability, is the question whether its publication will be
30 permitted—not even whether it is intrinsically good or evil, moral or immoral, but whether some roving Methodist preacher, self-commissioned to keep watch on letters, will read indecency into it. Not a week passes that I do not decline some sound and honest piece of work for no other reason. I have a long list of such things by American authors, well-devised, well-imagined, well-executed, respectable as human documents and as works of art—but
40 never to be printed in mine or any other American magazine. It includes four or five short stories of the very first rank, and the best one-act play yet done, to my knowledge, by an American. All of these pieces would go into type at once on the Continent; no sane man would think of objecting to them; they are no more obscene, to a normal adult, than his own bare legs. But they simply cannot be printed in the United States, with the law what it is
50 and the courts what they are.

I know many other editors. All of them are in the same boat. Some of them try to get around the difficulty by pecksniffery more or less open—for example, by fastening a moral purpose upon works of art, and hawking them as uplifting. Others, facing the intolerable fact, yield to it with resignation. And if they didn't? Well, if one of them didn't, any professional moralist could go before a police magistrate, get a warrant upon a simple affidavit, raid the
60 office of the offending editor, seize all the magazines in sight, and keep them impounded until after the disposition of the case. Editors cannot afford to take this risk. Magazines are perishable goods. Even if, after a trial has been had, they are returned, they are worthless save as waste paper. And what may be done with copies found in the actual office of publication may be done too with copies found on newsstands, and not only in one city, but in two,
70 six, a dozen, a hundred. All the costs and burdens of the contest are on the defendant. Let him be acquitted with honour, and invited to dinner by the judge, he has yet lost his property, and the Comstock hiding behind the warrant cannot be made to pay. In this concealment, indeed, lurk many sinister things—not forgetting personal enmity and business rivalry. The actual complainant is seldom uncovered; comstockery, taking on a semi-judicial
80 character, throws its chartered immunity around the whole process. A hypothetical outrage? By no means. It has been perpetrated, in one American city or another, upon fully half of the magazines of general circulation published today. Its possibility sticks in the consciousness of every editor and publisher like a recurrent glycosuria.

But though the effects of comstockery are thus abominably insane and irritating, the fact
90 is not to be forgotten that, after all, the thing is no more than an effect itself. The fundamental causes of all the grotesque (and often half-fabulous) phenomena flowing out of it are to be sought in the habits of mind of the American people. They are, as I have shown, be-

54. **for . . . as uplifting.** For example, the magazine which printed David Graham Phillips' *Susan Lenox: Her Fall and Rise* as a serial prefaced it with a moral encomium by the Rev. Charles H. Parkhurst. Later, when the novel appeared in book form, the Comstocks began an action to have it suppressed and forced the publisher to bowdlerize it. (Author's note.)   80. **comstockery . . . glycosuria.** An account of a typical prosecution, arbitrary, unintelligent, and disingenuous, is to be found in "Sumner and Indecency," by Frank Harris, in *Pearson's Magazine* for June, 1917, p. 556. (Author's note.) 88. **glycosuria,** sugar in the urine, the classic symptom of diabetes.

sotted by moral concepts, a moral engrossment, a delusion of moral infallibility. In their
view of the arts they are still unable to shake
off the naïve suspicion of the Fathers. A work
of the imagination can justify itself, in their
sight, only if it show a moral purpose, and that
purpose must be obvious and unmistakable.
Even in their slow progress toward a revolt
against the ancestral Philistinism, they cling to
10 this ethical bemusement: a new gallery of pictures is welcomed as "improving," to hear Beethoven "makes one better." Any questioning of
the moral ideas that prevail—the principal business, it must be plain, of the novelist, the serious dramatist, the professed inquirer into human motives and acts—is received with the utmost hostility. To attempt such an enterprise is
to disturb the peace—and the disturber of the
peace, in the national view, quickly passes over
20 into the downright criminal.

These symptoms, it seems to me, are only
partly racial, despite the persistent survival of
that third-rate English strain which shows itself so ingenuously in the colonial spirit, the
sense of inferiority, the frank craving for praise
from home. The race, in truth, grows mongrel,
and the protest against that mongrelism only
serves to drive in the fact. But a mongrel race
is necessarily a race still in the stage of reach-
30 ing out for culture; it has not yet formulated
defensible standards; it must needs rest heavily upon the superstitions that go with inferiority. The Reformation brought Scotland among
the civilized nations, but it took Scotland a
century and a half to live down the Reformation. Dogmatism, conformity, Philistinism, the
fear of rebels, the crusading spirit; these are
the marks of an upstart people, uncertain of
their rank in the world and even of their direc-
40 tion. A cultured European, reading a typical

American critical journal, must needs conceive
the United States, says H. G. Wells, as "a vain,
garrulous and prosperous female of uncertain
age and still more uncertain temper, with un-
founded pretensions to intellectuality and an
ideal of refinement of the most negative description . . . the Aunt Errant of Christendom." There is always that blushful shyness,
that timorous uncertainty, broken by sudden
rages, sudden enunciations of impeccable doc- 50
trine, sudden runnings amuck. Formalism is
the hall-mark of the national culture, and sins
against the one are sins against the other. The
American is school-mastered out of gusto, out
of joy, out of innocence. He can never fathom
William Blake's notion that "the lust of the
goat is also to the glory of God." He must be
correct, or, in his own phrase, he must bust.

Via trita est tutissima. The new generation,
urged to curiosity and rebellion by its mount- 60
ing sap, is rigorously restrained, regimented,
policed. The ideal is vacuity, guilelessness, imbecility. "We are looking at this particular
book," said Comstock's successor of "The 'Genius,'" "from the standpoint of its harmful effect
on female readers of immature mind." To be
curious is to be lewd; to know is to yield to
fornication. Here we have the mediaeval doctrine still on its legs: a chance word may
arouse "a libidinous passion" in the mind of a 70
"modest" woman. Not only youth must be safeguarded, but also the "female," the untrust-
worthy one, the temptress. "Modest," is a euphemism; it takes laws to keep her "pure." The
"locks of chastity" rust in the Cluny Museum;
in place of them we have comstockery. . . .

But, as I have said in hymning Huneker,
there is yet the munyonic consolation. Time is

2. In . . . Fathers. For further discussions of this point consult "Art in America," by Aleister Crowley, *The English Review*, Nov., 1913; "Life, Art and America," by Theodore
Dreiser, *The Seven Arts*, Feb., 1917; and "The American;
His Ideas of Beauty," by H. L. Mencken, *The Smart Set*, Sept.,
1913. (Author's note.) 33. **Reformation . . . Scotland.**
Mencken refers here to the various religious conflicts in Scotland during the sixteenth and seventeenth centuries, culminating in the battles between the English and the Covenanters
in the reigns of Charles II (1660-1685) and William and Mary
(1688-1702). 35. **the Reformation.** *Vide The Cambridge
History of English Literature*, Vol. XI, p. 290. (Author's note.)
36. **Dogmatism . . . direction.** The point is discussed by H. V.
Routh in *The Cambridge History of English Literature*, Vol. XI,
p. 290. (Author's note.) 40. **A cultured . . . Christendom,**
in *Boon*, New York, George H. Doran Co., 1915. (Author's
note.)

42. **H. G. Wells,** prolific English writer (1866-1946) of short
stories, novels, and miscellaneous prose works. His *Outline of
History* (1920) is probably his best-known work; but his early
short stories show a vivid imagination concerning the possibilities of modern science. 59. **Via . . . tutissima,** the well-
worn way is the safest. 63. **"We . . . mind,"** in a letter to
Felix Shay, Nov. 24, 1916. (Author's note.) 75. **"locks of
chastity" . . . Museum.** The Cluny Museum is a former
monastery in Paris now a museum of medieval antiquities.
"Locks of chastity" were iron girdles, worn by women, which
when locked assured chaste conduct on the part of the woman.
77. **Huneker,** a noted American music, dramatic, and art
critic (1860-1921), with a cosmopolitan viewpoint and a
brilliant prose style. His critical specialties were Ibsen and
Nietzsche in nineteenth-century literature and Chopin in nineteenth-century music. 78. **munyonic consolation.** "Professor" Munyon was a famous quack doctor whose panaceas
were known all over the country during the early years of the
present century. The "professor's" stern, pompadoured figure
with upraised arm, proclaiming that "there is still hope," appears in almost any advertising section in the newspapers and
magazines of the Gay Nineties or the Naughty Naughts.

a great legalizer, even in the field of morals. We have yet no delivery, but we have at least the beginnings of a revolt, or, at all events, of a protest. We have already reached, in Howells, our Hannah More; in Clemens, our Swift;

5. **More . . . Southey.** Hannah More (1745–1833) was a friend of Samuel Johnson's circle, a verse-writer and witty conversationalist, a writer of Puritanic persuasion on moral and religious subjects, and a noted practical philanthropist. William Cowper (1731–1800) was a noted English writer of light didactic verse, serious moral epistles in poetry, deeply religious hymns (the famous *Olney Hymns*), some satire, and a charming correspondence. George Crabbe (1754–1832), author of *The Village* and other serious poems, was a rather harsh critic of society and the ills of the industrial age. Robert Southey (1774–1843), friend of Wordsworth and Coleridge, was a feeble poet of vast pretensions; but he was Poet Laureate in his time and a stronghold of conservative politics and artistic ideals. Both his politics and ideals were violently hated by younger romantic writers like Byron and Shelley.

in Henry James, our Horace Walpole; in Woodberry, Robinson *et al.*, our Cowpers, Southeys and Crabbes; perhaps we might even make a composite and call it our Johnson. We are sweating through our Eighteenth Century, our era of sentiment, our spiritual measles. Maybe a new day is not quite so far off as it seems to be, and with it we may get our Hardy, our Conrad, our Swinburne, our Thoma, our Moore, our Meredith and our Synge. 10

14. **Thoma.** Ludwig Thoma (1867–1921) was a German satirical novelist, editor, and playwright, noted for his attacks upon social prejudices and religion. His best-known works are the novel *Andreas Vost* (1905; 1910) and the three plays *Magdalena* (1912), a tragedy, and *Moral* (1909) and *Die Lokalbahn* (1902), social comedies.

❦ English Romantic Individualism

WILLIAM BUTLER YEATS

The last major poet of the romantic tradition, William Butler Yeats, was born in Sandymount near Dublin, June 13, 1865. The families of his mother, Susan Pollexfen Yeats, and his father, John Butler Yeats, a minor pre-Raphaelite painter, came from Sligo, and it was in this part of Ireland that their son spent some of the most memorable summers of his childhood. When Yeats was still young, his family moved to London, where he went to school until he was fifteen. In *Reveries* he described the day school, the Godolphin, Hammersmith, as rough and cheap, and added:

I had a harassed life, and got many a black eye and had many outbursts of grief and rage. . . .
I was ashamed of my lack of courage, for I wanted to be like my grandfather, who thought so little of danger that he had jumped overboard in the Bay of Biscay after an old hat.

Nevertheless, Yeats was not entirely unhappy.

He made friends who, because he looked so thin and poetic, not only were devoted to him personally but engaged their mothers in the process of trying to feed him.

The family returned to Ireland and the boy attended the Erasmus Smith High School in Dublin, and there, despite his ignorance of Irish politics—due in part to his father's feeling of superiority to them—he felt at home. About him were his mother's relatives and the magical Irish scenery; for source books he had the Irish legends and fairy tales. He was soaking up the material for his own poetry, and at nineteen he had begun his career.

As early as his eighteenth year, Yeats was writing many of the poems which were to appear in *The Wanderings of Oisin* (1889), a book which established the young man as a lyric poet of somewhat the same tradition as Arthur Symons and Ernest Dowson. During the nineties Yeats met the Symbolist poet

Stéphane Mallarmé in Paris; and Arthur Symons, engaged in translations of the French Symbolists, introduced his friend to their writings. Yeats was a founder of the Rhymers' Club and was recognized as an esthete, in agreement with the school of writers who promoted the Art for Art's Sake Movement. This movement, in rebellion against late Victorianism, emphasized the idea that poetry should be an impression, a mood, the expression of the poet's personal emotions, and never a statement of idea, never a vehicle of philosophy or of social theory.

After he had dabbled briefly in French Symbolism, Yeats soon found in Irish mythology and folklore the images which most accurately project his poetic moods. "The Shadowy Horses," "Cuchulain Fighting the Waves"—all the creatures of Irish mythology, some of them unfamiliar even to Irish readers, seemed a treasury of symbols ready to Yeats' hand. He soon came under that cultural movement known as the Irish Renaissance, and together with Lady Gregory and Synge he became interested in restoring to Ireland a sense of her own rich and heroic early culture, even a knowledge of her language. Almost totally unconcerned with Irish politics, the young and idealistic Yeats saw the theater as the vehicle which could give back to the Irish a feeling of nationalistic dignity.

Yeats was now writing both short and long lyrics and poetic dramas, and his books were appearing regularly. He had, moreover, found the lovely and fiery Maud Gonne, with whom he was to be in love, at least in his imagination, all his life. The tall, dramatic young woman became one of the most active of the Irish revolutionists, valuing the nationalist struggle above her personal happiness and crushing Yeats' hopes of marriage. He was to carry her picture always in his heart, and it was to serve as the image and the symbol of beauty, the core around which clustered all the other ecstatic emotions so necessary to a poet who would create the heightened counterpart of reality.

At the turn of the century, however, Yeats became dissatisfied with his imaginative escapism and began trying to eliminate from his poetry the mistiness and the rhetoric. He had

found that he could not live forever in fairyland, and had begun to examine the differences between the two worlds of experience, the imaginative and the real. At this point, Yeats began to develop a poetic method. Almost by himself, he was actually examining the links between the conscious and the subconscious. His youth and his romantic conditioning behind him, he was no longer the young poet that George Moore had pictured

> striding to and forth at the back of a dress circle, a long black cloak drooping from his shoulders, a soft black sombrero on his head, a voluminous black silk tie flowing from his collar, loose black trousers dragging untidily over his long, heavy feet.

Back of him now lay the years of his idealistic love of Maud Gonne. She was becoming more and more involved in Irish politics; in 1903 she married John MacBride, an officer of the Irish Revolutionary Army who was later executed in the Easter Rising of 1916. Although as the new century began Yeats was still immersed in the Irish theater and its controversies, and was to be for some years, other less artistic responsibilities were coming to him.

Because his books never earned him more than two hundred pounds a year until he was fifty, he had to learn the harsh realities of life. He had even to accept rather tiresome public office. His had been a slow maturing, but he had been observant. Now he began to rid himself of vagueness of language and vagueness of experience. He announced that he believed in a kind of racial memory which one could tap by brooding deeply. He made the central image of Maud Gonne the image of that moment of belief in beauty by which the poet is sustained. His poetry became more and more a record of his reactions to fact, hard and real, compared with his imaginative vision of deep, powerful human passions.

He was by no means the first poet to choose the image of a woman as the image of beauty in art. Shelley, for example, had done this. Yeats pointed out that he did not choose to preserve the ideal by knowing it only from afar. He would record the fact. Consequently, he pictured Maud Gonne and himself as growing older, but also, as recalled in a kind of imaginative flashback, as young, sensitive, and strangely beautiful.

Actually, Yeats was using modern psychology. Through a deliberate probing of memory he was bringing into conjunction what was actually taking place and the dream of perfection, aristocratic and contemplative, in which he had believed in his youth. His language was growing more prosaic, he was being less prodigal in symbols, his attention was more and more fixed on the actual, but he was sustaining his grand manner in the use of language and symbols now through sheer intensity and exaltation. The result was a clear and fired verse, free of all unnecessary ornamentation, moving brilliantly between comments on politics and science and the process of aging and the dramatic play of feeling of poetic life. Beginning with *The Green Helmet* in 1910, continuing through *The Wild Swans at Coole* in 1919, and extending to some of his last books, *The Tower* (1928) and *The Winding Stair* (1929), Yeats established his mature manner firmly. He was no longer a descriptive lyricist of minor moods, but a major poet, a dramatic lyricist of extraordinary imaginative vision.

At fifty-two Yeats had married Georgie Lees, who for some time had been his secretary. He was growing older and he seemed to fear more than anything else the loss of his great poetic intensity. Under his wife's influence he began to investigate, in apparent earnestness, the realm of the supernatural, in which he had always been interested. A few days after their marriage his wife had done some automatic writing, and soon Yeats was caught up in séances and the invocation of spirits. How much of all this either of them believed is uncertain, but Yeats found it stimulating to further reading, and it seems possible that his wife led him to read such philosophers as might so stimulate him.

In *A Vision* Yeats tells of his investigations into spiritualism, and confesses that the voices heard, whether real or not, served to prolong his passionate convictions as to the part the super-rational mind plays in poetic creation. He drew up for himself graphs of the movement of the mind away from innocence, through sophistication, and back again to a higher inno-

cence. He solemnly placed under the sign of the moon all writers who dredged the subjective mind—Blake, for example; and under the sign of the sun those who lived or wrote objectively, as did the eighteenth-century poets. Between these extremes lay many literary figures. In his later poems Yeats frequently mentions these gyres, or graphs, and always, one notes, he finds most to his liking characters who move through those sections of his graphs which are indicative of the passionate, subjective, and emotional response to the events of life.

Many of his late poems are debates, in a sense, between the two sides of himself, the realist and the dreamer. Even in his last poems he upheld passion as eternal and turned to create his own myths, using as the characters of his poems the people he himself had created imaginatively. He saw the vulgarity of the actual, later to be immortalized by Eliot, but he never regarded it as truth which could imprison the imaginative mind.

In later life Yeats was active in Irish politics. For a time he served as superintendent of schools in Ireland, and he was a member of the Irish Senate between 1922 and 1928. He died in France in 1939. Two volumes of reminiscences, *Reveries* (1915) and *The Trembling of the Veil* (1922), were combined in 1926 as *Autobiographies,* not a factual account of his life, but a rich and beautiful narrative of the impressions and facts which had formed a poet's mind.

The list of Yeats' books is long; most of his writing is now to be found in collected volumes. His *Collected Poems* were published in 1933, and a posthumous *Last Poems and Plays* appeared in 1940.

In one sense, Yeats' work was all of a piece, despite the two periods in it. He believed art flourished only in an old and aristocratic culture. He never, in fact, felt close kinship with the common people. This is why, toward the end of his life, he wrote poems against any change; poems which indicated that if the choice must be made, he leaned more toward the view that authority and tradition make history than toward the view held by many that the people themselves, in their economic emergencies, may direct it.

He Remembers Forgotten Beauty

WHEN my arms wrap you round I press
    My heart upon the loveliness
That has long faded from the world;
The jewelled crowns that kings have hurled
In shadowy pools, when armies fled;   5
The love tales wrought with silken thread
By dreaming ladies upon cloth
That had made fat the murderous moth;
The roses that of old time were
Woven by ladies in their hair;   10
The dew-cold lilies ladies bore
Through many a sacred corridor
Where such grey clouds of incense rose
That only the gods' eyes did not close:
For that pale breast and lingering hand   15
Come from a more dream-heavy land,
A more dream-heavy hour than this;
And when you sigh from kiss to kiss
I hear white Beauty sighing, too,
For hours when all must fade like dew;   20
But flame on flame, deep under deep,
Throne over throne, where in half sleep
Their swords upon their iron knees,
Brood her high lonely mysteries.

The Leaders of the Crowd

THEY must to keep their certainty accuse
    All that are different of a base intent;
Pull down established honour; hawk for news
Whatever their loose phantasy invent
And murmur it with bated breath, as though
The abounding gutter had been Helicon   6
Or calumny a song. How can they know
Truth flourishes where the student's lamp has
    shone,
And there alone, that have no solitude?
So the crowd come they care not what may
    come.   10

The poems of William Butler Yeats are reprinted from *Collected Poems*, copyright, 1933, by The Macmillan Company, publishers, and used with their permission.
He Remembers Forgotten Beauty. The poet gives here the credo of the late romantics who remember beauty, once felt as absolute, now known as dream.
The Leaders of the Crowd. One of many poems expressing Yeats' distrust of the crowd or the group in action. He consistently believed that the artist must be aristocratic and separate.
6. Helicon, or Mount Zagara, a mountain in Boeotia, Greece, traditionally the abode of the Muses.

They have loud music, hope every day re-
    newed
And heartier loves; that lamp is from the tomb.

The Cold Heaven

SUDDENLY I saw the cold and rook-delighting
    Heaven
That seemed as though ice burned and was but
    the more ice,
And thereupon imagination and heart were
    driven
So wild that every casual thought of that and
    this
Vanished, and left but memories, that should
    be out of season   5
With the hot blood of youth, of love crossed
    long ago;
And I took all the blame out of all sense and
    reason,
Until I cried and trembled and rocked to and
    fro,
Riddled with light. Ah! when the ghost begins
    to quicken,
Confusion of the death-bed over, is it sent   10
Out naked on the roads, as the books say, and
    stricken
By the injustice of the skies for punishment?

Broken Dreams

THERE is grey in your hair.
    Young men no longer suddenly catch their
    breath
When you are passing;
But maybe some old gaffer mutters a blessing
Because it was your prayer   5
Recovered him upon the bed of death.
For your sole sake—that all heart's ache have
    known,
And given to others all heart's ache,
From meagre girlhood's putting on

The Cold Heaven, another of Yeats' many poems in which the imagination recalls the passion for beauty, the poet's vision, once felt in youth. It ends on the question whether after death one must again be punished by knowledge of the contrast between reality and vision.
Broken Dreams, one of Yeats' many poems on love (probably the woman here, as so frequently, is Maud Gonne). The poem is typical of Yeats' use of the romantic image of the woman to symbolize beauty, and of his modernity in examining not only the dream but the fact.

Burdensome beauty—for your sole sake   10
Heaven has put away the stroke of her doom,
So great her portion in that peace you make
By merely walking in a room.

Your beauty can but leave among us
Vague memories, nothing but memories.   15
A young man when the old men are done
    talking
Will say to an old man, 'Tell me of that lady
The poet stubborn with his passion sang us
When age might well have chilled his blood.'

Vague memories, nothing but memories,   20
But in the grave all, all, shall be renewed.
The certainty that I shall see that lady
Leaning or standing or walking
In the first loveliness of womanhood,
And with the fervour of my youthful eyes,   25
Has set me muttering like a fool.

You are more beautiful than any one,
And yet your body had a flaw:
Your small hands were not beautiful,
And I am afraid that you will run   30
And paddle to the wrist
In that mysterious, always brimming lake
Where those that have obeyed the holy law
Paddle and are perfect. Leave unchanged
The hands that I have kissed   35
For old sakes' sake.
The last stroke of midnight dies.
All day in the one chair
From dream to dream and rhyme to rhyme I
    have ranged
In rambling talk with an image of air: 40
Vague memories, nothing but memories.

Easter, 1916

I HAVE met them at close of day
  Coming with vivid faces
From counter or desk among grey
Eighteenth-century houses.
I have passed with a nod of the head   5
Or polite meaningless words,

Easter, 1916. On Easter Sunday, 1916, the Irish Republican
forces seized vantage points in Dublin, but the rising was
ruthlessly repressed by the British. Yeats disagreed entirely
with those who believed that violence and revolution would
help Ireland. He hated those who aroused the people. Yet his
is some of the great revolutionary poetry when, as here, his
imagination beholds the commonplace grown into martyrdom.

Or have lingered awhile and said
Polite meaningless words,
And thought before I had done
Of a mocking tale or a gibe   10
To please a companion
Around the fire at the club,
Being certain that they and I
But lived where motley is worn:
All changed, changed utterly: 15
A terrible beauty is born.

That woman's days were spent
In ignorant good-will,
Her nights in argument
Until her voice grew shrill.   20
What voice more sweet than hers
When, young and beautiful,
She rode to harriers?
This man had kept a school
And rode our wingèd horse;   25
This other his helper and friend
Was coming into his force;
He might have won fame in the end,
So sensitive his nature seemed,
So daring and sweet his thought.   30
This other man I had dreamed
A drunken, vainglorious lout.
He had done most bitter wrong
To some who are near my heart,
Yet I number him in the song;   35
He, too, has resigned his part
In the casual comedy;
He, too, has been changed in his turn,
Transformed utterly:
A terrible beauty is born.   40

Hearts with one purpose alone
Through summer and winter seem
Enchanted to a stone
To trouble the living stream.
The horse that comes from the road,   45
The rider, the birds that range
From cloud to tumbling cloud,
Minute by minute they change;
A shadow of cloud on the stream
Changes minute by minute;   50
A horse-hoof slides on the brim,
And a horse plashes within it;
The long-legged moor-hens dive,
And hens to moor-cocks call;
Minute by minute they live: 55
The stone's in the midst of all.

Too long a sacrifice
Can make a stone of the heart.
O when may it suffice?
That is Heaven's part, our part   60
To murmur name upon name,
As a mother names her child
When sleep at last has come
On limbs that had run wild.
What is it but nightfall?   65
No, no, not night but death;
Was it needless death after all?
For England may keep faith
For all that is done and said.
We know their dream; enough   70
To know they dreamed and are dead;
And what if excess of love
Bewildered them till they died?
I write it out in a verse—
MacDonagh and MacBride   75
And Connolly and Pearse
Now and in time to be,
Wherever green is worn,
Are changed, changed utterly:
A terrible beauty is born.   80

No Second Troy

WHY SHOULD I blame her that she filled
    my days
With misery, or that she would of late
Have taught to ignorant men most violent
    ways,
Or hurled the little streets upon the great,
Had they but courage equal to desire?   5
What could have made her peaceful with a
    mind
That nobleness made simple as a fire,
With beauty like a tightened bow, a kind
That is not natural in an age like this,
Being high and solitary and most stern?   10
Why, what could she have done, being what
    she is?
Was there another Troy for her to burn?

75. **Macdonagh,** Thomas MacDonagh, Irish poet and Republican, executed after the rising. **MacBride,** Maud Gonne's husband, executed after the rising. 76. **Connolly,** James Connolly, Irish Republican leader, desperately wounded during the rising and later executed. **Pearse,** Patrick Pearse, Irish Republican leader of the rising, executed after it had been suppressed.
No Second Troy. 12. **Troy.** "Helen could not be Helen but for beleaguered Troy"—Yeats, *A Vision,* 1937 (p. 268).

The Second Coming

TURNING and turning in the widening gyre
    The falcon cannot hear the falconer:
Things fall apart: the centre cannot hold;
Mere anarchy is loosed upon the world,
The blood-dimmed tide is loosed, and every-
    where   5
The ceremony of innocence is drowned;
The best lack all conviction, while the worst
Are full of passionate intensity.

Surely some revelation is at hand;
Surely the Second Coming is at hand.   10
The Second Coming! Hardly are those words
    out
When a vast image out of *Spiritus Mundi*
Troubles my sight: somewhere in sands of the
    desert
A shape with lion body and the head of a man,
A gaze blank and pitiless as the sun,   15
Is moving its slow thighs, while all about it
Reel shadows of the indignant desert birds.
The darkness drops again; but now I know
That twenty centuries of stony sleep   19
Were vexed to nightmare by a rocking cradle,
And what rough beast, its hour come round at
    last,
Slouches towards Bethlehem to be born?

Sailing to Byzantium

I

THAT is no country for old men. The young
    In one another's arms, birds in the trees,
—Those dying generations—at their song,
The salmon-falls, the mackerel-crowded seas,
Fish, flesh, or fowl, commend all summer long
Whatever is begotten, born, and dies.   6
Caught in that sensual music all neglect
Monuments of unageing intellect.

The Second Coming, a curiously prophetic poem of the end of an era. Yeats knew of Spengler's theories in *The Decline of the West* and in his later years he reflected, as he saw again the approach of violence, that an age was ending. The poem is on the chaos of the present, particularly the chaos resulting from the separation of imagination and fact.
1. **gyre,** ring, circle, spiral, or vortex. The obsolete names for the gerfalcon were *gyrer* and *gyrfalcon.* 12. *Spiritus Mundi,* the spirit of the world, the great memory where all history and experience are stored.
Sailing to Byzantium. This poem is about the poet's old age. Since the world in which he lives is no country for the old (with its imagery of youth), he would sail into the imaginative. In the last two stanzas he explains what he might see there, how he would never choose to be mortal again but would become something with the permanence of, for example, art.

II

An aged man is but a paltry thing,
A tattered coat upon a stick, unless   10
Soul clap its hands and sing, and louder sing
For every tatter in its mortal dress,
Nor is there singing school but studying
Monuments of its own magnificence;
And therefore I have sailed the seas and come
To the holy city of Byzantium.   16

III

O sages standing in God's holy fire
As in the gold mosaic of a wall,
Come from the holy fire, perne in a gyre,
And be the singing-masters of my soul.   20
Consume my heart away; sick with desire
And fastened to a dying animal
It knows not what it is; and gather me
Into the artifice of eternity.

IV

Once out of nature I shall never take   25
My bodily form from any natural thing,
But such a form as Grecian goldsmiths make
Of hammered gold and gold enamelling
To keep a drowsy Emperor awake;
Or set upon a golden bough to sing   30
To lords and ladies of Byzantium
Of what is past, or passing, or to come.

A Dialogue of Self and Soul

I

M*y Soul.* I summon to the winding ancient
stair;
Set all your mind upon the steep ascent,

16. **Byzantium.** "I think if I could be given a month of antiquity and leave to spend it where I chose, I would spend it in Byzantium a little before Justinian opened St. Sophia and closed the Academy of Plato." (*A Vision*, p. 279.) Byzantium, later called Constantinople, is now Istanbul. 19. **perne in a gyre.** The gyre, as fully explained in *A Vision*, is one of the poet's ways of designating movement from center outward and back to center, from subjective or emotional to objective or rational and back. Since he regarded the subjective as the seat of all poetry, if the mind, brooding upon the real, returned to the subjective, he felt that all thought, all history, move in much the same way. The phrase here means "turn in the gyre from outer to inner, and take over the sick soul of an old man." *A Dialogue of Self and Soul,* one of a number of poems in which Yeats views the two sides of the question whether to hold to the sensuous and continuously passionate in the flesh, or to relinquish it and rely more on the spiritual. Neither is rejected, but in the end the poet asserts that, however defeating life proves, he would live it over again.

Upon the broken, crumbling battlement,
Upon the breathless starlit air,   4
Upon the star that marks the hidden pole;
Fix every wandering thought upon
That quarter where all thought is done:
Who can distinguish darkness from the soul?
My Self. The consecrated blade upon my knees
Is Sato's ancient blade, still as it was,   10
Still razor-keen, still like a looking-glass
Unspotted by the centuries;
That flowering, silken, old embroidery, torn
From some court-lady's dress and round
The wooden scabbard bound and wound,   15
Can, tattered, still protect, faded adorn.
My Soul. Why should the imagination of a man
Long past his prime remember things that are
Emblematical of love and war?
Think of ancestral night that can,   20
If but imagination scorn the earth
And intellect its wandering
To this and that and t'other thing,
Deliver from the crime of death and birth.
My Self. Montashigi, third of his family, fashioned it   25
Five hundred years ago, about it lie
Flowers from I know not what embroidery—
Heart's purple—and all these I set
For emblems of the day against the tower
Emblematical of the night,   30
And claim as by a soldier's right
A charter to commit the crime once more.
My Soul. Such fullness in that quarter overflows
And falls into the basin of the mind
That man is stricken deaf and dumb and blind,   35
For intellect no longer knows
Is from the *Ought*, or *Knower* from the *Known*—
That is to say, ascend to Heaven;
Only the dead can be forgiven;   39
But when I think of that my tongue's a stone.

II

My Self. A living man is blind and drinks his drop.
What matter if the ditches are impure?

10. **Sato.** Sato's sword was apparently a Japanese sword which Yeats kept in his tower. Such swords bear the names of both the owner (Sato) and the maker, in this case Montashigi.

What matter if I live it all once more?
Endure that toil of growing up;
The ignominy of boyhood; the distress   45
Of boyhood changing into man;
The unfinished man and his pain
Brought face to face with his own clumsi-
            ness;

The finished man among his enemies?—   49
How in the name of Heaven can he escape
That defiling and disfigured shape
The mirror of malicious eyes
Casts upon his eyes until at last
He thinks that shape must be his shape?
And what's the good of an escape   55
If honour find him in the wintry blast?

I am content to live it all again
And yet again, if it be life to pitch
Into the frog-spawn of a blind man's ditch,
A blind man battering blind men;   60
Or into that most fecund ditch of all,
The folly that man does
Or must suffer, if he woos
A proud woman not kindred of his soul.

I am content to follow to its source,   65
Every event in action or in thought;
Measure the lot; forgive myself the lot!
When such as I cast out remorse
So great a sweetness flows into the breast
We must laugh and we must sing,   70
We are blest by everything,
Everything we look upon is blest.

WALTER DE LA MARE

Perhaps more keenly than any other poet of his day, Walter de la Mare has caught the nostalgia for the past. His is a world of delicate beauty where all objects are seen in a ghostly half-light. He is a poet homesick for the vanished values such as love, faith, or a belief in the perfection of this life or the next. His childhood was spent in the older Victorian world where man's supremacy and spiritual integrity were unquestioned, his adulthood in the modern world of commercialism. As an adult artist he stresses, therefore, the pain of separation from that sense of fresh loveliness and of renewed beauty and faith which a child knows.

De la Mare was born in Charlton, Kent, April 25, 1873, the son of James Edward de la Mare, a churchwarden, and Lucy Sophia Browning de la Mare, thought to be related to Robert Browning. He received his elementary education at St. Paul's Cathedral Choir School in London and in 1890 took a position with the London branch of the Anglo-American Oil Company, a subsidiary of the Standard Oil Company of America, as a compiler of statistics and bookkeeper.

De la Mare wrote a great deal during the early years, though it was not until 1902 that his *Songs of Childhood* was published under the pseudonym "Walter Ramal." Two years later came the novel *Henry Brocken*, which was warmly received, and then in 1906, *Poems*. These poems won him a hundred-pound-a-year grant from the government, enabling him to give up his job and devote himself seriously to writing. He retired to Taplow, near London, and by 1930 he had published over twenty-five volumes of poetry and prose—among them *The Return* (1910); *Peacock Pie* (1913); *Motley and Other Poems* (1918); *Collected Poems 1910–1918* (1920); *Memoirs of a Midget* (1921), which won the James Tait Black Memorial Prize; *The Veil and Other Poems* (1921); *Come Hither,* an anthology of verse (1923); *Broomsticks* (1925); *On the Edge* (1930); and *The Eighteen-Eighties* (1930). Later books of importance are a highly illuminating study of childhood called *Early One Morning* (1935); *Collected Poems* (1941, 1944, and 1945); *Time Passes and Other Poems* (1942); *Love* (1943); *The Burning Glass* (1945); *Dutch Cheese and Other Stories* (1946); and *Rhymes and Verses*, collected poems for children (1947).

These works have brought him just fame. His sensitive intuition, his grace and craftsmanship, have given his work enduring qualities. From the desk of the bookkeeper have come prose and poetry that are unsurpassed for their imaginative beauty. De la Mare's late poems on death and on the distress of the war period have still the faith in sensitivity as reason for living.

The Listeners

"Is there anybody there?" said the Traveler,
  Knocking on the moonlit door;
And his horse in the silence champed the grasses
  Of the forest's ferny floor.
And a bird flew up out of the turret,   5
  Above the Traveler's head:
And he smote upon the door again a second time;
  "Is there anybody there?" he said.
But no one descended to the Traveler;
  No head from the leaf-fringed sill   10
Leaned over and looked into his gray eyes,
  Where he stood perplexed and still.
But only a host of phantom listeners
  That dwelt in the lone house then   14
Stood listening in the quiet of the moonlight
  To that voice from the world of men:
Stood thronging the faint moonbeams on the dark stair,
  That goes down to the empty hall,
Hearkening in an air stirred and shaken
  By the lonely Traveler's call.   20
And he felt in his heart their strangeness,
  Their stillness answering his cry,
While his horse moved, cropping the dark turf,
  'Neath the starred and leafy sky;
For he suddenly smote on the door, even   25
  Louder, and lifted his head:—
"Tell them I came, and no one answered,
  That I kept my word," he said.

The poems of Walter de la Mare are reprinted from *Collected Poems* by Walter de la Mare. Reproduced by permission of Henry Holt and Company. Copyright, 1941, by Walter de la Mare.
The Listeners. De la Mare, disliking the materialistic world in which he lives, has written many poems describing the search of the imagination for the true meaning of life. "The Listeners" is a legend of any sensitive man's search for spiritual significance not apparent in our daily life. One notes, however, that the traveler after truth is not answered, although the title suggests that his voice and his question are not unheard.

Never the least stir made the listeners,
  Though every word he spake   30
Fell echoing through the shadowiness of the still house
  From the one man left awake:
Ay, they heard his foot upon the stirrup,
  And the sound of iron on stone,   34
And how the silence surged softly backward,
  When the plunging hoofs were gone.

The Last Coachload

(TO COLIN)

Crashed through the woods that lumbering
  Coach. The dust
Of flinted roads bepowdering felloe and hood.
Its gay paint cracked, its axles red with rust,
It lunged, lurched, toppled through a solitude

Of whispering boughs, and feathery, nid-nod grass.   5
Plodded the fetlocked horses. Glum and mum,
Its ancient Coachman recked not where he was,
Nor into what strange haunt his wheels were come.

Crumbling the leather of his dangling reins;
Worn to a cow's tuft his stumped, idle whip;
Sharp eyes of beast and bird in the trees' green lanes   11
Gleamed out like stars above a derelict ship.

'Old Father Time—Time—Time!' jeered twittering throat.
A squirrel capered on the leader's rump,   14
Slithered a weasel, peered a thief-like stoat,
In sandy warren beat on the coney's thump.

Mute as a mammet in his saddle sate
The hunched Postilion, clad in magpie trim;
Buzzed the bright flies around his hairless pate;
Yaffle and jay squawked mockery at him.   20

Yet marvellous peace and amity breathed there.
Tranquil the labyrinths of this sundown wood.

The Last Coachload. De la Mare's nostalgia for a world of greater imaginative intensity than our natural world leads him to write poems in which death is an escape. The coach, painted as a child might imagine it, bears its passengers toward death. 15. **stoat,** the ermine. 17. **mammet,** idol. 20. **Yaffle,** woodpecker.

Musking its chaces, bloomed the brier-rose
    fair;
Spellbound as if in trance the pine-trees stood.

Through moss and pebbled rut the wheels
    rasped on;   25
That Ancient drowsing on his box. And still
The bracken track with glazing sunbeams
    shone;
Laboured the horses, straining at the hill. . . .

But now—a verdurous height with eve-shade
    sweet;
Far, far to West the Delectable Mountains
    glowed.   30
Above, Night's canopy; at the horses' feet
A sea-like honied waste of flowers flowed.

There fell a pause of utter quiet. And—
Out from one murky window glanced an eye,
Stole from the other a lean, groping hand,   35
The padded door swung open with a sigh.

And—*Exeunt Omnes!* None to ask the fare—
A myriad human Odds in a last release
Leap out incontinent, snuff the incensed air;
A myriad parched-up voices whisper,
    'Peace.'   40

On, on, and on—a stream, a flood, they flow.
O wondrous vale of jocund buds and bells!
Like vanishing smoke the rainbow legions
    glow,
Yet still the enravished concourse sweeps and
    swells.

All journeying done. Rest now from lash and
    spur—   45
Laughing and weeping, shoulder and elbow—
    'twould seem
That Coach capacious all Infinity were,
And these the fabulous figments of a dream.

Mad for escape; frenzied each breathless mote,
Lest rouse the Old Enemy from his death-still
    swoon,   50
Lest crack that whip again—they fly, they float,
Scamper, breathe—'Paradise!' abscond, are
    gone. . . .

23. **Musking,** infusing with odor. **chaces,** hunting grounds.
27. **bracken track,** road covered with fern. 29. **verdurous,**
covered with green foliage. 30. **Delectable Mountains,** the
luxuriant mountains in *Pilgrim's Progress,* from which the City
of Heaven could be seen. 37. *Exeunt Omnes!* All out!

I Sit Alone

I SIT alone,
  And clear thoughts move in me,
Pictures, now near, now far,
Of transient fantasy.
Happy I am, at peace   5
In my own company.

Yet life is a dread thing, too,
Dark with horror and fear.
Beauty's fingers grow cold,
Sad cries I hear,   10
Death with a stony gaze
Is ever near.

Lost in myself I hide
From the cold unknown:
Lost, like a world cast forth   15
Into space star-sown:
And the songs of the morning are stilled,
And delight in them flown.

So even the tender and dear
Like phantoms through memory stray—   20
Creations of sweet desire,
That faith can alone bid stay:
They cast off the cloak of the real
And vanish away.

Only love can redeem   25
This truth, that delight;
Bring morning to blossom again
Out of plague-ridden night;
Restore to the lost the found,
To the blinded, sight.   30

Sotto Voce

(TO EDWARD THOMAS)

THE HAZE of noon waned silver-grey
  The soundless mansion of the sun;
The air made visible in his ray,
Like molten glass from furnace run,
Quivered o'er heat-baked turf and stone   5

"I Sit Alone" from *The Fleeting and Other Poems* by Walter de
la Mare, reprinted by permission of Eric S. Pinker and Adrienne
Morrison, Inc.
Sotto Voce, softly, as to one's self, in an undertone. De la
Mare is recording here a conversation about beauty between
himself and Edward Thomas, one of the best pastoral poets
of this century, who died during World War I. The significance
of the last lines is that the nightingale, or beauty, sings even
when the poet is dead.

And the flower of the gorse burned on—
Burned softly as gold of a child's fair hair
Along each spiky spray, and shed
Almond-like incense in the air
Whereon our senses fed.   10

At foot—a few sparse harebells: blue
And still as were the friend's dark eyes
That dwelt on mine, transfixèd through
With sudden ecstatic surmise.

'Hst!' he cried softly, smiling, and lo,   15
Stealing amidst that maze gold-green,
I heard a whispering music flow
From guileful throat of bird, unseen:—

So delicate the straining ear
Scarce carried its faint syllabling   20
Into a heart caught-up to hear
That inmost pondering
Of bird-like self with self. We stood,
In happy trance-like solitude,
Hearkening a lullay grieved and sweet—   25
As when on isle uncharted beat
'Gainst coral at the palm-tree's root,
With brine-clear, snow-white foam afloat,
The wailing, not of water or wind—
A husht, far, wild, divine lament,   30
When Prospero his wizardry bent
Winged Ariel to bind. . . .

Then silence, and o'er-flooding noon.
I raised my head; smiled too. And he—
Moved his great hand, the magic gone—   35
Gently amused to see
My ignorant wonderment. He sighed.
'It was a nightingale,' he said,
'That *sotto voce* cons the song
He'll sing when dark is spread;   40
And Night's vague hours are sweet and long,
And we are laid abed.'

Old Susan

WHEN Susan's work was done, she'd sit
With one fat guttering candle lit,
And window opened wide to win

The sweet night air to enter in;
There, with a thumb to keep her place   5
She'd read, with stern and wrinkled face.
Her mild eyes gliding very slow
Across the letters to and fro,
While wagged the guttering candle flame   9
In the wind that through the window came.
And sometimes in the silence she
Would mumble a sentence audibly,
Or shake her head as if to say,
"You silly souls, to act this way!"
And never a sound from night I'd hear,   15
Unless some far-off cock crowed clear;
Or her old shuffling thumb should turn
Another page; and rapt and stern,
Through her great glasses bent on me,
She'd glance into reality;   20
And shake her round old silvery head,
With—"You!—I thought you was in bed!"—
Only to tilt her book again,
And rooted in Romance remain.

The Dreamer

O THOU who giving helm and sword,
  Gav'st, too, the rusting rain,
And starry dark's all tender dews
    To blunt and stain:

Out of the battle I am sped,   5
    Unharmed, yet stricken sore;
A living shape amid whispering shades
    On Lethe's shore.

No trophy in my hands I bring,
    To this sad, sighing stream,   10
The neighings and the trumps and cries
    Were but a dream.

Traitor to life, of life betrayed:
    O, of thy mercy deep,
A dream my all, the all I ask   15
    Is sleep.

---

25. **lullay,** old form of *lullaby*. 31. **Prospero,** in *The Tempest*
the Duke of Milan, shipwrecked on an island, where he engaged in enchantments. 32. **Ariel,** the sprightly and tricky
spirit who aided Prospero in all his magic.

The Dreamer. 8. **Lethe,** in Greek myth the Stream of Oblivion in the Underworld, from which souls drank before passing
to Elysium, that they might forget all earthly sorrows.

Peace

Night is o'er England, and the winds are
   still;
Jasmine and honeysuckle steep the air;
Softly the stars that are all Europe's fill
Her heaven-wide dark with radiancy fair;   4
The shadowed moon now waxing in the west
Stirs not a rumour in her tranquil seas;

Peace. Probably written after the First World War, but published in 1938, perhaps with foreboding. De la Mare is not given to writing poems which are indirect comments on the state of the nation.

Mysterious sleep has lulled her heart to rest,
Deep even as theirs beneath her churchyard
   trees.

Secure, serene; dumb now the night-hawk's
   threat;   9
The guns' low thunder drumming o'er the tide;
The anguish pulsing in her stricken side . . . .
All is at peace. . . . But, never, heart, forget:
For this her youngest, best, and bravest died,
These bright dews once were mixed with
   bloody sweat.

JOHN GALSWORTHY

One of the most readable as well as soundest interpreters of the society of industrial England during the late nineteenth and early twentieth centuries was John Galsworthy. His versatility no less than his fecundity in literature was unusual. His collected poems were published in 1934. He wrote many essays and sketches, such as those included in *The Inn of Tranquillity* (1912) and other later works. But the types of literature which were most useful to him in the utterance of his opinions and points of view are the novel and the drama. His poetry is negligible; his rank as an essayist is only fairly notable; but his position in his two favorite types is a distinguished one.

Galsworthy was born in Coombe, Surrey, in 1867, of an old Devonshire County family. It is not surprising that his work should show, among other things, a natural understanding of the feelings and attitudes of the landed gentry or men of property. He was educated at Harrow, where he made a name for himself as an athlete, and at New College, Oxford. He studied law and was admitted to the bar in 1890 but never cared for practice. Since he had money enough to obviate the necessity of an immediate occupation, he traveled extensively and read with equal extensiveness the works of Dickens, Turgenev, De Maupassant, Anatole France, and Tolstoy—all noted novelists. Galsworthy in consequence determined upon writing as a profession; he mingled with writers and later took pleasure in the thought that he had helped start at least one writer on a brilliant career—Joseph Conrad.

In the opening years of the present century Galsworthy was living in the wild, inhospitable, but thoroughly romantic region of Dartmoor in Devonshire and trying his wings as a professional man of letters. He felt a serious call to such a vocation: "Art," he wrote, "is the one form of human energy which really works for union and destroys the barriers between man and man. It is the continual, unconscious replacement of one self by another." His first novel, *Jocelyn* (1899), and its successor, *Villa Rubein* (1900), were published under the pseudonym of John Sinjohn. Galsworthy's name did not emerge until *The Island Pharisees* (1904) and *The Man of Property* (1906).

The first three of these novels were not distinctive and are today virtually forgotten. But in *The Man of Property* Galsworthy made his initial contribution to one of the most impressive fictional panoramas of the twentieth century, *The Forsyte Saga*, which was not published as a unit until 1922. The idea had been suggested to him some time before in the course of a brief novelette, *The Salvation of a Forsyte*, a work not usually included in the saga proper. The story of the Forsytes was to occupy Galsworthy off and on for the next quarter-century. The original saga was extended after 1922 by the addition of a half-dozen more stories, so that the legend is not complete until a year or so before Galsworthy's death in 1933; and his last novel, *One More River* (1933), deals with people who had appeared in minor rôles in the Forsyte novels. In the first Forsyte series were three novels, *The Man of Property* (1906), *In Chancery* (1920), and *To Let* (1921), a continuous sequence interrupted by two novelettes, or "interludes," *The Indian Summer of a Forsyte* (1920) and *Awakening* (1921). The second series treated of the newer generation of Forsytes, and the same general technique was observed—the novels were *The White Monkey* (1924), *The Silver Spoon* (1926), and *The Swan Song* (1928); the interludes this time were *The Silent Wooing* (1925) and *Passersby* (1927). At the conclusion of the entire double series come two books of short sketches—shavings from the workshop, so to speak—*On Forsyte 'Change* (1930) and *Forsytes, Pendyces, and Others* (1935). The gallery of Forsytes and their descendants both direct and collateral extends from the early Victorian period well into the twentieth century—almost a hundred years; and the shifting tastes, moral standards, even economic values of the succession of generations—the change from property owner to renter or buyer on the installment plan—are told with fidelity to truth, sympathetic insight, beauty of phrase, and occasional high seriousness. Some critics have seen in the work only "a manor-house hall hung with Rembrandts," but Galsworthy has been more than a pictorial delineator. He has drawn his characters well and thrown them into high relief against the background of modern industrial England, and he has made them live. Of course there are other Galsworthy novels; many prefer something like *The Patrician* (1911), *The Dark Flower* (1913), or *One More River* (1933). But posterity is likely to consider *The Forsyte Saga* as Galsworthy's most massive and most permanent achievement.

Attention to his novels must not blind the reader to the fact that Galsworthy was an inveterate and often powerful playwright. In nearly all his plays he is a social critic, particularly interested in the class struggle, though he can scarcely be called a propagandist, rather an interested and sympathetic bystander. His favorite formula is the ironic presentation of a character crushed by some circumstance in itself unimportant but magnified into irresistible significance by the importance which society puts upon it. His picture of society is that of an impersonal, unscrupulous, unfeeling, and often ruthless power that batters down all who get in its way. In so far as he exhibits partiality toward his characters, Galsworthy is likely to bestow it upon the weak or unfortunate character caught between society and the industrial scene.

The catalogue of Galsworthy's works for the stage is long—nearly twenty in as many years. The three most powerful are *Strife* (1909), on labor and capital in a small Welsh mining town; *Justice* (1910), on the inscrutable ways of the law; and *Loyalties* (1922), on social prejudice. But any one of the following will repay reading: *The Silver Box* (1906); *Joy* (1907); *Fraternity* (1909); *The Eldest Son* (1912); *The Little Man* (1915); *The Mob* (1915); *A Bit o' Love* (1916); *The Pigeon* (1916); *The Skin Game* (1920); *The Family Man* (1921); *Windows* (1922); *Old English* (1924); *The Forest* (1924); *The Show* (1925); *Escape* (1926); and *The Roof* (1931).

The fictional bent in Galsworthy's work is shown in several admirable volumes of short stories: *A Sheaf* (1916); *Beyond* (1917); *Another Sheaf* (1919); *Five Tales* (1919); *The Burning Spear* (1923); *Captures* (1923); and *Caravan* (1925), in addition to the two volumes of Forsyte sketches already noted. Sometimes these stories verge upon the character-essay, such as those in *Tatterdemalion* (1920). His typical essays in *The Inn of Tranquillity* have already been mentioned; there are also *A Commentary* (1916); *Addresses in America* (1919); *Castles in Spain* (1927); *The Flowering Wilderness* (1932); and *Candelabra* (1933).

Galsworthy has the urbanity combined with the attention to form and style that characterized the nineteenth-century writer. But he is living in the twentieth century, and he is fully aware of the impact of the new order upon the old. More than that, he is the social commentator; and however much he is of the older generation born and bred, his value as a contemporary commentator is none the less genuine.

At times he is the mellow romanticist, and usually he is the sentimentalist; but his sense of human injustice is keen and real, as his sense of human character is broad. He never lapses from essential dignity in his account of men and women of the industrial world, the dominating characters in our social scene.

Loyalties

PERSONS OF THE PLAY

CHARLES WINSOR, *owner of Meldon Court, near Newmarket*
LADY ADELA, *his wife*
FERDINAND DE LEVIS, *young, rich, and new*
TREISURE, *Winsor's butler*
GENERAL CANYNGE, *a Racing Oracle*
MARGARET ORME, *a Society Girl*
CAPTAIN RONALD DANCY, D.S.O., *Retired*
MABEL, *his wife*
INSPECTOR DEDE, *of the County Constabulary*
ROBERT, *Winsor's footman*
A CONSTABLE, *attendant on Dede*
AUGUSTUS BORRING, *a Clubman*
LORD ST. ERTH, *a Peer of the Realm*
A FOOTMAN, *of the Club*
MAJOR COLFORD, *a Brother Officer of Dancy's*
EDWARD GRAVITER, *a Solicitor*
A YOUNG CLERK, *of Twisden & Graviter's*
GILMAN, *a Large Grocer*
JACOB TWISDEN, *Senior Partner of Twisden & Graviter*
RICARDOS, *an Italian, in Wine*

ACT I

SCENE I

The dressing-room of CHARLES WINSOR, owner of Meldon Court, near Newmarket; about eleven-thirty at night. The room has pale grey walls, unadorned; the curtains are drawn over a window Back Left Centre. A bed lies along the wall, Left. An open door,

Reprinted from *Loyalties* by John Galsworthy, copyright, 1922, by Charles Scribner's Sons; Used by permission.

Right Back, leads into LADY ADELA's bedroom; a door, Right Forward, into a long corridor, on to which abut rooms in a row, the whole length of the house's left wing. WINSOR's dressing-table, with a light over it, is Stage Right of the curtained window. Pyjamas are laid out on the bed, which is turned back. Slippers are handy, and all the usual gear of a well-appointed bed-dressing-room. CHARLES WINSOR, a tall, fair, good-looking man about thirty-eight, is taking off a smoking jacket.

WINSOR. Hallo! Adela!
VOICE of LADY ADELA (*From her bedroom*). Hallo!
WINSOR. In bed?
VOICE of LADY ADELA. No.
She appears in the doorway in under-garment and a wrapper. She, too, is fair, about thirty-five, rather delicious, and suggestive of porcelain.
WINSOR. Win at Bridge?
LADY ADELA. No fear.
WINSOR. Who did?
LADY ADELA. Lord St Erth and Ferdy de Levis. 10
WINSOR. That young man has too much luck—the young bounder won two races to-day; and he's as rich as Crœsus.
LADY ADELA. Oh! Charlie, he did look so exactly as if he'd sold me a carpet when I was paying him.
WINSOR (*Changing into slippers*). His father did sell carpets, wholesale, in the City.
LADY ADELA. Really? And you say I haven't intuition! (*With a finger on her lips*). Mori- 20 son's in there.
WINSOR (*Motioning towards the door, which she shuts*). Ronny Dancy took a tenner off him, anyway, before dinner.
LADY ADELA. No! How?
WINSOR. Standing jump on to a bookcase four feet high. De Levis had to pay up, and sneered at him for making money by parlour tricks. That young Jew gets himself disliked.
LADY ADELA. Aren't you rather prejudiced? 30
WINSOR. Not a bit. I like Jews. That's not against him—rather the contrary these days. But he pushes himself. The General tells me he's deathly keen to get into the Jockey Club.

(*Taking off his tie*). It's amusing to see him trying to get round old St Erth.

LADY ADELA. If Lord St Erth and General Canynge backed him he'd get in if he *did* sell carpets!

WINSOR. He's got some pretty good horses. (*Taking off his waistcoat*). Ronny Dancy's on his bones again, I'm afraid. He had a bad day. When a chap takes to doing parlor stunts for a bet—it's a sure sign. What made him chuck the Army?

LADY ADELA. He says it's too dull, now there's no fighting.

WINSOR. Well, he can't exist on backing losers.

LADY ADELA. Isn't it just like him to get married now? He really is the most reckless person.

WINSOR. Yes. He's a queer chap. I've always liked him, but I've never quite made him out. What do you think of his wife?

LADY ADELA. Nice child; awfully gone on him.

WINSOR. Is *he?*

LADY ADELA. Quite indecently—both of them. (*Nodding towards the wall, Left*). They're next door.

WINSOR. Who's beyond them?

LADY ADELA. De Levis; and Margaret Orme at the end. Charlie, do you realise that the bathroom out there has to wash those four?

WINSOR. I know.

LADY ADELA. Your grandfather was crazy when he built this wing; six rooms in a row with balconies like an hotel, and only one bath —if we hadn't put ours in.

WINSOR (*Looking at his watch*). Half-past eleven. (*Yawns*). Newmarket always makes me sleepy. You're keeping Morison up.

LADY ADELA *goes to the door, blowing a kiss.*

CHARLES *goes up to his dressing-table and begins to brush his hair, sprinkling on essence. There is a knock on the corridor door.* Come in.

DE LEVIS *enters, clad in pyjamas and flowered dressing-gown. He is a dark, good-looking, rather Eastern young man. His face is long and disturbed.* Hallo! De Levis! Anything I can do for you?

DE LEVIS (*In a voice whose faint exoticism is broken by a vexed excitement*). I say, I'm awfully sorry, Winsor, but I thought I'd better tell you at once. I've just had—er—rather a lot of money stolen.

WINSOR. What! (*There is something of outrage in his tone and glance, as who should say: "In my house?"*) How do you mean, *stolen?*

DE LEVIS. I put it under my pillow and went to have a bath; when I came back it was gone.

WINSOR. Good Lord! How much?

DE LEVIS. Nearly a thousand—nine hundred and seventy, I think.

WINSOR. Phew! (*Again the faint tone of outrage, that a man should have so much money about him*).

DE LEVIS. I sold my Rosemary filly to-day on the course to Kentman the bookie, and he paid me in notes.

WINSOR. What? That weed Dancy gave you in the Spring?

DE LEVIS. Yes. But I tried her pretty high the other day; and she's in the Cambridgeshire. I was only out of my room a quarter of an hour, and I locked my door.

WINSOR (*Again outraged*). You *locked*——

DE LEVIS (*Not seeing the fine shade*). Yes, and had the key here. (*He taps his pocket.*) Look here! (*He holds out a pocket-book.*) It's been stuffed with my shaving papers.

WINSOR (*Between feeling that such things don't happen, and a sense that he will have to clear it up*). This is damned awkward, De Levis.

DE LEVIS (*With steel in his voice*). Yes. I should like it back.

WINSOR. Have you got the numbers of the notes?

DE LEVIS. No.

WINSOR. What were they?

DE LEVIS. One hundred, three fifties, and the rest tens and fives.

WINSOR. What d'you want me to do?

DE LEVIS. Unless there's anybody you think——

WINSOR (*Eyeing him*). Is it likely?

DE LEVIS. Then I think the police ought to see my room. It's a lot of money.

WINSOR. Good Lord! We're not in Town; there'll be nobody nearer than Newmarket at this time of night—four miles.

The door from the bedroom is suddenly opened and LADY ADELA *appears. She has on a lace cap over her finished hair, and the wrapper.*

LADY ADELA (*Closing the door*). What is it? Are you ill, Mr De Levis?

WINSOR. Worse; he's had a lot of money stolen. Nearly a thousand pounds.

LADY ADELA. Gracious! Where?

DE LEVIS. From under my pillow, Lady Adela—my door was locked—I was in the bathroom.

LADY ADELA. But how fearfully thrilling!

10 WINSOR. Thrilling! What's to be done? He wants it back.

LADY ADELA. Of course! (*With sudden realisation*). Oh! But—— Oh! it's quite too unpleasant!

WINSOR. Yes! What am I to do? Fetch the servants out of their rooms? Search the grounds? It'll make the devil of a scandal.

DE LEVIS. Who's next to me?

LADY ADELA (*Coldly*). Oh! Mr De Levis!

20 WINSOR. Next to you? The Dancys on this side, and Miss Orme on the other. What's that to do with it?

DE LEVIS. They may have heard something.

WINSOR. Let's get them. But Dancy was downstairs when I came up. Get Morison, Adela! No, look here! When *was* this exactly? Let's have as many alibis as we can.

DE LEVIS. Within the last twenty minutes, certainly.

30 WINSOR. How long has Morison been up with you?

LADY ADELA. I came up at eleven, and rang for her at once.

WINSOR (*Looking at his watch*). Half an hour. Then she's all right. Send her for Margaret and the Dancys—there's nobody else in this wing. No; send her to bed. We don't want gossip. D'you mind going yourself, Adela?

LADY ADELA. Consult General Canynge,

40 Charlie.

WINSOR. Right. Could you get him too? D'you really want the police, De Levis?

DE LEVIS (*Stung by the faint contempt in his tone of voice*). Yes, I do.

WINSOR. Then, look here, dear! Slip into my study and telephone to the police at Newmarket. There'll be somebody there; they're sure to have drunks. I'll have Treisure up, and speak to him. (*He rings the bell.*)

LADY ADELA *goes out into her room and closes the door.*

WINSOR. Look here, De Levis! This isn't an 50 hotel. It's the sort of thing that doesn't happen in a decent house. Are you sure you're not mistaken, and didn't have them stolen on the course?

DE LEVIS. Absolutely. I counted them just before putting them under my pillow; then I locked the door and had the key here. There's only one door, you know.

WINSOR. How was your window?

DE LEVIS. Open. 60

WINSOR (*Drawing back the curtains of his own window*). You've got a balcony like this. Any sign of a ladder or anything?

DE LEVIS. No.

WINSOR. It must have been done from the window, unless someone had a skeleton key. Who knew you'd got that money? Where did Kentman pay you?

DE LEVIS. Just around the corner in the further paddock. 70

WINSOR. Anybody about?

DE LEVIS. Oh, yes!

WINSOR. Suspicious?

DE LEVIS. I didn't notice anything.

WINSOR. You must have been marked down and followed here.

DE LEVIS. How would they know my room?

WINSOR. Might have got it somehow. (*A knock from the corridor*). Come in.

TREISURE, *the Butler, appears, a silent, grave man of almost supernatural conformity.* DE LEVIS *gives him a quick, hard look, noted and resented by* WINSOR.

TREISURE (*To* WINSOR). Yes, sir? 80

WINSOR. Who valets Mr De Levis?

TREISURE. Robert, sir.

WINSOR. When was he up last?

TREISURE. In the ordinary course of things, about ten o'clock, sir.

WINSOR. When did he go to bed?

TREISURE. I dismissed at eleven.

WINSOR. But did he go?

TREISURE. To the best of my knowledge. Is there anything *I* can do, sir? 90

WINSOR (*Disregarding a sign from* DE LEVIS). Look here, Treisure, Mr De Levis has had a large sum of money taken from his bedroom within the last half hour.

TREISURE. Indeed, sir!

WINSOR. Robert's quite all right, isn't he?

TREISURE. He is, sir.

DE LEVIS. How do you know?

TREISURE'S *eyes rest on* DE LEVIS.

TREISURE. I am a pretty good judge of character, sir, if you'll excuse me.

WINSOR. Look here, De Levis, eighty or ninety notes must have been pretty bulky. You didn't have them on you at dinner?

DE LEVIS. No.

WINSOR. Where did you put them?

DE LEVIS. In a boot, and the boot in my suitcase, and locked it.

TREISURE *smiles faintly.*

WINSOR (*Again slightly outraged by such precautions in his house*). And you found it locked—and took them from there to put under your pillow?

DE LEVIS. Yes.

WINSOR. Run your mind over things, Treisure—has any stranger been about?

TREISURE. No, sir.

WINSOR. This seems to have happened between 11:15 and 11:30. Is that right? (DE LEVIS *nods.*) Any noise—anything outside, anything suspicious anywhere?

TREISURE (*Running his mind—very still*). No, sir.

WINSOR. What time did you shut up?

TREISURE. I should say about eleven-fifteen, sir. As soon as Major Colford and Captain Dancy had finished billiards. What was Mr De Levis doing out of his room, if I may ask, sir?

WINSOR. Having a bath; with his room locked and the key in his pocket.

TREISURE. Thank you, sir.

DE LEVIS (*Conscious of indefinable suspicion*). Damn it! What do you mean? I *was*.

TREISURE. I beg your pardon, sir.

WINSOR (*Concealing a smile*). Look here, Treisure, it's infernally awkward for everybody.

TREISURE. It is, sir.

WINSOR. What do you suggest?

TREISURE. The proper thing, sir, I suppose, would be a cordon and a complete search—in our interests.

WINSOR. I entirely refuse to suspect anybody.

TREISURE. But if Mr De Levis feels otherwise, sir?

DE LEVIS (*Stammering*). I? All I know is—the money was there, and it's gone.

WINSOR (*Compunctious*). Quite! It's pretty sickening for you. But so it is for anybody else. However, we must do our best to get it back for you.

A knock on the door.

WINSOR. Hallo!

TREISURE *opens the door, and* GENERAL CANYNGE *enters.*

Oh! It's you, General. Come in. Adela's told you?

GENERAL CANYNGE *nods. He is a slim man of about sixty, very well preserved, intensely neat and self-contained, and still in evening dress. His eyelids droop slightly, but his eyes are keen and his expression astute.*

WINSOR. Well, General, what's the first move?

CANYNGE (*Lifting his eyebrows*). Mr De Levis presses the matter?

DE LEVIS (*Flicked again*). Unless you think it's too plebeian of me, General Canynge—a thousand pounds.

CANYNGE (*Drily*). Just so! Then we must wait for the police, Winsor. Lady Adela has got through to them. What height are these rooms from the ground, Treisure?

TREISURE. Twenty-three feet from the terrace, sir.

CANYNGE. Any ladders near?

TREISURE. One in the stables, sir, very heavy. No others within three hundred yards.

CANYNGE. Just slip down, and see whether that's been moved.

TREISURE. Very good, General.

He goes out.

DE LEVIS (*Uneasily*). Of course, he—— I suppose you——

WINSOR. We do.

CANYNGE. You had better leave this in our hands, De Levis.

DE LEVIS. Certainly; only, the way he——

WINSOR (*Curtly*). Treisure has been here since he was a boy. I should as soon suspect myself.

DE LEVIS (*Looking from one to the other—with sudden anger*). You seem to think——! What was I to do? Take it lying down and let whoever it is get clear off? I suppose it's natural to want my money back?

CANYNGE *looks at his nails;* WINSOR *out of the window.*

WINSOR (*Turning*). Of course, De Levis!

DE LEVIS (*Sullenly*). Well, I'll go to my room. When the police come, perhaps you'll let me know. (*He goes out.*)

WINSOR. Phew! Did you ever see such a dressing-gown?

The door is opened. LADY ADELA *and* MARGARET ORME *come in. The latter is a vivid young lady of about twenty-five in a vivid wrapper; she is smoking a cigarette.*

LADY ADELA. I've told the Dancys—she was in bed. And I got through to Newmarket, Charles, and Inspector Dede is coming like the wind on a motorcycle.

MARGARET. Did he say "like the wind," Adela? He must have imagination. Isn't this gorgeous? Poor little Ferdy!

WINSOR (*Vexed*). You might take it seriously, Margaret; it's pretty beastly for us all. What time did *you* come up?

MARGARET. I came up with Adela. Am I suspected, Charles? How thrilling!

WINSOR. Did you hear anything?

MARGARET. Only little Ferdy splashing.

WINSOR. And saw nothing?

MARGARET. Not even that, alas!

LADY ADELA (*With a finger held up*). Leste! un peu leste! Oh! Here are the Dancys. Come in, you two!

MABEL *and* RONALD DANCY *enter. She is a pretty young woman with bobbed hair, fortunately, for she has just got out of bed, and is in her nightgown and a wrapper.* DANCY *is in his smoking jacket. He has a pale, determined face with high cheekbones, small, deep-set dark eyes, reddish crisp hair, and looks like a horseman.*

WINSOR. Awfully sorry to disturb you, Mrs Dancy; but I suppose you and Ronny haven't heard anything. De Levis's room is just beyond Ronny's dressing-room, you know.

MABEL. I've been asleep nearly half an hour, and Ronny's only just come up.

CANYNGE. Did you happen to look out of your window, Mrs Dancy?

MABEL. Yes. I stood there quite five minutes.

CANYNGE. When?

MABEL. Just about eleven, I should think. It was raining hard then.

CANYNGE. Yes, it's just stopped. You saw nothing?

MABEL. No.

DANCY. What time does he say the money was taken?

WINSOR. Between the quarter and half past. He'd locked his door and had the key with him.

MARGARET. How quaint! Just like an hotel. Does he put his boots out?

LADY ADELA. Don't be so naughty, Meg.

CANYNGE. When exactly did *you* come up, Dancy?

DANCY. About ten minutes ago. I'd only just got into my dressing-room before Lady Adela came. I've been writing letters in the hall since Colford and I finished billiards.

CANYNGE. You weren't up for anything in between?

DANCY. No.

MARGARET. The mystery of the grey room.

DANCY. Oughtn't the grounds to be searched for footmarks?

CANYNGE. That's for the police.

DANCY. The deuce! Are they coming?

CANYNGE. Directly.

A knock.

Yes?

TREISURE *enters.*

Well?

TREISURE. The ladder has not been moved, General. There isn't a sign.

WINSOR. All right. Get Robert up, but don't say anything to him. By the way, we're expecting the police.

TREISURE. I trust they will not find a mare's nest, sir, if I may say so.

He goes.

WINSOR. De Levis has got wrong with Treisure. (*Suddenly*). But, I say, what would any of us have done if *we'd* been in his shoes?

MARGARET. A thousand pounds? I can't even conceive having it.

DANCY. We probably shouldn't have found it out.

LADY ADELA. No—but if we had.

DANCY. Come to you—as he did.

WINSOR. Yes; but there's a way of doing things.

CANYNGE. We shouldn't have wanted the police.

MARGARET. No. That's it. The hotel touch.

LADY ADELA. Poor young man; I think we're rather hard on him.

WINSOR. He sold that weed you gave him, Dancy, to Kentman, the bookie, and these were the proceeds.

DANCY. Oh!

10 WINSOR. He'd tried her high, he said.

DANCY (*Grimly*). He would.

MABEL. Oh! Ronny, what bad luck!

WINSOR. He must have been followed here. (*At the window*). After rain like that, there ought to be footmarks.

The splutter of a motorcycle is heard.

MARGARET. Here's the wind!

WINSOR. What's the move now, General?

CANYNGE. You and I had better see the Inspector in De Levis's room.

20 WINSOR (*To the others*). If you'll all be handy, in case he wants to put questions for himself.

MARGARET. I hope he'll want me; it's just too thrilling.

DANCY. I hope he won't want me; I'm dog-tired. Come on, Mabel.

He puts his arm in his wife's.

CANYNGE. Just a minute, Charles.

He draws close to WINSOR *as the others are departing to their rooms.*

WINSOR. Yes, General?

CANYNGE. We must be careful with this In-
30 spector fellow. If he pitches hastily on somebody in the house it'll be very disagreeable.

WINSOR. By Jove! It *will*.

CANYNGE. We don't want to rouse any ridiculous suspicion.

WINSOR. Quite. (*A knock*). Come in!

TREISURE *enters*.

TREISURE. Inspector Dede, sir.

WINSOR. Show him in.

TREISURE. Robert is in readiness, sir; but I could swear he knows nothing about it.

40 WINSOR. All right.

TREISURE *reopens the door, and says: "Come in, please." The* INSPECTOR *enters, blue, formal, moustachioed, with a peaked cap in his hand.*

WINSOR. Good-evening, Inspector. Sorry to have brought you out at this time of night.

INSPECTOR. Good evenin', sir. Mr Winsor? You're the owner here, I think?

WINSOR. Yes. General Canynge.

INSPECTOR. Good evenin', General. I understand, a large sum of money.

WINSOR. Yes. Shall we go straight to the room it was taken from? One of my guests, Mr De Levis. It's the third room on the left. 50

CANYNGE. We've not been in there yet, Inspector; in fact, we've done nothing, except to find out that the stable ladder has not been moved. We haven't even searched the grounds.

INSPECTOR. Right, sir; I've brought a man with me.

They go out.

SCENE II (*A few minutes later*)

The bedroom of DE LEVIS *is the same in shape as* WINSOR'S *dressing-room, except that there is only one door—to the corridor. The furniture, however, is differently arranged; a small four-poster bedstead stands against the wall, Right Back, jutting into the room. A chair, on which* DE LEVIS's *clothes are thrown, stands at its foot. There is a dressing-table against the wall to the left of the open windows, where the curtains are drawn back and a stone balcony is seen. Against the wall to the right of the window is a chest of drawers, and a washstand is against the wall, Left. On a small table to the right of the bed an electric reading lamp is turned up, and there is a light over the dressing-table. The* INSPECTOR *is standing plumb centre looking at the bed, and* DE LEVIS *by the back of the chair at the foot of the bed.* WINSOR *and* CANYNGE *are close to the door, Right Forward.*

INSPECTOR (*Finishing a note*). Now, sir, if this is the room as you left it for your bath, just show us exactly what you did after takin' the pocket book from the suit case. Where was 60 that, by the way?

DE LEVIS (*Pointing*). Where it is now—under the dressing-table.

He comes forward to the front of the chair, opens the pocket-book, goes through the pretence of counting his shaving papers, closes the pocket-book, takes it to the head of the bed and slips it under the pillow. Makes the motion of taking up his pyjamas, crosses below the INSPECTOR *to the washstand, takes up a bath sponge, crosses to the door, takes out the key, opens the door.*

INSPECTOR (*Writing*). We now have the room as it was when the theft was committed. Reconstruct accordin' to 'uman nature, gentlemen, assumin' the thief to be in the room, what would he try first?—the clothes, the dressin'-table, the suit case, the chest of drawers, and last the bed.

He moves accordingly, examining the glass on the dressing-table, the surface of the suit cases, and the handles of the drawers, with a spy-glass, for finger-marks.

CANYNGE (*Sotto voce to* WINSOR). The order would have been just the other way.

The INSPECTOR *goes on hands and knees and examines the carpet between the window and the bed.*

10 DE LEVIS. Can I come in again?

INSPECTOR (*Standing up*). Did you open the window, sir, or was it open when you first came in?

DE LEVIS. I opened it.

INSPECTOR. Drawin' the curtains back first?

DE LEVIS. Yes.

INSPECTOR (*Sharply*). Are you sure there was nobody in the room already?

DE LEVIS (*Taken aback*). I don't know. I 20 never thought. I didn't look under the bed, if you mean that.

INSPECTOR (*Jotting*). Did not look under bed. Did you look under it after the theft?

DE LEVIS. No, I didn't.

INSPECTOR. Ah! Now, what *did* you do after you came back from your bath? Just give us that precisely.

DE LEVIS. Locked the door and left the key in. Put back my sponge, and took off my dress-30 ing-gown and put it there. (*He points to the footrails of the bed.*) Then I drew the curtains, again.

INSPECTOR. Shutting the window?

DE LEVIS. No. I got into bed, felt for my watch to see the time. My hand struck the pocket-book, and somehow it felt thinner. I took it out, looked into it, and found the notes gone, and these shaving papers instead.

INSPECTOR. Let me have a look at those, sir. 40 (*He applies the spy-glasses.*) And then?

DE LEVIS. I think I just sat on the bed.

INSPECTOR. Thinkin' and cursin' a bit, I suppose. Ye-es?

DE LEVIS. Then I put on my dressing-gown and went straight to Mr Winsor.

INSPECTOR. Not lockin' the door?

DE LEVIS. No.

INSPECTOR. Exactly. (*With a certain finality*). Now, sir, what time did you come up?

DE LEVIS. About eleven. 50

INSPECTOR. Precise, if you can give it me.

DE LEVIS. Well, I *know* it was eleven-fifteen when I put my watch under my pillow, before I went to the bath, and I suppose I'd been about a quarter of an hour undressing. I should say after eleven, if anything.

INSPECTOR. Just undressin'? Didn't look over your bettin' book?

DE LEVIS. No.

INSPECTOR. No prayers or anything? 60

DE LEVIS. No.

INSPECTOR. Pretty slippy with your undressin' as a rule?

DE LEVIS. Yes. Say five past eleven.

INSPECTOR. Mr Winsor, what time did the gentleman come to you?

WINSOR. Half-past eleven.

INSPECTOR. How do you fix that, sir?

WINSOR. I'd just looked at the time, and told my wife to send her maid off. 70

INSPECTOR. Then we've got it fixed between 11:15 and 11:30. (*Jots*). Now, sir, before we go further I'd like to see your butler and the footman that valets this gentleman.

WINSOR (*With distaste*). Very well, Inspector; only—my butler has been with us from a boy.

INSPECTOR. Quite so. This is just clearing the ground, sir.

WINSOR. General, d'you mind touching that 80 bell?

CANYNGE *rings a bell by the bed.*

INSPECTOR. Well, gentlemen, there are four possibilities. Either the thief was here all the time, waiting under the bed, and slipped out after this gentleman had gone to Mr Winsor. Or he came in with a key that fits the lock; and I'll want to see all the keys in the house. Or he came in with a skeleton key and out by the window, probably droppin' from the balcony. Or he came in by the window with a 90 rope or ladder and out the same way. (*Point-*

ing). There's a footmark here from a big boot which has been out of doors since it rained.

CANYNGE. Inspector—you—er—walked up to the window when you first came into the room.

INSPECTOR (*Stiffly*). I had not overlooked that, General.

CANYNGE. Of course.

A knock on the door relieves a certain tension.

WINSOR. Come in.

The footman ROBERT, *a fresh-faced young man, enters, followed by* TREISURE.

10 INSPECTOR. You valet Mr—Mr De Levis, I think?

ROBERT. Yes, sir.

INSPECTOR. At what time did you take his clothes and boots?

ROBERT. Ten o'clock, sir.

INSPECTOR (*With a pounce*). Did you happen to look under his bed?

ROBERT. No, sir.

INSPECTOR. Did you come up again, to bring 20 the clothes back?

ROBERT. No, sir; they're still downstairs.

INSPECTOR. Did you come up again for anything?

ROBERT. No, sir.

INSPECTOR. What time did you go to bed?

ROBERT. Just after eleven, sir.

INSPECTOR (*Scrutinising him*). Now, be careful. Did you go to bed at all?

ROBERT. No, sir.

30 INSPECTOR. Then why did you say you did? There's been a theft here, and anything you say may be used against you.

ROBERT. Yes, sir. I meant, I went to my room.

INSPECTOR. Where is your room?

ROBERT. On the ground floor, at the other end of the right wing, sir.

WINSOR. It's the extreme end of the house from this, Inspector. He's with the other two 40 footmen.

INSPECTOR. Were you there alone?

ROBERT. No, sir. Thomas and Frederick was there too.

TREISURE. That's right; I've seen them.

INSPECTOR (*Holding up his hand for silence*). Were you out of the room again after you went in?

ROBERT. No, sir.

INSPECTOR. What were you doing, if you didn't go to bed? 50

ROBERT (*To* WINSOR). Beggin' your pardon, sir, we were playin' Bridge.

INSPECTOR. Very good. You can go. I'll see *them* later on.

ROBERT. Yes, sir. They'll say the same as me.

He goes out, leaving a smile on the face of all except the INSPECTOR *and* DE LEVIS.

INSPECTOR (*Sharply*). Call him back.

TREISURE *calls "Robert," and the* FOOTMAN *re-enters.*

ROBERT. Yes, sir?

INSPECTOR. Did you notice anything particular about Mr De Levis's clothes?

ROBERT. Only that they were very good, 60 sir.

INSPECTOR. I mean—anything peculiar?

ROBERT (*After reflection*). Yes, sir.

INSPECTOR. Well?

ROBERT. A pair of his boots this evenin' was reduced to one, sir.

INSPECTOR. What did you make of that?

ROBERT. I thought he might have thrown the other at a cat or something.

INSPECTOR. Did you look for it? 70

ROBERT. No, sir; I meant to draw his attention to it in the morning.

INSPECTOR. Very good.

ROBERT. Yes, sir. (*He goes again.*)

INSPECTOR (*Looking at* DE LEVIS). Well, sir, there's *your* story corroborated.

DE LEVIS (*Stiffly*). I don't know why it should need corroboration, Inspector.

INSPECTOR. In my experience, you can never have too much of that. (*To* WINSOR). I under- 80 stand there's a lady in the room on this side (*pointing Left*) and a gentleman on this (*pointing Right*). Were they in their rooms?

WINSOR. Miss Orme was; Captain Dancy not.

INSPECTOR. Do they know of the affair?

WINSOR. Yes.

INSPECTOR. Well, I'd just like the keys of their doors for a minute. My man will get them.

He goes to the door, opens it, and speaks to a constable in the corridor.

(*To* TREISURE). You can go with him.

TREISURE *goes out.*

In the meantime I'll just examine the balcony. 90

He goes out on the balcony, followed by DE LEVIS.

WINSOR (*To* CANYNGE). Damn De Levis

and his money! It's deuced invidious, all this, General.

CANYNGE. The Inspector's no earthly.

There is a simultaneous re-entry of the IN-SPECTOR from the balcony and of TREISURE and the CONSTABLE from the corridor.

CONSTABLE (*Handing key*). Room on the left, sir. (*Handing key*). Room on the right, sir.

The INSPECTOR tries the keys in the door, watched with tension by the others. The keys fail.

INSPECTOR. Put them back.

Hands keys to CONSTABLE, who goes out, followed by TREISURE.

I'll have to try every key in the house, sir.

WINSOR. Inspector, do you really think it
10 necessary to disturb the whole house and knock up all my guests? It's most disagreeable, all this, you know. The loss of the money is not such a great matter. Mr De Levis has a very large income.

CANYNGE. You could get the numbers of the notes from Kentman the bookmaker, Inspector; he'll probably have the big ones, anyway.

INSPECTOR (*Shaking his head*). A bookie. I don't suppose he will, sir. It's come and go
20 with them, all the time.

WINSOR. We don't want a Meldon Court scandal, Inspector.

INSPECTOR. Well, Mr Winsor, I've formed my theory.

As he speaks, DE LEVIS comes in from the balcony.

And I don't say to try the keys is necessary to it; but strictly, I ought to exhaust the possibilities.

WINSOR. What do you say, De Levis? D'you want everybody in the house knocked up so
30 that their keys can be tried?

DE LEVIS (*Whose face, since his return, expresses a curious excitement*). No, I don't.

INSPECTOR. Very well, gentlemen. In my opinion the thief walked in before the door was locked, probably during dinner; and was under the bed. He escaped by dropping from the balcony—the creeper at that corner (*he points stage Left*) has been violently wrenched. I'll go down now, and examine the grounds,
40 and I'll see you again, sir. (*He makes another entry in his note-book*). Good-night, then, gentlemen!

CANYNGE. Good-night!

WINSOR (*With relief*). I'll come with you, Inspector.

He escorts him to the door, and they go out.

DE LEVIS (*Suddenly*). General, I know who took them.

CANYNGE. The deuce you do! Are you following the Inspector's theory?

DE LEVIS (*Contemptuously*). That ass! (*Pull-* 5 *ing the shaving papers out of the case*). No! The man who put those there was clever and cool enough to wrench that creeper off the balcony, as a blind. Come and look here, General. (*He goes to the window, the GENERAL follows. DE LEVIS points stage Right.*) See the rail of my balcony, and the rail of the next? (*He holds up the cord of his dressing-gown, stretching his arms out.*) I've measured it with this. Just over seven feet, that's all! If a man can 60 take a standing jump on to a narrow bookcase four feet high and balance there, he'd make nothing of that. And, look here! (*He goes out on the balcony and returns with a bit of broken creeper in his hand, and holds it out into the light.*) Someone's stood on that—the stalk's crushed—the inner corner too, where he'd naturally stand when he took his jump back.

CANYNGE (*After examining it—stiffly*). That 70 other balcony is young Dancy's, Mr De Levis; a soldier and a gentleman. This is an extraordinary insinuation.

DE LEVIS. Accusation.

CANYNGE. What!

DE LEVIS. I have intuitions, General; it's in my blood. I see the whole thing. Dancy came up, watched me into the bathroom, tried my door, slipped back into his dressing-room, saw my window was open, took that jump, sneaked 80 the notes, filled the case up with these, wrenched the creeper there (*He points stage Left*) for a blind, jumped back, and slipped downstairs again. It didn't take him four minutes altogether.

CANYNGE (*Very gravely*). This is outrageous, De Levis. Dancy says he was downstairs all the time. You must either withdraw unreservedly, or I must confront you with him.

DE LEVIS. If he'll return the notes and apologise, I'll do nothing—except cut him in future. He gave me that filly, you know, as a hopeless weed, and he's been pretty sick ever since, that he was such a flat as not to see how good she was. Besides, he's hard up, I know.

CANYNGE (*After a vexed turn up and down the room*). It's mad, sir, to jump to conclusions like this.

DE LEVIS. Not so mad as the conclusion Dancy jumped to when he lighted on my balcony.

CANYNGE. Nobody could have taken this money who did not know you had it.

DE LEVIS. How do you know that he didn't?

CANYNGE. Do you know that he did?

DE LEVIS. I haven't the least doubt of it.

CANYNGE. Without any proof. This is very ugly, De Levis. I must tell Winsor.

DE LEVIS (*Angrily*). Tell the whole blooming lot. You think I've no feelers, but I've felt the atmosphere here, I can tell you, General. If I were in Dancy's shoes and he in mine, your tone to me would be very different.

CANYNGE (*Suavely frigid*). I'm not aware of using any tone, as you call it. But this is a private house, Mr De Levis, and something is due to our host and to the *esprit de corps* that exists among gentlemen.

DE LEVIS. Since when is a thief a gentleman? Thick as thieves—a good motto, isn't it?

CANYNGE. That's enough! (*He goes to the door, but stops before opening it.*) Now, look here! I have some knowledge of the world. Once an accusation like this passes beyond these walls no one can foresee the consequences. Captain Dancy is a gallant fellow, with a fine record as a soldier; and only just married. If he's as innocent as—Christ—mud will stick to him, unless the real thief is found. In the old days of swords, either you or he would not have gone out of this room alive. If you persist in this absurd accusation, you will *both* of you go out of this room dead in the eyes of Society: you for bringing it, he for being the object of it.

DE LEVIS. Society! Do you think I don't know that I'm only tolerated for my money? Society can't add injury to insult and have my money as well, that's all. If the notes are restored I'll keep my mouth shut; if they're not, I shan't. I'm certain I'm right. I ask nothing better than to be confronted with Dancy; but, if you prefer it, deal with him in your own way—for the sake of your *esprit de corps*.

CANYNGE. 'Pon my soul, Mr De Levis, you go too far.

DE LEVIS. Not so far as I shall go, General Canynge, if those notes aren't given back.

WINSOR *comes in.*

WINSOR. Well, De Levis, I'm afraid that's all we can do for the present. So very sorry this should have happened in my house.

CANYNGE (*After a silence*). There's a development, Winsor. Mr De Levis accuses one of your guests.

WINSOR. What?

CANYNGE. Of jumping from his balcony to this, taking the notes, and jumping back. I've done my best to dissuade him from indulging the fancy—without success. Dancy must be told.

DE LEVIS. You can deal with Dancy in your own way. All I want is the money back.

CANYNGE (*Drily*). Mr De Levis feels that he is only valued for his money, so that it is essential for him to have it back.

WINSOR. Damn it! This is monstrous, De Levis. I've known Ronald Dancy since he was a boy.

CANYNGE. You talk about adding injury to insult, De Levis. What do you call such treatment of a man who gave you the mare out of which you made this thousand pounds?

DE LEVIS. I didn't want the mare; I took her as a favour.

CANYNGE. With an eye to possibilities, I venture to think—the principle guides a good many transactions.

DE LEVIS (*As if flicked on a raw spot*). In my race, do you mean?

CANYNGE (*Coldly*). I said nothing of the sort.

DE LEVIS. No; you don't *say* these things, any of you.

CANYNGE. Nor did I think it.

DE LEVIS. Dancy does.

WINSOR. Really, De Levis, if this is the way you repay hospitality——

DE LEVIS. Hospitality that skins my feelings and costs me a thousand pounds!

CANYNGE. Go and get Dancy, Winsor; but don't say anything to him.

WINSOR *goes out.*

CANYNGE. Perhaps you will kindly control yourself and leave this to me.

DE LEVIS *turns to the window and lights a cigarette.* WINSOR *comes back, followed by* DANCY.

CANYNGE. For Winsor's sake, Dancy, we don't want any scandal or fuss about this affair. We've tried to make the police understand that. To my mind the whole thing turns on our finding who knew that De Levis had this money. It's about that we want to consult you.

WINSOR. Kentman paid De Levis round the corner in the further paddock, he says.

DE LEVIS *turns round from the window, so that he and* DANCY *are staring at each other.*

CANYNGE. Did you hear anything that throws light, Dancy? As it was your filly originally, we thought perhaps you might.

DANCY. I? No.

CANYNGE. Didn't you hear of the sale on the course at all?

DANCY. No.

CANYNGE. Then you can't suggest any one who could have known? Nothing else was taken, you see.

DANCY. De Levis is known to be rolling, as I am known to be stony.

CANYNGE. There are a good many people still rolling, besides Mr De Levis, but not many people with so large a sum in their pocket-books.

DANCY. He won two races.

DE LEVIS. Do you suggest that I bet in ready money?

DANCY. I don't know how you bet, and I don't care.

CANYNGE. You can't help us, then?

DANCY. No, I can't. Anything else? (*He looks fixedly at* DE LEVIS.)

CANYNGE (*Putting his hand on* DANCY's *arm*). Nothing else, thank you, Dancy.

DANCY *goes.* CANYNGE *puts his hand up to his face. A moment's silence.*

WINSOR. You see, De Levis? He didn't even know you'd got the money.

DE LEVIS. Very conclusive.

WINSOR. Well! You *are*——

There is a knock on the door, and the IN-SPECTOR *enters.*

INSPECTOR. I'm just going, gentlemen. The grounds, I'm sorry to say, have yielded nothing. It's a bit of a puzzle.

CANYNGE. You've searched thoroughly?

INSPECTOR. We have, General. I can pick up nothing near the terrace.

WINSOR (*After a look at* DE LEVIS, *whose face expresses too much*). H'm! You'll take it up from the other end, then, Inspector?

INSPECTOR. Well, we'll see what we can do with the bookmakers about the numbers, sir. Before I go, gentlemen—you've had time to think it over—there's no one you suspect in the house, I suppose?

DE LEVIS's *face is alive and uncertain.* CAN-YNGE *is staring at him fixedly.*

WINSOR (*Emphatically*). No.

DE LEVIS *turns and goes out on to the balcony.*

INSPECTOR. If you're coming in to the racing to-morrow, sir, you might give us a call. I'll have seen Kentman by then.

WINSOR. Right you are, Inspector. Good-night, and many thanks.

INSPECTOR. You're welcome, sir.

He goes out.

WINSOR. Gosh! I thought that chap (*With a nod toward the balcony*) was going to—! Look here, General, we *must* stop his tongue. Imagine it going the rounds. They may never find the real thief, you know. It's the very devil for Dancy.

CANYNGE. Winsor! Dancy's sleeve was damp.

WINSOR. How d'you mean?

CANYNGE. Quite damp. It's been raining.

The two look at each other.

WINSOR. I—I don't follow—— (*His voice is hesitative and lower, showing that he does.*)

CANYNGE. It was coming down hard; a minute out in it would have been enough—— (*He motions with his chin towards the balcony.*)

WINSOR (*Hastily*). He must have been out on his balcony since.

CANYNGE. It stopped before I came up, half an hour ago.

WINSOR. He's been leaning on the wet stone, then.

CANYNGE. With the outside of the *upper* part of the arm?

WINSOR. Against the wall, perhaps. There may be a dozen explanations. (*Very low and with great concentration*). I entirely and absolutely refuse to believe anything of the sort against Ronald Dancy—in my house. Dash it, General, we must do as we'd be done by. It hits us all—it hits us all. The thing's intolerable.

10 CANYNGE. I agree. Intolerable. (*Raising his voice*). Mr De Levis!

DE LEVIS *returns into view, in the centre of the open window.*

CANYNGE (*With cold decision*). Young Dancy was an officer and is a gentleman; this insinuation is pure supposition, and you must not make it. Do you understand me?

DE LEVIS. My tongue is still mine, General, if my money isn't!

CANYNGE (*Unmoved*). Must not. You're a member of three Clubs, you want to be mem-
20 ber of a fourth. No one who makes such an insinuation against a fellow-guest in a country house, except on absolute proof, can do so without complete ostracism. Have we your word to say nothing?

DE LEVIS. Social blackmail? H'm!

CANYNGE. Not at all—simple warning. If you consider it necessary in your interests to start this scandal—no matter how, we shall consider it necessary in ours to dissociate ourselves com-
30 pletely from one who so recklessly disregards the unwritten code.

DE LEVIS. Do you think your code applies to me? Do you, General?

CANYNGE. To anyone who aspires to be a gentleman, sir.

DE LEVIS. Ah! But you haven't known *me* since I was a boy.

CANYNGE. Make up your mind.

A pause.

DE LEVIS. I'm not a fool, General. I know
40 perfectly well that you can get me outed.

CANYNGE (*Icily*). Well?

DE LEVIS (*Sullenly*). I'll say nothing about it, unless I get more proof.

CANYNGE. Good! We have implicit faith in Dancy.

There is a moment's encounter of eyes; the GENERAL'S *steady, shrewd, impassive;* WINSOR'S *angry and defiant;* DE LEVIS'S *mocking, a little triumphant, malicious. Then* CANYNGE *and* WINSOR *go to the door, and pass out.*

DE LEVIS (*To himself*). Rats!

ACT II

SCENE I (*Three weeks later*)

Afternoon, three weeks later, in the card room of a London Club. A fire is burning, Left. A door, Right, leads to the billiard-room. Rather Left of Centre, at a card table, LORD ST ERTH, *an old John Bull, sits facing the audience; to his right is* GENERAL CANYNGE, *to his left* AUGUSTUS BORRING, *an essential Clubman, about thirty-five years old, with a very slight and rather becoming stammer or click in his speech. The fourth Bridge player,* CHARLES WINSOR, *stands with his back to the fire.*

BORRING. And the r-rub.

WINSOR. By George! You do hold cards, Borring.

ST. ERTH (*Who has lost*). Not a patch on 50 the old whist—this game. Don't know why I play it—never did.

CANYNGE. St Erth, shall we raise the flag for whist again?

WINSOR. No go, General. You can't go back on pace. No getting a man to walk when he knows he can fly. The young men won't look at it.

BORRING. Better develop it so that t-two can sit out, General. 60

ST. ERTH. We ought to have stuck to the old game. Wish I'd gone to Newmarket, Canynge, in spite of the weather.

CANYNGE (*Looking at his watch*). Let's hear what's won the Cambridgeshire. Ring, won't you, Winsor?

WINSOR *rings.*

ST. ERTH. By the way, Canynge, young De Levis was blackballed.

CANYNGE. What?

ST. ERTH. I looked in on my way down. 70

CANYNGE *sits very still, and* WINSOR *utters a disturbed sound.*

BORRING. But of c-course he was, General. What did you expect?

A FOOTMAN *enters.*

FOOTMAN. Yes, my lord?

ST. ERTH. What won the Cambridgeshire?

FOOTMAN. Rosemary, my lord. Sherbet second; Barbizon third. Nine to one the winner.

WINSOR. Thank you. That's all.

FOOTMAN *goes.*

BORRING. Rosemary! And De Levis sold her! But he got a good p-price, I suppose.

The other three look at him.

ST. ERTH. Many a slip between price and pocket, young man.

CANYNGE. Cut! (*They cut.*)

BORRING. I say, is that the yarn that's going round about his having had a lot of m-money stolen in a country house? By Jove! He'll be pretty s-sick.

WINSOR. You and I, Borring.

He sits down in CANYNGE's *chair, and the* GENERAL *takes his place by the fire.*

BORRING. Phew! Won't Dancy be mad! He gave that filly away to save her keep. He was rather pleased to find somebody who'd take her. Kentman must have won a p-pot. She was at thirty-threes a fortnight ago.

ST. ERTH. All the money goes to fellows who don't know a horse from a haystack.

CANYNGE (*Profoundly*). And care less. Yes! We want men racing to whom a horse means something.

BORRING. I thought the horse m-meant the same to everyone, General—chance to get the b-better of one's neighbor.

CANYNGE (*With feeling*). The horse is a noble animal, sir, as you'd know if you'd owed your life to them as often as I have.

BORRING. They always try to *take* mine, General. I shall never belong to the noble f-fellowship of the horse.

ST. ERTH (*Drily*). Evidently. Deal!

As BORRING *begins to deal the door is opened and* MAJOR COLFORD *appears—a lean and moustached cavalryman.*

BORRING. Hallo, C-Colford.

COLFORD. General!

Something in the tone of his voice brings them all to a standstill.

COLFORD. I want your advice. Young De Levis in there (*He points to the billiard-room from which he has just come*) has started a blasphemous story——

CANYNGE. One moment. Mr Borring, d'you mind——

COLFORD. It makes no odds, General. Four of us in there heard him. He's saying it was Ronald Dancy robbed him down at Winsor's. The fellow's mad over losing the price of that filly now she's won the Cambridgeshire.

BORRING (*All ears*). Dancy! Great S-Scott!

COLFORD. Dancy's in the Club. If he hadn't been I'd have taken it on myself to wring the bounder's neck.

WINSOR *and* BORRING *have risen.* ST ERTH *alone remains seated.*

CANYNGE (*After consulting* ST ERTH *with a look*). Ask De Levis to be good enough to come in here. Borring, you might see that Dancy doesn't leave the Club. We shall want him. Don't say anything to him, and use your tact to keep people off.

BORRING *goes out, followed by* COLFORD.

WINSOR. Result of hearing he was black-balled—pretty slippy.

CANYNGE. St Erth, I told you there was good reason when I asked you to back young De Levis. Winsor and I knew of this insinuation; I wanted to keep his tongue quiet. It's just wild assertion; to have it bandied about was unfair to Dancy. The duel used to keep people's tongues in order.

ST. ERTH. H'm! It never settled anything, except who could shoot straightest.

COLFORD (*Re-appearing*). De Levis says he's nothing to add to what he said to you before, on the subject.

CANYNGE. Kindly tell him that if he wishes to remain a member of this Club he must account to the Committee for such a charge against a fellow-member. Four of us are here, and form a quorum.

COLFORD *goes out again.*

ST. ERTH. Did Kentman ever give the police the numbers of those notes, Winsor?

WINSOR. He only had the numbers of two—the hundred, and one of the fifties.

ST. ERTH. And they haven't traced 'em?

WINSOR. Not yet.

As he speaks, DE LEVIS *comes in. He is in a highly-coloured, not to say excited state.* COLFORD *follows him.*

DE LEVIS. Well, General Canynge! It's a little too strong all this—a little too strong. (*Under emotion his voice is slightly more exotic.*)

CANYNGE (*Calmly*). It is obvious, Mr De Levis, that you and Captain Dancy can't both remain members of this Club. We ask you for an explanation before requesting one resignation or the other.

DE LEVIS. You've let me down.

CANYNGE. What?

DE LEVIS. Well, I shall tell people that you and Lord St Erth backed me up for one Club, and asked me to resign from another.

CANYNGE. It's a matter of indifference to me, sir, what you tell people.

ST. ERTH (*Drily*). You seem a venomous young man.

DE LEVIS. I'll tell you what seems to me venomous, my lord—chasing a man like a pack of hounds because he isn't your breed.

CANYNGE. You appear to have your breed on the brain, sir. Nobody else does, so far as I know.

DE LEVIS. Suppose I had robbed Dancy, would you chase him out for complaining of it?

COLFORD. My God! If you repeat that——

CANYNGE. Steady, Colford!

WINSOR. You make this accusation that Dancy stole your money in my house on no proof—no proof; and you expect Dancy's friends to treat you as if you were a gentleman! That's too strong, if you like!

DE LEVIS. No proof? Kentman told me at Newmarket yesterday that Dancy *did* know of the sale. He told Goole, and Goole says that he himself spoke of it to Dancy.

WINSOR. Well—if he did?

DE LEVIS. Dancy told you he *didn't* know of it in General Canynge's presence, and mine. (*To* CANYNGE). You can't deny that, if you want to.

CANYNGE. Choose your expressions more nicely, please!

DE LEVIS. Proof! Did they find any footmarks in the grounds below that torn creeper? Not a sign! You saw how he can jump; he won ten pounds from me that same evening betting on what he knew was a certainty. That's your Dancy—a common sharper!

CANYNGE (*Nodding towards the billiard-room*). Are those fellows still in there, Colford?

COLFORD. Yes.

CANYNGE. Then bring Dancy up, will you? But don't say anything to him.

COLFORD (*To* DE LEVIS). You may think yourself damned lucky if he doesn't break your neck.

He goes out. The three who are left with DE LEVIS *avert their eyes from him.*

DE LEVIS (*Smouldering*). I have a memory, and a sting too. Yes, my lord—since you are good enough to call me venomous. (*To* CANYNGE). I quite understand—I'm marked for Coventry now, whatever happens. Well, I'll take Dancy with me.

ST. ERTH (*To himself*). This Club has always had a decent, quiet name.

WINSOR. Are you going to retract, and apologise in front of Dancy and the members who heard you?

DE LEVIS. No fear!

ST. ERTH. You must be a very rich man, sir. A jury is likely to take the view that money can hardly compensate for an accusation of that sort.

DE LEVIS *stands silent.*

CANYNGE. Courts of law require proof.

ST. ERTH. He can make it a criminal action.

WINSOR. Unless you stop this at once, you may find yourself in prison. *If you can stop it, that is.*

ST. ERTH. If I were young Dancy, nothing should induce me.

DE LEVIS. But you didn't steal my money, Lord St Erth.

ST. ERTH. You're deuced positive, sir. So far as I could understand it, there were a dozen ways you could have been robbed. It seems to me you value other men's reputations very lightly.

DE LEVIS. Confront me with Dancy and give me fair play.

WINSOR (*Aside to* CANYNGE). Is it fair to Dancy not to let him know?

CANYNGE. Our duty is to the Club now, Winsor. We must have this cleared up.

COLFORD *comes in, followed by* BORRING *and* DANCY.

ST. ERTH. Captain Dancy, a serious accusation has been made against you by this gentle-

117

man in the presence of several members of the Club.

DANCY. What is it?

ST. ERTH. That you robbed him of that money at Winsor's.

DANCY (*Hard and tense*). Indeed! On what grounds is he good enough to say that?

DE LEVIS (*Tense too*). You gave me that filly to save yourself her keep, and you've been mad 10 about it ever since; you knew from Goole that I had sold her to Kentman and been paid in cash, yet I heard you myself deny that you knew it. You had the next room to me, and you can jump like a cat, as we saw that evening; I found some creepers crushed by a weight on my balcony on that side. When I went to the bath your door was open, and when I came back it was shut.

CANYNGE. That's the first we have heard 20 about the door.

DE LEVIS. I remembered it afterwards.

ST. ERTH. Well, Dancy?

DANCY (*With intense deliberation*). I'll settle this matter with any weapons, when and where he likes.

ST. ERTH (*Drily*). It can't be settled that way—you know very well. You must take it to the Courts, unless he retracts.

DANCY. Will you retract?

30 DE LEVIS. Why did you tell General Canynge you didn't know Kentman had paid me in cash?

DANCY. Because I didn't.

DE LEVIS. Then Kentman and Goole lied— for no reason?

DANCY. That's nothing to do with me.

DE LEVIS. If you were downstairs all the time, as you say, why was your door first open and then shut?

40 DANCY. Being downstairs, how should I know? The wind, probably.

DE LEVIS. I should like to hear what your wife says about it.

DANCY. Leave my wife alone, you damned Jew!

ST. ERTH. Captain Dancy!

DE LEVIS (*White with rage*). Thief!

DANCY. Will you fight?

DE LEVIS. You're very smart—dead men tell 50 no tales. No! Bring your action, and we shall see.

DANCY *takes a step towards him, but* CANYNGE *and* WINSOR *interpose.*

ST. ERTH. That'll do, Mr De Levis; we won't keep you. (*He looks round.*) Kindly consider your membership suspended till this matter has been threshed out.

DE LEVIS (*Tremulous with anger*). Don't trouble yourselves about my membership. I resign it. (*To* DANCY). You called me a damned Jew. My race was old when you were all sav- 60 ages. I am proud to be a Jew. *Au revoir*, in the Courts.

He goes out, and silence follows his departure.

ST. ERTH. Well, Captain Dancy?

DANCY. If the brute won't fight, what am I to do, sir?

ST. ERTH. We've told you—take action, to clear your name.

DANCY. Colford, you saw me in the hall writing letters after our game.

COLFORD. Certainly I did; you were there 70 when I went to the smoking-room.

CANYNGE. How long after you left the billiard-room?

COLFORD. About five minutes.

DANCY. It's impossible for me to prove that I was there all the time.

CANYNGE. It's for De Levis to prove what he asserts. You heard what he said about Goole?

DANCY. If he told me, I didn't take it in.

ST. ERTH. This concerns the honour of the Club. Are you going to take action? 80

DANCY (*Slowly*). That is a very expensive business, Lord St Erth, and I'm hard up. I must think it over. (*He looks round from face to face.*) Am I to take it that there is a doubt in your minds, gentlemen?

COLFORD (*Emphatically*). No.

CANYNGE. That's not the question, Dancy. This accusation was overheard by various members, and we represent the Club. If you don't take action, judgment will naturally go by 90 default.

DANCY. I might prefer to look on the whole thing as beneath contempt.

He turns and goes out. When he is gone there is an even longer silence than after DE LEVIS's *departure.*

ST. ERTH (*Abruptly*). I don't like it.

WINSOR. I've known him all his life.

118

COLFORD. You may have my head if he did it, Lord St Erth. He and I have been in too many holes together. By Gad! My toe itches for that fellow's butt end.

BORRING. I'm sorry; but has he t-taken it in quite the right way? I should have thought—hearing it s-suddenly——

COLFORD. Bosh!

WINSOR. It's perfectly damnable for him.

ST. ERTH. More damnable if he did it, Winsor.

BORRING. The Courts are b-beastly distrustful, don't you know.

COLFORD. His word's good enough for me.

CANYNGE. We're as anxious to believe Dancy as you, Colford, for the honour of the Army and the Club.

WINSOR. Of course, he'll bring a case, when he's thought it over.

ST. ERTH. What are we to do in the meantime?

COLFORD. If Dancy's asked to resign, you may take my resignation too.

BORRING. I thought his wanting to f-fight him a bit screeny.

COLFORD. Wouldn't you have wanted a shot at the brute? A law court? Pah!

WINSOR. Yes. What'll be his position even if he wins?

BORRING. Damages, and a stain on his c-character.

WINSOR. Quite so, unless they find the real thief. People always believe the worst.

COLFORD (*Glaring at* BORRING). They do.

CANYNGE. There *is* no decent way out of a thing of this sort.

ST. ERTH. No. (*Rising*). It leaves a bad taste. I'm sorry for young Mrs Dancy—poor woman!

BORRING. Are you going to play any more?

ST. ERTH (*Abruptly*). No, sir. Good night to you. Canynge, can I give you a lift?

He goes out, followed by CANYNGE.

BORRING (*After a slight pause*). Well, I shall go and take the t-temperature of the Club.

He goes out.

COLFORD. Damn that effeminate stammering chap! What can we do for Dancy, Winsor?

WINSOR. Colford! (*A slight pause*). The General felt his coat sleeve that night, and it was wet.

COLFORD. Well! What proof's that? No, by

George! An old school-fellow, a brother officer, and a pal.

WINSOR. If he did do it——

COLFORD. He didn't. But if he did, I stick to him, and see him through it, if I could.

WINSOR *walks over to the fire, stares into it, turns round and stares at* COLFORD, *who is standing motionless.*

COLFORD. Yes, by God!

SCENE II (*The following morning*)

Morning of the following day. The DANCYS' *flat. In the sitting-room of this small abode* MABEL DANCY *and* MARGARET ORME *are sitting full face to the audience, on a couch in the centre of the room, in front of the imaginary window. There is a fireplace, Left, with fire burning; a door below it, Left; and a door on the Right, facing the audience, leads to a corridor and the outer door of the flat, which is visible. Their voices are heard in rapid exchange; then as the curtain rises, so does* MABEL.

MABEL. But it's monstrous!

MARGARET. Of course! (*She lights a cigarette and hands the case to* MABEL, *who, however, sees nothing but her own thoughts.*) De Levis might just as well have pitched on me, except that I can't jump more than six inches in these skirts.

MABEL. It's wicked. Yesterday afternoon at the Club, did you say? Ronny hasn't said a word to me. Why?

MARGARET (*With a long puff of smoke*). Doesn't want you bothered.

MABEL. But—Good heavens!—Me!

MARGARET. Haven't you found out, Mabel, that he isn't exactly communicative? No desperate character is.

MABEL. Ronny?

MARGARET. Gracious! Wives *are* at a disadvantage, especially early on. You've never hunted with him, my dear. I have. He takes more sudden decisions than any man I ever knew. He's taking one now, I'll bet.

MABEL. That beast, De Levis! I was in our room next door all the time.

MARGARET. Was the door into Ronny's dressing-room open?

MABEL. I don't know; I—I think it was.

MARGARET. Well, you can say so in Court any way. Not that it matters. Wives are liars by law.

MABEL (*Staring down at her*). What do you mean—Court?

MARGARET. My dear, he'll have to bring an action for defamation of character, or whatever they call it.

MABEL. Were they talking of this last night at the Winsors'?

MARGARET. Well, you know a dinner-table, Mabel—Scandal is heaven-sent at this time of year.

MABEL. It's terrible, such a thing—terrible!

MARGARET (*Gloomily*). If only Ronny weren't known to be so broke.

MABEL (*With her hands to her forehead*). I can't realize—I simply can't. If there's a case would it be all right afterwards?

MARGARET. Do you remember St Offert—cards? No, you wouldn't—you were in high frocks. Well, St Offert got damages, but he also got the hoof, underneath. He lives in Ireland. There isn't the slightest connection, so far as I can see, Mabel, between innocence and reputation. Look at me!

MABEL. We'll fight it tooth and nail!

MARGARET. Mabel, you're pure wool, right through; everybody's sorry for you.

MABEL. It's for *him* they ought——

MARGARET (*Again handing the cigarette-case*). Do smoke, old thing.

MABEL *takes a cigarette this time, but does not light it.*

It isn't altogether simple. General Canynge was there last night. You don't mind my being beastly frank, do you?

MABEL. No. I want it.

MARGARET. Well, he's all for *esprit de corps* and that. But he was awfully silent.

MABEL. I hate half-hearted friends. Loyalty comes before everything.

MARGARET. Ye-es; but loyalties cut up against each other sometimes, you know.

MABEL. I *must* see Ronny. D'you mind if I go and try to get him on the telephone?

MARGARET. Rather not.

MABEL *goes out by the door Left.*

Poor kid!

She curls herself into a corner of the sofa, as if trying to get away from life. The bell rings.

MARGARET *stirs, gets up, and goes out into the corridor, where she opens the door to* LADY ADELA WINSOR, *whom she precedes into the sitting-room.*

Enter the second murderer! D'you know that child knew nothing?

LADY ADELA. Where is she?

MARGARET. Telephoning. Adela, if there's going to be an action, we shall be witnesses. I shall wear black georgette with an écru hat. Have you ever given evidence?

LADY ADELA. Never.

MARGARET. It must be too frightfully thrilling.

LADY ADELA. Oh! Why did I ever ask that wretch De Levis? I used to think him pathetic. Meg—did you know—Ronald Dancy's coat was wet? The General happened to feel it.

MARGARET. So that's why he was so silent.

LADY ADELA. Yes; and after the scene in the Club yesterday he went to see those bookmakers, and Goole—what a name!—is sure he told Dancy about the sale.

MARGARET (*Suddenly*). I don't care. He's my third cousin. Don't you feel you *couldn't*, Adela?

LADY ADELA. Couldn't—what?

MARGARET. Stand for De Levis against one of ourselves?

LADY ADELA. That's very narrow, Meg.

MARGARET. Oh! I know lots of splendid Jews, and I rather liked little Ferdy; but when it comes to the point—! *They* all stick together; why shouldn't we? It's in the blood. Open your jugular, and see if you haven't got it.

LADY ADELA. My dear, my great grandmother was a Jewess. I'm very proud of her.

MARGARET. Inoculated. (*Stretching herself*). Prejudices, Adela—or are they loyalties—I don't know—criss-cross—we all cut each other's throats from the best of motives.

LADY ADELA. Oh! I shall remember that. Delightful! (*Holding up a finger*). You got it from Bergson, Meg. Isn't he wonderful?

MARGARET. Yes; have you ever read him?

LADY ADELA. Well—No. (*Looking at the bedroom door*). That poor child! I quite agree. I shall tell everybody it's ridiculous. You don't really think Ronald Dancy——?

MARGARET. I don't know, Adela. There are people who simply can't live without danger.

I'm rather like that myself. They're all right when they're getting the D.S.O. or shooting man-eaters; but if there's no excitement going, they'll make it—out of sheer craving. I've seen Ronny Dancy do the maddest things for no mortal reason except the risk. He's had a past, you know.

LADY ADELA. Oh! Do tell!

MARGARET. He did splendidly in the war, of course, because it suited him; but—just before —don't you remember—a very queer bit of riding?

LADY ADELA. No.

MARGARET. Most dare-devil thing—but not quite. You must remember—it was awfully talked about. And then, of course, right up to his marriage——

She lights a cigarette.

LADY ADELA. Meg, you're very tantalising!

MARGARET. A foreign-looking girl—most plummy. Oh! Ronny's got charm—this Mabel child doesn't know in the least what she's got hold of!

LADY ADELA. But they're so fond of each other!

MARGARET. That's the mistake. The General isn't mentioning the coat, is he?

LADY ADELA. Oh, no! It was only to Charles.

MABEL *returns.*

MARGARET. Did you get him?

MABEL. No; he's not at Tattersall's, nor at the Club.

LADY ADELA *rises and greets her with an air which suggests bereavement.*

LADY ADELA. Nobody's going to believe this, my dear.

MABEL (*Looking straight at her*). Nobody who does need come here, or trouble to speak to *us* again.

LADY ADELA. That's what I was afraid of; you're going to be defiant. Now don't! Just be perfectly natural.

MABEL. So easy, isn't it? I could kill anybody who believes such a thing.

MARGARET. You'll want a solicitor, Mabel. Go to old Mr Jacob Twisden.

LADY ADELA. Yes; he's so comforting.

MARGARET. He got my pearls back once—without loss of life. A frightfully good fireside manner. Do get him here, Mabel, and have a heart-to-heart talk, all three of you!

MABEL (*Suddenly*). Listen! There's Ronny!

DANCY *comes in.*

DANCY (*With a smile*). Very good of you to have come.

MARGARET. Yes. We're just going. Oh! Ronny, this is quite too—— (*But his face dries her up; and sidling past, she goes.*)

LADY ADELA. Charles sent his—love—— (*Her voice dwindles on the word, and she, too, goes.*)

DANCY (*Crossing to his wife*). What have they been saying?

MABEL. Ronny! Why didn't you tell me?

DANCY. I wanted to see De Levis again first.

MABEL. That wretch! How dare he? Darling!

She suddenly clasps and kisses him. He does not return the kiss, but remains rigid in her arms, so that she draws away and looks at him. It's hurt you awfully, I know.

DANCY. Look here, Mabel! Apart from that muck—this is a ghastly tame-cat sort of life. Let's cut it and get out to Nairobi. I can scare up the money for that.

MABEL (*Aghast*). But how can we? Everybody would say——

DANCY. Let them! We shan't be here.

MABEL. I couldn't bear people to think——

DANCY. I don't care a damn what people think—monkeys and cats. I never could stand their rotten menagerie. Besides, what does it matter how I act; if I bring an action and get damages—if I pound him to a jelly—it's all no good! I can't *prove* it. There'll be plenty of people unconvinced.

MABEL. But they'll find the real thief.

DANCY (*With a queer little smile*). Will staying here help them to do that?

MABEL (*In a sort of agony*). Oh! I couldn't —it looks like running away. We *must* stay and fight it!

DANCY. Suppose I didn't get a verdict—you never can tell.

MABEL. But you must—I was there all the time, with the door open.

DANCY. Was it?

MABEL. I'm almost sure.

DANCY. Yes. But you're my wife.

MABEL (*Bewildered*). Ronny, I don't understand—suppose I'd been accused of stealing pearls!

DANCY (*Wincing*). I can't.

MABEL. But I might—just as easily. What would you think of me if I ran away from it?

DANCY. I see. (*A pause*). All right! You shall have a run for your money. I'll go and see old Twisden.

MABEL. Let me come! (DANCY *shakes his head.*) Why not? I can't be happy a moment unless I'm fighting this.

DANCY *puts out his hand suddenly and grips hers.*

DANCY. You *are* a little brick!

10 MABEL (*Pressing his hand to her breast and looking into his face*). Do you know what Margaret called you?

DANCY. No.

MABEL. A desperate character.

DANCY. Ha! I'm not a tame cat, any more than she.

The bell rings. MABEL *goes out to the door and her voice is heard saying coldly:*

MABEL. Will you wait a minute, please? *Returning.*

It's De Levis—to see you. (*In a low voice*). Let me see him alone first. Just for a minute! Do!

20 DANCY (*After a moment's silence*). Go ahead!

He goes out into the bedroom.

MABEL (*Going to the door, Right*). Come in. DE LEVIS *comes in, and stands embarrassed.* Yes?

DE LEVIS (*With a slight bow*). Your husband, Mrs. Dancy?

MABEL. He is in. Why do you want to see him?

DE LEVIS. He came round to my rooms just now, when I was out. He threatened me yes-

30 terday. I don't choose him to suppose I'm afraid of him.

MABEL (*With a great and manifest effort at self-control*). Mr De Levis, you are robbing my husband of his good name.

DE LEVIS (*Sincerely*). I admire your trustfulness, Mrs Dancy.

MABEL (*Staring at him*). How can you do it? What do you want? What's your motive? You can't possibly believe that my husband is

40 a *thief!*

DE LEVIS. Unfortunately.

MABEL. How dare you? How dare you? Don't you know that I was in our bedroom all the time with the door open? Do you accuse me too?

DE LEVIS. No, Mrs Dancy.

MABEL. But you do. I must have seen, I must have heard.

DE LEVIS. A wife's memory is not very good when her husband is in danger.   50

MABEL. In other words, I'm lying.

DE LEVIS. No. Your wish is mother to your thought, that's all.

MABEL (*After staring again with a sort of horror, turns to get control of herself. Then turning back to him*). Mr De Levis, I appeal to you as a gentleman to behave to us as you would we should behave to you. Withdraw this wicked charge, and write an apology that Ronald can show.   60

DE LEVIS. Mrs Dancy, I am not a gentleman, I am only a—damned Jew. Yesterday I might possibly have withdrawn to spare you. But when my race is insulted I have nothing to say to your husband, but as he wishes to see me, I've come. Please let him know.

MABEL (*Regarding him again with that look of horror—slowly*). I think what you are doing is too horrible for words.

DE LEVIS *gives her a slight bow, and as he does so* DANCY *comes quickly in, Left. The two men stand with the length of the sofa between them.* MABEL, *behind the sofa, turns her eyes on her husband, who has a paper in his right hand.*

DE LEVIS. You came to see me.   70

DANCY. Yes. I want you to sign this.

DE LEVIS. I will sign nothing.

DANCY. Let me read it: "I apologise to Captain Dancy for the reckless and monstrous charge I made against him, and I retract every word of it."

DE LEVIS. Not much!

DANCY. You will sign.

DE LEVIS. I tell you this is useless. I will sign nothing. The charge is true; you wouldn't be   80 playing this game if it weren't. I'm going. You'll hardly try violence in the presence of your wife; and if you try it anywhere else—look out for yourself.

DANCY. Mabel, I want to speak to him alone.

MABEL. No, no!

DE LEVIS. Quite right, Mrs. Dancy. Black and tan swashbuckling will only make things worse for him.

DANCY. So you shelter behind a woman, do   90 you, you skulking cur!

DE LEVIS *takes a step, with fists clenched and*

eyes blazing. DANCY, *too, stands ready to spring
—the moment is cut short by* MABEL *going
quickly to her husband.*

MABEL. Don't, Ronny. It's undignified! He
isn't worth it.

DANCY *suddenly tears the paper in two, and
flings it into the fire.*

DANCY. Get out of here, you swine!

DE LEVIS *stands a moment irresolute, then,
turning to the door, he opens it, stands again
for a moment with a smile on his face, then
goes.* MABEL *crosses swiftly to the door, and
shuts it as the outer door closes. Then she
stands quite still, looking at her husband—her
face expressing a sort of startled suspense.*

DANCY (*Turning and looking at her*). Well!
Do you agree with him?

MABEL. What do you mean?

DANCY. That I wouldn't be playing this
game unless——

MABEL. Don't! You hurt me!

10 DANCY. Yes. You don't know much of me,
Mabel.

MABEL. Ronny!

DANCY. What did you say to that swine?

MABEL (*Her face averted*). That he was
robbing *us.* (*Turning to him suddenly*). Ronny
—you—didn't? I'd rather know.

DANCY. Ha! I thought that was coming.

MABEL (*Covering her face*). Oh—how horrible of me—how horrible!

20 DANCY. Not at all. The thing looks bad.

MABEL (*Dropping her hands*). If *I* can't believe in you, who can? (*Going to him, throwing her arms round him, and looking up into
his face*). Ronny! If all the world—*I'd* believe
in you. You know I would.

DANCY. That's all right, Mabs! That's all
right! (*His face, above her head, is contorted
for a moment, then hardens into a mask.*)
Well, what shall we do?

30 MABEL. Oh! Let's go to that lawyer—let's go
at once!

DANCY. All right. Get your hat on.

MABEL *passes him, and goes into the bedroom, Left.* DANCY, *left alone, stands quite still,
staring before him. With a sudden shrug of his
shoulders he moves quickly to his hat and takes
it up just as* MABEL *returns, ready to go out.
He opens the door; and crossing him, she stops
in the doorway, looking up with a clear and
trustful gaze as the* CURTAIN *falls.*

ACT III

SCENE I (*Three months later*)

Three months later. Old MR JACOB TWISDEN'S
*Room, at the offices of Twisden & Graviter,
in Lincoln's Inn Fields, is spacious, with two
large windows at back, a fine old fireplace,
Right, a door below it, and two doors, Left.
Between the windows is a large table sideways to the window wall, with a chair in the
middle on the right-hand side, a chair
against the wall, and a client's chair on the
left-hand side.*

GRAVITER, TWISDEN'S *much younger partner, is
standing in front of the right-hand window
looking out on to the Fields, where the
lamps are being lighted, and a taxi's engine
is running down below. He turns his san-
guine, shrewd face from the window towards a grandfather clock, between the
doors, Left, which is striking "four." The
door, Left Forward, is opened.*

YOUNG CLERK (*Entering*). A Mr Gilman, sir,
to see Mr Twisden.

GRAVITER. By appointment?

YOUNG CLERK. No, sir. But important, he
says.

GRAVITER. I'll see him.

The CLERK *goes.*

GRAVITER *sits right of table. The* CLERK *returns, ushering in an oldish* MAN, *who looks
what he is, the proprietor of a large modern
grocery store. He wears a dark overcoat and
carries a pot hat. His gingery-grey moustache
and mutton-chop whiskers give him the expression of a cat.*

GRAVITER (*Sizing up his social standing*).
Mr Gilman? Yes.

GILMAN (*Doubtfully*). Mr Jacob Twisden? 40

GRAVITER (*Smiling*). His partner. Graviter
my name is.

GILMAN. Mr Twisden's not in, then?

GRAVITER. No. He's at the Courts. They're
just up; he should be in directly. But he'll be
busy.

GILMAN. Old Mr Jacob Twisden—I've heard
of him.

GRAVITER. Most people have.

A pause.

GILMAN. It's this Dancy-De Levis case that's 50
keepin' him at the Courts, I suppose?

123

GRAVITER *nods.*

Won't be finished for a day or two?

GRAVITER *shakes his head.*

No. Astonishin' the interest taken in it.

GRAVITER. As you say.

GILMAN. The Smart Set, eh? This Captain Dancy got the D.S.O., didn't he?

GRAVITER *nods.*

Sad to have a thing like that said about you. I thought he gave his evidence well; and his wife too. Looks as if this De Levis had got some private spite. *Searchy la femme,* I said to Mrs Gilman only this morning, before I——

GRAVITER. By the way, sir, what is your business?

GILMAN. Well, my business here—No, if you'll excuse me, I'd rather wait and see old Mr Jacob Twisden. It's delicate, and I'd like his experience.

GRAVITER (*With a shrug*). Very well; then, perhaps, you'll go in there. *He moves towards the door, Left Back.*

GILMAN. Thank you. (*Following*). You see, I've never been mixed up with the law——

GRAVITER (*Opening the door*). No?

GILMAN. And I don't want to begin. When you do, you don't know where you'll stop, do you? You see, I've only come from a sense of duty; and—other reasons.

GRAVITER. Not uncommon.

GILMAN (*Producing card*). This is my card. Gilman's—several branches, but this is the 'ead.

GRAVITER (*Scrutinising card*). Exactly.

GILMAN. Grocery—I daresay you know me; or your wife does. They say old Mr Jacob Twisden refused a knighthood. If it's not a rude question, why was that?

GRAVITER. Ask him, sir; ask him.

GILMAN. I said to my wife at the time, "He's holdin' out for a baronetcy."

GRAVITER *closes the door with an exasperated smile.*

YOUNG CLERK (*Opening the door, Left Forward*). Mr Winsor, sir, and Miss Orme.

They enter, and the CLERK *withdraws.*

GRAVITER. How d'you do, Miss Orme? How do you do, Winsor?

WINSOR. Twisden not back, Graviter?

GRAVITER. Not yet.

WINSOR. Well, they've got through De Levis's witnesses. Sir Frederic was at the very top of his form. It's looking quite well. But I hear they've just subpoenaed Canynge after all. His evidence is to be taken to-morrow.

GRAVITER. Oho?

WINSOR. I said Dancy ought to have called him.

GRAVITER. We considered it. Sir Frederic decided that he could use him better in cross-examination.

WINSOR. Well! I don't know that. Can I go and see him before he gives evidence to-morrow?

GRAVITER. I should like to hear Mr Jacob on that, Winsor. He'll be in directly.

WINSOR. They had Kentman, and Goole, the Inspector, the other bobby, my footman, Dancy's banker, and his tailor.

GRAVITER. Did we shake Kentman or Goole?

WINSOR. Very little. Oh! by the way, the numbers of those two notes were given, and I see they're published in the evening papers. I suppose the police wanted that. I tell you what I find, Graviter—a general feeling that there's something behind it all that doesn't come out.

GRAVITER. The public wants its money's worth—always does in these Society cases; they brew so long beforehand, you see.

WINSOR. They're looking for something lurid.

MARGARET. When I was in the box, I thought they were looking for me. (*Taking out her cigarette case*). I suppose I mustn't smoke, Mr Graviter?

GRAVITER. Do!

MARGARET. Won't Mr Jacob have a fit?

GRAVITER. Yes, but not till you've gone.

MARGARET. Just a whiff. (*She lights a cigarette.*)

WINSOR (*Suddenly*). It's becoming a sort of Dreyfus case—people taking sides quite outside the evidence.

MARGARET. There are more of the chosen in Court every day. Mr Graviter, have you noticed the two on the jury?

GRAVITER (*With a smile*). No; I can't say——

MARGARET. Oh! but quite distinctly. Don't you think they ought to have been challenged?

GRAVITER. De Levis might have challenged the other ten, Miss Orme.

MARGARET. Dear me, now! I never thought of that.

As she speaks, the door Left Forward is

opened and old MR JACOB TWISDEN *comes in. He is tallish and narrow, sixty-eight years old, grey, with narrow little whiskers curling round his narrow ears, and a narrow bow ribbon curling round his collar. He wears a long, narrow-tailed coat, and strapped trousers on his narrow legs. His nose and face are narrow, shrewd, and kindly. He has a way of narrowing his shrewd and kindly eyes. His nose is seen to twitch and sniff.*

TWISDEN. Ah! How are you, Charles? How do you do, my dear?

MARGARET. Dear Mr Jacob, I'm smoking. Isn't it disgusting? But they don't allow it in Court, you know. Such a pity! The Judge might have a hookah. Oh! wouldn't he look sweet—the darling!

TWISDEN (*With a little, old-fashioned bow*). It does not become everybody as it becomes you, Margaret.

MARGARET. Mr Jacob, how charming!

With a slight grimace she puts out her cigarette.

GRAVITER. Man called Gilman waiting in there to see you specially.

TWISDEN. Directly. Turn up the light, would you, Graviter?

GRAVITER (*Turning up the light*). Excuse me.

He goes.

WINSOR. Look here, Mr Twisden——

TWISDEN. Sit down; sit down, my dear.

And he himself sits behind the table, as a cup of tea is brought in to him by the YOUNG CLERK, *with two Marie biscuits in the saucer.* Will you have some, Margaret?

MARGARET. No, dear Mr Jacob.

TWISDEN. Charles?

WINSOR. No, thanks.

The door is closed.

TWISDEN (*Dipping a biscuit in the tea*). Now, then?

WINSOR. The General knows something which on the face of it looks rather queer. Now that he's going to be called, oughtn't Dancy to be told of it, so that he may be ready with his explanation, in case it comes out?

TWISDEN (*Pouring some tea into the saucer*). Without knowing, I can't tell you.

---

s.d. **Marie biscuits,** thin tea-biscuits.

WINSOR *and* MARGARET *exchange looks, and* TWISDEN *drinks from the saucer.*

MARGARET. Tell him, Charles.

WINSOR. Well! It rained that evening at Meldon. The General happened to put his hand on Dancy's shoulder, and it was damp.

TWISDEN *puts the saucer down and replaces the cup in it. They both look intently at him.*

TWISDEN. I take it that General Canynge won't say anything he's not compelled to say.

MARGARET. No, of course; but Mr Jacob, they might ask; they know it rained. And he is such a George Washington.

TWISDEN (*Toying with a pair of tortoise-shell glasses*). They didn't ask either of *you.* Still—no harm in your telling Dancy.

WINSOR. I'd rather *you* did it, Margaret.

MARGARET. I daresay. (*She mechanically takes out her cigarette-case, catches the lift of* TWISDEN'S *eyebrows, and puts it back.*)

WINSOR. Well, we'll go together. I don't want Mrs Dancy to hear.

MARGARET. Do tell me, Mr Jacob; is he going to win?

TWISDEN. I think so, Margaret; I think so.

MARGARET. It'll be too frightful if he doesn't get a verdict, after all this. But I don't know what we shall do when it's over. I've been sitting in that Court all these three days, watching, and it's made me feel there's nothing we like better than seeing people skinned. Well, bye-bye, bless you!

TWISDEN *rises and pats her hand.*

WINSOR. Half a second, Margaret. Wait for me.

She nods and goes out.

Mr Twisden, what do you really think?

TWISDEN. I am Dancy's lawyer, my dear Charles, as well as yours.

WINSOR. Well, can I go and see Canynge?

TWISDEN. Better not.

WINSOR. If they get that out of him, and recall me, am I to say he told me of it at the time?

TWISDEN. You didn't feel the coat yourself? And Dancy wasn't present? Then what Canynge told you is not evidence. *We'll* stop your being asked.

WINSOR. Thank goodness. Good-bye!

WINSOR *goes out.*

TWISDEN, *behind his table, motionless, taps*

his teeth with the eyeglasses in his narrow, well-kept hand. After a long shake of his head and a shrug of his rather high shoulders he sniffs, goes to the window and opens it. Then crossing to the door, Left Back, he throws it open and says:

TWISDEN. At your service, sir.

GILMAN *comes forth, nursing his pot hat.* Be seated.

TWISDEN *closes the window behind him, and takes his seat.*

GILMAN (*Taking the client's chair, to the left of the table*). Mr Twisden, I believe? My name's Gilman, head of Gilman's Department Stores. You have my card.

TWISDEN (*Looking at the card*). Yes. What can we do for you?

GILMAN. Well, I've come to you from a sense 10 of duty, sir, and also a feelin' of embarrassment. (*He takes from his breast pocket an evening paper.*) You see, I've been followin' this Dancy case—it's a good deal talked of in Putney—and I read this at half-past two this afternoon. To be precise, at 2:25. (*He rises and hands the paper to* TWISDEN, *and with a thick gloved forefinger indicates a passage.*) When I read these numbers, I 'appened to remember givin' change for a fifty-pound note— 20 don't often 'ave one in, you know—so I went to the cash-box out of curiosity, to see that I 'adn't got it. Well, I 'ad; and here it is. (*He draws out from his breast pocket and lays before* TWISDEN *a fifty-pound banknote.*) It was brought in to change by a customer of mine three days ago, and he got value for it. Now, that's a stolen note, it seems, and you'd like to know what I did. Mind you, that customer of mine I've known 'im—well—eight or nine years; 30 an Italian he is—wine salesman, and so far's I know, a respectable man—foreign-lookin', but nothin' more. Now, this was at 'alf-past two, and I was at my head branch at Putney, where I live. I want you to mark the time, so as you'll see I 'aven't wasted a minute. I took a cab and I drove straight to my customer's private residence in Putney, where he lives with his daughter—Ricardos his name is, Paolio Ricardos. They tell me there that he's at his busi- 40 ness shop in the City. So off I go in the cab again, and there I find him. Well, sir, I showed this paper to him and I produced the note.

"Here," I said, "you brought this to me and you got value for it." Well, that man was taken aback. If I'm a judge, Mr Twisden, he was taken aback, not to speak in a guilty way, but he was, as you might say, flummoxed. "Now," I said to him, "where did you get it—that's the point?" He took his time to answer, and then he said: "Well, Mr Gilman," he said, "you 50 know me; I am an honourable man. I can't tell you offhand, but I am above the board." He's foreign, you know, in his expressions. "Yes," I said, "that's all very well," I said, "but here I've got a stolen note and you've got the value for it. Now I tell you," I said, "what I'm going to do; I'm going straight with this note to Mr Jacob Twisden, who's got this Dancy De Levis case in 'and. He's a well-known Society lawyer," I said, "of great experience." "Oh!" he 60 said, "that is what you do?"—funny the way he speaks! "Then I come with you!"—And I've got him in the cab below. I want to tell you everything before he comes up. On the way I tried to get something out of him, but I couldn't—I could *not.* "This is very awkward," I said at last. "It is, Mr Gilman," was his reply; and he began to talk about his Sicilian claret— a very good wine, mind you; but under the circumstances it seemed to me uncalled for. 70 Have I made it clear to you?

TWISDEN (*Who has listened with extreme attention*). Perfectly, Mr Gilman. I'll send down for him.

He touches a hand-bell.

The YOUNG CLERK *appears at the door, Left Forward.*

A gentleman in a taxi—waiting. Ask him to be so good as to step up. Oh! and send Mr Graviter here again.

The YOUNG CLERK *goes out.*

GILMAN. As I told you, sir, I've been followin' this case. It's what you might call piquant. And I should be very glad if it came 80 about that this helped Captain Dancy. I take an interest, because, to tell you the truth, (*Confidentially*) I don't like—well, not to put too fine a point upon it—'Ebrews. They work harder; they're more sober; they're honest; and they're everywhere. I've nothing against them; but the fact is—they get *on* so.

TWISDEN (*Cocking an eye*). A thorn in the flesh, Mr Gilman.

GILMAN. Well, I prefer my own countrymen, and that's the truth of it.

As he speaks, GRAVITER *comes in by the door, Left Forward.*

TWISDEN (*Pointing to the newspaper and the note*). Mr Gilman has brought this, of which he is holder for value. His customer, who changed it three days ago, is coming up.

GRAVITER. The fifty-pounder. I see.

His face is long and reflective.

YOUNG CLERK (*Entering*). Mr. Ricardos, sir.

He goes out.

RICARDOS *is a personable, Italian-looking man in a frock coat, with a dark moustachioed face and dark hair a little grizzled. He looks anxious, and bows.*

TWISDEN. Mr Ricardos? My name is Jacob
10 Twisden. My partner. (*Holding up a finger, as* RICARDOS *would speak*). Mr Gilman has told us about this note. You took it to him, he says, three days ago; that is, on Monday, and received cash for it?

RICARDOS. Yes, sare.

TWISDEN. You were *not* aware that it was stolen?

RICARDOS (*With his hand to his breast*). Oh! no, sare.

20 TWISDEN. You received it from——?

RICARDOS. A minute, sare; I would weesh to explain—(*With an expressive shrug*) in private.

TWISDEN (*Nodding*). Mr Gilman, your conduct has been most prompt. You may safely leave the matter in our hands, now. Kindly let us retain this note; and ask for my cashier as you go out and give him (*He writes*) this. He will reimburse you. We will take any necessary steps ourselves.

30 GILMAN (*In slight surprise, with modest pride*). Well, sir, I'm in your 'ands. I must be guided by you, with your experience. I'm glad you think I acted rightly.

TWISDEN. Very rightly, Mr Gilman—very rightly. (*Rising*). Good-afternoon!

GILMAN. Good-afternoon, sir. Good-afternoon, gentlemen! (*To* TWISDEN). I'm sure I'm very 'appy to have made your acquaintance, sir. It's a well-known name.

40 TWISDEN. Thank you.

GILMAN *retreats, glances at* RICARDOS, *and turns again.*

GILMAN. I suppose there's nothing else I ought to do, in the interests of the law? I'm a careful man.

TWISDEN. If there is, Mr Gilman, we will let you know. We have your address. You may make your mind easy; but don't speak of this. It might interfere with Justice.

GILMAN. Oh! I shouldn't dream of it. I've no wish to be mixed up in anything conspicuous. That's not my principle at all. Good-day, gen- 50 tlemen.

He goes.

TWISDEN (*Seating himself*). Now, sir, will you sit down.

But RICARDOS *does not sit; he stands looking uneasily across the table at* GRAVITER.
You may speak out.

RICARDOS. Well, Mr Tweesden and sare, this matter is very serious for me, and very delicate —it concairns my honour. I am in a great difficulty.

TWISDEN. When in difficulty—complete frankness, sir. 60

RICARDOS. It is a family matter, sare, I——

TWISDEN. Let me be frank with you. (*Telling his points off on his fingers*). We have your admission that you changed this stopped note for value. It will be our duty to inform the Bank of England that it has been traced to you. You will have to account to them for your possession of it. I suggest to you that it will be far better to account frankly to us.

RICARDOS (*Taking out a handkerchief and* 70 *quite openly wiping his hands and forehead*). I received this note, sare, with others, from a gentleman, sare, in settlement of a debt of honour, and I know nothing of where he got them.

TWISDEN. H'm! that is very vague. If that is all you can tell us, I'm afraid——

RICARDOS. Gentlemen, this is very painful for me. It is my daughter's good name——

He again wipes his brow.

TWISDEN. Come, sir, speak out! 80

RICARDOS (*Desperately*). The notes were a settlement to her from this gentleman, of whom she was a great friend.

TWISDEN (*Suddenly*). I am afraid we must press you for the name of the gentleman.

RICARDOS. Sare, if I give it to you, and it does 'im 'arm, what will my daughter say? This is a bad matter for me. He behaved well to her; and she is attached to him still; sometimes she is crying yet because she lost him. And now we betray him, perhaps, who knows? This is very unpleasant for me. (*Taking up the paper*). Here it gives the number of another note—a 'undred-pound note. I 'ave that too.

He takes a note from his breast pocket.

GRAVITER. How much did he give you in all?

RICARDOS. For my daughter's settlement one thousand pounds. I understand he did not wish to give a check because of his marriage. So I did not think anything about it being in notes, you see.

TWISDEN. When did he give you this money?

RICARDOS. The middle of Octobare last.

TWISDEN (*Suddenly looking up*). Mr Ricardos, was it Captain Dancy?

RICARDOS (*Again wiping his forehead*). Gentlemen, I am so fond of my daughter. I have only the one, and no wife.

TWISDEN (*With an effort*). Yes, yes; but I must know.

RICARDOS. Sare, if I tell you, you will give me your good word that my daughter shall not hear of it?

TWISDEN. So far as we are able to prevent it —certainly.

RICARDOS. Sare, I trust you.—It was Captain Dancy.

A long pause.

GRAVITER (*Suddenly*). Were you blackmailing him?

TWISDEN (*Holding up his hand*). My partner means, did you press him for this settlement?

RICARDOS. I did think it my duty to my daughter to ask that he make compensation to her.

TWISDEN. With threats that you would tell his wife?

RICARDOS (*With a shrug*). Captain Dancy was a man of honour. He said: "Of course I will do this." I trusted him. And a month later I did remind him, and he gave me this money for her. I do not know where he got it—I do not know. Gentlemen, I have invested it all on her—every penny, except this note, for which I had the purpose to buy her a necklace. That is the swearéd truth.

TWISDEN. I must keep this note. (*He touches the hundred-pound note.*) You will not speak of this to anyone. I may recognise that you were a holder for value received—others might take a different view. Good-day, sir. Graviter, see Mr Ricardos out, and take his address.

RICARDOS (*Pressing his hands over the breast of his frock coat—with a sigh*). Gentlemen, I beg you—remember what I said. (*With a roll of his eyes*). My daughter—I am not happee. Good-day.

He turns and goes out slowly, Left Forward, followed by GRAVITER.

TWISDEN (*To himself*). Young Dancy!

He pins the two notes together and places them in an envelope, then stands motionless except for his eyes and hands, which restlessly express the disturbance within him.

GRAVITER *returns, carefully shuts the door, and going up to him, hands him* RICARDO'S *card.*

(*Looking at the card*). Villa Benvenuto. This will have to be verified, but I'm afraid it's true. That man was not acting.

GRAVITER. What's to be done about Dancy?

TWISDEN. Can you understand a gentleman——?

GRAVITER. I don't know, sir. The war loosened "form" all over the place. I saw plenty of that myself. And some men have no moral sense. From the first I've had doubts.

TWISDEN. We can't go on with the case.

GRAVITER. Phew! . . . (*A moment's silence*). Gosh! It's an awful thing for his wife.

TWISDEN. Yes.

GRAVITER (*Touching the envelope*). Chance brought this here, sir. That man won't talk—he's too scared.

TWISDEN. Gilman.

GRAVITER. Too respectable. If De Levis got those notes back, and the rest of the money, anonymously?

TWISDEN. But the case, Graviter; the case.

GRAVITER. I don't believe this alters what I've been thinking.

TWISDEN. Thought is one thing—knowledge another. There's duty to our profession. Ours is a fine calling. On the good faith of solicitors a very great deal hangs.

He crosses to the hearth as if warmth would help him.

GRAVITER. It'll let him in for a prosecution. He came to us in confidence.

TWISDEN. Not as against the law.

GRAVITER. No. I suppose not. (*A pause*). By Jove, I don't like losing this case. I don't like the admission we backed such a wrong 'un.

TWISDEN. Impossible to go on. Apart from ourselves, there's Sir Frederic. We must disclose to him—can't let him go on in the dark. Complete confidence between solicitor and counsel is the essence of professional honour.

GRAVITER. What are you going to do, then, sir?

TWISDEN. See Dancy at once. Get him on the 'phone.

GRAVITER (*Taking up the telephone*). Get me Captain Dancy's flat. . . . What? . . . (*To* TWISDEN). Mrs Dancy is here. That's *à propos* with a vengeance. Are you going to see her, sir?

TWISDEN (*After a moment's painful hesitation*). I must.

GRAVITER (*Telephoning*). Bring Mrs Dancy up.

He turns to the window.

MABEL DANCY *is shown in, looking very pale.* TWISDEN *advances from the fire, and takes her hand.*

MABEL. Major Colford's taken Ronny off in his car for the night. I thought it would do him good. I said I'd come round in case there was anything you wanted to say before to-morrow.

TWISDEN (*Taken aback*). Where have they gone?

MABEL. I don't know, but he'll be home before ten o'clock to-morrow. Is there anything?

TWISDEN. Well, I'd like to see him before the Court sits. Send him on here as soon as he comes.

MABEL (*With her hand to her forehead*). Oh! Mr Twisden, when will it be over? My head's getting awful sitting in that Court.

TWISDEN. My dear Mrs Dancy, there's no need at all for you to come down to-morrow; take a rest and nurse your head.

MABEL. Really and truly?

TWISDEN. Yes; it's the very best thing you can do.

GRAVITER *turns his head, and looks at them unobserved.*

MABEL. How do you think it's going?

TWISDEN. It went very well to-day; very well indeed.

MABEL. You must be awfully fed up with us.

TWISDEN. My dear young lady, that's our business.

He takes her hand.

MABEL's *face suddenly quivers. She draws her hand away, and covers her lips with it.* There, there! You want a day off badly.

MABEL. I'm so tired of—! Thank you so much for all you're doing. Good night! Good night, Mr Graviter!

GRAVITER. Good night, Mrs Dancy.

MABEL *goes.*

GRAVITER. D'you know, I believe she knows.

TWISDEN. No, no! She believes in him implicitly. A staunch little woman. Poor thing!

GRAVITER. Hasn't that shaken you, sir? It has me.

TWISDEN. No, no! I—I can't go on with the case. It's breaking faith. Get Sir Frederic's chambers.

GRAVITER (*Telephoning, and getting a reply, looks round at* TWISDEN). Yes?

TWISDEN. Ask if I can come round and see him.

GRAVITER (*Telephoning*). Can Sir Frederic spare Mr Twisden a few minutes now if he comes round? (*Receiving reply*). He's gone down to Brighton for the night.

TWISDEN. H'm! What hotel?

GRAVITER (*Telephoning*). What's his address? What. . . ? (*To* TWISDEN). The Bedford.

TWISDEN. I'll go down.

GRAVITER (*Telephoning*). Thank you. All right.

He rings off.

TWISDEN. Just look out the trains down and up early to-morrow.

GRAVITER *takes up an A B C, and* TWISDEN *takes up the Ricardos card.*

TWISDEN. Send to this address in Putney, verify the fact that Ricardos has a daughter, and give me a trunk call to Brighton. Better go yourself, Graviter. If you see her, don't say anything, of course—invent some excuse. (GRAVITER *nods.*) I'll be up in time to see Dancy.

GRAVITER. By George! I feel bad about this.

s.d. *A B C*, the Alphabetical Railway Guide, the combined time-table of British railroads.

TWISDEN. Yes. But professional honour comes first. What time is that train?

(*He bends over the A B C.*)

SCENE II (*Next morning*)

The same room on the following morning at ten-twenty-five, by the Grandfather clock.

The YOUNG CLERK *is ushering in* DANCY, *whose face is perceptibly harder than it was three months ago, like that of a man who has lived under great restraint.*

DANCY. He wanted to see me before the Court sat.

YOUNG CLERK. Yes, sir. Mr Twisden will see you in one minute. He had to go out of town last night.

He prepares to open the waiting-room door.

DANCY. Were *you* in the war?

YOUNG CLERK. Yes.

10   DANCY. How can you stick this?

YOUNG CLERK (*With a smile*). My trouble was to stick that, sir.

DANCY. But you get no excitement from year's end to year's end. It'd drive me mad.

YOUNG CLERK (*Shyly*). A case like this is pretty exciting. I'd give a lot to see us win it.

DANCY (*Staring at him*). Why? What is it to you?

YOUNG CLERK. I don't know, sir. It's—it's like

20   football—you want your side to win. (*He opens the waiting-room door. Expanding*). You see some rum starts, too, in a lawyer's office in a quiet way.

DANCY *enters the waiting-room, and the* YOUNG CLERK, *shutting the door, meets* TWISDEN *as he comes in, Left Forward, and takes from him overcoat, top hat, and a small bag.*

YOUNG CLERK. Captain Dancy's waiting, sir.

He indicates the waiting-room.

TWISDEN (*Narrowing his lips*). Very well. Mr Graviter gone to the Courts?

YOUNG CLERK. Yes, sir.

TWISDEN. Did he leave anything for me?

YOUNG CLERK. On the table, sir.

30   TWISDEN (*Taking up an envelope*). Thank you.

The CLERK *goes.*

TWISDEN (*Opening the envelope and reading*). "All corroborates." H'm! (*He puts it in his pocket and takes out of an envelope the two notes, lays them on the table, and covers*

them with a sheet of blotting-paper; stands a moment preparing himself, then goes to the door of the waiting-room, opens it, and says:) Now, Captain Dancy. Sorry to have kept you waiting.   40

DANCY (*Entering*). Winsor came to me yesterday about General Canynge's evidence. Is that what you wanted to speak to me about?

TWISDEN. No. It isn't that.

DANCY (*Looking at his wrist watch*). By me it's just on the half-hour, sir.

TWISDEN. Yes. I don't want you to go to the Court.

DANCY. Not?

TWISDEN. I have very serious news for you.   50

DANCY (*Wincing and collecting himself*). Oh!

TWISDEN. These two notes. (*He uncovers the notes.*) After the Court rose yesterday we had a man called Ricardos here. (*A pause*). Is there any need for me to say more?

DANCY (*Unflinching*). No. What now?

TWISDEN. Our duty is plain; we could not go on with the case. I have consulted Sir Frederic. He felt—he felt that he must throw up his brief,   60 and he will do that the moment the Court sits. Now I want to talk to you about what you're going to do.

DANCY. That's very good of you, considering.

TWISDEN. I don't pretend to understand, but I imagine that you may have done this in a moment of reckless bravado, feeling, perhaps, that as you gave the mare to De Levis, the money was by rights as much yours as his.

Stopping DANCY, *who is about to speak, with a gesture.*

To satisfy a debt of honour to this—lady; and,   70 no doubt, to save your wife from hearing of it from the man Ricardos. Is that so?

DANCY. To the life.

TWISDEN. It was mad, Captain Dancy, mad! —But the question now is: What do you owe to your wife? She doesn't dream—I suppose?

DANCY (*With a twitching face*). No.

TWISDEN. We can't tell what the result of this collapse will be. The police have the theft in hand. They may issue a warrant. The money   80 could be refunded, and the costs paid—somehow that can all be managed. But it may not help. In any case, what end is served by your staying in the country? You can't save your honour—that's gone. You can't save your wife's peace of mind. If she sticks to you—do you think she will?

DANCY. Not if she's wise.

TWISDEN. Better go! There's a war in Morocco.

DANCY (*With a bitter smile*). Good old Morocco!

TWISDEN. Will you go, then, at once, and leave me to break it to your wife?

10 DANCY. I don't know yet.

TWISDEN. You must decide quickly, to catch a boat train. Many a man has made good. You're a fine soldier.

DANCY. There are alternatives.

TWISDEN. Now, go straight from this office. You've a passport, I suppose; you won't need a *visa* for France, and from there you can find means to slip over. Have you got money on you? (DANCY *nods*.) We will see what we can
20 do to stop or delay proceedings.

DANCY. It's all damned kind of you. (*With difficulty*). But I must think of my wife. Give me a few minutes.

TWISDEN. Yes, yes; go in there and think it out.

He goes to the door, Right, and opens it.
DANCY *passes him and goes out.* TWISDEN *rings a bell and stands waiting.*

CLERK (*Entering*). Yes, sir?

TWISDEN. Tell them to call a taxi.

CLERK (*Who has a startled look*). Yes, sir. Mr Graviter has come in, sir, with General
30 Canynge. Are you disengaged?

TWISDEN. Yes.

The CLERK *goes out, and almost immediately* GRAVITER *and* CANYNGE *enter.*
Good-morning, General. (*To* GRAVITER). Well?

GRAVITER. Sir Frederic got up at once and said that since the publication of the numbers of those notes, information had reached him which forced him to withdraw from the case. Great sensation, of course. I left Bromley in charge. There'll be a formal verdict for the defendant, with costs. Have you told Dancy?

40 TWISDEN. Yes. He's in there deciding what he'll do.

CANYNGE (*Grave and vexed*). This is a dreadful thing, Twisden. I've been afraid of it all along. A soldier! A gallant fellow, too. What on earth got into him?

TWISDEN. There's no end to human nature, General.

GRAVITER. You can see queerer things in the papers, any day.

CANYNGE. That poor young wife of his! Win-
50 sor gave me a message for you, Twisden. If money's wanted quickly to save proceedings, draw on him. Is there anything I can do?

TWISDEN. I've advised him to go straight off to Morocco.

CANYNGE. I don't know that an asylum isn't the place for him. He must be off his head at moments. That jump—crazy! He'd have got a verdict on that alone—if they'd seen those balconies. I was looking at them when I was
60 down there last Sunday. Daring thing, Twisden. Very few men, on a dark night—He risked his life twice. That's a shrewd fellow—young De Levis. He spotted Dancy's nature.

The YOUNG CLERK *enters.*

CLERK. The taxi's here, sir. Will you see Major Colford and Miss Orme?

TWISDEN. Graviter—No; show them in.

The YOUNG CLERK *goes.*

CANYNGE. Colford's badly cut up.

MARGARET ORME *and* COLFORD *enter.*

COLFORD (*Striding forward*). There must be some mistake about this, Mr Twisden.   70

TWISDEN. Hssh! Dancy's in there. He's admitted it.

Voices are subdued at once.

COLFORD. What? (*With emotion*). If it were my own brother, I couldn't feel it more. But—damn it! What right had that fellow to chuck up the case—without letting him know, too. I came down with Dancy this morning, and he knew nothing about it.

TWISDEN (*Coldly*). That was unfortunately unavoidable.   80

COLFORD. Guilty or not, you ought to have stuck to him—it's not playing the game, Mr Twisden.

TWISDEN. You must allow me to judge where my duty lay, in a very hard case.

COLFORD. I thought a man was safe with his solicitor.

CANYNGE. Colford, you don't understand professional etiquette.

COLFORD. No, thank God!   90

TWISDEN. When you have been as long in your profession as I have been in mine, Major Colford, you will know that duty to your calling outweighs duty to friend or client.

COLFORD. But I serve the Country.

131

TWISDEN. And I serve the Law, sir.

CANYNGE. Graviter, give me a sheet of paper. I'll write a letter for him.

MARGARET (*Going up to* TWISDEN). Dear Mr Jacob—pay De Levis. You know my pearls —put them up the spout again. Don't let Ronny be——

TWISDEN. Money isn't the point, Margaret.

MARGARET. It's ghastly! It really is.

10 COLFORD. I'm going in to shake hands with him.

He starts to cross the room.

TWISDEN. Wait! We want him to go straight off to Morocco. Don't upset him. (*To* COLFORD *and* MARGARET). I think you had better go. If, a little later, Margaret, you could go round to Mrs Dancy——

COLFORD. Poor little Mabel Dancy! It's perfect hell for her.

They have not seen that DANCY *has opened the door behind them.*

DANCY. It is!

They all turn round in consternation.

20 COLFORD (*With a convulsive movement*). Old boy!

DANCY. No good, Colford. (*Gazing round at them*). Oh! clear out. I can't stand commiseration—and let me have some air.

TWISDEN *motions to* COLFORD *and* MARGARET *to go; and as he turns to* DANCY, *they go out.* GRAVITER *also moves towards the door. The* GENERAL *sits motionless.* GRAVITER *goes out.*

TWISDEN. Well?

DANCY. I'm going home, to clear things up with my wife. General Canynge, I don't quite know why I did the damned thing. But I did, and there's an end of it.

30 CANYNGE. Dancy, for the honor of the Army, avoid further scandal if you can. I've written a letter to a friend of mine in the Spanish War Office. It will get you a job in their war.

CANYNGE *closes the envelope.*

DANCY. Very good of you. I don't know if I can make use of it.

CANYNGE *stretches out the letter, which* TWISDEN *hands to* DANCY, *who takes it.* GRAVITER *re-opens the door.*

TWISDEN. What is it?

GRAVITER. De Levis is here.

TWISDEN. De Levis? Can't see him.

DANCY. Let him in!

After a moment's hesitation TWISDEN *nods, and* GRAVITER *goes out. The three wait in silence with their eyes fixed on the door, the* GENERAL *sitting at the table,* TWISDEN *by his chair,* DANCY *between him and the door Right.* DE LEVIS *comes in and shuts the door. He is advancing towards* TWISDEN *when his eyes fall on* DANCY, *and he stops.*

TWISDEN. You wanted to see me?

DE LEVIS (*Moistening his lips*). Yes. I came to say that—that I overheard—I am afraid a warrant is to be issued. I wanted you to realise —it's not *my* doing. I'll give it no support. I'm content. I don't want my money. I don't even want costs. Dancy, do you understand?

DANCY *does not answer, but looks at him with nothing alive in his face but his eyes.*

TWISDEN. We are obliged to you, sir. It was good of you to come.

DE LEVIS (*With a sort of darting pride*). Don't mistake me. I didn't come here because I feel Christian; I am a Jew. I will take no money—not even that which was stolen. Give it to a charity. I'm proved right. And now I'm done with the damned thing. Good morning!

He makes a little bow to CANYNGE *and* TWISDEN, *and turns to face* DANCY, *who has never moved. The two stand motionless, looking at each other, then* DE LEVIS *shrugs his shoulders and walks out. When he is gone there is a silence.*

CANYNGE (*Suddenly*). You heard what he said, Dancy. You have no time to lose.

But DANCY *does not stir.*

TWISDEN. Captain Dancy?

Slowly, without turning his head, rather like a man in a dream, DANCY *walks across the room, and goes out.*

SCENE III (*A few minutes later*)

The DANCYS' *sitting-room, a few minutes later.* MABEL DANCY *is sitting alone on the sofa with a newspaper on her lap; she is only just up, and has a bottle of smelling-salts in her hand. Two or three other newspapers are dumped on the arm of the sofa. She topples the one off her lap and takes up another as if she couldn't keep away from them; drops it in turn, and sits staring before her, sniffing at the salts. The door, Right, is opened and* DANCY *comes in.*

132

MABEL (*Utterly surprised*). Ronny! Do they want me in Court?

DANCY. No.

MABEL. What is it, then? Why are you back?

DANCY. Spun.

MABEL (*Blank*). Spun? What do you mean? What's spun?

DANCY. The case. They've found out through those notes.

10 MABEL. Oh! (*Staring at his face*). Who?

DANCY. Me!

MABEL (*After a moment of horrified stillness*). Don't, Ronny! Oh! No! Don't!

She buries her face in the pillows of the sofa. DANCY *stands looking down at her.*

DANCY. Pity you wouldn't come to Africa three months ago.

MABEL. Why didn't you tell me then? I would have gone.

DANCY. You wanted this case. Well, it's fallen down.

20 MABEL. Oh! Why didn't I face it? But I couldn't—I *had* to believe.

DANCY. And now you can't. It's the end, Mabel.

MABEL (*Looking up at him*). No.

DANCY *goes suddenly on his knees and seizes her hand.*

DANCY. Forgive me!

MABEL (*Putting her hand on his head*). Yes; oh, yes. I think I've known a long time, really. Only—why? What made you?

DANCY (*Getting up and speaking in jerks*).

30 It was a crazy thing to do; but, damn it, I was only looting a looter. The money was as much mine as his. A decent chap would have offered me half. You didn't see the brute look at me that night at dinner as much as to say: "You blasted fool!" It made me mad. That wasn't a bad jump—twice over. Nothing in the war took quite such nerve. (*Grimly*). I rather enjoyed that evening.

MABEL. But—money! To keep it!

40 DANCY (*Sullenly*). Yes, but I had a debt to pay.

MABEL. To a woman?

DANCY. A debt of honour—it wouldn't wait.

MABEL. It was—it was to a woman. Ronny, don't lie any more.

DANCY (*Grimly*). Well! I wanted to save your knowing. I'd promised a thousand. I had

a letter from her father that morning, threatening to tell you. All the same, if that tyke hadn't jeered at me for parlour tricks!—But what's the 50 good of all this now? (*Sullenly*). Well—it may cure you of loving me. Get over that, Mab; I never was worth it—and I'm done for!

MABEL. The woman—have you—since——?

DANCY (*Energetically*). No! You supplanted her. But if you'd known I was leaving a woman for you, you'd never have married me.

He walks over to the hearth.

MABEL *too gets up. She presses her hands to her forehead, then walks blindly round to behind the sofa and stands looking straight in front of her.*

MABEL (*Coldly*). What has happened, exactly?

DANCY. Sir Frederic chucked up the case. 60 I've seen Twisden; they want me to run for it to Morocco.

MABEL. To the war there?

DANCY. Yes. There's to be a warrant out.

MABEL. A prosecution? Prison? Oh, go! Don't wait a minute! Go!

DANCY. Blast them!

MABEL. Oh, Ronny! Please! Please! Think what you'll want. I'll pack. Quick! No! Don't wait to take things. Have you got money? 70

DANCY (*Nodding*). This'll be good-bye, then!

MABEL (*After a moment's struggle*). Oh! No! No, no! I'll follow—I'll come out to you there.

DANCY. D'you mean you'll stick to me?

MABEL. Of course I'll stick to you.

DANCY *seizes her hand and puts it to his lips.* *The bell rings.*

MABEL (*In terror*). Who's that?

The bell rings again. DANCY *moves towards the door.*

No! Let *me!*

She passes him and steals out to the outer door of the flat, where she stands listening. The bell rings again. She looks through the slit of the letter-box. While she is gone DANCY *stands quite still, till she comes back.*

MABEL. Through the letter-box—I can see— It's—it's police. Oh! God! . . . Ronny! I can't 80 bear it.

DANCY. Heads up, Mab! Don't show the brutes!

MABEL. Whatever happens, I'll go on loving

you. If it's prison—*I'll wait.* Do you understand? I don't care what you did—I don't care! I'm just the same. I will be just the same when you come back to me.

DANCY (*Slowly*). That's not in human nature.

MABEL. It is. It's in *me*.

DANCY. I've crocked up your life.

MABEL. No, no! Kiss me!

A long kiss, till the bell again startles them apart, and there is a loud knock.

DANCY. They'll break the door in. It's no
10 good—we must open. Hold them in check a little. I want a minute or two.

MABEL (*Clasping him*). Ronny! Oh, Ronny! It won't be for long—I'll be waiting! I'll be waiting—I swear it.

DANCY. Steady, Mab! (*Putting her back from him*). Now!

He opens the bedroom door, Left, and stands waiting for her to go. Summoning up her courage, she goes to open the outer door. A sudden change comes over DANCY's *face; from being stony it grows almost maniacal.*

DANCY (*Under his breath*). No! No! By God! No!

He goes out into the bedroom, closing the door behind him.

MABEL *has now opened the outer door, and disclosed* INSPECTOR DEDE *and the* YOUNG CONSTABLE *who were summoned to Meldon Court on the night of the theft, and have been witnesses in the case. Their voices are heard.*

MABEL. Yes?
20 INSPECTOR. Captain Dancy in, madam?

MABEL. I am not quite sure—I don't think so.

INSPECTOR. I wish to speak to him a minute. Stay here, Grover. Now, madam!

MABEL. Will you come in while I see?

She comes in, followed by the INSPECTOR.

INSPECTOR. I should think you must be sure, madam. This is not a big place.

MABEL. He was changing his clothes to go out. I think he has gone.

INSPECTOR. What's that door?
30 MABEL. To our bedroom.

INSPECTOR (*Moving towards it*). He'll be in there, then.

MABEL. What do you want, Inspector?

INSPECTOR (*Melting*). Well, madam, it's no use disguising it. I'm exceedingly sorry, but I've a warrant for his arrest.

MABEL. Inspector!

INSPECTOR. I'm sure I've every sympathy for you, madam; but I must carry out my instructions.
40 MABEL. And break my heart?

INSPECTOR. Well, madam, we're—we're not allowed to take that into consideration. The Law's the Law.

MABEL. Are you married?

INSPECTOR. I am.

MABEL. If you—your wife——

The INSPECTOR *raises his hand, deprecating.* (*Speaking low*). Just half an hour! Couldn't you? It's two lives—two whole lives! We've
50 only been married four months. Come back in half an hour. It's such a little thing—nobody will know. Nobody. Won't you?

INSPECTOR. Now, madam—you must know my duty.

MABEL. Inspector, I beseech you—just half an hour.

INSPECTOR. No, no—don't you try to undermine me—I'm sorry for you; but don't you try
60 it!

He tries the handle, then knocks at the door.

DANCY'S VOICE. One minute!

INSPECTOR. It's locked. (*Sharply*). Is there another door to that room? Come, now!

The bell rings.
(*Moving towards the door, Left; to the* CONSTABLE). Who's that out there?

CONSTABLE. A lady and gentleman, sir.

INSPECTOR. What lady and—Stand by, Grover!

DANCY'S VOICE. All right! You can come in
70 now.

There is the noise of a lock being turned. And almost immediately the sound of a pistol shot in the bedroom. MABEL *rushes to the door, tears it open, and disappears within, followed by the* INSPECTOR, *just as* MARGARET ORME *and* COLFORD *come in from the passage, pursued by the* CONSTABLE. *They, too, all hurry to the bedroom door and disappear for a moment; then* COLFORD *and* MARGARET *reappear, supporting* MABEL, *who faints as they lay her on the sofa.* COLFORD *takes from her hand an envelope, and tears it open.*

COLFORD. It's addressed to *me*.

He reads it aloud to MARGARET *in a low voice.*

"DEAR COLFORD,—This is the only decent thing I can do. It's too damned unfair to her. It's only another jump. A pistol keeps faith. Look after her. Colford—my love to her, and you."

MARGARET *gives a sort of choking sob, then, seeing the smelling bottle, she snatches it up, and turns to revive* MABEL.

COLFORD. Leave her! The longer she's unconscious, the better.

INSPECTOR (*Re-entering*). This is a very serious business, sir.

10 COLFORD (*Sternly*). Yes, Inspector; you've done for my best friend.

INSPECTOR. I, sir? He shot himself.

COLFORD. Hari-kari.

INSPECTOR. Beg pardon?

COLFORD. (*He points with the letter to* MABEL.) For her sake, and his own.

INSPECTOR (*Putting out his hand*). I'll want that, sir.

COLFORD (*Grimly*). You shall have it read at the inquest. Till then—it's addressed to me, 20 and I stick to it.

INSPECTOR. Very well, sir. Do you want to have a look at him?

COLFORD *passes quickly into the bedroom, followed by the* INSPECTOR. MARGARET *remains kneeling beside* MABEL. COLFORD *comes quickly back.* MARGARET *looks up at him. He stands very still.*

COLFORD. Neatly—through the heart.

MARGARET (*Wildly*). Keeps faith! We've all done that. It's not enough.

COLFORD (*Looking down at* MABEL). All right, old boy!

(*The Curtain falls.*)

❦ Romantic Historians

LYTTON STRACHEY

The most arresting figure in the modern history of English biography, Giles Lytton Strachey was one of those frequent cases of an author with inclinations toward one kind of writing who achieved great success in another. Born to a family of acknowledged literary interests— one cousin was John Strachey (p. 821)— Strachey matriculated at Trinity College, Cambridge, where he indulged in the composing of facile, undistinguished verse, and expressed the desire to write both plays and novels. He soon came to have doubts about his powers in either the fictional or dramatic field, turning instead to critical literary history in his first published work, *Landmarks in French Literature* (1912).

While this work was scarcely noteworthy, it indicated to Strachey the direction in which his efforts might most successfully be turned. As he was a man of independent means, he was able to devote himself to further reading and study for several years. The fruits of his study are apparent in the brilliant *Eminent Victorians* (1918), a series of four pungent and satirical biographical sketches of people prominent in Victorian England though not of the first rank in importance—Cardinal Manning, Thomas Arnold, Florence Nightingale, and General "Chinese" Gordon. His next work, *Queen Victoria* (1921), is by general consent his masterpiece, a landmark in modern biographical writing. Although *Pope* (1925) and *Elizabeth and Essex* (1928) were two excellent performances, they did not manage to achieve the remarkable blend of caustic wit, breadth of understanding, and romantic sympathy (which, however, never allows for an idealization of the subject) to be found in *Queen Victoria*. Miscellanies, such as *Portraits in Miniature* (1931) and *Characters and Commentaries* (1933), while they contain memorable pages, represent a general decline in the author's powers.

Strachey was noted for his sociability among the group of writers and critics at his home in Bloomsbury; to many, however, he seemed to be querulous, arrogant, and gossiping. The answer to the riddle lies in the fact that Strachey had a marked personal approach both to people and to ideas. His biographies are intensely subjective, and have both the strength and weakness that derive from the personal point of view. But they are generally accurate as to facts; the only true quarrel with them may be in reference to the interpretation of those facts. They are concise, satirical, often mordantly so; they savor more of the French than the English temperament. Strachey is, indeed, a neoclassicist intellectually, which enables him to treat a figure like Alexander Pope with understanding, *con amore*, and gives him a hate for the Victorian which lends a razor edge to his writings about England in the nineteenth century. But he is also a romantic and nostalgic soul, so that even when he is expressing his personal dislike he has sentimental twitches about the Victorians; in spite of himself, he comes to fall in love with Queen Victoria. The result is that, although he is the most remarkable and inimitable of all the "debunking" biographers of the 1920's, he cannot dismiss his characters as negligible mortals. In the catalogue they go for men and women, whatever their shortcomings; and so, while Strachey is a satirist in biography, he is also a human biographer.

from Queen Victoria

IX. Old Age

I

MEANWHILE in Victoria's private life many changes and developments had taken place. With the marriages of her elder children her family circle widened; grandchildren appeared; and a multitude of new domestic interests sprang up. The death of King Leopold— in 1865—had removed the predominant figure of the older generation, and the functions he had performed as the center and adviser of a large group of relatives in Germany and in 10 England devolved upon Victoria. These functions she discharged with unremitting industry, carrying on an enormous correspondence, and following with absorbed interest every detail in the lives of the ever-ramifying cousinhood. And she tasted to the full both the joys and the pains of family affection. She took a particular delight in her grandchildren, to whom she showed an indulgence which their parents had not always enjoyed, though, even to her 20 grandchildren, she could be, when the occasion demanded it, severe. The eldest of them, the little Prince Wilhelm of Prussia, was a remarkably headstrong child; he dared to be impertinent even to his grandmother; and once, when she told him to bow to a visitor at Osborne, he disobeyed her outright. This would not do; the order was sternly repeated, and the naughty boy, noticing that his kind grandmamma had suddenly turned into a most terri- 30 fying lady, submitted his will to hers, and bowed very low indeed.

It would have been well if all the Queen's domestic troubles could have been got over as easily. Among her more serious distresses was the conduct of the Prince of Wales. The young

Reprinted from *Queen Victoria* by Lytton Strachey, copyright, 1925, by Harcourt, Brace and Company; reprinted by permission.
6. **King Leopold,** Leopold I (1790–1865), King of the Belgians and Victoria's uncle. 23. **Prince Wilhelm,** later Emperor William II of Germany (1859–1941), who as ruler of the German people precipitated World War I. 26. **Osborne,** on the Isle of Wight, a royal dwelling during most of Queen Victoria's reign and the scene of her death in 1901. 36. **Prince of Wales,** later King Edward VII of England (1841–1910), who succeeded his mother.

man was now independent and married; he had shaken the parental yoke from his shoulders; he was positively beginning to do as he liked. Victoria was much perturbed, and her worst fears seemed to be justified when in 1870 he appeared as a witness in a society divorce case. It was clear that the heir to the throne had been mixing with people of whom she did not at all approve. What was to be done? She saw that it was not only her son that was to blame—that it was the whole system of society; and so she despatched a letter to Mr. Delane, the editor of *The Times,* asking him if he would "frequently *write* articles pointing out the *immense* danger and evil of the wretched frivolity and levity of the views and lives of the Higher Classes." And five years later Mr. Delane did write an article upon that very subject. Yet it seemed to have very little effect.

Ah! if only the Higher Classes would learn to live as she lived in the domestic sobriety of her sanctuary at Balmoral! For more and more did she find solace and refreshment in her Highland domain; and twice yearly, in the spring and in the autumn, with a sigh of relief, she set her face northwards, in spite of the humble protests of Ministers, who murmured vainly in the royal ears that to transact the affairs of State over an interval of six hundred miles added considerably to the cares of government. Her ladies, too, felt occasionally a slight reluctance to set out, for, especially in the early days, the long pilgrimage was not without its drawbacks. For many years the Queen's conservatism forbade the continuation of the railway up Deeside, so that the last stages of the journey had to be accomplished in carriages. But, after all, carriages had their good points; they were easy, for instance, to get in and out of, which was an important consideration, for the royal train remained for long immune from modern conveniences, and when it drew up, on some border moorland, far from any platform, the high-bred dames were

obliged to descend to earth by the perilous foot-board, the only pair of folding steps being reserved for Her Majesty's saloon. In the days of crinolines such moments were sometimes awkward; and it was occasionally necessary to summon Mr. Johnstone, the short and sturdy Manager of the Caledonian Railway, who, more than once, in a high gale and drenching rain with great difficulty "pushed up"—as he himself described it—some unlucky Lady Blanche or Lady Agatha into her compartment. But Victoria cared for none of these things. She was only intent upon regaining, with the utmost swiftness, her enchanted Castle, where every spot was charged with memories, where every memory was sacred, and where life was passed in an incessant and delightful round of absolutely trivial events.

And it was not only the place that she loved; she was equally attached to "the simple mountaineers," from whom, she said, "she learnt many a lesson of resignation and faith." Smith and Grant and Ross and Thompson—she was devoted to them all; but beyond the rest, she was devoted to John Brown. The Prince's gillie had now become the Queen's personal attendant—a body servant from whom she was never parted, who accompanied her on her drives, waited on her during the day, and slept in a neighboring chamber at night. She liked his strength, his solidity, the sense he gave her of physical security; she even liked his rugged manners and his rough unaccommodating speech. She allowed him to take liberties with her which would have been unthinkable from anybody else. To bully the Queen, to order her about, to reprimand her—who could dream of venturing upon such audacities? And yet, when she received such treatment from John Brown, she positively seemed to enjoy it. The eccentricity appeared to be extraordinary; but, after all, it is no uncommon thing for an autocratic dowager to allow some trusted indispensable servant to adopt towards her an attitude of authority which is jealously forbidden to relatives or friends: the power of a depend-

---

13. **Mr. Delane,** John T. Delane (1817–1879), editor of *The London Times* and one of the most judicial journalists of the century.   23. **Balmoral,** Balmoral Castle in Aberdeenshire, Scotland, a favorite vacationing-place of Victoria and Albert.

71. **gillie,** originally an attendant to a Gaelic chieftain, used now in Scotland for a manservant to a gentleman who is on a hunting or fishing expedition.

ant still remains, by a psychological sleight-of-hand, one's own power, even when it is exercised over oneself. When Victoria meekly obeyed the abrupt commands of her henchman to get off her pony or put on her shawl, was she not displaying, and in the highest degree, the force of her volition? People might wonder; she could not help that; this was the manner in which it pleased her to act, and there was an end of it. To have submitted her judgment to a son or a Minister might have seemed wiser or more natural; but if she had done so, she instinctively felt, she would indeed have lost her independence. And yet upon somebody she longed to depend. Her days were heavy with the long process of domination. As she drove in silence over the moors she leaned back in the carriage, oppressed and weary; but what a relief!—John Brown was behind on the rumble, and his strong arm would be there for her to lean upon when she got out.

He had, too, in her mind, a special connection with Albert. In their expeditions the Prince had always trusted him more than any one; the gruff, kind, hairy Scotsman was, she felt, in some mysterious way, a legacy from the dead. She came to believe at last—or so it appeared—that the spirit of Albert was nearer when Brown was near. Often, when seeking inspiration over some complicated question of political or domestic import, she would gaze with deep concentration at her late husband's bust. But it was also noticed that sometimes in such moments of doubt and hesitation Her Majesty's looks would fix themselves upon John Brown.

Eventually, the "simple mountaineer" became almost a state personage. The influence which he wielded was not to be overlooked. Lord Beaconsfield was careful, from time to time, to send courteous messages to "Mr. Brown" in his letters to the Queen, and the French Government took particular pains to provide for his comfort during the visits of the English Sovereign to France. It was only natural that among the elder members of the royal family he should not have been popular, and

that his failings—for failings he had, though Victoria would never notice his too acute appreciation of Scotch whiskey—should have been the subject of acrimonious comment at Court. But he served his mistress faithfully, and to ignore him would be a sign of disrespect in her biographer. For the Queen, far from making a secret of her affectionate friendship, took care to publish it to the world. By her orders two gold medals were struck in his honor; on his death, in 1883, a long and eulogistic obituary of him appeared in the *Court Circular;* and a Brown memorial brooch—of gold, with the late gillie's head on one side and the royal monogram on the other—was designed by Her Majesty for presentation to her Highland servants and cottagers, to be worn by them on the anniversary of his death, with a mourning scarf and pins. In the second series of extracts from the Queen's *Highland Journals,* published in 1884, her "devoted personal attendant and faithful friend" appears upon almost every page, and is in effect the hero of the book. With an absence of reticence remarkable in royal persons, Victoria seemed to demand, in this private and delicate matter, the sympathy of the whole nation; and yet—such is the world!—there were those who actually treated the relations between their Sovereign and her servant as a theme for ribald jests.

II

The busy years hastened away; the traces of Time's unimaginable touch grew manifest; and old age, approaching, laid a gentle hold upon Victoria. The grey hair whitened; the mature features mellowed; the short firm figure amplified and moved more slowly, supported by a stick. And, simultaneously, in the whole tenor of the Queen's existence an extraordinary transformation came to pass. The nation's attitude towards her, critical and even hostile as it had been for so many years, altogether changed; while there was a corresponding alteration in the temper of Victoria's own mind.

Many causes led to this result. Among them were the repeated strokes of personal misfortune which befell the Queen during a cruelly short space of years. In 1878 the Princess Alice, who had married in 1862 the Prince

40. **Lord Beaconsfield,** Benjamin Disraeli (1804–1881), one of the great figures in nineteenth-century European statesmanship. He was prime minister in 1868 and from 1874 to 1880; he worked tirelessly for the cause of British imperialism.

Louis of Hesse-Darmstadt, died in tragic circumstances. In the following year the Prince Imperial, the only son of the Empress Eugénie, to whom Victoria, since the catastrophe of 1870, had become devotedly attached, was killed in the Zulu War. Two years later, in 1881, the Queen lost Lord Beaconsfield, and, in 1883, John Brown. In 1884 the Prince Leopold, Duke of Albany, who had been an invalid from birth, died prematurely, shortly after his marriage. Victoria's cup of sorrows was indeed overflowing; and the public, as it watched the widowed mother weeping for her children and her friends, displayed a constantly increasing sympathy.

An event which occurred in 1882 revealed and accentuated the feelings of the nation. As the Queen, at Windsor, was walking from the train to her carriage, a youth named Roderick Maclean fired a pistol at her from a distance of a few yards. An Eton boy struck up Maclean's arm with an umbrella before the pistol went off; no damage was done, and the culprit was at once arrested. This was the last of a series of seven attempts upon the Queen—attempts which, taking place at sporadic intervals over a period of forty years, resembled one another in a curious manner. All, with a single exception, were perpetrated by adolescents, whose motives were apparently not murderous, since, save in the case of Maclean, none of their pistols was loaded. These unhappy youths, who, after buying their cheap weapons, stuffed them with gunpowder and paper, and then went off, with the certainty of immediate detection, to click them in the face of royalty, present a strange problem to the psychologist. But, though in each case their actions and their purposes seemed to be so similar, their fates were remarkably varied. The first of them, Edward Oxford, who fired at Victoria within a few months of her marriage, was tried for high treason, declared to

be insane, and sent to an asylum for life. It appears, however, that this sentence did not commend itself to Albert, for when, two years later, John Francis committed the same offense, and was tried upon the same charge, the Prince pronounced that there was no insanity in the matter. "The wretched creature," he told his father was "not out of his mind, but a thorough scamp." "I hope," he added, "his trial will be conducted with the greatest strictness." Apparently it was; at any rate, the jury shared the view of the Prince, the plea of insanity was set aside, and Francis was found guilty of high treason and condemned to death; but, as there was no proof of an intent to kill or even to wound, this sentence, after a lengthened deliberation between the Home Secretary and the Judges, was commuted for one of transportation for life. As the law stood, these assaults, futile as they were, could only be treated as high treason; the discrepancy between the actual deed and the tremendous penalties involved was obviously grotesque; and it was, besides, clear that a jury, knowing that a verdict of guilty implied a sentence of death, would tend to the alternative course, and find the prisoner not guilty but insane—a conclusion which, on the face of it, would have appeared to be the more reasonable. In 1842, therefore, an Act was passed making any attempt to hurt the Queen a misdemeanor, punishable by transportation for seven years, or imprisonment, with or without hard labor, for a term not exceeding three years—the misdemeanant, at the discretion of the Court, "to be publicly or privately whipped, as often, and in such manner and form, as the Court shall direct, not exceeding thrice." The four subsequent attempts were all dealt with under this new law; William Bean, in 1842, was sentenced to eighteen months' imprisonment; William Hamilton, in 1849, was transported for seven years; and, in 1850, the same sentence was passed upon Lieutenant Robert Pate, who struck the Queen on the head with his cane in Piccadilly. Pate, alone among these delinquents, was of mature years; he had held a commission in the Army, dressed himself as a dandy, and was, the Prince declared, "manifestly deranged." In 1872 Arthur O'Connor, a youth of seventeen, fired an unloaded pistol at

1. **tragic circumstances.** Princess Alice caught diphtheria from one of her children during an epidemic which scourged her household, an extremely common occurrence during the nineteenth century. 3. **Eugénie,** the Empress Eugénie (1826–1920), wife of Napoleon III of France, who presided over the so-called "Second Empire" of the French nation (1852–1870). 4. **catastrophe of 1870,** a reference to the Franco-Prussian War of that year, which brought about the defeat of France, the collapse of Napoleon III's "Second Empire," and the emergence of Germany as an imperial world power.

the Queen outside Buckingham Palace; he was immediately seized by John Brown, and sentenced to one year's imprisonment and twenty strokes of the birch rod. It was for his bravery upon this occasion that Brown was presented with one of his gold medals. In all these cases the jury had refused to allow the plea of insanity; but Roderick Maclean's attempt in 1882 had a different issue. On this occasion the pistol was found to have been loaded, and the public indignation, emphasized as it was by Victoria's growing popularity, was particularly great. Either for this or for some other reason the procedure of the last forty years was abandoned, and Maclean was tried for high treason. The result was what might have been expected; the jury brought in a verdict of "not guilty, but insane"; and the prisoner was sent to an asylum during Her Majesty's pleasure. Their verdict, however, produced a remarkable consequence. Victoria, who doubtless carried in her mind some memory of Albert's disapproval of a similar verdict in the case of Oxford, was very much annoyed. What did the jury mean, she asked, by saying that Maclean was not guilty? It was perfectly clear that he was guilty—she had seen him fire off the pistol himself. It was in vain that Her Majesty's constitutional advisers reminded her of the principle of English law which lays down that no man can be found guilty of a crime unless he be proved to have had a criminal intention. Victoria was quite unconvinced. "If that is the law," she said, "the law must be altered": and altered it was. In 1883 an Act was passed changing the form of the verdict in cases of insanity, and the confusing anomaly remains upon the Statute Book to this day.

But it was not only through the feelings—commiserating or indignant—of personal sympathy that the Queen and her people were being drawn more nearly together; they were beginning, at last, to come to a close and permanent agreement upon the conduct of public affairs. Mr. Gladstone's second administration (1880–85) was a succession of failures, ending in disaster and disgrace; liberalism fell into discredit with the country, and Victoria per-

ceived with joy that her distrust of her Ministers was shared by an ever-increasing number of her subjects. During the crisis in the Sudan, the popular temper was her own. She had been among the first to urge the necessity of an expedition to Khartoum, and, when the news came of the catastrophic death of General Gordon, her voice led the chorus of denunciation which raved against the Government. In her rage, she despatched a fulminating telegram to Mr. Gladstone, not in the usual cypher, but open; and her letter of condolence to Miss Gordon, in which she attacked her Ministers for breach of faith, was widely published. It was rumored that she had sent for Lord Hartington, the Secretary of State for War, and vehemently upbraided him. "She rated me," he was reported to have told a friend, "as if I'd been a footman." "Why didn't she send for the butler?" asked his friend. "Oh," was the reply, "the butler generally manages to keep out of the way on such occasions."

But the day came when it was impossible to keep out of the way any longer. Mr. Gladstone was defeated, and resigned. Victoria, at a final interview, received him with her usual amenity, but, besides the formalities demanded by the occasion, the only remark which she made to him of a personal nature was to the effect that she supposed Mr. Gladstone would now require some rest. He remembered with regret how, at a similar audience in 1874, she had expressed her trust in him as a supporter of the throne; but he noted the change without surprise. "Her mind and opinions," he wrote in his diary afterwards, "have since that day been seriously warped."

Such was Mr. Gladstone's view; but the majority of the nation by no means agreed with him; and, in the General Election of 1886, they showed decisively that Victoria's politics were identical with theirs by casting forth the contrivers of Home Rule—that abom-

45. **Mr. Gladstone,** William Ewart Gladstone (1809–1898), prime minister 1868–74 and 1880–85, the most noted leader of the English liberals.

51. **Sudan,** the region of northeast Africa south of Egypt along the Nile valley. The tribesmen of this locality, under the fanatical leadership of Mohammed Ahmed (1843?–1885), the Mahdi, began a Holy War in the mid-1880's. An English force under General "Chinese" Gordon was sent out to put down the disturbance; but Gordon received inadequate support from the government, was cut off and besieged in the city of Khartoum, and was slain there early in 1885. 91. **Home Rule.** The problem of Home Rule, or autonomy, for Ireland was a vital question in British domestic policy in the 1870's and 1880's. Gladstone favored it but was defeated on the issue. The matter was still agitating the country on the eve of World War I.

ination of desolation—into outer darkness, and placing Lord Salisbury in power. Victoria's satisfaction was profound. A flood of new unwonted hopefulness swept over her, stimulating her vital spirits with a surprising force. Her habit of life was suddenly altered; abandoning the long seclusion which Disraeli's persuasions had only momentarily interrupted, she threw herself vigorously into a multitude of public activities. She appeared at drawing-rooms, at concerts, at reviews; she laid foundation-stones; she went to Liverpool to open an international exhibition, driving through the streets in her open carriage in heavy rain amid vast applauding crowds. Delighted by the welcome which met her everywhere, she warmed to her work. She visited Edinburgh, where the ovation of Liverpool was repeated and surpassed. In London, she opened in high state the Colonial and Indian Exhibition at South Kensington. On this occasion the ceremonial was particularly magnificent; a blare of trumpets announced the approach of Her Majesty; the "National Anthem" followed; and the Queen, seated on a gorgeous throne of hammered gold, replied with her own lips to the address that was presented to her. Then she rose, and, advancing upon the platform with regal port, acknowledged the acclamations of the great assembly by a succession of curtseys, of elaborate and commanding grace.

Next year was the fiftieth of her reign, and in June the splendid anniversary was celebrated in solemn pomp. Victoria, surrounded by the highest dignitaries of her realm, escorted by a glittering galaxy of kings and princes, drove through the crowded enthusiasm of the capital to render thanks to God in Westminster Abbey. In that triumphant hour the last remaining traces of past antipathies and past disagreements were altogether swept away. The Queen was hailed at once as the mother of her people and as the embodied symbol of their imperial greatness; and she responded to the double sentiment with all the ardor of her spirit. England and the people of England, she knew it, she felt it, were, in some wonderful and yet quite simple manner, *hers*.

2. **Salisbury,** Robert Viscount Salisbury (1830–1903), prime minister 1886–92 and 1895–1902.

Exultation, affection, gratitude, a profound sense of obligation, an unbounded pride—such were her emotions; and, coloring and intensifying the rest, there was something else. At last, after so long, happiness—fragmentary, perhaps, and charged with gravity, but true and unmistakable none the less—had returned to her. The unaccustomed feeling filled and warmed her consciousness. When, at Buckingham Palace again, the long ceremony over, she was asked how she was, "I am very tired, but very happy," she said.

III

And so, after the toils and tempests of the day, a long evening followed—mild, serene, and lighted with a golden glory. For an unexampled atmosphere of success and adoration invested the last period of Victoria's life. Her triumph was the summary, the crown, of a greater triumph—the culminating prosperity of a nation. The solid splendor of the decade between Victoria's two jubilees can hardly be paralleled in the annals of England. The sage counsels of Lord Salisbury seemed to bring with them not only wealth and power, but security; and the country settled down, with calm assurance, to the enjoyment of an established grandeur. And—it was only natural—Victoria settled down too. For she was a part of the establishment—an essential part as it seemed—a fixture—a magnificent, immovable sideboard in the huge saloon of state. Without her the heaped-up banquet of 1890 would have lost its distinctive quality—the comfortable order of the substantial unambiguous dishes, with their background of weighty glamor, half out of sight.

Her own existence came to harmonize more and more with what was around her. Gradually, imperceptibly, Albert receded. It was not that he was forgotten—that would have been impossible—but that the void created by his absence grew less agonizing, and even, at last, less obvious. At last Victoria found it possible to regret the bad weather without immediately reflecting that her "dear Albert always said we could not alter it, but must leave it as it was"; she could even enjoy a good breakfast without considering how "dear Albert" would have liked the buttered eggs. And, as

141

that figure slowly faded, its place was taken, inevitably, by Victoria's own. Her being, revolving for so many years round an external object, now changed its motion and found its center in itself. It had to be so: her domestic position, the pressure of her public work, her indomitable sense of duty, made anything else impossible. Her egotism proclaimed its rights. Her age increased still further the surround-10 ing deference; and her force of character, emerging at length in all its plenitude, imposed itself absolutely upon its environment by the conscious effort of an imperious will.

Little by little it was noticed that the outward vestiges of Albert's posthumous domination grew less complete. At court the stringency of mourning was relaxed. As the Queen drove through the Park in her open carriage with her Highlanders behind her, nursery-maids can-20 vassed eagerly the growing patch of violet velvet in the bonnet with its jet appurtenances on the small bowing head.

It was in her family that Victoria's ascendancy reached its highest point. All her offspring were married; the number of her descendants rapidly increased; there were many marriages in the third generation; and no fewer than thirty-seven of her great-grandchildren were living at the time of her death. A 30 picture of the period displays the royal family collected together in one of the great rooms at Windsor—a crowded company of more than fifty persons, with the imperial matriarch in their midst. Over them all she ruled with a most potent sway. The small concerns of the youngest aroused her passionate interest; and the oldest she treated as if they were children still. The Prince of Wales, in particular, stood in tremendous awe of his mother. She had 40 steadily refused to allow him the slightest participation in the business of government; and he had occupied himself in other ways. Nor could it be denied that he enjoyed himself— out of her sight; but, in that redoubtable presence, his abounding manhood suffered a miserable eclipse. Once, at Osborne, when, owing to no fault of his, he was too late for a dinner party, he was observed standing behind a pillar and, wiping the sweat from his forehead, 50 trying to nerve himself to go up to the Queen. When at last he did so, she gave him a stiff nod, whereupon he vanished immediately behind another pillar, and remained there until the party broke up. At the time of this incident the Prince of Wales was over fifty years of age.

It was inevitable that the Queen's domestic activities should occasionally trench upon the domain of high diplomacy; and this was especially the case when the interests of her eld-60 est daughter, the Crown Princess of Prussia, were at stake. The Crown Prince held liberal opinions; he was much influenced by his wife; and both were detested by Bismarck, who declared with scurrilous emphasis that the Englishwoman and her mother were a menace to the Prussian State. The feud was still further intensified when, on the death of the old Emperor (1888), the Crown Prince succeeded to the throne. A family entanglement brought on 70 a violent crisis. One of the daughters of the New Empress had become betrothed to Prince Alexander of Battenberg, who had lately been ejected from the throne of Bulgaria owing to the hostility of the Tsar. Victoria, as well as the Empress, highly approved of the match. Of the two brothers of Prince Alexander, the elder had married another of her granddaughters, and the younger was the husband of her daughter, the Princess Beatrice; she was de-80 voted to the handsome young man; and she was delighted by the prospect of the third brother—on the whole the handsomest, she thought, of the three—also becoming a member of her family. Unfortunately, however, Bismarck was opposed to the scheme. He perceived that the marriage would endanger the friendship between Germany and Russia, which was vital to his foreign policy, and he announced that it must not take place. A fierce 90 struggle between the Empress and the Chancellor followed. Victoria, whose hatred of her daughter's enemy was unbounded, came over to Charlottenburg to join in the fray. Bismarck, over his pipe and lager, snorted out his alarm.

68. old Emperor . . . throne. The "old Emperor" is William I of Prussia (1798–1888), the first Hohenzollern to rule over a united Germany. The Crown Prince is the Emperor Frederick III, who succeeded William I in 1888 but reigned for only three months before his sudden death. 85. Bismarck, Otto von Bismarck (1815–1898), generally regarded as the German statesman most responsible for the growth of modern Germany from a union of petty states to an integrated imperialistic world power.

The Queen of England's object, he said, was clearly political—she wished to estrange Germany and Russia—and very likely she would have her way. "In family matters," he added, "she is not used to contradiction"; she would "bring the parson with her in her traveling bag and the bridegroom in her trunk, and the marriage would come off on the spot." But the man of blood and iron was not to be thwarted so easily, and he asked for a private interview with the Queen. The details of their conversation are unknown; but it is certain that in the course of it Victoria was forced to realize the meaning of resistance to that formidable personage, and that she promised to use all her influence to prevent the marriage. The engagement was broken off; and in the following year Prince Alexander of Battenberg united himself to Fräulein Loisinger, an actress at the court theater of Darmstadt.

But such painful incidents were rare. Victoria was growing very old; with no Albert to guide her, with no Beaconsfield to inflame her, she was willing enough to abandon the dangerous questions of diplomacy to the wisdom of Lord Salisbury, and to concentrate her energies upon objects which touched her more nearly and over which she could exercise an undisputed control. Her home—her court—the monuments at Balmoral—the livestock at Windsor—the organization of her engagements—the supervision of the multitudinous details of her daily routine—such matters played now an even greater part in her existence than before. Her life passed in an extraordinary exactitude. Every moment of her day was mapped out beforehand; the succession of her engagements was immutably fixed; the dates of her journeys —to Osborne, to Balmoral, to the South of France, to Windsor, to London—were hardly altered from year to year. She demanded from those who surrounded her a rigid precision in details, and she was preternaturally quick in detecting the slightest deviation from the rules which she had laid down. Such was the irresistible potency of her personality, that anything but the most implicit obedience to her wishes was felt to be impossible; but sometimes somebody was unpunctual; and unpunctuality was one of the most heinous of sins. Then her displeasure—her dreadful displeasure—became all too visible. At such moments there seemed nothing surprising in her having been the daughter of a martinet.

But these storms, unnerving as they were while they lasted, were quickly over, and they grew more and more exceptional. With the return of happiness, a gentle benignity flowed from the aged Queen. Her smile, once so rare a visitant to those saddened features, flitted over them with an easy alacrity; the blue eyes beamed; the whole face, starting suddenly from its pendulous expressionlessness, brightened and softened and cast over those who watched it an unforgettable charm. For in her last years there was a fascination in Victoria's amiability which had been lacking even from the vivid impulse of her youth. Over all who approached her—or very nearly all—she threw a peculiar spell. Her grandchildren adored her; her ladies waited upon her with a reverential love. The honor of serving her obliterated a thousand inconveniences—the monotony of a court existence, the fatigue of standing, the necessity for a superhuman attentiveness to the minutiae of time and space. As one did one's wonderful duty one could forget that one's legs were aching from the infinitude of the passages at Windsor, or that one's bare arms were turning blue in the Balmoral cold.

What, above all, seemed to make such service delightful was the detailed interest which the Queen took in the circumstances of those around her. Her absorbing passion for the comfortable commonplaces, the small crises, the recurrent sentimentalities of domestic life constantly demanded wider fields for its activity; the sphere of her own family, vast as it was, was not enough; she became the eager confidante of the household affairs of her ladies; her sympathies reached out to the palace domestics; even the housemaids and scullions —so it appeared—were the objects of her searching inquiries, and of her heartfelt solicitude when their lovers were ordered to a foreign station, or their aunts suffered from an attack of rheumatism which was more than usually acute.

Nevertheless the due distinctions of rank were immaculately preserved. The Queen's mere presence was enough to insure that; but, in addition, the dominion of court etiquette was paramount. For that elaborate code, which had kept Lord Melbourne stiff upon the sofa and ranged the other guests in silence about the round table according to the order of precedence, was as punctiliously enforced as ever. Every evening after dinner, the hearth-rug, sacred to royalty, loomed before the profane in inaccessible glory, or, on one or two terrific occasions, actually lured them magnetically forward to the very edge of the abyss. The Queen, at the fitting moment, moved towards her guests; one after the other they were led up to her; and, while dualogue followed dualogue in constraint and embarrassment, the rest of the assembly stood still, without a word. Only in one particular was the severity of the etiquette allowed to lapse. Throughout the greater part of the reign the rule that ministers must stand during their audiences with the Queen had been absolute. When Lord Derby, the Prime Minister, had an audience of Her Majesty after a serious illness, he mentioned it afterwards, as a proof of the royal favor, that the Queen had remarked, "How sorry she was she could not ask him to be seated." Subsequently, Disraeli, after an attack of gout and in a moment of extreme expansion on the part of Victoria, had been offered a chair; but he had thought it wise humbly to decline the privilege. In her later years, however, the Queen invariably asked Mr. Gladstone and Lord Salisbury to sit down.

Sometimes the solemnity of the evening was diversified by a concert, an opera, or even a play. One of the most marked indications of Victoria's enfranchisement from the thralldom of widowhood had been her resumption—after an interval of thirty years—of the custom of commanding dramatic companies from London to perform before the Court at Windsor. On such occasions her spirits rose high. She loved acting; she loved a good plot; above all, she loved a farce. Engrossed by everything that passed upon the stage she would follow, with childlike innocence, the unwinding of the story; or she would assume an air of knowing superiority and exclaim in triumph, "There! You didn't expect *that*, did you?" when the *dénouement* came. Her sense of humor was of a vigorous though primitive kind. She had been one of the very few persons who had always been able to appreciate the Prince Consort's jokes; and, when those were cracked no more, she could still roar with laughter, in the privacy of her household, over some small piece of fun—some oddity of an ambassador, or some ignorant Minister's *faux pas*. When the jest grew subtle she was less pleased; but, if it approached the confines of the indecorous, the danger was serious. To take a liberty called down at once Her Majesty's most crushing disapprobation; and to say something improper was to take the greatest liberty of all. Then the royal lips sank down at the corners, the royal eyes stared in astonished protrusion, and in fact the royal countenance became inauspicious in the highest degree. The transgressor shuddered into silence, while the awful "We are not amused" annihilated the dinner table. Afterwards, in her private entourage, the Queen would observe that the person in question was, she very much feared, "not discreet"; it was a verdict from which there was no appeal.

In general, her esthetic tastes had remained unchanged since the days of Mendelssohn, Landseer, and Lablache. She still delighted in the roulades of Italian opera; she still demanded a high standard in the execution of a pianoforte duet. Her views on painting were decided; Sir Edwin, she declared, was perfect; she was much impressed by Lord Leighton's manners; and she profoundly distrusted Mr. Watts. From time to time she ordered engraved portraits to be taken of members of the royal family; on these occasions she would have the first proofs submitted to her, and, having inspected them with minute particularity, she would point out their mistakes to the artists, indicating at the same time how they might be corrected. The artists invariably discovered that Her Majesty's suggestions were

---

2. **Lord Melbourne,** William Lamb, Lord Melbourne (1779–1848), prime minister at the time of Victoria's accession in 1837; he was of great assistance to the young Queen in instructing her as to her duties and official functions. 20. **Lord Derby,** prime minister in 1852, 1858, and 1866–67.

77. **Landseer,** Sir Edwin H. Landseer (1802–1873), particularly famous for his paintings of animals. **Lablache,** Luigi Lablache (1794–1858), one of the celebrated operatic and concert bassos of the age. 82. **Lord Leighton . . . Watts,** Baron Frederick Leighton (1830–1896) and George F. Watts (1817–1904), noted English painters and sculptors.

of the highest value. In literature her interests were more restricted. She was devoted to Lord Tennyson; and, as the Prince Consort had admired George Eliot, she perused *Middlemarch:* she was disappointed. There is reason to believe, however, that the romances of another female writer, whose popularity among the humbler classes of Her Majesty's subjects was at one time enormous, secured, no less, the approval of Her Majesty. Otherwise she did not read very much.

Once, however, the Queen's attention was drawn to a publication which it was impossible for her to ignore. *The Greville Memoirs,* filled with a mass of historical information of extraordinary importance, but filled also with descriptions, which were by no means flattering, of George IV, William IV, and other royal persons, was brought out by Mr. Reeve. Victoria read the book, and was appalled. It was, she declared, a "dreadful and really scandalous book," and she could not say "how *horrified* and *indignant*" she was at Greville's "indiscretion, indelicacy, ingratitude towards friends, betrayal of confidence and shameful disloyalty towards his Sovereign." She wrote to Disraeli to tell him that in her opinion it was "*very important* that the book should be severely censured and discredited." "The tone in which he speaks of royalty," she added, "is unlike anything one sees in history even, and is most reprehensible." Her anger was directed with almost equal vehemence against Mr. Reeve for his having published "such an abominable book," and she charged Sir Arthur Helps to convey to him her deep displeasure. Mr. Reeve, however, was impenitent. When Sir Arthur told him that, in the Queen's opinion, "the book degraded royalty," he replied:

"Not at all; it elevates it by the contrast it offers between the present and the defunct state of affairs." But this adroit defense failed to make any impression upon Victoria; and Mr. Reeve, when he retired from the public service, did not receive the knighthood which custom entitled him to expect. Perhaps if the Queen had known how many caustic comments upon herself Mr. Reeve had quietly suppressed in the published *Memoirs,* she would have been almost grateful to him; but, in that case, what would she have said of Greville? Imagination boggles at the thought. As for more modern essays upon the same topic, Her Majesty, it is to be feared, would have characterized them as "not discreet."

But as a rule the leisure hours of that active life were occupied with recreations of a less intangible quality than the study of literature or the appreciation of art. Victoria was a woman not only of vast property but of innumerable possessions. She had inherited an immense quantity of furniture, of ornaments, of china, of plate, of valuable objects of every kind; her purchases, throughout a long life, made a formidable addition to these stores; and there flowed in upon her, besides, from every quarter of the globe, a constant stream of gifts. Over this enormous mass she exercised an unceasing and minute supervision, and the arrangement and the contemplation of it, in all its details, filled her with an intimate satisfaction. The collecting instinct has its roots in the very depths of human nature; and, in the case of Victoria, it seemed to owe its force to two of her dominating impulses—the intense sense, which had always been hers, of her own personality, and the craving which, growing with the years, had become in her old age almost an obsession, for fixity, for solidity, for the setting up of palpable barriers against the outrages of change and time. When she considered the multitudinous objects which belonged to her, or, better still, when, choosing out some section of them as the fancy took her, she actually savored the vivid richness of their individual qualities, she saw herself deliciously reflected from a million facets, felt herself magnified miraculously over a boundless area, and was well pleased. That was just as it should be; but then came the dismaying thought—every-

7. **female writer.** Strachey is not at all explicit at this point. Two of the most likely candidates for the title of most popular woman writer of the latter half of the century would be *Ouida* (pseudonym of Louise de la Ramée, 1839–1908) and Marie Corelli (1864–1924).   19. **Mr. Reeve.** *The Greville Memoirs* was the name given to the collection of diary- and journal-material written by Charles Cavendish Fulke Greville (1794–1865) and entrusted by him to the journalist Henry Reeve (1813–1895), to be published a reasonable time after Greville's death. In the memoirs are detailed, intimate accounts, of great value, covering the reigns of two of the most incompetent kings of recent British history and also the early reign of Victoria. Reeve published the book in separate parts (1875, 1885, and 1887).   35. **Sir Arthur Helps,** a clerk of the Privy Council and dilettante in literature, who helped to publish the addresses of the Prince Consort and the journals of Queen Victoria (1813–1875).

thing slips away, crumbles, vanishes; Sèvres dinner-services get broken; even golden basins go unaccountably astray; even one's self, with all the recollections and experiences that make up one's being, fluctuates, perishes, dissolves. . . . But no! It could not, should not be so! There should be no changes and no losses! Nothing should ever move—neither the past nor the present—and she herself least of all! And so the tenacious woman, hoarding her valuables, decreed their immortality with all the resolution of her soul. She would not lose one memory or one pin.

She gave orders that nothing should be thrown away—and nothing was. There, in drawer after drawer, in wardrobe after wardrobe, reposed the dresses of seventy years. But not only the dresses—the furs and the mantles and subsidiary frills and the muffs and the parasols and the bonnets—all were ranged in chronological order, dated and complete. A great cupboard was devoted to the dolls; in the china room at Windsor a special table held the mugs of her childhood, and her children's mugs as well. Mementoes of the past surrounded her in serried accumulations. In every room the tables were powdered thick with the photographs of relatives; their portraits, revealing them at all ages, covered the walls; their figures, in solid marble, rose up from pedestals, or gleamed from brackets in the form of gold and silver statuettes. The dead, in every shape—in miniatures, in porcelain, in enormous life-size oil-paintings—were perpetually about her. John Brown stood upon her writing-table in solid gold. Her favorite horses and dogs, endowed with a new durability, crowded round her footsteps. Sharp, in silver gilt, dominated the dinner table; Boy and Boz lay together among unfading flowers, in bronze. And it was not enough that each particle of the past should be given the stability of metal or of marble: the whole collection, in its arrangement, no less than its entity, should be immutably fixed. There might be additions, but there might never be alterations. No chintz might change, no carpet, no curtain, be replaced by another; or, if long use at last made it necessary, the stuffs and the patterns must be so identically reproduced that the keenest eye might not detect the difference. No new picture could be hung upon the walls at Windsor, for those already there had been put in their places by Albert, whose decisions were eternal. So, indeed, were Victoria's. To insure that they should be the aid of the camera was called in. Every single article in the Queen's possession was photographed from several points of view. These photographs were submitted to Her Majesty, and when, after careful inspection, she had approved of them, they were placed in a series of albums, richly bound. Then, opposite each photograph, an entry was made, indicating the number of the article, the number of the room in which it was kept, its exact position in the room and all its principal characteristics. The fate of every object which had undergone this process was henceforth irrevocably sealed. The whole multitude, once and for all, took up its steadfast station. And Victoria, with a gigantic volume or two of the endless catalogue always beside her, to look through, to ponder upon, to expatiate over, could feel, with a double contentment, that the transitoriness of this world had been arrested by the amplitude of her might.

Thus the collection, ever multiplying, ever encroaching upon new fields of consciousness, ever rooting itself more firmly in the depths of instinct, became one of the dominating influences of that strange existence. It was a collection not merely of things and of thoughts, but of states of mind and ways of living as well. The celebration of anniversaries grew to be an important branch of it—of birthdays and marriage days and death days, each of which demanded its appropriate feeling, which, in its turn, must be itself expressed in an appropriate outward form. And the form, of course—the ceremony of rejoicing or lamentation—was stereotyped with the rest: it was part of the collection. On a certain day, for instance, flowers must be strewn on John Brown's monument at Balmoral; and the date of the yearly departure for Scotland was fixed by that fact. Inevitably it was around the central circumstance of death—death, the final witness to human mutability—that these commemorative cravings clustered most thickly. Might not even death itself be humbled, if one could recall enough?—if one asserted, with a sufficiently passionate and reiterated emphasis, the eternity of love? Accordingly, every bed in which Victoria slept had attached to it, at the back, on the right-hand side, above the pillow, a photograph of the head and shoulders of Albert as he lay dead, surmounted by a wreath of immortelles. At Balmoral, where memories came crowding so closely, the solid signs of memory appeared in surprising profusion. Obelisks, pyramids, tombs, statues, cairns, and seats of inscribed granite, proclaimed Victoria's dedication to the dead. There, twice a year, on the days that followed her arrival, a solemn pilgrimage of inspection and meditation was performed. There, on August 26—Albert's birthday—at the foot of the bronze statue of him in Highland dress, the Queen, her family, her Court, her servants, and her tenantry, met together and in silence drank to the memory of the dead. In England the tokens of remembrance pullulated hardly less. Not a day passed without some addition to the multifold assemblage—a gold statuette of Ross, the piper—a life-sized marble group of Victoria and Albert, in medieval costume, inscribed upon the base with these words: "Allured to brighter worlds and led the way"—a granite slab in the shrubbery at Osborne, informing the visitor of "Waldmann: the very favorite little dachshund of Queen Victoria; who brought him from Baden, April, 1872; died, July 11, 1881."

At Frogmore, the great mausoleum, perpetually enriched, was visited almost daily by the Queen when the Court was at Windsor. But there was another, a more secret and a hardly less holy shrine. The suite of rooms which Albert had occupied in the Castle was kept forever shut away from the eyes of any save the most privileged. Within those precincts everything remained as it had been at the Prince's death; but the mysterious preoccupation of Victoria had commanded that her husband's clothing should be laid afresh, each evening, upon the bed, and that, each evening, the water should be set ready in the basin, as if he were still alive; and this incredible rite was performed with scrupulous regularity for nearly forty years.

Such was the inner worship; and still the flesh obeyed the spirit; still the daily hours of labor proclaimed Victoria's consecration of

30. **Frogmore**, near Windsor Castle, the site of the Mausoleum of the Prince Consort, Albert.

duty and to the ideal of the dead. Yet, with the years, the sense of self-sacrifice faded; the natural energies of that ardent being discharged themselves with satisfaction into the channel of public work; the love of business which, from her girlhood, had been strong within her, reasserted itself in all its vigor, and, in her old age, to have been cut off from her papers and her boxes would have been, not a relief, but an agony to Victoria. Thus, though toiling Ministers might sigh and suffer, the whole process of government continued, till the very end, to pass before her. Nor was that all; ancient precedent had made the validity of an enormous number of official transactions dependent upon the application of the royal sign-manual; and a great proportion of the Queen's working hours was spent in this mechanical task. Nor did she show any desire to diminish it. On the contrary, she voluntarily resumed the duty of signing commissions in the army, from which she had been set free by Act of Parliament, and from which, during the years of middle life, she had abstained. In no case would she countenance the proposal that she should use a stamp. But, at last, when the increasing pressure of business made the delays of the antiquated system intolerable, she consented that, for certain classes of documents, her oral sanction should be sufficient. Each paper was read aloud to her, and she said at the end "Approved." Often, for hours at a time, she would sit, with Albert's bust in front of her, while the word "Approved" issued at intervals from her lips. The word came forth with a majestic sonority; for her voice now—how changed from the silvery treble of her girlhood!—was a contralto, full and strong.

IV

The final years were years of apotheosis. In the dazzled imagination of her subjects Victoria soared aloft towards the regions of divinity through a nimbus of purest glory. Criticism fell dumb; deficiencies which, twenty years earlier, would have been universally admitted, were now as universally ignored. That the nation's idol was a very incomplete representative of the nation was a circumstance that was hardly noticed, and yet it was conspicuously true. For the vast changes which, out of the

England of 1837, had produced the England of 1897, seemed scarcely to have touched the Queen. The immense industrial development of the period, the significance of which had been so thoroughly understood by Albert, meant little indeed to Victoria. The amazing scientific movement, which Albert had appreciated no less, left Victoria perfectly cold. Her conception of the universe, and of man's place in it, and of the stupendous problems of nature and philosophy remained, throughout her life, entirely unchanged. Her religion was the religion which she had learnt from the Baroness Lehzen and the Duchess of Kent. Here, too, it might have been supposed that Albert's views might have influenced her. For Albert, in matters of religion, was advanced. Disbelieving altogether in evil spirits, he had had his doubts about the miracle of the Gadarene Swine. Stockmar, even, had thrown out, in a remarkable memorandum on the education of the Prince of Wales, the suggestion that while the child "must unquestionably be brought up in the creed of the Church of England," it might nevertheless be in accordance with the spirit of the times to exclude from his religious training the inculcation of a belief in "the supernatural doctrines of Christianity." This, however, would have been going too far; and all the royal children were brought up in complete orthodoxy. Anything else would have grieved Victoria, though her own conceptions of the orthodox were not very precise. But her nature, in which imagination and subtlety held so small a place, made her instinctively recoil from the intricate ecstasies of High Anglicanism; and she seemed to feel most at home in the simple faith of the Presbyterian Church of Scotland. This was what might have been expected; for Lehzen was the daughter of a Lutheran pastor, and the Lutherans and the Presbyterians have much in common. For many years Dr. Norman Macleod, an innocent Scotch minister, was her principal spiritual adviser;

and, when he was taken from her, she drew much comfort from quiet chats about life and death with the cottagers at Balmoral. Her piety, absolutely genuine, found what it wanted in the sober exhortations of old John Grant and the devout saws of Mrs. P. Farquharson. They possessed the qualities, which, as a child of fourteen, she had so sincerely admired in the Bishop of Chester's "Exposition of the Gospel of St. Matthew"; they were "just plain and comprehensible and full of truth and good feeling." The Queen, who gave her name to the Age of Mill and of Darwin, never got any further than that.

From the social movements of her time Victoria was equally remote. Towards the smallest no less than towards the greatest changes she remained inflexible. During her youth and middle age smoking had been forbidden in polite society, and so long as she lived she would not withdraw her anathema against it. Kings might protest; bishops and ambassadors, invited to Windsor, might be reduced, in the privacy of their bedrooms, to lie full-length upon the floor and smoke up the chimney—the interdict continued. It might have been supposed that a female sovereign would have lent her countenance to one of the most vital of all the reforms to which her epoch gave birth—the emancipation of women—but, on the contrary, the mere mention of such a proposal sent the blood rushing to her head. In 1870, her eye having fallen upon the report of a meeting in favor of Women's Suffrage, she wrote to Mr. Martin in royal rage—"The Queen is most anxious to enlist every one who can speak or write to join in checking this mad, wicked folly of 'Woman's Rights,' with all its attendant horrors, on which her poor feeble sex is bent, forgetting every sense of womanly feeling and propriety. Lady —— ought to get a *good whipping*. It is a subject which makes the Queen so furious that she cannot contain herself. God created men and women different—then let them remain each in their own position. Tennyson has some beautiful lines on the difference of men and women in 'The Princess.' Woman

---

13. **Baroness Lehzen,** Louise Lehzen of Coburg, Victoria's girlhood governess. 14. **Duchess of Kent,** Victoria's mother (1786–1861). 19. **Gadarene Swine.** Cf. Mark 5:1–15, the account of how Jesus drove from a "possessed" man a legion of unclean spirits, which entered into a herd of swine; the swine ran to the sea and were drowned. 20. **Stockmar,** Christian Friedrich Stockmar (1787–1863), a German diplomatist in the service of Prince Albert, who was adviser to both him and Queen Victoria in the early years of their married life.

78. **Mr. Martin,** Leopold C. Martin, a miscellaneous writer and journalist, whose wife was the sister of Sir John Tenniel, the celebrated cartoonist for *Punch* and illustrator of Lewis Carroll's *Alice in Wonderland* and *Through the Looking-Glass*.

would become the most hateful, heartless, and disgusting of human beings were she allowed to unsex herself; and where would be the protection which man was intended to give the weaker sex? The Queen is sure that Mrs. Martin agrees with her." The argument was irrefutable; Mrs. Martin agreed; and yet the canker spread.

In another direction Victoria's comprehension of the spirit of her age has been constantly asserted. It was for long the custom for courtly historians and polite politicians to compliment the Queen upon the correctness of her attitude towards the Constitution. But such praises seem hardly to be justified by the facts. In her later years Victoria more than once alluded with regret to her conduct during the Bedchamber crisis, and let it be understood that she had grown wiser since. Yet in truth it is difficult to trace any fundamental change either in her theory or her practice in constitutional matters throughout her life. The same despotic and personal spirit which led her to break off the negotiations with Peel is equally visible in her animosity towards Palmerston, in her threats of abdication to Disraeli, and in her desire to prosecute the Duke of Westminster for attending a meeting upon Bulgarian atrocities. The complex and delicate principles of the Constitution cannot be said to have come within the compass of her mental faculties; and in the actual developments which it underwent during her reign she played a passive part. From 1840 to 1861 the power of the Crown steadily increased in England; from 1861 to 1901 it steadily declined. The first process was due to the influence of the Prince Consort, the second to that of a series of great Ministers. During the first Victoria was in effect a mere accessory; during the second the threads of power, which Albert had so laboriously collected, inevitably fell from her hands into the vigorous grasp of Mr. Gladstone, Lord Beaconsfield, and Lord Salisbury. Perhaps, ab-

sorbed as she was in routine, and difficult as she found it to distinguish at all clearly between the trivial and the essential, she was only dimly aware of what was happening. Yet, at the end of her reign, the Crown was weaker than at any other time in English history. Paradoxically enough, Victoria received the highest eulogiums for assenting to a political evolution, which, had she completely realized its import, would have filled her with supreme displeasure.

Nevertheless it must not be supposed that she was a second George III. Her desire to impose her will, vehement as it was, and unlimited by any principle, was yet checked by a certain shrewdness. She might oppose her Ministers with extraordinary violence; she might remain utterly impervious to arguments and supplications; the pertinacity of her resolution might seem to be unconquerable; but, at the very last moment of all, her obstinacy would give way. Her innate respect and capacity for business, and perhaps, too, the memory of Albert's scrupulous avoidance of extreme courses, prevented her from ever entering an *impasse*. By instinct she understood when the facts were too much for her, and to them she invariably yielded. After all, what else could she do?

But if, in all these ways, the Queen and her epoch were profoundly separated, the points of contact between them also were not few. Victoria understood very well the meaning and the attractions of power and property, and in such learning the English nation, too, had grown to be more and more proficient. During the last fifteen years of the reign—for the short Liberal Administration of 1892 was a mere interlude—imperialism was the dominant creed of the country. It was Victoria's as well. In this direction, if in no other, she had allowed her mind to develop. Under Disraeli's tutelage the British Dominions over the seas had come to mean much more to her than ever before, and, in particular, she had grown enamored of the East. The thought of India fascinated her; she set to, and learnt a little Hindustani; she engaged some Indian servants, who became her inseparable attendants, and one of whom, Munshi Abdul Karim, eventually almost succeeded to the position which had once been John Brown's. At the same time, the imperialist temper of the nation invested her office with a

17. **Bedchamber crisis.** Shortly after her marriage to the Prince Consort, Victoria gave herself up to domestic life and yet attempted to hold the reins of government and dictate to her ministers. It was Albert himself who managed to show Victoria the despotic nature of her attitude. 24. **Peel,** Sir Robert Peel (1788–1850), once prime minister (1834–35) and an exceptionally able administrator of internal affairs. 25. **Palmerston,** Viscount Palmerston, prime minister (1855–65), an uncompromising nationalist and rather a strong-armed diplomat.

new significance exactly harmonizing with her own inmost proclivities. The English polity was in the main a common-sense structure; but there was always a corner in it where common-sense could not enter—where, somehow or other, the ordinary measurements were not applicable and the ordinary rules did not apply. So our ancestors had laid it down, giving scope, in their wisdom, to that mystical element which, as it seems, can never quite be eradicated from the affairs of men. Naturally it was in the Crown that the mysticism of the English polity was concentrated—the Crown, with its venerable antiquity, its sacred associations, its imposing spectacular array. But, for nearly two centuries, common-sense had been predominant in the great building, and the little, unexplored, inexplicable corner had attracted small attention. Then, with the rise of imperialism, there was a change. For imperialism is a faith as well as a business; as it grew, the mysticism in English public life grew with it; and simultaneously a new importance began to attach to the Crown. The need for a symbol —a symbol of England's might, of England's worth, of England's extraordinary and mysterious destiny—became felt more urgently than ever before. The Crown was that symbol: and the Crown rested upon the head of Victoria. Thus it happened that while by the end of the reign the power of the sovereign had appreciably diminished, the prestige of the sovereign had enormously grown.

Yet this prestige was not merely the outcome of public changes; it was an intensely personal matter, too. Victoria was the Queen of England, the Empress of India, the quintessential pivot round which the whole magnificent machine was revolving—but how much more besides! For one thing, she was of a great age— an almost indispensable qualification for popularity in England. She had given proof of one of the most admired characteristics of the race —persistent vitality. She had reigned for sixty years, and she was not out. And then, she was a character. The outlines of her nature were firmly drawn, and, even through the mists which envelop royalty, clearly visible. In the popular imagination her familiar figure filled, with satisfying ease, a distinct and memorable

place. It was, besides, the kind of figure which naturally called forth the admiring sympathy of the great majority of the nation. Goodness they prized above every other human quality; and Victoria, who had said that she would be good at the age of twelve, had kept her word. Duty, conscience, morality—yes! in the light of those high beacons the Queen had always lived. She had passed her days in work and not in pleasure—in public responsibilities and family cares. The standard of solid virtue which had been set up so long ago amid the domestic happiness of Osborne had never been lowered for an instant. For more than half a century no divorced lady had approached the precincts of the Court. Victoria, indeed, in her enthusiasm for wifely fidelity, had laid down a still stricter ordinance: she frowned severely upon any widow who married again. Considering that she herself was the offspring of a widow's second marriage, this prohibition might be regarded as an eccentricity; but, no doubt, it was an eccentricity on the right side. The middle classes, firm in the triple brass of their respectability, rejoiced with a special joy over the most respectable of Queens. They almost claimed her, indeed, as one of themselves; but this would have been an exaggeration. For, though many of her characteristics were most often found among the middle classes, in other respects—in her manners, for instance—Victoria was decidedly aristocratic. And, in one important particular, she was neither aristocratic nor middle-class: her attitude toward herself was simply regal.

Such qualities were obvious and important; but, in the impact of a personality, it is something deeper, something fundamental and common to all its qualities, that really tells. In Victoria, it is easy to discern the nature of this underlying element: it was a peculiar sincerity. Her truthfulness, her single-mindedness, the vividness of her emotions and her unrestrained expression of them, were the varied forms which this central characteristic assumed. It was her sincerity which gave her at once her impressiveness, her charm, and her absurdity. She moved through life with the imposing certitude of one to whom concealment was impossible—either towards her surroundings or towards herself. There she was, all of her—the Queen of England, complete and obvious; the world might take her or leave her; she had nothing more to show, or to explain, or to modify; and, with her peerless carriage, she swept along her path. And not only was concealment out of the question; reticence, reserve, even dignity itself, as it sometimes seemed, might be very well dispensed with. As Lady Lyttleton said: "There is a transparency in her truth that is very striking—not a shade of exaggeration in describing feelings or facts; like very few other people I ever knew. Many may be as true, but I think it goes often along with some reserve. She talks all out; just as it is, no more and no less." She talked all out; and she wrote all out, too. Her letters, in the surprising jet of their expression, remind one of a turned-on tap. What is within pours forth in an immediate, spontaneous rush. Her utterly unliterary style has at least the merit of being a vehicle exactly suited to her thoughts and feelings; and even the platitude of her phraseology carries with it a curiously personal flavor. Undoubtedly it was through her writings that she touched the heart of the public. Not only in her *Highland Journals,* where the mild chronicle of her private proceedings was laid bare without a trace either of affectation or of embarrassment, but also in those remarkable messages to the nation which, from time to time, she published in the newspapers, her people found her very close to them indeed. They felt instinctively Victoria's irresistible sincerity, and they responded. And in truth it was an endearing trait.

The personality and the position, too—the wonderful combination of them—that, perhaps, was what was finally fascinating in the case. The little old lady, with her white hair and her plain mourning clothes, in her wheeled chair or her donkey-carriage—one saw her so; and then—close behind—with their immediate suggestion of singularity, of mystery, and of power —the Indian servants. That was the familiar vision, and it was admirable; but, at chosen moments, it was right that the widow of Windsor should step forth apparent Queen. The last and the most glorious of such occasions was the Jubilee of 1897. Then, as the splendid procession passed along, escorting Victoria through the thronged reechoing streets of London on her progress of thanksgiving in St. Paul's Cathedral, the greatness of her realm and the adoration of her subjects blazed out together. The tears welled to her eyes, and, while the multitude roared round her, "How kind they are to me! How kind they are!" she repeated over and over again. That night her message flew over the Empire: "From my heart I thank my beloved people. May God bless them!" The long journey was nearly done. But the traveler, who had come so far, and through such strange experiences, moved on with the old unfaltering step. The girl, the wife, the aged woman, were the same: vitality, conscientiousness, pride, and simplicity were hers to the latest hour.

X. The End

The evening had been golden; but, after all, the day was to close in cloud and tempest. Imperial needs, imperial ambitions, involved the country in the South African War. There were checks, reverses, bloody disasters; for a moment the nation was shaken, and the public distresses were felt with intimate solicitude by the Queen. But her spirit was high, and neither her courage nor her confidence wavered for a moment. Throwing herself heart and soul into the struggle, she labored with redoubled vigor, interested herself in every detail of the hostilities, and sought by every means in her power to render service to the national cause. In April, 1900, when she was in her eighty-first year, she made the extraordinary decision to abandon her annual visit to the South of France, and to go instead to Ireland, which had provided a particularly large number of recruits to the armies in the field. She stayed for three weeks in Dublin, driving through the streets, in spite of the warnings of her advisers, without an armed escort; and the visit was a complete success. But, in the course of it, she began, for the first time, to show signs of the fatigue of age.

72. **South African War,** generally known as the Boer War.

For the long strain and the unceasing anxiety, brought by the war, made themselves felt at last. Endowed by nature with a robust constitution, Victoria, though in periods of depression she had sometimes supposed herself an invalid, had in reality throughout her life enjoyed remarkably good health. In her old age, she had suffered from a rheumatic stiffness of the joints, which had necessitated the use of a
10 stick, and, eventually, a wheeled chair; but no other ailments attacked her, until, in 1898, her eyesight began to be affected by incipient cataract. After that, she found reading more and more difficult, though she could still sign her name, and even, with some difficulty, write letters. In the summer of 1900, however, more serious symptoms appeared. Her memory, in whose strength and precision she had so long prided herself, now sometimes deserted her;
20 there was a tendency toward aphasia; and, while no specific disease declared itself, by the autumn there were unmistakable signs of a general physical decay. Yet, even in these last months, the strain of iron held firm. The daily work continued; nay, it actually increased; for the Queen, with an astonishing pertinacity, insisted upon communicating personally with an ever-growing multitude of men and women who had suffered through the war.
30 By the end of the year the last remains of her ebbing strength had almost deserted her; and through the early days of the opening century it was clear that her dwindling forces were only kept together by an effort of will. On January 14, she had at Osborne an hour's interview with Lord Roberts, who had returned victorious from South Africa a few days before. She inquired with acute anxiety into all the details of the war; she appeared to sus-
40 tain the exertion successfully; but, when the audience was over, there was a collapse. On the following day her medical attendants recognized that the state was hopeless; and yet, for two days more, the indomitable spirit fought on; for two days more she discharged

the duties of a Queen of England. But after that there was an end of working; and then, and not till then, did the last optimism of those about her break down. The brain was failing, and life was gently slipping away. Her family 50 gathered round her; for a little more she lingered, speechless and apparently insensible; and, on January 22, 1901, she died.

When, two days previously, the news of the approaching end had been made public, astonished grief had swept over the country. It appeared as if some monstrous reversal of the course of nature was about to take place. The vast majority of her subjects had never known a time when Queen Victoria had not been 60 reigning over them. She had become an indissoluble part of their whole scheme of things, and that they were about to lose her appeared a scarcely possible thought. She herself, as she lay blind and silent, seemed to those who watched her to be divested of all thinking—to have glided already, unawares, into oblivion. Yet, perhaps, in the secret chambers of consciousness, she had her thoughts, too. Perhaps her fading mind called up once more the shad- 70 ows of the past to float before it, and retraced, for the last time, the vanished visions of that long history—passing back and back, through the cloud of years, to older and ever older memories—to the spring woods at Osborne, so full of primroses for Lord Beaconsfield—to Lord Palmerston's queer clothes and high demeanor, and Albert's face under the green lamp, and Albert's first stag at Balmoral, and Albert in his blue and silver uniform, and the 80 Baron coming in through a doorway, and Lord M. dreaming at Windsor with the rooks cawing in the elm-trees, and the Archbishop of Canterbury on his knees in the dawn, and the old King's turkey-cock ejaculations, and Uncle Leopold's soft voice at Claremont, and Lehzen with the globes, and her mother's feathers sweeping down towards her, and a great old repeater-watch of her father's in its tortoise-shell case, and a yellow rug, and some friendly 90 flounces of sprigged muslin, and the trees and the grass at Kensington.

36. **Lord Roberts,** Frederick S. R. Roberts (1832–1914), who had distinguished himself in the Afghan War of 1879–80, was the most successful leader of the British armed forces in the Boer War and was rewarded by a peerage.

85. **old King's.** The sovereign referred to is William IV of England, Victoria's predecessor on the throne.

PHILIP GUEDALLA

One of the most graceful and pleasing of modern historians, Philip Guedalla combined the literary style of a well-educated Englishman with the romantic imagination of the Latin, for he was of Spanish extraction on his father's side. He was born in London on March 12, 1889, attended Rugby and then Balliol College, Oxford, and distinguished himself from the beginning as a scholar. In 1911 he was president of the Oxford Union Society, which was a virtual acknowledgment that he was considered the best debater at Oxford. His taste was not all for history and dialectics, however; while he was at the university he published two works, *Ignes Fatui: a book of parodies* (1911), and *Metri Gratia*, a more serious effort in both verse and prose (1911). In the following year he graduated with a First in Modern History and in 1913 took a degree of Master of Arts. After leaving Oxford he assumed at once the profession of barrister at the Inner Temple in London; and when the First World War broke out he served his country and his profession at one and the same time, first as legal adviser to the Contracts Department, the War Office, and the Ministry of Munitions, and then as an organizer and later a secretary of the Flax Control Board (1917–20). Even during these busy years he managed to write a little, notably a history, *The Partition of Europe: 1715–1815* (1914), and after the war he resumed his writing, but it was not until 1923 that he retired from the legal profession to devote his time to composition. Subsequently he held various business connections and was a director of the Ibero-American Institute of Great Britain, as well as a member of the Cinematographic Films Council on the British Board of Trade. Several times he stood unsuccessfully for Parliament. The greater part of his activity, however, was devoted to a copious stream of historical writings mingled with occasional literary criticism and miscellaneous essays.

Following the close of the First World War, Guedalla produced two essay collections, *Supers and Supermen* (1920) and *The Industrial Future* (1921). But these were not in his characteristic vein. That vein he struck, rather, when he turned to straightforward historiography in *The Second Empire* (1922), which is one of the best present-day accounts of nineteenth-century France. Scattered through his writings are shorter biographical sketches and occasional lectures. The full list is too long to give here, but it includes *Masters and Men* (1923); *A Gallery* (1924), a long series of sketches of prominent authors and statesmen either contemporary or near-contemporary; *A Council of Industry* (1925); *Napoleon and Palestine* (1925), the story of one of the early campaigns of Napoleon; *Independence Day* (1926; American title, *Fathers of the Revolution*), two extremely sympathetic studies of the American struggle for independence; *Palmerston* (1926), probably the most scholarly of his full-length biographies; *Conquistador* (1926), a descriptive account of the Americas, subtitled "an American fantasia"; *Gladstone and Palmerston* (1928); *Bonnet and Shawl* (1928), a series of short biographies of famous wives in the nineteenth century, including the Mesdames Carlyle, Gladstone, Arnold, Disraeli, Tennyson, and Palmerston among historical figures, and the mythical wives of Henry James, Swinburne, and the Goncourt brothers as fictional characters; *The Missing Muse* (1929); *The Duke* (1931), generally known in the United States as *Wellington*; *Argentine Tango* (1932), in which his love of the Spanish-American finds brilliant expression; *The Queen and Mr. Gladstone* (1933); *The Hundred Days* (1934), the tale of Napoleon from his return from Elba to Waterloo; and *The Hundred Years* (1936), one of his finest performances, embracing the history of the Western World, as exemplified by its critical years, from the accession of Victoria in 1837 to the days of the growing international tension in 1937. To these should be added in particular *The Hundredth Year* (1939), a special study of the year 1936, in which the spotlight is played upon King Edward VIII of England, and a wartime (1941) biography of Winston Churchill. Guedalla died on December 13, 1944.

The impressive list of his writings shows precisely where Guedalla excelled as a historian. Few men of his time knew more about the nineteenth century, that remarkable—and greatly underestimated—century which lies behind our contemporary era. But there is more to Guedalla's work than a masterful grasp of facts and a perception of the currents of human activities. His manner of presenting his materials is extremely effective—suave, polished, concentrated, ironic, yet completely understanding in reference to the human motives, the failings, and the strengths that underlie all history. His romantic coloring, to be sure, does not recommend itself to the objective historian, who complains often that Guedalla is not accurate; but few argue against the essential truth of his overall picture. But perhaps it is better to let Guedalla speak for himself. The historian, he averred,

is, when all is said, one cell in the world's memory of itself; he, too, like the lamented Proust, rides off *à la recherche du temps perdu*. And if the quest is to succeed, he must reconstruct the past, set old breezes stirring once again, and—most elusive miracle of all—bring the dead back to life. His business is to write about dead men; but if he is to do his duty, he should remember that they were not always dead. For he is not concerned to embalm them, but to resurrect, to set them moving, catch the tone of their voices, tilt of their heads, and posture of the once living men. . . . The past should, for the historian, be his present. He must never write from the angle of today, but almost always from the angle of contemporaries with the events that he describes. . . . When his reader is set dreaming of the past, the historian has done his work, only provided that the dream be true. For then *temps perdu* has become *temps retrouvé*, and the quest is ended.

from The Hundred Years

1861

1. ST. PETERSBURG

THE RUSSIAN winter was half over; and the rust-red palace by the Neva still faced the yellow amphitheatre of the General Staff across the square. The rank classicism of a bronze quadriga in sharp outline on the pale February sky crowned their building and celebrated Czar Alexander's victories over Napoleon, whilst in the rooms downstairs his successor's officers considered the best method of repairing the less satisfactory operations of the Crimean War. The last indignities endured by Sebastopol were five years behind them now. The gorges of the Caucasus, where their advancing Cossacks slowly shepherded the last defenders towards the south, fixed their attention; and they considered the reports of columns operating far to the south-east in Turkestan towards Tashkent, as Russia developed her slow southward thrust into the sun. The ministry next door, where the spectacled Prince Gortchakoff peered at draft protocols, was busy with the last finesse of diplomacy. But behind the rich rococo of the Winter Palace their imperial master's mind was less occupied with diplomatic fencing or the unhurrying advance

"1861" from *The Hundred Years*, by Philip Guedalla, copyright 1936, 1937 by Doubleday, Doran & Company, Inc.
2. rust-red . . . Neva, the famous Winter Palace of the Czars, situated on the left bank of the Neva River. **5. quadriga,** in Roman art a figure of a car or chariot drawn by four horses abreast. **7. Czar . . . Napoleon.** The campaign of Napoleon against Czar Alexander I of Russia in 1812 ended disastrously for the French emperor. He was forced to retreat from Moscow in the dead of winter and lost a large part of his army in the process. **10. Crimean War,** a war undertaken against the Russians by the allied British and French forces. Its chief purpose was to prevent the spread of Russia into Asia Minor, the domination of Turkey by that country, and the consequent threat to the colonial aspirations of Britain and France, at that time the two most powerful nations in Europe. The war began in 1854 and lasted until the Treaty of Paris (1856). Russia was temporarily checked and forbidden to fortify the Black Sea ports or to attempt any control of Turkey. As a result she pushed her expansion southward and eastward into the Caucasian mountains and Turkestan, only to find herself, at the end of the nineteenth century, threatening the frontiers of British India. **21. Gortchakoff,** Alexander Michaelovitch Gortchakoff (1798–1883), at this time minister of foreign affairs for Russia; later he became chancellor (prime minister) of the Russian empire and was until the advent of Bismarck the most influential figure in European diplomacy. **23. imperial master,** Alexander II, Czar of Russia from 1855 to 1881. He was much the most far-seeing and well-intentioned of the latter-day Romanoffs; but ironically enough he was the only one to be assassinated by revolutionists until the shooting of Nicholas II and his family in 1918.

of Russian armies into Central Asia than with the haunting problems of his own dominions. They had haunted him since boyhood, when he learnt that there was nothing in the Bible that could be held to justify the institution of slavery as it was practised by his father's subjects. This conclusion was not displaced by anything that he had seen of them upon his early travels; and when he succeeded to the vast, discouraged empire while British guns were thundering outside Sebastopol, he faced the problem with a deep conviction that Emancipation must be conceded freely from above, unless it was to come chaotically from below. For it was equally repugnant to his conscience and to the march of history that a contemporary of Queen Victoria should reign over forty-seven million white slaves. He showed the way by the prompt liberation of all human beings owned by the Crown. But Russia still remained a nation of slave-owners, no less than the enlightened citizens beyond the Atlantic in those Southern States of which (to their dismay) Mr. Lincoln had just been elected President. For private property in human beings persisted on the everlasting Russian plain no less than in Virginia; and in 1861, by an odd chance, the destiny of both slave-states was settled.

There is an unchanging rhythm in Russian history, which compels an alternation of unsuccessful wars abroad with uncomfortable jerks at home. For Russian wars are mostly unsuccessful; and they are usually followed by an acceleration of internal politics that leads to grave events. A military empire can scarcely thrive upon an unsustaining diet of defeat; and as Russian armies were generally beaten except when they were used against their fellow-subjects or a backward race, their operations rarely added to the glory of the imperial régime. For nothing is more undeserved than the respectful apprehension with which the world has long consented to regard the Russians as a military menace, since their operations normally exhibit a devastating incompetence. At intervals in the last hundred years the Russian state embarked upon a war; and since it was quite unsupported by the requisite efficiency in arms, the war almost invariably ended in disaster. This recurrent accident was followed in

each case by an unpleasant quickening of its domestic discontents; and to each military defeat succeeded an uncomfortable period of civil strain, until the final shock was so severe as to destroy the whole fabric of the nation's life. In spite of a delusive air of massive strength, that rhythm of alternating defeat and disorder was invariable. The tread of Russian armies seemed to shake the ground of Europe, and neighbours muttered nervously about 'the Colossus of the North.' But each war ended in defeat; and each defeat brought revolution nearer.

In 1861 a kindly ruler had anticipated the unrest that was bound to follow the discouragement of the Crimean War by launching an immense reform; and whilst officials struggled with the endless detail of Emancipation, the Czar plodded up and down his territories to stimulate the better impulses of his slave-holding subjects. They stood in ample need of such encouragement, since the impending loss of all their human capital formed anything but an attractive prospect for those cheerful *boyars*, whose fantastic opulence had made them the *rastas* of the first years of the nineteenth century; and their enthusiasm for the emancipation of their serfs was scarcely equal to their royal master's. But he persisted bravely, making speeches, reading memoranda, travelling, arguing with unenthusiastic ministers, until Emancipation gradually emerged from the uncertain hands of drafting committees on to the table of the Council of State. Its form was not ideal, since the new freedom of the Russian peasant was unaccompanied by any corresponding distribution of the Russian land, and the vast land-hunger of forty million rustics remained unsatisfied. But as his pen traced Alexander's signature beneath the Rescript of Emancipation on a winter day in 1861, the Russian Empire moved slowly forward towards freedom. Their liberation was not yet complete; and the inadequacy of the step may have been detected by the curl of a class-conscious lip, since abject poverty persisted

75. **boyars**, members of the Russian aristocracy next to the ruling family. As a recognized unit they were abolished by Peter the Great in the eighteenth century, but the term is used here generally for the land-owning aristocrats. 77. **rastas**. The term is used in general for any new-rich aristocracy; here, however, it is virtually synonymous with the *boyars* just described.

155

in the place from which slavery had been removed. But when the Czar's hand lifted from
the paper, there were no more serfs in Russia,
though there were not yet free men. For beyond the palace windows the Fortress of St.
Peter and St. Paul still lifted a slim, gilded
finger skywards in its eternal warning.

2. CHARLESTON, S. C.

A low outline lay off the shore. Beyond the
city spires and warehouses, beyond the watch-
10 ing houses on the Battery where all Charleston
strolled on cool evenings it lay like a dismasted
ship across the harbour mouth. Inland the little
balconies behind their blinds surveyed the
shaded alleys of the town, and tall, pillared
porches beneath the empty grace of a white
pediment withdrew with dignity behind the
rusted tracery of iron gates to dream of a lost
age among the flowers or to look bravely out
across the water, as the Ashley River crept
20 past Charleston to the sea. The spring tides set
the palmetto swamps whispering up-river; and
shrouded trees along the country roads were
veiled in a dim fog of hanging moss or shadowed an unlikely blaze of flowers, where a
gentle angle of the river elbowed an incomparable garden. The bright flowers burned in
the Carolina spring; gray moss hung dimly
from the live-oaks; and at Charleston, where
the hours struck slowly from St. Philip's and
30 St. Michael's, the unpleasant outline of the fort
hung midway between sea and sky.

It hung there shadowing their world, an angular reminder, as the Stars and Stripes ran up
each morning on Fort Sumter's flagstaff, that
the United States continued to exist, whatever Southern eloquence might say; and all the
lightnings of that fatal gift played round the
uneasy question. It was an awkward problem,
since there were other forts in Charleston Har-
40 bour and they flew another flag. For South
Carolina in solemn session at St. Andrew's Hall

5. **Fortress . . . St. Paul,** the great cathedral founded in 1703
by Peter the Great.   29. **St. Philip's and St. Michael's,**
two famous Episcopal churches in Charleston.   41. **St. Andrew's Hall . . . chaperons.** St. Andrew's Hall in Charleston
was the scene of the many balls and concerts offered by the
St. Cecelia Society of that city. The hall itself was originally
the headquarters of the St. Andrew Society, one of the oldest
benevolent societies in the American colonies. In this hall on
December 20, 1860 the South Carolina legislature passed a
declaration of secession from the Federal Union.

upon the velvet chairs sacred at other times to
Charleston chaperons had seceded from the
Union. Their reasons were a shade obscure. A
growing feeling that the South was challenged
in its age-long mastery of the United States
disturbed them. It was unthinkable that regions which had provided Presidents and ministers in such profusion should be outnumbered
in the nation. Their sons had been its leaders 50
for so long; the Senate was their private forum
and West Point their training school; they officered its army, made its laws, and commanded
its ships. Their self-esteem was pardonable since
the country was beyond a doubt their United
States. But would it always be? That was the
disturbing question; and the uncomfortable
feeling stole through the South that the United
States were not so safe as they had been for
Southern elements. The Union grew less con- 60
genial, as its balance was disturbed by immigration and the thrust of its new populations
towards the West. Industrial expansion in the
North imposed new fiscal policies, in which
the needs of Southern cotton-growers were not
the sole consideration. For the United States
were changing fast; and it was highly doubtful
to the Southern mind how long the country
would continue to be their United States.

Besides, an irritating tendency of Northern 70
thought and speech had dared to question the
sole basis of the South's existence. They were
a community of cotton-growers living by slave
labour; and the noisy challenge of the North
was too threatening to be ignored, since slavery was the foundation of their economics, and
the whole life of the South hung by a thread
of cotton. The Northern challenge was anything but academic, as it took the form of
Abolitionist corroborees, at which philanthro- 80
pists of either sex, discarding all restraints of
courtesy or fact, lashed one another into par-
oxysms of denunciation that left the South,
never deficient in repartee, under the dangerous impression that a fair proportion of its fellow-citizens were "hot as the hellish passions of
their own black hearts, foul as streams from
the sewers of Pandemonium." This duel of
abuse, unpromising for the prospects of national harmony, passed from the platform into 90
politics; and a long struggle opened on the

thorny topics of escaping slaves, State jurisdiction, and the future of slavery in the new
Territories, culminating in the demented heroism of John Brown's half-witted foray at Harper's Ferry.

But the gravest consequence of the protracted controversy was a growing sense of
isolation in the South. Its apologists were conscientiously instructed that "the rest of Chris-
10 tendom stands united against us, and are almost unanimous in pronouncing a verdict of
condemnation"; its bread-winners believed that
they were bound to live by means of which
their fellow-countrymen could not approve;
and, human perversity being what it was, the
Southern mind sought compensation for this
disparagement in a vast expansion of Southern
self-esteem. For if they had been proud before,
they were ten times prouder now. Always ro-
20 mantic, the Southern mind had long been subject to illusions as to the aristocratic nature of
its origins and way of life. Watering a tenacious Cavalier tradition with a minimum of
Cavalier blood, it was always prone to see
a belle in every woman and a gallant gentleman in every man. An allied hallucination implied that the ownership of land was in some
occult way a patent of nobility; and this, once
predicted, entitled land-owners to contemn the
30 base commercial classes of the North in favour of *independent* South Carolina *country
gentlemen,* the nearest to *noblemen* of any
possible class in America." Their reading served
to add fuel to this fire, since it was said that
they absorbed vast quantities of fiction from
the chivalrous pen of Walter Scott, imported to
the South in car-load lots; and gentlemen in
pleasant houses on the Ashley River began to
see themselves as belted knights who might be
40 called upon at any moment to defend the Holy
Sepulchre against the paynim hosts.

Few moods are more unfriendly to clear
thinking than a crusading temper; and as the
South grew more self-conscious, it was fortified
by the last absurdity of all, race-theory. For,

exasperated by Yankee self-righteousness and
the facile caricature of *Uncle Tom's Cabin,* it
was not content to tell the North that its
"priesthood prostitutes itself to a level with the
blackguard, and enters the field of secular poli- 50
tics, in the spirit of a beer-house bully," adding
without unnecessary chivalry that Northern
womanhood, "deserting their nurseries, stroll
over the country as politico-moral reformers,
delivering lewd lectures upon the beauties of
free-love or spiritualism, or writing yellow-back
literature, so degraded in taste, so prurient in
passion, so false in fact, so wretched in execution, and so vitiating to the morals of mothers
in the land, as almost to force them to bring 60
up daughters without virtue and sons without
bravery." But Southern vanity found a more
convincing explanation of its fatal disagree-
ment with the North, since it began to be convinced that "the Cavaliers, Jacobites, and Hu-
guenots, who settled the South, naturally hate,
condemn, and despise the Puritans who settled
the North. The former are master races; the
latter a slave race, descendants of the Saxon
serfs." Pursuing their researches, Southern gen- 70
ealogists detected a monopoly of Norman
blood among themselves; and where Norman
blood was present, it was pardonable to expect
a Norman Conquest, which might take the
form either of regenerated United States or
of "a vast, opulent, happy and glorious slave-
holding Republic throughout tropical America." Such were the unhealthy dreams engendered in the South by Northern disapproval
and an unpleasant sense of isolation.   80

These tendencies were deepened and accelerated by the Presidential election of 1860,
which emphasised the shrinkage of their influence by sending Lincoln to the White House.
The South was horrified; and the wild diagnosis of a Richmond journal informed thoughtful
Virginians that "with Lincoln comes something
worse than slang, rowdyism, brutality, and all
moral filth; something worse than the rag and
tag of Western grog-shops and Yankee facto- 90
ries. . . . With all those comes the daring and

---

24. **Cavalier blood.** The Carolinas trace their origin from the
Cavalier supporters of King Charles I of England, and the
king's name is in the name of the colonies. Actually, however,
there was a large influx of Huguenot and other stocks later.

65. **Jacobites,** the name given to the supporters of the Stuarts
after the abdication of James II of England (1688); the word
is derived from *Jacobus,* Latin for *James.*

reckless leader of Abolitionists." Before that prospect the last thread of Southern self-restraint snapped, and South Carolina seceded from the Union. Its life had always been a little isolated, and now the isolation was past bearing. So the Palmetto flag was substituted for the Stars and Stripes; and up-country gentlemen came riding into town, prepared for knightly deeds. They drilled with gusto, though most Southerners believed that there would be no fighting. For Southern honour had been satisfied by secession; and if Southern honour had been satisfied, there was no more to be said. The North was far away, and Northern honour was less susceptible. Indeed, it had already survived a shot fired upon its flag by eager Southerners, as a Federal supply ship came steaming into Charleston Harbour with stores for the little garrison. But it was always possible that the North might entertain a preference for the continuance of the United States, though the Palmetto flag waved gaily over Charleston; and the unpleasant outline of Fort Sumter, vaguely seen across three miles of water, hung midway between sea and sky.

It shadowed Charleston; and it shadowed Washington as well, since the national situation was full of explosive possibilities so long as an isolated harbour fort was held by Union troops, while the surrounding forces marched behind the flag of a seceding State. The Northern mind was anything but clear as to the immediate problem. But few governments are so long-suffering as to submit indefinitely to armed rebellion within their territories; and whatever resolutions might be passed by the representatives of South Carolina, there could not be the slightest doubt that until recently they had formed part of the United States. That was an essential point in Northern eyes, as Northern loyalty was growing capable of something larger than allegiance to a single State. To traders with interests in a dozen States the Union was something more than a constitutional formality, since it created the territorial unit within which they were at liberty to operate. It was impossible for Northerners to trade with the expanding West without developing a national conception of the Union transcending their municipal attachment to the State in which they lived. Commerce, in fine, enlarged their loyalties and, finding them New Yorkers, made them Americans. Besides, a fair proportion of their population had escaped from Europe with the simple objective of a fresh start in a new country and without local predilections on the subject of States, however admirable, with whose names they were largely unfamiliar; and to recent immigrants the United States meant infinitely more than any of their components.

Upon this background of Union sentiment bewildered gentlemen at Washington surveyed the awkward problem of the South in the winter days of 1861, as six more States followed the perilous example of South Carolina and Southern delegates trooped into the State House at Montgomery, Alabama, to make solemn speeches beneath its curving galleries and vote a new constitution for the Confederate States of America. Mr. Jefferson Davis walked across from the first White House of the Confederacy for his Inaugural beneath the grave, approving eyes of Southern gentlemen. His eyes were grave as well; for when the telegram had come announcing that he was to be their President, he could hardly bring himself to tell his wife and Mrs. Davis, when she saw the look that clouded his lean handsomeness, felt sure the telegram contained bad news. They cheered him as he spoke, since hardly one of them saw war as the inevitable end of their proceedings. The Southern *pundonor* demanded their secession, and it was widely assumed that they would be allowed to go in peace. This hopeful view prevailed among the delegates at Montgomery, and it was significant that the post offices of the new Confederacy were ordered to conform peacefully to official routine by accounting to Washington until the June half-year of 1861. But Mr. Davis was less cheerful; and beyond the cheers he "saw troubles and thorns innumerable. We are without machinery, without means, and are threatened by a powerful opposition." And as he spoke from the tall steps between the great fluted pillars of that Southern portico, he

83. *pundonor*, contracted from the Spanish *punto de honor*, "point of honor."

looked down the long avenue between the balconies and shaded porches of comfortable Alabama houses and the endless vista that led straight to Gettysburg, the 'Bloody Angle,' and the long agony in the winter trenches of Petersburg.

What was to happen next? Bewildered Washington, faced with an exodus of Southerners, balanced uneasily between the two alternatives of coercion and acquiescence. As the first meant civil war and heroics were less fashionable north of the Mason and Dixon Line, there was a considerable tendency to play for time, murmuring wistfully to the seceded States, "Wayward Sisters, depart in peace." But time might prove to be an awkward ally, so long as the unpleasant riddle of Fort Sumter was unsolved. Nobody seemed to know the answer; and it was anything but simple to devise a satisfactory finale for the piece which had marooned Major Anderson and eighty-four fellow-creatures in the Union service upon an island in a neighbourhood by which the Union had been vociferously repudiated. Charleston's notion of a happy ending was an interlude of Southern chivalry, in which the garrison was given free access to food supplies while gallant planters toiled beside their slaves at the revetments of the new Southern batteries, followd by a spirited *dénouement* enabling everyone to display gallantry and ending with the Palmetto waving unchallenged over South Carolina. Washington's requirements were less spirited, if something could be worked out that was reasonably dignified and did not involve an inadmissible surrender. There was no desire to turn the fortress guns on Charleston in a wild effort to recall it to its late allegiance. Even the Abolitionists inclined to leave the South in a disgraceful solitude, and the most vocal of them doubted whether the Union had any "right to a soldier in Fort Sumter." No government, however, can desert subordinates; and since withdrawal would be tantamount to an admission that the Confederacy was sovereign in South Carolina, Lincoln and his colleagues resolved that the embarrassed fort must be revictualled. A flotilla of supply ships loaded stores at the Brooklyn Navy Yard and sailed for the South.

But the decision hardly lay with Washington, where Secretary Seward aired his evident superiority to the new President. For a ring of Southern guns, controlled by the Confederacy, was trained upon the lonely fort from every angle of the harbour; and the decisive word in the imbroglio must be spoken at Montgomery. Scarcely more inclined than Washington to precipitate a civil war, the South found it less easy to avoid heroic attitudes. Mr. Davis in his White House on the Alabama River was no more belligerent than Mr. Lincoln in his other White House on the Potomac. But strong language and the use of arms came more easily in Southern latitudes; and there was something to be said for a decisive action which might stimulate Virginia, still hanging in the wind, to march with the Confederacy. So an official telegram from Montgomery ordered the dashing Beauregard, in command at Charleston, to reduce the fort if it would not surrender. Anderson refused, adding the welcome information that if he were let alone, he would be starved out in three days. Southern punctilio required the date and hour of his evacuation; but when he gave both with a further undertaking that his guns would not be used in the interval unless fresh supplies or orders came from his government, his answer was found insufficient and he was duly warned that the shore batteries would open fire. Nothing more unreal could be imagined than the situation of Fort Sumter, where three days of starvation, if Anderson could be believed, would solve the problem. But Southern etiquette, enamoured of the duel, imposed a meaningless exchange; and if it was to be avoided, Beauregard was unhappy in his choice of intermediaries, since

---

4. **'Bloody Angle,'** the name given to a section of the battlefield of Spotsylvania Court House where, on May 11 and 12, 1864, was fought one of the bloodiest battles of the Civil War. 5. **Petersburg,** the Virginia city besieged by Grant as part of the final campaign for the investment and capture of Richmond, during the winter of 1864–65. 29. **revetment,** a facing of stone to reinforce a trench or embankment.

52. **Seward . . . President.** For a time after the election of Lincoln, Secretary of State Seward, who had been a candidate for the Republican nomination in the same convention that named Lincoln, was inclined to patronize the rustic figure from the Illinois prairies.

at least one of them was spoiling for a fight which would "put Virginia in the Southern Confederacy in less than an hour by Shrewsbury clock." (The language of Falstaff was not inappropriate on those martial lips.) The cartel was carried to the reluctant Anderson; and Charleston waited for the duel to begin at dawn. The little pillared houses waited in the night; still gardens by the silent river, where
10 tall trees stood listening in their long draperies of smoky moss, lay waiting for the dawn, whilst all the watchers on the waterfront strained through the darkness and the lonely fort, hulldown across the harbour-mouth, hung midway between the night sky and the black waters of the bay.

It hung there as the darkness turned to dawn; and as the fort hung between night and day, the United States—mile after mile across
20 the continent from silent beaches in New England to the last promontory that looked down on the Pacific—hung midway between peace and war. Fourscore years of growth had made them the most hopeful fact in the world of 1861, where the Emperor Napoleon III aired his slightly reminiscent splendors, Czar Alexander II his good intentions, and Lord Palmerston his firm conviction that the not too recent past was good enough for him, as well as for
30 the subjects of Queen Victoria. It was, to some extent, a retrospective age in which men took their last glance at the receding outlines of the eighteenth century. Some took it, like Lord Palmerston, with unconcealed regret, while more progressive figures like Garibaldi or Cavour drew inspiration from those principles of nationality and secularism which were the last bequest of the departed century. Dedicated to the proposition that all men were created equal

(and no less eighteenth-century in their initial 40 inspiration), the United States had seemed to point to a more modern future in which trade would rule the peaceful scene and states vie only in prosperity. Trade, indeed, was not confined to the United States; but elsewhere it conducted itself a shade apologetically beneath the borrowed grandeur of a Second Empire title or discreetly ranged in its appointed place in the Victorian hierarchy, halfway between the upper levels of the landed gentry or 50 the cathedral close and the last indignity of manual work. Beyond the Atlantic it was more unashamed. Society was simpler, and there were less categories to embarrass the pursuit of happiness. Achievement was the only test in a new country, success the sole nobility; and even government, preserved elsewhere as a hereditary mystery, was there a simple exercise by the people of the people's right. Small wonder that a fair proportion of the world looked 60 enviously at the United States, at the vast opportunity and the consoling featurelessness of the social scene. Repellent to romantics—did not Disraeli titter that American society was like "the best society in Manchester"?—it was a standing inspiration to Radicals with its hopeful indication of a future in which a man could call his soul (and a fair amount of his property) his own. That was the commonplace sublimity of the American experiment, which had 70 dedicated half a continent to peaceful work; and on that spring night in 1861 the whole experiment hung midway between peace and war.

This interruption of its ordered growth seemed so uncalled for. Faced with the cruel fact, subsequent attempts to rationalise the haphazard course of events have represented the conflict between North and South as irrepressible. For there is always a temptation to 80 assign ineluctable causes to chance happenings, since history is infinitely more impressive when it is inevitable. One cannot draw lessons from pure accidents. Besides, it would be too bitter to attribute all the misery that followed to an unhappy chance. Yet there was no compelling reason in economics or sociology for the war

---

3. **Shrewsbury clock.** "But we rose both at an instant and fought a long hour by Shrewsbury clock," spoken by Falstaff in *I Henry IV*, V, iv, 153–4. 5. **cartel,** a letter of challenge or defiance. 25. **Napoleon III,** see note 3, p. 139. 27. **Palmerston,** see note 25, p. 149. 35. **Garibaldi,** Giuseppe Garibaldi (1807–1882), the active military leader and among the most prominent social agitators for the independence of Italy, which was ultimately achieved in 1870; he was one of the most devoted patriots of which history has record. **Cavour,** Camillo Benso di Cavour (1810–1861), another leader for Italian independence; but his great contributions to the cause were in the fields of diplomacy. Both men were much impressed by the American Declaration of Independence, which has sometimes been called "the triumphant fruit of eighteenth-century rational thinking."

64. **Disraeli,** see note 40, p. 138. 81. **ineluctable,** irresistible.

between the States, and the tragic outcome was almost completely lacking in Marxian inevitability. The North had no quarrel with the South for mastery of a disputed country, since the true lines of the United States ran east and west across the continent. Their duel, if there had ever been one, ended when the South was outflanked by the march of time, the westward march that sent the wagons creaking overland across the Plains; and as the tide of population set westward towards California and the steel ribbon of the railroads crept behind the advancing fringe, the South was relegated past recall to a secondary place in the United States. That was a process of history which could not be revised by force of arms; and the unhappy outcome of the war did little more than emphasise it.

Yet there was one incalculable consequence that outweighed all the suffering, since the ensuing agony ensured for all time the unchallenged unity of the United States. That was a fact of deep significance for America and later, as their influence began to radiate, for the world beyond the ocean. For the cruel price exacted from the war-time generation purchased the continuance of that immense community. Its unity could not be challenged now without sacrilege; and so long as its growing millions lived and worked in peace from the Great Lakes to the Rio Grande, something more precious to mankind than comfort was preserved, since government of the people, by the people, for the people, could not perish from the earth.

A tragic generation paid the price in four years of gunfire and fratricide; and what a price it was. It paid it marching through the midsummer dust along the unshaded roads that ended in the little wooded hills along the Bull Run where Beauregard sent the startled Federals streaming back to Washington in the first flurry of the war, or beside the Rappahannock flowing tidily between its ridges whilst Lee parried the Northern thrust at Fredericksburg, or under the wide skies that looked down on the sloping fields in front of Richmond where the South turned to bay behind its shallow breastworks, scooped in the thirsty, sandy soil along the vast, untidy water-line of the Chickahominy. It paid where the small rounded hills of Tennessee climb steeply to the Ridge, the straight-backed Pyrenean Ridge above the gleaming levels of a river of blue steel that runs beneath the cliffs at Chattanooga, and beside the great angle of the river where Vicksburg peers across the broad and gleaming shield of the Mississippi and the tall shoulder of the river-fortress stands in a sort of tangled Devonshire, a moist green country of amazing verdure and tall trees growing out of their own reflections in still swamps that echoed with the dull discharges of Grant's batteries until the fortress guns fell silent and the Northern gunboats could run clear from Memphis to New Orleans and an incomparable tongue at Washington announced that "the Father of Waters goes again unvexed to the sea." It paid in heat and cold, by night and day, for four bitter years as the slow struggle swayed across the country and the South writhed in an unyielding grip. The red earth of Georgia saw them go by, as the Northern thrust went deeper into the South and Sherman, a little wild-eyed, told them grimly to prepare the people for his coming; and the black waters of the Yorktown peninsula, that invite the noiseless onset of canoes between the silent pine-poles, reflected their marching columns. The open country beyond Gettysburg, where men spent their lives with reckless prodigality, had felt the furthest ripple of the Southern wave; and later as the angry tide receded, it drew slowly nearer to the green hollows and bare uplands of the last Southern stronghold, where Richmond watched from its brown escarpments and the news, the last unbelievable news, came to Mr. Davis in his pew at St. Paul's, and Lee trailed westward towards Lynchburg under the wide skies, watched by the friendly slopes of the Blue Ridge through which Jackson had so often slipped out of the Valley to startle Washington or to scare unsuspecting Federals by a sudden apparition on their unguarded flank. But now there was no Jackson, and no Stuart to go riding round the Northern rear and cut the

2. **Marxian inevitability.** Marx believed in an inevitable conflict between the classes of society which would result finally in the destruction of the capitalistic system.

telegraphs; only a road winding before him past the little Court House and down the slope towards the Appomattox. Grant came towards him up the road, and the two men walked together to a house. Finding no table there, they strolled up a brick path into another small dwelling-house that stood a little back from the highway. So the two soldiers sat talking; and all round them the easy slopes lay under the clear April light. The woods were full of halted men, and on the distant sky the Blue Ridge looked down in pity at the South's surrender.

But that was still four years away, as Charleston waited for the dawn and the black muzzles of the Southern guns tilted towards the silent fort. Grant was a dusty salesman somewhere in the West, and Sherman had come north from the superintendent's desk of an academy in Louisiana, and Lee in a dim room at Arlington was facing the harsh syllogism of his conflicting duties as a Virginian and a commissioned officer of the United States. Even the President was still a shadowy almost an unknown figure with a distressing tendency to damp excited callers with homely answers in a Western drawl that struck them sometimes as a little clownish. For the incomparable voice at Washington had not yet found the full compass of its utterance that still hangs on the air with the clear purity of a struck bell, from its deep note of consecration in a new birth of freedom to the dying fall of his last purpose to proceed with malice toward none, with charity for all, with firmness in the right, as God gives us to see the right. . . . That was still hidden in the night, as the sky began to pale behind Fort Sumter. A gun thudded; a shell whined across a mile of water; and the war began. It was about half-past four in the morning of April 12, 1861.

3. OSBORNE

The short December day was over, and beyond the lighted windows the Solent swung drearily in the night. Inside the house a royal figure swathed in crêpe dragged wretchedly about the silent rooms and "felt as if living in a dreadful dream." The children were all there (she had one of them to sleep with her); and her uncle Leopold from Brussels had proposed himself, which was an immense comfort to her, as he could do so much in telling people what they ought to do. But, in justice to them, it was only fair to say that they were all doing it in the most exemplary manner. Lord Palmerston himself seemed quite heartbroken; nothing could be more attentive than her other ministers; the faithful Household far surpassed all standards of devoted sympathy; and though she had not strength to read them yet, the tributes of a wider circle enshrined her darling in the grateful memory of an afflicted people, who *"might perhaps"* (as she wrote a little ruefully) "have shown this *more* during his lifetime." But that could not be mended now; and as Bertie and the children tiptoed about the silent house, she felt utterly alone.

It has always been a lonely business to be Queen of England. The royal solitude, perhaps, had thrilled her just a little on that first morning twenty-four years ago at Kensington. But she had soon mitigated it with the alleviation of an incomparable partnership, and the royal solitude became a solitude of two. For the Queen needed somebody to lean on; and through twenty happy years of married life she leaned increasingly upon her husband. A clinging nature taught her to play ivy to his oak; and his grave affection had impelled the deliberate creation in himself of a sense of public duty which enabled him to bear the burden. For twenty years of perfect harmony the weight of monarchy was carried on two pairs of shoulders, its heavy correspondence despatched from two royal writing-tables standing side by side, and its grave decisions taken by two minds that worked as one. A rare felicity for once enabled two persons to lead a single life and, sharing opinions and pastimes, to perform one royal functionary's work with the united energies of two. But that was over now. A dragging chill that turned suddenly to typhoid fever had ended it; and the Queen, shattered by three dreadful weeks at Windsor

---

43. **the Solent.** The Isle of Wight, on which was situated the royal palace of Osborne, is a small island a few miles off the southern coast of England, separated from the mainland on its northwestern quarter by a strait, known as the Solent.

49. **uncle Leopold,** see note 6, p. 136. 65. **Bertie,** the Prince of Wales (1841–1910), later King Edward VII of Great Britain, who succeeded Victoria in 1901.

Castle, was utterly alone. Indeed, bereavement left her in something worse than solitude. For she had lost a portion of herself; and the Prince Consort's death, which widowed her, came almost with the shock of amputation.

The broken woman looked hopefully towards a personal Nirvana of reunion with her lost husband. Meanwhile there was the cheerless prospect of her remaining days on earth.
10 She hoped sincerely that they would be few, quite overlooking the unhappy circumstance that she would be forty-three next birthday and was exceptionally robust; and she could hardly doubt that they would be uniformly wretched, now that the sun round which her life revolved had been withdrawn. But even in the first abandonment of her self-pity there were indications of a programme that was highly creditable to her strength of character.
20 For in an age when widowhood was frequently accompanied by the deliberate collapse of a sort of spiritual suttee, the Queen preferred a more courageous attitude. As she must live— and she announced her firm resolve that nothing should be done by her to make her any worse than she already was—her life should be his monument, her actions a reflection of his mind, her reign a prolongation of his influence upon the country in whose service he had
30 worn himself to death. That became the burden of her grief—"to *follow* in *everything all* HIS *wishes, great and small."* His views were now her law, his plans the programme of her life; and it was some consolation, since in the daily effort to divine his mind upon each problem she could feel him near to her still.

This spectral dyarchy was now to govern England; and if England only knew what was good for it, all would be for the best. Lord
40 Palmerston was most obliging now, and he had highly sympathetic colleagues. Lord Russell had been more than kind; the amiable Granville had enjoyed her confidence for years; and

Mr. Gladstone had always been a favourite with the Prince, since he was by far the ablest pupil of Sir Robert Peel, who was Prince Albert's *beau idéal* of a British statesman. Built upon somewhat less forbidding lines, the old Prime Minister exhaled an air of comfort, as

Agricultural meetings he holds by the ears, 50
Through their pacings puts Hampshire Volunteers,
Or with Rowcliffe takes up the gloves for fun,
This elderly evergreen, Palmerston.
Sing hey, my brisk John Palmerston!
Sing ho, my blithe John Palmerston!
Let Tory and Radical own they've none
To compare with my jaunty John Palmerston.
He'll resist the gale, or he'll bow to the storm—
He'll patronise Bright, or he'll chaff Reform— 60
Make a Shafts'bury Bishop, or poke his fun
At original sin, will John Palmerston . . .

This amiable veteran appeared to hold domestic politics in a cheerful equilibrium that was unfriendly to disturbances in either sense. It was years now since Russell had introduced a Reform Bill; and progressive persons muttered darkly in corners, echoing the unfriendly sentiments of Mr. Bright, who came nearer to blasphemy on the subject of Lord 70 Palmerston than upon any other topic. But, after all, the Government had sent that paladin of progress, Mr. Cobden, to negotiate a Commercial Treaty with the French; the harvest of Free Trade was gathered steadily in growing manufactures and expanding shipping; and Mr. Gladstone's Budgets were a treatise in annual instalments upon the last word in modern finance. This homage to the future amply satisfied the exigencies of a sense 80 of progress, while more stable elements felt few misgivings on the subject of a Cabinet adorned by the controlling presence of Lord

---

7. **Nirvana,** in Hindu philosophy the state of complete self-abnegation, in which the believer achieves a perfect union with the absolute whence he came. 37. **dyarchy,** a dual form of government, or rule by two. Victoria and her husband Albert had been virtually joint rulers for a good many years before his death. 41. **Russell,** John Earl Russell (1792–1878), colonial secretary and then prime minister (1846–52). 42. **Granville,** George Leveson-Gower Granville (1815–1891), foreign secretary under Russell, later president of the council, and, like Russell, leader of the Liberal Party.

44. **Gladstone,** see note 45, p. 140. 46. **Sir Robert Peel,** see note 24, p. 149. 60. *Bright,* John Bright (1811–1889), a Quaker and industrial leader, ardent supporter of free trade, member of Parliament, and noted as one of the few prominent men in public life in Britain who favored the Union cause during the American Civil War; he was a strong political opponent of Palmerston. 67. **Reform Bill.** Russell had been instrumental in the passing of the Reform Act of 1832, the first in the series of three parliamentary acts to extend suffrage in Britain and revise the system of representation. 73. **Cobden,** Richard Cobden (1804–1865), "the apostle of free trade," a prominent cotton manufacturer and member of Parliament.

Palmerston, whose long career was reassuring in its mere chronology. Had he not presided in the War Department when Lord Wellington was in the Peninsula and drafted protocols for Talleyrand to read when Metternich was in his heyday? There was small risk of unexpected innovation from such a quarter; and though Palmerston moved with the times, there was no fear that he would ever find himself in ad-10 vance of them.

That dangerous prerogative belonged to impatient Radicals and to their eloquent recruit, the Chancellor of the Exchequer. For Mr. Gladstone's fatal logic impelled him to erect economy into an idol, whose worship interfered with the customary financial sacrifices on the altar of national defence, and to explore the possibilities of a wider franchise without the nervous inhibitions of an older generation.
20 Small wonder that his leader murmured that there would be strange doings when Gladstone had his place. But until then his fellow-countrymen reposed in Palmerstonian security. In twenty years the national income assessed to tax had risen from one hundred and fifty-six millions to two hundred and twenty-one; in six years the export trade climbed from a volume of one hundred and thirty millions to one hundred and eighty-eight; and a thrifty cornucopia
30 distributed the fruits of this expansion in such judicious benefits as cheap books, cheap claret, and cheap railway-fares. It was an age of high profits and high principles; and every year the tide of comfort mounted higher. As the Prime Minister wrote proudly, "Gentlemen's Houses are better and more extensively provided than was formerly the Case. Tenant Farmers are not disposed to live in the Houses which were held good enough for their Predecessors; and the

Labourers have had provided for them Habita-40 tions which would have satisfied the Smock Frock Farmer of former Times." Life was less picturesque; but it was infinitely more enjoyable under a new commercial class soberly resolved to keep what it had got and to get as much more as the unfolding opportunities of business would permit. It was the culmination of bourgeois ethics in a paradise of orderly self-seeking. Less material ideals were safely relegated to art and letters, which soared (with 50 Mr. Tennyson) towards the stars without the sobering necessity of making both ends meet. But beyond Farringford and the less airy dwellings where young Pre-Raphaelites adored the wan perfection of Miss Siddal England was severely practical, a nation happily absorbed in the excitements of Palmerstonian prosperity, as new factories with taller chimneys spread a wider pall of smoke and the countryside contracted before the advancing tide of brick and 60 the new stucco palaces of recent wealth exhibited the strange profusion of their ornament and the Victorian age stood at its most Victorian.

But though there was small cause for worry in the state of things at home, the scene in 1861 was more disquieting abroad. The Continent had lived for forty years under the dispensation of the peace-treaties of Vienna. Those powerful incantations averted war for upwards of a gen-70 eration; but the settlement was not immortal, and its authority had gradually evaporated before the rise of forces which the treaty system had not taken into account. The omission was deliberate. For it was not to be expected that

3. **Wellington . . . Peninsula.** During the Napoleonic wars Wellington first made himself famous by the conduct of the Peninsular Campaign from 1808 through 1813; by this long series of operations the French were driven out of Portugal and the Spanish peninsula, and the tide began to turn against Napoleon. 5. **Talleyrand.** Charles Maurice, Prince of Talleyrand-Perigord (1754–1838), a brilliant French diplomatist under the leaders of the French Revolution and the Emperor Napoleon, and Clemens Wenzel Lother, Prince von Metternich (1773–1859), an equally famous Austrian statesman, were the chief agents in the "Holy Alliance," an association of European powers formed after Waterloo and the Treaty of Paris (1815) to make the world safe for autocracy; the alliance represented the inevitable reaction against a quarter-century of revolution and its effects. 13. **Chancellor of the Exchequer.** Gladstone had been appointed to this post in 1852.

53. **Farringford,** home of Tennyson and his family on the Isle of Wight in 1853; although he later built a home at Aldworth, Sussex, he constantly revisited Farringford in the autumn. 54. **Pre-Raphaelites . . . Siddal.** The Pre-Raphaelites were a school of artists and poets in nineteenth-century England whose artistic ideals of simplicity, symbolic suggestion, and medieval mysticism were blended with a devotion to the sensuous, worthy of John Keats. (See p. 25.) By many of their contemporary critics they were condemned as "fleshly." But in Dante Gabriel Rossetti (1828–1882) and William Morris (1834–1896) they produced at least two considerable poets. Rossetti, his brother William, and his sister Christina were in a way the guiding spirits of the literary aspects of this movement—at least at the beginning; and Elizabeth Siddal, who later became Dante Rossetti's wife, was their model in both painting and poetry. 69. **peace-treaties of Vienna.** The Congress of Vienna, which began in 1815, effected a readjustment of Europe following the defeat of Napoleon and established the Holy Alliance (see l. 5 and note). Talleyrand and Metternich were the chief movers of these Vienna treaties; but Robert Stewart Castlereagh (1769–1822; p. 165) was the English representative.

Prince Metternich and Lord Castlereagh would respect the right of populations to choose their own allegiance, since in their view the principle of nationality had (like the Rights of Man) been one of the flamboyant pretexts behind which the late French aggression had marched across Europe; and what loyal Austrian could doubt that Hapsburgs were no less entitled to rule over Czechs, Italians, and Magyars than
10 over Viennese? This misapprehension was corrected by a few decades of old-fashioned government, in which paternalism verged upon domestic tyranny. Under this stimulus the vogue of romance, with its accompanying taste for the revival of long-vanished national glories, acquired the urgency of current politics and combined with the deferred explosion of ideas upon the risky topic of self-government, which the receding tide of French revolution-
20 ary influence had left in the subsoil of European consciousness. The results were most unsettling for a treaty system founded upon anything rather than the principle of nationality, and the settlement was promptly challenged at a dozen points across the Continent. Poles, Italians, Hungarians, and Czechs questioned the dictates of Vienna; and though their effort to reverse the settlement was crushed in 1848, their questions were unanswered. The chal-
30 lenge still persisted; and the fitful light of freedom burned in Italy, until the guarded flame of a few secret societies became a noble blaze of national resurgence in the strong hands of Garibaldi and Cavour. The French successfully asserted a still more categorical denial of the treaty system, when a nephew of the Emperor whom the treaties had deposed became their ruler; and the enigmatic presence of Napoleon III was now the main focus of
40 unsettlement in Europe. His restless diplomacy —Palmerston wrote to a colleague that "the Emperor's mind seems as full of schemes as a warren is full of rabbits"—broke the long peace and violated the traditional alignment of the ex-Allied Powers hallowed by the Holy Alliance, when he ranged England on his side against the Czar in the strange imbroglio of the Crimean War. In 1859 his revolutionary sym-

pathies made French armies, by which Austrian resistance was broken at Magenta and 50 Solferino, the main instruments of Italian liberation; and he was perpetually hoping for a European conference to bring the treaties of 1815 up to date, a proposal which elicited from Palmerston the bland response that "those who hold their estates under a good title, now nearly half a century old, might not be particularly desirous of having it brought under discussion with all the alterations which good-natured neighbours might wish to suggest in 60 their boundaries." But the Continental equilibrium was no longer balanced on the faded formulae of those forgotten instruments. For though Poland was still a hope, Italy was a reality; and the Continent appeared to be controlled by a more fluid element, constituted by the slow-moving impulses of Napoleon III.

His dictatorship wore the accustomed air of permanence, since all dictatorships invariably look as if they would last for ever. France, 70 skilfully alarmed by the imaginary imminence of the *Spectre rouge* in 1851, had fled to the shelter of his name; and one more Bonaparte ensured the continuity of national life at the modest price of a complete suspension of all political activity. After the wild uproar of 1848 a welcome silence settled on French politics, and public business was transacted by his nominees. Refreshed by this repose, the national intelligence began to interest itself once 80 more in its own affairs; and the Imperial dictatorship endeavoured to respond by a slight relaxation of its political authority approximating roughly to the Parliamentary liberties conceded to her subjects by Queen Elizabeth.

72. *Spectre rouge,* the red specter, i.e., fear of radical government. The wave of political revolt that passed over Europe in 1848 was the first strong manifestation of Marxian ideologies, which founded socialism and the extreme forms of which bred communism and syndicalism (cf. pp. 623 ff.). As a result of this "red scare" France dropped her Second Republic (1851) and accepted Napoleon III and the Second Empire. 85. **Elizabeth.** Actually it would be possible to maintain that Guedalla has presented the wrong interpretation here. In theory, Parliament, under the Tudor sovereigns of England, had the right to veto any proposal by the Crown; but the Tudors, who were very astute, saw to it that Parliament was so constituted as to be a rubber-stamp of approval to all royal acts. The issue as to whether Parliament or the Crown was supreme never was allowed to come up. The Stuarts, who followed the Tudors in the seventeenth century, were not so clever; they allowed the issue to be raised, and the result was not only the Civil War of the 1640's but the Bill of Rights in 1689, which established the supremacy of Parliament.

8. **Hapsburgs,** the ruling dynasty in the Austrian Empire.

This stage in a dictator's life is always the most precarious, since the steep ladder of dictatorship, often so easy to ascend, is infinitely harder to come down; and the descent is often faster and leads further than the climber meant. The Second Empire was gently launched upon this incline which, its director hoped, might bring it to the safe levels of Parliamentary government. But in the event the slope proved too severe for the brittle fabric of his authority; and when it ultimately reached the bottom, there was no Emperor.

Some touch of the uncertainty involved in that delicate transition already blurred the sharp outline of the Empire and of the long shadow which it cast across the Continent. France was still paramount in 1861, and its slow-spoken Emperor behind his big moustache was still the leading figure in the world. But would they always be? The flaring lights of Paris were still turned up as high as they had ever been; but, by the mournful destiny of all dictators, they must either burn still higher or go out.

That was the difficulty. He could not force the note of French supremacy for ever. It had been comparatively simple for a man of more intelligence than was usual among monarchs to dominate the Continental scene. His policies bore more relation to the modern world; his armies jingled spurs and trailed their scabbards more gallantly, and their proud Imperial emblems—the great N's on their sabretaches, the tall bearskins of his grenadiers, and the dull gleam of the *Cuirassiers* in their big helmets— were a sobering reminder of the long columns which had once marched across the world to victory behind their eagles; even his fleet alarmed Lord Palmerston into a paroxysm of coast-defence and set the Poet Laureate writing lyrics for the Volunteers. But the Emperor could hardly force the note for ever; and there were other voices on the Continent which might break in upon his solo. A warning murmur sounded, as he held the centre of the

stage after the Austrian defeat at Solferino. For the Prussians began massing troops behind the Rhine, since (in a shrewd diagnosis) they would "regard any serious defeat of Austria in Italy, or anything that should seriously endanger her position in the Quadrilateral, as a danger to the left flank of the German position." True their mobilisation was extremely faulty; the Prussian army of 1859 was still the army of von Bonin and an exceedingly imperfect instrument of war. But that would soon be remedied, if von Moltke and von Roon could have their way; and it was an unpleasing revelation that there was a German point of view, since hitherto the Continent had got on pleasantly enough without one.

The Hapsburg mosaic had formed the highly decorative centre of a still richer tessellation, in which assorted German states were loosely assembled in the vague pattern of a Germanic Confederation. It was little more than a diplomatic convenience, which bore faint traces of its feudal origins; and there were few facilities for the application of a German point of view to the formation of a German policy. The German soul, if it existed, was unsatisfied in the field of politics. As one of them had written, he "could not say abroad, 'I am a German,' could not pride himself that the German flag was flying from his vessel, could have no German consul in time of need, but had to explain, 'I am a Hessian, a Darmstädter, a Buckebürger: my Fatherland was once a great and powerful country, now it is shattered into eight and thirty splinters.'" The lively transformation-scenes of 1848 had included among the less satisfactory exhibits of that year of sudden impulses and swift retreats a sketch of German unity. But it was almost equally defective in time, *personnel,* and place,

41. **lyrics for the Volunteers,** particularly such poems as Tennyson's "Third of February, 1852" and "Britons, Guard Your Own," both written on the occasion of Napoleon III's *coup d'état* of December 1851 which resulted in the proclaiming of the Second Empire.

51. **Quadrilateral,** a section of northern Italy occupied by the Austrians, formed by lines connecting the four Italian towns of Verona, Peschiera, Legnago, and Mantua. 55. **von Bonin,** Eduard von Bonin (1793–1865), war minister of Prussia 1858–59. 57. **von Moltke,** Helmuth Karl Bernhard, Count von Moltke (1800–1891), the builder of the modern German army and a powerful stimulus to the militaristic spirit of prewar imperial Germany. He was the brilliant leader of the Prussians against Austria in 1866 and against France in 1870 and was generally regarded as the leading military strategist of his time. **von Roon,** Albrecht Theodor Emil von Roon (1803–1879), a lesser cog in the same military machine.

since no amount of well-intentioned eloquence could turn a Frankfort Parliament into the operative centre of a new Germany or convert the unstable personality of King Frederick William IV into its champion against the forces of reaction. Besides, the forces of reaction had an awkward way of triumphing in 1848; and as the dawn faded, Germany relapsed once more into its aboriginal multiplicity. But even that might be remedied, if the Germans followed the heartening example of Italy; and in December, 1861, King William intimated that Prussia might appear in the part played in Italy by Piedmont. His rehearsals for the *rôle* took the form of an elaborate reorganisation and rearmament of the Prussian army. But the chief performer was still a diplomat abroad with a capacity for pointed sayings and an amazing taste in liquor. For Count von Bismarck had the unclouded vision and the simple ruthlessness by which the Frederician tradition might be continued. The Prussian kingdom had originally been raised from feudal unimportance by one thin-lipped monarch, who kept the flame of war burning through half the eighteenth century in order to maintain a naked theft of Austrian territory; and if his work was to be resumed, Europe would become a less pleasant place to live in than it had been. That was the worst (for Europe) of the emergence of a German point of view.

The masters of the Continent in 1861 were largely untroubled by these forebodings, since Napoleon was vaguely favourable to the creation of a Prussian counterpoise to Austria, and in spite of all that Prince Albert and Count Stockmar wrote Lord Palmerston could never be prevailed upon to take a German state altogether seriously. Indeed, his main preoccupations as the year went out were transatlantic. For the Civil War was on, and neutrality is never easy for maritime powers. A Northern cruiser had committed the inexcusable irregularity of stopping a British mail-steamer and removing four Southern passengers by force. The names of Captain Wilkes, the *Trent*, and Messrs. Slidell and Mason acquired a feverish notoriety, as a sharp argument proceeded between Washington and Downing Street. War-correspondents hopefully began to study the American campaign of 1812, and the Guards sailed for Canada. Lord Palmerston dropped in one evening at the Confederate offices in Suffolk Street, Pall Mall, and had a most exciting talk about the possibilities of armed Franco-British intervention to stop the war; and Lincoln in his yokel phase was slightly irritating to the Queen's minister at Washington with a vague assurance, when pressed about the burning question, "Oh, that'll be got along with." But the Cabinet was cautious; the law was on their side; a draft despatch of Russell's was discreetly modified, toned down still further by the Prince Consort's failing hand, and rendered even milder by a last revision in Cabinet; and as Secretary Seward intimated that his prisoners would be set free, the war-cloud passed. That anxious piece of drafting had been the Prince's last public work. Now the Queen was quite alone in the bewildering solitude of Palmerstonian England and the Europe of the Second Empire, alone among her crowding memories of his ideals that had been so noble and his opinions that had been so precise; and the short winter afternoon was over, as the tide ran mournfully through Spithead beneath the windows of the house that he had built.

4. **Frederick William IV,** ruler of Prussia 1840–1861, an absolutist monarch who tried to throw himself against the advance of constitutional government. He was succeeded by his brother William, who became the first emperor of modern Germany under the title of William I. 14. **Piedmont,** a section of northern Italy, embracing the aforementioned "Quadrilateral." 21. **Frederician tradition.** Frederick II (1712–1786), king of Prussia, commonly known as Frederick the Great, was a rigorous, ambitious, and unscrupulous imperialist who raised Prussia from a fifth-rate European state to a position of world power, largely through the seizure of Silesia from Austria (1745) and by the Seven Years' War (1756–63) which saw him ultimately gain many important concessions from France, Austria, and Russia, against all three of which he had been engaged. In spite of his ruthlessness, however, he possessed much constructive insight. 27. **theft . . . territory,** the seizure of Silesia. 37. **Stockmar,** see note 20, p. 148.

46. **Wilkes . . . Mason.** On November 8, 1861, the British steamer *Trent*, bound from Havana to England and having on board John Slidell and James M. Mason, the newly appointed Confederate ambassadors to London and Paris respectively, was stopped by the American man-of-war *San Jacinto*. Charles Wilkes, captain of the *San Jacinto*, boarded the *Trent* in flagrant violation of international law, seized the Confederate emissaries, and took them into custody. The event caused a sensation; and Britain threatened war against the United States. Ultimately the American government apologized, Slidell and Mason were set free, and the crisis passed. But the incident did nothing to ameliorate relations between the Federal Government and Great Britain, and intensified British official sympathy and support for the Confederacy.

✿ The Conflict Between Emotion and Reason

EDNA ST. VINCENT MILLAY

Edna Millay is among the best known, most widely read women poets of today. She is that contradiction in terms, a poet who is a best seller. In 1923 her *The Harp Weaver* won the Pulitzer Prize for poetry; her lyrics have appeared in most of the more important American periodicals; and her libretto for the opera *The King's Henchman* (1927), for which the music was composed by Deems Taylor, is one of the few contemporary American works to have been presented at the Metropolitan in New York City.

Miss Millay was born on February 22, 1892, and received her early education in the schools of two small Maine communities, Rockland and Camden. As her early work indicates, her formative artistic influences were the classical masters of verse. The publication of "Renascence" in the anthology *The Lyric Year* (1912) first made her talent known. At once a benefactor provided tuition at Vassar, and there Miss Millay received an A.B. degree in 1917, the year of the publication of her first volume, *Renascence and Other Poems*.

Supporting herself in Greenwich Village by penning short stories under the name Nancy Boyd, Miss Millay soon became the toast of her generation. She wrote no longer in her earlier vein of innocence and spiritual experience. Hers were the age-old emotional themes—death, love, unfaithfulness—expressed with a modernity that America found at once startling and refreshing. In *A Few Figs from Thistles* (1920), *Second April* (1921), and *The Harp Weaver and Other Poems* (1923), Miss Millay boldly waved the banner of the feminist movement, upholding woman's right to love when and whom she pleases.

In a decade when the dominant intellectual and literary direction was best charted by T. S. Eliot's *Waste Land* (cf. p. 237), Edna Millay reformulated for her generation the seventeenth-century philosophy of "Gather ye rosebuds while ye may," of living in the pleasure of the moment, broadening this credo to include women as well as men. *Aria da Capo,* a play written in 1920, sounded the poet's hatred of war and strife, which she traced allegorically to the greed of individuals; and in the same piece she mocked the superficialities of the current intellectual fashions. Stirred by what she felt was the injustice of the Sacco-Vanzetti trial, Miss Millay with other liberals marched in protest against the execution of the men in 1927. Her poem *Justice Denied in Massachusetts* is based on the trial.

The Buck in the Snow appeared in 1928, *Selected Poems for Young People* in 1929, *Fatal Interview* in 1931, *Wine from These Grapes* in 1934, translations from Baudelaire's *Flowers of Evil* in 1936, *Conversation at Midnight* in 1937, *Huntsman, What Quarry?* in 1939, *Make Bright the Arrows* in 1940, *Collected Sonnets* in 1941, and *Collected Lyrics* in 1943. First interested in verse drama at Vassar, Miss Millay later joined the Provincetown Players, as both a playwright and an actress. In 1921 three of her plays were published: *Two Slatterns and a King; Moral Interlude; The Lamp and the Bell.* In 1923 Miss Millay married Eugen Jan Boissevain, an importer, and settled in the Berkshires, where she lived until her death in 1950.

Miss Millay's poetry is literary in imagery. The strongest personal note in it is the feminist. The Elizabethans and seventeenth-century poets are her masters in form, but her subject matter is more modern. Like the esthetes of the 1890's in England, she believed in sheer intensity of feeling as reason enough for writing.

168

She built no philosophy and drew no conclusions concerning the more universal values of life. In her later poems she confessed that both pain and pleasure, the two stimuli of her lyricism, were dulled for her by maturity and that she could not conjure up emotions about which to write. Her later work, though technically often expert, seems more artificial than her earlier. Love was always her chief subject matter, and one cannot forever be falling in or out of love. She continued, even in her humorous and satirical study of our modern scene, *Conversation at Midnight,* really an ardent individualist.

From time to time she reacted poetically to a current situation. She visited Spain in 1937 and wrote favorably of the Loyalists. World War II aroused her to write a good deal of popular verse on the tragedy of war; such poems as "There Are No Islands Any More" (1940), "lines written," as she said, "in passion and in deep concern for England, France and my own country," and "The Murder of Lidice" (1942), were printed in our most popular magazines and were presented over the radio. The latest of these was "Poem and Prayer for an Invading Army," written for the National Broadcasting Company and read by Ronald Colman on D-Day, June 6, 1944. Essentially, they are not her best work. The best of her poetry was completed when she published *Second April.*

Miss Millay, by becoming the voice of the anarchistic and Bohemian proclaimers of art for art's sake, was caught in a trap from which she never escaped. Having limited herself to crying out for woman's right to live intensely, to love, and to be creative in the arts, she was later forced to resort to the pretense of continuous youth, to repeated manifestoes that she could still live in the intense moment of physical love. The result was that she seemed never to have grown up.

While the phase of feminism which attracted her most—abandonment to feeling, to anti-puritanism—gave way to the vast movement for equal rights and the right to work, Miss Millay had to remain her rebellious self. She will be remembered for her early work, which is typical of the individualistic and romantic revolt of the women poets between 1915 and 1925.

Mariposa

Butterflies are white and blue
In this field we wander through.
Suffer me to take your hand.
Death comes in a day or two.

All the things we ever knew 5
Will be ashes in that hour,
Mark the transient butterfly,
How he hangs upon the flower.

Suffer me to take your hand.
Suffer me to cherish you 10
Till the dawn is in the sky.
Whether I be false or true,
Death comes in a day or two.

Elegy before Death

There will be rose and rhododendron
When you are dead and under ground;
Still will be heard from white syringas
Heavy with bees, a sunny sound;

Still will the tamaracks be raining 5
After the rain has ceased, and still
Will there be robins in the stubble,
Brown sheep upon the warm green hill.

Spring will not ail nor autumn falter;
Nothing will know that you are gone, 10
Saving alone some sullen plough-land
None but yourself sets foot upon;

Saving the may-weed and the pig-weed
Nothing will know that you are dead,—
These, and perhaps a useless wagon 15
Standing beside some tumbled shed.

Oh, there will pass with your great passing
Little of beauty not your own,—
Only the light from common water,
Only the grace from simple stone!

Dirge without Music

I am not resigned to the shutting away of
loving hearts in the hard ground.
So it is, and so it will be, for so it has been,
time out of mind:

Into the darkness they go, the wise and the
  lovely. Crowned
With lilies and with laurel they go; but I am
  not resigned.   4

Lovers and thinkers, into the earth with you.
Be one with the dull, the indiscriminate dust.
A fragment of what you felt, of what you knew,
A formula, a phrase remains,—but the best is
  lost.

The answers quick and keen, the honest look,
  the laughter, the love,—
They are gone. They are gone to feed the roses.
  Elegant and curled   10
Is the blossom. Fragrant is the blossom. I
  know. But I do not approve.
More precious was the light in your eyes than
  all the roses of the world.

Down, down, down into the darkness of the
  grave
Gently they go, the beautiful, the tender, the
  kind;
Quietly they go, the intelligent, the witty, the
  brave.   15
I know. But I do not approve. And I am not resigned.

Sonnet

Euclid alone has looked on Beauty bare.
  Let all who prate of beauty hold their
  peace,

"Sonnet," from *The Harp Weaver and Other Poems*, published
by Harper & Brothers. Copyright, 1920, 1921, 1922, 1923, by
Edna St. Vincent Millay.
Sonnet. Euclid wrote a treatise on geometry about 300 B.C. Miss
Millay is treating here of abstract beauty or beauty of line, as
opposed to a more fleshly beauty.

And lay them prone upon the earth and cease
To ponder on themselves, the while they stare
At nothing, intricately drawn nowhere   5
In shapes of shifting lineage; let geese
Gabble and hiss, but heroes seek release
From dusty bondage into luminous air.
O blinding hour, O holy, terrible day,
When first the shaft into his vision shone   10
Of light anatomized! Euclid alone
Has looked on Beauty bare. Fortunate they
Who, though once only and then but far away,
Have heard her massive sandal set on stone.

The Plum Gatherer

The angry nettle and the mild
  Grew together under the blue-plum trees.
I could not tell as a child
  Which was my friend of these.   4
Always the angry nettle in the skirt of his sister
  Caught my wrist that reached over the
  ground,
Where alike I gathered,—for the one was sweet
  and the other wore a frosty dust—
The broken plum and the sound.

The plum-trees are barren now and the black
  knot is upon them,
That stood so white in the spring.   10
I would give, to recall the sweetness and the
  frost of the lost blue plums,
Anything, anything.
I thrust my arm among the grey ambiguous
  nettles, and wait.
But they do not sting.

ELINOR WYLIE

Elinor Hoyt Wylie was thirty-four when she
came to New York in 1920 and began to publish her poetry. A year later her first book, *Nets
to Catch the Wind*, appeared—a slight little
volume containing some verse which indicated
a sensitive mind and a gift for verse form.

  She was born in Somerville, New Jersey,

September 3, 1885. Her father, Henry Hoyt,
was Solicitor General in Theodore Roosevelt's
administration. Her childhood was spent, therefore, in Washington, D. C., where she made
her début. Her early life was the usual one of
a young girl in society. Two other Hoyt children became well-known: Henry was an Amer-

ican painter of some note; Nancy, a novelist. But for Elinor nothing mattered so much as did poetry. She began writing when she was young and was known as "the infant Keats" at Miss Baldwin's School in Bryn Mawr, Pennsylvania. Later she went to the Holton Arms School in Washington. As early as 1912 a book of her poems was privately printed for her in London by her mother. None of this early work, however, satisfied the mature poet, and none is included in her collected poems. Her first marriage, to Philip S. Hichborn, ended in separation, and she went to England, renouncing the social world of her girlhood. Some four years after the death of her first husband she married Horace Wylie, whose name she used in writing. In 1923 she divorced her second husband and married William Rose Benét, the poet. They settled in New York, and from that time on she devoted herself entirely to writing.

Elinor Wylie now began writing novels as well as poetry. She spent her summers in England, sometimes in London, sometimes in a rural village. She felt herself closely identified with Shelley, as her novel *Orphan Angel* (1926) indicates, and in England she always visited Half Moon Street where the romantic poet once lived. From early womanhood Mrs. Wylie had suffered from high blood pressure, and for many years she knew that she might die at any time. This, however, did not prevent her from working very hard at her four novels: *Jennifer Lorn* (1923); *Venetian Glass Nephew* (1925); *Orphan Angel* (1926); and *Mr. Hodge and Mr. Hazard* (1928). Her prose was delicate and hard, but it was a poet's prose. Neither her first, thin little book, nor *Black Armour* (1923), nor *Trivial Breath* (1928) would have made her a permanent figure in American letters. Her last book—mailed for publication, it is said, the night she suddenly died of the paralysis which had long threatened her and which in 1928 had paralyzed her face—is her one truly fine piece of work. This book, *Angels and Earthly Creatures*, published after her death (December 16, 1928) at forty-three, contains her best love sonnets and several long lyrics of maturity and dignity. In this last volume her poetry, which had always been chiseled and a little cold, became warm and human. Her collected poems were published in 1932.

She was part of the romantic era in American poetry in which, for a time, this country felt it had come upon a renaissance of its own. But, unlike Edna Millay, who is the most typical woman poet of this period, Mrs. Wylie did not live for sensations alone. She had an analytical mind and examined whatever she felt, sometimes even cruelly dissecting her own emotions. She was beautiful—tall and slender, with reddish-brown hair and brown eyes. As an artist she had the same typical fastidiousness her appearance indicated. She was no ardent feminist, proclaiming as did Miss Millay the same freedom for woman as for man. The subtler shades of feeling, the harder and more brilliant qualities of objects are presented in her lyrical imagery. She stands between the poets of pure sensibility and the intellectual poets of the period beginning around 1925.

Hymn to Earth

FAREWELL, incomparable element,
    Whence man arose, where he shall not return;
And hail, imperfect urn
Of his last ashes, and his firstborn fruit;
Farewell, the long pursuit,   5
And all the adventures of his discontent;
The voyages which sent
His heart averse from home:
Metal of clay, permit him that he come
To thy slow-burning fire as to a hearth;   10
Accept him as a particle of earth.

Fire, being divided from the other three,
It lives removed, or secret at the core;
Most subtle of the four,
When air flies not, nor water flows,   15

The poems of Elinor Wylie are reprinted from *Collected Poems* by permission of and special arrangement with Alfred A. Knopf, Inc., authorized publishers.
Hymn to Earth. According to the philosophy that preceded the discovery of modern chemistry, the world had been composed from varying admixtures of the four initial elements, i.e., water, fire, air, earth. Water becomes the symbol of life learned through sorrow; fire, the creative energy of man which dies; air, the spirit of man; and earth, that element which receives him as dust when he dies.

It disembodied goes,
Being light, elixir of the first decree,
More volatile than he;
With strength and power to pass
Through space, where never his least atom
      was;   20
He has no part in it, save as his eyes
Have drawn its emanation from the skies.

A wingless creature heavier than air,
He is rejected of its quintessence;
Coming and going hence,   25
In the twin minutes of his birth and death,
He may inhale as breath,
As breath relinquish heaven's atmosphere,
Yet in it have no share,
Nor can survive therein   30
Where its outer edge is filtered pure and thin:
It doth but lend its crystal to his lungs
For his early crying, and his final songs.

The element of water has denied
Its child; it is no more his element;   35
It never will relent;
Its silver harvests are more sparsely given
Than the rewards of heaven,
And he shall drink cold comfort at its side:
The water is too wide: 40
The seamew and the gull
Feather a nest made soft and pitiful
Upon its foam; he has not any part
In the long swell of sorrow at its heart.

Hail and farewell, beloved element,   45
Whence he departed, and his parent once;
See where thy spirit runs
Which for so long hath had the moon to wife;
Shall this support his life
Until the arches of the waves be bent   50
And grow shallow and spent?
Wisely it cast him forth
With his dead weight of burdens nothing
      worth,
Leaving him, for the universal years,
A little seawater to make his tears.   55

Hail, element of earth, receive thy own,
And cherish, at thy charitable breast,
This man, this mongrel beast:
He ploughs the sand, and, at his hardest need,
He sows himself for seed;   60
He ploughs the furrow, and in this lies down
Before the corn is grown;

Between the apple bloom
And the ripe apple is sufficient room
In time, and matter, to consume his love   65
And make him parcel of a cypress grove.

Receive him as thy lover for an hour
Who will not weary, by a longer stay,
The kind embrace of clay;
Even within thine arms he is dispersed   7c
To nothing, as at first;
The air flings downward from its four-quar-
      tered tower
Him whom the flames devour;
At the full tide, at the flood,
The sea is mingled with his salty blood: 75
The traveller dust, although the dust be vile,
Sleeps as thy lover for a little while.

from **One Person**

III

"CHILDREN and dogs are subject to my
      power,"
You said, and smiled, and I beside you smiled,
Perceiving my unwisdom of a child,
My courage of a wolf new-taught to cower:
Upon the grass, beneath the falling flower,   5
I saw my spirit silent and beguiled
Standing at gaze; a brute no longer wild;
An infant wearied by the difficult hour.

And am I not your child who has come home?
And am I not your hound for faithfulness?   10
Put forth your hand, put forth your hand to
      bless
A creature stricken timorous and dumb,
Who now regards you with a lover's eyes
And knows that you are merciful and wise.

V

The little beauty that I was allowed—
The lips new-cut and coloured by my sire,
The polished hair, the eyes' perceptive fire—
Has never been enough to make me proud:
For I have moved companioned by a cloud,   5
And lived indifferent to the blood's desire
Of temporal loveliness in vain attire:
My flesh was but a fresh-embroidered shroud.

Now do I grow indignant at the fate
Which made me so imperfect to compare   19

With your degree of noble and of fair;
Our elements are the farthest skies apart;
And I enjoin you, ere it is too late,
To stamp your superscription on my heart.

X

When I perceive the sable of your hair
Silvered, and deep within those caverns are
Your eyesockets, a double-imaged star,
And your fine substance fretted down by care,
Then do I marvel that a woman dare   5
Prattle of mortal matters near and far
To one so wounded in demonic war
Against some prince of Sirius or Altair.

How is it possible that this hand of clay,   9
Though white as porcelain, can contrive a
     touch
So delicate it shall not hurt too much?
What voice can my invention find to say
So soft, precise, and scrupulous a word
You shall not take it for another sword?

XI

"Before I die, let me be happy here."
The glass of heaven was split, and by that
     token
I knew the bubble of my heart had broken;
The cool and chaste, the iridescent sphere,

Filled, in that vernal season of the year,   5
With sapling's blood, the beechen and the
     oaken
And the green willow's; when the word was
     spoken
This innocence did faint and disappear.

So have I lost my only wedding dower,   9
The veins of spring, enclosed within my heart,
Traced small in silver like a celestial chart;
And I am vanished in the leaf and flower,
Since, at your voice, my body's core and pith
Dissolves in air, and is destroyed forthwith.

XVII

Upon your heart, which is the heart of all
My late discovered earth and early sky,
Give me the dearest privilege to die;
Your pity for the velvet of my pall;
Your patience for my grave's inviolate wall;   5
And for my passing bell, in passing by,
Your voice itself, diminished to a sigh
Above all other sounds made musical.

Meanwhile I swear to you I am content
To live without a sorrow to my name;   10
To live triumphant, and to die the same,
Upon the fringes of this continent,
This map of Paradise, this scrap of earth
Wheron you burn like flame upon a hearth.

LOUISE BOGAN

Louise Bogan was born at Livermore Falls, Maine, August 11, 1897, of Irish-American parentage. Her education was begun in the New England country schools and completed at the Girls' Latin School in Boston. At nineteen she married Curt Alexander, who died in 1920. They had one daughter. Later she married Raymond Holden, from whom she is now divorced.

Since 1919 Miss Bogan has lived most of the time in New York City, although one year was spent in Vienna, another in Santa Fe, New Mexico, and two years (1933 and 1937) abroad on Guggenheim Fellowships. In 1944 she was appointed Fellow in American Letters at the Library of Congress, and in 1945–46 she was appointed to the Chair of Poetry in English. Since 1931 Miss Bogan has been the poetry critic of *The New Yorker*. Her career as a critic is a long and distinguished one, including reviewing for *The Nation* and *The New Republic* and writing articles for several of the literary magazines.

High-spirited and witty, Miss Bogan is well

known in literary circles. Her early poetry is concerned largely with woman's relationship to man but not in terms as self-revealing or as sentimental as Miss Millay's. Precisely analytical, Miss Bogan shows how feeling and the analytical mind contradict each other, and how mind can destroy feeling. Her later and more mature work turns to less personal themes. She writes with fine craftsmanship of her response to beauty. Some of her best poetry is an ironic and psychologically acute study of the minds of other poets.

Her published books are *Body of This Death* (1923), *Dark Summer* (1929), *The Sleeping Fury* (1937), and *Poems and New Poems* (1941).

Medusa

I HAD come to the house, in a cave of trees,
  Facing a sheer sky.
Everything moved,—a bell hung ready to strike,
Sun and reflection wheeled by.

When the bare eyes were before me   5
And the hissing hair,
Held up at a window, seen through a door.
The stiff bald eyes, the serpents on the fore-
    head
Formed in the air.

This is a dead scene forever now.   10
Nothing will ever stir.
The end will never brighten it more than this,
Nor the rain blur.

The water will always fall, and will not fall,
And the tipped bell make no sound.   15
The grass will always be growing for hay
Deep on the ground.

And I shall stand here like a shadow
Under the great balanced day,

"Medusa," "The Frightened Man," "Women," and "The Alchemist" from *Body of This Death* by Louise Bogan, reprinted by permission of Robert M. McBride & Company.
Medusa, in Greek mythology one of three Gorgons, winged monsters with claws of bronze and serpents for hair, whose appearance turned all beholders to stone.

My eyes on the yellow dust, that was lifting in
    the wind,   20
And does not drift away.

The Frightened Man

IN FEAR of the rich mouth
  I kissed the thin,—
Even that was a trap
To snare me in.

Even she, so long   5
The frail, the scentless,
Is becoming strong
And proves relentless.

O, forget her praise,
And how I sought her   10
Through a hazardous maze
By shafted water.

Women

WOMEN have no wilderness in them,
  They are provident instead,
Content in the tight hot cell of their hearts
To eat dusty bread.

They do not see cattle cropping red winter
    grass,   5
They do not hear
Snow water going down under culverts
Shallow and clear.

They wait, when they should turn to journeys,
They stiffen, when they should bend.   10
They use against themselves that benevolence
To which no man is friend.

They cannot think of so many crops to a field
Or of clean wood cleft by an axe.
Their love is an eager meaninglessness   15
Too tense, or too lax.
They hear in every whisper that speaks to
    them
A shout and a cry.
As like as not, when they take life over their
    door-sills
They should let it go by.   20

The Alchemist

I BURNED my life, that I might find
  A passion wholly of the mind,
Thought divorced from eye and bone,
Ecstasy come to breath alone.
I broke my life, to seek relief   5
From the flawed light of love and grief.

With mounting beat the utter fire
Charred existence and desire.
It died low, ceased its sudden thresh.
I had found unmysterious flesh—   10
Not the mind's avid substance—still
Passionate beyond the will.

Hypocrite Swift

H YPOCRITE Swift now takes an eldest daugh-
  ter.
He lifts Vanessa's hand. Cudsho, my dove!
Drink Wexford ale and quaff down Wexford
  water
But never love.   4

He buys new caps; he and Lord Stanley ban
Hedge-fellows who have neither wit nor
  swords.
He turns his coat; Tories are in; Queen Anne
Makes twelve new lords.

The Alchemist. Alchemy, the chemistry of the Middle Ages, was mainly devoted to the vain effort to transform baser metals into gold. Miss Bogan here indicates that she (like many other intellectual poets of this period) attempted to exchange the passion of the heart for that of the mind, only to find that the heart (or emotion) was the source of poetry.
"Hypocrite Swift," "The Sleeping Fury," "Henceforth from the Mind," and "Song for a Lyre," from *The Sleeping Fury,* copyright, 1937, by Charles Scribner's Sons; reprinted by permission.
1. **Swift,** etc. When Jonathan Swift, the great eighteenth-century satirist, left Ireland to live in London, he daily wrote Esther Johnson his *Journal to Stella.* This journal was written in what Swift called his "little language," a code of telescoped words easily translated. The journal is the monument of the Dean's curious love, never consummated in marriage so far as the records show, for Stella, who was his former pupil. In London, Swift lived for a time in the home of a Mrs. Vanhomrigh, whose daughter, Esther, called "Vanessa" by Swift, became deeply attached to him. In general, the poet takes exception to Swift's hypocrisy in his treatment of both Stella and Vanessa. 2. **Cudsho,** a sort of exclamation which Swift occasionally uses and which is probably equivalent to our slang "Oh, nuts" or "Oh, yeah." 3. **Wexford,** a county in Ireland where Stella sometimes went to drink the waters. 6. **Hedge-fellows,** low-class fellows, scoundrels whom Swift snubbed. 7. **Queen Anne,** the English sovereign (1703–14) during Swift's brief term of success in London. Swift was ambitious and hoped for great favors from the Queen, but she only made him Dean of St. Patrick's in Dublin, and he never forgave her for this. The Whigs and Tories were the dominating political parties of the day. As an opportunist, Swift changed parties in the hope of gaining preferment and a bishopric from the Queen by supporting her party, the Tories. Stanley (l. 5), Peterborough (l. 17), and Fountain (l. 17) were lords of the Queen's court.

The town mows hay in hell; he swims in the
  river;
His giddiness returns; his head is hot.   10
Berries are clean, while peaches dam the giver
(Though grapes do not).

Mrs. Vanhomrigh keeps him safe from the
  weather.
Preferment pulls his periwig askew.
Pox takes belittlers; do the willows feather?   15
God keep you.

Stella spells ill; Lords Peterborough and Foun-
  tain
Talk politics; the Florence wine went sour.
Midnight: two different clocks, here and in
  Dublin
Give out the hour.   20

On walls at court, long gilded mirrors gaze.
The parquet shines; outside the snow falls
  deep.
Venus, the Muses stare above the maze.
Now sleep.

Dream the mixed, fearsome dream. The satiric
  word   25
Dies in its horror. Wake, and live by stealth.
The bitter quatrain forms, is here, is heard,
Is wealth.

What care I; what cares saucy Presto? Stir   29
The bed-clothes; hearten up the perishing fire.
Hypocrite Swift sent Stella a green apron
And dead desire.

To My Brother

KILLED: HAUMONT WOOD: OCTOBER, 1918

O YOU so long dead,
  You masked and obscure,

9. **The town . . . hell,** Swift's reference to the heat of the summer. 11. **Berries, etc.** Swift blamed his mysterious attacks of giddiness on the eating of fruit. He could eat berries and grapes without harmful results, but peaches seemed to cause after-effects. These attacks of giddiness, which sprang from a source not definitely known, increased and resulted finally in his madness. 15. **Pox takes belittlers,** a curse upon those who belittle me. 23. **the maze,** the network of paths at Hampton Court. There may not have been statuary overlooking the maze; the figures of the Muses and Venus were added by the poet to make a fuller picture. 29. **What . . . Presto,** an actual quotation from the *Journal. Presto* was the name by which Swift referred to himself in the *Journal's* "little language."
"To My Brother" and "Roman Fountain" copyright 1935 The New Yorker Magazine, Inc. Reprinted from *The Sleeping Fury* by Louise Bogan; Copyright, 1937, by Charles Scribner's Sons; Used by permission.
To My Brother. Miss Bogan's brother was killed in action in Haumont Wood shortly before World War I ended. The poem is a bitter comment on the fact that the war changed nothing and brought not peace but further wars.

I can tell you, all things endure:
The wine and the bread;

The marble quarried for the arch;   5
The iron become steel;
The spoke broken from the wheel;
The sweat of the long march;

The hay-stacks cut through like loaves
And the hundred flowers from the seed;
All things indeed   11
Though struck by the hooves

Of disaster, of time due,
Of fell loss and gain,
All things remain,   15
I can tell you, this is true.

Though burned down to stone
Though lost from the eye,
I can tell you, and not lie,—
Save of peace alone.   20

The Sleeping Fury

YOU ARE here now,
Who were so loud and feared, in a symbol
    before me,
Alone and asleep, and I at last look long upon
    you.

Your hair fallen on your cheek, no longer in
    the semblance of serpents,
Lifted in the gale; your mouth, that shrieked
    so, silent.   5
You, my scourge, my sister, lie asleep, like a
    child,
Who, after rage, for an hour quiet, sleeps out
    its tears.

The days close to winter
Rough with strong sound. We hear the sea and
    the forest,   9
And the flames of your torches fly, lit by others,

Ripped by the wind, in the night. The black
    sheep for sacrifice
Huddle together. The milk is cold in the jars.

All to no purpose, as before, the knife whetted
    and plunged,
The shout raised, to match the clamor you
    have given them.
You alone turn away, not appeased; unaltered,
    avenger.   15

Hands full of scourges, wreathed with your
    flames and adders
You alone turned away, but did not move from
    my side,
Under the broken light, when the soft nights
    took the torches.

At thin morning you showed, thick and wrong
    in that calm,
The ignoble dream and the mask, sly, with slits
    at the eyes,   20
Pretence and half-sorrow, beneath which a
    coward's hope trembled.

You uncovered at night, in the locked stillness
    of houses,
False love due the child's heart, the kissed-out
    lie, the embraces,
Made by the two who for peace tenderly
    turned to each other.

You who know what we love, but drive us to
    know it;   25
You with your whips and shrieks, bearer of
    truth and solitude;
You who give, unlike men, to expiation your
    mercy.

Dropping the scourge when at last the
    scourged advances to meet it,
You, when the hunted turns, no longer remain
    the hunter
But stand silent and wait, at last returning his
    gaze.   30

Beautiful now as a child whose hair, wet with
    rage and tears
Clings to its face. And now I may look upon
    you,
Having once met your eyes. You lie in sleep
    and forget me.
Alone and strong in my peace, I look upon you
    in yours.

The Sleeping Fury. According to ancient Greek beliefs the Furies, or Eumenides, punished all offenses against human society; above all, murder of relatives. But they were not without benevolent and beneficent attributes. When the sinner had expiated his crime, they were ready to forgive. Black sheep were sacrificed to them (in Athens) at night by the light of torches. A festival was held in their honor every year, with offerings of milk and honey mixed with water—no wine. Miss Bogan says of the purpose of her poem: "I suppose the Fury in my poem is really a mother-domination complex, which has finally been overcome."

Roman Fountain

UP FROM the bronze, I saw
Water without a flaw
Rush to its rest in air,
Reach to its rest, and fall.

Bronze of the blackest shade,   5
An element man-made,
Shaping upright the bare
Clear gouts of water in air.

O, as with arm and hammer,
Still it is good to strive   10
To beat out the image whole,
To echo the shout and stammer
When full-gushed waters, alive
Strike on the fountain's bowl
After the air of summer.   15

Henceforth, from the Mind

HENCEFORTH, from the mind,
For your whole joy, must spring
Such joy as you may find
In any earthly thing,
And every time and place   5
Will take your thought for grace.

Henceforth, from the tongue,
From shallow speech alone,
Comes joy you thought, when young,
Would bring you to the bone,   10
Would pierce you to the heart
And spoil its stop and start.

Henceforth, from the Mind. This poem is the poet's mature statement that the material of art must be gathered not so much from the sensations as from all which the mind has digested.

Henceforward, from the shell,
Wherein you heard, and wondered
At oceans like a bell   15
So far from ocean sundered—
A smothered sound that sleeps
Long lost within lost deeps,

Will chime you change and hours,
The shadow of increase,   20
Will sound you flowers
Born under troubled peace—
Henceforth, henceforth
Will echo sea and earth.

Song for a Lyre

THE LANDSCAPE where I lie
Again from boughs sets free
Summer; all night must fly
In wind's obscurity
The thick, green leaves that made   5
Heavy the August shade.

Soon, in the pictured night,
Returns—as in a dream
Left after sleep's delight—
The shallow autumn stream: 10
Softly awake, its sound
Poured on the chilly ground.

Soon fly the leaves in throngs;
O love, though once I lay
Far from its sound, to weep,   15
When night divides my sleep,
When stars, the autumn stream,
Stillness, divide my dream,
Night to your voice belongs.

Song for a Lyre. This lyric is nostalgic for a more youthful period in life when love gave more assurance than the later landscape of emotion does.

LÉONIE ADAMS

Léonie Adams was born in Brooklyn, New York, December 9, 1899. Her immediate ancestors came from Maryland and Virginia, but her paternal grandmother was a Venezuelan. Shy and quick of speech, small and dark-haired, Miss Adams reflects her Latin American ancestry. After attending the public schools in Brooklyn, she entered Barnard College and was graduated in 1922. When asked why so much of her poetry is, in a sense, nature poetry, she replied that she had been raised in a Brooklyn back yard. She and her sisters were never allowed to play on the streets, and could only peer wistfully at the other children from the lower windows of their old brownstone house. Miss Adams had never been in the subway until she went to college. Each weekend her father escorted her home from Barnard.

Despite this parental watchfulness, she met many of the younger literary people and did her share of seeing the Village with her friends. While she was still an undergraduate, *The New Republic* printed her poem "April Mortality." Soon she was regarded as one of the best of the younger poets. By this time her family had moved to Hillburn, New York, near Suffern, and lived in a large house surrounded by some of the wildest country to be found in New York. These hills and forests are often reflected in her poetry.

In 1924, Léonie Adams was on the editorial board of *Measure*, a poetry magazine which had a lively and a brief career. Then came recognition of a wider order. Her first book, *Those Not Elect*, was published in 1925 and was immediately praised highly. In 1928 she was granted a Guggenheim Fellowship, which was renewed in 1929. During these years she lived in London, Oxford, and Paris. Always a fine linguist, she was able during this period abroad to complete her knowledge of conversational French.

Returning to New York, Miss Adams taught at New York University, where she met and married the well-known critic William Troy. After a brief period of teaching at Sarah Lawrence, she and her husband went to Bennington College in Vermont.

Her second book, *High Falcon*, appeared in 1929. Miss Adams is now finishing a selected volume of her poems which will contain many new and longer lyrics as well as some poems from her two earlier volumes. Recently she taught creative writing at Rutgers and Columbia University. She has edited for the Limited Editions Club a collection of translations from François Villon's lyrics, including translations of her own; and she and her husband are now contributing to a collection of translations from the prose and poetry of the French poet Paul Valéry. Others of her translations

are to be found in *The Lyrics of François Villon* (1933). She was appointed Consultant in Poetry to the Library of Congress for 1948–49.

Miss Adams' work is difficult to place. She is, in a way, a modern mystic, a mystic who relies not on the sense of the other world but on the conviction that mortal beauty, earthly loveliness is itself eternal. In no sense does this poet deny modern science or modern thought, with which she is fully conversant. Her poetry, arising out of the images of nature, interprets the complexities of the human heart as a part of the brave and continuous cycle of life. All life is to be fully tasted and to be understood. She is never personal or sentimental: whatever pattern her feeling takes in verse, it is related to the feeling of all sensitive people. She grew up loving the poetry of Yeats; later she studied Blake and taught his work. She also knows the metaphysical poets well. Many of her poems revolve around the old dualism of body and soul, the sensitive and the insensitive, but only as this dualism heightens the conviction that life is good. Her rare music and her keen, almost unique perception help to make her one of our most distinguished modern American lyricists.

Death and the Lady

DEATH to the Lady said,
While she to dancing-measure still
Would move, while beauties on her lay,
Simply as dews the buds do fill,
Death said, "Stay!   5
Tell me, Lady,
If in your breast the lively breath
May flicker for a little space,
What ransom will you give to Death,
Lady?" he said.   10
"Oh not one joy, oh not one grace,
And what is your will to my will?
I can outwit parched fancies still,"
To Death said the Lady.

"Death and the Lady," "Those Not Elect," "Pity of the Heavens," and "To The Waterfront Pigeons," from *Those Not Elect*, reprinted by permission of Robert M. McBride & Company.

Death to that Lady said,   15
When blood went numb and wearily,
"In innocency dear breath you drew,
And marrow and bloom you rendered me."
She said, "True."
"How now, Lady?"   20
"My heart sucked up its sweet at will,
Whose scent, when substance' sweet is past,
Is lovely still, is lovely still,
Death," she said.
"For bones' reprieve the dreams go last.   25
Soon, soon, your flowery show did part,
But preciously I cull the heart."
Death said to the Lady.

Death to that Lady said,
"Is then not all our bargain done?   30
Or why do you beckon me so fast,
To chaffer for a skeleton
Flesh must cast,
Ghostly lady?"
"For, Death, that I would have you drain 35
From my dead heart the blood that stands
So chilly in the withered vein,
And, Death," she said,
"Give my due bones into your hands."
"Beauties I claim at morning-prime,   40
But the lack-lustre in good time,"
Death said to the Lady.

Those Not Elect

NEVER, being damned, see Paradise.
  The heart will sweeten at its look;
Nor hell was known, till Paradise
Our senses shook.

Never hear angels at laughter,   5
For how comports with grief to know
Wisdom in heaven bends to laughter, laughter,
Laughter upon woe?

Never fall dreaming on celestials,
Lest, bound in a ruinous place,   10
You turn to wander with celestials
Down holy space.

Never taste that fruit with the soul
Whereof the body may not eat,
Lest flesh at length lay waste the soul   15
In its sick heat.

Pity of the Heavens

LIGHT all day from heaven was streaming,
  But the last hour gathered earth with light,
Seeping the darkened air with a blue color;
And now the stars from the lofty brow of the
      night
Regard the earth, regard the withering land; 5
And now fair snow comes dropping over her
      bosom,
Sky touching earth with a chaste hand.

Earth bears no more the print of her creatures'
      feet;
Dark breast, no more the glittering waters
      start;
The hare and the doe are uncherished in the
      wood;   10
She is numb, there is bitter armor on her
      heart.

But how profoundly would the heavens caress
      her,
With pity that hardly is reckoned from eye to
      eye,
And mouth on mouth is untold.
The amity of the skies has left their touch   15
So light, so pure, so cold.

O bosom carven upon the roses and pleasures,
Heaven cannot unlock your passions and your
      mirth,
But have you not perceived those eyes, mourn-
      ful and bright,
How you are cherished by the countenance of
      the skies;   20
Is it not much, O earth?

To the Waterfront Pigeons

CEASE to preen, O shining pigeons!
  A jewel eye and breast of quiet,
Rainbow neck, will purchase here
Never nest nor wholesome diet.

What would these with muck and soot?   5
Or to what mortal use bestead

17. **O bosom, etc.,** an image of the earth or life frozen but
still beautiful in the light of spiritual contemplation.
To the Waterfront Pigeons. The city pigeons here are symbols of beauty in modern times.

Dainty steppings and a foot
Coral-pink and ringleted?

Did you look, O airish flock,
Now when only breath comes cheap,   10
For one dirty drudging dock
Seven exquisites to keep?

Sweetings, then you have not known
How Beauty that the waters bred
Creeps up battered and alone   15
To precarious cup and bread.

Beauty's self, your holy mother,
Here sits not to a goddess' share.
She must live like any other
With no way but being fair.   20

Stealing up the morning alleys,
And who to tell she is not fraud?
Mortals now are grimly pressed,
That make Beauty to a bawd.

Ghostly Tree

O   BEECH, unbind your yellow leaf, for deep
    The honeyed time lies sleeping, and lead
        shade
Seals up the eyelids of its golden sleep.
Long are your flutes, chimes, little bells, at rest,
And here is only the cold scream of the fox,
Only the hunter following on the hound;   6
While your quaint-plumaged,
The bird that your green summer boughs
        lapped round,
Bends south its soft bright breast.

Before the winter and the terror break,   10
Scatter the leaf that broadened with the rose
Not for a tempest, but a sigh, to take.
Four nights to exorcise the thing that stood
Bound by these frail which dangle at your
        branch,

23. **Mortals . . . pressed.** This line and the following express
the idea that beauty today is valued only commercially.
"Ghostly Tree," "Bell Tower," "The River in the Meadows,"
"Evening Sky," "Sundown," "Country Summer," "Lullaby,"
"Send Forth the High Falcon," "Caryatid," and "The Mount"
from *High Falcon* (1929), reprinted by permission of The John
Day Company.
Ghostly Tree. 4. **Long,** etc., images of the leaves in the
full richness of summer.   14. **frail,** use of adjective instead
of noun—frail leaves or images of summer. The word "thing"
(l. 13) means life or fulfillment which must be renounced because of the coming in of winter. The syntax here is difficult
and the idea merely suggested, not stated. The theme of the
poem is that beauty should be renounced without struggle.

They ran a frosty dagger to its heart;   15
And it, wan substance,
No more remembered it might cry or start
Or stain a point with blood.

Bell Tower

I   HAVE seen, O desolate one, the voice has its
        tower,
The voice also, builded at secret cost,
Its temple of precious tissue. Not silent then
Forever—casting silence in your hour.

There marble boys are leant from the light
        throat,   5
Thick locks that hang with dew and eyes dew-
        lashed,
Dazzled with morning, angels of the wind,
With ear a-point to the enchanted note.   8

And these at length shall tip the hanging bell,
And first the sound must gather in deep bronze,
Till, rarer than ice, purer than a bubble of gold,
It fill the sky to beat on an airy shell.

The River in the Meadows

C   RYSTAL parting the meads,
    A boat drifted up it like a swan.
Tranquil, lovely, its bright front to the
        waters,
A slow swan is gone.

Full waters, O flowing silver,   5
Pure, level with the clover,
It will stain drowning a star,
With the moon it will brim over.

Running through lands dewy and shorn,
Cattle stoop at its brink,   10
And every fawny-colored throat
Will sway its bells and drink.

I saw a boat sailing the river
With a tranced gait. It seemed
Loose by a spell from its moorings,   15
Or a thing the helmsman dreamed.

Bell Tower. The image of the voice (within the tower of the
throat) is related to Yeats' image of the poet's tower, the place
from which the poet may speak his message about life. Miss
Adams connects the physical image of the poet speaking
imaginatively with the physical image of an actual tower.
The River in the Meadows. This image of the boat is that
of the imagination of man's creative spirit which can be injured
by pain. The idea is that the imagination springs from the
heart's and mind's happiness and fulfillment.

They said it would carry no traveller,
But the vessel would go down,
If a heart were heavy-winged,
Or the bosom it dwelt in stone.

Evening Sky

How NOW are we tossed about by a windy
heaven,
The eye that scans it madded to discern
In a single quarter all the wild ravage of light,
Amazing light to quiver and suddenly turn
Before the stormy demon fall of night;   5
And yet west spaces saved celestial
With silver sprinklings of the anointed sun.
The eye goes up for certitude,
Driven hither and thither on that shifty scene
To the dome closing like impenetrable hoar,
And down from the cold zenith drops abashed;
O desolation rent by intolerable blue   12
Of the living heaven's core,
Nor death itself at last the heavenly whim.
For how can an eye sustain   15
To watch heaven slain and quickening, or do
To stretch in its little orbit and contain
Sky balancing chaos in an inconstant rim?

Sundown

THIS is the time lean woods shall spend
A steeped-up twilight, and the pale evening drink,
And the perilous roe, the leaper to the west
brink,
Trembling and bright to the caverned cloud
descend.

Now shall you see pent oak gone gusty and
frantic,   5
Stooped with dry weeping, ruinously unloosing
The sparse disheveled leaf, or reared and toss-
ing
A dreary scarecrow bough in funeral antic.

Aye, tatter you and rend,
Oak heart, to your profession mourning; not
obscure   10
The outcome, not crepuscular; on the deep
floor
Sable and gold match lustres and contend.

And rags of shrouding will not muffle the slain.
This is the immortal extinction, the priceless
wound
Not to be staunched. The live gold leaks be-
yond,   15
And matter's sanctified, dipped in a gold stain.

Country Summer

Now THE rich cherry, whose sleek wood
And top with silver petals traced,
Like a strict box its gems encased,
Has split from out that cunning lid,
All in an innocent green round,   5
Those melting rubies which it hid;
With moss ripe-strawberry-encrusted,
So birds get half, and minds lapse merry
To taste that deep-red, lark's-bite berry,
And blackcap bloom is yellow-dusted.   10

The wren that thieved it in the eaves
A trailer of the rose could catch
To her poor droopy sloven thatch,
And side by side with the wren's brood—
O lovely time of beggars' luck—   15
Opens the quaint and hairy bud;
And full and golden is the yield
Of cows that never have to house,
But all night nibble under boughs,
Or cool their sides in the moist field.   20

Into the rooms flow meadow airs,
The warm farm baking smell's blown round,
Inside and out, and sky and ground
Are much the same, the wishing star,
Hesperus, kind and early born,   25
Is risen only finger-far;
All stars stand close in summer air,
And tremble, and look mild as amber,
When wicks are lighted in the chamber,
You might say, stars were settling there.   30

Evening Sky. The first lines describe the storm and peace of
sky. Beginning with "The eye goes up" (l. 8), we see the poet
identifying her state of mind with that of the sky, in which
only a little blue is left, soon to be blotted out. And the final
question is really how the poet can keep faith with his vision
in a world symbolized by a sky "balancing chaos in an inconstant rim."
Sundown. This is a statement of faith in the sanctity of matter,
or mortal beauty. The poem begins with an image of sunset in
autumn, of beauty in death. The oak is addressed as a symbol
of permanent grief. In the last stanza the beauty of death
and grief is exalted. 3. perilous roe, really an image of light.

11. crepuscular, obscure, like twilight.
Country Summer. The poem begins with small images of summer, widening to larger images of its beauty, and in the last
two stanzas turns to the human wonder in, and love of, summer.

Now straightening from the flowery hay,
Down the still light the mowers look,
Or turn, because their dreaming shook,
And they waked half to other days,
When left alone in the yellow stubble   35
The rusty-coated mare would graze.
Yet thick the lazy dreams are born,
Another thought can come to mind,
But like the shivering of the wind,
Morning and evening in the corn.

Lullaby

Hush, lullay.
   Your treasures all
Encrust with rust,
Your trinket pleasures fall
      To dust.   5

Beneath the sapphire arch,
Upon the grassy floor,
Is nothing more
      To hold,
And play is over-old.   10
Your eyes
      In sleepy fever gleam,
Your lids droop
      To their dream.
You wander late alone,   15
The flesh frets on the bone,
Your love fails in your breast,
Here is the pillow.
      Rest.

Send Forth the High Falcon

Send forth the high falcon flying after the
   mind
To topple it from its cold cloud:
The beak of the falcon to pierce it till it fall
Where the simple heart is bowed.
O in wild innocence it rides   5
The rare ungovernable element,
But once it sways to terror and descent,
The marches of the wind are its abyss,

Send Forth the High Falcon. The falcon is the image of
hunting or exploring. Its flight to topple the mind to the subjective regions of the emotions or heart is a flight to create art.
For only through fusion of mind and emotion can the poet work.
This poem is an answer to the poets who talk of creating poetry
as an intellectual process.

No wind staying it upward of the breast—
Let mind be proud for this,   10
And ignorant from what fabulous cause it
      dropt,
And with how learned a gesture the un-
      schooled heart
Shall lull both terror and innocence to rest.

Caryatid

Not at midnight, not at morning, O sweet
   city,
Shall we come in at your portal, but this girl,
   your servant,
Bearing on her head a broken stone,
In the body shaped to this, the throat and
   bosom
Poised no less for the burden now the temple
   is fallen,   5
Tells the white Athenian wonder overthrown.

There is no clasp which stays beauty forever.
Time has undone her, from porphyry, from
   bronze.
She is winged every way and will not rest;
But the gesture of the lover shall remain long
   after,   10
Where lovely and imponderable there leans
A weight more grave than marble on the
   breast.

The Mount

No, I have tempered haste,
   The joyous traveller said,
The steed has passed me now
Whose hurrying hooves I fled.
My spectre rides thereon,   5
I learned what mount he has,
Upon what summers fed,

Caryatid. The figure of the girl or caryatid (a Greek column
in the form of a female figure used to support an entablature)
is the figure of a woman who has loved and keeps the posture
or attitude of love even if the lover goes (and the temple of
love decays).   8. **porphyry,** a rock that because of its high
polish is used as an ornamental stone. The ancient Greeks and
Romans quarried a great deal of it for columns, pavements,
and interior decorations.
The Mount. Desire or impulse to perfection in fulfillment is
tempered now in the poet. This desire (imaged as the mount
or steed) she understands, and she knows too what it had
caused her to suffer. Meantime the creative process of her
own fulfillment which she has imagined, even as it passed her
by, remains pictured for her as immortal.

And wept to know again,
Beneath the saddle swung,
Treasure for whose great theft   10
This breast was wrung.
His bridle bells sang out,
I could not tell their chime,
So brilliantly he rings,
But called his name as Time.   15
His bin was morning light,
Those straws which gild his bed
Are of the fallen West.
Although green lands consume
Beneath their burning tread,   20
In everlasting bright
His hooves have rest.

Never Enough of Living

NEVER, my heart, is there enough of living,
Since only in thee is loveliness so sweet
    pain;
Only for thee the willows will be giving
Their quiet fringes to the dreaming river;
Only for thee so the light grasses ever   5
Are hollowed by the print of windy feet,
And breathe hill weather on the misty plain;
And were no rapture of them in thy beat,
For every hour of sky
Stillborn in gladness would the waters wear 10
Colors of air translucently,
And the stars sleep there.

Gently, my heart, nor let one moment ever
Be spilled from the brief fullness of thine urn.
Plunge in its exultation star and star,   15
Sea and plumed sea in turn.
O still, my heart, nor spill this moment ever.

"Never Enough of Living" from *Those Not Elect*, reprinted by
permission of Robert M. McBride & Company.

Grapes Making

NOON sun beats down the leaf; the noon
Of summer burns along the vine
And thins the leaf with burning air
Till from the under leaf is fanned
And down the woven vine the light.   5
Still the pleached leaves drop, layer on layer,
To wind the sun on either hand;
And echoes of the light are bound,
And hushed the blazing cheek of light,
The hurry of the breathless noon,   10
And from the thicket of the vine
The grape has pressed into its round.

The grape has pressed into its round
And swings, aloof chill green, clean won
Of light, between the sky and ground,   15
Those hid soft-flashing lamps yet blind,
Which yield an apprehended sun.
Fresh triumph in the courteous kind
That has more ways to be, and years,
And easy countless treasuries,   20
You whose all-told is still no sum,
Like a rich heart, well-said in sighs,
The careless autumn mornings come,
The grapes drop glimmering to the shears.

Now shady sod at heel piles deep;   25
An over-arching shade, the vine
Across the fall of noon is flung;
And here beneath the leaves is cast
A light to color noonday sleep,
While still, bemused, the grape is swung   30
Beneath the eyelids of the vine;
And deepening like a tender thought
Green moves along the leaf, and bright
The leaf above, and leaf has caught,
And emerald pierces day, and last   35
The faint leaf vanishes to light.

"Grapes Making" reprinted by permission of The John Day
Company.

Karl Hofer: Seated Man (Sitzender)
*The primitive yet sophisticated
style of this lithograph lends itself
admirably to the portrayal of a world
type as characteristic in its way as
Eliot's J. Alfred Prufrock. Hofer's work
was influenced by African sculpture*

PART TWO

The war

and the waste landers

THE PERIOD in literature discussed in the first essay and the period of the First World War and the Waste Landers cross each other in time. Many of the English writers who had separated life and literature were beyond the age of conscription in the first war and went on singing nostalgically about beauty. They clung to the memory of childhood as a period of heightened sensitivity or to the memory of the past and to the earlier conceptions of man's spiritual greatness. But the war which began in 1914 ended the belief that our civilization evolved easily into any utopia where man's intelligence had free play. As Henry James said in 1915, speaking for his generation as to the significance of the national hatreds now aroused, "To have to take it all for what the treacherous years were, all the while, really making for and *meaning*, is too tragic for any words." Like James, many a young artist had chosen to believe that our complex industrial system, whatever the inequalities it fostered, could be justified if it allowed the sensitive few, in particular the artists, their exhaustive imaginative researches.

185

But actually, as we have noted, despite the defense raised against it, disillusionment in literature had been growing since the nineties. In England the decline of faith had been slow and rather graceful; in America optimism had fed longer on our characteristic American individualism, our greater economic stability, and our traditional puritanism. Both puritanism and optimism provoked us to an extreme egotism concerning our future as free men in a long-boasted democracy. Moreover, while in England the tide of romantic enthusiasm ebbed, America still enjoyed a kind of naïve radicalism. Still believing herself to be at this time a nation of people completely different from Europeans, America until the First World War held no achievement beyond her. Between 1910 and 1917 many American artists, clergymen, and intellectuals wrote freely in favor of some sort of socialism, and their writings were published in our most popular magazines. The most enthusiastic radicals prophesied that Debs might become President. And indeed, in the election of 1920, when the Socialists had been largely suppressed and he himself was in prison, Debs did receive nearly a million votes for President. On the other hand, our decentralized government, stressing the rights of the states against the federal government, of town against state, of individual against town, encouraged us as a people to believe in individualism as a continuous possibility in political, intellectual, and cultural evolution.

While in England, Beauty, as she had been cultivated in literature in an attempt to ignore reality, continued to fix her eyes on nature and on man's glorious past, in America she still kept one eye on the strictly American future. Every new American movement gave her new hope. Beauty became a feminist. She was lionized by the women's clubs in the small towns of the Middle West. At times she even slightly resembled Mrs. Babbitt. Long after literature in England ceased to be completely concerned about "Art" and turned to a consideration of political difficulties as well, America, for the most part, continued to believe that perhaps finally she had reached artistic maturity. Such artists as fought for individualism here (even such as saw it beset by science or industrialism) were often very naïve.

America still loved her success stories, and her minor writers very often wrote them. But her more significant authors had not been so steadily optimistic. Even the writers of the late nineteenth century, like Henry James, and even, more exactly, the major figures of the early twentieth century, like Edwin Arlington Robinson, had rejected the businessman as hero, and most of the important writers had expressed fear that America's materialistic advance might defeat her artistic growth. Nevertheless, the war years did not force America toward the precipice of despair quite so rapidly as England. During and for some years after the war America was allowed a period of respite.

In that period, American literature for the first time took precedence over English literature. The poets who were shortly to set the form and theme of poetry, the novelists of the greatest vitality, were American, not English. From the period of the First World War until today, American literature has had a kind of physical and emotional energy lacking in the English literature of these years. Crude it may be, and often is, in its attempts at new style or in the treatment of new subject matter. But its very lack of tradition has allowed it freedom to explore new techniques and new scenes. While the English writers have clung to old ideas and old forms, American writers, believing in ever-expanding American horizons and not opposed to science, have searched out new aspects of Beauty and pursued her somewhat fugitive figure in and out of the tangled city alleys. They have refused to believe she could be found only in nature and have been delighted with such glimpses of her as might appear, even in the slum streets. Against an industrial backdrop, Beauty had her worshipers among the American writers.

The English writers meanwhile had not been able to forget that in their country Beauty had long had the lineaments of nobility, and that these lineaments, though aging, were still dear to the memory. Therefore, while the American writers optimistically enough, at least until the period of the depression, pictured her as inhabiting the new scenery of the city, in England Beauty remained only the symbol of memory of past glory.

✠ WORLD WAR I broke out for England in 1914. At once most of the traditional writers were silenced. John Masefield, considered one of the most modern poets in the period just preceding the war, became a conscientious objector and for some curious reason was later rewarded for this by being made Poet Laureate. He upheld all the old virtues and clung to the old ideal of Beauty. Although he claimed to be a realist descended from Chaucer, Masefield, who had shocked the English dons, was recognized by younger literary critics after the war as the typical English Victorian dressed in rough clothes. He wrote of low characters as if they were typical English idealists slightly misled and out at the elbow. But all his characters reform or die. That Masefield is actually a sentimentalist, for all his use of realistic situations, is indicated in such a passage as this:

Jimmy walked home with all his mind on fire,
One lovely face forever set in flame.
He shivered as he went, like tautened wire,
Surge after surge of shuddering in him came
And then swept out repeating the one sweet
  name
"Anna, oh Anna," to the evening star.
Anna was sipping whiskey in the bar.

While Masefield and those of his generation of writers continued upholding the old virtues, the young poets were in the trenches. And with the war, a feeling that had been growing up in America as well as in England of the helplessness of the individual in modern society began to be expressed everywhere. In both countries romantic naturalism curdled into pessimistic determinism. Biology and psychology already seemed to have denied the greatness and goodness of man as divinely created and directed. The war seemed to emphasize man's inhumanity to man; the idealism of the nineteenth century as to man's natural nobility did not seem to be proved by the facts. Skies were darkening and remaining dark. Soon a form of naturalism, different from the romantic nature worship of the nineteenth century, became current in the literature of all the English-speaking peoples.

It had the war as its immediate cause, but its fundamental cause was rooted in science and in economics. Already current in Europe, this form of naturalism was a philosophy which pictured man in a mechanical world, victimized by that world and by his own impulses as well. As the last nineteenth-century novelist, George Meredith, says, concerning this pessimistic form of naturalism, often called determinism, "the naturalist sees the hog in Nature, and takes Nature for the hog."

Such naturalism had developed in France long before the war. Now, as a result of the great loss of faith in moral or spiritual values brought about by the war, it crept quickly over England and America. It was, of course, an overcorrective to romantic individualism. Soon a number of younger writers were to describe all cities as sewers and all men as sex-driven creatures closely akin to the lower animals. Some years after the war, Joseph Wood Krutch surveyed with horror in his book *The Modern Temper* the results of such a view of civilization and mankind. He noted that the old form of tragedy, which results when an essentially noble character transgresses an immutable moral law by self-originating will, was no longer the tragedy with which the artists concerned themselves. There were no noble characters; there was no immutable moral law; and in man there was no self-originating will. Those artists who had been concerned with grief were forced now to turn to study grievances. Practically, it was no longer possible to write—since the writers conceived of life as pathetic and will-less—except of man's actions as predetermined by his glands or his psychological conditioning. Wherever they looked the artists concluded that man was frustrated and given over to an increasingly subjective self-examination and to Freudian engrossment in a sick individualism. The very industrial machine which man had created seemed, because of its complexity and its concern for success, to have become the enemy of all the sensitive people. Nor was there yet any assurance that the sciences of sociology and economics might be used so intelligently as to free man rather than to imprison him. Literature was, consequently, given over to an exhausting and exhaustive study of the self as thwarted and trapped.

The English war poets

Man's impotence in the face of economic forces was emphasized by the war. And war literature was on the whole pessimistic. Such of it as emphasized patriotism was very second-rate. There is in fact very little war poetry of any great value. Writers in the trenches are in no position to view life whole, and much war literature is propaganda. During World War I, one poet after another was hailed in England or America as a new star in the literary heavens; but many of these died, and those who lived were to come to feel that they had fought for nothing and to discover that their early poetry was naïve or warped.

Wilfred Owen, almost alone of the war poets, saw the tragedy clearly. That men would behave with magnificent bravery he knew. That they would act on false idealism he realized. He took the tragic view of the young men whose lives, like his own, were to be lost. Writing in a fairly traditional literary form, he stressed the dignity of the human spirit, victimized by causes it cannot justify and cannot end.

Siegfried Sassoon spent his war years circulating, even in the trenches, violently anti-war poetry. He stressed the ugliness, the filth, the degradation that war inflicted. He mocked the patriotism of the people who stayed at home. He became an agitator against the scheme of things which set one nation against another and maimed and disillusioned the youth of many lands. His poetry is, at times, almost propaganda, and he never believed in the slogan which inspired the more sentimental poets: that this was a war to end wars. Sassoon lived to return to England to write satires against the upper classes, whom he pictured as safe enough to pretend to patriotism. By nature a late romantic writer highly aware of the intellectual's inability to act politically, he has in recent years written verse not unlike his very early poetry in its expression of the beauty of the country life. And although he has never successfully recaptured the genteel illusions knocked out of him during the war years, he has come to see the Second World War as one

of self-preservation, but his recognition of this fact has not, at least in his poetry, led him to analyze the connection between the first war and the second.

Early post-war literature in America: experimentation in form

When the war was over, the young boys who had been thrown into it and who had lived wrote their autobiographies—books in which they examined what they had been before the war and what they were after it. Robert Graves, in his *Good-Bye to All That*, stresses the fact that English youth, nourished on ideas of honor, patriotism, and a worship of culture, was totally unprepared for the cataclysm which robbed it of all illusions. For Graves, the whole structure of idealism went down with the war. It crashed for most of the younger generation in England, who shortly were to be seen entering with less enthusiasm than the Americans into a Jazz Age of escape from thinking.

Meanwhile, America had entered the war under a President who, student of history that he was, saw in the struggle the dangers to world peace which were to be long disregarded, and found in the League of Nations, which he advocated, a possible means of avoiding another war. Although he pictured and popularized the war as a humanitarian crusade and although he was to be regarded as an idealistic leader and to be defeated both abroad and at home in his program, Wilson, it seems clear now, at least partially recognized the economic struggle which after his death would reach another climax in further wars and depressions. At the time of his leadership, however, the American people as yet understood almost nothing of the connection between their economic welfare and that of the world.

We were only a short time in the war and it had, therefore, relatively little direct influence upon our writers. Some sentimental fanfare about war poetry and the glories of dying for one's country was of course to be heard. A few minor poets fought in the war and a number of well-known literary names made it the subject of their early writing. E. E. Cummings wrote one of the better war novels, *The Enormous Room*, a study of the prisoners with whom he had been confined. Some of Archibald MacLeish's later works reflected his experiences in the war. Indeed, one finds in many of the now well-known writers the reflection of their youthful reactions to the brief experience of fighting abroad. The year and a half of war ended, it became apparent that most of the poetry written at this time had nothing to do with the military invasion. Our literature, however, profited by the struggle indirectly.

Soon much of the literary excitement which had developed in England just previous to the war was to be transplanted to America. While England lost a generation of artists, we suffered no such catastrophe. Consequently, from this time on, the artists of the more secure and prosperous America began to dominate English literature. The long period of recovery in England allowed for no immediate revival of the newer literary movements which in the prewar period had sprung up in English soil. Driven from England in 1914, the Imagists, for example, had been transplanted to flourish in America. Ezra Pound, self-exiled from America and living in England, was dethroned by Amy Lowell, and the Imagist school which he had originated began to be associated solely with this energetic and imposing critic; its poets began to be published widely in American magazines. A high percentage of the hubbub about the "new" poetry, Imagist and free verse, came after the war from American journals. It was such leaders as Amy Lowell who kept the controversy alive.

The Imagist credo stresses the need of new verse forms and rhythms to express new feelings concerning the industrial world. The Imagists are descended from the Symbolists in France, whom we have spoken of as influencing such a poet as Yeats. Where the Symbolists, however, used subjective imagery to portray familiar moods, the Imagists attempt to objectify personal feeling and to present a picture. But the danger in this technique is that a word picture by a poet may communicate very little. Poets are not painters. To Miss Lowell, for example, love may be pictured as a set of fruit jars. When she describes the fruit jars, however, many of her readers will not know she talks of love. Since pure objectivity was the mania of the Imagists, they did not allow themselves the statement of their emotions, except

through an image. Often the result was that they did not communicate.

The Imagist school created a tempest in a teapot in literary America during and after the war, but despite its influence on the early works of such important poets as Hart Crane, it is today very largely a dead school. Once the noise was over, critics pointed out that in their insistence both on free verse and on objectivity, actually the Imagists were not particularly original. Great free verse had been written even in the nineteenth century. A vast amount of broken-up prose printed as Imagist verse was not poetry at all, and soon the better poets returned to the more traditional form of verse in which they found it quite possible authentically to express the modern world. Today, although a few important poets like William Carlos Williams still make use of free verse and of the Imagist technique, they use it in no such stereotyped way as would have been insisted upon by the originators of the Imagist school itself.

American literature was experimenting in new forms at the time the war ended. After the Armistice the questioning and evasion which had been confined to the trenches, at least in their greatest intensity, spread over the world. And while literary schools rose and fell, in much of the literature of both England and America it seemed that morals, manners, and ideas of honor were thrown out the window. We had entered upon the Jazz Age, which was the inevitable reaction to military regimentation and disillusion. In England there was little literature. Many writers had died in the war; the survivors were busy attempting again to make some adjustment physically and mentally to normal ways of living. In America, where people were imbibing bathtub gin and where a general recklessness prevailed, some writers returned to stressing individualistic self-expression. But for the most part, American writers were busy describing man as the victim of the outer forces of industrialism or the inner forces of emotion. Here the reaction against romanticism was becoming stronger daily.

Theodore Dreiser was one of the first to trace life and conduct back to chemistry. Acclaimed after the war by Mencken, Dreiser (see Part II, p. 289) analyzed the creature called man. He was determined to keep nothing hidden. With the realistic technique of an

PORK and BEANS
DELICIOUS

HOT CAKES
THE KIND GRANDMOTHER
USED TO MAKE

Jules Pascin: Illustration for Paul Morand's Closed All Night
Pascin, who lived in many countries, has become thought of as an international artist.
This illustration shows such remarkable qualities of observation of the American scene
that one might think the artist had spent his formative years in America

American Zola, he insisted on examining all the facts of life which convention had ignored. A naturalist who chose to examine the individual without concern for anything but the truth, he accepted the fact that man is a creature of hidden instincts and desires, forced often into a violation of social conventions. Pity he had, and he fought against any judgment of men by the hypocritical standards of the middle class. He saw men as driven by three impulses: love of power, love of women, love of art. He presented man objectively and without apology, and he knew that the sensitive individual often loses in the fight for survival. Most of his characters have some social weakness and cannot conquer the bitter world into which they are born. The story presented in the text (p. 291) is a study of a man who has been unable to act against the social convention of marriage, who feels himself immoral in wishing for his wife's death, and who finds himself, once he is free, free only to die.

Sherwood Anderson, an American writer who began to be known about the time of the First World War, likewise accepted the allegation that man is often tricked by life and that life is usually ugly. Unlike Dreiser, however, Anderson studied almost exclusively the effects of the inner frustration which resulted from a crude and narrow environment and from the lingering of the puritan idea that man was born in sin. In discussing the position of an artist in America, he argued that the artist must escape from the world he hates. He must release his own instincts and be free to understand the curious ways in which repressed passion finds its outlet. Anderson stresses the common hunger for romance and fellowship, so often denied by our ways of living. Fundamentally he relied on a belief that man's instincts are more right than is any conventional pattern by which society restrains those instincts. Actually he was profoundly puritan in his anti-puritanism. That life often ends in futility, and that many personalities through repression become grotesques, Anderson saw. He was dealing with pathos rather than tragedy.

Everywhere among the writers, in short, even in America, where the artists had been largely undisturbed by the war, the conviction was growing that art would not justify the world as it was—its inequalities and injustices were too great. Dreiser foreshadowed the despair and social questioning that were soon to grip our writers, and Anderson blamed conventional thinking for denying the individual self-development. We come at this point to a scene commonly referred to as the Waste Land.

ELIOT DEFINES THE WASTE LAND

THE PERIOD can take its name from T. S. Eliot's poem *The Waste Land,* published in 1922. And it was Eliot who in both his criticism and his verse defined the intellectual and spiritual self-examination which was to dominate the literature of the period. Poetry, he indicated, was not the expression of a people or a folk living in a certain section of the country but a fine art, impersonal in statement, bookish in its sources. The poets became scholars exploring the golden past of art and letters. And why? Because the war generation of poets had lost faith in any manifestation of the present world. Eliot soon announced the theme of the sterility and vulgarity of this our present day. Eliot, moreover, developed a new method for writing verse, that of contrasting and comparing an older and, in memory, perfected world of the past with the newer, more chaotic world of the present. Promptly following in his footsteps, every lesser poet went intellectual and became depressed. Emotional spontaneity was soon lost in intellectual doubt and self-interrogation. If feeling dared assert itself at all in poetry, it was only as an outcry against intellectual skepticism. And so, early in the nineteen twenties, the new school of poets had exactly defined their methods and their subject matter. They prevailed and the romantics declined in popularity.

Eliot, born an American, brought up a puritan, thoroughly inoculated at Harvard against false ideals of material culture, had by this time removed himself to England, there to become the literary dictator of both countries. He, better than anyone else, summed up in his poetry the pessimism then current in the literature of both countries concerning the values of human life under industrialism. First of all he set out to negate all that the romantic poets had insisted upon as truth about life. In his early poems he attacked modern conceptions and observances of religion and of love. To him, religion was the opium of a materialistic age, and love was a pathological sickness. As for tragedy, there was none save the tragedy of being born. Once man was born, life was a living death to be gone through in utter boredom. Men had, he felt, lost their passion. If Eliot wrote a spring song, it was to state that spring no longer awakened man to delight. If he wrote a love song, it had to do with a bored young man in spats who could not make up his mind to declare himself on anything. Born of old American stock and associating with an intellectual and socially well established group, Eliot came to feel strongly that they, like their counterparts in England, lived merely to go South in the winter, to behave properly in the drawing room, to talk of culture, concerning which (in America at least) they really knew very little. Eliot, in a sense, was born old. He had wondered at the ripe age of twenty-three how he would look with a bald spot in the middle of his head. He shortly saw all life as a repetition of the same decadent attitudes. Conventional living, as he pictured it, led to monotony and to frustration of feeling. Modern man had no dignity, was no Prince Hamlet.

No! I am not Prince Hamlet, nor was meant to
    be;
Am an attendant lord, one that will do
To swell a progress, start a scene or two,
Advise the prince; no doubt, an easy tool,
Deferential, glad to be of use,
Politic, cautious and meticulous;
Full of high sentence, but a bit obtuse;
At times, indeed, almost ridiculous—
Almost, at times, the Fool.

191

For Eliot all value lay in the residue of art which the spiritual in man has created. And the only retreat, therefore, was the retreat to great books, by the reading of which human nobility may be recalled. Beauty for him was in the library or in the traditional church and there alone. Eliot, bored with the life of the upper middle class, a life spread too thin, could not enter the lower middle classes, whose vitality was greater. He saw in them and in the white-collar group no help whatsoever. Everything they stood for was "vulgar." Better, he felt, to live within the conventions of a scholar-gentleman than to live merely for material things. As for the laboring man, he confessed only ignorance and withdrawal from him. Eliot did not, of course, examine the possible economic basis of the common man's lack of interest in the cultural aspects of life.

Eliot developed in his poetry the use of what he called the "objective correlative." Wishing to write dramatic poetry in which he could voice his own sentiments through the mouths of others, he chose the character of J. Alfred Prufrock to symbolize a bored young man very much like himself, and Sweeney to symbolize the average man, working for money, the vulgarian. Prufrock, living in the drawing room, thought of his life as measured out in coffee spoons (coffee spoons here being the objective correlative for typical after-dinner boredom among sophisticated people), or he recalled ladies talking of Michelangelo, such talk being the objective correlative of all American pseudo-intellectual conversation. Eliot's objective correlative is, in other words, a symbol that expresses very briefly a whole group of associated ideas. But, unlike the symbols of the Symbolists, who expressed highly personal reactions in their images, Eliot's objective correlative is actually a social symbol. It sums up a social attitude characteristic and recognizable to anyone who knows the social pattern in which the group described lives.

In his poetry, Eliot uses inner monologues and lyrics to record moments of high emotional tension, all illustrative of the neurotic mood of his generation. *The Waste Land* (p. 237), a poem of only twenty pages, sums up the pessimism and spiritual defeat of the writers to whom, once the values formerly held true were relinquished, life appeared as merely a kind of progressive death. The scene, which symbolizes sterility, is the modern city with its gas tanks, dirty rivers, and slums, typical of what Eliot saw as the desert of contemporary culture. Throughout the poem Eliot is comparing our standardized living with the older pattern of life in which the individual felt himself important. Using such romantic symbols as spring, childhood delight, and love, the poet sets out in this work to indicate how our age negates the values of the earlier revolutionary and humanistic romantics. Within the city he places characters representative of the upper and lower social levels, and throughout the poem his own despair is voiced by these characters.

The Waste Land was proclaimed at once by many other writers in both England and America, where Eliot's theme was current, to be the great poem of modern doubt and despair. There was therefore a general disappointment on the part of some of those poets who rather enjoyed chaos and dark moods when Eliot, having thoroughly presented the spiritual dearth in modern life, moved out of his own Waste Land into the Anglo-Catholic Church. For those who had read closely, however, the violence of Eliot's hatred of modern life had indicated that here was a poet who could not endure to accept doubt or despair. Despite the fact that he had announced himself a classicist, Eliot's anguish over the loss of man's faith in ultimate values indicated that he was highly emotional. His, indeed, is merely the reverse side of the shield of romanticism. Hatred and repugnance are as much a passion as is love, and in denouncing twentieth-century sterility of feeling, Eliot indicated that he was essentially a religious person who upheld the values of the more authoritarian past. A believer in tradition, he sought a traditional church. Consequently, he now opposed to earth the possible beauty of heaven. Eliot in turn stated that he was a royalist in politics. This gentleman whose mind was furnished with quotations from books, who shuddered away from reality, held that the welfare of the world lay in the devotion of the very few highly sensitized individuals to spiritual truth. The common people were incapable, he was sure, of any such devotion. They needed both civil and spiritual leadership from the élite. Pursuing this same line of thought, he finally made, just before the Second World War, statements which seem obsessively concerned with racial purity.

Characteristically T. S. Eliot appears in his later poetry as a man who desires a kind of martyrdom if by it he may teach truth to the spiritual leaders with whom he now identifies himself. In his play *The Family Reunion,* he denounces the English gentry for their reliance upon material things, points out that they are dead, in truth, and identifies himself with his leading character, who is strongly possessed of a sense of sin and is fighting a quite unworldly battle in order that he may come again into a sense of grace. Eliot holds out always the idea of Christian crusade against economic determinism. His poems of the period just preceding and during the Second World War—some of his finest poetic work—are a reiteration of the idea that life is begun in sin and ends in sin, of a religious and philosophical search for "peace." Eliot has moved from exhausting doubt to exhaustive religious inquiry as to personal salvation, without which he thinks there can be no public salvation. Other poets have followed him through this move and on into that kind of artistic isolation and belief in the superior soul of the artist which frequently leads to an acceptance of a reactionary political position.

But not all poets of his period, however strong their emphasis on the selectivity of the artist, followed Eliot philosophically. Marianne Moore, of Eliot's generation and, as editor of *The Dial,* responsible for introducing him to literary America, is curiously unlike him in her own poetry. Eliot himself recently has introduced her *Selected Poems;* he places her as one of the greater poets of his day: "a descriptive poet rather than lyrical or dramatic," whose "poems form a small body of durable poetry written in our times in which an original sensibility and alert intelligence and deep feeling have been engaged in maintaining the life of the English language." What Eliot does not remark is that Marianne Moore's intelligence and feeling have engaged in maintaining the magic of the very reality of detail from which Eliot himself shied away. Miss Moore's agile and ironic mind, intent upon the minutiae which compose life, abstracts the personal from the real, the universal from the particular, with

an intellectual honesty. She has never separated Art from life, but has seen Art as rather the gift of seeing into the life of things. Nor is she without pity and terror as to what a depression and a war have meant. She has, indeed, recently published one of the important war poems of the Second World War (see p. 257), and side by side with it a fine metaphysical poem concerning the whole problem of our innocence and guilt in a war-torn world. (See p. 258.) She is never blind to the possibilities of poetry as sociological criticism. Miss Moore has remained the clear-thinking puritan who judges as she analyzes, and who finds in the slightest detail of observation a contribution to truth. Truth for her is beauty. Unlike Eliot, she has never denied her American and puritanic inheritance. There is for her no need to seek an escape, for there is no need for her to deny the factual and real world. She loves this world with a kind of intellectual passion, whether it be made up of the small animals she observes so accurately, the people she knows penetratingly, the miracles of science which she accepts, or the metaphysical speculations she comes upon as naturally as she observes any of the workings of the human mind.

Other poets of the Waste Land

Unlike Eliot, E. E. Cummings, not at all depressed by a world without illusions, finds the obvious contradictions in modern society on the whole funny. All his poetry save for a few satirical pieces is love poetry, but of two different types—romantic love poetry and poetry about passing affairs. Both forms of experience, momentarily at least, lull man into thinking life worth while. Cummings offers in opposition to complete disillusion the idea that the sensual experience of love remains. In another period he would undoubtedly have been a poet of romantic enthusiasms, but in the twentieth century he accepts the materialistic world, acknowledges man's descent from animals, and does handsprings to illustrate that this is all very comical. After the First World War he remained for a while among the expatriates in France, painting surrealist pictures and writing verse concerning personal impressions of what was generally considered to be a cockeyed world. When he returned home to live among the esthetes in Greenwich Village, Cummings continued to write poetry which stated his belief that in art anything might happen. He developed his own scheme of typography and punctuation, which supposedly indicates how the poem reads and what it means. He argues that neither man, God, nor the first person singular pronoun should be capitalized, since neither deity nor man is "important." Yet, obviously, he is himself an anarchistic believer in the rights of the artist as the only important rights worthy of defense at all.

To explain Cummings' typography completely and logically is impossible. If a poem winds all over the page and words are split into syllables printed on different lines, this may be because Cummings wishes us to realize that he is describing a sunset seen under a locomotive from a rear sleeper as a train makes a curve. But ordinarily his typography is not so easily explained. Cummings has a real love for eccentricity. For him two plus two is not four but five. He holds, in other words, that the irrational is one of the chief realms for poetic investigation. The "logic" of Marxian philosophy does not appeal to him. He is in truth the playboy of the Waste Land. Denying most permanent values in life, Cummings lives in the moment. He, too, is really a romantic. His return to a limited popularity since World War II is a symbol of disillusionment, individual anarchism, and escapism.

While Eliot puts on clerical vestments and Cummings does handsprings, Ezra Pound, acknowledged by Eliot to be his master in technique, puts on and takes off a series of "masks." Pound early shook the dust of America from his heels and went to dig in the loam of European literature. Always an inventor, he headed there one school of poetry after another. But his best poems are adaptations from the Greek, the Latin, the Provençal, and the Chinese poets. As Blackmur says in his essay, "The Masks of Ezra Pound," he is as a translator better than he is as an original poet. When his pupil Eliot became famous and surpassed his master, Pound turned into a red-haired fury who denounced in particular the general stupidity of all Americans. He sat himself down, moreover, to finish his *Cantos,* of which four had been published before *The Waste Land* appeared,

and which he felt would be a more final picture of the era of disillusionment that was Eliot's *Waste Land.* These *Cantos* are a mosaic of quotations drawn from every source possible. For Pound, like Eliot, uses quotations from past literature as symbolic of the beautiful, in contrast with the realistic vulgarity of the modern world.

Even when the *Cantos* are finished there is little likelihood that they will form so universal a picture of sterility as does Eliot's very brief poem, for Pound is never so universal nor so dramatic a poet as is Eliot. Much of his reaction to the modern scene is highly colored by his personal resentment of everything American, a resentment not always tempered by taste. Pound felt that the country of his birth never appreciated him, that what he regarded as an almost illiterate America could not possibly be aware of his superiority. Nor did his residence abroad assure him the praise which his growing egomania demanded. Acknowledged as master by many a modern poet, he had nevertheless been exceeded, for he lacked any consistency of belief. It was not too strange, therefore, that under the flattery of Mussolini he should have become a supporter of the fascist regime. Accused of treason, after the war he was legally declared insane. Now institutionalized in America, Pound has been allowed to publish his latest *Cantos,* with their indirect satire of the Roosevelt era, and many a little magazine has of late paid him homage. Some of those who praise him seem to agree with Pound's idea that the artist has no moral responsibility, save to himself.

One more important poet reacted to the modern world with violence. Finding no intensity possible to the average man living the average life, Robinson Jeffers betook himself to the farthermost point on the Pacific Coast to live his own life and build his own religion. Unlike Eliot, he rejected Christianity, regarding it as the religion of an enslaved people. He had explored thoroughly the teachings of Freud and the philosophy of Nietzsche, and from them he constructed a belief in a God of primitive beauty and of power. One after another of Jeffers' tragedies has to do with strong and primitive characters who assert their wills against all conventional laws of conduct. Only in so far as they violate the moral codes of conventional society do these characters approach a kind of godhood. Despising the ordinary standardized reactions to what is good or what is bad, Jeffers presents stories of individuals who will to act as they please, even if they end in death or insanity. Practically all of them in fact do die or go mad. Once they have declared themselves defiant individualists acting on their own principles, they have no practical part to play in life, and Jeffers as a dramatist has to get rid of them. The poet recognizes, of course, that not many people will follow his God of Violence as the god to worship. Despising modern civilization, Jeffers returns to the barbaric as the noble. When he says, "I can understand the guns and airplanes, the other conveniences leave me cold"; when he mocks those who would adjust our economics to the new abundance, and finally states boldly, "Blind war, compared to this kind of life [meaning the standardization of life in order that most people may enjoy more material wealth], has nobility, famine has dignity," he seems to espouse, if not the fascist centralization of government, at least the barbarism to which fascism leads. Jeffers, preferring isolation to conventional society, has fled from the industrialized East and stands staring out over the great Pacific Ocean. His predilection for violence and passion has led him to admire heroes as the makers of history; nevertheless, in the period of the Second World War, Jeffers took the position that we need not have entered. He saw in this war only the same social forces as had long denied man his natural greatness, the forces of a highly institutionalized, greedy, and standardized world. As an anarchistic individualist, Jeffers can believe in none of the social forces which may compel man to their will.

By this time it must be clear that the Waste Land mood formulated by Eliot was between 1925 and 1932 to be found in almost every section of America. Various reasons were given as to how it had come about. There were those, like the Southern agrarian writers, who insisted that health for America lay in the return to a gracious, less commercial, and more agrarian culture, and who connected the decline of art with the decline of the Southern aristocracy—this aristocracy being the only one which might be said to have resembled the earlier feudal aristocracy of Europe. Led by Allen Tate, the Southern agrarian writers, in rejection of the cosmopolitan city with its commercial overtones as not the proper home for art, returned to the agricultural South, in an endeavor there to find what roots they had in the American past with historical American tradition. They sought to live a simpler life, one more integrated with a culture. Not all of them, like Tate, emphasized the beauty and greatness of the past; not all of them wrote an *Ode to the Confederate Dead*. All of them had, however, come to the belief that a poet must have roots and must draw his sustenance from a sense of literary and historical tradition. And most of them saw in socialism only a furthering of the controls already exerted upon the individual by society, and in particular upon the artist, and therefore opposed it as an even more strident materialism than that which existed in the large cities. They sought to re-create the gentility of art and to explain the vulgarity of much American writing in terms of the vulgarity that the industrial age itself had created.

To be sure, at least one of the best poets among them, John Crowe Ransom, is not unaware of the slow fading of the flower of Southern gentility. Although Ransom dislikes industrialism, he places no great faith in the survival of Beauty in hoop skirts. His gentlemen are in bonds and his romantic Southern gentlewomen are as neurotic as their Northern counterparts. Nor was the Southern agrarian group of writers who had fled the commercial cities and transplanted themselves in the South long to remain there. Ransom, himself a Southerner, has of course drawn all his material from his own background. But soon Allen Tate and most of his followers, who, like him, had been part of the earlier Bohemian tradition of the twenties, returned to the East and to the center of the publishing world, there to become the editors of the *avant-garde* magazines. When the *Southern Review* ceased to be privately subsidized, it ceased to be printed. Despite the *Kenyon Review* and the *Sewanee Review,* in the publication of which Tate and others of this group played their part, despite the agrarian group's dream of building a literary center in the South, the East remained the literary center. And soon the Southern writers, by no means all of whom were actually of Southern ancestry, dispersed. Making no further attempt to define a culture proper to art geographically, they placed the emphasis upon an intellectual literary tradition. Something of the theory that art springs only from a culture which gives rise to an intellectual aristocracy still prevails in their estheticism. But their movement to turn the hands of the clock back and thus to repudiate the machine age, as William Morris earlier had suggested, has ceased to be localized. It was, indeed, always a part of the insistence on Art for Art's Sake, and a defense of art against materialism.

All in all, the poets seemed to be singing a melody of chaos, and only one or two sought a way out of the labyrinth of their own dramatized frustration. At home or abroad where they had fled to write, they reveled in the emotions of disillusionment and despair.

But finally one of the expatriates, Archibald MacLeish (almost alone at first), announced that poets and writers could but grow more rootless and obscure if, by remaining in foreign lands, as so many had after the First World War, or by being concerned with only the subjective and individualistic, they failed to take into account the real scene from whence they spring. MacLeish, in his *New Found Land*, announced that he must return to his native America. He advised the many other poets living particularly in Paris to cease dramatizing their exile, to cease studying and imitating the French poets, and to return home where they could mirror actual American developments. Nor was it long before MacLeish struck the new note of faith in the liberal movements he began to regard as expressive of the need of the American people. He was consequently one of the first poets to turn from themes of despair to a poetry advocating action against the will of the few and in favor of the will of the many. Quite naturally therefore, under Roosevelt, MacLeish later became rather more of a public man than a poet, a man identified with and active in promoting what he believed the liberal movements of his own day. In the more sociological, less personal poetry soon to spring up was to be found a conviction, never a part of the Waste Land repudiation of a commercial culture, that economic change itself might be a part of the history of a culture.

The language of the Waste Land poets

Although for the most part they use the conventional rhythms and stanzaic forms, the Waste Land poets as a whole employ images of defeat, and stress bones rather than stars, death rather than life. They recall the romantic imagery of nature, love, and passion only by way of contrast to the modern imagery of the industrial city. The hue and cry over simple diction died almost as soon as it had been raised by the Imagists. Poetic language became more complex because of the rapidly accumulating associations gathering around each newly introduced thought or object in a complex civilization. Attempting to record now all the subtle shades of reaction to city living and at the same time to keep in mind old reactions to the more peaceful country living, the poets employed whatever language might suit their purpose. Usually, in order to indicate what Beauty had been and what she was no longer, they contrasted passages in the rich poetic phraseology of the nineteenth century with blunt realistic or scientific statement of the twentieth century. In other words, even after the faith in individualism ceased to be the chief subject for poetry, the individualism continued to be displayed as a kind of virtuosity in form, in novelty, distortion, or shock expressed by the manipulation of language.

Novelists of the Waste Land

While all this was going on in poetry, the novelists too had come to believe man a victim of both outer and inner forces. As soon as this happened, characters such as had been completely defined in Victorian novels and had continued to move through early twentieth-century novels, acting out precisely the parts expected of them, disappeared. Once modern psychology was thoroughly studied, the authors' conception of what motivated human action became more complex, nor was this action defined as either simply good or simply bad. The capabilities of a character were consequently no longer seen as easily determinable.

A man's attention toward a woman in a Victorian novel is frequently, for example, depicted as being either virtuous or the reverse; either he is in love with her or he lusts after her or her money. Not so with the lover in the modern novel. He is not at all sure of the worth of love; he is aware that a woman can present all kinds of different surfaces. He is caught up in a kind of pessimism which makes any formal or social plan of life seem inadequate to his inner necessity. He may advance and retreat before the idea of marriage, and he frequently finds his own life and emotions more interesting than those of another person. The psychological novel had, of course, not been entirely unknown during the Victorian period. Henry James and Samuel Butler were aware of its possibilities, as had been the Russian novelists for fully fifty years. But as Freudian psychology became popular, the extent of our knowledge of psychology deepened. And, what is more important, Freudianism came to represent, with something like scientific assurance, the many reasons for our inability to adjust to those very social institutions which had long been felt to be restrictive of human interests and abilities. As the artist came to feel that he could not express or assimilate the complexities and contradictions in modern society, and could not entirely accept the conventionalized and social standards of behavior as right, Freudianism offered to him a new field, and in many ways a simpler one. He turned to study the subjective and inactive life, thus narrowing his observations to his own inner world and escaping for a time the need of analyzing the society which confused him.

The psychological movement in literature begins early in the twentieth century with a succession of autobiographical novels. The hero is seen growing up, loving his mother, resenting his father, going for the first time to school (where undoubtedly he will be made fun of by other children), getting religion, losing it perhaps in a university, falling in love, marrying or not marrying, becoming successful or unsuccessful, and, finally, dying. Many such novels were being written before the First World War.

Before that war, too, Virginia Woolf began writing her books in which no subjective sensation was too little to set down. Obviously, for Mrs. Woolf a character is built up by meticulous recording of all that goes on in the character's mind—in other words, of all that goes on in Mrs. Woolf's mind. The infinite minutiae of daily personal life are recorded, "the atoms as they fall upon the mind, in the order in which they fall, by tracing the pattern, however disconnected and incoherent it appears, which each sight or incident scores upon the consciousness." Thus Mrs. Woolf defines the quality of her own writing and of writers like James Joyce, in whose footsteps she follows. In *The Waves,* for example (p. 525), Mrs. Woolf tells the story of the life of six characters in images of the way in which these characters react to the sea. Nothing happens in the book except that the characters grow older and die, and we know that fact largely because the vividness of their impressions of the sea slowly fades. All six characters are obviously Mrs. Woolf herself in different states of awareness or sensitivity. The book has no plot but is a rather subtle record of various states of mind. Virginia Woolf's later books repeated her conviction that life is static save for the heightened drama of the hypersensitive individual mind in a world where calm and health were nowhere to be found.

The shift from a belief in character as consistent to the belief in character as really nonexistent—save as the novelist could record a series of impressions most likely to arise in a single person's mind—indicates that two forces had convinced the novelist that stories of the traditional variety in which people acted out their parts consistently were no longer true. Psychology was the first force. It taught that the inner life was more important than the outer and that one must record the stream-of-consciousness of any character as well as the character's actions.

The second force influencing the Waste Land novelist was the conviction that no one man's actions were important. For this reason writers neglected studies of action to concentrate on studies of the continuous or of the discontinuous personality. They wrote novels which were a series of isolated scenes, or isolated incidents, with only a spatio-temporal connection. No sooner had the lack of importance of the individual as an agent in society become a popular conception than the novelists stopped picturing society save as a kind of backdrop to which individuals reacted. Taking in a wider scope of material and observation than the poets, they of course saw many signs of disintegration in the social structure of both England and America. Those sturdy enough to analyze the social scene therefore reacted most often with distaste. The greater number of novelists, however, resorted to psychological analyses and in a way began to usurp the realm of the poets in their exposition of the subconscious. These novelists wrote out of the privacy of their own sensibilities. In the normal or the average they saw little reason for existence, and no dramatic tension. Value in human life lay, for them, in a retreat from action, in a concern solely for the interplay of desire and its frustration.

But first there had been Hemingway, perfectly aware of the loss of values brought about by the war, but expressing his repudiation of the real scene not so much by a retreat into the sensibilities as by an emphasis on meaningless action. His two novels of the war and its aftermath, *A Farewell to Arms* and *The Sun Also Rises,* pictured the individualistic desertion from meaningful action. World War I went on while his characters made love, drank too much, and talked too much about nothing. Most of his characters were derelicts of one type or another, and almost all were in some way impotent. His writers cannot write great books, nor can his painters paint great pictures; but they can keep moving, and thus escape from taking thought. In their way, they are portraits in prose of the same moral sterility that Eliot's Prufrock or Sweeney are in poetry. But their repudiation of the real scene through high-pitched action turns rather more toward self-destruction than toward personal salvation. Once the immediate post-war period was over, Hemingway turned more and more to stories of low-caste characters, because in them he found people for whom action was naturally an escape from futility. He became an indirect critic of society in his depiction of the injustices which force men to be killers or to waste their lives in dissipation. When we entered a period of comparative prosperity, some critics thought indeed that Hemingway's best work was finished. But it is apparent now that in *Death in the Afternoon* and *The Green Hills of Africa,* Hemingway was still presenting the drama of such action as intensified the feeling of being alive, because in it was imminent the possibility of death.

Soon history showed Hemingway another period of war and revolution, in which the matador and the good shot were not the only ones called upon to act. His book of short stories *The Fifth Column* placed him as one of the writers aware that individualism might be destroyed by the reactionary forces of society. The Spanish revolution gave him the background for a kind of individualistic heroism among guerrillas and for a story of love in the face of death, not totally unrelated to that in *A Farewell to Arms.* But whereas in *A Farewell to Arms* the hero found in the First World War no cause important enough to die for, Hemingway discovered in his novel of the Spanish revolution that man was willing to die for the cause of freedom. It is to be doubted whether Hemingway could have written as Malraux did, of the organized Loyalist forces and their martyrdom. His emphasis has always been on individualism, and although he seems to have come to the conclusion that no man can live alone, he has always presented what is essentially the lonely hero. The Spanish guerrillas, despite the worth of their action in the revolution, were not an organized group. They were akin, moreover, in their primitive passions, to some of Hemingway's earlier heroes. It is natural, therefore, that Hemingway should have chosen their form of warfare as his subject matter; it is natural also that his hero should be Robert Jordan, an American abroad seeking to die for an ideal he had not found at home. This is a marked change, but it does not obscure the fact that Hemingway's emphasis has always been on the disillusioned individual who, although he may find momentary relief in lust or love, still believes that he is of a lost generation and that any action against the forces that have exiled him is likely to be dangerous unto death.

Because sheer passion and intensity are negated in the normal patterns of living, Hemingway's men of action for the sake of action seem sometimes to be adolescently seeking a sense of the dramatic rather than promoting any ideals of human dignity. To die inert in a disintegrating world is to have no sense of life at all; but to live so self-destructively as to feel always the hot breath of death is, for Hemingway, to live intensely. If out of this intensity one furthers the cause of humanity, so much the better. It is on this persuasion that Hemingway moves out of the Waste Land into the period advocating social change.

Of all the writers of the Waste Land, F. Scott Fitzgerald is in certain ways the most typical. He, better than anyone else, pictures the smugness and seeming worthlessness of his own generation of intellectuals, the romanticism and futility even of their radicalism. He knew the rich, and he both loved and hated them. He was of an "old" family, and he understood the disintegration of many older families. He caught all the sheen, the interplay of light and shadow, of beauty and emptiness, that was the life of a small irresponsible segment of the population. He acknowledged that his subjects were careless people, utterly amoral despite their charm. It is clear that after his early novels concerned with these, the wealthy, the intelligent, the clever, he came slowly to feel that these, the élite and the moneyed, were destructive and vicious. Not that he had any great sympathy or understanding for those whom the rich destroyed: like Eliot, he shrank from the common man; but he felt that wit and beauty were possible in our society only to the greedy, and that hence both were cynical and spiritually dissolute. In *The Diamond as Big as the Ritz* he gave us an allegory of the gargantuan madness to which accumulation led, and certainly in his books we have a panorama of golden and white heroines become gilt, and Arrow collar heroes grown carelessly malicious. To understand the difference between portraits of decadence like Fitzgerald's and the work of writers who are concerned with making the world a better place, one should compare Fitzgerald's story *May Day* with Beachcroft's story *May Day Celebration* in Part III of this book. Fitzgerald's is more brilliant because it is more luminously able to mirror a many-faceted and falsely scintillating era. Beachcroft's story is a quiet presentation of the dignity with which a workingman and his wife defend their radical position. One has the dying glow of a world we all remember; the other presents a personal sacrifice for a world not yet born.

Less directly representative of the era than Fitzgerald, Katherine Anne Porter is nevertheless today recognized as one of our finest short-story writers. A master of understatement and of irony, she has given us stories of Mexico, of a decadent Europe facing disaster, and of the deep South. Never directly a social critic, she has nonetheless always been deeply concerned with the distortion of moral values possible in our culture. She is critical of our commercialism and even more critical of our lack of sensitivity to the spiritual needs in every heart. Recently it has become clear, as she has lectured on the responsibility of the artist, that she considers it the artist's duty to promote such conditions in society and in personal relationships as would lead to a greater humanitarianism. But for the most part her stories are tales of bitter and brilliant perception and of precise and quiet comment on the whole struggle that is the life pattern.

Another woman who is well known as a stylist is the late Willa Cather. Less subtle than Miss Porter and more imitative of such earlier American writers as Henry James, she became known through long and devoted work as one of our more disciplined writers. Her novels range from the robust and vital *My Ántonia* to

Eric Gill: Procession to the Cross
One of the greatest craftsmen of our time, Gill was closely associated with literary life, and did his most significant work in the designing and illustration of books

199

the stylized and philosophical *Death Comes for the Archbishop*—by some critics considered her masterpiece. Her preoccupation with style becomes at times rather tiresome; but when in her later books her concern with ideas released her from this preoccupation she proved less the artist. It is possible that her reputation is due to a great extent to her development of a lucid and precise form and a felicitous language.

Aldous Huxley is fairly representative of a whole generation of English novelists emphasizing in a somewhat more intellectual way than Hemingway and Fitzgerald the weariness, fatigue, skepticism, sophistication, and perversity of a generation which had no certitude offered it by its elders when it came out of the trenches. In Huxley there is a kind of desperation based on the feeling of being lost, of having no place and no anchorage in society. He is the grandson of Thomas Huxley, whose scientific optimism was in some ways responsible for the world which his grandson found waiting for him after the First World War. The belief in scientific progress without any consideration of how this progress was to be related to moral progress was largely responsible for the catastrophe of the war. Aldous Huxley brought to the novel a scientific background, and his *Point Counter Point* makes considerable use of scientific information. There is a lingering insistence upon the physical decay which leads to death and a remarkable picture of the upper classes of the literary intelligentsia in London after the war. The heroine is heartless and completely without any redeeming qualities. Philip Quarles in this book is Huxley himself, a character whose chief difficulty is a lack of sympathy with people. Other figures are Everard Webley, a thinly disguised portrait of Sir Oswald Mosley, the British fascist; a young communist; a biology research chemist; and a character patterned after D. H. Lawrence. This man, Mark Rampion, is so sympathetically treated that one feels Huxley would have liked to be possessed of the energy and passion of Lawrence, if at the same time he could have kept his own intellectual erudition. Huxley calls *Point Counter Point* a "novel of ideas," and the book dates because some of the ideas have ceased to be living issues. Continuing, however, to deal with ideas, Huxley wrote *Brave New World,* a picture of what the future

would be like if we continued to try to solve all of our difficulties through science. But in fact, in this scientific Utopia, scientifically conditioned, clothed, fed, and taught, people do not seem to find peace. In *Eyeless in Gaza,* Huxley again stresses the inability of the intellectual to feel anything save through the most sensational form of shock. His intellectual, surveying the world of social conflicts, decides upon a belief in pacifism. He remains an intellectual and a Waste Lander. In his later books, as in *Time Must Have a Stop,* Huxley turns to rather Oriental beliefs in quietism, and escapes from a scientific world which he completely denies is able to offer man peace. Like many others, he has grown religious and mystical. He finally rejects modern science and accepts only man's ability to deny reality and to live in a kind of spiritual quietism, outside both time and space.

D. H. Lawrence's statement, "We are prostituted, oh prostituted by life," is of course akin to the American novelist Sherwood Anderson's "Tricked, by gad, tricked by life and made a fool of." And the English novelist, like the American, tends to explain man's sad state as a result of a conflict between impulses and social conventions. More than anything else, Lawrence is interested in analyzing what he conceives to be the validity of the male's desire for power. The first step in obtaining this power is obviously, for Lawrence, that the male should conquer the female. Reacting against all the nineteenth century's romantic attitudes toward women which stressed their purity, Lawrence insists on interpreting the female as a kind of primitive Mother Earth. Education and financial freedom have given her an unsound release from the power of the male, before which power she actually desires to bow. Born of a working-class father and a mother more gently bred, Lawrence projected his own background into his books; in novel after novel either the man or the woman is of the upper class and must consequently be brought back to a simpler and more primitive passion for life through an opposing character from the lower class. In Lawrence there is an almost mystical love of the anti-intellectual, the primitive, and the emotionally urgent. For him the cure for the bored intellectual is that he return to passion, submerge himself as it were in the dark flow of the blood stream, get back to the womb of life.

Max Beckmann: In the Street Car
Beckmann sums up the whole period of life after the First World War.
"In the Streetcar" is one of many forceful prints
using the direct, brilliant line of the drypoint to convey
a scene which combines bitter humor with an almost sinister atmosphere

Out of Freud's insistence on a need for greater sexual freedom, D. H. Lawrence built a mystical philosophy. His was a form of primitivism which was in its essence really romantic. It acknowledged that man might be victimized by society or by his brain, but insisted nevertheless that his instincts could save him.

All of these novelists implied to a greater or lesser extent that man is a victim of society. Hemingway made his way out of one shell-shocked world into another and differently shell-shocked world. He saw that, given something to believe in, the derelicts of the First World War might accept action for purpose instead of resting on action as escape. Aldous Huxley argued first that man's action is determined by his body, and that the tragedy of the spirit is that it sooner or later succumbs to the flesh. His intellectuals are either freed from a sense of the fatality and implacability of the real by a reliance upon some mystical faith, or are destroyed by their reliance upon the material world. D. H. Lawrence, on the other hand,

censures modern society for its intellectual hypocrisy and emphasizes the primitive instincts. But one and all, these writers see modern life as lacking in spiritual vigor and society as decadent.

In James Joyce we have a writer who indicted modern civilization but who nevertheless insisted on the capacity of the human spirit to welcome the experiences of life. In his first well-known book, *A Portrait of the Artist as a Young Man,* he recalls Yeats' early attitude toward romantic beauty and asserts that for him beauty lies in further research into man's spiritual and intellectual development.

Michael Robartes remembers forgotten beauty and, when his arms wrap her round, he presses in his arms the loveliness which has long faded from the world. Not this. Not at all. I desire to press in my arms the loveliness which has not yet come into the world.

In *A Portrait of the Artist as a Young Man,* Joyce's style is fairly conservative. But in *Ulys-*

201

ses, his great work, he tried to record all that takes place in the minds of his leading characters within the space of twenty-four hours. In Bloom, who is the leading character of the section from *Ulysses* reprinted here, Joyce draws the normal man, the mean average of humanity. Bloom's intellect consists largely of absorption of cheap fiction, newspapers, and advertising. He has lost contact with nature, especially through his slight alienation from his wife Molly, the completely uninhibited, somewhat overripe opera singer. Opposed to Bloom is Stephen Dedalus, the intellectual and the artist. He is the Hamlet of our day, the refined mind of Ireland and of Europe formed by centuries of culture and tradition, a mind that is largely the product of the Church, upon which European culture was based for two thousand years. Throughout his modern wanderings, Stephen Dedalus is looking for a higher kind of paternity than that afforded him by his own father or the Church. He finds in Bloom, because Bloom is more closely related than himself to sensual nature, the father he is looking for; but this is only one step in his search for the real springs of life, flowing continuously, without reference to historical events. Concerning both Bloom and Dedalus we know everything that goes on, and what goes on is chiefly the flow of memory, images, passionate reactions, and brief moments of rational thinking in each person's mind.

Joyce brings to its climax the method of telling a story through the stream-of-consciousness technique. *Ulysses,* coming as it did at the end of a period of culture, may be thought of as a summary of the intellectual and emotional inheritance of western Europe. Because it stresses confusion, disorder, and incompleteness as all that one sees today in the culture of western Europe, it is a great criticism of modern civilization. For Joyce, even as for D. H. Lawrence in more mystical terms, it is to sensitivity and imaginative creativeness that man must return as a cure for the too great commercialism of his culture and for any growth within himself. Joyce's *Finnegans Wake* is his final study of the biological and psychological awareness of life as profoundly subjective. Joyce never rejects life itself; he probes the internal conflicts of body and spirit. He does reject social history and institutionalized forms of competitive society as destructive of the infinitely dramatic history of man's growth in awareness, which to him alone is significant.

Another pioneer of the stream-of-consciousness technique is Gertrude Stein. She regarded herself in fact as the leader in the movement to use language not for the precise statement of ideas but for the portrayal of the rhythms of consciousness. Words for her were very much what colors were to a painter, and by their arrangement could be made to convey typical attitudes of mind or typical emotions. Her attack upon the mediocrity of the middle-class consciousness was in fact an attack upon the typical middle-class use of language. By the use of words out of context, by destroying the typical sentence syntax, she satirized other literary forms as too conventional and the conventional literary emotions as trite. In both her poetry and her prose she sought an extreme modernity of expression. Entirely sympathetic with modern painting, she attempted to present through repetition and through design of words the emotional effects of the more primitive or the more abstract French painters. Hemingway is said to have been influenced by her, but Hemingway uses repetition and the monosyllable to portray speech and action. Miss Stein used speech and word, so she said, to show us the typical rhythms of certain states of mind, or certain types of people, or the reactions of people. Trained in medicine and psychology, she was for the most part interested chiefly in studies of the complex, contradictory, and individualistic mind. She was in general unconcerned with the movements of history and greatly concerned with the movements of art. Even during the period of the German occupation of France, her attitude was that all wars are the same war; but when the American soldiers entered France it became known that she was anti-German; and her humorous portrayal of the confused but democratic reactions of the American soldier in *Brewsie and Willie* indicated that she was still strongly aware of her Americanism. She was of course one of the chief figures among that group of artists, of whom Cummings was also one, who saw in the break-up of institutionalized forms of expression the possibility of expressing the artist's peculiar sensitivity.

These are some of the chief literary spokesmen of the Waste Land, those who cried havoc. Many of them have since, as we shall later make clear, come to seek religion, mysticism, or faith in some cause as a way of escaping their sense of doom and decadence. The lesser writers who follow the Waste Land tradition are legion. Nor can one place these writers too categorically. Sinclair Lewis, for example, described in Part I as critical of the American optimism of the 1920's, can perhaps best be classified as a satirist of mediocrity, of puritanism, even of himself. In this sense, he is of the Waste Land. He spoke no "open sesame" as a way out of the boredom of American commercialism. But Lewis can also be classed with the social critics. In *It Can't Happen Here* he attempted to attack fascism. And more recently, in *Kingsblood Royal,* in which a "white Protestant American" finds that one of his ancestors is a Negro, Lewis is, after a period of relaxing into Babbittry, again hitting hard at a very contemporary social evil, that of race prejudice. William Faulkner, likewise a novelist who is difficult to place, is most frequently referred to as a Waste Lander because of his treatment of abnormal psychology. Nevertheless, in *The Hamlet,* it is quite clear that Faulkner regards American commercialism and cutthroat competition as forces which breed cruel and low characters. In much of his later work Faulkner is, as a novelist, critical of all that in the South encourages race prejudice, fear, and hatred.

So it is that a number of novelists never directly advocating a better, more democratic, less power-mad, world nonetheless expose indirectly the evils in society. It is apparent then that although we pigeonhole these writers in chapters according to the dominating themes of their books, what is general throughout the entire twentieth-century esthetic expression is the artists' concern over the spiritual, artistic, and physical waste which, as they see it, the modern world demands for its perpetuation. The late Romantics wrote only of the death of values, the Waste Landers only of the hopelessness of action. But the writers of the 1930's who followed them insisted that a more stable economy giving security to everyone might transform disillusionment into hope. Their optimism was strangled, at least temporarily, by the Second World War; and the writers of the Age of Anxiety following this second war have, by and large, found even greater disillusionment concerning any immediate carrying out of a program for world peace and stability than did the writers immediately after the First World War. The reasons for this are many, as we shall see in our last chapter.

It is with the shades of disillusionment coloring the Waste Land psychology that we are now concerned, and these range from, let us say, deep purple to light gray. There are as many ways of curing the melancholy as there are melancholies. We have such figures as Thornton Wilder, earnest, puritanic, moralistic, turning to individualistic religion as one solution; turning in *Our Town* to the small community as the only safety against the commercial and immoral city; turning, if somewhat sentimentally, to the human heart and its hungers; turning finally to the whole question of progress in his play *The Skin of Our Teeth,* and therein denying progress in favor of some mystical idea of God's working through mysterious ways. We have also Ring Lardner, best known of the American humorists of this period, and the most realistic portrayer of the temporarily-believed-in success story of the 1920's. Lardner attempted to laugh disillusionment off and to take at its face value the belief in personal success as an end in itself. He ended by laughing bitterly at himself, as an example of the success story of the artist, for his life had been that. The basic belief in his own importance became in the end impossible, as did his belief in the myth of the Jazz Age, for neither he nor his protagonists had any past or any future—they had only vanity, and for a time the world looked pretty good, life was a quest for the jack pot, avarice was considered a virtue. "Gullible," in his travels from poverty to wealth, wrote his own success story throughout America.

But 1929 was around the corner and the belief in success was to fade, and egotism and vanity without intelligence were leading us to a catastrophe. Living merely with a blind belief in our progress landed us in the depression. Lardner's Mr. and Mrs. U.S.A. at last went financially bankrupt as they had always been spiritually. Lardner, who was highly gifted, finally lost faith in his own life as he lost faith in the meaning of the life around him; for this

Christian Rohlfs: The Prisoner
*Rohlfs is one of the earliest
of the German Expres-
sionists whose work is
just becoming known
in this country. This
woodcut avoids rigid-
ity and preciseness;
so strikingly are tragedy
and power expressed
that the honesty and
excellence of the tech-
nique are almost overlooked*

faith had been highly chauvinistic, highly personal, and was therefore ruinous. Even as they
succeed, Mr. and Mrs. America in their pragmatism have spiritually nowhere to go, and
Lardner's transference of the puritan insistence
on salvation to the blind insistence of the 1920's
on personal success gave us finally portraits of
a period blind to history, intent only on individual power, unconcerned with the welfare of
mankind. As a humorist, Lardner has been
called by some critics second only to Mark
Twain, but it has been the fate of our humorists who have relied on the myth of individual
greatness that they should find that greatness
finally dust.

Eugene O'Neill, primarily a Waste Lander,
began his career with sociological dramas of
sea life. As the Waste Land deepened, this
best-known dramatist of the period shifted to
Freudian studies of the struggle in the human
mind. He wrote the complicated study of inner
conflicts, *Strange Interlude.* He wrote also *The
Great God Brown,* one of his greatest in conception, though least perfect in execution. This
play, which deals with inner conflict and is
therefore chiefly Freudian, nevertheless hits on
the essential problem of man's difficulty in communicating with anyone else, even through love
or through business contact. Here is a major twentieth-century symbol for the diversity
caused by personal, occupational, and class differences which has left the twentieth-century

artist without an audience and without a universal message. It has seemed to leave not only the artist but each person isolated within his purely private desires or fears. Although even in the romantic nineteenth century it became customary to stress the loneliness of man as the prophetic artist's soul attempting to lead toward a greater belief in the perfectibility of mankind, it was not until the end of that century that the writer began to stress his own exile. Certainly he was not, as in the eighteenth century, a businessman and chronicler of business, nor as in the early nineteenth century an advocate of idealistic social revolutions. Mirror of what he saw, he yet repudiated much that he saw as inconsistent with all that was best and most sensitive in mankind. For the stress now was not upon the sensitive, but upon the successful. The twentieth century saw the theme of the artist as exile from his own society more and more stressed. This is one of the reasons for the insistence of our psychological critics of literature upon the problem of communication and for the increasing stress placed on semantics. That O'Neill seized upon this lack of communication between people as a major tragedy of our times is, therefore, interesting. *The Great God Brown* might have been a great play, had O'Neill thoroughly analyzed the problem he presented. Instead, the third act is largely mystical nonsense.

The Waste Land over, and World War II near, O'Neill turned to a nostalgia for the innocence of childhood in his play *Ah, Wilderness!* It was no far step from this to his recent post-World War II drama, *The Iceman Cometh*, in which he opposed the world of drama to the world of fact and proposed that man choose not fact but self-induced dream. It is said that his as yet unproduced plays bring him full circle back to his early religion as the only satisfactory answer to doubt concerning the values of life. He is, indeed, a Waste Lander dramatizing the problems of his period —Freudianism, mysticism, and religion—as retreats from many social problems. O'Neill is as characteristic of the Waste Land, although a much more serious artist, as is that English Beau Brummel, Noel Coward, with his drawing-room comedies, his disdain for morality or reason, and his feeling that only the "best" people can possibly be interesting. Coward has been the clever darling of our theater, a theater often emphasizing sophisticated, brittle, and cynical plots, avoiding the serious questions of the period between wars.

IN SUMMARY

❦ THE GENERAL OUTLOOK of the thinkers and writers of the Waste Land period is dark. Man has not yet seen clearly a way in which he may become dignified, a way in which the industry he has built may serve his needs. He is lonely as was the Hairy Ape in O'Neill's play. O'Neill, like most writers of this period, did not imply, as many authors of a later day were going to do, that man's real enemy is a class, not a girl nor an illusion of one's social inferiority.

All man's enormous knowledge of himself, as displayed in the rich, rhythmic, subjective penetration of man's mind in Joyce's *Finnegans Wake*, or in Huxley's analysis of man's scientific brain, or in Lewis' puzzlement as to what is wrong, was out of focus. This knowledge could not be used, as the Waste Land writers saw it, because this mechanistic machine-made world denied the spirit and the flesh. That man's inhumanity to man was due to economic instability first and spiritual emptiness second was the message of the next group of writers. To the Waste Landers, it seemed that a blindfolded world was singing, with Eliot,

> *This is the way the world ends*
> *This is the way the world ends*
> *This is the way the world ends*
> *Not with a bang but a whimper.*

But when at last it became inescapably clear that a period *can* end with a "bang," many of the Waste Land doubters preferred their boredom to war. Doubt at least had left them their personal lives to concentrate upon; it demanded of them no action in a world they saw no immediate way to redeem.   (E.L.W.)

WILFRED OWEN

Wilfred Owen was born at Plas Wilmot, Oswestry, England, March 18, 1893, and he was killed November 4, 1918, while attempting as a commander of the Artist's Rifles, O.T.C., to get his men across the Sambre Canal.

Owen, always in delicate health, was a dreamy, imaginative child. He was educated at the Birkenhead Institute and then at London University. As a boy of thirteen he had lived for a while in France, and after college in 1913 he went to Bordeaux as a private tutor, remaining there until 1915. He enlisted in 1915 and served in France until June 1917, when he was invalided home for fourteen months. He returned to the front, was awarded the Military Cross for gallantry, and was killed a week before the Armistice.

His hatred of war was as deep and as intense as his love for life, and his letters from the front are dramatic and cruel pictures:

> No Man's Land under snow is like the face of the moon, chaotic, crater-ridden, uninhabitable, awful, the abode of madness. . . . I was kept warm by the ardour of Life within me. I forgot hunger in the hunger for Life.

While he was convalescing at Craiglockhart, Owen met Siegfried Sassoon, who was in the same hospital. Owen remembered with gratitude his kindly help and urging:

> And you have *fixed* my Life—however short. You did not light me: I was always a mad comet; but you have fixed me. I spun round you a satellite for a month, but I shall swing out soon, a dark star in the orbit where you will blaze. It is some consolation to know that Jupiter himself sometimes swims out of ken.

Sassoon edited Owen's *Poems* in 1920. In 1931 Edmund Blunden edited *The Poems of Wilfred Owen*, which included many new poems and a memoir and notes. As late as 1941, when England was fighting for her life, an appraisal of Owen appeared in the *Poetry Review*.

The universal theme of the tragedy and pity of war which runs through Owen's poetry lifts it above the poetry of rhetorical patriotism. His poetry is filled with the restrained passion of revolt; he is crying out against the war that killed so many young men of genius. His own work, so rich with promise, fuses the horrible experiences of war with a stern wisdom about life and a belief in progress. While he proposed no panacea, he held that men hate war, and that such cataclysms are ruinous to all that is best in humankind.

Greater Love

Red lips are not so red
    As the stained stones kissed by the English dead.
Kindness of wooed and wooer
Seems shame to their love pure.
O Love, your eyes lose lure   5
    When I behold eyes blinded in my stead!

Your slender attitude
    Trembles not exquisite like limbs knife-skewed,

"Greater Love," "Apologia pro Poemate Meo," "Dulce et Decorum Est," "Disabled," "The End," and "Anthem for Doomed Youth" from *Poems* by Wilfred Owen. Published by the Viking Press, Inc., New York.

Rolling and rolling there
Where God seems not to care;   10
Till the fierce Love they bear
    Cramps them in death's extreme decrepi-
        tude.

Your voice sings not so soft,—
    Though even as wind murmuring
        through raftered loft,—
Your dear voice is not dear,   15
Gentle, and evening clear,
As theirs whom none now hear
    Now earth has stopped their piteous
        mouths that coughed.

Heart, you were never hot,
    Nor large, nor full like hearts made great
        with shot;   20
And though your hand be pale,
Paler are all which trail
Your cross through flame and hail:
    Weep, you may weep, for you may touch
        them not.

Apologia pro Poemate Meo

I, TOO, saw God through mud—
    The mud that cracked on cheeks when
        wretches smiled.
    War brought more glory to their eyes than
        blood,
    And gave their laughs more glee than
        shakes a child.

Merry it was to laugh there—   5
    Where death becomes absurd and life
        absurder.
    For power was on us as we slashed bones
        bare
    Not to feel sickness or remorse of murder.

I, too, have dropped off fear—   9
    Behind the barrage, dead as my platoon,
    And sailed my spirit surging, light and
        clear
    Past the entanglement where hopes lay
        strewn;

And witnessed exultation—
    Faces that used to curse me, scowl for
        scowl,   14

Apologia . . . Meo, apology for my poetry.

Shine and lift up with passion of oblation,
    Seraphic for an hour; though they were
        foul.

I have made fellowships—
    Untold of happy lovers in old song.
    For love is not the binding of fair lips
    With the soft silk of eyes that look and
        long,   20

By Joy, whose ribbon slips,—
    But wound with war's hard wire whose
        stakes are strong;
    Bound with the bandage of the arm that
        drips;
    Knit in the welding of the rifle-thong.

I have perceived much beauty   25
    In the hoarse oaths that kept our courage
        straight;
    Heard music in the silentness of duty;
    Found peace where shell-storms spouted
        reddest spate.

Nevertheless, except you share
    With them in hell the sorrowful dark of
        hell,   30
    Whose world is but the trembling of a
        flare,
    And heaven but as the highway for a
        shell,

You shall not hear their mirth:
    You shall not come to think them well
        content   34
    By any jest of mine. These men are worth
    Your tears: You are not worth their merri-
        ment.

Dulce et Decorum Est

BENT double, like old beggars under sacks,
    Knock-kneed, coughing like hags, we
        cursed through sludge,
Till on the haunting flares we turned our backs,
And towards our distant rest began to trudge.
Men marched asleep. Many had lost their
        boots,   5
But limped on, blood-shod. All went lame, all
        blind;

Dulce . . . Est, "It is sweet and honorable to die for one's country." Horace, *Odes,* III, 2, l. 13.

Drunk with fatigue; deaf even to the hoots
Of gas-shells dropping softly behind.

Gas! GAS! Quick, boys!—An ecstasy of fum-
    bling
Fitting the clumsy helmets just in time,   10
But someone still was yelling out and stum-
    bling
And flound'ring like a man in fire or lime.—
Dim through the misty panes and thick green
    light,
As under a green sea, I saw him drowning.
In all my dreams before my helpless sight   15
He plunges at me, guttering, choking, drown-
    ing.

If in some smothering dreams, you too could
    pace
Behind the wagon that we flung him in,
And watch the white eyes writhing in his face,
His hanging face, like a devil's sick of sin,   20
If you could hear, at every jolt, the blood
Come gargling from the froth-corrupted lungs
Bitten as the cud
Of vile, incurable sores on innocent tongues,—
My friend, you would not tell with such high
    zest   25
To children ardent for some desperate glory,
The old Lie: *Dulce et decorum est*
Pro patria mori.

Disabled

HE SAT in a wheeled chair, waiting for dark,
    And shivered in his ghastly suit of grey,
Legless, sewn short at elbow. Through the
    park
Voices of boys rang saddening like a hymn,
Voices of play and pleasure after day,   5
Till gathering sleep had mothered them from
    him.

About this time Town used to swing so gay
When glow-lamps budded in the light-blue
    trees
And girls glanced lovelier as the air grew dim,
—In the old times, before he threw away his
    knees.   10
Now he will never feel again how slim
Girls' waists are, or how warm their subtle
    hands,
All of them touch him like some queer disease.

There was an artist silly for his face,
For it was younger than his youth, last year.
Now he is old; his back will never brace;   16
He's lost his colour very far from here,
Poured it down shell-holes till the veins ran
    dry,
And half his lifetime lapsed in the hot race,
And leap of purple spurted from his thigh.   20
One time he liked a bloodsmear down his leg,
After the matches carried shoulder-high.
It was after football, when he'd drunk a peg,
He thought he'd better join. He wonders
    why . . .
Someone had said he'd look a god in kilts.   25

That's why; and maybe, too, to please his Meg,
Aye, that was it, to please the giddy jilts,
He asked to join. He didn't have to beg;
Smiling they wrote his lie; aged nineteen years.
Germans he scarcely thought of; and no fears
Of Fear came yet. He thought of jewelled hilts
For daggers in plaid socks; of smart salutes;   32
And care of arms; and leave; and pay arrears;
Esprit de corps; and hints for young recruits.
And soon, he was drafted out with drums and
    cheers.   35

Some cheered him home, but not as crowds
    cheer Goal.
Only a solemn man who brought him fruits
Thanked him; and then inquired about his
    soul.
Now, he will spend a few sick years in Insti-
    tutes,
And do what things the rules consider wise,
And take whatever pity they may dole.   41
To-night he noticed how the women's eyes
Passed from him to the strong men that were
    whole.
How cold and late it is! Why don't they come
And put him into bed? Why don't they come?

The End

AFTER the blast of lightning from the east,
    The flourish of loud clouds, the Chariot
    throne,
After the drums of time have rolled and ceased
And from the bronze west long retreat is
    blown,

2. **Chariot throne.** Apollo, who pulled the sun across the heavens, rode in a chariot.

Shall Life renew these bodies? Of a truth   5
All death will he annul, all tears assuage?
Or fill these void veins full again with youth
And wash with an immortal water age?

When I do ask white Age, he saith not so,—
"My head hangs weighed with snow."   10
And when I hearken to the Earth she saith
"My fiery heart sinks aching. It is death.
Mine ancient scars shall not be glorified
Nor my titanic tears the seas be dried."

Anthem for Doomed Youth

WHAT passing-bells for these who die as
  cattle?
Only the monstrous anger of the guns.

Only the stuttering rifles' rapid rattle
Can patter out their hasty orisons.   4
No mockeries for them; no prayers nor bells,
Nor any voice of mourning save the choirs,—
The shrill, demented choirs of wailing shells;
And bugles calling for them from sad shires.

What candles may be held to speed them
  all?
Not in the hands of boys, but in their eyes
Shall shine the holy glimmers of good-byes.   11
The pallor of girls' brows shall be their
  pall;
Their flowers the tenderness of patient minds,
And each slow dusk a drawing-down of
  blinds.

SIEGFRIED SASSOON

Siegfried Lorraine Sassoon was one of the young poets whose lives were to be influenced by the misery and futility of World War I. He was born September 8, 1886, into the distinguished English-Arabian-Jewish family of businessmen and bankers whose fascinating story is outlined in Cecil Roth's *The Sassoon Dynasty*. Siegfried was educated at Marlborough Grammar School and Clare College, Cambridge—a departure from tradition since Oxford is the university of the Sassoons.

His first collection, *Poems,* was published in 1902 while he was still in college. Between 1911 and 1916 he issued anonymously seven small privately printed volumes of verse. *The Old Huntsman and Other Poems* appeared in 1917, *Picture Show* in 1919, and *Satirical Poems* in 1926 and again in 1933 with five poems added. *Selected Poems* was published in 1925 and again in 1931; *Vigils* in 1935, *Rhymed Ruminations* in 1940, and *Poems Newly Selected 1916–35* in 1942. *Meredith,* a biography of the famous nineteenth-century poet and novelist, was published in 1948. Sassoon's *Collected Poems* appeared in the United States in 1949.

Sassoon enlisted early and saw over four years of service in battle, and won the Military Cross for bringing in the wounded under shellfire. He finally became a captain. In the spring of 1917 he was shot in the throat while leading a bombing party. While he constantly and recklessly led attack after attack, his hatred of war and his need of immediate expression made him write and circulate what we know as his war poems, opposed to the very war in which he was a hero. Some of them appeared in the pacifist *Cambridge Magazine* which was mailed to the front.

By July 1917, he refused to serve in the army. His statement was important enough to be read in Parliament:

I am making this statement because I believe that this war is being deliberately prolonged by those who have the power to end it. I am a soldier convinced that I am acting on behalf of soldiers. . . . I have seen and endured the suffering of the troops, and I can no longer be a party to prolong these sufferings for ends which I believe to be evil and unjust.

To save him from court-martial his friends had him adjudged insane and sent to Craiglockhart convalescent hospital in Edinburgh, where he met Wilfred Owen. He returned to active service, first in Palestine and then on the Western Front, where he was wounded in the head by one of his own men and finally invalided home. Faithful to his pledge to fight against war, Sassoon, without much political understanding, was active in the election campaign of the pacifist Snowden. Until its collapse, he was part of the international group of intellectuals, Clarte, organized by Henri Barbusse. In 1920 he traveled through the United States and Canada on an extended lecture tour, giving readings from his war poems at a number of universities.

Sassoon in his later poems turns to the verities of nature, truth, and love. Most notable are his later poems on his son, over whose life he broods tenderly. But more interesting than this later verse are his two series of autobiographies, one written as Sassoon, man of letters, and the other as George Sherston, gentleman. George Sherston's life is told in the anonymously published *Memoirs of a Fox-Hunting Man* (1928), *Memoirs of an Infantry Officer* (1930), and *Sherston's Progress* (1936). The three volumes were combined in 1937 as *The Complete Memoirs of George Sherston. The Old Century and Seven More Years* (1938) takes Sassoon's personal story up to 1907; *The Weald of Youth* (1924) covers the years 1909 to 1914; and *Siegfried's Journey* (1945) begins with 1916 and ends in 1920. The two streams were partly united in 1941 with the publication of *The Flower Show Match and Other Pieces*, which contained excerpts from both series.

These autobiographies, taken from a continuously kept diary, are proof of Sassoon's absorption in his dual personality, which is typical of any man sensitive to letters but caught in the prison of a conservative background. He became the voice of a generation of English boys gently bred and intellectually curious.

Sassoon's estimate of World War II is of greatest importance because in this war he was not a pacifist. He accepts the necessity of war when fascism is the enemy. "If I were asked to make a speech about war now," he writes in *Siegfried's Journey,*

it would consist of a couple of sentences. "The only effective answer that a poet can make to barbarism is poetry, for the only answer to death is the life of the spirit. Explosives cannot destroy the immaterial or dumbfound the utterance of inspiration."

Ex-Service

DERISION from the dead
Mocks armamental madness.
Redeem (each Ruler said)
Mankind. Men died to do it.
And some with glorying gladness   5
Bore arms for earth and bled:
But most went glumly through it
Dumbly doomed to rue it.

The darkness of their dying
Grows one with War recorded;   10
Whose swindled ghosts are crying
From shell-holes in the past,
Our deeds with lies were lauded,
Our bones with wrongs rewarded.
Dream voices these—denying   15
Dud laurels to the last.

Break silence. You have listened overlong
To muttering mind-wrought voices. Call for
          lights.
Prove these persistent haunting presences
          wrong   19
Who mock and stultify your days and nights.

Dawn comes, and re-creates the sleepless
          room;
And eyesight asks what arguing plagues exist.
But in that garret of uneasy gloom
Which is your brain, the presences persist.

"Ex-Service" and "Vigil in Spring" from *Vigils*, copyright, 1936; "On Reading the War Diary of a Defunct Ambassador," "Villa d'Este Gardens," and "The Case for the Miners" from *Satirical Poems*, copyright, 1926, by Siegfried Sassoon. Published by The Viking Press, Inc., New York.

Vigil in Spring

THE NIGHT air, smelling cold with spring,
   And the dark twigs of towering trees,—
When age remembers youth we bring
Aliveness back to us in these.
Leaning from windows on the gloom,   5
We are one with purpling woods and wet
Wild violets of our earth in whom
Aliveness wakes and wonders yet.
Inbreathed awareness, hushed and cold,
Of growth's annunciate thrust and thrill,   10
We lean from lifetime, growing old,
And feel your starlit magic still.

On Reading the War Diary of a Defunct Ambassador

SO THAT'S your Diary—that's your private
         mind
Translated into shirt-sleeved History. That
Is what diplomacy has left behind
For after-ages to peruse, and find
What passed beneath your elegant silk-hat.   5

You were a fine old gentleman; compact
Of shrewdness, charm, refinement and finesse.
Impeccable in breeding, taste and dress,
No diplomatic quality you lacked—
No tittle of ambassadorial tact.   10

I can imagine you among "the guns,"
Urbanely peppering partridge, grouse, or
         pheasant—
Guest of those infinitely privileged ones
Whose lives are padded, petrified, and pleas-
      ant.
I visualise you feeding off gold plate   15
And gossiping on grave affairs of State.

Now you're defunct; your gossip's gravely
         printed;
The world discovers where you lunched and
         dined
On such and such a day; and what was hinted

By ministers and generals far behind   20
The all-important conflict, carnage-tinted.

The world can read the rumours that you
         gleaned
From various Fronts; the well-known Names
         you met;
Each conference you attended and convened;
And (at appropriate moments) what you ate.
Thus (if the world's acute) it can derive   26
Your self, exact, uncensored and alive.

The world will find no pity in your pages;
No exercise of spirit worthy of mention;
Only a public-funeral grief-convention;   30
And all the circumspection of the ages.
But I, for one, am grateful, overjoyed,
And unindignant that your punctual pen
Should have been so constructively employed
In manifesting to unprivileged men   35
The visionless officialized fatuity
That once kept Europe safe for Perpetuity.

On Passing the New Menin Gate

WHO WILL remember, passing through this
         Gate,
The unheroic Dead who fed the guns?
Who shall absolve the foulness of their fate,—
Those doomed, conscripted, unvictorious ones?
   Crudely renewed, the Salient holds its own.
   Paid are its dim defenders by this pomp;   6
   Paid, with a pile of peace-complacent stone,
   The armies who endured that sullen swamp.

Here was the world's worst wound. And here
         with pride,
'Their name liveth for ever,' the Gateway
         claims.   10
Was ever an immolation so belied
As these intolerably nameless names?
Well might the Dead who struggled in the
         slime
Rise and deride this sepulchre of crime.

21. **carnage-tinted**, colored from the bloody slaughter of battle.
"On Passing the New Menin Gate" from *The Heart's Journey*, reprinted by permission of the author, William Heinemann, Ltd., and Harper & Brothers.
1. **Gate**. Menin Gate is an historic monument at the gate to the town of Menin, in Flanders, Belgium. 5. **Salient**, the trenches projecting farthest into the enemy's territory.

10. **annunciate**, proclamation of coming. (This is obviously poetic license—the use of a verb for an adjective.)

Villa d'Este Gardens

"Of course you saw the Villa d'Este Gardens,"
Writes one of my Italianistic friends.
Of course; of course; I saw them in October,
Spired with pinaceous ornamental gloom
Or that arboreal elegy the cypress. 5

Those fountains, too, "like ghosts of cy-
        presses";—
(That phrase occurred to me while I was
        leaning
On an old balustrade; imbibing sunset;
Wrapped in my verse vocation)—how they
        linked me
With Byron, Landor, Liszt, and Robert
        Browning! . . . 10
A *Liebestraum* of Liszt cajoled my senses.
My language favored Landor, chaste and for-
mal.
My intellect (though slightly in abeyance)
Functioned against a Byronistic background.
Then Browning jogged my elbow; bade me
        hob-nob 15
With some forgotten painter of dim frescoes
That haunt the Villa's intramural twilight.

While roaming in the Villa d'Este Gardens
I felt like that . . . and fumbled for my note-
        book.

The Case for the Miners

SOMETHING goes wrong with my synthetic
        brain
When I defend the Strikers and explain
My reasons for not blackguarding the Miners.
"*What do you know?*" exclaim my fellow-
        diners

(Peeling their plovers eggs or lifting glasses 5
Of mellowed *Château Rentier* from the table),
"*What do you know about the working
        classes?*"

I strive to hold my own; but I'm unable
To state the case succinctly. Indistinctly
I mumble about World-Emancipation, 10
Standards of Living, Nationalization
Of Industry; until they get me tangled
In superficial details; goad me on
To unconvincing vagueness. When we've
        wrangled
From soup to savoury, my temper's gone. 15

"*Why should a miner earn six pounds a week?*
Leisure! They'd only spend it in a bar!
Standard of life! You'll never teach them Greek,
Or make them more contented than they are!"
That's how my port-flushed friends discuss the
        Strike. 20
And that's the reason why I shout and splutter.
And that's the reason why I'd almost like
To see them hawking matches in the gutter.

Silent Service

NOW, MULTIFOLD, let Britain's patient power
        Be proven within us for the world to see.
None are exempt from service in this hour;
And vanquished in ourselves we dare not be.
    Now, for a sunlit future, we can show 5
    The clenched resolved endurance that defies
Daemons in dark—and toward that future go
With earth's defended freedom in our eyes.
    In every separate soul let courage shine—
    A kneeling angel holding faith's front-line. 10

May 23, 1940

1. *Villa d'Este Gardens,* the gardens surrounding the estate of
the d'Este family of Ferrara, a celebrated ducal family of the
Renaissance period.   4. **pinaceous,** full of pines.   10. **Byron
. . . Browning.** The poets and composer mentioned all lived
in Italy.   11. *Liebestraum,* a melodious waltz; a piano composition by Franz Liszt. The title means "A Dream of
Love."
The Case for the Miners. The title of the poem indicates
that Sassoon is making a plea for better conditions among the
miners to his middle-class friends, who have false ideas about
labor.

5. **plovers eggs,** a great table delicacy, being eaten by the
wealthy diners as they retort to the poet's argument for labor.
6. *Château Rentier,* a distinguished Bordeaux wine. "Château" signifies the castle or mansion of the estate on which the
wine was grown.   20. **port-flushed friends.** The poet emphasizes the fact that his friends have eaten and drunk much
while they make completely unintelligent comments on the
miners.
"Silent Service" from *Rhymed Ruminations* by Siegfried Sassoon, reprinted by permission of The Viking Press, New York.

WOODROW WILSON

Thomas Woodrow Wilson was born at Staunton, Virginia, December 28, 1856. He graduated from Princeton University in 1879, studying law later at the University of Virginia and at Johns Hopkins. From 1885 to 1888 he was on the faculty of Bryn Mawr College; from 1888 to 1890 he was professor of history at Wesleyan University. He became professor of jurisprudence and politics at Princeton in 1890, where he had great success as a teacher. In 1902 he was made president of Princeton, serving in that capacity until 1910, when he resigned to campaign successfully for the governorship of New Jersey. He resigned his governorship in 1913 to become the twenty-eighth President of the United States, having won this position after the torrid campaign of 1912 against Theodore Roosevelt and the incumbent William Howard Taft. He was reëlected in 1916.

The great events of his administrations included the revision of the tariff, the establishment of the parcel-post service, the recognition of the Chinese Republic, the institution of the Income Tax Law, the adoption of a constitutional amendment providing for the election of United States Senators by direct vote of the people, the enactment of alien land laws, the establishment of the Federal Reserve Banking system, the difficulties with Mexico, and—most important of all—the First World War. The conclusion of the war saw the emergence of his specific plans for world peace, the League of Nations, and the independence of small nations. These ideals are all seen shadowed forth in his Speech for Declaration of War Against Germany (April 2, 1917), which appears on the following pages.

President Wilson's state papers are marked by a high degree of literary excellence; he was an impressive wielder of phrases and expressed in unforgettable terms the hopes and aspirations of millions for peace and political, national integrity. His will, however, did not have its way with the American people; his is a great personal tragedy and perhaps a political one as well, yet we are concerned here primarily with his utterances as representing the voice of America militant in the year 1917.

Even before the close of his second administration President Wilson had suffered a physical collapse; the remaining years of his life were spent quietly in Washington, where he died peacefully in 1924.

Speech for Declaration of War Against Germany

(APRIL 2, 1917)

I HAVE called the Congress into extraordinary session because there are serious, very serious, choices of policy to be made, and made immediately, which it was neither right nor constitutionally permissible that I should assume the responsibility of making.

On the third of February last I officially laid before you the extraordinary announcement of the Imperial German Government that on and after the first day of February it was its purpose to put aside all restraints of law or of humanity and use its submarines to sink every vessel that sought to approach either the ports of Great Britain and Ireland or the western coasts of Europe or any of the ports controlled by the enemies of Germany within the Mediterranean. That had seemed to be the object of the German submarine warfare earlier in the war, but since April of last year the Imperial Government had somewhat restrained the commanders of its undersea craft in conformity with its promise then given to us that passen-

"Speech for Declaration of War Against Germany" reprinted by permission of Mrs. Woodrow Wilson.

ger boats should not be sunk and that due warning would be given to all other vessels which its submarines might seek to destroy, when no resistance was offered or escape attempted, and care taken that their crews were given at least a fair chance to save their lives in their open boats. The precautions taken were meager and haphazard enough, as was proved in distressing instance after instance in 10 the progress of the cruel and unmanly business, but a certain degree of restraint was observed. The new policy has swept every restriction aside. Vessels of every kind, whatever their flag, their character, their cargo, their destination, their errand, have been ruthlessly sent to the bottom without warning and without thought of help or mercy for those on board, the vessels of friendly neutrals along with those of belligerents. Even hospital ships and 20 ships carrying relief to the sorely bereaved and stricken people of Belgium, though the latter were provided with safe conduct through the proscribed areas by the German Government itself and were distinguished by unmistakable marks of identity, have been sunk with the same reckless lack of compassion or of principle.

I was for a little while unable to believe that such things would in fact be done by any gov- 30 ernment that had hitherto subscribed to the humane practices of civilized nations. International law had its origin in the attempt to set up some law which would be respected and observed upon the seas, where no nation had right of dominion and where lay the free highways of the world. By painful stage after stage has that law been built up, with meagre enough results, indeed, after all was accomplished that could be accomplished, but al- 40 ways with a clear view, at least, of what the heart and conscience of mankind demanded.

This minimum of right the German Government has swept aside under the plea of retaliation and necessity and because it had no weapons which it could use at sea except those which it is impossible to employ as it is employing them without throwing to the winds all scruples of humanity or of respect for the understandings that were supposed to under- 50 lie the intercourse of the world. I am not now thinking of the loss of property involved, immense and serious as that is, but only of the wanton and wholesale destruction of the lives of non-combatants, men, women, and children, engaged in pursuits which have always, even in the darkest periods of modern history, been deemed innocent and legitimate. Property can be paid for; the lives of peaceful and innocent people cannot be. The present German submarine warfare against commerce is a warfare 60 against mankind.

It is a war against all nations. American ships have been sunk, American lives taken, in ways which it has stirred us very deeply to learn of, but the ships and people of other neutral and friendly nations have been sunk and overwhelmed in the waters in the same way. There has been no discrimination. The challenge is to all mankind. Each nation must decide for itself how it will meet it. The choice 70 we make for ourselves must be made with a moderation of counsel and a temperateness of judgment befitting our character and our motives as a nation. We must put excited feeling away. Our motive will not be revenge or the victorious assertion of the physical might of the nation, but only the vindication of right, of human right, of which we are only a single champion.

When I addressed the Congress on the 80 twenty-sixth of February last I thought that it would suffice to assert our neutral rights with arms, our right to use the seas against unlawful interference, our right to keep our people safe against unlawful violence. But armed neutrality, it now appears, is impracticable. Because submarines are in effect outlaws when used as the German submarines have been used against merchant shipping, it is impossible to defend ships against their attacks as the 90 law of nations has assumed that merchantmen would defend themselves against privateers or cruisers, visible craft giving chase upon the open sea. It is common prudence in such circumstances, grim necessity indeed, to endeavor to destroy them before they have shown their own intention. They must be dealt with upon sight, if dealt with at all. The German Government denies the right of neutrals to use arms at all within the areas of the sea 100 which it has proscribed, even in the defense of rights which no modern publicist has ever before questioned their right to defend. The intimation is conveyed that the armed guards which we have placed on our merchant ships will be treated as beyond the pale of law and subject to be dealt with as pirates should be. Armed neutrality is ineffectual enough at best; in such circumstances and in the face of such pretensions it is worse than ineffectual; it is likely only to produce what it was meant to prevent; it is practically certain to draw us into the war without either the rights or the effectiveness of belligerents. There is one choice we cannot make, we are incapable of making: we will not choose the path of submission and suffer the most sacred rights of our Nation and our people to be ignored or violated. The wrongs against which we now array ourselves are no common wrongs; they cut to the very root of human life.

With a profound sense of the solemn and even tragical character of the step I am taking and of the grave responsibilities which it involves, but in unhesitating obedience to what I deem my constitutional duty, I advise that the Congress declare the recent course of the Imperial German Government to be in fact nothing less than war against the government and people of the United States; that it formally accept the status of belligerent which has thus been thrust upon it; and that it take immediate steps not only to put the country in a more thorough state of defense but also to exert all its power and employ all its resources to bring the Government of the German Empire to terms and end the war.

What this will involve is clear. It will involve the utmost practicable coöperation in counsel and action with the governments now at war with Germany, and, as incident to that, the extension to those governments of the most liberal financial credits, in order that our resources may so far as possible be added to theirs. It will involve the organization and mobilization of all the material resources of the country to supply the materials of war and serve the incidental needs of the Nation in the most abundant and yet the most economical and efficient way possible. It will involve the immediate full equipment of the navy in all respects but particularly in supplying it with the best means of dealing with the enemy's submarines. It will involve the immediate addition to the armed forces of the United States already provided for by law in case of war at least five hundred thousand men, who should, in my opinion, be chosen upon the principle of universal liability to service, and also the authorization of subsequent additional increments of equal force so soon as they may be needed and can be handled in training. It will involve also, of course, the granting of adequate credits to the Government, sustained, I hope, so far as they can equitably be sustained by the present generation, by well conceived taxation. I say sustained so far as is equitable by taxation, because it seems to me that it would be most unwise to base the credits, which will now be necessary, entirely on money borrowed. It is our duty, I most respectfully urge, to protect our people, so far as we may, against the very serious hardships and evils which would be likely to arise out of the inflation which would be produced by vast loans.

In carrying out the measures by which these things are to be accomplished we should keep constantly in mind the wisdom of interfering as little as possible in our own preparation and in the equipment of our military forces with the duty—for it will be a very practical duty— of supplying the nations already at war with Germany with the materials which they can obtain only from us or by our assistance. They are in the field, and we should help them in every way to be effective there.

I shall take the liberty of suggesting, through the several executive departments of the Government, for the consideration of your committees, measures for the accomplishment of the several objects I have mentioned. I hope that it will be your pleasure to deal with them as having been framed after very careful thought by the branch of the Government upon whom the responsibility for conducting the war and safeguarding the nation will most directly fall.

While we do these things, these deeply momentous things, let us be very clear, and make very clear to all the world what our motives and our objects are. My own thought has not been driven from its habitual and normal course by the unhappy events of the last two months, and I do not believe that the thought of the Nation has been altered or clouded by them. I have exactly the same things in mind now that I had in mind when I addressed the Senate on the twenty-second of January last; the same that I had in mind when I addressed the Congress on the third of February and on the twenty-sixth of February. Our object now, as then, is to vindicate the principles of peace and justice in the life of the world as against selfish and autocratic power and to set up amongst the really free and self-governed peoples of the world such a concert of purpose and of action as will henceforth insure the observance of those principles. Neutrality is no longer feasible or desirable where the peace of the world is involved and the freedom of its peoples, and the menace to that peace and freedom lies in the existence of autocratic governments backed by organized force which is controlled wholly by their will, not by the will of their people. We have seen the last of neutrality in such circumstances. We are at the beginning of an age in which it will be insisted that the same standards of conduct and of responsibility for wrong done shall be observed among nations and their governments that are observed among the individual citizens of civilized states.

We have no quarrel with the German people. We have no feeling toward them but one of sympathy and friendship. It was not upon their impulse that their government acted in entering this war. It was not with their previous knowledge or approval. It was a war determined upon as wars used to be determined upon in the old, unhappy days when peoples were nowhere consulted by their rulers and wars were provoked and waged in the interests of dynasties or of little groups of ambitious men who were accustomed to use their fellow men as pawns and tools.

Self-governed nations do not fill their neighbor States with spies or set the course of intrigue to bring about some critical posture of affairs which will give them an opportunity to strike and make conquest. Such designs can be successfully worked out only under cover and where no one has the right to ask questions. Cunningly contrived plans of deception or aggression, carried, it may be, from generation to generation, can be worked out and kept from the light only within the privacy of courts or behind the carefully guarded confidences of a narrow and privileged class. They are happily impossible where public opinion commands and insists upon full information concerning all the nation's affairs.

A steadfast concert for peace can never be maintained except by a partnership of democratic nations. No autocratic Government could be trusted to keep faith within it or observe its covenants. It must be a league of honor, a partnership of opinion. Intrigue would eat its vitals away; the plottings of inner circles who could plan what they would and render account to no one would be a corruption seated at its very heart. Only free peoples can hold their purpose and their honor steady to a common end and prefer the interests of mankind to any narrow interest of their own.

Does not every American feel that assurance has been added to our hope for the future peace of the world by the wonderful and heartening things that have been happening within the last few weeks in Russia? Russia was known by those who knew her best to have been always in fact democratic at heart in all the vital habits of her thought, in all the intimate relationships of her people that spoke their natural instinct, their habitual attitude toward life. The autocracy that crowned the summit of her political structure, long as it had stood and terrible as was the reality of its power, was not in fact Russian in origin, character, or purpose; and now it has been shaken off and the great, generous Russian people have been added, in all their naïve majesty and might, to the forces that are fighting for freedom in the world, for justice, and for peace. Here is a fit partner for a League of Honor.

One of the things that has served to convince us that the Prussian autocracy was not and could never be our friend is that from the very outset of the present war it has filled our unsuspecting communities, and even our offices of government, with spies and set criminal intrigues everywhere afoot against our national unity of counsel, our peace within and without, our industries and our commerce. Indeed, it is now evident that its spies were here even before the war began; and it is unhappily not a matter of conjecture, but a fact proved in our courts of justice, that the intrigues which have more than once come perilously near to disturbing the peace and dislocating the industries of the country, have been carried on at the instigation, with the support, and even under the personal direction of official agents of the Imperial Government, accredited to the Government of the United States.

Even in checking these things and trying to extirpate them we have sought to put the most generous interpretation possible upon them because we knew that their source lay, not in any hostile feeling or purpose of the German people toward us (who were, no doubt, as ignorant of them as we ourselves were), but only in the selfish designs of a Government that did what it pleased and told its people nothing. But they have played their part in serving to convince us at last that that Government entertains no real friendship for us, and means to act against our peace and security at its convenience. That it means to stir up enemies against us at our very doors the intercepted note to the German Minister at Mexico City is eloquent evidence.

We are accepting this challenge of hostile purpose because we know that in such a Government, following such methods, we can never have a friend; and that in the presence of its organized power, always lying in wait to accomplish we know not what purpose, there can be no assured security for the democratic Governments of the world. We are now about to accept the gage of battle with this natural foe to liberty and shall, if necessary, spend the whole force of the nation to check and nullify its pretensions and its power. We are glad, now that we see the facts with no veil of false pretense about them, to fight thus for the ultimate peace of the world and for the liberation of its peoples, the German peoples included: for the rights of nations great and small and the privilege of men everywhere to choose their way of life and of obedience. The world must be made safe for democracy. Its peace must be planted upon the tested foundations of political liberty. We have no selfish ends to serve. We desire no conquest, no dominion. We seek no indemnities for ourselves, no material compensation for the sacrifices we shall freely make. We are but one of the champions of the rights of mankind. We shall be satisfied when those rights have been made as secure as the faith and the freedom of nations can make them.

Just because we fight without rancor and without selfish object, seeking nothing for ourselves but what we shall wish to share with all free peoples, we shall, I feel confident, conduct our operations as belligerents without passion and ourselves observe with proud punctilio the principles of right and of fair play we profess to be fighting for.

I have said nothing of the Governments allied with the Imperial Government of Germany because they have not made war upon us or challenged us to defend our right and our honor. The Austro-Hungarian Government has, indeed, avowed its unqualified indorsement and acceptance of the reckless and lawless submarine warfare adopted now without disguise by the Imperial German Government, and it has therefore not been possible for this Government to receive Count Tarnowski, the Ambassador recently accredited to this Government by the Imperial and Royal Government of Austria-Hungary; but that Government has not actually engaged in warfare against citizens of the United States on the seas, and I take the liberty, for the present at least, of postponing a discussion of our relations with the authorities at Vienna. We enter this war only where we are clearly forced into it because there are no other means of defending our rights.

It will be all the easier for us to conduct ourselves as belligerents in a high spirit of right and fairness because we act without animus, not in enmity towards a people or with the desire to bring any injury or disadvantage upon them, but only in armed opposition to an irresponsible government which has thrown aside all considerations of humanity and of right and is running amuck. We are, let me say again, the sincere friends of the German people, and shall desire nothing so much as the early reëstablishment of intimate relations of mutual advantage between us,—however hard it may be for them, for the time being, to believe that this is spoken from our hearts. We have borne with their present Government through all these bitter months because of that

friendship,—exercising a patience and forbearance which would otherwise have been impossible. We shall, happily, still have an opportunity to prove that friendship in our daily attitude and actions towards the millions of men and women of German birth and native sympathy who live amongst us and share our life, and we shall be proud to prove it towards all who are in fact loyal to their neighbors and to
10 the Government in the hour of test. They are, most of them, as true and loyal Americans as if they had never known any other fealty or allegiance. They will be prompt to stand with us in rebuking and restraining the few who may be of a different mind and purpose. If there should be disloyalty, it will be dealt with with a firm hand of stern repression; but, if it lifts its head at all, it will lift it only here and there and without countenance except from a
20 lawless and malignant few.

It is a distressing and oppressive duty, Gentlemen of the Congress, which I have performed in thus addressing you. There are, it

may be, many months of fiery trial and sacrifice ahead of us. It is a fearful thing to lead this great peaceful people into war, into the most terrible and disastrous of all wars, civilization itself seeming to be in the balance. But the right is more precious than peace, and we shall fight for the things which we have always carried nearest our hearts,—for democracy, for the right of those who submit to authority to have a voice in their own Governments, for the rights and liberties of small nations, for a universal dominion of right by such a concert of free peoples as shall bring peace and safety to all nations and make the world itself at last free. To such a task we can dedicate our lives and our fortunes, everything that we are and everything that we have, with the pride of those who know that the day has come when America is privileged to spend her blood and her might for the principles that gave her birth and happiness and the peace which she has treasured. God helping her, she can do no other.

❦ Waste Land

EDITH SITWELL

Edith Louisa Sitwell is one of the most brilliant and provocative of women writers. She and her brothers, Sacheverell and Osbert, have written much about their once seemingly permanent world of landed estates, governesses, and nursemaids. Miss Sitwell has always presented this world in images which tell us that it is dead or dying, that its inhabitants have been driven from their peaceful, sheltered existence by the harshness of commercialism and industry. Her poetry is gently satirical of the aristocracy, yet half nostalgic too, presenting the past as if it were a faded tapestry with

the no longer quite reverenced motto, "God Bless Our Home."

Miss Sitwell was born in Scarborough, Yorkshire, England, in 1887, daughter of Sir George, fourth baronet, and Lady Ida Sitwell. Her imposing line of ancestry can be traced back to the Norman chiefs who came to England with William the Conqueror. The Sitwell estate at Renishaw Park has been in the family for over 600 years. Though her whole manner of life has been in accord with her surroundings, her thinking and her literary works have been those of an intellectual liberal.

She had private tutoring of a rambling sort and traveled in Italy and Spain. At twenty-four, while recuperating from the measles, she wrote her first poem, "Serenade." Her first published work, "Drowned Suns," appeared in the *London Mirror* a little later.

In 1914 she moved to London and began her serious participation in the literary movement; she published *The Mother and Other Poems* in 1915, and in 1916 edited *Wheels*, an annual anthology of verse. Such early works as *Clown's House* (1918), *Wooden Pegasus* (1920), and *Bucolic Comedies* (1923) express even in their titles the ironic treatment of her childhood memories. Her jazzed rhythms are deliberately chosen to evoke the mad post-war world which followed World War I. Constantly she opposes the cultural and idealistic values of the old world to the commercialism of the new. Offsetting the old pastoral scene is the surrealistic picture of the modern scene and its moods.

The poems which followed were even more autobiographical. She is *The Sleeping Beauty* (1924), whose waking is not romantic. *Troy Park* (1925) and *Rustic Elegies* (1927) both have something of the old in poetic setting. *Gold Coast Customs* (1929) is broadly satirical of the present-day emphasis on money rather than on human dignity. Her *Selected Poems* appeared in 1936 together with an introductory essay on her own poetry, her *Collected Poems* in 1930, *Poems New and Old* in 1940, *Street Songs* in 1942, *Green Song and Other Poems* in 1944, *The Song of the Cold* in 1945, and *Shadow of Cain* in 1947.

Among Miss Sitwell's several prose works are a biography, *Alexander Pope* (1930), *Bath* (1932), a book dealing with the life of the fashionable eighteenth-century health resort, and *Victoria of England* (1936). During World War II she brought out an anthology, *Planet and Glow Worm* (1944) in which she writes:

This . . . book . . . is meant for those whose "continual cares, fears, sorrows, dry brains," drive rest away; it contains some of the composing and calming beauties that in the compiler's own experience bring a happy sleep in their train.

Her recent "Still Falls the Rain" is a vivid poem on the tragic bombing of England. Her latest poems still impart through their fine phrasing her amazing nervous energy and impassioned love of life.

Edith Sitwell's chief technical trick is the interpretation of one sensuous feeling in terms of another sensuous feeling. "And wooden flowers that 'gin to cluck," for example, means not that flowers actually cluck but that from a kitchen maid's forlorn point of view, flowers look like the combs of chickens. Her imagery is always a reflection of the mind which she is evoking. To a romantic young stenographer, the seashore seems like a horsehair sofa appropriate for love. As unusual as Miss Sitwell's imagery are her rhythms, which seem to echo the contradictory ideas of the old and new embodied in her poems.

Aubade

JANE, Jane,
Tall as a crane,
The morning light creaks down again.

Comb your cockscomb-ragged hair;
Jane, Jane, come down the stair.   5

Each dull blunt wooden stalactite
Of rain creaks, hardened by the light,

Sounding like an overtone
From some lonely world unknown.

But the creaking empty light   10
Will never harden into sight,

Will never penetrate your brain
With overtones like the blunt rain.

The light would show (if it could harden)
Eternities of kitchen garden,   15

"Aubade," "Fox Trot," "Fleecing Time," "Poor Martha," and "Trio for Two Cats and a Trombone" from *Bucolic Comedies* and "Yesterday" from *Troy Park*, reprinted by permission of Gerald Duckworth & Co. Ltd.
Aubade, a song for morning performance. The whole poem is a dawn song as a kitchen maid feels it—a satire on the hymns to morning written in romantic vein.   1. **Jane.** Jane is a house-maid, and a morning song for her means drudgery.   6. **stalactite.** The rain is seen through Jane's eyes as coming down woodenly and monotonously.   10. **But . . . sight.** These two lines indicate that for Jane, the drudge, the light of morning will never mean vision or insight.   13. **With . . . rain.** Jane will never hear any romantic music in the rain.   15. **Eternities . . . garden.** Jane's idea of life is limited to kitchen gardens.

Cockscomb flowers that none will pluck,
And wooden flowers that 'gin to cluck.

In the kitchen you must light
Flames as staring, red and white

As carrots or as turnips, shining   20
Where the cold dawn light lies whining.

Cockscomb hair on the cold wind
Hangs limp, turns the milk's weak mind. . . .

    Jane, Jane,
    Tall as a crane,   25
    The morning light creaks down again!

Fox Trot

O^{LD} Sir
       Faulk,
    Tall as a stork,
Before the honeyed fruits of dawn were ripe,
    would walk   5
And stalk with a gun
The reynard-coloured sun
Among the pheasant-feathered corn the uni-
    corn has torn, forlorn the
Smock-faced sheep
Sit   10
  And
    Sleep,
Periwigged as William and Mary, weep . . .
"Sally, Mary, Mattie, what's the matter, why
    cry?"
The huntsman and the reynard-coloured sun
    and I sigh   15

"Oh, the nursery-maid Meg
With a leg like a peg
Chased the feathered dreams like hens and
    when they laid an egg
In the sheepskin
Meadows   20
Where
The serene King James would steer
Horse and hounds, then he
From the shade of a tree
Picked it up as spoil to boil for nursery tea,"
    said the mourners. In the   25
Corn, towers strain
Feathered tall as a crane,
And whistling down the feathered rain, old
    Noah goes again—
An old dull mome
With a head like a pome,   30
Seeing the world as a bare egg
Laid by the feathered air; Meg
Would beg three of these
For the nursery teas
Of Japhet, Shem, and Ham; she gave it   35
Underneath the trees
Where the boiling
      Water
        Hissed
Like the goose-king's feathered daughter—
    kissed   40
Pot and pan and copper kettle
Put upon their proper mettle
Lest the Flood begin again through these!

Fleecing Time

Q^{UEEN} VENUS, like a bunch of roses,
  Fat and pink, that splashed dew closes,

Underneath dark mulberry trees,
Wandered with the fair-haired breeze.

Among the dark leaves, preening wings,   5
Sit golden birds of light; each sings,

"Will you accept the blue muslin?"
As they peck the blackamoor mulberries' skin.

---

16. **Cockscomb flowers.** Cockscomb is a flowering plant with some features suggesting the comb of the cock; the image here, however, indicates that for Jane flowers appeal no more to the imagination than do chickens.   17. **And wooden . . . cluck.** This is an example of Miss Sitwell's use of imagery to record a state of mind through synaesthesia—the shifting of an image from one sense to another. She will use a sound image where one would expect a visual, a tactual where one would expect a taste image, or any such abrupt shift to record a strange impression.   21. **light lies whining.** Just as the flames in the stove resemble things to cook, like carrots or turnips, the dawn seems to Jane to resemble an unpleasant sound like whining. 22. **Cockscomb . . . mind,** a rather bad pun on how the drudge's appearance affects the milk, figuratively speaking, of course.
Fox Trot. The poem, written in fox-trot steps, is in light mockery of the Jazz Age in which we live. Each character sees life in images typical of his class or critical background in order to escape the idea (stated in the last line) that the world may end again, as in the legends of the Flood, by its own hypocrisy. 9. **Smock-faced,** effeminate-looking.

29. **mome,** fool.   30. **pome,** ball.   32. **Meg.** Her imagination runs to food.
Fleecing Time. The idea of Venus, symbolizing Love, here is treated as old-fashioned and eventually commercial. Venus is a fat lady who "fleeces" the lovers who come to her. All images are woolly, as if the idea of her were akin to a picture in an old sampler.   4. **fair-haired breeze,** a mocking image to indicate the voluptuousness of Venus and her setting. 7. **"Will . . . muslin?"** A nonsense line indicating that even the birds sing of love in terms of the gifts made to entice the loved one.

Then came a sheep like a sparkling cloud;
"Oh, ma'am, please ma'am, sleek me proud,   10

Come fleece and comb my golden wool
And do not mind, ma'am, if you pull!"

Her flocks came thick as the mulberries
That grow on the dark, clear mulberry trees,

As thick as the daisies in the sky . . .   15
Prince Paris, Adonis; as each passed by

She cried, "Come feed on buds as cold
As my fleeced lamb-tailed river's gold,

And you shall dance like each golden bird
Of light that sings in dark trees unheard,   20

And you shall skip like my lamb-tailed river,
In my buttercup fields for ever."

The lady Venus, with hair thick as wool,
Cried, "Come and be fleeced—each sheepish
    fool!"

Poor Martha

BY WHITE wool houses thick with sleep
Wherein pig-snouted small winds creep,

With our white muslin faces clean,
We slip to see what can be seen.

Those rustling corn-sheaves the gold stars   5
Drop grain between the window-bars

Among dark leaves all velvety—
(So seem the shadows) and we see

Crazed Martha tie up her brown hair
With the moon's blue ribbons, stare   10

At candles that are lit in vain—
They cannot penetrate her brain:

Their tinsel jargon seems to be
Incomprehensibility

To Martha's mind, though every word   15
Of hers they echo, like that bird

Of brilliant plumage, whose words please
The Indians by their bright-plumed seas.

The Fair's tunes bloom like myosotis
Smooth-perfumèd stephanotis;   20

We children come with twisted curls
Like golden corn-sheaves or fat pearls,

Like ondines in blue muslin dance
Around her; never once a glance

She gives us: "Can my love be true?   25
He promised he would bring me blue

Ribbons to tie up my brown hair.
He promised me both smooth and fair

That he would dive through brightest plumes
Of Indian seas for pearls, where glooms   30

The moon's blue ray; in her sleeping-chamber
Find me Thetis' fan of amber."

.   .   .   .   .

The candles preen and sleek their feathers . . .
"Pretty lady!" "Sweet June weathers."

But silence now lies all around   35
Poor Martha, since her love is drowned.

9. **Then . . . sheep,** the lover comes asking to be fleeced. 16. **Prince Paris,** the son of Priam, who awarded the prize of beauty to Aphrodite and carried off Helen of Troy, thus causing the Trojan War. **Adonis,** a youth beloved of Venus for his great beauty. Both Paris and Adonis are mentioned satirically as figures of great lovers. 17. **She . . . cold.** Venus offers only cold buds of love. 18. **As my . . . gold.** Since Venus fleeces her lovers, the river is presented in the image of a fleeced lamb-tail. The word "gold" here is used to indicate again that she will get what she can from her adorers.
Poor Martha. Martha represents someone whose belief in the older Victorian world of faith in love is dead. The fact that Martha is old and spiritually dead indicates Miss Sitwell's usual feeling that an old order of society is gone or to be seen today only in the grotesques of life. 1. **By . . . houses,** a picture of Martha and her Victorian world. She is old and crazy, and the scene in which she lives is drawn in images characteristic of her woolly mind; therefore the houses are such as one might see embroidered on a sampler, and the winds which creep around them have no force and are pigsnouted because Martha might have lived on a run-down farm. 3. **white muslin faces,** the washed faces (like the typical curtains of a small house such as Martha might have lived in) inquisitively peering to see what Martha's world is like. 5. **rustling corn-sheaves.** Martha sees her world as smug and beautiful and herself as young.

15. **To Martha's mind.** Martha thinks of her words as romantic. The next three stanzas go on with this idea. 19. **myosotis,** a plant like the forget-me-not. 20. **stephanotis,** a plant of the milkweed family. 23. **ondines,** water sprites. 32. **Thetis,** mother of Achilles, and a beautiful sea-nymph. It was at her wedding to Peleus that the race for the fairest was judged by Paris.

Trio for Two Cats and a Trombone

LONG steel grass—
  The white soldiers pass—
The light is braying like an ass.
See
The tall Spanish jade   5
With hair black as nightshade
Worn as a cockade!
Flee
Her eyes' gasconade
And her gown's parade   10
(as stiff as a brigade).
Tee-hee!
The hard and braying light
Is zebra'd black and white
It will take away the slight   15
And free
Tinge of the mouth-organ sound
(Oyster-stall notes) oozing round
Her flounces as they sweep the ground.
The   20
Trumpet and the drum
And the martial cornet come
To make the people dumb—
But we
Won't wait for sly-foot night   25
(Moonlight, watered milk-white, bright)
To make clear the declaration
Of our Paphian vocation
Beside the castanetted sea
Where stalks Il Capitaneo   30
Swaggart braggadocio
Sword and moustachio—
He
Is green as a cassada
And his hair is an armada.   35
To the jade "Come kiss me harder"

He called across the battlements as she
Heard our voices thin and shrill
As the steely grasses' thrill
Or the sound of the onycha   40
When the phoca has the pica
In the palace of the Queen Chinee!

Yesterday

(TO HELEN)

SWEET was my childish life to me
  Like the first spring dream of a hawthorn
      tree.
Every night an ancient crone
Crookèd, silver-flowered as a thorn
Came as quietly as the moon   5
Through the frosty night with her old lanthorn
And put my childish self to bed
With all the dreams that nest in my head.
And the moon's shadows were silvery seen
As hawthorn blossoms, perfumed flowers,   10
The glamour of beauty that never has been,
With petals falling through the night hours;
And as the old crone spoke to me
Night seemed a flowering Chinese wave
Which bore me to each cloudy cave   15
Where there are mysteries none may see
In far Thibet and Persia; words
Grow into lands unknown where birds
Are singing in an unknown tongue
Of loveliness for ever young.   20
Then in the morning an aged sage
Tall and thin as a cloudy cage
Came, and we looked below at the eaves
Where cool airs float like lotus leaves
And the crystal grass-blades of the rain   25
Tremble to music once again.
He said, "We are wingless, can only infer
What even the smallest birds can see.
Outside in their nests they begin to be,—
A spark of fire and grass-like frondage   30
In crystal eggs as hard as the air,—
They break, as instinct from earth-bondage
When man was sightless, before thoughts
      were.

Trio for . . . Trombone. This poem is a mockery of the world of romantic faith and its absolutes, such as love. The romantic emotions are represented in a cheap jazz version. The poem as a whole plays on images of sound, as the title suggests. First the Spanish jade appears, then trumpet and drum take up the musical theme, and the lover appears. The last three lines are sheer nonsense, and the words "onycha," "phoca," and "pica" are used first for sound and secondly to state that such things occur in our modern world which according to the poet is completely upside down and where anything can happen.
9. **gasconade,** boasting.   13. **hard . . . light,** the harshness of light. Here is an example of Miss Sitwell's method of using one sensuous impression to explain another. This is an image of sound used to picture a visual impression, the physical effect of light.   28. **Paphian,** prostitute.   30. **Il Capitaneo,** the captain.   34. **cassada,** a tropical herb from which bread is made, here used to describe humorously the lover Il Capitaneo.
35. **armada,** an armed fleet; but here the image refers to the Spanish background of the gentleman and his steel-like hair.

40. **onycha,** a species of mussel.   41. **phoca,** a genus of seal. **pica,** a magpie, or a vitiated appetite.
Yesterday. This is a typical theme of Miss Sitwell's—nostalgia for a lost beauty or youth which she knew as a member of the aristocracy.   14. **flowering Chinese wave.** To the romantic eyes of youth, night seemed to resemble the Chinese picture of a wave.   32. **They . . . earth-bondage.** The bird breaking the shell is compared to the instinctive way in which the spirit breaks from earthy things.

And the music that birds know, to me is un-
    heard
Though my head seems the egg of an extinct
    bird   35
And my hair seems the crystal grass-blades of
    the rain
Upon the forlorn blue cliffs of the Day
Trembling and growing to music again.
But my heart still dreams that the warmth of
    spring
Will stir in its thickets, begin to sing   40
In the lonely crystal egg of my head—
Though it seems all the lovely wings are dead
And only pity and love are left
In my wintry heart, of its wings bereft."

Though I am lonely now and old,   45
Those rare birds with their strange songs bless
My heart with spring's warm loveliness,—
It never withered grows nor cold,—
For the unfledged thoughts within my brain
Sing in their sad and wintry nest,—   50
Singing their loveliest, singing their best
Of a world that is yet undreamt, unborn,
Where never a shade is of cruelty or scorn,—
Those wild birds sing in an unknown tongue
Of blossoming worlds for ever young.

Lullaby

Though the world has slipped and gone,
    Sounds my loud discordant cry
Like the steel birds' song on high:
"Still one thing is left—the Bone!"
Then out danced the Babioun.   5

She sat in the hollow of the sea—
A socket whence the eye's put out—
She sang to the child a lullaby
(The steel birds' nest was thereabout).

"Do, do, do, do—   10
Thy mother's hied to the vaster race:
The Pterodactyl made its nest
And laid a steel egg in her breast—

34. And . . . unheard. Man today cannot hear the music of
instinct or emotion.
"Lullaby" and "Still Falls the Rain" from *Street Songs*, reprinted by permission of the author.
Lullaby, a lullaby to an era ended, to man's return to animalism because war has made him brute. The spirit of Christ is
again betrayed; man has reverted to a condition of barbarism.
3. steel birds, one of several references to the cruel images of
war, or possible attack. 5. out . . . Babioun, an epigram
by Ben Jonson, here used as a nonsense phrase. 12. Pterodactyl. The reference is to Hitler's attack on Poland in September 1939.

Under the Judas-coloured sun.
She'll work no more, nor dance, nor moan, 15
And I am come to take her place
Do, do.

There's nothing left but earth's low bed—
(The Pterodactyl fouls its nest):
But steel wings fan thee to thy rest, 20
And wingless truth and larvae lie
And eyeless hope and handless fear—
All these for thee as toys are spread,
Do—do—

Red is the bed of Poland, Spain, 25
And my mother's breast, who has grown wise
In that fouled nest. If she could rise,
Give birth again,

In wolfish pelt she'd hide thy bones
To shield thee from the world's long cold, 30
And down on all fours shouldst thou crawl
For thus from no height canst thou fall—
Do, do.

She'd give no hands: there's nought to hold
And nought to make: there's dust to sift, 35
But no food for the hands to lift.
Do, do.

Heed my ragged lullaby,
Fear not living, fear not chance;
All is equal—blindness, sight, 40
There is no depth, there is no height;
Do, do,

The Judas-coloured sun is gone,
And with the Ape thou art alone—
Do,   45
  Do."

Still Falls the Rain

(THE RAIDS, 1940. NIGHT AND DAWN)

Still falls the Rain—
  Dark as the world of man, black as our
    loss—
Blind as the nineteen hundred and forty nails
Upon the Cross.

Still falls the Rain   5
With a sound like the pulse of the heart that is
    changed to the hammer-beat
In the Potter's Field, and the sound of the im-
    pious feet

25. Spain. By the time this poem was written, dictatorship had
triumphed in Spain and executions were continuous.

On the Tomb:

> Still falls the Rain

In the Field of Blood where the small hopes
    breed and the human brain   10
Nurtured its greed, that worm with the brow
    of Cain.

Still falls the Rain
At the feet of the Starved Man hung upon the
    Cross.
Christ that each day, each night, nails there,
           have mercy on us—
On Dives and on Lazarus: 15
Under the Rain the sore and the gold are as
    one.

Still falls the Rain—
Still falls the Blood from the Starved Man's
    wounded Side:
He bears in His Heart all wounds,—those of
    the light that died,

The last faint spark   20
In the self-murdered heart, the wounds of the
    sad uncomprehending dark,
The wounds of the baited bear,—
The blind and weeping bear whom the keepers
    beat
On his helpless flesh . . . the tears of the
    hunted hare.

Still falls the Rain—   25
Then—O Ile leape up to my God: who pulles
    me doune—
See, see where Christ's blood streames in the
    firmament:
It flows from the Brow we nailed upon the tree
Deep to the dying, to the thirsting heart
That holds the fires of the world,—dark-
    smirched with pain   30
As Caesar's laurel crown.

Then sounds the voice of One who like the
    heart of man
Was once a child who among beasts has lain—
"Still do I love, still shed my innocent light,
    my Blood, for thee."

15. **Dives . . . Lazarus,** a reference to the rich man and the
beggar in the parable in Luke 16:19–31. After death the beggar
went to his heavenly reward in Abraham's bosom, the rich man
to Hell.

'Green Flows the River of Lethe . . . O'

GREEN flows the river of Lethe—O
    Long Lethe river
Where the fire was in the veins—and grass is
    growing
Over the fever—
The green grass growing. . . .   5

I stood near the Cities of the Plains
And the young girls were chasing their hearts
    like the gay butterflies
Over the fields of summer—
O evanescent velvets fluttering your wings
Like winds and butterflies on the Road from
    Nothing to Nowhere!   10

But in the summer drought
I fled, for I was a Pillar of Fire, I was Destruc-
    tion
Unquenched, incarnate and incarnadine.

I was Annihilation
Yet white as the Dead Sea, white as the Cities
    of the Plains.   15
For I listened to the noontide and my veins
That threatened thunder and the heart of roses.

I went the way I would—
But long is the terrible Street of the Blood
That had once seemed only part of the sum-
    mer redness: 20
It stretches for ever, and there is no turning
But only fire, annihilation, burning.

I thought the way of the Blood would never
    tire
But now only the red clover
Lies over the breath of the lion and the mouth
    of the lover—   25

And green flows Lethe river—O
Long Lethe river
Over Gomorrah's city and the fire. . . .

"Green Flows the River of Lethe . . . O," "Green Song," and
"Invocation," from *Green Songs*, reprinted by permission of
the author.
"Green . . . O." This is a lyric which, with biblical overtones,
indicates that even as Sodom and Gomorrah burned of their
own evil, man today has carried that evil forward and we are
again in a world bathed in blood. Around us flows the river of
Hades forever green and renewed, forever signifying oblivion.
1. **Lethe,** the river of forgetfulness; in Greek mythology all
who came to Hades had to drink of its waters. 6. **Cities of
the Plains,** Sodom and Gomorrah, Admah and Zeboiim, the
cities destroyed as punishment for their sins. (Genesis 10:19
and 13, 14, 18, and 19.) 12. **Pillar of Fire,** a reference to the
pillar of fire which led the children of Israel through the wilderness.

Green Song

TO DAVID HORNER

AFTER the long and portentous eclipse of the
        patient sun
The sudden spring began
With the bird-sounds of Doom in the egg, and
        Fate in the bud that is flushed with the
        world's fever—
But those bird-songs have trivial voices and
        sound not like thunder,
And the sound when the bud bursts is no more
        the sound of the worlds that are
        breaking.—   5
But the youth of the world, the lovers, said, 'It
        is Spring!
And we who were black with the winter's
        shade, and old,
See the emeralds are awake upon the branches
And grasses, bird-blood leaps within our veins
And is changed to emeralds like the sap in the
        grasses.   10
The beast-philosopher hiding in the orchards,
Who had grown silent from the world's long
        cold
Will tell us the secret of how Spring began
In the young world before the Fall of Man.
For you are the young spring earth   15
And I, O Love, your dark and lowering
        heaven.'

But an envious ghost in the spring world
Sang to them a shrunken song
Of the world's right and wrong—   19
Whispered to them through the leaves, 'I wear
The world's cold for a coat of mail
Over my body bare—
I have no heart to shield my bone
But with the world's cold am alone—
And soon your heart, too, will be gone—   25
My day's darling.'

The naked Knight in the coat of mail
Shrieked like a bird that flies through the
        leaves—
The dark bird proud as the Prince of the Air,
'I am the world's last love . . . Beware—   30
Young girl, you press your lips to lips

That are already cold—
For even the bright earthly dress
Shall prove, at last, unfaithfulness.

His country's love will steal his heart—   35
To you it will turn cold
When foreign earth lies on the breast
Where your young heart was wont to rest
Like leaves upon young leaves, when warm
        was the green spray,
And warm was the heart of youth, my day's
        darling.   40
And if that ghost return to you—
(The dead disguised as a living man)
Then I will come like Poverty
And wear your face, and give your kiss,   44
And shrink the world, and that sun the heart
Down to a penny's span:

For there is a sound you heard in youth,
A flower whose light is lost—
There is a faith and a delight—
They lie at last beneath my frost   50
When I am come like Time that all men, faiths,
        loves, suns defeat,
My frost despoils the day's young darling.

For the young heart like the spring wind grows
        cold
And the dust, the shining racer, is overtaking
The laughing young people who are running
        like fillies   55
The golden ladies and the ragpickers
And the foolish companions of spring, the wild
        wood lilies.'

But the youth of the world said, 'Give me your
        golden hand
That is but earth, yet it holds the lands of
        heaven
And you are the sound of the growth of spring
        in the heart's deep core,   60
The hawthorn-blossoming boughs of the stars
        and the young orchards' emerald lore.'

And hearing that, the poor ghost fled like the
        winter rain—
Sank into greenish dust like the fallen moon
Or the sweet green dust of the lime-flowers
        that will be blossoming soon—
And spring grew warm again—   65

No more the accusing light, revealing the rank-
        ness of Nature,

Green Song. In a mood almost of ecstasy Miss Sitwell insists
on the eternality, the permanence of the life cycle. She sees in a
warlike earth and a dismantled personal life, even in so dark a
period as the war, the return of spring, of renewed passion, and
of love.

All motives and desires and lack of desire
In the human heart, but loving all life, it comes
    to bless
Immortal things in their poor earthly dress—
The blind of life beneath the frost of their
    great winter   70
And those for whom the winter breaks in
    flower
And summer grows from a long-shadowed kiss.
And Love is the vernal equinox in the veins
When the sun crosses the marrow and pith of
    the heart   74
Among the veridian smells, the green rejoicing.
All names, sounds, faiths, delights, and duties
    lost
Return to the hearts of men, those households
    of high heaven.
And voices speak in the woods as from a nest
Of leaves—they sing of rest,   79
And love, and toil, the rhythms of their lives,
Singing how winter's dark was overcome,
And making plans for tomorrow as though yes-
    terday
Had never been, nor the lonely ghost's old sor-
    row,
And Time seemed but the beat of heart to
    heart,
And Death the pain of earth turning to spring
    again   85
When lovers meet after the winter rain.
And when we are gone, they will see in the
    great mornings
Born of our lives, some memory of us, the
    golden stalk
Of the young long-petalled flower of the sun
    in the pale air
Among the dew. . . . Are we not all of the
    same substance,   90
Men, planets and earth, born from the heart of
    darkness,
Returning to darkness, the consoling mother,
For the short winter sleep—O my calyx of the
    flower of the world, you the spirit
Moving upon the waters, the light on the
    breast of the dove.

76. **All . . . lost.** "'I wept for names, sounds, faiths, delights, and duties lost'—taken from a poem on Cowley's wish to retire to the Plantations."—Dorothy Wordsworth, *Grasmere Journal*, May 8, 1802. (Author's note.)

Invocation

FOR ALEC AND MERULA GUINNESS

I WHO was once a golden woman like those
    who walk
In the dark heavens—but am now grown old
And sit by the fire, and see the fire grow cold,
Watch the dark fields for a rebirth of faith and
    of wonder.

The turning of Ixion's wheel the day   5
Ceased not, yet sounds no more the beat of the
    heart
But only the sound of ultimate Darkness fall-
    ing
And of the Blind Samson at the Fair, shaking
    the pillars of the world and emptily
    calling.

For the gardeners cried for rain, but the high
    priests howled   9
For a darker rain to cool the delirium of gold
And wash the sore of the world, the heart of
    Dives,
Raise wheat for the hunger that lies in the soul
    of the poor—
Then came the thunderous darkness

And the fly-like whispering of small hopes,
    small fears,
The gossips of mean Death—gadflies and gnats,
    the summer world: 15
The small and gilded scholars of the Fly
That feed upon the crowds and their dead
    breath
And buzz and stink where the bright heroes
    die
Of the dust's rumours and the old world's fe-
    vers.
Then fell the world in winter.   20

But I, a golden woman like the corn goddess
Watch the dark fields, and know when spring
    begins

Invocation. In commenting on her own old age, Miss Sitwell here is reviewing the turns in historical events that she has seen, and is praying that this last period of war may mean a return to true love between men and nations. She prays that we may be freed of the sin of having killed our own brothers. 1. **Alec Guinness,** an English poet. 5. **Ixion's wheel.** In Greek mythology Ixion, king of the Lapithes, was given refuge on Olympus by Zeus. He made love to Hera, but Zeus substituted a phantom for her, and Centaurs were born of the union. As a punishment, Ixion was chained to an ever-turning fiery wheel in Hades. 8. **Blind Samson,** the giant Samson, blinded and working at the mill in Gaza, until his hair grew and his strength returned, enabling him to pull down the pillars.

To the sound of the heart and the planetary
    rhythm,
Fires in the heavens and in the hearts of men,
Young people and young flowers come out in
    the darkness.   25

And where are they going? How should I
    know? I see only
The hierarchies love the young people—the
    Swan has given his snows
And Berenice her wild mane to make their
    fair hair,
And speaking of love are the voices that come
    from the darkness: 29

Of the nobler love of Man for his brother Man,
And of how the creeds of the world shall no
    more divide them
But every life be that of a country Fate
Whose wheel had a golden woof and warp, the
    Day—
Woven of threads of the common task; and
    light
Tells to that little child the humble dust   35
Tales of the old world's holiness, finds veins
    of ore
In the unripe wheat-ear; and the common fire
That drops with seeds like the Sun's, is fallen
    from the long-leaved planets.

So when the winter of the world and Man's
    fresh Fall
When democratic Death feared no more the
    heart's coldness   40
Shall be forgotten,
O Love, return to the dying world, as the light
Of morning, shining in all regions, latitudes
And households of high heaven within the heart.

Be then our visible world, our world invisible!
Throughout our day like the laughing flames
    of the Sun   46
Lie on our leaves of life, your heat infusing
Deep in the amber blood of the smooth tree.
The panic splendour of the animal
Is yours—O primal Law   50
That rules the blood (the solar ray in the
    veins)—

The fire of the hearth, the household Deity
That shines not, nor does it burn, destroy like
    fire,
But nourishes with its endless wandering
Like that of the Golden Ones in the high
    heavens.   55

Rule then the spirit working in dark earth
As the Sun and Planets rule the husbandman—
O pride that in each semitone
Of amber blood and bone
Proclaims the splendour that arose from the
    first Dark!   60

Be too the ear of wheat to the Lost Men
Who ask the city stones if they are bread
And the stones of the city weep . . .
                     You, the lost days
When all might still be hoped for, and the light
Laid gold in the unhopeful path of the poor— 66
The shrunken darkness in the miser's heart.

Now falls the night of the world:—O Spirit
    moving upon the waters
Your peace instil   69
In the animal heat and splendour of the blood—
The hot gold of the sun that flames in the night
And knows not down-going
But moves with the revolutions in the heavens.

The thunders and the fires and acclamations
Of the leaves of spring are stilled, but in the
    night   75
The Holy Ghost speaks in the whispering leaves.
O wheat-ear shining like a fire and the bright
    gold,
O water brought from far to the dying gardens!
Bring peace to the famine of the heart and lips,
And to the Last Man's loneliness   80
Of those who dream they can bring back sight
    to the blind!

You are the Night
When the long hunt for Nothing is at rest
In the Blind Man's Street, and in the human
    breast
The hammer of Chaos is stilled.   85
                     Be then the sleep
When Judas gives again the childish kiss
That once his mother knew—and wash the stain
From the darkened hands of the universal Cain.

---

28. **Berenice,** an Egyptian princess of the third century B.C.,
who, according to Catullus, sacrificed her hair to Arsinoë for
her husband's safe return from the war. The hair was said to
have become the constellation *Coma Berenices.*

87. **Judas . . . kiss.** Judas Iscariot indicated Christ to his
captors by kissing him.

T. S. ELIOT

Thomas Stearns Eliot, who was to define better than any other single poet the period between the wars, was born in St. Louis, September 26, 1888, of a distinguished Boston family which included such names as President Charles W. Eliot of Harvard. Both the Eliot family and the poet's maternal ancestors, the Stearns family, were deeply rooted in the New England tradition and in early American history. It is clear to the careful reader that this ancestry profoundly influenced Eliot's poetry. Eliot's mother, Charlotte Stearns Eliot (1843–1930), was herself a writer, author of a poetic drama, *Savonarola*.

Eliot lived in St. Louis until he was eighteen, attended briefly first the Smith Academy of Washington University and then Milton Academy in Massachusetts, and entered Harvard in 1906. A superior student, he topped a class which had many brilliant and subsequently famous members. After taking his M.A. in 1911, he went to Paris for a year's study at the Sorbonne. Returning to Harvard, he continued his graduate work in philosophy but did not accept a doctor's degree. A year at Merton College, Oxford, followed an interval of European travel, and in 1915 Eliot married and settled in England. His first job in London was as a teacher at the Highgate School; then for a time he was a clerk in Lloyds Bank. Finally, in 1917, he became assistant editor of Ezra Pound's periodical, *The Egoist*. Pound and his poetry had a strong influence on Eliot, and his first prose volume, *Ezra Pound, His Metric and Poetry* (1917), indicated how much he had learned from the man to whom he has always deferred as his master. Eliot's first poems, *Prufrock and Other Observations*, also appeared in 1917; in 1919 came *Poems*, and in 1920 *Ara Vos Prec* and his earliest important essays, *Three Critical Essays*. His reputation as a literary critic was unassailable from the time of the publication of *The Sacred Wood* in 1920.

With *The Waste Land* (1922) Eliot became the leading poet of his generation. This work won him the two-thousand-dollar *Dial* prize, and when it was reprinted in America the critics recognized Eliot as the poet who best summed up the disillusionment of a postwar generation and, what is more, made clear in his social symbols the sterility of our civilization. Although the more conservative critics objected to the voluminous footnotes, the psychoanalysis, and the use of mythology, Eliot in this poem—even in the title—named and mapped the emotional geography of most of the writers between the two world wars. *The Waste Land* was soon widely translated and has influenced French and Spanish literature, just as the Symbolist poets Laforgue, Corbière, and Baudelaire, as well as Dante, Dryden, the Elizabethan dramatists, and the early metaphysical poets, had influenced both Eliot's earlier and his more mature works. Eliot's poetic method and its juxtaposition of old values and new have already been spoken of (p. 191).

The year of *The Waste Land* had seen the establishment of Eliot's magazine *The Criterion*, which until he discontinued it in 1938 was influential in directing the trends of modern literature. Meanwhile Eliot became associated with the British publishing house of Faber & Faber, of which he is still a director. This position enabled him to select important newcomers in poetry and criticism.

In keeping with his naturalization as a British subject in 1927, Eliot became a professed, ardent Anglo-Catholic. More than that, he explicitly declared himself, in the Preface to *For Lancelot Andrewes* (a series of essays on style and order published in 1928) as "an Anglo-Catholic in religion, a classicist in literature, and a royalist in politics." Already he had disappointed those who had seen in him the leader of the lost generation; a close reading of *The Waste Land* itself indicated his horror of a skeptical and commercial world. Once again he led the way, this time away from the Waste Land and toward religion. His later poetry is devoted entirely to the theme of repentance, in which one sees the intellectual man reaching toward, if never quite achieving, spiritual rest in a traditional faith.

It was clear that Eliot meant seriously his declaration of classicism in literature; but this was scarcely a new stand. He had always shown an interest in the classical models of form, balance, symmetry, intellectuality, and restraint, and even in college had been strongly sympathetic toward the ideals of Harvard's Irving Babbitt.

This insistence upon form was accompanied, however, by skill in so modifying the older traditional forms as to make them his own. For example, the interior monologue can be traced back to Shakespeare; but its psychoanalytical overtones in Eliot are modern. Despite his devoted interpretation of the neoclassical in English literature, it could nevertheless be argued that there is much of romanticism in Eliot's nostalgia for the past, since for him the past, at least as it is to be found in libraries, is the Golden Age. Viewed in this light, his turning to the traditional in religion seems inevitable.

As for the avowed political royalism, it is strongly expressed in *The Idea of a Christian Society* (1940), in which Eliot proposes the national or state church as the source of governmental and cultural authority. He has stated his opinion that a mixture of races, and particularly the introduction of an "internationally minded race," into a culture, is dangerous. In some of his early poems the Jew—the "international" Jew—is chosen to symbolize the degradation of commercialism. Moreover, all his poetry gives a clear picture of a man who would avoid contact with ordinary people.

During the recent war Eliot wrote the last of his *Quartets*, and these were published in collected form in 1943. They are repetitious but beautiful lyrical summaries of his defeatism and his desire for emotional security and wholeness to be gained through the Church. Politically Eliot certainly did not hold that the war was necessary. What was necessary for England, as he saw it, he had stated earlier in *The Rock* (1934), and again in *Murder in the Cathedral* (1935)—namely, a return to the earlier Christian and spiritual values. There are indications that the last war, for him, was the purgation necessary to a commercial, individu-

alistic, non-religious society. Although he gives no direct political advice, his argument seems to be that only by repentance and by acceptance of our fate, and perhaps by the martyrdom of our spiritual leaders, can this world be saved.

For all of his outward superciliousness it is obvious that Eliot is a driven man, and completely convinced of his arguments. In his plays, written in modified forms of the old Greek dramas, he is intensely concerned about modern morals and the modern spiritual emptiness. In the end of *Murder in the Cathedral* we see his accusing finger pointed at us, and in *Family Reunion* we perceive the earnestness with which he considers even a kind of personal martyrdom.

In addition to those already mentioned, T. S. Eliot's collections of essays include *Andrew Marvell* (1922), *Dante* (1929), *Tradition and Experiment in Present-Day Literature* (1929), *Thoughts After Lambeth* (1931), *Selected Essays, 1917–1932* (1932), *John Dryden* (1932), *The Use of Poetry and the Use of Criticism* and *After Strange Gods* (1933), *Elizabethan Essays* (1934), *Essays Ancient and Modern* (1936), *Milton* (1947), and *Notes Toward the Definition of Culture* (1949). His first play, *Sweeney Agonistes,* appeared in 1932. Other volumes of his poetry are *Poems* (1919), *Poems, 1909–1925* (1925), *Ash-Wednesday* (1930), *Collected Poems, 1909–1935* (including *Burnt Norton*, 1936), *East Coker* (1940), *The Dry Salvages* (1941), and *Little Gidding* (1942).

In 1948 Eliot received the Nobel Prize in Literature for "his pioneering work in modern poetry."

from The Sacred Wood

Tradition and the Individual Talent

I

IN ENGLISH writing we seldom speak of tradition, though we occasionally apply its name in deploring its absence. We cannot refer to "the tradition" or to "a tradition"; at most, we employ the adjective in saying that the poetry of So-and-so is "traditional" or even "too tradi-

"Tradition and the Individual Talent" from *The Sacred Wood,* reprinted by permission of the author and Methuen & Co., Ltd.

tional." Seldom, perhaps, does the word appear except in a phrase of censure. If otherwise, it is vaguely approbative, with the implication, as to the work approved, of some pleasing archaeological reconstruction. You can hardly make the word agreeable to English ears without this comfortable reference to the reassuring science of archaeology.

Certainly the word is not likely to appear in our appreciations of living or dead writers. Every nation, every race, has not only its own creative, but its own critical turn of mind; and is even more oblivious of the shortcomings and limitations of its critical habits than of those of its creative genius. We know, or think we know, from the enormous mass of critical writing that has appeared in the French language the critical method or habit of the French; we only conclude (we are such unconscious people) that the French are "more critical" than we, and sometimes even plume ourselves a little with the fact, as if the French were the less spontaneous. Perhaps they are; but we might remind ourselves that criticism is as inevitable as breathing, and that we should be none the worse for articulating what passes in our minds when we read a book and feel an emotion about it, for criticizing our own minds in their work of criticism. One of the facts that might come to light in this process is our tendency to insist, when we praise a poet, upon those aspects of his work in which he least resembles anyone else. In these aspects or parts of his work we pretend to find what is individual, what is the peculiar essence of the man. We dwell with satisfaction upon the poet's difference from his predecessors, especially his immediate predecessors; we endeavour to find something that can be isolated in order to be enjoyed. Whereas if we approach a poet without this prejudice we shall often find that not only the best, but the most individual parts of his work may be those in which the dead poets, his ancestors, assert their immortality most vigorously. And I do not mean the impressionable period of adolescence, but the period of full maturity.

Yet if the only form of tradition, of handing down, consisted in following the ways of the immediate generation before us in a blind or timid adherence to its successes, "tradition" should positively be discouraged. We have seen many such simple currents soon lost in the sand; and novelty is better than repetition. Tradition is a matter of much wider significance. It cannot be inherited, and if you want it you must obtain it by great labour. It involves, in the first place, the historical sense, which we may call nearly indispensable to anyone who would continue to be a poet beyond his twenty-fifth year; and the historical sense involves a perception not only of the pastness of the past, but of its presence; the historical sense compels a man to write not merely with his own generation in his bones, but with a feeling that the whole of the literature of Europe from Homer and within it the whole of the literature of his own country has a simultaneous existence and composes a simultaneous order. This historical sense, which is a sense of the timeless as well as of the temporal and of the timeless and of the temporal together, is what makes a writer traditional. And it is at the same time what makes a writer most acutely conscious of his place in time, of his contemporaneity.

No poet, no artist of any art, has his complete meaning alone. His significance, his appreciation is the appreciation of his relation to the dead poets and artists. You cannot value him alone; you must set him, for contrast and comparison, among the dead. I mean this as a principle of aesthetic, not merely historical, criticism. The necessity that he shall conform, that he shall cohere, is not one-sided; what happens when a new work of art is created is something that happens simultaneously to all the works of art which preceded it. The existing monuments form an ideal order among themselves, which is modified by the introduction of the new (the really new) work of art among them. The existing order is complete before the new work arrives; for order to persist after the supervention of novelty, the *whole* existing order must be, if ever so slightly, altered; and so the relations, proportions, values of each work of art toward the whole are readjusted; and this is conformity between the old and the new. Whoever has approved this idea of order, of the form of European, of English literature, will not find it preposterous that the past should be altered by the present as much as the present is directed by the past. And the poet who is aware of this will be aware of great difficulties and responsibilities.

In a peculiar sense he will be aware also that he must inevitably be judged by the standards of the past. I say judged, not amputated, by them; not judged to be as good as, or worse or better than, the dead; and certainly not judged by the canons of dead critics. It is a judgment, a comparison, in which two things are measured by each other. To conform merely would be for the new work not really to conform at all; it would not be new, and would therefore not be a work of art. And we do not quite say that the new is more valuable because it fits in; but its fitting in is a test of its value—a test, it is true, which can only be slowly and cautiously applied, for we are none of us infallible judges of conformity. We say: it appears to conform, and is perhaps individual, or it appears individual, and may conform; but we are hardly likely to find that it is one and not the other.

To proceed to a more intelligible exposition of the relation of the poet to the past: he can neither take the past as a lump, an indiscriminate bolus, nor can he form himself wholly on one or two private admirations, nor can he form himself wholly upon one preferred period. The first course is inadmissible, the second is an important experience of youth, and the third is a pleasant and highly desirable supplement. The poet must be very conscious of the main current, which does not at all flow invariably through the most distinguished reputations. He must be quite aware of the obvious fact that art never improves, but that the material of art is never quite the same. He must be aware that the mind of Europe—the mind of his own country—a mind which he learns in time to be much more important than his own private mind—is a mind which changes, and that this change is a development which abandons nothing en route, which does not superannuate either Shakespeare, or Homer, or the rock drawing of the Magdalenian draughtsmen. That this development, refinement per-

haps, complication certainly, is not, from the point of view of the artist, any improvement. Perhaps not even an improvement from the point of view of the psychologist or not to the extent which we imagine; perhaps only in the end based upon a complication in economics and machinery. But the difference between the present and the past is that the conscious present is an awareness of the past in a way and to an extent which the past's awareness of itself cannot show.

Some one said: "The dead writers are remote from us because we *know* so much more than they did." Precisely, and they are that which we know.

I am alive to a usual objection to what is clearly part of my programme for the *métier* of poetry. The objection is that the doctrine requires a ridiculous amount of erudition (pedantry), a claim which can be rejected by appeal to the lives of poets in any pantheon. It will even be affirmed that much learning deadens or perverts poetic sensibility. While, however, we persist in believing that a poet ought to know as much as will not encroach upon his necessary receptivity and necessary laziness, it is not desirable to confine knowledge to whatever can be put into a useful shape for examinations, drawing-rooms, or the still more pretentious modes of publicity. Some can absorb knowledge, the more tardy must sweat for it. Shakespeare acquired more essential history from Plutarch than most men could from the whole British Museum. What is to be insisted upon is that the poet must develop or procure the consciousness of the past and that he should continue to devolop this consciousness throughout his career.

What happens is a continual surrender of himself as he is at the moment to something which is more valuable. The progress of an artist is a continual self-sacrifice, a continual extinction of personality.

There remains to define this process of depersonalization and its relation to the sense of

46. **Magdalenian draughtsmen,** the men who drew in the Magdalenian Age. The name "Magdalenian" is applied to a stage of the Stone Age and is named from the archaeological remains found at La Madeleine in the Dordogne, France. The Magdalenian workmen used tools of horn and bone and reached a high quality of craftsmanship before the end of the period.

80. **Plutarch,** the great Greek biographer who flourished during the first century A.D. His major work is the "Parallel Lives" of twenty-three Greeks and twenty-three Romans. The work was translated into French during the Renaissance and from the French into English by Sir Thomas North (1579). North's translation was Shakespeare's chief source of classical learning; it was from the "Lives" that he derived material for his *Julius Caesar, Coriolanus,* and *Antony and Cleopatra.*

tradition. It is in this depersonalization that art may be said to approach the condition of science. I shall, therefore, invite you to consider, as a suggestive analogy, the action which takes place when a bit of finely filiated platinum is introduced into a chamber containing oxygen and sulphur dioxide.

II

Honest criticism and sensitive appreciation is directed not upon the poet but upon the poetry. If we attend to the confused cries of the newspaper critics and the susurrus of popular repetition that follows, we shall hear the names of poets in great numbers; if we seek not Blue-book knowledge but the enjoyment of poetry, and ask for a poem, we shall seldom find it. In the last article I tried to point out the importance of the relation of the poem to other poems by other authors, and suggested the conception of poetry as a living whole of all the poetry that has ever been written. The other aspect of this Impersonal theory of poetry is the relation of the poem to its author. And I hinted, by an analogy, that the mind of the mature poet differs from that of the immature one not precisely in any valuation of "personality," not being necessarily more interesting, or having "more to say," but rather by being a more finely perfected medium in which special, or very varied, feelings are at liberty to enter into new combinations.

The analogy was that of the catalyst. When the two gases previously mentioned are mixed in the presence of a filament of platinum, they form sulphurous acid. This combination takes place only if the platinum is present; nevertheless the newly formed acid contains no trace of platinum, and the platinum itself is apparently unaffected; has remained inert, neutral, and unchanged. The mind of the poet is the shred of platinum. It may partly or exclusively operate upon the experience of the man himself; but, the more perfect the artist, the more completely separate in him will be the man who suffers and the mind which creates; the more perfectly will the mind digest and transmute the passions which are its material.

The experience, you will notice, the elements which enter the presence of the transforming catalyst, are of two kinds: emotions and feelings. The effect of a work of art upon the person who enjoys it is an experience different in kind from any experience not of art. It may be formed out of one emotion, or may be a combination of several; and various feelings, inhering for the writer in particular words or phrases or images, may be added to compose the final result. Or great poetry may be made without the direct use of any emotion whatever: composed out of feelings solely. Canto XV of the *Inferno* (Brunetto Latini) is a working up of the emotion evident in the situation; but the effect, though single as that of any work of art, is obtained by considerable complexity of detail. The last quatrain gives an image, a feeling attaching to an image, which "came," which did not develop simply out of what precedes, but which was probably in suspension in the poet's mind until the proper combination arrived for it to add itself to. The poet's mind is in fact a receptacle for seizing and storing up numberless feelings, phrases, images, which remain there until all the particles which can unite to form a new compound are present together.

If you compare several representative passages of the greatest poetry you see how great is the variety of types of combination, and also how completely any semi-ethical criterion of "sublimity" misses the mark. For it is not the "greatness," the intensity, of the emotions, the components, but the intensity of the artistic process, the pressure, so to speak, under which the fusion takes place, that counts. The episode of Paolo and Francesca employs a definite emotion, but the intensity of the poetry is something quite different from whatever intensity in the supposed experience it may give the impression of. It is no more intense, furthermore, than Canto XXVI, the voyage of Ulysses, which has not the direct dependence upon an emotion. Great variety is possible in the process

11. **susurrus,** rustling whisper.

61. **Brunetto Latini,** a great Florentine scholar of the thirteenth century and master of the Italian poet Dante Alighieri (1265–1321). Dante admired greatly Brunetto's learning but deplored his worldliness and vices and so depicts him in Canto XV of the *Inferno* among those who are being punished for violence against themselves, against art, against life, or against God and man. 85. **Paolo and Francesca.** The tragic story of these two lovers, ill-starred in life and condemned after death to whirl about in Hell on the ceaseless blasts of unsatisfied desire, is told with matchless simplicity and great art by Dante in his *Inferno*, Canto V, 75 ff.

of transmutation of emotion: the murder of Agamemnon, or the agony of Othello, gives an artistic effect apparently closer to a possible original than the scenes from Dante. In the *Agamemnon*, the artistic emotion approximates to the emotion of an actual spectator; in *Othello* to the emotion of the protagonist himself. But the difference between art and the event is always absolute; the combination which is the murder of Agamemnon is probably as complex as that which is the voyage of Ulysses. In either case there has been a fusion of elements. The ode of Keats contains a number of feelings which have nothing particular to do with the nightingale, but which the nightingale, partly, perhaps, because of its attractive name, and partly because of its reputation, served to bring together.

The point of view which I am struggling to attack is perhaps related to the metaphysical theory of the substantial unity of the soul: for my meaning is, that the poet has, not a "personality" to express, but a particular medium, which is only a medium and not a personality, in which impressions and experiences combine in peculiar and unexpected ways. Impressions and experiences which are important for the man may take no place in the poetry, and those which become important in the poetry may play quite a negligible part in the man, the personality.

I will quote a passage which is unfamiliar enough to be regarded with fresh attention in the light—or darkness—of these observations:

And now methinks I could e'en chide myself
For doting on her beauty, though her death
Shall be revenged after no common action.
Does the silkworm expend her yellow labours
For thee? For thee does she undo herself?
Are lordships sold to maintain ladyships
For the poor benefit of a bewildering minute?
Why does yon fellow falsify highways,
And put his life between the judge's lips,
To refine such a thing—keeps horse and men
To beat their valours for her? . . .

In this passage (as is evident if it is taken in its context) there is a combination of positive and negative emotions: an intensely strong attraction toward beauty and an equally intense fascination by the ugliness which is contrasted with it and which destroys it. This balance of contrasted emotion is in the dramatic situation to which the speech is pertinent, but that situation alone is inadequate to it. This is, so to speak, the structural emotion, provided by the drama. But the whole effect, the dominant tone, is due to the fact that a number of floating feelings, having an affinity to this emotion by no means superficially evident, have combined with it to give us a new art emotion.

It is not in his personal emotions, the emotions provoked by particular events in his life, that the poet is in any way remarkable or interesting. His particular emotions may be simple, or crude, or flat. The emotion in his poetry will be a very complex thing, but not with the complexity of the emotions of people who have very complex or unusual emotions in life. One error, in fact, of eccentricity in poetry is to seek for new human emotions to express; and in this search for novelty in the wrong place it discovers the perverse. The business of the poet is not to find new emotions, but to use the ordinary ones and, in working them up into poetry, to express feelings which are not in actual emotions at all. And emotions which he has never experienced will serve his turn as well as those familiar to him. Consequently, we must believe that "emotion recollected in tranquillity" is an inexact formula. For it is neither emotion, nor recollection, nor, without distortion of meaning, tranquillity. It is a concentration, and a new thing resulting from the

1. **Agamemnon,** a hero of the Greeks in the Trojan War. After the sack of Troy he returned to his home in Argos, where he was murdered by his faithless wife Clytemnestra and her lover Aegisthus. Subsequently this murder was avenged by Agamemnon's son, Orestes. The tragic story was the subject of a play by Aeschylus (525-456 B.C.). 35. **And now methinks, etc.,** spoken by Vindici in the dark and dismal *The Revenger's Tragedy* (1607) by Cyril Tourneur (1575?-1626), III, v, 71-82.

79. **"emotion . . . tranquillity,"** Wordsworth's explanation of the poetic process. The passage describing this process is found in Wordsworth's *Preface* to the *Lyrical Ballads* (1800): "I have said that poetry is the spontaneous overflow of powerful feelings: it takes its origin from emotion recollected in tranquillity; the emotion is contemplated till, by a species of reaction, the tranquillity gradually disappears, and an emotion, kindred to that which was before the subject of contemplation, is gradually produced, and does itself actually exist in the mind. In this mood successful composition generally begins, and in a mood similar to this it is carried on; but the emotion, of whatever kind and in whatever degree, from various causes, is qualified by various pleasures, so that in describing any passions whatsoever which are voluntarily described, the mind will, upon the whole, be in a state of enjoyment."

concentration, of a very great number of experiences which to the practical and active person would not seem to be experiences at all; it is a concentration which does not happen consciously or of deliberation. These experiences are not "recollected," and they finally unite in an atmosphere which is "tranquil" only in that it is a passive attending upon the event. Of course this is not quite the whole
10 story. There is a great deal, in the writing of poetry, which must be conscious and deliberate. In fact, the bad poet is usually unconscious where he ought to be conscious, and conscious where he ought to be unconscious. Both errors tend to make him "personal." Poetry is not a turning loose of emotion, but an escape from emotion; it is not the expression of personality, but an escape from personality. But, of course, only those who have person-
20 ality and emotions know what it means to want to escape from these things.

III

ὁ δὲ νοῦς, ἴσως, θειότερόν τι καὶ ἀπαθές ἐστιν

This essay proposes to halt at the frontier of metaphysics or mysticism, and confine itself to such practical conclusions as can be applied by the responsible person interested in poetry. To divert interest from the poet to the poetry is a laudable aim: for it would conduce to a juster estimation of actual poetry, good
30 and bad. There are many people who appreciate the expression of sincere emotion in verse, and there is a smaller number of people who can appreciate technical excellence. But very few know when there is expression of *significant* emotion, emotion which has its life in the poem and not in the history of the poet. The emotion of art is impersonal. And the poet cannot reach this impersonality without surrendering himself wholly to the work to be
40 done. And he is not likely to know what is to be done unless he lives in what is not merely the present, but the present moment of the past, unless he is conscious, not of what is dead, but of what is already living.

22. ὁ . . . ἐστιν, "Possibly the mind is too divine, and is therefore unaffected," quoted from Aristotle's *On the Soul*, I, iv (translation by W. S. Hett).

The Love Song of J. Alfred Prufrock

S'io credesse che mia risposta fosse
A persona che mai tornasse al mondo,
Questa fiamma staria senza piu scosse.
Ma perciocche giammai di questo fondo
Non torno vivo alcun, s'i'odo il vero,
Senza tema d'infamia ti rispondo.

LET us go then, you and I,
When the evening is spread out against the sky
Like a patient etherised upon a table;
Let us go, through certain half-deserted streets,
The muttering retreats   5
Of restless nights in one-night cheap hotels
And sawdust restaurants with oyster-shells:
Streets that follow like a tedious argument
Of insidious intent   9
To lead you to an overwhelming question . . .
Oh, do not ask, "What is it?"
Let us go and make our visit.

In the room the women come and go
Talking of Michelangelo.

The yellow fog that rubs its back upon the window-panes,   15
The yellow smoke that rubs its muzzle on the window-panes
Licked its tongue into the corners of the evening,
Lingered upon the pools that stand in drains,

The poetry of T. S. Eliot is reprinted from *Collected Poems 1909–1935*, by T. S. Eliot, copyright, 1936, by Harcourt, Brace and Company, reprinted by permission of Harcourt, Brace and Company.
The Love . . . Prufrock. J. Alfred Prufrock is the symbol of a wealthy young man, blasé, intellectual, sensitive, but completely incapable of action. The poem is a fragment of his soliloquy as he walks the streets at evening, reluctant to come to a decision about love—or, for that matter, about anything. He imagines bits of typical conversation, typical drawing-room scenes; he thinks of death. And with death forever in mind, love and intellectual inquiry grow empty; life is an ironic picture, a meaningless pattern endlessly repeated everywhere. The epigraph indicates Eliot's view of life's futility, since death is inevitable. Since man no longer imagines he can conquer death, no longer believes he can bend the universe to his will, he is, for all his contemplation of death (as in the Lazarus symbol, l. 94) or of life, mediocre, and his actions and decisions are therefore inconsequential.
S'io . . . rispondo, If I could believe that my answer might be to a person who should ever return into the world, this flame would stand without more quiverings; but inasmuch as, if I hear the truth, never from this depth did any living man return, without fear of infamy I answer thee. (*Inferno*, Canto XXVII, ll. 61–66)   14. **Michelangelo,** here used as a symbol for conversation on art.

Let fall upon its back the soot that falls from
   chimneys,   19
Slipped by the terrace, made a sudden leap,
And seeing that it was a soft October night,
Curled once about the house, and fell asleep.

And indeed there will be time
For the yellow smoke that slides along the
   street,
Rubbing its back upon the window-panes;   25
There will be time, there will be time
To prepare a face to meet the faces that you
   meet;
There will be time to murder and create,
And time for all the works and days of hands
That lift and drop a question on your plate;
Time for you and time for me,   31
And time yet for a hundred indecisions,
And for a hundred visions and revisions,
Before the taking of a toast and tea.

In the room the women come and go   35
Talking of Michelangelo.

And indeed there will be time
To wonder, "Do I dare?" and, "Do I dare?"
Time to turn back and descend the stair,
With a bald spot in the middle of my hair—   40
[They will say: "How his hair is growing
   thin!"]
My morning coat, my collar mounting firmly to
   the chin,
My necktie rich and modest, but asserted by a
   simple pin—
[They will say: "But how his arms and legs
   are thin!"]
Do I dare   45
Disturb the universe?
In a minute there is time
For decisions and revisions which a minute
   will reverse.

For I have known them all already, known
   them all:—
Have known the evenings, mornings, after-
   noons,   50
I have measured out my life with coffee spoons;
I know the voices dying with a dying fall
Beneath the music from a farther room.

49. **For I have . . . all.** Compare with the figure of Tiresias
in *The Waste Land.*

So how should I presume?

And I have known the eyes already, known
   them all—   55
The eyes that fix you in a formulated phrase,
And when I am formulated, sprawling on a
   pin,
When I am pinned and wriggling on the wall,
Then how should I begin
To spit out all the butt-ends of my days and
   ways?   60
And how should I presume?

And I have known the arms already, known
   them all—
Arms that are braceleted and white and bare
[But in the lamplight, downed with light brown
   hair!]
Is it perfume from a dress   65
That makes me so digress?
Arms that lie along a table, or wrap about a
   shawl.
   And should I then presume?
   And how should I begin?

. . . .

Shall I say, I have gone at dusk through narrow
   streets   70
And watched the smoke that rises from the
   pipes
Of lonely men in shirt-sleeves, leaning out of
   windows? . . .

I should have been a pair of ragged claws
Scuttling across the floors of silent seas.

. . . .

And the afternoon, the evening, sleeps so
   peacefully!   75
Smoothed by long fingers,
Asleep . . . tired . . . or it malingers,
Stretched on the floor, here beside you and me.
Should I, after tea and cakes and ices,
Have the strength to force the moment to its
   crisis?   80
But though I have wept and fasted, wept and
   prayed,
Though I have seen my head (grown slightly
   bald) brought in upon a platter,
I am no prophet—and here's no great matter;
I have seen the moment of my greatness flicker,

82. **my head,** a reference to the execution of St. John the
Baptist.

And I have seen the eternal Footman hold my
    coat, and snicker,   85
And in short, I was afraid.

And would it have been worth it, after all,
After the cups, the marmalade, the tea,
Among the porcelain, among some talk of you
    and me,
Would it have been worth while,   90
To have bitten off the matter with a smile,
To have squeezed the universe into a ball
To roll it toward some overwhelming question,
To say: "I am Lazarus, come from the dead,
Come back to tell you all, I shall tell you all"—
If one, settling a pillow by her head,   96
    Should say: "That is not what I meant at all.
    That is not it, at all."

And would it have been worth it, after all,
Would it have been worth while,   100
After the sunsets and the dooryards and the
    sprinkled streets,
After the novels, after the teacups, after the
    skirts that trail along the floor—
And this, and so much more?—
It is impossible to say just what I mean!
But as if a magic lantern threw the nerves in
    patterns on a screen: 105
Would it have been worth while
If one, settling a pillow or throwing off a shawl,
And turning toward the window, should say:
    "That is not it at all,
    That is not what I meant, at all."   110

.   .   .   .   .

No! I am not Prince Hamlet, nor was meant to
    be;
Am an attendant lord, one that will do
To swell a progress, start a scene or two,
Advise the prince; no doubt, an easy tool,
Deferential, glad to be of use,   115
Politic, cautious, and meticulous;
Full of high sentence, but a bit obtuse;
At times, indeed, almost ridiculous—
Almost, at times, the Fool.

I grow old . . . I grow old . . .   120
I shall wear the bottoms of my trousers rolled.

Shall I part my hair behind? Do I dare to eat
    a peach?

94. **Lazarus,** the young man who was resurrected by Christ
(John 11).   111. **Prince Hamlet.** A conscious renunciation
of the position of the young man who sees himself as the principal figure in a tragedy.

I shall wear white flannel trousers, and walk
    upon the beach.
I have heard the mermaids singing, each to
    each.

I do not think that they will sing to me.   125

I have seen them riding seaward on the waves
Combing the white hair of the waves blown
    back
When the wind blows the water white and
    black.

We have lingered in the chambers of the sea
By sea-girls wreathed with seaweed red and
    brown   130
Till human voices wake us, and we drown.

Sweeney among the Nightingales

ὤμοι πέπληγμαι καιρίαν πληγὴν ἔσω.

A PENECK SWEENEY spreads his knees
  Letting his arms hang down to laugh,
The zebra stripes along his jaw
Swelling to maculate giraffe.

The circles of the stormy moon   5
Slide westward toward the River Plate,
Death and the Raven drift above
And Sweeney guards the hornèd gate.

Gloomy Orion and the Dog   9
Are veiled; and hushed the shrunken seas;
The person in the Spanish cape
Tries to sit on Sweeney's knees

Slips and pulls the table cloth
Overturns a coffee-cup,
Reorganised upon the floor   15
She yawns and draws a stocking up;

Sweeney Among the Nightingales. Eliot here pictures the
revels of a coarsely sensual man in whose slow brain there is
perhaps only a dim awareness that his companions are plotting
against him. The feeling of impending disaster subtly hinted
at in the poem is reinforced by the epigraph, a quotation from
Aeschylus' *Agamemnon:* "Alas! I am stricken by a timely blow
within"—the words which Agamemnon "cried aloud" (l. 38)
as his faithless wife, Clytemnestra, and her lover, Aegisthus,
killed him. The nightingales (symbolizing beauty) sing near
the convent (symbolizing religious intensity) just as they might
have sung at the time of Agamemnon's betrayal.   **6. River
Plate,** the estuary between Argentina and Uruguay.
7. **Death and the Raven.** The raven is traditionally a bird
of ill omen.   **8. hornèd gate,** possibly the crescent moon,
or possibly one of the two Gates of Dreams, through one of
which, the ivory, passed dreams of illusion, while through the
other, the horn, passed the dreams which came true.   **9. Orion
and the Dog,** the constellations Orion, the Hunter, and Sirius,
the Dog Star.

The silent man in mocha brown
Sprawls at the window-sill and gapes;
The waiter brings in oranges
Bananas figs and hothouse grapes;   20
The silent vertebrate in brown
Contracts and concentrates, withdraws;
Rachel *née* Rabinovitch
Tears at the grapes with murderous paws;

She and the lady in the cape   25
Are suspect, thought to be in league;
Therefore the man with heavy eyes
Declines the gambit, shows fatigue,

Leaves the room and reappears
Outside the window, leaning in,   30
Branches of wistaria
Circumscribe a golden grin;

The host with someone indistinct
Converses at the door apart,
The nightingales are singing near   35
The Convent of the Sacred Heart,

And sang within the bloody wood
When Agamemnon cried aloud,
And let their liquid siftings fall
To stain the stiff dishonoured shroud.   40

The Hippopotamus

*Similiter et omnes revereantur Diaconos, ut
mandatum Jesu Christi; et Episcopum, ut Jesum
Christum, existentem filium Patris; Presbyteros
autem, ut concilium Dei et conjunctionem Apos-
tolorum. Sine his Ecclesia non vocatur; de quibus
suadeo vos sic habeo.*
        S. Ignatii Ad Trallianos.
*And when this epistle is read among you,
cause that it be read also in the church of the
Laodiceans.*

THE BROAD-BACKED hippopotamus
Rests on his belly in the mud;
Although he seems so firm to us
He is merely flesh and blood.

The Hippopotamus. One of Eliot's earlier works, this poem
is one of his purest satires on religion and on the contradictions
implied in the belief that the church (Protestant, in this case,
since such are the quotations from the hymnal) is immortal,
while man is mortal and must eat and sleep. *Similiter . . .
habeo.* In like manner, let all reverence the Deacons as Jesus
Christ, and the Bishop as the Father, and the Presbyters as
the Council of God, and the assembly of the Apostles. Without
these there is no Church. Concerning all which I am persuaded
that ye think after the same manner.   1. **The broad-backed
hippopotamus.** This first verse derives largely from a poem,
"L'Hippopotame," by Théophile Gautier (1811–72).

Flesh and blood is weak and frail,   5
Susceptible to nervous shock;
While the True Church can never fail
For it is based upon a rock.

The hippo's feeble steps may err
In compassing material ends,   10
While the True Church need never stir
To gather in its dividends.

The 'potamus can never reach
The mango on the mango-tree;
But fruits of pomegranate and peach   15
Refresh the Church from over sea.

At mating time the hippo's voice
Betrays inflexions hoarse and odd,
But every week we hear rejoice
The Church, at being one with God.   20

The hippopotamus's day
Is passed in sleep; at night he hunts;
God works in a mysterious way—
The Church can sleep and feed at once.

I saw the 'potamus take wing   25
Ascending from the damp savannas,
And quiring angels round him sing
The praise of God, in loud hosannas.

Blood of the Lamb shall wash him clean
And him shall heavenly arms enfold,   30
Among the saints he shall be seen
Performing on a harp of gold.

He shall be washed as white as snow,
By all the martyr'd virgins kist,
While the True Church remains below   35
Wrapt in the old miasmal mist.

The Waste Land

[The intellectual atmosphere of the years following the First World War seemed to be characterized by an increasing despair, cynicism,
and spiritual emptiness. In 1922 Eliot combined erudition, pessimism, and nostalgia for
the distant past to produce *The Waste Land*,
in which he applied the ancient legend of the

Holy Grail to his own period. The poem caught the imagination of the times, and its title was quickly adopted to describe the contemporary scene.

The Waste Land is neither plainly discernible allegory nor straightforward narrative, but rather a tissue of associations, tags, and quotations, bursts of conversation, descriptions, and fragmentary interior monologues, loosely held within the framework of the Grail legend and its primitive counterparts. As Eliot points out, the mythology of the Waste Land and much of the imagery with which he defines the period between wars are to be found in the late Jessie L. Weston's *From Ritual to Romance* (1920), a study of the anthropological and religious sources of the legend of the Holy Grail. The gist of the ancient stories is that when a monarch known as the Fisher King was mysteriously wounded in the genital organs, the land over which he ruled became barren and dry, to be reclaimed only if a knight (an agent of purity) should arrive and heal the King. A miraculous vessel—or sometimes a cup and a lance—figured in many of the versions.

This story was closely connected with the fertility rites of a number of ancient religions. Outliving its sources, it formed a link between these pre-Christian ceremonies of vegetation and fertility and the later Christian festivals of rebirth (such as Easter), and finally was absorbed into the medieval Arthurian romances; the vessel was identified with the holy chalice supposedly used by Christ at the Last Supper with the disciples. In the symbolism of the old allegory, the cup and lance represented the sexual organs, but the Christian story interpreted them as symbolic of holiness and purity. (It is to be remembered that Eliot had in mind the sexual as well as the religious significance of the symbols which figure in the old legend.)

In the Grail romances the knight who comes to heal the wounded King Joseph of Arimathea is variously identified as Gawain, Galahad, and —most often in the stories to which Eliot refers —Percival. The questing knight must endure terrible trials of flesh and spirit in order to reach the Chapel Perilous in the center of the Waste Land; there he is to face his greatest trial, after which he can attain the castle and

heal the King, thereby healing as well the land and the people and restoring spiritual intensity and fertility.

The recollection of spring and young love which opens the first part of the poem is followed by an intimation of the drought and desolation to come in Part V. Among the successive speakers one recurring voice seems to be that of the protagonist, the man whose agonized quest for spiritual salvation is the theme of the poem. The clairvoyant Madame Sosostris represents those who try astrology instead of religious intensity, fortunetelling instead of metaphysical speculation. In her brief speech she foreshadows the later events of the poem. Through Madame Sosostris, Eliot introduces the Tarot prophetic cards, whose four suits—cup, lance, dish, and sword—bear symbols which figure in the Grail legend. Part I closes lyrically on a description of London wherein the protagonist broods over man's earlier conceptions of his heroic greatness and the later symbols of his fall from grace.

Part II begins with a descriptive passage which is a rich fabric of allusions to romance and mythology and quotations from Shakespeare, Ovid, Milton, and Vergil. Amid the splendor of her boudoir a wealthy woman is fretful, oblivious of her luxurious surroundings, peevishly critical of her lover (with whom she shares nothing but the commonplaces of their society), and above all bored, almost to the extent of being frightened, at the emptiness of her life. The scene then shifts to a pub where a gossiping woman weaves a sordid tale of infidelity, abortion, and faded marriage—ugly symbols of the same sterility among the poorer people as that which renders bleak and monotonous the opulence and beauty of the wealthy woman's life. Throughout this part, Eliot has in mind Thomas Middleton's *Women Beware Woman* and his other play, *A Game at Chesse,* the plot of which involves action in which a widow is kept occupied while her daughter-in-law is violated.

"The Fire Sermon" makes use of two of the symbolic meanings of fire: fire as spiritual intensification and fire as the destroyer of lust. The fire of love is conspicuously absent. The Thames of Spenser's Wedding Hymns is now the scene of tawdry affairs. Love is commercialized and boring; the creative passion is denied, and our civilization must perish. But from a parody of a classical myth, and from a comic song, Eliot's associations return sharply to the Grail theme with a recollection of a scene of innocence and devotion, the ceremonial foot-washing in Verlaine's *Parsifal* (and the chorus of children in Wagner's opera).

Section Four is almost a direct translation of the last stanza of one of Eliot's earlier poems, *Dans le Restaurant*. In relation to the rest of the poem it is a kind of summing up, for as Eliot says, Mr. Eugenides melts into Phlebas, and Phlebas into Ferdinand, Prince of Naples. And all their voyages of exploration end in death. An interesting analysis of this section has been presented by Grover Smith:

The meaning of the name Phlebas, by which the Phoenician is known in "Death by Water," is derived, I am disposed to think, from the Greek *phléps, phlébos*, a vein. This would fit very well with the common expression "vein of commerce" in connection with the Phoenician's rôle as a trader. But even more remarkable is the fact that the Greek word has another meaning, which is the same as that of *phallós*—a most rewarding fact, if it confirms my theory that the Phoenician Sailor represents the commerce of *lust* as well as the commerce of materialism.

So it is, I think, that "Death by Water" should be explicated. This death is a death of the soul, though a rebirth of the body in the course of biological re-transformation. Such a rebirth is in no wise satisfactory to men desiring personal life after death. But, to retain identity after death, only one way is indicated—salvation through Christ. One must find the "Hanged Man," as neither Madame Sosostris, nor Ferdinand, nor Mr. Eugenides, nor the Phoenician Sailor can do. It will be remembered that the Sibyl, in the passage . . . quoted by Mr. Eliot as his epigraph to *The Waste Land*, wishes, more than anything else, *to be dead*. Yet she, participating in the poem through the seers, Tiresias and Madame Sosostris, can find no means of escaping from her prison (she is kept in a bottle, because, like Tithonus, she has

asked for prolonged life but not prolonged youth, and has shriveled to dwarfish size). The prison of Tiresias and Madame Sosostris is the Waste Land. . . . they are bound to an existence that periodically, by physical death, enters new incarnations or vegetable forms, but they have no spiritual rebirth *out of the world*, though they would leave it, as the Sibyl would leave her flask. The death they desire is more than the simple extinction longed for by the Sibyl: it is a death that shall bring life *in their own identity*. The means to this are obvious. These people, as I interpret *The Waste Land*, must turn from the errors of lust and materialism, and must find grace. They can do so, no matter who they are. . . . "Gentile *or* Jew"—to whom Saint Paul assures, in Romans II:

Tribulation and anguish, upon every soul of man that doeth evil; of the Jew first, and also of the Gentile;

But glory, honour, and peace, to every man that worketh good; to the Jew first, and also to the Gentile:

For there is no respect of persons with God.

Phlebas is a Phoenician, a Semite; but his example can teach anyone, as can the antithetical example of Christ, to seek liberation from the Waste Land of no purpose and no peace.*

The fifth section is a statement that the Grail cannot be reached. In a beautiful lyric passage we are told that our age has no water (the source of rebirth) but only rock, and that the rocks themselves are empty of the old symbolism, in which they were often the home of the gods. The protagonist, searching for the Grail in a kind of hallucination, feels death as if it were walking beside him. In a hysterical prophecy he sees the world as upside down, and when at last he reaches the Chapel it is empty and he hears the cock-crow which is a symbol of betrayal. Abruptly Eliot names three keys to grace: to give of ourselves with feeling, which we cannot do; to sympathize and thereby come in contact with others, an act of which we are no longer capable; to control ourselves, which we attempt but fail to do. These words

* From "Eliot's 'Death by Water'" by Grover C. Smith, reprinted from *Accent*, Summer 1946, by permission of the author and *Accent*.

—*give, sympathize, control*—are taken from the Sanskrit prayer. (As Cleanth Brooks has pointed out, Eliot uses Sanskrit words at this point not only because of their onomatopoetic value as thunder sounds, but because they furnish yet another link with the old legends; for Sanskrit was the language of the earliest religions which centered around the fertility rites.) But the three words have lost their ability to give us grace and left us exiled in our loneliness. The will and the spirit are dead. But although he has read the rites, it is clear in the last section of the poem that Eliot is not resigned to an acceptance of such spiritual desolation. He prays for grace and for the peace that passes understanding.

One of the aspects of its construction which make a careful study of the poem especially rewarding is Eliot's use of a rich and varied imagery, not only to render a series of literal pictures but to convey deeper and more symbolic meanings. Certain themes recur and are elaborated at various levels of meaning. Of the several motifs which dominate the imagery of *The Waste Land,* water (whether present or absent) is perhaps the most important. Its significance arises primarily, of course, from the primitive religious rites at the very source of the Grail legend. For water's life-giving properties were the core of early tribal religions in agricultural communities; and the Tarot cards, which appear in the poem and are also connected with the Grail story, were originally used in ancient Egypt for prophesying the rising of the Nile. Many images of water are woven into the poem: of water as an instrument of fertility; as an agent of purification—washing away stain and sin; as a cooling, healing, thirst-abating liquid. The Thames, a modern Nile, flows through the earlier parts of the poem, and related imagery of ships, bridges, fishermen, and ocean commerce pervades every section. Similarly, the poem contains extended images of light, shadow, and color, of birth and death, and of the changing seasons.

Although by most of the early critics *The Waste Land* was called the great poem of doubt, there is in it much fierce repudiation of a world without values. It was inevitable that Eliot should after this summarizing of our ste-rility turn to fields of religious inquiry. From here on he was concerned with the search for grace. He became an Anglo-Catholic and sought through the traditional church the means of both personal and social salvation.]

The Waste Land

"NAM Sibyllam quidem Cumis ego ipse oculis meis vidi in ampulla pendere, et cum illi pueri dicerent: Σιβυλλα τί θέλεις; respondebat illa: ἀποθανεῖν θέλω."

> For Ezra Pound
> *il miglior fabbro*

I. THE BURInAL OF THE DEAD

APRIL is the cruellest month, breeding
Lilacs out of the dead land, mixing
Memory and desire, stirring
Dull roots with spring rain.
Winter kept us warm, covering

Earth in forgetful snow, feeding
A little life with dried tubers.
Summer surprised us, coming over the Starnbergersee
With a shower of rain; we stopped in the colonnade,   9
And went on in sunlight, into the Hofgarten,
And drank coffee, and talked for an hour.
Bin gar keine Russin, stamm' aus Litauen, echt deutsch.

Nam . . . θέλω." [Yes, and I myself, with my own eyes, saw the Sibyl of Cumae hanging in a cage; and when the boys jeered at her, "Sibyl, what do you want?" she answered, "I want to die." (Petronius, *Satyricon,* Chap. 37 : 48)]. *il miglior fabbro,* [the greatest maker, i.e., the great master.] 'Not only the title, but the plan and a good deal of the incidental symbolism of the poem were suggested by Miss Jessie L. Weston's book on the Grail legend: *From Ritual to Romance* (Cambridge). Indeed, so deeply am I indebted, Miss Weston's book will elucidate the difficulties of the poem much better than my notes can do; and I recommend it (apart from the great interest of the book itself) to any who think such elucidation of the poem worth the trouble. To another work of anthropology I am indebted in general, one which has influenced our generation profoundly; I mean *The Golden Bough;* I have used especially the two volumes *Adonis, Attis, Osiris.* Anyone who is acquainted with these works will immediately recognize in the poem certain references to vegetation ceremonies. [The notes here given are Eliot's; notes supplied by the editors are enclosed in brackets.]
The Burial of the Dead. [The poem opens in spring, to develop the idea that April, the month of rebirth, is cruel to those who would keep emotional forgetfulness and to whom death is attractive. The characters speak in a kind of reverie. The first group consists of the bored wealthy woman and her contemporaries.] 12. **Bin . . . deutsch,** I am no Russian, I come from Litau, true German.

And when we were children, staying at the
    archduke's,
My cousin's, he took me out on a sled,
And I was frightened. He said, Marie,   15
Marie, hold on tight. And down we went.
In the mountains, there you feel free.
I read, much of the night, and go south in the
    winter.
What are the roots that clutch, what branches
    grow
Out of this stony rubbish? Son of man,   20
You cannot say, or guess, for you know only
A heap of broken images, where the sun beats,
And the dead tree gives no shelter, the cricket
    no relief,
And the dry stone no sound of water. Only
There is shadow under this red rock,   25
(Come in under the shadow of this red rock),
And I will show you something different from
    either
Your shadow at morning striding behind you
Or your shadow at evening rising to meet you;
I will show you fear in a handful of dust.   30
      Frisch weht der Wind
      Der Heimat zu
      Mein Irisch Kind,
      Wo weilest du?
"You gave me hyacinths first a year ago;   35
"They called me the hyacinth girl."
—Yet when we came back, late, from the Hya-
    cinth garden,
Your arms full, and your hair wet, I could not

Speak, and my eyes failed, I was neither
Living nor dead, and I knew nothing,   40
Looking into the heart of light, the silence.
Oed' und leer das Meer.
Madame Sosostris, famous clairvoyante,
Had a bad cold, nevertheless   44
Is known to be the wisest woman in Europe,
With a wicked pack of cards. Here, said she,
Is your card, the drowned Phoenician Sailor,
(Those are pearls that were his eyes. Look!)
Here is Belladonna, the Lady of the Rocks,
The lady of situations.   50
Here is the man with three staves, and here
    the Wheel,
And here is the one-eyed merchant, and this
    card,
Which is blank, is something he carries on his
    back,
Which I am forbidden to see. I do not find
The Hanged Man. Fear death by water.   55
I see crowds of people, walking round in a
    ring.
Thank you. If you see dear Mrs. Equitone,
Tell her I bring the horoscope myself:
One must be so careful these days.

Unreal City,   60
Under the brown fog of a winter dawn,

---

20. Son of man. Cf. Ezekiel II, i. [The reference is to Ezekiel, and as the passage unfolds, also to the Ecclesiastes. Ezekiel 2:1: And he said unto me, Son of man, stand upon thy feet, and I will speak unto thee.]   **23.** [Ecclesiastes 12:1: Remember now thy Creator in the days of thy youth, while the evil days come not, nor the years draw nigh, when thou shalt say, I have no pleasure in them, etc.]   **31. *Frisch . . . du.*** V. Tristan und Isolde, I, verses 5–8. [Fresh blows the wind to the homeland; my Irish child, where do you tarry? (Wagner.) The song is one of innocent love, sung by the sailors carrying Isolde to Cornwall and Tristan. This quotation is in contrast to l. 42 *Oed' und leer das Meer*, from the same opera, and the latter quotation in a sense answers the first, for the phrase "My Irish child, where dwellest thou?" is answered by the idea that love is absent and that the sea is wide and empty.]   **37. Yet . . . garden.** [Eliot uses the hyacinth not only as a spring flower of regeneration, but also in the light of the myth of Apollo's love for Hyacinthus, who was in a sense himself a spring god. When by accident Hyacinthus was killed by Apollo, his blood colored the flower now called the hyacinth. The whole impact of the story, the protagonist of the poem now remembers, is the impact of a memory which for a moment seems to bring about a kind of spiritual rebirth.]

42. *Oed' . . . Meer.* Id. III, verse 24: Sea, desolate and empty.   **46. wicked pack of cards.** I am not familiar with the exact constitution of the Tarot pack of cards, from which I have obviously departed to suit my own convenience. The Hanged Man, a member of the traditional pack, fits my purpose in two ways: because he is associated in my mind with the Hanged God of Frazer, and because I associate him with the hooded figure in the passage of the disciples to Emmaus in Part V. The Phoenician Sailor and the Merchant appear later; also the "crowds of people," and Death by Water is executed in Part IV. The Man with Three Staves (an authentic member of the Tarot pack) I associate, quite arbitrarily, with the Fisher King himself. [Madame Sosostris, as a clairvoyante engaged not in religious prophecy but in fortunetelling, is a symbol of the degeneration of our belief in religion. It is by a reference to the Tarot cards that Eliot begins to introduce the characters in his poem, all of whom are representative of the kind of secularization in which the modern world has trapped us.]   **48. Those are pearls:** [*The Tempest*, I, 2. Ariel's song:
      Full fathom five thy father lies;
        Of his bones are coral made;
      Those are pearls that were his eyes:
        Nothing of him that doth fade
      But doth suffer a sea-change
      Into something rich and strange. . . .]
60. Unreal City. Cf. Baudelaire:
    "Fourmillante cité, cité pleine de rêves,
    "Où le spectre en plein jour raccroche le passant."
              Fleurs du Mal, The Seven Old Men.
[Swarming city, city full of dreams,
Where the ghost walks in daylight with the passer-by.]

A crowd flowed over London Bridge, so many,
I had not thought death had undone so many.
Sighs, short and infrequent, were exhaled,
And each man fixed his eyes before his feet.
Flowed up the hill and down King William
    Street,   66
To where Saint Mary Woolnoth kept the hours
With a dead sound on the final stroke of nine.
There I saw one I knew, and stopped him,
    crying: "Stetson!
"You who were with me in the ships at Mylae!
"That corpse you planted last year in your
    garden,   71
"Has it begun to sprout? Will it bloom this
    year?
"Or has the sudden frost disturbed its bed?
"Oh keep the Dog far hence, that's friend to
    men,
"Or with his nails he'll dig it up again!   75
"You! hypocrite lecteur!—mon semblabie,—mon
    frère!"

63. **I . . . many.** Cf. Inferno III, 55–57:
               "Si lunga tratta
    di gente, ch'io non avrei mai creduto
    che morte tanta n'avesse disfatta."
               [so long a train
    of people, that I should not have believed
    that death had undone so many. . . .]
64. **Sighs . . . exhaled.** Cf. Inferno IV, 25–27:
    "Quivi, secondo che per ascoltare,
    "non avea pianto, ma' che di sospiri,
    "che l'aura eterna facevan tremare."
    [No grumbling could be heard, but that of sighs
    Which made a trembling of the outer air.]
68. **dead . . . nine.** A phenomenon which I have often noticed.
70. **You . . . Mylae!** [Mylae is the ancient name of Milayyo which is a seaport on the northern coast of Sicily. In 260 B.C. Duilius won the first Roman naval victory over the Carthaginians in the bay of Mylae. According to Eliot's interpretation, this was a trade war, as was World War I. In a kind of hallucination the protagonist is asking of one who was with him in the war whether the sacrifice symbol (as of the god's sacrifice to bring the New Year, or the sacrifice involved in war) has indicated that it could bring on a renascence. Ironically, as the passage develops, it is indicated that there will be no rebirth.]   74. Cf. the Dirge in Webster's *White Devil:*
    [Call for the robin redbreast and the wren,
    Since o'er shady groves they hover,
    And with leaves and flowers do cover
    The friendless bodies of unburied men.

    Call unto his funeral dole
    The ant, the field-mouse, and the mole,
    To rear him hillocks that shall keep him warm,
    And, when gay tombs are robbed, sustain no harm;
    But keep the wolf far thence, that's foe to men,
    For with his nails he'll dig it up again.]
Eliot turns the wolf into the dog, possibly because he wished to imply that it is those who would seem to be friends to men who might destroy their hope of regeneration.]   76. **You . . . frère.** V. Baudelaire, Preface to *Fleurs du Mal.* [You! hypocrite reader,—my double,—my brother!]

II. A GAME OF CHESS

The Chair she sat in, like a burnished throne,
Glowed on the marble, where the glass
Held up by standards wrought with fruited
    vines
From which a golden Cupidon peeped out
(Another hid his eyes behind his wing)   81
Doubled the flames of sevenbranched cande-
    labra
Reflecting light upon the table as
The glitter of her jewels rose to meet it,
From satin cases poured in rich profusion;   85
In vials of ivory and coloured glass
Unstoppered, lurked her strange synthetic per-
    fumes,
Unguent, powdered, or liquid—troubled, con-
    fused
And drowned the sense in odours; stirred by
    the air
That freshened from the window, these as-
    cended   90
In fattening the prolonged candle-flames,
Flung their smoke into the laquearia,
Stirring the pattern on the coffered ceiling.
Huge sea-wood fed with copper
Burned green and orange, framed by the col-
    oured stone,   95
In which sad light a carvèd dolphin swam.
Above the antique mantel was displayed
As though a window gave upon the sylvan
    scene

A Game of Chess. [The general reference is that life is a game of chess in which the outcome is arbitrary and, as can be seen from the quotation taken from Middleton's *Women Beware Women,* that life is a kind of rape of the emotions. Women no longer, like Cleopatra, have variety, are no longer willing to give up a kingdom for love. This is why we are introduced first to a woman who in her dressing room has assembled carvings and paintings of the heroic and the magnificent now no longer meaningful. The slight overtones here of Milton's *Paradise Lost,* the one word of the *Aeneid,* and the story of the passion of Dido grant, by juxtaposition with the idea of boredom in the modern age, the ironic contrast between the past and the present which the poet wishes to emphasize. The whole passage has to do with the commercialism now connected with sex as well as with trade, and the loss of the spiritual value of love.]   77. **The chair, etc.** Cf. *Antony and Cleopatra,* II, ii, line 190: [the passage which begins,
    The barge she sat in, like a burnished throne,
    Burned on the water. . . .]
92. **Laquearia.** V. *Aeneid,* I, 726:
    dependent lychni laquearibus aureis incensi,
et noctem flammis funalia vincunt.
    [from the gold-coffered ceiling hang the lamps
New-lighted, and the torches vanquish night with their flames.]
98. **sylvan scene,** V. Milton, *Paradise Lost,* IV. 140 [Milton's description of the Garden of Eden].

The change of Philomel, by the barbarous king
So rudely forced; yet there the nightingale
Filled all the desert with inviolable voice   101
And still she cried, and still the world pursues,
"Jug Jug" to dirty ears.
And other withered stumps of time
Were told upon the walls; staring forms   105
Leaned out, leaning, hushing the room en-
    closed.
Footsteps shuffled on the stair.
Under the firelight, under the brush, her hair
Spread out in fiery points
Glowed into words, then would be savagely
    still.   110

"My nerves are bad to-night. Yes, bad. Stay
    with me.
"Speak to me. Why do you never speak. Speak.
    "What are you thinking of? What thinking?
    What?
"I never know what you are thinking. Think."

I think we are in rats' alley   115
Where the dead men lost their bones.

"What is that noise?"
                The wind under the door.
"What is that noise now? What is the wind
    doing?"
                Nothing again nothing. 120
                    "Do
"You know nothing? Do you see nothing? Do
    you remember
"Nothing?"

    I remember
Those are pearls that were his eyes.   125
"Are you alive, or not? Is there nothing in your
    head?"
                                  But

O O O O that Shakespeherian Rag—
It's so elegant

So intelligent   130
"What shall I do now? What shall I do?"
"I shall rush out as I am, and walk the street
"With my hair down, so. What shall we do to-
    morrow?
"What shall we ever do?"   134
                The hot water at ten.
And if it rains, a closed car at four.
And we shall play a game of chess,
Pressing lidless eyes and waiting for a knock
    upon the door.

When Lil's husband got demobbed, I said—
I didn't mince my words, I said to her myself,
HURRY UP PLEASE ITS TIME   141
Now Albert's coming back, make yourself a
    bit smart.
He'll want to know what you done with that
    money he gave you
To get yourself some teeth. He did, I was
    there.   144
You have them all out, Lil, and get a nice set,
He said, I swear, I can't bear to look at you.
And no more can't I, I said, and think of poor
    Albert,
He's been in the army four years, he wants a
    good time,
And if you don't give it him, there's others will,
    I said.   149
Oh is there, she said. Something o' that, I said.
Then I'll know who to thank, she said, and give
    me a straight look.
HURRY UP PLEASE ITS TIME
If you don't like it you can get on with it, I
    said.
Others can pick and choose if you can't.
But if Albert makes off, it won't be for lack of
    telling.   155
You ought to be ashamed, I said, to look so
    antique.
(And her only thirty-one.)
I can't help it, she said, pulling a long face,
It's them pills I took, to bring it off, she said.
(She's had five already, and nearly died of
    young George.)   160
The chemist said it would be all right, but I've
    never been the same.
You *are* a proper fool, I said.

99. the change . . . king. V. Ovid, *Metamorphoses*, VI, Philomela. [Philomel was changed to a nightingale to escape from the barbarous king, a rape which continues in our modern Waste Land as the change in tense in the line, *and still she cried, and still the world pursues.* . . .] 100. the nightingale. Cf. Part III, l. 204. 108. Under . . . still. [The line has an overtone of prophecy which will be meaningless; something of a Cassandra image.] 115. I never . . . Think. Cf. Part III, l. 195. 116. I think . . . bones. [After musing that even death is sterile, the protagonist remembers the death that was transformed into something strange and rare, and therefore re-calls (l. 125) Ariel's song in *The Tempest*.] 118. The wind . . . door. Cf. Webster: "Is the wind in that door still?" 126. Are . . . head. Cf. Part I, l. 37, 48. 128. O . . . Rag. [This is a deliberate jazzing and vulgarizing of the Shake-spearian notion of death as a transmigration into something beautiful.]

138. Pressing . . . door. Cf. the game of chess in Middleton's *Women Beware Women*, Act 2, Scene 2. 141. Hurry . . . time, [the traditional words of an English bartender at closing time.]

Well, if Albert won't leave you alone, there it
    is, I said,
What you get married for if you don't want
    children?
HURRY UP PLEASE ITS TIME   165
Well, that Sunday Albert was home, they had
    a hot gammon,
And they asked me in to dinner, to get the
    beauty of it hot—
HURRY UP PLEASE ITS TIME
HURRY UP PLEASE ITS TIME
Goonight Bill. Goonight Lou. Goonight May.
    Goonight.   170
Ta ta. Goonight. Goonight.
Good night, ladies, good night, sweet ladies,
    good night, good night.

III. THE FIRE SERMON

The river's tent is broken: the last fingers of
    leaf
Clutch and sink into the wet bank. The wind
Crosses the brown land, unheard. The nymphs
    are departed.   175
Sweet Thames, run softly, till I end my song.
The river bears no empty bottles, sandwich
    papers,
Silk handkerchiefs, cardboard boxes, cigarette
    ends
Or other testimony of summer nights. The
    nymphs are departed.
And their friends, the loitering heirs of city di-
    rectors;   180
Departed, have left no addresses.
By the waters of Leman I sat down and
    wept . . .
Sweet Thames, run softly till I end my song,
Sweet Thames, run softly, for I speak not loud
    or long.
But at my back in a cold blast I hear   135
The rattle of the bones, and chuckle spread
    from ear to ear.
A rat crept softly through the vegetation
Dragging its slimy belly on the bank
While I was fishing in the dull canal

172. **Good night, ladies,** etc. [See Ophelia's song, *Hamlet*, V, 5, the song of a woman defeated in love.]   176. **Sweet . . . song.** V. Spenser, *Prothalamion.* [The refrain of *Prothalamion* (marriage song): Sweet Themmes, run softly till I end my song, a wedding hymn of the day in which love was thought to be permanent and constructive.]   182. **By the waters.** [Psalm 137: "By the rivers of Babylon, there we sat down, yea, we wept. . . ."]

On a winter evening round behind the gas-
    house   190
Musing upon the king my brother's wreck
And on the king my father's death before him.
White bodies naked on the low damp ground
And bones cast in a little low dry garret,   194
Rattled by the rat's foot only, year to year.
But at my back from time to time I hear
The sound of horns and motors, which shall
    bring
Sweeney to Mrs. Porter in the spring.
O the moon shone bright on Mrs. Porter
And on her daughter   200
They wash their feet in soda water
*Et O ces voix d'enfants, chantant dans la
    coupole!*

Twit twit twit
Jug jug jug jug jug jug
So rudely forc'd.   205
Tereu

Unreal City
Under the brown fog of a winter noon
Mr. Eugenides, the Smyrna merchant
Unshaven, with a pocket full of currants   210
C.i.f. London: documents at sight,
Asked me in demotic French
To luncheon at the Cannon Street Hotel
Followed by a weekend at the Metropole.
At the violet hour, when the eyes and back
Turn upward from the desk, when the human
    engine waits   216
Like a taxi throbbing waiting,

192. **And . . . him.** Cf. *The Tempest*, I, ii. [Sitting on a bank Weeping against the king my father's wreck.]   196. **But . . . hear.** Cf. Marvell, *To His Coy Mistress.* [But at my back I always hear Time's winged chariot, hurrying near.]   197. **The sound . . . bring.** Cf. Day, *Parliament of Bees:* "When of the sudden, listening, you shall hear, "A noise of horns and hunting, which shall bring "Actaeon to Diana in the spring, "Where all shall see her naked skin . . ."   199. **the moon,** etc. I do not know the origin of the ballad from which these lines are taken: it was reported to me from Sydney, Australia.   202. *Et . . . coupole.* V. Verlaine, *Parsifal.* ["And O these voices of children singing in the choir-loft." Here again is a memory image in contrast to the present-day vulgarization of any love.]   203. **Twit twit twit,** simply a repetition of the nightingale song, vulgarized, and a hint again of the rape of Philomela.   209. **Mr. Eugenides,** [the Phoenician Sailor in the Tarot pack who carried something on his back which the fortuneteller could not make out.]   211. **C.i.f.** The currants were quoted at a price "carriage and insurance free to London"; and the Bill of Lading, etc., were to be handed to the buyer upon payment of the sight draft.

I Tiresias, though blind, throbbing between
    two lives,
Old man with wrinkled female breasts, can see
At the violet hour, the evening hour that
    strives   220
Homeward, and brings the sailor home from
    sea,
The typist home at teatime, clears her break-
    fast, lights
Her stove, and lays out food in tins.
Out of the window perilously spread
Her drying combinations touched by the sun's
    last rays,   225
On the divan are piled (at night her bed)
Stockings, slippers, camisoles, and stays.
I Tiresias, old man with wrinkled dugs
Perceived the scene, and foretold the rest—
I too awaited the expected guest.   230
He, the young man carbuncular, arrives,

A small house agent's clerk, with one bold
    stare,
One of the low on whom assurance sits
As a silk hat on a Bradford millionaire.   234
The time is now propitious, as he guesses,
The meal is ended, she is bored and tired,
Endeavours to engage her in caresses
Which still are unreproved, if undesired.
Flushed and decided, he assaults at once;
Exploring hands encounter no defence;   240
His vanity requires no response,
And makes a welcome of indifference.
(And I Tiresias have foresuffered all
Enacted on this same divan or bed;
I who have sat by Thebes below the wall   245
And walked among the lowest of the dead.)
Bestows one final patronising kiss,
And gropes his way, finding the stairs un-
    lit . . .

She turns and looks a moment in the glass,
Hardly aware of her departed lover;   250
Her brain allows one half-formed thought to
    pass:
"Well now that's done: and I'm glad it's over."
When lovely woman stoops to folly and
Paces about her room again, alone,   254
She smoothes her hair with automatic hand,
And puts a record on the gramophone.

"This music crept by me upon the waters"
And along the Strand, up Queen Victoria
    Street.
O City city, I can sometimes hear   259
Beside a public bar in Lower Thames Street,
The pleasant whining of a mandoline
And a clatter and a chatter from within
Where fishmen lounge at noon: where the walls
Of Magnus Martyr hold
Inexplicable splendour of Ionian white and
    gold.   265

218. Tiresias. Tiresias, although a mere spectator and not indeed a "character," is yet the most important personage in the poem, uniting all the rest. Just as the one-eyed merchant, seller of currants, melts into the Phoenician Sailor, and the latter is not wholly distinct from Ferdinand Prince of Naples, so all the women are one woman, and the two sexes meet in Tiresias. What Tiresias *sees*, in fact, is the substance of the poem. The whole passage from Ovid is of great anthropological interest:

   '. . . Cum Iunone iocos et maior vestra profecto est
   Quam, quae contingit maribus, dixisse, 'voluptas.'
   Illa negat; placuit quae sit sententia docti
   Quaerere Tiresiae: venus huic erat utraque nota.
   Nam duo magnorum viridi coeuntia silva
   Corpora serpentum baculi violaverat ictu
   Deque viro factus, mirabile, femina septem
   Egerat autumnos; octavo rursus eosdem
   Vidit et 'est tua si tanta potentia plagae,'
   Dixit 'ut auctoris sortem in contraria mutet,
   Nunc quoque vos feriam!' percussis anguibus isdem
   Forma prior rediit genetivaque venit imago.
   Arbiter hic igitur sumptus de lite iocosa
   Dicta Iovis firmat; gravius Saturnia iusto
   Nec pro materia fertur doluisse suique
   Iudicis aeterna damnavit lumina nocte,
   At pater omnipotens (neque enim licet inrita cuiquam
   Facta dei fecisse deo) pro lumine adempto
   Scire futura dedit poenamque levavit honore.

[. . . It happened that Jove, heated with wine, laid care aside to jest with Juno in an idle hour. "I insist," he said, "that your pleasure in love is greater than that we (male gods) enjoy." She disagreed. So they decided to ask the judgment of wise Tiresias. He knew love from both sides. For once, having outraged two huge serpents mating in the forest, with a blow of his stick, he had, wonderful to say, been changed from a man into a woman, and in that shape he spent seven years. In the eighth year he saw the same serpents again and said, "Since in striking you there is such magic power as to change the nature of the giver of the blow, now I will strike you again." So saying, he struck the serpents and was restored to his former state and became as he was born. Therefore, being asked to arbitrate the cheerful quarrel of the gods, he took Jove's side. Saturnia (Juno) was, they say, grieved more deeply either than she should have been, or the issue deserved, and condemned the judge to perpetual blindness, but the eternal father gave Tiresias the power to know the future in return for his loss of sight. **220. At the violet hour, etc.** This may not appear as exact as Sappho's lines, but I had in mind the "longshore" or "dory" fisherman, who returns at nightfall. [Sappho's poem to the evening star.]

253. When lovely woman, etc. V. Goldsmith, the song in *The Vicar of Wakefield*:

    [When lovely woman stoops to folly
       and finds too late that men betray
      What charm can soothe her melancholy,
        What art can wash her guilt away?]

257. This . . . waters. V. *The Tempest*, as above. (I, 2)
263. Where . . . noon. [This is one of Eliot's few hints that there may be moments of innocence in the lives of simple people at the foot of the church of Magnus Martyr. Both the innocence and the church are old, and have a spirituality which the modern scene lacks, but both are also in a sense relics.] **264. Magnus Martyr.** The interior of St. Magnus Martyr is to my mind one of the finest among Wren's interiors. See *The Proposed Demolition of Nineteen City Churches*: (P. S. King & Son, Ltd.)

The river sweats
Oil and tar
The barges drift
With the turning tide
Red sails   270
Wide
To leeward, swing on the heavy spar.
The barges wash
Drifting logs
Down Greenwich reach   275
Past the Isle of Dogs.
          Weialala leia
          Wallala leialala

Elizabeth and Leicester
Beating oars   280
The stern was formed
A gilded shell
Red and gold
The brisk swell
Rippled both shores   285
Southwest wind
Carried down stream
The peal of bells
White towers
          Weialala leia   290
          Wallala leialala

"Trams and dusty trees.
Highbury bore me. Richmond and Kew
Undid me. By Richmond I raised my
     knees   294
Supine on the floor of a narrow canoe."

"My feet are at Moorgate, and my heart
Under my feet. After the event
He wept. He promised 'a new start.'
I made no comment. What should I re-
     sent?"

"On Margate Sands.   300
I can connect
Nothing with nothing.
The broken fingernails of dirty hands.
My people humble people who expect
Nothing."   305
          la la

To Carthage then I came
Burning burning burning burning
O Lord Thou pluckest me out
O Lord Thou Pluckest   310

burning

IV. DEATH BY WATER

Phlebas the Phoenician, a fortnight dead,
Forgot the cry of gulls, and the deep sea swell
And the profit and loss.
                    A current under sea   315
Picked his bones in whispers. As he rose and
     fell
He passed the stages of his age and youth
Entering the whirlpool.
                    Gentile or Jew
O you who turn the wheel and look to wind-
     ward,   320
Consider Phlebas, who was once handsome and
     tall as you.

V. WHAT THE THUNDER SAID

After the torchlight red on sweaty faces
After the frosty silence in the gardens
After the agony in stony places
The shouting and the crying   325
Prison and palace and reverberation
Of thunder of spring over distant mountains

266. **The river sweats.** The Song of the (three) Thames-daughters begins here. From line 292 to 306 inclusive they speak in turn. V. *Götterdämmerung*, III, i; the Rhine daughters. [There is, in the story of the Rhine daughters, a story of rape also, and this hint of the secularization of love flows over into the Elizabeth and Leicester scene, a scene of seduction which came to nothing.]   279. **Elizabeth and Leicester.** V. Froude, *Elizabeth*, Vol. I, ch. iv, letter of De Quadra to Philip of Spain: "In the afternoon we were in a barge, watching the games on the river. (The queen) was alone with Lord Robert and myself on the poop, when they began to talk nonsense, and went so far that Lord Robert at last said, as I was on the spot there was no reason why they should not be married if the queen pleased."   293. **Highbury . . . me.** Cf. *Purgatorio*, V, 133:

      "Ricorditi di me, che son la Pia;
      Siena mi fe', disfecemi Maremma."
      ["Remember me, who am la Pia;
      Sienna made me, Maremma unmade me."]

307. **To . . . came.** V. St. Augustine's *Confessions:* "to Carthage then I came, where a cauldron of unholy loves sang all about mine ears." 308. **Burning . . . burning.** The complete text of the Buddha's Fire Sermon (which corresponds in importance to the Sermon on the Mount) from which these words are taken, will be found translated in the late Henry Clarke Warren's *Buddhism in Translation* (Harvard Oriental Series). Mr. Warren was one of the great pioneers of Buddhist studies in the Occident. [The protagonist here is still praying that he be freed of the fire of lust; but he is not yet free.] 312. **Phlebas . . . dead.** From St. Augustine's *Confessions* again. The collocation of these two representatives of eastern and western asceticism, as the culmination of this part of the poem, is not an accident.   322. **After the torchlight.** In the first part of Part V three themes are employed: the journey to Emmaus, the approach to the Chapel Perilous (see Miss Weston's book) and the present decay of eastern Europe. [This section is a reminiscence of the betrayal of Christ in the Garden of Gethsemane.]

He who was living is now dead
We who were living are now dying
With a little patience   330

Here is no water but only rock
Rock and no water and the sandy road
The road winding above among the mountains
Which are mountains of rock without water
If there were water we should stop and drink
Amongst the rock one cannot stop or think   336
Sweat is dry and feet are in the sand
If there were only water amongst the rock
Dead mountain mouth of carious teeth that
          cannot spit
Here one can neither stand nor lie nor sit   340
There is not even silence in the mountains
But dry sterile thunder without rain
There is not even solitude in the mountains
But red sullen faces sneer and snarl
From doors of mudcracked houses   345
          If there were water
   And no rock
   If there were rock
   And also water
   And water   350
   A spring
   A pool among the rock
   If there were the sound of water only
   Not the cicada
   And dry grass singing   355
   But sound of water over a rock
   Where the hermit-thrush sings in the pine
          trees
   Drip drop drip drop drop drop drop
   But there is no water

Who is the third who walks always beside you?
When I count, there are only you and I to-
          gether   360
But when I look ahead up the white road

There is always another one walking beside you
Gliding wrapt in a brown mantle, hooded
I do not know whether a man or a woman
—But who is that on the other side of you?   365

What is that sound high in the air
Murmur of maternal lamentation
Who are those hooded hordes swarming
Over endless plains, stumbling in cracked earth
Ringed by the flat horizon only   370
What is the city over the mountains
Cracks and reforms and bursts in the violet air
Falling towers
Jerusalem Athens Alexandria
Vienna London   375
Unreal

A woman drew her long black hair out tight
And fiddled whisper music on those strings
And bats with baby faces in the violet light
Whistled, and beat their wings   380
And crawled head downward down a black-
          ened wall
And upside down in air were towers
Tolling reminiscent bells, that kept the hours
And voices singing out of empty cisterns and
          exhausted wells.

In this decayed hole among the mountains   385
In the faint moonlight, the grass is singing
Over the tumbled graves, about the chapel
There is the empty chapel, only the wind's
          home.
It has no windows, and the door swings,
Dry bones can harm no one.   390
Only a cock stood on the rooftree
Co co rico co co rico
In a flash of lightning. Then a damp gust
Bringing rain

331. **Here . . . rock.** [In this lyrical scene of agony and sterility, the hint is always that the rock or the material will give
forth no water; that there is no spring of life.]   357. **hermit-thrush.** This *Turdus aonalaschkae pallasii*, the hermit-
thrush which I have heard in Quebec County. Chapman
says (*Handbook of Birds of Eastern North America*), "it is
most at home in secluded woodland and thickety retreats . . .
its notes are not remarkable for variety or volume, but in
purity and sweetness of tone and exquisite modulation they
are unequalled." Its "water-dripping song" is justly celebrated.
360. **When I count, etc.** The following lines were stimulated
by the account of one of the Antarctic expeditions (I forget
which, but I think one of Shackleton's): it was related that the
party of explorers, at the extremity of their strength, had the
constant delusion that there was *one more member* than could
actually be counted. [In the journey to Emmaus the disciples
who have left Christ in the grave see someone beside them
whose face is hidden. They do not recognize the risen God—
in other words, they do not recognize the impulse to rebirth.]

366-76. **What is that sound.** Cf. Hermann Hesse, *Blick ins
Chaos:* "Schon ist halb Europa, schon ist zumindest der halbe
Osten Europas auf dem Wege zum Chaos, fährt betrunken im
heiligem Wahn am Abgrund entlang und singt dazu, singt
betrunken und hymnisch wie Dmitri Karamasoff sang. Ueber
diese Lieder lacht der Bürger beleidigt, der Heilige und Seher
hört sie mit Tränen." [*A Look at Chaos:* Already half of Europe,
already at least half of Eastern Europe, is on the way to Chaos,
travelling drunken in an illusion of holy ecstasy, along the edge
of the abyss, and celebrating this by singing, singing drunken
hymns, as Dmitri Karamasoff (cf. Dostoevsky) sang. Over
these songs the insulted burgher laughs, the saint and the seer
hear them in tears.]   377. **A woman . . . tight.** [Here again
is a hysterical Cassandra image of a prophecy of a world upside
down and sterile.]   391. **Only . . . rooftree.** [The crow of the
cock is an ominous warning.]

Ganga was sunken, and the limp leaves   395
Waited for rain, while the black clouds
Gathered far distant, over Himavant.
The jungle crouched, humped in silence.
Then spoke the thunder
Da   400
Datta: what have we given?
My friend, blood shaking my heart
The awful daring of a moment's surrender
Which an age of prudence can never retract
By this, and this only, we have existed   405
Which is not to be found in our obituaries
Or in memories draped by the beneficent spider
Or under seals broken by the lean solicitor
In our empty rooms
Da   410
Dayadhvam: I have heard the key
Turn in the door once and turn once only
We think of the key, each in his prison
Thinking of the key, each confirms a prison
Only at nightfall, aethereal rumours   415
Revive for a moment a broken Coriolanus
Da
Damyata: The boat responded
Gaily, to the hand expert with sail and oar
The sea was calm, your heart would have
    responded   420
Gaily, when invited, beating obedient
To controlling hands

              I sat upon the shore

Fishing, with the arid plain behind me
Shall I at least set my lands in order?   425
London Bridge is falling down falling down
    falling down
Poi s'ascose nel foco che gli affina
Quando fiam uti chelidon—O swallow swallow
Le Prince d'Aquitaine à la tour abolie
These fragments I have shored against my
    ruins   430
Why then Ile fit you. Hieronymo's mad againe.
Datta. Dayadhvam. Damyata.
    Shantih   shantih   shantih

Ash Wednesday

[*Ash Wednesday* is Eliot's first long analytical and personal poem concerning his own religious conversion. It is supposedly a study in the way in which a highly poetic and intellectual mind sloughs off (or attempts to) its earthly delights and its doubts in concern that the spirit be saved. Doubtless the poet may have so intended it. Eliot's honesty is so great, however, that the poem presents an outcry for grace, a plea for pardon and redemption through the church, meanwhile indicating that neither the skeptical mind (so apparent in Eliot's earlier poems) nor the poetic sensitivity is easily relinquished.

The poem begins with a statement of a turn in Eliot's own position, his decision not to return to the infirm glory of life, and with his prayer to God for mercy. He argues that his

395. Ganga . . . leaves. [The storm breaks, but only the thunder speaks; we are given three cues as to our possible escape from sterility, but none of these methods of escape can be used by the protagonist.]   **401. Datta, dayadhvam, damyata.** (Give, sympathise, control). The fable of the meaning of the Thunder is found in the *Brihadaranyaka—Upanishad,* 5, I. A translation is found in Deussen's *Sechzig Upanishads des Veda,* p. 489.   **407. beneficent spider.** Cf. Webster, *The White Devil,* V. vi:

                    ". . . they'll remarry
    Ere the worm pierce your winding-sheet, ere the spider
    Make a thin curtain for your epitaphs."
411. I have . . . key. Cf. *Inferno,* XXXIII, 46:
        "ed io sentii chiavar l'uscio di sotto
        all'orribile torre."
["and below I heard the outlet of the horrible tower locked up."] Also F. H. Bradley, *Appearance and Reality,* p. 346. "My external sensations are no less private to myself than are my thoughts or my feelings. In either case my experience falls within my own circle, a circle closed on the outside; and, with all its elements alike, every sphere is opaque to the others which surround it. . . . In brief, regarded as an existence which appears in a soul, the whole world for each is peculiar and private to that soul."   **416. Coriolanus.** [Roman general and hero of Shakespeare's play, whose pride, combined with the ingratitude of the citizens, exiled him from Rome. He joined the enemy, the Volscians, and attacked Rome. The arguments of his Roman mother, wife, and son persuaded him to spare the city, and on his return the Volscians killed him.]

424. Fishing . . . me. V. Weston: *From Ritual to Romance;* chapter on the Fisher King.   **427. Poi . . . affina.** V. *Purgatorio,* XXVI, 148:
    "'Ara vos prec per aquella valor
    'Que vos guida al som de l'escalina,
    'sovegna vos a temps de ma dolor.'
    Poi s'ascose nel foco che gli affina."
    ["Now I pray you by that goodness
    Which guides you to the summit of the stair
    In good time remember my pain."
    Then he dived back into that fire which refines them.]
428. Quando . . . chelidon. V. *Pervigilium Veneris.* Cf. Philomela in Parts II and III: [She is singing: I am silent. When will spring awake in me? When shall I be like the swallow and from dumb distress be free?]   **429. Le Prince . . . abolie.** V. Gerard de Nerval, Sonnet *El Desdichado.* [I am the gloomy one—the widower,—the unconsoled, . . . The Prince of Aquitaine at the ruined tower.]   **431. Hieronymo's mad againe.** V. Kyd's *Spanish Tragedy.* [This puzzling reference to the Spanish tragedy may mean that since *Hieronymo's mad againe* for a purpose, like Hamlet, the poet has been mad for the purpose of disclosing reality, from which he now turns, and in the words of the Sanskrit prayer asks release.]   **433. Shantih.** Repeated as here, a formal ending to an Upanishad. "The Peace which passeth understanding" is our equivalent to this word.

poetic wings no longer carry him as before, that he is convinced he is a sinner and must repent. The theme of the second section is "dust to dust"—the destruction of the body and the willingness to relinquish the human form if some greater sense of permanence can be obtained than the bones have afforded. The third section has to do with the ascent of three stairs, as one escapes the flesh. On the first stair it is impossible to think of oneself save in one's human shape, on the second stair the image of old age forces one to relinquish the life of the flesh, on the third stair one relinquishes what is most dear, the sensual perceptions, the poet's delight in the image. The fourth section, in more mystical terms, tells of being led out of the images of fleshly life, away from even the pagan images of poetic delight in order that one, after the exile of the flesh, may know again the fertile, the replenishing, and the spiritual. The fifth section is a development of the opposing ideas of reality: the Word of God, the word from which all others flow, and the word of man lost, who must again seek the spiritual truth since he has walked in darkness and denied the voice of truth and God; the poet is led toward redemption by the veiled sister. He himself has found it difficult to surrender his doubts, he himself has denied between the rocks—the altars of the primitive gods, now empty of all sacrifice. These same rocks appear also in *The Waste Land*. The sixth section repeats with a slight but important variation the theme of the first. The poet sees the images of the white sails of poetic exploration, he recalls the poetic delights of the senses, the smell of all that is earthly. He is now at that time of tension which calls for dying and for birth (spiritual birth). And so again, the image of life (the Virgin, the spirit of water or of all fertility) is the image called up before him. He must be spiritually reborn or he is indeed dead; he prays for grace that he may be forgiven and saved.

The poem, explained in greater detail in the footnotes, is, as a whole, a curiously honest story of the struggle to relinquish the cherished weapon of a poetic intelligence in order, through the church (Anglo-Catholic), to attain to grace in God. It is a poem of conflict and repentance rather than of straight religious ecstasy.]

I

BECAUSE I do not hope to turn again
Because I do not hope
Because I do not hope to turn
Desiring this man's gift and that man's scope
I no longer strive to strive towards such
      things   5
(Why should the agèd eagle stretch its wings?)
Why should I mourn
The vanished power of the usual reign?

Because I do not hope to know again
The infirm glory of the positive hour   10
Because I do not think
Because I know I shall not know
The one veritable transitory power
Because I cannot drink
There, where trees flower, and springs flow, for
      there is nothing again   15

Because I know that time is always time
And place is always and only place
And what is actual is actual only for one time
And only for one place
I rejoice that things are as they are and   20
I renounce the blessèd face
And renounce the voice
Because I cannot hope to turn again
Consequently I rejoice, having to construct
      something
Upon which to rejoice   25

1. **Because . . . again,** A direct translation of Guido Cavalcanti, "perch'io non spero di torna grammai." But there is probably some connection with Lancelot Andrewes' sermon on "Turn ye even unto me, saith the Lord," the opening words of the Epistle for Ash Wednesday: "Now at this time is the turning of the year. . . . Everything now turning that we also would make it our time to turn to God. . . . Upon this turning, *cardo vertitur*, the hinge turns, of our well and evil doing for ever. . . . Repentance itself is nothing but a kind of circling. . . . Which circle consists of two turnings. . . . First a turn wherein we look forward to God and with our whole heart resolve to turn to Him. Then a turn again wherein we look backward to our sins wherein we have turned from God. . . . The wheel turns apace, and if we turn not the rather these turnings may overtake us." 4. **Desiring . . . scope.** "Desiring this man's art and that man's scope," Shakespeare, *Sonnet XXIX*. 6. **Why . . . wings.** The intention of the eagle as an image here may have something in common with Baudelaire's intention in his poem, *L'Albatros*, as described by Eliot in his essay on the French poet, but the connotations are primarily religious. The Psalmist said, "Thy youth shall be renewed as the eagle's," and since the Middle Ages the eagle has been the symbol of Baptismal grace. There is also a connection with Dante's dream of the Eagle, *Purgatorio*, ix, and with the fact that, in the Medieval Bestiaries, the aged eagle flew up into the circle of fire where his feathers were burned off and he fell into a fountain of water, to come out with his youth restored. 10. **The infirm . . . hour.** The whole of this passage is opposed to the last clause of the Lord's Prayer, "For thine is the kingdom, the power, and the glory, for ever and ever." (There may also be a subconscious echo of "The uncertain glory of an April day," *Two Gentlemen of Verona*, I, 3, 1:85).

And pray to God to have mercy upon us
And I pray that I may forget
These matters that with myself I too much
    discuss
Too much explain
Because I do not hope to turn again   30
Let these words answer
For what is done, not to be done again
May the judgement not be too heavy upon us

Because these wings are no longer wings to fly
But merely vans to beat the air   35
The air which is now thoroughly small and dry
Smaller and dryer than the will
Teach us to care and not to care
Teach us to sit still

Pray for us sinners now and at the hour of our
    death   40
Pray for us now and at the hour of our death.

II

Lady, three white leopards sat under a juniper-
    tree
In the cool of the day, having fed to satiety
On my legs my heart my liver and that which
    had been contained   44
In the hollow round of my skull. And God said
Shall these bones live? shall these
Bones live? And that which had been contained

In the bones (which were already dry) said
    chirping:
Because of the goodness of this Lady
And because of her loveliness, and because   50
She honours the Virgin in meditation,
We shine with brightness. And I who am here
    dissembled
Proffer my deeds to oblivion, and my love
To the posterity of the desert and the fruit of
    the gourd.
It is this which recovers   55
My guts the strings of my eyes and the indi-
    gestible portions
Which the leopards reject. The Lady is with-
    drawn
In a white gown, to contemplation, in a white
    gown.
Let the whiteness of bones atone to forgetful-
    ness.
There is no life in them. As I am forgotten   60
And would be forgotten, so I would forget
Thus devoted, concentrated in purpose. And
    God said
Prophesy to the wind, to the wind only for
    only
The wind will listen. And the bones sang chirp-
    ing   64
With the burden of the grasshopper, saying
Lady of silences
Calm and distressed
Torn and most whole
Rose of memory
Rose of forgetfulness   70
Exhausted and life-giving
Worried reposeful
The single Rose
Is now the Garden
Where all loves end   75
Terminate torment

35. **But merely . . . air.** The fans of a winnowing machine are called vans.   40. **Pray . . . death,** the Angelical Salutation in the Catholic Mass, "Ora pro nobis."   42. **Lady.** Cf. T. S. Eliot's essay on Dante: "In the Earthly Paradise Dante encounters a lady named Matilda, whose identity need not at first bother us." **three white leopards.** Cf. T. S. Eliot's essay on Dante: "I do not recommend, in first reading the first canto of the *Inferno*, worrying about the identity of the Leopard, the Lion, or the She-Wolf. It is really better, at the start, not to know or care what they do mean. What we should consider is not so much the meaning of the images, but the reverse process, that which led a man having an idea to express it in images. We have to consider the type of mind which by nature and *practice* tended to express itself in allegory; and for a competent poet, allegory means *clear visual images*." Dante's beasts derive from Jeremiah 5 : 6: "wherefore a lion out of the forest shall slay them, and a wolf of the evenings shall spoil them, a leopard shall watch over their cities: every one that goeth out thence shall be torn in pieces: because their transgressions are many, and their backslidings are increased." Eliot's leopards are clearly agents of good, while Dante's animals are sinister. **a juniper-tree.** Elijah "came and sat down under a juniper-tree." I Kings, 19 : 4. But as well as with this tree, under which Elijah despaired, there may also be a connection with the Grimm's fairy tale, *The Juniper Tree*, under which Marlinchen buried the little boy's bones.   45. **In . . . skull.** In this section the passages dealing with the destruction of the body are connected with Baudelaire's poem *Voyage à Cythère*.   46. **Shall these bones live?** "Thus saith the Lord God unto these bones; Behold, I will cause breath to enter into you, and ye shall live." Ezekiel 37 : 5.

54. **the fruit of the gourd.** "Thou hast had pity on the gourd." Jonah 4 : 10.   63. **Prophesy to the wind.** "Prophesy unto the wind, prophesy, son of man." Ezekiel 37 : 9.   65. **With . . . grasshopper.** "and the grasshopper shall be a burden, and desire shall fail." Ecclesiastes 12 : 5.   69. **Rose of memory.** One of the titles of the Virgin Mary is *Rosa Mystica*, and in the *Paradiso* she is the "Rose in which the Word Divine made itself flesh."   73. **The single Rose.** Christ, who is the Rose of Sharon. Dante saw the whole of the saints in Paradise as the petals of one white rose. See also George Herbert, *Church-Rents and Schisms:*
    Brave rose (alas!) where art thou? in the chair
    Where thou didst lately so triumph and shine
    A worm doth sit, whose many feet and hair
    Are the more foul, the more thou wert divine.
74. **Is now the Garden.** There is probably a reference here to the Garden of Gethsemane, where Christ prayed all night before his betrayal.

Of love unsatisfied
The greater torment
Of love satisfied
End of the endless   80
Journey to no end
Conclusion of all that
Is inconclusible
Speech without word and
Word of no speech   85
Grace to the Mother
For the Garden
Where all love ends.

Under a juniper-tree the bones sang, scattered
    and shining
We are glad to be scattered, we did little good
    to each other,   90
Under a tree in the cool of the day, with the
    blessing of sand,
Forgetting themselves and each other, united
In the quiet of the desert. This is the land
    which ye
Shall divide by lot. And neither division nor
    unity
Matters. This is the land. We have our inher-
    itance.   95

III

At the first turning of the second stair
I turned and saw below
The same shape twisted on the banister
Under the vapour in the fetid air
Struggling with the devil of the stairs who
    wears   100
The deceitful face of hope and of despair.

At the second turning of the second stair
I left them twisting, turning below;
There were no more faces and the stair was
    dark,
Damp, jaggèd, like an old man's mouth drivel-
    ling, beyond repair,   105
Or the toothed gullet of an agèd shark.

81. **Journey to no end.** Compare with the end of "The Journey of the Magi." 93. **This . . . lot.** "This is the land which ye shall divide by lot unto the tribes of Israel for inheritance, and these are their portions, saith the Lord God." Ezekiel 48 : 29. 96. **the second stair.** The reference to the stairs in this section is also to *Purgatorio*, xxvi, 145–7:

    I pray you by that Goodness which doth deign
    To guide you to the summit of this stair
    Bethink you in due season of my pain.

However, also, "O my dove, that art in the clefts of the rock, in the secret places of the stairs, let me see thy countenance." Song of Solomon 2 : 14.

At the first turning of the third stair
Was a slotted window bellied like the fig's
    fruit
And beyond the hawthorn blossom and a pas-
    ture scene   109
The broadbacked figure drest in blue and green
Enchanted the maytime with an antique flute.
Blown hair is sweet, brown hair over the
    mouth blown,
Lilac and brown hair;
Distraction, music of the flute, stops and steps
    of the mind over the third stair,
Fading, fading; strength beyond hope and de-
    spair   115
Climbing the third stair.
Lord, I am not worthy
Lord, I am not worthy

        but speak the word only.

IV

Who walked between the violet and the violet
Who walked between   121
The various ranks of varied green
Going in white and blue, in Mary's colour,
Talking of trivial things
In ignorance and in knowledge of eternal
    dolour   125
Who moved among the others as they walked,
Who then made strong the fountains and made
    fresh the springs

Made cool the dry rock and made firm the sand
In blue of larkspur, blue of Mary's colour,
Sovegna vos   130

Here are the years that walk between, bearing
Away the fiddles and the flutes, restoring
One who moves in the time between sleep and
    waking, wearing

112. **Blown hair is sweet.** Richard Eberhardt has suggested that there may be a reminiscence here of Tennyson's "The Lotus Eaters":

    There is a sweet music here that softer falls
    Than petals from blown roses on the grass.

It is equally probable, however, that it is a reminiscence of Ernest Dowson, for whose work Eliot has great admiration. 117. **Lord, I am not worthy.** "The centurion answered and said, Lord, I am not worthy that thou shouldest come under my roof: but speak the word only, and my servant shall be healed." Matthew 8 : 8. 123. **in Mary's colour,** a reminiscence of the paintings of the Italians and of the English Pre-Raphaelites who always depicted Mary in white and blue. 130. **Sovegna vos.** See note to l. 96; "sovegna vos" means "bethink you" or "be mindful."

White light folded, sheathed about her, folded.
The new years walk, restoring   135
Through a bright cloud of tears, the years, re-
    storing
With a new verse the ancient rhyme. Redeem
The time. Redeem
The unread vision in the higher dream
While jewelled unicorns draw by the gilded
    hearse.   140
The silent sister veiled in white and blue
Between the yews, behind the garden god,
Whose flute is breathless, bent her head and
    signed but spoke no word

But the fountain sprang up and the bird sang
    down
Redeem the time, redeem the dream   145
The token of the word unheard, unspoken

Till the wind shake a thousand whispers from
    the yew

And after this our exile

                    V

If the lost word is lost, if the spent word is
    spent
If the unheard, unspoken   150
Word is unspoken, unheard;
Still is the unspoken word, the Word unheard,
The Word without a word, the Word within
The world and for the world;
And the light shone in darkness and   155
Against the Word the unstilled world still
    whirled
About the centre of the silent Word.

O my people, what have I done unto thee.

134. **White . . . her.** Dante frequently uses the image of a
figure swathed [*fasciato*] in light or joy.   140. **jewelled unicorns.** These unicorns may derive from Cavalcanti, or from
one of the Florentine engravings of the Triumphs of Petrarch,
where the car in the Triumph of Chastity is drawn by unicorns:
traditionally, the unicorn was captured by a Virgin, and was
the symbol of virtue.   142. **the yews.** The yew-tree is traditionally the tree planted in English church-yards, being
described by Sir Thomas Browne as "an emblete of Resurrection from its perpetual verdure."   148. **And . . . exile,** from
the prayer *Salve Regina* which follows the celebration of the
Catholic Mass: "To thee do we send up our sighs mourning
and weeping in this valley of tears; turn, then, most gracious
advocate, thine eyes of mercy towards us; and after this our
exile, show unto us the blessed fruit of the womb, Jesus."
153. **Word without a word.** The whole of this passage is a
variation on John 1: 1–14; But also "The word within a word,
unable to speak a word," a phrase from Lancelot Andrewes,
quoted by Eliot in his essay *For Lancelot Andrewes.*   158. **O
. . . thee,** a quotation from Micah 6:3.

Where shall the word be found, where will the
    word
Resound? Not here, there is not enough silence
Not on the sea or on the islands, not   161
On the mainland, in the desert or the rain land,
For those who walk in darkness
Both in the day time and in the night time
The right time and the right place are not here
No place of grace for those who avoid the face
No time to rejoice for those who walk among
    noise and deny the voice   167

Will the veiled sister pray for
Those who walk in darkness, who chose thee
    and oppose thee.
Those who are torn on the horn between season
    and season, time and time, between
Hour and hour, word and word, power and
    power, those who wait   171
In darkness? Will the veiled sister pray
For children at the gate
Who will not go away and cannot pray:
Pray for those who chose and oppose   175

    O my people, what have I done unto thee.

Will the veiled sister between the slender
Yew trees pray for those who offend her
And are terrified and cannot surrender
And affirm before the world and deny between
    the rocks   180
In the last desert between the last blue rocks
The desert in the garden the garden in the
    desert
Of drouth, spitting from the mouth the with-
    ered apple-seed.

    O my people.

163. **For those . . . darkness.** The Bible is full of references
to those who walk in darkness, as "when by his light I walked
through darkness" (Job 29 : 3), and "that walketh in darkness
and hath no light" (Isaiah 9 : 2). Other references are Psalms
82: 5; Psalms 91: 6; Ecclesiastes 2: 14; Isaiah 59: 9; John 8: 12;
John 12: 35; I John 1: 6; I John 2: 11.   167. **deny the voice,**
perhaps a reference to "Jesus said unto him, Verily I say unto
thee, That this night, before the cock crow, thou shalt deny
me thrice. Peter said unto him, Though I should die with thee,
yet will I not deny thee. Likewise also said all the disciples."
(Matthew 26: 34–35.)   169. **who . . . thee.** "He that is not
with me is against me." (Matthew 12: 30.)   170. **torn on the
horn,** the image of destruction, as if by a bull.   180. **affirm
. . . rocks.** There may be a reference here to the story of
Leonardo's *The Madonna of the Rocks* which affirmed in the
painting of the rocks geological theories he could not express
in writing to the world, as it was heretical to oppose the Biblical and Aristotelian concepts of the creation. See also note 167.
182. **The desert in the garden.** "He will make . . . her desert
like the garden of the Lord." (Isaiah 51: 3.)   183. **the withered apple-seed.** Probably there is some connection between
the seed and the fruit of the Tree of Knowledge, traditionally
an apple.

VI

Although I do not hope to turn again   185
Although I do not hope
Although I do not hope to turn

Wavering between the profit and the loss
In this brief transit where the dreams cross
The dreamcrossed twilight between birth and
          dying   190
(Bless me father) though I do not wish to wish
          these things
From the wide window towards the granite
          shore
The white sails still fly seaward, seaward flying
Unbroken wings

And the lost heart stiffens and rejoices   195
In the lost lilac and the lost sea voices
And the weak spirit quickens to rebel
For the bent golden-rod and the lost sea smell
Quickens to recover
The cry of quail and the whirling plover   200
And the blind eye creates
The empty forms between the ivory gates

191. **Bless me father.** The opening formula of the confession,
"Bless me father, for I have sinned."   193. **seaward.** "And
his will is our peace: it is that sea to which all moves that it
createth and that nature maketh." (Dante, *Purgatorio*, III, 85.)
The landscape here is that of New England which appears
later in *The Dry Salvages*.   200. **The cry . . . plover**, more
reminiscences of New England fauna. See also "A wind from
the Lord . . . brought quails." (Numbers 11:31.)   202. **the
ivory gates.** The ivory gates appear in Greek legend, but
there may also be a memory of the Soldiers' Song from J. E.
Flecker's *Hassan:* "We storm at your ivory gates."

And smell renews the salt savour of the sandy
          earth

This is the time of tension between dying and
          birth   204
The place of solitude where three dreams cross
Between blue rocks
But when the voices shaken from the yew-tree
          drift away
Let the other yew be shaken and reply.

Blessèd sister, holy mother, spirit of the foun-
          tain, spirit of the garden,   209
Suffer us not to mock ourselves with falsehood
Teach us to care and not to care
Teach us to sit still
Even among these rocks,
Our peace in His will
And even among these rocks   215
Sister, mother
And spirit of the river, spirit of the sea,
Suffer me not to be separated

And let my cry come unto Thee.

214. **Our . . . will**, a translation from Dante's "la sua volun-
tade e nostra pace." The whole of this passage is reminiscent
of Bernard's Prayer to Mary in the last Canto of the *Paradiso*.
218. **Suffer . . . separated**, the ancient prayer *Anima Christi*,
"Suffer me not to be separated from Thee."   219. **And . . .
Thee.** "Let my cry come near before thee, O Lord," Psalm
119 : 169, a prominent response in the Catholic Mass ritual.

MARIANNE MOORE

Marianne Moore, although she has long been
a poet and was connected early with the famous literary magazine, *The Dial*, has only recently received the full acclaim she has deserved. She was born in St. Louis in 1887, was
graduated from Bryn Mawr College in 1909,
for a time taught stenography, and then for
several years was a librarian in New York.
From 1925 to 1929 she was a member of the
editorial staff of *The Dial*. She had begun publication in English journals in 1920 and her first

collection of poems was published by the Egoist Press. In 1924 a book of her poems, under
the title of *Observations*, was published in
America. Recently T. S. Eliot, in his essay introducing her collected poems, praised Miss
Moore as one of the few moderns to deserve
immortality.

Her poetry is intellectual but also highly sensitive, not that type of verse in which a wide
range of knowledge is used merely as display,
but poetry in which an analytic eye, a sensi-

tive ironic emotion, and a fine intelligence play over reality. She says of herself,

> I have learned, I feel, from trade journals and technical books that were a pleasure to me, and that seemed, from their obligation to exposit accurately, effective as writing; John Mc-Graw's *How to Play Baseball,* Christy Mathewson's *Pitching in a Pinch,* Harold Baynes's manual on dogs, articles in the *Journal of Natural History,* for in my work I have been influenced also by fondness for outdoor life, tennis and sailing in particular—the latter, vicariously in the person of my brother more than in my own right . . . I admit that in anything I have written, I have never achieved what satisfied me. In writing, it is my one principle that nothing is too much trouble.

Such a remark indicates the kind of eclectic and refined intelligence and keen observation with which Miss Moore made the whole of her world her field, from which she could choose material for her poetic commentaries. Her poetry is a poetry of what one might call brilliant conversation. She has a fine command of the sentence in verse. She deals with the significant idea or fact, allowing her feelings concerning what she is discussing or the larger implications of her subject to rise from the almost jewel precision of what she has said. She chooses from life such objects as will give significance or moral relish to the eternal questions as to why we live at all, and what life and sensitivity are about. But in her, there is never any romantic escapism, only a rigorous, almost microscopic observation of what each experience, little or great, has meant. It is as if, like Emily Dickinson, Marianne Moore had faced each special experience and given us her personal reaction. But her poetry is evidence that she meets each experience, not only intuitively, as did Emily Dickinson, but with the full weight of an almost encyclopedic reading behind her. In other words, she is a highly sophisticated, in the best sense of the word, and a learned puritan, believing that in the intelligent and personal relation of each man to fact is also his relation to eternity. Not orthodoxly religious, she indicates in such poems as "What Are Years" that she has thoroughly considered the problems of how to make the soul strong, and finds that in self-expression, which is the artist's duty, one escapes the captivity of the lowly by making it creative.

Miss Moore has never married. She lived many years with her mother, who died in 1947, through what might seem to some people an uneventful life. But since for her every book is an experience, and since she can, through books, vicariously encompass the world, there is in her work no sense of a narrow existence. Alfred Kreymborg describes the young Marianne Moore as an astonishing person with titian hair, a brilliant complexion and a mellifluous flow of polysyllables which held listeners in awe. Still slender and aristocratic, and clad usually in rather severe black, she continues to command every group with which she comes in contact. For all of her Victorian appearance, she is almost electrically alert to whatever she participates in. Her recent books, *What Are Years* (1941) and *The Selected Poems* (1935) and the little volume *Nevertheless* (1944), have proved that Miss Moore has a completely established place in American letters. She has moreover written some of the great war poetry, not directly on the action so much as on the historical and spiritual guilt which brought the war about.

No Swan So Fine

No water so still as the
   dead fountains of Versailles.' No swan,
with swart blind look askance
and gondoliering legs, so fine
   as the chintz china one with fawn-   5
brown eyes and toothed gold
collar on to show whose bird it was.

Lodged in the Louis Fifteenth
   candelabrum-tree of cockscomb-
tinted buttons, dahlias,   10
sea-urchins, and everlastings,
   it perches on the branching foam
of polished sculptured
flowers—at ease and tall. The king is dead.

"No Swan So Fine," "When I Buy Pictures," and "To Military Progress" from *Selected Poems* by Marianne Moore, used by permission of The Macmillan Company.
No Swan So Fine. 1. No . . . Versailles. "There is no water so still as the dead fountains of Versailles." (Percy Phillip, *New York Times Magazine,* May 10, 1931.) 2. No swan, etc. A pair of Louis XV candelabra with Dresden figures of swans belonging to Lord Balfour. (Author's notes.)

When I Buy Pictures

OR WHAT is closer to the truth,
   when I look at that of which I may regard
     myself as the imaginary possessor,
I fix upon what would give me pleasure in my
     average moments:
the satire upon curiosity in which no more is
     discernible
than the intensity of the mood: 5
or quite the opposite—the old thing, the me-
     diaeval decorated hat-box,
in which there are hounds with waists dimin-
     ishing like the waist of the hour-glass,
and deer and birds and seated people;
it may be no more than a square of parquetry;
     the literal biography perhaps,
in letters standing well apart upon a parch-
     ment-like expanse;   10
an artichoke in six varieties of blue; the snipe-
     legged hieroglyphic in three parts;
the silver fence protecting Adam's grave, or
     Michael taking Adam by the wrist.
Too stern an intellectual emphasis upon this
     quality or that detracts from one's
     enjoyment.
It must not wish to disarm anything; nor may
     the approved triumph easily be hon-
     oured—
that which is great because something else is
     small.   15
It comes to this: of whatever sort it is,
it must be 'lit with piercing glances into the life
     of things';
it must acknowledge the spiritual forces which
     have made it.

To Military Progress

YOU USE your mind
   Like a millstone to grind
     Chaff.
You polish it
And with your warped wit   5
     Laugh

At your torso,
Prostrate where the crow
     Falls
On such faint hearts   10
As its god imparts,
     Calls

And claps its wings
Till the tumult brings
     More   15
Black minute-men
To revive again,
     War

At little cost.
They cry for the lost   20
     Head
And seek their prize
Till the evening sky's
     Red.

What Are Years?

WHAT is our innocence,
   what is our guilt? All are
naked, none is safe. And whence
is courage: the unanswered question,
the resolute doubt,—   5
dumbly calling, deafly listening—that
in misfortune, even death,
     encourages others
     and in its defeat, stirs

     the soul to be strong? He   10
sees deep and is glad; who
     accedes to mortality
and in his imprisonment, rises
upon himself as
the sea in a chasm, struggling to be   15
free and unable to be,
     in its surrendering
     finds its continuing.

So he who strongly feels,
behaves. The very bird,   20
     grown taller as he sings, steels
his form straight up. Though he is captive,
his mighty singing
says, satisfaction is a lowly
thing, how pure a thing is joy.   25
     This is mortality,
     this is eternity.

12. **silver ... grave.** "A silver fence was erected by Constantine to enclose the grave of Adam." *Literary Digest* 5th January, 1918, descriptive paragraph with photograph. 17. **lit ... glances,** A. R. Gordon: *The Poets of the Old Testament* (Hodder and Stoughton). (Author's notes.)

Four Quartz Crystal Clocks

THERE are four vibrators, the world's exact-
    est clocks;
and these quartz time-pieces that tell
    time intervals to other clocks,
these workless clocks work well;
and all four, independently the   5
    same, are there in the cool Bell
        Laboratory time

vault. Checked by a comparator with Arlington,
    they punctualize the "radio,
cinema," and "presse,"—a group the   10
    Giraudoux truth-bureau
of hoped-for accuracy has termed
    "instruments of truth." We know—
        as Jean Giraudoux says   14

certain Arabs have not heard—that Napoleon
    is dead; that a quartz prism when
the temperature changes, feels
    the change and that the then
electrified alternate edges
    oppositely charged, threaten   20
        careful timing; so that

this water-clear crystal as the Greeks used to
    say,
    this "clear ice" must be kept at the
same coolness. Repetition, with
    the scientist, should be   25
synonymous with accuracy.

The lemur-student can see
    that an aye-aye is not

an angwan-tibo, potto, or loris. The sea-
    side burden should not embarrass   30
the bell-buoy with the buoy-ball
    endeavoring to pass
hotel patronesses; nor could a
    practiced ear confuse the glass
        eyes for taxidermists   35

with eye-glasses from the optometrist. And as
    MEridian-7 1, 2
1, 2 gives, each fifteenth second
    in the same voice, the new
data—"The time will be" so and so—   40
    you realize that "when you
        hear the signal," you'll be

hearing Jupiter or jour pater, the day god—
    the salvaged son of Father Time—
telling the cannibal Chronos   45
    (eater of his proxime
newborn progeny) that punctual-
    ity is not a crime.

The Student

IN AMERICA," began
 the lecturer, "everyone must have a
degree. The French do not think that
all can have it, they don't say everyone
    must go to college." We   5
do incline to feel
    that although it may be unnecessary

to know fifteen languages,
one degree is not too much. With us, a
school—like the singing tree of which   10
the leaves were mouths singing in concert—is

Four . . . Clocks. The poet comments here, drawing chiefly on scientific theory, on Time's inevitability. Ironically, though man can build the clock that controls all clocks, and though man has precise time, he cannot escape the punctuality of death. **1. four . . . clocks.** Bell Telephone leaflet, 1939, "*The World's Most Accurate Clocks:* In the Bell Telephone Laboratories in New York, in a 'time vault' whose temperature is maintained within 1/100 of a degree, at 41° Centigrade, are the most accurate clocks in the world—the four quartz crystal clocks . . . When properly cut and inserted in a suitable circuit, they will control the rate of electric vibration to an accuracy of one part in a million. . . . When you call MEridian 7–1212 for correct time you get it every 15 seconds." (Author's note.) **11. Giraudoux . . . truth.** "Appeler à l'aide d'un camouflage ces instruments faits pour la verité qui sont la radio, le cinéma, la presse?"—Une allocution radio-diffusée de M. Giraudoux aux Françaises à propos de Sainte Catherine; the Figaro, November, 1939. ("To call to the aid of deception these instruments of truth, such as the radio, the moving pictures, the press."—A radio speech by M. Giraudoux to French women in regard to St. Catherine.) (Author's note.) **14. Jean Giraudoux,** French author, 1882–1944, who was French Commissioner of Information before World War II. **15. certain . . . dead.** "J'ai traversé voilà un an des pays arabes ou l'on ignorait encore que Napoléon était mort." ("For a year I travelled through Arabic countries where the people still did not know that Napoleon was dead.") **23. "clear ice."** The ancients believed that crystal was petrified ice.

27. lemur. The true lemur is a small animal of nocturnal habits found only in Madagascar. **28. aye-aye,** one of the lemurs. **29. angwan-tibo,** a tailless West African lemur. **potto,** a lemuroid, the West African slow-lemur. **loris,** a lemuroid found in Siam. These references to lemurs are references to being exact. **43. jour pater,** day father or day god. **45. cannibal Chronos.** Rhea, mother of Zeus, hid him from Chronos, who "devoured all his children except Jupiter (air), Neptune (water), and Pluto (the grave). These Time cannot consume." (Brewer's *Dictionary of Phrase and Fable.*) Chronos, from the Greek word for *time.*
The Student is a witty commentary on American education. The poet uses quotations to make the point that some think education is never ended, some that it makes us bookworms, some that the student needs patience above all things, some that he needs a free mind and his own opinion. The notes here given are Miss Moore's. **1. "In America."** Les Idéals de l'Education Française; lecture, December 3, 1931, by M. Auguste Desclos, Director-adjoint, Office National des Universités et Ecoles Françaises de Paris. **10. the singing tree.** Each leaf was a mouth, and every leaf joined in concert (*Arabian Nights' Entertainment*).

both a tree of knowledge
and of liberty,—
    seen in the unanimity of college

mottoes, *lux et veritas,*   15
Christo et ecclesiae, sapiet
felici. It may be that we
have not knowledge, just opinions, that we
    are undergraduates,
not students; we know   20
    we have been told with smiles, by expatriates

of whom we had asked "When will
your experiment be finished?" "Science
is never finished." Secluded
from domestic strife, Jack Bookworm led a   25
    college life, says Goldsmith;
and here also as
    in France or Oxford, study is beset with

dangers,—with bookworms, mildews,
and complaisancies. But someone in New   30
England has known enough to say
the student is patience personified,
    is a variety
of hero, "patient
    of neglect and of reproach,"—who can "hold
        by   35

himself." You can't beat hens to
make them lay. Wolf's wool is the best of wool,
but it cannot be sheared because
the wolf will not comply. With knowledge as
    with the wolf's surliness,   40
the student studies
    voluntarily, refusing to be less

than individual. He
"gives his opinion and then rests on it;"
he renders service when there is   45
no reward, and is too reclusive for
    some things to seem to touch
him, not because he
    has no feeling but because he has so much.

In Distrust of Merits

STRENGTHENED to live, strengthened to die for
    medals and position victories?
They're fighting and fighting, fighting the blind
    man who thinks he sees,—
who cannot see that the enslaver is   5
enslaved; the hater, harmed. O shining O
    firm star, O tumultuous
        ocean lashed till small things go
    as they will, the mountainous
        wave makes us who look, know   10

depth. Lost at sea before they fought! O
    star of David, star of Bethlehem,
O black imperial lion
    of the Lord—emblem
of a risen world—be joined at last, be   15
joined. There is hate's crown beneath which
        all is
    death; there's love's without which none
        is king; the blessed deeds bless
    the halo. As contagion
        of sickness makes sickness,   20

contagion of trust can make trust. They're
    fighting in deserts and caves, one by
one, in battalions and squadrons;
    they're fighting that I
may yet recover from the disease, My   25
self; some have it lightly, some will die. "Man's
    wolf to man" and we devour
        ourselves. The enemy could not
    have made a greater breach in our
        defenses. One pilot-   30

ing a blind man can escape him, but
    Job disheartened by false comfort knew
that nothing can be so defeating
    as a blind man who
can see. O alive who are dead, who are   35
proud not to see, O small dust of the earth
    that walks so arrogantly,

15. *lux et veritas,* light and truth, the motto of Yale.
16. *Christo et ecclesiae,* the motto of Harvard.   23. "Science ... finished," Professor Einstein to an American
student, *New York Times.* 25. Jack Bookworm, in Goldsmith's *The Double Transformation.*   33. a variety of hero,
Emerson in *The American Scholar:* "There can be no scholar
without the heroic mind"; "let him hold by himself . . . patient
of neglect, patient of reproach."   37. Wolf's wool. Edmund
Burke, November, 1781, in reply to Fox: "There is excellent
wool on the back of a wolf and therefore he must be sheared.
But will he comply?"   44. gives his opinion. Henry McBride
in the *New York Sun,* December 12, 1931: "Dr. Valentiner . . .
has the typical reserve of the student. He does not enjoy the
active battle of opinion that invariably rages when a decision
is announced that can be weighed in great sums of money. He
gives his opinion firmly and rests upon that."

"In Distrust of Merits" and "Keeping Their World Large,"
from *Nevertheless* by Marianne Moore, used by permission of
The Macmillan Company.
In ... Merits. The poet here comments on the tendency in
wartime to justify our position. Her prayer is that all religions
(since men of many religions fight under the same flag) may
come under the flag of love, not hate. She remarks on man's
historic cruelty to man, and refers to the story of Job to prove
that we are the more blind because we can see but cannot see
far enough. Finally, she points to the sacrifice of life, to the
necessary and agonizing patience of the soldier, insisting that
none of this sacrifice will gain us anything unless we conquer
the evil within ourselves.   13. O black imperial lion. In
Christian symbolism the lion anciently represented Christ.
32. Job, Hebrew prophet whose "comforters" brought him
nothing but bad news.

trust begets power and faith is
an affectionate thing. We
    vow, we make this promise   40
to the fighting—it's a promise—"We'll
    never hate black, white, red, yellow, Jew,
Gentile, Untouchable." We are
    not competent to   44
make our vows. With set jaw they are fighting,
fighting, fighting,—some we love whom we
        know,
some we love but know not—that
    hearts may feel and not be numb
It cures me; or am I what
    I can't believe in? Some   50

in snow, some on crags, some in quicksands,
    little by little, much by much, they
are fighting fighting fighting that where
    there was death there may
be life. "When a man is prey to anger,   55
he is moved by outside things; when he holds
    his ground in patience patience
      patience, that is action or
beauty," the soldier's defense
    and hardest armor for   60

the fight. The world's an orphans' home. Shall
    we never have peace without sorrow?
without pleas of the dying for
    help that won't come? O
quiet form upon the dust, I cannot   65
look and yet I must. If these great patient
    dyings—all these agonies
      and woundbearings and bloodshed—
can teach us how to live, these
    dyings were not wasted.   70

Hate-hardened heart, O heart of iron,
    iron is iron till it is rust.
There never was a war that was
    not inward; I must
fight till I have conquered in myself what   75
causes war, but I would not believe it.
    I inwardly did nothing.
      O Iscariotlike crime!
    Beauty is everlasting
      and dust is for a time.   80

Keeping Their World Large

> All too literally, their flesh and their
> spirit are our shield.
> *New York Times,* June 7, 1944

I SHOULD like to see that country's tiled bed-
    rooms,
stone patios
    and ancient wells: Rinaldo
Caramonica's the cobbler's, Frank Sblendorio's
    and Dominick Angelastro's country—   5
    the grocer's, the iceman's, the dancer's—
      the
beautiful Miss Damiano's; wisdom's

and all angels' Italy, this Christmas Day
this Christmas year.
    A noiseless piano, an   10
innocent war, the heart that acts against itself.
    Here,
    each unlike and all alike, could
    so many—stumbling, falling, multiplied
till bodies lay as ground to walk on—say   14

"If Christ and the apostles died in vain, I'll
die in vain with them"?
    When the very heart was a prayer
against this way of victory, stem after stem
    of what we call the tree—set, row   19
    on row; that forest of white crosses; the
vision makes us faint. My eyes won't close to
    it. While
the knife was lifted, Isaac the offering
lay mute.
    These, laid like animals for sacrifice,
like Isaac on the mount, were their own sub-
    stitute.   25
    And must they all be harmed by those
    whom they have saved? Tears that don't
    fall are what
they wanted. Belief in belief marching

---

55. **When a man is prey, etc.** In a series of lectures on immortality at the Brooklyn Institute several years ago, Professor Hocking quoted General Chiang Kai-Shek as saying:
"When a man is prey to passion he is moved by outside things,
but when he holds to his course in patience, that is action."
(Author's note.)

Keeping Their World Large. The poet is speaking of Italy,
used as ground for the fight against Germany, as our troops
invaded and fought there. This country, which in the First
World War was our ally, is seen by the poet in this war as
having been led into a battle for which the people had no heart.
She loves it for its simplicity, its ability to fight against poverty.
All too literally, etc. The phrase is quoted from the Rev.
James Gordon Gilkey.   **8. Christmas Day.** Despite the date
on the apposite quotation, this poem would appear to have
been written on Christmas, 1944.   **22. Isaac,** the beloved
son whom Abraham believed he had been ordered to sacrifice.

marching marching—all alone, all similar, spurning pathos, 30
    clothed in fear—marching to death marching to life; it was like the cross, is like the cross.
    Keeping their world large, that silent marching marching marching and this silence

32. **cross,** a reference to the crucifixion.

for which there is no description are 35
    the voices of fighters with no rests between, who would not yield;
    whose spirits and whose bodies all too literally were our shield, are still our shield.
    They fought the enemy, we fight 40
    fat living and self-pity. Shine O shine unfalsifying sun, on this sick scene.

EZRA POUND

Ezra Loomis Pound, a distant relative of Henry Wadsworth Longfellow, was born in Hailey, Idaho, October 30, 1885. He entered the University of Pennsylvania as a special student at fifteen and finally graduated from Hamilton College in 1905 with the degree of Ph.B. He returned to the University of Pennsylvania on a fellowship in Romance languages, for which he had a remarkable aptitude, and was an instructor there from 1905 to 1907, receiving his M.A. in 1906. Before he left for Europe to get material for a dissertation on the Spanish playwright Lope de Vega, he was an instructor at Wabash College, Crawfordsville, Indiana, for four months.

Pound remained in Europe from 1907 until 1939, when a visit to this country was cut short on the advice of his friends who thought his open defense of fascism might get him into trouble. He set the example for those prejudiced poets in exile who left the United States after World War I in protest against what they thought was our lack of culture and tradition. In light of Pound's later development it is important to record that he was one of the first to cover up his attack on democracy by complaining against the poverty of esthetic response in America.

For a year after he went abroad, Pound traveled through Spain, Italy, and Provence. In Venice he published his first book of poems, *A Lume Spento* (1908). He then went to England and lived in London for about ten years. Here he did translations, lectured, and contributed to the *Fortnightly Review, The Dial,* and *Poetry. Personae* and *Exultations* were published in 1909, and in 1914 he edited the first anthology of Imagist verse. While he considers himself the founder of the Imagist school, the wealthier and more energetic Amy Lowell later appropriated leadership of the Imagists. Until 1919 Pound was foreign correspondent of *Poetry,* and from 1917 to 1919 London editor of *The Little Review.* In 1920 he moved to Paris for four years and then on to Rapallo, Italy, working on his *Cantos* and contributing occasionally to magazines. The year Pound was given the Dial Award, 1927, he and Pascal Covici founded *The Exile.*

Among Pound's published works are *Provença* (1910), *Ripostes* (1912), *Lustra* (1916, 1917), *Quia Pauper Amavi* (1919), *Poems 1918–1921* (1921), *Personae* (1926), *Selected Poems* (1928) with an introduction by T. S. Eliot; *A Draft of XXX Cantos* (1933), *Eleven New Cantos* (1934), *The Fifth Decad of Cantos* (1937), *Cantos LII–LXXI* (1940), and *The Pisan Cantos* (Nos. 74–84, 1948). All eighty-four of the completed cantos were collected in one volume in 1948. Some of his prose works are: *A B C of Economics* (1933), *A B C of Reading* (1934), *Guide to Kulchur* (1938), and his radio broadcasts to the United States during World War II, for which he was indicted for treason.

His prose works are confused, rather violent, and snobbish statements as to what every well-educated man should know and what by implication every American does not know. Pound has consistently denounced his American reviewers and the American reading public, despite various kinds of recognition he received here. After Pearl Harbor he insisted on staying in Italy, refusing to sail on the *Drottningholm*, which carried American citizens from the Axis countries in 1943. Instead, he became a fascist radio propagandist for the Italian government, specializing in short wave broadcasts to the United States calling upon us to surrender. Early in 1946 he was brought from Italy to stand trial for treason. A plea of insanity was made, and on the advice of eminent doctors Pound was committed to an institution. Since his commitment for insanity, he has been allowed to publish further poems, the themes of which are not precisely democratic.

Pound's dislike of the American people is not a recent development. It had been expressed in numerous early essays and letters, for example, some of his imaginary letters of Walter Villerant to Mrs. Bland Burn, dealing with the future of art.

Unfortunately the turmoil of Letts, Finns, Esthonians, Cravats, Niberians, Nubians, Algerians, sweeping along Eighth Avenue in the splendor of the vigorous unwashed animality will not help us. They are the America of tomorrow. . . . It is rubbish to say "art of the people lies behind us." The populace was paid to attend Greek drama. It would have gone to cinemas instead, had cinemas then existed. Art begins with the artist. It goes first to the very few; and next, to the few very very idle. Even Journalism and advertising can not reverse this law.

His work continues to be honored by various little magazines in this country. In 1949 he was awarded the first annual thousand-dollar Bollingen Prize for his *Pisan Cantos*.

Dance Figure

FOR THE MARRIAGE IN CANA OF GALILEE

Dark eyed,
O woman of my dreams,
Ivory sandaled,
There is none like thee among the dancers,
None with swift feet.   5

I have not found thee in the tents,
In the broken darkness.
I have not found thee at the well-head
Among the women with pitchers.

Thine arms are as a young sapling under the
    bark;   10
Thy face as a river with lights.

White as an almond are thy shoulders;
As new almonds stripped from the husk.
They guard thee not with eunuchs;
Not with bars of copper.   15

Gilt turquoise and silver are in the place of thy
    rest.
A brown robe, with threads of gold woven in
    patterns, hast thou gathered about thee,
O Nathat-Ikanaie, "Tree-at-the-river."

As a rillet among the sedge are thy hands upon
    me;
Thy fingers a frosted stream.   20

Thy maidens are white like pebbles;
Their music about thee!

There is none like thee among the dancers;
None with swift feet.

Ancient Music

Winter is icummen in,
    Lhude sing Goddamm,
Raineth drop and staineth slop,
And how the wind doth ramm!
        Sing: Goddamm.   5

"Dance Figure," "Ancient Music," and "Exile's Letter" from *Personae* by Ezra Pound, reprinted by permission of Liveright Publishing Corporation.
1. **Cana of Galilee.** Jesus and his mother were at a wedding in Cana of Galilee, and Jesus turned the water into wine. This was the beginning of Christ's miracles in Galilee.   19. **rillet,** small stream.
Ancient Music. This is a parody on "Sumer is icumen in," a medieval lyric.

Skiddeth bus and sloppeth us,
An ague hath my ham.
Freezeth river, turneth liver,
   Damn you, sing: Goddamm.
Goddamm, Goddamm, 'tis why I am, God-
  damm,   10
   So 'gainst the winter's balm.
Sing goddamm, damm, sing Goddamm,
Sing goddamm, sing goddamm, DAMM.

Exile's Letter

To So-Kin of Rakuyo, ancient friend, Chan-
 cellor of Gen.
Now I remember that you built me a special
 tavern
By the south side of the bridge at Ten-Shin.
With yellow gold and white jewels, we paid
 for songs and laughter
And we were drunk for month on month, for-
 getting the kings and princes.   5
Intelligent men came drifting in from the sea
 and from the west border,
And with them, and with you especially
There was nothing at cross purpose,
And they made nothing of sea-crossing or of
 mountain-crossing,
If only they could be of that fellowship, 10
And we all spoke out our hearts and minds,
 and without regret.
And then I was sent off to South Wei, smoth-
 ered in laurel groves,
And you to the north of Raku-hoku,
Till we had nothing but thoughts and mem-
 ories in common.
And then, when separation had come to its
 worst,   15
We met, and travelled into Sen-Go,
Through all the thirty-six folds of the turning
 and twisting waters,
Into a valley of the thousand bright flowers,
That was the first valley;
And into ten thousand valleys full of voices
 and pine-winds.   20
And with silver harness and reins of gold,

Out came the East of Kan foreman and his
 company.
And there came also the "True man" of Shiyo
 to meet me,
Playing on a jewelled mouth-organ.
In the storied houses of San-Ko they gave us
 more Sennin music,   25
Many instruments, like the sound of young
 phoenix broods.
The foreman of Kan Chu, drunk, danced be-
 cause his long sleeves wouldn't keep
 still
With that music playing,
And I, wrapped in brocade, went to sleep with
 my head on his lap,
And my spirit so high it was all over the
 heavens,   30
And before the end of the day we were scat-
 tered like stars, or rain.
I had to be off to So, far away over the waters,
You back to your river-bridge.

And your father, who was brave as a leopard,
Was governor in Hei Shu, and put down the
 barbarian rabble.   35
And one May he had you send for me, despite
 the long distance.
And what with broken wheels and so on, I
 won't say it wasn't hard going,
Over roads twisted like sheep's guts.
And I was still going, late in the year, in the
 cutting wind from the North,
And thinking how little you cared for the cost,
 and you caring enough to pay it. 40
And what a reception:
Red jade cups, food well set on a blue jew-
 elled table,
And I was drunk, and had no thought of re-
 turning.
And you would walk out with me to the west-
 ern corner of the castle,
To the dynastic temple, with water about it
 clear as blue jade,   45
With boats floating, and the sound of mouth-
 organs and drums.

Exile's Letter. This is a poem adapted for the most part by Pound from the Chinese of Rihaku, from the notes of the late Ernest Fenollosa and the decipherings of Professors Mori and Agiga. Rihaku was a Chinese poet of the eighth century.

23. **"True man,"** a man transformed into a genius or super-natural being. 25. **Sennin music,** supernatural or fairy music. 45. **dynastic temple,** ancestral temple of the imperial household.

With ripples like dragon-scales, going grass
    green on the water,
Pleasure lasting, with courtezans, going and
    coming without hindrance,
With the willow flakes falling like snow,
And the vermilioned girls getting drunk about
    sunset,   50
And the water, a hundred feet deep, reflecting
    green eyebrows
—Eyebrows painted green are a fine sight in
    young moonlight,
Gracefully painted—
And the girls singing back at each other,
Dancing in transparent brocade,   55
And the wind lifting the song, and interrupt-
    ing it,
Tossing it up under the clouds.
        And all this comes to an end.
        And is not again to be met with.
I went up to the court for examination,   60

Tried Layu's luck, offered the Choyo song,
And got no promotion,
        and went back to the East Mountains
        White-headed.
And once again, later, we met at the South
    bridge-head.   65
And then the crowd broke up, you went north
    to San palace,
And if you ask how I regret that parting:
It is like the flowers falling at Spring's end
    Confused, whirled in a tangle.
What is the use of talking, and there is no end
    of talking,   70
There is no end of things in the heart.
I call in the boy,
Have him sit on his knees here
        To seal this,
And send it a thousand miles, thinking.

61. **Layu,** probably some Chinese figure thought to bring good luck to examination candidates.

ROBINSON JEFFERS

John Robinson Jeffers' family is pre-revolutionary American, except for a paternal grandfather from North Ireland. Jeffers, who was born January 10, 1887, in Pittsburgh, was first taken abroad at the age of five. From the ages of twelve to fifteen he lived in Europe, attending schools there. During the summers he took walking trips with his father in the Swiss Alps. At fifteen he returned to America and entered Occidental College, Los Angeles, from which he graduated at eighteen. Later he spent some time studying at the University of Southern California, the University of Zurich, and a medical school in Los Angeles. In 1914 he received a legacy which left him free to devote his time to literature. He has published many books since 1925, when he began to be known as a dramatic and narrative poet. Among these are *The Women at Point Sur* (1927), *Cawdor* (1928), *Dear Judas* (1929), *Descent to the Dead* (1931), *Give Your Heart to the Hawks* (1933), *Solstice* (1935), *Such Counsels You Gave to Me* (1937); *The Selected Poetry of Robinson Jeffers* (1938), *Be*

Angry at the Sun (1941), and *The Double Axe and Other Poems* (1948).

Not until he published *Roan Stallion* in 1925, the first of his many narrative and dramatic poems, was Robinson Jeffers known to any considerable number of readers. He was then about forty and had published books of more conventional poems—*Flagons and Apples* (1912), *Californians* (1916), and even one long narrative, *Tamar* (1924), later a part of the *Roan Stallion* volume. These, however, had not created much favorable comment. Once Jeffers became known as the poet of strange stories in which Freudian symbolism and a kind of primitivism mingled with violent drama, he attracted considerable attention. California claimed him for her own, for he had settled in Carmel and built his house there out of worn boulders of gray Santa Lucia granite, on a low bluff a hundred feet from the foam line of the Pacific. This home, which he shares with his wife, Una Call Kuster, whom he married in 1913, and their twin sons born in 1916, is a copy of an old Tudor barn in Surrey. Practically unaided, moreover, Jeffers built himself a thirty-foot tower of the same ocean boulders. The ground floor belonged to the twins, Garth and Donnan, and the second floor to Mrs. Jeffers; the third floor is Jeffers' own studio, a tiny cell with a table and chair. The outlook from the tower, which took seven years to build, is very beautiful. Jeffers' passion for stone-masonry, tree planting, and swimming, his strong vigorous body, and his rather unusually chiseled face have made him the truly picturesque poet. His desire, however, has been always for a quiet life, and he hates meddlers.

Repudiating our commercial civilization, Jeffers has turned to stories of the backwoods Californians, for him the people in whom primitive passion has most play. Actually, his characters are not the simple people of the California hills but types he has himself created. Like the characters of Greek tragedy they are committed to violence. Indeed, all of Jeffers' stories show the influence of Greek tragedy and of Freud's theories of psychology. Each character is a symbol. In his poetry man is the creative force; woman, usually, the force necessary for the conservation of the race. Man, Jeffers believes, has been imprisoned by institutions and by the need of making money. He should try to free himself of the usual mold of human-

ity and become again a superman. He must reject society and reject the God of Love represented by the Christian God. He can become free only by identifying himself with the true Nature god, the god of storm, violence, and action who frees man from the usual codes of law and from the modern stereotyped way of living.

He believes, too, that in committing violent acts man may be seeking to identify himself with the violence of nature, may be allowing his impulses proper play, and may become free. Jeffers read much of Nietzsche and absorbed the theory that only through passionate individualism was man great. Such a philosophy leads him to believe, politically, in a rather dangerous individual anarchism, almost fascist indeed. With any theory of society which emphasizes complete equality among men he will have nothing to do. Jeffers desires tragic terror and high-pitched emotion.

During World War II he was openly antiwar. Such an attitude is an ironic corollary to the personal violence running through his poetry. All that he can conclude from the historic victory over world fascism is that we must return to the Nietzschean patterns of belief and culture wherein the individual remains sole dictator of his acts.

Meditation on Saviors

I

WHEN I considered it too closely, when I wore it like an element and smelt it like water,
  Life is become less lovely, the net nearer than the skin, a little troublesome, a little terrible.

I pledged myself awhile ago not to seek refuge, neither in death nor in a walled garden,
In lies nor gated loyalties, nor in the gates of contempt, that easily lock the world out of doors.

Here on the rock it is great and beautiful, here on the foam-wet granite sea-fang it is easy to
    praise
                                                                                                5
Life and water and the shining stones: but whose cattle are the herds of the people that one
    should love them?

"Meditation on Saviors" from *Cawdor and Other Poems;* "Night," "Promise of Peace," and "The Tower beyond Tragedy" from *Roan Stallion, Tamar and Other Poems;* "The Trap" from *Solstice;* reprinted by permission of Random House, Inc., New York. "Shine, Empire" and "Black-Out" from *Be Angry at the Sun* by Robinson Jeffers, copyright, 1941, by Robinson Jeffers, reprinted by permission of Random House, Inc.

Meditation on Saviors. This is Jeffers' statement of his lack of identification with the common people, of his supreme individualism. He dislikes the fact that men who should be in his mind supermen and powerful, lean either on the Christian God who counsels humility or on humanitarian social philosophies.

If they were yours, then you might take a cattle-breeder's delight in the herds of the future. Not
    yours.
Where the power ends let love, before it sours to jealousy. Leave the joys of government to
    Caesar.

Who is born when the world wanes, when the brave soul of the world falls on decay in the
    flesh increasing   9
Comes one with a great level mind, sufficient vision, sufficient blindness, and clemency for love.

This is the breath of rottenness I smelt; from the world waiting, stalled between storms, de-
    caying a little,
Bitterly afraid to be hurt, but knowing it cannot draw the savior Caesar but out of the blood-
    bath.

The apes of Christ lift up their hands to praise love: but wisdom without love is the present
    savior,
Power without hatred, mind like a many-bladed machine subduing the world with deep indif-
    ference.

The apes of Christ itch for a sickness they have never known; words and the little envies will
    hardly   15
Measure against that blinding fire behind the tragic eyes they have never dared to confront.

II

Point Lobos lies over the hollowed water like a humped whale swimming to shoal; Point Lobos
Was wounded with that fire; the hills at Point Sur endured it; the palace at Thebes; the hill
    Calvary.

Out of incestuous love power and then ruin. A man forcing the imaginations of men,
Possessing with love and power the people: a man defiling his own household with impious
    desire.   20

King Oedipus reeling blinded from the palace doorway, red tears pouring from the torn pits
Under the forehead; and the young Jew writhing on the domed hill in the earthquake, against
    the eclipse

Frightfully uplifted for having turned inward to love the people:—that root was so sweet Oh,
    dreadful agonist?—
I saw the same pierced feet, that walked in the same crime to its expiation; I heard the same
    cry.

A bad mountain to build your world on. Am I another keeper of the people, that on my own
    shore,   25
On the gray rock, by the grooved mass of the ocean, the sicknesses I left behind me concern me?

Here where the surf has come incredible ways out of the splendid west, over the deeps
Light nor life sounds forever; here where enormous sundowns flower and burn through color
    to quietness;

---

8. **Caesar,** that is, a dictator. 12. **blood-bath,** revolution. 17. **Point Lobos,** near Carmel, California, where Jeffers lives.
21. **Oedipus,** the King of Thebes, who blinded himself in remorse. 22. **domed hill,** Calvary, where Christ was crucified.

Then the ecstasy of the stars is present? As for the people, I have found my rock, let them find
    theirs.
Let them lie down at Caesar's feet and be saved; and he in his time reap their daggers of grati-
    tude.
        30

III

Yet I am the one made pledges against the refuge contempt, that easily locks the world out of
    doors.
This people as much as the sea-granite is part of the God from whom I desire not to be fugitive.

I see them: they are always crying. The shored Pacific makes perpetual music, and the stone
    mountains
Their music of silence, the stars blow long pipings of light: the people are always crying in their
    hearts.

One need not pity; certainly one must not love. But who has seen peace, if he should tell them
    where peace
        35
Lives in the world . . . they would be powerless to understand; and he is not willing to be re-
    involved.

IV

How should one caught in the stone of his own person dare tell the people anything but relative
    to that?
But if a man could hold in his mind all the conditions at once, of man and woman, of civilized

And barbarous, of sick and well, of happy and under torture, of living and dead, of human and
    not
Human, and dimly all the human future:—what should persuade him to speak? And what could
    his words change?
        40

The mountain ahead of the world is not forming but fixed. But the man's words would be fixed
    also,
Part of that mountain, under equal compulsion; under the same present compulsion in the iron
    consistency.

And nobody sees good or evil but out of a brain a hundred centuries quieted, some desert
Prophet's, a man humped like a camel, gone mad between the mud-walled village and the
    mountain sepulchres.

V

Broad wagons before sunrise bring food into the city from the open farms, and the people are
    fed.
        45
They import and they consume reality. Before sunrise a hawk in the desert made them their
    thoughts.

VI

Here is an anxious people, rank with suppressed blood-thirstiness. Among the mild and unwar-
    like
Gautama needed but live greatly and be heard, Confucius needed but live greatly and be heard.

31. **Yet I . . . doors,** Jeffers' statement that he has not allowed himself to retire from life because of his contempt of men.
37. **How should . . . that?** How can anyone judge save for himself?   46. **They import . . . thoughts,** a comment on our
materialistic way of living and (in the image of a hawk) the idea that man really exists only through remembered ideas of freedom.   47. **Here is, etc.** A belief in great men of history is here stated.   48. **Gautama,** Buddha.

This people has not outgrown blood-sacrifice, one must writhe on the high cross to catch at
their memories;
The price is known. I have quieted love; for love of the people I would not do it. For power I
would do it.   50

—But that stands against reason: what is power to a dead man, dead under torture?—What is
power to a man
Living, after the flesh is content? Reason is never a root, neither of act nor desire.

For power living I would never do it; they are not delightful to touch, one wants to be separate. For power
After the nerves are put away underground, to lighten the abstract unborn children toward
peace . . .

A man might have paid anguish indeed. Except he had found the standing sea-rock that even
this last   55
Temptation breaks on; quieter than death but lovelier; peace that quiets the desire even of
praising it.

VII

Yet look: are they not pitiable? No: if they lived forever they would be pitiable:
But a huge gift reserved quite overwhelms them at the end; they are able then to be still and
not cry.

And having touched a little of the beauty and seen a little of the beauty of things, magically
grow   59
Across the funeral fire or the hidden stench of burial themselves into the beauty they admired,

Themselves into the God, themselves into the sacred steep unconsciousness they used to mimic
Asleep between lamp's death and dawn, while the last drunkard stumbled homeward down the
dark street.

They are not to be pitied but very fortunate; they need no savior, salvation comes and takes
them by force,
It gathers them into the great kingdoms of dust and stone, the blown storms, the stream's-end
ocean.

With this advantage over their granite grave-marks, of having realized the petulant human consciousness   65
Before, and then the greatness, the peace: drunk from both pitchers: these to be pitied? These
not fortunate?

But while he lives let each man make his health in his mind, to love the coast opposite humanity
And so be freed of love, laying it like bread on the waters; it is worst turned inward, it is best
shot farthest.

Love, the mad wine of good and evil, the saint's and murderer's, the mote in the eye that makes
its object
Shine the sun black; the trap in which it is better to catch the inhuman God than the hunter's
own image.

50. **love**, "the mad wine of good and evil"; love of people or personal love is either good or evil but always blinding.

Night

THE EBB slips from the rock, the sunken
    Tide-rocks lift streaming shoulders
Out of the slack, the slow west
Sombering its torch; a ship's light
Shows faintly, far out,   5
Over the weight of the prone ocean
On the low cloud.

Over the dark mountain, over the dark pine-
    wood,
Down the long dark valley along the shrunken
    river,
Returns the splendor without rays, the shining
    of shadow,   10
Peace-bringer, the matrix of all shining and
    quieter of shining.
Where the shore widens on the bay she opens
    dark wings
And the ocean accepts her glory. O soul wor-
    shipful of her
You like the ocean have grave depths where
    she dwells always,
And the film of waves above that takes the sun
    takes also   15
Her, with more love. The sun-lovers have a
    blonde favorite,
A father of lights and noises, wars, weeping
    and laughter,
Hot labor, lust and delight and the other blem-
    ishes. Quietness
Flows from her deeper fountain; and he will
    die; and she is immortal.

Far off from here the slender   20
Flocks of the mountain forest
Move among stems like towers
Of the old redwoods to the stream,
No twig crackling; dip shy
Wild muzzles into the mountain water   25
Among the dark ferns.

O passionately at peace you being secure will
    pardon
The blasphemies of glowworms, the lamp in
    my tower, the fretfulness

Night, a statement of Jeffers' identification with the vast and
powerful forces of nature—his own variety of pantheism or a
faith in the deity expressed by violence in nature, after which
comes peace.   3. **slack,** the period between high and low tide.
28. **The . . . glowworms,** night, a pantheistic symbol of peace
following upon tumult. Such peace or oblivion is asked to pardon lights on earth and in the heavens.

Of cities, the crescents of the planets, the
    pride of the stars.
This August night in a rift of cloud Antares
    reddens,   30
The great one, the ancient torch, a lord among
    lost children,
The earth's orbit doubled would not girdle his
    greatness, one fire
Globed, out of grasp of the mind enormous;
    but to you O night
What? Not a spark? What flicker of a spark in
    the faint far glimmer
Of a lost fire dying in the desert, dim coals of
    a sand-pit the Bedouins   35
Wandered from a dawn . . . Ah singing
    prayer to what gulfs tempted
Suddenly are you more lost? To us the near-
    hand mountain
Be a measure of height, the tide-worn cliff at
    the sea-gate a measure of continuance.

The tide, moving the night's
Vastness with lonely voices,   40
Turns, the deep dark-shining
Pacific leans on the land,
Feeling his cold strength
To the outmost margins: you Night will resume
The stars in your time.   45

O passionately at peace when will that tide
    draw shoreward?
Truly the spouting fountains of light, Antares,
    Arcturus,
Tire of their flow, they sing one song but they
    think silence.
The striding winter giant Orion shines, and
    dreams darkness.
And life, the flicker of men and moths and the
    wolf on the hill,   50
Though furious for continuance, passionately
    feeding, passionately
Remaking itself upon its mates, remembers
    deep inward
The calm mother, the quietness of the womb
    and the egg,
The primal and the latter silences: dear Night
    it is memory
Prophesies, prophecy that remembers, the
    charm of the dark.   55
And I and my people, we are willing to love
    the four-score years
Heartily; but as a sailor loves the sea, when the
    helm is for harbor.

Have men's minds changed,
Or the rock hidden in the deep of the waters of
the soul
Broken the surface? A few centuries   60
Gone by, was none dared not to people
The darkness beyond the stars with harps and
habitations.
But now, dear is the truth. Life is grown
sweeter and lonelier,
And death is no evil.

Promise of Peace

THE HEADS of strong old age are beautiful
Beyond all grace of youth. They have
strange quiet,
Integrity, health, soundness, to the full
They've dealt with life and been attempered
by it.   4
A young man must not sleep; his years are war
Civil and foreign but the former's worse;
But the old can breathe in safety now that they
are
Forgetting what youth meant, the being per-
verse,
Running the fool's gauntlet and being cut
By the whips of the five senses. As for me,   10
If I should wish to live long it were but
To trade those fevers for tranquillity,
Thinking though that's entire and sweet in the
grave
How shall the dead taste the deep treasure
they have?

The Trap

I AM NOT well civilized, really alien here:
trust me not.
I can understand the guns and the airplanes,
The other conveniences leave me cold.

"We must adjust our economics to the new
abundance . . ."
Of what? Toys: motors, music-boxes,   5
Paper, fine clothes, leisure, diversion.

I honestly believe (but really an alien here:
trust me not)
Blind war, compared to this kind of life,
Has nobility, famine has dignity.

The Trap. Jeffers will accept any intensity rather than the
commonplace or monotonous. He thinks men's scientific development and economic thoughts have led them only into the
idea of the leveling off of all differences in individuality.

Be happy, adjust your economics to the new
abundance;   10
One is neither saint nor devil, to wish
The intolerable nobler alternative.

from The Tower beyond Tragedy

CASSANDRA

IF ANYWHERE in the world
Were a tower with foundations, or a treas-
ure-chamber
With a firm vault, or a walled fortress
That stood on the years, not staggering, not
moving   4
As the mortar were mixed with wine for water
And poppy for lime: they reel, they are all
drunkards,
The piled strengths of the world: no pyramid
In bitter Egypt in the desert
But skips at moonrise; no mountain
Over the Black Sea in awful Caucasus   10
But whirls like a young kid, like a bud of the
herd,
Under the hundredth star: I am sick after
steadfastness
Watching the world cataractlike
Pour screaming onto steep ruins: for the wings
of prophecy
God once my lover give me stone sandals   15
Planted on stone: he hates me, the God, he
will never
Take home the gift of the bridleless horse
The stallion, the unbitted stallion: the bed
Naked to the sky on Mount Ida,
The soft clear grass there,   20
Be blackened forever, may vipers and Greeks
In that glen breed
Twisting together, where the God
Come golden from the sun
Gave me for a bride-gift prophecy and I took
it for a treasure: 25
I a fool, I a maiden,
I would not let him touch me though love of
him maddened me
Till he fed me that poison, till he planted that
fire in me,
The girdle flew loose then.

The Tower beyond Tragedy tells of Orestes' and Electra's
killing of Clytemnestra, their mother, a theme widely used in
Greek classical drama. It is used here as a kind of allegory to
imply that modern man must free himself from institutionalized
ideas of right and wrong if he is again to become great. The
prophecy here is of the complete instability of the modern world.
1. Cassandra, see note, p. 44. 18. stallion, in this poem the
symbol of creative energy.

Shine, Empire

POWERFUL and armed, neutral in the midst of madness, we might have held the whole world's
    balance and stood
Like a mountain in a wind. We were misled and took sides. We have chosen to share the crime
    and the punishment.

Perhaps justly, being part of Europe. Three thousand miles of ocean would hardly wash out the
    stains
Of all that mish-mash, blood, language, religion, snobbery. Three thousand miles in a ship
    would not make Americans.

I have often in weak moments thought of this people as something higher than the natural run
    of the earth.
I was quite wrong; we are lower. We are the people who hope to win wars with money as we
    win elections.   5

Hate no one. Roosevelt's intentions were good, and Hitler is a patriot. They have split the
    planet into two millstones
That will grind small and bloody; but still let us keep some dignity, these days are tragic, and
    fight without hating.

It is war, and no man can see an end of it. We must put freedom away and stiffen into bitter
    empire.
All Europe was hardly worth the precarious freedom of one of our states: what will her ashes
    fetch?   10

If I were hunting in the Ventana canyons again with my strong sons, and to sleep under stars,
I should be happy again. It is not time for happiness. Happy the blind, the witless, the dead.

Now, thoroughly compromised, we aim at world rule, like Assyria, Rome, Britain, Germany,
    to inherit those hordes
Of guilt and doom. I am American, what can I say but again, "Shine, perishing republic?" . . .
    Shine, empire.

Black-Out

THE WAR that we have carefully for years provoked
    Comes on us unprepared, amazed and indignant. Our warships are shot
Like sitting ducks and our planes like nest-birds, both our coasts ridiculously panicked,
And our leaders make orations. This is the people
That hopes to impose on the whole planetary world   5
An American peace.
        (Oh, we'll win our war. My money on amazed Gulliver
And his horse-pistols.)
            Meanwhile our prudent officers

Shine, Empire is one of Jeffers' several poems against World War II. He was, in general, isolationist, refusing to take sides, regarding man's madness and civilization's emphasis on money as the reasons for desire for power. Before the discussion of imperialistic motivation for war was general he pointed out how war makes for an empire-like centering of power. **11. Ventana canyons,** canyons in the Point Lobos section of California, where Jeffers lives and which he makes the constant stark and tragic backdrop for action in his poetry.
Black-Out. The poem expresses Jeffers' anti-war mood. Earlier he had said that if it were a choice between socialism and leveling out society and a centralized idea of power, he would choose power rather than mediocrity. **7. amazed Gulliver.** The hero of Jonathan Swift's satire found that despite his weapons, he was no match for the Lilliputians.

Have cleared the coast-long ocean of ships and fishing-craft, the sky of planes, the windows of
    light: these clearings
Make a strange beauty. Watch the wide sea, there is nothing human, the gulls have it. Watch
    the wide sky,   10
All day clean of machines, only at dawn and dusk a military hawk passes
High on patrol. Walk at night on the shore,
The pretty firefly spangle that used to line it
Perfectly silent, shut are the shops, mouse-dark the houses.
            Here the prehuman dignity of night   15
Stands, as it was and will be again. Oh beautiful
Darkness and silence, the two eyes that see God. Great staring eyes.

E. E. CUMMINGS

Edward Estlin Cummings was born in Cambridge, Massachusetts, October 14, 1894, the son of Edward and Rebecca Haswell (Clarke) Cummings. His father was a professor at Harvard and Radcliffe and later a Unitarian clergyman in Boston. The younger Edward received his B.A. from Harvard in 1915, his M.A. in 1916. In 1917 he joined the Norton Harjes Ambulance Division and was sent overseas, driving an ambulance for six months. Then for some epistolary indiscretion he was sentenced to prison. He was sent home soon after and became a private in Camp Devens, Massachusetts. In 1922 he published *The Enormous Room*, a study of a prison which indicated clearly his disillusionment concerning war. *Tulips and Chimneys*, his first book of verse, was published in 1923. In 1926 he published a book of verse called *is 5*, to which he wrote a preface stating that he was interested in making poems, that poets rejoiced in the irresistible fact that for them 2 times 2 is often 5. *Him*, a poetic play concerning man as artist, man as lover, and man as an ordinary and often vulgar human being, was published in 1927. Other books of verse, entitled *&, XLI Poems* (1925), *W. (Viva)* (1931), *No Thanks* (1935), and *New Poems*, were privately printed and later made available to the general public in *Collected Poems* (1938). In 1931 Cummings published a book of his paintings and drawings entitled *C.I.O.P.W.*, meaning charcoal, ink, oil, pencil, and water color. *Eimi* (1933), written in prose and poetry, dealt with his trip to Rus-

sia. He criticized the Soviet Union because he felt that it afforded no variety of impressions. *Tom*, a ballet on the theme of *Uncle Tom's Cabin*, appeared in 1935, and *1 x 1* was published in 1944. In 1946 he wrote *Santa Claus*, and an introduction to George Herriman's *Krazy Kat*, analyzing the perversity of Krazy Kat.

The later Cummings remains a romanticist and perhaps also something of a snob, disliking any attempt to bring order in our chaotic times. Today he more frequently attacks and mocks democracy, the middle class, the common foibles, and the common people. He lingers in that last fortress of the Art for Art's Sake movement, intellectual anarchism which tries to be superior to everything and everyone normal and usual. Here, in Cummings, as in other poets who believe as he does, one sees a fear masked in disdain for the common people; the desire is strong in him to believe in the artist's superiority.

Cummings has been famous for his special use of typography to indicate, in general, how a poem reads. Believing that poetry is today seldom read aloud, he seeks to present to the eyes by means of broken line-links, curious punctuation, and capitalization the rhythm of the poem and the special importance of certain words. He argues that typography should indicate the meaning of the poet, and he therefore breaks all the rules of conventional poetic stanzas. His sonnets, for example, although they scan perfectly, may be printed in more than fourteen lines, when the reader's eye can supposedly catch the significance of the poem better if the regular five-foot line is broken and printed as two or more lines. Like many of the modern poets Cummings uses lower-case letters for such words as *i* and *god* to indicate that neither individual nor deity is today allowed any particular reverence. Actually, his peculiarities of punctuation, capitalization, and typography follow no set rules. His idiosyncrasies express his individuality and his philosophy. The world is for him a place in which all truths are questionable, an amusing, many-sided place for one who has no particular faith and likes contradiction. Cummings is, as he describes himself, a tightrope artist balancing three chairs—the man, the lover, the artist, while the world below him watches. In other words, he is an ardent individualist and a romantic who writes love poetry either of a romantic vein or of a purely sensual vein. In his satiric poems Cummings is intent on laughing at the home, religion, patriotism, and at all our revered institutions.

He was the wit and the clown in the poetry of World War I, the humorist idling in the Waste Land. During the New Deal period little was written on or about him, and it has taken the growing disillusionment since VJ-Day to bring Cummings into the limelight again. Today he is becoming again the vogue: brittle, brilliant, non-intellectual, almost naughty, always non-democratic because of his horror of middle-class mores, singing romantically of a cockeyed world where rich and poor by their very contradictions should give the poet a point of departure for imagery. For Cummings perversity is enough.

One VI

Jimmie's got a goil
                goil
                    goil,
                        Jimmie
's got a goil and
she coitnly can shimmie

"One VI," "Two XI," "One XI" from *is 5*, and "LI" from *W*, by E. E. Cummings, reprinted by permission of Liveright Publishing Corporation.

when you see her shake
            shake
                shake,
                    when
you see her shake a   5
shimmie how you wish that you was Jimmie.

Oh for such a gurl
            gurl
                gurl,
                    oh
for such a gurl to
be a fellow's twistandtwirl

talk about your Sal-
            Sal-
                Sal-,
                    talk   10
about your Salo
-mes but gimmie Jimmie's gal.

Two XI

My sweet old etcetera
aunt lucy during the recent

war could and what
is more did tell you just
what everybody was fighting   5
for,
my sister

isabel created hundreds
(and
hundreds) of socks not to   10
mention shirts fleaproof earwarmers

etcetera wristers etcetera, my
mother hoped that

i would die etcetera
bravely of course my father used   15
to become hoarse talking about how it was
a privilege and if only he
could meanwhile my

self etcetera lay quietly
in the deep mud et   20

11. **Salome.** Salome danced so beautifully before King Herod that he granted her the head of John the Baptist. Here the name is used humorously to indicate that "Jimmie's gal" is a better dancer than Salome.

271

cetera
(dreaming,
et
   cetera, of
Your smile 25
eyes knees and of your Etcetera)

One XI

Nobody loses all the time

i had an uncle named
Sol who was a born failure and
nearly everybody said he should have gone
into vaudeville perhaps because my Uncle Sol
could 5
sing McCann He Was A Diver on Xmas Eve
like Hell Itself which
may or may not account for the fact that my
Uncle

Sol indulged in that possibly most inexcusable
of all to use a highfalootin phrase
luxuries that is or to 10
wit farming and be
it needlessly
added

my Uncle Sol's farm
failed because the chickens 15
ate the vegetables so
my Uncle Sol had a
chicken farm till the
skunks ate the chickens when

my Uncle Sol 20
had a skunk farm but
the skunks caught cold and
died and so
my Uncle Sol imitated the
skunks in a subtle manner 25

or by drowning himself in the watertank
but somebody who'd given my Uncle Sol a
Victor
Victrola and records while he lived presented to
him upon the auspicious occasion of his de-
cease a
scrumptious not to mention splendiferous funeral with 30
tall boys in black gloves and flowers and everything and

i remember we all cried like the Missouri
when my Uncle Sol's coffin lurched because
somebody pressed a button
(and down went 35
my Uncle
Sol

and started a worm farm)

LI

A clown's smirk in the skull of a baboon
(where once good lips stalked or eyes
firmly stirred)
my mirror gives me, on this afternoon;
i am a shape that can but eat and turd
e'er with the dirt death shall him vastly gird,
a coward waiting clumsily to cease 6
whom every perfect thing meanwhile doth
miss;
a hand's impression in an empty glove,
a soon forgotten tune, a house for lease.
i have never loved you dear as now i love 10

behold this fool who, in the month of June,
having of certain stars and planets heard,
rose very slowly in a tight balloon
until the smallening world became absurd;
him did an archer spy (whose aim had erred
never) and by that little trick or this 16
he shot the aeronaut down, into the abyss
—and wonderfully i fell through the green
groove
of twilight, striking into many a piece.
i have never loved you dear as now i love 20

god's terrible face, brighter than a spoon,
collects the image of one fatal word;
so that my life (which liked the sun and the
moon)
resembles something that has not occurred:
i am a birdcage without any bird, 25
a collar looking for a dog, a kiss
without lips; a prayer lacking any knees
but something beats within my shirt to prove
he is undead who, living, noone is.
i have never loved you dear as now i love. 30

LI. The modern man's emptiness or monotony of life is expressed here as redeemed only by the romantic faith in love
akin to that of Aucassin (the hero of "Aucassin and Nicolette,"
a twelfth-century Provençal love-story), who preferred hell to
heaven because in hell he would find the fair ladies and brave
knights of medieval courtship. For Cummings, love, either
romantic or casual, is reason enough to find life worth while.

Hell (by most humble me which shall increase)
open thy fire! for i have had some bliss
of one small lady upon earth above;
to whom i cry, remembering her face,
i have never loved you dear as now i love   35

It Was a Goodly Co

IT WAS a goodly co
which paid to make man free
(for man is enslaved by a dread dizziz
and the sooner it's over the sooner to biz
don't ask me what it's pliz)   5

then up rose bishop budge from kew
a anglican was who
(with a rag and a bone and a hank of hair)'d
he picked up a thousand pounds or two
and he smote the monster merde   10

then up rose pride and up rose pelf
and ghibelline and guelph
and ladios and laddios
(on radios and raddios)
did save man from himself   15

ye duskiest despot's goldenest gal
did wring that dragon's tail
(for men must loaf and women must lay)

and she gave him a desdemonial
that took his breath away   20

all history oped her teeming womb
said demon for to doom
yea (fresh complexions being oke
with him) one william shakespeare broke
the silence of the tomb   25

then up rose mr lipshits pres
(who always nothing says)
and he kisséd the general menedjerr
and they smokéd a robert burns cigerr
to the god of things like they err   30

All Ignorance Toboggans into Know

ALL IGNORANCE toboggans into know
and trudges up to ignorance again:
but winter's not forever, even snow
melts; and if spring should spoil the game,
        what then?

all history's a winter sport or three: 5
but were it five, i'd still insist that all
history is too small for even me;
for me and you, exceedingly too small.

Swoop (shrill collective myth) into thy grave
merely to toil the scale to shrillerness   10
per every madge and mabel dick and dave
—tomorrow is our permanent address

and there they'll scarcely find us (if they do,
we'll move away still further: into now)

WALLACE STEVENS

As disillusioned concerning any ultimate values in life as are most of the Waste Land
school of poets, Wallace Stevens uses rich
poetic imagery and lyrical rhythms to stress
the fact that man still dreams of the older romantic faiths in love and beauty, while his

mind mocks at, and denies, these faiths. In his
earlier work this poet was concerned almost
entirely with recording sensuously the nostal-
gias for beauty, perfection, and spiritual intensity which haunt modern man and particularly the artist living in a skeptical world. In

his more recent books, however, Stevens has become aware of the revolutionary faith which leads many artists to criticize this society and to believe that human beings can change it.

Wallace Stevens was born October 2, 1879, in Reading, Pennsylvania. His father was a lawyer of Dutch descent, and his mother came of Pennsylvania Germans. He was educated at Harvard, admitted to the New York bar in 1904, and practiced law in New York until 1916. He then moved to Hartford, Connecticut, where he is now vice-president of the Hartford Accident and Indemnity Company. He is married and has one child, a daughter.

His published volumes of verse are *Harmonium* (1923); *Ideas of Order* (1935); *Owl's Clover* (1936); *The Man with the Blue Guitar and Other Poems* (1937); *Parts of a World* (1942); *Notes Toward a Supreme Fiction* (1942); *Transport to Summer* (1947); and *Three Academic Pieces: The Realm of Resemblance. Someone Puts a Pineapple Together. Of Ideal Time and Choice* (1948).

The *Harmonium* poems for the most part are devoted to the theme of the boredom modern man finds in a world in which spiritual intensities are not largely taken seriously. Stevens puzzles continuously in his later books over which reality it is that stimulates the artist and brings him to the creation of a work—the actual world from which he draws his material or the dream world which he builds to oppose the imperfections in life as he observes it all about him. The "blue guitar," for example, is a symbol of the creative imagination which changes and perfects the world as the poet allows himself to use it. Stevens, in other words, is awake to the fact that the artist must observe the real scene even when, as today, that scene is difficult to imagine as beautiful. In *Ideas of Order* the poet considers the various concepts of beauty held by artist and non-artist. The separation between life and art and the reasons for their separation cause him to ponder again and again the philosophical problem of what is or is not real. This is the central philosophical problem of Stevens' latest poems. He also considers the hero and examines the reality of our idea of the hero, who serves as a symbol of leadership in times of war.

The Paltry Nude Starts on a Spring Voyage

BUT NOT on a shell, she starts,
Archaic, for the sea.
But on the first-found weed
She scuds the glitters,
Noiselessly, like one more wave.   5

She too is discontent
And would have purple stuff upon her arms,
Tired of the salty harbors,
Eager for the brine and bellowing
Of the high interiors of the sea.   10

The wind speeds her,
Blowing upon her hands
And watery back.
She touches the clouds, where she goes
In the circle of her traverse of the sea.   15

Yet this is meagre play
In the scurry and water-shine,
As her heels foam—
Not as when the goldener nude
Of a later day   20

Will go, like the centre of sea-green pomp,
In an intenser calm,
Scullion of fate,
Across the spick torrent, ceaselessly,
Upon her irretrievable way.

"The Paltry Nude Starts on a Spring Voyage," "The Emperor of Ice-Cream," "Peter Quince at the Clavier," "Disillusionment of Ten O'clock," "The Worms at Heaven's Gate," and "Cortège for Rosenbloom" reprinted from *Harmonium* by Wallace Stevens; "A Fading of the Sun" reprinted from *Ideas of Order* by Wallace Stevens; I–IV reprinted from *The Man with the Blue Guitar,* by Wallace Stevens. By permission of and special arrangement with Alfred A. Knopf, Inc., authorized publishers. *The Paltry Nude, etc.* Stevens says there is nothing mythological about the "paltry nude." The image was suggested to him when he saw the nudes used as figureheads of whaling boats. The poem treats of the spring goddess (or the nude) as unhappy and desirous of leaving her harbor. This goddess represents man's creative spirit—a spirit which in our day has languished. The poem ends with lines which suggest that in some distant time this creative spirit, or goddess, will exchange her "meagre play" for renewed "pomp," for journeys swift and far.

The Emperor of Ice-Cream

CALL the roller of big cigars,
The muscular one, and bid him whip
In kitchen cups concupiscent curds.
Let the wenches dawdle in such dress
As they are used to wear, and let the boys   5
Bring flowers in last month's newspapers.
Let be be finale of seem.
The only emperor is the emperor of ice-cream.

Take from the dresser of deal,
Lacking the three glass knobs, that sheet   10
On which she embroidered fantails once
And spread it so as to cover her face.
If her horny feet protrude, they come
To show how cold she is, and dumb.
Let the lamp affix its beam.   15
The only emperor is the emperor of ice-cream.

Peter Quince at the Clavier

I

JUST as my fingers on these keys
Make music, so the selfsame sounds
On my spirit make a music, too.

Music is feeling, then, not sound;
And thus it is that what I feel,   5
Here in this room, desiring you,

Thinking of your blue-shadowed silk,
Is music. It is like the strain
Waked in the elders by Susanna.

Of a green evening, clear and warm,   10
She bathed in her still garden, while
The red-eyed elders watching, felt

The basses of their beings throb
In witching chords, and their thin blood
Pulse pizzicati of Hosanna.   15

II

In the green water, clear and warm,
Susanna lay.

She searched
The touch of springs,
And found   20
Concealed imaginings.
She sighed,
For so much melody.

Upon the bank, she stood
In the cool   25
Of spent emotions.
She felt, among the leaves,
The dew
Of old devotions.

She walked upon the grass,   30
Still quavering.
The winds were like her maids,
On timid feet,
Fetching her woven scarves,
Yet wavering.   35

A breath upon her hand
Muted the night.
She turned—
A cymbal crashed,
And roaring horns.   40

III

Soon, with a noise like tambourines,
Came her attendant Byzantines.

They wondered why Susanna cried
Against the elders by her side;

And as they whispered, the refrain   45
Was like a willow swept by rain.

The Emperor of Ice-Cream. The whole poem is an ironic comment on the meaninglessness of death in our modern society. 1. **Call . . . cigars.** The command here is—let life go on in its usual vulgar way.   2. **bid . . . concupiscent curds,** let the vulgar gentleman whip up lustfully appetizing drinks. 7. **Let . . . seem,** a play upon words meaning "let whatever actually is be accepted." 16. **The only . . . ice-cream,** a comment on the fact that in our jazz age the only ruler is a symbol of physical satisfaction.
Peter Quince, etc. The poem compares the emotions aroused by music with those aroused by love. The story of Susanna symbolizes innocence beset by sophistication. The Biblical story is used for illustration of the way in which purity of mood may be sullied. The last stanza expresses the poet's belief that the beauty and innocence of the body is immortal in its influence upon the sensitive mind.   9. **Susanna,** the wife of Joachim, a Jewish man of rank, who was spied upon by the elders of the community in her husband's absence. When one of them accosted her and was spurned, he maliciously denounced her to her husband, who believed that she had been unfaithful. She was condemned to death for adultery. Daniel proved her innocence and turned the criminal charges on the elders themselves.

36. **A breath . . . night.** These two lines indicate change in Susanna due to the fact that the elders have entered. 42. **Came . . . Byzantines,** referring to the story of Susanna in the Apocrypha, in which mention is made of Susanna's maids but not of their being Byzantine. The word here is probably used for rime.

Anon, their lamps' uplifted flame
Revealed Susanna and her shame.

And then, the simpering Byzantines
Fled, with a noise like tambourines.   50

IV

Beauty is momentary in the mind—
The fitful tracing of a portal;
But in the flesh it is immortal.

The body dies; the body's beauty lives.
So evenings die, in their green going,   55
A wave, interminably flowing.
So gardens die, their meek breath scenting
The cowl of winter, done repenting.
So maidens die, to the auroral
Celebration of a maiden's choral.   60

Susanna's music touched the bawdy strings
Of those white elders; but, escaping,
Left only Death's ironic scraping.
Now, in its immortality, it plays
On the clear viol of her memory,   65
And makes a constant sacrament of praise.

Disillusionment of Ten O'clock

THE HOUSES are haunted
By white night-gowns.
None are green,
Or purple with green rings,
Or green with yellow rings,   5
Or yellow with blue rings.
None of them are strange,
With socks of lace
And beaded ceintures.
People are not going   10
To dream of baboons and periwinkles.
Only, here and there, an old sailor,
Drunk and asleep in his boots,
Catches tigers
In red weather.

The Worms at Heaven's Gate

OUT OF the tomb, we bring Badroulbadour,
Within our bellies, we her chariot.
Here is an eye. And here are, one by one,
The lashes of that eye and its white lid.
Here is the cheek on which that lid declined,
And, finger after finger, here, the hand,   6
The genius of that cheek. Here are the lips,
The bundle of the body and the feet.

.   .   .   .   .   .

Out of the tomb we bring Badroulbadour.

Cortège for Rosenbloom

NOW, THE WRY Rosenbloom is dead
And his finical carriers tread,
On a hundred legs, the tread
Of the dead.
Rosenbloom is dead.   5

They carry the wizened one
Of the color of horn
To the sullen hill,
Treading a tread
In unison for the dead.   10

Rosenbloom is dead.
The tread of the carriers does not halt
On the hill, but turns
Up the sky.
They are bearing his body into the sky.   15

It is the infants of misanthropes
And the infants of nothingness
That tread
The wooden ascents
Of the ascending of the dead.   20

It is turbans they wear
And boots of fur
As they tread the boards
In a region of frost,
Viewing the frost;   25

---

52. **tracing of a portal.** The meaning here is that beauty is a brief memory like an image of a door opening into new scenes but quickly closing.   57. **So gardens, etc.,** an autumnal image of death.
Disillusionment of Ten O'clock, an ironic comment on the fact that modern man has no dreams. All life is leveled out to the commonplace. Only the drunkard can be romantic.   9. **ceintures,** girdles or belts.   11. **periwinkles,** any of various snails, including edible European species.

The Worms at Heaven's Gate.   1. **Badroulbadour.** According to Wallace Stevens, this is a version of the Arab word *bedr* given by Edward Lane in his translation of *The Arabian Nights.* The French version seems to be *Badoure.* The author has taken the meaning to be "full moon" or "full moons," to signify death.
Cortège for Rosenbloom. Rosenbloom, unimportant in life, is ironically shown to be important in his funeral procession—a procession toward death—which all take pompously and without much belief in an after world. The rhythm is that of a death march.

To a chirr of gongs
And a chitter of cries
And the heavy thrum
Of the endless tread
That they tread;   30

To a jangle of doom
And a jumble of words
Of the intense poem
Of the strictest prose
Of Rosenbloom.   35

And they bury him there,
Body and soul,
In a place in the sky.
The lamentable tread!
Rosenbloom is dead.

A Fading of the Sun

WHO CAN think of the sun costuming
　　　clouds
When all people are shaken
Or of night endazzled, proud,
When people awaken
And cry and cry for help?   5

The warm antiquity of self,
Everyone, grows suddenly cold.
The tea is bad, bread sad.
How can the world so old be so mad
That the people die?   10

If joy shall be without a book
It lies, themselves within themselves,
If they will look
Within themselves
And will not cry for help,   15

Within as pillars of the sun,
Supports of night. The tea,
The wine is good. The bread,
The meat is sweet.
And they will not die.

"A Fading of the Sun" reprinted from *Ideas of Order* by Wallace
Stevens, I–IV reprinted from *The Man with the Blue Guitar*
by Wallace Stevens, by permission of and special arrangement
with Alfred A. Knopf, Inc., authorized publishers.
A Fading of the Sun, a comment on the civilization we live in
and the poet's need to believe in joy even when the sun fades
or the world darkens—an image of our modern chaos.   3. endazzled, bespangled.   6. The warm . . . self, the ancient
feeling of the importance of one's self.

from The Man with the Blue Guitar

I

THE MAN bent over his guitar,
A shearsman of sorts. The day was green.

They said, "You have a blue guitar,
You do not play things as they are."

The man replied, "Things as they are   5
Are changed upon the blue guitar."

And they said then, "But play, you must,
A tune beyond us, yet ourselves,

A tune upon the blue guitar
Of things exactly as they are."   10

II

I cannot bring a world quite round,
Although I patch it as I can.

I sing a hero's head, large eye
A bearded bronze, but not a man,

Although I patch him as I can   15
And reach through him almost to man.

If to serenade almost to man
Is to miss, by that, things as they are,

Say that it is the serenade
Of a man that plays a blue guitar.   20

III

Ah, but to play man number one,
To drive the dagger in his heart,

To lay his brain upon the board
And pick the acrid colors out,

To nail his thought across the door,   25
Its wings spread wide to rain and snow,

To strike his living hi and ho,
To tick it, tock it, turn it true,

To bang it from a savage blue,
Jangling the metal of the strings . . .   30

From *The Man with the Blue Guitar*. The poet is talking
here of the way in which the poetic imagination makes use of
and changes reality. The blue guitar is a symbol of the creative
imagination. Stevens often chooses musical instruments to
symbolize certain types of poetic composition. In his *Harmonium* the poetry is very rhythmical. In "The Man with the
Blue Guitar" the verse is conversational, as if spoken to the
accompaniment of chords played upon a guitar.   2. shearsman, one who clips something from something else. In this
case it is a reference to the poet, who clips poetry from life.

IV

So that's life, then: things as they are?
It picks its way on the blue guitar.

A million people on one string?
And all their manner in the thing,

And all their manner, right and wrong,   35
And all their manner, weak and strong?

The feelings crazily, craftily call,
Like a buzzing of flies in autumn air,

And that's life, then: things as they are,
This buzzing of the blue guitar.

from **Examination of the Hero in a Time of War**

THE IMMENSE poetry of war and the poetry of a work of the imagination are two different things. In the presence of the violent reality of war, consciousness takes the place of the imagination. And consciousness of an immense war is a consciousness of fact. If that is true, it follows that the poetry of war as a consciousness of the victories and defeats of nations, is a consciousness of fact, but of heroic
10 fact, of fact on such a scale that the mere consciousness of it affects the scale of one's thinking and constitutes a participating in the heroic.

It has been easy to say in recent times that everything tends to become real, or, rather, that everything moves in the direction of reality, that is to say, in the direction of fact. We leave fact and come back to it, come back to what we wanted fact to be, not to what it was, not to what it has too often remained. The poetry of a work of the imagination constantly illustrates the fundamental and endless struggle with fact. It goes on everywhere, even in the periods that we call peace. But in war, the desire to move in the direction of fact as we want it to be and to move quickly is overwhelming.

Nothing will ever appease this desire except a consciousness of fact as everyone is at least satisfied to have it be.

I

FORCE is my lot and not pink-clustered
   Roma ni Avignon ni Leyden,
And cold, my element.   Death is my
Master and, without light, I dwell. There   4
The snow hangs heavily on the rocks, brought
By a wind that seeks out shelter from snow.
   Thus
Each man spoke in winter. Yet each man spoke of
The brightness of arms, said Roma wasted
In its own dirt, said Avignon was
Peace in a time of peace, said Leyden   10
Was always the other mind. The brightness
Of arms, the will opposed to cold, fate
In its cavern, wings subtler than any mercy,
These were the psalter of their sibyls.

II

The Got whome we serve is able to deliver   15
Us. Good chemistry, good common man, what
Of that angelic sword? Creature of
Ten times ten times dynamite, convulsive
Angel, convulsive shatterer, gun,   19
Click, click, the Got whom we serve is able,
Still, still to deliver us, still magic,
Still moving yet motionless in smoke, still
One with us, in the heaved-up noise, still
Captain, the man of skill, the expert
Leader, the creator of bursting color   25

Parts I–VI and XVI of "Examination of the Hero in a Time of War." Reprinted from *Parts of a World* by Wallace Stevens by permission of Alfred A. Knopf, Inc. copyright 1942 by Wallace Stevens.

Examination of . . . War, a long ironic poem about what heroism consists of. The poem begins with the philosophic reflection on the difference between fact and fiction, and moves into pure parody of the military spirit. In Section III the poet points to the fact that war sharpens our observation and draws us away from the old clichés about heroes. He indicates that no moment of sublimation through art equals the intensity of the moment of combat. Section IV reflects that virtuosity in war is like any other virtuosity. Section V states that for the common man, heroism lies in the daily life. Section VI asks what would lead, were it not for our imagination concerning heroism, and concludes that the familiar must lead. (Sections VII-XV are here omitted.) Section VII again points up the choices of war or peace, and the fact that few are suited to be immortalized. In Section VIII Stevens shifts to the idea that no hero is actual, that every hero is symbolic, and he continues in the next section to state that it is our ideal of heroism that changes any man. Section X questions how far the wind moves in shifting from reality to symbolism of reality. Section XI stresses the persuasiveness of the military parade to death. Section XII returns to Stevens' consistent inquiry into the difference between the image and the thing imaged. This continues into the thirteenth section, where the poet states that since the act and the actor are not divided, the actor is, in a sense, always anonymous. Section XIV argues that it is always the universal conception of heroism which defines heroic action. Section XV implies that man never exceeds what he is, save through symbols of himself. Section XVI repeats the familiar cycle of hero-as-man becoming hero-as-symbol, and returning to hero-as-man.

1. **not . . . Leyden.** Not . . . Rome nor Avignon nor Leyden. Stevens, in contrasting the present-day hero's sense of living always as if under force (in a century of two wars and depressions) indicates that in such an era heroism cannot act in the good faith expressed in the war songs of the period of the decline of Rome, the reign of the Popes at Avignon, when they were forced to leave Rome, or at the siege of Leyden. In these earlier wars man's will was not directed toward a sense of fatality or death, as now.

and rainbow sortilege, the savage weapon
Against enemies, against the prester,
Presto, whose whispers prickle the spirit.

III

They are sick of each old romance, returning,
Of each old revolving dance, the music   30
Like a euphony in a museum
Of euphonies, a skin from Nubia,
A helio-horn. How strange the hero
To this accurate, exacting eye. Sight
Hangs heaven with flash drapery. Sight   35
Is a museum of things seen. Sight,
In war, observes each man profoundly.
Yes. But these sudden sublimations
Are to combat what his exaltations
Are to the unaccountable prophet or   40
What any fury to its noble centre.

IV

To grasp the hero, the eccentric
On a horse, in a plane, at the piano—
At the piano, scales, arpeggios
And chords, the morning exercises,   45
The afternoon's reading, the night's reflection,
That's how to produce a virtuoso.
The drill of a submarine. The voyage
Beyond the oyster-beds, indigo
Shadow, up the great sea and downward   50
And darkly beside the vulcanic
Sea-tower, sea-pinnacles, sea-mountain.
The signal . . . The sea-tower, shaken,
Sways slightly and the pinnacles frisson.
The mountain collapses. Chopiniana.   55

V

The common man is the common hero.
The common hero is the hero.
Imprimatur. But then there's common fortune,
Induced by what you will: the entrails
Of a cat, twelve dollars for the devil,   60
A kneeling woman, a moon's farewell;
And common fortune, induced by nothing,
Unwished for, chance, the merest riding
Of the wind, rain in a dry September,
The improvisations of the cuckoos   65

26. **sortilege,** sorcery. 33. **helio-horn,** probably a primitive horn to announce the rising of the sun. 54. **frisson,** shiver.
55. **Chopiniana,** pertaining to the music of Chopin. The poet means that he is playing over the idea of what the hero consists of with the same kind of virtuosity as a pianist might have at his instrument or the warrior at his. 58. **Imprimatur,** to sanction or approve. The poet simply means, "Well, suppose we sanction this." He then goes on to question, however, whether it is enough to state that the common hero is the hero.

In a clock-shop. . . . Soldier, think, in the
    darkness,
Repeating your appointed paces
Between two neatly measured stations,
Of less neatly measured common-places.

VI

Unless we believe in the hero, what is there
To believe? Incisive what, the fellow   71
Of what good. Devise. Make him of mud,
For every day. In a civiler manner,
Devise, devise, and make him of winter's
Iciest core, a north star, central   75
In our oblivion, of summer's
Imagination, the golden rescue:
The bread and wine of the mind, permitted
In an ascetic room, its table
Red as a red table-cloth, its windows   80
West Indian, the extremest power
Living and being about us and being
Ours, like a familiar companion.

XVI

Each false thing ends. The bouquet of summer
Turns blue and on its empty table   85
It is stale and the water is discolored.
True autumn stands then in the doorway.
After the hero, the familiar
Man makes the hero artificial.
But was the summer false? The hero?   90
How did we come to think that autumn
Was the veritable season, that familiar
Man was the veritable man? So
Summer, jangling the savagest diamonds and
Dressed in its azure-doubled crimsons,   95
May truly bear its heroic fortunes
For the large, the solitary figure.

How Red the Rose
That is the Soldier's Wound

How RED the rose that is the soldier's
    wound,
The wounds of many soldiers, the wounds of
    all
The soldiers that have fallen, red in blood,

78. **the bread . . . mind,** a reference to the Communion supper, meaning that to partake of the sacrament of the belief in heroism is what we live by.
"How Red the Rose That Is the Soldier's Wound" Part VII of "Esthétique du Mal." Reprinted from *Transport to Summer* by Wallace Stevens by permission of Alfred A. Knopf, Inc. copyright 1947 by Wallace Stevens.

The soldier of time grown deathless in great
   size.

A mountain in which no ease is ever found, 5
Unless indifference to deeper death
Is ease, stands in the dark, a shadows' hill,
And there the soldier of time has deathless rest.

Concentric circles of shadows, motionless
Of their own part, yet moving on the wind, 10
Form mystical convolutions in the sleep
Of time's red soldier deathless on his bed.

The shadows of his fellows ring him round
In the high night, the summer breathes for
   them
Its fragrance, a heavy somnolence, and for him,
For the soldier of time, it breathes a summer
   sleep, 16

In which his wound is good because life was.
No part of him was ever part of death.
A woman smoothes her forehead with her hand
And the soldier of time lies calm beneath that
   stroke. 20

JOHN CROWE RANSOM

John Crowe Ransom is one of the foremost critics and poets in a group known as the agrarian distributionists, who believe that people should live in the cultural traditions of their regions. Together with Allen Tate, Robert Penn Warren, Katherine Anne Porter, and others, Ransom is part of the scattered and varied number of those artists who would substitute a naïve provincialism for modern industrial society, who would in a sense replace belief in society with tradition. Most of this group, in the period following the Art for Art's Sake Bohemian movement in New York, returned to the country looking for "tradition," claiming that the equivalent of cultured Europe could be found only in New England and the South, for the industrial world could give no continuity to poets and writers. But New England has long been industrialized, and the "aristocratic" South claimed the allegiance of these traditionalists despite the fact that the history of the old families and idle, leisured people of the Slave South revealed no literature to give much substance, texture, or inspiration to their own.

Born in Pulaski, Tennessee, in 1888, Ransom was educated at Vanderbilt University and as a Rhodes Scholar at Oxford. He taught at Vanderbilt, served in World War I, studied abroad on a Guggenheim Fellowship, and at present is Professor of English at Kenyon College. He has been connected with such magazines as the *Southern Review* and *Sewanee Review*, and was one of the founders of *The Fugitive*, a magazine of verse, and of the *Kenyon Review*, of which he is at present the editor. Among his volumes of verse are *Chills and Fever* (1924), *Poems about God* (1919), *Two Gentlemen in Bonds* (1927), and *Selected Poems* (1948). His chief books of criticism are *The World's Body* (1938), and *The New Criticism* (1941). Of *The New Criticism* Louise Bogan wrote:

> Mr. Ransom's is a very tense book. It is so tied up that no real definition and no cool exposition of "the new criticism" ever come through. Mr. Ransom is so determined to haggle with his material as he goes along that his neatly articulated "objective cognitions," his "structures," and his "textures" dissolve, in the end, into a confused blur.

In the introduction Ransom himself said,

> Poetry is the kind of knowledge by which we must know what we have arranged that we shall not know otherwise. . . . Men become poets, or at least they read poets, in order to atone for having been hard and practical men and hard theoretical scientists.

In Ransom's poetry we have the irony which is also critical of what exists. He believes, as does Edith Sitwell in England, that the gentry in both countries are decadent, introspective, and inactive, that their very intricacy, although interesting, is sick. As Ransom grieves over the lost richness of the southern pre-Civil War culture, he is also more aware than his more militant agrarian friends that this past is irreparably gone. His belief in the continuity of an agrarian culture as opposed to the meanness and the apparent chaos of industrial culture does not blind him to many keen analyses of the modern world. He belongs with the Waste Land poets whose essential theme is nostalgia for the past and ironic disillusionment with the present.

Spectral Lovers

By NIGHT they haunted a thicket of April mist,
As out of the rich ground strangely come to birth,
Else two immaculate angels fallen on earth.
Lovers they knew they were, but why unclasped, unkissed?
Why should two lovers go frozen asunder in fear? 5
And yet they were, they were.

Over the shredding of an April blossom
Her thrilling fingers touched him quick with care;
Of many delicate postures she cast a snare;
But for all the red heart beating in the pale bosom, 10
Her face as of cunningly tinctured ivory
Was hard with an agony.

Stormed by the little batteries of an April night,
Passionate being the essences of the field,
Should the penetrable walls of the crumbling prison yield 15
And open her treasure to the first clamorous knight?

"Spectral Lovers," "The Tall Girl," "April Treason," and "Here Lies a Lady" reprinted from *Chills and Fever;* "Two in August" and "Survey of Literature" reprinted from *Two Gentlemen in Bonds,* by John Crowe Ransom; by permission of and special arrangement with Alfred A. Knopf, Inc., authorized publishers.
Spectral Lovers. The poem is a study in the psychology of young lovers. **1. By night . . . earth.** The first three lines picture young and innocent love walking in April.

"This is the mad moon, and must I surrender all?
If he but ask it, I shall."

And gesturing largely to the very moon of Easter,
Mincing his steps, and swishing the jubilant grass, 20
And beheading some field-flowers that had come to pass,
He had reduced his tributaries faster,
Had not considerations pinched his heart
Unfitly for his art.

"Am I reeling with the sap of April like a drunkard? 25
Blessed is he that taketh this richest of cities;
But it is so stainless, the sack were a thousand pities;
This is that marble fortress not to be conquered,
Lest its white peace in the black flame turn to tinder
And an unutterable cinder." 30

They passed me once in April, in the mist.
No other season is it, when one walks and discovers
Two clad in the shapes of angels, being spectral lovers,
Trailing a glory of moon-gold and amethyst,
Who touched their quick fingers fluttering like a bird 35
Whose songs shall never be heard.

The Tall Girl

The Queens of Hell had lissome necks to crane
At the tall girl approaching with long tread
And, when she was caught up even with them, nodded:
"If the young miss with gold hair might not disdain, 4
We would esteem her company over the plain,
To profit us all where the dogs will be out barking;
And we'll walk by the windows where the young men are working
And to-morrow we will all come home again."

22. He had reduced . . . art, an image to indicate that the young man would have come more quickly to a statement of his emotion had he not remembered the innocence of the girl.

But the Queen of Heaven on the other side of
    the road
In the likeness, I hear, of a fine motherly
    woman   10
Made a wry face, despite it was so common
To be worsted by the smooth ladies of hell,
And crisped her sweet tongue: "This never will
    come to good!
Just an old woman, my pet, that wishes you
    well."

April Treason

So he put her in his picture
  Of a lady he was painting,
Put her lips, which smiled but faintly,
And her eyes, which levelled quaintly,
While her length of limb and noble Roman
    bust,   5
These he copied as he must.

And she was a perfect model,
Never restless with her features,
Never agitating greatly,
More than still and less than stately,   10
Till he knew that he could limn the dream
    aright
In his honest Northern light.

He had nearly done his portrait,
But there came a day in April;
There was treachery come winging   15
On the dust of flowers springing;
It was not a day for artist to play host
Lest the man come uppermost.

And he knew that he was changed,
Was changed the wintry lady.   20
It was but their way of speaking,
It was but their way of looking,
But the cunning all had fled his fingertips;
So he bent and kissed her lips.

Then for all his giddy pulses   25
He laid grim hands on the picture,
And he trampled it with loathing,
Flung it many miles to nothing,
And it screamed to wake the devils as it fell
Till it thundered into hell.   30

Then a silence straightway took them
And they paced the woodland homeward.
What a bitter noon in April
(It was April, it was April)   34
As she touched his fleeting fingers cold as ice
And recited, "It was nice!"

Two in August

Two that could not have lived their single
    lives
As can some husbands and wives
Did something strange: they tensed their vocal
    chords
And attacked each other with silences and
    words
Like catapulted stones and arrowed knives.   5

Dawn was not yet; night is for loving or sleep-
    ing,
Sweet dreams or safekeeping;
Yet he of the wide brows that were used to
    laurel
And she, the famed for gentleness, must
    quarrel,   9
Furious both of them, and scared, and weeping.

How sleepers groan, twitch, wake to such a
    mood
Is not well understood,
Nor why two entities grown almost one
Should rend and murder trying to get undone,
With individual tigers in their blood.   15

In spring's luxuriant weather had the bridal
Transpired, nor had the growing parts been
    idle,
Nor was it easily dissolved;
Therefore they tugged but were still inter-
    volved,   19
With pain prodigious. The exploit was suicidal.

She in terror fled from the marriage chamber
Circuiting the dark room like a string of amber
Round and round and back,
And would not light one lamp against the
    black,
And heard the clock that clanged: Remember,
    Remember.   25

And he must tread barefooted the dim lawn,
Soon he was up and gone;
High in the trees the night-mastered birds
    were crying
With fear upon their tongues, no singing nor
    flying
Which are their lovely attitudes by dawn.   30

Whether those bird-cries were of heaven or hell
There is no way to tell;
In the long ditch of darkness the man walked
Under the hackberry trees where the birds
    talked
With words too sad and strange to syllable.

Survey of Literature

IN ALL the good Greek of Plato
I lack my roast beef and potato.

A better man was Aristotle,
Pulling steady on the bottle.

I dip my hat to Chaucer   5
Swilling soup from his saucer,

And to Master Shakespeare
Who wrote big on small beer.

The abstemious Wordsworth
Subsisted on a curd's-worth,   10

But a slick one was Tennyson,
Putting gravy on his venison.

What these men had to eat and drink
Is what we say and what we think.

The flatulence of Milton   15
Came out of wry Stilton.

Sing a song for Percy Shelley,
Drowned in pale lemon jelly,

And for precious John Keats,
Dripping blood of pickled beets.   20

Survey of Literature. The poem points out that the favorite drink and food of various earlier poets may have had something to do with the way in which these poets composed and ends with a statement that the modern poet has no food and must write with no dinner. References are to Aristotle's wine-drinking; Chaucer's table manners; Shakespeare's beer; Wordsworth's abstemiousness; Tennyson's comfortable living; Milton's love of Stilton, an English cheese; Shelley's delicacy; Keats' tuberculosis; and Blake's emphasis on sweetness and light. The poem points out that the body cannot be separated from the soul, even in the artist.

Then there was poor Willie Blake,
He foundered on sweet cake.

God have mercy on the sinner
Who must write with no dinner,

No gravy and no grub,   25
No pewter and no pub,

No belly and no bowels,
Only consonants and vowels.

Here Lies a Lady

HERE lies a lady of beauty and high degree.
  Of chills and fever she died, of fever and
    chills,
The delight of her husband, her aunts, an in-
    fant of three,
And of medicos marvelling sweetly on her ills.

For either she burned, and her confident eyes
    would blaze,   5
And her fingers fly in a manner to puzzle their
    heads—
What was she making? Why, nothing; she sat
    in a maze
Of old scraps of laces, snipped into curious
    shreds—

Or this would pass, and the light of her fire
    decline
Till she lay discouraged and cold as a thin stalk
    white and blown,   10
And would not open her eyes, to kisses, to
    wine;
The sixth of these states was her last; the cold
    settled down.

Sweet ladies, long may ye bloom, and toughly
    I hope ye may thole,
But was she not lucky? In flowers and lace and
    mourning,
In love and great honour we bade God rest her
    soul   15
After six little spaces of chill, and six of burn-
    ing.

Here Lies a Lady, a satirical poem on the emptiness of the aristocratic life.

JOSEPH WOOD KRUTCH

It would be well worth while to hear George Bernard Shaw's comment on the fact that his play, *Man and Superman,* turned a potential engineer and mathematician into a literary critic and college professor. The victim—or beneficiary—of this lively modern drama was Joseph Krutch. Krutch was born in Knoxville, Tennessee, on November 25, 1893. He attended the secondary schools in that city and then the University of Tennessee, where he graduated in 1915. It was as a freshman that he made his first acquaintance with the genius of Shaw; he shaped his college course thereafter to make himself into a literary analyst. After leaving the University of Tennessee, he took his master's degree at Columbia (1916) and served there as instructor during the following year. The First World War interrupted his academic career; for a time he was in the Psychological Corps of the United States Army.

With the cessation of hostilities, Krutch received a traveling fellowship from Columbia and spent the year 1919–20 in Europe. Then for a while he was assistant professor of English at the Brooklyn Polytechnic Institute and finally took his degree of doctor of philosophy from Columbia (1923). He was dramatic critic and associate editor of *The Nation* from 1924 until 1932, when he joined the board of editors of the periodical. He remained on the board until 1937. Meanwhile he was lecturer at Vassar (1924–25), associate professor of journalism at Columbia University (1925–31), lecturer for the New School for Social Research (1932–37), and finally professor of English at Columbia (1937–   ). In 1926, along with the late Zona Gale, the novelist; the late Glenn Frank, the miscellaneous prose-writer and political dabbler; and Carl Van Doren, literary student and critic, Krutch founded the Literary Guild of America and served on its editorial board. The function of this organization has been essentially a critical one; it has sponsored the publication and dissemination of contemporary literature which it

has adjudged valuable. Krutch rounded out these manifold activities by holding a Guggenheim Fellowship during the year 1930 for the continuation of his study of esthetics. The fruit of this study was *Experience and Art* (1932).

Krutch's first book was his doctoral dissertation, *Comedy and Conscience after the Restoration* (1924). He next contributed "Modern Love and Modern Fiction" (1925) to a collection of essays by various people on our changing mind. *Edgar Allan Poe; A Study in Genius* (1926), a readable and persuasive biography and critique of the American poet, has manifest limitations because of its over-emphasis on a certain set psychology of motive in Poe's soul. Very likely *The Modern Temper* (1929) will be the most lasting of his works so far as the general reader is concerned; it is "a statement of the modern intellectual who has weighed and rejected the moral, esthetic, and other values of his predecessors and who finds only in the pursuit of knowledge that which makes life worth living." *Living Philosophies* (1931); *Experience and Art* (1932), a study of the aspects of the esthetics of literature; and *Was Europe a Success?* (1934) are shrewd, rather pungent, and thoroughly attractive contributions. But they add little to Krutch's stature. For the more technical student of literature and literary craftsmanship, Krutch's more "professional" work is valuable—such pieces as his scholarly editions of Congreve's *Comedies* (1927), of *Nine Plays* by Eugene O'Neill (1932), and of Marcel Proust's *Remembrance of Things Past* (1934); also his *Five Masters; a Study in the Mutations of the Novel* (1930), analyses of the work of Boccaccio, Cervantes, Richardson, Stendhal, and Proust. He has also distinguished himself by such contributions as the *American Drama since 1918* (1939) and *Representative American Dramas* (1941). Two later biographical studies are *Samuel Johnson* (1944) and *Henry David Thoreau* (1948).

As would be expected from his background,

training, and intellectual leanings, Krutch's work has been entirely of a critical nature. He has always been interested in philosophy, so that he is particularly fond of the philosophical analysis in his critiques—a type of criticism at which he excels. On the other hand, his application of modern psychology to his material seems less successful, because he has had difficulty in breaking the spell which Freudian psychology has cast over him. His study of Poe, for example, which is probably his most ambitious work, has been hampered by the attitude that Poe is best explained on the ground that he suffered an Oedipus complex, or mother-fixation. As usual with such psychoanalytical considerations, the theory is far too simple and fails to take into account other facts. Krutch is, however, a stimulating writer, although his outlook upon modern art and life is extremely disquieting; he believes, with Oswald Spengler, in the decline and failure of Western civilization. Perhaps such an outlook is unduly limited, but the fact remains that Krutch is right more often than he is wrong; and in any event his point of view is thoroughly representative of the years which produced it.

---

from **The Modern Temper**

The Tragic Fallacy

THROUGH the legacy of their art the great ages have transmitted to us a dim image of their glorious vitality. When we turn the pages of a Sophoclean or a Shakespearean tragedy we participate faintly in the experience which created it and we sometimes presumptuously say that we "understand" the spirit of these works. But the truth is that we see them, even at best and in the moments when our souls expand most nearly to their dimensions, through a glass darkly.

It is so much easier to appreciate than to create that an age too feeble to reach the

heights achieved by the members of a preceding one can still see those heights towering above its impotence, and so it is that, when we perceive a Sophocles or a Shakespeare soaring in an air which we can never hope to breathe, we say that we can "appreciate" them. But what we mean is that we are just able to wonder, and we can never hope to participate in the glorious vision of human life out of which they were created—not even to the extent of those humbler persons for whom they were written; for while to us the triumphant voices come from far away and tell of a heroic world which no longer exists, to them they spoke of immediate realities and revealed the inner meaning of events amidst which they still lived.

When the life has entirely gone out of a work of art come down to us from the past, when we read it without any emotional comprehension whatsoever and can no longer even imagine why the people for whom it was intended found it absorbing and satisfying, then, of course, it has ceased to be a work of art at all and has dwindled into one of those deceptive "documents" from which we get a false sense of comprehending through the intellect things which cannot be comprehended at all except by means of a kinship of feeling. And though all works from a past age have begun in this way to fade there are some, like the great Greek or Elizabethan tragedies, which are still halfway between the work of art and the document. They no longer can have for us the immediacy which they had for those to whom they originally belonged, but they have not yet eluded us entirely. We no longer live in the world which they represent, but we can half imagine it and we can measure the distance which we have moved away. We write no tragedies today, but we can still talk about the tragic spirit of which we would, perhaps, have no conception were it not for the works in question.

An age which could really "appreciate" Shakespeare or Sophocles would have something comparable to put beside them—something like them, not necessarily in form, or spirit, but at least in magnitude—some vision of life which would be, however different, equally ample and passionate. But when we move to put a modern masterpiece beside them, when we seek to compare them with, let

us say, a *Ghosts* or a *Weavers,* we shrink as from the impulse to commit some folly and we feel as though we were about to superimpose Bowling Green upon the Great Prairies in order to ascertain which is the larger. The question, we see, is not primarily one of art but of the two worlds which two minds inhabited. No increased powers of expression, no greater gift for words, could have transformed Ibsen into
10 Shakespeare. The materials out of which the latter created his works—his conception of human dignity, his sense of the importance of human passions, his vision of the amplitude of human life—simply did not and could not exist for Ibsen, as they did not and could not exist for his contemporaries. God and Man and Nature had all somehow dwindled in the course of the intervening centuries, not because the realistic creed of modern art led us to seek out
20 mean people, but because this meanness of human life was somehow thrust upon us by the operation of that same process which led to the development of realistic theories of art by which our vision could be justified.

Hence, though we still apply, sometimes, the adjective "tragic" to one or another of these modern works of literature which describe human misery and which end more sadly even than they begin, the term is a misnomer since
30 it is obvious that the works in question have nothing in common with the classical examples of the genre and produce in the reader a sense of depression which is the exact opposite of that elation generated when the spirit of a Shakespeare rises joyously superior to the outward calamities which he recounts and celebrates the greatness of the human spirit whose travail he describes. Tragedies, in that only sense of the word which has any distinctive
40 meaning, are no longer written in either the dramatic or any other form and the fact is not to be accounted for in any merely literary terms. It is not the result of any fashion in literature or of any deliberation to write about human nature or character under different as-

pects, any more than it is of either any greater sensitiveness of feeling which would make us shrink from the contemplation of the suffering of Medea or Othello or of any greater optimism which would make us more likely to see life in more cheerful terms. It is, on the contrary, the result of one of those enfeeblements of the human spirit not unlike that described in the previous chapter of this essay, and a further illustration of that gradual weakening of man's confidence in his ability to impose upon the phenomenon of life an interpretation acceptable to his desires which is the subject of the whole of the present discussion.

To explain that fact and to make clear how the creation of classical tragedy did consist in the successful effort to impose such a satisfactory interpretation will require, perhaps, the special section which follows, although the truth of the fact that it does impose such an interpretation must be evident to any one who has ever risen from the reading of *Oedipus* or *Lear* with that feeling of exultation which comes when we have been able, by rare good fortune, to enter into its spirit as completely as it is possible for us of a remoter and emotionally enfeebled age to enter it. Meanwhile one anticipatory remark may be ventured. If the plays and the novels of today deal with littler people and less mighty emotions, it is not because we have become interested in commonplace souls and their unglamorous adventures but because we have come, willy-nilly, to see the soul of man as commonplace and its emotions as mean.

1. **Ghosts . . . Weavers.** *Ghosts* (1881), Ibsen's powerful drama on the subject of hereditary disease, shares the honor with the same playwright's *A Doll's House* (1879) of having revolutionized contemporary drama and instituted the long line of distinguished realistic problem- or thesis-plays. *The Weavers* (1892), by the German dramatist Gerhardt Hauptmann (1862–1946), is an equally impressive play about the working-classes.
4. **Bowling Green,** originally the bowling-green for the city of New York.

54. **previous . . . essay.** In Chapter IV of *The Modern Temper,* entitled "Love—or the Life and Death of a Value," Krutch discusses the sublimation of sex in literature and art, as the Victorians saw the matter; he observes that contemporary literature has rejected this sublimation and rejoices in the realistic and even biological presentation of sex. As a result, Krutch thinks, "For the more skeptical of the Victorians, love performed some of the functions of the God whom they had lost. Faced with it, many of even the most hard-headed turned, for the moment, mystical. They found themselves in the presence of something which awoke in them that sense of reverence which nothing else claimed, and something to which they felt, even in the very depths of their being, that an unquestioning loyalty was due. For them love, like God, demanded all sacrifices; but like Him, also, it rewarded the believer by investing all the phenomena of life with a meaning not yet analyzed away. We have grown used—more than they—to a Godless universe, but we are not yet accustomed to one which is loveless as well, and only when we have so become shall we realize what atheism really means."

II

Tragedy, said Aristotle, is the "imitation of noble actions," and though it is some twenty-five hundred years since the dictum was uttered there is only one respect in which we are inclined to modify it. To us "imitation" seems a rather naïve word to apply to that process by which observation is turned into art, and we seek one which would define or at least imply the nature of that interposition of the personality of the artist between the object and the beholder which constitutes his function and by means of which he transmits a modified version, rather than a mere imitation, of the thing which he has contemplated.

In the search for this word the estheticians of romanticism invented the term "expression" to describe the artistic purpose to which apparent imitation was subservient. Psychologists, on the other hand, feeling that the artistic process was primarily one by which reality is modified in such a way as to render it more acceptable to the desires of the artist, employed various terms in the effort to describe that distortion which the wish may produce in vision. And though many of the newer critics reject both romanticism and psychology, even they insist upon the fundamental fact that in art we are concerned, not with mere imitation, but with the imposition of some form upon the material which it would not have if it were merely copied as a camera copies.

Tragedy is not, then, as Aristotle said, the *imitation* of noble actions, for, indeed, no one knows what a *noble* action is or whether or not such a thing as nobility exists in nature apart from the mind of man. Certainly the action of Achilles in dragging the dead body of Hector around the walls of Troy and under the eyes of Andromache, who had begged to be allowed to give it decent burial, is not to us a noble action, though it was such to Homer, who made it the subject of a noble passage in a noble poem. Certainly, too, the same action might

conceivably be made the subject of a tragedy and the subject of a farce, depending upon the way in which it was treated; so that to say that tragedy is the *imitation* of a *noble* action is to be guilty of assuming, first, that art and photography are the same, and, second, that there may be something inherently noble in an act as distinguished from the motives which prompted it or from the point of view from which it is regarded.

And yet, nevertheless, the idea of nobility is inseparable from the idea of tragedy, which cannot exist without it. If tragedy is not the imitation or even the modified representation of noble actions it is certainly a representation of actions *considered* as noble, and herein lies its essential nature, since no man can conceive it unless he is capable of believing in the greatness and importance of man. Its action is usually, if not always, calamitous, because it is only in calamity that the human spirit has the opportunity to reveal itself triumphant over the outward universe which fails to conquer it; but this calamity in tragedy is only a means to an end and the essential thing which distinguishes real tragedy from those distressing modern works sometimes called by its name is the fact that it is in the former alone that the artist has found himself capable of considering and of making us consider that his people and his actions have that amplitude and importance which make them noble. Tragedy arises then when, as in Periclean Greece or Elizabethan England, a people fully aware of the calamities of life is nevertheless serenely confident of the greatness of man, whose mighty passions and supreme fortitude are revealed when one of these calamities overtakes him.

To those who mistakenly think of it as something gloomy or depressing, who are incapable of recognizing the elation which its celebration of human greatness inspires, and who, therefore, confuse it with things merely miserable or pathetic, it must be a paradox that the happiest, most vigorous, and most confident ages which the world has ever known —the Periclean and the Elizabethan—should be exactly those which created and which most

1. **"imitation . . . actions."** The full statement of this definition, as found in Aristotle's *Poetics* (translation by S. N. Butcher), is as follows: "Tragedy, then, is an imitation of an action that is serious, complete, and of a certain magnitude; in language embellished with each kind of artistic ornament, the several kinds being found in separate parts of the play; in the form of action, not narration; through pity and terror effecting the purgation of these emotions."

76. **Periclean Greece,** Greece in the Age of Pericles, the peak of Athenian civilization (fifth century B.C.).

relished the mightiest tragedies; but the paradox is, of course, resolved by the fact that tragedy is essentially an expression, not of despair, but of the triumph over despair and of confidence in the value of human life. If Shakespeare himself ever had that "dark period" which his critics and biographers have imagined for him, it was at least no darkness like that bleak and arid despair which some10times settles over modern spirits. In the midst of it he created both the elemental grandeur of Othello and the pensive majesty of Hamlet and, holding them up to his contemporaries, he said in the words of his own Miranda, "Oh, rare new world that hath *such* creatures in it."

All works of art which deserve their name have a happy end. This is indeed the thing which constitutes them art and through which they perform their function. Whatever the20character of the events, fortunate or unfortunate, which they recount, they so mold or arrange or interpret them that we accept gladly the conclusion which they reach and would not have it otherwise. They may conduct us into the realm of pure fancy where wish and fact are identical and the world is remade exactly after the fashion of the heart's desire or they may yield some greater or less allegiance to fact; but they must always reconcile us in30one way or another to the representation which they make and the distinctions between the genres are simply the distinctions between the means by which this reconciliation is effected.

Comedy laughs the minor mishaps of its characters away; drama solves all the difficulties which it allows to arise; and melodrama, separating good from evil by simple lines, distributes its rewards and punishments in accordance with the principles of a naïve justice40which satisfied the simple souls of its audience, which are neither philosophical enough to question its primitive ethics nor critical enough to object to the way in which its neat events violate the laws of probability. Tragedy, the greatest and the most difficult of the arts, can adopt none of these methods; and yet it must reach its own happy end in its own way. Though its conclusion must be, by its premise, outwardly

calamitous, though it must speak to those who know that the good man is cut off and that the50fairest things are the first to perish, yet it must leave them, as *Othello* does, content that this is so. We must be and we are glad that Juliet dies and glad that Lear is turned out into the storm.

Milton set out, he said, to justify the ways of God to man, and his praise, if it be interpreted broadly enough, may be taken as describing the function of all art, which must in some way or other, make the life which it seems to rep-60resent satisfactory to those who see its reflection in the magic mirror, and it must gratify or at least reconcile the desires of the beholder, not necessarily, as the naïver exponents of Freudian psychology maintain, by gratifying individual and often eccentric wishes, but at least by satisfying the universally human desire to find in the world some justice, some meaning, or, at the very least, some recognizable order. Hence it is that every real tragedy,70however tremendous it may be, is an affirmation of faith in life, a declaration that even if God is not in his Heaven, then at least Man is in his world.

We accept gladly the outward defeats which it describes for the sake of the inward victories which it reveals. Juliet died, but not before she had shown how great and resplendent a thing love could be; Othello plunged the dagger into his own breast, but not before he had revealed80that greatness of soul which makes his death seem unimportant. Had he died in the instant when he struck the blow, had he perished still believing that the world was as completely black as he saw it before the innocence of Desdemona was revealed to him, then, for him at least, the world would have been merely damnable, but Shakespeare kept him alive long enough to allow him to learn his error and hence to die, not in despair, but in the full ac-90ceptance of the tragic reconciliation to life. Perhaps it would be pleasanter if men could believe what the child is taught—that the good are happy and that things turn out as they should—but it is far more important to be able

---

14. **"Oh, rare new world, etc.,"** spoken by Miranda in Shakespeare's *The Tempest*, V, i, 183–184. The more common reading is "brave" for "rare."

56. **justify . . . man,** found in Milton's *Paradise Lost*, Book I, 26. 73. **God . . . world,** paraphrased from Browning's *Pippa Passes*, Part I, 226–227:

> "God's in his Heaven!
> All's right with the world!"

to believe, as Shakespeare did, that however much things in the outward world may be awry, man has, nevertheless, splendors of his own and that, in a word, Love and Honor and Glory are not words but realities.

Thus for the great ages tragedy is not an expression of despair but the means by which they saved themselves from it. It is a profession of faith, and a sort of religion; a way of looking at life by virtue of which it is robbed of its pain. The sturdy soul of the tragic author seizes upon suffering and uses it only as a means by which joy may be wrung out of existence, but it is not to be forgotten that he is enabled to do so only because of his belief in the greatness of human nature and because, though he has lost the child's faith in life, he has not lost his far more important faith in human nature. A tragic writer does not have to believe in God, but he must believe in man.

And if, then, the Tragic Spirit is in reality the product of a religious faith in which, sometimes at least, faith in the greatness of God is replaced by faith in the greatness of man, it serves, of course, to perform the function of religion, to make life tolerable for those who participate in its beneficent illusion. It purges the souls of those who might otherwise despair and it makes endurable the realization that the events of the outward world do not correspond 30 with the desires of the heart, and thus, in its own particular way, it does what all religions do, for it gives a rationality, a meaning, and a justification to the universe. But if it has the strength it has also the weakness of all faiths, since it may—nay, it must—be ultimately lost as reality, encroaching further and further into the realm of imagination, leaves less and less room in which that imagination can build its refuge. 40

THEODORE DREISER

Seldom does a writer of prominence leave the world more direct information about himself, his life, his hopes, his inmost desires, than Theodore Dreiser has done. In his self-revealing passages, as in all his work, there is a tireless mining up of truth however unpalatable and a dogged desire to explore all possible implications of that truth. With a frankness which transcends completely the Victorian tradition, Dreiser tells us in three long narratives—*Dawn* (1931), *A Traveler at Forty* (1913), and *A Book about Myself* (1922)—all that the average reader would feel he had a right to know about Theodore Dreiser.

Dreiser was born in Terre Haute, Indiana, on August 27, 1871. His father was a strict Catholic; the son explains that he never knew "a narrower, more hide-bound religionist, nor one more tender and loving in his narrow way." His mother was "a happy, hopeful animal; an open, uneducated, wondering, dreamy mind; a pagan mother, taken over into the Catholic church at marriage." There were some brothers and sisters, one of whom, Paul Dresser, achieved some fame as a popular musician; but Dreiser does not seem to have enjoyed his relations with the family as a whole.

He was educated in the public schools of Warsaw, Indiana. At sixteen he was in Chicago looking for a job. He found one with a hardware company, but it did not last long. At eighteen he was studying at the University of Indiana, but such was the economic pressure that he had to leave shortly after the beginning of his sophomore year. He then returned to Chicago and became a clerk in a real estate office, later a collector for a furniture house. But all this time he was craving literary work of some sort. The desire to write, on the part of a boy who as a mere child had been entranced by the comparatively mild stimulation of Oliver Goldsmith, was too strong for him. He gave up his collecting of bills for furniture and entered newspaper work.

His career as a journalist lasted nearly twenty years. He was first a reporter on the

Chicago Daily Globe (1892), then dramatic editor and traveling correspondent for the *St. Louis Globe-Democrat* (1892–93) and later for the *St. Louis Republic* (1893–94). In 1894 Dreiser went to New York to try his wings. After some difficulties, this adventure proved successful. At first (from 1895 to 1898) he was editor of *Every Month*, a music magazine. For several years he was employed as a free-lance journalist, contributing to most of the important periodicals of the day. Such pieces of Dreiseriana as have survived from that period are literary critiques. In 1905 he returned to editorship, managing first *Smith's Magazine*, then the *Broadway Magazine* (1906–07); and he finally became editor-in-chief of the Butterick publications, a syndicate of women's magazines, the best-known member of which was the late popular and effective *Delineator*. After his retirement from this post in 1910, Dreiser devoted himself to writing.

As editor of the Butterick publications, Dreiser was most cautious and conservative. Yet his first novel, *Sister Carrie* (1900), the realistic story of a girl "with a past," had been banned shortly after its publication. For eleven years thereafter Dreiser was silent except for writing incidental to his editorship. Then in 1911 appeared *Jennie Gerhardt*, a novel the theme of which was almost the same as that of *Sister Carrie*. There were loud growls of disapprobation from the conservative members of the reading public; but this time Dreiser was undeterred. He began a "trilogy of desire," a projected trio of novels to illustrate the two great lusts in a man's life—the lust for power and the lust for women. Two of these, *The Financier* (1912) and *The Titan* (1914), were completed and made a sensation; the overpowering figure of ruthless Frank Cowperwood was the embodiment of all that was unscrupulous and selfish in society. (The third, *The Stoic*, was published posthumously in 1947. That it fell short of the others in power may be due to the fact that Dreiser never quite finished it.) *The 'Genius'* (1915), on a theme similar to that of the two preceding works —indeed, it is in effect a third member of the trilogy—portrayed the weak-willed but avid and thick-skinned artist Eugene Witla. So great was the outcry upon the publication of *The 'Genius'* that the novel was banned, but not be-

fore a much publicized court action, in which nearly five hundred contemporary writers petitioned the court in favor of the book (p. 79, n. 14). This was the so-called Dreiser Protest (1916). Once again Dreiser turned his glance away from the novel to other kinds of writing. He turned out some plays—a collection of short dramas, *Plays of the Natural and Supernatural* (1916), and a four-act tragedy, *The Hand of the Potter* (1919)–which were often intrinsically of interest but extremely deficient in dramatic force. He described what was for the time a considerable adventure—an automobile trip from New York to Indianapolis—*A Hoosier Holiday* (1916). He wrote two volumes of short stories, which exhibit many of his virtues in small compass and, from their comparative brevity, have avoided some of his worst faults —*Free and Other Stories* (1918) and *Twelve Men* (1919). Not the least significant of his works in this period were the two books of essays, *Hey-Rub-a-dub-dub!* (1920) and *The Color of a Great City* (1923), in which his social inquisitiveness and essential sympathy for humanity—and of course his pessimistic atmosphere—come impressively to the fore.

In 1906 a murder had shaken Oneida County in the state of New York. A young man named Gillette had been accused of drowning his mistress, Grace Brown; he was convicted and eventually electrocuted. Dreiser made this incident the basis of a long novel, *An American Tragedy* (1925). The protagonist, renamed Clyde Griffiths, is traced by Dreiser with infinite patience from his adolescence to his death in the electric chair. No detail is spared to show how Griffiths' unfortunate early environment was responsible for grave weaknesses in his character, so that he turned from a sensitive youth into an ambitious, weak-kneed opportunist. Whether he deliberately caused the girl to drown, or merely allowed her to perish when he might have rescued her, is never quite clear. But in effect Dreiser is indicting society, not its miserable victim. The entire trial of Griffiths is given in full detail; it is as if Dreiser had transcribed the records of the trial of Gillette. In great part that is precisely what he did. Naturally the book made a profound impression. But it is interesting to compare the situation here with what had happened with *Sister Carrie* a quarter of a century before. To be sure, some cities banned *An American Tragedy*, notably Boston, which was, as usual, in the grip of a peculiarly short-sighted type of Comstockery (p. 84, n. 83). The novel, however, has been generally hailed as Dreiser's masterpiece. Huge and formless as it is, there is little doubt that such a judgment is the correct one.

After *An American Tragedy* Dreiser did not produce a novel of importance until his posthumous novel, *The Bulwark* (1946), which appeared several months after his death December 28, 1945. *The Bulwark* is, in fact, a surprisingly effective novel of life in a Quaker community—the complete antithesis of *An American Tragedy* or of the other novels which went before. In the meantime, Dreiser traveled to Russia—whence his *Dreiser Looks at Russia* (1928)—and lived quietly at New York, and in Southern California, where he died. His trip to Russia was made, as he puts it, "to know America better." He was both repelled and attracted by Russia; but eventually the rigid totalitarian censorship disillusioned him sadly. He returned to the United States with more faith in "the land of the free" than he had felt before; at least life here was "no worse" than in Russia. Later he wrote a brochure on the thesis that America was "worth saving" (1941).

For the rest, he collected some of his earlier work and produced some new items—*A Gallery of Women* (1929), a series of portraits of women "worth noticing," which might be called a collection of brief novelettes; *Fine Furniture* (1930); and *Tragic America* (1932), which is a kind of supplement to *Dreiser Looks at Russia*, with further overtones induced by the spectacle of the great depression of the 1930's; and some poems, *Moods* (1926), "cadenced and declaimed," and *Epitaph* (1930). There is nothing in these, or in his final novel, to suggest that Dreiser did not reach his zenith of significant accomplishment in *An American Tragedy*.

"One is hounded," said Dreiser in *Hey-Rub-a-dub-dub!*, "by the thought that as with individuals so with nations; some are born fools, live fools, and die fools. And may not America perchance be one such? One hopes not. But . . ." There is no denying Dreiser's moral earnestness and his passion for truth. He is, therefore, a supreme realist in substance, with romantic yearnings which collide disastrously with his sense of fact and produce in consequence bitterness and pessimism. Furthermore, he is handicapped by an atrocious style, one well guaranteed because of its muddiness to drive an academic mind frantic and to offend an esthetic mind with its singular awkwardness of phrase, its astonishing gaucherie of vocabulary, its frequent inadequacy of expression. As one critic has observed, Dreiser writes "as if he had learned the English language only last Tuesday." There is little beauty in Dreiser's work, but there emerge great fidelity of observation, complete sincerity, and a lumbering, massive power that transcend his esthetic limitations. His contribution to American letters has been a notable one of great influence; he has helped particularly to establish the case-history as one of the significant forms of contemporary American fiction.

Free

THE LARGE and rather comfortable apartment of Rufus Haymaker, architect, in Central Park West, was very silent. It was scarcely dawn yet, and at the edge of the park, over the way, looking out from the front windows which graced this abode and gave it its charm, a stately line of poplars was still shrouded in a gray morning mist. From his bedroom at one end of the hall, where, also, a glimpse of the park was to be had, came Mr. Haymaker at 10 this early hour to sit by one of these broader windows and contemplate these trees and a small lake beyond. He was very fond of Nature in its manifold art forms—quite poetic, in fact.

He was a tall and spare man of about sixty, not ungraceful, though slightly stoop-shouldered, with heavy overhanging eyebrows and hair, and a short, professionally cut gray mustache and beard, which gave him a severe and yet agreeable presence. For the present he was 20 clad in a light-blue dressing gown with silver cords, which enveloped him completely. He had thin, pale, long-fingered hands, wrinkled

"Free" from *Free and Other Stories* by Theodore Dreiser, reprinted by permission of Simon and Schuster, Inc.

at the back and slightly knotted at the joints, which bespoke the artist, in mood at least, and his eyes had a weary and yet restless look in them.

For only yesterday Doctor Storm, the family physician, who was in attendance on his wife, ill now for these three weeks past with a combination of heart lesion, kidney poisoning and neuritis, had taken him aside and said very softly and affectionately, as though he were trying to spare his feelings: "To-morrow, Mr. Haymaker, if your wife is no better I will call in my friend, Doctor Grainger, whom you know, for a consultation. He is more of an expert in these matters of the heart"—the heart, Mr. Haymaker had time to note ironically—"than I am. Together we will make a thorough examination, and then I hope we will be better able to say what the possibilities of her recovery really are. It's been a very trying case, a very stubborn one, I might say. Still, she has a great deal of vitality and is doing as well as could be expected, all things considered. At the same time, though I don't wish to alarm you unnecessarily—and there is no occasion for great alarm yet—still I feel it my duty to warn you that her condition is very serious indeed. Not that I wish you to feel that she is certain to die. I don't think she is. Not at all. Just the contrary. She may get well, and probably will, and live all of twenty years more." (Mentally Mr. Haymaker sighed a purely spiritual sigh.) "She has fine recuperative powers, so far as I can judge, but she has a bad heart, and this kidney trouble has not helped it any. Just now, when her heart should have the least strain, it has the most.

"She is just at the point where, as I may say, things are in the balance—day or two, or three or four at the most, ought to show which way things will go. But, as I have said before, I do not wish to alarm you unnecessarily. We are not nearly at the end of our tether. We haven't tried blood transfusion yet, and there are several arrows to that bow. Besides, at any moment she may respond more vigorously to medication than she has heretofore—especially in connection with her kidneys. In that case the situation would be greatly relieved at once.

"However, as I say, I feel it my duty to speak to you in this way in order that you may be mentally prepared for any event, because in such an odd combination as this the worst may happen at any time. We never can tell. As an old friend of yours and Mrs. Haymaker's, and knowing how much you two mean to each other"—Mr. Haymaker merely stared at him vacantly—"I feel it my duty to prepare you in this way. We all of us have to face these things. Only last year I lost my dear Matilda, my youngest child, as you know. Just the same, as I say, I have the feeling that Mrs. Haymaker is not really likely to die soon, and that we—Doctor Grainger and myself—will still be able to pull her through. I really do."

Doctor Storm looked at Mr. Haymaker as though he were very sorry for him—an old man long accustomed to his wife's ways and likely to be made very unhappy by her untimely end; whereas Mr. Haymaker, though staring in an almost sculptural way, was really thinking what a farce it all was, what a dull mixture of error and illusion on the part of all. Here he was, sixty years of age, weary of all this, of life really—a man who had never been really happy in all the time that he had been married; and yet here was his wife, who from conventional reasons believed that he was or should be, and who on account of this was serenely happy herself, or nearly so. And this doctor, who imagined that he was old and weak and therefore in need of this loving woman's care and sympathy and understanding! Unconsciously he raised a deprecating hand.

Also his children, who thought him dependent on her and happy with her; his servants and her and his friends thinking the same thing, and yet he really was not. It was all a lie. He was unhappy. Always he had been unhappy, it seemed, ever since he had been married—for over thirty-one years now. Never in all that time, for even so much as a single day, had he ever done anything but long, long, long, in a pale, constrained way—for what, he scarcely dared think—not to be married any more—to be free—to be as he was before ever he saw Mrs. Haymaker.

And yet being conventional in mood and training and utterly domesticated by time and conditions over which he seemed not to have much control—nature, custom, public opinion, and the like, coming into play as forces—he had drifted, had not taken any drastic action. No, he had merely drifted, wondering if time, accident or something might not interfere and straighten out his life for him, but it never had. Now weary, old, or rapidly becoming so, he condemned himself for his inaction. Why hadn't he done something about it years before? Why hadn't he broken it up before it was too late, and saved his own soul, his longing for life, color? But no, he had not. Why complain so bitterly now?

All the time the doctor had talked this day before he had wanted to smile a wry, dry, cynical smile, for in reality he did not want Mrs. Haymaker to live—or at least at the moment he thought so. He was too miserably tired of it all. And so now, after nearly twenty-four hours of the same unhappy thought, sitting by this window looking at a not distant building which shone faintly in the haze, he ran his fingers through his hair as he gazed, and sighed.

How often in these weary months, and even years, past—ever since he and his wife had been living here, and before—had he come to these or similar windows while she was still asleep, to sit and dream! For some years now they had not even roomed together, so indifferent had the whole state become; though she did not seem to consider that significant, either. Life had become more or less of a practical problem to her, one of position, place, prestige. And yet how often, viewing his life in retrospect, had he wished that his life had been as sweet as his dreams—that his dreams had come true.

After a time on this early morning, for it was still gray, with the faintest touch of pink in the east, he shook his head solemnly and sadly, then rose and returned along the hall to his wife's bedroom, at the door of which he paused to look where she lay seriously ill, and beside her in an armchair, fast asleep, a trained nurse who was supposedly keeping the night vigil ordered by the doctor, but who no doubt was now very weary. His wife was sleeping also—very pale, very thin now, and very weak. He felt sorry for her at times, in spite of his own weariness; now, for instance. Why need he have made so great a mistake so long ago? Perhaps it was his own fault for not having been wiser in his youth. Then he went quietly on to his own room, to lie down and think.

Always these days, now that she was so very ill and the problem of her living was so very acute, the creeping dawn thus roused him—to think. It seemed as though he could not really sleep soundly any more, so stirred and distrait was he. He was not so much tired or physically worn as mentally bored or disappointed. Life had treated him so badly, he kept thinking to himself over and over. He had never had the woman he really wanted, though he had been married so long, had been faithful, respectable and loved by her, in her way. "In her way," he half quoted to himself as he lay there.

Presently he would get up, dress and go down to his office as usual if his wife were not worse. But—but, he asked himself—would she be? Would that slim and yet so durable organism of hers—quite as old as his own, or nearly so—break under the strain of this really severe illness? That would set him free again, and nicely, without blame or comment on him. He could then go where he chose once more, do as he pleased—think of that—without let or hindrance. For she was ill at last, so very ill, the first and really great illness she had endured since their marriage. For weeks now she had been lying so, hovering, as it were, between life and death, one day better, the next day worse, and yet not dying, and with no certainty that she would, and yet not getting better either. Doctor Storm insisted that it was a leak in her heart which had suddenly manifested itself which was causing all the real trouble. He was apparently greatly troubled as to how to control it.

During all this period Mr. Haymaker had been, as usual, most sympathetic. His manner toward her was always soft, kindly, apparently tender. He had never really begrudged her anything—nothing certainly that he could afford. He was always glad to see her and the children humanly happy—though they, too, largely on account of her, he thought, had proved a disappointment to him—because he had always sympathized with her somewhat unhappy youth, narrow and stinted; and yet he had never been happy himself, either, never in all the time that he had been married. If she had endured much, he kept telling himself when he was most unhappy, so had he, only it was harder perhaps for women to endure things than men—he was always willing to admit that—only also she had had his love, or thought she had, an actual spiritual peace, which he had never had. She knew she had a faithful husband. He felt that he had never really had a wife at all, not one that he could love as he knew a wife should be loved. His dreams as to that!

Going to his office later this same day—it was in one of those tall buildings that face Madison Square—he had looked first, in passing, at the trees that line Central Park West, and then at the bright wall of apartment houses facing it, and meditated sadly, heavily. Here the sidewalks were crowded with nursemaids and children at play, and in between them, of course, the occasional citizen loitering or going about his errands. The day was so fine, so youthful, as spring days will seem at times. As he looked, especially at the children, and the young men bustling office-ward, mostly in new spring suits, he sighed and wished that he were young once more. Think how brisk and hopeful they were! Everything was before them. They could still pick and choose—no age or established conditions to stay them. Were any of them, he asked himself for the thousandth time, it seemed to him, as wearily connected as he had been at their age? Did they each have a charming young wife to love—one of whom they were passionately fond—such a one as he had never had; or did they not?

Wondering, he reached his office on one of the topmost floors of one of those highest buildings commanding a wide view of the city, and surveyed it wearily. Here were visible the two great rivers of the city, its towers and spires and far-flung walls. From these sometimes, even yet, he seemed to gain a patience to live, to hope. How in his youth all this had inspired him—or that other city that was then. Even now he was always at peace here, so much more so than in his own home, pleasant as it was. Here he could look out over this great scene and dream or he could lose the memory in his work that his love-life had been a failure. The great city, the buildings he could plan or supervise, the efficient help that always surrounded him—his help, not hers—aided to take his mind off himself and that deep-seated inner ache or loss.

The care of Mr. Haymaker's apartment during his wife's illness and his present absence throughout the day, devolved upon a middle-aged woman of great seriousness, Mrs. Elf-

ridge by name, whom Mrs. Haymaker had employed years before; and under her a maid of all work, Hester, who waited on table, opened the door, and the like; and also at present two trained nurses, one for night and one for day service, who were in charge of Mrs. Haymaker. The nurses were both bright, healthy, blue-eyed girls, who attracted Mr. Haymaker and suggested all the youth he had never had—without really disturbing his poise. It would seem as though that could never be any more.

In addition, of course, there was the loving interest of his son Wesley and his daughter Ethelberta—whom his wife had named so in spite of him—both of whom had long since married and had children of their own and were living in different parts of the great city. In this crisis both of them came daily to learn how things were, and occasionally to stay for the entire afternoon or evening, or both. Ethelberta had wanted to come and take charge of the apartment entirely during her mother's illness, only Mrs. Haymaker, who was still able to direct, and fond of doing so, would not hear of it. She was not so ill but that she could still speak, and in this way could inquire and direct. Besides, Mrs. Elfridge was as good as Mrs. Haymaker in all things that related to Mr. Haymaker's physical comfort, or so she thought.

If the truth will come out—as it will in so many pathetic cases—it was never his physical so much as his spiritual or affectional comfort that Mr. Haymaker craved. As said before, he had never loved Mrs. Haymaker, or certainly not since that now long-distant period back in Muskegon, Michigan, where both had been born and where they had lived and met at the ages, she of fifteen, he of seventeen. It had been, strange as it might seem now, a love match at first sight with them. She had seemed so sweet, a girl of his own age or a little younger, the daughter of a local chemist. Later, when he had been forced by poverty to go out into the world to make his own way, he had written her much, and imagined her to be all that she had seemed at fifteen, and more—a dream among fair women. But Fortune, slow in coming to his aid and fickle in fulfilling his dreams, had brought it about that for several years more he had been compelled to stay away nearly all of the time, unable to marry her; during which period, unknown to himself really, his own point of view had altered. How it had happened he could never tell really, but so it was. The great city, larger experiences—while she was still enduring the smaller ones—other faces, dreams of larger things, had all combined to destroy it or her; only he had not quite realized it then. He was always so slow in realizing the full import of the immediate thing, he thought.

That was the time, as he had afterwards told himself—how often!—that he should have discovered his mistake and stopped. Later it always seemed to become more and more impossible. Then, in spite of some heartache to her and some distress to himself, no doubt, all would be well for him now. But no; he had been too inexperienced, too ignorant, too bound by all the conventions and punctilio of his simple Western world. He thought an engagement, however unsatisfactory it might come to seem afterward, was an engagement, and binding. An honorable man would not break one—or so his country moralists argued.

Yes, at that time he might have written her, he might have told her, then. But he had been too sensitive and kindly to speak of it. Afterward it was too late. He feared to wound her, to undo her, to undo her life. But now—now—look at his! He had gone back on several occasions before marriage, and might have seen and done and been free if he had had but courage and wisdom—but no; duty, order, the belief of the region in which he had been reared, and of America—what it expected and what she expected and was entitled to—had done for him completely. He had not spoken. Instead, he had gone on and married her without speaking of the change in himself, without letting her know how worse than ashes it had all become. God, what a fool he had been! how often since he had told himself over and over.

Well, having made a mistake it was his duty perhaps, at least according to current beliefs, to stick by it and make the best of it;—a bargain was a bargain in marriage, if nowhere else—but still that had never prevented him from being unhappy. He could not prevent that himself. During all these long years, therefore, owing to these same conventions—what people would think and say—he had been compelled to live with her, to cherish her, to pretend to be happy with her—"another perfect union," as he sometimes said to himself. In reality he had been unhappy, horribly so. Even her face wearied him at times, and her presence, her mannerisms. Only this other morning Doctor Storm, by his manner indicating that he thought him lonely, in danger of being left all alone and desperately sad and neglected in case she died had irritated him greatly. Who would take care of him? his eyes had seemed to say—and yet he himself wanted nothing so much as to be alone for a time, at least, in this life, to think for himself, to do for himself, to forget this long, dreary period in which he had pretended to be something that he was not.

Was he never to be rid of the dull round of it, he asked himself now, never before he himself died? And yet shortly afterward he would reproach himself for these very thoughts, as being wrong, hard, unkind—thoughts that would certainly condemn him in the eyes of the general public, that public which made reputations and one's general standing before the world.

During all this time he had never even let her know—no, not once—of the tremendous and soul-crushing sacrifice he had made. Like the Spartan boy, he had concealed the fox gnawing at his vitals. He had not complained. He had been, indeed, the model husband, as such things go in conventional walks. If you doubted it look at his position, or that of his children; or his wife—her mental and physical comfort, even in her illness, her unfailing belief that he was all he should be! Never once apparently, during all these years, had she doubted his love or felt him to be unduly unhappy—or, if not that exactly, if not fully accepting his love as something that was still at a fever heat, the thing it once was—still believing that he found pleasure and happiness in being with her, a part of the home which together they had built up, these children they had reared, comfort in knowing that it would endure to the end! To the end! During all these years she had gone on molding his and her lives—as much as that was possible in his case—and those of their children, to suit herself; and thinking all the time that she was doing what he wanted or at least what was best for him and them.

How she adored convention! What did she not think she knew in regard to how things ought to be—mainly what her old home surroundings had taught her, the American idea of this, that and the other. Her theories in regard to friends, education of the children, and so on, had in the main prevailed, even when he did not quite agree with her; her desires for certain types of pleasure and amusement, of companionship, and so on, were conventional types always and had also prevailed. There had been little quarrels, of course, always had been —what happy home is free of them?—but still he had always given in, or nearly always, and had acted as though he were satisfied in so doing.

But why, therefore, should he complain now, or she ever imagine, or ever have imagined, that he was unhappy? She did not, had not. Like all their relatives and friends of the region from which they sprang, and here also— and she had been most careful to regulate that, courting whom she pleased and ignoring all others—she still believed most firmly, more so than ever, that she knew what was best for him, what he really thought and wanted. It made him smile most wearily at times.

For in her eyes—in regard to him, at least, not always so with others, he had found—marriage was a sacrament, sacrosanct, never to be dissolved. One life, one love. Once a man had accepted the yoke or even asked a girl to marry him it was his duty to abide by it. To break an engagement, to be unfaithful to a wife, even unkind to her—what a crime, in her eyes! Such people ought to be drummed out of the world. They were really not fit to live—dogs, brutes!

And yet, look at himself—what of him? What of one who had made a mistake in regard to all this? Where was his compensation to come from, his peace and happiness? Here on earth or only in some mythical heaven—that odd, angelic heaven that she still believed in? What a farce! And all her friends and his would think he would be so miserable now if she died, or at least ought to be. So far had asinine convention and belief in custom carried the world. Think of it!

But even that was not the worst. No; that was not the worst, either. It had been the gradual realization coming along through the years that he had married an essentially small, narrow woman who could never really grasp his point of view—or, rather, the significance of his dreams or emotions—and yet with whom, nevertheless, because of this original promise or mistake, he was compelled to live. Grant her every quality of goodness, energy, industry, intent—as he did freely—still there was this; and it could never be adjusted, never. Essentially, as he had long since discovered, she was narrow, ultraconventional, whereas he was an artist by nature, brooding and dreaming strange dreams and thinking far-off things which she did not or could not understand or did not sympathize with, save in a general and very remote way. The nuances of his craft, the wonders and subtleties of forms and angles—had she ever realized how significant these were to him, let alone to herself? No, never. She had not the least true appreciation of them—never had had. Architecture? Art? What could they really mean to her, desire as she might to appreciate them? And he could not now go elsewhere to discover that sympathy. No. He had never really wanted to, since the public and she would object, and he thinking it half evil himself.

Still, how was it, he often asked himself, that Nature could thus allow one conditioned or equipped with emotions and seekings such as his, not of an utterly conventional order, to seek out and pursue one like Ernestine, who was not fitted to understand him or to care what his personal moods might be? Was love truly blind, as the old saw insisted, or did Nature really plan, and cleverly, to torture the artist mind—as it did the pearl-bearing oyster with a grain of sand—with something seemingly inimical, in order that it might produce beauty? Sometimes he thought so. Perhaps the many interesting and beautiful buildings he had planned—the world called them so, at least —had been due to the loving care he lavished on them, being shut out from love and beauty elsewhere. Cruel Nature, that cared so little for the dreams of man—the individual man or woman!

At the time he had married Ernestine he was really too young to know exactly what it was he wanted to do or how it was he was going to feel in the years to come; and yet there was no one to guide him, to stop him. The custom of the time was all in favor of this dread disaster.

Nature herself seemed to desire it—mere children being the be-all and the end-all of everything, everywhere. Think of that as a theory! Later, when it became so clear to him what he had done, and in spite of all the conventional thoughts and conditions that seemed to bind him to this fixed condition, he had grown restless and weary, but never really irritable. No, he had never become that.

Instead he had concealed it all from her, persistently, in all kindness; only this hankering after beauty of mind and body in ways not represented by her had hurt so—grown finally almost too painful to bear. He had dreamed and dreamed of something different until it had become almost an obsession. Was it never to be, that something different, never, anywhere, in all time? What a tragedy! Soon he would be dead and then it would never be anywhere—anymore! Ernestine was charming, he would admit, or had been at first, though time had proved that she was not charming to him either mentally or physically in any compelling way; but how did that help him now? How could it? He had actually found himself bored by her for more than twenty-seven years now, and this other dream growing, growing, growing—until—

But now he was old, and she was dying, or might be, and it could not make so much difference what happened to him or to her; only it could, too, because he wanted to be free for a little while, just for a little while, before he died.

To be free! free!

One of the things that had always irritated him about Mrs. Haymaker was this, that in spite of his determination never to offend the social code in any way—he had felt for so many reasons, emotional as well as practical, that he could not afford so to do—and also in spite of the fact that he had been tortured by this show of beauty in the eyes and bodies of others, his wife, fearing perhaps in some strange psychic way that he might change, had always tried to make him feel or believe—premeditatedly and of a purpose, he thought—that he was not the kind of man who would be attractive to women; that he lacked some physical fitness, some charm that other men had, which would cause all young and really charming women to turn away from him. Think of it! He to whom so many women had turned with questioning eyes!

Also that she had married him largely because she had felt sorry for him! He chose to let her believe that, because he was sorry for her. Because other women had seemed to draw near to him at times in some appealing or seductive way she had insisted that he was not even a cavalier, let alone a Lothario; that he was ungainly, slow, uninteresting—to all women but her!

Persistently, he thought, and without any real need, she had harped on this, fighting chimeras, a chance danger in the future; though he had never given her any real reason, and had never even planned to sin against her in any way—never. She had thus tried to poison his own mind in regard to himself and his art—and yet—and yet—Ah, those eyes of other women, their haunting beauty, the flitting something they said to him of infinite, inexpressible delight. Why had his life been so very hard?

One of the disturbing things about all this was the iron truth which it had driven home, namely, that Nature, unless it were expressed or represented by some fierce determination within, which drove one to do, cared no whit for him or any other man or woman. Unless one acted for oneself, upon some stern conclusion nurtured within, one might rot and die spiritually. Nature did not care. "Blessed be the meek"—yes. Blessed be the strong, rather, for they made their own happiness. All these years in which he had dwelt and worked in this knowledge, hoping for something but not acting, nothing had happened, except to him, and that in an unsatisfactory way. All along he had seen what was happening to him; and yet held by convention he had refused to act always, because somehow he was not hard enough to act. He was not strong enough, that was the real truth—had not been. Almost like a bird in a cage, an animal peeping out from behind bars, he had viewed the world of free thought and freer action. In many a drawing-room, on the street, or in his own home even, had he not looked into an eye, the face of someone who seemed to offer understanding, to know, to sympathize, though she might not have, of course; and yet religiously and moralistically, like an anchorite, because of duty and current belief and what people would say and think, Ernestine's position and faith in him, her comfort, his career and that of the children—he had put them all aside, out of his mind, forgotten them almost, as best he might. It had been hard at times, and sad, but so it had been.

And look at him now, old, not exactly feeble yet—no, not that yet, not quite!—but life weary and almost indifferent. All these years he had wanted, wanted—wanted—an understanding mind, a tender heart, the some one woman— she must exist somewhere—who would have sympathized with all the delicate shades and meanings of his own character, his art, his spiritual as well as his material dreams—And yet look at him! Mrs. Haymaker had always been with him, present in the flesh or the spirit, and —so—

Though he could not ever say that she was disagreeable to him in a material way—he could not say that she had ever been that exactly—still she did not correspond to his idea of what he needed, and so—Form had meant so much to him, color; the glorious perfectness of a glorious woman's body; for instance, the color of her thoughts, moods—exquisite they must be, like his own at times; but no, he had never had the opportunity to know one intimately. No, not one, though he had dreamed of her so long. He had never even dared whisper this to any one, scarcely to himself. It was not wise, not socially fit. Thoughts like this would tend to social ostracism in his circle, or rather hers— for had she not made the circle?

And here was the rub with Mr. Haymaker, at least, that he could not make up his mind whether in his restlessness and private mental complaints he were not even now guilty of a great moral crime in so thinking. Was it not true that men and women should be faithful in marriage whether they were happy or not? Was there not some psychic law governing this matter of union—one life, one love—which made the thoughts and the pains and the subsequent sufferings and hardships of the individual, whatever they might be, seem unimportant? The churches said so. Public opinion and the law seemed to accept this. There were so many problems, so much order to be disrupted, so much pain caused, many insoluble problems where children were concerned—if

people did not stick. Was it not best, more blessed—socially, morally, and in every other way important—for him to stand by a bad bargain rather than to cause so much disorder and pain, even though he lost his own soul emotionally? He had thought so—or at least he had acted as though he thought so—and yet—How often had he wondered over this!

Take, now, some other phases. Granting first that Mrs. Haymaker had, according to the current code, measured up to the requirements of a wife, good and true, and that at first after marriage there had been just enough of physical and social charm about her to keep his state from becoming intolerable, still there was this old ache; and then newer things which came with the birth of the several children: First Elwell—named after a cousin of hers, not his— who had died only two years after he was born; and then Wesley; and then Ethelberta. How he had always disliked that name!—largely because he had hoped to call her Ottilie, a favorite name of his; or Janet, after his mother.

Curiously the arrival of these children and the death of poor little Elwell at two had somehow, in spite of his unrest, bound him to this matrimonial state and filled him with a sense of duty, and pleasure even—almost entirely apart from her, he was sorry to say—in these young lives; though if there had not been children, as he sometimes told himself, he surely would have broken away from her; he could not have stood it. They were so odd in their infancy, those little ones, so troublesome and yet so amusing—little Elwell, for instance, whose nose used to crinkle with delight when he would pretend to bite his neck, and whose gurgle of pleasure was so sweet and heart-filling that it positively thrilled and lured him. In spite of his thoughts concerning Ernestine— and always in those days they were rigidly put down as unmoral and even evil, a certain unsocial streak in him perhaps which was against law and order and social well-being—he came to have a deep and abiding feeling for Elwell. The latter, in some chemic, almost unconscious way, seemed to have arrived as a balm to his misery, a bandage for his growing wound—sent by whom, by what, how? Elwell had seized upon his imagination, and so his heartstrings— had come, indeed, to make him feel understanding and sympathy there in that little child; to supply, or seem to at least, what he lacked in the way of love and affection from one whom he could truly love. Elwell was never so happy apparently as when snuggling in his arms, not Ernestine's, or lying against his neck. And when he went for a walk or elsewhere there was Elwell always ready, arms up, to cling to his neck. He seemed, strangely enough, inordinately fond of his father, rather than his mother, and never happy without him. On his part, Haymaker came to be wildly fond of him—that queer little lump of a face, suggesting a little of himself and of his own mother, not so much of Ernestine, or so he thought, though he would not have objected to that. Not at all. He was not so small as that. Toward the end of the second year, when Elwell was just beginning to be able to utter a word or two, he had taught him that silly old rhyme which ran "There were three kittens," and when it came to "and they shall have no—" he would stop and say to Elwell, "What now?" and the latter would gurgle "puh!"—meaning, of course, pie.

Ah, those happy days with little Elwell, those walks with him over his shoulder or on his arm, those hours in which of an evening he would rock him to sleep in his arms! Always Ernestine was there, and happy in the thought of his love for little Elwell and her, her more than anything else perhaps; but it was an illusion—that latter part. He did not care for her even then as she thought he did. All his fondness was for Elwell, only she took it as evidence of his growing or enduring affection for her—another evidence of the peculiar working of her mind. Women were like that, he supposed—some women.

And then came that dreadful fever, due to some invading microbe which the doctors could not diagnose or isolate, infantile paralysis perhaps; and little Elwell had finally ceased to be as flesh and was eventually carried forth to the lorn, disagreeable graveyard near Woodlawn. How he had groaned internally, indulged in sad, despondent thoughts concerning the futility of all things human, when this had happened! It seemed for the time being as if all color and beauty had really gone out of his life for good.

"Man born of woman is of few days and full of troubles," the preacher whom Mrs. Haymaker had insisted upon having into the house at the time of the funeral had read. "He fleeth also as a shadow and continueth not."

Yes; so little Elwell had fled, as a shadow, and in his own deep sorrow at the time he had come to feel the first and only sad, deep sympathy for Ernestine that he had ever felt since marriage; and that because she had suffered so much—had lain in his arms after the funeral and cried so bitterly. It was terrible, her sorrow. Terrible—a mother grieving for her first-born! Why was it, he had thought at the time, that he had never been able to think or make her all she ought to be to him? Ernestine at this time had seemed better, softer, kinder, wiser, sweeter than she had ever seemed; more worthy, more interesting than ever he had thought her before. She had slaved so during the child's illness, stayed awake night after night, watched over him with such loving care—done everything, in short, that a loving human heart could do to rescue her young from the depths; and yet even then he had not really been able to love her. No, sad and unkind as it might seem, he had not. He had just pitied her and thought her better, worthier! What cursed stars disordered the minds and moods of people so? Why was it that these virtues of people, their good qualities, did not make you love them, did not really bind them to you, as against the things you could not like? Why? He had resolved to do better in his thoughts, but somehow, in spite of himself, he had never been able so to do.

Nevertheless, at that time he seemed to realize more keenly than ever her order, industry, frugality, a sense of beauty within limits, a certain laudable ambition to do something and be somebody—only, only he could not sympathize with her ambitions, could not see that she had anything but a hopelessly commonplace and always unimportant point of view. There was never any flare to her, never any true distinction of mind or soul. She seemed always in spite of anything he might say or do, hopelessly to identify doing and being with money and current opinion—neighborhood public opinion, almost—and local social position, whereas he knew that distinguished doing might as well be connected with poverty and shame and disgrace as with these other things —wealth and station, for instance; a thing which she could never quite understand apparently, though he often tried to tell her, much against her mood always.

Look at the cases of the great artists! Some of the greatest architects right here in the city, or in history, were of peculiar, almost disagreeable, history. But no, Mrs. Haymaker could not understand anything like that, anything connected with history, indeed—she hardly believed in history, its dark, sad pages, and would never read it, or at least did not care to. And as for art and artists—she would never have believed that wisdom and art understanding and true distinction might take their rise out of things necessarily low and evil—never.

Take now, the case of young Zingara. Zingara was an architect like himself, whom he had met more than thirty years before, here in New York, when he had first arrived, a young man struggling to become an architect of significance, only he was very poor and rather unkempt and disreputable-looking. Haymaker had found him several years before his marriage to Ernestine in the dark offices of Pyne & Starboard, Architects, and had been drawn to him definitely; but because he smoked all the time and was shabby as to his clothes and had no money—why, Mrs. Haymaker, after he had married her, and though he had known Zingara nearly four years, would have none of him. To her he was low, and a failure, one who would never succeed. Once she had seen him in some cheap restaurant that she chanced to be passing, in company with a drabby-looking maid, and that was the end.

"I wish you wouldn't bring him here any more, dear," she had insisted; and to have peace he had complied—only, now look. Zingara had since become a great architect, but now of course, owing to Mrs. Haymaker, he was definitely alienated. He was the man who had since designed the Æsculapian Club; and Symphony Hall with its delicate façade; as well as the tower of the Wells Building, sending its sweet lines so high, like a poetic thought or dream. But Zingara was now a dreamy recluse like himself, very exclusive, as Haymaker had long since come to know, and indifferent as to what people thought or said.

But perhaps it was not just obtuseness to certain of the finer shades and meanings of life, but an irritating aggressiveness at times, backed only by her limited understanding, which caused her to seek and wish to be here, there and the other place; wherever, in her mind, the truly successful—which meant nearly always the materially successful of a second or third rate character—were, which irritated him most of all. How often had he tried to point out the difference between true and shoddy distinction—the former rarely connected with great wealth.

But no. So often she seemed to imagine such queer people to be truly successful, when they were really not—usually people with just money, or a very little more.

And in the matter of rearing and educating and marrying their two children, Wesley and Ethelberta, who had come after Elwell—what peculiar pains and feelings had not been involved in all this for him. In infancy both of these had seemed sweet enough, and so close to him, though never quite so wonderful as Elwell. But, as they grew, it seemed somehow as though Ernestine had come between him and them. First, it was the way she had raised them, the very stiff and formal manner in which they were supposed to move and be, copied from the few new-rich whom she had chanced to meet through him—and admired in spite of his warnings. That was the irony of architecture as a profession—it was always bringing such queer people close to one, and for the sake of one's profession, sometimes, particularly in the case of the young architect, one had to be nice to them. Later, it was the kind of school they should attend. He had half imagined at first that it would be the public school, because they both had begun as simple people; but no, since they were prospering it had to be a private school for each, and not one of his selection, either—or hers, really—but one to which the Barlows and the Westervelts, two families of means with whom Ernestine had become intimate, sent their children and therefore thought excellent!

The Barlows! Wealthy, but, to him, gross and mediocre people who had made a great deal of money in the manufacture of patent medicines out West, and who had then come to New York to splurge, and had been attracted to Ernestine—not him particularly, he imagined—because Haymaker had built a town house for them, and also because he was gain-

ing a fine reputation. They were dreadful really, so *gauche*, so truly dull; and yet somehow they seemed to suit Ernestine's sense of fitness and worth at the time, because, as she said, they were good and kind—like her Western home folks; only they were not really. She just imagined so. They were worthy enough people in their way, though with no taste. Young Fred Barlow had been sent to the ex-
10 pensive Gaillard School for Boys, near Morristown, where they were taught manners and airs, and little else, as Haymaker always thought, though Ernestine insisted that they were given a religious training as well. And so Wesley had to go there—for a time, anyhow. It was the best school.

And similarly, because Mercedes Westervelt, senseless, vain little thing, was sent to Briarcliff School, near White Plains, Ethelberta had to
20 go there. Think of it! It was all so silly, so pushing. How well he remembered the long, delicate campaign which preceded this, the logic and tactics employed, the importance of it socially to Ethelberta, the tears and cajolery. Mrs. Haymaker could always cry so easily, or seem to be on the verge of it, when she wanted anything; and somehow, in spite of the fact that he knew her tears were unimportant, or timed and for a purpose, he could never stand
30 out against them, and she knew it. Always he felt moved or weakened in spite of himself. He had no weapon wherewith to fight them, though he resented them as a part of the argument. Positively Mrs. Haymaker could be as sly and as ruthless as Machiavelli himself at times, and yet believe all the while that she was tender, loving, self-sacrificing, generous, moral and a dozen other things, all of which led to the final achievement of her own aims.
40 Perhaps this was admirable from one point of view, but it irritated him always. But if one were unable to see him—or herself—their actual disturbing inconsistencies, what were you to do?

And again, he had by then been married so long that it was almost impossible to think of throwing her over, or so it seemed at the time. They had reached the place then where they had supposedly achieved position together, though in reality it was all his—and not such
50 position as he was entitled to, at that. Ernestine —and he was thinking this in all kindness— could never attract the ideal sort. And anyhow,

the mere breath of a scandal between them, separation or unfaithfulness, which he never really contemplated, would have led to endless bickering and social and commercial injury, or so he thought. All her strong friends—and his, in a way—those who had originally been his clients, would have deserted him. Their wives, their own social fears, would have compelled 60 them to ostracize him! He would have been a scandal-marked architect, a brute for objecting to so kind and faithful and loving a wife. And perhaps he would have been, at that. He could never quite tell, it was all so mixed and tangled.

Take, again, the marriage of his son Wesley into the de Gaud family—George de Gaud *père* being nothing more than a retired real-estate speculator and promoter who had money, but 70 nothing more; and Irma de Gaud, the daughter, being a gross, coarse, sensuous girl, physically attractive no doubt, and financially reasonably secure, or so she had seemed; but what else? Nothing, literally nothing; and his son had seemed to have at least some spiritual ideals at first. Ernestine had taken up with Mrs. George de Gaud—a miserable, narrow creature, so Haymaker thought—largely for Wesley's sake, he presumed. Anyhow, everything had 80 been done to encourage Wesley in his suit and Irma in her toleration, and now look at them! De Gaud *père* had since failed and left his daughter practically nothing. Irma had been interested in anything but Wesley's career, had followed what she considered the smart among the new-rich—a smarter, wilder, newer new-rich than ever Ernestine had fancied, or could. To-day she was without a thought for anything besides teas and country clubs and theaters—and 90 what else?

And long since Wesley had begun to realize it himself. He was an engineer now, in the employ of one of the great construction companies, a moderately successful man. But even Ernestine, who had engineered the match and thought it wonderful, was now down on her. She had begun to see through her some years ago, when Irma had begun to ignore her; only before it was always the de Gauds here, and 100 the de Gauds there. Good gracious, what more could any one want than the de Gauds—Irma de Gaud, for instance? Then came the concealed dissension between Irma and Wesley,

301

and now Mrs. Haymaker insisted that Irma had held, and was holding Wesley back. She was not the right woman for him. Almost— against all her prejudices—she was willing that he should leave her. Only, if Haymaker had broached anything like that in connection with himself!

And yet Mrs. Haymaker had been determined, because of what she considered the position of the de Gauds at that time, that Wesley should marry Irma. Wesley now had to slave at mediocre tasks in order to have enough to allow Irma to run in so-called fast society of a second or third rate. And even at that she was not faithful to him—or so Haymaker believed. There were so many strange evidences. And yet Haymaker felt that he did not care to interfere now. How could he? Irma was tired of Wesley, and that was all there was to it. She was looking elsewhere, he was sure.

Take but one more case, that of Ethelberta. What a name! In spite of all Ernestine's determination to make her so successful and thereby reflect some credit on her had she really succeeded in so doing? To be sure, Ethelberta's marriage was somewhat more successful financially than Wesley's had proved to be, but was she any better placed in other ways? John Kelso—"Jack," as she always called him—with his light ways and lighter mind, was he really any one!—anything more than a waster? His parents stood by him no doubt, but that was all; and so much the worse for him. According to Mrs. Haymaker at the time, he, too, was an ideal boy, admirable, just the man for Ethelberta, because the Kelsos, *père* and *mère*, had money. Homer Kelso had made a kind of fortune in Chicago in the banknote business, and he had settled in New York, about the time that Ethelberta was fifteen, to spend it. Ethelberta had met Grace Kelso at school.

And now see! She was not unattractive, and had some pleasant albeit highly affected, social ways; she had money, and a comfortable apartment in Park Avenue; but what had it all come to? John Kelso had never done anything really, nothing. His parents' money and indulgence and his early training for a better social state had ruined him if he had ever had a mind that amounted to anything. He was idle, pleasure-loving, mentally indolent, like Irma de Gaud. Those two should have met and married, only they could never have endured each other. But how Mrs. Haymaker had courted the Kelsos in her eager and yet diplomatic way, giving teas and receptions and theater parties; and yet he had never been able to exchange ten significant words with either of them, or the younger Kelsos either. Think of it!

And somehow in the process Ethelberta, for all his early affection and tenderness and his still kindly feeling for her, had been weaned away from him and had proved a limited and conventional girl, somewhat like her mother, and more inclined to listen to her than to him —though he had not minded that really. It had been the same with Wesley before her. Perhaps, however, a child was entitled to its likes and dislikes, regardless.

But why had he stood for it all, he now kept asking himself. Why? What grand results, if any, had been achieved? Were their children so wonderful?—their lives? Would he not have been better off without her—his children better, even, by a different woman?—hers by a different man? Wouldn't it have been better if he had destroyed it all, broken away? There would have been pain, of course, terrible consequences, but even so he would have been free to go, to do, to reorganize his life on another basis. Zingara had avoided marriage entirely— wise man. But no, no; always convention, that long list of reasons and terrors he was always reciting to himself. He had allowed himself to be pulled round by the nose, God only knows why, and that was all there was to it. Weakness, if you will, perhaps; fear of convention; fear of what people would think and say.

Always now he found himself brooding over the dire results to him of all this respect on his part for convention, moral order, the duty of keeping society on an even keel, of not bringing disgrace to his children and himself and her, and yet ruining his own life emotionally by so doing. To be respectable had been so important that it had resulted in spiritual failure for him. But now all that was over with him, and Mrs. Haymaker was ill, near to death, and he was expected to wish her to get well, and be happy with her for a long time yet! Be happy! In spite of anything he might wish or think he ought to do, he couldn't. He couldn't even wish her to get well.

It was too much to ask. There was actually

a haunting satisfaction in the thought that she might die now. It wouldn't be much, but it would be something—a few years of freedom. That was something. He was not utterly old yet, and he might have a few years of peace and comfort to himself still—and—and—That dream—that dream—though it might never come true now—it couldn't really—still—still— He wanted to be free to go his own way once more, to do as he pleased, to walk, to think, to brood over what he had not had—to brood over what he had not had! Only, only, whenever he looked into her pale sick face and felt her damp limp hands he could not quite wish that, either; not quite, not even now. It seemed too hard, too brutal—only—only—So he wavered.

No; in spite of her long-past struggle over foolish things and in spite of himself and all he had endured or thought he had, he was still willing that she should live; only he couldn't wish it exactly. Yes, let her live if she could. What matter to him now whether she lived or died? Whenever he looked at her he could not help thinking how helpless she would be without him, what a failure at her age, and so on. And all along, as he wryly repeated to himself, she had been thinking and feeling that she was doing the very best for him and her and the children!—that she was really the ideal wife for him, making every dollar go as far as it would, every enjoyment yield the last drop for them all, every move seeming to have been made to their general advantage! Yes, that was true. There was a pathos about it, wasn't there? But as for the actual results—!

The next morning, the second after his talk with Doctor Storm, found him sitting once more beside his front window in the early dawn, and so much of all this, and much more, was coming back to him, as before. For the thousandth or the ten-thousandth time, as it seemed to him, in all the years that had gone, he was concluding again that his life was a failure. If only he were free for a little while just to be alone and think, perhaps to discover what life might bring him yet; only on this occasion his thoughts were colored by a new turn in the situation. Yesterday afternoon, because Mrs. Haymaker's condition had grown worse, the consultation between Grainger and Storm was held, and to-day sometime transfusion was

to be tried, that last grim stand taken by physicians in distress over a case; blood taken from a strong ex-cavalryman out of a position, in this case, and the best to be hoped for, but not assured. In this instance his thoughts were as before wavering. Now supposing she really died, in spite of this? What would he think of himself then? He went back after a time and looked in on her where she was still sleeping. Now she was not so strong as before, or so she seemed; her pulse was not so good, the nurse said. And now as before his mood changed in her favor, but only for a little while. For later, waking, she seemed to look and feel better.

Later he came up to the dining room, where the nurse was taking her breakfast, and seating himself beside her, as was his custom these days, asked: "How do you think she is to-day?"

He and the night nurse had thus had their breakfasts together for days. This nurse, Miss Filson, was such a smooth, pink, graceful creature, with light hair and blue eyes, the kind of eyes and color that of late, and in earlier years, had suggested to him the love time or youth that he had missed.

The latter looked grave, as though she really feared the worst but was concealing it.

"No worse, I think, and possibly a little better," she replied, eying him sympathetically. He could see that she too felt that he was old and in danger of being neglected. "Her pulse is a little stronger, nearly normal now, and she is resting easily. Doctor Storm and Doctor Grainger are coming, though, at ten. Then they'll decide what's to be done. I think if she's worse that they are going to try transfusion. The man has been engaged. Doctor Storm said that when she woke to-day she was to be given strong beef tea. Mrs. Elfridge is making it now. The fact that she is not much worse, though, is a good sign in itself, I think."

Haymaker merely stared at her from under his heavy gray eyebrows. He was so tired and gloomy, not only because he had not slept much of late himself but because of this sawing to and fro between his varying moods. Was he never to be able to decide for himself what he really wished? Was he never to be done with this interminable moral or spiritual problem? Why could he not make up his mind on the side of moral order, sympathy, and be at peace? Miss Filson pattered on about other heart cases, how so many people lived years and years after they were supposed to die of heart lesion; and he meditated as to the grayness and strangeness of it all, the worthlessness of his own life, the variability of his own moods. Why was he so? How queer—how almost evil, sinister—he had become at times; how weak at others. Last night as he had looked at Ernestine lying in bed, and this morning before he had seen her, he had thought if she only would die—if he were only really free once more, even at this late date. But then when he had seen her again this morning and now when Miss Filson spoke of transfusion, he felt sorry again. What good would it do him now? Why should he want to kill her? Could such evil ideas go unpunished either in this world or the next? Supposing his children could guess! Supposing she did die now—and he wished it so fervently only this morning—how would he feel? After all, Ernestine had not been so bad. She had tried, hadn't she?—only she had not been able to make a success of things, as he saw it, and he had not been able to love her, that was all. He reproached himself once more now with the hardness and the cruelty of his thoughts.

The opinion of the two physicians was that Mrs. Haymaker was not much better and that this first form of blood transfusion must be resorted to—injected straight via a pump—which should restore her greatly provided her heart did not bleed it out too freely. Before doing so, however, both men once more spoke to Haymaker, who in an excess of self-condemnation insisted that no expense must be spared. If her life was in danger, save it by any means —all. It was precious to her, to him and to her children. So he spoke. Thus he felt that he was lending every force which could be expected of him, aside from fervently wishing for her recovery, which even now, in spite of himself, he could not do. He was too weary of it all, the conventional round of duties and obligations. But if she recovered, as the physicians seemed to think she might if transfusion were tried, if she gained even, it would mean that he would have to take her away for the summer to some quiet mountain resort—to be with her hourly during the long period in which she would be recovering. Well, he would do it.

He would be bored of course, as usual, but it would be too bad to have her die when she could be saved. Yes, that was true. And yet—

He went down to his office again and in the meantime this first form of transfusion was tried, and proved a great success, apparently. She was much better, so the day nurse phoned at three; very much better. At five-thirty Mr. Haymaker returned, no unsatisfactory word having come in the interim, and there she was, resting on a raised pillow, if you please, and looking so cheerful, more like her old self than he had seen her in some time.

At once then his mood changed again. They were amazing, these variations in his own thoughts, almost chemic, not volitional, decidedly peculiar for a man who was supposed to know his own mind—only did one, ever? Now she would not die. Now the whole thing would go on as before. He was sure of it. Well, he might as well resign himself to the old sense of failure. He would never be free now. Everything would go on as before, the next and the next day the same. Terrible! Though he seemed glad—really grateful, in a way, seeing her cheerful and hopeful once more—still the obsession of failure and being once more bound forever returned now. In his own bed at midnight he said to himself: "Now she will really get well. All will be as before. I will never be free. I will never have a day—a day! Never!"

But the next morning, to his surprise and fear or comfort, as his moods varied, she was worse again; and then once more he reproached himself for his black thoughts. Was he not really killing her by what he thought? he asked himself—these constant changes in his mood? Did not his dark wishes have power? Was he not as good as a murderer in his way? Think, if he had always to feel from now on that he had killed her by wishing so! Would not that be dreadful—an awful thing really? Why was he this way? Could he not be human, kind?

When Doctor Storm came at nine-thirty, after a telephone call from the nurse, and looked grave and spoke of horses' blood as being better, thicker than human blood—not so easily bled out of the heart when injected as a serum—Haymaker was beside himself with self-reproaches and sad, disturbing fear. His dark, evil thoughts of last night and all these days had done this, he was sure. Was he really a murderer at heart, a dark criminal, plotting her death?—and for what? Why had he wished last night that she would die? Her case must be very desperate.

"You must do your best," he now said to Doctor Storm. "Whatever is needful—she must not die if you can help it."

"No, Mr. Haymaker," returned the latter sympathetically, "all that can be done will be done. You need not fear. I have an idea that we didn't inject enough yesterday, and anyhow human blood is not thick enough in this case. She responded, but not enough. We will see what we can do to-day."

Haymaker, pressed with duties, went away, subdued and sad. Now once more he decided that he must not tolerate these dark ideas any more, must rid himself of these black wishes, whatever he might feel. It was evil. They would eventually come back to him in some dark way, he might be sure. They might be influencing her. She must be allowed to recover if she could without any opposition on his part. He must now make a further sacrifice of his own life, whatever it cost. It was only decent, only human. Why should he complain now, anyhow, after all these years! What difference would a few more years make? He returned at evening, consoled by his own good thoughts and a telephone message at three to the effect that his wife was much better. This second injection had proved much more effective. Horses' blood was plainly better for her. She was stronger, and sitting up again. He entered at five, and found her lying there pale and weak, but still with a better light in her eye, a touch of color in her cheeks—or so he thought—more force, and a very faint smile for him, so marked had been the change. How great and kind Doctor Storm really was! How resourceful! If she would only get well now! If this dread siege would only abate! Doctor Storm was coming again at eight.

"Well, how are you, dear?" she asked, looking at him sweetly and lovingly, and taking his hand in hers.

He bent and kissed her forehead—a Judas kiss, he had thought up to now, but not so to-night. To-night he was kind, generous—anxious, even, for her to live.

"All right, dearest; very good indeed. And how are you? It's such a fine evening out. You ought to get well soon so as to enjoy these spring days."

"I'm going to," she replied softly. "I feel so much better. And how have you been? Has your work gone all right?"

He nodded and smiled and told her bits of news. Ethelberta had phoned that she was coming, bringing violets. Wesley had said he would be here at six, with Irma! Such-and-such people had asked after her. How could he have been so evil, he now asked himself, as to wish her to die? She was not so bad—really quite charming in her way, an ideal wife for some one, if not him. She was as much entitled to live and enjoy her life as he was to enjoy his; and after all she was the mother of his children, had been with him all these years. Besides, the day had been so fine—it was now —a wondrous May evening. The air and sky were simply delicious. A lavender haze was in the air. The telephone bell now ringing brought still another of a long series of inquiries as to her condition. There had been so many of these during the last few days, the maid said, and especially to-day—and she gave Mr. Haymaker a list of names. See, he thought, she had even more friends than he, being so good, faithful, worthy. Why should he wish her ill?

He sat down to dinner with Ethelberta and Wesley when they arrived, and chatted quite gayly—more hopefully than he had in weeks. His own varying thoughts no longer depressing him, for the moment he was happy. How were they? What were the children all doing? At eight-thirty Doctor Storm came again, and announced that he thought Mrs. Haymaker was doing very well indeed, all things considered.

"Her condition is fairly promising, I must say," he said. "If she gets through another night or two comfortably without falling back I think she'll do very well from now on. Her strength seems to be increasing a fraction. However, we must not be too optimistic. Cases of this kind are very treacherous. To-morrow we'll see how she feels, whether she needs any more blood."

He went away, and at ten Ethelberta and

Wesley left for the night, asking to be called if she grew worse, thus leaving him alone once more. He sat and meditated. At eleven, after a few moments at his wife's bedside—absolute quiet had been the doctor's instructions these many days—he himself went to bed. He was very tired. His varying thoughts had afflicted him so much that he was always tired, it seemed—his evil conscience, he called it—but to-night he was sure he would sleep. He felt better about himself, about life. He had done better, to-day. He should never have tolerated such dark thoughts. And yet—and yet—and yet—

He lay on his bed near a window which commanded a view of a small angle of the park, and looked out. There were the spring trees, as usual, silvered now by the light, a bit of lake showing at one end. Here in the city a bit of sylvan scenery such as this was so rare and so expensive. In his youth he had been so fond of water, any small lake or stream or pond. In his youth, also, he had loved the moon, and to walk in the dark. It had all, always, been so suggestive of love and happiness, and he had so craved love and happiness and never had it. Once he had designed a yacht club, the base of which suggested waves. Once, years ago, he had thought of designing a lovely cottage or country house for himself and some new love—that wonderful one—if ever she came and he were free. Now—now—the thought at such an hour and especially when it was too late, seemed sacrilegious, hard, cold, unmoral, evil. He turned his face away from the moonlight and sighed, deciding to sleep and shut out these older and darker and sweeter thoughts if he could, and did.

Presently he dreamed, and it was as if some lovely spirit of beauty—that wondrous thing he had always been seeking—came and took him by the hand and led him out, out by dimpling streams and clear rippling lakes and a great, noble highway where were temples and towers and figures in white marble. And it seemed as he walked as if something had been, or were, promised him—a lovely fruition to something which he craved—only the world toward which he walked was still dark or shadowy, with something sad and repressing about it, a haunting sense of a still darker distance. He

was going toward beauty apparently, but he was still seeking, seeking, and it was dark there when—

"Mr. Haymaker! Mr. Haymaker!" came a voice—soft, almost mystical at first, and then clearer and more disturbing, as a hand was laid on him. "Will you come at once? It's Mrs. Haymaker!"

On the instant he was on his feet seizing the blue silk dressing gown hanging at his bed's head, and adjusting it as he hurried. Mrs. Elfridge and the nurse were behind him, very pale and distrait, wringing their hands. He could tell by that that the worst was at hand. When he reached the bedroom—her bedroom—there she lay as in life—still, peaceful, already limp, as though she were sleeping. Her thin, and as he sometimes thought, cold lips were now parted in a faint, gracious smile, or trace of one. He had seen her look that way, too, at times; a really gracious smile, and wise, wiser than she was. The long, thin, graceful hands were open, the fingers spread slightly apart as though she were tired, very tired. The eyelids, too, rested wearily on tired eyes. Her form, spare as always, was outlined clearly under the thin coverlets. Miss Filson, the night nurse, was saying something about having fallen asleep for a moment, and waking only to find her so. She was terribly depressed and disturbed, possibly because of Doctor Storm.

Haymaker paused, greatly shocked and moved by the sight—more so than by anything since the death of little Elwell. After all, she had tried, according to her light. But now she was dead—and they had been together so long! He came forward, tears of sympathy springing to his eyes, then sank down beside the bed on his knees so as not to disturb her right hand where it lay.

"Ernie, dear," he said gently. "Ernie—are you really gone?" His voice was full of sorrow; but to himself it sounded false, traitorous.

He lifted the hand and put it to his lips sadly, then leaned his head against her, thinking of his long, mixed thoughts these many days, while both Mrs. Elfridge and the nurse began wiping their eyes. They were so sorry for him, he was so old now!

After a while he got up—they came forward to persuade him at last—looking tremendously sad and distrait, and asked Mrs. Elfridge and the nurse not to disturb his children. They could not aid her now. Let them rest until morning. Then he went back to his own room and sat down on the bed for a moment, gazing out on the same silvery scene that had attracted him before. It was dreadful. So then his dark wishing had come true at last? Possibly his black thoughts had killed her after all. Was that possible? Had his voiceless prayers been answered in this grim way? And did she know now what he had really thought? Dark thought. Where was she now? What was she thinking now if she knew? Would she hate him —haunt him? It was not dawn yet, only two or three in the morning, and the moon was still bright. And in the next room she was lying, pale and cool, gone forever now out of his life.

He got up after a time and went forward into that pleasant front room where he had so often loved to sit, then back into her room to view the body again. Now that she was gone, here more than elsewhere, in her dead presence, he seemed better able to collect his scattered thoughts. She might see or she might not —might know or not. It was all over now. Only he could not help but feel a little evil. She had been so faithful, if nothing more, so earnest in behalf of him and of his children. He might have spared her these last dark thoughts of these last few days. His feelings were so jumbled that he could not place them half the time. But at the same time the ethics of the past, of his own irritated feelings and moods in regard to her, had to be adjusted somehow before he could have peace. They must be adjusted, only how—how? He and Mrs. Elfridge had agreed not to disturb Doctor Storm any more to-night. They were all agreed to get what rest they could against the morning.

After a time he came forward once more to the front room to sit and gaze at the park. Here, perhaps, he could solve these mysteries for himself, think them out, find out what he did feel. He was evil for having wished all he had, that he knew and felt. And yet there was his own story, too—his life. The dawn was breaking by now; a faint grayness shaded the east and dimly lightened this room. A tall pier mirror between two windows now revealed him to himself—spare, angular, disheveled, his beard and hair astray and his eyes weary. The figure he made here as against his dreams of a happier life, once he were free, now struck him forcibly. What a farce! What a failure! Why should he, of all people, think of future happiness in love, even if he were free? Look at his reflection here in this mirror. What a picture—old, grizzled, done for! Had he not known that for so long? Was it not too ridiculous? Why should he have tolerated such vain thoughts? What could he of all people hope for now? No thing of beauty would have him now. Of course not. That glorious dream of his youth was gone forever. It was a mirage, an *ignis fatuus*. His wife might just as well have lived as died, for all the difference it would or could make to him. Only, he was really free just the same, almost as it were in spite of his varying moods. But he was old, weary, done for, a recluse and ungainly.

Now the innate cruelty of life, its blazing ironic indifference to him and so many grew rapidly upon him. What had he had? What all had he not missed? Dismally he stared first at his dark wrinkled skin; the crow's-feet at the sides of his eyes; the wrinkles across his forehead and between the eyes; his long, dark, wrinkled hands—handsome hands they once were, he thought; his angular, stiff body. Once he had been very much of a personage, he thought, striking, forceful, dynamic—but now! He turned and looked out over the park where the young trees were, and the lake, to the pinking dawn—just a trace now—a significant thing in itself at this hour surely—the new dawn, so wondrously new for younger people —then back at himself. What could he wish for now—what hope for?

As he did so his dream came back to him— that strange dream of seeking and being led and promised and yet always being led forward into a dimmer, darker land. What did that mean? Had it any real significance? Was it all to be dimmer, darker still? Was it typical of his life? He pondered.

"Free!" he said after a time. "Free! I know now how that is. I am free now, at last! Free! . . . Free! . . . Yes—free . . . to die!"

So he stood there ruminating and smoothing his hair and his beard.

SHERWOOD ANDERSON

The "Bohemian" life of a self-made writer is best explained by the author himself. Fortunately Sherwood Anderson has given us two fascinating pieces of autobiography, *A Story-Teller's Story* (1924) and *Tar, a Midwest Childhood* (1927), which are not only highly illuminating as far as the personality of the author himself is concerned but also essential to a proper comprehension of his aims and objectives in literature. Anderson was born September 13, 1876, in Camden, Ohio. His father was of Scotch-Irish descent; his mother was partly Italian. His family was a wandering gypsy sort of tribe; the father "lovable," "improvident," "colorful," "no-account," to use some of the son's own frank epithets, "the sort of a man who should have been a novelist." Apparently the Andersons moved from one small Ohio town to another as debts became increasingly oppressive. No two of the eight brothers and sisters of Sherwood Anderson were born in the same place. Most of Anderson's boyhood, however, was spent in Clyde, Ohio. His schooling was highly irregular and in any case ceased in a formal way when he was twelve years old; it was necessary for him to go to work to keep the wheels of the family running. He was for a while a timekeeper on a public construction job, a worker in various factories, a snapper-up of odd jobs, a drifter.

His drifting carried him to Chicago in 1893, where the same unsystematic routine was continued. The Spanish War gave him an opportunity for a soldier's transient fame; he served in Cuba, and when he returned, he found himself "something of a hero." Eventually he married and settled down as the manager of a paint factory in Elyria, Ohio. He also began to write; one day, dissatisfied to the point of disgust with the status of the labor-capital relationship in this country, he walked out of his office and did not return, first having made some inane remark that launched the rumor (heartily desired by Anderson) that he was crazy. He never avoided this charge.

Back to Chicago he went, where his brother was a portrait painter. Through him he met Theodore Dreiser (p. 289), Carl Sandburg (p. 567), Ben Hecht, Floyd Dell, and others of the famous Chicago group, none of whom is now living in the Middle West. "Windy McPherson's Son," his first short story, was favorably received by the group but caused moral qualms among many publishers. It finally appeared in 1916. A nervous breakdown led Anderson to try a rest cure in the Ozarks, where he wrote a novel; but upon more careful reading he was so annoyed with it that he threw the manuscript out of a train window. *Marching Men* (1917), a story of factory conditions, and *Mid-American Chants* (1918), a volume of Whitmanesque verse, gained him some recognition, most of it unfavorable. But *Winesburg, Ohio* (1919) the critics acclaimed as a fine picture of a small town in the Middle West, a town that was a composite of Camden, Clyde, Elyria, and others of the numerous towns that Anderson had known so intimately as an adolescent. The work, a series of mordant tales and sketches, was compared to Edgar Lee Masters' *Spoon River Anthology* (1915) and later to Sinclair Lewis' *Main Street* (1920) as remarkable pictures of the life of the American midwestern bourgeois. Anderson was likened to the great Russian nineteenth-century writers Dostoievski (1821–81) and Chekhov (1860–1904). Actually he had never read either of them. At the time his chief literary authorities were, instead, the Old Testament, the works of that eccentric novelist of gypsy life, George Borrow (1803–81), notably his *Lavengro* and *The Bible in Spain,* and the works of D. H. Lawrence (p. 412).

Anderson then made a trip abroad (1921) and a stay in New Orleans. But he was still restless. Ultimately he came to Smyth County, Virginia, where in the little town of Marion he established two newspapers, one Democratic in politics and the other Republican, took quarters for himself in some rooms over his printing-shop, puttered about the press at all hours, and became a country sage, philosopher, poet, and social and economic critic. Early in 1941 he began a tour of Central and South America as an unofficial kind of ambassador of good will, but was taken ill suddenly and died at Colón, Panama, on March 8, 1941.

After *Winesburg, Ohio,* which looms more and more as his best work, Anderson produced a moderately long series of miscellaneous writings. His two autobiographical works have already been mentioned. In addition there are the novels *Poor White* (1920), *Many Marriages* (1923), *Dark Laughter* (1925), *Beyond Desire* (1933), and *Kit Brandon* (1936). A strand frequently noticed in these is the relation of the black and the white races. There are some notable volumes of short stories—*The Triumph of the Egg* (1921); *Horses and Men* (1923); and *Death in the Woods* (1933), the first stories in each of which are required reading for the Anderson enthusiast. There are collections of essays or philosophical dicta like *A New Testament* (1927), which contains some verse as well. *No Swank* (1934) gives the author's impressions of well-known people. *Hello Towns!* (1929); *The American County Fair* (1930); *Perhaps Women* (1931), "a record of thoughts, of feelings in the presence of something amazing in modern life—the machine"; and *Puzzled America* (1935) can be described as sociological essays. Anderson even attempted (1937) some plays, usually dramatizations of previous stories like "The Triumph of the Egg" or scenes from *Winesburg, Ohio.*

Anderson's early contact with the Bible no doubt explains the simplicity of his style and narrative. At times this simplicity palls; it leaves the impression that the writer is merely assuming naïveté. Of naïveté there is plenty in Anderson's work, however, and it is a real, rustic, homespun type of naïveté. He is most successful when he writes about the country, the small town, the laborer in either. As a delineator of metropolitan life, he is a failure. He is inclined toward the neurotic and the pessimistic; but when he comes to portray the neurotic adolescent, he is remarkably sympathetic and true to life. Frequently he merely maunders, and he is usually prolix, at times beyond endurance. He is an earnest student of the social and economic ills that beset the mid-region

of the United States. There is not a trace of the academic, however, in Anderson, nor of the pretentious; he flaunts a kind of triumphant bourgeois attitude or proletarianism that does not always seem genuine because he is morally out of step with the bourgeoisie. He remains, none the less, an important phenomenon of the early 1920's; and although his later work failed to fulfill the promise of his earlier, he has been a significant figure in the liberation of recent American letters from the conventional and the pharisaical. But as one critic has remarked, there is in Sherwood Anderson "too much smug subscribing to the sentiments of the popular song, 'Hallelujah! I'm a bum!' "

Sophistication

IT WAS early evening of a day in the late fall and the Winesburg County Fair had brought crowds of country people into town. The day had been clear and the night came on warm and pleasant. On the Trunion Pike, where the road after it left town stretched away between berry fields now covered with dry brown leaves, the dust from passing wagons arose in clouds. Children, curled into little balls, slept on the straw scattered on wagon beds. Their 10 hair was full of dust and their fingers black and sticky. The dust rolled away over the fields and the departing sun set it ablaze with colors.

In the main street of Winesburg crowds filled the stores and the sidewalks. Night came on, horses whinnied, the clerks in the stores ran madly about, children became lost and cried lustily, an American town worked terribly at the task of amusing itself. 20

Pushing his way through the crowds in Main Street, young George Willard concealed himself in the stairway leading to Doctor Reefy's office and looked at the people. With feverish eyes he watched the faces drifting past under the store lights. Thoughts kept coming into his head and he did not want to think. He stamped impatiently on the wooden steps and looked sharply about. "Well, is she going to stay with him all day? Have I done all this waiting for nothing?" he muttered.

George Willard, the Ohio village boy, was fast growing into manhood and new thoughts had been coming into his mind. All that day, amid the jam of people at the Fair, he had gone about feeling lonely. He was about to leave Winesburg to go away to some city where he hoped to get work on a city newspaper and he felt grown up. The mood that had taken possession of him was a thing known to men and unknown to boys. He felt old and a little tired. Memories awoke in him. To his mind his new sense of maturity set him apart, made of him a half-tragic figure. He wanted someone to understand the feeling that had taken possession of him after his mother's death.

There is a time in the life of every boy when he for the first time takes the backward view of life. Perhaps that is the moment when he crosses the line into manhood. The boy is walking through the street of his town. He is thinking of the future and of the figure he will cut in the world. Ambitions and regrets awake within him. Suddenly something happens; he stops under a tree and waits as for a voice calling his name. Ghosts of old things creep into his consciousness; the voices outside of himself whisper a message concerning the limitations of life. From being quite sure of himself and his future he becomes not at all sure. If he be an imaginative boy a door is torn open and for the first time he looks out upon the world, seeing, as though they marched in procession before him, the countless figures of men who before his time have come out of nothingness into the world, lived their lives and again disappeared into nothingness. The sadness of sophistication has come to the boy. With a little gasp he sees himself as merely a leaf blown by the wind through the streets of his village. He knows that in spite of all the stout talk of his fellows he must live and die in uncertainty, a thing blown by the winds, a thing destined like corn to wilt in the sun. He shivers and looks eagerly about. The eighteen years he has lived seem but a moment, a breathing space in the long march of humanity. Already he hears death calling. With all his heart he wants to come close to some other human, touch some-

one with his hands, be touched by the hand of another. If he prefers that the other be a woman, that is because he believes that a woman will be gentle, that she will understand. He wants, most of all, understanding.

When the moment of sophistication came to George Willard, his mind turned to Helen White, the Winesburg banker's daughter. Always he had been conscious of the girl growing into womanhood as he grew into manhood. Once on a summer night when he was eighteen, he had walked with her on a country road and in her presence had given way to an impulse to boast, to make himself appear big and significant in her eyes. Now he wanted to see her for another purpose. He wanted to tell her of the new impulses that had come to him. He had tried to make her think of him as a man when he knew nothing of manhood and now he wanted to be with her and to try to make her feel the change he believed had taken place in his nature.

As for Helen White, she also had come to a period of change. What George felt, she in her young woman's way felt also. She was no longer a girl and hungered to reach into the grace and beauty of womanhood. She had come home from Cleveland, where she was attending college, to spend a day at the Fair. She also had begun to have memories. During the day she sat in the grandstand with a young man, one of the instructors from the college, who was a guest of her mother's. The young man was of a pedantic turn of mind and she felt at once he would not do for her purpose. At the Fair she was glad to be seen in his company as he was well dressed and a stranger. She knew that the fact of his presence would create an impression. During the day she was happy, but when night came on she began to grow restless. She wanted to drive the instructor away, to get out of his presence. While they sat together in the grandstand and while the eyes of former schoolmates were upon them, she paid so much attention to her escort that he grew interested. "A scholar needs money. I should marry a woman with money," he mused.

Helen White was thinking of George Willard even as he wandered gloomily through the crowds thinking of her. She remembered the summer evening when they had walked together and wanted to walk with him again. She thought that the months she had spent in the city, the going to theatres and the seeing of great crowds wandering in lighted thoroughfares, had changed her profoundly. She wanted him to feel and be conscious of the change in her nature.

The summer evening together that had left its mark on the memory of both the young man and woman had, when looked at quite sensibly, been rather stupidly spent. They had walked out of town along a country road. Then they had stopped by a fence near a field of young corn and George had taken off his coat and let it hang on his arm. "Well, I've stayed here in Winesburg—yes—I've not yet gone away but I'm growing up," he said. "I've been reading books and I've been thinking. I'm going to try to amount to something in life.

"Well," he explained, "that isn't the point. Perhaps I'd better quit talking."

The confused boy put his hand on the girl's arm. His voice trembled. The two started to walk back along the road to town. In his desperation George boasted, "I'm going to be a big man, the biggest that ever lived here in Winesburg," he declared. "I want you to do something, I don't know what. Perhaps it is none of my business. I want you to try to be different from other women. You see the point. It's none of my business I tell you. I want you to be a beautiful woman. You see what I want."

The boy's voice failed and in silence the two came back into town and went along the street to Helen White's house. At the gate he tried to say something impressive. Speeches he had thought out came into his head, but they seemed utterly pointless. "I thought—I used to think—I had it in my mind you would marry Seth Richmond. Now I know you won't," was all he could find to say as she went through the gate and toward the door of her house.

On the warm fall evening as he stood in the stairway and looked at the crowd drifting through Main Street, George thought of the talk beside the field of young corn and was ashamed of the figure he had made of himself. In the street the people surged up and down like cattle confined in a pen. Buggies and wagons almost filled the narrow thoroughfare. A band played and small boys raced along the sidewalk, diving between the legs of men. Young men with shining red faces walked awkwardly about with girls on their arms. In a room above one of the stores, where a dance was to be held, the fiddlers tuned their instruments. The broken sounds floated down through an open window and out across the murmur of voices and the loud blare of the horns of the band. The medley of sounds got on young Willard's nerves. Everywhere, on all sides, the sense of crowding, moving life closed in about him. He wanted to run away by himself and think. "If she wants to stay with that fellow she may. Why should I care? What difference does it make to me?" he growled and went along Main Street and through Hern's grocery into a side street.

George felt so utterly lonely and dejected that he wanted to weep but pride made him walk rapidly along, swinging his arms. He came to Westley Moyer's livery barn and stopped in the shadows to listen to a group of men who talked of a race Westley's stallion, Tony Tip, had won at the Fair during the afternoon. A crowd had gathered in front of the barn and before the crowd walked Westley, prancing up and down and boasting. He held a whip in his hand and kept tapping the ground. Little puffs of dust arose in the lamplight. "Hell, quit your talking," Westley exclaimed. "I wasn't afraid, I knew I had 'em beat all the time. I wasn't afraid."

Ordinarily George Willard would have been intensely interested in the boasting of Moyer, the horseman. Now it made him angry. He turned and hurried away along the street. "Old windbag," he sputtered. "Why does he want to be bragging? Why don't he shut up?"

George went into a vacant lot and as he hurried along, fell over a pile of rubbish. A nail protruding from an empty barrel tore his trousers. He sat down on the ground and swore. With a pin he mended the torn place and then arose and went on. "I'll go to Helen White's house, that's what I'll do. I'll walk right in. I'll say that I want to see her. I'll walk right in and sit down, that's what I'll do," he declared, climbing over a fence and beginning to run.

.   .   .   .   .

On the veranda of Banker White's house Helen was restless and distraught. The instructor sat between the mother and daughter. His talk wearied the girl. Although he had also been raised in an Ohio town, the instructor began to put on the airs of the city. He wanted to appear cosmopolitan. "I like the chance you have given me to study the background out of which most of our girls come," he declared. "It was good of you, Mrs. White, to have me down for the day." He turned to Helen and laughed. "Your life is still bound up with the life of this town?" he asked. "There are people here in whom you are interested?" To the girl his voice sounded pompous and heavy.

Helen arose and went into the house. At the door leading to a garden at the back she stopped and stood listening. Her mother began to talk. "There is no one here fit to associate with a girl of Helen's breeding," she said.

Helen ran down a flight of stairs at the back of the house and into the garden. In the darkness she stopped and stood trembling. It seemed to her that the world was full of meaningless people saying words. Afire with eagerness she ran through a garden gate and turning a corner by the banker's barn, went into a little side street. "George! Where are you, George?" she cried, filled with nervous excitement. She stopped running, and leaned against a tree to laugh hysterically. Along the dark little street came George Willard, still saying words. "I'm going to walk right into her house. I'll go right in and sit down," he declared as he came up to her. He stopped and stared stupidly. "Come on," he said and took hold of her hand. With hanging heads they walked away along the street under the trees. Dry leaves rustled under foot. Now that he had found her George wondered what he had better do and say.

.   .   .   .   .   .

At the upper end of the fair ground, in Winesburg, there is a half decayed old grandstand. It has never been painted and the boards are all warped out of shape. The fair ground stands on top of a low hill rising out of the valley of Wine Creek and from the grandstand one can see at night, over a cornfield, the lights of the town reflected against the sky.

George and Helen climbed the hill to the fair ground, coming by the path past Waterworks Pond. The feeling of loneliness and iso-

lation that had come to the young man in the crowded streets of his town was both broken and intensified by the presence of Helen. What he felt was reflected in her.

In youth there are always two forces fighting in people. The warm unthinking little animal struggles against the thing that reflects and remembers, and the older, the more sophisticated thing had possession of George Willard. Sensing his mood, Helen walked beside him filled with respect. When they got to the grandstand they climbed up under the roof and sat down on one of the long bench-like seats.

There is something memorable in the experience to be had by going into a fair ground that stands at the edge of a Middle Western town on a night after the annual fair has been held. The sensation is one never to be forgotten. On all sides are ghosts, not of the dead, but of living people. Here, during the day just passed, have come the people pouring in from the town and the country around. Farmers with their wives and children and all the people from the hundreds of little frame houses have gathered within these board walls. Young girls have laughed and men with beards have talked of the affairs of their lives. The place has been filled to overflowing with life. It has itched and squirmed with life and now it is night and the life has all gone away. The silence is almost terrifying. One conceals oneself standing silently beside the trunk of a tree and what there is of a reflective tendency in his nature is intensified. One shudders at the thought of the meaninglessness of life while at the same instant, and if the people of the town are his people, one loves life so intensely that tears come into the eyes.

In the darkness under the roof of the grandstand, George Willard sat beside Helen White and felt very keenly his own insignificance in the scheme of existence. Now that he had come out of town where the presence of the people stirring about, busy with a multitude of affairs, had been so irritating the irritation was all gone. The presence of Helen renewed and refreshed him. It was as though her woman's hand was assisting him to make some minute readjustment of the machinery of his life. He began to think of the people in the town where he had always lived with something like reverence. He had reverence for Helen. He wanted to love and to be loved by her, but he did not want at the moment to be confused by her womanhood. In the darkness he took hold of her hand and when she crept close put a hand on her shoulder. A wind began to blow and he shivered. With all his strength he tried to hold and to understand the mood that had come upon him. In that high place in the darkness the two oddly sensitive human atoms held each other tightly and waited. In the mind of each was that same thought. "I have come to this lonely place and here is this other," was the substance of the thing felt.

In Winesburg the crowded day had run itself out into the long night of the late fall. Farm horses jogged away along lonely country roads pulling their portion of weary people. Clerks began to bring samples of goods in off the sidewalk and lock the doors of stores. In the Opera House a crowd had gathered to see a show and further down Main Street the fiddlers, their instruments tuned, sweated and worked to keep the feet of youth flying over a dance floor.

In the darkness of the grandstand Helen White and George Willard remained silent. Now and then the spell that held them was broken and they turned and tried in the dim light to see into each other's eyes. They kissed but that impulse did not last. At the upper end of the fair ground a half dozen men worked over horses that had raced during the afternoon. The men had built a fire and were heating kettles of water. Only their legs could be seen as they passed back and forth in the light. When the wind blew the little flames of the fire danced crazily about.

George and Helen arose and walked away into the darkness. They went along a path past a field of corn that had not yet been cut. The wind whispered among the dry corn blades. For a moment during the walk back into town the spell that held them was broken. When they had come to the crest of Waterworks Hill they stopped by a tree and George again put his hands on the girl's shoulders. She embraced him eagerly and then again they drew quickly back from that impulse. They stopped kissing and stood a little apart. Mutual respect grew big in them. They were both embarrassed and to relieve their embarrassment dropped into the animalism of youth. They laughed and began to pull and haul at each other. In some way chastened and purified by the mood they had been in they became, not man and woman, not boy and girl, but excited little animals.

It was so they went down the hill. In the darkness they played like two splendid young things in a young world. Once, running swiftly forward, Helen tripped George and he fell. He squirmed and shouted. Shaking with laughter, he rolled down the hill. Helen ran after him. For just a moment she stopped in the darkness. There is no way of knowing what woman's thoughts went through her mind but, when the bottom of the hill was reached and she came up to the boy, she took his arm and walked beside him in dignified silence. For some reason they could not have explained they had both got from their silent evening together the thing needed. Man or boy, woman or girl, they had for a moment taken hold of the thing that makes the mature life of men and women in the modern world possible.

WILLA CATHER

Among the prominent women writers of the present generation—and there have been a great many of them—Willa Sibert Cather has earned a secure and honorable position as one who was an excellent stylist as well as a sympathetic interpreter of humanity. She was born on December 7, 1876, near Winchester, Vir- ginia. Her family had been in this country for two full generations before her; they had originally emigrated from Ireland but were Englishmen who had been granted land in Ireland for their loyalty to the Stuart cause far back in the seventeenth century. In 1884 Willa Cather was taken by her parents to a ranch in Nebraska, where she experienced, at an impressionable age, the openness and simplicity of life on the prairie. Many of her companions were children of immigrants who were hastening to gain whatever profit they could from the fast-disappearing western frontier. Miss Cather was taught at home, for there were no elementary schools in the neighborhood; she herself tells us how as a child she read the classics at night to her two grandmothers. Finally she matriculated at the University of Nebraska, where she worked her way through college by filling a position on a Lincoln newspaper. She graduated in 1895.

Life on a prairie farm was not what she wanted to lead indefinitely; so Miss Cather departed to a more sophisticated community where there might be music and art and greater opportunity for self-expression. She went to Pittsburgh and joined the staff of the Pittsburgh *Daily Leader,* staying there until 1901. In that year she accepted the headship of the English department of the Allegheny High School.

It was about this same time that Miss Cather began to write. First some of her poems began to appear in various magazines; these were collected and printed in 1903 under the title *April Twilights.* These poems were delicate and derivative. Then came, two years later, a collection of short stories, *The Troll Garden.* These artistically written narratives won their author many favorable reviews. As an immediate consequence she was offered an editorship on *McClure's Magazine* (1906); then, and for some half-dozen years thereafter, this magazine was one of the most energetic and fearless periodicals in the country, and its fiction was of excellent standard. Miss Cather accepted the offer and was so successful in her relationship with the magazine that she was its managing editor from 1908 to 1912. It was while she was with *McClure's* that she first traveled extensively abroad. But whenever the opportunity offered, she preferred to return to Wyoming and Nebraska; she was homesick for her prairies.

In 1912 Miss Cather terminated her connection with *McClure's* and devoted herself to writing. Her work was never remarkable in bulk but was of a uniformly high degree of excellence; and her literary following has always

been reliable and devoted. Her life was uneventful; most of it was spent in the Middle West and the Southwest. She surrounded herself with books, with paintings of the many lands she had visited, and with photographs of the musicians and writers she had met. After 1920 her efforts were given more to the novel than to the short story, but she worked felicitously in both mediums. Included among her volumes of short stories are *The Troll Garden* (1905); *Youth and the Bright Medusa* (1920); *Obscure Destinies* (1932); and a charming series of personal reminiscences couched in the form of short stories, *Not under Forty* (1936). (Her last collection, *The Old Beauty and Others,* appeared posthumously in 1948.) Her novels are *The Bohemian Girl* (1912); *Alexander's Bridge* (1912); *O Pioneers!* (1913); *The Song of the Lark* (1915); *My Ántonia* (1918); *One of Ours* (1922), which won the Pulitzer Prize for novels in that year; *A Lost Lady* (1923); *The Professor's House* (1925); *My Mortal Enemy* (1926); *Death Comes for the Archbishop* (1927), probably her masterpiece; *Shadows on the Rock* (1931); *Lucy Gayheart* (1935); and *Sapphira and the Slave-Girl* (1940). Miss Cather died in New York City on April 24, 1947.

In addition to honorary degrees from various American universities, Miss Cather was awarded (1933) the "Prix Fémina Américaine" for "distinguished literary achievement." It should be remarked that she had two major interests in her writing. One of these was, of course, the creation of human characters, particularly those living in an environment with which she was familiar. So with the settlers of *O Pioneers!* the immigrants of *My Ántonia,* the Indians, Mexicans, and half-breeds of *Death Comes for the Archbishop.* The other literary interest of Miss Cather was her style. She always expressed herself in an unusually lucid, direct manner, yet with great flexibility and finish. She tended to develop, however, a simplicity which is sometimes exaggerated and austere; and her preoccupation with style therefore imparted a certain thinness to her later works, even when, as in *Shadows on the Rock,* she invested her work with historical garments. Her best work undoubtedly comprises those books which began with *O Pioneers!* and ended with *Death Comes for the*

Archbishop. In these there is a quiet approach to life, fully sensitive to its beauty but not ignoring the mean, ignoble, and ungracious. She is realistic implicitly rather than explicitly but is none the less effective because she leaves much to the reader's imagination. To take but one example: it is quite possible to argue that "The Sculptor's Funeral," from *Youth and the Bright Medusa,* is as strong an indictment of the petty cruelties and drabness of a small midwestern town as is Sinclair Lewis' *Main Street,* with its flood of ruthless photographic minutiae. It is surely more artistic than Lewis' novel and more exhilarating to the reader, provided always that he can see for himself what Miss Cather sees but does not tell. One must have something in him of the craftsman fully to appreciate a craftsman.

The Sculptor's Funeral

A GROUP of the townspeople stood on the station siding of a little Kansas town, awaiting the coming of the night train, which was already twenty minutes overdue. The snow had fallen thick over everything; in the pale starlight the line of bluffs across the wide, white meadows south of the town made soft, smoke-coloured curves against the clear sky. The men on the siding stood first on one foot and then on the other, their hands thrust deep into their trousers pockets, their overcoats open, their shoulders screwed up with the cold; and they glanced from time to time toward the southeast, where the railroad track wound along the river shore. They conversed in low tones and moved about restlessly, seeming uncertain as to what was expected of them. There was but one of the company who looked as if he knew exactly why he was there, and he kept conspicuously apart; walking to the far end of the platform, returning to the station door, then pacing up the track again, his chin sunk in the high collar of his overcoat, his burly shoulders drooping forward, his gait

"The Sculptor's Funeral" reprinted from *Youth and the Bright Medusa* by Willa Cather, by permission of and special arrangement with Alfred A. Knopf, Inc., authorized publishers.

heavy and dogged. Presently he was approached by a tall, spare, grizzled man clad in a faded Grand Army suit, who shuffled out from the group and advanced with a certain deference, craning his neck forward until his back made the angle of a jack-knife three-quarters open.

"I reckon she's a-goin' to be pretty late agin tonight, Jim," he remarked in a squeaky falsetto. "S'pose it's the snow?"

"I don't know," responded the other man with a shade of annoyance, speaking from out an astonishing cataract of red beard that grew fiercely and thickly in all directions.

The spare man shifted the quill toothpick he was chewing to the other side of his mouth. "It ain't likely that anybody from the East will come with the corpse, I s'pose," he went on reflectively.

"I don't know," responded the other, more curtly than before.

"It's too bad he didn't belong to some lodge or other. I like an order funeral myself. They seem more appropriate for people of some repytation," the spare man continued, with an ingratiating concession in his shrill voice, as he carefully placed his toothpick in his vest pocket. He always carried the flag at the G.A.R. funerals in the town.

The heavy man turned on his heel, without replying, and walked up the siding. The spare man rejoined the uneasy group. "Jim's ez full ez a tick, ez ushel," he commented commiseratingly.

Just then a distant whistle sounded, and there was a shuffling of feet on the platform. A number of lanky boys, of all ages, appeared as suddenly and slimily as eels wakened by the crack of thunder; some came from the waiting-room, where they had been warming themselves by the red stove, or half asleep on the slat benches; others uncoiled themselves from baggage trucks or slid out of express wagons. Two clambered down from the driver's seat of a hearse that stood backed up against the siding. They straightened their stooping shoulders and lifted their heads, and a flash of momentary animation kindled their dull eyes at that cold, vibrant scream, the worldwide call for men. It stirred them like the note of a trumpet, just as it had often stirred the man who was coming home tonight, in his boyhood.

The night express shot, red as a rocket, from out the eastward marsh lands and wound along the river shore under the long lines of shivering poplars that sentinelled the meadows, the escaping steam hanging in grey masses against the pale sky and blotting out the Milky Way. In a moment the red glare from the headlight streamed up the snow-covered track before the siding and glittered on the wet, black rails. The burly man with the dishevelled red beard walked swiftly up the platform toward the approaching train, uncovering his head as he went. The group of men behind him hesitated, glanced questioningly at one another, and awkwardly followed his example. The train stopped, and the crowd shuffled up to the express car just as the door was thrown open, the man in the G.A.R. suit thrusting his head forward with curiosity. The express messenger appeared in the doorway, accompanied by a young man in a long ulster and travelling cap.

"Are Mr. Merrick's friends here?" inquired the young man.

The group on the platform swayed uneasily. Philip Phelps, the banker, responded with dignity: "We have come to take charge of the body. Mr. Merrick's father is very feeble and can't be about."

"Send the agent out here," growled the express messenger, "and tell the operator to lend a hand."

The coffin was got out of its rough-box and down on the snowy platform. The townspeople drew back enough to make room for it and then formed a close semicircle about it, looking curiously at the palm leaf which lay across the black cover. No one said anything. The baggage man stood by his truck, waiting to get at the trunks. The engine panted heavily, and the fireman dodged in and out among the wheels with his yellow torch and long oil-can, snapping the spindle boxes. The young Bostonian, one of the dead sculptor's pupils who had come with the body, looked about him helplessly. He turned to the banker, the only one of that black, uneasy, stoop-shouldered group who seemed enough of an individual to be addressed.

"None of Mr. Merrick's brothers are here?" he asked uncertainly.

The man with the red beard for the first time stepped up and joined the others. "No, they have not come yet; the family is scattered. The body will be taken directly to the house." He stooped and took hold of one of the handles of the coffin.

"Take the long hill road up, Thompson; it will be easier on the horses," called the liveryman as the undertaker snapped the door of the hearse and prepared to mount to the driver's seat.

Laird, the red-bearded lawyer, turned again to the stranger: "We didn't know whether there would be any one with him or not," he explained. "It's a long walk, so you'd better go up in the hack." He pointed to a single battered conveyance, but the young man replied stiffly: "Thank you, but I think I will go up with the hearse. If you don't object," turning to the undertaker, "I'll ride with you."

They clambered up over the wheels and drove off in the starlight up the long, white hill toward the town. The lamps in the still village were shining from under the low, snow-burdened roofs; and beyond, on every side, the plains reached out into emptiness, peaceful and wide as the soft sky itself, and wrapped in a tangible, white silence.

When the hearse backed up to a wooden sidewalk before a naked, weather-beaten frame house, the same composite, ill-defined group that had stood upon the station siding was huddled about the gate. The front yard was an icy swamp, and a couple of warped planks, extending from the sidewalk to the door, made a sort of rickety footbridge. The gate hung on one hinge, and was opened wide with difficulty. Steavens, the young stranger, noticed that something black was tied to the knob of the front door.

The grating sound made by the casket, as it was drawn from the hearse, was answered by a scream from the house; the front door was wrenched open, and a tall, corpulent woman rushed out bareheaded into the snow and flung herself upon the coffin, shrieking: "My boy, my boy! And this is how you've come home to me!"

As Steavens turned away and closed his eyes with a shudder of unutterable repulsion, another woman, also tall, but flat and angular, dressed entirely in black, darted out of the house and caught Mrs. Merrick by the shoulders, crying sharply: "Come, come, mother; you musn't go on like this!" Her tone changed to one of obsequious solemnity as she turned to the banker: "The parlour is ready, Mr. Phelps."

The bearers carried the coffin along the narrow boards, while the undertaker ran ahead with the coffin-rests. They bore it into a large, unheated room that smelled of dampness and disuse and furniture polish, and set it down under a hanging lamp ornamented with jingling glass prisms and before a "Rogers group" of John Alden and Priscilla, wreathed with smilax. Henry Steavens stared about him with the sickening conviction that there had been a mistake, and that he had somehow arrived at the wrong destination. He looked at the clover-green Brussels, the fat plush upholstery, among the hand-painted china placques and panels and vases, for some mark of identification,—for something that might once conceivably have belonged to Harvey Merrick. It was not until he recognized his friend in the crayon portrait of a little boy in kilts and curls, hanging above the piano, that he felt willing to let any of these people approach the coffin.

"Take the lid off, Mr. Thompson; let me see my boy's face," wailed the elder woman between her sobs. This time Steavens looked fearfully, almost beseechingly into her face, red and swollen under its masses of strong, black, shiny hair. He flushed, dropped his eyes, and then, almost incredulously, looked again. There was a kind of power about her face—a kind of brutal handsomeness, even; but it was scarred and furrowed by violence, and so coloured and coarsened by fiercer passions that grief seemed never to have laid a gentle finger there. The long nose was distended and knobbed at the end, and there were deep lines on either side of it; her heavy, black brows almost met across her forehead, her teeth were large and square, and set far apart—teeth that could tear. She filled the room; the men were

obliterated, seemed tossed about like twigs in an angry water, and even Steavens felt himself being drawn into the whirlpool.

The daughter—the tall, raw-boned woman in crepe, with a mourning comb in her hair which curiously lengthened her long face — sat stiffly upon the sofa, her hands, conspicuous for their large knuckles, folded in her lap, her mouth and eyes drawn down, solemnly awaiting the opening of the coffin. Near the door stood a mulatto woman, evidently a servant in the house, with a timid bearing and an emaciated face pitifully sad and gentle. She was weeping silently, the corner of her calico apron lifted to her eyes, occasionally suppressing a long, quivering sob. Steavens walked over and stood beside her.

Feeble steps were heard on the stairs, and an old man, tall and frail, odorous of pipe smoke, with shaggy, unkept grey hair and a dingy beard, tobacco stained about the mouth, entered uncertainly. He went slowly up to the coffin and stood rolling a blue cotton handkerchief between his hands, seeming so pained and embarrassed by his wife's orgy of grief that he had no consciousness of anything else.

"There, there, Annie, dear, don't take on so," he quavered timidly, putting out a shaking hand and awkwardly patting her elbow. She turned and sank upon his shoulder with such violence that he tottered a little. He did not even glance toward the coffin, but continued to look at her with a dull, frightened, appealing expression, as a spaniel looks at the whip. His sunken cheeks slowly reddened and burned with miserable shame. When his wife rushed from the room, her daughter strode after her with set lips. The servant stole up to the coffin, bent over it for a moment, and then slipped away to the kitchen, leaving Steavens, the lawyer, and the father to themselves. The old man stood looking down at his dead son's face. The sculptor's splendid head seemed even more noble in its rigid stillness than in life. The dark hair had crept down upon the wide forehead; the face seemed strangely long, but in it there was not that repose we expect to find in the faces of the dead. The brows were so drawn that there were two deep lines above the beaked nose, and the chin was thrust forward defiantly. It was as though the strain of life had

14. **"Rogers group."** John Rogers (1829–1904), an American sculptor, was noted for his group-sculptures; most of these had to do with the American Civil War, especially "The Slave Auction" (1859), but a few had to do with other subjects of American history or legend. The statues were heavily sentimentalized, and their appeal was strictly middle-class.

been so sharp and bitter that death could not at once relax the tension and smooth the countenance into perfect peace—as though he were still guarding something precious, which might even yet be wrested from him.

The old man's lips were working under his stained beard. He turned to the lawyer with timid deference: "Phelps and the rest are comin' back to set up with Harve, ain't they?" he asked. "Thank 'ee, Jim, thank 'ee." He brushed the hair back gently from his son's forehead. "He was a good boy, Jim; always a good boy. He was ez gentle ez a child and the kindest of 'em all—only we didn't none of us ever onderstand him." The tears trickled slowly down his beard and dropped upon the sculptor's coat.

"Martin, Martin! Oh, Martin! come here," his wife wailed from the top of the stairs. The old man started timorously: "Yes, Annie, I'm coming." He turned away, hesitated, stood for a moment in miserable indecision; then reached back and patted the dead man's hair softly, and stumbled from the room.

"Poor old man, I didn't think he had any tears left. Seems as if his eyes would have gone dry long ago. At his age nothing cuts very deep," remarked the lawyer.

Something in his tone made Steavens glance up. While the mother had been in the room, the young man had scarcely seen any one else; but now, from the moment he first glanced into Jim Laird's florid face and blood-shot eyes, he knew that he had found what he had been heartsick at not finding before—the feeling, the understanding, that must exist in some one, even here.

The man was red as his beard, with features swollen and blurred by dissipation, and a hot, blazing blue eye. His face was strained —that of a man who is controlling himself with difficulty—and he kept plucking at his beard with a sort of fierce resentment. Steavens, sitting by the window, watched him turn down the glaring lamp, still its jangling pendants with an angry gesture, and then stand with his hands locked behind him, staring down into the master's face. He could not help wondering what link there had been between the porcelain vessel and so sooty a lump of potter's clay.

From the kitchen an uproar was sounding; when the dining-room opened, the import of it was clear. The mother was abusing the maid for having forgotten to make the dressing for the chicken salad which had been prepared for the watchers. Steavens had never heard anything in the least like it; it was injured, emotional, dramatic abuse, unique and masterly in its excruciating cruelty, as violent and unrestrained as had been her grief of twenty minutes before. With a shudder of disgust the lawyer went into the dining-room and closed the door into the kitchen.

"Poor Roxy's getting it now," he remarked when he came back. "The Merricks took her out of the poor-house years ago; and if her loyalty would let her, I guess the poor old thing could tell tales that would curdle your blood. She's the mulatto woman who was standing in here a while ago, with her apron to her eyes. The old woman is a fury; there never was anybody like her. She made Harvey's life a hell for him when he lived at home; he was so sick ashamed of it. I never could see how he kept himself sweet."

"He was wonderful," said Steavens slowly, "wonderful; but until tonight I have never known how wonderful."

"That is the eternal wonder of it, anyway; that it can come even from such a dung heap as this," the lawyer cried, with a sweeping gesture which seemed to indicate much more than the four walls within which they stood.

"I think I'll see whether I can get a little air. The room is so close I am beginning to feel rather faint," murmured Steavens, struggling with one of the windows. The sash was stuck, however, and would not yield, so he sat down dejectedly and began pulling at his collar. The lawyer came over, loosened the sash with one blow of his red fist and sent the window up a few inches. Steavens thanked him, but the nausea which had been gradually climbing into his throat for the last half hour left him with but one desire—a desperate feeling that he must get away from this place with what was left of Harvey Merrick. Oh, he comprehended well enough now the quiet bitterness of the smile that he had seen so often on his master's lips!

Once when Merrick returned from a visit home, he brought with him a singularly feeling and suggestive bas-relief of a thin, faded old woman, sitting and sewing something pinned to her knee; while a full-lipped, full-blooded little urchin, his trousers held up by a single gallows, stood beside her, impatiently twitching her gown to call her attention to a butterfly he had caught. Steavens, impressed by the tender and delicate modelling of the thin, tired face, had asked him if it were his mother. He remembered the dull flush that had burned up in the sculptor's face.

The lawyer was sitting in a rocking-chair beside the coffin, his head thrown back and his eyes closed. Steavens looked at him earnestly, puzzled at the line of the chin, and wondering why a man should conceal a feature of such distinction under that disfiguring shock of beard. Suddenly, as though he felt the young sculptor's keen glance, Jim Laird opened his eyes.

"Was he always a good deal of an oyster?" he asked abruptly. "He was terribly shy as a boy."

"Yes, he was an oyster, since you put it so," rejoined Steavens. "Although he could be very fond of people, he always gave one the impression of being detached. He disliked violent emotion; he was reflective, and rather distrustful of himself—except, of course, as regarded his work. He was sure enough there. He distrusted men pretty thoroughly and women even more, yet somehow without believing ill of them, yet somehow without believing ill of them. He was determined, indeed, to believe the best; but he seemed afraid to investigate."

"A burnt dog dreads the fire," said the lawyer grimly, and closed his eyes.

Steavens went on and on, reconstructing that whole miserable boyhood. All this raw, biting ugliness had been the portion of the man whose mind was to become an exhaustless gallery of beautiful impressions—so sensitive that the mere shadow of a poplar leaf flickering against a sunny wall would be etched and held there for ever. Surely, if ever a man had the magic word in his finger tips, it was Merrick. Whatever he touched, he revealed its holiest secret; liberated it from enchantment and restored it to its pristine loveliness. Upon whatever he had come in contact with, he had left a beautiful record of the experience—a sort of ethereal signature; a scent, a sound, a colour that was his own.

Steavens understood now the real tragedy of his master's life; neither love nor wine, as many had conjectured; but a blow which had fallen earlier and cut deeper than anything else could have done—a shame not his, and yet so unescapably his, to hide in his heart from his very boyhood. And without—the frontier warfare; the yearning of a boy, cast ashore upon a desert of newness and ugliness and sordidness, for all that is chastened and old, and noble with traditions.

At eleven o'clock the tall, flat woman in black announced that the watchers were arriving, and asked them to "step into the dining-room." As Steavens rose, the lawyer said dryly: "You go on—it'll be a good experience for you. I'm not equal to that crowd tonight; I've had twenty years of them."

As Steavens closed the door after him he glanced back at the lawyer, sitting by the coffin in the dim light, with his chin resting on his hand.

The same misty group that had stood before the door of the express car shuffled into the dining-room. In the light of the kerosene lamp they separated and became individuals. The minister, a pale, feeble-looking man with white hair and blond chin-whiskers, took his seat beside a small side table and placed his Bible upon it. The Grand Army man sat down behind the stove and tilted his chair back comfortably against the wall, fishing his quill toothpick from his waistcoat pocket. The two bankers, Phelps and Elder, sat off in a corner behind the dinner-table, where they could finish their discussion of the new usury law and its effect on chattel security loans. The real estate agent, an old man with a smiling, hypocritical face, soon joined them. The coal and lumber dealer and the cattle shipper sat on opposite sides of the hard-coal burner, their feet on the nickel-work. Steavens took a book from his pocket and began to read. The talk around him ranged through various topics of local interest while the house was quieting down. When it was clear that the members of the family were in bed, the Grand Army man hitched his shoulders and, untangling his long legs, caught his heels on the rounds of his chair.

"S'pose there'll be a will, Phelps?" he queried in his weak falsetto.

The banker laughed disagreeably, and began trimming his nails with a pearl-handled pocket-knife.

"There'll scarcely be any need for one, will there?" he queried in his turn.

The restless Grand Army man shifted his position again, getting his knees still nearer his chin. "Why, the ole man says Harve's done right well lately," he chirped.

The other banker spoke up. "I reckon he means by that Harve ain't asked him to mortgage any more farms lately, so as he could go on with his education."

"Seems like my mind don't reach back to a time when Harve wasn't bein' edycated," tittered the Grand Army man.

There was a general chuckle. The minister took out his handkerchief and blew his nose sonorously. Banker Phelps closed his knife with a snap. "It's too bad the old man's sons didn't turn out better," he remarked with reflective authority. "They never hung together. He spent money enough on Harve to stock a dozen cattle-farms, and he might as well have poured it into Sand Creek. If Harve had stayed at home and helped nurse what little they had, and gone into stock on the old man's bottom farm, they might all have been well fixed. But the old man had to trust everything to tenants and was cheated right and left."

"Harve never could have handled stock none," interposed the cattleman. "He hadn't it in him to be sharp. Do you remember when he bought Sander's mules for eight-year olds, when everybody in town knew that Sander's father-in-law give 'em to his wife for a wedding present eighteen years before, an' they was full-grown mules then?"

The company laughed discreetly, and the Grand Army man rubbed his knees with a spasm of childish delight.

"Harve never was much account for anything practical, and he shore was never fond of work," began the coal and lumber dealer. "I mind the last time he was home; the day he left, when the old man was out to the barn helpin' his hand hitch up to take Harve to the train, and Cal Moots was patchin' up the fence; Harve, he come out on the step and sings out, in his lady-like voice: 'Cal Moots, Cal Moots! please come cord my trunk.'"

"That's Harve for you," approved the Grand Army man. "I kin hear him howlin' yet, when he was a big feller in long pants and his mother used to whale him with a rawhide in the barn for lettin' the cows git foundered in the corn-field when he was drivin' 'em home from pasture. He killed a cow of mine that-a-way onct —a pure Jersey and the best milker I had, an' the ole man had to put up for her. Harve, he was watchin' the sun set acrost the marshes when the anamile got away."

"Where the old man made his mistake was in sending the boy East to school," said Phelps, stroking his goatee and speaking in a deliberate, judicial tone. "There was where he got his head full of nonsense. What Harve needed, of all people, was a course in some first-class Kansas City business college."

The letters were swimming before Steavens' eyes. Was it possible that these men did not understand, that the palm on the coffin meant nothing to them? The very name of their town would have remained for ever buried in the postal guide had it not been now and again mentioned in the world in connection with Harvey Merrick's. He remembered what his master had said to him on the day of his death, after the congestion of both lungs had shut off any probability of recovery, and the sculptor had asked his pupil to send his body home. "It's not a pleasant place to be lying while the world is moving and doing and bettering," he had said with a feeble smile, "but it rather seems as though we ought to go back to the place we came from, in the end. The towns-people will come in for a look at me; and after they have had their say, I shan't have much to fear from the judgment of God!"

The cattleman took up the comment. "Forty's young for a Merrick to cash in; they usually hang on pretty well. Probably he helped it along with whiskey."

"His mother's people were not long lived, and Harvey never had a robust constitution," said the minister mildly. He would have liked to say more. He had been the boy's Sunday-school teacher, and had been fond of him; but he felt that he was not in a position to speak. His own sons had turned out badly, and it was not a year since one of them had made his last trip home in the express car, shot in a gambling-house in the Black Hills.

"Nevertheless, there is no disputin' that Harve frequently looked upon the wine when it was red, also variegated, and it shore made an oncommon fool of him," moralized the cattleman.

Just then the door leading into the parlour rattled loudly and everyone started involuntarily, looking relieved when only Jim Laird came out. The Grand Army man ducked his head when he saw the spark in his blue, bloodshot eye. They were all afraid of Jim; he was a drunkard, but he could twist the law to suit his client's needs as no other man in all western Kansas could do, and there were many who tried. The lawyer closed the door behind him, leaned back against it and folded his arms, cocking his head a little to one side. When he assumed this attitude in the courtroom, ears were always pricked up, as it usually foretold a flood of withering sarcasm.

"I've been with you gentlemen before," he began in a dry, even tone, "when you've sat by the coffins of boys born and raised in this town; and, if I remember rightly, you were never any too well satisfied when you checked them up. What's the matter, anyhow? Why is it that reputable young men are as scarce as millionaires in Sand City? It might almost seem to a stranger that there was some way something the matter with your progressive town. Why did Ruben Sayer, the brightest young lawyer you ever turned out, after he had come home from the university as straight as a die, take to drinking and forge a check and shoot himself? Why did Bill Merrit's son die of the shakes in a saloon in Omaha? Why was Mr. Thomas's son, here, shot in a gambling-house? Why did young Adams burn his mill to beat the insurance companies and go to the pen?"

The lawyer paused and unfolded his arms, laying one clenched fist quietly on the table. "I'll tell you why. Because you drummed nothing but money and knavery into their ears from the time they wore knickerbockers; because you carped away at them as you've been carping here tonight, holding our friends Phelps and Elder up to them for their models, as our grandfathers held up George Washington and John Adams. But the boys were young, and raw at the business you put them to, and how could they match coppers with such artists as Phelps and Elder? You wanted them to be successful rascals; they were only unsuccessful ones—that's all the difference. There was only one boy ever raised in this borderland between ruffianism and civilization who didn't come to grief, and you hated Harvey Merrick more for winning out than you hated all the other boys who got under the wheels. Lord, Lord, how you did hate him! Phelps, here, is fond of saying that he could buy and sell us all out any time he's a mind to; but he knew Harve wouldn't have given a tinker's damn for his bank and all his cattle farms put together; and a lack of appreciation, that way, goes hard with Phelps.

"Old Nimrod thinks Harve drank too much; and this from such as Nimrod and me!

"Brother Elder says Harve was too free with the old man's money—fell short in filial consideration, maybe. Well, we can all remember the very tone in which brother Elder swore his own father was a liar, in the county court; and we all know that the old man came out of that partnership with his son as bare as a sheared lamb. But maybe I'm getting personal, and I'd better be driving ahead at what I want to say."

The lawyer paused a moment, squared his heavy shoulders, and went on: "Harvey Merrick and I went to school together, back East. We were dead in earnest, and we wanted you all to be proud of us some day. We meant to be great men. Even I, and I haven't lost my sense of humour, gentlemen, I meant to be a great man. I came back here to practise, and I found you didn't in the least want me to be a great man. You wanted me to be a shrewd lawyer—oh, yes! Our veteran here wanted me to get him an increase of pension, because he had dyspepsia; Phelps wanted a new county survey that would put the widow Wilson's little bottom farm inside his south line; Elder wanted to lend money at 5 per cent a month, and get it collected; and Stark here wanted to wheedle old women up in Vermont into investing their annuities in real-estate mortgages that are not worth the paper they are written on. Oh, you needed me hard enough, and you'll go on needing me!

"Well, I came back here and became the damned shyster you wanted me to be. You pretend to have some sort of respect for me; and yet you'll stand up and throw mud at Harvey Merrick, whose soul you couldn't dirty and whose hands you couldn't tie. Oh, you're a discriminating lot of Christians! There have been times when the sight of Harvey's name in some Eastern paper has made me hang my head like a whipped dog; and, again, times when I liked to think of him off there in the world, away from all this hog-wallow, climbing the big, clean up-grade he'd set for himself.

"And we? Now that we've fought and lied and sweated and stolen, and hated as only the disappointed strugglers in a bitter, dead little Western town know how to do, what have we got to show for it? Harvey Merrick wouldn't have given one sunset over your marshes for all you've got put together, and you know it. It's not for me to say why, in the inscrutable wisdom of God, a genius should ever have been called from this place of hatred and bitter waters; but I want this Boston man to know that the drivel he's been hearing here tonight is the only tribute any truly great man could have from such a lot of sick, side-tracked, burnt-dog,

land-poor sharks as the here-present financiers of Sand City—upon which town may God have mercy!"

The lawyer thrust out his hand to Steavens as he passed him, caught up his overcoat in the hall, and had left the house before the Grand Army man had had time to lift his ducked head and crane his long neck about at his fellows.

Next day Jim Laird was drunk and unable to attend the funeral services. Steavens called twice at his office, but was compelled to start East without seeing him. He had a presentiment that he would hear from him again, and left his address on the lawyer's table; but if Laird found it, he never acknowledged it. The thing in him that Harvey Merrick had loved must have gone underground with Harvey Merrick's coffin; for it never spoke again, and Jim got the cold he died of driving across the Colorado mountains to defend one of Phelps's sons who had got into trouble out there by cutting government timber.

KATHERINE ANNE PORTER

Katherine Anne Porter may have published relatively few works, but these have been hailed universally as among the most finished examples of the short story in contemporary fiction. She was born in Indian Creek, Texas, May 15, 1894. Her girlhood was spent in Texas and Louisiana, and her education came chiefly from small southern convent schools. She tells us that since her first acquaintance with the alphabet, writing has been the absorbing interest of her life; but she did not seek publication until she was nearly thirty; rather, she destroyed much of what she had written before that time. Her isolation from contacts with celebrated writers gave her an independence which is one of the most marked characteristics of her writing and enabled her to avoid the inevitable cliques and groups which lead to artistic and esthetic bias of one kind or another.

She has traveled much in the United States and abroad; in 1931 she held a Guggenheim Fellowship which she used for writing on the

Continent. By this time her stories had already begun to appear in such dissimilar magazines as *Century, transition, New Masses, Scribner's,* and *Hound and Horn.* Even these earlier works exhibited a surprising maturity of execution, range of interests, and strength of attack upon her central problem or situation. Virtually all of her stories have raised a social challenge in the minds of discriminating readers. Her style has always been direct and sinewy, with nothing of the "arty" or the over-delicate poses of many modern short-story writers. The best of them will probably be found in her three major collections of tales: *Flowering Judas* (1935); *Pale Horse, Pale Rider* (1939); and *The Leaning Tower* (1944).

My whole attempt [she writes] has been to discover and understand human motives, human feeling, to make a distillation of what human relations and experiences my mind has been able to absorb. I have never known an uninteresting human being, and I have never known two alike; there are broad classifications and deep similarities, but I am interested in one thumb-print.

In other words, she cares little for large generalizations, which she believes must inevitably turn out to be false.

If so, she has found that her individuals add up to a disconcerting whole, for the strange disease of modern life seems to have infected most of them, especially those of the younger generation. Her two finest stories, "Pale Horse, Pale Rider" and "The Leaning Tower" (the title-stories of two of her collections named above), are frankly pessimistic in tone: the first is the story of a girl brought back from a nearly fatal illness to realize that her life, pillaged by the death of someone who meant much to her, must continue to be lived for whatever empty virtues it may still possess; the second is a powerful picture of decadent Europe in the days before the fascistic disaster which engulfed it. On the other hand, others among her stories give glimpses often of the lighter side of life, although they are never devoid of some degree of poignancy. Katherine Anne Porter can evoke a mood in the manner of Katherine Mansfield (p. 425), although with infinitely more rugged and healthy qualities; she can write of graft and corruption in modern society with an outright naturalistic zest; she can catch the nostalgia of the older generation in the South (black as well as white) in charming sentimental tones. Primarily, however, she writes like herself, not like someone else.

A Day's Work

THE DULL scrambling like a giant rat in the wall meant the dumb-waiter was on its way up, the janitress below hauling on the cable. Mrs. Halloran paused, thumped her iron on the board, and said, "There it is. Late. You could have put on your shoes and gone around

the corner and brought the things an hour ago. I can't do everything."

Mr. Halloran pulled himself out of the chair, clutching the arms and heaving to his feet slowly, looking around as if he hoped to find crutches standing near. "Wearing out your socks, too," added Mrs. Halloran. "You ought either go barefoot outright or wear your shoes over your socks as God intended," she said. "Sock feet. What's the good of it, I'd like to know? Neither one thing nor the other."

She unrolled a salmon-colored chiffon nightgown with cream-colored lace and broad ribbons on it, gave it a light flirt in the air, and spread it on the board. "God's mercy, look at that indecent thing," she said. She thumped the iron again and pushed it back and forth over the rumpled cloth. "You might just set the things in the cupboard," she said, "and not leave them around on the floor. You might just."

Mr. Halloran took a sack of potatoes from the dumb-waiter and started for the cupboard in the corner next the icebox. "You might as well take a load," said Mrs. Halloran. "There's no need on earth making a half-dozen trips back and forth. I'd think the poorest sort of man could well carry more than five pounds of potatoes at one time. But maybe not."

Her voice tapped on Mr. Halloran's ears like wood on wood. "Mind your business, will you?" he asked, not speaking to her directly. He carried on the argument with himself. "Oh, I couldn't do that, Mister Honey," he answered in a dull falsetto. "Don't ever ask me to think of such a thing, even. It wouldn't be right," he said, standing still with his knees bent, glaring bitterly over the potato sack at the scrawny strange woman he had never liked, that one standing there ironing clothes with a dirty look on her whole face like a suffering saint. "I may not be much good any more," he told her in his own voice, "but I still have got wits enough to take groceries off a dumb-waiter, mind you."

"That's a miracle," said Mrs. Halloran. "I'm thankful for that much."

"There's the telephone," said Mr. Halloran, sitting in the armchair again and taking his pipe out of his shirt pocket.

"I heard it as well," said Mrs. Halloran, sliding the iron up and down over the salmon-colored chiffon.

"It's for you, I've no further business in this world," said Mr. Halloran. His little greenish eyes glittered; he exposed his two sharp dog-teeth in a grin.

"You could answer it. It could be the wrong number again or for somebody downstairs," said Mrs. Halloran, her flat voice going flatter, even.

"Let it go in any case," decided Mr. Hallo-ran, "for my own part, that is." He struck a match on the arm of his chair, touched off his pipe, and drew in his first puff while the telephone went on with its nagging.

"It might be Maggie again," said Mrs. Halloran.

"Let her ring, then," said Mr. Halloran, settling back and crossing his legs.

"God help a man who won't answer the telephone when his own daughter calls up for a word," commented Mrs. Halloran to the ceiling, "and she in deep trouble, too, with her husband treating her like a dog about the money, and sitting out late nights in saloons with that crowd from the Little Tammany Association. He's getting into politics now with the McCorkery gang. No good will come of it, and I told her as much."

"She's no troubles at all, her man's a sharp fellow who will get ahead if she'll let him alone," said Mr. Halloran. "She's nothing to complain of, I could tell her. But what's a father?" Mr. Halloran cocked his head toward the window that opened on the brick-paved areaway and crowed like a rooster, "What's a father these days and who would heed his advice?"

"You needn't tell the neighbors, there's disgrace enough already," said Mrs. Halloran. She set the iron back on the gas ring and stepped out to the telephone on the first stair landing. Mr. Halloran leaned forward, his thin, red-haired hands hanging loosely between his knees, his warm pipe sending up its good decent smell right into his nose. The woman hated the pipe and the smell; she was a woman born to make any man miserable. Before the depression, while he still had a good job and prospects of a raise, before he went on relief, before she took in fancy washing and ironing, in the Good Days Before, God's pity, she didn't exactly keep her mouth shut, there wasn't a word known to man she couldn't find an an-

swer for, but she knew which side her bread was buttered on, and put up with it. Now she was, you might say, buttering her own bread and she never forgot it for a minute. And it's her own fault we're not riding round today in a limousine with ash trays and a speaking tube and a cut-glass vase for flowers in it. It's what a man gets for marrying one of these holy women. Gerald McCorkery had told him as much, in the beginning.

"There's a girl will spend her time holding you down," Gerald had told him. "You're putting your head in a noose will strangle the life out of you. Heed the advice of one who wishes you well," said Gerald McCorkery. This was after he had barely set eyes on Lacey Mahaffy one Sunday morning in Coney Island. It was like McCorkery to see that in a flash, born judge of human nature that he was. He could look a man over, size him up, and there was an end to it. And if the man didn't pass muster, McCorkery could ease him out in a way that man would never know how it happened. It was the secret of McCorkery's success in the world.

"This is Rosie, herself," said Gerald that Sunday in Coney Island. "Meet the future Mrs. Gerald J. McCorkery." Lacey Mahaffy's narrow face had gone sour as whey under her big straw hat. She barely nodded to Rosie, who gave Mr. Halloran a look that fairly undressed him right there. Mr. Halloran had thought, too, that McCorkery was picking a strange one; she was good-looking all right, but she had the smell of a regular little Fourteenth Street hustler if Halloran knew anything about women. "Come on," said McCorkery, his arm around Rosie's waist, "let's all go on the roller coaster." But Lacey would not. She said, "No, thank you. We didn't plan to stay, and we must go now." On the way home Mr. Halloran said, "Lacey, you judge too harshly. Maybe that's a nice girl at heart; hasn't had your opportunities." Lacey had turned upon him a face ugly as an angry cat's, and said, "She's a loose, low woman, and 'twas an insult to introduce her to me." It was a good while before the pretty fresh face that Mr. Halloran had fallen in love with returned to her.

Next day in Billy's Place, after three drinks each, McCorkery said, "Watch your step, Halloran; think of your future. There's a straight

324

good girl I don't doubt, but she's no sort of mixer. A man getting into politics needs a wife who can meet all kinds. A man needs a woman knows how to loosen her corsets and sit easy."

Mrs. Halloran's voice was going on in the hall, a steady dry rattle like old newspapers blowing on a park bench. "I told you before it's no good coming to me with your troubles now. I warned you in time but you wouldn't listen. . . . I told you just how it would be, I tried my best. . . . No, you couldn't listen, you always knew better than your mother. . . . So now all you've got to do is stand by your married vows and make the best of it. . . . Now listen to me, if you want himself to do right you have to do right first. The woman has to do right first, and then if the man won't do right in turn it's no fault of hers. You do right whether he does wrong or no, just because he does wrong is no excuse for you."

"Ah, will you hear that?" Mr. Halloran asked the areaway in an awed voice. "There's a holy terror of a saint for you."

". . . the woman has to do right first, I'm telling you," said Mrs. Halloran into the telephone, "and then if he's a devil in spite of it, why she has to do right without any help from him." Her voice rose so the neighbors could get an earful if they wanted. "I know you from old, you're just like your father. You must be doing something wrong yourself or you wouldn't be in this fix. You're doing wrong this minute, calling over the telephone when you ought to be getting your work done. I've got an iron on, working over the dirty nightgowns of a kind of woman I wouldn't soil my foot on if I'd had a man to take care of me. So now you do up your housework and dress yourself and take a walk in the fresh air. . . ."

"A little fresh air never hurt anybody," commented Mr. Halloran loudly through the open window. "It's the gas gets a man down."

"Now listen to me, Maggie, that's not the way to talk over the public wires. Now you stop that crying and go and do your duty and don't be worrying me any more. And stop saying you're going to leave your husband, because where will you go, for one thing? Do you want to walk the streets or set up a laundry in your kitchen? You can't come back here, you'll stay with your husband where you belong. Don't be a fool, Maggie. You've got your living,

and that's more than many a woman better than you has got. Yes, your father's all right. No, he's just sitting here, the same. God knows what's to become of us. But you know how he is, little he cares. . . . Now remember this, Maggie, if anything goes wrong with your married life it's your own fault and you needn't come here for sympathy. . . . I can't waste any more time on it. Good-by."

Mr. Halloran, his ears standing up for fear of missing a word, thought how Gerald J. McCorkery had gone straight on up the ladder with Rosie; and for every step the McCorkerys took upward, he, Michael Halloran, had taken a step downward with Lacey Mahaffy. They had started as greenhorns with the same chances at the same time and the same friends, but McCorkery had seized all his opportunities as they came, getting in steadily with the Big Shots in ward politics, one good thing leading to another. Rosie had known how to back him up and push him onward. The McCorkerys for years had invited him and Lacey to come over to the house and be sociable with the crowd, but Lacey would not.

"You can't run with that fast set and drink and stay out nights and hold your job," said Lacey, "and you should know better than to ask your wife to associate with that woman." Mr. Halloran had got into the habit of dropping around by himself, now and again, for McCorkery still liked him, was still willing to give him a foothold in the right places, still asked him for favors at election time. There was always a good lively crowd at the McCorkerys, wherever they were; for they moved ever so often to a better place, with more furniture. Rosie helped hand around the drinks, taking a few herself with a gay word for everybody. The player piano or the victrola would be going full blast, with everybody dancing, all looking like ready money and a bright future. He would get home late these evenings, back to the same little cold-water walk-up flat, because Lacey would not spend a dollar for show. It must all go into savings against old age, she said. He would be full of good food and drink, and find Lacey, in a bungalow apron, warming up the fried potatoes once more, cross and bitterly silent, hanging her head and frowning at the smell of liquor on his breath. "You might at least eat the potatoes when I've fried them and waited all this time," she would say. "Ah, eat them yourself, they're none of mine," he would snarl in his disappointment with her, and with the life she was leading him.

He had believed with all his heart for years that he would one day be manager of one of the G. and I. chain grocery stores he worked for, and when that hope gave out there was still his pension when they retired him. But two years before it was due they fired him, on account of the depression, they said. Overnight he was on the sidewalk, with no place to go with the news but home. "Jesus," said Mr. Halloran, still remembering that day after nearly seven years of idleness.

The depression hadn't touched McCorkery. He went on and on up the ladder, giving beefsteaks and beanfests and beer parties for the boys in Billy's Place, standing in with the right men and never missing a trick. At last the Gerald J. McCorkery Club chartered a whole boat for a big excursion up the river. It was a great day, with Lacey sitting at home sulking. After election Rosie had her picture in the papers, smiling at McCorkery; not fat exactly, just a fine figure of a woman with flowers pinned on her spotted fur coat, her teeth as good as ever. Oh, God, there was a girl for any man's money. Mr. Halloran saw out of his eye-corner the bony stooped back of Lacey Mahaffy, standing on one foot to rest the other like a tired old horse, leaning on her hands waiting for the iron to heat.

"That was Maggie, with her woes," she said.

"I hope you gave her some good advice," said Mr. Halloran. "I hope you told her to take up her hat and walk out on him."

Mrs. Halloran suspended the iron over a pair of pink satin panties. "I told her to do right and leave wrong-doing to the men," she said, in her voice like a phonograph record running down. "I told her to bear with the trouble God sends as her mother did before her."

Mr. Halloran gave a loud groan and knocked out his pipe on the chair arm. "You would ruin the world, woman, if you could, with your wicked soul, treating a new-married girl as if she had no home and no parents to come to. But she's no daughter of mine if she sits there peeling potatoes, letting a man run over her. No daughter of mine and I'll tell her so if she—"

"You know well she's your daughter, so hold your tongue," said Mrs. Halloran, "and if she heeded you she'd be walking the streets this minute. I brought her up an honest girl, and an honest woman she's going to be or I'll take her over my knee as I did when she was little. So there you are, Halloran."

Mr. Halloran leaned far back in his chair and felt along the shelf above his head until his fingers touched a half-dollar he had noticed there. His hand closed over it, he got up instantly and looked about for his hat.

"Keep your daughter, Lacey Mahaffy," he said, "she's none of mine but the fruits of your long sinning with the Holy Ghost. And now I'm off for a little round and a couple of beers to keep my mind from dissolving entirely."

"You can't have that dollar you just now sneaked off the shelf," said Mrs. Halloran. "So you think I'm blind besides? Put it back where you found it. That's for our daily bread."

"I'm sick of bread daily," said Mr. Halloran. "I need beer. It was not a dollar, but a half-dollar as you know well."

"Whatever it was," said Mrs. Halloran, "it stands instead of a dollar to me. So just drop it."

"You've got tomorrow's potatoes sewed up in your pocket this minute, and God knows what sums in that black box wherever you hide it, besides the life savings," said Mr. Halloran. "I earned this half-dollar on relief, and it's going to be spent properly. And I'll not be back for supper, so you'll save on that, too. So long, Lacey Mahaffy. I'm off."

"If you never come back, it will be all the same," said Mrs. Halloran, not looking up.

"If I came back with a pocket full of money, you'd be glad to see me," said Mr. Halloran.

"It would want to be a great sum," said Mrs. Halloran.

Mr. Halloran shut the door behind him with a fine slam.

He strolled out into the clear fall weather, a late afternoon sun warming his neck and brightening the old red-brick, high-stooped houses of Perry Street. He would go after all these years to Billy's Place, he might find some luck there. He took his time, though, speaking to the neighbors as he went. "Good afternoon, Mr. Halloran." "Good afternoon to you, Missis Caffery." . . . "It's fine weather for the time of year, Mr. Gogarty." "It is indeed, Mr. Hallo-ran." Mr. Halloran thrived on these civilities, he loved to flourish his hat and give a hearty good day like a man who has nothing on his mind. Ah, there was the young man from the G. and I. store around the corner. He knew what kind of job Mr. Halloran once held there. "Good day, Mr. Halloran." "Good day to you, Mr. McInerny, how's business holding up with you?" "Good for the times, Mr. Halloran, that's the best I can say." "Things are not getting any better, Mr. McInerny." "It's the truth we are all hanging on by the teeth now, Mr. Hal-loran."

Soothed by this acknowledgment of man's common misfortune Mr. Halloran greeted the young cop at the corner. The cop, with his quick eyesight, was snatching a read from a newspaper on the stand across the sidewalk. "How do you do, Young O'Fallon," asked Mr. Halloran, "is your business lively these days?"

"Quiet as the tomb itself on this block," said Young O'Fallon. "But that's a sad thing about Connolly, now." His eyes motioned toward the newspaper.

"Is he dead?" asked Mr. Halloran; "I haven't been out until now, I didn't see the papers."

"Ah, not yet," said Young O'Fallon, "but the G-men are after him, it looks they'll get him surely this time."

"Connolly in bad with the G-men? Holy Je-sus," said Mr. Halloran, "who will they go after next? The meddlers."

"It's that numbers racket," said the cop. "What's the harm, I'd like to know? A man must get his money from somewhere when he's in politics. They oughta give him a chance."

"Connolly's a great fellow, God bless him, I hope he gives them the slip," said Mr. Hallo-ran, "I hope he goes right through their hands like a greased pig."

"He's smart," said the cop. "That Connolly's a smooth one. He'll come out of it."

Ah, will he though? Mr. Halloran asked him-self. Who is safe if Connolly goes under? Wait till I give Lacey Mahaffy the news about Con-nolly. I'll like seeing her face the first time in twenty years. Lacey kept saying, "A man is a downright fool must be a crook to get rich. Plenty of the best people get rich and do no harm by it. Look at the Connollys now, good practical Catholics with nine children and more

to come if God sends them, and Mass every day, and they're rolling in wealth richer than your McCorkerys with all their wickedness." So there you are, Lacey Mahaffy, wrong again, and welcome to your pious Connollys. Still and all it was Connolly who had given Gerald Mc-Corkery his start in the world; McCorkery had been publicity man and then campaign man-ager for Connolly, in the days when Connolly had Tammany in the palm of his hand and the sky was the limit. And McCorkery had begun at the beginning, God knows. He was running a little basement place first, rent almost noth-ing, where the boys of the Connolly Club and the Little Tammany Association, just the mere fringe of the district, you might say, could drop in for quiet evenings for a game and a drink along with the talk. Nothing low, nothing but what was customary, with the house tak-ing a cut on the winnings and a fine profit on the liquor, and holding the crowd together. Many was the big plan hatched there came out well for everybody. For everybody but myself, and why was that? And when McCorkery says to me, "You can take over now and run the place for the McCorkery Club," ah, there was my chance and Lacey Mahaffy wouldn't hear of it, and with Maggie coming on just then it wouldn't do to excite her.

Mr. Halloran went on, following his feet that knew the way to Billy's Place, head down, not speaking to passersby any more, but talk-ing it out with himself again, again. What a track to go over seeing clearly one by one the crossroads where he might have taken a differ-ent turn that would have changed all his for-tunes; but no, he had gone the other way and now it was too late. She wouldn't say a thing but "It's not right and you know it, Halloran," so what could a man do in all? Ah, you could have gone on with your rightful affairs like any other man, Halloran, it's not the woman's place to decide such things; she'd have come round once she saw the money, or a good whack on the backsides would have put her in her place. Never had mortal woman needed a good wal-loping worse than Lacey Mahaffy, but he could never find it in his heart to give it to her for her own good. That was just another of your many mistakes, Halloran. But there was always the life-long job with the G. and I. and peace in the house more or less. Many a man envied

327

me in those days I remember, and I was resting
easy on the savings and knowing with that and
the pension I could finish out my life with some
little business of my own. "What came of
that?" Mr. Halloran inquired in a low voice,
looking around him. Nobody answered. You
know well what came of it, Halloran. You
were fired out like a delivery boy, two years
before your time was out. Why did you sit
10 there watching the trick being played on others before you, knowing well it could happen
to you and never quite believing what you saw
with your own eyes? G. and I. gave me my
start, when I was green in this country, and
they were my own kind or I thought so. Well,
it's done now. Yes, it's done now, but there
was all the years you could have cashed in on
the numbers game with the best of them, helping collect the protection money and taking
20 your cut. You could have had a fortune by
now in Lacey's name, safe in the bank. It was
good quiet profit and none the wiser. But
they're wiser now, Halloran, don't forget; still
it's a lump of grief and disappointment to swallow all the same. The game's up with Connolly, maybe; Lacey Mahaffy had said, "Numbers is just another way of stealing from the
poor, and you weren't born to be a thief like
that McCorkery." Ah, God, no, Halloran, you
30 were born to rot on relief and maybe that's
honest enough for her. That Lacey—A fortune
in her name would have been no good to me
whatever. She's got all the savings tied up,
such as they are, she'll pinch and she'll starve,
she'll wash dirty clothes first, she won't give up
a penny to live on. She has stood in my way,
McCorkery, like a skeleton rattling its bones,
and you were right about her, she has been my
ruin. "Ah, it's not too late yet, Halloran," said
40 McCorkery, appearing plain as day inside Mr.
Halloran's head with the same old face and
way with him. "Never say die, Halloran. Elections are coming on again, it's a busy time for
all, there's work to be done and you're the very
man I'm looking for. Why didn't you come to
me sooner, you know I never forget an old
friend. You don't deserve your ill fortune, Halloran," McCorkery told him; "I said so to others and I say it now to your face, never did
50 man deserve more of the world than you, Halloran, but the truth is, there's not always enough

good luck to go round; but it's your turn now,
and I've got a job for you up to your abilities
at last. For a man like you, there's nothing to
it at all, you can toss it off with one hand tied,
Halloran, and good money in it. Organization
work, just among your own neighbors, where
you're known and respected for a man of your
word and an old friend of Gerald McCorkery.
Now look, Halloran," said Gerald McCorkery, 60
tipping him the wink, "do I need to say more?
It's voters in large numbers we're after, Halloran, and you're to bring them in, alive or
dead. Keep your eye on the situation at all
times and get in touch with me when necessary. And name your figure in the way of
money. And come up to the house sometimes,
Halloran, why don't you? Rosie has asked me
a hundred times, 'Whatever went with Halloran, the life of the party?' That's the way you 70
stand with Rosie, Halloran. We're in a two-
story flat now with green velvet curtains and
carpets you can sink to your shoetops in, and
there's no reason at all why you shouldn't have
the same kind of place if you want it. With
your gifts, you were never meant to be a poor
man."

Ah, but Lacey Mahaffy wouldn't have it,
maybe. "Then get yourself another sort of
woman, Halloran, you're a good man still, find 80
yourself a woman like Rosie to snuggle down
with at night." Yes, but McCorkery, you forget
that Lacey Mahaffy had legs and hair and eyes
and a complexion fit for a chorus girl. But
would she do anything with them? Never.
Would you believe there was a woman
wouldn't take off all her clothes at once even to
bathe herself? What a hateful thing she was
with her evil mind thinking everything was a
sin, and never giving a man a chance to show 90
himself a man in any way. But she's faded
away now, her mean soul shows out all over
her, she's ugly as sin itself now, McCorkery.
"It's what I told you would happen," said Mc-
Corkery, "but now with the job and the money
you can go your ways and let Lacey Mahaffy
go hers." I'll do it, McCorkery. "And forget
about Connolly. Just remember I'm my own
man and always was. Connolly's finished, but
I'm not. Stronger than ever, Halloran, with 100
Connolly out of the way. I saw this coming
long ever ago, Halloran, I got clear of it. They

don't catch McCorkery with his pants down, Halloran. And I almost forgot . . . Here's something for the running expenses to start. Take this for the present, and there's more to come. . . ."

Mr. Halloran stopped short, a familiar smell floated under his nose: the warm beer-and-beefsteak smell of Billy's Place, sawdust and onions, like any other bar maybe, but with something of its own besides. The talk within him stopped also as if a hand had been laid on his mind. He drew his fist out of his pocket almost expecting to find green money in it. The half dollar was in his palm. "I'll stay while it lasts and hope McCorkery will come in."

The moment he stepped inside his eye lighted on McCorkery standing at the bar pouring his own drink from the bottle before him. Billy was mopping the bar before him idly, and his eye, swimming toward Halloran, looked like an oyster in its own juice. McCorkery saw him too. "Well, blow me down," he said, in a voice that had almost lost its old County Mayo ring, "if it ain't my old sidekick from the G. and I. Step right up, Halloran," he said, his poker-face as good as ever, no man ever saw Gerald McCorkery surprised at anything. "Step up and name your choice."

Mr. Halloran glowed suddenly with the warmth around the heart he always had at the sight of McCorkery, he couldn't put a name on it, but there was something about the man. Ah, it was Gerald all right, the same, who never forgot a friend and never seemed to care whether a man was rich or poor, with his face of granite and his eyes like blue agates in his head, a rock of a man surely. There he was, saying "Step right up," as if they had parted only yesterday; portly and solid in his expensive-looking clothes, as always; his hat a darker gray than his suit, with a devil-may-care roll to the brim, and nothing sporting, mind you. All first-rate, well made, and the right thing for him, more power to him. Mr. Halloran said, "Ah, McCorkery, you're the one man on this round earth I hoped to see today, but I says to myself, maybe he doesn't come round to Billy's Place so much nowadays."

"And why not?" asked McCorkery, "I've been coming around to Billy's Place for twenty-five years now, it's still headquarters for the old guard of the McCorkery Club, Halloran." He took in Mr. Halloran from head to foot in a flash of a glance and turned toward the bottle.

"I was going to have a beer," said Mr. Halloran, "but the smell of that whiskey changes my mind for me." McCorkery poured a second glass, they lifted the drinks with an identical crook of the elbow, a flick of the wrist at each other.

"Here's to crime," said McCorkery, and "Here's looking at you," said Mr. Halloran, merrily. Ah, to hell with it, he was back where he belonged, in good company. He put his foot on the rail and snapped down his whiskey, and no sooner was his glass on the bar than McCorkery was filling it again. "Just time for a few quick ones," he said, "before the boys get here." Mr. Halloran downed that one, too, before he noticed that McCorkery hadn't filled his own glass. "I'm ahead of you," said McCorkery, "I'll skip this one."

There was a short pause, a silence fell around them that seemed to ooze like a fog from somewhere deep in McCorkery, it was suddenly as if he had not really been there at all, or hadn't uttered a word. Then he said outright: "Well, Halloran, let's have it. What's on your mind?" And he poured two more drinks. That was McCorkery all over, reading your thoughts and coming straight to the point.

Mr. Halloran closed his hand round his glass and peered into the little pool of whiskey. "Maybe we could sit down," he said, feeling weak-kneed all at once. McCorkery took the bottle and moved over to the nearest table. He sat facing the door, his look straying there now and then, but he had a set, listening face as if he was ready to hear anything.

"You know what I've had at home all these years," began Mr. Halloran, solemnly, and paused.

"Oh, God, yes," said McCorkery with simple good-fellowship. "How is herself these days?"

"Worse than ever," said Mr. Halloran, "but that's not it."

"What is it, then, Halloran?" asked McCorkery, pouring drinks. "You know well you can speak out your mind to me. Is it a loan?"

"No," said Mr. Halloran. "It's a job."

"Now that's a different matter," said McCorkery. "What kind of a job?"

Mr. Halloran, his head sunk between his shoulders, saw McCorkery wave a hand and nod at half a dozen men who came in and ranged themselves along the bar. "Some of the boys," said McCorkery. "Go on." His face was tougher, and quieter, as if the drink gave him a firm hold on himself. Mr. Halloran said what he had planned to say, had said already on the way down, and it still sounded reasonable and right to him. McCorkery waited until he had finished, and got up, putting a hand on Mr. Halloran's shoulder. "Stay where you are, and help yourself," he said, giving the bottle a little push, "and anything else you want, Halloran, order it on me. I'll be back in a few minutes, and you know I'll help you out if I can."

Halloran understood everything but it was through a soft warm fog, and he hardly noticed when McCorkery passed him again with the men, all in that creepy quiet way like footpads on a dark street. They went into the back room, the door opened on a bright light and closed again, and Mr. Halloran reached for the bottle to help himself wait until McCorkery should come again bringing the good word. He felt comfortable and easy as if he hadn't a bone or muscle in him, but his elbow slipped off the table once or twice and he upset his drink on his sleeve. Ah, McCorkery, is it the whole family you're taking on with the jobs? For my Maggie's husband is in now with the Little Tammany Association. "There's a bright lad will go far and I've got my eye on him, Halloran," said the friendly voice of McCorkery in his mind, and the brown face, softer than he remembered it, came up clearly behind his closed eyes.

"Ah, well, it's like myself beginning all over again in him," said Mr. Halloran, aloud, "besides my own job that I might have had all this time if I'd just come to see you sooner."

"True for you," said McCorkery in a merry County Mayo voice, inside Mr. Halloran's head, "and now let's drink to the gay future for old times' sake and be damned to Lacey Mahaffy." Mr. Halloran reached for the bottle but it skipped sideways, rolled out of reach like a creature, and exploded at his feet. When he stood up the chair fell backward from under him. He leaned on the table and it folded up under his hands like cardboard.

"Wait now, take it easy," said McCorkery, and there he was, real enough, holding Mr. Halloran braced on the one side, motioning with his hand to the boys in the back room, who came out quietly and took hold of Mr. Halloran, some of them, on the other side. Their faces were all Irish, but not an Irishman Mr. Halloran knew in the lot, and he did not like any face he saw. "Let me be," he said with dignity, "I came here to see Gerald J. McCorkery, a friend of mine from old times, and let not a thug among you lay a finger upon me."

"Come on, Big Shot," said one of the younger men, in a voice like a file grating, "come on now, it's time to go."

"That's a fine low lot you've picked to run with, McCorkery," said Mr. Halloran, bracing his heels against the slow weight they put upon him toward the door, "I wouldn't trust one of them far as I could throw him by the tail."

"All right, all right, Halloran," said McCorkery. "Come on with me. Lay off him, Finnegan." He was leaning over Mr. Halloran and pressing something into his right hand. It was money, a neat little roll of it, good smooth thick money, no other feel like it in the world, you couldn't mistake it. Ah, he'd have an argument to show Lacey Mahaffy would knock her off her feet. Honest money with a job to back it up. "You'll stand by your given word, McCorkery, as ever?" he asked, peering into the rock-colored face above him, his feet weaving a dance under him, his heart ready to break with gratitude.

"Ah, sure, sure," said McCorkery in a loud hearty voice with a kind of curse in it. "Crisakes, get on with him, do." Mr. Halloran found himself eased into a taxicab at the curb, with McCorkery speaking to the driver and giving him money. "So long, Big Shot," said one of the thug faces, and the taxicab door thumped to. Mr. Halloran bobbed about on the seat for a while, trying to think. He leaned forward and spoke to the driver. "Take me to my friend Gerald J. McCorkery's house," he said, "I've got important business. Don't pay any attention to what he said. Take me to his house."

"Yeah?" said the driver, without turning his head. "Well, here's where you get out, see? Right here." He reached back and opened the door. And sure enough, Mr. Halloran was standing on the sidewalk in front of the flat in

Perry Street, alone except for the rows of garbage cans, the taxicab hooting its way around the corner, and a cop coming toward him, plainly to be seen under the street light.

"You should cast your vote for McCorkery, the poor man's friend," Mr. Halloran told the cop, "McCorkery's the man who will get us all off the spot. Stands by his old friends like a maniac. Got a wife named Rosie. Vote for McCorkery," said Mr. Halloran, working hard at his job, "and you'll be Chief of the Force when Halloran says the word."

"To hell with McCorkery, that stooge," said the cop, his mouth square and sour with the things he said and the things he saw and did every night on that beat. "There you are drunk again, Halloran, shame to you, with Lacey Mahaffy working her heart out over the washboard to buy your beer."

"It wasn't beer and she didn't buy it, mind you," said Mr. Halloran, "and what do you know about Lacey Mahaffy?"

"I knew her from old when I used to run errands for St. Veronica's Altar Society," said the cop, "and she was a great one, even then. Nothing good enough."

"It's the same today," said Mr. Halloran, almost sober for a moment.

"Well, go on up now and stay up till you're fit to be seen," said the cop, censoriously.

"You're Johnny Maginnis," said Mr. Halloran, "I know you well."

"You should know me by now," said the cop.

Mr. Halloran worked his way upstairs partly on his hands and knees, but once at his own door he stood up, gave a great blow on the panel with his fist, turned the knob and surged in like a wave after the door itself, holding out the money toward Mrs. Halloran, who had finished ironing and was at her mending.

She got up very slowly, her bony hand over her mouth, her eyes starting out at what she saw. "Ah, did you steal it?" she asked. "Did you kill somebody for that?" the words grated up from her throat in a dark whisper. Mr. Halloran glared back at her in fear.

"Suffering Saints, Lacey Mahaffy," he shouted until the whole houseful could hear him, "haven't ye any mind at all that you can't see your husband has had a turn of fortune and a job and times are changed from tonight? Stealing, is it? That's for your great friends the

Connollys with their religion. Connolly steals, but Halloran is an honest man with a job in the McCorkery Club, and money in pocket."

"McCorkery, is it?" said Mrs. Halloran, loudly too. "Ah, so that's the whole family, young and old, wicked and innocent, taking their bread from McCorkery, at last. Well, it's no bread of mine, I'll earn my own as I have, you can keep your dirty money to yourself, Halloran, mind you I mean it."

"Great God, woman," moaned Mr. Halloran, and he tottered from the door to the table, to the ironing board, and stood there, ready to weep with rage, "haven't you a soul even that you won't come along with your husband when he's riding to riches and glory on the Tiger's back itself, with everything for the taking and no questions asked?"

"Yes, I have a soul," cried Mrs. Halloran, clenching her fists, her hair flying. "Surely I have a soul and I'll save it yet in spite of you. . . ."

She was standing there before him in a kind of faded gingham winding sheet, with her dead hands upraised, her dead eyes blind but fixed upon him, her voice coming up hollow from the deep tomb, her throat thick with grave damp. The ghost of Lacey Mahaffy was threatening him, it came nearer, growing taller as it came, the face changing to a demon's face with a fixed glassy grin. "It's all that drink on an empty stomach," said the ghost, in a hoarse growl. Mr. Halloran fetched a yell of horror right out of his very boots, and seized the flatiron from the board. "Ah, God damn you, Lacey Mahaffy, you devil, keep away, keep away," he howled, but she advanced on air, grinning and growling. He raised the flatiron and hurled it without aiming, and the specter, whoever it was, whatever it was, sank and was gone. He did not look, but broke out of the room and was back on the sidewalk before he knew he had meant to go there. Maginnis came up at once. "Hey there now, Halloran," he said, "I mean business this time. You get back upstairs or I'll run you in. Come along now, I'll help you get there this time, and that's the last of it. On relief the way you are, and drinking your head off."

Mr. Halloran suddenly felt calm, collected; he would take Maginnis up and show him just what had happened. "I'm not on relief any more, and if you want any trouble, just call on my friend, McCorkery. He'll tell you who I am."

"McCorkery can't tell me anything about you I don't know already," said Maginnis. "Stand up there now." For Halloran wanted to go up again on his hands and knees.

"Let a man be," said Mr. Halloran, trying to sit on the cop's feet. "I killed Lacey Mahaffy at last, you'll be pleased to hear," he said, looking up into the cop's face. "It was high time and past. But I did not steal the money."

"Well, ain't that just too bad," said the cop, hauling him up under the arms. "Chees, why'n't you make a good job while you had the chance? Stand up now. Ah, hell with it, stand up or I'll sock you one."

Mr. Halloran said, "Well, you don't believe it so wait and see."

At that moment they both glanced upward and saw Mrs. Halloran coming downstairs. She was holding to the rail, and even in the speckled hall-light they could see a great lumpy clout of flesh standing out on her forehead, all colors. She stopped, and seemed not at all surprised.

"So there you are, Officer Maginnis," she said. "Bring him up."

"That's a fine welt you've got over your eye this time, Mrs. Halloran," commented Officer Maginnis, politely.

"I fell and hit my head on the ironing board," said Mrs. Halloran. "It comes of overwork and worry, day and night. A dead faint, Officer Maginnis. Watch your big feet there, you thriving, natural fool," she added to Mr. Halloran. "He's got a job now, you mightn't believe it, Officer Maginnis, but it's true. Bring him on up, and thank you."

She went ahead of them, opened the door, and led the way to the bedroom through the kitchen, turned back the covers, and Officer Maginnis dumped Mr. Halloran among the quilts and pillows. Mr. Halloran rolled over with a deep groan and shut his eyes.

"Many thanks to you, Officer Maginnis," said Mrs. Halloran.

"Don't mention it, Mrs. Halloran," said Officer Maginnis.

When the door was shut and locked, Mrs. Halloran went and dipped a large bath towel under the kitchen tap. She wrung it out and tied several good hard knots in one end and tried it out with a whack on the edge of the table. She walked in and stood over the bed and brought the knotted towel down in Mr. Halloran's face with all her might. He stirred and muttered, ill at ease. "That's for the flatiron, Halloran," she told him, in a cautious voice as if she were talking to herself, and whack, down came the towel again. "That's for the half-dollar," she said, and whack, "that's for your drunkenness—" Her arm swung around regularly, ending with a heavy thud on the face that was beginning to squirm, gasp, lift itself from the pillow and fall back again, in a puzzled kind of torment. "For your sock feet," Mrs. Halloran told him, whack, "and your laziness, and this is for missing Mass and—" here she swung half a dozen times—"that is for your daughter and your part in her. . . ."

She stood back breathless, the lump on her forehead burning in its furious colors. When Mr. Halloran attempted to rise, shielding his head with his arms, she gave him a push and he fell back again. "Stay there and don't give me a word," said Mrs. Halloran. He pulled the pillow over his face and subsided again, this time for good.

Mrs. Halloran moved about very deliberately. She tied the wet towel around her head, the knotted end hanging over her shoulder. Her hand ran into her apron pocket and came out again with the money. There was a five-dollar bill with three one-dollar bills rolled in it, and the half-dollar she had thought spent long since. "A poor start, but something," she said, and opened the cupboard door with a long key. Reaching in, she pulled a loosely fitted board out of the wall, and removed a black-painted metal box. She unlocked this, took out one five-cent piece from a welter of notes and coins. She then placed the new money in the box, locked it, put it away, replaced the board, shut the cupboard door and locked that. She went out to the telephone, dropped the nickel in the slot, asked for a number, and waited.

"Is that you, Maggie? Well, are things any better with you now? I'm glad to hear it. It's late to be calling, but there's news about your father. No, no, nothing of that kind, he's got a job. I said a *job*. Yes, at last, after all my urging him onward. . . . I've got him bedded down to sleep it off so he'll be ready to work tomorrow. . . . Yes, it's political work, toward the election time, with Gerald McCorkery. But that's no harm, getting votes and all, he'll be in the open air and it doesn't mean I'll have to associate with low people, now or ever. It's clean enough work, with good pay; if it's not just what I prayed for, still it beats nothing, Maggie. After all my trying . . . it's like a miracle. You see what can be done with patience and doing your duty, Maggie. Now mind you do as well by your own husband."

SINCLAIR LEWIS

Erratic and uneven as the works may be, forming a bold and lunging kind of satire which misses its target almost as often as it hits the mark, the all-around contribution of Sinclair Lewis to the writing of his generation is of such high excellence that American literature could never do without it, for in many respects Lewis has been the foremost reporter of American life and thought in the 1920's. His delineation of the small midwestern town in *Main Street* and his portrayal of the average American businessman in *Babbitt* have done more than give to the world outside America, for better or for worse, its stock conception of American small towns and American businessmen; they have actually contributed two names to the English language which bid fair to abide. Few thoughtful critics, therefore, have dissented from the judgment of the committee which awarded him the Nobel Prize in Literature for 1930.

Sinclair Lewis was born February 7, 1885, in Sauk Centre, Minnesota, a small town which, in spite of his protestations to the contrary, gave him much of his material for "Gopher Prairie" in *Main Street*, just as the career of his father served in part as a model for that of the likable Doctor Kennicott in the same novel. He attended Yale and eventually took his degree from that institution in 1908. But he was a restless, adventurous type of youth who wanted nothing better than to free-lance. He tried unsuccessfully to get a job working on the Panama Canal; he managed rather inauspiciously to be initiated into the occupation of newspaper reporter, first in Iowa and then in California. It was not that he was temperamentally unable to endure the constraints necessarily placed upon any employee of a journalistic enterprise (as a matter of fact, he was a competent editor on the staff of the George H. Doran publishing house until 1916); it was rather that, as a superb individualist, he preferred the kind of schooling which a rolling stone is obliged to receive.

Encouraged by the sale of some short stories, he settled for a time in New York as a free-lance writer. It must be said here that his short stories are derivative and unimpressive, although one occasionally hears still of "Young Man Axelbrod" from *Free Air* (1919). This is the pathetic tale of an old midwestern farmer who goes to Yale for an autumnal college education, only to be rebuffed by the academic life and to return to his home, wiser but not necessarily sadder, because he has met a young esthete who on one occasion gave him a glimpse of the beauty of poetry and music not to be found in a classroom. It was with *Main Street* (1920), however, that Sinclair Lewis rocketed into prominence. He had settled himself down to write a novel in which he would say precisely what he wanted to say, without fear or favor. The result was an original, witty, satirical, and devastating picture of a drab middlewestern small town (which, however, might be a small town anywhere in America) and of the futile efforts of a rather neurotic, "cultured" doctor's wife to rouse Gopher Prairie from its smug intellectual and spiritual apathy; the book sold a half-million copies and made its author an international figure. It is in reality a work which fits neatly into a prevailing pattern of the time, for its objectives are not unlike those of Edgar Lee Masters' *Spoon River Anthology* (1915), Sherwood Anderson's *Winesburg, Ohio* (p. 308), or Willa Cather's *Youth and the Bright Medusa* (1920), to take but three prominent examples.

If *Main Street* threw a merciless spotlight on the small American town, *Babbitt* (1922) did the same for the American city and its worship of business, as typified by George F. Babbitt and his colleagues. Minneapolis has been suggested as the prototype for Zenith; actually, however, any American city except one of truly cosmopolitan nature will fit the outlines as well. Babbitt, like Carol Kennicott in *Main Street,* has his aspirations and his desire to get away from his prosaic and materialistic environment; but he does not know how to make his escape, and so sinks back into domestic desuetude, with the disillusioned reflection that, with all his efforts, he has made perhaps "a quarter of an inch out of a possible hundred rods." Withal, Babbitt is a kindly and basically sympathetic figure, for all his ignorance and stupidity. Similarly, Martin Arrowsmith, the protagonist of *Arrowsmith* (1925), must fight a long and rather inconclusive struggle between two great factions of his chosen profession of medicine—the cold, objective scientist for science's sake and the practical healer who regards research as only a means to an end. The medical profession in general is soundly rapped in *Arrowsmith,* with no diminution in the author's powers of mordant humor, scorn of hypocrisy, and hatred of the untutored masses, who seem unaware that they remain untutored. But in *Arrowsmith,* especially in its later pages, there emerges an often lavish romanticism which is at the bottom of Sinclair Lewis's mind—a romanticism which often approaches pure sentimentality.

Elmer Gantry (1927) is a vicious attack upon the disingenuous, self-seeking, animalistic preacher—it is not fair to call him a minister of the gospel—and upon the evangelical charlatans of whom America seems to have more than its proper share. The book contains many memorable scenes of typical Lewisian quality; but as a whole the novel is an angry one—too angry, in fact, to make for good satire as satire. For it is essential that a satirist keep his temper in writing satire, otherwise his work degenerates too easily into invective and name-calling; to blow the trumpet too hard is to blow flat notes. *Dodsworth* (1929) is a rather prosaic return to a calmer tone, and its portrayal of a silly, empty-headed, and trivial wife is one that will never be out of date.

The awarding of the Nobel Prize to Lewis was a fitting tribute to his talent; but it ironically rang down the curtain on most of the author's dynamic achievement. The novels which followed—*Ann Vickers* (1933), *Work of Art* (1934), *The Prodigal Parents* (1938), and *Bethel Merriday* (1940)—show a great decline. They are written with less skill and less suppleness; their humor is less spontaneous; and their characterization more vague and fuzzy. Indeed, *The Prodigal Parents* has been termed by some critics an outright reversal of *Babbitt,* which is generally considered Lewis' best work. At any rate, there is no better example of the astonishing gap between his best work and his worst work than these two novels. On the other hand, *Cass Timberlane* (1945) is an improvement; yet technically it is not even so good as *Dodsworth,* to say nothing of the earlier novels; and intellectually it has not advanced even a quarter of an inch beyond 1929. *Kingsblood Royal* (1947) treated in the *Main Street* manner Main Street's racial discrimination. *The God-Seeker* (1949) is a somewhat unconvincing attempt in the field of the historical novel, with the Middle West of the nineteenth century as background.

Lewis died in Italy in 1951, and his body was returned for burial at Sauk Centre. His early work, which was, on the whole, brilliant, remains his best. Its surface realism, at least, is unapproached in American letters. Lewis always held a great admiration for Theodore Dreiser (p. 289), which implies that he had been influenced by Dreiser. But while Dreiser is a psychological student in his realism, Lewis is more successful as the photographer of a psychological behaviorism. His effects, indeed, are likely to be most useful when they remain scenic effects. As a philosopher of human conduct he does not cut a distinguished figure. And he has probably written with too much detail and too many words. But as a reporter he had courage, skill, infernal cleverness at mimicry, and—best of all—power; and that power, whatever his detractors may say, was not all destructive. He has, to be sure, been attacked as vitri-olically as H. L. Mencken (p. 67), with whom he had a great deal in common; and small town people, businessmen, hotel-managers, doctors, lawyers, ministers, and social workers all have protested that he was grossly unfair to their individual occupations and professions. But he made Gopher Prairie and Zenith first squirm and then examine themselves ruefully, which is a sure sign that his criticism, especially in its more destructive aspects, struck home. In his savage political novel, *It Can't Happen Here* (1935), he warned the United States of the dangers of fascism and, incidentally, contributed another phrase to modern American thought.

As a child of the 1920's which he, paradoxically enough, somehow managed to remain, Sinclair Lewis neatly wrapped up American life in its raw, physical, and ineffably smug bourgeois state and placed it in a pigeon-hole, where future social historians will undoubtedly find it an invaluable ingredient for their chronicle of twentieth-century American civilization. The package does not contain everything, but it is a singularly rich and valuable gift to posterity.

from **Babbitt**

CHAPTER I

I

THE TOWERS of Zenith aspired above the morning mist; austere towers of steel and cement and limestone, sturdy as cliffs and delicate as silver rods. They were neither citadels nor churches, but frankly and beautifully of-fice-buildings.

The mist took pity on the fretted structures of earlier generations: the Post Office with its shingle-tortured mansard, the red brick mina-rets of hulking old houses, factories with stingy and sooted windows, wooden tenements col-ored like mud. The city was full of such gro-tesqueries, but the clean towers were thrusting

From *Babbitt*, by Sinclair Lewis, copyright, 1922, by Harcourt, Brace and Company, Inc.

them from the business center, and on the farther hills were shining new houses, homes—they seemed—for laughter and tranquillity.

Over a concrete bridge fled a limousine of long sleek hood and noiseless engine. These people in evening clothes were returning from an all-night rehearsal of a Little Theater play, [20] an artistic adventure considerably illuminated by champagne. Below the bridge curved a railroad, a maze of green and crimson lights. The New York Flyer boomed past, and twenty lines of polished steel leaped into the glare.

In one of the skyscrapers the wires of the Associated Press were closing down. The telegraph operators wearily raised their celluloid eye-shades after a night of talking with Paris and Peking. Through the building crawled the [30] scrubwomen, yawning, their old shoes slap-ping. The dawn mist spun away. Cues of men with lunch-boxes clumped toward the immen-sity of new factories, sheets of glass and hol-low tile, glittering shops where five thousand men worked beneath one roof, pouring out the honest wares that would be sold up the Eu-phrates and across the veldt. The whistles rolled out in greeting a chorus cheerful as the April dawn; the song of labor in a city built— [40] it seemed—for giants.

II

There was nothing of the giant in the aspect of the man who was beginning to awaken on the sleeping-porch of a Dutch Colonial house in that residential district of Zenith known as Floral Heights.

His name was George F. Babbitt. He was forty-six years old now, in April, 1920, and he made nothing in particular, neither butter nor shoes nor poetry, but he was nimble in the [50] calling of selling houses for more than people could afford to pay.

His large head was pink, his brown hair thin and dry. His face was babyish in slum-ber, despite his wrinkles and the red spectacle-dents on the slopes of his nose. He was not fat but he was exceedingly well fed; his cheeks were pads, and the unroughened hand which lay helpless upon the khaki-colored blanket was slightly puffy. He seemed prosperous, ex- [60] tremely married and unromantic; and alto-gether unromantic appeared this sleeping-porch, which looked on one sizable elm, two respectable grass-plots, a cement driveway, and a corrugated iron garage. Yet Babbitt was again dreaming of the fairy child, a dream more romantic than scarlet pagodas by a silver sea.

For years the fairy child had come to him. Where others saw but Georgie Babbitt, she discerned gallant youth. She waited for him, in the darkness beyond mysterious groves. When at last he could slip away from the crowded house he darted to her. His wife, his clamoring friends, sought to follow, but he escaped, the girl fleet beside him, and they crouched together on a shadowy hillside. She was so slim, so white, so eager! She cried that he was gay and valiant, that she would wait for him, that they would sail—

Rumble and bang of the milk-truck.

Babbitt moaned, turned over, struggled back toward his dream. He could see only her face now, beyond misty waters. The furnace-man slammed the basement door. A dog barked in the next yard. As Babbitt sank blissfully into a dim warm tide, the paper-carrier went by whistling, and the rolled-up *Advocate* thumped the front door. Babbitt roused, his stomach constricted with alarm. As he relaxed, he was pierced by the familiar and irritating rattle of some one cranking a Ford: snap-ah-ah, snap-ah-ah, snap-ah-ah. Himself a pious motorist, Babbitt cranked with the unseen driver, with him waited through taut hours for the roar of the starting engine, with him agonized as the roar ceased and again began the infernal patient snap-ah-ah—a round, flat sound, a shivering cold-morning sound, a sound infuriating and inescapable. Not till the rising voice of the motor told him that the Ford was moving was he released from the panting tension. He glanced once at his favorite tree, elm twigs against the gold patina of sky, and fumbled for sleep as for a drug. He who had been a boy very credulous of life was no longer greatly interested in the possible and improbable adventures of each new day.

He escaped from reality till the alarm-clock rang, at seven-twenty.

III

It was the best of nationally advertised and quantitatively produced alarm-clocks, with all modern attachments, including cathedral chime, intermittent alarm, and a phosphorescent dial. Babbitt was proud of being awakened by such a rich device. Socially it was almost as creditable as buying expensive cord tires.

He sulkily admitted now that there was no more escape, but he lay and detested the grind of the real-estate business, and disliked his family, and disliked himself for disliking them. The evening before, he had played poker at Vergil Gunch's till midnight, and after such holidays he was irritable before breakfast. It may have been the tremendous home-brewed beer of the prohibition-era and the cigars to which that beer enticed him; it may have been resentment of return from this fine, bold man-world to a restricted region of wives and stenographers, and of suggestions not to smoke so much.

From the bedroom beside the sleeping-porch, his wife's detestably cheerful "Time to get up, Georgie boy," and the itchy sound, the brisk and scratchy sound, of combing hairs out of a stiff brush.

He grunted; he dragged his thick legs, in faded baby-blue pajamas, from under the khaki blanket; he sat on the edge of the cot, running his fingers through his wild hair, while his plump feet mechanically felt for his slippers. He looked regretfully at the blanket—forever a suggestion to him of freedom and heroism. He had bought it for a camping trip which had never come off. It symbolized gorgeous loafing, gorgeous cursing, virile flannel shirts.

He creaked to his feet, groaning at the waves of pain which passed behind his eyeballs. Though he waited for their scorching recurrence, he looked blurrily out at the yard. It delighted him, as always; it was the neat yard of a successful business man of Zenith, that is, it was perfection, and made him also perfect. He regarded the corrugated iron garage. For the three-hundred-and-sixty-fifth time in a year he reflected, "No class to that tin shack. Have to build me a frame garage. But by golly it's the only thing on the place that isn't up-to-date!" While he stared he thought of a community garage for his acreage development, Glen Oriole. He stopped puffing and jiggling. His arms were akimbo. His petulant, sleep-swollen face was set in harder lines. He suddenly seemed capable, an official, a man to contrive, to direct, to get things done.

On the vigor of his idea he was carried down the hard, clean, unused-looking hall into the bathroom.

Though the house was not large it had, like all houses on Floral Heights, an altogether royal bathroom of porcelain and glazed tile and metal sleek as silver. The towel-rack was a rod of clear glass set in nickel. The tub was long enough for a Prussian Guard, and above the set bowl was a sensational exhibit of toothbrush holder, shaving-brush holder, soap-dish, sponge-dish, and medicine-cabinet, so glittering and so ingenious that they resembled an electrical instrument board. But the Babbitt whose god was Modern Appliances was not pleased. The air of the bathroom was thick with the smell of a heathen toothpaste. "Verona been at it again! 'Stead of sticking to Lilidol, like I've re-peat-ed-ly asked her, she's gone and gotten some confounded stinkum stuff that makes you sick!"

The bath-mat was wrinkled and the floor was wet. (His daughter Verona eccentrically took baths in the morning, now and then.) He slipped on the mat, and slid against the tub. He said "Damn!" Furiously he snatched up his tube of shaving-cream, furiously he lathered, with a belligerent slapping of the unctuous brush, furiously he raked his plump cheeks with a safety-razor. It pulled. The blade was dull. He said, "Damn—oh—oh—damn it!"

He hunted through the medicine-cabinet for a packet of new razor-blades (reflecting, as invariably, "Be cheaper to buy one of these dinguses and strop your own blades") and when he discovered the packet, behind the round box of bicarbonate of soda, he thought ill of his wife for putting it there and very well of himself for not saying "Damn." But he did say it, immediately afterward, when with wet and soap-slippery fingers he tried to remove the horrible little envelope and crisp clinging oiled paper from the new blade.

Then there was the problem, oft-pondered, never solved, of what to do with the old blade, which might imperil the fingers of his young. As usual, he tossed it on top of the medicine-cabinet, with a mental note that some day he must remove the fifty or sixty other blades that

were also temporarily piled up there. He finished his shaving in a growing testiness increased by his spinning headache and by the emptiness of his stomach. When he was done, his round face smooth and streamy and his eyes stinging from soapy water, he reached for a towel. The family towels were wet, wet and clammy and vile, all of them wet, he found, as he blindly snatched them—his own face-towel, his wife's, Verona's, Ted's, Tinka's, and the lone bath-towel with the huge welt of initial. Then George F. Babbitt did a dismaying thing. He wiped his face on the guest-towel! It was a pansy-embroidered trifle which always hung there to indicate that the Babbitts were in the best Floral Heights society. No one had ever used it. No guest had ever dared to. Guests secretively took a corner of the nearest regular towel.

He was raging, "By golly, here they go and use up all the towels, every doggone one of 'em, and they use 'em and get 'em all wet and sopping, and never put out a dry one for me—of course, I'm the goat!—and then I want one and—I'm the only person in the doggone house that's got the slightest doggone bit of consideration for other people and thoughtfulness and consider there may be others that may want to use the doggone bathroom after me and consider—"

He was pitching the chill abominations into the bath-tub, pleased by the vindictiveness of that desolate flapping sound; and in the midst his wife serenely trotted in, observed serenely, "Why Georgie dear, what are you doing? Are you going to wash out the towels? Why, you needn't wash out the towels. Oh, Georgie, you didn't go and use the guest-towel, did you?"

It is not recorded that he was able to answer.

For the first time in weeks he was sufficiently roused by his wife to look at her.

IV

Myra Babbitt—Mrs. George F. Babbitt—was definitely mature. She had creases from the corners of her mouth to the bottom of her chin, and her plump neck bagged. But the thing that marked her as having passed the line was that she no longer had reticences before her husband, and no longer worried about not having reticences. She was in a petticoat now, and corsets which bulged, and unaware of being seen in bulgy corsets. She had become so dully habituated to married life that in her full matronliness she was as sexless as an anemic nun. She was a good woman, a kind woman, a diligent woman, but no one, save perhaps Tinka her ten-year-old, was at all interested in her or entirely aware that she was alive.

After a rather thorough discussion of all the domestic and social aspects of towels she apologized to Babbitt for his having an alcoholic headache; and he recovered enough to endure the search for a B.V.D. undershirt which had, he pointed out, malevolently been concealed among his clean pajamas.

He was fairly amiable in the conference on the brown suit.

"What do you think, Myra?" He pawed at the clothes hunched on a chair in their bedroom, while she moved about mysteriously adjusting and patting her petticoat and, to his jaundiced eye, never seeming to get on with her dressing. "How about it? Shall I wear the brown suit another day?"

"Well, it looks awfully nice on you."

"I know, but gosh, it needs pressing."

"That's so. Perhaps it does."

"It certainly could stand being pressed, all right."

"Yes, perhaps it wouldn't hurt it to be pressed."

"But gee, the coat doesn't need pressing. No sense in having the whole darn suit pressed, when the coat doesn't need it."

"That's so."

"But the pants certainly need it, all right. Look at them—look at those wrinkles—the pants certainly do need pressing."

"That's so. Oh, Georgie, why couldn't you wear the brown coat with the blue trousers we were wondering what we'd do with them?"

"Good Lord! Did you ever in all my life know me to wear the coat of one suit and the pants of another? What do you think I am? A busted bookkeeper?"

"Well, why don't you put on the dark gray suit today, and stop in at the tailor and leave the brown trousers?"

"Well, they certainly need—Now where the devil is that gray suit? Oh, yes, here we are."

He was able to get through the other crises of dressing with comparative resoluteness and calm.

His first adornment was the sleeveless dimity B.V.D. undershirt, in which he resembled a small boy humorlessly wearing a cheesecloth tabard at a civic pageant. He never put on B.V.D.'s without thanking the God of Progress that he didn't wear tight, long, old-fashioned undergarments, like his father-in-law and partner, Henry Thompson. His second embellishment was combing and slicking back his hair. It gave him a tremendous forehead, arching up two inches beyond the former hair-line. But most wonder-working of all was the donning of his spectacles.

There is character in spectacles—the pretentious tortoise-shell, the meek pince-nez of the school teacher, the twisted silver-framed glasses of the old villager. Babbitt's spectacles had huge, circular, frameless lenses of the very best glass; the ear-pieces were thin bars of gold. In them he was the modern business man; one who gave orders to clerks and drove a car and played occasional golf and was scholarly in regard to Salesmanship. His head suddenly appeared not babyish but weighty, and you noted his heavy, blunt nose, his straight mouth and thick, long upper lip, his chin overfleshy but strong; with respect you beheld him put on the rest of his uniform as a Solid Citizen.

The gray suit was well cut, well made, and completely undistinguished. It was a standard suit. White piping on the V of the vest added a flavor of law and learning. His shoes were black laced boots, good boots, honest boots, standard boots, extraordinarily uninteresting boots. The only frivolity was in his purple knitted scarf. With considerable comment on the matter to Mrs. Babbitt (who, acrobatically fastening the back of her blouse to her skirt with a safety-pin, did not hear a word he said), he chose between the purple scarf and a tapestry effect with stringless brown harps among blown palms, and into it he thrust a snakehead pin with opal eyes.

A sensational event was changing from the brown suit to the gray the contents of his pockets. He was earnest about these objects. They were of eternal importance, like baseball or the Republican Party. They included a fountain pen and a silver pencil (always lacking a supply of new leads) which belonged in the righthand upper vest pocket. Without them he would have felt naked. On his watch-chain were a gold penknife, silver cigar-cutter, seven keys (the use of two of which he had forgotten), and incidentally a good watch. Depending from the chain was a large, yellowish elk's-tooth—proclamation of his membership in the Brotherly and Protective Order of Elks. Most significant of all was his loose-leaf pocket note-book, that modern and efficient note-book which contained the addresses of people whom he had forgotten, prudent memoranda of postal money-orders which had reached their destinations months ago, stamps which had lost their mucilage, clippings of verses by T. Cholmondeley Frink and of the newspaper editorials from which Babbitt got his opinions and his polysyllables, notes to be sure and do things which he did not intend to do, and one curious inscription—D.S.S.D.M.Y.P.D.F.

But he had no cigarette-case. No one had ever happened to give him one, so he hadn't the habit, and people who carried cigarette-cases he regarded as effeminate.

Last, he stuck in his lapel the Boosters' Club button. With the conciseness of great art the button displayed two words: "Boosters—Pep!" It made Babbitt feel loyal and important. It associated him with Good Fellows, with men who were nice and human, and important in business circles. It was his V.C., his Legion of Honor ribbon, his Phi Beta Kappa key.

With the subtleties of dressing ran other complex worries. "I feel kind of punk this morning," he said. "I think I had too much dinner last evening. You oughtn't to serve those heavy banana fritters."

"But you asked me to have some."

"I know, but—I tell you, when a fellow gets past forty he has to look after his digestion. There's a lot of fellows that don't take proper care of themselves. I tell you at forty a man's a fool or his doctor—I mean, his own doctor. Folks don't give enough attention to this matter of dieting. Now I think—Course a man

ought to have a good meal after the day's work, but it would be a good thing for both of us if we took lighter lunches."

"But Georgie, here at home I always do have a light lunch."

"Mean to imply I make a hog of myself, eating down-town? Yes, sure! You'd have a swell time if you had to eat the truck that new steward hands out to us at the Athletic Club! But I certainly do feel out of sorts, this morning. Funny, got a pain down here on the left side—but no, that wouldn't be appendicitis, would it? Last night, when I was driving over to Verg Gunch's, I felt a pain in my stomach, too. Right here it was—kind of a sharp shooting pain. I—Where'd that dime go to? Why don't you serve more prunes at breakfast? Of course I eat an apple every evening—an apple a day keeps the doctor away—but still, you ought to have more prunes, and not all these fancy doo-dads."

"The last time I had prunes you didn't eat them."

"Well, I didn't feel like eating 'em, I suppose. Matter of fact, I think I did eat some of 'em. Anyway—I tell you it's mighty important too—I was saying to Verg Gunch, just last evening, most people don't take sufficient care of their diges—"

"Shall we have the Gunches for our dinner, next week?"

"Why sure; you bet."

"Now see here, George: I want you to put on your nice dinner-jacket that evening."

"Rats! The rest of 'em won't want to dress."

"Of course they will. You remember when you didn't dress for the Littlefields' supper-party, and all the rest did, and how embarrassed you were."

"Embarrassed, hell! I wasn't embarrassed. Everybody knows I can put on as expensive a Tux. as anybody else, and I should worry if I don't happen to have it on sometimes. All a darn nuisance, anyway. All right for a woman, that stays around the house all the time, but when a fellow's worked like the dickens all day, he doesn't want to go and hustle his head off getting into the soup-and-fish for a lot of folks that he's seen in just reg'lar ordinary clothes that same day."

"You know you enjoy being seen in one. The other evening you admitted you were glad I'd insisted on your dressing. You said you felt a lot better for it. And oh, Georgie, I do wish you wouldn't say 'Tux.' It's 'dinner-jacket.'"

"Rats, what's the odds?"

"Well, it's what all the nice folks say. Suppose Lucile McKelvey heard you calling it a 'Tux.'"

"Well, that's all right now! Lucile McKelvey can't pull anything on me! Her folks are common as mud, even if her husband and her dad are millionaires! I suppose you're trying to rub in *your* exalted social position! Well, let me tell you that your revered paternal ancestor, Henry T., doesn't even call it a 'Tux.'! He calls it a 'bobtail jacket for a ringtail monkey,' and you couldn't get him into one unless you chloroformed him!"

"Now don't be horrid, George."

"Well, I don't want to be horrid, but Lord! you're getting as fussy as Verona. Ever since she got out of college she's been too rambunctious to live with—doesn't know what she wants —well, I know what she wants!—all she wants is to marry a millionaire, and live in Europe, and hold some preacher's hand, and simultaneously at the same time stay right here in Zenith and be some blooming kind of a socialist agitator or boss charity-worker or some damn thing! Lord, and Ted is just as bad! He wants to go to college, and he doesn't want to go to college. Only one of the three that knows her own mind is Tinka. Simply can't understand how I ever came to have a pair of shillyshallying children like Rone and Ted. I may not be any Rockefeller or James J. Shakespeare, but I certainly do know my own mind, and I do keep right on plugging along in the office and—Do you know the latest? Far as I can figure out, Ted's new bee is he'd like to be a movie actor and— And here I've told him a hundred times, if he'll go to college and law-school and make good, I'll set him up in business and—Verona just exactly as bad. Doesn't know what she wants. Well, well, come on! Aren't you ready yet? The girl rang the bell three minutes ago."

V

Before he followed his wife, Babbitt stood at the westernmost window of their room. This residential settlement, Floral Heights, was on a rise; and though the center of the city was three miles away—Zenith had between three and four hundred thousand inhabitants now— he could see the top of the Second National Tower, an Indiana limestone building of thirty-five stories.

Its shining walls rose against April sky to a simple cornice like a streak of white fire. Integrity was in the tower, and decision. It bore its strength lightly as a tall soldier. As Babbitt stared, the nervousness was soothed from his face, his slack chin lifted in reverence. All he articulated was "That's one lovely sight!" but he was inspired by the rhythm of the city; his love of it renewed. He beheld the tower as a temple-spire of the religion of business, a faith passionate, exalted, surpassing common men; and as he clumped down to breakfast he whistled the ballad "Oh, by gee, by gosh, by jingo" as though it were a hymn melancholy and noble.

CHAPTER II

I

Relieved of Babbitt's bumbling and the soft grunts with which his wife expressed the sympathy she was too experienced to feel and much too experienced not to show, their bedroom settled instantly into impersonality.

It gave on the sleeping-porch. It served both of them as dressing-room, and on the coldest nights Babbitt luxuriously gave up the duty of being manly and retreated to the bed inside, to curl his toes in the warmth and laugh at the January gale.

The room displayed a modest and pleasant color-scheme, after one of the best standard designs of the decorator who "did the interiors" for most of the speculative-builders' houses in Zenith. The walls were gray, the woodwork white, the rug a serene blue; and very much like mahogany was the furniture— the bureau with its great clear mirror, Mrs. Babbitt's dressing-table with toilet-articles of almost solid silver, the plain twin beds, between them a small table holding a standard electric bedside lamp, a glass for water, and a standard bedside book with colored illustrations—what particular book it was cannot be ascertained, since no one had ever opened it. The mattresses were firm but not hard, triumphant modern mattresses which had cost a great deal of money; the hot-water radiator was of exactly the proper scientific surface for the cubic contents of the room. The windows were large and easily opened, with the best catches and cords, and Holland roller-shades guaranteed not to crack. It was a masterpiece among bedrooms, right out of Cheerful Modern Houses for Medium Incomes. Only it had nothing to do with the Babbitts, nor with any one else. If people had ever lived and loved here, read thrillers at midnight and lain in beautiful indolence on a Sunday morning, there were no signs of it. It had the air of being a very good room in a very good hotel. One expected the chambermaid to come in and make it ready for people who would stay but one night, go without looking back, and never think of it again.

Every second house in Floral Heights had a bedroom precisely like this.

The Babbitts' house was five years old. It was all as competent and glossy as this bedroom. It had the best of taste, the best of inexpensive rugs, a simple and laudable architecture, and the latest conveniences. Throughout, electricity took the place of candles and slatternly hearth-fires. Along the bedroom baseboard were three plugs for electric lamps, concealed by little brass doors. In the halls were plugs for the vacuum cleaner, and in the living-room plugs for the piano lamp, for the electric fan. The trim dining-room (with its admirable oak buffet, its leaded-glass cupboard, its creamy plaster walls, its modest scene of a salmon expiring upon a pile of oysters) had plugs which supplied the electric percolator and the electric toaster.

In fact there was but one thing wrong with the Babbitt house: It was not a home.

II

Often of a morning Babbitt came bouncing and jesting in to breakfast. But things were mysteriously awry today. As he pontifically trod the upper hall he looked into Verona's bedroom and protested, "What's the use of giving the family a high-class house when they don't appreciate it and tend to business and get down to brass tacks?"

He marched upon them: Verona, a dumpy brown-haired girl of twenty-two, just out of Bryn Mawr, given to solicitudes about duty and sex and God and the unconquerable bagginess of the gray sports-suit she was now wearing. Ted—Theodore Roosevelt Babbitt—a decorative boy of seventeen. Tinka—Katherine —still a baby at ten, with radiant red hair and a thin skin which hinted of too much candy and too many ice cream sodas. Babbitt did not show his vague irritation as he tramped in. He really disliked being a family tyrant, and his nagging was as meaningless as it was frequent. He shouted at Tinka, "Well, kittiedoolie!" It was the only pet name in his vocabulary, except the "dear" and "hon." with which he recognized his wife, and he flung it at Tinka every morning.

He gulped a cup of coffee in the hope of pacifying his stomach and his soul. His stomach ceased to feel as though it did not belong to him, but Verona began to be conscientious and annoying, and abruptly there returned to Babbitt the doubts regarding life and families and business which had clawed at him when his dream-life and the slim fairy girl had fled.

Verona had for six months been filing-clerk at the Gruensberg Leather Company offices, with a prospect of becoming secretary to Mr. Gruensberg and thus, as Babbitt defined it, "getting some good out of your expensive college education till you're ready to marry and settle down."

But now said Verona: "Father! I was talking to a classmate of mine that's working for the Associated Charities—oh, Dad, there's the sweetest little babies that come to the milk-station there!—and I feel as though I ought to be doing something worth while like that."

"What do you mean 'worth while'? If you get to be Gruensberg's secretary—and maybe you would, if you kept up your shorthand and didn't go sneaking off to concerts and talk-fests every evening—I guess you'll find thirty-five or forty bones a week worth while!"

"I know, but—oh, I want to—contribute—I wish I were working in a settlement-house. I wonder if I could get one of the department-stores to let me put in a welfare-department with a nice rest-room and chintzes and wicker chairs and so on and so forth. Or I could—"

"Now you look here! The first thing you got to understand is that all this uplift and flipflop and settlement-work and recreation is nothing in God's world but the entering wedge for socialism. The sooner a man learns he isn't going to be coddled, and he needn't expect a lot of free grub and, uh, all these free classes and flipflop and doodads for his kids unless he earns 'em, why, the sooner he'll get on the job and produce—produce—produce! That's what the country needs, and not all this fancy stuff that just enfeebles the will-power of the working man and gives his kids a lot of notions above their class. And you—if you'd tend to business instead of fooling and fussing—All the time! When I was a young man I made up my mind what I wanted to do, and stuck to it through thick and thin, and that's why I'm where I am today, and—Myra! What do you let the girl chop the toast up into these dinky little chunks for? Can't get your fist onto 'em. Half cold, anyway!"

Ted Babbitt, junior in the great East Side High School, had been making hiccup-like sounds of interruption. He blurted now, "Say, Rone, you going to—"

Verona whirled. "Ted! Will you kindly not interrupt us when we're talking about serious matters!"

"Aw, punk," said Ted judicially. "Ever since somebody slipped up and let you out of college, Ammonia, you been pulling these nut conversations about what-nots and so-on-and-so-forths. Are you going to—I want to use the car tonight."

Babbitt snorted, "Oh, you do! May want it myself!" Verona protested, "Oh, you do, Mr. Smarty! I'm going to take it myself!" Tinka wailed, "Oh, papa, you said maybe you'd drive us down to Rosedale!" and Mrs. Babbitt, "Careful, Tinka, your sleeve is in the butter." They glared, and Verona hurled, "Ted, you're a perfect pig about the car!"

"Course you're not! Not a-tall!" Ted could be maddeningly bland. "You just want to grab it off, right after dinner, and leave it in front of some skirt's house all evening while you sit and gas about lite'ature and the high-

brows you're going to marry—if they'd only propose!"

"Well, Dad oughtn't to *ever* let you have it! You and those beastly Jones boys drive like maniacs. The idea of your taking the turn on Chautauqua Place at forty miles an hour!"

"Aw, where do you get that stuff! You're so darn scared of the car that you drive up-hill with the emergency brake on!"

"I did not! And you—Always talking about how much you know about motors, and Eunice Littlefield told me you said the battery fed the generator!"

"You—why, my good woman, you don't know a generator from a differential." Not unreasonably was Ted lofty with her. He was a natural mechanic, a maker and tinkerer of machines; he lisped in blueprints for the blueprints came.

"That'll do now!" Babbitt flung in mechanically, as he lighted the gloriously satisfying first cigar of the day and tasted the exhilarating drug of the *Advocate-Times* headlines.

Ted negotiated: "Gee, honest, Rone, I don't want to take the old boat, but I promised couple o' girls in my class I'd drive 'em down to the rehearsal of the school chorus, and, gee, I don't want to, but a gentleman's got to keep his social engagements."

"Well, upon my word! You and your social engagements! In high school!"

"Oh, ain't we select since we went to that hen college! Let me tell you there isn't a private school in the state that's got as swell a bunch as we got in Gamma Digamma this year. There's two fellows that their dads are millionaires. Say, gee, I ought to have a car of my own, like lots of the fellows."

Babbitt almost rose. "A car of your own! Don't you want a yacht, and a house and lot? That pretty near takes the cake! A boy that can't pass his Latin examinations, like any other boy ought to, and he expects me to give him a motor-car, and I suppose a chauffeur, and an areoplane maybe, as a reward for the hard work he puts in going to the movies with Eunice Littlefield! Well, when you see me giving you—"

Somewhat later, after diplomacies, Ted persuaded Verona to admit that she was merely going to the Armory, that evening, to see the dog and cat show. She was then, Ted planned, to park the car in front of the candy-store across from the Armory and he would pick it up. There were masterly arrangements regarding leaving the key, and having the gasoline tank filled; and passionately, devotees of the Great God Motor, they hymned the patch on the spare inner-tube, and the lost jack-handle.

Their truce dissolving, Ted observed that her friends were "a scream of a bunch—stuck-up gabby four-flushers." His friends, she indicated, were "disgusting imitation sports, and horrid little shrieking ignorant girls." Further: "It's disgusting of you to smoke cigarettes, and so on and so forth, and those clothes you've got on this morning, they're too utterly ridiculous —honestly, simply disgusting."

Ted balanced over to the low beveled mirror in the buffet, regarded his charms, and smirked. His suit, the latest thing in Old Eli Togs, was skin-tight, with skimpy trousers to the tops of his glaring tan boots, a chorus-man waistline, pattern of an agitated check, and across the back a belt which belted nothing. His scarf was an enormous black silk wad. His flaxen hair was ice-smooth, pasted back without parting. When he went to school he would add a cap with a long vizor like a shovel-blade. Proudest of all was his waistcoat, saved for, begged for, plotted for; a real Fancy Vest of fawn with polka dots of a decayed red, the points astoundingly long. On the lower edge of it he wore a high-school button, a class button, and a fraternity pin.

And none of it mattered. He was supple and swift and flushed; his eyes (which he believed to be cynical) were candidly eager. But he was not over-gentle. He waved his hand at poor dumpy Verona and drawled: "Yes, I guess we're pretty ridiculous and disgusticulus, and I rather guess our new necktie is some smear!"

Babbitt barked: "It is! And while you're admiring yourself, let me tell you that it might add to your manly beauty if you wiped some of that egg off your mouth!"

Verona giggled, momentary victor in the greatest of Great Wars, which is the family war. Ted looked at her hopelessly, then shrieked at Tinka: "For the love o' Pete, quit pouring the whole sugar bowl on your corn flakes!"

When Verona and Ted were gone and Tinka upstairs, Babbitt groaned to his wife: "Nice family, I must say! I don't pretend to be any baa-lamb, and maybe I'm a little cross-grained at breakfast sometimes, but the way they go on jab-jab-jabbering, I simply can't stand it. I swear, I feel like going off some place where I can get a little peace. I do think after a man's spent his lifetime trying to give his kiddies a chance and a decent education, it's pretty discouraging to hear them all the time scrapping like a bunch of hyenas and never—and never— Curious; here in the paper it says—Never silent for one mom—Seen the morning paper yet?"

"No, dear." In twenty-three years of married life, Mrs. Babbitt had seen the paper before her husband just sixty-seven times.

"Lots of news. Terrible big tornado in the South. Hard luck, all right. But this, say, this is corking! Beginning of the end for those fellows! New York Assembly has passed some bills that ought to completely outlaw the socialists! And there's an elevator-runners' strike in New York and a lot of college boys are taking their places. That's the stuff! And a mass-meeting in Birmingham's demanded that this Mick agitator, this fellow De Valera, be deported. Dead right, by golly! All these agitators paid with German gold anyway. And we got no business interfering with the Irish or any other foreign government. Keep our hands strictly off. And there's another well-authenticated rumor from Russia that Lenin is dead. That's fine. It's beyond me why we don't just step in there and kick those Bolshevik cusses out."

"That's so," said Mrs. Babbitt.

"And it says here a fellow was inaugurated mayor in overalls—a preacher, too! What do you think of that!"

"Humph! Well!"

He searched for an attitude, but neither as a Republican, a Presbyterian, an Elk, nor a real-estate broker did he have any doctrine about preacher-mayors laid down for him, so he grunted and went on. She looked sympathetic and did not hear a word. Later she would read the headlines, the society columns, and the department store advertisements.

"What do you know about this! Charley Mc-Kelvey still doing the sassiety stunt as heavy as ever. Here's what that gushy woman reporter says about last night:

"Never is Society with the big, big S more flattered than when they are bidden to partake of good cheer at the distinguished and hospitable residence of Mr. and Mrs. Charles L. McKelvey as they were last night. Set in its spacious lawns and landscaping, one of the notable sights crowning Royal Ridge, but merry and homelike despite its mighty stone walls and its vast rooms famed for their decoration, their home was thrown open last night for a dance in honor of Mrs. McKelvey's notable guest, Miss J. Sneeth of Washington. The wide hall is so generous in its proportions that it made a perfect ballroom, its hardwood floor reflecting the charming pageant above its polished surface. Even the delights of dancing paled before the alluring opportunities for tête-à-têtes that invited the soul to loaf in the long library before the baronial fireplace, or in the drawing-room with its deep comfy armchairs, its shaded lamps just made for a sly whisper of pretty nothings all a deux; or even in the billiard room where one could take a cue and show a prowess at still another game than that sponsored by Cupid and Terpsichore."

There was more, a great deal more, in the best urban journalistic style of Miss Elnora Pearl Bates, the popular society editor of the *Advocate-Times*. But Babbitt could not abide it. He grunted. He wrinkled the newspaper. He protested: "Can you beat it! I'm willing to hand a lot of credit to Charley McKelvey. When we were in college together he was just as hard up as any of us, and he's made a million good bucks out of contracting and hasn't been any dishonester or bought any more city councils than was necessary. And that's a good house of his—though it ain't any 'mighty stone walls' and it ain't worth the ninety thousand it cost him. But when it comes to talking as though Charley McKelvey and all that booze-hoisting set of his are any blooming bunch of, of, of Vanderbilts, why, it makes me tired!"

Timidly from Mrs. Babbitt: "I would like to see the inside of their house, though. It must be lovely. I've never been inside."

"Well, I have! Lots of—couple of times. To see Chaz about business deals, in the evening.

It's not so much. I wouldn't *want* to go there to dinner with that gang of, of high-binders. And I'll bet I make a whole lot more money than some of those tin-horns that spend all they got on dress-suits and haven't got a decent suit of underwear to their name! Hey! What do you think of this!"

Mrs. Babbitt was strangely unmoved by the tidings from the Real Estate and Building column of the *Advocate-Times*:

Ashtabula Street, 496—J. K. Dawson
to Thomas Mullaly,
April 17, 15.7 x 112.2, mtg. $4000 . . . . Nom.

And this morning Babbitt was too disquieted to entertain her with items from Mechanics' Liens, Mortgages Recorded, and Contracts Awarded. He rose. As he looked at her his eyebrows seemed shaggier than usual. Suddenly:

"Yes, maybe—Kind of shame to not keep in touch with folks like the McKelveys. We might try inviting them to dinner, some evening. Oh, thunder, let's not waste our good time thinking about 'em! Our little bunch has a lot liver times than all those plutes. Just compare a real human like you with these neurotic birds like Lucile McKelvey—all highbrow talk and dressed up like a plush horse! You're a great old girl, hon.!"

He covered his betrayal of softness with a complaining: "Say, don't let Tinka go and eat any more of that poison nut-fudge. For Heaven's sake, try to keep her from ruining her digestion. I tell you, most folks don't appreciate how important it is to have a good digestion and regular habits. Be back 'bout usual time, I guess."

He kissed her—he didn't quite kiss her—he laid unmoving lips against her unflushing cheek. He hurried out to the garage, muttering: "Lord, what a family! And now Myra is going to get pathetic on me because we don't train with this millionaire outfit. Oh, Lord, sometimes I'd like to quit the whole game. And the office worry and detail just as bad. And I act cranky and—I don't mean to, but I get—So darn tired!"

F. SCOTT FITZGERALD

The melancholy young men and women of the Jazz Age had one of their most fearless and accomplished interpreters on this side of the Atlantic in F. Scott Fitzgerald. A distant relative of the author of "The Star-Spangled Banner," Francis Scott Key Fitzgerald was born in St. Paul, Minnesota, on September 24, 1896. He always was interested in writing. Throughout his schooldays at St. Paul Academy and later at Newman School in Hackensack, New Jersey, he scribbled industriously and with merit, though with great detriment to his study of subjects other than English. At Newman School he conceived a passion, happily rather transient, for the writing of musical comedies. This passion manifested itself, none the less, throughout his first year at Princeton, where, according to his own word, he spent all the available time in the composing of a show to be produced by the famous Princeton Triangle Club. As a result, "I failed in algebra, trigonometry, coördinate geometry, and hygiene," though the show went on. With the entrance of America into World War I, Fitzgerald left Princeton and joined the army, rising to the rank of first lieutenant in the infantry. He saw no service overseas.

While he was serving on the staff of Brigadier General Ryan in New York, Fitzgerald found time amid the multitudinous petty duties of a staff-officer to write a novel by making use of all his leisure time on Saturdays and Sundays. The novel, *The Romantic Egoist,* was praised for its originality by the publishers to whom he submitted it; but it was nevertheless rejected. Fitzgerald now tried to get a berth with a New York newspaper but failed to do so. Eventually he became an advertising writer in New York at ninety dollars a month; later he commented bitterly upon the number and the nature of the advertising slogans he wrote for the doubtful delectation of people in the subway or on the trolleys. After a compara-

tively short turn at this occupation he gave up and returned to St. Paul, where he immediately fell to writing another novel, *This Side of Paradise* (1920). The book was an immediate success; and when he followed it up with two effective volumes of short stories, *Flappers and Philosophers* (1920) and *Tales of the Jazz Age* (1922), his position as one of the most promising of rising young American authors was believed to be assured. *The Beautiful and Damned* (1922), another arresting novel whose title defines at once the quality of Fitzgerald's characters and the attitude they show toward life, seemed to make the assurance doubly sure.

Unhappily the promise faded. Not that Fitzgerald, during these disappointing years, was either inactive or unadventurous. He tried his fortune with a play, *The Vegetable; or From President to Postman* (1923). It was a flat failure and cost its author much in dollars as well as in prestige. One more novel, *Tender Is the Night* (1934), was almost a fiasco. Two volumes of short stories, *All the Sad Young Men* (1926) and *Taps at Reveille* (1935), in spite of their comparatively late date, assumed a merely historical interest. Except for one other novel, in the same vein as its predecessors and fully as competent, Fitzgerald did not maintain the standard of his earlier works. This novel, *The Great Gatsby* (1925), was written while he was vacationing in Italy and on the French Riviera; but it treats, as usual with Fitzgerald, of the Long Island smart set of the 1920's.

But Fitzgerald's untimely death, on December 22, 1940, and the attention directed to his then unfinished novel, *The Last Tycoon,* awakened interest in his undoubted talents, an interest which was heightened by the somewhat wry discovery that conditions after the First World War—Fitzgerald's favorite theme —were disconcertingly similar to conditions after the Second World War. And so Fitzgerald, far from being a museum piece, was actually a vital writer about pressing post-war social problems.

In the long run, however, "historical" is precisely the word to indicate Fitzgerald's general significance in the story of American letters. He could write fluently; he had a sharp eye for realism; he knew the milieu of which he wrote; he had a more than adequate sense of humor and an excellent instinct for proportion and total effect. In other words, he was a most gifted writer, and his virtues will always be welcome among fiction-writers. Yet his subject-matter is limited. He knows handsome, affluent young men and women of the smarter social sets derived ultimately from collegiate and country-club cliques; he knows their psychology, their motives, and their souls—where souls can be discerned. While he is dealing with New York City and Long Island (or Westchester) society of the period after the First World War and during the years of the depression, he is the master supreme. But when he tries other themes and other environments, he fails. He lacks the brilliance, the cleverness, and the all-round information of Aldous Huxley (p. 469), to whom he has sometimes been compared. In retrospect he appears, for all the brave glitter and romantic settings of his stories, as one of the most desolate of the Waste Landers. He is, in his superior talents and potentially great powers, as indispensable a part of the Jazz Age as Clara Bow and her "It," collegiate super-plus-fours, and the Charleston. The terrible intellectual and moral sterility of this band of beautiful and damned he has demonstrated in a way that deserves to be remembered.

May Day

THERE had been a war fought and won and the great city of the conquering people was crossed with triumphant arches and vivid with thrown flowers of white, red, and rose. All through the long spring days the returning sol-

"May Day" from *Tales of the Jazz Age*, reprinted by permission of Charles Scribner's Sons.

diers marched up the chief highway behind the strump of drums and the joyous, resonant wind of the brasses, while merchants and clerks left their bickerings and figurings and, crowding to the windows, turned their white-bunched faces gravely upon the passing battalions.

Never had there been such splendor in the great city, for the victorious war had brought plenty in its train, and the merchants had flocked thither from the South and West with their households to taste of all the luscious feasts and witness the lavish entertainments prepared—and to buy for their women furs against the next winter and bags of golden mesh and varicolored slippers of silk and silver and rose satin and cloth of gold.

So gaily and noisily were the peace and prosperity impending hymned by the scribes and poets of the conquering people that more and more spenders had gathered from the provinces to drink the wine of excitement, and faster and faster did the merchants dispose of their trinkets and slippers until they sent up a mighty cry for more trinkets and more slippers in order that they might give in barter what was demanded of them. Some even of them flung up their hands helplessly, shouting:

"Alas! I have no more slippers! and alas! I have no more trinkets! May heaven help me, for I know not what I shall do!"

But no one listened to their great outcry, for the throngs were far too busy—day by day, the foot-soldiers trod jauntily the highway and all exulted because the young men returning were pure and brave, sound of tooth and pink of cheek, and the young women of the land were virgins and comely both of face and of figure.

So during all this time there were many adventures that happened in the great city, and, of these, several—or perhaps one—are here set down.

I

At nine o'clock on the morning of the first of May, 1919, a young man spoke to the room clerk at the Biltmore Hotel, asking if Mr. Philip Dean were registered there, and if so, could he be connected with Mr. Dean's rooms. The inquirer was dressed in a well-cut, shabby suit. He was small, slender, and darkly handsome; his eyes were framed above with unusually long eyelashes and below with the blue semicircle of ill health, this latter effect heightened by an unnatural glow which colored his face like a low, incessant fever.

Mr. Dean was staying there. The young man was directed to a telephone at the side.

After a second his connection was made; a sleepy voice hello'd from somewhere above.

"Mr. Dean?"—this very eagerly—"it's Gordon, Phil. It's Gordon Sterrett. I'm downstairs. I heard you were in New York and I had a hunch you'd be here."

The sleepy voice became gradually enthusiastic. Well, how was Gordy, old boy! Well, he certainly was surprised and tickled! Would Gordy come right up, for Pete's sake!

A few minutes later Philip Dean, dressed in blue silk pajamas, opened his door and the two young men greeted each other with a half-embarrassed exuberance. They were both about twenty-four, Yale graduates of the year before the war; but there the resemblance stopped abruptly. Dean was blond, ruddy, and rugged under his thin pajamas. Everything about him radiated fitness and bodily comfort. He smiled frequently, showing large and prominent teeth.

"I was going to look you up," he cried enthusiastically. "I'm taking a couple of weeks off. If you'll sit down a sec I'll be right with you. Going to take a shower."

As he vanished into the bathroom his visitor's dark eyes roved nervously around the room, resting for a moment on a great English travelling bag in the corner and on a family of thick silk shirts littered on the chairs amid impressive neckties and soft woollen socks.

Gordon rose and, picking up one of the shirts, gave it a minute examination. It was of very heavy silk, yellow, with a pale blue stripe —and there were nearly a dozen of them. He stared involuntarily at his own shirt-cuffs—they were ragged and linty at the edges and soiled to a faint gray. Dropping the silk shirt, he held his coat-sleeves down and worked the frayed shirt-cuffs up till they were out of sight. Then he went to the mirror and looked at himself with listless, unhappy interest. His tie, of former glory, was faded and thumb-creased—it served no longer to hide the jagged button-holes of his collar. He thought, quite without amusement, that only three years before he

had received a scattering vote in the senior elections at college for being the best-dressed man in his class.

Dean emerged from the bathroom polishing his body.

"Saw an old friend of yours last night," he remarked. "Passed her in the lobby and couldn't think of her name to save my neck. That girl you brought up to New Haven senior year."

Gordon started.

"Edith Bradin? That whom you mean?"

"'At's the one. Damn good-looking. She's still sort of a pretty doll—you know what I mean: as if you touched her she'd smear."

He surveyed his shining self complacently in the mirror, smiled faintly, exposing a section of teeth.

"She must be twenty-three anyway," he continued.

"Twenty-two last month," said Gordon absently.

"What? Oh, last month. Well, I imagine she's down for the Gamma Psi dance. Did you know we're having a Yale Gamma Psi dance to-night at Delmonico's? You better come up, Gordy. Half of New Haven'll probably be there. I can get you an invitation."

Draping himself reluctantly in fresh underwear, Dean lit a cigarette and sat down by the open window, inspecting his calves and knees under the morning sunshine which poured into the room.

"Sit down, Gordy," he suggested, "and tell me all about what you've been doing and what you're doing now and everything."

Gordon collapsed unexpectedly upon the bed; lay there inert and spiritless. His mouth, which habitually dropped a little open when his face was in repose, became suddenly helpless and pathetic.

"What's the matter?" asked Dean quickly.

"Oh, God!"

"What's the matter?"

"Every God damn thing in the world," he said miserably. "I've absolutely gone to pieces, Phil. I'm all in."

"Huh?"

"I'm all in." His voice was shaking.

Dean scrutinized him more closely with appraising blue eyes.

"You certainly look all shot."

"I am. I've made a hell of a mess of everything." He paused. "I'd better start at the beginning—or will it bore you?"

"Not at all; go on." There was, however, a hesitant note in Dean's voice. This trip East had been planned for a holiday—to find Gordon Sterrett in trouble exasperated him a little.

"Go on," he repeated, and then added half under his breath, "Get it over with."

"Well," began Gordon unsteadily, "I got back from France in February, went home to Harrisburg for a month, and then came down to New York to get a job. I got one—with an export company. They fired me yesterday."

"Fired you?"

"I'm coming to that, Phil. I want to tell you frankly. You're about the only man I can turn to in a matter like this. You won't mind if I just tell you frankly, will you, Phil?"

Dean stiffened a bit more. The pats he was bestowing on his knees grew perfunctory. He felt vaguely that he was being unfairly saddled with responsibility; he was not even sure he wanted to be told. Though never surprised at finding Gordon Sterrett in mild difficulty, there was something in this present misery that repelled him and hardened him, even though it excited his curiosity.

"Go on."

"It's a girl."

"Hm." Dean resolved that nothing was going to spoil his trip. If Gordon was going to be depressing, then he'd have to see less of Gordon.

"Her name is Jewel Hudson," went on the distressed voice from the bed. "She used to be 'pure,' I guess, up to about a year ago. Lived here in New York—poor family. Her people are dead now and she lives with an old aunt. You see it was just about the time I met her that everybody began to come back from France in droves—and all I did was to welcome the newly arrived and go on parties with 'em. That's the way it started, Phil, just from being glad to see everybody and having them glad to see me."

"You ought to've had more sense."

"I know," Gordon paused, and then continued listlessly. "I'm on my own now, you know, and Phil, I can't stand being poor. Then came this darn girl. She sort of fell in love with me

for a while and, though I never intended to get so involved, I'd always seem to run into her somewhere. You can imagine the sort of work I was doing for those exporting people—of course, I always intended to draw; do illustrating for magazines; there's a pile of money in it."

"Why didn't you? You've got to buckle down if you want to make good," suggested Dean with cold formalism.

"I tried, a little, but my stuff's crude. I've got talent, Phil; I can draw—but I just don't know how. I ought to go to art school and I can't afford it. Well, things came to a crisis about a week ago. Just as I was down to about my last dollar this girl began bothering me. She wants some money; claims that she can make trouble for me if she doesn't get it."

"Can she?"

"I'm afraid she can. That's one reason I lost my job—she kept calling up the office all the time, and that was sort of the last straw down there. She got a letter all written to send to my family. Oh, she's got me, all right. I've got to have some money for her."

There was an awkward pause. Gordon lay very still, his hands clenched by his side.

"I'm all in," he continued, his voice trembling. "I'm half crazy, Phil. If I hadn't known you were coming East, I think I'd have killed myself. I want you to lend me three hundred dollars."

Dean's hands, which had been patting his bare ankles, were suddenly quiet—and the curious uncertainty playing between the two became taut and strained.

After a second Gordon continued:

"I've bled the family until I'm ashamed to ask for another nickel."

Still Dean made no answer.

"Jewel says she's got to have two hundred dollars."

"Tell her where she can go."

"Yes, that sounds easy, but she's got a couple of drunken letters I wrote her. Unfortunately she's not at all the flabby sort of person you'd expect."

Dean made an expression of distaste.

"I can't stand that sort of woman. You ought to have kept away."

"I know," admitted Gordon wearily.

"You've got to look at things as they are. If you haven't got money you've got to work and stay away from women."

"That's easy for you to say," began Gordon, his eyes narrowing. "You've got all the money in the world."

"I most certainly have not. My family keep darn close tab on what I spend. Just because I have a little leeway I have to be extra careful not to abuse it."

He raised the blind and let in a further flood of sunshine.

"I'm not a prig, Lord knows," he went on deliberately. "I like pleasure—and I like a lot of it on a vacation like this, but you're—you're in awful shape. I never heard you talk just this way before. You seem to be sort of bankrupt—morally as well as financially."

"Don't they usually go together?"

Dean shook his head impatiently.

"There's a regular aura about you that I don't understand. It's a sort of evil."

"It's an air of worry and poverty and sleepless nights," said Gordon, rather defiantly.

"I don't know."

"Oh, I admit I'm depressing. I depress myself. But, my God, Phil, a week's rest and a new suit and some ready money and I'd be like—like I was. Phil, I can draw like a streak, and you know it. But half the time I haven't had the money to buy decent drawing materials—and I can't draw when I'm tired and discouraged and all in. With a little ready money I can take a few weeks off and get started."

"How do I know you wouldn't use it on some other woman?"

"Why rub it in?" said Gordon quietly.

"I'm not rubbing it in. I hate to see you this way."

"Will you lend me the money, Phil?"

"I can't decide right off. That's a lot of money and it'll be darn inconvenient for me."

"It'll be hell for me if you can't—I know I'm whining, and it's all my own fault but—that doesn't change it."

"When could you pay it back?"

This was encouraging. Gordon considered. It was probably wisest to be frank.

"Of course, I could promise to send it back next month, but—I'd better say three months. Just as soon as I start to sell drawings."

"How do I know you'll sell any drawings?"

A new hardness in Dean's voice sent a faint chill of doubt over Gordon. Was it possible that he wouldn't get the money?

"I supposed you had a little confidence in me."

"I did have—but when I see you like this I begin to wonder."

"Do you suppose if I wasn't at the end of my rope I'd come to you like this? Do you think I'm enjoying it?" He broke off and bit his lip, feeling that he had better subdue the rising anger in his voice. After all, he was the suppliant.

"You seem to manage it pretty easily," said Dean angrily. "You put me in the position where, if I don't lend it to you, I'm a sucker—oh, yes, you do. And let me tell you it's no easy thing for me to get hold of three hundred dollars. My income isn't so big but that a slice like that won't play the deuce with it."

He left his chair and began to dress, choosing his clothes carefully. Gordon stretched out his arms and clenched the edges of the bed, fighting back a desire to cry out. His head was splitting and whirring, his mouth was dry and bitter and he could feel the fever in his blood resolving itself into innumerable regular counts like a slow dripping from a roof.

Dean tied his tie precisely, brushed his eyebrows, and removed a piece of tobacco from his teeth with solemnity. Next he filled his cigarette case, tossed the empty box thoughtfully into the waste basket, and settled the case in his vest pocket.

"Had breakfast?" he demanded.

"No; I don't eat it any more."

"Well, we'll go out and have some. We'll decide about that money later. I'm sick of the subject. I came East to have a good time.

"Let's go over to the Yale Club," he continued moodily, and then added with an implied reproof: "You've given up your job. You've got nothing else to do."

"I'd have a lot to do if I had a little money," said Gordon pointedly.

"Oh, for Heaven's sake drop the subject for a while! No point in glooming on my whole trip. Here, here's some money."

He took a five-dollar bill from his wallet and tossed it over to Gordon, who folded it carefully and put it in his pocket. There was an added spot of color in his cheeks, an added glow that was not fever. For an instant before they turned to go out their eyes met and in that instant each found something that made him lower his own glance quickly. For in that instant they quite suddenly and definitely hated each other.

II

Fifth Avenue and Forty-fourth Street swarmed with the noon crowd. The wealthy, happy sun glittered in transient gold through the thick windows of the smart shops, lighting upon mesh bags and purses and strings of pearls in gray velvet cases; upon gaudy feather fans of many colors; upon the laces and silks of expensive dresses; upon the bad paintings and the fine period furniture in the elaborate show rooms of interior decorators.

Working-girls, in pairs and groups and swarms, loitered by these windows, choosing their future boudoirs from some resplendent display which included even a man's silk pajamas laid domestically across the bed. They stood in front of the jewelry stores and picked out their engagement rings, and their wedding rings and their platinum wrist watches, and then drifted on to inspect the feather fans and opera cloaks; meanwhile digesting the sandwiches and sundaes they had eaten for lunch.

All through the crowd were men in uniform, sailors from the great fleet anchored in the Hudson, soldiers with divisional insignia from Massachusetts to California, wanting fearfully to be noticed, and finding the great city thoroughly fed up with soldiers unless they were nicely massed into pretty formations and uncomfortable under the weight of a pack and rifle.

Through this medley Dean and Gordon wandered; the former interested, made alert by the display of humanity at its frothiest and gaudiest; the latter reminded of how often he had been one of the crowd, tired, casually fed, overworked, and dissipated. To Dean the struggle was significant, young, cheerful; to Gordon it was dismal, meaningless, endless.

In the Yale Club they met a group of their former classmates who greeted the visiting Dean vociferously. Sitting in a semicircle of lounges and great chairs, they had a highball all around.

Gordon found the conversation tiresome and interminable. They lunched together *en masse*, warmed with liquor as the afternoon began. They were all going to the Gamma Psi dance that night—it promised to be the best party since the war.

"Edith Bradin's coming," said some one to Gordon. "Didn't she used to be an old flame of yours? Aren't you both from Harrisburg?"

"Yes." He tried to change the subject. "I see her brother occasionally. He's sort of a socialistic nut. Runs a paper or something here in New York."

"Not like his gay sister, eh?" continued his eager informant. "Well, she's coming tonight with a junior named Peter Himmel."

Gordon was to meet Jewel Hudson at eight o'clock—he had promised to have some money for her. Several times he glanced nervously at his wrist watch. At four, to his relief, Dean rose and announced that he was going over to Rivers Brothers to buy some collars and ties. But as they left the Club another of the party joined them, to Gordon's great dismay. Dean was in a jovial mood now, happy, expectant of the evening's party, faintly hilarious. Over in Rivers' he chose a dozen neckties, selecting each one after long consultations with the other man. Did he think narrow ties were coming back? And wasn't it a shame that Rivers' couldn't get any more Welsh Margotson collars? There never was a collar like the "Covington."

Gordon was in something of a panic. He wanted the money immediately. And he was now inspired also with a vague idea of attending the Gamma Psi dance. He wanted to see Edith—Edith whom he hadn't met since one romantic night at the Harrisburg Country Club just before he went to France. The affair had died, drowned in the turmoil of the war and quite forgotten in the arabesque of these three months, but a picture of her, poignant, debonnaire, immersed in her own inconsequential chatter, recurred to him unexpectedly and brought a hundred memories with it. It was Edith's face that he had cherished through college with a sort of detached yet affectionate admiration. He had loved to draw her—around his room had been a dozen sketches of her— playing golf, swimming—he could draw her pert, arresting profile with his eyes shut.

They left Rivers' at five-thirty and paused for a moment on the sidewalk.

"Well," said Dean genially, "I'm all set now. Think I'll go back to the hotel and get a shave, haircut, and massage."

"Good enough," said the other man; "I think I'll join you."

Gordon wondered if he was to be beaten after all. With difficulty he restrained himself from turning to the man and snarling out, "Go on away, damn you!" In despair he suspected that perhaps Dean had spoken to him, was keeping him along in order to avoid a dispute about the money.

They went into the Biltmore—a Biltmore alive with girls—mostly from the West and South, the stellar débutantes of many cities gathered for the dance of a famous fraternity of a famous university. But to Gordon they were faces in a dream. He gathered together his forces for a last appeal, was about to come out with he knew not what, when Dean suddenly excused himself to the other man and taking Gordon's arm led him aside.

"Gordy," he said quickly, "I've thought the whole thing over carefully and I've decided that I can't lend you that money. I'd like to oblige you, but I don't feel I ought to—it'd put a crimp in me for a month."

Gordon, watching him dully, wondered why he had never before noticed how much those upper teeth projected.

"—I'm mighty sorry, Gordon," continued Dean, "but that's the way it is."

He took out his wallet and deliberately counted out seventy-five dollars in bills.

"Here," he said, holding them out, "here's seventy-five; that makes eighty all together. That's all the actual cash I have with me, besides what I'll actually spend on the trip."

Gordon raised his clenched hand automatically, opened it as though it were a tongs he was holding, and clenched it again on the money.

"I'll see you at the dance," continued Dean. "I've got to get along to the barber shop."

"So-long," said Gordon in a strained and husky voice.

"So-long."

Dean began to smile, but seemed to change his mind. He nodded briskly and disappeared.

But Gordon stood there, his handsome face awry with distress, the roll of bills clenched tightly in his hand. Then, blinded by sudden tears, he stumbled clumsily down the Biltmore steps.

III

About nine o'clock of the same night two human beings came out of a cheap restaurant in Sixth Avenue. They were ugly, ill-nourished, devoid of all except the very lowest form of intelligence, and without even that animal exuberance that in itself brings color into life; they were lately vermin-ridden, cold, and hungry in a dirty town of a strange land; they were poor, friendless, tossed as driftwood from their births, they would be tossed as driftwood to their deaths. They were dressed in the uniform of the United States Army, and on the shoulder of each was the insignia of a drafted division from New Jersey, landed three days before.

The taller of the two was named Carrol Key, a name hinting that in his veins, however thinly diluted by generations of degeneration, ran blood of some potentiality. But one could stare endlessly at the long, chinless face, the dull, watery eyes, and high cheek-bones, without finding a suggestion of either ancestral worth or native resourcefulness.

His companion was swart and bandy-legged, with rat-eyes and a much-broken nose. His defiant air was obviously a pretense, a weapon of protection borrowed from that world of snarl and snap, of physical bluff and physical menace, in which he had always lived. His name was Gus Rose.

Leaving the café they sauntered down Sixth Avenue, wielding toothpicks with great gusto and complete detachment.

"Where to?" asked Rose, in a tone which implied that he would not be surprised if Key suggested the South Sea Islands.

"What you say if we can getta holda some liquor?" Prohibition was not yet. The ginger in the suggestion was caused by the law forbidding the selling of liquor to soldiers.

Rose agreed enthusiastically.

"I got an idea," continued Key, after a moment's thought, "I got a brother somewhere."

"In New York?"

"Yeah. He's an old fella." He meant that he was an elder brother. "He's a waiter in a hash joint."

"Maybe he can get us some."

"I'll say he can!"

"B'lieve me, I'm goin' to get this darn uniform off me to-morra. Never get me in it again, neither. I'm goin' to get some regular clothes."

"Say, maybe I'm not."

10 As their combined finances were something less than five dollars, this intention can be taken largely as a pleasant game of words, harmless and consoling. It seemed to please both of them, however, for they reinforced it with chuckling and mention of personages high in biblical circles, adding such further emphasis as "Oh, boy!" "You know!" and "I'll say so!" repeated many times over.

The entire mental pabulum of these two men 20 consisted of an offended nasal comment extended through the years upon the institution —army, business, or poorhouse—which kept them alive, and toward their immediate superior in that institution. Until that very morning the institution had been the "government" and the immediate superior had been the "Cap'n" —from these two they had glided out and were now in the vaguely uncomfortable state before they should adopt their next bondage. They 30 were uncertain, resentful, and somewhat ill at ease. This they hid by pretending an elaborate relief at being out of the army, and by assuring each other that military discipline should never again rule their stubborn, liberty-loving wills. Yet, as a matter of fact, they would have felt more at home in a prison than in this newfound and unquestionable freedom.

Suddenly Key increased his gait. Rose, looking up and following his glance, discovered a 40 crowd that was collecting fifty yards down the street. Key chuckled and began to run in the direction of the crowd; Rose thereupon also chuckled and his short bandy legs twinkled beside the long, awkward strides of his companion.

Reaching the outskirts of the crowd they immediately became an indistinguishable part of it. It was composed of ragged civilians somewhat the worse for liquor, and of soldiers representing many divisions and many stages of 50 sobriety, all clustered around a gesticulating little Jew with long black whiskers, who was waving his arms and delivering an excited but succinct harangue. Key and Rose, having wedged themselves into the approximate parquet, scrutinized him with acute suspicion, as his words penetrated their common consciousness.

"—What have you got outa the war?" he was crying fiercely. "Look arounja, look arounja! 60 Are you rich? Have you got a lot of money offered you?—no; you're lucky if you're alive and got both your legs; you're lucky if you came back an' find your wife ain't gone off with some other fella that had the money to buy himself out of the war! That's when you're lucky! Who got anything out of it except J. P. Morgan an' John D. Rockerfeller?"

At this point the little Jew's oration was interrupted by the hostile impact of a fist upon 70 the point of his bearded chin and he toppled backward to a sprawl on the pavement.

"God damn Bolsheviki!" cried the big soldier-blacksmith who had delivered the blow. There was a rumble of approval, the crowd closed in nearer.

The Jew staggered to his feet, and immediately went down again before a half-dozen reaching-in fists. This time he stayed down, breathing heavily, blood oozing from his lip 80 where it was cut within and without.

There was a riot of voices, and in a minute Rose and Key found themselves flowing with the jumbled crowd down Sixth Avenue under the leadership of a thin civilian in a slouch hat and the brawny soldier who had summarily ended the oration. The crowd had marvellously swollen to formidable proportions and a stream of more non-committal citizens followed it along the sidewalks lending their moral sup- 90 port by intermittent huzzas.

"Where we goin'?" yelled Key to the man nearest him.

His neighbor pointed up to the leader in the slouch hat.

"That guy knows where there's a lot of 'em! We're goin' to show 'em!"

"We're goin' to show 'em!" whispered Key delightedly to Rose, who repeated the phrase rapturously to a man on the other side. 100

Down Sixth Avenue swept the procession, joined here and there by soldiers and marines, and now and then by civilians, who came up with the inevitable cry that they were just out of the army themselves, as if presenting it as a card of admission to a newly formed Sporting and Amusement Club.

Then the procession swerved down a cross street and headed for Fifth Avenue and the word filtered here and there that they were bound for a Red meeting at Tolliver Hall.

"Where is it?"

The question went up the line and a moment later the answer floated back. Tolliver Hall was down on Tenth Street. There was a bunch of other sojers who was goin' to break it up and was down there now!

But Tenth Street had a faraway sound and at the word a general groan went up and a score of the procession dropped out. Among these were Rose and Key, who slowed down to a saunter and let the more enthusiastic sweep on by.

"I'd rather get some liquor," said Key as they halted and made their way to the sidewalk amid cries of "Shell hole!" and "Quitters!"

"Does your brother work around here?" asked Rose, assuming the air of one passing from the superficial to the eternal.

"He oughta," replied Key. "I ain't seen him for a coupla years. I been out to Pennsylvania since. Maybe he don't work at night anyhow. It's right along here. He can get us some o'right if he ain't gone."

They found the place after a few minutes' patrol of the street—a shoddy tablecloth restaurant between Fifth Avenue and Broadway. Here Key went inside to inquire for his brother George, while Rose waited on the sidewalk.

"He ain't here no more," said Key emerging. "He's a waiter up to Delmonico's."

Rose nodded wisely, as if he'd expected as much. One should not be surprised at a capable man changing jobs occasionally. He knew a waiter once—there ensued a long conversation as they walked as to whether waiters made more in actual wages than in tips—it was decided that it depended upon the social tone of the joint wherein the waiter labored. After having given each other vivid pictures of millionaires dining at Delmonico's and throwing away fifty-dollar bills after their first quart of champagne, both men thought privately of becoming waiters. In fact, Key's narrow brow was secreting a resolution to ask his brother to get him a job.

"A waiter can drink up all the champagne those fellas leave in bottles," suggested Rose with some relish, and then added as an afterthought, "Oh, boy!"

By the time they reached Delmonico's it was half past ten, and they were surprised to see a stream of taxis driving up to the door one after the other and emitting marvelous, hatless young ladies, each one attended by a stiff young gentleman in evening clothes.

"It's a party," said Rose with some awe. "Maybe we better not go in. He'll be busy."

"No, he won't. He'll be o'right."

After some hesitation they entered what appeared to them to be the least elaborate door and, indecision falling upon them immediately, stationed themselves nervously in an inconspicuous corner of the small dining-room in which they found themselves. They took off their caps and held them in their hands. A cloud of gloom fell upon them and both started when a door at one end of the room crashed open, emitting a comet-like waiter who streaked across the floor and vanished through another door on the other side.

There had been three of these lightning passages before the seekers mustered the acumen to hail a waiter. He turned, looked at them suspiciously, and then approached with soft catlike steps, as if prepared at any moment to turn and flee.

"Say," began Key, "say, do you know my brother? He's a waiter here."

"His name is Key," annotated Rose.

Yes, the waiter knew Key. He was upstairs, he thought. There was a big dance going on in the main ballroom. He'd tell him.

Ten minutes later George Key appeared and greeted his brother with the utmost suspicion; his first and most natural thought being that he was going to be asked for money.

George was tall and weak chinned, but there his resemblance to his brother ceased. The waiter's eyes were not dull, they were alert and twinkling, and his manner was suave, indoor, and faintly superior. They exchanged formalities. George was married and had three

353

children. He seemed fairly interested, but not impressed by the news that Carrol had been abroad in the army. This disappointed Carrol.

"George," said the younger brother, these amenities having been disposed of, "we want to get some booze, and they won't sell us none. Can you get us some?"

George considered.

"Sure. Maybe I can. It may be half an hour, though."

"All right," agreed Carrol, "we'll wait."

At this Rose started to sit down in a convenient chair, but was hailed to his feet by the indignant George.

"Hey! Watch out, you! Can't sit down here! This room's all set for a twelve o'clock banquet."

"I ain't goin' to hurt it," said Rose resentfully. "I been through the delouser."

"Never mind," said George sternly, "if the head waiter seen me here talkin' he'd romp all over me."

"Oh."

The mention of the head waiter was full explanation to the other two; they fingered their overseas caps nervously and waited for a suggestion.

"I tell you," said George, after a pause, "I got a place you can wait; you just come here with me."

They followed him out of the far door, through a deserted pantry and up a pair of dark winding stairs, emerging finally into a small room chiefly furnished by piles of pails and stacks of scrubbing brushes, and illuminated by a single dim electric light. There he left them, after soliciting two dollars and agreeing to return in half an hour with a quart of whiskey.

"George is makin' money, I bet," said Key gloomily as he seated himself on an inverted pail. "I bet he's making fifty dollars a week."

Rose nodded his head and spat.

"I bet he is, too."

"What'd he say the dance was of?"

"A lot of college fellas. Yale College."

They both nodded solemnly at each other.

"Wonder where that crowda sojers is now?"

"I don't know. I know that's too damn long to walk for me."

"Me too. You don't catch me walkin' that far."

Ten minutes later restlessness seized them.

"I'm goin' to see what's out here," said Rose, stepping cautiously toward the other door.

It was a swinging door of green baize and he pushed it open a cautious inch.

"See anything?"

For answer Rose drew in his breath sharply.

"Doggone! Here's some liquor I'll say!"

"Liquor?"

Key joined Rose at the door, and looked eagerly.

"I'll tell the world that's liquor," he said, after a moment of concentrated gazing.

It was a room about twice as large as the one they were in—and in it was prepared a radiant feast of spirits. There were long walls of alternating bottles set along two white covered tables; whiskey, gin, brandy, French and Italian vermouths, and orange juice, not to mention an array of syphons and two great empty punch bowls. The room was as yet uninhabited.

"It's for this dance they're just starting," whispered Key; "hear the violins playin'? Say, boy, I wouldn't mind havin' a dance."

They closed the door softly and exchanged a glance of mutual comprehension. There was no need of feeling each other out.

"I'd like to get my hands on a coupla those bottles," said Rose emphatically.

"Me too."

"Do you suppose we'd get seen?"

Key considered.

"Maybe we better wait till they start drinkin' 'em. They got 'em all laid out now, and they know how many of them there are."

They debated this point for several minutes. Rose was all for getting his hands on a bottle now and tucking it under his coat before any one came into the room. Key, however, advocated caution. He was afraid he might get his brother in trouble. If they waited till some of the bottles were opened it'd be all right to take one, and everybody'd think it was one of the college fellas.

While they were still engaged in argument George Key hurried through the room and, barely grunting at them, disappeared by way of the green baize door. A minute later they heard several corks pop, and then the sound of cracking ice and splashing liquid. George was mixing the punch.

The soldiers exchanged delighted grins.

"Oh, boy!" whispered Rose.

George reappeared.

"Just keep low, boys," he said quickly. "I'll have your stuff for you in five minutes."

He disappeared through the door by which he had come.

As soon as his footsteps receded down the stairs, Key, after a cautious look, darted into the room of delights and reappeared with a bottle in his hand.

"Here's what I say," he said, as they sat radiantly digesting their first drink. "We'll wait till he comes up, and we'll ask him if we can't just stay here and drink what he brings us—see. We'll tell him we haven't got any place to drink it—see. Then we can sneak in there whenever there ain't nobody in that there room and tuck a bottle under our coats. We'll have enough to last us a coupla days—see?"

"Sure," agreed Rose enthusiastically. "Oh, boy! And if we want to we can sell it to sojers any time we want to."

They were silent for a moment thinking rosily of this idea. Then Key reached up and unhooked the collar of his O.D. coat.

"It's hot in here, ain't it?"

Rose agreed earnestly.

"Hot as hell."

IV

She was still quite angry when she came out of the dressing-room and crossed the intervening parlor of politeness that opened onto the hall—angry not so much at the actual happening which was, after all, the merest commonplace of her social existence, but because it had occurred on this particular night. She had no quarrel with herself. She had acted with that correct mixture of dignity and reticent pity which she always employed. She had succinctly and deftly snubbed him.

It had happened when their taxi was leaving the Biltmore—hadn't gone half a block. He had lifted his right arm awkwardly—she was on his right side—and attempted to settle it snugly around the crimson fur-trimmed opera cloak she wore. This in itself had been a mistake. It was inevitably more graceful for a young man attempting to embrace a young lady of whose acquiescence he was not certain, to first put his far arm around her. It avoided that awkward movement of raising the near arm.

His second *faux pas* was unconscious. She had spent the afternoon at the hairdresser's; the idea of any calamity overtaking her hair was extremely repugnant—yet as Peter made his unfortunate attempt the point of his elbow had just faintly brushed it. That was his second *faux pas*. Two were quite enough.

He had begun to murmur. At the first murmur she had decided that he was nothing but a college boy—Edith was twenty-two, and anyhow, this dance, first of its kind since the war, was reminding her, with the accelerating rhythm of its associations, of something else—of another dance and another man, a man for whom her feelings had been little more than a sad-eyed, adolescent mooniness. Edith Bradin was falling in love with her recollection of Gordon Sterrett.

So she came out of the dressing-room at Delmonico's and stood for a second in the doorway looking over the shoulders of a black dress in front of her at the groups of Yale men who flitted like dignified black moths around the head of the stairs. From the room she had left drifted out the heavy fragrance left by the passage to and fro of many scented young beauties—rich perfumes and the fragile memory-laden dust of fragrant powders. This odor drifting out acquired the tang of cigarette smoke in the hall, and then settled sensuously down the stairs and permeated the ballroom where the Gamma Psi dance was to be held. It was an odor she knew well, exciting, stimulating, restlessly sweet—the odor of a fashionable dance.

She thought of her own appearance. Her bare arms and shoulders were powdered to a creamy white. She knew they looked very soft and would gleam like milk against the black backs that were to silhouette them to-night. The hairdressing had been a success; her reddish mass of hair was piled and crushed and creased to an arrogant marvel of mobile curves. Her lips were finely made of deep carmine; the irises of her eyes were delicate, breakable blue, like china eyes. She was a complete, infinitely delicate, quite perfect thing of beauty, flowing in an even line from a complex coiffure to two small slim feet.

She thought of what she would say tonight at this revel, faintly presaged already by the sound of high and low laughter and slippered footsteps, and movements of couples up and down the stairs. She would talk the language she had talked for many years—her line—made up of the current expressions, bits of journalese and college slang strung together into an intrinsic whole, careless, faintly provocative, delicately sentimental. She smiled faintly as she heard a girl sitting on the stairs near her say: "You don't know the half of it, dearie!"

And as she smiled her anger melted for a moment, and closing her eyes she drew in a deep breath of pleasure. She dropped her arms to her side until they were faintly touching the sleek sheath that covered and suggested her figure. She had never felt her own softness so much nor so enjoyed the whiteness of her own arms.

"I smell sweet," she said to herself simply, and then came another thought—"I'm made for love."

She liked the sound of this and thought it again; then in inevitable succession came her new-born riot of dreams about Gordon. The twist of her imagination which, two months before, had disclosed to her her unguessed desire to see him again, seemed now to have been leading up to this dance, this hour.

For all her sleek beauty, Edith was a grave, slow-thinking girl. There was a streak in her of that same desire to ponder, of that adolescent idealism that had turned her brother socialist and pacifist. Henry Bradin had left Cornell, where he had been an instructor in economics, and had come to New York to pour the latest cures for incurable evils into the columns of a radical weekly newspaper.

Edith, less fatuously, would have been content to cure Gordon Sterrett. There was a quality of weakness in Gordon that she wanted to take care of; there was a helplessness in him that she wanted to protect. And she wanted someone she had known a long while, someone who had loved her a long while. She was a little tired; she wanted to get married. Out of a pile of letters, half a dozen pictures and as many memories, and this weariness, she had decided that next time she saw Gordon their relations were going to be changed. She would say something that would change them. There

was this evening. This was her evening. All evenings were her evenings.

Then her thoughts were interrupted by a solemn undergraduate with a hurt look and an air of strained formality who presented himself before her and bowed unusually low. It was the man she had come with, Peter Himmel. He was tall and humorous, with horned-rimmed glasses and an air of attractive whimsicality. She suddenly rather disliked him—probably because he had not succeeded in kissing her.

"Well," she began, "are you still furious at me?"

"Not at all."

She stepped forward and took his arm.

"I'm sorry," she said softly. "I don't know why I snapped out that way. I'm in a bum humor to-night for some strange reason. I'm sorry."

"S'all right," he mumbled. "Don't mention it."

He felt disagreeably embarrassed. Was she rubbing in the fact of his late failure?

"It was a mistake," she continued, on the same consciously gentle key. "We'll both forget it." For this he hated her.

A few minutes later they drifted out on the floor while the dozen swaying, sighing members of the specially hired jazz orchestra informed the crowded ballroom that "if a saxophone and me are left alone why then two is com-pan-ee!"

A man with a mustache cut in.

"Hello," he began reprovingly. "You don't remember me."

"I can't just think of your name," she said lightly—"and I know you so well."

"I met you up at—" His voice trailed disconsolately off as a man with very fair hair cut in. Edith murmured a conventional "Thanks, loads —cut in later," to the inconnu.

The very fair man insisted on shaking hands enthusiastically. She placed him as one of the numerous Jims of her acquaintance—last name a mystery. She remembered even that he had a peculiar rhythm in dancing and found as they started that she was right.

"Going to be here long?" he had breathed confidentially.

She leaned back and looked up at him.

"Couple of weeks."

"Where are you?"

"Biltmore. Call me up some day."

"I mean it," he assured her. "I will. We'll go to tea."

"So do I—Do."

A dark man cut in with intense formality.

"You don't remember me, do you?" he said gravely.

"I should say I do. Your name's Harlan."

"No-ope. Barlow."

"Well, I knew there were two syllables anyway. You're the boy that played the ukulele so well up at Howard Marshall's house party."

"I played—but not—"

A man with prominent teeth cut in. Edith inhaled a slight cloud of whiskey. She liked men to have had something to drink; they were so much more cheerful, and appreciative and complimentary—much easier to talk to.

"My name's Dean, Philip Dean," he said cheerfully. "You don't remember me, I know, but you used to come up to New Haven with a fellow I roomed with senior year, Gordon Sterrett."

Edith looked up quickly.

"Yes, I went up with him twice—to the Pump and Slipper and the Junior prom."

"You've seen him, of course," said Dean carelessly. "He's here to-night. I saw him just a minute ago."

Edith started. Yet she had felt sure he would be here.

"Why, no, I haven't—"

A fat man with red hair cut in.

"Hello, Edith," he began.

"Why—hello there—"

She slipped, stumbled lightly.

"I'm sorry, dear," she murmured mechanically.

She had seen Gordon—Gordon very white and listless, leaning against the side of a doorway, smoking and looking into the ballroom. Edith could see that his face was thin and wan —that the hand he raised to his lips with a cigarette was trembling. They were dancing quite close to him now.

"—They invite so darn many extra fellas that you—" the short man was saying.

"Hello, Gordon," called Edith over her partner's shoulder. Her heart was pounding wildly.

His large dark eyes were fixed on her. He took a step in her direction. Her partner turned her away—she heard his voice bleating—

"—but half the stags get lit and leave before long, so—"

Then a low tone at her side.

"May I, please?"

She was dancing suddenly with Gordon, one of his arms around her; she felt it tighten spasmodically; felt his hand on her back with the fingers spread. Her hand holding the little lace handkerchief was crushed in his.

"Why, Gordon," she began breathlessly.

"Hello, Edith."

She slipped again—was tossed forward by her recovery until her face touched the black cloth of his dinner coat. She loved him—she knew she loved him—then for a minute there was silence while a strange feeling of uneasiness crept over her. Something was wrong.

Of a sudden her heart wrenched, and turned over as she realized what it was. He was pitiful and wretched, a little drunk, and miserably tired.

"Oh—" she cried involuntarily.

His eyes looked down at her. She saw suddenly that they were blood-streaked and rolling uncontrollably.

"Gordon," she murmured, "we'll sit down; I want to sit down."

They were nearly in mid-floor, but she had seen two men start toward her from opposite sides of the room, so she halted, seized Gordon's limp hand and led him bumping through the crowd, her mouth tight shut, her face a little pale under her rouge, her eyes trembling with tears.

She found a place high up on the soft-carpeted stairs, and he sat down heavily beside her.

"Well," he began, staring at her unsteadily, "I certainly am glad to see you, Edith."

She looked at him without answering. The effect of this on her was immeasurable. For years she had seen men in various stages of intoxication, from uncles all the way down to chauffeurs, and her feelings had varied from amusement to disgust, but here for the first time she was seized with a new feeling—an unutterable horror.

"Gordon," she said accusingly and almost crying, "you look like the devil."

He nodded. "I've had trouble, Edith."

"Trouble?"

"All sorts of trouble. Don't you say anything

to the family, but I'm all gone to pieces. I'm a mess, Edith."

His lower lip was sagging. He seemed scarcely to see her.

"Can't you—can't you," she hesitated, "can't you tell me about it, Gordon? You know I'm always interested in you."

She bit her lip—she had intended to say something stronger, but found at the end that she couldn't bring it out.

Gordon shook his head dully. "I can't tell you. You're a good woman. I can't tell a good woman the story."

"Rot," she said, defiantly. "I think it's a perfect insult to call any one a good woman in that way. It's a slam. You've been drinking, Gordon."

"Thanks." He inclined his head gravely. "Thanks for the information."

"Why do you drink?"

"Because I'm so damned miserable."

"Do you think drinking's going to make it any better?"

"What you doing—trying to reform me?"

"No; I'm trying to help you, Gordon. Can't you tell me about it?"

"I'm in an awful mess. Best thing you can do is to pretend not to know me."

"Why, Gordon?"

"I'm sorry I cut in on you—it's unfair to you. You're a pure woman—and all that sort of thing. Here, I'll get someone else to dance with you."

He rose clumsily to his feet, but she reached up and pulled him down beside her on the stairs.

"Here, Gordon. You're ridiculous. You're hurting me. You're acting like a—like a crazy man—"

"I admit it. I'm a little crazy. Something's wrong with me, Edith. There's something left me. It doesn't matter."

"It does; tell me."

"Just that. I was always queer—little bit different from other boys. All right in college, but now it's all wrong. Things have been snapping inside me for four months like little hooks on a dress, and it's about to come off when a few more hooks go. I'm very gradually going loony."

He turned his eyes full on her and began to laugh, and she shrank away from him.

"What *is* the matter?"

"Just me," he repeated. "I'm going loony. This whole place is like a dream to me—this Delmonico's—"

As he talked she saw he had changed utterly. He wasn't at all light and gay and careless—a great lethargy and discouragement had come over him. Revulsion seized her, followed by a faint, surprising boredom. His voice seemed to come out of a great void.

"Edith," he said. "I used to think I was clever, talented, an artist. Now I know I'm nothing. Can't draw, Edith. Don't know why I'm telling you this."

She nodded absently.

"I can't draw, I can't do anything. I'm poor as a church mouse." He laughed, bitterly and rather too loud. "I've become a damn beggar, a leech on my friends. I'm a failure. I'm poor as hell."

Her distaste was growing. She barely nodded this time, waiting for her first possible cue to rise.

Suddenly Gordon's eyes filled with tears.

"Edith," he said, turning to her with what was evidently a strong effort at self-control, "I can't tell you what it means to me to know there's one person left who's interested in me."

He reached out and patted her hand, and involuntarily she drew it away.

"It's mighty fine of you," he repeated.

"Well," she said slowly, looking him in the eye, "any one's always glad to see an old friend—but I'm sorry to see you like this, Gordon."

There was a pause while they looked at each other, and the momentary eagerness in his eyes wavered. She rose and stood looking at him, her face quite expressionless.

"Shall we dance?" she suggested, coolly.

—Love is fragile—she was thinking—but perhaps the pieces are saved, the things that hovered on lips, that might have been said. The new love words, the tendernesses learned, are treasured up for the next lover.

V

Peter Himmel, escort to the lovely Edith, was unaccustomed to being snubbed; having been snubbed, he was hurt and embarrassed, and ashamed of himself. For a matter of two months he had been on special delivery terms with Edith Bradin, and knowing that the one excuse and explanation of the special delivery letter is its value in sentimental correspondence, he had believed himself quite sure of his ground. He searched in vain for any reason why she should have taken this attitude in the matter of a simple kiss.

Therefore when he was cut in on by the man with the mustache he went out into the hall and, making up a sentence, said it over to himself several times. Considerably deleted, this was it:

"Well, if any girl ever led a man on and then jolted him, she did—and she has no kick coming if I go out and get beautifully boiled."

So he walked through the supper room into a small room adjoining it, which he had located earlier in the evening. It was a room in which there were several large bowls of punch flanked by many bottles. He took a seat beside the table which held the bottles.

At the second highball, boredom, disgust, the monotony of time, the turbidity of events, sank into a vague background before which glittering cobwebs formed. Things became reconciled to themselves, things lay quietly on their shelves; the troubles of the day arranged themselves in trim formation and at his curt wish of dismissal, marched off and disappeared. And with the departure of worry came brilliant, permeating symbolism. Edith became a flighty, negligible girl, not to be worried over; rather to be laughed at. She fitted like a figure of his own dream into the surface world forming about him. He himself became in a measure symbolic, a type of the continent bacchanal, the brilliant dreamer at play.

Then the symbolic mood faded and as he sipped his third highball his imagination yielded to the warm glow and he lapsed into a state similar to floating on his back in pleasant water. It was at this point that he noticed that a green baize door near him was open about two inches, and that through the aperture a pair of eyes were watching him intently.

"Hm," murmured Peter calmly.

The green door closed—and then opened again—a bare half inch this time.

"Peek-a-boo," murmured Peter.

The door remained stationary and then he became aware of a series of tense intermittent whispers.

"One guy."

"What's he doin'?"

"He's sittin' lookin'."

"He better beat it off. We gotta get another li'l' bottle."

Peter listened while the words filtered into his consciousness.

"Now this," he thought, "is most remarkable."

He was excited. He was jubilant. He felt that he had stumbled upon a mystery. Affecting an elaborate carelessness he arose and walked around the table—then, turning quickly, pulled open the green door, precipitating Private Rose into the room.

Peter bowed.

"How do you do?" he said.

Private Rose set one foot slightly in front of the other, poised for fight, flight, or compromise.

"How do you do?" repeated Peter politely.

"I'm o'right."

"Can I offer you a drink?"

Private Rose looked at him searchingly, suspecting possible sarcasm.

"O'right," he said finally.

Peter indicated a chair.

"Sit down."

"I got a friend," said Rose, "I got a friend in there." He pointed to the green door.

"By all means let's have him in."

Peter crossed over, opened the door and welcomed in Private Key, very suspicious and uncertain and guilty. Chairs were found and the three took their seats around the punch bowl. Peter gave them each a highball and offered them a cigarette from his case. They accepted both with some diffidence.

"Now," continued Peter easily, "may I ask why you gentlemen prefer to lounge away your leisure hours in a room which is chiefly furnished, as far as I can see, with scrubbing brushes. And when the human race has progressed to the stage where seventeen thousand chairs are manufactured on every day except Sunday—" he paused. Rose and Key regarded him vacantly. "Will you tell me," went on Peter, "why you choose to rest yourselves on articles intended for the transportation of water from one place to another?"

At this point Rose contributed a grunt to the conversation.

"And lastly," finished Peter, "will you tell me why, when you are in a building beautifully hung with enormous candelabra, you prefer to spend these evening hours under one anemic electric light?"

Rose looked at Key; Key looked at Rose. They laughed; they laughed uproariously; they found it was impossible to look at each other without laughing. But they were not laughing with this man—they were laughing at him. To them a man who talked after this fashion was either raving drunk or raving crazy.

"You are Yale men, I presume," said Peter, finishing his highball and preparing another.

They laughed again.

"Na-ah."

"So? I thought perhaps you might be members of that lowly section of the university known as the Sheffield Scientific School."

"Na-ah."

"Hm. Well, that's too bad. No doubt you are Harvard men, anxious to preserve your incognito in this—this paradise of violet blue, as the newspapers say."

"Na-ah," said Key scornfully, "we was just waitin' for somebody."

"Ah," exclaimed Peter, rising and filling their glasses, "very interestin'. Had a date with a scrublady, eh?"

They both denied this indignantly.

"It's all right," Peter reassured them, "don't apologize. A scrublady's as good as any lady in the world. Kipling says, 'Any lady and Judy O'Grady under the skin.'"

"Sure," said Key, winking broadly at Rose.

"My case, for instance," continued Peter, finishing his glass. "I got a girl up here that's spoiled. Spoildest darn girl I ever saw. Refused to kiss me; no reason whatsoever. Led me on deliberately to think sure I want to kiss you and then plunk! Threw me over! What's the younger generation comin' to?"

"Say tha's hard luck," said Key—"that's awful hard luck."

"Oh, boy!" said Rose.

"Have another?" said Peter.

"We got in a sort of a fight for a while," said Key after a pause, "but it was too far away."

"A fight?—tha's stuff!" said Peter, seating himself unsteadily. "Fight 'em all! I was in the army."

"This was with a Bolshevik fella."

"Tha's stuff!" exclaimed Peter, enthusiastic. "That's what I say! Kill the Bolshevik! Exterminate 'em!"

"We're Americuns," said Rose, implying a sturdy, defiant patriotism.

"Sure," said Peter. "Greatest race in the world! We're all Americuns! Have another."

They had another.

VI

At one o'clock a special orchestra, special even in a day of special orchestras, arrived at Delmonico's, and its members, seating themselves arrogantly around the piano, took up the burden of providing music for the Gamma Psi Fraternity. They were headed by a famous flute-player, distinguished throughout New York for his feat of standing on his head and shimmying with his shoulders while he played the latest jazz on his flute. During his performance the lights were extinguished except for the spotlight on the flute-player and another roving beam that threw flickering shadows and changing kaleidoscopic colors over the massed dancers.

Edith had danced herself into that tired, dreamy state habitual only with débutantes, a state equivalent to the glow of a noble soul after several long highballs. Her mind floated vaguely on the bosom of the music; her partners changed with the unreality of phantoms under the colorful shifting dusk, and to her present coma it seemed as if days had passed since the dance began. She had talked on many fragmentary subjects with many men. She had been kissed once and made love to six times. Earlier in the evening different undergraduates had danced with her, but now, like all the more popular girls there, she had her own entourage —that is, half a dozen gallants had singled her out or were alternating her charms with those of some other chosen beauty; they cut in on her in regular, inevitable succession.

Several times she had seen Gordon—he had been sitting a long time on the stairway with his palm to his head, his dull eyes fixed at an infinite speck on the floor before him, very depressed, he looked, and quite drunk—but Edith each time had averted her glance hurriedly. All that seemed long ago; her mind was passive now, her senses were lulled to trance-like sleep; only her feet danced and her voice talked on in hazy sentimental banter.

But Edith was not nearly so tired as to be incapable of moral indignation when Peter Himmel cut in on her, sublimely and happily drunk. She gasped and looked up at him.

"Why, *Peter!*"

"I'm a li'l stewed, Edith."

"Why, Peter, you're a *peach*, you are! Don't you think it's a bum way of doing—when you're with me?"

Then she smiled unwillingly, for he was looking at her with owlish sentimentality varied with a silly spasmodic smile.

"Darlin' Edith," he began earnestly, "you know I love you, don't you?"

"You tell it well."

"I love you—and I merely wanted you to kiss me," he added sadly.

His embarrassment, his shame, were both gone. She was a mos' beautiful girl in whole worl'. Mos' beautiful eyes, like stars above. He wanted to 'pologize—firs', for presuming try to kiss her; second, for drinking—but he'd been so discouraged 'cause he had thought she was mad at him—

The red-fat man cut in, and looking up at Edith smiled radiantly.

"Did you bring any one?" she asked.

No. The red-fat man was a stag.

"Well, would you mind—would it be an awful bother for you to—to take me home tonight?" (This extreme diffidence was a charming affectation on Edith's part—she knew that the red-fat man would immediately dissolve into a paroxysm of delight.)

"Bother? Why, good Lord, I'd be darn glad to! You know I'd be darn glad to."

"Thanks *loads*. You're awfully sweet."

She glanced at her wrist-watch. It was half-past one. And, as she said "half-past one" to herself, it floated vaguely into her mind that her brother had told her at luncheon that he worked in the office of his newspaper until after one-thirty every evening.

Edith turned suddenly to her current partner.

"What street is Delmonico's on, anyway?"

"Street? Oh, why Fifth Avenue, of course."

"I mean, what cross street?"

"Why—let's see—it's on Forty-fourth Street."

This verified what she had thought. Henry's office must be across the street and just around the corner, and it occurred to her immediately that she might slip over for a moment and surprise him, float in on him, a shimmering marvel in her new crimson opera cloak and "cheer him up." It was exactly the sort of thing Edith revelled in doing—an unconventional, jaunty thing. The idea reached out and gripped at her imagination—after an instant's hesitation she had decided.

"My hair is just about to tumble entirely down," she said pleasantly to her partner; "would you mind if I go and fix it?"

"Not at all."

"You're a peach."

A few minutes later, wrapped in her crimson opera cloak, she flitted down a side-stairs, her cheeks glowing with excitement at her little adventure. She ran by a couple who stood at the door—a weak-chinned waiter and an over-rouged young lady, in hot dispute—and opening the outer door stepped into the warm May night.

VII

The over-rouged young lady followed her with a brief, bitter glance—then turned again to the weak-chinned waiter and took up her argument.

"You better go up and tell him I'm here," she said defiantly, "or I'll go up myself."

"No, you don't!" said George sternly.

The girl smiled sardonically.

"Oh, I don't, don't I? Well, let me tell you I know more college fellas and more of 'em know me, and are glad to take me out on a party, than you ever saw in your whole life."

"Maybe so—"

"Maybe so," she interrupted. "Oh, it's all right for any of 'em like that one that just ran out—God knows where *she* went—it's all right for them that are asked here to come or go as they like—but when I want to see a friend they have some cheap, ham-slinging, bring-me-a-doughnut waiter to stand here and keep me out."

"See here," said the elder Key indignantly, "I can't lose my job. Maybe this fella you're talkin' about doesn't want to see you."

361

"Oh, he wants to see me all right."

"Anyways, how could I find him in all that crowd?"

"Oh, he'll be there," she asserted confidently. "You just ask anybody for Gordon Sterrett and they'll point him out to you. They all know each other, these fellas."

She produced a mesh bag, and taking out a dollar bill handed it to George.

"Here," she said, "here's a bribe. You find him and give him my message. You tell him if he isn't here in five minutes I'm coming up."

George shook his head pessimistically, considered the question for a moment, wavered violently, and then withdrew.

In less than the allotted time Gordon came down-stairs. He was drunker than he had been earlier in the evening and in a different way. The liquor seemed to have hardened on him like a crust. He was heavy and lurching—almost incoherent when he talked.

"'Lo, Jewel," he said thickly. "Came right away. Jewel, I couldn't get that money. Tried my best."

"Money nothing!" she snapped. "You haven't been near me for ten days. What's the matter?"

He shook his head slowly.

"Been very low, Jewel. Been sick."

"Why didn't you tell me if you were sick? I don't care about the money that bad. I didn't start bothering you about it at all until you began neglecting me."

Again he shook his head.

"Haven't been neglecting you. Not at all."

"Haven't! You haven't been near me for three weeks, unless you been so drunk you didn't know what you were doing."

"Been sick, Jewel," he repeated, turning his eyes upon her wearily.

"You're well enough to come and play with your society friends here all right. You told me you'd meet me for dinner, and you said you'd have some money for me. You didn't even bother to ring me up."

"I couldn't get any money."

"Haven't I just been saying that doesn't matter? I wanted to see *you*, Gordon, but you seem to prefer your somebody else."

He denied this bitterly.

"Then get your hat and come along," she suggested.

Gordon hesitated—and she came suddenly close to him and slipped her arms around his neck.

"Come on with me, Gordon," she said in a half whisper. "We'll go over to Devineries' and have a drink, and then we can go up to my apartment."

"I can't, Jewel—"

"You can," she said intensely.

"I'm sick as a dog!"

"Well, then, you oughtn't to stay here and dance."

With a glance around him in which relief and despair were mingled, Gordon hesitated; then she suddenly pulled him to her and kissed him with soft, pulpy lips.

"All right," he said heavily. "I'll get my hat."

VIII

When Edith came out into the clear blue of the May night she found the Avenue deserted. The windows of the big shops were dark; over their doors were drawn great iron masks until they were only shadowy tombs of the late day's splendor. Glancing down toward Forty-second Street she saw a commingled blur of lights from the all-night restaurants. Over on Sixth Avenue the elevated, a flare of fire, roared across the street between the glimmering parallels of light at the station and streaked along into the crisp dark. But at Forty-fourth Street it was very quiet.

Pulling her cloak close about her Edith darted across the Avenue. She started nervously as a solitary man passed her and said in a hoarse whisper—"Where bound, kiddo?" She was reminded of a night in her childhood when she had walked around the block in her pajamas and a dog had howled at her from a mystery-big back yard.

In a minute she had reached her destination, a two-story, comparatively old building on Forty-fourth, in the upper window of which she thankfully detected a wisp of light. It was bright enough outside for her to make out the sign beside the window—the *New York Trumpet*. She stepped inside a dark hall and after a second saw the stairs in the corner.

Then she was in a long, low room furnished with many desks and hung on all sides with file copies of newspapers. There were only two occupants. They were sitting at different ends of the room, each wearing a green eye-shade and writing by a solitary desk light.

For a moment she stood uncertainly in the doorway, and then both men turned around simultaneously and she recognized her brother.

"Why, Edith!" He rose quickly and approached her in surprise, removing his eye-shade. He was tall, lean, and dark, with black, piercing eyes under very thick glasses. They were far-away eyes that seemed always fixed just over the head of the person to whom he was talking.

He put his hands on her arms and kissed her cheek.

"What is it?" he repeated in some alarm.

"I was at a dance across at Delmonico's, Henry," she said excitedly, "and I couldn't resist tearing over to see you."

"I'm glad you did." His alertness gave way quickly to a habitual vagueness. "You oughtn't to be out alone at night though, ought you?"

The man at the other end of the room had been looking at them curiously, but at Henry's beckoning gesture he approached. He was loosely fat with little twinkling eyes, and, having removed his collar and tie, he gave the impression of a Middle-Western farmer on a Sunday afternoon.

"This is my sister," said Henry. "She dropped in to see me."

"How do you do?" said the fat man, smiling.

"My name's Bartholomew, Miss Bradin. I know your brother has forgotten it long ago."

Edith laughed politely.

"Well," he continued, "not exactly gorgeous quarters we have here, are they?"

Edith looked around the room.

"They seem very nice," she replied. "Where do you keep the bombs?"

"The bombs?" repeated Bartholomew, laughing. "That's pretty good—the bombs. Did you hear her, Henry? She wants to know where we keep the bombs. Say, that's pretty good."

Edith swung herself onto a vacant desk and sat dangling her feet over the edge. Her brother took a seat beside her.

"Well," he asked, absent-mindedly, "how do you like New York this trip?"

"Not bad. I'll be over at the Biltmore with the Hoyts until Sunday. Can't you come to luncheon to-morrow?"

He thought a moment.

"I'm especially busy," he objected, "and I hate women in groups."

"All right," she agreed, unruffled. "Let's you and me have luncheon together."

"Very well."

"I'll call for you at twelve."

Bartholomew was obviously anxious to return to his desk, but apparently considered that it would be rude to leave without some parting pleasantry.

"Well"—he began awkwardly.

They both turned to him.

"Well, we—we had an exciting time earlier in the evening."

The two men exchanged glances.

"You should have come earlier," continued Bartholomew, somewhat encouraged. "We had a regular vaudeville."

"Did you really?"

"A serenade," said Henry. "A lot of soldiers gathered down there in the street and began to yell at the sign."

"Why?" she demanded.

"Just a crowd," said Henry, abstractedly. "All crowds have to howl. They didn't have anybody with much initiative in the lead, or they'd probably have forced their way in here and smashed things up."

"Yes," said Bartholomew, turning again to Edith, "you should have been here."

He seemed to consider this a sufficient cue for withdrawal, for he turned abruptly and went back to his desk.

"Are the soldiers all set against the Socialists?" demanded Edith of her brother. "I mean do they attack you violently and all that?"

Henry replaced his eye-shade and yawned.

"The human race has come a long way," he said casually, "but most of us are throwbacks; the soldiers don't know what they want, or what they hate, or what they like. They're used to acting in large bodies, and they seem to have to make demonstrations. So it happens to be against us. There've been riots all over the city to-night. It's May Day, you see."

"Was the disturbance here pretty serious?"

"Not a bit," he said scornfully. "About twenty-five of them stopped in the street about nine o'clock, and began to bellow at the moon."

"Oh"—She changed the subject. "You're glad to see me, Henry?"

"Why, sure."

"You don't seem to be."

"I am."

"I suppose you think I'm a—a waster. Sort of the World's Worst Butterfly."

Henry laughed.

"Not at all. Have a good time while you're young. Why? Do I seem like the priggish and earnest youth?"

10 "No—" She paused, "—but somehow I began thinking how absolutely different the party I'm on is from—from all your purposes. It seems sort of—of incongruous, doesn't it?—me being at a party like that, and you over here working for a thing that'll make that sort of party impossible ever any more, if your ideas work."

"I don't think of it that way. You're young, and you're acting just as you were brought up 20 to act. Go ahead—have a good time."

Her feet, which had been idly swinging, stopped and her voice dropped a note.

"I wish you'd—you'd come back to Harrisburg and have a good time. Do you feel sure that you're on the right track—"

"You're wearing beautiful stockings," he interrupted. "What on earth are they?"

"They're embroidered," she replied, glancing down. "Aren't they cunning?" She raised 30 her skirt and uncovered slim, silk-sheathed calves. "Or do you disapprove of silk stockings?"

He seemed slightly exasperated, bent his dark eyes on her piercingly.

"Are you trying to make me out as criticizing you in any way, Edith?"

"Not at all—"

She paused. Bartholomew had uttered a grunt. She turned and saw that he had left his 40 desk and was standing at the window.

"What is it?" demanded Henry.

"People," said Bartholomew, and then after an instant: "Whole jam of them. They're coming from Sixth Avenue."

"People?"

The fat man pressed his nose to the pane.

"Soldiers, by God!" he said emphatically. "I had an idea they'd come back."

Edith jumped to her feet, and running over 50 joined Bartholomew at the window.

"There's a lot of them!" she cried excitedly. "Come here, Henry!"

Henry readjusted his shade, but kept his seat.

"Hadn't we better turn out the lights?" suggested Bartholomew.

"No. They'll go away in a minute."

"They're not," said Edith, peering from the window. "They're not even thinking of going away. There's more of them coming. Look— there's a whole crowd turning the corner of Sixth Avenue."

By the yellow glow and blue shadows of the street lamp she could see the sidewalk was crowded with men. They were mostly in uniform, some sober, some enthusiastically drunk, and over the whole swept an incoherent clamor and shouting.

Henry rose, and going to the window exposed himself as a long silhouette against the office lights. Immediately the shouting became a steady yell, and a rattling fusillade of small missiles, corners of tobacco plugs, cigarette-boxes, and even pennies beat against the window. The sounds of the racket now began floating up the stairs as the folding doors revolved.

"They're coming up!" cried Bartholomew.

Edith turned anxiously to Henry.

"They're coming up, Henry."

From down-stairs in the lower hall their cries were now quite audible.

"—God damn Socialists!"

"Pro-Germans! Boche-lovers!"

"Second floor, front! Come on!"

"We'll get the sons—"

The next five minutes passed in a dream. Edith was conscious that the clamor burst suddenly upon the three of them like a cloud of rain, that there was a thunder of many feet on the stairs, that Henry had seized her arm and drawn her back toward the rear of the office. Then the door opened and an overflow of men were forced into the room—not the leaders, but simply those who happened to be in front.

"Hello, Bo!"

"Up late, ain't you?"

"You an' your girl. Damn *you!*"

She noticed that two very drunken soldiers had been forced to the front, where they

---

84. **Boche-lovers.** *Boche*, a French slang term shortened from *caboche*, "square-" or "hammer-head," was an uncomplimentary epithet applied to the Germans during World War I.

wobbled fatuously—one of them was short and dark, the other was tall and weak of chin.

Henry stepped forward and raised his hands. "Friends!" he said.

The clamor faded into a momentary stillness, punctuated with mutterings.

"Friends!" he repeated, his far-away eyes fixed over the heads of the crowd, "you're injuring no one but yourselves by breaking in here to-night. Do we look like rich men? Do we look like Germans? I ask you in all fairness—"

"Pipe down!"

"I'll say you do!"

"Say, who's your lady friend, buddy?"

A man in civilian clothes, who had been pawing over a table, suddenly held up a newspaper.

"Here it is!" he shouted. "They wanted the Germans to win the war!"

A new overflow from the stairs was shouldered in and of a sudden the room was full of men all closing around the pale little group at the back. Edith saw that the tall soldier with the weak chin was still in front. The short dark one had disappeared.

She edged slightly backward, stood close to the open window, through which came a clear breath of cool night air.

Then the room was a riot. She realized that the soldiers were surging forward, glimpsed the fat man swinging a chair over his head—instantly the lights went out, and she felt the push of warm bodies under rough cloth, and her ears were full of shouting and trampling and hard breathing.

A figure flashed by her out of nowhere, tottered, was edged sideways, and of a sudden disappeared helplessly out through the open window with a frightened, fragmentary cry that died staccato on the bosom of the clamor. By the faint light streaming from the building backing on the area Edith had a quick impression that it had been the tall soldier with the weak chin.

Anger rose astonishingly in her. She swung her arms wildly, edged blindly toward the thickest of the scuffling. She heard grunts, curses, and muffled impact of fists.

"Henry!" she called frantically, "Henry!"

Then, it was minutes later, she felt suddenly that there were other figures in the room.

She heard a voice, deep, bullying, authoritative; she saw yellow rays of light sweeping here and there in the fracas. The cries became more scattered. The scuffling increased and then stopped.

Suddenly the lights were on and the room was full of policemen, clubbing left and right. The deep voice boomed out:

"Here now! Here now! Here now!"

And then:

"Quiet down and get out! Here now!"

The room seemed to empty like a washbowl. A policeman fast-grappled in the corner released his hold on his soldier antagonist and started him with a shove toward the door. The deep voice continued. Edith perceived now that it came from a bull-necked police captain standing near the door.

"Here now! This is no way! One of your own sojers got shoved out of the back window an' killed hisself!"

"Henry!" called Edith, "Henry!"

She beat wildly with her fists on the back of the man in front of her; she brushed between two others; fought, shrieked, and beat her way to a very pale figure sitting on the floor close to a desk.

"Henry," she cried passionately, "what's the matter? What's the matter? Did they hurt you?"

His eyes were shut. He groaned and then looking up said disgustedly—

"They broke my leg. My God, the fools!"

"Here now!" called the police captain. "Here now! Here now!"

IX

"Childs', Fifty-ninth Street," at eight o'clock of any morning differs from its sisters by less than the width of their marble tables or the degree of polish on the frying-pans. You will see there a crowd of poor people with sleep in the corners of their eyes, trying to look straight before them at their food so as not to see the other poor people. But Childs', Fifty-ninth, four hours earlier is quite unlike any Childs' restaurant from Portland, Oregon, to Portland, Maine. Within its pale but sanitary walls one finds a noisy medley of chorus girls, college boys, débutantes, rakes, *filles de joie*— a not unrepresentative mixture of the gayest of Broadway, and even of Fifth Avenue.

In the early morning of May the second it was unusually full. Over the marble-topped tables were bent the excited faces of flappers whose fathers owned individual villages. They were eating buckwheat cakes and scrambled eggs with relish and gusto, an accomplishment that it would have been utterly impossible for them to repeat in the same place four hours later.

Almost the entire crowd were from the Gamma Psi dance at Delmonico's except for several chorus girls from a midnight revue who sat at a side table and wished they'd taken off a little more make-up after the show. Here and there a drab, mouse-like figure, desperately out of place, watched the butterflies with a weary, puzzled curiosity. But the drab figure was the exception. This was the morning after May Day, and celebration was still in the air.

Gus Rose, sober but a little dazed, must be classed as one of the drab figures. How he had got himself from Forty-fourth Street to Fifty-ninth Street after the riot was only a hazy half-memory. He had seen the body of Carrol Key put in an ambulance and driven off, and then he had started up town with two or three soldiers. Somewhere between Forty-fourth Street and Fifty-ninth Street the other soldiers had met with some women and disappeared. Rose had wandered to Columbus Circle and chosen the gleaming lights of Childs' to minister to his craving for coffee and doughnuts. He walked in and sat down.

All around him floated airy, inconsequential chatter and high-pitched laughter. At first he failed to understand, but after a puzzled five minutes he realized that this was the aftermath of some gay party. Here and there a restless, hilarious young man wandered fraternally and familiarly between the tables, shaking hands indiscriminately and pausing occasionally for a facetious chat, while excited waiters, bearing cakes and eggs aloft, swore at him silently, and bumped him out of the way. To Rose, seated at the most inconspicuous and least crowded table, the whole scene was a colorful circus of beauty and riotous pleasure.

He became gradually aware, after a few moments, that the couple seated diagonally across from him, with their backs to the crowd, were not the least interesting pair in the room.

The man was drunk. He wore a dinner coat with a dishevelled tie and shirt swollen by spillings of water and wine. His eyes, dim and bloodshot, roved unnaturally from side to side. His breath came short between his lips.

"He's been on a spree!" thought Rose.

The woman was almost if not quite sober. She was pretty, with dark eyes and feverish high color, and she kept her active eyes fixed on her companion with the alertness of a hawk. From time to time she would lean and whisper intently to him, and he would answer by inclining his head heavily or by a particularly ghoulish and repellent wink.

Rose scrutinized them dumbly for some minutes, until the woman gave him a quick, resentful look; then he shifted his gaze to two of the most conspicuously hilarious of the promenaders who were on a protracted circuit of the tables. To his surprise he recognized in one of them the young man by whom he had been so ludicrously entertained at Delmonico's. This started him thinking of Key with a vague sentimentality, not unmixed with awe. Key was dead. He had fallen thirty-five feet and split his skull like a cracked cocoanut.

"He was a darn good guy," thought Rose mournfully. "He was a darn good guy, o'right. That was awful hard luck about him."

The two promenaders approached and started down between Rose's table and the next, addressing friends and strangers alike with jovial familiarity. Suddenly Rose saw the fair-haired one with the prominent teeth stop, look unsteadily at the man and girl opposite, and then begin to move his head disapprovingly from side to side.

The man with the blood-shot eyes looked up.

"Gordy," said the promenader with the prominent teeth, "Gordy."

"Hello," said the man with the stained shirt thickly.

Prominent Teeth shook a finger pessimistically at the pair, giving the woman a glance of aloof condemnation.

"What'd I tell you, Gordy?"

Gordon stirred in his seat.

"Go to hell!" he said.

Dean continued to stand there shaking his finger. The woman began to get angry.

"You go away!" she cried fiercely. "You're drunk, that's what you are!"

"So's he," suggested Dean, staying the motion of his finger and pointing it at Gordon.

Peter Himmel ambled up, owlish now and oratorically inclined.

"Here now," he began as if called upon to deal with some petty dispute between children. "Wha's all trouble?"

"You take your friend away," said Jewel tartly. "He's bothering us."

"Wha's 'at?"

"You heard me!" she said shrilly. "I said to take your drunken friend away."

Her rising voice rang out above the clatter of the restaurant and a waiter came hurrying up.

"You gotta be more quiet!"

"That fella's drunk," she cried. "He's insulting us."

"Ah-ha, Gordy," persisted the accused. "What'd I tell you." He turned to the waiter. "Gordy an' I friends. Been tryin' help him, haven't I, Gordy?"

Gordy looked up.

"Help me? Hell, no!"

Jewel rose suddenly, and seizing Gordon's arm assisted him to his feet.

"Come on, Gordy!" she said, leaning toward him and speaking in a half whisper. "Let's us get out of here. This fella's got a mean drunk on."

Gordon allowed himself to be urged to his feet and started toward the door. Jewel turned for a second and addressed the provoker of their flight.

"I know all about *you!*" she said fiercely. "Nice friend you are, I'll say. He told me about you."

Then she seized Gordon's arm, and together they made their way through the curious crowd, paid their check, and went out.

"You'll have to sit down," said the waiter to Peter after they had gone.

"What's 'at? Sit down?"

"Yes—or get out."

Peter turned to Dean.

"Come on," he suggested. "Let's beat up this waiter."

"All right."

They advanced toward him, their faces grown stern. The waiter retreated.

Peter suddenly reached over to a plate on the table beside him and picking up a handful of hash tossed it into the air. It descended as a languid parabola in snowflake effect on the heads of those near by.

"Hey! Ease up!"

"Put him out!"

"Sit down, Peter!"

"Cut out that stuff!"

Peter laughed and bowed.

"Thank you for your kind applause, ladies and gents. If someone will lend me some more hash and a tall hat we will go on with the act."

The bouncer bustled up.

"You've gotta get out!" he said to Peter.

"Hell, no!"

"He's my friend!" put in Dean indignantly.

A crowd of waiters were gathering. "Put him out!"

"Better go, Peter."

There was a short struggle and the two were edged and pushed toward the door.

"I got a hat and a coat here!" cried Peter.

"Well, go get 'em and be spry about it!"

The bouncer released his hold on Peter, who, adopting a ludicrous air of extreme cunning, rushed immediately around to the other table, where he burst into derisive laughter and thumbed his nose at the exasperated waiters.

"Think I just better wait a l'il longer," he announced.

The chase began. Four waiters were sent around one way and four another. Dean caught hold of two of them by the coat, and another struggle took place before the pursuit of Peter could be resumed; he was finally pinioned after overturning a sugarbowl and several cups of coffee. A fresh argument ensued at the cashier's desk, where Peter attempted to buy another dish of hash to take with him and throw at policemen.

But the commotion upon his exit proper was dwarfed by another phenomenon which drew admiring glances and a prolonged involuntary "Oh-h-h!" from every person in the restaurant.

The great plate-glass front had turned to a deep creamy blue, the color of a Maxfield Parrish moonlight—a blue that seemed to press close upon the pane as if to crowd its way into the restaurant. Dawn had come up in Columbus Circle, magical, breathless dawn, silhouetting the great statue of the immortal Christopher, and mingling in a curious and uncanny manner with the fading yellow electric light inside.

x

Mr. In and Mr. Out are not listed by the census-taker. You will search for them in vain through the social register or the births, marriages, and deaths, or the grocer's credit list. Oblivion has swallowed them and the testimony that they ever existed at all is vague and shadowy, and inadmissible in a court of law. Yet I have it upon the best authority that for a brief space Mr. In and Mr. Out lived, breathed, answered to their names and radiated vivid personalities of their own.

During the brief span of their lives they walked in their native garments down the great highway of a great nation; were laughed at, sworn at, chased, and fled from. Then they passed and were heard of no more.

They were already taking form dimly, when a taxicab with the top open breezed down Broadway in the faintest glimmer of May dawn. In this car sat the souls of Mr. In and Mr. Out discussing with amazement the blue light that had so precipitately colored the sky behind the statue of Christopher Columbus, discussing with bewilderment the old, gray faces of the early risers which skimmed palely along the street like blown bits of paper on a gray lake. They were agreed on all things, from the absurdity of the bouncer in Childs' to the absurdity of the business of life. They were dizzy with the extreme maudlin happiness that the morning had awakened in their glowing souls. Indeed, so fresh and vigorous was their pleasure in living that they felt it should be expressed by loud cries.

"Ye-ow-ow!" hooted Peter, making a megaphone with his hands—and Dean joined in with a call that, though equally significant and symbolic, derived its resonance from its very inarticulateness.

"Yoho! Yea! Yoho! Yo-buba!"

Fifty-third Street was a bus with a dark, bobbed-hair beauty atop; Fifty-second was a street cleaner who dodged, escaped, and sent up a yell of "Look where you're aimin'!" in a pained and grieved voice. At Fiftieth Street a group of men on a very white sidewalk in front of a very white building turned to stare after them, and shouted:

"Some party, boys!"

At Forty-ninth Street Peter turned to Dean. "Beautiful morning," he said gravely, squinting up his owlish eyes.

"Probably is."

"Go get some breakfast, hey?"

Dean agreed—with additions.

"Breakfast and liquor."

"Breakfast and liquor," repeated Peter, and they looked at each other, nodding. "That's logical."

Then they both burst into loud laughter.

"Breakfast and liquor! Oh, gosh!"

"No such thing," announced Peter.

"Don't serve it? Ne'mind. We force 'em serve it. Bring pressure bear."

"Bring logic bear."

The taxi cut suddenly off Broadway, sailed along a cross street, and stopped in front of a heavy tomb-like building in Fifth Avenue.

"What's idea?"

The taxi-driver informed them that this was Delmonico's.

This was somewhat puzzling. They were forced to devote several minutes to intense concentration, for if such an order had been given there must have been a reason for it.

"Somep'm 'bouta coat," suggested the taxi-man.

That was it. Peter's overcoat and hat. He had left them at Delmonico's. Having decided this, they disembarked from the taxi and strolled toward the entrance arm in arm.

"Hey!" said the taxi-driver.

"Huh?"

"You better pay me."

They shook their heads in shocked negation.

"Later, not now—we give orders, you wait."

The taxi-driver objected; he wanted his money now. With the scornful condescension of men exercising tremendous self-control they paid him.

Inside Peter groped in vain through a dim, deserted check-room in search of his coat and derby.

"Gone, I guess. Somebody stole it."

"Some Sheff student."

"All probability."

"Never mind," said Dean, nobly. "I'll leave mine here too—then we'll both be dressed the same."

He removed his overcoat and hat and was hanging them up when his roving glance was caught and held magnetically by two large squares of cardboard tacked to the two coatroom doors. The one on the left-hand door bore the word "In" in big black letters, and the one on the right-hand door flaunted the equally emphatic word "Out."

"Look!" he exclaimed happily—

Peter's eyes followed his pointing finger.

"What?"

"Look at the signs. Let's take 'em."

"Good idea."

"Probably pair very rare an' valuable signs. Probably come in handy."

Peter removed the left-hand sign from the door and endeavored to conceal it about his person. The sign being of considerable proportions, this was a matter of some difficulty. An idea flung itself at him, and with an air of dignified mystery he turned his back. After an instant he wheeled dramatically around, and stretching out his arms displayed himself to the admiring Dean. He had inserted the sign in his vest, completely covering his shirt front. In effect, the word "In" had been painted upon his shirt in large black letters.

"Yoho!" cheered Dean. "Mister In."

He inserted his own sign in like manner.

"Mister Out!" he announced triumphantly. "Mr. In meet Mr. Out."

They advanced and shook hands. Again laughter overcame them and they rocked in a shaken spasm of mirth.

"Yoho!"

"We probably get a flock of breakfast."

"We'll go—go to the Commodore."

Arm in arm they sallied out the door, and turning east in Forty-fourth Street set out for the Commodore.

As they came out a short dark soldier, very pale and tired, who had been wandering listlessly along the sidewalk, turned to look at them.

He started over as though to address them, but as they immediately bent on him glances of withering unrecognition, he waited until they had started unsteadily down the street, and then followed at about forty paces, chuckling to himself and saying, "Oh, boy!" over and over under his breath, in delighted anticipatory tones.

Mr. In and Mr. Out were meanwhile exchanging pleasantries concerning their future plans.

"We want liquor; we want breakfast. Neither without the other. One and indivisible." 60

"We want both 'em!"

"Both 'em!"

It was quite light now, and passers-by began to bend curious eyes on the pair. Obviously they were engaged in a discussion, which afforded each of them intense amusement, for occasionally a fit of laughter would seize upon them so violently that, still with their arms interlocked, they would bend nearly double. 70

Reaching the Commodore, they exchanged a few spicy epigrams with the sleepy-eyed doorman, navigated the revolving door with some difficulty, and then made their way through a thinly populated but startled lobby to the dining-room, where a puzzled waiter showed them an obscure table in a corner. They studied the bill of fare helplessly, telling over the items to each other in puzzled mumbles. 80

"Don't see any liquor here," said Peter reproachfully.

The waiter became audible but unintelligible.

"Repeat," continued Peter, with patient tolerance, "that there seems to be unexplained and quite distasteful lack of liquor upon bill of fare."

"Here!" said Dean confidently, "let me handle him." He turned to the waiter—"Bring us— 90 bring us—" he scanned the bill of fare anxiously. "Bring us a quart of champagne and a —a—probably ham sandwich."

The waiter looked doubtful.

"Bring it!" roared Mr. In and Mr. Out in chorus.

The waiter coughed and disappeared. There was a short wait during which they were subjected without their knowledge to a careful scrutiny by the head-waiter. Then the champagne arrived, and at the sight of it Mr. In 100 and Mr. Out became jubilant.

"Imagine their objecting to us having champagne for breakfast—jus' imagine."

They both concentrated upon the vision of such an awesome possibility, but the feat was too much for them. It was impossible for their joint imaginations to conjure up a world where any one might object to any one else having champagne for breakfast. The waiter drew the cork with an enormous *pop*—and their glasses immediately foamed with pale yellow froth.

"Here's health, Mr. In."

"Here's the same to you, Mr. Out."

The waiter withdrew; the minutes passed; the champagne became low in the bottle.

"It's—it's mortifying," said Dean suddenly.

"Wha's mortifying?"

"The idea their objecting us having champagne breakfast."

"Mortifying?" Peter considered. "Yes, tha's word—mortifying."

Again they collapsed into laughter, howled, swayed, rocked back and forth in their chairs, repeating the word "mortifying" over and over to each other—each repetition seeming to make it only more brilliantly absurd.

After a few more gorgeous minutes they decided on another quart. Their anxious waiter consulted his immediate superior and this discreet person gave implicit instructions that no more champagne should be served. Their check was brought.

Five minutes later, arm in arm, they left the Commodore and made their way through a curious, staring crowd along Forty-second Street, and up Vanderbilt Avenue to the Biltmore. There, with sudden cunning, they rose to the occasion and traversed the lobby, walking fast and standing unnaturally erect.

Once in the dining-room they repeated their performance. They were torn between intermittent convulsive laughter and sudden spasmodic discussions of politics, college, and the sunny state of their dispositions. Their watches told them that it was now nine o'clock, and a dim idea was born in them that they were on a memorable party, something that they would remember always. They lingered over the second bottle. Either of them had only to mention the word "mortifying" to send them both into riotous gasps. The dining-room was whirring and shifting now; a curious lightness permeated and rarefied the heavy air.

They paid their check and walked out into the lobby.

It was at this moment that the exterior doors revolved for the thousandth time that morning, and admitted into the lobby a very pale young beauty with dark circles under her eyes, attired in a much-rumpled evening dress. She was accompanied by a plain stout man, obviously not an appropriate escort.

At the top of the stairs this couple encountered Mr. In and Mr. Out.

"Edith," began Mr. In, stepping toward her hilariously and making a sweeping bow, "darling, good morning."

The stout man glanced questioningly at Edith, as if merely asking her permission to throw this man summarily out of the way.

"'Scuse familiarity," added Peter, as an afterthought. "Edith, good morning."

He seized Dean's elbow and impelled him into the foreground.

"Meet Mr. In, Edith, my bes' frien'. Inseparable. Mr. In and Mr. Out."

Mr. Out advanced and bowed; in fact, he advanced so far and bowed so low that he tipped slightly forward and only kept his balance by placing a hand lightly on Edith's shoulder.

"I'm Mr. Out, Edith," he mumbled pleasantly, "'Smisterin Misterout."

"'Smisterinanout," said Peter proudly.

But Edith stared straight by them, her eyes fixed on some infinite speck in the gallery above her. She nodded slightly to the stout man, who advanced bull-like and with a sturdy brisk gesture pushed Mr. In and Mr. Out to either side. Through this alley he and Edith walked.

But ten paces farther on Edith stopped again—stopped and pointed to a short, dark soldier who was eyeing the crowd in general, and the tableau of Mr. In and Mr. Out in particular, with a sort of puzzled, spellbound awe.

"There," cried Edith. "See there!"

Her voice rose, became somewhat shrill. Her pointing finger shook slightly.

"There's the soldier who broke my brother's leg."

There were a dozen exclamations; a man in a cutaway coat left his place near the desk and advanced alertly; the stout person made a sort of lightning-like spring toward the short, dark soldier, and then the lobby closed around the little group and blotted them from the sight of Mr. In and Mr. Out.

But to Mr. In and Mr. Out this event was merely a parti-colored iridescent segment of a whirring, spinning world.

They heard loud voices; they saw the stout man spring; the picture suddenly blurred.

Then they were in an elevator bound skyward.

"What floor, please?" said the elevator man.

"Any floor," said Mr. In.

"Top floor," said Mr. Out.

"This is the top floor," said the elevator man.

"Have another floor put on," said Mr. Out.

"Higher," said Mr. In.

"Heaven," said Mr. Out.

XI

In a bedroom of a small hotel just off Sixth Avenue Gordon Sterrett awoke with a pain in the back of his head and a sick throbbing in all his veins. He looked at the dusky gray shadows in the corners of the room and at a raw place on a large leather chair in the corner where it had long been in use. He saw clothes, dishevelled, rumpled clothes on the floor and he smelt stale cigarette smoke and stale liquor. The windows were tight shut. Outside the bright sunlight had thrown a dust-filled beam across the sill—a beam broken by the head of the wide wooden bed in which he had slept. He lay 30 very quiet—comatose, drugged, his eyes wide, his mind clicking wildly like an unoiled machine.

It must have been thirty seconds after he perceived the sunbeam with the dust on it and the rip on the large leather chair that he had the sense of life close beside him, and it was another thirty seconds after that before he realized that he was irrevocably married to Jewel Hudson. 40

He went out half an hour later and bought a revolver at a sporting goods store. Then he took a taxi to the room where he had been living on East Twenty-seventh Street, and, leaning across the table that held his drawing materials, fired a cartridge into his head just behind the temple.

ERNEST HEMINGWAY

"A remarkable talent for writing in an author who is now a forty-year-old adolescent." This harsh but not inaccurate judgment of the work of Ernest Hemingway ten years ago is another way of stating that he is one of the most important members of the large group of writers whose emotional and moral perceptions have been limited by the two World Wars. Hemingway's life was completely bound up with these great conflicts at the critical times in his development as a writer, and he has never been able to shed the crushing disillusionment, the sadistic cruelty, and the stunted spiritual growths that were engendered on the battlefields of Europe.

Ernest Hemingway was born in Oak Park, Illinois, on July 21, 1898. His father was a physician, who often took his little son on his professional visits. The experiences of the lad on these tours of mercy were later reflected in his first collection of short stories, *In Our Time*. Most of young Hemingway's boyhood was spent in Michigan; he attended the public schools, where he was a popular athlete and distinguished himself particularly in football and boxing. The nature of those two violent and popular sports is singularly appropriate to the nature of Hemingway the later writer.

For a time he was a reporter on the *Kansas City Star*. But the First World War shed its fatal fascination upon him as it did upon many another American youth. He did not wait for the United States to enter the conflict but went overseas as a volunteer worker in an ambulance unit. Later he enlisted in the Italian Arditi, served at the front, participated in the disastrous rout of the Italians at Caporetto (October 1917), and was wounded severely.

He emerged from the war with a silver plate in his shoulder, two Italian war decorations—the Medaglia d'Argente al Valore Militare and the Croce di Guerra—and a thorough emotional battering. On his return to the United States he resumed his newspaper work, becoming a reporter on the *Toronto Star* (1919) and later its foreign correspondent, with headquarters in Paris. He was present at the difficulties cast up by the French colonial and mandatory policies in Syria, other parts of the Near East, and northern Africa. While he was stationed abroad, he enjoyed sports along with writing and became incidentally initiated into the gentle pastime of bullfighting—as a spectator, of course.

His professional literary career, apart from his newspaper work, began while he was in Paris. *Three Stories and Ten Poems* appeared there in 1923; it was followed by *In Our Time* (1924), his first impressive collection of short stories. A later editor of this book remarks in his Preface that *In Our Time* "has the whole of Hemingway in it already." In a sense this statement is true—there is the penchant for the macabre, the romantic soliloquizing over dead love, the bullfight, the maudlin intoxication, the "feeling good" in a purely sensual manner, and the violent death that we can always find somewhere in a Hemingway story if the story is long enough. But at the same time Hemingway has, since that early work, developed a maturity of technique and grasp of his style that have made him one of the most vivid writers of fiction since Kipling.

He returned to the United States in 1926 and since that time has moved about constantly, living for a time in Florida, in Wyoming, abroad in France and Italy, and in Mexico. He has always disliked New York City and has avoided it; his phobia in regard to the metropolis resembles that of D. H. Lawrence and O'Neill. His periods of writing have been punctuated by fishing, hunting, and roughing it. In recent years his most spectacular adventure has been his stay as war correspondent and thrill-seeker in the Spanish Civil War, which began in 1936; his sympathies here, along with those of most writers interested, were with the Loyalist government.

Hemingway's output has been comparatively small but, thanks to his vigor and effectiveness as a writer, extremely influential. In addition to the two collections of short stories already noted, there are *Men Without Women* (1927), *Winner Take Nothing* (1933), and *The Fifth Column and the First Forty-Nine Stories* (1938), besides numerous miscellaneous stories and screeds contributed to periodicals like *The Transatlantic Review, This Quarter, Scribner's, Esquire, The Atlantic Monthly,* and *The New Republic*—widely divergent magazines with surprisingly different tastes and standards. Many of Hemingway's non-fictional writings exhibit a strong revolutionary quality; but thus far he is clearly more important as a member of the "Lost Generation" than as a revolutionist of the thirties. This fact is nowhere better demonstrated than in his impressively dynamic novels, *The Torrents of Spring* (1926), *The Sun Also Rises* (1926), and *A Farewell to Arms* (1929). The last of these, one of his two most celebrated novels and in many ways his best, recounts the experiences of a soldier in the Italian army and his tragic love for a nurse; the story of the retreat of the Italians from Caporetto is tense, dramatic, rushing narrative. *Death in the Afternoon* (1932) is a philosophical piece on the subject of bullfighting with considerable sentimental twaddle about the glory of killing; nothing can justify better the charge that Hemingway was emotionally not yet full-grown. *The Green Hills of Africa* (1935) needs no comment save a notice of its locale and offers nothing new in subject-matter. *To Have and Have Not* (1937) is a somewhat muddy novel of a man who has lived beyond the law and meets an unnatural death, yet whose sense of moral justice is not sufficiently developed for him to refrain from whining that he has never had a chance.

Aside from *A Farewell to Arms,* the novel of Hemingway most likely to live longest is *For Whom the Bell Tolls* (1940), a graphic, poignant, at times sadistic, at times mawkish, but generally powerful novel about a young American who sacrifices himself in the Spanish Civil War. That the novel could ever live as long as the magnificent sentence from the meditation by John Donne (1573–1631) from which its title is derived is more than dubious; but as a document of the tragic war, the preliminary struggle before the Second World War, it easily surpasses John Dos Passos' *Adventures of a Young Man* (1939), on the same subject.

It has been observed that Hemingway summarizes the essential contradictions of the Waste Landers (pp. 191–205). He is, in stern American parlance, hard-boiled on the surface; but he can on occasion be tender-hearted, although in a rough and rather grudging way. At times he creates the impression that his hardness is either a pose or a defense mechanism. For the rest, however, he is thoroughly disillusioned but with a kind of athletic hopefulness. His themes are simple; his characters far from subtle; his style direct, colloquial, pungent, staccato; his vocabulary realistic, harsh, though producing the effect of the remarkably natural, particularly in dialogue. But as yet he has not been able to break away from the spell woven by his character, Lieutenant Henry, in *A Farewell to Arms*:

> I was always embarrassed by the words sacred, glorious, and sacrifice and the expression in vain. We heard them . . . and read them . . . now for a long time, and I had seen nothing sacred, and the things that were glorious had no glory and the sacrifices were like the stockyards at Chicago if nothing was done with the meat except to bury it. There were many words that you could not stand to hear and finally only the names of places had dignity.

The Killers

THE DOOR of Henry's lunch-room opened and two men came in. They sat down at the counter.

"What's yours?" George asked them.

"I don't know," one of the men said. "What do you want to eat, Al?"

"The Killers" from *Men Without Women*, reprinted by permission of Charles Scribner's Sons.

"I don't know," said Al. "I don't know what I want to eat."

Outside it was getting dark. The street-light came on outside the window. The two men at the counter read the menu. From the other end of the counter Nick Adams watched them. He had been talking to George when they came in.

"I'll have a roast pork tenderloin with apple sauce and mashed potatoes," the first man said.

"It isn't ready yet."

"What the hell do you put it on the card for?"

"That's the dinner," George explained. "You can get that at six o'clock."

George looked at the clock on the wall behind the counter.

"It's five o'clock."

"The clock says twenty minutes past five," the second man said.

"It's twenty minutes fast."

"Oh, to hell with the clock," the first man said. "What have you got to eat?"

"I can give you any kind of sandwiches," George said. "You can have ham and eggs, bacon and eggs, liver and bacon, or a steak."

"Give me chicken croquettes with green peas and cream sauce and mashed potatoes."

"That's the dinner."

"Everything we want's the dinner, eh? That's the way you work it."

"I can give you ham and eggs, bacon and eggs, liver—"

"I'll take ham and eggs," the man called Al said. He wore a derby hat and a black overcoat buttoned across the chest. His face was small and white and he had tight lips. He wore a silk muffler and gloves.

"Give me bacon and eggs," said the other man. He was about the same size as Al. Their faces were different, but they were dressed like twins. Both wore overcoats too tight for them. They sat leaning forward, their elbows on the counter.

"Got anything to drink?" Al asked.

"Silver beer, bevo, ginger-ale," George said.

"I mean you got anything to *drink*?"

"Just those I said."

"This is a hot town," said the other. "What do they call it?"

"Summit."

"Ever hear of it?" Al asked his friend.

"No," said the friend.

"What do you do here nights?" Al asked.

"They eat the dinner," his friend said. "They all come here and eat the big dinner."

"That's right," George said.

"So you think that's right?" Al asked George.

"Sure."

"You're a pretty bright boy, aren't you?"

"Sure," said George.

"Well, you're not," said the other little man. "Is he, Al?"

"He's dumb," said Al. He turned to Nick. "What's your name?"

"Adams."

"Another bright boy," Al said. "Ain't he a bright boy, Max?"

"The town's full of bright boys," Max said.

George put the two platters, one of ham and eggs, the other of bacon and eggs, on the counter. He set down two side-dishes of fried potatoes and closed the wicket into the kitchen.

"Which is yours?" he asked Al.

"Don't you remember?"

"Ham and eggs."

"Just a bright boy," Max said. He leaned forward and took the ham and eggs. Both men ate with their gloves on. George watched them eat.

"What are *you* looking at?" Max looked at George.

"Nothing."

"The hell you were. You were looking at me."

"Maybe the boy meant it for a joke, Max," Al said.

George laughed.

"*You* don't have to laugh," Max said to him. "*You* don't have to laugh at all, see?"

"All right," said George.

"So he thinks it's all right." Max turned to Al. "He thinks it's all right, that's a good one."

"Oh, he's a thinker," Al said. They went on eating.

"What's the bright boy's name down the counter?" Al asked Max.

"Hey, bright boy," Max said to Nick. "You go around on the other side of the counter with your boy friend."

"What's the idea?" Nick asked.

"There isn't any idea."

"You better go around, bright boy," Al said. Nick went around behind the counter.

"What's the idea?" George asked.

"None of your damned business," Al said. "Who's out in the kitchen?"

"The nigger."

"What do you mean the nigger?"

"The nigger that cooks."

"Tell him to come in."

"What's the idea?"

"Tell him to come in."

"Where do you think you are?"

"We know damn well where we are," the man called Max said. "Do we look silly?"

"You talk silly," Al said to him. "What the hell do you argue with this kid for? Listen," he said to George, "tell the nigger to come out here."

"What are you going to do to him?"

"Nothing. Use your head, bright boy. What would we do to a nigger?"

George opened the slit that opened back into the kitchen. "Sam," he called. "Come in here a minute."

The door to the kitchen opened and the nigger came in. "What was it?" he asked. The two men at the counter took a look at him.

"All right, nigger. You stand right there," Al said.

Sam, the nigger, standing in his apron, looked at the two men sitting at the counter. "Yes, sir," he said. Al got down from his stool.

"I'm going back to the kitchen with the nigger and bright boy," he said. "Go on back to the kitchen, nigger. You go with him, bright boy." The little man walked after Nick and Sam, the cook, back into the kitchen. The door shut after them. The man called Max sat at the counter opposite George. He didn't look at George but looked in the mirror that ran along back of the counter. Henry's had been made over from a saloon into a lunch-counter.

"Well, bright boy," Max said, looking into the mirror, "why don't you say something?"

"What's it all about?"

"Hey, Al," Max called, "bright boy wants to know what it's all about."

"Why don't you tell him?" Al's voice came from the kitchen.

"What do you think it's all about?"

"I don't know."

"What do you think?"

Max looked into the mirror all the time he was talking.

"I wouldn't say."

"Hey, Al, bright boy says he wouldn't say what he thinks it's all about."

"I can hear you, all right," Al said from the kitchen. He had propped open the slit that dishes passed through into the kitchen with a catsup bottle. "Listen, bright boy," he said from the kitchen to George. "Stand a little further along the bar. You move a little to the left, Max." He was like a photographer arranging for a group picture.

"Talk to me, bright boy," Max said. "What do you think's going to happen?"

George did not say anything.

"I'll tell you," Max said. "We're going to kill a Swede. Do you know a big Swede named Ole Andreson?"

"Yes."

"He comes here to eat every night, don't he?"

"Sometimes he comes here."

"He comes here at six o'clock, don't he?"

"If he comes."

"We know all that, bright boy," Max said. "Talk about something else. Ever go to the movies?"

"Once in a while."

"You ought to go to the movies more. The movies are fine for a bright boy like you."

"What are you going to kill Ole Andreson for? What did he ever do to you?"

"He never had a chance to do anything to us. He never even seen us."

"And he's only going to see us once," Al said from the kitchen.

"What are you going to kill him for, then?" George asked.

"We're killing him for a friend. Just to oblige a friend, bright boy."

"Shut up," said Al from the kitchen. "You talk too goddam much."

"Well, I got to keep bright boy amused. Don't I, bright boy?"

"You talk too damn much," Al said. "The nigger and my bright boy are amused by themselves. I got them tied up like a couple of girl friends in the convent."

"I suppose you were in a convent."

"You never know."

"You were in a kosher convent. That's where you were."

George looked up at the clock.

"If anybody comes in you tell them the cook is off, and if they keep after it, you tell them you'll go back and cook yourself. Do you get that, bright boy?"

"All right," George said. "What you going to do with us afterwards?"

"That'll depend," Max said. "That's one of those things you never know at the time."

George looked up at the clock. It was a quarter past six. The door from the street opened. A street-car motorman came in.

"Hello, George," he said. "Can I get supper?"

"Sam's gone out," George said. "He'll be back in about half an hour."

"I'd better go up the street," the motorman said. George looked at the clock. It was twenty minutes past six.

"That was nice, bright boy," Max said. "You're a regular little gentleman."

"He knew I'd blow his head off," Al said from the kitchen.

"No," said Max. "It ain't that. Bright boy is nice. He's a nice boy. I like him."

At six-fifty-five George said: "He's not coming."

Two other people had been in the lunch-room. Once George had gone out to the kitchen and made a ham-and-egg sandwich "to go" that a man wanted to take with him. Inside the kitchen he saw Al, his derby hat tipped back, sitting on a stool beside the wicket with the muzzle of a sawed-off shotgun resting on the ledge. Nick and the cook were back to back in the corner, a towel tied in each of their mouths. George had cooked the sandwich, wrapped it up in oiled paper, put it in a bag, brought it in, and the man had paid for it and gone out.

"Bright boy can do everything," Max said. "He can cook and everything. You'd make some girl a nice wife, bright boy."

"Yes?" George said. "Your friend, Ole Andreson, isn't going to come."

"We'll give him ten minutes," Max said.

Max watched the mirror and the clock. The

hands of the clock marked seven o'clock, and then five minutes past seven.

"Come on, Al," said Max. "We better go. He's not coming."

"Better give him five minutes," Al said from the kitchen.

In the five minutes a man came in, and George explained that the cook was sick.

"Why the hell don't you get another cook?" the man asked. "Aren't you running a lunch-counter?" He went out.

"Come on, Al," Max said.

"What about the two bright boys and the nigger?"

"They're all right."

"You think so?"

"Sure. We're through with it."

"I don't like it," said Al. "It's sloppy. You talk too much."

"Oh, what the hell," said Max. "We got to keep amused, haven't we?"

"You talk too much, all the same," Al said. He came out from the kitchen. The cut-off barrels of the shotgun made a slight bulge under the waist of his too tight-fitting overcoat. He straightened his coat with his gloved hands.

"So long, bright boy," he said to George. "You got a lot of luck."

"That's the truth," Max said. "You ought to play the races, bright boy."

The two of them went out the door. George watched them, through the window, pass under the arc-light and cross the street. In their tight overcoats and derby hats they looked like a vaudeville team. George went back through the swinging-door into the kitchen and untied Nick and the cook.

"I don't want any more of that," said Sam, the cook. "I don't want any more of that."

Nick stood up. He had never had a towel in his mouth before.

"Say," he said. "What the hell?" He was trying to swagger it off.

"They were going to kill Ole Andreson," George said. "They were going to shoot him when he came in to eat."

"Ole Andreson?"

"Sure."

The cook felt the corners of his mouth with his thumbs.

"They all gone?" he asked.

"Yeah," said George. "They're gone now."

"I don't like it," said the cook. "I don't like any of it at all."

"Listen," George said to Nick. "You better go see Ole Andreson."

"All right."

"You better not have anything to do with it at all," Sam, the cook, said. "You better stay way out of it."

"Don't go if you don't want to," George said.

"Mixing up in this ain't going to get you anywhere," the cook said. "You stay out of it."

"I'll go see him," Nick said to George. "Where does he live?"

The cook turned away.

"Little boys always know what they want to do," he said.

"He lives up at Hirsch's rooming-house," George said to Nick.

"I'll go up there."

Outside the arc-light shone through the bare branches of a tree. Nick walked up the street beside the car-tracks and turned at the next arc-light down a side-street. Three houses up the street was Hirsch's rooming-house. Nick walked up the two steps and pushed the bell. A woman came to the door.

"Is Ole Andreson here?"

"Do you want to see him?"

"Yes, if he's in."

Nick followed the woman up a flight of stairs and back to the end of a corridor. She knocked on the door.

"Who is it?"

"It's somebody to see you, Mr. Andreson," the woman said.

"It's Nick Adams."

"Come in."

Nick opened the door and went into the room. Ole Andreson was lying on the bed with all his clothes on. He had been a heavyweight prizefighter and he was too long for the bed. He lay with his head on two pillows. He did not look at Nick.

"What was it?" he asked.

"I was up at Henry's," Nick said, "and two fellows came in and tied up me and the cook, and they said they were going to kill you."

It sounded silly when he said it. Ole Andreson said nothing.

"They put us out in the kitchen," Nick went on. "They were going to shoot you when you came in to supper."

Ole Andreson looked at the wall and did not say anything.

"George thought I better come and tell you about it."

"There isn't anything I can do about it," Ole Andreson said.

"I'll tell you what they were like."

"I don't want to know what they were like," Ole Andreson said. He looked at the wall. "Thanks for coming to tell me about it."

"That's all right."

Nick looked at the big man lying on the bed.

"Don't you want me to go and see the police?"

"No," Ole Andreson said. "That wouldn't do any good."

"Isn't there something I could do?"

"No. There ain't anything to do."

"Maybe it was just a bluff."

"No. It ain't just a bluff."

Ole Andreson rolled over toward the wall.

"The only thing is," he said, talking toward the wall, "I just can't make up my mind to go out. I been in here all day."

"Couldn't you get out of town?"

"No," Ole Andreson said. "I'm through with all that running around."

He looked at the wall.

"There ain't anything to do now."

"Couldn't you fix it up some way?"

"No. I got in wrong." He talked in the same flat voice. "There ain't anything to do. After a while I'll make up my mind to go out."

"I better go back and see George," Nick said.

"So long," said Ole Andreson. He did not look toward Nick. "Thanks for coming around."

Nick went out. As he shut the door he saw Ole Andreson with all his clothes on, lying on the bed looking at the wall.

"He's been in his room all day," the land-lady said down-stairs. "I guess he don't feel well. I said to him: 'Mr. Andreson, you ought to go out and take a walk on a nice fall day like this,' but he didn't feel like it."

"He doesn't want to go out."

"I'm sorry he don't feel well," the woman said. "He's an awfully nice man. He was in the ring, you know."

"I know it."

"You'd never know it except from the way his face is," the woman said. They stood talking just inside the street door. "He's just as gentle."

"Well, good-night, Mrs. Hirsch," Nick said.

"I'm not Mrs. Hirsch," the woman said. "She owns the place. I just look after it for her. I'm Mrs. Bell."

"Well, good-night, Mrs. Bell," Nick said.

"Good-night," the woman said.

Nick walked up the dark street to the corner under the arc-light, and then along the car-tracks to Henry's eating-house. George was inside, back of the counter.

"Did you see Ole?"

"Yes," said Nick. "He's in his room and he won't go out."

The cook opened the door from the kitchen when he heard Nick's voice.

"I don't even listen to it," he said and shut the door.

"Did you tell him about it?" George asked.

"Sure. I told him but he knows what it's all about."

"What's he going to do?"

"Nothing."

"They'll kill him."

"I guess they will."

"He must have got mixed up in something in Chicago."

"I guess so," said Nick.

"It's a hell of a thing."

"It's an awful thing," Nick said.

They did not say anything. George reached down for a towel and wiped the counter.

"I wonder what he did?" Nick said.

"Double-crossed somebody. That's what they kill them for."

"I'm going to get out of this town," Nick said.

"Yes," said George. "That's a good thing to do."

"I can't stand to think about him waiting in the room and knowing he's going to get it. It's too damned awful."

"Well," said George, "you better not think about it."

RING LARDNER

Ring Lardner was born Ringgold Wilmer Lardner, at Niles, Michigan, on March 6, 1885. He died in New York City on September 25, 1933. Between these two dates, much too close together, lay a life dedicated almost entirely to journalism. He actually began as a student of engineering at the Armour Institute, but soon found an opening on the South Bend *Times* as a miscellaneous reporter of police courts, moving pictures, and sports events. After some service with Chicago newspapers, he emerged as a sports correspondent on the spring training trips of the Chicago White Sox; and it was this experience which gave him his start as a writer of parts. In 1914 he began to send to the *Saturday Evening Post* a series of satirical sketches about a boastful, crude, but well-intentioned and likable rookie pitcher, which were published in 1916 under the title of *You Know Me, Al.*

The success of these stories was great. They were written in the form of letters—an ancient device which has always been effective because it affords so many excellent opportunities for personal revelations and analysis of character—and they made use in highly realistic form of the unrivaled color and picturesqueness of the professional baseball players' language. After more writing of this general nature, which helped to establish Lardner as perhaps the leading humorist of America at the time, he stepped into a much larger field. *How to Write Short Stories* (1924), a collection of tales, and a similar volume, *The Love Nest* (1926), showed that Lardner was a satirist of the first rank—bitter and disillusioned and misanthropic toward all forms of pretense (and life is mostly pretense), yet endowed with a remarkable surface humor which made the author in the minds of the unthinking reader only a very funny man.

A somewhat insane autobiography, *The Story of a Wonder Man* (1927), was followed by two dramatic efforts, both of which may be called successful as plays, although in both instances Lardner received the help of professional men of the theater. *Elmer the Great*, written in collaboration with the noted showman George M. Cohan (1928), brings to Broadway the baseball hero; *June Moon* (1930), written with George S. Kaufman, is an amusing extravaganza which hits at all the sentimental drama that was ever written.

In the years following his ill-health and premature death, Lardner's stature has grown steadily. It is obviously unfair to consider him merely a talented journalist who began as a sports writer and was never able to shake off his pedestrian beginnings. As a master of the racy vernacular of present-day America, he is unsurpassed in any case; and as the unrelenting foe of the four-flusher he is superb. His hatred of man and woman is often closer to that of Jonathan Swift than that of any other writer, English or American, since Mark Twain; yet, like most misanthropes, he has the compensating power of attracting people both by his writing and his personality. And he is artist enough to achieve his goal by implicit suggestion rather than by outright accusation and reproach.

Champion

An example of the mystery story. The mystery is how it came to get printed.

MIDGE KELLY scored his first knockout when he was seventeen. The knockee was his brother Connie, three years his junior and a cripple. The purse was a half dollar given to the younger Kelly by a lady whose electric had just missed bumping his soul from his frail little body.

Connie did not know Midge was in the house, else he never would have risked laying the prize on the arm of the least comfortable chair in the room, the better to observe its shining beauty. As Midge entered from the kitchen, the crippled boy covered the coin with his hand, but the movement lacked the speed requisite to escape his brother's quick eye.

"Watcha got there?" demanded Midge.

"Nothin'," said Connie.

"You're a one legged liar!" said Midge.

He strode over to his brother's chair and grasped the hand that concealed the coin.

"Let loose!" he ordered.

Connie began to cry.

"Let loose and shut up your noise," said the elder, and jerked his brother's hand from the chair arm.

The coin fell onto the bare floor. Midge pounced on it. His weak mouth widened in a triumphant smile.

"Nothin', huh?" he said. "All right, if it's nothin' you don't want it."

"Give that back," sobbed the younger.

"I'll give you a red nose, you little sneak! Where'd you steal it?"

"I didn't steal it. It's mine. A lady give it to me after she pretty near hit me with a car."

"It's a crime she missed you," said Midge.

Midge started for the front door. The cripple picked up his crutch, rose from his chair with difficulty, and, still sobbing, came toward Midge. The latter heard him and stopped.

"You better stay where you're at," he said.

"I want my money," cried the boy.

"I know what you want," said Midge.

Doubling up the fist that held the half dollar, he landed with all his strength on his brother's mouth. Connie fell to the floor with a thud, the crutch tumbling on top of him. Midge stood beside the prostrate form.

"Is that enough?" he said. "Or do you want this, too?"

And he kicked him in the crippled leg.

"I guess that'll hold you," he said.

There was no response from the boy on the floor. Midge looked at him a moment, then at the coin in his hand, and then went out into the street, whistling.

An hour later, when Mrs. Kelly came home from her day's work at Faulkner's Steam Laundry, she found Connie on the floor, moaning. Dropping on her knees beside him, she called him by name a score of times. Then she got

up and, pale as a ghost, dashed from the house. Dr. Ryan left the Kelly abode about dusk and walked toward Halsted Street. Mrs. Dorgan spied him as he passed her gate.

"Who's sick, Doctor?" she called.

"Poor little Connie," he replied. "He had a bad fall."

"How did it happen?"

"I can't say for sure, Margaret, but I'd almost bet he was knocked down."

"Knocked down!" exclaimed Mrs. Dorgan. "Why, who—?"

"Have you seen the other one lately?"

"Michael? No, not since mornin'. You can't be thinkin'—"

"I wouldn't put it past him, Margaret," said the doctor gravely. "The lad's mouth is swollen and cut, and his poor, skinny little leg is bruised. He surely didn't do it to himself and I think Helen suspects the other one."

"Lord save us!" said Mrs. Dorgan. "I'll run over and see if I can help."

"That's a good woman," said Doctor Ryan, and went on down the street.

Near midnight, when Midge came home, his mother was sitting at Connie's bedside. She did not look up.

"Well," said Midge, "what's the matter?"

She remained silent. Midge repeated his question.

"Michael, you know what's the matter," she said at length.

"I don't know nothin'," said Midge.

"Don't lie to me, Michael. What did you do to your brother?"

"Nothin'."

"You hit him."

"Well, then, I hit him. What of it? It ain't the first time."

Her lips pressed tightly together, her face like chalk, Ellen Kelly rose from her chair and made straight for him. Midge backed against the door.

"Lay off'n me, Ma. I don't want to fight no woman."

Still she came on breathing heavily.

"Stop where you're at, Ma," he warned.

There was a brief struggle and Midge's mother lay on the floor before him.

"You ain't hurt, Ma. You're lucky I didn't land good. And I told you to lay off'n me."

"God forgive you, Michael!"

Midge found Hap Collins in the showdown game at the Royal.

"Come on out a minute," he said.

Hap followed him out on the walk.

"I'm leavin' town for a w'ile," said Midge.

"What for?"

"Well, we had a little run-in up to the house. The kid stole a half buck off'n me, and when I went after it he cracked me with his crutch. So I nailed him. And the old lady came at me with a chair and I took it off'n her and she fell down."

"How is Connie hurt?"

"Not bad."

"What are you runnin' away for?"

"Who the hell said I was runnin' away? I'm sick and tired o' gettin' picked on; that's all. So I'm leavin' for a w'ile and I want a piece o' money."

"I ain't only got six bits," said Happy.

"You're in bad shape, ain't you? Well, come through with it."

Happy came through.

"You oughtn't to hit the kid," he said.

"I ain't astin' you who can I hit," snarled Midge. "You try to put somethin' over on me and you'll get the same dose. I'm goin' now."

"Go as far as you like," said Happy, but not until he was sure that Kelly was out of hearing.

Early the following morning, Midge boarded a train for Milwaukee. He had no ticket, but no one knew the difference. The conductor remained in the caboose.

On a night six months later, Midge hurried out of the "stage door" of the Star Boxing Club and made for Duane's saloon, two blocks away. In his pocket were twelve dollars, his reward for having battered up one Demon Dempsey through the six rounds of the first preliminary. It was Midge's first professional engagement in the manly art. Also it was the first time in weeks that he had earned twelve dollars.

On the way to Duane's he had to pass Niemann's. He pulled his cap over his eyes and increased his pace until he had gone by. Inside Niemann's stood a trusting bartender, who for ten days had staked Midge to drinks and allowed him to ravage the lunch on a promise to come in and settle the moment he was paid for the "prelim."

Midge strode into Duane's and aroused the napping bartender by slapping a silver dollar on the festive board.

"Gimme a shot," said Midge.

The shooting continued until the wind-up at the Star was over and part of the fight crowd joined Midge in front of Duane's bar. A youth in the early twenties, standing next to young Kelly, finally summoned sufficient courage to address him.

"Wasn't you in the first bout?" he ventured.

"Yeh," Midge replied.

"My name's Hersch," said the other.

Midge received the startling information in silence.

"I don't want to butt in," continued Mr. Hersch, "but I'd like to buy you a drink."

"All right," said Midge, "but don't overstrain yourself."

Mr. Hersch laughed uproariously and beckoned to the bartender.

"You certainly gave that wop a trimmin' tonight," said the buyer of the drink, when they had been served. "I thought you'd kill him."

"I would if I hadn't let up," Midge replied. "I'll kill 'em all."

"You got the wallop all right," the other said admiringly.

"Have I got the wallop?" said Midge. "Say, I can kick like a mule. Did you notice them muscles in my shoulders?"

"Notice 'em? I couldn't help from noticin' 'em," said Hersch. "I says to the fella settin' alongside o' me, I says: 'Look at them shoulders! No wonder he can hit,' I says to him."

"Just let me land and it's good-by, baby," said Midge. "I'll kill 'em all."

The oral manslaughter continued until Duane's closed for the night. At parting, Midge and his new friend shook hands and arranged for a meeting the following evening.

For nearly a week the two were together almost constantly. It was Hersch's pleasant rôle to listen to Midge's modest revelations concerning himself, and to buy every time Midge's glass was empty. But there came an evening when Hersch regretfully announced that he must go home to supper.

"I got a date for eight bells," he confided. "I could stick till then, only I must clean up and put on the Sunday clo'es, 'cause she's the prettiest little thing in Milwaukee."

"Can't you fix it for two?" asked Midge.

"I don't know who to get," Hersch replied. "Wait, though. I got a sister and if she ain't busy, it'll be O.K. She's no bum for looks herself."

So it came about that Midge and Emma Hersch and Emma's brother and the prettiest little thing in Milwaukee foregathered at Wall's and danced half the night away. And Midge and Emma danced every dance together, for though every little onestep seemed to induce a new thirst of its own, Lou Hersch stayed too sober to dance with his own sister.

The next day, penniless at last in spite of his phenomenal ability to make someone else settle, Midge Kelly sought out Doc Hammond, matchmaker for the Star, and asked to be booked for the next show.

"I could put you on with Tracy for the next bout," said Doc.

"What's they in it?" asked Midge.

"Twenty if you cop," Doc told him.

"Have a heart," protested Midge. "Didn't I look good the other night?"

"You looked all right. But you aren't Freddie Welsh yet by a consid'able margin."

"I ain't scared of Freddie Welsh or none of 'em," said Midge.

"Well, we don't pay our boxers by the size of their chests," Doc said. "I'm offerin' you this Tracy bout. Take it or leave it."

"All right; I'm on," said Midge, and he passed a pleasant afternoon at Duane's on the strength of his booking.

Young Tracy's manager came to Midge the night before the show.

"How do you feel about this go?" he asked.

"Me?" said Midge. "I feel all right. What do you mean, how do I feel?"

"I mean," said Tracy's manager, "that we're mighty anxious to win, 'cause the boy's got a chanct in Philly if he cops this one."

"What's your proposition?" asked Midge.

"Fifty bucks," said Tracy's manager.

"What do you think I am, a crook? Me lay down for fifty bucks. Not me!"

"Seventy-five, then," said Tracy's manager.

The market closed on eighty and the details were agreed on in short order. And the next night Midge was stopped in the second round by a terrific slap on the forearm.

This time Midge passed up both Niemann's and Duane's, having a sizable account at each place, and sought his refreshment at Stein's farther down the street.

When the profits of his deal with Tracy were gone, he learned, by first-hand information from Doc Hammond and the matchmakers at the other "clubs," that he was no longer desired for even the cheapest of preliminaries. There was no danger of his starving or dying of thirst while Emma and Lou Hersch lived. But he made up his mind, four months after his defeat by Young Tracy, that Milwaukee was not the ideal place for him to live.

"I can lick the best of 'em," he reasoned, "but there ain't no more chanct for me here. I can maybe go east and get on somewheres. And besides—"

But just after Midge had purchased a ticket to Chicago with the money he had "borrowed" from Emma Hersch "to buy shoes," a heavy hand was laid on his shoulders and he turned to face two strangers.

"Where are you goin', Kelly?" inquired the owner of the heavy hand.

"Nowheres," said Midge. "What the hell do you care?"

The other stranger spoke:

"Kelly, I'm employed by Emma Hersch's mother to see that you do right by her. And we want you to stay here till you've done it."

"You won't get nothin' but the worst of it, monkeying with me," said Midge.

Nevertheless, he did not depart for Chicago that night. Two days later, Emma Hersch became Mrs. Kelly, and the gift of the groom, when once they were alone, was a crushing blow on the bride's pale cheek.

Next morning, Midge left Milwaukee as he had entered it—by fast freight.

"They's no use kiddin' ourself any more," said Tommy Haley. "He might get down to thirty-seven in a pinch, but if he done below that a mouse could stop him. He's a welter; that's what he is and he knows it as well as I do. He's growed like a weed in the last six mont's. I told him, I says, 'If you don't quit growin' they won't be nobody for you to box, only Willard and them.' He says, 'Well, I wouldn't run away from Willard if I weighed twenty pounds more.'"

"He must hate himself," said Tommy's brother.

"I never seen a good one that didn't," said Tommy. "And Midge is a good one; don't make no mistake about that. I wisht we could of got Welsh before the kid growed so big. But it's too late now. I won't make no holler, though, if we can match him up with the Dutchman."

"Who do you mean?"

"Young Goetz, the welter champ. We mightn't not get so much dough for the bout itself, but it'd roll in afterward. What a drawin' card we'd be, 'cause the people pays their money to see the fella with the wallop, and that's Midge. And we'd keep the title just as long as Midge could make the weight."

"Can't you land no match with Goetz?"

"Sure, 'cause he needs the money. But I've went careful with the kid so far and look at the results I got! So what's the use of takin' a chanct? The kid's comin' every minute and Goetz is going back faster'n big Johnson did. I think we could lick him now; I'd bet my life on it. But six mont's from now they won't be no risk. He'll of licked hisself before that time. Then all as we'll have to do is sign up with him and wait for the referee to stop it. But Midge is so crazy to get at him now that I can't hardly hold him back."

The brothers Haley were lunching in a Boston hotel. Dan had come down from Holyoke to visit with Tommy and to watch the latter's protégé go twelve rounds, or less, with Bud Cross. The bout promised little in the way of a contest, for Midge had twice stopped the Baltimore youth and Bud's reputation for gameness was all that had earned him the date. The fans were willing to pay the price to see Midge's hay-making left, but they wanted to see it used on an opponent who would not jump out of the ring the first time he felt its crushing force. But Cross was such an opponent, and his willingness to stop boxing-gloves with his eyes, ears, nose, and throat had long enabled him to escape the horrors of honest labor. A game boy was Bud, and he showed it in his battered, swollen, discolored face.

"I should think," said Dan Haley, "that the kid'd do whatever you tell him after all you done for him."

"Well," said Tommy, "he's took my dope pretty straight so far, but he's so sure of hisself that he can't see no reason for waitin'. He'll do what I say, though; he'd be a sucker not to."

"You got a contrac' with him?"

"No, I don't need no contrac'. He knows it was me that drug him out o' the gutter and he ain't goin' to turn me down now, when he's got the dough and bound to get more. Where'd he of been at if I hadn't listened to him when he first come to me? That's pretty near two years ago now, but it seems like last week. I was settin' in the s'loon acrost from the Pleasant Club in Philly, waitin' for McCann to count the dough and come over, when this little bum blowed in and tried to stand the house off for a drink. They told him nothin' doin' and to beat it out o' there, and then he seen me and come over to where I was settin' and ast me wasn't I a boxin' man and I told him who I was. Then he ast me for money to buy a shot and I told him to set down and I'd buy it for him.

"Then we got talkin' things over and he told me his name and told me about fightin' a couple o' prelims out to Milwaukee. So I says, 'Well, boy, I don't know how good or how rotten you are, but you won't never get nowheres trainin' on that stuff.' So he says he'd cut it out if he could get on in a bout, and I says I would give him a chanct if he played square with me and didn't touch no more to drink. So we shook hands and I took him up to the hotel with me and give him a bath and the next day I bought him some clo'es. And I staked him to eats and sleeps for over six weeks. He had a hard time breakin' away from the polish, but finally I thought he was fit and I give him his chanct. He went on with Smiley Sayer and stopped him so quick that Smiley thought sure he was poisoned.

"Well, you know what he's did since. The only beatin' in his record was by Tracy in Milwaukee before I got hold of him, and he's licked Tracy three times in the last year.

"I've gave him all the best of it in a money way and he's got seven thousand bucks in cold storage. How's that for a kid that was in the gutter two years ago? And he'd have still more yet if he wasn't so nuts over clo'es and got to stop at the good hotels and so forth."

"Where's his home at?"

"Well, he ain't really got no home. He came from Chicago and his mother canned him out o' the house for bein' no good. She give him a raw deal, I guess, and he says he won't have nothin' to do with her unless she comes to him first. She's got a pile o' money, he says, so he ain't worryin' about her."

The gentleman under discussion entered the café and swaggered to Tommy's table, while the whole room turned to look.

Midge was the picture of health despite a slightly colored eye and an ear that seemed to have no opening. But perhaps it was not his healthiness that drew all eyes. His diamond horse-shoe tie pin, his purple cross-striped shirt, his orange shoes and his light blue suit fairly screamed for attention.

"Where you been?" he asked Tommy. "I been lookin' all over for you."

"Set down," said his manager.

"No time," said Midge. "I'm goin' down to the w'arf and see 'em unload the fish."

"Shake hands with my brother Dan," said Tommy.

Midge shook with the Holyoke Haley.

"If you're Tommy's brother, you're O.K. with me," said Midge, and the brothers beamed with pleasure.

Dan moistened his lips and murmured an embarrassed reply, but it was lost on the young gladiator.

"Leave me take twenty," Midge was saying. "I prob'ly won't need it, but I don't like to be caught short."

Tommy parted with a twenty dollar bill and recorded the transaction in a small black book the insurance company had given him for Christmas.

"But," he said, "it won't cost you no twenty to look at them fish. Want me to go along?"

"No," said Midge hastily. "You and your brother here prob'ly got a lot to say to each other."

"Well," said Tommy, "don't take no bad money and don't get lost. And you better be back at four o'clock and lay down a w'ile."

"I don't need no rest to beat this guy," said Midge. "He'll do enough layin' down for the both of us."

And laughing even more than the jest called for, he strode out through the fire of admiring and startled glances.

The corner of Boylston and Tremont was the nearest Midge got to the wharf, but the lady awaiting him was doubtless a more dazzling sight than the catch of the luckiest Massachusetts fisherman. She could talk, too—probably better than the fish.

"O you Kid!" she said, flashing a few silver teeth among the gold. "O you fighting man!"

Midge smiled up at her.

"We'll go somewheres and get a drink," he said. "One won't hurt."

In New Orleans, five months after he had re-arranged the map of Bud Cross for the third time, Midge finished training for his championship bout with the Dutchman.

Back in his hotel after the final workout, Midge stopped to chat with some of the boys from up north, who had made the long trip to see a champion dethroned, for the result of this bout was so nearly a foregone conclusion that even the experts had guessed it.

Tommy Haley secured the key and the mail and ascended to the Kelly suite. He was bathing when Midge came in, half hour later.

"Any mail?" asked Midge.

"There on the bed," replied Tommy from the tub.

Midge picked up the stack of letters and postcards and glanced them over. From the pile he sorted out three letters and laid them on the table. The rest he tossed into the wastebasket. Then he picked up the three and sat for a few moments holding them, while his eyes gazed off into space. At length he looked again at the three unopened letters in his hand; then he put one in his pocket and tossed the other two at the basket. They missed their target and fell on the floor.

"Hell!" said Midge, and stooping over picked them up.

He opened one postmarked Milwaukee and read:

Dear Husband:

I have wrote to you so manny times and got no anser and I dont know if you ever got them, so I am writeing again in the hopes you will get this letter and anser. I dont like to bother you with my trubles and I would not only for the baby and I am not asking you should write to me but only send a little money and I am

383

not asking for myself but the baby has not been well a day since last Aug. and the dr. told me she cant live much longer unless I give her better food and thats impossible the way things are. Lou has not been working for a year and what I make dont hardley pay for the rent. I am not asking for you to give me any money, but only you should send what I loaned when convenient and I think it amts. to about $36.00.

10 Please try and send that amt. and it will help me, but if you cant send the whole amt. try and send me something.

Your wife,
EMMA.

Midge tore the letter into a hundred pieces and scattered them over the floor.

"Money, money, money!" he said. "They must think I'm made o' money. I s'pose the old woman's after it too."

20 He opened his mother's letter:

dear Michael Connie wonted me to rite and say you must beet the dutchman and he is sur you will and wonted me to say we wont you to rite and tell us about it, but I gess you havent no time to rite or we herd from you long beffore this but I wish you would rite jest a line or 2 boy becaus it wuld be better for Connie then a barl of medisin. It wuld help me to keep things going if you send me money now and

30 then when you can spair it but if you cant send no money try and fine time to rite a letter onley a few lines and it will please Connie. jest think boy he hasent got out of bed in over 3 yrs. Connie says good luck.

Your Mother,
ELLEN F. KELLY.

"I thought so," said Midge. "They're all alike."

The third letter was from New York. It
40 read:

HON:—This is the last letter you will get from me before your champ, but I will send you a telegram Saturday, but I can't say as much in a telegram as in a letter and I am writeing this to let you know I am thinking of you and praying for good luck.

Lick him good hon and don't wait no longer than you have to and don't forget to wire me

as soon as its over. Give him that little old left of yours on the nose hon and don't be afraid of 50 spoiling his good looks because he couldn't be no homlier than he is. But don't let him spoil my baby's pretty face. You won't will you hon.

Well hon I would give anything to be there and see it, but I guess you love Haley better than me or you wouldn't let him keep me away. But when your champ hon we can do as we please and tell Haley to go to the devil.

Well hon I will send you a telegram Satur- 60 day and I almost forgot to tell you I will need some more money, a couple hundred say and you will have to wire it to me as soon as you get this. You will won't you hon.

I will send you a telegram Saturday and remember hon I am pulling for you.

Well good-by sweetheart and good luck.

GRACE.

"They're all alike," said Midge. "Money, money, money." 70

Tommy Haley, shining from his ablutions, came in from the adjoining room.

"Thought you'd be layin' down," he said.

"I'm goin' to," said Midge, unbuttoning his orange shoes.

"I'll call you at six and you can eat up here without no bugs to pester you. I got to go down and give them birds their tickets."

"Did you hear from Goldberg?" asked Midge. 80

"Didn't I tell you? Sure; fifteen weeks at five hundred, if we win. And we can get a guarantee o' twelve thousand, with privileges either in New York or Milwaukee."

"Who with?"

"Anybody that'll stand up in front of you. You don't care who it is, do you?"

"Not me. I'll make 'em all look like a monkey."

"Well you better lay down aw'ile." 90

"Oh, say, wire two hundred to Grace for me, will you? Right away; the New York address."

"Two hundred! You just sent her three hundred last Sunday."

"Well, what the hell do you care?"

"All right, all right. Don't get sore about it. Anything else?"

"That's all," said Midge, and dropped onto the bed.

"And I want the deed done before I come back," said Grace as she rose from the table, "You won't fall down on me, will you, hon?"

"Leave it to me," said Midge. "And don't spend no more than you have to."

Grace smiled a farewell and left the café. Midge continued to sip his coffee and read his paper.

They were in Chicago and they were in the middle of Midge's first week in vaudeville. He had come straight north to reap the rewards of his glorious victory over the broken down Dutchman. A fortnight had been spent in learning his act, which consisted of a gymnastic exhibition and a ten minutes' monologue on the various excellences of Midge Kelly. And now he was twice daily turning 'em away at the Madison Theater.

His breakfast over and his paper read, Midge sauntered into the lobby and asked for his key. He then beckoned to a bell-boy, who had been hoping for that very honor.

"Find Haley, Tommy Haley," said Midge. "Tell him to come up to my room."

"Yes, sir, Mr. Kelly," said the boy, and proceeded to break all his former records for diligence.

Midge was looking out of his seventh-story window when Tommy answered the summons.

"What'll it be?" inquired his manager.

There was a pause before Midge replied.

"Haley," he said, "twenty-five per cent's a whole lot o' money."

"I guess I got it comin', ain't I?" said Tommy.

"I don't see how you figger it. I don't see where you're worth it to me."

"Well," said Tommy. "I didn't expect nothin' like this. I thought you was satisfied with the bargain. I don't want to beat nobody out o' nothin', but I don't see where you could have got anybody else that would of did all I done for you."

"Sure, that's all right," said the champion. "You done a lot for me in Philly. And you got good money for it, didn't you?"

"I ain't makin' no holler. Still and all, the big money's still ahead of us yet. And if it hadn't

of been for me, you wouldn't of never got within grabbin' distance."

"Oh, I guess I could of went along all right," said Midge. "Who was it that hung that left on the Dutchman's jaw, me or you?"

"Yes, but you wouldn't been in the ring with the Dutchman if it wasn't for how I handled you."

"Well, this won't get us nowheres. The idear is that you ain't worth no twenty-five per cent now and it don't make no diff'rence what come off a year or two ago."

"Don't it?" said Tommy. "I'd say it made a whole lot of difference."

"Well, I say it don't and I guess that settles it."

"Look here, Midge," Tommy said, "I thought I was fair with you, but if you don't think so, I'm willin' to hear what you think is fair. I don't want nobody callin' me a Sherlock. Let's go down to business and sign up a contrac'. What's your figger?"

"I ain't namin' no figger," Midge replied. "I'm sayin' that twenty-five's too much. Now what are you willin' to take?"

"How about twenty?"

"Twenty's too much," said Kelly.

"What ain't too much?" asked Tommy.

"Well, Haley, I might as well give it to you straight. They ain't nothin' that ain't too much."

"You mean you don't want me at no figger?"

"That's the idear."

There was a minute's silence. Then Tommy Haley walked toward the door.

"Midge," he said, in a choking voice, "you're makin' a big mistake, boy. You can't throw down your best friends and get away with it. That damn woman will ruin you."

Midge sprang from his seat.

"You shut your mouth!" he stormed. "Get out o' here before they have to carry you out. You been spongin' off o' me long enough. Say one more word about the girl or about anything else and you'll get what the Dutchman got. Now get out!"

And Tommy Haley, having a very vivid memory of the Dutchman's face as he fell, got out.

Grace came in later, dropped her numerous bundles on the lounge and perched herself on the arm of Midge's chair.

"Well?" she said.

"Well," said Midge, "I got rid of him."

"Good boy!" said Grace. "And now I think you might give me that twenty-five per cent."

"Besides the seventy-five you're already gettin'?" said Midge.

"Don't be no grouch, hon. You don't look pretty when you're grouchy."

"It ain't my business to look pretty," Midge replied.

"Wait till you see how I look with the stuff I bought this mornin'!"

Midge glanced at the bundles on the lounge.

"There's Haley's twenty-five per cent," he said, "and then some."

The champion did not remain long without a manager. Haley's successor was none other than Jerome Harris, who saw in Midge a better meal ticket than his popular-priced musical show had been.

The contract, giving Mr. Harris twenty-five per cent of Midge's earnings, was signed in Detroit the week after Tommy Haley had heard his dismissal read. It had taken Midge just six days to learn that a popular actor cannot get on without the ministrations of a man who thinks, talks, and means business. At first Grace objected to the new member of the firm, but when Mr. Harris had demanded and secured from the vaudeville people a one-hundred dollar increase in Midge's weekly stipend, she was convinced that the champion had acted for the best.

"You and my missus will have some great old times," Harris told Grace. "I'd of wired her to join us here, only I seen the Kid's bookin' takes us to Milwaukee next week, and that's where she is."

But when they were introduced in the Milwaukee hotel, Grace admitted to herself that her feeling for Mrs. Harris could hardly be called love at first sight. Midge, on the contrary, gave his new manager's wife the many times over and seemed loath to end the feast of his eyes.

"Some doll," he said to Grace when they were alone.

"Doll is right," the lady replied, "and sawdust where her brains ought to be."

"I'm li'ble to steal that baby," said Midge, and he smiled as he noted the effect of his words on his audience's face.

On Tuesday of the Milwaukee week the champion successfully defended his title in a bout that the newspapers never reported. Midge was alone in his room that morning when a visitor entered without knocking. The visitor was Lou Hersch.

Midge turned white at the sight of him.

"What do you want?" he demanded.

"I guess you know," said Lou Hersch. "Your wife's starvin' to death and your baby's starvin' to death and I'm starvin' to death. And you're dirty with money."

"Listen," said Midge, "if it wasn't for you, I wouldn't never saw your sister. And, if you ain't man enough to hold a job, what's that to me? The best thing you can do is keep away from me."

"You give me a piece o' money and I'll go."

Midge's reply to the ultimatum was a straight right to his brother-in-law's narrow chest.

"Take that home to your sister."

And after Lou Hersch had picked himself up and slunk away, Midge thought: "It's lucky I didn't give him my left or I'd of croaked him. And if I'd hit him in the stomach, I'd of broke his spine."

There was a party after each evening performance during the Milwaukee engagement. The wine flowed freely and Midge had more of it than Tommy Haley ever would have permitted him. Mr. Harris offered no objection, which was possibly just as well for his own physical comfort.

In the dancing between drinks, Midge had his new manager's wife for a partner as often as Grace. The latter's face as she floundered round in the arms of the portly Harris, belied her frequent protestations that she was having the time of her life.

Several times that week, Midge thought Grace was on the point of starting the quarrel he hoped to have. But it was not until Friday night that she accommodated. He and Mrs. Harris had disappeared after the matinee and when Grace saw him again at the close of the night show, she came to the point at once.

"What are you tryin' to pull off?" she demanded.

"It's none o' your business, is it?" said Midge.

"You bet it's my business; mine and Harris's. You cut it short or you'll find out."

"Listen," said Midge, "have you got a mortgage on me or somethin'? You talk like we was married."

"We're goin' to be, too. And tomorrow's as good a time as any."

"Just about," Midge said. "You got as much chanct o' marryin' me tomorrow as the next day or next year and that ain't no chanct at all."

"We'll find out," said Grace.

"You're the one that's got somethin' to find out."

"What do you mean?"

"I mean I'm married already."

"You lie!"

"You think so, do you? Well, s'pose you go to this here address and get acquainted with my missus."

Midge scrawled a number on a piece of paper and handed it to her. She stared at it unseeingly.

"Well," said Midge, "I ain't kiddin' you. You go there and ask for Mrs. Michael Kelly, and if you don't find her, I'll marry you tomorrow before breakfast."

Still Grace stared at the scrap of paper. To Midge it seemed an age before she spoke again.

"You lied to me all this w'ile."

"You never ast me was I married. What's more, what the hell diff'rence did it make to you? You got a split, didn't you? Better'n fifty-fifty."

He started away.

"Where you goin'?"

"I'm goin' to meet Harris and his wife."

"I'm goin' with you. You're not goin' to shake me now."

"Yes, I am, too," said Midge quietly. "When I leave town tomorrow night, you're going to stay here. And if I see where you're goin' to make a fuss, I'll put you in a hospital where they'll keep you quiet. You can get your stuff tomorrow mornin' and I'll slip you a hundred bucks. And then I don't want to see no more o' you. And don't try and tag along now or I'll have to add another K.O. to the old record."

When Grace returned to the hotel that night, she discovered that Midge and the Harrises had moved to another. And when Midge left town the following night, he was again without a manager, and Mr. Harris was without a wife.

Three days prior to Midge Kelly's ten-round bout with Young Milton in New York City, the sporting editor of *The News* assigned Joe Morgan to write two or three thousand words about the champion to run with a picture lay-out for Sunday.

Joe Morgan dropped in at Midge's training quarters Friday afternoon. Midge, he learned, was doing road work, but Midge's manager, Wallie Adams, stood ready and willing to supply reams of dope about the greatest fighter of the age.

"Let's hear what you've got," said Joe, "and then I'll try to fix up something."

So Wallie stepped on the accelerator of his imagination and shot away.

"Just a kid; that's all he is; a regular boy. Get what I mean? Don't know the meanin' o' bad habits. Never tasted liquor in his life and would prob'ly get sick if he smelled it. Clean livin' put him up where he's at. Get what I mean? And modest and unassumin' as a school girl. He's so quiet you wouldn't never know he was round. And he'd go to jail before he'd talk about himself.

"No job at all to get him in shape, 'cause he's always that way. The only trouble we have with him is gettin' him to light into these poor bums they match him up with. He's scared he'll hurt somebody. Get what I mean? He's tickled to death over this match with Milton, 'cause everybody says Milton can stand the gaff. Midge'll maybe be able to cut loose a little this time. But the last two bouts he had, the guys hadn't no business in the ring with him, and he was holdin' back all the w'ile for the fear he'd kill somebody. Get what I mean?"

"Is he married?" inquired Joe.

"Say, you'd think he was married to hear him rave about them kiddies he's got. His fam'ly's up in Canada to their summer home and Midge is wild to get up there with 'em. He thinks more o' that wife and them kiddies than all the money in the world. Get what I mean?"

"How many children has he?"

"I don't know, four or five, I guess. All boys and every one of 'em a dead ringer for their dad."

"Is his father living?"

"No, the old man died when he was a kid. But he's got a grand old mother and a kid brother out in Chi. They're the first ones he thinks about after a match, them and his wife
10 and kiddies. And he don't forget to send the old woman a thousand bucks after every bout. He's going to buy her a new home as soon as they pay him off for this match."

"How about his brother? Is he going to tackle the game?"

"Sure, and Midge says he'll be a champion before he's twenty years old. They're a fightin' fam'ly and all of 'em honest and straight as a die. Get what I mean? A fella that I can't tell
20 you his name come to Midge in Milwaukee onct and wanted him to throw a fight and Midge give him such a trimmin' in the street that he couldn't go on that night. That's the kind he is. Get what I mean?"

Joe Morgan hung around the camp until Midge and his trainers returned.

"One o' the boys from *The News*," said Wallie by way of introduction. "I been givin' him your fam'ly hist'ry."

30 "Did he give you good dope?" he inquired.

"He's some historian," said Joe.

"Don't call me no names," said Wallie smiling. "Call us up if they's anything more you want. And keep your eyes on us Monday night. Get what I mean?"

The story in Sunday's *News* was read by thousands of lovers of the manly art. It was well written and full of human interest. Its slight inaccuracies went unchallenged, though three readers, besides Wallie Adams and Midge 40 Kelly, saw and recognized them. The three were Grace, Tommy Haley and Jerome Harris and the comments they made were not for publication.

Neither the Mrs. Kelly in Chicago nor the Mrs. Kelly in Milwaukee knew that there was such a paper as the New York *News*. And even if they had known of it and that it contained two columns of reading matter about Midge, neither mother nor wife could have bought it. 50 For *The News* on Sunday is a nickel a copy.

Joe Morgan could have written more accurately, no doubt, if instead of Wallie Adams, he had interviewed Ellen Kelly and Connie Kelly and Emma Kelly and Lou Hersch and Grace and Jerome Harris and Tommy Haley and Hap Collins and two or three Milwaukee bartenders.

But a story built on their evidence would never have passed the sporting editor. 60

"Suppose you can prove it," that gentleman would have said, "it wouldn't get us anything but abuse to print it. The people don't want to see him knocked. He's champion."

EUGENE O'NEILL

Eugene Gladstone O'Neill was born in New York City, October 6, 1888. His father was James O'Neill, a well-known actor of his day, who was especially famous for his rôle of Edmond Dantes in the dramatization of Dumas's novel, *The Count of Monte Cristo*. The first seven years of the younger O'Neill's life were spent in the larger towns of the United States, where his father went on his theatrical tours. Later the boy attended various Catholic schools, eventually graduating from Betts Academy at Stamford, Connecticut (1906). He matriculated at Princeton but left after a year because of a breach of college discipline.

For a time he served as secretary with a New York mail-order house; but a business life was not for him. Nor did his first marriage in 1909 succeed in settling him. Instead he developed a pronounced case of wanderlust. The years 1909–10 were spent on a gold-prospecting trip to Honduras. A sea voyage took him as far south as Buenos Aires, where he spent several months in a kind of waterfront existence. This vagabondage gave him invaluable first-hand material, which he was later to use most effectively in his plays. Eventually he turned up in New Orleans without either a job or the prospects of one; by good fortune his father's theatrical company was then playing in the city, and the son was enabled to return somewhat in the manner of the Prodigal. For a short time thereafter he acted as assistant manager to the troupe (1910). But the need for some kind of literary occupation was manifesting itself. As one means of satisfying this instinct he took a position as reporter on the New London (Connecticut) *Telegraph* (1911).

The New London job was interrupted by the unforeseen onset of tuberculosis, which forced upon O'Neill a five months' stay in a sanitarium at Wallingford, Connecticut, and imposed upon him the necessity of a carefully regimented life. His experience there has been painted unforgettably in the pathetic little play, *The Straw* (1921). During the long hours of his stay at Wallingford he began "thinking it over." Obviously his conclusion was to adopt playwriting for his career—it was in his blood and heritage anyway—and to submit to the discipline necessary to a success in his chosen field. His knowledge of the practical theater had been intimate from his boyhood, but he desired a sterner training in dramatic theory. He therefore enrolled at Harvard for study in Professor George P. Baker's famous English 47 (Workshop) course (1914–15). Following the completion of the course he spent some time in Greenwich Village, which in that very year (1915) was beginning to gain a national reputation as a breeding-place for the younger distinguished literary lights.

The summer of 1915, however, took him to Cape Cod, near the famous artists' colony at Provincetown, Massachusetts. Here the Provincetown Players were beginning to make a name for themselves in the new experimental American drama. O'Neill and this association of players found themselves mutually beneficial; at least the association, by producing *Thirst* and *Bound East for Cardiff*, published in 1916 as *Provincetown Plays*, made O'Neill known to a small, advanced public and put him on his feet as a dramatist, while in O'Neill the players found a fresh dramatic talent endowed with power and an intuitive compre-

hension of what makes for the dramatic. The Provincetown Players moved to New York for the winter of 1916–17, and during the next three or four years produced no less than ten plays, most of them short one-acters, from the pen of the rising young author. Of these ten, O'Neill published three through the sympathetic coöperation of the *Smart Set* magazine, then under the editorship of Henry L. Mencken (p. 67) and George Jean Nathan. These three plays, all inspired by O'Neill's experience as a seafarer, were *The Long Voyage Home* (1917), *Ile* (1918), and *The Moon of the Caribbees* (1918). All are short; all are pathetic if not downright tragic; and the last of the three has a poignant climax which is lyrical in its emotional force.

O'Neill's apprenticeship had now been fully served. *Beyond the Horizon*, which followed (1920), was his first full-length play to have a general success. It won the Pulitzer Prize for Drama in that same year. More effective, however, were the next three plays, *The Emperor Jones* (1921), a powerful study of disintegrating terror in the mind of a simple Negro; *The Hairy Ape* (1922), the tragedy of a stoker on a transatlantic liner who realizes his position among the misfits of society; and *Anna Christie* (1922), the touching account of the misfortunes a bargeman's daughter suffered because she had once been a prostitute. The last-named of these three plays again won for the author a Pulitzer Prize and in addition the gold medal annually awarded a drama by the National Institute of Arts and Letters. The high dramatic standard of these three plays was not maintained, however, in any of those immediately following. There was *Desire Under the Elms* (1924), a morbid study of degeneration in a New England scene (O'Neill has always had the commonly held but poorly based prejudice against New England and its people), which more or less deserved the Broadway quip that it should have been called "Lust Under the Shingles." *Marco Millions* (1924) and *The Great God Brown* (1925) were only moderately successful; in the second of these plays O'Neill adopted the venerable symbolism of the mask for all his characters to indicate their essential hypocrisies. *Lazarus Laughed* (1926) and *Dynamo* (1928), indictments of our machine age and its pharisaical qualities, succeeded no better.

The dramatist now proceeded to a bold innovation—the dramatic trilogy, in which the production of all three plays is made at the same performance with only brief intermissions. *Strange Interlude* (1928), the drama of an oversexed female and her mates, is a monument to the Jazz Age; it is good, though attenuated, theater, and is particularly noteworthy for its technique, which includes an audacious use of the soliloquy and the aside, two well-known devices of Elizabethan drama. *Mourning Becomes Electra* (1931) is, like its predecessor, a trilogy but it is a much more remarkable performance. It goes to New England for its setting. Its theme is essentially the tragic Greek theme of guilt washed out in blood; its overtones are deep, morbid, and unnatural, sounding as they do the degeneration of a family into incest and violence. Yet it is grim, austere, and magnificent.

Thus far in his career O'Neill had won a reputation as a strong, original dramatist of pessimism and gloom; and critics, while recognizing his genius, pointed out his essential one-sidedness in no uncertain terms. As if to refute those critics, O'Neill now turned to a charmingly nostalgic, sentimental domestic comedy, *Ah! Wilderness* (1932), as different from his earlier plays as black from white. It seemed, indeed, that we had come to a new stage in the author's development. *Days Without End* (1933) was virtually a failure and can be ignored. After that fiasco, O'Neill spent the next dozen years in seclusion, working on an entire chain of new plays. Only two plays of this chain have appeared at the present time: *The Iceman Cometh* (1946) and *Moon for the Misbegotten,* which was presented briefly on the road in 1947 but which never reached Broadway. Ill health had put an end to O'Neill's writing several years before his death in 1953.

O'Neill was by nature a reticent, retiring individual, sensitive to the point of withdrawing from society for long periods. He avoided the city at all times and saw only three of his own plays on the stage. He summered on Cape Cod in a small shack near Provincetown, miles from civilization; he rusticated in Bermuda and in France; he went around the world on sea voyages. He remained, in spite of the inevitable dating of many of his plays, an isolated but impressive figure, whose achievement in his chosen field, while far from consistent, is on the whole solid and unshakable. In spite of his occasional sentimentality and his dim view of the human psyche, he richly deserved the award of the Nobel Prize in Literature in 1936; and he still stands as unquestionably the most arresting American playwright of the 1920's.

The Hairy Ape

A COMEDY OF ANCIENT AND MODERN LIFE IN EIGHT SCENES

CHARACTERS

ROBERT SMITH, "YANK"
PADDY
LONG
MILDRED DOUGLAS
HER AUNT
SECOND ENGINEER
A GUARD
A SECRETARY OF AN ORGANIZATION
STOKERS, LADIES, GENTLEMEN, ETC.

SCENES

SCENE I: *The firemen's forecastle of an ocean liner—an hour after sailing from New York.*

SCENE II: *Section of promenade deck, two days out—morning.*

SCENE III: *The stokehole. A few minutes later.*

SCENE IV: *Same as Scene I. Half an hour later.*

SCENE V: *Fifth Avenue, New York. Three weeks later.*

SCENE VI: *An island near the city. The next night.*

SCENE VII: *In the city. About a month later.*

SCENE VIII: *In the city. Twilight of the next day.*

The Hairy Ape is reprinted by permission of Random House, Inc., New York.

SCENE ONE

SCENE—*The firemen's forecastle of a transatlantic liner an hour after sailing from New York for the voyage across. Tiers of narrow, steel bunks, three deep, on all sides. An entrance in rear. Benches on the floor before the bunks. The room is crowded with men, shouting, cursing, laughing, singing—a confused, inchoate uproar swelling into a sort of unity, a meaning—the bewildered, furious, baffled defiance of a beast in a cage. Nearly all the men are drunk. Many bottles are passed from hand to hand. All are dressed in dungaree pants, heavy ugly shoes. Some wear singlets, but the majority are stripped to the waist.*

The treatment of this scene, or of any other scene in the play, should by no means be naturalistic. The effect sought after is a cramped space in the bowels of a ship, imprisoned by white steel. The lines of bunks, the uprights supporting them, cross each other like the steel framework of a cage. The ceiling crushes down upon the men's heads. They cannot stand upright. This accentuates the natural stooping posture which shoveling coal and the resultant over-development of back and shoulder muscles have given them. The men themselves should resemble those pictures in which the appearance of Neanderthal Man is guessed at. All are hairy-chested, with long arms of tremendous power, and low, receding brows above their small, fierce, resentful eyes. All the civilized white races are represented, but except for the slight differentiation in color of hair, skin, eyes, all these men are alike.

The curtain rises on a tumult of sound. YANK *is seated in the foreground. He seems broader, fiercer, more truculent, more powerful, more sure of himself than the rest. They respect his superior strength—the grudging respect of fear. Then, too, he represents to them a self-expression, the very last word in what they are, their most highly developed individual.*

VOICES. Gif me trink dere, you!
    'Ave a wet!
    Salute!

Gesundheit!
Skoal!
Drunk as a lord, God stiffen you!
Here's how!
Luck!
Pass back that bottle, damn you!
Pourin' it down his neck!
Ho, Froggy! Where the devil have you been?
La Touraine.
I hit him smash in yaw, py Gott!
Jenkins—the First—he's a rotten swine—
And the coppers nabbed him—and I run—
I like peer better. It don't pig head gif you.
A slut, I'm sayin'! She robbed me aslape—
To hell with 'em all!
You're a bloody liar!
Say dot again! (*Commotion. Two men about to fight are pulled apart.*)
No scrappin' now!
Tonight—
See who's the best man!
Bloody Dutchman!
Tonight on the for'ard square.
I'll bet on Dutchy.
He packa da wallop, I tella you!
Shut up, Wop!
No fightin', maties. We're all chums, ain't we?
(*A voice starts bawling a song.*)
"Beer, beer, glorious beer!
Fill yourself right up to here."

YANK (*For the first time seeming to take notice of the uproar about him, turns around threateningly—in a tone of contemptuous authority*). Choke off dat noise! Where d'yuh get dat beer stuff? Beer, hell! Beer's for goils—and Dutchmen. Me for somep'n wit a kick to it! Gimme a drink, one of youse guys. (*Several bottles are eagerly offered. He takes a tremendous gulp at one of them; then, keeping the bottle in his hand, glares belligerently at the owner, who hastens to acquiesce in this robbery by saying—*) All righto, Yank. Keep it and have another. (YANK *contemptuously turns his back on the crowd again. For a second there is an embarrassed silence. Then—*)

VOICES. We must be passing the Hook.
    She's beginning to roll to it.
    Six days in hell—and then Southamp-
        ton.
    Py Yesus, I vish somepody take my
        first vatch for me!
    Gittin' seasick, Square-head?
    Drink up and forget it!
    What's in your bottle?
10   Gin.
    Dot's nigger trink.
    Absinthe? It's doped. You'll go off
        your chump, Froggy!
    Cochon!
    Whisky, that's the ticket!
    Where's Paddy?
    Going asleep.
    Sing us that whisky song, Paddy.

(*They all turn to an old, wizened Irishman who is dozing, very drunk, on the benches forward. His face is extremely monkey-like with all the sad, patient pathos of that animal in his small eyes.*)
    Singa da song, Caruso Pat!
20   He's gettin' old. The drink is too
        much for him.
    He's too drunk.

PADDY (*Blinking about him, starts to his feet resentfully, swaying, holding on to the edge of a bunk*). I'm never too drunk to sing. 'Tis only when I'm dead to the world I'd be wishful to sing at all. (*With a sort of sad contempt.*) "Whisky Johnny," ye want? A chanty, ye want? Now that's a queer wish from the ugly like of
30 you, God help you. But no mather. (*He starts to sing in a thin, nasal, doleful tone*):

Oh, whisky is the life of man!
    Whisky! O Johnny! (*They all join in on this.*)
Oh, whisky is the life of man!
    Whisky for my Johnny! (*Again chorus*).
Oh, whisky drove my old man mad!
    Whisky! O Johnny!
Oh, whisky drove my old man mad!
40   Whisky for my Johnny!

YANK (*Again turning around scornfully*). Aw hell! Nix on dat old sailing ship stuff! All dat bull's dead, see? And you're dead, too, yuh damned old Harp, on'y yuh don't know it.

Take it easy, see. Give us a rest. Nix on de loud noise. (*With a cynical grin*). Can't youse see I'm tryin' to t'ink?

ALL (*Repeating the word after him as one with the same cynical amused mockery*). Think! (*The chorused word has a brazen me-* 50 *tallic quality as if their throats were phonograph horns. It is followed by a general uproar of hard, barking laughter.*)

VOICES. Don't be cracking your head wit ut, Yank.
    You gat headache, py yingo!
    One thing about it—it rhymes with drink!
    Ha, ha, ha!
    Drink, don't think! 60
    Drink, don't think!
    Drink, don't think! (*A whole chorus of voices has taken up this refrain, stamping on the floor, pounding on the benches with fists.*)

YANK (*Taking a gulp from his bottle—good-naturedly*). Aw right. Can de noise. I got yuh de foist time. (*The uproar subsides. A very drunken sentimental tenor begins to sing*):

"Far away in Canada, 70
    Far across the sea,
There's a lass who fondly waits
    Making a home for me——"

YANK (*Fiercely contemptuous*). Shut up, yuh lousy boob! Where d'yuh get dat tripe? Home? Home, hell! I'll make a home for yuh! I'll knock yuh dead. Home! T'hell wit home! Where d'yuh get dat tripe? Dis is home, see? What d'yuh want wit home? (*Proudly*). I runned away from mine when I was a kid. On'y 80 too glad to beat it, dat was me. Home was lickings for me, dat's all. But yuh can bet your shoit no one ain't never licked me since! Wanter try it, any of youse? Huh! I guess not. (*In a more placated but still contemptuous tone*). Goils waitin' for yuh, huh? Aw, hell! Dat's all tripe. Dey don't wait for no one. Dey'd double-cross yuh for a nickel. Dey're all tarts, get me? Treat 'em rough, dat's me. To hell wit 'em. Tarts, dat's what, de whole bunch of 'em. 90

LONG (*Very drunk, jumps on a bench excitedly, gesticulating with a bottle in his hand*). Listen 'ere, Comrades. Yank 'ere is right. 'E says this 'ere stinkin' ship is our 'ome. And 'e says as 'ome is 'ell. And 'e's right! This is 'ell. We lives in 'ell, Comrades—and right enough we'll die in it. (*Raging*). And who's ter blame, I arsks yer? We ain't. We wasn't born this rotten way. All men is born free and ekal. That's in the bleedin' Bible, maties. But what d'they care for the Bible—them lazy, bloated swine what travels first cabin? Them's the ones. They dragged us down 'til we're on'y wage slaves in the bowels of a bloody ship, sweatin', burnin' up, eatin' coal dust! Hit's them's ter blame—the damned Capitalist clarss! (*There had been a gradual murmur of contemptuous resentment rising among the men until now he is interrupted by a storm of catcalls, hisses, boos, hard laughter.*)

VOICES. Turn it off!
  Shut up!
  Sit down!
  Closa da face!
  Tamn fool! (*Etc.*)

YANK (*Standing up and glaring at* LONG). Sit down before I knock yuh down! (LONG *makes haste to efface himself.* YANK *goes on contemptuously.*) De Bible, huh? De Cap'tlist class, huh? Aw nix on dat Salvation Army-Socialist bull. Git a soapbox! Hire a hall! Come and be saved, huh? Jerk us to Jesus, huh? Aw g'wan! I've listened to lots of guys like you, see. Yuh're all wrong. Wanter know what I t'ink? Yuh ain't no good for no one. Yuh're de bunk. Yuh ain't got no noive, get me? Yuh're yellow, dat's what. Yellow, dat's you. Say! What's dem slobs in de foist cabin got to do wit us? We're better men dan dey are, ain't we? Sure! One of us guys could clean up de whole mob wit one mit. Put one of 'em down here for one watch in de stokehole, what'd happen? Dey'd carry him off on a stretcher. Dem boids don't amount to nothin'. Dey're just baggage. Who makes dis old tub run? Ain't it us guys? Well den, we belong, don't we? We belong and dey don't. Dat's all. (*A loud chorus of approval.* YANK *goes on.*) As for dis bein' hell—aw, nuts! Yuh lost your noive, dat's what. Dis is a man's job, get me? It belongs. It runs dis tub. No stiffs need apply. But yuh're a stiff, see? Yuh're yellow, dat's you.

VOICES (*With a great hard pride in them*).
  Righto!
  A man's job!

Talk is cheap, Long.
He never could hold up his end.
Divil take him!
Yank's right. We make it go.
Py Gott, Yank say right ting!
We don't need no one cryin' over us.
Makin' speeches.
Throw him out!
Yellow!
Chuck him overboard!
I'll break his jaw for him!
(*They crowd around* LONG *threateningly.*)

YANK (*Half good-natured again—contemptuously*). Aw, take it easy. Leave him alone. He ain't woith a punch. Drink up. Here's how, whoever owns dis. (*He takes a long swallow from his bottle. All drink with him. In a flash all is hilarious amiability again, back-slapping, loud talk, etc.*)

PADDY (*Who has been sitting in a blinking, melancholy daze—suddenly cries out in a voice full of old sorrow*). We belong to this, you're saying? We make the ship to go, you're saying? Yerra then, that Almighty God have pity on us! (*His voice runs into the wail of a keen, he rocks back and forth on his bench. The men stare at him, startled and impressed in spite of themselves.*) Oh, to be back in the fine days of my youth, ochone! Oh, there was fine beautiful ships them days—clippers wid tall masts touching the sky—fine strong men in them— men that was sons of the sea as if 'twas the mother that bore them. Oh, the clean skins of them, and the clear eyes, the straight backs and full chests of them! Brave men they was, and bold men surely! We'd be sailing out, bound down round the Horn maybe. We'd be making sail in the dawn, with a fair breeze, singing a chanty song wid no care to it. And astern the land would be sinking low and dying out, but we'd give it no heed but a laugh, and never a look behind. For the day that was, was enough, for we was free men—and I'm thinking 'tis only slaves do be giving heed to the day that's gone or the day to come—until they're old like me. (*With a sort of religious exaltation*). Oh, to be scudding south again wid the power of the Trade Wind driving her on steady through the nights and the days! Full sail on her! Nights and days! Nights when

the foam of the wake would be flaming wid
fire, when the sky'd be blazing and winking
wid stars. Or the full of the moon maybe.
Then you'd see her driving through the gray
night, her sails stretching aloft all silver and
white, not a sound on the deck, the lot of us
dreaming dreams, till you'd believe 'twas no
real ship at all you was on but a ghost ship like
the *Flying Dutchman* they say does be roam-
10 ing the seas forevermore widout touching a
port. And there was the days, too. A warm sun
on the clean decks. Sun warming the blood of
you, and wind over the miles of shiny green
ocean like strong drink to your lungs. Work—
aye, hard work—but who'd mind that at all?
Sure, you worked under the sky and 'twas work
wid skill and daring to it. And wid the day
done, in the dog watch, smoking me pipe at
ease, the lookout would be raising land maybe,
20 and we'd see the mountains of South Americy
wid the red fire of the setting sun painting
their white tops and the clouds floating by
them! (*His tone of exaltation ceases. He goes
on mournfully.*) Yerra, what's the use of talking? 'Tis a dead man's whisper. (*To* YANK *resentfully*). 'Twas them days men belonged to
ships, not now. 'Twas them days a ship was
part of the sea, and a man was part of a ship,
and the sea joined all together and made it one.
30 (*Scornfully*). Is it one wid this you'd be, Yank
—black smoke from the funnels smudging the
sea, smudging the decks—the bloody engines
pounding and throbbing and shaking—wid divil
a sight of sun or a breath of clean air—choking
our lungs wid coal dust—breaking our backs
and hearts in the hell of the stokehole—feeding the bloody furnace—feeding our lives along
wid the coal, I'm thinking—caged in by steel
from a sight of the sky like bloody apes in the
40 Zoo! (*With a harsh laugh*). Ho-ho, divil mend
you! Is it to belong to that you're wishing? Is
it a flesh and blood wheel of the engines you'd
be?

9. *Flying Dutchman.* According to an old legend a Dutch sea-
captain, detained for an intolerable while from rounding the
Cape of Good Hope by adverse winds, swore that he would sail
round the Cape if it took until doomsday. For this rash oath he
was condemned by the fates to travel restlessly for eternity
unless he could find some woman who would be true to him
until death. The ghost-ship of the Flying Dutchman is probably
the most noted supernatural ship of marine legendry. The story
is told in Wagner's opera, *The Flying Dutchman* (*Der Fliegende
Holländer*). 18. dog watch, a watch of two hours aboard ship,
from 4 to 6 P.M. and from 6 to 8 P.M., unlike the usual four-
hour watches.

YANK (*Who had been listening with a contemptuous sneer, barks out the answer*). Sure
ting! Dat's me. What about it?

PADDY (*As if to himself—with great sorrow*).
Me time is past due. That a great wave wid
sun in the heart of it may sweep me over the
side sometime I'd be dreaming of the days
that's gone!

YANK. Aw, yuh crazy Mick! (*He springs to
his feet and advances on Paddy threateningly
—then stops, fighting some queer struggle
within himself—lets his hands fall to his sides—
contemptuously.*) Aw, take it easy. Yuh're aw
right, at dat. Yuh're bugs, dat's all—nutty as a
cuckoo. All dat tripe yuh been pullin'—Aw,
dat's all right. On'y it's dead, get me? Yuh don't
belong no more, see. Yuh don't get de stuff.
Yuh're too old. (*Disgustedly*). But aw say,
come up for air onct in a while, can't yuh? See
what's happened since yuh croaked. (*He suddenly burst forth vehemently, growing more
and more excited.*) Say! Sure! Sure I meant it!
What de hell—Say, lemme talk! Hey! Hey, you
old Harp! Hey, youse guys! Say, listen to me
—wait a moment—I gotta talk, see. I belong
and he don't. He's dead but I'm livin'. Listen
to me! Sure I'm part of de engines! Why de
hell not? Dey move, don't dey? Dey're speed,
ain't dey? Dey smash trou, don't dey? Twenty-
five knots a hour! Dat's goin' some! Dat's new
stuff! Dat belongs! But him, he's too old. He
gets dizzy. Say listen. All dat crazy tripe about
nights and days; all dat crazy tripe about stars
and moons; all dat crazy tripe about suns and
winds, fresh air and de rest of it—Aw hell, dat's
all a dope dream! Hittin' de pipe of de past,
dat's what he's doin'. He's old and don't belong no more. But me, I'm young! I'm in de
pink! I move wit it! It, get me! I mean de ting
dat's de guts of all dis. It ploughs trou all de
tripe he's been sayin'. It blows dat up! It
knocks dat dead! It slams dat offen de face of
de oith! It, get me! De engines and de coal
and de smoke and all de rest of it! He can't
breathe and swallow coal dust, but I kin, see?
Dat's fresh air for me! Dat's food for me! I'm
new, get me? Hell in de stokehole? Sure! It
takes a man to work in hell. Hell, sure, dat's
my fav'rite climate. I eat it up! I git fat on it!
It's me makes it hot! It's me makes it roar! It's
me makes it move! Sure, on'y for me everyting

stops. It all goes dead, get me? De noise and smoke and all de engines movin' de woild, dey stop. Dere ain't nothin' no more! Dat's what I'm sayin'. Everyting else dat makes de woild move, somep'n makes it move. It can't move without somep'n else, see? Den yuh get down to me. I'm at de bottom, get me! Dere ain't nothin' foither. I'm de end! I'm de start! I start somep'n and de woild moves! It—dat's me!—de new dat's moiderin' de old! I'm de ting in coal dat makes it boin; I'm steam and oil for de engines; I'm de ting in noise dat makes yuh hear it; I'm smoke and express trains and steamers and factory whistles; I'm de ting in gold dat makes money! And I'm what makes iron into steel! Steel, dat stands for de whole ting! And I'm steel—steel—steel! I'm de muscles in steel, de punch behind it! (*As he says this he pounds with his fist against the steel bunks. All the men roused to a pitch of frenzied self-glorification by his speech, do likewise. There is a deafening metallic roar, through which* YANK's *voice can be heard bellowing.*) Slaves, hell! We run de whole woiks. All de rich guys dat tink dey're somep'n, dey ain't nothin'! Dey don't belong. But us guys, we're in de move, we're at de bottom, de whole ting is us! (PADDY *from the start of* YANK's *speech has been taking one gulp after another from his bottle, at first frightenedly, as if he were afraid to listen, then desperately, as if to drown his senses, but finally has achieved complete indifferent, even amused, drunkenness.* YANK *sees his lips moving. He quells the uproar with a shout.*) Hey, youse guys, take it easy! Wait a moment! De nutty Harp is sayin' somep'n.

PADDY (*Is heard now—throws his head back with a mocking burst of laughter*). Ho-ho-ho-ho-ho——

YANK (*Drawing back his fist, with a snarl*). Aw! Look out who yuh're givin' the bark!

PADDY (*Begins to sing the "Miller of Dee" with enormous good nature*).

"I care for nobody, no, not I,
And nobody cares for me."

YANK (*Good-natured himself in a flash, interrupts* PADDY *with a slap on the bare back like a report*). Dat's de stuff! Now yuh're gettin' wise to somep'n. Care for nobody, dat's de dope! To hell wit 'em all! And nix on nobody else carin'. I kin care for myself, get me! (*Eight bells sound, muffled, vibrating through the steel walls as if some enormous brazen gong were imbedded in the heart of the ship. All the men jump up mechanically, file through the door silently close upon each other's heels in what is very like a prisoners' lockstep.* YANK *slaps* PADDY *on the back.*) Our watch, yuh old Harp! (*Mockingly*). Come on down in hell. Eat up de coal dust. Drink in de heat. It's it, see! Act like yuh liked it, yuh better—or croak yuhself.

PADDY (*With jovial defiance*). To the divil wid it! I'll not report this watch. Let thim log me and be damned. I'm no slave the like of you. I'll be sittin' here at me ease, and drinking, and thinking, and dreaming dreams.

YANK (*Contemptuously*). Tinkin' and dreamin', what'll that get yuh? What's tinkin' got to do wit it? We move, don't we? Speed, ain't it? Fog, dat's all you stand for. But we drive trou dat, don't we? We split dat up and smash trou—twenty-five knots a hour! (*Turns his back on* PADDY *scornfully*). Aw, yuh make me sick! Yuh don't belong! (*He strides out the door in rear.* PADDY *hums to himself, blinking drowsily.*)

(Curtain)

SCENE TWO

SCENE—*Two days out. A section of the promenade deck.* MILDRED DOUGLAS *and her aunt are discovered reclining in deck chairs. The former is a girl of twenty, slender, delicate, with a pale, pretty face marred by a self-conscious expression of disdainful superiority. She looks fretful, nervous and discontented, bored by her own anemia. Her aunt is a pompous and proud—and fat—old lady. She is a type even to the point of a double chin and lorgnettes. She is dressed pretentiously, as if afraid her face alone would never indicate her position in life.* MILDRED *is dressed all in white.*

The impression to be conveyed by this scene is one of the beautiful, vivid life of the sea all about—sunshine on the deck in a great flood, the fresh sea wind blowing across it. In the midst of this, these two incongruous, artificial figures, inert and dis-

*harmonious, the elder like a gray lump of
dough touched up with rouge, the younger
looking as if the vitality of her stock had
been sapped before she was conceived, so
that she is the expression not of its life
energy but merely of the artificialities that
energy had won for itself in the spending.*

MILDRED (*Looking up with affected dream-
iness*). How the black smoke swirls back
against the sky! Is it not beautiful?

AUNT (*Without looking up*). I dislike smoke
of any kind.

MILDRED. My great-grandmother smoked a
pipe—a clay pipe.

AUNT (*Ruffling*). Vulgar!

MILDRED. She was too distant a relative to
10 be vulgar. Time mellows pipes.

AUNT (*Pretending boredom but irritated*).
Did the sociology you took up at college teach
you that—to play the ghoul on every possible
occasion, excavating old bones? Why not let
your great-grandmother rest in her grave?

MILDRED (*Dreamily*). With her pipe beside
her—puffing in Paradise.

AUNT (*With spite*). Yes, you are a natural
born ghoul. You are even getting to look like
20 one, my dear.

MILDRED (*In a passionless tone*). I detest
you, Aunt. (*Looking at her critically*). Do you
know what you remind me of? Of a cold pork
pudding against a background of linoleum
tablecloth in the kitchen of a—but the possibilities are wearisome. (*She closes her eyes.*)

AUNT (*With a bitter laugh*). Merci for your
candor. But since I am and must be your chaperon—in appearance—at least—let us patch up
30 some sort of armed truce. For my part you
are quite free to indulge any pose of eccentricity that beguiles you—as long as you observe the amenities——

MILDRED (*Drawling*). The inanities?

AUNT. (*Going on as if she hadn't heard*).
After exhausting the morbid thrills of social
service work on New York's East Side—how
they must have hated you, by the way, the
poor that you made so much poorer in their
40 own eyes!—you are now bent on making your
slumming international. Well, I hope White-

chapel will provide the needed nerve tonic. Do
not ask me to chaperon you there, however. I
told your father I would not. I loathe deformity. We will hire an army of detectives and you
may investigate everything—they allow you to
see.

MILDRED (*Protesting with a trace of genuine earnestness*). Please do not mock at my attempts to discover how the other half lives.
Give me credit for some sort of groping sincerity in that at least. I would like to help
them. I would like to be of some use in the
world. Is it my fault I don't know how? I
would like to be sincere, to touch life somewhere. (*With weary bitterness*). But I'm afraid
I have neither the vitality nor integrity. All
that was burnt out in our stock before I was
born. Grandfather's blast furnaces, flaming
to the sky, melting steel, making millions—
then father keeping those home fires burning,
making more millions—and little me at the tail-
end of it all. I'm a waste product in the Bes-
semer process—like the millions. Or rather, I
inherit the acquired trait of the by-product,
wealth, but none of the energy, none of the
strength of the steel that made it. I am sired
by gold and damned by it, as they say at the
race track—damned in more ways than one.
(*She laughs mirthlessly.*)

AUNT (*Unimpressed—superciliously*). You
seem to be going in for sincerity today. It isn't
becoming to you, really—except as an obvious
pose. Be as artificial as you are, I advise.
There's a sort of sincerity in that, you know.
And, after all, you must confess you like that
better.

MILDRED (*Again affected and bored*). Yes,
I suppose I do. Pardon me for my outburst.
When a leopard complains of its spots, it must
sound rather grotesque. (*In a mocking tone*).
Purr, little leopard. Purr, scratch, tear, kill,
gorge yourself and be happy—only stay in the
jungle where your spots are camouflage. In a
cage they make you conspicuous.

AUNT. I don't know what you are talking
about.

MILDRED. It would be rude to talk about
anything to you. Let's just talk. (*She looks at
her wrist watch.*) Well, thank goodness, it's
about time for them to come for me. That
ought to give me a new thrill, Aunt.

AUNT (*Affectedly troubled*). You don't mean

---

41. **Whitechapel,** a district in the eastern portion of the city
of London, noted for its squalid slums.

to say you're really going? The dirt—the heat must be frightful——

MILDRED. Grandfather started as a puddler. I should have inherited an immunity to heat that would make a salamander shiver. It will be fun to put it to the test.

AUNT. But don't you have to have the captain's—or someone's—permission to visit the stokehole?

MILDRED (*With a triumphant smile*). I have it—both his and the chief engineer's. Oh, they didn't want to at first, in spite of my social service credentials. They didn't seem a bit anxious that I should investigate how the other half lives and works on a ship. So I had to tell them that my father, the president of Nazareth Steel, chairman of the board of directors of this line, had told me it would be all right.

AUNT. He didn't.

MILDRED. How naïve age makes one! But I said he did, Aunt. I even said he had given me a letter to them—which I had lost. And they were afraid to take the chance that I might be lying. (*Excitedly*). So it's ho! for the stokehole. The second engineer is to escort me. (*Looking at her watch again*). It's time. And here he comes, I think. (*The* SECOND ENGINEER *enters. He is a husky, fine-looking man of thirty-five or so. He stops before the two and tips his cap, visibly embarrassed and ill-at-ease.*)

SECOND ENGINEER. Miss Douglas?

MILDRED. Yes. (*Throwing off her rugs and getting to her feet*). Are we all ready to start?

SECOND ENGINEER. In just a second, ma'am. I'm waiting for the Fourth. He's coming along.

MILDRED (*With a scornful smile*). You don't care to shoulder this responsibility alone, is that it?

SECOND ENGINEER (*Forcing a smile*). Two are better than one. (*Disturbed by her eyes, glances out to sea—blurts out*). A fine day we're having.

MILDRED. Is it?

SECOND ENGINEER. A nice warm breeze——

MILDRED. It feels cold to me.

SECOND ENGINEER. But it's hot enough in the sun——

MILDRED. Not hot enough for me. I don't like Nature. I was never athletic.

SECOND ENGINEER (*Forcing a smile*). Well, you'll find it hot enough where you're going.

MILDRED. Do you mean hell?

SECOND ENGINEER (*Flabbergasted, decides to laugh*). Ho-ho! No, I mean the stokehole.

MILDRED. My grandfather was a puddler. He played with boiling steel.

SECOND ENGINEER (*All at sea—uneasily*). Is that so? Hum, you'll excuse me, ma'am, but are you intending to wear that dress?

MILDRED. Why not?

SECOND ENGINEER. You'll likely rub against oil and dirt. It can't be helped.

MILDRED. It doesn't matter. I have lots of white dresses.

SECOND ENGINEER. I have an old coat you might throw over——

MILDRED. I have fifty dresses like this. I will throw this one into the sea when I come back. That ought to wash it clean, don't you think?

SECOND ENGINEER (*Doggedly*). There's ladders to climb down that are none too clean—and dark alleyways——

MILDRED. I will wear this very dress and none other.

SECOND ENGINEER. No offense meant. It's none of my business. I was only warning you—

MILDRED. Warning? That sounds thrilling.

SECOND ENGINEER (*Looking down the deck —with a sigh of relief*). There's the Fourth now. He's waiting for us. If you'll come——

MILDRED. Go on. I'll follow you. (*He goes.* MILDRED *turns a mocking smile on her aunt.*) An oaf—but a handsome, virile oaf.

AUNT (*Scornfully*). Poser!

MILDRED. Take care. He said there were dark alleyways—

AUNT (*In the same tone*). Poser!

MILDRED (*Biting her lips angrily*). You are right. But would that my millions were not so anemically chaste!

AUNT. Yes, for a fresh pose I have no doubt you would drag the name of Douglas in the gutter!

MILDRED. From which it sprang. Good-by, Aunt. Don't pray too hard that I may fall into the fiery furnace.

AUNT. Poser!

MILDRED (*Viciously*). Old hag! (*She slaps her aunt insultingly across the face and walks off, laughing gaily.*)

AUNT (*Screams after her*). I said poser!

(*Curtain*)

SCENE THREE

SCENE—*The stokehole. In the rear, the dimly outlined bulks of the furnaces and boilers. High overhead one hanging electric bulb sheds just enough light through the murky air laden with coal dust to pile up masses of shadows everywhere. A line of men, stripped to the waist, is before the furnace doors. They bend over, looking neither to right nor left, handling their shovels as if they were part of their bodies, with a strange, awkward, swinging rhythm. They use the shovels to throw open the furnace doors. Then from these fiery round holes in the black a flood of terrific light and heat pours full upon the men who are outlined in silhouette in the crouching, inhuman attitudes of chained gorillas. The men shovel with a rhythmic motion, swinging as on a pivot from the coal which lies in heaps on the floor behind to hurl it into the flaming mouths before them. There is a tumult of noise—the brazen clang of the furnace doors as they are flung open or slammed shut, the grating, teeth-gritting grind of steel against steel, of crunching coal. This clash of sound stuns one's ears with its rending dissonance. But there is order in it, rhythm, a mechanical regulated recurrence, a tempo. And rising above all, making the air hum with the quiver of liberated energy, the roar of leaping flames in the furnaces, the monotonous throbbing beat of the engines.*

As the curtain rises, the furnace doors are shut. The men are taking a breathing spell. One or two are arranging the coal behind them, pulling it into more accessible heaps. The others can be dimly made out leaning on their shovels in relaxed attitudes of exhaustion.

PADDY (*From somewhere in the line—plaintively*). Yerra, will this divil's own watch nivir end? Me back is broke. I'm destroyed entirely.

YANK (*From the center of the line—with exuberant scorn*). Aw, yuh make me sick! Lie down and croak, why don't yuh? Always beefin', dat's you! Say, dis is a cinch! Dis was made for me! It's my meat, get me! (*A whistle is blown—a thin, shrill note from somewhere overhead in the darkness.* YANK *curses without resentment.*) Dere's dat damn engineer crackin' de whip. He tinks we're loafin'.

PADDY (*Vindictively*). God stiffen him!

YANK (*In an exultant tone of command*). Come on, youse guys! Git into de game! She's gittin' hungry! Pile some grub in her. Trow it into her belly! Come on now, all of youse! Open her up! (*At this last all the men, who have followed his movements of getting into position, throw open their furnace doors with a deafening clang. The fiery light floods over their shoulders as they bend round for the coal. Rivulets of sooty sweat have traced maps on their backs. The enlarged muscles form bunches of high light and shadow.*)

YANK (*Chanting a count as he shovels without seeming effort*). One—two—tree—— (*His voice rising exultantly in the joy of battle*). Dat's de stuff! Let her have it! All togedder now! Sling it into her! Let her ride! Shoot de piece now! Call de toin on her! Drive her into it! Feel her move! Watch her smoke! Speed, dat's her middle name! Give her coal, youse guys! Coal, dat's her booze! Drink it up, baby! Let's see yuh sprint! Dig in and gain a lap! Dere she go-o-es. (*This last in the chanting formula of the gallery gods at the six-day bike race. He slams his furnace door shut. The others do likewise with as much unison as their wearied bodies will permit. The effect is of one fiery eye after another being blotted out with a series of accompanying bangs.*)

PADDY (*Groaning*). Me back is broke. I'm bate out—bate—— (*There is a pause. Then the inexorable whistle sounds again from the dim regions above the electric light. There is a growl of cursing rage from all sides.*)

YANK (*Shaking his fist upward—contemptuously*). Take it easy dere, you! Who d'yuh tinks runnin' dis game, me or you? When I git ready, we move. Not before! When I git ready, get me!

VOICES (*Approvingly*). That's the stuff!
Yank tal him, py golly!
Yank ain't afeerd.
Goot poy, Yank!
Give him hell!
Tell 'im 'e's a bloody swine!
Bloody slave-driver!

YANK (*Contemptuously*). He ain't got no noive. He's yellow, get me? All de engineers is

398

yellow. Dey got streaks a mile wide. Aw, to hell with him! Let's move, youse guys. We had a rest. Come on, she needs it! Give her pep! It ain't for him. Him and his whistle, dey don't belong. But we belong, see! We gotter feed de baby! Come on! (*He turns and flings his furnace door open. They all follow his lead. At this instant the* SECOND *and* FOURTH ENGINEERS *enter from the darkness on the left with* MILDRED *between them. She starts, turns paler, her pose is crumbling, she shivers with fright in spite of the blazing heat, but forces herself to leave the* ENGINEERS *and take a few steps near the men. She is right behind* YANK. *All this happens quickly while the men have their backs turned.*)

YANK. Come on, youse guys! (*He is turning to get coal when the whistle sounds again in a peremptory, irritating note. This drives* YANK *into a sudden fury. While the other men have turned full around and stopped dumbfounded by the spectacle of* MILDRED *standing there in her white dress,* YANK *does not turn far enough to see her. Besides, his head is thrown back, he blinks upward through the murk trying to find the owner of the whistle, he brandishes his shovel murderously over his head in one hand, pounding on his chest, gorilla-like, with the other, shouting.*) Toin off dat whistle! Come down outa dere, yuh yellow, brass-buttoned, Belfast bum, yuh! Come down and I'll knock yer brains out! Yuh lousy, stinkin', yellow mut of a Catholic-moiderin' bastard! Come down and I'll moider yuh! Pullin' dat whistle on me, huh? I'll show yuh! I'll crash yer skull in! I'll drive yer teet' down yer throat! I'll slam yer nose trou de back of yer head! I'll cut yer guts out for a nickel, yuh lousy boob, yuh dirty, crummy, muck-eatin' son of a—— (*Suddenly he becomes conscious of all the other men staring at something directly behind his back. He whirls defensively with a snarling, murderous growl, crouching to spring, his lips drawn back*

over his teeth, his small eyes gleaming ferociously. He sees* MILDRED, *like a white apparition in the full light from the open furnace doors. He glares into her eyes, turned to stone. As for her, during his speech she has listened, paralyzed with horror, terror, her whole personality crushed, beaten in, collapsed, by the terrific impact of this unknown, abysmal brutality, naked and shameless. As she looks at his gorilla face, as his eyes bore into hers, she utters a low, choking cry and shrinks away from him, putting both hands up before her eyes to shut out the sight of his face, to protect her own. This startles* YANK *to a reaction. His mouth falls open, his eyes grow bewildered.*)

MILDRED (*About to faint—to the* ENGINEERS, *who now have her one by each arm—whimperingly*). Take me away! Oh, the filthy beast! (*She faints. They carry her quickly back, disappearing in the darkness at the left, rear. An iron door clangs shut. Rage and bewildered fury rush back on* YANK. *He feels himself insulted in some unknown fashion in the very heart of his pride. He roars.*) God damn yuh! (*And hurls his shovel after them at the door which has just closed. It hits the steel bulkhead with a clang and falls clattering on the steel floor. From overhead the whistle sounds again in a long, angry, insistent command.*)

(*Curtain*)

SCENE FOUR

SCENE—*The firemen's forecastle.* YANK'S *watch has just come off duty and had dinner. Their faces and bodies shine from a soap and water scrubbing but around their eyes, where a hasty dousing does not touch, the coal dust sticks like black make-up, giving them a queer, sinister expression.* YANK *has not washed either face or body. He stands out in contrast to them, a blackened, brooding figure. He is seated forward on a bench in the exact attitude of Rodin's* "The Thinker." The others, most of them smoking pipes, are staring at* YANK *half-apprehen-*

---

31. **Belfast . . . bastard.** If the engineer came from Belfast, he came from Northern Ireland, which is populated chiefly by Protestant Scotch-Irish. The county of Ulster has never been willing to join politically with Eire; and there has always been intense feeling between the two sections of the island, dating from the time when William of Orange became King of England (William III, co-ruler with Mary) in 1689, defeated the deposed Catholic James II and his Irish allies at the Battle of the Boyne (1690), and established the since unbroken line of Anglican kings on the throne of England. Sometimes the Protestants of Ireland are known as Orangemen.

* *Rodin*, Auguste Rodin (1840–1917), a French sculptor, whose "The Thinker" is probably the best-known piece of contemporary sculpture.

sively, as if fearing an outburst; half-amusedly, as if they saw a joke somewhere that tickled them.

VOICES. He ain't ate nothin'.
  Py golly, a fallar gat to gat grub in him.
  Divil a lie.
  Yank feeda da fire, no feeda da face.
  Ha-ha.
  He ain't even washed hisself.
  He's forgot.
  Hey, Yank, you forgot to wash.

10 YANK (*Sullenly*). Forgot nothin'! To hell wit washin'.

VOICES. It'll stick to you.
  It'll get under your skin.
  Give yer the bleedin' itch, that's wot.
  It makes spots on you—like a leopard.
  Like a piebald nigger, you mean.
  Better wash up, Yank.

20   You sleep better.
  Wash up, Yank.
  Wash up! Wash up!

YANK (*Resentfully*). Aw say, youse guys. Lemme alone. Can't youse see I'm tryin' to tink?

ALL (*Repeating the word after him as one with cynical mockery*). Think! (*The word has a brazen, metallic quality as if their throats were phonograph horns. It is followed by a chorus*

30 *of hard, barking laughter.*)

YANK (*Springing to his feet and glaring at them belligerently*). Yes, tink! Tink, dat's what I said! What about it? (*They are silent, puzzled by his sudden resentment at what used to be one of his jokes.* YANK *sits down again in the same attitude of "The Thinker."*)

VOICES. Leave him alone.
  He's got a grouch on.
  Why wouldn't he?

40 PADDY (*With a wink at the others*). Sure I know what's the matther. 'Tis aisy to see. He's fallen in love, I'm telling you.

ALL (*Repeating the word after him as one with cynical mockery*). Love! (*The word has a brazen, metallic quality as if their throats were phonograph horns. It is followed by a chorus of hard, barking laughter.*)

YANK (*With a contemptuous snort*). Love, hell! Hate, dat's what. I've fallen in hate, get me? 50

PADDY (*Philosophically*). 'Twould take a wise man to tell one from the other. (*With a bitter, ironical scorn, increasing as he goes on*). But I'm telling you it's love that's in it. Sure what else but love for us poor bastes in the stokehole would be bringing a fine lady, dressed like a white quane, down a mile of ladders and steps to be havin' a look at us? (*A growl of anger goes up from all sides.*)

LONG (*Jumping on a bench—hecticly*). Hin- 6 sultin' us! Hinsultin' us, the bloody cow! And them bloody engineers! What right 'as they got to be exhibitin' us 's if we was bleedin' monkeys in a menagerie? Did we sign for hinsults to our dignity as 'onest workers? Is that in the ship's articles? You kin bloody well bet it ain't! But I knows why they done it. I arsked a deck steward 'o she was and 'e told me. 'Er old man's a bleedin' millionaire, a bloody Capitalist! 'E's got enuf bloody gold to sink this 7 bleedin' ship! 'E makes arf the bloody steel in the world! 'E owns this bloody boat! And you and me, Comrades, we're 'is slaves! And the skipper and mates and engineers, they're 'is slaves! And she's 'is bloody daughter and we're all 'er slaves, too! And she gives 'er orders as 'ow she wants to see the bloody animals below decks and down they takes 'er! (*There is a roar of rage from all sides.*)

YANK (*Blinking at him bewilderedly*). Say! 8 Wait a moment! Is all dat straight goods?

LONG. Straight as string! The bleedin' steward as waits on 'em, 'e told me about 'er. And what're we goin' ter do, I arsks yer? 'Ave we got ter swaller 'er hinsults like dogs? It ain't in the ship's articles. I tell yer we got a case. We kin go to law——

YANK (*With abysmal contempt*). Hell! Law!

ALL (*Repeating the word after him as one with cynical mockery*). Law! (*The word has a brazen metallic quality as if their throats were phonograph horns. It is followed by a chorus of hard, barking laughter.*)

LONG (*Feeling the ground slipping from under his feet—desperately*). As voters and citizens we kin force the bloody governments——

YANK (*With abysmal contempt*). Hell! Governments!

ALL (*Repeating the word after him as one with cynical mockery*). Governments! (*The word has a brazen metallic quality as if their throats were phonograph horns. It is followed by a chorus of hard, barking laughter.*)

LONG (*Hysterically*). We're free and equal in the sight of God——

YANK (*With abysmal contempt*). Hell! God!

ALL (*Repeating the word after him as one with cynical mockery*). God! (*The word has a brazen metallic quality as if their throats were phonograph horns. It is followed by a chorus of hard, barking laughter.*)

YANK (*Witheringly*). Aw, join de Salvation Army!

ALL. Sit down! Shut up! Damn fool! Sea-lawyer! (LONG *slinks back out of sight.*)

PADDY (*Continuing the trend of his thoughts as if he had never been interrupted—bitterly*). And there she was standing behind us, and the Second pointing at us like a man you'd hear in a circus would be saying: In this cage is a queerer kind of baboon than ever you'd find in darkest Africy. We roast them in their own sweat—and be damned if you won't hear some of thim saying they like it! (*He glances scornfully at* YANK.)

YANK (*With a bewildered uncertain growl*). Aw!

PADDY. And there was Yank roarin' curses and turning round wid his shovel to brain her—and she looked at him, and him at her——

YANK (*Slowly*). She was all white. I tought she was a ghost. Sure.

PADDY (*With heavy, biting sarcasm*). 'Twas love at first sight, divil a doubt of it! If you'd seen the endearin' look on her pale mug when she shriveled away with her hands over her eyes to shut out the sight of him! Sure, 'twas as if she'd seen a great hairy ape escaped from the Zoo!

YANK (*Stung—with a growl of rage*). Aw!

PADDY. And the loving way Yank heaved his shovel at the skull of her, only she was out the door! (*A grin breaking over his face*). 'Twas touching, I'm telling you! It put the touch of home, swate home in the stokehole. (*There is a roar of laughter from all.*)

YANK (*Glaring at* PADDY *menacingly*). Aw, choke dat off, see!

PADDY (*Not heeding him—to the others*). And her grabbin' at the Second's arm for protection. (*With a grotesque imitation of a woman's voice*). Kiss me, Engineer dear, for it's dark down here and me old man's in Wall Street making money! Hug me tight, darlin', for I'm afeerd in the dark and me mother's on deck makin' eyes at the skipper! (*Another roar of laughter*).

YANK (*Threateningly*). Say! What yuh tryin' to do, kid me, yuh old Harp?

PADDY. Divil a bit! Ain't I wishin' myself you'd brained her?

YANK (*Fiercely*). I'll brain her! I'll brain her yet, wait 'n' see! (*Coming over to* PADDY *slowly*). Say, is dat what she called me—a hairy ape?

PADDY. She looked it at you if she didn't say the word itself.

YANK (*Grinning horribly*). Hairy ape, huh? Sure! Dat's de way she looked at me, aw right. Hairy ape! So dat's me, huh? (*Bursting into rage—as if she were still in front of him*). Yuh skinny tart! Yuh white-faced bum, yuh! I'll show yuh who's a ape! (*Turning to the others, bewilderment seizing him again*). Say, youse guys. I was bawlin' him out for pullin' de whistle on us. You heard me. And den I seen youse lookin' at somep'n and I tought he'd sneaked down to come up in back of me, and I hopped round to knock him dead wit de shovel. And dere she was wit de light on her! Christ, yuh coulda pushed me over with a finger! I was scared, get me? Sure! I tought she was a ghost, see? She was all in white like dey wrap around stiffs. You seen her. Kin yuh blame me? She didn't belong, dat's what. And den when I come to and seen it was a real skoit and seen de way she was lookin' at me—like Paddy said—Christ, I was sore, get me? I don't stand for dat stuff from nobody. And I flung de shovel—on'y she'd beat it. (*Furiously*). I wished it'd banked her! I wished it'd knocked her block off!

LONG. And be 'anged for murder or 'lectrocuted? She ain't bleedin' well worth it.

YANK. I don't give a damn what! I'd be square wit her, wouldn't I? Tink I wanter let her put somep'n over on me? Tink I'm goin' to let her git away wit dat stuff? Yuh don't know me! No one ain't never put nothin' over on me and got away wit it, see!—not dat kind of stuff

—no guy and no skoit neither! I'll fix her! Maybe she'll come down again——

VOICE. No chance, Yank. You scared her out of a year's growth.

YANK. I scared her? Why de hell should I scare her? Who de hell is she? Ain't she de same as me? Hairy ape, huh? (*With his old confident bravado*). I'll show her I'm better'n her, if she on'y knew it. I belong and she don't, see! I move and she's dead! Twenty-five knots a hour, dat's me! Dat carries her but I make dat. She's on'y baggage. Sure! (*Again bewilderedly*). But, Christ, she was funny lookin'! Did yuh pipe her hands? White and skinny. Yuh could see de bones through 'em. And her mush, dat was dead white, too. And her eyes, dey was like dey'd seen a ghost. Me, dat was! Sure! Hairy ape! Ghost, huh? Look at dat arm! (*He extends his right arm, swelling out the great muscles.*) I coulda took her wit dat, wit just my little finger even, and broke her in two. (*Again bewilderedly*). Say, who is dat skoit, huh? What is she? What's she come from? Who made her? Who give her de noive to look at me like dat? Dis ting's got my goat right. I don't get her. She's new to me. What does a skoit like her mean, huh? She don't belong, get me! I can't see her. (*With growing anger*). But one ting I'm wise to, aw right, aw right! Youse all kin bet your shoits I'll git even wit her. I'll show her if she tinks she—She grinds de organ and I'm on de string, huh? I'll fix her! Let her come down again and I'll fling her in de furnace! She'll move den! She won't shiver at nothin', den! Speed, dat'll be her! She'll belong den! (*He grins horribly.*)

PADDY. She'll never come. She's had her belly-full, I'm telling you. She'll be in bed now, I'm thinking, wid ten doctors and nurses feedin' her salts to clean the fear out of her.

YANK (*Enraged*). Yuh tink I made her sick, too, do yuh? Just lookin' at me, huh? Hairy ape, huh? (*In a frenzy of rage*). I'll fix her! I'll tell her where to git off! She'll git down on her knees and take it back or I'll bust de face offen her! (*Shaking one fist upward and beating on his chest with the other*). I'll find yuh! I'm comin', d'yuh hear? I'll fix yuh, God damn yuh! (*He makes a rush for the door.*)

VOICES. Stop him!
    He'll get shot!
    He'll murder her!

Trip him up!
Hold him!
He's gone crazy!
Gott, he's strong!
Hold him down!
Look out for a kick!
Pin his arms!

(*They have all piled on him and, after a fierce struggle, by sheer weight of numbers have borne him to the floor just inside the door.*)

PADDY (*Who has remained detached*). Kape him down till he's cooled off. (*Scornfully*). Yerra, Yank, you're a great fool. Is it payin' attention at all you are to the like of that skinny sow widout one drop of rale blood in her?

YANK (*Frenziedly, from the bottom of the heap*). She done me doit! She done me doit, didn't she? I'll git square wit her! I'll get her some way! Git offen me, youse guys! Lemme up! I'll show her who's a ape!

(*Curtain*)

SCENE FIVE

SCENE—*Three weeks later. A corner of Fifth Avenue in the Fifties on a fine Sunday morning. A general atmosphere of clean, well-tidied, wide street; a flood of mellow, tempered sunshine; gentle, genteel breezes. In the rear, the show windows of two shops, a jewelry establishment on the corner, a furrier's next to it. Here the adornments of extreme wealth are tantalizingly displayed. The jeweler's window is gaudy with glittering diamonds, emeralds, rubies, pearls, etc., fashioned in ornate tiaras, crowns, necklaces, collars, etc. From each piece hangs an enormous tag from which a dollar sign and numerals in intermittent electric lights wink out the incredible prices. The same in the furrier's. Rich furs of all varieties hang there bathed in a downpour of artificial light. The general effect is of a background of magnificence cheapened and made grotesque by commercialism, a background in tawdry disharmony with the clear light and sunshine on the street itself.*

Up the side street YANK and LONG come swaggering. LONG is dressed in shore clothes, wears a black Windsor tie, cloth cap. YANK is in his dirty dungarees. A fireman's cap *with black peak is cocked defiantly on the side of his head. He has not shaved for days and around his fierce, resentful eyes—as around those of* LONG *to a lesser degree—the black smudge of coal dust still sticks like make-up. They hesitate and stand together at the corner, swaggering, looking about them with a forced, defiant contempt.*

LONG (*Indicating it all with an oratorical gesture*). Well, 'ere we are. Fif' Avenoo. This 'ere's their bleedin' private lane, as yer might say. (*Bitterly.*) We're trespassers 'ere. Proletarians keep orf the grass!

YANK (*Dully*). I don't see no grass, yuh boob. (*Staring at the sidewalk*). Clean, ain't it? Yuh could eat a fried egg offen it. The white wings got some job sweepin' dis up. (*Looking up and down the avenue—surlily*). Where's all de white-collar stiffs yuh said was here—and de skoits—*her* kind?

LONG. In church, blarst 'em! Arskin' Jesus to give 'em more money.

YANK. Choich, huh? I useter go to choich onct—sure—when I was a kid. Me old man and woman, dey made me. Dey never went demselves, dough. Always got too big a head on Sunday mornin', dat was dem. (*With a grin*). Dey was scrappers for fair, bot' of dem. On Satiday nights when dey bot' got a skinful dey could put up a bout oughter been staged at de Garden. When dey got trough dere wasn't a chair or table wit a leg under it. Or else dey bot' jumped on me for somep'n. Dat was where I loined to take punishment. (*With a grin and a swagger*). I'm a chip offen de old block, get me?

LONG. Did yer old man follow the sea?

YANK. Naw. Worked along shore. I runned away when me old lady croaked wit de tremens. I helped at truckin' and in de market. Den I shipped in de stokehole. Sure. Dat belongs. De rest was nothin'. (*Looking around him*). I ain't never seen dis before. De Brooklyn waterfront, dat was where I was dragged up. (*Taking a deep breath*). Dis ain't so bad at dat, huh?

LONG. Not bad? Well, we pays for it wiv our bloody sweat, if yer wants to know!

YANK (*With sudden angry disgust*). Aw, hell! I don't see no one, see—like her. All dis gives me a pain. It don't belong. Say, ain't dere a back room around dis dump? Let's go shoot a ball. All dis is too clean and quiet and dolled-up, get me? It gives me a pain.

LONG. Wait and yer'll bloody well see——

YANK. I don't wait for no one. I keep on de move. Say, what yuh drag me up here for, anyway? Tryin' to kid me, yuh simp, yuh?

LONG. Yer wants to get back at 'er, don't yer? That's what yer been sayin' every bloomin' hour since she hinsulted yer.

YANK (*Vehemently*). Sure ting I do! Didn't I try to get even wit her in Southampton? Didn't I sneak on de dock and wait for her by de gangplank? I was goin' to spit in her pale mug, see! Sure, right in her pop-eyes! Dat woulda made me even, see? But no chanct. Dere was a whole army of plain-clothes bulls around. Dey spotted me and gimme de bum's rush. I never seen her. But I'll git square wit her yet, you watch! (*Furiously*). De lousy tart! She tinks she kin get away with moider— but not wid me! I'll fix her! I'll tink of a way!

LONG (*As disgusted as he dares to be*). Ain't that why I brought yer up 'ere—to show yer? Yer been lookin' at this 'ere 'ole affair wrong. Yer been actin' an' talkin' 's if it was all a bleedin' personal matter between yer and that bloody cow. I wants to convince yer she was on'y a representative of 'er clarss. I wants to awaken yer bloody clarss consciousness. Then yer'll see it's 'er clarss yer've got to fight, not 'er alone. There's a 'ole mob of 'em like 'er, Gawd blind 'em!

YANK (*Spitting on his hands—belligerently*). De more de merrier when I gits started. Bring on de gang!

LONG. Yer'll see 'em in arf a mo', when that church lets out. (*He turns and sees the window display in the two stores for the first time.*) Blimey! Look at that, will yer? (*They both walk back and stand looking in the jeweler's.* LONG *flies into a fury.*) Just look at this 'ere bloomin' mess! Just look at it! Look at the bleedin' prices on 'em—more'n our 'ole bloody stokehole makes in ten voyages sweatin' in 'ell! And they—'er and 'er bloody clarss—buys 'em for toys to dangle on 'em! One of these 'ere would buy scoff for a starvin' family for a year!

YANK. Aw, cut de sob stuff! T' hell wit de starvin' family! Yuh'll be passin' de hat to me next. (*With naïve admiration*). Say, dem tings is pretty, huh? Bet yuh dey'd hock for a piece of change aw right. (*Then turning away, bored*). But, aw hell, what good are dey? Let 'er have 'em. Dey don't belong no more'n she does. (*With a gesture of sweeping the jewelers into oblivion*). All dat don't count, get me?

LONG (*Who has moved to the furrier's—indignantly*). And I s'pose this 'ere don't count neither—skins of poor, 'armless animals slaugh-
10 tered so as 'er and 'ers can keep their bleedin' noses warm!

YANK (*Who has been staring at something inside—with queer excitement*). Take a slant at dat! Give it de once-over! Monkey fur—two t'ousand bucks! (*Bewilderedly*). Is dat straight goods—monkey fur? What de hell——?

LONG (*Bitterly*). It's straight enuf. (*With grim humor*). They wouldn't bloody well pay that for a 'airy ape's skin—no, nor for the 'ole
20 livin' ape with all 'is 'ead, and body, and soul thrown in!

YANK (*Clenching his fists, his face growing pale with rage as if the skin in the window were a personal insult*). Trowin' it up in my face! Christ! I'll fix her!

LONG (*Excitedly*). Church is out. 'Ere they come, the bleedin' swine. (*After a glance at* YANK's *lowering face—uneasily*). Easy goes, Comrade. Keep yer bloomin' temper. Remem-
30 ber force defeats itself. It ain't our weapon. We must impress our demands through peaceful means—the ·votes of the on-marching proletarians of the bloody world!

YANK (*With abysmal contempt*). Votes, hell! Votes is a joke, see. Votes for women! Let dem do it!

LONG (*Still more uneasily*). Calm, now. Treat 'em wiv the proper contempt. Observe the bleedin' parasites but 'old yer 'orses.
40 YANK (*Angrily*). Git away from me! Yuh're yellow, dat's what. Force, dat's me! De punch, dat's me every time, see! (*The crowd from church enter from the right, sauntering slowly and affectedly, their heads held stiffly up, looking neither to right nor left, talking in toneless, simpering voices. The women are rouged, calcimined, dyed, overdressed to the nth degree. The men are in Prince Alberts, high hats, spats, canes, etc. A procession of gaudy mari-
50 onettes, yet with something of the relentless horror of Frankenstein monsters in their detached, mechanical unawareness.*)

VOICES. Dear Doctor Caiaphas! He is so sincere!

What was the sermon? I dozed off.

About the radicals, my dear—and the false doctrines that are being preached.

We must organize a hundred per cent American bazaar. 60

And let everyone contribute one one-hundredth per cent of their income tax.

What an original idea!

We can devote the proceeds to rehabilitating the veil of the temple.

But that has been done so many times.

YANK (*Glaring from one to the other of them —with an insulting snort of scorn*). Huh! Huh! 70 (*Without seeming to see him, they make wide detours to avoid the spot where he stands in the middle of the sidewalk.*)

LONG (*Frightenedly*). Keep yer bloomin' mouth shut, I tells yer.

YANK (*Viciously*). G'wan! Tell it to Sweeney! (*He swaggers away and deliberately lurches into a top-hatted gentleman, then glares at him pugnaciously.*) Say, who d'yuh tink yuh're bumpin'? Tink yuh own de oith? 80

GENTLEMAN (*Coldly and affectedly*). I beg your pardon. (*He has not looked at* YANK *and passes on without a glance, leaving him bewildered.*)

LONG (*Rushing up and grabbing* YANK's *arm*). 'Ere! Come away! This wasn't what I meant. Yer'll 'ave the bloody coppers down on us.

YANK (*Savagely—giving him a push that sends him sprawling*). G'wan! 9

LONG (*Picks himself up—hysterically*). I'll pop orf then. This ain't what I meant. And whatever 'appens, yer can't blame me. (*He slinks off left.*)

YANK. T' hell wit youse! (*He approaches a lady—with a vicious grin and a smirking wink.*) Hello, Kiddo. How's every little ting? Got anyting on for tonight? I know an old boiler down to de docks we kin crawl into. (*The lady stalks by without a look, without a change of* 10

53. **Caiaphas.** The name has probably been suggested by that of the high priest of the Jews who "gave counsel to the Jews, that it was expedient that one man should die for the people" (John 18:14) and furthered the prosecution of Jesus.

pace. YANK *turns to others—insultingly.*) Holy smokes, what a mug! Go hide yuhself before de horses shy at yuh. Gee, pipe de heine on dat one! Say, youse, yuh look like de stoin of a ferry-boat. Paint and powder! All dolled up to kill! Yuh look like stiffs laid out for de bone-yard! Aw, g'wan, de lot of youse! Yuh give me de eye-ache. Yuh don't belong, get me! Look at me, why don't youse dare? I belong, dat's me! (*Pointing to a skyscraper across the street which is in process of construction—with bravado*). See dat building goin' up dere? See de steel work? Steel, dat's me! Youse guys live on it and tink yuh're somep'n. But I'm *in* it, see! I'm de hoistin' engine dat makes it go up! I'm it—de inside and bottom of it! Sure! I'm steel and steam and smoke and de rest of it! It moves—speed—twenty-five stories up—and me at de top and bottom—movin'! Youse simps don't move. Yuh're on'y dolls I winds up to see 'im spin. Yuh're de garbage, get me—de leav-ins—de ashes we dump over de side! Now, what 'a' yuh gotta say? (*But as they seem neither to see nor hear him, he flies into a fury.*) Bums! Pigs! Tarts! Bitches! (*He turns in a rage on the men, bumping viciously into them but not jar-ring them the least bit. Rather it is he who re-coils after each collision. He keeps growling.*) Git off de oith! G'wan, yuh bum! Look where yuh're goin', can't yuh? Git outa here! Fight, why don't yuh? Put up yer mits! Don't be a dog! Fight or I'll knock yuh dead! (*But, with-out seeming to see him, they all answer with mechanical affected politeness, "I beg your pardon." Then at a cry from one of the women, they all scurry to the furrier's window.*)

THE WOMAN (*Ecstatically, with a gasp of de-light*). Monkey fur! (*The whole crowd of men and women chorus after her in the same tone of affected delight.*) Monkey fur!

YANK (*With a jerk of his head back on his shoulders, as if he had received a punch full in the face—raging*). I see yuh, all in white! I see yuh, yuh white-faced tart, yuh! Hairy ape, huh? I'll hairy ape yuh! (*He bends down and grips at the street curbing as if to pluck it out and hurl it. Foiled in this, snarling with pas-sion, he leaps to the lamp-post on the corner and tries to pull it up for a club. Just at that mo-ment a bus is heard rumbling up. A fat, high-hatted, spatted gentleman runs out from the side street. He calls out plaintively.*) Bus! Bus!

Stop there! (*And runs full tilt into the bending, straining* YANK, *who is bowled off his balance.*)

YANK (*Seeing a fight—with a roar of joy as he springs to his feet*). At last! Bus, huh! I'll bust yuh! (*He lets drive a terrific swing, his fist landing full on the fat gentleman's face. But the gentleman stands unmoved as if nothing had happened.*)   60

GENTLEMAN. I beg your pardon. (*Then irri-tably*). You have made me lose my bus. (*He claps his hands and begins to scream.*) Officer! Officer! (*Many police whistles shrill out on the instant and a whole platoon of policemen rush in on* YANK *from all sides. He tries to fight but is clubbed to the pavement and fallen upon. The crowd at the window have not moved or noticed this disturbance. The clanging gong of the patrol wagon approaches with a clamoring   70 din.*)

(*Curtain*)

SCENE SIX

SCENE—*Night of the following day. A row of cells in the prison on Blackwell's Island. The cells extend back diagonally from right front to left rear. They do not stop, but disappear in the dark background as if they ran on, numberless, into infinity. One electric bulb from the low ceiling of the narrow corridor sheds its light through the heavy steel bars of the cell at the extreme front and reveals part of the interior.* YANK *can be seen within, crouched on the edge of his cot in the atti-tude of Rodin's "The Thinker." His face is spotted with black and blue bruises. A blood-stained bandage is wrapped around his head.*

YANK (*Suddenly starting as if awakening from a dream, reaches out and shakes the bars —aloud to himself, wonderingly*). Steel. Dis is de Zoo, huh? (*A burst of hard, barking laugh-ter comes from the unseen occupants of the cells, runs back down the tier, and abruptly ceases.*)

VOICES (*Mockingly*). The Zoo? That's a new name for this coop—a damn good   80 name!

Steel, eh? You said a mouthful. This is the old iron house.

405

Who is that boob talkin'?

He's the bloke they brung in out of his head. The bulls had beat him up fierce.

YANK (*Dully*). I musta been dreamin'. I tought I was in a cage at de Zoo—but de apes don't talk, do dey?

VOICES (*With mocking laughter*). You're in a cage aw right.

A coop!

A pen!

A sty!

A kennel! (*Hard laughter—a pause*). Say, guy! Who are you? No, never mind lying. What are you?

Yes, tell us your sad story. What's your game?

What did they jug yuh for?

YANK (*Dully*). I was a fireman—stokin' on de liners. (*Then with a sudden rage, rattling his cell bars*). I'm a hairy ape, get me? And I'll bust youse all in de jaw if yuh don't lay off kiddin' me.

VOICES. Huh! You're a hard boiled duck, ain't you!

When you spit, it bounces! (*Laughter*).

Aw, can it. He's a regular guy. Ain't you?

What did he say he was—a ape?

YANK (*Defiantly*). Sure ting! Ain't dat what youse all are—apes? (*A silence. Then a furious rattling of bars from down the corridor*).

A VOICE (*Thick with rage*). I'll show yuh who's a ape, yuh bum!

VOICES. Ssshh! Nix!

Can de noise!

Piano!

You'll have the guard down on us!

YANK (*Scornfully*). De guard? Yuh mean de keeper, don't yuh? (*Angry exclamations from all the cells*).

VOICE (*Placatingly*). Aw, don't pay no attention to him. He's off his nut from the beatin'-up he got. Say, you guy! We're waitin' to hear what they landed you for—or ain't yuh tellin'?

YANK. Sure, I'll tell youse. Sure! Why de hell not? On'y—youse won't get me. Nobody gets me but me, see? I started to tell de Judge and all he says was: "Toity days to tink it over." Tink it over! Christ, dat's all I been doin' for weeks! (*After a pause*). I was tryin' to git even wit someone, see?—someone dat done me doit.

VOICES (*Cynically*). De old stuff, I bet. Your goil, huh?

Give yuh the double-cross, huh?

That's them every time!

Did yuh beat up de odder guy?

YANK (*Disgustedly*). Aw, yuh're all wrong! Sure dere was a skoit in it—but not what youse mean, not dat old tripe. Dis was a new kind of skoit. She was dolled up all in white—in de stokehole. I tought she was a ghost. Sure. (*A pause*).

VOICES (*Whispering*). Gee, he's still nutty.

Let him rave. It's fun listenin'.

YANK (*Unheeding—groping in his thoughts*). Her hands—dey was skinny and white like dey wasn't real but painted on somep'n. Dere was a million miles from me to her—twenty-five knots a hour. She was like some dead ting de cat brung in. Sure, dat's what. She didn't belong. She belonged in de window of a toy store, or on de top of a garbage can, see! Sure! (*He breaks out angrily.*) But would yuh believe it, she had de noive to do me doit. She lamped me like she was seein' somep'n broke loose from de menagerie. Christ, yuh'd oughter seen her eyes! (*He rattles the bars of his cell furiously.*) But I'll get back at her yet, you watch! And if I can't find her I'll take it out on de gang she runs wit. I'm wise to where dey hangs out now. I'll show her who belongs! I'll show her who's in de move and who ain't. You watch my smoke!

VOICES (*Serious and joking*). Dat's de talkin'!

Take her for all she's got!

What was this dame, anyway? Who was she, eh?

YANK. I dunno. First cabin stiff. Her old man's a millionaire, dey says—name of Douglas.

VOICES. Douglas? That's the president of the Steel Trust, I bet.

Sure. I seen his mug in de papers.

He's filthy with dough.

VOICE. Hey, feller, take a tip from me. If you want to get back at that dame, you better join the Wobblies. You'll get some action then.

YANK. Wobblies? What de hell's dat?

VOICE. Ain't you ever heard of the I. W. W.?

YANK. Naw. What is it?

VOICE. A gang of blokes—a tough gang. I been readin' about 'em today in the paper. The guard give me the *Sunday Times*. There's a long spiel about 'em. It's from a speech made in the Senate by a guy named Senator Queen. (*He is in the cell next to* YANK's. *There is a rustling of paper.*) Wait'll I see if I got light enough and I'll read you. Listen. (*He reads.*) "There is a menace existing in this country today which threatens the vitals of our fair Republic—as foul a menace against the very lifeblood of the American Eagle as was the foul conspiracy of Cataline against the eagles of ancient Rome!"

VOICE (*Disgustedly*). Aw, hell! Tell him to salt de tail of dat eagle!

VOICE (*Reading*). "I refer to that devil's brew of rascals, jailbirds, murderers and cutthroats who libel all honest working-men by calling themselves the Industrial Workers of the World; but in the light of their nefarious plots, I call them the Industrious *Wreckers* of the World!"

YANK (*With vengeful satisfaction*). Wreckers, dat's de right dope! Dat belongs! Me for dem!

VOICE. Ssshh! (*Reading*). "This fiendish organization is a foul ulcer on the fair body of our Democracy——"

VOICE. Democracy, hell! Give him the boid, fellers—the raspberry! (*They do.*)

VOICE. Ssshh! (*Reading*). "Like Cato I say to this Senate, the I. W. W. must be destroyed! For they represent an ever-present dagger pointed at the heart of the greatest nation the world has ever known, where all men are born free and equal, with equal opportunities to all, where the Founding Fathers have guaranteed to each one happiness, where Truth, Honor,

Liberty, Justice, and the Brotherhood of Man are a religion absorbed with one's mother's milk, taught at our father's knee, sealed, signed, and stamped upon in the glorious Constitution of these United States!" (*A perfect storm of hisses, catcalls, boos, and hard laughter*).

VOICES (*Scornfully*). Hurrah for de Fort' of July!
Pass de hat!
Liberty!
Justice!
Honor!
Opportunity!
Brotherhood!

ALL (*With abysmal scorn*). Aw, hell!

VOICE. Give that Queen Senator guy the bark! All togedder now—one—two—tree—— (*A terrific chorus of barking and yapping*).

GUARD (*From a distance*). Quiet there, youse —or I'll git the hose. (*The noise subsides.*)

YANK (*With growling rage*). I'd like to catch dat senator guy alone for a second. I'd loin him some trute!

VOICE. Ssshh! Here's where he gits down to cases on the Wobblies. (*Reads*). "They plot with fire in one hand and dynamite in the other. They stop not before murder to gain their ends, nor at the outraging of defenseless womanhood. They would tear down society, put the lowest scum in the seats of the mighty, turn Almighty God's revealed plan for the world topsy-turvy, and make of our sweet and lovely civilization a shambles, a desolation where man, God's masterpiece, would soon degenerate back to the ape!"

VOICE (*To* YANK). Hey, you guy. There's your ape stuff again.

YANK (*With a growl of fury*). I got him. So dey blow up tings, do dey? Dey turn tings round, do dey? Hey, lend me dat paper, will yuh?

VOICE. Sure. Give it to him. On'y keep it to yourself, see. We don't wanter listen to no more of that slop.

VOICE. Here you are. Hide it under your mattress.

YANK (*Reaching out*). Tanks. I can't read much but I kin manage. (*He sits, the paper in the hand at his side, in the attitude of Rodin's "The Thinker." A pause. Several snores from down the corridor. Suddenly* YANK *jumps to his*

---

14. **Cataline . . . Rome.** The name is more commonly spelled *Catiline*. Lucius Sergius Catiline (108–62 B.C.) was governor of Africa under the Roman republic and wished to become consul, but his corrupt practices in office and in private life blocked this ambition. Much disgruntled, he organized a conspiracy against the life of the great orator, Cicero (106–43 B.C.). Cicero, in a series of speeches in the Senate, revealed the conspiracy to the Roman government; as a result, Catiline was forced to flee the city. An army was sent after him and finally encountered his forces in Etruria; Catiline was defeated and slain after a hard struggle. 33. **Cato.** Marcus Porcius Cato, the Elder (234–149 B.C.), was a violent foe of Rome's great rival, Carthage, and repeatedly preached that "*Cartago delenda est*," "Carthage must be destroyed." He is considered one of the greatest of Roman orators.

feet with a furious groan as if some appalling thought had crashed on him—bewilderedly.) Sure—her old man—president of de Steel Trust —makes half de steel in de world—steel—where I tought I belonged—drivin' trou—movin'—in dat—to make *her*—and cage me in for her to spit on! Christ! (*He shakes the bars of his cell door till the whole tier trembles. Irritated, protesting exclamations from those awakened or*
10 *trying to get to sleep.*) He made dis—dis cage! Steel! *It* don't belong, dat's what! Cages, cells, locks, bolts, bars—dat's what it means!—holdin' me down wit him at de top! But I'll drive trou! Fire, dat melts it! I'll be fire—under de heap— fire dat never goes out—hot as hell—breakin' out in de night—— (*While he has been saying this last he has shaken his cell door to a clanging accompaniment. As he comes to the "breakin' out" he seizes one bar with both hands and,*
20 *putting his two feet up against the others so that his position is parallel to the floor like a monkey's, he gives a great wrench backwards. The bar bends like a licorice stick under his tremendous strength. Just at this moment the* PRISON GUARD *rushes in, dragging a hose behind him.*)

GUARD (*Angrily*). I'll loin youse bums to wake me up! (*Sees* YANK). Hello, it's you, huh? Got the D. T's, hey? Well, I'll cure 'em. I'll
30 drown your snakes for yuh! (*Noticing the bar*). Hell, look at dat bar bended! On'y a bug is strong enough for dat!

YANK (*Glaring at him*). Or a hairy ape, yuh big yellow bum! Look out! Here I come! (*He grabs another bar.*)

GUARD (*Scared now—yelling off left*). Toin de hose on, Ben!—full pressure! And call de others—and a straitjacket! (*The curtain is falling. As it hides* YANK *from view, there is a*
40 *splattering smash as the stream of water hits the steel of* YANK's *cell.*)

(*Curtain*)

SCENE SEVEN

SCENE—*Nearly a month later. An I. W. W. local near the waterfront, showing the interior of a front room on the ground floor, and the street outside. Moonlight on the narrow street, buildings massed in black shadow. The interior of the room, which is general as-* sembly room, office, and reading room, resembles some dingy settlement boys' club. A desk and high stool are in one corner. A table with papers, stacks of pamphlets, chairs about it, is at center. The whole is decidedly cheap, banal, commonplace and unmysterious as a room could well be. The Secretary is perched on the stool making entries in a large ledger. An eye shade casts his face into shadows. Eight or ten men, longshoremen, iron workers, and the like, are grouped about the table. Two are playing checkers. One is writing a letter. Most of them are smoking pipes. A big signboard is on the wall at the rear, "Industrial Workers of the World—Local No. 57."*

YANK (*Comes down the street outside. He is dressed as in Scene Five. He moves cautiously, mysteriously. He comes to a point opposite the door; tiptoes softly up to it, listens, is impressed by the silence within, knocks carefully, as if he were guessing at the password to some secret rite. Listens. No answer. Knocks again a bit louder. No answer. Knocks impatiently much louder.*)

SECRETARY (*Turning around on his stool*). What the hell is that—someone knocking? (*Shouts*). Come in, why don't you? (*All the men in the room look up.* YANK *opens the door slowly, gingerly, as if afraid of an ambush. He looks around for secret doors, mystery, is taken aback by the commonplaceness of the room and the men in it, thinks he may have gotten in the wrong place, then sees the signboard on the wall and is reassured.*)

YANK (*Blurts out*). Hello.

MEN (*Reservedly*). Hello.

YANK (*More easily*). I tought I'd bumped into de wrong dump.

SECRETARY (*Scrutinizing him carefully*). Maybe you have. Are you a member?

YANK. Naw, not yet. Dat's what I come for— to join.

SECRETARY. That's easy. What's your job— longshore?

YANK. Naw. Fireman—stoker on de liners.

SECRETARY (*With satisfaction*). Welcome to our city. Glad to know you people are waking up at last. We haven't got many members in your line.

YANK. Naw. Dey're all dead to de woild.

SECRETARY. Well, you can help to wake 'em. What's your name? I'll make out your card.

YANK (*Confused*). Name? Lemme tink.

SECRETARY (*Sharply*). Don't you know your own name?

YANK. Sure; but I been just Yank for so long —Bob, dat's it—Bob Smith.

SECRETARY (*Writing*). Robert Smith. (*Fills out the rest of card*). Here you are. Cost you half a dollar.

YANK. Is dat all—four bits? Dat's easy. (*Gives the Secretary the money*).

SECRETARY (*Throwing it in drawer*). Thanks. Well, make yourself at home. No introductions needed. There's literature on the table. Take some of those pamphlets with you to distribute aboard ship. They may bring results. Sow the seed, only go about it right. Don't get caught and fired. We got plenty out of work. What we need is men who can hold their jobs—and work for us at the same time.

YANK. Sure. (*But he still stands, embarrassed and uneasy.*)

SECRETARY (*Looking at him—curiously*). What did you knock for? Think we had a coon in uniform to open doors?

YANK. Naw. I tought it was locked—and dat yuh'd wanter give me the once-over trou a peephole or somep'n to see if I was right.

SECRETARY (*Alert and suspicious but with an easy laugh*). Think we were running a crap game? That door is never locked. What put that in your nut?

YANK (*With a knowing grin, convinced that this is all camouflage, a part of the secrecy*). Dis burg is full of bulls, ain't it?

SECRETARY (*Sharply*). What have the cops got to do with us? We're breaking no laws.

YANK (*With a knowing wink*). Sure. Youse wouldn't for woilds. Sure. I'm wise to dat.

SECRETARY. You seem to be wise to a lot of stuff none of us knows about.

YANK (*With another wink*). Aw, dat's aw right, see. (*Then made a bit resentful by the suspicious glances from all sides*). Aw, can it! Youse needn't put me trou de toid degree. Can't youse see I belong? Sure! I'm reg'lar. I'll stick, get me? I'll shoot de woiks for youse. Dat's why I wanted to join in.

SECRETARY (*Breezily, feeling him out*). That's the right spirit. Only are you sure you understand what you've joined? It's all plain and aboveboard; still, some guys get a wrong slant on us. (*Sharply*). What's your notion of the purpose of the I. W. W.?

YANK. Aw, I know all about it.

SECRETARY (*Sarcastically*). Well, give us some of your valuable information.

YANK (*Cunningly*). I know enough not to speak outa my toin. (*Then resentfully again*). Aw, say! I'm reg'lar. I'm wise to de game. I know yuh got to watch your step wit a stranger. For all youse know, I might be a plain-clothes dick, or somep'n, dat's what yuh're tinkin', huh? Aw, forget it! I belong, see? Ask any guy down to de docks if I don't.

SECRETARY. Who said you didn't?

YANK. After I'm 'nitiated, I'll show yuh.

SECRETARY (*Astounded*). Initiated? There's no initiation.

YANK (*Disappointed*). Ain't there no pass-word—no grip nor nothin'?

SECRETARY. What'd you think this is—the Elks—or the Black Hand?

YANK. De Elks, hell! De Black Hand, dey're a lot of yellow backstickin' Ginees. Naw. Dis is a man's gang, ain't it?

SECRETARY. You said it! That's why we stand on our two feet in the open. We got no secrets.

YANK (*Surprised but admiringly*). Yuh mean to say yuh always run wide open—like dis?

SECRETARY. Exactly.

YANK. Den yuh sure got your noive wit youse!

SECRETARY (*Sharply*). Just what was it made you want to join us? Come out with that straight.

YANK. Yuh call me? Well, I got noive, too! Here's my hand. Yuh wanter blow tings up, don't yuh? Well, dat's me! I belong!

SECRETARY (*With pretended carelessness*). You mean change the unequal conditions of society by legitimate direct action—or with dynamite?

YANK. Dynamite! Blow it offen de oith—steel —all de cages—all de factories, steamers, buildings, jails—de Steel Trust and all dat makes it go.

SECRETARY. So—that's your idea, eh? And did you have any special job in that line you wanted to propose to us? (*He makes a sign to *the men, who get up cautiously one by one and group behind* YANK.)

YANK (*Boldly*). Sure, I'll come out wit it. I'll show youse I'm one of de gang. Dere's dat millionaire guy, Douglas——

SECRETARY. President of the Steel Trust, you mean? Do you want to assassinate him?

YANK. Naw, dat don't get yuh nothin'. I mean blow up de factory, de woiks, where he
10 makes de steel. Dat's what I'm after—to blow up de steel, knock all de steel in de woild up to de moon. Dat'll fix tings! (*Eagerly, with a touch of bravado*). I'll do it by me lonesome! I'll show yuh! Tell me where his woiks is, how to git there, all de dope. Gimme de stuff, de old butter—and watch me do de rest! Watch de smoke and see it move! I don't give a damn if dey nab me—long as it's done! I'll soive life for it—and give 'em de laugh! (*Half to himself*).
20 And I'll write her a letter and tell her de hairy ape done it. Dat'll square tings.

SECRETARY (*Stepping away from* YANK). Very interesting. (*He gives a signal. The men, huskies all, throw themselves on* YANK *and before he knows it they have his legs and arms pinioned. But he is too flabbergasted to make a struggle, anyway. They feel him over for weapons.*)

MAN. No gat, no knife. Shall we give him
30 what's what and put the boots to him?

SECRETARY. No. He isn't worth the trouble we'd get into. He's too stupid. (*He comes closer and laughs mockingly in* YANK's *face.*) Ho-ho! By God, this is the biggest joke they've put up on us yet. Hey, you Joke! Who sent you—Burns or Pinkerton? No, by God, you're such a bonehead I'll bet you're in the Secret Service! Well, you dirty spy, you rotten agent provocator, you can go back and tell whatever
40 skunk is paying you blood-money for betraying your brothers that he's wasting his coin. You couldn't catch a cold. And tell him that all he'll ever get on us, or ever has got, is just his own sneaking plots that he's framed up to put us in jail. We are what our manifesto says we are, neither more nor less—and we'll give him a copy of that any time he calls. And as for you —— (*He glares scornfully at* YANK, *who is sunk*

in an oblivious stupor.) Oh, hell, what's the use of talking? You're a brainless ape. 50

YANK (*Aroused by the word to fierce but futile struggles*). What's dat, yuh Sheeny bum, yuh!

SECRETARY. Throw him out, boys. (*In spite of his struggles, this is done with gusto and éclat. Propelled by several parting kicks,* YANK *lands sprawling in the middle of the narrow cobbled street. With a growl he starts to get up and storm the closed door, but stops bewildered by the confusion in his brain, patheti-* 60 *cally impotent. He sits there, brooding, in as near to the attitude of Rodin's "Thinker" as he can get in his position.*)

YANK (*Bitterly*). So dem boids don't tink I belong, neider. Aw, to hell with 'em! Dey're in de wrong pew—de same old bull—soapboxes and Salvation Army—no guts! Cut out an hour offen de job a day and make me happy! Gimme a dollar more a day and make me happy! Tree square a day, and cauliflowers in de front yard 70 —ekal rights—a woman and kids—a lousy vote —and I'm all fixed for Jesus, huh? Aw, hell! What does dat get yuh? Dis ting's in your inside, but it ain't your belly. Feedin' your face —sinkers and coffee—dat don't touch it. It's way down—at de bottom. Yuh can't grab it, and yuh can't stop it. It moves, and everything moves. It stops and de whole woild stops. Dat's me now—I don't tick, see?—I'm a busted Ingersoll, dat's what. Steel was me, and I owned de 80 woild. Now I ain't steel, and de woild owns me. Aw, hell! I can't see—it's all dark, get me? It's all wrong! (*He turns a bitter mocking face up like an ape gibbering at the moon.*) Say, youse up dere, Man in de Moon, yuh look so wise, gimme de answer, huh? Slip me de inside dope, de information right from de stable—where do I get off at, huh?

A POLICEMAN (*Who has come up the street in time to hear this last—with grim humor*). 90 You'll get off at the station, you boob, if you don't get up out of that and keep movin'.

YANK (*Looking up at him—with a hard, bitter laugh*). Sure! Lock me up! Put me in a cage! Dat's de on'y answer yuh know. G'wan, lock me up!

POLICEMAN. What you been doin'?

YANK. Enuf to gimme life for! I was born, see? Sure, dat's de charge. Write it in de blotter. I was born, get me! 100

---

36. **Burns or Pinkerton.** Allan Pinkerton (1819–84) was a Scottish-born American detective who founded a great detective agency and promoted the American Secret Service; William J. Burns (1861–1932) was a later, lesser counterpart.

POLICEMAN (*Jocosely*). God pity your old woman! (*Then matter-of-fact*). But I've no time for kidding. You're soused. I'd run you in but it's too long a walk to the station. Come on now, get up, or I'll fan your ears with this club. Beat it now! (*He hauls* YANK *to his feet.*)

YANK (*In a vague mocking tone*). Say, where do I go from here?

POLICEMAN (*Giving him a push—with a grin, indifferently*). Go to hell.

(*Curtain*)

SCENE EIGHT

SCENE—*Twilight of the next day. The monkey house at the Zoo. One spot of clear gray light falls on the front of one cage so that the interior can be seen. The other cages are vague, shrouded in shadow from which chatterings pitched in a conversational tone can be heard. On the one cage a sign from which the word "gorilla" stands out. The gigantic animal himself is seen squatting on his haunches on a bench in much the same attitude as Rodin's "Thinker."* YANK *enters from the left. Immediately a chorus of angry chattering and screeching breaks out. The gorilla turns his eyes but makes no sound or move.*

YANK (*With a hard, bitter laugh*). Welcome to your city, huh? Hail, hail, de gang's all here! (*At the sound of his voice the chattering dies away into an attentive silence.* YANK *walks up to the gorilla's cage and, leaning over the railing, stares in at its occupant, who stares back at him, silent and motionless. There is a pause of dead stillness. Then* YANK *begins to talk in a friendly confidential tone, half-mockingly, but with a deep undercurrent of sympathy.*) Say, yuh're some hard-lookin' guy, ain't yuh? I seen lots of tough nuts dat de gang called gorillas, but yuh're de foist real one I ever seen. Some chest yuh got, and shoulders, and dem arms and mits! I bet yuh got a punch in eider fist dat'd knock 'em all silly! (*This with genuine admiration. The gorilla, as if he understood, stands upright, swelling out his chest and pounding on it with his fist.* YANK *grins sympathetically.*) Sure, I get yuh. Yuh challenge de whole woild, huh? Yuh got what I was

sayin' even if yuh muffed de woids. (*Then bitterness creeping in*). And why wouldn't yuh get me? Ain't we both members of de same club—de Hairy Apes? (*They stare at each other—a pause—then* YANK *goes on slowly and bitterly.*) So yuh're what she seen when she looked at me, de white-faced tart! I was you to her, get me? On'y outa de cage—broke out—free to moider her, see? Sure! Dat's what she tought. She wasn't wise dat I was in a cage, too—worser'n yours—sure—a damn sight—'cause you got some chanct to bust loose—but me—— (*He grows confused.*) Aw, hell! It's all wrong, ain't it? (*A pause*). I s'pose yuh wanter know what I'm doin' here, huh? I been warmin' a bench down to de Battery—ever since last night. Sure. I seen de sun come up. Dat was pretty, too—all red and pink and green. I was lookin' at de skyscrapers—steel—and all de ships comin' in, sailin' out, all over de oith—and dey was steel, too. De sun was warm, dey wasn't no clouds, and dere was a breeze blowin'. Sure, it was great stuff. I got it aw right—what Paddy said about dat bein' de right dope—on'y I couldn't get *in* it, see? I couldn't belong in dat. It was over my head. And I kept tinkin'—and den I beat it up here to see what youse was like. And I waited till dey was all gone to git yuh alone. Say, how d'yuh feel sittin' in dat pen all de time, havin' to stand for 'em comin' and starin' at yuh—de white-faced, skinny tarts and de boobs what marry 'em—makin' fun of yuh, laughin' at yuh, gittin' scared of yuh—damn 'em! (*He pounds on the rail with his fist. The gorilla rattles the bars of his cage and snarls. All the other monkeys set up an angry chattering in the darkness.* YANK *goes on excitedly.*) Sure! Dat's de way it hits me, too. On'y yuh're lucky, see? Yuh don't belong wit 'em and yuh know it. But me, I belong wit 'em—but I don't, see? Dey don't belong wit me, dat's what. Get me? Tinkin' is hard—— (*He passes one hand across his forehead with a painful gesture. The gorilla growls impatiently.* YANK *goes on gropingly.*) It's dis way, what I'm drivin' at. Youse can sit and dope dream in de past, green woods, de jungle and de rest of it. Den yuh belong and dey don't. Den yuh kin laugh at 'em, see? Yuh're de champ of de woild. But me—I ain't got no past to tink in, nor nothin' dat's comin', on'y what's now—and dat don't belong. Sure, you're de best off! Yuh

411

can't tink, can yuh? Yuh can't talk neider. But I kin make a bluff at talkin' and tinkin'—a'most git away wit it—a'most!—and dat's where de joker comes in. (*He laughs.*) I ain't on oith and I ain't in heaven, get me? I'm in de middle tryin' to separate 'em, takin' all de woist punches from bot' of 'em. Maybe dat's what dey call hell, huh? But you, yuh're at de bottom. You belong! Sure! Yuh're de on'y one in de woild dat does, yuh lucky stiff! (*The gorilla growls proudly.*) And dat's why dey gotter put yuh in a cage, see? (*The gorilla roars angrily.*) Sure! Yuh get me. It beats it when you try to tink it or talk it—it's way down—deep—behind —you 'n' me we feel it. Sure! Bot' members of dis club! (*He laughs—then in a savage tone.*) What de hell! T' hell wit it! A little action, dat's our meat! Dat belongs! Knock 'em down and keep bustin' 'em till dey croaks yuh wit a gat—wit steel! Sure! Are yuh game? Dey've looked at youse, ain't dey—in a cage? Wanter get even? Wanter wind up like a sport 'stead of croakin' slow in dere? (*The gorilla roars an emphatic affirmative.* YANK *goes on with a sort of furious exaltation.*) Sure! Yuh're reg'lar! Yuh'll stick to de finish! Me 'n' you, huh?—bot' members of dis club! We'll put up one last star bout dat'll knock 'em offen deir seats! Dey'll have to make de cages stronger after we're trou! (*The gorilla is straining at his bars, growling, hopping from one foot to the other.* YANK *takes a jimmy from under his coat and forces the lock on the cage door. He throws this open.*) Pardon from de governor! Step out and shake hands! I'll take yuh for a walk down Fif' Avenoo. We'll knock 'em offen de oith and croak wit de band playin'. Come on, Brother. (*The gorilla scrambles gingerly out of his cage.*

Goes to YANK *and stands looking at him.* YANK *keeps his mocking tone—holds out his hand.*) Shake—de secret grip of our order. (*Something, the tone of mockery, perhaps, suddenly enrages the animal. With a spring he wraps his huge arms around* YANK *in a murderous hug. There is a crackling snap of crushed ribs—a gasping cry, still mocking, from* YANK.) Hey, I didn't say kiss me! (*The gorilla lets the crushed body slip to the floor; stands over it uncertainly, considering; then picks it up, throws it in the cage, shuts the door, and shuffles off menacingly into the darkness at left. A great uproar of frightened chattering and whimpering comes from the other cages. Then* YANK *moves, groaning, opening his eyes, and there is silence. He mutters painfully.*) Say—dey oughter match him—with Zybszko. He got me, aw right. I'm trou. Even him didn't tink I belonged. (*Then, with sudden passionate despair*). Christ, where do I get off at? Where do I fit in? (*Checking himself as suddenly*). Aw, what de hell! No squawkin', see! No quittin', get me! Croak wit your boots on! (*He grabs hold of the bars of the cage and hauls himself painfully to his feet—looks around him bewilderedly—forces a mocking laugh.*) In de cage, huh? (*In the strident tones of a circus barker*). Ladies and gents, step forward and take a slant at de one and only—(*His voice weakened*)—one and original—Hairy Ape from de wilds of—— (*He slips in a heap on the floor and dies. The monkeys set up a chattering, whimpering wail. And, perhaps, the Hairy Ape at last belongs.*)

(*Curtain*)

56. **Zybszko.** Stanislaus Zybszko, a Pole, was heavy-weight wrestling champion of the world during the second decade of the present century.

D. H. LAWRENCE

David Herbert Lawrence was born September 11, 1885, at Eastwood, Nottinghamshire, the son of a coal miner, who hated the boy, drank to excess, and beat his wife. The domestic environment of the boy was, to put it mildly, undesirable; and so he took refuge in books, for which he showed early a veritable passion, and in writing of all kinds. He attended the Nottingham High School, was for a while a clerk, and taught in various places, finally coming to temporary rest at Croydon, a suburb of London (1908). His adolescent scribbling had been encouraged by a friendly neighbor girl (the "Miriam" of *Sons and Lovers*). She copied out five of his poems and sent them to *The English Review,* where they were accepted by no less a person than that stern critic of style, Ford Madox Ford. Indeed, Ford was so impressed that he arranged with young Lawrence for a novel; this was published in 1911 as *The White Peacock.* As first novels go, it was a most promising effort.

Lawrence was on one occasion invited to the home of an old Nottinghamshire acquaintance, Ernest Weekley, the present lexicographer and authority on English proper names. Lawrence repaid his host's hospitality by promptly falling in love with Mrs. Weekley, who had been Frieda von Richthofen, sister of Manfred von Richthofen, later to be renowned as Germany's most distinguished aviator in the First World War. The two eloped from under the nose of the husband and went to the Continent, where Lawrence's second novel, *The Trespasser* (1912), was completed and where they spent the winter "penniless" in Italy. Lawrence's first book of poems, *Love Poems and Others* (1913), appeared next; it contains charming romantic poetry with an unusual gift of passion and sense of color.

In the meantime Lawrence and Frieda had married, following her divorce from Weekley. Back in England, Lawrence worked feverishly on his new novel, *Sons and Lovers* (1913), which was ultimately extremely successful, although it was rejected by the first publisher approached as " a dirty book." The first part of this novel, probably the better part, is autobiographical and is a very poignant human study; the whole novel, painting in striking colors the depressing background from which Lawrence grew, is a masterpiece. About this time Lawrence met J. Middleton Murry and his wife, Katherine Mansfield (p. 425), both of whom encouraged him greatly in his writing. Another brief visit to Italy followed; but the war had broken out when the Lawrences returned, and the entire four years of the great conflict Lawrence spent at different places in England, wandering about in poor health, always away from the great cities, which he hated and dreaded. Three times he tried to enlist; and as many times he was rejected as tubercular. But these war years were far from unproductive. *The Rainbow* (1915) caused a sensation; it was the first of Lawrence's novels to present tense sex situations in frank, unashamed language, and it dwelt far more than *Sons and Lovers* upon the problems of sex. There is little cause for wonder that the novel was condemned in the English-speaking world of 1915. In the following year Lawrence was in Cornwall, where *Look! We Have Come Through* (1917), a volume of poems on his life with Frieda, added fuel to the fire of controversy kindled by *The Rainbow.* Moreover, his frequent perambulations about the Cornish countryside and his dark, rather sinister appearance led to his being suspected as a German spy. He found it wiser to move away from Cornwall. In 1918 he nearly died of influenza.

On the whole, these years in England had been anything but happy for Lawrence. After the Armistice, he left the country (1919) and, except for a few very brief visits, never returned. Italy was his first resting-place; he lived at Capri and in Sicily from 1920 to 1922, producing some short stories, an excellent novel— *Women in Love* (1920)—and a book on history—*Movements in European History* (1921) —under the rather transparent pseudonym of Lawrence H. Davidson. The juxtaposition of the academic study and the story of purple passion is not too remarkable in Lawrence's case; all his life there was in him a triangular conflict involving the teacher, the moralist, and the pagan.

Leaving Italy in 1922, Lawrence began a kind of vagabondage around the world. First he went to Ceylon, then to Australia, then to San Francisco via New Zealand and Tahiti. His ultimate destination, he planned, was to be the artists' colony at Taos, New Mexico, where his devoted admirer, Mabel Dodge Luhan, was waiting for him and Frieda to appear. Lawrence's general hope was that at Taos he might build a new social existence, a hope reminiscent of the idealistic dreams of Rousseau and Coleridge. "Let us all live together," he wrote, "and create a new world." He and Frieda settled on the Del Monte ranch, seventeen miles from Taos. But this terrestrial paradise was rent with strife; Mabel Luhan and Frieda Lawrence became jealous of each other, and Lawrence himself was annoyed by the presence of Mabel Luhan. In the winter of 1923 he took refuge for a time at Chapala, near Guadalajara, Mexico. The following year he went on a flying trip back to Europe, whence he returned to Taos, pulling in tow one Dorothy Brett, a close friend of the late Katherine Mansfield. Again, conditions in the New Mexican paradise were far from harmonious, and so he wintered once more in Mexico, this time at Oaxaca.

Lawrence's departure from the United States (1925) was an admission that his social dream had been dissipated, for he never returned. Instead, he went to Italy and the French Riviera, dabbled in painting, made the acquaintance of Aldous Huxley (p. 469), wrote, and tried to fight off the advance of tuberculosis. He was now seriously ill; but he found time nevertheless to do a large amount of miscellaneous writing and to create an international literary scandal with *Lady Chatterley's Lover* (1928), a novel which he himself regarded as "the best of all"—a novel recounting the love of an English lady for her lodge-keeper, told in the bluntest possible language liberally powdered with all the four-letter Anglo-Saxon monosyllables which would make it unacceptable to the general public. It was immediately banned; and, unlike Joyce's *Ulysses* (p. 503), it has not yet broken through the ban. Lawrence was, nevertheless, outraged by this reception of his novel and did little more of importance, dying rather suddenly near Nice, France, on March 2, 1930.

Lawrence himself saw a three-stage development in his work; the first stage comprises those works written before he left England for his peregrinations abroad; the second is covered by those works he composed abroad with a foreign background; and the third embraces the books from his pen during his last years in Italy and on the French Riviera. But the differences among these three stages are more or less external. Of the novels of the first stage Lawrence preferred *Sons and Lovers;* of the second stage, *Women in Love. Lady Chatterley's Lover,* from the third stage, he considered, as has been said, his best performance. In retrospect, however, it seems that *Sons and Lovers* is likely to remain his masterpiece; it has greater balance, greater comprehensiveness, and greater universality than the others. To give all one's attention to Lawrence's novels, however, is unfair to the author. He wrote many distinctive short stories, many beautiful poems and stimulating essays. He even attempted some plays. The complete list of his works is impressive as to length and, when one has observed strictly Lawrence's limitations as an author, impressive as to general achievement. The novels comprise *The White Peacock* (1911); *The Trespasser* (1912); *Sons and Lovers* (1913); *The Rainbow* (1915); *The Lost Girl* (1920); *Women in Love* (1920); *Aaron's Rod* (1922); *Kangaroo* (1923); *The Boy in the Bush* (1924), written in collaboration with M. L. Skinner; *St. Mawr* (1925); *The Plumed Serpent* (1925), the best of his novels inspired by his stay in America; *Lady Chatterley's Lover* (1928); and *The Virgin and the Gypsy* (1930). Among his volumes of poetry are *Love Poems and Others* (1913); *Amores* (1916); *Look! We Have Come Through* (1917); *New Poems* (1918); *Tortoises* (1921); *Birds, Beasts, and Flowers* (1923); *Collected Poems* (1928); *Pansies* (1929); *Nettles* (1930); *Last Poems* (1933); and *Selected Poems* (1948). The short stories are to be found in *The Prussian Officer* (1914); *England, My England* (1922); *The Ladybird* (1923), known in the United States from the title of its first story as *The Captain's Doll;* *Glad Ghosts* (1926); *The Woman Who Rode Away* (1928); *The Man Who Died* (1929); and three posthumous volumes—*The Lovely Lady* (1933); *Love Among the Haystacks* (1933); and *Christ in the Tyrol* (1933). His three plays—*The Widowing of Mrs. Holroyd* (1914), *Touch and Go* (1920), and *David* (1926)—were collected in 1933. The rather considerable body of prose nonfiction consists of travel sketches—*Twilight in Italy* (1916); *The Sea and Sardinia* (1921); *Mornings in Mexico* (1927); and *Etruscan Places* (1927)—and general essays—*Psychoanalysis and the Unconscious* (1921); *Movements in European History* (1921); *Fantasia of the Unconscious* (1922); *Studies in Classical American Literature* (1923); *Pornography and Obscenity* (1930), prompted by his experience with publishing *Lady Chatterley's Lover;* and *Apocalypse* (1931).

Scarcely had Lawrence been buried before J. Middleton Murry published a memoir of Lawrence, entitled *Son of Woman,* in which he proclaimed that Lawrence suffered severely from an Oedipus complex, that the image of his mother, the victim of her drunken husband, was constantly before the son and that in consequence the son was obsessed with sex and was unable to find happiness with any woman. It must be conceded that, judging by Lawrence's own words and the implications of *Sons and Lovers*, there was more basis of fact in Murry's theory than there was, let us say, in Krutch's explanation of Edgar Allan Poe's vagaries (p. 284). But not unnaturally Frieda Lawrence made an angry retort, vehemently remarking that Murry's statement was "a beastly thing to say with me still alive," and all of Lawrence's friends, particularly those from the large female sector, lifted their voices in a chorus of protest. On the other side of the question is the fact that Lawrence's letters were edited by Aldous Huxley (1932), who is believed to have drawn his characters the Rampions, in *Point Counter Point* (p. 470), from Lawrence and Frieda; in his commentary on these letters Huxley refers to Lawrence as "no Bohemian; a provincial, an inspired provincial with puritan leanings." Somewhere between the viewpoints of Murry and Huxley the truth probably lies concealed by the smoke screen of passionate discussion which this unusual man invariably calls forth.

Lawrence's life was restless and inconclusive, and he shows the effects of his constant travels in the variety of scene in his many works. His experiences in Ceylon, in Australia, and in Mexico give him locales which he can describe in brilliant contrast to those of his stories of English life. But essentially he remains unchanged in the theme of these stories, and is thus limited. No writer of the day has better illustrated the preoccupation with sex so characteristic of the Jazz Age than D. H. Lawrence. The struggle of the human being in love caused by the physical expression of his love on the one hand and its spiritual phase on the other is what lies at the core of all his work. The sociological leveling which he hopes for in his later novels seems to be, after all, merely a proposed solution to this struggle. And, unfortunately for Lawrence's peace of mind and for the worth of his net achievement, he can never decide upon the philosophical viewpoint which his characters should adopt. He gropes and

suffers, and his characters with him. Consequently there is in his work the itch of an unsatisfied longing, partly physical and partly spiritual. His characters are harried by moral scruples, by social pressures, by lust—"they would and they would not." They, like their creator, are appallingly deficient in a sense of humor.

But, if this philosophical torment seems inevitable in Lawrence, and if he seems to be unable to escape from the waste land in which he finds himself—still, few can deny his power of expression, his passionate warmth, his vividness of language, and his sense of futility and tragedy. In substance he may be a puritan, as some will have it; more often, however, he gives the impression of a naïve and quixotic but at the same time decadent tilter against windmills and scatterer of sheep. In manner he is a fine artist. But he could not take sex for granted and proceed from that point.

The Lovely Lady

AT SEVENTY-TWO, Pauline Attenborough could still sometimes be mistaken, in the half-light, for thirty. She really was a wonderfully preserved woman, of perfect *chic*. Of course, it helps a great deal to have the right frame. She would be an exquisite skeleton, and her skull would be an exquisite skull, like that of some Etruscan woman, with feminine charm still in the swerve of the bone and the pretty naïve teeth.   10

Mrs. Attenborough's face was of the perfect oval and slightly flat type that wears best. There is no flesh to sag. Her nose rode serenely in its finely bridged curve. Only her big grey eyes were a tiny bit prominent on the surface of her face, and they gave her away most. The bluish lids were heavy, as if they ached sometimes with the strain of keeping the eyes beneath them arch and bright; and at the corners of the eyes were fine little wrinkles which   20 would slacken with haggardness, then be pulled up tense again, to that bright, gay look, like a Leonardo woman who really could laugh outright.

Her niece Cecilia was perhaps the only person in the world who was aware of the invisible little wire which connected Pauline's eye-wrinkles with Pauline's will power. Only Cecilia *consciously* watched the eyes go haggard and old and tired, and remain so, for hours; until Robert came home. Then, ping!—the mysterious little wire that worked between Pauline's will and her face went taut; the weary, haggard, prominent eyes suddenly began to gleam; the eyelids arched; the queer curved eyebrows, which floated in such frail arches on Pauline's forehead, began to gather a mocking significance, and you had the *real* lovely lady, in all her charm.

She really had the secret of everlasting youth; that is to say, she could don her youth again like an eagle. But she was sparing of it. She was wise enough not to try being young for too many people. Her son Robert, in the evenings, and Sir Wilfred Knipe sometimes in the afternoon to tea; then occasional visitors on Sunday, when Robert was home; for these she was her lovely and changeless self, that age could not wither, nor custom stale; so bright and kindly and yet subtly mocking, like Mona Lisa who knew a thing or two. But Pauline knew more, so she needn't be smug at all, she could laugh that lovely mocking Bacchante laugh of hers, which was at the same time never malicious, always good-naturedly tolerant, both of virtues and vices. The former, of course, taking much more tolerating. So she suggested, roguishly.

Only with her niece Cecilia she did not trouble to keep up the glamor. Ciss was not very observant, anyhow; and more than that, she was plain; more still, she was in love with Robert; and most of all, she was thirty, and dependent on her Aunt Pauline. Oh, Cecilia! Why make music for her?

Cecilia, called by her aunt and by her cousin Robert just Ciss, like a cat spitting, was a big dark-complexioned pug-faced young woman who very rarely spoke, and, when she did, couldn't get it out. She was the daughter of a poor Congregational minister who had been, while he lived, brother to Ronald, Aunt Pauline's husband. Ronald and the Congregational minister were both well dead, and Aunt Pauline had had charge of Ciss for the last five years.

They lived all together in a quite exquisite though rather small Queen Anne house some twenty-five miles out of town, secluded in a little dale, and surrounded by small but very quaint and pleasant grounds. It was an ideal place and an ideal life for Aunt Pauline, at the age of seventy-two. When the kingfishers flashed up the little stream in the garden, going under the alders, something still flashed in her heart. She was that kind of woman.

Robert, who was two years older than Ciss, went every day to town, to his chambers in one of the Inns. He was a barrister, and, to his secret but very deep mortification, he earned about a hundred pounds a year. He simply *couldn't* get above that figure, though it was rather easy to get below it. Of course, it didn't matter. Pauline had money. But then what was Pauline's was Pauline's, and, though she could give almost lavishly, still, one was always aware of having a *lovely* and *undeserved* present made to one: presents are so much nicer when they are undeserved, Aunt Pauline would say.

Robert too was plain, and almost speechless. He was medium-sized, rather broad and stout, though not fat. Only his creamy, clean-shaven face was rather fat and sometimes suggestive of an Italian priest, in its silence and its secrecy. But he had grey eyes like his mother but very shy and uneasy, not bold like hers. Perhaps Ciss was the only person who fathomed his awful shyness and *malaise*, his habitual feeling that he was in the wrong place: almost like a soul that has got into the wrong body. But he never did anything about it. He went up to his chambers, and read law. It was, however, all the weird old processes that interested him. He had, unknown to everybody but his mother, a quite extraordinary collection of old Mexican legal documents, reports of processes and trials, pleas, accusations, the weird and awful mixture of ecclesiastical law and common law in seventeenth-century Mexico. He had started a study in this direction through coming across a report of a trial of two English sailors, for murder, in Mexico in 1620, and he had gone on, when the next document was an accusation against a Don Miguel Estrada for seducing one of the nuns of the Sacred Heart Convent in Oaxaca in 1680.

Pauline and her son Robert had wonderful evenings with these old papers. The lovely lady knew a little Spanish. She even looked a trifle Spanish herself, with a high comb and a marvelous dark brown shawl embroidered in thick silvery silk embroidery. So she would sit at the perfect old table, soft as velvet in its deep brown surface, a high comb in her hair, ear-rings with dropping pendants in her ears, her arms bare and still beautiful, a few strings of pearls round her throat, a puce velvet dress on, and this or another beautiful shawl, and by candlelight she looked, yes, a Spanish highbred beauty of thirty-two or three. She set the candles to give her face just the chiaroscuro she knew suited her; her high chair that rose behind her face was done in old green brocade, against which her face emerged like a Christmas rose.

They were always three at table; and they always drank a bottle of champagne: Pauline two glasses, Ciss two glasses, Robert the rest. The lovely lady sparkled and was radiant. Ciss, her black hair bobbed, her broad shoulders in a very nice and becoming dress that Aunt Pauline had helped her to make, stared from her aunt to her cousin and back again, with rather confused, mute, hazel eyes, and played the part of an audience suitably impressed. She *was* impressed, somewhere, all the time. And even rendered speechless by Pauline's brilliancy, even after five years. But at the bottom of her consciousness were the data of as weird a document as Robert ever studied: all the things she knew about her aunt and cousin.

Robert was always a gentleman, with an old-fashioned punctilious courtesy that covered his shyness quite completely. He was, and Ciss knew it, more confused than shy. He was worse than she was. Cecilia's own confusion dated from only five years back—Robert's must have started before he was born. In the lovely lady's womb he must have felt *very* confused.

He paid all his attention to his mother, drawn to her as a humble flower to the sun. And yet, priest-like, he was all the time aware, with the tail of his consciousness, that Ciss was there, and that she was a bit shut out of it,

and that something wasn't right. He was aware of the third consciousness in the room. Whereas, to Pauline, her niece Cecilia was an appropriate part of her own setting, rather than a distinct consciousness.

Robert took coffee with his mother and Ciss in the warm drawing-room, where all the furniture was so lovely, all collectors' pieces—Mrs. Attenborough had made her own money, dealing privately in pictures and furniture and rare things from barbaric countries—and the three talked desultorily till about eight or half-past. It was very pleasant, very cosy, very homely even: Pauline made a real home cosiness out of so much elegant material. The chat was simple and nearly always bright. Pauline was her *real* self, emanating a friendly mockery and an odd, ironic gaiety. Till there came a little pause.

At which Ciss always rose and said good-night and carried out the coffee tray, to prevent Burnett from intruding any more.

And then! Oh, then, the lovely glowing intimacy of the evening, between mother and son, when they deciphered manuscripts and discussed points, Pauline with that eagerness of a girl, for which she was famous. And it was quite genuine. In some mysterious way she had *saved up* her power for being thrilled, in connexion with a man. Robert, solid, rather quiet and subdued, seemed like the elder of the two: almost like a priest with a young girl pupil. And that was rather how he felt.

Ciss had a flat for herself just across the court-yard, over the old coachhouse and stables. There were no horses. Robert kept his car in the coachhouse. Ciss had three very nice rooms up there, stretching along in a row one after another, and she had got used to the ticking of the stable clock.

But sometimes she did not go up to her rooms. In the summer she would sit on the lawn, and from the open window of the drawing-room upstairs she would hear Pauline's wonderful heart-searching laugh. And in the winter the young woman would put on a thick coat and walk slowly to the little balustraded bridge over the stream, and then look back at the three lighted windows of that drawing-room where mother and son were so happy together.

Ciss loved Robert, and she believed that Pauline intended the two of them to marry: when she was dead. But poor Robert, he was so convulsed with shyness already, with man or woman. What would he be when his mother was dead?—in a dozen more years. He would be just a shell, the shell of a man who had never lived.

The strange unspoken sympathy of the young with one another, when they are overshadowed by the old, was one of the bonds between Robert and Ciss. But another bond, which Ciss did not know how to draw tight, was the bond of passion. Poor Robert was by nature a passionate man. His silence and his agonized, though hidden, shyness were both the result of a secret physical passionateness. And how Pauline could play on this! Ah, Ciss was not blind to the eyes which he fixed on his mother, eyes fascinated yet humiliated, full of shame. He was ashamed that he was not a man. And he did not love his mother. He was fascinated by her. Completely fascinated. And for the rest, paralyzed in a life-long confusion.

Ciss stayed in the garden till the lights leapt up in Pauline's bedroom—about ten o'clock. The lovely lady had retired. Robert would now stay another hour or so, alone. Then he too would retire. Ciss, in the dark outside, sometimes wished she could creep up to him and say: "Oh, Robert! It's all wrong!" But Aunt Pauline would hear. And anyhow, Ciss couldn't do it. She went off to her own rooms, once more, and so for ever.

In the morning, coffee was brought up on a tray to each of the three relatives. Ciss had to be at Sir Wilfred Knipe's at nine o'clock, to give two hours' lessons to his little granddaughter. It was her sole serious occupation, except that she played the piano for the love of it. Robert set off to town about nine. And, as a rule, Aunt Pauline appeared to lunch, though sometimes not until tea-time. When she appeared, she looked fresh and young. But she was inclined to fade rather quickly, like a flower without water, in the daytime. Her hour was the candle hour.

So she always rested in the afternoon. When the sun shone, if possible she took a sun bath. This was one of her secrets. Her lunch was very light, she could take her sun-and-air bath before noon or after, as it pleased her. Often it was in the afternoon, when the sun shone very warmly into a queer little yew-walled square just behind the stables. Here Ciss stretched out the lying-chair and rugs, and put the light parasol handy in the silent little enclosure of thick dark yew hedges beyond the red walls of the unused stables. And hither came the lovely lady with her book. Ciss then had to be on guard in one of her own rooms, should her aunt, who was very keen-eared, hear a footstep.

One afternoon it occurred to Cecilia that she herself might while away this rather long afternoon by taking a sun bath. She was growing restive. The thought of the flat roof of the stable buildings, to which she could climb from a loft at the end, started her on a new adventure. She often went on to the roof: she had to, to wind up the stable clock, which was a job she had assumed to herself. Now she took a rug, climbed out under the heavens, looked at the sky and the great elm-tops, looked at the sun, then took off her things and lay down perfectly serenely, in a corner of the roof under the parapet, full in the sun.

It was rather lovely, to bask all one's length like this in warm sun and air. Yes, it was very lovely! It even seemed to melt some of the hard bitterness of her heart, some of that core of unspoken resentment which never dissolved. Luxuriously, she spread herself, so that the sun should touch her limbs fully, fully. If she had no other lover, she should have the sun! She rolled voluptuously. And suddenly, her heart stood still in her body, and her hair almost rose on end as a voice said very softly, musingly in her ear:

"No, Henry dear! It was not my fault you died instead of marrying that Claudia. No, darling. I was quite, quite willing for you to marry her, unsuitable though she was."

Cecilia sank down on her rug powerless and perspiring with dread. That awful voice, so soft, so musing, yet so unnatural. Not a human voice at all. Yet there must, there must be someone on the roof! Oh! how unspeakably awful!

She lifted her weak head and peeped across the sloping leads. Nobody! The chimneys were far too narrow to shelter anybody. There was nobody on the roof. Then it must be someone in the trees, in the elms. Either that, or terror unspeakable, a bodiless voice! She reared her head a little higher:

And as she did so, came the voice again:

"No, darling! I told you you would tire of her in six months. And you see, it was true, dear. It was true, true, true! I wanted to spare you that. So it wasn't I who made you feel weak and disabled, wanting that very silly Claudia; poor thing, she looked so woebegone afterwards! Wanting her and not wanting her, you got *yourself* into that perplexity, my dear. I only warned you. What else could I do? And you lost your spirit and died without ever knowing me again. It was bitter, bitter——"

The voice faded away. Cecilia subsided weakly on to her rug, after the anguished tension of listening. Oh, it was awful. The sun shone, the sky was blue, all seemed so lovely and afternoony and summery. And yet, oh, horror!—she was going to be forced to believe in the supernatural! And she loathed the supernatural, ghosts and voices and rappings and all the rest.

But that awful creepy bodiless voice, with its rusty sort of whisper of an overtone! It had something so fearfully familiar in it too! and yet was so utterly uncanny. Poor Cecilia could only lie there unclothed, and so all the more agonizingly helpless, inert, collapsed in sheer dread.

And then she heard the thing sigh! A deep sigh that seemed weirdly familiar, yet was not human. "Ah, well; ah, well, the heart must bleed! Better it should bleed than break. It is grief, grief! But it wasn't my fault, dear. And Robert could marry our poor dull Ciss tomorrow, if he wanted her. But he doesn't care about it, so why force him into anything!" The sounds were very uneven, sometimes only a husky sort of whisper. Listen! Listen!

Cecilia was about to give vent to loud and piercing screams of hysteria, when the last two sentences arrested her. All her caution and her cunning sprang alert. It was Aunt Pauline! It must be Aunt Pauline, practising ventriloquism or something like that! What a devil she was!

Where was she? She must be lying down there, right below where Cecilia herself was lying. And it was either some fiend's trick of ventriloquism, or else thought transference that conveyed itself like sound. The sounds were very uneven. Sometimes quite inaudible, some-

times only a brushing sort of noise. Ciss listened intently. No, it could not be ventriloquism. It was worse, some form of thought transference. Some horror of that sort. Cecilia still lay weak and inert, terrified to move, but she was growing calmer, with suspicion. It was some diabolic trick of that unnatural woman.

But *what a devil* of a woman! She even knew that she, Cecilia, had mentally accused her of killing her son Henry. Poor Henry was Robert's elder brother, twelve years older than Robert. He had died suddenly when he was twenty-two, after an awful struggle with himself, because he was passionately in love with a young and very good-looking actress, and his mother had humorously despised him for the attachment. So he had caught some sudden ordinary disease, but the poison had gone to his brain and killed him, before he ever regained consciousness. Ciss knew the few facts from her own father. And lately, she had been thinking that Pauline was going to kill Robert as she had killed Henry. It was clear murder: a mother murdering her sensitive sons, who were fascinated by her: the Circe!

"I suppose I may as well get up," murmured the dim unbreaking voice. "Too much sun is as bad as too little. Enough sun, enough love thrill, enough proper food, and not too much of any of them, and a woman might live for ever. I verily believe for ever. If she absorbs as much vitality as she expends! Or perhaps a trifle more!"

It was certainly Aunt Pauline! How, how horrible! She, Ciss, was hearing Aunt Pauline's thoughts. Oh, how ghastly! Aunt Pauline was sending out her thoughts in a sort of radio, and she, Ciss, had to *hear* what her aunt was thinking. How ghastly! How insufferable! One of them would surely have to die.

She twisted as she lay inert and crumpled, staring vacantly in front of her. Vacantly! Vacantly! And her eyes were staring almost into a hole. She was staring into it unseeing, a hole going down in the corner from the lead gutter. It meant nothing to her. Only it frightened her a little more.

When suddenly out of the hole came a sigh and a last whisper. "Ah, well! Pauline! Get up, it's enough for today!"—Good God! Out of the hole of the rain-pipe! The rain-pipe was acting as a speaking-tube! Impossible! No, quite possible. She had read of it even in some book. And Aunt Pauline, like the old and guilty woman she was, talked aloud to herself. That was it!

A sullen exultance sprang into Ciss's breast. *That* was why she would never have anybody, not even Robert, in her bedroom. That was why she never dozed in a chair, never sat absent-minded anywhere, but went to her room, and kept to her room, except when she roused herself to be alert. When she slackened off, she talked to herself! She talked in a soft crazy little voice, to herself. But she was not crazy. It was only her thoughts murmuring themselves aloud.

So she had qualms about poor Henry! Well, she might have! Ciss believed that Aunt Pauline had loved her big, handsome, brilliant first-born much more than she loved Robert, and that his death had been a terrible blow and a chagrin to her. Poor Robert had been only ten years old when Henry died. Since then he had been the substitute.

Ah, how awful!

But Aunt Pauline was a strange woman. She had left her husband when Henry was a small child, some years even before Robert was born. There was no quarrel. Sometimes she saw her husband again, quite amicably, but a little mockingly. And she even gave him money.

For Pauline earned all her own. Her father had been a Consul in the East and in Naples, and a devoted collector of beautiful and exotic things. When he died, soon after his grandson Henry was born, he left his collection of treasures to his daughter. And Pauline, who had really a passion and a genius for loveliness, whether in texture or form or color, had laid the basis of her fortune on her father's collection. She had gone on collecting, buying where she could, and selling to collectors and to museums. She was one of the first to sell old, weird African wooden figures to the museums, and ivory carvings from New Guinea. She bought Renoir as soon as she saw his pictures. But not Rousseau. And all by herself, she made a fortune.

After her husband died, she had not married again. She was not even *known* to have had lovers. If she did have lovers, it was not among

44. **Renoir,** Pierre Auguste Renoir (1841–1919), probably the most distinguished of French painters of the Impressionist school.   45. **Rousseau,** Pierre Etienne Theodore Rousseau (1812–67), French painter of romantic persuasion.

the men who admired her most and paid her devout and open attendance. To these she was a "friend."

Cecilia slipped on her clothes and caught up her rug, hastening carefully down the ladder to the loft. As she descended she heard the ringing musical call: "All right, Ciss!" which meant that the lovely lady was finished, and returning to the house. Even her voice was marvellously young and sonorous, beautifully balanced and self-possessed. So different from the little voice in which she talked to herself. *That* was much more the voice of an old woman.

Ciss hastened round to the yew enclosure, where lay the comfortable chaise-longue with the various delicate rugs. Everything Pauline had was choice, to the fine straw mat on the floor. The great yew walls were beginning to cast long shadows. Only in the corner, where the rugs tumbled their delicate colors, was there hot, still sunshine.

The rugs folded up, the chair lifted away, Cecilia stooped to look at the mouth of the rain-pipe. There it was, in the corner, under a little hood of masonry and just projecting from the thick leaves of the creeper on the wall. If Pauline, lying there, turned her face towards the wall, she would speak into the very mouth of the hole. Cecilia was reassured. She had heard her aunt's thoughts indeed, but by no uncanny agency.

That evening, as if aware of something, Pauline was a little quicker than usual, though she looked her own serene, rather mysterious self. And after coffee she said to Robert and Ciss: "I'm so sleepy. The sun has made me so sleepy. I feel full of sunshine like a bee. I shall go to bed, if you don't mind. You two sit and have a talk."

Cecilia looked quickly at her cousin.

"Perhaps you would rather be alone," she said to him.

"No, no," he replied. "Do keep me company for a while, if it doesn't bore you."

The windows were open, the scent of the honeysuckle wafted in, with the sound of an owl. Robert smoked in silence. There was a sort of despair in the motionless, rather squat body. He looked like a caryatid bearing a weight.

"Do you remember Cousin Henry?" Cecilia asked him suddenly.

He looked up in surprise.

"Yes, very well," he said.

"What did he look like?" she said, glancing into her cousin's big secret-troubled eyes, in which there was so much frustration.

"Oh, he was handsome; tall and fresh-colored, with mother's soft brown hair." As a matter of fact, Pauline's hair was gray. "The ladies admired him very much; he was at all the dances."

"And what kind of character had he?"

"Oh, very good-natured and jolly. He liked to be amused. He was rather quick and clever, like mother, and very good company."

"And did he love your mother?"

"Very much. She loved him too—better than she does me, as a matter of fact. He was so much more nearly her idea of a man."

"Why was he more her idea of a man?"

"Tall—handsome—attractive, and very good company—and would, I believe, have been very successful at law. I'm afraid I am merely negative in all those respects."

Ciss looked at him attentively, with her slow-thinking hazel eyes. Under his impassive mask, she knew he suffered.

"Do you think you are so much more negative than he?" she said.

He did not lift his face. But after a few moments he replied:

"My life, certainly, is a negative affair."

She hesitated before she dared ask him:

"And do you mind?"

He did not answer her at all. Her heart sank.

"You see, I am afraid my life is as negative as yours is," she said. "And I'm beginning to mind bitterly. I'm thirty."

She saw his creamy, well-bred hand tremble.

"I suppose," he said, without looking at her, "one will rebel when it is too late."

That was queer, from him.

"Robert," she said, "do you like me at all?"

She saw his dusky creamy face, so change-less in its folds, go pale.

"I am very fond of you," he murmured.

"Won't you kiss me? Nobody ever kisses me," she said pathetically.

He looked at her, his eyes strange with fear and a certain haughtiness. Then he rose and came softly over to her, and kissed her gently on the cheek.

"It's an awful shame, Ciss!" he said softly.

She caught his hand and pressed it to her breast.

"And sit with me sometime in the garden," she said, murmuring with difficulty. "Won't you?"

He looked at her anxiously and searchingly.

"What about mother?" he said.

Ciss smiled a funny little smile, and looked into his eyes. He suddenly flushed crimson, turning aside his face. It was a painful sight.

"I know," he said, "I am no lover of women."

He spoke with sarcastic stoicism against himself, but even she did not know the shame it was to him.

"You never try to be!" she said.

Again his eyes changed uncannily.

"Does one have to try?" he said.

"Why, yes! One never does anything if one doesn't try."

He went pale again.

"Perhaps you are right," he said.

In a few minutes she left him, and went to her rooms. At least, she had tried to take off the everlasting lid from things.

The weather continued sunny, Pauline continued her sun baths, and Ciss lay on the roof eavesdropping in the literal sense of the word. But Pauline was not to be heard. No sound came up the pipe. She must be lying with her face away into the open. Ciss listened with all her might. She could just detect the faintest, faintest murmur away below, but no audible syllable.

And at night, under the stars, Cecilia sat and waited in silence, on the seat which kept in view the drawing-room windows and the side door into the garden. She saw the light go up in her aunt's room. She saw the lights at last go out in the drawing-room, And she waited. But he did not come. She stayed on in the darkness half the night, while the owl hooted. But she stayed alone.

Two days she heard nothing, her aunt's thoughts were not revealed, and at evening nothing happened. Then the second night, as she sat with heavy, helpless persistence in the garden, suddenly she started. He had come out. She rose and went softly over the grass to him.

"Don't speak," he murmured.

And in silence, in the dark, they walked down the garden and over the little bridge to the paddock, where the hay, cut very late, was in cock. There they stood disconsolate under the stars.

"You see," he said, "how can I ask for love, if I don't feel any love in myself. You know I have a real regard for you——"

"How can you feel any love, when you never feel anything?" she said.

"That is true," he replied.

10 And she waited for what next.

"And how can I marry?" he said. "I am a failure even at making money. I can't ask my mother for money."

She sighed deeply.

"Then don't bother yet about marrying," she said. "Only love me a little. Won't you?"

He gave a short laugh.

"It sounds so atrocious, to say it is hard to begin," he said.

20 She sighed again. He was so stiff to move.

"Shall we sit down a minute?" she said. And then as they sat on the hay, she added: "May I touch you? Do you mind?"

"Yes, I mind! But do as you wish," he replied, with that mixture of shyness and queer candor which made him a little ridiculous, as he knew quite well. But in his heart there was almost murder.

She touched his black, always tidy hair with 30 her fingers.

"I suppose I shall rebel one day," he said again, suddenly.

They sat some time till it grew chilly. And he held her hand fast, but he never put his arms round her. At last she rose and went indoors, saying good night.

The next day, as Cecilia lay stunned and angry on the roof, taking her sunbath, and becoming hot and fierce with sunshine, sud- 40 denly she started. A terror seized her in spite of herself. It was the voice.

"*Caro, caro, tu non l'hai visto!*" it was murmuring away, in a language Cecilia did not understand. She lay and writhed her limbs in the sun, listening intently to words she could not follow. Softly, whisperingly, with infinite caressiveness and yet with that subtle, insidious arrogance under its velvet, came the voice,

murmuring in Italian: "*Bravo, si, molto bravo, poverino, ma uomo come te non lo sara mai,* 50 *mai, mai!*" Oh, especially in Italian Cecilia heard the poisonous charm of the voice, so caressive, so soft and flexible, yet so utterly egoistic. She hated it with intensity as it sighed and whispered out of nowhere. Why, why should it be so delicate, so subtle and flexible and beautifully controlled, while she herself was so clumsy! Oh, poor Cecilia, she writhed in the afternoon sun, knowing her own clownish clumsiness and lack of suavity, in compari- 60 son.

"No, Robert dear, you will never be the man your father was, though you have some of his looks. He was a marvellous lover, soft as a flower yet piercing as a humming-bird. No, Robert dear, you will never know how to serve a woman as Monsignor Mauro did. *Cara, cara mia bellissima, ti ho aspettato come l'agonizzante aspetta la morte, morte deliziosa, quasi quasi troppo deliziosa per un' anima umana—* 70 Soft as a flower, yet probing like a hummingbird. He gave himself to a woman as he gave himself to God. Mauro! Mauro! How you loved me!"

The voice ceased in reverie, and Cecilia knew what she had guessed before, that Robert was not the son of her Uncle Ronald, but of some Italian.

"I am disappointed in you, Robert. There is no poignancy in you. Your father was a Jes- 80 uit, but he was the most perfect and poignant lover in the world. You are a Jesuit like a fish in a tank. And that Ciss of yours is the cat fishing for you. It is less edifying even than poor Henry."

Cecilia suddenly bent her mouth down to the tube, and said in a deep voice:

"Leave Robert alone! Don't kill him as well."

There was a dead silence, in the hot July afternoon that was lowering for thunder. Ce- 90 cilia lay prostrate, her heart beating in great thumps. She was listening as if her whole soul were an ear. At last she caught the whisper:

"Did someone speak?"

She leaned again to the mouth of the tube.

49. *Bravo . . . mai.* Beloved . . . yes, there is none like you . . . wonderful, yes, wonderful, poor sweetheart, there will never be a man like you, never, never. 67. *Cara . . . umana.* Beloved, most beautiful . . . I have awaited you as the dying awaits death, delicious death, . . . as if . . . as if it were almost too wonderful for a human being.

42. *Caro . . . visto,* Beloved, you didn't see him.

"Don't kill Robert as you killed me," she said with a slow enunciation, and a deep but small voice.

"Ah!" came the sharp little cry. "Who is that speaking?"

"Henry!" said the deep voice.

There was dead silence. Poor Cecilia lay with all the use gone out of her. And there was dead silence. Till at last came the whisper:

"I didn't kill Henry. No, NO! Henry, surely you can't blame me! I loved you, dearest. I only wanted to help you."

"You killed me!" came the deep, artificial, accusing voice. "Now, let Robert live. Let him go! Let him marry!"

There was a pause.

"How very, very awful!" mused the whispering voice. "Is it possible, Henry, you are a spirit, and you condemn me?"

"Yes! I condemn you!"

Cecilia felt all her pent-up rage going down that rain-pipe. At the same time, she almost laughed. It was awful.

She lay and listened and listened. No sound! As if time had ceased, she lay inert in the weakening sun. The sky was yellowing. Quickly she dressed herself, went down, and out to the corner of the stables.

"Aunt Pauline!" she called discreetly. "Did you hear thunder?"

"Yes! I am going in. Don't wait," came a feeble voice.

Cecilia retired, and from the loft watched, spying, as the figure of the lovely lady, wrapped in a lovely wrap of old blue silk, went rather totteringly to the house.

The sky gradually darkened, Cecilia hastened in with the rugs. Then the storm broke. Aunt Pauline did not appear to tea. She found the thunder trying. Robert also did not arrive till after tea, in the pouring rain. Cecilia went down the covered passage to her own house, and dressed carefully for dinner, putting some white columbines at her breast.

The drawing-room was lit with a softly shaded lamp. Robert, dressed, was waiting, listening to the rain. He too seemed strangely crackling and on edge. Cecilia came in, with the white flowers nodding at her breast. Robert was watching her curiously, a new look on his face. Cecilia went to the bookshelves near the door and was peering for something, listening acutely. She heard a rustle, then the door softly opening. And as it opened, Ciss suddenly switched on the strong electric light by the door.

Her aunt, in a dress of black lace over ivory color, stood in the doorway. Her face was made up, but haggard with a look of unspeakable irritability, as if years of suppressed exasperation and dislike of her fellow-men had suddenly crumpled her into an old witch.

"Oh, aunt!" cried Cecilia.

"Why, mother, you're a little old lady!" came the astounded voice of Robert; like an astonished boy; as if it were a joke.

"Have you only just found it out?" snapped the old woman venomously.

"Yes! Why, I thought——" his voice trailed out in misgiving.

The haggard, old Pauline, in a frenzy of exasperation, said:

"Aren't we going down?"

She had never even noticed the excess of light, a thing she shunned. And she went downstairs almost tottering.

At table she sat with her face like a crumpled mask of unspeakable irritability. She looked old, very old, and like a witch. Robert and Cecilia fetched furtive glances at her. And Ciss, watching Robert, saw that he was so astonished and repelled by his mother's looks, that he was another man.

"What kind of a drive home did you have?" snapped Pauline, with an almost gibbering irritability.

"It rained, of course," he said.

"How clever of you to have found that out!" said his mother, with the grisly grin of malice that had succeeded her arch smirk.

"I don't understand," he said with quiet suavity.

"It's apparent," said his mother, rapidly and sloppily eating her food.

She rushed through the meal like a crazy dog, to the utter consternation of the servant. And the moment it was over, she darted in a queer, crab-like way upstairs. Robert and Cecilia followed her, thunderstruck, like two conspirators.

"You pour the coffee. I loathe it! I'm going! Good night!" said the old woman, in a succession of sharp shots. And she scrambled out of the room.

There was a dead silence. At last he said:

"I'm afraid mother isn't well. I must persuade her to see a doctor."

"Yes!" said Cecilia.

The evening passed in silence. Robert and Ciss stayed on in the drawing-room, having lit a fire. Outside was cold rain. Each pretended to read. They did not want to separate. The evening passed with ominous mysteriousness, yet quickly.

At about ten o'clock, the door suddenly opened, and Pauline appeared, in a blue wrap. She shut the door behind her and came to the fire. Then she looked at the two young people in hate, real hate.

"You two had better get married quickly," she said in an ugly voice. "It would look more decent; such a passionate pair of lovers!"

Robert looked up at her quietly.

"I thought you believed that cousins should not marry, mother," he said.

"I do! But you're not cousins. Your father was an Italian priest." Pauline held her daintily slippered foot to the fire, in an old coquettish gesture. Her body tried to repeat all the old graceful gestures. But the nerve had snapped, so it was a rather dreadful caricature.

"Is that really true, mother?" he asked.

"True! What do you think? He was a distinguished man, or he wouldn't have been my lover. He was far too distinguished a man to have had you for a son. But that joy fell to me."

"How unfortunate all round," he said slowly.

"Unfortunate for you? *You* were lucky. It was *my* misfortune," she said acidly to him.

She was really a dreadful sight, like a piece of lovely Venetian glass that had been dropped, and gathered up again in horrible, sharp-edged fragments.

Suddenly she left the room again.

For a week it went on. She did not recover. It was as if every nerve in her body had suddenly started screaming in an insanity of discordance. The doctor came, and gave her sedatives, for she never slept. Without drugs, she never slept at all, only paced back and forth in her room, looking hideous and evil, reeking with malevolence. She could not bear to see either her son or her niece. Only when either of them came, she asked in pure malice:

"Well! When's the wedding? Have you celebrated the nuptials yet?"

At first Cecilia was stunned by what she had done. She realized vaguely that her aunt, once a definite thrust of condemnation had penetrated her beautiful armor, had just collapsed squirming inside her shell. It was too terrible. Ciss was almost terrified into repentance. Then she thought: This is what she always was. Now let her live the rest of her days in her true colors.

But Pauline would not live long. She was literally shrivelling away. She kept her room, and saw no one. She had her mirrors taken away.

Robert and Cecilia sat a good deal together. The jeering of the mad Pauline had not driven them apart, as she had hoped. But Cecilia dared not confess to him what she had done.

"Do you think your mother ever loved anybody?" Ciss asked him tentatively, rather wistfully, one evening.

He looked at her fixedly.

"Herself!" he said at last.

"She didn't even *love* herself," said Ciss. "It was something else—what was it?" She lifted a troubled, utterly puzzled face to him.

"Power!" he said curtly.

"But what power?" she asked. "I don't understand."

"Power to feed on other lives," he said bitterly. "She was beautiful, and she fed on life. She has fed on me as she fed on Henry. She put a sucker into one's soul, and sucked up one's essential life."

"And don't you forgive her?"

"No."

"Poor Aunt Pauline!"

But even Ciss did not mean it. She was only aghast.

"I *know* I've got a heart," he said, passionately striking his breast. "But it's almost sucked dry. I *know* people who want power over others."

Ciss was silent; what was there to say?

And two days later, Pauline was found dead in her bed, having taken too much veronal, for her heart was weakened. From the grave even she hit back at her son and her niece. She left Robert the noble sum of one thousand pounds; and Ciss one hundred. All the rest, with the nucleus of her valuable antiques, went to form the "Pauline Attenborough Museum."

KATHERINE MANSFIELD

The art of the short story, that perennial among literary types, had many talented practitioners during World War I and the years immediately following. But none of them can be considered so much a specialist in the type as one woman whose brief life and limited writings were colored by illness, the fear of death, and a constant search for spiritual as well as bodily well-being. Katherine Mansfield was born Kathleen Beauchamp, daughter of a local banker, in Wellington, New Zealand, October 14, 1888. Her childhood was spent in nearby Karori, where she attended the village school and, at the age of nine, first manifested her talent by winning a prize in English composition and publishing a story in a local periodical. At thirteen she was sent to complete her education at Queen's College, London, where she edited the college magazine. She often regarded the five years there as wasted, for to her, education was attainable only through living and observing. For a time during her college years she was as much interested in music as in literature, and she became an excellent cellist. Returning to New Zealand in 1906, she found colonial life dull and confining, and after much pleading was at last permitted to go back to England.

Miss Mansfield had by now determined on writing as a career; but unfortunately the simple, deceptively naïve style of her short stories did not attract publishers. Unable to sell her work, she took minor parts in a traveling opera company to supplement the small allowance from her father. Traveling and living in uncertain conditions in cheap boarding houses undermined her health, and she went to Germany to recover. A series of short stories, "In a German Pension," written at this time, was published in *The New Age*, bringing her a little money and the opportunity for further contributions to the magazine. She managed to eke out her income by reviewing books for the *Westminster Gazette*.

In 1911, through her connection with *The New Age*, Miss Mansfield met her future husband, J. Middleton Murry, with whom she joined in the editorship of *Rhythm* (later *The Blue Review*), a little magazine which lasted about eighteen months. During its lifetime it published a number of her stories; but after its collapse in 1913—the year, incidentally, she and Murry were married—she wrote no more for several years. Meanwhile, her constant fear that she would die suddenly of heart disease was exaggerated by continuing poor health, and she went to Paris for medical advice. Now began the wandering from one health resort to another which was to continue until her death in 1923.

In 1915, back at home in wartime London, Katherine Mansfield was visited by her brother, Leslie, on leave from the army. Their happy reminiscing about childhood in New Zealand rekindled her love of storytelling. When Leslie Beauchamp was killed in action shortly after this reunion, she wrote, ". . . I feel I have a duty to perform to the lovely time when we were both alive. I want to write about it, and he wanted me to." And at Bandol, in southern France, that autumn, she began to write again, producing this time a long story of childhood, part of which was then published as *Prelude*, the complete version being brought out posthumously as *The Aloe*.

J. Middleton Murry and D. H. Lawrence had meanwhile founded the magazine *Signature*, and to this, when she came back to England, Miss Mansfield contributed under the pseudonym of Matilda Berry. A severe attack of pleurisy in December 1917 prompted her to return to Bandol; but she found it ravaged by war, and as a result of the neglect and strain she suffered there and on her return journey through bombarded Paris, her pleurisy developed into the tuberculosis which eventually proved fatal.

Despite recurrent bouts of illness and the rigorous treatments she underwent in her search for health, Katherine Mansfield continued to write and publish. In 1919 her husband became editor of the London *Athenaeum,* and she regularly submitted literary criticism and short stories to that review. Her reputation was growing; even as recognition came, however, she stopped writing and began a serious self-examination, seeking to overcome what she seemed to regard as the falseness of her previous life and to grasp the truth which would enable her to write finer and greater things. Although this spiritual bent was calming to her neuroticism, such otherworldliness had an adverse effect upon the progress of her disease, for she was inclined to neglect the advice of her physicians. In the autumn of 1922 she went to Fontainebleau, where the Russian mystic Gurdieff had established a kind of spiritual brotherhood. There she was happy and at peace; but suddenly, on January 9, 1923, she died. The epitaph over her grave at Avon, near Fontainebleau, is a quotation from *Henry IV* which also appears on the title page of *Bliss and Other Stories:* "But I tell you, my lord fool, out of this nettle, danger, we pluck this flower, safety."

Since Miss Mansfield's art was of the kind that matures with the years, we may justifiably regard her net achievement as incomplete, just as one of her most characteristic stories, "The Doves' Nest," is incomplete. She was a nervous and hypersensitive creature, as even a superficial reading of her very interesting *Journal* will reveal. At times she is a brooding sick woman, at other times a volatile spirit. Always she loved life; always her mind was amazingly mercurial and plastic, and her receptivity to impressions startling. A curious poignancy and tenderness pervade her writing. Beginning a story was always difficult for her; but once under way, it went in a headlong rush, and an exciting period of elation and tension followed its completion. Something of that *élan* is conveyed to the coldest of readers by her *Journal* and letters.

Most of her stories are set in New Zealand or on the Riviera. But locale means little, for action means little in Katherine Mansfield's writing; she is far more interested in the spiritual aspects of the story than in technical details, and she certainly is more absorbed in creating an atmosphere, a mood, a psychology than in developing narrative incident. "The greatest literature of all," she once wrote,

the literature that scarcely exists has not merely an esthetic object, nor merely a didactic object, but in addition a creative object: that of subjecting its readers to a real and at the same time illuminating experience. Major literature, in short, is an initiation into truth.

Chekhov, Wordsworth, Coleridge, Milton, Dickens, and Proust were her favorite authors; and her own art is often reminiscent of Chekhov's. But the essential part of her limited product has a fragile personality all its own, suffused by a delicate beauty that cannot well be imitated.

Katherine Mansfield's stories are collected in *In a German Pension* (1911); *Bliss* (1920); *The Garden Party* (1922); *The Doves' Nest* (1923); *Something Childish* (1924); *The Aloe* (1930); *Selected Stories* (1930); and *Short Stories* (1937). Some of her poems, not at all remarkable, were published in 1923; and her extremely intelligent critical work was grouped under the title *Novels and Novelists* (1930). *The Journal* (1927), *Letters* (1928), and *Scrapbook* (1939) complete the list.

The Doves' Nest

AFTER lunch Milly and her mother were sitting as usual on the balcony beyond the salon, admiring for the five hundredth time the stocks, the roses, the small, bright grass beneath the palms, and the oranges against a wavy line of blue, when a card was brought them by Marie. Visitors at the Villa Martin were very rare. True, the English clergyman, Mr. Sandiman, had called, and he had come a second time with his wife to tea. But an awful 10 thing had happened on that second occasion. Mother had made a mistake. She had said "More tea, Mr. Sandybags?" Oh, what a frightful thing to have happened! How could she have done it? Milly still flamed at the thought. And he had evidently not forgiven them; he'd never come again. So this card put them both into a flutter.

Mr. Walter Prodger, they read. And then an American address, so very much abbreviated that neither of them understood it. Walter Prodger? But they'd never heard of him. Mother looked from the card to Milly.

"Prodger, dear?" she asked mildly, as though helping Milly to a slice of a never-before-tasted pudding.

And Milly seemed to be holding her plate back in the way she answered "I—don't—know, Mother."

"These are the occasions," said Mother, becoming a little flustered, "when one does so feel the need of our dear English servants. Now if I could just say, 'What is he like, Annie?' I should know whether to see him or not. But he may be some common man, selling something—one of those American inventions for peeling things, you know, dear. Or he may even be some kind of foreign sharper." Mother winced at the hard, bright little word as though she had given herself a dig with her embroidery scissors.

But here Marie smiled at Milly and murmured "C'est un très beau Monsieur."

"What does she say, dear?"

"She says he looks very nice, Mother."

"Well, we'd better—" began Mother. "Where is he now I wonder."

Marie answered "In the vestibule, Madame."

In the hall! Mother jumped up, seriously alarmed. In the hall, with all those valuable little foreign things that didn't belong to them scattered over the tables.

"Show him in, Marie. Come, Milly, come dear. We will see him in the salon. Oh, why isn't Miss Anderson here?" almost wailed Mother.

But Miss Anderson, Mother's new companion, never was on the spot when she was wanted. She had been engaged to be a comfort, a support to them both. Fond of travelling, a cheerful disposition, a good packer and so on. And then, when they had come all this way and taken the Villa Martin and moved in,

30. "C'est . . . Monsieur," "It's a very fine gentleman."

she had turned out to be a Roman Catholic. Half her time, more than half, was spent wearing out the knees of her skirts in cold churches. It was really too . . .

The door opened. A middle-aged clean-shaven, very well dressed stranger stood bowing before them. His bow was stately. Milly saw it pleased Mother very much; she bowed her Queen Alexandra bow back. As for Milly, she never could bow. She smiled, feeling shy, but deeply interested. 60

"Have I the pleasure," said the stranger very courteously, with a strong American accent, "of speaking with Mrs. Wyndham Fawcett?"

"I am Mrs. Fawcett," said Mother, graciously, "and this is my daughter, Mildred."

"Pleased to meet you, Miss Fawcett." And the stranger shot a fresh, chill hand at Milly, who grasped it just in time before it was gone again. 70

"Won't you sit down?" said Mother, and she waved faintly at all the gilt chairs.

"Thank you, I will," said the stranger.

Down he sat, still solemn, crossing his legs, and, most surprisingly, his arms as well. His face looked at them over his dark arms as over a gate.

"Milly, sit down, dear."

So Milly sat down, too, on the Madame Recamier couch, and traced a filet lace flower 80 with her finger. There was a little pause. She saw the stranger swallow; Mother's fan opened and shut.

Then he said "I took the liberty of calling, Mrs. Fawcett, because I had the pleasure of your husband's acquaintance in the States when he was lecturing there some years ago. I should like very much to renoo our—well— I venture to hope we might call it friendship. Is he with you at present? Are you expecting 90 him out? I noticed his name was not mentioned in the local paper. But I put that down to a foreign custom, perhaps—giving precedence to the lady."

And here the stranger looked as though he might be going to smile.

79. **Madame Recamier,** Jeanne Françoise Julie Adelaide Bernard Récamier (1777–1849), an accomplished French society leader noted for her sparkling wit and gay *salons.* The long divan-like couch was named in honor of these *salons.* 88. **renoo.** As is usually the case when English writers try to reproduce American pronunciation or language tricks, the results are not particularly convincing.

But as a matter of fact it was extremely awkward. Mother's mouth shook. Milly squeezed her hands between her knees, but she watched hard from under her eyebrows. Good, noble little Mummy! How Milly admired her as she heard her say, gently and quite simply, "I am sorry to say my husband died two years ago."

Mr. Prodger gave a great start. "Did he?" He thrust out his under lip, frowned, pondered. "I am truly sorry to hear that, Mrs. Fawcett. I hope you'll believe me when I say I had no idea your husband had . . . passed over."

"Of course." Mother softly stroked her skirt.

"I do trust," said Mr. Prodger, more seriously still, "that my inquiry didn't give you too much pain."

"No, no. It's quite all right," said the gentle voice.

But Mr. Prodger insisted. "You're sure? You're positive?"

At that Mother raised her head and gave him one of her still, bright, exalted glances that Milly knew so well. "I'm not in the least hurt," she said, as one might say it from the midst of the fiery furnace.

Mr. Prodger looked relieved. He changed his attitude and continued. "I hope this regrettable circumstance will not deprive me of your—"

"Oh, certainly not. We shall be delighted. We are always so pleased to know any one who—" Mother gave a little bound, a little flutter. She flew from her shadowy branch on to a sunny one. "Is this your first visit to the Riviera?"

"It is," said Mr. Prodger. "The fact is I was in Florence until recently. But I took a heavy cold there—"

"Florence so damp," cooed Mother.

"And the doctor recommended I should come here for the sunshine before I started for home."

"The sun is so very lovely here," agreed Mother, enthusiastically.

"Well, I don't think we get too much of it," said Mr. Prodger, dubiously, and two lines showed at his lips. "I seem to have been sitting around in my hotel more days than I care to count."

"Ah, hotels are so very trying," said Mother, and she drooped sympathetically at the thought of a lonely man in an hotel. . . . "You are alone here?" she asked, gently, just in case . . . one never knew . . . it was better to be on the safe, the tactful side.

But her fears were groundless.

"Oh, yes, I'm alone," cried Mr. Prodger, more heartily than he had spoken yet, and he took a speck of thread off his immaculate trouser leg. Something in his voice puzzled Milly. What was it?

"Still, the scenery is so very beautiful," said Mother, "that one really does not feel the need of friends. I was only saying to my daughter yesterday I could live here for years without going outside the garden gate. It is all so beautiful."

"Is that so?" said Mr. Prodger, soberly. He added, "You have a very charming villa." And he glanced round the salon. "Is all this antique furniture genuine, may I ask?"

"I believe so," said Mother. "I was certainly given to understand it was. Yes, we love our villa. But of course it is very large for two, that is to say three, ladies. My companion, Miss Anderson, is with us. But unfortunately she is a Roman Catholic, and so she is out most of the time."

Mr. Prodger bowed as one who agreed that Roman Catholics were very seldom in.

"But I am so fond of space," continued Mother, "and so is my daughter. We both love large rooms and plenty of them—don't we, Milly?"

This time Mr. Prodger looked at Milly quite cordially and remarked, "Yes, young people like plenty of room to run about."

He got up, put one hand behind his back, slapped the other upon it and went over to the balcony.

"You've a view of the sea from here," he observed.

The ladies might well have noticed it; the whole Mediterranean swung before the windows.

"We are so fond of the sea," said Mother, getting up, too.

Mr. Prodger looked towards Milly. "Do you see those yachts, Miss Fawcett?"

Milly saw them.

"Do you happen to know what they're doing?" asked Mr. Prodger.

What they were doing? What a funny question! Milly stared and bit her lip.

"They're racing!" said Mr. Prodger, and this time he did actually smile at her.

"Oh, yes, of course," stammered Milly. "Of course they are." She knew that.

"Well, they're not always at it," said Mr. Prodger, good-humouredly. And he turned to Mother and began to take a ceremonious farewell.

"I wonder," hesitated Mother, folding her little hands and eyeing him, "if you would care to lunch with us—if you would not be too dull with two ladies. We should be so very pleased."

Mr. Prodger became intensely serious again. He seemed to brace himself to meet the luncheon invitation. "Thank you very much, Mrs. Fawcett. I should be delighted."

"That will be very nice," said Mother, warmly. "Let me see. Today is Monday—isn't it, Milly? Would Wednesday suit you?"

Mr. Prodger replied, "It would suit me excellently to lunch with you on Wednesday, Mrs. Fawcett. At *mee-dee,* I presume, as they call it here."

"Oh, no! We keep our English times. At one o'clock," said Mother.

And that being arranged, Mr. Prodger became more and more ceremonious and bowed himself out of the room.

Mother rang for Marie to look after him, and a moment later the big glass hall-door shut.

"Well!" said Mother. She was all smiles. Little smiles like butterflies, alighting on her lips and gone again. "That was an adventure, Milly, wasn't it, dear? And I thought he was such a very charming man, didn't you?"

Milly made a little face at Mother and rubbed her eye.

"Of course you did. You must have, dear. And his appearance was so satisfactory—wasn't it?" Mother was obviously enraptured. "I mean he looked so very well kept. Did you notice his hands? Every nail shone like a diamond. I must say I do like to see . . ."

She broke off. She came over to Milly and patted her big collar straight.

"You do think it was right of me to ask him to lunch—don't you, dear?" said Mother pathetically.

Mother made her feel so big, so tall. But she was tall. She could pick Mother up in her arms. Sometimes, rare moods came when she did. Swooped on Mother who squeaked like a mouse and even kicked. But not lately. Very seldom now. . . .

"It was so strange," said Mother. There was the still, bright, exalted glance again. "I suddenly seemed to hear Father say to me 'Ask him to lunch.' And then there was some—warning. . . . I think it was about the wine. But that I didn't catch—very unfortunately," she added, mournfully. She put her hand on her breast; she bowed her head. "Father is still so near," she whispered.

Milly looked out of the window. She hated Mother going on like this. But of course she couldn't say anything. Out of the window there was the sea and the sunlight silver on the palms, like water dripping from silver oars. Milly felt a yearning—what was it?—it was like a yearning to fly.

But Mother's voice brought her back to the salon, to the gilt chairs, the gilt couches, sconces, cabinets, the tables with the heavy-sweet flowers, the faded brocade, the pink-spotted Chinese dragons on the mantelpiece and the two Turks' heads in the fireplace that supported the broad logs.

"I think a leg of lamb would be nice, don't you, dear?" said Mother. "The lamb is so very small and delicate just now. And men like nothing so much as plain roast meat. Yvonne prepares it so nicely, too, with that little frill of paper lace round the top of the leg. It always reminds me of something—I can't think what. But it certainly makes it look very attractive indeed."

§

Wednesday came. And the flutter that Mother and Milly had felt over the visiting card extended to the whole villa. Yes, it was not too much to say that the whole villa thrilled and fluttered at the idea of having a man to lunch. Old, flat-footed Yvonne came waddling back from market with a piece of gorgonzola in so perfect a condition that when she found Marie in the kitchen she flung down her great basket, snatched the morsel up and held it, rustling in its paper, to her quivering bosom.

"J'ai trouvé un morceau de gorgonzola," she panted, rolling up her eyes as though she invited the heavens themselves to look down upon it. "J'ai un morceau de gorgonzola ici pour un prince, ma fille." And hissing the word "prr-ince" like lightning, she thrust the morsel under Marie's nose. Marie, who was a delicate
10 creature, almost swooned at the shock.

"Do you think," cried Yvonne, scornfully, "that I would ever buy such cheese *pour ces dames?* Never. Never. *Jamais de ma vie.*" Her sausage finger wagged before her nose, and she minced in a dreadful imitation of Mother's French, "We have none of us large appetites, Yvonne. We are very fond of boiled eggs and mashed potatoes and a nice, plain salad. Ah-Bah!" With a snort of contempt she flung
20 away her shawl, rolled up her sleeves, and began unpacking the basket. At the bottom there was a flat bottle which, sighing, she laid aside.

"De quoi pour mes cors," said she.

And Marie, seizing a bottle of Sauterne and bearing it off to the dining-room murmured, as she shut the kitchen door behind her, "Et voilà pour les cors de Monsieur!"

The dining-room was a large room panelled in dark wood. It had a massive mantelpiece
30 and carved chairs covered in crimson damask. On the heavy, polished table stood an oval glass dish decorated with little gilt swags. This dish, which it was Marie's duty to keep filled with fresh flowers, fascinated her. The sight of it gave her a *frisson*. It reminded her always, as it lay solitary on the dark expanse, of a little tomb. And one day, passing through the long windows on to the stone terrace and down the steps into the garden she had the
40 happy thought of so arranging the flowers that they would be appropriate to one of the ladies on a future tragic occasion. Her first creation had been terrible. *Tomb of Mademoiselle Anderson* in black pansies, lily-of-the-valley, and

a frill of heliotrope. It gave her a most intense, curious pleasure to hand Miss Anderson the potatoes at lunch, and at the same time to gaze beyond her at her triumph. It was like (*O ciel!*), it was like handing potatoes to a corpse.

The *Tomb of Madame* was on the contrary almost gay. Foolish little flowers, half yellow, half blue, hung over the edge, wisps of green trailed across, and in the middle there was a large scarlet rose. *Cœur saignant*, Marie had called it. But it did not look in the least like a *cœur saignant*. It looked flushed and cheerful, like Mother emerging from the luxury of a warm bath.

Milly's, of course, was all white. White stocks, little white rose-buds, with a sprig or two of dark box edging. It was Mother's favorite.

Poor innocent! Marie, at the sideboard, had to turn her back when she heard Mother exclaim, "Isn't it pretty, Milly? Isn't it sweetly pretty? Most artistic. So original." And she had said to Marie, "C'est très joli, Marie. Très original."

Marie's smile was so remarkable that Milly, peeling a tangerine, remarked to Mother, "I don't think she likes you to admire them. It makes her uncomfortable."

But today—the glory of her opportunity made Marie feel quite faint as she seized her flower scissors. *Tombeau d'un beau Monsieur.* She was forbidden to cut the orchids that grew round the fountain basin. But what were orchids for if not for such an occasion? Her fingers trembled as the scissors snipped away. They were enough; Marie added two small sprays of palm. And back in the dining-room she had the happy idea of binding the palm together with a twist of gold thread deftly torn off the fringe of the dining-room curtains. The effect was superb. Marie almost seemed to see her *beau Monsieur*, very small, very small, at the bottom of the bowl, in full evening dress with a ribbon across his chest and his ears white as wax.

What surprised Milly, however, was that Miss Anderson should pay any attention to Mr. Prodger's coming. She rustled to breakfast in

3. "**J'ai . . . gorgonzola,**" "I've found a piece of gorgonzola."
6. "**J'ai . . . fille,**" "I've a piece of gorgonzola here (fit) for a prince, little girl." 12. "**pour ces dames,**" "for these ladies."
13. "**Jamais . . . vie,**" "Never in my life." 23. "**De . . . cors,**" "Something for my corns." 26. "**Et . . . Monsieur!**" "Something for the gentleman's corns!" It is quite possible, however, that Marie is punning on the word *cor*. She may mean "Something for the gentleman's horns," referring to the old folk-belief that a man whose wife was unfaithful to him grew horns on his head. 35. **frisson,** thrill.

48. *O ciel!* Heavens! 54. *Cœur saignant,* bleeding heart. 67. "*C'est . . . original.*" "It's very pretty, Marie. Very original." 75. *Tombeau . . . Monsieur,* tomb of a fine gentleman.

her best black silk blouse, her Sunday blouse, with the large, painful-looking crucifix dangling over the front. Milly was alone when Miss Anderson entered the dining-room. This was unfortunate, for she always tried to avoid being left alone with Miss Anderson. She could not say exactly why; it was a feeling. She had the feeling that Miss Anderson might say something about God, or something fearfully intimate. Oh, she would sink through the floor if such a thing happened; she would expire. Supposing she were to say "Milly, do you believe in our Lord?" Heavens! It simply didn't bear thinking about.

"Good-morning, my dear," said Miss Anderson, and her fingers, cold, pale, like church candles, touched Milly's cheeks.

"Good-morning, Miss Anderson. May I give you some coffee?" said Milly, trying to be natural.

"Thank you, dear child," said Miss Anderson, and laughing her light, nervous laugh, she hooked on her eyeglasses and stared at the basket of rolls. "And is it today that you expect your guest?" she asked.

Now why did she ask that? Why pretend when she knew perfectly well? That was all part of her strangeness. Or was it because she wanted to be friendly? Miss Anderson was more than friendly; she was genial. But there was always this something. Was she spying? People said at school that Roman Catholics spied. . . . Miss Anderson rustled, rustled about the house like a dead leaf. Now she was on the stairs, now in the upstairs passage. Sometimes, at night, when Milly was feverish, she woke up and heard that rustle outside her door. Was Miss Anderson looking through the keyhole? And one night she actually had the idea that Miss Anderson had bored two holes in the wall above her head and was watching her from there. The feeling was so strong that next time she went into Miss Anderson's room her eyes flew to the spot. To her horror a large picture hung there. Had it been there before? . . .

"Guest?" The crisp breakfast roll broke in half at the word.

"Yes, I think it is," said Milly, vaguely, and her blue, flower-like eyes were raised to Miss Anderson in a vague stare.

"It will make quite a little change in our little party," said the much-too-pleasant voice. "I confess I miss very much the society of men. I have had such a great deal of it in my life. I think that ladies by themselves are apt to get a little—h'm—h'm . . ." And helping herself to cherry jam, she spilt it on the cloth.

Milly took a large, childish bite out of her roll. There was nothing to reply to this. But how young Miss Anderson made her feel! She made her want to be naughty, to pour milk over her head or make a noise with a spoon.

"Ladies by themselves," went on Miss Anderson, who realized none of this, "are very apt to find their interests limited."

"Why?" said Milly, goaded to reply. People always said that; it sounded most unfair.

"I think," said Miss Anderson, taking off her eyeglasses and looking a little dim, "it is the absence of political discussion."

"Oh, politics!" cried Milly, airily. "I hate politics. Father always said—" But here she pulled up short. She crimsoned. She didn't want to talk about Father to Miss Anderson.

"Oh! Look! Look! A butterfly!" cried Miss Anderson, softly and hastily. "Look, what a darling!" Her own cheeks flushed a slow red at the sight of the darling butterfly fluttering so softly over the glittering table.

That was very nice of Miss Anderson—fearfully nice of her. She must have realized that Milly didn't want to talk about Father and so she had mentioned the butterfly on purpose. Milly smiled at Miss Anderson as she never had smiled at her before. And she said in her warm, youthful voice, "He is a duck, isn't he? I love butterflies. I think they are great lambs."

§

The morning whisked away as foreign mornings do. Mother had half decided to wear her hat at lunch.

"What do you think, Milly? Do you think as head of the house it might be appropriate? On the other hand one does not want to do anything at all extreme."

"Which do you mean, Mother? Your mushroom or the jampot?"

"Oh, not the jampot, dear." Mother was quite used to Milly's name for it. "I somehow don't feel myself in a hat without a brim. And

to tell you the truth I am still not quite certain whether I was wise in buying the jampot. I cannot help the feeling that if I were to meet Father in it he would be a little too surprised. More than once lately," went on Mother quickly, "I have thought of taking off the trimming, turning it upside down, and making it into a nice little workbag. What do you think, dear? But we must not go into it now, Milly.
10 This is not the moment for such schemes. Come on to the balcony. I have told Marie we shall have coffee there. What about bringing out that big chair with the nice, substantial legs for Mr. Prodger? Men are so fond of nice, substantial . . . No, not by yourself, love! Let me help you."

When the chair was carried out Milly thought it looked exactly like Mr. Prodger. It *was* Mr. Prodger admiring the view.

20 "No, don't sit down on it. You mustn't," she cried hastily, as Mother began to subside. She put her arm through Mother's and drew her back into the salon.

Happily, at that moment there was a rustle and Miss Anderson was upon them. In excellent time, for once. She carried a copy of the *Morning Post*.

"I have been trying to find out from this," said she, lightly tapping the newspaper with
30 her eyeglasses, "whether Congress is sitting at present. But unfortunately after reading my copy right through, I happened to glance at the heading and discovered it was five weeks' old."

Congress! Would Mr. Prodger expect them to talk about Congress? The idea terrified Mother. Congress! The American parliament, of course, composed of senators—grey-bearded old men in frock coats and turn-down collars,
40 rather like missionaries. But she did not feel at all competent to discuss them.

"I think we had better not be too intellectual," she suggested, timidly, fearful of disappointing Miss Anderson, but more fearful still of the alternative.

"Still, one likes to be prepared," said Miss Anderson. And after a pause she added softly, "One never knows."

Ah, how true that is! One never does. Miss
50 Anderson and Mother seemed both to ponder this truth. They sat silent, with head bent, as though listening to the whisper of the words.

432

"One never knows," said the pink-spotted dragons on the mantelpiece and the Turks' heads pondered. Nothing is known—nothing. Everybody just waits for things to happen as they were waiting there for the stranger who came walking towards them through the sun and shadow under the budding plane trees, or driving, perhaps, in one of the small, cotton-covered cabs. . . . An angel passed over the Villa Martin. In that moment of hovering silence something beseeching seemed to lift, seemed to offer itself, as the flowers in the salon, uplifted, gave themselves to the light.

Then Mother said, "I hope Mr. Prodger will not find the scent of the mimosa too powerful. Men are not fond of flowers in a room as a rule. I have heard it causes actual hay-fever in some cases. What do you think, Milly? Ought we perhaps—" But there was no time to do anything. A long firm trill sounded from the hall door. It was a trill so calm and composed and unlike the tentative little push they gave the bell that it brought them back to the seriousness of the moment. They heard a man's voice; the door clicked and shut again. He was inside. A stick rattled on the table. There was a pause, and then the door handle of the salon turned and Marie, in frilled muslin cuffs and an apron shaped like a heart, ushered in Mr. Prodger.

Only Mr. Prodger after all? But whom had Milly expected to see? The feeling was there and gone again that she would not have been surprised to see somebody quite different, before she realized this wasn't quite the same Mr. Prodger as before. He was smarter than ever; all brushed, combed, shining. The ears that Marie had seen white as wax flashed as if they had been pink enamelled. Mother fluttered up in her pretty little way, so hoping he had not found the heat of the day too trying to be out in . . . but happily it was a little early in the year for dust. Then Miss Anderson was introduced. Milly was ready this time for that fresh hand, but she almost gasped; it was so very chill. It was like a hand stretched out to you from the water. Then together they all sat down.

"Is this your first visit to the Riviera?" asked Miss Anderson, graciously, dropping her handkerchief.

"It is," answered Mr. Prodger composedly,

and he folded his arms as before. "I was in Florence until recently, but I caught a heavy cold—"

"Florence so—" began Mother, when the beautiful brass gong, that burned like a fallen sun in the shadows of the hall, began to throb. First it was a low muttering, then it swelled, it quickened, it burst into a clash of triumph under Marie's sympathetic fingers. Never had they been treated to such a performance before. Mr. Prodger was all attention.

"That's a very fine gong," he remarked approvingly.

"We think it is so very Oriental," said Mother. "It gives our little meals quite an Eastern flavour. Shall we . . ."

Their guest was at the door bowing.

"So many gentlemen and only one lady," fluttered Mother. "What I mean is the boot is on the other shoe. That is to say—come, Milly, come, dear." And she led the way to the dining-room.

Well, there they were. The cold, fresh napkins were shaken out of their charming shapes and Marie handed the omelette. Mr. Prodger sat on Mother's right, facing Milly, and Miss Anderson had her back to the long windows. But after all—why should the fact of their having a man with them make such a difference? It did; it made all the difference. Why should they feel so stirred at the sight of that large hand outspread, moving among the wine glasses? Why should the sound of that loud, confident "Ah-hm!" change the very look of the dining-room? It was not a favourite room of theirs as a rule; it was overpowering. They bobbed uncertainly at the pale table with a curious feeling of exposure. They were like those meek guests who arrive unexpectedly at the fashionable hotel, and are served with whatever may be ready, while the real luncheon, the real guests lurk important and contemptuous in the background. And although it was impossible for Marie to be other than deft, nimble and silent, what heart could she have in ministering to that most uninspiring of spectacles—three ladies dining alone?

Now all was changed. Marie filled their glasses to the brim as if to reward them for some marvellous feat of courage. These timid English ladies had captured a live lion, a real one, smelling faintly of eau de cologne, and

with a tip of handkerchief showing, white as a flake of snow.

"He is worthy of it," decided Marie, eyeing her orchids and palms.

Mr. Prodger touched his hot plate with appreciative fingers.

"You'll hardly believe it, Mrs. Fawcett," he remarked, turning to Mother, "but this is the first hot plate I've happened on since I left the States. I had begun to believe that there were two things that just weren't to be had in Europe. One was a hot plate and the other was a glass of cold water. Well, the cold water one can do without; but a hot plate is more difficult. I'd got so discouraged with the cold wet ones I encountered everywhere that when I was arranging with Cook's Agency about my room here I explained to them 'I don't care what the expense may be. But for mercy's sake find me a hotel where I can get a hot plate by ringing for it.'"

Mother, though outwardly all sympathy, found this a little bewildering. She had a momentary vision of Mr. Prodger ringing for hot plates to be brought to him at all hours. Such strange things to want in any numbers.

"I have always heard the American hotels are so very well equipped," said Miss Anderson. "Telephones in all the rooms and even tape machines."

Milly could see Miss Anderson reading that tape machine.

"I should like to go to America awfully," she cried, as Marie brought in the lamb and set it before Mother.

"There's certainly nothing wrong with America," said Mr. Prodger, soberly. "America's a great country. What are they? Peas? Well, I'll just take a few. I don't eat peas as a rule. No, no salad, thank you. Not with the hot meat."

"But what makes you want to go to America?" Miss Anderson ducked forward, smiling at Milly, and her eyeglasses fell into her plate, just escaping the gravy.

Because one wants to go everywhere, was the real answer. But Milly's flower-blue gaze rested thoughtfully on Miss Anderson as she said, "The ice-cream. I adore ice-cream."

"Do you?" said Mr. Prodger, and he put down his fork; he seemed moved. "So you're fond of ice-cream, are you, Miss Fawcett?"

82. **tape,** ticker tape.

Milly transferred her dazzling gaze to him. It said she was.

"Well," said Mr. Prodger quite playfully, and he began eating again, "I'd like to see you get it. I'm sorry we can't manage to ship some across. I like to see young people have just what they want. It seems right, somehow."

Kind man! Would he have any more lamb?

Lunch passed so pleasantly, so quickly, that
10 the famous piece of gorgonzola was on the table in all its fatness and richness before there had been an awkward moment. The truth was that Mr. Prodger proved most easy to entertain, most ready to chat. As a rule men were not fond of chat as Mother understood it. They did not seem to understand that it does not matter very much what one says; the important thing is not to let the conversation drop. Strange! Even the best men ignored that sim-
20 ple rule. They refused to realize that conversation is like a dear little baby that is brought in to be handed round. You must rock it, nurse it, keep it on the move if you want it to keep smiling. What could be simpler? But even Father . . . Mother winced away from memories that were not as sweet as memories ought to be.

All the same she could not help hoping that Father saw what a successful little lunch party
30 it was. He did so love to see Milly happy, and the child looked more animated than she had done for weeks. She had lost that dreamy expression, which, though very sweet, did not seem natural at her age. Perhaps what she wanted was not so much Easton's Syrup as taking out of herself.

"I have been very selfish," thought Mother, blaming herself as usual. She put her hand on Milly's arm; she pressed it gently as they rose
40 from the table. And Marie held the door open for the white and grey figure; for Miss Anderson, who peered shortsightedly, as though looking for something; for Mr. Prodger who brought up the rear, walking stately, with the benign air of a Monsieur who had eaten well.

§

Beyond the balcony, the garden, the palms and the sea lay bathed in quivering brightness.

35. **Easton's Syrup,** a common spring tonic of the patent-medicine variety.

Not a leaf moved; the oranges were little worlds of burning light. There was the sound of grasshoppers ringing their tiny tambourines, and the hum of bees as they hovered, as though to taste their joy in advance, before burrowing close into the warm wide-open stocks and roses. The sound of the sea was like a breath, was like a sigh.

Did the little group on the balcony hear it? Mother's fingers moved among the black and gold coffee-cups; Miss Anderson brought the most uncomfortable chair out of the salon and sat down. Mr. Prodger put his large hand on to the yellow stone ledge of the balcony and remarked gravely, "This balcony rail is just as hot as it can be."

"They say," said Mother, "that the greatest heat of the day is at about half-past two. We have certainly noticed it is very hot then."

"Yes, it's lovely then," murmured Milly, and she stretched out her hand to the sun. "It's simply baking!"

"Then you're not afraid of the sunshine?" said Mr. Prodger, taking his coffee from Mother. "No, thank you. I won't take any cream. Just one lump of sugar." And he sat down balancing the little, chattering cup on his broad knee.

"No, I adore it," answered Milly, and she began to nibble the lump of sugar. . . .

from **The Journal**

1919

JANUARY 1. J. came to bed at ten minutes to twelve. Said he: "Don't go to sleep before the New Year." I lay holding my watch. I think I did go to sleep for a moment. The window was wide open and I looked out and over a big soft hollow, with a sprinkle of lights between. Then the hour struck: the bells rang—hooter, sirens, horns, trumpets sounded. The church organ pealed out (reminding me of Hans An-

"1919" reprinted from *The Journal* by Katherine Mansfield by permission of and special arrangement with Alfred A. Knopf, Inc., authorized publishers.
1. **J.,** J. Middleton Murry, the author's husband (cf. headnote above, p. 425). 9. **Hans Andersen,** Hans Christian Andersen (1805–75), Danish poet and novelist, particularly known for his fairy tales. Miss Mansfield may have been referring to his story "The Red Shoes."

dersen) and an Australian called *Coo—ee*. (I longed to reply.) I wanted L. M. to hear and to see. I called loudly to her ever so many times, but she had "chosen" to take a bath. . . .

May 19. 6 p.m. I wish I had some idea of how old this note book is. The writing is very faint and far away. Now it is May 1919. Six o'clock. I am sitting in my own room thinking of Mother: I want to cry. But my thoughts are beautiful and full of gaiety. I think of *our* house, *our* garden, *us* children—the lawn, the gate, and Mother coming in. "Children! Children!" I really only ask for time to write it all —time to write my books. Then I don't mind dying. I live to write. The lovely world (God, how lovely the external world is!) is there and I bathe in it and am refreshed. But I feel as though I had a DUTY, someone has set me a task which I am bound to finish. Let me finish it: let me finish it without hurrying—leaving all as fair as I can. . . .

My little Mother, my star, my courage, my *own*. I seem to dwell in her now. We live in *the same world*. Not quite this world, not quite another. I do not care for people: and the idea of fame, of being a success,—that's nothing, less than nothing. I love my family and a few others dearly, and I love, in the old—in the ancient way, through and through, my husband.

Not a soul knows where she is. She goes slowly, thinking it all over, wondering how she can express it *as she wants to*—asking for time and for peace.

Escape

She was sure I would be cold and as usual tried to make of my departure une petite affaire sérieuse. I always try to thieve out, steal out. I should like to let myself down from a window, or just withdraw like a ray of light.

"Are you sure you won't have your cape . . . etc. etc. etc.?"

Her attitude made me quite sure. I went out. At the corner the flying, gay, eager wind ran at me. It was too much to bear. I went on for a yard or two, shivering—then I came home. I slipped the Yale key into the lock like a thief, shut the door *dead* quiet. Up she came, up the stairs.

"So it *was* too cold, after all!"

I couldn't answer or even look at her. I had to turn my back and pull off my gloves. Said she:

"I have a blouse-pattern here I want to show you."

At that I crept upstairs, came into my room, and shut the door. It was a miracle she did not follow. . . .

What is there in all this to make me HATE her so? What do you see? She has known me try to get in and out without anyone knowing it dozens of times—that is true. I have even *torn* my heart out and told her how it hurts my last little defences to be questioned—how it makes me feel just for the moment an independent being, to be allowed to go and come unquestioned. But that is just "Katie's funniness. She doesn't mean it, of course. . . ."

We hardly spoke at lunch. When it was over she asked me again if she might show me the pattern. I felt so ill, it seemed to me that even a hen could see at a side glance of its little leaden eye how ill I felt. I don't remember what I said. But in she came and put before me—something. Really, I hardly know what it was. "Let the little dressmaker help you," I said. But there was nothing to say.

She murmured: "Purple chiffon front neck sleeves." I don't know. Finally I asked her to take it away.

"What *is* it, Katie? Am I interrupting your work?"

"Yes, we'll call it that."

Being Alone

Saturday. This joy of being alone. What is it? I feel so gay and at peace—the whole house takes the air. Lunch is ready. I have a baked egg, apricots and cream, cheese straws and black coffee. How delicious! A baby meal! Mother shares it with me. Athenaeum is asleep and then awake on the studio sofa. He has a silver spoon of cream—then hides under the sofa frill and puts out a paw for my finger. I gather the dried leaves from the plant in the

1. Coo-ee, a cry of the Australian bushman, made to attract attention, later imitated by the white settlers, and now used as a common greeting by Australians everywhere.   2. L. M., the friend of Miss Mansfield who was her companion through much of her last illness.   34. She, L. M.   35. une . . . sérieuse, a serious affair.

87. Athenaeum, the cat.

435

big white bowl, and because I *must* play with something, I take an orange up to my room and throw it and catch it as I walk up and down. . . .

[This note appears later, re-written, in the following form.]

Saturday. Peaceful and gay. The whole house takes the air. Athenaeum is asleep and then awake on the studio sofa. He has a silver
10 spoonful of my cream at lunch time—then hides under the sofa frill and plays the game of the Darting Paw. I gather the dried leaves from the plant in the big white bowl; they are powdered with silver. There is nobody in the house, and yet whose is this faint whispering? On the stairs there are tiny spots of gold—tiny footprints. . . .

Geraniums

The red geraniums have bought the garden over my head. They are there, established,
20 back in the old home, every leaf and flower unpacked and in its place—and quite determined that no power on earth will ever move them again. Well, *that* I don't mind. But why should they make me feel a stranger? Why should they ask me every time I go near: "And what are you doing in a London garden?" They burn with arrogance and pride. And I am the little Colonial walking in the London garden patch—allowed to look, per-
30 haps, but not to linger. If I lie on the grass they positively shout at me: "Look at her, lying on *our* grass, pretending she lives here, pretending this her garden, and that tall back of the house, with the windows open and the coloured curtains lifting, is her house. She is a stranger—an alien. She is nothing but a little girl sitting on the Tinakori hills and dreaming: 'I went to London and married an Englishman and we lived in a tall grave house with red
40 geraniums and white daisies in the garden at the back.' *Im*-pudence!"

[This note appears later, re-written, in the following form.]

The red geraniums have bought the garden over my head and taken possession. They are settled in, every leaf and flower unpacked and in its place, and never do they mean to move again! Well—that I could bear. But why because I've let them in should they throw me out? They won't even let me lie on the grass without their shouting: "*Im*-pudence!"

A Dream

Sometimes I glance up at the clock. Then I know I am expecting Chummie. The bell peals. I run out on to the landing. I hear his hat and stick thrown on to the hall-table. He runs up the stairs, three at a time. "Hullo, darling!" But I can't move—I can't move. He puts his arm around me, holding me tightly, and we kiss—a long, firm, family kiss. And the kiss means: We are of the same blood; we have absolute confidence in each other; we love; all is well; nothing can ever come between us.

We come into my room. He goes over to the glass. "By Jove, I am hot." Yes, he is very hot. A deep childish colour shows in his cheeks, his eyes are brilliant, his lips burn, he strokes the hair back from his forehead with the palm of his hand. I pull the curtains together and the room is shadowy. He flings himself down on the sommier and lights a cigarette, and watches the smoke, rising so slowly.

"Is that better?" I ask.

"Perfect, darling—simply perfect. The light reminds me of. . . ."

And then the dream is over and I begin working again.

England

The two brothers were on one side of the room, I on the other. R. sat on the floor inclined towards J. J. lay on the stickle-back, very idly.

"If you could have your wish, where would you be?"

First he thought a café in some foreign town . . . in Spain . . . no, in Grenoble, perhaps . . . sitting listening to music and watching

---

5. **This note . . . form.** This and succeeding bracketed entries are notes by J. Middleton Murry, the editor of Miss Mansfield's journal. 37. **Tinakori hills,** in New Zealand, near Miss Mansfield's birthplace.

53. **Chummie,** Miss Mansfield's brother, Leslie Beauchamp, whose untimely death in the First World War exerted a considerable influence over her writing (cf. headnote above, p. 425). 70. **sommier,** day-bed.

the people. We are just passing through. . . . There is a lake and a river near. . . . But then, NO. A farmhouse in Sussex—some good old furniture—knocking about in the garden—rolling the lawn, perhaps—yes, rolling the lawn. An infant—two good servants. And then, when it grew dark—to go in, have some milk, then I go to my study and you to yours and work for about an hour and a half and then trundle off to bed. I would like to earn my living, but *not* by writing. I feel that my talent as a writer isn't a great one—I'll have to be careful of it. . . . Yes, that's what I'd like. No new places —no new things. I don't *want* them. Would you like that?

I felt his brother was with him, the brother inclined towards him, understanding and sharing that life—the homestead on the Downs—his English country—the sober quiet. . . .

"Would you like that?"

No, I don't want that. No, I don't want England. England is of no use to me. What do I mean by that? I mean there never has been—never will be—any rapprochement between us, *never.* . . . The lack of its *appeal*—that is what I chiefly hate. I would not care if I never saw the English country again. Even in its flowering I feel deeply antagonistic to it, and I will never change.

A Good Beginning

May 30. First comes L. M. I give her orders. Ask her to supervise the maid till Monday. 'Be gentle with her: help her to make the beds; and just tell her how everything must be.' Then in detail I sketch out the maid's programme. 'Send Ralph, please.' Ralph arrives. I arrange the food. Then settle all that must be done, coercing Ralph, putting her mind in order if I can, making her see the bright side of things, sending her away (I hope) feeling important and happy.

I go upstairs to see Maud, to say good-morning, to hope 'she will be happy.' "Just take things gently; I'll quite understand that you can't get into our ways at once. Ask Miss B. and the cook for what you want. But if you wish to see me, don't hesitate to come in. I was so glad you were early." She was very reassured. Her eyes shone (she's only a little girl). She said it was like the country. As she walked up from the tram the birds sang "something beautiful." This instead of the 'long drag up the hill' was cheering. I left her happy. I know I did.

Downstairs just to say Good-day to Mrs. Moody and to say there were some flowers for her to take home. The good creature was on her knees polishing and saying it was such a fine day. Bless her 60 years! We had a little joke or two and I came away.

L. M. again—just for a moment to say: "As you have a machine, don't hem dusters by hand as I see you are doing. Keep your energies for something *important!*"

Then I sit down to work, and there comes a steady, pleasant vibration from the ship. If only I could always control these four women like this! I must learn to.

May 31. *Work*. Shall I be able to express one day my love of work—my desire to be a better writer—my longing to take greater pains. And the passion I feel. It takes the place of religion—it *is* my religion—of people—I create my people: of 'life'—it *is* Life. The temptation is to kneel before it, to adore, to prostrate myself, to stay too long in a state of ecstasy before the *idea* of it. I must be more busy about my master's business.

Oh, God! The sky is filled with the sun, and the sun is like music. The sky is full of music. Music comes streaming down these great beams. The wind touches the harp-like trees, shakes little jets of music—little shakes, little trills from the flowers. The shape of every flower is like a sound. My hands open like five petals. Praise Him! Praise Him! No, I am overcome; I am dazed; it is too much to bear.

A little fly has dropped by mistake into the huge sweet cup of a magnolia. Isaiah (or was it Elisha?) was caught up into Heaven in a chariot of fire *once*. But when the weather is divine and I am free to work, such a journey is positively nothing.

18. **Downs,** the Sussex Downs, rolling land on the top or side of a raised shelf, terminating to the south in the cliffs along the English Channel.   35–59. **Ralph, etc.,** various servants in the household of the Murrys at Hampstead, where Miss Mansfield was spending the winter.

65. **ship,** of her inspiration.   88. **Isaiah, etc.** It was Elijah, and neither Isaiah nor Elisha, who was caught up to Heaven in a chariot of fire.

The Angel of Mercy

May. The day the housemaid had to leave because her husband 'didn't want her to work
no more' and, to consolidate his authority, had
punched her so hard in the neck that she had a
great red swelling under ear, the cook became
a kind of infallible being,—an angel of mercy.
Nothing was too much for her. Stairs were
rays of light up which she floated. She wore
her cap differently: it gave her the air of a
10 hospital nurse. Her voice changed. She suggested puddings as though they were compresses: whiting, because they were so 'delicate and harmless.' Trust me! Lean on me!
There is nothing I cannot do! was her attitude.
Every time she left me, she left me for her
mysterious reasons—to lay out the body again
and again—to change the stiffened hand—to
pull the paper frill over the ominous spot appearing.

The Cook

20 The cook is evil. After lunch I trembled so
that I had to lie down on the sommier—thinking about her. I meant—when she came up to
see me—to say *so much* that she'd have to go.
I waited, playing with the wild kitten. When
she came, I said it all, and more, and *she* said
how sorry she was and agreed and apologised
and quite understood. She stayed at the door,
plucking at a d'oyley. "Well, I'll see it doesn't
happen in the future. I *quite* see what you
30 mean."

So the serpent still slept between us. Oh!
why won't she turn and speak her mind. This
pretence of being fond of me! I believe she
thinks she is. There is something in what L. M.
says: she is not consciously evil. She is a
FOOL, of course. I have to do all the managing and all the explaining. I have to cook
everything before she cooks it. I believe she
thinks she is a treasure . . . no, wants to
40 think it. At bottom she knows her corruptness.
There are moments when it comes to the surface, comes out, like a stain, in her face. Then
her eyes are like the eyes of a woman-prisoner
—a creature looking up as you enter her cell
and saying: 'If you'd know what a hard life
I've had you wouldn't be surprised to see me
here.'

[This appears again in the following form.]

Cook to See Me

As I opened the door, I saw her sitting in
the middle of the room, hunched, still. . . .
She got up, obedient, like a prisoner when you
enter a cell. And her eyes said, as a prisoner's
eyes say, "Knowing the life I've had, I'm the
last to be surprised at finding myself here."

The Cook's Story

Her first husband was a pawnbroker. He
learned his trade from her uncle, with whom
she lived, and was more like her big brother
than anything else from the age of thirteen.
After he had married her they prospered. He
made a perfect pet of her—they used to say.
His sisters put it that he made a perfect fool
of himself over her. When their children were
fifteen and nine he urged his employers to take
a man into their firm—a great friend of his—
and persuaded them; really went security for
this man. When she saw the man she went all
over cold. She said, Mark me, you've not done
right: no good will come of this. But he
laughed it off. Time passed: the man proved a
villain. When they came to take stock, they
found all the stock was false: he'd sold everything. This preyed on her husband's mind,
went on preying, kept him up at night, made
a changed man of him, he went mad as you
might say over figures, worrying. One evening,
sitting in his chair, very late, he *died* of a clot
of blood on the brain.

She was left. Her big boy was old enough
to go out, but the little one was still not more
than a baby: he was so nervous and delicate.
The doctors had never let him go to school.

One day her brother-in-law came to see her
and advised her to sell her home and get
some work. All that keeps you back, he said,
is little Bert. Now, I'll advise you to place a
certain sum with your solicitors for him and
put him out—in the country. He said he'd take
him. I did as he advised. But, funny! I never
heard a word from the child after he'd gone. I
used to ask why he didn't write, and they said,
when he can write a decent letter you shall
have it—not before. That went on for a twelve-
month, and I found afterwards he'd been writing all the time, grieving to be took away, and

they'd never sent his letters. Then quite sudden his uncle wrote and said he must be taken away. He'd done the most awful things—things I couldn't find you a name for—he'd turned *vicious*—he was a little criminal! What his uncle said was I'd spoiled the child and he was going to make a man of him, and he'd beaten him and half starved him and when he was frightened at night and screamed, he turned him out into the New Forest and made him sleep under the branches. My big boy went down to see him. Mother, he says, you wouldn't know little Bert. He can't speak. He won't come near anybody. He starts off if you touch him; he's like a little beast. And, oh dear, the things he'd done! Well, you hear of people doing those things before they're put into orphanages. But when I heard that and thought it was the same little baby his father used to carry into Regent's Park bathed and dressed of a Sunday morning—well, I felt my religion was going from me.

I had a terrible time trying to get him into an orphanage. I begged for three months before they would take him. Then he was sent to Bisley. But after I'd been to see him there, in his funny clothes and all—I could see 'is misery. I was in a nice place at the time, cook to a butcher in a large way in Kensington, but that poor child's eyes—they used to follow me —and a sort of shivering that came over him when people went near.

Well, I had a friend that kept a boarding house in Kensington. I used to visit her, and a friend of hers, a big well-set-up fellow, quite the gentleman, an engineer who worked in a garage, came there very often. She used to joke and say he wanted to walk me out. I laughed it off till one day she was very serious. She said, You're a very silly woman. He earns good money; he'd give you a home and you could have your little boy. Well, he was to speak to me next day and I made up my mind to listen. Well, he did, and he couldn't have put it nicer. I can't give you a house to start with, he said, but you shall have three good

rooms and the kid, and I'm earning good money and shall be more.

A week after, he come to me. I can't give you any money this week, he says, there's things to pay for from when I was single. But I daresay you've got a bit put by. And I was a fool, you know, I didn't think it funny. Oh yes, I said, I'll manage. Well, so it went on for three weeks. We'd arranged not to have little Bert for a month because, he said, he wanted me to himself, and he was so fond of him. A big fellow, he used to cling to me like a child and call me mother.

After three weeks was up I hadn't a penny. I'd been taking my jewels and best clothes to put away to pay for him until he was straight. But one night I said, Where's my money? He just up and gave me such a smack in the face I thought my head would burst. And that began it. Every time I asked him for money he beat me. As I said, I was very religious at the time, used to wear a crucifix under my clothes and couldn't go to bed without kneeling by the side and saying my prayers—no, not even the first week of my marriage. Well, I went to a clergyman and told him everything and he said, My child, he said, I am very sorry for you, but with God's help, he said, it's your duty to make him a better man. You say your first husband was so good. Well, perhaps God has kept this trial for you until now. I went home—and that very night he tore my crucifix off and hit me on the head when I knelt down. He said he wouldn't have me say my prayers; it made him wild. I had a little dog at the time I was very fond of, and he used to pick it up and shout, I'll teach it to say its prayers, and beat it before my eyes—until—well, such was the man he was.

Then one night he came in the worse for drink and fouled the bed. I couldn't stand it. I began to cry. He gave me a hit on the ear and I fell down, striking my head on the fender. When I came to, he was gone. I ran out into the street just as I was—I ran as fast as I could, not knowing where I was going— just dazed—my nerves were gone. And a lady found me and took me to her home and I was there three weeks. And after that I never went back. I never even told my people. I found work, and not till months after I went to see

10. **New Forest,** a heavily wooded section in Hampshire, England.   20. **Regent's Park,** a favorite park in the center of London.   26. **Bisley,** a town in Gloucestershire, England. 29. **Kensington,** a rather well-to-do section of London. 38. **walk me out,** court me.

my sister. Good gracious! she says, we all thought you was murdered! And I never see him since. . . .

Those were dreadful times. I was so ill, I could scarcely hardly work and of course I couldn't get my little boy out. He had to grow up in it. And so I had to start all over again. I had nothing of his, nothing of mine. I lost it all except my marriage lines. Somehow I re-
10 membered them just as I was running out that night and put them in my boddy—sort of an instinct as you might say.

J. digs the garden as though he were exhuming a hated body or making a hole for a loved one.

The ardent creature spent more than half her time in church praying to be delivered from temptation. But God grew impatient at last and caused the door to be shut against her.
20 "For Heaven's sake," said he, "give the temptation a chance!"

It's raining, but the air is soft, smoky, warm. Big drops patter on the languid leaves, the tobacco flowers lean over. Now there is a rustle in the ivy. Wingley has appeared from the garden next door; he bounds from the wall. And delicately, lifting his paws, pointing his ears, very afraid that big wave will overtake him, he wades over the lake of green grass.

30 "Mr. Despondency's daughter, Muchafraid, went through the water singing."

She said: "I don't feel in the least afraid. I feel like a little rock that the rising tide is going to cover. You won't be able to see me . . . big waves . . . but they'll go down again. I shall be there—winking bright."

Oh, what sentimental toshery!

June 10. I have discovered that I cannot burn the candle at one end and write a book with
40 the other.

Life without *work*—I would commit suicide. Therefore work is more important than life.

June 21. Bateson and his love of the louse for its own sake. Pedigree lice. £100 a year from the Royal Institute: a large family: desperately poor: but he never notices. The lives he saved in the Balkan war with shaving and Thymol. Cases reduced from 7000 to 700. No reward, not even an O.B.E. He dissects them, finds their glands and so on, keeps them in tiny boxes; they feed on his arm. The louse and the bedbug.

Hydatids: the Australian who got them: handfuls of immature grapes. They attack the liver. In the human body they reproduce indefinitely. When they are passed and a sheep is attacked by them, they develop *hooks* and become long worms.

The Egyptian disease: a parasite which attacks the veins and arteries and causes fluxion —constant bleeding. It is another egg drunk in water. After it has been in man the only thing it can affect is a water-snail. It goes through an entirely new cycle of *being* until it can attack man again. *Dysentery:* another parasite.

Hydrophobia: the virus from the dog is taken and a rabbit is infected. That rabbit is used to infect another rabbit: the 2nd a 3rd, and so on, until you get a rabbit who is practically *pure* virus. The spinal cords are then taken from these rabbits and dried by a vacuum. The result is pounded up fine into an emulsion: 1st rabbit, 2nd rabbit, 3rd rabbit, etc., and the patient is injected progressively till at last he receives a dose which, if he had not been prepared to resist it, would kill him outright. The disease develops very slowly; the treatment is very expensive. Symptoms are a profuse shiny bubbling saliva, and gasping and groaning as in gas-poisoning. No barking, no going on all fours.

In lockjaw the jaw does not lock.

Pasteur was a very dreamer of dreamers. Human beings are a *side-line* to science.

All this I talked over with Sorapure, June 21. His point of view about medicine seems to me *just completely right*. I'd willingly let him take off my head, look inside, and pop it

---

11. **boddy,** bodice.   13. **J. . . . garden.** The cook's story has stopped with the preceding sentence.   16. **The ardent creature, etc.** This and the next four paragraphs are merely notes (possibly for future use in stories) that unexpectedly sprinkle the pages of Miss Mansfield's journal from time to time.

43. **Bateson,** a scientist acquaintance of the Murrys; his particular specialty at this time was typhus fever and the relation of the louse to the disease. The notes on diseases that follow here represent some conversation between Miss Mansfield and her doctor.   49. **O.B.E.,** Officer (of the Order) of the British Empire.   85. **Sorapure,** at that time Miss Mansfield's physician.

440

on again, if he thought it might assist future generations. Quite the right man to have at one's dying bedside. He'd get me at any rate so interested in the process—gradual loss of sensitiveness, coldness in the joints, etc.—I'd lie there thinking: this is very valuable to know; I must make a note of this.

As he stood at the door talking: "Nothing is incurable; it's all a question of *time*. What seems so useless today may be just that link which will make all plain to a future generation. . . ." I had a sense of the *larger breath*, of the mysterious lives within lives, and the Egyptian parasite beginning its new cycle of being in a water-snail affected me like a *great* work of art. No, that's not what I mean. It made me feel how *perfect* the world is, with its worms and hooks and ova, how incredibly perfect. There is the sky and the sea and the shape of a lily, and there is all this other as well. The *balance* how perfect! (*Salut*, Tchehov!) I would not have the one without the other.

The clocks are striking ten. Here in my room the sky looks lilac; in the bath-room it is like the skin of a peach. Girls are laughing.

I have consumption. There is still a great deal of moisture (*and* pain) in my BAD lung. But I do not care. I do not want anything I could not have. Peace, solitude, time to write my books, beautiful external life to watch and ponder—no more. O, I'd like a child as well—a baby boy; *mais je demande trop!*

[Part of this note appears again in the following form.]

As he stood at the door he said quietly, "Nothing is incurable. What seems so useless today may be the link that will make all plain tomorrow." We had been discussing hydatids, the Egyptian parasite that begins its cycle of existence being in a water-snail and the effects of hydrophobia. He smiled gently. There was nothing to be alarmed or shocked or surprised at. It was all a question of knowing these things as they should be known and not other-

wise. But he said none of this and went off to his next case. . . .

At breakfast time a mosquito and a wasp came to the edge of the honey dish to drink. The mosquito was a lovely little high stepping gazelle, but the wasp was a fierce roaring tiger. Drink, my darlings!

When the coffee is cold L. M. says: These things have to happen sometimes. And she looks mysterious and important, as if as a matter of fact she had known all along that this was a cold coffee day.

What I felt was, he said, that I wasn't in the whole of myself at all. I'd got locked in, somehow, in some little . . . top room in my mind, and strangers had got in—people I'd never seen before were making free of the rest of it. There was a dreadful feeling of confusion, chiefly that, and . . . vague noises—like things being moved—changed about—in my head. I lit the candle and sat up and in the mirror I saw a dark, brooding, strangely lengthened face.

"The feeling roused by the cause is more important than the cause itself. . . ." That is the kind of thing I like to say to myself as I get into the train. And then, as one settles into the corner—"For example"—or "Take—for instance . . ." It's a good game for *one*.

She fastens on a white veil and hardly knows herself. Is it becoming or is it not becoming? Ah, who is there to say. There is a lace butterfly on her left cheek and a spray of flowers on her right. Two dark bold eyes stare through the mesh—Surely not hers. Her lips tremble; faint, she sinks on her bed. And now she doesn't want to go. Must she? She is being driven out of the flat by those bold eyes. Out you go. Ah, how cruel! (*Second Violin.*)

But her hand is large and cold with big knuckles and short square nails. It is not a little velvet hand that sighs, that yields—faints dead away and has to be revived again only to faint once more. (*S.V.*)

---

21. *Salut*, Tchehov! The preceding sentence is a good illustration of the philosophy of life shown in the short stories of Anton Chekhov (1860–1904). Miss Mansfield would not have beauty without ugliness, life without disease and death. 33. *mais . . . trop!* But I'm asking too much.

46. he, her doctor.　74. She fastens, etc., a note which contains a situation in Miss Mansfield's story "Second Violin." More notes used in this story follow immediately, as well as some sketches of dreams and imaginings that never came to story-form (Cinderella; Two Climates; Indoo Weather; Mrs. Nightingale; Et in Arcadia Ego).

What do I want? she thought. What do I really want more than anything else in the world? If I had a wishing ring or Ali Baba's lamp—no, it wasn't Ali Baba—it was—Oh, what did it matter! Just supposing some one came. . . . "I am here to grant your dearest wish." And she saw, vaguely, a fluffy little creature with a silver paper star on a wand—a school fairy. . . . What should I say? It was cold in the kitchen, cold and dim. The tap dripped slowly, as tho' the water were half frozen. . . . (S.V.)

Miss Todd and Miss Hopper were second violins. Miss Bray was a viola.

Midday strikes on various bells—some velvety soft, some languid, some regretful, and one impatient—a youthful bell ringing high and quick above the rest. He thought joyfully: That's the bell for me! . . .

Cinderella

Oh, my sisters—my beautiful Peacock-proud sisters—have pity on me as I sit with my little broom beside the cold ashes while you dance at the Prince's party. But why—is the Fairy Godmother, the coach, the plumes and glass slippers just—faery—and all the rest of the story deeply, deeply true? Fate I suppose—Fate. It had to be. These things happen so. La réponse: Poor old girl—of course she is awfully sorry for her, but she does become a bore—doesn't she? There's no getting away from it.

When they got into bed together her feet rushed to greet his like little puppies that had been separated all day from their brothers. And first they chased one another and played and nudged gently. But then, they settled down, curled up, twined together under the clothes (like puppies on a warm hearth rug) and went to sleep.

Dark Bogey is a little inclined to jump into the milk jug to rescue the fly.

Fairylike, the fire rose in two branched flames like the golden antlers of some enchanted stag.

So he sat there, burning the letters, and each time he cast a fresh packet on the flame, his shadow, immense, huge, leapt out of the wall opposite him. It looked, sitting so stiff and straight, like some horrible old god, toasting his knees at the flames of the sacrifice.

Two Climates

I'd always rather be in a place that is too hot rather than one that's too cold. But I'd always rather be with people who loved me too little rather than with people who loved me too much.

"She has made her bed," said Belle—"she must lie on it." I reflected thankfully that in this case that would be no hardship—on the contrary, indeed. I hoped it was what they were both longing to do. . . .

North Africa. The whole valley is smothered in little white lilies. You never saw such a sight! They make me feel so wretchedly homesick. They smell just like dear old Selfridge's.

Souvent j'ai dit à mon mari: Nous en prenons un? Et il me dit: Ah, non, non, ma pauvre femme. Notre petit moment pour jouer est passé. Je ne peux rien faire que de rester dans un chaise en faisant des grimaces, et ça fait trembler plus que ça ne fait rire un petit enfant.

When I read Dr. Johnson, I feel like a little girl sitting at the same table. My eyes grow round. I don't only listen; I take him in *immensely.*

"Don't you think it would be marvellous," she said, "to have just one person in one's life to whom one could tell everything?" She leant forward, put down her cup, but stayed bent forward touching the spoon against the saucer. She looked up—"Or is it just childish of me— just absurd to want such a thing? . . . All the same," she leaned back, smiling, "childish or not—how wonderful it would be—how wonderful! to feel—from this person, this one person —I really don't need to hide anything. It would be such heavenly happiness!" she cried, sud-

---

63. **Selfridge's,** a noted department store in London. 64. **Souvent . . . enfant.** Often I have said to my husband, "Will we have one?" And he says to me, "No, my poor wife. Our little moment to play has passed. I can do nothing but stay in a chair and make faces, and that will make a little baby tremble rather than laugh. 75. **"Don't you think, etc."** It is not clear whether this is an imaginary scene or a real one. The speech might be that of some caller in the Murrys' house. The sardonic situation, however, is effective, whether real or imaginary.

denly, "it would make life so . . ." she got up, went to the window, looked out vaguely and turned round again. She laughed. "It's a queer thing," she said, "I've always believed in the possibility—and yet—in reality . . . Take R. and me, for instance." And here she flung back in a chair and leant back, still she was laughing but her body leaned to the chair as though exhausted. "I tell him everything. You know we're . . . rather different from most people. What I mean is—don't laugh—we love each other simply tremendously—we're everything to each other! In fact he's the one person on earth for me—and yet," she shut her eyes and bit her lip as though she wanted to stop laughing herself: "try, try, try as I can—there's always just one secret—just one—that never can be told—that mocks me." And then for a moment she lay still. . . .

Indoo Weather: A Dream

"It's what you might call indoo weather," said the little man.

"Oh, really. . . . Why that?" said I, vaguely.

He did not answer. The two polished knobs of his behind shone as he leaned over feeding the black seams of the boat with a brown twist.

The day was dull, steaming; there was a blackness out at sea; the heavy waves came tolling. On the sea grasses the large bright dew fell not. The little man's hammer went tap-tap.

L. M. snorted, threw up her head, stamped her feet on the wet sand, scrambled to a boulder, tore at some sea-poppies, dug them in her hat, held the hat away, looked, scornful, wrenched them out again.

I looked and felt vague as a king.

"Spades and buckets is round the point with the lobster catch." The hammer tapped. He explained that all the lovers would be sent away alive in sacks if they were not given a sharp *stang* with one of these. It was an ordinary grey and red garden trowel. L. M. went off to save their lives, but not joyfully. She walked heavy, her head down, beating the trowel against her side.

We were alone. The watcher appeared. He stood always in profile, his felt hat turned up at the side, a patch on the eye nearest us. His curved pipe fell from his jaws.

"Hi, Missy," he shouted to me. "Why don't you give us a bit of a show out there?"

The little man remonstrated. The sea was like a mass of half-set jelly. On the horizon it seemed ages fell.

"Come on, Missy!" bawled the watcher. I took off my clothes, stepped to the edge and was drawn in. I tried to catch the stumps of an old wharf, but slime filled my nails and I was sucked out. They watched.

Suddenly there came, winnowing landward, an enormous skinny skeleton of a Hindoo, standing upright. A tattered pink and white print coat flapped about his stiff outstretched arms. He had cloth of the same with a fringe of spangles over his head. He stood upright because of the immense sweeping broom of wood growing waist-high. "Help! Help!" I called.

The noise of the hammer came, and I felt the watcher's patched profile. A huge unbreakable wave lifted him, tipped him near. His shadow lay even, on the surface of the dusty water—a squat head and two giant arms. It broadened into a smile.

Strangers

I saw S. as a little fair man with a walrus moustache, a bowler much too small for him and an ancient frock coat that he keeps buttoning and unbuttoning. D.B. saw him as a grave gentleman with big black whiskers. Anyhow, there he was at the end of a dark tunnel, either coming towards us or walking away. . . . That started us on a fascinating subject. There are the people in D.B.'s life I've never seen (very few) and the immense number in mine that he has only heard of. What did they look like to us? And then, before we meet anyone while they are still far too far off to be seen we begin to build an image . . . how true is it? It's queer how well one gets to know this stranger; how often you've watched him before the other comes to take his place. . . . I can even imagine someone keeping their "first impression"—*in spite of* the other.

July

Tedious Brief Adventure of K.M.

A Doctor who came from Jamaica
Said: "This time I'll mend her or break her.
I'll plug her with serum.

And if she can't bear 'em
I'll call in the next undertaker."

His *locum tenens,* Doctor Byam,
Said: "Right oh, old fellow, we'll try 'em,
For I'm an adept, O,
At pumping in strepto
Since I was a surgeon in Siam."

The patient, who haled from New Zealing,
Said: "Pray don't consider my feeling,
10   Provided you're certain
  'Twill not go on hurtin',
I'll lie here and smile at the ceiling."

These two very bloodthirsty men
Injected five million, then ten,
  But found that the strepto
  Had suddenly crept to
Her feet—and the worst happened then!

Any day you may happen to meet
Her alone in the Hampstead High Street
20   In a box on four wheels
  With a whistle that squeals;
And her hands do the job of her feet.

[In September 1919 K.M. went to San
Remo, and, after a few weeks, took a little furnished cottage—the "Casetta"—at Ospedaletti
near by. I was with her in San Remo, but returned to England to my work as editor of
The Athenaeum as soon as she was settled into
the "Casetta" with L.M. For a time K.M. was
30 very happy; but then illness and isolation and
the everlasting sound of the sea began to depress her.]

Mrs. Nightingale: A Dream

November. Walking up a dark hill with high
iron fences at the sides of the road and immense trees over. I was looking for a midwife,
Mrs. Nightingale. A little girl, barefoot, with a
handkerchief over her head pattered up and
put her chill hand in mine; she would lead me.

A light showed from a general shop. Inside
40 a beautiful fair angry young woman directed
me up the hill and to the right.

"You should have believed *me!*" said the
child, and dug her nails into my palm.

23. **San Remo,** a town on the Italian Riviera, just across the
Franco-Italian border in the province of Liguria.

There reared up a huge wall with a blank
notice plastered on it. That was the house. In
a low room, sitting by a table, a dirty yellow
and black rug on her knees, an old hag sat.
She had a grey handkerchief on her head. Beside her on the table was a jar of onions and
a fork. I explained. She was to come to mother. 50
Mother was very delicate: her eldest daughter
was thirty-one and she had heart disease. "So
please come at once."

"Has she any adhesions?" muttered the old
hag, and she speared an onion, ate it and
rubbed her nose.

"Oh, yes"—I put my hands on my breast—
"many, many plural adhesions."

"Ah, that's bad, that's very bad," said the
old crone, hunching up the rug so that through 60
the fringe I saw her square slippers. "But I
can't come. I've a case at four o'clock."

At that moment a healthy, bonny young
woman came in with a bundle. She sat down
by the midwife and explained, "Jinnie has had
hers already." She unwound the bundle too
quickly: a new-born baby with round eyes fell
forward on her lap. I felt the pleasure of the
little girl beside me—a kind of quiver. The
young woman blushed and lowered her voice. 70
"I got her to . . ." And she paused to find a
very *medical private* word to describe washing. . . . "To *navigate* with a bottle of English
water," she said, "but it isn't all away yet."

Mrs. Nightingale told me to go to the friend,
Madame Léger, who lived on the terrace with
a pink light before her house. I went. The terrace of houses was white and grey-blue in the
moonlight with dark pines down the road. I
saw the exquisite pink light. But just then 80
there was a clanking sound behind me, and
there was the little girl, bursting with breath-
lessness dragging in her arms a huge black
bag. "Mrs Nightingale says you forgot this."

So *I* was the midwife. I walked on thinking:
"I'll go and have a look at the poor little soul.
But it won't be for a long time yet."

Et in Arcadia Ego

To sit in front of the little wood fire, your
hands crossed in your lap and your eyes closed

88. *Et . . . Ego,* And I (was) in Arcadia. Arcadia was, in classical tradition, an idyllic place of open country inhabited by
shepherds and their flocks, a perfect resort for the pastoral poet.

—to fancy you see again upon your eyelids all the dancing beauty of the day, to feel the flame on your throat as you used to imagine you felt the spot of yellow when Bogey held a buttercup under your chin . . . when breathing is such delight that you are almost afraid to breathe—as though a butterfly fanned its wings upon your breast. Still to taste the warm sunlight that melted in your mouth; still to smell the white waxy scent that lay upon the jonquil fields and the wild spicy scent of the rosemary growing in little tufts among the red rocks close to the brim of the sea. . . .

The moon is rising but the reluctant day lingers upon the sea and sky. The sea is dabbled with a pink the colour of unripe cherries, and in the sky there is a flying yellow light like the wings of canaries. Very stubborn and solid are the trunks of the palm trees. Springing from their tops the stiff green bouquets seem to cut into the evening air and among them, the blue gum trees, tall and slender with sickle-shaped leaves and drooping branches half blue, half violet. The moon is just over the mountain behind the village. The dogs know she is there; already they begin to howl and bark. The fishermen are shouting and whistling to one another as they bring in their boats, some young boys are singing in half-broken voices down by the shore, and there is a noise of children crying, little children with burnt cheeks and sand between their toes being carried to bed. . . .

I am tired, blissfully tired. Do you suppose that daisies feel blissfully tired when they shut for the night and the dews descend upon them?

Death

December 15. When I had gone to bed I realised what it was that had caused me to "give way." It was the effort of being up, with a heart that won't work. Not my lungs at all. My despair simply disappeared—yes, simply. The weather was lovely. Every morning the sun came in and drew more squares of golden light on the wall, I looked round my bed on to a sky like silk. The day opened slowly, slowly like a flower, and it held the sun long, long before it slowly, slowly folded. Then my homesickness went. I not only didn't want to be in England,

I began to love Italy, and the thought of it— the sun—even when it was too hot—always the sun—and a kind of *wholeness* which was good to bask in.

All these two years I have been obsessed by the fear of death. This grew and grew and grew gigantic, and this it was that made me cling so, I think. Ten days ago it went, I care no more. It leaves me perfectly cold. . . . Life either stays or goes.

I must put down here a dream. The first night I was in bed here, *i.e.*, after my first day in bed, I went to sleep. And suddenly I felt my whole body *breaking up*. It broke with a violent shock—an earthquake—and it broke like glass. A long terrible shiver, you understand— the spinal cord and the bones and every bit and particle quaking. It sounded in my ears a low, confused din, and there was a sense of floating greenish brilliance, like broken glass. When I awoke I thought that there had been a violent earthquake. But all was still. It slowly dawned upon me—the conviction that in that dream I died. I shall go on living now—it may be for months, or for weeks or days or hours. Time is not. In that dream I died. The *spirit* that is the enemy of death and quakes so and is so tenacious was shaken out of me. I am (December 15, 1919) a dead woman, and *I don't care*. It might comfort others to know that one gives up caring; but they'd not believe any more than I did until it happened. And, oh, how strong was its hold upon me! How I *adored* life and *dreaded* death!

I'd like to write my books and spend some happy time with J. (not very much faith withal) and see L. in a sunny place and pick violets—all kinds of flowers. I'd like to do heaps of things, really. But I don't mind if I do not do them. . . . Honesty (why?) is the only thing one seems to prize beyond life, love, death, everything. It alone remaineth. O you who come after me, will you believe it? At the end *truth* is the only thing *worth having*: it's more thrilling than love, more joyful and more passionate. It simply can*not* fail. All else fails. I, at any rate, give the remainder of my life to it and it alone.

December 17. I'd like to write a *long, long* story on this and call it "Last Words to Life."

One *ought* to write it. And another on the subject of HATE.

December. It often happens to me now that when I lie down to sleep at night, instead of getting drowsy, I feel more wakeful and, lying here in bed, I begin to *live* over either scenes from real life or imaginary scenes. It's not too much to say that they are almost hallucinations: they are marvellously vivid. I lie on my right side and put my left hand up to my forehead as though I were praying. This seems to induce the state. Then, for instance, it is 10:30 p.m. on a big liner in mid ocean. People are beginning to leave the Ladies' Cabin. Father puts his head in and asks if "one of you would care for a walk before you turn in. It's glorious up on deck." That begins it. I am *there.* Details: Father rubbing his gloves, the cold air—the *night* air, the pattern of everything, the feel of the brass stair-rail and the rubber stairs. Then the deck—the pause while the cigar is lighted, the look of all in the moonlight, the *steadying* hum of the ship, the first officer on deck, so far aloft the bells, the steward going into the smoking-room with a tray, stepping over the high, brass-bound step. . . . All these things are far realer, more in detail, *richer* than life. And I believe I could go on until. . . . There's *no end* to it.

I can do this about everything. Only there are no personalities. Neither am I there personally. People are only part of the silence, *not* of the pattern—vastly different from that—part of the *scheme.* I could always do this to a certain extent; but it's only since I was really ill that this—shall we call it?—"consolation prize" has been given to me. My God! it's a marvellous thing.

I can call up certain persons—Doctor S. for instance. And then I remember how I used to say to J. and R. "He was looking very beautiful today." I did not know what I was saying. But when I so summon him and see him "in relation," he *is* marvellously beautiful. There again he comes complete, to every detail, to the shape of his thumbs, to looking over his glasses, his lips as he writes, and particularly in all connected with putting the needle into the syringe. . . . I relive all this at will.

"Any children?" he said, taking his stethoscope as I struggled with my nightgown.

"No, no children."

But what would he have said if I'd told him that until a few days ago I had had a little child, aged five and three quarters, of indeterminate sex? Some days it was a boy. For two years now it had very often been a little girl. . . .

December. Surely I do know more than other people: I have suffered more, and endured more. I know how they long to be happy, and how precious is an atmosphere that is loving, a *climate* that is not frightening. Why do I not try to bear this in mind, and try to cultivate my garden? Now I descend to a strange place among strangers. Can I not make myself felt as a real personal force? (why should you?) Ah, but I *should.* I have had experiences unknown to them. I should by now have learnt C.'s obiter dictum—how true it might be. It *must* be.

[Towards the end of December, worried by the depression of her letters, I went to Ospedaletti for a fortnight to see K. M.]

December 30. Calm day. In garden read early poems in Oxford Book. Discussed our future library. In the evening read Dostoevsky. In the morning discussed the importance of 'eternal life.' Played our famous Stone Game (Cape Sixpence and Cornwall).

December 31. Long talk over house. Foster said I could walk. Sea sounded like an island sea. Happy. Lovely fire in my bedroom. Succès éclatant avec demon before dinner. Listened to Wingley's fiddle. The wooden bed.

70. **obiter dictum,** an incidental opinion or remark. 77. **Dostoevsky,** Feodor Dostoievski (1821–81), generally considered the supreme realist among the many great Russian writers of fiction during the nineteenth century; his best-known works are *Crime and Punishment* (1866) and *The Brothers Karamazov* (1880). 79. **Stone . . . Cornwall.** The Stone Game was simple. You placed a largish stone at the extreme edge of a cliff, sat down about ten yards away and shied smaller stones at it. The one who first toppled it over received sixpence from the other. Hence the name, Cape Sixpence, which we gave to the cliff near Bandol where we first played the game. (Author's note.) 81. **Foster,** one of Miss Mansfield's many doctors. 84. **éclatant,** resounding, brilliant.

SOMERSET MAUGHAM

William Somerset Maugham was educated to the profession of medicine, made a fortune in the writing of plays, and will probably go down to posterity as a gifted novelist and teller of short stories. He was born January 25, 1874, in Paris, where his father was a councilor at the British Embassy. The boy's early childhood was passed in Paris; between the ages of ten and thirteen he lived in England and attended King's School at Canterbury. Later he studied at the University of Heidelberg and dabbled in painting in Paris. But his parents had intended him for the career of a physician or surgeon; in consequence he spent several years at St. Thomas Hospital in London, where he eventually took his degree and became a member of the Royal College of Surgeons. Actually his practice was as unsubstantial as was Galsworthy's practice of law (p. 102).

It was while he was still at St. Thomas Hospital that he wrote his first novel, *Liza of Lambeth,* a naturalistic study of the slums of London. This novel shocked many by its uncompromising, photographic realism and by its "morbid" interest in the pathology, physical and psychological, of its characters. Yet Maugham was merely doing what his older French contemporary Emile Zola (1840–1902) had accomplished more successfully. *Liza of Lambeth* (1897) was not a great novel, but it showed the "medical student" attitude toward life that Maugham has never completely outgrown. Three more novels followed, *The Making of a Saint* (1898), *Orientations* (1899), and *The Hero* (1901); none of these made any stir, but they determined for Maugham that his calling should be that of a man of letters.

He now turned to the drama, and his first play, in one act, was written in German and produced in Berlin—*Schiffbrüchig* (1902). He continued to struggle to gain recognition and obtained moderate success with two novels, *Mrs. Craddock* (1902) and *Merry-Go-Round* (1904), and a play, *A Man of Honour* (1903); but his first real success on the stage came with *Lady Frederick* (1907). This play and the success of three farces, *Penelope* (1909), *Jack Straw* (1912), and *Mrs. Dot* (1912), rounded out the apprentice period of Maugham's writing. Thereafter he was to gain distinction.

During the First World War Maugham was a secret agent for the British government; the experiences he underwent at this time formed the basis of his later best-seller, *British Agent* (1928), known in England under the title *Ashenden.* But his great success of the war years was his excellent *Of Human Bondage* (1915), generally acclaimed as his masterpiece. It is a powerful novel of a young medical student and his difficulties in getting adjusted both to his profession and to the hazards of his emotional and sexual life. Except for some minor changes the novel is largely autobiographical and goes back to Maugham's own unhappy childhood experiences in school, as well as to his own days at St. Thomas Hospital.

Between 1915 and 1919 his writing struck a calm. When the war was over, he traveled—he has always been a globe-trotter—and made a visit to the South Seas, to determine wherein lay their great fascination. He stayed for some time in Tahiti. The result was *The Moon and Sixpence* (1919), a novel of the South Seas based primarily upon the life of the French artist Paul Gauguin (1848–1903), a work which was so frank in respect to Tahitian life that it was banned in the island. But Maugham had struck a peculiarly rich vein of story material in the Orient and one for which he was unusually fitted. *The Trembling of a Leaf* (1921) and *On a Chinese Screen* (1922), two volumes of admirable short stories, and *East of Suez* (1922), a grim play, followed in rapid succession and established Maugham as the most important interpreter of the white man gone native in those multifarious tropical way-stations east of Suez, "where the best is like the worst." *The Painted Veil* (1925), a full-length novel, and *The Casuarina Tree* (1926) continued the line, with the author's power undiminished. A little by-path in Maugham's works is *Andalusia* (1920), an account of his travels in Spain, which prompted *Don Fernando* (1935), "a variation on Spanish themes," a glorified history and travel-book combined. His other account of a journey, *The Gentleman in the Parlour* (1930), again within the Oriental periphery, is one of the best of its kind.

All this time Maugham had been piling up hit after hit on the stage, so that he has been regarded as the most financially fortunate of contemporary British dramatists. His plays number nearly thirty, all of them marked by wit, a brilliant cynicism, and superb dramatic craftsmanship. The best are probably *The Circle* (1921), *Our Betters* (1923), and *The Letter* (1927). *Rain,* written by John Colton and Randolph Clemence, based on Maugham's story "Miss Thompson" (p. 449), made a sensation in the United States because of its daring theme and the superior acting of the late Jeanne Eagels. *The Letter* is another Maugham story set in dramatic form. Other plays written in this period which are worth mentioning are *Caesar's Wife* (1919), *The Constant Wife* (1927), *The Sacred Flame* (1928), *The Breadwinner* (1930), *For Services Rendered* (1932), and *Sheppey* (1933).

Of recent years Maugham has been writing in a quieter, more reflective mood, but still with plenty of satirical zest. *Cakes and Ale,* while classifiable as a novel, is largely literary reminiscence and has caused many heartburns because of its thinly veiled attacks upon Thomas Hardy (1840-1928) and Hugh Walpole (1884-1941). *First Person Singular* (1931) is in the same vein. *Strictly Personal* (1941) is Maugham's account of his experiences in France and of his escape at the time of the Nazi breakthrough. *The Summing-Up* (1938) is an excellent retrospect, in which Maugham is quite willing to appraise himself ruthlessly and wittily. Several collections of essays, ranging from *Books and You* (1940) to a staid enough *Introduction to Modern English and American Literature* (1943) and a rather ambitious *Great Novelists and Their Novels* (1948) show that Maugham is essentially a brilliant conversationalist in prose.

And to date he has continued as well a steady flow of fiction: short-story collections such as *The Mixture as Before* (1940), *East and West* (1941), and *Creatures of Circumstance* (1947), some of which contain reprints of earlier stories, some of which are new; and five novels, *The Christmas Holiday* (1939), *The Hour Before the Dawn* (1942), *The Razor's Edge* (1944), *Then and Now* (1946), and *Catalina* (1948). Of these novels *The Razor's Edge,* the tale of a besmirched young idealist in search of a peace which he can find only in mystic religion, is probably the best. Although it is in no way comparable in worth to *Of Human Bondage,* it is certainly far superior to the general run of contemporary fiction.

As for the general artistic achievement of Maugham, there is no reason to suppose that he will be able to modify it much in the future. He has won a secure place in British fiction of the present generation and has earned the sobriquet, "the English Maupassant." In a sense this is fair enough—granting Maugham's undoubted originality—for he has the same terse style, the same dramatic economy and vigor, the same penetrating wit, the same shameless cynicism, the same brilliant craftsmanship, the same headlong love of adventurous incident, the same faint odor of the sewer. It is perhaps unfortunate that he should be thought of so often as a writer who paints the depressing picture of white men—missionaries preferred—succumbing to the lure of the tropics under the double compulsion of enervating heat and unremitting rain; or of white women becoming morally degraded and criminal for the same reasons. He has done other things and done them well. But he has none to blame but himself for the popular concept of his work; he must in all justice be put in the category of the pessimist (and a not too healthy one, either), a brilliant painter of the Waste Land.

Miss Thompson

IT WAS nearly bed-time and when they awoke next morning land would be in sight. Dr. Macphail lit his pipe and, leaning over the rail, searched the heavens for the Southern Cross. After two years at the front and a wound that had taken longer to heal than it should, he was glad to settle down quietly at Apia for twelve months at least, and he felt already better for the journey. Since some of the passengers were leaving the ship next day at Pago-Pago they had had a little dance that evening and in his ears hammered still the harsh notes of the mechanical piano. But the deck was quiet at last. A little way off he saw his wife in a long chair talking with the Davidsons, and he strolled over to her. When he sat down under the light and took off his hat you saw that he had very red hair, with a bald patch on the crown, and the red, freckled skin which accompanies red hair; he was a man of forty, thin, with a pinched face, precise and rather pedantic; and he spoke with a Scotch accent in a very low, quiet voice.

Between the Macphails and the Davidsons, who were missionaries, there had arisen the intimacy of shipboard, which is due to propinquity rather than to any community of taste. Their chief tie was the disapproval they shared of the men who spent their days and nights in the smoking-room playing poker or bridge and drinking. Mrs. Macphail was not a little flattered to think that she and her husband were the only people on board with whom the Davidsons were willing to associate, and even the doctor, shy but no fool, half unconsciously acknowledged the compliment. It was only because he was of an argumentative mind that in their cabin at night he permitted himself to carp.

"Mrs. Davidson was saying she didn't know how they'd have got through the journey if it hadn't been for us," said Mrs. Macphail, as she neatly brushed out her transformation. "She said we were really the only people on the ship they cared to know."

"I shouldn't have thought a missionary was such a big bug that he could afford to put on frills."

"It's not frills. I quite understand what she means. It wouldn't have been very nice for the Davidsons to have to mix with all that rough lot in the smoking-room."

"The founder of their religion wasn't so exclusive," said Dr. Macphail with a chuckle.

"I've asked you over and over again not to joke about religion," answered his wife. "I shouldn't like to have a nature like yours, Alec. You never look for the best in people."

He gave her a sidelong glance with his pale, blue eyes, but did not reply. After many years of married life he had learned that it was more conducive to peace to leave his wife with the last word. He was undressed before she was, and climbing into the upper bunk he settled down to read himself to sleep.

When he came on deck next morning they were close to land. He looked at it with greedy eyes. There was a thin strip of silver beach rising quickly to hills covered to the top with luxuriant vegetation. The coconut trees, thick and green, came nearly to the water's edge, and among them you saw the grass houses of the Samoans; and here and there, gleaming white, a little church. Mrs. Davidson came and stood beside him. She was dressed in black and wore round her neck a gold chain, from which dangled a small cross. She was a little woman, with brown, dull hair very elaborately arranged, and she had prominent blue eyes behind invisible *pince-nez*. Her face was long, like a sheep's, but she gave no impression of foolishness, rather of extreme alertness; she had the quick movements of a bird. The most remarkable thing about her was her voice, high, metallic, and without inflection; it fell on the ear with a hard monotony, irritating to the nerves like the pitiless clamour of the pneumatic drill.

"This must seem like home to you," said Dr. Macphail, with his thin, difficult smile.

"Miss Thompson" (sometimes known as "The Trembling of a Leaf") from *The Trembling of a Leaf*, by W. Somerset Maugham, copyright 1921 by Doubleday, Doran & Company, Inc.
7. **Apia,** on Upolu Island in the Samoan group and the capital of British Samoa. 10. **Pago-Pago,** or Pango-Pango, the chief settlement on Tutuila Island in the Samoan group; this island belongs to the United States.

43. **transformation,** here used in the sense of artificial hair, worn by women of the 1920's and before as part of their hairdress.

449

"Ours are low islands, you know, not like these. Coral. These are volcanic. We've got another ten days' journey to reach them."

"In these parts that's almost like being in the next street at home," said Dr. Macphail facetiously.

"Well, that's rather an exaggerated way of putting it, but one does look at distances differently in the South Seas. So far you're right." Dr. Macphail sighed faintly.

"I'm glad we're not stationed here," she went on. "They say this is a terribly difficult place to work in. The steamers' touching makes the people unsettled; and then there's the naval station; that's bad for the natives. In our district we don't have difficulties like that to contend with. There are one or two traders, of course, but we take care to make them behave, and if they don't we make the place so hot for them they're glad to go."

Fixing the glasses on her nose she looked at the green island with a ruthless stare.

"It's almost a hopeless task for the missionaries here. I can never be sufficiently thankful to God that we are at least spared that."

Davidson's district consisted of a group of islands to the north of Samoa; they were widely separated and he had frequently to go long distances by canoe. At these times his wife remained at their headquarters and managed the mission. Dr. Macphail felt his heart sink when he considered the efficiency with which she certainly managed it. She spoke of the depravity of the natives in a voice which nothing could hush, but with a vehemently unctuous horror. Her sense of delicacy was singular. Early in their acquaintance she had said to him:

"You know, their marriage customs when we first settled in the islands were so shocking that I couldn't possibly describe them to you. But I'll tell Mrs. Macphail and she'll tell you."

Then he had seen his wife and Mrs. Davidson, their deckchairs close together, in earnest conversation for about two hours. As he walked past them backwards and forwards for the sake of exercise, he had heard Mrs. Davidson's agitated whisper, like the distant flow of a mountain torrent, and he saw by his wife's open mouth and pale face that she was enjoying an alarming experience. At night in their cabin she repeated to him with bated breath all she had heard.

"Well, what did I say to you?" cried Mrs. Davidson, exultant next morning. "Did you ever hear anything more dreadful? You don't wonder that I couldn't tell you myself, do you? Even though you are a doctor?"

Mrs. Davidson scanned his face. She had a dramatic eagerness to see that she had achieved the desired effect.

"Can you wonder that when we first went there our hearts sank? You'll hardly believe me when I tell you it was impossible to find a single good girl in any of the villages."

She used the word *good* in a severely technical manner.

"Mr. Davidson and I talked it over, and we made up our minds the first thing to do was to put down the dancing. The natives were crazy about dancing."

"I was not averse to it myself when I was a young man," said Dr. Macphail.

"I guessed as much when I heard you ask Mrs. Macphail to have a turn with you last night. I don't think there's any real harm if a man dances with his wife, but I was relieved that she wouldn't. Under the circumstances I thought it better that we should keep to ourselves."

"Under what circumstances?"

Mrs. Davidson gave him a quick look through her *pince-nez*, but did not answer his question.

"But among white people it's not quite the same," she went on, "though I must say I agree with Mr. Davidson, who says he can't understand how a husband can stand by and see his wife in another man's arms, and as far as I'm concerned I've never danced a step since I married. It's not only immoral in itself, but it distinctly leads to immorality. However, I'm thankful to God that we stamped it out, and I don't think I'm wrong in saying that no one has danced in our district for eight years."

But now they came to the mouth of the harbour and Mrs. Macphail joined them. The ship turned sharply and steamed slowly in. It was a great land-locked harbour big enough to hold a fleet of battleships; and all around it rose, high and steep, the green hills. Near the entrance, getting such breeze as blew from the sea, stood the governor's house in a garden. The Stars and Stripes dangled languidly from a flagstaff. They passed two or three trim bungalows, and a tennis court, and then they came to the quay with its warehouses. Mrs. Davidson pointed out the schooner, moored two or three hundred yards from the side, which was to take them to Apia. There was a crowd of eager, noisy, and good-humoured natives come from all parts of the island, some from curiosity, others to barter with the travellers on their way to Sydney; and they brought pineapples and huge bunches of bananas, *tapa* cloths, necklaces of shells or sharks' teeth, *kava*-bowls, and models of war canoes. American sailors, neat and trim, clean-shaven and frank of face, sauntered among them, and there was a little group of officials. While their luggage was being landed the Macphails and Mrs. Davidson watched the crowd. Dr. Macphail looked at the yaws from which most of the children and the young boys seemed to suffer, disfiguring sores like torpid ulcers, and his professional eyes glistened when he saw for the first time in his experience cases of elephantiasis, men going about with a huge, heavy arm or dragging along a grossly disfigured leg. Men and women wore the *lava-lava*.

"It's a very indecent costume," said Mrs. Davidson. "Mr. Davidson thinks it should be prohibited by law. How can you expect people to be moral when they wear nothing but a strip of red cotton round their loins?"

"It's suitable enough to the climate," said the doctor, wiping the sweat off his head.

Now that they were on land the heat, though it was so early in the morning, was already oppressive. Closed in by its hills, not a breath of air came in to Pago-Pago.

"In our islands," Mrs. Davidson went on in her high-pitched tones, "we've practically eradicated the *lava-lava*. A few old men still continue to wear it, but that's all. The women have all taken to the Mother Hubbard, and the men wear trousers and singlets. At the very beginning of our stay Mr. Davidson said in one of his reports: the inhabitants of these islands will

never be thoroughly Christianized till every boy of more than ten years is made to wear a pair of trousers."

But Mrs. Davidson had given two or three of her birdlike glances at heavy grey clouds that came floating over the mouth of the harbour. A few drops began to fall.

"We'd better take shelter," she said.

They made their way with all the crowd to a great shed of corrugated iron, and the rain began to fall in torrents. They stood there for some time and then were joined by Mr. Davidson. He had been polite enough to the Macphails during the journey, but he had not his wife's sociability, and had spent much of his time reading. He was a silent, rather sullen man, and you felt that his affability was a duty that he imposed upon himself Christianly; he was by nature reserved and even morose. His appearance was singular. He was very tall and thin, with long limbs loosely jointed; hollow cheeks and curiously high cheek-bones; he had so cadaverous an air that it surprised you to notice how full and sensual were his lips. He wore his hair very long. His dark eyes, set deep in their sockets, were large and tragic; and his hands with their big, long fingers, were finely shaped; they gave him a look of great strength. But the most striking thing about him was the feeling he gave you of suppressed fire. It was impressive, and vaguely troubling. He was not a man with whom any intimacy was possible.

He brought now unwelcome news. There was an epidemic of measles, a serious and often fatal disease among the Kanakas, on the island, and a case had developed among the crew of the schooner which was to take them on their journey. The sick man had been brought ashore and put in hospital on the quarantine station, but telegraphic instructions had been sent from Apia to say that the schooner would not be allowed to enter the harbour till it was certain no other member of the crew was affected.

"It means we shall have to stay here for ten days at least."

"But I'm urgently needed at Apia," said Dr. Macphail.

"That can't be helped. If no more cases develop on board, the schooner will be allowed to sail with white passengers, but all native traffic is prohibited for three months."

13. *tapa* cloths, cloths made from the bark of the paper mulberry tree.   14. *kava*-bowls, vessels used to serve *kava*, an intoxicating drink made from the root of an Australasian pepper-plant.

"Is there a hotel here?" asked Mrs. Macphail.

Davidson gave a low chuckle.

"There's not."

"What shall we do then?"

"I've been talking to the governor. There's a trader along the front who has rooms that he rents, and my proposition is that as soon as the rain lets up we should go along there and see what we can do. Don't expect comfort. You've just got to be thankful if we get a bed to sleep on and a roof over our heads."

But the rain showed no sign of stopping, and at length with umbrellas and waterproofs they set out. There was no town, but merely a group of official buildings, a store or two, and at the back, among the coconut trees and plantains, a few native dwellings. The house they sought was about five minutes' walk from the wharf. It was a frame house of two storeys, with broad verandahs on both floors and a roof of corrugated iron. The owner was a half-caste named Horn, with a native wife surrounded by little brown children, and on the ground-floor he had a store where he sold canned goods and cottons. The rooms he showed them were almost bare of furniture. In the Macphails' there was nothing but a poor, worn bed with a ragged mosquito net, a rickety chair, and a washstand. They looked round with dismay. The rain poured down without ceasing.

"I'm not going to unpack more than we actually need," said Mrs. Macphail.

Mrs. Davidson came into the room as she was unlocking a portmanteau. She was very brisk and alert. The cheerless surroundings had no effect on her.

"If you'll take my advice you'll get a needle and cotton and start right in to mend the mosquito net," she said, "or you'll not be able to get a wink of sleep tonight."

"Will they be very bad?" asked Dr. Macphail.

"This is the season for them. When you're asked to a party at Government House at Apia you'll notice that all the ladies are given a pillow-slip to put their—their lower extremities in."

"I wish the rain would stop for a moment," said Mrs. Macphail. "I could try to make the place comfortable with more heart if the sun were shining."

"Oh, if you wait for that, you'll wait a long time. Pago-Pago is about the rainiest place in the Pacific. You see, the hills and that bay, they attract the water, and one expects rain at this time of year any way."

She looked from Macphail to his wife, standing helplessly in different parts of the room, like lost souls, and she pursed her lips. She saw that she must take them in hand. Feckless people like that made her impatient, but her hands itched to put everything in order which came so naturally to her.

"Here, you give me a needle and cotton and I'll mend that net of yours, while you go on with your unpacking. Dinner's at one. Dr. Macphail, you'd better go down to the wharf and see that your heavy luggage has been put in a dry place. You know what these natives are, they're quite capable of storing it where the rain will beat in on it all the time."

The doctor put on his waterproof again and went downstairs. At the door Mr. Horn was standing in conversation with the quartermaster of the ship they had just arrived in and a second-class passenger whom Dr. Macphail had seen several times on board. The quartermaster, a little, shrivelled man, extremely dirty, nodded to him as he passed.

"This is a bad job about the measles, doc," he said. "I see you've fixed yourself up already."

Dr. Macphail thought he was rather familiar, but he was a timid man and he did not take offence easily.

"Yes, we've got a room upstairs."

"Miss Thompson was sailing with you to Apia, so I've brought her along here."

The quartermaster pointed with his thumb to the woman standing by his side. She was twenty-seven perhaps, plump, and in a coarse fashion pretty. She wore a white dress and a large white hat. Her fat calves in white cotton stockings bulged over the tops of long white boots in glacé kid. She gave Macphail an ingratiating smile.

"The feller's tryin' to soak me a dollar and a half a day for the meanest sized room," she said in a hoarse voice.

"I tell you she's a friend of mine, Jo," said the quartermaster. "She can't pay more than a dollar, and you've sure got to take her for that."

The trader was fat and smooth and quietly smiling.

"Well, if you put it like that, Mr. Swan, I'll see what I can do about it. I'll talk to Mrs. Horn and if we think we can make a reduction we will."

"Don't try to pull that stuff with me," said Miss Thompson. "We'll settle this right now. You get a dollar a day for the room and not one bean more."

Dr. Macphail smiled. He admired the effrontery with which she bargained. He was the sort of man who always paid what he was asked. He preferred to be over-charged than to haggle. The trader sighed.

"Well, to oblige Mr. Swan I'll take it."

"That's the goods," said Miss Thompson. "Come right in and have a shot of hooch. I've got some real good rye in that grip if you'll bring it along, Mr. Swan. You come along too, doctor."

"Oh, I don't think I will, thank you," he answered. "I'm just going down to see that our luggage is all right."

He stepped out into the rain. It swept in from the opening of the harbour in sheets and the opposite shore was all blurred. He passed two or three natives clad in nothing but the *lava-lava*, with huge umbrellas over them. They walked finely, with leisurely movements, very upright; and they smiled and greeted him in a strange tongue as they went by.

It was nearly dinner-time when he got back, and their meal was laid in the trader's parlour. It was a room designed not to live in but for purposes of prestige, and it had a musty, melancholy air. A suite of stamped plush was arranged neatly round the walls, and from the middle of the ceiling, protected from the flies by yellow tissue paper, hung a gilt chandelier. Davidson did not come.

"I know he went to call on the governor," said Mrs. Davidson, "and I guess he's kept him to dinner."

A little native girl brought them a dish of Hamburger steak, and after a while the trader came up to see that they had everything they wanted.

"I see we have a fellow lodger, Mr. Horn," said Dr. Macphail.

"She's taken a room, that's all," answered the trader. "She's getting her own board."

He looked at the two ladies with an obsequious air.

"I put her downstairs so she shouldn't be in the way. She won't be any trouble to you."

"Is it someone who was on the boat?" asked Mrs. Macphail.

"Yes, ma'am, she was in the second cabin. She was going to Apia. She has a position as cashier waiting for her."

"Oh!"

When the trader was gone Macphail said:

"I shouldn't think she'd find it exactly cheerful having her meals in her room."

"If she was in the second cabin I guess she'd rather," answered Mrs. Davidson. "I don't exactly know who it can be."

"I happened to be there when the quartermaster brought her along. Her name's Thompson."

"It's not the woman who was dancing with the quartermaster last night?" asked Mrs. Davidson.

"That's who it must be," said Mrs. Macphail. "I wondered at the time what she was. She looked rather fast to me."

"Not good style at all," said Mrs. Davidson.

They began to talk of other things, and after dinner, tired with their early rise, they separated and slept. When they awoke, though the sky was still grey and the clouds hung low, it was not raining and they went for a walk on the high road which the Americans had built along the bay.

On their return they found that Davidson had just come in.

"We may be here for a fortnight," he said irritably. "I've argued it out with the governor, but he says there is nothing to be done."

"Mr. Davidson's just longing to get back to his work," said his wife, with an anxious glance at him.

"We've been away for a year," he said, walking up and down the verandah. "The mission has been in charge of native missionaries and I'm terribly nervous that they've let things slide. They're good men. I'm not saying a word against them, God-fearing, devout, and truly Christian men—their Christianity would put many so-called Christians at home to the blush —but they're pitifully lacking in energy. They can make a stand once, they can make a stand twice, but they can't make a stand all the time. If you leave a mission in charge of a native missionary, no matter how trustworthy he seems, in course of time you'll find he's let abuses creep in."

Mr. Davidson stood still. With his tall, spare form, and his great eyes flashing out of his pale face, he was an impressive figure. His sincerity was obvious in the fire of his gestures and in his deep, ringing voice.

"I expect to have my work cut out for me. I shall act and I shall act promptly. If the tree
10 is rotten it shall be cut down and cast into the flames."

And in the evening after the high tea which was their last meal, while they sat in the stiff parlour, the ladies working and Dr. Macphail smoking his pipe, the missionary told them of his work in the islands.

"When we went there they had no sense of sin at all," he said. "They broke the commandments one after the other and never knew
20 they were doing wrong. And I think that was the most difficult part of my work, to instil into the natives the sense of sin."

The Macphails knew already that Davidson had worked in the Solomons for five years before he met his wife. She had been a missionary in China, and they had become acquainted in Boston, where they were both spending part of their leave to attend a missionary congress. On their marriage they had been appointed to
30 the islands in which they had laboured ever since.

In the course of all the conversations they had had with Mr. Davidson one thing had shone out clearly and that was the man's unflinching courage. He was a medical missionary, and he was liable to be called at any time to one or other of the islands in the group. Even the whaleboat is not so very safe a conveyance in the stormy Pacific of the wet sea-
40 son, but often he would be sent for in a canoe, and then the danger was great. In cases of illness or accident he never hesitated. A dozen times he had spent the whole night bailing for his life, and more than once Mrs. Davidson had given him up for lost.

"I'd beg him not to go sometimes," she said, "or at least to wait till the weather was more settled, but he'd never listen. He's obstinate, and when he's once made up his mind, nothing can move him."
50

"How can I ask the natives to put their trust in the Lord if I am afraid to do so myself?" cried Davidson. "And I'm not, I'm not. They know that if they send for me in their trouble I'll come if it's humanly possible. And do you think the Lord is going to abandon me when I am on his business? The wind blows at His bidding and the waves toss and rage at His word."

Dr. Macphail was a timid man. He had
60 never been able to get used to the hurtling of the shells over the trenches, and when he was operating in an advanced dressing-station the sweat poured from his brow and dimmed his spectacles in the effort he made to control his unsteady hand. He shuddered a little as he looked at the missionary.

"I wish I could say that I've never been afraid," he said.

"I wish you could say that you believed in
70 God," retorted the other.

But for some reason, that evening the missionary's thoughts travelled back to the early days he and his wife had spent on the islands.

"Sometimes Mrs. Davidson and I would look at one another and the tears would stream down our cheeks. We worked without ceasing, day and night, and we seemed to make no progress. I don't know what I should have done without her then. When I felt my heart
80 sink, when I was very near despair, she gave me courage and hope."

Mrs. Davidson looked down at her work, and a slight colour rose to her thin cheeks. Her hands trembled a little. She did not trust herself to speak.

"We had no one to help us. We were alone, thousands of miles from any of our own people, surrounded by darkness. When I was broken and weary she would put her work
90 aside and take the Bible and read to me till

9. **"If . . . flames,"** "Therefore every tree which bringeth not forth good fruit is hewn down, and cast into the fire."— Matthew 3 : 10.   24. **Solomons,** a large archipelago of Polynesian islands running from 4 to 12 degrees south latitude and from 154 to 164 east longitude. Before World War I they were divided between British and German ownership; after the war Germany's portion was turned over to Japan.

57. **"The wind . . . word,"** "Fear ye not me?" saith the Lord; "will ye not tremble at my presence, which have placed the sand for the bound of the sea by a perpetual decree, that it cannot pass it; and though the waves thereof toss themselves, yet can they not prevail; though they roar, yet can they not pass over it?"—Job 5 : 22.

peace came and settled upon me like sleep upon the eyelids of a child, and when at last she closed the book she'd say: 'We'll save them in spite of themselves.' And I felt strong again in the Lord, and I answered: 'Yes, with God's help I'll save them. I must save them.'"

He came over to the table and stood in front of it as though it were a lectern.

"You see, they were so naturally depraved that they couldn't be brought to see their wickedness. We had to make sins out of what they thought were natural actions. We had to make it a sin, not only to commit adultery and to lie and thieve, but to expose their bodies, and to dance and not to come to church. I made it a sin for a girl to show her bosom and a sin for a man not to wear trousers."

"How?" asked Dr. Macphail, not without surprise.

"I instituted fines. Obviously the only way to make people realize that an action is sinful is to punish them if they commit it. I fined them if they didn't come to church, and I fined them if they danced. I fined them if they were improperly dressed. I had a tariff, and every sin had to be paid for either in money or work. And at last I made them understand."

"But did they never refuse to pay?"

"How could they?" asked the missionary.

"It would be a brave man who tried to stand up against Mr. Davidson," said his wife, tightening her lips.

Dr. Macphail looked at Davidson with troubled eyes. What he heard shocked him, but he hesitated to express his disapproval.

"You must remember that in the last resort I could expel them from their church membership."

"Did they mind that?"

Davidson smiled a little and gently rubbed his hands.

"They couldn't sell their copra. When the men fished they got no share of the catch. It meant something very like starvation. Yes, they minded quite a lot."

"Tell him about Fred Ohlson," said Mrs. Davidson.

The missionary fixed his fiery eyes on Dr. Macphail.

"Fred Ohlson was a Danish trader who had been in the islands a good many years. He was a pretty rich man as traders go, and he wasn't very pleased when we came. You see, he'd had things very much his own way. He paid the natives what he liked for their copra, and he paid in goods and whiskey. He had a native wife, but he was flagrantly unfaithful to her. He was a drunkard. I gave him a chance to mend his ways, but he wouldn't take it. He laughed at me."

Davidson's voice fell to a deep bass as he said the last words, and he was silent for a minute or two. The silence was heavy with menace.

"In two years he was a ruined man. He'd lost everything he'd saved in a quarter of a century. I broke him, and at last he was forced to come to me like a beggar and beseech me to give him a passage back to Sydney."

"I wish you could have seen him when he came to see Mr. Davidson," said the missionary's wife. "He had been a fine, powerful man, with a lot of fat on him, and he had a great big voice, but now he was half the size, and he was shaking all over. He'd suddenly become an old man."

With abstracted gaze Davidson looked out into the night. The rain was falling again.

Suddenly from below came a sound, and Davidson turned and looked questioningly at his wife. It was the sound of a gramophone, harsh and loud, wheezing out a syncopated tune.

"What's that?" he asked.

Mrs. Davidson fixed her *pince-nez* more firmly on her nose.

"One of the second-class passengers has a room in the house. I guess it comes from there."

They listened in silence, and presently they heard the sound of dancing. Then the music stopped, and they heard the popping of corks and voices raised in animated conversation.

"I daresay she's giving a farewell party to her friends on board," said Dr. Macphail. "The ship sails at twelve, doesn't it?"

Davidson made no remark, but he looked at his watch.

"Are you ready?" he asked his wife.

She got up and folded her work.

"Yes, I guess I am," she answered.

"It's early to go to bed yet, isn't it?" said the doctor.

"We have a good deal of reading to do," explained Mrs. Davidson. "Wherever we are, we read a chapter of the Bible before retiring for the night and we study it with the commentaries, you know, and discuss it thoroughly. It's a wonderful training for the mind."

The two couples bade one another goodnight. Dr. and Mrs. Macphail were left alone. For two or three minutes they did not speak.

10 "I think I'll go and fetch the cards," the doctor said at last.

Mrs. Macphail looked at him doubtfully. Her conversation with the Davidsons had left her a little uneasy, but she did not like to say that she thought they had better not play cards when the Davidsons might come in at any moment. Dr. Macphail brought them and she watched him, though with a vague sense of guilt, while he laid out his patience. Below the

20 sound of revelry continued.

It was fine enough next day, and the Macphails, condemned to spend a fortnight of idleness at Pago-Pago, set about making the best of things. They went down to the quay and got out of their boxes a number of books. The doctor called on the chief surgeon of the naval hospital and went round the beds with him. They left cards on the governor. They passed Miss Thompson on the road. The doctor took

30 off his hat, and she gave him a "Good morning, doc," in a loud, cheerful voice. She was dressed as on the day before, in a white frock, and her shiny white boots with their high heels, her fat legs bulging over the tops of them, were strange things on that exotic scene.

"I don't think she's very suitably dressed, I must say," said Mrs. Macphail. "She looks extremely common to me."

When they got back to their house, she was

40 on the verandah playing with one of the trader's dark children.

"Say a word to her," Dr. Macphail whispered to his wife. "She's all alone here, and it seems rather unkind to ignore her."

Mrs. Macphail was shy, but she was in the habit of doing what her husband bade her.

"I think we're fellow lodgers here," she said, rather foolishly.

"Terrible, ain't it, bein' cooped up in a one-

50 horse burg like this?" answered Miss Thompson. "And they tell me I'm lucky to have gotten a room. I don't see myself livin' in a native

456

house, and that's what some have to do. I don't know why they don't have a hotel."

They exchanged a few more words. Miss Thompson, loud-voiced and garrulous, was evidently quite willing to gossip, but Mrs. Macphail had a poor stock of small talk and presently she said:

"Well, I think we must go upstairs."

In the evening when they sat down to their high-tea Davidson on coming in said:

"I see that woman downstairs has a couple of sailors sitting there. I wonder how she's gotten acquainted with them."

"She can't be very particular," said Mrs. Davidson.

They were all rather tired after the idle, aimless day.

"If there's going to be a fortnight of this I don't know what we shall feel like at the end of it," said Dr. Macphail.

"The only thing to do is to portion out the day to different activities," answered the missionary. "I shall set aside a certain number of hours to study and a certain number to exercise, rain or fine—in the wet season you can't afford to pay any attention to the rain—and a certain number to recreation."

Dr. Macphail looked at his companion with misgiving. Davidson's programme oppressed him. They were eating Hamburger steak again. It seemed the only dish the cook knew how to make. Then below the gramophone began. Davidson started nervously when he heard it, but said nothing. Men's voices floated up. Miss Thompson's guests were joining in a well-known song and presently they heard her voice too, hoarse and loud. There was a good deal of shouting and laughing. The four people upstairs, trying to make conversation, listened despite themselves to the click of glasses and the scrape of chairs. More people had evidently come. Miss Thompson was giving a party.

"I wonder how she gets them all in," said Mrs. Macphail, suddenly breaking into a medical conversation between the missionary and her husband.

It showed whither her thoughts were wandering. The twitch of Davidson's face proved that, though he spoke of scientific things, his mind was busy in the same direction. Suddenly, while the doctor was giving some experience of practice on the Flanders front, rather prosily, he sprang to his feet with a cry.

"What's the matter, Alfred?" asked Mrs. Davidson.

"Of course! It never occurred to me. She's out of Iwelei."

"She can't be."

"She came on board at Honolulu. It's obvious. And she's carrying on her trade here. Here."

He uttered the last word with a passion of indignation.

"What's Iwelei?" asked Mrs. Macphail.

He turned his gloomy eyes on her and his voice trembled with horror.

"The plague spot of Honolulu. The Red Light district. It was a blot on our civilization."

Iwelei was on the edge of the city. You went down side streets by the harbour, in the darkness, across a rickety bridge, till you came to a deserted road, all ruts and holes, and then suddenly you came out into the light. There was parking room for motors on each side of the road, and there were saloons, tawdry and bright, each one noisy with its mechanical piano, and there were barbers' shops and tobacconists. There was a stir in the air and a sense of expectant gaiety. You turned down a narrow alley, either to the right or to the left, for the road divided Iwelei into two parts, and you found yourself in the district. There were rows of little bungalows, trim and neatly painted in green, and the pathway between them was broad and straight. It was laid out like a garden-city. In its respectable regularity, its order and spruceness, it gave an impression of sardonic horror; for never can the search for love have been so systematized and ordered. The pathways were lit by a rare lamp, but they would have been dark except for the lights that came from the open windows of the bungalows. Men wandered about, looking at the women who sat at their windows, reading or sewing, for the most part taking no notice of the passers-by; and like the women they were of all nationalities. There were Americans, sailors from the ships in port, enlisted men off the gunboats, sombrely drunk, and soldiers from the regiments, white and black, quartered on the island; there were Japanese, walking in twos and threes; Hawaiians, Chi-

nese in long robes, and Filipinos in preposterous hats. They were silent and as it were oppressed. Desire is sad.

"It was the most crying scandal of the Pacific," exclaimed Davidson vehemently. "The missionaries had been agitating against it for years, and at last the local press took it up. The police refused to stir. You know their argument. They say that vice is inevitable and consequently the best thing is to localize and control it. The truth is, they were paid. Paid. They were paid by the saloon-keepers, paid by the bullies, paid by the women themselves. At last they were forced to move."

"I read about it in the papers that came on board in Honolulu," said Dr. Macphail.

"Iwelei, with its sin and shame, ceased to exist on the very day we arrived. The whole population was brought before the justices. I don't know why I didn't understand at once what that woman was."

"Now you come to speak of it," said Mrs. Macphail, "I remember seeing her come on board only a few minutes before the boat sailed. I remember thinking at the time she was cutting it rather fine."

"How dare she come here!" cried Davidson indignantly. "I'm not going to allow it."

He strode towards the door.

"What are you going to do?" asked Macphail.

"What do you expect me to do? I'm going to stop it. I'm not going to have this house turned into—into . . ."

He sought for a word that should not offend the ladies' ears. His eyes were flashing and his pale face was paler still in his emotion.

"It sounds as though there were three or four men down there," said the doctor. "Don't you think it's rather rash to go in just now?"

The missionary gave him a contemptuous look and without a word flung out of the room.

"You know Mr. Davidson very little if you think the fear of personal danger can stop him in the performance of his duty," said his wife.

She sat with her hands nervously clasped, a spot of colour on her high cheek bones, listening to what was about to happen below. They all listened. They heard him clatter down the wooden stairs and throw open the door. The singing stopped suddenly, but the gramophone continued to bray out its vulgar tune. They heard Davidson's voice and then the noise of something heavy falling. The music stopped. He had hurled the gramophone on the floor. Then again they heard Davidson's voice, they could not make out the words, then Miss Thompson's, loud and shrill, then a confused clamour as though several people were shouting together at the top of their lungs. Mrs. Davidson gave a little gasp, and she clenched her hands more tightly. Dr. Macphail looked uncertainly from her to his wife. He did not want to go down, but he wondered if they expected him to. Then there was something that sounded like a scuffle. The noise now was more distinct. It might be that Davidson was being thrown out of the room. The door was slammed. There was a moment's silence and they heard Davidson come up the stairs again. He went to his room.

"I think I'll go to him," said Mrs. Davidson. She got up and went out.

"If you want me, just call," said Mrs. Macphail, and then when the other was gone: "I hope he isn't hurt."

"Why couldn't he mind his own business?" said Dr. Macphail.

They sat in silence for a minute or two and then they both started, for the gramophone began to play once more, defiantly, and mocking voices shouted hoarsely the words of an obscene song.

Next day Mrs. Davidson was pale and tired. She complained of headache, and she looked old and wizened. She told Mrs. Macphail that the missionary had not slept at all; he had passed the night in a state of frightful agitation and at five had got up and gone out. A glass of beer had been thrown over him and his clothes were stained and stinking. But a sombre fire glowed in Mrs. Davidson's eyes when she spoke of Miss Thompson.

"She'll bitterly rue the day when she flouted Mr. Davidson," she said. "Mr. Davidson has a wonderful heart and no one who is in trouble has ever gone to him without being comforted, but he has no mercy for sin, and when his righteous wrath is excited he's terrible."

"Why, what will he do?" asked Mrs. Macphail.

"I don't know, but I wouldn't stand in that creature's shoes for anything in the world."

Mrs. Macphail shuddered. There was something positively alarming in the triumphant assurance of the little woman's manner. They were going out together that morning, and they went down the stairs side by side. Miss Thompson's door was open, and they saw her in a bedraggled dressing-gown, cooking something in a chafing-dish.

"Good morning," she called. "Is Mr. Davidson better this morning?"

They passed her in silence, with their noses in the air, as if she did not exist. They flushed, however, when she burst into a shout of derisive laughter. Mrs. Davidson turned on her suddenly.

"Don't you dare to speak to me," she screamed. "If you insult me I shall have you turned out of here."

"Say, did I ask Mr. Davidson to visit with me?"

"Don't answer her," whispered Mrs. Davidson hurriedly.

They walked on till they were out of earshot.

"She's brazen, brazen," burst from Mrs. Davidson.

Her anger almost suffocated her.

And on their way home they met her strolling towards the quay. She had all her finery on. Her great white hat with its vulgar, showy flowers was an affront. She called out cheerily to them as she went by, and a couple of American sailors who were standing there grinned as the ladies set their faces to an icy stare. They got in just before the rain began to fall again.

"I guess she'll get her fine clothes spoilt," said Mrs. Davidson with a bitter sneer.

Davidson did not come in till they were half way through dinner. He was wet through, but he would not change. He sat, morose and silent, refusing to eat more than a mouthful, and he stared at the slanting rain. When Mrs. Davidson told him of their two encounters with Miss Thompson he did not answer. His deepening frown alone showed that he had heard.

"Don't you think we ought to make Mr. Horn turn her out of here?" asked Mrs. Davidson. "We can't allow her to insult us."

"There doesn't seem to be any other place for her to go," said Macphail.

"She can live with one of the natives."

"In weather like this a native hut must be a rather uncomfortable place to live in."

"I lived in one for years," said the missionary.

When the little native girl brought in the fried bananas which formed the sweet they had every day, Davidson turned to her.

"Ask Miss Thompson when it would be convenient for me to see her," he said.

The girl nodded shyly and went out.

"What do you want to see her for, Alfred?" asked his wife.

"It's my duty to see her. I won't act till I've given her every chance."

"You don't know what she is. She'll insult you."

"Let her insult me. Let her spit on me. She has an immortal soul, and I must do all that is in my power to save it."

Mrs. Davidson's ears rang still with the harlot's mocking laughter.

"She's gone too far."

"Too far for the mercy of God?" His eyes lit up suddenly and his voice grew mellow and soft. "Never. The sinner may be deeper in sin than the depth of hell itself, but the love of the Lord Jesus can reach him still."

The girl came back with the message.

"Miss Thompson's compliments and as long as Rev. Davidson don't come in business hours she'll be glad to see him any time."

The party received it in stony silence, and Dr. Macphail quickly effaced from his lips the smile which had come upon them. He knew his wife would be vexed with him if he found Miss Thompson's effrontery amusing.

They finished the meal in silence. When it was over the two ladies got up and took their work. Mrs. Macphail was making another of the innumerable comforters which she had turned out since the beginning of the war, and the doctor lit his pipe. But Davidson remained in his chair and with abstracted eyes stared at the table. At last he got up and without a word went out of the room. They heard him go down and they heard Miss Thompson's defiant "Come in" when he knocked at the door. He remained with her for an hour. And Dr. Macphail watched the rain. It was beginning to get on his nerves. It was not like our soft English rain that drops gently on the earth; it was un-merciful and somehow terrible; you felt in it the malignancy of the primitive powers of nature. It did not pour, it flowed. It was like a deluge from heaven, and it rattled on the roof of corrugated iron with a steady persistence that was maddening. It seemed to have a fury of its own. And sometimes you felt that you must scream if it did not stop, and then suddenly you felt powerless, as though your bones had suddenly become soft; and you were miserable and hopeless.

Macphail turned his head when the missionary came back. The two women looked up.

"I've given her every chance. I have exhorted her to repent. She is an evil woman."

He paused, and Dr. Macphail saw his eyes darken and his pale face grow hard and stern.

"Now I shall take the whips with which the Lord Jesus drove the usurers and the money changers out of the Temple of the Most High."

He walked up and down the room. His mouth was close set, and his black brows were frowning.

"If she fled to the uttermost parts of the earth I should pursue her."

With a sudden movement he turned round and strode out of the room. They heard him go downstairs again.

"What is he going to do?" asked Mrs. Macphail.

"I don't know." Mrs. Davidson took off her *pince-nez* and wiped them. "When he is on the Lord's work I never ask him questions."

She sighed a little.

"What is the matter?"

"He'll wear himself out. He doesn't know what it is to spare himself."

Dr. Macphail learnt the first results of the missionary's activity from the half-caste trader in whose house they lodged. He stopped the doctor when he passed the store and came out to speak to him on the stoop. His fat face was worried.

"The Rev. Davidson has been at me for letting Miss Thompson have a room here," he said, "but I didn't know what she was when I rented it to her. When people come and ask if I can rent them a room all I want to know is if they've the money to pay for it. And she paid me for hers a week in advance."

Dr. Macphail did not want to commit himself.

"When all's said and done it's your house. We're very much obliged to you for taking us in at all."

Horn looked at him doubtfully. He was not certain yet how definitely Macphail stood on the missionary's side.

"The missionaries are in with one another," he said, hesitatingly. "If they get it in for a trader he may just as well shut up his store and quit."

"Did he want you to turn her out?"

"No, he said so long as she behaved herself he couldn't ask me to do that. He said he wanted to be just to me. I promised she shouldn't have no more visitors. I've just been and told her."

"How did she take it?"

"She gave me Hell."

The trader squirmed in his old ducks. He had found Miss Thompson a rough customer.

"Oh, well, I daresay she'll get out. I don't suppose she wants to stay here if she can't have anyone in."

"There's nowhere she can go, only a native house, and no native'll take her now, not now that the missionaries have got their knife in her."

Dr. Macphail looked at the falling rain.

"Well, I don't suppose it's any good waiting for it to clear up."

In the evening when they sat in the parlour Davidson talked to them of his early days at college. He had had no means and had worked his way through by doing odd jobs during the vacations. There was silence downstairs. Miss Thompson was sitting in her little room alone. But suddenly the gramophone began to play. She had set it on in defiance, to cheat her loneliness, but there was no one to sing, and it had a melancholy note. It was like a cry for help. Davidson took no notice. He was in the middle of a long anecdote and without change of expression went on. The gramophone continued. Miss Thompson put on one reel after another. It looked as though the silence of the night were getting on her nerves. It was breathless and sultry. When the Macphails went to bed they could not sleep. They lay side by side with their eyes wide open, listening to the cruel singing of the mosquitoes outside their curtain.

"What's that?" whispered Mrs. Macphail at last.

They heard a voice, Davidson's voice, through the wooden partition. It went on with a monotonous, earnest insistence. He was praying aloud. He was praying for the soul of Miss Thompson.

Two or three days went by. Now when they passed Miss Thompson on the road she did not greet them with ironic cordiality or smile; she passed with her nose in the air, a sulky look on her painted face, frowning, as though she did not see them. The trader told Macphail that she had tried to get lodging elsewhere, but had failed. In the evening she played through the various reels of her gramophone, but the pretense of mirth was obvious now. The ragtime had a cracked, heart-broken rhythm as though it were a one-step of despair. When she began to play on Sunday Davidson sent Horn to beg her to stop at once since it was the Lord's day. The reel was taken off and the house was silent except for the steady pattering of the rain on the iron roof.

"I think she's getting a bit worked up," said the trader next day to Macphail. "She don't know what Mr. Davidson's up to and it makes her scared."

Macphail had caught a glimpse of her that morning and it struck him that her arrogant expression had changed. There was in her face a hunted look. The half-caste gave him a sidelong glance.

"I suppose you don't know what Mr. Davidson is doing about it?" he hazarded.

"No, I don't."

It was singular that Horn should ask him that question, for he also had the idea that the missionary was mysteriously at work. He had an impression that he was weaving a net around the woman, carefully, systematically, and suddenly, when everything was ready, would pull the strings tight.

"He told me to tell her," said the trader, "that if at any time she wanted him she only had to send and he'd come."

"What did she say when you told her that?"

"She didn't say nothing. I didn't stop. I just said what he said I was to and then I beat it. I thought she might be going to start weepin'."

"I have no doubt the loneliness is getting on her nerves," said the doctor. "And the rain—

460

that's enough to make anyone jumpy," he continued irritably. "Doesn't it ever stop in this confounded place?"

"It goes on pretty steady in the rainy season. We have three hundred inches in the year. You see, it's the shape of the bay. It seems to attract the rain from all over the Pacific."

"Damn the shape of the bay," said the doctor.

He scratched his mosquito bites. He felt very short-tempered. When the rain stopped and the sun shone, it was like a hot-house, seething, humid, sultry, breathless, and you had a strange feeling that everything was growing with a savage violence. The natives, blithe and childlike by reputation, seemed then, with their tattooing and their dyed hair, to have something sinister in their appearance; and when they pattered along at your heels with their naked feet you looked back instinctively. You felt they might at any moment come behind you swiftly and thrust a long knife between your shoulder blades. You could not tell what dark thoughts lurked behind their wide-set eyes. They had a little the look of ancient Egyptians painted on a temple wall, and there was about them the terror of what is immeasurably old.

The missionary came and went. He was busy, but the Macphails did not know what he was doing. Horn told the doctor that he saw the governor every day, and once Davidson mentioned him. "He looks as if he had plenty of determination," he said, "but when you come down to brass tacks he has no backbone."

"I suppose that means he won't do exactly what you want," suggested the doctor facetiously.

The missionary did not smile.

"I want him to do what's right. It shouldn't be necessary to persuade a man to do that."

"But there may be differences of opinion about what is right."

"If a man had a gangrenous foot would you have patience with anyone who hesitated to amputate it?"

"Gangrene is a matter of fact."

"And Evil?"

What Davidson had done soon appeared. The four of them had just finished their midday meal, and they had not yet separated for the siesta which the heat imposed on the ladies and on the doctor. Davidson had little patience with the slothful habit. The door was suddenly flung open and Miss Thompson came in. She looked round the room and then went up to Davidson.

"You low-down skunk, what have you been saying about me to the governor?"

She was spluttering with rage. There was a moment's pause. Then the missionary drew forward a chair.

"Won't you be seated, Miss Thompson? I've been hoping to have another talk with you."

"You poor low-life bastard."

She burst into a torrent of insult, foul and insolent. Davidson kept his grave eyes on her.

"I'm indifferent to the abuse you think fit to heap on me, Miss Thompson," he said, "but I must beg you to remember that ladies are present."

Tears by now were struggling with her anger. Her face was red and swollen as though she were choking.

"What has happened?" asked Dr. Macphail.

"A feller's just been in here and he says I gotter beat it on the next boat."

Was there a gleam in the missionary's eyes? His face remained impassive.

"You could hardly expect the governor to let you stay here under the circumstances."

"You done it," she shrieked. "You can't kid me. You done it."

"I don't want to deceive you. I urged the governor to take the only possible step consistent with his obligations."

"Why couldn't you leave me be? I wasn't doin' you no harm."

"You may be sure that if you had I should be the last man to resent it."

"Do you think I want to stay on in this poor imitation of a burg? I don't look no busher, do I?"

"In that case I don't see what cause of complaint you have," he answered.

She gave an inarticulate cry of rage and flung out of the room. There was a short silence.

"It's a relief to know that the governor has acted at last," said Davidson finally. "He's a weak man and he shilly-shallied. He said she was only here for a fortnight anyway, and if she went on to Apia that was under British jurisdiction and had nothing to do with him."

The missionary sprang to his feet and strode across the room.

"It's terrible the way the men who are in authority seek to evade their responsibility. They speak as though evil that was out of sight ceased to be evil. The very existence of that woman is a scandal and it does not help matters to shift it to another of the islands. In the end I had to speak straight from the shoulder."

Davidson's brow lowered, and he protruded his firm chin. He looked fierce and determined.

"What do you mean by that?"

"Our mission is not entirely without influence at Washington. I pointed out to the governor that it wouldn't do him any good if there was a complaint about the way he managed things here."

"When has she got to go?" asked the doctor, after a pause.

"The San Francisco boat is due here from Sydney next Tuesday. She's to sail on that."

That was in five days' time. It was next day, when he was coming back from the hospital where for want of something better to do Macphail spent most of his mornings, that the half-caste stopped him as he was going upstairs.

"Excuse me, Dr. Macphail, Miss Thompson's sick. Will you have a look at her?"

"Certainly."

Horn led him to her room. She was sitting in a chair idly, neither reading nor sewing, staring in front of her. She wore her white dress and the large hat with the flowers on it. Macphail noticed that her skin was yellow and muddy under her powder, and her eyes were heavy.

"I'm sorry to hear you're not well," he said.

"Oh, I ain't sick really. I just said that, because I just had to see you. I've got to clear on a boat that's going to 'Frisco."

She looked at him and he saw that her eyes were suddenly startled. She opened and clenched her hands spasmodically. The trader stood at the door, listening.

"So I understand," said the doctor.

She gave a little gulp.

"I guess it ain't very convenient for me to go to 'Frisco just now. I went to see the governor yesterday afternoon, but I couldn't get to him. I saw the secretary, and he told me I'd got to take that boat and that was all there was to it. I just had to see the governor, so I waited outside his house this morning, and when he come out I spoke to him. He didn't want to speak to me, I'll say, but I wouldn't let him shake me off, and at last he said he hadn't no objection to my staying here till the next boat to Sydney if the Rev. Davidson will stand for it."

She stopped and looked at Dr. Macphail anxiously.

"I don't know exactly what I can do," he said.

"Well, I thought maybe you wouldn't mind asking him. I swear to God I won't start anything here if he'll just only let me stay. I won't go out of the house if that'll suit him. It's no more'n a fortnight."

"I'll ask him."

"He won't stand for it," said Horn. "He'll have you out on Tuesday, so you may as well make up your mind to it."

"Tell him I can get work in Sydney, straight stuff, I mean. 'Taint asking very much."

"I'll do what I can."

"And come and tell me right away, will you? I can't set down to a thing till I get the dope one way or the other."

It was not an errand that much pleased the doctor, and, characteristically perhaps, he went about it indirectly. He told his wife what Miss Thompson had said to him and asked her to speak to Mrs. Davidson. The missionary's attitude seemed rather arbitrary and it could do no harm if the girl were allowed to stay in Pago-Pago another fortnight. But he was not prepared for the result of his diplomacy. The missionary came to him straightway.

"Mrs. Davidson tells me that Thompson has been speaking to you."

Dr. Macphail, thus directly tackled, had the shy man's resentment at being forced out into the open. He felt his temper rising, and flushed.

"I don't see that it can make any difference if she goes to Sydney rather than to San Francisco, and so long as she promises to behave while she's here it's dashed hard to persecute her."

The missionary fixed him with his stern eyes.

"Why is she unwilling to go back to San Francisco?"

"I didn't enquire," answered the doctor with some asperity. "And I think one does better to mind one's own business."

Perhaps it was not a very tactful answer.

"The governor has ordered her to be deported by the first boat that leaves the island. He's only done his duty and I will not interfere. Her presence is a peril here."

"I think you're very harsh and tyrannical."

The two ladies looked up at the doctor with some alarm, but they need not have feared a quarrel, for the missionary smiled gently.

"I'm terribly sorry you should think that of me, Dr. Macphail. Believe me, my heart bleeds for that unfortunate woman, but I'm only trying to do my duty."

The doctor made no answer. He looked out of the window sullenly. For once it was not raining and across the bay you saw nestling among the trees the huts of a native village.

"I think I'll take advantage of the rain stopping to go out," he said.

"Please don't bear me malice because I can't accede to your wish," said Davidson, with a melancholy smile. "I respect you very much, doctor, and I should be sorry if you thought ill of me."

"I have no doubt you have a sufficiently good opinion of yourself to bear mine with equanimity," he retorted.

"That's one on me," chuckled Davidson.

When Dr. Macphail, vexed with himself because he had been uncivil to no purpose, went downstairs, Miss Thompson was waiting for him with her door ajar.

"Well," she said, "have you spoken to him?"

"Yes, I'm sorry, he won't do anything," he answered, not looking at her in his embarrassment.

But then he gave her a quick glance, for a sob broke from her. He saw that her face was white with fear. It gave him a shock of dismay. And suddenly he had an idea.

"But don't give up hope yet. I think it's a shame the way they're treating you and I'm going to see the governor myself."

"Now?"

He nodded. Her face brightened.

"Say, that's real good of you. I'm sure he'll let me stay if you speak for me. I just won't do a thing I didn't ought all the time I'm here."

Dr. Macphail hardly knew why he had made up his mind to appeal to the governor. He was perfectly indifferent to Miss Thompson's affairs, but the missionary had irritated him, and with him temper was a smouldering thing. He

found the governor at home. He was a large, handsome man, a sailor, with a grey toothbrush moustache; and he wore a spotless uniform of white drill.

"I've come to see you about a woman who's lodging in the same house as we are," he said. "Her name's Thompson."

"I guess I've heard nearly enough about her, Dr. Macphail," said the governor, smiling. "I've given her the order to get out next Tuesday and that's all I can do."

"I wanted to ask you if you couldn't stretch a point and let her stay here till the boat comes in from San Francisco so that she can go to Sydney. I will guarantee her good behaviour."

The governor continued to smile, but his eyes grew small and serious.

"I'd be very glad to oblige you, Dr. Macphail, but I've given the order and it must stand."

The doctor put the case as reasonably as he could, but now the governor ceased to smile at all. He listened sullenly, with averted gaze. Macphail saw that he was making no impression.

"I'm sorry to cause any lady inconvenience, but she'll have to sail on Tuesday and that's all there is to it."

"But what difference can it make?"

"Pardon me, doctor, but I don't feel called upon to explain my official actions except to the proper authorities."

Macphail looked at him shrewdly. He remembered Davidson's hint that he had used threats, and in the governor's attitude he read a singular embarrassment.

"Davidson's a damned busybody," he said hotly.

"Between ourselves, Dr. Macphail, I don't say that I have formed a very favourable opinion of Mr. Davidson, but I am bound to confess that he was within his rights in pointing out to me the danger that the presence of a woman of Miss Thompson's character was to a place like this where a number of enlisted men are stationed among a native population."

He got up and Dr. Macphail was obliged to do so too.

"I must ask you to excuse me. I have an engagement. Please give my respects to Mrs. Macphail."

The doctor left him crestfallen. He knew

that Miss Thompson would be waiting for him, and unwilling to tell her himself that he had failed, he went into the house by the back door and sneaked up the stairs as though he had something to hide.

At supper he was silent and ill-at-ease, but the missionary was jovial and animated. Dr. Macphail thought his eyes rested on him now and then with triumphant good-humour. It struck him suddenly that Davidson knew of his visit to the governor and of its ill success. But how on earth could he have heard of it? There was something sinister about the power of that man. After supper he saw Horn on the verandah and, as though to have a casual word with him, went out.

"She wants to know if you've seen the governor," the trader whispered.

"Yes. He wouldn't do anything. I'm awfully sorry, I can't do anything more."

"I knew he wouldn't. They daren't go against the missionaries."

"What are you talking about?" said Davidson affably, coming out to join them.

"I was just saying there was no chance of your getting over to Apia for at least another week," said the trader glibly.

He left them, and the two men returned into the parlour. Mr. Davidson devoted one hour after each meal to recreation. Presently a timid knock was heard at the door.

"Come in," said Mrs. Davidson, in her sharp voice.

The door was not opened. She got up and opened it. They saw Miss Thompson standing at the threshold. But the change in her appearance was extraordinary. This was no longer the flaunting hussy who had jeered at them in the road, but a broken, frightened woman. Her hair, as a rule so elaborately arranged, was tumbling untidily over her neck. She wore bedroom slippers and a skirt and blouse. They were unfresh and bedraggled. She stood at the door with the tears streaming down her face and did not dare to enter.

"What do you want?" said Mrs. Davidson harshly.

"May I speak to Mr. Davidson?" she said in a choking voice.

The missionary rose and went towards her.

"Come right in, Miss Thompson," he said in cordial tones. "What can I do for you?"

She entered the room.

"Say, I'm sorry for what I said to you the other day an' for—for everythin' else. I guess I was a bit lit up. I beg pardon."

"Oh, it was nothing. I guess my back's broad enough to bear a few hard words."

She stepped towards him with a movement that was horribly cringing.

"You've got me beat. I'm all in. You won't make me go back to Frisco?"

His genial manner vanished and his voice grew on a sudden hard and stern.

"Why don't you want to go back there?"

She cowered before him.

"I guess my people live there. I don't want them to see me like this. I'll go anywhere else you say."

"Why don't you want to go back to San Francisco?"

"I've told you."

He leaned forward, staring at her, and his great, shining eyes seemed to try to bore into her soul. He gave a sudden gasp.

"The penitentiary."

She screamed, and then she fell at his feet, clasping his legs.

"Don't send me back there. I swear to you before God I'll be a good woman. I'll give all this up."

She burst into a torrent of confused supplication and the tears coursed down her painted cheeks. He leaned over her and, lifting her face, forced her to look at him.

"Is that it, the penitentiary?"

"I beat it before they could get me," she gasped. "If the bulls grab me it's three years for mine."

He let go his hold of her and she fell in a heap on the floor, sobbing bitterly. Dr. Macphail stood up.

"This alters the whole thing," he said. "You can't make her go back when you know this. Give her another chance. She wants to turn over a new leaf."

"I'm going to give her the finest chance she's ever had. If she repents let her accept her punishment."

She misunderstood the words and looked up. There was a gleam of hope in her heavy eyes.

"You'll let me go?"

"No. You shall sail for San Francisco on Tuesday."

She gave a groan of horror and then burst into low, hoarse shrieks which sounded hardly human, and she beat her head passionately on the ground. Dr. Macphail sprang to her and lifted her up.

"Come on, you mustn't do that. You'd better go to your room and lie down. I'll get you something."

He raised her to her feet and partly dragging her, partly carrying her, got her downstairs. He was furious with Mrs. Davidson and with his wife because they made no effort to help. The half-caste was standing on the landing and with his assistance he managed to get her on the bed. She was moaning and crying. She was almost insensible. He gave her a hypodermic injection. He was hot and exhausted when he went upstairs again.

"I've got her to lie down."

The two women and Davidson were in the same positions as when he had left them. They could not have moved or spoken since he went.

"I was waiting for you," said Davidson, in a strange, distant voice. "I want you all to pray with me for the soul of our erring sister."

He took the Bible off a shelf, and sat down at the table at which they had supped. It had not been cleared, and he pushed the tea-pot out of the way. In a powerful voice, resonant and deep, he read to them the chapter in which is narrated the meeting of Jesus Christ with the woman taken in adultery.

"Now kneel with me and let us pray for the soul of our dear sister, Sadie Thompson."

He burst into a long, passionate prayer in which he implored God to have mercy on the sinful woman. Mrs. Macphail and Mrs. Davidson knelt with covered eyes. The doctor, taken by surprise, awkward and sheepish, knelt too. The missionary's prayer had a savage eloquence. He was extraordinarily moved, and as he spoke the tears ran down his cheeks. Outside, the pitiless rain fell, fell steadily, with a fierce malignity that was all too human.

At last he stopped. He paused for a moment and said:

"We will now repeat the Lord's prayer."

They said it and then, following him, they rose from their knees. Mrs. Davidson's face was pale and restful. She was comforted and at peace, but the Macphails felt suddenly bashful. They did not know which way to look.

"I'll just go down and see how she is now," said Dr. Macphail.

When he knocked at her door it was opened for him by Horn. Miss Thompson was in a rocking-chair, sobbing quietly.

"What are you doing there?" exclaimed Macphail. "I told you to lie down."

"I can't lie down. I want to see Mr. Davidson."

"My poor child, what do you think is the good of it? You'll never move him."

"He said he'd come if I sent for him."

Macphail motioned to the trader.

"Go and fetch him."

He waited with her in silence while the trader went upstairs. Davidson came in.

"Excuse me for asking you to come here," she said, looking at him sombrely.

"I was expecting you to send for me. I knew the Lord would answer my prayer."

They stared at one another for a moment and then she looked away. She kept her eyes averted when she spoke.

"I've been a bad woman. I want to repent."

"Thank God! thank God! He has heard our prayers."

He turned to the two men.

"Leave me alone with her. Tell Mrs. Davidson that our prayers have been answered."

They went out and closed the door behind them.

"Gee whiz," said the trader.

That night Dr. Macphail could not get to sleep till late, and when he heard the missionary come upstairs he looked at his watch. It was two o'clock. But even then he did not go to bed at once, for through the wooden partition that separated their rooms he heard him praying aloud, till he himself, exhausted, fell asleep.

When he saw him next morning he was surprised at his appearance. He was paler than ever, tired, but his eyes shone with an inhuman fire. It looked as though he were filled with an overwhelming joy.

"I want you to go down presently and see Sadie," he said. "I can't hope that her body is better, but her soul—her soul is transformed."

The doctor was feeling wan and nervous.

31. **Jesus . . . adultery,** as told in John 8 : 3–11.

"You were with her very late last night," he said.

"Yes, she couldn't bear to have me leave her."

"You look as pleased as Punch," the doctor said irritably.

Davidson's eyes shone with ecstasy.

"A great mercy has been vouchsafed me. Last night I was privileged to bring a lost soul to the loving arms of Jesus."

Miss Thompson was again in the rocking-chair. The bed had not been made. The room was in disorder. She had not troubled to dress herself, but wore a dirty dressing-gown, and her hair was tied in a sluttish knot. She had given her face a dab with a wet towel, but it was all swollen and creased with crying. She looked a drab.

She raised her eyes dully when the doctor came in. She was cowed and broken.

"Where's Mr. Davidson?" she asked.

"He'll come presently if you want him," answered Macphail acidly. "I came here to see how you were."

"Oh, I guess I'm O.K. You needn't worry about that."

"Have you had anything to eat?"

"Horn brought me some coffee."

She looked anxiously at the door.

"D'you think he'll come down soon? I feel as if it wasn't so terrible when he's with me."

"Are you still going on Tuesday?"

"Yes, he says I've got to go. Please tell him to come right along. You can't do me any good. He's the only one as can help me now."

"Very well," said Dr. Macphail.

During the next three days the missionary spent almost all his time with Sadie Thompson. He joined the others only to have his meals. Dr. Macphail noticed that he hardly ate.

"He's wearing himself out," said Mrs. Davidson pitifully. "He'll have a breakdown if he doesn't take care, but he won't spare himself."

She herself was white and pale. She told Mrs. Macphail that she had had no sleep. When the missionary came upstairs from Miss Thompson he prayed till he was exhausted, but even then he did not sleep for long. After an hour or two he got up and dressed himself, and went for a tramp along the bay. He had strange dreams.

"This morning he told me that he'd been dreaming about the mountains of Nebraska," said Mrs. Davidson.

"That's curious," said Dr. Macphail.

He remembered seeing them from the windows of the train when he crossed America. They were like huge mole-hills, rounded and smooth, and they rose from the plain abruptly. Dr. Macphail remembered how it struck him that they were like a woman's breasts.

Davidson's restlessness was intolerable even to himself. But he was buoyed up by a wonderful exhilaration. He was tearing out by the roots the last vestiges of sin that lurked in the hidden corners of that poor woman's heart. He read with her and prayed with her.

"It's wonderful," he said to them one day at supper. "It's a true rebirth. Her soul, which was black as night, is now pure and white like the new-fallen snow. I am humble and afraid. Her remorse for all her sins is beautiful. I am not worthy to touch the hem of her garment."

"Have you the heart to send her back to San Francisco?" said the doctor. "Three years in an American prison. I should have thought you might have saved her from that."

"Ah, but don't you see? It's necessary. Do you think my heart doesn't bleed for her? I love her as I love my wife and my sister. All the time that she is in prison I shall suffer all the pain that she suffers."

"Bunkum," cried the doctor impatiently.

"You don't understand because you're blind. She's sinned, and she must suffer. I know what she'll endure. She'll be starved and tortured and humiliated. I want her to accept the punishment of man as a sacrifice to God. I want her to accept it joyfully. She has an opportunity which is offered to very few of us. God is very good and merciful."

Davidson's voice trembled with excitement. He could hardly articulate the words that tumbled passionately from his lips.

"All day I pray with her and when I leave her I pray again, I pray with all my might and main, so that Jesus may grant her this great mercy. I want to put in her heart the passionate desire to be punished so that at the end, even if I offered to let her go, she would refuse. I want her to feel that the bitter punishment of prison is the thank-offering that she places at the feet of our Blessed Lord, who gave His life for her."

The days passed slowly. The whole household, intent on the wretched, tortured woman downstairs, lived in a state of unnatural excitement. She was like a victim that was being prepared for the savage rites of a bloody idolatry. Her terror numbed her. She could not bear to let Davidson out of her sight; it was only when he was with her that she had courage, and she hung upon him with a slavish dependence. She cried a great deal, and she read the Bible, and prayed. Sometimes she was exhausted and apathetic. Then she did indeed look forward to her ordeal, for it seemed to offer an escape, direct and concrete, from the anguish she was enduring. She could not bear much longer the vague terrors which now assailed her. With her sins she had put aside all personal vanity, and she slopped about her room, unkempt and dishevelled, in her tawdry dressing-gown. She had not taken off her nightdress for four days, nor put on stockings. Her room was littered and untidy. Meanwhile the rain fell with a cruel persistence. You felt that the heavens must at last be empty of water, but still it poured down, straight and heavy, with a maddening iteration, on the iron roof. Everything was damp and clammy. There was mildew on the walls and on the boots that stood on the floor. Through the sleepless nights the mosquitoes droned their angry chant.

"If it would only stop raining for a single day it wouldn't be so bad," said Dr. Macphail.

They all looked forward to the Tuesday when the boat for San Francisco was to arrive from Sydney. The strain was intolerable. So far as Dr. Macphail was concerned, his pity and his resentment were alike extinguished by his desire to be rid of the unfortunate woman. The inevitable must be accepted. He felt he would breathe more freely when the ship had sailed. Sadie Thompson was to be escorted on board by a clerk in the governor's office. This person called on the Monday evening and told Miss Thompson to be prepared at eleven in the morning. Davidson was with her.

"I'll see that everything is ready. I mean to come on board with her myself."

Miss Thompson did not speak.

When Dr. Macphail blew out his candle and crawled cautiously under his mosquito curtains, he gave a sigh of relief.

"Well, thank God that's over. By this time tomorrow she'll be gone."

"Mrs. Davidson will be glad too. She says he's wearing himself to a shadow," said Mrs. Macphail. "She's a different woman."

"Who?"

"Sadie. I should never have thought it possible. It makes one humble."

Dr. Macphail did not answer, and presently he fell asleep. He was tired out, and he slept more soundly than usual.

He was awakened in the morning by a hand placed on his arm, and starting up, saw Horn by the side of his bed. The trader put his finger on his mouth to prevent any exclamation from Dr. Macphail and beckoned to him to come. As a rule he wore shabby ducks, but now he was barefoot and wore only the *lava-lava* of the natives. He looked suddenly savage, and Dr. Macphail, getting out of bed, saw that he was heavily tattooed. Horn made him a sign to come on to the verandah. Dr. Macphail got out of bed and followed the trader out.

"Don't make a noise," he whispered. "You're wanted. Put on a coat and some shoes. Quick."

Dr. Macphail's first thought was that something had happened to Miss Thompson.

"What is it? Shall I bring my instruments?"

"Hurry, please, hurry."

Dr. Macphail crept back into the bedroom, put on a waterproof over his pajamas, and a pair of rubber-soled shoes. He rejoined the trader, and together they tiptoed down the stairs. The door leading out to the road was open and at it were standing half a dozen natives.

"What is it?" repeated the doctor.

"Come along with me," said Horn.

He walked out and the doctor followed him. The natives came after them in a little bunch. They crossed the road and came on to the beach. The doctor saw a group of natives standing round some object at the water's edge. They hurried along, a couple of dozen yards perhaps, and the natives opened out as the doctor came up. The trader pushed him forwards. Then he saw, lying half in the water and half out, a dreadful object, the body of Davidson. Dr. Macphail bent down—he was not a man to lose his head in an emergency—and turned the body over. The throat was cut from ear to ear, and in the right hand was still the razor with which the deed was done.

"He's quite cold," said the doctor. "He must have been dead some time."

"One of the boys saw him lying there on his way to work just now and came and told me. Do you think he did it himself?"

"Yes. Someone ought to go for the police."

Horn said something in the native tongue, and two youths started off.

"We must leave him here till they come," said the doctor.

"They mustn't take him into my house. I won't have him in my house."

"You'll do what the authorities say," replied the doctor sharply. "In point of fact I expect they'll take him to the mortuary."

They stood waiting where they were. The trader took a cigarette from a fold in his *lava-lava* and gave one to Dr. Macphail. They smoked while they stared at the corpse. Dr. Macphail could not understand.

"Why do you think he did it?" asked Horn.

The doctor shrugged his shoulders. In a little while native police came along, under the charge of a marine, with a stretcher, and immediately afterwards a couple of naval officers and a naval doctor. They managed everything in a businesslike manner.

"What about the wife?" said one of the officers.

"Now that you've come I'll go back to the house and get some things on. I'll see that it's broken to her. She'd better not see him till he's been fixed up a little."

"I guess that's right," said the naval doctor.

When Dr. Macphail went back he found his wife nearly dressed.

"Mrs. Davidson's in a dreadful state about her husband," she said to him as soon as he appeared. "He hasn't been to bed all night. She heard him leave Miss Thompson's room at two, but he went out. If he's been walking about since then he'll be absolutely dead."

Dr. Macphail told her what had happened and asked her to break the news to Mrs. Davidson.

"But why did he do it?" she asked, horror-stricken.

"I don't know."

"But I can't. I can't."

"You must."

She gave him a frightened look and went out. He heard her go into Mrs. Davidson's room. He waited a minute to gather himself together and then began to shave and wash. When he was dressed he sat down on the bed and waited for his wife. At last she came.

"She wants to see him," she said.

"They've taken him to the mortuary. We'd better go down with her. How did she take it?"

"I think she's stunned. She didn't cry. But she's trembling like a leaf."

"We'd better go at once."

When they knocked at her door Mrs. Davidson came out. She was very pale, but dry-eyed. To the doctor she seemed unnaturally composed. No word was exchanged, and they set out in silence down the road. When they arrived at the mortuary Mrs. Davidson spoke.

"Let me go in and see him alone."

They stood aside. A native opened a door for her and closed it behind her. They sat down and waited. One or two white men came and talked to them in undertones. Dr. Macphail told them again what he knew of the tragedy. At last the door was quietly opened and Mrs. Davidson came out. Silence fell upon them.

"I'm ready to go back now," she said.

Her voice was hard and steady. Dr. Macphail could not understand the look in her eyes. Her pale face was very stern. They walked back slowly, never saying a word, and at last they came round the bend on the other side of which stood their house. Mrs. Davidson gave a gasp, and for a moment they stopped still. An incredible sound assaulted their ears. The gramophone which had been silent for so long was playing, playing ragtime loud and harsh.

"What's that?" cried Mrs. Macphail with horror.

"Let's go on," said Mrs. Davidson.

They walked up the steps and entered the hall. Miss Thompson was standing at her door, chatting with a sailor. A sudden change had taken place in her. She was no longer the cowed drudge of the last days. She was dressed in all her finery, in her white dress, with the high shiny boots over which her fat legs bulged in their cotton stockings; her hair was

468

elaborately arranged; and she wore that enormous hat covered with gaudy flowers. Her face was painted, her eyebrows were boldly black, and her lips were scarlet. She held herself erect. She was the flaunting queen that they had known at first. As they came in she broke into a loud, jeering laugh; and then, when Mrs. Davidson involuntarily stopped, she collected the spittle in her mouth and spat. Mrs. Davidson cowered back, and two red spots rose suddenly to her cheeks. Then, covering her face with her hands, she broke away and ran quickly up the stairs. Dr. Macphail was outraged. He pushed past the woman into her room.

"What the devil are you doing?" he cried. "Stop that damned machine."

He went up to it and tore the record off. She turned on him.

"Say, doc, you can that stuff with me. What the hell are you doin' in my room?"

"What do you mean?" he cried. "What d'you mean?"

She gathered herself together. No one could describe the scorn of her expression or the contemptuous hatred she put into her answer.

"You men! You filthy, dirty pigs! You're all the same, all of you. Pigs! Pigs!"

Dr. Macphail gasped. He understood.

ALDOUS HUXLEY

Aldous Leonard Huxley is the grandson of Thomas Huxley (1825–95), the great scientist and missionary for the propagation of scientific faith, "Darwin's bulldog." His maternal great-uncle was Matthew Arnold (1822–88), perhaps the most distinguished English literary critic of the nineteenth century. Aldous Huxley has at various times written much about himself. He was born in London on July 26, 1894. His education at Eton, he says, was interrupted by a serious eye affliction that has bothered him ever since; but this interruption was probably more than ordinarily fortunate for him, he believes, because it prevented him from becoming the complete English public school gentleman and particularly because it turned him aside from the paths of medicine which he had been expected to follow. To the great religion of science that his family had recently believed in and to which his brother Julian subscribed, Aldous Huxley was sympathetic by instinct. But professionally he has been an apostate. He went to Oxford, where he graduated (1916) with honors in English literature, and after some rather haphazard work in a government office and in teaching, he joined (1919) the editorial staff of the *Athenaeum* under the leadership of J. Middleton Murry (p. 425), husband of Katherine Mansfield (p. 425) and in-

timate of D. H. Lawrence (p. 412). For a time Huxley did the general versatile potboiling that falls to the lot of a miscellaneous journalist—he wrote criticisms of the current drama, art, and music, and he reviewed novels. His recreations and hobbies were all centered in the art of solitary reading, if we are to take his word for it. But he obviously traveled as well as read. Indeed, he has lived much of his time in Italy, and most of his novels have been written there.

Huxley began his literary career by editing an anthology of Oxford poetry (1916) and has subsequently written some poetry of his own, including *The Burning Wheel* (1916); *Jonah* (1917), which contains poetry in French as well as in English; *The Defeat of Youth* (1918); *Leda* (1920); and *Arabia Infelix* (1929). As might be expected from a reading of his better-known prose, Huxley's verse is bitter and disillusioned, with a certain air of the unwholesome, even the decadent. As for his prose narrative, it matters little whether one considers his short stories or his novels, for both types represent him and his attitude toward life equally well. Among his volumes of short stories must be included *Limbo* (1920), seven characteristic narratives; *Mortal Coils* (1922); *The Little Mexican and Other Stories* (1924), published in the United States as *Young Archimedes and Other Sketches; Two or Three Graces* (1926); and *Brief Candles* (1930). The novels, which naturally made a much more forceful impact upon the reading public—and are, also, much more garrulous and diffuse—are *Crome Yellow* (1921), written, so the author says, in the mock-romantic style of Thomas Love Peacock (1785–1866), although the comparison is not obvious; *Antic Hay* (1923), a novel which, Huxley asserts, "dramatizes with relentless logic the necessary implications, in terms of life, of the skepticism of Thomas Huxley—skepticism battening at the vitals of animal faith"; and *Those Barren Leaves* (1925), which calls for no special comment. The novel generally considered his masterpiece, *Point Counter Point* (1928), is a completely heartless, excessively loquacious, and audaciously brilliant satire on his contemporary London, although the sickness eating at the souls of his characters is by no means a local *malaise*. *A Brave New World* (1932), equally devastating, is almost equally effective. The cycle of mordant novels was more or less rounded out by *Eyeless in Gaza* (1936). *After Many a Summer Dies the Swan* (1940), which is a magnificent satire on the vagaries of a certain section of Southern Californian culture, shows the depressing consequences of a successful attempt to find the secret of immortality in a diet of carp's intestines. But here Huxley gives many of the pages of the novel over to a discussion of man and his place in the scheme of things. This semi-religious questing is in keeping with his intellectual character throughout the 1930's, as evinced in his many essays. *Grey Eminence* (1941), a biography of Father Joseph, the seventeenth-century French mystic and statesman, confidant of the great Cardinal Richelieu, has many of the unmistakable traits of a religious novel. Again, *Time Must Have a Stop* (1944) is almost a summation of the two contrary aspects of Huxley's mercurial mind: the first portion of this novel is in the old satirical vein; the latter part is of strong mystic tendency. In *Ape and Essence* (1948) Huxley's pessimism predicts a shattering atomic war which reduces its survivors to the fearful worship of evil as the primal world force.

To many critics, Huxley's contributions as a writer are more valuable in the field of the essay than in the field of prose fiction. His interest in nonfictional prose during the past dozen years is clear evidence of the fact that he has become dissatisfied with the purely mechanistic attitude toward life which characterized his early novels. Like T. S. Eliot, he turns from the Waste Land into a realm of serious moral and religious purpose, although he cannot be content to drop anchor in a fixed creed. There is at best great difficulty in distinguishing between Huxley the novelist and Huxley the didactic commentator. Both are the complete and polished product of the post-World-War-I generation in England.

His essays date as far back as 1923, when *On the Margin* was published. Following this came the travel essays included under the bizarre title of *Jesting Pilate* (1923); *Do What You Will* (1929); *The Holy Face and Other Essays* (1929); *Vulgarity in Literature* (1930); *Music at Night* (1931); *Texts and Pretexts* (1932), an anthology of criticism; *Beyond the Mexique Bay* (1934); *The Olive Tree and Other Essays* (1936); *An Encyclopedia of Pacifism* (1937); *Ends and Means* (1937), perhaps the most revealing of all; *The Art of Seeing* (1942), born of his own painful experiences with eye trouble; *Science, Liberty, and Peace* (1944); and *The Perennial Philosophy* (1945).

Huxley is always learned and not in the least loath to parade this learning; he is witty and makes a fetish of the well-turned phrase roasted in the flame of a searing cynicism. Sometimes his desire to be clever at all costs leads him into painful lapses from good or even passable taste. Particularly significant is his preoccupation with the scientific in general and the medical in particular; his characters are virtually test-tube specimens, and he surveys them with the same degree of detachment as that with which any conscientious scientist observes his laboratory material.

In Huxley's stories, therefore, human beings behave as their physical organism prompts them to act; and if they think, they think in terms of a large, divine, and completely uncomfortable skepticism. In extreme moments they touch absolute negation, and most of them, even in their spiritual crises, leave the impression that it is solely their body chemistry, their endocrine glands, that drive them along. This at least was true of Huxley's work through the 1920's and the early 1930's. This gaudy sophomoric brilliance, however, then began to subside, and in its place appeared a more chastened mood, a search for values of a spiritual nature, pointing to a more balanced and hence more abiding achievement by the author. *Ends and Means,* in its subtitle, indicates the general trend of the later Huxley; it is "the inquiry into the nature of ideals and into the methods employed for their realization." Where Huxley will eventually come out is not for us to say, for, like every important writer, he shows the invaluable ability to change and develop. Unquestionably he has a brilliant mind and razor-keen perceptions; as his humanity deepens, he becomes ever a greater author.

The Rest Cure

SHE WAS a tiny woman, dark-haired and with grey-blue eyes, very large and arresting in a small pale face. A little girl's face, with small, delicate features, but worn—prematurely; for Mrs. Tarwin was only twenty-eight; and the big, wide-open eyes were restless and unquietly bright. "Moira's got nerves," her husband would explain when people enquired why she wasn't with him. Nerves that couldn't stand 10 the strain of London or New York. She had to take things quietly in Florence. A sort of rest cure. "Poor darling!" he would add in a voice that had suddenly become furry with sentiment; and he would illuminate his ordinarily rather blankly intelligent face with one of those lightning smiles of his—so wistful and tender and charming. Almost too charming, one felt uncomfortably. He turned on the charm and the wistfulness like electricity. Click! his face 20 was briefly illumined. And then, click! the light went out again and he was once more the

blankly intelligent research student. Cancer was his subject.

Poor Moira! Those nerves of hers! She was full of caprices and obsessions. For example, when she leased the villa on the slopes of Bellosguardo, she wanted to be allowed to cut down the cypresses at the end of the garden. "So terribly like a cemetery," she kept repeating to old Signor Bargioni. Old Bargioni was 30 charming, but firm. He had no intention of sacrificing his cypresses. They gave the finishing touch of perfection to the loveliest view in all Florence; from the best bedroom window you saw the dome and Giotto's tower framed between their dark columns. Inexhaustibly loquacious, he tried to persuade her that cypresses weren't really at all funereal. For the Etruscans, on the contrary (he invented this little piece of archaeology on the spur of the 40 moment) the cypress was a symbol of joy; the feasts of the vernal equinox concluded with dances round the sacred tree. Boecklin, it was true, had planted cypresses on his Island of the Dead. But then Boecklin, after all . . . And if she really found the trees depressing, she could plant nasturtiums to climb up them. Or roses. Roses, which the Greeks . . .

"All right, all right," said Moira Tarwin hastily. "Let's leave the cypresses." 50

That voice, that endless flow of culture and foreign English! Old Bargioni was really terrible. She would have screamed if she had had to listen a moment longer. She yielded in mere self-defence.

"*E la Tarwinnè?*" questioned Signora Bargioni when her husband came home.

He shrugged his shoulders. "*Una donnina piuttosto sciocca,*" was his verdict.

Rather silly. Old Bargioni was not the only 60 man who had thought so. But he was one of the not so many who regarded her silliness as a fault. Most of the men who knew her were

---

26. **Bellosguardo,** heights not far from the city of Florence, Italy.   35. **dome . . . tower,** on the cathedral at Florence. Giotto (1276–1336), the great Florentine painter, was distinguished in his later life as an architect as well; he was responsible for the west front of the cathedral and for its campanile, or bell-tower.   44. **Island of the Dead,** a famous picture by the Swiss painter, Arnold Boecklin (1827–1901), which portrays the dead being ferried to a mysterious-appearing island. 58. "*Una . . . sciocca,*" "a rather silly little woman." Many of these Italian phrases Huxley translates immediately afterwards in his text.

---

charmed by it; they adored while they smiled. In conjunction with that tiny stature, those eyes, that delicate childish face, her silliness inspired avuncular devotions and protective loves. She had a faculty for making men feel, by contrast, agreeably large, superior and intelligent. And as luck, or perhaps as ill luck, would have it, Moira had passed her life among men who were really intelligent and what is called superior. Old Sir Watney Croker, her grandfather, with whom she had lived ever since she was five (for her father and mother had both died young) was one of the most eminent physicians of his day. His early monograph on duodenal ulcers remains even now the classical work on the subject. Between one duodenal ulcer and another Sir Watney found leisure to adore and indulge and spoil his little granddaughter. Along with fly-fishing and metaphysics she was his hobby. Time passed; Moira grew up, chronologically; but Sir Watney went on treating her as a spoilt child, went on being enchanted by her birdy chirrupings and ingenuousnesses and impertinent *enfant-terrible-isms*. He encouraged, he almost compelled her to preserve her childishness. Keeping her a baby in spite of her age amused him. He loved her babyish and could only love her so. All those duodenal ulcers—perhaps they had done something to his sensibility, warped it a little, kept it somehow stunted and unadult, like Moira herself. In the depths of his unspecialized, unprofessional being Sir Watney was a bit of a baby himself. Too much preoccupation with the duodenum had prevented this neglected instinctive part of him from fully growing up. Like gravitates to like; old baby Watney loved the baby in Moira and wanted to keep the young woman permanently childish. Most of his friends shared Sir Watney's tastes. Doctors, judges, professors, civil servants—every member of Sir Watney's circle was professionally eminent, a veteran specialist. To be asked to one of his dinner parties was a privilege. On these august occasions Moira had always, from the age of seventeen, been present, the only woman at the table. Not really a woman, Sir Watney explained; a child. The veteran specialists were all her indulgent uncles. The more childish she was, the better they liked her. Moira gave them pet names. Professor Stagg, for example, the neo-Hegelian, was Uncle Bonzo; Mr. Justice Gidley was Giddy Goat. And so on. When they teased, she answered back impertinently. How they laughed! When they started to discuss the Absolute or Britain's Industrial Future, she interjected some deliciously irrelevant remark that made them laugh even more heartily. Exquisite! And the next day the story would be told to colleagues in the law courts or the hospital, to cronies at the Athenaeum. In learned and professional circles Moira enjoyed a real celebrity. In the end she had ceased not only to be a woman; she had almost ceased to be a child. She was hardly more than their mascot.

At half-past nine she left the dining-room, and the talk would come back to ulcers and Reality and Emergent Evolution.

"One would like to keep her as a pet," John Tarwin had said as the door closed behind her on that first occasion he dined at Sir Watney's.

Professor Broadwater agreed. There was a little silence. It was Tarwin who broke it.

"What's your feeling," he asked, leaning forward with that expression of blank intelligence on his eager, sharp-featured face, "what's *your* feeling about the validity of experiments with artificially grafted tumours as opposed to natural tumours?"

Tarwin was only thirty-three and looked even younger among Sir Watney's veterans. He had already done good work, Sir Watney explained to his assembled guests before the young man's arrival, and might be expected to do much more. An interesting fellow too. Had been all over the place—tropical Africa, India, North and South America. Well off. Not tied to an academic job to earn his living. Had worked here in London, in Germany, at the Rockefeller Institute in New York, in Japan. Enviable opportunities. A great deal to be said for a private income. "Ah, here you are, Tarwin. Good evening. No, not at all late. This is Mr. Justice Gidley, Professor Broadwater, Professor Stagg and—bless me! I hadn't noticed

52. **neo-Hegelian**, a modern follower of the philosophy of George Wilhelm Friedrich Hegel (1770–1831); its basis was the Hegelian dialectic, according to which reflective thinking can arrange all the categories, or necessary conceptions of reason, in an order of development that corresponds to the actual order in development of all reality. It represents, therefore, an attempt to effect a compromise between idealistic and rational thinking.

you, Moira; you're really too ultra-microscopic —my granddaughter." Tarwin smiled down at her. She was really ravishing.

Well, now they had been married five years, Moira was thinking, as she powdered her face in front of the looking-glass. Tonino was coming to tea; she had been changing her frock. Through the window behind the mirror one looked down between the cypress trees on to Florence—a jumble of brown roofs, and above them, in the midst, the marble tower and the huge, upleaping, airy dome. Five years. It was John's photograph in the leather travelling-frame that made her think of her marriage. Why did she keep it there on the dressing-table? Force of habit, she supposed. It wasn't as though the photograph reminded her of days that had been particularly happy. On the contrary. There was something, she now felt, slightly dishonest about keeping it there. Pretending to love him when she didn't. . . . She looked at it again. The profile was sharp and eager. The keen young research student intently focused on a tumour. She really liked him better as a research student than when he was having a soul, or being a poet or a lover. It seemed a dreadful thing to say—but there it was: the research student was of better quality than the human being.

She had always known it—or, rather not known, felt it. The human being had always made her rather uncomfortable. The more human, the more uncomfortable. She oughtn't ever to have married him, of course. But he asked so persistently; and then he had so much vitality; everybody spoke so well of him; she rather liked his looks; and he seemed to lead such a jolly life, travelling about the world; and she was tired of being a mascot for her grandfather's veterans. There were any number of such little reasons. Added together, she had fancied they would be the equivalent of the one big, cogent reason. But they weren't; she had made a mistake.

Yes, the more human, the more uncomfortable. The disturbing way he turned on the beautiful illumination of his smile! Turned it on suddenly, only to switch it off again with as little warning when something really serious, like cancer or philosophy, had to be discussed. And then his voice, when he was talking about

Nature, or Love, or God, or something of that sort—furry with feeling! The quite unnecessarily moved and tremulous way he said good-bye! "Like a Landseer dog," she told him once, before they were married, laughing and giving a ludicrous imitation of his too heart-felt "Good-bye, Moira." The mockery hurt him. John prided himself as much on his soul and his feelings as upon his intellect; as much on his appreciation of Nature and his poetical love-longings as upon his knowledge of tumours. Goethe was his favourite literary and historical character. Poet and man of science, deep thinker and ardent lover, artist in thought and in life—John saw himself in the rich part. He made her read *Faust* and *Wilhelm Meister*.

Moira did her best to feign the enthusiasm she did not feel. Privately she thought Goethe a humbug.

"I oughtn't to have married him," she said to her image in the glass, and shook her head.

John was the pet-fancier as well as the loving educator. There were times when Moira's childishnesses delighted him as much as they had delighted Sir Watney and his veterans, when he laughed at every naïveté or impertinence she uttered, as though it were a piece of the most exquisite wit; and not only laughed, but drew public attention to it, led her on into fresh infantilities and repeated the stories of her exploits to any one who was prepared to listen to them. He was less enthusiastic, however, when Moira had been childish at his expense, when her silliness had in any way compromised *his* dignity or interests. On these occasions he lost his temper, called her a fool, told her she ought to be ashamed of herself. After which, controlling himself, he would become grave, paternal, pedagogic. Moira would be made to feel, miserably, that she wasn't worthy of him. And finally he switched on the smile and made it all up with caresses that left her like a stone.

"And to think," she reflected, putting away her powder-puff, "to think of my spending all that time and energy trying to keep up with him."

All those scientific papers she had read, those outlines of medicine and physiology,

55. **Landseer.** See note 77, p. 144.

those text-books of something or other (she couldn't even remember the name of the science), to say nothing of all that dreary stuff by Goethe! And then all the going out when she had a headache or was tired! All the meeting of people who bored her, but who were really, according to John, so interesting and important! All the travelling, the terribly strenuous sight-seeing, the calling on distinguished foreigners and their generally less distinguished wives! It was difficult for her to keep up even physically—her legs were so short and John was always in such a hurry. Mentally, in spite of all her efforts, she was always a hundred miles behind.

"Awful!" she said aloud.

Her whole marriage had really been awful. From that awful honeymoon at Capri, when he had made her walk too far, too fast, uphill, only to read her extracts from Wordsworth when they reached the *Aussichtspunkt;* when he had talked to her about love and made it, much too frequently, and told her the Latin names of the plants and butterflies—from that awful honeymoon to the time when, four months ago, her nerves had gone all to pieces and the doctor had said that she must take things quietly, apart from John. Awful! The life had nearly killed her. And it wasn't (she had come at last to realize), it wasn't really a life at all. It was just a galvanic activity, like the twitching of a dead frog's leg when you touch the nerve with an electrified wire. Not life, just galvanized death.

She remembered the last of their quarrels, just before the doctor had told her to go away. John had been sitting at her feet, with his head against her knee. And his head was beginning to go bald! She could hardly bear to look at those long hairs plastered across the scalp. And because he was tired with all that microscope work, tired and at the same time (not having made love to her, thank goodness! for more than a fortnight) amorous, as she could tell by the look in his eyes, he was being very sentimental and talking in his furriest voice about Love and Beauty and the necessity for being like Goethe. Talking till she felt like screaming aloud. And at last she could bear it no longer.

21. *Aussichtspunkt,* point of view; that is, here, the point at which the full effect of their vista would be revealed to them.

474

"For goodness sake, John," she said in a voice that was on the shrill verge of being out of control, "be quiet!"

"What *is* the matter?" He looked up at her questioningly, pained.

"Talking like that!" She was indignant. "But you've never loved anybody, outside yourself. Nor felt the beauty of anything. Any more than that old humbug Goethe. You know what you *ought* to feel when there's a woman about, or a landscape; you know what the best people feel. And you deliberately set yourself to feel the same, out of your head."

John was wounded to the quick of his vanity. "How can you say that?"

"Because it's true, it's true. You only live out of your head. And it's a bald head too," she added, and began to laugh, uncontrollably.

What a scene there had been! She went on laughing all the time he raged at her; she couldn't stop.

"You're hysterical," he said at last; and then he calmed down. The poor child was ill. With an effort he switched on the expression of paternal tenderness and went to fetch the sal volatile.

One last dab at her lips, and there! she was ready. She went downstairs to the drawing-room, to find that Tonino had already arrived —he was always early—and was waiting. He rose as she entered, bowed over her outstretched hand and kissed it. Moira was always charmed by his florid, rather excessive Southern good manners. John was always too busy being the keen research student or the furry-voiced poet to have good manners. He didn't think politeness particularly important. It was the same with clothes. He was chronically ill-dressed. Tonino, on the other hand, was a model of dapper elegance. That pale grey suit, that lavender-coloured tie, those piebald shoes of white kid and patent leather— marvellous!

One of the pleasures or dangers of foreign travel is that you lose your class-consciousness. At home you can never, with the best will in the world, forget it. Habit has rendered your own people as immediately legible as your own language. A word, a gesture is sufficient; your man is placed. But in foreign parts your fellows are unreadable. The less obvious products of upbringing—all the subtler refinements, the finer shades of vulgarity—escape your notice. The accent, the inflexion of voice, the vocabulary, the gestures tell you nothing. Between the duke and the insurance clerk, the profiteer and the country gentleman, your inexperienced eye and ear detect no difference. For Moira, Tonino seemed the characteristic flower of Italian gentility. She knew, of course, that he wasn't well off; but then, plenty of the nicest people are poor. She saw in him the equivalent of one of those younger sons of impoverished English squires—the sort of young man who advertises for work in the Agony Column of the *Times*. "Public School education, sporting tastes; would accept any well-paid position of trust and confidence." She would have been pained, indignant, and surprised to hear old Bargioni describing him, after their first meeting, as "*il tipo del parruchiere napoletano*"—the typical Neapolitan barber. Signora Bargioni shook her head over the approaching scandal and was secretly delighted.

As a matter of actual fact Tonino was not a barber. He was the son of a capitalist—on a rather small scale, no doubt; but still a genuine capitalist. Vasari senior owned a restaurant at Pozzuoli and was ambitious to start a hotel. Tonino had been sent to study the tourist industry with a family friend who was the manager of one of the best establishments in Florence. When he had learnt all the secrets, he was to return to Pozzuoli and be the managing director of the rejuvenated boarding-house which his father was modestly proposing to rechristen the Grand Hotel Ritz-Carlton. Meanwhile, he was an underworked lounger in Florence. He had made Mrs. Tarwin's acquaintance romantically, on the highway. Driving, as was her custom, alone, Moira had run over a nail. A puncture. Nothing is easier than changing wheels—nothing, that is to say, if you have sufficient muscular strength to undo the nuts which hold the punctured wheel to its axle. Moira had not. When Tonino came upon her, ten minutes after the mishap, she was sitting on the running-board of her car, flushed and dishevelled with her efforts, and in tears. "*Una signora forestiera.*" At the café that evening Tonino recounted his adventure with a certain rather fatuous self-satisfaction. In the

small bourgeoisie in which he had been brought up, a Foreign Lady was an almost fabulous creature, a being of legendary wealth, eccentricity, independence. "*Inglese,*" he specified. "*Giovane,*" and "*bella, bellissima.*" His auditors were incredulous; beauty, for some reason, is not common among the specimens of English womanhood seen in foreign parts. "*Ricca,*" he added. That sounded less intrinsically improbable; foreign ladies were all rich, almost by definition. Juicily, and with unction, Tonino described the car she drove, the luxurious villa she inhabited.

Acquaintance had ripened quickly into friendship. This was the fourth or fifth time in a fortnight that he had come to the house.

"A few poor flowers," said the young man in a tone of soft, ingratiating apology; and he brought forward his left hand, which he had been hiding behind his back. It held a bouquet of white roses.

"But how kind of you!" she cried in her bad Italian. "How lovely!" John never brought flowers to any one; he regarded that sort of thing as rather nonsensical. She smiled at Tonino over the blossoms. "Thank you a thousand times."

Making a deprecating gesture, he returned her smile. His teeth flashed pearly and even. His large eyes were bright, dark, liquid, and rather expressionless, like a gazelle's. He was exceedingly good-looking. "White roses for the white rose," he said.

Moira laughed. The compliment was ridiculous, but it pleased her all the same.

Paying compliments was not the only thing Tonino could do. He knew how to be useful. When, a few days later, Moira decided to have the rather dingy hall and dining-room redistempered, he was invaluable. It was he who haggled with the decorator, he who made scenes when there were delays, he who interpreted Moira's rather special notions about colours to the workmen, he who superintended their activities.

"If it hadn't been for you," said Moira gratefully, when the work was finished, "I'd have been hopelessly swindled and they wouldn't have done anything properly."

It was such a comfort, she reflected, having a man about the place who didn't always have something more important to do and think

27. **Pozzuoli,** a suburb of Naples.

about; a man who could spend his time being useful and a help. Such a comfort! And such a change! When she was with John, it was she who had to do all the tiresome, practical things. John always had his work, and his work took precedence of everything, including her convenience. Tonino was just an ordinary man, with nothing in the least superhuman about either himself or his functions. It was a great relief.

Little by little Moira came to rely on him for everything. He made himself universally useful. The fuses blew out; it was Tonino who replaced them. The hornets nested in the drawing-room chimney; heroically Tonino stank them out with sulphur. But his speciality was domestic economy. Brought up in a restaurant, he knew everything there was to be known about food and drink and prices. When the meat was unsatisfactory, he went to the butcher and threw the tough beefsteak in his teeth, almost literally. He beat down the extortionate charges of the green-grocer. With a man at the fish market he made a friendly arrangement whereby Moira was to have the pick of the soles and the red mullet. He bought her wine for her, her oil—wholesale, in huge glass demi-johns; and Moira, who since Sir Watney's death could have afforded to drink nothing cheaper than Pol Roger 1911 and do her cooking in imported yak's butter, exulted with him in long domestic conversations over economies of a farthing a quart or a shilling or two on a hundredweight. For Tonino the price and the quality of victuals and drink were matters of gravest importance. To secure a flask of Chianti for five lire ninety instead of six lire was, in his eyes, a real victory; and the victory became a triumph if it could be proved that the Chianti was fully three years old and had an alcohol content of more than fourteen per cent. By nature Moira was neither greedy nor avaricious. Her upbringing had confirmed her in her natural tendencies. She had the disinterestedness of those who have never known a shortage of cash; and her abstemious indifference to the pleasures of the table had never been tempered by the housewife's preoccupation with other people's appetites and digestions. Never; for Sir Watney had kept a professional housekeeper, and with John Tarwin, who anyhow

hardly noticed what he ate, and thought that women ought to spend their time doing more important and intellectual things than presiding over kitchens, she had lived for the greater part of their married life in hotels or service flats, or else in furnished rooms and in a chronic state of picnic. Tonino revealed to her the world of markets and the kitchen. Still accustomed to thinking, with John, that ordinary domestic life wasn't good enough, she laughed at first at his earnest preoccupation with meat and halfpence. But after a little she began to be infected by his almost religious enthusiasm for housekeeping; she began to discover that meat and halfpence were interesting after all, that they were real and important—much more real and important, for example, than reading Goethe when one found him a bore and a humbug. Tenderly brooded over by the most competent of solicitors and brokers, the late Sir Watney's fortune was bringing in a steady five per cent. free of tax. But in Tonino's company Moira could forget her bank balance. Descending from the financial Sinai on which she had been lifted so high above the common earth, she discovered, with him, the preoccupations of poverty. They were curiously interesting and exciting.

"The prices they ask for fish in Florence!" said Tonino, after a silence, when he had exhausted the subject of white roses. "When I think how little we pay for octopus at Naples! It's scandalous!"

"Scandalous!" echoed Moira with an indignation as genuine as his own. They talked, interminably.

Next day the sky was no longer blue, but opaquely white. There was no sunshine, only a diffused glare that threw no shadows. The landscape lay utterly lifeless under the dead and fishy stare of heaven. It was very hot, there was no wind, the air was hardly breathable and as though woolly. Moira woke up with a headache, and her nerves seemed to have an uneasy life of their own, apart from hers. Like caged birds they were, fluttering and starting

75. **Sinai,** originally the mountain of northwestern Arabia where Moses was given the tablets of the Lord which represented the Ten Commandments, the core of Mosaic law; see Exodus 19. Metaphorically, the term is used here for an eminence that transcends mere earthly affairs.

and twittering at every alarm; and her aching, tired body was their aviary. Quite against her own wish and intention she found herself in a temper with the maid and saying the unkindest things. She had to give her a pair of stockings to make up for it. When she was dressed, she wanted to write some letters; but her fountain-pen made a stain on her fingers and she was so furious that she threw the beastly thing out of the window. It broke to pieces on the flagstones below. She had nothing to write with; it was too exasperating. She washed the ink off her hands and took out her embroidery frame. But her fingers were all thumbs. And then she pricked herself with the needle. Oh, so painfully! The tears came into her eyes; she began to cry. And having begun, she couldn't stop. Assunta came in five minutes later and found her sobbing. "But what is it, signora?" she asked, made most affectionately solicitous by the gift of the stockings. Moira shook her head. "Go away," she said brokenly. The girl was insistent. "Go away," Moira repeated. How could she explain what was the matter when the only thing that had happened was that she had pricked her finger? Nothing was the matter. And yet everything was the matter, everything.

The everything that was the matter resolved itself finally into the weather. Even in the best of health Moira had always been painfully conscious of the approach of thunder. Her jangled nerves were more than ordinarily sensitive. The tears and furies and despairs of this horrible day had a purely meteorological cause. But they were none the less violent and agonizing for that. The hours passed dismally. Thickened by huge black clouds, the twilight came on in a sultry and expectant silence, and it was prematurely night. The reflection of distant lightnings, flashing far away below the horizon, illuminated the eastern sky. The peaks and ridges of the Apennines stood out black against the momentary pale expanses of silvered vapour and disappeared again in silence; the attentive hush was still unbroken. With a kind of sinking apprehension—for she was terrified of storms—Moira sat at her window, watching the black hills leap out against the silver and die again, leap out and die. The flashes brightened; and then, for the first time, she heard the

approaching thunder, far off and faint like the whisper of the sea in a shell. Moira shuddered. The clock in the hall struck nine, and, as though the sound were a signal prearranged, a gust of wind suddenly shook the magnolia tree that stood at the crossing of the paths in the garden below. Its long stiff leaves rattled together like scales of horn. There was another flash. In the brief white glare she could see the two funereal cypresses writhing and tossing as though in the desperate agitation of pain. And then all at once the storm burst catastrophically, it seemed, directly overhead. At the savage violence of that icy downpour Moira shrank back and shut the window. A streak of white fire zig-zagged fearfully just behind the cypresses. The immediate thunder was like the splitting and fall of a solid vault. Moira rushed away from the window and threw herself on the bed. She covered her face with her hands. Through the continuous roaring of the rain the thunder crashed and reverberated, crashed again and sent the fragments of sound rolling unevenly in all directions through the night. The whole house trembled. In the window-frames the shaken glasses rattled like the panes of an old omnibus rolling across the cobbles.

"Oh God, Oh God," Moira kept repeating. In the enormous tumult her voice was small and, as it were, naked, utterly abject.

"But it's too stupid to be frightened." She remembered John's voice, his brightly encouraging, superior manner. "The chances are thousands to one against your being struck. And anyhow, hiding your head won't prevent the lightning from . . ."

How she hated him for being so reasonable and right! "Oh God!" There was another. "God, God, God. . . ."

And then suddenly a terrible thing happened; the light went out. Through her closed eyelids she saw no longer the red of translucent blood, but utter blackness. Uncovering her face, she opened her eyes and anxiously looked round—on blackness again. She fumbled for the switch by her bed, found it, turned and turned; the darkness remained impenetrable.

"Assunta!" she called.

And all at once the square of the window was a suddenly uncovered picture of the garden, seen against a background of mauve-white sky and shining down-pouring rain.

"Assunta!" Her voice was drowned in a crash that seemed to have exploded in the very roof. "Assunta, Assunta!" In a panic she stumbled across the grave-dark room to the door. Another flash revealed the handle. She opened. "Assunta!"

Her voice was hollow above the black gulf of the stairs. The thunder exploded again above her. With a crash and a tinkle of broken glass one of the windows in her room burst open. A blast of cold wind lifted her hair. A flight of papers rose from her writing-table and whirled with crackling wings through the darkness. One touched her cheek like a living thing and was gone. She screamed aloud. The door slammed behind her. She ran down the stairs in terror, as though the fiend were at her heels. In the hall she met Assunta and the cook coming towards her, lighting matches as they came.

"Assunta, the lights!" She clutched the girl's arm.

Only the thunder answered. When the noise subsided Assunta explained that the fuses had all blown out and that there wasn't a candle in the house. Not a single candle, and only one more box of matches.

"But then we shall be left in the dark," said Moira hysterically.

Through the three blackly reflecting windows of the hall three separate pictures of the streaming garden revealed themselves and vanished. The old Venetian mirrors on the walls blinked for an instant into life, like dead eyes briefly opened.

"In the dark," she repeated with an almost mad insistence.

"Aie!" cried Assunta, and dropped the match that had begun to burn her fingers. The thunder fell on them out of a darkness made denser and more hopeless by the loss of light.

When the telephone bell rang, Tonino was sitting in the managerial room of his hotel, playing cards with the proprietor's two sons and another friend. "Someone to speak to you, Signor Tonino," said the underporter, looking in. "A lady." He grinned significantly.

Tonino put on a dignified air and left the room. When he returned a few minutes later, he held his hat in one hand and was buttoning up his rain-coat with the other.

"Sorry," he said. "I've got to go out."

"Go out?" exclaimed the others incredulously. Beyond the shuttered windows the storm roared like a cataract and savagely exploded. "But where?" they asked. "Why? Are you mad?"

Tonino shrugged his shoulders, as though it were nothing to go out into a tornado, as though he were used to it. The *signora forestiera*, he explained, hating them for their inquisitiveness; the Tarwin—she had asked him to go up to Bellosguardo at once. The fuses . . . not a candle in the house . . . utterly in the dark . . . very agitated . . . nerves. . . .

"But on a night like this. . . . But you're not the electrician." The two sons of the proprietor spoke in chorus. They felt, indignantly, that Tonino was letting himself be exploited.

But the third young man leaned back in his chair and laughed. "*Vai, caro, vai,*" he said, and then, shaking his finger at Tonino knowingly, "*Ma fatti pagare per il tuo lavoro,*" he added. "Get yourself paid for your trouble." Berto was notoriously the lady-killer, the tried specialist in amorous strategy, the acknowledged expert. "Take the opportunity." The others joined in his rather unpleasant laughter. Tonino also grinned and nodded.

The taxi rushed splashing through the wet deserted streets like a travelling fountain. Tonino sat in the darkness of the cab ruminating Berto's advice. She was pretty, certainly. But somehow—why was it?—it had hardly occurred to him to think of her as a possible mistress. He had been politely gallant with her—on principle almost, and by force of habit—but without really wanting to succeed; and when she had shown herself unresponsive, he hadn't cared. But perhaps he ought to have cared, perhaps he ought to have tried harder. In Berto's world it was a sporting duty to do one's best to seduce every woman one could. The most admirable man was the man with the greatest number of women to his credit. Really lovely, Tonino went on to himself, trying to work up an enthusiasm for the sport. It would be a triumph to be proud of. The more so as she was a foreigner. And very rich. He thought with inward satisfaction of that big car, of the house, the servants, the silver.

72. "*Vai . . . vai,*" "Go ahead, my dear chap, go ahead!"

"*Certo*," he said to himself complacently, "*mi vuol bene.*" She liked him; there was no doubt of it. Meditatively he stroked his smooth face; the muscles stirred a little under his fingers. He was smiling to himself in the darkness; naïvely, an ingenuous prostitute's smile. "*Moira*," he said aloud. ."*Moira. Strano, quel nome. Piuttosto ridicolo.*"

It was Moira who opened the door for him. She had been standing at the window, looking out, waiting and waiting.

"Tonino!" She held out both her hands to him; she had never felt so glad to see any one.

The sky went momentarily whitish-mauve behind him as he stood there in the open doorway. The skirts of his rain-coat fluttered in the wind; a wet gust blew past him, chilling her face. The sky went black again. He slammed the door behind him. They were in utter darkness.

"Tonino, it was too sweet of you to have come. Really too . . ."

The thunder that interrupted her was like the end of the world. Moira shuddered. "Oh God!" she whimpered; and then suddenly she was pressing her face against his waistcoat and crying, and Tonino was holding her and stroking her hair. The next flash showed him the position of the sofa. In the ensuing darkness he carried her across the room, sat down and began to kiss her tear-wet face. She lay quite still in his arms, relaxed, like a frightened child that has at last found comfort. Tonino held her, kissing her softly again and again. "*Ti amo, Moira,*" he whispered. And it was true. Holding her, touching her in the dark, he did love her. "*Ti amo.*" How profoundly! "*Ti voglio un bene immenso,*" he went on, with a passion, a deep warm tenderness born almost suddenly of darkness and soft blind contact. Heavy and warm with life, she lay pressed against him. Her body curved and was solid under his hands, her cheeks were rounded and cool, her eyelids rounded and tremulous and tear-wet, her mouth so soft, so soft under his touching lips. "*Ti amo, ti amo.*" He was breathless with love, and it was as though there were a hollowness at the center of his being, a void of desiring tenderness that longed to be filled, that could only be filled by her, an emptiness that drew her towards him, into him, that drank her as an empty vessel eagerly drinks the water. Still, with closed eyes, quite still she lay there in his arms, suffering herself to be drunk up by his tenderness, to be drawn into the yearning vacancy of his heart, happy in being passive, in yielding herself to his soft insistent passion.

"*Fatti pagare, fatti pagare.*" The memory of Berto's words transformed him suddenly from a lover into an amorous sportsman with a reputation to keep up and records to break. "*Fatti pagare.*" He risked a more intimate caress. But Moira winced so shudderingly at the touch that he desisted, ashamed of himself.

"*Ebbene,*" asked Berto when, an hour later, he returned, "did you mend the fuses."

"Yes, I mended the fuses."

"And did you get yourself paid?"

Tonino smiled an amorous sportsman's smile. "A little on account," he answered, and at once disliked himself for having spoken the words, disliked the others for laughing at them. Why did he go out of his way to spoil something which had been so beautiful? Pretexting a headache, he went upstairs to his bedroom. The storm had passed on, the moon was shining now out of a clear sky. He opened the window and looked out. A river of ink and quicksilver, the Arno flowed whispering past. In the street below the puddles shone like living eyes. The ghost of Caruso was singing from a gramophone, far away on the other side of the water. "*Stretti, stretti, nell' estasì d'amor. . . .*" Tonino was profoundly moved.

The sky was blue next morning, the sunlight glittered on the shiny leaves of the magnolia tree, the air was demurely windless. Sitting at her dressing-table, Moira looked out and wondered incredulously if such things as storms were possible. But the plants were broken and prostrate in their beds; the paths were strewn with scattered leaves and petals. In spite of the soft air and the sunlight, last night's horrors had been more than a bad dream.

Moira sighed and began to brush her hair. Set in its leather frame, John Tarwin's profile confronted her, brightly focused on imaginary tumours. Her eyes fixed on it. Moira went on

7. "*Strano . . . ridicolo,*" "Strange, that name. A wee bit ridiculous." 34. "*Ti amo,*" "I love you." 37. "*Ti . . . immenso,*" "I want the best for you."

65. "*Ebbene,*" "Well?" 83. "*Stretti . . . d'amor,*" "pressed tight in the joys of love."

mechanically brushing her hair. Then, suddenly, interrupting the rhythm of her movements, she got up, took the leather frame and, walking across the room, threw it up, out of sight, on to the top of the high wardrobe. There! She returned to her seat and, filled with a kind of frightened elation, went on with her interrupted brushing.

When she was dressed, she drove down to the town and spent an hour at Settepassi's, the jewelers. When she left, she was bowed out on to the Lungarno like a princess.

"No, don't smoke those," she said to Tonino that afternoon as he reached for a cigarette in the silver box that stood on the drawing-room mantelpiece. "I've got a few of those Egyptian ones you like. Got them specially for you." And, smiling, she handed him a little parcel.

Tonino thanked her profusely—too profusely, as was his custom. But when he had stripped away the paper and saw the polished gold of a large cigarette-case, he could only look at her in an embarrassed and enquiring amazement.

"Don't you think it's rather pretty?" she asked.

"Marvellous! But is it . . ." He hesitated. "Is it for me?"

Moira laughed with pleasure at his embarrassment. She had never seen him embarrassed before. He was always the self-possessed young man of the world, secure and impregnable within his armour of Southern good manners. She admired that elegant carapace. But it amused her for once to take him without it, to see him at a loss, blushing and stammering like a little boy. It amused and it pleased her; she liked him all the more for being the little boy as well as the polished and socially competent young man.

"For me?" she mimicked, laughing. "Do you like it?" Her tone changed; she became grave. "I wanted you to have something to remind you of last night." Tonino took her hands and silently kissed them. She had received him with such off-handed gaiety, so nonchalantly, as though nothing had happened, that the tender references to last night's happenings (so carefully prepared as he walked up the hill) had

remained unspoken. He had been afraid of saying the wrong thing and offending her. But now the spell was broken—and by Moira herself. "One oughtn't to forget one's good actions," Moira went on, abandoning him her hands. "Each time you take a cigarette out of this case, will you remember how kind and good you were to a silly ridiculous little fool?"

Tonino had had time to recover his manners. "I shall remember the most adorable, the most beautiful . . ." Still holding her hands, he looked at her for a moment in silence, eloquently. Moira smiled back at him. "Moira!" And she was in his arms. She shut her eyes and was passive in the strong circle of his arms, soft and passive against his firm body. "I love you, Moira." The breath of his whispering was warm on her cheek. *"Ti amo."* And suddenly his lips were on hers again, violently, impatiently kissing. Between the kisses his whispered words came passionate to her ears. *"Ti amo pazzamente . . . piccina . . . tesoro . . . amore . . . cuore . . ."* Uttered in Italian, his love seemed somehow specially strong and deep. Things described in a strange language themselves take on a certain strangeness. *"Amami, Moira, amami. Mi ami un po?"* He was insistent. "A little, Moira—do you love me a little?"

She opened her eyes and looked at him. Then, with a quick movement, she took his face between her two hands, drew it down and kissed him on the mouth. "Yes," she whispered, "I love you." And then, gently, she pushed him away. Tonino wanted to kiss her again. But Moira shook her head and slipped away from him. "No, no," she said with a kind of peremptory entreaty. "Don't spoil it all now."

The days passed, hot and golden. Summer approached. The nightingales sang unseen in the cool of the evening.

"L'ussignuolo," Moira whispered softly to herself, as she listened to the singing. *"L'ussignuolo."* Even the nightingales were subtly better in Italian. The sun had set. They were sitting in the little summer-house at the end of the garden, looking out over the darkening landscape. The white-walled farms and villas

---

12. **Lungarno,** a main thoroughfare in Florence, running along the banks of the River Arno.   33. **carapace,** the hard case or shell of an animal.

70. *"Ti . . . cuore,"* "I love you, madly . . . little . . . treasure . . . love . . . heart."

on the slope below stood out almost startlingly clear against the twilight of the olive trees, as though charged with some strange and novel significance. Moira sighed. "I'm so happy," she said; Tonino took her hand. "Ridiculously happy." For, after all, she was thinking, it *was* rather ridiculous to be so happy for no valid reason. John Tarwin had taught her to imagine that one could only be happy when one was doing something "interesting" (as he put it), or associating with people who were "worth while." Tonino was nobody in particular, thank goodness! And going for picnics wasn't exactly "interesting" in John's sense of the word; nor was talking about the respective merits of different brands of cars; nor teaching him to drive; nor going shopping; nor discussing the problem of new curtains for the drawing-room; nor, for that matter, sitting in the summer-house and saying nothing. In spite of which, or because of which, she was happy with an unprecedented happiness. "Ridiculously happy," she repeated.

Tonino kissed her hand. "So am I," he said. And he was not merely being polite. In his own way he was genuinely happy with her. People envied him sitting in that magnificent yellow car at her side. She was so pretty and elegant, so foreign too; he was proud to be seen about with her. And then the cigarette case, the gold-mounted, agate-handled cane she had given him for his birthday. . . . Besides, he was really very fond of her, really, in an obscure way, in love with her. It was not for nothing that he had held and caressed her in the darkness of that night of thunder. Something of that deep and passionate tenderness, born suddenly of the night and their warm sightless contact, still remained in him—still remained even after the physical longings she then inspired had been vicariously satisfied. (And under Berto's knowing guidance they *had* been satisfied, frequently.) If it hadn't been for Berto's satirical comments on the still platonic nature of his attachment, he would have been perfectly content.

"*Alle donne,*" Berto sententiously generalized, "*piace sempre la violenza.* They long to be raped. You don't know how to make love, my poor boy." And he would hold up his own achievements as examples to be followed. For Berto, love was a kind of salacious vengeance on women for the crime of their purity.

Spurred on by his friend's mockeries, Tonino made another attempt to exact full payment for his mending of the fuses on the night of the storm. But his face was so soundly slapped, and the tone in which Moira threatened never to see him again unless he behaved himself was so convincingly stern, that he did not renew his attack. He contented himself with looking sad and complaining of her cruelty.

But in spite of his occasionally long face, he was happy with her. Happy like a fireside cat. The car, the house, her elegant foreign prettiness, the marvellous presents she gave him, kept him happily purring.

The days passed and the weeks. Moira would have liked life to flow on like this for ever, a gay bright stream with occasional reaches of calm sentimentality but never dangerously deep or turbulent, without fall or whirl or rapid. She wanted her existence to remain for ever what it was at this moment—a kind of game with a pleasant and emotionally exciting companion, a playing at living and loving. If only this happy playtime could last for ever!

It was John Tarwin who decreed that it should not. "ATTENDING CYTOLOGICAL CONGRESS ROME WILL STOP FEW DAYS ON WAY ARRIVING THURSDAY LOVE JOHN." That was the text of the telegram Moira found awaiting her on her return to the villa one evening. She read it and felt suddenly depressed and apprehensive. Why did he want to come? He would spoil everything. The bright evening went dead before her eyes; the happiness with which she had been brimming when she returned with Tonino from that marvellous drive among the Apennines was drained out of her. Her gloom retrospectively darkened the blue and golden beauty of the mountains, put out the bright flowers, dimmed the day's laughter and talk. "Why does he want to come?" Miserably and resentfully, she wondered. "And what's going to happen, what's going to happen?" She felt cold and rather breathless and almost sick with the questioning apprehension.

John's face, when he saw her standing there at the station, lit up instantaneously with all its hundred-candle-power tenderness and charm.

"My darling!" His voice was furry and tremulous. He leaned towards her; stiffening, Moira suffered herself to be kissed. His nails, she noticed disgustedly, were dirty.

The prospect of a meal alone with John had appalled her; she had asked Tonino to dinner. Besides, she wanted John to meet him. To have kept Tonino's existence a secret from John would have been to admit that there was something wrong in her relations with him. And there wasn't. She wanted John to meet him just like that, naturally, as a matter of course. Whether he'd like Tonino when he'd met him was another question. Moira had her doubts. They were justified by the event. John had begun by protesting when he heard that she had invited a guest. Their first evening— how could she? The voice trembled—fur in a breeze. She had to listen to outpourings of sentiment. But finally, when dinner-time arrived, he switched off the pathos and became once more the research student. Brightly enquiring, blankly intelligent, John cross-questioned his guest about all the interesting and important things that were happening in Italy. What was the real political situation? How did the new educational system work? What did people think of the reformed penal code? On all these matters Tonino was, of course, far less well-informed than his interrogator. The Italy he knew was the Italy of his friends and his family, of shops and cafés and girls and the daily fight for money. All that historical, impersonal Italy, of which John so intelligently read in the high-class reviews, was utterly unknown to him. His answers to John's questions were childishly silly. Moira sat listening, dumb with misery.

"What *do* you find in that fellow?" her husband asked, when Tonino had taken his leave. "He struck me as quite particularly uninteresting."

Moira did not answer. There was a silence. John suddenly switched on his tenderly, protectively, yearningly marital smile. "Time to go to bed, my sweetheart," he said. Moira looked up at him and saw in his eyes that expression she knew so well and dreaded. "My sweetheart," he repeated, and the Landseer dog was also amorous. He put his arms round her and bent to kiss her face. Moira shuddered—but

helplessly, dumbly, not knowing how to escape. He led her away.

When John had left her, she lay awake far into the night, remembering his ardours and his sentimentalities with a horror that the passage of time seemed actually to increase. Sleep came at last to deliver her.

Being an archaeologist, old Signor Bargioni was decidedly "interesting."

"But he bores me to death," said Moira when, next day, her husband suggested that they should go to see him. "That voice! And the way he goes on and on! And that beard! And his wife!"

John flushed with anger. "Don't be childish," he snapped out, forgetting how much he enjoyed her childishness when it didn't interfere with his amusements or his business. "After all," he insisted, "there's probably no man living who knows more about Tuscany in the Dark Ages."

Nevertheless, in spite of darkest Tuscany, John had to pay his call without her. He spent a most improving hour, chatting about Romanesque architecture and the Lombard kings. But just before he left, the conversation somehow took another turn; casually, as though by chance, Tonino's name was mentioned. It was the *signora* who had insisted that it should be mentioned. Ignorance, her husband protested, is bliss. But Signora Bargioni loved scandal, and being middle-aged, ugly, envious, and malicious, was full of righteous indignation against the young wife and of hypocritical sympathy for the possibly injured husband. Poor Tarwin, she insisted—he ought to be warned. And so, tactfully, without seeming to say anything in particular, the old man dropped his hints.

Walking back to Bellosguardo, John was uneasily pensive. It was not that he imagined that Moira had been, or was likely to prove, unfaithful. Such things really didn't happen to oneself. Moira obviously liked the uninteresting young man; but, after all, and in spite of her childishness, Moira was a civilized human being. She had been too well brought up to do anything stupid. Besides, he reflected, remembering the previous evening, remembering all the years of their marriage, she had no temperament; she didn't know what passion was, she was utterly without sensuality. Her native childishness would reinforce her principles. Infants may be relied on to be pure; but not (and this was what troubled John Tarwin) worldly-wise. Moira wouldn't allow herself to be made love to; but she might easily let herself be swindled. Old Bargioni had been very discreet and noncommittal; but it was obvious that he regarded this young fellow as an adventurer, out for what he could get. John frowned as he walked, and bit his lip.

He came home to find Moira and Tonino superintending the fitting of the new cretonne covers for the drawing-room chairs.

"Carefully, carefully," Moira was saying to the upholsterer as he came in. She turned at the sound of his footsteps. A cloud seemed to obscure the brightness of her face when she saw him; but she made an effort to keep up her gaiety. "Come and look, John," she called. "It's like getting a very fat old lady into a very tight dress. Too ridiculous!"

But John did not smile with her; his face was a mask of stony gravity. He stalked up to the chair, nodded curtly to Tonino, curtly to the upholsterer, and stood there watching the work as though he were a stranger, a hostile stranger at that. The sight of Moira and Tonino laughing and talking together had roused in him a sudden and violent fury. "Disgusting little adventurer," he said to himself ferociously behind his mask.

"It's a pretty stuff, don't you think?" said Moira. He only grunted.

"Very modern too," added Tonino. "The shops are very modern here," he went on, speaking with all the rather touchy insistence on up-to-dateness which characterizes the inhabitants of an under-bathroomed and over-monumented country.

"Indeed?" said John sarcastically.

Moira frowned. "You've no idea how helpful Tonino has been," she said with a certain warmth.

Effusively Tonino began to deny that she had any obligation towards him. John Tarwin interrupted him. "Oh, I've no doubt he was helpful," he said in the same sarcastic tone and with a little smile of contempt.

There was an uncomfortable silence. Then Tonino took his leave. The moment he was gone, Moira turned on her husband. Her face was pale, her lips trembled.

"How dare you speak to one of my friends like that?" she asked in a voice unsteady with anger.

John flared up. "Because I wanted to get rid of the fellow," he answered; and the mask was off, his face was nakedly furious. "It's disgusting to see a man like that hanging round the house. An adventurer. Exploiting your silliness. Sponging on you."

"Tonino doesn't sponge on me. And anyhow, what do you know about it?"

He shrugged his shoulders. "One hears things."

"Oh, it's those old beasts, is it?" She hated the Bargionis, *hated* them. "Instead of being grateful to Tonino for helping me! Which is more than you've ever done, John. You, with your beastly tumours and your rotten old *Faust!*" The contempt in her voice was blasting. "Just leaving me to sink or swim. And when somebody comes along and is just humanly decent to me, you insult him. And you fly into a rage of jealousy because I'm normally grateful to him."

John had had time to readjust his mask. "I don't fly into any sort of rage," he said, bottling his anger and speaking slowly and coldly. "I just don't want you to be preyed upon by handsome, black-haired young pimps from the slums of Naples."

"John!"

"Even if the preying *is* done platonically," he went on. "Which I'm sure it is. But I don't want to have even a platonic pimp about." He spoke coldly, slowly, with the deliberate intention of hurting her as much as he could. "How much has he got out of you so far?"

Moira did not answer, but turned and hurried from the room.

Tonino had just got to the bottom of the hill, when a loud insistent hooting made him turn round. A big yellow car was close at his heels.

"Moira!" he called in astonishment. The car came to a halt beside him.

"Get in," she commanded almost fiercely, as though she were angry with him. He did as he was told.

483

"But where did you think of going?" he asked.

"I don't know. Anywhere. Let's take the Bologna road into the mountains."

"But you've got no hat," he objected, "no coat."

She only laughed and, throwing the car into gear, drove off at full speed. John spent his evening in solitude. He began by reproaching himself. "I oughtn't to have spoken so brutally," he thought, when he heard of Moira's precipitate departure. What tender, charming things he would say, when she came back, to make up for his hard words! And then, when she'd make peace, he would talk to her gently, paternally about the dangers of having bad friends. Even the anticipation of what he would say to her caused his face to light up with a beautiful smile. But when, three-quarters of an hour after dinner-time, he sat down to a lonely and overcooked meal, his mood had changed. "If she wants to sulk," he said to himself, "why, let her sulk." And as the hours passed, his heart grew harder. Midnight struck. His anger began to be tempered by a certain apprehension. Could anything have happened to her? He was anxious. But all the same he went to bed, on principle, firmly. Twenty minutes later he heard Moira's step on the stairs and then the closing of her door. She was back; nothing had happened; perversely, he felt all the more exasperated with her for being safe. Would she come and say good-night? He waited.

Absently, meanwhile, mechanically, Moira had undressed. She was thinking of all that had happened in the eternity since she had left the house. That marvellous sunset in the mountains! Every westward slope was rosily gilded; below them lay a gulf of blue shadow. They had stood in silence, gazing.

"Kiss me, Tonino," she had suddenly whispered, and the touch of his lips had sent a kind of delicious apprehension fluttering under her skin. She pressed herself against him; his body was firm and solid within her clasp. She could feel the throb of his heart against her cheek, like something separately alive. Beat, beat, beat—and the throbbing life was not the life of the Tonino she knew, the Tonino who laughed and paid compliments and brought flowers; it was the life of some mysterious and separate power. A power with which the familiar individual Tonino happened to be connected, but almost irrelevantly. She shuddered a little. Mysterious and terrifying. But the terror was somehow attractive, like a dark precipice that allures. "Kiss me, Tonino, kiss me." The light faded; the hills died away into featureless flat shapes against the sky. "I'm cold," she said at last, shivering. "Let's go." They dined at a little inn, high up between the two passes. When they drove away, it was night. He put his arm around her and kissed her neck, at the nape, where the cropped hair was harsh against his mouth. "You'll make me drive into the ditch," she laughed. But there was no laughter for Tonino. "Moira, Moira," he repeated; and there was something like agony in his voice. "Moira." And finally, at his suffering entreaty, she stopped the car. They got out. Under the chestnut trees, what utter darkness!

Moira slipped off her last garment and, naked before the mirror, looked at her image. It seemed the same as ever, her pale body; but in reality it was different, it was new, it had only just been born.

John still waited, but his wife did not come. "All right then," he said to himself, with a spiteful little anger that disguised itself as a god-like and impersonal serenity of justice; "let her sulk if she wants to. She only punishes herself." He turned out the light and composed himself to sleep. Next morning he left for Rome and the Cytological Congress without saying good-bye; that would teach her. But "Thank goodness!" was Moira's first reflection when she heard that he had gone. And then, suddenly, she felt rather sorry for him. Poor John! Like a dead frog, galvanized; twitching, but never alive. He was pathetic really. She was so rich in happiness that she could afford to be sorry for him. And in a way she was even grateful to him. If he hadn't come, if he hadn't behaved so unforgivably, nothing would have happened between Tonino and herself. Poor John! But all the same he was hopeless.

Day followed bright serene day. But Moira's life no longer flowed like the clear and shallow stream it had been before John's coming. It was turbulent now, there were depths and darknesses. And love was no longer a game with a pleasant companion; it was violent, all-absorbing, even rather terrible. Tonino became for her a kind of obsession. She was haunted by him—by his face, by his white teeth and his dark hair, by his hands and limbs and body. She wanted to be with him, to feel his nearness, to touch him. She would spend whole hours stroking his hair, ruffling it up, rearranging it fantastically, on end, like a golliwog's, or with hanging fringes, or with the locks twisted up into horns. And when she had contrived some specially ludicrous effect, she clapped her hands and laughed, laughed, till the tears ran down her cheeks. "If you could see yourself now!" she cried. Offended by her laughter, "You play with me as though I were a doll," Tonino would protest with a rather ludicrous expression of angry dignity. The laughter would go out of Moira's face and with a seriousness that was fierce, almost cruel, she would lean forward and kiss him, silently, violently, again and again.

Absent, he was still unescapably with her, like a guilty conscience. Her solitudes were endless meditations on the theme of him. Sometimes the longing for his tangible presence was too achingly painful to be borne. Disobeying all his injunctions, breaking all her promises, she would telephone for him to come to her, she would drive off in search of him. Once, at about midnight, Tonino was called down from his room at the hotel by a message that a lady wanted to speak to him. He found her sitting in the car. "But I couldn't help it. I simply couldn't help it!" she cried to excuse herself and mollify his anger. Tonino refused to be propitiated. Coming like this in the middle of the night! It was madness, it was scandalous! She sat there, listening, pale and with trembling lips and the tears in her eyes. He was silent at last. "But if you knew, Tonino," she whispered, "if you only knew . . ." She took his hand and kissed it, humbly.

Berto, when he heard the good news (for Tonino proudly told him at once) was curious to know whether the *signora forestiera* was as cold as northern ladies were proverbially supposed to be.

"*Macchè!*" Tonino protested vigorously. On the contrary. For a long time the two young sportsmen discussed the question of amorous temperatures, discussed it technically, professionally.

Tonino's raptures were not so extravagant as Moira's. So far as he was concerned, this sort of thing had happened before. Passion with Moira was not diminished by satisfaction, but rather, since the satisfaction was for her so novel, so intrinsically apocalyptic, increased. But that which caused her passion to increase produced in his a waning. He had got what he wanted; his night-begotten, touch-born longing for her (dulled in the interval and diminished by all the sporting love-hunts undertaken with Berto) had been fulfilled. She was no longer the desired and unobtainable, but the possessed, the known. By her surrender she had lowered herself to the level of all the other women he had ever made love to; she was just another item in the sportsman's grand total.

His attitude towards her underwent a change. Familiarity began to blunt his courtesy; his manner became offhandedly marital. When he saw her after an absence, "*Ebbene, tesoro,*" he would say in a genially unromantic tone, and pat her once or twice on the back or shoulder, as one might pat a horse. He permitted her to run her own errands and even his. Moira was happy to be his servant. Her love for him was, in one at least of its aspects, almost abject. She was dog-like in her devotion. Tonino found her adoration very agreeable so long as it expressed itself in fetching and carrying, in falling in with his suggestions, and in making him presents. "But you mustn't, my darling, you shouldn't," he protested each time she gave him something. Nevertheless, he accepted a pearl tie-pin, a pair of diamond and enamel links, a half-hunter on a gold and platinum chain. But Moira's devotion expressed itself also in other ways. Love demands as much as it gives. She wanted so much—his heart, his physical presence, his caresses, his confidences, his time, his fidelity. She was tyrannous in her adoring abjection. She pestered him with devotion. Tonino was bored and irritated by her excessive love. The omniscient Berto, to whom he carried his troubles, advised him to take a strong line. Women, he pronounced, must be kept in their places, firmly. They love one all the better if they are a little maltreated.

48. "*Macchè!*" "But no!"

485

Tonino followed his advice and pretexting work and social engagements, reduced the number of his visits. What a relief to be free of her importunity! Disquieted, Moira presented him with an amber cigar-holder. He protested, accepted it, but gave her no more of his company in return. A set of diamond studs produced no better effect. He talked vaguely and magniloquently about his career and the necessity for unremitting labour; that was his excuse for not coming more often to see her. It was on the tip of her tongue, one afternoon, to say that *she* would be his career, would give him anything he wanted, if only . . . But the memory of John's hateful words made her check herself. She was terrified lest he might make no difficulties about accepting her offer. "Stay with me this evening," she begged, throwing her arms round his neck. He suffered himself to be kissed.

"I wish I could stay," he said hypocritically. "But I have some important business this evening." The important business was playing billiards with Berto.

Moira looked at him for a moment in silence; then, dropping her hands from his shoulders, turned away. She had seen in his eyes a weariness that was almost a horror.

Summer drew on; but in Moira's soul there was no inward brightness to match the sunshine. She passed her days in a misery that was alternately restless and apathetic. Her nerves began once more to lead their own irresponsible life apart from hers. For no sufficient cause and against her will, she would find herself uncontrollably in a fury, or crying, or laughing. When Tonino came to see her, she was almost always, in spite of all her resolutions, bitterly angry or hysterically tearful. "But why do I behave like this?" she would ask herself despairingly. "Why do I say such things? I'm making him hate me." But the next time he came, she would act in precisely the same way. It was as though she were possessed by a devil. And it was not her mind only that was sick. When she ran too quickly upstairs, her heart seemed to stop beating for a moment and there was a whirling darkness before her eyes. She had an almost daily headache, lost appetite, could not digest what she ate. In her thin sallow face her

eyes became enormous. Looking into the glass, she found herself hideous, old, repulsive. "No wonder he hates me," she thought, and she would brood, brood for hours over the idea that she had become physically disgusting to him, disgusting to look at, to touch, tainting the air with her breath. The idea became an obsession, indescribably painful and humiliating.

"*Questa donna!*" Tonino would complain with a sigh, when he came back from seeing her. Why didn't he leave her, then? Berto was all for strong measures. Tonino protested that he hadn't the courage; the poor woman would be too unhappy. But he also enjoyed a good dinner and going for drives in an expensive car and receiving sumptuous additions to his wardrobe. He contented himself with complaining and being a Christian martyr. One evening his old friend Carlo Menardi introduced him to his sister. After that he bore his martyrdom with even less patience than before. Luisa Menardi was only seventeen, fresh, healthy, provocatively pretty, with rolling black eyes that said all sorts of things and an impertinent tongue. Tonino's business appointments became more numerous than ever. Moira was left to brood in solitude on the dreadful theme of her own repulsiveness.

Then, quite suddenly, Tonino's manner towards her underwent another change. He became once more assiduously tender, thoughtful, affectionate. Instead of hardening himself with a shrug of indifference against her tears, instead of returning anger for hysterical anger, he was patient with her, was lovingly and cheerfully gentle. Gradually, by a kind of spiritual infection, she too became loving and gentle. Almost reluctantly—for the devil in her was the enemy of life and happiness—she came up again into the light.

"My dear son," Vasari senior had written in that eloquent and disquieting letter, "I am not one to complain feebly of Destiny; my whole life has been one long act of Faith and unshatterable Will. But there are blows under which even the strongest man must stagger—blows which . . ." The letter rambled on for pages in the same style. The hard unpleasant fact that emerged from under the eloquence was that

59. "*Questa donna!*" "What a woman!"

Tonino's father had been speculating on the Naples stock exchange, speculating unsuccessfully. On the first of the next month he would be required to pay out some fifty thousand francs more than he could lay his hands on. The Grand Hotel Ritz-Carlton was doomed; he might even have to sell the restaurant. Was there anything Tonino could do?

"Is it possible?" said Moira with a sigh of happiness. "It seems too good to be true." She leaned against him; Tonino kissed her eyes and spoke caressing words. There was no moon; the dark-blue sky was thickly constellated; and, like another starry universe gone deliriously mad, the fire-flies darted, alternately eclipsed and shining, among the olive trees. "Darling," he said aloud and wondered if this would be a propitious moment to speak. "Piccina mia." In the end he decided to postpone matters for another day or two. In another day or two, he calculated, she wouldn't be able to refuse him anything.

Tonino's calculations were correct. She let him have the money, not only without hesitation, but eagerly, joyfully. The reluctance was all on his side, in the receiving. He was almost in tears as he took the cheque, and the tears were tears of genuine emotion. "You're an angel," he said, and his voice trembled. "You've saved us all." Moira cried outright as she kissed him. How could John have said those things? She cried and was happy. A pair of silver-backed hair brushes accompanied the cheque —just to show that the money had made no difference to their relationship. Tonino recognized the delicacy of her intention and was touched. "You're too good to me," he insisted, "too good." He felt rather ashamed.

"Let's go for a long drive to-morrow," she suggested.

Tonino had arranged to go with Luisa and her brother to Prato. But so strong was his emotion, that he was on the point of accepting Moira's invitation and sacrificing Luisa.

"All right," he began, and then suddenly thought better of it. After all, he could go out with Moira any day. It was seldom that he had

a chance of jaunting with Luisa. He struck his forehead, he made a despairing face. "But what am I thinking of!" he cried. "To-morrow's the day we're expecting the manager of the hotel company from Milan."

"But must you be there to see him?"

"Alas."

It was too sad. Just how sad Moira only fully realized the next day. She had never felt so lonely, never longed so ardently for his presence and affection. Unsatisfied, her longings were an unbearable restlessness. Hoping to escape from the loneliness and ennui with which she had filled the house, the garden, the landscape, she took out the car and drove away at random, not knowing whither. An hour later she found herself at Pistoia, and Pistoia was as hateful as every other place; she headed the car homewards. At Prato there was a fair. The road was crowded; the air was rich with a haze of dust and the noise of brazen music. In a field near the entrance to the town, the merry-go-round revolved with a glitter in the sunlight. A plunging horse held up the traffic. Moira stopped the car and looked about her at the crowd, at the swings, at the whirling round-abouts, looked with a cold hostility and distaste. Hateful! And suddenly there was Tonino sitting on a swan in the nearest merry-go-round, with a girl in pink muslin sitting in front of him between the white wings and the arching neck. Rising and falling as it went, the swan turned away out of sight. The music played on. But poor poppa, poor poppa, he's got nothin' at all. The swan reappeared. The girl in pink was looking back over her shoulder, smiling. She was very young, vulgarly pretty, shining and plumped with health. Tonino's lips moved; behind the wall of noise what was he saying? All that Moira knew was that the girl laughed; her laughter was like an explosion of sensual young life. Tonino raised his hand and took hold of her bare brown arm. Like an undulating planet, the swan once more wheeled away out of sight. Meanwhile, the plunging horse had been quieted, the traffic had begun to move forward. Behind her a horn

18. "Piccina mia," "My little one." 42. Prato, a town about ten miles northwest of Florence.

64. Pistoia, a town about twenty miles from Florence, beyond Prato.

tooted insistently. But Moira did not stir. Something in her soul desired that the agony should be repeated and prolonged. Hoot, hoot, hoot! She paid no attention. Rising and falling, the swan emerged once more from eclipse. This time Tonino saw her. Their eyes met; the laughter suddenly went out of his face. "*Porco madonna!*" shouted the infuriated motorist behind her. "Can't you move on?" Moira threw the car into gear and shot forward along the dusty road.

The cheque was in the post; there was still time, Tonino reflected, to stop the payment of it.

"You're very silent," said Luisa teasingly, as they drove back towards Florence. Her brother was sitting in front, at the wheel; he had no eyes at the back of his head. But Tonino sat beside her like a dummy.

"Why are you so silent?"

He looked at her, and his face was grave and stonily unresponsive to her bright and dimpling provocations. He sighed; then, making an effort, he smiled, rather wanly. Her hand was lying on her knee, palm upwards, with a pathetic look of being unemployed. Dutifully doing what was expected of him, Tonino reached out and took it.

At half-past six he was leaning his borrowed motor-cycle against the wall of Moira's villa. Feeling like a man who is about to undergo a dangerous operation, he rang the bell.

Moira was lying on her bed, had lain there ever since she came in; she was still wearing her dustcoat, she had not even taken off her shoes. Affecting an easy cheerfulness, as though nothing unusual had happened, Tonino entered almost jauntily.

"Lying down?" he said in a tone of surprised solicitude. "You haven't got a headache, have you?" His words fell, trivial and ridiculous, into abysses of significant silence. With a sinking of the heart, he sat down on the edge of the bed, he laid a hand on her knee. Moira did not stir, but lay with averted face, remote and unmoving. "What is it, my darling?" He patted her soothingly. "You're not upset because I

7. "*Porco madonna!*" "Pig of a woman!"

went to Prato, are you?" he went on, in the incredulous voice of a man who is certain of a negative answer to his question. Still she said nothing. This silence was almost worse than the outcry he had anticipated. Desperately, knowing it was no good, he went on to talk about his old friend, Carlo Menardi, who had come round in his car to call for him; and as the director of the hotel company had left immediately after luncheon—most unexpectedly—and as he'd thought Moira was certain to be out, he had finally yielded and gone along with Carlo and his party. Of course, if he'd realized that Moira hadn't gone out, he'd have asked her to join them. For his own sake her company would have made all the difference.

His voice was sweet, ingratiating, apologetic. "A black-haired pimp from the slums of Naples." John's words reverberated in her memory. And so Tonino had never cared for her at all, only for her money. That other woman . . . She saw again that pink dress, lighter in tone than the sleek, sunburnt skin; Tonino's hand on the bare brown arm; that flash of eyes and laughing teeth. And meanwhile he was talking on and on, ingratiatingly; his very voice was a lie.

"Go away," she said at last, without looking at him.

"But, my darling . . ." Bending over her, he tried to kiss her averted cheek. She turned and, with all her might, struck him in the face.

"You little devil!" he cried, made furious by the pain of the blow. He pulled out his handkerchief and held it to his bleeding lip. "Very well, then." His voice trembled with anger. "If you want me to go, I'll go. With pleasure." He walked heavily away. The door slammed behind him.

But perhaps, thought Moira, as she listened to the sound of his footsteps receding on the stairs, perhaps it hadn't really been as bad as it looked; perhaps she had misjudged him. She sat up; on the yellow counterpane was a little circular red stain—a drop of his blood. And it was she who had struck him.

"Tonino!" she called; but the house was silent. "Tonino!" Still calling, she hurried downstairs, through the hall, out on to the porch. She was just in time to see him riding off through the gate on his motor-cycle. He was steering with one hand; the other still pressed a handkerchief to his mouth.

"Tonino, Tonino!" But either he didn't, or else he wouldn't hear her. The motor-cycle disappeared from view. And because he had gone, because he was angry, because of his bleeding lip, Moira was suddenly convinced that she had been accusing him falsely, that the wrong was all on her side. In a state of painful, uncontrollable agitation she ran to the garage. It was essential that she should catch him, speak to him, beg his pardon, implore him to come back. She started the car and drove out.

"One of these days," John had warned her, "you'll go over the edge of the bank, if you're not careful. It's a horrible turning."

Coming out of the garage door, she pulled the wheel hard over as usual. But too impatient to be with Tonino, she pressed the accelerator at the same time. John's prophecy was fulfilled. The car came too close to the edge of the bank; the dry earth crumbled and slid under its outer wheels. It tilted horribly, tottered for a long instant on the balancing point, and went over.

But for the ilex tree, it would have gone crashing down the slope. As it was, the machine fell only a foot or so and came to rest, leaning drunkenly sideways with its flank against the bole of the tree. Shaken, but quite unhurt, Moira climbed over the edge of the car and dropped to the ground. "Assunta! Giovanni!" The maids, the gardener came running. When they saw what had happened, there was a small babel of exclamations, questions, comments.

"But can't you get it on to the drive again?" Moira insisted to the gardener; because it was necessary, absolutely necessary, that she should see Tonino at once.

Giovanni shook his head. It would take at least four men with levers and a pair of horses. . . .

"Telephone for a taxi, then," she ordered Assunta and hurried into the house. If she remained any longer with those chattering people, she'd begin to scream. Her nerves had come to a separate life again; clenching her fists, she tried to fight them down.

Going up to her room, she sat down before the mirror and began, methodically and with deliberation (it was her will imposing itself on her nerves) to make up her face. She rubbed a little red on to her pale cheeks, painted her lips, dabbed on the powder. "I must look presentable," she thought and put on her smartest hat. But would the taxi never come? She struggled with her impatience. "My purse," she said to herself. "I shall need some money for the cab." She was pleased with herself for being so full of foresight, so coolly practical in spite of her nerves. "Yes, of course; my purse."

But where was the purse? She remembered so clearly having thrown it on to the bed when she came in from her drive. It was not there. She looked under the pillow, lifted the counterpane. Or perhaps it had fallen on the floor. She looked under the bed; the purse wasn't there. Was it possible that she hadn't put it on the bed at all? But it wasn't on her dressing-table, or on the mantelpiece, or on any of the shelves, or in any of the drawers of her wardrobe. Where, where, where? And suddenly a terrible thought occurred to her. Tonino. . . . Was it possible? The seconds passed. The possibility became a dreadful certainty. A thief as well as . . . John's words echoed in her head. "Black-haired pimp from the slums of Naples, black-haired pimp from the slums. . . ." And a thief as well. The bag was made of gold chainwork; there were more than four thousand lire in it. A thief, a thief. . . . She stood quite still, strained, rigid, her eyes staring. Then something broke, something seemed to collapse within her. She cried aloud as though under a sudden intolerable pain.

The sound of the shot brought them running upstairs. They found her lying face downwards across the bed, still faintly breathing. But she was dead before the doctor could come up from the town. On a bed standing, as hers stood, in an alcove, it was difficult to lay out the body. When they moved it out of its recess, there was the sound of a hard, rather metallic fall. Assunta bent down to see what had dropped.

"It's her purse," she said. "It must have got stuck between the bed and the wall."

NOEL COWARD

Teddington, Middlesex, was the birthplace in 1899 of the most versatile English dramatist of the 1920's and 1930's, Noel Pierce Coward. Coward's father was associated with a London firm of music publishers, and later traveled as a salesman of pianos. His mother early encouraged her son's evident dramatic and musical talents, somewhat at the expense of his formal schooling. The boy made his first professional appearance on the stage in 1910, and thereafter energetically pursued a theatrical career. Called up for military service in 1918, he found his way into the Artists' Rifles O.T.C., but a head injury during training kept him hospitalized for most of his term in the Army.

Soon after he was released from the service, Coward became interested in another aspect of the theater, and at eighteen he wrote his first full-length play, *I'll Leave It to You,* which was unsuccessfully staged in 1920. After several equally short-lived and light-hearted ventures, he produced in 1923 a serious work which finally brought him recognition as a dramatist. *The Vortex* is a powerful play of a young decadent in the 1920's and of his equally decadent mother—a sort of twentieth-century Hamlet disillusioned by Gertrude and her immorality. Despite the seriousness of the drama, Coward had opportunity to display plenty of his characteristic wit, of much the same paradoxical nature as that of Oscar Wilde and George Bernard Shaw. It was this wittiness which he proceeded to develop to a high excellence in the sophisticated drawing-room comedies which followed *The Vortex.* Among the better known of these, *Hay Fever* (1925) has long been one of Coward's favorites, although it is one of his few plays in which there is no suitable rôle for himself. In *Private Lives* (1930), Coward presents the unusual situation of a divorced couple's meeting on their respective second honeymoons, and abandoning their new mates for each other—at least temporarily. *Design for Living* (1933) is a typically iconoclastic Coward comedy in which

two men are so devoted to the same woman and to each other that they arrange an unorthodox *ménage à trois.* Not quite so strong is *Blithe Spirit* (1941), which depicts the nagging and haunting of a couple by the man's deceased first wife; all three are united in death, with somewhat appalling prospects. *Present Laughter* (1943) is in some ways a satiric caricature of Coward himself, but the brittle sophistication already begins to appear a little dated. Though the tone in all these comedies is clever, light, even flippant, and brilliantly satirical of society, there is an undertone of the cynical and amoral that will not be suppressed. Yet Coward would insist that the various outrageous situations offered in these plays are never intended to apply to society in general but only to the characters immediately concerned in the plays.

With the feeling for convincing staging and the ability to construct felicitously entertaining dialogue which have made his plays so popular, Coward has combined a third talent—the ability to compose appealing music—to produce a number of successful operettas and musical comedies. The best remembered of these are probably *Bittersweet* (1929) and *Conversation Piece* (1934). In these Coward demonstrates his versatility by creating an atmosphere of sentiment which yet manages to avoid mawkishness. *Cavalcade* (1931) and *This Happy Breed* (1943) are nostalgic panorama-plays; each describes events in the lives of an English family—the first, a family of culture in the first generation of the twentieth century; the second, a middle-class family between the First and Second World Wars. The collection of one-act plays, *Tonight at 8:30* (1936), represents a sort of summation of Coward's work; they range from farce to brutal satire to tender romance, and each of the eight is an example of Coward's fine craftsmanship.

Coward, as he admits in his autobiography, *Present Indicative,* is frankly egocentric; and his self-importance is reflected in the occasional showiness, arrogance, and affectation of some of his work. Yet he succeeds in being the most effective writer of English drama since Oscar Wilde and the earlier works of George Bernard Shaw: he has greater versatility than Wilde and he is a better dramatic craftsman than Shaw. Few can deny that his writing is marked by an unusual combination of wit, humor, insight, and fundamental professional sincerity.

Fumed Oak

A Comedy in Two Scenes

CHARACTERS

HENRY GOW
DORIS, *his wife*
ELSIE, *his daughter*
MRS. ROCKETT, *his mother-in-law*

SCENE I—*Morning*
SCENE II—*Evening*

The action of the play passes in the sitting-room of the Gows' house in South London. The time is the present day.

SCENE I

The Gows' sitting-room is indistinguishable from several thousand other suburban sitting-rooms. The dominant note is refinement. There are French windows at the back opening on to a narrow lane of garden. These are veiled discreetly by lace curtains set off by a pelmet and side pieces of rather faded blue casement cloth. There is a tiled fireplace on the right; an upright piano between it and the window; a fumed oak sideboard on the left and, below it, a door leading to the hall, the stairs of the front door. There is a fumed oak dining-room suite consisting of a table, and six chairs; a sofa; an armchair in front of the fire; a radio, and a plentiful sprinkling over the entire room of ornaments and framed photographs.
When the curtain rises it is about eight-thirty on a spring morning. Rain is trickling down

the windows and breakfast is laid on the table.
MRS. ROCKETT *is seated in the armchair by the fire; on a small table next to her is a cup of tea, and a work-basket. She is a fattish grey-looking woman dressed in a blouse and skirt and a pepper and salt jumper of artificial silk. Her pince-nez snap in and out of a little clip on her bosom and her feet are bad which necessitates the wearing of large quilted slippers in the house.*
DORIS, *aged about thirty-five, is seated at the table reading a newspaper propped up against the cruet. She is thin and anæmic and whatever traces of past prettiness she might have had are obscured by the pursed-up, rather sour geniality of her expression. She wears a nondescript coat-frock, a slave bangle and a necklace of amber glass beads.*
ELSIE, *her daughter aged about fourteen, is sitting opposite to her, cutting her toast into strips in order to dip them into her boiled egg. She is a straight-haired ordinary-looking girl dressed in a navy blue school dress with a glacé red leather waist belt.*
There is a complete silence broken only by the occasional rattle of a spoon in a cup or a sniffle from ELSIE *who has a slight head cold.*
HENRY GOW *comes into the room. He is tall and spare, neatly dressed in a blue serge suit. He wears rimless glasses and his hair is going grey at the sides and thin on the top. He sits down at the table without a word.*
DORIS *automatically rises and goes out, returning in a moment with a plate of haddock which she places in front of him and resumes her place.* HENRY *pours himself out some tea.* DORIS, *without looking at him, being immersed in the paper, passes him the milk and sugar.*
The silence continues until ELSIE *breaks it.*

ELSIE. Mum?
DORIS. What?
ELSIE. When can I put my hair up?
DORIS (*Snappily*). When you're old enough.
ELSIE. Gladys Pierce is the same age as me and she's got hers up.
DORIS. Never you mind about Gladys Pierce, get on with your breakfast.
ELSIE. I don't see why I can't have it cut. That would be better than nothing.   10

This remark is ignored.

Maisie Blake had hers cut last week and it looks lovely.

DORIS. Never you mind about Maisie Blake neither. She's common.

ELSIE. Miss Pritchard doesn't think so. Miss Pritchard likes Maisie Blake a lot, she said it looked ever so nice.

DORIS (*Irritably*). What?

ELSIE. Her hair.

DORIS. Get on with your breakfast. You'll be late.

ELSIE (*Petulantly*). Oh, Mum——

DORIS. And stop sniffling. Sniffle sniffle sniffle! Haven't you got a handkerchief?

ELSIE. Yes, but it's a clean one.

DORIS. Never mind, use it.

MRS. ROCKETT. The child can't help having a cold.

DORIS. She can blow her nose, can't she, even if she has got a cold?

ELSIE (*Conversationally*). Dodie Watson's got a terrible cold, she's had it for weeks. It went to her chest and then it went back to her head again.

MRS. ROCKETT. That's the worst of schools, you're always catching something.

ELSIE. Miss Pritchard's awful mean to Dodie Watson, she said she'd had enough of it.

DORIS. Enough of what?

ELSIE. Her cold.

There is silence again which is presently shattered by the wailing of a baby in the house next door.

MRS. ROCKETT. There's that child again. It kept me awake all night.

DORIS. I'm very sorry, I'm sure.

MRS. ROCKETT (*Fiddling in her work-basket*). I wasn't blaming you.

DORIS. The night before last it was the hot-water pipes.

MRS. ROCKETT. You ought to have them seen to.

DORIS. You know as well as I do you can't stop them making that noise every now and then.

MRS. ROCKETT (*Threading a needle*). I'm sure I don't know why you don't get a plumber in.

DORIS (*Grandly*). Because I do not consider it necessary.

MRS. ROCKETT. You would if you slept in my room—gurgle gurgle gurgle all night long—it's all very fine for you, you're at the end of the passage.

DORIS (*With meaning*). You don't have to sleep there.

MRS. ROCKETT. What do you mean by that?

DORIS. You know perfectly well what I mean.

MRS. ROCKETT (*With spirit*). Listen to me, Doris Gow. I've got a perfect right to complain if I want to and well you know it. It isn't as if I was staying here for nothing.

DORIS. I really don't know what's the matter with you lately, Mother, you do nothing but grumble.

MRS. ROCKETT. Me, grumble! I like that, I'm sure. That's rich, that is.

DORIS. Well, you do. It gives me a headache.

MRS. ROCKETT. You ought to do something about those headaches of yours. They seem to pop on and off at the least thing.

DORIS. And I wish you wouldn't keep passing remarks about not staying here for nothing.

MRS. ROCKETT. Well, it's true, I don't.

DORIS. Anyone would think we was taking advantage of you.

MRS. ROCKETT. Well, they wouldn't be far wrong.

DORIS. Mother, how can you! You're not paying a penny more than you can afford.

MRS. ROCKETT. I never said I was. It isn't the money, it's the lack of consideration.

DORIS. Pity you don't go and live with Nora for a change.

MRS. ROCKETT. Nora hasn't got a spare room.

DORIS. Phyllis has, a lovely one, looking out over the railway. I'm sure her hot-water pipes wouldn't annoy you, there isn't hot water in them.

MRS. ROCKETT. Of course, if I'm not wanted here, I can always go to a boarding-house or a private hotel.

DORIS. Catch you!

MRS. ROCKETT. I'm not the sort to outstay my welcome anywhere——

DORIS. Oh, for heaven's sake don't start that again——

MRS. ROCKETT (*Addressing the air*). It seems as though some of us had got out of bed the wrong side this morning.

ELSIE. Mum, can I have some more toast?

DORIS. No.

ELSIE. I could make it myself over the kitchen fire.

DORIS. No, I tell you. Can't you understand plain English? You've had quite enough and you'll be late for school.

MRS. ROCKETT. Never mind, Elsie, here's twopence, you can buy yourself a sponge-cake at Barret's.

ELSIE (*Taking the twopence*). Thanks, Grandma.

DORIS. You'll do no such thing, Elsie. I'm not going to have a child of mine stuffing herself with cake in the middle of the High Street.

MRS. ROCKETT (*Sweetly*). Eat it in the shop, dear.

DORIS. Go on, you'll be late.

ELSIE. Oh, Mum, it's only ten to.

DORIS. Do as I tell you.

ELSIE. Oh, all right.

She goes sullenly out of the room and can be heard scampering noisily up the stairs.

MRS. ROCKETT (*Irritatingly*). Poor little soul.

DORIS. I'll trouble you not to spoil Elsie, Mother.

MRS. ROCKETT. Spoil her! I like that. Better than half starving her.

DORIS (*Hotly*). Are you insinuating——

MRS. ROCKETT. I'm not insinuating anything. Elsie's getting a big girl, she only had one bit of toast for her breakfast and she used that for her egg. I saw her.

DORIS. It's none of your business and in future I'd be much obliged if you'd keep your twopences to yourself.

MRS. ROCKETT (*Hurt*). Very well, of course if I'm to be abused every time I try to bring a little happiness into the child's life——

DORIS. Anyone would think I ill-treated her the way you talk.

MRS. ROCKETT. You certainly nag her enough.

DORIS. I don't do any such thing and I wish you'd be quiet.

She flounces up from the table and goes over to the window, where she stands drumming her fingers on the pane. HENRY *quietly appropriates the newspaper she has flung down.*

MRS. ROCKETT (*Unctuously*). There's no need to lose your temper.

DORIS. I am not losing my temper.

MRS. ROCKETT. If I'd known when you were Elsie's age what you were going to turn out like I'd have given you what for, I can tell you.

DORIS. Pity you didn't, I'm sure.

MRS. ROCKETT. One thing, I never stinted any of my children.

DORIS. I wish you'd leave me to bring up my own child in my own way.

MRS. ROCKETT. That cold's been hanging over her for weeks and a fat lot you care——

DORIS. I've dosed her for it, haven't I? The whole house stinks of Vapex. What more can I do?

MRS. ROCKETT. She ought to have had Doctor Bristow last Saturday when it was so bad. He'd have cleared it up in no time.

DORIS. You and your Doctor Bristow.

MRS. ROCKETT. Nice thing if it turned to bronchitis. Mrs. Henderson's Muriel got bronchitis, all through neglecting a cold; the poor child couldn't breathe, they had to have two kettles going night and day——

DORIS. I suppose your precious Doctor Bristow told you that.

MRS. ROCKETT. Yes, he did, and what's more he saved the girl's life, you ask Mrs. Henderson.

DORIS. Catch me asking Mrs. Henderson anything, not likely, stuck up thing——

MRS. ROCKETT. Mrs. Henderson's a very nice lady-like woman; just because she's quiet and a bit reserved you say she's stuck up——

DORIS. Who does she think she is, anyway, Lady Mountbatten?

MRS. ROCKETT. Really, Doris, you make me tired sometimes, you do really.

DORIS. If you're so fond of Mrs. Henderson it's a pity you don't see more of her. I notice you don't go there often.

MRS. ROCKETT (*With dignity*). I go when I am invited.

DORIS (*Triumphantly*). Exactly.

MRS. ROCKETT. She's not the kind of woman that likes people dropping in and out all the time. We can't all be Amy Fawcetts.

DORIS. What's the matter with Amy Fawcett?

ELSIE *comes into the room wearing a mackintosh and a tam-o'-shanter. She stamps over to the piano and begins to search untidily through the pile of music on it.*

MRS. ROCKETT. Well, she's common for one thing, she dyes her hair for another, and she's a bit too free and easy all round for my taste.

DORIS. She doesn't put on airs, anyway.

MRS. ROCKETT. I should think not, after the sort of life she's led.

DORIS. How do you know what sort of a life she's led?

MRS. ROCKETT. Everybody knows, you only have to look at her; I'm a woman of the world, I am, and you can't pull the wool over my eyes——

DORIS. Don't untidy everything like that, what are you looking for?

ELSIE. 'The Pixie's Parade'; I had it last night.

DORIS. If it's the one with the blue cover it's at the bottom.

ELSIE. It isn't—oh, dear, Miss Pritchard will be mad at me if I can't find it.

MRS. ROCKETT. Perhaps you put it in your satchel, dear, here, let me look—— (She opens ELSIE's satchel, which is hanging over the back of a chair and fumbles in it.) Is this it?

ELSIE. Oh, yes; thanks Grandma.

DORIS. Go along now, for heaven's sake, you'll be late.

ELSIE. Oh, all right, Mum. Good-bye, Mum, good-bye, Grandma, good-bye, Dad.

HENRY. Good-bye.

MRS. ROCKETT. Good-bye, dear, give Grandma a kiss.

ELSIE does so.

DORIS. Don't dawdle on the way home.

ELSIE. Oh, all right, Mum.

She goes out. The slam of the front door shakes the house.

DORIS (Irritably). There now.

MRS. ROCKETT (With studied politeness). If you are going down to the shops this morning, would it be troubling you too much to get me a reel of white cotton?

DORIS. I thought you were coming with me.

MRS. ROCKETT. I really don't feel up to it.

DORIS. I'll put it on my list.

She takes a piece of paper out of the sideboard drawer and scribbles on it.

MRS. ROCKETT. If it's out of your way, please don't trouble, it'll do another time.

DORIS. Henry, it's past nine.

HENRY (Without looking up). I know.

DORIS. You'll be late.

HENRY. Never mind.

DORIS. That's a nice way to talk, I must say.

MRS. ROCKETT. I'm sure if my Robert had ever lazed about like that in the mornings, I'd have thought the world had come to an end.

DORIS. Henry'll do it once too often, mark my words.

MRS. ROCKETT (Biting off her thread). Well, that corner's finished.

DORIS (To HENRY). You'll have to move now, I've got to clear.

HENRY (Rising—absently). All right.

MRS. ROCKETT. Where's Ethel?

DORIS. Doing the bedroom.

She takes a tray which is leaning against the wall by the sideboard and proceeds to stack the breakfast things on to it.

HENRY quietly goes out of the room.

DORIS. Look at that wicked waste.

Throws more scraps in fire.

MRS. ROCKETT. What's the matter with him?

DORIS. Don't ask me, I'm sure I couldn't tell you.

MRS. ROCKETT. He came in very late last night, I heard him go into the bathroom. (There is a pause.) That cistern makes a terrible noise.

DORIS. Does it indeed!

MRS. ROCKETT. Yes, it does.

DORIS (Slamming the teapot on the tray). Very sorry, I'm sure.

MRS. ROCKETT. Where'd he been?

DORIS. How do I know?

MRS. ROCKETT. Didn't you ask him?

DORIS. I wouldn't demean myself.

MRS. ROCKETT. Been drinking?

DORIS. No.

MRS. ROCKETT. Sounded very like it to me, all that banging about.

DORIS. You know Henry never touches a drop.

MRS. ROCKETT. I know he says he doesn't.

DORIS. Oh, do shut up, Mother, we're not all like father.

MRS. ROCKETT. You watch your tongue, Doris Gow, don't let me hear you saying anything against the memory of your poor father.

DORIS. I wasn't.

MRS. ROCKETT (Belligerently). Oh yes, you were, you were insinuating again.

DORIS (*Hoisting up the tray*). Father drank and you know it—everybody knew it.

MRS. ROCKETT. You're a wicked woman.

DORIS. It's true.

MRS. ROCKETT. Your father was a gentleman, which is more than your husband will ever be, with all his night-classes and his book reading—night-classes indeed!

DORIS. Who's insinuating now?

MRS. ROCKETT (*Angrily*). I am, and I'm not afraid to say so.

DORIS. What of it?

MRS. ROCKETT (*With heavy sarcasm*). I suppose he was at a night-class last night?

DORIS (*Loudly*). Mind your own business.

HENRY *comes in wearing his mackintosh and a bowler hat.*

HENRY. What's up?

DORIS. Where were you last night?

HENRY. Why?

DORIS. Mother wants to know and so do I.

HENRY. I was kept late at the shop and I had a bit of dinner in town.

DORIS. Who with?

HENRY. Charlie Henderson.

He picks up the paper off the table and goes out. After a moment the front door slams.

The baby next door bursts into fresh wails.

MRS. ROCKETT. There goes that child again. It's my belief it's hungry.

DORIS. Wonder you don't go and give it twopence to buy sponge-cake.

She pulls the door open with her foot and goes out with the tray as the lights fade on the scene.

SCENE II

It is about seven-thirty in the evening. ELSIE *is sitting at the piano practising with the loud pedal firmly down all the time.*

MRS. ROCKETT *is sitting in her chair by the fire, but she is dressed in her street things and wearing a black hat with a veil.*

DORIS, *also in street clothes, is clearing some paper patterns and pieces of material from the table.*

There is a cloth across the end of the table on which is set a loaf, a plate of cold ham, a saucer with two tomatoes in it, a bottle of A.1 *sauce and a teapot, teacup, sugar basin and milk jug.*

HENRY *comes in, taking off his mackintosh. He gives one look round the room and goes out into the hall again to hang up his things.* ELSIE *stops playing and comes over to* DORIS.

ELSIE. Can we go now?

DORIS. In a minute.

ELSIE. We'll miss the Mickey.

DORIS. Put on your hat and don't worry.

ELSIE (*Grabbing her hat from the sideboard*). Oh, all right.

HENRY *re-enters.*

DORIS. Your supper's all ready; the kettle's on the gas stove when you want it. We've had ours.

HENRY. Oh!

DORIS. And you needn't look injured, either.

HENRY. Very well.

DORIS. If you managed to get home a bit earlier it'd save a lot of trouble all round.

HENRY (*Amiably*). Sorry, dear.

DORIS. It's all very fine to be sorry, you've been getting later and later these last few weeks, they can't keep you overtime every night.

HENRY. All right, dear; I'll tell them.

DORIS. Here, Elsie, put these away in the cupboard.

She hands her a pile of material and pieces of paper. ELSIE *obediently takes them and puts them in the left-hand cupboard of the sideboard.*

HENRY (*Sitting at the table*). Cold ham, what a surprise!

DORIS (*Looking at him sharply*). What's the matter with it?

HENRY. I don't know, yet.

DORIS. It's perfectly fresh, if that's what you mean?

HENRY. Why are you all so dressed up?

ELSIE. We're going to the pictures.

HENRY. Oh, I see.

DORIS. You can put everything on the tray when you've finished and leave it in the kitchen for Ethel.

HENRY. Good old Ethel.

DORIS (*Surprised*). What?

HENRY. I said good old Ethel.

DORIS. Well, it sounded very silly, I'm sure.

MRS. ROCKETT (*Scrutinizing him*). What's the matter with you?

HENRY. Nothing, why?

MRS. ROCKETT. You look funny.

HENRY. I feel funny.

MRS. ROCKETT. Have you been drinking?

HENRY. Yes.

DORIS. Henry!

MRS. ROCKETT. I knew it.

10 HENRY. I had a whisky and soda in town and another one at the Plough.

DORIS (*Astounded*). What for?

HENRY. Because I felt like it.

DORIS. You ought to be ashamed of yourself.

HENRY. I'm going to have another one too, a bit later on.

DORIS. You'll do no such thing.

HENRY. That hat looks awful.

DORIS (*Furiously*). Don't you speak to me 20 like that.

HENRY. Why not?

DORIS (*Slightly nonplussed*). Because I won't have it, so there.

HENRY. It's a common little hat and it looks awful.

DORIS (*With an admirable effort at control*). Now listen to me, Henry Gow, the next time I catch you drinking and coming home here and insulting me, I'll——

30 HENRY (*Interrupting her gently*). What will you do, Dorrie?

DORIS (*Hotly*). I'll give you a piece of my mind, that's what I'll do.

HENRY. It'll have to be a very little piece, Dorrie, you can't afford much! (*He laughs delighted at his own joke.*)

DORIS. I'd be very much obliged if you'd kindly tell me what this means.

HENRY. I'm celebrating.

40 DORIS. What do you mean, celebrating? What are you talking about?

HENRY. To-night's our anniversary.

DORIS. Don't talk so soft; our anniversary's not until November.

HENRY. I don't mean that one. Tonight's the anniversary of the first time I had an affair with you and you got in the family way.

DORIS (*Shrieking*). Henry!

HENRY (*Delighted with his carefully calcu-50 lated effect*). Hurray!

DORIS (*Beside herself*). How dare you say such a dreadful thing, in front of the child, too.

HENRY (*In romantic tones*). Three years and a bit after that wonderful night our child was born! (*Lapsing into his normal voice*). Considering all the time you took forming yourself, Elsie, I'm surprised you're not a nicer little girl than you are.

DORIS. Go upstairs, Elsie.

HENRY. Stay here, Elsie.

DORIS. Do as I tell you.

ELSIE. But, Mum——

DORIS. Mother, take her for God's sake! There's going to be a row.

HENRY (*Firmly*). Leave her alone and sit down.

MRS. ROCKETT hesitates.

Sit down, I tell you.

MRS. ROCKETT (*Subsiding into a chair*). Well, I never, I——

HENRY (*Happily*). See? It works like a charm.

DORIS. A fine exhibition you're making of yourself, I must say.

HENRY. Not bad, is it? As a matter of fact I'm rather pleased with it myself.

DORIS. Go to bed!

HENRY. Stop ordering me about. What right have you got to nag at me and boss me? No right at all. I'm the one that pays the rent and works for you and keeps you. What do you give me in return, I'd like to know! Nothing! I sit through breakfast while you and mother wrangle. You're too busy being snappy and bad-tempered even to say good morning. I come home tired after working all day and ten to one there isn't even a hot dinner for me; here, see this ham? This is what I think of it! (*He throws it at her feet.*) And the tomatoes and the A.1 bloody sauce! (*He throws them too.*)

DORIS (*Screaming*). Henry! All over the carpet.

HENRY (*Throwing the butter-dish face downwards on the floor*). And that's what I think of the carpet, now then!

DORIS. That I should live to see this! That I should live to see the man I married make such a beast of himself!

HENRY. Stop working yourself up into a state, you'll need all your control when you've heard ▶ what I'm going to say to you.

DORIS. Look here——

HENRY. Sit down. We'll all sit down. I'm

afraid you'll have to miss the pictures for once.

DORIS. Elsie, you come with me.

MRS. ROCKETT. Yes, go on, Ducks.

She makes a movement towards the door, but HENRY *is too quick for her. He locks the door and slips the key into his pocket.*

HENRY. I've been dreaming of this moment for many years, and believe me it's not going to be spoiled for me by you running away.

DORIS (*On the verge of tears*). Let me out of this room.

HENRY. You'll stay where you are until I've had my say.

DORIS (*Bursting into tears and sinking down at the table*). Oh! Oh! Oh!——

ELSIE (*Starting to cry too*). Mum—oh, Mum——

HENRY. Here you, shut up, go and get the port out of the sideboard and give some to your mother—go on, do as I tell you.

ELSIE, *terrified and hypnotized into submission, goes to the sideboard cupboard and brings out a bottle of invalid port and some glasses, snivelling as she does so.* DORIS *continues to sob.*

That's right.

MRS. ROCKETT (*Quietly*). You drunken brute, you!

HENRY (*Cheerfully*). Worse than that, Mother, far worse. Just you wait and see.

MRS. ROCKETT (*Ignoring him*). Take some port, Dorrie, it'll do you good.

DORIS. I don't want any—it'd choke me——

HENRY (*Pouring some out*). Come on— here——

DORIS. Keep away from me.

HENRY. Drink it and stop snivelling.

DORIS. I'll never forgive you for this, never, never, never as long as I live!

She gulps down some port.

HENRY (*Noting her gesture*). That's better.

MRS. ROCKETT. Pay no attention, Dorrie, he's drunk.

HENRY. I'm not drunk. I've only had two whiskies and sodas, just to give me enough guts to take the first plunge. You'd never believe how scared I was, thinking it over in cold blood. I'm not scared any more, though, it's much easier than I thought it was going to be. My only regret is that I didn't come to the boil a long time ago, and tell you to your face, Dorrie, what I think of you, what I've been think-ing of you for years, and this horrid little kid, and that old bitch of a mother of yours.

MRS. ROCKETT (*Shrilly*). Henry Gow!

HENRY. You heard me, old bitch was what I said, and old bitch was what I meant.

MRS. ROCKETT. Let me out of this room, I'm not going to stay here and be insulted—I'm not——

HENRY. You're going to stay here just as long as I want you to.

MRS. ROCKETT. Oh, am I? We'll see about that——

With astonishing quickness she darts over to the window and manages to drag one open. HENRY *grabs her by the arm.*

HENRY. No, you don't.

MRS. ROCKETT. Let go of me.

DORIS. Oh, Mother, don't let the neighbours know all your business.

HENRY. Not on your life!

MRS. ROCKETT (*Suddenly screaming power-fully*). Help! Help! Police! Help! Mrs. Harri-son—help!——

HENRY *drags her away from the window, turns her round and gives her a light slap on the face, she staggers against the piano, mean-while he shuts the window again, locks it and pockets the key.*

DORIS (*Looking at him in horror*). Oh, God! Oh, my God!

ELSIE (*Bursting into tears again*). Oh, Mum, Mum, he hit Grandma! Oh, Mum——

She runs to DORIS, *who puts her arm round her protectively.*

MRS. ROCKETT (*Gasping*). Oh—my heart! I think I'm going to faint—oh—my heart——

HENRY. Don't worry, I'll bring you round if you faint——

MRS. ROCKETT. Oh—oh—oh, dear——

MRS. ROCKETT *slides on to the floor, percepti-bly breaking her fall by clinging on to the pi-ano stool.*

DORIS *jumps up from the table.*

DORIS. Mother!

HENRY. Stay where you are.

HENRY *goes to the sideboard and pours out a glass of water.* DORIS, *disobeying him, runs over to her mother.* ELSIE *wails.*

HENRY. Stand out of the way, Doris, we don't all want to get wet.

He approaches with the glass of water. MRS. ROCKETT *sits up weakly.*

497

MRS. ROCKETT (*In a far-away voice*). Where am I?

HENRY. Number Seventeen Cranworth Road, Clapham.

MRS. ROCKETT. Oh—oh, dear!

HENRY. Look here, Mother, I don't want there to be any misunderstanding about this. I liked slapping you just now, see? It was lovely, and if you don't behave yourself and keep quiet
10 I shall slap you again. Go and sit in your chair and remember if you feel faint the water's all ready for you.

He helps her up and escorts her to her chair by the fire. She collapses into it and looks at him balefully.

Now then. Sit down, Dorrie, you look silly standing about.

DORIS (*With a great effort at control*). Henry——

HENRY (*Slowly, but very firmly*). Sit down! And keep Elsie quiet or I'll fetch her one, too.

DORIS (*With dignity*). Come here, Elsie.
20 Shut up, will you!

She sits at the table, with ELSIE.

HENRY. That's right.

He walks round the room slowly and in silence, looking at them with an expression of the greatest satisfaction on his face. Finally he goes over to the fireplace; MRS. ROCKETT *jumps slightly as he approaches her, but he smiles at her reassuringly and lights a cigarette. Meanwhile* DORIS, *recovering from her fear, is beginning to simmer with rage, she remains still, however, watching.*

Now then. I'm going to start, quite quietly, explaining a few things to you.

DORIS. Enjoying yourself, aren't you.

HENRY. You've said it.

DORIS (*Gaining courage*). You'll grin on the other side of your face before I've done with you.

HENRY (*Politely*). Very likely, Dorrie, very
30 likely indeed!

DORIS. And don't you Dorrie me, either! Coming home here drunk, hitting poor mother and frightening Elsie out of her wits.

HENRY. Maybe it'll do her good, do 'em both good, a little excitement in the home. God knows, it's dull enough as a rule.

DORIS (*With biting sarcasm*). Very clever, oh, very clever, I'm sure.

HENRY. Fifteen, no sixteen years ago tonight, Dorrie, you and me had a little rough and tumble in your Aunt Daisy's house in Stansfield Road, do you remember?

DORIS. Henry——

HENRY (*Ignoring her*). We had the house to ourselves, it being a Sunday, your Aunt had popped over to the Golden Calf with Mr. Simmonds, the lodger, which, as the writers say, was her wont——

MRS. ROCKETT. This is disgusting; I won't listen to another word.

HENRY (*Rounding on her*). You will! Shut up!

DORIS. Pay no attention, Mother, he's gone mad.

HENRY. Let me see now, where was I? Oh yes, Stansfield Road. You had been after me for a long while, Dorrie, I didn't know it then, but I realized it soon after. You had to have a husband, what with Nora married and Phyllis engaged, both of them younger than you, you had to have a husband, and quick, so you fixed on me. You were pretty enough and I fell for it, hook, line and sinker; then, a couple of months later you'd told me you'd clicked, you cried a hell of a lot, I remember, said the disgrace would kill your mother if she ever found out. I didn't know then that it'd take a sight more than that to kill that leathery old mare——

MRS. ROCKETT (*Bursting into tears*). I won't stand it, I won't! I won't!

HENRY (*Rising above her sobs*). I expect you were in on the whole business, in a refined way, of course, you knew what was going on all right, you knew that Dorrie was no more in the family way than I was, but we got married; you both saw to that, and I chucked up all the plans I had for getting on, perhaps being a steward in a ship and seeing a bit of the world. Oh yes, all that had to go, and we settled down in rooms and I went into Ferguson's Hosiery.

DORIS. I've given you the best years of my life and don't you forget it.

HENRY. You've never given me the best of anything, not even yourself. You didn't even have Elsie willingly.

DORIS (*Wildly*). It's not true—stop up your ears, Elsie, don't listen to him; he's wicked—he's wicked——

HENRY (*Grimly*). It's true all right, and you know it as well as I do.

DORIS (*Shrilly*). It was only right that you married me. It was only fair! You took advantage of me, didn't you? You took away my innocence. It was only right that you paid for it.

HENRY. Come off it, Dorrie, don't talk so silly. I was the innocent one, not you. I found out you'd cheated me a long, long time ago, and when I found out, realized it for certain, I started cheating you. Prepare yourself, Dorrie, my girl, you're going to be really upset this time. I've been saving! Every week for over ten years I've been earning a little bit more than you thought I was. I've managed, by hook and by crook, to put by five hundred and seventy-two pounds—d'you hear me?—five hundred and seventy-two pounds!

MRS. ROCKETT (*Jumping to her feet*). Henry! You never have—it's not true——

DORIS (*Also jumping up*). You couldn't have —you'd have given it away—I should have found out——

HENRY. I thought that'd rouse you, but don't get excited, don't get worked up. I haven't got it on me, it's in the bank. And it's not for you, it's for me—all but fifty pounds of it, that much is for you, just fifty pounds, the last you'll ever get from me——

DORIS. Henry! You couldn't be so cruel! You couldn't be so mean!

HENRY. I've done what I think's fair and what I think's fair is a damn sight more than you deserve. I've transferred the freehold of this house into your name, so you'll always have a roof over your head—you can take in lodgers at a pinch, though God help the poor bastards if you do!

DORIS. Five hundred and seventy-two pounds! You've got all that and you're going to leave me to starve!

HENRY. Cut out the drama, Dorrie, and have a look at your mother's savings bank book—I bet you'll find she's got enough to keep you in comfort till the day you die. She soaked her old man plenty, I'm sure—before he took to soaking himself!

MRS. ROCKETT. It's a lie!

HENRY. Now listen to me, Mother Machree—you've 'ad one sock in the jaw this evening and you're not just asking for another, you're sitting up and begging for it.

MRS. ROCKETT. I'll have you up for assault. I'll have the police on you, my fine fellow!

HENRY. They'll have to be pretty nippy—my boat sails first thing in the morning.

DORIS (*Horrified*). Boat!

HENRY. I'm going away. I've got my ticket here in my pocket, and my passport. My passport photo's a fair scream, I wish I could show it to you, but I don't want you to see the nice new name I've got.

DORIS. You can't do it, I can have you stopped by law. It's desertion.

HENRY. That's right, Dorrie, you've said it. Desertion's just exactly what it is.

DORIS (*Breathlessly*). Where are you going, you've got to tell me. Where are you going?

HENRY. Wouldn't you like to know? Maybe Africa, maybe China, maybe Australia. There are lots of places in the world you know nothing about, Dorrie. You've often laughed at me for reading books, but I've found out a hell of a lot from books. There are islands in the South Seas for instance with cocoa palms and turtles and sunshine all the year round—you can live there for practically nothing, then there's Australia or New Zealand, with a little bit of capital I might start in a small way sheep-farming. Think of it; miles and miles of open country stretching as far as the eye can see—good food and fresh air—that might be very nice, that might suit me beautifully. Then there's South America. There are coffee plantations, there, and sugar plantations, and banana plantations. If I go to South America I'll send you a whole crate. 'Ave a banana, Dorrie! 'Ave a banana!

DORIS. Henry, listen to me, you can't do this dreadful thing, you can't! If you don't love me any more, think of Elsie.

HENRY (*Still in his dream*). Then there's the sea, not the sea we know at Worthing with the tide going in and out regular and the band playing on the pier. The real sea's what I mean. The sea that Joseph Conrad wrote about, and Rudyard Kipling and lots of other people too, a sea with whacking great waves and water spouts and typhoons and flying-fish and phosphorus making the foam look as if it was lit up. Those people knew a thing or two I can tell you. They knew what life could be like if you give it a chance. They knew there was a bit more to it than refinement and fumed oak and lace curtains and getting old and miserable with nothing to show for it. I'm a middle-aged man, but my health's not too bad taken all round. There's still time for me to see a little bit of real life before I conk out. I'm still fit enough to do a job of work—real work, mind you—not bowing and scraping and wearing myself out showing fussy old cows the way to the lace and the china ware and the bargain basement.

DORIS (*Hysterically*). God will punish you, you just see if He doesn't, you just see——

HENRY. God's been punishing me for fifteen years, it's high time He laid off me now. He's been punishing me good and proper for being damn fool enough to let you get your claws into me in the first place——

DORIS (*Changing tactics*). Henry, have pity, please don't be so cruel, please—please——

HENRY. And don't start weeping and wailing either, that won't cut any ice with me, I know what you're like, I know you through and through. You're frightened now, scared out of your wits, but give you half a chance and you'd be worse than ever you were. You're a bad lot, Dorrie, not what the world would call a bad lot, but what I call a bad lot. Mean and cold and respectable. Good-bye, Dorrie——

DORIS (*Flinging her arms round him and bursting into tears*). Listen to me, Henry, you've got to listen—you must. You can't leave us to starve, you can't throw us on to the streets —if I've been a bad wife to you, I'm sorry—I'll try to be better, really I will, I swear to God I will—— You can't do this, if you won't forgive me, think of Elsie, think of poor little Elsie——

HENRY. Poor little Elsie, my eye! I think Elsie's awful. I always have ever since she was little. She's never done anything but whine and snivel and try to get something for nothing——

ELSIE (*Wailing*). Oh, Mum, did you hear what he said? Oh, Dad, oh dear——

MRS. ROCKETT (*Comforting her*). There, there, dear, don't listen to him——

HENRY. Elsie can go to work in a year or so, in the meantime, Dorrie, you can go to work yourself, you're quite a young woman still and strong as an ox.—Here's your fifty pounds——

He takes an envelope out of his pocket and throws it on to the table. Then he goes towards the door. DORIS *rushes after him and hangs on to his arm.*

DORIS. Henry, Henry, you shan't go, you shan't——

HENRY (*Struggling with her*). Leave hold of me.

DORIS. Mother, mother—help—help me, don't let him go——

HENRY *frees himself from her and, taking her by the shoulders, forces her back into a chair, then he unlocks the door and opens it.*

HENRY. I'm taking my last look at you, Dorrie. I shall never see you again as long as I live——

DORIS. Mother! Oh God!—oh, my God!——

She buries her head in her arms and starts to sob loudly. ELSIE *runs and joins her, yelling.* MRS. ROCKETT *sits transfixed, staring at him murderously.*

HENRY (*Quietly*). Three generations. Grandmother, Mother and Kid. Made of the same bones and sinews and muscles and glands, millions of you, millions just like you. You're past it now, Mother, you're past the thick of the fray, you're nothing but a music-hall joke, a mother-in-law with a bit of money put by. Dorrie, the next few years will show whether you've got guts or not. Maybe what I'm doing to you will save your immortal soul in the long run, that'd be a bit of all right, wouldn't it? I doubt it, though; your immortal soul's too measly. You're a natural bully and a cheat, and I'm sick of the sight of you; I should also like to take this opportunity of saying that I hate that bloody awful slave bangle and I always have. As for you, Elsie, you've got a chance, it's a slim one, I grant you, but still it's a chance. If you learn to work and be independent and, when the time comes, give what you have to give freely and without demanding life-long payment for it, there's just a bit of hope that you'll turn into a decent human being. At all events, if you'll take one parting piece of advice from your cruel, ungrateful father, you'll spend the first money you ever earn on having your adenoids out. Good-bye, one and all. Nice to have known you!

The wails of DORIS *and* ELSIE *rise in volume as he goes jauntily out, slamming the door behind him.*

(*Curtain*)

✌ Explorers of the Subjective

JAMES JOYCE

James Joyce was born in Dublin on February 2, 1882, one of a large and not very prosperous family whose father was noted chiefly as a fine amateur tenor. James Joyce himself had an excellent voice and for a time considered seriously a professional musical career. The boy is reputed to have developed the writing habit at an early age; when only nine years old, he composed a pamphlet on Charles Stewart Parnell (1846–91), the fiery though unsuccessful leader for Irish independence. Young Joyce was educated at the Jesuit school of Clongowes Wood, then at Belvedere College, and finally at the Royal University in Dublin. Always he seemed the independent, solitary student with great intellectual acquisitiveness and more than the customary amount of self-assurance and sophomoric arrogance. He read copiously at all times; but his first great passion was for the Norwegian dramatist Henrik Ibsen (1828–1906). It was his essay on Ibsen, published in the *Fortnightly Review* (1899), which marked his real debut as an author. To read Ibsen with the proper degree of appreciation, Joyce learned Norwegian in a surprisingly short time; but he regarded this feat as no special achievement, and the fact is that he was always a remarkable linguist, having had command of no less than seventeen languages. In addition to Ibsen, Joyce was extremely fond of the English Elizabethan writers, with whom, in his forthrightness of language, his intellectual audacity, and his fearless delineation of character, he had a great bond of spiritual kinship.

Ireland was reaching the peak of her artistic renaissance at the turn of the century, largely because of the work of William Butler Yeats (p. 91), and nowhere was this renaissance more worth while than in the field of the drama. But Joyce was generally hostile to the efforts of his fellow-countrymen. There are few remarks in literary history more impudent than that attributed to Joyce upon the occasion of his first meeting Yeats; he allegedly said to the man nearly twenty years his senior, "We have met too late; you can learn nothing from me." But even if he did not say this, it represents well enough his attitude toward Yeats. His attack upon the Irish theater, delivered in *The Day of the Rabblement* (1901), meant the opening of an unclosable breach in the relations of Joyce and his Irish contemporaries, although he came later to admire greatly the plays of John Millington Synge (1871–1909), notably *Riders to the Sea* (1904). Yet Joyce found Ireland cramping to his intellectual comfort as did his character Stephen Dedalus in *A Portrait of the Artist As a Young Man,* and so he departed for the Continent. Except for a brief stay in Ireland during 1904 and intermittent visits from 1909 to 1912, Joyce spent the rest of his life in Europe. At first he was in Paris (1903–04). There he briefly studied medicine, but lack of funds prevented his continuing. His temporary return to Dublin was occasioned by the death of his mother in 1904; he made the most of this opportunity to gather material for his collection of short stories, *Dubliners,* which was not published until 1914. Once he had left Ireland again, he settled in Trieste, then a part of Austria-Hungary. In the meantime he had published *Chamber Music* (1907), a small volume of poems, rather delicately cast in the Elizabethan manner and decidedly unoriginal.

His return to Dublin in 1909 meant an unsuccessful experiment in the managing of a moving-picture theater and was otherwise unproductive, unless it be granted that the occasion was favorable for him to renew his impressions of Dublin and its inhabitants. Back in Trieste the First World War caught him; and he, a British subject on Austrian soil, was interned there. Later, however, he and his family were enabled to move to Switzerland, where he wrote an undistinguished play, *Exiles* (1915). In the meantime, as has been observed, *Dubliners* appeared; it contained many glimpses of real places and real people in Dublin and could have done little to endear him to the people of the Irish capital. The stories, however, are very effective—and effective in a distinctly orthodox style; there was as yet no sign of the radical in thought and manner which was to distinguish the later Joyce.

From February 1914 to September 1915, Joyce's first novel, *A Portrait of the Artist As a Young Man*, had been appearing serially in Ezra Pound's periodical, *The Egoist* (p. 259). The work was published in book form the next year (1916). (An earlier version of the *Portrait* was published as *Stephen Hero* in 1946.) It is an intensely autobiographical piece of writing; in Stephen Dedalus we have Joyce himself, embittered at the poverty and querulousness of his family, at what he considered the cant and worldliness of the Catholic Church, at the medieval nature of his teaching and upbringing. There are here many passages of great power and many examples of execrable taste which defy analysis. But for the first time Joyce had attained full stature.

The next few years saw the progressive advance of a serious eye disease which rendered Joyce subject to recurrent attacks of near or complete blindness and which ever after handicapped him severely in the carrying out of his work. With the coming of the Armistice, he and his family moved back to Trieste; but the post-war conditions there made the place extremely undesirable, and so the family moved back to Paris. Here Joyce stayed for most of the remainder of his life, working painfully and fitfully at his writing, making use of large scrawls in red pencil upon large sheets of paper and wearing an all-white costume to make his writing stand out in bolder relief, so that he could see what he was doing. He died rather suddenly, following an operation, in Zurich, Switzerland, on January 13, 1941.

Ulysses began as a serial in *The Little Review* of New York in March 1918, and continued until it was stopped by the authorities in August 1920. Subsequently it was published in Paris in book form (1922). This lengthy novel, one of the most varied and influential works of the twentieth century, has had a stormy career. It has been banned in many places at one time or another and did not get legally into the United States until 1933. It will be described later (pp. 503–06). Joyce's last work, a vast novel called for a long time *Work in Progress*, finally made its appearance under the title *Finnegans Wake*. It consists of five parts—*Anna Livia Plurabelle; Tales Told by Shem and Shaun; Haveth Childers Everywhere; The Mime of Mick, Nick, and the Maggies;* and *Storiella As She Is Syung. Finnegans Wake* was literally a work in progress for some fifteen years. It is impossible to determine its future. In a sense it is a fourth-dimensional work: all history, all time and space are telescoped and seen as the present. All the characters are multiple personalities. The language is virtually a new language; it is a kind of associational shorthand—the word is not so important for its objective meaning as for the image or images it can evoke in the author's mind because of some previous experience he underwent in association with that word. Hence the entire plan of Joyce's later writing, as illustrated by *Finnegans Wake,* is the *reductio ad absurdum* of the subjective; such a plan is bound to be unintelligible except to those who know the author's intimate thoughts on the material about which he is writing. There are set up, in other words, insuperable barriers between Joyce himself and his reader; and one of the fundamental factors in all writing—communication with another—is absent except where the reader has the insight or the intimate knowledge necessary to break down the barriers. All this is extremely illogical, of course, and seems certain to limit Joyce's usefulness as a writer; but it is, after all, only the natural result of the excessive growth of a favorite element of the romantic—self-portrayal through one's own imagination and emotions. The trouble is that to the average reader Joyce came no longer to portray.

There can be little doubt, however, that there are fine passages in *Ulysses* and extreme brilliance of a perverse order. Unquestionably Leopold Bloom and Stephen Dedalus are notable contributions to the gallery of English fictional characters. Almost as striking is Mrs. Bloom, a hearty, coarse, envigorating animal of a woman, "the twentieth-century incarnation of Chaucer's Wife of Bath." In one section of *Ulysses* Joyce has written imitations of the prose styles of all the major periods of English literature—an astonishing *tour de force*. But again, the author gets in the way of his readers; the novel is appallingly difficult reading as a whole, and many pages of drab dullness are there to take away the edge from the razor-like keenness of the frequent fine passages. The structure of the novel is entirely episodic and singularly lacking in dramatic force. It is evident that Joyce's genius lies in the bursts of poetic, minutely observing, Rabelaisian writing in isolated scenes—Stephen Dedalus walking along the shore in the early morning and thinking about a corpse; Mr. Bloom in his peripatetics about the streets of Dublin; the tantalizing behavior of Gerty MacDowell before Mr. Bloom on the beach; the amazing scenes in the brothel, which become the depiction of a twentieth-century Witches' Sabbath or *Walpurgisnacht;* the previously mentioned experiments in the parodying of historical English literary styles—which is infernally clever but, because of its very derivativeness, decadent; the unforgettable subconscious monologue of Mrs. Molly Bloom at the end of the novel.

As a writer Joyce is temperamentally without scruple in his choice of language. He has an impious boldness in his satire, so much so that to the more conservative orthodox thinkers he must stand as a monument of sin. In keeping with other realists of the present day, he has a complete willingness to use the four-letter Anglo-Saxon monosyllables of obscenity. Apart from these naturalistic expressions, Joyce frequently lapses from good taste in his choice of metaphors; and these lapses come when there is no very good reason for them. His learning—and it is considerable—is often used in a strained and obtrusive manner. But his conceptions of the stream of thought—conscious or subconscious—in his characters are nothing short of uncanny. He can give his own subconscious, for example, in Stephen Dedalus; but he can also give us two entirely separate examples of the subconscious in Mr. Bloom and his wife. In short, he is a great creative writer, whatever his shortcomings—and his influence upon almost all writers of fiction in the last two decades is thoroughgoing. One need mention only Virginia Woolf, Hemingway, Faulkner, and Thomas Wolfe as examples of the Joycean style and Joycean vocabulary. No longer is it intelligent to throw up one's hands in horror at the mention of Joyce's work, as did Paul Elmer More; Joyce has, for better or for worse, achieved that which will leave its mark upon English letters for a long time to come.

from Ulysses

[*Ulysses* is the record of a single day (June 16, 1904) in the lives of a few people in Dublin. The chief members of the cast of characters are (1) Leopold Bloom, an advertisement-canvasser of Jewish extraction; (2) Molly Bloom, *née* Marion Tweedy, his wife and a popular singer in Dublin; (3) Stephen Dedalus, the leading character in Joyce's *Portrait of the Artist As a Young Man* (p. 502), who was in that novel James Joyce himself. *Ulysses* is strictly episodic in structure, consisting of eighteen definite episodes written in almost as many different styles and making use of a variety of techniques even within a given episode. A brief indication of each of the episodes follows, with the approximate time of day at which each takes place.

1. (8 A.M.) Stephen Dedalus, who has just returned from a year in Paris (*vide* the biographical sketch of Joyce given on pp. 501 ff.) without having enlarged his "reality of experience," is discovered living in a disused tower overlooking Dublin Bay, in company with Buck Mulligan, a sardonic and loose-mouthed young medical student, and a silly Oxonian named Haines.

2. (10 A.M.) Stephen is giving a lesson in ancient history at Mr. Deasy's School for Boys. He is abstracted and unhappy—for he has been estranged from his family—and the implication is that he will not remain long in his present occupation.

3. (11 A.M.) Stephen, having finished with his class, is walking along the beach, meditating and following the restless flow of his mercurial mind, watching the rising tide which symbolizes the uprushing current of his own thoughts.

(These first three episodes are actually in the nature of an introduction; they represent a bridge between *A Portrait of the Artist As a Young Man* and *Ulysses*. For, as will be observed, there is coming a certain sympathy between Stephen and Mr. Bloom, however much they may differ in other respects; and so a detailed account of Stephen's mentality is part of the psychological background of *Ulysses*, where Mr. Bloom is, after all, the protagonist. We now come to the beginning of Mr. Bloom's wanderings, or Odyssey.)

4. (8 A.M.) Mr. Bloom is preparing his wife's breakfast at their home on Eccles Street. He goes out to get some kidney; on his return he hands his wife her mail. Molly Bloom is a lush, sensuous woman, a combination of Spanish, Jewish, and Irish. She is a hearty animal; her current lover is "Blazes" Boylan; and one of her morning letters is from him. Mr. Bloom knows of the intrigue but is unwilling or unable to act; he prefers to temporize.

5. (10 A.M.) Mr. Bloom starts off on his day's work. His first visit is to a branch post office, where he receives a *billet doux* from Martha Clifford. For Mr. Bloom is scarcely more faithful as a spouse than is his wife, except that his sins are more frequently sins of volition than of commission. On his way he stops to hear some music in All Hallows' Church and then proceeds to a chemist's shop, where he orders some face lotion for his wife; thence to a bath, where he revels in the warm scents and perfumes and forgets his mundane business errands.

6. (11 A.M.) Mr. Bloom, in company with Stephen Dedalus' father and some other sedate-appearing Dubliners, attends the funeral of Paddy Dignam. They ride far through the streets of the city—each man wrapped for most of the ride in his own thoughts—amid comparative silence. There is some embarrassment and friction among the group; but Paddy is eventually buried in sanctity, and the group takes up a subscription for the widow, a subscription to which Mr. Bloom contributes generously.

7. (Noon.) Mr. Bloom visits a newspaper office to arrange for an advertisement; Stephen Dedalus enters a short time after Mr. Bloom. (The two are drawing together.) Stephen has quit his job at Mr. Deasy's school and, flush with his salary check, invites the editor and his group to the nearby pub for drinks. Mr. Bloom, however, has gone on his way just before.

8. (1 P.M.) Mr. Bloom is hungry. He looks into a popular eating-place, but the sight reminds him of animals, and he withdraws, nauseated. About him in the streets are many notables, including AE (George Russell), the eminent Irish poet. Finally Mr. Bloom wanders into Davy Byrne's (an actual pub in Dublin) and tides over with a sandwich and some wine.

9. (2 P.M.) In a public library Stephen Dedalus is engaged in a rather intellectual, Plato-like dialogue with Buck Mulligan and Haines. Mr. Bloom is going in to look up an advertisement in a newspaper file and passes among the men as he goes out but does not make their acquaintance.

10. (3 P.M.) This episode is an amazing symphony of the sights and sounds of Dublin street life; it contains eighteen separate scenes, concluding with a procession of the Lord Lieutenant and his staff. Mr. Bloom, Stephen Dedalus, his father, his sister Dilly, and countless others wander in and out of the pages of this episode.

11. (4 P.M.) Mr. Bloom must eat. He has a luncheon at the Ormond Hotel; there he finds Stephen Dedalus' father and uncle dedicating their existence to wine, women, and song. At about this same time the adulterous intrigue between Mrs. Bloom and "Blazes" Boylan is being consummated at the house on Eccles Street.

12. (5 P.M.) Mr. Bloom wanders to a tavern where he is to meet his acquaintance Martin Cunningham, and where they are to ar-

range for Paddy Dignam's widow to receive her insurance. A drunken citizen in the tavern takes violent exception to the Hebraism of Mr. Bloom, and the latter beats a strategic retreat.

13. (8 P.M.) Mr. Bloom has been walking about for some time; he is hot and tired and goes down to the beach for some cool air. He is attracted by a girl on the beach, Gerty Mac-Dowell, and is mentally unfaithful to his wife. After Gerty's departure, he sits in the growing darkness and thinks of his earlier courtship of his wife.

14. (10 P.M.) Mr. Bloom goes to the Lying-In Hospital to visit a friend, Mina Purefoy, who has been delivered of a child. Stephen is in the internes' quarters carousing with Buck Mulligan and finally meets Mr. Bloom. As a matter of fact, Stephen is well on his way to being gloriously drunk; and Mr. Bloom, taking a paternal interest in the young man, decides to see him home. Thus Mr. Bloom takes, in part, the place of Stephen Dedalus' own father, from whom the son has been definitely estranged. So, in short, Stephen becomes the Telemachus to Mr. Bloom's Ulysses. The revelers go forth into the red-light district of Dublin, and Mr. Bloom follows to watch Stephen.

15. (Midnight.) The scene is a brothel. Stephen, under the influence of drink, joins with the exhausted Mr. Bloom in watching their secret thoughts and inmost desires materialize before them. This scene has been aptly called the Witches' Sabbath or Walpurgis Night Scene; there is about it a kind of devilish exorcization of evil that is remarkable, though it is fearfully difficult reading because of the variety of lyric, dramatic, and prose techniques employed.

16. (1 A.M.) Stephen does not want to return to the tower and Buck Mulligan. He decides to go home with Mr. Bloom. They stop on the way to take some coffee in a cabman's shelter, and they encounter a sailor, who spins several wild yarns before they see fit to leave him.

17. (2 A.M.) Finally in Mr. Bloom's kitchen they gulp down a cup of cocoa apiece and compare their experiences for the day. Not only that, the two, particularly Mr. Bloom, recall certain important events in their own lives. The technique here is that of a catechism. The personality and antecedents of Mr. Bloom are analyzed in scholastic fashion.

18. (That night.) Mr. Bloom is lying in bed beside his wife. In one of the most remarkable passages describing a stream of consciousness in all literature Mrs. Bloom expresses herself in a silent, unpunctuated monologue, "the refined quintessence of unrefined femininity." Mr. Bloom's wanderings have brought him back, not to a chaste Penelope, but to the adulterous bed of a faithless wife; his home proves to be only a hideous waste land. Yet in the triumphant assertion in the monologue of the female principle, the source of ever-recurring life, the novel ends on a ringing major chord.

No reading of *Ulysses* should be attempted without a prior reading of Homer's *Odyssey*. The Homeric parallels in Joyce's novel are multitudinous and at times most subtly concealed. Mr. Bloom (Ulysses) has lost his infant son; he finds his Telemachus in Stephen Dedalus, who, as has been observed, has repudiated his father. Each episode in the novel has for its key an incident or character in the *Odyssey*— (1) Stephen in the tower typifies Telemachus; (2) Stephen in the schoolroom, Nestor; (3) Stephen walking along the shore following the flux of his own mind, Proteus; (4) Mr. Bloom preparing his wife's breakfast represents the Calypso incident; (5) Mr. Bloom in the bath, the Lotus Eaters; (6) the funeral of Paddy Dignam, Ulysses' voyage to Hades; (7) the newspaper office, Aeolus; (8) the disgusting eaters at lunch, the Lestrygonians; (9) Stephen and his disputants in the public library, Scylla and Charybdis; (10) the streets of Dublin, the Wandering Rocks; (11) the father and uncle of Stephen Dedalus dining and bibbing in the Ormond Hotel, the Sirens; (12) the brawling Irishman who frightened Mr. Bloom away from the tavern, the Cyclops; (13) Gerty MacDowell and her seductiveness, Nausicaä; (14) the scene in the Lying-In Hospital, the Oxen of the Sun; (15) the scene in the brothel, Circe and her court; (16) the teller of tall stories in the cabman's shelter, Eumaeus; (17) the kitchen of the house in Eccles Street, Ithaca; (18) Molly Bloom, as pointed out above, Penelope. And the differences between the Homeric and Joycean parallels are nothing more than the differences between the Heroic Age of ancient Greece and twentieth-century occidental metropolitanism.

In each episode of *Ulysses* the parallelism with Homer is given in profuse detail. Thus, in the excerpt given below—Paddy Dignam's funeral (the descent to Hades)—the ripped-up roadway represents the approach to Hades; the Dodder River, the Liffey River, the Grand Canal, and the Royal Canal symbolize the four rivers of Hades; Paddy Dignam himself is the parallel to Elpenor, the member of Ulysses' crew who fell from a roof, was killed, and so preceded his companions to Hades. In fact, Joyce etymologizes "Elpenor" into "blazing face" (via the Semitic) and portrays Paddy Dignam in life as red-faced and bibulous. Martin Cunningham, with his "awful drunkard of a wife" ("setting up house for her time after time and then pawning the furniture on him every Saturday almost"), is to be likened to Sisyphus rolling the great rock uphill for eternity. The description of Father Coffey is clearly a shadowing forth of Cerberus. The caretaker, John O'Connell, is the personification of Pluto himself; his wife, unexpectedly fair spouse of a cold, impotent old man, is Proserpine. The monuments to O'Connell and Parnell are the shades of Hercules and Agamemnon. Apart from these Homeric recalls, the characters in this episode, as in many other parts of *Ulysses*, are drawn from Joyce's previous work—some from *A Portrait of the Artist As a Young Man*, some from *Dubliners*.

A realization of the immense virtuosity and academic erudition in Joyce's mind will emerge from even the following detached episode which has been reprinted, contrary to the general policy of the present work, not to represent the novel as a whole, but to exhibit a characteristic unit of James Joyce's writing. Yet however great the enthusiasm for the pyrotechnics of this work and the homage due the unquestioned influence of its brilliant writer, no praise can truly counterbalance the censure of Joyce's work explicit in the biographical and critical headnote given. In spite of a formidable battery of notes, keys, protocols, and ingenious guesswork on the part of the sympathetic reader, much of *Ulysses* remains deliberately and unjustifiably obscure.]

Martin Cunningham, first, poked his silk-hatted head into the creaking carriage and, entering deftly, seated himself. Mr Power stepped in after him, curving his height with care.

—Come on, Simon.

—After you, Mr Bloom said.

Mr Dedalus covered himself quickly and got in, saying:

—Yes, yes.

—Are we all here now? Martin Cunningham asked. Come along, Bloom.

Mr Bloom entered and sat in the vacant place. He pulled the door to after him and slammed it tight till it shut tight. He passed an arm through the armstrap and looked seriously from the open carriage window at the lowered blinds of the avenue. One dragged aside: an old woman peeping. Nose white-flattened against the pane. Thanking her stars she was passed over. Extraordinary the interest they take in a corpse. Glad to see us go we give them such trouble coming. Job seems to suit them. Huggermugger in corners. Slop

Section from *Ulysses* reprinted by permission of Random House, Inc., New York. Copyright, 1934, by the Modern Library, Inc.

The excerpt given here (pp. 84–111 of the original edition) represents the sixth episode of the novel. Mr. Bloom is attending the funeral of Paddy Dignam. The incident is told always from Mr. Bloom's point of view. Ordinary quotation marks are dispensed with. Unless definitely stated in the text, it is to be assumed that the thoughts presented in the "stream-of-consciousness" portions are those of Mr. Bloom. The men in the cab are under the constraint of the moment and only occasionally are their speeches of any significance. As for Mr. Bloom, his mind races along on all currents presented by the sights and sounds around him; his sensibilities and power of association are stimulated by the unhappy circumstances of the funeral itself. Reminiscences of his own life, snatches of popular songs, impressions of other people in his life, idle fancies about passing strangers, unbidden and fruitless speculations about life and death—all are cast up in his own mind without any conscious effort. To be noted especially is the recurrence of the bed in this episode: it is symbolic of the grave and sets the atmosphere for the piece. Stuart Gilbert, one of the keenest analysts of *Ulysses*, refers to the technique of this episode as "incubistic." 1. **Martin Cunningham.** The group in the carriage is composed of figures who appear elsewhere in *Ulysses;* but only Simon Dedalus, father of Stephen, is of any great importance. Martin Cunningham and Mr. Power appeared in Joyce's *Dubliners;* Mr. Dedalus is one of the most prominent figures in the *Portrait of the Artist As a Young Man.* Mr. Kernan and Hynes the reporter, who appear later in the episode, were also in *Dubliners.* 21. **Extraordinary . . . corpse.** Here begins the first of the many "stream-of-consciousness" passages in the episode. The sight of the curious old woman suggests to Bloom the whole function of women in the biological and social scene from birth to death; the thought of death suggests the laying out of the corpse and the presence of the undertaker. Such thought-progressions are too frequent and illogical and much too subjective to bear fuller comment. They should be accepted at face value.

about in slipperslappers for fear he'd wake. Then getting it ready. Laying it out. Molly and Mrs Fleming making the bed. Pull it more to your side. Our windingsheet. Never know who will touch you dead. Wash and shampoo. I believe they clip the nails and the hair. Keep a bit in an envelope. Grow all the same after. Unclean job.

All waited. Nothing was said. Stowing in the
10 wreaths probably. I am sitting on something hard. Ah, that soap in my hip pocket. Better shift it out of that. Wait for an opportunity.

All waited. Then wheels were heard from in front turning: then nearer: then horses' hoofs. A jolt. Their carriage began to move, creaking and swaying. Other hoofs and creaking wheels started behind. The blinds of the avenue passed and number nine with its craped knocker, door ajar. At walking pace.

20 They waited still, their knees jogging, till they had turned and were passing along the tramtracks. Tritonville road. Quicker. The wheels rattled rolling over the cobbled causeway and the crazy glasses shook rattling in the doorframes.

—What way is he taking us? Mr Power asked through both windows.

—Irishtown, Martin Cunningham said. Ringsend. Brunswick street.

30 Mr Dedalus nodded, looking out.

—That's a fine old custom, he said. I am glad to see it has not died out.

All watched awhile through their windows caps and hats lifted by passers. Respect. The carriage swerved from the tramtrack to the smoother road past Watery lane. Mr Bloom at gaze saw a lithe young man, clad in mourning, a wide hat.

—There's a friend of yours gone by, Dedalus,
40 he said.

—Who is that?

—Your son and heir.

—Where is he? Mr Dedalus said, stretching over, across.

The carriage, passing the open drains and mounds of ripped-up roadway before the tenement houses, lurched round the corner and,

swerving back to the tramtrack, rolled on noisily with chattering wheels. Mr Dedalus fell back, saying: 50

—Was that Mulligan cad with him? His *fidus Achates?*

—No, Mr Bloom said. He was alone.

—Down with his aunt Sally, I suppose, Mr Dedalus said, the Goulding faction, the drunken little costdrawer and Crissie, papa's little lump of dung, the wise child that knows her own father.

Mr Bloom smiled joylessly on Ringsend road. Wallace Bros the bottleworks. Dodder bridge. 60

Richie Goulding and the legal bag. Goulding, Collis and Ward he calls the firm. His jokes are getting a bit damp. Great card he was. Waltzing in Stamer street with Ignatius Gallaher on a Sunday morning, the landlady's two hats pinned on his head. Out on the rampage allnight. Beginning to tell on him now: that backache of his, I fear. Wife ironing his back. Thinks he'll cure it with pills. All breadcrumbs they are. About six hundred per cent 70 profit.

—He's in with a lowdown crowd, Mr Dedalus snarled. That Mulligan is a contaminated bloody doubledyed ruffian by all accounts. His name stinks all over Dublin. But with the help of God and His blessed mother I'll make it my business to write a letter one of those days to his mother or his aunt or whatever she is that will open her eyes as wide as a gate. I'll tickle his catastrophe, believe you me. 80

He cried above the clatter of the wheels.

—I won't have her bastard of a nephew ruin my son. A counterjumper's son. Selling tapes

---

51. *fidus Achates.* In Virgil's *Aeneid* "faithful Achates" was the constant companion of Aeneas. 54. **Sally, etc.** Simon Dedalus had married May Goulding. In the eleventh episode he is found dining with his brother-in-law, Goulding, at the Ormond Hotel. But it is obvious that Mr. Dedalus has little regard for his in-laws, as his unflattering references to the "Goulding faction" indicate. A *costdrawer* is apparently a disrespectful slang term about the equivalent of our "cashregister," i.e., a man interested solely in the grubbing of money. 60. **Dodder bridge,** over the River Dodder, one of the four waterways of Dublin used by Joyce to typify the four rivers of Hades. 68. **backache . . . profit.** The thought of Goulding's backache and his wife's home-made remedy of the hot flatiron causes Mr. Bloom to think of drugs, the comparative uselessness of pills ("all breadcrumbs"), and the immense profit a druggist can make on these pills. 79. **I'll . . . catastrophe,** quoted from Shakespeare's *II Henry IV*, II, i, 66. Falstaff is engaged in a quarrel with the hostess of a tavern. "Away, you scullion! you rampallian! you fustilarian! I'll tickle your catastrophe." *Catastrophe* is obviously used in an indecent sense. 83. **counterjumper,** a clerk.

---

42. **Your . . . heir,** Stephen Dedalus. Note the elder Dedalus' reactions. 46. **ripped-up . . . houses.** This detail is symbolic of the approach to Hades, represented by the graveyard. We have here a characteristic example of the Homeric recall.

in my cousin, Peter Paul M'Swiney's. Not likely.

He ceased. Mr Bloom glanced from his angry moustache to Mr Power's mild face and Martin Cunningham's eyes and beard, gravely shaking. Noisy selfwilled man. Full of his son. He is right. Something to hand on. If little Rudy had lived. See him grow up. Hear his voice in the house. Walking beside Molly in an Eton suit. My son. Me in his eyes. Strange feeling it would be. From me. Just a chance. Must have been that morning in Raymond terrace she was at the window, watching the two dogs at it by the wall of the cease to do evil. And the sergeant grinning up. She had that cream gown on with the rip she never stitched. Give us a touch, Poldy. God, I'm dying for it. How life begins.

Got big then. Had to refuse the Greystones concert. My son inside her. I could have helped him on in life. I could. Make him independent. Learn German, too.

—Are we late? Mr Power asked.

—Ten minutes, Martin Cunningham said, looking at his watch.

Molly. Milly. Same thing watered down. Her tomboy oaths. O jumping Jupiter! Ye gods and little fishes! Still, she's a dear girl. Soon be a woman. Mullingar. Dearest Papli. Young student. Yes, yes: a woman too. Life. Life.

The carriage heeled over and back, their four trunks swaying.

—Corny might have given us a more commodious yoke, Mr Power said.

—He might, Mr Dedalus said, if he hadn't that squint troubling him. Do you follow me?

He closed his left eye. Martin Cunningham began to brush away crustcrumbs from under his thighs.

—What is this, he said, in the name of God? Crumbs?

—Someone seems to have been making a picnic party here lately, Mr Power said.

All raised their thighs, eyed with disfavour the mildewed buttonless leather of the seats. Mr Dedalus, twisting his nose, frowned downward and said:

—Unless I'm greatly mistaken. What do you think, Martin?

—It struck me too, Martin Cunningham said.

Mr Bloom set his thigh down. Glad I took that bath. Feel my feet quite clean. But I wish Mrs Fleming had darned these socks better.

Mr Dedalus sighed resignedly.

—After all, he said, it's the most natural thing in the world.

—Did Tom Kernan turn up. Martin Cunningham asked, twirling the peak of his beard gently.

—Yes, Mr Bloom answered. He's behind with Ned Lambert and Hynes.

And Corny Kelleher himself? Mr Power asked.

—At the cemetery, Martin Cunningham said.

—I met M'Coy this morning, Mr Bloom said. He said he'd try to come.

The carriage halted short.

—What's wrong?

—We're stopped.

—Where are we?

Mr Bloom put his head out of the window.

—The grand canal, he said.

Gas works. Whooping cough they say it cures. Good job Milly never got it. Poor children! Doubles them up black and blue in convulsions. Shame really. Got off lightly with illness compared. Only measles. Flaxseed tea. Scarlatina influenza epidemics. Canvassing for death. Don't miss this chance. Dog's home over there. Poor old Athos! Be good to Athos, Leopold, is my last wish. Thy will be done. We obey them in the grave. A dying scrawl. He took it to heart, pined away. Quiet brute. Old men's dogs usually are.

A raindrop spat on his hat. He drew back and saw an instant of shower spray dots over the grey flags. Apart. Curious. Like through a colander. I thought it would. My boots were creaking I remember now.

—The weather is changing, he said quietly.

—A pity it did not keep up fine, Martin Cunningham said.

—Wanted for the country, Mr Power said. There's the sun again coming out.

---

8. **Rudy,** Mr. Bloom's little son, who had died in infancy. Observe once more the stream of consciousness inspired by the thought of the dead child.   9. **Molly,** Mr. Bloom's wife. 26. **Milly,** his daughter, Millicent, a shop assistant in Mullingar (in county West Meath, Ireland) who writes affectionately to *Dearest Papli.*

57. **Tom Kernan.** See p. 506, note to l. 1.   80. **Leopold . . . wish.** As observed later, Mr. Bloom's father, Rudolph Bloom the elder, committed suicide by taking poison. The incident is referred to several times in this episode.

Mr Dedalus peering through his glasses towards the veiled sun, hurled a mute curse at the sky.

—It's as uncertain as a child's bottom, he said.

—We're off again.

The carriage turned again its stiff wheels and their trunks swayed gently. Martin Cunningham twirled more quickly the peak of his beard.

—Tom Kernan was immense last night, he said. And Paddy Leonard taking him off to his face.

—O draw him out, Martin, Mr Power said eagerly. Wait till you hear him, Simon, on Ben Dollard's singing of *The Croppy Boy.*

—Immense, Martin Cunningham said pompously. *His singing of that simple ballad, Martin, is the most trenchant rendering I ever heard in the whole course of my experience.*

—Trenchant, Mr Power said laughing. He's dead nuts on that. And the retrospective arrangement.

—Did you read Dan Dawson's speech? Martin Cunningham asked.

—I did not then, Mr Dedalus said. Where is it?

—In the paper this morning.

Mr Bloom took the paper from his inside pocket. That book I must change for her.

—No, no, Mr Dedalus said quickly. Later on, please.

Mr Bloom's glance travelled down the edge of the paper, scanning the deaths. Callan, Coleman, Dignam, Fawcett, Lowry, Naumann, Peake, what Peake is that? is it the chap was in Crosbie and Alleyne's? no, Sexton, Urbright. Inked characters fast fading on the frayed breaking paper. Thanks to the Little Flower. Sadly missed. To the inexpressible grief of his. Aged 88 after a long and tedious illness. Month's mind Quinlan. On whose soul Sweet Jesus have mercy.

It is now a month since dear Henry fled
To his home up above in the sky
While his family weeps and mourns his loss
Hoping some day to meet him on high.

I tore up the envelope? Yes. Where did I put her letter after I read it in the bath? He patted his waistcoat pocket. There all right. 50 Dear Henry fled. Before my patience are exhausted.

National school. Meade's yard. The hazard. Only two there now. Nodding. Full as a tick. Too much bone in their skulls. The other trotting round with a fare. An hour ago I was passing there. The jarvies raised their hats.

A pointsman's back straightened itself upright suddenly against a tramway standard by Mr Bloom's window. Couldn't they invent 60 something automatic so that the wheel itself much handier? Well but that fellow would lose his job then? Well but then another fellow would get a job making the new invention?

Antient concert rooms. Nothing on there. A man in a buff suit with a crape armlet. Not much grief there. Quarter mourning. People in law, perhaps.

They went past the bleak pulpit of Saint Mark's, under the railway bridge, past the 70 Queen's theatre: in silence. Hoardings. Eugene Stratton. Mrs Bandman Palmer. Could I go to see *Leah* tonight, I wonder. I said I. Or the *Lily of Killarney?* Elster Grimes Opera Company. Big powerful change. Wet bright bills for next week. *Fun on the Bristol.* Martin Cunningham could work a pass for the Gaiety. Have to stand a drink or two. As broad as it's long.

He's coming in the afternoon. Her songs. 80

Plasto's. Sir Philip Crampton's memorial fountain bust. Who was he?

—How do you do? Martin Cunningham said, raising his palm to his brow in salute.

—He doesn't see us, Mr Power said. Yes, he does. How do you do?

—Who? Mr Dedalus asked.

48. I . . . envelope. Mr. Bloom, in the fifth episode, had begun his perambulations by visiting a post office, where he received a love letter from Martha Clifford, a stenographer with whom he is carrying on an affair. She knows him as "Henry Flower." She addresses him as "Henry" and encloses a little flower. The association of this with the obituary verse and the society of the Little Flower is obvious. 57. jarvies, cabdrivers. 58. pointsman, switchman on the elevated railway. 71. Hoardings, billboards. There follow the names of the plays or musical shows being advertised, with the names also of the actors participating. 80. He's . . . songs. "Blazes" Boylan, the impresario, is coming to Mr. Bloom's home that afternoon to show Mrs. Bloom some new songs for her to sing. She is a singer of some local reputation, as is seen below. When Boylan comes, the affair between him and Marion Bloom will be consummated. Observe that Mr. Bloom, seeing Boylan, is disturbed and turns to study his nails, with consequent embarrassing rumination.

15. Ben Dollard, a singer who appears in some of the pages of *Ulysses,* a former lover of Mrs. Bloom. 18. His . . . experience. Mr. Cunningham is quoting Kernan's critique of Ben Dollard's rendition of "that simple ballad," *The Croppy Boy;* hence the italics. 39. Little Flower, a memorial society in the Catholic Church.

—Blazes Boylan, Mr Power said. There he is airing his quiff. Just that moment I was thinking.

Mr Dedalus bent across to salute. From the door of the Red Bank the white disc of a straw hat flashed reply: passed.

Mr Bloom reviewed the nails of his left hand, then those of his right hand. The nails, yes. Is there anything more in him that they she sees? Fascination. Worst man in Dublin. That keeps him alive. They sometimes feel what a person is. Instinct. But a type like that. My nails. I am just looking at them: well pared. And after: thinking alone. Body getting a bit softy. I would notice that from remembering. What causes that I suppose the skin can't contract quickly enough when the flesh falls off. But the shape is there. The shape is there still. Shoulders. Hips. Plump. Night of the dance dressing. Shift stuck between the cheeks behind.

He clasped his hands between his knees and, satisfied, sent his vacant glance over their faces. Mr Power asked:

—How is the concert tour getting on, Bloom?

—O very well, Mr Bloom said. I hear great accounts of it. It's a good idea, you see . . .

—Are you going yourself?

—Well no, Mr Bloom said. In point of fact I have to go down to the county Clare on some private business. You see the idea is to tour the chief towns. What you lose on one you can make up on the other.

—Quite so, Martin Cunningham said. Mary Anderson is up there now.

—Have you good artists?

—Louis Werner is touring her, Mr Bloom said. O yes, we'll have all topnobbers. J. C. Doyle and John Mac Cormack, I hope and. The best, in fact.

—And Madame, Mr Power said, smiling. Last but not least.

Mr Bloom unclasped his hands in a gesture of soft politeness and clasped them. Smith O'Brien. Someone has laid a bunch of flowers there. Woman. Must be his death-day. For many happy returns. The carriage wheeling by Farrell's statue united noiselessly their unresisting knees.

Oot: a dullgarbed old man from the curbstone tendered his wares, his mouth opening: oot.

—Four bootlaces for a penny.

Wonder why he was struck off the rolls. Had his office in Hume street. Same house as Molly's namesake. Tweedy, crown solicitor for Waterford. Had that silk hat ever since. Relics of old decency. Mourning too. Terrible comedown, poor wretch! Kicked about like snuff at a wake. O'Callaghan on his last legs.

And *Madame.* Twenty past eleven. Up. Mrs Fleming is in to clean. Doing her hair, humming: *voglio e non vorrei.* No: *vorrei e non.* Looking at the tips of her hairs to see if they are split. *Mi trema un poco il.* Beautiful on that *tre* her voice is: weeping tone. A thrush. A throstle. There is a word throstle that expressed that.

His eyes passed lightly over Mr Power's goodlooking face. Greyish over the ears. *Madame:* smiling. I smiled back. A smile goes a long way. Only politeness perhaps. Nice fellow. Who knows is that true about the woman he keeps? Not pleasant for the wife. Yet they say, who was it told me, there is no carnal. You would imagine that would get played out pretty quick. Yes, it was Crofton met him one evening bringing her a pound of rumpsteak. What is this she was? Barmaid in Jury's. Or the Moira, was it?

They passed under the hugecloaked Liberator's form.

Martin Cunningham nudged Mr Power.

—Of the tribe of Reuben, he said.

A tall blackbearded figure, bent on a stick, stumping round the corner of Elvery's elephant house showed them a curved hand open on his spine.

—In all his pristine beauty, Mr Power said.

Mr Dedalus looked after the stumping figure and said mildly:

—The devil break the hasp of your back!

Mr Power, collapsing in laughter, shaded his

---

2. **quiff,** British slang for a man's well-oiled hair; it is related to *coif* and *coiffure.* 34. **Mary Anderson,** a noted actress of the older generation.

63. *voglio . . . vorrei . . . poco il,* from the famous duet, *La ci darem,* in Mozart's opera, *Don Giovanni,* I. "I would and yet I would not . . . my heart trembles a little." 81. **Liberator's form,** the statue of Daniel O'Connell; see p. 517, l. 24, and note. 84. **Reuben.** Reuben J. Dodd was a famous money-lender of Dublin; his son tried unsuccessfully to commit suicide in the River Liffey. 86. **Elvery's elephant house,** in Stuart Gilbert's phrase, a "nuance of evanescent local color . . . incomprehensible for most English and American readers and may become so, in course of time, even to Dubliners."

face from the window as the carriage passed Gray's statue.

—We have all been there, Martin Cunningham said broadly.

His eyes met Mr Bloom's eyes. He caressed his beard adding:

—Well, nearly all of us.

Mr Bloom began to speak with sudden eagerness to his companion's faces.

—That's an awfully good one that's going the rounds about Reuben J. and the son.

—About the boatman? Mr Power asked.

—Yes. Isn't it awfully good?

—What is that? Mr Dedalus asked. I didn't hear it.

—There was a girl in the case, Mr Bloom began, and he determined to send him to the isle of Man out of harm's way but when they were both. . . .

—What? Mr Dedalus asked. That confirmed bloody hobbledehoy is it?

—Yes, Mr Bloom said. They were both on the way to the boat and he tried to drown . . .

—Drown Barabbas! Mr Dedalus cried. I wish to Christ he did!

Mr Power sent a long laugh down his shaded nostrils.

—No, Mr Bloom said the son himself . . .

Martin Cunningham thwarted his speech rudely.

—Reuben J. and the son were piking it down the quay next the river on their way to the isle of Man boat and the young chiseller suddenly got loose and over the wall with him into the Liffey.

—For God's sake! Mr Dedalus exclaimed in fright. Is he dead?

—Dead! Martin Cunningham cried. Not he! A boatman got a pole and fished him out by the slack of the breeches and he was landed up to the father on the quay. More dead than alive. Half the town was there.

—Yes, Mr Bloom said. But the funny part is . . .

—And Reuben J., Martin Cunningham said,

gave the boatman a florin for saving his son's life.

A stifled sigh came from under Mr Power's hand.

—O, he did, Martin Cunningham affirmed. Like a hero. A silver florin.

—Isn't it awfully good? Mr Bloom said eagerly.

—One and eightpence too much, Mr Dedalus said drily.

Mr Power's choked laugh burst quietly in the carriage.

Nelson's pillar.

—Eight plums a penny! Eight for a penny!

—We had better look a little serious, Martin Cunningham said.

Mr Dedalus sighed.

—And then indeed, he said, poor little Paddy wouldn't grudge us a laugh. Many a good one he told himself.

—The Lord forgive me! Mr Power said, wiping his wet eyes with his fingers. Poor Paddy! I little thought a week ago when I saw him last and he was in his usual health that I'd be driving after him like this. He's gone from us.

—As decent a little man as ever wore a hat, Mr Dedalus said. He went very suddenly.

—Breakdown, Martin Cunningham said. Heart. He tapped his chest sadly.

Blazing face: redhot. Too much John Barleycorn. Cure for a red nose. Drink like the devil till it turns adelite. A lot of money he spent colouring it.

Mr Power gazed at the passing houses with rueful apprehension.

—He had a sudden death, poor fellow, he said.

—The best death, Mr Bloom said.

Their wide open eyes looked at him.

—No suffering, he said. A moment and all is over. Like dying in sleep. No-one spoke.

Dead side of the street this. Dull business by day, land agents, temperance hotel, Falconer's

11. **Reuben . . . son.** See p. 510, l. 84, and note.   17. **isle of Man,** a large island in the Irish Sea, northeast of Dublin.   24. **Barabbas.** When Christ was accused before Pilate, the latter, having examined the Savior, was willing to release him; but the Jews preferred to have released to them Barabbas, "Who for a certain sedition made in the city and for murder, was cast into prison" (Luke 23:19). According to John 18:40, Barabbas was a robber. At any rate, he was released, and Jesus was led to Calvary.

46. **florin,** two shillings (24 pence). Mr. Dedalus remarks that the florin was "one and eightpence too much"; in short, the son's life was worth no more than fourpence, or about the equivalent of "one thin dime."   58. **Nelson's pillar,** the monument to Horatio Lord Nelson (1758–1805), famous British admiral and victor at the Battle of Trafalgar, in which he was killed.   75. **Blazing face: redhot.** As observed before, Paddy Dignam is the Homeric recall of Elpenor, the member of Ulysses' crew who fell from the roof of Circe's palace and preceded his companions to Hades. His name has been derived from a Semitic root signifying "blazing face."   77. **adelite,** a kind of brick.

railway guide, civil service college, Gill's catholic club, the industrious blind. Why? Some reason. Sun or wind. At night too. Chummies and slaveys. Under the patronage of the late Father Mathew. Foundation stone for Parnell. Breakdown. Heart.

White horses with white frontlet plumes came round the Rotunda corner, galloping. A tiny coffin flashed by. In a hurry to bury. A mourning coach. Unmarried. Black for the married. Piebald for bachelors. Dun for a nun.

—Sad, Martin Cunningham said. A child.

A dwarf's face mauve and wrinkled like little Rudy's was. Dwarf's body, weak as putty, in a whitelined deal box. Burial friendly society pays. Penny a week for a sod of turf. Our. Little. Beggar. Baby. Meant nothing. Mistake of nature. If it's healthy it's from the mother. If not the man. Better luck next time.

—Poor little thing, Mr Dedalus said. It's well out of it.

The carriage climbed more slowly the hill of Rutland square. Rattle his bones. Over the stones. Only a pauper. Nobody owns.

—In the midst of life, Martin Cunningham said.

—But the worst of all, Mr Power said, is the man who takes his own life.

Martin Cunningham drew out his watch briskly, coughed and put it back.

—The greatest disgrace to have in the family, Mr Power added.

Temporary insanity, of course, Martin Cunningham said decisively. We must take a charitable view of it.

—They say a man who does it is a coward, Mr Dedalus said.

—It is not for us to judge, Martin Cunningham said.

Mr Bloom, about to speak, closed his lips again. Martin Cunningham's large eyes. Looking away now. Sympathetic human man he is. Intelligent. Like Shakespeare's face. Always a good word to say. They have no mercy on that here or infanticide. Refuse christian burial. They used to drive a stake of wood through his heart in the grave. As if it wasn't broken already. Yet sometimes they repent too late. Found in the riverbed clutching rushes. He looked at me. And that awful drunkard of a wife of his. Setting up house for her time after time and then pawning the furniture on him every Saturday almost. Leading him the life of the damned. Wear the heart out of a stone, that. Monday morning start afresh. Shoulder to the wheel. Lord, she must have looked a sight that night, Dedalus told me he was in there. Drunk about the place and capering with Martin's umbrella:

> —And they call me the jewel of Asia,
> Of Asia,
> The geisha.

He looked away from me. He knows. Rattle his bones.

That afternoon of the inquest. The red-labelled bottle on the table. The room in the hotel with hunting pictures. Stuffy it was. Sunlight through the slats on the Venetian blinds. The coroner's ears, big and hairy. Boots giving evidence. Thought he was asleep first. Then saw like yellow streaks on his face. Had slipped down to the foot of the bed. Verdict: overdose. Death by misadventure. The letter. For my son Leopold.

No more pain. Wake no more. Nobody owns.

The carriage rattled swiftly along Blessington street. Over the stones.

—We are going the pace, I think, Martin Cunningham said.

—God grant he doesn't upset us on the road, Mr Power said.

—I hope not, Martin Cunningham said. That will be a great race tomorrow in Germany. The Gordon Bennett.

—Yes, by Jove, Mr Dedalus said. That will be worth seeing, faith.

50. **awful drunkard . . . almost.** Cunningham's wife is his burden through life, just as Sisyphus in Hades "pressed a monstrous stone with hands and feet, striving to roll it towards the brow of a hill. But oft as he was about to hurl it over the top, the weight would drive him back; so once again to the plane rolled the stone, the pitiless thing. And he once more kept heaving and straining, and the sweat the while was pouring from his limbs, and the dust rose upwards from his head." 60. **And . . . geisha.** This and countless other verses in *Ulysses* represent popular songs and ballads of the day, some polite, others ribald. The *geisha* is the "entertainment-girl" of Japan. 69. **Boots,** in English usage the boy at a hotel or tavern whose job it is to polish the boots of the guests during the night. 84. **Gordon Bennett,** referring here to the famous races in the early history of automobiling, at which was presented as prize the Gordon Bennett Cup, awarded by the American newspaper-owner and sportsman, James Gordon Bennett.

46. **stake . . . grave.** In folklore, any corpse believed to house a demon or vampire was "laid" by driving a stake through the heart. Suicides, being regarded as sinful, were considered to be inspired by the devil; hence the refusal of Christian burial.

As they turned into Berkeley street a street-organ near the Basin sent over and after them a rollicking rattling song of the halls. Has anybody here seen Kelly? Kay ee double ell wy. Dead march from *Saul*. He's as bad as old Antonio. He left me on my ownio. Pirouette! The *Mater Misericordiae*. Eccles street. My house down there. Big place. Ward for incurables there. Very encouraging. Our Lady's Hospice for the dying. Dead house handy underneath. Where old Mrs Riordan died. They look terrible the women. Her feeding cup and rubbing her mouth with the spoon. Then the screen round her bed for her to die. Nice young student that was dressed that bite the bee gave me. He's gone over to the lying-in hospital they told me. From one extreme to the other.

The carriage galloped round a corner: stopped.

—What's wrong now?

A divided drove of branded cattle passed the windows, lowing, slouching by on padded hoofs, whisking their tails slowly on their clotted bony croups. Outside them and through them ran raddled sheep bleating their fear.

—Emigrants, Mr Power said.

—Huuuh! the drover's voice cried, his switch sounding on their flanks. Huuuh! Out of that!

Thursday of course. Tomorrow is killing day. Springers. Cuffe sold them about twenty-seven quid each. For Liverpool probably. Roast beef for old England. They buy up all the juicy ones. And then the fifth quarter is lost: All that raw stuff, hide, hair, horns. Comes to a big thing in a year. Dead meat trade. Byproducts of the slaughterhouses for tanneries, soap, margarine. Wonder if that dodge works now getting dicky meat off the train at Clonsilla.

The carriage moved on through the drove.

—I can't make out why the corporation doesn't run a tramline from the parkgate to the quays, Mr Bloom said. All those animals could be taken in trucks down to the boats.

—Instead of blocking up the thoroughfare, Martin Cunningham said. Quite right. They ought to.

—Yes, Mr Bloom said, and another thing I often thought is to have municipal funeral trams like they have in Milan, you know. Run the line out to the cemetery gates and have special trams, hearse and carriage and all. Don't you see what I mean?

—O that be damned for a story, Mr Dedalus said. Pullman car and saloon dining-room.

—A poor lookout for Corny, Mr Power added.

—Why? Mr Bloom asked, turning to Mr Dedalus. Wouldn't it be more decent than galloping two abreast?

—Well, there's something in that, Mr Dedalus granted.

—And, Martin Cunningham said, we wouldn't have scenes like that when the hearse capsized round Dunphy's and upset the coffin on to the road.

—That was terrible, Mr Power's shocked face said, and the corpse fell about the road. Terrible!

—First round Dunphy's, Mr Dedalus said, nodding. Gordon Bennett cup.

—Praises be to God! Martin Cunningham said piously.

Bom! Upset. A coffin bumped out on to the road. Burst open. Paddy Dignam shot out and rolling over stiff in the dust in a brown habit too large for him. Red face: grey now. Mouth fallen open. Asking what's up now. Quite right to close it. Looks horrid open. Then the insides decompose quickly. Much better to close up all the orifices. Yes, also. With wax. The sphincter loose. Seal up all.

—Dunphy's, Mr Power announced as the carriage turned right.

Dunphy's corner. Mourning coaches drawn up drowning their grief. A pause by the wayside. Tiptop position for a pub. Expect we'll pull up there on the way back to drink his health. Pass round the consolation. Elixir of life.

But suppose now it did happen. Would he bleed if a nail say cut him in the knocking about? He would and he wouldn't, I suppose. Depends on where. The circulation stops. Still some might ooze out of an artery. It would be better to bury them in red: a dark red.

In silence they drove along Phibsborough road. An empty hearse trotted by, coming from the cemetery: looks relieved.

Cross guns bridge: the royal canal.

Water rushed roaring through the sluices. A man stood on his dropping barge between

---

31. **quid,** slang for pounds sterling.   38. **dicky,** cheap. **Clonsilla,** a suburb of Dublin.

clamps of turf. On the towpath by the lock a slacktethered horse. Aboard of the *Bugabu*.

Their eyes watched him. On the slow weedy waterway he had floated on his raft coastward over Ireland drawn by a haulage rope past beds of reeds, over slime, mud-choked bottles, carrion dogs. Athlone, Mullingar, Moyvalley, I could make a walking tour to see Milly by the canal. Or cycle down. Hire some old crock, safety. Wren had one the other day at the auction but a lady's. Developing waterways. James M'Cann's hobby to row me o'er the ferry. Cheaper transit. By easy stages. Houseboats. Camping out. Also hearses. To heaven by water. Perhaps I will without writing. Come as a surprise, Leixlip, Clonsilla. Dropping down, lock by lock to Dublin. With turf from the midland bogs. Salute. He lifted his brown straw hat, saluting Paddy Dignam.

They drove on past Brian Boroimhe house. Near it now.

—I wonder how is our friend Fogarty getting on, Mr. Power said.

—Better ask Tom Kernan, Mr Dedalus said.

—How is that? Martin Cunningham said. Left him weeping I suppose.

—Though lost to sight, Mr Dedalus said, to memory dear.

The carriage steered left for Finglas road.

The stonecutter's yard on the right. Last lap. Crowded on the spit of land silent shapes appeared, white, sorrowful, holding out calm hands, knelt in grief, pointing. Fragments of shapes, hewn. In white silence: appealing. The best obtainable. Thos. H. Dennany, monumental builder and sculptor.

Passed.

On the curbstone before Jimmy Geary the sexton's an old tramp sat, grumbling, emptying the dirt and stones out of his huge dustbrown yawning boot. After life's journey.

Gloomy gardens then went by, one by one: gloomy houses.

Mr Power pointed.

—That is where Childs was murdered, he said. The last house.

So it is, Mr Dedalus said. A gruesome case, Seymour Bushe got him off. Murdered his brother. Or so they said.

—The crown had no evidence, Mr Power said.

—Only circumstantial, Martin Cunningham said. That's the maxim of the law. Better for ninety-nine guilty to escape than for one innocent person to be wrongfully condemned.

They looked. Murderer's ground. It passed darkly. Shuttered, tenantless, unweeded garden. Whole place gone to hell. Wrongfully condemned. Murder. The murderer's image in the eye of the murdered. They love reading about it. Man's head found in a garden. Her clothing consisted of. How she met her death. Recent outrage. The weapon used. Murderer is still at large. Clues. A shoelace. The body to be exhumed. Murder will out.

Cramped in this carriage. She mightn't like me to come that way without letting her know. Must be careful about women. Catch them once with their pants down. Never forgive you after. Fifteen.

The high railings of Prospects rippled past their gaze. Dark poplars, rare white forms. Forms more frequent, white shapes thronged amid the trees, white forms and fragments streaming by mutely, sustaining vain gestures on the air.

The felly harshed against the curbstone: stopped. Martin Cunningham put out his arm and, wrenching back the handle, shoved the door open with his knee. He stepped out. Mr Power and Mr Dedalus followed.

Change that soap now. Mr Bloom's hand unbuttoned his hip pocket swiftly and transferred the paperstuck soap to his inner handkerchief pocket. He stepped out of the carriage, replacing the newspaper his other hand still held.

Paltry funeral: coach and three carriages. It's all the same. Pallbearers, gold reins, requiem mass, firing a volley. Pomp of death. Beyond the hind carriage a hawker stood by his barrow of cakes and fruit. Simnel cakes those are, stuck together: cakes for the dead. Dogbiscuits. Who ate them? Mourners coming out.

He followed his companions. Mr Kernan and Ned Lambert followed, Hynes walking after them. Corny Kelleher stood by the opened hearse and took out the two wreaths. He handed one to the boy.

Where is that child's funeral disappeared to?

---

71. **Prospects,** Prospect Park.   91. **Simnel cakes,** a rich plum cake with a hard crust.

514

A team of horses passed from Finglas with toiling plodding tread, dragging through the funereal silence a creaking wagon on which lay a granite block. The waggoner marching at their head saluted.

Coffin now. Got here before us, dead as he is. Horse looking round at it with his plume skeowways. Dull eye: collar tight on his neck, pressing on a bloodvessel or something. Do they know what they cart out here every day? Must be twenty or thirty funerals every day. Then Mount Jerome for the protestants. Funerals all over the world everywhere every minute. Shovelling them under by the cartload doublequick. Thousands every hour. Too many in the world.

Mourners came out through the gates: woman and a girl. Leanjawed harpy, hard woman at a bargain, her bonnet awry. Girl's face stained with dirt and tears, holding the woman's arm looking up at her for a sign to cry. Fish's face, bloodless and livid.

The mutes shouldered the coffin and bore it in through the gates. So much dead weight. Felt heavier myself stepping out of that bath. First the stiff: then the friends of the stiff. Corny Kelleher and the boy followed with their wreaths. Who is that beside them? Ah, the brother-in-law.

All walked after.

Martin Cunningham whispered:

—I was in mortal agony with you talking of suicide before Bloom.

—What? Mr Power whispered. How so?

—His father poisoned himself, Martin Cunningham whispered. Had the Queen's hotel in Ennis. You heard him say he was going to Clare. Anniversary.

—O God! Mr Power whispered. First I heard of it. Poisoned himself!

He glanced behind him to where a face with dark thinking eyes followed towards the cardinal's mausoleum. Speaking.

—Was he insured? Mr Bloom asked.

—I believe so, Mr Kernan answered, but the policy was heavily mortgaged. Martin is trying to get the youngster into Artane.

—How many children did he leave?

—Five. Ned Lambert says he'll try to get one of the girls into Todd's.

—A sad case, Mr Bloom said gently. Five young children.

—A great blow to the poor wife, Mr Kernan added.

—Indeed yes, Mr Bloom agreed.

Has the laugh at him now.

He looked down at the boots he had blackened and polished. She had outlived him, lost her husband. More dead for her than for me. One must outlive the other. Wise men say. There are more women than men in the world. Condole with her. Your terrible loss. I hope you'll soon follow him. For Hindu widows only. She would marry another. Him? No. Yet who knows after? Widowhood not the thing since the old queen died. Drawn on a guncarriage. Victoria and Albert. Frogmore memorial mourning. But in the end she put a few violets in her bonnet. Vain in her heart of hearts. All for a shadow. Consort not even a king. Her son was the substance. Something new to hope for not like the past she wanted back, waiting. It never comes. One must go first: alone under the ground: and lie no more in her warm bed.

—How are you, Simon? Ned Lambert said softly, clasping hands. Haven't seen you for a month of Sundays.

—Never better. How are all in Cork's own town?

—I was down there for the Cork park races on Easter Monday, Ned Lambert said. Same old six and eightpence. Stopped with Dick Tivy.

—And how is Dick, the solid man?

—Nothing between himself and heaven, Ned Lambert answered.

—By the holy Paul! Mr Dedalus said in subdued wonder. Dick Tivy bald?

—Martin is going to get up a whip for the youngsters, Ned Lambert said, pointing ahead. A few bob a skull. Just to keep them going till the insurance is cleared up.

---

63. **Hindu . . . only.** According to ancient Hindu practice, the widow of a dead man was supposed to immolate herself on his funeral pyre.   67. **Victoria . . . mourning.** Albert, consort to Queen Victoria, died December 14, 1861, and was buried in a magnificent mausoleum at Frogmore, in the confines of Windsor Castle, near London.   74. **bed.** Note here as elsewhere the allusion to beds; the entire episode is based upon the allegory of the bed, the last resting place, the grave. The device is known technically as "incubism."   89. **whip**, slang for *contribution*.

23. **mutes**, professional mourners.   47. **Artane**, like **Todd's** (l. 50), prominent private schools in the Dublin district.

—Yes, yes, Mr Dedalus said dubiously. Is that the eldest boy in front?

—Yes, Ned Lambert said, with the wife's brother. John Henry Menton is behind. He put down his name for a quid.

—I'll engage he did, Mr Dedalus said. I often told poor Paddy he ought to mind that job. John Henry is not the worst in the world.

—How did he lose it? Ned Lambert asked. Liquor, what?

—Many a good man's fault, Mr Dedalus said with a sigh.

They halted about the door of the mortuary chapel. Mr Bloom stood behind the boy with the wreath, looking down at his sleek combed hair and the slender furrowed neck inside his brandnew collar. Poor boy! Was he there when the father? Both unconscious. Lighten up at the last moment and recognize for the last time. All he might have done. I owe three shillings to O'Grady. Would he understand? The mutes bore the coffin into the chapel. Which end is his head?

After a moment he followed the others in, blinking in the screened light. The coffin lay on its bier before the chancel four tall yellow candles at its corners. Always in front of us. Corny Kelleher, laying a wreath at each fore corner, beckoned to the boy to kneel. The mourners knelt here and there in praying desks. Mr Bloom stood behind near the font and, when all had knelt dropped carefully his unfolded newspaper from his pocket and knelt his right knee upon it. He fitted his black hat gently on his left knee and, holding its brim, bent over piously.

A server, bearing a brass bucket with something in it, came out through a door. The whitesmocked priest came after him tidying his stole with one hand, balancing with the other a little book against his toad's belly. Who'll read the book? I, said the rook.

They halted by the bier and the priest began to read out of his book with a fluent croak.

Father Coffey. I knew his name was like a coffin. *Dominenamine*. Bully about the muzzle he looks. Bosses the show. Muscular christian. Woe betide anyone that looks crooked at him: priest. Thou art Peter. Burst sideways like a sheep in clover Dedalus says he will. With a belly on him like a poisoned pup. Most amusing expressions that man finds. Hhhn: burst sideways.

—*Non intres in judicium cum servo tuo, Domine.*

Makes them feel more important to be prayed over in Latin. Requiem mass. Crape weepers. Blackedged notepaper. Your name on the altarlist. Chilly place this. Want to feed well, sitting in there all the morning in the gloom kicking his heels waiting for the next please. Eyes of a toad too. What swells him up that way? Molly gets swelled after cabbage. Air of the place maybe. Looks full of bad gas. Must be an infernal lot of bad gas round the place. Butchers for instance: They get like raw beefsteaks. Who was telling me? Mervyn Brown. Down in the vaults of saint Werburgh's lovely old organ hundred and fifty they have to bore a hole in the coffins sometimes to let out the bad gas and burn it. Out it rushes: blue. One whiff of that and you're a goner.

My kneecap is hurting me. Ow. That's better.

The priest took a stick with a knob at the end of it out of the boy's bucket and shook it over the coffin. Then he walked to the other end and shook it again. Then he came back and put it back in the bucket. As you were before you rested. It's all written down: he has to do it.

—*Et ne nos inducas in tentationem.*

The server piped the answers in the treble. I often thought it would be better to have boy servants. Up to fifteen or so. After that of course . . .

Holy water that was, I expect. Shaking sleep out of it. He must be fed up with that job, shaking that thing over all the corpses they trot up. What harm if he could see what he was shaking it over. Every mortal day a fresh batch: middleaged men, old women, children, women dead of childbirth, men with beards, baldheaded business men, consumptive girls with

---

37. **A server, etc.** Mr. Bloom is not a Catholic; as his mental observations reveal, the details of the ritual are new to him.
45. **Father Coffey . . . sideways.** The entire description of Father Coffey, with his "bully . . . muzzle," his "belly on him like a poisoned pup," is considered a Homeric recall of Cerberus, the three-headed hound that guarded the approach to the lower world.

54. *Non . . . Domine,* Enter not into judgment against thy servant, O Lord! 82. *Et . . . tentationem,* And lead us not into temptation.

little sparrow's breasts. All the year round he prayed the same thing over them all and shook water on top of them: sleep. On Dignam now.

—*In paradisum.*

Said he was going to paradise or is in paradise. Says that over everybody. Tiresome kind of a job. But he has to say something.

The priest closed his book and went off, followed by the server. Corny Kelleher opened the sidedoors and the gravediggers came in, hoisted the coffin again, carried it out and shoved it on their cart. Corny Kelleher gave one wreath to the boy and one to the brother-in-law. All followed them out of the sidedoors into the mild grey air. Mr Bloom came last, folding his paper again into his pocket. He gazed gravely at the ground till the coffincart wheeled off to the left. The metal wheels ground the gravel with a sharp grating cry and the pack of blunt boots followed the barrow along a lane of sepulchres.

The ree the ra the ree the ra the roo. Lord. I mustn't lilt here.

—The O'Connell circle, Mr Dedalus said about him.

Mr Power's soft eyes went up to the apex of the lofty cone.

—He's at rest, he said, in the middle of his people, old Dan O'. But his heart is buried in Rome. How many broken hearts are buried here, Simon!

—Her grave is over there, Jack, Mr Dedalus said. I'll soon be stretched beside her. Let Him take me whenever He likes.

Breaking down, he began to weep to himself quietly, stumbling a little in his walk. Mr Power took his arm.

—She's better where she is, he said kindly.

—I suppose so, Mr Dedalus said with a weak gasp. I suppose she is in heaven if there is a heaven.

Corny Kelleher stepped aside from his rank and allowed the mourners to plod by.

—Sad occasions, Mr Kernan began politely.

Mr Bloom closed his eyes and sadly twice bowed his head.

—The others are putting on their hats, Mr Kernan said. I suppose we can do so too. We are the last. This cemetery is a treacherous place.

They covered their heads.

—The reverend gentleman read the service too quickly, don't you think? Mr. Kernan said with reproof.

Mr Bloom nodded gravely, looking in the quick bloodshot eyes. Secret eyes, secret searching eyes. Mason, I think: not sure. Beside him again. We are the last. In the same boat. Hope he'll say something else.

Mr Kernan added:

—The service of the Irish church, used in Mount Jerome, is simpler, more impressive, I must say.

Mr Bloom gave prudent assent. The language of course was another thing.

Mr Kernan said with solemnity:

—*I am the resurrection and the life.* That touches a man's inmost heart.

—It does, Mr Bloom said.

Your heart perhaps but what price the fellow in the six feet by two with his toes to the daisies? No touching that. Seat of the affections. Broken heart. A pump after all, pumping thousands of gallons of blood every day. One fine day it gets bunged up and there you are. Lots of them lying around here: lungs, hearts, livers. Old rusty pumps: damn the thing else. The resurrection and the life. Once you are dead you are dead. That last day idea. Knocking them all up out of their graves. Come forth, Lazarus! And he came fifth and lost the job. Get up! Last day! Then every fellow mousing around for his liver and his lights and the rest of his traps. Find damn all of himself that morning. Pennyweight of powder in a skull. Twelve grammes one pennyweight. Troy measure.

Corny Kelleher fell into step at their side.

—Everything went off A 1, he said. What?

He looked on them from his drawling eye.

---

24. **O'Connell circle.** Daniel O'Connell, called the Liberator, and the Uncrowned Monarch of Ireland, was a famous Irish orator and patriot (1775–1847). His efforts to achieve Irish independence were fruitless in his lifetime, but he was instrumental in freeing the Catholics of Britain from the disabilities they had suffered since the Revolution of 1688. He was very much of an agitator during the difficult depression years of the 1840's, and was finally arrested and tried for sedition. The sentence against him was ultimately reversed, but his health was broken by his fourteen months' imprisonment. A trip to Italy did him no good, and he died in Genoa (not Rome).

81. **Lazarus,** in the New Testament the brother of Mary and Martha. He died and was resurrected by Jesus' ringing "Lazarus, come forth!" (John 11:43).

Policeman's shoulders. With your tooraloom tooraloom.

—As it should be, Mr Kernan said.

—What? Eh? Corny Kelleher said.

Mr Kernan assured him.

—Who is that chap behind with Tom Kernan? John Henry Menton asked. I know his face.

Ned Lambert glanced back.

10 —Bloom, he said, Madam Marion Tweedy that was, is, I mean, the soprano. She's his wife.

—O, to be sure, John Henry Menton said. I haven't seen her for some time. She was a fine-looking woman. I danced with her, wait, fifteen seventeen golden years ago, at Mat Dillons, in Roundtown. And a good armful she was.

He looked behind through the others.

20 —What is he? he asked. What does he do? Wasn't he in the stationery line? I fell foul of him one evening, I remember, at bowls.

Ned Lambert smiled.

—Yes, he was, he said, in Wisdom Hely's. A traveller for blottingpaper.

—In God's name, John Henry Menton said, what did she marry a coon like that for? She had plenty of game in her then.

—Has still, Ned Lambert said. He does some 30 canvassing for ads.

John Henry Menton's large eyes stared ahead.

The barrow turned into a side lane. A portly man, ambushed among the grasses, raised his hat in homage. The gravediggers touched their caps.

—John O'Connell, Mr Power said, pleased. He never forgets a friend.

Mr O'Connell shook all their hands in si-40 lence. Mr Dedalus said:

—I am come to pay you another visit.

—My dear Simon, the caretaker answered in a low voice. I don't want your custom at all.

Saluting Ned Lambert and John Henry Menton he walked on at Martin Cunningham's side, puzzling two keys at his back.

—Did you hear that one, he asked them, about Mulcahy from the Coombe?

—I did not, Martin Cunningham said.

50 They bent their silk hats in concert and Hynes inclined his ear. The caretaker hung his

thumbs in the loops of his gold watch chain and spoke in a discreet tone to their vacant smiles.

—They tell the story, he said, that two drunks came out here one foggy evening to look for the grave of a friend of theirs. They asked for Mulcahy from the Coombe and were told where he was buried. After traipsing about in the fog they found the grave, sure enough. One 60 of the drunks spelt out the name: Terence Mulcahy. The other drunk was blinking up at a statue of our Saviour the widow had got put up.

The caretaker blinked up at one of the sepulchres they passed. He resumed:

—And, after blinking up at the sacred figure, *Not a bloody bit like the man*, says he. *That's not Mulcahy*, says he, *whoever done it.*

Rewarded by smiles he fell back and spoke 70 with Corny Kelleher, accepting the dockets given him, turning them over and scanning them as he walked.

—That's all done with a purpose, Martin Cunningham explained to Hynes.

—I know, Hynes said, I know that.

—To cheer a fellow up, Martin Cunningham said. It's pure goodheartedness: damn the thing else.

Mr Bloom admired the caretaker's prosper- 80 ous bulk. All want to be on good terms with him. Decent fellow, John O'Connell, real good sort. Keys: like Keyes's ad: no fear of anyone getting out, no passout checks. *Habeas corpus.* I must see about that ad after the funeral. Did I write Ballsbridge on the envelope I took to cover when she disturbed me writing to Martha? Hope it's not chucked in the dead letter office. Be the better of a shave. Grey spouting beard. That's the first sign when the hairs come 90 out grey and temper getting cross. Silver threads among the grey. Fancy being his wife. Wonder how he had the gumption to propose to any girl. Come out and live in the graveyard. Dangle that before her. It might thrill her first. Courting death . . . Shades of night hovering here with all the dead stretched about. The shadows of the tombs when churchyards yawn and Daniel O'Connell must be a de-

93. **gumption . . . girl.** John O'Connell, the caretaker, is the Homeric recall of Pluto, king of Hades. Pluto was forced to resort to abduction to get his bride, Proserpine.

scendant I suppose who is this used to say he was a queer breedy man great catholic all the same like a big giant in the dark. Will o' the wisp. Gas of graves. Want to keep her mind off it to conceive at all. Women especially are so touchy. Tell her a ghost story in bed to make her sleep. Have you ever seen a ghost? Well, I have. It was pitchdark night. The clock was on the stroke of twelve. Still they'd kiss all right if properly keyed up. Whores in Turkish graveyards. Learn anything if taken young. You might pick up a young widow here. Men like that. Love among the tombstones. Romeo. Spice of pleasure. In the midst of death we are in life. Both ends meet. Tantalising for the poor dead. Smell of grilled beefsteaks to the starving gnawing their vitals. Desire to grig people. Molly wanting to do it at the window. Eight children he has anyway.

He has seen a fair share go under in his time, lying around him field after field. Holy fields. More room if they buried them standing. Sitting or kneeling you couldn't. Standing? His head might come up some day above ground in a landslip with his hand pointing. All honeycombed the ground must be: oblong cells. And very neat he keeps it too, trim grass and edgings. His garden Major Gamble calls Mount Jerome. Well so it is. Ought to be flowers of sleep. Chinese cemeteries with giant poppies growing produce the best opium Mastiansky told me. The Botanic Gardens are just over there. It's the blood sinking in the earth gives new life. Same idea those jews they said killed the christian boy. Every man his price. Well preserved fat corpse gentlemen, epicure, invaluable for fruit garden. A bargain. By carcass of William Wilkinson, auditor and accountant, lately deceased, three pounds thirteen and six. With thanks.

I daresay the soil would be quite fat with corpse manure, bones, flesh, nails, charnelhouses. Dreadful. Turning green and pink, decomposing. Rot quick in damp earth. The lean old ones tougher. Then a kind of a tallowy kind of a cheesy. Then begin to get black, tre-

acle oozing out of them. Then dried up. Deadmoths. Of course the cells or whatever they are go on living. Changing about. Live for ever practically. Nothing to feed on feed on themselves.

But they must breed a devil of a lot of maggots. Soil must be simply swirling with them. Your head it simply swurls. Those pretty little seaside gurls. He looks cheerful enough over it. Gives him a sense of power seeing all the others go under first. Wonder how he looks at life. Cracking his jokes too: warms the cockles of his heart. The one about the bulletin. Spurgeon went to heaven 4 a.m. this morning. 11 p.m. (closing time). Not arrived yet. Peter. The dead themselves the men anyhow would like to hear an odd joke or the women to know what's in fashion. A juicy pear or ladies' punch, hot, strong and sweet. Keep out of the damp. You must laugh sometimes so better do it that way. Gravediggers in *Hamlet*. Shows the profound knowledge of the human heart. Daren't joke about the dead for two years at least. *De mortuis nil nisi prius*. Go out of mourning first. Hard to imagine his funeral. Seems a sort of a joke. Read your own obituary notice they say you live longer. Gives you second wind. New lease of life.

—How many have you for tomorrow? the caretaker asked.

—Two, Corny Kelleher said. Half ten and eleven.

The caretaker put the papers in this pocket. The barrow had ceased to trundle. The mourners split and moved to each side of the hole, stepping with care round the graves. The gravediggers bore the coffin and set its nose on the brink, looping the bands round it.

Burying him. We come to bury Caesar. His ides of March or June. He doesn't know who is here nor care.

Now who is that lankylooking galoot over there in the macintosh? Now who is he I'd like to know? Now, I'd give a trifle to know who he

---

34. Same . . . boy. There are several legends in medieval literature treating of the murder of a little Christian boy by Jews; the best known is the case of little Hugh of Lincoln, mentioned in the Waverly Annals for the year 1255. It is the subject of an extremely widespread cycle of popular ballads, a saint's legend (St. Hugh), and Chaucer's very effective *Prioress's Tale*.

54. swurls. The pronunciation of the word suggests to Mr. Bloom the spelling given here. The refrain of the popular song from which this and the following sentence are derived appears more than once in *Ulysses*. **69. De . . . prius.** The original saying is the Latin proverb, *De mortuis nil nisi bonum,* (Say) nothing but good concerning the dead. But Mr. Bloom is reminded by the *nisi* of the legal phrase, *nisi prius.* The phrase is used in any legal case involving an issue of fact and declares that such case must be tried at Westminster (London) *unless* the case has *first* been tried in the county where it originated.

519

is. Always someone turns up you never dreamt of. A fellow could live on his lonesome all his life. Yes, he could. Still he'd have to get someone to sod him after he died though he could dig his own grave. We all do. Only man buries. No ants too. First thing strikes anybody. Bury the dead. Say Robinson Crusoe was true to life. Well then Friday buried him. Every Friday buries a Thursday if you come to look
10 at it.

O, poor Robinson Crusoe,
How could you possibly do so?

Poor Dignam! His last lie on the earth in his box. When you think of them all it does seem a waste of wood. All gnawed through. They could invent a handsome bier with a kind of panel sliding let it down that way. Ay but they might object to be buried out of another fellow's. They're so particular. Lay me in my na-
20 tive earth. Bit of clay from the holy land. Only a mother and deadborn child ever buried in the one coffin. I see what it means, I see. To protect him as long as possible even in the earth. The Irishman's house is his coffin. Embalming in catacombs, mummies, the same idea.

Mr Bloom stood far back, his hat in his hand, counting the bared heads. Twelve. I'm thirteen. No. The chap in the macintosh is thir-
30 teen. Death's number. Where the deuce did he pop out of? He wasn't in the chapel, that I'll swear. Silly superstition that about thirteen.

Nice soft tweed Ned Lambert has in that suit. Tinge of purple. I had one like that when we lived in Lombard street west. Dressy fellow he was once. Used to change three suits in the day. Must get that grey suit of mine turned by Mesias. Hello. It's dyed. His wife I forgot he's not married or his landlady ought
40 to have picked out those threads for him.

The coffin dived out of sight, eased down by the men straddled on the gravetrestles. They struggle up and out: and all uncovered. Twenty.

Pause.

If we were all suddenly somebody else.

Far away a donkey brayed. Rain. No such ass. Never see a dead one, they say. Shame of death. They hide. Also poor papa went away.
50 Gentle sweet air blew round the bared heads

in a whisper. Whisper. The boy by the gravehead held his wreath with both hands staring quietly in the black open space. Mr Bloom moved behind the portly kindly caretaker. Well cut frockcoat. Weighing them up perhaps to see which will go next. Well it is a long rest. Feel no more. It's the moment you feel. Must be damned unpleasant. Can't believe it at first. Mistake must be: someone else. Try the house opposite. Wait, I wanted to I haven't yet. Then darkened deathchamber. Light they want. Whispering around you. Would you like to see a priest? Then rambling and wandering. Delirium all you hid all your life. The death struggle. His sleep is not natural. Press his lower eyelid. Watching is his nose pointed is his jaw sinking are the soles of his feet yellow. Pull the pillow away and finish it off on the floor since he's doomed. Devil in that picture of sinner's death showing him a woman. Dying to embrace her in his shirt. Last act of *Lucia. Shall I nevermore behold thee?* Bam! expires. Gone at last. People talk about you a bit: forget you. Don't forget to pray for him. Remember him in your prayers. Even Parnell. Ivy day dying out. Then they follow: dropping into a hole one after the other.

We are praying now for the repose of his soul. Hoping you're well and not in hell. Nice change of air. Out of the fryingpan of life into the fire of purgatory.

Does he ever think of the hole waiting for himself? They say you do when you shiver in the sun. Someone walking over it. Callboy's warning. Near you. Mine over there towards Finglas, the plot I bought. Mamma poor mamma, and little Rudy.

The gravediggers took up their spades and flung heavy clods of clay in on the coffin. Mr

72. *Lucia . . . thee.* In Donizetti's opera, *Lucia di Lammermoor*, the hero, Edgardo, hearing that Lucia is dead, commits suicide by stabbing himself. Before he dies he sings this aria (*Tu che spiegasti*), one of the most beautiful in romantic Italian opera. 75. **Parnell.** Charles Stewart Parnell (1846–1891) was the most prominent leader of the Irish nationalists after the death of O'Connell (cf. p. 517, note to l. 24). He was a member of Parliament for County Meath and won the support of Prime Minister Gladstone in his struggle for recognition of the Irish nation. Unfortunately he was involved first in charges of forgery—from which he was completely exonerated—and then, more seriously, in a divorce scandal. He died suddenly under the shadow of the proceedings, his party split, and his objectives far from realized. Ivy day is observed among the Parnellites on October 9, the anniversary of Parnell's death; on this day a memorial procession and ceremony is held; the scene is Glasnevin Cemetery in Dublin, where Paddy Dignam is being buried (cf. p. 521, note to l. 80).

Bloom turned his face. And if he was alive all the time? Whew! By Jingo, that would be awful! No, no: he is dead, of course. Of course he is dead. Monday he died. They ought to have some law to pierce the heart and make sure or an electric clock or a telephone in the coffin and some kind of a canvas airhole. Flag of distress. Three days. Rather long to keep them in summer. Just as well to get shut of them as soon as you are sure there's no.

The clay fell softer. Begin to be forgotten. Out of sight, out of mind.

The caretaker moved away a few paces and put on his hat. Had enough of it. The mourners took heart of grace, one by one, covering themselves without show. Mr Bloom put on his hat and saw the portly figure make its way deftly through the maze of graves. Quietly, sure of his ground, he traversed the dismal fields.

Hynes jotting down something in his notebook. Ah, the names. But he knows them all. No: coming to me.

—I am just taking the names, Hynes said below his breath. What is your christian name? I'm not sure.

—L, Mr Bloom said. Leopold. And you might put down M'Coy's name too. He asked me to.

—Charley, Hynes said writing. I know. He was on the *Freeman* once.

So he was before he got the job in the morgue under Louis Byrne. Good idea a post-mortem for doctors. Find out what they imagine they know. He died on a Tuesday. Got the run. Levanted with the cash of a few ads. Charley, you're my darling. That was why he asked me to. O well, does no harm. I saw to that, M'Coy. Thanks, old chap: much obliged. Leave him under an obligation: costs nothing.

—And tell us, Hynes said, do you know that fellow in the, fellow was over there in the . . .

He looked around.

—Macintosh. Yes, I saw him, Mr Bloom said. Where is he now?

—Macintosh, Hynes said, scribbling. I don't know who he is. Is that his name?

He moved away, looking about him.

—No, Mr Bloom began, turning and stopping. I say, Hynes!

Didn't hear. What? Where has he disappeared to? Not a sign. Well of all the. Has anybody here seen? Kay ee double ell. Become invisible. Good Lord, what became of him?

A seventh gravedigger came beside Mr Bloom to take up an idle spade.

—O, excuse me!

He stepped aside nimbly.

Clay, brown, damp, began to be seen in the hole. It rose. Nearly over. A mound of damp clods rose more, rose, and the gravediggers rested their spades. All uncovered again for a few instants. The boy propped his wreath against a corner: the brother-in-law his on a lump. The gravediggers put on their caps and carried their earthy spades towards the barrow. Then knocked the blades lightly on the turf: clean. One bent to pluck from the haft a long tuft of grass. One, leaving his mates, walked slowly on with shouldered weapon, its blade blue-glancing. Silently at the gravehead another coiled the coffinband. His navelcord. The brother-in-law, turning away, placed something in his free hand. Thanks in silence. Sorry, sir: trouble. Headshake. I know that. For yourselves just.

The mourners moved away slowly, without aim, by devious paths, staying awhile to read a name on a tomb.

—Let us go round by the chief's grave, Hynes said. We have time.

—Let us, Mr Power said.

They turned to the right, following their slow thoughts. With awe Mr Power's blank voice spoke:

—Some say he is not in that grave at all. That the coffin was filled with stones. That one day he will come again.

Hynes shook his head.

—Parnell will never come again, he said. He's there, all that was mortal of him. Peace to his ashes.

Mr Bloom walked unheeded along his grove by saddened angels, crosses, broken pillars, family vaults, stone hopes praying with upcast

---

36. **Levanted,** embezzled.

72. **navelcord,** the umbilicus. In *Ulysses* it symbolizes the link in the chain of lives and the reincarnation of life.   80. **chief's grave,** Parnell's (cf. p. 520, note to l. 75). Parnell was a Protestant, and his burial in Glasnevin Cemetery is remarkable.

eyes, old Ireland's hearts and hands. More sensible to spend the money on some charity for the living. Pray for the repose of the soul of. Does anybody really? Plant him and have done with him. Like down a coalshoot. Then lump them together to save time. All soul's day. Twenty-seventh I'll be at his grave. Ten shillings for the gardener. He keeps it free of weeds. Old man himself. Bent down double with his shears clipping. Near death's door. Who passed away. Who departed this life. As if they did it of their own accord. Got the shove, all of them. Who kicked the bucket. More interesting if they told you what they were. So and so, wheelwright. I travelled for cork lino. I paid five shillings in the pound. Or a woman's with her saucepan. I cooked good Irish stew. Eulogy in a country churchyard it ought to be that poem of whose is it Wordsworth or Thomas Campbell. Entered into rest the protestants put it. Old Dr Murren's. The great physician called him home. Well it's God's acre for them. Nice country residence. Newly plastered and painted. Ideal spot to have a quiet smoke and read the *Church Times.* Marriage ads they never try to beautify. Rusty wreaths hung on knobs, garlands of bronzefoil. Better value that for the money. Still, the flowers are more poetical. The other gets rather tiresome, never withering. Expresses nothing. Immortelles.

A bird sat tamely perched on a poplar branch. Like stuffed. Like the wedding present alderman Hooper gave us. Hu! Not a budge out of him. Knows there are no catapults to let fly at him. Dead animal even sadder. Silly-Milly burying the little dead bird in the kitchen matchbox, a daisy-chain and bits of broken chainies on the grave.

The Sacred Heart that is: showing it. Heart on his sleeve. Ought to be sideways and red it should be painted like a real heart. Ireland was dedicated to it or whatever that. Seems anything but pleased. Why this infliction? Would birds come then and peck like the boy with the basket of fruit but he said no because they ought to have been afraid of the boy. Apollo that was.

How many! All these here once walked

round Dublin. Faithful departed. As you are now so once were we.

Besides how could you remember everybody? Eyes, walk, voice. Well, the voice, yes: gramophone. Have a gramophone in every grave or keep it in the house. After dinner on a Sunday. Put on poor old greatgrandfather Kraahraark! Hellohellohello amawfullyglad kraark awfullygladaseeragain hellohello amarawf kopthsth. Remind you of the voice like the photograph reminds you of the face. Otherwise you couldn't remember the face after fifteen years, say. For instance who? For instance some fellow that died when I was in Wisdom Hely's.

Rtststr! A rattle of pebbles. Wait. Stop.

He looked down intently into a stone crypt. Some animal. Wait. There he goes.

An obese grey rat toddled along the side of the crypt, moving the pebbles. An old stager: greatgrandfather: he knows the ropes. The grey alive crushed itself in under the plinth, wriggled itself in under it. Good hidingplace for treasure.

Who lives there? Are laid the remains of Robert Emery. Robert Emmet was buried here by torchlight, wasn't he? Making his rounds.

Tail gone now.

One of those chaps would make short work of a fellow. Pick the bones clean no matter who it was. Ordinary meat for them. A corpse is meat gone bad. Well and what's cheese? Corpse of milk. I read in that *Voyages in China* that the Chinese say a white man smells like a corpse. Cremation better. Priests dead against it. Devilling for the other firm. Wholesale burners and Dutch oven dealers. Time of the plague. Quicklime fever pits to eat them. Lethal chamber. Ashes to ashes. Or bury at sea. Where is that Parsee tower of silence? Eaten by birds. Earth, fire, water. Drowning they say is the pleasantest. See your whole life in a flash. But being brought back to life no. Can't bury in the air however. Out of a flying machine. Wonder does the news go about whenever a

---

16. **lino,** linoleum.   18. **Eulogy . . . Campbell.** Actually it was Thomas Gray (1716–1771) who wrote "Elegy Written in a Country Churchyard" (1751), probably the best-known poem of the eighteenth century.

75. **Robert Emmet,** one of the earliest of the Irish workers for national independence; he attempted to seize the arsenal at Dublin and begin a general revolution, but his support melted away. He was finally captured and executed (1803), at the age of 26.   89. **Parsee . . . silence.** In Bombay, India, the large colony of Parsees (descended from the ancient Zoroastrians, or Fire-worshipers of Persia, also called the Magi) placed their dead in open towers; birds of prey ate the flesh from the bodies.

fresh one is let down. Underground communication. We learned that from them. Wouldn't be surprised. Regular square feed for them. Flies come before he's well dead. Got wind of Dignam. They wouldn't care about the smell of it. Salt-white crumbling mush of corpse: smell, taste like raw white turnips.

The gates glimmered in front: still open. Back to the world again. Enough of this place. Brings you a bit nearer every time. Last time I was here was Mrs Sinico's funeral. Poor papa too. The love that kills. And even scraping up the earth at night with a lantern like that case I read of to get at fresh buried females or even putrefied with running gravesores. Give you the creeps after a bit. I will appear to you after death. You will see my ghost after death. My ghost will haunt you after death. There is another world after death named hell. I do not like that other world she wrote. No more do I. Plenty to see and hear and feel yet. Feel live warm beings near you. Let them sleep in their maggoty beds. They are not going to get me this innings. Warm beds: warm fullblooded life.

Martin Cunningham emerged from a sidepath, talking gravely.

Solicitor, I think. I know his face. Menton. John Henry, solicitor, commissioner for oaths and affidavits. Dignam used to be in his office. Mat Dillon's long ago. Jolly Mat convivial evenings. Cold fowl, cigars, the Tantalus glasses. Heart of gold really. Yes, Menton. Got

19. **I . . . world.** Mr. Bloom is thinking of a sentence from Martha Clifford's letter, "I do not like that other world." 32. **Tantalus,** a kind of locked case or cellaret for wines and liquors. 33. **Got . . . out,** became annoyed.

his rag out that evening on the bowling green because I sailed inside him. Pure fluke of mine: the bias. Why he took such a rooted dislike to me. Hate at first sight. Molly and Floey Dillon linked under the lilactree, laughing. Fellow always like that, mortified if women are by.

Got a dinge in the side of his hat. Carriage 40 probably.

—Excuse me, sir, Mr Bloom said beside them. They stopped.

—Your hat is a little crushed, Mr Bloom said, pointing.

John Henry Menton stared at him for an instant without moving.

—There, Martin Cunningham helped, pointing also.

John Henry Menton took off his hat, bulged 50 out the dinge and smoothed the nap with care on his coatsleeve. He clapped the hat on his head again.

—It's all right now, Martin Cunningham said.

John Henry Menton jerked his head down in acknowledgment.

—Thank you, he said shortly.

They walked on towards the gates. Mr Bloom, chapfallen, drew behind a few paces so as not to overhear. Martin laying down the law. 60 Martin could wind a sappyhead like that round his little finger without his seeing it.

Oyster eyes. Never mind. Be sorry after perhaps when it dawns on him. Get the pull over him that way.

Thank you. How grand we are this morning.

64. **Get . . .him,** get back at him.

VIRGINIA WOOLF

A brilliant, sensitive, and spiritual descendant of the Victorian intellectuals, Virginia Woolf developed into one of the most distinguished and, at the same time, controversial writers of her day. Endowed with a fluid, delicate, yet vigorous style and a poetic insight greater perhaps than that of any other English-speaking novelist of the present generation, she has taken her place just below James Joyce as a portrayer of the mercurial powers and the fitful restlessness of the twentieth-century mind.

Mrs. Woolf was born, like Joyce, in 1882; her father was the noted critic Sir Leslie Stephen, editor of *The Cornhill Magazine* and *The Dictionary of National Biography.* By birth and marriage she was related to Thackeray, Darwin, and John Addington Symonds. She began her writing as a book reviewer for the *London Times Literary Supplement*. With her husband, Leonard Woolf, she established the Hogarth Press, which enabled the Woolfs to gather together a group of intellectuals which included the novelists E. M. Forster and V. Sackville-West, the Sitwells (p. 218), the biographer Lytton Strachey (p. 135), and the economist John Maynard Keynes.

Her first two novels, *The Voyage Out* (1915) and *Night and Day* (1919), are of no great moment, though in the latter we find unmistakable signs of Mrs. Woolf's unquenchable interest in the symbolic. In 1919, however, she began to read James Joyce's *Ulysses* (p. 503), then coming out in *The Little Review*, and a few years later the works of Marcel Proust. The effect of these two powerful creative minds upon her work was, as she put it, "a memorable catastrophe." Four novels from her pen, undoubtedly the works on which her fame will rest, show undoubted evidence of the influences of Joyce and Proust—*Jacob's Room* (1922); *Mrs. Dalloway* (1925); *To the Lighthouse* (1927); and *The Waves* (1931), to which an earlier volume of sketches, *Monday or Tuesday* (1921) serves as an admirable introduction. Among her non-fictional works, the general reader will find *The Common Reader* (1925) and *The Second Common Reader* (1932) the most valuable.

We may term these four novels just mentioned "stream-of-consciousness" novels, although the phrase is too loose and too simplifying to afford an accurate definition. *Jacob's Room* is the world of a young man—his sojourn at Cambridge; his travels; his life in London; his studies abroad; his death in the First World War. But we see Jacob only through the other people about him—that is, through his "room." *Mrs. Dalloway*, covering a time-span of only twelve temporal hours, compresses the lives of many people into that short period, in a manner similar in objectives though not in methods to Joyce's *Ulysses*.

The theory that emerges from *Mrs. Dalloway* in particular is one of Virginia Woolf's favorite theses: everything that happened to Mrs. Dalloway and everything she did in those twelve hours were shaped by what had happened to her and what she had done before. The past, the present, and, it is to be inferred, the future are all part of a single piece, though we are never told this in so many words. And as it was for Mrs. Dalloway, so is it for everything and everybody in twentieth-century British civilization about her.

In *To the Lighthouse*, a family vacationing in the Hebrides plans an excursion to a lighthouse. For one reason or another, the excursion is never made. Years later, the little boy, once so disappointed, visits the lighthouse as a young man, only to be disillusioned. Time has had its way with the lighthouse, with the home of the Ramsays, with the young man himself. Time, in effect, is the real protagonist of this novel, which remains probably the most powerful and certainly the most moving of all Mrs. Woolf's works.

The Waves is a difficult novel because Mrs. Woolf, in her quest after the life of the human mentality, has cast aside all semblance of conventional structure. Six friends, at different points in their progress from birth to death, are caught and fixed by a series of soliloquies which imply rather than explain what has happened to them. The integrating element here is the sea (a symbol for Time), to which Mrs. Woolf has addressed a series of beautiful poetic prose interludes which illustrate remarkably her essentially lyrical nature. But the language throughout is the author's, not the characters'. Characterization, in fact, so essential to the conventional concept of a novel, has been subordinated to an interpretation of the universality of human spiritual experience.

Further into this intangible kingdom Virginia Woolf could not go; and her last two novels, *The Years* (1937) and *Between the Acts* (1941), are more conventional and much less effective, although in *The Years* the ravages of time are dominating forces. Freakish but brilliant is her prose fantasy, *Orlando* (1928), a historical study of the English scene from the time of Queen Elizabeth to the present, in which the hero moves through English history and English literature, changing sex on one occasion in order to bring into the picture the essential feminine elements in life. *Orlando* illustrates, moreover, a second favorite idea of Virginia Woolf—namely, that there are many potential beings wrapped up in every individual human being. *Flush* (1933), the biography of Elizabeth Barrett Browning's little spaniel, may be dismissed as a charming tour de force. *Three Guineas* (1938) is notable for its passionate hatred for war, that inhuman institution which afflicts mankind, the awful being whose face is the face of death.

The almost mystic blending of time and personality in Mrs. Woolf's novels should be buttressed in the reader's mind with her love of life—a gift at once beautiful, painful, and paradoxical—and her faith in life in which death, an ever-present fact, is only an incident. The life of the mind and the interplay of many human personalities, moving horizontally in a space-time relationship and vertically in a psychological projection in which the limitations of time and space no longer exist—these constitute Virginia Woolf's natural kingdom. Thus it may take only a few seconds to wind a watch; but in those few seconds the mind can flash back and forth over a whole lifetime, playing over the lives of innumerable other human beings—indeed over all Eternity. Reality, as most people understand the term, becomes then far more than a materialistic fact. The lighthouse to which the young boy aspired was a beautiful, unattained figment; the lighthouse which the young man visited proved to be a mean, prosaic thing—yet both, as Virginia Woolf sees it, had true reality. Her blending of the tangible and intangible is marvelously delicate but, once understood, hauntingly impressive.

Unfortunately, she cared little about the common middle-class problems of existence and survival, in which dreams are too often rudely displaced by vulgar and prostituting compromises. Hers was an aristocratic, poetic, essentially romantic intelligence which, because it regarded life as a "translucent envelope" which contains us all, found all attempts to grip life in concrete terms uncertain and unsatisfying. For all Virginia Woolf's instinctive faith in life and in the integrity of human personality, the cruel physical horrors of the Second World War were too much for her. On March 28, 1941, she drowned herself in a Sussex stream, in a brave decision to compromise no longer in her choice between death and insanity.

from The Waves

[The novel is written in sections; each section is a series of monologues by the main characters. The course of the lives of these characters is indicated in a prose-poem prefixed to each of the sections, in which the sun symbolizes their lives, and the pressing waves the inevitable passage of time, which will ultimately triumph over all. In the following section, therefore, it should be remembered that the characters are speaking from a time somewhat 10 past the middle of their lives.]

T*HE SUN no longer stood in the middle of the sky. Its light slanted, falling obliquely. Here it caught on the edge of a cloud and burnt it into a slice of light, a blazing island on which no foot could rest. Then another cloud was caught in the light and another and another, so that the waves beneath were arrow-struck with fiery feathered darts that shot erratically across the quivering blue.* 20

The topmost leaves of the tree were crisped in the sun. They rustled stiffly in the random breeze. The birds sat still save that they flicked their heads sharply from side to side. Now they paused in their song as if glutted with sound, as if the fullness of midday had gorged them. The dragon-fly poised motionless over a reed then shot its blue stitch further through the air. The far hum in the distance seemed made of the broken tremor of fine wings danc- 30 *ing up and down on the horizon. The river water held the reeds now fixed as if glass had hardened round them; and then the glass wavered and the reeds swept low. Pondering, sunken headed the cattle stood in the fields and cumbrously moved one foot and then another. In the bucket near the house the tap stopped dripping, as if the bucket were full, and then the tap dripped one, two, three separate drops in succession.* 40

The windows showed erratically spots of burning fire, the elbow of one branch, and then some tranquil space of pure clarity. The blind hung red at the window's edge and within the room daggers of light fell upon chairs and tables making cracks across their lacquer and polish. The green pot bulged enormously, with its white window elongated in its side. Light driving darkness before it spilt itself profusely upon the corners and bosses; and yet heaped up darkness in mounds of unmoulded shape.

The waves massed themselves, curved their backs and crashed. Up spurted stones and shingle. They swept round the rocks, and the spray, leaping high, spattered the walls of a cave that had been dry before, and left pools inland, where some fish, stranded, lashed its tail as the wave drew back.

"I have signed my name," said Louis, "already twenty times. I, and again I, and again I. Clear, firm, unequivocal, there it stands, my name. Clear-cut and unequivocal am I too. Yet a vast inheritance of experience is packed in me. I have lived thousands of years. I am like a worm that has eaten its way through the wood of a very old oak beam. But now I am compact; now I am gathered together this fine morning.

"The sun shines from a clear sky. But twelve o'clock brings neither rain nor sunshine. It is the hour when Miss Johnson brings me my letters in a wire tray. Upon these white sheets I indent my name. The whisper of leaves, water running down gutters, green depths flecked with dahlias and zinnias; I, now a duke, now Plato, companion of Socrates; the tramp of dark men and yellow men migrating east, west, north and south; the eternal procession, women going with attaché cases down the Strand as they went once with pitchers to the Nile; all the furled and close-packed leaves of my many-folded life are now summed in my name; incised cleanly and barely on the sheet. Now a full-grown man; now upright standing in sun or rain, I must drop heavy as a hatchet and cut the oak with my sheer weight, for if I deviate, glancing this way, or that way, I shall fall like snow and be wasted.

"I am half in love with the typewriter and the telephone. With letters and cables and brief but courteous commands on the telephone to Paris, Berlin, New York I have fused my many lives into one; I have helped by my assiduity and decision to score those lines on the map there by which the different parts of the world are laced together. I love punctually at ten to come into my room; I love the purple glow of the dark mahogany; I love the table and its sharp edge; and the smooth-running drawers. I love the telephone with its lip stretched to my whisper, and the date on the wall; and the engagement book. Mr. Prentice at four; Mr. Eyres sharp at four-thirty.

"I like to be asked to come to Mr. Burchard's private room and report on our commitments to China. I hope to inherit an armchair and a Turkey carpet. My shoulder is to the wheel; I roll the dark before me, spreading commerce where there was chaos in the far parts of the world. If I press on, from chaos making order, I shall find myself where Chatham stood, and Pitt, Burke, and Sir Robert Peel. Thus I expunge certain stains, and erase old defilements; the woman who gave me a flag from the top of the Christmas tree; my accent; beatings and other tortures; the boasting boys; my father, a banker at Brisbane.

"I have read my poet in an eating-house, and, stirring my coffee, listened to the clerks making bets at the little tables, watched the women hesitating at the counter. I said that nothing should be irrelevant, like a piece of brown paper dropped casually on the floor. I said their journeys should have an end in view; they should earn their two pound ten a week at the command of an august master; some hand, some robe, should fold us about in the evening. When I have healed these fractures and comprehended these monstrosities so that they need neither excuse nor apology which both waste our strength, I shall give back to the street and the eating-shop what they lost when they fell on these hard times and broke on these stony beaches. I shall assemble a few words and forge round us a hammered ring of beaten steel.

"But now I have not a moment to spare. There is no respite here, no shadow made of quivering leaves, or alcove to which one can retreat from the sun, to sit, with a lover, in the cool of the evening. The weight of the world is on our shoulders; its vision is through our eyes;

if we blink or look aside, or turn back to finger what Plato said or remember Napoleon and his conquests, we inflict on the world the injury of some obliquity. This is life; Mr. Prentice at four; Mr. Eyres at four-thirty. I like to hear the soft rush of the lift and the thud with which it stops on my landing and the heavy male tread of responsible feet down the corridors. So by dint of our united exertions we send ships to the remotest parts of the globe; replete with lavatories and gymnasiums. The weight of the world is on our shoulders. This is life. If I press on, I shall inherit a chair and a rug; a place in Surrey with glass houses, and some rare conifer, melon, or flowering tree which other merchants will envy.

"Yet I still keep my attic room. There I open the usual little book; there I watch the rain glisten on the tiles till they shine like a policeman's waterproof; there I see the broken windows in poor people's houses; the lean cats; some slattern squinting in a cracked looking-glass as she arranges her face for the street corner; there Rhoda sometimes comes. For we are lovers.

"Percival has died; (he died in Egypt; he died in Greece; all deaths are one death). Susan has children; Neville mounts rapidly to the conspicuous heights. Life passes. The clouds change perpetually over our houses. I do this, do that, and again do this and then that. Meeting and parting, we assemble different forms, make different patterns. But if I do not nail these impressions to the board and out of the many men in me make one; exist here and now and not in streaks and patches, like scattered snow wreaths of far mountains; and ask Miss Johnson as I pass through the office about the movies and take my cup of tea and accept also my favorite biscuit; then I shall fall like snow and be wasted.

"Yet when six o'clock comes and I touch my hat to the commissionaire, being always too effusive in ceremony since I desire so much to be accepted; and struggle, leaning against the wind, buttoned up, with my jaws blue and my eyes running water, I wish that a little typist would cuddle on my knees; I think that my favorite dish is liver and bacon; and so am apt to wander to the river, to the narrow streets where there are frequent public-houses, and the shadows of ships passing at the end of the street, and women fighting. But I say to myself, recovering my sanity, Mr. Prentice at four; Mr. Eyres at four-thirty. The hatchet must fall on the block; the oak must be cleft to the center. The weight of the world is on my shoulders. Here is the pen and the paper; on the letters in the wire basket I sign my name, I, I, and again I."

"Summer comes, and winter," said Susan. "The seasons pass. The pear fills itself and drops from the tree. The dead leaf rests on its edge. But steam has obscured the window. I sit by the fire watching the kettle boil. I see the pear tree through the streaked steam on the window-pane.

"Sleep, sleep, I croon, whether it is summer or winter, May or November. Sleep I sing—I, who am unmelodious and hear no music save rustic music when a dog barks, a bell tinkles, or wheels crunch upon the gravel. I sing my song by the fire like an old shell murmuring on the beach. Sleep, sleep, I say, warning off with my voice all who rattle milk-cans, fire at rooks, shoot rabbits, or in any way bring the shock of destruction near this wicker cradle, laden with soft limbs, curled under a pink coverlet.

"I have lost my indifference, my blank eyes, my pear-shaped eyes that saw to the root. I am no longer January, May or any other season, but am all spun to a fine thread round the cradle, wrapping in a cocoon made of my own blood the delicate limbs of my baby. Sleep, I say, and feel within me uprush some wilder, darker violence, so that I would fell down with one blow any intruder, any snatcher, who should break into this room and wake the sleeper.

"I pad about the house all day long in apron and slippers, like my mother who died of cancer. Whether it is summer, whether it is winter, I no longer know by the moor grass, and the heath flower; only by the steam on the window-pane, or the frost on the window-pane. When the lark peels high his ring of sound and it falls through the air like an apple paring, I stoop; I feed my baby. I, who used to walk through beech woods noting the jay's feather

527

turning blue as it falls, past the shepherd and the tramp, who stared at the woman squatted beside a tilted cart in a ditch, go from room to room with a duster. Sleep, I say, desiring sleep to fall like a blanket of down and cover these weak limbs; demanding that life shall sheathe its claws and gird its lightning and pass by, making of my own body a hollow, a warm shelter for my child to sleep in. Sleep, I say, sleep.
Or I go to the window, I look at the rook's high nest; and the pear tree. 'His eyes will see when mine are shut,' I think. 'I shall go mixed with them beyond my body and shall see India. He will come home, bringing me trophies to be laid at my feet. He will increase my possessions.'

"But I never rise at dawn and see the purple drops in the cabbage leaves; the red drops in the roses. I do not watch the setter nose in a circle, or lie at night watching the leaves hide the stars and the stars move and the leaves hang still. The butcher calls; the milk has to be stood under a shade lest it should sour.

"Sleep, I say, sleep, as the kettle boils and its breath comes thicker and thicker issuing in one jet from the spout. So life fills my veins. So life pours through my limbs. So I am driven forward, till I could cry, as I move from dawn to dusk opening and shutting, 'No more, I am glutted with natural happiness.' Yet more will come, more children; more cradles, more baskets in the kitchen and hams ripening; and onions glistening; and more beds of lettuce and potatoes. I am blown like a leaf by the gale; now brushing the wet grass, now whirled up. I am glutted with natural happiness; and wish sometimes that the fullness would pass from me and the weight of the sleeping house rise, when we sit reading, and I stay the thread at the eye of my needle. The lamp kindles a fire in the dark pane. A fire burns in the heart of the ivy. I see a lit-up street in the evergreens. I hear traffic in the brush of the wind down the lane, and broken voices, and laughter, and Jinny who cries as the door opens, 'Come, Come!'

"But no sound breaks the silence of our house, where the fields sigh close to the door. The wind washes through the elm trees; a moth hits the lamp; a cow lows; a crack of sound starts in the rafter, and I push my thread through the needle and murmur, 'Sleep.'"

"Now is the moment," said Jinny. "Now we have met, and have come together. Now let us talk, let us tell stories. Who is he? Who is she? I am infinitely curious and do not know what is to come. If you, whom I meet for the first time, were to say to me, 'The coach starts at four from Piccadilly,' I would not stay to fling a few necessaries in a bandbox, but would come at once.

"Let us sit here under the cut flowers, on the sofa by the picture. Let us decorate our Christmas tree with facts and again with facts. People are so soon gone; let us catch them. That man there, by the cabinet; he lives, you say, surrounded by china pots. Break one and you shatter a thousand pounds. And he loved a girl in Rome and she left him. Hence the pots, old junk found in lodging-houses or dug from the desert sands. And since beauty must be broken daily to remain beautiful, and he is static, his life stagnates in a china sea. It is strange, though; for once as a young man, he sat on damp ground and drank rum with soldiers.

"One must be quick and add facts deftly, like toys to a tree, fixing them with a twist of the fingers. He stoops, how he stoops, even over an azalea. He stoops over the old woman even, because she wears diamonds in her ears, and, bundling about her estate in a pony carriage, directs who is to be helped, what tree felled, and who turned out tomorrow. (I have lived my life I must tell you all these years and I am now past thirty, perilously, like a mountain goat leaping from crag to crag; I do not settle long anywhere; I do not attach myself to one person in particular; but you will find that if I raise my arm, some figure at once breaks off and will come.) And that man is a judge; and that man is a millionaire, and that man, with the eyeglass, shot his governess through the heart with an arrow when he was ten years old. Afterwards he rode through deserts with dispatches, took part in revolutions and now collects materials for a history of his mother's family, long settled in Norfolk. That little man with a blue chin has a right hand that is withered. But why? We do not know. That woman, you whisper discreetly, with the pearl pagodas hanging from her ears, was the pure flame who lit the life of one of our statesmen; now since his death she sees ghosts, tells fortunes, and has adopted a coffee-colored youth whom she calls the Messiah. That man with the drooping moustache, like a cavalry officer, lived a life of the utmost debauchery (it is all in some memoir) until one day he met a stranger in a train who converted him between Edinburgh and Carlisle by reading the Bible.

"Thus, in a few seconds, deftly, adroitly, we decipher the hieroglyphs written on other people's faces. Here, in this room, are the abraded and battered shells cast on the shore. The door goes on opening. The room fills and fills with knowledge, anguish, many kinds of ambition, much indifference, some despair. Between us, you say, we could build cathedrals, dictate policies, condemn men to death, and administer the affairs of several public offices. The common fund of experience is very deep. We have between us scores of children of both sexes, whom we are educating, going to see at school with the measles, and bringing up to inherit our houses. In one way or another we make this day, this Friday, some by going to the Law Courts; others to the city; others to the nursery; others by marching and forming fours. A million hands stitch, raise hods with bricks. The activity is endless. And tomorrow it begins again; tomorrow we make Saturday. Some take train for France; others ship for India. Some will never come into this room again. One may die tonight. Another will beget a child. From us every sort of building, policy, venture, picture, poem, child, factory, will spring. Life comes; life goes; we make life. So you say.

"But we who live in the body see with the body's imagination things in outline. I see rocks in bright sunshine. I cannot take these facts into some cave and, shading my eyes, grade their yellows, blues, umbers into one substance. I cannot remain seated for long. I must jump up and go. The coach may start from Piccadilly. I drop all these facts—diamonds, withered hands, china pots and the rest of it, as a monkey drops nuts from its naked paws. I cannot tell you if

life is this or that. I am going to push out into the heterogeneous crowd. I am going to be buffeted; to be flung up, and flung down, among men, like a ship on the sea.

"For now my body, my companion, which is always sending its signals, the rough black 'No,' the golden 'Come' in rapid running arrows of sensation, beckons. Some one moves. Did I raise my arm? Did I look? Did my yellow scarf with the strawberry spots float and signal? He has broken from the wall. He follows. I am pursued through the forest. All is rapt, all is nocturnal and the parrots go screaming through the branches. All my senses stand erect. Now I feel the roughness of the fibre of the curtain through which I push; now I feel the cold iron railing and its blistered paint beneath my palm. Now the cool tide of darkness breaks its waters over me. We are out of doors. Night opens; night traversed by wandering moths; night hiding lovers roaming to adventure. I smell roses; I smell violets; I see red and blue just hidden. Now gravel is under my shoes; now grass. Up reel the tall backs of houses guilty with lights. All London is uneasy with flashing lights. Now let us sing our love song—Come, come, come. Now my gold signal is like a dragon-fly flying taut. Jug, jug, jug, I sing like the nightingale whose melody is crowded in the too narrow passage of her throat. Now I hear the crash and rending of boughs and the crack of antlers as if the beasts of the forest were all hunting, all rearing high and plunging down among the thorns. One has pierced me. One is driven deep within me. And velvet flowers and leaves whose coolness has been stood in water wash me round, and sheathe me, embalming me."

"Why, look," said Neville, "at the clock ticking on the mantelpiece? Time passes, yes. And we grow old. But to sit with you, alone with you, here in London, in this firelit room, you there, I here, is all. The world ransacked to its uttermost ends, and all its heights stripped and gathered of their flowers holds no more. Look at the firelight running up and down the gold thread in the curtain. The fruit it circles droops heavy. It falls on the toe of your boot, it gives your face a red rim—I think it is the firelight and not your face; I think those are books against the wall, and that a curtain, and that perhaps an arm-chair. But when you come everything changes. The cups and saucers changed when you came in this morning. There can be no doubt, I thought, pushing aside the newspaper, that our mean lives, unsightly as they are, put on splendour and have meaning only under the eyes of love.

"I rose. I had done my breakfast. There was the whole day before us, and as it was fine, tender, noncommittal, we walked through the Park to the Embankment, along the Strand to St. Paul's, then to the shop where I bought an umbrella, always talking, and now and then stopping to look. But can this last? I said to myself, by a lion in Trafalgar Square, by the lion seen once and for ever;—so I revisit my past life, scene by scene, there is an elm tree, and there lies Percival. For ever and ever, I swore. Then darted in the usual doubt. I clutched your hand. You left me. The descent into the Tube was like death. We were cut up, we were dissevered by all those faces and the hollow wind that seemed to roar down there over desert boulders. I sat staring in my own room. By five I knew that you were faithless. I snatched the telephone and the buzz, buzz, buzz of its stupid voice in your empty room battered my heart down, when the door opened and there you stood. That was the most perfect of our meetings. But these meetings, these partings, finally destroy us.

"Now this room seems to me central, something scooped out of the eternal night. Outside lines twist and intersect, but round us, wrapping us about. Here we are centred. Here we can be silent, or speak without raising our voices. Did you notice that and then that? we say. He said that, meaning. . . . She hesitated, and I believe suspected. Anyhow, I heard voices, a sob on the stair late at night. It is the end of their relationship. Thus we spin round us infinitely fine filaments and construct a system. Plato and Shakespeare are included, also quite obscure people, people of no importance whatsoever. I hate men who wear crucifixes on the left side of their waistcoats. I hate ceremonies and lamentations and the sad figure of Christ trembling beside another trembling and sad figure. Also the pomp and the indifference

and the emphasis, always on the wrong place, of people holding forth under chandeliers in full evening dress, wearing stars and decorations. Some spray in a hedge, though, or a sunset over a flat winter field, or again the way some old woman sits, arms akimbo, in an omnibus with a basket—those we point at for the other to look at. It is so vast an alleviation to be able to point for another to look at. And then not to talk. To follow the dark paths of the mind and enter the past, to visit books, to brush aside their branches and break off some fruit. And you take it and marvel, as I take the careless movements of your body and marvel at its ease, its power—how you fling open windows and are dexterous with your hands. For alas! my mind is a little impeded, it soon tires; I fall damp, perhaps disgusting, at the goal.

"Alas! I could not ride about India in a sunhelmet and return to a bungalow. I cannot tumble, as you do, like half-naked boys on the deck of a ship, squirting each other with hosepipes. I want this fire, I want this chair. I want some one to sit beside after the day's pursuit and all its anguish, after its listenings, and its waitings, and its suspicions. After quarreling and reconciliation I need privacy—to be alone with you, to set this hubbub in order. For I am as neat as a cat in my habits. We must oppose the waste and deformity of the world, its crowds eddying round and round disgorged and trampling. One must slip paper-knives, even, exactly through the pages of novels, and tie up packets of letters neatly with green silk, and brush up the cinders with a hearth broom. Everything must be done to rebuke the horror of deformity. Let us read writers of Roman severity and virtue; let us seek perfection through the sand. Yes, but I love to slip the virtue and severity of the noble Romans under the grey light of your eyes, and dancing grasses and summer breezes and the laughter and shouts of boys at play—of naked cabin-boys squirting each other with hose-pipes on the decks of ships. Hence I am not a disinterested seeker, like Louis, after perfection through the sand. Colours always stain the page; clouds pass over it. And the poem, I think, is only your voice speaking. Alcibiades, Ajax, Hector and Percival are also you. They loved riding, they risked

their lives wantonly, they were not great readers either. But you are not Ajax or Percival.
They did not wrinkle their noses and scratch
their foreheads with your precise gesture. You
are you. That is what consoles me for the lack
of many things—I am ugly, I am weak—and the
depravity of the world, and the flight of youth
and Percival's death, and bitterness and ran-
cour and envies innumerable.

"But if one day you do not come after break- 10
fast, if one day I see you in some looking-glass
perhaps looking after another, if the telephone
buzzes and buzzes in your empty room, I
shall then, after unspeakable anguish, I shall
then—for there is no end to the folly of the human heart—seek another, find another, you.
Meanwhile, let us abolish the ticking of time's
clock with one blow. Come closer."

GERTRUDE STEIN

Probably the most controversial of contemporary writers, regarded as a genius by some, a
mumbling idiot by others, Gertrude Stein was
a famous expatriate who considered herself definitely an American, though her trips to these
shores were infrequent and brief.

She was born in Allegheny, Pennsylvania,
February 3, 1874, daughter of wealthy parents,
Daniel and Amelia (Keyser) Stein. She attended Radcliffe College (1893–97), where
she was a favorite pupil in psychology of William James, and studied at Johns Hopkins Medical School (1897–1902) but did not take a
degree. Instead, as she had an independent
income, she went to Paris to live. She occupied
the same apartment in the Montparnasse section for over thirty years, was known as a hospitable hostess and a connoisseur of modern
painting, and was the center of a select artistic
group which included such early friends as Picasso, Matisse, Braque, and Gris. During the
First World War Miss Stein and her secretary,
Alice B. Toklas, were decorated by the French
government for their work as supply drivers
for the American Fund for French Wounded.
They remained in France throughout the recent
war. When American forces reached Paris, the
G.I.'s and Miss Stein were mutually enthusiastic; her admiration of them and her resurgence of patriotism are expressed in *Wars I
Have Seen* (1945) and the posthumous *Brewsie and Willie* (1947). She died at Neuilly,
near Paris, July 27, 1946.

Miss Stein's published works gave rise to
much comment. She developed a technique of
using words for their rhythm and volume
rather than directly for their dictionary meaning. She was interested in presenting the way
in which the subconscious mind records experience, often allowing groups of words to swim
into the consciousness without any logical reason. Her aim was to set down the flow of consciousness intermingled with the larger stream
of subconscious imagery or sound. The effect
of words broken from their usual meaning or
usual syntax within a sentence fascinated her.
An example of this, from *Sacred Emily*, is,
"Birds measure birds measure stores birds
measure stores measure birds measure." In her
lectures Miss Stein could be perfectly logical,
and she was possessed of a brilliant mind. But
her contact with the modern painters strengthened her feeling that literature, to be renewed
in its force, must break the old molds and that
in it, as in painting, the mental processes of
the artist must be allowed fairly free expression. Communication of a precise theme or idea
was of less importance to her, therefore, than
the suggestion of a highly individual reaction
of life presented through words which for the
artist, if not for the reader always, express an
experience. Her attempt to portray the highly
individual and particularized movement of any
certain person's consciousness (the flow of the
mind which differentiates one mind from another) led Miss Stein to the development of

531

what sometimes is criticized as a very eccentric style. Her use of monosyllabic words influenced Hemingway. Hemingway, however, chooses to tell a story and keeps, therefore, to ordinary syntax. Miss Stein was interested not in telling a story but in presenting a state of mind. She regarded each individual psychology as unique, and she was entirely cheerful about psychological diversities.

The works of Gertrude Stein include *Three Lives* (1908); *Tender Buttons* (1915); *Geography and Plays* (1922); *Making of Americans* (1925); *Useful Knowledge* (1928); *Acquaintance with Description* (1929); *Ten Portraits* (1930); *Lucy Church Amiably* (1930); *Before the Flowers of Friendship Faded Friendship Faded* (1931); *How to Write* (1931); *Operas and Plays* (1932); *Matisse, Picasso and Gertrude Stein* (1932); *The Autobiography of Alice B. Toklas* (1933); *Four Saints in Three Acts* (1934); *Portraits and Prayers* (1934); *Lectures in America* (1935); *Narration* (1936); *Geographical History of America* (1936); *Everybody's Autobiography* (1937).

---

from **Four Saints in Three Acts**

[Gertrude Stein's writing has most frequently been defined as "automatic writing." In her earlier writing Miss Stein seemed interested in getting down the contradictory ideas and images of the subjective mind. Gradually, as we have seen, she came to represent in words, so used in a sentence as to be divorced from their usual meaning and by almost mesmeristic repetition, not so much the emotional images of the subconscious as the motion of the mind half way between thinking and dreaming. In short stories such as "Miss Furr and Miss Skeene" the repetitive rigmarole, as Edmund Wilson says, is admirable to render the monotony and insipidity of the feminine lives which are being narrated. In Miss Stein's later works Wilson believed that she had gone so far in using words solely for the pure purpose of suggestion that she no longer really suggested. The trouble with using words so abstractly is that words

have meanings and we cannot help remembering them. Words used purely as symbols of the way in which the mind moves in ripples of consciousness still retain their accustomed meanings, and any complete discussion of Miss Stein's use of words would lead us to a discussion of the nature of language itself and the mysteries of human psychology, subjects about which even the philosophers are in the dark.

Miss Stein wrote the libretto of *Four Saints in Three Acts* especially for stage production. The lines printed here were assigned on the stage to many voices and sung antiphonally. In the modern stage production of *Four Saints* all the theatrical elements were developed in conjunction with each other. Music composer, libretto-writer, costume, scene and lighting designers, choreographer and director, in coöperation with the cast, worked together. In consistency of expression—regardless of the mystery of what was being expressed—the production succeeded magnificently. It was felt that white actors might be self-conscious, stiff in the presentation of Miss Stein's lines, and all Negro actors were chosen. Thus an entire cast made up in a uniform warm brown paint and costumed in vivid reds, blues, and greens sang and danced and pantomimed in incomprehensible but individually pleasing fragments against a delightful, if apparently unrelated, backdrop of pale blue and cellophane. Docile spectators who submitted uncomplainingly to Miss Stein's symbolistic libretto observed that the opera produced in them sensual stimulations, all in the lighter vein, ranging from amusement to delight. Spectators made of sterner stuff, who would not relinquish preconceived ideas of operatic procedure, were outraged by the altogether nonrational nature of Miss Stein's fare.

Four Saints was first presented in New York on February 20, 1934. Here follow excerpts from reviews representing the various critical responses to the piece. Lawrence Gilman, in the *New York Herald Tribune*:

So far as the listener is concerned, Miss Stein really contributes very little to the total effect, apart from the occasional emergence of such famous triumphs of the intellect and the imagination as the fantasia on "Pigeons on the grass, alas" and the deathless variations on "Let Lucy Lily Lily Lucy Lucy let Lucy," which were delightedly hailed by last night's assemblage.

George Stevens, in the *Saturday Review of Literature:*

"Pigeons on the grass, alas," is pigeon English.

Kenneth Burke in *The Nation:*

I should like to discourse easily and familiarly on the plot of Stein's piece, but must admit that I cannot. The words show evidence of a private planfulness which makes them more difficult to fathom than if they were written under gas.

John Anderson in the *New York Journal:*

The theory of this sort of tommyrot is that music needs only words for its singing, and that the words need not make sense as long as they fulfill the ideas of sound. It may be all right as a theory. Lewis Carroll's "Jabberwocky" in *Alice in Wonderland* is a classic example of this idea in its purest form. The trouble with Miss Stein is that she does not play fair. She does not keep her scheme within the limits she herself has laid down. She violates the spirit and mood of her intention repeatedly by using lines which come so close to making sense that they focus the attention on the meaning and not the sound, thereby upsetting the whole project. She uses, for instance, a line which sounds magnificent when sung, though it means nothing. "Pigeons on the grass, alas." But Miss Stein wants to have her cake and eat it, too. So now and then a line connects with grammar, and you get, on top of the one about "pigeons on the grass, alas," a line that runs "If they are not pigeons, what are they?" This blatant question is cheap vaudeville humor, and the honesty of the whole thing is violated over and over again by this sort of silliness.

Stark Young in *The New Republic:*

Four Saints is as essential theater the most important event of our season . . . for one reason because it is the most delightful and joyous— and delight is the fundamental in all art great or small . . . it is important because it is theater and flies off the ground.

Four Saints closed after a short run, but popu-

lar curiosity ran so high in April of 1934 that the piece was recalled to Broadway for a second engagement. Actually the performance was interesting for its pageantry and choreography if for nothing else.]

ACT II

PIGEONS on the grass alas.
Pigeons on the grass alas.
Short longer grass short longer longer shorter yellow grass Pigeons large pigeons on the shorter longer yellow grass alas pigeons on the grass.
If they were not pigeons what were they.
If they were not pigeons on the grass alas what were they. He had heard of a third and he asked about it it was a magpie in the sky. 10
If a magpie in the sky on the sky can not cry if the pigeon on the grass alas can alas and to pass the pigeon on the grass alas and the magpie in the sky on the sky and to try and to try alas on the grass alas the pigeon on the grass the pigeon on the grass and alas. They might be very well very well very well they might be they might be very well they might be very well very well they might be.
Let Lucy Lily Lily Lucy Lucy let Lucy Lucy 20
Lily Lily Lily Lily Lily let Lily Lucy Lucy let Lily. Let Lucy Lily.

SCENE ONE

Saint Ignatius and please please please please.

SCENE ONE

One and one.

SCENE ONE

Might they be with they be with them might they be with them. Never to return to distinctions.
Might they be with them with they be with they be with them.   30
Saint Ignatius. In line and in in line please say it first in line.
Saint Ignatius

	When it is ordinarily
and	thoughtful and making
friends.	it be when they were

wishing at one time insatiably and with re-

Act II from *Four Saints in Three Acts*, reprinted by permission of Random House, Inc., New York.

nounced where where ware and wear wear
with them with them and where where will it
be as long as long as they might with it with it
individually removing left to it when it very
well well way well and crossed crossed in articu-
lately minding what you do.

He asked for a distant magpie as if they
made a difference.

He asked for a distant magpie as if he asked
for a distant magpie as if that made a difference.

He asked as if that made a difference.

He asked for a distant magpie.

As if that made a difference he asked for a
distant magpie as if that made a difference. He
asked as if that made a difference. A distant
magpie. He asked for a distant magpie. He
asked for a distant magpie.

Saint Ignatius. Might be admired for himself
alone.

Saint Chavez. Saint Ignatius might be admired for himself alone and because of that it
might be as much as any one could desire.

Saint Chavez. Because of that it might be as
much as any one could desire.

Saint Chavez. Because of that because it
might be as much as any one could desire it
might be that it could be done as easily as because it might very much as if precisely why
they were carried.

Saint Ignatius. Left when there was precious
little to be asked by the ones who were overwhelmingly particular about what they were
adding to themselves by means of their arrangements which might be why they went
away and came again.

It is every once in a while very much what
they pleased.

In a minute.

Saint Ignatius. In a minute by the time that
it is graciously gratification and might it be
with them to be with them to be with them to
be to be windowed.

As seen as seen.

Saint Ignatius surrounded by them.

Saint Ignatius and one of two.

Saint Chavez might be with them at that
time. All of them. Might be with them at that
time.

All of them might be with them all of them
at that time.

Might be with them at that time all of them
might be with them at that time.

SCENE II

It is very easy to love alone. Too much too
much. There are very sweetly very sweetly
Henry very sweetly Rene very sweetly many
very sweetly. They are very sweetly many very
sweetly Rene very sweetly there are many very
sweetly.

There is a difference between Barcelona and
Avila. What difference.

SCENE

There is a difference between Barcelona and
Avila.

There is a difference between Barcelona.

SCENE IV

And no more.

SCENE V

Saint Ignatius. Left to left left to left left to
left. Left right left left right left left to left!

When they do change to.

Saint Vincent. Authority for it.

Saint Gallo. By this clock o'clock. By this
clock, by this clock by this clock o'clock.

Saint Ignatius. Foundationally marvellously
aboundingly illimitably with it as a circumstance. Fundamentally and saints fundamentally and saints and fundamentally and saints.

One Saint. Whose has whose has whose has
ordered needing white and green as much as
orange and with grey and how much and as
much and as much and as a circumstance.

Saint Therese. Intending to be intending to
intending to to to to to. To do it for me.

Saint Ignatius. Two and two.

SCENE V

Alive.

SCENE VI

With Seven.

SCENE VII

With eight.

SCENE VIII

Ordinary pigeons and trees.

If a generation all the same between forty and fifty as as. As they were and met. Was it tenderness and seem. Might it be as well as mean with in.

Ordinary pigeons and trees. This is a setting which is as soon which is as soon which is as soon ordinary setting which is as soon which is as soon and noon.

Saint Therese. In face of in face of might make milk sung sung face to face face in face place in place in place of face to face. Milk sung.

Saint Ignatius. Once in a while and where and where around around is a sound and around is a sound and around is a sound and around. Around is a sound around is a sound around is a sound around is a sound around and around. Around differing from anointed now. Now differing from anointed now. Now differing differing. Now differing from anointed now. Now when there is left and with it integrally with it integrally withstood within without with out with drawn and in as much as if it could be withstanding what in might might be so.

Many might be comfortabler. This is very well known now. When this you see remember me. It was very well known to every one.

Might and right very well to do. It is all colored by a straw straw laden.

Very nearly with it with it soon soon as said.

Having asked additionally theirs instead.

Once in a minute.

In a minute.

One two three as are are and are are are to be are with them are with them are with them with are with are with with it.

Miss Furr and Miss Skeene

HELEN FURR had quite a pleasant home. Mrs. Furr was quite a pleasant woman. Mr. Furr was quite a pleasant man. Helen Furr had quite a pleasant voice a voice quite worth cultivating. She did not mind working. She worked to cultivate her voice. She did not find it gay living in the same place where she

had always been living. She went to a place where some were cultivating something, voices and other things needing cultivating. She met Georgine Skeene there who was cultivating her voice which some thought was quite a pleasant one. Helen Furr and Georgine Skeene lived together then. Georgine Skeene liked travelling. Helen Furr did not care about travelling, she liked to stay in one place and be gay there. They were together then and travelled to another place and stayed there and were gay there.

They stayed there and were gay there, not very gay there, just gay there. They were both gay there, they were regularly working there both of them cultivating their voices there, they were both gay there. Georgine Skeene was gay there and she was regular, regular in being gay, regular in not being gay, regular in being a gay one who was one not being gay longer than was needed to be one being quite a gay one. They were both gay then there and both working there then.

They were in a way both gay there where there were many cultivating something. They were both regular in being gay there. Helen Furr was gay there, she was gayer and gayer there and really she was just gay there, she was gayer and gayer there, that is to say she found ways of being gay there that she was using in being gay there. She was gay there, not gayer and gayer, just gay there, that is to say she was not gayer by using the things she found there that were gay things, she was gay there, always she was gay there.

They were quite regularly gay there, Helen Furr and Georgine Skeene, they were regularly gay there where they were gay. They were very regularly gay.

To be regularly gay was to do every day the gay thing that they did every day. To be regularly gay was to end every day at the same time after they had been regularly gay. They were regularly gay. They were gay every day. They ended every day in the same way, at the same time, and they had been every day regularly gay.

The voice Helen Furr was cultivating was quite a pleasant one. The voice Georgine Skeene was cultivating was, some said, a better one. The voice Helen Furr was cultivating she

cultivated and it was quite completely a pleasant enough one then, a cultivated enough one then. The voice Georgine Skeene was cultivating she did not cultivate too much. She cultivated it quite some. She cultivated and she would sometime go on cultivating it and it was not then an unpleasant one, it would not be then an unpleasant one, it would be a quite richly enough cultivated one, it would be quite
10 richly enough to be a pleasant enough one.

They were gay where there were many cultivating something. The two were gay there, were regularly gay there. Georgine Skeene would have liked to do more travelling. They did some travelling, not very much travelling, Helen Furr did not care about doing travelling, she liked to stay in a place and be gay there.

They stayed in a place and were gay there,
20 both of them stayed there, they stayed together there, they were gay there, they were regularly gay there.

They went quite often, not very often, but they did go back to where Helen Furr had a pleasant enough home and then Georgine Skeene went to a place where her brother had quite some distinction. They both went, every few years, went visiting to where Helen Furr had quite a pleasant home. Certainly Helen
30 Furr would not find it gay to stay, she did not find it gay, she said she would not stay, she said she did not find it gay, she said she would not stay where she did not find it gay, she said she found it gay where she did stay and she did stay there where very many were cultivating something. She did stay there. She always did find it gay there.

She went to see them where she had always been living and where she did not find it gay.
40 She had a pleasant home there, Mrs. Furr was a pleasant enough woman, Mr. Furr was a pleasant enough man, Helen told them and they were not worrying, that she did not find it gay living where she had always been living.

Georgine Skeene and Helen Furr were living where they were both cultivating their voices and they were gay there. They visited where Helen Furr had come from and then they went to where they were living where
50 they were then regularly living.

There were some dark and heavy men there then. There were some who were not so heavy and some who were not so dark. Helen Furr and Georgine Skeene sat regularly with them. They sat regularly with the ones who were dark and heavy. They sat regularly with the ones who were not so dark. They sat regularly with the ones that were not so heavy. They sat with them regularly, sat with some of them. They went with them regularly went with them. They were regular then, they were gay then, they were where they wanted to be then where it was gay to be then, they were regularly gay then. There were men there then who were dark and heavy and they sat with them with Helen Furr and Georgine Skeene and they went with them with Miss Furr and Miss Skeene, and they went with the heavy and dark men Miss Furr and Miss Skeene went with them, and they sat with them, Miss Furr and Miss Skeene sat with them, and there were other men, some were not heavy men and they sat with Miss Furr and Miss Skeene and Miss Furr and Miss Skeene sat with them, and there were other men who were not dark men and they sat with Miss Furr and Miss Skeene and Miss Furr and Miss Skeene sat with them. Miss Furr and Miss Skeene went with them and they went with Miss Furr and Miss Skeene, some who were not heavy men, some who were not dark men. Miss Furr and Miss Skeene sat regularly, they sat with some men. Miss Furr and Miss Skeene went and there were some men with them. There were men and Miss Furr and Miss Skeene went with them, went somewhere with them, went with some of them.

Helen Furr and Georgine Skeene were regularly living where very many were living and cultivating in themselves something. Helen Furr and Georgine Skeene were living very regularly then, being very regular then in being gay then. They did then learn many ways to be gay and they were then being gay being quite regular in being gay, being gay and they were learning little things, little things in ways of being gay, they were very regular then, they were learning very many little things in ways of being gay, they were being gay and using these little things they were learning to have to be gay with regularly gay with then and they were gay the same amount they had been gay. They were quite gay, they were quite regular, they were learning little things, gay little things, they were gay inside them the same amount they had been gay, they were gay the same length of time they had been gay every day.

They were regular in being gay, they learned little things that are things in being gay, they learned many little things that are things in being gay, they were gay every day, they were regular, they were gay, they were gay the same length of time every day, they were gay, they were quite regularly gay.

Georgine Skeene went away to stay two months with her brother. Helen Furr did not go then to stay with her father and her mother. Helen Furr stayed there where they had been regularly living the two of them and she would then certainly not be lonesome, she would go on being gay. She did go on being gay. She was not any more gay but she was gay longer every day than they had been being gay when they were together being gay. She was gay then quite exactly the same way. She learned a few more little ways of being in being gay. She was quite gay and in the same way, the same way she had been gay and she was gay a little longer in the day, more of each day she was gay. She was gay longer every day than when the two of them had been being gay. She was gay quite in the way they had been gay, quite in the same way.

She was not lonesome then, she was not at all feeling any need of having Georgine Skeene. She was not astonished at this thing. She would have been a little astonished by this thing but she knew she was not astonished at anything and so she was not astonished at this thing not astonished at not feeling any need of having Georgine Skeene.

Helen Furr had quite a completely pleasant voice and it was quite well enough cultivated and she could use it and she did use it but then there was not any way of working at cultivating a completely pleasant voice when it has become a quite completely well enough cultivated one, and there was not much use in using it when one was not wanting it to be helping to make one a gay one. Helen Furr was not needing using her voice to be a gay one. She was gay then and sometimes she used her voice and she was not using it very often. It was quite completely enough cultivated and it was quite completely a pleasant one and she did not use it very often. She was then, she was quite exactly as gay as she had been, she was gay a little longer in the day than she had been.

She was gay exactly the same way. She was never tired of being gay that way. She had learned very many little ways to use in being gay. Very many were telling about using other ways in being gay. She was gay enough, but was always gay exactly the same way, she was always learning little things to use in being gay, she was telling about using other ways in being gay, she was telling about learning other ways in being gay, she was learning other ways in being gay, she would be using other ways in being gay, she would always be gay in the same way, when Georgine Skeene was there not so long each day as when Georgine Skeene was away.

She came to using many ways in being gay, she came to use every way in being gay. She went on living where many were cultivating something and she was gay, she had used every way to be gay.

They did not live together then Helen Furr and Georgine Skeene. Helen Furr lived there the longer where they had been living regularly together. Then neither of them were living there any longer. Helen Furr was living somewhere else then and telling some about being gay and she was gay then and she was living quite regularly then. She was regularly gay then. She was quite regular in being gay then. She remembered all the little ways of being gay. She used all the little ways of being gay. She was quite regularly gay. She told many then the way of being gay, she taught very many then little ways they could use in being gay. She was living very well, she was gay then, she went on living then, she was regular in being gay, she always was living very well and was gay very well and was telling about little ways one could be learning to use in being gay, and later was telling them quite often, telling them again and again.

Ada

Barnes Colhard did not say he would not do it but he did not do it. He did it and then he did not do it, he did not ever think about it. He just thought some time he might do something.

His father Mr. Abram Colhard spoke about it to every one and very many of them spoke to Barnes Colhard about it and he always listened to them.

Then Barnes fell in love with a very nice girl and she would not marry him. He cried then, his father Mr. Abram Colhard comforted him and they took a trip and Barnes promised he would do what his father wanted him to be doing. He did not do the thing, he thought he would do another thing, he did not do the other thing, his father Mr. Colhard did not want him to do the other thing. He really did not do anything then. When he was a good deal older he married a very rich girl. He had thought perhaps he would not propose to her but his sister wrote to him that it would be a good thing. He married the rich girl and she thought he was the most wonderful man and one who knew everything. Barnes never spent more than the income of the fortune he and his wife had then, that is to say they did not spend more than the income and this was a surprise to very many who knew about him and about his marrying the girl who had such a large fortune. He had a happy life while he was living and after he was dead his wife and children remembered him.

He had a sister who also was successful enough in being one being living. His sister was one who came to be happier than most people come to be in living. She came to be a completely happy one. She was twice as old as her brother. She had been a very good daughter to her mother. She and her mother had always told very pretty stories to each other. Many old men loved to hear her tell these stories to her mother. Every one who ever knew her mother liked her mother. Many were sorry later that not every one liked the daughter. Many did like the daughter but not every one as every one had liked the mother. The daughter was charming inside in her, it did not show outside in her to every one, it certainly did to some. She did sometimes think her mother would be pleased with a story that did not please her mother, when her mother later was sicker the daughter knew that there were some stories she could tell her that would not please her mother. Her mother died and really mostly altogether the mother and the daughter had told each other stories very happily together.

The daughter then kept house for her father and took care of her brother. There were many relations who lived with them. The daughter did not like them to live with them and she did not like them to die with them. The daughter, Ada they had called her after her grandmother who had delightful ways of smelling flowers and eating dates and sugar, did not like it at all then as she did not like so much dying and she did not like any of the living she was doing then. Every now and then some old gentlemen told delightful stories to her. Mostly then there were not nice stories told by any one then in her living. She told her father Mr. Abram Colhard that she did not like it at all being one being living then. He never said anything. She was afraid then, she was one needing charming stories and happy telling of them and not having that thing she was always trembling. Then every one who could live with them were dead and there were then the father and the son a young man then and the daughter coming to be that one then. Her grandfather had left some money to them each one of them. Ada said she was going to use it to go away from them. The father said nothing then, then he said something and she said nothing then, then they both said nothing and then it was that she went away from them. The father was quite tender then, she was his daughter then. He wrote her tender letters then, she wrote him tender letters then, she never went back to live with him. He wanted her to come and she wrote him tender letters then. He liked the tender letters she wrote to him. He wanted her to live with him. She answered him by writing tender letters to him and telling very nice stories indeed in them. He wrote nothing and then he wrote again and there was some waiting and then he wrote tender letters again and again.

She came to be happier than anybody else who was living then. It is easy to believe this thing. She was telling some one, who was loving every story that was charming. Some one who was living was almost always listening. Some one who was loving was almost always listening. That one who was loving was almost always listening. That one who was loving was telling about being one then listening. That one being loving was then telling stories having a beginning and a middle and an ending. That one was then one always completely listening. Ada was then one and all her living then one completely telling stories that were charming, completely listening to stories having a beginning and a middle and an ending. Trembling was all living, living was all loving, some one was then the other one. Certainly this one was loving this Ada then. And certainly Ada all her living then was happier in living than any one else who ever could, who was, who is, who ever will be living.

PART THREE

"Chorus for Survival"

George Grosz: The Survivor
*This drawing, the subject of which
Grosz has also used in a prize-winning
painting, presents the artist in his
most mature and typical manner*

THE FIRST WORLD WAR over, England went about the business of recovery at home and abroad. The dole was instituted, and other attempts were made to put labor back on its feet while at the same time keeping it from gaining too much power. Violent resistance in Ireland and civil disobedience in India were dealt with. The Conservative cabinet in 1924 gave way briefly to a Labour ministry headed by Ramsay MacDonald; but this new government was far from dangerously radical. It put through only a few mild and necessary changes to stabilize the home economy and instigated no startling reforms in either England's foreign policy or her attitude toward her Empire. And in the long run, as always before, conservative England muddled through. The monarchy, although for centuries merely a symbol, has nevertheless been taken for granted by the English people. Even labor governments might rise and fall, while the royal family—as familiar a part of English life as boiled mutton—still held the general imagination. Royalty, which does not come and go as do American presidents, spelled to the English a kind of glamour, the glamour of English tradition and of stability. The seem-

540

ingly unshakable grip of the English conservatives in the years following the war was fortified by the monarchy, fortified too by the Church, the landed gentry, and doubtless by the English industrialists, who had known the Empire as part of their security. England with her Empire could not profess the same self-sufficiency that America could still claim. England knew that her trade and her industries depended on other lands. Foreign trade was her life blood; and within her islands there was not enough of the oil and other resources needed for her manufactures. Empire policy and home

prosperity, in so far as the government thought, were linked with conservatism. So it was that the conservatives, symbolized in the late 1930's by Chamberlain with his umbrella and his promise of "peace in our time," came back to power in England.

In more volatile America, without any fixed symbol of a long tradition or of an ancient culture, in an America still believing herself a young nation with a comparatively short history, opinion after the war swung back and forth between radical ideas and more conservative programs. Even before Woodrow Wilson

541

died the more liberal commentators on the war had suggested that such idealism as he had apparently acted upon, both in leading America into war and in promoting the League of Nations, had been premature. The more radical journalists suggested that we had fought a war in which only industrialists and arms manufacturers had benefited, that we had been outwitted by the European politicians in our endeavors to promote world unity. Soon America, willingly enough, retreated into her traditional isolationism, her policy of high tariffs, and her convictions that she should support herself and keep free of European entanglements. Although even the elected Republicans knew that foreign trading was necessary to American industrial expansion, America remained a far more self-supporting nation than England.

America, moreover, had been little hurt by the war. The loss of life had not been so great as to affect adversely the national psychology. Actually there had been more deaths from the influenza epidemic than from the fighting. Industrially the country was more powerful than ever before. Thus, even as American radicals were being aroused to new enthusiasms and starry-eyed hopes for socialism by the revolutionary developments in Russia, the United States returned to a more conservative and isolationist policy, and entered a period of prosperity which shortly became a period of long, though not permanent, boom. In the widespread optimism of the boom period, labor struggles and celebrated causes such as that of Sacco and Vanzetti were generally forgotten, and not until the stock-market crash of 1929 did the critics of capitalism—the "industrial Cassandras," as they had long been called—emerge from their ten years of lethargy to make themselves clearly heard.

Individualists reject society

During the Waste Land period most of the writers had seemed to be lying on their backs and groaning or whimpering about the sad state of human life without value or direction. They did not trace their disillusion, however, to economic insecurity or injustice, but by and large gave their sense of confusion and skepticism a moral justification in terms of frustrated individualism, in terms of society's lack of appreciation of culture or of anything esthetic. Artists blamed the materialism of society for thwarting the sensitivity on which art thrived. Dreiser had been among the first to describe man as conditioned by the social machine, American genius as commercialized and trapped. Late in his life he was to turn to Communism as a cure for what he looked upon as the American tragedy of inequality and commercialism—the "tragedy" that he had emphasized much earlier in his novel.

Meantime, unlike Dreiser, who pioneered in social criticism, many other writers indulged in greater and greater emphasis on individualism, and spoke of the artist as unique, isolated, a law unto himself, unanswerable to a society which did not appreciate him. T. S. Eliot, whose symbols had so characterized the whole of the Waste Land, probably had not realized at first that he was rejecting society. Nevertheless, there is in Eliot, as we have noted in Part II, the clearest possible set of symbols of a bored society and a decadent culture. Finally, driven by his despair over such a society, Eliot turned from it as subject matter to argue for the rebuilding of a Christian civilization. His worship of the traditional and his individualistic penitence for his years of irony and doubt led him to accept Anglo-Catholicism. Hating all conflict and confusion, Eliot leaned more and more toward the idea that the best of cultures are not those of such new countries as are settled by many peoples. To quote exactly:

*The population should be homogeneous; where two or more cultures exist in the same place they are likely either to be fiercely self-conscious or both to become adulterate. What is still more important is unity of religious background. . . .**

Here again his emphasis is, as always, upon a consistent tradition.

Following to some extent in Eliot's footsteps, many of the older writers sought various methods of escape from a world which they be-

* *After Strange Gods*, pp. 19–20 (Harcourt, Brace).

lieved to be without values. These escapes ranged from religious conversions to an even more morbid individualism than had dominated the Waste Land period. As Mario Praz pointed out in *The Romantic Agony*, romanticism was now running into all kinds of excesses, sadistic and masochistic. But even while these escapes and excesses were going on, the depression was the actual reality in which the younger writers were being forced to function. College graduates were jobless, students were forced to leave school without completing an education, and the harsh facts of its own existence forced youth in general to shake off morbid individualism and to try to assimilate the tragedy of the real scene. The younger writers, therefore, came shortly to feel that what ailed them was not explainable solely in personal or Freudian terms; too many people suffered with them. The trouble, they felt, was with society. Many of them knew economic privation, and instead of mumbling about private frustrations, or holding themselves to be the humanistic priests of a dying culture, they began to use loud-speakers to instruct the world concerning the contradictions they had observed in contemporary society.

The depression stirs younger writers to interest in society

By 1931 millions were unemployed in America. Groups of American intellectuals had been turning left at more or less regular intervals since 1840; and our American intellectuals of the 1930's, with an exuberant faith in our revolutionary history, found in the depression cause to turn again in the direction of socialism (a form of society which had existed in early utopian colonies here and a form of society in which Lincoln, for example, had seen some value). They began energetically to read the left-wing magazines, the writings of Marx, or interpretations—good or bad—of Marxian doctrines.

Meantime the typical solid American businessman went on his way, trying to rebuild his lessening fortunes, sure that this depression, like others, was just part of something called

the "business cycle" and would pass. As the years of unemployment went on, however, the lower middle class teetered up and down between the stability of the upper middle class and the considerable insecurity of the laboring class. A good many former "businessmen" were glad to become manual laborers and receive wages. Many, however, remained jobless.

Slowly the first crisis, in which almost anything could have happened in America, eased off. With Roosevelt as President, various remedial acts were passed. Labor unions completely destroyed after the First World War were slowly rebuilt, and it was not long before "labor's Magna Charta," the Wagner Act, was passed. Soon office workers, who had clung to the idea that their white collars distinguished them from the denim-shirted working class, decided they needed some organization. Newspapermen, for example, formed their Guild, and other organizations of professional people were founded.

During the early years after the crash one cure after another was suggested for the serious economic difficulties in which America now found herself. Much of the literature was concerned with arguments as to how to survive. It is for this reason that we have used the title of Horace Gregory's book of poems *Chorus for Survival* for this chapter. Quite aside from the remedial methods used by the President in his New Deal, every group offered in book form its answer to the economic riddle. Engineers argued that as technocrats they could best take over production. Intellectuals proposed, from time to time, that their superior intelligence (particularly as economic theorists) should be used in governing. All manner of books outlining all manner of cure-alls—political, economic, and spiritual—were published and many became popular.

Even some of the artists, the priests of culture, felt they could direct the nation—at least spiritually. During the years of the depression, however, many of the older artists who had relied so strongly on their exclusiveness, their superiority to organized society (obviously because society offered them neither fixed spiritual values nor economic security), fought any tendency to use their art to change the society which oppressed them and insisted that they continued to believe that the artist should withdraw still further from participation in action.

But despite the reactionary turning away from life on the part of the older artists, the younger writers soon sensed the urgency of the times. They realized that the interest in the possible remedies for our economic distress was symptomatic of two new attitudes current in America. A growing sense of social responsibilities extended for the first time for most Americans beyond their immediate communities, and appreciation of the threat to American life in Europe's post-war turmoil slowly became more general. Who had escaped the "now it can be told" literature of the post-war period? Who had not learned from the many books debunking the war that America's skirts were not entirely clean? Much of the idealism with which Americans had entered the First World War was dissipated soon after it was over. In

its place was growing a skepticism, not always healthy. So long as the boom lasted we could enjoy literature debunking ourselves and still feel safe, but with the depression this enjoyment and this literature ended. Soon our writers and intellectuals began to follow historic events more closely. The Chinese Revolution in 1926 had seemed remote; the Civil War in Spain in 1936 was reason for the choosing of sides. Americans were listening to radios and watching Europe with alarm. As liberal movements grew and labor unions reorganized, our intellectuals ceased to be insular. Before the actual crash of 1929 our hysterical optimism had not been punctured, but with the crash it was completely deflated. From then on, intelligent people realized that for American writers as for English writers, there were no islands any more. Conditions and events that affected artists in Europe inevitably affected those in England and in the United States as well.

LITERATURE AS EXPLORATION OF SOCIAL CONDITIONS

❦ During England's slow recovery from the war and America's rise to what proved to be an artificial prosperity, followed immediately by her plunge into the depression, the older writers of both countries continued to mourn the past or to move uneasily away from the new social criticism in prose and poetry. Such English war poets as were alive had gone home, but they had produced remarkably little after the war. Siegfried Sassoon, for example, violently anti-war in the First World War, came home to satirize English society, to write poetry expressing the wish that he could identify himself with "strikers" and "workers," but poetry which indicated that to act politically was beyond him. Aldous Huxley sailed for America and finally took himself to Hollywood and to New Mexico. Soon he wrote books denouncing science as an answer to human problems, and grew more and more concerned with metaphysical and religious questions as to the reason for life. Virginia Woolf continued to write increasingly exhaustive studies of hypersensitivity and complete inaction, until in *The Years* she pic-

tured the English aristocracy as beginning and ending life in the same armchair, before the same teakettle. One after another, the older writers, each in his or her way, emphasized the writer's inability to take action within a social scene which so refuted for the imaginative mind any consistent desire for order.

Meantime, biography became popular in both England and America. Some of the more conservative biographers at this time seem to have been trying to sum up the virtues of the past in rather sentimental fashion, while the determinedly modern ones (like Lytton Strachey in his lives of Queen Victoria and Queen Elizabeth) appeared to be reviewing all great leaders in the disillusioning light of current historical, biological, or psychological theories. The day of worshiping the old and the great was nearly over. There was still nostalgia, but there was also the reverse—a sticking out of the tongue at all the sacredly old. While the writers who had survived the war period returned uneasily to the old manner of living, the Waste Landers more loudly insisted that progress was non-existent, that society was moronic, that intensity of feeling could be aroused, if indeed it could be aroused at all, only by the psychologically abnormal.

Writers in England and America analyze their world

By the time it had become apparent both in England and in America that the Versailles Treaty opened the way to new wars, writers in general began to analyze the world in which they found themselves. Soon there were a few books about workers like *Love on the Dole* by Walter Greenwood and some rather sentimental treatments in England of the Welsh

coal miners or of other laboring groups, such as Richard Llewellyn's *How Green Was My Valley*. And finally, although it may seem a bit odd now in view of the author's political change of heart, there was John Strachey's *The Coming Struggle for Power,* a work hailed in England and in America as a brilliant analysis of the rise and decline of capitalism. This book influenced in particular such American and English intellectuals as were not easily reached through the simpler, more direct left-wing pamphlets. Strachey was both an aristocrat and an intellectual. He seemed in no way dangerous; he was able, moreover, to present the history of the development of capitalism and the background of our economic crisis without resorting to statistics or relying upon complicated theories of

Leopoldo Mendez: Rich Man, Poor Man
The work of Leopoldo Mendez springs from the primitive nineteenth-century artists like Posada. Mendez has brought the technique of wood engraving to a high degree of perfection

economics. In *The Coming Struggle for Power*, after presenting the history of capitalism, Strachey argued in favor of Communism. This stand he was later to refute even for himself. Shortly after the book's publication, however, he toured the universities of his own country and of America as that intriguing combination, gentleman and radical, advocating profound social change. The arguments of *The Coming Struggle for Power* were fortified by a brilliant analysis of historical facts; he wrote well and at the same time simply; he made the snowballing of capitalism into monopolistic capitalism and into internationally monopolistic capitalism seem the perfect explanation of how depressions came to pass.

Americans in particular, never too strongly given to political analysis, took to John Strachey with great enthusiasm. Strachey, moreover, pointed to the fascism already in existence as the last breastwork flung up by embattled capitalism—this explained the new European war clouds. He pointed to highly militarized Italy and shortly to Hitler taking power in Germany and building, with some English and American financial backing, the totalitarian state. He intimated that the big financiers were holding together, that they had a true "united front." When the German totalitarian state extended its power over Central Europe, Strachey followed his first book with a series of volumes analyzing and fairly accurately forecasting the dangers of fascism to his own country, and later even to America. Reading his and other liberal, or even radical, books as a way of seeking to understand what had happened first to those on the dole in England, second to those out of work during the depression in America, many liberals and intellectuals in both countries came to think more than ever before along lines sympathetic to Marxism.

Artists face the real scene

Meantime, with or without any specific reading in economic theories, the artists knew they were jobless and poor. Poets and prose writers began to emphasize the influences of society on man. Even Freudian psychology, long a great influence on literature, began to change its color. Particularly during the 1920's much attention had been paid on all levels of literature and conversation to the theories of Freud regarding the profound influence of early childhood experiences on adult personality and behavior, and the existence of the "unconscious," the deeply buried memories and desires the repression of which affected man's conscious thoughts and actions. One of the criticisms of Freudianism was that it was essentially a "middle-class psychology"; that the behavior patterns it described and interpreted were limited to the middle class; that it regarded personal and family conditions as the sole causes of man's ills, and took no notice of culture, immediate social environment, or economic and racial backgrounds. With the coming of the depression pure Freudian theory, at least in relation to literature, fell into some disrepute, and the Freudianism which remained was modified by sociology and economics.

As the 1930's moved on, many artists who had previously lived outside the more workaday society—in Greenwich Village, on farms, in colonies of thatch-roofed cottages—found these retreats from civilization no longer satisfying. They seemed to symbolize the artists' defeat as well as their exile. Now, with the rise of dictators and prophecies of world disaster, writers began eagerly to reëxamine the actual world. Some, of course, did turn to religion, some did take temporary refuge in an increased emphasis on Freudianism, but most faced the real scene at last. The English writers still carried the classics under their arms, still held to the traditional in form. The Americans were not so burdened. But both the English and American literary investigators began an eager search for new material.

Impatient with the emphasis on abstract beauty and the detached passion of the mind so much talked about during the Waste Land period, and feeling that these matters were no longer of the first significance, many authors soon found new characters and new plots among the lives of the working people. They found new explanations of man's dilemma also in economic history. People, they argued, had the right to live and to earn a living. The writers began to realize that even as Roosevelt said in 1941 in his "Four Freedoms" speech,

The basic things expected by our people of their political and economic systems are simple. They are: equality of opportunity for youth and for others; jobs for those who can work; security for those who need it; the ending of special privilege for the few; the preservation of civil liberties for all; the enjoyment of the fruits of scientific progress in a wider and constantly rising standard of living.

AMERICAN POETS OBSERVE SOCIAL CONDITIONS

As early as 1915, certain Americans had begun to write of the working people. Carl Sandburg refused to flee from dirty Chicago. He argued that machines were not to blame for the situation in which men found themselves. In the right hands machinery and the machine economy could, he knew, be beneficial. There was, to be sure, something romantic in his enthusiasm for industrial America; Sandburg insisted too often, perhaps, on the conventional response of the poet to the beauty of the city streets.

Carl Sandburg did not need to seek far for material; he was the child of a Scandinavian immigrant laborer, and the environment and language of the common people were familiar to him. That he deliberately studied it, its inflections and its imagery, is also true. His style and philosophy seemed to combine in curious mixture Walt Whitman's nineteenth-century enthusiasm for democracy and Sinclair Lewis' contemporary satire of our "herd life." He did not accept Whitman's assumption that complete individualism and complete equality are both possible in America, and he did not fail to develop his own ideas or his own forms; indeed, he became a pioneer of a style which influenced, and was imitated by, many a younger writer. His prose, as exemplified in the monumental six-volume biography of Lincoln, also reflects the rhythms and the images of the common speech. Sandburg was a socialist; he felt, and still feels, that there are inequalities and waste in capitalism. He knows that the mass of the people often fare badly. He particularly hates those who fatten off the struggle between rich and poor. He believes the people should inherit the earth. Not an isolated intellectual but a poet of the folk and himself a workingman, Sandburg knows first hand the injustices of our industrial life. He has never been afraid to speak as a public man, to use his art as propaganda. This is probably why the theme of much of his poetry is life in the large cities as it is lived by the ordinary person who must work for his bread. He always upholds the dignity of labor and despises those who clip coupons. For all these reasons, Sandburg, under Roosevelt, became an ardent New Dealer, to work as a Washington newspaper columnist, a journalist for freedom.

Vachel Lindsay preaches the gospel of beauty

As popular as Sandburg during the same early period of sociological criticism was Vachel Lindsay, America's minstrel singer. But Lindsay's economic and social background was somewhat different from Sandburg's. Lindsay's father rather disapproved of his poetic son and would not subsidize his art. His deeply religious, artistic mother felt that art and religion were one; she concentrated on teaching her son that he could save the world through personal goodness and through art. Lindsay's formal education was conventional and left him with a large store of almost entirely undigested knowledge; added to this was the naïve idealism absorbed from his home training. He became an emotional, almost evangelical reformer. At first, as if to the tom-tom beat of the street-corner religious meeting, he sang of the possible greatness of his country once the people in it would return to innocence. Later, feeling that his early rhythms were becoming popular for their own sake and not for the message the words set to them were meant to convey, he assumed the solemn tone of the preacher. But always his message was that godliness and artistry were one and the same, that if Americans would relinquish their desire for financial success and become the pure in spirit, the worshipers of beauty and of goodness, our cities would not be dens of sin, but would instead become the temples of holiness and of brotherly love. In a language almost entirely middle class and with a mediocrity of expression which he and he alone raised to a curious poetic pitch (clichés and padded phrases in his thrusting rhythm rang with feverish commands and spiritual messages to the effect that God, beauty, and democracy were one) he preached what he felt was the gospel of the future.

The gist of Lindsay's message was to be found in his opposing symbols: the spider Mammon (greed and competition), an evil symbol, was always for him antithetical to the butterfly of beauty (the symbol of exploration and of good). In Lindsay's never quite mature mind was a conglomeration of all he had read of the teachings of the great religious leaders. He wanted Christian incense burners over the city hall, he wanted God in the market place, and most of all he wanted the eternal lotus flower of dream and delight. He wanted America's idealism to cleanse America of commercialism. His myth-making grew from his feeling of identity with our pioneer American exuberance. But it was getting late for buffaloes to wander on our plains, late for Johnny Appleseed to find space to sow his orchards, late for such adolescent hero worship as this poet's of a motley group of American leaders. Lindsay truly represented, nevertheless, something powerfully American, a kind of blind faith in our earlier and more revolutionary symbols—in leadership and democracy, in love and in power—symbols possibly contradictory if one examined them too closely in the light of modern developments.

A psychiatrist might have described Lindsay's idealism and yearnings for reform as a messianic complex. But these aspects of his personality are in a way curiously representative of the American ideal. Periodically, America has held that she could save the world. She has never thought through the contradictions between her early idealism and revolutionary fervor and, on the other hand, her growing desire for power. When economically secure she holds that she is the child of nineteenth-century idealism. Insecure, she grows more reactionary. But it has long been one of America's great hopes that her own history need not repeat exactly the pattern of class distinctions so long existent in England and in the countries of Europe. Lindsay held to all of the incoherent liberal and religious American ideals which ran contrary to American commercialism. He was a middle-western puritan who lived through the economic madness of the 1910's and 1920's. Popular for his picturesque poetry recitals during which he half-danced, half-shouted his verse, he spent his life on railroad trains, lecturing everywhere to support his family, until it began to seem to him that his was a voice in the American wilderness. Then he committed suicide. Lindsay was able to make the myths of America part of our twentieth-century consciousness, but his map of the American future was a curious and confused blur. The signposts on his road to progress bore the names of everything in religious faith, occidental or oriental, and many of the slogans for social reform.

Hart Crane creates new symbols of man and machines

Another poet who because of his highly sensitive nature might at this time have remained in the ivory tower refused in his earliest work the abnegation of reality which this implied. Hart Crane as early as 1926 had published *White Buildings* and become known as a poet who disliked Eliot's negation of the passion of living. Entirely familiar with Eliot's theories, Crane nevertheless sought beauty in modern life. He felt, as few others did, that there was much new that the poet must absorb—the whole machine age. He was aware that to do this was not easy. Crane saw new reason for faith in man's creative genius exemplified in machinery, in the beauty of the modern city, its towers, its bridges. He fought against those who argued that science had routed poetry. Crane had worked in a wartime munitions plant at the age of fifteen and he disagreed with the discouraged poets who thought the First World War had ended the poet's power of imaginative vision.

Soon I. A. Richards was to state in an essay that poetry was no longer to thrive, since it relied upon pseudo-truth and not scientific truth for its emotional appeal. Crane insisted,

on the contrary, that poetic truth was a kind of super-rational truth concerning the as-yet-unknown, the deeply felt, the necessary to the heart and mind of man. The modern poet, he felt, must nevertheless absorb the truths of science and industry in order to know what greater truths of imagination sprang from these:

The function of poetry in a Machine Age is identical to function in any other age; and its capacities for presenting the most complete synthesis of human values remain essentially immune from any of the so-called inroads of

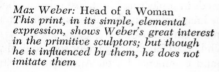
Max Weber: Head of a Woman
This print, in its simple, elemental expression, shows Weber's great interest in the primitive sculptors; but though he is influenced by them, he does not imitate them

science. The emotional stimulus of machinery is on an entirely different psychic plane from that of poetry. Its only menace lies in its capacities for facile entertainment, so easily accessible as to arrest the development of any but the most negligible esthetic responses. The ultimate influence of machinery in this respect remains to be seen; its firm entrenchment in our lives has already produced a series of challenging new responsibilities for the poet.

For unless poetry can absorb the machine, i.e., acclimatize it as naturally and casually as trees, cattle, galleons, castles and all other human associations of the past, then poetry has failed of its full contemporary function. This process does not infer any program of lyrical pandering to the taste of those obsessed by the importance of machinery; nor does it essentially involve even the specific mention of a single mechanical contrivance. It demands, however, along with the traditional qualifications of the poet, an extraordinary capacity for surrender, at least temporarily, to the sensations of urban life. This presupposes, of course, that the poet possesses sufficient spontaneity and gusto to convert this experience into positive terms.*

Obviously, great physical energy and great sensitivity are necessary to a poet who would absorb the sensations of urban life. The poet who surrenders only to the sensations of the rose garden or the cow pasture is not likely to be so easily exhausted, or so overstimulated, so stretched in creative tension as is the poet who rides on subways, stays up half the night at Harlem dance halls, sleeps briefly, and gets up to earn his living at a depressing and incompatible eight-hour job. Crane, although physically strong, was a highly neurotic person.

As a poet, Crane's first problem was to develop the images and symbols which would convey the emotions of modern life. This meant that he had to create almost a new language. Always he had to associate an old symbol with a new—the boat, a symbol of exploration, with the airplane; sunlight, a symbol of illumination, with the acetylene torch. He must so em-

* From the essay written by Hart Crane from Oliver M. Saylers' Symposium, *Revolt in the Arts* (Brentano's, 1930), reprinted by permission of Coward-McCann, Inc.

ploy industrial language as to make it poetic. He willed, moreover, to look forward, not backward. The world which Eliot pictured as commercial and bored Crane saw as a world in which men working anonymously together created a new kind of beauty. For him the past had led into the greatness of the present, which in turn could lead into a greater future. Reaching out always to assimilate and penetrate the new, Crane willed to think that the potentialities of man were, as yet, almost untapped. Sometimes he pictured these potentialities with clear historical perspective, and sometimes with a kind of romantic mysticism.

His attempts to find a fresh imagery and to express new ideas often made Crane's poetry extremely obscure. Since both his language and his message as to the limitlessness of man's ability to create a world were new, Crane depended very largely on language to create out of itself a vision which he wished to project. Consequently, when his language evokes the exaltation he felt, and is at the same time sufficiently close to his real scheme of reference (the astounding beauty and energy of the modern city), then he succeeds in projecting his almost religious belief in the imagination as able always to affirm man's eternal greatness.

While Carl Sandburg gave us sociological satires and commentaries on American industrial life, and Vachel Lindsay transformed puritan idealism into evangelistic shouts for reform, Crane crossed swords with Eliot's despair and projected against Eliot's defeatism and subsequent reliance upon traditional religion a new faith in beauty as man-made, rather than God-made. Crane was a modern romantic who felt the greatness of man's anonymous work. And although he never saw the men from whose worn shoulders it sprang, he saw the bridge they made, working collectively, as a symbol of communication between men, cities, and continents.

Spotlight on social investigation

The pessimistic and optimistic reactions to the world which the poets were presenting had their sociological theorists. Even before the First World War, Bertrand Russell had proposed shorter hours of labor, better education, and a slow evolution, in general, toward socialism. Randolph Bourne, the American idol of college liberals during the first war, had written essays, sometimes political and sometimes literary, against such ideas of power and such weaknesses on the part of the intellectuals as led to war. He died in 1918, pilloried indeed by the war madness, but not before he had in his *Untimely Papers* influenced many liberals and some who were not so liberal to think favorably concerning socialism.

When President Wilson carried his fight for the League of Nations to the people and lost, when the immediate post-war optimism faded, the American writers, as had the English earlier, fixed their eyes more and more on the social scene. From then until the rumblings of a second war, we had many books of social investigation. The new searchlight for the writer was modern sociology. The lives of the "robber barons" were laid not too prettily bare in book after book. The journalists watched the rise of dictatorships. The psychologists meantime noted the growth of modern neuroses, and such novelists as Huxley, who found these neuroses due to science, grew skeptical of what the scientific world held for man. Literature widened its horizons, circle after circle, and everywhere historical events impinged upon imaginative vision.

Methods of propaganda also became the subject of investigation, and from the period of the depression on, both American and English writers more exactly, if more pessimistically, analyzed what was being done to the human mind by political manipulation. They had been instructed, moreover, as to the meaning of fascism by a few writers like Kenneth Burke, who earlier had turned his thoughtful attention to *Mein Kampf*.

Some of our journalists, philosophers, and critics attempted to clarify the real scene, as it has unrolled before us, and to give us a new perspective. And so it came about that the creative writers, whatever vision of man's lot they presented, were forced into an awareness of actual events and of the main currents of political and economic thinking. No poet, and for that matter no fiction writer, has escaped the sociological searchlight, and the relation of literature and society has consequently become clearer. Sandburg, Lindsay, and Crane came early on the scene and were the forerunners of the new school of poetry which sprang up with the depression in America.

American poets criticize society

These poets were called "left-wing," or "radical," or "proletarian," according to who did the tagging. Actually, they were young, jobless, and acutely aware of the relationship between economics and personal life. Unlike Eliot, they could not be physically comfortable and superior in boredom; Eliot, they believed, had pronounced the last rites of a generation optimistically believing that artists could exist apart from their society. In truth, these poets were physically confronted by the fact of poverty—not just spiritual poverty, such as Eliot had mourned over, but fear and hunger—and they had a consequent identification with others in the same predicament. Of middle-class background, they found themselves with no appreciable income, not even a furnished room; and certainly no ivory tower was given them rent-free. At employment agencies, on park benches, perhaps with only a nickel for coffee, they found themselves in a harsh reality and they turned to analyze what might be wrong in our society.

During the depression, poetry was the dominant literature of both England and America. The depression in England had been more or less continuous between wars, and had therefore not been felt as the shock it was to Americans after the boom; at any rate, artists in both countries faced for themselves and for a good many others an economic scarcity. They could not continue to study decadence, inhaling its sometimes rich perfumes. They had to leave their hideouts, whether of Freudian self-examination or romantic illusion, and walk the streets to get work. Liking it or not, they were no longer the special class they had felt themselves to be in the Waste Land period; they were just people in a highly industrialized world in crisis. This may explain why poetry became more popular than prose. For the economic crisis had made the strongest instinctive tendency of this period's artists that of survival. And "poetry," as the late "Christopher Caudwell" (Christopher St. John Sprigg) wrote in *Illusion and Reality*,

is an expression of freedom which is inherent in man's timeless unity in society; it is interested in society as the sun and guardian of common instinctive tendencies. Poetry speaks of love, death, hope, sorrow, despair, as all experience them. Unlike the novel, which is an expression of freedom which men seek not in their unity but in their differences of their repulsions from clashes with concrete motions against other individuals different from themselves. . . .

Poetry, to paraphrase Caudwell briefly, is a "tribal cry."

The "tribal cry" of the depression years, particularly in America, was for bread. There was a "unity" of belief that the bare economic necessities were of utmost importance. Consequently, all the frustrated values of individualism so rehearsed by the Waste Land writers were for the time being lost in the cry for universal salvation. Although the Waste Land had not been a congenial environment for writers who had consistently despised commercialism and materialism, it had all too frequently appeared a necessary evil: after all, they argued, a rich society alone could afford a top soil, however thin, for art. Now the "necessary evil" became economic chaos; even shrinking from the purely material was a luxury. Therefore, they said, there were questions to be asked: was there something wrong with capitalism; why did not so large an industrial machine produce enough to give jobs to and feed and clothe its workers? If man could bring about the machine age with its tremendous capacities for comfort, why could he not control more directly what he produced?

The writers, like other citizens, began to argue these questions. They relinquished their attitudes of spiritual superiority and antagonism to economic determinism and wrote prose and poetry (in particular, poetry) about the economic failures and the possible economic cures and changes necessary to make life endurable. They shifted from the individualistic values of the Waste Land toward an emphasis on more broadly humanitarian values. The aristocratic dislike of the vulgar and sometimes, hence, of the common man, was replaced by a love of justice (sometimes, unfortunately, with a consequent debasing of esthetic standards); the emphasis on death as an escape from boredom and materialism shifted into an examination of the causes for which man might be willing to give his life to better humanity. The intensity about individual salvation became an intensity about social betterment.

Economics and politics frequently enter poetry when they directly affect our physical lives. This explains why economics and politics now play so striking a part in contemporary European (in particular Spanish) and South American poetry. But although America had a revolutionary background, she had, until the depression, largely forgotten it. Even when the depression struck, Americans were still an optimistic and non-political people, much less trained in the observation of historical events and world problems than were the English. But together with the boom which helped to create it, the American Renaissance, with its romantic individualism and its hope for continuous prosperity, ended. The lost generation, which had come home to build an American art, found it had to turn its attention to the economic crisis. Some of its poets, like Archibald MacLeish, for example, stopped insisting on the vulgarity of our commercial culture as unproductive of art, and became enthusiastic about liberal movements and about the governmental changes being made by the Roosevelt administration.

New ends and new imagery in poetry

So general was the first enthusiasm for sociological criticism, in fact, that our poets were in danger of making poetry into a formula or into straight propaganda. The shift away from the individualistic values of the Waste Land to the humanitarian values of the depression called, indeed, for new poetic language. The only language proposing direct social change was Marxian and its terminology was still strange, at least to the average poet. The poets' audience, moreover, was used to the older imagery of esthetic response, and conditioned to a subjective and personal imagery. In using the Marxian ideology and its imagery in poetry the poets therefore were using words and emotions on the whole still unfamiliar, disagreed with by many, and therefore calling forth a mixed response. Indeed, since poetry is condensed and has no time to argue, poets usually have to rely on what Caudwell defines as "public truth," or the general body of accepted feeling and fact through which we communicate. The public truth of the depression was that of sheer economic necessity, but as yet there was no accepted truth as to the way of obtaining jobs and food for all. The crisis was a fact, but the cures conceived for it were contradictory. Even those poets who had read enough to have followed the history of socialism were themselves conditioned by capitalism and had as their audience a multitude who had never criticized their own way of life. Not until the depression had the more revolutionary social philosophies at all inflamed the poetic imagination; not until the depression had many of the poets, or their audience, attempted to understand the Marxist philosophy. Then, as always, it was the young and adventurous writers who attempted to state the newer revolutionary theories concerning, for example, the "class struggle." Some of their attempts were overly obvious: a poem describing an iceberg suddenly becomes a poem about the submerged two thirds of society; a poem about a rescue becomes a poem about a Communist teaching his comrade how to come ashore in the socialist world. Few of these early revolutionary poems made use of a language universal enough to call upon the radical fervor for change, potentially always existent even in America. But despite the novelty and the artificiality of much of the language employed by the more ardent radical poets there was, by 1931, a poet on every soapbox.

One of these so-called soapbox poets was Kenneth Fearing, whose solution to the problem of finding images to communicate his message was similar to that used by Carl Sandburg in some of his most successful poems. Instead of identifying himself solely with the proletariat in an attempt to project the vision of a better world for the common people, Fearing chose, as Sandburg had earlier, to satirize the middle class in their own language. Satire is always of the familiar, since what is satirized must be recognizable. And Fearing gave back to the middle class, in journalese and urban slang, what he believed were their essential empty-mindedness and stupid self-assurance. Because of the economic chaos, his verse was recognized as a half-angry, half-humorous attack, but he was always understood. As time went on and the crisis lessened, Fearing, indeed, became more and more popular with the very people he caricatured. Today he is a well-known *New Yorker* poet. He has asked not only for a world of "paid-up bills" but for one in which we can still have at least whimsical reminders of our old romantic dreams. Although he tried once or twice to present a picture of a new, just, and free world, he has in general been happier in satirizing our "herd" life. His talent is little better today than it was in the depression, but he remains popular. He learned from Sandburg his use of free verse and his method of handling the language, but his rhythms are moderately reflective of the staccato and conflicting emotions of the depression.

It is not surprising that many of the depression poets became the novelists and poets of the Second World War. They were the right age; they were anti-fascist; and they saw and felt more clearly than many what the war was about. Typical of them was Alfred Hayes. More journalist than artist, Hayes was well known in the depression for his verse on such topics as unemployment; like many of these young poets, he was soon caught up in the war. His experiences in Italy with the army of occupation provided material for his poems and for his novel *All Thy Conquests*, which was published in 1946. Hayes is a facile writer, but his plots are somewhat sentimentalized.

Another poet of the depression years is Muriel Rukeyser, who found a distorted world when she left Vassar College. She associates herself with the dispossessed. Her most moving early poems were lyrics on her divorcement from the middle-class attitudes of her family. Like many other poets, she turned to examine critically the emphasis put on social and financial position. Becoming convinced that only a socialist world made sense, she wrote poetry to arouse readers to this conviction. She toured the United States; in *U. S. 1* are her poems on the contradictions between the life of the wealthy and the life of the poor seen along the great highway. Her poetry of the depression merged into still better anti-fascist poetry during the war period. Since the Second World War she has written more reflective lyric verse (*The Green Wave*, 1947) about the inevitable conflict in a mind aware of both personal and social problems.

Sol Funaroff, an ardent Communist poet who died in poverty, and Edwin Rolfe, who fought in Spain and again in the Second World War, are both dominantly Marxist poets. Rolfe is a good example of a poet who has had difficulty in communicating his own political enthusiasm, because what for him is public truth appears to the majority to be little more than propaganda. Such words as "comrade" and "proletariat," which to him were emotionally charged and expressed high aims, were for his readers controversial and possibly unpleasant. Rolfe has rendered a service to American poetry, however, by translating the excellent highly political verse of the Spanish and South American left-wing poets which has recently come to influence a number of English and American poets.

The self-styled left-wing poets enjoyed considerable popularity for several years. But the times were changing rapidly. Like the early romantics of the eighteenth century, who had expressed the romantic tendency in neoclassical verse forms, some of these poets used an older form and an older imagery to express a new social philosophy. The greater number of them were from "average" families, and the sterile speech of the middle class clung so closely to them that it was difficult for them to use any other kind of language in their poetry. This limited their power to communicate their new ideas concerning social change. Furthermore,

there was, as we have already pointed out, little identification between writers and laborers, and although some writers attempted this identification intellectually, they had been formed emotionally by their particular social environments. As a matter of fact, no real literature of the laboring class had at this period time to mature, for the era of the depression was soon to become the pre-war period. Moreover, despite the brief enthusiasm for socialist ideas of world betterment, the leaning toward socialism in America was not strong. Few people were convinced of the necessity of even mild social changes here; consequently the writers had actually no accepted "public truth" to communicate. So finally, along with much of the propaganda for change circulated in the early 1930's, the "soapbox poetry" of the depression years disappeared as the Roosevelt program for the correction of social evils began to better economic conditions.

Negro Americans contribute to the literature of social protest

From Colonial times on, Negro Americans had contributed significantly to the literature as well as to the other cultural elements of the country. Because other minority groups have not had the same racial and cultural continuity, there is no other literature of a minority group which has become so important a part of the body of American literature while at the same time retaining its distinctive characteristics. The Negro's religious intensity and his struggle for freedom naturally served as his most significant themes.

An important section of the poetry of social protest had come from the Negro poets. Despite efforts to dispel intolerance, the New Deal was unable to overcome the prejudice and ignorance which had long hemmed these people in. Negroes are always among the first and most seriously affected in any crisis. Discrimination against them has had a long history. It is natural, therefore, that their artists should have written of their economic plight when that plight was gravest.

Langston Hughes, among many others, saw

Pablo Picasso: Illustration for Balzac's
Le chef d'oeuvre inconnu
Here is remarkably skillful use of the
wood block to reproduce the qualities of
a brush-and-ink drawing

the "Negro problem" as related to the problems of the working class, and wrote of them in the blues rhythms common to Negro songs. Sterling Brown chose a larger canvas, although he was by no means unaware of the Negro's unfortunate economic position. He uses the folk forms, the ballad and the tall tale, to present half-humorous, half-tragic stories of persecution. He invents Negro heroes in stature very like Paul Bunyan, heroes whose verse narratives convey with irony and a little humor the fear and disorder under which the Negro must live. Brown, a college professor, has written sociological treatises on the subject of race prejudice. He sees the Negro problem as related to the struggle of the laboring class as a whole. His poetry became popular in the years of the depression and has remained the authentic vehicle of the singing speech of a people. He is

perhaps the most talented of the contemporary Negro poets.

Interest broadens to world politics

We have seen that in all the depression poetry, with its leanings toward socialism and toward much greater equality, a new content and new direction of thought are opposed in some degree to the traditional American belief in free competition. However, the leftward movement of poetic thought did not continue indefinitely. The depression poets may have been right in believing that the world was at a crossroads, but they were overly optimistic as to any peaceful evolution toward socialism. Even as the slow recovery began, the symptoms of another world war were becoming evident. It was not long before "radicals" became less concerned with economic maladjustments and joined hands with moderate liberals in opposing fascism. It was, consequently, those poets who had remained closely in the stream of tradition and never turned propagandist who most unobtrusively bridged the gap between the poetry of strictly personal emotion and poetry in which the social scene affected personal emotion. David Schubert, for example, wrote verse in which he connected his childhood experience of poverty and insecurity with his adult fear of personal and economic catastrophe. Ben Belitt, too, comes upon the acceptance of human dignity through the necessity of understanding adversity.

Most of the older poets, conditioned by a more prosperous period, were less directly sympathetic with the proletariat than were the younger. But William Carlos Williams as a physician recognized the plight of his own patients. As a physician, indeed, he had long drawn his material directly from the lives of the common people. In his work in the clinics he came close to the poor and was moved deeply by their will to live. Consequently, combining his vocation and his avocation, he pictures the common people as instruments of change and as the core of creative energy. In his early long poem *The Wanderer,* which like Wordsworth's *Prelude* is a history of how he became a poet, he points out first that the poet must describe nature not as a retreat, but as that out of which the farmer struggles to create his livelihood; second, that the poet must love all the people, the poor and the hideous as well as the beautiful; and third, that the poet must see in labor organization the implement of a people. In *Paterson: Book I,* Williams images man as made by and making his community. Because his life has allowed him no divorcement from the economic factors which mold life, Williams, now in his sixties, is one of our more progressive poets. His well-known short stories and his novels also portray the economic forces in our society which condition our people. Williams believes that the insistence on money has vitiated the wealthy and left the poor as the only vessels of creative vitality, though they too, of course, may be thwarted and devitalized by the ills of an acquisitive society.

American novelists and playwrights analyze social problems

The novelists of the Waste Land had summed up a period. Their novels, very like poetry, were studies of a sensitive mood. They had rejected action and turned to study what is often the natural subject matter of poetry, or as Virginia Woolf says, to study "the whole heredity of instincts, glands and thought channellings of man's general timeless unity." Their heroes were either will-less pigmies or Freudian cases in the process of self-analysis. The emphasis was on spiritual decadence and never upon the sociological. With the depression, however, and the increasing awareness of a need for action to insure survival, novelists found significance in a new kind of plot, a new kind of hero; the novel of action and the novel of sociological criticism were born.

The chief technical problem for the depression novelists was the problem of how to make group action exciting. For years interest had centered on the peculiarly individualistic hero and his complicated psychology. Now the novelist must write, notebook in hand, about the conditions under which people worked and lived. From Henry James on down, the novelist seldom liked the businessman, and only a few writers, like Sinclair Lewis, had concerned themselves with him. Still fewer had treated of the working man as hero. The sociological novelist had to examine the forces in society which made both the businessman and the working man its tools. For dramatic appeal and dynamic action there were such subjects as revolutions abroad and the struggle of the labor unions at home.

Actually it was a French writer, André Malraux, who produced what was probably the most famous novel of revolution. This was *Man's Fate,* the story of the ill-fated Chinese Revolution of 1926. It bears mention here because of its influence on American and English novelists of this period. With noteworthy skill Malraux peopled his novel with characters having subtle personal attachments, psychological complexities, yet serving each as a symbol—though not a stereotype—of some phase of social action. The theme of *Man's Fate* is an intensely serious contemplation of human dignity as the only condition under which it is possible to live. Its hero is not the passive man of the earlier Waste Land novels but the hero engaged in dramatic action against forces greater than himself—not the inactive and pathetic but the tragic hero.

The novel of social action sweeps the country

There had been earlier novelists, like Dreiser, who had pictured man as a socially conditioned animal; there had been earlier attacks upon our competitive and acquisitive drives. Sinclair Lewis, as we have noted, had satirized the Babbitts; but for all that he hated in babbittry, he tended to blame institutions, not those who controlled them. Not until the period following the Second World War was Lewis aroused to accusation.

In the depression the novelist began to look at the world about him. Self-pity gave way in him to social pity, and consequently to social action. Therefore he turned to social criticism. Novels were written about strikes, about racial discrimination, about poverty and joblessness and the endless personal problems which attended these social phenomena. The dramatic human conflict was now interpreted most frequently as a conflict between the common man and a blind and greedy minority.

During the depression John Steinbeck, whose earliest books had been escapist, discovered the novel of social action. He made the strike leader his hero in *In Dubious Battle*. He turned to examine the deplorable condition of the migratory workers in California in *Grapes of Wrath*. He studied the lumpen proletariat in *Of Mice and Men;* but in this book it becomes obvious that he is more interested in the Freudian than in the sociological novel. Indeed, his fascination with Freudianism has distorted his study of fascism, *The Moon Is Down,* and in *Tortilla Flat* it is apparent that Steinbeck's natural medium is a gentler form of Tobacco Road literature. Steinbeck, like such other writers as Erskine Caldwell and Robert Cantwell, is on the whole more interested in simple, even slightly backward people than he is in labor organiza-

tions or intellectuals. He finds it easier to present as human the simpler communities, with their homely and eccentric characters, than to treat of socially necessary action as politically led. There is a possibility, indeed, as Steinbeck seems to indicate in *The Wayward Bus*, that he might escape from the perils and confusion of social theorizing. Steinbeck is broadly humanitarian, but he is also somewhat romantic in his love of the "people," and he has held to no singular point of view as a social critic. Some critics feel that he is a lesser writer, since unlike most great novelists he has no single and obsessive theme.

James Farrell rose to prominence as a novelist during the depression with his studies of the lower middle-class Irish in Chicago. His first important books were novels of delinquent, disease-ridden youth directly affected by economic instability. More able to record than to invent, Farrell in *Studs Lonigan* proved both his strength and his deficiency as a novelist. He knew best the religious discussions, the family rows, the younger generation's bewilderment, as part of his own experience. When he attempted to portray intellectual and mature characters, he failed. His type of novel is often referred to as "cesspool" literature: literature exposing the conditions under which the less fortunate in our cities live. Once the exposure is made, no very specific cure is offered for the disease. To be sure, Farrell seemed at first to lean vaguely toward Communism, but of such leanings he has more than repented. Today he more often takes violent issue with what he terms "stalinist" ideas.

Another novelist much discussed for his attempts to picture the whole of America is John Dos Passos. He too wished to get away from the highly individualistic themes of the Waste Landers. His book on the First World War, *Three Soldiers,* is still spoken of as one of his best, but he soon turned his attention to developing new techniques for presenting a broad canvas. His "Camera Eye" and "Newsreel" are both tricks of form for changing time and place rapidly. His fiction is episodic, as he conceives our lives to be. In *Manhattan Transfer* and *U.S.A.* he gives us what he thinks to be the real America, commercial, sprawling, contradictory, a scene in which personal lives flare briefly into prominence only to die down into obscurity. Obviously, Dos Passos thought of capitalism as distorting our lives; obviously he is now against the doctrine of economic determinism, as shown in his recent novel *The Grand Design;* but he offers no cure. He wants Life to be FREE, and he is almost Calvinistic in his fury against any controls. His later work, consequently, is violently anti-Communist. He has become the defender of free individualism.

The primitivists—romantic and sociological

In the late 1920's and the early 1930's there emerged another school of writing which purported to be social criticism—we might call it the school of American primitivism. Erskine Caldwell has remained the leader of this. The world such writers as Caldwell and Robert Cantwell examined (that world which, as we have said, Steinbeck finally chose as his own) was composed of simple people spawned in our backwoods. These people are amoral, anti-puritanic, and vulgar, dramatically but noncommittally sadistic. They are both humorous and pathetic. The authors who handled this Tobacco Road literature did so, perhaps, in part because they felt a kind of superiority to their characters, or because they felt that the abnormal was more interesting than the normal. These novels often rely on the pure picturesqueness of the primitive.

One section of our country lent itself especially to writers interested in the primitive: this was the South. And it was the South which gave birth to William Faulkner, one of our more important novelists. Faulkner is an intensely subjective psychological writer who never tries to beautify what he pictures. Hardly a character in his books could be said to be "normal." His primitives of the south are clearly conditioned by race suppression, fear, and economic distress. In his scene, a bored and decadent aristocracy lives close upon a depressed poor, nor is it long before the keener minds among his poor learn the cheap commercial strivings once practiced by his aristocracy. They even vulgarize and make more violent these strivings. While Faulkner's fine old families either go mad or die, his poor, mean in spirit, inherit the earth. With the skill of a detective-story writer, he constructs an involved and endless series of horrible incidents, the resolution of which is unclear until the book ends. Faulkner's scenes are of Exodus, rather than of Genesis. His characters dash across the landscape, Negro pursued by white, or white by white, or inner man by outer man. Faulkner's South is peopled as in a long nightmare from which one would like to awaken but cannot. The madness constantly mounts until in one of his best novels, *The Hamlet,* Faulkner points to economic greed and fear as that which destroys any people and any culture.

Another chronicler of the South was Thomas Wolfe, a late romantic who was by the very exuberance of his nature incapable of being a Waste Lander. All Wolfe's writing is in a sense autobiographical. With Whitmanesque fervor he embraced America, and like Whitman he seems to have felt himself to be typical of much that was America. He wanted to know everything and to experience everything. His theme, that of a poor boy escaping a small southern environment and a closely knit, rather ignorant family in order to come to the big city and be an artist, is a typical American success story, not unlike some of those written in the romantic twenties. Wolfe felt the energy of man and of his own great country. A large man, he liked large canvases. His novels are full of kaleidoscopic events, of redundant hates and redundant prejudices. Much of his prose has a pseudo-Shelleyan flavor. Nevertheless, his novels are impressive; they practically burst their covers. Through the eyes of their sensitive but always somewhat adolescent chronicler we see the American people as exuberant and untried as Wolfe himself. It is probably for this reason that Wolfe has such a large following. His optimism, his joy in life and experience, even his somewhat immature enthusiasms to encompass all experience, are in a way typical of the still young, sometimes undirected strength which America possesses. His excitement over the emotional experience of growing up, his appetite for knowledge convey themselves particularly to younger readers, and many an older

Henri Matisse: Illustration for Mallarmé's poem "Brise Marine" Matisse's delicate etchings succeed in combining the qualities of decoration and illustration without obtruding on the poems of Mallarmé which they were designed to accompany

reader seems to find in him an antidote for the more learned skepticism typical of many other writers of his period. However, it is not entirely strange that something about Wolfe's grandiose manner pleased Hitler. This author's power lay in a kind of titanic myth-making; Hitler too built his tall tales, for self and national exploitation. Wolfe finally went to Germany and saw fascism. He rejected all it stood for, immediately; for despite its grandioseness his myth was of a childishly innocent, incoherent, and humane democracy. Wolfe, for all his egotism, loved ordinary people and felt himself to be of them.

All these novelists in one way or another, consciously or unconsciously, write fiction which has sociological overtones. But in the actual depression years it was the younger novelists who most specifically attacked the themes of racial discrimination or political planning. Richard Wright placed squarely before us the Negro so frustrated and so mistreated as to become a criminal. Almost every character in Wright's *Native Son* is a clear social symbol. There is the well-intentioned white philanthropist who lives off the Negro slums; the gentle and blind aristocratic woman; the bored daughter, taking up any form of excitement; and there is Bigger, the hero, child of poverty, who gains his only manhood through the act of killing. The intent of the book is clear, the plot is swift. Only in the end does the book falter, when rather ponderously the novelist tries to indicate Bigger's awakening to the friendship offered him by the radicals. *Native Son* is an indictment of a society, but even in this novel there is some indication that Wright is more involved in introspection and in his dislike of being a Negro than he is interested in presenting a cure for the resentment between white and black. *Black Boy* is a completely autobiographical account of society's injustice to the Negro artist. There is in this account much self-adulation and self-pity, and today most critics consider Wright's early short stories his best work.

The theater of the 1930's reflects contemporary issues

There were other novels of this time, definitely propagandistic in nature. The excitement and the stimulus of thinking in larger circles gave birth to many new books. Although little of this literature has left its artistic landmark, it nevertheless was wholly typical of the early thirties. Not until our slow economic recovery began, even as the shadow of war appeared, did the social critics shift from an analysis of the depression to an analysis of fascism. Under the encouragement of the W.P.A. art in all fields had begun to thrive, so luxuriantly as to indicate what economic security or succor might do for the artistic growth of America. Not only were many novels written, but even more plays were produced. The experimental theater revitalized the classic *Doctor Faustus* of Marlowe, granted Eliot's *Murder in the Cathedral* a large audience, and gave us many plays in which the workingman emerged as hero. So intensely aware were the authors of many of these plays of their desire to project the need of economic change, that the government came to feel that the theater was perhaps being used politically. Since we were still in crisis, some censorship was felt necessary. In later comments upon the First World War there had

been *Johnny Johnson* by Paul Green, the theme of which was the essential madness of a war world. There had been Irwin Shaw's *Bury the Dead*, which asserted man's right to live. On the theme of strikes there had been Clifford Odets' *Waiting for Lefty*. On the actual crisis there had been Archibald MacLeish's play called *Panic*. Moreover, our stage was also being invaded by the work of the left-wing English poets. There was much talk about the return of poetic drama. Auden and Isherwood gave us *The Dog Beneath the Skin*, a long allegory about an English squire who identifies himself with the underdog. Everywhere were new forms and new themes, even new types of theaters which went directly to the people. The low price of tickets brought a large audience, excited by the realization that the theater was speaking of the actual events which influenced their lives.

All this activity went on until W.P.A. disappeared. Then Shaw and Odets found jobs in Hollywood; MacLeish became Librarian of Congress and entered on a career of administrative service in the government; and all that was left of an artistic rebirth were Saroyan, with his theme of confusion and contradiction as the spice of life, and Maxwell Anderson, who seemed to be saying serious things while he allowed us to rest on our dream that God was in His heaven and all was well with the world. Shortly, the popular Lillian Hellman turned from the native scene of *The Little Foxes* and the criticism of economic blindness to write her anti-fascist play, *Watch on the Rhine*, which won the New York Drama Critics Circle award in 1941. When the war actually broke over us, the theater became a vehicle of amusement.

The plays which were most popular at that time were those which were intended to relieve the strain felt by people, not necessarily to enlighten audiences or awaken them to awareness of the world situation. Most of these productions were light comedy, musical comedy, and murder mysteries—the kind of entertainment often scornfully termed "escapist." But now and then there appeared, in experimental theaters and even on Broadway, a serious anti-fascist drama.

ENGLISH WRITERS AND THE SOCIAL SCENE

When England, taking cognizance of her economic situation after the First World War, saw her conservatives fall from power, saw the rise and fall of a Labour government, and realized her difficulties with the Empire, she moved moderately through such social changes as were necessary. She kept her dole, she went through no such inflation as did America. Never did her intellectuals indicate the flamboyant optimism and the consequent violent disillusion that caught up the intellectuals in America. English writers were for the most part aware of their disillusion as a *class* disillusion and as a continuous development from Victorianism on through the Bohemian revolt of the nineties into the economic struggles of the twentieth century.

The greater number of England's older novelists continued after the first war to write of the retreat from nineteenth-century values. Some, like Huxley, stressed the disillusion concerning any scientific or purely intellectual answer as to the real needs of mankind; others, like Virginia Woolf, emphasized the neurotic hypersensitivity of the cultured. Most of the older writers' themes were continuations of themes already in English literature and heavily played upon in European literature. Such novelists as attempted to write of the English proletariat —the term so frequently used in the 1930's to describe the great group of wage-earners—approached the matter from a broadly humanitarian basis also traditional to English thought, for from Dickens down the problem of the poor never entirely disappears from English literature. Fabian Socialism of the mild evolutionary variety had long concerned the English writers. But only a few proletarian novels did appear, so called because they treated of a class society and of the problems of an actual industrial proletariat. Moreover, liberals like Beachcroft (see p. 814) began to advocate the rights of the English workers and to project their endeavors to better themselves.

Truth to tell, few English writers were dogmatically concerned with the philosophy of Marxism. The war writers came home to repudiate the schooling and the idealism which had thrown them blindly into the struggle for power. But no bubble had burst, no rainbow had shattered; the conflict between commercialism and culture had been continuous and was now regarded simply as a fight to the death for one or the other. England had a long tradition of political thinking far more consistently promoted among her intellectuals than among American intellectuals. She had a literary tradition of polemic satire and of argument in every form which the younger writers could appropriate as vehicles for their attacks upon contemporary problems. From the seventeenth century on, England had had her Miltons, her Swifts, her Butlers, her Popes, her revolutionary Shelleys and Byrons. And while the English novel had most particularly recorded the rise, the control, and the decline in power of the upper middle class, English poetry had been more consistently inclined to record the changing political policies and philosophies of both Europe and England. Although American writers had been slow to incorporate the main trends of European thought, and had been given to a kind of provincialism which although refreshing was also very insular, English writers had long been molded by the chief European philosophical, economic, and historical trends.

Younger post-war poets turn leftward

Actually, it was the English poets who wrote the chief credos of the post-war time of stress. With Shelleyan enthusiasm they sought visions of better worlds, with Byronic vehemence they attacked their own class and their own shifting culture. With the same general enlargement of horizons as had stimulated the early romantics of the eighteenth century, they turned to examine the condition of the common people. Nevertheless, the consistency of their poetry depends upon the violence with which they criticized the very cultural backgrounds from which

Pablo Picasso: Illustration for Balzac's Le chef d'oeuvre inconnu
*This engraving shows how Picasso's classic linear style
can be transcribed by the wood engraver as well as by the etcher*

they came. As W. H. Auden, the most brilliant of these poets, points out, these poets knew the emptiness and corruptness of their own conditioning.

There is one great psychological class division in English society, the division between those who have been educated at public school [equivalent of American private preparatory schools] and those who have not; and it is impossible for a foreigner to realize how profound the division is.

Some six percent of the population from the age of eight to the age of twenty-one spend three-quarters of each year away from home in small communities made up exclusively of members of their own class and sex. In the best of these communities they receive excellent academic education. But academic education is neither the whole nor the chief aim of these schools. The beliefs they inculcate are summed up by Mr. Connolly thus:

1. Character is more important than Intellect.
2. Intellect is usually found without Character. (Oscar Wilde.)
3. Best of all is Character plus Prettiness. Prettiness alone is suspect, like intellect alone, but prettiness that is good at games is safe.

From the six percent who undergo this education come most of England's rulers and writers. It is impossible to understand modern English literature until one realizes that most English writers are rebels against the way they are educated, and it is impossible to understand the strength of the English ruling class until one realizes where it comes from.*

Auden, himself of the class so educated, became the spokesman of the new school of poets and of a disintegrating upper class. With his followers, Day Lewis, MacNeice, Spender, and others, he first turned to embrace the political philosophy of Communism. He tried to reverse the Waste Land values. He spoke for brotherhood, for love, for a socialist future. His was an intellectual conversion, and the contradictions between it and his social conditioning were part of his poetic equipment. While Spender, in the critical volume *The Destructive Element*, announced the new literary creed of the left, Auden, often called a contemporary Byron, exploited social criticism in verse. He and his satellites rejected their pompous fathers and their social mothers and took to airplanes to look over the brave new world. In brilliant Don Juan stanzas, Auden described his travels in revolutionary countries and his hatred of English stuffiness. Spender pointed out the conflict between social action and the escapist poetic dreams. Day Lewis wrote calls to action. MacNeice talked of slums and factories.

Disillusionment attacks the intellectual "radicals"

But soon, alas, the idealism of these English poets played them false. The revolution they had been led to expect was not gloriously around the corner. A new world was not being born just over the border. The mills of history were grinding very slowly and very drearily toward new world conflicts. When nothing happened, when the intellectuals did not march down the streets with banners, when the process of social change began to prove bloody, and

* From a review of Cyril Connolly's *Enemies of Promise* in *The New Republic*, April 26, 1939. Reprinted by permission of W. H. Auden and *The New Republic*.

perhaps when, most of all, the need for political action began to interfere with the quieter and more contemplative life of observation and feeling to which they were conditioned, many English intellectual poets became discouraged in their attempts to change the world through the lyric word. They had seen China, Spain, and Germany under fascism. They were not unaware that there were some fascist forces in England. They were thoroughly disillusioned, most of all about an "intellectual" revolution. Of the masses they knew little or nothing. Between their class and the working class there was a great chasm.

Auden, who had led the way in developing the poetry of social comment and had always been skeptical of ultimate values and fascinated by the inner conflicts apparent in his own social group, wrote of the experiences personal to himself, to his friends, and in a sense to a whole generation caught between wars. In his poetry the typical English scene is visible only as from the rear platform of a train whose destination is unknown. These things are seen as they fall forward in kaleidoscopic patterns of destruction while the poet stares down the lengthening track of history. Auden is convinced that the destruction is due to economic war between the powers and his greatest concern is for the sensitive who perish in it. While for Eliot the tea party symbolizes merely a boring intermission in a boring life, for Auden it is the last rite before the violent death of the guests.

Completely disillusioned as to his ability to prevent the cataclysm, Auden, whose radicalism had been primarily idealistic and in part a nostalgia for stability, gave up and left for America. In essence he was capable only of recording change and not of promoting action to change the social scene. His real devotion was to the art of stating the case for his own kind. Uprooted from his own background, he soon argued his devotion to art as against politics. His scene was no longer intimate to him; he could not record the situation in America, for America had not formed him. In his later phase he has consequently flirted with religious symbols as another pattern of idealism than the social. Dominantly he remains the skeptical poet, concerned with the contradictions between the emotions and the mind. Recently in a lecture he stated that his position is akin to that of the Existentialists (see p. 859), a group whose post-war philosophy is even more emphatic about the divorcement of the artist from action and the enmity between the individual and society than was the so-called philosophy of the Art for Art's Sake group (see p. 25).

The poets whose names were associated with Auden's have, for the most part, all softened their social criticism. Spender, in the Home Guard during the war period, continues to use as his real scene the incidents of the war itself as illustrative both of the hopes of the liberals and of the sense of guilt that everyone in the war must feel. MacNeice has sharpened his poetry emotionally by concerning himself with the dramatic events of the war, and Isherwood remains the chronicler of the decline of belief and morals, and of action as escape from thought.

Ideas and new poetic language

These English poets have faced a number of difficulties. Their poetry is a poetry of ideas; its form is that of the essay in verse. They have had to emotionalize a language of ideas, political and economic, and juxtapose it with the language of personal experience. Their symbols are not always easily understood by those who have not lived among the English gentry. It must be noted that the language of history and political science, as well as that of Freud and Jung, is more familiar to the well-educated English group than it is to most American middle-class poets. Therefore it is not astonishing that while Eliot defined a spiritual Waste Land, it remained for Auden and his followers to define a historical Waste Land. Eliot, American by birth and puritan by ancestry, of an earlier generation than Auden, saw as the only antithesis to materialism the regeneration of man through the spirit. Auden, trained in the political thinking of the English upper classes and conditioned by the long years of economic crisis, saw that man's materialistic knowledge might benefit him.

Contemporary English poetry has affected the American literary group so strongly that almost overnight we have developed a poetry in which historical and political symbols play an important part. It is to be noted, however, that since they have learned their political imagery from the English, our poets sometimes apply English political symbols to the native American scene. Much American poetry having to do with political feeling makes little or no use of the language of the true American laboring class.

IN SUMMARY

❦ THE LATE 1920's and the 1930's in both England and America brought to writing a distinct shift in fundamental values. In general this was a shift from concern with highly individualistic problems to concern with social problems. The search for freedom, for example, ceased to be treated as a purely personal rebellion against the status quo of manners and morals, Victorian or Puritan, and became an outcry for freedom for all peoples, and in particular for freedom from want. Individualistic love was extended to a feeling of love for mankind. Life ceased to be only a study of alternating boredoms and high moments of sensitivity and became life with a purpose, the social purpose of making existence humane and dig-

Pablo Picasso: Horse and Bull, *Illustration for Balzac's* Le chef d'oeuvre inconnu
The illustrations for Balzac's famous story were executed in Picasso's
pure, linear, so-called classic style, combining the serene clarity
of Ingres with strong emotional content

nified. Death, which had been discussed in the Waste Land either as the final escape or as merely the inch-by-inch process of living until the cells died, became death for what one believed in—even unto martyrdom. The past was not in these later years thought of as the golden, the heroic, the lost because of modern commercialism, but as that from which the present proceeded; and the present was history in the making.

The "island of self" so much dissected and elaborated upon by the Waste Landers became the social self in action for its own safety and enlargement. Subjective individualism ceased to be the refuge of those disgusted with commercialism. Immersion in real action and the dramatic emotions resulting therefrom were the new materials of the artist. The picture of the artist as a rebel, a hypersensitive neurotic,

an exile, a mad genius gave way to the picture of an artist as an intelligent and sensitive recorder of the events of his own times. Man's enemy was no longer, as in the Waste Land, pictured as some vague, arbitrary social machine which crushed the spiritual longing, but a wastefully handled economy. Many an artist came to believe that art could be sustained only in a society which had solved its economic problems and where these problems consequently were not the main concern.

But soon the period of economic depression moved into the pre-war and then into the war period, and the outcry for economic justice became a seeming outcry for democracy against fascism. Most pseudo-Marxist idealism was blotted out by an aroused nationalism. The internal difficulties of each nation were suppressed. History was spinning off under our feet

565

and the literary revolution by the word alone was forced to give way to preparation for war, both by word and by sword. As the new faith in social change was replaced by militant anti-fascism, some of the radical writers of the period of economic chaos were called to arms.

Writing in the 1890's, Charles S. Pierce, whom such thinkers as William James and John Dewey have placed in the forefront of the great seminal minds of our times, had said prophetically of the period now ended:

The twentieth century, in its latter half, shall surely see the deluge-tempest burst upon the social order—to clear upon a world as deep in ruin as that greed-philosophy has long plunged it into guilt.

And so it was that events in the period of the depression forced the revolutionary writers to take up arms against the greed-philosophy which even the best of the nineteenth-century writers had condemned as ruinous to all intellectual and spiritual achievement.   [E.L.W.]

Forerunners

CARL SANDBURG

Sandburg the reporter, the folk-ballad singer, and the poet are irrevocably the same person—the man who has popularized the sectional ideas and ideals of the United States. With a background of Swedish ancestry he has experienced rather than inherited his Americanism. Each of his varied jobs and professions has influenced his poetry. His keen observation, his quick sympathy, and his political awareness have enriched it.

Carl Sandburg was born in Galesburg, Illinois, January 6, 1878. His father, a Swede named August Johnson, changed his name to Sandburg because his pay envelopes were frequently confused with those of several other August Johnsons. Between thirteen and seventeen, Carl worked on a milk wagon, was a porter in a barber shop, a scene-shifter in a cheap theater, a truck-handler in a brickyard, and a turner-apprentice in a pottery. At seventeen he went West, riding baggage cars and generally bumming his way. He washed dishes in hotels in Kansas City, Omaha, Denver; worked in the Kansas wheat fields; canvassed paint stores; and finally returned to Galesburg and apprenticed himself to a house-painter.

When the Spanish-American War broke out in 1898, Sandburg, anxious for adventure, enlisted with the Sixth Illinois Volunteers Infantry and went to Puerto Rico, where he served for eight months. A fellow soldier got him interested in furthering his education. Accordingly he used his hundred dollars mustering-out pay for his first year's tuition at Lombard College in Galesburg. He supplemented his expenses by working as tutor, bell-ringer, and janitor of the gymnasium. These tasks made little, if any, inroads on his tremendous vitality,

for in addition he was captain of the college basketball team and later editor-in-chief of the college monthly and annual magazines.

After graduation in 1902, his immediate concern was to earn a living, and he became a salesman for Underwood and Underwood, traveling about the country selling films. In 1904 his first book of verse, *In Reckless Ecstasy*, was published. During the next few years he was successively advertising manager for a department store, district organizer for the Social Democratic party of Wisconsin, and newspaper reporter in Milwaukee. From 1910 to 1912 he was secretary to the mayor of Milwaukee. In 1917 he joined the staff of the *Chicago Daily News* and in 1918 was sent to Norway and Sweden as correspondent of the Newspaper Enterprise Association. When he returned home after the Armistice, he became an editorial writer for the *Daily News*. In 1908 Sandburg married Lillian Steichen, sister of the well-known photographer, Edward Steichen.

During all these years of active and varied work Sandburg continued to write poetry. *Chicago Poems* was published in 1916 and established his name as a poet. *Cornhuskers* appeared in 1918; *Smoke and Steel*, 1920; *Slabs of the Sunburnt West*, 1922; *Selected Poems*, edited by Rebecca West, 1926; *The American Songbag*, a compilation of ballads, 1927; *Good Morning, America*, 1928; *Early Moon*, 1930; and *The People, Yes* (1936). This last book states his optimism concerning the people's will to live during the years of the depression.

Meantime Sandburg had won the hearts of American children with his *Rootabaga Stories* (1922) and other juvenile books. The biography of Abraham Lincoln begun in *The*

Prairie Years (1926) was finally, in 1939, finished with the publication of *The War Years,* for which in 1940 Sandburg received the Pulitzer Prize. His *Home Front Memo* (1943) is a collection of pamphlets, speeches, broadcasts, and poems. Collaborating with Frederick Hill Meserve he published in 1944 *The Photographs of Abraham Lincoln.* And in 1948 he entered the field of historical fiction with *Remembrance Rock.*

Sandburg supported the New Deal; he had always been a citizen poet, from the time he covered the race riots in Chicago as labor editor of the *Chicago Daily News.* (His columns were later reprinted in his book *The Chicago Race Riots, July, 1919.*) During World War II Sandburg was a columnist for the *Chicago Daily Times,* and he was often in Washington, conferring with President Roosevelt. He is said sometimes to have helped the President with his speeches.

Sandburg's use of folk speech and folkways derives from his belief that art is from and of the people. His hatred of exploiters and his love of the common people cause him to satirize the worst and praise the best in our American way of life. From him the younger Marxian poets of the depression years learned their techniques as he, in his time, had learned much from the democratic Walt Whitman.

The symphonic studies of American industrial life, like *Smoke and Steel,* are the first panoramas in poetry of the world we live in. Sandburg is tender and ironic, critical and sentimental, with as many soft spots as the average American. Beginning with studies of the Middle West's people and their ways, he has extended his canvas to depict all America.

Chicago

H OG BUTCHER for the World,
  Tool Maker, Stacker of Wheat,
Player with Railroads and the Nation's Freight Handler;
Stormy, husky, brawling,
City of the Big Shoulders:

They tell me you are wicked, and I believe them; for I have seen your painted women under the
    gas lamps luring the farm boys.
And they tell me you are crooked, and I answer: Yes, it is true I have seen the gunman kill and
    go free to kill again.
And they tell me you are brutal, and my reply is: On the faces of women and children I have seen
    the marks of wanton hunger.
And having answered so I turn once more to those who sneer at this my city, and I give them
    back the sneer and say to them:
Come and show me another city with lifted head singing so proud to be alive and coarse and
    strong and cunning.   10
Flinging magnetic curses amid the toil of piling job on job, here is a tall bold slugger set vivid
    against the little soft cities;
Fierce as a dog with tongue lapping for action, cunning as a savage pitted against the wilderness,
        Bareheaded,
        Shovelling,
        Wrecking,   15
        Planning,
        Building, breaking, rebuilding,

Under the smoke, dust all over his mouth, laughing with white teeth,
Under the terrible burden of destiny laughing as a young man laughs,
Laughing even as an ignorant fighter laughs who has never lost a battle,   20
Bragging and laughing that under his wrist is the pulse, and under his ribs the heart of the
    people,
                        Laughing!
Laughing the stormy, husky, brawling laughter of Youth, half-naked, sweating, proud to be Hog
    Butcher, Tool Maker, Stacker of Wheat, Player with Railroads and Freight Handler to
    the Nation.

To a Contemporary Bunkshooter

YOU COME along . . . tearing your shirt . . . yelling about Jesus.
    Where do you get that stuff?
    What do you know about Jesus?
Jesus had a way of talking soft and outside of a few bankers and higher-ups among the con men
    of Jerusalem everybody liked to have this Jesus around because he never made any fake
    passes and everything he said went and he helped the sick and gave the people hope.
You come along squirting words at us, shaking your fist and call us all dam fools so fierce the
    froth slobbers over your lips . . . always blabbing we're all going to hell straight off and
    you know all about it.   5

I've read Jesus' words. I know what he said. You don't throw any scare into me. I've got your
    number. I know how much you know about Jesus.
He never came near clean people or dirty people but they felt cleaner because he came along. It
    was your crowd of bankers and business men and lawyers hired the sluggers and murder-
    ers who put Jesus out of the running.
I say the same bunch backing you nailed the nails into the hands of this Jesus of Nazareth. He
    had lined up against him the same crooks and strong-arm men now lined up with you pay-
    ing your way.

This Jesus was good to look at, smelled good, listened good. He threw out something fresh and
    beautiful from the skin of his body and the touch of his hands wherever he passed along.
You slimy bunkshooter, you put a smut on every human blossom in reach of your rotten breath
    belching about hell-fire and hiccupping about this Man who lived a clean life in Galilee.
When are you going to quit making the carpenters build emergency hospitals for women and girls
    driven crazy with wrecked nerves from your gibberish about Jesus?—I put it to you again:
    Where do you get that stuff? What do you know about Jesus?   11

Go ahead and bust all the chairs you want to. Smash a whole wagon-load of furniture at every
    performance. Turn sixty somersaults and stand on your nutty head. If it wasn't for the
    way you scare the women and kids I'd feel sorry for you and pass the hat.
I like to watch a good four-flusher work, but not when he starts people puking and calling for the
    doctors.
I like a man that's got nerve and can pull off a great original performance, but you—you're only a
    bug-house pedlar of secondhand gospel — you're only shoving out a phoney imitation of
    the goods this Jesus wanted free as air and sunlight.

Bunkshooter, William Ashley (1863–1935), called Billy Sunday. A professional baseball player turned evangelist, he claimed to
have preached to more people (80,000,000) than any other man in the history of Christendom, and he was largely responsible for
the introduction of Prohibition. His creed was of the "there'll be pie in the sky, when you die" variety.

You tell people living in shanties Jesus is going to fix it up all right with them by giving them mansions in the skies after they're dead and the worms have eaten 'em.   15

You tell $6 a week department store girls all they need is Jesus; you take a steel trust wop, dead without having lived, grey and shrunken at forty years of age, and you tell him to look at Jesus on the cross and he'll be all right.

You tell poor people they don't need any more money on pay day and even if it's fierce to be out of a job, Jesus'll fix that up all right, all right—all they gotta do is take Jesus the way you say.

I'm telling you Jesus wouldn't stand for the stuff you're handing out. Jesus played it different. The bankers and lawyers of Jerusalem got their sluggers and murderers to go after Jesus just because Jesus wouldn't play their game. He didn't sit in with the big thieves.

I don't want a lot of gab from a bunkshooter in my religion.

I won't take my religion from any man who never works except with his mouth and never cherishes any memory except the face of the woman on the American silver dollar.   20

I ask you to come through and show me where you're pouring out the blood of your life.

I've been to this suburb of Jerusalem they call Golgotha, where they nailed Him, and I know if the story is straight it was real blood ran from His hands and the nailholes, and it was real blood spurted in red drops where the spear of the Roman soldier rammed in between the ribs of this Jesus of Nazareth.

Prairie

I WAS BORN on the prairie, and the milk of its wheat, the red of its clover, the eyes of its women, gave me a song and a slogan.

Here the water went down, the icebergs slid with gravel, the gaps and the valleys hissed, and the black loam came, and the yellow sandy loam.

Here between the sheds of the Rocky Mountains and the Appalachians, here now a morning star fixes a fire sign over the timber claims and cow pastures, the corn belt, the cotton belt, the cattle ranches.

Here the grey geese go five hundred miles and back with a wind under their wings honking the cry for a new home.

Here I know I will hanker after nothing so much as one more sunrise or a sky moon of fire doubled to a river moon of water.   5

The prairie sings to me in the forenoon and I know in the night I rest easy in the prairie arms, on the prairie heart.

. . .

After the sunburn of the day
handling a pitchfork at a hayrack,
after the eggs and biscuit and coffee,
the pearl-grey haystacks
in the gloaming
are cool prayers
to the harvest hands.

In the city among the walls the overland passenger train is choked and the pistons hiss and the wheels curse.

"Prairie," "Psalm of Those Who Go Forth before Daylight," and "Cool Tombs" from *Cornhuskers* by Carl Sandburg, reprinted by permission of Henry Holt and Company.

On the prairie the overland flits on phantom wheels and the sky and the soil between them muffle the pistons and cheer the wheels.

. . .

I am here when the cities are gone.
I am here before the cities come.   10
I nourish the lonely men on horses.
I will keep the laughing men who ride iron.
I am dust of men.

The running water babbled to the deer, the cottontail, the gopher.   15
You came in wagons, making streets and schools,
Kin of the axe and rifle, kin of the plough and horse,
Singing *Yankee Doodle, Old Dan Tucker, Turkey in the Straw,*
You in the coonskin cap at a log house door hearing a lone wolf howl,
You at a sod house door reading the blizzards and chinooks let loose from Medicine Hat,   20
I am dust of your dust, as I am brother and mother
To the copper faces, the worker in flint and clay,
The singing women and their sons a thousand years ago
Marching single file the timber and the plain.
I hold the dust of these amid changing stars.   25
I last while old wars are fought, while peace broods mother-like,
While new wars arise and the fresh killings of young men.
I fed the boys who went to France in great dark days.
Appomattox is a beautiful word to me and so is Valley Forge and the Marne and Verdun,
I who have seen the red births and the red deaths   30
Of sons and daughters, I take peace or war, I say nothing and wait.

Have you seen a red sunset drip over one of my cornfields, and the shore of night stars, the wave lines of dawn up a wheat valley?
Have you heard my threshing crews yelling in the chaff of a strawpile and the running wheat of the wagonboards, my cornhuskers, my harvest hands hauling crops, singing dreams of women, worlds, horizons?

. . .

    Rivers cut a path on flat lands.
    The mountains stand up.
    The salt oceans press in   35
    And push on the coast lines.
    The sun, the wind, bring rain
    And I know what the rainbow writes across the east or west
        in a half-circle:
    A love-letter pledge to come again.   40

. . .

    Towns on the Soo Line,
    Towns on the Big Muddy,
    Laugh at each other for cubs
    And tease as children.

Omaha and Kansas City, Minneapolis and St. Paul, sisters in a house together, throwing slang, growing up.   45

571

Towns in the Ozarks, Dakota wheat towns, Wichita, Peoria, Buffalo, sisters throwing slang,
    growing up.

. . .

Out of prairie-brown grass crossed with a streamer of wigwam smoke—out of a smoke pillar, a
    blue promise—out of wild ducks woven in greens and purples—
Here I saw a city rise and say to the peoples round world: Listen, I am strong, I know what I
    want.
Out of log houses and stumps—canoes stripped from tree sides—flatboats coaxed with an axe from
    the timber claims—in the years when the red and the white men met—the houses and
    streets rose.

A thousand red men cried and went away to new places for corn and women: a million white
    men came and put up skyscrapers, threw out rails and wires, feelers to the salt sea: now
    the smokestacks bite the skyline with stub teeth.   50

In an early year the call of a wild duck woven in greens and purples: now the riveter's chatter,
    the police patrol, the song-whistle of the steamboat.

To a man across a thousand years I offer a handshake.
I say to him: Brother, make the story short, for the stretch of a thousand years is short.

. . .

What brothers these in the dark?
What eaves of skyscrapers against a smoke moon?   55
These chimneys shaking on the lumber shanties
When the coal boats plough by on the river—
The hunched shoulders of the grain elevators—
The flame sprockets of the sheet steel mills
And the men in the rolling mills with their shirts off   60
Playing their flesh arms against the twisting wrists of steel:

        what brothers these
        in the dark
        of a thousand years?

. . .

A headlight searches a snowstorm.
A funnel of white lights shoots from over the pilot of the Pioneer Limited crossing Wisconsin.

In the morning hours, in the dawn,
The sun puts out the stars of the sky   65
And the headlight of the Limited train.

The fireman waves his hand to a country school teacher on a bobsled.
A boy, yellow hair, red scarf and mittens, on the bobsled, in his lunch box a pork chop sandwich
    and a V of gooseberry pie.

The horses fathom a snow to their knees.
Snow hats are on the rolling prairie hills.   70
The Mississippi bluffs wear snow hats.

. . .

Keep your hogs on changing corn and mashes of grain, O farmerman.
        Cram their insides till they waddle on short legs
        Under the drums of bellies, hams of fat.
        Kill your hogs with a knife slit under the ear.   75
        Hack them with cleavers.
        Hang them with hooks in the hind legs.

. . .

A wagonload of radishes on a summer morning.
Sprinkles of dew on the crimson-purple balls.
The farmer on the seat dangles the reins on the rumps of dapple-grey horses.   80
The farmer's daughter with a basket of eggs dreams of a new hat to wear to the country fair.

. . .

On the left- and right-hand side of the road,
        Marching corn—
I saw it knee high weeks ago—now it is head high—tassels of red silk creep at the ends of the ears.

. . .

I am the prairie, mother of men, waiting.
They are mine, the threshing crews eating beefsteak, the farmboys driving steers to the railroad
    cattle pens.   85
They are mine, the crowds of people at a Fourth of July basket picnic, listening to a lawyer read
    the Declaration of Independence, watching the pinwheels and Roman candles at night,
    the young men and women two by two hunting the bypaths and kissing bridges.
They are mine, the horses looking over a fence in the frost of late October saying good-morning
    to the horses hauling wagons of rutabaga to market.
They are mine, the old zigzag rail fences, the new barb wire.

. . .

The cornhuskers wear leather on their hands.
There is no let-up to the wind.
Blue bandanas are knotted at the ruddy chins.   90

Falltime and winter apples take on the smoulder of the five-o'clock November sunset: falltime,
    leaves, bonfires, stubble, the old things go, and the earth is grizzled.
The land and the people hold memories, even among the anthills and the angleworms, among
    the toads and woodroaches—among gravestone writings rubbed out by the rain—they keep
    old things that never grow old.

The frost loosens corn husks.
The sun, the rain, the wind
        loosen corn husks.
The men and women are helpers.   95
They are all cornhuskers together.
I see them late in the western evening
        in a smoke-red dust.

. . .

The phantom of a yellow rooster flaunting a scarlet comb, on top of a dung pile crying hallelujah
 to the streaks of daylight,
The phantom of an old hunting dog nosing in the underbrush for muskrats, barking at a coon in
 a treetop at midnight, chewing a bone, chasing his tail round a corncrib,   100
The phantom of an old workhorse taking the steel point of a plough across a forty-acre field in
 spring, hitched to a harrow in summer, hitched to a wagon among cornshocks in fall,
These phantoms come into the talk and wonder of people on the front porch of a farmhouse late
 summer nights.
'The shapes that are gone are here,' said an old man with a cob pipe in his teeth one night in
 Kansas with a hot wind on the alfalfa.

Look at six eggs
In a mocking-bird's nest.   105

Listen to six mocking-birds
Flinging follies of O-be-joyful
Over the marshes and uplands.

Look on songs
Hidden in eggs.   110

   . . .

When the morning sun is on the trumpet-vine blossoms, sing at the kitchen pans: Shout All Over
 God's Heaven.
When the rain slants on the potato hills and the sun plays a silver shaft on the last shower, sing
 to the bush at the backyard fence: Mighty Lak a Rose.
When the icy sleet pounds on the storm windows and the house lifts to a great breath, sing for
 the outside hills: The Ole Sheep Done Know the Road, the Young Lambs Must Find the
 Way.

Spring slips back with a girl face calling always: 'Any new songs for me? Any new songs?'

O prairie girl, be lonely, singing, dreaming, waiting—your lover comes—your child comes—the
 years creep with toes of April rain on new-turned sod.   115
O prairie girl, whoever leaves you only crimson poppies to talk with, whoever puts a good-bye
 kiss on your lips and never comes back—
There is a song deep as the falltime redhaws, long as the layer of black loam we go to, the shine
 of the morning star over the corn belt, the wave line of dawn up a wheat valley.

   . . .

O prairie mother, I am one of your boys.
I have loved the prairie as a man with a heart shot full of pain over love.
Here I know I will hanker after nothing so much as one more sunrise or a sky moon of fire dou-
 bled to a river moon of water.   120

   . . .

I speak of new cities and new people.
I tell you the past is a bucket of ashes.

574

I tell you yesterday is a wind gone down, a sun dropped in the west.
I tell you there is nothing in the world only an ocean of to-morrows, a sky of to-morrows.

I am a brother of the cornhuskers who say at sundown:
          To-morrow is a day. 125

Psalm of Those Who Go Forth Before Daylight

THE POLICEMAN buys shoes slow and careful; the teamster buys gloves slow and careful; they take care of their feet and hands; they live on their feet and hands.

The milkman never argues; he works alone and no one speaks to him; the city is asleep when he is on the job; he puts a bottle on six hundred porches, and calls it a day's work; he climbs two hundred wooden stairways; two horses are company for him; he never argues.

The rolling-mill men and the sheet-steel men are brothers of cinders; they empty cinders out of their shoes after the day's work; they ask their wives to fix burnt holes in the knees of their trousers; their necks and ears are covered with a smut; they scour their necks and ears; they are brothers of cinders.

Cool Tombs

WHEN Abraham Lincoln was shovelled into the tombs, he forgot the copperheads and the assassin . . . in the dust, in the cool tombs.

And Ulysses Grant lost all thought of con men and Wall Street, cash and collateral turned ashes . . . in the dust, in the cool tombs.

Pocahontas' body, lovely as a poplar, sweet as a red haw in November or a pawpaw in May, did she wonder? does she remember? . . . in the dust, in the cool tombs?

Take any streetful of people buying clothes and groceries, cheering a hero or throwing confetti and blowing tin horns . . . tell me if the lovers are losers . . . tell me if any get more than the lovers . . . in the dust . . . in the cool tombs.

Smoke and Steel

SMOKE of the fields in spring is one,
Smoke of the leaves in autumn another.
Smoke of a steel-mill roof or a battleship funnel,
They all go up in a line with a smokestack,
Or they twist . . . in the slow twist . . . of the wind. 5

If the north wind comes they run to the south.
If the west wind comes they run to the east.
      By this sign
        all smokes
        know each other. 10
Smoke of the fields in spring and leaves in autumn,

Smoke and Steel. A free-verse, almost symphonic poem of the voices of industry pitted against the voices of men who make steel. It is one of Sandburg's great poems, best expressive of his knowledge of the contradictions in capitalism and of the faith even the simple workingman places in it. This is a hymn to industry, but it is also a deeply ironic comment on the steel cities and magnates who build our empire and often starve our people. In the end, as always, Sandburg pictures the mills as he, the poet, sees them.

Smoke of the finished steel, chilled and blue,
By the oath of work they swear: "I know you."

Hunted and hissed from the center
Deep down long ago when God made us over,
Deep down are the cinders we came from—
You and I and our heads of smoke.

. . . . . .

Some of the smokes God dropped on the job
Cross on the sky and count our years
And sing in the secrets of our numbers;
Sing their dawns and sing their evenings,
Sing an old log-fire song:
            You may put the damper up,
            You may put the damper down,
            The smoke goes up the chimney just the same.

Smoke of a city sunset skyline,
Smoke of a country dusk horizon—
            They cross on the sky and count our years.

. . . .

Smoke of a brick-red dust
            Winds on a spiral
            Out of the stacks
For a hidden and glimpsing moon.
This, said the bar-iron shed to the blooming mill,
This is the slang of coal and steel.
The day-gang hands it to the night-gang,
The night-gang hands it back.

Stammer at the slang of this—
Let us understand half of it.
            In the rolling mills and sheet mills,
            In the harr and boom of the blast fires,
            The smoke changes its shadow
            And men change their shadow;
            A nigger, a wop, a bohunk changes.

            A bar of steel—it is only
Smoke at the heart of it, smoke and the blood of a man.
A runner of fire ran in it, ran out, ran somewhere else,
And left—smoke and the blood of a man
And the finished steel, chilled and blue.

So fire runs in, runs out, runs somewhere else again,
And the bar of steel is a gun, a wheel, a nail, a shovel,
A rudder under the sea, a steering-gear in the sky;
And always dark in the heart and through it,
            Smoke and the blood of a man.
Pittsburg, Youngstown, Gary—they make their steel with men.

15

20

25

30

35

40

45

50

576

In the blood of men and the ink of chimneys 55
The smoke nights write their oaths:
Smoke into steel and blood into steel;
Homestead, Braddock, Birmingham, they make their steel with men.
Smoke and blood is the mix of steel.

       The birdmen drone 60
       in the blue; it is steel
       a motor sings and zooms.

   .   .   .   .

Steel barb-wire around The Works.
Steel guns in the holsters of the guards at the gates of The Works.
Steel ore-boats bring the loads clawed from the earth by steel, lifted and lugged by arms of steel,
    sung on its way by the clanking clam-shells. 65
The runners now, the handlers now, are steel; they dig and clutch and haul; they hoist their au-
    tomatic knuckles from job to job; they are steel making steel.
Fire and dust and air fight in the furnaces; the pour is timed, the billets wriggle; the clinkers are
    dumped:
Liners on the sea, skyscrapers on the land; diving steel in the sea, climbing steel in the sky.

   .   .   .   .

Finders in the dark, you Steve with a dinner bucket, you Steve clumping in the dusk on the side-
    walks with an evening paper for the woman and kids, you Steve with your head wonder-
    ing where we all end up—
Finders in the dark, Steve: I hook my arm in cinder sleeves; we go down the street together; it is
    all the same to us; you Steve and the rest of us end on the same stars; we all wear a hat in
    hell together, in hell or heaven.
  Smoke nights now, Steve. 70
  Smoke, smoke, lost in the sieves of yesterday;
  Dumped again to the scoops and hooks today.
  Smoke like the clocks and whistles, always.
      Smoke nights now. 75
      To-morrow something else.

   .   .   .   .

Luck moons come and go:
Five men swim in a pot of red steel.
Their bones are kneaded into the bread of steel:
Their bones are knocked into coils and anvils 80
And the sucking plungers of sea-fighting turbines.
Look for them in the woven frame of a wireless station.

So ghosts hide in steel like heavy-armed men in mirrors.
Peepers, skulkers—they shadow-dance in laughing tombs.
They are always there and they never answer. 85

One of them said: "I like my job, the company is good to me, America is a wonderful country."
One: "Jesus, my bones ache; the company is a liar; this is a free country, like hell."
One: "I got a girl, a peach; we save up and go on a farm and raise pigs and be the boss ourselves."
And the others were roughneck singers a long ways from home.
Look for them back of a steel vault door. 90

They laugh at the cost.
They lift the birdmen into the blue.
It is steel a motor sings and zooms.

In the subway plugs and drums,
In the slow hydraulic drills, in gumbo or gravel,   95
Under dynamo shafts in the webs of armature spiders.
They shadow-dance and laugh at the cost.

    .   .   .   .

The ovens light a red dome.
Spools of fire wind and wind.
Quadrangles of crimson sputter.   100
The lashes of dying maroon let down.
Fire and wind wash out the slag.
Forever the slag gets washed in fire and wind.

The anthem learned by the steel is:
      Do this or go hungry.   105
Look for our rust on a plow.
Listen to us in a threshing-engine razz.
Look at our job in the running wagon wheat.

    .   .   .   .

Fire and wind wash at the slag.
Box-cars, clocks, steam-shovels, churns, pistons, boilers, scissors—   110
Oh, the sleeping slag from the mountains, the slag-heavy pig-iron will go down many roads.
Men will stab and shoot with it, and make butter and tunnel rivers, and mow hay in swaths, and
    slit hogs and skin beeves, and steer airplanes across North America, Europe, Asia, round
    the world.

Hacked from a hard rock country, broken and baked in mills and smelters, the rusty dust waits
Till the clean hard weave of its atoms cripples and blunts the drills chewing a hole in it.
The steel of its plinths and flanges is reckoned, O God, in one-millionth of an inch.   115

    .   .   .   .

Once when I saw the curves of fire, the rough scarf women dancing,
Dancing out of the flues and smoke-stacks—flying hair of fire, flying feet upside down;
Buckets and baskets of fire exploding and chortling, fire running wild out of the steady and fas-
    tened ovens;
Sparks cracking a harr-harr-huff from a solar-plexus of rock-ribs of the earth taking a laugh for
    themselves;
Ears and noses of fire, gibbering gorilla arms of fire, gold mud-pies, gold bird-wings, red jackets
    riding purple mules, scarlet autocrats tumbling from the humps of camels, assassinated
    czars straddling vermillion balloons;   120
I saw then the fires flash one by one: good-by: then smoke, smoke;
And in the screens the great sisters of night and cool stars, sitting women arranging their hair,
Waiting in the sky, waiting with slow easy eyes, waiting and half-murmuring:
    "Since you know all
    and I know nothing,   125
    tell me what I dreamed last night."

    .   .   .   .

Pearl cobwebs in the windy rain,
in only a flicker of wind,
are caught and lost and never known again.

A pool of moonshine comes and waits,
but never waits long: the wind picks up
loose gold like this and is gone.   130

A bar of steel sleeps and looks slant-eyed
on the pearl cobwebs, the pools of moonshine;
sleeps slant-eyed a million years,
sleeps with a coat of rust, a vest of moths,   135
a shirt of gathering sod and loam.

The wind never bothers . . . a bar of steel.
The wind picks only . . pearl cobwebs . . pools of moonshine.

They All Want to Play Hamlet

THEY all want to play Hamlet.
They have not exactly seen their fathers killed
Nor their mothers in a frame-up to kill,
Nor an Ophelia dying with a dust gagging the heart,
Not exactly the spinning circles of singing golden spiders,
Not exactly this have they got at nor the meaning of flowers—O flowers, flowers slung by a danc-   5
    ing girl—in the saddest play the inkfish, Shakespeare, ever wrote;
Yet they all want to play Hamlet because it is sad like all actors are sad and to stand by an open
    grave with a joker's skull in the hand and then to say over slow and say over slow wise,
    keen, beautiful words masking a heart that's breaking, breaking,
This is something that calls and calls to their blood.
They are acting when they talk about it and they know it is acting to be particular about it and
    yet: They all want to play Hamlet.

The Sins of Kalamazoo

THE SINS of Kalamazoo are neither scarlet nor crimson.
The sins of Kalamazoo are a convict gray, a dishwater drab.
And the people who sin the sins of Kalamazoo are neither scarlet nor crimson.
They run to drabs and grays—and some of them sing they shall be washed whiter than snow—and
    some: We should worry.

They All . . . Hamlet, a reiteration of the well-known idea that all young men see themselves as the tragic Prince of Denmark in Shakespeare's play. See T. S. Eliot, "The Love Song of J. Alfred Prufrock," p. 234.   2. **fathers killed.** Hamlet's father was killed by his uncle.   3. **mothers.** Gertrude, Hamlet's mother, married his uncle.   4. **Ophelia.** Ophelia, who loves Hamlet, goes mad and drowns herself, after the famous speech in which she distributes flowers.
The Sins of Kalamazoo. Kalamazoo, because of its name often used as typical of the growing small American town, is for the poet typical also of our American philosophies and attitudes—either commercially iconoclastic or idealistic, or sometimes like the poet's (he always walks into his poems) poetic in that it rises from the real to the abstract.

Yes, Kalamazoo is a spot on the map   5
And the passenger trains stop there
And the factory smokestacks smoke
And the grocery stores are open Saturday nights
And the streets are free for citizens who vote
And inhabitants counted in the census.   10
Saturday night is the big night.
    Listen with your ears on a Saturday night in Kalamazoo
    And say to yourself: I hear America, I hear, *what* do I hear?

Main street there runs through the middle of the town
And there is a dirty postoffice   15
And a dirty city hall
And a dirty railroad station
And the United States flag cries, cries the Stars and Stripes to the four winds on Lincoln's birth-
    day and the Fourth of July.

Kalamazoo kisses a hand to something far off.
Kalamazoo calls to a long horizon, to a shivering silver angel, to a creeping mystic what-is-it.   20
"We're here because we're here," is the song of Kalamazoo.
"We don't know where we're going but we're on our way," are the words.
There are hound dogs of bronze on the public square, hound dogs looking far beyond the public
    square.

Sweethearts there in Kalamazoo
Go to the general delivery window of the postoffice   25
And speak their names and ask for letters
And ask again, "Are you sure there is nothing for me?
I wish you'd look again—there must be a letter for me."

And sweethearts go to the city hall
And tell their names and say, "We want a license."   30
And they go to an installment house and buy a bed on time and a clock
And the children grow up asking each other, "What can we do to kill time?"

They grow up and go to the railroad station and buy tickets for Texas, Pennsylvania, Alaska.
"Kalamazoo is all right," they say. "But I want to see the world."
And when they have looked the world over they come back saying it is all like Kalamazoo.   35

The trains come in from the east and hoot for the crossings,
And buzz away to the peach country and Chicago to the west
Or they come from the west and shoot on to the Battle Creek breakfast bazaars
And the speedbug heavens of Detroit.

"I hear America, I hear, *what* do I hear?"   40
Said a loafer lagging along on the sidewalks of Kalamazoo,
Lagging along and asking questions, reading signs.

Oh yes, there is a town named Kalamazoo,
A spot on the map where the trains hesitate.
I saw the sign of a five and ten cent store there   45
And the Standard Oil Company and the International Harvester
And a graveyard and a ball grounds

And a short order counter where a man can get a stack of wheats
And a pool hall where a rounder leered confidential like and said:
"Lookin' for a quiet game?"   50

The loafer lagged along and asked,
"Do you make guitars here?
Do you make boxes the singing wood winds ask to sleep in?
Do you rig up strings the singing wood winds sift over and sing low?"
The answer: "We manufacture musical instruments here."   55

Here I saw churches with steeples like hatpins,
Undertaking rooms with sample coffins in the show window
And signs everywhere satisfaction is guaranteed,
Shooting galleries where men kill imitation pigeons,
And there were doctors for the sick,   60
And lawyers for people waiting in jail,
And a dog catcher and a superintendent of streets,
And telephones, water-works, trolley cars,
And newspapers with a splatter of telegrams from sister cities of Kalamazoo the round world
    over.

And the loafer lagging along said: 65
Kalamazoo, you ain't in a class by yourself;
I seen you before in a lot of places.
If you are nuts America is nuts.
        And lagging along he said bitterly:
        Before I came to Kalamazoo I was silent.   70
        Now I am gabby, God help me, I am gabby.

Kalamazoo, both of us will do a fadeaway.
I will be carried out feet first
And time and the rain will chew you to dust
And the winds blow you away.   75
And an old, old mother will lay a green moss cover on my bones
And a green moss cover on the stones of your postoffice and city hall.

    Best of all
I have loved your kiddies playing run-sheep-run
And cutting their initials on the ball ground fence.   80
They knew every time I fooled them who was fooled and how.

    Best of all
I have loved the red gold smoke of your sunsets;
I have loved a moon with a ring around it
Floating over your public square;   85
I have loved the white dawn frost of early winter silver
And purple over your railroad tracks and lumber yards.

    The wishing heart of you I loved, Kalamazoo.
        I sang bye-lo, bye-lo to your dreams.
I sang bye-lo to your hopes and songs.   90
I wished to God there were hound dogs of bronze on your public square,
Hound dogs with bronze paws looking to a long horizon with a shivering silver angel, a creep-
    ing mystic what-is-it.

581

from **The People, Yes**

14

THE PEOPLE is Everyman, everybody.
Everybody is you and me and all others.
What everybody says is what we all say.
 And what is it we all say?

Where did we get these languages?   5
Why is your baby-talk deep in your blood?
What is the cling of the tongue
To what it heard with its mother-milk?

They cross on the ether now.
They travel on high frequencies   10
Over the border-lines and barriers
Of mountain ranges and oceans.
When shall we all speak the same language?
And do we want to have all the same language?
Are we learning a few great signs and pass-
 words?   15
Why should Everyman be lost for words?
The questions are put every day in every
 tongue:
    "Where you from, Stranger?
    Where were you born?
    Got any money?   20
    What do you work at?
    Where's your passport?
    Who are your people?"

Over the ether crash the languages.
 And the people listen.   25
As on the plain of Howdeehow they listen.
 They want to hear.
They will be told when the next war is ready.
The long wars and the short wars will come on
 the air,
How many got killed and how the war ended
And who got what and the price paid   31
And how there were tombs for the Unknown
 Soldier,
 The boy nobody knows the name of,

From *The People, Yes*, by Carl Sandburg, copyright, 1936,
by Harcourt, Brace & Co., Inc.
The People, Yes. This is a section from a complete book in
which, in the very language of the people, rich or poor, eastern,
middle western, or southern, the poet expresses his own, and
what he believes to be their, faith in life, in progressive thought,
in the need for greater equality and justice. The poem is a
summary of Sandburg's idealistic socialism politically, and
it is as well a realistic, homely presentation of the average
citizen's way of philosophizing and meeting life's emergencies.
In the end, the poet says that the people (despite war or any
catastrophe) will win their rights, will insist on affirming life's
values, if for no other reason than that they wish to live. As a
folklorist, Sandburg knew the people, their idiom, their groping
thoughts, their fantasies and faiths.

The boy whose great fame is that of the masses,
The millions of names too many to write on a
 tomb,   35
The heroes, the cannonfodder, the living tar-
 gets,
The mutilated and sacred dead,
The people, yes.

Two countries with two flags
are nevertheless one land, one blood, one people—   40
 can this be so?
And the earth belongs to the family of man?
 can this be so?

The first world war came and its cost was laid
 on the people.
The second world war—the third—what will be
 the cost?   45
And will it repay the people for what they pay?

15

From the people the countries get their armies.
By the people the armies are fed, clothed,
 armed.
Out of the smoke and ashes of the war
The people build again their two countries
 with two flags
Even though sometimes it is one land, one
 blood, one people.   5

Hate is a vapor fixed and mixed.
Hate is a vapor blown and thrown.
And the war lasts till the hate dies down
And the crazy Four Horsemen have handed
 the people
Hunger and filth and a stink too heavy to
 stand.   10
Then the earth sends forth bright new grass
And the land begins to breathe easy again
Though the hate of the people dies slow and
 hard.
 Hate is a lingering heavy swamp mist.

And the bloated horse carcass points four feet
 to the sky   15
And the tanks and caterpillar tractors are buried deep in shell holes
And rust flakes the big guns and time rots the
 gas masks on skeleton faces:

Deep in the dirt the dynamite threw them with
     an impersonal detonation: war is "Oh!"
     and "Ah!": war is "Ugh!"

          And after the strife of war
          begins the strife of peace.   20

25

"You do what you must—this world and then
     the next—one world at a time."
The grain gamblers and the price manipulators
     and the stock-market players put their
     own twist on the text: In the sweat of
     thy brow shalt thou eat thy bread.
The day's work in the factory, mill, mine—the
     whistle, the bell, the alarm clock, the
     timekeeper and the paycheck, your
     number on the assembly line, what the
     night shift says when the day shift
     comes—the blood of years paid out for
     finished products proclaimed on bill-
     boards yelling at highway travellers in
     green valleys—
These are daily program items, values of blood
     and mind in the everyday rituals of the
     people.

107

The people will live on.
The learning and blundering people will live
     on.
     They will be tricked and sold and again
     sold
And go back to the nourishing earth for root-
     holds,
     The people so peculiar in renewal and
     comeback,   5
You can't laugh off their capacity to take
     it.
The mammoth rests between his cyclonic
     dramas.

The people so often sleepy, weary, enigmatic,
is a vast huddle with many units saying:
     "I earn my living.   10
     I make enough to get by
     and it takes all my time.
     If I had more time
     I could do more for myself
     and maybe for others.   15

I could read and study
and talk things over
and find out about things.
It takes time.
I wish I had the time."   20

The people is a tragic and comic two-face:
hero and hoodlum: phantom and gorilla twisting to moan with a gargoyle mouth: "They
buy me and sell me . . . it's a game . . .
sometime I'll break loose . . ."   25
     Once having marched
     Over the margins of animal necessity,
     Over the grim line of sheer subsistence
          Then man came
     To the deeper rituals of his bones,   30
     To the lights lighter than any bones,
     To the time for thinking things over,
     To the dance, the song, the story,
     Or the hours given over to dreaming,
          Once having so marched.   35

Between the finite limitations of the five senses
and the endless yearnings of man for the be-
          yond
the people hold to the humdrum bidding of
          work and food
while reaching out when it comes their way
for lights beyond the prison of the five senses,
for keepsakes lasting beyond any hunger or
          death.   41
     This reaching is alive.
The panderers and liars have violated and
          smutted it.
     Yet this reaching is alive yet
     for lights and keepsakes.   45

     The people know the salt of the sea
     and the strength of the winds
     lashing the corners of the earth.
     The people take the earth   49
     as a tomb of rest and a cradle of hope.
     Who else speaks for the Family of Man?
     They are in tune and step
     with constellations of universal law.

     The people is a polychrome,
     a spectrum and a prism   55
     held in a moving monolith,
     a console organ of changing themes,

a clavilux of color poems
wherein the sea offers fog
and the fog moves off in rain   60
and the labrador sunset shortens
to a nocturne of clear stars
serene over the shot spray
of northern lights.

The steel mill sky is alive.   65
The fire breaks white and zigzag
shot on a gun-metal gloaming.
Man is a long time coming.
Man will yet win.   69
Brother may yet line up with brother:

This old anvil laughs at many broken hammers.
There are men who can't be bought.
The fireborn are at home in fire.
The stars make no noise.
You can't hinder the wind from blowing.
Time is a great teacher.   76
Who can live without hope?

In the darkness with a great bundle of grief
the people march.
In the night, and overhead a shovel of stars
for keeps, the people march:
"Where to? what next?"

VACHEL LINDSAY

Nicholas Vachel Lindsay is often referred to as America's minstrel poet, because he brought his poetry directly to the people; and indeed a large measure of Lindsay's popularity was due to his own distinctive and unforgettable readings of his work. But although his rhythmic chants fascinated audiences, his ideas failed to convert them, and the poetic career which had begun with such high hopes for a new world of beauty, purity, and brotherhood ended in despair and disillusion.

Lindsay was born in Springfield, Illinois, November 10, 1879. His father was one of the town's better known physicians, a practical man who always viewed his son's career with some concern. His mother, who herself indulged in the minor arts of painting china and burning wood, was convinced that only by uniting art and religion could the spiritual vigor of America be re-created. It was undoubtedly she who directed her son into his early enthusiasm for drawing. Lindsay was a dreamy child who took himself very seriously. He played minor parts in his mother's Sunday school dramas, in which Cupid and Jesus were sometimes on the same stage. Quite early he came to believe himself appointed to redeem

the world, which he saw as given over to the spider Mammon and to a kind of drab, mass-produced ugliness. His diaries and letters indicate that the boy was perhaps too ingrown, too much impressed with himself as the uncorrupted savior of a people who thoroughly enjoy the ways of the flesh. The diaries written while Lindsay attended Hiram College are the rather terrifying record of the undigested reading and enthusiasms of an adolescent who believed he must know everything in order to consecrate himself to the work he was to do.

Three years at college were followed by three years in Chicago, working and attending night classes at the Art Institute. Against his father's wishes, Lindsay went to New York in 1904 to study at the New York Art School. He had no money, and earned his living at all manner of odd jobs. His drawings, although psychologically clear portrayals of his religious and esthetic enthusiasms, were not great, and they were somewhat obscure. In order to explain them, Lindsay began to write poetry to accompany them. And since he was determined that his creed of beauty should reach the people, he copied the poems and drawings on post cards and began to peddle them in drugstores, restaurants, and bars for a few pennies apiece. They met every kind of reception; some people thought Lindsay mad, others bought out of amusement. Meanwhile, the young man was eating badly and living poorly. "I was beaten," he said later, "but I couldn't go home beaten. You can't, you know, so I made up my mind to be a tramp and a beggar." So it was that he started on his trips through the West, reciting his poetry, staying at farmhouses—never at wealthy homes—where he could do a little work for his supper. In general he found the country people friendly. In the summer of 1912, he walked from Illinois to New Mexico, distributing verses from his little book, *Rhymes to Be Traded for Bread,* and lecturing for the YMCA and other organizations.

When Harriet Monroe printed "General William Booth Enters into Heaven" in *Poetry* in January 1913, and wrote an account of its author as a folk-poet—something which various editors were then trying to discover—Vachel Lindsay became known. Lecture tours to the colleges followed, and he began to develop his "higher vaudeville" technique for conveying his great message. He usually began his lecture with the strenuous "Kallyope Yell," a poem reproducing circus noises and enthusiasms. The college youngsters would answer him with their college yell, and he would be off into one of the strangest performances that any poet ever gave, singing, shouting, and dancing his poems. Lindsay was a tall, lanky man, with a beautiful head, great range of voice, and evangelistic intensity. For some years, because of these really great performances, he was unusually popular as a reader. His *The Art of the Moving Picture* (1915) is the first important book on the moving picture as a popular art. *A Handy Guide for Beggars* (1916) is a witty commentary on the things Lindsay saw during his cross-country tours. His great jazz poems, "The Congo," "The Santa Fé Trail," and "The Chinese Nightingale," written at this time, added to his fame. But perhaps because he found that his audiences were not taking his religious messages to heart and were more interested in his jazz rhythms and his exciting readings, or perhaps merely because his physical energies began to ebb, he turned from the jazz poems to

naïve, rather trite rhymes about how people should live. With *The Golden Whales of California* (1920), his popular appeal diminished. Because his books did not provide a living, he was forced to continue with his eternal lecturing. Lindsay was increasingly depressed by this and his belief that his audiences were not following him in his teachings; he began to feel as if they came merely to see something odd. By the time *Collected Poems* was published in 1923, his career was already headed downhill.

Lindsay's greatest talent had been his ability to re-create American myths. Despite his inherited puritanism, he wrote in the tradition of the tall tale. In his rhythmic yawps about Johnny Appleseed's sowing of the orchards over the American plain, in his songs about the rush of the buffalo, in his poems on the days of Lincoln, Lindsay satisfied our desire for an American tradition. At times too he was successful in making everyone from Bryan to Theodore Roosevelt seem to be the great leaders of a new, energetic, and democratic America. But his visions of a free democracy with individualistic leaders were denied by the complexity of Lindsay's own time.

The poet could not arouse enthusiasm for the Temperance Union or for making over city halls into pure citadels of democratic religions. He could describe Lincoln's anger at the new bloodshed; but the First World War did not stop because of his poem. He could explain that women would enjoy housework if they danced in Greek robes while doing it. He could print *The Golden Book of Springfield, Illinois* as a kind of bible for the citizens; but his own townsmen were not proud of him. He could post illustrated placards on back fences, urging Americans to turn away from commercialism and greed; he could tell why he voted the Socialist ticket, or why every soul was a circus; but people in the 1920's went on playing the stock market and trying to get richer quicker. Lindsay, in short, was moving against the historical stream. He had dedicated himself to being a prophet of a new age in which individualism would mean morality and artistic sensitivity; but he had fewer and fewer disciples. Vachel Lindsay's story in some ways seems to illustrate how a highly commercial age can stifle and eventually kill the idealistic poet. It is true that he was naïve and that his interpretation of history was mythological rather than accurate; it is also true that he tried to reach the people and failed. He illustrates the conflict between materialistic drives and the compulsions of a sensitive person. It might be said that Lindsay's poetic vices are sometimes his virtues, as for example when the noticeable poverty of speech in some poems becomes in others a fine poetry springing from our simple everyday language. His mythmaking ability developed because of his own childlike faith in and enthusiasm for the tall tales of our early history. Jazz rhythm, taken indirectly from the American Negro, was the folk rhythm into which he could best cast an almost perpetually adolescent enthusiasm for heroic bygone days and American patterns of leadership.

In 1925, in his middle years, Lindsay married Elisabeth Connors. They lived for a time in the West, but eventually returned to Springfield and settled there. Although Lindsay's talent was waning, he continued to write and lecture, but his books *Going-to-the-Stars* (1926) and *Every Soul Is a Circus* (1929) were badly received. Gradually it became difficult for him to earn a living. Lecturing to unresponsive audiences tried him more and more. The gap between what he had believed the world could be and what it really was became all too evident. Lindsay's mind was giving way, and on December 5, 1931, after an unsuccessful lecture tour, he killed himself by swallowing acid. Only after his death did the public, which had begun to ignore him, realize that it had lost an important poet.

It is interesting to compare Lindsay and Sandburg. Both wished to make the world a better place to live; both believed they were Socialists. But Sandburg came from a laboring-class background, knew the common language, and was in contact with the working people themselves. Lindsay, on the other hand, was of more well-to-do parentage, and had within him all the confusions which may befall the liberal and the evangelist. Despite his idealism and enthusiasm, he was never able really to understand the people, and he never really matured.

The Chinese Nightingale

A SONG IN CHINESE TAPESTRIES

"How, HOW," he said. "Friend Chang," I said,
"San Francisco sleeps as the dead—
Ended license, lust and play:
Why do you iron the night away?
Your big clock speaks with a deadly sound,   5
With a tick and a wail till dawn comes round.
While the monster shadows glower and creep,
What can be better for man than sleep?"

"I will tell you a secret," Chang replied;
"My breast with vision is satisfied,   10
And I see green trees and fluttering wings,
And my deathless bird from Shanghai sings."
Then he lit five firecrackers in a pan.
"Pop, pop," said the firecrackers, "cra-cra-crack."
He lit a joss stick long and black.   15
Then the proud gray joss in the corner stirred;
On his wrist appeared a gray small bird,
And this was the song of the gray small bird:
"Where is the princess, loved forever,
Who made Chang first of the kings of men?"

And the joss in the corner stirred again;   21
And the carved dog, curled in his arms, awoke,
Barked forth a smoke-cloud that whirled and
    broke.
It piled in a maze round the ironing-place,
And there on the snowy table wide   25
Stood a Chinese lady of high degree,
With a scornful, witching, tea-rose face. . . .
Yet she put away all form and pride,
And laid her glimmering veil aside
With a childlike smile for Chang and for me.

The walls fell back, night was aflower,   31
The table gleamed in a moonlit bower,
While Chang, with a countenance carved of
    stone,
Ironed and ironed, all alone.
And thus she sang to the busy man Chang: 35
"Have you forgotten . . .
Deep in the ages, long, long ago,

The poems of Lindsay are reprinted from *Collected Poems* by Vachel Lindsay by permission of The Macmillan Company, publishers.
The Chinese Nightingale. Lindsay's knowledge (despite wide but confused readings) was always undigested. Here, without any real oriental scholarship, is a poem, supposedly about oriental feeling, in which the romantic idea of love is very clear. Lindsay loved *The Chinese Nightingale*, and thought it one of his best poems—perhaps because it combines rich oriental images with western images, and is also a plea that the poor sublimate their poverty.

I was your sweetheart, there on the sand—
Storm-worn beach of the Chinese land?
We sold our grain in the peacock town—   40
Built on the edge of the sea-sands brown—
Built on the edge of the sea-sands brown. . . .

When all the world was drinking blood
From the skulls of men and bulls
And all the world had swords and clubs of
      stone,   45
We drank our tea in China beneath the sacred
      spice-trees,
And heard the curled waves of the harbor moan.
And this gray bird, in Love's first spring,
With a bright-bronze breast and a bronze-
      brown wing,
Captured the world with his carolling.   50
Do you remember, ages after,
At last the world we were born to own?
You were the heir of the yellow throne—
The world was the field of the Chinese man
And we were the pride of the Sons of Han?   55
We copied deep books and we carved in jade,
And wove blue silks in the mulberry shade. . . ."

"I remember, I remember
That Spring came on forever,
That Spring came on forever,"   60
Said the Chinese nightingale.

My heart was filled with marvel and dream,
Though I saw the western street-lamps gleam,
Though dawn was bringing the western day,
Though Chang was a laundryman ironing
      away. . . .   65
Mingled there with the streets and alleys,
The railroad-yard and the clock-tower bright,
Demon clouds crossed ancient valleys;
Across wide lotus-ponds of light
I marked a giant firefly's flight.   70

And the lady, rosy-red,
Flourished her fan, her shimmering fan,
Stretched her hand toward Chang, and said:
"Do you remember,
Ages after,   75
Our palace of heart-red stone?
Do you remember
The little doll-faced children
With their lanterns full of moon-fire,
That came from all the empire   80
Honoring the throne?—

The loveliest fête and carnival
Our world had ever known?
The sages sat about us
With their heads bowed in their beards,   85
With proper meditation on the sight.
Confucius was not born;
We lived in those great days
Confucius later said were lived aright. . . .
And this gray bird, on that day of spring,   90
With a bright-bronze breast, and a bronze-
      brown wing,
Captured the world with his carolling.
Late at night his tune was spent.
Peasants,
Sages,   95
Children,
Homeward went,
And then the bronze bird sang for you and me.
We walked alone. Our hearts were high and
      free.
I had a silvery name, I had a silvery name,   100
I had a silvery name—do you remember
The name you cried beside the tumbling sea?"

Chang turned not to the lady slim—
He bent to his work, ironing away;
But she was arch, and knowing and glowing,
For the bird on his shoulder spoke for him.   106

"Darling . . . darling . . . darling . . . dar-
      ling . . ."
Said the Chinese nightingale.

The great gray joss on the rustic shelf,
Rakish and shrewd, with his collar awry,   110
Sang impolitely, as though by himself,
Drowning with his bellowing the nightingale's
      cry:
"Back through a hundred, hundred years
Hear the waves as they climb the piers,
Hear the howl of the silver seas,   115
Hear the thunder.
Hear the gongs of holy China
How the waves and tunes combine
In a rhythmic clashing wonder,
Incantation old and fine: 120
   'Dragons, dragons, Chinese dragons,
   Red firecrackers, and green firecrackers
   And dragons, dragons, Chinese dragons.' "

Then the lady, rosy-red,
Turned to her lover Chang and said: 125

587

"Dare you forget that turquoise **dawn**
When we stood in our mist-hung velvet lawn,
And worked a spell this great joss taught
Till a God of the Dragons was charmed and
      caught?
From the flag high over our palace home   130
He flew to our feet in rainbow-foam—
A king of beauty and tempest and thunder
Panting to tear our sorrows asunder.
A dragon of fair adventure and wonder.
We mounted the back of that royal slave   135
With thoughts of desire that were noble and
      grave.
We swam down the shore to the dragon-moun-
      tains,
We whirled to the peaks and the fiery fountains.
To our secret ivory house we were borne.
We looked down the wonderful wing-filled re-
      gions   140
Where the dragons darted in glimmering legions.
Right by my breast the nightingale sang;
The old rhymes rang in the sunlit mist
That we this hour regain—
Song-fire for the brain.   145
When my hands and my hair and my feet you
      kissed,
When you cried for your heart's new pain,
What was my name in the dragon-mist,
In the rings of rainbowed rain?"

"Sorrow and love, glory and love,"   150
Said the Chinese nightingale.
"Sorrow and love, glory and love,"
Said the Chinese nightingale.

And now the joss broke in with his song:
"Dying ember, bird of Chang,   155
Soul of Chang, do you remember?—
Ere you returned to the shining harbor
There were pirates by ten thousand
Descended on the town   159
In vessels mountain-high and red and brown,
Moon-ships that climbed the storms and cut the
      skies.
On their prows were painted terrible bright eyes.
But I was then a wizard and a scholar and a
      priest;
I stood upon the sand;
With lifted hand I looked upon them   165
And sunk their vessels with my wizard eyes,
And the stately lacquer-gate made safe again.
Deep, deep below the bay, the seaweed and the
      spray,

Embalmed in amber every pirate lies,
Embalmed in amber every pirate lies."   170
Then this did the noble lady say:
"Bird, do you dream of our home-coming day
When you flew like a courier on before
From the dragon-peak to our palace-door,   174
And we drove the steed in your singing path—
The ramping dragon of laughter and wrath:
And found our city all aglow,
And knighted this joss that decked it so?
There were golden fishes in the purple river
And silver fishes and rainbow fishes.   180
There were golden junks in the laughing river,
And silver junks and rainbow junks:
There were golden lilies by the bay and river,
And silver lilies and tiger-lilies,
And tinkling wind-bells in the gardens of the
      town   185
By the black-lacquer gate
Where walked in state
The kind king Chang
And his sweetheart mate. . . .
With his flag-born dragon   190
And his crown of pearl . . . and . . . jade,
And his nightingale reigning in the mulberry
      shade,
And sailors and soldiers on the sea-sands brown,
And priests who bowed them down to your song—
By the city called Han, the peacock town,   195
By the city called Han, the nightingale town,
The nightingale town."

Then sang the bird, so strangely gay,
Fluttering, fluttering, ghostly and gray,
A vague, unravelling, final tune,   200
Like a long unwinding silk cocoon;
Sang as though for the soul of him
Who ironed away in that bower dim:—
    "I have forgotten
      Your dragons great,   205
      Merry and mad and friendly and bold.
Dim is your proud lost palace-gate.
I vaguely know
There were heroes of old,
Troubles more than the heart could hold,   210
There were wolves in the woods
Yet lambs in the fold,
Nests in the top of the almond tree. . . .
The evergreen tree . . . and the mulberry
      tree . . .
Life and hurry and joy forgotten,   215
Years on years I but half-remember . . .

Man is a torch, then ashes soon,
May and June, then dead December,
Dead December, then again June.
Who shall end my dream's confusion?   220
Life is a loom, weaving illusion . . .
I remember, I remember
There were ghostly veils and laces . . .
In the shadowy bowery places . . .
With lovers' ardent faces   225
Bending to one another,
Speaking each his part.
They infinitely echo
In the red cave of my heart.
'Sweetheart, sweetheart, sweetheart,'   230
They said to one another.
They spoke, I think, of perils past.
They spoke, I think, of peace at last.
One thing I remember:
Spring came on forever,   235
Spring came on forever,"
Said the Chinese nightingale.

Abraham Lincoln Walks at Midnight

(In Springfield, Illinois)

IT IS PORTENTOUS, and a thing of state
That here at midnight, in our little town
A mourning figure walks, and will not rest,
Near the old court-house pacing up and down,

Or by his homestead, or in shadowed yards   5
He lingers where his children used to play,
Or through the market, on the well-worn stones
He stalks until the dawn-stars burn away.

A bronzed, lank man! His suit of ancient black,
A famous high top-hat and plain worn shawl
Make him the quaint great figure that men
       love,   11
The prairie-lawyer, master of us all.

He cannot sleep upon his hillside now.
He is among us:—as in times before!
And we who toss and lie awake for long   15
Breathe deep, and start, to see him pass the
       door.

His head is bowed. He thinks on men and
       kings.
Yea, when the sick world cries, how can he
       sleep?   18
Too many peasants fight, they know not why,
Too many homesteads in black terror weep.

The sins of all the war-lords burn his heart.
He sees the dreadnaughts scouring every main.
He carries on his shawl-wrapped shoulders
       now
The bitterness, the folly and the pain.

He cannot rest until a spirit-dawn   25
Shall come;—the shining hope of Europe free:
The league of sober folk, the Workers' Earth,
Bringing long peace to Cornland, Alp and Sea.

It breaks his heart that kings must murder still,
That all his hours of travail here for men   30
Seem yet in vain. And who will bring white
       peace
That he may sleep upon his hill again?

The Leaden-Eyed

LET NOT young souls be smothered out before
       They do quaint deeds and fully flaunt their
       pride.
It is the world's one crime its babes grow dull,
Its poor are ox-like, limp and leaden-eyed.   4

Not that they starve, but starve so dreamlessly,
Not that they sow, but that they seldom reap,
Not that they serve, but have no gods to serve,
Not that they die but that they die like sheep.

John L. Sullivan, the Strong Boy of Boston

(Inscribed to Louis Untermeyer and Robert Frost)

WHEN I WAS nine years old, in 1889,
       I sent my love a lacy Valentine.
Suffering boys were dressed like Fauntleroys,
While Judge and Puck in giant humor vied.

Abraham Lincoln Walks at Midnight. Lincoln practiced law at Springfield (Lindsay's birthplace) until he became President of the United States; after his assassination his body was taken there, and his home and monument are places of pilgrimage. The poem is clearly Lindsay's bitter comment on the First World War.
John . . . Boston. 3. **Fauntleroys.** The velvet-clad boy hero of Frances Eliza Hodgson Burnett's *Little Lord Fauntleroy* (1886) became a symbol of the soft and pampered child. 4. **Judge and Puck,** well-known comic magazines of the period.

The Gibson Girl came shining like a bride   5
To spoil the cult of Tennyson's Elaine.
Louisa Alcott was my gentle guide. . . .
Then . . .
I heard a battle trumpet sound.
Nigh New Orleans   10
Upon an emerald plain
John L. Sullivan
The strong boy
Of Boston
Fought seventy-five red rounds with Jake Kilrain.   15

In simple sheltered 1889
Nick Carter I would piously deride.
Over the Elsie Books I moped and sighed.
St. Nicholas Magazine was all my pride,
While coarser boys on cellar doors would slide.   20
The grown-ups bought refinement by the pound.
Rogers groups had not been told to hide.
E. P. Roe had just begun to wane.
Howells was rising, surely to attain!
The nation for a jamboree was gowned.—   25
Her hundredth year of roaring freedom crowned.
The British Lion ran and hid from Blaine
The razzle-dazzle hip-hurrah from Maine.
The mocking bird was singing in the lane. . . .
Yet . . .   30
"East side, west side, all around the town   *To be sung.*
The tots sang: 'Ring a rosie—'   *Let the*
'London Bridge is falling down.'"   *audience join*
   in softly on
And . . .   *this tune,*
John L. Sullivan   *wherever it*   35
The strong boy   *appears.*
Of Boston
Broke every single rib of Jake Kilrain.

In dear provincial 1889,
Barnum's bears and tigers could astound.   40
Ingersoll was called a most vile hound,
And named with Satan, Judas, Thomas Paine!
Robert Elsmere riled the pious brain.
Phillips Brooks for heresy was fried.
Boston Brahmins patronized Mark Twain.   45
The baseball rules were changed. That was a gain.

6. **Elaine,** a fragile character in *Idylls of the King.* She might be considered to represent Tennyson's ideal of virginal beauty. 12. **John L. Sullivan** (1858–1918), American pugilist and heavyweight champion of the world. 15. **seventy-five red rounds.** The fight between Kilrain and Sullivan in Mississippi in 1889 was the last "bare-knuckled" fight before the use of gloves and the present boxing rules were established. According to the old rules, a round ended whenever one fighter dropped to his knees. The entire seventy-five round fight lasted two hours and sixteen minutes. 17. **Nick Carter,** hero (and pseudonym of the author, Frederick V. R. Dey) of a series of dime novels of the late nineteenth century. 18. **Elsie Books,** Martha Finley's series of pious and sentimental girls' books of the same period. 19. **St. Nicholas Magazine,** the famous children's magazine (1873–1939) founded and first edited by Mary Mapes Dodge. 22. **Rogers groups.** See note l. 14, p. 317. 23. **E. P. Roe** (1838–88), American clergyman and novelist, writer of stories of romantic adventure. 24. **Howells,** William Dean Howells (1837–1920), American novelist, critic, and editor. 27. **Blaine,** James Gillespie Blaine (1830–93), American statesman. In 1881, as secretary of state, he had bitter dealings with the British government over the Panama Canal. 41. **Ingersoll,** Robert Green Ingersoll (1833–99), American orator and lawyer, known as "the great agnostic." 43. **Robert Elsmere,** a novel by Mrs. Humphry Ward (1851–1920) concerning the inward religious conflicts of a young clergyman. 44. **Phillips Brooks** (1835–93), American Protestant Episcopal bishop. 45. **Boston Brahmins,** the upper crust of New England society—Lowells, Cabots, and other "first families."

Pop Anson was our darling, pet and pride.
Native sons in Irish votes were drowned.
Tammany once more escaped its chain.
Once more each raw saloon was raising Cain.
The mocking bird was singing in the lane. . . .   50
Yet . . .
"East side, west side, all around the town
The tots sang: 'Ring a rosie'
'London Bridge is falling down.'"
And . . .   55
John L. Sullivan
The strong boy
Of Boston
Finished the ring career of Jake Kilrain.   60

In mystic, ancient 1889,
Wilson with pure learning was allied.
Roosevelt gave forth a chirping sound.
Stanley found old Emin and his train.
Stout explorers sought the pole in vain.   65
To dream of flying proved a man insane.
The newly rich were bathing in champagne.
Van Bibber Davis, at a single bound
Displayed himself, and simpering glory found.
John J. Ingalls, like a lonely crane   70
Swore and swore, and stalked the Kansas plain.
The Cronin murder was the ages' stain.
Johnstown was flooded, and the whole world cried.
We heard not of Louvain nor of Lorraine,
Or a million heroes for their freedom slain.   75
Of Armageddon and the world's birth-pain—
The League of Nations, the new world allied,
With Wilson, crucified, then justified.
We *thought* the world would loaf and sprawl and mosey.
The gods of Yap and Swat were sweetly dozy.   80
We *thought* the far-off gods of Chow had died.
The mocking bird was singing in the lane. . . .
Yet . . .
"East side, west side, all around the town
The tots sang: 'Ring a rosie'   85
'London Bridge Is Falling Down.'"
And . . .
John L. Sullivan knocked out Jake Kilrain.

47. **Pop Anson,** Adrian Constantine Anson (1852–1922), American baseball player, the greatest figure of his day in the game. 49. **Tammany.** Tammany Hall is the headquarters of the New York County Democratic organization. Thomas Nast, political cartoonist of the period, used the tiger as a symbol of the power wielded by Tammany Hall. 62. **Wilson.** In 1889 Woodrow Wilson was still a teacher and had not yet entered the political arena. 63. **Roosevelt.** In 1889 Theodore Roosevelt was appointed to the Civil Service Commission. 64. **Stanley.** Sir Henry Morton Stanley (1841–1904), famous English explorer, in 1889 headed an expedition to extricate Emin Pasha, governor of the Egyptian Sudan, from the Lado Enclave and bring him to confer about annexation of territory to the Congo Free State. 68. **Van Bibber Davis,** Richard Harding Davis (1864–1916), American novelist and journalist. His account of the Johnstown flood brought him a position on the New York *Evening Sun,* and he became the most famous war correspondent of his generation. The Van Bibber stories which he wrote gave him his nickname. 70. **John J. Ingalls** (1833–1900), Kansan senator whose opposition to all progressive legislation brought about his defeat in 1890. 72. **Cronin murder,** current news in 1889. 73. **Johnstown,** Cambria County, Pennsylvania. The dam above the city broke on May 31, 1889, and many people were drowned in the resultant flood. 74. **Louvain,** Belgian city with a famous university, sacked by the Germans after its surrender in August 1914. **Lorraine,** the disputed territory generally called Alsace-Lorraine, restored to the French after World War I. 80. **The gods . . . died,** a reference to the peacefulness of Japan in 1889 before there was talk of the "Yellow Peril."

The Eagle That Is Forgotten

(John P. Altgeld. Born December 30, 1847;
  died March 12, 1902)

SLEEP softly . . . eagle forgotten . . . under the stone.
Time has its way with you there, and the clay
    has its own.

"We have buried him now," thought your foes,
    and in secret rejoiced.
They made a brave show of their mourning,
    their hatred unvoiced.
They had snarled at you, barked at you,
    foamed at you day after day.   5
Now you were ended. They praised you, . . .
    and laid you away.

The others that mourned you in silence and terror and truth,
The widow bereft of her crust, and the boy
    without youth,
The mocked and the scorned and the wounded,
    the lame and the poor
That should have remembered forever, . . .
    remember no more.   10

Where are those lovers of yours, on what name
    do they call
The lost, that in armies wept over your funeral
    pall?
They call on the names of a hundred high-valiant ones,
A hundred white eagles have risen the sons of
    your sons,
The zeal in their wings is a zeal that your
    dreaming began   15
The valor that wore out your soul in the service of man.

Sleep softly, . . . eagle forgotten, . . . under
    the stone,
Time has its way with you there and the clay
    has its own.
Sleep on, O brave-hearted, O wise man, that
    kindled the flame—
To live in mankind is far more than to live in a
    name,   20
To live in mankind, far, far more . . . than to
    live in a name.

John P. Altgeld, Governor of Illinois 1892–97, whose efforts
in behalf of progressive labor legislation made him one of the
most controversial figures of his time.

General William Booth Enters into Heaven

(*To be sung to the tune of "The Blood of the
  Lamb" with indicated instrument*)

I

(*Bass drum beaten loudly.*)

BOOTH led boldly with his big bass drum—
    (Are you washed in the blood of the
        Lamb?)
The Saints smiled gravely and they said: "He's
    come."
(Are you washed in the blood of the Lamb?)
Walking lepers followed, rank on rank,   5
Lurching bravos from the ditches dank,
Drabs from the alleyways and drug fiends
    pale—
Minds still passion-ridden, soul-powers frail:—
Vermin-eaten saints with moldy breath,
Unwashed legions with the ways of Death— 10
(Are you washed in the blood of the Lamb?)

(*Banjos.*)

Every slum had sent its half-a-score
The round world over. (Booth had groaned for
    more.)
Every banner that the wide world flies
Bloomed with glory and transcendent dyes.   15
Big-voiced lasses made their banjos bang,
Tranced, fanatical they shrieked and sang:—
"Are you washed in the blood of the Lamb?"
Hallelujah! It was queer to see   19
Bull-necked convicts with that land make free.
Loons with trumpets blowed a blare, blare,
    blare
On, on upward thro' the golden air!
(Are you washed in the blood of the Lamb?)

II

(*Bass drum slower and softer.*)

Booth died blind and still by faith he trod,
Eyes still dazzled by the ways of God.   25
Booth led boldly, and he looked the chief
Eagle countenance in sharp relief,
Beard a-flying, air of high command
Unabated in that holy land.

(*Sweet flute music.*)

Jesus came from out the court-house door,   30

General William Booth Enters into Heaven. Lindsay
himself believed in evangelistic revivals of faith and tried to
make his poetry serve this purpose. It was natural, therefore,
that he should praise Booth. *"The Blood of the Lamb,"* the
most famous of all Salvation Army hymns. 1. **Booth** (1829–
1912), English religious leader and founder of the Salvation
Army. He was blind when he died.

Stretched his hands above the passing poor.
Booth saw not, but led his queer ones there
Round and round the mighty court-house
  square.
Then, in an instant all that blear review
Marched on spotless, clad in raiment new.   35
The lame were straightened, withered limbs
  uncurled
And blind eyes opened on a new, sweet world.

  (*Bass drum louder.*)
Drabs and vixens in a flash made whole!
Gone was the weasel-head, the snout, the jowl!
Sages and sibyls now, and athletes clean,   40
Rulers of empires, and of forests green!

  (*Grand chorus of all instruments. Tambou-
rines to the foreground.*)
The hosts were sandalled, and their wings were
  fire!
(Are you washed in the blood of the Lamb?)
But their noise played havoc with the angel-
  choir.
(Are you washed in the blood of the Lamb?)
Oh, shout Salvation! It was good to see   46
Kings and Princes by the Lamb set free.
The banjos rattled and the tambourines
Jing-jing-jingled in the hands of Queens.

  (*Reverently sung, no instruments.*)
And when Booth halted by the curb for prayer

He saw his Master thro' the flag-filled air.   51
Christ came gently with a robe and crown
For Booth the soldier, while the throng knelt
  down.
He saw King Jesus. They were face to face,
And he knelt a-weeping in that holy place.   55
Are you washed in the blood of the Lamb?

A Dirge for a Righteous Kitten

(*To be intoned, all but the two italicized lines,
which are to be spoken in a snappy, matter-of-
fact way*)

DING-DONG, ding-dong, ding-dong.
Here lies a kitten good, who kept
A kitten's proper place.
He stole no pantry eatables,
Nor scratched the baby's face.   5
He let the alley-cats alone.
He had no yowling vice.
His shirt was always laundried well,
He freed the house of mice.
Until his death he had not caused   10
His little mistress tears,
He wore his ribbon prettily,
He washed behind his ears.
Ding-dong, ding-dong, ding-dong.

The Santa-Fé Trail (A Humoresque)

  (I asked the old Negro: "What is that bird that sings so well?" He answered: "That is the Rachel-
Jane." "Hasn't it another name—lark or thrush, or the like?" "No. Jus' Rachel-Jane.")

I. In Which a Racing Auto Comes from the East

THIS is the order of the music of the morning:—
  First, from the far East comes but a crooning.
The crooning turns to a sunrise singing.
Hark to the *calm*-horn, *balm*-horn, *psalm*-horn.
Hark to the *faint*-horn, *quaint*-horn, *saint*-horn. . . .   5

*To be sung
delicately, to
an improvised
tune.*

Hark to the *pace*-horn, *chase*-horn, *race*-horn.
And the holy veil of the dawn has gone.
Swiftly the brazen car comes on.
It burns in the East as the sunrise burns.
I see great flashes where the far trail turns.   10

*To be sung
or read with
great speed.*

Santa Fé Trail. The poem is one of the most famous examples of Lindsay's myth-building ability. Here he sees America as if circled by cars which, like Apollo's chariot, will eventually circle the world. But the poet, although not unenthusiastic about the equality of travel and modern wanderlust, prefers to tramp over the country—his way of observing and of contemplation. 8. **brazen car.** In Greek mythology, the sun was Apollo's chariot, and here Lindsay has tied the image up with the headlights of a racing automobile.

Its eyes are lamps like the eyes of dragons.
It drinks gasoline from big red flagons.
Butting through the delicate mists of the morning,
It comes like lightning, goes past roaring.
It will hail all the windmills, taunting, ringing,   15
Dodge the cyclones,
Count the milestones,
On through the ranges the prairie-dog tills—
Scooting past the cattle on the thousand hills. . . .
Ho for the tear-horn, scare-horn, dare-horn,   20   *To be read or*
Ho for the gay-horn, bark-horn, bay-horn.   *sung in a roll-*
Ho for Kansas, land that restores us   *ing bass, with*
When houses choke us, and great books bore us!   *some delibera-*
Sunrise Kansas, harvesters' Kansas,   *tion.*
A million men have found you before us.   25
A million men have found you before us.

II. In Which Many Autos Pass Westward

I want live things in their pride to remain.   *In an even,*
I will not kill one grasshopper vain   *deliberate,*
Though he eats a hole in my shirt like a door.   *narrative*
I let him out, give him one chance more.   30   *manner.*
Perhaps, while he gnaws my hat in his whim,
Grasshopper lyrics occur to him.

I am a tramp by the long trail's border,
Given to squalor, rags and disorder.
I nap and amble and yawn and look,   35
Write fool-thoughts in my grubby book,
Recite to the children, explore at my ease,
Work when I work, beg when I please,
Give crank-drawings, that make folks stare
To the half-grown boys in the sunset glare,   40
And get me a place to sleep in the hay
At the end of a live-and-let-live day.

I find in the stubble of the new-cut weeds
A whisper and a feasting, all one needs:
The whisper of the strawberries, white and red   45
Here where the new-cut weeds lie dead.

But I would not walk all alone till I die
Without some life-drunk horns going by.
And up round this apple-earth they come
Blasting the whispers of the morning dumb:—   50
Cars in a plain realistic row.
And fair dreams fade
When the raw horns blow.

On each snapping pennant
A big black name:—   55
The careering city
Whence each car came.

They tour from Memphis, Atlanta, Savannah,
Tallahassee and Texarkana.
They tour from St. Louis, Columbus, Manistee,   60   *Like a train-*
They tour from Peoria, Davenport, Kankakee.   *caller in a*
Cars from Concord, Niagara, Boston,   *Union Depot.*
Cars from Topeka, Emporia, and Austin.
Cars from Chicago, Hannibal, Cairo.
Cars from Alton, Oswego, Toledo.   65
Cars from Buffalo, Kokomo, Delphi,
Cars from Lodi, Carmi, Loami.
Ho for Kansas, land that restores us
When houses choke us, and great books bore us!
While I watch the highroad   70
And look at the sky,
While I watch the clouds in amazing grandeur
Roll their legions without rain
Over the blistering Kansas plain—
While I sit by the milestone   75
And watch the sky,
The United States
Goes by.

Listen to the iron-horns, ripping, racking.   *To be given*
Listen to the quack-horns, slack and clacking.   80   *very harshly,*
Way down the road, trilling like a toad,   *with a*
Here comes the *dice*-horn, here comes the *vice*-horn,   *snapping ex-*
Here comes the *snarl*-horn, *brawl*-horn, *lewd*-horn,   *plosiveness.*
Followed by the *prude*-horn, bleak and squeaking:—
(Some of them from Kansas, some of them from Kansas.)   85
Here comes the *hod*-horn, *plod*-horn, *sod*-horn,
Nevermore-to-*roam*-horn, *loam*-horn, *home*-horn.
(Some of them from Kansas, some of them from Kansas.)
    Far away the Rachel-Jane
    Not defeated by the horns   90
    Sings amid a hedge of thorns:—
    "Love and life,   *To be read or*
    Eternal youth—   *sung, well-*
    Sweet, sweet, sweet, sweet,   *nigh in a*
    Dew and glory,   95   *whisper.*
    Love and truth,
    Sweet, sweet, sweet, sweet."
WHILE SMOKE-BLACK FREIGHTS ON THE DOUBLE-TRACKED RAILROAD,   *Louder and*
DRIVEN AS THOUGH BY THE FOUL FIEND'S OX-GOAD,   *louder,*
SCREAMING TO THE WEST COAST, SCREAMING TO THE EAST,   100   *faster and*
CARRY OFF A HARVEST, BRING BACK A FEAST,   *faster.*
AND HARVESTING MACHINERY AND HARNESS FOR THE BEAST,
THE HAND-CARS WHIZ, AND RATTLE ON THE RAILS,
THE SUNLIGHT FLASHES ON THE TIN DINNER-PAILS.
And then, in an instant, ye modern men,   105   *In a rolling*
Behold the procession once again,   *bass, with*

58. Memphis, Atlanta, a catalogue of American place names on the road west, notable for their fine sound.

The United States goes by!
Listen to the iron-horns, ripping, racking,
Listen to the *wise*-horn, desperate-to-*advise* horn,
Listen to the *fast*-horn, *kill*-horn, *blast*-horn. . . .   110
      Far away the Rachel-Jane
      Not defeated by the horns
      Sings amid a hedge of thorns:—
      "Love and life,
      Eternal youth,   115
      Sweet, sweet, sweet, sweet,
      Dew and glory,
      Love and truth.
      Sweet, sweet, sweet, sweet."
The mufflers open on a score of cars   120
With wonderful thunder,
CRACK, CRACK, CRACK,
CRACK-CRACK, CRACK-CRACK,
CRACK, CRACK, CRACK,
Listen to the gold-horn . . .   125
Old-horn . . .
Cold horn . . .
And all of the tunes, till the night comes down
On hay-stack, and ant-hill, and wind-bitten town.
Then far in the west, as in the beginning,   130
Dim in the distance, sweet in retreating,
Hark to the faint-horn, quaint-horn, saint-horn,
Hark to the calm-horn, balm-horn, psalm-horn. . . .

They are hunting the goals that they understand:—
San-Francisco and the brown sea-sand.   135
My goal is the mystery the beggars win.
I am caught in the web the night-winds spin.
The edge of the wheat-ridge speaks to me.
I talk with the leaves of the mulberry tree.
And now I hear, as I sit all alone   140
In the dusk, by another big Santa-Fé stone,
The souls of the tall corn gathering round
And the gay little souls of the grass in the ground.
Listen to the tale the cottonwood tells.
Listen to the windmills, singing o'er the wells.   145
Listen to the whistling flutes without price
Of myriad prophets out of paradise.
Harken to the wonder
That the night-air carries. . . .
Listen . . . to . . . the . . . whisper . . .   150
Of . . . the . . . prairie . . . fairies
      Singing o'er the fairy plain:—
      "Sweet, sweet, sweet, sweet.
      Love and glory,
      Stars and rain,   155
      Sweet, sweet, sweet, sweet. . . ."

*increasing
deliberation.*

*With a snap-
ping explo-
siveness.*

*To be sung or
read well-
nigh in a
whisper.*

*To be brawled
in the begin-
ning with a
snapping
explosiveness,
ending in a
languorous
chant.*

*To be sung to
exactly the
same whispered
tune as the
first five lines.*

*This section
beginning
sonorously,
ending in a
languorous
whisper.*

*To the same
whispered tune
as the Rachel-
Jane song—
but very slowly.*

596

HART CRANE

Harold Hart Crane was born on July 21, 1899, at Garretsville, Ohio. His parents, Clarence A. and Grace Edna (Hart) Crane, were from well-to-do families of New England stock. Both parents were of unstable temperament, and from earliest childhood the boy was subjected to family quarrels. Made shy by the emotional insecurity of his home, he felt himself set apart from other children, and his school days in Warren and later in Cleveland were lonely.

At fourteen Hart Crane began to write poetry. In 1916 *Bruno's Bohemia*, a Greenwich Village publication, carried his first printed poem. Convinced by this success that poetry would be his lifework, he was happy to leave high school before his courses were finished. His father and mother permanently separated that same year and Hart, who had always taken his mother's side, for a time made his home with her. To lighten the strain upon his mother's income he at once found work in a print shop. Later, however, with his father's aid he was sent to New York to prepare for admission to Columbia. He attended art showings and concerts, displaying in his indifference toward the issues of the First World War his real inability to analyze the effect of society upon himself.

Shortly he was engrossed in his own study of the poetry of his contemporaries and of Marlowe, Webster, Donne, and Blake. He examined with acute critical intelligence the little magazines then introducing the current poets. Although in the next ten years his work was to appear in almost all these publications— *The Measure, The Double Dealer, The Little Review, The Gargoyle, The Criterion, The Broom, Secession, The Pagan, The Dial*—Crane never subscribed for long, if at all, to any established esthetic dictum.

Crane was already beginning his own first sustained work when T. S. Eliot's *Waste Land* appeared in 1922. He acknowledged Eliot as one of the greatest of modern poets, but his reaction to Eliot's study of disillusionment and decay was that "after this perfection of death nothing is possible but a motion of some kind." Crane saw immediately that once a fine poet had dramatized our modern emotional and mental chaos, that work was finished. It was, then, the duty of another poet to try to see beyond chaos to some new synthesis of values. It was probably in reaction to Eliot that Crane turned to Whitman for a statement of belief in America.

The years between 1918 and 1925, although they brought Crane maturity of style, brought him also economic and emotional harassment. Friends seemed to lose faith in him, family troubles increased, and he suffered alternately from want of work and from the stultification of his creative power because of the need of earning a living. He turned his hand to such varied employments as riveter in a Lake Erie shipyard, packer in his father's confectionery warehouse, reporter on the Cleveland *Plain Dealer*, salesman and manager in his father's tea-rooms, and later, writer of advertising copy in Cleveland and New York. In order to blast poetry out of his weary head in the evenings, he formed the enduring habit of writing under the double stimulation of wine and of music played on the portable phonograph he carried everywhere. The misery of the intervals between periods of creative work was intensified by the longings of a morbidly insecure personality for a permanent home. Crane's drinking bouts and debaucheries became increasingly violent as he became more disillusioned with the love affairs his nature continually demanded. Yet it is significant that he never wished to join his expatriate literary friends in post-war Paris.

While he was living at Columbia Heights, Brooklyn, and daily crossing the Brooklyn Bridge, the theme of *The Bridge* grew in him. The entire work was to re-create the major forces in the development of American civilization. In the winter of 1925–26, which Crane was enabled to spend in the artists' colony of

Patterson, New York, through the financial aid of the art patron Otto Kahn, the actual composition of *The Bridge* was begun. In June 1926 he sailed to his grandparents' plantation on the Isle of Pines, near Cuba. There three fourths of the poem was written; sections of it were published abroad in both *The Broom* and *The Criterion*. The collection *White Buildings* was published in the fall of the same year.

A savage hurricane demolished his grandparents' home, and Crane returned to New York in October, the period of creativity which had produced his greatest work at end. Although he now found himself considered the leading poet of his generation by the critics he most respected, in the next two years his life was more erratic and dissipated and more driven by money needs than ever before. He began to suffer from insomnia, and he seemed to lose faith in his own vision of humanity and in his ability to meet again the high standard of the unfinished *Bridge*. In the spring of 1928 he lived with his mother in California, but a bitter quarrel concluded his visit. He went to London and Paris, but it was not until his return to New York in December 1929 that he could bring himself to complete *The Bridge* (1930), grinding out for the most part certain poor sections to meet a printer's deadline.

After a period of desperation worse than any preceding, Crane came to friendly terms with his father and worked about his father's inn at Chagrin Falls, near Cleveland. Here he led a happy, active, and simple life, and very easily abstained from liquor. Awarded a Guggenheim Fellowship, he determined to go to Mexico, where he planned to compose a poetic drama of the conquest. But inspiration did not come, and as ever he was wretched in new surroundings. Although he did write one poem, "The Broken Tower," in his high magnificent style, the friends of whom he had asked criticism, not knowing his desperate need for assurance, delayed their replies too long. His drunken violences reached new heights of self-torment and abuse of those who loved him. In April 1932, learning from his stepmother that the entire estate of his father (who had died the year before) might be swallowed by a lawsuit, he set sail for New York. On board he continued his drinking. Shortly before noon on April 26, he walked to the stern of the ship and vaulted over the railing into the wake. His body was not recovered. His third volume, *Collected Poems,* appeared posthumously in 1933.

Although critical opinion is not in complete agreement concerning Hart Crane, many important critics acknowledge that despite his obscurity he is one of our most significant poets. Philip Horton's biography, from which this résumé has been taken, explains in detail the poet's psychology and analyzes his way of working. R. P. Blackmur's *The Double Agent* contains an essay minutely analyzing certain of Crane's difficult poems. There has been considerable literary comment concerning Crane's use of the Samuel Greenberg poems, only recently published by New Directions. These writings of a sensitive but psychotic youth who died early were of course known to Crane, but Crane's use of certain images taken from them is entirely un-imitative.

That Crane is obscure to the average reader cannot be denied. He was fundamentally a lyric poet working with complex images. His *Bridge*, although Crane thought of it as an epic about America, breaks into a number of long lyrics. Some of the most intelligent remarks about this book, and about Crane's poetry in general, are made in Ben Belitt's unpublished essay on Crane:

> Among the possible explanations for the failure of Hart Crane's *The Bridge* is the surmise that Crane, as a miniaturist, was never at home in the "epical" form. In general, his tools are the tools of the miniaturist, narrow and delicate edges for cutting in intaglio, mineral surfaces to take light strangely and deflect it glancingly. . . . The stroke is at once a line and a form; no sooner does the blade depress the surface, than it converts its bias into a plane, and its plane into a facet. Its complexity is at least twofold, for it not only is a complexity of lines, but of surfaces as well. It is from the interplay of line with surface, that the design as a whole communicates its "meanings."
>
> Obviously, such a technique is at odds with the formal exigencies of the "epic" which moves in perspectives rather than planes, and masses rather than facets, and in which the individual stroke is not final, but fluid. Yet when one returns from the analogy to the subject with which it is concerned, one discovers that Crane was

598

capable of something more than the devices of the miniaturist. It is impossible to read such sections of *The Bridge* as "Ave Maria" and "The Tunnel" for example without feeling that the poet's vision was almost the reverse of the miniaturists, that, indeed, its long rebounding cadences and breathing rhythms were the product of a "massive" rather than a linear energy.

Belitt goes on to point out that Crane's confusions are often confusions of focus in which mass obscures detail, and detail, mass. "Crane's poetry," he states, "is poetry in which ideas are caught up and wrenched out of their lodging, subjected to change in speeds and changing stature." That Crane was caught by his own images and by their double or triple significances and associations is evident in all his work. As Belitt says, "His world is a dream world whose dimensional integers are in continual flux." In such a world, time expands and contracts according to the poet's emotional state. Despite Crane's sense of flux and change, he wished to state an affirmative attitude toward life and a belief in a synthesis of values. As a symbol of the unity in all men's lives, he chose man's anonymous power to create. And in seeking an image of this power he selected the bridge, created by all men working together. He saw it, even as Whitman saw the railroad, as a symbol of time and space, of unity between past and present, and between various phases of American life. Crane's was the logic of the dreamer which has no validity outside the dream. Actually his world was one of chaos to which he reacted violently. His poetry consequently is greatest for its powerful lyrical intensity and for the amazing variety and explosiveness of its imagery. He had been born into the wrong period to accomplish what he wished, to carry into this century Whitman's faith in democratic brotherhood. The democracy which Whitman prophesied had become a capitalistic society; there was no dream of socialism. Crane could see that scientific advancements had made it necessary for men to work together in order to create great cities, with their bridges and other means of communication. He wrote of man's scientific creations, but he had no vision of man's mass power to change his world, and he died before any revolutionary faith was prevalent among the artists.

He stands, therefore, between the school of poets who sang of man's spiritual poverty and the school who sing of man's will to bring about social change. He affirms man's greatness by emphasizing the greatness of his works, not the greatness of man himself.

Lachrymae Christi

WHITELY, while benzine
　Rinsings from the moon
Dissolve all but the windows of the mills
(Inside the sure machinery
Is still　　　　　　　　　　　　　　　5
And curdled only where a sill
Sluices its one unyielding smile)

Immaculate venom binds
The fox's teeth, and swart
Thorns freshen on the year's　　　　　10
First blood. From flanks unfended,
Twanged red perfidies of spring
Are trillion on the hill.

And the nights opening
Chant pyramids,—　　　　　　　　　15
Anoint with innocence,—recall
To music and retrieve what perjuries
Had galvanized the eyes.
　　　　　　　　　While chime
Beneath and all around

The poems of Hart Crane are reprinted from *Collected Poems* by permission of Liveright Publishing Corporation. *Lachrymae Christi*, Christ's tears. **1. Whitely . . . Rinsings.** The scene is a mill town in spring. Crane uses industrial images like "benzine rinsings" for moonlight to indicate the cleaning effect of the moon shining upon the mills, its light reflected on the windows. Inside the machinery is quiet, save for a sill or sluice in which water is running. "Sill" (l. 6) means threshold, and Crane here means the line over which the water flows. The only motion in the factory is the sluice, which catches and reflects the moonlight. **8. Immaculate venom.** A paraphrase of this stanza may be given as follows: a cleansing poison (the moonlight) has stopped the machinery (the fox's teeth), and swart thorns, suggestive of the thorns worn by the crucified Christ (rather than flowers), indicate that spring is here. Along the hill these thorns twang (rather than sing) perfidies or lies (rather than the truth) of spring. The poet is deliberately using imagery contradictory to the usual sentimental images of spring. **14. And . . . opening**, a mystical assertion of the beauty of the night and of the poet's vision of beauty, despite the ugliness of the town. **15. Chant pyramids.** The night sings of mystery, and anoints with innocence, despite the fact that perjuries (lies against beauty, or the realities of this industrial scene) have galvanized (plated with metal) the eyes and blinded them to true beauty.

Distilling clemencies,—worms' 20
Inaudible whistle, tunneling
Not penitence
But song, as these
Perpetual fountains, vines,—

Thy Nazarene and tinder eyes. 25

(Let sphinxes from the ripe
Borage of death have cleared my tongue
Once and again; vermin and rod
No longer bind. Some sentient cloud
Of tears flocks through the tendoned loam: 30
Betrayed stones slowly speak.)

Names peeling from Thine eyes
And their undimming lattices of flame,
Spell out in palm and pain
Compulsion of the year, O Nazarene. 35

Lean long from sable, slender boughs,
Unstanched and luminous. And as the nights
Strike from Thee perfect spheres,
Lift up in lilac-emerald breath the grail
of earth again—
                    Thy face 40
From charred and riven stakes, O
Dionysus, Thy
Unmangled target smile.

To Brooklyn Bridge

How many dawns, chill from his rippling
    rest
The seagull's wings shall dip and pivot him,
Shedding white rings of tumult, building high
Over the chained bay waters Liberty—

Then, with inviolate curve, forsake our eyes
As apparitional as sails that cross 6
Some page of figures to be filed away;
—Till elevators drop us from our day . . .

I think of cinemas, panoramic sleights
With multitudes bent toward some flashing
    scene 10
Never disclosed, but hastened to again,
Foretold to other eyes on the same screen;

And Thee, across the harbor, silver-paced
As though the sun took step of thee, yet left
Some motion ever unspent in thy stride,— 15
Implicitly thy freedom staying thee!

Out of some subway scuttle, cell or loft
A bedlamite speeds to thy parapets,
Tilting there momently, shrill shirt ballooning,
A jest falls from the speechless caravan. 20

20. **worms' Inaudible whistle.** This is probably one of Crane's complex images in which two ideas are associated —the idea of worms tunneling through the soil toward light, and the idea of underground trains running between different sections of the mill.   25. **Thy . . . eyes.** Note the word "tinder" (inflammable substance), an image of Christ's eyes, always to be relit by any new conception of beauty.   26. **(Let sphinxes . . . speak.).** The poet prays to be resurrected also, to speak as a sphinx might or as one come back from death might. He wishes to be freed of the gravestones. R. P. Blackmur, in his book *The Double Agent*, says of this passage: "It is syntax rather than grammar that is obscure. I take it that 'let' is here a somewhat homemade adjective and that Crane is making a direct statement, so that the problem is to construe the right meanings of the right words in the right references; which will be an admirable exercise in exegesis, but an exercise only. The applicable senses of 'let' are these: neglected or weary, permitted or prevented, hired, and let in the sense that blood is let. [*Editor's note*: It seems possible that "let" here may mean "allow" and be a verb.] Sphinxes are inscrutable, have secrets, propound riddles to travellers and strangle those who cannot answer. 'Borage' has at least three senses: something rough (in sound suggestive of barrage and barrier), a blue-flowered, hairy-leaved plant, and a cordial made from the plant. *The Shorter Oxford Dictionary* quotes this jingle from Hooker: 'I Borage always bring courage.' One guess is that Crane meant something to the effect that if you meditate enough on death it has the same bracing and warming effect as drinking a cordial, so that the riddles of life (or death) are answered. But something very near the contrary may have been intended; or both. In any case a guess is ultimately worthless because, with the defective syntax, the words do not verify it. Crane had a profound feeling for the hearts of words, and how they beat and cohabited, but here they overtopped him; the meanings in the words themselves are superior to the use to which he put them. The operation of selective cross-pollination not only failed but was not even rightly attempted. The language remains in the condition of that which it was intended to express: in the flux of intoxicated sense; whereas the language of the other lines of this poem here examined—the language, not the sense—is disintoxicated and candid. The point is that the quality of Crane's success is also the quality of his failure, and the distinction is perhaps by the hair of accident." As this intricate explanation of Blackmur's indicates, this passage is one of the more difficult in Crane, who, at times, used words for their sound value rather than for precise meaning. 34. **Spell . . . pain,** a reference to the suffering prior to the Resurrection and to Palm Sunday.

36. **Lean . . . sable.** The images here suggest the crucifixion and the old druidical sacrifices. The images of Christ and Dionysus, both images of resurrection, are used interchangeably, to indicate how although life is constantly sacrificed, it rises again.   41. **riven,** split.   42. **Dionysus,** Bacchus, god of wine and drama and spring.
To Brooklyn Bridge. 1. **How many dawns . . . Liberty.** The image of the sea-gull in flight (true freedom) is presented as against the image of the Statue of Liberty (false freedom). 8. **Till . . . day.** The gull is contrasted with our mechanical flight in elevators.   9. **I think . . . screen.** This stanza describes the poet's reflection on the monotony of most lives in the modern city. To city dwellers the moving-picture "screen" is a prophecy of a dream place never attained and an image of sentimental emotion.   13. **And . . . thee!** This is an image of the quietness and dignity of the Bridge, of its motion in stillness.   17. **Out . . . caravan.** This stanza presents the silly gesture of a suicide jumping from the Bridge and the resulting reaction of the crowd that sees this.

Down Wall, from girder into street noon leaks,
A rip-tooth of the sky's acetylene;
All afternoon the cloud-flown derricks turn . . .
Thy cables breathe the North Atlantic still.

And obscure as that heaven of the Jews,   25
Thy guerdon . . . Accolade thou dost bestow
Of anonymity time cannot raise:
Vibrant reprieve and pardon thou dost show.

O harp and altar, of the fury fused,
(How could mere toil align thy choiring
        strings!)   30
Terrific threshold of the prophet's pledge,
Prayer of pariah, and the lover's cry,—

Again the traffic lights that skim thy swift
Unfractioned idiom, immaculate sigh of stars,
Beading thy path—condense eternity: 35
And we have seen night lifted in thine arms.

Under thy shadow by the piers I waited;
Only in darkness is thy shadow clear.
The City's fiery parcels all undone,
Already snow submerges an iron year . . .

O Sleepless as the river under thee,   41
Vaulting the sea, the prairies' dreaming sod,
Unto us lowliest sometime sweep, descend
And of the curveship lend a myth to God.

---

21. Down . . . still. This stanza pictures the swift passage of the city day on Wall Street (financial center of the country). The enduring strength of the Bridge is contrasted with the flight of time.   **25. And . . . guerdon.** The guerdon (reward) is as obscure in its intellectual beauty as the heaven of the Jews. After a stanza almost purely descriptive, the poet begins here to use the language of religious exaltation. He states his faith that art such as is created by men working anonymously together to erect modern beauty (the Bridge) is reason enough for believing in man's holiness. Crane was unwilling to restrict the idea of art to the fine arts. He saw in our modern industrial age new expressions of the creative imagination as man worked scientifically and esthetically to build towers, bridges, and airplanes.   **26. Accolade . . . raise,** meaning that accolade (the act of knighting) is bestowed on anonymous creative work which time will not destroy.   **28. Vibrant reprieve,** thrilling pardon. Here Crane unites the idea of the vibrancy of the Bridge with the religious thrill of pardon, implying that since man is capable of creating beauty in this scientific age, he may be pardoned his materialism.   **29. O harp and altar.** Here the Bridge is both physically described and presented as a religious symbol.   **30. (How . . . strings!).** The poet asks how toil could create such beauty.   **31. Terrific . . . cry.** Here the Bridge is addressed as a prophet's pledge and the prayer of an outcast and a lover's cry, all symbols of things which endure.   **33. Again . . . arms,** an exact picture of the lighted Bridge and at the same time a further statement of the eternal endurance of beauty.   **37. Under thy shadow, etc.** In these last two stanzas the poet places himself near the pier of the Bridge in order to see its full shadow. Around him the city lights up (as if it were a Christmas tree). The poet imagines the Bridge extending itself further and further over sea and over prairie, continuing forever. He asks that it, with its beautiful curves, be considered a modern myth symbolic of man's spiritual integrity.

For the Marriage of Faustus and Helen

"And so we may arrive by Talmud skill
And profane Greek to raise the building up
Of Helen's house against the Ismaelite,
King of Thogarma, and his habergeons
Brimstony, blue and fiery; and the force
Of King Abaddon, and the beast of Cittim;
Which Rabbi David Kimchi, Onkelos,
And Aben Ezra do interpret Rome."
                    —THE ALCHEMIST

I

THE MIND has shown itself at times
Too much the baked and labeled dough
Divided by accepted multitudes.
Across the stacked partitions of the day—
Across the memoranda, baseball scores,   5
The stenographic smiles and stock quotations
Smutty wings flash out equivocations.

The mind is brushed by sparrow wings;
Numbers, rebuffed by asphalt, crowd
The margins of the day, accent the curbs,   10
Convoying divers dawns on every corner
To druggist, barber and tobacconist,
Until the graduate opacities of evening
Take them away as suddenly to somewhere
Virginal perhaps, less fragmentary, cool.   15

    *There is the world dimensional for those
    untwisted by the love of things irrecon-
    cilable. . .*

For the Marriage, etc. The poem uses the image of Faust as a symbol of the modern scientific or skeptical mind. The image of Helen represents modern civilization as typified by a large city, probably New York. Helen (the metropolitan city) is wooed by Faustus (skeptical modern man). The poem opens with a statement of the confusion in our daily life. With the line "There is the world dimensional . . ." (l. 16) the poet states his faith that even for the modern man or poet there can be a synthesis of values. The poem goes on then recording images of a poet's awareness of city beauty, and the first section closes with a declaration of the poet's love for the metropolis. The second section opens with what is apparently a Harlem or primitive dance scene. The poet would accept the modern nuances and nervosities of city life. The third section is a ride through the city at dawn in which a sense of death is given. With line 112, "We did not ask for that, but have survived," the poet embraces the intricacy of beauty in our age—a beauty which comes out of man's researches in the past and will be extended by his researches into the future. "The imagination spans beyond despair" (l. 134) is a line which begins the poet's statement of his belief in man's creative power or his power to love, despite commercialism.
The Alchemist, a play by Ben Jonson (1573-1637). This quotation is a part of a chant calling upon the secret, or esoteric, spirits in the art of alchemy.
1. The mind, etc. These first two stanzas describe the average mind of modern man taken up by baseball scores, etc., brushed by sparrow wings (brief imaginary moments), and sometimes arriving at peace in the gradual cloudiness of evening.

And yet, suppose some evening I forgot
The fare and transfer, yet got by that way
Without recall,—lost yet poised in traffic.   19
Then I might find your eyes across an aisle,
Still flickering with those prefigurations—
Prodigal, yet uncontested now,
Half-riant before the jerky window frame.

There is some way, I think, to touch   24
Those hands of yours that count the nights
Stippled with pink and green advertisements.
And now, before its arteries turn dark,
I would have you meet this bartered blood.
Imminent in his dream, none better knows   29
The white wafer cheek of love, or offers words
Lightly as moonlight on the eaves meets snow.

Reflective conversion of all things
At your deep blush, when ecstasies thread
The limbs and belly, when rainbows spread
Impinging on the throat and sides . . .   35
Inevitable, the body of the world
Weeps in inventive dust for the hiatus
That winks above it, bluet in your breasts.

The earth may glide diaphanous to death;
But if I lift my arms it is to bend   40
To you who turned away once, Helen, know-
        ing
The press of troubled hands, too alternate
With steel and soil to hold you endlessly.
I meet you, therefore, in that eventual flame
You found in final chains, no captive then—   45
Beyond their million brittle, bloodshot eyes;
White, through white cities passed on to as-
        sume
That world which comes to each of us alone.

Accept a lone eye riveted to your plane,   49
Bent axle of devotion along companion ways
That beat, continuous, to hourless days—
One inconspicuous, glowing orb of praise.

II

Brazen hypnotics glitter here;
Glee shifts from foot to foot,
Magnetic to their tremolo.   55
This crashing opéra bouffe,
Blest excursion! this ricochet
From roof to roof—
Know, Olympians, we are breathless
While nigger cupids scour the stars!   60

A thousand light shrugs balance us
Through snarling hails of melody.
White shadows slip across the floor
Splayed like cards from a loose hand;
Rhythmic ellipses lead into canters   65
Until somewhere a rooster banters.

Greet naïvely—yet intrepidly
New soothings, new amazements
That cornets introduce at every turn—
And you may fall downstairs with me   70
With perfect grace and equanimity.
Or, plaintively scud past shores
Where, by strange harmonic laws
All relatives, serene and cool,
Sit rocked in patent armchairs.   75

O, I have known metallic paradises
Where cuckoos clucked to finches
Above the deft catastrophes of drums.
While titters hailed the groans of death
Beneath gyrating awnings I have seen   80
The incunabula of the divine grotesque.
This music has a reassuring way.

The siren of the springs of guilty song—
Let us take her on the incandescent wax
Striated with nuances, nervosities   85
That we are heir to: she is still so young,
We cannot frown upon her as she smiles,
Dipping here in this cultivated storm
Amid slim skaters of the gardened skies.

17. **And yet, etc.** In this stanza the poet imagines himself on an elevated train, noticing the beauty of the city (like that of a "half-riant" [l. 23], i.e., laughing, girl), and he continues in the next stanza to speak of the beauty of the city as if the city were a woman and he the lover who would meet her at least in his dream.   28. **bartered blood.** Although his life (blood) has been sold to purchase bread in a commercial society, none knows better than he the beauty of love.   32. **Reflective conversion, etc.** This stanza continues to picture chiefly in images of light the beauty of the city (always as if it were a feminine body).   38. **bluet,** a delicate blue meadow flower. 39. **The earth, etc.** This and the last stanza are the poet's statement of almost religious devotion to the beauty of the city, a beauty which cannot be held endlessly or made captive, but can be realized only in moments of peculiar penetration.

53. **Brazen hypnotics, etc.** This whole section has to do with an impression of a Harlem dance scene. The poet exults in the various rhythms.   57. **ricochet.** The rhythm of the dance in music is pictured as rebounding from roof to roof.   67. **Greet naïvely,** etc. The next three stanzas are mere impressions of the effect of music upon the mind.   76. **O, I have . . . death,** the melody of the music like birdsongs contrasted with the drums which suggest death.   80. **Beneath gyrating awnings,** an impression of the dancehall looking like the birthplace of the grotesque in life.   83. **The siren,** Helen, or the city, pictured as a flapper to be taken out to dance.

III

Capped arbiter of beauty in this street   90
That narrows darkly into motor dawn,—
You, here beside me, delicate ambassador
Of intricate slain numbers that arise
In whispers, naked of steel;
                              religious gunman!   94
Who faithfully, yourself, will fall too soon,
And in other ways than as the wind settles
On the sixteen thrifty bridges of the city:
Let us unbind our throats of fear and pity.

                              We even,
Who drove speediest destruction
In corymbulous formations of mechanics,—   100
Who hurried the hill breezes, spouting malice
Plangent over meadows, and looked down
On rifts of torn and empty houses
Like old women with teeth unjubilant
That waited faintly, briefly and in vain: 105

We know, eternal gunman, our flesh remem-
          bers
The tensile boughs, the nimble blue plateaus,
The mounted, yielding cities of the air!
That saddled sky that shook down vertical
Repeated play of fire—no hypogeum   110
Of wave or rock was good against one hour.

We did not ask for that, but have survived,
And will persist to speak again before
All stubble streets that have not curved   114
To memory, or known the ominous lifted arm
That lowers down the arc of Helen's brow
To saturate with blessing and dismay.

A goose, tobacco and cologne—
Three-winged and gold-shod prophecies of
          heaven,   119
The lavish heart shall always have to leaven
And spread with bells and voices, and atone
The abating shadows of our conscript dust.

Anchises' navel, dripping of the sea,—
The hands Erasmus dipped in gleaming tides,
Gathered the voltage of blown blood and vine;
Delve upward for the new and scattered wine,
O brother-thief of time, that we recall.   127
Laugh out the meager penance of their days
Who dare not share with us the breath re-
          leased,
The substance drilled and spent beyond re-
          pair   130
For golden, or the shadow of gold hair.

Distinctly praise the years, whose volatile
Blamed bleeding hands extend and thresh the
          height
The imagination spans beyond despair,
Outpacing bargain, vocable and prayer.

Chaplinesque

WE MAKE our meek adjustments,
          Contented with such random consola-
tions
As the wind deposits
In slithered and too ample pockets.

For we can still love the world, who find   5
A famished kitten on the step, and know
Recesses for it from the fury of the street,
Or warm torn elbow coverts.

90. **Capped arbiter, etc.** The poet has presented a Harlem night scene as a picture of the Jazz Age of the twenties. Now in section three he addresses his companion, Gorham Munson, a conservative critic with whom Crane was staying. "Capped arbiter" is a direct reference to the academic cap, typical of such scholars. The critic is pictured as shooting down other writers as he himself will in time be, figuratively speaking, killed. He is the religious gunman who arrives home at dawn with the poet. He is called religious because he, as a humanist, slays for what he considers an ideal the less moralistic poets of the younger generation. The second stanza is the picture of the youth of the twenties who lived by sensation and who knew the war and its destruction. 100. **corymbulous,** having an indeterminate number of blossomings. 102. **Plangent,** resounding noisily. 107. **tensile,** stretched out. The picture here is of nature as seen from an airplane, one such as a youth who had been in air warfare might remember. 110. **hypogeum,** subterranean part of the building. This whole stanza is concluded with a statement that the youth of the twenties took no shelter against experience, hid underground from no single hour's excitement. 112. **We did not ask,** youth does not ask certainty but feeds on excitement. 114. **stubble,** covered with remnants of the past. The whole stanza means that all memories of the past will be added to by modern creative writers who will persist in giving new interpretations of Helen (such interpretations as Crane, for example, gives in this entire poem).

118. **A goose . . . cologne,** a reference to the forms of gratification acceptable to the middle class and to the bourgeois critic contrasted in the last three lines of the stanza with ideas of the lavish spending of life characteristic of the young poet. 123. **Anchises,** the father of Aeneas by Venus. He was carried from burning Troy out into the sea on his son's shoulders. Crane uses the reference as an indication of the glory of Greek civilization carried into Rome. 124. **Erasmus,** Dutch philosopher and scholar (1466?–1536). Crane uses him as a figure to symbolize the beginning of the Renaissance. He was one of the scholars who crossed the sea and brought culture to England. In other words, both Anchises and Erasmus symbolize the spread of art into new fields, and Crane indicates in the last four lines of this stanza that the high-spirited youth of the twenties will further art. 132. **Distinctly . . . years, etc.** Crane praises the years of the past, which, even though they record suffering, record also how the imagination spans beyond despair.
Chaplinesque. If the reader will keep in mind Chaplin's characteristic gestures in the moving pictures, he will see that in this poem Chaplin is used as the symbol of the modern man's disillusionments and ways of getting through life without any assurance of its value here or hereafter. 4. **slithered,** ragged. The picture here is of Chaplin's typical costume with its large pockets always empty. 8. **coverts,** shelters. The reference again is to the tenderness with which Chaplin protects weaker things than himself, even though he is always down and out.

We will sidestep, and to the final smirk
Dally the doom of that inevitable thumb   10
That slowly chafes its puckered index toward
    us,
Facing the dull squint with what innocence
And what surprise!

And yet these fine collapses are not lies   14
More than the pirouettes of any pliant cane;
Our obsequies are, in a way, no enterprise.
We can evade you, and all else but the heart:
What blame to us if the heart live on.

The game enforces smirks; but we have seen
The moon in lonely alleys make   20
A grail of laughter of an empty ash can,
And through all sound of gaiety and quest
Have heard a kitten in the wilderness.

The Hurricane

Lo, LORD, Thou ridest!
  Lord, Lord, Thy swifting heart

Naught stayeth, naught now bideth
But's smithereened apart!

Ay! Scripture flee'th stone!   5
Milk-bright, Thy chisel wind

Rescindeth flesh from bone
To quivering whittlings thinned—

Swept—whistling straw! Battered,
Lord, e'en boulders now out-leap   10

Rock sockets, levin-lathered!
Nor, Lord, may worm out-deep

Thy drum's gambade, its plunge abscond!
Lord God, while summits crashing

Whip sea-kelp screaming on blond   15
Sky-seethe, high heaven dashing—

Thou ridest to the door, Lord!
Thou bidest wall nor floor, Lord!

The Broken Tower

THE BELL-ROPE that gathers God at dawn
  Dispatches me as though I dropped down
    the knell
Of a spent day—to wander the cathedral lawn
From pit to crucifix, feet chill on steps from hell.

Have you not heard, have you not seen that
    corps   5
Of shadows in the tower, whose shoulders sway

9. We will sidestep, etc. This stanza is a picture of Chaplin's dodging the thumb of a policeman pointed in his direction, and the thumb for the modern man is, of course, death. In other words, we smirk and pretend innocence, although we know we face death.   **14. And, etc.** This stanza gives pictures of two of Chaplin's favorite attitudes, his sudden collapses when overcome by a situation and his way of pirouetting his cane when he escapes from any danger. These two attitudes are characteristic of modern man, whose prayers are a task of no importance and who lives by accepting whatever comes, evading most things but unable to stop feeling.   **19. The game enforces smirks, etc.** Life enforces smirks, but nevertheless modern man sees beauty, though somewhat humorously, in an empty ashcan which may recall to him the image of the Holy Grail sought by King Arthur's knights. And he may hear, instead of a voice in the wilderness, a Biblical reference to the voice of God, a kitten in the wilderness, or the small voice of pity.
The Hurricane. This poem, written after Crane had experienced a hurricane on the Isle of Pines, is an attempt to get down in words the motion of the storm. The rhythm is an imitation of that most commonly employed by Gerard Manley Hopkins, a poet of the second half of the nineteenth century. Hopkins developed a system of accented rhythm and alliteration related to that used in early Anglo-Saxon poetry.   **5. Scripture flee'th stone,** a reference to the fact that the stone on which the Ten Commandments were carved was broken; here used as an image of the world broken by the hurricane.

11. levin-lathered, lathered with lightning.   **13. gambade,** flourish. **abscond,** escape. The whole passage here means that nothing may escape from the noise of the whirlwind's thunder.   **15. Whip sea-kelp . . . dashing.** Sea weed which makes the water look blond seems to boil as high as heaven.
The Broken Tower. This is the last important poem Crane wrote. It was finished not long before he committed suicide. The theme of the poem is that the poet feels himself to have been destroyed by the intensity of his imagination. The first four stanzas, in which many images of bells are used, refer to the imagination which destroys the tower (or the body). The body is shattered, as it were, by the poet's attempt to present his vision. In a letter to the editor Crane said that Léonie Adams' "Bell Tower" (p. 180) inspired him to write this. This was before he left New Mexico. Apparently the poem had been in his mind for some time, for there is some argument as to just when it was written. In a letter to the *New English Weekly* after Crane's death, to refute Gorham Munson's statement that the poem had been composed several years earlier, Lesley Simpson left a record of its immediate genesis: "I was with Hart Crane in Taxco, Mexico, the morning of January 27, this year," [1932] he wrote, "when he first conceived the idea of 'The Broken Tower.' The night before, being troubled with insomnia, he had risen before daybreak and walked down to the village square. It so happened that one of the innumerable Indian fiestas was to be celebrated that day, and Hart met the old Indian bell-ringer who was on his way down to the church. He and Hart were old friends, and he brought Hart up into the tower with him to help ring the bells. As Hart was swinging the clapper of the great bell, half drunk with its mighty music, the swift tropical dawn broke over the mountains. The sublimity of the scene and the thunder of the bells woke in Hart one of those gusts of joy of which only he was capable. He came striding up the hill afterwards in a sort of frenzy, refused his breakfast, and paced up and down the porch impatiently waiting for me to finish my coffee. Then he seized my arm and bore me off to the plaza where we sat in the shadow of the church, Hart the while pouring out a magnificent cascade of words. It was a Hart Crane I had never known and an experience I shall never forget." (*Hart Crane*, by Philip Horton, p. 292.)
1. The bell-rope, etc. This stanza and the next are physical descriptions of Crane's response to hearing the bells rung in the tower.

Antiphonal carillons launched before
The stars are caught and hived in the sun's ray?

The bells, I say, the bells break down their
    tower;
And swing I know not where. Their tongues en-
    grave   10
Membrane through marrow, my long-scattered
    score
Of broken intervals. . . . And I, their sexton
    slave!

Oval encyclicals in canyons heaping
The impasse high with choir. Banked voices
    slain!   14
Pagodas, campaniles with reveilles outleaping—
O terraced echoes prostrate on the plain! . . .

And so it was I entered the broken world
To trace the visionary company of love, its
    voice
An instant in the wind (I know not whither
    hurled)   19
But not for long to hold each desperate choice.

My word I poured. But was it cognate, scored

Of that tribunal monarch of the air
Whose thigh embronzes earth, strikes crystal
    Word
In wounds pledged once to hope—cleft to de-
    spair?   24

The steep encroachments of my blood left me
No answer (could blood hold such a lofty tower
As flings the question true?)—or is it she
Whose sweet mortality stirs latent power?—

And through whose pulse I hear, counting the
    strokes
My veins recall and add, revived and sure   30
The angelus of wars my chest evokes:
What I hold healed, original now, and
    pure . . .

And builds, within, a tower that is not stone
(Not stone can jacket heaven)—but slip
Of pebbles—visible wings of silence sown   35
In azure circles, widening as they dip

The matrix of the heart, lift down the eye
That shrines the quiet lake and swells a
    tower . . .
The commodious, tall decorum of that sky
Unseals her earth, and lifts love in its shower.

Van Winkle

MACADAM, gun-grey as the tunny's belt,
    Leaps from Far Rockaway to Golden Gate:
Listen! the miles a hurdy-gurdy grinds—
Down gold arpeggios mile on mile unwinds.

Times earlier, when you hurried off to school
—It is the same hour though a later day—

Streets
spread past
store and
factory—
sped by sun-
light and her
5 *smile . . .*

7. **Antiphonal,** song sung responsively. **carillons,** bells so rung as to be a musical instrument.   10. **Their tongues engrave, etc.** Beginning here Crane describes his own identification with the experience of hearing the bells. The bells seem to him his own emotions which he can ring.   13. **encyclical,** a circular letter to all connected with the Church. In this case Crane means the message which the song of the bells carries.   15. **Pagoda,** sacred tower. **campanile,** bell tower. **reveille,** the song and signal of day.
17. **And so, etc.** Beginning here Crane indicates that he (as poet) like the sexton entered the world to ring bells (write poems) about love and faith, but that these poems or songs could not long indicate his spiritual vision. In time the poetic intensity of his imagination seemed indeed to destroy his physical health, and while he was still young, he felt both mind and body failing him.
21. **My word . . . despair,** a stanza which states that he sang, but that the song was dissipated on the air, while the religious word, had he been able to state it, would have been hope rather than despair. **cognate,** kindred.   25. **The steep . . . answer.** Emotions left him no answer.   26. **could blood . . . power?** Can emotions present truth, do emotions still stir latent power?   29. **And through whose pulse, etc.** His emotions still recall the old song of hope, despite the fact that there are conflicting feelings in him concerning his vision.   31. **angelus of wars.** The angelus is the ringing of bells to call people to prayer. In other words, this phrase means that desires or prayers have struggled against one another in the poet before he could proclaim truth.   33. **And builds, etc.** The poet builds his own spiritual tower.   37. **The matrix . . . shower.** The formative qualities of the heart (or emotional feelings) command the poet to understand the whole scene of earth and heaven and to declare that love is the greatest power of the imagination.
Van Winkle, here used as the muse of memory, the connection between past and present, between childhood and harsher adult reality.   1. **Macadam . . . Gate,** a reference to the road, gray as a tuna fish, stretching from Far Rockaway, a beach resort on Long Island, New York, to San Francisco (on the Golden Gate).   3. **hurdy-gurdy . . . Smith.** A hand organ begins playing arpeggios, and the poet begins to remember school days—such figures as Pizarro (a Spanish adventurer who fought the Incas of Peru and conquered), Cortez (the Spanish conqueror of Mexico), Priscilla Mullins, and Captain John Smith.

You walked with Pizarro in a copybook,
And Cortez rode up, reining tautly in—
Firmly as coffee grips the taste,—and away!

There was Priscilla's cheek close in the wind,   10
And Captain Smith, all beard and certainty,
And Rip Van Winkle bowing by the way,—
"Is this Sleepy Hollow, friend—?" And he—

Like
memory, she
is time's
truant, shall
take you by
the hand . . .

And Rip forgot the office hours,
                        and he forgot the pay;
            Van Winkle sweeps a tenement
                        way down on Avenue A,—   15

The grind-organ says . . . Remember, remember
The cinder pile at the end of the backyard
Where we stoned the family of young
Garter snakes under . . . And the monoplanes
We launched—with paper wings and twisted   20
Rubber bands . . . Recall—recall
                        the rapid tongues
That flittered from under the ash heap day
After day whenever your stick discovered
Some sunning inch of unsuspecting fibre—
It flashed back at your thrust, as clean as fire.   25

And Rip was slowly made aware
            that he, Van Winkle, was not here
    nor there. He woke and swore he'd seen Broadway
            a Catskill daisy chain in May—

So memory, that strikes a rhyme out of a box
Or splits a random smell of flowers through glass—
Is it the whip stripped from the lilac tree   30
One day in spring my father took to me,
Or is it the Sabbatical, unconscious smile
My mother almost brought me once from church
And once only, as I recall—?

It flickered through the snow screen, blindly   35
It forsook her at the doorway, it was gone
Before I had left the window. It
Did not return with the kiss in the hall.

Macadam, gun-grey as the tunny's belt,
Leaps from Far Rockaway to Golden Gate. . . .   40
Keep hold of that nickel for car-change, Rip,—
Have you got your *"Times"*—?
And hurry along, Van Winkle—it's getting late!

---

15. **Avenue A,** an avenue of the lower East Side of New York, a slum district. The line indicates humorously that Van Winkle today would be poor.   16. **The grind-organ, etc.** The poem continues with images of childhood and only in the last three lines swings back to images of adulthood and of going to work in the morning.

RANDOLPH BOURNE

The pathetic brief life of a cripple was Randolph Silliman Bourne's; but he lived long enough to establish his name as one of the best of contemporary American essayists—small though the total volume of his work may be—and his dreams of a future America that would be a refuge for the entire world have come to have an appositeness that justifies his position as a prophet of our latter day. He was born May 30, 1886, at Bloomfield, New Jersey, and was educated at the local public schools. For a time he had the rather unusual occupation of reading proof in the offices of an automatic-piano music company, but as soon as possible he entered Columbia University, where he graduated in 1912. In college he distinguished himself as a scholar and as the editor of the local literary monthly magazine. In 1913 he took the master's degree at Columbia. He had already attracted the attention of Professors Woodbridge and Dewey of Columbia, the latter an extremely influential philosopher and educator whose work in modern progressive education has been of first importance. Bourne served as an instructor and assistant in philosophy at Columbia and contributed to numerous periodicals, among them *The Dial, The New Republic, The Yale Review, The Columbia University Quarterly, The Masses,* and *Seven Arts.* But he became discontented with Dewey's more or less pragmatic viewpoint and turned into a radical—a tendency which caused him much trouble during the First World War, for his radicalness was translated into the most complete type of pacifism. Indeed, the magazine *Seven Arts* was suspended in 1917 because of its anti-war policy, which Bourne had done much to shape. Unhappy and spiritually out of tune with the times, Bourne was a victim of the great influenza epidemic in the last year of the war, dying on December 22, 1918.

His writing first gained notice shortly after his graduation from Columbia. *Youth and Life* (1913) was a series of many-sided, tender, keen, and extremely sensitive essays, which be-lied the author's ugly physical appearance and diffident manner. The essays, moreover, were written in a fluid, limpid style that was the envy of his friends and the despair of his imitators. For a time, while he was working with Dewey, Bourne undertook some educational surveys, of which *The Gary Schools* (1916) and *Education and Living* (1917) bear direct evidence. But these rather objective studies do not represent the real Bourne. *Towards an Enduring Peace* (1916), on the other hand, is a passionate plea for harmony among all peoples; only its inappropriate date prevented it from being a great success. For the rest, Bourne's literary work is posthumous. Two volumes of essays survived him—the first, *Untimely Papers,* was edited by his friend, the poet James Oppenheim, in 1919; the second, *The History of a Literary Radical,* edited by Van Wyck Brooks (p. 59) in 1920, is generally regarded as Bourne's most significant work. The essays from this book illustrate Bourne's chief virtues—a beautiful style, a firm belief in the vitality and positiveness of all great literature, and the clear vision of a melting-pot that does indeed melt. A dreamer Bourne proved himself to be; but his dreams are probably merging into realities, and it can never be said that he has writ in water. An Anglo-Saxon by birth and breeding, he was a cosmopolitan by instinct, a lover of the beautiful by cultivation, and a sympathetic humanitarian by divine compulsion.

The History of a Literary Radical

FOR A man of culture, my friend Miro began his literary career in a singularly unpromising way. Potential statesmen in log-cabins might miraculously come in touch with all the great books of the world, but the days of

Miro's young school life were passed in innocence of Homer or Dante or Shakespeare, or any of the other traditional mind-formers of the race. What Miro had for his nourishment, outside the Bible, which was a magical book that you must not drop on the floor, or his school-readers, which were like lightning flashes of unintelligible scenes, was the literature that his playmates lent him—exploits of British sol-
10 diers in Spain and the Crimea, the death-defying adventures of young filibusters in Cuba and Nicaragua. Miro gave them a languid perusing, and did not criticize their literary style. *Huckleberry Finn* and *Tom Sawyer* somehow eluded him until he had finished college, and no fresher tale of adventure drifted into his complacent home until the era of *Richard Carvel* and *Janice Meredith* sharpened his wits and gave him a vague feeling that there was such a thing as
20 literary art. The classics were stiffly enshrined behind glass doors that were very hard to open —at least Hawthorne and Irving and Thackeray were there, and Tennyson's and Scott's poems —but nobody ever discussed them or looked at them. Miro's busy elders were taken up with the weekly *Outlook* and *Independent* and *Christian Week*, and felt they were doing much for Miro when they provided him and his sister with *St. Nicholas* and *The Youth's Companion*.
30 It was only that Miro saw the black books looking at him accusingly from the case, and a rudimentary conscience, slipping easily over from Calvinism to culture, forced him solemnly to grapple with *The Scarlet Letter* or *Marmion*. All he remembers is that the writers of these books he browsed among used a great many words and made a great fuss over shadowy offenses and conflicts and passions that did not even stimulate his imagination with sufficient
40 force to cause him to ask his elders what it was all about. Certainly the filibusters were easier.

At school Miro was early impressed with the vast dignity of the literary works and names he was compelled to learn. Shakespeare and Goethe and Dante lifted their plaster heads frowningly above the teacher's, as they perched on shelves about the room. Much was said of the greatness of literature. But the art of phonetics and the complications of grammar
50 swamped Miro's early school years. It was not until he reached the High School that literature began really to assume that sacredness which he had heretofore felt only for Holy Scripture. His initiation into culture was made almost a religious mystery by the conscientious and harassed teacher. As the Deadwood Boys and Henty and David Harum slipped away from Miro's soul in the presence of Milton's "Comus" and Burke's "On Conciliation," a cultural devoutness was engendered in him that never really died. At first it did not take Miro beyond the stage where your conscience is strong enough to make you uncomfortable, but not strong enough to make you do anything about it. Miro did not actually become an omnivorous reader of great books. But he was filled with a rich grief that the millions pursued cheap and vulgar fiction instead of the best that has been thought and said in the world. Miro indiscriminately bought cheap editions of the English classics and read them with a certain patient incomprehension.

As for the dead classics, they came to Miro from the hands of his teachers with a prestige even vaster than the books of his native tongue. No doubt ever entered his head that four years of Latin and three years of Greek, an hour a day, were the important preparation he needed for his future as an American citizen. No doubt ever hurt him that the world into which he would pass would be a world where, as his teacher said, Latin and Greek were a solace to the aged, a quickener of taste, a refreshment after manual labor, and a clue to the general knowledge of all human things. Miro would as soon have doubted the rising of the sun as have doubted the wisdom of these serious, puckered women who had the precious manipulation of his cultural upbringing in their charge. Miro was a bright, if a rather vague, little boy, and a fusion of brightness and docility gave him

---

57. **Henty,** George A. Henty (1832–1903), a famous war correspondent of the mid-nineteenth century and the author of a great number of historical novels for boys, in their day extremely popular. **David Harum,** the leading character in the novel of the same name (1896) by Edward Noyes Westcott (1847–98). David Harum was a shrewd, kindly, humorous middle-class American of New York State, the epitome of the homely qualities that are dear to the average American. The novel was very popular in its own day and for a generation thereafter. 68. **best . . . world,** from the definition of criticism by Matthew Arnold, the great English critic (1822–88). "My own definition of criticism: *a disinterested endeavor to learn and propagate the best that is known and thought in the world.*" The sentence as quoted here is found in Arnold's "The Function of Criticism at the Present Time" from *Essays in Criticism* (1865); but the phrase is a favorite one with its author and can be found in several places in his works.

high marks in the school where we went together.

No one ever doubted that these marks expressed Miro's assimilation of the books we pored over. But he told me later that he had never really known what he was studying. Caesar, Virgil, Cicero, Xenophon, Homer were veiled and misty experiences to him. His mind was a moving present, obliterating each day what it had read the day before, and piercing into a no more comprehended future. He could at no time have given any intelligible account of Aeneas' wanderings or what Cicero was really inveighing against. *The Iliad* was even more obscure. The only thing which impressed him deeply was an expurgated passage, which he looked up somewhere else and found to be about Mars and Venus caught in the golden bed. Caesar seemed to be at war, and Xenophon wandering somewhere in Asia Minor, with about the same lengthiness and hardship as Miro suffered in reading him. The trouble, Miro thought afterwards, was that these books were to his mind flickering lights in a vast jungle of ignorance. He does not remember marvelling at the excessive dulness of the stories themselves. He plodded his faithful way, using them as his conscientious teachers did, as exercises in language. He looked on Virgil and Cicero as essentially problems in disentangling words which had unaccountably gotten into a bizarre order, and in recognizing certain rather amusing and ingenious combinations, known as "constructions." Why these words took so irritating an order Miro never knew, but he always connected the problem with those algebraic puzzles he had elsewhere to unravel. Virgil's words were further complicated by being arranged in lines which one had to "scan." Miro was pleased with the rhythm, and there were stanzas that had a roll of their own. But the inexorable translating that had to go on tore all this fabric of poetry to pieces. His translations were impeccable, but, as he never wrote them down, he had never before his eyes the consecutive story.

Translations Miro never saw. He knew that they were implements of deadly sin that boys used to cheat with. His horror of them was such as a saint might feel towards a parody of the Bible. Just before Miro left school, his sister in a younger class began to read a prose transla-

tion of *The Odyssey*, and Miro remembers the scorn with which he looked down on so sneaking an entrance into the temple of light. He knew that not everyone could study Latin and Greek, and he learned to be proud of his knowledge. When at last he had passed his examinations for college—his Latin composition and grammar, his syntax and his sight-reading, and his Greek composition and grammar, his Greek syntax and sight-reading, and his translation of Gallic battles and Anabatic frosts, and Dido's farewell and Cicero's objurgations—his zealous rage did not abate. He even insisted on reading the *Bucolics*, while he was away on his vacation, and a book or two in *The Odyssey*. His family was a little chilled by his studiousness, but he knew well that he was laying up cultural treasures in heaven, where moth and rust do not corrupt, neither do thieves break in and steal.

Arrived at college, Miro expended his cultural interests on the approved lines. He read Horace and Plato, Lysias and Terence, impartially, with faithful conscience. Horace was the most exciting because of the parodies that were beginning to appear in the cleverer newspapers. Miro scarcely knew whether to be amused or shocked at *Odi Persicos* or *Integer Vitae* done into current slang. The professors, mild-mannered men who knew their place and kept it, never mentioned these impudent adventures, but for Miro it was the first crack in his Ptolemaic system of reverences. There came a time when his mind began to feel replete, when this heavy pushing through the opaque

63. **Anabatic,** of or pertaining to the *Anabasis,* the title given by the Greek historian and educator Xenophon (430–355? B.C.) to his narrative of the expedition undertaken by Cyrus the younger against his brother Artaxerxes of Persia (401 B.C.). The campaign was brought to a conclusion by the famous retreat of the ten thousand Greeks. 66. **Bucolics,** the *Eclogues* of the Roman poet Virgil (70–19 B.C.). They are charming pastoral poems; the fourth of these, which paints a kind of golden age to come, brought Virgil great fame as a seer. For this reason he was hailed throughout the Middle Ages as a seer. 75. **Horace . . . Terence.** Horace (65–8 B.C.), the Roman lyric and satiric poet, and Plato (428–347 B.C.), the great Greek philosopher, are perhaps too well-known to need comment here. Lysias (459?–378 B.C.) was an important orator and rhetorician of ancient Athens; Terence (190?–159 B.C.) was one of the two prominent Roman writers of comedy whose works have survived. 80. **Odi . . . Vitae,** the titles of two of Horace's most famous odes. *Odi Persicos* is the first phrase of Ode 38, Book I; *Integer Vitae,* that of Ode 22, Book I. 85. **Ptolemaic system,** the ancient system of cosmology, which conceived of the earth as flat and the center of the universe around which the sun and other heavenly bodies revolved. Bourne is using the expression metaphorically here to represent something antedated and thoroughly discredited by present-day science.

medium of dead language began to fatigue him. He should have been able to read fluently, but there were always turning up new styles, new constructions, to plague him. Latin became to him like a constant diet of beefsteak, and Greek like a constant diet of fine wheaten bread. They lost their taste. These witty poets and ostentatious orators—what were they all about? What was their background? Where did they fit into Miro's life? The professors knew some history, but what did that history mean? Miro found himself surfeited and dissatisfied. He began to look furtively at translations to get some better English than he was able to provide. The hair-splittings of Plato began to bore him when he saw them in crystal-clear English, and not muffled in the original Greek. His apostasy had begun.

It was not much better in his study of English literature. Miro was given a huge anthology, a sort of press-clipping bureau of *belles-lettres*, from Chaucer to Arthur Symons. Under the direction of a professor who was laying out a career for himself as poet—or "modern singer," as he expressed it—the class went briskly through the centuries sampling their genius and tasting the various literary flavors. The enterprise reminded Miro of those books of woollen samples which one looks through when one is to have a suit of clothes made. But in this case, the student did not even have the pleasure of seeing the suit of clothes. All that was expected of him, apparently, was that he should become familiar, from these microscopic pieces, with the different textures and patterns. The great writers passed before his mind like figures in a crowded street. There was no time for preferences. Indeed the professor strove diligently to give each writer his just due. How was one to appreciate the great thoughts and the great styles if one began to choose violently between them, or attempt any discrimination on grounds of their peculiar congeniality for one's own soul? Criticism had to spurn such subjectivity, scholarship could not be wilful. The neatly arranged book of "readings," with its medicinal doses of inspiration, became the symbol of Miro's education.

These early years of college did not deprive Miro of his cultural loyalty, but they deadened his appetite. Although almost inconceivably docile, he found himself being bored. He had come from school a serious boy, with more than a touch of priggishness in him, and a vague aspiration to be a "man of letters." He found himself becoming a collector of literary odds-and-ends. If he did not formulate this feeling clearly, he at least knew. He found that the literary life was not as interesting as he had expected. He sought no adventures. When he wrote, it was graceful lyrics or polite criticisms of William Collins or Charles Lamb. These canonized saints of culture still held the field for Miro, however. There was nothing between them and that popular literature of the day that all good men bemoaned. Classic or popular, "highbrow" or "lowbrow," this was the choice, and Miro unquestioningly took the orthodox heaven. In 1912 the most popular of Miro's English professors had never heard of Galsworthy, and another was creating a flurry of scandal in the department by recommending Chesterton to his classes. It would scarcely have been in college that Miro would have learned of an escape from the closed dichotomy of culture. Bored with the "classic," and frozen with horror at the "popular," his career as a man of culture must have come to a dragging end if he had not been suddenly liberated by a chance lecture which he happened to hear while he was at home for the holidays.

The literary radical who appeared before the Lyceum Club of Miro's village was none other than Professor William Lyon Phelps, and it is to that evening of cultural audacity Miro thinks he owes all his later emancipation. The lecturer grappled with the "modern novel," and tossed Hardy, Tolstoi, Turgenev, Meredith,

62. **William Collins,** one of the so-called pre-romantic poets in English literature (1721–59), who was particularly noted for his "Ode to Evening" (1746), a delicate and beautiful lyric dedicated to the beauties of twilight. 73. **Chesterton.** Gilbert Keith Chesterton (1874–1936) was a prominent essayist, literary critic, detective-story writer, and even at times a poet. His prose style was noted for its fondness for antithesis and paradox. Chesterton was in his last years a convert to Catholicism; and this conversion affected adversely the balance, proportion, and sense of values in his later work. 75. **dichotomy,** division into two parts. 84. **William Lyon Phelps,** "Billy" Phelps (1865–), for years a beloved professor of English at Yale. He was an influential teacher of undergraduates and did valuable pioneer work in the scholarship of the English romantic age of the early nineteenth century. With his recent retirement, and for some years before, he has been in great demand as a lecturer, preacher, and expert in bonhommerie.

22. **Arthur Symons,** a poet, critic, and art-lover (1865–1945), of Welsh extraction, who was a leading light in the esthetic decadent group of the 1890's, a lecturer on French poetry of the last century, an editor of Shakespeare.

even Trollope, into the minds of the charmed audience with such effect that the virgin shelves of the village library were ravished for days to come by the eager minds upon whom these great names dawned for the first time. *Jude the Obscure* and *Resurrection* were of course kept officially away from the vulgar, but Miro managed to find *Smoke* and *Virgin Soil* and *Anna Karenina* and *The Warden* and *A Pair of Blue Eyes* and *The Return of the Native*. Later at college he explored the forbidden realms. It was as if some devout and restless saint had suddenly been introduced to the Apocrypha. A new world was opened to Miro that was neither "classic" nor "popular," and yet which came to one under the most unimpeachable auspices. There was, at first, it is true, an air of illicit adventure about the enterprise. The lecturer who made himself the missionary of such vigorous and piquant doctrine had the air of being a heretic, or at least a boy playing out of school. But Miro himself returned to college a cultural revolutionist. His orthodoxies crumbled. He did not try to reconcile the new with the old. He applied pick and dynamite to the whole structure of the canon. Irony, humor, tragedy, sensuality suddenly appeared to him as literary qualities in forms that he could understand. They were like oxygen to his soul.

If these qualities were in the books he had been reading, he had never felt them. The expurgated sample-books he had studied had passed too swiftly over the Elizabethans to give him a sense of their lustiness. Miro immersed himself voluptuously in the pessimism of Hardy. He fed on the poignant torture of Tolstoi. While he was reading *Resurrection,* his class in literature was making an "intensive" study of Tennyson. It was too much. Miro rose in revolt. He foreswore literary courses forever, dead rituals in which anaemic priests mumbled their trite critical commentary. Miro did not know that to naughtier critics even Mr. Phelps might eventually seem a pale and timid Gideon, himself stuck in moral sloughs. He was grateful enough for that blast of trumpets which made his own scholastic walls fall down.

The next stage in Miro's cultural life was one of frank revolt. He became as violent as a here-

tic as he had been docile as a believer. Modern novels merely started the rift that widened into modern ideas. The professors were of little use. Indeed, when Miro joined a group of radicals who had started a new college paper, a relentless vendetta began with the teachers. Miro and his friends threw over everything that was mere literature. Social purpose must shine from any writing that was to rouse their enthusiasm. Literary flavor was to be permissible only where it made vivid high and revolutionary thought. Tolstoi became their god, Wells their high priest. Chesterton infuriated them. They wrote violent assaults upon him which began in imitation of his cool paradoxicality and ended in incoherent ravings. There were so many enemies to their new fervor that they scarcely knew where to begin. There were not only the old tables of stone to destroy, but there were new and threatening prophets of the eternal verities who had to be exposed. The nineteenth century which they had studied must be weeded of its nauseous moralists. The instructors consulted together how they might put down the revolt, and bring these sinners back to the faith of cultural scripture.

It was of no avail. In a short time Miro had been converted from an aspiration for the career of a cultivated "man of letters" to a fiery zeal for artistic and literary propaganda in the service of radical ideas. One of the results of this conversion was the discovery that he really had no standards of critical taste. Miro had been reverential so long that he had felt no preferences. Everything that was classic had to be good to him. But now that he had thrown away the books that were stamped with the mark of the classic mint, and was dealing with the raw materials of letters, he had to become a critic and make selection. It was enough that a book should be radical. Some of the books he read, though impeccably revolutionary as to ideas, were clearly poor as literature. His muffled taste began to assert itself. He found himself impressionable where before he had been only mildly acquisitive. The literature of revolt and free speculation fired him into a state of spiritual explosiveness. All that he read now stood out in brighter colors and in sharper outlines than before. As he reached a better balance, he began to feel the vigor of literary form, the value of sincerity and freshness of

45. **Gideon.** In the Old Testament Gideon, youngest son of Joash, was helpful in overthrowing the worship of Baal and restoring the altars of Jehovah. The story is told in Judges 6–8.

style. He began to look for them keenly in everything he read. It was long before Miro realized that enthusiasm not docility had made him critical. He became a little proud of his sensitive and discriminating reactions to the modern and the unsifted.

This pursuit had to take place without any help from the college. After Miro graduated, it is true that it became the fashion to study literature as the record of ideas and not merely as a canon of sacred books to be analyzed, commented upon, and absorbed. But no dent was made upon the system in Miro's time, and, the inventory of English criticism not going beyond Stevenson, no college course went beyond Stevenson. The Elizabethans had been exhumed and fumigated, but the most popular attention went to the gallery of Victorians, who combined moral soundness with literary beauty, and were therefore considered wholesome food for young men. The instructors all remained in the state of reverence which saw all things good that had been immemorially taught. Miro's own teacher was a fragile, earnest young man, whose robuster parents had evidently seized upon his nature as a fortunate pledge of what the family might produce in the way of an intellectual flower that should surpass in culture and gentility the ambitions of his parents. His studiousness, hopeless for his father's career as grocer, had therefore been capitalized into education.

The product now shone forth as one of the most successful and promising younger instructors in the department. He knew his subject. Card-indexes filled his room, covering in detail the works, lives, and deaths of the illustrious persons whom he expounded, as well as everything that had been said about them in the way of appreciation or interpretation. An endless number of lectures and courses could be made from this bountiful store. He never tried to write himself, but he knew all about the different kinds of writing, and when he corrected the boys' themes he knew infallibly what to tell them to avoid. Miro's vagaries scandalized his teacher all the more because during his first year in college Miro had been generally noticed as one with the proper sobriety and scholarly patience to graduate into a similar priestly calling. Miro found scant sympathy in the young man. To the latter, literary studies were a science not an art, and they were to be treated with somewhat the same cold rigor of delimitation and analysis as any other science. Miro felt his teacher's recoil at the idea that literature was significant only as the expression of personality or as an interpretation of some social movement. Miro saw how uneasy he became when he was confronted with current literature. It was clear that Miro's slowly growing critical sense had not a counterpart in the scholastic mind.

When Miro and his friends abandoned literary studies, they followed after the teachers of history and philosophy, intellectual arenas of which the literary professors seemed scandalously ignorant. At this ignorance Miro boiled with contempt. Here were the profitable clues that would give meaning to dusty literary scholarship, but the scholars had not the wits to seize them. They lived along, playing what seemed to Miro a rather dreary game, when they were not gaping reverently at ideas and forms which they scarcely had the genuine personality to appreciate. Miro felt once and for all free of these mysteries and reverences. He was to know the world as it has been and as it is. He was to put literature into its proper place, making all "culture" serve its apprenticeship for him as interpretation of things larger than itself, of the course of individual lives and the great tides of society.

Miro's later cultural life is not without interest. When he had finished college and his architectural course, and was making headway in his profession, his philosophy of the intellectual life began to straighten itself out. Rapid as his surrender of orthodoxy had been, it had taken him some time to live down that early education. He found now that he would have to live down his heresies also, and get some coherent system of tastes that was his own and not the fruit of either docility or the zeal of propaganda.

The old battles that were still going on helped Miro to realize his modern position. It was a queer, musty quarrel, but it was enlisting minds from all classes and of all intellectual fibers. The "classics" were dying hard, as Miro recognized whenever he read, in the magazines, attacks on the "new education." He found that professors were still taken seriously who declared in passion that without the universal study of the Latin language in American schools all conceptions of taste, standards, criticism, the historic sense itself, would vanish from the earth. He found that even as late as 1917 professional men were gathering together in solemn conclave and buttressing the "value of the classics" with testimonials from "successful men" in a variety of vocations. Miro was amused at the fact that the mighty studies once pressed upon him so uncritically should now require, like the patent medicines, testimonials as to their virtue. Bank presidents, lawyers, and editors had taken the Latin language regularly for years, and had found its effects painless and invigorating. He could not escape the unconscious satire that such plump and prosperous Americans expressed when they thought it admirable to save their cherished intellectual traditions in any such fashion.

Other conservatives Miro saw to be abandoning the line of opposition to science, only to fall back on the line of a defensive against "pseudo-science," as they seemed to call whatever intellectual interests had not yet become indubitably reputable. It was a line which would hold them rather strongly for a time, Miro thought, because so many of the cultural revolutionists agreed with them in hating some of these arrogant and mechanical psychologies and sociologies that reduced life to figures or organisms. But Miro felt also how obstructive was their fight. If the "classics" had done little for him except to hold his mind in an uncomprehending prison, and fetter his spontaneous taste, they seemed to have done little more for even the thorough scholars. When professors had devoted scholarly lives to the "classics" only to exhibit in their own polemics none of the urbanity and intellectual command which were supposed by the believer somehow to rub off automatically on the faithful student, Miro had to conclude an absence of causal connection between the "classics" and the able modern mind. When, moreover, critical power or creative literary work became almost extinct among these defenders of the "old education," Miro felt sure that a revolution was needed in the materials and attitudes of "culture."

The case of the defenders was all the weaker because their enemies were not wanton infidels, ignorant of the holy places they profaned.

They were rather cultural "Modernists," reforming the church from within. They had the classic background, these young vandals, but they had escaped from its flat and unoriented surface. Abreast of the newer objective, impersonal standards of thinking, they saw the weakness of these archaic minds which could only appeal to vested interests in culture and testimonials from successful men.

The older critics had long since disavowed the intention of discriminating among current writers. These men, who had to have an academy to protect them, lumped the younger writers of verse and prose together as "anarchic" and "naturalistic," and had become, in these latter days, merely peevish and querulous, protesting in favor of standards that no longer represented our best values. Every one, in Miro's time, bemoaned the lack of critics, but the older critics seemed to have lost all sense of hospitality and to have become tired and a little spitefully disconsolate, while the newer ones were too intent on their crusades against puritanism and philistinism to have time for a constructive pointing of the way.

Miro had a very real sense of standing at the end of an era. He and his friends had lived down both their old orthodoxies of the classics and their new orthodoxies of propaganda. Gone were the priggishness and self-consciousness which had marked their teachers. The new culture would be more personal than the old, but it would not be held as a personal property. It would be democratic in the sense that it would represent each person's honest, spontaneous taste. The old attitude was only speciously democratic. The assumption was that if you pressed your material long enough and winningly enough upon your culturable public, they would acquire it. But the material was something handed down, not grown in the garden of their own appreciations. Under these conditions the critic and appreciator became a mere impersonal register of orthodox opinion. The cultivated person, in conforming his judgments to what was authoritatively taught him, was really a member of the herd—a cultivated herd, it is true, but still a herd. It was the mass that spoke through the critic and not his own discrimination. These authoritative judgments might, of course, have come—probably had come—to the herd through discerning critics, but in Miro's time judgment in the schools had petrified. One believed not because one felt the original discernment, but because one was impressed by the weight and reputability of opinion. At least so it seemed to Miro.

Now just as the artists had become tired of conventions and were breaking through into new and personal forms, so Miro saw the younger critics breaking through these cultural conventions. To the elders the result would seem mere anarchy. But Miro's attitude did not want to destroy, it merely wanted to rearrange the materials. He wanted no more second-hand appreciations. No one's cultural store was to include anything that one could not be enthusiastic about. One's acquaintance with the best that had been said and thought should be encouraged—in Miro's ideal school—to follow the lines of one's temperament. Miro, having thrown out the old gods, found them slowly and properly coming back to him. Some would always repel him, others he hoped to understand eventually. But if it took wisdom to write the great books, did it not also take wisdom to understand them? Even the Latin writers he hoped to recover, with the aid of translations. But why bother with Greek when you could get Euripides in the marvellous verse of Gilbert Murray? Miro was willing to believe that no education was complete without at least an inoculation of the virus of the two orthodoxies that he was transcending.

As Miro looked around the American scene, he wondered where the critics were to come from. He saw, on the one hand, Mr. Mencken and Mr. Dreiser and their friends, going heavily forth to battle with the Philistines, glorying in pachydermatous vulgarisms that hurt the polite and cultivated young men of the old school. And he saw these violent critics, in their rage against puritanism, becoming themselves moralists, with the same bigotry and tastelessness as their enemies. No, these would never do. On the other hand, he saw Mr. Stuart P. Sherman, in his youthful if somewhat belated ardor, revolting so conscientiously against the "natural-

ism" and crude expression of current efforts that, in his defense of *belles-lettres*, of the fine tradition of literary art, he himself became a moralist of the intensest brand, and as critic plumped for Arnold Bennett, because that clever man had a feeling for the proprieties of human conduct. No, Mr. Sherman would do even less adequately. His fine sympathies were as much out of the current as was the specious classicism of Professor Shorey. He would have to look for the critics among the young men who had an abounding sense of life, as well as a feeling for literary form. They would be men who had not been content to live on their cultural inheritance, but had gone out into the modern world and amassed a fresh fortune of their own. They would be men who were not squeamish, who did not feel the delicate differences between "animal" and "human" conduct, who were enthusiastic about Mark Twain and Gorki as well as Romain Rolland, and at the same time were thrilled by Copeau's theater.

Where was a better program for culture, for any kind of literary art? Culture as a living effort, a driving attempt both at sincere expression and at the comprehension of sincere expression wherever it was found! Appreciation to be as far removed from the "I know what I like!" as from the textbook impeccability of taste! If each mind sought its own along these lines, would not many find themselves agreed? Miro insisted on liking Amy Lowell's attempt to outline the tendencies in American poetry in a

---

51. **Arnold Bennett.** Enoch Arnold Bennett (1867–1931) gained fame as a novelist through *The Old Wives' Tale* (1908) and the Clayhanger novels, which included *Clayhanger* (1910), *Hilda Lessways* (1911), and *These Twain* (1916). The novels are laid in the pottery section of the Midlands in England; they are realistic and almost callously objective.   56. **Shorey, Paul Shorey** (1857–1934), professor of Greek at Bryn Mawr (1885–92) and later at Chicago (1892–1934), noted for his scholarly work in Plato and Horace. Bourne is probably referring here, however, to Shorey's *Assault on Humanism* (1917), one of the most able defenses of the classics in their losing fight of the present generation.   67. **Gorki.** Maxim Gorki (1868–1936) was the last of the great Russian fiction-writers born in the nineteenth century. His name is also indelibly associated with the Russian Revolution of 1917. The best-known of his works is probably *The Lower Depths* (1923); he is celebrated for his power and vivid naturalistic writing. **Romain Rolland** (1866–1943), as a professor at the Sorbonne, made great contributions to the teaching of the history of art and music. He wrote probably the greatest biography of Beethoven (1903) and a long trilogy, *Jean-Christophe* (1904–12), the fictitious life of a nineteenth-century German musician. Rolland was awarded the Nobel Prize for Literature in 1915.   68. **Copeau's theater.** Jacques Copeau (1879–1947), a playwright and theatrical producer, did much to revivify the French drama immediately before and after the First World War. His most important single contribution to this renaissance came with the founding of the Théâtre du Vieux-Colombier.

---

38. **pachydermatous,** literally "thick-skinned." The pachyderms are a family of quadrupeds notable for their tough, armored hide; the hippopotamus and rhinoceros are good examples. In current American sports jargon, a pachyderm is the name for a heavy-weight wrestler.   44. **Stuart P. Sherman,** a brilliant American critic (1881–1926), a militant opponent of Mencken and what Mencken represented (p. 67).

form which made clear the struggles of contemporary men and women with the tradition and against "every affectation of the mind." He began to see in the new class-consciousness of poets the ending of that old division which "culture" made between the chosen people and the gentiles. We were now to form little pools of workers and appreciators of similar temperaments and tastes. The little magazines that were starting up became voices for these new communities of sentiment. Miro thought that perhaps at first it was right to adopt a tentative superciliousness towards the rest of the world, so that both Mr. Mencken with his shudders at the vulgar Demos and Mr. Sherman with his obsession with the sanely and wholesomely American might be shut out from influence. Instead of fighting the Philistine in the name of freedom, or fighting the vulgar iconoclast in the name of wholesome human notions, it might be better to write for one's own band of comprehenders, in order that one might have something genuine with which to appeal to both the mob of the "bourgeois" and the ferocious vandals who had been dividing the field among them. Far better a quarrel among these intensely self-conscious groups than the issues that had filled *The Atlantic* and *The Nation* with their dreary obsolescence. Far better for the mind that aspired towards "culture" to be told not to conform or worship, but to search out its group, its own temperamental community of sentiment, and there deepen appreciations through sympathetic contact.

It was no longer a question of being hospitable towards the work of other countries. Miro found the whole world open to him, in these days, through the enterprise of publishers. He and his friends felt more sympathetic with certain groups in France and Russia than they did with the variegated "prominent authors" of their own land. Winston Churchill as a novelist came to seem more of an alien than Artzybashev. The fact of culture being international had been followed by a sense of its being. The old cultural attitude had been hospitable

enough, but it had imported its alien culture in the form of "comparative literature." It was hospitable only in trying to mould its own taste to the orthodox canons abroad. The older American critic was mostly interested in getting the proper rank and reverence for what he borrowed. The new critic will take what suits his community of sentiment. He will want to link up not with the foreign canon, but with that group which is nearest in spirit with the effort he and his friends are making. The American has to work to interpret and portray the life he knows. He cannot be international in the sense that anything but the life in which he is saturated, with its questions and its colors, can be the material for his art. But he can be international—and must be—in the sense that he works with a certain hopeful vision of a "young world," and with certain ideal values upon which the younger men, stained and revolted by war, in all countries are agreeing.

Miro wonders sometimes whether the direction in which he is tending will not bring him around the circle again to a new classicism. The last stage in the history of the man of culture will be that "classic" which he did not understand and which his mind spent its youth in overthrowing. But it will be a classicism far different from that which was so unintelligently handed down to him in the American world. It will be something worked out and lived into. Looking into the future he will have to do what Van Wyck Brooks calls "inventing a usable past." Finding little in the American tradition that is not tainted with sweetness and light and burdened with the terrible patronage of bourgeois society, the new classicist will yet rescue Thoreau and Whitman and Mark Twain and try to tap through them a certain eternal human tradition of abounding vitality and moral freedom, and so build out the future. If the classic means power with restraint, vitality with harmony, a fusion of intellect and feeling, and a keen sense of the artistic conscience, then the revolutionary world is coming out into the classic. When Miro sees behind the minds of *The Masses* group a desire for form and for expressive beauty, and sees the radicals following Jacques Copeau and reading Chekhov, he smiles at the thought of the American critics, young and old, who do not know yet that they are dead.

---

42. **Winston Churchill** (1871–), an American historical novelist of the early years of the century, known especially for *Richard Carvel* (1899), *The Crisis* (1901), and one or two sociological novels, such as *Coniston* (1906), an attack on civic corruption, and *The Inside of the Cup* (1913).   43. **Artzybashev**, a lesser Russian novelist and dramatist (1878–1927).

FREDERICK LEWIS ALLEN

The years between the two World Wars were the time of a great increase in the quantity of historical and biographical writing. At first, in keeping with the general revolt against the standards of the Victorian and Edwardian eras and earlier, these writings exhibited a violent reaction from the respectful, near-worshiping treatments accorded their subjects by nineteenth-century historians and biographers. There was, in other words, a great deal of the "debunking" type of historical writing, with occasionally serious lapses in good taste and constant wandering from the sound attitude of the objective historian. As this tendency, however, spent its force in the early 1930's, a more mature treatment took its place. Historians became once more interested in the portrayal of their scene primarily for its human implications; but they became also meticulous as to their sources and skeptical as to the preconceived ideas about their subject matter. The present resources for research and historical scholarship being what they are, the writer of history and biography today has an immense advantage over his predecessors in the opportunity for truth and comprehensive, accurate treatment; and present-day writers are clearly making the most of their opportunities.

A good example of this type of writer who was not, however, an academician is Frederick Lewis Allen, who was born in Boston, July 5, 1890, the son of a minister, and studied at Harvard, graduating in 1912 and taking a master's degree in the following year. From 1912 to 1914 he was an assistant in the English Department at Harvard; then he turned with definite success to magazine work. He became first an assistant editor of *The Atlantic Monthly* (1914–16) and then managing editor of *The Century Magazine* (1916–17), but his journalistic career was interrupted by the First World War. He served on the Council of National Defense until the close of the war (1917–19). For the next four years Allen was Secretary of the Corporation at Harvard, but left this post in 1923 to resume his work in the magazine world. He became an assistant editor for *Harper's Magazine* in 1923 and associate editor in 1931. He continued with that magazine until shortly before he died in 1954.

In the course of his associations with these periodicals Allen contributed various articles on miscellaneous topics. But it was *Only Yesterday* (1931) and *Since Yesterday* (1942), informal histories of the 1920's and 1930's from Armistice Day in 1918 to the outbreak of war between Nazi Germany and the Western powers in 1939, which were his best achievements. They are brilliantly conceived and compellingly written studies of the Jazz Age and the years of depression and bear a remarkable fascination for any thinking man who has lived in these two perplexing decades. Less striking and less general in its appeal is *The Lords of Creation* (1935), which the author describes as "the story of the immense financial and corporate expansion which took place in the United States between the depression of the 1890's and the crisis of the 1930's." No one else writing about America at the present time can catch the essentially dramatic in the newspaper headlines of some single day in history as could Allen; and the endless implications and linkages of every daily event, however obscure, are the matters that he made absorbing.

from Only Yesterday

CHAPTER ONE

Prelude: May, 1919

IF TIME were suddenly to turn back to the earliest days of the Post-war Decade, and you were to look about you, what would seem strange to you? Since 1919 the circumstances of American life have been transformed—yes, but exactly how?

Chapter One from *Only Yesterday* by Frederick Lewis Allen, reprinted by permission of Harper & Brothers.

Let us refresh our memories by following a moderately well-to-do young couple of Cleveland or Boston or Seattle or Baltimore—it hardly matters which—through the routine of an ordinary day in May, 1919. (I select that particular date, six months after the Armistice of 1918, because by then the United States had largely succeeded in turning from the ways of war to those of peace, yet the profound alterations wrought by the Post-war Decade had hardly begun to take place.) There is no better way of suggesting what the passage of a few years has done to change you and me and the environment in which we live.

From the appearance of Mr. Smith as he comes to the breakfast table on this May morning in 1919, you would hardly know that you are not in the nineteen-thirties (though you might, perhaps, be struck by the narrowness of his trousers). The movement of men's fashions is glacial. It is different, however, with Mrs. Smith.

She comes to breakfast in a suit, the skirt of which—rather tight at the ankles—hangs just six inches from the ground. She has read in *Vogue* the alarming news that skirts may become even shorter, and that "not since the days of the Bourbons has the woman of fashion been visible so far above the ankle"; but six inches is still the orthodox clearance. She wears low shoes now, for spring has come; but all last winter she protected her ankles either with spats or with high laced "walking-boots," or with high patent-leather shoes with contrasting buckskin tops. Her stockings are black (or tan, perhaps, if she wears tan shoes); the idea of flesh-colored stockings would appal her. A few minutes ago Mrs. Smith was surrounding herself with an "envelope chemise" and a petticoat; and from the thick ruffles on her undergarments it was apparent that she was not disposed to make herself more boyish in form than ample nature intended.

Mrs. Smith may use powder, but she probably draws the line at paint. Although the use of cosmetics is no longer, in 1919, considered *prima facie* evidence of a scarlet career, and sophisticated young girls have already begun to apply them with some bravado, most well-brought-up women still frown upon rouge. The beauty-parlor industry is in its infancy; there are a dozen hair-dressing parlors for every beauty parlor, and Mrs. Smith has never heard of such dark arts as that of face-lifting. When she puts on her hat to go shopping she will add a veil pinned neatly together behind her head. In the shops she will perhaps buy a bathing-suit for use in the summer; it will consist of an outer tunic of silk or cretonne over a tight knitted undergarment—worn, of course, with long stockings.

Her hair is long, and the idea of a woman ever frequenting a barber shop would never occur to her. If you have forgotten what the general public thought of short hair in those days, listen to the remark of the manager of the Palm Garden in New York when reporters asked him, one night in November, 1918, how he happened to rent his hall for a pro-Bolshevist meeting which had led to a riot. Explaining that a well-dressed woman had come in a fine automobile to make arrangements for the use of the auditorium he added, "Had we noticed then, as we do now, that she had short hair, we would have refused to rent the hall." In Mrs. Smith's mind, as in that of the manager of the Palm Garden, short-haired women, like long-haired men, are associated with radicalism, if not with free love.

The breakfast to which Mr. and Mrs. Smith sit down may have been arranged with a view to the provision of a sufficient number of calories—they need only to go to Childs' to learn about calories—but in all probability neither of them has ever heard of a vitamin.

As Mr. Smith eats, he opens the morning paper. It is almost certainly not a tabloid, no matter how rudimentary Mr. Smith's journalistic tastes may be: for although Mr. Hearst has already experimented with small-sized picture papers, the first conspicuously successful tabloid is yet to be born. Not until June 26, 1919, will the New York *Daily News* reach the newsstands, beginning a career that will bring its daily circulation in one year to nearly a quarter of a million, in five years to over four-fifths of a million, and in ten years to the amazing total of over one million three hundred thousand.

Strung across the front page of Mr. Smith's paper are headlines telling of the progress of the American navy seaplane, the NC-4, on its flight across the Atlantic *via* the Azores. That flight is the most sensational news story of May, 1919. (Alcock and Brown have not yet crossed

the ocean in a single hop; they will do it a few weeks hence, eight long years ahead of Lindbergh.) But there is other news, too: of the Peace Conference at Paris, where the Treaty is now in its later stages of preparation; of the successful oversubscription of the Victory Loan ("Sure, we'll finish the job!" the campaign posters have been shouting); of the arrival of another transport with soldiers from overseas; of
10 the threat of a new strike; of a speech by Mayor Ole Hanson of Seattle denouncing that scourge of the times, the I. W. W.; of the prospects for the passage of the Suffrage Amendment, which it is predicted will enable women to take "a finer place in the national life"; and of Henry Ford's libel suit against the Chicago *Tribune*— in the course of which he will call Benedict Arnold a writer, and in reply to the question, "Have there been any revolutions in this coun-
20 try?" will answer, "Yes, in 1812."

If Mr. Smith attends closely to the sporting news, he may find obscure mention of a young pitcher and outfielder for the Boston Red Sox named Ruth. But he will hardly find the Babe's name in the headlines. (In April, 1919, Ruth made one home run; in May two, but the season was much further advanced before sporting writers began to notice that he was running up a new record for swatting—twenty-nine
30 home runs for the year; the season had closed before the New York Yankees, seeing gold in the hills, bought him for $125,000; and the summer of 1920 had arrived before a man died of excitement when he saw Ruth smash a ball into the bleachers, and it became clear that the mob had found a new idol. In 1919, the veteran Ty Cobb, not Ruth, led the American League in batting.)

The sporting pages inform Mr. Smith that
40 Rickard has selected Toledo as the scene of a forthcoming encounter between the heavyweight champion, Jess Willard, and another future idol of the mob, Jack Dempsey. (They met, you may recall, on the Fourth of July, 1919, and sober citizens were horrified to read that 19,650 people were so depraved as to sit in a boiling sun to watch Dempsey knock out the six-foot-six-inch champion in the third round. How would the sober citizens have felt
50 if they had known that eight years later a

Dempsey-Tunney fight would bring in more than five times as much money in gate receipts as this battle of Toledo?) In the sporting pages there may be news of Bobby Jones, the seventeen-year-old Southern golf champion, or of William T. Tilden, Jr., who is winning tennis tournaments here and there, but neither of them is yet a national champion. And even if Jones were to win this year he would hardly become a great popular hero; for although golf 6 is gaining every day in popularity, it has not yet become an inevitable part of the weekly ritual of the American business man. Mr. Smith very likely still scoffs at "grown men who spend their time knocking a little white ball along the ground"; it is quite certain that he has never heard of plus fours; and if he should happen to play golf he had better not show his knickerbockers in the city streets, or small boys will shout to him, "Hey, get some men's pants!" 7

Did I say that by May, 1919, the war was a thing of the past? There are still reminders of it in Mr. Smith's paper. Not only the news from the Peace Conference, not only the item about Sergeant Alvin York being on his way home; there is still that ugliest reminder of all, the daily casualty list.

Mr. and Mrs. Smith discuss a burning subject, the High Cost of Living. Mr. Smith is hoping for an increase in salary, but meanwhile the 8 family income seems to be dwindling as prices rise. Everything is going up—food, rent, clothing, and taxes. These are the days when people remark that even the man without a dollar is fifty cents better off than he once was, and that if we coined seven-cent pieces for streetcar fares, in another year we should have to discontinue them and begin to coin fourteen-cent pieces. Mrs. Smith, confronted with an appeal from Mr. Smith for economy, reminds him that 9 milk has jumped since 1914 from nine to fifteen cents a quart, sirloin steak from twenty-seven to forty-two cents a pound, butter from thirty-

75. **Sergeant Alvin York.** Alvin York, a corporal in the American army, led his squad to the capture of 132 Germans in a skirmish near Château-Thierry on October 8, 1918. For this he gained a promotion to sergeant, an honorary colonelship in the national guard of his native Tennessee, and the Congressional Medal of Honor. He was considered America's greatest individual war-hero. Subsequently he toured the country, went into vaudeville, and then sank into obscurity until World War II.

two to sixty-one cents a pound, and fresh eggs from thirty-four to sixty-two cents a dozen. No wonder people on fixed salaries are suffering, and colleges are beginning to talk of applying the money-raising methods learned during the Liberty Loan campaigns to the increasing of college endowments. Rents are almost worse than food prices, for that matter; since the Armistice there has been an increasing shortage of houses and apartments, and the profiteering landlord has become an object of popular hate along with the profiteering middleman. Mr. Smith tells his wife that "these profiteers are about as bad as the I. W. W.'s." He could make no stronger statement.

Breakfast over, Mr. Smith gets into his automobile to drive to the office. The car is as likely to be a Lexington, a Maxwell, a Briscoe, or a Templar as to be a Dodge, Buick, Chevrolet, Cadillac, or Hudson, and it surely will not be a Chrysler; Mr. Chrysler has just been elected first vice-president of the General Motors Corporation. Whatever the make of the car, it stands higher than the cars of the nineteen-thirties; the passengers look down upon their surroundings from an imposing altitude. The chances are nine to one that Mr. Smith's automobile is open (only 10.3 per cent of the cars manufactured in 1919 were closed). The vogue of the sedan is just beginning. Closed cars are still associated in the public mind with wealth; the hated profiteer of the newspaper cartoon rides in a limousine.

If Mr. Smith's car is one of the high, hideous, but efficient model T Fords of the day, let us watch him for a minute. He climbs in by the right-hand door (for there is no left-hand door by the front seat), reaches over to the wheel, and sets the spark and throttle levers in a position like that of the hands of a clock at ten minutes to three. Then, unless he has paid extra for a self-starter, he gets out to crank. Seizing the crank in his right hand (carefully, for a friend of his once broke his arm cranking), he slips his left forefinger through a loop of wire that controls the choke. He pulls the loop of wire, he revolves the crank mightily, and as the engine at last roars, he leaps to the trembling running-board, leans in, and moves the spark and throttle to twenty-five minutes of two. Perhaps he reaches the throttle before the engine falters into silence, but if it is a cold morning perhaps he does not. In that case, back to the crank again and the loop of wire. Mr. Smith wishes Mrs. Smith would come out and sit in the driver's seat and pull that spark lever down before the engine has time to die.

Finally he is at the wheel with the engine roaring as it should. He releases the emergency hand-brake, shoves his left foot against the low-speed pedal, and as the car sweeps loudly out into the street, he releases his left foot, lets the car into high gear, and is off. Now his only care is for that long hill down the street; yesterday he burned his brake on it, and this morning he must remember to brake with the reverse pedal, or the low-speed pedal, or both, or all three in alternation. (Jam your foot down on any one of the three pedals and you slow the car.)

Mr. Smith is on the open road—a good deal more open than it will be a decade hence. On his way to work he passes hardly a third as many cars as he will pass in 1929; there are less than seven million passenger cars registered in the United States in 1919, as against over twenty-three million cars only ten years later. He is unlikely to find many concrete roads in his vicinity, and the lack of them is reflected in the speed regulations. A few states like California and New York permit a rate of thirty miles an hour in 1919, but the average limit is twenty (as against thirty-five or forty in 1931). The Illinois rate of 1919 is characteristic of the day; it limits the driver to fifteen miles in residential parts of cities, ten miles in built-up sections, and six miles on curves. The idea of making a hundred-mile trip in two and a half hours —as will constantly be done in the nineteen-thirties by drivers who consider themselves conservative—would seem to Mr. Smith perilous, and with the roads of 1919 to drive on he would be right.

In the course of his day at the office, Mr. Smith discusses business conditions. It appears that things are looking up. There was a period of uncertainty and falling stock prices after the Armistice, as huge government contracts were canceled and plants which had been running overtime on war work began to throw off men by the thousand, but since then conditions have been better. Everybody is talking about the bright prospects for international trade and American shipping. The shipyards are running full tilt. There are too many strikes going on, to be sure; it seems as if the demands of labor for higher and higher wages would never be satisfied, although Mr. Smith admits that in a way you can't blame the men, with prices still 10 mounting week by week. But there is so much business activity that the men being turned out of army camps to look for jobs are being absorbed better than Mr. Smith ever thought they would be. It was back in the winter and early spring that there was so much talk about the ex-service men walking the streets without work; it was then that *Life* ran a cartoon which represented Uncle Sam saying to a soldier, "Nothing is too good for you, my boy! What 20 would you like?" and the soldier answering, "A job." Now the boys seem to be sifting slowly but surely into the ranks of the employed, and the only clouds on the business horizon are strikes and Bolshevism and the dangerous wave of speculation in the stock market.

"Bull Market Taxes Nerves of Brokers," cry the headlines in the financial pages, and they speak of "Long Hours for Clerks." Is there a familiar ring to those phrases? Does it seem 30 natural to you, remembering as you do the Big Bull Market of 1928 and 1929, that the decision to keep the Stock Exchange closed over the 31st of May, 1919, should elicit such newspaper comments as this: "The highly specialized machine which handles the purchase and sales of stocks and bonds in the New York market is fairly well exhausted and needs a rest"? Then listen: in May, 1919, it was a long series of *million-and-a-half-share* days which was 40 causing financiers to worry and the Federal Reserve Board to consider issuing a warning against speculation. During that year a new record of six two-million-share days was set up, and on only 145 days did the trading amount to over a million shares. What would Mr. Smith and his associates think if they were to be told that within eleven years there would

occur a sixteen-million-share day; and that they would see the time when three-million-share days would be referred to as "virtual stagna- 50 tion" or as "listless trading by professionals only, with the general public refusing to become interested"? The price of a seat on the New York Stock Exchange in 1919 ranged between $60,000 and a new high record of $110,-000; it would be hard for Mr. Smith to believe that before the end of the decade seats on the Exchange would fetch a half million.

In those days of May, 1919, the record of daily Stock Exchange transactions occupied 60 hardly a newspaper column. The Curb Market record referred to trading on a real curb—to that extraordinary market in Broad Street, New York, where boys with telephone receivers clamped to their heads hung out of windows high above the street and grimaced and wig-wagged through the din to traders clustered on the pavement below. And if there was anything Mrs. Smith was certain not to have on her mind as she went shopping, it was the price 70 of stocks. Yet the "unprecedented bull market" of 1919 brought fat profits to those who participated in it. Between February 15th and May 14th, Baldwin Locomotive rose from 72 to 93, General Motors from 130 to 191, United States Steel from 90 to 104½, and International Mercantile Marine common (to which traders were attracted on account of the apparently boundless possibilities of shipping) from 23 to 47⅝.

When Mr. Smith goes out to luncheon, he 80 has to proceed to his club in a roundabout way, for a regiment of soldiers just returned from Europe is on parade and the central thoroughfares of the city are blocked with crowds. It is a great season for parades, this spring of 1919. As the transports from Brest swing up New York Harbor, the men packed solid on the decks are greeted by Mayor Hylan's Committee of Welcome, represented sometimes by the Mayor's spruce young secretary, Grover Wha- 90 len, who in later years is to reduce welcoming to a science and raise it to an art. New York City has built in honor of the home-coming troops a huge plaster arch in Fifth Avenue at Madison Square, toward the design of which forty artists are said to have contributed. ("But the result," comments the New York *Tribune*,

---

17. **Life.** The original magazine *Life* was the most famous of American humorous weeklies; and in its way it did for the American public what *Punch* did for the English. In the 1930's, however, it fell on evil days. The present photograph-tabloid *Life* bears not the slightest resemblance to its predecessor.

97. **Tribune,** now the New York *Herald-Tribune.*

sadly, "suggests four hundred rather than forty. It holds everything that was ever on an arch anywhere, the lay mind suspects, not forgetting the horses on top of a certain justly celebrated Brandenburg Gate.") Farther up the Avenue, before the Public Library, there is a shrine of pylons and palms called the Court of the Heroic Dead, of whose decorative effect the *Tribune* says, curtly, "Add perils of death." A few blocks to the north an arch of jewels is suspended above the Avenue "like a net of precious stones, between two white pillars surmounted by stars"; on this arch colored searchlights play at night with superb effect. The Avenue is hung with flags from end to end; and as the Twenty-Seventh Division parades under the arches the air is white with confetti and ticker tape, and the sidewalks are jammed with cheering crowds. Nor is New York alone in its enthusiasm for the returning soldiers; every other city has its victory parade, with the city elders on the reviewing stand and flags waving and the bayonets of the troops glistening in the spring sunlight and the bands playing "The Long, Long Trail." Not yet disillusioned, the nation welcomes its heroes—and the heroes only wish the fuss were all over and they could get into civilian clothes and sleep late in the mornings and do what they pleased, and try to forget.

Mr. and Mrs. Smith have been invited to a tea dance at one of the local hotels, and Mr. Smith hurries from his office to the scene of revelry. If the hotel is up to the latest wrinkles, it has a jazz-band instead of the traditional orchestra for dancing, but not yet does a saxophone player stand out in the foreground and contort from his instrument that piercing music, "endlessly sorrowful yet endlessly unsentimental, with no past, no memory, no future, no hope," which William Bolitho called the *Zeitgeist* of the Post-war Age. The jazz band plays "I'm Always Chasing Rainbows," the tune which Harry Carroll wrote in wartime after Harrison Fisher persuaded him that Chopin's "Fantasie Impromptu" had the makings of a good ragtime tune. It plays, too, "Smiles" and "Dardanella" and "Hindustan" and "Japanese Sandman" and "I Love You Sunday," and that other song whch is to give the Post-war Decade one of its most persistent and wearisome slang phrases, "I'll Say She Does." There are a good many military uniforms among the fox-trotting dancers. There is one French officer in blue; the days are not past when a foreign uniform adds the zest of war-time romance to any party. In the more dimly lighted palm-room there may be a juvenile petting party or two going on, but of this Mr. and Mrs. Smith are doubtless oblivious. F. Scott Fitzgerald has yet to confront a horrified republic with the Problem of the Younger Generation.

After a few dances, Mr. Smith wanders out to the bar (if this is not a dry state). He finds there a group of men downing Bronxes and Scotch highballs, and discussing with dismay the approach of prohibition. On the 1st of July the so-called Wartime Prohibition Law is to take effect (designed as a war measure, but not signed by the President until after the Armistice), and already the ratification of the Eighteenth Amendment has made it certain that prohibition is to be permanent. Even now, distilling and brewing are forbidden. Liquor is therefore expensive, as the frequenters of midnight cabarets are learning to their cost. Yet here is the bar, still quite legally doing business. Of course there is not a woman within eyeshot of it; drinking by women is unusual in 1919, and drinking at a bar is an exclusive masculine prerogative. Although Mr. and Mrs. Smith's hosts may perhaps serve cocktails before dinner this evening, Mr. and Mrs. Smith have never heard of cocktail parties as a substitute for tea parties.

As Mr. Smith stands with his foot on the brass rail, he listens to the comments on the coming of prohibition. There is some indignant talk about it, but even here the indignation is by no means unanimous. One man, as he tosses off his Bronx, says that he'll miss his liquor for a time, he supposes, but he thinks "his boys will be better off for living in a world where there is no alcohol"; and two or three others agree with him. Prohibition has an overwhelming majority behind it throughout the United States; the Spartan fervor of war-time has not yet cooled. Nor is there anything iron-

---

5. **Brandenburg Gate.** The Brandenburg Gate, at the entrance to the famous avenue Unter den Linden, in Berlin, is in the very heart of official Berlin and is indelibly associated with the pride and pomp of the Hohenzollerns.   30. **try to forget.** Compare the idea in this sentence with the situation in Fitzgerald's "May Day" (p. 346).   41. *Zeitgeist*, the spirit of the age.

ical in the expressed assumption of these men that when the Eighteenth Amendment goes into effect, alcohol will be banished from the land. They look forward vaguely to an endless era of actual drought.

At the dinner party to which Mr. and Mrs. Smith go that evening, some of the younger women may be bold enough to smoke, but they probably puff their cigarettes self-consciously, even defiantly. (The national consumption of cigarettes in 1919, excluding the very large sizes, is less than half of what it will be by 1930.)

After dinner the company may possibly go to the movies to see Charlie Chaplin in *Shoulder Arms* or Douglas Fairbanks in *The Knickerbocker Buckaroo* or Mary Pickford in *Daddy Long Legs,* or Theda Bara, or Pearl White, or Griffith's much touted and much wept-at *Broken Blossoms.* Or they may play auction bridge (not contract, of course). Mah Jong, which a few years hence will be almost obligatory, is still over the horizon. They may discuss such best sellers of the day as *The Four Horsemen of the Apocalypse,* Tarkington's *The Magnificent Ambersons,* Conrad's *Arrow of Gold,* Brand Whitlock's *Belgium,* and Wells's *The Undying Fire.* (The *Outline of History* is still unwritten.) They may go to the theater: the New York successes of May, 1919, include "Friendly Enemies," "Three Faces East," and "The Better 'Ole," which have been running ever since war-time and are still going strong, and also "Listen, Lester," Gillette in "Dear Brutus," Frances Starr in "Tiger! Tiger!" and—to satisfy a growing taste for bedroom farce—such tidbits as "Up in Mabel's Room." The Theater Guild is about to launch its first drama, Ervine's "John Ferguson." The members of the senior class at Princeton have just voted "Lightnin'" their favorite play (after "Macbeth" and "Hamlet," for which they cast the votes expected of educated men), and their favorite actresses, in order of preference, are Norma Talmadge, Elsie Ferguson, Marguerite Clark, Constance Talmadge, and Madge Kennedy.

One thing the Smiths certainly will not do this evening. They will not listen to the radio.

For there is no such thing as radio broadcasting. Here and there a mechanically inclined boy has a wireless set, with which, if he knows the Morse code, he may listen to messages from ships at sea and from land stations equipped with sending apparatus. The radiophone has been so far developed that men flying in an airplane over Manhattan have talked with other men in an office-building below. But the broadcasting of speeches and music—well, it was tried years ago by DeForest, and "nothing came of it." Not until the spring of 1920 will Frank Conrad of the Westinghouse Company of East Pittsburgh, who has been sending out phonograph music and baseball scores from the barn which he has rigged up as a spare-time research station, find that so many amateur wireless operators are listening to them that a Pittsburgh newspaper has had the bright idea of advertising radio equipment "which may be used by those who listen to Dr. Conrad's programs." And not until this advertisement appears will the Westinghouse officials decide to open the first broadcasting station in history in order to stimulate the sale of their supplies.

One more word about Mr. and Mrs. Smith and we may dismiss them for the night. Not only have they never heard of radio broadcasting; they have never heard of Coué, the Dayton Trial, cross-word puzzles, bathing-beauty contests, John J. Raskob, racketeers, Teapot Dome, Coral Gables, the *American Mercury,* Sacco and Vanzetti, companionate marriage, brokers' loan statistics, Michael Arlen, the Wall Street explosion, confession magazines, the Hall-Mills case, Radio stock, speakeasies, Al Capone, automatic traffic lights, or Charles A. Lindbergh.

The Post-war Decade lies before them.

---

24. **best sellers** . . . *Outline of History. The Four Horsemen of the Apocalypse* was a crude but effective war-novel by the Spaniard Blasco Ibáñez (1867–1928); Brand Whitlock as a novelist is now forgotten but not the fact that he was Minister to Belgium under Woodrow Wilson and did great services to humanity in his work for Belgian war-relief (as did Herbert Hoover); H. G. Wells has already been mentioned (p. 90, note to l. 42) as a kind of lay prophet of imaginative science—in this field his *Outline of History* (1922) was his most notable contribution.

78. **Coué.** Emile Coué (1857–1926) was a French pharmacist and psychotherapist; his therapeutic formula, "Day by day in every way I am getting better and better," was extremely popular as a spiritual corrective for the horrible effects of the war on the public mind. Many of the other persons or events alluded to in this sentence have been touched upon in "Passing in Review" (pp. 1–21); in a literary way Michael Arlen, the pen name of Dikyan Kuyumjian (an English writer of Armenian extraction), deserves note for his brief but meteoric success in sophisticated popular fiction with his novel (later dramatized as a vehicle for Katharine Cornell), *The Green Hat.*

BERTRAND RUSSELL

One of the leading exponents of philosophy in our day, Bertrand Arthur William, Lord Russell, has distinguished himself in other fields of knowledge and has written on a variety of subjects—political, scientific, social, and economic. He was born on May 18, 1872, at Trelleck, in Wales. His grandfather was Lord John Russell (1792–1878), prime minister of England (1846–52) and a noted liberal, whose great contribution to English history was the leading part he played in passing through Parliament the Reform Bill of 1832—an act which meant the revision of British suffrage and the gradual emergence of Britain as a democratic power. Bertrand Russell was left an orphan at three and was brought up by his grandmother at Pembroke Lodge, Richmond Park, where he was privately instructed, to the great benefit of his knowledge of French and German. At Trinity College, Cambridge, where he graduated in 1894, he won honors in mathematics and moral sciences. For a time he worked in the British Embassy at Paris and traveled in Germany; then he settled in Haslemere, on the southern border of Surrey. As a result of his visit to Germany he published his first work, *German Social Democracy,* in 1896. This analysis of social and political conditions marks one of his many intellectual interests. A second, in mathematics, is evidenced by his *Essay on the Foundations of Geometry* (1897). Shortly thereafter he turned to still another field in his *Philosophy of Leibnitz,* published in 1902. Eventually he was able to move with equal ease from one field to another. The range of his subsequent writings has been most unusual.

For a few years he was a lecturer at Trinity College, Cambridge, during which period he made frequent visits to the Continent. The First World War brought him into difficulties. Always an avowed pacifist and an extreme liberal, if not a radical, in politics, Russell found himself a conscientious objector; and his activities as such brought him a fine of one hundred pounds (as a result of which some of his private library was attached), the cancellation of his lectureship at Cambridge, and, last but not least, a six months' sentence in prison (1918). At the same time he was refused the opportunity to leave England and accept an appointment at Harvard. But the sojourn in jail gave him leisure to complete his *Introduction to Mathematical Philosophy* (1918). Incidentally, the work which had concentrated attention upon his pacifism was *Principles of Social Reconstruction* (1917), published in the United States under the title *Why Men Fight.* This work has remained one of his best known and most influential.

After the close of the war Russell devoted himself to writing and lecturing for a year or so. He was, however, much interested in the sequelae of the Russian Revolution, and so traveled to Russia—whence his *Practice and Theory of Bolshevism* (1920). He proceeded from Russia to China, where he served for a year as lecturer at the then University of Peking. A severe illness nearly cost him his life; and he returned to England (1921) much broken in health. The same year saw the dissolution of his first marriage and a second marriage—this time to Dora Black, herself a sociologist and author of *The Right to Be Happy* (1927). Russell's lectures in China formed the basis for his *Analysis of Mind* (1921). During the next several years he became greatly interested in practical politics and twice stood unsuccessfully for Parliament as a member of the Liberal Party. But his great contribution to the intellectual life of these years was the founding (1927) by himself and his wife of a nursery school based on most progressive ideas, to which he devoted himself whole-heartedly. His principles of education rested primarily upon personal contacts with his pupils and the inculcation of habits of practical behavior rather than the learning of mere theory.

Russell's older brother died in 1931 and left him the earldom which had been originally bestowed upon his grandfather. This elevation to the peerage, of course, gave him a seat in the House of Lords; and he gladly accepted the responsibility, declaring that he would devote himself henceforth to social problems, particularly those of divorce and the distribution of wealth. Such, in effect, he has done; and he has published almost every year a work in which scholarship, worldly wisdom, and humanitarian idealism are blended in almost equal proportions. In the winter of 1938–39 he was a Visiting Professor of Philosophy at the University of Chicago; in the fall of 1939 he became a lecturer at the University of California; in 1940 he occupied similar posts at Harvard and the College of the City of New York. To the last-named institution, however, Russell's views on sex and religion were not acceptable, and his appointment was revoked. He became a lecturer in history at the Barnes Foundation in Merion, Pennsylvania (1941), where he still maintains residence.

From the impressive catalogue of Russell's works it is impossible to mention more than a few; yet even so it is difficult to do justice to the author. Besides those already mentioned, we must note *Principles of Mathematics* (1903); *Principia Mathematica* (1910), written in collaboration with the brilliant English mathematician A. N. Whitehead; *Problems of Philosophy* (1911), still a standard textbook for elementary courses in philosophy; *Our Knowledge of the External World as a Field for Scientific Method in Philosophy* (1914); *Justice in War Time* (1916), the first of his troublemaking tracts; *Political Ideals* (1917); *Mysticism and Logic* (1919); *Proposed Roads to Freedom* (1918; 1919; 1926); *The Problem of China* (1922); *The A.B.C. of Atoms* (1923); *A Prospectus of Industrial Civilization* (1923); *Icarus, or the Future of Science* (1924); *The A.B.C. of Relativity* (1925); *What I Believe* (1925); *On Education* (1926); *The Analysis of Matter* (1927); *An Outline of Philosophy* (1927); *Sceptical Essays* (1928); *Marriage and Morals* (1929); *On the Evils Due to Fear* (1929); *The Conquest of Happiness* (1930); *The Scientific Outlook,* known in the United States as *The Meaning of Science* (1931); *Education and the Social Order,* known in the United States as *Education and the Modern World* (1932); *Freedom and Organization, 1814–1914* (1934); *Religion and Science* (1935); *In Praise of Idleness* (1935),

a venture into the familiar essay; *Which Way to Peace?* (1936); *Power, a New Social Analysis* (1938), inspired by the spectacle of the supreme executive power of the modern European dictator; and many others.

Philosophically, Russell has been consistently a monist and a materialist, an anti-mystic with leanings toward pragmatism and behaviorism. Sociologically, he is an advanced individualist. He has been most useful, generally speaking, as a brilliant popularizer of science and sociology. But he is far too magnificent a scholar to be dismissed thus cavalierly. He is an unquestionably distinguished teacher and lecturer. His analysis of Marxian philosophy in *Proposed Roads to Freedom,* for example, should be read by anyone who wishes to know the principles of present-day revolutionism. Yet Russell is no agitator. He has an exceptionally keen academic mind, clear and incisive; and his presentations are notably dispassionate. One cannot, on the other hand, accuse him of over-objectivity. Scientist as he is by instinct—his early mathematical training is no doubt responsible for his precision—he is nevertheless willing at all times to recognize the importance of human personality; as he says in *The Meaning of Science,*

> the scientific society in its pure form is incompatible with the pursuit of truth, with love, with art, with every ideal that men have hitherto cherished. If such a society is ever created, it will therefore probably perish through the fact that the individuals composing it will find life unbearable.

---

from **Proposed Roads to Freedom**

I

Marx and Socialist Doctrine

SOCIALISM, like everything else that is vital, is rather a tendency than a strictly definable body of doctrine. A definition of Socialism is sure either to include some views which many would regard as not Socialistic, or to exclude

"Marx and Socialist Doctrine" from *Proposed Roads to Freedom,* reprinted by permission of George Allen & Unwin, Ltd. and Henry Holt and Company.

others which claim to be included. But I think we shall come nearest to the essence of Socialism by defining it as the advocacy of communal ownership of land and capital. Communal ownership may mean ownership by a democratic State, but cannot be held to include ownership by any State which is not democratic. Communal ownership may also be understood, as Anarchist Communism understands it, in the sense of ownership by the free association of the men and women in a community without those compulsory powers which are necessary to constitute a State. Some Socialists expect communal ownership to arrive suddenly and completely by a catastrophic revolution, while others expect it to come gradually, first in one industry, then in another. Some insist upon the necessity of completeness in the acquisition of land and capital by the public, while others would be content to see lingering islands of private ownership, provided they were not too expensive or powerful. What all forms have in common is democracy and the abolition, virtual or complete, of the present capitalistic system. The distinction between Socialists, Anarchists and Syndicalists turns largely upon the kind of democracy which they desire. Orthodox Socialists are content with parliamentary democracy in the sphere of government, holding that the evils apparent in this form of constitution at present would disappear with the disappearance of capitalism. Anarchists and Syndicalists, on the other hand, object to the whole parliamentary machinery, and aim at a different method of regulating the political affairs of the community. But all alike are democratic in the sense that they aim at abolishing every kind of privilege and every kind of artificial inequality: all alike are champions of the wage-earner in existing society. All three also have much in common in their economic doctrine. All three regard capital and the wages system as a means of exploiting the laborer in the interests of the possessing classes, and hold that communal ownership, in one form or another, is the only means of bringing freedom to the producers. But within the framework of this common doctrine there are many divergences, and even among those who are strictly to be called Socialists, there is a very considerable diversity of schools.

Socialism as a power in Europe may be said to begin with Marx. It is true that before his time there were Socialist theories, both in England and in France. It is also true that in France, during the revolution of 1848, Socialism for a brief period acquired considerable influence in the State. But the Socialists who preceded Marx tended to indulge in Utopian dreams and failed to found any strong or stable political party. To Marx, in collaboration with Engels, are due both the formulation of a coherent body of Socialist doctrine, sufficiently true or plausible to dominate the minds of vast numbers of men, and the formation of the International Socialist movement, which has continued to grow in all European countries throughout the last fifty years.

In order to understand Marx's doctrine, it is necessary to know something of the influences which formed his outlook. He was born in 1818 at Trèves in the Rhine Provinces, his father being a legal official, a Jew who had nominally accepted Christianity. Marx studied jurisprudence, philosophy, political economy and history at various German universities. In philosophy he imbibed the doctrines of Hegel, who was then at the height of his fame, and something of these doctrines dominated his thought throughout his life. Like Hegel, he saw in history the development of an Idea. He conceived the changes in the world as forming a logical development, in which one phase passes by revolution into another, which is its antithesis—a conception which gave to his views a certain hard abstractness, and a belief in revolution rather than evolution. But of Hegel's more definite doctrines Marx retained nothing after his youth. He was recognized as a brilliant student, and might have had a prosperous career as a professor or an official, but his interest in politics and his Radical views led him into more arduous paths. Already in 1842 he became editor of a newspaper, which was suppressed by the Prussian Government early in the following year on account of its advanced

80. **Hegel.** Georg Wilhelm Friedrich Hegel (1770–1831), author of *The Science of Logic* (1812), was one of the leading philosophers during the romantic age of the early nineteenth century. The basic assumption of Hegel's philosophy is the Hegelian dialectic, which enables reflective thinking to arrange all the categories, or necessary conceptions of reason, in an order of development that corresponds precisely to the actual order in development of all reality. Sometimes the system of Hegel is known as absolute idealism.

opinions. This led Marx to go to Paris, where he became known as a Socialist and acquired a knowledge of his French predecessors. (Chief among these were Fourier and Saint-Simon, who constructed somewhat fantastic Socialistic ideal commonwealths. Proudhon, with whom Marx had some not wholly friendly relations, is to be regarded as a forerunner of the Anarchists rather than of orthodox Socialism.) Here in the year 1844 began his lifelong friendship with Engels, who had been hitherto in business in Manchester, where he had become acquainted with English Socialism and had in the main adopted its doctrines. In 1845 Marx was expelled from Paris and went with Engels to live in Brussels. There he formed a German Working Men's Association and edited a paper which was their organ. Through his activities in Brussels he became known to the German Communist League in Paris, who, at the end of 1847, invited him and Engels to draw up for them a manifesto, which appeared in January, 1848. This is the famous "Communist Manifesto," in which for the first time Marx's system is set forth. It appeared at a fortunate moment. In the following month, February, the revolution broke out in Paris, and in March it spread to Germany. Fear of the revolution led the Brussels Government to expel Marx from Belgium, but the German revolution made it possible for him to return to his own country. In Germany he again edited a paper, which again led him into a conflict with the authorities, increasing in severity as the reaction gathered force. In June, 1849, his paper was sup-

pressed, and he was expelled from Prussia. He returned to Paris, but was expelled from there also. This led him to settle in England—at that time an asylum for friends of freedom—and in England, with only brief intervals for purposes of agitation, he continued to live until his death in 1883.

The bulk of his time was occupied in the composition of his great book, "Capital." His other important work during his later years was the formation and spread of the International Working Men's Association. From 1849 onward the greater part of his time was spent in the British Museum, accumulating, with German patience, the materials for his terrific indictment of capitalist society, but he retained his hold on the International Socialist movement. In several countries he had sons-in-law as lieutenants, like Napoleon's brothers, and in the various internal contests that arose his will generally prevailed.

The most essential of Marx's doctrines may be reduced to three: first, what is called the materialistic interpretation of history; second, the law of the concentration of capital; and, third, the class-war.

1. *The Materialistic Interpretation of History.*—Marx holds that in the main all the phenomena of human society have their origin in material conditions, and these he takes to be embodied in economic systems. Political constitutions, laws, religions, philosophies—all these he regards as, in their broad outlines, expressions of the economic *régime* in the society that gives rise to them. It would be unfair to represent him as maintaining that the conscious economic motive is the only one of importance; it is rather that economics molds character and opinion, and is thus the prime source of much that appears in consciousness to have no connection with them. He applies his doctrine in particular to two revolutions, one in the past, the other in the future. The revolution in the past is that of the bourgeoisie against feudalism, which finds its expression, according to him, particularly in the French Revolution. The one in the future is the revolution of the wage-

---

3. **predecessors.** Marx mentions the English Socialists with praise in *The Poverty of Philosophy* (1847). They, like him, tend to base their arguments upon a Ricardian theory of value, but they have not his scope or erudition or scientific breadth. Among them may be mentioned Thomas Hodgskin (1787–1869), originally an officer in the Navy, but dismissed for a pamphlet critical of the methods of naval discipline, author of *Labour Defended Against the Claims of Capital* (1825), and other works; William Thompson (1785–1833), author of *Inquiry into the Principles of Distribution of Wealth Most Conducive to Human Happiness* (1824), and *Labour Rewarded* (1825); and Piercy Ravenstone, from whom Hodgskin's ideas are largely derived. Perhaps more important than any of these was Robert Owen. (Author's note.) 6. **Proudhon.** Pierre Joseph Proudhon (1809–65), a French political and social radical, was one of the leaders in the French Revolution of 1848 which established the short-lived Second Republic. His radicalism, however, was too much for even the revolutionists; he spent three years in prison during the republic and in 1852 left France and settled in Belgium, where he remained a focal point of social and political reform.

---

44. **"Capital."** The first and most important volume appeared in 1867; the other two volumes were published posthumously (1885 and 1894). (Author's note.)

earners, or proletariat, against the bourgeoisie, which is to establish the Socialist Commonwealth. The whole movement of history is viewed by him as necessary, as the effect of material causes operating upon human beings. He does not so much advocate the Socialist revolution as predict it. He holds, it is true, that it will be beneficent, but he is much more concerned to prove that it must inevitably come. The same sense of necessity is visible in his exposition of the evils of the capitalist system. He does not blame capitalists for the cruelties of which he shows them to have been guilty; he merely points out that they are under an inherent necessity to behave cruelly so long as private ownership of land and capital continues. But their tyranny will not last forever, for it generates the forces that must in the end overthrow it.

2. *The Law of the Concentration of Capital.* —Marx pointed out that capitalist undertakings tend to grow larger and larger. He foresaw the substitution of trusts for free competition, and predicted that the number of capitalist enterprises must diminish as the magnitude of single enterprises increased. He supposed that this process must involve a diminution, not only in the number of businesses, but also in the number of capitalists. Indeed, he usually spoke as though each business were owned by a single man. Accordingly, he expected that men would be continually driven from the ranks of the capitalists into those of the proletariat, and that the capitalists, in the course of time, would grow numerically weaker and weaker. He applied this principle not only to industry but also to agriculture. He expected to find the landowners growing fewer and fewer while their estates grew larger and larger. This process was to make more and more glaring the evils and injustices of the capitalist system, and to stimulate more and more the forces of opposition.

3. *The Class War.*—Marx conceives the wage-earner and the capitalist in a sharp antithesis. He imagines that every man is, or must soon become, wholly the one or wholly the other. The wage-earner, who possesses nothing, is exploited by the capitalists, who possess everything. As the capitalist system works itself

out and its nature becomes more clear, the opposition of bourgeoisie and proletariat becomes more and more marked. The two classes, since they have antagonistic interests, are forced into a class war which generates within the capitalist *régime* internal forces of disruption. The working men learn gradually to combine against their exploiters, first locally, then nationally, and at last internationally. When they have learned to combine internationally they must be victorious. They will then decree that all land and capital shall be owned in common; exploitation will cease; the tyranny of the owners of wealth will no longer be possible; there will no longer be any division of society into classes, and all men will be free.

All these ideas are already contained in the "Communist Manifesto," a work of the most amazing vigor and force, setting forth with terse compression the titanic forces of the world, their epic battle, and the inevitable consummation. Their work is of such importance in the development of Socialism and gives such an admirable statement of the doctrines set forth at greater length and with more pedantry in "Capital," that its salient passages must be known by anyone who wishes to understand the hold which Marxian Socialism has acquired over the intellect and imagination of a large proportion of working-class leaders.

"A spectre is haunting Europe," it begins, "the spectre of Communism. All the Powers of old Europe have entered into a holy alliance to exorcise this spectre—Pope and Czar, Metternich and Guizot, French Radicals and German police-spies. Where is the party in opposition

84. **Metternich.** Clemens Wenzel Lother, Prince von Metternich (1773–1859), Austrian statesman during the Napoleonic era, became one of the champions of the autocratic reaction in Europe following the Treaty of Paris (1815). This treaty sealed Napoleon's fate after his defeat at Waterloo. Metternich then became one of the motivating forces in the Holy Alliance, a coalition of Britain, Austria, and Royalist France "to make the world safe for autocracy." Metternich's reactionism, however, brought about his downfall in the Austrian revolution of 1848; he spent the next few years in England as a political exile; but in 1851 he returned to Vienna and until his death exercised much influence over the young emperor Franz Joseph. 85. **Guizot,** François Pierre Guillaume Guizot (1787–1874), a French historian and statesman, author of the impressive *History of France.* Later he entered politics with greater success than his early dabbling had augured; he rose to be prime minister for a short time in 1848. The revolutionary movement in that year cut his ministerial duties short, for Guizot was very much of a conservative. He retired to Normandy and resumed his scholarly career.

that has not been decried as communistic by its opponents in power? Where the Opposition that has not hurled back the branding reproach of Communism against the more advanced opposition parties, as well as against its reactionary adversaries?"

The existence of a class war is nothing new: "The history of all hitherto existing society is the history of class struggles." In these strug-
10 gles the fight "each time ended, either in a revolutionary re-constitution of society at large, or in the common ruin of the contending classes."

"Our epoch, the epoch of the bourgeoisie . . . has simplified the class antagonisms. Society as a whole is more and more splitting up into two great hostile camps, into two great classes directly facing each other: Bourgeoisie and Proletariat." Then follows a history of the fall of feudalism, leading to a description of
20 the bourgeoisie as a revolutionary force. "The bourgeoisie, historically, has played a most revolutionary part." "For exploitation, veiled by religious and political illusions, it has substituted naked, shameless, direct, brutal exploitation." "The need of a constantly expanding market for its products chases the bourgeoisie over the whole surface of the globe." "The bourgeoisie, during its rule of scarce one hundred years, has created more massive and more
30 colossal productive forces than have all preceding generations together." Feudal relations became fetters: "They had to be burst asunder; they were burst asunder. . . . A similar movement is going on before our own eyes." "The weapons with which the bourgeoisie felled feudalism to the ground are now turned against the bourgeoisie itself. But not only has the bourgeoisie forged the weapons that bring death to itself; it has also called into existence
40 the men who are to wield those weapons—the modern working class—the proletarians."

The causes of the destitution of the proletariat are then set forth. "The cost of production of a workman is restricted, almost entirely, to the means of subsistence that he requires for his maintenance and for the propagation of his race. But the price of a commodity, and therefore also of labor, is equal to the cost of production. In proportion, therefore, as the repul-
50 siveness of the work increases, the wage de-

creases. Nay more, in proportion as the use of machinery and diversion of labor increases, in the same proportion the burden of toil also increases."

"Modern industry has converted the little workshop of the patriarchal master into the great factory of the industrial capitalist. Masses of laborers, crowded into the factory, are organized like soldiers. As privates of the industrial army they are placed under the command of a perfect hierarchy of officers and sergeants. Not only are they slaves of the bourgeois class, and of the bourgeois State, they are daily and hourly enslaved by the machine, by the overlooker, and, above all, by the individual bourgeois manufacturer himself. The more openly this despotism proclaims gain to be its end and aim, the more petty, the more hateful, and the more embittering it is."

The Manifesto tells next the manner of growth of the class struggle. "The proletariat goes through various stages of development. With its birth begins its struggle with the bourgeoisie. At first the contest is carried on by individual laborers, then by the workpeople of a factory, then by the operatives of one trade, in one locality, against the individual bourgeois who directly exploits them. They direct their attacks not against the bourgeois conditions of production, but against the instruments of production themselves."

"At this stage the laborers still form an incoherent mass scattered over the whole country, and broken up by their mutual competition. If anywhere they unite to form more compact bodies, this is not yet the consequence of their own active union, but of the union of the bourgeoisie, which class, in order to attain its own political ends, is compelled to set the whole proletariat in motion, and is moreover yet, for a time, able to do so."

"The collisions between individual workmen and individual bourgeois take more and more the character of collisions between two classes. Thereupon the workers begin to form combinations (Trades Unions) against the bourgeois; they club together in order to keep up the rate of wages; they found permanent associations in order to make provision beforehand for these occasional revolts. Here and there the contest 1 breaks out into riots. Now and then the workers are victorious, but only for a time. The real fruit of their battles lies, not in the immediate result, but in the ever-expanding union of the workers. This union is helped on by the improved means of communication that are created by modern industry, and that place the workers of different localities in contact with one another. It was just this contact that was needed to centralize the numerous local struggles, all of the same character, into one national struggle between classes. But every class struggle is a political struggle. And that union, to attain which the burghers of the Middle Ages, with their miserable highways, required centuries, the modern proletarians, thanks to railways, achieve in a few years. This organization of the proletarians into a class, and consequently into a political party, is continually being upset again by the competition between the workers themselves. But it ever rises up again, stronger, firmer, mightier. It compels legislative recognition of particular interests of the workers, by taking advantage of the divisions among the bourgeoisie itself."

"In the conditions of the proletariat, those of old society at large are already virtually swamped. The proletarian is without property; his relation to his wife and children has no longer anything in common with the bourgeois family-relations; modern industrial labor, modern subjection to capital, the same in England as in France, in America as in Germany, has stripped him of every trace of national character. Law, morality, religion, are to him so many bourgeois prejudices, behind which may lurk in ambush just as many bourgeois interests. All the preceding classes that got the upper hand, sought to fortify their already acquired status by subjecting society at large to their conditions of appropriation. The proletarians cannot become masters of the productive forces of society, except by abolishing their own previous mode of appropriation, and thereby also every other previous mode of appropriation. They have nothing of their own to secure and to fortify; their mission is to destroy all previous securities for, and insurances of, individual property. All previous historical movements were movements of minorities, or in the interest of minorities. The proletarian movement is the self-conscious, independent movement of the immense majority, in the interest of the immense majority. The proletariat, the lowest stratum of our present society, cannot stir, cannot raise itself up, without the whole superincumbent strata of official society being sprung into the air."

The Communists, says Marx, stand for the proletariat as a whole. They are international. 60 "The Communists are further reproached with desiring to abolish countries and nationality. The working men have no country. We cannot take from them what they have not got."

The immediate aim of the Communists is the conquest of political power by the proletariat. "The theory of the Communists may be summed up in the single sentence: Abolition of private property."

The materialistic interpretation of history is 70 used to answer such charges as that Communism is anti-Christian. "The charges against Communism made from a religious, a philosophical, and, generally, from an ideological standpoint, are not deserving of serious examination. Does it require deep intuition to comprehend that man's ideas, views, and conceptions, in one word, man's consciousness, changes with every change in the conditions of his material existence, in his social relations, 80 and in his social life?"

The attitude of the Manifesto to the State is not altogether easy to grasp. "The executive of the modern State," we are told, "is but a Committee for managing the common affairs of the whole bourgeoisie." Nevertheless, the first step for the proletariat must be to acquire control of the State. "We have seen above, that the first step in the revolution by the working class, is to raise the proletariat to the position of rul- 90 ing class, to win the battle of democracy. The proletariat will use its political supremacy to wrest, by degrees, all capital from the bourgeoisie, to centralize all instruments of production in the hands of the State, i.e., of the proletariat organized as the ruling class; and to increase the total of productive forces as rapidly as possible."

The Manifesto passes on to an immediate program of reform, which would in the first in- 100 stance much increase the power of the existing State, but it is contended that when the Socialist revolution is accomplished, the State, as we know it, will have ceased to exist. As Engels says, elsewhere, when the proletariat seizes the power of the State "it puts an end to all differences of class and antagonisms of class, and consequently also puts an end to the State as a State." Thus, although State Socialism might, in fact, be the outcome of the proposals of Marx and Engels, they cannot themselves be accused of any glorification of the State.

The Manifesto ends with an appeal to the wage-earners of the world to rise on behalf of Communism. "The Communists disdain to conceal their views and aims. They openly declare that their ends can be attained only by the forcible overthrow of all existing social conditions. Let the ruling classes tremble at a Communistic revolution. The proletarians have nothing to lose but their chains. They have a world to win. Working men of all countries, unite!"

In all the great countries of the Continent, except Russia, a revolution quickly followed on the publication of the Communist Manifesto, but the revolution was not economic or international, except at first in France. Everywhere else it was inspired by the ideas of nationalism. Accordingly, the rulers of the world, momentarily terrified, were able to recover power by fomenting the enmities inherent in the nationalist idea, and everywhere, after a very brief triumph, the revolution ended in war and reaction. The ideas of the Communist Manifesto appeared before the world was ready for them, but its authors lived to see the beginnings of the growth of that Socialist movement in every country, which has passed on with increasing force, influencing Governments more and more, dominating the Russian Revolution, and perhaps capable of achieving at no very distant date that international triumph to which the last sentences of the Manifesto summon the wage-earners of the world.

Marx's *magnum opus*, "Capital," added bulk and substance to the theses of the Communist Manifesto. It contributed the theory of surplus value, which professed to explain the actual mechanism of capitalist exploitation. This doctrine is very complicated and is scarcely tena-

ble as a contribution to pure theory. It is rather to be viewed as a translation into abstract terms of the hatred with which Marx regarded the system that coins wealth out of human lives, and it is in this spirit, rather than in that of disinterested analysis, that it has been read by its admirers. A critical examination of the theory of surplus value would require much difficult and abstract discussion of pure economic theory without having much bearing upon the practical truth or falsehood of Socialism; it has therefore seemed impossible within the limits of the present volume. To my mind the best parts of the book are those which deal with economic facts, of which Marx's knowledge was encyclopaedic. It was by these facts that he hoped to instil into his disciples that firm and undying hatred that should make them soldiers to the death in the class war. The facts which he accumulates are such as are practically unknown to the vast majority of those who live comfortable lives. They are very terrible facts, and the economic system which generates them must be acknowledged to be a very terrible system. A few examples of his choice of facts will serve to explain the bitterness of many Socialists:—

"Mr. Broughton Charlton, county magistrate, declared, as chairman of a meeting held at the Assembly Rooms, Nottingham, of the 14th January, 1860, 'that there was an amount of privation and suffering among that portion of the population connected with the lace trade, unknown in other parts of the kingdom, indeed, in the civilized world. . . . Children of nine or ten years are dragged from their squalid beds at two, three, or four o'clock in the morning and compelled to work for a bare subsistence until ten, eleven, or twelve at night, their limbs wearing away, their frames dwindling, their faces whitening, and their humanity absolutely sinking into a stone-like torpor, utterly horrible to contemplate.'

"Three railway men are standing before a London coroner's jury—a guard, an engine-driver, a signalman. A tremendous railway ac-

78. **"Mr. Broughton Charlton . . . contemplate."** Vol. I, p. 227. (Author's note.)   94. **"Three . . . labor-power."** Vol. I, pp. 237, 238. (Author's note.)

cident has hurried hundreds of passengers into another world. The negligence of the employes is the cause of the misfortune. They declare with one voice before the jury that ten or twelve years before, their labor only lasted eight hours a day. During the last five or six years it has been screwed up to 14, 18, and 20 hours, and under a specially severe pressure of holiday-makers, at times of excursion trains, it often lasted 40 or 50 hours without a break. They were ordinary men, not Cyclops. At a certain point their labor-power failed. Torpor seized them. Their brain ceased to think, their eyes to see. The thoroughly 'respectable' British jurymen answered by a verdict that sent them to the next assizes on a charge of manslaughter, and, in a gentle 'rider' to their verdict, expressed the pious hope that the capitalistic magnates of the railways would, in future, be more extravagant in the purchase of a sufficient quantity of labor-power, and more 'abstemious,' more 'self-denying,' more 'thrifty,' in the draining of paid labor-power.

"In the last week of June, 1863, all the London daily papers published a paragraph with the 'sensational' heading, 'Death from simple over-work.' It dealt with the death of the milliner, Mary Anne Walkley, twenty years of age, employed in a highly respectable dressmaking establishment, exploited by a lady with the pleasant name of Elise. The old, often-told story was once more recounted. This girl worked, on an average, 16½ hours, during the season often 30 hours, without a break, whilst her failing labor-power was revived by occasional supplies of sherry, port, or coffee. It was just now the height of the season. It was necessary to conjure up in the twinkling of an eye the gorgeous dresses for the noble ladies bidden to the ball in honor of the newly-imported Princess of Wales. Mary Anne Walkley had worked without intermission for 26½ hours, with 60 other girls, 30 in one room, that only afforded ⅓ of the cubic feet of air required for them. At night, they slept in pairs in one of the stifling holes into which the bedroom was divided by partitions of board. And this was one of the best millinery establishments in London. Mary Anne Walkley fell ill on the Friday, died on Sunday, without, to the astonishment of 50 Madame Elise, having previously completed the work in hand. The doctor, Mr. Keys, called too late to the death bed, duly bore witness before the coroner's jury that 'Mary Anne Walkley had died from long hours of work in an over-crowded workroom, and a too small and badly ventilated bedroom.' In order to give the doctor a lesson in good manners, the coroner's jury thereupon brought in a verdict that 'the deceased had died of apoplexy, but there 60 was reason to fear that her death had been accelerated by over-work in an over-crowded workroom, etc.' 'Our white slaves,' cried the 'Morning Star,' the organ of the free-traders, Cobden and Bright, 'our white slaves, who are toiled into the grave, for the most part silently pine and die.'

"Edward VI: A statute of the first year of his reign, 1547, ordains that if anyone refuses to work, he shall be condemned as a slave to 70 the person who has denounced him as an idler. The master shall feed his slave on bread and water, weak broth and such refuse meat as he thinks fit. He has the right to force him to do any work, no matter how disgusting, with whip and chains. If the slave is absent a fortnight, he is condemned to slavery for life and is to be branded on forehead or back with the letter S; if he runs away thrice, he is to be executed as a felon. The master can sell him, bequeath him, 80 let him out on hire as a slave, just as any other personal chattel or cattle. If the slaves attempt anything against the masters, they are also to be executed. Justices of the peace, on information, are to hunt the rascals down. If it hap-

---

24. **"In . . . die."** Vol. I, pp. 239, 240. (Author's note.)
41. **Princess of Wales,** later Queen Alexandra of England (1844–1925), consort of King Edward VII and daughter-in-law of Queen Victoria, mother of King George V, and grandmother of King Edward VIII and King George VI.

65. **Cobden.** Richard Cobden (1804–65) was an English economist who advocated imperial expansion but decried the use of armed force in bringing this about. He was a violent opponent of the British Corn Laws and aided greatly in their repeal (1846). He was several times returned to Parliament. In addition to his parliamentary duties, he was a tireless lecturer and traveler. **Bright.** John Bright (1811–89), another member of Parliament, was an ardent supporter of free trade, a man of great skill in all forms of public discussion; he was especially friendly to the Union cause during the American Civil War. 68. **"Edward VI . . . 'roundsmen.' "** Vol. I, pp. 758, 759. (Author's note.)

pens that a vagabond has been idling about for three days, he is to be taken to his birthplace, branded with a redhot iron with the letter V on the breast and be set to work, in chains, in the streets or at some other labor. If the vagabond gives a false birthplace, he is then to become the slave for life of this place, of its inhabitants, or its corporation, and to be branded with an S. All persons have the right to take away the children of the vagabonds and to keep them as apprentices, the young men until the 24th year, the girls until the 20th. If they run away, they are to become up to this age the slaves of their masters, who can put them in irons, whip them, etc., if they like. Every master may put an iron ring around the neck, arms or legs of his slave, by which to know him more easily and to be more certain of him. The last part of this statute provides that certain poor people may be employed by a place or by persons, who are willing to give them food and drink and to find them work. This kind of parish-slaves was kept up in England until far into the 19th century under the name of 'roundsmen.'"

Page after page and chapter after chapter of facts of this nature, each brought up to illustrate some fatalistic theory which Marx professes to have proved by exact reasoning, cannot but stir into fury any passionate working-class reader, and into unbearable shame any possessor of capital in whom generosity and justice are not wholly extinct.

Almost at the end of the volume, in a very brief chapter, called "Historical Tendency of Capitalist Accumulation," Marx allows one moment's glimpse of the hope that lies beyond the present horror:—

"As soon as this process of transformation has sufficiently decomposed the old society from top to bottom, as soon as the laborers are turned into proletarians, their means of labor into capital, as soon as the capitalist mode of production stands on its own feet, then the further socialization of labor and further transformation of the land and other means of production into socially exploited and, therefore,

39. "As soon as . . . expropriated." Vol. I, pp. 788, 789. (Author's note.)

common means of production, as well as the further expropriation of private proprietors, takes a new form. That which is now to be expropriated is no longer the laborer working for himself, but the capitalist exploiting many laborers. This expropriation is accomplished by the action of the immanent laws of capitalistic production itself, by the centralization of capital. One capitalist always kills many and in hand with this centralization, or this expropriation of many capitalists by few, develop, on an ever extending scale, the co-operative form of the labor-process, the conscious technical application of science, the methodical cultivation of the soil, the transformation of the instruments of labor into instruments of labor only usable in common, the economizing of all means of production by their use as the means of production of combined, socialized labor, the entanglement of all peoples in the net of the world-market, and with this, the international character of the capitalistic régime. Along with the constantly diminishing number of the magnates of capital, who usurp and monopolize all advantages of this process of transformation, grows the mass of misery, oppression, slavery, degradation, exploitation; but with this, too, grows the revolt of the working-class, a class always increasing in numbers, and disciplined, united, organized by the very mechanism of the process of capitalist production itself. The monopoly of capital becomes a fetter upon the mode of production, which has sprung up and flourished along with, and under it. Centralization of the means of production and socialization of labor at last reach a point where they become incompatible with their capitalist integument. This integument is burst asunder. The knell of capitalist private property sounds. The expropriators are expropriated."

That is all. Hardly another word from beginning to end is allowed to relieve the gloom, and in this relentless pressure upon the mind of the reader lies a great part of the power which this book has acquired.

Two questions are raised by Marx's work: First, Are his laws of historical development true? Second, Is Socialism desirable? The second of these questions is quite independent of the first. Marx professes to prove that Socialism *must* come, but scarcely concerns himself to argue that when it comes it will be a good thing. It may be, however, that if it comes, it will be a good thing, even though all Marx's arguments to prove that it must come should be at fault. In actual fact, time has shown many flaws in Marx's theories. The development of the world has been sufficiently like his prophecy to prove him a man of very unusual penetration, but has not been sufficiently like to make either political or economic history exactly such as he predicted that it would be. Nationalism, so far from diminishing, has increased, and has failed to be conquered by the cosmopolitan tendencies which Marx rightly discerned in finance. Although big businesses have grown bigger and have over a great area reached the stage of monopoly, yet the number of shareholders in such enterprises is so large that the actual number of individuals interested in the capitalist system has continually increased. Moreover, though large firms have grown larger, there has been a simultaneous increase in firms of medium size. Meanwhile the wage-earners, who were, according to Marx, to have remained at the bare level of subsistence at which they were in the England of the first half of the nineteenth century, have instead profited by the general increase of wealth, though in a lesser degree than the capitalists. The supposed iron law of wages has been proved untrue, so far as labor in civilized countries is concerned. If we wish now to find examples of capitalist cruelty analogous to those with which Marx's book is filled, we shall have to go for most of our material to the Tropics, or at any rate to regions where there are men of inferior races to exploit. Again: the skilled worker of the present day is an aristocrat in the world of labor. It is a question with him whether he shall ally himself with the unskilled worker against the capitalist, or with the capitalist against the unskilled worker. Very often he is himself a capitalist in a small way, and if he is not so individually, his trade union or his friendly society is pretty sure to be so. Hence the sharpness of the class war has not been maintained. There are gradations, intermediate ranks between rich and poor, instead of the

clear-cut logical antithesis between the workers who have nothing and the capitalists who have all. Even in Germany, which became the home of orthodox Marxianism and developed a powerful Social-Democratic party, nominally accepting the doctrine of "Das Kapital" as all but verbally inspired, even there the enormous increase of wealth in all classes in the years preceding the war led Socialists to revise their beliefs and to adopt an evolutionary rather than a revolutionary attitude. Bernstein, a German Socialist who lived long in England, inaugurated the "Revisionist" movement which at last conquered the bulk of the party. His criticisms of Marxian orthodoxy are set forth in his "Evolutionary Socialism." Bernstein's work, as is common in Broad Church writers, consists largely in showing that the Founders did not hold their doctrines so rigidly as their followers have done. There is much in the writings of Marx and Engels that cannot be fitted into the rigid orthodoxy which grew up among their disciples. Bernstein's main criticisms of these disciples, apart from such as we have already mentioned, consist in a defense of piecemeal action as against revolution. He protests against the attitude of undue hostility to Liberalism which is common among Socialists, and he blunts the edge of the Internationalism which undoubtedly is part of the teachings of Marx. The workers, he says, have a Fatherland as soon as they become citizens, and on this basis he defends that degree of nationalism which the war has since shown to be prevalent in the ranks of Socialists. He even goes so far as to maintain that European nations have a right to tropical territory owing to their higher civilization. Such doctrines diminish revolutionary ardor and tend to transform Socialists into a left wing of the Liberal Party. But the increasing prosperity of wage-earners before the war made these developments inevi-

66. **"Evolutionary Socialism,"** *Die Voraussetzungen des Sozialismus und die Aufgaben der Sozial-Demokratie.* In March, 1914, Bernstein delivered a lecture in Budapest in which he withdrew from several of the positions he had taken up (vide Budapest "Volksstimme," March 19, 1914). (Author's note.)
67. **Broad Church,** a party of the Anglican Church, which might be defined as the left wing of that institution. It was particularly active in the second half of the nineteenth century

table. Whether the war will have altered conditions in this respect, it is as yet impossible to know. Bernstein concludes with the wise remark: "We have to take working men as they are. And they are neither so universally paupers as was set out in the Communist Manifesto, nor so free from prejudices and weaknesses as their courtiers wish to make us believe."

Bernstein represents the decay of Marxian orthodoxy from within. Syndicalism represents an attack against it from without, from the standpoint of a doctrine which professes to be even more radical and more revolutionary than that of Marx and Engels. The attitude of Syndicalists to Marx may be seen in Sorel's little book, "La Décomposition du Marxisme," and in his larger work, "Reflections on Violence," authorized translation by T. E. Hulme (Allen & Unwin, 1915). After quoting Bernstein, with approval in so far as he criticises Marx, Sorel proceeds to other criticisms of a different order. He points out (what is true) that Marx's theoretical economics remain very near to Manchesterism: the orthodox political economy of his youth was accepted by him on many points on which it is now known to be wrong. According to Sorel, the really essential thing in Marx's teaching is the class war. Whoever keeps this alive is keeping alive the spirit of Socialism much more truly than those who adhere to the letter of Social-Democratic orthodoxy. On the basis of the class war, French Syndicalists developed a criticism of Marx which goes much deeper than those that we have been hitherto considering. Marx's views on historical development may have been in a greater or less degree mistaken in fact, and yet the economic and political system which he sought to create might be just as desirable as his followers suppose. Syndicalism, however, criticises, not only Marx's views of fact, but also the goal at which he aims and the general nature of the means which he recommends. Marx's ideas were formed at a time when democracy did not yet exist. It was in the very year in which "Das Kapital" appeared that urban working men first got the vote in England and universal suffrage was granted by Bismarck in Northern Germany. It was natural that great hopes should

be entertained as to what democracy would achieve. Marx, like the orthodox economists, imagined that men's opinions are guided by a more or less enlightened view of economic self-interest, or rather of economic class interest. A long experience of the workings of political democracy has shown that in this respect Disraeli and Bismarck were shrewder judges of human nature than either Liberals or Socialists. It has become increasingly difficult to put trust in the State as a means to liberty, or in political parties as instruments sufficiently powerful to force the State into the service of the people. The modern State, says Sorel, "is a body of intellectuals, which is invested with privileges, and which possesses means of the kind called political for defending itself against the attacks made on it by other groups of intellectuals, eager to possess the profits of public employment. Parties are constituted in order to acquire the conquest of these employments, and they are analogous to the State."

Syndicalists aim at organizing men, not by party, but by occupation. This, they say, alone represents the true conception and method of the class war. Accordingly they despise all *political* action through the medium of Parliament and elections: the kind of action that they recommend is direct action by the revolutionary syndicate or trade union. The battle-cry of industrial versus political action has spread far beyond the ranks of French Syndicalism. It is to be found in the I. W. W. in America, and among Industrial Unionists and Guild Socialists in Great Britain. Those who advocate it, for the most part, aim also at a different goal from that of Marx. They believe that there can be no adequate individual freedom where the State is all-powerful, even if the State be a Socialist one. Some of them are out-and-out Anarchists, who wish to see the State wholly abolished; others only wish to curtail its authority. Owing to this movement, opposition to Marx, which from the Anarchist side existed from the first, has grown very strong. It is this opposition in its older form that will occupy us in our next chapter.

64. The modern State . . . to the State. *La Décomposition du Marxisme,* p. 53. (Author's note.)

HORACE GREGORY

Horace Victor Gregory was born April 10, 1898, in Milwaukee, Wisconsin. There he attended the German-English Academy and the Milwaukee School of Fine Arts. After his graduation from the University of Wisconsin in 1923 he went to New York and began working as a free-lance writer on *The New Republic, The Nation, The Atlantic Monthly, Hound and Horn,* and the *Herald Tribune.* In 1925 he married Marya Zaturenska, the poet, and they have two children. Since 1934 he has been a lecturer on poetry and criticism at Sarah Lawrence College, Bronxville, New York.

Known as a critic and poet, Gregory won *Poetry* magazine's Lyric Prize in 1928, its Helen Haire Levinson Prize in 1934. He published *Chelsea Rooming House* in 1930, *No Retreat* in 1931, and *Chorus for Survival* in 1935. All these books of poetry were clearly inspired by an awareness of the suffering of the poor, by a knowledge of the evils of our society. However, Gregory came more and more under the influence of T. S. Eliot, who had admired his poetry; slowly his identification (perhaps always intellectual) with the workers waned and his picture became the American version of the intellectual chaos, the defeatism of the late twenties. Like Eliot, Gregory sought out as refuge first the traditional past, and finally religion. He has not become, as far as is known, Anglo-Catholic, but his *Poems* (1930–41) indicate his concentration on personal salvation or integration, his resting on art for art's sake, his retreat from any poetic comment on the social scene. Possibly his early ill health and struggle for position only temporarily identified

him with the all-too-evident problems of the depression years. Today, together with Eliot and Auden, he holds that poets are non-participants in any action save that of writing poetry.

As a Latin scholar, Gregory translated in 1931 the *Poems of Catullus.* In 1933 he wrote an interpretation of D. H. Lawrence called *Pilgrim of the Apocalypse;* and in 1944 he published a kind of poetic credo called *The Shield of Achilles. A History of American Poetry, 1900–1940,* on which he and his wife collaborated, was published in 1946. He edited *Critical Remarks on the Metaphysical Poets,* by Samuel Johnson and others (1946).

O Metaphysical Head

THE MAN was forever haunted by his head,
this John Brown's body head—
John Brown's body lies—
John Brown's body lies—
John Brown's body lies—   5
its head goes marching on—
triumphant, bowing to its friends,
lost in a crowd, then bright as dawn

The poems of Horace Gregory are reprinted from *Chelsea Rooming House* by permission of Covici Friede, Inc.
O Metaphysical Head. Here one sees the poet trace gradually the complete mechanization of life through the loss of glory formally symbolized by man's mind or head. Finally the head becomes merely a machine collecting pennies in a subway. "Metaphysical Head" means the transcendental qualities of a head, for everything is possible that can be conceived.

found again, shining through streets,
laughing, happy by god, drunk, merry old
      head,   10
two cocktails and a bottle of champagne
lighting the dark corners in its brain.

A taxi. Home. O, metaphysical head,
the world is too small for it,
barefooted, naked in a bedroom. Bed.   15
It is awake, remembering, thinking:
(I have seen this head too often,
this too-familiar head, yet it changes,
      changes. . . .
I have seen this young Caesar head
rising above a summer hill, bland and omnipo-
      tent,   20
to meet its love, to see her rise
to this head and with closing eyes
and open lips drinking
the head down until
its brain enters her body   25
and its will
becomes her will.)

And now, the head goes rolling down the hill,
(uxorious head)
rolls into darkness, sleeps: 30
grows large in dreams, serene, awful,
becomes God, opens its mighty lips
crying, *Let there be light
in this dream.* Let all
all the women who have not worshipped   35
this head come naked and ashamed before it,
suffering their little children
to come unto it.
Pity for little children,
conceived in sin,   40
not fathered by this head
but from the needs
of other men.

Awake again, rising from the dream
into the bedroom, eyelids closed,   45
the head lost in space,
fixed in ecstatic peace,
senses warm, fluid in the body,
but the head, the wingèd, haloed head gone,

19. **I have seen . . . head, etc.** The poet here speaks especially
of the sense of power man has in youth. This sense of power is
quickly destroyed by the necessity a man feels to support his
family. In this day and age love has its price.

gone where all godheads go,   50
singing, *Heaven, heaven.* . . .

         No,
found somewhere in a gutter,
pitiful, blind, sallow.
(And curious friends examine it,   55
saying, It shall never rise again,
poor fellow.
Put it away.
It hurts us.
Poor fellow,   60
no words were made to say
how sad we feel. An ugly head—
see what's become of John—
we're sorry, but we must be moving on.)

The head gone. Irrevocably gone,   65
no longer magnificent, the speaker of the word,
divine, exalted, tilting backward in a barber's
      chair,
august, revered,
floating above a glass-topped desk,
making its power heard   70
roaring into a telephone,
then brisk, attentive,
meeting its clients and its creditors,
then finally tired, meditating restfully
on the flat bosoms of its stenographers,   75
on the undetermined virginity of its stenogra-
      phers.

There would be no offices for headless men,
no girls, nor wives,
only the subway entrances where one may
      stand
unseeing (almost unseen)   80
with right arm raised, the index finger of the
      hand
pointing where the head had been,
the left hand catching pennies.

*John Brown's body goes
begging underground,*   85
John Brown's body—
(No one would dare look at the creature;
it could stand,
a monument for years,
headless, quiet,   90
forever catching pennies
in its hand.)

O Mors Aeterna

BE for a little while eternal,
singing with all the songs in your body
but making no sound.

The Rose of Sharon singing in an old city
was eternal suddenly   5
for a little while.

And the mountains fell away
and the city sank into earth again
and the voices of dead men came from the
            ground
crying, Incest and poverty and murder   10
(all in the many dead years
that had sent them into the earth)
but now rising, crying against the world
and mortal sun and moon and stars,
against life and the masters   15
in purple victories, clothed with iron wars.

For a little while
the Rose of Sharon sang eternally
until the city came round her again
and there was no sound.

Columbo Dominico

COLUMBO Dominico
dead on Minetta Street
is no finality,
even with a regiment of bullets in his back,
is no end of things;   5
maybe the cops got him (he was out of work,
vagrant, selling bad booze)
maybe his brother, maybe his girl
shouting: *You go to hell, get out of here,
good bye, Dominico*   10
and Dominico, surprised, unsteady,

leaping into eternal aether
crying: Viva, viva anarchy!

Here is no end of things.
Even a frozen outpost of the Salvation Army
walking down the winter street,   16
seeing Dominico,
quickens his feet,
lifts up his watery eyes and sings:
Jesus saves and his sweet breath   20
wakens all the sinners in the halls of death
and his eyes shine bright and his heart beats
            warm
as he gathers all the sinners in the crook of his
            arm.
Jesus saves, Jesus saves.
Here is no finality.   25
Dominico dead
mingles with all the dead,
his gigantic shade
(an elbow leaning on the Woolworth Tower)
pierces lovestruck Dante with a shoulder blade
and spits upon the trembling purpled face   31
that once was Nero's and the elder Morgan's,
vaulted into space,
it strides with Robespierre,
kisses Marat   35
and sleeps, relaxed, with Lesbia for an hour.

There is no end of things . . .
Angelo Gorini and Tony Bruno (out of work,
vagrant, selling bad booze)
the cops got them for killing   40
Columbo Dominico.
Angelo Gorini and Tony Bruno, falling,
slipping into death, calling
out: *By Jesus Christ, we didn't do it,*
viva, viva anarchy,   45
we love the red flag!

Longface Mahoney Discusses Heaven

IF SOMEONE said, *Escape,*
let's get away from here,
you'd see snow mountains thrown
against the sky,
cold, and you'd draw your breath and feel   5
air like cold water going through your veins,

O Mors Aeterna, a prayer for something (death, at least) eternal in this modern world of flux and change. **4. Rose of Sharon,** the flower which blooms on the plains of Jaffa; in reality a white narcissus, symbol of prosperity.
Columbo Dominico, any poverty-stricken Italian killed on Minetta Street (in Greenwich Village, New York) because he is an outcast. His life and death are insignificant, but the poet indicates that once dead his knowledge of Dante and his hatred of ancient tyrants like Nero, Emperor of Rome, or modern capitalists like Morgan, the founder of an international private banking house, dignify him. He may even identify himself with Robespierre, a French revolutionary leader, executed, and Marat, a French revolutionary leader killed by Charlotte Corday. Finally Dominico sleeps with Lesbia, the name used by Catullus for his mistress.

Longface Mahoney Discusses Heaven. Longface Mahoney's idea of heaven is merely a hotel bedroom with a girl—an escape from the life of a man who lives, none too honestly, by his wits in this modern world.

but you'd be free, up so high,
or you'd see a row of girls dancing on a beach
with tropic trees and a warm moon
and warm air floating under your clothes   10
and through your hair.
Then you'd think of heaven
where there's peace, away from here
and you'd go someplace unreal
where everybody goes after something hap-
          pens,   15
set up in the air, safe, a room in a hotel.
A brass bed, military hair brushes,
a couple of coats, trousers, maybe a dress
on a chair or draped on the floor.
This room is not on earth, feel the air,   20
warm like heaven and far away.

This is a place
where marriage nights are kept
and sometimes here you say, Hello
to a neat girl with you   25
and sometimes she laughs
because she thinks it's funny to be sitting here

for no reason at all, except perhaps,
she likes you daddy.
Maybe this isn't heaven but near   30
to something like it,
more like love coming up in elevators
and nothing to think about, except, o god,
you love her now and it makes no difference
if it isn't spring. All seasons are warm   35
in the warm air
and the brass bed is always there.

If you've done something
and the cops get you afterwards, you
can't remember the place again,   40
away from cops and streets—
it's all unreal—
the warm air, a dream
that couldn't save you now.
No one would care   45
to hear about it,
it would be heaven
far away, dark and no music,
not even a girl there.

WILLIAM CARLOS WILLIAMS

William Carlos Williams likes to view his life in a prosaic fashion, yet it has been a rich and important one. He was born September 18, 1883, at Rutherford, New Jersey, where he still lives and practices medicine. His father was English, his mother a Puerto Rican who had studied painting in Paris and was responsible for her children's interest in the arts. Williams was educated in the public schools of Rutherford and in New York City and Geneva, Switzerland, and graduated from the Medical School of the University of Pennsylvania. Here he met Ezra Pound, with whom he became fast friends; the American Imagist poet Hilda Doolittle; and the painter Charles Demuth, with whom he likewise formed a lifelong friendship. After his internship in New York he attended the University of Leipzig. He visited London, then went to Sicily, where his brother, who had

won the Prix de Rome in architecture, was then living.

In 1923 Williams and his wife made a six-month trip through Europe, visiting Paris, Vienna, and Italy, where he again studied medicine. Some time later they traveled to Switzerland, where they took their two boys to school. It is important that this man, although closely connected in friendship and thought with many artists living abroad, was always quick to return to America.

Whereas his mother expressed herself in painting, William Carlos Williams felt that words were a more explicit manner of expression. While none of his works has brought large material returns, they have always won the serious consideration of critics. The published verse volumes are: *Poems* (1909); *The Tempers* (1913); *Kora in Hell: Improvisations*

(1920); *Sour Grapes* (1921); *Spring and All* (1923); *Collected Poems, 1921–1931* (1934); *The Complete Collected Poems of William Carlos Williams, 1906–1938* (1938); *Paterson: Book I* (1946); and *Paterson: Book II* (1948); *Selected Poems* (1948); and *Clouds, Aigeltinger, Russia, and Other Verse* (1949). Of his prose, *White Mule* was published in 1937, and *Life Along the Passaic River* in 1938.

Some of the critics have felt that *Paterson: Book I* is his greatest poem. Its subject, as Randall Jarrell puts it, is "How can you tell the truth about things?—that is, how can you find language so close to the world that the world can be represented and understood in it?" Williams' plea in his poetry is for the "green" of life which cancels out the "red" of any purely esthetic impression.

He has continued to follow the path marked out in his earlier autobiographical poem "The Wanderer," where the poet with his Muse, a homely old woman, and his phoenix, an ordinary crow, first becomes acquainted with Nature. He finds Nature not romantic but difficult, as those who wrest a living from her know. Next, he meets all kinds of human beings, ugly as well as beautiful, and comes to love them all. A strike scene in Paterson prompts him to hint that the poets have failed the people. At last he is ready to be baptized in the dirty Passaic River, and out of this baptism is reborn the modern poet. *Paterson: Book I* is not far from the theme of this earlier poem; the problem of art and reality is the same.

William Carlos Williams began as an imagist, and he has always objectified his emotions by picturing them. Poem after poem takes the form of a series of imagistic notations, recording the details of an experience. The poet notes that a smile is like a knife. He describes a cat carefully releasing a hind foot from a flower pot. Always he sees life vividly and realistically. He sets down an actual observation together with his poetic response to what he has seen. The scene of his poems is the scene of his daily life; and these poems are in a sense an imaginative mind's notations of intense moments arising during even the most ordinary daily routine. Because he wishes to record speech rather than song, he uses free verse.

In general, Williams has identified his vocation and avocation. As a practicing physician who does much charity work, he makes his observations the subject matter of both his prose and his poetry. In his poetry one can trace the life of a man among men, of a doctor with a deep understanding of the variability in human nature and with a firm faith that the laboring people are robust enough and desirous enough of life to bring about better social conditions.

The Lonely Street

SCHOOL is over. It is too hot
to walk at ease. At ease
in light frocks they walk the streets
to while the time away.
They have grown tall. They hold   5
pink flames in their right hands.
In white from head to foot,
with sidelong, idle look—
in yellow, floating stuff,
black sash and stockings—   10
touching their avid mouths
with pink sugar on a stick—
like a carnation each holds in her hand—
they mount the lonely street.

Overture to a Dance of Locomotives

I

MEN WITH picked voices chant the names
of cities in a huge gallery: promises
that pull through descending stairways
to a deep rumbling.
        The rubbing feet   5
of those coming to be carried quicken a
grey pavement into soft light that rocks
to and fro, under the domed ceiling,

"The Lonely Street" and "Overture to a Dance of Locomotives" from *Sour Grapes*. Copyright, 1920, by the Four Seas Co. Used by permission of Bruce Humphries, Inc., Boston.
The Lonely Street. The poem is a picture of adolescence, of youth sucking the lollypop of life. The images of adolescence are all indicative of the psychology of this period in life when youth feels its own importance. 6. **pink flames,** an image of life taken from the candy sticks the youngsters held.
Overture, etc. Here in rhythm and image is a story of any large railroad station from which one departs on journeys. The significance of the poem is in its suggestion that our lives are an "overture" to a journey.

across and across from pale
earthcoloured walls of bare limestone.   10

Covertly the hands of a great clock
go round and round! Were they to
move quickly and at once the whole
secret would be out and the shuffling
of all ants be done forever.   15
A leaning pyramid of sunlight, narrowing
out at a high window, moves by the clock:
disaccordant hands straining out from
a center: inevitable postures infinitely
repeated—   20

                    II

Two—twofour—twoeight!
Porters in red hats run on narrow platforms.
This way ma'am!
                    —important not to take
the wrong train!   25
                    Lights from the concrete
ceiling hang crooked but—
                    Poised horizontal
on glittering parallels the dingy cylinders
packed with a warm glow—inviting entry—   30
pull against the hour. But brakes can
hold a fixed posture till—
                    The whistle!

Not twoeight. Not twofour. Two!

Gliding windows. Colored cooks sweating   35
in a small kitchen. Taillights—

In time: twofour!
In time: twoeight!

—rivers are tunneled: trestles
cross oozy swamplands: wheels repeating   40
the same gesture remain relatively
stationary: rails forever parallel
return on themselves infinitely.
                    The dance is sure.

The Trees

THE TREES—being trees
thrash and scream
guffaw and curse—

"The Trees" and "The Wind Increases" from *Imagist Anthology* (1930), reprinted by permission of Covici Friede, Inc.
The Trees, a humorous study of the noise of trees in wind. The trees really are symbols of man, blown about, chilled, losing his imagination concerning such things as satyrs and maenads as he grows scientific and philosophic.

640

wholly abandoned
damning the race of men—   5

Christ, the bastards
haven't even sense enough
to stay out in the rain—

Wha ha ha ha

Wheeeeee   10
clacka tacka tacka
tacka tacka
wha ha ha ha ha
ha ha ha

knocking knees, buds   15
bursting from each pore
even the trunk's self
putting out leafheads—

Loose desire!
we naked cry to you—   20
"Do what you please."

You cannot!

—ghosts
sapped of strength

wailing at the gate   25
heartbreak at the bridgehead—
desire
dead in the heart

haw haw haw haw
—and memory broken   30

wheeeeee

There were never satyrs
never maenads
never eagle-headed gods—
These were men   35
from whose hands sprung
love
bursting the wood—

Trees their companions
—a cold wind winterlong   40
in the hollows of our flesh
icy with pleasure—

no part of us untouched

The Wind Increases

THE HARRIED
earth is swept.
The trees
the tulip's bright
tips   5
sidle and
toss—
Loose your love
to flow

Blow!   10

Good Christ what is
a poet—if any
exists?

a man
whose words will   15
bite
their way
home—being actual
having the form
of motion   20

At each twigtip

new
upon the tortured
body of thought
gripping   25
the ground
a way
to the last leaftip

Late for Summer Weather

HE HAS on
an old light grey Fedora
She a black beret

He a dirty sweater
She an old blue coat   5
that fits her tight

Grey flapping pants
Red skirt and
broken down black pumps

Fat   Lost   Ambling   10
nowhere through
the upper town they kick

their way through
heaps of
fallen maple leaves   15

still green—and
crisp as dollar bills
Nothing to do. Hot cha!

The Yachts

CONTEND in a sea which the land partly encloses
shielding them from the too heavy blows
of an ungoverned ocean which when it chooses

tortures the biggest hulls, the best man knows
to pit against its beatings, and sinks them pitilessly.   5
Mothlike in mists, scintillant in the minute

brilliance of cloudless days, with broad belly-
ing sails
they glide to the wind tossing green water
from their sharp prows while over them the
crew crawls

antlike, solicitously grooming them, releasing,
making fast as they turn, lean far over and
having   11
caught the wind again, side by side, head for
the mark.

In a well guarded arena of open water surrounded by
lesser and greater craft which, sycophant,
lumbering
and flittering follow them, they appear youthful, rare   15

as the light of a happy eye, live with the grace
of all that in the mind is feckless, free and
naturally to be desired. Now the sea which
holds them

is moody, lapping their glossy sides, as if feeling
for some slightest flaw but fails completely.   20
Today no race. Then the wind comes again.
The yachts

The Wind Increases. The poem is a study in rhythm to
represent the rhythm of the wind.   11. **Good Christ . . .
motion.** Here Williams states that the poet must swing words
into new motions.
"Late for Summer Weather" and "The Yachts" from *An Early
Martyr* (1935), reprinted by permission of The Alcestis Press.

The Yachts. The yachts, which symbolize the privileged
class, as they skim over inland waters, are contrasted with the
biggest hulls—the underprivileged, or the laboring, class, exposed to the cruelest buffetings of heavy seas. In the end the
yachts are shown skimming safe into harbor over drowned
bodies from the wrecked, because unprotected, bigger hulls.

641

move, jockeying for a start, the signal is set
  and they
are off. Now the waves strike at them but they
  are too
well made, they slip through, though they take
  in canvas.

Arms with hands grasping seek to clutch at the
  prows.   25
Bodies thrown recklessly in the way are cut
  aside.
It is a sea of faces about them in agony, in
  despair

until the horror of the race dawns staggering
  the mind,
the whole sea become an entanglement of
  watery bodies
lost to the world bearing what they cannot
  hold. Broken   30

beaten, desolate, reaching from the dead to be
  taken up
they cry out, failing, failing! their cries rising
in waves still as the skillful yachts pass over.

St. Francis Einstein of the Daffodils

ON THE FIRST VISIT OF PROFESSOR
EINSTEIN TO THE UNITED STATES
IN THE SPRING OF 1921

S WEET land"
  at last!
out of the sea—
the Venusremembering wavelets
rippling with laughter—   5
freedom

for the daffodils!
—in a tearing wind
that shakes
the tufted orchards—   10
Einstein, tall as a violet
in the lattice-arbor corner
is tall as
a blossomy peartree

O Samos, Samos   15
dead and buried. Lesbia
a black cat in the freshturned
garden. All dead.
All flesh they sung
is rotten   20
Sing of it no longer—

Side by side young and old
take the sun together—
maples, green and red
  yellowbells   25
and the vermilion quinceflower
together—

The peartree
with foetid blossoms
sways its high topbranches   30
with contrary motions
and there are both pinkflowered
and coralflowered peachtrees
in the bare chickenyard
of the old Negro   35
with white hair who hides
poisoned fish-heads
here and there
where stray cats find them—
find them   40

Spring days
swift and mutable
winds blowing four ways
hot and cold
shaking the flowers—   45

28. **until . . . mind.** From here on the poet indicates the horror of the race which at first he had described as beautiful. "St. Francis Einstein of the Daffodils" from *Adam and Eve and the City* (1936), reprinted by permission of The Alcestis Press.
St. Francis Einstein of the Daffodils. Professor Albert Einstein is compared to St. Francis of Assisi because both walked humbly, and by communion with nature discovered laws unknown to the average man. St. Francis, living in an age of miracles, could, according to legend, talk with animals and plants. Einstein discovered laws which upset all known scientific hypotheses concerning the movement of one natural body in respect to another. Williams probably thinks of such a discovery as Einstein's as a modern miracle. The poem begins with Einstein's coming to the new land to teach and lecture in 1921, the year he received the Nobel Prize. The second stanza indicates that the old world is dead, as are old ideas. The rest of the poem is in images of spring which symbolize Einstein's new theories. 4. **Venusremembering wavelets.** One conception of Venus is found in the statue of her by an Athenian artist, Cleomenes, titled Venus Anadyomene. The sculpture shows her rising from the sea. It is the most youthful of all her statues.

11. **Einstein,** the world's greatest physicist, born at Ulm, Württemberg, Germany, of German-Swiss parentage, March 14, 1879. The work by which he is best known is his theory of relativity, which he first made known to the public in 1905 and which was generally accepted by 1915, after it was put to the severe test of being mathematically checked by a solar eclipse visible in the South Seas. The general principle of this law is: To the laws of nature may be given such a mathematical form as will be independent of the relative condition displayed by the observer. In 1933 Hitler deprived him of his post in Berlin, and he became Professor of Mathematics at Princeton. He is now an American citizen.   15. **Samos,** an ancient island in the Aegean Sea.   16. **Lesbia,** the name which the poet Catullus gave to one of the favorites in his poems.

Now the northeast wind
moving in fogs leaves the grass
cold and dripping. The night
is dark. But in the night
the southeast wind approaches.   50
The owner of the orchard
lies in bed
with open windows
and throws off his covers
one by one

from **Paterson: Book 1**

1.

Paterson lies in the valley under the Passaic
    Falls
its spent waters forming the outline of his back.
    He
lies on his right side, head near the thunder
of the waters filling his dreams! Eternally
    asleep,
his dreams walk about the city where he per-
    sists   5
incognito. Butterflies settle on his stone ear.
Immortal he neither moves nor rouses and is
    seldom

From *Paterson: Book I* by William Carlos Williams, reprinted
by permission of the publisher, New Directions.
Paterson: Book 1. This is the first part of a long poem in four
parts—that a man in himself is a city, beginning, seeking,
achieving and concluding his life in ways which the various
aspects of a city may embody—if imaginatively conceived—
any city, all the details of which may be made to voice his most
intimate convictions. Part One introduces the elemental character of the place. The Second Part [comprises] the modern
replicas. Three will seek a language to make them vocal, and
Four, the river below the falls, will be reminiscent of episodes—
all that any one man may achieve in a lifetime. (Author's
note.)

seen, though he breathes and the subtleties of
    his machinations
drawing their substance from the noise of the
    pouring river
animate a thousand automatons, Who because
    they   10
neither know their sources nor the sills of their
disappointments walk outside their bodies aim-
    lessly for the most part,
locked and forgot in their desires—unroused.

—Say it, no ideas but in things—   14
nothing but the blank faces of the houses
and cylindrical trees
bent, forked by preconception and acci-
    dent—
split, furrowed, creased, mottled, stained—
secret—into the body of the light!   19

From above, higher than the spires, higher
even than the office towers, from oozy fields
abandoned to grey beds of dead grass,
black sumac, withered weed-stalks,
mud and thickets cluttered with dead leaves—
the river comes pouring in above the city   25
and crashes from the edge of the gorge
in a recoil of spray and rainbow mists—

(What common language to unravel?
. . combed into straight lines
from that rafter of a rock's   30
lip.)

A man like a city and a woman like a flower
—who are in love. Two women. Three women.
Innumerable women, each like a flower.
                                            But
only one man—like a city.

STERLING BROWN

Sterling Allen Brown was born in Washington,
D.C., May 1, 1901; he was educated in the
public schools of Washington and at Williams
College, from which he received his A.B. in
1922. At Harvard the following year he took
his master's degree in English, and later, his
Ph.D. Before taking his doctorate he taught
at Virginia Seminary and College, Lynchburg,
Virginia, at Lincoln University in Missouri, and
at Fisk University. After 1929 he was a member of the faculty of Howard University in
Washington, where he still lectures; he has re-

cently been Visiting Professor of English at Vassar College. During the summer of 1946 he taught at the University of Minnesota as participant in Tremaine McDowell's Program of American Studies. After completing his work on *An American Dilemma* (1944), the published report of a study of the Negro in America sponsored by the Carnegie Foundation and directed by Gunnar Myrdal, Brown was asked by a New York publisher to write a book on the South, on which he is now working. In April 1947 he gave a series of lectures at the New School for Social Research.

In all his writing, Brown's purpose is to interpret authentically the life of the American Negro in the American scene, North and South. He has lived and traveled among his own people in the South, at times risking his personal safety to get accurate social data for his records and for his poetry. When the Federal Writers' Project was in existence, Brown was Editor on Negro Affairs. Together with Arthur P. Davis and Ulysses Lee he edited in 1941 *The Negro Caravan.* Awarded the Guggenheim Fellowship for creative writing in 1937, he published *The Negro in American Fiction* (1937) and *Negro Poetry and Drama* (1937).

His first book of poetry, *Southern Road* (1932), had made him one of the leading Negro poets. His second and as yet unpublished book, *No Hiding Place*, in verse and prose, treats the Negro "problem" as one of several minority problems.

Some of Sterling Brown's poems, written in ballad meter, present Negro characters who speak in a modified regional dialect. Slim Greer, who first appears in *Southern Road*, develops into a Negro Paul Bunyan in the second volume, *No Hiding Place*. Through Slim Greer's yarns we begin to understand the bitterness and the suffering as well as the humor and the spirit of fun inherent in the Negro people. Since jazz rhythms and blues songs are not in key with Brown's quiet satire, he seldom uses them. He is concerned more with representing the Negro raconteur than with depicting the Negro singer. In commenting on the life of the educated Negro, he uses, appropriately, the speech rhythms of the American poet. Through his scholarly contributions to Negro history and his widely read poetry Sterling Brown has brought honor to his country and to his people.

Transfer

I

IT MUST have been that the nigger was
    tongue-tied,
Or absent-minded, or daft with the heat,
But howsoeverbeit he didn't say sir,
So they took and bounced him out on the street.

And then the motorman brained him with his
    crank,   5
And the conductor clubbed him with his gun,
But before they could place the nickels on his
    eyes,
The cops rushed up to see justice done.

The city-court judge was merciful to him: 9
Gave him just four years and suspended his fine,
For bruising white knuckles, inciting to riot,
And holding up traffic on the Peachtree line.

When the boy came to, he was still right
    skittish,
They figured they had got him rid of his harm,
By beating his head, and displacing his jaw-
    bone,   15
So they made him a trusty on the prison-farm.

II

But one day a red sun beat on the red hills
As he was in the pasture, haltering a mare,
And something went snap in his trusty old head
And he started a-riding away from there.   20

When he got to Atlanta, the folks took him in,
And fed him and clothed him, and hid him
    away;
And let him out only when the cops disappear
From the streets of Darktown at the dusk of
    day:

Then he goes to the car-stop and takes his stand,
And some call him daffy, and some call him
    smart,   26
But all have heard the one text he's been
    preaching,
And some have the whole sermon down by
    heart:

"I stayed in my place, and my place stayed wid
    me,
Took what was dished, said I liked it fine:
Figgered they would see that I warn't no
    trouble,   31
Figgered this must be the onliest line.

"Transfer," "Old Lem," "Conjured," "Colloquy," and "Glory, Glory" are reprinted by permission of the author.

"But this is the wrong line we been ridin',
This route doan git us where we got to go.
Got to git transferred to a new direction.   35
We can stand so much, then doan stan no mo'."

Old Lem

I TALKED to old Lem
And old Lem said:
    "They weigh the cotton
    They store the corn
        We only good enough   5
        To work the rows;
    They run the commissary
    They keep the books
        We gotta be grateful
        For being cheated;   10
    Whippersnapper clerks
    Call us out of our name
        We got to say mister
        To spindling boys
    They make our figgers   15
    Turn somersets
        We buck in the middle
        Say, 'Thankyuh, sah.'
            They don't come by ones
            They don't come by twos   20
            But they come by tens.

    "They got the judges
    They got the lawyers
    They got the jury-rolls
    They got the law   25
            They don't come by ones
    They got the sheriffs
    They got the deputies
            They don't come by twos
    They got the shotguns   30
    They got the rope
        We git the justice
        In the end
            And they come by tens.

    "Their fists stay closed   35
    Their eyes look straight
        Our hands stay open
        Our eyes must fall
            They don't come by ones
    They got the manhood   40
    They got the courage
            They don't come by twos
    We got to slink around,
    Hangtailed hounds.

They burn us when we dogs   45
They burn us when we men
        They come by tens . . . .

    "I had a buddy
    Six foot of man
    Muscled up perfect   50
    Game to the heart
            They don't come by ones
    Outworked and outfought
    Any man or two men
            They don't come by twos   55
    He spoke out of turn
    At the commissary
    They gave him a day
    To git out the county.
    He didn't take it.   60
    He said, 'Come and git me.'
    And they came and got him.
            And they come by tens.
    He stayed in the county.
    He lays there dead.   65
            They don't come by ones
            They don't come by twos
            But they come by tens."

Conjured

SHE DONE put huh little hands
On de back uh my head;
I cain't git away from her
Twill I'm dead.

"She done laid huh little body   5
Beneaf' my breast,
And I won't never
Git no rest.

"She done been in my arms
Twill de break of day   10
Won't never
Git away . . . .

"She done put huh little shoes
Underneaf my bed
Never git away from her   15
Twill I'm dead.

"Won't want to leave her
Then," he said.
"Oh, baby, gotta lay
So long   20
Alone . . ."

Colloquy

(BLACK WORKER AND WHITE WORKER)

IT'S BEEN a long time since we got together,
    Sam."
"A long time? I don't know when we did befo'."
"Sure you remember when we was kids,
Long time ago?"

"I recollec' how you chased me and my
    brothers   5
Out of de crick; an' I recollec' when
You rocked us through Cottontown clean cross
    de railroad—
We didn't get together, then.

"We didn't get together 'cause we niggers ran
    too fast.
We knew we'd keep our health a little better
    if we run,   10
That's about all de gettin' together
You an' me's ever done."

"Reckon you'se right—we 'uns been tarnation
    onery,
But we didn't know no better, an' that time's
    past.
I got to stop my pitchin' rocks, an' you—you
    got to trust me,   15
An' not run away so fas'.

"The bosses got us both where de bosses want
    us
An' dey's squeezin' us both an' dey won't let go.
We gotta get together, we gotta jerk from
    under
Or else we are goners, bo."   20

"I coulda told you, long ago, Mist' Charlie,
Bein' onery wan't no way you should behave,
When both of us got more'n our share of
    misery
From rockin' cradle to de lastin' grave."   24

"Shake hands, Sam. We'll be buddies now,
An' do our scrappin' side by side from this."
"Well, here's my hand. I never gave it before,
Scared I might draw back a wrist.

"But dere's hard times comin'—wuss'n hard
    times now,
An' in de hard times dat I recollec'   30
De whites stood together on top of our
    shoulders
An' give it to us square in de neck.

"So I tells you like de bull frog say unto de
    eagle,
Flyin' cross de stone quarry high in de sky,
Don't do it, big boy, don't do it to me—   35
Not when we'se up so high . . ."

Bitter Fruit of the Tree

THEY SAID to my grandmother: "Please do
    not be bitter,"
When they sold her first-born and let the sec-
    ond die,
When they drove her husband till he took to
    the swamplands,
And brought him home bloody and beaten at
    last.
They told her, "It is better you should not be
    bitter,   5
Some must work and suffer so that we, who
    must, can live,
Forgiving is noble, you must not be heathen
    bitter;
These are your orders: you *are* not to be
    bitter."
And they left her shack for their porticoed
    house.

They said to my father: "Please do not be
    bitter,"   10
When he ploughed and planted a crop not his,
When he weatherstripped a house that he
    could not enter,
And stored away a harvest he could not enjoy.
They answered his questions: "It does not con-
    cern you,
It is not for you to know, it is past your un-
    derstanding,   15
All you need know is: you must not be bitter."
And they laughed on their way to reckon the
    crop.
And my father walked over the wide gar-
    nered acres
Where a cutting wind warned him of the cold
    to come.

They said to my brother: "Please do not be
    bitter,   20
Is it not sad to see the old place go to ruin?
The eaves are sprung and the chimney tower
    is leaning,

"Bitter Fruit of the Tree" is reprinted by permission of the
author and *The Nation.*

The sills, joists, and columns are rotten in the
    core;
The blinds hang crazy and the shingles blow
    away,
The fields have gone back to broomsedge and
    pine,   25
And the soil washes down the red gulley scars.
With so much to be done, there's no time for
    being bitter;
Your father made it for us, it is up to you to
    save it,
What is past is over, and you should not be
    bitter."
But my brother is bitter, and he does not hear.

Slim in Hell

I

SLIM GREER went to heaven;
    St. Peter said, "Slim,
You been a right good boy."
    An' he winked at him.

        "You been a travelin' rascal   5
        In yo' day.
        You kin roam once mo';
            Den you comes to stay.

"Put dese wings on yo' shoulders,
    An' save yo' feet."   10
Slim grin, and he speak up
    "Thankye, Pete."

        Den Peter say, "Go
        To Hell an' see,
        All dat is doing, and   15
            Report to me.

"Be sure to remember
    How everything go."
Slim say, "I be seein' yuh
    On de late watch, bo."   20

        Slim got to cavortin',
        Swell as you choose,
        Like Lindy in de "Spirit
            Of St. Louis Blues!"

"Slim in Hell" from *Folk-Say IV*, edited by B. A. Botkin
(University of Oklahoma Press, 1932). Copyright 1932 by
B. A. Botkin.

He flew an' he flew,   25
    Till at last he hit
A hangar wid de sign readin'
    DIS IS IT.

        Den he parked his wings,
        An' strolled aroun'   30
        Gettin' used to his feet
        On de solid ground.

II

Big bloodhound came aroarin'
    Like Niagry Falls,
Sicked on by white devils   35
    In overhalls.

Now Slim warn't scared,
    Cross my heart, it's a fac',
An' de dog went on a bayin'
    Some po' devil's track.   40

        Den Slim saw a mansion
        An' walked right in;
        De Devil looked up
        Wid a sickly grin.

"Suttinly didn't look   45
    Fo' you, Mr. Greer,
How it happen you comes
    To visit here?"

        Slim say—"Oh, jes' thought
        I'd drap by a spell."   50
        "Feel at home, seh, an' here's
        De keys to hell."

Den he took Slim around,
    An' showed him people
Raisin' hell as high as   55
    De First Church Steeple.

        Lots of folks fightin'
        At de roulette wheel,
        Like old Rampart Street,
        Or leastwise Beale.   60

Showed him bawdy houses
    An' cabarets,
Slim thought of New Orleans
    An' Memphis days.

        Each devil was busy   65
        Wid a devilish broad,
        An' Slim cried, "Lawdy,
        Lawd, Lawd, Lawd."

Took him in a room
   Where Slim see   70
De Baptist preacher wid a brownskin
   On each knee.

       Showed him giant stills,
         Going everywhere,
       Wid a passel of devils,   75
         Stretched dead drunk there.

Den he took him to de furnace
   Dat some devils was firing,
Hot as hell, an' Slim start
   A mean presspirin';   80

       White devils wid pitchforks
         Threw black devils on,
       Slim thought he'd better
         Be gittin' along.

An' he say—"Dis makes   85
   Me think of home—
Vicksburg, Little Rock, Jackson,
   Waco, and Rome."

       Den de devil gave Slim
         De big Ha-Ha;   90
       An' turned into a cracker,
         Wid a sheriff's star.

Slim ran fo' his wings,
   Lit out from de groun'
Hauled it back to St. Peter,   95
   Safety boun'.

         III

       St. Peter said, "Well,
         You got back quick.
       How's de devil? An' what's
         His latest trick?"   100

An' Slim say, "Peter,
   I really cain't tell,
De place was Dixie
   Dat I took for hell."

       Then Peter say, "You must   105
         Be crazy, I vow,
       Where'n hell dja think Hell *was*,
         Anyhow?

"Git on back to de yearth,
   Cause I got de fear,   110
You'se a leetle too dumb,
   Fo' to stay up here . . ."

Break of Day

BIG JESS fired on the Alabama Central,
  Man in full, babe, man in full.
Been throwing on coal for Mister Murphy
From times way back, baby, times way back.

Big Jess had a pleasing woman, name of
    Mamie,   5
Sweet-hipted mama, sweet-hipted Mame;
Had a boy growing up for to be a fireman,
Just like his pa, baby, like his pa.

Out by the roundhouse Jess had his cabin,
Longside the tracks, babe, long the tracks,   10
Jess pulled the whistle when they high-balled
    past it
"I'm on my way, baby, on my way."

Crackers craved the job what Jess was holding,
Times right tough, babe, times right tough,
Warned Jess to quit his job for a white man,
Jess he laughed, baby, he jes' laughed.   16

He picked up his lunch-box, kissed his sweet
    woman,
Sweet-hipted mama, sweet-hipted Mame,
His son walked with him to the white-washed
    palings,
"Be seeing you soon, son, see you soon."   20

Mister Murphy let Big Jess talk on the whistle
"So long sugar baby, so long babe";
Train due back in the early morning
Breakfast time, baby, breakfast time.

Mob stopped the train crossing Black Bear
    Mountain   25
Shot rang out, babe, shot rang out.
They left Big Jess on the Black Bear Moun-
    tain,
Break of day, baby, break of day.

Sweet Mame sits rocking, waiting for the
    whistle
Long past due, babe, long past due.   30
The grits are cold, and the coffee's boiled
    over,
But Jess done gone, baby; he done gone.

"Break of Day" is reprinted by permission of the author and *The New Republic*.

Glory, Glory

WHEN Annie Mae Johnson condescends to
        take the air,
Give up all your business, make haste to get
        there,
Glory oh glory, get there, be there.

The last time I saw Annie on the avenue,
She held up traffic for an hour or two.   5
The green light refused, absolutely, to go off
        at all;
And the red light and the amber nearly popped
        the glass,
When Annie walked by, they came on so fast,
Then stayed on together twenty minutes after
        she went past;
And it took three days for to get them duly
        timed again.   10
Even so, they palpitated every now and then.

A driver of a coal truck turned his head around,
Watching her walk and knocked an old man
        down,
Old man's weak eyes had been dazzled by the
        gorgeous sight;
Po' man collapsed and he heaved a sigh,   15
Said, "Lord, I'm willin' at the last to die,
Cause my state is blessed, everything's all right,
Happy, Lord, happy, yes happy am I."

Saw a Rock Creek Bridge car jump off the
        track,
Do the shim-sham shimmy and come reeling
        back;   20

Saw a big steam roller knocked clean off its
        base,
When it got itself together, the little Austin
        had its place.

Ambulance came a-clanging, the fire truck
        banging,
Police patrol a-sailing, the sirens all wailing,
Parked any whichaway and turned their head-
        lights high,   25
With their engines just a purring, till Annie
        Mae tipped on by.

Folks gathered from the manors, swarmed in
        from the alleys,
Deserted their pool-rooms, rushed out of their
        lodges,
Some took taxis to get them to the place on
        time;
Way the preachers left their congregations was
        a holy crime.   30
Twixt Uncle Ham's sonny boys and Aunt
        Hagar's daughters
Just like Daddy Moses through the Red Sea
        Waters,
Annie Johnson made a path, as she laid it on
        the frazzling line;
The dark waves parted, and then they closed
        in behind.   34

Aaanh, Lord, when Annie Mae lays it down,
If you want to take the census proper, better
        come around.

KENNETH FEARING

Born in Chicago in 1902 and educated there,
Kenneth Fearing stems from the same scene as
did Sandburg, from whom he is, as a poet, directly descended. After his graduation from the
University of Wisconsin he wrote for the *Chicago Herald and Examiner* and the pulps, reviewed later for the *New Masses,* the *Nation,*
the *New Republic,* and frequently for *The New
Yorker.* He is married to Rachel Meltzer and
they have a son.

Fearing's poetry is of a socially critical kind
prominent first in the depression years. His
books *Angel Arms* (1929), *Poems* (1935),
Dead Reckoning (1938), *Collected Poems*
(1940), *Afternoon of a Pawnbroker* (1943),
and *Stranger at Coney Island* (1948) have had,
however, a kind of popularity not granted the
more serious political criticism in verse. For
Fearing is primarily a satirist of the middle
class. One can satirize only such groups as have

achieved a certain success, only patterns of life which are well known. Fearing's free verse, in a jargon composed of images from the radio, newspapers, and Wall Street journals, sketches a waste land more recent than T. S. Eliot's and one we all inhabit. He presents us all as bundles of conditioned reflexes, will-less, half comical and half pathetic—the mechanical men of a mechanical age. With this rather cynical and yet somewhat sentimental approach to our troubles it is easy to feel kinship. Consequently Fearing (at first clearly Marxist in his approach) has become acceptable to such sophisticated publications as *The New Yorker*. He is a cartoonist given rather to emphasizing the general stupidity of our conditioning than to suggesting how to correct it. When, as in "Denoument," he tries to give us symbols of faith, of change and correction, he often fails. His symbols of the existing society are exact, but those of a better society do not come clear. Unable to present any clear political philosophy, he can and does present the cockeyed world as deadening to sensitivity. Like Sandburg in certain poems, he is a great debunker, but he has not Sandburg's certain faith in the people. Fearing escapes often into fantasy, as in "Afternoon of a Pawnbroker"; often, too, he fails to take seriously subjects which need serious consideration, as in his poem on Martin Dies. His poetry is very clever but not very profound.

Denoument

1

Sky, be blue, and more than blue; wind, be flesh and blood; flesh and blood, be deathless;
    walls, streets, be home;
    desire of millions, become more real than warmth and breath and strength and bread;
    clock, point to the decisive hour and, hour without name when stacked and waiting murder fades, dissolves, stay forever as the world grows new;

Truth, be known, be kept forever, let the letters, letters, souvenirs, documents, snapshots, bills be found at last, be torn away from a world of lies, be kept as final evidence, transformed forever into more than truth;
    change, change, rows and rows and rows of figures, spindles, furrows, desks, change into paid-up rent and let the paid-up rent become South Sea music;   5
    magic film, unwind, unroll, unfold in silver on that million mile screen, take us all, bear us again to the perfect denoument,

Where everything lost, needed, each forgotten thing, all that never happens, gathers at last into a dynamite triumph, a rainbow peace, a thunderbolt kiss,
    for you, the invincible, and I, grown older, and he, the shipping clerk, and she, an underweight blond journeying home in the last express.

2

But here is the body found lying face down in a burlap sack, strangled in the noose jerked shut by these trussed and twisted and frantic arms;
    but here are the agents come to seize the bed;   10
    but here is the vase holding saved-up cigarstore coupons, and here is a way to save on cigars and to go without meat;

"Denoument," "Dirge," and "Obituary" by Kenneth Fearing are reprinted from *Poems* (Dynamo Press, 1935) by permission of the author.
Denoument (climax), in the poet's phraseology, a contrast between man's desire for beauty and significance in life and death and the actual completely inconsequential pattern of modern life and death. The idea of a new society of justice to the workingman is contrasted toward the end of the poem with the reality of a modern world ready for war.

but here is the voice that strikes around the world, "My friends . . . my friends," issues
from the radio and thunders "My friends" in newsreel close-ups, explodes across headlines, "Both rich and poor, my friends, must sacrifice," re-echoes, murmuring, through
hospitals, deathcells, "My friends . . . my friends . . . my friends . . . my friends
. . ."

And who, my friend, are you?
Are you the one who leaped to the blinds of the cannon-ball express? Or are you the one
who started life again with three dependents and a pack of cigarettes?

But how can these things be made finally clear in a postmortem room with the lips taped shut
and the blue eyes cold, wide, still, blind, fixed beyond the steady glare of electric lights,
through the whitewashed ceiling and the crossmounted roof, past the drifting clouds?

Objection, over-ruled, exception, proceed: 16

Was yours the voice heard singing one night in a flyblown, sootbeamed, lost and forgotten Santa
Fe saloon? Later bellowing in rage? And you boiled up a shirt in a Newark furnished
room? Then you found another job, and pledged not to organize or go on strike?

We offer this union book in evidence. We offer these rent receipts in evidence. We offer in evidence this vacation card marked, "This is the life. Regards to all."

You, lodge member, protestant, crossborn male, the placenta discolored, at birth, by syphilis,
you, embryo four inches deep in the seventh month,
among so many, many sparks struck and darkened at conception,   20
which were you,
you, six feet tall on the day of death?

Then you were at no time the senator's son? Then you were never the beef king's daughter, married in a storm of perfume and music and laughter and rice?
And you are not now the clubman who waves and nods and vanishes to Rio in a special
plane?
But these are your lungs, scarred and consumed? These are your bones, still marked by
rickets? These are your pliers? These are your fingers, O master mechanic, and these
are your cold, wide, still, blind eyes?   25

The witness is lying, lying, an enemy, my friends, of Union Gas and the home:

But how will you know us, wheeled from the icebox and stretched upon the table with the belly
slit wide and the entrails removed, voiceless as the clippers bite through ligaments and
flesh and nerves and bones,
but how will you know us, attentive, strained, before the director's desk, or crowded in line
in front of factory gates,
but how will you know us through ringed machinegun sights as we run and fall in gas-
mask, steel helmet, flame-tunic, uniform, bayonet, pack,   29
but how will you know us, crumbled into ashes, lost in air and water and fire and stone,
how will you know us, now or any time, who will ever know that we have lived or died?

And this is the truth? So help you God, this is the truth? The truth in full, so help you God? So
help you God?

12. **"My friends,"** introductory words of address often used by Franklin D. Roosevelt in his addresses to the American people.
14. **one who leaped . . . cigarettes?** The author seems to have been running through a number of newspaper items, one concerning a man who leaped in front of a cannon-ball express, another concerning a man who started life again.   16. **Objection, over-
ruled.** The poet, in a phrase recalled from parliamentary procedure, turns from the idea of death to further ideas about life.
19. **crossborn,** born to bear a cross, or to suffer. **placenta,** main part of the afterbirth, in childbirth.   26. **Union Gas,** a utility
company.

But the pride that was made of iron and could not be broken, what has become of it, what
has become of the faith that nothing could destroy, what has become of the deathless
hope,
you, whose ways were yours alone, you, the one like no one else, what have you done with
the hour you swore to remember, where is the hour, the day, the achievement that
would never die?

Morphine. Veronal. Veronal. Morphine. Morphine. Morphine. Morphine.   35

Leaflets, scraps, dust, match-stubs strew the linoleum that leads upstairs to the union hall, the
walls of the basement workers' club are dim and cracked and above the speaker's
stand Vanzetti's face shows green, behind closed doors the committee-room is a fog of
smoke,

Who are these people?

All day the committee fought like cats and dogs and twelve of Mr. Kelly's strongarm men pa-
trolled the aisles that night, them blackjack guys get ten to twenty bucks a throw, the
funds were looted, sent to Chicago, at the meeting the section comrade talked like a
fool, more scabs came through in trucks guarded by police,
workers of the world, workers of the world, workers of the world,

Who are these people and what do they want, can't they be decent, can't they at least be calm
and polite,   40
besides the time is not yet ripe, it might take years, like Mr. Kelly said, years,

Decades black with famine and red with war, centuries on fire, ripped wide,

Who are these people and what do they want, why do they walk back and forth with signs that
say "Bread Not Bullets," what do they mean "They Shall Not Die" as they sink in
clouds of poison gas and fall beneath clubs, hooves, rifles, fall and do not rise, arise,
unite,
never again these faces, arms, eyes, lips,

Not unless we live, and live again,   45
return, everywhere alive in the issue that returns, clear as light that still descends from a
star long cold, again alive and everywhere visible through and through the scene that
comes again, as light on moving water breaks and returns, heard only in the words, as
millions of voices become one voice, seen only in millions of hands that move as one,

Look at them gathered, raised, look at their faces, clothes, who are these people, who are these
people,
what hand scrawled large in the empty prison cell "I have just received my sentence of
death. Red Front," whose voice screamed out in the silence "Arise"?

And all along the waterfront, there, where rats gnaw into the leading platforms, here, where
the wind whips at warehouse corners, look, there, here,
everywhere huge across the walls and gates "Your party lives,"   50
where there is no life, no breath, no sound, no touch, no warmth, no light but the lamp that
shines on a trooper's drawn and ready bayonet.

35. **Veronal,** a mild narcotic.   36. **Vanzetti,** a laborer of Plymouth, Massachusetts, who, with Nicola Sacco, was convicted of a
murder charge in South Braintree, Massachusetts, and never retried though later evidence proving his innocence was brought to
light. He was executed (p. 7).   38. **Mr. Kelly,** Edward J. Kelly, Mayor of Chicago 1933–47. **strongarm men,** special police.
48. **"Arise,"** first word of the song of the international communists, "Arise, ye prisoners of starvation."

Dirge

1-2-3 was the number he played but today the number came 3-2-1;
    bought his Carbide at 30 and it went to 29; had the favorite at Bowie but the track was
        slow—

O, executive type, would you like to drive a floating power, knee-action, silk-upholstered six?
    Wed a Hollywood star? Shoot the course in 58? Draw to the ace, king, jack?
      O, fellow with a will who won't take no, watch out for three cigarettes on the same, single
        match; O, democratic voter born in August under Mars, beware of liquidated rails—

Denoument to denoument, he took a personal pride in the certain, certain way he lived his own,
    private life,   5
    but nevertheless, they shut off his gas; nevertheless, the bank foreclosed; nevertheless, the
        landlord called; nevertheless, the radio broke,

And twelve o'clock arrived just once too often,
    just the same he wore one grey tweed suit, bought one straw hat, drank one straight Scotch,
        walked one short step, took one long look, drew one deep breath,
    just one too many,

And wow he died as wow he lived,   10
    going whop to the office and blooie home to sleep and biff got married and bam had chil-
        dren and oof got fired,
    zowie did he live and zowie did he die,

With who the hell are you at the corner of his casket, and where the hell we going on the right-
        hand silver knob, and who the hell cares walking second from the end with an Ameri-
        can Beauty wreath from why the hell not,

Very much missed by the circulation staff of the *New York Evening Post*; deeply, deeply
    mourned by the B.M.T.,

Wham, Mr. Roosevelt; pow, Sears Roebuck, awk, big dipper; bop, summer rain;   15
    bong, Mr., bong, Mr., bong, Mr., bong.

Obituary

TAKE him away, he's as dead as they die.
    Hear that ambulance bell, his eyes are staring straight at death.
    Look at the fingers growing stiff, touch the face already cold, see the stars in the sky, look
        at the stains on the street,

Look at the ten-ton truck that came rolling along fast and stretched him out cold,

Dirge, a poem about modern life lived by chance and ended by chance—a statement of our own lack of importance and of how ridiculously life passes. The whole poem is a satire on modern civilization. 1. **1-2-3 . . . played,** the "numbers" played especially in New York, where the betting is based on the last digits of the volume of business in the New York Stock Exchange. Bets are placed at great odds on the appearance of the right combination of these numbers. 2. **Carbide,** Union Carbide, an industrial corporation. **Bowie,** a racetrack in Bowie, Maryland. 3. **Shoot . . . 58?** Par on a golf course usually varies from 68 strokes to 72. 3. **executive type,** a satiric comment on the materialistic desires of a man. 4. **democratic voter,** a satiric comment on a superstitious belief in astrology. 5. **Denoument to denoument,** moving from one outcome to another. 14. *New York Evening Post,* a liberal New York City evening newspaper. **B.M.T.,** Brooklyn-Manhattan Transit System.
Obituary. The poem is a satirical statement of the modern disregard for human life. A man dies on the streets. The poet remarks ironically that the small change in his pocket might be given to the Standard Oil (l. 9) or the People's Gas (l. 11); that the key to his flat might be handed over to the D.A.R. (Daughters of the American Revolution) (l. 10); his socks to the Guggenheim Fund (an endowment by a wealthy mining family to award fellowships to those doing worthy work in creative arts); and other possessions to the Morgans (one of the wealthiest families in America), to Mr. Hoover, Republican President of the United States (1928–32), to Gene Tunney (former heavy-weight boxing champion of the world), to Will Hays (former censor of the motion-picture industry), to Al Capone (former Chicago underworld chieftain), and to the I.R.T. (Interborough Rapid Transit Company of New York City). Obviously this jazz poem on death emphasizes the fact that modern man has no intimate friends but is known only to those institutions which he is forced to support.

Then turn out his pockets and make the crowd move on.   5
    Sergeant, what was his name? What's the driver's name? What's your name, sergeant?
    Go through his clothes,
    take out the cigars, the money, the papers, the keys, take everything there is,

And give the dollar and a half to the Standard Oil. It was his true-blue friend.   9
    Give the key of his flat to the D.A.R. They were friends of his, the best a man ever had.
    Take out the pawnticket, wrap it, seal it, send it along to the People's Gas. They were life-
        long pals. It was more than his brother. They were just like twins.

Give away the shoes,
    give his derby away. Donate his socks to the Guggenheim fund,
    let the Morgans hold the priceless bills, and leaflets, and racing tips under lock and key,
    and give Mr. Hoover the pint of gin.   15
    Because they're all good men. And they were friends of his.

Don't forget Gene Tunney. Don't forget Will Hays. Don't forget Al Capone. Don't forget the
        I.R.T.
    Give them his matches to remember him by.
    They lived with him, in the same old world. And they're good men, too.
That's all, sergeant. There's nothing else, lieutenant. There's no more, captain.   20
    Pick up the body, feed it, shave it, find it another job.

Have a cigar, driver?
    Take two cigars.
    You were his true-blue pal.

Cracked Record Blues

IF YOU watch it long enough you can see the clock move,
If you try hard enough you can hold a little water in the palm of your hand,
If you listen once or twice you know it's not the needle, or the tune, but a crack in the record
    when sometimes a phonograph falters and repeats, and repeats, and repeats, and re-
    peats—

And if you think about it long enough, long enough, long enough, long enough then every-
    thing is simple and you can understand the times,
You can see for yourself that the Hudson still flows, that the seasons change as ever, that love
    is always love,   5
Words still have a meaning, still clear and still the same;
You can count upon your fingers that two plus two still equals, still equals, still equals, still
    equals—
There is nothing in this world that should bother the mind.

"Cracked Record Blues" (originally published in *The New Yorker*) and "Afternoon of a Pawnbroker" from *Afternoon of a Pawn-broker and Other Poems*, by Kenneth Fearing, copyright, 1943, by Kenneth Fearing. Reprinted by permission of Harcourt, Brace & Co., Inc.
Cracked Record Blues. Fearing likens our whole method of feeling and thinking in these days to a cracked record constantly repeating the same phrase.

Because the mind is a common sense affair filled with common sense answers to common sense
    facts,
It can add up, can add up, can add up, can add up earthquakes and subtract them from fires,
It can bisect an atom or analyze the planets— 11
All it has to do is to, do is to, do is to, do is to start at the beginning and continue to the end.

Afternoon of a Pawnbroker

STILL they bring me diamonds, diamonds, always diamonds,
Why don't they pledge something else for a change, if they must have loans, other than those
    diamond clasps and diamond rings,
Rubies, sapphires, emeralds, pearls,
Ermine wraps, silks and satins, solid gold watches and silver plate and violins two hundred years
    old,
And then again diamonds, diamonds, the neighborhood diamonds I have seen so many times be-
    fore, and shall see so many times again? 5

Still I remember the strange afternoon (it was a season of extraordinary days and nights) when
    the first of the strange customers appeared,
And he waited, politely, while Mrs. Nunzio redeemed her furs, then he stepped to the counter
    and he laid down a thing that looked like a trumpet,
In fact, it was a trumpet, not mounted with diamonds, not plated with gold or even silver, and
    I started to say: "We can't use trumpets—"
But a light was in his eyes,
And after he was gone, I had the trumpet. And I stored it away. And the name on my books was
    Gabriel. 10

It should be made clear my accounts are always open to the police, I have nothing to conceal,
I belong, myself, to the Sounder Business Principles League,
Have two married daughters, one of them in Brooklyn, the other in Cleveland,
And nothing like this had ever happened before.
How can I account for my lapse of mind? 15
All I can say is, it did not seem strange. Not at the time. Not in that neighborhood. And not in
    that year.

And the next to appear was a man with a soft, persuasive voice,
And a kindly face, and the most honest eyes I have ever seen, and ears like arrows, and a pointed
    beard,
And what he said, after Mrs. Case had pledged her diamond ring and gone, I cannot now en-
    tirely recall,
But when he went away I found I had an apple. An apple, just an apple. 20
"It's been bitten," I remember that I tried to argue. But he smiled, and said in his quiet voice:
    "Yes, but only once."
And the strangest thing is, it did not seem strange. Not strange at all.

And still those names are on my books.
And still I see listed, side by side, those incongruous, and not very sound securities:
(1) Aladdin's lamp (I must have been mad), (1) Pandora's box, (1) Magic carpet, 25
(1) Fountain of youth (in good condition), (1) Holy Grail, (1) Invisible man (the only article
    never redeemed, and I cannot locate him), and others, others, many others,
And still I recall how my storage vaults hummed and crackled, from time to time, or sounded
    with music, or shot forth flame,

And I wonder, still, that the season did not seem one of unusual wonder, not even different—not
   at the time.

And still I think, at intervals, why didn't I, when the chance was mine, drink just once from that
   Fountain of youth?
Why didn't I open that box of Pandora?   30
And what if Mr. Gabriel, who redeemed his pledge and went away, should some day decide to
   blow on his trumpet?
Just one short blast, in the middle of some busy afternoon?

But here comes Mr. Barrington, to pawn his Stradivarius.
And here comes Mrs. Case, to redeem her diamond ring.

JOHN DOS PASSOS

One of the most uncompromising realists of American fiction, John Dos Passos was something of a sensation during the 1920's and 1930's, although his productivity and his reputation have both fallen off markedly in recent years. The reason for this decline is probably that fiction is his real métier, whereas social comment (in which he is unfortunately chiefly interested) is something he can make only in uncertain tones. In short, he is better as the inspired reporter of personal lives than as the would-be clear-headed commentator on the social scene.

Dos Passos was born in Chicago on January 14, 1896; his father was a lawyer of Portuguese extraction. As a boy John Dos Passos lived in many places—in Europe, in Washington, D.C., in Virginia. He graduated from Harvard in 1916 and went to Spain shortly thereafter to begin the study of architecture. The First World War, however, brought him into military service, first as an independent ambulance driver and then, after induction, in the Medical Corps as a private. After the war was over, he worked as a newspaper correspondent in Spain, Mexico, and the Near East; but he eventually gravitated to the United States and became a professional writer of miscellaneous talents. His experiences in the war were the great shaping influence in his fiction; his adventures as a correspondent led him to write some highly original books of travel; his pursuit of journalism in general inspired the writing of some plays. Under the general promptings of the subjective he even wrote some feeble verse. *Three Plays* (1934) illustrates best his dramatic gifts, which are not of great worth; *Route Number One* (1943) and a work preliminary to it, *The Ground We Stand On* (1941), illustrate his occasionally effective combination of travelogue and social criticism.

However, it is the pungent series of novels, written between 1917 and 1939, which makes of Dos Passos an important and useful member of the Waste Land group. In their total effect these novels are defeatist, but they have many powerful pages and in some instances a fresh, if somewhat confusing, technique. This is the device of the Newsreel and the Camera-Eye; the first correlates the action of the story with current events by means of newspaper headlines, and the second is virtually an impressionistically poetic Greek chorus on the action of the story. Illustration serves the purpose better than objective definition.

We can ignore *One Man's Initiation* (1917), for its substance is treated far more effectively in *Three Soldiers* (1922), still considered by many who participated in the great conflict as the most realistic novel dealing with the First World War. It is the record of the bitterly disillusioning experience of the private soldier, similar to William Faulkner's *Soldier's Pay* and the Stallings-Anderson play, *What Price Glory?*,

656

oth of which appeared at about the same
time. *Manhattan Transfer* brings us back to
America; here Dos Passos struck his real stride
in domestic satire. *The 42nd Parallel* (1930),
Nineteen Nineteen (1932), and *The Big Money* (1936) follow the plan and devices of *Manhattan Transfer* on an epic scale. Combined in
1937 into a trilogy under the title *U.S.A.*, they
are clearly Dos Passos' masterpiece. They trace
the lives of certain widely dissimilar people
through the First World War and beyond,
bringing together these lives at various tangential points, avoiding battle-scenes but concentrating on the scenes behind the lines, embittering the characters, encompassing them
with the shades of the prison-house that is
life—a harsh indictment not so much of these
characters as of the environment in which
they are obliged to live and make the most
of it.

A similar study is *The Grand Design* (1949),
which examines the lives of a number of Americans under the New Deal of the Rooseveltian
era. The outcome of this study is the same, only
this time the reader is often left with the feeling that the subjects of Dos Passos' case-history
are even more unworthy of the mighty events
going on about them than the mediocre characters in *U.S.A.*

Dos Passos has always evinced a sympathy
for the oppressed—a sympathy which allied him
for a while with radical groups and radical ideologies. But he has never been a "party" man,
and *The Adventures of a Young Man* (1939)
was a definite debunking of both sides involved
in the Spanish Civil War. Fundamentally, it
would seem, Dos Passos is an individualist of
liberal tendencies, but he is not an extremist,
not a propagandist as such, not a crusader, not
a missionary. He is the unsatisfied observer of
life without much of a clear program, but an
observer who believes that the little men have
been let down badly by the big men, and he
can see no hope for humanity until the little
men have been heard and their cause accepted.
Yet he sees that these mortals are neither heroic nor glamorous—a less glamorous writer
than Dos Passos would be hard to find. His
frankness is often brutal, his details often clinical; but his sincerity and his power are apparent to all but the incurably prejudiced.

from U.S.A.: The 42nd Parallel

Newsreel I

It was that emancipated race
That was chargin up the hill
Up to where them insurrectos
Was afightin fit to kill

CAPITAL CITY'S CENTURY CLOSED

GENERAL MILES with his gaudy uniform and
spirited charger was the center for all eyes
especially as his steed was extremely restless.
Just as the band passed the Commanding General his horse stood upon his hind legs and was 10
almost erect. General Miles instantly reined in
the frightened animal and dug in his spurs in
an endeavor to control the horse which to the
horror of the spectators, fell over backwards
and landed squarely on the Commanding General. Much to the gratification of the people
General Miles was not injured but considerable
skin was scraped off the flank of the horse. Almost every inch of General Miles's overcoat
was covered with the dust of the street and be- 20
tween the shoulders a hole about an inch in diameter was punctured. Without waiting for
anyone to brush the dust from his garments
General Miles remounted his horse and reviewed the parade as if it were an everyday
occurrence.

The incident naturally attracted the attention of the crowd, and this brought to notice
the fact that the Commanding General never
permits a flag to be carried past him without 30
uncovering and remaining so until the colors
have passed

And the Captain bold of Company B
Was afightin in the lead
Just like a trueborn soldier he
Of them bullets took no heed

From *U.S.A.*, copyright, 1937, by John Dos Passos, and reprinted by permission of the author.
Newsreel I. A series of impressionistic glimpses of the American scene as gathered from a glance at the morning headlines
or featured stories in the morning newspaper. The impressions
of the times are further heightened by the inclusion of lines
from some popular song or songs of the day (see lines 2–6,
25–29, etc.). 6. **General Miles,** Nelson A. Miles (1839–
1925), famous for his rôle in the Indian Wars of the 1870's and
1880's and for his work as a staff-leader in the Spanish-American
War.

OFFICIALS KNOW NOTHING OF VICE

Sanitary trustees turn water of Chicago River into drainage canal LAKE MICHIGAN SHAKES HANDS WITH THE FATHER OF THE WATERS German zuchter-verein singing contest for canary-birds opens the fight for bimetallism at the ratio of 16 to 1 has not been lost says Bryan

BRITISH BEATEN AT MAFEKING

10 *For there's many a man been murdered*
in Luzon

CLAIMS ISLANDS FOR ALL TIME

Hamilton Club Listens to Oratory by Ex-Congressman Posey of Indiana

NOISE GREETS NEW CENTURY

LABOR GREETS NEW CENTURY

CHURCHES GREET NEW CENTURY

Mr. McKinley is hard at work in his office
20 when the new year begins.

NATION GREETS CENTURY'S DAWN

Responding to a toast, Hail Columbia! at the Columbia Club banquet in Indianapolis, Ind., ex-President Benjamin Harrison said in part: I have no argument to make here or anywhere against territorial expansion; but I do not, as some do, look upon territorial expansion as the safest and most attractive avenue of national development. By the advantages of abundant
30 and cheap coal and iron, of an enormous overproduction of food products and of invention and economy in production, we are now leading by the nose the original and the greatest of the colonizing nations.

Society Girls Shocked: Danced with Detectives

For there's many a man been murdered in
Luzon and Mindanao

GAIETY GIRLS MOBBED IN NEW JERSEY

One of the lithographs of the leading lady represented her in less than Atlantic City bathing costume, sitting on a red-hot stove; in one hand she held a brimming glass of wine, in the other ribbons drawn over a pair of rampant lobsters.

For there's many a man been murdered in
Luzon and Mindanao
and in Samar

In responding to the toast, "The Twentieth Century," Senator Albert J. Beveridge said in part: *The twentieth century will be American. American thought will dominate it. American progress will give it color and direction. American deeds will make it illustrious.*

Civilization will never lose its hold on Shanghai. Civilization will never depart from Hongkong. The gates of Peking will never again be closed to the methods of modern man. The regeneration of the world, physical as well as moral, has begun, and revolutions never move backwards.

There's been many a good man murdered in the Philippines
Lies sleeping in some lonesome grave.

The Camera Eye (1)

when you walk along the street you have to step carefully always on the cobbles so as not to step on the bright anxious grassblades
easier if you hold Mother's hand and hang on it that way you can kick up your toes but walking fast you have to tread on too many grassblades the poor hurt green tongues shrink under your feet   maybe thats why those people are so angry and follow us shaking their fists   they're throwing stones grownup people throwing stones She's walking fast and we're running her pointed toes sticking out

---

9. **Mafeking,** a town in South Africa noted as the scene of a famous siege during the Boer War, a siege from which the beleaguered British were finally delivered by a relief force under the command of Generals Roberts and Kitchener (May 1900). When the news of the relief of Mafeking reached London, the popular celebration was so violent that for some time thereafter the term "to maffick" meant unrestrained revelry in the streets.

65. **The Camera Eye.** These sections represent glimpses from the life of an outsider—in some cases the author himself, in some cases only a fictitious character—which suggest the mood of both the foregoing and the following narratives. In this instance the glimpse is that of a little boy caught in the Boer War within Boer territory.

sharp among the poor trodden grassblades under the shaking folds of the brown cloth dress Englander   a pebble tinkles along the cobbles

Quick darling quick in the postcard shop its quiet the angry people are outside and cant come in   non nein nicht englander amerikanisch americain   Hoch Amerika Vive l'Amerique She laughs My dear they had me right frightened

war on the veldt Kruger Bloemfontein Ladysmith and Queen Victoria an old lady in a pointed lace cap sent chocolate to the soldiers at Christmas

under the counter it's dark and the lady the nice Dutch lady who loves Americans and has relations in Trenton shows you postcards that shine in the dark pretty hotels and palaces
      O que c'est beau schön prittie prittie
      and the moonlight ripple ripple under a bridge and the little reverbères are alight in the dark under the counter and the little windows of hotels around the harbor   O que c'est beau la lune
      and the big moon

Mac

When the wind set from the silver factories across the river the air of the gray fourfamily frame house where Fainy McCreary was born was choking all day with the smell of whaleoil soap. Other days it smelt of cabbage and babies and Mrs. McCreary's washboilers. Fainy could never play at home because Pop, a lame cavechested man with a whispy blondegray mustache, was nightwatchman at the Chadwick Mills and slept all day. It was only round five o'clock that a curling whiff of tobacco smoke would seep through from the front room into the kitchen. That was a sign that Pop was up and in good spirits, and would soon be wanting his supper.

Then Fainy would be sent running out to one of two corners of the short muddy street of identical frame houses where they lived.

To the right it was half a block to Finley's

where he would have to wait at the bar in a forest of mudsplattered trouserlegs until all the rank brawling mouths of grownups had been stopped with beers and whiskeys. Then he would walk home, making each step very carefully, with the handle of the pail of suds cutting into his hand.

To the left it was half a block to Maginnis's Fancy Groceries, Home and Imported Products. Fainy liked the cardboard Cream of Wheat darkey in the window, the glass case with different kinds of salami in it, the barrels of potatoes and cabbages, the brown smell of sugar, sawdust, ginger, kippered herring, ham, vinegar, bread, pepper, lard.

"A loaf of bread, please, mister, a half pound of butter and a box of ginger snaps."

Some evenings when Mom felt poorly, Fainy had to go further; round the corner past Maginnis's, down Riverside Avenue where the trolley ran, and across the red bridge over the little river that flowed black between icy undercut snowbanks in winter, yellow and spuming in the spring thaws, brown and oily in summer. Across the river all the way to the corner of Riverside and Main, where the drugstore was, lived Bohunks and Polaks. Their kids were always fighting with the kids of the Murphys and O'Haras and O'Flanagans who lived on Orchard Street.

Fainy would walk along with his knees quaking, the medicine bottle in its white paper tight in one mittened hand. At the corner of Quince was a group of boys he'd have to pass. Passing wasn't so bad; it was when he was about twenty yards from them that the first snowball would hum by his ear. There was no comeback. If he broke into a run, they'd chase him. If he dropped the medicine bottle he'd be beaten up when he got home. A soft one would plunk on the back of his head and the snow began to trickle down his neck. When he was a half a block from the bridge he'd take a chance and run for it.

"Scared cat . . . Shanty Irish . . . Bowlegged Murphy . . . Running home to tell the cop" . . . would yell the Polak and Bohunk kids between snowballs. They made their snowballs hard by pouring water on them and leaving them to freeze overnight; if one of those hit him it drew blood.

1. **Kruger . . . Ladysmith,** Stephanus Johannes Paulus Kruger, "Oom Paul" (1825–1904), was the last President of the Boer Republic in the Transvaal and the leader of the Boers against the British. He was driven into exile with the collapse of organized Boer resistance in 1901. **Bloemfontein** and **Ladysmith** were two towns where bloody battles took place in this war. 21. **reverbères,** street-lamps.

The backyard was the only place you could really feel safe to play in. There were broken-down fences, dented garbage cans, old pots and pans too nearly sieves to mend, a vacant chickencoop that still had feathers and droppings on the floor, hogweed in summer, mud in winter; but the glory of the McCreary's backyard was Tony Harriman's rabbit hutch, where he kept Belgian hares. Tony Harriman was a consumptive and lived with his mother on the ground floor left. He wanted to raise all sorts of other small animals too, raccoons, otter, even silver fox, he'd get rich that way. The day he died nobody could find the key to the big padlock on the door of the rabbit hutch. Fainy fed the hares for several days by pushing in cabbage and lettuce leaves through the double thickness of chickenwire. Then came a week of sleet and rain when he didn't go out in the yard. The first fine day, when he went to look, one of the hares was dead. Fainy turned white; he tried to tell himself the hare was asleep, but it lay gawkily stiff, not asleep. The other hares were huddled in a corner looking about with twitching noses, their big ears flopping helpless over their backs. Poor hares; Fainy wanted to cry. He ran upstairs to his mother's kitchen, ducked under the ironing board and got the hammer out of the drawer in the kitchen table. The first time he tried he mashed his finger, but the second time he managed to jump the padlock. Inside the cage there was a funny, sour smell. Fainy picked the dead hare up by its ears. Its soft white belly was beginning to puff up, one dead eye was scaringly open. Something suddenly got hold of Fainy and made him drop the hare in the nearest garbage can and run upstairs. Still cold and trembling, he tiptoed out onto the back porch and looked down. Breathlessly he watched the other hares. By cautious hops they were getting near the door of the hutch into the yard. One of them was out. It sat up on its hind legs, limp ears suddenly stiff. Mom called him to bring her a flatiron from the stove. When he got back to the porch the hares were all gone.

That winter there was a strike in the Chadwick Mills and Pop lost his job. He would sit all day in the front room smoking and cursing: "Ablebodied man by Jesus, if I couldn't lick any one of those damn Polaks with my crutch

tied behind my back . . . I says so to Mr. Barry; I ain't goin' to join no strike. Mr. Barry, a sensible quiet man, a bit of an invalid, with a wife an' kiddies to think for. Eight years I've been watchman, an' now you give me the sack to take on a bunch of thugs from a detective agency. The dirty pug-nosed son of a bitch."

"If those damn lousy furreners hadn't a walked out," somebody would answer soothingly.

The strike was not popular on Orchard Street. It meant that Mom had to work harder and harder, doing bigger and bigger boilersful of wash, and that Fainy and his older sister Milly had to help when they came home from school. And then one day Mom got sick and had to go back to bed instead of starting in on the ironing, and lay with her round white creased face whiter than the pillow and her watercreased hands in a knot under her chin. The doctor came and the district nurse, and all three rooms of the flat smelt of doctors and nurses and drugs, and the only place Fainy and Milly could find to sit was on the stairs. There they sat and cried quietly together. Then Mom's face on the pillow shrank into a little creased white thing like a rumpled up handkerchief and they said that she was dead and took her away.

The funeral was from the undertaking parlors on Riverside Avenue on the next block. Fainy felt very proud and important because everybody kissed him and patted his head and said he was behaving like a little man. He had a new black suit on, too, like a grownup suit with pockets and everything, except that it had short pants. There were all sorts of people at the undertaking parlors he had never been close to before, Mr. Russell, the butcher and Father O'Donnell and Uncle Tim O'Hara who'd come on from Chicago, and it smelt of whisky and beer like at Finley's. Uncle Tim was a skinny man with a knobbed red face and blurry blue eyes. He wore a loose black silk tie that worried Fainy, and kept leaning down suddenly, bending from the waist as if he was going to close up like a jackknife, and whispering in a thick voice in Fainy's ear.

"Don't you mind 'em, old sport, they're bunch o' bums and hypocrytes, stewed to th ears most of 'em already. Look at Fathe

'Donnell the fat swine already figurin' up the
burial fees. But don't you mind 'em, remember
you're an O'Hara on your mother's side. I don't
mind 'em, old sport, and she was my own sister
by birth and blood."

When they got home he was terribly sleepy
and his feet were cold and wet. Nobody paid
any attention to him. He sat whimpering on the
edge of the bed in the dark. In the front room
there were voices and a sound of knives and
forks, but he didn't dare go in there. He curled
up against the wall and went to sleep. Light in
his eyes woke him up. Uncle Tim and Pop were
standing over him talking loud. They looked
funny and didn't seem to be standing very
steady. Uncle Tim held the lamp.

"Well, Fainy, old sport," said Uncle Tim
waving the lamp a perilous wave over Fainy's
head. "Fenian O'Hara McCreary, sit up and
take notice and tell us what you think of our
proposed removal to the great and growing city
of Chicago. Middletown's a terrible bitch of a
dump if you ask me . . . Meanin' no offense,
John . . . But Chicago . . . Jesus God, man,
when you get there you'll think you've been
dead and nailed up in a coffin all these years."

Fainy was scared. He drew his knees up to
his chin and looked tremblingly at the two big
swaying figures of men lit by the swaying lamp.
He tried to speak but the words dried up on
his lips.

"The kid's asleep, Tim, for all your speechi-
fin' . . . Take your clothes off, Fainy, and
get into bed and get a good night's sleep. We're
leavin' in the mornin'."

And late on a rainy morning, without any
breakfast, with a big old swelltop trunk tied
on with rope joggling perilously on the roof of
the cab that Fainy had been sent to order from
Hodgeson's Livery Stable, they set out. Milly
was crying. Pop didn't say a word but sucked
on an unlit pipe. Uncle Tim handled everything, making little jokes all the time that nobody laughed at, pulling a roll of bills out of
his pocket at every juncture, or taking great
gurgling sips out of the flask he had in his
pocket. Milly cried and cried. Fainy looked out
with big dry eyes at the familiar streets, all
suddenly odd and lopsided, that rolled past the
cab; the red bridge, the scabshingled houses
where the Polaks lived, Smith's and Smith's

corner drug store . . . there was Billy Hogan
just coming out with a package of chewing
gum in his hand. Playing hookey again. Fainy
had an impulse to yell at him, but something
froze it . . . Main with its elms and streetcars, blocks of stores round the corner of
Church, and then the fire department. Fainy
looked for the last time into the dark cave
where shone entrancingly the brass and copper curves of the engine, then past the cardboard fronts of the First Congregational
Church, The Carmel Baptist Church, St. Andrew's Episcopal Church built of brick and set
catercornered on its lot instead of straight with
a stern face to the street like the other churches,
then the three castiron stags on the lawn in
front of the Commercial House, and the resi-
dences, each with its lawn, each with its scroll-
saw porch, each with its hydrangea bush. Then
the houses got smaller, and the lawns disappeared; the cab trundled round past Simpson's
Grain and Feed Warehouse, along a row of
barbershops, saloons and lunchrooms, and they
were all getting out at the station.

At the station lunchcounter Uncle Tim set
everybody up to breakfast. He dried Milly's
tears and blew Fainy's nose in a big new
pockethandkerchief that still had the tag on
the corner and set them to work on bacon and
eggs and coffee. Fainy hadn't had coffee before, so the idea of sitting up like a man and
drinking coffee made him feel pretty good.
Milly didn't like hers, said it was bitter. They
were left all alone in the lunchroom for sometime with the empty plates and empty coffee
cups under the beady eyes of a woman with
the long neck and pointed face of a hen who
looked at them disapprovingly from behind the
counter. Then with an enormous, shattering
rumble, sludgepuff sludge . . . puff, the train
came into the station. They were scooped up
and dragged across the platform and through a
pipesmoky car and before they knew it the
train was moving and the wintry russet Connecticut landscape was clattering by.

The Camera Eye (2)

we hurry wallowing like in a boat in the
musty stablesmelling herdic cab. He kept say-

97. *The Camera Eye* (2). The scene is a railroad train going
north from Washington to New York.

ing What would you do Lucy if I were to invite one of them to my table? They're very
lovely people Lucy the colored people and He
had cloves in a little silver box and a rye
whisky smell on his breath hurrying to catch
the cars to New York

and She was saying Oh dolly I hope we wont
be late and Scott was waiting with the tickets
and we had to run up the platform of the Sev-
10 enth Street Depot and all the little cannons
kept falling out of the Olympia and everybody
stooped to pick them up and the conductor
Allaboard lady quick lady

they were little brass cannons and were
bright in the sun on the platform of the Seventh Street Depot and Scott hoisted us all up
and the train was moving and the engine bell
was ringing and Scott put in your hand a little handful of brass tiny cannons just big
20 enough to hold the smallest size red firecracker
at the battle of Manila Bay and said Here's the
artillery Jack

and He was holding forth in the parlor car
Why Lucy if it were necessary for the cause of
humanity I would walk out and be shot any
day you would Jack wouldn't you? wouldn't
you porter? who was bringing apollinaris and
He had a flask in the brown grip where the
silk initialed handkerchiefs always smelt of bay
30 rum

and when we got to Havre de Grace He said
Remember Lucy we used to have to ferry across
the Susquehanna before the bridge was built

and across Gunpowder Creek too

Mac

Russet hills, patches of woods, farmhouses,
cows, a red colt kicking up its heels in a pasture, rail fences, streaks of marsh.

"Well, Tim, I feel like a whipped cur . . .
So long as I've lived, Tim, I've tried to do the
40 right thing," Pop kept repeating in a rattling
voice. "And now what can they be asayin'
about me?"

"Jesus God, man, there was nothin' else you
could do, was there? What the devil can you
do if you haven't any money and haven't any
job and a lot o' doctors and undertakers and
landlords come round with their bills and you
with two children to support?"

"But I've been a quiet and respectable man,

steady and misfortunate ever since I married
and settled down. And now what'll they be
thinkin' of me sneakin' out like a whipped cur?"

"John, take it from me that I'd be the last
one to want to bring disrespect on the dead
that was my own sister by birth and blood . . .
But it ain't your fault and it ain't my fault . . .
it's the fault of poverty, and poverty's the fault
of the system . . . Fenian, you listen to Tim
O'Hara for a minute and Milly you listen too,
cause a girl ought to know these things just as
well as a man and for once in his life Tim
O'Hara's tellin' the truth . . . It's the fault of
the system that don't give a man the fruit of his
labor . . . The only man that gets anything
out of capitalism is a crook, an' he gets to be a
millionaire in short order . . . But an honest
workin' man like John or myself we can work
a hundred years and not leave enough to bury
us decent with."

Smoke rolled white in front of the window
shaking out of its folds trees and telegraph
poles and little square shingleroofed houses
and towns and trolleycars, and long rows of
buggies with steaming horses standing in line.

"And who gets the fruit of our labor, the
goddam business men, agents, middlemen who
never did a productive piece of work in their
life."

Fainy's eyes are following the telegraph
wires that sag and soar.

"Now, Chicago ain't no paradise, I can promise you that, John, but it's a better market for a
workin' man's muscle and brains at present
than the East is . . . And why, did you ask
me why . . . ? Supply and demand, they need
workers in Chicago."

"Tim, I tellyer I feel like a whipped cur."

"It's the system, John, it's the goddam lousy
system."

A great bustle in the car woke Fainy up. It
was dark. Milly was crying again. He didn't
know where he was.

"Well, gentlemen," Uncle Tim was saying,
"we're about to arrive in little old New York."

In the station it was light; that surprised
Fainy, who thought it was already night. He
and Milly were left a long time sitting on a
suitcase in the waitingroom. The waitingroom
was huge, full of unfamiliarlooking people
scary like people in picturebooks. Milly kept
crying.

"Hey, Milly, I'll biff you one if you don't stop crying."

"Why?" whined Milly, crying all the more.

Fainy stood as far away from her as possible so that people wouldn't think they were together. When he was about ready to cry himself Pop and Uncle Tim came and took them and the suitcase into the restaurant. A strong smell of fresh whisky came from their breaths, and they seemed very bright around the eyes. They all sat at a table with a white cloth and a sympathetic colored man in a white coat handed them a large card full of printing.

"Let's eat a good supper," said Uncle Tim, "if it's the last thing we do on this earth."

"Damn the expense," said Pop, "it's the system that's to blame."

"To hell with the Pope," said Uncle Tim. "We'll make a social-democrat out of you yet."

They gave Fainy fried oysters and chicken and icecream and cake, and when they all had to run for the train he had a terrible stitch in his side. They got into a day-coach that smelt of coalgas and armpits. "When are we going to bed?" Milly began to whine. "We're not going to bed," said Uncle Tim airily. "We're going to sleep right here like little mice . . . like little mice in a cheese." "I doan like mice," yelled Milly with a new flood of tears as the train started.

Fainy's eyes smarted; in his ears was the continuous roar, the clatter clatter over crossings, the sudden snarl under bridges. It was a tunnel, all the way to Chicago it was a tunnel. Opposite him Pop's and Uncle Tim's faces looked red and snarling, he didn't like the way they looked, and the light was smoky and jiggly and outside it was all a tunnel and his eyes hurt and wheels and rails roared in his ears and he fell asleep.

When he woke up it was a town and the train was running right through the main street. It was a sunny morning. He could see people going about their business, stores, buggies and spring-wagons standing at the curb, newsboys selling newspapers, wooden Indians outside of cigarstores. At first he thought he was dreaming, but then he remembered and decided it must be Chicago. Pop and Uncle Tim were asleep on the seat opposite. Their mouths were open, their faces were splotched and he didn't like the way they looked. Milly was curled up

with a wooly shawl all over her. The train was slowing down, it was a station. If it was Chicago they ought to get off. At that moment the conductor passed, an old man who looked a little like Father O'Donnell.

"Please, mister, is this Chicago?" "Chicago's a long way off yet, son," said the conductor without smiling. "This is Syracuse." 60

And they all woke up, and for hours and hours the telephone poles went by, and towns, frame houses, brick factories with ranks and ranks of glittering windows, dumping grounds, trainyards, plowed land, pasture, and cows, and Milly got trainsick and Fainy's legs felt like they would drop off from sitting in the seat so long; some places it was snowing and some places it was sunny, and Milly kept getting sick and smelt dismally of vomit, and it 70 got dark and they all slept; and light again, and then the towns and the framehouses and the factories all started drawing together, humping into warehouses and elevators, and the trainyards spread out as far as you could see and it was Chicago.

But it was so cold and the wind blew the dust so hard in his face and his eyes were so stuck together by dust and tiredness that he couldn't look at anything. After they had 80 waited round a long while, Milly and Fainy huddled together in the cold, they got on a streetcar and rode and rode. They were so sleepy they never knew exactly where the train ended and the streetcar began. Uncle Tim's voice went on talking proudly excitedly, Chicago, Chicago, Chicago. Pop sat with his chin on his crutch. "Tim, I feel like a whipped cur."

Fainy lived ten years in Chicago.

At first he went to school and played base- 90 ball on back lots on Saturday afternoons, but then came his last commencement, and all the children sang *My Country, 'Tis Of Thee,* and school was over and he had to go to work. Uncle Tim at that time had his own jobprinting shop on a dusty side street off North Clark in the ground floor of a cranky old brick building. It only occupied a small section of the building that was mostly used as a warehouse and was famous for its rats. It had a single wide 100 plateglass window made resplendent by gold Old English lettering: TIMOTHY O'HARA, JOB PRINTER.

"Now, Fainy, old sport," said Uncle Tim,

"you'll have a chance to learn the profession from the ground up." So he ran errands, delivered packages of circulars, throwaways, posters, was always dodging trolleycars, ducking from under the foamy bits of big truckhorses, bumming rides on deliverywagons. When there were no errands to run he swept out under the presses, cleaned type, emptied the office wastepaper basket, or, during rush times, ran round 10 the corner for coffee and sandwiches for the typesetter, or for a small flask of bourbon for Uncle Tim.

Pop puttered round on his crutch for several years, always looking for a job. Evenings he smoked his pipe and cursed his luck on the back stoop of Uncle Tim's house and occasionally threatened to go back to Middletown. Then one day he got pneumonia and died quietly at the Sacred Heart Hospital. It was about 20 the same time that Uncle Tim bought a linotype machine.

Uncle Tim was so excited he didn't take a drink for three days. The floorboards were so rotten they had to build a brick base for the linotype all the way up from the cellar. "Well, when we get another one we'll concrete the whole place," Uncle Tim told everybody. For a whole day there was no work done. Everybody stood around looking at the tall black in- 30 tricate machine that stood there like an organ in a church. When the machine was working and the printshop filled with the hot smell of molten metal, everybody's eyes followed the quivering inquisitive arm that darted and flexed above the keyboard. When they handed round the warm shiny slugs of type the old German typesetter who for some reason they called Mike pushed back his glasses on his forehead and cried, "Fifty-five years a printer, and now 40 when I'm old I'll have to carry hods to make a living."

The first print Uncle Tim set up on the new machine was the phrase: Workers of the world unite; you have nothing to lose but your chains.

When Fainy was seventeen and just beginning to worry about skirts and ankles and girls' underwear when he walked home from work in the evening and saw the lights of the city bright against the bright heady western sky, there 50 was a strike in the Chicago printing trades. Tim O'Hara had always run a union shop and did all the union printing at cost. He even got

up a handbill signed, A Citizen, entitled An Ernest Protest, which Fainy was allowed to set up on the linotype one evening after the operator had gone home. One phrase stuck in Fainy's mind, and he repeated it to himself after he had gone to bed that night: It is time for all honest men to band together to resist the ravages of greedy privilege.

The next day was Sunday, and Fainy went along Michigan Avenue with a package of the handbills to distribute. It was a day of premature spring. Across the rotting yellow ice on the lake came little breezes that smelt unexpectedly of flowers. The girls looked terribly pretty and their skirts blew in the wind and Fainy felt the spring blood pumping hot in him, he wanted to kiss and to roll on the ground and to run out across the icecakes and to make speeches from the tops of telegraph poles and to vault over trolleycars; but instead he distributed handbills and worried about his pants being frayed and wished he had a swell looking suit and a swell looking girl to walk with.

"Hey, young feller, where's your permit to distribute them handbills?" It was a cop's voice growling in his ear. Fainy gave the cop one look over his shoulder, dropped the handbills and ran. He ducked through between the shiny black cabs and carriages, ran down a side street and walked and walked and didn't look back until he managed to get across a bridge just before the draw opened. The cop wasn't following him anyway.

He stood on the curb a long time with the whistle of a peanutstand shrilling derisively in his ear.

That night at supper his uncle asked him about the handbills.

"Sure I gave 'em out all along the lakeshore . . . A cop tried to stop me but I told him right where to get off." Fainy turned burning red when a hoot went up from everybody at the table. He filled up his mouth with mashed potato and wouldn't say any more. His aunt and his uncle and their three daughters all laughed and laughed. "Well, it's a good thing you ran faster than the cop," said Uncle Tim "else I should have had to bail you out and that would have cost money."

The next morning early Fainy was sweeping out the office, when a man with a face like raw steak walked up the steps; he was smoking thin black stogy of a sort Fainy had never seen before. He knocked on the ground glass door.

"I want to speak to Mr. O'Hara, Timothy O'Hara."

"He's not here yet, be here any minute now, sir. Will you wait?"

"You bet I'll wait." The man sat on the edge of a chair and spat, first taking the chewed end of the stogy out of his mouth and looking at it meditatively for a long time. When Tim O'Hara came the office door closed with a bang. Fainy hovered nervously around, a little bit afraid the man might be a detective following up the affair of the handbills. Voices rose and fell, the stranger's voice in short rattling tirades, O'Hara's voice in long expostulating clauses, now and then Fainy caught the word foreclose, until suddenly the door flew open and the stranger shot out, his face purpler than ever. On the iron stoop he turned and pulling a new stogy from his pocket, lit it from the old one; growling the words through the stogy and the blue puff of smoke, he said, "Mr. O'Hara, you have twenty-four hours to think it over . . . A word from you and proceedings stop immediately." Then he went off down the street leaving behind him a long trail of rancid smoke.

A minute later, Uncle Tim came out of the office, his face white as paper. "Fenian, old sport," he said, "you go get yourself a job. I'm going out of business . . . Keep a weather eye open. I'm going to have a drink." And he was drunk for six days. By the end of that time a number of meeklooking men appeared with summonses, and Uncle Tim had to sober up enough to go down to the court and put in a plea of bankruptcy.

Mrs. O'Hara scolded and stormed, "Didn't I tell you, Tim O'Hara, no good'll ever come with your fiddlin' round with these godless labor unions and social-democrats and knights of labor, all of 'em drunk and loafin' bums like yourself, Tim O'Hara. Of course the master printers ud have to get together and buy up your outstandin' paper and squash you, and serve you right too, Tim O'Hara, you and your godless socialistic boosin' ways only they might have thought of your poor wife and her helpless wee babes, and now we'll starve all of us together, us and the dependents and hangers on you've brought into the house."

"Well, I declare," cried Fainy's sister Milly. "If I haven't slaved and worked my fingers to the bone for every piece of bread I've eaten in this house," and she got up from the breakfast table and flounced out of the room. Fainy sat there while the storm raged above his head; then he got up, slipping a corn muffin into his pocket as he went. In the hall he found the "help wanted" section of the Chicago *Tribune*, took his cap and went out into a raw Sunday morning full of churchbells jangling in his ears. He boarded a streetcar and went out to Lincoln Park. There he sat on a bench for a long time munching the muffin and looking down the columns of advertisements: Boy Wanted. But they none of them looked very inviting. One thing he was bound, he wouldn't get another job in a printing shop until the strike was over. Then his eye struck

> Bright boy wanted with amb. and lit. taste, knowledge of print. and pub. business. Conf. sales and distrib. proposition $15 a week apply by letter P.O. Box 1256b

Fainy's head suddenly got very light. Bright boy, that's me, ambition and literary taste . . . Gee, I must finish *Looking Backward* . . . and jez, I like reading fine, an' I could run a linotype or set up print if anybody'd let me. Fifteen bucks a week . . . pretty soft, ten dollars' raise. And he began to write a letter in his head, applying for the job.

DEAR SIR (MY DEAR SIR)
   or maybe GENTLEMEN,
      In applying for the position you offer in today's Sunday *Tribune* I want to apply, (allow me to state) that I'm seventeen years old, no, nineteen, with several years' experience in the printing and publishing trades, ambitious and with excellent knowledge and taste in the printing and publishing trades,

no, I can't say that twice . . . And I'm very anxious for the job . . . As he went along it got more and more muddled in his head.

He found he was standing beside a peanut wagon. It was cold as blazes, a razor wind was shrieking across the broken ice and the black patches of water of the lake. He tore out the ad and let the rest of the paper go with the wind. Then he bought himself a warm package of peanuts.

Newsreel II

> *Come on and hear*
> *Come on and hear*
> *Come on and hear*

In his address to the Michigan state Legislature the retiring governor, Hazen S. Pingree, said in part: I make the prediction that unless those in charge and in whose hands legislation is reposed do not change the present system of inequality, there will be a bloody revolution in
10 less than a quarter of a century in this great country of ours.

CARNEGIE TALKS OF HIS EPITAPH

> *Alexander's Ragtime Band*
> *It is the best*
> *It is the best*

the luncheon which was served in the physical laboratory was replete with novel features. A miniature blastfurnace four feet high was on the banquet table and a narrow gauge railroad
20 forty feet long ran round the edge of the table. Instead of molten metal the blastfurnace poured hot punch into small cars on the railroad. Icecream was served in the shape of railroad ties and bread took the shape of locomotives.

Mr. Carnegie, while extolling the advantages of higher education in every branch of learning, came at last to this conclusion: Manual labor has been found to be the best foundation for the greatest work of the brain.

30 ## VICE PRESIDENT EMPTIES A BANK

> *Come on and hear*
> *Alexander's Ragtime Band*
> *It is the best*
> *It is the best*

brother of Jesse James declares play picturing him as bandit trainrobber and outlaw is demoralizing district battle ends with polygamy, according to an investigation by Salt Lake ministers, still practiced by Mormons clubwomen
40 gasp

> *It is the best band in the land*

say circus animals only eat Chicago horsemeat Taxsale of Indiana lots marks finale of World's Fair boom uses flag as ragbag killed on

cannibal isle keeper falls into water and sealions attack him.

The launch then came alongside the half deflated balloon of the aerostat which threatened at any moment to smother Santos Dumont. The latter was half pulled and half clambered over 5 the gunwale into the boat.

The prince of Monaco urged him to allow himself to be taken on board the yacht to dry himself and change his clothes. Santos Dumont would not leave the launch until everything that could be saved had been taken ashore, then, wet but smiling and unconcerned, he landed amid the frenzied cheers of the crowd.

The Camera Eye (3)

O qu'il a des beaux yeux said the lady in the seat opposite but She said that was no way to 6 talk to children and the little boy felt all hot and sticky but it was dusk and the lamp shaped like half a melon was coming on dim red and the train rumbled and suddenly I've been asleep and it's black dark and the blue tassel bobs on the edge of the dark shade shaped like a melon and everywhere there are pointed curved shadows (the first time He came He brought a melon and the sun was coming in through the tall lace windowcurtains and when 7 we cut it the smell of melons filled the whole room) No don't eat the seeds deary they give you appendicitis

but you're peeking out of the window into the black rumbling dark suddenly ranked with squat chimneys and you're scared of the black smoke and the puffs of flame that flare and fade out of the squat chimneys   Potteries dearie they work there all night   Who works there all night?   Workingmen and 8 people like that laborers travailleurs greasers
     you were scared

but now the dark was all black again the lamp in the train and the sky and everything had a blueblack shade on it and She was telling a story about

Longago   Beforetheworldsfair   Beforeyouwereborn and they went to Mexico on a private car on the new international line and the men shot antelope off the back of the train and big 9 rabbits jackasses they called them and once one night Longago Beforetheworldsfair Beforeyouwereborn one night Mother was so frightened on account of all the rifleshots but it was all-right turned out to be nothing but a little shooting they'd been only shooting a greaser that was all

that was in the early days

Lover of Mankind

Debs was a railroad man, born in a weather-boarded shack at Terre Haute.

He was one of ten children.

His father had come to America in a sailing-ship in '49,

an Alsatian from Colmar; not much of a money-maker, fond of music and reading,

he gave his children a chance to finish public school and that was about all he could do.

At fifteen Gene Debs was already working as a machinist on the Indianapolis and Terre Haute Railway.

He worked as locomotive fireman,

clerked in a store

joined the local of the Brotherhood of Locomotive Firemen, was elected secretary, traveled all over the country as organizer.

He was a tall shamblefooted man, had a sort of gusty rhetoric that set on fire the railroad workers in their pineboarded halls

made them want the world he wanted,

a world brothers might own

where everybody would split even:

I am not a labor leader. I don't want you to follow me or anyone else. If you are looking for a Moses to lead you out of the capitalist wilderness you will stay right where you are. I would not lead you into this promised land if I could, because if I could lead you in, someone else would lead you out.

That was how he talked to freighthandlers and gandywalkers, to firemen and switchmen and engineers, telling them it wasn't enough to organize the railroadmen, that all workers must be organized, that all workers must be organized in the workers' cooperative commonwealth.

Locomotive fireman on many a long night's run,

under the smoke a fire burned him up, burned in gusty words that beat in pineboarded halls; he wanted his brothers to be free men.

6. **Debs,** Eugene Victor Debs (1855–1926), a prominent American Socialist.

That was what he saw in the crowd that met him at the Old Wells Street Depot when he came out of jail after the Pullman strike, 50

those were the men that chalked up nine hundred thousand votes for him in nineteen twelve and scared the frockcoats and the top-hats and diamonded hostesses at Saratoga Springs, Bar Harbor, Lake Geneva with the bogy of a socialist president.

But where were Gene Debs' brothers in nineteen eighteen when Woodrow Wilson had him locked up in Atlanta for speaking against war,

where were the big men fond of whisky and 60 fond of each other, gentle rambling tellers of stories over bars in small towns in the Middle West,

quiet men who wanted a house with a porch to putter around and a fat wife to cook for them, a few drinks and cigars, a garden to dig in, cronies to chew the rag with

and wanted to work for it

and others to work for it;

where were the locomotive firemen and en- 70 gineers when they hustled him off to Atlanta Penitentiary?

And they brought him back to die in Terre Haute

to sit on his porch in a rocker with a cigar in his mouth,

beside him American Beauty roses his wife fixed in a bowl,

and the people of Terre Haute and the people in Indiana and the people of the Middle 80 West were fond of him and afraid of him and thought of him as an old kindly uncle who loved them, and wanted to be with him and to have him give them candy,

but they were afraid of him as if he had contracted a social disease, syphilis or leprosy, and thought it was too bad,

but on account of the flag

and prosperity

and making the world safe for democracy, 90

they were afraid to be with him,

or to think much about him for fear they might believe him;

for he said:

While there is a lower class I am of it, while there is a criminal class I am of it, while there is a soul in prison I am not free.

WILBUR DANIEL STEELE

Wilbur Daniel Steele began as a painter, and he has written a few one-act plays and a novel or two; but it is in the medium of the short story that he has achieved his greatest success, a success he well deserves, for his variety and power in that field have been nothing less than remarkable.

It was appropriate that he should have been born (March 17, 1886) in Greensboro, North Carolina, the home of O. Henry. There is apparent a certain kinship between these two short-story writers; both are versatile and both are, in one way or another, tricksters. But O. Henry was primarily an entertainer, whereas Steele has a penetrating satirical approach which gives him a far stronger grasp upon realities than his more popular and flashy colleague.

Steele graduated from the University of Denver in 1907 and proceeded at once to his art studies—in Boston, Paris, and New York. His first short story appeared in *The Atlantic Monthly* in 1912. He was a naval correspondent in the First World War. For the rest of the time he has traveled and assumed the life of the professional writer, composing systematically and carefully, in full self-dedication to his art and craft, but obviously a well-balanced, normal worker. The really significant fact in his biography is that he studied art and painted, because his short stories are a most arresting blend of the impressionistic and the romantic with the realism and irony of the bitter commentator. There are both beauty and cruelty in his work, as well as a strangeness which is not freakish, a disquieting mood which is not merely shocking—and always an originality which expresses itself with firmness and courage. His evocation of a mood has been compared, sometimes unfavorably, with that of Katherine Mansfield; but his masculine power often has the ability to make Miss Mansfield's moods extremely pallid, which may not be art but is assuredly life.

Among the many stories by Steele, the following are the most noteworthy volumes: *The Shame Dance* (1923); *Urkey Island* (1926); *The Man Who Saw Through Heaven* (1927)— in many ways his best work; and *Tower of Sand* (1929). His plays were collected in 1924; of these *The Giant's Stair* is still performed. Two novels, *Sound of Rowlocks* (1938) and *That Girl from Memphis* (1945), are less significant, although the latter has had much popular success. His best short stories were gathered together in a collection in 1946.

What Do You Mean—Americans?

THEY live in the country of the old—old houses, old stands, old men. Already they dream, and this is their dream, that when they are gone the tides, which seem to eat deeper into the Cove each year, will just come on up one spring and carry what's left of Cape Cod down under the water of the Seven Seas that in its youth it conquered, its work and its glory done. And that will be before long now, for there are only a few folks left.

You can count the families on one hand. There are the Whites and the Fullers in the Hollow, the Rogerses at the Bog, the Brewster brothers at the Cove. That's about all now in this tenuous, half-drowned, seven-mile wrist of the Cape. Of the Whites and Rogerses there are four generations, in the Fuller house three: the latter ends run pretty puttering, though, and pretty thin.

If it's a far cry from the Edward Fuller who came ashore to say his prayers, chase Indians, and leave his name on the Pilgrim Tablet over in Provincetown, down to Eddie Fuller, yawning and attending to his pimples behind the post-office boxes at the Center—if it's a far cry from these dreadless "subjects of the dread sovereign" down to the youthless White youths, flivver rattling to their fevered merry-makings at Wellfleet or Eastham, their galvanic deadfrog dancing, their drug-store tipple, and their radio jazz—if there's a gap there, there's a gap almost as wide and quite as melancholy between these tag ends of the stock and a generation still living under the roofs with them—Sam White and Benjie Fuller in the Hollow, Ember Rogers at the Bog, Andy and Isaiah Brewster at the Cove—men who fetched Kennebec ice cakes to Calcutta and brought new China tea up the Thames in the *Sea Glory* and the *A. J. Stowell* two weeks ahead of London's own East-Indiamen in the days that were days.

In those days the Cape bred women too. Look at Molly, Andy Brewster's wife, that's dead and gone. Then look at the Molly Brewster of today. She keeps house for her great-grandfather Andy and his brother Isaiah at the Cove, and what house she keeps! Well, it's not the way the other Molly did it sixty years ago. Bread baked in Boston, beans baked in Chicago, cake in cardboard from goodness-knows where! She hasn't the time, she says.

Hasn't the time! Those two old men fathom the sad, deep, literal truth of that. She hasn't the time. She came too late, the sands too nearly run. After her the deluge; so why take pains? What's the use of forethought, with nothing to come? What's the use of character, never to be handed down? What's the use even of appearances? Studying her secretly from beneath their watery lids, they comprehend. That is why, then, she speaks a language of strange, daring, slipshod words; why her gestures are all immoderate and her songs out of tune; why she goes about unabashed in skirts as short and lips as red as a California harlot in the days of gold. That is why she is never at home evenings, darning or quilting under the sitting-room lamp, but off as soon as ever the supper dishes are stacked, with a pat and a fling and a mouth of rebellion, flitting the devil alone knows where in the dark of the country of the old.

"Let us eat, drink, and be merry. . . ." Poor girl!

She hasn't the time even to care about the company she keeps. This strikes deepest into the hearts of Andy and Isaiah. Their pride is bitter. To think of these two blond vikings of the republic who carried the Stars and Stripes around a wondering world, who came home to fetch good, honest Indies rum ashore under the dark of the Cove like the free men they were, and went up to the meeting house in their Sabbath beavers to worship the God of Massachusetts as only free men may—to think of them having to sit, shackled to their rockers by the weight of their proud years, and watch the remnant of their line and population going, without visibly caring, to the dogs!

They would have called him a dog in their time, or at least "one of them niggers of some sort."

He comes out of the deepening shadows. Whence he comes, in that narrow land where there are only Rogerses and Brewsters, the Fullers and the Whites, who can say? Andy and Isaiah can't. When they try, their minds close up.

Their minds do that of late years. More and more easily. When, at the ice-cream feast of the Dorcases last Autumn, the two old fellows undertook in mournful gaiety to twit the schoolma'am upon the dwindling of her flock, and when she looked puzzled (for all the world) and told them that, land alive! they weren't to worry, she had her hands full, and would have them a sight fuller, she guessed, before they got around to putting in the new primary room —when she said that, Isaiah looked at Andy and Andy at Isaiah, one winked and the other cackled, and their minds, like wary clam shells, closed up tight. "Primary room!" They weren't to be taken in by jokes like that. They were too smart.

He comes out of the deepening shadows, his approach heralded, long before he is seen, by the sounding boards of the hills that gather down to the Cove, the clank of a loose brake beam, the whine of gritted springs, gaskets wheezing. A curious centaur, head and shoulders and busy arms of a man, body of an ungroomed half-ton truck; so from their rockers

on the porch behind the mosquito-netting they always see him, Jimmy the Greek. So he careens to a halt under the antique, uneasy willows in the blue-brown shadow cast by Sheep Hill; so he snorts, backs, swerves, caracoles, pawing the sand, gamboling in the twilight of these Yankee gods; so he rears there, breathing heavily with his pitted cylinders, peering glassily with his one large rectangular eye at the
10 house beyond the turf, the house native and noble, solid and broad and low, with a roof like another slope of the gray Pamet moors. So, unbudging from his hybrid shell, he calls through the dusk: "Molly to home?"

Neither Andy nor Isaiah answers. Rock, rock, rock, their chairs and their dry bones creaking, their eyes meeting, full of repugnance, rebellion, appeal. They'd have their tongues cut out before they'd speak.

20 No need. Molly has answered herself: "Yep, just a second I'll be with yu, Jim, old kid."

She passes out between the rockers, hatless, free of elbow, wanton of stocking, neither mother of tomorrow nor daughter of yesterday.

"Where you bound for, Molly?" Andy writhes. He feels degraded.

"Where you bound?" Isaiah writhes. He too had sworn never to ask again.

"Oh, nowheres. Up to the dance at Chatham,
30 that's all. Oh, for the love, Jimmy, can that honking, will yu! I'm on my way! Now, Daddies, run, climb in your beds like good boys. Sound sleep, sweet dreams!"

Sleep! Dreams! The mockery!

Their rockers are still. Leaning forward, squeezing the chair arms with their vein-corded fists, they follow the iron flight of the centaur, cast back in fainter and fainter reverberations from the folded moor sides, careen-
40 ing farther away, deeper away in the mists of the falling night.

He's going up Graveyard Hill now. If only their legs could run as swiftly as their minds. He's abreast of the old Snow place now. Thrrmmm! Whine and wheeze! An abominable whisper threading the valleys. It's louder for an instant as though a door in the hills had opened. He's crossing the marsh at the Center now, this what-is-he? This Greek. This what's-
50 his-name? J. Krenk, General Trucking. Jimmy the Greek. And Molly Brewster!

Anger, reckless and helpless, sweeps them.

Let him take her. Let him take her back to his lemon-peddling, olive-stinking, two-for-a-nickel Levant ports. Then let her see!

Then let her think of those white women, the other Mollys, her mothers!

Memories submerge the two men; their tantrum passes and gives place to nostalgia; they turn cowards, feeling themselves abandoned, 60 defeated at last. The mosquito bar is a cage, oppressing their lungs and bringing to their skins a faint, chill sweat. Moved by a common impulse, they get up and rush out. They have forgotten their hats, and Isaiah's head is as bald as a porpoise. What matter? Their rheumatics! Their hearts! What odds?

Where are they going, hoisting their feet so industriously along the clam-shell metal of this road? Where and why? 70

"We might drop around and see Sam White a minute, the night's so fine."

"So we might. I hear tell he was ailin' a trifle yesterday."

Two shafts of light, streaming from nowhere, wheel across the dark. Two orbs, sudden and blinding, fetch up with a snort to eye the vivid old men.

"Here they are now," comes a voice out of the creature. 80

"Why," gasps Andy, "if 't'ain't the White boys!" Isaiah, blinking into the headlights, lifts a reedy voice: "We was bound over your way, boys."

"Well, ma said we should stop by and tell you, and save you the trip. It'll be Friday at two, the fun'ral."

The monster squats there on its rubber haunches, purring, reading their stupid faces. After a little it says: "You'd heard about gran'- 90 pa, hadn't you? Went last evenin', quiet, no pain. And it's Friday at two." Presently it gives them over for dumb ones, bounces around in the road and streams off up the vale, leaving their eyes full of stars.

"Sam!" says one.

"Sam!" says the other. That's all.

Perhaps it's the way it happened, the stage effects; perhaps it's something long predestined in the calendar of their years. No matter, 100 the night has turned a corner and become apocalyptic.

Sam White is gone.

In silence they plod back. They plod back toward the cage of the netting, the eighty-year prison of the dark house. Sleep. Dreams.

But, no-sir! Not by a dang sight, they won't. They bolt the road and flee it at right angles across the tricky footing of the poverty-grass. *"They seek water, and die in the open."* That's rats.

But why all this? They knew Sam had to go sooner or later and give over his much of room to the returning wilderness and the climbing tides. Just as they know that Benjie and Ember will have to give over theirs, and they themselves, and let the tired Cape go down. Didn't they know that?

They're silly, but you can't argue it. It's something in this night, something let loose, something that pursues and climbs up their legs like a travesty of strength, another childhood. So they clamber for all they're worth, in silence, their mouths open, as if it were true that the valley behind was filling up with the flood.

They look back when they reach the crest of Sheep Hill, and from the height they see the country familiar to them, rod by rod of its folded moors, its dunes and winding marshes, spread of a sudden fantastic and pixy-peopled under this night. Will-o'-the-wisps and ghost-fires.

There's John Champion's house, under the shoulder of Finback, a mile to the east. John died a good twenty years ago, and his daughter's family moved to Iowa. Yet there looks to be a light in it, a goblin cheer. Dave Burch passed on in the nineties; his children live in Los Angeles; the homestead, hidden under the cottonwoods in the Flat, opens an eye in distant banshee mockery. And there again. As if there were people, populations! And there again. Like a lamp on Borneo Plain!

There's one element that never betrays, but always plays fair. If the land is playing tricks' with your eyes, old fellows, turn them to the sea.

Across the water the sky toward Boston shows a late loom of dusk, doubled upside down in the mirroring plain. Not far offshore, across the mouth of the Cove, a fisherman sails, his dim masts erect in the meager breeze. Farther distant, toward the lights on Provincetown shore, a monster lies at rest on the sea.

So the sea too is corruptible tonight; even the sea. It abides Leviathan. Leviathan blowing a leaden, lazy spout; prodigious creature, ink-black, and incandescent-striped.

"She come in weeth engine trouble," says a voice.

There's another watcher on Sheep Hill. He arises from a beach-plum bush at their feet, headless, because he has his coat shawlwise over his head.

"I never seen her before, thees ship, and that's funny because my boy goes een her, and she's lak a city, he says. Fifty-nine t'ousand ton! What do you know about that?"

What, indeed, do they know about that? Except that the night is trying to play them another trick. Painting that shadow on the shadows out there, enormous; as though a master and a mate of an incomparable *Sea Glory* were to be taken in by jest as thin as that, a ship enormous as eighty *Sea Glories* on one keel!

"I tell you," says the shade, "these Englishmann, these Germann, they got notheeng on us now. One day us Americans we weel be as beeg a shipping nation as they is on the sea; you watch."

It's too rare. Andy and Isaiah open their mouths to chuckle, and before they can chuckle, a hot, contemptuous anger has got in their throats instead.

"Who are *you?*" they cry, and "Where you from?" Those voices that rang, full-winded, absolute, over the decks of the white clippers of the years when the world rubbed its eyes. Echoes now.

Echoes, yes, but echoes still puissant. The headless Jack-in-the-box sounds fetched aback and ill at ease.

"Wh-wh-who am I? Well, I guess you know me, Meester Brewster. You know Manuel Braganza. You seen me round plentee, I guess. Since five year I got thees old Champion place back here, crost from Jimmee the Greek. I guess you know *me*, all right."

"Nope."

"You don't know Manuel Brag—don't know Manny the Lisbon?"

671

"Never hear the name. Never!"

"You—you—never hear o' my boy Johnee?"

"Johnnie who?"

Silence. That has done for him. It has done for them too; done wonders. Their feet are solid on their own hill again and they begin to tower. Men against bogies, men will win every time.

It's true. The spook hasn't a word. Presently
10 he begins to fade before their eyes, a receding whisper of sand. Across the hilltop and down the slope the long, black, dismembered torso vanishes degree by degree into the dark above the invisible Cove.

Give these old fellows an inch and they'll take a mile. The impulse to pursue, to rout him sevenfold, to crow, to pile it on, is too strong. Nor is it altogether this that hauls them to the sandy precipice where he disappeared. Tri-
20 umph has given sudden rein to memories; their feet are in old paths; their tongues wag.

"Remember that night the revenue man came snoopin'?"

"Remember the skiff bottom-up on the beach with the three bar'ls of rum under it, and me under it with 'em and my legs caught out by the gun'l, full in view?"

"Rec'lect the brig hove to out there, 'bout where that fisherman lays now?"

30 "The *Abraham*, wa'n't it? And Ezra Small?"

They pause. Pause? Where are they? What in the name of Jehoshaphat are they doing here, old flies, clinging midway of the precipitous sand? This much is certain: if they don't catch their death one way they'll catch it another.

They pause. Hunkering down in little sand slides, they gaze at the becalmed schooner. In the cobweb starlight it might truly be the
40 *Abraham*, and Captain Ezra prowling the deck and chewing his whisker and wondering what's wrong with the Brewster boys ashore. They gaze at the pool of the inlet below them, and there the starlight, chasing the ripples, weaves silver stuff of dreams, mesmeric, fluent. The gods are young.

"Rec'lect that night, eh?"

"Remember Molly. . . ."

Molly! A subconscious discord. A rift of syn-
50 copation, dilute, galvanic; a painted mouth, an empty head; a half-ton truck, a Greek.

No, though! By thunder, no! *Molly*, they're talking of *Molly*!

She was the wife of one, the sister-in-law of the other. Years have almost outlawed that inequality. To each she comes back all comeliness, all docile bravery, all grace. A woman of those days.

"Remember Molly that night, Isaiah? You couldn't see her, though, and you stuck under the skiff; the way she come trippin' down from nowheres, fetch one look at your boots croppin' out like a hamstrung turtle, set down on the skiff, tidied her skirts out over, and set there gazing at the stars as soberlike as if she was in the habit of stargazin' every night with a shotgun laid across her lap. Nor you couldn't see the way old Revenue Perkins eyed her and hesitated, scrawn out his neck and fetch to a halt."

"I heard him, though, Andy; promise you that. 'Pleasant evenin', Mis' Brewster!' 'Pleasant evenin', Mr. Perkins!' 'I'm aimin' to have a look in under that skiff, if you don't mind, Mis' Brewster?' 'In which case, Mr. Perkins, you're aimin' to do something you ain't able; not so long's I'm settin' on to it.' 'In which case, Mis' Brewster, I shall have the law on to the lot of you—' 'In which case, Mr. Perkins, I'll have something a sight quicker actin' than the law on to *you*, sir.' (With that I hear the gun butt easin' up along the garboard strake.) 'Quit it, Molly Brewster,' says Perkins. 'Git, Eben Perkins,' says Molly, 'and git quick!' "

"And Revenue gat! I *guess* he gat!"

"Never hear the last of it, did he? Nor come snoopin' *this* way again, eh?"

"Feared o' meetin' up with Molly! Heh-heh!"

"The gentlest and abidin'est of women! Heh-heh-heh!"

The gentlest, the abidingest of women! What homage could be more precious to the heroine of long ago than this cachinnation of old men, this mirth flung out in thready challenge to reconquering nothingness and the prowling powers of the dark?

The dark answers, coagulating in another shade at their feet, downhill.

"What you doin' here, you guys?"

Their mouths dry and fall agape.

"Well, I v-v-vow!" bleats Isaiah, and Andy echoes him: "I vow!"

"Oh," breathes the shade, "I know now. It's old Isaiah and old Andy."

"But who—in—in—are *you?*"

"Don't you rec'nize me? It's Tony Fuller from the Coast Guard. You know me."

"Tony!" They see their chance. "Tony *Fuller!"* The impostor is delivered into their hands. Their voices break high. "There wa'n't never a man—there's been Eds and Ezras, Johns and Jonathans—but never a man amongst the Fullers called by any such nigger name, such a lemon-peddlin' name, as 'Tony.' No-sir-ee!"

The haunt chuckles, rubbing his lips with a spectral sleeve.

"Try Farquiera then; that's my family name when they come from the Azores. Or if you're bent on crackin' your jaws, try 'em on this guy Sob-lef-sky—Sub-lof-sky—whatever 'tis. He's down in the road to the left, waitin'; so you get along now, quiet, and tell him I sent you, and he'll leave you through. Skedaddle, my boys; clear out o' here!"

If there is one there are a dozen retorts, just at their scandalized lips; arrogant laughter, withering old quarter-deck oaths. Dumbly, though, sending down a whispering lace of sand, like autumnal spiders, they flee as they are told, not knowing why. They get off the cliff, their own cliff, not knowing how; a lichenous ground is underfoot, then a streak half clay, then, nuts. A wind, a slow draft redolent of clam and weed, bears them along; an air familiar as the years of their youth, turned secret and queer. It bears them into the mouth of a hollow floored with blackness and roofed with stars. Sergeant Belkar Soblievski of the State Police snaps on the headlight of his motorcycle and examines them with his yellow cornucopia of flame.

"You're out late, my friends." Then, not meaning the light-blistered couple to stand there all night, he says in a kindlier tone: "Go right on, the way you were going, my fathers, and keep your mouths shut, and no harm done. Good night."

It is some moments before he snaps off the snooping light. Behind Isaiah and Andy, across the wheel track to the Eden of their ancestral Cove, the ray hangs horizontal, like a lazy angel's flaming sword.

Here come the willows out of the hill. There's a moon somewhere under the eastern ocean, and its foreglow, refracting from the zenith, describes with faint silver the slopes of the roof, the two fat chimneys, the fence.

So it's home they're coming after all.

Their boots drag; soul and body they're beat, the pair of them, dead beat.

The house opens and swallows them. No need of a lamp; they can find their beds in the dark. Mind the table, Isaiah. Take care of that swayed door; it's got to be fixed, no two ways. Here's the chair for Andy, and here's the chair for Isaiah, to drape their coats and trousers over, their shirts and drawers.

There's nothing left but sleep, then. Sound sleep. Sweet dreams.

Isaiah, the youngster of the two, lies on his back, toes up, wide awake. Andy, across the room, lies toes up too, counting sheep. One sheep over the fence; two sheep over the fence; three sheep over the fence. There's a nigger-looking fellow herding them. Land! he's got no head. Manny the Lisbon! That's a dirty port, Lisbon. And he had the gall to say—this headless Portugee Eyetalian fly-by-night—

What's that? There! Again! Passing like spirit footfalls across the turf outside!

The hall clock is still—still these years—but Molly's alarm clock sends in a tinny cheeping from the kitchen. Where can Molly be?

Five sheep over the fence; six sheep over the—

"What's that? Andy!"

"Yes, Isaiah?"

Isaiah slides out of bed, tiptoes across the chamber, creeps in beside his elder brother. Neither of them says anything. It's nearly seventy years since Isaiah did that. But neither of them speaks.

They're not used to lying awake. It's this night. This night of supernal license, weird air quakes, invasions crepuscular and fleering of little peoples from beyond the pale.

Seven sheep over the fence—

"What's wrong, boy?"

"I hear a mosquito in the room, dang him, and I can't sleep."

"Pshaw, Isaiah, now you turn over and shut your eyes and—" Andy sits bolt up, a listener. "Hark!"

Thud! A fault in the atmosphere, small, echo-less. A gunshot, unmistakable. Thud! Thud! Thud! An imponderable fusillade.

Is it ghosts, in this land of the dead? Memories? All inside the brain?

Andy tries Isaiah: "Isaiah, did you hear anything?"

The youngster lies there with the quilt tight over his chest. It's a terrible thing, when you've
10 been equal to anything and everything, to find yourself suddenly like this. His voice comes as thin as eel grass:

"Where's that girl?"

It's too much for Andy, and he joins in: "Why don't she ever come home? What's she thinkin' on, this hour of the night?"

" 'Tain't decent, Andy. What'll folks say?"

"What does she care for that?"

"What does she care if she keeps us wakin'
20 for her?"

"Who are *we*, anyhow? What do *we* 'mount to?"

"What does anything 'mount to these days; anything but cavortin' about with foreigners, dancin', huggin' maybe, carryin' on, forgettin' your religion, your elders, your upbringing—anything to make the time go quick?"

"And devil take the hindmost!"

There's a cry, chambered in a distance. The
30 devil taking the hindmost, perhaps. The empty moors and dunes where men used to live give it out; one lone articulation, anger, terror, mortal pain, who can tell from the spent whisper creeping in through the Brewster blinds?

"A-n-d-y, I wish—I wish that girl was to home."

"I—I wish she was."

The shame of it, confessed at last, mutually, out loud! Isaiah Brewster, who in the name of
40 the Great Republic stood up on his feet and told the portbashaw of the Emperor of Siam to go to Jericho! Andy Brewster, who with his own hands put half his crew in irons at the height of the Seventy-one Typhoon! The two of them now, praying nothing but the sound of Molly's dance shoes on the floor beyond the wall; the comfort of even Molly's doomsday youthfulness under the roof with them!

Prayers aren't half-ton trucks, though, for
50 beggars to ride.

Or are they? Wait!

Isaiah is up now, sitting as bolt and gray as Andy.

Another mosquito? No. Hardly louder than a mosquito, to be sure, and oddly like the insect's silky whine—that whine of springs and beams and gaskets, all in one, a mile away.

" 'Tis him!"

" 'Tis! 'Tis!"

"He's to the marsh now—or—or no—"

"N-n-no—no—Isaiah!"

"You mean it don't sound like 'twas on—"

" 'Tain't on. 'Tain't on any road I know of, Isaiah. That's clear to the north'rd somewheres. Sounds to me—"

"Sounds to me like it was all adrift somewheres up Borneo Plain—"

Thud! The shadow of the phantom of a shot! That's gone. So is the whine, like the whir of a nighthawk planing back into the night again.

"Isaiah," says Andy, "you lay down and go to sleep. This is foolishness."

Five minutes, up they knife again.

A step. A clandestine sole on the porch. A sneaking tread.

Andy wouldn't speak for a million dollars; neither would Isaiah.

"Molly!" they call in the same breath.

No answer. Only the scratch of a match, out the kitchen way.

"Molly Brewster!"

The match goes out. More footfalls. Odd footfalls. Odd chills.

Who? What?

The second match is at the very foot of their bed, a blinding nimbus. In the nimbus there are two eyes, a lean, green-brown face, a hat like an inverted flower pot made of kinky wool.

"You gaht ahny rags, say?"

When Isaiah was mate in the Boston fruit-bark *Hope Wade* he used once a year to load figs at Smyrna. He used to sit in an armchair on the house within one spit of the rail and keep those natives going as only a Cape man could, with alternate volleys of truculence and wit. "If there's one thing I'd love to see before I die," he used to say, "it's one of you lazy heathen Turk-fellahs tryin' to earn a meal in the town of Pamet, Barnstable County, Mass. If there's one thing I'd love!"

It comes back to Isaiah, every fatal syllable.

The white rims widen around his eyes. He begins to speak.

"You're that Turk—"

"Curse the Toork! He kelled my fahther, my mahther, my brahther!"

"No-sir, though, no-sir, all foolin', you're the one—the one folks c-c-calls the Turk—that comes by sellin' carpets. You are so!"

A frown withers the green-brown face.

10 "You gaht ahny rags, say? You gaht ahny rags?"

The match burns a finger and sails away in two red stars, blown by an Asian oath. In reverse the business of footfalls reenacted, across the kitchen, across the porch.

The night has overreached itself. "Got any rags?" That's a joke.

There's a glimmer of moon through the cracks in the blinds. In the wraith of light Andy
20 lifts on an elbow and studies supine Isaiah. The youngster lies with his head cracked back, as though by a blow, his mouth open, the shape of a black egg, and his whisker thrust straight up in the air. He's not dead, though; he's asleep.

Andy lies back and summons all his resolution. Resolutely he envisions sheep, just such sheep as Dave Burch used to run on Borneo Plain, matted gray-brown bodies and slender
30 legs snapping under them. Over the stone wall they go. One sheep over; two sheep over; three sheep over; four—or was it five?—five—six sheep—

When he awakens it is with a gulp and a kick.

Who's that? By the bed there, towering in the new gray?

It's Isaiah. It's the youngster, getting his pants on.

"I can't stand it," says Isaiah, his teeth aclatter.

"What is it now?"

"I don't know. My Godfrey, if I knowed, I —there! Hark to that!"

"That trompin' like?"

"Trompin', yes. Trompin', skitterin', skutter-in' all about, whisperin' too, and groanin' into the bargain. There now! Will y'hark?"

"In the wood house. Or more like Molly's room. Mebby it's Molly."

"I want to know."

"Or cats."

"I want to know."

Andy fumbles his pale legs out of the quilt and into his trousers. They go in stocking feet, carrying their boots. In the kitchen Andy pauses.

"Molly come home?"

"Never hear her."

"You been asleep, though."

"I ain't. Not one blessed wink, and that's 60 true. No-sir, everything I seen, I seen. There's niggers and heathen and all manner of islanders and dagoes spiritin' about, this night. Andy, there was a Turk come into our room, and I seen him with my own two eyes. So I ain't been asleep."

"I'll look in her room, anyway, on the chance."

Holding his breath, he edges open Molly's 70 door. His head disappears. It reappears, the cheeks collapsing with relief.

"By glory, she *be*. Here all this time, to bed, asleep. Us fools!"

Side by side, holding the door open, they gaze into the little chamber, cave-lit with the seepage of dawn, perfumed with violet water, tar soap, carnation powder, fiber-silk stockings, and all the faint, mingled emanations from frocks and underthings—the rectangular gray 80 whiteness of the bed—the dark spot of a head averted on the pillow.

"Don't wake 'er."

"No; easy's the word; take care."

The old fools!

"Molly!" breathes Andy, just once. Just to try.

The head on the pillow flops over. The heads in the door thrust out.

Black eyes study them from the pillow, hyp- 90 notized.

Jimmy the Greek!

If he is hypnotized, what are they?

It was in this room, in that bed, that Molly White Brewster died, on Cleveland's election day. It was through that window her soul went to heaven.

They can do nothing but stare; stare at the bureau, holy of holies, untidy, intimate; a pot of cold cream, a ribbon, a note, a garter, a 100 kitten of combings, a man's plaid cap; stare at the bed, the pillow, the solitary presence there, obscurely begotten, horde-born, Mediterranean.

They open their mouths to roar like lions; in the hush they bleat.

"Where's M-M-Molly?"

He holds them with black-and-white eyes; he has lost his tongue.

"Wh-wh-wh-where's *Molly?*"

10 It's Molly that answers, Molly's feet askip on the porch behind them, the wind of her coming across the kitchen, the fling of her arms brushing them aside like wraiths.

Worse than wraiths! Of a sudden something beyond accounting happens. In Molly's bedroom they've always kept the old paper, spotty and faded as it is; funny old paper, peopled by Venetian boatmen and early Victorian trees. And now between two breaths Andy and 20 Isaiah are pictures with the boatmen and memories with the trees. It is as though still visible, no one saw them; as though reality had abandoned them and gone out into the middle of the room.

Molly is real; they're not. Tag end of a race and a tradition, her docked hair tousled, her shoes streaked with mud from another county, hem of a torn petticoat at the trail, she's flesh alive; a tradition and a race beginning.

30 She's on the bed's edge, hip and elbow, one wild hand in Jimmy Krenk's black curls, combwise, questioning, and her breath against his cheek.

"Y'all right, kid? Tell me quicker'n quick: Y'all right?"

"Are *you* all right, Moll; you tell *me?*"

"You should worry about me! Do I look sick?"

"But, Moll—"

40 "Shush, kid, I know. I look like a homemade hangover, I know I do, but you got to consider a hundred 'n' thirty miles in that bus of yours is no *thé dansant* for a fair young thing, is it now? 'Specially the last fifteen of 'em on a rim. Cheer up; I'll look good when I get a shot of coffee in me. And don't worry about the stuff; I got it all safe and dark to you-know-who, you-know-where, thirty-one cases, check, and you couldn't have made it snappier 50 yourself, you poor angel, and that's that. And the bus is back in Costa's g'rage with the old

plates on—and the clutch afloat—and that phony rear shoe gone to hell and that's that. And that motorcycle egg was into Yarmouth Hospital at three, I just got word at the marsh, with his right arm out of commish. And that's that."

"Was it you, Moll? Was it you plugged the guy, same's Turkey says?"

"Well, if I didn't, there's been some awful 60 mistake. I picked up your gun when you dropped it, and I was peeved. But say, don't get me talkin'—"

"Listen, Moll, tell me somethin'. Was it you carried me up here from the Cove, same's Turkey says?"

"Well, Turkey helped some—as quick as he—"

"Where was the other guys?"

"Busy, don't you forget. Who'd' you s'pose 70 got the cop crowd trailed off down Truro way? Jazzy work for a while. But now, Jim, how's the bean?"

"Bean's bright."

It's the strangest sensation, being a Venetian boatman inked on moldy wall paper, harkening to unintelligible tongues.

"And the leg?"

"Absitively perfect limb."

"Turkey got it bandaged right? That petti- 80 coat of mine I slammed on—"

"Coold not find ahny rahgs."

Reality spreads with the growing dawn. It's the Armenian himself, down on his hams on the carpet beyond the bed.

"No rags? Turkey, you're a bird! But listen —my God! You mean to say that plugged leg is still—Oh, you poor lamb! Now, listen, Jim; I'll go as easy, as easy, but I got to give it a look." 90

The painted boatmen close their painted eyes. Their painted ears they can not close. Earth swarms. Their painted minds they can not get quite shut. Murmurs. Fragments. The land of the old, the turncoat, teems with pitiless voices of the young. Rumors creep in through the windows.

"Doc and the priest ought to be coming—"

"—No, Gabriel phoned the priest he needn't come. Jim's all right." 10

"He'll be all right, that is, if we can keep him doggo for a spell—"

"—But what they'll say up-Cape when he

don't show up at shortstop for the Legion in the Barnstable game next Sunday—"

"Oh, we can bull through it somehow—Hey, what's that?"

Another kind of a murmur; a high, faint throbbing in the air.

"Molly! Inside there! Here comes Doc Bader from Provincetown. I guess it's him, anyway; it sounds like Gaspa's seaplane. I'll slide up to the pond and show him the way."

Still another note, within the room, this one, half crooning:

"Good kid, did I hurt? Oh, good kid, I tried to be so gentle—"

"Gentle, Moll? Don't talk. You're the gentlest ever; and you're more'n the gentlest; you're the beautifulest, and you're more'n the beautifulest; you're the straightest, bravest—"

"Bravest! Quit kiddin', you Greek idiot. I been frightened sober; I'm still scared weak. Take hold of me and hang onto me tight, tight."

"I got yu, tight. All there is, though, I hate to be a bother here."

"Bother! That's a good line. It's my house, isn't it, Jimmy dearie? And seeing we're going to get married Friday, where's the diff?"

(Friday at two!)

The Venetian boatmen end their fading by fading quite away, out of the bedroom, out of the house.

It's a fog-dawn, the light from the sun-tipped hills coming down at every angle, through the pearly smother. It's as if the night, in place of ending, had just bleached out. Albino darkness. White shades. The veil is troubled by them, half-glimpsed and gone; white shades of youth, black-eyed and swarthy, sallow and gray-eyed.

Once more Andy and Isaiah flee the canopy of the willows and puff up Sheep Hill. The mist dilutes; at the height they find the sun and air. And the sea, Leviathan gone. The honest sea.

They flop on a timber and gaze at it. By and by Isaiah points a finger at the wedge of the Cove, still in the shadow below them.

"By cricky, she goes fast these days, Andy."

He is resolved to see it, and he sees it; the marsh growing an estuary, the estuary a strait, a worm of blue salt water eating ever and ever more hungrily into the entrails of the dead

Cape. "By cricky, 'twon't be many years till you can sail a vessel straight through the Hollow to the back side."

"Where do you get that stuff?" inquires a voice from behind the brothers. They won't have it. They won't hear.

"'Twa'n't so many years ago," says Andy in resolute musing, "there was beach plums growin' out there where them breakers are now."

"The hell there was!" A shadow falls across them, and out over their heads, blue and amber, floats the cloud of a cigaret. It's Frankie Silvado, the surfman from Pamet Station, and he has a purple mustache and dark, live, ardent eyes. He might have yellow eyes and green whiskers for all Andy and Isaiah: they won't see him and they don't see him.

Andy clears an indomitable throat: "Accordin' to my calc'lations, Isaiah, the way she's sinkin' now—"

"That's a lovely pipe, that is," persists the tactless shade. "I been patrollin' this shore ten years and more, and I used to have to walk on the cliff because the tide was all over where them grass flats is now. You old geezers ain't up with the times, or you'd know all this land is makin' all the while. There was a pr'fessor lectured to Provincetown last summer, and he says, like's not, it'll be all dry ground from here clean to Plymouth shore one day, with woods, like's not, and farms, and cities—"

Cities! The brothers are betrayed. From one to the other passes a sage and soundless guffaw.

"Though," adds Silvado, "I don't know what kind o' people there'll be to live in 'em, the way things are goin' now with this Cape crowd, gettin' to be smugglers—runnin' in liquor off these West Indie vessels for all they're worth—women as bad as the men, too, accordin' to what Tony Fuller says he seen last night. I tell you the truth, I don't know what this country of ourn is comin' to."

By and by Andy turns an eye on Isaiah, and once more, with dogmatic patience, clears his throat.

"As I was sayin'—the way she's sinkin' now —and the way they're droppin' off—Sam yesterday—like's not you or me tomorrow—'twon't be so long now before there won't be any left hereabouts."

"Any what?"

Curse and double curse that Ginny! Like drops of water on the skull it grows suddenly too much.

"Any folks!" cried Isaiah.

"Any folks?"

Now they upend on their reedy legs and face him and lash out at him.

"Any—any—*Americans!*"

In the white pouring of the sunshine, as they watch greedily the effect of that brutal blow, the red mottles go out of their cheeks. Now, at last, they are terrified. This fellow doesn't even know what they're driving at.

"What do you mean?" he puzzles. "What do you mean—*Americans?*"

THOMAS WOLFE

Fundamentally Thomas Wolfe, a lonely, lovable giant of a man—physically, intellectually, and spiritually—is the supreme example in his generation of the poetic quester after life and its meaning. He possessed an enormous hunger for human experience; an insatiable curiosity about people and things; an intoxication with both the beauty of living and its hideous cruelties. *Look Homeward, Angel* and *Of Time and the River* are drenched with a nostalgic sadness and an almost futile bewilderment about all that is ugly and base and pathetic. *The Web and the Rock* and *You Can't Go Home Again* strike the reader as the writings of an affirmationist rather than of a Waste Lander. Even in these, however, there lie a smoldering ache and a sense of tears.

Thomas Wolfe was born in Asheville, North Carolina, on October 3, 1900. His boyhood was the not unusual American boyhood of paper routes and public schooling. But his father, a stonecutter, was a man of sensitive tastes and a phenomenal memory of the past century, and a man who encouraged the boy to become a voracious reader of history and fiction. The son not only admired his father as a man but revered him as representative of the America of past generations, the America which had set its seal upon our present-day civilization. It is not surprising, therefore, that the father-symbol is one of Wolfe's favorites.

Wolfe matriculated at the University of North Carolina at an unusually early age (1915), and took part there in the customary college journalistic activities. In fact, his first published work was a play which appeared in the second series of *Carolina Folk Plays* (1924). During the First World War, Wolfe worked for a time in the shipyards at Norfolk, but he returned to take his degree at North Carolina in 1920. At this time he was interested primarily in becoming a dramatist, and so he went to Harvard for the famous "47 Workshop" course in practical drama given by the late George P. Baker ("Professor Hatcher" in *Of Time and the River*). His plays made no impression upon New York theatrical producers, however, and Wolfe earned his living meanwhile by teaching English at New York University. A trip abroad brought him into contact with the writings of James Joyce, among others, which contact not only shaped his bent toward prose fiction but influenced greatly his essentially intense, subjective style.

He had been working on a "first novel" for some time before it could interest a publisher sufficiently to be placed. Even so, the manuscript of the novel was so undisciplined and its structure so sprawling and amorphous that for a while the author despaired of ever bringing it out. But *Look Homeward, Angel* (1929), when it finally appeared, was a spectacular success. As in the case of virtually everything Thomas Wolfe ever wrote, this novel was basically autobiographical; it projected the life of Eugene Gant, that is to say, Thomas Wolfe, from his boyhood in Catawba (Asheville in extremely thin disguise), and it crowded its pages with innumerable characters and scenes and frequent rhapsodies of sheer blank-verse lyricism. Wolfe may not have pleased his home town, but in general he pleased the critics, for the novel is tremendously alive, observing of life in the most searching detail, superficially realistic—almost naturalistic—but fundamentally romantic, and blessed with a style which, while it was often a mere flow of words, was more frequently poetic and haunting.

On the strength of the royalties which *Look Homeward, Angel* brought to the author, Wolfe was able to devote himself thenceforth to writing. But it was six years before the second volume in the splendid tetralogy, the fictional life-story of Thomas Wolfe himself, was forthcoming. This was *Of Time and the River* (1935), which carries Eugene Gant through his days at Harvard, New York University and New York City, and England. In the meantime the author had been abroad again, chiefly in Paris—where, according to that fine autobiography of his artistic life, *The Story of a Novel* (1936), he nearly perished of sheer loneliness. He had also written two other works—the minor *Portrait of Bascom Hawke* (1932), which is negligible; and the excellent collection of short stories, *From Death to Morning* (1935), which Wolfe believed contained some of his best writing.

The great tetralogy was completed by *The Web and the Rock* (1939) and *You Can't Go Home Again* (1940), both of which, it will be noted, were published after the author's untimely death on September 15, 1938. If George Webber has now replaced Eugene Gant as the protagonist, because he is supposedly more representative of man in the mass, the substitution should fool no one. The triple identity is still true: Eugene Gant equals George Webber equals Thomas Wolfe. In these novels Wolfe is in Europe or he is back in Brooklyn and New York; he is worrying about the Nazi menace or about the American way. He meets people; he loves some and hates others. But he has gradually come to believe that no return to Tradition or Memory or the Enchantment of Buried Time can bring a satisfactory answer. "You can't go back to them," for man's home still lies in the veiled future. The same attitude is apparent in many of the sketches published posthumously in *The Hills Beyond* (1941).

Unsatisfied Thomas Wolfe's craving and lifelong hunger for the secret of life may be, but it is the very reverse of the inarticulate. Wolfe was an enormously copious writer; the critics have often remarked upon his "intemperate excess" of words and thoughts and appetites. None can well deny, however, his magnificent romanticism, his almost Whitmanesque love of the American tradition, which even the grosser defects of American civilization and the surrounding waste land can never quite destroy. And his vividness of spiritual eyesight is transmitted directly to his writings—he is an amazing reporter of individual scenes and situations, a masterful meeter and handler of crowds of individuals, an almost unscrupulous wielder of power of the poignant, the pathetic, the tragic, the unforgettable.

from **Look Homeward, Angel**

XXX

THERE was at Dixieland a girl named Laura James. She was twenty-one years old. She looked younger. She was there when he came back.

Laura was a slender girl, of medium height, but looking taller than she was. She was very firmly moulded: she seemed fresh and washed and clean. She had thick hair, very straight and blonde, combed in a flat bracelet around her small head. Her face was white, with small freckles. Her eyes were soft, candid, cat-green. Her nose was a little too large for her face: it was tilted. She was not pretty. She dressed very simply and elegantly in short plaid skirts and waists of knitted silk.

She was the only young person at Dixieland. Eugene spoke to her with timid hauteur. He thought her plain and dull. But he began to sit with her on the porch at night. Somehow, he began to love her.

He did not know that he loved her. He talked to her arrogantly and boastfully as they sat in the wooden porch-swing. But he breathed the clean perfume of her marvellous young body. He was trapped in the tender cruelty of her clear green eyes, caught in the subtle net of her smile.

Laura James lived in the eastern part of the

Reprinted from Chapters 30 and 31 of *Look Homeward, Angel* by Thomas Wolfe; copyright, 1929, by Charles Scribner's Sons; used by permission

State, far east even of Pulpit Hill, in a little town built on a salt river of the great coastal plain. Her father was a wealthy merchant—a wholesale provisioner. The girl was an only child: she spent extravagantly.

Eugene sat on the porch rail one evening and talked to her. Before, he had only nodded, or spoken stiffly a word or two. They began haltingly, aware painfully of gaps in their conversation.

"You're from Little Richmond, aren't you?" he said.

"Yes," said Laura James, "do you know any one from there?"

"Yes," said he. "I know John Bynum and a boy named Ficklen. They're from Little Richmond, aren't they?"

"Oh, Dave Ficklen! Do you know him? Yes. They both go to Pulpit Hill. Do you go there?"

"Yes," he said, "that's where I knew them."

"Do you know the two Barlow boys? They're Sigma Nus," said Laura James.

He had seen them. They were great swells, football men.

"Yes, I know them," he said, "Roy Barlow and Jack Barlow."

"Do you know 'Snooks' Warren? He's a Kappa Sig."

"Yes. They call them Keg Squeezers," said Eugene.

"What fraternity are you?" said Laura James.

"I'm not any," he said painfully. "I was just a Freshman this year."

"Some of the best friends I have never joined fraternities," said Laura James.

They met more and more frequently, without arrangement, until by silent consent they met every night upon the porch. Sometimes they walked along the cool dark streets. Sometimes he squired her clumsily through the town, to the movies, and later, with the uneasy pugnacity of youth, past the loafing cluster at Wood's. Often he took her to Woodson Street, where Helen secured for him the cool privacy of the veranda. She was very fond of Laura James.

"She's a nice girl. A lovely girl. I like her. She's not going to take any beauty prizes, is she?" She laughed with a trace of good-natured ridicule.

He was displeased.

"She looks all right," he said. "She's not as ugly as you make out."

But she *was* ugly—with a clean lovely ugliness. Her face was freckled lightly, over her nose and mouth: her features were eager, unconscious, turned upward in irregular pertness. But she was exquisitely made and exquisitely kept: she had the firm young line of Spring, budding, slender, virginal. She was like something swift, with wings, which hovers in a wood—among the feathery trees suspected, but uncaught, unseen.

He tried to live before her in armor. He showed off before her. Perhaps, he thought, if he were splendid enough, she would not see the ugly disorder and meanness of the world he dwelt in.

Across the street, on the wide lawn of the Brunswick—the big brick gabled house that Eliza once had coveted—Mr. Pratt, who crawled in that mean world in which only a boarding-house husband can exist, was watering wide green spaces of lawn with a hose. The flashing water motes gleamed in the red glare of sunset. The red light fell across the shaven pinched face. It glittered on the buckles of his arm-bands. Across the walk, on the other lobe of grass, several men and women were playing croquet. There was laughter on the vine-hid porch. Next door, at the Belton, the boarders were assembled on the long porch in bright hash-house chatter. The comedian of the Dixie Ramblers arrived with two chorus girls. He was a little man, with the face of a weasel and no upper teeth. He wore a straw hat with a striped band, and a blue shirt and collar. The boarders gathered in around him. In a moment there was shrill laughter.

Julius Arthur sped swiftly down the hill, driving his father home. He grinned squintly and flung his arm up in careless greeting. The prosperous lawyer twisted a plump Van Dyked face on a wry neck curiously. Unsmiling, he passed.

A Negress in the Brunswick struck on the several bells of a Japanese gong. There was a scramble of feet on the porch; the croquet players dropped their mallets and walked rapidly toward the house. Pratt wound his hose over a wooden reel.

A slow bell-clapper in the Belton sent the

guests in a scrambling drive for the doors. In a moment there was a clatter of heavy plates and a loud foody noise. The guests on the porch of Dixieland rocked more rapidly, with low mutters of discontent.

Eugene talked to Laura in thickening dusk, sheeting his pain in pride and indifference. Eliza's face, a white blur in the dark, came up behind the screen.

"Come on out, Mrs. Gant, and get a breath of fresh air," said Laura James.

"Why no-o, child. I can't now. Who's that with you?" she cried, obviously flustered. She opened the door. "Huh? Heh? Have you seen 'Gene? Is it 'Gene?"

"Yes," he said. "What's the matter?"

"Come here a minute, boy," she said.

He went into the hall.

"What is it?" he asked.

"Why, son, what in the world! I don't know. You'll have to do something," she whispered, twisting her hands together.

"What is it, mama? What are you talking about?" he cried irritably.

"Why—Jannadeau's just called up. Your papa's on a rampage again and he's coming this way. Child! There's no telling what he'll do. I've all these people in the house. He'll ruin us." She wept. "Go and try to stop him. Head him off if you can. Take him to Woodson Street."

He got his hat quickly and ran through the door.

"Where are you going?" asked Laura James. "Are you going off without supper?"

"I've got to go to town," he said. "I won't be long. Will you wait for me?"

"Yes," she said.

He leaped down on the walk just as his father lurched in from the street by the high obscuring hedge that shut the house from the spacious yard of the attorney Hall. Gant reeled destructively, across a border of lilies, on to the lawn, and strode for the veranda. He stumbled, cursing, on the bottom step and plunged forward in a sprawl upon the porch. The boy jumped for him, and half dragged, half lifted his great drunken body erect. The boarders shrank into a huddle with a quick scattering of chairs: he greeted them with a laugh of howling contempt.

"Are you there? I say, are you there? The lowest of the low—boarding-house swine! Merciful God! What a travesty! A travesty on Nature! That it should come to this!"

He burst into a long peal of maniacal laughter.

"Papa! Come on!" said Eugene in a low voice. He took his father cautiously by the sleeve. Gant flung him half across the porch with a gesture of his hand. As he stepped in again swiftly, his father struck at him with a flailing arm. He evaded the great mowing fist without trouble, and caught the falling body, swung from its own pivot, in his arms. Then quickly, before Gant could recover, holding him from behind, he rushed him toward the door. The boarders scattered away like sparrows. But Laura James was at the screen before him: she flung it open.

"Get away! Get away!" he cried, full of shame and anger. "You stay out of this." For a moment he despised her for seeing his hurt.

"Oh, let me help you, my dear," Laura James whispered. Her eyes were wet, but she was not afraid.

Father and son plunged chaotically down the wide dark hall, Eliza, weeping and making gestures, just before them.

"Take him in here, boy. Take him in here," she whispered, motioning to a large bedroom on the upper side of the house. Eugene propelled his father through a blind passage of bathroom, and pushed him over on the creaking width of an iron bed.

"You damned scoundrel!" Gant yelled, again trying to reap him down with the long arm, "let me up or I'll kill you!"

"For God's sake, papa," he implored angrily, "try to quiet down. Every one in town can hear you."

"To hell with them!" Gant roared. "Mountain Grills—all of them, fattening upon my heart's-blood. They have done me to death, as sure as there's a God in heaven."

Eliza appeared in the door, her face contorted by weeping.

"Son, can't you do something to stop him?" she said. "He'll ruin us all. He'll drive every one away."

Gant struggled to stand erect when he saw her. Her white face stirred him to insanity.

"There it is! There! There! Do you see! The fiend-face I know so well, gloating upon my misery. Look at it! Look! Do you see its smile of evil cunning? Greeley, Will, The Hog, The Old Major! The Tax Collector will get it all, and I shall die in the gutter!"

"If it hadn't been for me," Eliza began, stung to retaliation, "you'd have died there long ago."

"Mama, for God's sake!" the boy cried. "Don't stand there talking to him! Can't you see what it does to him! Do something, in heaven's name! Get Helen! Where is she?"

"I'll make an end to it all!" Gant yelled, staggering erect. "I'll do for us both now."

Eliza vanished.

"Yes, sir, papa. It's going to be all right," Eugene began soothingly, pushing him back on the bed again. He dropped quickly to his knees, and began to draw off one of Gant's soft tongueless shoes, muttering reassurances all the time: "Yes, sir. We'll get you some good hot soup and put you to bed in a jiffy. Everything's going to be all right," the shoe came off in his hand and, aided by the furious thrust of his father's foot, he went sprawling back.

Gant got to his feet again and, taking a farewell kick at his fallen son, lunged toward the door. Eugene scrambled up quickly, and leaped after him. The two men fell heavily into the roughly grained plaster of the wall. Gant cursed, flailing about clumsily at his tormentor. Helen came in.

"Baby!" Gant wept, "they're trying to kill me. O Jesus, do something to save me, or I perish."

"You get back in that bed," she commanded sharply, "or I'll knock your head off."

Very obediently he suffered himself to be led back to bed and undressed. In a few minutes she was sitting beside him with a bowl of smoking soup. He grinned sheepishly as she spooned it into his opened mouth. She laughed —almost happily—thinking of the lost and irrevocable years. Suddenly, before he slept, he lifted himself strongly from the pillows that propped him, and, with staring eyes, called out in savage terror:

"Is it a cancer? I say, is it a cancer?"

"Hush!" she cried. "No. Of course not! Don't be foolish."

He fell back exhausted, with eyes closed. But they knew that it was. He had never been told. The terrible name of his malady was never uttered save by him. And in his heart he knew—what they all knew and never spoke of before him—that it was, it was a cancer. All day, with fear-stark eyes, Gant had sat, like a broken statue, among his marbles, drinking. It was a cancer.

The boy's right hand bled very badly across the wrist, where his father's weight had ground it into the wall.

"Go wash it off," said Helen. "I'll tie it up for you."

He went into the dark bathroom and held his hand under a jet of lukewarm water. A very quiet despair was in his heart, a weary peace that brooded too upon the house of death and tumult, that flowed, like a soft exploring wind, through its dark halls, bathing all things quietly with peace and weariness. The boarders had fled like silly sheep to the two houses across the street: they had eaten there, they were clustered there upon the porches, whispering. And their going brought him peace and freedom, as if his limbs had been freed from a shackling weight. Eliza, amid the slow smoke of the kitchen, wept more quietly over the waste of supper; he saw the black mournful calm of the Negress's face. He walked slowly up the dark hall, with a handkerchief tied loosely round his wound. He felt suddenly the peace that comes with despair. The sword that pierces very deep had fared through the folds of his poor armor of pride. The steel had sheared his side, had bitten to his heart. But under his armor he had found himself. No more than himself could be known. No more than himself could be given. What he was—he was: evasion and pretense could not add to his sum. With all his heart he was glad.

By the door, in the darkness, he found Laura James.

"I thought you had gone with the others," he said.

"No," said Laura James, "how is your father?"

"He's all right now. He's gone to sleep," he answered. "Have you had anything to eat?"

"No," she said, "I didn't want it."

"I'll bring you something from the kitchen," he said. "There's plenty there." In a moment he added: "I'm sorry, Laura."

"What are you sorry for?" she asked.

He leaned against the wall limply, drained of his strength at her touch.

"Eugene. My dear," she said. She pulled his drooping face down to her lips and kissed him. "My sweet, my darling, don't look like that."

All his resistance melted from him. He seized her small hands, crushing them in his hot fingers, and devouring them with kisses.

"My dear Laura! My dear Laura!" he said in a choking voice. "My sweet, my beautiful Laura! My lovely Laura! I love you, I love you." The words rushed from his heart, incoherent, unashamed, foaming through the broken levees of pride and silence. They clung together in the dark, with their wet faces pressed mouth to mouth. Her perfume went drunkenly to his brain; her touch upon him shot through his limbs a glow of magic; he felt the pressure of her narrow breasts, eager and lithe, against him with a sense of fear—as if he had dishonored her—with a sickening remembrance of his defilement.

He held between his hands her elegant small head, so gloriously wound with its thick bracelet of fine blonde hair, and spoke the words he had never spoken—the words of confession, filled with love and humility.

"Don't go! Don't go! Please don't go!" he begged. "Don't leave, dear. Please!"

"Hush!" she whispered. "I won't go! I love you, my dear."

She saw his hand, wrapped in its bloody bandage; she nursed it gently with soft little cries of tenderness. She fetched a bottle of iodine from her room and painted the stinging cut with a brush. She wrapped it with clean strips of fine white cloth, torn from an old waist, scented with a faint and subtle perfume.

Then they sat upon the wooden swing. The house seemed to sleep in darkness. Helen and Eliza came presently from its very quiet depth.

"How's your hand, 'Gene?" Helen asked.

"It's all right," he said.

"Let me see! O-ho, you've got a nurse now, haven't you?" she said, with a good laugh.

"What's that? What's that? Hurt his hand? How'd you do that? Why, here—say—I've got the very thing for it, son," said Eliza, trying to bustle off in all directions.

"Oh, it's all right now, mama. It's been fixed," he said wearily, reflecting that she had the very thing always too late. He looked at Helen grinning:

"God bless our Happy Home!" he said.

"Poor old Laura!" she laughed, and hugged the girl roughly with one hand. "It's too bad you have to be dragged into it."

"That's all right," said Laura. "I feel like one of the family now anyhow."

"He needn't think he can carry on like this," said Eliza resentfully. "I'm not going to put up with it any longer."

"Oh forget about it!" said Helen wearily. "Good heavens, mama. Papa's a sick man. Can't you realize that?"

"Pshaw!" said Eliza scornfully. "I don't believe there's a thing in the world wrong with him but that vile licker. All his trouble comes from that."

"Oh—how ridiculous! How ridiculous! You can't tell me!" Helen exclaimed angrily.

"Let's talk about the weather," said Eugene.

Then they all sat quietly, letting the darkness soak into them. Finally Helen and Eliza went back into the house: Eliza went unwillingly, at the girl's insistence, casting back the doubtful glimmer of her face upon the boy and girl.

The wasting helve of the moon rode into heaven over the bulk of the hills. There was a smell of wet grass and lilac, and the vast brooding symphony of the million-noted little night things, rising and falling in a constant ululation, and inhabiting the heart with steady unconscious certitude. The pallid light drowned out the stars, it lay like silence on the earth, it dripped through the leafy web of the young maples, printing the earth with swarming moths of elvish light.

Eugene and Laura sat with joined hands in the slowly creaking swing. Her touch shot through him like a train of fire: as he put his arm around her shoulders and drew her over to him, his fingers touched the live firm cup of her breast. He jerked his hand away, as if he had been stung, muttering an apology. Whenever she touched him, his flesh got numb and weak. She was a virgin, crisp like celery—his heart shrank away from the pollution of his touch upon her. It seemed to him that he was much the older, although he was sixteen, and she twenty-one. He felt the age of his loneliness and his dark perception. He felt the gray

wisdom of sin—a waste desert, but seen and known. When he held her hand, he felt as if he had already seduced her. She lifted her lovely face to him, pert and ugly as a boy's; it was inhabited by a true and steadfast decency, and his eyes were wet. All the young beauty in the world dwelt for him in that face that had kept wonder, that had kept innocency, that had lived in such immortal blindness to
10 the terror and foulness of the world. He came to her, like a creature who had travelled its life through dark space, for a moment of peace and conviction on some lonely planet, where now he stood, in the vast enchanted plain of moonlight, with moonlight falling on the moon-flower of her face. For if a man should dream of heaven and, waking, find within his hand a flower as token that he had really been there—what then, what then?

20 "Eugene," she said presently, "how old are you?"

His vision thickened with his pulse. In a moment he answered with terrible difficulty.

"I'm—just sixteen."

"Oh, you child!" she cried. "I thought you were more than that!"

"I'm—old for my age," he muttered. "How old are you?"

"I'm twenty-one," she said. "Isn't it a pity?"
30 "There's not much difference," he said. "I can't see that it matters."

"Oh, my dear," she said. "It does! It matters so much!"

And he knew that it did—how much he did not know. But he had his moment. He was not afraid of pain, he was not afraid of loss. He cared nothing for the practical need of the world. He dared to say the strange and marvellous thing that had bloomed so darkly in
40 him.

"Laura," he said, hearing his low voice sound over the great plain of the moon, "let's always love each other as we do now. Let's never get married. I want you to wait for me and to love me forever. I am going all over the world. I shall go away for years at a time; I shall become famous, but I shall always come back to you. You shall live in a house away in the mountains, you shall wait for me, and keep
50 yourself for me. Will you?" he said, asking for her life as calmly as for an hour of her time.

"Yes, dear," said Laura in the moonlight, "I will wait for you forever."

She was buried in his flesh. She throbbed in the beat of his pulses. She was wine in his blood, a music in his heart.

"He has no consideration for you or any one else," Hugh Barton growled. He had returned late from work at his office, to take Helen home. "If he can't do better than this, we'll find 60 a house of our own. I'm not going to have you get down sick on account of him."

"Forget about it," Helen said. "He's getting old."

They came out on the veranda.

"Come down to-morrow, honey," she said to Eugene. "I'll give you a real feed. Laura, you come too. It's not always like this, you know." She laughed, fondling the girl with a big hand.

They coasted away downhill. 70

"What a lovely girl your sister is," said Laura James. "Aren't you simply crazy about her?"

Eugene made no answer for a moment.

"Yes," he said.

"She is about you. Any one can see that," said Laura.

In the darkness he caught at his throat.

"Yes," he said.

The moon quartered gently across heaven. 80 Eliza came out again, timidly, hesitantly.

"Who's there? Who's there?" she spoke into the darkness. "Where's 'Gene? Oh! I didn't know! Are you there, son?" She knew very well.

"Yes," he said.

"Why don't you sit down, Mrs. Gant?" asked Laura. "I don't see how you stand that hot kitchen all day long. You must be worn out."

"I tell you what!" said Eliza, peering dimly 90 at the sky. "It's a fine night, isn't it? As the fellow says, a night for lovers." She laughed uncertainly, then stood for a moment in thought.

"Son," she said in a troubled voice, "why don't you go to bed and get some sleep? It's not good for you staying up till all hours like this."

"That's where I should be," said Laura James, rising.

"Yes, child," said Eliza. "Go get your beauty 100

sleep. As the saying goes, early to bed and early to rise——"

"Let's all go, then. Let's all go!" said Eugene impatiently and angrily, wondering if she must always be the last one awake in that house.

"Why law, no!" said Eliza, "I can't, boy. I've all those things to iron."

Beside him, Laura gave his hand a quiet squeeze, and rose. Bitterly, he watched his loss.

"Good-night, all. Good-night, Mrs. Gant."

"Good-night, child."

When she had gone, Eliza sat down beside him, with a sigh of weariness.

"I tell you what," she said. "That feels good. I wish I had as much time as some folks, and could sit out here enjoying the air." In the darkness, he knew her puckering lips were trying to smile.

"Hm!" she said, and caught his hand in her rough palm. "Has my baby gone and got him a girl?"

"What of it? What if it were true?" he said angrily. "Haven't I a right as much as any one?"

"Pshaw!" said Eliza. "You're too young to think of them. I wouldn't pay any attention to them, if I were you. Most of them haven't an idea in the world except going out to parties and having a good time. I don't want my boy to waste his time on them."

He felt her earnestness beneath her awkward banter. He struggled in a chaos of confused fury, trying for silence. At last he spoke in a low voice, filled with his passion:

"We've got to have something, mama. We've got to have something, you know. We can't go on always alone—alone."

It was dark. No one could see. He let the gates swing open. He wept.

"I know!" Eliza agreed hastily. "I'm not saying——"

"My God, my God, where are we going? What's it all about? He's dying—can't you see it? Don't you know it? Look at his life. Look at yours. No light, no love, no comfort—nothing." His voice rose frantically: he beat on his ribs like a drum. "Mama, mama, in God's name, what is it? What do you want? Are you going to strangle and drown us all? Don't you own enough? Do you want more string? Do you want more bottles? By God, I'll go around collecting them if you say so." His voice had risen almost to a scream. "But tell me what you want. Don't you own enough? Do you want the town? What is it?"

"Why, I don't know what you're talking about, boy," said Eliza angrily. "If I hadn't tried to accumulate a little property none of you would have had a roof to call your own, for your papa, I can assure you, would have squandered everything."

"A roof to call our own!" he yelled, with a crazy laugh. "Good God, we haven't a bed to call our own. We haven't a room to call our own. We have not a quilt to call our own that might not be taken from us to warm the mob that rocks upon this porch and grumbles."

"Now, you may sneer at the boarders all you like—" Eliza began sternly.

"No," he said. "I can't. There's not breath or strength enough in me to sneer at them all I like."

Eliza began to weep.

"I've done the best I could!" she said. "I'd have given you a home if I could. I'd have put up with anything after Grover's death, but he never gave me a moment's peace. Nobody knows what I've been through. Nobody knows, child. Nobody knows."

He saw her face in the moonlight, contorted by an ugly grimace of sorrow. What she said, he knew, was fair and honest. He was touched deeply.

"It's all right, mama," he said painfully. "Forget about it! I know."

She seized his hand almost gratefully and laid her white face, still twisted with her grief, against his shoulder. It was the gesture of a child: a gesture that asked for love, pity, and tenderness. It tore up great roots in him, bloodily.

"Don't!" he said. "Don't, mama! Please!"

"Nobody knows," said Eliza. "Nobody knows. I need some one too. I've had a hard life, son, full of pain and trouble." Slowly, like a child again, she wiped her wet weak eyes with the back of her hand.

Ah, he thought, as his heart twisted in him full of wild pain and regret, she will be dead some day and I shall always remember this. Always this. This.

They were silent a moment. He held her rough hand tightly, and kissed her.

"Well," Eliza began, full of cheerful prophecy, "I tell you what: I'm not going to spend my life slaving away here for a lot of boarders. They needn't think it. I'm going to set back and take things as easy as any of them." She winked knowingly at him. "When you come home next time, you may find me living in a big house in Doak Park. I've got the lot—the best lot out there for view and location, far better than the one W. J. Bryan has. I made the trade with old Dr. Doak himself, the other day. Look here! What about it!" She laughed. "He said, 'Mrs. Gant, I can't trust any of my agents with you. If I'm to make anything on this deal, I've got to look out. You're the sharpest trader in this town.' 'Why, pshaw! Doctor,' I said (I never let on I believed him or anything), 'all I want is a fair return on my investment. I believe in every one making his profit and giving the other fellow a chance. Keep the ball a-rolling!' I said, laughing as big as you please. 'Why, Mrs. Gant!' he said—" She was off on a lengthy divagation, recording with an absorbed gusto the interminable minutiæ of her transaction with the worthy Quinine King, with the attendant phenomena, during the time, of birds, bees, flowers, sun, clouds, dogs, cows, and people. She was pleased. She was happy.

Presently, returning to an abrupt reflective pause, she said: "Well, I may do it. I want a place where my children can come to see me and bring their friends, when they come home."

"Yes," he said, "yes. That would be nice. You mustn't work all your life."

He was pleased at her happy fable: for a moment he almost believed in a miracle of redemption, although the story was an old one to him.

"I hope you do," he said. "It would be nice. . . . Go on to bed now, why don't you, mama? It's getting late." He rose. "I'm going now."

"Yes, son," she said, getting up. "You ought to. Well, good-night." They kissed with a love, for the time, washed clean of bitterness. Eliza went before him into the dark house.

But before he went to bed, he descended to the kitchen for matches. She was still there, beyond the long littered table, at her ironing board, flanked by two big piles of laundry. At his accusing glance she said hastily:

"I'm a-going. Right away. I just wanted to finish up these towels."

He rounded the table, before he left, to kiss her again. She fished into a button-box on the sewing-machine and dug out the stub of a pencil. Gripping it firmly above an old envelope, she scrawled out on the ironing board a rough mapping. Her mind was still lulled in its project.

"Here, you see," she began, "is Sunset Avenue, coming up the hill. This is Doak Place, running off here at right angles. Now this corner-lot here belongs to Dick Webster; and right here above it, at the very top is——"

Is, he thought, staring with dull interest, the place where the Buried Treasure lies. Ten paces N.N.E. from the Big Rock, at the roots of the Old Oak Tree. He went off into his delightful fantasy while she talked. What if there *was* a buried treasure on one of Eliza's lots? If she kept on buying, there might very well be. Or why not an oil-well? Or a coal-mine? These famous mountains were full (they said) of minerals. 150 Bbl. a day right in the backyard. How much would that be? At $3.00 a Bbl., there would be over $50.00 a day for every one in the family. The world is ours!

"You see, don't you?" she smiled triumphantly. "And right there is where I shall build. That lot will bring twice its present value in five years."

"Yes," he said, kissing her. "Good-night, mama. For God's sake, go to bed and get some sleep."

"Good-night, son," said Eliza.

He went out and began to mount the dark stairs. Benjamin Gant, entering at this moment, stumbled across a mission-chair in the hall. He cursed fiercely, and struck at the chair with his hand. Damn it! Oh damn it! Mrs. Pert whispered a warning behind him, with a fuzzy laugh. Eugene paused, then mounted softly the carpeted stair, so that he would not be heard, entering the sleeping-porch at the top of the landing on which he slept.

He did not turn on the light, because he disliked seeing the raw blistered varnish of the dresser and the bent white iron of the bed. It sagged, and the light was dim—he hated dim lights, and the large moths, flapping blindly around on their dusty wings. He undressed in the moon. The moonlight fell upon the earth like a magic unearthly dawn. It wiped away all rawness, it hid all sores. It gave all common and familiar things—the sagging drift of the barn, the raw shed of the creamery, the rich curve of the lawyer's crab-apple trees—a uniform bloom of wonder. He lighted a cigarette, watching its red glowing suspiration in the mirror, and leaned upon the rail of his porch, looking out. Presently, he grew aware that Laura James, eight feet away, was watching him. The moonlight fell upon them, bathing their flesh in a green pallor, and steeping them in its silence. Their faces were blocked in miraculous darkness, out of which, seeing but unseen, their bright eyes lived. They gazed at each other in that elfin light, without speaking. In the room below them, the light crawled to his father's bed, swam up the cover, and opened across his face, thrust sharply upward. The air of the night, the air of the hills, fell on the boy's bare flesh like a sluice of clear water. His toes curled in to grip wet grasses.

On the landing, he heard Mrs. Pert go softly up to bed, fumbling with blind care at the walls. Doors creaked and clicked. The house grew solidly into quiet, like a stone beneath the moon. They looked, waiting for a spell and the conquest of time. Then she spoke to him—her whisper of his name was only a guess at sound. He threw his leg across the rail, and thrust his long body over space to the sill of her window, stretching out like a cat. She drew her breath in sharply, and cried out softly, "No! No!" but she caught his arms upon the sills and held him as he twisted in.

Then they held each other tightly in their cool young arms, and kissed many times with young lips and faces. All her hair fell down about her like thick corn-silk, in a sweet loose wantonness. Her straight dainty legs were clad in snug little green bloomers, gathered in by an elastic above the knee.

They were locked limb to limb; he kissed the smooth sheen of her arms and shoulders—the passion that numbed his limbs was governed by a religious ecstasy. He wanted to hold her, and go away by himself to think about her.

He stooped, thrusting his arm under her knees, and lifted her up exultantly. She looked at him frightened, holding him more tightly.

"What are you doing?" she whispered. "Don't hurt me."

"I won't hurt you, my dear," he said. "I'm going to put you to bed. Yes. I'm going to put you to bed. Do you hear?" He felt he must cry out in his throat for joy.

He carried her over and laid her on the bed. Then he knelt beside her, putting his arm beneath her and gathering her to him.

"Good-night, my dear. Kiss me good-night. Do you love me?"

"Yes." She kissed him. "Good-night, my darling. Don't go back by the window. You may fall."

But he went, as he came, reaching through the moonlight exultantly like a cat. For a long time he lay awake, in a quiet delirium, his heart thudding fiercely against his ribs. Sleep crept across his senses with goose-soft warmth: the young leaves of the maples rustled, a cock sounded his distant elfin minstrelsy, the ghost of a dog howled. He slept.

He awoke with a high hot sun beating in on his face through the porch awnings. He hated to awake in sunlight. Some day he would sleep in a great room that was always cool and dark. There would be trees and vines at his windows, or the scooped-out lift of the hill. His clothing was wet with night-damp as he dressed. When he went downstairs he found Gant rocking miserably upon the porch, his hand gripped over a walking-stick.

"Good-morning," he said, "how do you feel?"

His father cast his uneasy flickering eyes on him, and groaned.

"Merciful God! I'm being punished for my sins."

"You'll feel better in a little," said Eugene. "Did you eat anything?"

"It stuck in my throat," said Gant, who had eaten heartily. "I couldn't swallow a bite. How's your hand, son?" he asked very humbly.

"Oh, it's all right," said Eugene quickly. "Who told you about my hand?"

"She said I had hurt your hand," said Gant sorrowfully.

"Ah-h!" said the boy angrily. "No. I wasn't hurt."

Gant leaned to the side and, without looking, clumsily, patted his son's uninjured hand.

"I'm sorry for what I've done," he said. "I'm a sick man. Do you need money?"

"No," said Eugene, embarrassed. "I have all I need."

"Come to the office to-day, and I'll give you something," said Gant. "Poor child, I suppose you're hard up."

But instead, he waited until Laura James returned from her morning visit to the city's bathing-pool. She came with her bathing-suit in one hand, and several small packages in the other. More arrived by Negro carriers. She paid and signed.

"You must have a lot of money, Laura?" he said. "You do this every day, don't you?"

"Daddy gets after me about it," she admitted, "but I love to buy clothes. I spend all my money on clothes."

"What are you going to do now?"

"Nothing—whatever you like. It's a lovely day to do something, isn't it?"

"It's a lovely day to do nothing. Would you like to go off somewhere, Laura?"

"I'd love to go off somewhere with you," said Laura James.

"That is the idea, my girl. That is the idea," he said exultantly, in throaty and exuberant burlesque. "We will go off somewhere alone— we will take along something to eat," he said lusciously.

Laura went to her room and put on a pair of sturdy little slippers. Eugene went into the kitchen.

"Have you a shoe-box?" he asked Eliza.

"What do you want that for?" she said suspiciously.

"I'm going to the bank," he said ironically. "I wanted something to carry my money in." But immediately he added roughly:

"I'm going on a picnic."

"Huh? Hah? What's that you say?" said Eliza. "A picnic? Who are you going with? That girl?"

"No," he said heavily, "with President Wilson, the King of England, and Dr. Doak. We're going to have lemonade—I've promised to bring the lemons."

"I'll vow, boy," said Eliza fretfully. "I don't like it—your running off this way when I need you. I wanted you to make a deposit for me, and the telephone people will disconnect me if I don't send them the money to-day."

"O mama! For God's sake!" he cried, annoyed. "You always need me when I want to go somewhere. Let them wait! They can wait a day!"

"It's overdue," she said. "Well, here you are. I wish I had time to go off on picnics." She fished a shoe-box out of a pile of magazines and newspapers that littered the top of a low cupboard.

"Have you got anything to eat?"

"We'll get it," he said, and departed.

They went down the hill, and paused at the musty little grocery around the corner on Woodson Street, where they bought crackers, peanut butter, currant jelly, bottled pickles, and a big slice of rich yellow cheese. The grocer was an old Jew who muttered jargon into a rabbi's beard as if saying a spell against Dybbuks. The boy looked closely to see if his hands touched the food. They were not clean.

On their way up the hill, they stopped for a few minutes at Gant's. They found Helen and Ben in the dining-room. Ben was eating breakfast, bending, as usual, with scowling attention, over his coffee, turning from eggs and bacon almost with disgust. Helen insisted on contributing boiled eggs and sandwiches to their provision: the two women went back into the kitchen. Eugene sat at table with Ben, drinking coffee.

"O-oh my God!" Ben said at length, yawning wearily. He lighted a cigarette. "How's the Old Man this morning?"

"He's all right, I think. Said he couldn't eat breakfast."

"Did he say anything to the boarders?"

" 'You damned scoundrels! You dirty Mountain Grills! Whee—!' That was all."

Ben snickered quietly.

"Did he hurt your hand? Let's see."

"No. You can't see anything. It's not hurt," said Eugene, lifting his bandaged wrist.

"He didn't hit you, did he?" asked Ben sternly.

"Oh no. Of course not. He was just drunk. He was sorry about it this morning."

"Yes," said Ben, "he's always sorry about it— after he's raised all the hell he can." He drank deeply at his cigarette, inhaling the smoke as if in the grip of a powerful drug.

"How'd you get along at college this year, 'Gene?" he asked presently.

"I passed my work. I made fair grades—if that's what you mean. I did better—this Spring," he added, with some difficulty. "It was hard getting started—at the beginning."

"You mean last Fall?"

Eugene nodded.

"What was the matter?" said Ben, scowling at him. "Did the other boys make fun of you?"

"Yes," said Eugene, in a low voice.

"Why did they? You mean they didn't think you were good enough for them? Did they look down on you? Was that it?" said Ben savagely.

"No," said Eugene, very red in the face. "No. That had nothing to do with it. I look funny, I suppose. I looked funny to them."

"What do you mean you look funny?" said Ben pugnaciously. "There's nothing wrong with you, you know, if you didn't go around looking like a bum. In God's name," he exclaimed angrily, "when did you get that hair cut last? What do you think you are: the Wild Man from Borneo?"

"I don't like barbers!" Eugene burst out furiously. "That's why! I don't want them to go sticking their damned dirty fingers in my mouth. Whose business is it, if I never get my hair cut?"

"A man is judged by his appearance to-day," said Ben sententiously. "I was reading an article by a big business man in *The Post* the other day. He says he always looks at a man's shoes before he gives him a job."

He spoke seriously, haltingly, in the same way that he read, without genuine conviction. Eugene writhed to hear his fierce condor prattle this stale hash of the canny millionaires, like any obedient parrot in a teller's cage. Ben's voice had a dull flat quality as he uttered these admirable opinions: he seemed to grope behind it all for some answer, with hurt puzzled eyes. As he faltered along, with scowling intensity, through a success-sermon, there was something poignantly moving in his effort: it was the effort of his strange and lonely spirit to find some entrance into life—to find success, position, companionship. And it was as if, spelling the words out with his mouth, a settler in the Bronx from the fat Lombard plain, should try to unriddle the new world by deciphering the World Almanac, or as if some woodsman,

trapped by the winter, and wasted by an obscure and terrible disease, should hunt its symptoms and its cure in a book of Household Remedies.

"Did the Old Man send you enough money to get along on?" Ben asked. "Were you able to hold your own with the other boys? He can afford it, you know. Don't let him stint you. Make him give it to you, 'Gene."

"I had plenty," said Eugene, "all that I needed."

"This is the time you need it—not later," said Ben. "Make him put you through college. This is an age of specialization. They're looking for college-trained men."

"Yes," said Eugene. He spoke obediently, indifferently, the hard bright mail of his mind undinted by the jargon: within, the Other One, who had no speech, saw.

"So get your education," said Ben, scowling vaguely. "All the Big Men—Ford, Edison, Rockefeller—whether they had it or not, say it's a good thing."

"Why didn't you go yourself?" said Eugene curiously.

"I didn't have any one to tell me," said Ben. "Besides, you don't think the Old Man would give me anything, do you?" He laughed cynically. "It's too late now."

He was silent a moment; he smoked.

"You didn't know I was taking a course in advertising, did you?" he asked, grinning.

"No. Where?"

"Through the Correspondence School," said Ben. "I get my lessons every week. I don't know," he laughed diffidently, "I must be good at it. I make the highest grades they have—98 or 100 every time. I get a diploma, if I finish the course."

A blinding mist swam across the younger brother's eyes. He did not know why. A convulsive knot gathered in his throat. He bent his head quickly and fumbled for his cigarettes. In a moment he said:

"I'm glad you're doing it. I hope you finish, Ben."

"You know," Ben said seriously, "they've turned out some Big Men. I'll show you the testimonials some time. Men who started with nothing: now they're holding down big jobs."

"I hope you do," said Eugene.

"So, you see you're not the only College Man around here," said Ben with a grin. In a moment, he went on gravely: "You're the last hope, 'Gene. Go on and finish up, if you have to steal the money. The rest of us will never amount to a damn. Try to make something out of yourself. Hold your head up! You're as good as any of them—a damn sight better than these little pimps about town." He became very
10 fierce; he was very excited. He got up suddenly from the table. "Don't let them laugh at you! By God, we're as good as they are. If any of them laughs at you again, pick up the first damn thing you get your hand on and knock him down. Do you hear?" In his fierce excitement he snatched up the heavy carving steel from the table and brandished it.

"Yes," said Eugene awkwardly. "I think it's going to be all right now. I didn't know how
20 to do at first."

"I hope you have sense enough now to leave those old hookers alone?" said Ben very sternly. Eugene made no answer. "You can't do that and be anything, you know. And you're likely to catch everything. This looks like a nice girl," he said quietly, after a pause. "For heaven's sake, fix yourself up and try to keep fairly clean. Women notice that, you know. Look after your fingernails, and keep your clothes
30 pressed. Have you any money?"

"All I need," said Eugene, looking nervously toward the kitchen. "Don't, for God's sake!"

"Put it in your pocket, you little fool," Ben said angrily, thrusting a bill into his hand. "You've got to have some money. Keep it until you need it."

Helen came out on the high front porch with them as they departed. As usual, she had added a double heaping measure to what they needed.
40 There was another shoe-box stuffed with sandwiches, boiled eggs, and fudge.

She stood on the high step-edge, with a cloth wound over her head, her gaunt arms, pitted with old scars, akimbo. A warm sunny odor of nasturtiums, loamy earth, and honeysuckle washed round them its hot spermy waves.

"O-ho! A-ha!" she winked comically. "I know something! I'm not as blind as you think, you
50 know—" She nodded with significant jocularity,

her big smiling face drenched in the curious radiance and purity that occasionally dwelt so beautifully there. He thought always, when he saw her thus, of a sky washed after rain, of wide crystalline distances, cool and clean.

With a rough snigger she prodded him in the ribs:

"Ain't love grand! Ha-ha-ha-ha! Look at his face, Laura." She drew the girl close to her in a generous hug, laughing, Oh, with laughing pity, and as they mounted the hill, she stood there, in the sunlight, her mouth slightly open, smiling, touched with radiance, beauty, and wonder.

They mounted slowly toward the eastern edge of town, by the long upward sweep of Academy Street, which bordered the Negro settlement sprawled below it. At the end of Academy Street, the hill loomed abruptly; a sinuous road, well paved, curved up along the hillside to the right. They turned into this road, mounting now along the eastern edge of Niggertown. The settlement fell sharply away below them, rushing down along a series of long clay streets. There were a few frame houses by the roadside: the dwellings of Negroes and poor white people, but these became sparser as they mounted. They walked at a leisurely pace up the cool road speckled with little dancing patches of light that filtered through the arching trees and shaded on the left by the dense massed foliage of the hill. Out of this green loveliness loomed the huge raw turret of a cement reservoir: it was streaked and blotted coolly with water-marks. Eugene felt thirsty. Further along, the escape from a small reservoir roared from a pipe in a foaming hawser, as thick as a man's body.

They climbed sharply up, along a rocky trail, avoiding the last long corkscrew of the road, and stood in the gap, at the road's summit. They were only a few hundred feet above the town: it lay before them with the sharp nearness of a Sienese picture, at once close and far. On the highest ground, he saw the solid masonry of the Square, blocked cleanly out in light and shadow, and a crawling toy that was a car, and men no bigger than sparrows. And about the Square was the treeless brick jungle of business—cheap, ragged, and ugly, and beyond all this, in indefinite patches, the houses where all the people lived, with little bright raw ulcers of suburbia further off, and the healing and concealing grace of fair massed trees. And below him, weltering up from the hollow along the flanks and shoulders of the hill, was Niggertown. There seemed to be a kind of centre at the Square, where all the cars crawled in and waited, yet there was no purpose anywhere.

But the hills were lordly, with a plan. Westward, they widened into the sun, soaring up from buttressing shoulders. The town was thrown up on the plateau like an encampment: there was nothing below him that could resist time. There was no idea. Below him, in a cup, he felt that all life was held: he saw it as might one of the old schoolmen writing in monkish Latin a Theatre of Human Life; or like Peter Breughel, on one of his swarming pictures. It seemed to him suddenly that he had not come up on the hill from the town, but that he had come out of the wilderness like a beast, and was staring now with steady beast-eye at this little huddle of wood and mortar which the wilderness must one day repossess, devour, cover over.

The seventh from the top was Troy—but Helen had lived there; and so the German dug it up.

They turned from the railing, with recovered wind, and walked through the gap, under Philip Roseberry's great arched bridge. To the left, on the summit, the rich Jew had his castle, his stables, his horses, his cows, and his daughters. As they went under the shadow of the bridge Eugene lifted his head and shouted. His voice bounded against the arch like a stone. They passed under and stood on the other side of the gap, looking from the road's edge down into the cove. But they could not yet see the cove, save for green glimmers. The hillside was thickly wooded, the road wound down its side in a white perpetual corkscrew. But they could look across at the fair wild hills on the other side of the cove, cleared half-way up their flanks with ample field and fenced meadow, and forested above with a billowing sea of greenery.

The day was like gold and sapphires: there was a swift flash and sparkle, intangible and multifarious, like sunlight on roughened water, all over the land. A rich warm wind was blowing, turning all the leaves back the same way, and making mellow music through all the lutestrings of flower and grass and fruit. The wind moaned, not with the mad fiend-voice of winter in harsh boughs, but like a fruitful woman, deep-breasted, great, full of love and wisdom; like Demeter unseen and hunting through the world. A dog bayed faintly in the cove, his howl spent and broken by the wind. A cowbell tinkled gustily. In the thick wood below them the rich notes of birds fell from their throats, straight down, like nuggets. A woodpecker drummed on the dry unbarked bole of a blasted chestnut-tree. The blue gulf of the sky was spread with light massy clouds: they cruised like swift galleons, tacking across the hills before the wind, and darkening the trees below with their floating shadows.

The boy grew blind with love and desire: the cup of his heart was glutted with all this wonder. It overcame and weakened him. He grasped the girl's cool fingers. They stood leg to leg, riven into each other's flesh. Then they left the road, cutting down across its loops along steep wooded paths. The wood was a vast green church; the bird-cries fell like plums. A great butterfly, with wings of blue velvet streaked with gold and scarlet markings, fluttered heavily before them in freckled sunlight, tottering to rest finally upon a spray of dogwood. There were light skimming noises in the dense undergrowth to either side, the swift bullet-shadows of birds. A garter snake, greener than wet moss, as long as a shoelace and no thicker than a woman's little finger, shot across the path, its tiny eyes bright with terror, its small forked tongue playing from its mouth like an electric spark. Laura cried out, drawing back in sharp terror; at her cry he snatched up a stone in a wild lust to kill the tiny creature that shot at them, through its coils, the old snake-fear, touching them with beauty, with horror, with something supernatural. But the snake glided away into the undergrowth and, with a feeling of strong shame, he threw the stone away. "They won't hurt you," he said.

At length, they came out above the cove, at a forking of the road. They turned left, to the north, toward the upper and smaller end. To the south, the cove widened out in a rich little

691

Eden of farm and pasture. Small houses dotted the land, there were green meadows and a glint of water. Fields of young green wheat bent rhythmically under the wind; the young corn stood waist-high, with light clashing blades. The chimneys of Rheinhart's house showed above its obscuring grove of maples; the fat dairy-cows grazed slowly across the wide pastures. And further below, half tree-
10 and-shrub-hidden, lay the rich acres of Judge Webster Tayloe. The road was thickly coated with white dust; it dipped down and ran through a little brook. They crossed over on white rocks, strewn across its bed. Several ducks, scarcely disturbed by their crossing, waddled up out of the clear water and re-garded them gravely, like little children in white choir aprons. A young country fellow clattered by them in a buggy filled with empty
20 milk-cans. He grinned with a cordial red face, saluting them with a slow gesture, and leaving behind an odor of milk and sweat and butter. A woman, in a field above them, stared curiously with shaded eyes. In another field, a man was mowing with a scythe, moving into the grass like a god upon his enemies, with a reaping hook of light.

They left the road near the head of the cove, advancing over the fields on rising ground to
30 the wooded cup of the hills. There was a pow-erful masculine stench of broad dock-leaves, a hot weedy odor. They moved over a pathless field, knee-high in a dry stubbly waste, gath-ering on their clothes clusters of brown cockle-burrs. All the field was sown with hot odorous daisies. Then they entered the wood again, mounting until they came to an island of tender grass, by a little brook that fell down from the green hill along a rocky ferny bed in
40 bright cascades.

"Let's stop here," said Eugene. The grass was thick with dandelions: their poignant and wordless odor studded the earth with yellow magic. They were like gnomes and elves, and tiny witchcraft in flower and acorn.

Laura and Eugene lay upon their backs, looking up through the high green shimmer of leaves at the Caribbean sky, with all its fleet of cloudy ships. The water of the brook made a
50 noise like silence. The town behind the hill lay in another unthinkable world. They forgot its pain and conflict.

"What time is it?" Eugene asked. For, they had come to a place where no time was. Laura held up her exquisite wrist, and looked at her watch.

"Why!" she exclaimed, surprised. "It's only half-past twelve!"

But he scarcely heard her.

"What do I care what time it is!" he said huskily, and he seized the lovely hand, bound with its silken watch-cord, and kissed it. Her long cool fingers closed around his own; she drew his face down to her mouth.

They lay there, locked together, upon that magic carpet, in that paradise. Her gray eyes were deeper and clearer than a pool of clear water; he kissed the little freckles on her rare skin; he gazed reverently at the snub tilt of her nose; he watched the mirrored dance of the sparkling water over her face. All of that magic world—flower and field and sky and hill, and all the sweet woodland cries, sound and sight and odor—grew into him, one voice in his heart, one tongue in his brain, harmonious, ra-diant, and whole—a single passionate lyrical noise.

"My dear! Darling! Do you remember last night?" he asked fondly, as if recalling some event of her childhood.

"Yes," she gathered her arms tightly about his neck, "why do you think I could forget it?"

"Do you remember what I said—what I asked you to do?" he insisted eagerly.

"Oh, what are we going to do? What are we going to do?" she moaned, turning her head to the side and flinging an arm across her eyes.

"What is it? What's the matter? Dear!"

"Eugene—my dear, you're only a child. I'm so old—a grown woman."

"You're only twenty-one," he said. "There's only five years' difference. That's nothing."

"Oh!" she said. "You don't know what you're saying. It's all the difference in the world."

"When I'm twenty, you'll be twenty-five. When I'm twenty-six, you'll be thirty-one. When I'm forty-eight, you'll be fifty-three. What's that?" he said contemptuously. "Noth-ing."

"Everything," she said, "everything. If I were sixteen, and you twenty-one it would be nothing. But you're a boy and I'm a woman. When you're a young man I'll be an old maid; when you grow old I shall be dying. How do you know where you'll be, what you'll be do-ing five years from now?" she continued in a moment. "You're only a boy—you've just started college. You have no plans yet. You don't know what you're going to do."

"Yes, I do!" he yelled furiously. "I'm going to be a lawyer. That's what they're sending me for. I'm going to be a lawyer, and I'm going into politics. Perhaps," he added with gloomy pleasure, "you'll be sorry then, after I make a name for myself." With bitter joy he foresaw his lonely celebrity. The Governor's Mansion. Forty rooms. Alone. Alone.

"You're going to be a lawyer," said Laura, "and you're going everywhere in the world, and I'm to wait for you, and never get married. You poor kid!" She laughed softly. "You don't know what you're going to do."

He turned a face of misery on her; bright-ness dropped from the sun.

"You don't care?" he choked. "You don't care?" He bent his head to hide his wet eyes.

"Oh, my dear," she said, "I do care. But peo-ple don't live like that. It's like a story. Don't you know that I'm a grown woman? At my age, dear, most girls have begun to think of getting married. What—what if I had begun to think of it, too?"

"Married!" The word came from him in a huge gasp of horror as if she had mentioned the abominable, proposed the unspeakable. Then, having heard the monstrous suggestion, he immediately accepted it as a fact. He was like that.

"So! That's it!" he said furiously. "You're go-ing to get married, eh? You have fellows, have you? You go out with them, do you? You've known it all the time, and you've tried to fool me."

Nakedly, with breast bare to horror, he scourged himself, knowing in the moment that the nightmare cruelty of life is not in the re-mote and fantastic, but in the probable—the horror of love, loss, marriage, the ninety sec-onds treason in the dark.

"You have fellows—you let them feel you. They feel your legs, they play with your breasts, they—" His voice became inaudible through strangulation.

"No. No, my dear. I haven't said so," she rose swiftly to a sitting position, taking his hands. "But there's nothing unusual about get-ting married, you know. Most people do. Oh, my dear! Don't look like that! Nothing has hap-pened. Nothing! Nothing!"

He seized her fiercely, unable to speak. Then he buried his face in her neck.

"Laura! My dear! My sweet! Don't leave me alone! I've been alone! I've always been alone!"

"It's what you want, dear. It's what you'll always want. You couldn't stand anything else. You'd get so tired of me. You'll forget this ever happened. You'll forget me. You'll forget—for-get."

"Forget! I'll never forget! I won't live long enough."

"And I'll never love any one else! I'll never leave you! I'll wait for you forever! Oh, my child, my child!"

They clung together in that bright moment of wonder, there on the magic island, where the world was quiet, believing all they said. And who shall say—whatever disenchantment follows—that we ever forget magic, or that we can ever betray, on this leaden earth, the apple-tree, the singing, and the gold? Far out beyond that timeless valley, a train, on the rails for the East, wailed back its ghostly cry: life, like a fume of painted smoke, a broken wrack of cloud, drifted away. Their world was a sing-ing voice again: they were young and they could never die. This would endure.

He kissed her on her splendid eyes; he grew into her young Mænad's body, his heart numbed deliciously against the pressure of her narrow breasts. She was as lithe and yielding to his sustaining hand as a willow rod—she was bird-swift, more elusive in repose than the dancing water-motes upon her face. He held her tightly lest she grow into the tree again, or be gone amid the wood like smoke.

Come up into the hills, O my young love. Return! O lost, and by the wind grieved, ghost, come back again, as first I knew you in the timeless valley, where we shall feel ourselves anew, bedded on magic in the month of June. There was a place where all the sun went glis-tering in your hair, and from the hill we could have put a finger on a star. Where is the day that melted into one rich noise? Where the music of your flesh, the rhyme of your teeth, the dainty languor of your legs, your small firm arms, your slender fingers, to be bitten like an apple, and the little cherry-teats of your white breasts? And where are all the tiny wires of finespun maidenhair? Quick are the mouths of earth, and quick the teeth that fed upon this loveliness. You who were made for music, will hear music no more: in your dark house the winds are silent. Ghost, ghost, come back from that marriage that we did not foresee, return not into life, but into magic, where we have never died, into the enchanted wood, where 10 we still lie, strewn on the grass. Come up into the hills, O my young love: return. O lost, and by the wind grieved, ghost, come back again.

XXXI

One day, when June was coming to its end, Laura James said to him:

"I shall have to go home next week." Then, seeing his stricken face, she added, "but only for a few days—not more than a week."

"But why? The summer's only started. You will burn up down there."

20 "Yes. It's silly, I know. But my people expect me for the Fourth of July. You know, we have an enormous family—hundreds of aunts, cousins, and in-laws. We have a family reunion every year—a great barbecue and picnic. I hate it. But they'd never forgive me if I didn't come."

Frightened, he looked at her for a moment.

"Laura! You're coming back, aren't you?" he said quietly.

30 "Yes, of course," she said. "Be quiet."

He was trembling violently; he was afraid to question her more closely.

"Be quiet," she whispered, "quiet!" She put her arms around him.

He went with her to the station on a hot mid-afternoon. There was a smell of melted tar in the streets. She held his hand beside her in the rattling trolley, squeezing his fingers to give him comfort, and whispering from time to 40 time:

"In a week! Only a week, dear."

"I don't see the need," he muttered. "It's over 400 miles. Just for a few days."

He passed the old one-legged gateman on the station platform very easily, carrying her baggage. Then he sat beside her in the close green heat of the pullman until the train should go. A little electric fan droned uselessly above

the aisle; a prim young lady whom he knew arranged herself amid the bright new leather of her bags. She returned his greeting elegantly, with a shade of refined hauteur, then looked out the window again, grimacing eloquently at her parents who gazed at her raptly from the platform. Several prosperous merchants went down the aisle in expensive tan shoes that creaked under the fan's drone.

"Not going to leave us, are you, Mr. Morris?"

"Hello, Jim. No, I'm running up to Richmond for a few days." But even the gray weather of their lives could not deaden the excitement of that hot chariot to the East.

" 'Board!"

He got up trembling.

"In a few days, dear." She looked up, taking his hand in her small gloved palms.

"You will write as soon as you get there? Please!"

"Yes. To-morrow—at once."

He bent down suddenly and whispered, "Laura—you will come back. You will come back!"

She turned her face away and wept bitterly. He sat beside her once more; she clasped him tightly as if he had been a child.

"My dear, my dear! Don't forget me ever!"

"Never. Come back. Come back."

The salt print of her kiss was on his mouth, his face, his eyes. It was, he knew, the guttering candle-end of time. The train was in motion. He leaped blindly up the passage with a cry in his throat.

"Come back again!"

But he knew. Her cry followed him, as if he had torn something from her grasp.

Within three days he had his letter. On four sheets of paper, bordered with victorious little American flags, this:

"My dear: I got home at half-past one, just too tired to move. I couldn't sleep on the train at all last night, it seemed to get hotter all the way down. I was so blue when I got here, I almost cried. Little Richmond is too ghastly for words—everything burned up and every one gone away to the mountains or the sea. How can I ever stand it even for a week!" (Good! he thought. If the weather holds, she will come back all the sooner.) "It would be heaven now to get one breath of mountain air. Could you

find your way back to our place in the valley again?" (Yes, even if I were blind, he thought.) "Will you promise to look after your hand until it gets well? I worried so after you had gone, because I forgot to change the bandage yesterday. Daddy was glad to see me: he said he was not going to let me go again but, don't worry, I'll have my own way in the end. I always do. I don't know any one at home any more—all the boys have enlisted or gone to work in the shipyards at Norfolk. Most of the girls I know are getting married, or married already. That leaves only the kids." (He winced. As old as I am, maybe older.) "Give my love to Mrs. Barton, and tell your mother I said she must not work so hard in that hot kitchen. And all the little cross-marks at the bottom are for you. Try to guess what they are.
                                        LAURA."

He read her prosy letter with rigid face, devouring the words more hungrily than if they had been lyrical song. She would come back! She would come back! Soon.

There was another page. Weakened and relaxed from his excitement, he looked at it. There he found, almost illegibly written, but at last in her own speech, as if leaping out from the careful aimlessness of her letter, this note:

"July 4.

"Richard came yesterday. He is twenty-five, works in Norfolk. I've been engaged to him almost a year. We're going off quietly to Norfolk to-morrow and get married. My dear! My dear! I couldn't tell you! I tried to, but I couldn't. I didn't want to lie. Everything else was true. I meant all I said. If you hadn't been so young, but what's the use of saying that? Try to forgive me, but please don't forget me. Good-by and God bless you. Oh, my darling, it was heaven! I shall never forget you."

When he had finished the letter, he re-read it, slowly and carefully. Then he folded it, put it in his inner breast-pocket, and leaving Dixieland, walked for forty minutes, until he came up in the gap over the town again. It was sunset. The sun's vast rim, blood-red, rested upon the western earth, in a great field of murky pollen. It sank beyond the western ranges. The clear sweet air was washed with gold and pearl. The vast hills melted into purple solitudes:

they were like Canaan and rich grapes. The motors of cove people toiled up around the horse-shoe of the road. Dusk came. The bright winking lights in the town went up. Darkness melted over the town like dew: it washed out all the day's distress, the harsh confusions. Low wailing sounds came faintly up from Niggertown.

And above him the proud stars flashed into heaven: there was one, so rich and low, that he could have picked it, if he had climbed the hill beyond the Jew's great house. One, like a lamp, hung low above the heads of men returning home. (O Hesperus, you bring us all good things.) One had flashed out the light that winked on him the night that Ruth lay at the feet of Boaz; and one on Queen Isolt; and one on Corinth and on Troy. It was night, vast brooding night, the mother of loneliness, that washes our stains away. He was washed in the great river of night, in the Ganges tides of redemption. His bitter wound was for the moment healed in him: he turned his face upward to the proud and tender stars, which made him a god and a grain of dust, the brother of eternal beauty and the son of death —alone, alone.

"Ha-ha-ha-ha-ha!" Helen laughed huskily, prodding him in the ribs. "Your girl went and got married, didn't she? She fooled you. You got left."

"Wh-a-a-a-t!" said Eliza banteringly, "has my boy been—as the fellow says" (she sniggered behind her hand) "has my boy been—a-courtin'?" She puckered her lips in playful reproach.

"Oh, for God's sake," he muttered angrily. "What fellow says!"

His scowl broke into an angry grin as he caught his sister's eye. They laughed.

"Well, 'Gene," said the girl seriously, "forget about it. You're only a kid yet. Laura is a grown woman."

"Why, son," said Eliza with a touch of malice, "that girl was fooling you all the time. She was just leading you on."

"Oh, stop it, please."

"Cheer up!" said Helen heartily. "Your time's coming. You'll forget her in a week. There are plenty more, you know. This is puppy love.

Show her that you're a good sport. You ought to write her a letter of congratulation."

"Why, yes," said Eliza, "I'd make a big joke of it all. I wouldn't let on to her that it affected me. I'd write her just as big as you please and laugh about the whole thing. I'd show them! That's what I'd——"

"Oh, for God's sake!" he groaned, starting up. "Leave me alone, won't you?"

10 He left the house.

But he wrote the letter. And the moment after the lid of the mail-box clanged over it, he was writhen by shame. For it was a proud and boastful letter, salted with scatterings of Greek, Latin, and English verse, quotable scraps, wrenched into the text without propriety, without accuracy, without anything but his pitiful and obvious desire to show her his weight in the point of his wit, the depth of his 20 learning. She would be sorry when she knew her loss! But, for a moment at the end, his fiercely beating heart stormed through:

" . . . and I hope he's worth having you— he can't deserve you, Laura; no one can. But if he knows what he has, that's something. How lucky he is! You're right about me—I'm too young. I'd cut off my hand now for eight or ten years more. God bless and keep you, my dear, dear Laura.

"Something in me wants to burst. It keeps 30 trying to, but it won't, it never has. O God! If it only would! I shall never forget you. I'm lost now and I'll never find the way again. In God's name write me a line when you get this. Tell me what your name is now—you never have. Tell me where you're going to live. Don't let me go entirely, I beg of you, don't leave me alone."

He sent the letter to the address she had given him—to her father's house. Week melted 40 into week: his life mounted day by day in a terrible tension to the delivery of the mail, morning and afternoon, fell then into a miasmic swamp when no word came. July ended. The summer waned. She did not write. . . .

WILLIAM FAULKNER

Out of a background of military men, state governors, and southern politicians came William Faulkner (or Falkner as he now prefers to spell it), whose popular reputation is largely that of a portrayer of degeneracy in southern society both high and low. He was born in New Albany, Mississippi, on September 25, 1897. A half-century or so before, his great-grandfather William Faulkner had written an extremely popular romantic novel, *The White Rose of Memphis,* redolent of magnolia blossoms and ecstatic about the womanhood of the South. It would be highly diverting to hear the great-grandfather's comments on his great-grand-son's novels. At first, however, William Faulkner the younger did nothing to indicate that he was going to be an *enfant terrible* of contemporary letters. While he was still a child, his family moved to Oxford, Mississippi, where the Faulkner home still stands. During the First World War Faulkner joined the Canadian Fly-

ing Corps; and by the time of the Armistice he had risen to the rank of lieutenant. After the Armistice he returned to Mississippi and attended the state university (1919–21).

For a time Faulkner lived in New Orleans with Sherwood Anderson (p. 308). The two men had rather a tempestuous time of it. But Faulkner found an opportunity to satisfy his natural, hereditary instinct for writing. His first novel, *Soldier's Pay* (1926), was written in New Orleans, as were several short stories, which were published in the *New Orleans Times-Picayune. Soldier's Pay,* which is the inevitable realistic novel by the returned soldier with literary ambitions, attracted little attention. A small volume of poetry, *The Marble Faun* (1924), dating in composition from this same general period, attracted even less. Indeed, neither this volume nor a subsequent one, *The Green Bough* (1933), demands further consideration; Faulkner is not one of our major poets. But the short stories, vivid, naturalistic, brutal to the point of morbidity, and impregnated with a haunting atmosphere of the unnatural—even of the monstrous—brought their author considerable notice. This notice deepened into a sharp admiration or a strong dislike —according to the tastes of the individual critic —as *Sartoris* (1929), a novel, took its place in the growing list of Faulkner's peculiarly pungent writings.

It was *The Sound and the Fury* (1929), a powerful novel of the decay of a southern family, that lifted Faulkner into the ranks of the major contemporary American fiction-writers. There followed the repellently fascinating *As I Lay Dying* (1930), the story of a degenerate family transporting the corpse of their mother across the state to her home for burial. *Sanctuary* (1931), a grisly tale of the violation of a southern college girl by a group of reprobate moonshiners, whom she had intruded upon for the sake of a drink, won for Faulkner perhaps the greatest fame of any of his works. An effective collection of short stories, *These Thirteen* (1931), and a less significant story, *Idyll in the Desert* (1931), rounded out the first period of Faulkner's career. His work throughout this period had been extreme in subject matter, violent, harshly staccato, and experimental in form and technique—in short, he represented an advanced stage of the disease of the Waste Lander.

Many of these characteristics are still to be found in Faulkner's later work, which can be said to begin with the novel *Light in August* (1932). In spite of the surface realism and sordidness of his earlier work, Faulkner, in his insistence upon the emotional effect of his materials on the reader and in his emphasis upon the strange, the wayward, and the intangible, has shown the tendencies of a romanticist; and these tendencies are strengthening upon him. *Light in August,* for example, ends upon a positive note of female triumph vaguely reminiscent of the conclusion to James Joyce's *Ulysses* (p. 503). *Pylon* (1934), a novel associated with the lives of those who make their living in the air, is bawdy, crude, and bizarre but self-assertive; *Dr. Martino and Other Stories* (1934) contains short stories that manage to achieve a considerable degree of moral affirmation. *Absalom! Absalom!* (1936), on the other hand, is something of a retrogression in tone; it is a bewildering novel of incest and insanity, and wallows in blood and degradation. Its difficult prose style is strongly influenced by that of Joyce's *Ulysses,* with its fourth-dimensional devices, its contempt of stylistic coherence or the conventional means of communication with the reader. Apparently Faulkner was not satisfied with the experiment; he returned to an extremely lucid, almost naïve style and substance in *The Unvanquished* (1938), a book of tales dedicated to the tradition of the Lost Cause. *The Wild Palms* (1939) is gritty in substance and style but portrays in powerful language and with something of an epic sweep the struggle for existence among neurotic folk along the banks and valleys of the Mississippi River. *The Hamlet* (1940) is a loosely linked collection of episodes. In *Go Down, Moses* (1942) are a group of short stories centering about a simple family. *Intruder in the Dust* appeared in 1948, and in this novel the author indicates that he is capable of straightforward writing without a loss of vividness and power.

Where Faulkner will ultimately arrive, none can say. It is clear, however, that he has outgrown in part the sophomoric desire merely to shock; and his world of characters, choked as it may often be by the mephitic mists of abnormality, contributes nevertheless something hard, definite, and vital to the social scene. That Faulkner is tending more and more to the revolutionary in thought and technique can scarcely be denied; but he is still groping. For the general reader he remains a startling phenomenon; there are times when he appears to write as he does out of sheer perversity. But he cannot be ignored or flouted as a libeler of southern civilization; he would probably have written in the same manner about the same kind of people no matter where he had lived— and it may be conceded that he would have found similar material in any given locality of these United States. He is a sore trial to the southern agrarians (p. 195), no doubt, and in any case he has thus far tended to exaggerate in a suspiciously self-conscious way; but no amount of personal bias can deny him his rightful place as one of the most striking writers of fiction in contemporary America.

Go Down, Moses

I

THE FACE was black, smooth, impenetrable; the eyes had seen too much. The negroid hair had been treated so that it covered the skull like a cap, in a single neat-ridged sweep, with the appearance of having been lacquered, the part trimmed out with a razor, so that the head resembled a bronze head, imperishable and enduring. He wore one of those sports costumes called ensembles in the men's shop
10 advertisements, shirt and trousers matching and cut from the same fawn-colored flannel, and they had cost too much and were draped too much, with too many pleats; and he half lay on the steel cot in the steel cubicle just outside which an armed guard had stood for twenty hours now, smoking cigarettes and answering in a voice which was anything under the sun but a southern voice or even a Negro voice, the questions of the spectacled young white
20 man sitting with a broad census-taker's portfolio on the steel stool opposite:

"Samuel Worsham Beauchamp. Twenty-six. Born in the country near Jefferson, Mississippi. No family. No—"

"Wait." The census-taker wrote rapidly. "That's not the name you were sen— lived under in Chicago."

The other snapped the ash from the cigarette. "No. It was another guy killed the cop."
30 "All right. Occupation—"

"Getting rich too fast."

"—none." The census-taker wrote rapidly. "Parents."

"Sure. Two. I dont remember them. My grandmother raised me."

"What's her name? Is she still living?"

"I dont know. Mollie Worsham Beauchamp. If she is, she's on Carothers Edmonds' farm seventeen miles from Jefferson, Mississippi. That
40 all?"

The census-taker closed the portfolio and stood up. He was a year or two younger than the other. "If they don't know who you are here, how will they know—how do you expect to get home?"

The other snapped the ash from the cigarette, lying on the steel cot in the fine Hollywood clothes and a pair of shoes better than the census-taker would ever own. "What will that matter to me?" he said.

So the census-taker departed; the guard locked the steel door again. And the other lay on the steel cot smoking until after a while they came and slit the expensive trousers and shaved the expensive coiffure and led him out of the cell.

II

On that same hot, bright July morning the same hot bright wind which shook the mulberry leaves just outside Gavin Stevens' window blew into the office too, contriving a semblance of coolness from what was merely motion. It fluttered among the county-attorney business on the desk and blew in the wild shock of prematurely white hair of the man who sat behind it—a thin, intelligent, unstable face, a rumpled linen suit from whose lapel a Phi Beta Kappa key dangled on a watch chain —Gavin Stevens, Phi Beta Kappa, Harvard, Ph.D., Heidelberg, whose office was his hobby, although it made his living for him, and whose serious vocation was a twenty-two-year-old unfinished translation of the Old Testament back into classic Greek. Only his caller seemed impervious to it, though by appearance she should have owned in that breeze no more of weight and solidity than the intact ash of a scrap of burned paper—a little old Negro woman with a shrunken, incredibly old face beneath a white headcloth and a black straw hat which would have fitted a child.

"Beauchamp?" Stevens said. "You live on Mr Carothers Edmonds' place."

"I done left," she said. "I come to find my boy." Then, sitting on the hard chair opposite him and without moving, she began to chant. "Roth Edmonds sold my Benjamin. Sold him in Egypt. Pharaoh got him—"

"Wait," Stevens said. "Wait, Aunty." Because memory, recollection, was about to mesh and click. "If you don't know where your grandson is, how do you know he's in trouble? Do you mean that Mr Edmonds has refused to help you find him?"

"It was Roth Edmonds sold him," she said. "Sold him in Egypt. I dont know whar he is.

I just knows Pharaoh got him. And you the Law. I wants to find my boy."

"All right," Stevens said. "I'll try to find him. If you're not going back home, where will you stay in town? It may take some time, if you dont know where he went and you haven't heard from him in five years."

"I be staying with Hamp Worsham. He my brother."

"All right," Stevens said. He was not surprised. He had known Hamp Worsham all his life, though he had never seen the old Negress before. But even if he had, he still would not have been surprised. They were like that. You could know two of them for years; they might even have worked for you for years, bearing different names. Then suddenly you learn by pure chance that they are brothers or sisters.

He sat in the hot motion which was not breeze and listened to her toiling slowly down the steep outside stairs, remembering the grandson. The papers of that business had passed across his desk before going to the District Attorney five or six years ago—Butch Beauchamp, as the youth had been known during the single year he had spent in and out of the city jail: the old Negress' daughter's child, orphaned of his mother at birth and deserted by his father, whom the grandmother had taken and raised, or tried to. Because at nineteen he had quit the country and come to town and spent a year in and out of jail for gambling and fighting, to come at last under serious indictment for breaking and entering a store.

Caught red-handed, whereupon he had struck with a piece of iron pipe at the officer who surprised him and then lay on the ground where the officer had felled him with a pistol-butt, cursing through his broken mouth, his teeth fixed into something like furious laughter through the blood. Then two nights later he broke out of jail and was seen no more—a youth not yet twenty-one, with something in him from the father who begot and deserted him and who was now in the State Penitentiary for manslaughter—some seed not only violent but dangerous and bad.

And that's who I am to find, save, Stevens thought. Because he did not for one moment doubt the old Negress' instinct. If she had also been able to divine where the boy was and what his trouble was, he would not have been surprised, and it was only later that he thought to be surprised at how quickly he did find where the boy was and what was wrong.

His first thought was to telephone Carothers Edmonds, on whose farm the old Negress' husband had been a tenant for years. But then, according to her, Edmonds had already refused to have anything to do with it. Then he sat perfectly still while the hot wind blew in his wild white mane. Now he comprehended what the old Negress had meant. He remembered now that it was Edmonds who had actually sent the boy to Jefferson in the first place: he had caught the boy breaking into his commissary store and had ordered him off the place and had forbidden him ever to return. *And not the sheriff, the police,* he thought. *Something broader, quicker in scope.* . . . He rose and took his old fine worn panama and descended the outside stairs and crossed the empty square in the hot suspension of noon's beginning, to the office of the county newspaper. The editor was in—an older man but with hair less white than Stevens', in a black string tie and an old-fashioned boiled shirt and tremendously fat.

"An old nigger woman named Mollie Beauchamp," Stevens said. "She and her husband live on the Edmonds place. It's her grandson. You remember him—Butch Beauchamp, about five or six years ago, who spent a year in town, mostly in jail, until they finally caught him breaking into Rouncewell's store one night? Well, he's in worse trouble than that now. I dont doubt her at all. I just hope, for her sake as well as that of the great public whom I represent, that his present trouble is very bad and maybe final too—"

"Wait," the editor said. He didn't even need to leave his desk. He took the press association flimsy from its spike and handed it to Stevens. It was datelined from Joliet, Illinois, this morning:

Mississippi Negro, on eve of execution for murder of Chicago policeman, exposes alias by completing census questionnaire. Samuel Worsham Beauchamp—

Five minutes later Stevens was crossing again the empty square in which noon's hot suspension was that much nearer. He had thought that he was going home to his boarding house for the noon meal, but he found that he was not. *'Besides, I didn't lock my office door,'* he thought. Only, how under the sun she could have got to town from those seventeen miles. She may even have walked. "So it seems I didn't mean what I said I hoped," he said aloud, mounting the outside stairs again, out of the hazy and now windless sunglare, and entered his office. He stopped. Then he said,

"Good morning, Miss Worsham."

She was quite old, too—thin, erect, with a neat, old-time piling of white hair beneath a faded hat of thirty years ago, in rusty black, with a frayed umbrella faded now until it was green instead of black. He had known her too all his life. She lived alone in the decaying house her father had left her, where she gave lessons in china-painting and, with the help of Hamp Worsham, descendant of one of her father's slaves, and his wife, raised chickens and vegetables for market.

"I came about Mollie," she said. "Mollie Beauchamp. She said that you—"

He told her while she watched him, erect on the hard chair where the old Negress had sat, the rusty umbrella leaning against her knee. On her lap, beneath her folded hands, lay an old-fashioned beaded reticule almost as big as a suitcase. "He is to be executed tonight."

"Can nothing be done? Mollie's and Hamp's parents belonged to my grandfather. Mollie and I were born in the same month. We grew up together as sisters would."

"I telephoned," Stevens said. "I talked to the Warden at Joliet, and to the District Attorney in Chicago. He had a fair trial, a good lawyer—of that sort. He had money. He was in a business called numbers, that people like him make money in." She watched him, erect and motionless. "He is a murderer, Miss Worsham. He shot that policeman in the back. A bad son of a bad father. He admitted, confessed it afterward."

"I know," she said. Then he realized that she was not looking at him, not seeing him at least. "It's terrible."

"So is murder terrible," Stevens said. "It's better this way." Then she was looking at him again.

"I wasn't thinking of him. I was thinking of Mollie. She mustn't know."

"Yes," Stevens said. "I have already talked with Mr Wilmoth at the paper. He has agreed not to print anything. I will telephone the Memphis paper, but it's probably too late for that. . . . If we could just persuade her to go on back home this afternoon, before the Memphis paper. . . . Out there, where the only white person she ever sees is Mr Edmonds, and I will telephone him; and even if the other darkies should hear about it, I'm sure they wouldn't. And then maybe in about two or three months I could go out there and tell her he is dead and buried somewhere in the North. . . ." This time she was watching him with such an expression that he ceased talking; she sat there, erect on the hard chair, watching him until he had ceased.

"She will want to take him back home with her," she said.

"Him?" Stevens said. "The body?" She watched him. The expression was neither shocked nor disapproving. It merely embodied some old, timeless, female affinity for blood and grief. Stevens thought: *She has walked to town in this heat. Unless Hamp brought her in the buggy he peddles eggs and vegetables from.*

"He is the only child of her oldest daughter, her own dead first child. He must come home."

"He must come home," Stevens said as quietly. "I'll attend to it at once. I'll telephone at once."

"You are kind." For the first time she stirred, moved. He watched her hands draw the reticule toward her, clasping it. "I will defray the expenses. Can you give me some idea—?"

He looked her straight in the face. He told the lie without batting an eye, quickly and easily. "Ten or twelve dollars will cover it. They will furnish a box and there will be only the transportation."

"A box?" Again she was looking at him with that expression curious and detached, as though he were a child. "He is her grandson, Mr Stevens. When she took him to raise, she gave him my father's name—Samuel Worsham. Not just a box, Mr Stevens. I understand that can be done by paying so much a month."

"Not just a box," Stevens said. He said it in exactly the same tone in which he had said He must come home. "Mr Edmonds will want to help, I know. And I understand that old Luke

Beauchamp has some money in the bank. And if you will permit me—"

"That will not be necessary," she said. He watched her open the reticule; he watched her count onto the desk twenty-five dollars in frayed bills and coins ranging down to nickels and dimes and pennies. "That will take care of the immediate expenses. I will tell her— You are sure there is no hope?"

"I am sure. He will die tonight."

"I will tell her this afternoon that he is dead then."

"Would you like for me to tell her?"

"I will tell her," she said.

"Would you like for me to come out and see her, then, talk to her?"

"It would be kind of you." Then she was gone, erect, her feet crisp and light, almost brisk, on the stairs, ceasing. He telephoned again, to the Illinois warden, then to an undertaker in Joliet. Then once more he crossed the hot, empty square. He had only to wait a short while for the editor to return from dinner.

"We're bringing him home," he said. "Miss Worsham and you and me and some others. It will cost—"

"Wait," the editor said. "What others?"

"I don't know yet. It will cost about two hundred. I'm not counting the telephones; I'll take care of them myself. I'll get something out of Carothers Edmonds the first time I catch him; I don't know how much, but something. And maybe fifty around the square. But the rest of it is you and me, because she insisted on leaving twenty-five with me, which is just twice what I tried to persuade her it would cost and just exactly four times what she can afford to pay—"

"Wait," the editor said. "Wait."

"And he will come in on Number Four the day after tomorrow and we will meet it, Miss Worsham and his grandmother, the old nigger, in my car and you and me in yours. Miss Worsham and the old woman will take him back home, back where he was born. Or where the old woman raised him. Or where she tried to. And the hearse out there will be fifteen more, not counting the flowers—"

"Flowers?" the editor cried.

"Flowers," Stevens said. "Call the whole thing two hundred and twenty-five. And it will probably be mostly you and me. All right?"

"No, it aint all right," the editor said. "But it don't look like I can help myself. By Jupiter," he said, "even if I could help myself, the novelty will be almost worth it. It will be the first time in my life I ever paid money for copy I had already promised before hand I won't print."

"Have already promised before hand you will not print," Stevens said. And during the remainder of that hot and now windless afternoon, while officials from the city hall, and justices of the peace and bailiffs come fifteen and twenty miles from the ends of the county, mounted the stairs to the empty office and called his name and cooled their heels a while and then went away and returned and sat again, fuming, Stevens passed from store to store and office to office about the square— merchant and clerk, proprietor and employee, doctor dentist lawyer and barber—with his set and rapid speech: "It's to bring a dead nigger home. It's for Miss Worsham. Never mind about a paper to sign: just give me a dollar. Or a half a dollar then. Or a quarter then."

And that night after supper he walked through the breathless and star-filled darkness to Miss Worsham's house on the edge of town and knocked on the paintless front door. Hamp Worsham admitted him—an old man, belly-bloated from the vegetables on which he and his wife and Miss Worsham all three mostly lived, with blurred old eyes and a fringe of white hair about the head and face of a Roman general.

"She expecting you," he said. "She say to kindly step up to the chamber."

"Is that where Aunt Mollie is?" Stevens said.

"We all dar," Worsham said.

So Stevens crossed the lamplit hall (he knew that the entire house was still lighted with oil lamps and there was no running water in it) and preceded the Negro up the clean, paintless stairs beside the faded wallpaper, and followed the old Negro along the hall and into the clean, spare bedroom with its unmistakable faint odor of old maidens. They were all there, as Worsham had said—his wife, a tremendous light-colored woman in a bright turban leaning in the door, Miss Worsham erect again on a hard straight chair, the old Negress sitting in the only rocking chair beside the hearth on

701

which even tonight a few ashes smoldered faintly.

She held a reed-stemmed clay pipe but she was not smoking it, the ash dead and white in the stained bowl; and actually looking at her for the first time, Stevens thought: *Good Lord, she's not as big as a ten-year-old child.* Then he sat too, so that the four of them—himself, Miss Worsham, the old Negress and her brother

10 —made a circle about the brick hearth on which the ancient symbol of human coherence and solidarity smoldered.

"He'll be home the day after tomorrow, Aunt Mollie," he said. The old Negress didn't even look at him; she never had looked at him.

"He dead," she said. "Pharaoh got him."

"Oh yes, Lord," Worsham said. "Pharaoh got him."

"Done sold my Benjamin," the old Negress

20 said. "Sold him in Egypt." She began to sway faintly back and forth in the chair.

"Oh yes, Lord," Worsham said.

"Hush," Miss Worsham said. "Hush, Hamp."

"I telephoned Mr Edmonds," Stevens said. "He will have everything ready when you get there."

"Roth Edmonds sold him," the old Negress said. She swayed back and forth in the chair. "Sold my Benjamin."

30 "Hush," Miss Worsham said. "Hush, Mollie. Hush now."

"No," Stevens said. "No he didn't Aunt Mollie. It wasn't Mr Edmonds. Mr Edmonds didn't—" *But she cant hear me,* he thought. She was not even looking at him. She never had looked at him.

"Sold my Benjamin," she said. "Sold him in Egypt."

"Sold him in Egypt," Worsham said.

40 "Roth Edmonds sold my Benjamin."

"Sold him to Pharaoh."

"Sold him to Pharaoh and now he dead."

"I'd better go," Stevens said. He rose quickly. Miss Worsham rose too, but he did not wait for her to precede him. He went down the hall fast, almost running; he did not even know whether she was following him or not. *Soon I will be outside,* he thought. *Then there will be air, space, breath.* Then he could hear her be-

50 hind him—the crisp, light, brisk yet unhurried feet as he had heard them descending the

stairs from his office, and beyond them the voices:

"Sold my Benjamin. Sold him in Egypt."

"Sold him in Egypt. Oh yes, Lord."

He descended the stairs, almost running. It was not far now; now he could smell and feel it: the breathing and simple dark, and now he could manner himself to pause and wait, turning at the door, watching Miss Worsham as she followed him to the door—the high, white, erect, old-time head approaching through the old-time lamplight. Now he could hear the third voice, which would be that of Hamp's wife—a true constant soprano which ran without words beneath the strophe and antistrophe of brother and sister:

"Sold him in Egypt and now he dead."

"Oh yes, Lord. Sold him in Egypt."

"Sold him in Egypt."

"And now he dead."

"Sold him to Pharaoh."

"And now he dead."

"I'm sorry," Stevens said. "I ask you to forgive me. I should have known. I shouldn't have come."

"It's all right," Miss Worsham said. "It's our grief."

And on the next bright hot day but one the hearse and the two cars were waiting when the southbound train came in. There were more than a dozen cars, but it was not until the train came in that Stevens and the editor began to notice the number of people, Negroes and whites both. Then, with the idle white men and youths and small boys and probably half a hundred Negroes, men and women too, watching quietly, the Negro undertaker's men lifted the gray-and-silver casket from the train and carried it to the hearse and snatched the wreaths and floral symbols of man's ultimate and inevitable end briskly out and slid the casket in and flung the flowers back and clapped-to the door.

Then, with Miss Worsham and the old Negress in Stevens' car with the driver he had hired and himself and the editor in the editor's, they followed the hearse as it swung into the long hill up from the station, going fast in a whining lower gear until it reached the crest, going pretty fast still but with an unctuous, an almost bishoplike purr until it slowed into the square, crossing it, circling the Confederate monument and the courthouse while the merchants and clerks and barbers and professional men who had given Stevens the dollars and half-dollars and quarters and the ones who had not, watched quietly from doors and upstairs windows, swinging then into the street which at the edge of town would become the country road leading to the destination seventeen miles away, already picking up speed again and followed still by the two cars containing the four people—the high-headed erect white woman, the old Negress, the designated paladin of justice and truth and right, the Heidelberg Ph.D.—in formal component complement to the Negro murderer's catafalque: the slain wolf.

When they reached the edge of town the hearse was going quite fast. Now they flashed past the metal sign which said Jefferson. Corporate Limit, and the pavement vanished, slanting away into another long hill, becoming gravel. Stevens reached over and cut the switch, so that the editor's car coasted, slowing as he began to brake it, the hearse and the other car drawing rapidly away now as though in flight, the light and unrained summer dust spurting from beneath the fleeing wheels; soon they were gone. The editor turned his car clumsily, grinding the gears, sawing and filling until it was back in the road facing town again.

Then he sat for a moment, his foot on the clutch.

"Do you know what she asked me this morning, back there at the station?" he said.

"Probably not," Stevens said.

"She said, 'Is you gonter put hit in de paper?'"

"What?"

"That's what I said," the editor said. "And she said it again: 'Is you gonter put hit in de paper? I wants hit all in de paper. All of hit.' And I wanted to say, 'If I should happen to know how he really died, do you want that in too?' And by Jupiter, if I had and if she had known what we know even, I believe she would have said yes. But I didn't say it. I just said, 'Why, you couldn't read it, Aunty.' And she said, 'Miss Belle will show me whar to look and I can look at hit. You put hit in de paper. All of hit.'"

"Oh," Stevens said. *Yes,* he thought. *It doesn't matter to her now. Since it had to be and she couldn't stop it, and now that it's all over and done and finished, she doesn't care how he died. She just wanted him home, but she wanted him to come home right. She wanted that casket and those flowers and the hearse and she wanted to ride through town behind it in a car.* "Come on," he said. "Let's get back to town. I haven't seen my desk in two days."

JAMES T. FARRELL

Because he has shown conclusively that he is potentially a distinguished writer of fiction in the naturalistic vein, excelling in a field which has never been a favorite among the English-speaking peoples, James Thomas Farrell continues to be one of the most controversial figures in contemporary letters. He was born in Chicago, January 27, 1904, attended St. Cyril's High School and De Paul Academy in that city, and matriculated at the University of Chicago, although he did not complete work for a degree. Like John Steinbeck (p. 713), he then moved about from one occupation to another, in Chicago and New York—according to his own account, he wrapped shoes in a chain shoe store, served as clerk in an express office, toiled as an attendant in a filling station, worked as salesman for a chain cigar company, acted as a promotional agent for a publishing company, and had his fill of drudging for an undertaker. Much of his experience in these various trades will account for the remarkable verisimilitude of his writing.

In 1932, with the publication of *Young*

Lonigan, Farrell attracted nation-wide attention. This characteristic novel was followed by two others, *The Young Manhood of Studs Lonigan* (1934) and *Judgment Day* (1935); the three went to comprise the Studs Lonigan trilogy, which still remains the most solid accomplishment to be entered to Farrell's credit. It is the somber, fearless, and powerful account of an unsympathetic but pathetically aspiring child of the Irish city bourgeoisie in Chicago. When Studs Lonigan, still a young man, dies of pneumonia, the implication in Farrell's novel is clear that "cut is the branch that might have grown full straight." But Studs is never strong enough to overcome his sordid, brutal, cheap, ignorant, bigoted, and parochial environment.

Farrell's plans, however, envisage far more than a Studs Lonigan. He tells us that he has in mind more than a score of works—consisting of short stories, novels, and plays—which taken together, and treating of a loosely interrelated group of people from the same district of Chicago, will exhibit "a sense of American life as I have seen it, as I have imagined it and as I have reflected upon and evaluated it." One group of novels, associated in a multiple panel like the Studs Lonigan trilogy, includes *No Star Is Lost* (1938), *A World I Never Made* (1939), and *Father and Son* (1940). The protagonist in these novels is Danny O'Neill, a boy with no better family background than that of Studs Lonigan, but with the ideals, the courage, and the energy to make a successful break with his environment and to win out over his social handicaps. We are to assume that this second group of novels, not yet complete, is more distinctly autobiographical than the Studs Lonigan trilogy. In both groups, however, there are certain well-patterned types of lower middle-class Americans. There are the pimps, the wastrels, the hoodlums, and the prostitutes of the American underworld; there are the quarrelsome, bickering, and uncomprehending relatives, limited in outlook or weak in moral stamina or downright vicious, who act as the true adversaries of Studs Lonigan and Danny O'Neill. There is also the Catholic Church, which apparently is to Farrell perhaps the greatest handicap of all to overcome.

Subsidiary stories or novels such as *Gas House McGinty* (1935), *Calico Shoes and Other Stories* (1937), *Guillotine Party and Other Stories* (1935), *Ellen Rogers* (1941), and *$1,000 a Week and Other Stories* (1942), stress the same theme of social frustration as the novels do; but they are neither so significant nor so powerful as the works already mentioned. Farrell's talents operate more successfully in the novel than in the short story.

The author's progress, however, has not been so rapid as his early admirers had hoped. His possibilities remain great, of course, because of his remarkable observation and the ability to transfer this observation effectively to paper, because of his masterfully realistic dialogue and the fundamental strength and sinew of his social concepts and his documentation. But Farrell is repetitious; he piles up far more detail than is necessary; he is still in such violent protest against the limitations of the society which he is painting that he cannot speak well for the other side of life and living (granted always that many of his targets deserve to be attacked). In short, like nearly all naturalists in fiction, he overstates his case. He seems to be somewhat in need of a change of scene and of a new set of characters which will be characters rather than types, however easily recognizable those types may be. *The Road Between* (1949) shows that Farrell is still in search of a new philosophy of life.

Nevertheless, Farrell manages to mask his anger with a deceptively objective style; and his indictments are not easily to be dismissed. To some he must appear as a Fifth Columnist, boring from within; to others he must seem a courageous tilting knight; to still others he is only a sensational filth-monger. Yet any sober reader will see that his effects are revolting rather than pornographic. And many of the things he has said needed to be said.

Reverend Father Gilhooley

I

*D*omine, non sum dignis. . . .

Albert Schaeffer, from the sixth grade, sounded the sanctuary bell, its echoes knelling through the hush of Saint Patrick's barn-like church. Heads lowered in pews, and closed fists beat against suddenly contrite breasts. Low, sweet organ tones flowed, and Miss Molly O'Callaghan sang.

Agnus Dei, qui tollis peccata mundi,
Agnus Dei. . . .

Communicants slowly and solemnly marched to the altar rail, heads bent, lips forming prayers, hands palmed together in stiff prayerfulness. Father Gilhooley, the corpulent, ruddy-faced, bald, gray-fringed pastor, choked his Latin, mumbled. Miss O'Callaghan's voice lifted, evoking and spreading through the church a spirit of murmuring contrition, a deep and feelingful Catholic humility.

Oh, Lord, I am not worthy
That Thou shouldst come to me,
But speak the words of comfort
And my spirit healed shall be.

Father Gilhooley descended from the altar carrying the golden chalice. His Irish blood, plunged with pride, pride in his ascent to the priesthood from his lowly Irish peasant origins, pride in his power to change flour and water into the Real Presence and to carry it comfortingly to penitents and sorely troubled sinners.

Oh, Lord, I am not worthy. . . .

The cassocked acolyte shoved the silver communion plate under the fat chin of the first communicant. The priest extracted a wafer of unleavened bread with his consecrated fingers, crossed it in the air, and placed it on the outthrust tongue, muttering simultaneously:

Corpus Domini nostri Jesu Christi custodiat animam tuam in vitam aeternam.

Twenty-year-old Peggy Collins knelt at the altar rail, her dark eyes closed, her pert round face lifted, her tongue stuck out. She waited, praying please to God and the Blessed Virgin to guide her and aid her and give her the grace and courage to see and to do what was right in the eyes of Heaven. The priest laid the host on her tongue and swept along.

Corpus Domini nostri Jesu Christi custodiat animam tuam in vitam aeternam.

Oh, Lord, I am not worthy. . . .

II

"Gee, I'll have to hurry. I'm going to be late at the office," Peggy Collins said, entering the kitchen, home from the eight o'clock mass.

"Well, the food is here. You can make your own breakfast and not be expecting me to be waiting on you hand and foot," Mrs. Collins, a beefy and coarse-faced woman, said, frowning as she talked.

Peggy turned on the gas under the coffeepot.

"When you're my age, I hope you won't be expected to slave for ungrateful children."

"Oh, Mother, please, now! I've just come from receiving Holy Communion. Please let's not quarrel!"

"And little good it'll do you!"

"Why, Mother!" Peggy exclaimed, turning toward her mother with a pained expression.

"Don't talk to me, you that would disgrace me in the eyes of the parish, and before a holy man, a breathing saint of God like Father Gilhooley. Well, you mark my words. There's never the day's luck that will shine on you and yours. I only hope that the day will come when your children won't turn their backs on you the way mine have on me," the mother slobbered.

"Oh, Mother, let's not be silly!"

"So, it's silly I am! She with her airs and her primping and powdering and cooing and billing for a black devil of a Protestant. So, it's silly I am!"

Peggy poured coffee, buttered a slice of white bread, and sat down at the kitchen table.

"Marry a black devil out of Hell! A Protestant!" the mother exclaimed sarcastically, standing over Peggy with her hands on her hefty hips. "Setting yourself against the wishes of one of God's noble men. Disgracing your home and your hard-working father, and me, your mother, who bore you, and washed your diapers, and raised you."

"I'm not doing anything wrong, and you can't talk to me like that! I'm not a child or a baby any more," Peggy said, struggling to check a flow of tears.

"Why, the priest of God won't even marry you. He knows your ilk. Ah, the day will come! The day will come when you'll regret what you're doing to your poor mother. And when it does, I only hope that your heart does not ache as my poor heart aches, and that the curse of God will not be put on your soul."

Mrs. Collins followed Peggy to her bedroom and to the front door.

"Go, you whore, and never come back for all that I may care!"

Peggy slammed the door and went down the stairs sobbing.

III

"Mary, God has given us another spring day," Father Gilhooley floridly said as he expanded comfortably in a chair. His housekeeper set an ample breakfast on the table before him, and he said Grace before eating heartily. As he slowly stirred his coffee, Mary ushered in a boy of about twelve who stood by the entrance, blushing and breathless with awe.

"What's the trouble, son?"

"Father . . . can . . . can you give me Holy Communion?" the boy asked.

"But you know, son, mass is at eight o'clock."

With several stuttering lapses, the boy exclaimed that he was making the nine first Fridays for a very special intention, and this morning the alarm clock had not worked, so he hadn't woke up until around eight-twenty. He'd run all the way to church, but had arrived after Holy Communion. He was terribly worried for fear that his Fridays be broken, and he looked pleadingly at the priest.

Father Gilhooley answered that there were no more hosts and he couldn't consecrate any because he had already said mass.

"Father, does a spiritual communion count?" the boy said with timid hope, fumbling with his cap as he spoke. "When I was running to church, all the way, I tried to think of God and holy things, and keep my mind on them and imagine that I was receiving Holy Communion."

Beaming broadly, the priest reassured the boy, instructing him to receive Holy Communion on the following morning. He called the lad to him, patted his head, and gave him a nickel.

"God bless you, son!" the priest said as the boy left.

Slowly drinking his coffee, a glow of gratification spread through the pastor. For had not this small incident been another demonstration of the power of God and the Church to enflame young hearts with piety? And he and his assistants and the good sisters teaching in the parish schools, they were all doing their work well in the Master's vineyard. The seeds of faith planted in that lad's heart would sprout forth a thousandfold in rich spiritual fruits lovely to the sight of God Almighty. His name was Colahan, and his father ran a drug store at Sixty-first and Vernon. A good family. Mr. Colahan was a good man and he had contributed fifty dollars to last Sunday's Easter Collection. And the lad was just the type that God would call to His holy altar. He was reminded, too, that he should instruct the sisters to talk on vocations to the graduating class until the end of the school term in June. And he would deliver a sermon on the subject one of these Sundays. Also, Father Donegan and Father Marcel could go over to the classrooms. For one of his few disappointments at Saint Patrick's was that not one of its sons from the parish school had yet been ordained. He believed that the parish school should be sending two or three boys, at least, from each graduating class to Quigley Seminary to start studying for the priesthood. This was an aim that required cooperation and concentration.

After breakfast, he read his morning mail in his small office. Several letters from needy parishioners requesting funds were marked off for Father Donegan's attention, and he would refer them to a Catholic charity organization. He opened a vituperative letter from an anti-Catholic, unsigned, and he cast it in his waste basket with the word *bigot*. He knew that he was a minister of God's true Church, and that Christ Himself had built the Church upon the rock of Peter, promising that the gates of Hell would not prevail against it. Such missives could not shake him. His face suddenly broke into a beaming smile as he picked up several letters containing delayed donations to the Easter Collection. But two were five-dollar checks from families which could have well afforded at least twenty-five. Another was from a politician giving fifty dollars when twice that amount would not have hurt him. His flock was made up of people who were good and generous, but some of them required to be more strongly impressed with a sense of their duty to contribute to the support of their pastor. And he would have to remember that when he spoke on the next regular collection. That reminded him that he ought soon again to be delivering that sermon of his: *Mother Church; Why She Is the Only True One.* It was one of his best sermons. And since he had three shelves of the works of Longfellow, Shakespeare, and the other great literary masters, he would have to be looking through them to find a few apt quotations for his sermons. No harm in making them more erudite.

His mail read, he seated himself in a deep and comfortable chair, and discovered, as usual, that the morning paper was full of dismaying items. Ah, the age was sinful and pagan. Prohibition and bootleggers and gangsters, and the younger generation running wild, promiscuous dances, assaults on women, people going blind and dying in the streets from moonshine . . . ah, yes, a sinful and pagan age. Still, he knew that the people of his flock were much better Catholics than those in many a parish. And why? He was not immodest, no, he was only recognizing a true fact when he thought that it was his own example before them, his teaching and guidance in sermons and the confessional. He knew, too, that he was a much more conscientious shepherd than Kiley from Saint Rose's church. And Kiley wouldn't be a Monsignor today if he hadn't shown off and put on airs. Well, no one could accuse Father Gilhooley of advancing himself by showing off and playing politics.

But that Collins girl? She still seemed determined to marry that Protestant scamp after all his dissuasion, after he had talked to her parents, explained to her, given counsel that not only was the fruit of his own long experience but also of the Church's two thousand years of wisdom. And she, only a chit of a thing. Well, they had come from Kiley's parish. What else could he expect? And her whole family had given only five dollars to the Easter Collection. If Kiley paid less attention to the Cathedral on the north side, and more to his own people, and if her parents had raised the girl properly, instilling in her respect for authority and her elders, and a proper fear of the Almighty, she wouldn't be crossing him now to the endangerment of her immortal soul. Well, he had told her, and he would not permit the marriage. It was a bad business. Ah, a bad business.

He read his office for the day, and then walked to look out the window with a drifting glance. Below him was the large rectangular-shaped parish yard. It was to the right of the church building and ringed with an iron picket fence, a half block of land alive with spring greenness. Soon the building on this ground would be started. Soon men would be digging, preparing to lay the foundation for one of the most beautiful churches in the whole city of Chicago. With pride and gratification, he continued to stand by his window, his hands in his trouser pockets beneath his cassock, his dream bursting like a rocket in his mind. When he had come to this parish in 1900 there had been nothing, only a handful of the faithful, and he had celebrated his first mass on a winter Sunday morning in a vacant and chilly store on Sixty-first Street. This parish, it was the work of his own hand, and his own heart, and his own mind, and his own soul, and his own faith, the dedication of his life, which he had given to God. And he had been happy here in this vineyard of the Master. Now his greatest happiness and triumph lay ahead of him. He prayed God to permit him to witness it. But God would. God had preserved his health to this date. Ah, yes, he had built up the present parish and school, and now it was free of debt. Saint Patrick's was one of the few parishes in the city totally free of debt. Of that he was certain. And with the slowly accumulating sinking fund he had established for the new church, and the drive for funds that he was now almost ready to launch, he would build an edifying house of the Lord, a monument to stand in the Creator's honor long after, years and years after, he would have returned to the dust from whence he had come. This dream and this hope, it was his life, his life's blood, and the mere contemplation of it intoxicated him with a sweet elation and pleasure. It would be a church second to none, the envy of pastors throughout the diocese, a temple and a house of beauty and worship that would make the Cardinal Archbishop take notice of him. Perhaps then and on the merits of his work he would be made . . . Monsignor Gilhooley. He could visualize himself in this parish, in the new church which would draw rich and well-to-do people to the neighborhood. He could imagine himself in the rear of the church at late Sunday masses when the people would file out, inspired after the mass and by the beauty of the church, going home to happy dinners with the word and fear of God in their hearts, nodding and smiling to him as they left. Ah!

The thought of that chit of a Collins girl again broke upon him. She, only eighteen years old, and to keep coming back at him, wasting his time with her begging and pleading after he had given her his final word. That chit of a girl! Well, he would not sanction the marriage to a Protestant. But now he had lost, beyond recapturing, that splendid vision he had just experienced. He turned from the window.

IV

"Gee, Kid, you look fagged out. Why are you so sad?" Madge said to Peggy as they sat munching chicken-salad sandwiches and sipping malted milks for lunch in a crowded and noisy Loop ice-cream parlor.

"I'm terribly worried, Madge."

"I hope it's not your darling Graham again."

"It's serious. Graham's a dear. I adore him. But it's just the same awful trouble. It makes me feel just awful. I saw Father Gilhooley with my mother again last night, and he still refuses to let us get married. And my mother sides with him, too, and we had such a terrible fight this morning. I left the house with the jitters, and cried halfway downtown on the elevated train."

"You're taking it too seriously, Collins. I'd like to see anybody pull that kind of a trick on me! I'd just like to see them! Come on, Kid, snap out of it. Tell them you've got your own life to live, and if they don't like the way you live it, they can lump it."

"But Madge, dear, you know if you're not married in the church it's not marriage at all, and then it will be living in mortal sin. He won't publish the banns and marry us, and my mother keeps throwing fits. Gee, Kid, I'm going nearly crazy."

"You poor kid! Now don't cry."

"I can't help it. I love Graham. And he's so sweet and kind to me. If I had to give him up, I don't know what I'd do. I'd just go and throw myself in the lake, I guess, because then I wouldn't care about anything any more."

"Listen, Kiddo, don't pay any attention to them. Take my advice, dearie, and you and Graham just step down to the City Hall, and then let them jaw their ears off. God isn't a school teacher or a fierce old giant, and He isn't going to go punishing people just because they love each other and are honest about it. You and Graham just go away and get married. It isn't hocus pocus that some old fool says that counts and makes you married. It's what you and Graham feel inside your hearts."

"Madge, darling, you're not a Catholic, and you just don't understand."

"Well, if that's what it means to be a Catholic, I'm glad I'm not one."

"Madge, please, don't say that!"

Madge shrugged her shoulders in a gesture of resignation.

"Of course, Peg, it isn't my business, but honestly, I can't understand why you let an old fossil of a priest who doesn't know what it's all about go sticking his nose in your business the way you do."

"But if we're not married in the church, it'll be living in sin."

"Oh, don't be a fool, Peg!"

V

The pastor partook of a sufficient luncheon with Father Donegan, the wiry, thin, energetic blond assistant pastor who was in his early thirties. After suggesting to his assistant that they should start a drive to turn the minds of boys and girls in the school to the subject of vocations, Father Gilhooley mentioned the Collins girl. Father Donegan, speaking with careful reserve, suggested that the only course of action, he feared, was to publish the banns and marry the couple.

"Pat, I shall not!" Father Gilhooley said with stern stubbornness, meaning will for shall.

"Father, you know, naturally, that I agree with you in toto on the question of mixed marriages. But in this case, the girl being as set and as determined as she is, I think that marriage is the lesser of the two evils involved."

"Pat, it's a bad business. What she needs is for her mother to give her a hiding that will drive some sense into that flighty little head of hers," the pastor said as a prelude to filling his mouth with steak until his cheeks bulged. Chewing, he added, "I shall not permit it!"

Father Donegan knew the uselessness of reply. He recalled with silent and frustrated anger two fairly recent run-ins he had had with Father Gilhooley. He had tried to persuade him that instead of preaching sermons and asking for contributions repeatedly, they might raise money for the new church by holding bazaars that would also serve the added purpose of giving the parishioners a good time and welding them together socially. And Father Gilhooley had disapproved because the raffles held at bazaars constituted, in his mind, gambling, and he feared demoralizing the parish and setting a bad example for the young. Father Donegan had tried, also, to convince the pastor that they should organize a parish young people's society and conduct clean dances in the parish auditorium. But the auditorium was on consecrated ground, so Father Gilhooley had refused.

Now Father Donegan continued eating. Father Gilhooley was in authority. And the assistant was living in his own agony of doubts and temptations. He was beginning to see that the priesthood was the wrong place for him. The cancer of doubt, doubt even of the existence of the very God he served, was poisoning him almost to madness. He was drinking more and more, and he would not always be able to hide it. Sooner or later he would face a showdown. He would even, possibly, have to face the choice of a future of hypocrisy or else the road of an unfrocked priest, marked and scarred and defamed on every side, and almost totally unfitted for any worldly occupation. And the issue raised by the Collins girl only strengthened his doubts, adding one more instance to the contradictions between the raw life of emotions and passions and sins and waywardness poured into his ears in the confessional, and the dogmatization of life in the formal philosophy of the Church. He looked almost enviously at Father Gilhooley, who was so corpulently contented, the fires of the flesh now dead embers, with gluttony and eating his only sin. Did the complacency on that blown ruddy face extend clean through to the man's soul? Was it sainthood or a barricade of fat around his spirit? Anyway, he had not the energy to try convincing his pastor. He was drained by his own internal struggles. His will was paralyzed.

Quickly finishing his luncheon, he left on the pretext of working over next Sunday's sermon.

VI

At three-thirty, Father Gilhooley left the parish house for his afternoon stroll. Walking, he gazed at the fenced-in grounds where he would build his new church. In a few years now, when there would be a Eucharistic Congress in Chicago, his beautiful new house of worship would be an honor to God, a credit to himself, a tribute to the faith he served. It would be a mark of such beauty that thousands of visitors would come to behold its wonders. Visiting clergymen, bishops, perhaps even the Papal Delegate, would view it, and after that he would take a trip to the old country, and he might go, too, as a Monsignor. He stepped into his church and thought, as if in fresh discovery, that it was very rapidly becoming increasingly inadequate for the needs of the parish. His new church would make the neighborhood grow, attracting to it the best types of well-to-do Catholics. It would be a rich parish. And Monsignor Gilhooley, wouldn't he then outshine Kiley!

As he stood thus in the rear of his church, his dreams and his visions alive within him, he saw a small boy leave a pew, hastily genuflect without touching his knee to the flooring, bless himself at the holy water font with his left hand, and bound through the swinging doors. Father Gilhooley quickly followed and called the lad back.

"Good afternoon, Father," the boy timidly muttered, retracing his steps up the church stairs.

Answering the priest's questions, the boy said that he was William Markham in the sixth grade of the parish school. Father Gilhooley promptly recalled that the only contribution from a Markham to the Easter Collection had been two dollars.

"Did Sister ever teach you how to bless yourself?" the priest sternly asked.

"Yes, Father."

He ordered the boy to demonstrate. William slowly and correctly made the sign of the cross. Father Gilhooley told him that he should always bless himself with his right hand, and

709

when he genuflected in the presence of the Blessed Sacrament his knee should touch the floor.

The pastor stopped in at Strunsky's drug store for a cigar. The pinched druggist, aware that Father Gilhooley's displeasure could decrease his business, obsequiously nodded agreement to the priest's platitudes, and in parting they agreed on the weather. Several passing laborers and school boys tipped their hats and caps to him, and he acknowledged the greeting with a dignified nod. Women parishioners greeted him with smiles and salutations which could have been no more humble had he been one of the Twelve Apostles. He paused to discuss the weather with the attractive and smartly dressed Mrs. Freeman. Her husband, a manufacturer of tennis rackets, had contributed a hundred dollars to the Easter Collection. Patting her youngster's head, he told her what a fine healthy child she had. She said she hoped it would grow up to be as good a man and a priest as the one who had baptized him. Beaming over the compliment, Father Gilhooley said that he knew with the good home influences in which the child was being reared, he was certain the baby would develop and one day be a tribute both to its parents and to Saint Patrick's parish. She thanked him, and they parted. A black-shawled, hunched little Irish woman with a shrivelled face almost bent her back in bowing to him. Superstitious admiration and reverence brought life, even freshness, into her small, suspicious eyes. She again humbly bowed, and mumbled, a foreign phrase learned by rote.

"Ga lob Jasus Christe."

The homage paid to him as a man of God was warming, gratifying. This peasant woman, with her simple faith and humility, stirred in him memories of his own Irish mother. Ah, that she were alive to see her son today. He prided himself his ascent from lowly origins, his race. Had not the Irish preserved the faith in the face of oppression? And did not the Church owe a great credit to those simple Irish mothers who had been the backbone of Catholicism in Ireland, the women out of whose wombs heroic and sainted priests had come? If only the young chits of girls these days

would learn the great simple lessons of truth from their Irish mothers and grandmothers! Chits of girls like the Collins one, with her powder and lipstick, and her thinking she loved a Protestant.

He called the woman grandmother, said that it was a fine day, and told her how well and how young she looked. Passing on, his good humor lushly expanded, and again he grew proud in the dignity of his office. He walked like a great man. Only again the recollection of that Collins girl threatening to cross him bobbed annoyingly in his mind, and his cheeks flushed from anger.

I'll permit none of it! he vowed to himself.

Strolling back with an afternoon paper under his arm, he met Father Georgiss, the pastor of Saint Sofia's, the Greek Catholic Church across from Saint Patrick's. Father Georgiss was a bearded, dark-browed man who always looked at Father Gilhooley with a roguish and enigmatic twinkle in his eyes. Scholarly, urbane, skeptical, even cosmopolitan alongside of the Roman Catholic priest, he usually managed to impress an uneasiness, even a sense of inferiority, upon Father Gilhooley. Father Georgiss' church was larger and more impressive than Saint Patrick's, but seeing him, Father Gilhooley insisted to himself that it wasn't beautiful. Too Oriental. Too sensuous. The two clergymen spoke to each other with excessive politeness, and Father Gilhooley assuaged his falling pride by casually remarking that very soon now he would let out the contracts and begin operations on his church. Father Georgiss congratulated him, but again there was that disconcerting look in his eyes. He accepted Father Gilhooley's invitation to drop over some evening for a chat. He said that he was busy these days pursuing his studies of Byzantine civilization. It was a great civilization, and it had saved Christianity for centuries from the Turks, and Father Gilhooley should read of it. Father Gilhooley said he would like to have Father Georgiss tell him of it, thinking silently that with all this Greek priest's reading of history he could not see the truth and the simple necessity of the dogma of Papal infallibility. They parted politely, agreeing that God had given them splendid weather.

VII

Peggy sat on the steps before the box-like yellow apartment building on Prairie Avenue where the Collins family lived. She studiously looked into her purse mirror, and dabbed her face to mask the evidence that she had been crying. She hated her mother. That was an awful thought. But she didn't care! She didn't. She hated her! She did! And it was all so silly. This business of Catholics and Protestants. Graham's little finger was worth more than any number of Catholic boys she knew. And he was good and decent. Good to her. And she didn't care. She loved him. He had such nice eyes, she dreamed about his eyes, and his lips, and she was always thinking she saw him on the street. She loved him. She wanted to love him with all of herself forever, and forever, and her mother and Father Gilhooley were so silly about it. They must have never been in love. Because she knew that she couldn't help herself, and she would love Graham even if her soul would burn for all eternity in Hell. And God! He couldn't be like Father Gilhooley and want her to give up Graham. And the way her mother had cut up at the supper table! So silly. Oh, she just wanted to be away from it all and to be alone with her Graham.

And she was going to see Father Gilhooley and tell him he would just have to marry them. And again tears came to her eyes. Because maybe it was too late now. Maybe religion had already been thrown between them like some terrible shadow, and gee, she was afraid that they could never be happy together. She couldn't give him up, and she didn't want to, and . . . she saw him swinging along the street, so tall, so handsome. She tried to dry her tears.

VIII

Father Gilhooley was contented, at peace with himself, at peace with the world, at peace with his God, after his hearty supper. When his sense of almost somnolent well-being was disturbed by Mary who told him that that Collins girl was back again, he frowned. He said, sternly, that he wouldn't see her, and followed his housekeeper into the small reception room where Peggy and Graham waited.

"Good evening, Father!" Peggy said meekly and with respect.

"Good evening, Father!" Graham said, restrained.

"Good evening, my girl! Good evening, sir! Be seated!" Father Gilhooley curtly said.

"Father . . ." Peggy began in a hesitant manner.

"I am a very busy man. I do not see, for the life of me, why you return to waste my time after I have told you definitely and finally that I cannot permit such a marriage in my parish."

"But, Father, what can we do? We can't get married in another parish," Peggy said, despair creeping into her voice.

"I have already explained my reasons fully to both of you. I have nothing personally against this young man, Mr. . . . ah . . ."

"McIntosh," Peggy volunteered.

"Mr. McIntosh, my decision is not personal and directed against you. I am opposed to mixed marriages on principle and on reflection after long years of experience as a clergyman. I have learned that oil and water do not mix. And this applies to the marriage of persons of different religions. I have witnessed the irreparable evil and the ruination of souls that results from mixed marriages. This I have already explained to you young people. If I sanction this marriage, others will come, and you two will set a bad example for all the young people of my parish. I am not the kind of a person who waits to lock his stable door after the horse has been stolen."

"But, Father, suppose I had been insincere and pretended to be converted. Then you could not have objected to our marriage. Because I have chosen not to be a hypocrite you refuse to let us be married in your church," Graham said, controlling his voice, but the expression in his eyes was hard, as if they were knifing the priest.

"Sir, that is a matter for your own conscience. My action is impersonal, and I am thinking not simply of your temporal happiness, but of the soul of this girl which has been placed in my care, since I happen to be her pastor, and thus her spiritual guardian. And also, I am thinking of the souls of many more young people like her in my parish. I am older than you two people, and I am drawing on long experience, and the wisdom of my church through long years and centuries of history when I speak. You two are young, and you are letting yourselves be blinded by what you call love. I am older than you, and I see more. I see the danger to this girl's immortal soul, and to the souls of any offspring you might have."

"But, Father, Graham, Mr. McIntosh, is perfectly willing to let our children be raised Catholic, and he will not interfere with my fulfilling my religious obligations," Peggy said, blushing.

"My dear girl, a house divided against itself will fall. A home cannot be built unless there is sympathy and understanding erected on the religion of God. There cannot be sympathy unless both parties see eye to eye on religion, because religion is the foundation stone of the Catholic home."

"But Father, we love each other!" Peggy exclaimed impulsively, almost despairingly, and Graham glanced at her with raised eyebrows, pained.

"You young people take my advice. Forget this marriage, and stay away from each other for six months. Then come back to see me and see if I am not right. Mixed marriages are the principal cause of the pagan evil of divorce which spreads through the world these days like a cancer, and in so many cases it paves a sure road to Hell. I have given my decision, my dear girl, because I am your pastor, responsible to Almighty God for your soul."

"But Father. . . ." Peggy exclaimed, startled, ready to cry.

"Father, you can't stop us!" Graham said, his face white, set.

"There is nothing further for me to say. Good evening!" Father Gilhooley said, arising and leaving the room with a swish of his cassock.

IX

From a window he saw them pass slowly, arm in arm, under a lamplight, and move on, their figures growing vague in the spring dusk. His blood rose. He frowned, reassuring himself that he was right, and acting wisely for the best interests of both of them and in accordance with the dictates and spirit of God and of God's True Church. And in his whole time as a pastor at Saint Patrick's no one had ever crossed him as this chit of a girl had.

I'll have none of it, he told himself in rising fury.

His anger cooled. You could take a horse to water, but you couldn't make him drink. He had done his best to explain and guide the girl, and under the circumstances he was forced to recognize that marriage was the lesser evil. But he felt, sure as the summer followed the spring, certain as the night succeeded the day, that the girl was paving the road to her own perdition. He called Father Donegan and instructed him to telephone the girl in the morning and arrange all the details. But he would not perform the marriage as the girl had requested when she had first come to him.

He returned to the window. They were gone somewhere with their love and their hugging and kissing. The spring night now was quilted and shadowed the yard, and he could hear voices and street sounds through the opened window. He thought again of how gray towers would rise above this quiet and darkened grass, piercing the blue heavens of God on nights like this one. The gray towers of his magnificent church, with vaulted nave, marble pillars, a grand organ, a marble altar imported from Italy, stained glass windows, hand-carved woodwork, a marble pulpit from which he would deliver the first sermon to be preached in the new church, packed with faithful parishioners for the first mass. He could see how the edifice, in stone and steel and wood and marble, would stand in beauty and inspiration to goodness and the doing of God's holy Will amongst his flock . . . and it would make him Monsignor Gilhooley.

But that chit of a girl! Suddenly he enjoyed the realization that she was making for herself a fiery bed in the eternal flames of Hell. A slip of a girl crossing him who might some day even be . . . Bishop Gilhooley.

He turned from the window, the excitement of his dream ebbing in his mind. And for the first time in his long pastorhood he knew that he had been . . . defeated.

JOHN STEINBECK

John Steinbeck is California born and has been associated primarily with the civilization of the California valleys and bays. His experience has been varied, imparting to his writings a range of treatment which has made it difficult to appraise his social, political, or economic views. Born in Salinas in 1902 and educated in local schools and at Stanford University, he has been by turns a newspaper reporter, a painter, a chemist, a caretaker on a rich man's estate, a surveyor, and a fruit-picker. Out of these dissimilar occupations he has acquired a rich background, which his facility of style and innate sense of narrative have translated into arresting writing.

Steinbeck's first published novel, *Cup of Gold*, appeared in 1929. In addition to numerous short stories, he has produced several novels, four of which have brought about a certain amount of controversy. *Tortilla Flat* (1935) is a homey, comfortable, somewhat sentimental story of the problems of life confronting a group of *paisanos* in California; *Of Mice and Men* (1937) is the pathetic story of two men—one a feeble-minded giant and the other a smart, normal young man with the romantic desire to settle down on a little farm—whose dream of a friendly participation in this farm is shattered when the feeble-minded Lennie accidentally kills a woman; *The Grapes of Wrath* (1939), by common consent Steinbeck's masterpiece, is the saga of the Joad family of Oklahoma, who migrate from the dust-bowl to find work among the fruit-pickers of California, only to meet a hostile reception from those already established in the work in California; and *The Moon Is Down* (1942), a tale of the Norwegians' warfare against the occupying Germans. His more recent books, such as *Cannery Row* (1944), *The Wayward Bus* (1947), and *The Pearl* (1948), indicate a return to primitivism and an abandonment of the social criticism implicit in such earlier works as *In Dubious Battle* (1936) and *The Grapes of Wrath*.

Steinbeck, for all his surface realism, is essentially a romantic writer, in the particular sense that he possesses a deep humanitarianism which is instinctive rather than rational, a mystic kind of religious prompting, and a primary sympathy for the underdog. All these easily recognizable qualities he clothes in a straightforward prose style, often somewhat meretricious, but generally sincere and frequently eloquent. In his longer works, which, however, are likely to be his chief monuments, he is successful at characterization but not so successful at the handling of plot, because he relies too heavily upon melodrama. His use of dialogue is realistic enough, but occasionally there is about it an artificial kind of toughness. All things considered, however, he has been a stimulating writer in the literature of the 1930's, for the attention he has drawn to the dubious fortunes of the worker if for nothing else.

The Chrysanthemums

THE HIGH gray-flannel fog of winter closed off the Salinas Valley from the sky and from all the rest of the world. On every side it sat like a lid on the mountains and made of the great valley a closed pot. On the broad, level land floor the gang plows bit deep and left the black earth shining like metal where the shares had cut. On the foothill ranches across the Salinas River, the yellow stubble fields seemed to be bathed in pale cold sun- 10 shine, but there was no sunshine in the valley now in December. The thick willow scrub along the river flamed with sharp and positive yellow leaves.

It was a time of quiet and of waiting. The air was cold and tender. A light wind blew up from the southwest so that the farmers were mildly hopeful of a good rain before long; but fog and rain do not go together.

Across the river, on Henry Allen's foothill ranch, there was little work to be done, for the hay was cut and stored and the orchards were plowed up to receive the rain deeply when it should come. The cattle on the higher slopes were becoming shaggy and rough-coated.

Elisa Allen, working in her flower garden, looked down across the yard and saw Henry, her husband, talking to two men in business suits. The three of them stood by the tractor shed, each man with one foot on the side of the little Fordson. They smoked cigarettes and studied the machine as they talked.

Elisa watched them for a moment and then went back to her work. She was thirty-five. Her face was lean and strong and her eyes were as clear as water. Her figure looked blocked and heavy in her gardening costume, a man's black hat pulled low down over her eyes, clodhopper shoes, a figured print dress almost completely covered by a big corduroy apron with four big pockets to hold the snips, the trowel and scratcher, the seeds and the knife she worked with. She wore heavy leather gloves to protect her hands while she worked.

She was cutting down the old year's chrysanthemum stalks with a pair of short and powerful scissors. She looked down toward the men by the tractor shed now and then. Her face was eager and mature and handsome; even her work with the scissors was over-eager, over-powerful. The chrysanthemum stems seemed too small and easy for her energy.

She brushed a cloud of hair out of her eyes with the back of her glove, and left a smudge of earth on her cheek in doing it. Behind her stood the neat white farm house with red geraniums close-banked around it as high as the windows. It was a hard-swept looking little house, with hard-polished windows, and a clean mud-mat on the front steps.

Elisa cast another glance toward the tractor shed. The strangers were getting into their Ford coupe. She took off a glove and put her strong fingers down into the forest of new green chrysanthemum sprouts that were growing around the old roots. She spread the leaves and looked down among the close-growing stems. No aphids were there, no sowbugs or snails or cutworms. Her terrier fingers destroyed such pests before they could get started.

Elisa started at the sound of her husband's voice. He had come near quietly, and he leaned over the wire fence that protected her flower garden from cattle and dogs and chickens.

"At it again," he said. "You've got a strong new crop coming."

Elisa straightened her back and pulled on the gardening glove again. "Yes. They'll be strong this coming year." In her tone and on her face there was a little smugness.

"You've got a gift with things," Henry observed. "Some of those yellow chrysanthemums you had this year were ten inches across. I wish you'd work out in the orchard and raise some apples that big."

Her eyes sharpened. "Maybe I could do it, too. I've a gift with things, all right. My mother had it. She could stick anything in the ground and make it grow. She said it was having planters' hands that knew how to do it."

"Well, it sure works with flowers," he said.

"Henry, who were those men you were talking to?"

"Why, sure, that's what I came to tell you. They were from the Western Meat Company. I sold those thirty head of three-year-old steers. Got nearly my own price, too."

"Good," she said. "Good for you."

"And I thought," he continued, "I thought how it's Saturday afternoon, and we might go into Salinas for dinner at a restaurant, and then to a picture show—to celebrate, you see."

"Good," she repeated. "Oh, yes. That will be good."

Henry put on his joking tone. "There's fights tonight. How'd you like to go to the fights?"

"Oh, no," she said breathlessly. "No, I wouldn't like fights."

"Just fooling, Elisa. We'll go to a movie. Let's see. It's two now. I'm going to take Scotty and bring down those steers from the hill. It'll take us maybe two hours. We'll go in town about five and have dinner at the Cominos Hotel. Like that?"

"Of course I'll like it. It's good to eat away from home."

"All right, then. I'll go get up a couple of horses."

She said, "I'll have plenty of time to transplant some of these sets, I guess."

She heard her husband calling Scotty down by the barn. And a little later she saw the two men ride up the pale yellow hillside in search of the steers.

There was a little square sandy bed kept for rooting the chrysanthemums. With her trowel she turned the soil over and over, and smoothed it and patted it firm. Then she dug ten parallel trenches to receive the sets. Back at the chrysanthemum bed she pulled out the little crisp shoots, trimmed off the leaves of each one with her scissors and laid it on a small orderly pile.

A squeak of wheels and plod of hoofs came from the road. Elisa looked up. The country road ran along the dense bank of willows and cottonwoods that bordered the river, and up this road came a curious vehicle, curiously drawn. It was an old spring-wagon, with a round canvas top on it like the cover of a prairie schooner. It was drawn by an old bay horse and a little gray-and-white burro. A big stubble-bearded man sat between the cover flaps and drove the crawling team. Underneath the wagon, between the hind wheels, a lean and rangy mongrel dog walked sedately. Words were painted on the canvas, in clumsy, crooked letters. "Pots, pans, knives, sisors, lawn mores, Fixed." Two rows of articles, and the triumphantly definitive "Fixed" below. The black paint had run down in little sharp points beneath each letter.

Elisa, squatting on the ground, watched to see the crazy, loose-jointed wagon pass by. But it didn't pass. It turned into the farm road in front of her house, crooked old wheels skirling and squeaking. The rangy dog darted from between the wheels and ran ahead. Instantly the two ranch shepherds flew out at him. Then all three stopped, and with stiff and quivering tails, with taut straight legs, with ambassadorial dignity, they slowly circled, sniffing daintily. The caravan pulled up to Elisa's wire fence and stopped. Now the newcomer dog,

feeling out-numbered, lowered his tail and retired under the wagon with raised hackles and bared teeth.

The man on the wagon seat called out, "That's a bad dog in a fight when he gets started."

Elisa laughed. "I see he is. How soon does he generally get started?"

The man caught up her laughter and echoed it heartily. "Sometimes not for weeks and weeks," he said. He climbed stiffly down, over the wheel. The horse and the donkey drooped like unwatered flowers.

Elisa saw that he was a very big man. Although his hair and beard were graying, he did not look old. His worn black suit was wrinkled and spotted with grease. The laughter had disappeared from his face and eyes the moment his laughing voice ceased. His eyes were dark, and they were full of the brooding that gets in the eyes of teamsters and of sailors. The calloused hands he rested on the wire fence were cracked, and every crack was a black line. He took off his battered hat.

"I'm off my general road, ma'am," he said. "Does this dirt road cut over across the river to the Los Angeles highway?"

Elisa stood up and shoved the thick scissors in her apron pocket. "Well, yes, it does, but it winds around and then fords the river. I don't think your team could pull through the sand."

He replied with some asperity. "It might surprise you what them beasts can pull through."

"When they get started?" she asked.

He smiled for a second. "Yes. When they get started."

"Well," said Elisa. "I think you'll save time if you go back to the Salinas road and pick up the highway there."

He drew a big finger down the chicken wire and made it sing. "I ain't in any hurry, ma'am. I go from Seattle to San Diego and back every year. Takes all my time. About six months each way. I aim to follow nice weather."

Elisa took off her gloves and stuffed them in the apron pocket with the scissors. She touched the under edge of her man's hat, searching for fugitive hairs. "That sounds like a nice kind of a way to live," she said.

He leaned confidentially over the fence. "Maybe you noticed the writing on my wagon.

I mend pots and sharpen knives and scissors. You got any of them things to do?"

"Oh, no," she said quickly. "Nothing like that." Her eyes hardened with resistance.

"Scissors is the worst thing," he explained. "Most people just ruin scissors trying to sharpen 'em, but I know how. I got a special tool. It's a little bobbit kind of thing, and patented. But it sure does the trick."

10 "No. My scissors are all sharp."

"All right, then. Take a pot," he continued earnestly, "a bent pot, or a pot with a hole. I can make it like new so you don't have to buy no new ones. That's a saving for you."

"No," she said shortly. "I tell you I have nothing like that for you to do."

His face fell to an exaggerated sadness. His voice took on a whining undertone. "I ain't had a thing to do today. Maybe I won't have no 20 supper tonight. You see I'm off my regular road. I know folks on the highway clear from Seattle to San Diego. They save their things for me to sharpen up because they know I do it so good and save them money."

"I'm sorry," Elisa said irritably. "I haven't anything for you to do."

His eyes left her face and fell to searching the ground. They roamed about until they came to the chrysanthemum bed where she had 30 been working. "What's them plants, ma'am?"

The irritation and resistance melted from Elisa's face. "Oh, those are chrysanthemums, giant whites and yellows. I raise them every year, bigger than anybody around here."

"Kind of a long-stemmed flower? Looks like a quick puff of colored smoke?" he asked.

"That's it. What a nice way to describe them."

"They smell kind of nasty till you get used 40 to them," he said.

"It's a good bitter smell," she retorted, "not nasty at all."

He changed his tone quickly. "I like the smell myself."

"I had ten-inch blooms this year," she said.

The man leaned farther over the fence. "Look. I know a lady down the road a piece, has got the nicest garden you ever seen. Got nearly every kind of flower but no chrysanthe-50 ums. Last time I was mending a copper-bottom washtub for her (that's a hard job but I do it good), she said to me, 'If you ever run acrost some nice chrysantheums I wish you'd try to get me a few seeds.' That's what she told me."

Elisa's eyes grew alert and eager. "She couldn't have known much about chrysanthemums. You *can* raise them from seed, but it's much easier to root the little sprouts you see there."

"Oh," he said. "I s'pose I can't take none to 6 her, then."

"Why yes you can," Elisa cried. "I can put some in damp sand, and you can carry them right along with you. They'll take root in the pot if you keep them damp. And then she can transplant them."

"She'd sure like to have some, ma'am. You say they're nice ones?"

"Beautiful," she said. "Oh, beautiful." Her eyes shone. She tore off the battered hat and 7 shook out her dark pretty hair. "I'll put them in a flower pot, and you can take them right with you. Come into the yard."

While the man came through the picket gate Elisa ran excitedly along the geranium-bordered path to the back of the house. And she returned carrying a big red flower pot. The gloves were forgotten now. She kneeled on the ground by the starting bed and dug up the sandy soil with her fingers and scooped it into 8 the bright new flower pot. Then she picked up the little pile of shoots she had prepared. With her strong fingers she pressed them into the sand and tamped around them with her knuckles. The man stood over her. "I'll tell you what to do," she said. "You remember so you can tell the lady."

"Yes, I'll try to remember."

"Well, look. These will take root in about a month. Then she must set them out, about a foot apart in good rich earth like this, see?" She lifted a handful of dark soil for him to look at. "They'll grow fast and tall. Now remember this: In July tell her to cut them down, about eight inches from the ground."

"Before they bloom?" he asked.

"Yes, before they bloom." Her face was tight with eagerness. "They'll grow right up again. About the last of September the buds will start." 1

She stopped and seemed perplexed. "It's the budding that takes the most care," she said hesitantly. "I don't know how to tell you." She looked deep into his eyes, searchingly. Her mouth opened a little, and she seemed to be listening. "I'll try to tell you," she said. "Did you ever hear of planting hands?"

"Can't say I have, ma'am."

"Well, I can only tell you what it feels like. It's when you're picking off the buds you don't want. Everything goes right down into your fingertips. You watch your fingers work. They do it themselves. You can feel how it is. They pick and pick the buds. They never make a mistake. They're with the plant. Do you see? Your fingers and the plant. You can feel that, right up your arm. They know. They never make a mistake. You can feel it. When you're like that you can't do anything wrong. Do you see that? Can you understand that?"

She was kneeling on the ground looking up at him. Her breast swelled passionately.

The man's eyes narrowed. He looked away self-consciously. "Maybe I know," he said. "Sometimes in the night in the wagon there—"

Elisa's voice grew husky. She broke in on him, "I've never lived as you do, but I know what you mean. When the night is dark—why, the stars are sharp-pointed, and there's quiet. Why, you rise up and up! Every pointed star gets driven into your body. It's like that. Hot and sharp and—lovely."

Kneeling there, her hand went out toward his legs in the greasy black trousers. Her hesitant fingers almost touched the cloth. Then her hand dropped to the ground. She crouched low like a fawning dog.

He said, "It's nice, just like you say. Only when you don't have no dinner, it ain't."

She stood up then, very straight, and her face was ashamed. She held the flower pot out to him and placed it gently in his arms. "Here. Put it in your wagon, on the seat, where you can watch it. Maybe I can find something for you to do."

At the back of the house she dug in the can pile and found two old and battered aluminum saucepans. She carried them back and gave them to him. "Here, maybe you can fix these."

His manner changed. He became professional. "Good as new I can fix them." At the back of his wagon he set a little anvil, and out of an oily tool box dug a small machine hammer. Elisa came through the gate to watch him while he pounded out the dents in the kettles. His mouth grew sure and knowing. At a difficult part of the work he sucked his underlip.

"You sleep right in the wagon?" Elisa asked.

"Right in the wagon, ma'am. Rain or shine I'm dry as a cow in there."

"It must be nice," she said. "It must be very nice. I wish women could do such things."

"It ain't the right kind of a life for a woman."

Her upper lip raised a little, showing her teeth. "How do you know? How can you tell?" she said.

"I don't know, ma'am," he protested. "Of course I don't know. Now here's your kettles, done. You don't have to buy no new ones."

"How much?"

"Oh, fifty cents will do. I keep my prices down and my work good. That's why I have all them satisfied customers up and down the highway."

Elisa brought him a fifty-cent piece from the house and dropped it in his hand. "You might be surprised to have a rival some time. I can sharpen scissors too. And I can beat the dents out of little pots. I could show you what a woman might do."

He put his hammer back in the oily box and shoved the little anvil out of sight. "It would be a lonely life for a woman, ma'am, and a scarey life, too, with animals creeping under the wagon all night." He climbed over the singletree, steadying himself with a hand on the burro's white rump. He settled himself in the seat, picked up the lines. "Thank you kindly, ma'am," he said. "I'll do like you told me; I'll go back and catch the Salinas road."

"Mind," she called, "if you're long in getting there, keep the sand damp."

"Sand, ma'am? . . . Sand? Oh, sure. You mean around the chrysantheums. Sure I will." He clucked his tongue. The beasts leaned luxuriously into their collars. The mongrel dog took his place between the back wheels. The wagon turned and crawled out the entrance road and back the way it had come, along the river.

Elisa stood in front of her wire fence watching the slow progress of the caravan. Her shoulders were straight, her head thrown back, her eyes half-closed, so that the scene came vaguely into them. Her lips moved silently, forming the words "Good-bye—good-bye." Then she whispered, "That's a bright direction. There's a glowing there." The sound of her whisper startled her. She shook herself free and looked about to see whether anyone had been listening. Only the dogs had heard. They lifted their heads toward her from their sleeping in the dust, and then stretched out their chins and settled asleep again. Elisa turned and ran hurriedly into the house.

In the kitchen she reached behind the stove and felt the water tank. It was full of hot water from the noonday cooking. In the bathroom she tore off her soiled clothes and flung them into the corner. And then she scrubbed herself with a little block of pumice, legs and thighs, loins and chest and arms, until her skin was scratched and red. When she had dried herself she stood in front of a mirror in her bedroom and looked at her body. She tightened her stomach and threw out her chest. She turned and looked over her shoulder at her back.

After a while she began to dress, slowly. She put on her newest underclothing and her nicest stockings and the dress which was the symbol of her prettiness. She worked carefully on her hair, penciled her eyebrows and rouged her lips.

Before she was finished she heard the little thunder of hoofs and the shouts of Henry and his helper as they drove the red steers into the corral. She heard the gate bang shut and set herself for Henry's arrival.

His step sounded on the porch. He entered the house calling, "Elisa, where are you?"

"In my room, dressing. I'm not ready. There's hot water for your bath. Hurry up. It's getting late."

When she heard him splashing in the tub, Elisa laid his dark suit on the bed, and shirt and socks and tie beside it. She stood his polished shoes on the floor beside the bed. Then she went to the porch and sat primly and stiffly down. She looked toward the river road where the willow-line was still yellow with frosted leaves so that under the huge gray fog they seemed a thin band of sunshine. This was the only color in the gray afternoon. She sat unmoving for a long time. Her eyes blinked rarely.

Henry came banging out of the door, shoving his tie inside his vest as he came. Elisa stiffened and her face grew tight. Henry stopped short and looked at her. "Why—why, Elisa. You look so nice!"

"Nice? You think I look nice? What do you mean by 'nice'?"

Henry blundered on. "I don't know. I mean you look different, strong and happy."

"I am strong? Yes, strong. What do you mean by 'strong'?"

He looked bewildered. "You're playing some kind of a game," he said helplessly. "It's a kind of a play. You look strong enough to break a calf over your knee, happy enough to eat it like a watermelon."

For a second she lost her rigidity. "Henry! Don't talk like that. You didn't know what you said." She grew complete again. "I'm strong," she boasted. "I never knew before how strong."

Henry looked down toward the tractor shed, and when he brought his eyes back to her, they were his own again. "I'll get out the car. You can put on your coat while I'm starting."

Elisa went into the house. She heard him drive to the gate and idle down his motor, and then she took a long time to put on her hat. She pulled it here and pressed it there. When Henry turned the motor off she slipped into her coat and went out.

The little roadster bounced along on the dirt road by the river, raising the birds and driving the rabbits into the brush. Two cranes flapped heavily over the willow-line and dropped into the river-bed.

Far ahead on the road Elisa saw a dark speck. She knew.

She tried not to look as they passed it, but her eyes would not obey. She whispered to herself sadly, "He might have thrown them off the road. That wouldn't have been much trouble, not very much. But he kept the pot," she explained. "He had to keep the pot. That's why he couldn't get them off the road."

The roadster turned a bend and she saw the caravan ahead. She swung full around toward her husband so she could not see the little covered wagon and the mismatched team as the car passed them.

In a moment it was over. The thing was done. She did not look back.

She said loudly, to be heard above the motor, "It will be good, tonight, a good dinner."

"Now you're changed again," Henry complained. He took one hand from the wheel and patted her knee. "I ought to take you in to dinner oftener. It would be good for both of us. We get so heavy out on the ranch."

"Henry," she asked, "could we have wine at dinner?"

"Sure we could. Say! That will be fine."

She was silent for a while; then she said, "Henry, at those prize fights, do the men hurt each other very much?"

"Sometimes a little, not often. Why?"

"Well, I've read how they break noses, and blood runs down their chests. I've read how the fighting gloves get heavy and soggy with blood."

He looked around at her. "What's the matter, Elisa? I didn't know you read things like that." He brought the car to a stop, then turned to the right over the Salinas River bridge.

"Do any women ever go to the fights?" she 20 asked.

"Oh, sure, some. What's the matter, Elisa? Do you want to go? I don't think you'd like it, but I'll take you if you really want to go."

She relaxed limply in the seat. "Oh, no. No. I don't want to go. I'm sure I don't." Her face was turned away from him. "It will be enough if we can have wine. It will be plenty." She turned up her coat collar so he could not see that she was crying weakly—like an old woman. 30

PAUL GREEN

Back with my own folks, and I mean black and white . . . I can't help feeling that they are experiencing life that no art can compass. . . . There among them I felt at home as I'll never feel at home elsewhere. The smell of their sweaty bodies, the gust of their indecent jokes, the knowledge of their twisted philosophies, the sight of their feet entangled among the pea vines and grass, their shouts, grunts, and belly-achings, the sun blistering down upon them and the rim of the sky enclosing them forever, all took me wholly, and I was one of them—neither black nor white, but one of them, children of the moist earth underfoot.

It was as an interpreter of Negro life in his native Carolina that Paul Eliot Green first made his name as a writer. The artlessness of the Negro, of which he speaks here, is in a measure his own artlessness, for he is technically a much less proficient playwright than many others. He was born near Lillington, North Carolina, on March 17, 1894. His parents were landowners and lived on their holdings not as tenant farmers but as proprietors; they earned their living from the farm, and Paul Green was one of those who worked in the fields to maintain that living. He has always been proud of the fact that he was once acclaimed a champion cottonpicker. He attended Buie's Creek Academy, taught for a couple of years thereafter, and enrolled at the University of North Carolina, "The Hill," in the class of 1920. During the summers he played semi-professional baseball to defray his college expenses. His first play was written while he was a freshman at the University; it was an unoriginal piece called *Surrender to the Enemy*, which considered the trite problem of the southern girl in love with a Yankee army captain and the inevitable family opposition. About this same time (1917) he published *Trifles of Thought*, a small volume of poems containing eulogies, epitaphs, war verse, and some Negro dialect in verse—honest but undistinguished writing.

The war interrupted both his college course and his writing; he served in the Engineering Corps, rising from private to second lieutenant. After the Armistice he returned to the University, where he graduated in 1921. He continued in graduate work at Chapel Hill during the next year and studied for another year at Cornell. In 1923 he returned to the University of North Carolina as a member of the faculty and has been in academic life ever since. His writing, however, has remained a brilliant avocation. Nearly all of it has been in the dramatic field, although he has published a book of sketches, *Wide Fields* (1928), two novels, *Laughing Pioneer* (1932) and *This Body the Earth* (1935), and a collection of short stories, *Salvation on a String* (1946). It is perhaps too soon to decide whether Green will develop as a novelist; he is as usual honest, sincere, and often deeply moving in these works. But as a playwright he has become one of the most original and significant of present-day American writers for the theater. A group of early one-acters was published in 1922 under the title of *Carolina Folk-Plays*. A second series of these was published in 1924. *The Lord's Will and Other Carolina Plays*, a third series of folk plays, appeared in 1925. The next collection, *Lonesome Road* (1926), had for its first play the one-act *In Abraham's Bosom*; this play was expanded later into seven scenes and was produced by the Provincetown Players in New York in 1926–27. Although it was not a popular hit, it won the Pulitzer Prize for Drama (1927). This, the best known of Green's plays, is a beautiful and tragic representation of the struggle of the black man to better himself. Abraham, the hero, has a white father who helps him to study. He succeeds in opening a small school for Negroes, but his efforts are thwarted by the prejudices of his environment —he is repudiated not only by the whites but by the blacks as well, and therein lies the tragedy. *The Field God* (1927) was produced shortly afterwards with some success. But the award of the Pulitzer Prize meant a revival of *In Abraham's Bosom*, much to the author's indignation. "This capitalizing of a windfall," cried Green to the manager, "is illegitimate and vulgar. Let *Abraham* rest with some dignity in his grave; there is a damnable cheapness about this sudden bestirring over the Pulitzer soup."

The comparative success of the play, however, certainly did nothing to discourage the author. He collected eleven of his one-act plays into a new volume, *In the Valley and Other Carolina Plays* (1928). He wrote two full-length plays, *Tread the Green Grass* (1929) and *The House of Connelly* (1931). The first of these is a fantastic interpretation of the growing insanity of a young country girl who has been nourished overmuch on folklore and folk religion. The second, *The House of Connelly*, was much more successful. In this play

Green attempted to portray the decadence of an old southern family and to describe the collision between this decadence, as personified by the heir, and lusty paganism, as exemplified by the field-woman Patsy Tate. The girl tries to inveigle Connelly into marriage so that she may acquire her share of the great estate. She succeeds in her plans. The social turmoil engendered by the character of Patsy Tate is painted again in the succeeding plays, *Roll, Sweet Chariot* (1934) and *Shroud My Body Down* (1935) and especially in *Hymn to the Rising Sun* (1935), a scorching attack upon a Georgia prison-camp, drawn in a picture which for sheer brutality has few equals in modern dramaturgy. The warden of the prison-camp in *Hymn to the Rising Sun*, however, for all his ferocity and his savage contempt for humanity, is baffled by his own situation; and the play ends with a tremendously ironic Fourth of July oration which exhibits Green's revolutionism in vivid colors.

This revolutionism, softened and mellowed but none the less mordant, appears again in *Johnny Johnson* (1936), a most affecting play of the idealist caught up in the meshes of a war-machine, entering the conflict with the words of Woodrow Wilson (p. 213) ringing in his ears, and trying to bring the war to an end through the sheer tenacity of his idealism, only to be broken by the pitiless will of society. For his idealism is considered insanity; he is immured in a "house of balm." The last scene of the play is unforgettable: the aging, broken Johnny, walking away in the twilight gloom, his shoulders still erect, whistling bravely in spite of the utter desolation about him. The form of the play is radical enough; it is a queer medley of musical comedy, farcical horseplay, weird melodrama, and poignant pathos. *The Lost Colony* (1937), presented each summer since that date on Roanoke Island, is a historical sketch, almost a masque, about Raleigh's Roanoke colony in North Carolina (1584–87). In recent years Green has devoted considerable time to the production of folk opera and the writing of motion-picture scripts.

"My theater," Green has written, "for the present is the published play. . . . The American professional stage is an industry and not an art as I had thought . . . it is a business run to the pattern of supply and demand. . . ." Green's plays make huge demands upon any theater, since they call for frequent changes of ingenious scenery. Their lines are often difficult; their language, the local patois of the Negro or the Rabelaisian vocabulary of the prison-camp or the easy colloquialism of an average man, is astonishingly varied and colorful. In a sense Green is not a dramatist so much as a poet of humanity; his imagination can treat human fantasy and human passions with equal warmth. He has a rugged sense of humor, a dynamic sense of character, and with it all a naïve charm that is never assumed or forced.

Johnny Johnson

Music by Kurt Weill

CAST

(*in order of their speech*)

His Honor, *the Mayor*
The Village Editor
Minny Belle Tompkins, *the sweetheart of Johnny Johnson*
Grandpa Joe, *her grandfather*
A Photographer
A Bicycle Messenger
Johnny Johnson, *a tombstone cutter and private citizen*
Anguish Howington, *rival to Johnny in business and love and owner of the Crystal Mineral Springs*
Aggie Tompkins, *Minny Belle's mother*
Captain Valentine, *a U. S. Army officer and formerly a movie stand-in*
Doctor McBray, *a major in the medical corps, formerly a veterinary surgeon and county health officer*
Private Jessel, *a stenographer at the recruiting office*
Sergeant Jackson, *the Captain's aide, an old army man and top-sergeant*
A Camp Doll
Corporal George, *formerly a waiter at Childs'*

Private Fairfax, *formerly a gangster*
Private Goldberger, *a junkman's apprentice*
Private Harwood, *a Texas cowpuncher*
Private Kearns, *a baseball pitcher*
Private O'Day, *a life-insurance salesman*
Private Svenson, *a Swedish farm-hand*
A West Point Lieutenant
An English Sergeant
A French Nurse
An Orderly
A Doctor
A Sister, *from the Organization for the Delight of Soldiers Disabled in Line of Duty (ODSDLD)*
The Chief of the Allied High Command
His Majesty, a King
A Belgian Major-General
The British Commander-in-Chief
A French Major-General
The French Premier
The American Commander-in-Chief
A Scottish Colonel
A Liaison Officer
A Second Liaison Officer
An American Priest
A German Priest
A Military Policeman
Doctor Mahodan, *a psychiatrist*
His Secretary
Dr. Frewd
Brother Thomas
Brother Claude
Brother George
Brother William
Brother Hiram
Brother Jim
Brother Theodore
Brother Henry
A Doctor
Anguish Howington's Secretary
An Attendant
Anguish Howington, Jr.
Soldiers

Neighbors, *men and women, young and old;* a Squad of English Soldiers, a Squad of German Soldiers, the English Premier, an Italian Brigadier-General, a Polish Colonel, Three Field Clerks, Several Orderlies, Hospital Directors, a Guard, *and* Attendants.

TIME

A few years ago as well as now

PLACE

Somewhere in America, somewhere in France, and somewhere in a House of Balm

SCENES

ACT I

SCENE 1. *A hilltop outside a small American town—April, 1917.*
SCENE 2. *The Tompkins home—several nights later.*
SCENE 3. *A recruiting office—the next day.*
SCENE 4. *New York harbor—a few nights later.*

ACT II

SCENE 1. *A road somewhere in France—a few weeks later.*
SCENE 2. *The front line trench—a week later.*
SCENE 3. *A ruined churchyard—an hour later.*
SCENE 4. *A hospital—a week later.*
SCENE 5. *The Château de Cent Fontaines, somewhere behind the lines—the same night.*
SCENE 6. *The edge of a great battle-field—the same night, just before dawn.*
SCENE 7. *No Man's Land—an hour later.*
SCENE 8. *The same—a few minutes later.*
SCENE 9. *New York harbor—a few weeks later.*

ACT III

SCENE 1. *A psychiatrist's office in the state hospital—a few days later.*
SCENE 2. *The forensic arena in the House of Balm—ten years later.*
SCENE 3. *A street—today.*

ACT ONE

SCENE I

"How sweetly friendship binds."

The curtain rises on the level and clean-swept top of a little hill. The ground is covered with a carpet of green grass, and at the right front a quaint young arbor-vitae tree is grow-

"**How . . . binds,**" the first line of a song of fellowship sung by the inmates of the House of Balm in Act III, scene II. It is more or less a paraphrase of the familiar hymn "Blest Be the Tie That Binds."

ing. In the middle background is a funereal obelisk-like monument about ten feet high and draped in a dark low-hanging cloth. At the left is a naïve and homemade example of the Star-Spangled Banner hanging down from a hoe-handle staff which stands stuck in the ground. It is a beautiful day in spring, and far beyond the obelisk and far beyond the scene stretches the blue and light-filled sky with here and there a tiny billowy cloud hanging motionless in it.

At the conclusion of the slightly mock-heroic overture the curtain goes up, revealing a group of villagers assembled on the little hilltop. They have just marched in and are taking their places around the monument. On the left are some eight or ten women, young and old. They are garbed in dark dresses and wear brown slat bonnets which shadow their faces, and each one holds a little United States flag in her hand. Some eight or ten men, young and old, stand on the right. They are dressed in ordinary sober clothes, and each holds his dark hat against his heart with one hand and in the other, like the women, a little flag. At the right front stands a little bow-legged swarthy man with a camera, and at the left front a young girl with a large wreath of flowers. To the right front and opposite the girl stands ANGUISH HOWINGTON *with a bottle of water in his hand. He is a long gangling young man resembling the stage undertaker type. To the rear and at the left of the monument stands* MINERVA TOMPKINS, *or* MINNY BELLE *to us. She is a vision of loveliness with her golden hair, baby limpid eyes, and doll-like face, and is dressed like a village May Queen. Her filmy white dress comes down to the ground to hide all except the toes of her tiny white shoes. Her shoulders are draped with a light blue scarf, and her golden hair is set off by a chaplet of pasture pinks. Clasped against her girlish bosom in her two white cotton-gloved hands is an object that looks like a small picture frame.* MINNY BELLE *is about twenty years old. Opposite to her and to the right of the obelisk stands* JOHNNY JOHNSON, *a quiet-mannered young fellow of twenty-five or six. He is dressed in a well-worn palm beach suit, soft checked shirt, blue tie, flat-topped straw hat, and square-toed russet shoes. He is of medium height, his face roundish and clean-shaven, his nose short and snubby, his eyes blue and mild, his whole appearance denoting*

*a gentle and complacent attitude toward both
his neighbors and the world in which he lives.
Between* MINNY BELLE *and the monument
stands* GRANDPA JOE, *an old man with a scraggly
graying mustache, dressed in a shrunk-up faded
blue-and-gray uniform of 1865, on the breast
of which is pinned a marksman's badge and
some sort of brass medal about the size of an
alarm clock dial. He wears an old dark felt hat
turned up at one side, and around his neck a
fiery red handkerchief as large as a towel, and
holds a bloodthirsty looking sabre in his hand.
Between* JOHNNY JOHNSON *and the obelisk
stands the* EDITOR *of "The County Argus," a
nondescript middle-aged man in a dark shiny-
sleeved seersucker suit, with spectacles, a
grimy collar and shoestring tie. Several huge
carpenter's pencils and a fountain pen resembling a small fire extinguisher show in his upper outside pocket. Standing on a little platform directly behind the* EDITOR *is the* MAYOR.
*He is an elderly fellow with a violet nose, and
dressed in an antediluvian swallow-tailed coat,
wing collar, swollen black tie, baggy striped
trousers and button shoes. In his lapel he wears
a big red rose. His old top hat and a big day
ledger rest on a little stand before him.*

*As the music in the orchestra stops, he holds
up one lean hand in a gesture that looks like a
combination raspberry and Fascist salute, and
begins his speech.*

MAYOR. Friends and fellow-citizens,
We are met this April sixth,
In the year of our Lord nineteen hundred and
    seventeen,
On an occasion most auspicious—
  (*At the pompous dignity in the* MAYOR'S
voice, JOHNNY *removes his hat, and* GRANDPA
JOE *salutes sharply with his sabre.*)
For we are gathered to commemorate
The anniversary of the founding of our town—
  (*Gesturing off to the left*).
Two hundred years ago today.
'Twas on this hilltop here—
This very site—
That our forefathers met to arbitrate
And sign a treaty with the Indians
Which ended strife and war.
With this eternal stone we mark that fact.
And at this moment let me pay respect
To Johnny Johnson here,

Our gentle-hearted friend and artisan
And tombstone carver of the skilful hand—
'Twas through his kindly zeal
That we at this late date
Erect this monument of peace—
Our thanks to Johnny Johnson.
  (*The villagers applaud warmly.*)
  JOHNNY (*With shy awkward acceptance as*
MINNY BELLE *looks admiringly over at him*). 60
Thanks, folks, thanky. (*Reaching out and shak-
ing hands with a little old lady in a black dress
and bonnet*). Howdy, Miz Smith.
  MIZ SMITH. Howdy, Johnny.
  MAYOR (*Continuing as* JOHNNY *turns back re-
spectfully*).
And now
Full meet it is that I speak forth my thoughts
Upon this vital subject—peace.
  (*Leaning forward*). 70
These are parlous times—
  (*To the* EDITOR).
Parlous times.
The war clouds belch and thunder over Eu-
    rope's sky
As if to swallow up the solid earth—
Where Germany and France and half the world
Do battle unto death.
The question now before th' American people
    is 80
Shall we take part or not—
  (*After an emphatic pause*).
I point you to our glorious president—
  (*He points in a general direction towards*
Washington.)
Who stands unshaken like a rock
And tells us nay—
We are too proud to fight—
For peace it is that's made our nation great
And peace that's made our village likewise 90
    what she is
Where each man loves his neighbor as himself
And puts his money in the bank on Monday
    morn.
  (*Cutting a sudden spasmodic step and be-
ginning to sing, his slightly cracked and nasal
voice filling the air as the orchestra strikes up a
soft and teasing accompaniment*).
    Over in Europe things are bad,
      A great big war is going on, 100
    And every day somebody's dad
    Has shot and killed somebody's son.
      —Turr-uble—turr-uble,

It's awful to think about,
  Oh frightful, oh shameful,
  America will stay out.
VILLAGERS.—Turr-uble—turr-uble,
  It's awful to think about.
MAYOR. They say in France a million odd
  Of souls have yielded up their lives,
  In Germany th' elect of God
  Have widowed more'n a million wives.
10   —Turr-uble—turr-uble,
  The woe and ruin and rout—
  Oh monstrous, oh horrible,
  America must stay out.
VILLAGERS.—Turr-uble—turr-uble,
  The woe and ruin and rout—
  Oh monstrous, oh horrible,
  America must stay out.
  (*With the exception of* JOHNNY *everybody has joined in with the singing.*)
20   MAYOR (*Continuing his speech*).
America must stay out.
  (*Some of the villagers nod agreement, and* JOHNNY *reaches gravely out and takes the wreath from the girl and places it at the foot of the monument. The* MAYOR *continues with deepening oratory.*)
What said th' immortal Washington?
No entangling alliances.
And James Monroe?
30 People of Europe stay over on your side.
You heard me.
  (*He looks around to see if the* EDITOR *is on the job with his pencil. He is.*)
And what does the great president of the
    United States say today—
Than whom there is none whom—ahem—?
He says that neutral we must be to the last
    ditch.
And what do I, your mayor, say?
40 I say the same.
  (*Pointing to* MINNY BELLE).
You all do well recall the matchless verse
Which lately in *The Argus* said——
  (*Pulling out his handkerchief, he violently blows his flaming nose.*)
EDITOR (*Intoning to his pad as he writes*).
"Democracy Advancing"—Minerva Tompkins.
  MINNY BELLE (*Beginning to sing from her framed verses as the orchestra strikes up and*
50 *the others join in*).
    Though Washington did fighting stand
      Embattled in the fray,

My children, 'twas that this great land
  Should know a happier day
  Of peace—peace—peace—
And then his flag was furled,
  Washington—Washington,
  The leader of the world.
(*The* MAYOR *now joins in with his nasal bleating.*)
  MAYOR *and the* VILLAGERS. And then when
    frightful carnage swept
  With red and direful gleam
Across our land 'twas Lincoln kept
  The vision and the dream
  Of peace—peace—peace,
And then his flag was furled,
  Lincoln, Abe Lincoln,
  The leader of the world.
MAYOR (*With great feeling*).
  And now today a mighty third
    Proclaims that men are free,
  'Tis Wilson with the golden word
    Of peace and liberty—
MAYOR *and the* VILLAGERS (*With* MINNY
BELLE's *voice fresh and clear above*).
  Of peace—peace—peace,
  And thus his flag is furled—
  Wilson, great Wilson,
  The leader of the world.
  (GRANDPA JOE *suddenly stands by the monument.*)
  GRANDPA JOE (*His eyes closed with intense reminiscence as he babbles*).
Up Chickamauga Hill we rode,
The bullets whizzed, and loud the shells they
    screamed—
Hold, hold, they cried, enough!
But on we sped and straight we flew
And never stopped until
We reached the parapet and grasped the flag
And brought the victory home.
This leg was crushed that day,
  (*Indicating his leg*).
This ear was sorely hacked,
  (*Indicating his ear*).
But praises to Almighty God,
Behind us came the riding fools
Of Barlow's cavalry—

99. **Barlow.** No doubt the author means General Francis C. Barlow (1834–96), who served with distinction in the Union army and later, as district attorney in New York City, prosecuted the Tammany chieftain "Boss" Tweed (1872–73). But there is no record of Barlow's having been present at the Battle of Chickamauga (September 19–20, 1863).

(*Letting out a sudden bloodthirsty yell*).
Yay-eh! Yay-eh! Yay-eh!
It's victory or die!

VILLAGERS (*Including the* MAYOR).
Yay-eh! Yay-eh! Yay-eh!
It's victory or die!

(JOHNNY *touches the* MAYOR *on the arm*.)

JOHNNY (*Quietly*). Say, your honor, are we for peace or war?

VILLAGERS. Peace, Johnny!

MAYOR (*Recovering himself*).
Why, yes of course—
Our hero of the Civil War
Always enthuses us—ahem—
And now before we unveil the monument and have our pictures made, I think we ought to hear a few words from the young man who carved this work of art—Johnny Johnson.

VILLAGERS. Speech, Johnny! Hooray for Johnny!

JOHNNY (*In hesitating embarrassment*). Aw shucks—I can't make a speech. I might say though, I think we've done a mighty good thing in putting up this monument. It's the biggest job I've ever done.—But then peace and arbitration's a big idea. I side with Woodrow Wilson on that. (*He stops.*)

MAYOR. He'll be glad to hear of it, Johnny.

JOHNNY. I reckon he's already heard of it. I wrote him a letter—(*The villagers applaud.*) —inviting him down to the unveiling—(*The applause is louder.*) But he hasn't come—not yet— (*Helplessly he twists his hat about in his hands.*) Well, that's about all. I am better at working with my hands than my tongue. (*Looking up admiringly*). But the Mayor now ——(*The* MAYOR *starts slightly.*)

MAYOR. And now we'll gather round the monument and have our picture made——

PHOTOGRAPHER (*Hopping out in front of his camera*). One moment, please. (*Everybody looks toward the camera and stiffens himself as the little guy runs around and sticks his head under the cloth. Immediately he bounds out again, grasps the shutter bulb and quavers.*) Here's the little bir-dee-ee! (*He presses the bulb and there is a flash, followed by a sharp explosion. A nervous shock goes through the crowd, and* MINNY BELLE *lets out a low scream.* JOHNNY *looks over at her paternally and smiles. The little guy jerks out the plate, reverses it, and grasps his bulb again.*) Once more, please.

(*The villagers with the exception of* JOHNNY *all get set again. The* PHOTOGRAPHER *presses the bulb but nothing happens. He hops around in front of the camera and begins working hurriedly at one of his gadgets. And now beginning softly in the orchestra and coming rapidly nearer is the tuh-blickety-blickety-blickety-blick of a galloping horse. The villagers gradually* 60 *take their eyes from the camera and begin looking at one another. The sound of the galloping horse grows louder in the orchestra. They all turn to look off at the left. Now the thundering hoofs are upon them, for it seems the scudding horse is coming into the scene. It does—a lanky barefoot boy with a tangle of grimy hair under a coca-cola cap, riding slowly on a ramshackle bicycle and gnawing the remnant of an ice-cream cone. He skids the machine a few inches* 70 *by dragging his heel on the ground, lets it fall out from under him, and then wanders over to the* MAYOR *and hands him up a big envelope, sealed with authoritative devices, which he pulls from his blouse.*)

BOY (*In a gosling voice*). Extry for his reverence the Mayor.

(*The* MAYOR *grabs the letter and rips open the envelope. Pulling down his spectacles he peers at the unwinding sheet of paper. Back* 80 *and forth he runs his eyes and then suddenly flings up his hand.*)

MAYOR (*Bellowing*). War is declared! (*For a moment he holds his hand so and then lets it fall with heavy finality. A low murmur runs through the villagers.*)

FIRST VILLAGER. War—war.

SECOND VILLAGER. What war? (*The* MAYOR *is peering at the paper and mumbling to himself as he tries to decipher it.*) 90

THIRD VILLAGER. Who're we fighting against?

MAYOR (*Now straightens up again, his shoulders squared in the grip of a sudden military feeling*).
And in this fateful hour, my friends,
America expects that every man shall do his
      duty.

GRANDPA JOE (*Giving his sabre a trembling swish through the air*).
Forward against the enemy— 100
Lead on. (*He begins hacking at an imaginary adversary before him, and* JOHNNY *steps nimbly out of the way.*)

JOHNNY (*Looking around in dolorous amaze-*

ment, at the growing excitement). Heigh, folks, we got to unveil the monument!

MAYOR (*Holding up his hand again in his raspberry and Fascist gesture*). Silence! (*Now beginning to read, his words running out in a low, voluble roll*). Now therefore I, Woodrow Wilson, by virtue of—and so on—so on—do hereby proclaim to all whom it may concern that a state of war exists—ahem—exists—be-
10 tween the United States and the Imperial German government, and I do specially direct all officers, civil or military, of the United States that they exercise vigilance and zeal in the discharge of duties incident to such a state of war—(*Looking over at* GRANDPA JOE). Our police force will take cognizance of these orders. (GRANDPA JOE *pulls out a whistle and blows a sharp and sudden blast.*)

GRANDPA JOE (*Gazing searchingly about him,*
20 *his voice hoarse with sudden ominousness*).
Be careful of what you say,
Be watchful of everyone,
All spies will be shot or hanged without mercy—
At the rising of the sun.

MAYOR (*Rolling up the long paper*).
In such an hour as this, my friends,
'Tis not for us to question why,
'Tis but for us to do and die—
I command each and every one of you to
30 meet me at the courthouse for a public reading.

EDITOR (*Again talking to his pad as he writes*). The president has called to arms—the nation answers to a man.

MAYOR (*Calling out again*).
Our democratic institutions stand endangered.
(*Shaking his fist at the* BOY).
Go ring the courthouse bell!

BOY. Sure. (*He turns and gets on his bicycle*
40 *and goes rolling off.*)

MAYOR. Volunteers, hold up your hands!
(*The hands of the men and women go up, with* GRANDPA JOE'S *sabre showing above them all. And even* ANGUISH *gets his hand slowly hoisted, for he like* JOHNNY *is under the watchful eye of* MINNY BELLE. *But* JOHNNY *does not raise his hand. The* MAYOR *peers over at him an instant.*) Johnny Johnson, where's your good right hand?

50 JOHNNY (*Hesitating*). Why—why—I thought we were all for peace.

MAYOR (*Bawling out*). These exercises are adjourned! (MINNY BELLE *stares at* JOHNNY *in querying reproachment.*)

JOHNNY. But folks—heigh, people—we've got to unveil the monument! Your Honor—heigh!——
(*The* MAYOR *makes no answer, for by this time he has hopped down from his perch and hurried over to the flag, pulled it up and begun waving it in the air.*)

MAYOR. Follow me to the courthouse! War! War!

MINNY BELLE (*Starting to sing as she and the* MAYOR *begin marching at the head of the rout*). And now the fateful hour has come—
(ANGUISH, *who has been watching his chance, steps to* MINNY BELLE'S *side, bows and smiles, waves his bottle and begins singing in a loud flat voice. Now they all sing, waving their little flags and swirling about the stage.*)

PEOPLE (*With the exception of* JOHNNY).
And now the fateful hour has come
And millions strong we rise
To fight for France and Belgium
And crush their enemies!—
—War! War! War!
Our banner flies unfurled—
(*The* MAYOR *waves the flag aloft.*)
America—America,
The leader of the world!
(*They go milling around, shouting and singing out at the right front, the little guy caught helplessly in the maelstrom and knocked this way and that as he and his camera are swept along. In an instant the scene is deserted save for* JOHNNY *who stares mournfully before him.*

And now the orchestra begins softly playing JOHNNY'S *theme melody. In the distance the singing and the shouting die away. A moment passes, and* MINNY BELLE'S *voice is heard off at the right—"Johnny!"—*JOHNNY *turns quickly around as* MINNY BELLE *comes running in. The orchestra, out of deference to her, suddenly stops.*)

MINNY BELLE (*In sharp petulance*). Whatever is the matter with you, Johnny? (*Hurrying over and getting him by the hand*). Come on, come on!

JOHNNY. But, Minny Belle——

MINNY BELLE (*Wiggling her childlike form up and down in a panic of nervous haste*).

Please—please—listen to the bell ringing——
(ANGUISH's *long lean figure comes hurrying in.*)

ANGUISH. The Mayor needs his ledger. (*He goes over to the monument, picks up the volume, and then turns back and slows up by* MINNY BELLE's *side.*)

MINNY BELLE (*Taking hold of* JOHNNY's *arm with one hand and* ANGUISH's *arm with the other*). Forward march—One—two—three—four——(*But* JOHNNY *balks.*)

JOHNNY. I can't just go now. (*Calling off to the left*). Heigh you, Mr. Fink—we want our pictures took!

MINNY BELLE (*Staring at him*). Oh, Johnny, surely you'll be the first to fly to the defense of your flag.

JOHNNY. But—why, I got all my work to attend to—(*Softly*)—and—and—(*He touches her shyly and lovingly on the arm.*) I've got other things to arrange for—for you and me. I'll tell you Wednesday night.

MINNY BELLE (*Hiding her face in her hands*). He can't mean it. His country needs him, and now he talks of personal happiness.

JOHNNY. Good gracious, Minny Belle, you don't expect me to do that—go off and enlist—and we don't even know what it's all about.

MINNY BELLE. We've declared war on Germany, that's what.

JOHNNY. And it ain't like Woodrow Wilson to do that. Why, he's been our first leader for peace. And now—(*Shaking his head*) I bet it's a false alarm.

ANGUISH (*Swallowing manfully and then speaking out boldly, as he raises his clenched fist*). I'll go—I'll be in No-Man's Land in a fortnight. Yes, that I will! (*His valor mounting*). They'll get a taste of my smoke—them Huns and Boches that rape—mistreat French ladies. Let me at 'em.

MINNY BELLE. Ah, listen!

ANGUISH. Yeh, dod-rot their souls!

MINNY BELLE. Yes, Anguish, yes.

ANGUISH. Dod-dum 'em, I say. (*Letting out a bloodthirsty gr-r-r*). Give me a gun and a bayonet—a gun and a bayonet is all I want.

MINNY BELLE (*Rapturously*). Hurrah!

JOHNNY (*Growling*). Yeh, hurrah! Anguish Howington won't ever see the sight of a German. He can run too fast.

ANGUISH. Here, now——

MINNY BELLE (*Stamping her tiny foot*). Stop it—stop it!

JOHNNY. Oh, Minny Belle, I'm sorry, but this buzzard here—(*Snapping at* ANGUISH). Take your hand off her arm. (ANGUISH *instinctively jerks away from* MINNY BELLE, *and then reaches out to take her hand, but she denies him that. In the distance a trumpet begins blowing "The Star-Spangled Banner."* JOHNNY *calls out.*) All right, Mr. Fink, we're ready for the pictures! (*Reaching out and taking* MINNY BELLE's *hand*). You and me, Minny Belle, one on either side of the tombstone.

MINNY BELLE (*Pulling her hand away*). No—most emphatically no.

JOHNNY. But I need the pictures for advertising the business.

MINNY BELLE (*Almost ready to weep with vexation*). Business—business—and our country called to war.

ANGUISH (*Taking his cue from* MINNY BELLE). Yes, he talks of business—and at such an hour!

JOHNNY (*Angrily again*). Yeh? You may not be talking it right now but you're thinking it. (*Scornfully*). And such a business!

ANGUISH (*Likewise angry again*). Well, selling mineral water is just as elevated as putting up tombstones. And there's a sight more money in it.

MINNY BELLE. Stop it! You boys promised not to quarrel over me again. (*She starts away at the right and then turns back.*) I'm not engaged to either of you. Remember that. (*She hurries tearfully away at the right.* ANGUISH *starts to follow after when* JOHNNY *darts in front of him.*)

JOHNNY. Now you listen to me, Anguish Howington, I want you to stay away from my girl.

ANGUISH (*Edging back*). Well, she's no more yours than mine.

JOHNNY. But she's gonna be.

ANGUISH (*With weak determination*). Not if I can help it.

JOHNNY. You—heard me—you—— (*He springs at* ANGUISH *who darts around behind the monument.*)

ANGUISH (*Defensively*). I got a right to love her.

JOHNNY. The hell you have! I love her myself.

(*He doubles up his left fist and starts toward him.*)

ANGUISH (*Pleadingly, as he peeps out from behind the monument*). Why—I—I thought you believed in settling things by arbitration, Johnny.

JOHNNY. This here's a different matter. (*He starts on toward* ANGUISH *and then stops and stares queryingly at the ground a moment as if suddenly confronted with a tough problem.* AN-GUISH *flies out at the left front.* JOHNNY *gazes quizzically after him, and then turning in vexation, pulls the draw-string hanging down from the monument. The drape rolls up and reveals the single word "peace" engraved in large letters on the stone.*)

Black Out

ACT ONE

SCENE II

"Keep the home fires burning."

The living-room of MINNY BELLE'S *house a few days after Scene I. The interior is a simple one and rather typical of the American rural village home of the year 1917. At the right center is a fireplace, with windows on each side set off by clean muslin curtains. At the right rear is a door that opens into the hall, at the left rear a combination day-bed and sofa, the kind that can be got from a cheap mail-order house on the instalment plan, and at the right and left front are doors that open into other rooms. In the center is an oval table of the same style as the sofa, and placed here and there about the room are several heavy imitation oak chairs of the same suite. Between the center-table and the sofa is a sewing machine. The floor is covered with clean straw matting and the walls with a bright flower-patterned wall paper. But though the room is typical and ordinary, the arrangement of the three framed poster portraits on the rear wall is not. For here we see the touch of an individual and patriotic hand. In the center of the wall hangs a large picture of Woodrow Wilson, on the right is a smaller picture of George Washington, and on the left likewise a picture of Abraham Lincoln.*

"**Keep . . . burning,**" the first line of the refrain of the extremely popular British (and Allied) song of World War I, "Keep the Home Fires Burning" by Ivor Novello.

Under the Washington picture is a semi-circular pasteboard slogan with these words—"He saved the colonies," under Lincoln's a second slogan—"He saved a nation," and under Wilson's portrait in larger letters—"Make the world safe for democracy." Further emphasis upon Wilson is given by a United States flag which drapes his portrait from above.

It is early evening, and the light that comes into the scene from the windows reveals GRAND-PA JOE *sitting just beyond the fireplace. He is working at some sort of contraption about two feet high which resembles a small Ferris wheel, and is dressed in a not too clean collarless white shirt, galluses and sleeve holders, a pair of dark trousers and old carpet slippers. His thin graying hair is pushed raggedly back from his smooth dome-like forehead, and his high ridged nose is set off with a pair of steel-rimmed spectacles which somewhat hide his dead dreamy eyes and give a homey comic touch to his face. In brief his whole get-up and personality are now no longer that of the blood-thirsty warrior but rather that of the quiet local inventor who is always on the verge of perfecting a new patent window-shade or a perpetual motion machine. In the case of* GRANDPA JOE, *it is the latter mysterious device which has him in thrall.*

When the curtain rises he is hypnotically engaged with his machine, hovering over it and fiddling with some screw, gadget, tooth or cog. AGGIE TOMPKINS, *with the responsible and somewhat harassed appearance of a housewife and bread earner, is sitting at the sewing machine. She is a stoutish middle-aged woman with a strong-jowled face, a thundering ample bosom, and a pair of capable arms.*

AGGIE (*Belching and looking angrily over at the bent back of the old man as she stops her sewing*). Father, how you can sit there working at that old perpetual motion machine and my Minny Belle running around town stark raving mad with the war fever—is more than I can see. I want you to talk to her. (GRANDPA JOE *makes no answer.*) You know what she did when she came in a while ago? (*Grimly biting off a thread*). Why, she stood up on her tiptoes and kissed that picture. Now anybody that'll kiss Woodrow Wilson——

GRANDPA JOE. I'd rather kiss him than that bearded fellow—er—Charles Evans Hughes.

AGGIE. I hadn't.

GRANDPA JOE. That's because you're a Republican.

AGGIE. It's not—If that low-down Johnny Johnson didn't like Wilson so much maybe I wouldn't mind. (*With a loud belch*). Ah, Lord, why don't Anguish come on with my mineral water.

GRANDPA JOE. Yeh, and if you don't quit drinking them slops you're going to rot out your insides, Aggie.

AGGIE. It's not slops. Anguish had his spring tested by experts. It says so in *The Argus*.

GRANDPA JOE. Yeh, and Johnny says that water's plumb poison to both man, bird, and beast. I'd believe him.

AGGIE (*Scornfully*). Of course he'd say that. He hates the very ground Anguish walks on.

GRANDPA JOE. And I don't blame him either —in a manner of speaking.

AGGIE. You listen to me, Father Joe. Anguish Howington is going somewhere in the world. But Johnny Johnson won't ever amount to a row of pins. (*Grimacing*). Too good— wishy-washy—no backbone.

GRANDPA JOE. That's what you think. Anyhow *I* like Johnny. A lot of people do.

AGGIE. You may like him, but you all laugh at him. Now you don't catch folks laughing at Anguish.

GRANDPA JOE. That's right, they don't get much fun out of him. (*He begins hammering on his machine.*)

AGGIE (*Singing defensively to herself as she sews, her voice suddenly grown mellifluous and free*).

My husband is dead,
God rest the poor man,
And I in his stead
Do all that I can,
Keeping body and soul
And the house from the dole—
  —Sing treddle, trid-treddle,
  The wheel it goes round.
I wash and I cook,
I sweep and I clean,
I once dreamt a dook
Had made me his queen,
But oh weary me,
Such things cannot be
  —Sing treddle, trid-treddle,
  The wheel it goes round.

(*She stands up and begins fitting her corset around her.* JOHNNY *appears at the rear door with a package in his hand.*)

JOHNNY. Howdy, you all.

AGGIE (*Dropping her corset from around her and glaring at him*). Oh, it's you!

GRANDPA JOE. Come in, Johnny. (JOHNNY *comes on into the room. He is dressed in the same clothes as before.* AGGIE *now busily begins folding up her mending and piling it on top of the machine.*)

AGGIE (*With a scissors snip in her voice*). And how is your tombstone business? Guess this war will kill it off.

JOHNNY. Well, can't be fair weather all the time—as the cuckoo said. (*With finality*). That's the way I've figured it out, Miz Tompkins. Still things are not so bad. (*Nodding gravely*). Miz Esther Smith has just ordered a nice piece of stone work.

AGGIE. Well, I'm glad to hear that. Her poor husband has been lying there in the graveyard these ten years with nothing but a plank headboard to mark his resting place.

JOHNNY. She only wanted me to put out twenty dollars for him. Then she decided to let her husband's headboard stand and take a sixty-dollar job for the cow.

AGGIE (*Throwing up her hands*). The cow!

JOHNNY. Yes'm, the one that used to give four gallons of milk a day, year in, year out. I had a mighty lot of respect for that cow. There's nothing like good milk for humanity, you know. (*With a genial pointed touch*). Better'n mineral water. (*Slapping his thigh as* AGGIE *stares at him*). Daggone, I was forgetting. I've got a little present for your birthday, Miz Tompkins. (AGGIE, *who has started out of the room at the left front, with her arms full of the clothes, turns back.*)

AGGIE (*Somewhat mollified*). For me?

JOHNNY. Yes ma'am. (*He is busy unwrapping the package.* AGGIE, *showing she is a bit touched by his thoughtfulness as well as curious, comes over nearer* JOHNNY.)

AGGIE. That's real nice of you, Johnny.

JOHNNY. Shucks, I was glad to do it. It's a jim-dandy piece of work, too. (*He now lifts out a small white tombstone and sets it on the center table.* AGGIE *stares at it in speechless horror.* JOHNNY *runs his hand lovingly over the carving.*) You see there's two hands a-shaking. Below that the word "Friendship." (*Looking around at her*). What's the matter, Miz Tompkins, don't you——?

AGGIE (*Her voice almost breaking with anger and chagrin*). So—you're already making a tombstone for me, are you? (*Fiercely*). Well, let me tell you, I'm not ready to die yet!

JOHNNY. Why Miz Tompkins, I didn't mean it that way——

10 AGGIE (*Yelling*). Don't Miz Tompkins me, you—you fool!

(*She turns and goes storming out at the left front, carrying the clothes with her.* JOHNNY *stares forlornly after her a moment, sighs, and begins wrapping up the tombstone again. A low chuckle breaks from* GRANDPA JOE *where he works.*)

GRANDPA JOE. She don't like you, Johnny.

JOHNNY (*Giving his shoulders a doleful*
20 *shrug*). Well, everybody to his own taste, as the goat said to the skunk.

GRANDPA JOE. It's Anguish she likes, the rising young business man. (JOHNNY *sits down with the tombstone in his lap and stares abstractedly at the floor.* GRANDPA JOE *looks over at his glum face.*) Come on now, don't worry about Aggie.

JOHNNY. I'm not worrying about her—especially. It's the war, Mr. Joe. I still can't make
30 heads or tails of it.

GRANDPA JOE. I didn't understand the Civil War but I fought in it—just the same.

JOHNNY. Yeh, and suppose you had been killed——

GRANDPA JOE. Then they'd a-raised me up a fine tombstone the way you did to peace.

JOHNNY. But what good would it do you and you dead as a door-nail?

GRANDPA JOE. Whew—no good, that's certain.
40 Say, you ain't afraid are you, Johnny?

JOHNNY. No, but if I had to die I'd like to know what I was dying for—(*Emphatically*). You're durn right I would.

GRANDPA JOE. You're getting sort of strong in your language, ain't you, Johnny?

JOHNNY. Yeh—I feel strong about it all, Mr. Joe. I tell you it's plain as the nose on your—my face—war is about the low-downest thing the human race could indulge in. Add up all the
50 good in it and it's still a total loss. There ought

to be some way of settling it by discussion—the way we do over in the Adelphi Debating Society, and not by killing. The more you fight and kill the worse it gets. You may conquer your enemy for a while but he or his friends only wait to grow strong again to come back at you. That's human nature. And what I can't understand about Wilson is—why all of a sudden he's willing to go out and kill a lot of people for some idea about freedom of the seas.

GRANDPA JOE. The sea has got to be free, Johnny—it's got to be free.

JOHNNY. Well, maybe it has, though after all you could look on it as nothing but a big pond. Now if I was out in a pond and Anguish passed by——

GRANDPA JOE. Anguish?

JOHNNY. Well, take anybody you don't like. And he tried to come in and contaminate the water, I'd raise a little disturbance all right, but I wouldn't try to kill him. No, we'd get out on the bank and——

GRANDPA JOE. Arbitrate, Johnny?

JOHNNY. Anyhow there wouldn't be any killing, at least I don't think so. (*Glumly*). There must be some other idea in Wilson's mind—for him and me's been seeing eye to eye all along. Maybe when *The Argus* comes out——

GRANDPA JOE. Well, you needn't worry so. You don't *have* to go fight, not yet you don't.

JOHNNY. Uh, that's just the trouble, Mr. Joe. I'm for peace and Minny Belle's for war. That's the long and short of it.

GRANDPA JOE (*Thoughtfully*). Uhm, you are in a kind of a jam, ain't you—in a manner of speaking? On the one hand—your principle, on the other—your—er—love?

JOHNNY (*Fervently*). Yes sir.

GRANDPA JOE. I'd drop principle.

JOHNNY. But I can't do what I don't believe in.

GRANDPA JOE. Then you're sunk—like the *Lusitania*.

JOHNNY (*Going heavily on*). If I could see some honest-to-God reason in this war—then I'd go quick as scat. Like if by going I could help—well—(*Deep in thought*) put an end to —sort of like the idea of—say, a war to put down war. You know what I mean. Sometimes you have to fight fire with fire. Then I'd feel the cause was worth it. For when it was over the democratic nations maybe could league up and unite for peace and—(*His voice dies out and for a moment he is silent. Then he turns to the old man.*) What is democracy, Mr. Joe?

GRANDPA JOE (*Hesitating and then speaking thoughtfully*). Democracy?—Well——

JOHNNY. I asked the Mayor and he said democracy is the principle of freedom—self-government—whatever that is.

GRANDPA JOE. He's right—that's what it is—the principle of liberty—to follow your own business like I do my perpetual motion machine and—be happy.

JOHNNY (*Staring at the portrait of Wilson*). Yes, but suppose in order to be happy, I want something and somebody else wants it——

(*He suddenly sets the package on the floor by the table and rises out of his seat just as* MINNY BELLE *enters at the right front. It is almost as if he were so sensitive to her presence that he can feel her nearness without even seeing or hearing her. She comes on into the room and* JOHNNY *holds a chair ready for her to sit down.* MINNY BELLE *is dressed in a trim blue coat-suit, the lace-collar of which is fastened with a little pin, and her golden hair is combed back into a becoming bob. She comes over and sits down in the chair which he holds for her.*)

GRANDPA JOE (*Suddenly beginning to sing in his flat cracked voice*).
When two are alone in a parlor at eve,
And a manly young arm waits inside of its
    sleeve
So anxious its duty to do and receive—
Then, Grandpa, it's skidoo for you—
    For you——

(*With a fond glance at the two, he goes nimbly out at the left front.* JOHNNY *in great glee, suddenly stands up, dusts off his chair, and then sits down again and begins fumbling sheepishly with his hat.*)

JOHNNY (*Presently*). You're—you're looking purty as a pink tonight, Minny Belle.

MINNY BELLE (*With a slight touch of coldness*). Thank you.

JOHNNY (*Furtively taking a small trinket from his pocket*). That locket come in the mail today. (*He reaches out and quickly lays it in her lap.*) When you open it—see—it's got a picture of me inside.

MINNY BELLE (*Examining it after a moment*). It's nice, Johnny—nice. (*She hesitates and then puts it on.*)

JOHNNY (*Joyously*). I knew you'd like it. (*He stares at her in speechless love and stammers.*) You—you ain't mad at me for quarrelling with that rapscallion Anguish?

MINNY BELLE (*As she pulls a tiny snow-white handkerchief from her sleeve and puts it demurely against her lips*). Please, Johnny—you know I can't ever stay mad with you.

JOHNNY (*Haltingly getting out a few more words*). You remember that night when I was here—two weeks ago?

MINNY BELLE. I remember.

JOHNNY. And I pointed out that verse in the song book. (*Looking about him*). Where is that book? It was here on the table.

MINNY BELLE. It's up in my room.

JOHNNY (*Gazing at her fondly, his face wreathed in a sudden beatific smile*). In your room, Minny Belle—where you sleep at night? (*His chair moves a bit nearer.*) You must remember what the song said. Something about—about how one person feels when separated from the other. (*Pulling out a pencil he writes in the palm of his hand and holds it out to her. She reads it and drops her eyes.*) You see— see what I mean—(*Spelling*). "L-o-n-g-i-n-g." (*Helplessly*). Oh, Minny Belle!

MINNY BELLE (*Looking off before her and beginning to sing softly*).
    Oh heart of love,
    The soul of all my yearning,
    Come back to me,
    My days are filled with pain,

JOHNNY (*Sliding his chair still nearer*). You sing it—almost like—like you meant it.

MINNY BELLE. My fondest thoughts
    To you are ever turning—
    Wild foolish hopes
    To have you back again.

JOHNNY. Why, you know it all by heart.

MINNY BELLE. Every sound along the street,
    Every voice I chance to hear,
    Every note of music sweet
    Sets me longing for you, dear.
      —Come back to me,

Oh, can't you hear me calling!
Lost is my life,
Alas, what can I do?
Shadows of night
Across my path are falling,
Frightened and lone
I die apart from you.

JOHNNY (*Rapturously*). Minny Belle, Minny Belle! (*By this time his chair is alongside of hers. He reaches over and takes her hand.*) Minny Belle—oh—you know what I want to say.

MINNY BELLE (*Singing again as she looks around at him with bright eyes and pink cheeks*).

Every footfall on the floor,
Every tip-tap on the stair—
Open wide I fling the door,
You are never standing there.
—Come back to me,
Oh, can't you hear me calling!
Lost is my life,
Alas, what can I do?
Shadows of night
Across my path are falling,
Frightened and lone
I die apart from you.

JOHNNY (*His words pouring out as he stands up, his hat falling unnoticed to the floor*). Like the song says, Minny Belle, you are the—(*He stutters, swallows the lump in his throat and struggles on.*) From that first day I saw you down there in the meat market—yes, my heart thumps like it will hurt when I think of you. When I'm carving my tombstones—my hammer going whick-whack—whick-whack—it's all in time to my heart beating out what I want to say—(*Pulling out his handkerchief and wiping his forehead*). And I can't say it——

MINNY BELLE (*Murmuring and likewise standing up*). Beautiful—beautiful how you talk so. (*She leans against him, and he puts his arms suddenly around her and stands stupefied with joy.*)

JOHNNY (*Brokenly*). My little—er—bird. (*Holding her from him he stares down into her averted face, and then bends over and kisses her tenderly on top of the head.*)

MINNY BELLE (*Clinging to him an instant*). Oh, Johnny——

JOHNNY (*In hushed wonder*). We're engaged. (*Spinning drunkenly about the room*). We're engaged. I'm the happiest man in all the world. Yay-eh! (*Turning ecstatically back to her*). And now can I ask you—ask you that other question? (*A tiny nod of her bright head says he may.*) When are we to be—(*His voice trembling over the word*) be married? What do you say to next week? We'll get his honor the Mayor to—to do it.

MINNY BELLE (*With ever the slightest movement away from him*). But we can't do that.

JOHNNY. Why not, Precious?

MINNY BELLE. It's the war—you've got to enlist.

JOHNNY (*His arms dropping down from her with a thud*). Great guns, I'd forgot all about the war! (*He stands gazing moodily at the floor.*)

MINNY BELLE (*Her handkerchief to her lips*). It will be hard to be separated from you—hard. But we both must endure it for our country's sake.

JOHNNY (*Wretchedly*). But, Minny Belle——

MINNY BELLE. At night I'll think of you there on the battle-field—under the vast and starry sky—think of you standing there with your rifle, a bulwark of strength.

JOHNNY (*Murmuring*). A bulwark of strength.—But, Minny Belle——

MINNY BELLE (*Her face already touched with the pain of woman's renunciation as she stares off into the air*). Like that other song says—(*Beginning to recite*).

Alone I'll wait
Steadfast and true,
My every thought
A thought of you—
Of you.

(*Half-singing as* JOHNNY *gazes yearningly at her*).

So go, my dear, and quickly now,
And then the cruel deed is done,
For parting is a sharper blow
Than absence, my beloved one.

(*Her voice now rising into a plaintive melody*).

Farewell, goodbye,
Goodbye, farewell,
No tears, no words
My love can tell—
Farewell.

(*She buries her face tearfully against his shoulder.*)

JOHNNY (*Pulling her tightly to him*). Don't cry, Minny Belle. It breaks my heart—oh, don't——

MINNY BELLE (*Gulping*). Be careful, won't you? Do be careful, Johnny, and come back safe.

JOHNNY. Sure—sure.—Oh—but look here, Minny Belle, you see I'm not really gone yet.——

MINNY BELLE (*Mournfully*). I know, Johnny, but what is one day, or two days? For then you are gone. It comes so quick.

JOHNNY. No, I just as well tell you, Minny Belle, I've not been able to make up my mind about this war yet. I've got some more thinking to do.

MINNY BELLE (*Starting to speak and then staring at him in sudden and pained surprise*). You mean—you mean you still hesitate?—(*His unhappy face betraying him*). After all I've promised? (*With a wail*). Oh. Johnny, you can't!

JOHNNY (*Pleadingly*). But, Minny Belle, listen. You know how it is. I've got to have a reason before I——

MINNY BELLE. Reason? (*Her voice almost breaking in a sob*). And I thought you—Oh, Johnny, you don't love me—no you don't.

JOHNNY (*With a groan*). My Lord! (*He looks helplessly about him as if seeking aid from the empty air.*) Maybe I can figure things out—maybe——

MINNY BELLE. Figure—figure—(*With a sob*). Then we're not engaged, we're not. I take it all back.

(*With heaving shoulders, her handkerchief stuffed against her mouth, she hurries into the room at the right and closes the door behind her.*)

JOHNNY (*Calling piteously after her*). Minny Belle! Minny Belle!

(*But there is no answer. For a while he stands in the middle of the room crushed and desolate. Presently he picks up his tombstone and goes slowly out at the rear. A moment passes and the door at the left front opens and ANGUISH HOWINGTON, carrying a large glass jug full of water, sticks his head in. He looks inquiringly about him and then knocks on the side of the wall.*)

ANGUISH (*Calling*). Mis' Agnes! Mis' Agnes! (MINNY BELLE's *grieving face looks out from the room at the right.*)

MINNY BELLE. Oh, it's you! (*She slams the door shut.*)

ANGUISH (*Knocking and calling*). Mis' Agnes! I've brung your mineral water at last! Mis' Agnes! (*The door at the rear opens and* AGGIE *enters. She is looking behind her.*)

AGGIE (*Reaching out a supplicating hand as she comes across the room*). Quick—quick—Anguish.

(ANGUISH *hurries over to her with the jug. She seizes it and, like a mighty toper drinking from the bung, holds it aloft and lets the life-giving fluid trickle down her throat. Then she sets the jug down, wipes her lips with her apron, and looks over at him, the anger and grief gradually passing from her face.*)

ANGUISH. I'm sorry to be so late, but I'm trying to wind up my business before I enlist.

AGGIE (*Sitting*). Uh-huh, and that's what I want to talk to you about. (*She gazes at him a moment and then continues.*) You're not going to enlist, Anguish.

ANGUISH (*With a questioning look, and then shaking his head glumly*). Don't see any way out of it. Minny Belle's determined that I——

AGGIE (*Leaning forward and speaking with deep confidentiality*). In the Civil War my Uncle Heck didn't enlist. Why? He melted down a whole beeswax candle, got himself a hollow reed, and blew the stuff into a hole he'd cut into his arm. From then until Grant captured Lee at Appomattox he had a bad case of St. Vitus Dance. He shook so bad that bringing the milk from the cowbarn he'd make the butter come. Yes, and Cousin Melchisidec, he hamstrung his left leg with a butcher knife.

ANGUISH (*Staring at her in fearful amazement as he drops down in a chair*). Lord upon me, you mean they done damage to theirselves with knives!

AGGIE. And Bud Lauderdale, an old sweetheart of Ma's, cut off his big toe with a grass hook. He limped bad the rest of his life and wore a special made shoe.

ANGUISH (*Aghast*). Merciful heavens!

AGGIE (*Shaking her head reminiscently*). Ah, they had nerve—Uncle Heck and Cousin Melchisidec and Bud Lauderdale. Brave men all, they were. (*Consolingly*). But you don't have to do damage to yourself to keep out of this war, Anguish. It's your eyes. Cataracts and scales—Anguish.

ANGUISH. Huh, Mis' Agnes?

AGGIE. You can hardly see from here to the door—Almost blind. I'll swear an affidavid for you. (*She gazes at him in silence.*)

ANGUISH (*A great ragged smile sliding around his slit of a mouth*). I see—I see. (*Suddenly rising and grasping her hand in thankfulness.*) You've saved my life—Ever since last Sunday when that English hero preached in
10 church I haven't slept a wink—(*Stiffening sharply and croaking in a hypnotic, sepulchral voice*).

"In Flanders Fields the poppies blow
Between the crosses row and row
That mark *my* place——"

AGGIE (*Rising*). I got a pair of cross-eyed glasses I used when the flues settled in my eyes. You wear 'em and if you're not blind now, you will be shortly. Come on into the kitchen.
20 (*She starts out at the left front, ANGUISH following; then suddenly she turns back, picks up the jug, and goes off drinking from it. For a moment the scene is empty except for a low note that scurries around in the orchestra like a mouse on the floor. Then there is a noise of thumping footsteps in the hall at the rear. The door is opened and JOHNNY comes running in with a newspaper in his hand.*)

JOHNNY (*Calling out wildly*). Minny Belle!
30 Minny Belle, say, I've got some wonderful news for you! (*MINNY BELLE comes in at the right front, with her hair hanging down. Her eyes are red from weeping. JOHNNY runs over to her.*) Minny Belle, I'm going to enlist. Listen, it's all here in *The Argus*. Wilson's proclamation. And now I'm ready to go. (*Reading enthusiastically*). "We have no quarrel with the German people. It's their leaders who are to blame. Drunk with military power and glory,
40 they are leading the democratic people of Germany as well as the whole world into senseless slaughter." (*With deep finality*). "This is a war to end war." Daggone, near 'bout my own words! (*He sweeps MINNY BELLE into his arms and kisses her on the lips.*)

Black Out

13. **"In Flanders . . . place,"** from the well-known war poem, "In Flanders Field" by the Canadian John McCrae (1871–1918). The poem, in the original, has *our* for *my* in line 3. But Anguish is waxing melodramatic.

ACT ONE

SCENE III

"Your Country needs another man—and that means you."

Interior of the recruiting office—a medium-sized room. At the right front is a door opening to the street outside, and at the left rear a door opening into an inner room. On the wall at the 5 *back is a wide flamboyant poster with the sign —"Recruiting Office Number 18,659." Plastered all around the walls are other flaming signs and posters calling upon American manhood to go and fight for its country. At the left front, diagonally placed, is a bare-topped office desk, and farther back toward the rear is another and smaller desk with a typewriter, behind which* PRIVATE JESSEL, *the stenographer, sits. Just to the right of him is a tall white weighing and measuring scale, and still farther* 6 *over at the right is a small table with a phonograph, the horn of which disappears through the wall toward the street. At the right front is a bench on which* CAPTAIN VALENTINE *and* SERGEANT JACKSON *sit, and in the exact center of the stage near the foot-lights a chair is placed facing outwards.*

When the curtain rises, PRIVATE JESSEL *is busily typewriting, his keys going in a whirring clatter of sound somewhat like a small mowing* 7 *machine, for his typewriter is of ancient model.* CAPTAIN VALENTINE *and* SERGEANT JACKSON, *facing the front, are reading a lurid magazine which carries the picture of a male movie star on its cover.* PRIVATE JESSEL *is a slender, nervous fellow with a pale burning eye, and is about twenty years old;* CAPTAIN VALENTINE *is a handsome man, some thirty years old, with a dark matinee-idol face, and is dressed in a spick and span uniform of the United States In-* 8 *fantry;* SERGEANT JACKSON *is shorter, with a scrubby bull-dog face and stubby upturned nose, and is about forty years old.*

For a moment after the curtain goes up PRIVATE JESSEL *clatters away at his work, and the* CAPTAIN *and the* SERGEANT *read their magazine, the* CAPTAIN'S *fingers going tap tap on the*

"Your . . . you," a familiar slogan on the war-recruiting posters, showing a female figure (Columbia) pointing sternly at the passer-by.

bench. *Then suddenly from the room at the left rear comes a low moaning cry. No one pays any attention to it.* SERGEANT JACKSON *bends closer to the magazine, snickers lewdly, and points to the page with extended forefinger. The* CAPTAIN *smiles and nods a languorous agreement to the joke. The* SERGEANT *now salutes the* CAPTAIN, *stretching his snaggle-toothed mouth in a grin, and drops his hand. He turns the page and the two of them read on. The* CAPTAIN's *voice rises out of his tapping into a low croon.*

CAPTAIN VALENTINE (*Singing abstractedly as he reads*).

What are you coming for
Into my private boudoir
Disturbing the sleep of a lady, an innocent
   one?
   So sorry, the soldier replied
   I'll honorably step outside,
I meant no offense in the least and 'twas only
   in fun.

(*And now the scene is suddenly split by a blood-curdling scream from the room at the left rear.* PRIVATE JESSEL *abruptly stops typing, and sits listening. The* CAPTAIN *continues his reading and singing.*)

Up spake the lady demure,
If fun and not robbery, sir,
Is what you intend then perchance and perhaps
   you may stay.
Nay, nay I confess on my oath
Most stiffly inclined to them both
Was my will, and they say with a will like my
   will there's a way.

(*And now* PRIVATE JESSEL *leans over and sets the phonograph playing, and we can hear the air in the street outside being flooded with the brassy band notes of the "Democracy March." The record has played only part way through when the door at the left rear opens and* DOCTOR MCBRAY, *a middle-aged, pot-gutted fellow wearing a medical corps major's uniform comes in, carrying a stethoscope in his hand and mopping his face exhaustedly. He gestures to the stenographer—who cuts off the record, steps swiftly back to his little desk, takes up his dictation pad and waits. The* MAJOR *stands mopping and scouring his hand around down in his coat collar. Again the*

door at the left rear opens and two giant private soldiers of the regular U. S. army come in bringing* ANGUISH HOWINGTON *between them. They are stripped to the waist and their great muscular torsos are tattooed most horribly, mainly with voluptuous women's figures. As for* ANGUISH, *or what there is left of him, he is stark naked except for a scanty hand-towel tied around his middle, and his bony shaking form is on the verge of collapse. His swollen red eyes are almost closed, his face is bathed in cold sweat, and he is panting hoarsely for breath. The soldiers drag him over to the chair and drop him into it, and step one to the left and one to the right and stand waiting, the while they pinch and wiggle the women's figures on their fore-arms.* ANGUISH *sits shivering and mumbling incoherently to himself.*)

DOCTOR MCBRAY (*Barking out to the stenographer as the* CAPTAIN *and the* SERGEANT *continue to read their magazine in unconcern*). Examination findings. (*Dictating rapidly, with a mixed jargon of veterinary and medical learning, and now and then shooting out a word of advice to* ANGUISH.) Venereal diseases—none—candidate claims virginity. Claim sustained. General diseases—none—needs feeding, short on his fodder and corn—(*Snapping his fingers*). —Chook—nutritious food, I mean. Nervous diseases—characteristic hysteria during use of pump. Nose and throat—foul. (*To* ANGUISH). Drench with turpentine and linseed oil. (AN-GUISH *bends his head over on his arms and begins to weep softly.*) Teeth show candidate to be about twenty-eight. (*Snapping his fingers again*). Sight—moon-eyed, almost blind. Combination diseases—leucoma, incipient cataract, granular conjunctivitis and God knows what. (*Yelling at* ANGUISH). Get out!

(ANGUISH *springs to his feet and stands cowering in terror. At a gesture from the doctor, the two giants seize him and hurl him through the door at the left rear.* MCBRAY *sits down at the desk on the left and sprawls himself forward exhaustedly on it. And now the handsome* CAPTAIN VALENTINE *is interested. He turns toward* MCBRAY *and speaks in a polite*

---

87. **leucoma,** a dense white opaque spot in the cornea of the eye, the result of inflammation or ulceration of the cornea.

stage voice, his manner that of a cross-mixture of Sherlock Holmes and Rudolph Valentino.)

CAPTAIN. It's all very well for you to turn down that fellow, Major, but I need another man to fill out my company.

MCBRAY. And pursuant thereof to General Order thirty-four thousand oh—oh—six, we've got to have him today. (*Grimly*). And let me tell you—the next fellow comes in here better
10 be a man.

(*He gestures to* PRIVATE JESSEL *who sets the phonograph playing again. The two giant privates come back into the room and take up the same position and business as before.*)

PRIVATE JESSEL (*Leaning out the door at the right and calling high above the music*). Next man! Next man! (*Everybody waits, the record plays, but no one comes in. With a low wheezy growl, the phonograph stops.*)
20 MCBRAY (*Savagely*). Don't they love their country in this lousy dump! Only three enlistments today.

PRIVATE JESSEL. There's that same fellow walking up and down.

SERGEANT (*Turning and looking back through the door*). He was there an hour ago.

MCBRAY. Get the—(*Clearing his throat*)— get him in here.

SERGEANT. That music hooked him. Here he
30 comes. (*The* MAJOR *rubs his hands gleefully and fits his stethoscope into his ears.*)

CAPTAIN (*Languidly, as he sits down to his magazine again*). Pass him if you possibly can, Major.

MCBRAY. If he lives, I will. (JOHNNY JOHNSON *enters and stops just inside the door. He is in smiling good humor and wears a new blue serge suit all pressed for the occasion. A red poppy blooms in his lapel and a little United
40 States flag is tucked into the band of his flat-topped straw hat.* MCBRAY *grunts with anticipated joy.*) Unh——

JOHNNY (*Removing his hat, giving them a benign smile, and beginning to shake hands around*). Well, folks, I've decided to do what Minny Belle said and enlist. Where's the paper I sign?

MCBRAY (*Motioning* JOHNNY *to a chair in the manner of a headwaiter welcoming an honored
50 guest to a table*). Come right in, sir, and make yourself at home.

SERGEANT JACKSON. We're tickled to death to see you.

JOHNNY. And I'm real glad to see you all. (*Turning toward the chair*). I came here last night, but the office was closed.

MCBRAY. Now ain't that too bad?

JOHNNY. Yes sir. But if you don't succeed at first—you know. And so—since this is a war to end war, I'm in it a hundred per cent strong. 60

MCBRAY. You are?

JOHNNY. You bet your tintype. But it's not against the common man I'm going to fight. No-siree. It's the German leaders. As Wilson says, drunk with military power and——

MCBRAY (*Chortling*). Good, good. (*Growling*). Sit down. (*The two privates step forward and, lifting him suddenly from the floor, slam him down in the chair.* JOHNNY *looks up at them in pained surprise.*) 7

JOHNNY. Heigh, you fellows are kinder rough, ain't you?

MCBRAY (*Chuckling in low malevolence*). Don't mind them son, it's just their little way.

JOHNNY (*Sharply*). Well, I don't like it.

SERGEANT JACKSON (*To the* CAPTAIN). He don't like it.

CAPTAIN VALENTINE (*Crooning*). Says he don't like it, but he will——

JOHNNY. Still if that's the way you initiate 8 folks into the army, then I suppose I'll have to stand it. It's all in the cause.

CAPTAIN VALENTINE (*Languorous as always*). And what cause is that, my friend?

JOHNNY. Why, democracy—world democracy —the biggest idea of modern times, including electricity.

(*They all stare at him with some show of interest.* PRIVATE JESSEL *lifts a sort of tripod easel from the corner and sets it between* JOHNNY *and* 9 MCBRAY *and slightly toward the rear, then stands waiting with his notebook in his hand.*)

MCBRAY (*In his barking manner again*). What's your name?

JOHNNY. Johnny Johnson.

MCBRAY (*As* PRIVATE JESSEL *writes*). Occupation?

JOHNNY. I'm an artist.

MCBRAY. Artist?

JOHNNY. At least that's what the Mayor 10 called me. Artist in stone—I make tombstones— tombstones for both people and animals. You know we don't properly appreciate our pets. They are about the best friends man ever——

MCBRAY (*Snapping*). Place of birth?

JOHNNY. I don't know.

MCBRAY. Don't know?

JOHNNY. You see, my daddy and mammy were sort of worthless and wandered around all over—from one poorhouse to another. I don't know where I was born. I was dragged from pillar to post——

MCBRAY (*To* PRIVATE JESSEL). Born—between pillar and post.

JOHNNY (*With a wide breaking laugh as he slaps his knee*). Daggone my hide, that's good!

MCBRAY. How old are you?

JOHNNY. Well, let me see.—According to the way my pappy figured it I ought to be about twenty-six come pumpkin time. He remembered there was a big frost on the ground——

MCBRAY (*Wagging his tired shaggy head and speaking in a soft query to the* CAPTAIN). My God, don't tell me he's crazy?

CAPTAIN VALENTINE (*Bored*). Let science decide it.

MCBRAY (*Loudly to* PRIVATE JESSEL). Army intelligence test number one—lowest grade. (PRIVATE JESSEL *now throws back a wide sheet of paper from the easel and reveals the illustrated example in test number one.*)

PRIVATE JESSEL. Look this way, Mr. Johnson. (JOHNNY *shifts himself around and stares at the easel. As* MCBRAY *calls off the questions,* PRIVATE JESSEL's *pencil points them out.*) First question——

MCBRAY. Cats are useful animals because— one, they catch mice; two, they are gentle; and three, because they are afraid of dogs. (*Whirling on him.*) Quick, Mr. Johnson, which is correct—one, two, or three?

PRIVATE JESSEL (*Looking at his wrist watch and counting off the seconds*). One—two— three—four——

SERGEANT JACKSON and CAPTAIN VALENTINE (*In unison*). Make it snappy, Mr. Johnson.

JOHNNY. Well, as a matter of fact, cats *ain't* useful. They're the worst pests in the world. Once I had a mocking-bird——

MCBRAY (*Controlling himself by grim will*). Mr. Johnson, I want you to understand that we are trying to find out whether you've got sense enough to be a soldier.

JOHNNY. Sure I have. You ain't blind.

MCBRAY (*Loudly—as he strikes the table with his fist*). Problem number two! (PRIVATE JESSEL *turns another sheet*). If you fell into a river and couldn't swim, would you—one, yell for help and try to scramble out; two, dive to the bottom and crawl out; or three, lie on your back and float until help came?

JOHNNY. How deep is the river? (MCBRAY 60 *wipes his dripping forehead with his sleeve.* PRIVATE JESSEL *turns over another leaf.*)

MCBRAY (*Hoarsely and with suppressed but withering scorn*). Maybe you forget, Mr. Johnson, that these tests are prepared by the psychological experts of the United States government and you're either crazy or you're not.

CAPTAIN VALENTINE (*Sweetly*). Yes, Mr. Johnson, we need another man immediately. Please tell us whether you're a lunatic. 70

JOHNNY (*Flaring up*). Now look here, you folks——

MCBRAY (*Intoning heavily*). Why is wheat better for food than corn?—Is it, one—because it—Chook—is it because, one—is it more nutritious, two, more expensive than nutrinsive—or because in a miller you can flound it gri-ner?— Ha-ha—— (*A sickly look spreads over his face.*)

JOHNNY. I catch your drift, neighbor. It all 80 depends. Now take a mule—he likes corn better for his food than he does wheat. Of course I like wheat better—that is, flour. But take a sheep now—he—likes grass. And a hog'll eat anything.

MCBRAY (*Flinging up his hands*). Po-leece! Po-leece!

JOHNNY (*Looking about him and grinning with sudden comprehension*). I know what you all are doing. You're playing riddles, ain't you? 90 I'm good at that. Me and my daddy used to play 'em. (*His words snapping out with stern authority*). Everybody get set—(*He pops his fingers dramatically, and with the exception of the two giant watchdogs everybody looks up with sudden attention. Even the exhausted* MCBRAY *raises his drooping head.*) If a hen and a half lays an egg and a half in a day and a half, how many eggs will three hens lay in one day? (*Pulling out a big brass watch and staring at* 100 *it*). Quick—one—two—(*They look at one another and then almost simultaneously all jerk out their pencils and set to figuring.*)—three, four—five— You give up?—Sure you do, takes a quick mind to answer that. Well a hen lays only one egg a day anyhow, so the answer is three eggs, that is, if they're three good hens. (*Popping his fingers.*) Here's another one. On your toes—If two snakes get hold of each other's tail and started swallowing and kept on swallowing how would they wind up?

10 MCBRAY (*In a spinning rhythm*). How would they wind up?—(*Suddenly waked out of* JOHNNY's *spell by his pencil breaking under his great figuring, and gasping.*) Nuts, that's how! (*Yelling*). Throw him out! (*The two privates start toward* JOHNNY, *but he darts around behind the easel.*)

JOHNNY (*Staring about him*). What you folks mean? I come here to enlist, I tell you. (*Running over to* MCBRAY, *his voice almost frantic*).
20 You can't turn me down, you can't. (*Aghast*). Lord, Minny Belle wouldn't ever speak to me again. No, no, I got to go fight—I want to help end this war. I got to go—I——

(*At a gesture from* MCBRAY, *the guards seize* JOHNNY *and drag him through the door at the left.* MCBRAY *staggers to his feet, feels blindly about him, and goes in after them.* SERGEANT JACKSON *shrugs his shoulders hopelessly.*)

SERGEANT JACKSON. Looks like we got to
30 spend another night in this burg.

CAPTAIN VALENTINE (*Beginning to croon again as he looks off into space*).

The days went happy by,
And the nights more merrily
But alas like my ditty most every good thing
has an end.
The Colonel came home from the wars——
(*He breaks off.*)

SERGEANT JACKSON (*Staring at his figuring*).
40 Say what *would* happen to them two snakes? (*A loud guttural cry comes from the left rear.*) That old horse doctor's giving him the works—ha-ha!

(*Suddenly the door flies open and one of the tattooed giants pitches headlong into the scene and lies groaning on the floor, with his hands over his face.* JOHNNY *springs in after him, bareheaded and his torn blue serge coat in his hand.*)

50 JOHNNY (*Shaking his left fist at the prostrate figure and roaring*). So you'd tear my blue

serge, would you? Well, let me tell you, I'm planning to get married in that coat—at least I was. (*They all stare at him in amazement. The giant moans and rolls on the floor.* JOHNNY *now looks down at him somewhat in sorrow.*) I got a mighty hard fist from chiseling tombstones, and I didn't mean to hit you such a blow in the face.

CAPTAIN VALENTINE (*With a courtly bow and sweet smile*). Crazy or not crazy, he's our man!

Black Out

ACT ONE

SCENE IV

"A light that lighteth men their way."

It is night. A prospect looking seaward from the entrance to the harbor of New York. The tips of a few dark branches frame the scene of an infinite ocean and starless sky. Far in the background stands the STATUE OF LIBERTY, *the upper part of her figure illuminated from a hidden light, and in her hand a brightly glowing beacon. Tall and majestic she stands, immovable, and brooding over the scene like some fabled apocalyptic figure.*

When the curtain rises, the orchestra is concluding a soft, harmonious arrangement of a lullaby. And then sliding across the background from right to left, a painted thing upon a painted ocean, comes the gray ghostly shape of a great warship with its threatening guns stuck forward like the antennae of some strange, primeval crustacean. It disappears at the left, and now in from the right and almost close enough to the ledge to be touched by an onlooker's hand come the curved rail and part of the deck of a passenger ship. Stretched out on the floor one after the other lie the sleeping forms of soldiers, their pale upturned faces bathed in the radiance of the moon, and looking like recumbent figures on a great slow-moving catafalque. Standing by the rail and partly obscured by his hanging blanket is JOHNNY JOHNSON, *dressed in an army union suit, and his rumpled hair gently caressed by a lit-*

"A light . . . way," suggested by Luke 2:32.

tle breeze. *He has just risen from his sleep and is staring in dreamy and silent awe at the far-away* STATUE.

JOHNNY (*After a moment, his words rising at first broken and almost indistinct*).
Think of it—
(*The motion of the rail and deck stops.*)
There you stand,
Like a picture in that history book I read.
Minny Belle said I'd see you so,
And now at last I have—
Your hand uplifted with a torch
Saying goodbye to us,
Good luck and bless you every one.
(*With hushed fervency*).
And God bless you,
O Mother of Liberty—
That's what you are,
A sort of mother to us all,
(*Saluting sharply*).
And we your sons.
And here tonight as we set forth
To fight the German Lords,
I raise my hand
(*He does so.*)
And swear a Bible oath
That Johnny Johnson—
That's my name,
You maybe haven't heard of me,
But some day soon you will—
I swear that neither by a look, a thought, or
        word,
Will I fail either you or Minny Belle.
And I will keep my character clean
And come back as I went—
Without a smirch.
(*More sternly and emphatically*).
And furthermore I swear
That I will never see your light again
Until I've helped to bring back peace—
And win this war which ends all wars.
And yet I'm not just sure
How it will come to pass,
But I will find a way,
And if the generals and the kings don't know
I'll show them how it's done,
For never yet has Johnny Johnson failed
To get an answer when he hunted for it.
I swear!
I swear!
And once an oath is made with me,

It's same as sealed and bound.
        (*Murmuring*).
Farewell, Mother,
And peaceful be thy dreams.
(*With his hand still at salute, he pulls his blanket around him and slowly sinks back to his rest. And only when he is stretched out like the other figures does he let his hand fall. A murmurous groan seems to run among the sleepers; they turn in their hard beds and lie still again.* JOHNNY's *voice rises once more in falling drowsy syllables.*)
Starlight, star-bright—
Goodbye, Minny Belle, my darling,
I sleep with your dear—picture—'gainst—my—
        heart.
(*The rail and the deck slowly move away at the left and disappear in a great engulfing shadow. The illuminated* STATUE *remains alone in the depths of the night, lonely and aloof as she holds her beacon up, and following with her sightless, stony stare the progress of the boat that carries* JOHNNY JOHNSON *out to sea.*)

Curtain

ACT TWO

SCENE I

"Lead, kindly Light."

The scene is a shadowy road somewhere in France behind the front lines. It is night. A slow cortège of dark twisted and anguished French soldiers is moving like a small funeral procession across the foreground of the scene from right to left. These are the wounded men returning from the front. A few black trees show against the dim light of the sky in the background. As the figures go limping and moving painfully by, a file of American soldiers in full war gear, including gas masks at the alert, are discerned moving along the upper level of the roadbank from left to right. They are going up to the front lines as the French-men are coming out. The wounded men— some blinded, some walking with the aid of crutches, some helped along by their more for-

"**Lead, kindly Light,**" the first line of the hymn "The Pillar of the Cloud" (1833) by John Henry, Cardinal Newman (1801-90).

tunate fellows—are chanting a low, mournful hymn of pain.

WOUNDED SOLDIERS. Nous sommes blessés,
Ayez pitié,
Aidez, aidez,
Nous sommes blessés.

(*The last of the file of American soldiers stops on the roadbank and stands looking sympathetically down as the end of the cortège*
10 *moves slowly out at the left. In the dim light of approaching dawn and silhouetted as he is against the sky we recognize the form of* JOHNNY JOHNSON. *He stands there in an attitude of great sorrow and sympathy as the orchestra plays out its Marche Dolorosa and the little bleating cries and mumbling words of pain break forth from the lips of the wounded men. When the last Frenchman has disappeared,* JOHNNY *straightens himself up, looks out be-*
20 *fore him, and raises his clenched fist as if making another covenant.*)

JOHNNY (*With grim and stern emphasis*). Lafayette, we are here! (*He turns, and with his bayoneted rifle held on left-handed guard before him, sets off running to the right.*)

Black Out

ACT TWO

SCENE II

"There is one spot forever England."

The scene represents the front line trench, with its parapet and kneeling ledge running zig-zag across the stage at the rear. Beyond the trench and leaning awkwardly against the sky
30 *the tops of a few scattered and broken wooden crosses show themselves. On one of them a little bird is sitting.*

When the curtain rises, CORPORAL GEORGE *and his squad of six men are standing on guard at an interval of a step apart with their backs to the audience, their rifles resting on the parapet and pointing out into No Man's Land. Sit-*

ting *on the ledge in each of the intervals is a sleepy English soldier in full marching equipment. Standing to the front and in profile to the audience is an English* SERGEANT.

The time is late afternoon of an early autumn day.

SERGEANT (*Showing a mouth gapped with snaggled teeth, as he continues his speech*). It's the big push, the big push you Yanks will be facing and me risking my life in the traffic of London. Gawd help me—Some of you'll come out of it alive. (*He hoists one foot up on a broken box, spits in his palm and begins polishing his shoe.*)

CORPORAL GEORGE (*Looking around*). Yeh?

SERGEANT. Things is quiet up here, too quiet. You can see the little larks sitting on the crosses out there. (*He gestures toward the rear. A noise is heard off at the left like the sound of a breaking board.* PERCY FAIRFAX *at the right rear suddenly fires off his rifle into the vastness of No Man's Land, his body recoiling backwards from the kick of the gun. The little bird disappears from the cross, and the English* SERGEANT *bounds around and stares at him angrily.*) Oh, it's Percival Fairfax, the Chicago bad man.

FAIRFAX (*Reloading his rifle and still staring straight ahead of him, his voice tremulous and frightened*). Yes, sir, I—I'm nervous, I guess. If it—this was killing cops I wouldn't mind it, but this silence—I can't stand it.

PRIVATE SVENSON (*A long horse-faced Swede*). You scare our little bird away.

CORPORAL GEORGE (*Softly*). The waiting— the waiting—that's what unnerves a man.

PRIVATE GOLDBERGER (*A little squabby Jew*). Yeh, it says so in the books—the waiting. (*And now the musical whing of a bullet is heard flying toward the men. The Americans duck their heads down, but the English sit as they are. The bullet strikes the parapet with a plop.*)

FAIRFAX. O-ooh, and that sniper, he keeps shooting at us!

GOLDBERGER (*Mannishly*). Aw, what the hell! (*He whirls around and begins grubbing in the bank, then holds up a little object triumphantly and jiggles it.*) Look-a-there—that bullet's hot enough to burn your hand. (*Going over to his place at the parapet he lifts the lid of an old box and drops the bullet in.*)

PRIVATE KEARNS (*A huge square-shouldered*

---

3. **Nous . . . aidez,** "We are wounded; have pity and help us." 15. **Dolorosa,** of pain and lament.
"There . . . England," from the sonnet "The Soldier" (1914) by the young English poet and soldier Rupert Brooke (1887-1915). The first three lines run
"If I should die, think only this of me
That there's some corner of a foreign field
That is forever England . . ."

fellow about twenty years old, chewing to-bacco). Abie here likes this war. He was a junk man back home.

PRIVATE GOLDBERGER. Yeh, and let me tell you there's plenty of junk up here. Beats the flats of Jersey all hollow.

PRIVATE O'DAY (*A short red-faced Irishman*). And prowling around some of these nights you're gonna get your head blowed off.

PRIVATE HARWOOD (*Sandy-haired and blue-eyed, about twenty-one, singing softly to him-self*).
Keep your head down, Allemand
Late last night, by the pale moonlight—
I saw you—
Heigh, Swede, how's your corn crop coming on?

PRIVATE SVENSON (*Gazing dolefully down at a little potted plant on the ledge beside him*). It can't grow—gas—too much in the air, I tank.

SERGEANT (*Staring around*). Is it m'ize he's got here?

PRIVATE O'DAY (*Sarcastically*). No, corn. He found it growing back there in a shellhole. Re-minds him of Iowa.

SERGEANT (*Resuming his spitting and pol-ishing*). Bless me, what queer birds—you Amer-icans!

PRIVATE O'DAY (*Belligerently*). Yeh? That's like an Englishman—everybody's queer but himself.

CORPORAL GEORGE (*Sternly*). Keep your shirt on, Pat.

SERGEANT (*With a sharp grunt*). Uhck—"Pat"—Irish be Gawd! (*The other English sol-diers snicker.*)

PRIVATE O'DAY. Yes, from Boston.

SERGEANT (*Calling loudly off at the left*). Private Johnson!—Where is that bloody skivvy?

PRIVATE KEARNS (*Spitting*). He'll be back.

PRIVATE FAIRFAX. He always comes back.

SERGEANT. Queer?—Anyway me lads, Eng-land never produced a specimen like your Johnny Johnson.

PRIVATE KEARNS. You're right about that.

SERGEANT. Yesterday he offered to set me up with a nice tombstone for a shilling.

13. **Keep your head . . . you,** the refrain of a popular song of the war days; in this country it was known as "Keep your head down, Fritzie Boy." 39. **skivvy,** a hare-brained, crazy fellow.

CORPORAL GEORGE. With epitaph?

SERGEANT. Cripes, that too.

PRIVATE HARWOOD. He's got epitaphs writ for everybody in the company, including the Captain and the Colonel.

PRIVATE GOLDBERGER (*Teasingly, as he indi-cates* PRIVATE FAIRFAX). Sold him one.

PRIVATE FAIRFAX (*With timid braggadocio*). Johnny says—he says—be prepared for the worst is the way to keep it from happening.

PRIVATE KEARNS (*Gloomily*). I wish there was some way of being prepared for that big battle the Sergeant talks about.

PRIVATE SVENSON. Yohnny Yohnson, he say maybe the war be over soon.

(*He bends down, peers at his corn and then dipping a handful of water up out of the bot-tom of the trench pours it around its roots.*)

SERGEANT (*With genial cruelty*). This war will last ten years.

PRIVATE FAIRFAX (*With a groan*). We might as well be dead then.

SERGEANT. The big blighters back home don't want it to end. Who'd they sell their mu-nitions to if we have peace? Ten years? It might last twenty.

PRIVATE O'DAY (*Still anxious to put salt in the split tail*). It would if you English had to win it. (*Defiantly*). Yeh, it's me talking.

SERGEANT (*Scornfully*). Yeh, and if talking meant anything, the Irish would rule the world —not England.

PRIVATE O'DAY (*Now doubling up his fists*). Is it a fight you want? Come on!

CORPORAL GEORGE (*Shouting*). Can it! Can it!

(*He jerks down his gun and steps between* O'DAY *and the* SERGEANT. *The* SERGEANT *tries to push by* CORPORAL GEORGE *as* JOHNNY *comes in from the left, staggering under a heavy load. In one hand he carries a huge battered tin bucket full of hot steaming tea, and over his shoulder a tow sack full of provisions. Like the other soldiers he wears a helmet and gas mask at the ready, but he is stripped to the waist, grimed and muddy, and in general is a poor specimen of democracy's champion. A big hole has been torn in the top of his helmet. But though he looks somewhat dirty he seems to be the same cheerful* JOHNNY *as before.*)

JOHNNY. Old England and Ireland fighting again?—Here's something to stop it—your tea!

741

(*At the word "tea" the English soldiers spring to their feet and along with the* SERGEANT *snap their drinking cups from their belts.* JOHNNY *drops the bag of provisions, and with a dipper in one hand and the can in the other pours each man a drink.*)

SERGEANT (*Joyously*). Ha-ha-ha—here's to everybody. Cheer up, Yanks, cheer up.

ENGLISH SOLDIERS. Ha-ha-ha-ha-ha—tea—tea!

10 SERGEANT (*Suddenly beginning to sing*).

Now, England is, as we all know,
A great and mighty nation
With power big as half the world
And colonies galore.
Her army and her navy too
They quite befit her station,
The watchdogs of her flag unfurled
From Bath to Singapore.

(*The English Soldiers join in the chorus.*)

20 Then hail—hail—hail!
All hail Britannia and her crown!
We lift our cups to thee—

(*They do so.*)

And drink thy health in bumpers down
Of tea, strong tea.

(*They all drink.*)

'Twas tea that raised her in her might,
At least that's our opinion.
And tea that made America—

30 Go read your history—
And fit it is that we unite
To further the dominion
Of freedom's laws and lead the way
For England and her tea.

ALL (*With the exception of* JOHNNY *and* PRIVATE O'DAY—*singing*).

Then hail! hail! hail!
All hail Britannia and her crown!
We lift our cups to thee

40 And drink thy health in bumpers down
Of tea—strong tea.

(*Their song ended, they drain down the last drop, snap their cups back in their belts, and stand ready to march away. Suddenly as if coming from underground at the back a faint and far-away chorus of foreign voices is heard answering like an echo.*)

VOICES. "Then hail! hail! hail!
All hail Britannia and her crown!

50 We lift our cups to thee!—"

CORPORAL GEORGE (*Softly, as they all listen*). Golly, them Heinies are answering us.

SERGEANT (*With quiet and forlorn reminiscence*). Last Christmas up here we were singing "Holy Night," and they done the same.

JOHNNY (*Snapping his fingers and turning inclusively around*). See there—good scouts like us, I been telling you.

SERGEANT. Well, good or bad, our business is to lick 'em. (*Shaking his shoulders mournfully.*) Everything shipshape, mates? 60

ENGLISH SOLDIERS (*Loudly as they pat their bellies*). Aye, sir.

SERGEANT. Right-face! (*They obey.*) Hip—hip—(*They start marching off. The* SERGEANT *salutes.*) Cheerio, Yanks—we turn this war over to you. And Johnson, if you capture old Hindenburg, let me know. (*But* JOHNNY *makes no reply, for he has already gone over and sat down on a box to the right of the can of tea* 70 *and begun figuring on a sheet of paper. The* SERGEANT *goes on out after his squad singing.*)

Then hail! hail! hail!
All hail Britannia and her crown!
We lift——

(*The American soldiers turn and watch them leave regretfully.*)

PRIVATE KEARNS. God, it's lonesome already.

PRIVATE O'DAY (*Furiously*). Just like the dirty English. As soon as they think a real 80 fight's coming on they march out and leave us holding the bag.

JOHNNY (*Still figuring*). Well, every jug's got to stand on its own bottom sometime—as my mammy said.

CORPORAL GEORGE (*Snapping*). Don't you start them old sayings again, Johnson, I'm sick of 'em.

JOHNNY. All right, sir, you're the boss, as the ox said to the yoke—— 90

CORPORAL GEORGE (*Yelling*). You heard me!

JOHNNY (*Humbly*). Sorry, sir.

(*And now the men come over and get their food out of the bag—a hunk of bread to each man and a can of bully beef. Then they turn around from their rifles and sit down on the ledge and begin eating.*)

PRIVATE KEARNS (*Scratching himself with his elbows*). Where did you learn them old sayings, Johnson—"As the minnow said to the 100

742

whale" and "If smell was all the goat would win," and all the rest of it?

JOHNNY. Huh? Oh, just picked them up.

PRIVATE SVENSON (*Throwing crumbs over the parapet*). Chick-chick-chick!

CORPORAL GEORGE. That little bird won't come back around here, Slim. He's got too much sense. (*Yawning*). I feel like I've stood watch forty hours. What time is it, Johnson? (JOHNNY *pulls out his big watch and looks at it, then begins to chuckle softly.*) What you laughing at?

JOHNNY. Back home there was a teamster—when you asked him what time it was, he'd say—— (*He stops.*)

CORPORAL GEORGE. Yeh, and what would he say?

JOHNNY. He'd say—Time all dogs was dead, ain't you sick? (*The soldiers laugh and* CORPORAL GEORGE *springs angrily to his feet.*)

CORPORAL GEORGE. Damn it, I told you not to pull any more of them cracks. (*Wagging his head, he sinks back on the parapet.*) For six years I was a head waiter in Childs'. I thought I'd met every kind of a crumb——

JOHNNY (*Now springing up*). I won't take any more of that. I'm not a crumb. (*He seizes his bayoneted rifle which has been leaning against the bank and starts toward* CORPORAL GEORGE.) You keep picking on me——

CORPORAL GEORGE (*With a shriek*). Stop that left-handed fool! (PRIVATE KEARNS *and* HARWOOD *jump up and get in front of him.*)

JOHNNY (*In a low hard voice*). Take it back, Corporal——

PRIVATE KEARNS (*Eyeing* JOHNNY). You better, Corp, you better.

CORPORAL GEORGE (*Muttering*). All right, I take it back. And put that gun down, Johnson. You're breaking orders by touching it anyhow.

(JOHNNY *waits a moment and then with a chuckle replaces the gun against the parapet, after which he sits down and sets to figuring again.*)

PRIVATE O'DAY (*After a moment's silence*). What you figuring on now, Old end-the-war?

CORPORAL GEORGE (*Satirically*). He's writing a letter to the general, again . . . I guess . . . or is it Minny Belle this time?

JOHNNY (*Quietly*). I'm figuring on a sort of document addressed to the German enlisted men.

CORPORAL GEORGE. Ho-ho! Will wonders never cease as the Rabbi said to the—(*With sour distaste*). Bah!

JOHNNY. Well, you'll never end this war if you don't try to.

CORPORAL GEORGE. And you think you can do that by writing letters. Wonderful, wonderful.

JOHNNY. Well we don't seem to be able to end it with guns. (PRIVATE HARWOOD *suddenly pushes his food away from him and picking up a rope from the ledge sits spinning it aimlessly.*)

PRIVATE HARWOOD (*Twirling his rope*). What I'd like to do would be to slip up on the Kaiser standing somewhere and lasso the crook. That'd stop the whole crazy business. (*He throws his lariat backward over his shoulder, jerks it, and begins pulling it in.*)

PRIVATE KEARNS (*Scratching himself savagely*). And what I wish is old Kaiser Bill had my cooties.

PRIVATE HARWOOD (*Springing up from the ledge and pulling on his lariat*). Heigh, I've hung something. (*He sticks his head quickly up and jerks it down again.*) God, it's a German soldier's leg—with a boot on!

(*He drops the rope and sits staring before him. With the exception of* JOHNNY *the others shoot their heads up, then jerk them down and sit in grim silence.* PRIVATE FAIRFAX *starts to whimper and pulls a little book from his pocket and begins to read.*)

JOHNNY. Yeah, there's legs and arms scattered all around. Down there where you cross that gully you can see 'em. Young arms and legs that used to throw rocks and walk about. (*Now once more comes the musical whing of the sniper's bullet. They all, except* JOHNNY, *duck their heads and then sit a moment in silence.*)

PRIVATE FAIRFAX (*As if to himself*). It says here in the Bible to love your enemies. How can a man do that? (*And now off at the right the voice of* CAPTAIN VALENTINE *is heard humming. He comes drifting slowly in, immaculately dressed as ever.*)

CAPTAIN VALENTINE (*Continuing his ballad*

as he gives the scene a thorough inspection).

    Woe, woe, cried the lady so fair
    The while she disrupted her hair—
Ha-ha laughed the colonel, you're guilty, I
    knew I'd unearth it.
    And the sergeant he too had his say
    Ere the rope took his brave life away—
(He breaks off his humming as they stand to attention.) At ease. *(They all relax. He con-*
10 *tinues in a fast sharp flow of words, unlike his former drawling.)* We've got orders to get this sniper. You can draw lots.

    JOHNNY *(Stepping forward)*. Is he a leader —a big man, sir?

    CAPTAIN VALENTINE. Right now he's more important to us than Hindenburg himself. He's got the provision train scared off that road down there.

    JOHNNY *(Saluting)*. I volunteer, sir.

20   CAPTAIN VALENTINE *(Turning and looking at him with a smile)*. That's very nice of you, Johnson, but you're too valuable a man to risk. *(He takes a box of matches from his pocket and strikes one of them, then reverses the ends of several matches and holds them out.)* The fellow who draws the burnt match goes for the sniper at dawn.

    JOHNNY. Can I draw, sir?

    CAPTAIN VALENTINE. Yes—last. *(He turns*
30 *and holds out his hand to* PRIVATE FAIRFAX, *who draws and lets out a glad cry.)*

    PRIVATE FAIRFAX. I didn't get it. *(*CAPTAIN VALENTINE *holds out his hand to* PRIVATE GOLD-BERGER. *He draws. From the look of relief he too is saved.)*

    JOHNNY *(Crowding up)*. I'm always lucky at such things. *(*CAPTAIN VALENTINE *holds his hand out to* PRIVATE HARWOOD.*)*

    PRIVATE HARWOOD *(Drawing)*. Ha-ha—I
40 don't go. *(Then* PRIVATE KEARNS *draws. He strikes the match joyously on his helmet and flings it down. And now* PRIVATE SVENSON *stands up trembling. He draws.)*

    PRIVATE SVENSON *(In a nervous tittering of relief)*. Ha-ha-hee-hee——

    CAPTAIN VALENTINE *(With an ironic groan)*. I see what's coming.

    JOHNNY *(Grinning)*. I told you so. *(He draws the last match and the* CAPTAIN *shakes*
50 *his head disgustedly.)*

    CAPTAIN VALENTINE. I'll say this for you, Johnson, whatever your drawbacks, cowardice is not one of them. *(Angrily)*. Tomorrow night I'm going to send some of you fellows out too.

    JOHNNY. Aw, you won't need to do that, sir.

    CAPTAIN VALENTINE. Lie down now and get some sleep—all of you. There's going to be a patrol directly in front of you. *(He gestures to the rear.)* Johnson, you can use your own judgment about the sniper.

    JOHNNY. Yes, sir.

    CORPORAL GEORGE. Attenshun. *(They all stand up, salute, and* CAPTAIN VALENTINE *starts away at the left. And now once more we hear the musical whinging of the sniper's bullet, followed by a loud yell off at the left. Everybody ducks, then straightens up again.* CAPTAIN VALENTINE *looks off and hurries away. They all resume their seats.)* I wonder who got hit that time? Well, Johnson, I suppose you'd better begin to wind up your earthly business.

    JOHNNY *(Now sitting down and cleaning the mud from his shoe with a stick)*. I will—about forty or fifty years from now, I hope.

    PRIVATE FAIRFAX *(Staring at him)*. You mean you're not scared?

    PRIVATE KEARNS. Ever notice these nuts?— They ain't scared.

    (By this time the shades of evening have begun to fall. The soldiers sit a moment in silence and then begin to make themselves comfortable on the ground and on the parapet ledge. JOHNNY *gets his old coat, brings it over and spreads it out close beside the can of tea. With the exception of* PRIVATE FAIRFAX *and* PRIVATE HARWOOD *they all stretch themselves out.* PRIVATE HARWOOD *pulls off his shirt and sits staring before him.)*

    PRIVATE FAIRFAX *(Beginning to read aloud from his Bible)*. "For God so loved the world that he gave his only begotten Son that whosoever believeth on Him should not perish but have everlasting life." *(He drops down on his knees in an attitude of prayer.* JOHNNY *looks around and breaks into a low chuckle.)*

    CORPORAL GEORGE *(Muttering as he lies down)*. I'll tell you this, Johnson, if I were in your shoes, I'd be praying too.

90. **"For God . . . life,"** from John 3:16.

JOHNNY. Human beings are funny, ain't they? —I was just thinking how the Germans are praying to the same God on their side too. (*With the exception of* PRIVATE HARWOOD *they all settle themselves for sleep.*)

PRIVATE HARWOOD (*Mournfully*). Getting on towards dark—just about this time the boys are rounding up the calves back home.

CORPORAL GEORGE. Yeh—back home—Good-night everybody.

JOHNNY (*Kissing a photograph and putting it in his shirt*). Good-night, Minny Belle—good-night.

PRIVATE KEARNS (*With a mock-smacking sound*). Good-night, Minny Belle, the mighty hero is thinking of you.

JOHNNY. Thank you, Private Kearns.

PRIVATE HARWOOD (*Beginning to unwrap his leggings and singing with wistful remembrance*).
Oh the Rio Grande—where the wind blows
    free
And the sun shines so clear and bright,
Where the trail is long, o'er the wide prairie
And the cowboy travels light.
Well it's saddle and boots
In sun and rain
And away, and watch me ride
Up along the canyon and over the plain.
Myself and my horse are one and the same
And one shadow runs beside.
    (*The men stir and murmur sleepily to themselves.*)
Oh life was dull but it happened so
A rodeo came one day.
I took my gal to see the show—
There stood my little bay.
I jumped in the saddle and grabbed the horn
And yelled to all around,
I'm the best damn cowpuncher ever was born,
And for Texas I am bound.
    (*A foggy twilight begins to envelop the scene.*)
Oh the Rio Grande—where the wind blows
    free——
    (*He lies down on the parapet. The lights slowly die out, and the scene is gradually enveloped in the gloom of night, with the sightless eyelid of the world slowly shutting out the sky. Far away as if under the rim of the earth*

the low growling of the mighty guns is heard. A moment passes. The muffled forms of the soldiers are dimly discerned as they sleep. Only the smiling blissful face of JOHNNY *is visible. In the orchestra the low melody of* MINNY BELLE'S *love song is playing, and far away from out of No Man's Land comes the faint indistinguishable whisper of her tender voice.*)

JOHNNY (*Murmuring*). Minny Belle—My honey-love!   60

    (*And now the gray illumination of* JOHNNY'S *face begins to die out, and* MINNY BELLE'S *song fades in air. As it fades the other sleepers are heard moaning and twisting in the grip of an uneasy dream. And on their now tortured faces appears the same gray illumination, but* JOHNNY'S *face remains in shadow. As if embodied forth by the restless sleepers' nightmare, the round muzzles of three great cannon push themselves slowly up over the parapet and* 70 *then out and out until their long threatening necks stretch above the recumbent figures.* MINNY BELLE'S *song has now died out from the orchestra and is supplanted by the growling croompy notes of the guns. They begin to sing in a queer outlandish trio harmony.*)

GUNS. Soldiers, soldiers—
Sleep softly now beneath the sky,
    Soldiers, soldiers—
Tomorrow under earth you lie.   80
We are the guns that you have meant
For blood and death.—Our strength is spent
Obedient to your stern intent—
    Soldiers, masters, men.

    Masters, masters,
Deep dark in earth as iron we slept,
    Masters, masters,
Till at your word to light we leapt.
We might have served a better will—
Ploughs for the field, wheels for the mill,   90
But you decreed that we must kill—
    Masters, soldiers, men.

    Soldiers, soldiers,
Sleep darkly now beneath the sky,
    Soldiers, soldiers—
No sound shall wake you where you lie,
No foe disturb your quiet bed
Where we stand watching overhead—

We are your tools—and you the dead!—
Soldiers, masters, men!

(*As the cannon song begins to die, the air is split by the musical tinkling of an alarm clock. As it continues to ring, the guns withdraw behind the parapet, their great muzzles slowly and sullenly sinking out of sight. The ringing of the clock stops, and* JOHNNY *sits up looking about him. Jerking his arms above his head, he* 10 *yawns and gapes and then gets to his feet.*)

CORPORAL GEORGE (*Mumbling*). What time is it, Johnson?

JOHNNY (*Looking up at the sky*). About three-thirty—by the ell and the yard. Go on and get your sleep.

(*He takes an old sock from his knapsack and begins to fit it over his face like a mask. Suddenly* PRIVATE FAIRFAX *lets out a scream, sits up and begins to beat wildly about him.*)

20 PRIVATE FAIRFAX. Catch him, catch him! (*The other soldiers sit up and beat at something in the trenches.*)

PRIVATE GOLDBERGER (*Lunging off to the left*). There he goes.

PRIVATE O'DAY. Whoo!—that bugger was big as a hog!

JOHNNY (*Still working with his mask*). Yeah, the rats get plenty to eat up here. I saw one yesterday squatted on a dead Australian's face. 30 (*For a while they all sit in disconsolate silence.*)

CORPORAL GEORGE. What in the devil are you doing now, Johnson?

JOHNNY. Camouflage. (*Now pulling an old poncho over his shoulders, he picks up the bread knife and begins whetting it on his palm. Then he goes over to the parapet, pulls in part of the lariat and cuts it off. The soldiers stare at him.*)

40 CORPORAL GEORGE. Don't tell me you're going after that sniper without a gun.

JOHNNY. This piece of rope and bread knife ought to do.

PRIVATE GOLDBERGER. Do you know where he hangs out?

JOHNNY. I've got an idea.

PRIVATE KEARNS. He's got ideas. (PRIVATE SVENSON *clambers up and comes over to* JOHNNY.)

50 PRIVATE SVENSON (*Grabbing his hand, his voice choked with emotion*). Goodbye, Yohnny. Be careful—uh—— (*He gulps.*)

JOHNNY. I will, Slim. (*Jauntily*). So long. I'll be back about sun-up. (*Stopping and calling back*). Better have some breakfast for that sniper, he'll be hungry. (*He goes away at the left.*)

PRIVATE SVENSON (*Blubbering*). He'll be killed!——

CORPORAL GEORGE. I hope so. Go to sleep. 60 (*They all lie down again.*)

Black Out

ACT TWO

SCENE III

"A new way to pay old debts."

It is near dawn, and the scene represents a shell-battered churchyard with a few broken tombstones about and a piece of ruined church tower distant in the background. The earth is covered with a thick tangle of grass about knee high. In the immediate center rear of the scene stands a huge black wooden statue of the 70 *Christ, leaning a bit awry and showing in its posture something of the beaten and agonized torture of an El Greco figure. While the orchestra continues to play the music of the stricken Redeemer,* JOHNNY *crawls in from the right front and secretes himself in the tall rank grass. A moment passes, the music continues, and then from the left rear the* SNIPER *enters, dodging behind tombstones and any bit of covering much in the manner of the Big Bad Wolf slip-* 80 *ping upon the house of the three little pigs. He comes to the base of the statue and looks appraisingly about him. He is a slender fellow with a rather large Kaiser Wilhelm mustache and an evil-looking helmet pulled low down over his forehead. Climbing up on a little platform built behind the statue, he opens a panel in the back of the Christ, crawls in and secretes himself, the door closing after him. And now as he worms his way further up inside the* 90 *dolorous figure, like an animal squeezing along*

"A . . . debts," the name of a comedy (1625) by the English playwright Philip Massinger (1583–1640). The expression is, however, more or less proverbial.
73. **El Greco,** a prominent Spanish painter (1545–1614), born Domenico Theotocopuli, probably in Crete, whence his nickname of "the Greek." He is noted for his gray atmosphere and his tendency toward a stiff delineation of the human figure, indicative of passion repressed within the subject.

inside a hollow tree, the statue shakes and wriggles with his weight. Then it grows still, the orchestra stops playing. And now through a great wounded hole in the breast of Christ where the heart should be, the ugly muzzle of a telescopic rifle with a silencer attached is pushed through. The muzzle comes to rest on the outstretched hand of the Redeemer. It seems to grow tense and the eye of the SNIPER can be seen shining out of the heart as he takes his sight. Suddenly the air is stricken with a muffled explosion and the bullet goes whinging on its musical way. JOHNNY bounds up out of the grass and rushing forward, flings his rope around the statue and draws it tight. Immediately a tremendous drumming sets up inside, and the wooden figure totters and sways and gesticulates like a live thing.

JOHNNY. Ha-ha—I got the dead wood on you this time—— (He ties the rope as the statue continues to shake and the drumming keeps up.)

SNIPER (In a high piteous voice as the figure bobs about). Kamerad! Kamerad!

JOHNNY. Yeah, and I'll Kamerad you, you Proosian devil! Drop that gun. (The statue gives a final buck and lunge.) Drop it, I tell you. (And now the rifle is pushed through the hole and falls to the ground.) Pistol too! You've got one. (A moment passes. And a mean-looking Luger with belt attached is disgorged from the heart and falls to the ground. JOHNNY unwinds his rope and stands aside as he flings open the door.) Come on out. (The SNIPER comes gingerly down, and as he steps to the earth JOHNNY lays his knife against the back of his neck.)

SNIPER (In a high treble cry). Ooh, um Gottes willen, tun Sie das nicht!

JOHNNY (Cuffing him about the head). You dirty stinking rascal! I've a good mind to cut your throat. Ain't you ashamed—using Jesus Christ like that!—and he a good man!

(He slaps his face again. The SNIPER drops down on the ground and buries his face in his hands. JOHNNY steps over, picks up the gun and the pistol and throws them out of reach towards the front and then stands over the SNIPER looking angrily down at him, wiping his sweaty face with his sleeve.)

SNIPER (Looking up as JOHNNY takes off his mask). Du lieber Himmel!

JOHNNY (Suddenly kicking him in the shins as he pulls off his helmet). Look-a-there—that hole. You shot at me yesterday!

SNIPER (Howling). Ow! Ow!

JOHNNY (Stamping down on one of his feet and mocking him). Ow! Ow! I ought to get me a switch and beat the lard out of you.

SNIPER (With piteous pleading). Bitte, bitte —— (He begins sobbing.)

JOHNNY (Staring at him malevolently). Stop that crying. (The SNIPER's sobs stop.)

SNIPER. Yes—yes, sir.

JOHNNY. Why, you speak English.

SNIPER. Yes, sir.

JOHNNY. Smart, mean and smart, you big guys.—What's happened to your mustache? (The SNIPER pushes his hanging lip piece quickly back but it comes off in his hand, revealing the lips and face of a beardless boy.)

JOHNNY (Throwing up his hands). Great Jehosaphat! You're just a boy!

BOY (Pushing back his helmet and wiping his forehead with his hand, disclosing his close-cropped boyish head). Yes, sir. (JOHNNY suddenly turns away and stands looking off deep in thought. The BOY watches him apprehensively.)

JOHNNY (In anger and disgust). That knocks me for a row of stumps—it does! (Turning back to him). Come over here by this pile of dirt. (He goes over and sits down. The BOY crawls along the ground and sits a few feet away from him.) Of all the ungodly things! How old are you?

BOY. Sixteen, sir.

JOHNNY. Sixteen— Hardly weaned. (After a pause). Is your mother living?

BOY. Yes—sir. (He bows his bare head over in his hands and begins to weep again.)

JOHNNY. Aw, don't do that— Aw—quit it. (He moves over a bit and puts his hand on the BOY's shoulder. With the back of his other hand he furtively wipes his own eyes. Turning to him again.) Why in the devil did you get into this war—young as you are?

BOY (His voice suddenly stronger). For Faterland and Kaiser, sir. (He salutes the air.)

---

37. um . . . nicht, "For God's sake, don't do that!"

51. Du . . . Himmel! "(Thou) good (dear) Heaven!" 59. Bitte, "Please!"

JOHNNY (*With an exclamation of impatience*). Nuts, as the monkey said! But never mind that— Don't you know it's for his own power and glory that the Kaiser sends such little boys as you out to die? (*As the* BOY *makes no answer*). Don't you believe that?

BOY (*Lowering his voice*). That's what Sergeant Mueller says. (*Quickly*). But he only talks it among the soldiers— (*Murmuring*). Ser-
10 geant Mueller.

JOHNNY. And he's right. (*After a moment's silence*). Who is this Sergeant Miller?

BOY (*Fervently*). He is kind and good— The best man in the world. He was my English teacher.

JOHNNY. He is—huh?

BOY. Yes, sir.

JOHNNY. And how does he feel about this war?

20 BOY (*Reluctantly*). Yes—yes, sir, he—hates it.

JOHNNY. Like you and me—huh?

BOY. May—bee.

JOHNNY. Hmn-n. (*After a moment*). Want some chewing gum. (*He hands the* BOY *a piece which he has drawn from his pocket.*) Put it in your mouth and chew—like me— Don't swallow it. (*The* BOY *does so.* JOHNNY *watches him with a sort of paternal geniality.*) Good? (*A tiny half-frightened smile breaks for an instant
30 over the* BOY's *white drawn face.* JOHNNY *pats him on the shoulder.*) What's your name, son?

BOY. Johann—Johann Lang. It means John— in English.

JOHNNY. I be jim-swingled! Why that's my name too—John. (*He reaches over and shakes the* BOY's *limp hand.*) Don't be afraid. I'm not going to hurt you.

JOHANN (*Now staring at him*). But the generals tell us you Americans cut and kill and
40 scalp and chop the German soldiers to pieces with knives.

JOHNNY. Ha-ha, they do!

JOHANN. Yes, sir, they all do— (*Hesitatingly*). The generals and the colonels in their speeches—the newspapers too.

JOHNNY. That's because the Kaiser's crowd tells 'em what to say.

JOHANN (*More confidingly as he chews*). But Herr Mueller says he don't believe it—to us
50 he says so. (*Eagerly*). He says he thinks you soldiers are like us—in the heart good. But he

don't know—he thinks so. (JOHNNY *sits looking off. Suddenly he slaps his knee.*)

JOHNNY. Say—it looks like me and this Miller fellow ought to get together on the war. (*He begins tapping his lip with his forefinger in deep thought. Young* JOHANN *watches him constantly, though now something of his first fright has disappeared.*)

JOHNNY. Pardon me, sir, but the sun will soon rise. Then it will be very dangerous for you here.

JOHNNY (*Turning to the* BOY). Suppose your friend Miller knew we American soldiers wanted to end this war the way he does, what do you think he'd do?

JOHANN (*Mournfully*). Aber, he cannot know that.

JOHNNY. Suppose he knew that we Americans deep down are the German people's friends—what do you think he'd want to do?

JOHANN. Stop fighting.

JOHNNY. He's a sensible man. (*Dumping some letters and folded papers from his pockets, he suddenly begins writing with a stub of a pencil, reading off some of the words as he does so.*) "Friend Miller, John Lang who brings this letter to you was captured by me, but I am sending him back——"

JOHANN (*With a cry*). You let me go! (*He springs forward and hugs* JOHNNY's *knees and then lies weeping on the ground, one of his hands touching* JOHNNY's *foot.*)

JOHNNY (*Smiling*). Yeah, that's right—(*Looking around towards the flaming horizon.*) and we got to hurry. (*Reading aloud again as he writes*). "—sending him back with these messages—um—um— See the enclosed speeches of Woodrow Wilson, also some by me which come quicker to the point. You and me have the same ideas about being friends and ending this war. John will tell you more. I must close on account of the sun coming up—
  Yours in friendship,
    Johnny Johnson,
      Private soldier."
(*Touching* JOHANN *on the shoulder*). Get up, son. (JOHANN *rises and stands wiping the tears of happiness from his eyes.*)

JOHANN. You—you really let me go?

JOHNNY (*Shoving several papers in an envelope and sticking them into* JOHANN's *pock-*

et). I'm sending you back, son, and I hope we end the war before it ends you. (JOHANN *grabs his hand and kisses it with wild joy.*)

JOHANN. Forgive me—the Colonel, he made me do it——

JOHNNY (*Pulling his hand sheepishly away*). Do what?

JOHANN (*With a gesture towards the figure of Christ*). Hide in there and shoot at you Americans. All the time after this I shoot in the air.

JOHNNY (*Quickly*). That's the idea. Tell friend Miller to spread the news among his soldiers—his friends—make copies of the speeches, distribute them everywhere. You'll hear from me again—somehow. Now quick—run—we're going to save a lot of lives.

(*He pushes him along.* JOHANN *grabs* JOHNNY's *hand once more, then embraces him and dashes away at the left rear.* JOHNNY *stares after him, waves his hand, and then picks up the rifle and the pistol and stands looking at the statue of Christ. He pulls off his helmet in humility and respect.* CAPTAIN VALENTINE *comes crawling in on his all-fours at the right front. He is humming softly to himself.* JOHNNY *gives a last look at the statue, gazes at the rifle and pistol in his hands, then shrugs his shoulders in a vague comment on the world and comes toward the front.* CAPTAIN VALENTINE *calls out in a low admiring voice.*)

CAPTAIN VALENTINE. You killed him!

JOHNNY (*In good humor*). No.

CAPTAIN VALENTINE (*Standing quickly up*). What! (*Looking off and then jerking out his pistol.*) Yonder—look out! (*Raging*). Oh, you fool!

JOHNNY (*Springing in front of him*). Don't you shoot him! (CAPTAIN VALENTINE *tries to dodge this way and that around* JOHNNY, *and finally gets in a shot over his shoulder.*)

CAPTAIN VALENTINE (*Raising his pistol as if to strike* JOHNNY *with the butt of it*). I missed him. (*Suddenly a burst of machine gun fire rattles out from the direction of the German trenches. The air is filled with a medley of whinging sounds and the plop of bullets striking against the earth. The* CAPTAIN *throws himself flat on his belly.* JOHNNY *darts forward to drop down beside him, then suddenly slaps his hand to his rump with a howl.* CAPTAIN VALEN-

TINE *laughs hysterically as* JOHNNY *sprawls down beside him.*) Ha-ha-ha, got you, did they? There is a just God after all!

JOHNNY (*Half-sobbing with anger and vexation, one hand still on his rump*). Ain't that a hell of a place to get shot! (*The* CAPTAIN *starts crawling off at the right front,* JOHNNY *crawling painfully after him.*)

Black Out

ACT TWO

SCENE IV

" 'Tis not so deep as a well—but 'tis enough.
'Twill serve."

The hospital. JOHNNY's *bed is in the foreground with an infinite row of beds painted on the background diminishing in the distance.* JOHNNY *is lying restless on his side with his face towards the audience. A young French* NURSE, *very chic and attractive in her French uniform, is trying to make him comfortable.*

NURSE (*Sitting down by him and beginning to sing*).

My Madelon of Paree
She laugh and dance and sing
To cheer the weary soldier
    At his homecoming.
A little room together,
An hour of love to spend,
Comme-ça, your arm around me,
    Oh—mon ami, my friend.

(JOHNNY *stirs and closes his eyes.*)

But she—ah—she remembers
That other love and joy,
The first, the best, the dearest,
    Tired soldier boy—
A narrow room alone now,
Rain on the roof above,
And he will sleep forever,
    Oh—mon ami, my love.

My Madelon of Paree
She does not sit and grieve,

" 'Tis . . . serve," from the final speeches of Mercutio in *Romeo and Juliet*. He has been mortally wounded by Tybalt and his partisans; Romeo remarks that his wound cannot be very bad; "Ay, ay," says Mercutio, "a scratch; marry, 'tis enough . . . 'tis not so deep as a well nor so wide as a church-door; but 'tis enough, 'twill serve." (*Romeo and Juliet*, III, 1, 96–101.)

But sings away her sorrow
    To cheer the soldier's leave.
For life is short and funny,
And love must have an end.
An hour may be forever—
    Oh—mon ami, my friend.

(*A fat middle-aged hospital* ORDERLY *comes in from the right and starts on across the scene.*)

10   JOHNNY (*Jerking up his head and calling out*). Any mail for me?

ORDERLY (*Chuckling*). Not even a letter from General Pershing. (*Laughing softly*). Hee-hee —how's the wound this morning?

JOHNNY (*Irately*). I've told you to lay off that subject.

ORDERLY. The doctor's coming to have another look at it in a minute.

JOHNNY (*Irritably*). Yeh—and I want to have 20 a look at him. He's got to let me out of here.

ORDERLY. Why in blazes you want to get back to the front is more than I can see. (*Wagging his head he goes on out at left.*)

NURSE (*Putting her hand on his forehead*). Forty times a day I say take it easy, bébé, you last longer.

JOHNNY. And how can I take it easy, and me with work to do in the trenches? (*He pulls a letter from under his pillow and begins read-* 30 *ing it.*)

NURSE (*Presently*). Johnny.

JOHNNY. Yeh.

NURSE (*Softly*). Don't you love me a—you say—little bit?

JOHNNY. There you go—back on that subject. Now look here—you know I'm an engaged man.

NURSE. Oui, but your Minny Belle—she is so far away——

JOHNNY (*Pressing the letter to his breast*). 40 She is here—close by—(*Reading his letter aloud to himself perhaps for the twentieth time*). "Every night when we meet in the church I think of you and pray for victory. I am sure the despicable Hun will soon be brought to their knees." (*The warmth dying out of his voice*). "Anguish has just come with his new motor truck to take me to the office— How many of the enemy have you killed? Goodbye till next time."

50   NURSE. I don't like Anguish.

JOHNNY. Nobody does.

NURSE. Maybe Minny Belle likes him?

JOHNNY (*Rearing up in bed*). I should say not. (*Grimacing he lies down again.*)

NURSE (*In a flutter of sympathy*). You must sleep—your fever will be worse.

JOHNNY (*Gruffly*). Fever or no fever, I got to go, I tell you. (*He turns over on his side.*)

NURSE (*After a moment, timidly*). Johnny?

JOHNNY. Unh-hunh. 60

NURSE. You don't mind—me loving you—a little? Comprenez-vous?

JOHNNY. I comprenez, all right, but it don't do me no good. You go try one of them fellows with boots and spurs.

(*A middle-aged* DOCTOR *wearing a goatee and carrying a black satchel in his hand enters from the left. Close behind him comes the* OR- DERLY *with a little cylinder-tank, about fifteen inches long and three inches in diameter in his* 70 *hand. They stop by* JOHNNY'*s bed.*)

DOCTOR (*Gesturing with an inclination of his head towards the* ORDERLY). Better give him a whiff, I guess.

JOHNNY (*As the* ORDERLY *steps to the head of his bed*). What for?

ORDERLY. It's laughing gas—make you feel good.

JOHNNY. I don't need any gas, or whatever it is. Go ahead. And then I want you to tell me 80 when you're going to turn me loose.

DOCTOR (*Opening his satchel*). Hm-m— At the proper time.

JOHNNY (*Vexatiously*). What time is that—as the owl said?

DOCTOR (*Sourly*). Maybe sooner than you expect, as the pill said—ah-oom—Turn over.

(*The* ORDERLY *lays his cylinder down on the bed and rolls up his sleeve. He and the* DOCTOR *now step behind the bed, bend down and be-* 90 *gin deftly dressing* JOHNNY'*s wound. The little* NURSE *pulls a waist-high screen from under the bed and sets it up in front of* JOHNNY; *after which she moves over to the right and stands looking off. And now entering from the right comes the* SISTER *of the Organization for the Delight of Disabled Soldiers. She is a tall, raw- boned, breezy woman of middle-age, over- dressed and slightly over-enthusiastic in her manner.*) 100

SISTER (*Gazing about her*). I vow! this will be bully for our show. The acoustics look good. (*Trying them*). Tra-la-la. (*To the* NURSE). How many brave buddies have we got here?

NURSE. Four thousand and sixty-four soldiers this morning, madame.

SISTER. That's a real break. There's nothing like a big audience to cheer the actor—I mean the soldier. I wish to speak to the head doctor.

NURSE (*Gesturing towards the screen*). He is busy.

SISTER (*Looking behind the* NURSE *at the bed, her voice filling with sudden sympathy*). Hello, how are you, buddy! (*Then springing back in confusion*). Oh—it's not decent— And I was mistaken. One of our brave buddies is a coward.

NURSE (*Stoutly*). Johnny Johnson is not a coward.

SISTER. Then how did he get shot where he did? (*The* DOCTOR *finishes with* JOHNNY, *straightens up and sees the* SISTER.)

DOCTOR (*Hurrying over and shaking her hands*). Delighted, delighted. (*To the* ORDERLY *who is covering* JOHNNY *with the sheet*). Run —notify the Colonel. We will have entertainment this evening. The Sister from the Organization for the Delight of Soldiers Disabled in the Line of Duty is here. (*At the rigmarole of words*, JOHNNY *raises himself up. The* ORDERLY *hurries away to do the* DOCTOR's *bidding leaving the little gas cylinder behind.*)

SISTER. You got my message——

DOCTOR. Yes-yes-yes.

SISTER. The piano and the stage?

DOCTOR. All arranged.

SISTER. Good. (*Looking approvingly around*). Wonderful hospital, doctor. Best I've seen on my tour.

DOCTOR (*Bowing low*). Thank you, thank you. They tell me so in higher quarters.

SISTER. Hmn-n. Everything so spick and span —so many beds. (*Sleepily*). I could lie right down. (JOHNNY *looks up watchfully*.)

DOCTOR (*Stiffly, as a military manner creeps over him*). Extra facilities are being provided for the great oncoming battle, madam.

JOHNNY (*Calling out*). Battle?—when is it to start, sir?

DOCTOR (*Turning to him*). My man, the ex-act hour is known only to the Allied High Command, but it will doubtless be soon—perhaps tomorrow.

JOHNNY (*Aghast*). Tomorrow?—And here I lie. (*His face full of pain*). And there will be thousands killed—thousands of boys killed. (*He begins fingering the little cylinder abstractedly.*)

DOCTOR. But we must be prepared to offer these sacrifices on the altar of freedom.

JOHNNY (*Starting violently up*). The more I hear of this freedom the less I like it.

SISTER (*Loudly*). I was right. He *is* a coward!

JOHNNY (*Angrily*). And old lady, you're full of prunes.

DOCTOR (*Sternly*). Lie down, young man. You do not know to whom you are talking to.

JOHNNY (*Wagging his head in pain as the* NURSE *comes over and lays her hand on his shoulder*). When I think of the fools running this world it near'bout sets me distracted. (*Frantically*). Can't somebody do something to put off this fight?

DOCTOR. This is the most opportune time. (*To the* SISTER). From yesterday's prisoners we learn that a spirit of rebellion has begun to spread among the German soldiers.

JOHNNY (*Crying out*). What! Say that again.

DOCTOR. And we must strike while the iron is hot. (*Taking the* SISTER's *arm*). Let me show you around.

JOHNNY (*Wildly*). Hooray! Hooray! It's working! Good for you, Sergeant Miller!— (*Gazing out at them in happy innocence*). He's a German friend of mine on the other side —thinks the same way I do. He and Johann. (*The* SISTER *looks at him in horror.*)

SISTER (*Bending down and glaring at him*). Not only a coward, but a—traitor! (JOHNNY *in fingering the gas cylinder suddenly lets loose a spray in her face.*)

DOCTOR. Heigh! (*He starts towards* JOHNNY, *then turns and steadies the* SISTER *who seems about to fall.*)

JOHNNY (*As he cuts off the hiss of escaping gas*). Excuse me—I'm excited—I'm—— (*A vacant look passes over the* SISTER's *countenance, and then she begins to laugh with a low infectious gurgle of fun.* JOHNNY *stares at her in amazement.*)

SISTER (*With a sudden whoop*). I feel good! I love everybody. I love you, my brave suffering hero!

DOCTOR. Never mind, it's only the gas.

(*She suddenly grabs* JOHNNY *and begins to manhandle him in an affectionate embrace. The* DOCTOR *and the young French* NURSE *spring forward and pull her off. The* SISTER *now begins cavorting about and flinging her long* 10 *shanks shamelessly before their gaze.*)

SISTER. I feel wonderful! I feel like flying. (*She begins a clattering tap dance, and then throws her arms around the* DOCTOR.) Come on, doctor, the show's ready to start.

DOCTOR. Young man, I'll attend to you later!

(*The* SISTER *goes dancing off at the left, pulling the* DOCTOR *with her.* JOHNNY *and the* NURSE *sit looking off at the left as the sound of the dancing dies out. Then* JOHNNY'S *gaze* 20 *comes back to the cylinder and he stares at it.*)

JOHNNY. You see what happened? One minute she wanted to shoot me and the next minute eat me with love. Wonderful stuff this laughing gas.

NURSE (*As* JOHNNY *keeps staring before him*). You sleep now.

JOHNNY. Pity they don't use laughing gas in the war instead of poison gas. (*Snapping his fingers*). Bring me my britches.

30 NURSE (*Alarmed, as she bends over him and tries to push him back*). No, Johnny! Mon Dieu!

JOHNNY (*As he looks at the* NURSE, *then suddenly lays himself back*). All right— (*The* NURSE *pulls the cover up and tucks him in.*)

NURSE (*Kissing him on the forehead*). 'S'right —a good boy. Good-night, Johnny.

JOHNNY (*Dreamily*). Good-night— (*She blows him a kiss from her fingers and goes* 40 *softly away at the right. A moment passes,* JOHNNY *cautiously raises his head, looks around and then slides his legs out of the bed. He pulls the sheet off and the gas tank falls to the floor.*) Guess I better take you along—might meet another fool. (*He picks the cylinder up, then crawls out, pajamas and all, through the open window at the right.*)

Black Out

ACT TWO

SCENE V

"In the multitude of counsellors there is safety."

The scene is a meeting of the Allied High Command in the Chateau de Cent Fontaines somewhere behind the lines. The setting is one of magnificence, mainly consisting of glass, red plush, and a flight of marble-columned stairs in the right rear. Running along the back is a glassed hall with potted palms and decorative flowers, and with a door opening inward.

When the curtain rises, the Allied High Command is sitting around a long table in the middle of the room. At the center, back of the table, sits the CHIEF OF THE COMBINED ALLIED FORCES. *He bears a striking resemblance to Marshal Foch. And at his right sits an* AMERICAN GENERAL, *the Commander of the American Expeditionary Forces, who just as obviously resembles General Pershing; and on his left sits the* COMMANDER-IN-CHIEF *of the British Expeditionary Forces, an almost exact replica of Marshal Sir Douglas Haig. On the* BRITISH COMMANDER'S *left sits a* BRITISH MAJOR-GENERAL *who resembles General Rawlinson, and on the* AMERICAN COMMANDER'S *right a* FRENCH MAJOR-GENERAL *who looks much like General Petain. At the left end of the table in profile to the audience sits a man in civilian clothes somewhat resembling the British Premier Lloyd George. At the other end of the table also in profile is another man in civilian clothes much like Clemenceau, the Tiger Premier of France. On the side of the table next to the audience sits a single lone figure in uniform somewhat resembling Albert, King of the Belgians, who throughout most of the military proceedings remains with bowed head, as if taking no interest in what goes on around him. At the left in the rear stand several staff officers—a* BELGIAN MAJOR-GENERAL, *a* BRITISH BRIGADIER-GENERAL, *a* SCOTTISH COLONEL *and a* POLISH COLONEL. *Behind each of the three central figures—the* CHIEF OF THE ALLIED FORCES, *the* BRITISH COMMANDER, *and the* AMERICAN COMMANDER— *stands a* FIELD CLERK *with a stenographic pad*

"**In . . . safety,**" from Proverbs 11:14. The same clause appears in Proverbs 24:6; and virtually the same idea in Proverbs 15:22.

in his hand. All of the officers are dressed in most élite uniforms and are plentifully decorated with medals, crosses, and orders of merit. Their field coats and caps are placed on a sofa near the stairway. Spread out on the table is a huge war map which the three military leaders are considering.

As these mighty keepers of men's destiny speak forth their arguments and plans with puppet pomp and solemn precision, the orchestra keeps up an accompaniment of wide-spaced chords with now and then an ironic figure played by the flute or oboe in between.

CHIEF OF THE ALLIED HIGH COMMAND (*Continuing with a slight accent as he gestures with his baton of Maréchal of France*).
The Flanders group of armies—hmmn—
Will march as we have said
Towards Brussels on the left,
The right towards Hal—
(*Saluting and addressing the* KING).
Your Majesty.
(*The* KING *without replying gestures with a long finger towards the* BELGIAN MAJOR-GENERAL *at the left rear*.)
BELGIAN MAJOR-GENERAL (*With his wooden salute*).
Poor Belgium understands and quite agrees—
What little part is left of her I mean——
BRITISH COMMANDER-IN-CHIEF (*With a low mutter*).
And plenty of her's left, I'm shuah—
Such as it is.
BELGIAN MAJOR-GENERAL (*With his hand on his sword*).
I did not catch the gentleman's remarks——
CHIEF (*Sternly*).
We're not concerned with private quarrels here.
The question is not reparations now,
Nor yet division of the spoils.
BRITISH COMMANDER. My speech was purely
    topographical.
(*The* BELGIAN MAJOR-GENERAL *bows*.)
CHIEF (*Looking around at the* BRITISH COMMANDER).
The mission of the British army, sir,
Will be to hurl th' invader's forces back
Toward Froidchapelle and Philippeville.
(*The* BRITISH COMMANDER *looks confusedly*

16. *Maréchal*, marshal, the highest office in the French army.

around and then turns to the ENGLISH MAJOR-GENERAL *at his side. The* MAJOR-GENERAL *looks uncertainly about him and then turns towards the* ENGLISH BRIGADIER-GENERAL *at the left*).
BRIGADIER-GENERAL (*Vacuously*).
Ha-ha—quite so—
To hurl th' invader's forces back.
CHIEF (*Briskly*).
It seems that everything goes well in hand.
(*The* FIELD CLERKS *continue writing rapidly. The one behind the* CHIEF *bends down and whispers in his ear. The* CHIEF *nods and continues*.)
—Right—goes well in hand—
Though we were much remiss in leaving out
Our allied friends—les braves Américains.
AMERICAN COMMANDER-IN-CHIEF (*Gruffly*).
Mistakes in such small matters will occur.
CHIEF (*Consulting his map again*).
Th' American forces will move south
Co-operating with the French armies—
The first, the fourth, the fifth, the tenth,
Maneuvring on both wings
To catch the Boches by surprise.
(*He looks questioningly at the* AMERICAN COMMANDER *who nods his head in slothful agreement. Then as the* CHIEF *gazes about the room for confirmation, everybody nods with the exception of the* KING. *The* CHIEF *now picks up a huge stamp and with three swift and sudden blows puts the final seal upon the orders before him. Then he rises and in even more puppet dignity than before addresses the assembly, while the orchestra keeps up its mock-solemn accompaniment*.)
And so, Messieurs,
The disposition of the Allied arms
Is—all—arranged,
And each man knows his task,
N'est-ce-pas?
(*They all nod.*)
And now the saddest subject possible—
The necessary loss of life
In this oncoming drive—
Are we prepared to suffer it—
As we have done so many times before?
THE ASSEMBLY (*Like one man with the exception of the* KING *and the* AMERICAN COMMANDER).
Oui!
We are!

CHIEF (*To the* KING).

Your majesty?

(*The* KING *again points his finger towards the* BELGIAN MAJOR-GENERAL *at the left.*)

BELGIAN MAJOR-GENERAL (*In a crisp mathematical voice*).

The rivers, mud, concrete, and wire,

Which Belgium's sons must struggle through

Force us to allow for heavy loss—

10 Some thirty thousand dead perhaps,

Some hundred and ten thousand wounded too.

(*The* CHIEF *stamps an order with his seal.*)

CHIEF. Your excellency of the British Isles?

(*The* BRITISH COMMANDER *leans towards the* ENGLISH MAJOR-GENERAL *who turns once more and looks to the left at the* ENGLISH BRIGADIER-GENERAL.)

BRIGADIER-GENERAL. More than a hundred

20 thousand killed

And thrice as many wounded, sir.

CHIEF (*Hollowly*).

Vive, vive!

Proud England's glory never shall grow dim

The while her sons can die so easily.

(*Once more he stamps an order.*)

BELGIAN MAJOR-GENERAL (*Piteously*).

But Belgium, sir, is such a little land,

So tiny and so small—

30 (*Beginning to figure on a piece of paper*).

But tiny though she is, who knows?

We may enlarge that figure some—to say—

Er—fifty thousand dead.

CHIEF. Bravo!

OTHERS. Bravo!

(*The* BELGIAN MAJOR-GENERAL *bows and looks at the* BRIGADIER-GENERAL.)

CHIEF (*Continuing as he addresses the* FRENCH MAJOR-GENERAL *at the left*).

40 Et vous, mon cher brave camarade!

FRENCH MAJOR-GENERAL (*Rising and glancing about him*).

We bow before the mighty English nation.

(*Pounding the table with his knuckles, his thin face working with pent-up emotions*).

If we lose more than eighty thousand dead

Revolt will spread and anarchy break out in

France! (*He sits down.*)

CHIEF (*Stamping another order with a*

50 bang).

Vraiment!

(*But now the* PREMIER OF FRANCE *stands up, his white mustache quivering with vexation and rage.*)

FRENCH PREMIER. Non, non, I say and still say non!

If England gives her hundred thousand dead,

La Belle France, my native land,

Can give her hundred thousand so the same.

(*He collapses suddenly in his chair.*)

VOICES. Vive la France!

FRENCH MAJOR-GENERAL. But England has more men to lose—

(*Loudly*).

—and why?—

(*Now on his feet again*).

Because the sons of France fell with their guns

The while the English let them fall—

At Ypres, Vimy Ridge and Mons they did.

ENGLISH PREMIER (*Springing up*).

The English soldiers are no fools.

They know well when to die—

(*Scornfully*).

Unlike the French who at Verdun

Lost half a million wasteful dead—

Perhaps a million if the truth were known.

(*And now the French and Belgian staff officers are on their feet and the* FRENCH PREMIER *sputters like a fire cracker in his chair.*)

OFFICERS. We protest!

BRITISH PREMIER. I see that's still a hornet's nest—

So let it lie—

I only wanted to make clear my point,

And no offense was meant.

(*He sits down. The* CHIEF *bangs on his table with his baton.*)

CHIEF. As allies in a sacred cause

I ask you to forget what's past—

(*To the French and Belgian officers*).

Please have no worry, mes amis,

69. **Ypres . . . Mons,** names of great battles on the western front during World War I. Mons, in Hainaut Province, Belgium, was the scene of the first important contact between British and German troops early in August 1914; the British were overwhelmed and driven back until the opening of the first Battle of the Marne (September 6, 1914). Ypres, in West Flanders, Belgium, saw innumerable battles between the British and Germans from 1914 to 1918; the last came during the great spring drive of the Germans from March to May, 1918. Vimy Ridge, in Pas-de-Calais, France, was the scene of a victory by the Canadian troops in 1917. 74. **Verdun,** a fortress-town in the department of Meuse, France, scene of a prolonged series of assaults by the Germans under the Crown Prince through the major portion of the summer of 1916. The position was held by the French in spite of appalling losses, and the battle ended in an eventual stalemate.

The course of tactics and control
Is safely in French hands.
Be seated.

(*They all sit down, and the* CHIEF *now turns to the* AMERICAN COMMANDER.)
Your estimated losses, sir?

AMERICAN COMMANDER (*Curtly*).
Very few, I hope.

(*Bending over the spread-out map*).
It seems we have right many trees
Along the sector where we fight—
I don't expect so many killed—
I say expect.

(*The generals and officers look at him in querying displeasure. The* BRITISH PREMIER *suddenly applauds, then stares morosely at the floor.*)
There's nothing better than a tree
Between you and machine gun fire—
Especially if it's big.

CHIEF (*Airily*).
Much so the poor benighted Indians used to fight. (*With a shrug*).
Where are they now?

AMERICAN COMMANDER. I hear they're living peaceful in the West
And doing well with copper mines and oil.

CHIEF (*With a more violent shrug*).
Tant pis!

(*His voice suddenly stern and authoritative.*)
Messieurs,
At this high moment and historic hour
We all stand up—stand up—stand up—

(*Everybody does so including the unhurrying* AMERICAN COMMANDER.)
Salute—

(*They all lift their hands and salute, staring straight towards the front.*)
Salute the coming of the early dawn
That marks the zero hour of doom,
The end of Germany.

VOICES. The end of Germany!

(*For a moment they all stand in silence while the orchestra continues its commenting chords. Suddenly the* CHIEF *barks out.*)
We meet upon the battlefield—
The Council is adjourned—
For breakfast——

(*They all rise and, with the exception of the*

29. Tant pis! "So much the worse!"

AMERICAN COMMANDER, *begin shaking one another's hand solemnly.* JOHNNY *appears on the stairway at the right rear. He is still dressed in his pajamas which are now muddy-legged. And under his arm he carries the little gas tank bundled up in the hospital sheet.*)

JOHNNY (*Calling out*). Say—say, you folks, don't break up just yet. (*He comes on down into the scene and stops at the right front. Everybody has whirled around and is staring at the bizarre newcomer in speechless amazement.*)

AMERICAN COMMANDER (*Blinking*). How did you get in here?

JOHNNY (*With a tired disarming smile*). Oh, but I didn't hurt your guards. They're down there in the bushes, all feeling fine. (*He chuckles and looks around at them.*) I know most of you. I've seen your pictures in the papers.

CHIEF. Arrest that man. (*The* FIELD CLERKS *start around the table toward him.* JOHNNY *steps toward the footlights, his hand on the concealed cylinder.*)

JOHNNY. Say—wait a minute.

AMERICAN COMMANDER. Gentlemen, he is one of my countrymen. I know him by his accent. (*He addresses* JOHNNY.) Young man, I ask you quietly to leave the room, otherwise these gentlemen here will have the pleasant duty of hanging you.

JOHNNY. No, they won't hang me, General. They'll thank me—all of you will—when I tell you what I've come for.

AMERICAN COMMANDER (*With a placating gesture around him*). And what have you come for?

JOHNNY. To help you end this war. (*Now edging closer to the footlights as the staff officers at the right and left rear take a step toward him.*) Yes, sir, I've been in communication with some of the German soldiers and they're about ready to stop this fighting. (*Triumphantly*). A rebellion is spreading.

CHIEF (*In a low voice to the* AMERICAN COMMANDER). Rebellion?—How did he know that?

JOHNNY. I know it all right.

AMERICAN COMMANDER (*With a smile as he gazes around him as much as to say, "He is harmless. We can spare him a moment or two."*). You do?

JOHNNY. Yes sir, I got direct news from the

755

German sniper I captured. (*The* CHIEF *and the* AMERICAN COMMANDER *look at each other.*)

AMERICAN COMMANDER. So you captured a German?

JOHNNY. Yes sir. He said the common soldiers wanted to be friends with us, and I sent him back with all kinds of messages saying we want to be friends too. And I tell you it's beginning to work. They're rebelling against the German war lords—already. What we got to do now is get millions of articles and speeches printed——

AMERICAN COMMANDER (*Abruptly*). Is your name by any chance—Johnson—Johnny Johnson?

JOHNNY (*With a sudden pleased grin*). Yes sir, that's me, and you never did answer my letters.

AMERICAN COMMANDER (*To the assembly*). There's nothing to fear, gentlemen, he's harmless.

CHIEF. The meeting is adjourned.

JOHNNY (*Springing frantically towards them*). But it's the truth, the truth I'm telling you. You've got to hold up this battle. I'll make my way into the German lines—I'll prove it. I'll do anything! You and the other generals can sign an order right now stopping the offensive. Then we get busy with prop—propaganda— words—words.—Yes sir, they're a lot more powerful than bullets if you speak them at the right time. And this is the right time. For the more the Germans read, the more they'll see the truth of what we say. And right now when they're worn out and sick of war they'll be glad to come to terms, and there won't be a dozen people killed. (*Turning vehemently to the* SCOTTISH COLONEL). Ain't there some truth in what I'm saying, ma'am?

COLONEL (*Blinking and hesitating*). Aye, there is. (*Then wadding up his kilt nervously as his confrères stare around at him*). I—er— mean—ha-ha-ha.

JOHNNY. That's right, you can always depend upon the women folks. Now, come on, let's use our heads—that's what they're for. Let's——

CHIEF (*Sternly to the staff officers*). Take him away!

JOHNNY (*Incredulously*). You mean—you don't believe what I'm saying? (*Crying out warningly as the staff officers move towards him*). Heigh, better not! (*Suddenly he shoots his gas cylinder out and holds it protectively in front of him.*)

KING (*In a low horror-struck voice as he points a quivering forefinger*). A bomb!

VOICES (*Softly*). A bomb.

JOHNNY (*Eying them*). Well— (*Then quickly*). Ho-ho, then suppose I have got a bomb. (*He takes a quick step forward and they all draw back from him and stand frightened and awed, and even the* AMERICAN COMMANDER *is stopped in his tracks.* JOHNNY *watches them in silence a moment and then continues with suppressed emotion.*) Now then maybe you'll listen to me. (*Anger creeping into his voice*). I was standing there listening to you all right and you were speaking of a pile of dead men in tomorrow's battle higher'n that big tower in Paris—poor dumb guys like me you're sending out to die—to be blown to pieces! (*With sudden rage*). All right, suppose I blow you to pieces with this-er-bomb. (*Yelling*). Sit down, King! (*He lifts his bundle menacingly.*)

KING (*Collapsing into his chair and calling piteously*). Gendarmes! Gendarmes!

(*And now all the others, with the exception of the* AMERICAN COMMANDER *who never takes his eyes off* JOHNNY, *sink down into their chairs and stare about them with fearful faces.*)

JOHNNY. So here you sit on your hind ends holy as God and make your plans—marking up your thousands of dead and dying like cold figures on a blackboard. Know what that means? I ask you—know what it means?—all these boys—young fellows like me—like what you used to be—going out to die—shot down— killed—murdered—to lie dead and stiff and rotten in a trench with rats and mud? We were meant for something better, I tell you! (*Vehemently*). We want to live, and you could let us live! We want to be let alone to do our work in peace—to have our homes—to raise our families—We want to look back someday and say our life has meant something—we have been happy and it was good to be born into this world. (*Pleadingly to the* AMERICAN COMMANDER *who has approached close to him*). You see what I mean, don't you—don't you? (*More quietly as he controls the trembling in his voice*). When you come right down to it

what sense is there in human beings trying to cut and tear and destroy one another like wild beasts in a jungle? There's no sense in it, is there? Is there! (*Stretching out his hands to all of them*). You're our leaders—you're all powerful over us—you tell us to die for freedom or a flag or our country or whatever crazy ideal it is —and we have to die. (*Half-sobbing as they look at him with cold authority-set faces*).
10 You'd rather live too, hadn't you? You'd rather be at home with your wives and children, hadn't you—living in peace the way men were meant to live? Then end this killing—end it now—(*Brokenly*). Only a second's time—a movement of your hand—a written word—and you could stop this war. Do it! Do it! (*Staring at them aghast as they look at him with dull baleful eyes*). But you don't listen. That Englishman was right. You don't want to end this
20 war. (*A queer baffled grieving in his voice*). There's something black and evil got into you —something blinded you—something——

(*He drops his head. Suddenly at a gesture from the* AMERICAN COMMANDER *several of the staff officers spring upon him. He turns quick as a flash and starts toward the stairway at the right rear, but the* FIELD CLERKS *head him off. And now as several of the officers close in upon him he suddenly unscrews the tank of gas and*
30 *sends it hissing and spraying into their faces. The officers gradually stop their pursuit, look at one another, and the expression of their faces changes. And now they begin to laugh.* JOHNNY *stares at them in astonishment, as do the great generals. Then as the latter rise and move toward him, he rushes around among them releasing the gas in their faces, taking time to squirt the* KING *a full dose.*)

KING (*Throwing up his hands in a loud clap-*
40 *ping.*) Ho-ho-ho!

OTHERS. Whoops!—wonnerful!—Merveilleux!

(*And now the* AMERICAN COMMANDER *breaks into a roar and slaps his side. The orchestra begins to play a sprightly tune, and the scene changes from one of solemn dignity into one of humor and gaiety. Several of the officers begin dancing their native dances—the* POLISH COLONEL *at the right doing a Polonaise, the* SCOTTISH COLONEL *at the left a Highland Fling, and*
50 *the American, English, and French officers tap dancing, waltzing, and minuetting.* JOHNNY

with the sheet wadded over his nose and mouth, stands gazing at them with questioning, puckered eyes. And now the BRITISH PREMIER *and the* FRENCH PREMIER *hop out into the middle of the room, and hooking their arms together cut a few steps like old men at a country dance. His* MAJESTY *the* KING *bows his head on the table like a great ungainly puppet and begins to laugh at some secret and mysterious* 60 *joke.*)

KING. Ho-ho-ho-ho!

OTHERS. Heh-heh-heh-heh. (*And now there is a general chorus of merry laughter, and even* JOHNNY *giggles a bit.*)

THE WHOLE ASSEMBLY (*With the exception of* JOHNNY).
Ha-ha-ha-ho-ho-ho-
Haw-haw-haw-
Hey-hey-hey-hey-hey-hey- 70
Hy-hy-hy-hee-hee-hee-
Hi-hi-hi-iiiiiiiiiii-ay!

(*The Frenchmen now kiss the Americans and the Americans kiss the Frenchmen, and then they all take hands and dance around the table like children around a maypole. As they whirl by, the* AMERICAN COMMANDER *grabs* JOHNNY'S *hand and pulls him into the dance. He moves with them, holding his sheet around him. The* AMERICAN COMMANDER *in a benevo-* 80 *lent outburst of feeling picks up his great-coat with its insigniae and puts it around* JOHNNY *and then follows by placing his cap on his head.*)

AMERICAN COMMANDER (*With a loud voice as he salutes*). General Johnny Johnson!

(*The dance suddenly stops, and the officers all crowd towards* JOHNNY, *click their heels and salute likewise, as they repress their laughter into bubbling giggles.*) 90

VOICES. Vive
Hooray } General Johnny
Hip, hip } Johnson!

CHIEF. What can we do for you, General?

JOHNNY (*Shaking his head groggily and returning their salute with his left hand, and then after a moment's hesitation barking out*). Stop this war!

AMERICAN COMMANDER. Just as you say, General. Tee-hee-hee—so you want this fight- 100 ing stopped? (*Turning around and calling to everybody*). General Johnson's right. This war is foolish, there's nothing to it but blood and murder.

VOICES. War is foolish! Let's stop it!

AMERICAN COMMANDER (*Embracing the* CHIEF). Old boy, we're going to stop this war. What you say?

CHIEF (*Clapping his hands*). Stop the war! (*A great burst of applause and cheering follows.*)

10 AMERICAN COMMANDER. We'll sign the order right now. (*He hurries over to the table, writes something, signs it and hands the pen to the* CHIEF *who also signs and stamps it. Then he gives the paper to* JOHNNY, *and calls out in a loud voice.*) Silence! (*The laughter dies down once more to suppressed giggles.*) We have signed an order stopping the offensive! General Johnson, see that it is carried out!

THE ASSEMBLY. Vive
20 Hooray } Johnny
Hip, hip } Johnson!

(*And now the orchestra resumes playing. The officers lift* JOHNNY *on their shoulders and march around the room, then place him on the table and stand applauding him.*)

VOICES. Speech, speech!

JOHNNY (*Blinking and passing his hand across his forehead as if to clear his mind*). There's not much to say, friends. Now that 30 we're going to stop the war, we'll all be home in time for Christmas to see old Santa Claus. Ain't that fine?

VOICES. Christmas! Christmas! Merry Christmas! (*And now they all start marching around the table again and singing, with the exception of* JOHNNY, *who hops down and disappears up the stairs the way he came.*)

ALL (*Singing as in a round*). We'll all be home for Christmas—a merry, merry Christmas! 40 (*A moment passes while the singing continues. The orchestra raises to a loud fortissimo and suddenly stops. Gradually the noise subsides, the generals and the others sink down in their seats and gaze about them in amazement. The* AMERICAN COMMANDER *looks at the* CHIEF's *scattered and windblown hair and the* CHIEF *looks at his disarray.*)

CHIEF (*In a hollow dazed voice*). What time is it?

50 AMERICAN COMMANDER (*Staring at his wrist watch*). Ten minutes till five.

CHIEF (*With a cry*). The offensive!

AMERICAN COMMANDER (*Springing out of his chair with a yell*). My God!—We gave him an order stopping the offensive! Catch that man! (*He and the* CHIEF *tear out through the door at the rear followed by the mad scramble of the others.*)

Black Out

ACT TWO

SCENE VI

"Still stands thine ancient sacrifice."

The scene is the edge of a great battle-field near dawn. In the foreground is a small dug- 60 *out opening into a raised eyebrow of the earth. By a shaded lantern light two liaison officers are discerned, one a* CAPTAIN, *talking into a field telephone, and the other a young* LIEUTENANT, *squatted by him, taking notes in a book. The orchestra accompaniment has continued.*

CAPTAIN (*Chanting into the phone*). North —first British army;
South—British six, two, one, three, four.

LIEUTENANT. Check. 70

CAPTAIN. French army toward Saint-Quentin.

LIEUTENANT. Check.

CAPTAIN. On the right the American army. Code—L E, prefix three, six S M.

LIEUTENANT. Check.

CAPTAIN. Zero hour—0 1 5 1 0.

LIEUTENANT. Check.

CAPTAIN. Three minutes now—
Three minutes—
Three minutes and the western front 80 From Calais to Sedan will go—
Over the top—
The zero hour falls.

LIEUTENANT (*Half-sobbing*). Check.

CAPTAIN. May heaven help our enemies—
In such an hour!

LIEUTENANT. Check.—And help us all!

(*And now off at the left we hear the singing command "Attention," then nearer at hand the command repeated, and then still nearer the* 90

"**Still . . . sacrifice,**" from "Recessional" (1897), by Rudyard Kipling. The full sentence reads
> "The tumult and the shouting dies;
> The captains and the kings depart;
> Still stands Thine ancient sacrifice,
> An humble and a contrite heart." (ll. 7–10.)

The occasion of the poem was the sixtieth anniversary of the accession of Queen Victoria.

command repeated. *The* CAPTAIN *and the* LIEU-
TENANT *look around and suddenly spring to
their feet as* JOHNNY JOHNSON *enters wrapped
in the* AMERICAN COMMANDER'S *overcoat, and
cap.)*

CAPTAIN (*Saluting and clicking his heels*).
Attenshun!

(*The* LIEUTENANT *quickly salutes, clicks his
heels likewise.* JOHNNY'S *hand is pushed into his
coat in an attitude somewhat resembling the
popular picture of Napoleon.*)

JOHNNY (*In a slightly disguised voice*). At
ease.

CAPTAIN (*Gasping*).
General—General—General—
The danger is too great—
Oh General!

JOHNNY (*In a still heavy voice*).
The General has no fear when his own men
    are involved.
Are you in touch with the different command-
    ers?

CAPTAIN. Everything's in order, sir—in order,
    sir—

(*Jerking his wrist watch by his eyes*).
Two minutes now—two minutes—
The barrage will begin—

LIEUTENANT (*With a moan*). Check.

JOHNNY. There'll be no barrage—no bombardment either.

(*With a bark*). The war is called off!

CAPTAIN (*With a shout*). What!

JOHNNY. Suspended until further orders—

(*Authoritatively*). In the name of the Allied
High Command. Here! (*He hands him the
signed order.*)

LIEUTENANT (*With a broken cry*). Thank
God, thank God.

(*Slightly hysterical*). We'll live to get back
home again.

(*Wildly*). We'll live! (*He runs over and
kisses* JOHNNY'S *hand, then whirls and embraces
the* CAPTAIN.)

JOHNNY. Quick—get the news on the wire.

CAPTAIN (*Now down on his knees and grind-
ing the telephone*). Hello, hello! Second Army
Corps, Second Army Corps—Ypres section,
General Godby—Hello. This is Varner—Varner
—L-two-V-O-seven. (*Reading from the order*).
Order urgent—Special invoice—Allied High
Command—Cancellation. Eight-four-three-two-
one. Code—Acceptive. G. O.

JOHNNY (*From the shadow where he
stands*). Talk sense!

CAPTAIN. General offensive will not take
place. Indefinite suspension of hostilities.

LIEUTENANT (*Running about and clapping
his hands*). Shall we send up the signals?

JOHNNY (*Shouting*). Send 'em up! Send 'em
up!   60

LIEUTENANT (*Rushing off at the right*).
Flares! Flares!

(BLACK OUT. *The orchestra plays the "Democracy March" fortissimo. The lights come up
again.* JOHNNY *is at the back looking off and
waving his sheet in the air. And now at the left
the sound of cheering is heard, coming nearer
as if underground. From a flare somewhere off
stage the scene of No Man's Land at the rear is
lighted up. The subterranean cheering seems to 70
pass across the stage. And now at the back as
if popping out of the ground several American
soldiers spring up on the parapet yelling and
waving their caps.*)

A SOLDIER. Hooray, the war is over! War is
over! (*Shouting across No Man's Land*).
Heigh, Heinie, where are you?

ANOTHER SOLDIER. Come on out, you boys!
We've quit fighting!

ANOTHER SOLDIER. Kommt d'raus! Kein Krieg 80
mehr!

(*And now as the orchestra plays, the figures
of several German soldiers, muddy and be-
grimed, appear at the left and right rear. The
Americans run forward and shake hands with
them. They slap one another on the back and
embrace affectionately, weeping with happiness. Suddenly off at the left a siren blows. The*
CAPTAIN *and* LIEUTENANT *look off.* JOHNNY *hops
across the trench and joins the German and 90
American soldiers at the rear. They salute him
and he goes among them shaking hands. And
now rushing in from the left come three or four
brigadier-generals and colonels with drawn pistols.*)

FIRST BRIGADIER (*Yelling and pointing toward* JOHNNY). Catch that man!

JOHNNY (*Coming over to the trench and
speaking sternly to the staff officers*). Get back
to headquarters, you fellows, or I'll slap you 100
under arrest.

SECOND BRIGADIER (*Raising his pistol*). Spy!
Spy! Kill him!

LIEUTENANT (*Stepping in front of him*). My

759

God, would you shoot the Commander-in-Chief? (*The soldiers spring protectingly around* JOHNNY.)

SECOND BRIGADIER. Commander-in-Chief!

JOHNNY (*Pushing his way through the soldiers and turning toward them*). Boys, do you want to stop this war?

SOLDIERS (*With some of the Germans crying "Ja, Ja!"*). Yes, General, great God, we say so!
10 End it right now. And let's go home. Home— Let's go home. (*A* COLONEL *springs suddenly over, jerks* JOHNNY'S *coat from him and at the same time another officer knocks off his cap.*)

COLONEL. Look at him! (*The soldiers stare at him in silent astonishment.*)

FIRST BRIGADIER (*To the liaison* CAPTAIN). Command the offensive to begin at once! (*He sticks an order into his hand. The* CAPTAIN *stares at the order, then springs to the tele-*
20 *phone and begins cranking.* JOHNNY *whirls about as the officers and soldiers start toward him, jumps down into the trench and disappears. The* FIRST BRIGADIER *yells to the soldiers.*) Back into your trenches! The battle is beginning!

(*The American soldiers look helplessly about. Both brigadiers now have their pistols drawn.*)

SECOND BRIGADIER. At "three" we fire. One—
30 two— (*He raises his pistol. The American soldiers jump down into the trenches.*)

CAPTAIN (*At the telephone*). G-O-eight-four-three-two-one cancelled. Forged orders. Work of spies.

LIEUTENANT (*Now weeping as he squats with his pad and pencil*). Check.

(*The German soldiers at the back turn and flee toward their trenches. But some of them never reach there, for the American machine*
40 *guns now begin their rat-tat-tat-tat-tat, and they are seen falling. The* CAPTAIN *continues yelling into the telephone.*)

CAPTAIN. At once! At once! (*As he looks at his watch.*) It is now exactly hours—0 5 1 0— Open fire!—Fire! (*Somewhere far away and as if beneath the earth, a great gun is fired. There is an instant of pause, and then the battle begins, with the music in the orchestra portraying its fury and violence.*)

Black Out

ACT TWO

SCENE VII

"There's many a mangled body, a blanket **for their** shroud."

A SERIES OF FLASHES—*by the light of bursting shells. The orchestra is now an organ playing the stately chant music of a church prayer, while in a nebulous circle of light at the extreme right front of the stage an* AMERICAN PRIEST *is seen standing above the members of his congregation who are bowed in prayer, and while at the left front a* GERMAN PRIEST *likewise stands above his praying flock. As the battle goes on and the organ plays, the two priests repeat in unison, the one in English, the other in German, the prayer "In Time of War and Tumults"—*

Almighty God, the supreme Governor of all things, whose power no creature is able to resist, to whom it belongeth justly to punish sinners, and to be merciful to those who truly repent; save and deliver us, we humbly beseech thee, from the hands of our enemies; that we, being armed with thy defense, may be preserved evermore from all perils, to glorify thee, who art the only giver of all victory; through the merit of thy Son, Jesus Christ our Lord. Amen.

FLASH 1

Two squads of horrible creatures in gas masks, German and American, flying to meet each other and fighting hand to hand.

Black Out

FLASH 2

Two men fighting, a German and an American, with bare fists choking and strangling each other, towering up over the footlights.

Black Out

FLASH 3

Two soldiers—an American and a German— tangled in a roll of barbed wire, gasping and frothing from burning gas, clasping the hand of friendship as they die.

Black Out

"There's . . . shroud." There does not seem to be **any** definite source for this line.

FLASH 4

A squad of Germans holding up their hands in surrender. An American on his belly in the foreground with a machine gun mowing them down.

Black Out

FLASH 5

A squad of American soldiers holding up their hands in surrender. A German machine-gunner in the foreground mowing them down.

Black Out

FLASH 6

JOHNNY JOHNSON, fleeing around in No Man's Land, bareheaded, his pajamas in tatters.

Black Out

FLASH 7

A young German praying at the foot of the black wooden statue of Christ. He rises to meet an American who enters with bayonet. They fight and the German is run through. An exploding shell kills the American. The statue totters and falls with a crash.

Black Out

FLASH 8

JOHNNY JOHNSON, holding the head of a dying man in his lap and giving him a drink of water.

(*And now the organ music and the entire scene gradually fade out with the long breathing word of the two priests—"Amen."*)

Black Out

ACT TWO

SCENE VIII

"Dulce et decorum est pro patria mori."

It is dawn over No Man's Land. In the dim light that shows a faint gray in the east we can discern the forms of dead men scattered about us as far as the eye can see, and in the background the mutilated and shattered figure of the Christ. And ever and anon from somewhere out of that vast stretch of ruined world come the feeble and begging cries of those who have not yet died. The music in the orchestra now is that of the wounded French soldiers in Scene I, Act Two, "Nous Sommes Blessés." In the middle foreground, sitting on the edge of the raised lip of a torn shell hole is JOHNNY JOHNSON. Stretched out at his feet is the form of a soldier, his pale face upturned in the gray light. The face is that of JOHANN the young sniper. JOHNNY is naked save for a torn piece of cloth tied around his middle. His body is marked with sweat and powder burns. For a while he sits staring down at the pale face, then reaching out he lays his hand on the soldier's forehead, moving the German helmet back from his head to do so.*

JOHNNY (*In a low voice*). Feel better now? (*There is no reply. He bends closer, puts his hand on the soldier's mouth, and then sits with his head and shoulders bowed and his hands clasped around his knees. His voice rises through his burnt swollen lips in a hoarse broken monologue.*) Two hundred thousand dead, five hundred thousand dead, a million dead.— And they have had their way, Johann. And all for what? And why? What for? (*Wagging his head*). Nobody knows—nobody! (*Far off in the background a voice calls piteously.*)

VOICE. Mother, mother. (*JOHNNY continues to stare before him.*)

JOHNNY. He'll quit calling soon, he'll quit calling and lie still—like you, Johann, lie still. And they killed you. I saw it happen. One of my own squad did it. He stuck a bayonet through you. (*Gasping*). I had the war stopped once. Maybe there's no sense in that. They said so. But you wouldn't say so—no, you wouldn't, would you? (*Stretching out his hands over the still figure with a loud cry*). Would you! (*And now two tall military police loom up in the darkness at the left. With their hands on their pistols they approach JOHNNY.*)

FIRST MILITARY POLICE. Are you Johnny Johnson?

JOHNNY (*Without looking around*). He's dead.

SECOND MILITARY POLICE. Are you Johnny Johnson? (*His head sags down on his breast.*)

FIRST MILITARY POLICE. In the name of the armies of Europe and America we arrest you!

Black Out

"**Dulce . . . mori,**" "It is sweet and fitting to die for one's country." The line is to be found in Horace's *Odes*, Book III, ii, 13.

ACT TWO

SCENE IX

"Hail, Mary full of grace."

A prospect looking out upon the entrance to New York harbor. In the distance the STATUE *of* LIBERTY *stands against the evening sky, but this time she is not illuminated. And now the same gray ghostly warship slides across the back of the scene but from left to right, and from the left comes the rail and the deck of the passenger ship again.* JOHNNY *is sitting at the rail with his back to the* STATUE *and staring*
10 *straight before him. A uniformed* GUARD *is standing at his side. The* GUARD *salutes and then touches* JOHNNY *on the shoulder and points to the* STATUE. *But* JOHNNY *keeps staring ahead of him. The rail and the deck pass out at the right and disappear into a great engulfing shadow without stopping.*

Curtain

ACT THREE

SCENE I

"Is there no balm in Gilead? Is there no physician there?"

A psychiatrist's office in the State Hospital. At the left front is a heavy door opening into a corridor. At the left a typewriter desk and to
20 *the right of that a larger desk with telephones, papers and so on. At the center rear another door opens to an inner room. At the right rear are several filing cases, and to the right front a third door opening toward the entrance hall.*

When the curtain rises DR. MAHODAN, *a melancholy middle-aged man, is seated at his desk looking through several folders of newspaper clippings, letters, and reports. The telephone rings. He picks up the receiver.*

30 DR. MAHODAN. Hello. (*Wearily*). Yes, this is the bureau of psychiatry—(*Listening a moment and then bawling out at the unknown speaker*). You're crazy! (*He hangs up the receiver and sits staring before him. Presently he begins to sing to himself, to a low tom-tom accompaniment in the orchestra.*)

"**Hail . . . grace,**" a translation of the opening lines of the *Ave Maria.*
"**Is . . . there?**" from Jeremiah 8:22.]

Back in the ages primitive
When souls with devils were posses't,
The witch man came and did his best
With yell and blow and expletive   4(
    And loudly beaten drum.
And up and down and round about
He whirled with fearful fetish rout
    And wild delirium.
But rarely did the patient live
Back in the ages primitive.
    (*Continuing with organ accompaniment*).
Back when the priests had things their way
They viewed insanity the same,
Though now they would invoke the name   5
Of heaven's hosts, and sing and pray
    In accents dolorous.
And if they failed to ease his pains,
They bound the poor soul down in chains,
    Condemned and infamous.
And there in dungeon cell he lay,
Back when the priests had things their way.
    (*And now the orchestra is jazzing a bit.*)
Today psychologists agree
The insane man is only sick,
The problem is psy-chi-a-trick,
See Jung and Adler, Freud and me,
    And we will analyze.
And though it hurts, we probe the ruts
Of mental pain that drives men nuts
And heal their lunacies.
And from their devils being free,
They all take up Psychiatry.
    (*The telephone rings again as a spinsterish looking stenographer appears from the rear with a glass of yellow liquid in her hand. She sets the glass down and picks up the receiver.*)
STENOGRAPHER. Dr. Mahodan's office—Yes, we're expecting him. (*Sitting down and holding her stenographic pad in readiness*). Take your medicine.
DR. MAHODAN. Yes—yes—— (*He gulps down some of the liquid and shudders.*)
STENOGRAPHER. Better this morning?
DR. MAHODAN. No, worse—(*Sadly*). Well, my business is to cure others, and not myself. (*Picking up a photograph and staring at it.*)

62. **Jung, Adler, Freud,** names of three of the most prominent psychologists of the present age. The most famous is the Austrian Sigmund Freud (1856–1939), who virtually founded the modern science of psychoanalytics and made special studies of the phenomena of dreams. But scarcely less influential have been Alfred Adler (1870–1937), another Austrian, and Carl Jung (1875–) of Switzerland.

And this Johnny Johnson looks like a difficult case to cure. (*As the* STENOGRAPHER *writes*). Rare, very, very rare. Only once in a generation does such a diseased personality occur. According to his record, he appears to be one of those naturals born into the world at rare intervals. You recall my monograph on Jesus, the rural prophet and will-less egocentric.—Same type, same type. (*Tapping the photograph* with his finger). You will notice one significant fact. He holds his rifle left-handed—the others do not. (*Musingly*). Also notice the discrepancy between his forehead and his chin. (*The telephone on the desk rings again. The* STENOGRAPHER *picks it up.*)

STENOGRAPHER. Dr. Mahodan.—Good—yes, send him right in.

DR. MAHODAN. You'd better fetch the orderlies.

STENOGRAPHER. Yes, sir.

(*She rises and goes to the heavy door at the left, unlocks it with a loud click and disappears beyond.* DR. MAHODAN *picks up a hand mirror and begins studying the interior of his mouth. The door at the right opens and* JOHNNY JOHNSON *is escorted in by his former guard. He wears his old oversized soldier's uniform, though now it is clean, and in general his whole appearance denotes his usual cheerfulness and complacency. He looks about the scene with interest as* DR. MAHODAN *rises and receives a large envelope from the guard.*)

DR. MAHODAN. Mr.—er——?

JOHNNY JOHNSON. Howdy, sir.

DR. MAHODAN. Have a seat, Mr.—er—Johnson. (JOHNNY *sits down and the guard retires towards the door at the right and stands waiting.*)

JOHNNY (*With a gentle disarming smile*). Yes sir, I don't mind sitting down. I had to give my seat to a lady on the train, and my feet hurt. (*The* STENOGRAPHER *re-enters. She looks keenly at* JOHNNY *and he rises out of his seat.*) Have my chair, ma'am.

STENOGRAPHER (*Startled*). Oh—no, thank you. (*She sits at her desk again and takes up a writing pad.*)

DR. MAHODAN (*As the* STENOGRAPHER *writes*). Were you seasick on the ocean, Mr. Johnson?

JOHNNY. Oh no, sir. Funny, I didn't get seasick either way.

DR. MAHODAN (*With a slight inclination of his head toward the* STENOGRAPHER). Perfect adjustment of sense organs as expected.

JOHNNY. Sir?

DR. MAHODAN. I was just speaking to the young lady.

JOHNNY. Excuse me. Could I ask you a question, Mr.—Mr.?

DR. MAHODAN (*Bowing slightly*). My name? Er—? (*Blankly and then getting the answer*). Ah—Mahodan, Dr. Mahodan.

JOHNNY. Glad to know you, sir. Has Minny Belle come yet?

GUARD (*Taking a step forward*). That's his fiancée, Doctor. He wanted her to know he was home from the war so I let him send her a telegram.

DR. MAHODAN. Hum-hum. Question of procedure. (*To* JOHNNY *soothingly*). No, she hasn't come yet.

JOHNNY (*Dolefully*). That's funny. I wonder if she'll be able to locate me here. It's such a big place.

DR. MAHODAN. Yes, it's quite large.

JOHNNY (*Looking around him*). It's one of the nicest jails I ever saw.

DR. MAHODAN (*As the* STENOGRAPHER *writes away*). This is not a jail, Mr.—er—Johnson. It's a hospital. (*And now several husky orderlies enter from the left in white uniforms. They take up their position by the door.* JOHNNY *looks at them with interest.*)

JOHNNY. Why, it is a jail too. I saw some bars beyond that door. (*He stares around with quizzical eyes.*) And why is he locking up?

DR. MAHODAN. That's all right. We do that as a matter of habit. (JOHNNY *stares at the floor now, saying nothing.* DR. MAHODAN'S *voice changes to a more professional curtness as he sits down and hands the* STENOGRAPHER *the envelope he has received from the guard.*) Usual six copies of these, please. (*Then turning to* JOHNNY). We've looked forward with interest to seeing you. You are quite a famous man in military circles.

JOHNNY (*Looking up now with a grin*). I'm the man that stopped the war if that's what you mean. (*Shaking his head glumly, the smile dying from his face*). But they wouldn't let it stay stopped. They're still killing each other and shooting over there right on. They've got everything bassackwards!

DR. MAHODAN (*With the faintest touch of amusement beginning to show in his eyes*). Bass what?

JOHNNY (*Chuckling*). Oh, shucks, that's just a word means the front part behind——

(DR. MAHODAN *stares at him and gradually the dour hardness of his face begins to break up into a wrinkly smile. As if infected by* JOHNNY's *chuckle, he throws back his head and laughs and then goes off into a paroxysm of sputtering and coughing. The astonished* STENOGRAPHER *hurries to him with the remainder of the medicine which he drains off.*)

DR. MAHODAN (*Dabbing his lips with a large white handkerchief*). Excuse me, I am not accustomed to laughter. (*Leaning forward eagerly*). Tell us more about your wonderful experiences.

JOHNNY (*Humbly*). I didn't have any experiences. I didn't even shoot my gun once.

DR. MAHODAN (*To the* STENOGRAPHER *who jumps to her pad and starts writing rapidly*). The superman complex through the technique of humility, which—(*Stopping and eyeing* JOHNNY *closely*). No—Cancel that.

JOHNNY. Sir?

DR. MAHODAN. I was addressing the young lady.

JOHNNY. I know you were. But it was about me.

DR. MAHODAN. Yes, and very complimentary. (*And now the door at the right opens and* MINNY BELLE *comes in. She is dressed in a little blue coat suit and cute hat and looks adorable, though somewhat pale and worn.*)

MINNY BELLE. Johnny——(*Springing up, he whirls around and grabs her.*)

JOHNNY (*Brokenly*). Minny Belle, Minny Belle!

(*His lips quiver with emotion, and tears come into his eyes. And now he pulls her into his arms and hugs her tight to him. Then he pushes her from him and stares at her with hungry, devouring eyes. For a moment he stands looking at her so, and then kisses her on the forehead.*)

MINNY BELLE. No—Johnny—please—these people!

JOHNNY (*Manfully*). Oh, it's all right. They already know we're engaged. (*Taking* MINNY BELLE *by the hand and turning toward the doctor*). This is Minny Belle, Dr. Mahodan. Yes, that's his name, Minny Belle. He says it is. And he seems like a fine man.

MINNY BELLE. I'm sorry I'm late, sir, but we had a puncture on the way.

JOHNNY. A puncture?

MINNY BELLE. Yes, Anguish was good enough to bring me over in his new car.

JOHNNY. Oh——

MINNY BELLE. You're all dressed out in your uniform. (*Gazing at him queryingly*). But why are you back? The war's not over yet.

JOHNNY. They decided to send me back here. (*Then quickly*). But it wasn't because I wasn't a good soldier. Maybe I was too good.

MINNY BELLE (*Stiffly*). But why did you come back so soon? (JOHNNY *says nothing.*) And how many Germans did you kill, Johnny?

JOHNNY. None, Minny Belle—not a single one.

MINNY BELLE. Oh, Johnny!

DR. MAHODAN. We are sorry to interrupt you, Mr.—er——

JOHNNY (*Prompting*).—Johnson.

DR. MAHODAN. Yes—I'd like to have a word with the young lady in private. Will you kindly go with these gentlemen—to another room for a moment?

JOHNNY (*Looking about him*). All right, sir. I'll be right back, Minny Belle. (*The orderlies come forward and escort* JOHNNY *out at the rear and close the door behind them.*)

DR. MAHODAN (*Gesturing* MINNY BELLE *to a seat*). My dear young lady, I have a very sorrowful duty to perform. (*Curtly, to the* STENOGRAPHER). You needn't write down everything I say. (*The* STENOGRAPHER *stops writing.*) Your fiancé will not be able to go home with you.

MINNY BELLE. What's the matter?

DR. MAHODAN. This is a home for mental cases. Does that mean anything to you?

MINNY BELLE. I—I thought it was strange—Johnny's being here but—(*With a sudden cry*). You don't mean there's something wrong—wrong with his mind?

DR. MAHODAN (*Gravely*). The psychological experts of the United States army say so. I have their reports here.

MINNY BELLE (*Crying out*). No, no, Johnny —he's a little peculiar in his way but——(*Her words die out and she sits staring horrified at the doctor.*)

DR. MAHODAN. To you it may not appear that anything is wrong. But to one skilled in the science of mental diseases it is apparent that—

(*The door at the rear suddenly opens and* JOHNNY *dashes in. He has been stripped of his* 10 *army coat and wears in its place the blue denim jacket of an inmate of the House of Balm. He is followed by the orderlies.*)

JOHNNY (*Hotly to* DR. MAHODAN *as he tears off his jacket and throws it down*). What's the meaning of this, sir? (*He stares from the* DOC- TOR *to* MINNY BELLE's *grieved face. She suddenly drops her head in her hands and begins sobbing.* JOHNNY *hurries over to her.*) Has this —this queer dick of a doctor done anything to 20 you, Minny Belle?

MINNY BELLE. Oh—oh—oh!

DR. MAHODAN. Unfortunately I had to tell her about your condition.

JOHNNY. What condition?

DR. MAHODAN. That you are sick.

JOHNNY. Sick? Why I never felt in better health—at least I did till I came into this place. (*Grabbing* MINNY BELLE's *hand*). Come on, we're going out of here!

30 MINNY BELLE (*With a wail*). Oh, Johnny! You can't.

JOHNNY. We'll see about that! (*The door at the right opens and* ANGUISH *sticks his head in. He is sportingly dressed, like the rising young business man he is.*)

ANGUISH. Did you call me, Minny Belle?

MINNY BELLE (*Looking at* JOHNNY, *wavering a moment and then pulling away from him and running over to* ANGUISH). They're go- 40 ing to keep Johnny here, Anguish.

ANGUISH (*As he takes hold of her arm*). Well, an asylum is where he belongs.

JOHNNY. Asylum! (*Whirling around*). Take your hand off her arm.

ANGUISH (*As* MINNY BELLE *clings to him*). Don't you let him get at me, folks.

DR. MAHODAN (*Raising a gently teasing finger*). Now, Mr.—er—Now, now——

JOHNNY (*Stopping as the orderlies take a* 50 *step towards him*). I see. They think I'm crazy. They're going to shut me up. (*Then turning to*

MINNY BELLE. *Pleadingly*). You can't—you can't think——

(MINNY BELLE *drops her head and begins to sob again.* ANGUISH *puts his arm protectingly around her. At a gesture from the doctor, he leads her away at the right and closes the door.* JOHNNY *stands staring at the floor like a man in a dream.* DR. MAHODAN *comes over and puts his hand kindly on his shoulder. Then he picks* 60 *up the jacket from the floor, and* JOHNNY *slowly holds out his arm for the sleeve.*)

DR. MAHODAN. I think you'll make a very interesting patient, Mr.—er—(*Blankly, then getting the answer*). Mr. Mahodan.

Black Out

ACT THREE

SCENE II

"Out of the mouths of babes and sucklings."

The forensic arena in the House of Balm— a sort of ordinary reading or club room with several rows of chairs at the center right and a little speaker's stand facing diagonally out- ward from the left rear. Above the speaker's 70 *stand hangs a beflagged picture of Woodrow Wilson and above that a big placard with the words "Adelphi Debating Society" on it. When the curtain rises some dozen or more elderly men are standing by their seats as they face the rostrum. Some of them have pencils and cheap writing tablets in their hands. They re- semble the ordinary type of American business men—railroad, bank, or insurance company di- rectors. On the rostrum sits* BROTHER THOMAS, 80 *a man who resembles a certain late Vice-Presi- dent of the United States, and to his left a pale-faced clerk type of man about thirty years old. Sitting on a lower level and to the right of the rostrum is* JOHNNY JOHNSON. JOHNNY *has aged much since we saw him last. He is dressed in an old collarless white shirt and a dark sack*

"Out . . . sucklings," "Out of the mouths of babes and suck- lings hast thou ordained strength because of thine enemies, that thou mightest still the enemy and the avenger" (Psalms 8:2). The same phrase is repeated in a slightly different sense in Matthew 21:16.
81. *Vice-President . . . States*, Thomas R. Marshall (1854– 1925), who served as vice-president in both of the administra- tions of Woodrow Wilson (1913–21).

*coat much too large for him, and his hair with
suspicious signs of grayness at the temples is
still unruly though brushed somewhat to one
side. Like the portrait above him he wears
spectacles though his are of the plain steel-
rimmed kind, and in an indefinite way he
seems to resemble the portrait. With a small
brush he is painting a wooden toy which he
holds in his hand.*

10 *The scene is somewhat cut off from the footlights by a low railing which crosses the front
of the stage and in the center of which is a little gate. Two uniformed hospital guards stand
one on either side of the scene at the front,
looking straight ahead of them and with their
arms folded akimbo.*

*It is ten years after the preceding scene. As
the curtain rises, the Brethren are concluding a
song. With the exception of* JOHNNY *everybody*
20 *is singing.*

BRETHREN (*As* BROTHER THOMAS *beats time
with his rubber gavel*).

How sweetly friendship binds—
Our hearts in brother love
With kindness of forgiving minds—
Life's sweetest pleasures prove.

For fled are hate and harm,
No foe seeks us to kill—
To all we stretch the open arm
30 Of welcome and good will.

(*Ending with a churchly long-drawn chant*).
—Amen.

(*They all sit down.* DR. FREWD, *an old
bearded gentleman wearing a linen duster,
springs up in the front row.*)

DR. FREWD (*Piping out gently*). Hurrah for
the President of the United States! (*And now
several of the other Brethren join in likewise,
while* BROTHER THOMAS *thumps on the table*
40 *with his soft gavel.*)

BRETHREN. Hurrah for Johnny Johnson!
(*They begin a gentle clapping.* JOHNNY, *smiling kindly at them, shushes them with downward gestures of his hands.*)

THOMAS (*Bowing to the old bearded brother*).
I'm sorry, Dr. Frewd, but you keep making the
same mistake. Johnny is not the President of
the United States. (*Turning to* JOHNNY). Are
you, Johnny?

50 JOHNNY (*Looking up at the portrait*). No.

(*The* SECRETARY *begins writing in a huge
ledger.*)

DR. FREWD (*Sitting down*). I stand corrected,
sir. (*Then rising again*). If Johnny Johnson's
not the President of the United States, he ought
to be. (*The old gentlemen nod an enthusiastic
agreement.*)

ANOTHER VOICE. That's true. As chairman of
the ways and means committee I say we ought
to elect him. 6

ANOTHER VOICE. As ex-secretary of war, I
say so.

JOHNNY (*With kindly firmness*). You all
honor me a lot but—Maybe you'd better get
on with the business. (*He resumes his painting.*)

ANOTHER VOICE. That's right—asylum rules
—get on with the business.

THOMAS. Call the roll, sir.

SECRETARY (*Intoning above the ledger*). 7
Brother Claude——

CLAUDE. Present.

SECRETARY. Brother George.

GEORGE. Present.

SECRETARY. Brother Henry——(*There is no
answer, and the members look about them. A
man resembling a well-known Senator from the
Northwest rises.*)

WILLIAM. The gentleman from Massachusetts is working on his speech. He will be here 8
at any moment. (*He sits down.*)

A VOICE. I thought he'd lost his voice in that
filibuster.

THOMAS (*Chuckling as he holds up his
gavel*). As Johnny says—who ever heard of a
politician losing his voice?

VOICES. That's right. Johnny knows.

ANOTHER VOICE. But I thought Massachusetts
had finished speaking. (*A man resembling a
certain Senator from the west coast rises in* 9
pompous importance.)

HIRAM. Like California the old Bay State is
never finished. Thar she blows—I mean stands.
(*He sits down as* WILLIAM *applauds.*)

SECRETARY (*With a questioning look at*

---

77. *Senator . . . Northwest,* William E. Borah of Idaho
(1865–1940), who served in the United States Senate for 34
years. He, as well as the next three figures satirized below
(Johnson, Theodore Roosevelt, and Lodge), was an implacable
foe of the League of Nations sponsored by Woodrow Wilson.
90. *Senator . . . coast,* Hiram W. Johnson of California
(1866–1945), like Borah, long something of an institution in
the United States Senate.

JOHNNY *which* JOHNNY *answers with a nod).*
Brother Hiram——

   HIRAM. Present.

   SECRETARY. Brother Jim——

   JIM. Present.

   SECRETARY *(With a slight change of tone).*
Brother Theodore——*(A man resembling a certain late President of the United States, with
his square teeth and mustache, rises. He has
an inflated rubber stick in his hand.)*

   THEODORE *(Waving his stick).* Both present
—me and my stick. *(He bows and sits down.)*

   THOMAS. Read the minutes of the last meeting.

   SECRETARY *(Beginning to intone more sonorously).* On December the twelfth the Adelphi
Debating Society met in weekly session assembled, same being the five hundred and fifteenth meeting of that order, and proceeded to
the business of voting upon their final draft of
the League of World Republics. This League
was passed by an overwhelming majority—
overwhelming majority——

   *(The door at the left rear opens and a lit-
tle man resembling a certain late Senator from
Massachusetts comes bustling in. Under one
arm he carries a load of books and in his hand
several sheets of paper.)*

   HENRY *(In a voice hoarse from too much
use).* One moment, gentlemen. *(He comes forward in front of the rostrum and drops his
book with a bang. The old gentlemen spring
out of their seats with a squeal, and* JOHNNY
*looks out at them nodding and smiling, and
under his influence they sit down again.)* This
infamous league cuts at the very base of our
democratic institutions. *(Someone makes a
loud raspberry noise and* HENRY *glares about
him.)* I am first and foremost an American. I
love the American flag, a flag devoted to the
principles of liberty, and the pursuit of happiness.

---

8. **President . . . States,** Theodore Roosevelt (1858–1919),
twenty-sixth president of the United States. The *inflated rubber
stick* is a burlesque of Roosevelt's famous mythical "big stick,"
with which he threatened and occasionally did mayhem upon
unruly "big business" and malefactors in public office. His
opposition to Wilson's pacific measures during the early days
of the First World War was celebrated.   25. **Senator from
Massachusetts,** Henry Cabot Lodge (1850–1924), American
historian and for years senior senator from Massachusetts;
he was the leader of the opposition to Wilson's attempts
to bring the United States into the League of Nations and
a bitter political and personal enemy of the President.

   A VOICE. And in this asylum we're all happy.

   HENRY. Not only did the great Washington
tell us to keep ourselves aloof and inviolable
in the service of——

   SECRETARY *(Spontaneously).* —Liberty. *(He
looks about him abashed and begins writing
hurriedly in the ledger.)*

   HENRY. I challenge these interruptions.
(Picking up a book, opening it, and reading).
"If this damnable document is foisted upon the
American people it will mark the beginning
and end of our nation." Who said that?

   THEODORE *(Rising again and bowing all
around).* I said it, and you all know me.

   HENRY *(Continuing).* Gentlemen, if we
allowed the sentimentality and romanticism of
our President ex-officio—and he is the real author of this covenant—*(Reaching around and
shaking hands).* Hello, Johnny—*(Continuing).*
—allow him to involve us in responsibility for
any and every unimportant quarrel in Europe,
we would find our strength wasted and the
great principles of——

   VOICES *(In unison).* —Liberty! Sit down!

   HENRY *(Turning towards the members, and
stretching out his hands emphatically).* Under
the rules governing this floor I have a right to
speak—and I exercise that right in a last appeal
to you to use your reason as—as—*(Croaking).*
My voice is failing—I have given my all in the
service of my country. *(He staggers and sits
down.)*

   WILLIAM. Look at this martyr. *(Rising to
applaud).* In his name I move the vote be re-
taken.

   THEODORE *(Rising).* Second the motion.

   SEVERAL VOICES. No! No!

   WILLIAM. The motion's before the house.

   THOMAS. Let me speak! *(The* SECRETARY
nods. HIRAM, THEODORE, *and* WILLIAM *murmur
to one another in disgruntlement.)* Gentlemen,
we've passed this covenant once and let's let it
stay passed. As Johnny says, don't chew your
tobacco twice.

   VOICES. That's right.

   WILLIAM *(Springing up under* HENRY's *urging).* But under the Constitution we have a
right to ask for a recount. *(He sits down.)*

   THOMAS. Brethren, it is obvious that a majority of people everywhere want some sort of
world co-operation which will bring peace and

happiness to mankind—in place of wars and misery which we have had too long.

VOICES. Hear, hear!

THOMAS. The disorganized and selfish nations of the earth—frightened, suspicious, hating one another—are waiting for someone to show them the way out of their dilemma. (*Gesturing toward the ledger*). And in this covenant we show them.

10 VOICES. We show them.

THOMAS. Every day the need for great statesmanship increases—(*Bowing to* JOHNNY).—while the terrors of war hang in the air. Remember the pictures Johnny showed us yesterday?—horrible pictures—(*Some of the old gentlemen shudder.*)—Little children all over the world are leaving their toys and their playthings, their marbles and their maypoles, to learn to wear gas masks and sleep in shell-and-

20 gas-proof dungeons. In this very town they're doing it.

SEVERAL BRETHREN (*Covering their faces with their hands*). Horrible! Horrible!

THEODORE (*Waving his rubber stick*). In time of peace prepare for war.

JOHNNY (*Chuckling*). Same old argument, Theodore. We answered that the other day, I thought.

SECRETARY (*Intoning*). Article nineteen, Sec-

30 tion six—inviolability of non-combatants.

THOMAS. Silence, Johnny's going to speak.

VOICES (*Eagerly*). That's right, Johnny, tell us a story.

JOHNNY (*As they listen attentively*). I'm no speaker. (*Lifting his hand as* THEODORE *starts to interrupt*). And I've already said what I believe on the subject. But Brother Theodore's old argument about every country having to have a big show-off army and navy to keep

40 peace reminds me of old Mr. Zollicoff's dog. Now that was a good dog—until one day Mr. Zollicoff dressed him up in a brass spiked collar. First thing you know that dog was showing off his spikes and fighting every other dog in the neighborhood. They finally had to kill him with a baseball bat. Now our constitution shows——

VOICES (*With gentle laughter*). That's right, Johnny. He speaks straight to the point, don't

50 he?

WILLIAM. We are not talking about dogs,

but of civilized men. (JOHNNY *smiles, shrugs his shoulders and resumes his work.*)

THOMAS. The Chair feels that men are same as dogs—when they start fighting one another. (*He looks at* JOHNNY *for confirmation.*) History shows it.

DR. FREWD. I beg to report that in this asylum we are civilized men. Put it in the minutes. (*He sits down amid applause.*) 60

THEODORE (*Doggedly*). Let's vote.

THOMAS (*Bowing in resignation*). All in favor of the League of World Republics as laid down—(*Gesturing towards the ledger*).—in our Constitution please signify the same by rising. (*The majority of the brethren rise.* JOHNNY *keeps his seat.*)

SECRETARY (*Beginning to count*). One—two—three—four—five—six—seven——(JOHNNY *leans over and whispers to* THOMAS.) 70

THOMAS. Will the gentleman from California there in the rear kindly make his vote clear? He seems to be in a crouching position.

HIRAM (*Straightening up*). I—I—all right, I'll vote for it, but I'll have a hard time explaining it to the folks back home.

THEODORE (*Staring at him*). You—you've sold Brother Henry out.

HIRAM (*Now rising in recovered dignity*). I was offered a price but I didn't sell. 80

HENRY (*Springing up and croaking*). As Abe Lincoln said—let the American people speak. And they won't accept your verdict. I've got a hundred postal cards—(*Feeling in his pocket*). —and I'm going to flood the country——

VOICES. Sit down! (*He stands wavering an instant and then collapses in his chair.*)

JOHNNY (*Gently but firmly as he stands up*). I think now we ought to make it unanimous, boys. What do you say, Henry? (*Henry makes* 90 *no answer.*) You'd feel better if you joined in. We've done a lot of good work here, and we've got a lot more to do. We all need to pull together.

SECRETARY. Section forty-three—the world must pull together.

JOHNNY. And you need to do it too—for your own good. Think how much happier all of us are since we started to work at something that interested us. We've forgot our own troubles 100 and we eat better, sleep better. And besides if we don't take up these big problems, who will?

In the outside world they don't seem to be interested any more. (*He looks smilingly at* HENRY.) Come on now.

HENRY (*Croaking gruffly*). No, no.

THOMAS. Dr. Frewd will just have to analyze him some more—I reckon. (HENRY *cowers in his seat as* DR. FREWD *steps nimbly to his side and begins a crouching down and lifting up pantomime. The brethren with the exception of* THOMAS *and* JOHNNY, *crowd around.*)

HENRY (*In a pleading mumble*). No—no—I'm a free individual—I'm—(*But as if against his will he is finally lifted to his feet. He receives their plaudits and handshakings with bowed head and deep emotion.*)

THOMAS (*Happily*). The League of World Republics is passed unanimously. This is an historic hour. (*Loud applause*).

DR. FREWD (*Crying out*). Hurrah for the League!

OLD GENTLEMAN (*Loudly*). Hurrah! (THOMAS *thumps with his rubber gavel.*)

THOMAS. We're making a little too much noise, brethren.

VOICES. All right.

THOMAS. The new chairman of the board is inspecting the hospital this morning and we want everything quiet.

SECRETARY. And he's a millionaire too.

VOICE (*From the rear*). We don't like millionaires.

ANOTHER VOICE. No, we don't.

JOHNNY. Millionaires ain't so bad, fellows. They have their troubles too as the lap dog said.

DR. FREWD. Hurrah for peace!

ANOTHER VOICE. Hurrah for peace! (DR. FREWD *stands up and lifting his arms begins to lead them in a song.*)

BRETHREN (*Singing as in a round, with* THOMAS *and the* CLERK *joining in*).
Come let us hymn a hymn to peace,
Jollily, merrily we will sing—
Loudly proclaiming wars shall cease,
Hark ye, how the bells go ting-ling-ling—

(*The guard at the right front reaches out on the wall and turns on a radio. A gentle and sleepy requiem is heard playing. Gradually the brethren stop their singing and sit down in their seats as if feeling the drowsy spell of some opiate.*)

JOHNNY (*Resuming his work*). That's right—rest a while—listen to the soft music—listen and rest a while——

THOMAS (*Mumbling*). The next question before the house is—Capital and Labor—Section one—(*He sinks down into his seat.*)—the man who works must share in—share in—

(*He bows his head over on the table. And now all the old men likewise bow their heads over and go to sleep.* JOHNNY *sits working at his toy as the scene of the Adelphi Debating Society begins to dim out. The soft music continues to play for a moment and then it too dies gradually away.*

Now entering slowly and dreamily from the right come the group of hospital directors on their tour of inspection. In front walks ANGUISH HOWINGTON, *carrying a cane and wearing a top silk hat, and by his side walks a young clinical-faced* DOCTOR. *Behind* ANGUISH *and the* DOCTOR *come five or six stout and well-dressed business men, a few orderlies, and a young man secretary dressed in a Crystal Mineral Water uniform.*)

DOCTOR (*Gesturing to the rear where only* JOHNNY *now is visible*).—And here we have developed a little debating society where some of our elderly patients engage in harmless talk.

ANGUISH (*Softly, mechanically, and almost dreamily*). Interesting idea.

DOCTOR. Owing to our limited means the equipment is poor, as you see.

ANGUISH (*To his secretary*). Make a note of that. (*The young man writes on his pad.*)

DOCTOR. Thank you, sir, thank you, sir. You have already been very generous.

ANGUISH. And Mrs. Howington and I will continue to be so. She has a deep interest in this institution.

DOCTOR. For which we are very grateful. I may mention that all of our staff use Crystal Mineral Water nightly—Before retiring we do so. (*Slightly bowing*). We find it very helpful.

ANGUISH (*Stiffening with a sense of greatness*). Millions find it helpful in these disordered times. (*Staring towards the rear*). Adelphi Debating Society—I used to belong to a society with the same name—in the old days. It wasn't very peaceful, though. There was a

769

fellow—Johnson—He was always creating friction. (*His voice dies out.*)

DOCTOR. But the founder of this society—you see him there—seems to be able to keep peace. In fact we have finally diagnosed his disease as peace monomania.

ANGUISH. It is dangerous?

DOCTOR (*Gravely*). Oh no—I shouldn't say so.

ANGUISH (*Still gazing towards the rear*). That fellow's face looks familiar.

DOCTOR. His name is Johnson too—Johnny Johnson.

ANGUISH. Oh yes. Yes, I remember now.

DOCTOR. We are thinking of letting him out in a few days.

ANGUISH (*Quickly*). Do you think it is safe?

DOCTOR. Oh quite, quite. It will be a loss to us too. He has a way with the patients—(*Hurriedly*). I mean everybody likes him.

(*Far off in the distance a musical gong begins to sound. The light comes up on the scene in the rear as if in time to the notes, and the old gentlemen rise sleepily from their chairs. The two attendants step over and stand by the little gate that opens in the railing, and* JOHNNY, *carrying his basket of toys and accompanied by the* SECRETARY *with the great ledger, leads them out.* ANGUISH *and the directors move slowly on across the foreground to the left.*)

ANGUISH (*Pointing off down the hall*). Those bars seem rather frail and old.

DOCTOR. They are, sir.

ANGUISH (*To the young fellow behind him with the pad*). Make a note of that.

DOCTOR. Thank you, sir.

(*At the sound of* ANGUISH's *voice* JOHNNY *stops, and the* SECRETARY *and the old gentleman move away at the right with the two attendants, leaving him behind. Suddenly he runs forward and pulls* ANGUISH *by the arm.*)

JOHNNY (*As* ANGUISH *turns coldly and puppetlike around*). Why, I hardly knew you, Anguish, in all them duds. (*The orderlies spring back and surround* ANGUISH.)

ANGUISH (*Manfully*). Never mind, my men——

JOHNNY (*Hesitating*). Tell me—have you got any news—about Minny Belle, I mean?

ANGUISH (*Pondering a moment gravely*). She's—er—well—very well.

JOHNNY. Golly, I'm glad to hear that. It's been so long since—I heard. (*Staring off an instant as if caught in a vague worry and then smiling around at* ANGUISH). She must be awful busy—yeh—tell her I will be seeing her—I hope—soon.

ANGUISH (*After a cruel and genteel pause*). You don't keep up with what is going on, do you?

JOHNNY. Well, we get the *International Digest* and that gives us the world news.

ANGUISH (*Coldly*). Miss Tompkins did me the honor some years ago of accepting *my* hand in marriage. (*He bows and moves on accompanied by the* DOCTOR, *the directors and attendants. As he goes out he points quietly towards Wilson's portrait with his cane.*) That picture there should be removed.

DOCTOR. It shall be, sir, at once. (*They all disappear at the left.* JOHNNY *stands with bent head looking at the floor. A moment passes and an* ATTENDANT *comes hurriedly in from the right.*)

ATTENDANT. Say, it's against the rules—even for you, Johnny—to fall out like this. Lunch is ready. (*He takes* JOHNNY *by the arm and then stares at him.*) You look kind of sick—anything wrong? (JOHNNY *makes no answer but continues looking at the floor. The* ATTENDANT, *touched by something in his face, speaks kindly to him.*) Can I get a doctor? (*Gazing carefully about him*). You can trust me.

JOHNNY (*Murmuring*). No, thanks.

ATTENDANT (*A little more confidentially*). I've got some good news for you, Johnny. You're going to be let out of here next week. It's a secret, but we know it. Don't it make you feel better?

JOHNNY (*Shaking his head*). No, I guess I'll —I'll stay here—now.

ATTENDANT. What!

JOHNNY. All—my friends—are here—my work too.

ATTENDANT. Yeh, but when they say you're ready to leave you got to leave. That's the law. (JOHNNY *says nothing, and the* ATTENDANT, *taking him by the arm, leads him away at the right.*)

Black Out

ACT THREE

SCENE III

"Whither have ye made a road?"

The scene is a street corner—projecting diagonally in at the right front. Stretching along the right towards the rear is an evergreen hedge with an imposing iron gate marked "Private." Behind the hedge in the distance and showing through the leafless winter trees is the high rim of a great pennanted stadium cutting horizontally across the sky. It is viewed from the rear, and from over this rim now and then comes the muted trumpet sound of a high hoarse hysterical voice haranguing a multitude. The words are cacophonous and are applauded now and then by a burst of martial band music, beaten drum, or the husky rainy-sounding cheers of thousands. Over at the left front is the corner of a red brick factory-like building.

When the curtain rises, JOHNNY JOHNSON— *now a man of forty-five or fifty but looking much older, though his face and manner are still cheery—is standing by a lightless iron lamp-post looking out before him. He is dressed in nondescript clothes, an old shapeless gray felt hat, a work shirt, dark coat and trousers, and heavy well-worn walking shoes. Hung by a string around his neck and held in front of him is a little tray like that with which street hawkers pursue their calling. Stray passers-by on their way to the stadium go down the street at the right every now and then.*

JOHNNY (*Keeping a watchful eye for any prospective customer as he sends his voice across the scene in a quavering call.*) Toy-ees! for sale! (*He waits a moment, looking about him and wiggling his feet to keep them warm. Then he calls again.*) Toy-ees!

(*And now coming down through the great iron gate is a little* BOY *about twelve years old, dressed in the new uniform of a boy scout. He stops and looks behind him.*)

BOY (*Calling*). Can I give the old man a nickel, Mother?

A WOMAN'S VOICE (*Beyond the gate*). Remember, nickels make dollars—as daddy says.

"**Whither . . . road?**" from I Samuel 27:10.

BOY. But I haven't done my scout's good deed for today. (MINNY BELLE *comes suddenly out through the gate. She is wrapped in furs and somewhat stout.*) May I, Mother?

MINNY BELLE. We're already late for the parade. (*She starts on down the street at the left rear.*)

JOHNNY (*Calling*). Nice little toy-ees for nice little girls and boy-ees! (*As if touched by some faint and far-off remembrance* MINNY BELLE *stops. She slowly and abstractedly opens her purse.*)

MINNY BELLE. All right, give him a nickel— He looks cold. (*The* BOY *takes the nickel and comes over to* JOHNNY.)

BOY (*Touching* JOHNNY *on the arm*). Here's the nickel, sir.

JOHNNY. What do you want?—A monkey or a dove?—Maybe this little terrapin. See—he can wiggle his legs when you pull the string. Look.

BOY (*Appraisingly*). Hmm—Maybe I might take a toy soldier.

JOHNNY (*Sternly*). No—no—I don't make soldiers.

BOY. Then I don't want anything.

JOHNNY. Here's your nickel.

BOY. Oh no, you must keep the nickel anyway. My daddy's rich.

JOHNNY (*Smilingly*). Is he?—That's nice. What's your name, son?

BOY. Anguish Howington, Junior.

JOHNNY (*After a moment's silence*). That's a nice name. (*And now as if conscious that* MINNY BELLE *is there in the distance he pulls up his coat collar and turns his face slightly away.*)

ANGUISH, JR. I'm named after my father. He's mayor of the town, you know.

JOHNNY. Is he? That's wonderful. I'm a sort of stranger here— So he's mayor of the town! And you're a boy scout?

ANGUISH, JR. Yes sir. And some day I'm going to be a soldier.

JOHNNY (*Quickly*). No, I wouldn't be that.

ANGUISH, JR. Why not?

JOHNNY. You could be—well, you could make things—or be a great doctor—or a good farmer—do something that would be of use to the world.

ANGUISH, JR. But daddy says that we're in for a terrible war and all the people have got

771

to be ready to keep the enemy from destroying us.

JOHNNY (*Staring out before him*). Ah——

MINNY BELLE (*Calling*). Come on!

JOHNNY. And—and how is your mother, son?

ANGUISH, JR. Why, she's all right. She's standing right over there. (*But* JOHNNY *keeps looking before him.*) Goodbye.

JOHNNY (*In a muffled voice*). Goodbye, son.
10 (*Little* ANGUISH *turns and runs back to his mother, elated by his charitable act.* MINNY BELLE *takes him by the hand and they go away at the left rear.* JOHNNY *gazes at the nickel in his hand and then raises his voice again in a call.*) Toy-ees for sale! Nice little—

(*His voice dies out and he stands staring before him. And now blaring suddenly in the air nearby, comes a sound of a brass band playing the "Democracy March."* JOHNNY *still stands*
20 *gazing before him. The rat-tat-tat-tat of the drums comes near him, and crossing the scene at the extreme left rear is the American Legion Drum Corps with a few bugles and pieces of brass. Two boy-scout flag-bearers go before, and behind them, several young men and women carrying banners and placards—"America First," "Be Prepared," and so forth. The parade passes on like a vision in a dream, but* JOHNNY *still looks before him with his old*

man's face and unblinking eyes. He shivers a bit, and his shoulders seem to sag.

(*By this time the gloom of approaching twilight has spread over the scene. The street lamp above his head gradually lights up, casting its nebulous halo over his shabby figure standing motionless as stone. Suddenly he begins to whistle low and aimlessly to himself—the theme melody of the play. For a moment he continues whistling; then giving his shoulders the faintest touch of a shrug, he turns and starts down the long street. He looks up now and then at the row of silent houses on his right*). Toy-ees! Toy-ees—for nice little girls and boys!

(*But nobody appears, no windows are opened, no smiling youthful faces appear, for all are gathered into the great stadium in the distance where the drear outlandish haranguer voice can still be heard continuing its queer clamor to the sky—"Gog-a-gog—Magog-a-gog." Yet even so,* JOHNNY JOHNSON *is not hushed by this strange voice booming through the world. As he disappears down the long street that leads from the great city into the country and beyond, he begins whistling his song again—a little more clearly now, a little more bravely.*)

Curtain

E. B. WHITE

Elwyn Brooks White was born in Mount Vernon, New York, on July 11, 1899. He graduated from Cornell University in 1921; and, after some experimenting in various kinds of odd jobs, he entered the field of journalism. He has always been associated in the popular mind with the brilliant success of *The New Yorker*, for which much of his characteristic work has been written, but he also has conducted a column in *Harper's Magazine*, "One Man's Meat," the contributions to which have added immeasurably to his stature as a first-class satirist of

the gentler rather than the harsher persuasion and an extremely shrewd commentator on American society of the hectic 1930's and later. He has written some capable light verse, best illustrated by the collection *The Fox of Peapack* (1938), and some fantasy-pieces like *Stuart Little* (1945). His prose style is whimsical, intensely personal, deceptively rambling but unusually straightforward in its impact; and his sense of humor, sometimes puckish, sometimes mordant, has always been one of his most effective assets.

from One Man's Meat

Walden

MISS NIMS, take a letter to Henry David Thoreau. Dear Henry: I thought of you the other afternoon as I was approaching Concord doing fifty on Route 62. That is a high speed at which to hold a philosopher in one's mind, but in this century we are a nimble bunch.

On one of the lawns in the outskirts of the village a woman was cutting the grass with a motorized lawn mower. What made me think of you was that the machine had rather got away from her, although she was game enough, and in the brief glimpse I had of the scene it appeared to me that the lawn was mowing the lady. She kept a tight grip on the handles, which throbbed violently with every explosion of the one-cylinder motor, and as she sheered around bushes and lurched along at a reluctant trot behind her impetuous servant, she looked like a puppy who had grabbed something that was too much for him. Concord hasn't changed much, Henry; the farm implements and the animals still have the upper hand.

I may as well admit that I was journeying to Concord with the deliberate intention of visiting your woods; for although I have never knelt at the grave of a philosopher nor placed wreaths on moldy poets, and have often gone a mile out of my way to avoid some place of historical interest, I have always wanted to see Walden Pond. The account which you left of your sojourn there is, you will be amused to learn, a document of increasing pertinence; each year it seems to gain a little headway, as the world loses ground. We may all be transcendental yet, whether we like it or not. As our common complexities increase, any tale of individual simplicity (and yours is the best written and the cockiest) acquires a new fascination; as our goods accumulate, but not our well-being, your report of an existence without material adornment takes on a certain awkward credibility.

My purpose in going to Walden Pond, like yours, was not to live cheaply or to live dearly there, but to transact some private business with the fewest obstacles. Approaching Concord, doing forty, doing forty-five, doing fifty, the steering wheel held snug in my palms, the highway held grimly in my vision, the crown of the road now serving me (on the righthand curves), now defeating me (on the lefthand curves), I began to rouse myself from the stupefaction which a day's motor journey induces. It was a delicious evening, Henry, when the whole body is one sense, and imbibes delight through every pore, if I may coin a phrase. Fields were richly brown where the harrow, drawn by the stripped Ford, had lately sunk its teeth; pastures were green; and overhead the sky had that same everlasting great look which you will find on Page 144 of the Oxford pocket edition. I could feel the road entering me, through tire, wheel, spring, and cushion; shall I not have intelligence with earth, too? Am I not partly leaves and vegetable mold myself?—a man of infinite horsepower, yet partly leaves.

Stay with me on 62 and it will take you into Concord. As I say, it was a delicious evening. The snake had come forth to die in a bloody S on the highway, the wheel upon its head, its bowels flat now and exposed. The turtle had come up too to cross the road and die in the attempt, its hard shell smashed under the rubber blow, its intestinal yearning (for the other side of the road) forever squashed. There was a sign by the wayside which announced that the road had a "cotton surface." You wouldn't know what that is, but neither, for that matter, did I. There is a cryptic ingredient in many of our modern improvements—we are awed and pleased without knowing quite what we are enjoying. It is something to be traveling on a road with a cotton surface.

The civilization round Concord to-day is an odd distillation of city, village, farm, and manor. The houses, yards, fields look not quite suburban, not quite rural. Under the bronze beech and the blue spruce of the departed baron grazes the milch goat of the heirs. Under the porte-cochère stands the reconditioned station wagon; under the grape arbor sit the puppies for sale. (But why do men degenerate ever? What makes families run out?)

It was June and everywhere June was publishing her immemorial stanza; in the lilacs, in the syringa, in the freshly edged paths and the sweetness of moist beloved gardens, and the little wire wickets that preserve the tulips' front. Farmers were already moving the fruits of their toil into their yards, arranging the rhubarb, the asparagus, the strictly fresh eggs on the painted stands under the little shed roofs with the patent shingles. And though it was almost a hundred years since you had taken your ax and started cutting out your home on Walden Pond, I was interested to observe that the philosophical spirit was still alive in Massachusetts; in the center of a vacant lot some boys were assembling the framework of a rude shelter, their whole mind and skill concentrated in the rather inauspicious helter-skeleton of studs and rafters. They too were escaping from town, to live naturally, in a rich blend of savagery and philosophy.

That evening, after supper at the inn, I strolled out into the twilight to dream my shapeless transcendental dreams and see that the car was locked up for the night (first open the right front door, then reach over, straining, and pull up the handles of the left rear and the left front till you hear the click, then the handle of the right rear, then shut the right front but open it again, remembering that the key is still in the ignition switch, remove the key, shut the right front again with a bang, push the tiny keyhole cover to one side, insert key, turn, and withdraw). It is what we all do, Henry. It is called locking the car. It is said to confuse thieves and keep them from making off with the laprobe. Four doors to lock behind one robe. The driver himself never uses a laprobe, the free movement of his legs being vital to the operation of the vehicle; so that when he locks the car it is a pure and unselfish act. I have in my life gained very little essential heat from laprobes, yet I have ever been at pains to lock them up.

The evening was full of sounds, some of which would have stirred your memory. The robins still love the elms of New England villages at sundown. There is enough of the thrush in them to make song inevitable at the end of day, and enough of the tramp to make them hang round the dwellings of men. A robin, like many another American, dearly loves a white house with green blinds. Concord is still full of them.

Your fellow-townsmen were stirring abroad—not many afoot, most of them in their cars; and the sound which they made in Concord at evening was a rustling and a whispering. The sound lacks steadfastness and is wholly unlike that of a train. A train, as you know who lived so near the Fitchburg line, whistles once or twice sadly and is gone, trailing a memory in smoke, soothing to ear and mind. Automobiles, skirting a village green, are like flies that have gained the inner ear—they buzz, cease, pause, start, shift, stop, halt, brake, and the whole effect is a nervous polytone curiously disturbing.

As I wandered along, the toc toc of ping pong balls drifted from an attic window. In front of the Reuben Brown house a Buick was drawn up. At the wheel, motionless, his hat upon his head, a man sat, listening to Amos and Andy on the radio (it is a drama of many scenes and without an end). The deep voice of Andrew Brown, emerging from the car, although it originated more than two hundred miles away, was unstrained by distance. When you used to sit on the shore of your pond on Sunday morning, listening to the church bells of Acton and Concord, you were aware of the excellent filter of the intervening atmosphere. Science has attended to that, and sound now maintains its intensity without regard for distance. Properly sponsored, it goes on forever.

A fire engine, out for a trial spin, roared past Emerson's house, hot with readiness for public duty. Over the barn roofs the martins dipped and chittered. A swarthy daughter of an asparagus grower, in culottes, shirt, and bandanna, pedalled past on her bicycle. It was indeed a delicious evening, and I returned to the inn (I believe it was your house once) to rock with the old ladies on the concrete veranda.

Next morning early I started afoot for Walden, out Main Street and down Thoreau, past the depot and the Minuteman Chevrolet Company. The morning was fresh, and in a bean field along the way I flushed an agriculturalist, quietly studying his beans. Thoreau Street soon joined Number 126, an artery of the State. We number our highways nowadays, our speed being so great we can remember little of their quality or character and are lucky to remember their number. (Men have an indistinct notion that if they keep up this activity long enough all will at length ride somewhere, in next to no time.) Your pond is on 126.

I knew I must be nearing your woodland retreat when the Golden Pheasant lunchroom came into view—Sealtest ice cream, toasted sandwiches, hot frankfurters, waffles, tonics, and lunches. Were I the proprietor, I should add rice, Indian meal, and molasses—just for old time's sake. The Pheasant, incidentally, is for sale: a chance for some nature lover who wishes to set himself up beside a pond in the Concord atmosphere and live deliberately, fronting only the essential facts of life on Number 126. Beyond the Pheasant was a place called Walden Breezes, an oasis whose porch pillars were made of old green shutters sawed into lengths. On the porch was a distorting mirror, to give the traveler a comical image of himself, who had miraculously learned to gaze in an ordinary glass without smiling. Behind the Breezes, in a sun-parched clearing, dwelt your philosophical descendants in their trailers, each trailer the size of your hut, but all grouped together for the sake of congeniality. Trailer people leave the city, as you did, to discover solitude and in any weather, at any hour of the day or night, to improve the nick of time; but they soon collect in villages and get bogged deeper in the mud than ever. The camp behind Walden Breezes was just rousing itself to the morning. The ground was packed hard under the heel, and the sun came through the clearing to bake the soil and enlarge the wry smell of cramped housekeeping. Cushman's bakery truck had stopped to deliver an early basket of rolls. A camp dog, seeing me in the road, barked petulantly. A man emerged from one of the trailers and set forth with a bucket to draw water from some forest tap.

Leaving the highway I turned off into the woods toward the pond, which was apparent through the foliage. The floor of the forest was strewn with dried old oak leaves and *Transcripts*. From beneath the flattened popcorn wrapper (*granum explosum*) peeped the frail violet. I followed a footpath and descended to the water's edge. The pond lay clear and blue in the morning light, as you have seen it so many times. In the shallows a man's waterlogged shirt undulated gently. A few flies came out to greet me and convoy me to your cove, past the No Bathing signs on which the fellows and the girls had scrawled their names. I felt strangely excited suddenly to be snooping around your premises, tiptoeing along watchfully, as though not to tread by mistake upon the intervening century. Before I got to the cove I heard something which seemed to me quite wonderful: I heard your frog, a full, clear *troonk*, guiding me, still hoarse and solemn, bridging the years as the robins had bridged them in the sweetness of the village evening. But he soon quit, and I came on a couple of young boys throwing stones at him.

Your front yard is marked by a bronze tablet set in a stone. Four small granite posts, a few feet away, show where the house was. On top of the tablet was a pair of faded blue bathing trunks with a white stripe. Back of it is a pile of stones, a sort of cairn, left by your visitors as a tribute I suppose. It is a rather ugly little heap of stones, Henry. In fact the hillside itself seems faded, browbeaten; a few tall skinny pines, bare of lower limbs, a smattering of young maples in suitable green, some birches and oaks, and a number of trees felled by the last big wind. It was from the bole of one of these fallen pines, torn up by the roots, that I extracted the stone which I added to the cairn —a sentimental act in which I was interrupted by a small terrier from a nearby picnic group, who confronted me and wanted to know about the stone.

I sat down for a while on one of the posts of your house to listen to the bluebottles and the dragonflies. The invaded glade sprawled shabby and mean at my feet, but the flies were tuned to the old vibration. There were the remains of a fire in your ruins, but I doubt that it was yours; also two beer bottles trodden into the soil and become part of earth. A young oak had taken root in your house, and two or three ferns, unrolling like the ticklers at a banquet. The only other furnishings were a DuBarry pattern sheet, a page torn from a picture magazine, and some crusts in wax paper.

Before I quit I walked clear round the pond

and found the place where you used to sit on the northeast side to get the sun in the fall, and the beach where you got sand for scrubbing your floor. On the eastern side of the pond, where the highway borders it, the State has built dressing rooms for swimmers, a float with diving towers, drinking fountains of porcelain, and rowboats for hire. The pond is in fact a State Preserve, and carries a twenty-dollar fine

10 for picking wild flowers, a decree signed in all solemnity by your fellow-citizens Walter C. Wardwell, Erson B. Barlow, and Nathaniel I. Bowditch. There was a smell of creosote where they had been building a wide wooden stairway to the road and the parking area. Swimmers and boaters were arriving; bodies plunged vigorously into the water and emerged wet and beautiful in the bright air. As I left, a boatload of town boys were splashing about in mid-

20 pond, kidding and fooling, the young fellows singing at the tops of their lungs in a wild chorus:

> *Amer-ica, Amer-i-ca, God shed his grace on*
> *   thee,*
> *And crown thy good with brotherhood*
> *From sea to shi-ning sea!*

I walked back to town along the railroad, following your custom. The rails were expanding noisily in the hot sun, and on the slope of the road-bed the wild grape and the blackberry sent up their creepers to the track.

The expense of my brief sojourn in Concord was:

Canvas shoes	$1.95	
Baseball bat	.25	gifts to take back to a boy
Left-handed fielder's glove	1.25	
Hotel and meals	4.25	
In all	$7.70	

As you see, this amount was almost what you spent for food for eight months. I cannot defend the shoes or the expenditure for shelter and food: they reveal a meanness and grossness in my nature which you would find contemptible. The baseball equipment, however, is the kind of impediment with which you were never on even terms. You must remember that the house where you practiced the sort of economy which I respect was haunted only by mice and squirrels. You never had to cope with a shortstop.

❦ British Writers and the Social Scene

WYSTAN HUGH AUDEN

Wystan Hugh Auden is a product of what he himself calls "the upper six percent" of English society which is the governing and well-to-do class. In *Letters from Iceland* written in collaboration with Louis MacNeice, he describes himself: "My passport says I'm five feet and eleven, with hazel eyes and fair (it's tow-like)

hair, that I was born in York in 1907, with no distinctive markings anywhere." He is the son of a retired medical officer, George Augustus Auden, and Constance Rosalie (Bicknell) Auden. He received an excellent education, going from Gresham's School, Holt, to Christ College, Oxford. In his undergraduate days he supported left-wing politics, and later, together with Stephen Spender, C. Day Lewis, and others, supported the communist position in politics. All these English poets were intellectually, although not always emotionally, convinced of the decline of their own class and in general of the validity of the Marxist philosophy. That they were too idealistic in their visions of an easy change many of them later acknowledged, but for a time they led the English and American left-wing writers in issuing critical proclamations on the position of the artist in contemporary society. They attacked the bourgeois and envisioned a better world. But World War II put an end to their hopes for enduring brotherhood, and they reacted accordingly, each in his own way.

By this time Auden had published several volumes of poetry of unusual merit: *Poems* (1930); *The Orators* (1932); *The Dance of Death* (1933); *The Dog Beneath the Skin*, a poetic play written with Christopher Isherwood (1935); *Letters from Iceland* with Louis MacNeice (1937); and *The Ascent of F 6* with Christopher Isherwood (1936). He also wrote with Isherwood *Journey to a War* (1939), an account of their travels through revolutionary China. This, like *Letters from Iceland,* is a mixture of poetry and prose.

All these poems sparkle with Auden's keen wit, which sometimes turns to broad satire of current events. Constantly he stresses the decline of the middle class and the boredom of the life it leads. He analyzes keenly the vacuity of the social pattern and the personal neuroses developing therefrom. In his poetry are all the conflicts and personal and social values characteristic of the thirties.

Auden had been awarded the King's gold medal in 1937 for the best poetry of the year. But he was becoming disillusioned with his political faith in peaceful change. In 1939, with the signs of coming war about him, he turned to the United States. He had married Erika Mann, the daughter of the anti-fascist novelist Thomas Mann, and he soon sought American citizenship. His period of political poetry was over and, disillusioned in the possibilities of the poet's ability to lead a society, he became an advocate, although a late one, of the idea that the artist should be devoted only to his art.

He published *On the Frontier* (1938), a melodrama in three acts written with Christopher Isherwood; *Another Time,* more poems, in 1940; and *The Double Man* in 1941. This last is an exhaustive examination of the dualism between good and evil, of the split between body and soul, reviving the old medieval dichotomy in a violently skeptical and individualist manner. His *Collected Poetry* was published in 1945, as was *For the Time Being.* In 1947 *The Age of Anxiety,* subsequently awarded the Pulitzer Prize, appeared.

Auden drove an ambulance in Spain in the Spanish Civil War. He has been compared to Byron, who as an ardent individualist demanded freedom for himself almost more than for others, and yet died in the Greek national liberation. But in fighting for a new world Auden has so mourned for the imagined loss of the real values of the old that he cannot clearly see a new world coming. This lack of understanding and faith forces him as it did Eliot to return to the semi-philosophical and religious pattern of belief.

The young intellectual who rejects a world that has rejected him finds companionship more easily among the few than among the many. Auden's imagery reflects a constant terror; it is a caricature of values obviously dear to him. He sees how swiftly the past recedes; he knows what the rapidly nearing future brings; but he retreats from the inevitable act of will and of social participation in bringing to birth the new. For him there are two "islands," England and the Self—both isolated. He gestures toward unity, but fixes finally on redemption for the Self through art alone. His later poems therefore become less and less Marxist, more religious and metaphysical. It is easier to resolve the schism between good and evil, or at least to explain it, through the contradictions of the inner self and their momentary resolution, than it is to resolve the schism between the old world and the new. After flirting briefly with Catholicism (for his is essentially a very skeptical mind) Auden announced himself as an existentialist, a man participating in but never a part of anything, not even fully of nature.

from On This Island

IX

THE EARTH turns over, our side feels the cold,
And life sinks choking in the wells of trees;
The ticking heart comes to a standstill, killed,
The icing on the pond waits for the boys.
Among the holly and the gifts I move,   5
The carols on the piano, the glowing hearth,
All our traditional sympathy with birth,
Put by your challenge to the shifts of love.

Your portrait hangs before me on the wall   9
And there what view I wish for, I shall find,
The wooded or the stony—though not all
The painter's gifts can make its flatness round—
Through the blue irises the heaven of failures,
The mirror world where logic is reversed,   14
Where age becomes the handsome child at last,
The glass sea parted for the country sailors.

Where move the enormous comics, drawn from
        life;
My father as an Airedale and a gardener,
My mother chasing letters with a knife:
You are not present as a character.   20
—Only the family have speaking parts—
You are a valley or a river bend,
The one an aunt refers to as a friend,
The tree from which the weasel racing starts.

False; but no falser than the world it matches,
Love's daytime kingdom which I say you rule,
The total state where all must wear your
        badges,   27
Keep order perfect as a naval school:
Noble emotions organized and massed
Line the straight flood-lit tracks of memory   30
To cheer your image as it flashes by;
All lust at once informed on and suppressed.

Yours is the only name expressive there,
And family affection the one in cypher;
Lay-out of hospital and street and square   35
That comfort to the homesick children offer:

As I, their author, stand between these dreams,
Son of a nurse and doctor, loaned a room,
Your would-be lover who has never come
In the great bed at midnight to your arms.   40

Such dreams are amorous; they are indeed:
But no one but myself is loved in these,
And time flies on above the dreamer's head,
Flies on, flies on, and with your beauty flies.
All things he takes and loses but conceit,   45
The Alec who can buy the life within,
License no liberty except his own,
Order the fireworks after the defeat.

Language of moderation cannot hide;
My sea is empty and the waves are rough: 50
Gone from the map the shore where childhood
        played
Tight-fisted as a peasant, eating love;
Lost in my wake the archipelago,
Islands of self through which I sailed all day,
Planting a pirate's flag, a generous boy;   55
And lost the way to action and to you.

Lost if I steer. Gale of desire may blow
Sailor and ship past the illusive reef,
And I yet land to celebrate with you
Birth of a natural order and of love;   60
With you enjoy the untransfigured scene,
My father down the garden in his gaiters,
My mother at her bureau writing letters,
Free to our favours, all our titles gone.

X

Now from my window-sill I watch the night
The church clock's yellow face, the green pier
        light
Burn for a new imprudent year;
The silence buzzes in my ear;
The jets in both the dormitories are out.   5

Under the darkness nothing seems to stir;
The lilac bush like a conspirator
Shams dead upon the lawn and there
Above the flagstaff the Great Bear
Hangs as a portent over Helensburgh.   10

But deaf to prophecy or China's drum
The blood moves strangely in its moving home,

IX, X, XVII, and XXX from *On This Island*, reprinted by
permission of Random House, Inc., New York.
IX. The whole poem is a contrast between the former active
and progressive life of a man of Auden's class and the life of
Auden himself living in the dying age of the middle class.
9. Your portrait . . . me. The portrait is an idealized image
of the past, perhaps of a person and scenes which symbolized
to the child a life of security and love.   **17. Where move . . .
comics,** images of the child's parents and background.

49. Language . . . hide, etc. The poet himself contrasts his
highly personal life with the greater life of the ancestor mentioned in the first stanzas.
X. **10. Helensburgh,** a town on the coast of Scotland, Dum-
bartonshire.   **11. But deaf, etc.** Man now looks further than
England's imperialism or his own life.

Diverges, loops to travel further
Than the long still shadow of the father,
Though to the valley of regret it come.   15

Now in this season when the ice is loosened,
In scrubbed laboratories research is hastened
And cameras at the growing wood
Are pointed; for the long lost good,
Desire like a police-dog is unfastened.   20

O Lords of limit, training dark and light
And setting a tabu 'twixt left and right:
The influential quiet twins
From whom all property begins,
Look leniently upon us all to-night.   25

Oldest of masters, whom the schoolboy fears
Failing to find his pen, to keep back tears,
Collecting stamps and butterflies
Hoping in some way to appease
The malice of the erratic examiners.   30

No one has seen you. None can say of late,
'Here—you can see the marks—they lay in wait.'
But in my thoughts to-night you seem
Forms which I saw once in a dream,
The stocky keepers of a wild estate.   35

With guns beneath your arms, in sun and wet
At doorways posted or on ridges set,
By copse or bridge we know you there
Whose sleepless presences endear
Our peace to us with a perpetual threat.   40

We know you moody, silent, sensitive,
Quick to be offended, slow to forgive,
But to your discipline the heart
Submits when we have fallen apart
Into the isolated personal life.   45

Look not too closely, be not over-quick;
We have no invitation, but we are sick,
Using the mole's device, the carriage
Of peacock or rat's desperate courage,
For we shall only pass you by a trick.   50

At the end of my corridor are boys who dream
Of a new bicycle or winning team;

On their behalf guard all the more
This late-maturing Northern shore,   54
Who to their serious season must shortly come.

Give them spontaneous skill at holding rein,
At twisting dial, or at making fun,
That these may never need our craft,
Who, awkward, pasty, feeling the draught,   59
Have health and skill and beauty on the brain.

The clocks strike ten: the tea is on the stove;
And up the stair come voices that I love.
Love, satisfaction, force, delight,
To these players of Badminton to-night,
To Favel, Holland, sprightly Alexis give.   65

Deeper towards the summer the year moves on.
And what if the starving visionary have seen
The carnival within our gates,
Your bodies kicked about the streets,   69
We need your power still: use it, that none

O from this table break uncontrollably away
Lunging, insensible to injury,
Dangerous in the room, or out wild-
-ly spinning like a top in the field,
Mopping and mowing through the sleepless
          day.

XVII

Here on the cropped grass of the narrow ridge
          I stand,
A fathom of earth, alive in air,
Aloof as an admiral on the old rocks,
          England below me:
Eastward across the Midland plains   5
An express is leaving for a sailor's country;
Westward is Wales
Where on clear evenings the retired and rich
From the French windows of their sheltered
          mansions   9
See the Sugarloaf standing, an upright sentinel
          Over Abergavenny.

When last I stood here I was not alone; happy
Each thought the other, thinking of a crime,

21. O Lords, etc., a prayer to the mere chances of life—the
symbols of modern man's destiny—to the forces that limit a
life led in the present conflict of social forces.   26. Oldest of
masters, etc., a reference to "O Lords of limit" (l. 21), to
any master or instrument of correction (such as those a schoolboy grows up under) who lays fear upon a life. So today the
knowledge of the forces of society lays that fear.

65. Favel, Holland ... Alexis, names of Auden's pupils.
70. that none, etc. The poet sees the future which may destroy
his radical friends.
XVII. The first stanza gives the scene in which the poem is
composed, and the poet on his ridge can apparently see various
aspects of class divisions in England and Wales.   10. Sugarloaf, a mountain on the side of Abergavenny.   11. Abergavenny, a market-town in Monmouthshire, England, a west
border county.

And England to our meditations seemed
    The perfect setting: 15
But now it has no innocence at all;
It is the isolation and the fear,
    The mood itself;
It is the body of the absent lover,
An image to the would-be hero of the soul, 20
The little area we are willing to forgive
    Upon conditions.

For private reasons I must have the truth, re-
    member
These years have seen a boom in sorrow;
The presses of idleness issued more despair 25
    And it was honoured,
Gross Hunger took on more hands every month,
Erecting here and everywhere his vast
    Unnecessary workshops;
Europe grew anxious about her health, 30
Combines tottered, credits froze,
And business shivered in a banker's winter
    While we were kissing.

To-day no longer occupied like that, I give
The children at the open swimming pool 35
Lithe in their first and little beauty
    A closer look;
Follow the cramped clerk crooked at his desk,
The guide in shorts pursuing flowers
    In their careers;   40
A digit of the crowd, would like to know
Them better whom the shops and trams are full
    of,
The little men and their mothers, not plain but
    Dreadfully ugly.

Deaf to the Welsh wind now, I hear arising 45
From lanterned gardens sloping to the river
Where saxophones are moaning for a com-
    forter,
    From Gaumont theatres
Where fancy plays on hunger to produce
The nobler robber, ideal of boys, 50
    And from cathedrals,
Luxury liners laden with souls,
Holding to the east their hulls of stone,
The high thin rare continuous worship
    Of the self-absorbed.   55

Here, which looked north before the Cambrian
    alignment,
Like the cupped hand of the keen excavator
Busy with bones, the memory uncovers
    The hopes of time;
Of empires stiff in their brocaded glory, 60
The luscious lateral blossoming of woe
    Scented, profuse;
And of intercalary ages of disorder
When, as they prayed in antres, fell
Upon the noblest in the country night 65
    Angel assassins.

Small birds above me have the grace of those
    who founded
The civilization of the delicate olive,
Learning the laws of love and sailing
    On the calm Aegean;   70
The hawk is the symbol of the rule by thirst,
The central state controlling the canals;
    And the blank sky
Of the womb's utter peace before
The cell, dividing, multiplied desire, 75
And raised instead of death the image
    Of the reconciler.

And over the Cotswolds now the thunder mut-
    ters:
'What little of the truth your seers saw 79
They dared not tell you plainly but combined
    Assertion and refuge
In the common language of collective lying,
In codes of a bureau, laboratory slang
    And diplomats' French.
The relations of your lovers were, alas, picto-
    rial;   85
The treasure that you stole, you lost; bad luck
It brought you, but you cannot put it back
    Now with caresses.

'Already behind you your last evening hastens
    up
And all the customs your society has chosen 90

56. **Cambrian alignment,** a rock formation in Wales which pertains to the Molluscan age in geology (Cambria is the ancient name for Wales). 63. **intercalary,** inserted or introduced among others in the calendar, therefore meaning here periods of disorder introduced among periods of order in society. 64. **antres,** caves. 66. **Angel assassins,** probably a reference to bombings from airplanes. 68. **The civilization . . . olive.** The general meaning is that other civilizations, like the Greek, have perished. 71. **The hawk . . . symbol.** England's civilization may perish likewise. 78. **Cotswolds,** range of hills running through Gloucestershire. 79. **What little,** etc. Leaders of England have not been honest in stating the political and economic situation.

23. **the truth,** meaning pictures of England's condition today. 48. **Gaumont,** leading British motion-picture producer and owner of one of the largest chains of motion-picture theaters.

Harden themselves into the unbreakable
   Habits of death.
Has not your long affair with death
Of late become increasingly more serious;
   Do you not find   95
Him growing more attractive every day?
You shall go under and help him with the
   crops,
Be faithful to him, and to your friends
   Remain indifferent.'   99

And out of the turf the bones of war continue;
'Know then, cousin, the major cause of our collapse
Was a distortion in the human plastic by luxury produced,

Never higher than in our time were the vital advantages;
To matter entire, to the unbounded vigours of
   the instrument,
To all logical precision we were the rejoicing
   heirs.   105

But pompous, we assumed their power to be
   our own,
Believed machines to be our hearts' spontaneous fruit,
Taking our premises as shoppers take a tram.

While the disciplined love which alone could
   have employed these engines
Seemed far too difficult and dull, and when hatred promised   110
An immediate dividend, all of us hated.

Denying the liberty we knew quite well to be
   our destiny,
It dogged our steps with its accusing shadow
Until in every landscape we saw murder ambushed.   114

Unable to endure ourselves, we sought relief
In the insouciance of the soldier, the heroic sex-
   ual pose
Playing at fathers to impress the little ladies,

Call us not tragic; falseness made farcical our
   death:
Nor brave; ours was the will of the insane to
   suffer

By which since we could not live we gladly
   died: 120
And now we have gone for ever to our foolish
   graves.'

The Priory clock chimes briefly and I recollect
I am expected to return alive
My will effective and my nerves in order
   To my situation.   125
'The poetry is in the pity,' Wilfred said,
And Kathy in her journal, 'To be rooted in life,
   That's what I want.'
These moods give no permission to be idle,
For men are changed by what they do;   130
And through loss and anger the hands of the
   unlucky
Love one another.

XXX
(TO CHRISTOPHER ISHERWOOD)

August for the people and their favourite is-
   lands.
Daily the steamers sidle up to meet
The effusive welcome of the pier, and soon,
The luxuriant life of the steep stone valleys,
The sallow oval faces of the city   5
Begot in passion or good-natured habit,
Are caught by waiting coaches, or laid bare
Beside the undiscriminating sea.

Lulled by the light they live their dreams of
   freedom;   9
May climb the old road twisting to the moors,
Play leap frog, enter cafés, wear
The tigerish blazer and the dove-like shoe.
The yachts upon the little lake are theirs,
The gulls ask for them, and to them the band
Makes its tremendous statements; they control
The complicated apparatus of amusement.   16

All types that can intrigue the writer's fancy,
Or sensuality approves, are here.
And I, each meal-time with the families,
The animal brother and his serious sister,   20
Or after breakfast on the urned steps watching

115. **Unable . . . ladies.** Capitalism, Auden implies, brings war and a decadent individualism.

122. **Priory,** a monastic house presided over by a prior or prioress, next in dignity below an abbey. 126. **Wilfred,** the poet Wilfred Owen (p. 206), who wrote chiefly on war. 127. **Kathy,** Katherine Mansfield (p. 425). 129. **These moods . . . another.** The modern radical must act against the decay he sees around him.
XXX. 1. **August, etc.** The poem opens with pictures of vacation periods and of the poet on vacation. 21. **urned,** having large, decorative urns at the sides.

The defeated and disfigured marching by,
Have thought of you, Christopher, and wished
    beside me
Your squat spruce body and enormous head.

Nine years ago, upon that southern island   25
Where the wild Tennyson became a fossil,
Half-boys, we spoke of books and praised
The acid and austere, behind us only
The stuccoed suburb and expensive school.
Scented our turf, the distant baying   30
Nice decoration to the artist's wish;
Yet fast the deer was flying through the wood.

Our hopes were set still on the spies' career,
Prizing the glasses and the old felt hat,
And all the secrets we discovered were   35
Extraordinary and false; for this one coughed
And it was gasworks coke, and that one
    laughed
And it was snow in bedrooms; many wore wigs,
The coastguard signalled messages of love,
The enemy were sighted from the Norman
    tower.   40

Five summers pass and now we watch
The Baltic from a balcony: the word is love.
Surely one fearless kiss would cure
The million fevers, a stroking brush   44
The insensitive refuse from the burning core.
Was there a dragon who had closed the works
While the starved city fed it with the Jews?
Then love would tame it with his trainer's look.

Pardon the studied taste that could refuse   49
The golf-house quick one and the rector's tea;
Pardon the nerves the thrushes could not
    soothe,
Yet answered promptly the no-subtler lure
To private joking in a panelled room,
The solitary vitality of tramps and madmen;
Believed the whisper in the double bed: 55
Pardon for these and every flabby fancy.

For now the moulding images of growth
That made our interest and us, are gone.
Louder to-day the wireless roars
Its warnings and its lies, and it's impossible   60
Among the well-shaped cosily to flit,
Or longer to desire about our lives
The beautiful loneliness of the banks, or find
The stoves and resignations of the frozen plains.

The close-set eyes of mother's boy   65
Saw nothing to be done; we look again:
See Scandal praying with her sharp knees up,
And Virtue stood at Weeping Cross,
The green thumb to the ledger knuckled down,
And Courage to his leaking ship appointed,   70
Slim Truth dismissed without a character,
And gaga Falsehood highly recommended.

Greed showing shamelessly her naked money,
And all Love's wondering eloquence debased
To a collector's slang, Smartness in furs,   75
And Beauty scratching miserably for food,
Honour self-sacrificed for Calculation,
And Reason stoned by Mediocrity,
Freedom by Power shockingly maltreated,
And Justice exiled till Saint Geoffrey's Day.   80

So in this hour of crisis and dismay,
What better than your strict and adult pen
Can warn us from the colours and the consola-
    tions,
The showy arid works, reveal   84
The squalid shadow of academy and garden,
Make action urgent and its nature clear?
Who give us nearer insight to resist
The expanding fear, the savaging disaster?

This then my birthday wish for you, as now
From the narrow window of my fourth-floor
    room   90
I smoke into the night, and watch reflections
Stretch in the harbour. In the houses
The little pianos are closed, and a clock strikes.
And all sway forward on the dangerous flood
Of history, that never sleeps or dies,   95
And, held one moment, burns the hand.

25. **that southern island,** the Isle of Wight, off the southern coast of England, where Tennyson lived, retired from the world to steep himself in Arthurian traditions, in order to write his *Idylls of the King.* Here Auden and Isherwood as youths spent a vacation. Isherwood collaborated with Auden on some of his poetic dramas. (See p. 776.)   26. **Tennyson . . . fossil.** Auden is in effect stating that the later truly Victorian Tennyson writing on legendary subjects is less interesting than the earlier and more emotional Tennyson. In 1946 Auden edited a selection of Tennyson's poems.   42. **the word is love.** Auden is sketching in his and Isherwood's dream that love might solve both personal and social problems.   46. **dragon . . . Jews.** The dragon is Hitler, and the reference to the Jews is to his persecution of them.

57. **images of growth,** etc. Now the youthful images of growth have faded, and a sense of security in life which these young men had as members of the upper middle class is gone. Neither nature ("beautiful loneliness of the banks") nor isolation from society can convince the modern poet that much is not wrong with the world.   80. **And Justice . . . Day.** The venerable Bede, historian, mentions Saint Geoffrey (642–716) as an administrator of "extraordinary diligence, unrivaled in piety."   81–96. **So in . . . hand.** The last two stanzas record the condition of society today.

Epilogue

'O WHERE are you going?' said reader to rider,
'That valley is fatal when furnaces burn,
Yonder's the midden whose odours will madden,
That gap is the grave where the tall return.'

'O do you imagine,' said fearer to farer,   5
'That dusk will delay on your path to the pass,
Your diligent looking discover the lacking
Your footsteps feel from granite to grass?'

'O what was that bird,' said horror to hearer,
'Did you see that shape in the twisted trees?   10
Behind you swiftly the figure comes softly,
The spot on your skin is a shocking disease?'

'Out of this house'—said rider to reader
'Yours never will'—said farer to fearer   14
'They're looking for you'—said hearer to horror
As he left them there, as he left them there.

from Poems

III

SINCE you are going to begin to-day
Let us consider what it is you do.
You are the one whose part it is to lean,
For whom it is not good to be alone.
Laugh warmly turning shyly in the hall   5
Or climb with bare knees the volcanic hill,
Acquire that flick of wrist and after strain
Relax in your darling's arms like a stone
Remembering everything you can confess,   9
Making the most of firelight, of hours of fuss;
But joy is mine not yours—to have come so far,
Whose cleverest invention was lately fur;
Lizards my best once who took years to breed,
Could not control the temperature of blood.
To reach that shape for your face to assume,   15
Pleasure to many and despair to some,
I shifted ranges, lived epochs handicapped
By climate, wars, or what the young men kept,
Modified theories on the types of dross;
Altered desire and history of dress.   20

You in the town now call the exile fool
That writes home once a year as last leaves fall,

Think—Romans had a language in their day
And ordered roads with it, but it had to die:
Your culture can but leave—forgot as sure   25
As place-name origins in favourite shire—
Jottings for stories, some often-mentioned Jack,
And references in letters to a private joke,
Equipment rusting in unweeded lanes,
Virtues still advertised on local lines;   30
And your conviction shall help none to fly,
Cause rather a perversion on next floor.

Not even is despair your own, when swiftly
Comes general assault on your ideas of safety:
That sense of famine, central anguish felt   35
For goodness wasted at peripheral fault,
Your shutting up the house and taking prow
To go into the wilderness to pray,
Means that I wish to leave and to pass on,
Select another form, perhaps your son;   40
Though he reject you, join opposing team
Be late or early at another time,
My treatment will not differ—he will be tipped,
Found weeping, signed for, made to answer,
    topped.
Do not imagine you can abdicate;   45
Before you reach the frontier you are caught;
Others have tried it and will try again
To finish that which they did not begin:
Their fate must always be the same as yours,
To suffer the loss they were afraid of, yes,   50
Holders of one position, wrong for years.

IX

It's no use raising a shout.
No, Honey, you can cut that right out.
I don't want any more hugs;
Make me some fresh tea, fetch me some rugs.
Here am I, here are you: 5
But what does it mean? What are we going to
    do?

A long time ago I told my mother
I was leaving home to find another:
I never answered her letter
But I never found a better.   10
Here am I, here are you:
But what does it mean? What are we going to
    do?

"Epilogue" reprinted from *Poems* by permission of Random House, Inc., New York.
Epilogue. The poem, which is from Auden's extraordinary early "Charade," is a study of the conflict between the spirit of man which dares to advance into danger and social struggle and the instinct of man to preserve himself. 3. **midden**, pile of refuse.
III and IX from *Poems*, reprinted by permission of Random House, Inc., New York.

33. **Not even, etc.** Personal despair in times so chaotic as these is impossible, nor will personal goodness help to correct social evil. If this generation does not take the responsibility, the next must. 51. **Holders . . . position**, intellectuals and middle-class thinkers.
IX, a satirical statement of modern man's defeat in the contemporary scene which destroys all illusion of his greatness.

It wasn't always like this?
Perhaps it wasn't, but it is.
Put the car away; when life fails,   15
What's the good of going to Wales?
Here am I, here are you:
But what does it mean? What are we going to
    do?

In my spine there was a base;
And I knew the general's face: 20
But they've severed all the wires,
And I can't tell what the general desires.
Here am I, here are you:
But what does it mean? What are we going to
    do?

In my veins there is a wish,   25
And a memory of fish:
When I lie crying on the floor,
It says, 'You've often done this before.'
Here am I, here are you:
But what does it mean? What are we going to
    do?   30

A bird used to visit this shore:
It isn't going to come any more.
I've come a very long way to prove
No land, no water, and no love.
Here am I, here are you: 35
But what does it mean? What are we going to
    do?

from Letter to Lord Byron

(AN EXCERPT FROM PART IV)

THE GREAT WAR had begun: but masters'
    scrutiny
And fists of big boys were the war to us;

Excerpt from "Letter to Lord Byron" from *Letters from Iceland*
by W. H. Auden and Louis MacNeice, reprinted by permission
of Random House, Inc., New York.

Even as Byron, exiled from England, wrote his *Don Juan*,
a "quietly facetious" satire about his own English education
to indicate how sheltered English youth may break free into
experiences guaranteed to shock the conventional English middle class, Auden (in Iceland) writes of his youth. His long
letter is a modification of the *Don Juan* stanza (for the most
part an eight-line stanza, while Auden's is a seven, closing
with a couplet). Byron, the romantic individualist of the
nineteenth-century revolutionary movement, hated the stuffiness of English society and believed in individual freedom.
Auden is sometimes called a modern Byron. He had declared
himself, however, a communist, and although some of his posturing seems individualistic, his revolutionary theories were
of this century and not of the nineteenth.

It was as harmless as the Indian Mutiny,
    A beating from the Head was dangerous.
But once when half the form put down *Bel-*
    lus,   5
We were accused of that most deadly sin,
Wanting the Kaiser and the Huns to win.

The way in which we really were affected
    Was having such a varied lot to teach us.   9
The best were fighting, as the King expected,
    The remnant either elderly grey creatures,
    Or characters with most peculiar features.
Many were raggable, a few were waxy,
One had to leave abruptly in a taxi.

Surnames I must not write—O Reginald,   15
    You at least taught us that which fadeth not,
Our earliest visions of the great wide world;
    The beer and biscuits that your favourites
      got,
    Your tales revealing you a first-class shot,
Your riding breeks, your drama called *The*
    Waves,   20
A few of us will carry to our graves.

'Half a lunatic, half a knave.' No doubt
    A holy terror to the staff at tea;
A good headmaster must have soon found out
    Your moral character was all at sea;   25
    I question if you'd got a pass degree:
But little children bless your kind that knocks
Away the edifying stumbling blocks.

How can I thank you? For it only shows   29
    (Let me ride just this once my hobby-horse),
There're things a good headmaster never
      knows.
    There must be sober schoolmasters, of
      course,
    But what a prep school really puts across
Is knowledge of the world we'll soon be lost in:
To-day it's more like Dickens than Jane Austen.

I hate the modern trick, to tell the truth,   36
    Of straightening out the kinks in the young
      mind,
Our passion for the tender plant of youth,
    Our hatred for all weeds of any kind.

3. **Indian Mutiny,** the great revolt of the Bengal Army
in 1857 which led in 1858 to the transference of the government of India from the East India Company to the Crown.
5. **form,** grade, in English schools. ***Bellus,*** Latin for pleasant
happening, rather than *Bellum,* war.   20. **breeks,** breeches,
trousers.

Slogans are bad: the best that I can find   40
Is this: 'Let each child have that's in our care
As much neurosis as the child can bear.'

In this respect, at least, my bad old Adam is
Pigheadedly against the general trend;   44
And has no use for all these new academies
Where readers of the better weeklies send
The child they probably did not intend,
To paint a lampshade, marry, or keep pigeons,
Or make a study of the world religions.

Goddess of bossy underlings, Normality!   50
What murders are committed in thy name!
Totalitarian is thy state Reality,
Reeking of antiseptics and the shame
Of faces that all look and feel the same.   54
Thy Muse is one unknown to classic histories,
The topping figure of the hockey mistress.

From thy dread Empire not a soul's exempted:
More than the nursemaids pushing prams in
    parks,
By thee the intellectuals are tempted,
O, to commit the treason of the clerks,   60
Bewitched by thee to literary sharks.
But I must leave thee to thy office stool,
I must get on now to my public school.

Men had stopped throwing stones at one an-
    other,
Butter and Father had come back again;   65
Gone were the holidays we spent with Mother
In furnished rooms on mountain, moor, and
    fen;
And gone those summer Sunday evenings,
    when
Along the seafronts fled a curious noise,
'Eternal Father,' sung by three young boys.   70

Nation spoke Peace, or said she did, with na-
    tion;
The sexes tried their best to look the same;
Morals lost value during the inflation,
The great Victorians kindly took the blame:
Visions of Dada to the Post-War came,   75

Sitting in cafés, nostrils stuffed with bread,
Above the recent and the straight-laced dead.

I've said my say on public schools elsewhere:
Romantic friendship, prefects, bullying,   79
I shall not deal with, c'est une autre affaire.
Those who expect them, will get no such
    thing,
It is the strictly relevant I sing.
Why should they grumble? They've the Greek
    Anthology.
And all the spicier bits of Anthropology.   84

We all grow up the same way, more or less;
Life is not known to give away her presents;
She only swops. The unself-consciousness
That children share with animals and peas-
    ants
Sinks in the 'stürm und drang' of Adoles-
    cence.
Like other boys I lost my taste for sweets,   90
Discovered sunsets, passion, God, and Keats.

I shall recall a single incident
No more. I spoke of mining engineering
As the career on which my mind was bent,
But for some time my fancies had been veer-
    ing;   95
Mirages of the future kept appearing;
Crazes had come and gone in short, sharp
    gales,
For motor-bikes, photography, and whales.

But indecision broke off with a clean-cut end
One afternoon in March at half-past three
When walking in a ploughed field with a
    friend;   101
Kicking a little stone, he turned to me
And said, 'Tell me, do you write poetry?'
I never had, and said so, but I knew
That very moment what I wished to do.   105

Without a bridge passage this leads me straight
Into the theme marked 'Oxford' on my score
From pages twenty-five to twenty-eight.
Aesthetic trills I'd never heard before
Rose from the strings, shrill poses from the
    cor;   110
The woodwind chattered like a pre-war Rus-
    sian,

---

58. pram, English term for baby carriage.   **59. intellectuals
. . . treason of the clerks,** a reference to the idea that all
intellectuals are tempted to write.   **67. fen,** marshy land,
meadows.   **75. Dada,** Dadaism, a movement in modern art
which sprang into being about 1920, the basis of which was to
show how unrelated objects could be massed into one composition and take on form with meaning. Some of the artists in this
movement went to extremes, forming compositions of kitchen
utensils, buttons, and other incongruous objects. The movement
was short-lived, but many of its ideas have been carried over
into surrealism.

79. prefect, monitor in English schools.   **80. c'est une autre
affaire,** that is something else.   **89. 'stürm und drang,'**
storm and stress.   **110. cor,** horn.

'Art' boomed the brass, and 'Life' thumped the
    percussion.

A raw provincial, my good taste was tardy,
    And Edward Thomas I as yet preferred;
I was still listening to Thomas Hardy   115
    Putting divinity about a bird;
    But Eliot spoke the still unspoken word;
For gasworks and dried tubers I forsook
The clock at Grantchester, the English rook.

All youth's intolerant certainty was mine as
    I faced life in a double-breasted suit;   121
I bought and praised but did not read Aquinas,
    At the *Criterion's* verdict I was mute,
    Though Arnold's I was ready to refute;
And through the quads dogmatic words rang
    clear,   125
'Good poetry is classic and austere.'

So much for Art. Of course Life had its pas-
    sions too;
    The student's flesh like his imagination
Makes facts fit theories and has fashions too.
    We were the tail, a sort of poor relation 130
    To that debauched, eccentric generation
That grew up with their fathers at the War,
And made new glosses on the noun Amor.

Three years passed quickly while the Isis went
    Down to the sea for better or for worse;   135
Then to Berlin, not Carthage, I was sent
    With money from my parents in my purse,

And ceased to see the world in terms of
    verse.
I met a chap called Layard and he fed
New doctrines into my receptive head.   140

Part came from Lane, and part from D. H.
    Lawrence;
    Gide, though I didn't know it then, gave
    part.
They taught me to express my deep abhorrence
    If I caught anyone preferring Art   144
    To Life and Love and being Pure-in-Heart.
I lived with crooks but seldom was molested;
The Pure-in-Heart can never be arrested.

He's gay; no bludgeonings of chance can spoil
    it,
    The Pure-in-Heart loves all men on a par,
And has no trouble with his private toilet;   150
    The Pure-in-Heart is never ill; catarrh
    Would be the yellow streak, the brush of tar;
Determined to be loving and forgiving,   153
I came back home to try and earn my living.

The only thing you never turned your hand to
    Was teaching English in a boarding school.
To-day it's a profession that seems grand to
    Those whose alternative's an office stool;
    For budding authors it's become the rule.
To many an unknown genius postmen bring
Typed notices from Rabbitarse and String.   161

The Head's M.A., a bishop is a patron,
    The assistant staff is highly qualified;
Health is the care of an experienced matron,
    The arts are taught by ladies from outside;
    The food is wholesome and the grounds are
    wide;   166
Their aim is training character and poise,
With special coaching for the backward boys.

I found the pay good and had time to spend it,
    Though others may not have the good luck
    I did: 170
For You I'd hesitate to recommend it;

114. Edward Thomas, the modern English pastoral poet
who encouraged Robert Frost to publish his first book in
England and who was killed at the close of World War I.
117. Eliot. Auden in this line is parodying a line of T. S. Eliot's
religious poem *Ash-Wednesday.* **118. gasworks . . . tubers.**
Auden here satirizes Eliot's typical imagery of an ugly and
sterile civilization. References to gasworks and dried tubers
are to be found in Eliot's poem *The Waste Land.* Auden indicates in this stanza that while he was young he wrote in the
tradition of Thomas Hardy and Rupert Brooke, rather than
in the modern tradition. **119. clock at Grantchester.** Cf.
Rupert Brooke's poem "The Old Vicarage, Grantchester,"
l. 138: "oh! yet Stands the Church clock at ten to three?"
122. Aquinas. St. Thomas Aquinas (1225?–74), an Italian
philosopher and Dominican monk, whose great work *Summa
Totius Philosophiae* was a vast synthesis of the moral and political sciences and one of the greatest monuments of the medieval
mind. Aquinas argues the superiority of Catholic doctrine over
classic Greek morality. **123. Criterion,** the name of the
critical magazine edited by T. S. Eliot, publishing scholarly
articles on various medieval scholastics as well as modern writers. This magazine suspended publication in 1939. **124. Arnold,** Matthew Arnold (1822–88), English writer and critic.
125. quads, quadrangles or grassy squares around which
Oxford colleges are built. **134. Isis,** local name for the
upper course of the Thames River in England. **136. Berlin,
not Carthage,** an ironic touch that he was sent to the seat
of fascism, and not as Byron was to Carthage, the oldest seat
of learning.

139. Layard, John Layard, anthropologist, author of *The Stone
Men of Maleluka.* **141. Lane,** Homer Lane, an American
psychologist. Auden was interested especially in Lane's theories
of the psychological causes of disease. **D. H. Lawrence,** an
English writer (p. 413) who believed in the return to a primitive
life and to love as the basis of the emotions. **142. Gide,** André
Gide, a French novelist who deals with the abnormal in sex
and who in later life has written on revolutionary matters.
161. Rabbitarse and String, Gabbitas, Thring & Co., Ltd.,
an English school agency.

Several have told me that they can't abide
  it.
  Still, if one tends to get a bit one-sided,
It's pleasant as it's easy to secure
The hero worship of the immature.   175

More, it's a job, and jobs to-day are rare:
All the ideals in the world won't feed us
Although they give our crimes a certain air.
  So barons of the press who know their
    readers
  Employ to write their more appalling
    leaders,   180
Instead of Satan's horned and hideous minions,
Clever young men of liberal opinions.

Which brings me up to nineteen-thirty-five;
  Six months of film work is another story
I can't tell now. But, here I am, alive   185
  Knowing the true source of that sense of
    glory
That still surrounds the England of the Tory,
Come only to the rather tame conclusion
That no man by himself has life's solution.

I know—the fact is really not unnerving—   190
  That what is done is done, that no past dies,
That what we see depends on who's observing,
  And what we think on our activities.
  That envy warps the virgin as she dries
But 'Post coitum, homo tristis' means   195
The lover must go carefully with the greens.

The boat has brought me to the landing-stage,
  Up the long estuary of mud and sedges;
The line I travel has the English gauge;   199
  The engine's shadow vaults the little hedges;
  And summer's done. I sign the usual pledges
To be a better poet, better man;
I'll really do it this time if I can.

I'm home again, and goodness knows to what,
  To read the papers and to earn my bread;
I'm home to Europe where I may be shot;   206
  'I'm home again,' as William Morris said,
  'And nobody I really care for's dead.'
I've got a round of visits now to pay,
So I must finish this another day.

Spain 1937

YESTERDAY all the past. The language of size
  Spreading to China along the trade-routes; the diffusion
      Of the counting-frame and the cromlech;
Yesterday the shadow-reckoning in the sunny climates.

Yesterday the assessment of insurance by cards,
  The divination of water; yesterday the invention   5
      Of cart-wheels and clocks, the taming of
Horses; yesterday the bustling world of the navigators.

Yesterday the abolition of fairies and giants;
  The fortress like a motionless eagle eyeing the valley,   10
      The chapel built in the forest;
Yesterday the carving of angels and of frightening gargoyles.

183. **Which brings, etc.** Auden worked for the General Post Office in England, writing the commentaries, in verse, for the famous documentaries *Coal-Face* and *Night Mail*.   195. **'Post ... tristis,'** after cohabitation man is sad. "Spain 1937," "Refugee Blues," "New Year Letter," "Commentary," and "For the Time Being," from *Collected Poems*, copyright, 1945, by W. H. Auden; reprinted by permission of Random House, Inc.
Spain 1937. When the Spanish Civil War broke out in 1936, it seemed clear to many that it gave a microcosmic view of the struggle between the forces of reaction and progress. In this poem Auden contrasts the idea that man has been progressing with the blunt fact that a struggle against the ideals of human beings is taking place at that very moment.   3. **counting-frame,** the abacus, an ancient instrument used for working out mathematical problems. **cromlech,** megalithic structure consisting of two or more upright stones supporting a single flat one.   5. **insurance by cards,** the use of the Tarot pack or other fortunetelling cards to ascertain the probable good or evil outcome of some project. See T. S. Eliot, *The Waste Land*, p. 237.   6. **divination of water.** Water-diviners take in their hands a slender rod which is supposed to twitch violently when above hidden water.

The trial of heretics among the columns of stone;
Yesterday the theological feuds in the taverns
          And the miraculous cure at the fountain;   **15**
Yesterday the Sabbath of Witches. But today the struggle.

Yesterday the installation of dynamos and turbines;
The construction of railways in the colonial desert;
          Yesterday the classic lecture
On the origin of Mankind. But today the struggle.   **20**

Yesterday the belief in the absolute value of Greek;
The fall of the curtain upon the death of a hero;
          Yesterday the prayer to the sunset,
And the adoration of madmen. But today the struggle.

As the poet whispers, startled among the pines   **25**
Or, where the loose waterfall sings, compact, or upright
          On the crag by the leaning tower:
"O my vision. O send me the luck of the sailor."

And the investigator peers through his instruments
At the inhuman provinces, the virile bacillus   **30**
          Or enormous Jupiter finished:
"But the lives of my friends. I inquire, I inquire."

And the poor in their fireless lodgings dropping the sheets
Of the evening paper: "Our day is our loss. O show us
          History the operator, the   **35**
Organiser, Time the refreshing river."

And the nations combine each cry, invoking the life
That shapes the individual belly and orders
          The private nocturnal terror:
"Did you not found once the city state of the sponge,   **40**

"Raise the vast military empires of the shark
And the tiger, establish the robin's plucky canton?
          Intervene. O descend as a dove or
A furious papa or a mild engineer: but descend."

And the life, if it answers at all, replies from the heart   **45**
And the eyes and the lungs, from the shops and squares of the city:
          "O no, I am not the Mover,
Not today, not to you. To you I'm the

"Yes-man, the bar-companion, the easily-duped:
I am whatever you do; I am your vow to be   **50**
          Good, your humorous story;
I am your business voice; I am your marriage.

---

16. the Sabbath of Witches, the "Sabbath" or gathering of witches to meet their master, the devil.   **20. the origin of Mankind,** the idea of Evolution expressed by Charles Darwin in the *Origin of Species* (1859) contrasted with the present reactionary struggle. **21. Greek,** the belief of English schoolmasters that the teaching of a dead language was of great disciplinary value to the student. **44. A furious papa.** Mankind longs for a savior, even a tyrannical one. These stanzas have referred to various ideas of creation by a deity.

"What's your proposal? To build the Just City? I will.
I agree. Or is it the suicide pact, the romantic
      Death? Very well, I accept, for
I am your choice, your decision: yes, I am Spain."   55

Many have heard it on remote peninsulas,
On sleepy plains, in the aberrant fishermen's islands,
      In the corrupt heart of the city;
Have heard and migrated like gulls or the seeds of a flower.   60

They clung like burrs to the long expresses that lurch
Through the unjust lands, through the night, through the alpine tunnel;
      They floated over the oceans;
They walked the passes: they came to present their lives.

On that arid square, that fragment nipped off from hot   65
Africa, soldered so crudely to inventive Europe,
      On that tableland scored by rivers,
Our fever's menacing shapes are precise and alive.

Tomorrow, perhaps, the future: the research on fatigue
And the movements of packers; the gradual exploring of all the   70
      Octaves of radiation;
Tomorrow the enlarging of consciousness by diet and breathing.

Tomorrow the rediscovery of romantic love;
The photographing of ravens; all the fun under
      Liberty's masterful shadow;   75
Tomorrow the hour of the pageant-master and the musician.

Tomorrow, for the young the poets exploding like bombs,
The walks by the lake, the winter of perfect communion;
      Tomorrow the bicycle races
Through the suburbs on summer evenings: but today the struggle.   80

Today the inevitable increase in the chances of death;
The conscious acceptance of guilt in the fact of murder;
      Today the expending of powers
On the flat ephemeral pamphlet and the boring meeting.

Today the makeshift consolations; the shared cigarette;   85
The cards in the candle-lit barn and the scraping concert,
      The masculine jokes; today the
Fumbled and unsatisfactory embrace before hurting.

The stars are dead; the animals will not look:
We are left alone with our day, and the time is short and   90
      History to the defeated
May say Alas but cannot help or pardon.

56. **I am Spain.** The life, which is also God, is mankind, and, in turn, mankind is Spain: "No man is an island."   61. **They . . . lives,** the International Brigade in Spain, composed of men from many countries who felt very strongly that the Civil War was not merely a domestic struggle, but one in which mankind as a whole was involved.   69. **Tomorrow.** The suggestion is that the future may allow us to return to all these little and great things which make life worth living, but the implication is that in the defeat of Spain, which is also that of mankind, these things will be lost.

Refugee Blues

SAY THIS city has ten million souls,
Some are living in mansions, some are living
in holes:
Yet there's no place for us, my dear, yet there's
no place for us.

Once we had a country and we thought it fair,
Look in the atlas and you'll find it there: 5
We cannot go there now, my dear, we cannot
go there now.

In the village churchyard there grows an old
yew,
Every spring it blossoms anew:
Old passports can't do that, my dear, old passports can't do that.

The consul banged the table and said;   10
"If you've got no passport you're officially
dead":
But we are still alive, my dear, but we are still
alive.

Went to a committee; they offered me a chair;
Asked me politely to return next year:
But where shall we go today, my dear, but
where shall we go today?   15

Came to a public meeting; the speaker got up
and said:
"If we let them in, they will steal our daily
bread";
He was talking of you and me, my dear, he was
talking of you and me.

Thought I heard the thunder rumbling in the
sky;
It was Hitler over Europe, saying: "They must
die";   20
O we were in his mind, my dear, O we were in
his mind.

Saw a poodle in a jacket fastened with a pin,
Saw a door opened and a cat let in:
But they weren't German Jews, my dear, but
they weren't German Jews.

Went down the harbour and stood upon the
quay,   25
Saw the fish swimming as if they were free:

Only ten feet away, my dear, only ten feet
away.

Walked through a wood, saw the birds in the
trees;
They had no politicians and sang at their ease:
They weren't the human race, my dear, they
weren't the human race.   30

Dreamed I saw a building with a thousand
floors,
A thousand windows and a thousand doors;
Not one of them was ours, my dear, not one of
them was ours.

Stood on a great plain in the falling snow;
Ten thousand soldiers marched to and fro: 35
Looking for you and me, my dear, looking for
you and me.

from **New Year Letter**

(January 1, 1940)

WE HOPED; we waited for the day
The State would wither clean away,
Expecting the Millennium
That theory promised us would come,
It didn't. Specialists must try   5
To detail all the reasons why;
Meanwhile at least the layman knows
That none are lost so soon as those
Who overlook their crooked nose,
That they grow small who imitate   10
The mannerisms of the great,
Afraid to be themselves, or ask
What acts are proper to their task,
And that a tiny trace of fear
Is lethal in man's atmosphere.   15
The rays of Logos take effect,
But not as theory would expect,
For, sterile and diseased by doubt,
The dwarf mutations are thrown out
From Eros' weaving centrosome.   20

O Freedom still is far from home,
For Moscow is as far as ROME

"Refugee Blues" ("Song—XXVIII") copyright, 1939 The New
Yorker Magazine, Inc.
Refugee Blues. In this poem Auden uses a variation of the
typical blues form for the purpose of expressing the situation
of the German-Jewish refugee, who was the victim of the
economic fears of the countries which should have welcomed
him, just as much as he was the victim of Hitler's ideas.

New Year Letter. Auden here is discussing the essential split
in personalities like his own—that between intellectual radicalism and instinctive conservatism. He indicates that many
young enthusiasts will settle back into the comfort of their
earlier habits and beliefs. Nevertheless, only the young can
bring truth and justice into existence. But since his generation
is caught between two sets of values, it must reason from the
older morals to the newer vision. 16. **Logos,** the word as law.
20. **Eros.** This passage, with its use of genetical imagery and
phraseology, states that love does not follow a theoretical
pattern, but rejects its misfits. 22. **Moscow . . . Rome . . .
Paris,** the ideological distances are as great as the geographical.

Or PARIS. Once again we wake
With swimming heads and hands that shake
And stomachs that keep nothing down.   25
Here's where the devil goes to town
Who knows that nothing suits his book
So well as the hang-over look,
That few drunks feel more awful than
The Simon-pure Utopian.   30
He calls at breakfast in the role
Of blunt but sympathetic soul:
"Well, how's our Socialist this morning?
I could say 'Let this be a warning,'
But no, why should I? Students must   35
Sow their wild oats at times or bust.
Such things have happened in the lives
Of all the best Conservatives.
I'll fix you something for your liver."
And thus he sells us down the river.   40
Repenting of our last infraction
We seek atonement in reaction
And cry, nostalgic like a whore,
"I was a virgin still at four."
Perceiving that by sailing near   45

The Hegelian whirlpool of Idea
Some foolish aliens have gone down,
Lest our democracy should drown
We'd wreck her on the solid rock
Of genteel anarchists like Locke,   50
Wave at the mechanised barbarian
The vorpal sword of an Agrarian.

O how the devil who controls
The moral asymmetric souls
The either-ors, the mongrel halves   55
Who find truth in a mirror, laughs.
Yet time and memory are still
Limiting factors on his will;
He cannot always fool us thrice,
For he may never tell us lies,   60
Just half-truths we can synthesise.
So, hidden in his hocus-pocus,
There lies the gift of double focus,
That magic lamp which looks so dull
And utterly impractical   65
Yet, if Aladdin use it right,
Can be a sesame to light.

from In Time of War

Commentary

SEASON inherits legally from dying season;
Protected by the wide peace of the sun, the planets
Continue their circulations; and the galaxy

Is free for ever to revolve like an enormous biscuit:
With all his engines round him and the summer flowers,   5
Little upon his little earth, man contemplates

The universe of which he is both judge and victim;
A rarity in an uncommon corner, gazes
On the great trackways where his tribe and truth are nothing.

Certainly the growth of the fore-brain has been a success: 10
He has not got lost in a backwater like the lampshell
Or the limpet; he has not died out like the super-lizards.

30. **Simon-pure Utopian.** Psychologically, the puritan or the idealist suffers most from a hangover, because of his feeling of guilt. The reference is to Sir Thomas More's *Utopia* (1516).   46. **Hegelian** (See note 80, p. 625).   50. **Locke.** John Locke (1632–1704) maintained that moral judgments were man's voluntary reactions to human or divine law.   52. **The vorpal sword.** "He took his vorpal sword in hand," Lewis Carroll, "Jabberwocky." **Agrarian.** The idea that an agricultural society is at war with mechanized; in Carroll's poem the snicker-snack of the vorpal blade alters nothing—the poem ends as it began.   55. **The either-ors.** The split man contains within himself the answer to his predicaments.   64. **magic lamp.** Aladdin's wonderful lamp, in the fairy tale, was unusable until rubbed, when it granted any wish.
Commentary. This poem was part of *Journey to a War*, a book about China written by Auden in collaboration with Christopher Isherwood. It deals with the development of man above the beasts, and with his failure to organize a life for himself, especially in reference to the Sino-Japanese war. A history of the failure of civilizations includes, here, a general condemnation of the western and specifically British ideas of power, and calls for a world of real unity.   10. **fore-brain,** the development of man's power to walk upright and to reason.

His boneless worm-like ancestors would be amazed
At the upright position, the breasts, the four-chambered heart,
The clandestine evolution in the mother's shadow.   15

"Sweet is it," say the doomed, "to be alive though wretched,"
And the young emerging from the closed parental circle,
To whose uncertainty the certain years present

Their syllabus of limitless anxiety and labour,
At first feel nothing but the gladness of their freedom,   20
Are happy in the new embraces and the open talk.

But liberty to be and weep has never been sufficient;
The winds surround our griefs, the unfenced sky
To all our failures is a taciturn unsmiling witness.

And not least here, among this humorous and hairless people   25
Who like a cereal have inherited these valleys:
Tarim nursed them; Thibet was the tall rock of their protection,

And where the Yellow River shifts its course, they learnt
How to live well, though ruin threatened often.
For centuries they looked in fear towards the northern defiles,   30

But now must turn and gather like a fist to strike
Wrong coming from the sea, from those whose paper houses
Tell of their origin among the coral islands;

Who even to themselves deny a human freedom,
And dwell in the estranging tyrant's vision of the earth   35
In a calm stupor under their blood-spotted flag.

Here danger works a civil reconciliation,
Interior hatreds are resolved upon this foreign foe,
And will-power to resist is growing like a prosperous city.

For the invader now is deadly and impartial as a judge: 40
Down country footpaths, from each civic sky,
His anger blows alike upon the rich, and all

Who dwell within the crevices of destitution,
On those with a laborious lifetime to recall, and those,
The innocent and short whose dreams contain no children.   45

While in an international and undamaged quarter,
Casting our European shadows on Shanghai,
Walking unhurt among the banks, apparently immune

Below the monuments of an acquisitive society,
With friends and books and money and the traveller's freedom,   50
We are compelled to realize that our refuge is a sham.

25. **humorous and hairless people,** the Chinese.   27. **Tarim,** a river in the central Sinkiang province of China.   28. **the Yellow River.** The Hwang River runs for 2700 miles from its Thibetan source into the Gulf of Chihli.   33. **coral islands,** the Japanese, at that time carrying aggression far into China.   42. **rich.** The Japanese invaders made no distinctions.   47. **Shanghai,** a great cosmopolitan city with a large International Settlement. Shanghai, built from the riches taken out of China, did not at that time seem to be concerned in the war.

For this material contest that has made Hongkew
A terror and a silence, and Chapei a howling desert,
Is but the local variant of a struggle in which all,

The elderly, the amorous, the young, the handy and the
        thoughtful,   55
Those to whom feeling is a science, those to whom study
Of all that can be added and compared is a consuming love,

With those whose brains are empty as a school in August,
And those in whom the urge to action is so strong
They cannot read a letter without whispering, all   60

In cities, deserts, ships, in lodgings near the port,
Discovering the past of strangers in a library,
Creating their own future on a bed, each with his treasure,

Self-confident among the laughter and the *petits verres,*
Or motionless and lonely like a moping cormorant,   65
In all their living are profoundly implicated.

This is one sector and one movement of the general war
Between the dead and the unborn, the Real and the Pretended,
Which for the creature who creates, communicates, and chooses,

The only animal aware of lack of finish,   70
In essence is eternal. When we emerged from holes
And blinked in the warm sunshine of the Laufen Ice Retreat,

Thinking of Nature as a close and loyal kinsman,
On every acre the opponents faced each other,
And we were far within the zone where casualties begin.   75

Now in a world that has no localized events,
Where not a tribe exists without its dossier,
And the machine has taught us how, to the Non-Human,

That unprogressive blind society that knows
No argument except the absolute and violent veto,   80
Our colours, creeds and sexes are identical,

The issue is the same. Some uniforms are new,
Some have changed sides; but the campaign continues:
Still unachieved is *Jen,* the Truly Human.

This is the epoch of the Third Great Disappointment: 85
The First was the collapse of that slave-owning empire
Whose yawning magistrate asked, "What is truth?"

Upon its ruins rose the Plainly Visible Churches:

52. **Hongkew,** the American Concession district of Shanghai.   53. **Chapei,** Chinese section of Shanghai.   64. *petits verres,* literally "little glasses," i.e., cocktails and drinks.   72. **Laufen Ice Retreat,** the period of man's emergence from the purely animal state.   77. **dossier.** Each tribe has been catalogued and recorded.   78. **the Non-Human,** the mechanistic concept of the universe.   84. **Jen,** or Zen, the Buddhist concept of the universe.   86. **slave-owning empire,** Rome. The question "What is truth?" was put to Christ by Pontius Pilate, who, as Francis Bacon said, "did not wait for an answer."   88. **Plainly Visible Churches,** the medieval period, when civilization was controlled by the Church of Rome without much dissent.

Men camped like tourists under their tremendous shadows,
United by a common sense of human failure,   90

Their certain knowledge only of the timeless fields
Where the Unchanging Happiness received the faithful,
And the Eternal Nightmare waited to devour the doubters.

In which a host of workers, famous and obscure,
Meaning to do no more than use their eyes,   95
Not knowing what they did, then sapped belief;

Put in its place a neutral dying star,
Where Justice could not visit. Self was the one city,
The cell where each must find his comfort and his pain,

The body nothing but a useful favourite machine   100
To go upon errands of love and to run the house,
While the mind in its study spoke with its private God.

But now that wave which already was washing the heart,
When the cruel Turk stormed the gates of Constantine's city,
When Galileo muttered to himself, "*sed movet*,"   105

And Descartes thought, "I am because I think,"
Today, all spent, is silently withdrawing itself:
Unhappy he or she who after it is sucked.

Never before was the Intelligence so fertile,
The Heart more stunted. The human field became   110
Hostile to brotherhood and feeling like a forest.

Machines devised by harmless clergymen and boys
Attracted men like magnets from the marl and clay
Into towns on the coal-measures, to a kind of freedom,

Where the abstinent with the landless drove a bitter bargain,   115
But sowed in that act the seeds of an experienced hatred,
Which, germinating long in tenement and gas-lit cellar,

Is choking now the aqueducts of our affection.
Knowledge of their colonial suffering has cut off
The Hundred Families like an attack of shyness;   120

The apprehensive rich pace up and down
Their narrow compound of success; in every body
The ways of living are disturbed; intrusive as a sill,

Fear builds enormous ranges casting shadows,

---

97. **a neutral dying star.** The earth, like other astral bodies, is slowly dying.   104. **the cruel Turk,** Mohammed II, who, in 1453, sacked Constantinople, named after Constantine the Great (288?–337), the first Christian Roman Emperor.   105. **Galileo,** Galileo Galilei (1564–1642), great Italian physicist and astronomer, whose theory of bodies in motion was in conflict with the accepted Aristotelian concept. He was tried by the Inquisition and on being acquitted is said to have muttered under his breath: "E pur si muove" or "Sed movet," i.e., "All the same it does move."   106. **Descartes,** René Descartes (1596–1650), French philosopher and scientist. His most famous statement, the basis of his philosophy, "Cogito, ergo sum," is translated here.   115. **the abstinent,** a reference to those landowners, as in Ireland, who drew large incomes from estates they never visited, paid by men whom they never knew.   120. **The Hundred Families,** those who, by blood, consider themselves the aristocracy.

Heavy, bird-silencing, upon the outer world,   125
Hills that our grief sighs over like a Shelley, parting
All that we feel from all that we perceive,
Desire from Data; and the Thirteen gay Companions
Grow sullen now and quarrelsome as mountain tribes.

We wander on the earth, or err from bed to bed   130
In search of home, and fail, and weep for the lost ages
Before Because became As If, or rigid Certainty

The Chances Are. The base hear us, and the violent
Who long to calm our guilt with murder, and already
Have not been slow to turn our wish to their advantage.   135

On every side they make their brazen offer:
Now in that Catholic country with the shape of Cornwall,
Where Europe first became a term of pride,

North of the Alps where dark hair turns to blonde,
In Germany now loudest, land without a centre   140
Where the sad plains are like a sounding rostrum,

And on these tidy and volcanic summits near us now,
From which the Black Stream hides the Tuscarora Deep,
The voice is quieter but the more inhuman and triumphant.

By wire and wireless, in a score of bad translations,   145
They give their simple message to the world of man:
"Man can have Unity if Man will give up Freedom.

The State is real, the Individual is wicked;
Violence shall synchronize your movements like a tune,
And Terror like a frost shall halt the flood of thinking.   150

Barrack and bivouac shall be your friendly refuge,
And racial pride shall tower like a public column
And confiscate for safety every private sorrow.

Leave Truth to the police and us; we know the Good;
We build the Perfect City time shall never alter;   155
Our Law shall guard you always like a cirque of mountains,

Your ignorance keep off evil like a dangerous sea;
You shall be consummated in the General Will,
Your children innocent and charming as the beasts."

All the great conquerors sit upon their platform,   160
Lending their sombre weight of practical experience:
Ch'in Shih Huang Ti, who burnt the scholars' books,

---

128. Desire from Data, the separation of emotion from the mathematical fact. **the Thirteen gay Companions,** Christ and the Twelve Apostles.   **137. Catholic country,** Italy.   **142. these tidy . . . Deep,** a reference to Japan. The U.S.S. *Tuscarora* took soundings at a point off Japan where the Pacific Ocean is 4655 fathoms deep. The place gets its name from the ship.   **162. Ch'in Shih Huang Ti,** Chinese ruler of the Ch'in Dynasty (256–207 B.C.), who united China, but who also destroyed the classics of the preceding dynasty, the Chou.

Chaka the mad, who segregated the two sexes,
And *Genghis Khan,* who thought mankind should be destroyed,
And *Diocletian* the administrator, make impassioned speeches.   **165**

Napoleon claps who found religion useful,
And all who passed deception of the People, or who said
Like Little *Frederick,* "I shall see that it is done."

While many famous clerks support their programme:
Plato the good, despairing of the average man,   **170**
With sad misgiving signs their manifesto;

Shang-tzu approves their principle of Nothing Private;
The author of *The Prince* will heckle; *Hobbes* will canvass,
With generalizing *Hegel* and quiet *Bosanquet.*

And every family and every heart is tempted: **175**
The earth debates; the Fertile Crescent argues;
Even the little towns upon the way to somewhere,

Those desert flowers the aeroplane now fertilizes,
Quarrel on this; in England far away,
Behind the high tides and the navigable estuaries;   **180**

In the Far West, in absolutely free America,
In melancholy Hungary, and clever France
Where ridicule has acted a historic rôle,

And here where the rice-grain nourishes these patient households
The ethic of the feudal citadel has impregnated,   **185**
Thousands believe, and millions are half-way to a conviction.

Nor do our leaders help; we know them now
For humbugs full of vain dexterity, invoking
A gallery of ancestors, pursuing still the mirage

Of long dead grandeurs whence the interest has absconded,   **190**
As Fahrenheit in an odd corner of great Celsius' kingdom
Might mumble of the summers measured once by him.

Yet all the same we have our faithful sworn supporters
Who never lost their faith in knowledge or in man,
But worked so eagerly that they forgot their food   **195**

---

163. **Chaka,** Zulu chieftain, who between 1818 and 1820 ravaged large parts of what is now Natal, leaving large areas without a single inhabitant. 164. **Genghis Khan** (1162–1227), Mongol conqueror whose campaigns were noted for their brutality. 165. **Diocletian** (245–313), Roman emperor who persecuted the Christians.   166. **Napoleon** (1769–1821) obtained permission from the Pope to assume the crown and, later, for the annulment of his marriage to Josephine.   168. **Frederick,** Frederick the Great (1712–86), king who made Prussia a great state.   173. **The author,** Niccolo di Bernardo Machiavelli (1469–1527), author of *The Prince,* which laid down the requisites of the successful ruler. **Hobbes,** Thomas Hobbes (1588–1679), English philosopher whose most famous book, *The Leviathan,* argued that primitive man lived in anarchy and had to surrender his rights to create a state.   174. **Hegel.** (See note 80, p. 625). **Bosanquet,** Bernard Bosanquet (1848–1923), English philosopher who wrote several books on the state and the individual.   191. **Fahrenheit,** Gabriel Daniel Fahrenheit (1686–1736), German physicist who substituted mercury for alcohol in the thermometer, and invented the scale called after him. **Celsius,** Anders Celsius (1701–44), Swedish astronomer who invented the centigrade thermometer.

And never noticed death or old age coming on,
Prepared for freedom as *Kuo Hsi* for inspiration,
Waiting it calmly like the coming of an honoured guest.

Some looked at falsehood with the candid eyes of children,
Some had a woman's ear to catch injustice,   200
Some took Necessity, and knew her, and she brought forth Freedom.

Some of our dead are famous, but they would not care:
Evil is always personal and spectacular,
But goodness needs the evidence of all our lives,

And, even to exist, it must be shared as truth,   205
As freedom or as happiness. (For what is happiness
If not to witness joy upon the features of another?)

They did not live to be remembered specially as noble,
Like those who cultivated only cucumbers and melons
To prove that they were rich; and when we praise their names,   210

They shake their heads in warning, chiding us to give
Our gratitude to the Invisible College of the Humble,
Who through the ages have accomplished everything essential.

And stretch around our struggle as the normal landscape,
And mingle, fluent with our living, like the winds and waters,   215
The dust of all the dead that reddens every sunset;

Giving us courage to confront our enemies,
Not only on the Grand Canal, or in Madrid,
Across the campus of a university city,

But aid us everywhere, that in the lovers' bedroom,   220
The white laboratory, the school, the public meeting,
The enemies of life may be more passionately attacked.

And, if we care to listen, we can always hear them:
"Men are not innocent as beasts and never can be,
Man can improve but never will himself be perfect,   225

Only the free have disposition to be truthful,
Only the truthful have the interest to be just,
Only the just possess the will-power to be free.

For common justice can determine private freedom,
As a clear sky can tempt men to astronomy,   230
Or a peninsula persuade them to be sailors.

You talked of Liberty, but were not just; and now
Your enemies have called your bluff; for in your city,
Only the man behind the rifle had free-will.

---

197. ***Kuo Hsi,*** Chinese landscape painter (1020–90) of the Sung Dynasty.   218. **Grand Canal,** great canal of eastern China, connecting the Yangtze River with the Peiho; scene of much fighting in the Sino-Japanese war.   219. **university city.** A particularly fierce battle of the Spanish war took place in a new University of Madrid project, almost completely destroying it.

One wish is common to you both, the wish to build 235
A world united as that Europe was in which
The flint-faced exile wrote his three-act comedy.

Lament not its decay; that shell was too constricting:
The years of private isolation had their lesson,
And in the interest of intelligence were necessary. 240

Now in the clutch of crisis and the bloody hour
You must defeat your enemies or perish, but remember,
Only by those who reverence it can life be mastered;

Only a whole and happy conscience can stand up
And answer their bleak lie; among the just, 245
And only there, is Unity compatible with Freedom."

Night falls on China; the great arc of travelling shadow
Moves over land and ocean, altering life:
Thibet already silent, the packed Indias cooling,

Inert in the paralysis of caste. And though in Africa 250
The vegetation still grows fiercely like the young,
And in the cities that receive the slanting radiations

The lucky are at work, and most still know they suffer.
The dark will touch them soon: night's tiny noises
Will echo vivid in the owl's developed ear, 255

Vague in the anxious sentry's; and the moon look down
On battlefields and dead men lying, heaped like treasure,
On lovers ruined in a brief embrace, on ships

Where exiles watch the sea: and in the silence
The cry that streams out into the indifferent spaces, 260
And never stops or slackens, may be heard more clearly,

Above the everlasting murmur of the woods and rivers,
And more insistent than the lulling answer of the waltzes,
Or hum of printing-presses turning forests into lies;

As now I hear it, rising round me from Shanghai, 265
And mingling with the distant mutter of guerrilla fighting,
The voice of Man: "O teach us to outgrow our madness.

Ruffle the perfect manners of the frozen heart,
And once again compel it to be awkward and alive,
To all it suffered once a weeping witness. 270

Clear from the head the masses of impressive rubbish;
Rally the lost and trembling forces of the will,
Gather them up and let them loose upon the earth,

Till, as the contribution of our star, we follow
The clear instructions of that Justice, in the shadow 275
Of Whose uplifting, loving, and constraining power
All human reasons do rejoice and operate."

237. **three-act comedy,** the *Divine Comedy* of Dante Alighieri.

from **For the Time Being**

II

Narrator

IF, on account of the political situation,
There are quite a number of homes without
    roofs, and men
Lying about in the countryside neither drunk
    nor asleep,
If all sailings have been cancelled till further
    notice,   4
If it's unwise now to say much in letters, and if,
Under the subnormal temperatures prevailing,
The two sexes are at present the weak and the
    strong,
That is not at all unusual for this time of year.
If that were all we should know how to man-
    age. Flood, fire,
The desiccation of grasslands, restraint of
    princes,   10
Piracy on the high seas, physical pain and fiscal
    grief,
These after all are our familiar tribulations,
And we have been through them all before,
    many, many times.
As events which belong to the natural world
    where
The occupation of space is the real and final
    fact   15
And time turns round itself in an obedient cir-
    cle,
They occur again and again but only to pass
Again and again into their formal opposites,
From sword to ploughshare, coffin to cradle,
    war to work,
So that, taking the bad with the good, the pat-
    tern composed   20

By the ten thousand odd things that can possi-
    bly happen
Is permanent in a general average way.

Till lately we knew of no other, and between
    us we seemed
To have what it took—the adrenal courage of
    the tiger,
The chameleon's discretion, the modesty of the
    doe,   25
Or the fern's devotion to spacial necessity:
To practise one's peculiar civic virtue was not
So impossible after all; to cut our losses
And bury our dead was really quite easy: That
    was why
We were always able to say: "We are children
    of God,   30
And our Father has never forsaken His people."

But then we were children: That was a mo-
    ment ago,
Before an outrageous novelty had been intro-
    duced
Into our lives. Why were we never warned?
    Perhaps we were.
Perhaps that mysterious noise at the back of the
    brain   35
We noticed on certain occasions—sitting alone
In the waiting room of the country junction,
    looking
Up at the toilet window—was not indigestion
But this Horror starting already to scratch Its
    way in?
Just how, just when It succeeded we shall nev-
    er know: 40
We can only say that now It is there and that
    nothing
We learnt before It was there is now of the
    slightest use,
For nothing like It has happened before. It's as
    if
We had left our house for five minutes to mail
    a letter,
And during that time the living room had
    changed places   45
With the room behind the mirror over the fire-
    place;
It's as if, waking up with a start, we discovered
Ourselves stretched out flat on the floor, watch-
    ing our shadow
Sleepily stretching itself at the window. I mean

Narrator, If . . . situation. . . . This is a brilliant section of
the longer poem *For the Time Being*, written as a memorial to
the poet's mother, Constance Rosalie Auden. The poem is a subtle psychological analysis of the poet's growing sense of the
meaninglessness of all his conditioned reactions to life, of his
growing horror of the vacuity in existence as the political and
religious values he has held to be true seem to fade. The poet
analyzes human loneliness, deepening as he seeks truth (having
given up his sense of the importance of participating in action
or in social observances), as he asks himself, "Where may the
immortal centre be, the nameless place from which life and
death become terminals in a cycle of living?" The poet does
not, however, by the end of this poem (which continues its
religious inquiry in further poems of the same volume) find
an answer which gives him hope and faith. As a result, he is
forced to extemporize life.

That the world of space where events re-occur
    is still there,   50
Only now it's no longer real; the real one is no-
    where
Where time never moves and nothing can ever
    happen:
I mean that although there's a person we know
    all about
Still bearing our name and loving himself as be-
    fore,
That person has become a fiction; our true ex-
    istence   55
Is decided by no one and has no importance to
    love.

That is why we despair; that is why we
    would welcome
The nursery bogey or the winecellar ghost, why
    even
The violent howling of winter and war has be-
    come
Like a juke-box tune that we dare not stop. We
    are afraid   60
Of pain but more afraid of silence; for no night-
    mare
Of hostile objects could be as terrible as this
    Void.
This is the Abomination. This is the wrath of
    God.

STEPHEN SPENDER

Stephen Spender was born May 28, 1909, of German, Jewish, and English lineage, son of Violet (Schuster) Spender and Edward Harold Spender, author, journalist, and lecturer. As a small child he was interested in painting and printing, and when he became a little older he set up his own printing press and supported himself by printing chemist's labels. At nineteen he went to University College, Oxford, but found life there hostile to his temperament. However, after traveling around the Continent for a while, he returned to Oxford and completed his work in 1931. While an undergraduate, he published *Twenty Poems*. His first substantial book was *Poems* (1933). In 1935 he published the long anti-fascist poem *Vienna*. *The Destructive Element* (1935) spoke for the whole younger generation of poets who felt a need for Marxism yet who also believed that action destroys the poet. He was accepted by the public as the spokesman for the group which then included W. H. Auden, C. Day Lewis, Louis MacNeice, and others.

Forward from Liberalism, a politico-poetic credo, was published in 1937, and *Trial of a Judge* appeared in 1938. At the International Writers' Conference held in Spain in 1937, Spender met and became the close friend of the great French novelist and anti-fascist, André Malraux. When World War II began, Spender was editing the British magazine *Horizon* with Cyril Connolly. During the war he worked in an official capacity for the Churchill government. His own war service was largely with the home guard. He continued to write and publish verse: *The Still Centre* appeared in 1941 and *Ruins and Visions* in 1942; *Citizens in War and After* was published in 1945; *European Witness* and *Poems of Dedication* in 1946; and *Returning to Vienna* in 1947. With his wife and son, Spender is now living in the United States; recently he taught at Sarah Lawrence College, and he has made lecture tours through the country.

Though Stephen Spender has never completely rejected his idealist vision of socialism, he is turning more and more in his later poems to personal subjects. Always something of a romantic, he seems to have grown tired of the long wait for perfect brotherhood.

from Poems

I

H<small>E WILL</small> watch the hawk with an indifferent
    eye
    Or pitifully;
Nor on those eagles that so feared him, now
    Will strain his brow;
Weapons men use, stone, sling and strong-
    thewed bow   5
    He will not know.

This aristocrat, superb of all instinct.
    With death close linked
Had paced the enormous cloud, almost had
    won
    War on the sun;   10
Till now, like Icarus mid-ocean-drowned,
    Hands, wings, are found.

XII

My parents kept me from children who were
    rough
And who threw words like stones and who wore
    torn clothes.
Their thighs showed through rags. They ran in
    the street
And climbed cliffs and stripped by the country
    streams.   4

I feared more than tigers their muscles like iron
And their jerking hands and their knees tight
    on my arms.
I feared the salt coarse pointing of those boys
Who copied my lisp behind me on the road.

They were lithe, they sprang out behind
    hedges
Like dogs to bark at our world. They threw
    mud   10
And I looked another way, pretending to smile.
I longed to forgive them, yet they never
    smiled.

I, XII, XIII, XVI, XXV, XXIII, XXXIII from *Poems*, copyright, 1934, by Modern Library, Inc. Reprinted by permission of Random House, Inc.
11. **Icarus** (he who in Greek mythology tried to fly from Crete but who, when the heat melted his wings, dropped into the ocean) here is associated with man's creative instinct or ability to invent, which may come to a bad end as when, in war, airplanes are used to destroy.
XII, the comment of a middle-class person who realizes how he was separated from people—especially from the working people.

XIII

What I expected was
Thunder, fighting,
Long struggles with men
And climbing.
After continual straining   5
I should grow strong;
Then the rocks would shake
And I should rest long.

What I had not foreseen
Was the gradual day   10
Weakening the will
Leaking the brightness away,
The lack of good to touch
The fading of body and soul
Like smoke before wind   15
Corrupt, unsubstantial.

The wearing of Time,
And the watching of cripples pass
With limbs shaped like questions
In their odd twist,   20
The pulverous grief
Melting the bones with pity,
The sick falling from earth—
These, I could not foresee.

For I had expected always   25
Some brightness to hold in trust,
Some final innocence
To save from dust;
That, hanging solid,
Would dangle through all   30
Like the created poem
Or the dazzling crystal.

XVI

Moving through the silent crowd
Who stand behind dull cigarettes
These men who idle in the road,
I have the sense of falling light.

They lounge at corners of the street   5
And greet friends with a shrug of shoulder
And turn their empty pockets out,
The cynical gestures of the poor.

XIII, a comment on the idea that society is changed not by dramatic effort but by daily suffering.   21. **pulverous,** poetic license for *pulverizing.*

Now they've no work, like better men
Who sit at desks and take much pay   10
They sleep long nights and rise at ten
To watch the hours that drain away.

I'm jealous of the weeping hours
They stare through with such hungry eyes.
I'm haunted by these images,   15
I'm haunted by their emptiness.

XXV

The Funeral

DEATH is another milestone on their way.
With laughter on their lips and with winds
      blowing round them
They record simply
How this one excelled all others in making driv-
      ing belts.

This is festivity, it is the time of statistics   5
When they record what one unit contributed:
They are glad as they lay him back in the earth
And thank him for what he gave them.

They walk home remembering the straining red
      flags,
And with pennons of song still fluttering
      through their blood   10
They speak of the world state
With its towns like brain-centres and its pulsing
      arteries.

They think how one life hums, revolves and
      toils,
One cog in a golden and singing hive: 14
Like spark from fire, its task happily achieved,
It falls away quietly.

No more are they haunted by the individual
      grief
Nor the crocodile tears of European genius,
The decline of a culture
Mourned by scholars who dream of the ghosts
      of Greek boys.

The Funeral. The funeral is in Russia, probably. The dead man is dignified by the fact that he was a good workman and could make driving belts.

XXIII

I Think Continually of Those Who Were Truly Great

I THINK continually of those who were truly
      great.
Who, from the womb, remembered the soul's
      history
Through corridors of light where the hours are
      suns
Endless and singing. Whose lovely ambition
Was that their lips, still touched with fire,   5
Should tell of the Spirit clothed from head to
      foot in song.
And who hoarded from the Spring branches
The desires falling across their bodies like
      blossoms.

What is precious is never to forget
The essential delight of the blood drawn from
      ageless springs   10
Breaking through rocks in worlds before our
      earth.
Never to deny its pleasure in the morning
      simple light
Nor its grave evening demand for love.
Never to allow gradually the traffic to smother
With noise and fog the flowering of the spirit.

Near the snow, near the sun, in the highest
      fields   16
See how these names are fêted by the waving
      grass
And by the streamers of white cloud
And whispers of wind in the listening sky.
The names of those who in their lives fought
      for life   20
Who wore at their hearts the fire's centre.
Born of the sun they travelled a short while
      towards the sun,
And left the vivid air signed with their honour.

XXXIII

Not Palaces, an Era's Crown

NOT PALACES, an era's crown
Where the mind dwells, intrigues, rests;
The architectural gold-leaved flower
From people ordered like a single mind,

Not . . . Crown. The poet argues that he would build no images of power or past dignity, but rather of love, justice, and equality in life. Such images are denied by those of a war period.

I build. This only what I tell: 5
It is too late for rare accumulation
For family pride, for beauty's filtered dusts;
I say, stamping the words with emphasis,
Drink from here energy and only energy,
As from the electric charge of a battery, 10
To will this Time's change.
Eye, gazelle, delicate wanderer,
Drinker of horizon's fluid line;
Ear that suspends on a chord
The spirit drinking timelessness; 15
Touch, love, all senses;
Leave your gardens, your singing feasts,
Your dreams of suns circling before our sun,
Of heaven after our world.
Instead, watch images of flashing brass 20
That strike the outward sense, the polished will
Flag of our purpose which the wind engraves.
No spirit seek here rest. But this: No man
Shall hunger: Man shall spend equally. 24
Our goal which we compel: Man shall be man.

—That programme of the antique Satan
Bristling with guns on the indented page
With battleship towering from hilly waves:
For what? Drive of a ruining purpose
Destroying all but its age-long exploiters. 30
Our programme like this, yet opposite,
Death to the killers, bringing light to life.

Two Armies

DEEP in the winter plain, two armies
Dig their machinery, to destroy each other.
Men freeze and hunger. No one is given leave
On either side, except the dead, and wounded.
These have their leave; while new battalions
     wait 5
On time at last to bring them violent peace.

All have become so nervous and so cold
That each man hates the cause and distant
     words
Which brought him here, more terribly than
     bullets. 9
Once a boy hummed a popular marching song,

"Two Armies" and "Ultima Ratio Regum" from *Ruins and Visions*, copyright, 1942, by Stephen Spender, reprinted by permission of Random House, Inc.
Two Armies. Written during the period of the "phony war," the first year of World War II. Reference to colonialism is made in the fifth stanza as a symbol of man's dependence on man.

Once a novice hand flapped the salute;
The voice was choked, the lifted hand fell,
Shot through the wrist by those of his own side.

From their numb harvest all would flee, except
For discipline drilled once in an iron school
Which holds them at the point of a revolver. 16
Yet when they sleep, the images of home
Ride wishing horses of escape
Which herd the plain in a mass unspoken
     poem. 19

Finally, they cease to hate: for although hate
Bursts from the air and whips the earth like hail
Or pours it up in fountains to marvel at,
And although hundreds fall, who can connect
The inexhaustible anger of the guns
With the dumb patience of these tormented
     animals? 25

Clean silence drops at night when a little walk
Divides the sleeping armies, each
Huddled in linen woven by remote hands.
When the machines are stilled, a common suf-
     fering
Whitens the air with breath and makes both
     one 30
As though these enemies slept in each other's
     arms.

Only the lucid friend to aerial raiders,
The brilliant pilot moon, stares down
Upon the plain she makes a shining bone 34
Cut by the shadow of many thousand bones.
Where amber clouds scatter on no-man's-land
She regards death and time throw up
The furious words and minerals which kill life.

Ultima Ratio Regum

THE GUNS spell money's ultimate reason
In letters of lead on the spring hillside.
But the boy lying dead under the olive trees
Was too young and too silly
To have been notable to their important eye. 5
He was a better target for a kiss.

When he lived, tall factory hooters never sum-
     moned him.

Ultima Ratio Regum, the ultimate reason of kings. Money (or power) is the reason for war.

Nor did restaurant plate-glass doors revolve to
    wave him in.
His name never appeared in the papers.
The world maintained its traditional wall   10
Round the dead with their gold sunk deep as a
    well,
Whilst his life, intangible as a Stock Exchange
    rumour, drifted outside.

O too lightly he threw down his cap
One day when the breeze threw petals from
    the trees.
The unflowering wall sprouted with guns,   15
Machine-gun anger quickly scythed the grasses;
Flags and leaves fell from hands and branches;
The tweed cap rotted in the nettles.

Consider his life which was valueless
In terms of employment, hotel ledgers, news
    files.   20
Consider. One bullet in ten thousand kills a
    man.
Ask. Was so much expenditure justified
On the death of one so young and so silly
Lying under the olive trees, O world, O death?

from The Destructive Element

XIII

Writers and Manifestos

I A. RICHARDS writes, in his *Science and Poetry*, that 'over whole tracts of natural emotional response we are today like a bed of dahlias whose sticks have been removed.' The sticks
are our beliefs. In his note on *The Waste Land*
he adds that 'a sense of desolation, of uncertainty, of futility, of the groundlessness of aspirations, of the vanity of endeavour, and a
thirst for a life-giving water which seems sud-
10 denly to have failed, are the signs in consciousness of this necessary reorganization of our
lives.' Eliot 'has given a perfect emotive description of a state of mind which is probably
inevitable for a while to all meditative minds.'

This state of mind is a state of complete un-
belief. 'In the destructive element immerse.
That is the way,' he approvingly quotes. James
('Thank God, I have no opinions.') Yeats

From *The Destructive Element*, by Stephen Spender, reprinted
by permission of Jonathan Cape Ltd.

('Things fall apart; the centre cannot hold;
    Mere anarchy is loosed upon the world.')

and Eliot (in *The Waste Land*) all stood on the
verge of this destructive element, but decided
not to go in. But the important fact is that it is
there, that it is *realized*. It is realized in Yeats's
mythology, in James's desperate individualism,
in Eliot's retreat to the Anglo-Catholic Church.

The question is whether this despairing stage
is now over, whether it is now possible for the
artist to discover a system of values that are
not purely subjective and individualistic, but
objective and social; real in the world of a society *outside* the artist in the same way as Nature is real.

In spite of the attempts of various imperialist poets to carry on a buccaneering tradition,
the nationalist European state does not provide a sense of historic purposiveness: it does
not convince one of its reality. The history of
nationalities which we see around us, which we
live in, is not a full tide bearing us forward;
ours is not an Elizabethan age. On the contrary,
the trend of contemporary history, so far from
giving us direction, has not even the merit of
being obvious. It does not decide our attitude;
we have to adopt some analytic attitude towards it. We may, for example, simply think of
Europe in terms of War. A war carried on, it is
true, by political and economic means, after
the combatants, who are exhausted, have
stopped fighting. Nevertheless a war of victorious allies (with whatever shifting alliances)
holding down forcibly a defeated enemy, and
waiting anxiously and preparedly for the moment when he will rise and start to fight again.
This is a time then when anyone who is anxious
to avert such a protracted world war will have
to work very hard to undermine the whole system of armed alliances. If we hope to go on existing, if we want a dog's chance of a right to
breathe, to go on being able to write, it seems
that we have got to make some choice outside
the private entanglements of our personal life.
We have got to try somehow to understand that
objective life moving down on us like a glacier,
but which, after all, is essentially not a glacier,
is an historic process, the life of people like ourselves, and therefore our 'proper study.'

The point is that it is almost impossible for
an artist to-day—a believing artist, one who is

not simply an individualist-anarchist—to live entirely in the present, because the present is chaotic. If we want beliefs, or even a view of history, we must either turn back to the past, or we must exercise our imaginations to some degree, so that we live in the future.

It is not a question of sticks for dahlias. The answer to that remark is, "Don't be a dahlia, and you won't need a stick." It is a question of
10 what in the widest sense is going to be the social or political subject of writing. If the subject of writing is political justice and political freedom, it is no longer possible with consistency to be a writer who satirizes a small clique of literary dilettanti; who insists on regarding only the surface of his characters, who prides himself only on the eye; and on having an eye which ignores the more emotive centres. Literary fascism goes with political fascism. If,
20 then, one believes that freedom, justice and other moral qualities are desirable; if one wants to write about these things (I am not saying or even implying that one should want to do so); if one conceives that the subject of writing is the moral life of one's time, in the same way as the subject of Greek Tragedy is moral, and *Everyman* is a morality, and the subject of *Tao Te Ching* is the art of ruling and being ruled; then today one is in a very difficult situation.
30 The precise difficulty is to write about this moral life in a way that is significant: to find the real moral subject. The emphasis of our realistic tradition is entirely on the reality of externals: of nature, of mechanics, of acts. If one speaks of any other kind of reality one is suspected of a kind of idealism, which is rightly suspect: of projecting one's own hopes and fears, of inventing dreams in which one fulfils translated sexual wishes. Yet the fact remains
40 that certain manifestations of what I call moral life are perfectly real: as real as chairs and tables, and far more dangerously alive than most human beings. Indeed, if they are neglected, they draw attention to themselves in wars and revolutions. Such realities are the lust for power, the sense of guilt; and the most overwhelming of all is a life which is much larger than individuals, the whole life of the time, larger

even than the personal life, and threatening to destroy the personal life if it is not realized and 50 given room to develop.

I call all this as a subject 'moral' rather than 'psychological,' because I am concerned with a whole series of conflicts which contribute to the stream of contemporary life. I am not concerned with the sense of guilt and the lust for power, analytically, but with the direction of society produced by the complex of all of these. On the whole, then, to call this general tendency the 'moral' life rather than the 'psycho- 60 logical' life seems, paradoxically, the more impartial term. For if I call it 'psychological,' I am bound to analyse and condemn certain undesirable elements—the sense of guilt, and the lust for power. If I call it moral I am simply concerned with understanding the whole tendency, and accepting that as the resolved and deepest life of our time.

'We can no longer permit life to be shaped by a personified ideal, we must serve with all 70 our faculties some actual thing,' Yeats has written in a recent preface. This seems to me true. The 'actual thing' is the true moral or widely political subject that must be realized by contemporary literature, if that literature is itself to be moral and serious: that is to say, if it is to be the true successor of James. Any other art will tend to become a 'personified ideal.' The weakness of Lawrence is in this tendency. He wrote about a kind of life which was seri- 80 ous and real; but whereas he meant to write about people, about the life around him, he tended, as he went on, only to write about himself. For, in his search for values, he invented a way of life that did not betray those values: but, most unfortunately, it was only possible to himself. It was the outcome of a personal struggle, and the result dangerously bordered on the 'personified ideal.'

It seems, then, that the position of writers 90 who are endeavouring to serve some 'actual thing'—that is, who are endeavouring to write about it—is worth considering. Cecil Day Lewis has said:

'Yet living here,
As between two massing powers I live
Whom neutrality cannot save
Nor occupation cheer.

27. **Tao Te Ching,** the body of mystically religious, economic, political, and social doctrines attributed to Lao-Tzu (*ca.* 600 B.C.) and popularly known as Taoism, an essential part of Chinese civilization.

79. **Lawrence,** D. H. Lawrence (p. 412).   93. **Cecil Day Lewis,** see p. 776.

None such shall be left alive:
The innocent wing is soon shot down
And private stars fade in the blood-red dawn
Where two worlds strive.

The red advance of life
Contracts pride, calls out the common blood,
Beats song into a single blade,
Makes a depth-charge of grief.

10 Move then with new desires,
For when we used to build and love
Is no man's land, and only ghosts can live
Between two fires.'

The poem asserts that two worlds exist and are fighting: the striving worlds are obviously intended to represent the class war, or at all events the rivalry between revolution and reaction. This contest is so important that neutrality is impossible. 'The innocent wing is soon shot down, And private stars fade in the blood-red 20 dawn.' The poet is evidently on the side of 'The red advance of life,' because he believes that 'only ghosts can live between two fires.'

The poem, then, is not only about Communism: it also has a propagandist element: it argues, and some of the argument is, to say the least, controversial. For example, the simplification of issues might seem to some people premature, if not grotesque. But this does not really affect the real claim of the poet to value. 30 The implicit assertion of the poem is that it is about realities: that the struggle between two worlds is *real*—as real as the descriptions of environment in novels—that the material of the poem is life.

If I am right in saying that the struggle of Communism or Socialism against the anti-Socialist forces of the whole world exists, I think that the reader, in judging left-wing literature, must not judge it in the same way as he argues 40 against Communism. It is not a question of whether he thinks the premises are false, but of whether the premises are about realities, in the sense that there are political and moral realities which are more enduring than the external world of literary realism. What he should ask is—Does this Communist approach lead to a greater and more fundamental understanding of the struggle affecting our whole life to-day?

Now, one of the chief claims of Communism 50 as a political creed is that it is materialist. The materialist conception of history, the theory of surplus value, the idea of crystallized labour;

all these are solids, they are material subject-matter and yet move in the world of ideas. The writer who grasps anything of Marxist theory, feels that he is moving in a world of reality, and in a purposive world, not merely a world of obstructive and oppressive *things*.

Lastly, it is as well to remember that perhaps the most fundamental of all beliefs illustrated 60 by drama and poetry, in all history, is the idea of justice. We live in an age when we have become conscious of great social injustice, of the oppression of one class by another, of nationalities by other nations. Communism, or Socialism in its completed form, offers a just world—a world in which wealth is more equally distributed, and the grotesque accumulation of wealth by individuals is dispersed: in which nations have no interest in destroying each 70 other in the manner of modern war, because the system of competitive trade controlled by internecine and opposed capitalist interests is abolished.

These aims are so broad and so just that no amount of abuse and sneering can affect the people who hold them. It is no use telling me, for example, that I am a bourgeois-intellectual, that I know nothing, or next to nothing, of the proletariat. All that and a lot more may be true. 80 The point is, though, that if I desire social justice I am not primarily concerned with myself, I am concerned with bringing into being a world quite external to my own interests; in the same way as when one writes a poem one is allowing the poem to have its own, impersonal, objective being; one is not shoving oneself into it.

The Socialist artist is concerned with realizing in his own work the ideas of a classless so- 90 ciety: that is to say, applying those ideas to the life around him, and giving them their reality. He is concerned with a change of heart.

He is not primarily concerned with ways and means, and he is not paralysed by the argument that the economic system is rigid. The economic system was made for man, and not man for the economic system; so that if man changes—that is to say, if he has a new and strong conception of justice—the economic system will 100 also change.

It also follows that the writer is primarily interested in man, and not in systems, not even in a good economic system. Systems are rigid, and they must always be forced externally—by external criticism—to change. In that sense, art, because it insists on human values, is a criticism of life.

Good architecture is a criticism of slums. Good painting is a criticism of the pictures we have, the clothes we wear, all the appearances with which we surround ourselves. Good poetry is a criticism of language, of the way in which we express ourselves, the direction of our thoughts, the words we hand down to our children. Our industrial civilization has proved almost impervious to that criticism of life which we find in architecture, painting, music, and poetry. Art has been resisted, and the artists have been driven to form cliques with a private language and private jokes. But no system can afford to be without a criticism of art. The whole point of artists adopting a revolutionary position, is that their interests may become social, and not anti-social, and that their criticism may help to shape a new society.

When one considers the position of artists in a Socialist state, it is well, therefore, to remember that the art which has 'roots in the masses' must be free to tell the truth and to criticize life. Lenin said, 'Art belongs to the people. It ought to extend with deep roots into the very thick of the broad toiling masses. It ought to be intelligible to these masses and loved by them. And it ought to unify the feeling, thought and will of these masses, elevate them. It ought to arouse and develop artists among them.'

A democratic art has always been popular with certain writers, who have appealed in their work from a small set of fellow artists to the people. The point of such an appeal is that by widening his audience the artist also widens and deepens his subject-matter; he draws strength from deeper roots. The writer who is starving because he cannot reach any audience but a small clique, and who finds the whole literature, painting and music of his time a prey to the same cliquiness, will suspect that there is something wrong with our sectarian literature. Now, whatever may be the faults of Russian writers to-day, they do at least reach a wide audience, and they do succeed in writing about matters which passionately concern the people. In order to awaken this wide interest they don't play down to their audience in the fashion of our popular writers.

Nevertheless, Russian literature suffers, or has until recently suffered, from its own sectarianism, which consisted in the establishment of what amounted to a monopoly of publishing and criticism by a small group of writers who formed an organization called RAPP (Russian Association of Proletarian Writers). The business of this union, and of various companion societies was to insist on the proletarianization of art, and to persecute artists who were not correct in their party ideology. Max Eastman has written a book, called *Artists in Uniform*, which is an extremely prejudiced account of the activities of RAPP. He is clearly carrying on a bitter personal vendetta against the editors of the American Communist periodical, *New Masses*, which he finds to be subservient to Moscow. He is also a Trotskyist, and a violent critic of the Stalin dictatorship. He draws attention to all the blunders of RAPP, but he does not emphasize that some writers have been well treated. For example, he ignores Nekrassov, and he is so anxious to prove that RAPP has destroyed all literary talent in the Soviet, that Gladkov, to take one example, is not mentioned in his book. In spite of these defects of over-statement, the indictment he draws up is alarming and, in some ways, almost overwhelming. There are many examples of persecution by RAPP. The suicides of Yessenin and Maiakovsky may have been inevitable, since their faulty 'individualism' perhaps made it, in any case, impossible for them to adapt themselves to the revolution. Far more serious is the case of Zamyatin, whose novel, *We*, was not published in the Soviet, but was pirated in a Prague *émigré* magazine: this misfortune was used as a frame-up against Zamyatin; and he was compelled to live in exile. Romanov, who is well known in England for his novel, *Three Pairs of Silk Stockings*, was so unfortunate as to receive a favourable review in the London *New Statesman*, in which the reviewer remarked that it was a mystery that Romanov's book should be allowed to appear in Soviet Russia. The mystery did not cease, but Romanov was compelled to recant publicly. Another writer, Pilnyak, on being charged with counter-revolutionary tendencies, managed to make an art of humiliating himself and begging for Marxist instruction: he has become one of the most prosperous writers in the Union.

Since RAPP no longer exists, Eastman's indictment may seem irrelevant, because I do not suppose that even the Soviet Government would now defend RAPP's actions. But he holds that matters are now little, if at all, better, and that RAPP was only liquidated because its destructive function was completely performed. The next few years will show whether or not this accusation is just: but meanwhile Eastman's charges should be read and considered. It is not enough to dismiss him as a counter-revolutionary, if what he says is true. The following principles were dictated to the Kharkov literary congress, a meeting of Communist writers from every part of the world, by Auerbach, a young representative of the bureaucracy.

(1) Art is a class weapon.

(2) Artists are to abandon 'individualism' and the fear of strict 'discipline' as petty bourgeois attitudes.

(3) Artistic creation is to be systematized, organized, 'collectivized,' and carried out according to the plans of a central staff like any other soldierly work.

(4) This is to be done under the 'careful and yet firm guidance of the Communist Party.'

(5) Artists and writers of the rest of the world are to learn how to make proletarian art by studying the experience of the Soviet Union.

(6) 'Every proletarian artist must be a dialectical materialist. The method of creative art is the method of dialectic materialism.'

(7) 'Proletarian literature is not necessarily created by the proletariat, it can also be created by man writers from the petty bourgeoisie,' and one of the chief duties of the proletarian writer is to help the non-proletarian writers 'overcome their petty bourgeois character and accept the viewpoint of the proletariat.'

It is evident that the aim of this manifesto is to convert art into an instrument that can be used for party purposes. It is not the business of the artist to see, but to conform. He must not be a two-edged instrument which might turn against the party. It is his business to go where he is sent and to observe what he is told.

There is not the least doubt that a great many Communists look on art purely as a party instrument. To take a small instance, I read in a proposed manifesto sent by Alec Brown to *Left Review*, that 'during the initial period of our magazine [it is] most important to carry on rigorous criticism of all highbrowism, intellectualism, abstract rationalism, and similar dilettantism.' And what do these abusive terms mean, one may ask? The answer is only too simple: it is everything that WE happen not to agree with ideologically.

It may be argued that there is a severe censorship now in almost every European country except Russia, and that even in England there is no longer any great freedom of speech. But there is a great difference between even the severest and most stupefying censorship and the attempt to regard art as a mere instrument in party hands, which is illustrated in the Kharkov manifesto. The difference is that censorship cuts or bans books when they are already written: the principles laid down in this manifesto order the manner in which books should be written, what they should be about, and what attitude the writer should adopt to his subject. No censorship has ever gone so far as this. This instrumentalization permits too the rise of a school of critics whose business simply is to apply the canon. To attack writers because they are bourgeois, because their novels, if they are about life as they know it, are not proletarian, or, if they are about the working-classes, because their attitude is not revolutionary enough. In July 1934, an article appeared in *New Masses* attacking Auden, Day Lewis, and myself, because we were aristocrats, athletes, and so on. Auden's parents, it said, were Welsh squires, and we were all of exalted birth. Of course there was no word of truth in these attacks, in fact there was no fact at all in the whole article that was not invented. In any case, the facts, even if true, would to most people have seemed irrelevant. But not to this essayist. His business was to prove that we were aristocrats, and then to show that our verse was counter-revolutionary. His humble duty was to discredit us, and that he performed, quite regardless of any sense of truth. In Russia, a few years ago, such attacks were a commonplace, and there was no appeal against them.

Against this, one must set some statements

---

16. **of the bureaucracy.** "See Chap. I of *Artists in Uniform* by Max Eastman." (Author's note.)

52. **Left Review**, No. 3, December, 1934. (Author's note.)

by writers and critics in *Literature of the Peoples of the U.S.S.R.*, Vols. 7–8. Some of the declarations here seem admirable and honest. For instance, A. Selivenovsky, in an essay on the *Poetry of Socialism*, says: 'To become an artist of socialism means, if you come from the intelligentsia, that not only must you be convinced that the ideas of socialism are correct, but that you must alter your previously-formed poetic style. It means that you must overcome and discard many of your former ideas about life: you must change your way of looking at the world. But this alteration does not imply, of course, that the subject-matter, imagery, and style of the poet of socialism is made to lose all individuality, is reduced to complete uniformity. This is far from the case. The fact is that it is socialism that ensures the all-round development and growth of the human individual.'

This seems to me excellent. Good too is V. Kaverin's essay on literature and science, in which he pleads for a more scientific subject-matter in modern literature. C. Zelinsky is narrower: 'Criticism acquires a function of a principally intellectual-educational order: to struggle against the heritage of capitalism and consciousness by exposing it in art.' However, he has hard, almost sinister things to say of Voronsky, a figure of the recent past. 'Voronsky based his conception of art on the works of Tolstoy and Proust, writers in whose work direct observation is most prominent. In such a system of views, however, the very core of the Marxian conception of literature, its very heart, class activity, was lost. It was not by chance, therefore, that Voronsky proved to be allied with Trotskyism.'

Even officially, the position of literature in Communist society is extremely controversial. All I want to emphasize here is that if one is on the side of the greatest possible degree of freedom, if one insists that one should write as one cares and about what one wishes, one is not a traitor to the Socialist cause. No system is complete in itself as a solution of the bad system which it supersedes. If there is to be any sort of freedom or improvement, one has got to push and even sometimes fight the systems one most approves of. Unless artists insist on their right to criticize, to be human, and even 'humanitarian,' Communism will become a frozen era, another ice age.

Lastly, the view of Lenin was not at all that of a bureaucrat. Polonsky, in his *Outline of the Literary Movement of the Revolutionary Epoch*, relates how he pencilled comments on an article by Pletnev, *On the Ideological Front*, which was printed in *Pravda*, Sept. 27th, 1922. '"The creation of a new proletarian *class* culture is the fundamental goal of the Proletcult," wrote Pletnev. "Ha, ha!" There are many other comments and remarks, such as "human!" and "What a mess!" surviving. In two places he writes "Bunk."'

58. *Pravda* . . . 1922. Polonsky's article forms an appendix to Max Eastman's book. (Author's note.)

HUGH MacDIARMID

"Hugh MacDiarmid" is the pseudonym of the Scottish writer Christopher Murray Grieve, a man whose foremost interest has always been in Scottish Nationalist and labor movements.

The son of working-class parents, Christopher Grieve was born in Dumfriesshire, Scotland, August 11, 1892, and was educated at Edinburgh University. While a student he joined the socialist movement and the Independent Labour party, remaining an active member of the latter for over twenty years. After leaving college he embarked on journalism and became editor of various newspapers in Scotland, London, and South Wales. In Wales he ran a newspaper for the South Wales Miners' Federation. His first published work was *Rural Reform* in 1922, a Fabian Society publication of which he was co-author with Sidney Webb and others. During the First World War he served in Salonika for two years with the Royal Army Medical Corps, and then in Italy and France. For the last year of the war he was in the Indian General Hospital in Marseilles. After the war he concerned himself in the contemporary movement to express Scottish Nationalism in literature; founded the Scottish Centre of the International P.E.N., a society of writers; and represented Scotland as guest of honor at the Tailteann Games in Dublin and at P.E.N. Congresses in Vienna and The Hague. When he joined the Communist party of Great Britain, he was expelled from the National party of Scotland, and in 1937 he was expelled from the Communist party for his advocacy of Scottish separatism, though he was later reinstated when the Communist party had come to agree with his views on Scottish autonomy.

In 1936 he received a national testimonial signed by almost every living Scottish writer and many other well-known and distinguished people, testifying to his high poetic genius and his great services to Scottish arts and affairs. He is married to Valda Trevlyn and he lives on one of the North Islands of the Shetland group. Among his works are *Penny Wheep* (1926); *Albyn, or Scotland and the Future* (1927); *First Hymn to Lenin and Other Poems* (1931); and *Second Hymn to Lenin and Other Poems* (1935). *Speaking for Scotland,* a selection of his poems, has appeared in the United States. Until the beginning of World War II, he lived in the Orkney Islands. During the war he worked as a fitter in a shipyard. Since then he has become the center of the group of Scottish poets—among them Douglas Young, Sidney Goodsir Smith, and Maurice Lindsay—who are published by the house of William Maclellan in Glasgow, and whose periodical is Lindsay's *Poetry—Scotland.*

Hugh MacDiarmid carries forward the criticism of society implicit in many of Robert Burns' poems. Using a modified Scots dialect, he urges the Scottish workingmen's rights as against those of the upper classes. As a communist, he finds in Lenin a figure to admire. His subject matter is intended to arouse the poorer Scottish people to a sense of their own human dignity and potential rights. He has no false sentimentality about the poor, knowing the lack of learning and absence of moral standards resulting from extremes of poverty, but he sees them as people whose desire to live is strong enough to force them to fight for their existence.

A word should be said about MacDiarmid's Scottish language; this is not a spoken tongue, belonging to any single dialect or district. It is a purely literary language, as was that used by Robert Burns, and has been derived largely from the publication of Jameson's *Dictionary of Scottish Tongue.* It is called "synthetic Scots."

A Dog's Life

"TELL me," I asked a cripple who goes on all fours
Like a dog, pads on his hands, "Don't poor souls like you
Feel the need to believe in something beyond this world
Far more than we others do?"

"No. Not with a life like mine," he replied.   5
"It's not we who need God. He could tell us no more
If he does exist than we understand already
And are thankful for."

At the Cenotaph

ARE THE living so much use
That we need to mourn the dead?
Or would it yield better results
To reverse their rôles instead?
The millions slain in the War—   5
Untimely, the best of our seed?—
Would the world be any the better
If they were still living indeed?
The achievements of such as are
To the notion lend no support;   10

"A Dog's Life," "At the Cenotaph," and "Second Hymn to Lenin" from *Second Hymn to Lenin and Other Poems* (Stanley Nott, Ltd., 1935); "Parley of Beasts" and "Your Immortal Memory, Burns!" from *Penny Wheep* (William Blackwood & Sons, Ltd., 1937), reprinted by permission of the author.
A Dog's Life. With acknowledgments to Par Lagerkvist. (Author's note.) Lagerkvist is a modern Swedish writer, born in 1891, who has written a poem on this idea.   1. **a cripple**, a symbol of the underdog, or the wage-earning class.
Cenotaph, monument to the dead; a reference to the Cenotaph in London.

The whole history of life and death
Yields no scrap of evidence for't.—
Keep going to your wars, you fools, as of yore;
I'm the civilisation you're fighting for.

Second Hymn to Lenin

(EXCERPT)

Oh, it's nonsense, nonsense, nonsense,
Nonsense at this time o' day
That breid-and-butter problems
S'ud be in ony man's way.

They s'ud be like the tails we tint   5
On leavin' the monkey stage;
A' maist folk fash aboot's alike
Primaeval to oor age.

We're grown-up that haena yet
Put bairnly things aside   10
—A' that's material and moral—
And oor new state described.

Sport, love, and parentage,
Trade, politics, and law
S'ud be nae mair to us than braith   15
We hardly ken we draw.

Freein' oor poo'ers for greater things,
And feg's there's plenty o' them,
Tho' wha's still trammelt in alow
Canna be tenty o' them—

Parley of Beasts

Auld Noah was at hame wi' them a',
The lion and the lamb,
Pair by pair they entered the Ark
And he took them as they cam'.

If twa o' ilka beist there is   5
Into this room súd come,

Wad I cúd welcome them like him,
And no' staun' gowpin' dumb!

Be chief wi' them and they wi' me
And a' wi' ane anither   10
As Noah and his couples were
There in the Ark thegither.

It's fain I'd mell wi' tiger and tit
Wi' elephant and eel,
But noo-a-days e'en wi' ain's se   15
At hame it's hard to feel.

Your Immortal Memory, Burns!

Thought may demit
Its functions fit
While still to thee, O Burns,
The punctual stomach of thy people turns.

Most folks agree   5
That poetry
Is of no earthly use
Save thine—which yields at least this Annual
          Excuse!

Other cults die:
But who'll deny   10
That you your mob in thrall
Will keep, O Poet Intestinal?

From wame to wame
Wags on your fame,
Once more through all the world   15
On fronts of proud abdomena unfurled.

These be thy train,
No-Soul and No-Brain,
And Humour-Far-From-It,   19
Bunkum and Bung, Swallow-all and Vomit.

Palate and Paunch,
Enthusiasts staunch,
Gladly aver again,
"Behold one poet did not live in vain!"

"But us no Buts!"   25
Cry Gullet and Guts

Second Hymn to Lenin. The poem points out that it is nonsense that such matters as bread-and-butter problems, trade, politics, and law should prevent the human mind from advancement and progress.   5. *s'ud*, should. *tint*, shed. 7. *A'*, everything. *maist*, most. *fash*, worry.   9. *haena*, have not.   10. *bairnly*, childish.   16. *ken*, know.   17. *poo'ers*, powers.   18. *feg's*, Faith! (an interjection).   19. *trammelt*, caught. *alow*, in a blaze.   20. *tenty*, cautious.
Parley of Beasts. The general meaning of the poem is that it is hard to feel at home even with one's self in this modern world, although one may desire to mix with all classes.   5. **ilka**, each.

8. **gowpin'**, gaping.   9. **chief wi'**, friendly with.   13. **mell**, mix with. **tit**, small bird.
Your Immortal, etc. MacDiarmid continues the Burns tradition in praising the humble folk and is critical of the early romantic poet only because Burns' love and drinking songs (poetry of the intestines) are popular and his songs about the poor not so seriously considered as they should be in the light of their social significance.

Whose parrots of souls
Resemble a clever ventriloquist's dolls.

Be of good cheer
Since once a year   30
Poetry is not too pure
A savoury for shopkeepers to endure!

And, dined and wined,
Solicitors find
Their platitudes assume   35
The guise of intuitions that illume

The hidden heart
Of Human Art
And strike in ignorance
On wonders of unpredicated chance.   40

A boozy haze
Enchants your lays
And Gluttony for a change
Finds Genius within accosting range,

And cottons on!   45
—Thy power alone
The spectacle attests
Of drunken bourgeois on the Muses' breasts!

Only thy star
Falls from afar   50
To swim into the ken
Of countless masses of befuddled men,

In their hearts' skies
Like barmaids' eyes
Glabrous to glitter till   55
Their minds like rockets shoot away and spill

These vivid clots
Of idiot thoughts
Wherewith our Scottish life
Is once a year incomparably rife!   60

.   .   .   .

Belly will praise
Thee all its days
And spread to all nations
Thy fame in belchings and regurgitations,

While mean minds soar   65
And hiccoughs adore
And butcher-meat faces
Triumphant, transfigured, example thy graces!

Killing No Murder

GREETINGS from the grave to you, my mur-
      derers!
I bear you no grudge for killing me.
Each one seeks to promote what he thinks the
      right,
And doubtless you think you did rightly.

You believe in your ancestors' teaching,   5
"I am the master and you the serf,"
And you regard being master as an honour,
A special privilege you inherit and deserve.

But I took my stand with the lowly
And passionately appealed to them too   10
To reply to your ancestors' descendants,
"We are no servants, no masters you."

Thus I injured you in your pride
And shook the people in their mad belief
That you are made of superior stuff,   15
Born to be rulers, with the world in fief.

I hurt your pride and you took your revenge.
We were both convinced we were right,
Serving the just cause as every man must
According to his light.   20

Then may my spilt blood help to decide
If your right or mine shall prevail;
Your injured pride or the people's suffering
At last in world-judgment turn the scale.

If the people's liberation fell   25
Overboard with the ballast of my poor life
Then your killing me matters little
And in vain from the start was my strife.

But if from my blood springs up
The seed which you did not will   30

"Killing No Murder," "Behind the Symbols," "Think Not
That I Forget," and "Reflections in an Ironworks" by Hugh
MacDiarmid, reprinted by his permission.
Killing No Murder. "A striking example of literary prophecy,
this poem is a free translation of the remarkable poem, 'Die
Stimme des Gemordeten,' from his volume, *Brennende Erde*
(*Burning Earth*), Munich, 1920, in which the manner of his
death fourteen years later was forecast by Erich Muhsam, the
Socialist writer, officially stated to have committed suicide in
the Oranienberg Concentration Camp, but actually murdered
by the Nazis. May the ultimate issue it predicts come as true
as the author's forecast of how he would die!" (Author's note.)

Then exultingly I'll praise the moment
When fear of me compelled you to kill.

For so murder's arm would become
An instrument in Freedom's great task
And in death even more than in life   35
I'd advance it—what more could I ask?

My murder would herald your end then,
My spirit live in your overthrow
And when the goal I sought is achieved
In the hearts of all free men glow.   40

So I leave it to time to show
Which of us shall triumph at last
—Community, or Money-and-Arms,
The glorious future or brutish past.

Enough! The death I have suffered   45
Has steeled my comrades anew to the fight,
Greetings from the grave to you, murderers!
The battle goes on. And who wins is right!

Behind the Symbols

LET THE hearts of my people be lifted up
Once more with the daily sight
Of an eagle wheeling on majestic vans
    That is our Scottish birthright.

Fill their lives again with the noblest form   5
    At liberty in Europe still—
The red stag pausing with lifted hoof
    On the sun-assailing hill.

For these are among Earth's glorious symbols
    To souls of men needing symbols yet   10
And a man must be well nourished on these
    To embrace the Infinite.

But the supreme spirit enters into all
    As an otter into its watery home
As if without dividing its flow   15
    And making no ripple, bubble, or foam.

Even so in the course of time I hope
My people will open their hearts until
They are like the lochs the hill-streams feed
    Forever—but cannot overspill.   20

Think Not That I Forget

THINK not that I forget a single pang
    Of all that folk have tholed,
Agonies and abominations beyond all telling,
    Sights to daunt the most bold.   4

There are buildings in every town where daily
    Unthinkable horrors take place.
I am the woman in cancer's toils,
    The man without a face.

I am all cruelty and lust and filth,
    Corruption and law-made crime—   10
The helpless prisoners badgered in their cells
    In every land and clime,

All "gallant soldiers" murdering for pay
    (Plus "little Belgium" or like affair)
And heroic airmen blithe to give   15
    Poor tribes Death from the air,

And all the hidden but no less hideous deeds
    Sound citizens are always privily at—
Only in the mean natures and vicious looks
    Of their children, themselves, or their under-
        lings caught.   20

Oh, there's as much of it in Great Britain here
    As in Sing-Sing or in Cayenne—
Differently disguised, of course, and hiding
    In the most "decent and God-fearing" men.

There is no horror history's ever known   25
    Mob passion or greedy fear wouldn't soon
Make them do over again—slovens and cowards
    Moving pig-eyed in their daily round.

Behind the Symbols. MacDiarmid is an insistent Scottish nationalist, and although left wing in his sympathies, more nationalist than radical. Here he is addressing his own people and hoping that they will see in the approach of socialism the greatness that can fulfill them, if they accept it.

Think Not That I Forget. The poem is simple in theme. It is the poet's statement of the guilt of the people who, through greed or ignorance, have hurt others. As a Marxist, although rather an individualist too, MacDiarmid wrote many poems of social protest.   14. **"little Belgium,"** slogan of the First World War: "Gallant Little Belgium."   16. **poor tribes,** reference to the Royal Air Force bombing of Frontier tribesmen in India.   22. **Sing-Sing,** New York State Penitentiary. **Cayenne,** French penal settlement.

They face nothing—their whole lives depend
  On ignorance and base contempt   30
For all that's worth-while in the powers of Man
  From any share in it exempt.

In the midst of plenty in poverty,—
  To Art no better than apes—
Think not that I am unaware   35
  Of one of their loathsome shapes.

Aristocratic sentiments?—Yes! But remember
  These Yahoos belong to no single class.
You'll find far more in proportion to numbers
  In palaces and west-end clubs than in the
    mass.   40

38. Yahoos, the "men" in the final part of Swift's *Gulliver's
Travels*.

Reflections in an Ironworks

WOULD you resembled the metal you work
   with,
Would the iron entered into your souls,
Would you became like steel on your own be-
  half!
You are still only putty that tyranny rolls
Between its fingers! You makers of bayonets
  and guns   5
For your own destruction! No wonder that
  those
Weapons you make turn on you and mangle
  and murder—
You fools who equip your otherwise helpless
  foes!

THOMAS OWEN BEACHCROFT

The relatively brief literary career of Thomas Owen Beachcroft is marked by an excellence of achievement unusual in one whose story-writing remains more or less an avocation. He was born at Bristol, England, on September 3, 1902, and was educated at near-by Clifton College (1912–20), an institution whose name in America has been made famous by Sir Henry Newbolt's much quoted schoolboy poem, "Clifton Chapel," a poem which is an embodiment of all the virtues—and some of the vices—of Victorian ideals of manhood. Beachcroft has, in his stories, however, been sufficiently unconventional and original in thought to remove any possible suspicion that he is a Victorian. His stories have been traditional in form, respectful of the conventions of the written word, yet astonishingly varied in their material and vivid in their treatment, so that the author has been likened to Rudyard Kipling in contemporary dress. Such a criticism, nevertheless, applies with aptness only to his striking qualities as a storyteller; Beachcroft is removed by even more than a generation of years from the view-

point of the celebrated prophet of Victorian imperialism.

At Clifton, Beachcroft distinguished himself both as an athlete and as a poet; at the close of his college career he had hoped to be a Don. Instead he found himself an announcer for the British Broadcasting Corporation. The step from this to professional journalism was easy, and he subsequently made himself a success as an advertiser. This is his vocation, but short-story writing has been his relaxation. He observes that he chose this particular form of fiction because he can turn out short stories at odd moments during a busy life. Many of his stories have been written on the top deck of a London bus. But there is nothing of the hurried or careless about them; they are well constructed, sharply limned as to character, and charged with an unusual amount of emotional appeal without recourse to sentimentality.

Beachcroft's published collections to date are *A Young Man in a Hurry* (1935), *You Must Break Out Sometimes* (1937), *Parents Left Alone* (1940), and *Collected Stories* (1946).

May-Day Celebrations

IT WOULD be about now they would be coming, Mabel thought, and her heart beat somewhat faster. Thomas's face was all about her, wherever she turned; changing, changing from the boy with black hair and violent ways to the elderly man with the patient look; the waiting look; and the eyes deeper and deeper set with something in them of failure, and something in them of sticking to it.

Now she saw the red and white cheeks he used to have in his 'teens; now the grey face with heavy lines, and the stubble turning grey, and the shaggy eyebrows—and his eyes, which looked tired.

She heard the band now in the distance—the marchers were coming into the gardens. The crowd grew more dense every moment, and tremors of excitement shuddered through it, like gusts of wind in high corn. Mabel was carried sideways against her will over towards the platforms and the banners. A dense crowd was waiting there for the marchers and the speakers.

There were two platforms under the trees at the corner of the gardens. Round them the red banners were stretched. Overhead clouds were racing in a stormy sky, and the branches threshing and weaving in the wind.

Mabel found herself carried in the crowd into the arms of an old friend. The two women greeted each other.

'It's a good muster,' said Mabel, 'The numbers are very good.'

'Who's going to speak? Is your husband speaking?'

Mabel shook her head.

'He's going to start it off,' she said. 'He's taking things a bit easy. This fellow Hardy's going to speak.'

The crowd was massed solid round the platforms now, and policemen's helmets seemed to float everywhere among the heads. And beyond the crowd she could see the heads and shoulders of mounted policemen gliding about. Mabel knew there were almost as many policemen as there were demonstrators and marchers. There always were at a big meeting.

There came a wavering cheer, taken up uncertainly here and there: and the marchers began to file past the platforms. On each side of 50 them marched a rank of policemen. Mabel saw first the bobbies' red faces, purple and red with the full blood of health—and their red, fleshy necks and their upright carriage; each man of them carrying his twelve and fourteen stone like a boy athlete. She saw beef as they went by: and roasting fires. She saw steaks sizzling in grills and frying-pans. She saw gravy, and crusty chunks of bread and butter and foaming pints of beer and stout. 60

Then she saw the marchers; and she was watching pale, ill faces, grey and yellowish: she saw the dragging feet and ragged clothes. Here and there a man squared his shoulders and stuck his jaw out. In every face she saw sadness and old despair: she saw the drawn lines that she had seen so often, and the patient, stern look of the men who were brave. She saw rain-soaked street corners, and men leaning motionless against street posts with the 70 rain drifting over the cobble-stones. The word *hunger* transfixed her like a spear, a pain that ached in her own body. Hunger marchers, she thought—men who marched under the banner of Hunger. They were hungry: and they marched because there was nothing else for them to do.

Leading a section, her Thomas passed, looking steadfastly ahead. She pushed her way with purpose now towards the platforms. 80 Thomas mounted the platform and held up his hand for silence. A hush fell.

For a moment or two he looked about him at the marchers. What were his feelings? Mabel knew he was not thinking of himself, nor of her, nor of anything but of them. As he waited and looked from one side to the other a low mutter of recognition began to arise; it was a rough growl of friendship that never rose to a cheer: something more friendly than a cheer. 90

"May-Day Celebrations" from *You Must Break Out Sometimes*, reprinted by permission of Boriswood, Ltd.

The reader is asked to compare this story with Fitzgerald's "May Day" (p. 346) as an illustration of the change which came over the status of the radical worker between 1919 and the 1930's.

56. stone, the usual unit of weight for persons and livestock in the British Isles; a stone is fourteen pounds.

Thomas's grave deeply lined face looked round on the crowd, and he held up a strong, square hand.

'Comrades,' said Thomas, with slow Lancashire emphasis, 'you know me well. You know something of what I have done for you in these thirty years. I wish it were more,' he suddenly cried, 'by God I wish it were more.'

A sudden silence spread now.

10 'I'm not come here to speak for myself,' Thomas went on more calmly. 'I want to present to you Mark Hardy. He has been to Russia. Once he talked with Lenin himself. He is going to speak of our plans for the coming year.'

Hardy stood up. He was a man of about thirty-five—over six feet. His face was thin and handsome, with deep-set eyes. His hair was black and untidy. He wore a black coat and trousers and a red shirt open at the throat.

20 Before speaking he suddenly flung off his coat—and held his two arms towards the crowd. The murmur of talk round the platform died away. He began to speak at once swiftly and in loud, clear tones that carried far and compelled the attention.

'Friends,' he said, 'comrades—fellow workers. During the last five years we have passed through a century of experience in our long struggle: events have moved: and we have 30 made a tremendous advance towards the inevitable downfall of capitalist misrule, and the building up of the workers' united and worldwide front.

'In this five years we have seen every capitalist country sucked far down in the economic maelstrom. We have seen their foundations splitting and cracking. We have seen the feverish and insane efforts of Nazi and Fascist reactionaries in their despairing effort to shore 40 them up.'

Mabel's mind began to wander: now she had seen the marchers and heard Thomas speak, she began to edge away towards the back of the crowd.

Presently a burst of applause called her mind back to the speaker. Hardy was saying:

'We are asked this year to celebrate King George's Jubilee. You know as well as I do that all this Empire hullabaloo in the lickspittle 50 press is propaganda: cold-blooded propaganda,

aimed to divert people's eyes from the sickening state of present affairs.

'What have we in truth to celebrate? First that after twenty-five years of the present reign we accept that millions of men in every capitalist country continue in permanent unemployment. A glorious achievement indeed! Millions of workers condemned to a standard of life that would be despised by primitive savages. Secondly, we celebrate that since 1926 Trade Unions have been placed in a weaker position than they have occupied since the days of Castlereagh, and the Six Acts. Another great capitalist victory! Thirdly, that England continues to exploit by bloodshed, force, and cruelty the Asiatic nations. Fourthly, that insane quarrels over the ill-gotten Imperialist gains among the nations lead us to the very brink of another horrible war, to which the workers will once again be driven: a war which brings to the workers nothing but torture, degradation, horror. And the next war will carry every fiendish device of slaying and torture into the workers' own homes among their women and children.'

Hardy poured all this out in a torrent of clear and unhesitating speech. Suddenly he paused and looked round. Then he went on with slow measured emphasis:

'Stop it: stop it before it is too late. Remember Invergordon. Think of the power of the massed will of the people, the same needs, the same enemies in every country. There is no hope for you in nationalism. . . .'

While he was speaking the sky darkened: clouds and gusty rain came spinning through the air. The trees swayed, and men tightened their collars round their throats.

'Let's go,' said Mabel to Beth. 'Let's get back.

62. **Castlereagh . . . Acts.** Robert Stewart, Viscount Castlereagh (1769–1822), was a British statesman, member of Parliament (1794), secretary of state (1805), and minister of war (1807). He was active in promoting the alliance against Napoleon in 1812. Despondent and broken in health he committed suicide in 1822, to the great delight of Lord Byron, who in his writing had been Castlereagh's most articulate enemy. Unquestionably Castlereagh was a corrupt politician. The Six Acts were a series of acts repressing the rights of the laborer, following the industrial unrest and rioting which led up to the Peterloo Massacre at Manchester in August 1819. Castlereagh favored these acts in spirit and in policy; he was, in consequence, roundly hated by the people as a whole, and returned this hate with interest. 80. **Invergordon,** a town in the shire of Ross and Cromarty, Scotland. There were some disputes over the water and electricity utilities here in 1930 and 1932.

I'd like to have some tea ready when Thomas comes in. He'll need some warming up.'

They slowly edged their way out of the crowd. When they reached its distant scattered fringe, they turned round and looked back. The outer groups of people were talking together: many were breaking off and going away as the rain came on. From here the voice of Hardy could still be faintly heard.

'This form of state will go: be assured of it: *war* will go . . .'

Nearer in round the platform the crowd pressed silent, unmoving. Mabel looked back at the platform, and saw Hardy using his arms as he spoke, though his voice no longer reached her: and she saw Thomas sitting beside him: and the crowd packed round them.

The platform seemed like a heart or core of life, sending its own pulse through the silent, waiting crowd that pressed round to drain life from it. Her mind became filled with the image: she saw it as a brazier of coals in the dark, and men pressing round it, with the light gleaming on their hands and faces and clothes: she saw it as the pay office at the mills when she was a girl, with scores of men struggling round to draw their money. She saw it as a multitude of flowing, changing pictures, with light breaking through the clouds. She saw it as a stone sending silent ripples across the surface of a pond.

Both women were silent as the 'bus took them away from the parks and shopping streets to the grime-covered parts of the town beyond the two railway stations, where there were factories and warehouses and poor men's homes.

Mabel led the way through the dark arches which carried one of the stations above the streets and houses. They came out into a street of small houses, which lay for ever under the shadow of the enormous viaduct. Their walls were crusted with sooty deposit, so thick that it fell away at the touch of a hand. The air was filled with smoke, white, grey, and brown. And the little houses shook to the unending clamour of the trains overhead.

Mabel led the way up a bare boarded passage and uncarpeted stairs: the walls of the passage were thick with railway grime. She had two rooms. When they got inside, Beth looked round at the linoleum, worn and polished, and at the bareness of everything. She was used to rooms in which beds and tables and upholstered chairs jostled against each other.

'We've got another room here,' said Mabel. 'This is only the sitting-room.'

She hung her mackintosh and hat on the door: she stooped down and put a penny in the gas meter and lit a small gas-ring for the kettle. They settled themselves to talk. They sat with their knees apart and their hands resting in the outspread laps. Mabel and Beth had led hard lives; but time had brought their bodies a roundness which gave a placid dignity to all they said and did.

'It's a grubby place, this,' Mabel said. She began to put out cups and plates. 'I hope you'll overlook my not spreading a cloth: it'd only be black by the end of tea. The blacks get in even with the windows shut.'

As she spoke a long goods train rumbled past, filling the room with clanking.

'I don't like living in Railway Street,' she went on. 'It ain't exactly my idea of a country cottage with nice roses to smell. But Thomas has got to find a place for his little printing press. It's what they call a platen. We can put it down in the basement on a stone floor here. It's not every street they'd let you have a printing press.'

'Does he print the *Worker's Clarion* on it?' said Beth.

'No; it wouldn't take that,' said Mabel. 'That's got much too big an affair—which is all to the good. But they want him to issue a lot of small pamphlets all the time.'

She opened a cupboard door and showed, instead of cups and saucers, piles of papers and pamphlets. A cascade of papers came sliding out on the floor: they began to fall from the shelves, manuscripts, printed sheets, blank paper, all confused together.

'What do you think of that for a larder?' said Mabel.

Beth shook her head.

'Well,' she said, after a long silence, 'you would have him.'

Mabel pushed the papers back into the cup-

72. **goods train,** freight-train.

board, moved another pile from a wooden chair, and sat down.

'Don't think I meant that for a complaint against Thomas, or the way we live,' she said. 'You're right. I would have him—and perhaps my people were doing right in trying to stop me. I was only nineteen. But I've never lived to regret it. I was quite right, Beth, young as I was. There are some things the young ones know. He's a good husband and a good man: and I say that after forty years of married life. What more can a woman say than that? How many can say that much?'

Beth nodded.

'Forty years, is it? We're getting old. I can remember it all so clear, too: as if it was only last year. It seems funny.'

They both fell to thinking of other days and times, far-off scenes, when they were young slim girls in white muslin who ran with flying feet; who were caught by the waist on summer nights.

Mabel began to put out a loaf and butter on the bare table top.

'You'll stay and have a bite, won't you?' she said. 'We don't live very high: but there's some bread and butter and jam: the butter's as cheap nowadays as the marge.'

'Unless you have the fivepenny marge,' said Beth.

Mabel went on talking as she set out the tea with slow, quiet movements.

'Mind you,' she said, 'my married life hasn't been all honey and jujubes. I'm not complaining. Why should I? But when a man lives for something beyond the ordinary things of life, home can't be his be-all and end-all.'

Beth nodded.

'That's it,' she said.

Mabel paused with a plate in her hand. 'But take yourself, too,' she said. 'It cuts all ways. Your Arthur's been a good steady worker always. But you haven't been too happy with him.'

Beth nodded again.

'To all outward appearances,' Beth said, slowly and decidedly, 'Arthur looks like a 'usband to be proud of. But there it is. I got

my crying over early in my married life. I did plenty of it then. He's a bully, that's the trouble: and he's never thought for anyone but himself. He's selfish to the bone. The first ten years of my marriage were all babies and black eyes.'

'There have been times when I've felt it hard, too,' said Mabel. 'I've never had what I should call a home. Never in all these forty years. I've had to see my young ones go hungry and cold, when they were little. And I've never been able to give them a farthing to help them now they're older. We never know where we may be from one week to the next. Years ago I used to cry, too, when Thomas's views and meetings kept getting him the sack from good jobs. Many's the time I've said to him, "What's the use of going on?" Then every time he got a new job I used to think to myself, "Now I'll have a proper home." But just as we was getting things together something always went bust. We've lived in fourteen different towns, let alone all the rooms: they're more than I can remember.'

'But he's settled in a good job now, isn't he?' said Beth. 'He's been there for a year or two.'

'Yes, we're really better off now than we've ever been yet. I'm really beginning to hope now that I'm going to get a home together. We'll be out of this pig-sty in a year. Thomas is beginning to take it easier now. He doesn't do so much—not all day and every day, like he used to.'

'Well, he's getting on in years,' said Beth.

'Yes, he says he feels he isn't in the forefront any more: he looks to leave things to the younger men. But he can still earn good money. He always could. He's a foreman compositor now on the *Morning News*—working on the advertisements. It's a good job. I'm beginning to think we'll settle down yet, Beth: I'll be asking you to see me in a nice little place one of these days, in a little peace and comfort.'

Beth nodded.

'I'm sure I need it,' said Mabel. 'The kettle's on the boil now. I'll make tea. If he's late, I can make some fresh.'

'Is that the fourpenny,' said Beth, 'from the Stores round the corner?'

'It's the threepence-halfpenny. Tell me what

34. **jujubes,** a sweetmeat of Oriental origin.

you think of it. The only thing I wonder is whether he'll ever be happy if he gives it up. His one grumble has always been 'e's never been able to do enough for the *cause*. He's said that every day for the last twenty years, I should think.'

'What did you think of that fellow's speech this afternoon?' asked Beth.

Mabel sat silent for a little while.

'He seems a nice enough man,' she said at length.

'Yes, but what about all that he was talking about?'

'I don't know quite what to make of it,' said Mabel. 'And I've heard enough speeches in my time. He always talks that sort of thing. He means it when he says it. But I don't quite trust it somehow. What's he got to do with it all? He's a chap with a lot of money behind him. In Thomas's young days it was a fight against the *owners*: men understood what they were making for—and knew who was against them. Thomas spoke to the men about their own towns and factories and homes, and what they'd better do next week: not about the whole of this world and kingdom come. I sometimes think speech-makers like him get so full of the new plans in front of them and all to that, they forget what these poor fellows want is just food and dry clothes.'

'But he's an important man, isn't he?' said Beth. 'He's been an M.P., hasn't he? He'll be somebody one of these days.'

'Yes, I daresay he'll be someone,' said Mabel, 'on one side or the other. But it can't mean the same to him as it did to my Thomas when he was a young man. Yet he pushes forward and takes the limelight—and Thomas takes a back seat.'

'Well,' said Beth, 'you oughtn't to mind that: only a moment ago you were saying you'd be thankful if only he would drop out of things a bit and keep a steady job for once.'

'Yes,' said Mabel, 'but sometimes I feel— seeing all the work he's done—giving his whole life to it—he deserves something a bit more out of it.'

'You persuade him to give it up,' said Beth, 'and have a little peace and quiet for once in your life. I saw a little house out our way in Welcome's Fields a week back. You could have got it on the money he's making now. Let him spend it on you and his home for once.'

Mabel drew breath and compressed her lips: then she let it out as a slow, thoughtful sigh.

'We'll see,' she said. 'We'll see what happens.'

'It's time you had your way for once,' said Beth. 'You take my advice.'

'Here he is,' Mabel said.

They heard his footsteps in the passage, then on the bare boards of the stairs.

Thomas came in and greeted his wife and Beth a little absently. He sat down on a chair with a grunt. He was dressed in a dark serge suit with a muffler at his neck. His grey hair was closely cut and his face, once full of fire and expression, had grown dour and set and stubborn.

'I'm getting old,' he said.

'That's just what we've been saying,' said Beth. 'We're all getting old.'

'I'll just have time for some tea,' said Thomas, 'then I want to get down to the paper. I shan't be back till we've put her to bed. I'll be back about one. Then I shall have a full day on to-morrow, till late again. I had to work it that way so as to get off this afternoon.'

'You'll be worn-out,' said Mabel.

'It won't be the first time,' said Thomas.

Beth said: 'You ought to think of your health a bit more at your age.'

'I've got better things to think of,' he said. 'Not for Mabel.'

Thomas ignored her answer. Presently she said good-bye and went.

'I wanted to get downstairs to-night,' Thomas said, 'We want another thousand of those Invergordon pamphlets. That's been doing good work. But I can't manage it now—it's too late. Then they're asking me to do Hardy's speech later on. My Vanguard Press is getting well known.'

'What did you think of that speech of Hardy's?' said Mabel. 'I only heard the first part.'

'It was good,' said Thomas. 'My job nowadays is to go and print what better men say. I sometimes think I've never really done anything worth while for our cause.'

'Don't be silly. Isn't it anything to have given your whole life to it?'

'I dunno . . .' Thomas began: but stopped.

Mabel started up.

There was a loud knock at the street door. They heard it pushed open, and the tread of two or three men in the passage.

'They're coming up here,' said Thomas. 'Hardy said he might come round.'

There was a loud knock at the door.

'Come in,' said Thomas. He went to the door and opened it.

When he did so a police constable stepped into the room: behind him a plain clothes detective.

They stared at Thomas for a moment, seeming to dwarf him by their height and heavy bulk.

'Well,' said Thomas, after a bit, 'any trouble?'

The detective stepped forward.

'There's no need for me to ask if you're Thomas Devlin,' he said, 'because I know you by sight.'

'Yes, I'm Thomas Devlin.'

'I'm afraid, Mr. Devlin, I've got a warrant here for your arrest—and a search warrant, too.'

'What for? I'm an honest man. There must be some mistake.'

'No mistake,' said the detective. 'You work a small hand press down in the basement here. Whoever's at the back of you, the imprint's yours.'

Thomas nodded.

'And you've been issuing a lot of very foolish pamphlets lately. There's one of my men downstairs just found a pile of these Invergordon leaflets—with your imprint on them. I've got to arrest you under the new Act. There's the warrant.'

There was a pause.

'Well,' said Thomas, 'do you want me to come with you now?'

'Yes,' said the detective.

'Can't you give me time to make a few arrangements first?'

'I must ask you to come at once, please. We don't want a crowd of people round here. And I must search this room before we go, too. I'm under orders to confiscate all the printed matter I find here.'

Mabel opened the cupboard door and showed the stores of pamphlets. In a surprisingly short time they had searched the room and made a clean sweep.

Thomas began to make rapid arrangements with Mabel.

'We're going to the Central Police Station,' he said. 'Will you tell them what's happened at the paper at once? Go and see them yourself. Then come along and we'll see what we can arrange about bail.'

'I wouldn't count on bail, Mr. Devlin,' said the detective. 'The authorities at headquarters aren't playing. I'm afraid this is a serious business for you.'

'I'll come, anyhow,' said Mabel.

Before going, Thomas kissed her and held her in his arms.

'It'll be all right,' he said.

'Good-bye,' said Mabel. 'I'll be along directly.'

The door closed: and she was alone.

She stood silent for a long time, thinking and seeing nothing.

Then she slowly walked to the window and pulled the curtains. How grimy they were. Then she sat down beside the table which still carried the remains of tea. Many pictures of her broken and tattered life passed before her. She saw her hopes of the future torn in ragged dirty pieces, fluttering away. She knew now that she would never have a home: that from now on she need never hope for a home. The pictures of the little house she had begun to see changed to pictures of rooms in worse and worse streets: to fierce poverty, bare boards, and fireless grates, to comfortless old age.

Yet she felt calm and almost joyful. She had seen the look in Thomas's eyes. She knew he was living through the proudest and happiest moments of his whole life. She fell to thinking of the red and white cheeks, the wild black hair, he used to have. And gradually her heart grew light.

For a long time she sat silent and still until the penny in the gas was used up and the fire flickered out into cold, lifeless grey. Then she rose and put on her mackintosh to go out again. It was still wet from the afternoon's rain.

JOHN STRACHEY

The family of the Stracheys has made something of a name for itself in contemporary England. Lytton Strachey (p. 135) was a distinguished biographer in the ironic manner of the twenties; his cousin St. Loe Strachey was editor of the London *Spectator*. St. Loe Strachey's son, Evelyn John St. Loe Strachey, has been the stormy petrel of the clan. He was born on October 21, 1901, and went to Eton, thence to Magdalen College, Oxford. His life since his Oxford days has been given over to politics and to social and political research. He stood for Parliament as early as 1924, when he was unsuccessful; but in 1929 he was elected a member of Parliament from a Birmingham district as a Labourite. In 1931 he tried for reëlection, this time as an independent, but was not victorious. In the meantime, however, his writings had begun to attract attention—his masterpiece, *The Coming Struggle for Power*, appeared in the following year; and Strachey found himself thenceforth greatly in demand as a lecturer. His career as an independent political and social scientist has been firmly established since that time; he has written several challenging books and a larger number of arresting articles.

The list of Strachey's major works is illuminating in its very titles—*Revolution by Reason* (1925), *The Workers' Control in the Russian Mining Industry* (1928), *The Coming Struggle for Power* (1932), *The Menace of Fascism* (1933), *The Nature of the Capitalist Crisis* (1935), *The Theory and Practice of Socialism* (1936), *What Are We To Do?* (1938), and *Socialism Moves Forward* (1945). Strachey was convinced that capitalism was doomed and must be replaced by a Marxist system. So pronounced were his utterances on the subject and so close his affiliations with the Communist party in the 1930's that he was denied admittance to the United States in 1935 and 1938—something of a *cause célèbre* in the annals of the Bureau of Immigration.

With the coming of World War II, Strachey broke away from the pacifist doctrines of communism and expressed an intense nationalism and a strong faith in Britain's ultimate victory. Some of his convictions are put forth in *A Faith to Fight For* (1940). In addition to public relations work and broadcasting, he served as an air raid warden, and from this experience came the collection of reportorial sketches *Post-D*, known in the United States as *Digging for Mrs. Miller*. When the Labour Party came to power in 1945 Strachey returned to Parliament. He was shortly appointed Under Secretary for Air, and in 1946 succeeded to the post of Minister of Food, the first ministerial change made by Prime Minister Attlee.

There is no doubt about Strachey's cocksureness and British assumption of the divine right; but much of what he prophesied has come to pass in a general way; and he deserves the greatest respect not only as a political and economic thinker but also as a writer, for his style is not only persuasive but vigorous, and he possesses that quality usually absent from the writings of an economist—vitality. But so far as his thesis is concerned, if capitalism is to survive, it must answer successfully the serious indictments which Strachey has brought in against it throughout the resounding pages of *The Coming Struggle for Power*. That a struggle between capitalism and Marxism, as Strachey outlines it, can ever end in anything but a compromise seems unlikely, although such a point of view is of course repugnant to the enthusiastic revolutionists, of whom Strachey was in the 1930's an excellent example.

Yet Strachey himself has receded somewhat from the extreme position he occupied at the time he wrote *The Coming Struggle for Power*, and as a responsible member of the Government he has learned many things which as a professional economist he would never have known.

from **The Coming Struggle for Power**

CHAPTER XX

The Future of Great Britain

IN THIS chapter, an attempt is made to exemplify the foregoing discussion of the nature of communism, by a sketch of the problems involved in the struggle of the workers to overthrow capitalism and establish communism in one particular state. The state selected must perforce be Great Britain, for lack of adequate first-hand knowledge of any other. The British position is of such crucial world importance, however, that our particular instance throws a good deal of light on the general rule.

It is not proposed to attempt a discussion of the tactics appropriate for a Communist party working in an old-established democracy such as Great Britain. The steady growth of the Communist parties of the West is clearly dependent upon the continued development of a tactic exactly appropriate to the conditions of those capitalist states in which the forms of democracy have been, hitherto, preserved. But such a tactic cannot, we may be sure, be worked out in paper propositions, however ingenious. It can only be evolved, and it is now being evolved, gradually and painfully as the result of the experiences of the Communist parties of the West, gathered in the course of long and obstinate struggles. Nor does the undoubted fact that the tactics of the class struggle must differ from place to place, indicate in the least that the fundamental antagonism of class interest is not everywhere the same. More-

over, nothing is more disgusting than to sneer or jeer at the efforts of the men and women who are engaged in finding the correct tactics for each particular set of conditions, at heavy cost to themselves and by the only possible method, the painful and laborious method of trial and error.

All that is attempted here is a summary of the general position of Great Britain in respect of the need for, and prospects of, the communist movement. It may be worth while first of all to enumerate those, in themselves quite obvious, factors which make Great Britain a particularly favourable ground for communism. For these factors are, naturally, ignored whenever possible by British capitalist opinion. We will then come to a discussion of those objections to the possibility of communist success in Great Britain of which we already hear so much, and of which we shall hear to an ever-increasing extent.

The principal factors which give a revolutionary working-class movement in Great Britain a basis of strength, unequalled anywhere else in the world are as follows:

First: in actual numbers, the British working class is immensely strong. The proportion of the population of Great Britain which consists in industrial workers is higher than the corresponding proportion in any other important state. Britain is by far the oldest and is still the most heavily industrialized of all the great states. In America, for example, about a third of the population is still directly or indirectly on the land. Of the British population, some-

31. **Moreover . . . error.** Lenin wrote: "The problem here" (in Britain that is) "as everywhere, consists in the ability to apply the general and fundamental principles of communism to the specific relations between classes and parties, to the specific conditions in the objective development toward communism—conditions which are peculiar to every separate country, and which one must be able to study, understand, and point out. . . .

"The main thing now is that the communists of each country should, in full consciousness, study both the fundamental problems of the struggle with opportunism and 'Left' doctrinairism, and the specific peculiarities, which this struggle inevitably assumes in each separate country, according to the idiosyncrasies of its politics, economics, culture, national composition (e.g., Ireland), its colonies, religious divisions, etc. Everywhere is felt an ever-widening and increasing dissatisfaction with the Second International, a dissatisfaction due to its opportunism and its incapacity to create a real leading centre, able to direct the international tactics of the revolutionary proletariat in the struggle for the world Soviet Repub-

lic. One must clearly realize that such a leading centre can, under no circumstances, be built after a single model, by a mechanical adjustment and equalization of the tactical rules of the struggle. The national and state differences, now existing between peoples and countries, will continue to exist for a very long time, even after the realization of the proletarian dictatorship on a world scale. Unity of international tactics in the communist labour movement everywhere demands, not the elimination of variety, not the abolition of the national peculiarities (this at the present moment is a foolish dream), but such an application of the fundamental principles of communism—Soviet power and the Dictatorship of the Proletariat —as will admit of the right modification of these principles, in their adaptation and application to national and national-state differences. The principal problem of this historical moment in which all advanced (and not only the advanced) countries now find themselves lies here; that specific national peculiarities must be studied, ascertained, and grasped before concrete attempts are made in any country to solve the aspects of the single international problem, to overcome opportunism and Left doctrinairism within the working-class movement, to overthrow the bourgeoisie, and to institute a Soviet Republic and proletarian dictatorship." (*Left Wing Communism*) (Author's note.)

thing like four-fifths is industrial and commercial, hardly one-fifth agricultural. Even Germany, which is also heavily industrialized, can show no nearly corresponding proportion. Nor is it necessary to emphasize the cardinal importance of this fact in estimating the possibility of the working class being able to establish their dictatorship in Britain. For it is always upon the urban industrial workers that the whole body of wage-earners must rely. The industrial workers alone can play the leading part in the revolt of all non-property-owning sections of the population.

Second: the level of technical and educational development of this enormous British industrial working class is very high, relatively to that of the working class of other capitalist states. The British workers, as they have shown, by their unparalleled practical achievements in building trade unions and a Social Democratic party, have unrivalled powers of organization. And there is no reason to suppose that they will not exhibit those powers in the building of a Communist party.

Third: the converse of the extreme industrialization of Britain is, of course, the smallness and unimportance of her agricultural population. Now the comparative insignificance of British agriculture is usually quoted as one of the greatest objections to the maintenance of a communist régime in Britain. We shall consider this objection in a moment. It is obvious, however, that the absence of any large class of agriculturists, owning their means of production, and living by operating them themselves, is an enormous initial advantage to the British communist movement. For such a class is necessarily conservative, and will almost always ally itself to the big capitalists. We may recall the part which the farmers and richer peasants have played in Europe, and which they have sought to play in Russia. They have proved everywhere the readiest instruments of the big capitalists, when these determined that the time had come to resort to methods of open violence in order to smash all working-class organizations. How great then is the advantage of the British workers in the fact that this agricultural class is in Britain comparatively insignificant in numbers.

Fourth: what agricultural interests do exist are sharply divided into two antagonistic classes. For it is the unique characteristic of British agriculture that it has not developed a system of small holdings, and consequently a peasant class. On the contrary, British agriculture at an early stage in its development created units of production, farms, that is, too big to be worked by a single family. Hence, there grew up a relatively large class of wage-earn- 60 ing agricultural laborers, landless workers, as bereft as any urban proletarian of the means of production. And the agricultural workers, to the number of some 800,000, are a genuine rural working class. It is true that they are today on the whole backward, intimidated by the farmers and landlords and an easy prey for the old capitalist parties. British social democracy has never been able to secure their votes. (Not that this is necessarily a sign of their 70 backwardness.) But everyone who knows anything of the British agricultural workers agrees that, ill paid, and still suffering all those petty oppressions characteristic of the exploitation of small masters, they have intense, if latent, class antagonisms. Nor must all, at any rate, of the smaller tenant farmers be placed on the side of reaction. The "direct action" which the British farmers have lately taken by the refusal of many of them to pay tithes for the upkeep of 80 the State Church shows that under the pressure of economic circumstances they can become a force hostile to the capitalist State. Hence, even that rural population which does exist in Britain is by no means a unitedly anti-working-class force. The agricultural workers in a time of crisis could certainly be relied upon by the urban workers, at least to neutralize the efforts on behalf of the capitalists of the farmers and landlords. 90

Thus, the intrinsic balance of class forces is certainly more favorable to the workers in Great Britain than in any other major capitalist state. Nor is this truth ignored by the leaders of the British ruling class. Behind all their endless talk of the impossibility of communism in England, of the special immunity of the good, honest, British workers from the communism microbe, there lurks the "anxiety neurosis" of men who know that their position is 100 especially insecure. And just occasionally, in moments of special tension, the anxiety of the most intelligent and best-informed leaders of the British capitalist class secures conscious expression. There is, for example, that well-known passage in one of Mr. Lloyd George's speeches in 1920, a passage which drew from Lenin the comment that Mr. Lloyd George was "not only a very clever man, but that he has learnt much from the Marxists." Mr. Lloyd George was arguing in favor of the necessity of his coalition of all the forces of the capitalist class into the then existing "National Government." Such a coalition was necessary, he told his audience, in order to combat the communist menace.

"If you go to the agricultural areas," he said, "I agree that you have the old party divisions as strong as ever; they are far removed from the danger. It does not walk in their lanes. But when they see it they will be as strong as some of these industrial constituencies now are. Four-fifths of this country is industrial and commercial; hardly one-fifth is agricultural. It is one of the things I have constantly in my mind when I think of the dangers of the future here. In France the population is agricultural, and you have a solid body of opinion which does not move very rapidly, and which is not easily excited by revolutionary movements. That is not the case here. This country is more top-heavy than any country in the world, and if it begins to rock, the crash here, for that reason, will be greater than in any other land."

We have already discussed the intrinsic assets and liabilities of the British capitalist position. (For, of course, the British workers are not either absolutely weak or strong; they are weak or strong relatively to the strength or weakness of the British capitalist class.) We concluded that while immediately the British capitalists had very great—in some respects unrivalled—remaining strength, yet their world position was foredoomed to decline. We saw that the wisest and most successful of their leaders realized this, and that all their efforts were directed to mitigating Britain's decline: that they realized, whether consciously or unconsciously, that any strong action taken with a view to a permanent and decisive restoration of the British position necessarily involved war with some other empire; and that such a war

held but the darkest prospects for Britain. But such considerations, although they are themselves decisive in the long run, do not necessarily help us much in estimating the balance of class forces which may be expected to arise in Britain in the near future.

Let us next attempt to estimate the assets possessed by the British workers during that critical period which must supervene immediately after the establishment of their dictatorship. The factors which we have hitherto considered are assets only from the point of view of the possibility of the attainment of working-class power. It is one thing, however, for the workers to take power and another for them to be able permanently to maintain it. Nevertheless it will, on examination, become apparent that the British workers have important assets for this second period. We may summarize these assets as follows:

First: that same generally high level of technical skill, educational standards, and political experience which we noticed as forming an important asset for the building up of a communist movement in Britain, as objective circumstances become more and more favorable, is an asset of even greater importance for the maintenance of working-class power, once it has been achieved. No one who has seen the immense difficulties which the Soviet Union has faced in consequence of the backward state of development which Tsardom had imposed upon the Russian workers, can doubt that the task of laying the foundations of a communist economy in Great Britain would be immeasurably simpler, chiefly on account of this particular factor. The British workers are probably the most generally capable in the world: they will be far less dependent than are the Russians upon middle-class technicians, some of whom may be unreliable, for the maintenance and development of their economic system. (It may well be expected, however, that a much larger proportion of British technicians, with the example of the scope for technical ability which the Soviet system gives, will rally to a working-class régime.) It is probably not too much to say that the British workers are capable themselves of running the British productive system. Nor is it merely a question of technical skill. Several generations of industrial experience undoubtedly give a reliability, a sense of order, a power of co-operation for large-scale production which the Russian workers, outside Leningrad and one or two other exceptional places, necessarily lacked.

Second: the geographical nature of Great Britain makes her an ideal country to which to apply the principles of a planned centralized economy. Her geographical area is so small, and her system of communications so complete that the problems of centralized control will be greatly simplified. Britain is the most compact large-scale productive unit in the world. Her industries have been brought by capitalism to the point where they simply cry out for unified control. Nor will there be in Britain anything like the difficulty in generalizing the organizing committee or council of each industry into a nation-wide planning commission, which existed in Russia.

Third: moreover, the actual quality and quantity of the technical equipment of Great Britain (though some of it is now beginning physically to deteriorate) is perhaps unparalleled anywhere in the world. Think for a moment of the transport facilities of Great Britain —perhaps the most important single factor in the economic life of a nation. Great Britain has a double system of inland transport, by rail, and road, each of which is perhaps comparable to the very best of the systems of any other country. Her railway system throws a close mesh over the country, and is still on the whole better maintained than are the railways of any other area (though the Ruhr area of Germany and parts of Belgium and Luxembourg have an even closer mesh of railway lines). Her roads, though not nearly so well designed as those of France, are better maintained and, again, have a closer mesh. Moreover, they are equipped not only with an immense fleet of lorries for the transport of all kinds of goods, but with a very large number of passenger coaches or omnibuses. It is true that some parts of Britain's inland canal system, once one of the finest in the world, have been allowed to fall into decay. But the system would be restored very easily and cheaply if it were not considered redundant. It is probably not too much to say

that either the road or the railways system of Great Britain could independently, and in the impossible event of the other being totally destroyed, carry on quite effectively the entire transport services of the community. The roads could certainly do so if they were supplemented by the extremely cheap transport of heavy raw materials, which is possible by canal. In addition, however, to these incomparable forms of inland transport, probably the best method of all for British bulk transport is by coastal steamer. For it is an important and often neglected economic fact that something like two-thirds of the population of Britain lives in seaport towns—in areas which can be reached by ocean-going ships. It is only necessary to compare these transport facilities, now so squandered by capitalism, with the meagre resources inherited by the Russian workers, to understand the advantages which a British workers' dictatorship would possess. And the remarkably high development of the British transport system is only an instance of the general development of British capital equipment. For example, another source of immense strength to a workers' dictatorship in Britain will be the unequalled development of the British machine-building industries. Britain can produce machinery of all sorts, and above all machine tools, the machines for making machines, better than any country in the world. Thus, damage to existing plant, or its obsolescence, are factors which can be eliminated with unexampled ease in Britain.

In some respects certain British industries, it is true, lag behind the best German, French, American, and now Russian, practice. For example, British blast furnaces are mostly of small capacity; the surface equipment of her coal mines is inadequate; her motor-car industry is largely carried on by firms too small to apply all the advantages of mass production. A good deal of the equipment of the Lancashire cotton industry needs replacement. But on the whole British industrial equipment is probably as good as any in the world. For if it has many

66. **ocean-going ships.** Manchester and the neighbouring Lancastrian towns fall into this category since the building of the Manchester ship canal. (Author's note.)

defects, so have the equipment of all other capitalist states. Certainly it represents a productive power which, if operated steadily, and at full capacity, as it would be operated by a working-class dictatorship, could, even without extension, produce a standard of life for the British population at present unrivalled in the whole world. For it is not any lack of the technical ability to produce which is to-day progressively bringing British industry to a standstill. It is that the existing social relationships, the impasse which British capitalism has reached, make it impossible to utilize her admirable productive equipment.

The fourth factor which would facilitate the task of maintaining and consolidating a working-class dictatorship in Britain (for a period sufficiently long, firmly to lay the foundations of communism) is the unrivalled inheritance of what one may call "cultural" and "amenity" equipment which will accrue to the British workers. For example, Britain has, on the whole, an extensive system of school buildings and general educational equipment: her public utility services are well developed: she has the nucleus of a comprehensive system of free lending libraries: a network of cinemas: a large number of wireless receiving sets and excellent transmitting stations. Again, there exist in London the largest and finest plants in the world for the production and distribution of daily newspapers on a vast scale. (It is sometimes forgotten that the big London dailies, because of their national distribution, have much larger circulations than any American newspapers. This is another instance of the advantages of the compactness of Britain.) It is, of course, quite impossible for the British working class to make use of these assets to even 1% of their possible value in existing conditions.

It is true that in another respect a British working-class dictatorship will be seriously handicapped. The housing conditions which it will inherit are abominable. It is not too much to say that one of the most urgent tasks of a working-class dictatorship in Britain will be the

rebuilding of whole areas of every city in the land. On the whole, however, the British workers will find themselves, once they have attained power, in an incomparably better material position than did the Russian workers. They will be able at once to devote a much higher proportion of their energies to the production of consumable goods, as distinct from capital goods, than could the Russians. They will be able to satisfy all the basic wants of the population at a much earlier stage. It is not too much to say that while the primary problem in Russia has been to construct the basic equipment necessary to a communist civilization, in Great Britain the workers' first task will be the adaptation of a rich inheritance to new uses.

All the foregoing considerations, however, apply to the situation of a workers' dictatorship in Great Britain regarded in isolation. Such a view is highly abstract. A workers' dictatorship in Great Britain could, in fact, only be, as we show below, a part of a widespread working-class assumption of power extending to considerable areas of Europe at least. It may be best, however, to discuss this subject, which raises the real prospects of communism in Britain, by coming to a discussion of the principal objections to the possibility of communist success which are always raised in British capitalist and social democratic circles.

The first of these objections represents the other aspect of the undoubted fact, which we have already discussed, that Britain is a highly industrial country in which agricultural production plays a relatively small part in the national economy. This fact is expressed by the oft-repeated cry of the spokesmen of British capitalism, a cry which, as the power of communism grows, will rise into an almost deafening shriek, that "Britain cannot feed herself." From determined fascists, bewildered liberals, and socialists finding excuses for the abandonment of socialism, this cry already resounds. It is impossible, unthinkable, mad, outrageous, we are told, for the British workers even to dream of taking power. For if they did so, Britain would starve in a few weeks. The capitalist countries would boycott us. We could not buy

22. **For . . . equipment.** Compared to what they might and ought to be, British schools are pitiable: compared to what the Russians inherited in 1917, they are superb. (Author's note.)

our food. We should all perish miserably. Every shade of opinion within British capitalism, from the Churchills on the Right to the disaffiliated pacifists of the I.L.P. on the Left, feel that with these magic words they have laid the communist spectre. What further need have we of witnesses? "Britain cannot feed herself" and— oh, what a relief—that settles the matter.

What importance have we to attach to this question? On examination, the whole thing boils down to one simple proposition: viz. that a working-class régime in Britain must be part of an international movement. And whoever dreamt of it being anything else? Is it not precisely because communism is in its very essence international: because it is a movement which can recognize no frontiers of race, of colour, or of territory, that all the Communist parties of the world are tightly bound together into the Third International? It might be impossible to maintain a workers' dictatorship in Britain against a united capitalist world. Already, however, such a world does not exist. Capitalism has lost control of Russia. Moreover, the remaining capitalist powers are at daggers drawn with each other, so that they have never yet been able to combine even against the Soviet Union. This does not mean that the problem of securing regular and uninterrupted supplies of raw materials and foodstuffs to a Britain in which the workers had taken power would not be an important one. (Incidentally a tremendous lot of nonsense is talked about the actual quantity of food produced in Britain. Taking one type of foodstuff with another, Britain produces about a five months' supply annually. And she habitually carries a stock of food adequate to last from two to three months.) But it would not be an impossible task, even in the case of Russia and Britain being the only two communist areas in an otherwise capitalist world. But is such a case likely to arise? It is

4. **I.L.P.,** The Independent Labour Party.   6. **What . . . matter.** Thus Professor Harold Laski, in his well-known little book entitled *Communism*, tells us that "the rupture of Anglo-American trade would be fatal to an English revolution." But still Professor Laski's fears and anxieties lead him to stranger statements still. We are told, for instance, that "an American communist revolution would have to cope with problems of distance which would probably render it abortive at a very early stage." What luck for Lenin that he had to deal with a handy little pocket handkerchief of a country like Russia! (Author's note.)

improbable that Britain will be the next place in which, after Russia, the conflict of class comes to the point of decision. As a matter of fact, history will probably record that the Kwangsi province of China was the first area of the world after Russia, in which a stable workers' Government was set up. For already (March 1931) some sixty million Chinese, according to the Shanghai correspondent of the London *Times* (who is not a communist sympathizer) are living under the rule of Soviets. Again, there are half a dozen points in Europe in which the capitalist crisis is more acute, and, naturally therefore, the communist movement is more developed, than it is in Britain. The workers will probably obtain power in Poland or Roumania or Spain or Hungary or Austria or Germany, for example, before they do so in Britain. And the overthrow of capitalism in one or more of these countries would immediately transform the international balance of power. Thus the whole picture of a communist Britain surrounded by a ring of hostile capitalist powers is a preposterously unreal one. It is a picture which could only be found convincing by people whose desires and fears combined to allow them to cherish any illusion which helped them to believe that communism in Britain was impossible.

One other form of this objection is sometimes raised. It is suggested that even though it is extremely probable that a communist Britain will not arise until most of the rest of Europe is also in the hands of the workers, and is thus in a position to form, with Russia, a self-supporting unit, the British Navy would be used by the British capitalists to blockade the coasts of Britain, prevent food supplies from reaching her, and so either starve to death the population of her great cities, or, if necessary, bombard them into submission. It is probable that less will be heard of this objection after the revelation of the true spirit of the British sailors at Invergordon in the autumn of 1931. It is quite clear that it would be utterly impossible to order British seamen to intercept food ships bound for British ports and so starve to death their own countrymen, including their own

85. **true spirit . . . 1931,** evidently a state secret.

wives and children. Still less could they be induced to lay waste British coastal cities by bombardment.

As a matter of fact, the real and urgent task which faces the revolutionary movement in Britain is to keep up with the forward surge of development which Communist parties the world over are experiencing as a result of the present crisis (1932) in capitalism. There is visible no danger of the British workers making such rapid progress as to become, materially or psychologically, ready to take power before the workers elsewhere are able to give them such assistance as will secure for them supplies essential to the maintenance of their power. This is not in any way to reflect on the intelligence and courage of the British workers, which will, we may be confident, in the end prove to be second to none. It is not to subscribe by implication to any absurd doctrine of there being an inherent incompatibility between communism and the psychology of Britons. It is merely another way of repeating that the crisis in capitalism is as yet less grave in Britain than it is in many other parts of the world. When the British workers find themselves at last face to face with the same inescapable realities which, for example, the German workers are beginning to face to-day, they will, it is safe to prophesy, show themselves not less, but (because of their high level of development) more ready and active to take the road of their salvation. In the meanwhile, during the period when the vast remaining resources of British imperialism still make Britain

1. **Still . . . bombardment.** The theorists of the British Independent Labour Party now use simple and direct appeals to funk as their chief anti-revolutionary propaganda. They tell us that revolution is now utterly impossible because of the nature of modern armaments. Thus a speaker at a 1932 I.L.P. Summer School told his audience that revolution was for ever impossible in Great Britain because power was now concentrated in the hands of the air force. And the air force could easily bomb "camps of the unemployed" out of existence. Why, in a revolutionary situation, the unemployed should go camping was not explained. And in the case of the bombing of cities, it may be asked how the pilots of the air force are to pick out revolutionaries as their targets from a height of ten thousand feet.

Actually modern developments in the technique of warfare have probably not affected the balance of class forces one way or the other. It is quite true that to-day no workers' revolution can hope to succeed unless it receives the aid of the workers in the armed forces of the State. But then this has been true for the last two hundred years, at least. The most cursory examination of all previous revolutions will show that their success has always been due to the disaffection of the workers in the ranks of the armed forces of the established order. (Author's note.)

one of the strongest links in the capitalist chain, the task of British workers is not to worry as to what would happen in the quite impossible event of their getting power before the workers of Europe were in a position to prevent their destruction by a vengeful world capitalism. Their task is to see to it, by every means in their power, that they are strong enough to prevent British capitalism from destroying those workers' dictatorships which will certainly be established elsewhere in the coming years. Nor indeed is this a question of the future. It is an urgently necessary task of to-day for which it is essential to mobilize the whole strength of the British working class. At the present moment, British capitalism is helping, as actively as its jealousy of Japan, its bickerings with France, and its fear of America will allow it, to suppress the Chinese Soviets, and to egg on Japan to attack the Soviet Union. To hamper and if possible to prevent action of this sort is an immediate task for the British workers. They must see to it by their present efforts that when the time for them to take power does come, there will be workers' Governments puissant to aid them both in Asia and in Europe.

The second great objection to the possibility of communist success, and this objection is raised not only by the British capitalist class, but by the capitalist classes of all the Western powers, is that in contradistinction to Russia, the capitalist classes of the West are so overwhelmingly strong in numbers, wealth, intelligence, skill, and power of organization, that the workers have no chance against them. Let us consider these supposed qualities of our capitalist classes. They are said to be, compared to the Russian capitalist class, extremely numerous. This is undeniable. But then the working class of the Western powers is also, compared to the Russian working class in 1917, extremely numerous. As a matter of fact, the proportion between the two classes is probably just about the same in the two areas. And, needless to say, it is the proportion alone which is relevant to the argument.

Again, we are told that the Western capitalist classes are far richer than was the Russian. Hence, they can command vastly greater resources both of propaganda and of intimidation; moreover, they can make expensive concessions to the workers if they ever find themselves temporarily in a tight place. In the first place, this difference of the greater wealth, and therefore power, of the capitalist classes of the West compared to the same classes in pre-1917 Russia, applies to their respective working classes to an equal degree. The Western workers, also, can command resources—by reason of their universal literacy for example—which were totally closed to the Russians. It may be objected with some force, however, that this factor at any rate is not merely a question of the relative strength and wealth of the two classes. For while the wealth of the capitalist classes of the Western states increases their strength for the purposes of class conflict in direct ratio, the higher standards of the Western working classes, as compared to the Russian workers in 1917, may weaken, if not their strength, at any rate their will for the same purpose. Hence, while it is quite unreal to suggest that the higher standards of both of the opposed classes in the West is an absolute gain to the capitalist class, yet it may be agreed that it has on this account some net gain. And, in fact, the workers have usually been able to take power at times and places where the material strength of both sides has been low: while capitalism has been strongest where the standard of life both of the workers and capitalist class has been high. An important qualification immediately arises, however. The worker's urge to struggle is not so much a question of any absolute standard of life, as of sudden changes in his standard. A sudden drop in the worker's standard of life is naturally always accompanied by a sharp increase of class antagonism: interestingly enough, however, a sudden increase of standards—more especially in the case of the increase being due, not to a rise in wage-rates, but to a temporary absorption of the unemployed into industry (owing to a war, let us say)—may also increase class antagonism. And this latter case, which can be easily substantiated historically (cf. conditions in the last stages of the war in Great Britain and for that matter in Russia) shows clearly the limited character of the advantage to the capitalist class of a high standard of life for the working class.

But the main criticism of the claim that the Western capitalist class is unassailably strong, even if we discount the foregoing qualifications altogether, is that its strength and wealth is visibly, obviously, and now rapidly, declining. Again, of course, this process has not gone anything like so far in Great Britain as in Germany or Central Europe, for example. But one has only to compare either the income or the capital possessed to-day by the capitalist class of all the capitalist states, with what it possessed as lately as 1929, to realize the magnitude of the fall. We shall be told no doubt that this is only temporary: that the slump will soon be over and that then everything will be normal again. Well, that may, or may not, be true. It is quite possible that the present conditions of acute crisis will pass: for if they do not, then in the opinion of leading capitalist authorities, from the Governor of the Bank of England downwards, world capitalism will cause such appalling misery to the workers as to produce immediate and decisive revolt. Let us suppose for a moment that the best hopes of the capitalist world are realized, and that the present crisis is overcome. Even in that event, it seems most unlikely that any boom comparable in magnitude, duration or stability to the period 1924–1929 will recur. The 1924–1929 boom itself was far less general, secure and vigorous than were the great pre-war booms of the heyday of capitalism. (In fact, in Great Britain, it was considered to be merely the mitigation of permanent depression.) In the same way it seems clear, from the amount of permanent and irreparable damage that this slump has already done to world capitalism, from the extent to which it has forced all the great states to disrupt the world free market, and from the degree to which it has sharpened imperialist antagonisms, that the next boom period, if it comes, will be comparatively short, patchy, hectic and unstable. In general, one may venture to prophesy that with the progressive break up of a unified world market, possessing a unified currency based on gold, or any other objective standard, the quality of "patchi-

70. **Governor . . . revolt.** Mr. Montagu Norman, the Governor of the Bank of England, in one of his more dramatic moments, prophesied that this would happen. His remark, however, was probably only made in an effort to impress the Americans and the French, in order to induce them to do what he told them. (Author's note.)

ness" in capitalist booms will become especially pronounced. Thus, we are probably entering a period in which, say, Great Britain will be enjoying a boom and, say, America will be in deep depression (or vice versa), while, in a third country, capitalism will have so disintegrated as to have driven the workers to take power. And not only will future booms, if any, be patchy as between country and country:
10 they will be patchy as between industry and industry in the same country. To demonstrate the gross intensification of the political instability of world capitalism which such conditions will produce would be to recapitulate the main argument of preceding chapters. It is clear that such conditions will create, on the one hand, the greatest possible disproportions between different branches of production, leading to world-wide economic catastrophes which
20 will make the present (1931–193?) slump look like a period of stable prosperity: and, on the other hand, will vastly exacerbate every imperialist antagonism and so speed up the coming of war. Moreover, the efforts at readjustment which capitalism will be forced to attempt in order to overcome these more violent crises must themselves become more and more violent. Unheard-of wage-cuts, the wholesale abolition of social services, the iron repression of
30 mass agitation, desperate attempts to crush the resistance of colonial peoples to intensified exploitation, will become the order of the day. In general, then, we may say that while there may be further periods of capitalist boom, they will have the characteristics which the philosopher Hobbes attributed to the life of primitive man—they will be nasty, brutish and short.

There does not seem to be room for doubt that, neglecting the periodic ups and downs of
40 the trade cycle, the whole trend of the wealth, and consequently of the strength, of the capitalist classes of the West is steeply downwards. Although it may be true that they are, in certain exceptionally favoured spots, such as Great Britain, still too strong to be overthrown by the workers, they will not long remain so. For the ruling classes of the West to pin their hopes of defeating the workers upon the fact that their wealth is incomparably greater than that
50 of the Russian ruling class in 1917, is to rely

on a wasting asset. Truly, the workers are not likely to achieve power in those places where the capitalist class is still very rich and strong: but then in one country after another the capitalist class is becoming progressively poorer and weaker.

There is one further factor which qualifies the power of the capitalist classes of the West. Their internal unity is by no means complete. What these classes now need for their self- 60 preservation is an iron conservatism. But some sections of these classes, the intelligentsia and salariat in particular, have long traditions of liberalism. These sections of the capitalist class are unfitted to enter upon the policy of repressive violence, which their class interest now urgently requires. It is true that up to a point these individuals unconsciously play a part very useful to the main mass of capitalist conservatism. For the propaganda of liberal, paci- 70 fist and equalitarian ideas, which they maintain, serves to cover up the otherwise naked reaction of the policy of all capitalist Governments to-day.

As, however, the situation grows more desperate, such a smoke-screen of liberalism may well become more of an embarrassment than an assistance to the governing class. For it hampers that freedom of swift and ruthless action which a hard-pressed class requires. Then 80 dawns the day of what we have called the advocates of action—the Mussolinis, the Churchills and the Hitlers. The "liberal-minded statesmen," the "enlightened intellectuals," the whole paraphernalia of constitutionalism, are bundled off the stage. It is at this point, when the final struggle approaches, when the economic situation has become desperate beyond anything which we in Great Britain have guessed at, that the Western capitalist class will begin seri- 90 ously to lose its cohesion. Some of those sections which possess long liberal traditions will simply oppose the new fascistic methods, without facing the fact that the only alternative to their employment is a surrender of power to a working-class dictatorship. Such liberal opposition may to a significant extent, hamper the forces of the capitalist class. Another and much smaller section of the ruling class, faced at last with inescapable choice, will break away 10 entirely and throw in its lot with the working class. Marx defined this process very clearly, as early as 1848.

"Finally," he wrote, "when the class war is about to be fought to a finish, disintegration of the ruling class and the old order of society becomes so active, so acute, that a small part of the ruling class breaks away to make common cause with the revolutionary class, the class which holds the future in its hands. Just as in former days, part of the nobility went over to the bourgeoisie, so now part of the bourgeoisie goes over to the proletariat. Especially does this happen in the case of some of the bourgeois ideologues, who have achieved a theoretical understanding of the historical movement as a whole."

(Incidentally, the last sentence of Marx sums up almost the whole duty of the honest intellectual of to-day. His duty is to master "the historical movement as a whole." If he does so he can have no possible doubt as to the necessity of throwing in his lot with the workers.)

The third "fatal" objection to the success of communism in Britain is, we are told, the "psychology" of the British workers. Stripped of a mass of quite meaningless nonsense about "the national psychology," this objection is an appeal to the fact—and it is a fact—that sections of the British workers have been strongly infected with a capitalist point of view. (There is nothing in the least peculiar to Britain about this phenomenon: it has occurred in America, in Holland, in Sweden, wherever, in fact, capitalism has been until quite recently fairly successful and prosperous. And the capitalist classes of such countries have solemnly assured themselves that "their" workers—their good-hearted British, Dutch, Swedish or American workers—have a heaven-sent immunity from the communist bacillus.) Now this third objection is obviously consequential upon the second. The permeation of strata of the British workers by a capitalist point of view is simply an expression of the wealth and strength which the British capitalists have hitherto enjoyed. And it is clear that if this wealth declines, so

4. "Finally . . . whole." Quoted from Marx's *Communist Manifesto;* see p. 626.

also will its former owners' hold upon the workers' minds. It is worth while, however, to examine the basis of the present degree of capitalist control over the workers' psychology. The permeation of the workers by capitalist ideas is effected in several ways. The essential basis is an ability to give some sections of the workers a taste of middle-class economic security and sufficiency. American capitalism probably did this in the years between 1923 and 1929 to the greatest extent. A locomotive engineer (or as we in Britain would say, an engine driver) on, say, the Pennsylvania Railroad, a plumber, or any building trade craftsman in New York City, really did in those years enjoy the standard of living of a distinctly successful retail tradesman in Great Britain.

Moreover, at an earlier stage, American capitalism was unrivalled at providing the second instrument for promoting a capitalist point of view amongst the workers: it actually did offer a certain significant number of opportunities for the workers to make money, leave their class and become fully fledged American property-owners, living by virtue of their ownership of the means of production. But although American capitalism exhibited both these characteristics to an unrivalled degree, it never exhibited them for so long a period or so consistently as did British capitalism. The British railway engine driver may never have owned a motor-car; but he may have been in the apparently secure possession of the basic necessities of middle-class comfort—a satisfactory house, ample food, good clothes, some pocket-money—for the whole of his life—and he may remember that his father, who was also an engine driver before him, had the same good fortune. In other words, British capitalism by reason of the immense super-profits of its empire was able to maintain in comparative comfort a "labour aristocracy" of skilled workers for several generations. And in its earlier period, it provided enough examples of workers rising into the ranks of the property-owning class seriously to affect the minds of the whole working class. Moreover, British capitalism kept up until very recently yet another method by which the most active and intelligent workers were systematically "declassed." It possessed a comparatively well-developed educational ladder, by which the cleverest sons of workers could climb to a higher education by means of scholarships, and then be absorbed into administrative posts (the Civil Service) or become teachers or technicians. The rungs of this ladder are now being cut away, however, by the educational axe. Moreover, the number of administrative and technical posts open to this class of candidate is now rapidly decreasing, with the contraction of British industry and the difficulties of British imperialism, involving the surrender of administrative posts to the native middle class. These characteristics of a given capitalism are the indispensable basis for a capitalist point of view amongst sections of the workers: but upon this basis the ruling class seeks to build a whole variety of institutions designed to confirm and spread its ideas. The same wealth which allows the capitalists to maintain a labour aristocracy in comfort enables them to organize all sorts of institutions for controlling the minds of the rest of the working class. Thus a whole section of the Press grows up, the function of which is to cater for the tastes and aspirations of the slum workers, tastes which capitalism itself has so brutally restricted. Every form of gambling—in Britain predominantly betting on horse-racing —is organized on the scale of a national industry: or, for unfortunate workers of more earnest tastes, "missions" of all sorts, religious, educational, and charitable are sent down to the slums: and now the great twin weapons of the cinema and the wireless are unsparingly used.

In general, we may conclude that these efforts at the permeation of the workers will not lack some success, so long as the capitalist class which is using them remains rich and powerful. But so soon as its wealth declines, so must its ability to maintain these mental controls over its workers. In the end, therefore, this third "fatal objection" to the success of communism in Britain, or in any of the Western capitalist States, boils down to a repetition of the fact that Western capitalism will not be overthrown so long as it remains rich, strong and successful. Let us admit this most readily. For the whole point at issue is the question of whether it is in fact possible for these national capitalisms to remain rich, strong and successful. The first half of this book was devoted to a demonstration which (it is submitted) drove us to the conclusion that the national capitalisms of the West could not in the nature of things permanently arrest their present decline. Hence, the capitalist point of view which is held by, for example, some sections of the British workers, and which at first sight does appear a formidable obstacle to the success of communism in Britain, will disappear, is indeed now disappearing, with great rapidity. For the economic basis of imperial super-profits by which it has alone been possible for the British ruling class to maintain it, is now also in progressive disintegration. (One factor which tends to maintain the hold of the capitalists over the workers' brains, is the efforts of the social democratic functionaries, whose role it is to perform just this service to the governing class. Even they, however, will not indefinitely be able to make the bricks of a capitalist point of view in the workers' minds, without the straw of a share of capitalist super-profits in the workers' pockets.)

We can now attempt a general estimate of the weight which should be attached to these three "fatal objections" to the success of communism in Great Britain. For while we have, it is submitted, shown the relative and temporary character of these objections, which the British capitalists naturally delude themselves into supposing are absolute and eternal, we are not for a moment denying that they exist. What has been shown, it is suggested, is that all three objections, the objection that "Britain cannot feed herself," the objection of the overwhelming power of the British capitalist class compared to the Russian capitalist class, and finally the objection of the capitalist psychology of the British workers, are all objections based on conditions which are more or less rapidly disappearing. A thing, however, must exist in order for it to be possible to disappear. Hence, these conditions certainly do to some extent exist to-day. We must ask, therefore, that most crucial and most difficult question, which we posed earlier in these pages—the quantitative question of "How long?" How long, for example, will these objections to the success of communism in Britain persist to a significant degree?

He would be no better than a charlatan who would pretend to give any precise answer to such a question. It has been one of the arguments of these pages that the general trend of human development has at last come within the range of human cognition: that we are at last beginning to know enough about the past to be able to produce the historic curve of events for a little distance into the future, with a margin of error not too great to make it useless to come to certain conclusions of a general character. (And there is no room for doubt that the refusal of all the theorists of the capitalist class to do so, has nothing whatever to do with the scientific caution which they profess, but is dependent upon the painful nature of the conclusions to which any serious appraisal of the facts would drive them.) But this does not mean that our knowledge is yet adequate for any but broad and general conclusions about the future.

Let us first give the fullest possible weight to the factors of strength in the capitalist position. There exists in Britain, no doubt, a certain tradition of social intercourse between the classes which, while it is in many respects markedly inferior to that of France or America, is very different from anything which was known in pre-war Russia or Germany. The long-continued expansion and the incomparable stability of British capitalism ever since 1850 have undoubtedly established traditions of class collaboration which are only gradually being broken down by the repeated shocks of the present governing class offensive against the workers. Such transitory, but still noticeable, social phenomena as these allow the members of the British capitalist class, fixing their eyes resolutely on these purely local British conditions, to convince themselves that the communist position, while perhaps strong in theory, has no application to Britain. Conditions such as these allow those trusted allies of the British capitalists, the members of the British Labour Party, to convince themselves that communist methods are useless for the purpose of appealing to British workers. And, in truth, if we concentrated our attention on the internal situation of Great Britain, on the balance of class forces within her shores; on the present psychology of her workers; on the abilities of her ruling class; on the obstructive strength of her social democracy; on the shifts and devices still open to all those who desire to maintain the rule of the capitalist class, we might be disposed to agree that the task before the British communist movement was very formidable, and that success must be long postponed.

But to confine our appraisal to the internal situation, though it is a common error even amongst genuine sympathizers with the workers' cause, leads to an estimate of the prospects of British communism totally at variance with reality. For we must never forget for one moment that British communism is part of a world-wide movement, the successes, or failures, of any part of which quickly react upon the prospect of all its other parts: and that British capitalism is, to a degree unparalleled by any other national capitalism, intertwined at a thousand vital points with the capitalism of the whole world. Thus, when we raise our eyes from our island, the shores of which have too often marked the limits of vision for British social theorists, the scene changes. If the British people were an independent isolated community inhabiting a little planet of their own (and yet, by some magical process, able to draw their present imperial tribute), then the rule of the British capitalists might not have reached by many years its inevitable term: by a mixture of class collaboration where that was possible, and of the unflinching repression of the workers (which British rulers have always known very well how to use when they had to) their days of privilege might have continued for some time yet.

How different is the real situation. Britain is but an island in a sea which encompasses the whole world. No special providence reserves for her a peculiar destiny. On the contrary, her immense imperial possessions, scattered in every quarter of the globe, make it certain that her fate will be especially dependent upon that of the rest of the world. And when we shift our appraisal to the prospects of communism and of capitalism on the world stage, a different picture presents itself to our eyes. Only in a few exceptional areas do we find anything at all comparable to the economic conditions which have allowed of the comparatively pacific class relationships which we discover in Britain. On the contrary, we find in area after area of the earth's surface a political situation dissimilar to that of Britain. We find that in such areas the capitalist class has not now, nor ever has had, sufficient wealth to impose its outlook upon considerable sections of the workers; that it has had neither the skill in collaboration nor the decision in repression, which has characterized the social policy of the British ruling class; that a dozen different political complications have forbidden the capitalist classes of such areas to devote themselves to the task of controlling their workers; that in many areas, as in the colonies of the great empires, the capitalist class is largely of another race and colour from the workers.

Those possibilities of subtle and imperceptible social re-adjustments which seem so real in Britain are utterly out of the question in most of the rest of the world, and consequently communist theory and communist methods are the only ones which apply to the social conditions of nine-tenths of the inhabited globe. And if this is the case, then we may be assured that in a very short while they will apply also to such countries as Great Britain. Britain has her own history and consequently her own peculiar characteristics: but if we suppose that she will be allowed to work out her destiny in isolation, unaffected by the events which are unfolding themselves in the rest of the world, then we delude ourselves. The truth is rather that Britain is quite peculiarly vulnerable to the reactions of events which may take place at the other side of the globe. Her whole economy is based to an unparalleled degree upon profits drawn from the exploitation of her Empire. Colonial revolts already menace essential parts of her system. The social reactions which are bound to follow the crash of the high-piled pyramid of her super-profits, may well be especially violent and sudden. If communist theory and practice is the only possible policy for the working class of the world as a whole, then it is the only possible policy for the workers of Great Britain also.

A. P. HERBERT

As *Punch, or the London Charivari* is to *The New Yorker,* so is Sir Alan Patrick Herbert to E. B. White (p. 772), although the two men are altogether dissimilar in personality and temperament. Herbert is a big, bluff, hearty type of Englishman not unlike, in appearance, the "man about town" whom he so deliciously satirizes. He was born in London in 1890 and graduated from New College, Oxford (1914). He served in the British Navy during the First World War until 1918, when he was wounded and discharged. For a time he studied law, but although he was admitted to the Bar in 1918 he never practiced. He has had two great professional associations in his life: with *Punch,* for which he began to contribute as early as 1919 and on the staff of which he became a steady writer; and with Parliament, in which he has represented the Oxford constituency since 1935. He was knighted in 1945.

Herbert has lived in a houseboat on the Thames, served as a brilliant fictional reporter in the Second World War, distinguished himself as an after-dinner speaker and as a writer of operetta librettos and comic verse, and been a champion of anti-prohibitionists and a fighter in the cause of good English, and a general essayist on the *mores* of contemporary England, with special emphasis upon the whys and wherefores of metropolitan city society. He has written several light novels, of which *The Water-Gypsies* (1930) is a particularly good example. His amusing and witty comments give at first the impression of being candied pills; but there is always medicine in his pills, as even his most light-hearted satires upon reading, club life, foreign affairs, the amusements of the London cockney, and golf players exhibit in great exuberance. His most solid and praiseworthy accomplishment as a member of Parliament, however, has been his work leading to the Matrimonial Causes Bill of 1937, which did a great deal to liberalize the antiquated laws of England pertaining to divorce.

from The Man about Town

The Court Theatre

GEORGE and I belong to that distinguished army of men who have been called to the Bar and failed to answer the call; and it is on the doings of such men in the great world that the reputation of the Bar for high intelligence is largely founded. Barristers flatter themselves that they see life in all its aspects—and this is true in the sense that the producers of French farces and drawing-room plays see it. When people liken the Law to good Drama they make a great mistake; but if they likened a distinguished lawyer to a bad dramatist they would in most cases hit the nail on the head. For each, apparently, lives in an entirely fictitious and histrionic world of his own, with a standard of conduct never met with in the world of men; and each makes a great deal of money out of it.

So we do our best to keep our practising colleagues in touch with real life, and now and then take a little lunch with them, and follow it up with a pleasant afternoon in the Chancery Court, listening to some learned men being quietly witty about Contingent Remainders and Executory Devises.

Our last visit was unfortunate. As, of course, you know, one Court, or set of Courts, transacts the kindred business of Probate, Divorce, and Admiralty; and there, under the common symbol of the gilt Anchor, the Freedom of the Seas and the Freedom of Divorce are gloriously upheld together. George and I were bent on hearing an interesting case concerning the rights and duties of a Cornish harbour-master in connection with the carcass of a dead whale. We approached a door marked "Counsel Only," and were admitted under protest. The court was curiously crowded, and a cloud of counsel hung listening intently inside the door. Young barristers are always ready to learn, and evidently the dead whale must have raised some nice legal point to have drawn so many from their work.

A man's voice, deep and vibrant with moral indignation, was heard to say: "DARLING, I AM LONELY WITHOUT YOU. COME BACK SOON. . . ."

"George," I gasped, "this is the wrong court!"

From *The Man About Town* by A. P. Herbert, reprinted by permission of Doubleday and Company, Inc.

"Yes, I knew that," whispered George. "That's Mrs. Plum in the box." And he gazed with rapture at Mrs. Plum.

More barristers came in, and now there was scarce standing-room. Yet this was none of your *causes célèbres*, and occupied next day a bare half-column in the morning papers. Mrs. Plum was comparatively unknown to the public. No, the "draw" was Sir Charles Gupp, K.C., and on him the attention of the barristers was fixed, their interest in the case being, of course, more purely technical than George's.

Sir Charles was conducting a "deadly cross-examination" of Mrs. Plum. Sir Charles specializes in murders and co-respondents, and either he is a superb actor or he has a mind like a sewer; in either case he earns about forty thousand pounds a year.

He said to Mrs. Plum:

"Did you write that, Mrs. Plum? You did? And on the 15th did you write to your husband in *these* terms: 'Darling Hubby,—Your Tootles misses you. Flo died yesterday, and it's raining hard'? You did? Ha!"

Sir Charles put his foot on the seat, rested his elbow on his knee and weighed his words.

"That was on the 15th. And on the 16th, the day after you sent that affectionate communication to your husband in India, you were *dancing the Foxtrot* with Mr. *Spry?*"

"One can't dance the Foxtrot alone," said Mrs. Plum.

"Exactly," said Sir Charles, with a very moral light in his eye. "And you and Mr. Spry—"

"What is a Foxtrot?" said the Judge.

"Melud," said Sir Charles, "it appears" (appears!) "to be a kind of dance, etc., etc."

"That was at the Palais de Danse, was it not?"

"Yes."

"Yes—I *thought* so."

"What is the Palais de Danse," said the Judge.

"Melud. . . . etc., etc."

"Now tell the jury when it was you first met Mr. Spry, will you please, Mrs. Plum?"

"I first *saw* him on the Underground, two years ago."

"Two years ago! That would be about six months after Mr. Plum sailed for India? Ye-es. And what happened when you met Mr. Spry on the Underground?"

"I didn't exactly meet him, Sir Charles. He gave me his seat."

"Oh, he gave you his seat, did he? Can you recall your conversation on that occasion?"

"He took off his hat and said, 'Won't you take my seat, Madam?'"

"*I see*," said Sir Charles in an encouraging tone, as one humouring a child into a confession of naughtiness. "And didn't it strike you as a little *odd*, Mrs. Plum, that this man, a Perfect Stranger to you, should come up and *accost* you in this manner?—No?—Oh!—Didn't it occur to you, as a married woman with a husband in India, that that perhaps was the kind of man your husband *would rather you didn't meet?* No? Well—very well," said Sir Charles tolerantly, and paused awhile to let the thing sink in. Then, with challenging severity: "And IN FACT you *did* meet him again? Quite soon?"

"Yes."

"Ah! How was that?"

"At an 'At Home.' It was a coincidence."

"Oh," said Sir Charles, "you met at an 'At Home'? And it was a coincidence?"

"Yes, it was a coincidence. We both knew Mrs. Gregor."

"I see," said Sir Charles, nodding kindly, "a coincidence. Tell the jury what happened then."

"Well, we were introduced, and—and——"

"Yes, Mrs. Plum?" said Sir Charles sharply, cocking his head like an exceedingly wicked robin.

"We talked," said Mrs. Plum.

"I thought people never talked when they were at home," said the Judge with a benevolent smile, and a roar of laughter shook the court.

"You *talked?*" said Sir Charles in a surprised tone. "Can you recall the subject of *that* conversation, Mrs. Plum?" And all of us realized that the previous conversation she had remembered had been somehow very, very damaging.

"No? Very well. What happened then? You went home? Alone? *Not* alone? *I* see. You went home with somebody else. Who was that, Mrs. Plum?"

"Mr. Spry saw me home."

"Mr. Spry? Wasn't that a little remarkable, Mrs. Plum? The first time you meet this man—

if we exclude the encounter on the Underground Railway—he takes you home from a *party*. Isn't that a little *odd*, Mrs. Plum? No?"

"It was a black fog and there were no cabs running." (*Laughter.*)

"O-o-h!" said the righteous man, standing bolt-upright. "So Mr. Spry took you home in a *fog*, did he? (*Snigger.*) And in the fog I daresay you took his arm, Mrs. Plum? (*Snigger.*) Or perhaps he took *yours?*" (*Loud laughter.*)

"Of *course*," said Mrs. Plum hotly. "You couldn't——"

"Of *course?*" And now Sir Charles was very stern. "Really, Mrs. Plum, that is hardly what you mean, is it? The first time you meet this man——"

"It was pitch-*black*," said Mrs. Plum. "You couldn't see your hand in front of your face."

"And you didn't see *his*, eh, Mrs. Plum?" snapped the learned wit, and again we roared with laughter, manly, vigorous, refreshing laughter.

"He didn't take my arm," said Mrs. Plum; "I took his."

"Ah, it wasn't too dark for *that?*" (*Laughter.*)

Sir Charles, like other K.C.'s, knows how to make the most of a good joke, and this was too good to be left alone.

"You couldn't have seen your hand in front of your face—but, of course, that wasn't where you *put* your hand, was it, Mrs. Plum?—(*Loud laughter.*)—Putting it in front of your face wouldn't have been quite so useful?" (*Laughter.*)

"No," said poor Mrs. Plum sullenly.

"Or so pleasant?—(*Laughter.*)—So you found this gentleman's arm without much difficulty, Mrs. Plum?—(*Laughter.*)—In spite of the fog? —(*Laughter.*)—And how long," said Sir Charles genially, for by now it was quite evident that Mrs. Plum was done for—"how long did this agreeable journey continue?" (*Laughter.*)

"About half an hour."

"Ah!" said Sir Charles profoundly.

✿ ✿ ✿ ✿ ✿

Oh, when we speak of the Divorce Court as disgusting, let us at least thank Heaven for the spotless mind and personality of Sir Charles Gupp, K.C.!

A *Little Riot*

I am one of those men who always know immediately what I think about everything. I have judgment and decision. Like some of the papers. I know at once whether a man is a Bolshevist or a Patriot. And I say so.

I am also a man of unusual personal courage.

So when I heard that a riot had been arranged to take place in Trafalgar Square I deliberately stayed in Trafalgar Square. I stayed near the entrance to the subway to the Tube.

I distrust the partisan accounts of riots. I distrust the Communist papers when they say that the capitalist police made a brutal and unprovoked assault on the demonstrators, felled three women, and threw a baby under an omnibus.

I distrust the other papers when they say that half the Unemployed had obviously been working full time for the past six months, and the remaining half were obviously alien enemies who had never worked at all and never would.

It was time for an impartial observer to observe a riot and discover the truth. I stood by my burrow and admired the scene. It was dusk. Trafalgar Square was beautiful and dim in a blue haze. The lights came out in the shops. Lord Nelson melted slowly into the mist. I reflected on him. The lions grew black and very large. Someone told me once that all the ground under the Nelson Column and under the lions and under the fountains and under the National Gallery is occupied by vast wine-cellars. I reflected on that.

I admired the policemen, the calm magnificent men; I admired their horses, shiny and magnificent, but not so calm. (What is it they put on horses to make them shine so?) The policemen have all put on an expression of calm to make the public think that nothing is going to happen. As I reflect on this, the rumor spreads that the rioters are approaching from the N.W.

A crowd collects, waiting for the riot to begin. The man next to me tells me that if I keep moving I shall not be arrested. So we keep moving. We move round and round the railings of the subway entrance, followed by a huge policeman. It is like Musical Chairs. It is awful

when we are on the far side, away from the steps; I feel sure that I shall be caught on that side when the music stops—or rather when the band begins to play. But my friend tells me that if I stop still for a moment I shall be arrested at sight. I am afraid he is a Bolshevist. But he is rather a nice one. He seems to like me. He takes me for a Bolshevist.

It is no good. I cannot move on any more. I am going to stand still. Now I shall be arrested.

The huge policeman is looking at me severely. A nice man. He is not going to arrest me after all. He seems to like me. He takes me for a Patriot.

Down the road comes the procession, cheering aggressively. They have been told they cannot have a meeting in the Square. They have been meeting for three hours in Hyde Park already. From my experience of meetings that should be enough for any man. Why should they have another meeting here, blocking the traffic on a week-day? Especially when they have been told not to. . . . I am for Law and Order.

But why not let them meet in the Square? They can't say anything redder than they said in the Park. And it is my experience that meetings obstruct traffic much less thoroughly than riots. I am for common sense.

Thank heaven, I know what I think about things.

The procession has become a Mob. The Mob has broken through the policemen. They have mounted the—what is it?—the lintel?—the plinth. They are booing unpleasantly at the policemen. They have raised the Red Flag. It is the Revolution. It is all up.

The poor policemen! I'm sorry for them. It is humiliating. My Bolshevist is delighted. He says they will never get "the boys" out of the Square now. There are too many.

"The boys" are being turned off the plinth by two policemen. They go very rapidly. It is not the Revolution after all.

There is a poor old Englishman arguing with my policeman. He is not a good arguer. He is almost crying. He says, "Why *shouldn't* I go in there? It's a place of recreation, ain't it?" The policeman says, "Gerreralong outer-this," and pushes him with a huge hand. I am a Bolshevist.

A dirty little alien is yowling like a wild cat at my policeman. I am a Patriot.

There is an ugly temper abroad; but nobody seems to know exactly what to do next. I am in an ugly temper too, but I know exactly what to do. I must get round these railings to the sub-way entrance; for I was caught on the wrong side. I knew it would happen.

Everybody about me is yowling aimlessly. My Bolshevist says suddenly, "Gaw! them something 'orses!" and bolts for the Tube. The horses are charging.

I stand firm. They are charging in the opposite direction. There they go, the calm magnificent men. They have drawn those terrible long staves, truncheons, or batons. They are hitting people on the head with them. They have knocked down an old man—the old man I saw just now. Shame! They have knocked down another man—the dirty little alien. Capital!

Why do they hit the people on the head? Those shiny horses are surely enough to make a man a Patriot.

They are enough for *me*. Goodness! they are charging this way. I am off. I surrender. I will read the *Morning Post*.—I promise.

I am down the steps. I am underground. Thank heaven! Now I am a Bolshevist again. Surely no horse will follow me down the sub-way.

Here is my Bolshevist friend again. We peer through the bottom of the railings at the flying hoofs of the policeman's horses. They strike fire from the pavement. It is picturesque—from underground.

I see two policemen with their heads cut open. Broken bottles! Ugh! No wonder they hit people on the head. I wonder if they hit the right man.

My friend says, "Ain't you glad you was born in England?" I answer, "Yes." He thinks I am ironical. He is pleased.

It is all over. The mob is cowed. I am cowed. We creep out. The Square is clear. We creep home. Wherever I creep there is a policeman on a huge horse. I cower in the doorway of a jeweller's shop. A policeman says "Move on there"; and he waves a hand to direct me to-wards the stern end of six other horses strung across the pavement. Policemen's horses are never supposed to kick or to tread on one's toes. I know that. But do the horses know it? I enter the jeweller's shop. I want to buy a diamond ring.

I emerge, having bought nothing. I creep home. I am glad I have discovered the truth. I am glad I know what I think about it all.

Do you?

Coral Island

(*A Novel for the Film*)

CHAPTER I. "UP ANCHOR"

It was sunset in the little harbour of Rumble, and the sloop *White Witch* was getting under way. The anchor was hove short, and in the catheads stood a young girl, busy with the pawl. The jib was already hoisted, and as

MARION TARVER

stepped aside to avoid being flung into the water by the flapping sail one saw that her hair was of pure gold.

By the mast stood a young Englishman, clean-limbed, limber, and slim; and now he hauled on the throat halyard, which was jammed in the jaws of the gaff, and now on the peak halyard, which was foul of the topping-lift.

"Anchor's a-trip," cried the girl; and "Hell!" replied her husband. For

JOHN TARVER

had that day taken Marion to wife in the little church upon the hill. And now, on the first of the ebb, they were putting out upon the sea of life. In this frail craft (fifteen tons displacement and forty feet over all) they were to voyage round the world and see strange things.

How strange they little knew.

THE SPIRIT OF DRAKE

And now they were away, these two, alone upon the ocean. The Needles light bore N.E. by E.¾E. astern. The *White Witch* bounded down the Channel of Old England, griping a little, for she carried too much weather-helm.

The girl sat at the tiller, her hair like spun gold in the last rays of the setting sun.

"I have forgotten the charts," said John at last, as he re-spoke his love. "We must go back."

"What matter?" cried the fearless girl. "There must be no turning back.

LOVE IS OUR CHART."

Their lips met.

A squall carried away the topsail.

"Luff," he said simply.

CHAPTER II. SHIPWRECK

With a gesture of despair, the man turned away from his contemplation of the empty sea, and his eye ranged for the thousandth time the yellow shore, empty also but for a few stray snapping turtles, salamanders, sea-frogs, and tropical newts. He was in rags, and his face bore the marks of hardship and suffering; but one could see that once, at least, he had been a clean-limbed limber young Englishman. His head ached, and he could not think clearly. His foot struck a broken spar on which was painted in large letters the words *White Witch*. He stared at it, uncomprehending. The words struck no answering chord of memory. What was the *White Witch*? And who, for the matter of that, was he? He remembered nothing but a tremendous concussion. Before that ALL WAS BLANK. He knew now that he was alone on the island. He had walked all round it, hallooing. No one had answered.

At that moment there was a rustle in the undergrowth of yams and upas-trees which fringed the shore. And there emerged on all fours a most beautiful girl. Her hair was like spun gold. She was dressed quite simply in the main-sheet of the *White Witch*, skilfully worked into a dress with torn fragments of the storm-jib, stitched together with pine needles.

She stared at him, frightened; and his face seemed to strike no answering chord of memory.

"Who are you?" he said.

"I do not know," she answered. "I have lost my memory."

"So have I."

"I heard you hallooing," she said, "but I was afraid to halloo back."

His jaw set.

"YOU NEED HAVE NO FEAR," he said.

She held out her hand with a frank gesture.

"PALS, EH?" she said.

"Pals," he replied.

CHAPTER III. CALM

That night he built her a rude hut with the trunks of catalpa-trees, flanked by great boulders which he carried from the shore, and lashed together with tarred string and reef-points from the wreckage of the *White Witch*. The roof was of raw hide, the property of two buck wapiti, which he killed by the power of the human eye and a few bad words in common use at sea. Over the whole he put two coats of boat-varnish and a layer of pitch. In three hours the hut was ready.

Himself, he slept rough in the long grass outside. It rained.

CHAPTER IV. PALS

The days slipped by. Boy and girl, like brother and sister, they did together the busy and exhausting work of an island, sharing its disappointments, its simple pleasures, as comrades, as companions, as pals.

The little camp grew. On the second day he built a laundry for her, diverting a river for the supply of water. On the third he built a cook-house, and constructed a rough oven out of an old anchor. On the fourth he caught two mountain-goats, and built a dairy. By the sixth day they seemed to lack nothing, and he sat down and thought.

Meanwhile, Marion was not idle. Milking the goats, feeding the turtles (she was very fond of animals)—always she sang at her work; and all day her bell-like voice was heard booming across the island. One day she rescued a young turtle which had ventured out of its depth.

Two things only disturbed the even tenor of their thoughts. They could not remember who they were. And no one came to take them away.

And every night John slept rough in the long grass, protecting his pal. And nearly always it rained.

CHAPTER V. DEEP WATER

One day, wandering through the forest with his home-made axe, the man caught sight of his reflection in a stream, and stood appalled. He had grown a beard.

Without hesitation, he diverted the stream. And on the way home he hacked off the beard.

"Why have you done that?" said the woman at late dinner. "I do not know," he replied, avoiding her frank gaze.

10 The next day she crept out to the stream and looked in it. What she saw there amazed her. She had not known that she was beautiful. She had forgotten all that. But her nose was shining.

She went back thoughtfully, and powdered her nose with a little flour which she had made from the bread-fruit. She did not know why she did this.

NATURE, THE GREAT TEACHER

That night, as John looked at her across the yams, some hidden chord of his being seemed
20 to vibrate. He glanced at her curiously. She wore the same frock still, and by now the main-sheet was sadly frayed; yet there was a something——. What was it?

"Pal," he said,

"YOU LOOK DIFFERENT TONIGHT.

What have you done?"

She made no reply. There are some secrets that must be for ever hidden from man, deep-locked in woman's breast.

30 "Tell me about your work," she said softly.

"Today," he said, "I built a beacon on Prospect Point. Tomorrow—but there, I'm boring you."

"Go on," she said gently. "Somehow I feel that one day you will do something much bigger than—than all this, something bigger than you have ever done."

Their eyes met. And suddenly he knew that they were Man and Woman—boy and girl no
40 longer. And he loved her—loved her

WITH EVERY FIBRE OF HIS BEING.

His pulses drummed. Come what might, she should never know.

The next day he cut down the greater part of the forest, and built a ten-foot stockade about the hut.

"Why have you done that?" she asked.

"Snakes," he said evasively.

Day by day the man worked harder. He had
50 built a dam, a breakwater, three cairns, and a semaphore. He had built a rough furnace and a rough harbour. Then from the hollow trunk of the banyan he began to build a rough boat. But this he kept from the woman. All day he worked with his hands, hoping thus to occupy his mind; and in the evening he spoke in loud tones, lest the drumming of his pulses should betray him.

Work! Work! If he did not work he knew
60 that one day he would blurt out

THE GHASTLY SECRET

of his love.

Sometimes he threw stones at her to conceal his passion.

How he worked! He gave names to every promontory, stream, and gully in the island. Along the hill-tops ran a chain of beacons, cairns, and rough signalling stations. Huts and workshops dotted the shore. The forest had nearly disappeared. The whole face of the is-
70 land was changed.

Thus once again in the long struggle between Man and Nature, man had been victorious.

And secretly the boat advanced.

One day he cut down the last tree and made a rough mast with it. From the bark he made a rude sail. The boat was ready. And now there was nothing more that he could do. With no manual labor to occupy him he would be
80 forced to speak his love. Unless the boat. . . .

He walked twice round the island, renaming the promontories.

He looked out to sea. There was nothing to be seen, nothing but coral reefs and the black fins of sharks. The island, like so many of its kind, was off the trade-routes. The boat was their only hope. . . .

He pushed the boat into the water. It sank immediately.
90 And now there was no way out—none.

He looked out to sea again. But yes, there *was* a way out.

LIFE—OR HONOUR?

CHAPTER VII. JETTISON

The woman was in the library, reading a rough book which he had made for her.

"I am going away," he said simply. "You will be safe now. I have killed the snake. If you should see a sail, depress the lever in Prospect Valley and twenty beacons will be immediately ignited. Good-bye."

"Where are you going?" she said.

"I judge that we are no great distance from some Continent or other," he replied. "I go to bring help."

"Can I not go with you?"

"THE BOAT WILL NOT HOLD TWO," he said evasively.

"I do not fear death," she said.

"I go to save you from

WORSE THAN DEATH."

"You are a very brave man," she answered, wondering.

"Good-bye, pal," he said and, turning on his heel, strode down to the shore.

She gave a choking cry.

"——!"

But he did not turn his head. And even now she could not reveal the secret he so little suspected.

East and West, from Piccadilly to the far Pacific,

A WOMAN'S HEART

is the same.

CHAPTER VIII. SALVAGE

When she saw him stride into the sea she guessed at once his desperate design. He intended to swim to the nearest Continent. At all costs he must be stopped. It was too far.

She ran down and followed him through the clear blue tropical water. The turtles scattered before her, uttering their curious flute-like cries. And suddenly she realized that she could not swim.

He was far out now, swimming strongly with both arms. But what was that, away to the west, black and sinister and flashing in the sun? Her blood ran cold. It was the fin of a shark.

Something nudged her. It was Tulip, her fa-vorite turtle, nosing for food; Tulip whose child she had befriended.

Quick as thought she jumped upon his back, and whispering in his ear urged the huge creature after her unsuspecting pal.

The intelligent beast seemed to realize that something was required of him and plied his flippers with a will.

And now began a grim race. The shark was swift, but he had farther to go; and Tulip was the fleetest turtle in all the Pacific.

Still the shark gained rapidly. Now he was close astern, and Marion could feel his hot breath on her shoulder. Leaning back she struck the cruel monster a stinging blow in the face with her open hand.

The shark bit his lip, reddening at the insult.

But the moment's delay was priceless. In an instant the man had vaulted on to the back of the turtle, and Tulip, with his double freight, was paddling briskly for the shore.

The shark, with a snarl of baffled rage, headed out to sea, and was never seen again.

CHAPTER IX. HAVEN

Their lips met.

CHAPTER X. TEMPTATION

Athwart the coral reef the blue sea murmured listlessly. The moon rose out of the ocean like some great sphere. The hum of the salamander thrilled languorous in the distance; and somewhere could be heard the sensuous cheeping of an axolotl.

They were alone with Nature.

The man's brow darkened. He tore himself from her arms.

"You did wrong to save my life," he said; "our lips must not meet again."

"We are alone with Nature," she replied. "We have flung off the artificial trappings of the world we knew. Before heaven we are man and wife.

"WHERE THERE IS NO SOCIETY THERE CAN BE NO SIN."

"Sin is not the product of society," he answered, "it concerns the soul."

Somewhere in the undergrowth a chipmunk mewed, calling to his mate. Along the chequered sand the fireflies glowed, lighting in a thousand windows

THE LAMPS OF LOVE.

But he—there came into his mind dim pictures of the past.

The playing-fields at Eton. . . . Roll-Call. . . . The Terrace of the House of Commons. . . . His mother. . . .

10 He did not know what these pictures were, or whence they came. But the figures in them, so noble and gracious, seemed to be speaking to him a message from a world which he did not remember in a language which he did not understand.

Ah, the pitiless irony of Fate! For it is written: Man may build bridges out of a dead tree, but he cannot at will construct a parson.

"Life without Honour is an empty thing," he said simply. "Good-night."

20 All night he roamed the island, renaming the promontories for the third time.

CHAPTER XI. INTERMEZZO

Years passed.

CHAPTER XII. MONSOON

How she bored him!

CHAPTER XIII. NOCTURNE

How he bored her!

CHAPTER XIV. THE DOLDRUMS

The dull conventional routine of the island. The way he killed snakes, over and over again. . . . The way she did her hair. Her cooking. . . .

CHAPTER XV. THE RESCUE

And in the morning a great steamer lay in 30 the bay, calling for water.

Captain Sampson, hard-bitten, upright, weather-beaten, type of the men who keep our ships afloat and our flag aflutter, looked John Tarver in the eyes.

"Before we weigh anchor for the white cliffs of England," he said, "I will ask you a straight question: What are your relations with this woman?"

John Tarver hung his head.

"Seven years ago," he said, "I kissed her on the lips."

A spasm of disgust passed over the tarred face before him.

"Put him in irons," said the Captain.

CHAPTER XVI. SCHEHEREZADE

The giant liner pounded over the ocean, eating up the miles. On the promenade-deck the richer passengers idled away their time with card-games and quoits. Butterflies. . . .

And down in the bilge John Tarver gnawed at his irons, alone with his shame. What a contrast! But he had broken the Unwritten Code of decent men, and he must pay the score. Ostracized by the first-class passengers, who pointedly shunned the hold in which he lay—but, Pah! he cared nothing for them. One face only rose in the gloom before him.

But with every revolution of the screw the day drew nearer when he would be handed over to the proper authorities at Southampton. He would never see her again.

Almost angrily he brushed the rats from his sleeve.

And on the bridge Captain Sampson passionately pressed his suit.

For a moment Marion was drawn by his rugged honesty and the glamour of his calling. He showed her the compass. He explained the Theory of the Tides.

"Be mine," he said, "and I will let you hold the wheel."

She was tempted.

Then there rose before her the image of the man who had shared so many perils with her; and she re-thrilled to the old spell.

"Captain," she said, "the day we cross the bar I will give you my reply."

Dark clouds were massing to windward.

"The glass is falling," he answered grimly.

CHAPTER XVII. TORNADO

The great ship was in the grip of a hurricane. In all his forty years at sea the Captain could not remember a wind of such velocity. Crouched behind the dodger, with all his skill he baffled the elements. The huge vessel quivered. The swimming-bath was closed. The squash-racquets competition was postponed.

The frightened passengers clustered in the rigging.

And how fared it with the lonely passenger below? She must go to him.

"Where is the bilge?" she asked the Chief Engineer.

"Take this lift, Madam," he said, with an admiring glance.

Alone she worked the dangerous electric lift. Alone she groped her way through the roaring hold.

John Tarver saw the light of her lantern flickering among the bales of pea nuts.

The ship lurched violently to starboard. Man and woman were flung together with a blinding concussion. Their heads met.

CHAPTER XVIII. CROSSING THE BAR

Something snapped in their brains. The veils of oblivion were lifted.

"Husband mine," she cried.

"Wife mine," he said.

PART FOUR

"The Age of Anxiety"

TO ATTEMPT to plot the main trends of literature from 1939 to the present is hazardous. Publishing, interrupted and redirected by war, is only now beginning to be normal. There are still many gaps in the artists' picture of a world unrolling all too violently before their eyes. Whatever the main trends of recent literature may be, they have not, of course, taken place in a vacuum, for no writer, however he may pretend to, has been able in recent years to withdraw from the cataclysmic instabilities of war and depression. It took us until the 1920's to estimate the effect of the First World War upon the artists' sensibilities. To comprehend

Pablo Picasso: Head of a Girl
*This lithograph is an example of
Picasso's work after the Second
World War, and demonstrates that age
and the critical times have not
diminished his great resourcefulness*

and present imaginatively the Second World War, much longer and much more clearly directive of historic change, will undoubtedly take years more. Therefore the last chapter of this book can be no more than a summary of what has survived from pre-war art and of what changes and hints of change we perceive as we move forward.

During the war period, journalism and reporting temporarily replaced, in good part, the creative arts. Nonfiction was most read. The moving pictures, perhaps better than any other art form, gave us the immediacy of living through the dramatic and tragic years. Moving

pictures sharpened the sense of man and machine as interdependent, and of man's growing awareness of his need of his fellow man for mere survival. Race, creed, or class ceased to divide when men were forced to act collectively or perish; and since in war the quarrel between esthetics and science has respite, since in war the airplane or the gun becomes, as it were, the heart beating in fear or in relief, literature came soon to reflect greater unity of action as well as more sensitivity to the machine age. Through our motor responses we were made familiar with the complex mechanisms, which although they clothe and feed us

845

may never in peace come under our hands, but which when they protect us are our very fingers. We were, moreover, unified in our emotions, as is necessary for survival in war. In literature as in life we reflected, therefore, less specialization and individualistic difference, more cohesiveness and collectiveness of action and belief.

But back of the unity, a conflict in social directions persisted between nation and nation, between class and class. And no sooner was the war over than this conflict began to reappear in our literature. A six-year period of anxiety and stress is not long enough to overcome a hundred and fifty years of conditioning, and the development of our society has long been such as to train us away from, rather than toward, collective feeling or action. Today literature again mirrors, startlingly, the sharpened conflict in ideology between nations and between groups. Already it is apparent that if in the nineteenth century, as Matthew Arnold remarked, we were at the end of one period and the birth of another, the prolonged lying-in is causing fear, the birth is dangerous and slow.

So it is that Auden, in his recent book of prose and poetry *The Age of Anxiety*, gives the proper title for our chapter on these years. A war of self-preservation fought without clear knowledge of the kind of peace desired has not dissipated the continuously darkening skepticism, the exile of man from society, pictured in both English and American literature from the First World War on down. For, as has been indicated, the last glow of the economic certainty of the industrial nineteenth century had scarcely faded in the sky when the twentieth century saw an ever-deepening questioning of ideas of progress formerly taken for granted, and saw a more and more involved analysis of, and skepticism concerning, the split between materialism on the one hand and utopian idealism on the other. Today the chasm between our belief in the machine and the uses to which we were putting it has become seemingly unbridgeable. Questions arising out of the first world conflict, indeed, seem likely to persist until some form of world stability and national unity, undivided by national or social differences, is achieved.

With nations differing today in their political philosophies and their economic programs, with the specter of fear arising between nation and nation, it is understandable why many of the post-war novels and poems show an even more complete break with any clear faith in man's future than after the First World War. Since the recent world conflict the bodies of anti-fascist literature have naturally come from such nations as suffered most from fascism. Not all the data on this are clear, particularly in regard to those nations whose literature we read in translation. Such countries as least felt the effects of a clear-cut fascism reflect in their literature the conflicts between the older beliefs in capitalism and the newer political beliefs suggested by the war—the need, for example, of world unity, the need of greater equality of opportunity.

Today much of our literature appears to move from a pre-war study of chaos into a post-war study of decay. A play like O'Neill's *The Iceman Cometh*, the theme of which is that in escape lies our only personal reality, and a novel like Malcolm Lowry's *Under the Volcano*, the theme of which is that "lilies (or empires) that fester smell far worse than weeds," are but two examples of the descriptions of decadence to which many of our post-war writers have turned. It begins to look as if the neurotic hero, so dominatingly the chief character in the literature between wars, is today undergoing a real psychotic breakdown, a kind of schizophrenia. Having come upon an age of violence, this leading character of recent literature is either overstimulated by action as a relief from his Waste Land boredom (as in the novels of the Hungarian-born Arthur Koestler, for example) or so incapable of action and repulsed by it as to become, like the typical protagonist in the later novels of Huxley, a quietist. The neurotic hero of *The Waste Land* (pale ghost of the Art for Art's Sake school) must now retreat completely from any contact with the real, or with an equal detachment must act, however nonsensical action seems, in order to feel sure that though he be a patient on the critical list, his disease is not necessarily fatal. This is, of course, not the whole story. Despite many recent signs of sickness, it is always possible that we are in these uncertain days just beginning our slow return to health, for only after crisis does a fever abate.

Many writers return to disillusionment

Many older critics and writers had predicted that a second war could produce only a literature of more cancerous decay. Some prominent writers, as World War II came on, retreated into religion, mysticism, or a kind of gangsterism of the mind in which they would willingly have scrapped the present world in order to return to what they regarded as the values destroyed by commercialism. Disillusioned with intellectual and idealistic utopianism, Auden, for example, had come to America, and to "the island of self"; Huxley, in Hollywood, in *Time Must Have a Stop* had got outside time and space. During the war the little magazines, the last strongholds of the esthetic élite, continued to shout, "We told you so," and to insist on the priesthood of art, while they took occasional excursions on rather circular political railroads. For, of course, the long quarrel going on during the 1930's between left and right in literature as well as politics did not die out immediately. In England, indeed, where the argument had reached a higher intellectual peak and had enjoyed more freedom of expression than in America, the quarrel as to whether the artist should ever take a stand as conformist or nonconformist continued to run until the outbreak of the Second World War.

Then the first reaction of some of the younger writers was to attack the art-for-art's-sake philosophy of the older writers. T. S. Eliot was one step ahead of this, for he declined to edit the *Criterion* and said sadly:

In the present state of public affairs, which has induced in myself a depression of spirits so different from any other experience of fifty years as to be a new emotion—I no longer feel the enthusiasm necessary to make a literary review what it should be. . . . This is not to suggest that I consider literature to be at this time, or at any other time, a matter of indifference. On the contrary, I feel that it is all the more essential that authors who are concerned with that small part of literature which is really creative—and seldom immediately popular—should apply themselves sedulously to their work, without abayment or sacrifice of their artistic standards of art on any pretext whatsoever.

Certainly his reign was under attack, and his personal pessimism and his arguments against the validity of democratic civilization were suspect. One reviewer in the *London Times* commented acidly:

Mr. Eliot is disdainful of many things, of most things. His poetry is the poetry of disdain—disdain of the tragic view of life, even of himself. He is becoming more and more like an embalmer of the nearly dead: he colours their masks with expert fingers to resemble life but only to resemble. On all their lips is the twisted smile of Prufrock . . .

Huxley too, chief exponent of intellectual skepticism, annoyed the English reviewers:

From an ivory and chromium-plated tower in California, Mr. Huxley has seen everything that man has made and, behold, it is not very good. So bad it is, indeed, so foolish or so vile are the things to which human beings have put their hand, that Mr. Huxley seems to wait for a different species of life to inherit the earth.

Novels of plot and action return to popularity

Disillusioned with their prophets of the period between wars, the British, like the Americans, turned to writers of action. But the first effects of this turn were indicative of the confusion in literary and political thought. Koestler, for example, was much read. He produced novel after novel in which the hero had all the moral indecision familiar to pre-war heroes, and yet was forced by events into arbitrary action. Such heroes were not much more than the familiar Waste Land Hamlets, moving out of boredom into hysteria. In other words, the need of action reintroduced plot into the story;

and political adventure-story writers like Koestler, or certain romantic individualists like Saroyan, since they did not abruptly break with the older traditions of the neurotic as hero, almost immediately caught the conditioned imagination of the average "liberal" reader.

Shortly, however, the war engulfed British publishing. From England there came only such cheaply printed magazines—some of them left-wing—and such pocket editions of old and modern fiction and poetry as could be carried by soldiers. Continental and South American literature had begun to appear in American editions even before the war; but once war fixed our attention, the poems of Federico García Lorca, killed by the Spanish Republicans in 1936, and of the South American political poet Pablo Neruda, attained popularity. And soon we began to watch for the literature of resistance which appeared in France. American writers, long acquainted with the historical-mindedness of the English poets, began to show that they were influenced by antifascist literature wherever it appeared.

Since the declaration of peace, in fact, there has been a spate of such literature in translation. And although the chief signs are not in that direction, and although the mainstream of literary thought still portrays the decline of a culture and a deepening decadence, there is indication already of an undercurrent of literature more international, social, and political in direction which may in time swell and change the direction of the main current. It seems possible that any further crisis, economic or military, could bring to flood strength the economic and political thinking which sprang from the depression of the 1930's.

How English and American literatures differ today

English writers have long been more political than have Americans; but although today, as one would expect, the English are more pro-socialist and more inclined to believe that this is the end of an era, the two literatures are more strongly related than ever before. Some minor distinctions can, however, be made between them. The same traditions have influenced both literatures, but cultural differences have made for minor distinctions in growth. The popularity of Freudian psychology, for example, turned both literatures to an interest in the subjective. But in America, Freudianism became an excessive antidote to puritanism, a kind of new morality, while in England it was a reaction against the burden of historical tradition and the lingering death of Victorianism. The English artist, often a member of a titled or wealthy family, used Freudianism as a weapon against what he regarded as the decadence and restrictions of his class. In T. S. Eliot are to be found both the anti-puritan and the sociological use of Freudian symbolism. Eliot saved himself from the rather indecent exposure of other American Freudians who, having worn too long the costume of puritanic restraints, chose rebelliously to go naked. Donning the attire of an English gentleman and an Anglo-Catholic, Eliot rejected his puritan desire for personal salvation. Thus he became the leader of both the American and the English artists who would reject active personal participation. He rejected, too, the real world for a retreat into speculative musings. Divorcement from the real world also led Virginia Woolf into an almost insane isolation. But literature of neuroticism and retreat could not continue to dominate in a period of real physical danger, and Eliot gave way in time to Auden, the twentieth-century Byron, a poet who, although like Eliot and Mrs. Woolf conditioned to Freudianism, became a man of action in his search for new social programs.

Optimism among American writers

Meanwhile, there persisted in America, never bombed and economically prosperous, the old belief in our ability to survive anything, flood, fire, or famine. This optimism, outcome as much of the puritan-bred insistence on our moral righteousness as of our lack of weariness, is reflected in our literature. American writers imitate every English literary trend, but they mirror less general disillusionment and weariness. We retain, for example, a belief in action, which most upper-class English writers seem to have relinquished, save for such observers as Auden, who records the change in scene. American writers indeed exploit violence in action rather than the elderly nostalgia, the cancerous frustration which seem to eat away the vitals of much English literature. One is forced to ask, however, whether such action—meaningless, sentimental, and monstrously exhausting—is any less evil a trend in art, which always mirrors its social milieu, than are a diseased rejection of action and a fatalistic folding of the hands. English literature today grows more masochistic, American more sadistic. The English tear at their own wounds, retire to pray against or to cry out over their own guilt, while the Americans, like children, escape self-condemnation by condemning others. We are the less civilized in our emotional reactions. The English poets who have come to America to enjoy large audiences have brought to us their cynicism, a cynicism produced by a long history, a cynicism which now, here, seems possible of repetition. But although many of our writers imitate the English class consciousness and historical sophistication, there remains in America a school of typically realistic American writers such as Hemingway, Dos Passos, and Faulkner.

Danger signals

Shortly after the rise of Hitler and the publication of his book, Kenneth Burke had turned his thoughtful attention to *Mein Kampf.* His study of the way in which Hitler supplied his people with a kind of religion whose god was power and the nationalist-fascist state and whose devil was internationalism—which could be personified as the radical, and in particular as the radical Jew, the man without a nation—indicated how easily good can be made to appear evil. He showed how Hitler turned the traditional religious and political symbols upside down; how, because he wished to preserve and further to concentrate capitalism, he tagged all the evils of capitalism as non-Aryan or Jewish; how thus he protected German monopolistic interests, and how while purporting to give the people a kind of socialism he gave them fascism. Burke noted how Hitler perverted nationalism into military nationalism and national pride into hatred of other nations.

But Burke's essay was most important in that it pointed to the ever more evident truth that any national idealism can be so perverted as to become an agent of aggression. He pointed out that to arouse the people to violence, the propagandists of any nation have but to create a symbolic enemy, upon whom they can fix all the evils within themselves; that once so purged of the consciousness of their own ignorance and injustice, a people is easily led by those in control into war. This is best done by associating some traditional ideas of persecution with any nation or group toward which one would direct the sword. Burke's is a keen analysis of the methods of propaganda.

Broadly speaking, however, there is little evidence that American writers have been re-educated by the events between wars. Postwar attacks on labor unions have aroused few literary protests. Save for a sprinkling of poems about the Spanish Civil War and a few anti-fascist novels, like Sinclair Lewis' *It Can't Happen Here,* written in 1935, or like Albert Maltz' *The Cross and the Arrow,* written during the war, little political passion is reflected in American art. Our persistent American optimism has long blinded us somewhat to the events of history.

Our historic blindness indeed almost ruined us. Japan struck while many of us still pictured the Orient as a land of cherry blossoms. With war in Europe and evidence of fascism at home, we could not believe, despite Sinclair Lewis, that it *could* happen here. Traditional isolationism and our pacifism, the strongest idealistic force between the wars, deluded us. While agents of fascist propaganda worked, while Hitler's *Mein Kampf* sold millions of copies, few bothered to define fascism. The fall of France startled us at last, and from that point on we grew more willing to consider the idea of war; but it took a sneak attack to catapult us into it. Then we saw most of our writers alerted to danger. No writer in America before 1938 had pictured, like Auden, every bush an ambush, every railroad station as one en route to death. Not even with England in the war could American writers feel the same terror as the English did. But quickly, after Pearl Harbor, the shadow of Auden's terror came over American writers too.

Jean Cocteau: Two Men at a Table with Dice and Glasses
*Cocteau as a writer has exerted great influence not only in his native country
but in England and America as well. His drawings, as simple and free
as script, are nevertheless essentially graphic and full of suggestion, and are
triumphs of the discriminating artist's selectivity of detail*

The war reflected in American writing

War declared, our older writers reacted as their earlier literary works had indicated they might. Jeffers applauded a violence which might end a materialistic civilization. Cummings, aristocratically annoyed with anything resembling the democratic "herd life," and consequently appalled by Russia, grew more bitter. Steinbeck, always sensitive to the spirit of the times, became an early anti-fascist, while some of the younger generation became more convinced that capitalism was at an end. With the actual coming of war here, the more obviously anarchistic writers and those who were against the war politically were temporarily quieted. After Russia entered the war as our ally, the flood of anti-Russian literature stopped. Ernest Hemingway, who between

wars had been forced to seek stimulus in bull-fights and lion hunting, became again in the 1940's the first important reporter of new wars. His books of the First World War had been studies of action in order to escape from thought. But when he wrote *To Have and Have Not,* on the theme that man could not live entirely apart from his fellow men; *The Fifth Column,* a study of fascism; and *For Whom the Bell Tolls,* his story of the Spanish Civil War, it was clear that Hemingway had found that action for a cause was more worthy than action for the mere purpose of rebellion against the average middle-class existence. An American Hemingway could never cogitate the violence of history without wishing to punch somebody's nose; a civilized English Auden, of course, might merely think things over.

The first reaction of the American publishers

to Pearl Harbor was to look frantically around for patriotic literature. This they did not at once find. A generation fathered by one war, born in an artificial boom, come into adulthood in a jobless depression—a generation fed on the literature, first, of skepticism, and later of social criticism, went into the war with no fanfare. MacLeish, in sackcloth and ashes, bewailed the fact that his, the lost generation, had demoralized the younger generation, which would now have to fight. He need not have worried. Whatever happened to them during the war, the younger generation had caught the idea of one united world. As children of the depression they also believed strongly in the fourth freedom, the freedom from want. Moreover, they had no American dream of success to lose. If only vaguely, they knew the economic factors of war. And so, with none of the idealism of their fathers, but with a bitter sense of reality, they accepted necessity.

Poetry, a form of literature which had dominated the depression, came early in the war period again into first place. Difficulties in publishing may have had something to do with this fact. Moreover, even as the cry for food can be a group cry, so also can the outcry for protection or in fear be collective: and as we have noted, social or group passions lend themselves better to poetry than to the novel, which is an instrument to portray contradictions in action and belief. War verse soon recorded a shift from individualistic to collective feeling, an awakening to a sense of what collective action meant, a sense of escaping from personal isolation, even from class. When men are aware that they live because others die, love of their fellows knows no specification. With war, the human passions long frustrated awoke, and the key of sympathy which Eliot could not use unlocked the hearts of men to each other. "Man crumbling in the crumbling brain of man," as Yvor Winters pictured him, found suddenly he must act or his hypersensitivity would become his burying ground.

However (as Bernstein puts it in "The Subjective War," *Mainstream*, Vol. I, No. I), "the outraged world pictured in books early in the century was shortly replaced by the picture of the outraged artist," and, throughout a Second World War fought without sharp decision, the outraged artist was clearly still very much with us. Although the war temporarily united us, temporarily drew the mass of people into disciplined action, its ending threw us not into isolation or pacifism as had World War I, but rather into a continuation of war psychology and problems of economic instability. Fiction published immediately after any war is of course in part ephemeral; too little of it, moreover, has appeared since the cessation of hostilities to enable us to feel that our picture is wholly accurate. But only a relatively small proportion of it is concerned with the political reasons for the war, or with the questions of reaction and progress.

In the later years of the fighting we had some contrived pictures of fascism abroad, but they were less powerful than the novels of countries which had been under fascism—like Silone's *Fontamara* and *Bread and Wine*, or a less important book, Anna Seghers' *The Seventh Cross*. American post-war fiction, as Bernstein notes, is for the most part concerned with a hero no less confused than he was presumed to be before the war was fought. Never taught what fascism was or is, often not clearly knowing what or why he fought, this hero indeed seems increasingly depressed by the absurdity of his world. During the war his immediate enemy was his superior officer. There are occasional studies of discrimination within the army (as in Robert MacLaughlin's *This Side of Angels*) but it is the soldiers' hatred of the brass hats (as in Edward Newhouse's *The Iron Chain*) which dominates most war stories. Seldom indeed does one find so clear a story as Irwin Shaw's "Act of Faith." There have been, of course, many short stories and novels like R. J. Lowry's *Casualty* and more recently the large-canvas, somewhat episodic war novel like *The Naked and the Dead* by Norman Mailer, *The Crusaders* by Stefan Heym, and *The Young Lions* by Irwin Shaw, concerning adjustments of sensitive individuals to war and its aftermath.

One important theme appearing constantly in recent fiction suggests clearly that we are attempting to take measure of our post-war scene. Novels and plays concerned with the Negro and with other social problems continue to be published. We have had many books like *The Gentle Bush* by Barbara Giles and Lewis' *Kingsblood Royal*, and plays like *Deep Are the*

Roots, On Whitman Avenue, and the highly symbolic play, *Death of a Salesman,* which insist that the enemy is in our midst and confront us with our ignorance, our stupid cruelty, our fight to feel superior. Apparently for a good many writers Hitler's race theories clarified the universal significance of the race prejudices which have long fed maggotlike on the healthy body of our thinking. And although it may seem odd, in a period in which so much art seems produced merely for amusement, that we should have at the top of our best-seller lists books on racial and religious discrimination, certainly this is a first sign of a kind of health.

The theater, which thoroughly reflected the ferment of the thirties, has recently given us war plays which pose moral questions. Outstanding among such plays in the first years of peace was Arthur Miller's *All My Sons.*

As for English fiction, its outlines are no more clear than are those of American post-war fiction. That economically harassed country has given us as yet few new novels or stories. There is still Christopher Isherwood, whose *Berlin Stories* has to do largely with pre-war Germany, that ghostly adventure ground for the effete young Englishman, who would as lief flirt with Communism as with Freudian complexities. Evelyn Waugh told in *Brideshead Revisited* the tale of a family, aristocratic and feeble, and its escape from decadence into Catholicism, but turned in *The Loved One* to elaborate satire of a rather morbid kind and in *Scott-King's Modern Europe* to a fanciful episode in a mythical totalitarianism. Alex Comfort, a brilliant novelist, able if he would to treat powerfully of the workingman and his machine, turns more and more to an outright creed of individual anarchy. And besides these there are the many skeptical journalists and

surveyors of Europe after the war, like Rebecca West in her *Black Lamb and Grey Falcon.* Meantime, the short stories in English magazines seem to deal with the oddities of living, whatever one's "class" may be, in bomb-shelled, rationed, and impoverished good old England, either in the big houses in which the remnants of the aristocracy wonder how they will get along without their servants, or in the little houses where economic demands forbid much profound anger or love.

Philip Toynbee tried, in an article entitled "The English Literary Scene" (in the *New Republic,* December 2, 1946) to outline post-war English literary trends. He pointed to the exodus of the artistic intellectuals to America and added:

Older writers could ignore the ideological issues for they had trained themselves to do so. The young reacted either with horror or enthusiasm but in neither case was the result particularly happy. Great English writers have been greatly preoccupied with public issues of their time (Milton, Byron, and Shelley) and there was no obvious reason why the anti-fascist or pro-fascist struggle should not have inspired great writing. It may be that it was too close, too overwhelming. . . .

The more general attitude is that the state is a dangerous and a touchy animal which should be left alone as much as possible. It is still very difficult to leave the animal alone, or rather to be left alone by it, but the artist's ambition is to slip unobtrusively out of its clutches.

What Toynbee here labels the desire to be left alone is, as we shall exemplify shortly, one of the dominating drives of our post-war artists, many of whom recently have come to define themselves as religious or as existentialist.

THE POST-WAR RELIGIOUS REVIVAL

AS WE HAVE previously said, it was Eliot who in the 1930's first turned from what he considered the emptiness and vulgarity of the modern world back to the Church. When he

became Anglo-Catholic, many of his young disciples followed him, and the religious movement in poetry swelled. In his repudiation of the commercial and the ordinary, Eliot apparently found the traditional in religion a solace. But, although his sincerity cannot be denied, his poems of conversion are more prayers to be taken away from the stresses and strains of the too sensitive self in a confused world than any affirmation of religious faith. Most of his religious poems are poems of repentance, of an anguished yearning toward martyrdom. His is no simple, joyous godliness. He is as haunted by himself as by his world. The sense of personal guilt in his work indicates that in seeking grace he is obsessed by what is sometimes called the death-wish. The world is too much with him, and heaven not easily come by. Always the process of departing from outer reality is in both his secular and religious poetry characteristically traced through. Whatever his theme, Eliot dramatizes the odyssey of the twentieth-century homeless self.

This odyssey had been entered on by most of the imaginative minds of the twentieth century, nor was it surprising that Auden, who in his early work had sensed no split between good and evil man, should turn from politics and war to investigate the religious. One world, by this time, had begun to stand against another world, the progressive against the reactionary—the chasm between was deepening. Always the homeless poet, Auden, only superficially Marxist at most, repented of his dreams of Utopia as Eliot had of his doubts, and sought, as Eliot had, to be made whole by turning to the traditional. Auden's wit and skepticism, however, remained his baggage; and although it was rumored that he flirted with Catholicism, it soon became evident that the Church and its theologies were but new lands to explore. It was shortly apparent that Auden would not be limited to any traditional religion; he turned to existentialism—new resting place for those whose religion is actually art and art only, or art as completely divorced from social reality. Like Eliot, as we have noted, Auden has his American disciples. Karl Shapiro is one of the best of them. Split in parentage between two religions, Shapiro, who had seen army service in the Pacific theater, turned after the war to investigate the same religious fields as Eliot and Auden. Soon, however, like Auden, he too appears to have rejected Catholicism for existentialism.

The quest for personal salvation

To put it simply, the Second World War poets, for the most part somewhat sheltered and totally unaware of the mass movements coexistent with their political speculations, were by the mounting historical violence following the political thirties thrown back upon more personal and less social means of salvation. The war soon plumped them, regardless of their previous political convictions, into that reality which they had long avoided. Many of them now fled contact with the real scene completely. It was simpler and safer, and perhaps more immediately artistically productive in a war period, to narrow vision again to the self and to inner conflict. World conflicts were too overwhelming. Only the outlines of another type of life, the religious, afforded a relief from the inhumane reality of war and of post-war struggle for position and power. Therefore dualism, which would explain the split between good and evil, became the subject of much poetic speculation; throughout the war, and with increasing impetus since the war, the religious movement in art has gained in momentum.

What the Waste Land poets had deplored was boredom; what these Second World War poets were thrown into was blind action—or so they thought. From meaningless action and a fear of it, some fled to religious contemplation. Since the last great synthesis had been the Christian, and since the poets sought unity in retreat from a world which seemed totally undirected, most of the converts were drawn either to Roman Catholicism or to Anglo-Catholicism. They were, in other words, devotees either of a centralized world church or of a state church, or of authority.

Robert Lowell: religion and rebellion

One of the most talented of the younger American poets converted to Catholicism was Robert Lowell, of the famous Lowells of Boston. His was a Catholicism directed in attack against the religion of his ancestors, especially against that God of love which transcendentalism had projected as the puritans stepped out of a difficult economy into a more prosperous and settled one. Lowell very clearly repudiates his own family. He pictures his elders as strong, long in dying, eaten by cancers, destroyed by the quest for gold. Possessed of a startling talent for metaphysical contrast, Lowell in image after image suggests that innocence is lost, that man has fallen, that chaos has come, that all humanity is sinful. For this poet Satan is loosed upon the earth again; Christ and an Old Testament God (not unlike Lowell's image of his father) dominate a world bathed in blood. For Lowell only a wrathful god explains man's sufferings today:

> Lord, from the lust and dust thy will destroys
> Raise an unblemished Adam who will see
> The limbs of the tormented chestnut tree
> Tingle, and hear the March-winds lift and
>   cry:
> "The Lord of Hosts will overshadow us."*

His world is in a bad way:

> But we are old, our fields are running wild
> Till Christ again turn wanderer and child.*

And Catholic history has come to the end of another cycle:

> On Troy's last days alas, the populous
> Shrines held carnival, and girls and boys
> Flung garlands to the wooden horse, so we
> Burrow into the lion's mouth today.*

Lowell became a conscientious objector after much thought. He did not believe there was any reason for fighting, since "Can war ever change my old into new man?" But his is not simply the religious mind fleeing world chaos. Clearly he connects boredom with the entire middle-class way of life. He is, moreover, highly Freudian, particularly in his poems of childhood, where the mother image appears as both violently repulsive and violently attractive. He frequently juxtaposes the sensuous ecstasy and the religious. Passion is for him both erotic and religious. He sees the father image and the God image as connected. There is something physiological in Lowell's images of the Christ child born in blood. Probably the war itself denies for this poet that we are "children of Light." Rather, we are children of

darkness in a land where "our money talks and multiplies the darkness." Lowell is both attracted and repelled by violence. His metaphysical lyrical poetry (rooted in the seventeenth-century metaphysical verse) is more tortured, more wrenched, more unresolved, actually, into any moment of faith than any of the religious poetry of the seventeenth century. In truth the gap between faith and doubt is greater now than it ever was; our knowledge winds us in a maze, we push uphill our own disbelief but it rolls back upon us. Lowell rejects completely the materialistic idea of progress. He chooses instead to present the dramatic terror of a guilt-haunted soul, of a world drenched in blood, as if for Judgment Day. Psychologically, his repugnance to the world of wars drives him to conceive of a God stern and ruthless, and of man as saving himself through guilt and suffering. His more recent work indeed indicates that Lowell has encountered doubts, that in his philosophy there is something of existentialism. Some of his late poems on religious subjects are frankly skeptical as to the power of the Catholic Church, in a modern competitive world, to preserve its old spiritual intensity.

A Catholic of a rather different variety from Lowell is the Irish poet Denis Devlin. He comes from a country where the people are simple and superstitious, backward through no fault of their own, dominated still by a certain kind of feudalism from which England long got rich payment. Many of his people are pathetically poor; most of them are devout Catholics. The Church affords them their greatest emotional outlet. And yet there is, between its security and comfort and their ignorance and poverty, a wide gap. Consequently, Devlin's emotions are split between irony and pity. His mood is one of love for the people, contradicted by dislike of the rich. Toward the Church he feels a kind of anguish. He deplores that it sometimes rules, as he seems to think, through superstitions, but holds that the Christian ideas of brotherhood, if properly interpreted, would be beneficial to mankind.

Roy Campbell: The Church Militant

South African-born Roy Campbell is another Catholic convert. Like the lyric and late-

---

* From "In the Attic" and "Christmas Eve under Hooker's Statue" from *Lord Weary's Castle* by Robert Lowell. Copyright 1944, 1946 by Robert Lowell. Reprinted by permission of publisher, Harcourt, Brace and Company, Inc.

Misch Kohn: Workman's Family at Table
*Here the artist, with delicacy and restraint, has made use of all of the resources
of his medium to produce a miniature scene full of vigor and social
content which for us today is evocative of the 1930's*

romantic poet Dylan Thomas, Campbell was crowded out of the literary scene by Auden and the political poets of the thirties, a fact which he has never forgotten or forgiven. His greatest hatred seems very personally directed toward the left-wing poets. He denounces poets who suggest utopias, promise the masses better conditions, and make reputations by being the voices of the more radical movements. He remarks on what he regards as the effeminacy and cowardice of these left-wing English poets who sit at home or flee to America while he himself fights in a war he does not believe in, merely because he does not like foreign aggression. His poetic star rose early and then was darkened by the stronger literary lights of the thirties. During the second war he was, probably of necessity, silent; his fascism was

then unpopular. But with the war over, he is not hesitating to make his point of view quite clear. His admiration for Hitler, his hatred of Russia, and his hero worship of Franco are quite explicit, as is also his violent anti-Semitism. What motivates him toward fascism is fairly clear. He makes the distinction, as did Hitler, between good and bad capitalism, the former being Christian, the latter Jewish, the former being of an old and aristocratic culture, the latter of the hoi polloi. It is evident that he was in Spain and fought in the Civil War with the Royalists. Perhaps his conversion to Catholicism was linked with his attraction to Franco's theories of government.

Campbell, in other words, is a poet whose chief emotions are admiration of himself and hatred of others, whose mood is satirical. In

855

vehement and startling imagery and with amazing rhetoric he indicates that he always prefers violent action to "the architecture of confusion" in which he believes the more humanitarian poets of the modern world live.

> Coining the opulence of Babbitts,
> Out of the cowardice of rabbits
> And mealy kisses of Iscariot,
> More plutocratic in their habits,
> The more they woo the proletariat.*

Certainly Campbell hotly rejects the middle-class world and its mediocre conceptions of justice, and, in a kind of self-adulation, he sneers at them. He plays himself up as the artist in action, as the warrior. His images of God are often the images of a great hero or military conqueror cleansing a world; and his images of love are equally violent. Now it is, of course, questionable whether hatred without anything to offset it is viable in poetry. The great poet Swift, for example, used it, but always intellectually and not too personally. His hatred was always offset by a passionate sense of man's essential worth. But for Campbell, there is only one side to the shield. He never justifies mankind; he is exhaustive in justifying himself. The image of the Church which appeals to him is a crusading Church whose power should rightly rule the world. All in all, Campbell seems caught up in a kind of egomania, furiously asserting his own superiority, perhaps because he doubts it. He is master of the barbed line, the far-fetched violent metaphor, the rapid ballad form of narrative. His poetic language is pregnant with military language and images, whatever the subject:

> Her eyelashes with jet-black sting
> Like scorpions curved, and dark as night
> The chevrons on her brow that spring
> Like feathers in a condor's wing
> Arch in their splendour in height.*

or:

> Between the Jewish Fascism of Russia
> And gentile Bolshevism farmed on Prussia,
> I see no difference save in their salutes.*

* From "The Clock in Spain" and "Jungle Eclogue" from *Talking Bronco*, copyright 1946 by Roy Campbell and reprinted with his permission.

His pictures of war, since war is not pretty and since he handles well a rapid-fire narrative, often have a horrible power. But, as Wilfred Owen said, "the poetry is in the pity," and of pity there is none in Campbell. His warlike picture of a Church militant in a destroyed world in which "one thing remains intact, The Cross," is terrifying. His is the voice of an irrational, anti-intellectual brutality which fascinates us today because it has its replica in our real world.

Toward a synthesis of religious and social philosophies

In contrast to Campbell, John Frederick Nims is a Roman Catholic of liberal and progressive ideas. There is in his work no tendency to divide the religious intensities from a more broadly humanitarian love of mankind. Nims tends to blame social conditions for the situation in which we find ourselves, and he does not condemn man to suffer forever in these conditions. The social machine which controls man, he argues, could be made to save him and to free his energy for religious or poetic speculation. Regarding man as both a religious and a social animal, Nims is not inclined to separate the two. And so he uses religion more for the brotherhood it teaches than for any metaphysical or psychological reëxamination of the intricacies of the human soul.

George Barker, Anglo-Catholic in faith, is better acquainted with the more progressive social philosophies than is, perhaps, even Nims. He is a modern philosophical poet who analyzes the laws of cause and effect and traces the growth of belief. With a kind of rigorous and intellectual line, Barker in long poems makes observations on personal, philosophical, and historical movements and comes finally to a conclusion which could be interpreted as Marxist:

> The past's absolution is the present's resolution.
> The equation is the interdependence of parts.

There is, however, a note of late romantic terror and sadness in much of Barker's poetry, for the "immensely sad land . . . where only the ghosts are good" because "the beast Still rules England with its scales of gold."

In other words, Nims and Barker have not turned to the religious world as an escape from the historical problems of our time. They have attempted to bring the religious into conjunction with these problems. Both are seeking, although in somewhat different ways, a new synthesis.

That one aspect of this religious movement is divorcement from a world too complex and destructive is evident in all religious poetry. As in James Agee, who states that intellectually he is a Communist but emotionally he is Catholic, one sees in many poets the hatred of contradiction and the urge toward unity which have reached a desperate pitch during and since the war. In earlier periods the contradictions were not so great and not so dangerous. Consequently, one did not, even in the seventeenth century, have so violently to repudiate the secular man in order to affirm the religious. But today, with nations quarreling, with the agents of propaganda in the hands of a few, intelligence seems useless and a morbid sense of personal guilt for life's evil is general to the sensitive. Artists who have no historical perspective turn to beating their breasts. They seek the reason why the powers of evil are loose, and since they have no instrument with which to analyze the social forces, they return to the old idea of original sin. The historian might find another reason for the social sense of sin which now prevails, but the fact remains that in the twentieth century of doubt and despair either the artist must believe in an earthly future which he can help to make nearer to his heart's desire, or he must turn the pages of past theologies and seek out older patterns of belief to give him security and comfort.

EXISTENTIALISM IN LITERATURE

❦ OF LATE, there has been much ado among writers about a movement known as existentialism. It is not difficult to understand why such a movement should reappear today in post-war literature. For existentialism is a philosophy which attracts the artists who would, in order to escape confusion, avoid participation in citizenship, who would, moreover, avoid the contradictions of life by a neurotic concern with guilt or with death.

All this had its beginning with the Danish philosopher, Soren Kierkegaard (1813–55) who wrote many volumes on the essential subjectivity of man, on man's need to exist solely within himself, not as a participator in a chaotic society. He spoke of the existential system and his philosophy consequently came to be called existentialism. It spread from Scandinavia to Germany, where it influenced Nietzsche, and in due course of time Nietzsche influenced Hitler. Existentialism, which in its emphasis on the individual as sole judge of his own actions was always anti-Marxist in conception and in influence, became a refuge for escapists and idealists, distrustful of the scientific studies of the patterns of human life. It pictures man as unique and a law unto himself, and in its post-Second-War form it has caught the imagination of writers who despair of making order out of the social and political chaos. Nor have they felt man to be happy in his anti-rational revolt. Here again Kierkegaard's position becomes, today, highly acceptable. For Kierkegaard held that men exist only by chance, that therefore they have no rights, that existence itself is absurd. With this assumed, man has, of course, no duties; he is supreme in his own fiction of the free individual and need not be forced to fit himself to the badly tailored suit of normality in social action. He lives, indeed, in a kind of supreme nakedness, like Narcissus, staring only at himself, at his own image fixed, not fluctuating, in the pool of the mind.

By being subjective, man (and his creator in fiction, the artist) can recede further and further from any impact with the ugly realities about him. After all, if life is absurd—and Kierkegaard argued that since it ends in death it is always absurd—everything is then purely personal and there are no laws of belief. Even an orthodox belief in the church, said Kierkegaard, can be seen to be absurd, since the church, being man-made, is a social institution which cannot teach truth. Only in his subjectivity is man able to search out the inner, the true God; only through apartness from action or society can he discover the meaning of himself, and therefore the meaning of a whole, or of God.

As for plunging into any sociological or political action—man so doing is, according to existentialism, impure. Man as wage earner, as voter, is merely an actor, not himself; he is real indeed only in nonparticipation. Furthermore—and this is important—because man faces death, he exists, according to Kierkegaard, always in a state of anxiety, in fear and in trembling, in constant tension before the contradictions of existence. This conception of man's perpetual state of anxiety and dread, and of his guilt too, is clearly applicable today in our post-war state of mind. It is symbolic, too, unfortunately, of our despair in a period without peace and plan. It is not surprising, then, that existentialism seems created especially for the tired Waste Land and pre-war writer, and that it seems fitted, precisely, also to the would-be radical writer who after a brief period of idealism fled everything political. Like Kierkegaard, these writers state their rejection of the world in social terms, denouncing the paradoxes of society, of money and position, as have many artists indeed in rising voices since the First World War. Most of them could say with Kierkegaard,

When I was young, I forgot to laugh. Later, when I opened my eyes and considered reality, I began to laugh and since then I have never stopped. I have seen that the important thing in life is to earn a living, that the end, to obtain a post as an official, that the delights of love consisted in marrying a rich woman, that the highest advancement of friendship was to lend each other money; that wisdom was public opinion; that enthusiasm consisted in making a speech, courage in risking a fine of ten crowns, benevolence in welcoming guests to dinner, piety in communicating once a year. I saw all this and laughed. *

Since history in periods of change interrupts any exhaustive inquiry into intense personal

* R. Cant, "Kierkegaard," *Church Quarterly Review*, Vol. 127, 1939, p. 279.

areas of vision, it is not strange that after a Second World War, inconclusive still, the writers should be more vocal in their philosophical retreat from a world which, at the moment, may seem to have no rhyme or reason. And if the later writers differ from those reacting to the First World War, it is because a second world conflict has darkened into considerably deeper skepticism the political idealism of the thirties. Today, there is a greater terror current than ever before because of the contradictions between our high concepts of man's dignity and our recognition of the recent fact of his degradation.

Kafka pictures the disintegration of society

During the last years of the second war and before existentialism was defined as a post-war movement, writers turned to the German Franz Kafka as a spiritual leader. In heightened revolt from the materialistic values always displeasing to the artist, and from the continuation of the war psychology, Kafka, never before described as existentialist, became the symbolic leader of this new philosophy of art. Kafka was a highly sensitive and intellectual Jew, whose ill health and neurotic personality made him an exile from society. His actual social position must have had much to do with his views, for it was he who analyzed, as Professor Berry Burgum says, "the complete bankruptcy of faith in the middle class." Even Proust and Mann, critical as they were of the bourgeoisie, had nevertheless conceded that class a kind of aging strength. It remained for Kafka to picture the middle class power as complete and spiritually destructive. His symbol, for example, of authority in *The Castle* is a symbol of the absurdly unapproachable; his symbol of justice in *The Trial* is that of an irrational and absurd persecution; and his symbols of America (in his novel *Amerika*) are all of a huge, vulgar, and mechanical country, of a country held up to ridicule as preposterous. Even the American "nature theater" as Kafka saw it allegorically is a conglomeration of sentimental and practical contradictions, a Hollywood dream of the return to the simple life. The world for Kafka was absurd, but ironically absurd. Over it hovered, for man, a meaningless and inescapable doom. It is no wonder then that during the war Kafka enjoyed a great literary revival, that dozens of his volumes and many biographies and critical studies concerning him appeared. One has but to remember Kafka's appalling story, "Metamorphosis," of a man who suddenly found that he had turned into an enormous cockroach, shocking even to his family, desperate within himself because of his hideousness, to understand how completely Kafka rejected individual man's position in humanity as honorable, how he was lonely and ostracized in a world which marked him as an insect. And if, in general, as Berry Burgum says, "all modern fiction in the late nineteenth century and in increasing proportions in the twentieth century came to reflect both constructive and disintegrating phases of contemporary society," certainly Kafka was master interpreter of our abstract and symbolic disintegration. Nor is it surprising that many twentieth-century writers, long supporters of art for art, long divorced from society, have discovered in Kafka a writer who with mathematical objectivity maps their exile.

Existentialism reintroduced in France

Since the war, several French writers, in particular Jean Paul Sartre and Simone de Beauvoir, have been most vocal in redefining existentialism and popularizing it as a literary movement. Sartre was active in the resistance movement because he said he wished to give man one more chance. In part, he explains this contradiction. Granting that materialism is the only myth suitable for revolutionary demands, he argues, however, that Communists are misleading the workers by claiming rights for them. Man has no rights, regardless of his class, except insofar as he transcends whatever system of society he lives under. This man can do, not by opposing any social system, but by declaring his freedom from it. Logically, it would seem to follow that being more frustrated under fascism, man would be required to do more "transcending" and therefore might better realize himself. But Sartre is not interested in such logic. He is interested, apparently, in

maintaining that man's moral problems are exclusive of his social problems. An example of this approach is his play *No Exit*. One of the characters is a collaborator, but Sartre is not concerned with the social evils of collaboration with the enemy. The only moral problem this character confronts is that of determining whether or not he is a coward. Again in Sartre's brilliant essay *Portrait of an Anti-Semite*, the author condemns anti-Semitism, not as an anti-social attitude but as a case of cowardice. For Sartre is concerned purely with questions of personal character and apparently does not believe that character is molded by society. Perhaps unconsciously, Sartre emphatically rejects the biological and sociological sciences. He seems to feel that to accept these makes for that human identification with other human beings which will not keep the artist apart from "soft, bare, disorderly masses, monstrous and obscene in their frightful nudity."

Withdrawal to "the island of self"

The artist has not always been separated from his society and he has never functioned best in nonconformity. There are, of course, single artists who are exceptions to every rule, but, in general, art has flourished best when the artist felt himself a member of his society able to use its language and to be understood by it. The conception of the artist as in a class by himself is new in the twentieth century; it is a rationalization of existing fact; never before have the drives of an era been so alien to the sensitive. It is not strange that in this post-war Age of Anxiety no artist has yet been able to make order out of the sometimes conflicting directions the era seems to have. Nor is any group of artists defining new trends in literature. What we have most clearly from our writers is a picture of greater decadence, of greater despair, than that given us after the First World War. The conflict in social movements is great, and the artist still, like Joyce, creates his own dream to avoid the nightmare of history. The complete rejection of the values of our commercial success by the most sensitive group among us is startling evidence that faith in our present system is questionable. Invariably it is the artist who records an age; in the long run, it is he who pronounces judgment upon it. Therefore, the fact that the artist now seems to separate himself more thoroughly than ever from society, or to express his revulsion from it, may point to a breakdown in our culture not yet known to the general public.

Today the existentialist movement, introduced by the French writers, has gained its disciples among English and American writers. One can point to its philosophy in Eugene O'Neill's *The Iceman Cometh* and in almost every novel or moving picture of alcoholic escape. And in modern poetry, the statement of man's exile and terror is everywhere explicit. Indeed, Auden's recent book, *The Age of Anxiety*, is an elaborate statement of his own belief in existentialism. This is a long poem, in which several men and women are able to communicate because they have loosened their tongues with alcohol. They discuss in a bar the general human dilemma. The poem is a weighty and often boring statement of the irrelevance of man in nature or in society. Auden begins his poem with a prose statement:

*When the historical process breaks down and armies organize with their embossed debates the ensuing void which they can never consecrate, when necessity is associated with horror and freedom with boredom, then it looks good to the bar business.**

Noting that in wartime everyone becomes a worshiper of chance, he then puts his characters through a kind of double exposure—the inner as opposed to the outer man. In a wine dream they move through a reëxamination of the seven ages of man (here following Shakespeare) and in so doing move also through the deceptions afforded by nineteenth-century romanticism, by twentieth-century Waste Land boredom, and by recent political utopianism. Always about them and breaking in upon their moments of clarity is the modern scene:

The scene has all the signs of a facetious culture,
Publishing houses, pawnshops and pay-toilets;
August and Graeco-Roman are the granite temples
Of the medicine men whose magic keeps this body

Politic free from fevers,
*Cancer and constipation.**

And always the four are attempting to open to each other the closed shutters of the inner self. Watching a world that is fallen, they would forget by sinking into alcoholic communication their essential isolation and their futility. But having, in recapitulation, surveyed their lives, these characters see man as a stranger to his world, still looking for some idea— be it Sherlock Holmes or God—to lead them and to unravel for them life's mystery. Since

*. . . human beings are, necessarily, actors who cannot become something before they have first pretended to be it; and they can be divided, not into the hypocritical and the sincere, but into the sane who know they are acting and the mad who do not,**

Auden finds that his characters can discover no sense of continuity, except in the moments of physical passion or in the moments of abstract philosophizing when the personal panic disappears and the mind insists on believing in "the whole subject of our *Not-Knowing*"— Auden's name for the God who is with us to the end and who puts us through our terrors so that we may not elude him. Louise Bogan reviews *The Age of Anxiety* as a "Christian" poem. Actually its Christianity is superimposed, arbitrarily, on the poet's cynical analysis of man's plight. Auden, who has in a number of his recent poems flirted with Christianity and its precepts with his usual brilliant cynicism, seems now to have accommodated himself to the deeper cynicism of existentialism. Auden's attitudes have been several: intellectual revolutionary, Catholic theologian, and now philosopher. Undeniably, however, Auden is consistent in his exhaustive cross-examination of the predicament of the outraged artist, for whom history is too slow a presentation of the creative dream of perfection, and for whom the church is no permanent solution since it cannot quiet the skeptic mind, to whom probably existentialism is merely new material for a brilliant but tired cross-examiner. As he moves into this new phase of inquiry, Auden has with him his inevitable younger disciples— such writers as like himself have ceased to believe in any social cure. But despite all this recent talk of existentialism it is to be doubted whether such a philosophy or literary movement is much more than a reflection of a war-born disillusionment, pessimism, and desire to withdraw from society.

Existentialism is not the only literary school, possibly abortive in nature, whose popularity is traceable to the war. The Apocalyptic poets of England (so named because of their reliance on the mystic vision), led by Henry Treece, insist that the state of art never coincides with fact. They welcome the destruction of the world, if through that destruction a deliberately worked up state of poetic tension can persist. If the poet moves between the real and the dream, the Apocalyptic poets, finding the real an abomination, would create in art a state of continuous self-induced irrationalism. This school is clearly related in its extravagance to a dying romanticism.

Summary

We have observed both in the existentialist movement and in the religious a strong note of protest against modern society. Although these literary movements are not directly political, they have, nevertheless, their political aspects. The existentialists have themselves pointed to the fact that their philosophical position gained a great following among a defeated people in Germany immediately after the First World War. And in the religious revival we have hints of a belief in a Christian crusade which acknowledgedly, even in medieval times, had its political aspect. Finally, we have seen that in both movements the artist retires from a society inimical to his development, and that a consistent anarchistic individualism is the dominating mood of much recent literature. The anarchistic novelist Alex Comfort makes clear the political consequence of the artist's repudiation of society when he writes:

Therefore now politically we guard ourselves as absolved. The State has consistently shown itself to be evil, in so far as we are able to understand evil. It has absolved us by rejecting individuality to which as artists we are obliged to cling, even though in retaining it we are forced to face the reality of personal death, the bitterest thought that any interpretive mind can face. We now accept no responsibility to any group, only to individuals. There are no corporate allegiances. All our politics are atomized.

It is not that as artists we have deserted society. It has deserted or ejected us, and we live on in contrast with it as tenants whom the landlord has not troubled to have thrown out. We have not seceded, but in clinging to personality we cling to something which everybody knows is the harbinger of death. They hate us for reminding them of it. They burrow deeper into society to lose sight of the fact which towers over them. Rather than face it, they become insane. This is the world in which art is placed. Fascism is a refuge from death in death. And Fascism epitomizes society.

Comfort, in other words, angered by what he considers the insane totalitarian or semi-totalitarian order characteristic of a society based on war and death, believes that the artist finds his personal regeneration in disobedience to the State.

* George Woodcock's article on Comfort, *Poetry Quarterly*, Summer, 1947.

POETS OF THE PRESENT

☞ THERE ARE a number of modern poets not easily catalogued as concerned either with the religious revival or with existentialism. Like Hart Crane after the First World War, there was Dylan Thomas after the second, affirming life. Thomas, frequently mentioned as one of the decadent romantics, is not, in truth, related to them at all. If he has anything in common with them, it is only his insistence on creative ecstasy as illumination. While the Apocalyptic poets want ecstasy in order to blind themselves to what they consider a dead world, Thomas is always insistent on creative ecstasy as a reason for renewed belief in life's general vitality. The most consistent images in his work imply his feeling for the continuity of life. Always in rhythmic ebb and flow, he moves out of the dark of despair into the green of life, using a curious mingling of druidical and Christian symbols to reiterate his theme of the inevitable resurrection after whatever dying there may have to be.

Thomas first began to publish when Auden so commanded the English poetic scene as to allow little room for the Welsh poet, so different from the essayist in verse. While Auden analyzed history and politics, Thomas conducted a Freudian inquiry into the growth of the imagination. His early poems were preoccupied with symbols of birth and of childhood. Soon these extended to inquiries concerning the adolescent emotions. As it was for Blake, with whose philosophy he has something in common, the good for Thomas has always been the creative. The sex drive and the insistence on fulfilling himself make man, for this poet, godlike, akin to the spirit of creation. Goodness, therefore, is for Thomas as for Blake sheer physical energy and not the intellectual power of judgment. For him the word and the image are divine. He creates wholeness and mystery from the sheer use of language.

Dylan Thomas' vitality and mysticism

One sees in many of the post-war poets a kinship to the seventeenth-century metaphysical school, a school which arose in a period of conflict between science and religion, a period in some ways, as many critics have noted, comparable to our own. But to Dylan Thomas, and to many of the moderns, the secular and the religious are not as contradictory as they were to the earlier metaphysical poets. For Thomas, indeed, the biological and the psychological are the basis of the religious. Whenever therefore he uses one of the metaphysical poems of the seventeenth century as springboard, his imagery is a conscious application of the recent Freudian symbols to the older ideas of conflict between the sensual and the saintly. Thomas' mysticism springs from his sensuality. Only Gerard Manley Hopkins, from whom he learned much, has somewhat the same interest in the constant flux and change of things in nature; but for Thomas, unlike Hopkins,

growth in nature and man is enough and need not be resolved into a religious permanence. If Thomas were to define God, probably he would define Him as that moment of creation or that act of becoming which is ecstasy. In other words, for Thomas, the poet is divine; he is the sea, the sun, the tree, the vine, the mother and the father. With something of Whitman's all-embraciveness Thomas expresses every aspect of energy, but he makes no such explicit catalogue as did Whitman of the variety of ways in which man exemplifies energy. He simplifies his inclusiveness by stating it only in metaphysical terms:

I let perhaps an image be 'made' emotionally in me and then apply to it what intellectual and critical forces I possess—let it breed another, let the image contradict the first, make, of the third image bred of the other two together, a fourth contradictory image, and let them all within my imposed informal limits conflict. . . . Out of the inevitable conflict of images—inevitable, because of the creative, re-creative, destructive and contradictory nature of the motivating center, the womb of war—I try to make that momentary peace which is a poem. . . .*

Such a statement indicates that Thomas is not so much interested in fusing the real with the poetic vision for enlightenment as he is in insisting upon the creative nature of words themselves.

Like Whitman, Thomas has had to reconcile the fact of war with his belief that men are not naturally self-destructive. While not always concerned with asserting historical progress, Thomas is as insistent as was D. H. Lawrence in asserting man's biological necessities. Therefore, although he was active in a civilian capacity in this last war, he writes no elegies, but argues, on the contrary, that "death shall have no dominion." Startlingly contrasted in his war poems are the violent images of carnage and of resurrection. His poems urge that although we seem to live in the exodus of one set of values, we should move toward the genesis of other values, that out of "your monstrous officers and decaying army" must spring more passionate life, groping out of present darkness toward light.

* From *The Selected Writings of Dylan Thomas*, XV, 1946.

But as to how this will take place, he has no answer. He merely evokes in language the feeling that for him, and for those who follow him, creative intensity can know no permanent destruction. Thomas seems to rely for his faith upon what he would call a divine madness, which creates the tension and the "willing suspension of disbelief" denied the more skeptical. He makes no attempt to use memory as the bridge between emotional conviction and realistic doubt. Energy is for Thomas what memory was for Yeats; and energy denies that we are a world seeking death. We can

doubt anything but physical passion, and Thomas would so charge words as to make them almost physically give birth to the moment of belief.

If one must place him historically, Thomas is, of course, a very late romantic, but in his romanticism he is akin, not to those poets who would escape from the world in order to hold to their dream, but to a poet like Hart Crane (see p. 596) who would integrate all that he could assimilate of modernity with his dream of man's possibilities. And even as Hart Crane

Joan Miro: Lithograph XXXII
Miro is a master in evoking satire and humor in the spectator, although his work leaves an impression of mordant and critical penetration

repudiated Eliot, Thomas repudiates Auden and the poets of logical inquiry. Thus he escapes from the ultimate exhaustion of living in the mind's courtroom by using the language of feeling and of faith in life.

Other young poets were not wholly romantic. Some of them feel the need of learning what history teaches. Some have learned objectivity from the poets obsessed with history in the thirties and some, like Hart Crane or Dylan Thomas, from the Symbolists, and yet they have refused to be drawn into the turgid waters of emotional subjectivity too deep to be understood. Instead they have wished to interpret the significance of the objective world together with its impact upon the sensitive mind. These poets look not inward nor unto heaven, nor do they rely on a blind faith that life will go on, come what may. They turn, although rather obliquely, to earth and man.

Younger poets examine man's place in society

Ben Belitt moved during the 1930's from Keatsian affirmation into a consciousness of a poetic task not unlike Hart Crane's. Crane realized in poetry the meaning of the instruments man had made through which man might communicate. But he did not wholly realize the economic problems facing man. Belitt is concerned with the relationship between art and modern man's place as an individual in a complex society. Not a political poet in the sense that Fearing is, he works always from inner resolution of feeling to the outer image of the world. He sees that waste consumes all, and that the image of poverty is man's moral ghost. He feels that the poet's duty is to heighten the humanity common to us all. When Belitt entered the war, therefore, his poetry and prose became a close examination of what happens to the individual thus thrust into collective action. Without petulance or the Audenesque attitudes of Karl Shapiro, Belitt records the effects of the draft and of the war as it changes a poet's consciousness. Here for Belitt was a crisis in which suffering had to serve not to enhance isolation but to enforce unity. The horror of personal obliteration in war, he felt, could be cast off either in the curi-

ous sense of power afforded by group action—a power which is in itself something of an opiate —or, better still, by reducing to art the impact of action on the imagination. Belitt saw in the war films a possible art form through which could be achieved the victory over horror and over death. Even so had Keats seen the figures on the Grecian urn.

Another poet who never avoided the sensitive recording of the present was David Schubert. A poverty-stricken childhood and delicate health urged Schubert on to attempt an early integration of his sense of loneliness and his sense of human dignity. In his psychological studies of childhood are reflected all the incongruities of our society, with its idealism and its ruthless materialism. Familiarity with the great Spanish poets Federico García Lorca and Rafael Alberti threw Schubert more directly into political reasoning, and although he never argued in any orthodox political way, he imaged in his verse a future contrasting with the present, which would exclude poverty. Before the war came he understood the fortress which might create war. He attempted to join the Army, but his health and his spirit were broken. Nevertheless, his last poems were his most humorously realistic, in their affirmations of the greatness of human capacities. He died before the war ended.

In James Agee, we have a mind accurate unto painfulness in its registering of the actual, a sensibility keyed to assimilate every shock of the present. There is in this poet an almost Christlike dedication to humble men. In *Let Us Now Praise Famous Men*, he gives us an account of long weeks spent living with the southern sharecroppers. As he came to know these people and brooded over them, they seemed all our society could signify in mistakenness. Agee almost repudiates modern culture in his passion to prove that the poor alone enter the kingdom of heaven. And he ends this study of the underprivileged with the strange plea that we should leave each other alone. Here he indicates the split in his own consciousness which he referred to when he described himself as intellectually Communist but emotionally Catholic. For him, the sharecroppers are creatures of a sure and simple sense of beauty and innocence. Any contact between them and our middle-class commercialism will destroy them. This certainly is not a Communist argument, but neither can it be said to be Catholic. It is, Agee says, anarchistic. In Agee we have all of modern life strikingly imaged as a betrayal of man's true self. Yet Agee's religion, like Belitt's, is really an expression of faith in man's sensitivity and in his innocence. Whatever darkens this sensitivity, be it history or poverty, is for Agee the inevitable crucifixion of the human spirit.

Elizabeth Bishop is a very different poet from these so far mentioned. Like her master, the more striking Marianne Moore, she is a poet wholly of observation. Logical, witty, and intelligent, she begins each poem with concrete observations, proceeding gradually to heighten, unify, and universalize upon them. The poem "Roosters" moves through many images of the familiar bird until he symbolizes betrayal before cockcrow, war, and a possible new era. Miss Bishop is less selective than Miss Moore. Her material is more familiar, more dramatic, her mind more concerned with politics and more specific in its references. There is little in modern consciousness that has escaped her. If she is not so intellectual and profound as Marianne Moore, she is more acutely aware of the modern scene.

Randall Jarrell, perhaps more than most poets, has grown with recent events. Before the war, he was little more than a rather destructively witty critic and a rather overly intellectual poet. He has emerged as one of the more important poets of World War II. He served in it, as did many others, but not without finding, even in combat, time to consider the historical developments in society which led us to conflict. Jarrell sees the whole mad drive of competition as that which has consumed all good in human nature. Somber, widely read, sensitive, and intelligent, he is passionately moved to pity for the blind average souls caught up in these ideas of progress, believing in them, only to be destroyed. Jarrell interprets the movements of social developments and the development of capitalism, and in his poem "The Wide Progress" asks whether we can justify the industrial revolution if it ends by merely making a commodity of man. The war he sees as sweeping all men,

irrespective of class distinctions, into the instinctive fears of death and into the collective action necessary to life. And he asks, over and over again, what it is we die for. But he is not defeated, nor is he indifferent. One sees in his sense of history and of man's development a passion for human freedom. Jarrell's vision is of a world less haunted by poverty and by war.

Stanley Kunitz' first volume of poetry, *Intellectual Things* (1930), had shown talent, but had proved him still given to what Yeats has called "the rhetoric of the will." Certain lines were too contrived, too constricted; the image and the emotion did not always blend. His second volume, *Passport to the War* (1944), proves Kunitz has outgrown his earlier faults and is today better able to reflect the emotions of the American Jew in wartime and during the growth of fascism than is any other American poet. The lyrics in this volume show a metaphysical mind, distinctly Hebraic, but moving always in conjunction with a twentieth-century social conscience. "Reflections by a Mailbox," for example, is a complete study of the Jewish-American consciousness. Because this war implied almost total destruction of the Jewish people in Europe, its impact on the Jewish mind was naturally terrific. Nevertheless, poets like Shapiro reflect comparatively little identification with the suffering of the Jews abroad, while poets like Delmore Schwartz so overstress the problem of being a Jew as to become almost lost in a maudlin self-pity. Kunitz neither separates himself from, nor loses himself in, his background. He is fully aware of the ancient culture as well as of American culture. His poem "The Hemorrhage" is unforgettable in its registering of violence on a mind long taught submission. In the poem "Father and Son" he expresses the affection and the separateness of two generations. He says to his father, "Instruct your son, whirling between two wars, in the Gemara of your gentleness," and he is, apparently, so instructed, for his lines reflect high moral conviction and the will to fight oppression without egotism, self-pity, or narrowness. Kunitz has given us one of our better books of war poetry, a book in which the concentration on individualism does not cloud the clear, progressive vision.

These are some of the poets whose emotion

865

and imagination fix on the present more than on the past. It should be pointed out that certain of the religious poets are almost equally preoccupied with the modern scene. Barker, for example, studies it closely, but with considerable horror of what the past meant. This causes him to create a gulf between the past and the present. He is not sure, in other words, as to what in the present might prove the progressive forces from which the future might develop. Yet he jumps at times into images which appear to project a socialist design. Nor can Dylan Thomas' biological urgencies, ex-

alted as they are, clearly delineate what passions or actions convince us that belief in life can overcome belief in death. Only in Louis MacNeice, and particularly in his war poems (*Springboard*), do we see a poet whose name was earlier associated with Marxist convictions analyzing the present as a stepping stone to a future in which the common man's position would be better generally. MacNeice's realism and his liking for the broad outlines of Marxism have kept him one of the most leftist of the English poets. Unlike Auden, MacNeice still affirms the need of an evolution toward socialism.

THE ARTIST AS INDIVIDUAL IN TODAY'S SOCIETY

❦ ONE THEME has absorbed most of the poets of the war period—that of estimating the changes in individual consciousness as man became a participant in action. Long accustomed as the artist has been to a faith in the individual as all-important, it is natural that he should show some anxiety concerning what he loses or gains by yielding to social concerns. The richness of individualism is, of course, justification for the artist's belief in it. Henry James, indeed, held that whatever the possible evils of our society might be, they were compensated for if it reared an aristocracy of art. When the first war broke, he knew, however, that this was not true. Since then, it has become clear to the thinking man that individualism is possible only in a stable and a progressive society. Once a society grows unstable, overemphasized individualism takes the form of a neurotic protest against society.

There is another interesting difference between English and American poets. In England, the poets, with few exceptions, come from the educated and governing upper class, and that class is politically minded. The English poet, therefore, is more familiar with political emotion and imagery than is the American. In America, politics has the stamp of big business, and all writers have for some time disliked the commercial in any form. Political language is therefore alien to the American poet. He has until recently not always been concerned even with American history, but in this he is changing. Robert Lowell, for example, begins with

the desire to find the meaning of his own life in terms of his puritanical heredity and of the changing environment of his forebears. American writers have, in fact, grown more interested in the development of our culture. Each section of the country brings forth writers who seek to interpret the cultural patterns from which they sprang. Nevertheless, no literature prophesying socialism is likely to spring up, unless history moves that way; and the mainstream of literature is a continuation of the Waste Land despair.

At such a time, it is probably good that Briton and American can still laugh. We have our *New Yorker* poets and short story writers who often mirror with an undertone of irony the crosscurrents of the day. England has John Betjeman, the leading light-verse writer, to survey the modern scene with its good and bad, its old and new, in sentimental amusement. Even when Betjeman is annoyed into upbraiding the very class whose voice he is, as he did in *In Westminster Abbey*, his rapier thrust is forgiven him:

> Gracious Lord, oh bomb the Germans
> Spare their women for Thy Sake,
> And if that is not too easy
> We will pardon Thy Mistake.
> But, gracious Lord, whatever shall be,
> Don't let anyone bomb me.*

* From *Slick, but not Streamlined* by John Betjeman. Copyright 1947 by John Betjeman. Reprinted by permission of Doubleday & Company, Inc.

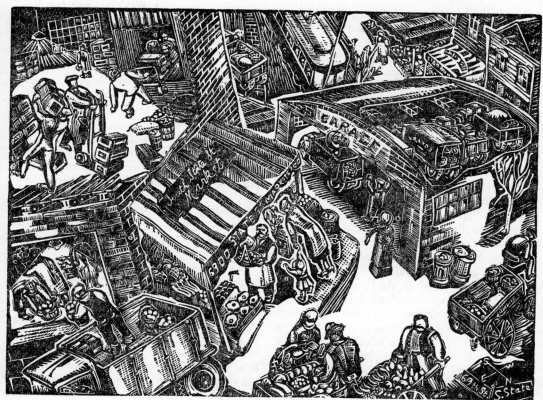

Adrian Troy: The Produce Market

In a composition confined almost to the limitations of a conventional design,
Adrian Troy, with nervous, intense, yet powerful, disposition of areas,
represents a scene in a great city in which what is commonplace
and bordering on the sordid becomes rich material for the artist

THE EMPHASIS ON CRITICISM AND ON FORM

THE PROPORTION OF criticism to creative literature is now high, and interest in form has increased from the period of the first war down. Nevertheless, this century, save for its elaboration of the subjective as against the objective, has given us no new art form. From Joyce onward, the worship of the word and of its overtones has spread, until it would seem that the word alone is god. And along with the writers, the students of semantics and the positivists have indicated our reliance on abstraction as more absorbing than any attempt to stretch the imagination. Books have been written to prove that given the word, the act will follow. I. A. Richards and Kenneth Burke and even William Empson are critics who imply that the word comes before the act. Such implication, though it shows some insight into what motivates us, puts the cart before the horse. It ignores the emotional and collective force of the inarticulate, who make language, first by acting, and then by labeling the act. Nevertheless, for the past fifteen years, the writers have found it more important to be interested in style than to be interested in subject matter. And although form has usually been supposed to spring from subject matter, it is treated by the critics more completely and as if it existed quite separately.

Both writers and critics, in other words, grow increasingly erudite and baroque. In the rise and fall of earlier literatures, the jewelled

867

and the precious have usually signified the end of an era. And it would seem that preoccupation with individual craftsmanship increases as the social scene becomes almost impossible of interpretation. In such a period the real is circumscribed by the symbol, and seems to exist only as the symbol: only when you name the object do you have it; otherwise it evades you.

Since the critics always thrive in a period of this type, we find ours flourishing. The little magazines are jammed with them; they jostle each other in their rediscoveries of all the older names. They believe in criticism for the sake of criticism; their tools are sharp but small. They carefully excavate, but seldom broadly interpret what they find. Most of them are so impressed with criticism as an end in itself that they snipe at anyone who takes the subject matter too seriously. And particularly they snipe at the newer sociological critics. Young poets must be interpreted in terms of older poets and older poetic forms, never in terms of what they try to say. The rules of thumb of a Tate, or a Ransom, or a Winters may limit all that is creative, and many of the younger artists today attempt to meet the critics' requirements, and become more conscious of technique than of vision. Meantime, in England Marxist criticism appears to be gaining in recognition. There Caudwell, who has appeared in America only through the International Publishers of New York, has been reprinted in an expensive edition, and the scholarly work of George Thomson (*Aeschylus and Athens*) which applies a sociological analysis to Greek literature, is taken seriously.

Meantime, much guesswork continues as to the future of our arts, though prophecy at this point seems futile. Whatever happens, we will probably not, as some believe, return to folk literature, unless, of course, after an atom war we are left in primitive homogeneity. Naïve literature, even in America, disappeared with regionalism, and attempts to resurrect it have not been fortunate. Today literature is international. Movements in literature travel faster than ever before. Forms carry over and are modified by the changes in the ideas they attempt to convey to the reader, but all the traditional techniques are now our literary inheritance.

We have remarked on the fact that after the first war the language of poetry was freshened by new imagery. In this respect it is interesting that a second world war has given us less of new imagery than we might have expected. If guns, tanks, and convoys appear, and of course, the constant imagery of the airplane, it is within the framework of history, within the emotional horror of a world at a brink. The quarrel between science and truth, recognized after the First World War, seems now tagged the quarrel between history and the individual. This may explain why the poetry of the second war names no concrete enemy. The enemy is not the German, but is a sense of division, at home as well as abroad.

IN SUMMARY

ALL IN ALL, the war has not simplified either the form or the subject matter of our literature. Our novels are all that the Waste Land novels were, and more elaborately. In poetry, a tortured and oblique use of imagery reflects the contradictions in the poet's mind. No new forms have developed, and it is possible that none will until the areas of our experience are better mapped, until, in other words, we know what path we are to take. (E. L. W.)

☞ "Peace in Our Time"

KENNETH BURKE

One of the most thoughtful and penetrating of present-day literary critics, Kenneth Burke brings to his work a gratifying combination of enthusiasm, scholarship, and a sound knowledge of the extremely important kindred fields of philosophy, history, and psychology. His intellectual interests are remarkably varied. Born in Pittsburgh on May 5, 1897, Burke was educated at Ohio State University and at Columbia, and settled into the career of a miscellaneous writer, contributing articles to numerous magazines. The subject which he seems to have chosen first to explore was sociology; he was a researcher at the Laura Spelman Rockefeller Memorial (1926–27) and did editorial work for the Bureau of Social Hygiene (1928–29). Music has always been one of his great loves, and he was a music critic, first for *The Dial* (1927–29) and later for *The Nation* (1934–36). He has been connected also with the New School for Social Research in New York, where he has lectured on the practice and theory of literary criticism, and with Bennington College, where he also lectured for several years. In 1928 Burke was awarded the *Dial* prize for distinguished work in American letters, and in 1935 he held a Guggenheim Fellowship. His activity as a writer of short stories, a poet, a translator, and an essayist has been nothing less than tireless.

Some of these many products of Burke's fertile intellect have been collected in part and amplified in other works, as in *The Philosophy of Literary Form* (1941), but much of his work can be found only in its original place in a periodical. *The White Oxen* (1924), his first ambitious publication, is a collection of short stories. *Counter-Statement* (1931) is largely literary criticism. *Towards a Better Life* (1932) is "a series of epistles and declamations," and can best be described as miscellaneous essays with a philosophical cast. *Permanence and Change, an Anatomy of Purpose* (1935) is a philosophical inquiry into the evolution of ethics and combines brilliantly Burke's interest in social matters with his philosophical and psychological virtuosity. *Attitudes Toward History* (1937) may be termed a study of the psychology of history or the psychological interpretation of historical events and personages; this kind of writing has occupied Burke especially of late, when historical events are being thrust under the nose of everyone. "The Rhetoric of Hitler's 'Battle'" is an excellent example of this preoccupation. *A Grammar of Motives,* which appeared in 1945, is the first volume of a projected trilogy, and consists of analyses of different kinds of writing which offer various interpretations of human motives.

Burke drank deep from the fountain of Marxism, but so thorough a student and so sound a scholar is he that this Marxism serves as little more than an intelligent and convenient approach to his writing. Possessing all the skepticism and the spirit of inquiry which characterize a scientific investigator, he has no blind faith in any dogma; he is not led to hysterical outbursts or even to passionate defenses. And he has the rare gift of making clear any topic over which his mind plays.

The Rhetoric of Hitler's "Battle"

THE APPEARANCE of *Mein Kampf* in unexpurgated translation has called forth far too many vandalistic comments. There are other ways of burning books than on the pyre— and the favorite method of the hasty reviewer is to deprive himself and his readers by inattention. I maintain that it is thoroughly vandalistic for the reviewer to content himself with the mere inflicting of a few symbolic wounds
10 upon this book and its author, of an intensity varying with the resources of the reviewer and the time at his disposal. Hitler's "Battle" is exasperating, even nauseating; yet the fact remains: If the reviewer but knocks off a few adverse attitudinizings and calls it a day, with a guaranty in advance that his article will have a favorable reception among the decent members of our population, he is contributing more to our gratification than to our enlightenment.

20 Here is the testament of a man who swung a great people into his wake. Let us watch it carefully; and let us watch it, not merely to discover some grounds for prophesying what political move is to follow Munich, and what move to follow that move, etc.; let us try also to discover what kind of "medicine" this medicine-man has concocted, that we may know, with greater accuracy, exactly what to guard against, if we are to forestall the concocting of
30 similar medicine in America.

Already, in many quarters of our country, we are "beyond" the stage where we are being saved from Nazism by our *virtues*. And Fascist integration is being staved off, rather, by the *conflicts among our vices*. Our vices cannot get together in a grand united front of prejudices;

and the result of this frustration, if or until they succeed in surmounting it, speaks, as the Bible might say, "in the name of" democracy. Hitler found a panacea, a "cure for what ails you," a 40 "snakeoil," that made such sinister unifying possible within his own nation. And he was helpful enough to put his cards face up on the table, that we might examine his hands. Let us, then, for God's sake, examine them. This book is the well of Nazi magic; crude magic, but effective. A people trained in pragmatism should want to inspect this magic.

I

Every movement that would recruit its followers from among many discordant and di- 50 vergent bands must have some spot towards which all roads lead. Each man may get there in his own way, but it must be the one unifying center of reference for all. Hitler considered this matter carefully, and decided that this center must be not merely a centralizing hub of *ideas*, but a Mecca geographically located towards which all eyes could turn at the appointed hours of prayer (or, in this case, the appointed hours of prayer-in-reverse, the hours 60 of vituperation). So he selected Munich, as the *materialization* of his unifying panacea. As he puts it:

The geo-political importance of a center of a movement cannot be overrated. Only the presence of such a center and of a place, bathed in the magic of a Mecca or a Rome, can at length give a movement that force which is rooted in the inner unity and in the recognition of a hand that represents this unity. 70

If a movement must have its Rome, it must also have its devil. For as Russell pointed out years ago, an important ingredient of unity in the Middle Ages (an ingredient that long did its unifying work despite the many factors driv-

"The Rhetoric of Hitler's 'Battle'" is reprinted by permission of the author and of *The Southern Review*.
24. **Munich**, the Munich Conference of September, 1938 (cf. "Passing in Review," p. 18). 35. **Our vices . . . democracy.** There is another aspect of vice that has on occasions come to the nation's assistance. I refer to our high development of the trained racketeer, who is always ready to bid for the control of any movement or organization sufficiently widespread to net a profit for unscrupulous insiders. And movements low in moral quality are the very first that succumb to such invasion. From that point on, the energies of the leaders are devoted primarily to the invention of new dues-paying schemes for shaking down the rank and file membership. And as a result of this merciless milking and mulcting, the movement is gradually dissipated and demoralized. Thus, the racketeer is a kind of unacknowledged guardian of the public welfare, as he zealously hastens the corruption of every organization that is corruptible and so hastens its collapse. Did not the Klan thus lose its strength, not through public resistance from without, but through the boring of the racketeer from within? It was obviously Satan-as-racketeer that Goethe had in mind, when char-

acterizing Mephistopheles as an ally of betterment: *ein Theil von jener Kraft, die stets das Böse will und stets das gute schafft.* (Author's note.)
46. **This book . . . this magic.** *Mein Kampf* is laborious reading—hence not likely of itself to produce much effect in America. Even in Germany its serviceableness probably resided less in its written form than in the uses to which it was put in Hitler's spoken improvisations. When one recalls the great cornerstone documents upon which political structures have been built in the past, one realizes all the more fully its dismalness. Yet it does provide us with an opportunity to examine the formula of prophecy, promise, and evasion which Hitler applied to the moulding of his people and himself. (Author's note.) 47. **pragmatism**, in philosophy the doctrine that practical results are the sole test of truth. 72. **Russell**, Bertrand Russell (p. 623).

ing towards disunity) was the symbol of a *common enemy*, the Prince of Evil himself. Men who can unite on nothing else can unite on the basis of a foe shared by all. Hitler himself states the case very succinctly:

As a whole, and at all times, the efficiency of the truly national leader consists primarily in preventing the division of the attention of a people, and always in concentrating it on a single enemy. The more uniformly the fighting will of a people is put into action, the greater will be the magnetic force of the movement and the more powerful the impetus of the blow. It is part of the genius of a great leader to make adversaries of different fields appear as always belonging to one category only, because to weak and unstable characters the knowledge that there are various enemies will lead only too easily to incipient doubts as to their own cause.

As soon as the wavering masses find themselves confronted with too many enemies, objectivity at once steps in, and the question is raised whether actually all the others are wrong and their own nation or their own movement alone is right.

Also with this comes the first paralysis of their own strength. Therefore, a number of essentially different enemies must always be regarded as one in such a way that in the opinion of the mass of one's own adherents the war is being waged against one enemy alone. This strengthens the belief in one's own cause and increases one's bitterness against the attacker.

As everyone knows, this policy was exemplified in his selection of an "international" devil, the "international Jew" (the Prince was international, universal, "catholic"). This *materialization* of a religious pattern is, I think, one terrifically effective weapon of propaganda in a period where religion has been progressively weakened by many centuries of capitalist materialism. You need but go back to the sermonizing of centuries to be reminded that religion had a powerful enemy long before organized atheism came upon the scene. Religion is based upon the "prosperity of poverty," upon the use of ways for converting our sufferings and handicaps into a good—but capitalism is based upon the prosperity of acquisitions, the only scheme of value, in fact, by which its proliferating store

of gadgets could be sold, assuming for the moment that capitalism had not got so drastically in its own way that it can't sell its gadgets even after it has trained people to feel that human dignity, the "higher standard of living," could be attained only by their vast private accumulation.

So, we have, as unifying step No. I, the international devil materialized, in the visible, point-to-able form of people with a certain kind of "blood," a burlesque of contemporary neo-positivism's ideal of meaning, which insists upon a *material* reference.

Once Hitler has thus essentialized his enemy, all "proof" henceforth is automatic. If you point out the enormous amount of evidence to show that the Jewish worker is at odds with the "international Jew stock exchange capitalist," Hitler replies with one hundred per cent regularity: That is one more indication of the cunning with which the "Jewish plot" is being engineered. Or would you point to "Aryans" who do the same as his conspiratorial Jews? Very well; that is proof that the "Aryan" has been "seduced" by the Jew.

The sexual symbolism that runs through Hitler's book, lying in wait to draw upon the responses of contemporary sexual values, is easily characterized: Germany in dispersion is the "dehorned Siegfried." The masses are "feminine." As such, they desire to be led by a dominating male. This male, as orator, woos them—and, when he has won them, he commands them. The rival male, the villainous Jew, would on the contrary "seduce" them. If he succeeds, he poisons their blood by intermingling with them. Whereupon, by purely associative con-

87. **Whereupon . . . democracy.** Tuberculosis, with which Hitler at one period was threatened, is thrown in for good measure. The symbolic connection between sexuality and tuberculosis in Thomas Mann's works may indicate that Hitler is here drawing upon something not quite haphazard, possibly by reason of the analogy between the "burning" of sex and the "burning" of tuberculosis fever, with its hectic flush—an intensity of desire commingled with a physical frailty in the gratification of it. We might also recall D. H. Lawrence, Octave Mirbeau's *Journal d'une Femme de Chambre*, and the use of the same theme in Gide's "Immoralist." An interesting kink, atop this continually recurrent theme of political control in terms of sexual love, is suggested by the fact that Hitler also stresses the total identification between the leader and his people. This would suggest, in a roundabout way, that the wooer, in wooing the people, is wooing himself. The thought might suggest why the Führer, dominating the feminine masses by his diction, has remained unmarried. Another lurid ingredient drawn upon throughout, and obviously connected psychologically with his racial theories, is the constant reference to blood-letting and blood-spilling. References to war are repeatedly materialized in such terms. (Author's note.)

nections of ideas, we are moved into attacks upon syphilis, prostitution, incest, and other similar misfortunes, which are introduced as a kind of "musical" argument when he is on the subject of "blood-poisoning" by intermarriage or, in its "spiritual" equivalent, by the infection of "Jewish" ideas, such as democracy.

The "medicinal" appeal of the Jew as scapegoat operates from another angle. The middle class contains, within the mind of each member, a duality: its members simultaneously have a cult of money and a detestation of this cult. When capitalism is going well, this conflict is left more or less in abeyance. But when capitalism is balked, it comes to the fore. Hence, there is "medicine" for the "Aryan" members of the middle class in the projective device of the scapegoat, whereby the "bad" features can be allocated to the "devil," and one can "respect himself" by a distinction between "good" capitalism and "bad" capitalism, with those of a different lodge being the vessels of the "bad" capitalism. It is doubtless the "relief" of this solution that spared Hitler the necessity of explaining just how the "Jewish plot" was to work out. Nowhere does this book, which is so full of war plans, make the slightest attempt to explain the steps whereby the triumph of "Jewish Bolshevism," which destroys *all* finance, will be the triumph of "*Jewish*" finance. Hitler well knows the point at which his "elucidations" should rely upon the lurid alone.

The question arises, in those trying to gauge Hitler: Was his selection of the Jew, as his unifying devil-function, a purely calculating act? Despite the quotation I have already given, I believe that it was *not*. The vigor with which he utilized it, I think, derives from a much more complex state of affairs. It seems that, when Hitler went to Vienna, in a state close to total poverty, he genuinely suffered. He lived among the impoverished; and he describes his misery at the spectacle. He was *sensitive* to it; and his way of manifesting this sensitiveness impresses me that he is, at this point, wholly genuine, as with his wincing at the broken family relationships caused by alcoholism, which he in turn relates to impoverishment. During this time he began his attempts at political theorizing; and his disturbance was considerably increased by the skill with which

Marxists tied him into knots. One passage in particular gives you reason, reading between the lines, to believe that the dialecticians of the class struggle, in their skill at blasting his muddled speculations, put him into a state of uncertainty that was finally "solved" by rage:

The more I argued with them, the more I got to know their dialectics. First they counted on the ignorance of their adversary; then, when there was no way out, they themselves pretended stupidity. If all this was of no avail, they refused to understand or they changed the subject when driven into a corner; they brought up truisms, but they immediately transferred their acceptance to quite different subjects, and, if attacked again, they gave way and pretended to know nothing exactly. Wherever one attacked one of these prophets, one's hands seized slimy jelly; it slipped through one's fingers only to collect again in the next moment. If one smote one of them so thoroughly that, with the bystanders watching, he could but agree, and if one thus thought he had advanced at least one step, one was greatly astonished the following day. The Jew did not in the least remember the day before, he continued to talk in the same old strain as if nothing had happened, and if indignantly confronted, he pretended to be astonished and could not remember anything except that his assertions had already been proved true the day before.

Often I was stunned.

One did not know what to admire more: their glibness of tongue or their skill in lying.

I gradually began to hate them.

At this point, I think, he is tracing the *spontaneous* rise of his anti-Semitism. He tells how, once he had discovered the "cause" of the misery about him, he could *confront it*. Where he had had to avert his eyes, he could now *positively welcome* the scene. Here his drastic structure of *acceptance* was being formed. He tells of the "internal happiness" that descended upon him.

This was the time in which the greatest change I was ever to experience took place in me.

From a feeble cosmopolite I turned into a fanatical anti-Semite, and thence we move, by one of those associational tricks which he brings forth at all strategic moments, into a vision of the end of the world—out of which in turn he emerges with his slogan: "I am acting in the sense of the Almighty Creator: *By warding off the Jews I am fighting for the Lord's work.*" (Italics his.)

He talks of this transition as a period of "double life," a struggle of "reason" and "reality" against his "heart." It was as "bitter" as it was "blissful." And finally, it was "reason" that won! Which prompts us to note that those who attack Hitlerism as a cult of the irrational should emend their statements to this extent: irrational it is, but it is carried on under the *slogan* of "Reason." Similarly, his cult of war is developed "in the name of" humility, love, and peace. Judged on a quantitative basis, Hitler's book certainly falls under the classification of hate. Its venom is everywhere, its charity is sparse. But the rationalized family tree for this hate situates it in "Aryan love." Some deepprobing German poets, whose work adumbrated the Nazi movement, did gravitate towards thinking *in the name of* war, irrational-

ity, and hate. But Hitler was not among them. After all, when it is so easy to draw a doctrine of war out of a doctrine of peace, why should the astute politician do otherwise, particularly when Hitler has slung together his doctrines, without the slightest effort at logical symmetry? Furthermore, Church thinking always got to its wars in Hitler's "sounder" manner; and the patterns of Hitler's thought are a bastardized or caricatured version of religious thought.

I spoke of Hitler's fury at the dialectics of those who opposed him when his structure was in the stage of scaffolding. From this we may move to another tremendously important aspect of his theory: his attack upon the *parliamentary*. For it is again, I submit, an important aspect of his medicine, in its function as medicine for him personally and as medicine for those who were later to identify themselves with him.

There is a "problem" in the parliament—and nowhere was this problem more acutely in evidence than in the pre-war Vienna that was to serve as Hitler's political schooling. For the parliament, at its best, is a "babel" of voices. There is the wrangle of men representing interests lying awkwardly on the bias across one another, sometimes opposing, sometimes vaguely divergent. Morton Prince's psychiatric study of "Miss Beauchamp," the case of a woman split into several sub-personalities at odds with one another, variously combining under hypnosis, and frequently in turmoil, is the allegory of a democracy fallen upon evil days. The parliament of the Habsburg Empire just prior to its collapse was an especially drastic instance of such disruption, such vocal diaspora, with

---

8. **He talks . . . "heart."** Other aspects of the career symbolism —Hitler's book begins: "Today I consider it my good fortune that Fate designated Braunau on the Inn as the place of my birth. For this small town is situated on the border between those two German States, the reunion of which seems, at least to us of the younger generation, a task to be furthered with every means our lives long," an indication of his "transitional" mind, that Wordsworth might have called the "borderer." He neglects to give the date of his birth, 1889, which is supplied by the editors. Again there is a certain "correctness" here, as Hitler was not "born" until many years later—but he does give the exact date of his war wounds, which were indeed formative. During his early years in Vienna and Munich, he forgoes protest, on the grounds that he is "nameless." And when his Party is finally organized and effective, he stresses the fact that his "nameless" period is over (i.e., he has shaped himself an identity). When reading in an earlier passage of his book some generalizations to the effect that one should not crystallize his political views until he is thirty, I made a note: "See what Hitler does at thirty." I felt sure that, though such generalizations may be dubious as applied to people as a whole, they must, given the Hitler type of mind (with his complete identification between himself and his followers) be valid statements about himself. One *should* do what he *did*. The hunch was verified: about the age of thirty Hitler, in a group of seven, began working with the Party that was to conquer Germany. I trace these steps particularly because I believe that the orator who has a strong sense of his own "rebirth" has this to draw upon when persuading his audiences that he is offering them the way to a "new life." However, I see no categorical objection to this attitude; its menace derives solely from the values in which it is exemplified. They may be wholesome or unwholesome. If they are unwholesome, but backed by conviction, the basic sincerity of the conviction acts as a sound virtue to reënforce a vice—and this combination is the most disastrous one that a people can encounter in a demagogue. (Author's note.)

50. **"babel."** "And the whole earth was of one language, and of one speech. And it came to pass, as they the descendants of Noah journeyed from the east, that they found a plain in the land of Shinar; and they dwelt there . . . And they said to one another, Go to, let us build a city and a tower, whose tops may reach unto heaven; and let us make us a name, lest we be scattered abroad upon the face of the whole earth. And the Lord came down to see the city and the tower, which the children of men builded. And the Lord said, Behold the people is one, and they have all one language; and this they begin to do: and now nothing will be restrained from them, which they have imagined to do. Go to, let us go down, and there confound their language, that they may not understand one another's speech. So the Lord scattered them abroad from thence upon the face of all the earth: and they left off to build the city. Therefore is the name of it called Babel, 'Confusion.'"—Genesis 11:1–9. 62. **diaspora,** dispersion.

movements that would reduce one to a disintegrated mass of fragments if he attempted to encompass the totality of its discordancies. So Hitler, suffering under the alienation of poverty and confusion, yearning for some integrative core, came to take this parliament as the basic symbol of all that he would move away from. He damned the tottering Habsburg Empire as a "State of Nationalities." The many conflicting voices of the spokesmen of the many political blocs arose from the fact that various separationist movements of a nationalistic sort had arisen within a Catholic imperial structure formed prior to the nationalistic emphasis and slowly breaking apart under its development. So, you had this Babel of voices; and, by the method of associative mergers, *using ideas as imagery*, it became tied up, in the Hitler rhetoric, with "Babylon," Vienna as the city of poverty, prostitution, immorality, coalitions, half-measures, incest, democracy (i.e., majority rule leading to "lack of personal responsibility"), death, internationalism, seduction, and anything else of a thumbs-down sort the associative enterprise cared to add on this side of the balance.

Hitler's way of treating the parliamentary babel, I am sorry to say, was at one important point not much different from that of the customary editorial in our own newspapers. Every conflict among the parliamentary spokesmen represents a corresponding conflict among the material interests of the groups for whom they are speaking. But Hitler did not discuss the babel from this angle. He discussed it on a purely *symptomatic* basis. The strategy of our orthodox press, in thus ridiculing the cacophonous verbal output of Congress, is obvious: by thus centering attack upon the *symptoms* of business conflict, as they reveal themselves on the dial of political wrangling, and leaving the underlying cause, the business conflicts themselves, out of the case, they can gratify the very public they would otherwise alienate: namely, the businessmen who are the activating members of their reading public. Hitler, however, went them one better. For not only did he stress the purely *symptomatic* attack here. He proceeded to search for the "cause." And this "cause," of course, he derived from his medicine, his racial theory by which he could give a non-economic interpretation of an economically engendered phenomenon.

Here again is where Hitler's corrupt use of religious patterns comes to the fore. Church thought, being primarily concerned with matters of the "personality," with problems of moral betterment, naturally, and I think rightly, stresses as a necessary feature the act of will upon the part of the individual. Hence its resistance to a purely "environmental" account of human ills. Hence its emphasis upon the "person." Hence its proneness to seek a non-economic explanation of economic phenomena. Hitler's proposal of a non-economic "cause" for the disturbances thus had much to recommend it from this angle. And, as a matter of fact, it was Lueger's Christian-Social Party in Vienna that taught Hitler the tactics of tying up a program of social betterment with an anti-Semitic "unifier." The two parties that he carefully studied at that time were this Catholic faction and Schoenerer's Pan-German group. And his analysis of their attainments and shortcomings, from the standpoint of demagogic efficacy, is an extremely astute piece of work, revealing how carefully this man used the current situation in Vienna as an experimental laboratory for the maturing of his plans.

His unification device, we may summarize, had the following important features:

(1) Inborn dignity. In both religious and humanistic patterns of thought, a "natural born" dignity of man is stressed. And this categorical dignity is considered to be an attribute of *all* men, if they will but avail themselves of it, by right thinking and right living. But Hitler gives this ennobling attitude an ominous twist by his theories of race and nation, whereby the "Aryan" is elevated above all others by the innate endowment of his blood, while other "races," in particular Jews and Negroes, are innately inferior. This sinister secularized revision of Christian theology thus puts the sense of dignity upon a fighting basis, requiring the conquest of "inferior races." After the defeat of Germany in the World War, there were especially strong emotional needs that this compensatory doctrine of an *inborn* superiority could gratify.

(2) *Projection* device. The "curative" process that comes with the ability to hand over one's ills to a scapegoat, thereby getting purification by dissociation. This was especially medicinal, since the sense of frustration leads to a self-questioning. Hence if one can hand over his infirmities to a vessel, or "cause," outside the self, one can battle an external enemy instead of battling an enemy within. And the greater one's internal inadequacies, the greater the amount of evils one can load upon the back of "the enemy." This device is furthermore given a semblance of reason because the individual properly realizes that he is not alone responsible for his condition. There *are* inimical factors in the scene itself. And he wants to have them "placed," preferably in a way that would require a minimum change in the ways of thinking to which he had been accustomed. This was especially appealing to the middle class, who were encouraged to feel that they could conduct their businesses without any basic change whatever, once the businessmen of a different "race" were eliminated.

(3) Symbolic rebirth. Another aspect of the two features already noted. The projective device of the scapegoat, coupled with the Hitlerite doctrine of inborn racial superiority, provides its followers with a "positive" view of life. They can again get the feel of *moving forward,* towards a *goal* (a promissory feature of which Hitler makes much). In Hitler, as the group's prophet, such rebirth involved a symbolic change of lineage. Here, above all, we see Hitler giving a malign twist to a benign aspect of Christian thought. For whereas the Pope, in the familistic pattern of thought basic to the Church, stated that the Hebrew prophets were the *spiritual ancestors* of Christianity, Hitler uses this same mode of thinking in reverse. He renounces this "ancestry" in a "materialistic" way by voting himself and the members of his lodge a different "blood stream" from that of the Jews.

(4) Commercial use. Hitler obviously here had something to sell—and it was but a question of time until he sold it (i.e., got financial backers for his movement). For it provided a *non-economic interpretation of economic ills.* As such, it served with maximum efficiency in deflecting the attention from the economic factors

involved in modern conflict; hence by attacking "Jew finance" instead of *finance,* it could stimulate an enthusiastic movement that left "Aryan" finance in control.

Never once, throughout his book, does Hitler deviate from the above formula. Invariably, he ends his diatribes against contemporary economic ills by a shift into an insistence that we must get to the "true" cause, which is centered in "race." The "Aryan" is "constructive"; the Jew is "destructive"; and the "Aryan," to continue his *construction,* must *destroy* the Jewish *destruction.* The Aryan, as the vessel of *love,* must *hate* the Jewish *hate.*

Perhaps the most enterprising use of his method is in his chapter, "The Causes of the Collapse," where he refuses to consider Germany's plight as in any basic way connected with the consequences of war. Economic factors, he insists, are "only of second or even third importance," but "political, ethical-moral, as well as factors of blood and race, are of the first importance." His rhetorical steps are especially interesting here, in that he begins by seeming to flout the national susceptibilities: "The military defeat of the German people is not an undeserved catastrophe, but rather a deserved punishment by eternal retribution." He then proceeds to present the military collapse as but a "consequence of moral poisoning, visible to all, the consequence of a decrease in the instinct of self-preservation . . . which had already begun to undermine the foundations of the people and the Reich many years before." This moral decay derived from "a sin against the blood and the degradation of the race," so its innerness was an outerness after all: the Jew, who thereupon gets saddled with a vast amalgamation of evils, among them being capitalism, democracy, pacifism, journalism, poor housing, modernism, big cities, loss of religion, half measures, ill health, and weakness of the monarch.

II

Hitler had here another important psychological ingredient to play upon. If a State is in economic collapse (and his theories, tentatively taking shape in pre-war Vienna, were but developed with greater efficiency in post-war Munich), you cannot possibly derive dignity from economic stability. Dignity must come first—and if you possess it, and implement it, from it may follow its economic counterpart. There is much justice to this line of reasoning, so far as it goes. A people in collapse, suffering under economic frustration and the defeat of nationalistic aspirations, with the very midrib 10 of their integrative efforts (the army) in a state of dispersion, have little other than some "spiritual" basis to which they could refer their nationalistic dignity. Hence, the categorical dignity of superior race was a perfect recipe for the situation. It was "spiritual" insofar as it was "above" crude economic "interests," but it was "materialized" at the psychologically "right" spot in that "the enemy" was something you could *see*.

20 Furthermore, you had the desire for unity, such as a discussion of class conflict, on the basis of conflicting interests, could not satisfy. The yearning for unity is so great that people are always willing to meet you halfway if you will give it to them by fiat, by flat statement, regardless of the facts. Hence, Hitler consistently refused to consider internal political conflict on the basis of conflicting interests. Here again, he could draw upon a religious pattern, 30 by insisting upon a *personal* statement of the relation between classes, the relation between leaders and followers, each group in its way fulfilling the same commonalty of interests, as the soldiers and captains of an army share a common interest in victory. People so dislike the idea of internal division that, where there is a real internal division, their dislike can easily be turned against the man or group who would so much as *name* it, let alone proposing 40 to act upon it. Their natural and justified resentment against internal division itself is turned against the diagnostician who states it as a *fact*. This diagnostician, it is felt, is the *cause* of the disunity he named.

Cutting in from another angle, therefore, we note how two sets of equations were built up, with Hitler combining or coalescing *ideas* the way a poet combines or coalesces *images*. On the one side, were the ideas, or images, of dis- 50 unity, centering in the parliamentary wrangle of the Habsburg "State of Nationalities." This

was offered as the antithesis of German nationality, which was presented in the curative imagery of unity, focused upon the glories of the Prussian Reich, with its Mecca now moved to "folkish" Vienna. For though Hitler at first attacked the many "folkish" movements, with their hankerings after a kind of Wagnerian mythology of Germanic origins, he subsequently took "folkish" as a basic word by which 60 to conjure. It was, after all, another non-economic basis of reference. At first we find him objecting to "those who drift about with the word 'folkish' on their caps," and asserting that "such a Babel of opinions cannot serve as the basis of a political fighting movement." But later he seems to have realized, as he well should, that its vagueness was a major point in its favor. So it was incorporated in the grand coalition of his ideational imagery, or imagistic 70 ideation; and Chapter XI ends with the vision of "a State which represents not a mechanism of economic considerations and interests, alien to the people, but a folkish organism."

So, as against the disunity equations, already listed briefly in our discussion of his attacks upon the parliamentary, we get a contrary purifying set; the wrangle of the parliamentary is to be stilled by the giving of *one* voice to the whole people, this to be the "inner 80 voice" of Hitler, made uniform throughout the German boundaries, as leader and people were completely identified with each other. In sum: Hitler's inner voice equals leader-people identification, equals unity, equals Reich, equals the Mecca of Munich, equals plow, equals sword,

83. **In sum . . . nation.** One could carry out the equations further, on both the disunity and unity side. In the esthetic field, for instance, we have expressionism on the thumbs-down side, as against esthetic hygiene on the thumbs-up side. This again is a particularly ironic moment in Hitler's strategy. For the expressionist movement was unquestionably a symptom of unhealthiness. It reflected the increasing alienation that went with the movement toward world war and the disorganization after the world war. It was "lost," vague in identity, a drastically accurate reflection of the response to material confusion, a pathetic attempt by sincere artists to make their wretchedness bearable at least to the extent that comes of giving it expression. And it attained its height during the period of wild inflation, when the capitalist world, which bases its morality of work and savings upon the soundness of its money structure, had this last prop of stability removed. The anguish, in short, reflected precisely the kind of disruption that made people *ripe* for a Hitler. It was the antecedent in a phrase of which Hitlerism was the consequent. But by thundering against this *symptom* he could gain persuasiveness, though attacking the very *foreshadowings of himself*. (Author's note.)

equals work, equals war, equals army as mid-rib, equals responsibility (the personal responsibility of the absolute ruler), equals sacrifice, equals the theory of "German democracy" (the free popular choice of the leader, who then accepts the responsibility, and demands absolute obedience in exchange for his sacrifice), equals love (with the masses as feminine), equals idealism, equals obedience to nature, equals race, nation.

And, of course, the two keystones of these opposite equations were Aryan "heroism" and "sacrifice" vs. Jewish "cunning" and "arrogance." Here again we get an astounding caricature of religious thought. For Hitler presents the concept of "Aryan" superiority, of all ways, in terms of "Aryan humility." This "humility" is extracted by a very delicate process that requires, I am afraid, considerable "good will" on the part of the reader who would follow it:

The Church, we may recall, had proclaimed an integral relationship between Divine Law and Natural Law. Natural Law was the expression of the Will of God. Thus, in the middle ages, it was a result of natural law, working through tradition, that some people were serfs and other people nobles. And every good member of the Church was "obedient" to this law. Everybody resigned himself to it. Hence, the serf resigned himself to his poverty, and the noble resigned himself to his riches. The monarch resigned himself to his position as representative of the people. And at times the Churchmen resigned themselves to the need of trying to represent the people instead. And the pattern was made symmetrical by the consideration that each traditional "right" had its corresponding "obligations." Similarly, the Aryan doctrine is a doctrine of resignation, hence of humility. It is in accordance with the laws of nature that the "Aryan blood" is superior to all other bloods. Also, the "law of the survival of the fittest" is God's law, working through natural law. Hence, if the Aryan blood has been vested with the awful responsibility of its inborn superiority, the bearers of this "culture-creating" blood must resign themselves to struggle in behalf of its triumph. Otherwise, the laws of God have been disobeyed, with human decadence as a result. We must fight, he says, in order to "deserve to be alive." The

Aryan "obeys" nature. It is only "Jewish arrogance" that thinks of "conquering" nature by democratic ideals of equality.

This picture has some nice distinctions worth following. The major virtue of the Aryan race was its instinct for self-preservation (in obedience to natural law). But the major vice of the Jew was his instinct for self-preservation; for, if he did not have this instinct to a maximum degree, he would not be the "perfect" enemy—that is, he wouldn't be strong enough to account for the ubiquitousness and omnipotence of his conspiracy in destroying the world to become its master.

How, then, are we to distinguish between the benign instinct of self-preservation at the roots of Aryanism, and the malign instinct of self-preservation at the roots of Semitism? We shall distinguish thus: The Aryan self-preservation is based upon *sacrifice*, the sacrifice of the individual to the group, hence, militarism, army discipline, and one big company union. But Jewish self-preservation is based upon individualism, which attains its cunning ends by the exploitation of peace. How, then, can such arrant individualists concoct the world-wide plot? By the help of their "herd instinct." By

51. **The Aryan . . . equality.** Hitler's own candidacy for leadership seems to have got strength from the conversion of guilt into power in this way: The guilt, revealed in the intensity and illogicality with which he projects all sin upon the persecuted "persecutor," the "seducer" of the people he would "woo," leads him to insist that the leader is one who takes personally upon himself full "responsibility" for the national well-being. This method is obviously spontaneous in the case of the prophet himself. But his henchmen use it automatically. Thus, one German paper, in discussing the Nazi invasion of Czechoslovakia, announces with automatic piety: "Germany does not shrink from assuming responsibilities for non-German peoples." (*New York Times*, March 16, 1939.) As for the scapegoat device: the overly efficient way in which every private or public ill has been handed over to the Jew has led to an ingenious popular use of this method in reverse. I have been told that when Germans want to criticize Hitler with less risk of imprisonment, they level their criticism at "Levine," saying, "Now, the trouble with Levine is this,"—or "Levine is wrong in such-and-such." And no one, of course, will mind your making objections to Levine. There seems evidence, in such sad decay of a noble invention, that its medicinal function is about over. Sophistication of this sort may well be further coached, unintentionally, by such zeal as that of the Nazi publisher who printed Heine's "Lorelei" with the ascription, "Author unknown." (Author's note.) 56. **The major . . . master.** If there were any use trying to catch Hitler in contradictions, one might properly ask what profit it would net the conspirators if they destroy the world they would master. And one does wonder why, if the Aryan blood is so damned all-powerful, it should fear mixing with non-Aryan blood. I should think that there would be a vast natural battle in the blood stream, and as a final result all the non-Aryan elements would have been killed off, as per the "law of the survival of the fittest." (Author's note.)

their sheer "herd instinct" individualists can band together for a common end. They have no real solidarity, but unite opportunistically to seduce the Aryan. Still, that brings up another technical problem. For we have been hearing much about the importance of the *person*. We have been told how, by the "law of the survival of the fittest," there is a sifting of people on the basis of their individual capac-
10 ities. We even have a special chapter of pure Aryanism: "The Strong Man Is Mightiest Alone." Hence, another distinction is necessary: The Jew represents individualism; the Aryan represents "super-individualism."

I had thought, when coming upon the "Strong Man Is Mightiest Alone" chapter, that I was going to find Hitler at his weakest. Instead, I found him at his strongest. (I am not referring to *quality*, but to *demagogic effective-*
20 *ness*.) For the chapter is not at all, as you might infer from the title, done in a "rise of Adolph Hitler" manner. Instead, it deals with the Nazis' gradual absorption of the many disrelated "folkish" groups. And it is managed throughout by means of a spontaneous identification between leader and people. Hence, the Strong Man's "aloneness" is presented as a *public* attribute, in terms of tactics for the struggle against the *Party's* dismemberment
30 under the pressure of rival saviors. There is no explicit talk of Hitler at all. And it is simply *taken for granted* that *his* leadership is the norm, and all other leaderships the abnorm. There is no "philosophy of the superman," in Nietzschean cast. Instead, Hitler's blandishments so integrate leader and people, commingling them so inextricably, that the politician does not even present himself as candidate. Somehow, the battle is over already, the

decision has been made. "German democracy" 40 has chosen. And the deployments of politics are, you might say, the chartings of Hitler's private mind translated into the vocabulary of nationalistic events. He says *what he thought* in terms of *what parties did*.

Here, I think, we see the distinguishing quality of Hitler's method as an instrument of persuasion, with reference to the question whether Hitler is sincere or deliberate, whether his vision of the omnipotent conspirator has the 50 drastic honesty of paranoia or the sheer shrewdness of a demagogue trained in Realpolitik of the Machiavellian sort. Must we choose? Or may we not, rather, replace the "either—or" with a "both—and"? Have we not by now offered grounds enough for our contention that Hitler's sinister powers of persuasion derive from the fact that he spontaneously evolved his "cure-all" in response to inner necessities?

III

So much, then, was "spontaneous." It was 60 further channelized into the anti-Semitic pattern by the incentives he derived from the Catholic Christian-Social Party in Vienna itself. Add, now, the step into *criticism*. Not criticism in the "parliamentary" sense of doubt, of hearkening to the opposition and attempting to mature a policy in the light of counter-policies; but the "unified" kind of criticism that simply seeks for conscious ways of making one's position more "efficient," more thoroughly itself. 70 This is the kind of criticism at which Hitler was an adept. As a result, he could *spontane-*

16. **Strong Man . . . chapter.** Throughout his book Hitler says many insulting things about the inferiority of the people. This is in accordance with the "law of the survival of the fittest" as he understands it. That is: he treats this "law" from a purely competitive angle, as a way of weeding out the innately inferior and raising the innately superior to leadership. He does not seem to have examined the Darwinian sources, where he might have learned how, by natural selection, the human race developed coöperative traits that enabled it to gain mastery over non-human competition. But the surprising thing is that Hitler's repeated insults seem to have disturbed his followers not at all. Possibly because each felt that the attacks applied to "the other fellow." (Author's note.) 35. **Nietzschean cast.** In *Thus Spake Zarathustra* (1883–84) Nietzsche painted a picture of the superman (as much above man as man was above the beasts), whose magnificent characteristics Zarathustra sought to teach the people and urged them to emulate.

53. **Machiavellian sort.** I should not want to use the word "Machiavellian," however, without offering a kind of apology to Machiavelli. It seems to me that Machiavelli's "Prince" has more to be said in extenuation than is usually said of it. Machiavelli's strategy, as I see it, was something like this: He accepted the values of the Renaissance rule as a *fact*. That is: whether you like these values or not, they were there and operating, and it was useless to try persuading the ambitious ruler to adopt other values, such as those of the Church. These men believed in the cult of material power, and they had the power to implement their beliefs. With so much as "the given," could anything in the way of benefits for the people be salvaged? Machiavelli evolved a typical "Machiavellian" argument in favor of popular benefits, on the basis of the princes' own scheme of values, that is: the ruler to attain the maximum strength, requires the backing of the populace. That this backing be as *effective* as possible, the populace should be made as strong as possible. And that the populace be as strong as possible, they should be well treated. Their gratitude would further repay itself in the form of increased loyalty. It was Machiavelli's hope that, for this roundabout project, he would be rewarded with a well-paying office in the prince's administrative bureaucracy. (Author's note.)

ously turn to a scapegoat mechanism, and he could, by conscious planning, perfect the symmetry of the solution towards which he had spontaneously turned.

This is the meaning of Hitler's diatribes against "objectivity." "Objectivity" is interference-criticism. What Hitler wanted was the kind of criticism that would be a pure and simple coefficient of power, enabling him to go most effectively in the direction he had chosen. And the "inner voice" of which he speaks would henceforth dictate to him the greatest amount of realism, as regards the tactics of efficiency. For instance, having decided that the masses required certainty, and simple certainty, quite as he did himself, he later worked out a 25-point program as the platform of his National Socialist German Workers Party. And he resolutely refused to change one single item in this program, even for purposes of "improvement." He felt that the *fixity* of the platform was more important for propagandistic purposes than any revision of his slogans could be, even though the revisions in themselves had much to be said in their favor. The astounding thing is that, although such an attitude gave good cause to doubt the Hitlerite promises, he could explicitly explain his tactics in his book and still employ them without loss of effectiveness.

Hitler also tells of his technique in speaking, once the Nazi party had become effectively organized, and had its army of guards, or bouncers, to maltreat hecklers and throw them from the hall. He would, he recounts, fill his speech with *provocative* remarks, whereat his bouncers would promptly swoop down in flying formation, with swinging fists, upon anyone whom these provocative remarks provoked to answer. The efficiency of Hitlerism is the effi-

14. **For instance . . . effectiveness.** On this point, Hitler reasons as follows: "Here, too, one can learn from the Catholic Church. Although its structure of doctrines in many instances collides, quite unnecessarily, with exact science and research, yet it is unwilling to sacrifice even one little syllable of its dogmas. It has rightly recognized that its resistibility does not lie in a more or less great adjustment to the scientific results of the moment, which in reality are always changing, but rather in a strict adherence to dogmas, once laid down, which alone give the entire structure the character of creed. Today, therefore, the Catholic Church stands firmer than ever. One can prophesy that in the same measure in which the appearances flee, the Church itself, as the resting-pole in the flight of appearances, will gain more and more blind adherence." (Author's note.)

ciency of the one voice, implemented throughout a total organization. The trinity of government which he finally offers is: *popularity* of the leader, *force* to back the popularity, and popularity and force maintained together long enough to become backed by a *tradition.* Is such thinking spontaneous or deliberate—or is it not rather both?

Freud has given us a succinct paragraph that bears upon the spontaneous aspect of Hitler's persecution mania. (A persecution mania, I should add, different from the pure product in that it was constructed of *public* materials; all the ingredients Hitler stirred into his brew were already rife, with spokesmen and bands of followers, before Hitler "took them over." Both the pre-war and post-war periods were dotted with saviors, of nationalistic and "folkish" cast. This proliferation was analogous to the swarm of barter schemes and currency-tinkering that burst loose upon the United States after the crash of 1929. Also, the commercial availability of Hitler's politics was, in a low sense of the term, a *public* qualification, removing it from the realm of "pure" paranoia, where the sufferer develops a wholly *private* structure of interpretations.)

I cite from "Totem and Taboo":

Another trait in the attitude of primitive races towards their rulers recalls a mechanism which is universally present in mental disturbances, and is openly revealed in the so-called delusions of persecution. Here the importance of a particular person is extraordinarily heightened and his omnipotence is raised to the improbable in order to make it easier to attribute to him responsibility for everything painful which happens to the patient. Savages really do not act differently towards their rulers when they ascribe to them power over rain and shine, wind and weather, and then dethrone them or kill them because nature has disappointed their expectation of a good hunt or a ripe harvest. The prototype which the paranoiac reconstructs in his persecution mania is found in the relation of the child to its father. Such omnipotence is regularly attributed to the father in the imagination of the son, and distrust of the father has been shown to be intimately connected with the heightened esteem for him. When a paranoiac names a person of his acquaintance as his "persecutor," he thereby elevates him to the paternal succession and brings him under conditions which enable him to make him responsible for all the misfortune which he experiences.

I have already proposed my modifications of this account when discussing the symbolic change of lineage connected with Hitler's project of a "new way of life." Hitler is symbolically changing from the "spiritual ancestry" of the Hebrew prophets to the "superior" ancestry of "Aryanism," and has given his story a kind of bastardized modernization, along the lines of naturalistic, materialistic "science," by his fiction of the special "blood-stream." He is voting himself a new identity (something contrary to the wrangles of the Habsburg Babylon, a soothing national unity); whereupon the vessels of the old identity become a "bad" father, i.e., the persecutor. It is not hard to see how, as his enmity becomes implemented by the backing of an organization, the rôle of "persecutor" is transformed into the rôle of persecuted, as he sets out with his like-minded band to "destroy the destroyer."

Were Hitler simply a poet, he might have written a work with an anti-Semitic turn, and let it go at that. But Hitler, who began as a student of painting, and later shifted to architecture, himself treats his political activities as an extension of his artistic ambitions. He remained, in his own eyes, an "architect," building a "folkish" State that was to match, in political materials, the "folkish" architecture of Munich.

We might consider the matter this way (still trying, that is, to make precise the relationship between the drastically sincere and the deliberately scheming): Do we not know of many authors who seem, as they turn from the rôle of citizen to the rôle of spokesman, to leave one room and enter another? Or who has not, on occasion, talked with a man in private conversation, and then been almost startled at the transformation this man undergoes when addressing a public audience? And I know persons today, who shift between the writing of items in the class of academic, philosophic speculation to items of political pamphleteering, and whose entire style and method changes with this change of rôle. In this academic manner, they are cautious, painstaking, eager to present all significant aspects of the case they are considering; but when they turn to political pamphleteering, they hammer forth with vituperation, they systematically misrepresent the position of their opponent, they go into a kind of political trance, in which, during its throes, they throb like a locomotive; and behold, a moment later, the mediumistic state is abandoned, and they are the most moderate of men.

Now, one will find few pages in Hitler that one could call "moderate." But there are many pages in which he gauges resistances and opportunities with the "rationality" of a skilled advertising man planning a new sales campaign. Politics, he says, must be sold like soap—and soap is not sold in a trance. But he did have the experience of his trance, in the "exaltation" of his anti-Semitism. And later, as he became a successful orator (he insists that revolutions are made solely by the power of the spoken word), he had this "poetic" rôle to draw upon, plus the great relief it provided as a way of slipping from the burdens of logical analysis into the pure "spirituality" of vituperative prophecy. What more natural, therefore, than that a man so insistent upon unification would integrate this mood with less ecstatic moments, particularly when he had found the followers and the backers that put a price, both spiritual and material, upon such unification?

Once this happy "unity" is under way, one has a "logic" for the development of a method. One knows when to "spiritualize" a material issue, and when to "materialize" a spiritual one. Thus, when it is a matter of materialistic interests that cause a conflict between employer and employee, Hitler here disdainfully shifts to a high moral plane. He is "above" such low concerns. Everything becomes a matter of "sacrifice" and "personality." It becomes crass to treat employers and employees as different *classes* with a corresponding difference in the classification of their interests. Instead, relations between employer and employee must be on the "personal" basis of leader and follower, and "whatever may have a divisive effect in national life should be given a unifying effect through the army." When talking of national rivalries, however, he makes a very shrewd materialistic gauging of Britain and France with relation to Germany. France, he says, desires the "Balkanization of Germany" (i.e., its breakup into separationist movements—the "disunity" theme again) in order to maintain commercial hegemony on the continent. But Britain desires the "Balkanization of *Europe*," hence would favor a fairly strong and unified Germany, to use as a counter-weight against French hegemony. *German* nationality, however, is unified by the *spiritual* quality of Aryanism (that would produce the national organization via the Party) while this in turn is *materialized* in the myth of the blood-stream.

IV

What are we to learn from Hitler's book? For one thing, I believe that he has shown, to a very disturbing degree, the power of endless repetition. Every circular advertising a Nazi meeting had, at the bottom, two slogans: "Jews not admitted" and "War victims free." And the substance of Nazi propaganda was built about these two "complementary" themes. He describes the power of spectacle; insists that mass meetings are the fundamental way of giving the individual the sense of being protectively surrounded by a movement, the sense of "community." He also drops one wise hint that I wish the American authorities would take in treating Nazi gatherings. He says that the presence of a special Nazi guard, in Nazi uniforms, was of great importance in building up, among the followers, a tendency to place the center of authority in the Nazi party. I believe that we should take him at his word here, but use the advice in reverse, by insisting that, where Nazi meetings are to be permitted, they be policed by the constituted authorities alone, and that uniformed Nazi guards to enforce the law be prohibited.

And is it possible that an equally important feature of appeal was not so much in the repetitiousness *per se,* but in the fact that, by means of it, Hitler provided a "world view" for people who had previously seen the world but piecemeal? Did not much of his lure derive, once more, from the *bad* filling of a *good* need? Are not those who insist upon a purely *planless* working of the market asking people to accept far too slovenly a scheme of human purpose, a slovenly scheme that can be accepted so long as it operates with a fair degree of satisfaction, but becomes abhorrent to the victims of its disarray? Are they not then psychologically ready for a rationale, *any* rationale, if it but offer them some specious "universal" explanation? Hence, I doubt whether the appeal was in the sloganizing element alone (particularly as even slogans can only be hammered home, in speech after speech, and two or three hours at a stretch, by endless variations on the themes). And Hitler himself somewhat justifies my interpretation by laying so much stress upon the *half-measures* of the middle-class politicians, and the contrasting *certainty* of his own methods. He was not offering people a *rival* world view; rather, he was offering a world view to people who had no other to pit against it.

As for the basic Nazi trick: the "curative" unification by a fictitious devil-function, gradually made convincing by the sloganizing repetitiousness of standard advertising technique— the opposition must be as unwearying in the attack upon it. It may well be that people, in their human frailty, require an enemy as well as a goal. Very well: Hitlerism itself has provided us with such an enemy—and the clear example of its operation is guaranty that we have, in Hitler and all he stands for, no purely fictitious "devil-function" made to look like a world menace by rhetorical blandishments, but a reality whose ominousness is clarified by the record of its conduct to date. In selecting his brand of doctrine as our "scapegoat," and in tracking down its equivalents in America, we shall be at the very center of accuracy. The Nazis themselves have made the task of clarification easier. Add to them Japan and Italy, and you have *case histories* of Fascism for those who might find it more difficult to approach an understanding of its imperialistic drives by a vigorously economic explanation.

But above all, I believe, we must make it apparent that Hitler appeals by relying upon

58. **rationale,** a reasonable course of action.

a bastardization of fundamentally religious patterns of thought. In this, if properly presented, there is no slight to religion. There is nothing in religion proper that requires a Fascist state. There is much in religion, when misused, that does lead to a Fascist state. There is a Latin proverb, *"Corruptio optimi pessima,"* the corruption of the best is the worst. And it is the corruptors of religion who are a major menace
10 to the world today, in giving the profound patterns of religious thought a crude and sinister distortion.

Our job, then, our Anti-Hitler Battle, is to find all available ways of making the Hitlerite distortions of religion apparent, in order that politicians of his kind in America be unable to perform a similar swindle. The desire for unity is genuine and admirable. The desire for national unity, in the present state of the world,
20 is genuine and admirable. But this unity, if attained on a deceptive basis, by emotional trickeries that shift our criticism from the accurate locus of our troubles, is no unity at all. For, even if we are among those who happen to be "Aryans," we solve no problems even for ourselves by such solutions, since the factors pressing towards calamity remain. Thus, in Germany, after all the upheaval, we see nothing

beyond a drive for ever more and more upheaval, precisely because the "new way of 30
life" was no new way, but the dismally oldest
way of sheer deception—hence, after all the
"change," the factors driving towards unrest
are left intact, and even strengthened. True,
the Germans had the resentment of a lost war
to increase their susceptibility to Hitler's rhetoric. But in a wider sense, it has repeatedly
been observed, the whole world lost the War—
and the accumulating ills of the capitalist order
were but accelerated in their movements to- 40
wards confusion. Hence, here too there are the
resentments that go with frustration of men's
ability to work and earn. At that point a certain kind of industrial or financial monopolist
may, annoyed by the contrary voices of our
parliament, wish for the momentary peace of
one voice, amplified by social organization,
with all the others not merely quieted, but
given the quietus. So he might, under Nazi
promptings, be tempted to back a group of 50
gangsters, who, on becoming the political rulers
of the state, would protect him against the necessary demands of the workers. His gangsters,
then, would be his insurance against his workers. But who would be his insurance against his
gangsters?

FRANKLIN DELANO ROOSEVELT

Franklin Delano Roosevelt, the only man ever elected for four consecutive terms to the presidency of the United States, was born at Hyde Park, New York, on January 30, 1882. He was educated at Groton, at Harvard University, and at the Columbia University Law School. After having practiced law in New York for several years, he was twice elected to the New York State Senate; served as an assistant secretary of the Navy (1913–21); and was defeated for the vice-presidency in 1920, having run with James M. Cox, on the Democratic ticket, against Warren G. Harding and Calvin Coolidge. Undaunted by the infantile paralysis which struck in 1921 and left him lame, Roosevelt continued his political activity. He served

two terms as governor of New York (1929–33), and in 1932 was elected President. Despite some of the bitterest political controversy of our history, he was thrice reëlected to this office. (A discussion of the significant events in his three administrations is to be found in the introductory essay, pp. 10–13.) On April 12, 1945, less than three months after his fourth inaugural, he died of a cerebral hemorrhage at Warm Springs, Georgia.

Roosevelt was an eloquent and magnetic speaker; his language was rhythmic and colorful, his delivery compelling. Most of his public papers and addresses have been compiled and have appeared in a uniform edition (1940).

First Inaugural Address

(March 4, 1933)

I AM CERTAIN that my fellow Americans expect that on my induction into the Presidency I will address them with a candor and a decision which the present situation of our Nation impels. This is preeminently the time to speak the truth, the whole truth, frankly and boldly. Nor need we shrink from honestly facing conditions in our country today. This great Nation will endure as it has endured, will revive and will prosper. So, first of all, let me assert my firm belief that the only thing we have to fear is fear itself—nameless, unreasoning, unjustified terror which paralyzes needed efforts to convert retreat into advance. In every dark hour of our national life a leadership of frankness and vigor has met with that understanding and support of the people themselves which is essential to victory. I am convinced that you will again give that support to leadership in these critical days.

In such a spirit on my part and on yours we face our common difficulties. They concern, thank God, only material things. Values have shrunken to fantastic levels; taxes have risen; our ability to pay has fallen; government of all kinds is faced by serious curtailment of income; the means of exchange are frozen in the currents of trade; the withered leaves of industrial enterprise lie on every side; farmers find no markets for their produce; the savings of many years in thousands of families are gone.

More important, a host of unemployed citizens face the grim problem of existence, and an equally great number toil with little return. Only a foolish optimist can deny the dark realities of the moment.

Yet our distress comes from no failure of substance. We are stricken by no plague of locusts. Compared with the perils which our forefathers conquered because they believed and were not afraid, we have still much to be thankful for. Nature still offers her bounty and human efforts

have multiplied it. Plenty is at our doorstep, but a generous use of it languishes in the very sight of the supply. Primarily this is because rulers of the exchange of mankind's goods have failed through their own stubbornness and their own incompetence, have admitted their failure, and have abdicated. Practices of the unscrupulous money changers stand indicted in the court of public opinion, rejected by the hearts and minds of men.

True, they have tried; but their efforts have been cast in the pattern of an outworn tradition. Faced by failure of credit they have proposed only the lending of more money. Stripped of the lure of profit by which to induce our people to follow their fatal leadership, they have resorted to exhortations, pleading tearfully for restored confidence. They know only the rules of a generation of self-seekers. They have no vision, and when there is no vision the people perish.

The money changers have fled from their high seats in the temple of our civilization. We may now restore that temple to the ancient truths. The measure of the restoration lies in the extent to which we apply social values more noble than mere monetary profit.

Happiness lies not in the mere possession of money; it lies in the joy of achievement, in the thrill of creative effort. The joy and moral stimulation of work no longer must be forgotten in the mad chase of evanescent profits. These dark days will be worth all they cost us if they teach us that our true destiny is not to be ministered unto but to minister to ourselves and to our fellow men.

Recognition of the falsity of material wealth as the standard of success goes hand in hand with the abandonment of the false belief that public office and high political position are to be valued only by the standards of pride of place and personal profit; and there must be an end to a conduct in banking and in business which too often has given to a sacred trust the likeness of callous and selfish wrongdoing. Small wonder that confidence languishes, for it thrives only on honesty, on honor, on the sacredness of obligations, on faithful protection, on unselfish performance; without them it cannot live.

Restoration calls, however, not for changes

The collected public papers of Franklin Delano Roosevelt have been published by Random House, Inc.

in ethics alone. This Nation asks for action, and action now.

Our greatest primary task is to put people to work. This is no unsolvable problem if we face it wisely and courageously. It can be accomplished in part by direct recruiting by the Government itself, treating the task as we would treat the emergency of a war, but at the same time, through this employment, accomplishing greatly needed projects to stimulate and reorganize the use of our natural resources.

Hand in hand with this we must frankly recognize the over-balance of population in our industrial centers and, by engaging on a national scale in a redistribution, endeavor to provide a better use of the land for those best fitted for the land. The task can be helped by definite efforts to raise the values of agricultural products and with this the power to purchase the output of our cities. It can be helped by preventing realistically the tragedy of the growing loss through foreclosure of our small homes and our farms. It can be helped by insistence that the Federal, State, and local governments act forthwith on the demand that their cost be drastically reduced. It can be helped by the unifying of relief activities which today are often scattered, uneconomical, and unequal. It can be helped by national planning for and supervision of all forms of transportation and of communications and other utilities which have a definitely public character. There are many ways in which it can be helped, but it can never be helped merely by talking about it. We must act and act quickly.

Finally, in our progress toward a resumption of work we require two safeguards against a return of the evils of the old order: there must be a strict supervision of all banking and credits and investments, so that there will be an end to speculation with other people's money; and there must be provision for an adequate but sound currency.

These are the lines of attack. I shall presently urge upon a new Congress, in special session, detailed measures for their fulfillment, and I shall seek the immediate assistance of the several States.

Through this program of action we address ourselves to putting our own national house in order and making income balance outgo. Our international trade relations, though vastly important, are in point of time and necessity secondary to the establishment of a sound national economy. I favor as a practical policy the putting of first things first. I shall spare no effort to restore world trade by international economic readjustment, but the emergency at home cannot wait on that accomplishment.

The basic thought that guides these specific means of national recovery is not narrowly nationalistic. It is the insistence, as a first consideration, upon the interdependence of the various elements in and parts of the United States—a recognition of the old and permanently important manifestation of the American spirit of the pioneer. It is the way to recovery. It is the immediate way. It is the strongest assurance that the recovery will endure.

In the field of world policy I would dedicate this Nation to the policy of the good neighbor —the neighbor who resolutely respects himself and, because he does so, respects the rights of others—the neighbor who respects his obligations and respects the sanctity of his agreements in and with a world of neighbors.

If I read the temper of our people correctly, we now realize as we have never realized before our interdependence on each other; that we cannot merely take but we must give as well; that if we are to go forward, we must move as a trained and loyal army willing to sacrifice for the good of a common discipline, because without such discipline no progress is made, no leadership becomes effective. We are, I know, ready and willing to submit our lives and property to such discipline, because it makes possible a leadership which aims at a larger good. This I propose to offer, pledging that the larger purposes will bind upon us all as a sacred obligation with a unity of duty hitherto evoked only in time of armed strife.

With this pledge taken, I assume unhesitatingly the leadership of this great army of our people dedicated to a disciplined attack upon our common problems.

Action in this image and to this end is feasible under the form of government which we have inherited from our ancestors. Our Constitution is so simple and practical that it is possible always to meet extraordinary needs by changes in emphasis and arrangement without loss of essential form. That is why our constitutional system has proved itself the most superbly enduring political mechanism the modern world has produced. It has met every stress of vast expansion of territory, of foreign wars, of bitter internal strife, of world relations.

It is to be hoped that the normal balance of Executive and legislative authority may be wholly adequate to meet the unprecedented task before us. But it may be that an unprecedented demand and need for undelayed action may call for temporary departure from that normal balance of public procedure.

I am prepared under my constitutional duty to recommend the measures that a stricken Nation in the midst of a stricken world may require. These measures, or such other measures as the Congress may build out of its experience and wisdom, I shall seek, within my constitutional authority, to bring to speedy adoption.

But in the event that the Congress shall fail to take one of these two courses, and in the event that the national emergency is still critical, I shall not evade the clear course of duty that will then confront me. I shall ask the Congress for the one remaining instrument to meet the crisis—broad Executive power to wage a war against the emergency, as great as the power that would be given to me if we were in fact invaded by a foreign foe.

For the trust reposed in me I will return the courage and the devotion that befit the time. I can do no less.

We face the arduous days that lie before us in the warm courage of national unity; with the clear consciousness of seeking old and precious moral values; with the clean satisfaction that comes from the stern performance of duty by old and young alike. We aim at the assurance of a rounded and permanent national life.

We do not distrust the future of essential democracy. The people of the United States have not failed. In their need they have registered a mandate that they want direct, vigorous action. They have asked for discipline and direction under leadership. They have made me the present instrument of their wishes. In the spirit of the gift I take it.

In this dedication of a Nation we humbly ask the blessing of God. May He protect each and every one of us. May He guide me in the days to come.

Address at the University of Virginia

(June 10, 1940)

I NOTICE by the program that I am asked to address the class of 1940. I avail myself of that privilege. But I also take this very apt occasion to speak to many other classes that have graduated through all the years, classes that are still in the period of study, not alone in the schools of learning of the Nation, but classes that have come up through the great schools of experience; in other words a cross section of the country, just as you who graduate today are a cross section of the Nation as a whole.

Every generation of young men and women in America has questions to ask the world. Most of the time they are the simple but nevertheless difficult questions, questions of work to do, opportunities to find, ambitions to satisfy.

But every now and again in the history of the Republic a different kind of question presents itself—a question that asks, not about the future of an individual or even of a generation, but about the future of the country, the future of the American people.

There was such a time at the beginning of our history as a Nation. Young people asked themselves in those days what lay ahead, not for themselves, but for the new United States.

There was such a time again in the seemingly endless years of the War Between the States. Young men and young women on both sides of the line asked themselves, not what trades or professions they would enter, what lives they would make, but what was to become of the country they had known.

There is such a time again today. Again today the young men and the young women of America ask themselves with earnestness and with deep concern this same question: "What is to become of the country we know?"

Now they ask it with even greater anxiety than before. They ask, not only what the future holds for this Republic, but what the future holds for all peoples and all nations that have been living under democratic forms of Government—under the free institutions of a free people.

It is understandable to all of us that they should ask this question. They read the words of those who are telling them that the ideal of

individual liberty, the ideal of free franchise, the ideal of peace through justice, are decadent ideals. They read the word and hear the boast of those who say that a belief in force—force directed by self-chosen leaders—is the new and vigorous system which will overrun the earth. They have seen the ascendancy of this philosophy of force in nation after nation where free institutions and individual liberties were
10 once maintained.

It is natural and understandable that the younger generation should first ask itself what the extension of the philosophy of force to all the world would lead to ultimately. We see today in stark reality some of the consequences of what we call the machine age.

Where control of machines has been retained in the hands of mankind as a whole, untold benefits have accrued to mankind. For mankind
20 was then the master; and the machine was the servant.

But in this new system of force the mastery of the machine is not in the hands of mankind. It is in the control of infinitely small groups of individuals who rule without a single one of the democratic sanctions that we have known. The machine in hands of irresponsible conquerors becomes the master; mankind is not only the servant; it is the victim, too. Such mastery
30 abandons with deliberate contempt all the moral values to which even this young country for more than three hundred years has been accustomed and dedicated.

Surely the new philosophy proves from month to month that it could have no possible conception of the way of life or the way of thought of a nation whose origins go back to Jamestown and Plymouth Rock.

Conversely, neither those who spring from
40 that ancient stock nor those who have come hither in later years can be indifferent to the destruction of freedom in their ancestral lands across the sea.

Perception of danger to our institutions may come slowly or it may come with a rush and a shock as it has to the people of the United States in the past few months. This perception of danger has come to us clearly and overwhelmingly; and we perceive the peril in a
50 world-wide arena—an arena that may become so narrowed that only the Americas will retain the ancient faiths.

Some indeed still hold to the now somewhat obvious delusion that we of the United States can safely permit the United States to become a lone island, a lone island in a world dominated by the philosophy of force.

Such an island may be the dream of those who still talk and vote as isolationists. Such an island represents to me and to the overwhelm- 6 ing majority of Americans today a helpless nightmare of a people without freedom—the nightmare of a people lodged in prison, handcuffed, hungry, and fed through the bars from day to day by the contemptuous, unpitying masters of other continents.

It is natural also that we should ask ourselves how now we can prevent the building of that prison and the placing of ourselves in the midst of it. 7

Let us not hesitate—all of us—to proclaim certain truths. Overwhelmingly we, as a nation—and this applies to all the other American nations—are convinced that military and naval victory for the gods of force and hate would endanger the institutions of democracy in the western world, and that equally, therefore, the whole of our sympathies lies with those nations that are giving their life blood in combat against these forces. 8

The people and the Government of the United States have seen with the utmost regret and with grave disquiet the decision of the Italian Government to engage in the hostilities now raging in Europe.

More than three months ago the Chief of the Italian Government sent me word that because of the determination of Italy to limit, so far as might be possible, the spread of the European conflict, more than two hundred millions of 9 people in the region of the Mediterranean had been enabled to escape the suffering and the devastation of war.

I informed the Chief of the Italian Government that this desire on the part of Italy to prevent the war from spreading met with full sympathy and response on the part of the Government and the people of the United States, and I expressed the earnest hope of this Government and of this people that this policy on the 10 part of Italy might be continued. I made it clear that in the opinion of the Government of the United States any extension of hostilities in the region of the Mediterranean might result in a still greater enlargement of the scene of the conflict, the conflict in the Near East and in Africa and that if this came to pass no one could foretell how much greater the theater of the war eventually might become.

Again on a subsequent occasion, not so long ago, recognizing that certain aspirations of Italy might form the basis of discussions among the powers most specifically concerned, I offered, in a message addressed to the Chief of the Italian Government, to send to the Governments of France and of Great Britain such specific indications of the desires of Italy to obtain readjustments with regard to her position as the Chief of the Italian Government might desire to transmit through me. While making it clear that the Government of the United States in such an event could not and would not assume responsibility for the nature of the proposals submitted nor for agreements which might thereafter be reached, I proposed that if Italy would refrain from entering the war I would be willing to ask assurances from the other powers concerned that they would faithfully execute any agreement so reached and that Italy's voice in any future peace conference would have the same authority as if Italy had actually taken part in the war, as a belligerent.

Unfortunately to the regret of all of us and the regret of humanity, the Chief of the Italian Government was unwilling to accept the procedure suggested and he has made no counter proposal.

This Government directed its efforts to doing what it could to work for the preservation of peace in the Mediterranean area, and it likewise expressed its willingness to endeavor to cooperate with the Government of Italy when the appropriate occasion arose for the creation of a more stable world order, through the reduction of armaments, and through the construction of a more liberal international economic system which would assure to all powers equality of opportunity in the world's markets and in the securing of raw materials on equal terms.

I have likewise, of course, felt it necessary in my communications to Signor Mussolini to express the concern of the Government of the United States because of the fact that any extension of the war in the region of the Mediterranean would inevitably result in great prejudice to the ways of life and Government and to the trade and commerce of all the American Republics.

The Government of Italy has now chosen to preserve what it terms its "freedom of action" and to fulfill what it states are its promises to Germany. In so doing it has manifested disregard for the rights and security of other nations, disregard for the lives of the peoples of those nations which are directly threatened by this spread of the war; and has evidenced its unwillingness to find the means through pacific negotiations for the satisfaction of what it believes are its legitimate aspirations.

On this tenth day of June, 1940, the hand that held the dagger has struck it into the back of its neighbor.

On this tenth day of June, 1940, in this University founded by the first great American teacher of democracy, we send forth our prayers and our hopes to those beyond the seas who are maintaining with magnificent valor their battle for freedom.

In our American unity, we will pursue two obvious and simultaneous courses; we will extend to the opponents of force the material resources of this nation; and, at the same time, we will harness and speed up the use of those resources in order that we ourselves in the Americas may have equipment and training equal to the task of any emergency and every defense.

All roads leading to the accomplishment of these objectives must be kept clear of obstructions. We will not slow down or detour. Signs and signals call for speed—full speed ahead.

It is right that each new generation should ask questions. But in recent months the principal question has been somewhat simplified. Once more the future of the nation and of the American people is at stake.

We need not and we will not, in any way, abandon our continuing effort to make democracy work within our borders. We still insist on the need for vast improvements in our own social and economic life.

But that is a component part of national defense itself.

The program unfolds swiftly and into that program will fit the responsibility and the opportunity of every man and woman in the land to preserve his and her heritage in days of peril.

887

I call for effort, courage, sacrifice, devotion. Granting the love of freedom, all of these are possible.

And the love of freedom is still fierce and steady in the nation today.

War Message to Congress

(December 8, 1941)

YESTERDAY, December 7th, 1941—a date which will live in infamy—the United States of America was suddenly and deliberately attacked by naval and air forces of the Empire of Japan.

The United States was at peace with that nation, and, at the solicitation of Japan, was still in conversation with its government and its Emperor looking toward the maintenance of
10 peace in the Pacific. Indeed, one hour after Japanese air squadrons had commenced bombing in the American island of Oahu, the Japanese ambassador to the United States and his colleague delivered to our Secretary of State a formal reply to a recent American message. While this reply stated that it seemed useless to continue the existing diplomatic negotiations, it contained no threat or hint of war or of armed attack.

20 It will be recorded that the distance of Hawaii from Japan makes it obvious that the attack was deliberately planned many days or even weeks ago. During the intervening time the Japanese government has deliberately sought to deceive the United States by false statements and expressions of hope for continued peace.

The attack yesterday on the Hawaiian Islands has caused severe damage to American
30 naval and military forces. I regret to tell you that very many American lives have been lost. In addition, American ships have been re-

ported torpedoed on the high seas between San Francisco and Honolulu.

Yesterday the Japanese government also launched an attack against Malaya. Last night Japanese forces attacked Hong Kong. Last night Japanese forces attacked Guam. Last night Japanese forces attacked the Philippine Islands. Last night the Japanese attacked Wake Island. And this morning the Japanese attacked Midway Island.

Japan has, therefore, undertaken a surprise offensive extending throughout the Pacific area. The facts of yesterday and today speak for themselves. The people of the United States have already formed their opinions and well understand the implications to the very life and safety of our nation.

As Commander in Chief of the Army and Navy I have directed that all measures be taken for our defense, but always will our whole nation remember the character of the onslaught against us. No matter how long it may take us to overcome this premeditated invasion, the American people in their righteous might will win through to absolute victory. I believe that I interpret the will of the Congress and of the people when I assert that we will not only defend ourselves to the uttermost but will make it very certain that this form of treachery shall never again endanger us.

Hostilities exist. There is no blinking at the fact that our people, our territory, and our interests are in grave danger. With confidence in our armed forces, with the unbounded determination of our people, we will gain the inevitable triumph, so help us God.

I ask that the Congress declare that since the unprovoked and dastardly attack by Japan on Sunday, December 7th, 1941, a state of war has existed between the United States and the Japanese Empire.

WINSTON CHURCHILL

From the time of the German break-through in France (May 10, 1940) until the defeat of Germany (May 8, 1945), Winston Spencer Churchill, champion of the nineteenth-century conception of the British Empire, was the unquestioned and unquestionable leader of Great Britain. Born in London, September 30, 1874, Churchill was educated at Harrow and at the royal military academy, Sandhurst. In his young manhood, military service and journalism carried him to far places; and in 1906, as a member of the House of Commons, he entered on his public career.

In 1908 Churchill was appointed president of the Board of Trade, and remained in this post until 1910. Other appointments followed: he was Home Secretary (1910–11), First Lord of the Admiralty (1914–15), Secretary of State for War and Air (1918–21), Secretary of State for the Colonies (1921–22), Chancellor of the Exchequer (1924–29), and, finally, Prime Minister of Great Britain (1940–45), a position which he held until he was replaced by Clement Attlee when the Labour Party came to power. He is justly famous for the remarkably inspiring addresses with which he informed and heartened his countrymen throughout the years of conflict. These fine examples of oratory have been published in several volumes, and in 1948 Churchill began the publication of his memoirs of the war.

A Time to Dare and Endure

Speech at the Free Trade Hall, Manchester, January 27, 1940

WE HAVE been five months at war against the world's greatest military power and the world's greatest air power. When the war began in September most of us expected that very soon our cities would be torn and charred by explosion and fire, and few would have dared to plan for the end of January a splendid gathering such as I see before me here this afternoon. I know of nothing more remarkable in our long history than the willingness to encounter the unknown, and to face and endure whatever might be coming to us, which was shown in September by the whole mass of the people of this Island in the discharge of what they felt sure was their duty. There never was a war which seemed so likely to carry its terrors at once into every home, and there never was a war into which the whole people en-

From *Blood, Sweat, and Tears* by Winston Churchill, published by G. P. Putnam's Sons. Reprinted by permission.

tered with the same united conviction that, God helping, they could do no other. 20

This was no war planned and entered upon by a Government, or a class, or a Party. On the contrary, the Government laboured for peace to the very end; and during those last days the only fear in Britain was lest, weighted down by their awful responsibilities, they should fail to rise up to the height of the occasion. They did not fail, and the Prime Minister led us forward in one great body into a struggle against aggression and oppression, against wrong-doing, 30 faithlessness and cruelty, from which there can be no turning back. We cannot tell what the course of that struggle will be, into what regions it will carry us, how long it will last, or who will fall by the way. But we are sure that in the end right will win, that freedom will not be trampled down, that a truer progress will open, and a broader justice will reign. And we are determined to play our part worthily, faithfully, and to the end. 40

So far the war in the west has fallen almost solely upon the Royal Navy, and upon those parts of the Royal Air Force who give the Navy invaluable help. But I think you will agree that up to date the Navy has not failed the nation. Continual losses there have been, and continual losses there will be. When you remember that we have hundreds of warships always running risks upon the sea in order to protect thousands of British and neutral merchant ships 50 spread about the vast ocean spaces of the globe, or crowding into our Island's gateways, you will realize that we shall have to pay an unrelenting toll for the mastery of the seas. Many hundreds of Naval homes in our dockyard cities have been darkened by irreparable loss. I am sure the sympathy and affection of the British people goes out to our sailormen—Royal Navy, Merchant Marine, trawlers, mine-sweepers, fisherfolk, and all who love them and depend 60 upon them as they toil day by day and night by night upon the dangerous stormy waters, doing their duty with unrivaled skill and with cheerful, unquestioning courage, that we may eat our daily bread each day, and that our cause may prosper.

Let no one therefore be disheartened when he reads of daily losses, or listens to them reiterated by the B.B.C. Let all remember that now, at the end of five months of vehement 70

889

naval war, it is five hundred to one against any ship which obeys Admiralty instructions and joins a British convoy being sunk, and that out of nearly seven thousand five hundred ships convoyed, only fifteen have been lost; that our convoy system is becoming more refined and rapid as the weeks go by; that the volume of our imports and exports, inevitably checked by change from peace to war, is now steadily in-
10 creasing; that the ships we have captured and the ships we have built have almost made good the losses we have suffered; and that very important reinforcements are approaching both our Navy and our merchant shipping to meet new dangers and new assaults which may very easily come upon us in the future.

We are embarking upon a widespread system of rationing. That is not because there is danger of famine or because the Navy has not
20 done its part in keeping open the oceans, the seas and the harbors. We are rationing ourselves because we wish to save every ton of imports, to increase our output of munitions, and to maintain and extend our export trade, thus gaining the foreign credits wherewith to buy more munitions and more materials of war, in order that the whole life-energy of the British nation and of the British Empire, and of our Allies, may be directed to the last ounce, to
30 the last inch, to the task we have in hand. This is no time for ease and comfort. It is the time to dare and endure. That is why we are rationing ourselves, even while our resources are expanding. That is why we mean to regulate every ton that is carried across the sea and make sure that it is carried solely for the purpose of victory.

But now on this question of food let me turn from the sea to the land, and from those who
40 plow the main to those who plow, or should plow, the manor. In our national effort there is need for all kinds of activity, and there is room, or room must be found, for all—men and women, old and young—to serve in one way or another. We must plow up the land. We must organize agriculture, upon at least the 1918 scale. We must grow more food and accommodate ourselves as much as possible to eat the kind of food we can grow. The cost of living must, so
50 far as possible, be kept down by abundance of simple food and necessaries. In this way we

may lighten the task of the Navy, increase its mobility, and free its striking forces for offensive action.

I have no doubt that from time to time you ask yourselves the question: Why is it that we have not yet been attacked from the air? Why is it that those severe ordeals for which we had braced ourselves on the outbreak of war have not been imposed upon us during these long five months? It is a question I am always turning over in my mind, and, like so many questions in this war, it is difficult to answer. Is it that they are saving up for some orgy of frightfulness which will soon come upon us, or is it because so far they have not dared? Is it because they dread the superior quality of our fighter aircraft? Is it because they have feared the massive counterstroke which they would immediately receive from our powerful bombing force? No one can say for certain. But one thing is sure: it is not from any false sense of delicacy that they have so far refrained from subjecting us to this new and odious form of attack. Nor is it out of lovingkindness.

We know from what they did in Poland that there is no brutality or bestial massacre of civilians by air bombing which they would not readily commit if they thought it were for their advantage. But here is a chapter of war which they have not chosen to open upon us, because they cannot tell what may be written in its final pages. But then the question arises, Ought we to have begun? Ought we, instead of demonstrating the power of our Air Force by dropping leaflets all over Germany, to have dropped bombs? But there I am quite clear that our policy has been right.

In this peaceful country, governed by public opinion, democracy and Parliament, we were not as thoroughly prepared at the outbreak as this Dictator State whose whole thought was bent upon the preparation for war. Everyone knows how far better we are organized now, and how much stronger our defenses of all kinds are, than at the beginning of the war. We have striven hard to make the most of the time of preparation that has been gained, and there is no doubt that an enormous advance has been made both in the protection of the civil population and in the punishment which would be inflicted upon the raiders. Not only have our air defenses and shelters been substantially improved, but our armies at home and abroad, which are now very large, are steadily maturing in training and in quality; and the whole preparation of our munition industries under the spell of war has rolled forward with gathering momentum. Therefore I feel I was right in saying in one of my earliest broadcasts that if we reached the spring without any interruption of our sea-borne trade, and without anything happening on land or in the air, we should, in fact, have gained the opening campaign of the war.

We cannot, however, place in the field immediately the great armies which we need, and which we are determined to form, and for which millions of eager men stand ready. We have to increase very largely our manufacture of munitions and equipment of all kinds. The immense plants and factories needed can only gradually come into full production. We are of course much further ahead than we were at this time in the last war, and, guided by the experiences of that war, we ought to make far more rapid progress. But we have to make a huge expansion of our labour force, and especially of those capable of performing skilled or semi-skilled operations. Here we must specially count for aid and guidance upon our Labour colleagues and trade union leaders. I can speak with some knowledge of this, having presided over the former Ministry of Munitions in its culminating phase. Millions of new workers will be needed, and more than a million women must come boldly forward into our war industry—into the shell plants and munitions works, and into the aircraft factories.

If trade unionists, from patriotic or international motives, lay aside for the duration of the war any of the special craft usages which they have so carefully built up, they need have no fear that these will not be fully restored to them after the war is won. Nearly a million women were employed in the last war in 1918 under the Ministry of Munitions. They did all kinds of things that no one had ever expected them to do before, and they did them very well. But after the war was over they all went back home, and were no obstacles to the resumption of normal conditions of British life and labour. Without this expansion of labour, and

without allowing the women of Britain to enter the struggle, as they desire to do, we should fail utterly to bear our fair share of the burden which France and Britain have jointly assumed, and which we just now carry forward together to the end, or perish miserably in slavery and ruin.

During this time of war great powers are entrusted to the executive government. Nevertheless, we exercise them under the constant supervision of Parliament, and with a wide measure of free debate. We have a stern and resolute House of Commons, which is not likely at all to flag or weaken in the conflict upon which it entered unanimously, and I do not doubt it is a House of Commons which will not hesitate, if emergency requires it, to approve and to enforce all measures necessary for the safety of the State. During the last two hundred and fifty years the British Parliament has fought several great and long European wars with unwearied zeal and tenacity, and carried them all to a successful conclusion. In this war they are fighting not only for themselves, but for Parliamentary institutions wherever they have been set up all over the globe.

In our country public men are proud to be servants of the people. They would be ashamed to be their masters. Ministers of the Crown feel themselves strengthened by having at their side the House of Commons and the House of Lords sitting with great regularity, and acting as a continual stimulus to their activities. Of course, it is quite true that there is often severe criticism of the Government in both Houses. We do not resent the well-meant criticism of any man who wishes to win the war. We do not shrink from fair criticism, and that is the most dangerous of all. On the contrary, we take it earnestly to heart and seek to profit by it. Criticism in the body politic is like pain in the human body. It is not pleasant, but where would the body be without it? No health or sensibility would be possible without continued correctives and warnings of pain.

It is in this fear of criticism that the Nazi and Bolshevik dictatorships run their greatest risk. They silence all criticism by the concentration camp, the rubber truncheon, or the firing party. Thus the men at the top must very often only be fed with the facts which are palatable to them. Scandals, corruption and shortcomings are not exposed, because there are no independent voices. Instead of being exposed, they continue to fester behind the pompous frontage of the State. The men at the top may be very fierce and powerful, but their ears are deaf, their fingers are numb; they cannot feel their feet as they move forward in the fog and darkness of the immeasurable and the unknown. One of the things that this war is going to prove is whether in modern times the full strength of nations can be realized for war under totalitarian systems working through an Ogpu or a Gestapo. Certainly what we have seen of the Russian effort when opposed to the heroic Finns should give the British and French democracies and Parliaments additional confidence in their own struggle with the Nazi despotism.

Herr Hitler boasts that he has ninety millions under his rod, but nearly twenty of these millions have to be forcibly held down by the others. We and the French have eighty-five millions in our homelands, and twenty millions more in the British Dominions whose armies are hastening to the battle front; and besides this there are vast populations of men of other races who owe allegiance to the Crown or the French Republic spread about the surface of the globe whose sure instinct leads them to regard Nazism as a deadly menace to their future progress. All these inexhaustible resources will steadily and surely, through the command of the seas, be brought to bear upon the evil things whose wickedness has cast its shadow upon mankind and seeks to bar its forward march.

Let us look for a moment at what Nazi Germany inflicts upon the peoples she has subjugated to her rule. The German invaders pursue with every method of cultural, social and economic oppression their intention of destroying the Czech nation. Students are shot by scores and tormented in concentration camps by thousands. All the Czech universities have closed—amongst them the Charles University of Prague which, founded in 1348, was the first university of Central Europe; the clinics in Central Europe, the laboratories, the libraries of the Czech universities have been pillaged or destroyed. The works of their national writers have been removed from the public libraries. More than two thousand periodicals and newspapers have been suppressed. Prominent writers, artists and professors have been herded into the concentration camps. The public administration and judicature have been reduced to chaos. The Czech lands have been plundered, and every scrap of food and useful portable article carried off into Germany by organised brigandage or common theft. The property of the Churches is maladministered and engrossed by German commissars. A hundred thousand Czech workmen have been led off into slavery to be toiled to death in Germany. Eight millions of Czechs—a nation famous and recognizable as a distinct community for many centuries past in Europe—writhe in agony under the German and Nazi tyranny.

But everything that is happening to the Czechs pales in comparison with the atrocities which as I speak here this afternoon are being perpetrated upon the Poles. In German-occupied Poland the most hideous form of terrorism prevails. In this there are two distinct phases. In the first the Germans tried to cow the population by shooting individuals picked at random from the towns. At one place where they had decided to shoot thirty-five people they collected thirty-four, and then, finding themselves one short, went into a chemist's shop and seized the first person they saw to make up the tally. But later on they became more discriminating—they made careful search for the natural leaders of Polish life: the nobles, the landowners, the priests, as well as prominent workmen and peasants. It is estimated that upwards of fifteen thousand intellectual leaders have been shot. These horrible mass executions are a frequent occurrence. At one place three hundred were lined up against the wall; at another a group of drunken German officers are said to have shot seventy hostages in prison; at another a hundred and thirty-six Polish students, some of whom were only twelve or thirteen years old, were butchered. Torture has been used. Press gangs seize men and women in the streets and drive them off in droves to forced labour in Germany. Famine stalks not only amid the ruins of Warsaw, but far and wide throughout that ancient country which a few months ago was the home of a people of over thirty-five millions, with a history extending back far beyond anything that Germany can boast.

"The horror and inexcusable excesses committed on a helpless and homeless people," declared the Papal broadcasts from the Vatican on the 22nd of this month, "have been established by the unimpeachable testimony of eyewitnesses. The crowning iniquity,"—says the Vatican broadcast—"lies in the cynical suppression of all but the merest suggestion of religious worship in the lives of one of the most pious and devotional of the peoples of Europe." From these shameful records we may judge what our own fate would be if we fell into their clutches. But from them also we may draw the force and inspiration to carry us forward upon our journey and not to pause or rest till liberation is achieved and justice done.

Come then: let us to the task, to the battle, to the toil—each to our part, each to our station. Fill the armies, rule the air, pour out the munitions, strangle the U-boats, sweep the mines, plow the land, build the ships, guard the streets, succor the wounded, uplift the downcast, and honor the brave. Let us go forward together in all parts of the Empire, in all parts of the Island. There is not a week, nor a day, nor an hour to lose.

Prime Minister

Speech before the House of Commons,
May 13, 1940

ON FRIDAY evening last I received His Majesty's Commission to form a new Administration. It was the evident wish and will of Parliament and the nation that this should be conceived on the broadest possible basis and that it should include all Parties, both those who supported the late Government and also the Parties of the Opposition. I have completed the most important part of this task. A War Cabinet has been formed of five Members, representing, with the Opposition Liberals, the unity of the nation. The three Party Leaders have agreed to serve, either in the War Cabinet or in high executive office. The three Fighting Services have been filled. It was necessary that this should be done in one single day, on account of the extreme urgency and rigor of events. A number of other key positions were filled yesterday, and I am submitting a further list to His Majesty tonight. I hope to complete the appointment of the principal Ministers during tomorrow. The appointment of the other Ministers usually takes a little longer, but I trust that, when Parliament meets again, this part of my task will be completed, and that the Administration will be complete in all respects.

I considered it in the public interest to suggest that the House should be summoned to meet today. Mr. Speaker agreed, and took the necessary steps, in accordance with the powers conferred upon him by the Resolution of the House. At the end of the proceedings today, the Adjournment of the House will be proposed until Tuesday, 21st May, with, of course, provision for earlier meeting if need be. The business to be considered during that week will be notified to Members at the earliest opportunity. I now invite the House, by the Resolution which stands in my name, to record its approval of the steps taken and to declare its confidence in the new Government.

To form an Administration of this scale and complexity is a serious undertaking in itself, but it must be remembered that we are in the preliminary stage of one of the greatest battles in history, that we are in action at many points in Norway and in Holland, that we have to be prepared in the Mediterranean, that the air battle is continuous, and that many preparations have to be made here at home. In this crisis I hope I may be pardoned if I do not address the House at any length today. I hope that any of my friends and colleagues, or former colleagues, who are affected by the political reconstruction, will make all allowance for any lack of ceremony with which it has been necessary to act. I would say to the House, as I said to those who have joined this Government: "I have nothing to offer but blood, toil, tears, and sweat."

We have before us an ordeal of the most grievous kind. We have before us many, many long months of struggle and of suffering. You ask, What is our policy? I will say: "It is to wage war, by sea, land, and air, with all our might and with all the strength that God can give us; to wage war against a monstrous tyranny, never surpassed in the dark, lamentable catalogue of human crime. That is our policy." You ask, What is our aim? I can answer in one word: Victory—victory at all costs, victory in spite of all terror, victory however long and hard the road may be; for without victory there is no survival. Let that be realized; no survival for the British Empire, no survival for all that the British Empire has stood for; no survival for the urge and impulse of the ages, that mankind will move forward towards its goal. But I take up my task with buoyancy and hope. I feel sure that our cause will not be suffered to fail among men. At this time I feel entitled to claim the aid of all, and I say, "Come, then, let us go forward together with our united strength."

Dunkirk

Speech before the House of Commons, June 4, 1940

FROM the moment that the French defenses at Sedan and on the Meuse were broken at the end of the second week of May, only a rapid retreat to Amiens and the south could have saved the British and French Armies who had entered Belgium at the appeal of the Belgian King; but this strategic fact was not immediately realized. The French High Command hoped they would be able to close the gap, and the Armies of the north were under their orders. Moreover, a retirement of this kind would have involved almost certainly the destruction of the fine Belgian Army of over twenty divisions and the abandonment of the whole of Belgium. Therefore, when the force and scope of the German penetration were realized and when a new French Generalissimo, General Weygand, assumed command in place of General Gamelin, an effort was made by the French and British Armies in Belgium to keep on holding the right hand of the Belgians and to give their own right hand to a newly created French Army which was to have advanced across the Somme in great strength to grasp it.

However, the German eruption swept like a sharp scythe around the right and rear of the Armies of the north. Eight or nine armored di-

visions, each of about four hundred armored vehicles of different kinds, but carefully assorted to be complementary and divisible into small self-contained units, cut off all communications between us and the main French Armies. It severed our own communications for food and ammunition, which ran first to Amiens and afterwards through Abbeville, and it shore its way up the coast to Boulogne and Calais, and almost to Dunkirk. Behind this armored and mechanized onslaught came a number of German divisions in lorries, and behind them again there plodded comparatively slowly the dull brute mass of the ordinary German Army and German people, always so ready to be led to the trampling down in other lands of liberties and comforts which they have never known in their own.

I have said this armored scythe-stroke almost reached Dunkirk—almost but not quite. Boulogne and Calais were the scenes of desperate fighting. The Guards defended Boulogne for a while and were then withdrawn by orders from this country. The Rifle Brigade, the 60th Rifles, and the Queen Victoria's Rifles, with a battalion of British tanks and a thousand Frenchmen, in all about four thousand strong, defended Calais to the last. The British Brigadier was given an hour to surrender. He spurned the offer, and four days of intense street fighting passed before silence reigned over Calais, which marked the end of a memorable resistance. Only thirty unwounded survivors were brought off by the Navy, and we do not know the fate of their comrades. Their sacrifice, however, was not in vain. At least two armored divisions, which otherwise would have been turned against the British Expeditionary Force, had to be sent to overcome them. They have added another page to the glories of the light divisions, and the time gained enabled the Graveline water lines to be flooded and to be held by the French troops.

Thus it was that the port of Dunkirk was kept open. When it was found impossible for the Armies of the north to reopen their communications to Amiens with the main French Armies, only one choice remained. It seemed, indeed, forlorn. The Belgian, British and French Armies were almost surrounded. Their sole line of retreat was to a single port and to its neighboring beaches. They were pressed on every side by heavy attacks and far outnumbered in the air.

When, a week ago today, I asked the House to fix this afternoon as the occasion for a statement, I feared it would be my hard lot to announce the greatest military disaster in our long history. I thought—and some good judges agreed with me—that perhaps 20,000 or 30,000 men might be re-embarked. But it certainly seemed that the whole of the French First Army and the whole of the British Expeditionary Force north of the Amiens-Abbeville gap would be broken up in the open field or else would have to capitulate for lack of food and ammunition. These were the hard and heavy tidings for which I called upon the House and the nation to prepare themselves a week ago. The whole root and core and brain of the British Army, on which and around which we were to build, and are to build, the great British Armies in the later years of the war, seemed about to perish upon the field or to be led into an ignominious and starving captivity.

That was the prospect a week ago. But another blow which might well have proved final was yet to fall upon us. The King of the Belgians had called upon us to come to his aid. Had not this Ruler and his Government severed themselves from the Allies, who rescued their country from extinction in the late war, and had they not sought refuge in what has proved to be a fatal neutrality, the French and British Armies might well at the outset have saved not only Belgium but perhaps even Poland. Yet at the last moment, when Belgium was already invaded, King Leopold called upon us to come to his aid, and even at the last moment we came. He and his brave, efficient Army, nearly half a million strong, guarded our left flank and thus kept open our only line of retreat to the sea. Suddenly, without prior consultation, with the least possible notice, without the advice of his Ministers and upon his own personal act, he sent a plenipotentiary to the German Command, surrendered his Army, and exposed our whole flank and means of retreat.

I asked the House a week ago to suspend its judgment because the facts were not clear, but I do not feel that any reason now exists why we should not form our own opinions upon this pitiful episode. The surrender of the Belgian Army compelled the British at the shortest notice to cover a flank to the sea more than thirty miles in length. Otherwise all would have been cut off, and all would have shared the fate to which King Leopold had condemned the finest Army his country had ever formed. So in doing this and in exposing this flank, as anyone who followed the operations on the map will see, contact was lost between the British and two out of the three corps forming the First French Army, who were still farther from the coast than we were, and it seemed impossible that any large number of Allied troops could reach the coast.

The enemy attacked on all sides with great strength and fierceness, and their main power, the power of their far more numerous Air Force, was thrown into the battle or else concentrated upon Dunkirk and the beaches. Pressing in upon the narrow exit, both from the east and from the west, the enemy began to fire with cannon upon the beaches by which alone the shipping could approach or depart. They sowed magnetic mines in the channels and seas; they sent repeated waves of hostile aircraft, sometimes more than a hundred strong in one formation, to cast their bombs upon the single pier that remained, and upon the sand dunes upon which the troops had their eyes for shelter. Their U-boats, one of which was sunk, and their motor launches took their toll of the vast traffic which now began. For four or five days an intense struggle reigned. All their armored divisions—or what was left of them—together with great masses of infantry and artillery, hurled themselves in vain upon the ever-narrowing, ever-contracting appendix within which the British and French Armies fought.

Meanwhile, the Royal Navy, with the willing help of countless merchant seamen, strained every nerve to embark the British and Allied troops; two hundred and twenty light warships and six hundred and fifty other vessels were engaged. They had to operate upon the difficult coast, often in adverse weather, under an almost ceaseless hail of bombs and an increasing concentration of artillery fire. Nor were the seas, as I have said, themselves free from mines and torpedoes. It was in conditions such as

these that our men carried on, with little or no rest, for days and nights on end, making trip after trip across the dangerous waters, bringing with them always men whom they had rescued. The numbers they have brought back are the measure of their devotion and their courage. The hospital ships, which brought off many thousands of British and French wounded, being so plainly marked were a special target for
10 Nazi bombs; but the men and women on board them never faltered in their duty.

Meanwhile, the Royal Air Force, which had already been intervening in the battle, so far as its range would allow, from home bases, now used part of its main metropolitan fighter strength, and struck at the German bombers and at the fighters which in large numbers protected them. This struggle was protracted and fierce. Suddenly the scene has cleared, the
20 crash and thunder has for the moment—but only for the moment—died away. A miracle of deliverance, achieved by valor, by perseverance, by perfect discipline, by faultless service, by resource, by skill, by unconquerable fidelity, is manifest to us all. The enemy was hurled back by the retreating British and French troops. He was so roughly handled that he did not hurry their departure seriously. The Royal Air Force engaged the main strength of the
30 German Air Force, and inflicted upon them losses of at least four to one; and the Navy, using nearly a thousand ships of all kinds, carried over 335,000 men, French and British, out of the jaws of death and shame, to their native land and to the tasks which lie immediately ahead. We must be very careful not to assign to this deliverance the attributes of a victory. Wars are not won by evacuations. But there was a victory inside this deliverance, which
40 should be noted. It was gained by the Air Force. Many of our soldiers coming back have not seen the Air Force at work; they saw only the bombers which escaped its protective attack. They underrate its achievements. I have heard much talk of this; that is why I go out of my way to say this. I will tell you about it.

This was a great trial of strength between the British and German Air Forces. Can you conceive a greater objective for the Germans in
50 the air than to make evacuation from these beaches impossible, and to sink all these ships which were displayed, almost to the extent of thousands? Could there have been an objective of greater military importance and significance for the whole purpose of the war than this? They tried hard, and they were beaten back; they were frustrated in their task. We got the Army away; and they have paid fourfold for any losses which they have inflicted. Very large formations of German aeroplanes—and we 60 know that they are a very brave race—have turned on several occasions from the attack of one-quarter of their number of the Royal Air Force, and have dispersed in different directions. Twelve aeroplanes have been hunted by two. One aeroplane was driven into the water and cast away by the mere charge of a British aeroplane, which had no more ammunition. All of our types—the Hurricane, the Spitfire and the new Defiant—and all our pilots have been 70 vindicated as superior to what they have at present to face.

When we consider how much greater would be our advantage in defending the air above this Island against an overseas attack, I must say that I find in these facts a sure basis upon which practical and reassuring thoughts may rest. I will pay my tribute to these young airmen. The great French Army was very largely, for the time being, cast back and disturbed by 80 the onrush of a few thousands of armored vehicles. May it not also be that the cause of civilization itself will be defended by the skill and devotion of a few thousand airmen? There never has been, I suppose, in all the world, in all the history of war, such an opportunity for youth. The Knights of the Round Table, the Crusaders, all fall back into the past—not only distant but prosaic; these young men, going forth every morn to guard their native land and 90 all that we stand for, holding in their hands these instruments of colossal and shattering power, of whom it may be said that

"Every morn brought forth a noble chance
    And every chance brought forth a noble
        knight,"

94. "Every . . . knight," quoted, somewhat inaccurately, from Tennyson's *Morte d'Arthur*, ll. 230–231:
    When every morning brought a noble chance,
    And every chance brought out a noble knight.

deserve our gratitude, as do all of the brave men who, in so many ways and on so many occasions, are ready, and continue ready, to give life and all for their native land.

I return to the Army. In the long series of very fierce battles, now on this front, now on that, fighting on three fronts at once, battles fought by two or three divisions against an equal or somewhat larger number of the enemy, and fought fiercely on some of the old grounds that so many of us knew so well—in these battles our losses in men have exceeded 30,000 killed, wounded, and missing. I take occasion to express the sympathy of the House to all who have suffered bereavement or who are still anxious. The President of the Board of Trade is not here today. His son has been killed, and many in the House have felt the pangs of affliction in the sharpest form. But I will say this about the missing: We have had a large number of wounded come home safely to this country, but I would say about the missing that there may be very many reported missing who will come back home, some day, in one way or another. In the confusion of this fight it is inevitable that many have been left in positions where honor required no further resistance from them.

Against this loss of over 30,000 men, we can set a far heavier loss certainly inflicted upon the enemy. But our losses in material are enormous. We have perhaps lost one-third of the men we lost in the opening days of the battle of 21st March, 1918, but we have lost nearly as many guns—nearly one thousand—and all our transport, all the armored vehicles that were with the Army in the north. Their loss will impose a further delay on the expansion of our military strength. That expansion has not been proceeding as fast as we had hoped. The best of all we had to give had gone to the British Expeditionary Force, and although they had not the numbers of tanks and some articles of equipment which were desirable, they were a very well and finely equipped Army. They had the first-fruits of all that our industry had to give, and that is gone. And now here is this further delay. How long it will be, how long it will last, depends upon the exertions which we make in this Island. An effort the like of which

has never been seen in our records is now being made. Work is proceeding everywhere, night and day, Sundays and week days. Capital and Labor have cast aside their interests, rights, and customs and put them into the common stock. Already the flow of munitions has leaped forward. There is no reason why we should not in a few months overtake the sudden and serious loss that has come upon us, without retarding the development of our general program.

Nevertheless, our thankfulness at the escape of our Army and so many men, whose loved ones have passed through an agonizing week, must not blind us to the fact that what has happened in France and Belgium is a colossal military disaster. The French Army has been weakened, the Belgian Army has been lost, a large part of those fortified lines upon which so much faith had been reposed is gone, many valuable mining districts and factories have passed into the enemy's possession, the whole of the Channel ports are in his hands, with all the tragic consequences that follow from that, and we must expect another blow to be struck almost immediately at us or at France. We are told that Herr Hitler has a plan for invading the British Isles. This has often been thought of before. When Napoleon lay at Boulogne for a year with his flat-bottomed boats and his Grand Army, he was told by someone, "There are bitter weeds in England." There are certainly a great many more of them since the British Expeditionary Force returned.

The whole question of home defense against invasion is, of course, powerfully affected by the fact that we have for the time being in this Island incomparably more powerful military forces than we have ever had at any moment in this war or the last. But this will not continue. We shall not be content with a defensive war. We have our duty to our Ally. We have to reconstitute and build up the British Expeditionary Force once again, under its gallant Commander-in-Chief, Lord Gort. All this is in train; but in the interval we must put our defenses in this Island into such a high state of organization that the fewest possible numbers will be required to give effective security and that the largest possible potential of offensive effort may be realized. On this we are now engaged. It will be very convenient, if it be the desire of the House, to enter upon this subject in a secret Session. Not that the Government would necessarily be able to reveal in very great detail military secrets, but we like to have our discussions free, without the restraint imposed by the fact that they will be read the next day by the enemy; and the Government would benefit by views freely expressed in all parts of the House by Members with their knowledge of so many different parts of the country. I understand that some request is to be made upon this subject, which will be readily acceded to by His Majesty's Government.

We have found it necessary to take measures of increasing stringency, not only against enemy aliens and suspicious characters of other nationalities, but also against British subjects who may become a danger or a nuisance should the war be transported to the United Kingdom. I know there are a great many people affected by the orders which we have made who are the passionate enemies of Nazi Germany. I am very sorry for them, but we cannot, at the present time and under the present stress, draw all the distinctions which we should like to do. If parachute landings were attempted and fierce fighting attendant upon them followed, these unfortunate people would be far better out of the way, for their own sakes as well as for ours. There is, however, another class, for which I feel not the slightest sympathy. Parliament has given us the powers to put down Fifth Column activities with a strong hand, and we shall use these powers, subject to the supervision and correction of the House, without the slightest hesitation until we are satisfied, and more than satisfied, that this malignancy in our midst has been effectively stamped out.

Turning once again, and this time more generally, to the question of invasion, I would observe that there has never been a period in all these long centuries of which we boast when an absolute guarantee against invasion, still less against serious raids, could have been given to our people. In the days of Napoleon the same wind which would have carried his transports across the Channel might have driven away the blockading fleet. There was always the

chance, and it is that chance which has excited and befooled the imaginations of many Continental tyrants. Many are the tales that are told. We are assured that novel methods will be adopted, and when we see the originality of malice, the ingenuity of aggression, which our enemy displays, we may certainly prepare ourselves for every kind of novel stratagem and every kind of brutal and treacherous maneuver. I think that no idea is so outlandish that it should not be considered and viewed with a searching, but at the same time, I hope, with a steady eye. We must never forget the solid assurances of sea power and those which belong to air power if it can be locally exercised.

I have, myself, full confidence that if all do their duty, if nothing is neglected, and if the best arrangements are made, as they are being made, we shall prove ourselves once again able to defend our Island home, to ride out the storm of war, and to outlive the menace of tyranny, if necessary for years, if necessary alone. At any rate, that is what we are going to try to do. That is the resolve of His Majesty's Government—every man of them. That is the will of Parliament and the nation. The British Empire and the French Republic, linked together in their cause and in their need, will defend to the death their native soil, aiding each other like good comrades to the utmost of their strength. Even though large tracts of Europe and many old and famous States have fallen or may fall into the grip of the Gestapo and all the odious apparatus of Nazi rule, we shall not flag or fail. We shall go on to the end, we shall fight in France, we shall fight on the seas and oceans, we shall fight with growing confidence and growing strength in the air, we shall defend our Island, whatever the cost may be, we shall fight on the beaches, we shall fight on the landing grounds, we shall fight in the fields and in the streets, we shall fight in the hills; we shall never surrender, and even if, which I do not for a moment believe, this Island or a large part of it were subjugated and starving, then our Empire beyond the seas, armed and guarded by the British Fleet, would carry on the struggle until, in God's good time, the New World, with all its power and might, steps forth to the rescue and the liberation of the old.

I

ARNOLD J. TOYNBEE

Arnold Joseph Toynbee, born April 14, 1889, has deservedly won the position of the most distinguished historian of his generation. He was educated at Winchester and later at Balliol College, Oxford, becoming a tutor at Balliol until the outbreak of the First World War. He was engaged in government work during the war and was a member of the British Delegation at the Paris Peace Conference as a specialist on the Middle East. For five years, from 1919 to 1924, he was Professor of Byzantine and Modern Greek Literatures at the University of London; and since 1925 he has been Director of Study at the Royal Institute of International Affairs and Research Professor of International History at the University of London.

His works, beginning with *Nationality and the War* (1915), have been many—all dedicated to his profession of historian. Toynbee has been active not only as teacher and scholar but also as editor and director—his annual *Survey of International Affairs,* which began in 1924, has been an invaluable aid to all modern students of history. But his masterpiece is clearly the six-volume *A Study of History* (1934–39), which has been justly hailed as the most important modern work yet written on the philosophy of history. (A convenient one-volume version of this work, prepared by D. C. Somervell, appeared in 1947, and the collection of essays *Civilization on Trial* [1948] is in part an explanation of the theories and philosophy set forth in the *Study.*) In his magnum opus Toynbee sees the decline of human civilization, which asserts itself in unmistakable terms; but unlike Oswald Spengler, the great prophet of doom, Toynbee is international-minded. Besides, he admits the possibility, however slim, that mankind may somehow arise from its own present bewildered confusion and evolve into some kind of superior type.

WHAT WILL be singled out as the salient event of our time by future historians, centuries hence, looking back on the first half of the twentieth century and trying to see its activities and experiences in that just proportion which the time-perspective sometimes reveals? Not, I fancy, any of those sensational or tragic or catastrophic political and economic events which occupy the headlines of our newspapers and the foregrounds of our minds; not 10 wars, revolutions, massacres, deportations, famines, gluts, slumps, or booms, but something of which we are only half-conscious, and out of which it would be difficult to make a headline. The things that make good headlines attract our attention because they are on the surface of the stream of life, and they distract our attention from the slower, impalpable, imponderable movements that work below the surface and penetrate to the depths. But of course it is 20 really these deeper, slower movements that, in the end, make history, and it is they that stand out huge in retrospect, when the sensational passing events have dwindled, in perspective, to their true proportions.

Mental perspective, like optical perspective, comes into focus only when the observer has put a certain distance between himself and his object. When, for example, you are traveling by air from Salt Lake City to Denver, the near- 30 est view of the Rockies is not the best one. While you are actually over the mountains, you see nothing but a maze of peaks, ridges, gullies, and crags. It is not until you have left the mountains behind you and are looking back at them as you fly over the plains that they rise up before you in their magnificent order, range behind range. It is only then that you have a vision of the Rockies themselves.

With this vision in mind, I believe that fu- 40 ture historians will be able to see our age in better proportion than we can. What are they likely to say about it?

Future historians will say, I think, that the great event of the twentieth century was the impact of the Western Civilization upon all the other living societies of the world of that day. They will say of this impact that it was so powerful and so pervasive that it turned the lives of all its victims upside down and inside out—affecting the behavior, outlook, feelings, and beliefs of individual men, women, and children in an intimate way, touching chords in human souls that are not touched by mere external material forces—however ponderous and terrifying. This will be said, I feel sure, by historians looking back on our times even from as short a time hence as A.D. 2047.

What will the historians of A.D. 3047 say? If we had been living a century ago, I should have had to apologize for the fantastic conceit of pretending to speculate about anything that might be said or done at so immensely remote a date. Eleven hundred years was a very long time for people who believed that the world had been created in 4004 B.C. But I need not apologize today; for, since our grandfathers' time, there has been so great a revolution in our time scale that, if I were to try to plot out to scale, on one of these pages, a chart of the history of this planet since its birth, I should not be able to make so short a period as eleven hundred years visible to the naked eye.

The historians of A.D. 3047, then, may have something far more interesting than those of A.D. 2047 to say, because they, by their time, may know much more of the story of which we, today, are perhaps in a rather early chapter. The historians of A.D. 3047 will, I believe, be chiefly interested in the tremendous countereffects which, by that time, the victims will have produced in the life of the aggressor. By A.D. 3047, our Western Civilization, as we and our Western predecessors have known it, say, for the last twelve or thirteen hundred years, since its emergence out of the Dark Ages, may have been transformed, almost out of all recognition, by a counter-radiation of influences from the foreign worlds which we, in our day, are in the act of engulfing in ours—influences from Orthodox Christendom, from Islam, from Hinduism, from the Far East.

By A.D. 4047 the distinction—which looms large today—between the Western Civilization, as an aggressor, and the other civilizations, as its victims, will probably seem unimportant. When radiation has been followed by counter-radiation of influences, what will stand out will be a single great experience, common to the whole of mankind: the experience of having one's parochial social heritage battered to bits by collision with the parochial heritages of other civilizations, and then finding a new life—a new common life—springing up out of the wreckage. The historians of A.D. 4047 will say that the impact of the Western Civilization on its contemporaries, in the second half of the second millennium of the Christian Era, was the epoch-making event of that age because it was the first step toward the unification of mankind into one single society. By their time, the unity of mankind will perhaps have come to seem one of the fundamental conditions of human life—just part of the order of nature—and it may need quite an effort of imagination on their part to recall the parochial outlook of the pioneers of civilization during the first six thousand years or so of its existence. Those Athenians, whose capital city was no more than a day's walk from the farthest frontiers of their country, and those American contemporaries—or virtual contemporaries—of theirs, whose country you could fly across from sea to sea in sixteen hours—how could they behave (as we know they did behave) as if their own little country were the universe?

And the historians of A.D. 5047? The historians of A.D. 5047 will say, I fancy, that the importance of this social unification of mankind was not to be found in the field of technics and economics, and not in the field of war and politics, but in the field of religion.

II

Why do I venture on these prophecies about how the history of our own time will appear to people looking back at it several thousand years hence? Because we have about six thousand years of past history to judge by, since the first emergence of human societies of the species we call "civilizations."

Six thousand years is an almost infinitesimally short time compared to the age of the human race, of mammals, of life on earth, of the planetary system round our sun, of the sun itself, and of the star-cluster of which our sun is a not particularly conspicuous member. Still, for our present purpose, these last six thousand years—brief though they are—do provide us with other examples of the phenomenon we are studying—examples of encounters between different civilizations. In relation to some of these cases, we ourselves, in our day, are already enjoying the advantage—which the historians living in A.D. 3047 or 4047 are going to have in looking back at us—of knowing the whole story. It is with some of these past encounters in mind that I have been speculating on how our own encounter with our own contemporaries is likely to turn out.

Take the history of one of our predecessors, the Graeco-Roman civilization, and consider how this looks to us in the fairly distant perspective in which we are now able to see it:

As a result of the conquests of Alexander the Great and of the Romans, the Graeco-Roman civilization radiated over most of the old world —into India, into the British Isles, and even as far as China and Scandinavia. The only civilizations of that day which remained untouched by its influence were those of Mexico and Peru, so that its expansion was not incomparable to our own in extent and vigor. When we look back on the history of the Graeco-Roman world during the last four centuries B.C., it is this great movement of expansion and penetration that stands out now. The wars, revolutions, and economic crises that ruffled the surface of Graeco-Roman history during those centuries, and occupied so much of the attention of the men and women who were struggling to live through them, do not mean much to us now compared with that great tide of Greek cultural influence invading Asia Minor, Syria, Egypt, Babylonia, Persia, India, China.

But why does the Graeco-Roman impact on these other civilizations matter to us now? Because of the counterattack of these other civilizations on the Graeco-Roman World.

This counterattack was partly delivered in the same style as the original Graeco-Roman attack: that is, by force of arms. But we are not much interested today in the forlorn hope of Jewish armed resistance to Greek and Roman imperialism in Palestine; or in the successful counterattack of the Parthians and their Persian successors under the Sassanian Dynasty east of the Euphrates; or in the sensational victories of the early Muslim Arabs, who in the seventh century of the Christian era liberated the Middle East from Graeco-Roman rule in as short a number of years as it had taken Alexander the Great to conquer it a thousand years earlier.

But there was another counterattack, a nonviolent one, a spiritual one, which attacked and conquered, not fortresses and provinces, but hearts and minds. This attack was delivered by the missionaries of new religions which had arisen in the worlds which the Graeco-Roman civilization had attacked by force and submerged. The prince of these missionaries was Saint Paul, who, starting from Antioch, made the audacious march on Macedonia, Greece, and Rome which King Antiochus the Great had once attempted unsuccessfully. These religions were different in kind from the native religion of the Graeco-Roman world. The gods of Graeco-Roman paganism had been rooted in the soil of particular communities; they had been parochial and political: Athene Polias, Fortuna Praenestina, Dea Roma. The gods of the new religions that were making this non-violent counterattack on Greek and Roman hearts and minds had risen above their original local origins. They had become universal gods, with a message of salvation for all mankind, Jew and Gentile, Scythian and Greek. Or, to put this great historical event in religious terms, one might say that the One True God had taken this opportunity of the opening of men's minds through the collision and collapse of their old local traditions; He had taken advantage of this excruciating experience in order to illuminate these momentarily open minds with a fuller and truer vision of His nature and purpose than they had been capable of receiving before.

Take the two words "Jesus Christ," which are so very important for us, and which, we may venture to prophesy, will still be important for mankind two or three thousand years hence. These very words are witness to the en-

901

counter between a Graeco-Roman civilization and a Syrian civilization out of which Christianity came to birth. "Jesus" is the third person singular of a Semitic verb; "Christ" is the passive participle of a Greek verb. The double name testifies that Christianity was born into this world from a marriage between those two cultures.

Consider the four higher religions, with a world-wide mission, which exist in the world today: Christianity, Islam, Hinduism, and the Mahayana form of Buddhism which prevails in the Far East. All four are, historically, products of the encounter between the Graeco-Roman civilization and its contemporaries. Christianity and Islam arose as alternative responses of the Syrian world to Graeco-Roman penetration: Christianity a non-violent response, Islam a violent one. Mahayanian Buddhism and Hinduism are the gentle and the violent responses of the Hindu world to the same Graeco-Roman challenge.

Looking back on Graeco-Roman history today, about thirteen hundred years after the date when the Graeco-Roman civilization became extinct, we can see that, in this perspective, the most important thing in the history of the Graeco-Roman world is its meeting with other civilizations; and these encounters are important, not for their immediate political and economic consequences, but for their long-term religious consequences. This Graeco-Roman illustration, of which we know the whole story, also gives us some idea of the time-span of encounters between civilizations. The Graeco-Roman World's impact upon other contemporary civilizations, which corresponds to the modern Western World's impact on its own contemporaries since the turn of the fifteenth and sixteenth centuries, started with the conquests of Alexander the Great in the fourth century B.C.; and the Middle Eastern World was still translating the classical works of Greek philosophy and science some five or six centuries after the liberation of the Middle East from Graeco-Roman rule by the early Muslim Arabs in the seventh century of the Christian era. From the fourth century B.C. to the thirteenth century of the Christian era, it took the best part of sixteen hundred years for the encounter between the Graeco-Roman civilization and its contemporaries to work itself out.

Now measure against that span of sixteen hundred years the duration, to date, of the encounter between our modern Western Civilization and its contemporaries. One may say that this encounter began with the Ottoman attack on the homelands of the Western Civilization and with the great Western voyages of discovery at the turn of the fifteenth and sixteenth centuries of our era. That makes only four-and-a-half centuries to the present.

Let us assume, if you like, that people's hearts and minds move rather faster nowadays (though I know of no evidence that the unconscious part of the human psyche ever greatly varies its pace)—even so, it looks as if we were still only in an early chapter of the story of our encounter with the civilizations of Mexico and Peru and Orthodox Christendom and Islam and the Hindu world and the Far East. We are just beginning to see some of the effects of our action on them, but we have hardly begun to see the effects—which will certainly be tremendous—of their coming counteraction upon us.

It is only in our generation that we have seen one of the first moves in this counteroffensive, and we have found it very disturbing; whether we have liked it or not, we have felt it to be momentous. I mean, of course, the move made by the offshoot of Orthodox Christendom in Russia. It is momentous and disturbing not because of the material power behind it. The Russians, after all, do not yet possess the atom bomb; but they have already shown (and this is the point) the power to convert Western souls to a non-Western "ideology."

The Russians have taken up a Western secular social philosophy, Marxism; you might equally well call Marxism a Christian heresy, a leaf torn out of the book of Christianity, and treated as if it were the whole gospel. The Russians have taken up this Western heretical religion, transformed it into something of their own, and are now shooting it back at us. This is the first shot in the anti-Western counteroffensive; but this Russian counter-discharge in the form of Communism may come to seem a small affair when the probably far more potent civilizations of India and China respond in their turn to our Western challenge. In the long run India and China seem likely to produce much deeper effects on our Western life than Russia can ever hope to produce with her Communism. But even the comparatively feeble native civilization of Mexico is beginning to react. The revolution through which Mexico has been passing since A.D. 1910 may be interpreted as a first move to shake off the top-dressing of Western civilization which we imposed on Mexico in the sixteenth century; and what is happening today in Mexico may happen tomorrow in the seats of the native civilization of South America: in Peru, Bolivia, Ecuador, and Colombia.

III

Before leaving off, I must say a word about one question which I have begged up to this point, and that is: what do we mean by a "civilization"? Clearly, we do mean something, for even before we have tried to define what our meaning is, this classification of human societies—the Western Civilization, the Islamic, the Far Eastern, the Hindu, and so on—does seem to make sense. These names do call up distinct pictures in our minds in terms of religion, architecture, painting, manners, and customs. Still, it is better to try to get closer to what we mean by a term which we have already been working so hard. I believe I do know what I mean by a civilization; at least, I am sure I know how I have arrived at my own idea of it.

I mean, by a civilization, the smallest unit of historical study at which one arrives when one tries to understand the history of one's own country: the United States, say, or the United Kingdom. If you were to try to understand the history of the United States by itself, it would be unintelligible: you could not understand the part played in American life by federal government, representative government, democracy, industrialism, monogamy, Christianity, unless you looked beyond the bounds of the United States—out beyond her frontiers to Western Europe and the other overseas countries founded by West Europeans, and back beyond her local origins to the history of Western Europe in centuries before Columbus or Cabot had crossed the Atlantic. But, to make American history and institutions intelligible for practical purposes, you need not look beyond Western Europe into Eastern Europe or the Islamic world, nor behind the origins of our Western European civilization to the decline and fall of the Graeco-Roman civilization. These limits of time and space give us the intelligible unit of social life of which the United States or Great Britain or France or Holland is a part: call it Western Christendom, Western Civilization, Western Society, the Western World. Similarly, if you start from Greece or Serbia or Russia, and try to understand their histories, you arrive at an Orthodox Christendom or Byzantine World. If you start from Morocco or Afghanistan, and try to understand their histories, you arrive at an Islamic world. Start from Bengal or Mysore or Rajputana, and you find a Hindu world. Start from China or Japan and you find a Far Eastern world.

While the state of which we happen to be citizens makes more concrete and more imperious claims on our allegiance, especially in the present age, the civilization of which we are members really counts far more in our lives. And this civilization of which we are members includes—at most stages in its history—the citizens of other states besides our own. It is older than our own state: the Western Civilization is about thirteen hundred years old, whereas the Kingdom of England is only one thousand years old, the United Kingdom of England and Scotland less than two hundred and fifty, the United States not much more than one hundred and fifty. States are apt to have short lives and sudden deaths: the Western Civilization of which you and I are members may be alive centuries after the United Kingdom and the United States have disappeared from the political map of the world like their late contemporaries, the Republic of Venice and the Dual Monarchy of Austria-Hungary. This is one of the reasons why I have been asking you to look at history in terms of civilizations, and not in terms of states, and to think of states as rather subordinates and ephemeral political phenomena in the lives of the civilizations in whose bosoms they appear and disappear.

Hiroshima

I

JOHN HERSEY

Of John Hersey it need only be said that, though still comparatively young, he has stamped himself as probably the best reporter to come out of the turmoil of the Second World War.

He was born June 17, 1914, in Tientsin, China, where his parents were American missionaries. Hersey's parents returned to the United States when he was ten years old. He was educated at Hotchkiss School and at Yale University (1936), served for a season as secretary to Sinclair Lewis (p. 333), and then settled to the occupation of journalist. He was first a writer for *Time,* and later an editor; he was on the staff of *Life* and became a senior editor of that magazine. With the advent of World War II, Hersey was sent as a reporter to active zones in both the Pacific and European areas. He produced in rapid succession *Men on Bataan* (1942), which needs no comment; *Into the Valley* (1943), reporting the experiences of the Marine Corps in the South Pacific; and the highly successful *A Bell for Adano,* a novel which recounted the experiences of an American officer of the army of occupation in Italy with the townsfolk of a shattered Italian village (1943).

But it is doubtful whether John Hersey has done anything else comparable to *Hiroshima* (1946), the most graphic of all stories dealing with the atomic bomb and the conclusion of the war in Japan. This masterly history was produced first in the pages of *The New Yorker,* to which Hersey had been a frequent contributor. Little can be added to the horrible implications in the story of the destruction of Hiroshima, except to emphasize that this was, indeed, only the beginning, for the bomb dropped on Hiroshima on August 6, 1945, was but a crude and comparatively inoffensive weapon of destruction. No document has thus far made clearer the inescapable fact that history and civilization alike have reached a critical fork in the road.

A Noiseless Flash

AT EXACTLY fifteen minutes past eight in the morning, on August 6, 1945, Japanese time, at the moment when the atomic bomb flashed above Hiroshima, Miss Toshiko Sasaki, a clerk in the personnel department of the East Asia Tin Works, had just sat down at her place in the plant office and was turning her head to speak to the girl at the next desk. At that same moment, Dr. Masakazu Fujii was settling down cross-legged to read the Osaka *Asahi* on the porch of his private hospital, overhanging one of the seven deltaic rivers which divide Hiroshima; Mrs. Hatsuyo Nakamura, a tailor's widow, stood by the window of her kitchen, watching a neighbor tearing down his house because it lay in the path of an air-raid-defense fire lane; Father Wilhelm Kleinsorge, a German priest of the Society of Jesus, reclined in his underwear on a cot on the top floor of his order's three-story mission house, reading a Jesuit magazine, *Stimmen der Zeit;* Dr. Terufumi Sasaki, a young member of the surgical staff of the city's large, modern Red Cross Hospital, walked along one of the hospital corridors with a blood specimen for a Wassermann test in his hand; and the Reverend Mr. Kiyoshi Tanimoto, pastor of the Hiroshima Methodist Church, paused at the door of a rich man's house in Koi, the city's western suburb, and prepared to unload a handcart full of things he had evacuated from town in fear of the massive B-29 raid which everyone expected Hiroshima to suffer. A hundred thousand people were killed by the atomic bomb, and these six were among the survivors. They still wonder why they lived when so many others died. Each of them counts many small items of chance or volition—a step taken in time, a decision to go indoors, catching one streetcar instead of the next—that spared him. And now each knows that in the act of survival he lived a dozen lives and saw more death than he ever

Reprinted from *Hiroshima* by John Hersey by permission of Alfred A. Knopf, Inc. copyright, 1946, by John Hersey. Originally published in The New Yorker.

thought he would see. At the time, none of them knew anything.

THE REVEREND MR. TANIMOTO got up at five o'clock that morning. He was alone in the parsonage, because for some time his wife had been commuting with their year-old baby to spend nights with a friend in Ushida, a suburb to the north. Of all the important cities of Japan, only two, Kyoto and Hiroshima, had not been visited in strength by *B-san,* or Mr. B., as the Japanese, with a mixture of respect and unhappy familiarity, called the B-29; and Mr. Tanimoto, like all his neighbors and friends, was almost sick with anxiety. He had heard uncomfortably detailed accounts of mass raids on Kure, Iwakuni, Tokuyama, and other nearby towns; he was sure Hiroshima's turn would come soon. He had slept badly the night before, because there had been several air-raid warnings. Hiroshima had been getting such warnings almost every night for weeks, for at that time the B-29s were using Lake Biwa, northeast of Hiroshima, as a rendezvous point, and no matter what city the Americans planned to hit, the Superfortresses streamed in over the coast near Hiroshima. The frequency of the warnings and the continued abstinence of Mr. B. with respect to Hiroshima had made its citizens jittery; a rumor was going around that the Americans were saving something special for the city.

Mr. Tanimoto is a small man, quick to talk, laugh, and cry. He wears his black hair parted in the middle and rather long; the prominence of the frontal bones just above his eyebrows and the smallness of his mustache, mouth, and chin give him a strange, old-young look, boyish and yet wise, weak and yet fiery. He moves nervously and fast, but with a restraint which suggests that he is a cautious, thoughtful man. He showed, indeed, just those qualities in the uneasy days before the bomb fell. Besides having his wife spend the nights in Ushida, Mr. Tanimoto had been carrying all the portable things from his church, in the close-packed residential district called Nagaragawa, to a house that belonged to a rayon manufacturer in Koi, two miles from the center of town. The rayon man, a Mr. Matsui, had opened his then unoccupied estate to a large number of his friends and acquaintances, so that they might evacuate whatever they wished to a safe distance from the probable target area. Mr. Tanimoto had had no difficulty in moving chairs, hymnals, Bibles, altar gear, and church records by pushcart himself, but the organ console and an upright piano required some aid. A friend of his named Matsuo had, the day before, helped him get the piano out to Koi; in return, he had promised this day to assist Mr. Matsuo in hauling out a daughter's belongings. That is why he had risen so early.

Mr. Tanimoto cooked his own breakfast. He felt awfully tired. The effort of moving the piano the day before, a sleepless night, weeks of worry and unbalanced diet, the cares of his parish—all combined to make him feel hardly adequate to the new day's work. There was another thing, too: Mr. Tanimoto had studied theology at Emory College, in Atlanta, Georgia; he had graduated in 1940; he spoke excellent English; he dressed in American clothes; he had corresponded with many American friends right up to the time the war began; and among a people obsessed with a fear of being spied upon—perhaps almost obsessed himself—he found himself growing increasingly uneasy. The police had questioned him several times, and just a few days before, he had heard that an influential acquaintance, a Mr. Tanaka, a retired officer of the Toyo Kisen Kaisha steamship line, an anti-Christian, a man famous in Hiroshima for his showy philanthropies and notorious for his personal tyrannies, had been telling people that Tanimoto should not be trusted. In compensation, to show himself publicly a good Japanese, Mr. Tanimoto had taken on the chairmanship of his local *tonariguni,* or Neighborhood Association, and to his other duties and concerns this position had added the business of organizing air-raid defense for about twenty families.

Before six o'clock that morning, Mr. Tanimoto started for Mr. Matsuo's house. There he found that their burden was to be a *tansu,* a large Japanese cabinet, full of clothing and household goods. The two men set out. The morning was perfectly clear and so warm that the day promised to be uncomfortable. A few minutes after they started, the air-raid siren went off—a minute-long blast that warned of approaching planes but indicated to the people of Hiroshima only a slight degree of danger, since it sounded every morning at this time, when an American weather plane came over. The two men pulled and pushed the handcart through the city streets. Hiroshima was a fan-shaped city, lying mostly on the six islands formed by the seven estuarial rivers that branch out from the Ota River; its main commercial and residential districts, covering about four square miles in the center of the city, contained three-quarters of its population, which had been reduced by several evacuation programs from a wartime peak of 380,000 to about 245,000. Factories and other residential districts, or suburbs, lay compactly around the edges of the city. To the south were the docks, an airport, and the island-studded Inland Sea. A rim of mountains runs around the other three sides of the delta. Mr. Tanimoto and Mr. Matsuo took their way through the shopping center, already full of people, and across two of the rivers to the sloping streets of Koi, and up them to the outskirts and foothills. As they started up a valley away from the tight-ranked houses, the all-clear sounded. (The Japanese radar operators, detecting only three planes, supposed that they comprised a reconnaissance.) Pushing the handcart up to the rayon man's house was tiring, and the men, after they had maneuvered their load into the driveway and to the front steps, paused to rest awhile. They stood with a wing of the house between them and the city. Like most homes in this part of Japan, the house consisted of a wooden frame and wooden walls supporting a heavy tile roof. Its front hall, packed with rolls of bedding and clothing, looked like a cool cave full of fat cushions. Opposite the house, to the right of the front door, there was a large, finicky rock garden. There was no sound of planes. The morning was still; the place was cool and pleasant.

Then a tremendous flash of light cut across the sky. Mr. Tanimoto has a distinct recollection that it travelled from east to west, from the city toward the hills. It seemed a sheet of sun. Both he and Mr. Matsuo reacted in terror —and both had time to react (for they were 3,500 yards, or two miles, from the center of the explosion). Mr. Matsuo dashed up the front steps into the house and dived among the bedrolls and buried himself there. Mr. Tanimoto took four or five steps and threw himself between two big rocks in the garden. He bellied up very hard against one of them. As his face was against the stone, he did not see what happened. He felt a sudden pressure, and then splinters and pieces of board and fragments of tile fell on him. He heard no roar. (Almost no one in Hiroshima recalls hearing any noise of the bomb. But a fisherman in his sampan on the Inland Sea near Tsuzu, the man with whom Mr. Tanimoto's mother-in-law and sister-in-law were living, saw the flash and heard a tremendous explosion; he was nearly twenty miles from Hiroshima, but the thunder was greater than when the B-29's hit Iwakuni, only five miles away.)

When he dared, Mr. Tanimoto raised his head and saw that the rayon man's house had collapsed. He thought a bomb had fallen directly on it. Such clouds of dust had risen that there was a sort of twilight around. In panic, not thinking for the moment of Mr. Matsuo under the ruins, he dashed out into the street. He noticed as he ran that the concrete wall of the estate had fallen over—toward the house rather than away from it. In the street, the first thing he saw was a squad of soldiers who had been burrowing into the hillside opposite, making one of the thousands of dugouts in which the Japanese apparently intended to resist invasion, hill by hill, life for life; the soldiers were coming out of the hole, where they should have been safe, and blood was running from their heads, chests, and backs. They were silent and dazed.

Under what seemed to be a local dust cloud, the day grew darker and darker.

At nearly midnight, the night before the bomb was dropped, an announcer on the city's radio station said that about two hundred B-29's were approaching southern Honshu and advised the population of Hiroshima to evacuate to their designated "safe areas." Mrs. Hatsuyo Nakamura, the tailor's widow, who lived in the section called Nobori-cho and who had long had a habit of doing as she was told, got her three children—a ten-year-old boy, Toshio, an eight-year-old girl, Yaeko, and a five-year-old girl, Myeko—out of bed and dressed them and walked with them to the military area known as the East Parade Ground, on the northeast edge of the city. There she unrolled some mats and the children lay down on them. They slept until about two, when they were awakened by the roar of the planes going over Hiroshima.

As soon as the planes had passed, Mrs. Nakamura started back with her children. They reached home a little after two-thirty and she immediately turned on the radio, which, to her distress, was just then broadcasting a fresh warning. When she looked at the children and saw how tired they were, and when she thought of the number of trips they had made in the past weeks, all to no purpose, to the East Parade Ground, she decided that in spite of the instructions on the radio, she simply could not face starting out all over again. She put the children in their bedrolls on the floor, lay down herself at three o'clock, and fell asleep at once, so soundly that when planes passed over later, she did not waken to their sound.

The siren jarred her awake at about seven. She arose, dressed quickly, and hurried to the house of Mr. Nakamoto, the head of her Neighborhood Association, and asked him what she should do. He said that she should remain at home unless an urgent warning—a series of intermittent blasts of the siren—was sounded. She returned home, lit the stove in the kitchen, set some rice to cook, and sat down to read that morning's Hiroshima *Chugoku*. To her relief, the all-clear sounded at eight o'clock. She heard the children stirring, so she went and gave each of them a handful of peanuts and told them to stay on their bedrolls, because they were tired from the night's walk. She had hoped that they would go back to sleep, but the man in the house directly to the south began to make a terrible hullabaloo of hammering, wedging, ripping, and splitting. The prefectural government, convinced, as everyone in Hiroshima was, that the city would be attacked soon, had begun to press with threats and warnings for the completion of wide fire lanes, which, it was hoped, might act in conjunction with the rivers to localize any fires started by an incendiary raid; and the neighbor was reluctantly sacrificing his home to the city's safety. Just the day before, the prefecture had ordered all able-bodied girls from the secondary schools to spend a few days helping to clear these lanes, and they started work soon after the all-clear sounded.

Mrs. Nakamura went back to the kitchen, looked at the rice, and began watching the man next door. At first, she was annoyed with him for making so much noise, but then she was moved almost to tears by pity. Her emotion was specifically directed toward her neighbor, tearing down his home, board by board, at a time when there was so much unavoidable destruction, but undoubtedly she also felt a generalized, community pity, to say nothing of self-pity. She had not had an easy time. Her husband, Isawa, had gone into the Army just after Myeko was born, and she had heard nothing from or of him for a long time, until, on March 5, 1942, she received a seven-word telegram: "Isawa died an honorable death at Singapore." She learned later that he had died on February 15th, the day Singapore fell, and that he had been a corporal. Isawa had been a not particularly prosperous tailor, and his only capital was a Sankoku sewing machine. After his death, when his allotments stopped coming, Mrs. Nakamura got out the machine and began to take in piecework herself, and since then had supported the children, but poorly, by sewing.

As Mrs. Nakamura stood watching her neighbor, everything flashed whiter than any white she had ever seen. She did not notice what happened to the man next door; the reflex of a mother set her in motion toward her children. She had taken a single step (the house was 1,350 yards, or three-quarters of a mile, from the center of the explosion) when something picked her up and she seemed to fly into the next room over the raised sleeping platform, pursued by parts of her house.

Timbers fell around her as she landed, and a shower of tiles pommelled her; everything became dark, for she was buried. The debris did not cover her deeply. She rose up and freed herself. She heard a child cry, "Mother, help me!" and saw her youngest—Myeko, the five-year-old—buried up to her breast and unable to move. As Mrs. Nakamura started frantically to claw her way toward her baby, she could see or hear nothing of her other children.

IN THE DAYS right after the bombing, Dr. Masakazu Fujii, being prosperous, hedonistic, and at the time not too busy, had been allowing himself the luxury of sleeping until nine or nine-thirty, but fortunately he had to get up early the morning the bomb was dropped to see a house guest off on a train. He rose at six, and half an hour later walked with his friend to the station, not far away, across two of the rivers. He was back home by seven, just as the siren sounded its sustained warning. He ate breakfast and then, because the morning was already hot, undressed down to his underwear and went out on the porch to read the paper. This porch—in fact, the whole building—was curiously constructed. Dr. Fujii was the proprietor of a peculiarly Japanese institution: a private, single-doctor hospital. This building, perched beside and over the water of the Kyo River, and next to the bridge of the same name, contained thirty rooms for thirty patients and their kinfolk—for, according to Japanese custom, when a person falls sick and goes to a hospital, one or more members of his family go and live there with him, to cook for him, bathe, massage, and read to him, and to offer incessant familial sympathy, without which a Japanese patient would be miserable indeed. Dr. Fujii had no beds—only straw mats—for his patients. He did, however, have all sorts of modern equipment: an X-ray machine, diathermy apparatus, and a fine tiled laboratory. The structure rested two-thirds on the land, one-third on piles over the tidal waters of the Kyo. This overhang, the part of the building where Dr. Fujii lived, was queer-looking, but it was cool in summer and from the porch, which faced away from the center of the city, the prospect of the river, with pleasure boats drifting up and down it, was always refreshing. Dr. Fujii had occasionally had anxious moments when the Ota and its mouth branches rose to flood, but the piling was apparently firm enough and the house had always held.

Dr. Fujii had been relatively idle for about a month because in July, as the number of untouched cities in Japan dwindled and as Hiroshima seemed more and more inevitably a target, he began turning patients away, on the ground that in case of a fire raid he would not be able to evacuate them. Now he had only two patients left—a woman from Yano, injured in the shoulder, and a young man of twenty-five recovering from burns he had suffered when the steel factory near Hiroshima in which he worked had been hit. Dr. Fujii had six nurses to tend his patients. His wife and children were safe; his wife and one son were living outside Osaka, and another son and two daughters were in the country on Kyushu. A niece was living with him, and a maid and a manservant. He had little to do and did not mind, for he had saved some money. At fifty, he was healthy, convivial, and calm, and he was pleased to pass the evenings drinking whiskey with friends, always sensibly and for the sake of conversation. Before the war, he had affected brands imported from Scotland and America; now he was perfectly satisfied with the best Japanese brand, Suntory.

Dr. Fujii sat down cross-legged in his underwear on the spotless matting of the porch, put on his glasses, and started reading the Osaka Asahi. He liked to read the Osaka news because his wife was there. He saw the flash. To him—faced away from the center and looking at his paper—it seemed a brilliant yellow. Startled, he began to rise to his feet. In that moment (he was 1,550 yards from the center), the hospital leaned behind his rising and, with a terrible ripping noise, toppled into the river. The Doctor, still in the act of getting to his feet, was thrown forward and around and over; he was buffeted and gripped; he lost track of everything, because things were so speeded up; he felt the water.

Dr. Fujii hardly had time to think that he was dying before he realized that he was alive, squeezed tightly by two long timbers in a V across his chest, like a morsel suspended between two huge chopsticks—held upright, so that he could not move, with his head miraculously above water and his torso and legs in it.

The remains of his hospital were all around him in a mad assortment of splintered lumber and materials for the relief of pain. His left shoulder hurt terribly. His glasses were gone.

FATHER WILHELM KLEINSORGE, of the Society of Jesus, was, on the morning of the explosion, in rather frail condition. The Japanese wartime diet had not sustained him, and he felt the strain of being a foreigner in an increasingly xenophobic Japan; even a German, since the defeat of the Fatherland, was unpopular. Father Kleinsorge had, at thirty-eight, the look of a boy growing too fast—thin in the face, with a prominent Adam's apple, a hollow chest, dangling hands, big feet. He walked clumsily, leaning forward a little. He was tired all the time. To make matters worse, he had suffered for two days, along with Father Cieslik, a fellow-priest, from a rather painful and urgent diarrhea, which they blamed on the beans and black ration bread they were obliged to eat. Two other priests then living in the mission compound, which was in the Nobori-cho section—Father Superior LaSalle and Father Schiffer—had happily escaped this affliction.

Father Kleinsorge woke up about six the morning the bomb was dropped, and half an hour later—he was a bit tardy because of his sickness—he began to read Mass in the mission chapel, a small Japanese-style wooden building which was without pews, since its worshippers knelt on the usual Japanese matted floor, facing an altar graced with splendid silks, brass, silver, and heavy embroideries. This morning, a Monday, the only worshippers were Mr. Takemoto, a theological student living in the mission house; Mr. Fukai, the secretary of the diocese; Mrs. Murata, the mission's devoutly Christian housekeeper; and his fellow-priests. After Mass, while Father Kleinsorge was reading the Prayers of Thanksgiving, the siren sounded. He stopped the service and the missionaries retired across the compound to the bigger building. There, in his room on the ground floor, to the right of the front door, Father Kleinsorge changed into a military uniform which he had acquired when he was teaching at the Rokko Middle School in Kobe and which he wore during air-raid alerts. After an alarm, Father Kleinsorge always

went out and scanned the sky, and in this instance, when he stepped outside, he was glad to see only the single weather plane that flew over Hiroshima each day about this time. Satisfied that nothing would happen, he went in and breakfasted with the other Fathers on substitute coffee and ration bread, which, under the circumstances, was especially repugnant to him. The Fathers sat and talked awhile, until, at eight, they heard the all-clear. They went then to various parts of the building. Father Schiffer retired to his room to do some writing. Father Cieslik sat in his room in a straight chair with a pillow over his stomach to ease his pain, and read. Father Superior LaSalle stood at the window of his room, thinking. Father Kleinsorge went up to a room on the third floor, took off all his clothes except his underwear, and stretched out on his right side on a cot and began reading his *Stimmen der Zeit*.

After the terrible flash—which, Father Kleinsorge later realized, reminded him of something he had read as a boy about a large meteor colliding with the earth—he had time (since he was 1,400 yards from the center) for one thought: A bomb has fallen directly on us. Then, for a few seconds or minutes, he went out of his mind.

Father Kleinsorge never knew how he got out of the house. The next things he was conscious of were that he was wandering around in the mission's vegetable garden in his underwear, bleeding slightly from small cuts along his left flank; that all the buildings round about had fallen down except the Jesuits' mission house, which had long before been braced and double-braced by a priest named Gropper, who was terrified of earthquakes; that the day had turned dark; and that Murata-*san*, the housekeeper, was nearby, crying over and over, "*Shu Jesusu, awaremi tamai!* Our Lord Jesus, have pity on us!"

ON THE TRAIN on the way into Hiroshima from the country, where he lived with his mother, Dr. Terufumi Sasaki, the Red Cross Hospital surgeon, thought over an unpleasant nightmare he had had the night before. His mother's home was in Mukaihara, thirty miles from the city, and it took him two hours by train and tram to reach the hospital. He had slept uneasily all night and had wakened an hour earlier than usual, and, feeling sluggish and slightly feverish, had debated whether to go to the hospital at all; his sense of duty finally forced him to go, and he had started out on an earlier train than he took most mornings. The dream had particularly frightened him because it was so closely associated, on the surface at least, with a disturbing actuality. He was only twenty-five years old and had just completed his training at the Eastern Medical University, in Tsingtao, China. He was something of an idealist and was much distressed by the inadequacy of medical facilities in the country town where his mother lived. Quite on his own, and without a permit, he had begun visiting a few sick people out there in the evenings, after his eight hours at the hospital and four hours' commuting. He had recently learned that the penalty for practicing without a permit was severe; a fellow-doctor whom he had asked about it had given him a serious scolding. Nevertheless, he had continued to practice. In his dream, he had been at the bedside of a country patient when the police and the doctor he had consulted burst into the room, seized him, dragged him outside, and beat him up cruelly. On the train, he just about decided to give up the work in Mukaihara, since he felt it would be impossible to get a permit, because the authorities would hold that it would conflict with his duties at the Red Cross Hospital.

At the terminus, he caught a streetcar at once. (He later calculated that if he had taken his customary train that morning, and if he had had to wait a few minutes for the streetcar, as often happened, he would have been close to the center at the time of the explosion and would surely have perished.) He arrived at the hospital at seven-forty and reported to the chief surgeon. A few minutes later, he went to a room on the first floor and drew blood from the arm of a man in order to perform a Wassermann test. The laboratory containing the incubators for the test was on the third floor. With the blood specimen in his left hand, walking in a kind of distraction he had felt all morning, probably because of the dream and his restless night, he started along the main corridor on his way toward the stairs. He was one step beyond an open window when the light of the bomb was reflected, like a gi-

gantic photographic flash, in the corridor. He ducked down on one knee and said to himself, as only a Japanese would, "Sasaki, *gambare!* Be brave!" Just then (the building was 1,650 yards from the center), the blast ripped through the hospital. The glasses he was wearing flew off his face; the bottle of blood crashed against one wall; his Japanese slippers zipped out from under his feet—but otherwise, thanks to where he stood, he was untouched.

Dr. Sasaki shouted the name of the chief surgeon and rushed around to the man's office and found him terribly cut by glass. The hospital was in horrible confusion: heavy partitions and ceilings had fallen on patients, beds had overturned, windows had blown in and cut people, blood was spattered on the walls and floors, instruments were everywhere, many of the patients were running about screaming, many more lay dead. (A colleague working in the laboratory to which Dr. Sasaki had been walking was dead; Dr. Sasaki's patient, whom he had just left and who a few moments before had been dreadfully afraid of syphilis, was also dead.) Dr. Sasaki found himself the only doctor in the hospital who was unhurt.

Dr. Sasaki, who believed that the enemy had hit only the building he was in, got bandages and began to bind the wounds of those inside the hospital; while outside, all over Hiroshima, maimed and dying citizens turned their unsteady steps toward the Red Cross Hospital to begin an invasion that was to make Dr. Sasaki forget his private nightmare for a long, long time.

Miss Toshiko Sasaki, the East Asia Tin Works clerk, who is not related to Dr. Sasaki, got up at three o'clock in the morning on the day the bomb fell. There was extra housework to do. Her eleven-month-old brother, Akio, had come down the day before with a serious stomach upset; her mother had taken him to the Tamura Pediatric Hospital and was staying there with him. Miss Sasaki, who was about twenty, had to cook breakfast for her father, a brother, a sister, and herself, and—since the hospital, because of the war, was unable to provide food—to prepare a whole day's meals for her mother and the baby, in time for her father, who worked in a factory making rubber earplugs for artillery crews, to take the food by on his way to the plant. When she had finished and had cleaned and put away the cooking things, it was nearly seven. The family lived in Koi, and she had a forty-five-minute trip to the tin works, in the section of town called Kannonmachi. She was in charge of the personnel records in the factory. She left Koi at seven, and as soon as she reached the plant, she went with some of the other girls from the personnel department to the factory auditorium. A prominent local Navy man, a former employee, had committed suicide the day before by throwing himself under a train—a death considered honorable enough to warrant a memorial service, which was to be held at the tin works at ten o'clock that morning. In the large hall, Miss Sasaki and the others made suitable preparations for the meeting. This work took about twenty minutes.

Miss Sasaki went back to her office and sat down at her desk. She was quite far from the windows, which were off to her left, and behind her were a couple of tall bookcases containing all the books of the factory library, which the personnel department had organized. She settled herself at her desk, put some things in a drawer, and shifted papers. She thought that before she began to make entries in her lists of new employees, discharges, and departures for the Army, she would chat for a moment with the girl at her right. Just as she turned her head away from the windows, the room was filled with a blinding light. She was paralyzed by fear, fixed still in her chair for a long moment (the plant was 1,600 yards from the center).

Everything fell, and Miss Sasaki lost consciousness. The ceiling dropped suddenly and the wooden floor above collapsed in splinters and the people up there came down and the roof above them gave way; but principally and first of all, the bookcases right behind her swooped forward and the contents threw her down, with her left leg horribly twisted and breaking underneath her. There, in the tin factory, in the first moment of the atomic age, a human being was crushed by books.

II

The Fire

IMMEDIATELY after the explosion, the Reverend Mr. Kiyoshi Tanimoto, having run wildly out of the Matsui estate and having looked in wonderment at the bloody soldiers at the mouth of the dugout they had been digging, attached himself sympathetically to an old lady who was walking along in a daze, holding her head with her left hand, supporting a small boy of three or four on her back with her right, and crying, "I'm hurt! I'm hurt! I'm hurt!" Mr. Tanimoto transferred the child to his own back and led the woman by the hand down the street, which was darkened by what seemed to be a local column of dust. He took the woman to a grammar school not far away that had previously been designated for use as a temporary hospital in case of emergency. By this solicitous behavior, Mr. Tanimoto at once got rid of his terror. At the school, he was much surprised to see glass all over the floor and fifty or sixty injured people already waiting to be treated. He reflected that, although the all-clear had sounded and he had heard no planes, several bombs must have been dropped. He thought of a hillock in the rayon man's garden from which he could get a view of the whole of Koi—of the whole of Hiroshima, for that matter—and he ran back up to the estate.

From the mound, Mr. Tanimoto saw an astonishing panorama. Not just a patch of Koi, as he had expected, but as much of Hiroshima as he could see through the clouded air was giving off a thick, dreadful miasma. Clumps of smoke, near and far, had begun to push up through the general dust. He wondered how such extensive damage could have been dealt out of a silent sky; even a few planes, far up, would have been audible. Houses nearby were burning, and when huge drops of water the size of marbles began to fall, he half thought that they must be coming from the hoses of firemen fighting the blazes. (They were actually drops of condensed moisture falling from the turbulent tower of dust, heat, and fission fragments that had already risen miles into the sky above Hiroshima.)

Mr. Tanimoto turned away from the sight when he heard Mr. Matsuo call out to ask whether he was all right. Mr. Matsuo had been safely cushioned within the falling house by the bedding stored in the front hall and had worked his way out. Mr. Tanimoto scarcely answered. He had thought of his wife and baby, his church, his home, his parishioners, all of them down in that awful murk. Once more he began to run in fear—toward the city.

Mrs. Hatsuyo Nakamura, the tailor's widow, having struggled up from under the ruins of her house after the explosion, and seeing Myeko, the youngest of her three children, buried breast-deep and unable to move, crawled across the debris, hauled at timbers, and flung tiles aside, in a hurried effort to free the child. Then, from what seemed to be caverns far below, she heard two small voices crying, "*Tasukete! Tasukete!* Help! Help!"

She called the names of her ten-year-old son and eight-year-old daughter: "Toshio! Yaeko!" The voices from below answered.

Mrs. Nakamura abandoned Myeko, who at least could breathe, and in a frenzy made the wreckage fly above the crying voices. The children had been sleeping nearly ten feet apart, but now their voices seemed to come from the same place. Toshio, the boy, apparently had some freedom to move, because she could feel him undermining the pile of wood and tiles as she worked from above. At last she saw his head, and she hastily pulled him out by it. A mosquito net was wound intricately, as if it had been carefully wrapped, around his feet. He said he had been blown right across the room and had been on top of his sister Yaeko under the wreckage. She now said, from underneath, that she could not move, because there was something on her legs. With a bit more digging, Mrs. Nakamura cleared a hole above the child and began to pull her arm. "*Itai!* It hurts!" Yaeko cried. Mrs. Nakamura shouted. "There's not time now to say whether it hurts or not," and yanked her whimpering daughter up. Then she freed Myeko. The children were filthy and bruised, but none of them had a single cut or scratch.

Mrs. Nakamura took the children out into the street. They had nothing on but underpants, and although the day was very hot, she worried rather confusedly about their being cold, so she went back into the wreckage and burrowed underneath and found a bundle of clothes she had packed for an emergency, and she dressed them in pants, blouses, shoes, padded-cotton air-raid helmets called *boku-*

zuki, and even, irrationally, overcoats. The children were silent, except for the five-year-old, Myeko, who kept asking questions: "Why is it night already? Why did our house fall down? What happened?" Mrs. Nakamura, who did not know what had happened (had not the all-clear sounded?), looked around and saw through the darkness that all the houses in her neighborhood had collapsed. The house next door, which its owner had been tearing down to make way for a fire lane, was now very thoroughly, if crudely, torn down; its owner, who had been sacrificing his home for the community's safety, lay dead. Mrs. Nakamoto, wife of the head of the local air-raid-defense Neighborhood Association, came across the street with her head all bloody, and said that her baby was badly cut; did Mrs. Nakamura have any bandage? Mrs. Nakamura did not, but she crawled into the remains of her house again and pulled out some white cloth that she had been using in her work as a seamstress, ripped it into strips, and gave it to Mrs. Nakamoto. While fetching the cloth, she noticed her sewing machine; she went back in for it and dragged it out. Obviously, she could not carry it with her, so she unthinkingly plunged her symbol of livelihood into the receptacle which for weeks had been her symbol of safety—the cement tank of water in front of her house, of the type every household had been ordered to construct against a possible fire raid.

A nervous neighbor, Mrs. Hataya, called to Mrs. Nakamura to run away with her to the woods in Asano Park—an estate, by the Kyo River not far off, belonging to the wealthy Asano family, who once owned the Toyo Kisen Kaisha steamship line. The park had been designated as an evacuation area for their neighborhood. Seeing fire breaking out in a nearby ruin (except at the very center, where the bomb itself ignited some fires, most of Hiroshima's citywide conflagration was caused by inflammable wreckage falling on cook stoves and live wires), Mrs. Nakamura suggested going over to fight it. Mrs. Hataya said, "Don't be foolish. What if planes come and drop more bombs?" So Mrs. Nakamura started out for Asano Park with her children and Mrs. Hataya, and she carried her rucksack of emergency clothing, a blanket, an umbrella, and a suitcase of things she had cached in her air-raid shelter. Under many ruins, as they hurried along, they heard muffled screams for help. The only building they saw standing on their way to Asano Park was the Jesuit mission house, alongside the Catholic kindergarten to which Mrs. Nakamura had sent Myeko for a time. As they passed it, she saw Father Kleinsorge, in bloody underwear, running out of the house with a small suitcase in his hand.

RIGHT AFTER the explosion, while Father Wilhelm Kleinsorge, S.J., was wandering around in his underwear in the vegetable garden, Father Superior LaSalle came around the corner of the building in the darkness. His body, especially his back, was bloody; the flash had made him twist away from his window, and tiny pieces of glass had flown at him. Father Kleinsorge, still bewildered, managed to ask, "Where are the rest?" Just then, the two other priests living in the mission house appeared—Father Cieslik, unhurt, supporting Father Schiffer, who was covered with blood that spurted from a cut above his left ear and who was very pale. Father Cieslik was rather pleased with himself, for after the flash he had dived into a doorway, which he had previously reckoned to be the safest place inside the building, and when the blast came, he was not injured. Father LaSalle told Father Cieslik to take Father Schiffer to a doctor before he bled to death, and suggested either Dr. Kanda, who lived on the next corner, or Dr. Fujii, about six blocks away. The two men went out of the compound and up the street.

The daughter of Mr. Hoshijima, the mission catechist, ran up to Father Kleinsorge and said that her mother and sister were buried under the ruins of their house, which was at the back of the Jesuit compound, and at the same time the priests noticed that the house of the Catholic-kindergarten teacher at the front of the compound had collapsed on her. While Father LaSalle and Mrs. Murata, the mission housekeeper, dug the teacher out, Father Kleinsorge went to the catechist's fallen house and began lifting things off the top of the pile. There was not a sound underneath; he was sure the Hoshijima women had been killed. At last, under what had been a corner of the kitchen, he saw

Mrs. Hoshijima's head. Believing her dead, he began to haul her out by the hair, but suddenly she screamed, "*Itai! Itai!* It hurts! It hurts!" He dug some more and lifted her out. He managed, too, to find her daughter in the rubble and free her. Neither was badly hurt.

A public bath next door to the mission house had caught fire, but since there the wind was southerly, the priests thought their house would be spared. Nevertheless, as a precaution, Father Kleinsorge went inside to fetch some things he wanted to save. He found his room in a state of weird and illogical confusion. A first-aid kit was hanging undisturbed on a hook on the wall, but his clothes, which had been on other hooks nearby, were nowhere to be seen. His desk was in splinters all over the room, but a mere papier-mâché suitcase, which he had hidden under the desk, stood handle-side up, without a scratch on it, in the doorway of the room, where he could not miss it. Father Kleinsorge later came to regard this as a bit of Providential interference, inasmuch as the suitcase contained his breviary, the account books for the whole diocese, and a considerable amount of paper money belonging to the mission, for which he was responsible. He ran out of the house and deposited the suitcase in the mission air-raid shelter.

At about this time, Father Cieslik and Father Schiffer, who was still spurting blood, came back and said that Dr. Kanda's house was ruined and that fire blocked them from getting out of what they supposed to be the local circle of destruction to Dr. Fujii's private hospital, on the bank of the Kyo River.

DR. MASAKAZU FUJII's hospital was no longer on the bank of the Kyo River; it was in the river. After the overturn, Dr. Fujii was so stupefied and so tightly squeezed by the beams gripping his chest that he was unable to move at first, and he hung there about twenty minutes in the darkened morning. Then a thought which came to him—that soon the tide would be running in through the estuaries and his head would be submerged—inspired him to fearful activity; he wriggled and turned and exerted what strength he could (though his left arm, because of the pain in his shoulder, was useless), and before long he had freed himself from the vise. After a few moments' rest, he climbed onto the pile of timbers and, finding a long one that slanted up to the riverbank, he painfully shinnied up it.

Dr. Fujii, who was in his underwear, was now soaking and dirty. His undershirt was torn, and blood ran down it from bad cuts on his chin and back. In this disarray, he walked out onto Kyo Bridge, beside which his hospital
10 had stood. The bridge had not collapsed. He could see only fuzzily without his glasses, but he could see enough to be amazed at the number of houses that were down all around. On the bridge, he encountered a friend, a doctor named Machii, and asked in bewilderment, "What do you think it was?"

Dr. Machii said, "It must have been a *Molotoffano hanakago*"—a Molotov flower basket, the delicate Japanese name for the "bread bas-
20 ket," or self-scattering cluster of bombs.

At first Dr. Fujii could see only two fires, one across the river from his hospital site and one quite far to the south. But at the same time, he and his friend observed something that puzzled them, and which, as doctors, they discussed: although there were as yet very few fires, wounded people were hurrying across the bridge in an endless parade of misery, and many of them exhibited terrible burns
30 on their faces and arms. "Why do you suppose it is?" Dr. Fujii asked. Even a theory was comforting that day, and Dr. Machii stuck to his. "Perhaps because it was a Molotov flower basket," he said.

There had been no breeze earlier in the morning when Dr. Fujii had walked to the railway station to see his friend off, but now brisk winds were blowing every which way; here on the bridge the wind was easterly. New fires
40 were leaping up, and they spread quickly, and in a very short time terrible blasts of hot air and showers of cinders made it impossible to stand on the bridge any more. Dr. Machii ran to the far side of the river and along a still unkindled street. Dr. Fujii went down into the water under the bridge, where a score of people had already taken refuge, among them his servants, who had extricated themselves from the wreckage. From there, Dr. Fujii saw a
50 nurse hanging in the timbers of his hospital by her legs, and then another painfully pinned across the breast. He enlisted the help of some

of the others under the bridge and freed both of them. He thought he heard the voice of his niece for a moment, but he could not find her; he never saw her again. Four of his nurses and the two patients in the hospital died, too. Dr. Fujii went back into the water of the river and waited for the fire to subside.

THE LOT of Drs. Fujii, Kanda, and Machii right
60 after the explosion—and, as these three were typical, that of the majority of the physicians and surgeons of Hiroshima—with their offices and hospitals destroyed, their equipment scattered, their own bodies incapacitated in varying degrees, explained why so many citizens who were hurt went untended and why so many who might have lived died. Of a hundred and fifty doctors in the city, sixty-five were already dead and most of the rest were
70 wounded. Of 1,780 nurses, 1,654 were dead or too badly hurt to work. In the biggest hospital, that of the Red Cross, only six doctors out of thirty were able to function, and only ten nurses out of more than two hundred. The sole uninjured doctor on the Red Cross Hospital staff was Dr. Sasaki. After the explosion, he hurried to a storeroom to fetch bandages. This room, like everything he had seen as he ran through the hospital, was chaotic—bottles of
80 medicines thrown off shelves and broken, salves spattered on the walls, instruments strewn everywhere. He grabbed up some bandages and an unbroken bottle of mercurochrome, hurried back to the chief surgeon, and bandaged his cuts. Then he went out into the corridor and began patching up the wounded patients and the doctors and nurses there. He blundered so without his glasses that he took
90 a pair off the face of a wounded nurse, and although they only approximately compensated for the errors of his vision, they were better than nothing. (He was to depend on them for more than a month.)

Dr. Sasaki worked without method, taking those who were nearest him first, and he noticed soon that the corridor seemed to be getting more and more crowded. Mixed in with the abrasions and lacerations which most people in the hospital had suffered, he began to
100 find dreadful burns. He realized then that casualties were pouring in from outdoors. There

were so many that he began to pass up the lightly wounded; he decided that all he could hope to do was to stop people from bleeding to death. Before long, patients lay and crouched on the floors of the wards and the laboratories and all the other rooms, and in the corridors, and on the stairs, and in the front hall, and under the porte-cochère, and on the stone front steps, and in the driveway and courtyard, and for blocks each way in the streets outside. Wounded people supported maimed people; disfigured families leaned together. Many people were vomiting. A tremendous number of schoolgirls—some of those who had been taken from their classrooms to work outdoors, clearing fire lanes—crept into the hospital. In a city of two hundred and forty-five thousand, nearly a hundred thousand people had been killed or doomed at one blow; a hundred thousand more were hurt. At least ten thousand of the wounded made their way to the best hospital in town, which was altogether unequal to such a trampling, since it had only six hundred beds, and they had all been occupied. The people in the suffocating crowd inside the hospital wept and cried, for Dr. Sasaki to hear, *Sensei!* Doctor!," and the less seriously wounded came and pulled at his sleeve and begged him to go to the aid of the worse wounded. Tugged here and there in his stockinged feet, bewildered by the numbers, staggered by so much raw flesh, Dr. Sasaki lost all sense of profession and stopped working as a skillful surgeon and a sympathetic man; he became an automaton, mechanically wiping, daubing, winding, wiping, daubing, winding.

SOME OF the wounded in Hiroshima were unable to enjoy the questionable luxury of hospitalization. In what had been the personnel office of the East Asia Tin Works, Miss Sasaki lay doubled over, unconscious, under the tremendous pile of books and plaster and wood and corrugated iron. She was wholly unconscious (she later estimated) for about three hours. Her first sensation was of dreadful pain in her left leg. It was so black under the books and debris that the borderline between awareness and unconsciousness was fine; she apparently crossed it several times, for the pain seemed to come and go. At the moments when it was sharpest, she felt that her leg had been cut off somewhere below the knee. Later, she heard someone walking on top of the wreckage above her, and anguished voices spoke up, evidently from within the mess around her: "Please help! Get us out!"

FATHER KLEINSORGE stemmed Father Schiffer's spurting cut as well as he could with some bandage that Dr. Fujii had given the priests a few days before. When he finished, he ran into the mission house again and found the jacket of his military uniform and an old pair of gray trousers. He put them on and went outside. A woman from next door ran up to him and shouted that her husband was buried under her house and the house was on fire; Father Kleinsorge must come and save him.

Father Kleinsorge, already growing apathetic and dazed in the presence of the cumulative distress, said, "We haven't much time." Houses all around were burning, and the wind was now blowing hard. "Do you know exactly which part of the house he is under?" he asked.

"Yes, yes," she said. "Come quickly."

They went around to the house, the remains of which blazed violently, but when they got there, it turned out that the woman had no idea where her husband was. Father Kleinsorge shouted several times, "Is anyone there?" There was no answer. Father Kleinsorge said to the woman, "We must get away or we will all die." He went back to the Catholic compound and told the Father Superior that the fire was coming closer on the wind, which had swung around and was now from the north; it was time for everybody to go.

Just then, the kindergarten teacher pointed out to the priests Mr. Fukai, the secretary of the diocese, who was standing in his window on the second floor of the mission house, facing in the direction of the explosion, weeping. Father Cieslik, because he thought the stairs unusable, ran around to the back of the mission house to look for a ladder. There he heard people crying for help under a nearby fallen roof. He called to passers-by running away in the street to help him lift it, but nobody paid any attention, and he had to leave the buried ones to die. Father Kleinsorge ran inside the mission house and scrambled up the stairs, which were awry and piled with plaster and lathing, and called to Mr. Fukai from the doorway of his room.

Mr. Fukai, a very short man of about fifty, turned around slowly, with a queer look, and said, "Leave me here."

Father Kleinsorge went into the room and took Mr. Fukai by the collar of his coat and said, "Come with me or you'll die."

Mr. Fukai said, "Leave me here to die."

Father Kleinsorge began to shove and haul Mr. Fukai out of the room. Then the theological student came up and grabbed Mr. Fukai's feet, and Father Kleinsorge took his shoulders, and together they carried him downstairs and outdoors. "I can't walk!" Mr. Fukai cried. "Leave me here!" Father Kleinsorge got his paper suitcase with the money in it and took Mr. Fukai up pickaback, and the party started for the East Parade Ground, their district's 'safe area." As they went out of the gate, Mr. Fukai, quite childlike now, beat on Father Kleinsorge's shoulders and said, "I won't leave. I won't leave." Irrelevantly, Father Kleinsorge turned to Father LaSalle and said, "We have lost all our possessions but not our sense of humor."

The street was cluttered with parts of houses that had slid into it, and with fallen telephone poles and wires. From every second or third house came the voices of people buried and abandoned, who invariably screamed, with formal politeness, *Tasukete kure!* Help, if you please!" The priests recognized several ruins from which these cries came as the homes of friends, but because of the fire it was too late to help. All the way, Mr. Fukai whimpered, "Let me stay." The party turned right when they came to a block of fallen houses that was one flame. At Sakai Bridge, which would take them across to the East Parade Ground, they saw that the whole community on the opposite side of the river was a sheet of fire; they dared not cross and decided to take refuge in Asano Park, off to their left. Father Kleinsorge, who had been weakened for a couple of days by his bad case of diarrhea, began to stagger under his protesting burden, and as he tried to climb up over the wreckage of several houses that blocked their way to the park, he stumbled, dropped Mr. Fukai, and

plunged down, head over heels, to the edge of the river. When he picked himself up, he saw Mr. Fukai running away. Father Kleinsorge shouted to a dozen soldiers, who were standing by the bridge, to stop him. As Father Kleinsorge started back to get Mr. Fukai, Father LaSalle called out, "Hurry! Don't waste time!" So Father Kleinsorge just requested the soldiers to take care of Mr. Fukai. They said they would, but the little, broken man got away from them, and the last the priests could see of him, he was running back toward the fire.

MR. TANIMOTO, fearful for his family and church, at first ran toward them by the shortest route, along Koi Highway. He was the only person making his way into the city; he met hundreds and hundreds who were fleeing, and every one of them seemed to be hurt in some way. The eyebrows of some were burned off and skin hung from their faces and hands. Others, because of pain, held their arms up as if carrying something in both hands. Some were vomiting as they walked. Many were naked or in shreds of clothing. On some undressed bodies, the burns had made patterns— of undershirt straps and suspenders and, on the skin of some women (since white repelled the heat from the bomb and dark clothes absorbed it and conducted it to the skin), the shapes of flowers they had had on their kimonos. Many, although injured themselves, supported relatives who were worse off. Almost all had their heads bowed, looked straight ahead, were silent, and showed no expression whatever.

After crossing Koi Bridge and Kannon Bridge, having run the whole way, Mr. Tanimoto saw, as he approached the center, that all the houses had been crushed and many were afire. Here the trees were bare and their trunks were charred. He tried at several points to penetrate the ruins, but the flames always stopped him. Under many houses, people screamed for help, but no one helped; in general, survivors that day assisted only their relatives or immediate neighbors, for they could not comprehend or tolerate a wider circle of misery. The wounded limped past the screams, and Mr. Tanimoto ran past them. As a Christian he was filled with compassion for those who were trapped, and as a Japanese he was overwhelmed by the shame of being unhurt, and he prayed as he ran, "God help them and take them out of the fire."

He thought he would skirt the fire, to the left. He ran back to Kannon Bridge and followed for a distance one of the rivers. He tried several cross streets, but all were blocked, so he turned far left and ran out to Yokogawa, a station on a railroad line that detoured the city in a wide semicircle, and he followed the rails until he came to a burning train. So impressed was he by this time by the extent of the damage that he ran north two miles to Gion, a suburb in the foothills. All the way, he overtook dreadfully burned and lacerated people, and in his guilt he turned to right and left as he hurried and said to some of them, "Excuse me for having no burden like yours." Near Gion, he began to meet country people going toward the city to help, and when they saw him, several exclaimed, "Look! There is one who is not wounded." At Gion, he bore toward the right bank of the main river, the Ota, and ran down it until he reached fire again. There was no fire on the other side of the river, so he threw off his shirt and shoes and plunged into it. In midstream, where the current was fairly strong, exhaustion and fear finally caught up with him —he had run nearly seven miles—and he became limp and drifted in the water. He prayed, "Please, God, help me to cross. It would be nonsense for me to be drowned when I am the only uninjured one." He managed a few more strokes and fetched up on a spit downstream.

Mr. Tanimoto climbed up the bank and ran along it until, near a large Shinto shrine, he came to more fire, and as he turned left to get around it, he met, by incredible luck, his wife. She was carrying their infant son. Mr. Tanimoto was now so emotionally worn out that nothing could surprise him. He did not embrace his wife; he simply said, "Oh, you are safe." She told him that she had got home from her night in Ushida just in time for the explosion; she had been buried under the parsonage with the baby in her arms. She told how the wreckage had pressed down on her, how the baby had cried. She saw a chink of light, and by reaching up with a hand, she worked the hole bigger, bit by bit. After about half an hour, she heard the crackling noise of wood burning. At last the opening was big enough for her to push the baby out, and afterward she crawled out herself. She said she was now going out to Ushida again. Mr. Tanimoto said he wanted to see his church and take care of the people of his Neighborhood Association. They parted casually—as bewildered—as they had met.

Mr. Tanimoto's way around the fire took him across the East Parade Ground, which, being an evacuation area, was now the scene of a gruesome review: rank on rank of the burned and bleeding. Those who were burned moaned, *"Mizu, mizu!* Water, water!" Mr. Tanimoto found a basin in a nearby street and located a water tap that still worked in the crushed shell of a house, and he began carrying water to the suffering strangers. When he had given drink to about thirty of them, he realized he was taking too much time. "Excuse me," he said loudly to those nearby who were reaching out their hands to him and crying their thirst. "I have many people to take care of." Then he ran away. He went to the river again, the basin in his hand, and jumped down onto a sandspit. There he saw hundreds of people so badly wounded that they could not get up to go farther from the burning city. When they saw a man erect and unhurt, the chant began again: *"Mizu, mizu, mizu."* Mr. Tanimoto could not resist them; he carried them water from the river—a mistake, since it was tidal and brackish. Two or three small boats were ferrying hurt people across the river from Asano Park, and when one touched the spit, Mr. Tanimoto again made his loud, apologetic speech and jumped into the boat. It took him across to the park. There, in the underbrush, he found some of his charges of the Neighborhood Association, who had come there by his previous instructions, and saw many acquaintances, among them Father Kleinsorge and the other Catholics. But he missed Fukai, who had been a close friend. "Where is Fukai-*san?*" he asked.

"He didn't want to come with us," Father Kleinsorge said. "He ran back."

WHEN MISS SASAKI heard the voices of the people caught along with her in the dilapidation at the tin factory, she began speaking to them.

917

Her nearest neighbor, she discovered, was a high-school girl who had been drafted for factory work, and who said her back was broken. Miss Sasaki replied, "I am lying here and I can't move. My left leg is cut off."

Some time later, she again heard somebody walk overhead and then move off to one side, and whoever it was began burrowing. The digger released several people, and when he had
10 uncovered the high-school girl, she found that her back was not broken, after all, and she crawled out. Miss Sasaki spoke to the rescuer, and he worked toward her. He pulled away a great number of books, until he had made a tunnel to her. She could see his perspiring face as he said, "Come out, Miss." She tried. "I can't move," she said. The man excavated some more and told her to try with all her strength to get out. But books were heavy on her hips,
20 and the man finally saw that a book case was leaning on the books and that a heavy beam pressed down on the book case. "Wait," he said. "I'll get a crowbar."

The man was gone a long time, and when he came back, he was ill-tempered, as if her plight were all her fault. "We have no men to help you!" he shouted in through the tunnel. "You'll have to get out by yourself."

"That's impossible," she said. "My left leg
30 . . ." The man went away.

Much later, several men came and dragged Miss Sasaki out. Her left leg was not severed, but it was badly broken and cut and it hung askew below the knee. They took her out into a courtyard. It was raining. She sat on the ground in the rain. When the downpour increased, someone directed all the wounded people to take cover in the factory's air-raid shelters. "Come along," a torn-up woman said
40 to her. "You can hop." But Miss Sasaki could not move, and she just waited in the rain. Then a man propped up a large sheet of corrugated iron as a kind of lean-to, and took her in his arms and carried her to it. She was grateful until he brought two horribly wounded people—a woman with a whole breast sheared off and a man whose face was all raw from a burn—to share the simple shed with her. No one came back. The rain cleared and the
50 cloudy afternoon was hot; before nightfall the three grotesques under the slanting piece of twisted iron began to smell quite bad.

THE FORMER head of the Nobori-cho Neighborhood Association to which the Catholic priests belonged was an energetic man named Yoshida. He had boasted, when he was in charge of the district air-raid defenses, that fire might eat away all of Hiroshima but it would never come to Nobori-cho. The bomb blew down his house, and a joist pinned him by the 60 legs, in full view of the Jesuit mission house across the way and of the people hurrying along the street. In their confusion as they hurried past, Mrs. Nakamura, with her children, and Father Kleinsorge, with Mr. Fukai on his back, hardly saw him; he was just part of the general blur of misery through which they moved. His cries for help brought no response from them; there were so many people shouting for help that they could not hear him 7 separately. They and all the others went along. Nobori-cho became absolutely deserted, and the fire swept through it. Mr. Yoshida saw the wooden mission house—the only erect building in the area—go up in a lick of flame, and the heat was terrific on his face. Then flames came along his side of the street and entered his house. In a paroxysm of terrified strength, he freed himself and ran down the alleys of Nobori-cho, hemmed in by the fire 8 he had said would never come. He began at once to behave like an old man; two months later his hair was white.

As DR. FUJII stood in the river up to his neck to avoid the heat of the fire, the wind blew stronger and stronger, and soon, even though the expanse of water was small, the waves grew so high that the people under the bridge could no longer keep their footing. Dr. Fujii went close to the shore, crouched down, and 9 embraced a large stone with his usable arm. Later it became possible to wade along the very edge of the river, and Dr. Fujii and his two surviving nurses moved about two hundred yards upstream, to a sandspit near Asano Park. Many wounded were lying on the sand. Dr. Machii was there with his family; his daughter, who had been outdoors when the bomb burst, was badly burned on her hands and legs but fortunately not on her face. Al- 10 though Dr. Fujii's shoulder was by now terribly painful, he examined the girl's burns curiously. Then he lay down. In spite of the misery all around, he was ashamed of his appearance, and he remarked to Dr. Machii that he looked like a beggar, dressed as he was in nothing but torn and bloody underwear. Later in the afternoon, when the fire began to subside, he decided to go to his parental house, in the suburb of Nagatsuka. He asked Dr. Machii to join him, but the Doctor answered that he and his family were going to spend the night on the spit, because of his daughter's injuries. Dr. Fujii, together with his nurses, walked first to Ushida, where, in the partially damaged house of some relatives, he found first-aid materials he had stored there. The two nurses bandaged him and he them. They went on. Now not many people walked in the streets, but a great number sat and lay on the pavement, vomited, waited for death, and died. The number of corpses on the way to Nagatsuka was more and more puzzling. The Doctor wondered: Could a Molotov flower basket have done all this?

Dr. Fujii reached his family's house in the evening. It was five miles from the center of town, but its roof had fallen in and the windows were all broken.

ALL DAY, people poured into Asano Park. This private estate was far enough away from the explosion so that its bamboos, pines, laurel, and maples were still alive, and the green place invited refugees—partly because they believed that if the Americans came back, they would bomb only buildings; partly because the foliage seemed a center of coolness and life, and the estate's exquisitely precise rock gardens, with their quiet pools and arching bridges, were very Japanese, normal, secure; and also partly (according to some who were there) because of an irresistible, atavistic urge to hide under leaves. Mrs. Nakamura and her children were among the first to arrive, and they settled in the bamboo grove near the river. They all felt terribly thirsty, and they drank from the river. At once they were nauseated and began vomiting, and they retched the whole day. Others were also nauseated; they all thought (probably because of the strong odor of ionization, an "electric smell" given off by the bomb's fission) that they were sick from a gas the Americans had dropped. When Father Kleinsorge and the other priests came into the park, nodding to their friends as they passed, the Nakamuras were all sick and prostrate. A woman named Iwasaki, who lived in the neighborhood of the mission and who was sitting near the Nakamuras, got up and asked the priests if she should stay where she was or go with them. Father Kleinsorge said, "I hardly know where the safest place is." She stayed there, and later in the day, though she had no visible wounds or burns, she died. The priests went farther along the river and settled down in some underbrush. Father LaSalle lay down and went right to sleep. The theological student, who was wearing slippers, had carried with him a bundle of clothes, in which he had packed two pairs of leather shoes. When he sat down with the others, he found that the bundle had broken open and a couple of shoes had fallen out and now he had only two lefts. He retraced his steps and found one right. When he rejoined the priests, he said, "It's funny, but things don't matter any more. Yesterday, my shoes were my most important possessions. Today, I don't care. One pair is enough."

Father Cieslik said, "I know. I started to bring my books along, and then I thought, 'This is no time for books.'"

When Mr. Tanimoto, with his basin still in his hand, reached the park, it was very crowded, and to distinguish the living from the dead was not easy, for most of the people lay still, with their eyes open. To Father Kleinsorge, an Occidental, the silence in the grove by the river, where hundreds of gruesomely wounded suffered together, was one of the most dreadful and awesome phenomena of his whole experience. The hurt ones were quiet; no one wept, much less screamed in pain; no one complained; none of the many who died did so noisily; not even the children cried; very few people even spoke. And when Father Kleinsorge gave water to some whose faces had been almost blotted out by flash burns, they took their share and then raised themselves a little and bowed to him, in thanks.

Mr. Tanimoto greeted the priests and then looked around for other friends. He saw Mrs. Matsumoto, wife of the director of the Methodist School, and asked her if she was thirsty. She was, so he went to one of the pools in the Asano's rock gardens and got water for her in his basin. Then he decided to try to get back to his church. He went into Nobori-cho by the way the priests had taken as they escaped, but he did not get far; the fire along the streets was so fierce that he had to turn back. He walked to the riverbank and began to look for a boat in which he might carry some of the most severely injured across the river from Asano Park and away from the spreading fire. Soon he found a good-sized pleasure punt drawn up on the bank, but in and around it was an awful tableau—five dead men, nearly naked, badly burned, who must have expired more or less all at once, for they were in attitudes which suggested that they had been working together to push the boat down into the river. Mr. Tanimoto lifted them away from the boat, and as he did so, he experienced such horror at disturbing the dead—preventing them, he momentarily felt, from launching their craft and going on their ghostly way—that he said out loud, "Please forgive me for taking this boat. I must use it for others, who are alive." The punt was heavy, but he managed to slide it into the water. There were no oars, and all he could find for propulsion was a thick bamboo pole. He worked the boat upstream to the most crowded part of the park and began to ferry the wounded. He could pack ten or twelve into the boat for each crossing, but as the river was too deep in the center to pole his way across, he had to paddle with the bamboo, and consequently each trip took a very long time. He worked several hours that way.

Early in the afternoon, the fire swept into the woods of Asano Park. The first Mr. Tanimoto knew of it was when, returning in his boat, he saw that a great number of people had moved toward the riverside. On touching the bank, he went up to investigate, and when he saw the fire, he shouted, "All the young men who are not badly hurt come with me!" Father Kleinsorge moved Father Schiffer and Father La-Salle close to the edge of the river and asked people there to get them across if the fire came too near, and then joined Tanimoto's volunteers. Mr. Tanimoto sent some to look for buckets and basins and told others to beat the burning underbrush with their clothes; when utensils were at hand, he formed a bucket chain from one of the pools in the rock gardens. The team fought the fire for more than two hours, and gradually defeated the flames.

As Mr. Tanimoto's men worked, the frightened people in the park pressed closer and closer to the river, and finally the mob began to force some of the unfortunates who were on the very bank into the water. Among those driven into the river and drowned were Mrs. Matsumoto, of the Methodist School, and her daughter.

When Father Kleinsorge got back after fighting the fire, he found Father Schiffer still bleeding and terribly pale. Some Japanese stood around and stared at him, and Father Schiffer whispered, with a weak smile, "It is as if I were already dead." "Not yet," Father Kleinsorge said. He had brought Dr. Fujii's first-aid kit with him, and he had noticed Dr. Kanda in the crowd, so he sought him out and asked him if he would dress Father Schiffer's bad cuts. Dr. Kanda had seen his wife and daughter dead in the ruins of his hospital; he sat now with his head in his hands. "I can't do anything," he said. Father Kleinsorge bound more bandage around Father Schiffer's head, moved him to a steep place, and settled him so that his head was high, and soon the bleeding diminished.

The roar of approaching planes was heard about this time. Someone in the crowd near the Nakamura family shouted, "It's some Grummans coming to strafe us!" A baker named Nakashima stood up and commanded, "Everyone who is wearing anything white, take it off." Mrs. Nakamura took the blouses off her children, and opened her umbrella and made them get under it. A great number of people, even badly burned ones, crawled into bushes and stayed there until the hum, evidently of a reconnaissance or weather run, died away.

It began to rain. Mrs. Nakamura kept her children under the umbrella. The drops grew abnormally large, and someone shouted, "The Americans are dropping gasoline. They're going to set fire to us!" (This alarm stemmed from one of the theories being passed through the park as to why so much of Hiroshima had burned: it was that a single plane had sprayed gasoline on the city and then somehow set fire to it in one flashing moment.) But the drops were palpably water, and as they fell, the wind grew stronger and stronger, and suddenly—probably because of the tremendous convection set up by the blazing city—a whirlwind ripped through the park. Huge trees crashed down; small ones were uprooted and flew into the air. Higher, a wild array of flat things revolved in the twisting funnel—pieces of iron roofing, papers, doors, strips of matting. Father Kleinsorge put a piece of cloth over Father Schiffer's eyes, so that the feeble man would not think he was going crazy. The gale blew Mrs. Murata, the mission housekeeper, who was sitting close by the river, down the embankment at a shallow, rocky place, and she came out with her bare feet bloody. The vortex moved out onto the river, where it sucked up a waterspout and eventually spent itself.

After the storm, Mr. Tanimoto began ferrying people again, and Father Kleinsorge asked the theological student to go across and make his way out to the Jesuit Novitiate at Nagatsuka, about three miles from the center of town, and to request the priests there to come with help for Fathers Schiffer and LaSalle. The student got into Mr. Tanimoto's boat and went off with him. Father Kleinsorge asked Mrs. Nakamura if she would like to go out to Nagatsuka with the priests when they came. She said she had some luggage and her children were sick—they were still vomiting from time to time, and so, for that matter, was she—and therefore she feared she could not. He said he thought the fathers from the Novitiate could come back the next day with a pushcart to get her.

Late in the afternoon, when he went ashore for a while, Mr. Tanimoto, upon whose energy and initiative many had come to depend, heard people begging for food. He consulted Father Kleinsorge, and they decided to go back into town to get some rice from Mr. Tanimoto's Neighborhood Association shelter and from the mission shelter. Father Cieslik and two or three others went with them. At first, when they got among the rows of prostrate houses, they did not know where they were; the change was too sudden, from a busy city of two hundred and forty-five thousand that morning to a mere pattern of residue in the afternoon. The asphalt of the streets was still so soft and hot from the fires that walking was uncomfortable. They encountered only one person, a woman, who said to them as they passed, "My husband is in those ashes." At the

mission, where Mr. Tanimoto left the party, Father Kleinsorge was dismayed to see the building razed. In the garden, on the way to the shelter, he noticed a pumpkin roasted on the vine. He and Father Cieslik tasted it and it was good. They were surprised at their hunger, and they ate quite a bit. They got out several bags of rice and gathered up several other cooked pumpkins and dug up some potatoes that were nicely baked under the ground, and started back. Mr. Tanimoto rejoined them on the way. One of the people with him had some cooking utensils. In the park, Mr. Tanimoto organized the lightly wounded women of his neighborhood to cook. Father Kleinsorge offered the Nakamura family some pumpkin, and they tried it, but they could not keep it on their stomachs. Altogether, the rice was enough to feed nearly a hundred people.

Just before dark, Mr. Tanimoto came across a twenty-year-old girl, Mrs. Kamai, the Tanimotos' next-door neighbor. She was crouching on the ground with the body of her infant daughter in her arms. The baby had evidently been dead all day. Mrs. Kamai jumped up when she saw Mr. Tanimoto and said, "Would you please try to locate my husband?"

Mr. Tanimoto knew that her husband had been inducted into the Army just the day before; he and Mrs. Tanimoto had entertained Mrs. Kamai in the afternoon, to make her forget. Kamai had reported to the Chugoku Regional Army Headquarters—near the ancient castle in the middle of town—where some four thousand troops were stationed. Judging by the many maimed soldiers Mr. Tanimoto had seen during the day, he surmised that the barracks had been badly damaged by whatever it was that had hit Hiroshima. He knew he hadn't a chance of finding Mrs. Kamai's husband, even if he searched, but he wanted to humor her. "I'll try," he said.

"You've got to find him," she said. "He loved our baby so much. I want him to see her once more."

III

Details Are Being Investigated

EARLY IN THE evening of the day the bomb exploded, a Japanese naval launch moved slowly up and down the seven rivers of Hiroshima. It stopped here and there to make an announcement—alongside the crowded sandspits, on which hundreds of wounded lay; at the bridges, on which others were crowded; and eventually, as twilight fell, opposite Asano Park. A young officer stood up in the launch and shouted through a megaphone, "Be patient! A naval hospital ship is coming to take care of you!" The sight of the shipshape launch against the background of the havoc across the river; the unruffled young man in his neat uniform; above all, the promise of medical help—the first word of possible succor anyone had heard in nearly twelve awful hours—cheered the people in the park tremendously. Mrs. Nakamura settled her family for the night with the assurance that a doctor would come and stop their retching. Mr. Tanimoto resumed ferrying the wounded across the river. Father Kleinsorge lay down and said the Lord's Prayer and a Hail Mary to himself, and fell right asleep; but no sooner had he dropped off than Mrs. Murata, the conscientious mission housekeeper, shook him and said, "Father Kleinsorge! Did you remember to repeat your evening prayers?" He answered rather grumpily, "Of course," and he tried to go back to sleep but could not. This, apparently, was just what Mrs. Murata wanted. She began to chat with the exhausted priest. One of the questions she raised was when he thought the priests from the Novitiate, for whom he had sent a messenger in midafternoon, would arrive to evacuate Father Superior LaSalle and Father Schiffer.

THE MESSENGER Father Kleinsorge had sent —the theological student who had been living at the mission house—had arrived at the Novitiate, in the hills about three miles out, at half past four. The sixteen priests there had been doing rescue work in the outskirts; they had worried about their colleagues in the city but had not known how or where to look for them. Now they hastily made two litters out of poles and boards, and the student led half a dozen of them back into the devastated area. They worked their way along the Ota above the city; twice the heat of the fire forced them int the river. At Misasa Bridge, they encountered a long line of soldiers making a bizarre forced march away from the Chugoku Regional Army

Headquarters in the center of the town. All were grotesquely burned, and they supported themselves with staves or leaned on one another. Sick, burned horses, hanging their heads, stood on the bridge. When the rescue party reached the park, it was after dark, and progress was made extremely difficult by the tangle of fallen trees of all sizes that had been knocked down by the whirlwind that afternoon. At last—not long after Mrs. Murata asked her question—they reached their friends, and gave them wine and strong tea.

The priests discussed how to get Father Schiffer and Father LaSalle out to the Novitiate. They were afraid that blundering through the park with them would jar them too much on the wooden litters, and that the wounded men would lose too much blood. Father Kleinsorge thought of Mr. Tanimoto and his boat, and called out to him on the river. When Mr. Tanimoto reached the bank, he said he would be glad to take the injured priests and their bearers upstream to where they could find a clear roadway. The rescuers put Father Schiffer onto one of the stretchers and lowered it into the boat, and two of them went aboard with it. Mr. Tanimoto, who still had no oars, poled the punt upstream.

About half an hour later, Mr. Tanimoto came back and excitedly asked the remaining priests to help him rescue two children he had seen standing up to their shoulders in the river. A group went out and picked them up—two young girls who had lost their family and were both badly burned. The priests stretched them on the ground next to Father Kleinsorge and then embarked Father LaSalle. Father Cieslik thought he could make it out to the Novitiate on foot, so he went aboard with the others. Father Kleinsorge was too feeble; he decided to wait in the park until the next day. He asked the men to come back with a handcart, so that they could take Mrs. Nakamura and her sick children to the Novitiate.

Mr. Tanimoto shoved off again. As the boatload of priests moved slowly upstream, they heard weak cries for help. A woman's voice stood out especially: "There are people here about to be drowned! Help us! The water is rising!" The sounds came from one of the sandspits, and those in the punt could see, in the reflected light of the still-burning fires, a number of wounded people lying at the edge of the river, already partly covered by the flooding tide. Mr. Tanimoto wanted to help them, but the priests were afraid that Father Schiffer would die if they didn't hurry, and they urged their ferryman along. He dropped them where he had put Father Schiffer down and then started back alone toward the sandspit.

THE NIGHT was hot, and it seemed even hotter because of the fires against the sky, but the younger of the two girls Mr. Tanimoto and the priests had rescued complained to Father Kleinsorge that she was cold. He covered her with his jacket. She and her older sister had been in the salt water of the river for a couple of hours before being rescued. The younger one had huge, raw flash burns on her body; the salt water must have been excruciatingly painful to her. She began to shiver heavily, and again said it was cold. Father Kleinsorge borrowed a blanket from someone nearby and wrapped her up, but she shook more and more, and said again, "I am so cold," and then she suddenly stopped shivering and was dead.

MR. TANIMOTO found about twenty men and women on the sandspit. He drove the boat onto the bank and urged them to get aboard. They did not move and he realized that they were too weak to lift themselves. He reached down and took a woman by the hands, but her skin slipped off in huge, glove-like pieces. He was so sickened by this that he had to sit down for a moment. Then he got out into the water and, though a small man, lifted several of the men and women, who were naked, into his boat. Their backs and breasts were clammy, and he remembered uneasily what the great burns he had seen during the day had been like: yellow at first, then red and swollen, with the skin sloughed off, and finally, in the evening, suppurated and smelly. With the tide risen, his bamboo pole was now too short and he had to paddle most of the way across with it. On the other side, at a higher spit, he lifted the slimy living bodies out and carried them up the slope away from the tide. He had to keep consciously repeating to himself, "These are human beings." It took him

three trips to get them all across the river. When he had finished, he decided he had to have a rest, and he went back to the park.

As Mr. Tanimoto stepped up the dark bank, he tripped over someone, and someone else said angrily, "Look out! That's my hand." Mr. Tanimoto, ashamed of hurting wounded people, embarrassed at being able to walk upright, suddenly thought of the naval hospital ship, which had not come (it never did), and he had for a moment a feeling of blind, murderous rage at the crew of the ship, and then at all doctors. Why didn't they come to help these people?

DR. FUJII lay in dreadful pain throughout the night on the floor of his family's roofless house on the edge of the city. By the light of a lantern, he had examined himself and found: left clavicle fractured; multiple abrasions and lacerations of face and body, including deep cuts on the chin, back, and legs; extensive contusions on chest and trunk; a couple of ribs possibly fractured. Had he not been so badly hurt, he might have been at Asano Park, assisting the wounded.

BY NIGHTFALL, ten thousand victims of the explosion had invaded the Red Cross Hospital, and Dr. Sasaki, worn out, was moving aimlessly and dully up and down the stinking corridors with wads of bandage and bottles of mercurochrome, still wearing the glasses he had taken from the wounded nurse, binding up the worst cuts as he came to them. Other doctors were putting compresses of saline solution on the worst burns. That was all they could do. After dark, they worked by the light of the city's fires and by candles the ten remaining nurses held for them. Dr. Sasaki had not looked outside the hospital all day; the scene inside was so terrible and so compelling that it had not occurred to him to ask any questions about what had happened beyond the windows and doors. Ceilings and partitions had fallen; plaster, dust, blood, and vomit were everywhere. Patients were dying by the hundreds, but there was nobody to carry away the corpses. Some of the hospital staff distributed biscuits and rice balls, but the charnel-house smell was so strong that few were hungry. By three o'clock the next morning, after nineteen straight hours of his gruesome work, Dr. Sasaki was incapable of dressing another wound. He and some other survivors of the hospital staff got straw mats and went outdoors—thousands of patients and hundreds of dead were in the yard and on the driveway—and hurried around behind the hospital and lay down in hiding to snatch some sleep. But within an hour wounded people had found them; a complaining circle formed around them: "Doctors! Help us! How can you sleep?" Dr. Sasaki got up again and went back to work. Early in the day, he thought for the first time of his mother, at their country home in Mukaihara, thirty miles from town. He usually went home every night. He was afraid she would think he was dead.

NEAR THE spot upriver to which Mr. Tanimoto had transported the priests, there sat a large case of rice cakes which a rescue party had evidently brought for the wounded lying thereabouts but hadn't distributed. Before evacuating the wounded priests, the others passed the cakes around and helped themselves. A few minutes later, a band of soldiers came up, and an officer, hearing the priests speaking a foreign language, drew his sword and hysterically asked who they were. One of the priests calmed him down and explained that they were Germans—allies. The officer apologized and said that there were reports going around that American parachutists had landed.

The priests decided that they should take Father Schiffer first. As they prepared to leave, Father Superior LaSalle said he felt awfully cold. One of the Jesuits gave up his coat, another his shirt; they were glad to wear less in the muggy night. The stretcher bearers started out. The theological student led the way and tried to warn the others of obstacles, but one of the priests got a foot tangled in some telephone wire and tripped and dropped his corner of the litter. Father Schiffer rolled off, lost consciousness, came to, and then vomited. The bearers picked him up and went on with him to the edge of the city, where they had arranged to meet a relay of other priests, left him

with them, and turned back and got the Father Superior.

The wooden litter must have been terribly painful for Father LaSalle, in whose back scores of tiny particles of window glass were embedded. Near the edge of town, the group had to walk around an automobile burned and squatting on the narrow road, and the bearers on one side, unable to see their way in the darkness, fell into a deep ditch. Father LaSalle was thrown onto the ground and the litter broke in two. One priest went ahead to get a handcart from the Novitiate, but he soon found one beside an empty house and wheeled it back. The priests lifted Father LaSalle into the cart and pushed him over the bumpy road the rest of the way. The rector of the Novitiate, who had been a doctor before he entered the religious order, cleaned the wounds of the two priests and put them to bed between clean sheets, and they thanked God for the care they had received.

THOUSANDS of people had nobody to help them. Miss Sasaki was one of them. Abandoned and helpless, under the crude lean-to in the courtyard of the tin factory, beside the woman who had lost a breast and the man whose burned face was scarcely a face any more, she suffered awfully that night from the pain in her broken leg. She did not sleep at all; neither did she converse with her sleepless companions.

IN THE PARK, Mrs. Murata kept Father Kleinsorge awake all night by talking to him. None of the Nakamura family were able to sleep, either; the children, in spite of being very sick, were interested in everything that happened. They were delighted when one of the city's gas-storage tanks went up in a tremendous burst of flame. Toshio, the boy, shouted to the others to look at the reflection in the river. Mr. Tanimoto, after his long run and his many hours of rescue work, dozed uneasily. When he awoke, in the first light of dawn, he looked across the river and saw that he had not carried the festered, limp bodies high enough on the sandspit the night before. The tide had risen above where he had put them;

they had not had the strength to move; they must have drowned. He saw a number of bodies floating in the river.

EARLY THAT day, August 7th, the Japanese radio broadcast for the first time a succinct announcement that very few, if any, of the people most concerned with its content, the survivors in Hiroshima, happened to hear: "Hiroshima suffered considerable damage as the result of an attack by a few B-29s. It is believed that a new type of bomb was used. The details are being investigated." Nor is it probable that any of the survivors happened to be tuned in on a short-wave rebroadcast of an extraordinary announcement by the President of the United States, which identified the new bomb as atomic: "That bomb had more power than twenty thousand tons of TNT. It had more than two thousand times the blast power of the British Grand Slam, which is the largest bomb ever yet used in the history of warfare." Those victims who were able to worry at all about what had happened thought of it and discussed it in more primitive, childish terms— gasoline sprinkled from an airplane, maybe, or some combustible gas, or a big cluster of incendiaries, or the work of parachutists; but, even if they had known the truth, most of them were too busy or too weary or too badly hurt to care that they were the objects of the first great experiment in the use of atomic power, which (as the voices on the short wave shouted) no country except the United States, with its industrial know-how, its willingness to throw two billion gold dollars into an important wartime gamble, could possibly have developed.

MR. TANIMOTO was still angry at doctors. He decided that he would personally bring one to Asano Park—by the scruff of the neck, if necessary. He crossed the river, went past the Shinto shrine where he had met his wife for a brief moment the day before, and walked to the East Parade Ground. Since this had long before been designated as an evacuation area, he thought he would find an aid station there. He did find one, operated by an Army medical unit, but he also saw that its doctors were hopelessly overburdened, with thousands of patients sprawled among corpses across the field in front of it. Nevertheless, he went up to one of the Army doctors and said, as reproachfully as he could, "Why have you not come to Asano Park? You are badly needed there."

Without even looking up from his work, the doctor said in a tired voice, "This is my station."

"But there are many dying on the riverbank over there."

"The first duty," the doctor said, "is to take care of the slightly wounded."

"Why—when there are many who are heavily wounded on the riverbank?"

The doctor moved to another patient. "In an emergency like this," he said, as if he were reciting from a manual, "the first task is to help as many as possible—to save as many lives as possible. There is no hope for the heavily wounded. They will die. We can't bother with them."

"That may be right from a medical standpoint—" Mr. Tanimoto began, but then he looked out across the field, where the many dead lay close and intimate with those who were still living, and he turned away without finishing his sentence, angry now with himself. He didn't know what to do; he had promised some of the dying people in the park that he would bring them medical aid. They might die feeling cheated. He saw a ration stand at one side of the field, and he went to it and begged some rice cakes and biscuits, and he took them back, in lieu of doctors, to the people in the park.

THE MORNING, again, was hot. Father Kleinsorge went to fetch water for the wounded in a bottle and a teapot he had borrowed. He had heard that it was possible to get fresh tap water outside Asano Park. Going through the rock gardens, he had to climb over and crawl under the trunks of fallen pine trees; he found he was weak. There were many dead in the gardens. At a beautiful moon bridge, he passed a naked, living woman who seemed to have been burned from head to toe and was red all over. Near the entrance to the park, an Army doctor was working, but the only medicine he had was iodine, which he painted over cuts, bruises, slimy burns, everything—and by now everything that he painted had pus on it. Outside the gate of the park, Father Kleinsorge found a faucet that still worked—part of the plumbing of a vanished house—and he filled his vessels and returned. When he had given the wounded the water, he made a second trip. This time, the woman by the bridge was dead. On his way back with the water, he got lost on a detour around a fallen tree, and as he looked for his way through the woods, he heard a voice ask from the underbrush, "Have you anything to drink?" He saw a uniform. Thinking there was just one soldier, he approached with the water. When he had penetrated the bushes, he saw there were about twenty men, and they were all in exactly the same nightmarish state: their faces were wholly burned, their eyesockets were hollow, the fluid from their melted eyes had run down their cheeks. (They must have had their faces upturned when the bomb went off; perhaps they were anti-aircraft personnel.) Their mouths were mere swollen, pus-covered wounds, which they could not bear to stretch enough to admit the spout of the teapot. So Father Kleinsorge got a large piece of grass and drew out the stem so as to make a straw, and gave them all water to drink that way. One of them said, "I can't see anything." Father Kleinsorge answered, as cheerfully as he could, "There's a doctor at the entrance to the park. He's busy now, but he'll come soon and fix your eyes, I hope."

Since that day, Father Kleinsorge has thought back to how queasy he had once been at the sight of pain, how someone else's cut finger used to make him turn faint. Yet there in the park he was so benumbed that immediately after leaving this horrible sight he stopped on a path by one of the pools and discussed with a lightly wounded man whether it would be safe to eat the fat, two-foot carp that floated dead on the surface of the water. They decided, after some consideration, that it would be unwise.

Father Kleinsorge filled the containers a third time and went back to the riverbank. There, amid the dead and dying, he saw a young woman with a needle and thread mending her kimono, which had been slightly torn.

Father Kleinsorge joshed her. "My, but you're a dandy!" he said. She laughed.

He felt tired and lay down. He began to talk with two engaging children whose acquaintance he had made the afternoon before. He learned that their name was Kataoka; the girl was thirteen, the boy five. The girl had been just about to set out for a barbershop when the bomb fell. As the family started for Asano Park, their mother decided to turn back for some food and extra clothing; they became separated from her in the crowd of fleeing people, and they had not seen her since. Occasionally they stopped suddenly in their perfectly cheerful playing and began to cry for their mother.

It was difficult for all the children in the park to sustain the sense of tragedy. Toshio Nakamura got quite excited when he saw his friend Seichi Sato riding up the river in a boat with his family, and he ran to the bank and waved and shouted, "Sato! Sato!"

The boy turned his head and shouted, "Who's that?"

"Nakamura."

"Hello, Toshio!"

"Are you all safe?"

"Yes. What about you?"

"Yes, we're all right. My sisters are vomiting, but I'm fine."

Father Kleinsorge began to be thirsty in the dreadful heat, and he did not feel strong enough to go for water again. A little before noon, he saw a Japanese woman handing something out. Soon she came to him and said in a kindly voice, "These are tea leaves. Chew them, young man, and you won't feel thirsty." The woman's gentleness made Father Kleinsorge suddenly want to cry. For weeks, he had been feeling oppressed by the hatred of foreigners that the Japanese seemed increasingly to show, and he had been uneasy even with his Japanese friends. This stranger's gesture made him a little hysterical.

Around noon, the priests arrived from the Novitiate with the handcart. They had been to the site of the mission house in the city and had retrieved some suitcases that had been stored in the air-raid shelter and had also picked up the remains of melted holy vessels in the ashes of the chapel. They now packed Father Kleinsorge's papier-mâché suitcase and the things belonging to Mrs. Murata and the Nakamuras into the cart, put the two Nakamura girls aboard, and prepared to start out. Then one of the Jesuits who had a practical turn of mind remembered that they had been notified some time before that if they suffered property damage at the hands of the enemy, they could enter a claim for compensation with the prefectural police. The holy men discussed this matter there in the park, with the wounded as silent as the dead around them, and decided that Father Kleinsorge, as a former resident of the destroyed mission, was the one to enter the claim. So, as the others went off with the handcart, Father Kleinsorge said goodbye to the Kataoka children and trudged to a police station. Fresh, clean-uniformed policemen from another town were in charge, and a crowd of dirty and disarrayed citizens crowded around them, mostly asking after lost relatives. Father Kleinsorge filled out a claim form and started walking through the center of the town on his way to Nagatsuka. It was then that he first realized the extent of the damage; he passed block after block of ruins, and even after all he had seen in the park, his breath was taken away. By the time he reached the Novitiate, he was sick with exhaustion. The last thing he did as he fell into bed was request that someone go back for the motherless Kataoka children.

ALTOGETHER, Miss Sasaki was left two days and two nights under the piece of propped-up roofing with her crushed leg and her two unpleasant comrades. Her only diversion was when men came to the factory air-raid shelters, which she could see from under one corner of her shelter, and hauled corpses up out of them with ropes. Her leg became discolored, swollen, and putrid. All that time, she went without food and water. On the third day, August 8th, some friends who supposed she was dead came to look for her body and found her. They told her that her mother, father, and baby brother, who at the time of the explosion were in the Tamura Pediatric Hospital, where the baby was a patient, had all been given up as certainly dead, since the hospital was totally destroyed. Her friends then left her to think that piece of news over. Later, some men picked her up by the arms and legs and carried her quite a distance to a truck. For about an hour, the truck moved over a bumpy road, and Miss Sasaki, who had become convinced that she was dulled to pain, discovered that she was not. The men lifted her out at a relief station in the section of Inokuchi, where two Army doctors looked at her. The moment one of them touched her wound, she fainted. She came to in time to hear them discuss whether or not to cut off her leg; one said there was gas gangrene in the lips of the wound and predicted she would die unless they amputated, and the other said that was too bad, because they had no equipment with which to do the job. She fainted again. When she recovered consciousness, she was being carried somewhere on a stretcher. She was put aboard a launch, which went to the nearby island of Ninoshima, and she was taken to a military hospital there. Another doctor examined her and said that she did not have gas gangrene, though she did have a fairly ugly compound fracture. He said quite coldly that he was sorry, but this was a hospital for operative surgical cases only, and because she had no gangrene, she would have to return to Hiroshima that night. But then the doctor took her temperature, and what he saw on the thermometer made him decide to let her stay.

THAT DAY, August 8th, Father Cieslik went into the city to look for Mr. Fukai, the Japanese secretary of the diocese, who had ridden unwillingly out of the flaming city on Father Kleinsorge's back and then had run back crazily into it. Father Cieslik started hunting in the neighborhood of Sakai Bridge, where the Jesuits had last seen Mr. Fukai; he went to the East Parade Ground, the evacuation area to which the secretary might have gone, and looked for him among the wounded and dead there; he went to the prefectural police and made inquiries. He could not find any trace of the man. Back at the Novitiate that evening, the theological student, who had been rooming with Mr. Fukai at the mission house, told the priests that the secretary had remarked to him, during an air-raid alarm one day not long before the bombing, "Japan is dying. If there is a real air raid here in Hiroshima, I want to die with our country." The priests concluded that Mr. Fukai had run back to immolate himself in the flames. They never saw him again.

AT THE Red Cross Hospital, Dr. Sasaki worked for three straight days with only one hour's sleep. On the second day, he began to sew up the worst cuts, and right through the following night and all the next day he stitched. Many of the wounds were festered. Fortunately, someone had found intact a supply of *narucopon*, a Japanese sedative, and he gave it to many who were in pain. Word went around among the staff that there must have been something peculiar about the great bomb, because on the second day the vice-chief of the hospital went down in the basement to the vault where the X-ray plates were stored and found the whole stock exposed as they lay. That day, a fresh doctor and ten nurses came in from the city of Yamaguchi with extra bandages and antiseptics, and the third day another physician and a dozen more nurses arrived from Matsue—yet there were still only eight doctors for ten thousand patients. In the afternoon of the third day, exhausted from his foul tailoring, Dr. Sasaki became obsessed with the idea that his mother thought he was dead. He got permission to go to Mukaihara. He walked out to the first suburbs, beyond which the electric train service was still functioning, and reached home late in the evening. His mother said she had known he was all right all along; a wounded nurse had stopped by to tell her. He went to bed and slept for seventeen hours.

BEFORE DAWN on August 8th, someone entered the room at the Novitiate where Father Kleinsorge was in bed, reached up to the hanging light bulb, and switched it on. The sudden flood of light, pouring in on Father Kleinsorge's half sleep, brought him leaping out of bed, braced for a new concussion. When he realized what had happened, he laughed confusedly and went back to bed. He stayed there all day.

On August 9th, Father Kleinsorge was still tired. The rector looked at his cuts and said they were not even worth dressing, and if Father Kleinsorge kept them clean, they would heal in three or four days. Father Kleinsorge felt uneasy; he could not yet comprehend what he had been through; as if he were guilty of something awful, he felt he had to go back to the scene of the violence he had experienced. He got up out of bed and walked into the city. He scratched for a while in the ruins of the mission house, but he found nothing. He went to the sites of a couple of schools and asked after people he knew. He looked for some of the city's Japanese Catholics, but he found only fallen houses. He walked back to the Novitiate, stupefied and without any new understanding.

AT TWO minutes after eleven o'clock on the morning of August 9th, the second atomic bomb was dropped, on Nagasaki. It was several days before the survivors of Hiroshima knew they had company, because the Japanese radio and newspapers were being extremely cautious on the subject of the strange weapon.

ON AUGUST 9TH, Mr. Tanimoto was still working in the park. He went to the suburb of Ushida, where his wife was staying with friends, and got a tent which he had stored there before the bombing. He now took it to the park and set it up as a shelter for some of the wounded who could not move or be moved. Whatever he did in the park, he felt he was being watched by the twenty-year-old girl, Mrs. Kamai, his former neighbor, whom he had seen on the day the bomb exploded, with her dead baby daughter in her arms. She kept the small corpse in her arms for four days, even though it began smelling bad on the second day. Once, Mr. Tanimoto sat with her for a while, and she told him that the bomb had buried her under their house with the baby strapped to her back, and that when she had dug herself free, she had discovered that the baby was choking, its mouth full of dirt. With her little finger, she had carefully cleaned out the infant's mouth, and for a time the child had breathed normally and seemed all right; then suddenly it had died. Mrs. Kamai also talked about what a fine man her husband was, and again urged Mr. Tanimoto to search for him.

Since Mr. Tanimoto had been all through the city the first day and had seen terribly burned soldiers from Kamai's post, the Chugoku Regional Army Headquarters, everywhere, he knew it would be impossible to find Kamai, even if he were living, but of course he didn't tell her that. Every time she saw Mr. Tanimoto, she asked whether he had found her husband. Once, he tried to suggest that perhaps it was time to cremate the baby, but Mrs. Kamai only held it tighter. He began to keep away from her, but whenever he looked at her, she was staring at him and her eyes asked the same question. He tried to escape her glance by keeping his back turned to her as much as possible.

THE JESUITS took about fifty refugees into the exquisite chapel of the Novitiate. The rector gave them what medical care he could—mostly just the cleaning away of pus. Each of the Nakamuras was provided with a blanket and a mosquito net. Mrs. Nakamura and her younger daughter had no appetite and ate nothing; her son and other daughter ate, and lost, each meal they were offered. On August 10th, a friend, Mrs. Osaki, came to see them and told them that her son Hideo had been burned alive in the factory where he worked. This Hideo had been a kind of hero to Toshio, who had often gone to the plant to watch him run his machine. That night, Toshio woke up screaming. He had dreamed that he had seen Mrs. Osaki coming out of an opening in the ground with her family, and then he saw Hideo at his machine, a big one with a revolving belt, and he himself was standing beside Hideo, and for some reason this was terrifying.

ON AUGUST 10TH, Father Kleinsorge, having heard from someone that Dr. Fujii had been injured and that he had eventually gone to the summer house of a friend of his named Okuma, in the village of Fukawa, asked Father Cieslik if he would go and see how Dr. Fujii was. Father Cieslik went to Misasa station, outside Hiroshima, rode for twenty minutes on an electric train, and then walked for an hour and a half in a terribly hot sun to Mr. Okuma's house, which was beside the Ota River at the foot of a mountain. He found Dr. Fujii sitting in a chair in a kimono, applying compresses to his broken collarbone. The Doctor told Father Cieslik about having lost his glasses and said that his eyes bothered him. He showed the priest huge blue and green stripes where beams had bruised him. He offered the Jesuit first a cigarette and then whiskey, though it was only eleven in the morning. Father Cieslik thought it would please Dr. Fujii if he took a little, so he said yes. A servant brought some Suntory whiskey, and the Jesuit, the Doctor, and the host had a very pleasant chat. Mr. Okuma had lived in Hawaii, and he told some things about Americans. Dr. Fujii talked a bit about the disaster. He said that Mr. Okuma and a nurse had gone into the ruins of his hospital and brought back a small safe which he had moved into his air-raid shelter. This contained some surgical instruments, and Dr. Fujii gave Father Cieslik a few pairs of scissors and tweezers for the rector at the Novitiate. Father Cieslik was bursting with some inside dope he had, but he waited until the conversation turned naturally to the mystery of the bomb. Then he said he knew what kind of bomb it was; he had the secret on the best authority—that of a Japanese newspaperman who had dropped in at the Novitiate. The bomb was not a bomb at all; it was a kind of fine magnesium powder sprayed over the whole city by a single plane, and it exploded when it came into contact with the live wires of the city power system. "That means," said Dr. Fujii, perfectly satisfied, since after all the information came from a newspaperman, "that it can only be dropped on big cities and only in the daytime, when the tram lines and so forth are in operation."

AFTER FIVE days of ministering to the wounded in the park, Mr. Tanimoto returned, on August 11th, to his parsonage and dug around in the ruins. He retrieved some diaries and church records that had been kept in books and were only charred around the edges, as well as some cooking utensils and pottery. While he was at work, a Miss Tanaka came and said that her father had been asking for him. Mr. Tanimoto had reason to hate her father, the retired shipping-company official who, though he made a great show of his charity, was notoriously selfish and cruel, and who, just a few days before the bombing, had said openly to several people that Mr. Tanimoto was a spy for the Americans. Several times he had derided Christianity and called it un-Japanese. At the moment of the bombing, Mr. Tanaka had been walking in the street in front of the city's radio station. He received serious flash burns, but he was able to walk home. He took refuge in his Neighborhood Association shelter and from there tried hard to get medical aid. He expected all the doctors of Hiroshima to come to him, because he was so rich and so famous for giving his money away. When none of them came, he angrily set out to look for them; leaning on his daughter's arm, he walked from private hospital to private hospital, but all were in ruins, and he went back and lay down in the shelter again. Now he was very weak and knew he was going to die. He was willing to be comforted by any religion.

Mr. Tanimoto went to help him. He descended into the tomblike shelter and, when his eyes were adjusted to the darkness, saw Mr. Tanaka, his face and arms puffed up and covered with pus and blood, and his eyes swollen shut. The old man smelled very bad, and he moaned constantly. He seemed to recognize Mr. Tanimoto's voice. Standing at the shelter stairway to get light, Mr. Tanimoto read loudly from a Japanese-language pocket Bible: "For a thousand years in Thy sight are but as yesterday when it is past, and as a watch in the night. Thou carriest the children of men away as with a flood; they are as a sleep; in the morning they are like grass which groweth up. In the morning it flourisheth and groweth up; in the evening it is cut down, and withereth. For we are consumed by Thine anger and by Thy wrath are we troubled. Thou has set our iniquities before Thee, our secret sins in the light of Thy countenance. For all our days are passed away in Thy wrath: we spend our years as a tale that is told. . . ."

Mr. Tanaka died as Mr. Tanimoto read the psalm.

On August 11th, word came to the Ninoshima Military Hospital that a large number of military casualties from the Chugoku Regional Army Headquarters were to arrive on the is-

land that day, and it was deemed necessary to evacuate all civilian patients. Miss Sasaki, still running an alarmingly high fever, was put on a large ship. She lay out on deck, with a pillow under her leg. There were awnings over the deck, but the vessel's course put her in the sunlight. She felt as if she were under a magnifying glass in the sun. Pus oozed out of her wound, and soon the whole pillow was covered with it. She was taken ashore at Hatsukaichi, a town several miles to the southwest of Hiroshima, and put in the Goddess of Mercy Primary School, which had been turned into a hospital. She lay there for several days before a specialist on fractures came from Kobe. By then her leg was red and swollen up to her hip. The doctor decided he could not set the breaks. He made an incision and put in a rubber pipe to drain off the putrescence.

At the Novitiate, the motherless Kataoka children were inconsolable. Father Cieslik worked hard to keep them distracted. He put riddles to them. He asked, "What is the cleverest animal in the world?," and after the thirteen-year-old girl had guessed the ape, the elephant, the horse, he said, "No, it must be the hippopotamus," because in Japanese that animal is *kaba,* the reverse of *baka,* stupid. He told Bible stories, beginning, in the order of things, with the Creation. He showed them a scrapbook of snapshots taken in Europe. Nevertheless, they cried most of the time for their mother.

Several days later, Father Cieslik started hunting for the children's family. First, he learned through the police that an uncle had been to the authorities in Kure, a city not far away, to inquire for the children. After that, he heard that an older brother had been trying to trace them through the post office in Ujina, a suburb of Hiroshima. Still later, he heard that the mother was alive and was on Goto Island, off Nagasaki. And at last, by keeping a check on the Ujina post office, he got in touch with the brother and returned the children to their mother.

About a week after the bomb dropped, a vague, incomprehensible rumor reached Hiroshima—that the city had been destroyed by the energy released when atoms were somehow split in two. The weapon was referred to in this word-of-mouth report as *genshi bakudan* —the root characters of which can be translated as "original child bomb." No one understood the idea or put any more credence in it than in the powdered magnesium and such things. Newspapers were being brought in from other cities, but they were still confining themselves to extremely general statements, such as Domei's assertion on August 12th: "There is nothing to do but admit the tremendous power of this inhuman bomb." Already, Japanese physicists had entered the city with Lauritsen electroscopes and Neher electrometers; they understood the idea all too well.

ON AUGUST 12TH, the Nakamuras, all of them still rather sick, went to the nearby town of Kabe and moved in with Mrs. Nakamura's sister-in-law. The next day, Mrs. Nakamura, although she was too ill to walk much, returned to Hiroshima alone, by electric car to the outskirts, by foot from there. All week, at the Novitiate, she had worried about her mother, brother, and older sister, who had lived in the part of town called Fukuro, and besides, she felt drawn by some fascination, just as Father Kleinsorge had been. She discovered that her family were all dead. She went back to Kabe so amazed and depressed by what she had seen and learned in the city that she could not speak that evening.

A COMPARATIVE orderliness, at least, began to be established at the Red Cross Hospital. Dr. Sasaki, back from his rest, undertook to classify his patients (who were still scattered everywhere, even on the stairways). The staff gradually swept up the debris. Best of all, the nurses and attendants started to remove the corpses. Disposal of the dead, by decent cremation and enshrinement, is a greater moral responsibility to the Japanese than adequate care of the living. Relatives identified most of the first day's dead in and around the hospital. Beginning on the second day, whenever a patient appeared to be moribund, a piece of paper with his name on it was fastened to his clothing. The corpse detail carried the bodies to a clearing outside, placed them on pyres of wood from ruined houses, burned them, put some of the ashes in envelopes intended for exposed X-ray plates, marked the envelopes with the names of the deceased, and piled them, neatly and respectfully, in stacks in the main office. In a few days, the envelopes filled one whole side of the impromptu shrine.

IN Kabe, on the morning of August 15th, ten-year-old Toshio Nakamura heard an airplane overhead. He ran outdoors and identified it with a professional eye as a B-29. "There goes Mr. B!" he shouted.

One of his relatives called out to him, "Haven't you had enough of Mr. B?"

The question had a kind of symbolism. At almost that very moment, the dull, dispirited voice of Hirohito, the Emperor Tenno, was speaking for the first time in history over the radio: "After pondering deeply the general trends of the world and the actual conditions obtaining in Our Empire today, We have decided to effect a settlement of the present situation by resorting to an extraordinary measure. . . ."

Mrs. Nakamura had gone to the city again, to dig up some rice she had buried in her Neighborhood Association air-raid shelter. She got it and started back for Kabe. On the electric car, quite by chance, she ran into her younger sister, who had not been in Hiroshima the day of the bombing. "Have you heard the news?" her sister asked.

"What news?"

"The war is over."

"Don't say such a foolish thing, sister."

"But I heard it over the radio myself." And then, in a whisper, "It was the Emperor's voice."

"Oh," Mrs. Nakamura said (she needed nothing more to make her give up thinking, in spite of the atomic bomb, that Japan still had a chance to win the war), "in that case . . ."

SOME time later, in a letter to an American, Mr. Tanimoto described the events of that morning. "At the time of the Post-War, the marvelous thing in our history happened. Our Emperor broadcasted his own voice through radio directly to us, common people of Japan. Aug. 15th we were told that some news of great importance could be heard & all of us should hear it. So I went to Hiroshima railway station. There set a loud-speaker in the ruins of the station. Many civilians, all of them were in boundage, some being helped by shoulder of their daughters, some sustaining their injured feet by sticks, they listened to the broadcast and when they came to realize the fact that it was the Emperor, they cried with full tears in their eyes, 'What a wonderful blessing it is that Tenno himself call on us and we can hear his own voice in person. We are thoroughly satisfied in such a great sacrifice.' When they came to know the war was ended—that is, Japan was defeated, they, of course, were deeply disappointed, but followed after their Emperor's commandment in calm spirit, making whole-hearted sacrifice for the everlasting peace of the world—and Japan started her new way."

IV

Panic Grass and Feverfew

ON AUGUST 18TH, twelve days after the bomb burst, Father Kleinsorge set out on foot for Hiroshima from the Novitiate with his papier-mâché suitcase in his hand. He had begun to think that this bag, in which he kept his valuables, had a talismanic quality, because of the way he had found it after the explosion, standing handle-side up in the doorway of his room, while the desk under which he had previously hidden it was in splinters all over the floor. Now he was using it to carry the yen belonging to the Society of Jesus to the Hiroshima branch of the Yokohama Specie Bank, already reopened in its half-ruined building. On the whole, he felt quite well that morning. It is true that the minor cuts he had received had not healed in three or four days, as the rector of the Novitiate, who had examined them, had positively promised they would, but Father Kleinsorge had rested well for a week and considered that he was again ready for hard work. By now he was accustomed to the terrible scene through which he walked on his way into the city: the large rice field near the Novitiate, streaked with brown; the houses on the outskirts of the city, standing but decrepit, with broken windows and dishevelled tiles; and then, quite suddenly, the beginning of the four

square miles of reddish-brown scar, where nearly everything had been buffeted down and burned; range on range of collapsed city blocks, with here and there a crude sign erected on a pile of ashes and tiles ("Sister, where are you?" or "All safe and we live at Toyosaka"); naked trees and canted telephone poles; the few standing, gutted buildings only accentuating the horizontality of everything else (the Museum of Science and Industry, with its dome stripped to its steel frame, as if for an autopsy; the modern Chamber of Commerce Building, its tower as cold, rigid, and unassailable after the blow as before; the huge, low-lying, camouflaged city hall; the row of dowdy banks, caricaturing a shaken economic system); and in the streets a macabre traffic—hundreds of crumpled bicycles, shells of streetcars and automobiles, all halted in mid-motion. The whole way, Father Kleinsorge was oppressed by the thought that all the damage he saw had been done in one instant by one bomb. By the time he reached the center of town, the day had become very hot. He walked to the Yokohama Bank, which was doing business in a temporary wooden stall on the ground floor of its building, deposited the money, went by the mission compound just to have another look at the wreckage, and then started back to the Novitiate. About halfway there, he began to have peculiar sensations. The more or less magical suitcase, now empty, suddenly seemed terribly heavy. His knees grew weak. He felt excruciatingly tired. With a considerable expenditure of spirit, he managed to reach the Novitiate. He did not think his weakness was worth mentioning to the other Jesuits. But a couple of days later, while attempting to say Mass, he had an onset of faintness and even after three attempts was unable to go through with the service, and the next morning the rector, who had examined Father Kleinsorge's apparently negligible but unhealed cuts daily, asked in surprise, "What have you done to your wounds?" They had suddenly opened wider and were swollen and inflamed.

As she dressed on the morning of August 20th, in the home of her sister-in-law in Kabe, not far from Nagatsuka, Mrs. Nakamura, who had suffered no cuts or burns at all, though she had been rather nauseated all through the week she and her children had spent as guests of Father Kleinsorge and the other Catholics at the Novitiate, began fixing her hair and noticed, after one stroke, that her comb carried with it a whole handful of hair; the second time, the same thing happened, so she stopped combing at once. But in the next three or four days, her hair kept falling out of its own accord, until she was quite bald. She began living indoors, practically in hiding. On August 26th, both she and her younger daughter, Myeko, woke up feeling extremely weak and tired, and they stayed on their bedrolls. Her son and other daughter, who had shared every experience with her during and after the bombing, felt fine.

At about the same time—he lost track of the days, so hard was he working to set up a temporary place of worship in a private house he had rented in the outskirts—Mr. Tanimoto fell suddenly ill with a general malaise, weariness, and feverishness, and he, too, took to his bedroll on the floor of the half-wrecked house of a friend in the suburb of Ushida.

These four did not realize it, but they were coming down with the strange capricious disease which came later to be known as radiation sickness.

Miss Sasaki lay in steady pain in the Goddess of Mercy Primary School, at Hatsukaichi, the fourth station to the southwest of Hiroshima on the electric train. An internal infection still prevented the proper setting of the compound fracture of her lower left leg. A young man who was in the same hospital and who seemed to have grown fond of her in spite of her unremitting preoccupation with her suffering, or else just pitied her because of it, lent her a Japanese translation of de Maupassant, and she tried to read the stories, but she could concentrate for only four or five minutes at a time.

The hospitals and aid stations around Hiroshima were so crowded in the first weeks after the bombing, and their staffs were so variable, depending on their health and on the unpredictable arrival of outside help, that patients had to be constantly shifted from place to place. Miss Sasaki, who had already been moved three times, twice by ship, was taken at the end of August to an engineering school, also at Hatsukaichi. Because her leg did not improve but swelled more and more, the doctors at the school bound it with crude splints and took her by car, on September 9th, to the Red Cross Hospital in Hiroshima. This was the first chance she had had to look at the ruins of Hiroshima; the last time she had been carried through the city's streets, she had been hovering on the edge of unconsciousness. Even though the wreckage had been described to her, and though she was still in pain, the sight horrified and amazed her, and there was something she noticed about it that particularly gave her the creeps. Over everything—up through the wreckage of the city, in gutters, along the riverbanks, tangled among tiles and tin roofing, climbing on charred tree trunks—was a blanket of fresh, vivid, lush, optimistic green; the verdancy rose even from the foundations of ruined houses. Weeds already hid the ashes, and wild flowers were in bloom among the city's bones. The bomb had not only left the underground organs of plants intact; it had stimulated them. Everywhere were bluets and Spanish bayonets, goosefoot, morning glories and day lilies, the hairy-fruited bean, purslane and clotbur and sesame and panic grass and feverfew. Especially in a circle at the center, sickle senna grew in extraordinary regeneration, not only standing among the charred remnants of the same plant but pushing up in new places, among bricks and through cracks in the asphalt. It actually seemed as if a load of sickle-senna seed had been dropped along with the bomb.

At the Red Cross Hospital, Miss Sasaki was put under the care of Dr. Sasaki. Now, a month after the explosion, something like order had been reëstablished in the hospital; which is to say that the patients who still lay in the corridors at least had mats to sleep on and that the supply of medicines, which had given out in the first few days, had been replaced, though inadequately, by contributions from other cities. Dr. Sasaki, who had had one seventeen-hour sleep at his home on the third night, had ever since then rested only about six hours a night, on a mat at the hospital; he had lost twenty pounds from his very small body; he still wore the borrowed glasses.

Since Miss Sasaki was a woman and was so sick (and perhaps, he afterward admitted, just a little bit because she was named Sasaki), Dr. Sasaki put her on a mat in a semi-private room, which at that time had only eight people in it. He questioned her and put down on her record card, in the correct, scrunched-up German in which he wrote all his records: "*Mittel-grosse Patientin in gutem Ernährungszustand.* 10 *Fraktur am linken Unterschenkelknochen mit Wunde; Anschwellung in der linken Unterschenkelgegend. Haut und sichtbare Schleimhäute mässig durchblutet und kein Oedema,*" noting that she was a medium-sized female patient in good general health; that she had a compound fracture of the left tibia, with swelling of the left lower leg; that her skin and visible mucous membranes were heavily spotted with *petechiae,* which are hemorrhages about 20 the size of grains of rice, or even as big as soybeans; and, in addition, that her head, eyes, throat, lungs, and heart were apparently normal; and that she had a fever. He wanted to set her fracture and put her leg in a cast, but he had run out of plaster of Paris long since, so he just stretched her out on a mat and prescribed aspirin for her fever, and glucose intravenously and diastase orally for her undernourishment (which he had not entered on her 30 record because everyone suffered from it). She exhibited only one of the queer symptoms so many of his patients were just then beginning to show—the spot hemorrhages.

Dr. Fujii was still pursued by bad luck, which still was connected with rivers. Now he was living in the summer house of Mr. Okuma, in Fukawa. This house clung to the steep banks of the Ota River. Here his injuries seemed to make good progress, and he even began to 40 treat refugees who came to him from the neighborhood, using medical supplies he had retrieved from a cache in the suburbs. He noticed in some of his patients a curious syndrome of symptoms that cropped out in the third and fourth weeks, but he was not able to do much more than swathe cuts and burns. Early in September, it began to rain, steadily and heavily. The river rose. On September 17th, there came a cloudburst and then a typhoon, and 50 the water crept higher and higher up the bank.

Mr. Okuma and Dr. Fujii became alarmed and scrambled up the mountain to a peasant's house. (Down in Hiroshima, the flood took up where the bomb had left off—swept away bridges that had survived the blast, washed out streets, undermined foundations of buildings that still stood—and ten miles to the west, the Ono Army Hospital, where a team of experts from Kyoto Imperial University was studying the delayed affliction of the patients, suddenly 60 slid down a beautiful pine-dark mountainside into the Inland Sea and drowned most of the investigators and their mysteriously diseased patients alike.) After the storm, Dr. Fujii and Mr. Okuma went down to the river and found that the Okuma house had been washed altogether away.

BECAUSE so many people were suddenly feeling sick nearly a month after the atomic bomb was dropped, an unpleasant rumor began to 70 move around, and eventually it made its way to the house in Kabe where Mrs. Nakamura lay bald and ill. It was that the atomic bomb had deposited some sort of poison on Hiroshima which would give off deadly emanations for seven years; nobody could go there all that time. This especially upset Mrs. Nakamura, who remembered that in a moment of confusion on the morning of the explosion she had literally sunk her entire means of livelihood, 80 her Sankoku sewing machine, in the small cement water tank in front of what was left of her house; now no one would be able to go and fish it out. Up to this time, Mrs. Nakamura and her relatives had been quite resigned and passive about the moral issue of the atomic bomb, but this rumor suddenly aroused them to more hatred and resentment of America than they had felt all through the war.

Japanese physicists, who knew a great deal 90 about atomic fission (one of them owned a cyclotron), worried about lingering radiation at Hiroshima, and in mid-August, not many days after President Truman's disclosure of the type of bomb that had been dropped, they entered the city to make investigations. The first thing they did was roughly to determine a center by observing the side on which telephone poles all around the heart of the town were scorched; they settled on the torii gateway of 100 the Gokoku Shrine, right next to the parade ground of the Chugoku Regional Army Headquarters. From there, they worked north and south with Lauritsen electroscopes, which are sensitive to both beta particles and gamma rays. These indicated that the highest intensity of radioactivity, near the torii, was 4.2 times the average natural "leak" of ultra-short waves for the earth of that area. The scientists noticed that the flash of the bomb had discolored concrete to a light reddish tint, had scaled off the surface of granite, and had scorched certain other types of building material, and that consequently the bomb had, in some places, left prints of the shadows that had been cast by its light. The experts found, for instance, a permanent shadow thrown on the roof of the Chamber of Commerce Building (220 yards from the rough center) by the structure's rectangular tower; several others in the lookout post on top of the Hypothec Bank (2,050 yards); another in the tower of the Chugoku Electric Supply Building (800 yards); another projected by the handle of a gas pump (2,630 yards); and several on granite tombstones in the Gokoku Shrine (385 yards). By triangulating these and other such shadows with the objects that formed them, the scientists determined that the exact center was a spot a hundred and fifty yards south of the torii and a few yards southeast of the pile of ruins that had once been the Shima Hospital. (A few vague human silhouettes were found, and these gave rise to stories that eventually included fancy and precise details. One story told how a painter on a ladder was monumentalized in a kind of bas-relief on the stone façade of a bank building on which he was at work, in the act of dipping his brush into his paint can; another, how a man and his cart on the bridge near the Museum of Science and Industry, almost under the center of the explosion, were cast down in an embossed shadow which made it clear that the man was about to whip his horse.) Starting east and west from the actual center, the scientists, in early September, made new measurements, and the highest radiation they found this time was 3.9 times the natural "leak." Since radiation of at least a thousand times the natural "leak" would be required to cause serious effects on the human body, the

scientists announced that people could enter Hiroshima without any peril at all.

As soon as this reassurance reached the household in which Mrs. Nakamura was concealing herself—or, at any rate, within a short time, after her hair had started growing back again—her whole family relaxed their extreme hatred of America, and Mrs. Nakamura sent her brother-in-law to look for the sewing machine. It was still submerged in the water tank, and when he brought it home, she saw, to her dismay, that it was all rusted and useless.

By THE END of the first week in September, Father Kleinsorge was in bed at the Novitiate with a fever of 102.2, and since he seemed to be getting worse, his colleagues decided to send him to the Catholic International Hospital in Tokyo. Father Cieslik and the rector took him as far as Kobe and a Jesuit from that city took him the rest of the way, with a message from a Kobe doctor to the Mother Superior of the International Hospital: "Think twice before you give this man blood transfusions, because with atomic-bomb patients we aren't at all sure that if you stick needles in them, they'll stop bleeding."

When Father Kleinsorge arrived at the hospital, he was terribly pale and very shaky. He complained that the bomb had upset his digestion and given him abdominal pains. His white blood count was three thousand (five to seven thousand is normal), he was seriously anemic, and his temperature was 104. A doctor who did not know much about these strange manifestations—Father Kleinsorge was one of a handful of atomic patients who had reached Tokyo—came to see him, and to the patient's face he was most encouraging. "You'll be out of here in two weeks," he said. But when the doctor got out in the corridor, he said to the Mother Superior. "He'll die. All these bomb people die—you'll see. They go along for a couple of weeks and then they die."

The doctor prescribed suralimentation for Father Kleinsorge. Every three hours, they forced some eggs or beef juice into him, and they fed him all the sugar he could stand. They gave him vitamins, and iron pills and arsenic (in Fowler's solution) for his anemia. He confounded both the doctor's predictions; he neither died nor got up in a fortnight. Despite the fact that the message from the Kobe doctor deprived him of transfusions, which would have been the most useful therapy of all, his fever and his digestive troubles cleared up fairly quickly. His white count went up for a while, but early in October it dropped again, to 3,600; then, in ten days, it suddenly climbed above normal, to 8,800; and it finally settled at 5,800. His ridiculous scratches puzzled everyone. For a few days, they would mend, and then, when he moved around, they would open up again. As soon as he began to feel well, he enjoyed himself tremendously. In Hiroshima he had been one of thousands of sufferers; in Tokyo he was a curiosity. American Army doctors came by the dozen to observe him. Japanese experts questioned him. A newspaper interviewed him. And once, the confused doctor came and shook his head and said, "Baffling cases, these atomic-bomb people."

Mrs. Nakamura lay indoors with Myeko. They both continued sick, and though Mrs. Nakamura vaguely sensed that their trouble was caused by the bomb, she was too poor to see a doctor and so never knew exactly what the matter was. Without any treatment at all, but merely resting, they began gradually to feel better. Some of Myeko's hair fell out, and she had a tiny burn on her arm which took months to heal. The boy, Toshio, and the older girl, Yaeko, seemed well enough, though they, too, lost some hair and occasionally had bad headaches. Toshio was still having nightmares, always about the nineteen-year-old mechanic, Hideo Osaki, his hero, who had been killed by the bomb.

On his back with a fever of 104, Mr. Tanimoto worried about all the funerals he ought to be conducting for the deceased of his church. He thought he was just overtired from the hard work he had done since the bombing, but after the fever had persisted for a few days, he sent for a doctor. The doctor was too busy to visit him in Ushida, but he dispatched a nurse, who recognized his symptoms as those of mild radiation disease and came back from time to time to give him injections of Vitamin B_1. A Buddhist priest with whom Mr. Tanimoto was acquainted called on him and suggested that moxibustion might give him relief; the priest showed the pastor how to give himself the ancient Japanese treatment, by setting fire to a twist of the stimulant herb moxa placed on the wrist pulse. Mr. Tanimoto found that each moxa treatment temporarily reduced his fever one degree. The nurse had told him to eat as much as possible, and every few days his mother-in-law brought him vegetables and fish from Tsuzu, twenty miles away, where she lived. He spent a month in bed, and then went ten hours by train to his father's home in Shikoku. There he rested another month.

Dr. Sasaki and his colleagues at the Red Cross Hospital watched the unprecedented disease unfold and at last evolved a theory about its nature. It had, they decided, three stages. The first stage had been all over before the doctors even knew they were dealing with a new sickness: it was the direct reaction to the bombardment of the body, at the moment when the bomb went off, by neutrons, beta particles, and gamma rays. The apparently uninjured people who had died so mysteriously in the first few hours or days had succumbed in this first stage. It killed ninety-five per cent of the people within a half mile of the center, and many thousands who were farther away. The doctors realized in retrospect that even though most of these dead had also suffered from burns and blast effects, they had absorbed enough radiation to kill them. The rays simply destroyed body cells—caused their nuclei to degenerate and broke their walls. Many people who did not die right away came down with nausea, headache, diarrhea, malaise, and fever, which lasted several days. Doctors could not be certain whether some of these symptoms were the result of radiation or nervous shock. The second stage set in ten or fifteen days after the bombing. Its first symptom was falling hair. Diarrhea and fever, which in some cases went as high as 106, came next. Twenty-five to thirty days after the explosion, blood disorders appeared: gums bled, the white-blood-cell count dropped sharply, and *petechiae* appeared on the skin and mucous membranes. The drop in the number of white blood corpuscles reduced the patient's capacity to resist infection, so open wounds were unusually slow in healing and many of the sick developed sore throats and mouths. The two key symptoms, on which the doctors came to base their prognosis, were fever and the lowered white-corpuscle count. If fever remained steady and high, the patient's chances for survival were poor. The white count almost always dropped below four thousand; a patient whose count fell below one thousand had little hope of living. Toward the end of the second stage, if the patient survived, anemia, or a drop in the red blood count, also set in. The third stage was the reaction that came when the body struggled to compensate for its ills—when, for instance, the white count not only returned to normal but increased to much higher than normal levels. In this stage, many patients died of complications, such as infections in the chest cavity. Most burns healed with deep layers of pink, rubbery scar tissue, known as keloid tumors. The duration of the disease varied, depending on the patient's constitution and the amount of radiation he had received. Some victims recovered in a week; with others the disease dragged on for months.

As the symptoms revealed themselves, it became clear that many of them resembled the effects of overdoses of X-ray, and the doctors based their therapy on that likeness. They gave victims liver extract, blood transfusions, and vitamins, especially B_1. The shortage of supplies and instruments hampered them. Allied doctors who came in after the surrender found plasma and penicillin very effective. Since the blood disorders were, in the long run, the predominant factor in the disease, some of the Japanese doctors evolved a theory as to the seat of the delayed sickness. They thought that perhaps gamma rays, entering the body at the time of the explosion, made the phosphorus in the victims' bones radioactive, and that they in turn emitted beta particles, which, though they could not penetrate far through flesh, could enter the bone marrow, where blood is manufactured, and gradually tear it down. Whatever its source, the disease had some baffling quirks. Not all the patients exhibited all the main symptoms. People who suffered flash burns were protected, to a considerable extent, from radiation sickness. Those who had lain quietly for days or even hours after the bombing were much less liable to get sick than those who had been active. Gray hair seldom fell out. And,

as if nature were protecting man against his own ingenuity, the reproductive processes were affected for a time; men became sterile, women had miscarriages, menstruation stopped.

FOR TEN DAYS after the flood, Dr. Fujii lived in the peasant's house on the mountain above the Ota. Then he heard about a vacant private clinic in Kaitaichi, a suburb to the east of Hiroshima. He bought it at once, moved there, and hung out a sign inscribed in English, in honor of the conquerors:

M. FUJII, M.D.

MEDICAL & VENEREAL

Quite recovered from his wounds, he soon built up a strong practice, and he was delighted, in the evenings, to receive members of the occupying forces, on whom he lavished whiskey and practiced English.

GIVING Miss Sasaki a local anaesthetic of procaine, Dr. Sasaki made an incision in her leg on October 23rd, to drain the infection, which still lingered on eleven weeks after the injury. In the following days, so much pus formed that he had to dress the opening each morning and evening. A week later, she complained of great pain, so he made another incision; he cut still a third, on November 9th, and enlarged it on the twenty-sixth. All this time, Miss Sasaki grew weaker and weaker, and her spirits fell low. One day, the young man who had lent her his translation of de Maupassant at Hatsukaichi came to visit her; he told her that he was going back to Kyushu but that when he came back, he would like to see her again. She didn't care. Her leg had been so swollen and painful all along that the doctor had not even tried to set the fractures, and though an X-ray taken in November showed that the bones were mending, she could see under the sheet that her left leg was nearly three inches shorter than her right and that her left foot was turning inward. She thought often of the man to whom she had been engaged. Someone told her he was back from overseas. She wondered what he had heard about her injuries that made him stay away.

FATHER KLEINSORGE was discharged from the hospital in Tokyo on December 19th and took a train home. On the way, two days later, at Yokogawa, a stop just before Hiroshima, Dr. Fujii boarded the train. It was the first time the two men had met since before the bombing. They sat together. Dr. Fujii said he was going to the annual gathering of his family, on the anniversary of his father's death. When they started talking about their experiences, the Doctor was quite entertaining as he told how his places of residence kept falling into rivers. Then he asked Father Kleinsorge how he was, and the Jesuit talked about his stay in the hospital. "The doctors told me to be cautious," he said. "They ordered me to have a two-hour nap every afternoon."

Dr. Fujii said, "It's hard to be cautious in Hiroshima these days. Everyone seems to be so busy."

A NEW municipal government, set up under Allied Military Government direction, had gone to work at last in the city hall. Citizens who had recovered from various degrees of radiation sickness were coming back by the thousand—by November 1st, the population, mostly crowded into the outskirts, was already 137,-000, more than a third of the wartime peak —and the government set in motion all kinds of projects to put them to work rebuilding the city. It hired men to clear the streets, and others to gather scrap iron, which they sorted and piled in mountains opposite the city hall. Some returning residents were putting up their own shanties and huts, and planting small squares of winter wheat beside them, but the city also authorized and built four hundred one-family "barracks." Utilities were repaired —electric lights shone again, trams started running, and employees of the waterworks fixed seventy thousand leaks in mains and plumbing. A Planning Conference, with an enthusiastic young Military Government officer, Lieutenant John D. Montgomery, of Kalamazoo, as its adviser, began to consider what sort of city the new Hiroshima should be. The ruined city had flourished—and had been an inviting target—mainly because it had been one of the most important military-command and communications centers in Japan, and would have become the Imperial headquarters had the islands been invaded and Tokyo been captured.

Now there would be no huge military establishments to help revive the city. The Planning Conference, at a loss as to just what importance Hiroshima could have, fell back on rather vague cultural and paving projects. It drew maps with avenues a hundred yards wide and thought seriously of erecting a group of buildings as a monument to the disaster, and naming them the Institute of International Amity. Statistical workers gathered what figures they could on the effects of the bomb. They reported that 78,150 people had been killed, 13,983 were missing, and 37,425 had been injured. No one in the city government pretended that these figures were accurate—though the Americans accepted them as official—and as the months went by and more and more hundreds of corpses were dug up from the ruins, and as the number of unclaimed urns of ashes at the Zempoji Temple in Koi rose into the thousands, the statisticians began to say that at least a hundred thousand people had lost their lives in the bombing. Since many people died of a combination of causes, it was impossible to figure exactly how many were killed by each cause, but the statisticians calculated that about twenty-five per cent had died of direct burns from the bomb, about fifty per cent from other injuries, and about twenty per cent as a result of radiation effects. The statisticians' figures on property damage were more reliable: sixty-two thousand out of ninety thousand buildings destroyed, and six thousand more damaged beyond repair. In the heart of the city, they found only five modern buildings that could be used again without major repairs. This small number was by no means the fault of flimsy Japanese construction. In fact, since the 1923 earthquake, Japanese building regulations had required that the roof of each large building be able to bear a minimum load of seventy pounds per square foot, whereas American regulations do not normally specify more than forty pounds per square foot.

Scientists swarmed into the city. Some of them measured the force that had been necessary to shift marble gravestones in the cemeteries, to knock over twenty-two of the forty-seven railroad cars in the yards at Hiroshima station, to lift and move the concrete roadway on one of the bridges, and to perform other noteworthy acts of strength, and concluded that the pressure exerted by the explosion varied from 5.3 to 8.0 tons per square yard. Others found that mica, of which the melting point is 900° C., had fused on granite gravestones three hundred and eighty yards from the center; that telephone poles of *Cryptomeria japonica,* whose carbonization temperature is 240° C., had been charred at forty-four hundred yards from the center; and that the surface of gray clay tiles of the type used in Hiroshima, whose melting point is 1,300° C., had dissolved at six hundred yards; and, after examining other significant ashes and melted bits, they concluded that the bomb's heat on the ground at the center must have been 6,000° C. And from further measurements of radiation, which involved, among other things, the scraping up of fission fragments from roof troughs and drainpipes as far away as the suburb of Takasu, thirty-three hundred yards from the center, they learned some far more important facts about the nature of the bomb. General MacArthur's headquarters systematically censored all mention of the bomb in Japanese scientific publications, but soon the fruit of the scientists' calculations became common knowledge among Japanese physicists, doctors, chemists, journalists, professors, and, no doubt, those statesmen and military men who were still in circulation. Long before the American public had been told, most of the scientists and lots of non-scientists in Japan knew—from the calculations of Japanese nuclear physicists—that a uranium bomb had exploded at Hiroshima and a more powerful one, of plutonium, at Nagasaki. They also knew that theoretically one ten times as powerful—or twenty—could be developed. The Japanese scientists thought they knew the exact height at which the bomb at Hiroshima was exploded and the approximate weight of the uranium used. They estimated that, even with the primitive bomb used at Hiroshima, it would require a shelter of concrete fifty inches thick to protect a human being entirely from radiation sickness. The scientists had these and other details which remained subject to security in the United States printed and mimeographed and bound into little books. The Americans knew of the existence of these, but tracing them and seeing that they did not fall into the

wrong hands would have obliged the occupying authorities to set up, for this one purpose alone, an enormous police system in Japan. Altogether, the Japanese scientists were somewhat amused at the efforts of their conquerors to keep security on atomic fission.

LATE in February, 1946, a friend of Miss Sasaki's called on Father Kleinsorge and asked him to visit her in the hospital. She had been growing more and more depressed and morbid; she seemed little interested in living. Father Kleinsorge went to see her several times. On his first visit, he kept the conversation general, formal, and yet vaguely sympathetic, and did not mention religion. Miss Sasaki herself brought it up the second time he dropped in on her. Evidently she had had some talks with a Catholic. She asked bluntly, "If your God is so good and kind, how can he let people suffer like this?" She made a gesture which took in her shrunken leg, the other patients in her room, and Hiroshima as a whole.

"My child," Father Kleinsorge said, "man is not now in the condition God intended. He has fallen from grace through sin." And he went on to explain all the reasons for everything.

IT CAME to Mrs. Nakamura's attention that a carpenter from Kabe was building a number of wooden shanties in Hiroshima which he rented for fifty yen a month—$3.33, at the fixed rate of exchange. Mrs. Nakamura had lost the certificates for her bonds and other wartime savings, but fortunately she had copied off all the numbers just a few days before the bombing and had taken the list to Kabe, and so, when her hair had grown in enough for her to be presentable, she went to her bank in Hiroshima, and a clerk there told her that after checking her numbers against the records the bank would give her her money. As soon as she got it, she rented one of the carpenter's shacks. It was in Nobori-cho, near the site of her former house, and though its floor was dirt and it was dark inside, it was at least a home in Hiroshima, and she was no longer dependent on the charity of her in-laws. During the spring, she cleared away some nearby wreckage and planted a vegetable garden. She cooked with utensils and ate off plates she scavenged from the debris. She sent Myeko to the kindergarten which the Jesuits reopened, and the two older children attended Nobori-cho Primary School, which, for want of buildings, held classes out of doors. Toshio wanted to study to be a mechanic, like his hero, Hideo Osaki. Prices were high; by midsummer Mrs. Nakamura's savings were gone. She sold some of her clothes to get food. She had once had several expensive kimonos, but during the war one had been stolen, she had given one to a sister who had been bombed out in Tokuyama, she had lost a couple in the Hiroshima bombing, and now she sold her last one. It brought only a hundred yen, which did not last long. In June, she went to Father Kleinsorge for advice about how to get along, and in early August, she was still considering the two alternatives he suggested—taking work as a domestic for some of the Allied occupation forces, or borrowing from her relatives enough money, about five hundred yen, or a bit more than thirty dollars, to repair her rusty sewing machine and resume the work of a seamstress.

WHEN Mr. Tanimoto returned from Shikoku, he draped a tent he owned over the roof of the badly damaged house he had rented in Ushida. The roof still leaked, but he conducted services in the damp living room. He began thinking about raising money to restore his church in the city. He became quite friendly with Father Kleinsorge and saw the Jesuits often. He envied them their Church's wealth; they seemed to be able to do anything they wanted. He had nothing to work with except his own energy, and that was not what it had been.

THE SOCIETY OF JESUS had been the first institution to build a relatively permanent shanty in the ruins of Hiroshima. That had been while Father Kleinsorge was in the hospital. As soon as he got back, he began living in the shack, and he and another priest, Father Laderman, who had joined him in the mission, arranged for the purchase of three of the standardized "barracks," which the city was selling at seven thousand yen apiece. They put two together,

end to end, and made a pretty chapel of them; they ate in the third. When materials were available, they commissioned a contractor to build a three-story mission house exactly like the one that had been destroyed in the fire. In the compound, carpenters cut timbers, gouged mortises, shaped tenons, whittled scores of wooden pegs and bored holes for them, until all the parts for the house were in a neat pile; then, in three days, they put the whole thing together, like an Oriental puzzle, without any nails at all. Father Kleinsorge was finding it hard, as Dr. Fujii had suggested he would, to be cautious and to take his naps. He went out every day on foot to call on Japanese Catholics and prospective converts. As the months went by, he grew more and more tired. In June, he read an article in the Hiroshima *Chugoku* warning survivors against working too hard—but what could he do? By July, he was worn out, and early in August, almost exactly on the anniversary of the bombing, he went back to the Catholic International Hospital, in Tokyo, for a month's rest.

WHETHER or not Father Kleinsorge's answers to Miss Sasaki's questions about life were final and absolute truths, she seemed quickly to draw physical strength from them. Dr. Sasaki noticed it and congratulated Father Kleinsorge. By April 15th, her temperature and white count were normal and the infection in the wound was beginning to clear up. On the twentieth, there was almost no pus, and for the first time she jerked along a corridor on crutches. Five days later, the wound had begun to heal, and on the last day of the month she was discharged.

During the early summer, she prepared herself for conversion to Catholicism. In that period she had ups and downs. Her depressions were deep. She knew she would always be a cripple. Her fiancé never came to see her. There was nothing for her to do except read and look out, from her house on a hillside in Koi, across the ruins of the city where her parents and brother died. She was nervous, and any sudden noise made her put her hands quickly to her throat. Her leg still hurt; she rubbed it often and patted it, as if to console it.

IT TOOK six months for the Red Cross Hospital, and even longer for Dr. Sasaki, to get back to normal. Until the city restored electric power, the hospital had to limp along with the aid of a Japanese Army generator in its back yard. Operating tables, X-ray machines, dentist chairs, everything complicated and essential came in a trickle of charity from other cities. In Japan, face is important even to institutions, and long before the Red Cross Hospital was back to par on basic medical equipment, its directors put up a new yellow brick veneer façade, so the hospital became the handsomest building in Hiroshima—from the street. For the first four months, Dr. Sasaki was the only surgeon on the staff and he almost never left the building; then, gradually, he began to take an interest in his own life again. He got married in March. He gained back some of the weight he lost, but his appetite remained only fair; before the bombing, he used to eat four rice balls at every meal, but a year after it he could manage only two. He felt tired all the time. "But I have to realize," he said, "that the whole community is tired."

A YEAR after the bomb was dropped, Miss Sasaki was a cripple; Mrs. Nakamura was destitute; Father Kleinsorge was back in the hospital; Dr. Sasaki was not capable of the work he once could do; Dr. Fujii had lost the thirty-room hospital it took him many years to acquire, and had no prospects of rebuilding it; Mr. Tanimoto's church had been ruined and he no longer had his exceptional vitality. The lives of these six people, who were among the luckiest in Hiroshima, would never be the same. What they thought of their experiences and of the use of the atomic bomb was, of course, not unanimous. One feeling they did seem to share, however, was a curious kind of elated community spirit, something like that of the Londoners after their blitz—a pride in the way they and their fellow-survivors had stood up to a dreadful ordeal. Just before the anniversary, Mr. Tanimoto wrote in a letter to an American some words which expressed this feeling: "What a heartbreaking scene this was the first night! About midnight I landed on the riverbank. So many injured people lied on the ground that I made my way by striding over them. Repeating 'Excuse me,' I forwarded and carried a tub of water with me and gave a cup of water to each one of them. They raised their upper bodies slowly and accepted a cup of water with a bow and drunk quietly and, spilling any remnant, gave back a cup with hearty expression of their thankfulness, and said, 'I couldn't help my sister, who was buried under the house, because I had to take care of my mother who got a deep wound on her eye and our house soon set fire and we hardly escaped. Look, I lost my home, my family, and at last my-self bitterly injured. But now I have gotted my mind to dedicate what I have and to complete the war for our country's sake.' Thus they pledged to me, even women and children did the same. Being entirely tired I lied down on the ground among them, but couldn't sleep at all. Next morning I found many men and women dead, whom I gave water last night. But, to my great surprise, I never heard any one cried in disorder, even though they suffered in great agony. They died in silence, with no grudge, setting their teeth to bear it. All for the country!

"Dr. Y. Hiraiwa, professor of Hiroshima University of Literature and Science, and one of my church members, was buried by the bomb under the two storied house with his son, a student of Tokyo University. Both of them could not move an inch under tremendously heavy pressure. And the house already caught fire. His son said, 'Father, we can do nothing except make our mind up to consecrate our lives for the country. Let us give *Banzai* to our Emperor.' Then the father followed after his son, '*Tenno-heika, Banzai, Banzai, Banzai!*' In the result, Dr. Hiraiwa said, 'Strange to say, I felt calm and bright and peaceful spirit in my heart, when I chanted *Banzai* to Tenno.' Afterward his son got out and digged down and pulled out his father and thus they were saved. In thinking of their experience of that time Dr. Hiraiwa repeated, 'What a fortunate that we are Japanese! It was my first time I ever tasted such a beautiful spirit when I decided to die for our Emperor.'

"Miss Kayoko Nobutoki, a student of girl's

high school, Hiroshima Jazabuin, and a daughter of my church member, was taking rest with her friends beside the heavy fence of the Buddhist Temple. At the moment the atomic bomb was dropped, the fence fell upon them. They could not move a bit under such a heavy fence and then smoke entered into even a crack and choked their breath. One of the girls begun to sing *Kimi ga yo*, national anthem, and others followed in chorus and died. Meanwhile one of them found a crack and struggled hard to get out. When she was taken in the Red Cross Hospital she told how her friends died, tracing back in her memory to singing in chorus our national anthem. They were just 13 years old.

"Yes, people of Hiroshima died manly in the atomic bombing, believing that it was for Emperor's sake."

A surprising number of the people of Hiroshima remained more or less indifferent about the ethics of using the bomb. Possibly they were too terrified by it to want to think about it at all. Not many of them even bothered to find out much about what it was like. Mrs. Nakamura's conception of it—and awe of it—was typical. "The atom bomb," she would say when asked about it, "is the size of a matchbox. The heat of it is six thousand times that of the sun. It exploded in the air. There is some radium in it. I don't know just how it works, but when the radium is put together, it explodes." As for the use of the bomb, she would say, "It was war and we had to expect it." And then she would add, *"Shikata ga nai,"* a Japanese expression as common as, and corresponding to, the Russian word *"nichevo"*: "It can't be helped. Oh, well. Too bad." Dr. Fujii said approximately the same thing about the use of the bomb to Father Kleinsorge one evening, in German: *"Da ist nichts zu machen.* There's nothing to be done about it."

Many citizens of Hiroshima, however, continued to feel a hatred for Americans which nothing could possibly erase. "I see," Dr. Sasaki once said, "that they are holding a trial for war criminals in Tokyo just now. I think they ought to try the men who decided to use the bomb and they should hang them all."

Father Kleinsorge and the other German Jesuit priests, who, as foreigners, could be expected to take a relatively detached view, often discussed the ethics of using the bomb. One of them, Father Siemes, who was out at Nagatsuka at the time of the attack, wrote in a report to the Holy See in Rome: "Some of us consider the bomb in the same category as poison gas and were against its use on a civilian population. Others were of the opinion that in total war, as carried on in Japan, there was no difference between civilians and soldiers, and that the bomb itself was an effective force tending to end the bloodshed, warning Japan to surrender and thus to avoid total destruction. It seems logical that he who supports total war in principal cannot complain of a war against civilians. The crux of the matter is whether total war in its present form is justifiable, even when it serves a just purpose. Does it not have material and spiritual evil as its consequences which far exceed whatever good might result? When will our moralists give us a clear answer to this question?"

It would be impossible to say what horrors were embedded in the minds of the children who lived through the day of the bombing of Hiroshima. On the surface, their recollections, months after the disaster, were of an exhilarating adventure. Toshio Nakamura, who was ten at the time of the bombing, was soon able to talk freely, even gaily, about the experience, and a few weeks before the anniversary he wrote the following matter-of-fact essay for his teacher at Nobori-cho Primary School: "The day before the bomb, I went for a swim. In the morning, I was eating peanuts. I saw a light. I was knocked to little sister's sleeping place. When we were saved, I could only see as far as the tram. My mother and I started to pack our things. The neighbors were walking around burned and bleeding. Hataya-*san* told me to run away with her. I said I wanted to wait for my mother. We went to the park. A whirlwind came. At night a gas tank burned and I saw the reflection in the river. We stayed in the park one night. Next day I went to Taiko Bridge and met my girl friends Kikuki and Murakami. They were looking for their mothers. But Kikuki's mother was wounded and Murakami's mother, alas, was dead."

✌ The Religious Revival

ROBERT LOWELL

Robert Lowell, who was born in 1917 into the famous Lowell family of Boston, has rebelled against the traditions of his ancestors. Although he matriculated at Harvard, the "family school," he transferred to Kenyon College and received his B.A. there in 1940. Apparently in rebellion against the puritan beliefs traditional in his family, he became, while still young, a Catholic convert. He tried to enlist in the Army but was rejected; later he became a conscientious objector and served a prison term. Before this, apparently, he must have spent much time in Concord, for many of his poems are closely related to his New England background. His two books of poetry are *Land of Unlikeness* (1944) and the Pulitzer Prize-winning *Lord Weary's Castle* (1946). Even with the publication of the first book he became one of the most talked-about poets in America. Although his first volume of verse was criticized for its obscurity and for the strangeness of its imagery, Lowell was immediately recognized as a dramatic lyric poet of the first rank. The violence of his imagery, the richness of his knowledge—Freudian, historical, and religious—the anger and the awe which he can communicate, are all unique.

Since his second volume indicates a much firmer control of his medium, and since the recent poetry published in magazines proves further progress, it is probable that Lowell is one of the more promising figures in the new poetry. His involvement with the early traditions of America and with the growth of puritanism, as typified by the whole history of his family, has given him historical perspective. His purpose is to oppose to the Puritan God the Catholic conception of religion, which he sees as less narrow and as granting to the poet the emotional fulfillment he finds necessary as he moves from the sensual into the spiritual. Moreover, Lowell sees contradictions in the individualistic approach to God which Protestantism allows, and is not unaware of the fact that individualism and commercial competition have something in common. His is a rich mind, philosophically, and he juggles brilliantly the contradictions and complexities of the real world and of religious passion. Primarily he is a metaphysical poet, in whom the strange distortion of imagery reflects the deep gap between reality as it is and wholeness of feeling and conviction as a sensitive spirit envisions it.

Despite the fact that Lowell has been consistently concerned with the Catholic dogma, it is clear that his mind is very subtly speculative, that his is no simple acceptance of faith, no self-imposed retreat from reality; and since this is true, one wonders where so Freudian a mind may move next.

Between the Porch and the Altar

I. Mother and Son

MEETING his mother makes him lose ten
    years,
Or is it twenty? Time, no doubt, has ears
That listen to the swallowed serpent, wound
Into its bowels, but he thinks no sound

Between the Porch and the Altar. Here Lowell is using the image of a cathedral to describe the entrance into passion and the course toward its consummation. The poet, as a protagonist, considers the different stages in his discovery of the problem of evil, knowledge of sexual love. *I.* Lowell traces in Freudian terms the return to childhood's awareness of sin and shame which comes to adulthood when the mother-image of womanhood is recalled.

943

Is possible before her, he thinks the past   5
Is settled. It is honest to hold fast
Merely to what one sees with one's own eyes
When the red velvet curves and haunches rise
To blot him from the pretty driftwood fire's
Façade of welcome. Then the son retires   10
Into the sack and selfhood of the boy
Who clawed through fallen houses of his Troy,
Homely and human only when the flames
Crackle in recollection. Nothing shames
Him more than this uncoiling, counterfeit   15
Body presented as an idol. It
Is something in a circus, big as life,
The painted dragon, a mother and a wife
With flat glass eyes pushed at him on a stick;
The human mover crawls to make them click.
The forehead of her father's portrait peels   21
With rosy dryness, and the schoolboy kneels
To ask the benediction of the hand,
Lifted as though to motion him to stand,
Dangling its watch-chain on the Holy Book—
A little golden snake that mouths a hook.   26

II. Adam and Eve

The farmer sizzles on his shaft all day.
He is content and centuries away
From white-hot Concord, and he stands on
     guard.
Or is he melting down like sculptured lard?
His hand is crisp and steady on the plough.
I quarrelled with you, but am happy now   6
To while away my life for your unrest
Of terror. Never to have lived is best;
Man tasted Eve with death. I taste my wife
And children while I hold your hands. I knife
Their names into this elm. What is exempt? 11
I eye the statue with an awed contempt
And see the puritanical façade
Of the white church that Irish exiles made
For Patrick—that Colonial from Rome   15
Had magicked the charmed serpents from their
     home,
As though he were the Piper. Will his breath
Scorch the red dragon of my nerves to death?
By sundown we are on a shore. You walk
A little way before me and I talk,   20

12. **Troy**, used here as an example of betrayal. **II.** The struggle
between ignorance and purity on the one hand, and knowledge
and passion on the other, as in the Garden of Eden, is suggested.
Overtones of the conflict (in beliefs) in the poet's mind between
puritanism and Catholicism are also suggested. 15. **Patrick**, St.
Patrick, patron saint of Ireland; a Roman, he was captured by
pirates and enslaved in Ireland. He is said to have driven the
snakes out of Ireland.

Half to myself and half aloud. They lied,
My cold-eyed seedy fathers when they died,
Or rather threw their lives away, to fix
Sterile, forbidding nameplates on the bricks
Above a kettle. Jesus rest their souls!   25
You cry for help. Your market-basket rolls
With all its baking apples in the lake.
You watch the whorish slither of a snake
That chokes a duckling. When we try to kiss,
Our eyes are slits and cringing, and we hiss;
Scales glitter on our bodies as we fall.   31
The Farmer melts upon his pedestal.

III. Katherine's Dream

It must have been a Friday. I could hear
The top-floor typist's thunder and the beer
That you had brought in cases hurt my head;
I'd sent the pillows flying from my bed,
I hugged my knees together and I gasped.   5
The dangling telephone receiver rasped
Like someone in a dream who cannot stop
For breath or logic till his victim drop
To darkness and the sheets. I must have slept,
But still could hear my father who had kept
Your guilty presents but cut off my hair.   11
He whispers that he really doesn't care
If I am your kept woman all my life,
Or ruin your two children and your wife;
But my dishonor makes him drink. Of course
I'll tell the court the truth for his divorce.   16
I walk through snow into St. Patrick's yard.
Black nuns with glasses smile and stand on
     guard
Before a bulkhead in a bank of snow,
Whose charred doors open, as good people go
Inside by twos to the confessor. One   21
Must have a friend to enter there, but none
Is friendless in this crowd, and the nuns smile.
I stand aside and marvel; for a while
The winter sun is pleasant and it warms   25
My heart with love for others, but the swarms
Of penitents have dwindled. I begin
To cry and ask God's pardon of our sin.
Where are you? You were with me and are
     gone.
All the forgiven couples hurry on   30
To dinner and their nights, and none will stop.
I run about in circles till I drop
Against a padlocked bulkhead in a yard
Where faces redden and the snow is hard.

III. Here we get the mistress' consciousness of her sense of sin
and of her isolation in it.

IV. At the Altar

I sit at a gold table with my girl
Whose eyelids burn with brandy. What a whirl
Of Easter eggs is colored by the lights,
As the Norwegian dancer's crystalled tights   4
Flash with her naked leg's high-booted skate,
Like Northern Lights upon my watching plate.
The twinkling steel above me is a star;
I am a fallen Christmas tree. Our car
Races through seven red-lights—then the road
Is unpatrolled and empty, and a load   10
Of ply-wood with a tail-light makes us slow.
I turn and whisper in her ear. You know
I want to leave my mother and my wife,
You wouldn't have me tied to them for life . . .
Time runs, the windshield runs with stars. The
    past   15
Is cities from a train, until at last
Its escalating and black-windowed blocks
Recoil against a Gothic church. The clocks
Are tolling. I am dying. The shocked stones
Are falling like a ton of bricks and bones   20
That snap and splinter and descend in glass
Before a priest who mumbles through his Mass
And sprinkles holy water; and the Day
Breaks with its lightning on the man of clay,
Dies amara valde. Here the Lord   25
Is Lucifer in harness: hand on sword,
He watches me for Mother, and will turn
The bier and baby-carriage where I burn.

The Drunken Fisherman

Wallowing in this bloody sty,
    I cast for fish that pleased my eye
(Truly Jehovah's bow suspends
No pots of gold to weight its ends);
Only the blood-mouthed rainbow trout   5

Rose to my bait. They flopped about
My canvass creel until the moth
Corrupted its unstable cloth.

A calendar to tell the day;
A handkerchief to wave away   10
The gnats; a couch unstuffed with storm
Pouching a bottle in one arm;
A whiskey bottle full of worms;
And bedroom slacks: are these fit terms
To mete the worm whose molten rage   15
Boils in the belly of old age?

Once fishing was a rabbit's foot—
O wind blow cold, O wind blow hot,
Let suns stay in or suns step out:
Life danced a jig on the sperm-whale's spout—
The fisher's fluent and obscene   21
Catches kept his conscience clean.
Children, the raging memory drools
Over the glory of past pools.

Now the hot river, ebbing, hauls   25
Its bloody waters into holes;
A grain of sand inside my shoe
Mimics the moon that might undo
Man and Creation too; remorse,
Stinking, has puddled up its source;   30
Here tantrums thrash to a whale's rage.
This is the pot-hole of old age.

Is there no way to cast my hook
Out of this dynamited brook?
The Fisher's sons must cast about   35
When shallow waters peter out.
I will catch Christ with a greased worm,
And when the Prince of Darkness stalks
My bloodstream to its Stygian term . . .
On water the Man-Fisher walks.   40

The Exile's Return

There mounts in squalls a sort of rusty mire,
    Not ice, not snow, to leaguer the Hôtel
De Ville, where braced pig-iron dragons grip
The blizzard to their rigor mortis. A bell
Grumbles when the reverberations strip   5

IV. It seems possible that Lowell had in mind George Herbert's poem "The Altar," in which the seventeenth-century meta-physical poet described his heart as God's altar, carved by His hand through being made to know love and pain. The closing lines of this section suggest a reference to Robert Southwell's "The Burning Babe," a metaphysical poem in which innocence, Christ, is destroyed by lust but shines in flames of love risen again. Obviously, the whole poem concludes with the poet's rejecting the puritanic conceptions of morality though they persist in his deep sense of sin and damnation. 25. *Dies amara valde,* day of great bitterness.
The Drunken Fisherman. The poet uses the imagery of fishing (cf. Matthew 4:19) to describe life, which in youth is brimming with innocence and satisfaction with things earthly and material, but which, as the river of mortality ebbs, be-comes muddied with remorse and guilt. The hope of old age is for redemption through Christ—for a return to the innocence of childhood as expressed by fishing with a pole and worm instead of casting with rod and fly—and for refuge, in the sea of eternity, from sin and death.

15. **worm.** The overtone here is that of serpent or evil. 31. **whale.** The imagery throughout the poem is complex. Here, for example, Lowell may have had in mind Melville's *Moby Dick,* the white whale which brought death to many.   40. **On water . . . walks.** A return to faith is suggested in the accept-ance of a miracle (Christ's walking on the waters). **Man-Fisher,** Christ.
The Exile's Return. The poem is probably placed in Austria during the Second World War.   2. **Hôtel de Ville,** town hall.

The thatching from its spire,
The search-guns click and spit and split up
    timber
And nick the slate roofs on the Holstenwall
Where torn-up tilestones crown the victor. Fall
And winter, spring and summer, guns unlimber
And lumber down the narrow gabled street
Past your gray, sorry and ancestral house   12
Where the dynamited walnut tree
Shadows a squat, old, wind-torn gate and cows
The bristling podestà. You will not see   15
Strutting children or meet
The peg-leg and reproachful chancellor
With a forget-me-not in his button-hole
When the unseasoned liberators roll
Into the Market Square, ground arms before
The Rathaus; but already lily-stands   21
Burgeon the risen Rhineland, and a rough
Cathedral lifts its eye. Pleasant enough,
Voi ch'entrate, and your life is in your hands.

After the Surprising Conversions

September twenty-second, Sir: today
I answer. In the latter part of May,
Hard on our Lord's Ascension, it began
To be more sensible. A gentleman
Of more than common understanding, strict
In morals, pious in behavior, kicked   6
Against our goad. A man of some renown,
An useful, honored person in the town,
He came of melancholy parents; prone
To secret spells, for years they kept alone—
His uncle, I believe, was killed of it: 11
Good people, but of too much or little wit.
I preached one Sabbath on a text from Kings;
He showed concernment for his soul. Some
    things
In his experience were hopeful. He   15
Would sit and watch the wind knocking a tree
And praise this countryside our Lord has made.
Once when a poor man's heifer died, he laid
A shilling on the doorsill; though a thirst   19
For loving shook him like a snake, he durst

Not entertain much hope of his estate
In heaven. Once we saw him sitting late
Behind his attic window by a light
That guttered on his Bible; through that night
He meditated terror, and he seemed   25
Beyond advice or reason, for he dreamed
That he was called to trumpet Judgement
    Day
To Concord. In the latter part of May
He cut his throat. And though the coroner
Judged him delirious, soon a noisome stir   30
Palsied our village. At Jehovah's nod
Satan seemed more let loose amongst us:
    God
Abandoned us to Satan, and he pressed
Us hard, until we thought we could not rest
Till we had done with life. Content was gone.
All the good work was quashed. We were un-
    done.   36
The breath of God had carried out a planned
And sensible withdrawal from this land;
The multitude, once unconcerned with doubt,
Once neither callous, curious nor devout,   40
Jumped at broad noon, as though some peddler
    groaned
At it in its familiar twang: "My friend,
Cut your own throat. Cut your own throat.
    Now! Now!"
September twenty-second, Sir, the bough   44
Cracks with the unpicked apples, and at dawn
The small-mouth bass breaks water, gorged
    with spawn.

[The source is a sermon by Jonathan Edwards, *Narrative of Surprising Conversions* (full title: A Faithful Narrative of the Surprising Work of God, in the Conversion of many Hundred Souls, in Northampton, etc.). This narrative is a letter from Edwards to the Rev. Dr. Colman, of Boston, in which he gives a full account of an amazing phenomenon of conversions by the people in his, and surrounding, villages. Their conversion is merely to a belief in the power of God as expressed in the Bible. They became Christians. Lowell's poem follows almost word for word a paragraph written by Edwards about one particular case. September 22, 1763, as closely as can be made out, is the date of this episode. Lowell has converted a piece of prose into verse, nothing more, but by all

8. **Holstenwall,** town hall.   15. **podestà,** a Fascist city official.   21. **Rathaus,** town hall.   24. *Voi ch'entrate*, skiing term for the starting of a run.

means nothing less. Edwards' paragraph follows:

. . . In the latter part of May, it began to be very sensible that the Spirit of God was gradually withdrawing from us, and after this time Satan seemed to be more let loose, and raged in a dreadful manner. The first instance wherein it appeared, was a person putting an end to his life by cutting his throat. He was a gentleman of more than common understanding, of strict morals, religious in his behavior, and an useful and honourable person in the town; but was of a family that are exceedingly prone to the disease of melancholy, and his mother was killed with it. He had, from the beginning of this extraordinary time, been exceedingly concerned about the state of his soul, and there were some things in his experience that appeared very hopeful; but he durst entertain no hope concerning his own good estate. Towards the latter part of his time, he grew much discouraged, and melancholy grew amain upon him, till he was wholly overpowered by it, and was on a great measure past a capacity of receiving advice, or being reasoned with to any purpose. The devil took the advantage, and drove him into despairing thoughts. He was kept awake at nights meditating terror, so that he had scarce any sleep at all for a long time together; and it was observed at last, that he was scarcely well capable of managing his ordinary business, and was judged delirious by the coroner's inquest. The news of this extraordinarily affected the minds of people here, and struck them as it were with astonishment. After this, multitudes in this and other towns seemed to have it strongly suggested to them, and pressed upon them, to do as this person had done. And many who seemed to be under no melancholy, some pious persons, who had no special doubts or darkness about the goodness of their state—nor were under any special trouble or concern of mind about anything spiritual or temporal—had it urged upon them as if somebody had spoken to them. Cut your own throat, now is a good opportunity. Now! Now! So that they were obliged to fight with all their might to resist it, and yet no reason suggested to them why they should do it. (Jonathan Edwards— *Works,* Vol. IV, pp. 70–71)

This put a virtual end to the "amazing" conversions—as if the devil had taken the place of God.]

Christmas Eve under Hooker's Statue

TONIGHT a blackout. Twenty years ago
I hung my stocking on the tree, and hell's
Serpent entwined the apple in the toe
To sting the child with knowledge. Hooker's heels
Kicking at nothing in the shifting snow,   5
A cannon and a cairn of cannon balls
Rusting before the blackened Statehouse, know
How the long horn of plenty broke like glass
In Hooker's gauntlets. Once I came from Mass;

Now storm-clouds shelter Christmas, once again   10
Mars meets his fruitless star with open arms,
His heavy saber flashes with the rime,
The war-god's bronzed and empty forehead forms
Anonymous machinery from raw men;
The cannon on the Common cannot stun   15
The blundering butcher as he rides on Time—
The barrel clinks with holly. I am cold:
I ask for bread, my father gives me mould;

His stocking is full of stones. Santa in red   19
Is crowned with wizened berries. Man of war,
Where is the summer's garden? In its bed
The ancient speckled serpent will appear,
And black-eyed susan with her frizzled head.
When Chancellorsville mowed down the volunteer,   24
"All wars are boyish," Herman Melville said;
But we are old, our fields are running wild:
Till Christ again turn wanderer and child.

Christmas Eve under Hooker's Statue. The poet comments on America's spiritual degradation through its insistence on material success. He sees in Hooker a possible emblem of the Second World War, which he thinks of as a war of trade. On the day of Christ's birth, man gets, instead of plenty and stability, the gifts of war and death.   **Hooker,** Joseph Hooker (1814–79), Union general.   24. **Chancellorsville,** the scene of one of General Hooker's defeats in the Civil War, where Stonewall Jackson was mortally wounded.   25. **Herman Melville** (1819–91), American writer, author of *Moby Dick, Benito Cereno, Billy Budd,* etc.

GEORGE BARKER

The work of George Barker shows a familiarity with the writings of W. H. Auden; but the former poet is much more the complete romantic in his use of language. His imagery, though largely derived from history, is rich; and his phrasing is intricate, although he employs little of the word magic found in the poetry of, for example, Dylan Thomas. Barker's poems are highly thematic: he treats of history, albeit subjectively; and the religious theme is also present, for as an Anglo-Catholic he argues indirectly for the spiritual revitalization of our culture.

Barker was born in England in 1913 and was more or less self-educated. He traveled widely, and was teaching in Tokyo University when World War II broke out. He has spent some time in the United States, and his poems have appeared simultaneously in both England and this country. His first book in prose, *Alanna Autumnal,* appeared in 1933. In 1934 he published *30 Preliminary Poems,* and in 1935 *Poems* and a prose volume under the pseudonym "Janus." *Selected Poems* appeared in 1941, *Sacred and Secular Elegies* in 1944, and *Love Poems* in 1947.

Barker's political liberalism leads him to project what might otherwise remain purely personal religious emotion into arguments for relief from periods of war and economic depression. His poetry is at times a sort of panorama of historical images of betrayal; the principal emotions expressed are personal guilt and horror. He appears to see our time as a time of betrayal, an era in which man, despite his eloquence and intensity, is granted little opportunity to think or to feel.

Many of Barker's poems are long. He inclines more toward the narrative explanation of feeling than toward the condensation or crystallization of it. Many of his stanzas show the need for some pruning, and the intellectual and the emotional in him do not seem to be entirely integrated; but Barker is a complex poet who may in time attain clarity of expression in his writing.

Vision of England '38

I LAY, not in Malvern or Alexandra Palace
From where the southern sorrow of the
    horizon is seen
Encompassing more of misery than a tear's
    whole circle,
But in Brighton I lay in bed, and behind my
    head

The tremendous panoply of England fell verti-
    cal,   5
The historical curtain exuding blood on my pil-
    low;
Conspicuously suspended from diamonds of
    justice
Dredged from the depths of national despair.

Not sleeping not dreaming I saw the imperial
    procession
Flicker past my foot in postures of triumph or
    violence;   10

Vision of England. Thinking back over the history of England and of English leaders, and looking to such revolutionaries as Shelley and Wat Tyler for inspiration, the poet reviewing the past is told in the first section to be patient and to watch closely. In the second section, obviously prophetic of England's difficult period recently, he indicates that England has remained commercial and that this is not a virtue. In the third section the poet, touring the industrial areas and noting the symbols of war, wonders what such leaders as Alfred and Arthur would think of contemporary England. In the fourth section he suggests that his own generation is also to blame, that love has not been the guiding star of England, that fear and terror are abroad. In the fifth section the poem focuses on London, center of greed and of national pride. A prayer is given that after this war there may be more equality and less insistence on power among the English. **1. Malvern,** town in Worcestershire, England. An annual Dramatic Festival is held there. **Alexandra Palace,** in northwest London; headquarters of the British Broadcasting Corporation's television department. **4. Brighton,** English seaside resort town on the southeast coast, popularized by George IV when he was Prince of Wales, and remarkable for the ornate architecture of that period.

Some moved in shapes of gluttony or envy,
    others
Rode pride like lions, and some bore their own
    flowers.

I heard voices that whispered and voices that
    sang,
'Death is no glory,' or 'I shun not the fire.'
Three women came screaming, wringing hands,
    flying,   15
With crowns on their brows, the last of them
    Victoria.

Behind them, randy as the angry beast who
    craves
Dominion for its ball and sceptre, loped the
    Disraelian lion.
The three queens with its scions in their loins
Flew forward screaming, hunting for their
    graves.   20

Nor could I halt this parade of historical char-
    acter,
Not with a lifted hand and a cry, or an elec-
    tric candle;
Not with appeals or protests or references to
    authority:
The shuffling crowd streamed through in a
    bright dream.

O lamentable lips that ragged showed their
    burns,   25
As that beautiful youth with Saint Mary Red-
    cliffe in hand
Stepped forward and fell at my side and mur-
    mured:
'I warn you, not poison.'

Who took my hand and left an orchid there,
With the mark of his lips that parted their
    shapes   30
To speak a word of hope: was it salacious Oscar
Or the lost Orphic who coughed blood at Na-
    ples?

'Remember me, remember me,' cried the skull
That floated through with seaweed in its teeth.

15. **Three women,** presumably Queen Elizabeth, Queen Anne, and Queen Victoria.   17. **randy,** lustful.   18. **Disraelian.** See note 40, p. 138.   26. **beautiful . . . poison.** Thomas Chatterton (1752–70), a talented young poet who lived near the church of St. Mary Redcliffe at Bristol, committed suicide at seventeen by taking poison.   31. **Oscar,** Oscar Wilde (1865–1900).   32. **Orphic.** The music of the Greek Orpheus supposedly gave him power over all mortal things. The term here describes John Keats, who died of consumption at Naples. 33. **the skull,** a reference to Percy Bysshe Shelley, who was drowned at sea.

'Drowned in a sudden squall I found him there,
Waiting under the wave, God ambushed me
    there.'   36

Then I abandoned my attitude of ease on the
    bed
To touch the salt tear that the skull had shed:
And like a pearl it poised upon my hand, and I
Saw in its circle the temporal Harlequin dome.

Next the rhodomontade of the political opera
Shattered by gaze and daze as I saw enter   42
The onager, the serpent and the macaw,
Tussling together over the heart of man.

But what one tore or what all three ravaged,
Though the wounds bled, seemed to restore
Soon to its shape like a world after war,   47
And all that commemorates is the blood on the
    floor.

So I took Shelley's tear which like a single rain
Dropped into the blood that murmured at my
    feet: 50
And a ghost arose holding out its hands in
    pain,
Looking at me with eyes that supplicated fate.

'From tears and blood I spring in sorrow and
    anger,
The long anonymous inhabitant of dearth.   54
I'm Wat Tyler's wife and Robert Owen's lover,
From whom you also came starving at birth.

'Remember me when the rose is too close,
Or when the triumphant dove coos sweetly
Filling the world with love, do not forget me.
I shall be here, the tenant of my woes.'   60

'Wait,' I said slowly. 'Tell me why I,
Lying at night in my Brighton bed,
Receive the visitation of the conspicuously
    dead,
Terrifying me with their mad pageantry.'

He lifted his head like a lover to me,   65
Smiling with a secret that no words revealed:

38. **To touch . . . dome.** The poet sees in Shelley's tear the image of the temporal striped dome of life. "Life, like a dome of many-colored glass, stains the white radiance of Eternity." 43. **onager,** wild ass.   55. **Wat Tyler** (d. 1381), English rebel and reformer. Shelley's utopian idea of love is the same as that of Tyler or Owen. **Robert Owen** (1771–1853), British social reformer. Barker apparently refers to the wife and the lover as part of the anonymous background.

Then he said softly, 'Mystery is no mystery
When Time divests it of its present mists.

'Therefore wait with patience: you will see
More than the theatrical zodiac of history.
Look closely enough and life will show her
    source   71
From higher than Chilterns and a grander
    course.'

Then the rain tattooed the window. He was
    gone,
Leaving me alone in a room of time   74
So small that I filled it with a minute sigh,
For the host and the ghost were gone.

II

But I arose, with a star against my cheek
Roaring of winter with the tongues of Orion:
'The great winds rage in the mane of the lion,
But not great winds make the lion weak.'   80

Near me the sea in nocturnal lamentation
Shrouded itself in hoods and wept a shower,
Retreating in sorrow from the lion's locks
Where he lies emaciated on capital rocks.   84

Cassiopeia wept. I felt her brilliant sympathy
Falling upon me as I walked by the waves;
I looked up at her outstretched arms in the sky
Too far to reach me and too near for a grave.

Then a saint walked up out of the sea,
Dragging his death behind him like a boat   90
He had a rusty sword and he said to me:
'I killed an enormous monster, but the brute

'Still rules England with its scales of gold.
O my green girl given to the rape of the
    banker,   94
The careerist politician and the vague thinker,
Lie easy for one more night out in the cold.'

He gave me his sword with a long look,
Then turned, and returned to his death.
I glanced down at the iron in my hand, and
    found
The blueblooded point that bleeds a book.   100

So I lay down against Saint George's green girl

To keep her warm an hour in my arms.
To see us lying by the waves' whirl
The dove also wept among the Great Dog's
    curls.

But Peace is dear and cannot be bought with
    sleep,   105
Any more than Birmingham can keep peace in
    steel:
So as I lay between a dream and a sleep
A tongue licked me, and I saw it was a sheep.

'This green,' it said, 'this pleasant place,
Not yet is fit for the foot of Christ.   110
How can your word or your sword sleep
While the Thames is the sweat of the people?

'I am Blake who broke my mind on God.
I tell you he does not touch this world
Till the disease is scoured from the sod   115
By the blood of sin made fit for his hand.'

The touch of the tongue as the Lamb kissed
Fired my spirit with the bliss of fate
When the spirit senses the great ultimate   119
To which it toils through mystery and mist.

Alone on the dark beach I stood.
The teeth of the seas tore the shore.
'O immensely sad land,' I said, 'where
Only the ghosts are good.'

III

I ride my grief along the road   125
Leaving the littoral cities to their summer sins;
Brighton and Bournemouth with the pots of
    God
Brimming fire over the signs of the times.

But who could whistle or sing in the South
With its ramshackle witch-barns broken and
    ruined;   130
Where the disused thresher rusts among the li-
    chens,
And the brood scuttles in the kitchens?

So I went northward to Salisbury on Friday.
But on the bridge I encountered a figure

72. **Chilterns,** a range of chalk hills in England. 78. **Orion,** a spectacular winter constellation. Here the poet moves into images of blind power, suggesting that such power still rules England. 89. **a saint,** Saint George, the patron saint of England, who is usually depicted in the act of killing a dragon.

106. **Birmingham,** headquarters of the English steel and iron industry. 112. **Thames,** the river that flows through London and has been described as "liquid history." 113. **Blake,** William Blake (1757–1827), English poet, painter, visionary, and revolutionary; Blake condemned England for her insincerity and injustice. 117. **Lamb,** reference probably to Blake, but also to the fact that Christ is known as the Lamb. 126. **littoral,** pertaining to the seashore. 133. **Salisbury,** cathedral city in Wiltshire, England.

Who crossed me with a look and shook his
    head: 135
'It's market day but even so we are dead.

'I'm William Longspee who lies in stone
In the north aisle of the Cathedral:
All the semblance of Salisbury's life is a pall
Covering the famous faces of the dead and
    gone.   140

'There's nothing here but the mere loveliness
Of the long lost Gothic ache to heaven:
Like the lily in which the dead dress,
Salisbury is a beautiful funeral.'

And I saw the sweet alto of the spire sing up-
    ward   145
Like the long note of the God-mourning choir
Creating its tomb of music, or song's pyre
Over the bones of Salisbury in Wiltshire.

From the Bay of Swanage as I came down in
    Dorset
The shade of Alfred arose shaking a guilty
    hand;   150
He pointed westward to Weymouth and with a
    hoarse voice
Cried: 'See what a fatal gift I gave England!'

Manoeuvring over the broad water like gnats
The naval seaplanes and the giant cruisers
Spread their shadows over the boats and bath-
    ers   155
Who played in Weymouth Bay among the
    shadows.

Then I saw that they floated in blood and blos-
    soms,
The blood of the bathers, the blossoms of the
    boughs
That made the boats: under the dreadnought
    bosoms   159
Crushed and bruised under the huge bows.

Alfred arraigned. 'O my people, what have I
    done
Unto thee, unto thee! O Arthur, Arthur!

Go, boy, over to Glastonbury and ask for Ar-
    thur,
Ask there for Arthur. Say England needs a fa-
    ther.'

He struck the Georgian Memorial in the street
    with his hand   165
As I strike nettles, and left it in the gutter.
He sprang in the trough of a wave and floated
    away,
Went down muttering with his face in his
    hands.

And I heard the air full of the songs of swans.
So I went down westward to Abbotsbury,
    whose waters   170
Echo so many ends that here the swan's vale-
    diction
Dies in the morning and is never dead.

It is the native music of contemporary England
I reflected when wandering along the verge;
And awakens in me a music I understand,   175
The note of the swan who bleeds for her purge.

And though the purge shall bleed her in revo-
    lution,
Dry up her unhappy heart whence song arises,
Rupture that loveliness with mechanical con-
    tortion,   179
If she achieves her perfect peace, it is the prize.

IV

North also to the broad vowels and the moun-
    tains,
Leaving the melancholy swans who mourn for
    the nation,
I went towards Mount Rydal where the ex-
    hausted fountain
Gaped dry and salty over Wordsworth's memo-
    rial.

Here the sun detonated among Cumberland
    cymbals,   185
Reminding me of time and my own shadow:
How soon I shall lie easy, evaded the shambles,

137. **William Longspee,** Longespée, natural son of Henry II, who persuaded King John to sign Magna Charta, 1216. His tomb, with the effigy, is in Salisbury Cathedral.   150. **Alfred,** Alfred the Great (848–900), English king who conquered the Danes. The fatal gift he gives is nationalism.   162. **Arthur,** King Arthur, the central figure in Celtic and British mythology. He was the symbol of medieval unity and culture.

163. **Glastonbury,** town in Somersetshire, England. In legend it is the place where Joseph of Arimathea brought Christianity to England; it is also identified with the Isle of Avalon, where King Arthur and his queen are said to be buried.   170. **Abbotsbury,** English village.   177. **revolution.** The poet accepts the struggle of change in nature as revolutionary. 183. **Mount Rydal,** Wordsworth's house.   184. **Wordsworth.** Early in life Wordsworth believed strongly in revolution.

The tremendous pendulum of the stars and my
    own sorrow.   188

But then from the ground it arose, my shade,
Bearing the teeth that shook in my own jaw:
'I am you. Forget me. No more me. No more
Dallying with the Idalian in the glade.'

He swung his arm to the east, and there
Down the mountain path came a young
    woman,
Wearing a tawdry blouse and careless hair, 195
Who hurried as though pursued by a rumour.

'He's behind me! He's behind me!' she cried,
    running.
Then I caught her hand and drew her from
    the road.
'Who?'—and the pulse of her hand, drumming,
Answered, 'Fear is abroad! Fear is abroad!

'I am the North,' she said, 'whom the South fol-
    lows   201
Like bailiff or police who demand my money.
He caught me on the road and rifled my mine,
Took the gold from my teeth and left me hol-
    low.

'Yes, the South in his bowler and morning jack-
    et,   205
His leather satchel, and handkerchief in pock-
    et,
He called me a whore, but when he'd had his
    worth
Not a penny he paid me for the child I bring
    forth.'

She ran her hand through her hair. I saw
Jarrow on her third finger like a lead ring. 210
'Yes,' she said, 'he absconded after the war,
The husband for whom I wore flowers in the
    spring.

'Write it red in your lines, O write it red,
I starve with my children on the northern sea-
    board.   214
Warn well the pot-bellied and the over-fed,
I'll have their hearts to fill my echoing cup-
    board.'

Then the December star sprang over a rock,
Filling the lines of her face with livid silver;
And a filigree of lace flittered over her shoul-
    der,
Making her anger a monument of silver.   220

'Nevertheless Venus is lovely,' I said,
And heard Wordsworth turn over in his grave:
Windermere flashed in my face at the words,
Where it hung at her eye instead.

'Go down. Go down. The eagle's eyrie,   225
The angel's angle, the abandoned wife's hearth,
These are no places for the nose of the query.
Leave me to birth.'

But beside Windermere I shall move at night
When the West Wind blows into my window
The tresses of Venus where they wave their
    light,   231
Even though I come from a dream of splen-
    dour.

Not less strong than the indomitable rock,
Not less lovely than the lake and the star,
The wife of England roves in the North,   235
Among the derelict cities and the memories of
    war.

v

Last in the Eastern Marshes I made a way
From town to town over the bog and slough,
Where the quartz cathedrals guide the stray
Like pillars in plains or pins in cloth: 240

With against my left ear the advancing sea
Gnawing the shore near Cromer, and water
Fallen around like glass, where tulips brought
A false sunrise, here I could see

The angel of stone in the attitude of song   245
Flicked with a tint of guilt above Norwich;
But its story only asked that the city be made
    rich,
More gilt and glory and less right and wrong.

And a fox over Cambridge and a fish over Yar-
    mouth

192. **Idalian.** Idalia was an ancient town in Cyprus, a center of the worship of Aphrodite (Venus), goddess of love and beauty. 210. **Jarrow,** a shipbuilding town near Newcastle, known during the depression for Sir John Jarvis' efforts to revive industry, but famous earlier as the abode of the Venerable Bede, scholarly and saintly representative of medieval church culture. The picture is a hysterical one of the violence engendered in pursuit of progress.

221. **Venus,** the planet whose name derives from that of the Greek goddess of love. The meaning here is that love is still ours, despite starvation and violence. 223. **Windermere,** the largest lake in England, between Lancashire and Westmoreland. 242. **Cromer,** town on the northeast coast of Norfolk, England. 246. **Norwich,** county city of Norfolk, England. 249. **Cambridge,** county city of Cambridgeshire, England, and seat of the university. In a university or in a simple fishing town, youth is jailed. **Yarmouth,** Great Yarmouth in Norfolk, the headquarters of the herring fishing fleet.

Yapping and yawing for cash and credit: 250
Everywhere here I saw the larks of youth
Tethered to banks for a debit.

Then a sad yammering wormed along the air
Like underground mouths swarming in the sky,
          and I
Heard from the south arise like the rumour of
          despair,   255
The moan of the seven million in the capital
          city.

O London, magnificent monster in whose guts
The bishop lisps with notes and the poet writes
With penny words, whose hunger cannot glut
With glory or gluttony, on whom a world waits,

I saw you astride the South in coils   261

Of insatiable economic appetite:
Mauling the Sussex hills and the broad
Hampshire heath for a maudlin profit.

Where is the Cappadocian for that throat   265
To cut the health and wealth of England loose?
O Political Prince, from this rock release
The national man and woman, who groan!

I see him rise sweating from the North,   269
Up from the deep shaft or the steel yard:—
He comes down not drummed or crowned or
          starred,
But nevertheless inheritor of the earth.

O equitable stars hasten that liberation!

265. **Cappadocian.** The reference is to St. George, who was
probably a Cappadocian.

ROY CAMPBELL

In the realm of the savage, Roy Campbell as a
poet has considerable power; and since, moreover, a period of war lends itself to images of
violence, it cannot be denied that there is a
kind of terrible reality about some of his war
poetry. His is a verse of attack, reflecting fierce
antagonisms and sometimes devoted to abuse.
If his arguments are not logical, they are certainly those of a man obsessed, and his mood
of romantic fanaticism is not alien either to
some religious poetry or to some political
poetry. Even his love poems have a kind of
military imagery, and he has more nearly assimilated the military language for the purposes of poetic imagery than has many another,
more objective, poet.

Campbell was born in Durban, South Africa,
October 2, 1901, of Scottish parentage. When
he was not in school he lived in the wilds of
Natal and Rhodesia. Reaching college age, he
was sent to Oxford; but failing there to pass
the examinations, he went to France, took a
walking tour from Lyons to Marseilles, and
lived for a time among the Marseilles fishermen. Returning to England, he met and married Mary Garman, and retired with his wife to
a fisherman's cabin in the wilder part of Wales.

There Campbell, only nineteen, wrote his first
book, *The Flaming Terrapin*. He worked at odd
jobs among the fisher-folk, but soon returned
to South Africa, there to edit the monthly literary review *Voorslag*. When he lost this job, he
returned to England.

His individualistic and egotistic approach
to life may explain Campbell's evident annoyance with his own literary generation, and particularly with the learned left-wing poets, who
came by the large from aristocratic families. It
may also explain his feeling that he knows the
working people and what is best for them.
Campbell is ambitious. He has written consistently and published, after his first book of
poems, almost a book a year. *Adamastor*
(1930), a single poem, *Choosing a Mast*
(1931), the *Georgiad*, a satirical fantasy in
verse (1931), *Poems* (1932), a small pamphlet, *Pomegranates* (1932), a book on bullfighting called *Taurine Provence* (1932), and
Flowering Reeds (1933) are among his early
works. But soon the left-wing poets of England
won the stage and Campbell ceased to play
the important rôle he desired in literature. This
is significant, because there is always current
in his poetry a kind of personal disdain for men

of letters and a peculiar personal antipathy to poets like Auden and Spender.

When Spain became the theater of the first rivalry between democracy and fascism, Campbell went there. His poems indicate that he blamed the left-wing forces for all the miseries of Spain and despised the English poets who urged intervention and the English writers who came to fight for the Loyalists.

Campbell has engaged as an unrestrained individual in any action which attracted him imaginatively. In 1936 he published *Mithraic Emblems,* in 1937 *Broken Record,* in 1938 *Flowering Rifle,* a verse attack on the left, in 1941 *Sons of the Mistral;* and *Talking Bronco* appeared in 1946. During the Second World War he was not a popular poet in England because of his evident fascist leaning; but he was scarcely quiet. Until he was invalided home he served as an enlisted man in East and North Africa, although apparently more in a clerical capacity than he indicates. Upon returning to England he joined the British Broadcasting Company as a talks producer. He continued to write political and satirical poems explaining his position and arguing that he did not believe in the war since it was fought against the wrong foe, but that he preferred fighting with the English to fighting with, or being invaded by, alien fascists from abroad. As soon as the war ended he began again to publish poetry in which his anti-Semitism, as well as anti-Communism, is unmistakable.

The Volunteer's Reply to the Poet

('WILL IT BE SO AGAIN?')

. . . So the Soldier replied to the Poet,
Oh yes! it will all be the same,
But a bloody sight worse, and you know it
Since you have a hand in the game:
And you'll be the first in the racket   5

To sell us a similar dope,
Wrapped up in a rosier packet,
But noosed with as cunning a rope.
You coin us the catchwords and phrases
For which to be slaughtered; and then,   10
While thousands are blasted to blazes,
Sit picking your nose with your pen.
We know what you're bursting to tell us,
By heart. It is all very fine.   14
We must swallow the Bait that you sell us
And pay for your Hook and your Line.
But his pride for a soldier suffices
Since someone must carry the can;
In war, or depression, or crisis,
It's what you expect of a man.   20
But when we have come to the Isthmus
That bridges the Slump to the War.
We shall contact a new Father Christmas
Like the one we contacted before,
Deploring the one he replaces   25
Like you do (it's part of the show!)
But with those same mincing grimaces
And that mealy old kisser we know!
And he'll patent a cheap cornucopia
For all that our purse can afford,   30
And rent us a flat in Utopia
With dreams for our lodging and board.
And we'll hand in our Ammo and Guns
As we handed them in once before,
And he'll lock them up safe; till our sons   35
Are conscripted for Freedom once more.
We can die for our faith by the million
And laugh at our bruises and scars,
But hush! for the Poet-Civilian
Is weeping, between the cigars.   40
Mellifluous, sweeter than Cadbury's,
The M.O.I. Nightingale (Hush!)
Is lining his pockets with Bradburies
So his feelings come out with a rush,
For our woes are the cash in his kitty   45
When his voice he so kindly devotes
In sentiment, pathos, and pity,
To bringing huge lumps to the throats
Of our widows, and sweethearts, and trollops,
Since it sells like hot cakes to the town   50

41. **Cadbury's,** one of the best known English brands of chocolate. 42. **M.O.I.,** Ministry of Information; British equivalent of the Office of War Information. 43. **Bradburies,** pound notes, so called from the name of a cashier of the Bank of England whose signature used to appear upon all notes.

As he doles out the Goitre in dollops
And the public is gulping it down.
Oh well may he weep for the soldier,
Who weeps at a guinea a tear,   54
For although his invention gets mouldier,
It keeps him his job in the rear.
When my Mrs. the organ is wheeling
And my adenoids wheeze to the sky,
He will publish the hunger I'm feeling
And rake in his cheque with a sigh: 60
And when with a trayful of matches
And laces, you hawk in the street,
O comrades, in tatters and patches,
Rejoice! since we're in for a treat:
For when we have died in the gutter   65
To safeguard his income and state,
Be sure that the Poet will utter
Some beautiful thoughts on our Fate!

Dreaming Spires

Through villages of yelping tykes
With skulls on totem-poles, and wogs
Exclaiming at our motor bikes
With more amazement than their dogs:

Respiring fumes of pure phlogiston   5
On hardware broncos, half-machine,
With arteries pulsing to the piston
And hearts inducting gasolene:

Buckjumping over ruts and boulders,
The Centaurs of an age of steel,   10
Engrafted all save head and shoulders
Into the horsepower of the wheel—

We roared into the open country,
Scattering vultures, kites, and crows;
All Nature scolding our effrontery   15
In raucous agitation rose.

Zoology went raving stark
To meet us on the open track—
The whole riff-raff of Noah's Ark
With which the wilderness was black.   20

With kicks and whinnies, bucks and snorts,
Their circuses stampeded by:
A herd of wildebeest cavorts,
And somersaults against the sky:

Across the stripes of Zebras sailing,   25
The eyesight rattles like a cane
That's rattled down an area-railing
Until it blurs upon the brain.

The lions flee with standing hackles,
Leaving their feast before they've dined: 30
Their funeral poultry flaps and cackles
To share the breeze they feel behind.

Both wart- and road-hog vie together,
As they and we, petarding smoke,
Belly to earth and hell for leather,   35
In fumes of dust and petrol choke.

We catch the madness they have caught,
Stand in the footrests, and guffaw—
Till shadowed by a looming thought
And visited with sudden awe,   40

We close our throttles, clench the curb,
And hush the rumble of our tyres,
Abashed and fearful to disturb
The City of the Dreaming Spires—

The City of Giraffes!—a People   45
Who live between the earth and skies,
Each in his lone religious steeple,
Keeping a light-house with his eyes:

Each his own stairway, tower, and stylite,
Ascending on his saintly way   50
Up rungs of gold into the twilight
And leafy ladders to the day:

Chimneys of silence! at whose summit,
Like storks, the daydreams love to nest:
The Earth, descending like a plummet   55
Into the oceans of unrest,

They can ignore—whose nearer neighbour
The sun is, with the stars and moon
That on their hides, with learned labour,
Tattooed the hieroglyphic rune.   60

Muezzins that from airy pylons
Peer out above the golden trees
Where the mimosas fleece the silence
Or slumber on the drone of bees:

---

51. **Goitre.** Cf. "lumps," l. 48. **dollops,** gobs.
Dreaming Spires, a long roaring poem about a motorcycle
ride through the Sudan.   1. **tykes,** mongrel dogs; hence,
boorish people.   2. **wogs,** British slang for colored troops.
Probably first employed on Sudanese, whose hair resembled
that of a golliwog.   5. **phlogiston,** hypothetical principle of
fire, so called by De Stahl, 1702, long since shown to be erroneous.

23. **wildebeest,** large antelope.

Nought of this earth they see but flowers   65
Quilting a carpet to the sky
To where some pensive crony towers
Or Kilimanjaro takes the eye.

Their baser passions fast on greens
Where, never to intrude or push,   70
Their bodies live like submarines,
Far down beneath them, in the bush.

Around their heads the solar glories,
With their terrestrial sisters fly—
Rollers, and orioles, and lories,   75
And trogons of the evening sky.

Their bloodstream with a yeasty leaven
Exalts them to the stars above,
As we are raised, though not to heaven,
By drink—or when we fall in love.   80

By many a dismal crash and wreck
Our dreams are weaned of aviation,
But these have beaten (by a neck!)
The steepest laws of gravitation.

Some animals have all the luck,   85
Who hurl their breed in nature's throat—
Out of a gumtree by a buck,
Or escalator—by a goat!

When I have worked my ticket, pension,
And whatsoever I can bum,   90
To colonise the fourth dimension,
With my Beloved, I may come,

And buy a pair of stilts for both,
And hire a periscope for two,
To vegetate in towering sloth   95
Out here amongst these chosen few . . .

Or so my fancies seemed to sing
To see, across the gulf of years,
The soldiers of a reigning King
Confront those ghostly halberdiers.   100

But someone kicks his starter back:
Anachronism cocks its ears.
Like Beefeaters who've got the sack
With their own heads upon their spears;

Like Leftwing Poets at the hint   105
Of work, or danger, or the blitz,

Or when they catch the deadly glint
Of satire, swordplay of the wits,—

Into the dusk of leafy oceans
They fade away with phantom tread;   110
And changing gears, reversing notions,
The roar to Moshi roars ahead.

One Transport Lost

WHERE, packed as tight as space can fit
   them
The soldiers retch, and snore, and stink,
It was no bunch of flowers that hit them
And woke them up, that night, to drink.

Dashing the bulkheads red with slaughter,   5
In the steep wash that swept the hold,
Men, corpses, kitbags, blood, and water,
Colliding and commingling rolled.

Some clung, like flies, in fear and wonder,
Clutched to the crossbeams, out of reach,   10
Till sprayed from thence by jets of thunder
That spouted rumbling from the breach.

In this new world of blast and suction,
The bulk-head tilted to a roof;
Friend aided friend—but to destruction,   15
And valour seemed its own reproof.

Forced by the pent explosive airs
In the huge death-gasp of its shell,
Or sucked, like Jonah, by their prayers
From forth that spiracle of Hell—   20

The ones that catapulted from it
Saw the whole hull reverse its dome,
Then ram the depths, like some huge comet,
Flood-lit with phosphorus and foam.

The shark and grampus might reprieve,   25
After their jaunt upon a raft,
The few that got Survivors' Leave—
But those who perished would have laughed!

Their fiercest thirst they've quenched and
   cupped,
And smashed the glass (this life of slaves!);

---

68. **Kilimanjaro,** the highest mountain peak in Africa.
103. **Beefeaters,** traditional guardians of the Tower of London;
they wear a traditional and distinctive uniform.

112. **Moshi,** a city in Africa.
One Transport Lost, an account of the torpedoing of a
troopship. 25. **grampus,** a whale. 27. **Survivors' Leave,**
the furlough granted to those who were rescued from shipwreck
during World War II.

No hectoring Redcaps interrupt 31
Their fornication with the waves.

For us, this world of Joad and Julian,
The dithering of abortive schemes;
For them, the infinite, cerulean 35
Suspension of desires and dreams.

So save your Bait, you Bards and Thinkers!
For us who daren't refuse to chew
Hook, line, and swivel, trace and sinkers,
And rod and all, and like it too! 40

For them, the wave, the melancholy
Chant of the wind that tells no lies;
The breakers roll their funeral volley
To which the thundering cliff replies.

The black cape-hens in decent crêpe 45
Will mourn them till the Last Event;
The roaring headlands of the Cape
Are lions on their monument.

Monologue

No DISILLUSIONMENT can gravel,
A mercenary volunteer
Who joins an alien force, to travel
And fight, for fifty pounds a year.
A grizzled sergeant of the pommies, 5
A gaunt centurion of the wogs,
Can fall for no Utopian promise
The Bait of grasping demagogues.
Against the usurers of tears,
Fraternity, and all that dope, 10
I learned (while wet behind the ears)
The use of Nelson's telescope.
The Left Wing Prophet, Bard, and Seer,

Sleek Babbitts of the Age to Be,
Who farm this carnage from the rear 15
Have yet to find a fly on me.
I know the love that shares our fleeces,
The love that makes our thinkers fools,
The love of thirty silver pieces—
A soldier's value, or a mule's! 20
The same for all who trade in doves
And fatten on the world's distress,
The pedlars of fraternal loves,
And creeping Shylocks of the Press.
Against each rearguard propheteer 25
And Tartuffe from the M.O.I.,
Experience wads my dainty ear,
And through the solemn bluff, my eye,
For bayonet-practice, punching sawdust,
Lets in the glint I love to see— 30
For where the sacking gapes the broadest
The daylight laughs and winks at me!

I'm fighting for no better world
But for a worse—the blasted pit
Wherein the bones of this were hurled—
And our hegemony of it! 36
I'm fighting for a funkhole-warren
Of bureaucrats, who've come to stay,
Because I'd rather, than the foreign
Equivalent, it should be they. 40
We all become the thing we fight
Till differing solely in the palms
And fists that semaphore (to Right
Or Left) their imbecile salaams.
Each of the other, fifty times, 45
Will plagiarise the stock-in-trade
Of purges, massacres, and crimes,
Before their hatred is allayed.
For I have lived, of three crusades,
The heroism and the pathos, 50
Seen how the daft illusion fades,
And learned of victory the bathos.
But when the lava has been poured
Through huge ravines of change and loss,
Of all most hated or adored, 55
One thing remains intact, the Cross!
It is the rifle on one's shoulder
That galls one on the endless march:
It is the backward-rolling boulder

---

31. **Redcaps,** English army slang for military police, so called
from the red tops of their caps. 33. **Joad and Julian,** Dr.
C. E. M. Joad and Julian Huxley. The philosopher and biologist
were the two most popular members of the British Broadcasting
Corporation's "Brains Trust" program, similar to the American
"Information Please." 45. **cape-hens,** skuas; large black-
marked gulls. 46. **Last Event,** the Last Judgment.
Monologue. This satirical poem states Campbell's position as
that of one who does not like the English, but prefers them to the
tyranny against which they are fighting. 5. **pommies,** Australian term for British emigrants. As a South African, Campbell also employs the word. The Australian troops in World
War I used the word for all British troops. 12. **Nelson's
telescope.** At the battle of Cape St. Vincent, Nelson, when
informed that the Commander-in-Chief had ordered him to
withdraw his ship, is said to have raised his telescope to his
blind eye and remarked that he could not see the signal.
13. **Left Wing Prophet.** Campbell is well known for his
fanatical opposition to liberalism.

19. **silver pieces,** the traditional thirty pieces of silver for
which Judas is said to have betrayed Christ. 26. **Tartuffe,**
a hypocritical religious character in Molière's play of that name.
49. **three crusades,** World War I, the Spanish Civil War (where
Campbell was vociferously pro-Franco), and World War II.

We sisyphise with backs that arch: 60
It is the axle of our lorry,
This breakdown planet, bogged in mire:
It is the road we stamp and quarry,
As prisoners, on the sands of fire:
It is the iron that brands us men—   65
Both friend and enemy as one,
The sword of Victory, and then
The Victor's crutch, when all is done!
Field Marshals, Captains, and Lieutenants
And we poor gunfood of the ranks,   70
Carry it as a curse or penance
Whether with blasphemy or thanks;
Whether rebelliously, or knowing
And prizing it for what it's worth—
All Heaven upon our thews bestowing   75
The Atlas-burden of the Earth.

Let me be there to share the strain
And with the poorest pull my weight
As in the Catacombs of Spain
When all the world was Red with hate!

60. **sisyphise.** The image derives from the myth of Sisyphus, who was condemned to push a large stone to the top of a hill, only to have it roll down the hill again.

I know that all ideals miscarry,   81
That cowards use the blows we strike,
That liars aim the guns we carry
Screeching their hatred on the Mike.
Yet lest that burden touch the ground   85
I would be there to lift that prize,
And with the lowest conscript found
That ever 'Freedom' chained with lies,
Rather than feast on poor men's bones
And cheat the worker of his bread   90
With Judas-kisses, sighs, and groans,
Between the armchair and the bed.
I love the hard and stony track
Where humour flashes from the flint,
And though on crutches crawling back   95
Trussed like a turkey on a splint—
If you should ask what other joy
Amongst my fellow-slaves I found:
I dare not speak, I am a Goy—
One of the Christian Underground.   100
From there, whichever way they work us,
Will boomerang the last surprise—
Out of the red sands of the Circus
The great Cathedrals climbed the skies!

❧ A Search for the Inner Self

KARL SHAPIRO

Karl Shapiro's poems had begun to appear in magazines as early as 1934, and his first collection, *Poems,* was published in 1935; but it was not until 1941, the year he was drafted, that his work received real notice. In that year a group of his poems under the title "Noun" was included in *Five Young American Poets* and was favorably received. *Person, Place and Thing* appeared in 1942, while its author was serving as a corporal in the Medical Corps in New Guinea, and Shapiro was immediately pointed out as one of the first important poets of the Second World War. In *V-Letter and Other Poems* (1944) it was clear that his talent was deepening, and such critics as F. O. Matthiessen praised his work. He was called a native Auden—which is perhaps as much censure as it is praise—and it began to seem that he was being pushed so rapidly as to endanger his growth as a poet. *Essay on Rime* (1945), according to Conrad Aiken, put Shapiro at the head of his generation; but at the same time this tour de force, a long verse essay on such modern poets as Shapiro admired, revealed most of his failings. For the young poet frequently relies on the witty phrase or the clever idea, rather than upon penetration or understanding, and he is sometimes pretentious. At his best, however, and when most engrossed in himself, he is a good modern lyricist, tracing the changes within the individual life shattered by war. His talent may not be the greatest of his generation, but like Auden's it is a talent easily tuned to sing an age of lost ideals and the contradictions between reason and emotion.

Shapiro was born in Baltimore on November 10, 1913. As a student at the University of Virginia, 1932–33, and at Johns Hopkins University, 1936–40, he became thoroughly acquainted with the techniques of poetry. His early poems were more clever than convincing, but the war deepened his feeling and his understanding, in particular his understanding of himself as intellectual and artist. He has received a number of prizes which have kept him in the foreground as a literary figure: the Jeannette Sewell Davis Award in 1941, the Helen Haire Levinson Award in 1942, the Pulitzer Prize for poetry (for *V-Letter*) in 1944, and a Guggenheim Post-Service Fellowship in the same year. He is married to Evalyn Katz, who as his fiancée during the war helped to establish his reputation by getting his poems into the hands of the publishers. In 1946 he became Consultant in Poetry at the Library of Congress, and in 1947 took a teaching post at Johns Hopkins University in the city of his birth.

It appears from recent poems published in magazines that Shapiro, like Auden, has examined the religious emotion, only to reject Catholicism. He stressed the personal problem of divided parentage—his mother was Catholic, his father Jewish—in the long "Recapitulations" (in *Trial of a Poet,* 1947), and referred there to his parents, although not by name. As their son, Shapiro records two types of religious inquiry and indicates a stand—probably with the Existentialists.

Karl Shapiro's is a facile and witty poetry, but his stature will depend, in the long run, on whether he completely develops a medium unmistakably his own and on whether he attains real emotional depth.

Necropolis

EVEN in death they prosper; even in the
    death
Where lust lies senseless and pride fallow
The mouldering owners of rents and labor
Prosper and improve the high hill.

For theirs is the stone whose name is deepest
    cut;   5
Theirs the facsimile temple, theirs
The iron acanthus and the hackneyed Latin,
The boxwood rows and all the birds.

And even in death the poor are thickly herded
In intimate congestion under streets and alleys.
Look at the standard sculpture, the cheap   11
Synonymous slabs, the machined crosses.

Yes, even in death the cities are unplanned.
The heirs govern from the old centers;
They will not remove. And the ludicrous an-
    gels,   15
Remains of the poor, will never fly
But only multiply in the green grass.

University

TO HURT the Negro and avoid the Jew
    Is the curriculum. In mid-September
The entering boys, identified by hats,
Wander in a maze of mannered brick
      Where boxwood and magnolia brood   5
      And columns with imperious stance
      Like rows of ante-bellum girls
        Eye them, outlanders.

In whited cells, on lawns equipped for peace,
Under the arch, and lofty banister,   10
Equals shake hands, unequals blankly pass;
The exemplary weather whispers, 'Quiet, quiet'
      And visitors on tiptoe leave
      For the raw North, the unfinished West,
      As the young, detecting an advantage,
        Practice a face.   16

Necropolis, literally, city of the dead, a burial ground. The poem compares the burial ground of the wealthy with that of the poor. 7. **acanthus,** here, a formalized leaf of the acanthus tree, employed in the Corinthian order of architecture.

Where, on their separate hill, the colleges,
Like manor houses of an older law,
Gaze down embankments on a land in fee,
The Deans, dry spinsters over family plate,   20
    Ring out the English name like coin,
    Humor the snob and lure the lout.
    Within the precincts of this world
      Poise is a club.

But on the neighboring range, misty and high,
The past is absolute: some luckless race   26
Dull with inbreeding and conformity
Wears out its heart, and comes barefoot and
    bad
    For charity or jail. The scholar
    Sanctions their obsolete disease;   30
    The gentleman revolts with shame
      At his ancestor.

And the true nobleman, once a democrat,
Sleeps on his private mountain. He was one
Whose thought was shapely and whose dream
    was broad;   35
This school he held his art and epitaph.
    But now it takes from him his name,
    Falls open like a dishonest look,
    And shows us, rotted and endowed,
      Its senile pleasure.

The Twins

LIKENESS has made them animal and shy.
  See how they turn their full gaze left and
    right,
Seeking the other, yet not moving close;
Nothing in their relationship is gross,
But soft, conspicuous, like giraffes. And why
Do they not speak except by sudden sight?   6

Sisters kiss freely and unsubtle friends
Wrestle like lovers; brothers loudly laugh:
These in a dreamier bondage dare not touch.
Each is the other's soul and hears too much
The heartbeat of the other; each apprehends
The sad duality and the imperfect half.   12

The one lay sick, the other wandered free,
But like a child to a small plot confined
Walked a short way and dumbly reappeared.
Is it not all-in-all of what they feared,   16
The single death, the obvious destiny
That maims the miracle their will designed?

For they go emptily from face to face,
Keeping the instinctive partnership of birth
A ponderous marriage and a sacred name;   21
Theirs is the pride of shouldering each the
    same
The old indignity of Esau's race
And Dromio's denouement of tragic mirth.
        (*March 21, 1942. At sea*)

V-Letter

I LOVE you first because your face is fair,
  Because your eyes Jewish and blue,
Set sweetly with the touch of foreignness
Above the cheekbones, stare rather than dream.
Often your countenance recalls a boy   5
  Blue-eyed and small, whose silent mischief
Tortured his parents and compelled my hate
    To wish his ugly death.
Because of this reminder, my soul's trouble,
And for your face, so often beautiful,   10
    I love you, wish you life.

I love you first because you wait, because
  For your own sake, I cannot write
Beyond these words. I love you for these words
That sting and creep like insects and leave filth.
I love you for the poverty you cry   16
  And I bend down with tears of steel
That melt your hand like wax, not for this war
    The droplets shattering
Those candle-glowing fingers of my joy,   20
But for your name of agony, my love,
    That cakes my mouth with salt.

And all your imperfections and perfections
  And all your magnitude of grace
And all this love explained and unexplained
Is just a breadth. I see you woman-size   26
And this looms larger and more goddess-like
  Than silver goddesses on screens.
I see you in the ugliness of light,
    Yet you are beautiful,   30
And in the dark of absence your full length
Is such as meets my body to the full
    Though I am starved and huge.

The Twins.   23. **Esau's race.** Esau, the son of Isaac, sold his birthright to his twin brother, Jacob (Genesis 25 : 29–34). 24. **Dromio,** Dromio of Ephesus and Dromio of Syracuse, twin brothers, attendant on the twin Antipholuses, in Shakespeare's *Comedy of Errors.*
"V-Letter" by Karl Shapiro, copyright 1943 The New Yorker Magazine, Inc. Reprinted from *V-Letter and Other Poems* by Karl Shapiro by permission of Reynal and Hitchcock, Inc.

You turn me from these days as from a scene
    Out of an open window far   35
Where lies the foreign city and the war.
You are my home and in your spacious love
I dream to march as under flaring flags
    Until the door is gently shut.
Give me the tearless lesson of your pride,   40
    Teach me to live and die
As one deserving anonymity,
The mere devotion of a house to keep
    A woman and a man.

Give me the free and poor inheritance   45
    Of our own kind, not furniture
Of education, nor the prophet's pose,
The general cause of words, the hero's stance,
The ambitions incommensurable with flesh,
    But the drab makings of a room   50
Where sometimes in the afternoon of thought
    The brief and blinding flash
May light the enormous chambers of your will
And show the gracious Parthenon that time
    Is ever measured by.   55

As groceries in a pantry gleam and smile
    Because they are important weights
Bought with the metal minutes of your pay,
So do these hours stand in solid rows,
    The dowry for a use in common life.   60
    I love you first because your years
Lead to my matter-of-fact and simple death
    Or to our open marriage,
And I pray nothing for my safety back,
Not even luck, because our love is whole   65
    Whether I live or fail.

The Intellectual

*What should the wars do with these jigging
    fools?*

The man behind the book may not be man,
His own man or the book's or yet the time's,
But still be whole, deciding what he can
In praise of politics or German rimes;

But the intellectual lights a cigarette   5
And offers it lit to the lady, whose odd smile
Is the merest hyphen—lest he should forget
What he has been resuming all the while.

He talks to overhear, she to withdraw
To some interior feminine fireside   10
Where the back arches, beauty puts forth a
    paw
Like a black puma stretching in velvet pride,

Making him think of cats, a stray of which
Some days sets up a howling in his brain,
Pure interference such as this neat bitch   15
Seems to create from listening disdain.

But talk is all the value, the release,
Talk is the very fillip of an act,
The frame and subject of the masterpiece   19
Under whose film of age the face is cracked.

His own forehead glows like expensive wood,
But back of it the mind is disengaged,
Self-sealing clock recording bad and good
At constant temperature, intact, unaged.

But strange, his body is an open house   25
Inviting every passerby to stay;
The city to and fro beneath his brows
Wanders and drinks and chats from night to
    day.

Think of a private thought, indecent room   29
Where one might kiss his daughter before bed!
Life is embarrassed; shut the family tomb,
Console your neighbor for his recent dead;

Do something! die in Spain or paint a green
Gouache, go into business (Rimbaud did),
Or start another Little Magazine,   35
Or move in with a woman, have a kid.

Invulnerable, impossible, immune,
Do what you will, your will will not be done
But dissipate the light of afternoon
Till evening flickers like the midnight sun,   40

And midnight shouts and dies: I'd rather be
A milkman walking in his sleep at dawn

The Intellectual. The poem comments on the inability of the
intellectual to act. It is reminiscent of Eliot's early poems on
the boredom of the upper class; but Shapiro here argues for
decision as against indecision and retreat.

33. **die in Spain,** reference to the Spanish Civil War, in which
a considerable number of intellectuals were among those killed.
34. **Gouache,** a method of painting with opaque water colors.
Rimbaud, Arthur Rimbaud (1854–91), French poet, who
turned from poetry to become an ivory trader in Abyssinia.
35. **Little Magazine,** generic name for all small magazines,
usually run without financial backing and almost always
avant garde.

Bearing fat quarts of cream, and so be free,
Crossing alone and cold from lawn to lawn.

I'd rather be a barber and cut hair   45
Than walk with you in gilt museum halls,
You and the puma-lady, she so rare
Exhaling her silk soul upon the walls.

Go take yourselves apart, but let me be
The fault you find with everyman. I spit,   50
I laugh, I fight; and you, *l'homme qui rit,*
Swallow your stale saliva, and still sit.

Jew

THE NAME is immortal but only the name,
      for the rest
Is a nose that can change in the weathers of
      time or persist
Or die out in confusion or model itself on the
      best.

But the name is a language itself that is whis-
      pered and hissed
Through the houses of ages, and ever a lan-
      guage the same,   5
And ever and ever a blow on our heart like a
      fist.

And this last of our dream in the desert, O
      curse of our name,
Is immortal as Abraham's voice in our frag-
      ment of prayer
Adenai, Adenai, for our bondage of murder
      and shame!

And the word for the murder of Christ will dry
      out on the air   10
Though the race is no more and the temples
      are closed of our will
And the peace is made fast on the earth and
      the earth is made fair;

Our name is impaled in the heart of the world
      on a hill
Where we suffer to die by the hands of our-
      selves, and to kill.

Troop Train

IT STOPS the town we come through. Workers
      raise
Their oily arms in good salute and grin.
Kids scream as at a circus. Business men
Glance hopefully and go their measured way.
And women standing at their dumbstruck
      door   5
More slowly wave and seem to warn us back,
As if a tear blinding the course of war
Might once dissolve our iron in their sweet
      wish.

Fruit of the world, O clustered on ourselves
We hang as from a cornucopia   10
In total friendliness, with faces bunched
To spray the streets with catcalls and with
      leers.
A bottle smashes on the moving ties
And eyes fixed on a lady smiling pink   14
Stretch like a rubber-band and snap and sting
The mouth that wants the drink-of-water kiss.

And on through crummy continents and days,
Deliberate, grimy, slightly drunk we crawl,
The good-bad boys of circumstance and
      chance,   19
Whose bucket-helmets bang the empty wall
Where twist the murdered bodies of our
      packs
Next to the guns that only seem themselves.
And distance like a strap adjusted shrinks,
Tightens across the shoulder and holds firm.

Here is a deck of cards; out of this hand   25
Dealer, deal me my luck, a pair of bulls,
The right draw to a flush, the one-eyed jack.
Diamonds and hearts are red but spades are
      black,
And spades are spades and clubs are clovers—
      black.
But deal me winners, souvenirs of peace.   30
This stands to reason and arithmetic,
Luck also travels and not all come back.

---

51. *l'homme qui rit,* the man who laughs.
Jew. This poem is concerned with the Jews' eternal problem
of survival.   9. **Adenai,** Hebrew for *God.*

Troop Train.   20. **bucket-helmets,** helmets worn during
World War II.   26. **bulls . . . flush . . . jack,** terms for
cards in the game of poker.

Trains lead to ships and ships to death or
    trains,
And trains to death or trucks, and trucks to
    death,
Or trucks lead to the march, the march to
    death,   35

Or that survival which is all our hope;
And death leads back to trucks and trains and
    ships,
But life leads to the march, O flag! at last
The place of life found after trains and death
—Nightfall of nations brilliant after war.

❦ Poets of the Present

DYLAN THOMAS

The influence of Dylan Thomas on younger
poets today is strong, for he, like Hart Crane,
was in a sense a very late romantic whose faith
in man's creativeness did not waver in a
world where man's self-destructiveness is evident. Moreover, he is a symbolist whose use of
language and of association in thought is often
unique. Consequently, the youngest writers today often reject the influence of the intellectuals and wits like Auden and Shapiro, and
find in Thomas a new object of study and imitation.

Thomas, who was a documentary film editor
during the war and was later connected with
the British Broadcasting Company, was born
in Wales in 1914 and was educated at the
Swansea Grammar School. His first book, *Eighteen Poems,* was published in 1934 and his second, *Twenty-Five Poems,* in 1937. But this was
the period when Auden and his school more or
less dominated the English literary scene, and
the reputation of Thomas, who was promptly labeled a late romantic, suffered. By 1939, however, he was gaining prominence; that year
saw the publication of *The Map of Love* and
his first book to appear in America, *The World
I Breathe.* With the successive publication of
New Poems (1943), *Deaths and Entrances*
(1946), and a representation of both prose and

poetry, *Selected Writings* (1946), Thomas'
standing was firmly established.

Whether or not at the time of his sudden
death in 1953 Thomas was progressing toward
greater logical lucidity is a matter of disagree-
ment among critics. Dudley Fitts, for example,
pointed out that while the first poems showed
a "wild, disordered, super-Dali romanticism"
and a tendency to address himself "solely to
the aesthetes," his later work exhibits more
control. On the other hand, certain critics
have deplored this very thinning out of his
overrich imagery. It is clear, in any case, that
the experiences of the war, which hastened
the maturing of so many young poets, brought
to Thomas greater depth of emotion and an
enlarged scheme of reference. Although his
early poetry, combining the imagery of primitive Celtic rituals of rebirth and sacrifice with
references to the Christian symbols, treated
indeed all ecstasy as religious in the sense
that ecstasy touched on creation, his later work
is more realistic and more profound and faces
squarely the destructiveness of the war.

Some of Thomas' prose pieces, like *The Portrait of the Artist as a Young Dog* (1940), are
not profound but merely clever. This tale of a
young Welshman's adolescence is a slight
though graceful performance, with none of the

deep inner drama of Joyce's book, of which the title is obviously a parody. But in his poetry, when he describes the ecstatic incidents in the growth of a poet's mind, he achieves an intense lyricism; he affirms—often in metaphysical statements—the importance of the life force, the urge of life. Against all the nay-sayers to life, Thomas asserts the value of sensuous existence; even when considering the horrors of war he expresses a strong, almost biological belief in living intensely.

Thomas' first name means "the wave"; commonest among his symbols are those of water, tide, and light. He seems to delight, too, in using images of fertility and growth. Each of his poems gives a momentary sense of physical or spiritual power; even in picturing the startling and horrifying facts of war, Thomas refutes the arguments of skepticism. Some of his own statements about his technique hint at a reliance on the superrational and on a self-stimulation, a kind of poetic madness, for escape from the factual and chaotic world. One can trace in his romanticism the influence of Yeats, in his Freudianism the influence of Lawrence. He seemed to see the bard as a world prophet, as one who leads the people back to faith.

To-day, This Insect, and the World I Breathe

To-day, this insect, and the world I breathe,
　Now that my symbols have outelbowed
　　space,
Time at the city spectacles, and half
The dear, daft time I take to nudge the sentence,
In trust and tale have I divided sense,　　5
Slapped down the guillotine, the blood-red
　　double
Of head and tail made witnesses to this

"Today, This Insect, and the World I Breathe," "The Hand That Signed the Paper Felled a City," "When All My Five and Country Senses See," from *The World I Breathe* by Dylan Thomas, published by New Directions.
Today . . . Breathe. With his usual reliance on words as images out of which the idea is born, Thomas here is asserting that through the creative act of poetry he can create the magic of belief. Whatever the outward symbols of disaster, the poet should, Thomas feels, write of his madman's love of man and consequently bring this love to pass.

Murder of Eden and green genesis.

The insect certain is the plague of fables.

This story's monster has a serpent caul,　　10
Blind in the coil scrams round the blazing outline,
Measures his own length on the garden wall
And breaks his shell in the last shocked beginning;
A crocodile before the chrysalis,　　14
Before the fall from love the flying heartbone,
Winged like a sabbath ass this children's piece
Uncredited blows Jericho on Eden.

The insect fable is the certain promise.

Death: death of Hamlet and the nightmare
　　madmen,
An air-drawn windmill on a wooden horse,　　20
John's beast, Job's patience, and the fibs of vision,
Greek in the Irish sea the ageless voice:
'Adam I love, my madmen's love is endless,
No tell-tale lover has an end more certain,
All legends' sweethearts on a tree of stories,　　25
My cross of tales behind the fabulous curtain.'

The Hand That Signed the Paper Felled a City

The hand that signed the paper felled a city;
　Five sovereign fingers taxed the breath,
Doubled the globe of dead and halved a country;
These five kings did a king to death.　　4

The mighty hand leads to a sloping shoulder,
The finger joints are cramped with chalk;
A goose's quill has put an end to murder
That put an end to talk.

The hand that signed the treaty bred a fever,
And famine grew, and locusts came;　　10
Great is the hand that holds dominion over
Man by a scribbled name.

The five kings count the dead but do not soften
The crusted wound nor pat the brow;
A hand rules pity as a hand rules heaven;　　15
Hands have no tears to flow.

The Hand . . . City. The "hand" here becomes a symbol of pitiless and dictatorial power. The "city" probably refers to Munich.

When All My Five and Country Senses See

WHEN all my five and country senses see,
The fingers will forget green thumbs
and mark
How, through the halfmoon's vegetable eye,
Husk of young stars and handfull zodiac,
Love in the frost is pared and wintered by,   5
The whispering ears will watch love drummed
away
Down breeze and shell to a discordant beach,
And, lashed to syllables, the lynx tongue cry
That her fond wounds are mended bitterly.
My nostrils see her breath burn like a bush.   10

My one and noble heart has witnesses
In all love's countries, that will grope awake;
And when blind sleep drops on the spying
senses,
The heart is sensual, though five eyes break.

Fern Hill

NOW AS I was young and easy under the
apple boughs
About the lilting house and happy as the grass
was green,
The night above the dingle starry,
Time let me hail and climb
Golden in the heydays of his eyes,   5
And honoured among wagons I was prince of
the apple towns
And once below a time I lordly had the trees
and leaves
Trail with daisies and barley
Down the rivers of the windfall light.

And as I was green and carefree, famous
among the barns   10

When All . . . See. Since Thomas relies on a kind of madness of words to create mood, his writing is difficult to explain; but the poem is a cry for the return to the sensual as the only way of feeling and creating. Thomas always denies the validity of the rational mind.   **14. five eyes,** the five senses.
"Fern Hill," "Holy Spring," "Among Those Killed in the Dawn Raid," and "And Death Shall Have No Dominion" from *New Poems* by Dylan Thomas, published by New Directions.
Fern Hill. The Celtic poet's statement of youthful storing-up of feeling and images later to be used as poetry is not unlike Wordsworth's *Prelude* in intent, though very different in style and philosophy. It has to do with the poetic response to nature when the senses are played upon by its sensual aspect. Youth is, Thomas feels, not concerned with death.

About the happy yard and singing as the farm
was home,
In the sun that is young once only,
Time let me play and be
Golden in the mercy of his means,
And green and golden I was huntsman and
herdsman, the calves   15
Sang to my horn, the foxes on the hills barked
clear and cold,
And the sabbath rang slowly
In the pebbles of the holy streams.

All the sun long it was running, it was lovely,
the hay-
Fields high as the house, the tunes from the
chimneys, it was air,   20
And playing, lovely and watery
And fire green as grass.
And nightly under the simple stars
As I rode to sleep the owls were bearing the
farm away,
All the moon long I heard, blessed among
stables, the nightjars   25
Flying with the ricks, and the horses
Flashing into the dark.

And then to awake, and the farm, like a wan-
derer white
With the dew, come back, the cock on his
shoulder: it was all
Shining, it was Adam and maiden,   30
The sky gathered again
And the sun grew round that very day.
So it must have been after the birth of the
simple light
In the first, spinning place, the spellbound
horses walking warm
Out of the whinnying green stable   35
On to the fields of praise.

And honoured among foxes and pheasants by
the gay house
Under the new made clouds and happy as the
heart was long,
In the sun born over and over,
I ran my heedless ways,   40
My wishes raced through the house high
hay
And nothing I cared, at my sky blue trades,
that time allows
In all his tuneful turning so few and such
morning songs

Before the children green and golden
Follow him out of grace,   45

Nothing I cared, in the lamb white days, that
time would take me
Up to the swallow thronged loft by the shadow
of my hand,
In the moon that is always rising,
Nor that riding to sleep
I should hear him fly with the high fields
And wake to the farm forever fled from the
childless land.   51
Oh as I was young and easy in the mercy of
his means,
Time held me green and dying
Though I sang in my chains like the sea.

Holy Spring

O

OUT OF A bed of love
When that immortal hospital made one
more move to sooth
The cureless counted body,
And ruin and his causes
Over the barbed and shooting sea assured an
army   5
And swept into our wounds and
houses,
I climb to greet the war in which I have no
heart but only
That one dark I owe my light,
Call for confessor and wiser mirror but there
are none
To glow after the god stoning night
And I am struck as lonely as a holy maker by
the sun.   11

No

Praise that the spring time is all
Gabriel and radiant shrubbery as the morning
grows joyful
Out of the woebegone pyre   15
And the multitude's sultry tear turns cool on
the weeping wall,
My arising prodigal

Holy Spring. The poem expresses the poet's determination
to sing of spring, as have all poets who have loved the pattern
of life, and this determination persists despite the war, which
may mean the last spring.   **8. That one . . . light.** With
typically strange and contradictory use of words, Thomas is
saying that he has no real heart for war, but only gropingly,
and through his poetic vision, can he figure out the meaning
of the war era.   **14. Gabriel,** the angel who is to announce
the awakening of the dead and Judgment Day.

Sun the father his quiver full of the infants of
pure fire,
But blessed be hail and upheaval
That uncalm still it is sure alone to stand and
sing   20
Alone in the husk of man's home
And the mother and toppling house of the holy
spring,
If only for a last time.

Among Those Killed in the Dawn Raid Was a Man Aged One Hundred

WHEN the morning was waking over the
war
He put on his clothes and stepped out and he
died,
The locks yawned loose and a blast blew them
wide,
He dropped where he loved on the burst pave-
ment stone
And the funeral grains of the slaughtered floor.
Tell his street on its back he stopped a sun   6
And the craters of his eyes grew springshoots
and fire
When all the keys shot from the locks, and
rang.

Dig no more for the chains of his grey haired
heart.
The heavenly ambulance drawn by a wound
Assembling waits for the spades' ring on the
cage.   11
O keep his bones away from that common cart,
The morning is flying on the wings of his age
And a hundred storks perch on the sun's right
hand.

And Death Shall Have No Dominion

AND DEATH shall have no dominion.
Dead men naked they shall be one
With the man in the wind and the west moon;
When their bones are picked clean and the
clean bones gone,
They shall have stars at elbow and foot;   5

Among . . . Hundred. With the urgency of life as his main
theme, Thomas sees the very old man change in death into a
symbol of life which must go on, regardless of death.   **6. a
sun,** a life.   **14. And a hundred storks.** The storks are a
typical symbol of life reborn as the ancient die.

Though they go mad they shall be sane,
Though they sink through the sea they shall
    rise again;
Though lovers be lost love shall not;
And death shall have no dominion.

And death shall have no dominion.   10
Under the windings of the sea
They lying long shall not die windily;
Twisting on racks when sinews give way,
Strapped to a wheel, yet they shall not break;

Faith in their hands shall snap in two,   15
And the unicorn evils run them through;

Split all ends up they shan't crack;
And death shall have no dominion.

And death shall have no dominion.
No more may gulls cry at their ears   20
Or waves break loud on the seashores;
Where blew a flower may a flower no more
Lift its head to the blows of the rain;
Though they be mad and dead as nails,
Heads of the characters hammer through
    daisies;   25
Break in the sun till the sun breaks down,
And death shall have no dominion.

JAMES AGEE

James Agee, who was born in Knoxville, Tennessee, in 1909 and educated at Harvard, earns his living by writing and is today one of our best known motion-picture critics. He has published only one book of poems, *Permit Me Voyage*, which appeared in 1934 as one of the Yale Series of Younger Poets; but this book, like the single poems which have since appeared, clearly indicated that Agee had unusual talent.

In 1936 Agee, then a staff writer for *Fortune,* was sent with Walker Evans, photographer for the Farm Security Administration, to prepare an article for the magazine about the southern tenant farmers. He lived closely with these people for some time, and ended by becoming so infuriated with his scientific research as directed by the magazine, and so awakened to the gentleness and beauty as well as the poverty of the people he studied, that he wrote not only the commissioned article but, in a kind of passionate protest, his own book—published in 1941 as *Let Us Now Praise Famous Men.*

The effect of this book, in which Agee's emotional prose blends with Evans' eloquent photographs, is almost overwhelming. Agee sees the tenant farmers as with the camera's eye, but at the same time with a deep sense of humility and love. He probes the indignity with which innocent and helpless people are treated. As he pictures these impoverished folk whom a commercial civilization has robbed of a birthright, he attacks some of our unreasonable notions of morality, esthetics, education, and race prejudice. Agee's final plea is not so much for the betterment of these people as it is that man let man alone lest each of us harm the other.

As might have been expected, *Let Us Now Praise Famous Men* received contradictory criticism; and much that was said of it, good and bad, was true. It was said to be a structural failure, which in a sense it is. The lyric beauty of its prose was commended, its "objectionable passages" deplored. Many critics noted that the book was as much about Agee as about the tenant families. Agee probably knew this; he was attempting to lay himself open, as any sensitive man might, to all the feelings from which we usually shrink; he wanted to see life simple and naked and to face its ugliness and its beauty.

Most of Agee's later poems appeared in this book. They, as well as those used by Elizabeth Drew in *Directions in Modern Poetry* to illustrate the art of imagery, show Agee to be one of our most talented American poets. The condensation necessary to poetry does not permit Agee the confusion of emotional responses sometimes found in his prose. Similarly, although in prose he seems sometimes unable to integrate emotion and reasoning, he never errs in this respect in his poetry. Consequently, the latter is perhaps his best medium.

967

Sunday Afternoon: Outskirts of Knoxville, Tenn.

THERE, in the earliest and chary spring, the
dogwood flowers.

Unharnessed in the friendly sunday air
By the red brambles, on the river bluffs,
Clerks and their choices pair.

Thrive by, not near, masked all away by shrub
and juniper,   5
The ford v eight, racing the chevrolet.

They can not trouble her:

Her breasts, helped open from the afforded
lace,
Lie like a peaceful lake;
And on his mouth she breaks her gentleness: 10

Oh, wave them awake!

They are not of the birds. Such innocence
Brings us to break us only.
Theirs are not happy words.

We that are human cannot hope.   15
Our tenderest joys oblige us most.
No chain so cuts the bone; and sweetest silk
most shrewdly strangles.

How this must end, that now please love were
ended,
In kitchens, bedfights, silences, women's-pages,
Sickness of heart before goldlettered doors, 20
Stale flesh, hard collars, agony in antiseptic cor-
ridors,
Spankings, remonstrances, fishing trips, orange
juice,
Policies, incapacities, a chevrolet,
Scorn of their children, kind contempt ex-
changed,
Recalls, tears, second honeymoons, pity, 25
Shouted corrections of missed syllables,
Hot water bags, gallstones, falls down stairs,

Oldfashioned christmases, suspicions of theft,
Arrangements with morticians taken care of by
sons in law,
Small rooms beneath the gables of brick bunga-
low,   30
The tumbler smashed, the glance between
daughter and husband,
The empty body in the lonely bed
And, in the empty concrete porch, blown ash
Grandchildren wandering the betraying sun

Now, on the winsome crumbling shelves of the
horror   35
God show, God blind these children!

To Walker Evans

AGAINST time and the damages of the brain
Sharpen and calibrate. Not yet in full,
Yet in some arbitrated part
Order the façade of the listless summer.

Spies, moving delicately among the enemy, 5
The younger sons, the fools,
Set somewhat aside the dialects and the stained
skins of feigned madness,
Ambiguously signal, baffle, the eluded sentinel.

Edgar, weeping for pity, to the shelf of that
sick bluff,   9
Bring your blind father, and describe a little;
Behold him, part wakened, fallen among field
flowers shallow
But undisclosed, withdraw.

Not yet that naked hour when armed,
Disguise flung flat, squarely we challenge the
fiend.
Still, comrade, the running of beasts and the
ruining heaven   15
Still captive the old wild king.

"To Walker Evans" from *Let Us Now Praise Famous Men* by James Agee is used by permission of, and arrangement with, the publisher, Houghton Mifflin Company.
To Walker Evans. This poem appeared as the dedication of *Let Us Now Praise Famous Men* (1941). The poet indicates that this is the time (immediately before the war in which we were shortly to be engaged) when like the mad King Lear we try to believe in a possible truce (or a Munich) which will not last. **Walker Evans,** the well-known photographer who collaborated with James Agee in *Let Us Now Praise Famous Men.* 2. **calibrate,** to measure the caliber, the worth. 6. **younger sons.** The younger son, traditionally, had to make his own way in the world. 9. **Edgar,** the son of Gloucester, in *King Lear;* Gloucester had been blinded for his loyalty to Lear.

"Sunday Afternoon: Outskirts of Knoxville, Tenn." by James Agee is reprinted by permission of the author.
Sunday . . . Tenn. The poet is concerned with the innocence of lovers who do not stop to think of all the chores and little-nesses of married life.

BEN BELITT

Ben Belitt is a highly trained poet who has said of himself, ". . . the truth is I have no wisdom, except what is contained in my imagery, and am always exceeded by it." His masters have been Donne, Keats, and Hart Crane. His imagery has developed from that of a fairly typical youthful search for adjustment to that of a consistent inquiry into problems of human dignity and human redemption.

Belitt was born on May 2, 1911, in New York, where he lived until he was ten, when his family moved to Virginia. In 1928 he entered the University of Virginia, from which he received his A.B. in 1932, his M.A. in 1934. Until he left college Belitt had thought of himself as a prose writer and had actually published several short stories; but within a few years his primary interest had become the writing of poetry. In 1936 he shared with Charlotte Wilder the Shelley Memorial Award for meritorious achievement in the field of poetry. In that same year he became assistant literary editor of *The Nation*, resigning after two years to join the faculty of Bennington College, where he taught modern poetry and other subjects. His first book of poems, *The Five-Fold Mesh*, was published in 1938. During the summer of 1939, Belitt directed the choral reading of Hart Crane's "The Bridge" at Mills College, California.

When World War II came, Belitt was among those who were convinced that the writer's place was in the service if he was to understand his own generation. Drafted in 1942, he first served as a private in a police battalion, next studied Russian for special intelligence work then contemplated by the Army, and finally was transferred to an intelligence and reconnaissance platoon in the 89th Infantry Division, where in 1944, preparing for overseas movement, he suffered an attack of arthritis which led to his discharge. As a civilian, he wrote for the Signal Corps Photographic Center several technical manuals on photographic theory and equipment, and, as a scenario writer

in the Combat Films Branch of the Army's Historical Films Division, wrote, organized, and supervised cutting and continuity for a twenty-three-reel document which is now in the War Department archives on the Seventh Army's drive from Dijon to the German border.

In 1946 Belitt received a Guggenheim Post-Service Fellowship, and devoted the year to the writing of new poems and a short prose project entitled *School of the Soldier*, his first creative literary work since 1942. He returned to the University of Virginia to continue the work on his doctorate, which had not been completed when he left there in 1936. In 1947, he resumed his teaching at Bennington.

Belitt's poetry grows steadily in power and in the perception of some of the most intense problems the artist today must face. All the vivid experiences of the real scene, absorbed by him, focus and illuminate both his inner world and the outer world which has molded his imagination. Never obviously political or propagandist, he lets his image of "the world's waste scanted to a personal sin" define his position. His symbols in the early "Battery Park," for example, bring the poet out of his past into a new vision of the contemporary world. In the park at noon, a poet tries to understand himself through understanding the noontime sleepers around him. Is he a "hurler," an "athlete of vision," or is he a "sleeper," who struggles to break the dreamer's sleep?

That question remained unanswered until Belitt realized that the theme of some of his later poems was the "consent to violence" in order to understand the clash between the poet's dream and action—to understand collective strength and thus to return to the problem of free will resurrected, all the purer for its burial in reality. His later poems reject mysticism, sometimes approached in the earlier work, for participation in action, participation in order to abstract from that action the "victory over horror" attainable by projecting the experience as art.

Charwoman

(LOWER MANHATTAN—6:00 P.M.)

CLAPPING the door to, in the little light,
In the stair-fall's deepening plunge,
I see, in the slate dark, the lumped form, like
    a sponge,
Striking a rote erasure in the night—

And keep that figure; while a watery arc   5
Trembles and wanes in wetted tile, as if
It wrote all darkness down in hieroglyph
And spoke vendetta with a water-mark.

That shadowy flare shall presently define   9
A scuffed and hazardous wrist, a ruined jaw
Packed into goitre, like a pigeon's craw,
A bitten elbow webbed with a naphtha line;

While light shall lessen, blunting, by brute
    degrees,   13
The world's waste scanted to a personal sin,
Till all is darkness where her brush had been
And blinds the blackening marble by her knees.

.   .   .   .

I mark what way the dropping shaft-light
    went;   17
It flung the day's drowned faces out, and fell
Hasped like a coffin down a darkening well:
And poise on the shaft-way for my own
    descent.

"Tarry, Delight"

IN JACKAL country, in the gum and umber,
That bird broke blank to the eyebeam.
                      She sprang
The feathery braid, the maze of slumber,
She trod the timeless humors, and the brief;
Her wings leapt thorny out of upper rain,   5
And chalked to stillness in that sparkling plane,
On derelict claws she sang.

What heart's-ease, and what thinking angers?

Her wings drove, black on bright;
For pure delight   10
The cold throat like a lessening spindle shook.
She sang the enemy joy as it were grief
And, with a condor look,
A summer's space in blue,
Bore down the wreath like rue.

The Unregenerate

*"Escape for thy life; look not behind thee, neither
stay thou in all the plain; escape to the mountain
lest thou be consumed.
And Lot said unto them; Or not so, my Lord . . ."*

FLEEING its childhood havens
And spent with fast,
The heart will beg its bread, at last,
At the beaks of ravens.
It asks no sign, invokes no grace, save grief,   5
But, grappling the angels of its unbelief,
Gluts its long hunger on the venomous weed
And the strengthless vine,
Treads the tart berry in the hollow sheaf,
And sucks repose according to its need.   10

II

It comes to me now, more than ever purely,
How, fleeing the fabulous cities, one looked
    back,
To see, beyond the shafts of sulphurous rain,
The roofs of Sodom blazing red and black,
And, shadowing the plain,   15
The hand of God laid over, like a stain:
    Where shall the flesh find sanctuary
    From the hard query
    That looks forever toward the burning city

"The Unregenerate" and "Battery Park: High Noon" by Ben
Belitt reprinted by permission of the author.
"*Escape . . . Lord . . .*," Genesis 19:17. The quotation taken
from the story of Lot, ordered to escape from the doomed city
of Sodom, where corruption and vice ruled, is chosen by the
poet as appropriate to the situation in which modern man finds
himself. Much of the imagery is consequently biblical. The
whole poem deals with the spiritual struggle caused by man's
intellectual doubt of the worth of life, and his instinctive and
emotional need to make some adjustment or accept some faith
in beauty as overbalancing his knowledge of evil.   1. **Fleeing
. . . ravens.** The reference is to Elijah being fed by the ravens,
but the poet means that childhood faith allows the heart to
meet pain and finally to accept it as a part of all experience.
The heart, in other words, accepts whatever bread or comfort
is given it.   17. **Where . . . sanctuary.** Human life recognized as corrupt cannot sustain the heart.

"Charwoman" and "Tarry, Delight" reprinted from *The Five-
Fold Mesh* by Ben Belitt, by permission of and special arrangement with Alfred A. Knopf, Inc., authorized publishers.
"**Tarry, Delight.**" Here all the imagery of desolation is a
modern poet's statement that poetry can create delight from
grief, can spring from an intensity of doubt or horror.

And the mortal fault,   20
Probing the ashes of its wrath and pity,
Freezing the mind to salt?

How shall the hurt be healed, or the strayed,
    restored?

Pity alone shall not renew the vision,
Nor wrath avail to thaw the inclement cell   25
Whose winter seals the fountains of decision
And stays the freshet from the unreplenished
    well.
    Shall love suffice us, then,
    Our elder overlord—   29
    The mild messiah, and the gentle shepherd
    With shadowy sword,
    Folding the mole with the serpent, the raven
        with the wren,
    The lamb with the leopard,
    And man with men?

III

Not so, not so, my Lord!   35

Cherish this disbelief
For final truth, although the end be grief.
Reject the frail pretense,
The vexed surmise, the wistful inference,
And reckon as you can   40
The gordian equation of the doubt
That struck the godhead out
And found no fruitful integer in man.

Now it were valor to unbend the flesh,   44
Burst the bright harness of dissembling sense,
The fine and five-fold mesh,
And loose the inward wound to bleed afresh.
Look for no respite of the ravening part,
Nor dream of quarter there:
Thriftless as time, prodigal as air,   50
Deep in the laboring heart,
The wakeful blood, unbridled like a spring,
By devious streams is gathering
To spend its furious overflow again   54
Like fire, like foam, like equatorial rain . . .

---

41. The gordian . . . man. The adult man must recognize
and take for granted a doubt of the goodness of man or of life.
Once he does this, he can allow his senses their full reaction to
beauty as it comes. The instinctive life renews itself though it
recognizes that it must be checked always by the intellectual
doubt of its worth.   **43. integer,** completeness.

Let the heart accept this thing;
Confront it there.
The mind, though it delay, was long aware.

Battery Park: High Noon

Suddenly the old fancy has me!
                                    Suddenly,
Between flint and glitter, the leant leaf,
The formal blueness blooming over slate,
Struck into glass and plate,
The public tulips, treading meridian glare   5
In bronze and whalebone by the statue-bases
    Elude the Battery square,
        Turn, with a southern gesture, in remem-
            bered air,
            And claim a loved identity, like faces
. . .

2

Compute the season out of height and heat: 10
Cubes in the poised shaft dwindle; tackle
        moves;
Descending diners paddle into the grooves
And burst from bolts and belts upon the street.

Summer deploys upon the brims of hats;   14
Turns upon twill; affirms with colored drinks
A mimic solstice poised in flying inks
In Babylons of ribbons and cravats.

Here thoroughfares are blind upon the sea—
Enter the packed paths where the lanes con-
        verge
                                                19

Battery Park, a public park at the foot of Manhattan Island,
facing the harbor and the Statue of Liberty.   **1. Suddenly . . .
has me, etc.** The poet indicates here that his poem is to
move from images of the South (where his childhood was spent)
and his early ideas of beauty, to images of the Wall Street
district of New York City, where he has reached adulthood.
The first stanza presents a picture of Battery Park, its formal
blueness and public tulips and statues which recall on this
summer day the beauty of nature.   **14. Summer deploys . . .
cravats.** Having in the previous stanza noted movements of
machinery and elevators bringing lunchers to the street, the
poet here pictures summer as suggested by the light on the
brims of hats, by colored drinks catching bits of sunshine, and
by bright-colored ribbons and men's ties. "Babylons" is used
here in the plural both to suggest the overtone of the idea of
city and wickedness and also to suggest a confusion of ribbons
and cravats.   **18. Here thoroughfares . . . gallery.** The
poet notes that all paths converge in this park upon the sea
like arrows upon a target.

That drop the derelict stragglers by the surge,
Like targets in a shooting gallery;

In middle sleep, below the list of bells
That turn soft answers to a barge's brass,
These take their length in quarantines of grass,
Among the pigeons and the peanut shells.   25

Their capbrims crush out day. Fulfillments
leap,
Sudden as bludgeons, in a vacuum:
They answer to the pricking of a thumb,
And serve him more than slumber, who would
sleep.

(A stricter sleep I guess, with double dread,
Who waken now and dream these sleepers
dead—   31
And yet, these are my dream that dream the
lie,
And keep their sleep more deathfully than I.)
Bend then to seaward. The element you ask
Rarer than sea is, wantoner than time;   35
You bear it on you, strangely, like a mask,
And dream the sailing in a pantomime:

The element is blood; tired voyager, turn:
The reckoning you take is yet to learn.   39
Somber, at fullest flood, the continents ride,
And break their beaches in a sleeper's side.

3

Follow the loll of smoke, fallow over water,
The expense of power in retentive stone,

Where the barge takes the ripple with an organ
tone—   44
Over water, over roof, over catchpenny green,
Into time-to-come and what-has-been:

Into the wells of chimneys, into the smother of
cisterns,
Resin and amber shed on divided flame:
Into the quick of the burning, combustion's ve-
hement heart
Flying the summery floor,   50
Beating its pure pulse on the violet core—

Into the million years' flowering . . . the age-
less green . . .
The sunken frond
The charmed marine:
Time's incorruptible, biding, through char and
pulp   55
The ceaseless diamond.

O lost and mythic scene,
Move yet within this frame!
This is that angel, whether gem or flower—
Leaven and gum and flint—   60
Recalled from carbon in explicit power,
Whose massive slumber wears the pure impress
Of old renewal and first fruitfulness,
Pledging the fern's shape in primordial tinder,
Sealing, in herb and mint,   65
The healing in the cinder.

Measure again the ruinous floor of the world,
Beyond the parkpath and the seaward paling,
The equal faces, stunned with light and void,
Tranced as in surmise, lost between myth and
mood,   70
Derelict, decoyed,
In some astonished dream of sailing . . .

22. In middle sleep, etc. The lunchers, half asleep, near the
sea, and half hearing the bell of the boat, take naps on little
spaces of grass among the pigeons and peanut shells, their cap
brims over their eyes. They dream of fulfillment or sensation
which they will not know.   27. bludgeons, short hammer-like
clubs, an image of the half-dream of these human beings and
of the sensation which tricked them once they relaxed.   30. A
stricter sleep I guess, etc. The poet also dreams of life and of
the picture before him. His dream is of these sleepers on the
grass and of the meaning of their life.   34. Bend then to seaward, etc. The poet turns from the pictures of mankind to
the sea, and dreams of sailing from the past into the future to
envision the significance of all life.   38. The element . . .
learn. The poet states that in his deeper instincts, man has the
key to the significance of life, that he does not yet know where
he goes.   40. Somber, at fullest flood, etc. In a kind of
vision the poet seems to see the continents in the sea all con-
verging upon these sleepers and especially upon himself, to
give him, as it were, a picture of the map of the universe and
its meaning.

44. Where the barge takes, etc., an image of the whistle
of the barge, a sound which carries the imagination of the poet
into the future and the past.   45. catchpenny, showy, made
to attract buyers. The poet uses the image to indicate the little
plots of grass in Battery Park which seem restful but are not.
47–60. Into the wells, etc. Here several images of the city
are given to indicate the poet's sensuous perception of it as it
faces the sea ("the charmed marine"). The whole of the poet's
imaginative perception of the scene leads him to see life despite
individual images of corruption, moving toward perfection, or
the absolute ("the ceaseless diamond"). In such a heightened
state of imagination ("O lost and mythic scene") the poet
understands that vision ("that angel") and reality are one,
that carbon (of life) becomes diamond of vision.   67. Measure
again, etc. Addressing himself, the poet commands that he
again take account of the world, the park, the similar faces of
mankind, and see that man in a certain heightened mood is
always living over again the old myth of exploration or spiritual
research.

Soundstage

(U. S. Signal Corps Photographic Center:
1945)

1

CATWALK, backdrop, cable, girder, fly—
A schooner capsized:

              sea-fans of artifice
Buoyed in the middle currents, gelatin and foil,
Baskets of radiant cordage, geysers of frost,
Miraculous canvas in the glowing levels, glazed,
The backdrops weedy, like oil: 6

The ropes plunge and are lost,
Are parted like hair,
Where, at the summit, among crucibles of light,
Equilibrist Gulliver   10
Calls to the carpenters in a tightwire vertigo,
At the Archimedean center of deception, un-
    amazed.

And all that is, is film. Film is
The serpent in Eden garden, the cord in the
    chrysalis,

"Soundstage" by Ben Belitt reprinted from *The Virginia
Quarterly Review*, Winter 1947, by permission of the author and
The Virginia Quarterly Review.
Soundstage. The footnotes have been furnished by the poet.
1. **Catwalk.** The poem opens with a synthesis of under-water
imagery to suggest the submergence of reality in filmic effects.
The catwalk is a narrow footway suspended on scaffolds, for
moving from one part of the soundstage to another. **fly,** the
space over a stage above the proscenium from which effects are
lowered. 2. **sea-fans of artifice,** the webbing of canvas and
cord by which the scenery is suspended in mid-air—here likened
to under-water plant life. 3. **gelatin and foil.** Gelatin is
used in the emulsion of motion-picture film. Tin foil is employed
in reflectors which catch and direct the floodlights. Both suggest the semi-opacity of the under-water world. 4. **Baskets
... cordage.** The pulleys and cords which hold the scenic
effects in position are likened to the crow's-nest of a ship.
geysers of frost, the beams of high-powered floodlights directed into space. 10. **Equilibrist Gulliver.** To the man on
the summit, the carpenters would appear as Lilliputians. To
the carpenters below, however, he is precariously balanced like
a tightrope performer. 12. **Archimedean center,** a favorite
metaphor of Kierkegaard. It recalls the boast of the Greek
mathematician and inventor, Archimedes (287–212 B.C.):
"Give me but a place to stand [the "center of deception"]
and I will move the earth." In the present context it refers to
the artifices of the theater whereby reality is displaced and the
illusions of perspective realized. 13. **all that is, is film, etc.,**
a synthesis of highly diversified imagery in which all history is,
in effect, turned into film. The poet employs many images of
circuition—loops, arcs, spirals—which relate the filmic story
with the myths of the past and the events of World War II.
The film loop thus takes on the magical character of the spiral—
symbol of eternity—linking the curve of the serpent of Genesis
with the whorl of a cocoon (the "chrysalis"), the dove's flight
in the story of Noah, Ariadne's thread in the Labyrinth, the
Chinese Wall erected against the barbarian hordes, the lines of
latitude and longitude spanning the earth's circumference, the
path of the exploding shell, and finally, the "l"—presumably of
the unfinished word *love*—of the wounded machine-gunner with
the characteristic looped *l* shape of the film loop in the pro-
jector.

The bough in the dove's beak trying the del-
    uge,   15
The thread in the labyrinth;
The great wall of China, spanning the dynasties
Like a calligraphic symbol; meridians, staves,
Between the upper and nether ice-caps; trajec-
    tory
Of shell and tracer-bullet, phosphor and
    satchel-charge;   20
The looped "l" given to the paper poorly on the
    burning tripod
And the victory over horror is an image.

2

The boy in the uniform of Oberleutnant, the
    demoniac flier,
Will not bleed humanly from the papier-mache
    doorway. The door
Will not close truly on the plausible flight,   25
With leisure for vanity, vacancy, mania, the
    stunned recognition.
And mocking the human wish for asylum,
Spray-gun and saw, the jaw of the plier,
Have outpaced fable.

It is divertissement, after all.   30
What is stilted in canvas, jailed to the plywood
    wall,
Stabbed to the floor
With wing-screws and metal angles,
Melts into vaudeville in a whirl of velocipedes
And a yelping of trained poodles,   35
A swindle of spangles.
Only the scaffold gives stress to the weightless
    interior,
On the wrong side of the pattern: the artisan's
    touch of the actual.
Yet, teased out of thought,

20. **phosphor,** employed in the manufacture of explosives.
satchel-charge, a package of 25 or 50 pounds of dynamite used
for throwing through the gun-ports of pillboxes. 23. **Oberleutnant.** German: First Lieutenant—i.e., the actor playing the rôle of a Nazi aviator in the scenario being filmed.
24. **papier-mache,** mashed-up paper mixed with paste and
used in making theatrical props. 30. **divertissement,** a short
entertainment between the acts of a play. 33. **wing-screws
and metal angles,** devices for securing the stage sets to the
stage floor. 34. **velocipedes,** an image commenting on the
essential falsity of everything connected with film making.
The utter bathos of vaudeville is suggested by the metaphor
of the acrobatic velocipedist and the performing dogs.
37. **weightless interior,** i.e., the actual stage set itself is two-
dimensional—without substance of reality. 39. **teased out of
thought,** from Keats' "Ode on a Grecian Urn":
    "Thou, silent form! dost tease us out of thought
    As doth eternity."

The smiling divination of the Spool   40
Whirls forever in the large eye of Keats, heavy
   with film.
For even that Attic shape,
The bride of quietness brought to bed on the
   urn,
Was not more actual than this.
                And, in equivocal distance,
Necessitous armies close, image and spectacle
   wait,   45
And beat on the canvas door;
The fiction
Calls in the ripening crystal to existence,
Loud as myself—
          in deed, in ghost—

And bleeds in Agamemnon's color,   50
And is articulate.

Nightpiece

RISE, cleanly trust, divided star,
   And spend that delicate fraud upon the
   night—
A lover's instance, moving mindful air
To make its peace in dedicated light

Whose look is charnel. Lustres, intent and
   blind,   5

Give darkness downward with a glow like
   sheaves,
A gleaner's pittance, withered in the bind,
That keeps the summer godhead of the leaves:

And bends tremendous evening under it,
Doubles its theft within a lonely course,   10
Till eye and eye repeat the counterfeit
And shape the replenishing mercy at its source.

All else were ravage, a demon-gaze of terror:
The emblem blackened in the living head,
The eye, the image, and the image-bearer   15
Struck to an awe with smiling on the dead.

Therefore that bounty, which, however false,
Tenders survival and is purely given,
And lends the viewless prisms at its pulse
To make an easy legendry in heaven.   20

Restore that grace! Indeed, the look is grace
That deals this desert providence in air,
And lifts a death's head, burning, into place
To serve a lover's faith.
                Rise, carrion star.

Speech for Mary

(AFTER MICHELANGELO'S "PIETÀ")

I HAVE willed the event,
   At length, and confront the violent shape,
And break, on the pyx of my lap,
In the old, paschal posture, the obscene Inno-
   cent.

---

40. **divination of the Spool.** The image of the spool has com-
pounded many associations. It is connected with the spindle of
the Three Fates, the divination of Cassandra, and the reel on
which the film is unwound. The "Attic shape" and the "bride
of quietness" are quoted from the "Grecian Urn," to suggest
that the stilled image on the film and the stilled figures on the
urn are one. 48. **ripening crystal,** a reference not only to the
lens of the camera, but to the silver halide crystals which make
up the emulsion of the film. "Ripening" is a technical word for
the effect of light on these crystals to produce the photographic
image. 50. **Agamemnon.** The poet chose Agamemnon instead of Cassandra (whom he thought of, too) because he was
both a *seminal* figure in Greek tragedy—that is, his sacrifice
of Iphigenia was directly responsible for the "chain reaction" of
murders that motivate Clytemnestra and Electra and Orestes
—and because his situation is literally that of a soldier returning to a wrecked home after the Trojan Wars. Agamemnon's
"color" is, of course, blood.
"Nightpiece" reprinted by permission of the author.
Nightpiece. The full moon is here used as a traditional image
of love and a personal symbol of the imagination that remains
open to belief, even when the mind and the experience of the
poet can furnish no occasion for belief. The poem explores the
paradox whereby a "dead planet" can become an instrument
of light and survival. 1. **star.** The moon is a "divided star"
because of its constantly altering phases and because its total
surface is equally divided between light and darkness.
5. **charnel,** i.e., corpselike. The reflective surface is an extinct
planet.

11. **counterfeit.** The word restates the idea of the "fraud" of
line 2. The moon's light is not its own, but is reflected. It is
"doubled" on the retina of the observer, and its "counterfeit"
is thereby "repeated." 13. **ravage.** The moon, although dead,
lends its surface to a life principle (the sun) and animates both
the spaces of heaven and the faith of the lover. It directs man's
attention away from death (the "demon gaze of terror") and
renders life interpretable and orderly ("an easy legendry in
heaven"). 21. **grace.** The poet's plea is for a special providence, or act of compassion, by which the "death's head" of
the moon may be transformed into a principle of survival.
"Speech for Mary" and "Ditty: Moby Dick at Nantucket" are
reprinted by permission of the author, from *Southern Review.*
Speech for Mary. The primary meaning of the poem is that
through the destruction of innocence a kind of Godhood is
born, which, in the language of man, must suffer all things.
On another level of reference the poem is interpretable as a
comment on the necessity of violence and the imminence of
war, "the Roman platitude." **Michelangelo's "Pietà,"** a famous sculptural group by the Italian painter, sculptor, and poet,
which represents the crucified Christ after His descent from
the Cross. He is depicted in the typical posture of the Renaissance *pietà*—stretched out at length over the knees of the seated
Madonna. *Pietà* is the Italian formula for "The Sorrowing
Woman." 1. **the event,** Christ's suffering and crucifixion in
behalf of man, or World War II. 3. **pyx,** the covered vessel
in which the Host, or body of Christ, is kept. 4. **paschal
posture.** Christ's rôle of scapegoat is suggested by the image
of the paschal lamb.

The pure vocation of that younger rage— 5
Godhead, little with woe—
Must bend to the stone of my knees and take
    its wage
And measure that murderous anvil for the
    blow,

And die: for a mourning animal,
In a schoolboy's subterfuge of grief, 10
Taking the expedient kiss, the coronal
Maudlin with thorns, between the deaths of a
    thief.

Playfellow, go: it is the old exchange,
The Roman platitude;
And it shall leave you range 15
To puzzle, again, your pedant's idea of the
    good,
In a child's solitude.

Dance Piece

"*. . . at the still point, there the dance is.*"

(FOR MARTHA GRAHAM)

THE ERRAND into the maze,
    Emblem, the heel's blow upon space,
Speak of the need, and order the dancer's will:
But the dance is *still*. 4

For a surmise of rest, over the flight of the dial,
Between shock of the fall, shock of repose,

11. **kiss,** the kiss of Judas Iscariot, the betrayer. 12. **deaths
of a thief.** The two thieves between whom Christ was crucified
are merged into one to suggest the persistence of an eternal
pattern. 14. **Roman platitude;** refers either to the "Roman" pattern of conquest and violence; or on a second level, to
the historic query of the Roman procurator who asked of
Christ, "What is Truth?" A possible inference is that Christ
is now at liberty to consider the question—the "pedant's idea
of the good"—for all eternity.
"Dance Piece" and "Descent in a Parachute" by Ben Belitt
first appeared in *The Nation*, November 30, 1946, and are reprinted by permission of the author and *The Nation*.
Dance Piece. This poem, written for and about Martha Graham, internationally famous exponent of the modern dance,
is concerned only incidentally with the legend of the Maze. The
"maze" is primarily intended as the arena of terror and action,
which the artist enters in order to achieve the "stillness" of
his art and objectify his experience in ceremonial terms. Thus,
the dancer seeks to create a moment of significant stillness
which will make known the true meaning of her action. *at the
still point,* etc., from T. S. Eliot's *Burnt Norton*. **Martha
Graham.** Miss Graham's dance, entitled "Errand into the
Maze," was presented at the Ziegfeld Theatre in New York
City for the first time in the winter of 1946. 1. **maze.** In
Greek legend, Theseus entered the maze or labyrinth to defeat
the Minotaur at its center and rescue Ariadne, daughter of
the King of Crete. He was guided to Ariadne by a thread which
she released as she moved into the labyrinth.

The flesh, in its time, delivered itself to the
    trial,
And rose.
Suffrance: the lapse, the pause,
Were the will of the dance— 10
The movement-to-be, charmed from the shifts
    of the chance,
Intent on its cause.

And the terrible gift
Of the gaze, blind on its zenith, the wreath
Of the throat, the body's unwearied uplift, 15
Unmaking and making its death,

Were ripeness; and theme for return;
Were rest in the durance of matter:
The sleep of the musing begetter
And the poise in the urn. 20

Ditty: Moby Dick at Nantucket

I SAW, over the gun's bore this summer,
    In a trick of light,
The young boats with a dazed sail
And finical spars spanned tight
To charm the inland comer 5
By the cropped wave, with a child's guess of a
    whale—
And cheered, in a lucky charade,
For the white whale-hump and the spearer,
Playing the innocent fraud
Of the Death of the Terror 10
Till the sail drew nearer

18. **matter.** In the final stanzas the dancer's movement is
merged with the flight of atomic particles ("durance of matter"), the theme of procreation ("the musing begetter"), and
the tensions of the completed art object ("the poise in the
urn").
Ditty: Moby Dick at Nantucket. Visiting Nantucket, the poet
here associates the story of Melville's symbolic voyage in
search of the meaning of life and death with the symbol of the
gun guarding the coast during World War II. Even as Melville
found the whale, or death in life, and overcame its fabled terror,
so the poet sees in the blue bore of the gun the concrete image
of death, rising out of the waters of exploration, or life.
1. **bore.** The gun is pictured as rising from the sea, with its
bore—the hollow chamber through which the bullet is expelled
—facing the poet. It is equally a symbol of the time's violence
and the vacationer's sense of guilt and insecurity. 4. **finical.**
The word is here applied to the tension and delicacy of the
cordage that lashes the sails to the spars. 6. **whale.** In the
distance, the whiteness of the sail suggests the fin of the Great
White Whale rising from the sea. It was from Nantucket that
the whalers of *Moby Dick* began their seasonal voyages, and
the poet whimsically refers to the illusion as a child's reminiscence of the story. 7. **charade.** The sportive imagery is extended to include the parlor game of charades, in which the
title of a book is mutely enacted in pantomimic symbols.

And the fable went down
Under the waste dune
And the pat verge of the hedge,
And out of the water's edge,   15
Rose, in the cold salt, the blue bore of the gun.

Descent in a Parachute

LEANT, in his fall, to question his confident
      haste;
And moaned; and fumbled the cord on his
      broken navel:

And rose on his arm in his fall, thinking ease,
As, level under level,
In the brute and downward waste,   5
Crouched for the birth-blow, chin to his knees,
He grappled his breast for the ring of the bone,
      in his rage,
And opened his brows, like a cage. . . .

2.

A little troughing the void,
Tensing its folds in the vehement interim,   10
Buoying its silks, itself for a moment buoyed,
Out sprang the parachute brain to recover him:

"For how, in an element
Of flight and fracture, reckon rest and stress?
Or mark the stroke—and know it for descent,
Among the cleaving zones of the abyss?   16

"Hurler and sleeper, who journey yourself in
      your fall,

Time is a bowspan, space is a discus hurled:
You stand with the hurlers, under the vault of
      the skull,
And turn a considering surmise, like a world—

"And think to fall helpless; and turn on your
      arm in that dream,   21
Thinking the dream, chafing a word in sleep,
And rise on your arm to give the dream its
      name,
And tremble; and cannot break the dreamer's
      keep."

3.

And plunged; keeping childbirth, knees to his
      breast,   25
Beating his temples, parting a garland of bone,
A little flying the parachute heart as he
      passed—
A hand's-breadth of cordage, poised, like a
      thought, over stone:
And bent in the circles of narrow and wilder-
      ness air,
Sprang to the ring's verge, bursting its silks on
      the height;   30
Wheeled in the ravel; leant to the deepening
      blur,
As up, like explosion, the flint of the world
      struck his flight.

The Casualty

AND HAVE your answer, out of the instinct's
      need
To render its terror tangible.

                        For, howsoever shyly,
Under the soldier's compulsion, with a human
      gaze,

12. **fable.** The sail—and its illusory consolations—vanishes below the horizon and is replaced by the obsessive image of the
gun.
Descent in a Parachute. The theme here, as in "Dance
Piece" and "Soundstage," is the search for significant action—
for a union of the "flint" of the world and the "flight" of the
poet that will give reality to his deepest beliefs and an awareness
of the tragic pattern which they serve. The image of the parachute is employed in a twofold capacity. It signifies the total
intellectual resources of man that bring his will to bear on the
events and realities of the physical universe ("the parachute
brain") and the sensibility ("the parachute heart") whereby
man intuits the meaning of his existence.   6. **birth-blow.** The
flight downward is treated as a birth image. The parachutist
normally falls in the birth position: the ring that releases the
rip cord is likened to the navel, and the rip cord itself to the
umbilical cord.   12. **parachute brain.** The parachute, fully
opened, suggests in its convolutions the contours of the human
brain.   16. **abyss.** The abyss is the "bottomless pit" of experience, where, like Joseph in the well, man enacts the mythological ordeals of his history.   17. **Hurler and sleeper.** The
poet is both he who hurls himself into the imaginative experience of life and he who dreams of its mythical completion. He
interprets his descent actively as "hurler" and symbolically as
"sleeper." **fall.** The image here suggests the "fall" of man in
the theological sense, as well as the descent of the parachutist.

24. **dreamer's keep.** As in "Battery Park," Belitt here indicates that the poet is he who must name the dream, or the universal significance, or his action, not only for himself, but for
all men.
"The Casualty" by Ben Belitt, reprinted from *The Virginia
Quarterly Review*, 1947, by permission of the author and *The
Virginia Quarterly Review.*
The Casualty. The general significance of the poem is that
the poet must, in order to face the horror of his own generation,
render the terror of that generation tangible. He must consent
to violence, to separation from himself, and to participation in
action. Compassion must yield to the necessity of killing. Therefore the poet stares upon the face of Medusa from the pit or the
beastliness of the necessity.

Puzzling disaster at a time when terror was
    usual,   5
You bent to the bullet a consented will—
You ripened volition with that other deed,
Valor's improvization, the unselving act,
To force an unspeakable image from the maze.

Infantryman falling, falling always: the fall is
    forever.   10
Fall to your certainty, no longer compelled and
    alone,
Yielding the gun-stock to the compassionate
    image.

7. **that other deed,** the death, or self-sacrifice (the "unselving act"), of the soldier.   12. **the compassionate image,** i.e., the image of horror and the world's evil which is finally elaborated in the concluding lines of the poem. It is a "compassionate" image because it transforms the *nameless* horror of experience into a *known* horror, and thereby frees the mind of its obsessions.

Turn from the bomb-burst by the powerless
    river,
Forfeit in cross-fire, on inadmissive ground—
Who have become that host the night-march
    sought,   15
Terror's unique enigma, the time-serving will,
The shield whereon Medusa's manifest gaze
Glows like a boss and confronts its deliverer
In the bottomless pit and beast's face of the
    wound.

15. **that host.** The night-marchers recognize in the individual death the violence into which they march collectively.   17. **The shield.** The body of the soldier is likened to the shield in which the hero Perseus saw the reflected image of the Medusa, just as his wounds become the "bottomless pit" of Christian theology and the Medusa image itself. **Medusa;** in Greek legend the snake-haired woman who turned all who looked upon her face to stone. She was killed by Perseus, who looked only at her image in the polished face of his shield.

ELIZABETH BISHOP

Elizabeth Bishop was born in Worcester, Massachusetts, on February 8, 1911. She graduated from Vassar in 1934 and a year later her poetry first appeared in print, in an anthology of college verse called *Trial Balances* (1935). It was not long until her poems began to appear in *New Directions* and the *Partisan Review*. Nevertheless, she waited until 1946 to publish her first volume, *North and South*. This book, most of the poems in which were written before 1942, has made it evident that Miss Bishop is a poet of first rank. She is indeed a younger, if less profound and less academic, Marianne Moore. Her style is her own, but her observations and her method of moving from the particular to the general are like the older woman's.

For subject matter Miss Bishop draws from the reality in which we live and, in her late poems particularly, from the reality of the war period. In restrained and subtle imagery she projects selectively but accurately her feelings and responses. Her poetry moves and is dynamic; she has probably learned from the Imagists, but unlike them is not static. Hers is a painter's eye, but she also has intellectual curiosity. Not at all "feminine," in the bad sense of that word, and never merely sentimental, Miss Bishop can be both objective and passionate. Without shock she delivers us into contact with the actual, from which she draws her conclusions, the conclusions of a liberal and sensitive mind.

The fact that she has been able to devote herself wholly to her work and to live on a private income in a pleasant home in Key West has not made Miss Bishop eclectic. Instead, she has had time to mature slowly, to escape the mistakes of youth, and to observe closely the events of her own day. She is neither a defeatist nor an escapist, but a poet able to make crystal clear either her own emotions or the shock of war upon the average mind.

Cirque d'Hiver

ACROSS the floor flits the mechanical toy,
fit for a king of several centuries back.
A little circus horse with real white hair.
His eyes are glossy black.
He bears a little dancer on his back.　　5

She stands upon her toes and turns and turns.
A slanting spray of artificial roses
is stitched across her skirt and tinsel bodice.
Above her head she poses
another spray of artificial roses.　　10

His mane and tail are straight from Chirico.
He has a formal, melancholy soul.
He feels her pink toes dangle toward his back
along the little pole
that pierces both her body and her soul　　15

and goes through his, and reappears below,
under his belly, as a big tin key.
He canters three steps, then he makes a bow,
canters again, bows on one knee,　　19
canters, then clicks and stops and looks at me.

The poems of Elizabeth Bishop are reprinted from *North and South* by permission of the publisher, Houghton Mifflin Co. "Cirque d'Hiver" copyright 1940 The New Yorker Magazine, Inc.
Cirque d'Hiver, winter circus.　11. **Chirico,** Giorgio di Chirico, Italian painter; until about 1920, probably one of the greatest influences on modern painting.

The dancer, by this time, has turned her back.
He is the more intelligent by far.
Facing each other rather desperately—
his eye is like a star—　　24
we stare and say, 'Well, we have come this far.'

The Colder the Air

WE MUST admire her perfect aim,
this huntress of the winter air
whose level weapon needs no sight,
if it were not that everywhere
her game is sure, her shot is right.　　5
The least of us could do the same.

The chalky birds or boats stand still,
reducing her conditions of chance;
air's gallery marks identically
the narrow gallery of her glance.　　10
The target-center in her eye
is equally her aim and will.

Time's in her pocket, ticking loud
on one stalled second. She'll consult
not time nor circumstance. She calls　　15
on atmosphere for her result.
(It is this clock that later falls
in wheels and chimes of leaf and cloud.)

The Colder the Air. The title indicates that Elizabeth Bishop has in mind the general symbol of time as the huntress, sure of her aim, sure, indeed, almost as death is.

RANDALL JARRELL

Randall Jarrell's reputation was first established in the critical field, where his witty if cruel dissections of books amused the sophisticates and infuriated the authors. Such critics as Allen Tate and John Crowe Ransom almost at once approved of him and of his early poetry, which reflected the influence of the Southern agrarians.

Born in 1914, Jarrell has lived most of his life in Texas, Tennessee, and California.

When war broke out he enlisted in the Air Force, but early in 1942 "washed out" after thirty hours of flying. In this year, too, he published his first book of poems, *Blood for a*

Stranger, and was recognized at once as a poet of considerable power, although a little overweighted on the intellectual side. In 1945 his war poems began to appear and were collected in the volume *Little Friend, Little Friend.*

It was evident that the war had deepened Jarrell emotionally and that his was no mean talent. During his service he had apparently read widely and thought; he had shaken off the academic robes worn while he was an instructor at the University of Texas, had become immersed in history and in economic theory. He had discovered his own generation, had become at least vaguely aware of the Marxian philosophy, and was imaginatively fired by anger and fear. Emotionally he was convinced of the need of bettering man's world. No propagandist, he was aware of the conflicts in opinion in his own day. Free now of Audenesque snobbishness, he began to hit at the heart of the problem, for like Wilfred Owen he saw that in war the poetry was in the pity. He saw, as Owen did not, political implications of the catastrophe. Consequently his poem *The Wide Progress* is a major work in its summary of all that these last few years have clarified.

Jarrell is young and his career has just begun. Some of the poems in his latest book, *Losses* (1948), like "Place of Death" and "Camp in the Prussian Forest," prove that Jarrell, with unblinking bravery, is feeling out and illuminating and summarizing both the idealism and the sense of defeat to which sensitive minds are now subject. It is not unlikely that as a war poet his name will rank fairly high.

On the Railway Platform

THE REWARDED porters opening their smiles,
Grapes with a card, and the climate changing
From the sun of bathers to the ice of skis
Cannot hide it—journeys are journeys.

And, arrived or leaving, "Where am I going?"
All the travelers have wept; "is it once again
    only   6
The county I laughed at and nobody else?
The passage of a cell between two cells?"

No, the ends are hardly indifferent, the shadow
Falls from our beaches to the shivering floes,
The faces fail while we watch, and darkness
Sucks from the traveler his crazy kiss.   12

The tears are forming; and the leaver falls
Down tracks no wheel retraces, by the signs
Whose names name nothing, mean: Turn
    where you may,   15
You travel by the world's one way.

And the tears fall. What we leave we leave forever:
Time has no travelers. And journeys end in
No destinations we meant. And the strangers
Of all the future turn their helpless gaze   20

Past the travelers who cannot understand
That they have come back to tomorrow's city,
And wander all night through the unbuilt
    houses
And take from strangers their unmeant kisses.

Losses

IT was not dying: everybody died.
It was not dying: we had died before
In the routine crashes—and our fields
Called up the papers, wrote home to our folks,
And the rates rose, all because of us.   5
We died on the wrong page of the almanac,
Scattered on mountains fifty miles away;
Diving on haystacks, fighting with a friend,
We blazed up on the lines we never saw.
We died like ants or pets or foreigners.   10
(When we left high school nothing else had
    died
For us to figure we had died like.)

In our new planes, with our new crews, we
    bombed
The ranges by the desert or the shore,   14
Fired at towed targets, waited for our scores—
And turned into replacements and woke up
One morning, over England, operational.
It wasn't different: but if we died
It was not an accident but a mistake
(But an easy one for anyone to make).   20
We read our mail and counted up our missions—
In bombers named for girls, we burned
The cities we had learned about in school—
Till our lives wore out; our bodies lay among
The people we had killed and never seen.   25
When we lasted long enough they gave us
    medals;

When we died they said, "Our casualties were
    low."
They said, "Here are the maps"; we burned the
    cities.

It was not dying—no, not ever dying;   29
But the night I died I dreamed that I was dead,
And the cities said to me: "Why are you dying?
We are satisfied, if you are; but why did I die?"

Mail Call

THE LETTERS always just evade the hand.
    One skates like a stone into a beam, falls
    like a bird.
Surely the past from which the letters rise
Is waiting in the future, past the graves?
The soldiers are all haunted by their lives.   5

Their claims upon their kind are paid in paper
That establishes a presence, like a smell.
In letters and in dreams they see the world.
They are waiting: and the years contract   9
To an empty hand, to one unuttered sound—

The soldier simply wishes for his name.

The Soldier Walks under the Trees
of the University

THE WALLS have been shaded for so many
    years
By the green magnificence of these great lives
Their bricks are darkened till the end of time.
(Small touching whites in the perpetual
Darkness that saturates the unwalled world;   5
Saved from the sky by leaves, and from the
    earth by stone)
The pupils trust like flowers to the shades
And interminable twilight of these latitudes.

In our zone innocence is born in banks   9
And cultured in colonies the rich have sown:
The one is spared here what the many share

Mail Call. A war poem on the separation from one's own
identity and the consequent desire to reach back to the personal
life.
The Soldier . . . University. The poem is a comment on
a society that Jarrell feels educates the rich to see life idealisti-
cally and uses everyone for commerce; on a society which, for
all its theories of democratic education, denies the poor even
the four years of idealistic youth.

To write the histories that others are.
The oak escapes the storm that broke the reeds,
They read here; they read, too, of reeds,
Of storms; and are, almost, sublime   15
In their read ignorance of everything.

The poor are always—somewhere, but not here;
We learn of them where they and Guilt subsist
With Death and Evil: in books, in books, in
    books.
Ah, sweet to contemplate the causes, not the
    things!   20
The soul learns fortitude in libraries,
Enduring patience in another's pain,
And pity for the lives we do not change:
All that the world would be, if it were real.

When will the boughs break blazing from these
    trees,   25
The darkened walls float heavenward like soot?
The days when men say: "Where we look is
    fire—
The iron branches flower in my veins"?
In that night even to be rich is difficult,   29
The world is something even books believe,
The bombs fall all year long among the states,
And the blood is black upon the unturned
    leaves.

The Sick Nought

DO THE wife and baby travelling to see
    Your grey pajamas and sick worried face
Remind you of something, soldier? I remember
You convalescing washing plates, or mopping
The endless corridors your shoes had scuffed;
And in the crowded room you rubbed your
    cheek   6
Against your wife's thin elbow like a pony.
But you are something there are millions of.
How can I care about you much, or pick you
    out
From all the others other people loved   10
And sent away to die for them? You are a ticket
Someone bought and lost on, a stray animal:
You have lost even the right to be condemned.
I see you looking helplessly around, in histo-
    ries,

The Sick Nought. A bitter comment on the waste of war.
The symbol here is the convalescent soldier, who will probably
never be healed.

Bewildered with your terrible companions,
  Pain   15
And Death and Empire: what have you under-
  stood, to die?
Were you worth, soldiers, all that people said
To be spent so willingly? Surely your one the-
  ory, to live,
Is nonsense to the practice of the centuries.
What is demanded in the trade of states   20
But lives, but lives?—the one commodity.
To sell the lives we were too poor to use,
To lose the lives we were too weak to keep—
This was our peace, this was our war.

The Wide Prospect

W̲H̲O̲ ̲C̲O̲U̲L̲D̲ have figured, when the har-
  nesses improved
And men pumped kobolds from the coal's
  young seams
There to the west, on Asia's unrewarding
  cape—
The interest on that first raw capital?   4
The hegemony only the corpses have escaped?

When the earth turns, the serfs are eaten by the
  sheep;
The ploughland frees itself from men with
  deeds.
The old Adam sells his hours to an alderman
(Who adds them, in Arabic, down his black
  books);
Men learn it takes nine men to make a pin.   10

The star-led merchants steer with powder and
  with steel
Past dragonish waters, to the fabled world
Whose ignorant peoples tear the heart with
  stone.

Their lashed lines transport to the galleons'
  holds
New vegetables, tobacco, and the gold! the
  gold   15
That cracked our veins with credit, till the in-
  dices
Of old commodities were meaningless as
  Christ,
Till serf and lord were hammered into States
The lettered princes mortgaged for their lace
To lenders shrewder than Poor Richard, crude
  as Fate.   20

What traffickers, the captains! How the mer-
  chants war!
Beneath their blood and gilt swim like a shade
Black friars who survey with impartial eyes
The flames where Fathers or the heathen die,
Who bless alike the corpses and the Trade.   25

Here the horseman—steel, and backed with
  wings,
The salt sails rising from the centuries—
Holds laws: the tables flash like steel
Under the hollows of the high head, whitening
The eyes that watch unseeingly, like coins, 30

The deaths of the peoples. They are entered in
  his books;
For them he keeps, as God for Adam, work
And death and wisdom. They are money.
Their lives, enchanted to a thousand forms, 34
Are piled in holds for Europe; and their bones

Work out their ghostly years, despair, and die.
The mills rise from the sea. . . . The mother
  and the son
Stare past the ponies of the pit, to wheels
Beaten from their iron breath, to shuttles
Threading their gnarled unprofitable flesh like
  bones—   40

Whirled on pulleys to the knife, drayed to the
  shuttling tramps,

The Wide Prospect. The poet reflects on the ironic outcome
of the discovery of coal, and the invention of industrial implements. The outcome is, of course, the Industrial Revolution,
the growth of capitalism; and the final result is that man becomes the commodity to be consumed. Jarrell is following fairly
closely here a Marxian idea of the development of capitalism,
but his bitterness against all that capitalism has made of man
is, according to Marx, quite short-sighted. He sees progress, as
it has so far been known, as inimical to man.   6. **serfs . . .
sheep,** a reference to the decline of feudalism.   11. **star-led
merchants,** a reference to the early explorers, who sought gold.

17. **old commodities,** a reference to the coöperative state of
society, which disappeared when gold became the exchange.
23. **Black friars.** The reference is to the fact that the Church
followed where the merchant went.   26. **Here the horseman**
—**steel,** the Pegasus symbol industrialized.   28. **the tables
. . . steel,** a reference to the tables of God's laws, which now
have become mechanical laws.   30. **like coins,** a suggestion
that all values are reduced to commercial values.

Through post or mission, the long bolts of their
    lives
Run out, run out: the flesh lasts to those last
    isles
Where in mine and compound the man-eaters
    die
Under the cross of their long-eaten Kin.   45

42. **long . . . lives,** an image of the lives of workers as fabric
in the great machine of industry.

All die for all. And the planes rise from the
    years:
The years when, West or West, the cities burn,
And Europe is the colony of colonies—
When men see men once more the food of Man
And their bare lives His last commodity.

50. **His last commodity.** Man finally becomes the last commodity.

STANLEY KUNITZ

Stanley Kunitz identifies himself with the cultural history of his own people, a history which began in Europe and ended in this land of promise; and he has interpreted with great sensitivity the effects of war and distressful times upon the consciousness of the American Jew.

Born in Worcester, Massachusetts, on July 29, 1905, Kunitz attended the local schools and went on to receive both his B.A., *summa cum laude,* in 1925, and his M.A., in 1927, from Harvard. During college he had been a reporter and feature writer for the Worcester *Telegram,* but upon receiving his master's degree he went to New York, where he became editor of the *Wilson Library Bulletin,* a professional magazine for librarians. After an interval of European travel he returned to the Wilson Company to edit a number of biographical dictionaries which have become standard literary reference works; among the best known of these are *British Authors of the Nineteenth Century, American Authors (1600–1900),* and *Twentieth Century Authors.*

Meantime Kunitz was acquiring a reputation as a poet. His first book, *Intellectual Things* (1930), had shown authentic talent, musical subtlety, and fine observation of scene and feeling. Perhaps its only serious fault was an occasional reliance on rhetoric where im-

agination was called for. He continued to develop, and in the years before the war won a number of poetry prizes, including the Lloyd McKim Garrison Medal at Harvard and the Oscar Blumenthal Prize for lyrical poetry, given by the magazine *Poetry.*

In 1943 Kunitz was drafted for military service. He claims to hold the record for the longest time spent in basic training by a soldier of this war. Transferred from camp to camp, from hospital to hospital, he eventually reached a Headquarters Air Command, where he was assigned to edit the Information and Education Bulletin, conduct an orientation course, and lecture to the soldiers.

Discharged from the Army in 1945, Kunitz was awarded a Guggenheim Fellowship and spent the year 1946 in Santa Fe at work on a novel, until he accepted a teaching position at Bennington College, where he has remained.

His second book of poetry, *Passport to the War,* appeared in 1944 and showed great advancement over his first collection. It was, indeed, one of the best collections of verse dealing with the war to come from any American poet; and better than any other poet today Stanley Kunitz has made us aware of the Jewish sensitivity, rooted in history and aware of history's significance.

Approach of Autumn

THE EARLY violets we saw together,
Lifting their delicate swift heads
As if to dip them in the water, now wither.
Arching no more like thoroughbreds.

Slender and pale, they flee the rime   5
Of death: the ghosts of violets
Are running in a dream. Heart-flowering time
Decays, green goes, and the eye forgets.

Forgets? But what spring-blooded stock
Sprouts deathless violets in the skull   10
That, pawing on the hard and bitter rock
Of reason, make thinking beautiful?

Father and Son

NOW IN the suburbs and the falling light
I followed him, and now down sandy road
Whiter than bone-dust, through the sweet
Curdle of fields, where the plums
Dropped with their load of ripeness, one by
    one.   5
Mile after mile I followed, with skimming feet,
After the secret master of my blood,
Him, steeped in the odor of ponds, whose in-
    domitable love
Kept me in chains. Strode years; stretched into
    bird;
Raced through the sleeping country where I
    was young,   10
The silence unrolling before me as I came,
The night nailed like an orange to my brow.

How should I tell him my fable and the fears,
How bridge the chasm in a casual tone,   14
Saying, "The house, the stucco one you built,
We lost. Sister married and went from home,
And nothing comes back, it's strange, from
    where she goes.
I lived on a hill that had too many rooms:
Light we could make, but not enough of
    warmth,
And when the light failed, I climbed under the
    hill.   20
The papers are delivered every day;
I am alone and never shed a tear."

At the water's edge, where the smothering
    ferns lifted

Their arms, "Father!" I cried, "Return! You
    know
The way. I'll wipe the mudstains from your
    clothes;   25
No trace, I promise, will remain. Instruct
Your son, whirling between two wars,
In the Gemara of your gentleness,
For I would be a child to those who mourn
And brother to the foundlings of the field   30
And friend of innocence and all bright eyes.
O teach me how to work and keep me kind."

Among the turtles and the lilies he turned to
    me
The white ignorant hollow of his face.

Careless Love

WHO HAVE been lonely once
Are comforted by their guns.
Affectionately they speak
To the dark beauty, whose cheek
Beside their own cheek glows.   5
They are calmed by such repose,
Such power held in hand;
Their young bones understand
The shudder in that frame.
Without nation, without name,   10
They give the load of love,
And it's returned, to prove
How much the husband heart
Can hold of it: for what
This nymphomaniac enjoys   15
Inexhaustibly is boys.

The Hemorrhage

THE PEOPLE made a ring
Around the man in the park.
He was our banished king
Of blames and staunchless flows,
Exhibitor of the dark   5
Abominable rose;

Our chief, returned at last
From exile, with the grim

Father and Son. 28. **Gemara,** the commentary on the
Talmud, the writings of Jewish tradition.
The Hemorrhage. Using a symbolic figure of death, the poet
describes the coming impact of war on the people of this
country, who had hoped to evade the violence under which
their ancestors suffered.

Stamina of the lost,
To show his sovereign hurt. 10
Wildly we dreaded him
And the strong god of his heart

Escaping, crawling down
Ditches where papers blow,
Smearing the sills of the town, 15
Strangling the hydra-drains
Coiled under. Stop! We know
How much a man contains.

We picnicked all that day,
Dishonored signs that nayed us, 20
Pulled marigolds, were gay
Before the apes, smashed glass.
Rifles could not have made us
Keep off the bloody grass;

For we were sick of crimes 25
Against us, and the head
Pitched on the absorbing *Times,*
And no one to accuse,
And nothing paid for, and we read, 29
We read that day what blotted out the news.

Reflection by a Mailbox

WHEN I stand in the center of that man's
madness,
Deep in his trauma, as in the crater of a
wound,
My ancestors step from my American bones.
There's mother in a woven shawl, and that,
No doubt, is father picking up his pack 5

Reflection by a Mailbox. In a familiar setting the poet, waiting for his induction notice, thinks of the fate of his people in Europe, and wonders how the madness of war can be stopped and how the war itself will condition him.

For the return voyage through those dreadful
years
Into the winter of the raging eye.

One generation past, two days by plane away,
My house is dispossessed, my friends dispersed,
My teeth and pride knocked in, my people
game 10
For the hunters of man-skins in the warrens of
Europe,
The impossible creatures of an hysteriac's
dream
Advancing with hatchets sunk into their skulls
To rip the god out of the machines.

Are these the citizens of the new estate 15
To which the continental shelves aspire;
Or the powerful get of a dying age, corrupt
And passion-smeared, with fluid on their lips,
As if a soul had been given to petroleum? 19

How shall we uncreate that lawless energy?

Now I wait under the hemlock by the road
For the red-haired postman with the smiling
hand
To bring me my passport to the war.
Familiarly his car shifts into gear
Around the curve; he coasts up to my drive;
the day 25
Strikes noon; I think of Pavlov and his dogs
And the motto carved on the broad lintel of his
brain:
"Sequence, consequence, and again conse-
quence."

26. **Pavlov and his dogs.** Ivan Pavlov, the Russian scientist
(d. 1936) whose theories of human learning and motivation,
first developed through laboratory experiments on conditioned
reflexes in dogs, applied the concept of cause-and-effect to human psychology.

LOUIS MacNEICE

Louis MacNeice, one of the group of energetic poets who emerged from Oxford in the early 1930's, is of Northern Irish background and was born in Belfast on September 12, 1907. His father was Bishop of Down, Connor, and Dromore. Sent to England for his college years, MacNeice attended Marlborough College in Wiltshire and, from 1926 to 1930, Merton College, Oxford. For the six years following he was Lecturer in Classics at the University of Birmingham and in 1936 was appointed Lecturer in Greek at Bedford College for Women in the University of London.

In the summer of 1937 he went to Iceland

with W. H. Auden, the poet, to write with him *Letters from Iceland.* He had already published *Blind Fireworks* (1929); *Poems* (1935); *The Agamemnon of Aeschylus,* a verse translation (1936); and *Out of the Picture* (1937), a play. *I Crossed the Minch* (1938) is a travel book about the Hebrides; *The Earth Compels* (1938), a book of poems. He completed a critical book, *Modern Poetry,* and did much book-reviewing for the London press. He acknowledges authorship of a short-lived novel.

In his *Collected Poems (1925–1940)* it is possible to trace the stages in MacNeice's development, for the volume consists of some early work and some written even after the beginning of World War II. The later poems stress the social changes taking place in England as a result of the war. MacNeice was in the United States in 1940, but went back to England in the fall of that year to participate in his country's war effort. *Springboard* (1944) indicates a growth in his talent, and contains some of the best war poems written by an Englishman undergoing the ordeal and sensitive to the changes in temper of the people. *Holes in the Sky* appeared in 1948, and in the same year were published some of MacNeice's outstanding contributions to serious radio drama, *The Dark Tower and Other Radio Scripts.*

In general, MacNeice's poetry attempts to reconcile a personal psychology or approach to life with the Marxian theories of society. Unwilling to forego all we have learned from the writings on the mind of such psychologists as Freud and Jung, he treats his subjects both psychologically and sociologically.

Bagpipe Music

It's no go the merry-go-round, it's no go the rickshaw,
All we want is a limousine and a ticket for the peepshow.
Their knickers are made of crêpe-de-chine, their shoes are made of python,

Bagpipe Music. A poem written in the Outer Hebrides and published in MacNeice's book, *I Crossed the Minch.*

Their halls are lined with tiger rugs and their walls with heads of bison.

John MacDonald found a corpse, put it under the sofa,   5
Waited till it came to life and hit it with a poker,
Sold its eyes for souvenirs, sold its blood for whiskey,
Kept its bones for dumb-bells to use when he was fifty.

It's no go the Yogi-Man, it's no go Blavatsky,
All we want is a bank balance and a bit of skirt in a taxi.   10

Annie MacDougall went to milk, caught her foot in the heather,
Woke to hear a dance record playing of Old Vienna.
It's no go your maidenheads, it's no go your culture,
All we want is a Dunlop tyre and the devil mend the puncture.

The Laird o'Phelps spent Hogmannay declaring he was sober;   15
Counted his feet to prove the fact and found he had one foot over.
Mrs. Carmichael had her fifth, looked at the job with repulsion,
Said to the midwife 'Take it away; I'm through with overproduction.'

It's no go the gossip column, it's no go the Ceilidh,
All we want is a mother's help and a sugar-stick for the baby.   20

Willie Murray cut his thumb, couldn't count the damage,
Took the hide of an Ayrshire cow and used it for a bandage.
His brother caught three hundred cran when the seas were lavish,
Threw the bleeders back in the sea and went upon the parish.

9. **Yogi-Man,** symbol of modern man's escape here through esoteric religion. Perhaps, also, a faint pun on "bogyman." **Blavatsky,** another symbol of escape. Helen Petrovna Blavatsky (1831–91) was a celebrated Russian theosophist. 12. **Old Vienna,** another symbol of the Never-Never land. 14. **Dunlop tyre,** best known English make of automobile tire. 15. **Laird,** squire or lord of the manor. **Hogmannay,** Scottish festival of the New Year. 19. **Ceilidh,** Gaelic word, pronounced "Cailey"; a social gathering, often meaning loosely a community sing. 23. **cran,** measure of herring.

It's no go the Herring Board, it's no go the Bible,   25

All we want is a packet of fags when our hands are idle.

It's no go the picture palace, it's no go the stadium,

It's no go the country cot with a pot of pink geraniums.

It's no go the Government grants, it's no go the elections,

Sit on your arse for fifty years and hang your hat on a pension.   30

It's no go my honey love, it's no go my poppet;

Work your hands from day to day, the winds will blow the profit.

The glass is falling hour by hour, the glass will fall for ever,

But if you break the bloody glass you won't hold up the weather.

Bottleneck

NEVER to fight unless from a pure motive
And for a clear end was his unwritten rule
Who had been in books and visions to a progressive school
And dreamt of barricades, yet being observant
Knew that that was not the way things are: 5
This man would never make a soldier or a servant.

When I saw him last, carving the longshore mist
With an ascetic profile, he was standing
Watching the troopship leave, he did not speak
But from his eyes there peered a furtive footsore envy   10
Of these who sailed away to make an opposed landing—
So calm because so young, so lethal because so meek.

Where he is now I could not say; he will,
The odds are, always be non-combatant
Being too violent in soul to kill   15

25. **Herring Board,** control board instituted by the British government to buy fish from the herring fishermen, and insure them a living.   26. **fags,** English slang for cigarettes.
"Bottleneck" from *Springboard,* copyright 1945 by Random House, Inc., reprinted by permission of Random House, Inc.

Anyone but himself, yet in his mind
A crowd of odd components mutter and press
For compromise with fact, longing to be combined
Into a working whole but cannot jostle through
The permanent bottleneck of his highmindedness.

The Dark Tower

THE DARK TOWER is a parable play, belonging to that wide class of writings which includes *Everyman, The Faerie Queene,* and *The Pilgrim's Progress.* Though under the name of allegory this kind of writing is somewhat dismissed as outmoded, the clothed as distinct from the naked allegory is in fact very much alive. Obvious examples are *Peer Gynt* and the stories of Kafka but also in such books as *The Magic Mountain* by Thomas Mann, where the   10 disguise of "realism" is maintained and nothing happens that is quite inconceivable in life, it is still the symbolic core which makes the work important. My own impression is that pure "realism" is in our time almost played out, though most works of fiction of course will remain realistic *on the surface.* The single-track mind and the single-plane novel or play are almost bound to falsify the world in which we live. The fact that there is method in madness   20 and the fact that there is fact in fantasy (and equally fantasy in "fact") have been brought home to us not only by Freud and other psychologists but by events themselves. This being so, reportage can no longer masquerade as art. So the novelist, abandoning the "straight" method of photography, is likely to resort once more not only to the twist of plot but to all kinds of other twists which may help him to do justice to the world's complexity. Some element of parable therefore, far from making a   30 work thinner and more abstract, ought to make it more concrete. Man does after all live by symbols.

The dual-plane work will not normally be allegory in the algebraic sense: i.e., it will not be

"The Dark Tower" from *The Dark Tower and Other Radio Plays* by Louis MacNeice, reprinted by permission of the author and Faber & Faber, Ltd., publisher.

desirable or even possible to equate each of the outward and visible signs with a precise or rational inner meaning. Thus *The Dark Tower* was suggested to me by Browning's poem "Childe Roland to the Dark Tower Came," a work which does not admit of a completely rational analysis and still less adds up to any clear moral or message. This poem has the solidity of a dream; the writer of such a poem,
10 though he may be aware of the "meanings" implicit in his dream, must not take the dream to pieces, must present his characters concretely, must allow the story to persist as a story and not dwindle into a diagram. While I could therefore have offered here an explicit summary of those implicit "meanings" in *The Dark Tower* of which I myself was conscious, I am not doing so, because it might impair the impact of the play. I would merely say—for the
20 benefit of people like the *Daily Worker's* radio critic, who found the programme pointless and depressing—that in my opinion it is neither. *The Faerie Queene, The Pilgrim's Progress, Piers Plowman* and the early Moralities could not have been written by men without any beliefs. In an age which precludes the simple and militant faith of a Bunyan, belief (whether consciously formulated or not) still remains a *sine qua non* of the creative writer. I have my be-
30 liefs and they permeate *The Dark Tower*. But do not ask me what Ism it illustrates or what Solution it offers. You do not normally ask for such things in the single-plane work; why should they be forced upon something much more complex? "Why, look you now, how unworthy a thing you make of me!" What is life *useful* for anyway?

Comments on points of detail will be found at the end of the book. The best in this kind are
40 but shadows—and in print they are shadows of shadows. To help the reader to *hear* this piece, I will therefore add this: in production I got the actors to play their parts "straight," i.e., like flesh and blood (in dreams the characters are usually like flesh and blood too). Out of an excellent cast I am particularly grateful to Cyril Cusack for his most sensitive rendering of "Roland." And Benjamin Britten provided this programme with music which is, I think, the
50 best I have heard in a radio play. Without his music *The Dark Tower* lacks a dimension.

Opening Announcement

The Dark Tower. The programme which follows is a parable play—suggested by Robert Browning's poem "Childe Roland to the Dark Tower Came." The theme is the ancient but ever-green theme of the Quest—the dedicated adventure; the manner of presentation is that of a dream—but a dream that is full of mean-
60 *ing. Browning's poem ends with a challenge blown on a trumpet:*

> "And yet
> Dauntless the slughorn to my lips I set
> And blew. "Childe Roland to the Dark Tower came."

Note well the words, "And yet." Roland did not have to—he did not wish to—and yet in the end he came to: The Dark Tower.

(*A trumpet plays through the Challenge Call.*)

SERGEANT-TRUMPETER.
70 There now, that's the challenge. And mark this:
Always hold the note at the end.
GAVIN.
Yes, Sergeant-Trumpeter, yes.
ROLAND (*as a boy*).
Why need Gavin hold the note at the end?
SERGEANT-TRUMPETER.
Ach, ye're too young to know. It's all tradition.
ROLAND.
What's tradition, Sergeant-Trumpeter?
GAVIN.
80 Ask Mother that one (*with a half-laugh*). She knows.
SERGEANT-TRUMPETER.
Aye, *she* knows.
But run along, sonny. Leave your brother to practise.

(*The trumpet begins—but breaks off.*)

SERGEANT-TRUMPETER.
No, again.

(*The trumpet re-begins—breaks off.*)

SERGEANT-TRUMPETER.
Again.

(*The trumpet re-begins and is sustained.*)

987

SERGEANT-TRUMPETER.

> That's it now. But hold that last note —hold it!

(On the long last note the trumpet fades into the distance.)

ROLAND.

> Mother! What's tradition?

MOTHER.

> Hand me that album. No—the black one.

ROLAND.

> Not the locked one!

MOTHER.

> Yes, the locked one. I have the key. Now, Roland, sit here by me on the sofa.
> We'll look at them backwards.

ROLAND.

> Why must we look at them backwards?

MOTHER.

> Because then you may recognize— Now! You know who this is?

ROLAND.

> Why, that's my brother Michael. And here's my brother Henry. Michael and Henry and Denis and Roger and John!

(He speaks with the bright callousness of children.)

> Do you keep this album locked because they're dead?

MOTHER.

> No . . . not exactly. Now—can you guess who this is?

ROLAND.

> That's someone I saw in a dream once.

MOTHER.

> It must have been in a dream. He left this house three months before you were born.

ROLAND.

> Is it . . . is it my father?

MOTHER.

> Yes. And this is your grandfather. And this is his father— For the time being you needn't look at the rest;

> This book goes back through seven long generations
> As far as George the founder of the family.

ROLAND.

> And did they all die the same way?

MOTHER.

> They did, Roland. And now I've answered your question.

ROLAND *(already forgetting)*.

> What question, Mother?

(The trumpet call is heard in the distance.)

ROLAND.

> Ah, there's Gavin practising. He's got it right at last.

(The Call ends and Gavin appears.)

GAVIN *(excited)*.

> Mother! I know the challenge. When can I leave? Tomorrow?

MOTHER.

> Why not today, Gavin?

GAVIN.

> Today! But I haven't yet checked my equipment; I mean—for such a long journey I—

MOTHER.

> You will travel light, my son.

GAVIN.

> Well, yes . . . of course . . . today then.

ROLAND.

> Where are you going, Gavin?

GAVIN.

> Why, surely you know; I'm—

MOTHER.

> Hsh!

ROLAND.

> I know where he's going. Across the sea like Michael.

GAVIN.

> That's right, Roland. Across the big, bad sea. Like Michael and Henry and Denis and Roger and John. And after that through the Forest. And after that through the Desert.—

ROLAND.

> What's the Desert made of?

GAVIN.

> Well . . . I've never been there.

Some deserts are made of sand and
some are made of grit but—

MOTHER (*as if to herself*).

This one is made of doubts and dried-
up hopes.

ROLAND (*still bright*).

And what do you find at the other
end of the desert?

GAVIN.

Well, I . . . well . . .

MOTHER.

You can tell him.

GAVIN.

I find the Dark Tower.

(*The Dark Tower theme gives a musical transition to the schoolroom.*)

TUTOR.

Now, Master Roland, as this is our
first day of lessons
I trust I shall find you as willing a
pupil
As your six brothers before you.

ROLAND.

Did you like teaching my brothers?

TUTOR.

Like it? It was an honor.
It was teaching to some purpose.

ROLAND.

When's my brother Gavin coming
back?

TUTOR.

What!

ROLAND.

Gavin. When's he coming back?

TUTOR.

Roland . . .
I see I must start from the beginning.
I thought your mother'd have told
you but maybe being the youngest—

ROLAND.

What would my mother have told
me?

TUTOR.

You ask when your brother Gavin is
coming back?
You must get this straight from the
start:
Your family never come back.

(*Roland begins to interrupt.*)

TUTOR.

Now, now, now, don't let me scare
you.
Sit down on that stool and I'll try to
explain.
Now, Roland—
I said that to teach your brothers was
an honor.
Before your mother engaged me to
tutor John
I was an usher in a great city,
I taught two dozen lads in a class—
The sons of careerists—salesmen, mid-
dlemen, half-men,
Governed by greed and caution; it
was my job
To teach them enough—and only
enough—
To fit them for making money. Means
to a means.
But with your family it is a means to
an end.

ROLAND (*naively puzzled*).

My family don't make money?

TUTOR.

They make history.

ROLAND.

And what do you mean by an end?

TUTOR.

I mean—surely they told you?
I mean: the Dark Tower.

ROLAND.

Will *I* ever go to the Dark Tower?

TUTOR.

Of course you will. That is why I am
here.

ROLAND (*gaily*).

Oh well! That's different!

TUTOR.

It is.

ROLAND.

And that means I'll fight the Dragon?

TUTOR.

Yes—but let me tell you:
We call it the Dragon for short, it is
a nameless force
Hard to define—for no one who has
seen it,
Apart from those who have seen its
handiwork,
Has returned to give an account of it.

All that we know is there is something there
Which makes the Dark Tower dark and is the source
Of evil through the world. It is immortal
But men must try to kill it—and keep on trying
So long as we would be human.

ROLAND.

10   What would happen
If we just let it alone?

TUTOR.

Well . . . some of us would live longer; all of us
Would lead a degraded life, for the Dragon would be supreme
Over our minds as well as our bodies. Gavin—
And Michael and Henry and Denis and Roger and John—

20   Might still be here—perhaps your father too,
He would be seventy-five—but mark this well:
They would not be themselves. Do you understand?

ROLAND.

I'm not quite sure, I . . .

TUTOR.

You are still small. We'll talk of the Dragon later.
Now come to the blackboard and
30   we'll try some Latin.
You see this sentence?

ROLAND.

Per ardua . . .

TUTOR.

Per ardua ad astra.

ROLAND.

What does it mean?

TUTOR.

It does not go very well in a modern language.
We had a word 'honor'—but it is obsolete.
Try the word 'duty'; and there's an-
40   other word—
'Necessity.'

ROLAND.

Necessity! That's a bit hard to spell.

TUTOR.

You'll have to spell it, I fear. Repeat this after me:
N—

ROLAND.

N—

TUTOR.

E—

ROLAND.

E—

(As they spell it through, their voices dwindle away and a tolling bell grows up out of the 50 *distance.)*

SERGEANT-TRUMPETER.

Ah, God, there's the bell for Gavin.
He had the greatest power to his lungs of the lot of them.
And now he's another name in the roll of honor
Where Michael's is still new gold.
Five years it is—
Or would it be more like six—since we tolled for Michael?   60
Bells and trumpets, trumpets and bells,
I'll have to be learning the young one next;
Then he'll be away too and my lady will have no more.

MOTHER (*coldly; she has come up behind him*).

No more children, Sergeant-Trumpeter?

SERGEANT-TRUMPETER.

Ach, I beg your pardon. I didn't see you.   70

MOTHER.

No matter. But know this:
I have one more child to bear.
No, I'm not mad; you needn't stare at me, Sergeant.
This is a child of stone.

SERGEANT-TRUMPETER.

A child of . . . ?

MOTHER.

Stone. To be born on my death-bed.
No matter. I'm speaking in metaphor.

SERGEANT-TRUMPETER (*relieved to change the subject*).

That's all right, then. How's young Roland   80
Making out at his lessons?

MOTHER.

I don't know. Roland lacks concentration; he's not like my other sons,

He's almost flippant, he's always asking questions—

SERGEANT-TRUMPETER.

Ach, he's young yet.

MOTHER.

Gavin was his age once.

So were Michael and Henry and Denis and Roger and John.

They never forgot what they learnt.

10 And they asked no questions.

SERGEANT-TRUMPETER.

Ah well—by the time that Roland comes to me

When he's had his fill of theory and is all set for action,

In another half dozen years when he comes to learn the trumpet call—

MOTHER.

Hsh, don't talk of it now.

(*as if to herself*).

Let one bell toll at a time.

20 (*The bell recedes into nothing, covering a passage of years. Roland is now grown up.*)

TUTOR.

So ends our course on ethics. Thank you, Roland;

After all these years our syllabus is concluded.

You have a brain; what remains to be tried is your will.

Remember our point today: the sensitive man

30 Is more exposed to seduction. In six years

I have come to know you; you have a warm heart—

It is perhaps too warm for a man with your commission;

Therefore be careful. Keep to your one resolve,

Your single code of conduct, listen to no one

40 Who doubts your values—and above all, Roland,

Never fall in love—That is not for you.

If ever a hint of love should enter your heart,

You must arise and go. . . . That's it: Go!

Yes, Roland my son. Go quickly.

(*His last words fade slightly and Sylvie's voice fades in.*) 50

SYLVIE.

But why must you go so quickly? Now that the sun's come out.

ROLAND.

I have my lesson to learn.

SYLVIE.

You're always learning lessons!

I'll begin to think you prefer your books to me.

ROLAND.

Oh, but Sylvie, this isn't books any more.

SYLVIE.

Not books? Then—

ROLAND.

I'm learning to play the trumpet. 60

SYLVIE (*irritated*).

Whatever for? Roland, you make me laugh.

Is this another idea of your mother's?

I needn't ask. What's all this leading to?

ROLAND (*quietly*).

I could tell you, darling. But not today.

Today is a thing in itself—apart from the future.

Whatever follows, I will remember 70 this tree

With this dazzle of sun and shadow —and I will remember

The mayflies jigging above us in the delight

Of the dying instant—and I'll remember *you*

With the bronze lights in your hair.

SYLVIE.

Yes, darling; but why so sad?

There will be other trees and— 80

ROLAND.

Each tree is itself, each moment is itself,

Inviolable gifts of time . . . of God—

But you cannot take them with you.

SYLVIE.

Take them with you where?

ROLAND.

Kiss me, Sylvie. I'm keeping my teacher waiting.

(*The Challenge Call is played through once.*)

SERGEANT-TRUMPETER.

Nicely blown! Nicely blown!

You've graduated, my lad.

But remember—when I'm not here—hold the note at the end.

ROLAND (*a shade bitter*).

You mean when *I'm* not here.

SERGEANT-TRUMPETER.

Aye, you're right. But you are my last pupil,

I'll be shutting up shop, I want you to do me credit.

When you've crossed the sea and the desert and come to the place itself

I want you to do me credit when you unsling that horn.

ROLAND.

I hope I will.

(*He pauses; then slightly embarrassed.*)

ROLAND.

Sergeant?

SERGEANT-TRUMPETER.

Eh?

ROLAND.

Do you believe all this?

SERGEANT-TRUMPETER.

All what?

ROLAND.

Do you think that there really is any dragon to fight?

SERGEANT-TRUMPETER.

What are you saying! What was it killed Gavin?

And Michael and Henry and Denis and Roger and John,

And your father himself and his father before him and all of them back to George!

ROLAND.

I don't know but . . . nobody's *seen* this dragon.

SERGEANT-TRUMPETER.

Seen him? They've seen what he's done!

Have you never talked to Blind Peter?

I thought not. Cooped up here in the castle—

Inside this big black ring of smothering yew-trees—

You never mixed with the folk.

But before you leave—if you want a reason for leaving—

I recommend that you pay a call on Peter.

And his house is low; mind your head as you enter.

(*Another verbal transition.*)

BLIND PETER (*old and broken*).

That's right, sir; mind your head as you enter.

Now take that chair, it's the only one with springs,

I saved it from my hey-day. Well now, sir,

It's kind of you to visit me. I can tell

By your voice alone that you're your father's son;

Your handshake's not so strong though.

ROLAND.

Why, was my father—

BLIND PETER.

He had a grip of iron.

And what's more, sir, he had a will of iron.

And what's still more again, he had a conscience—

Which is something we all need. *I* should know!

ROLAND.

Why?

BLIND PETER.

Why what?

ROLAND.

Why do you sound so sad when you talk about having a conscience?

BLIND PETER.

Because his conscience is something a man can lose.

It's cold in here, I'll make a long story short.

Fifty years ago when I had my sight—

But the Dragon was loose at the time—

I had a job and a wife and a new-born child

And I believed in God. Until one day—

I told you the Dragon was loose at the time,

No one had challenged him lately; so he came out from his den—

What some people call the Tower—and creeping around

He got to our part of the world; nobody saw him of course,

There was just like a kind of a bad smell in the air

And everything went sour; people's mouths and eyes

Changed their look overnight—and the government changed too—

And as for me I woke up feeling different

And when I looked in the mirror that first morning

The mirror said 'Informer'!

ROLAND (*startled*).

Informer?

BLIND PETER.

Yes, sir. My new rôle.

They passed a pack of laws forbidding this and that

And anyone breaking 'em—the penalty was death.

I grew quite rich sending men to their death.

The last I sent was my wife's father.

ROLAND.

But . . . but did you believe in these laws?

BLIND PETER.

Believe? Aha! Did I believe in anything?

God had gone round the corner. I was acquiring riches.

But to make a long story short—

When they hanged my wife's father my wife took poison,

So I was left with the child. Then the child took ill—

Scared me stiff—so I sent for all the doctors,

I could afford 'em then—but they couldn't discover

Anything wrong in its body, it was more as if its soul

Was set on quitting—and indeed why not?

To be a human being, people agree, is difficult.

ROLAND.

Then the child . . . ?

BLIND PETER.

Quit.

Yes; she quit—but slowly.

I watched it happen. That's why now I'm blind.

ROLAND.

Why? You don't mean you yourself—

BLIND PETER.

When you've seen certain things, you don't want to see no more.

Tell me, sir. Are people's faces nowadays

As ugly as they were? You know what I mean: evil?

ROLAND.

No, not most of them. *Some*, I suppose—

BLIND PETER.

Those ones belong to the Dragon.

ROLAND (*exasperated*).

Why put the blame of everything on the Dragon?

Men have free choice, haven't they?

Free choice of good or evil—

BLIND PETER.

That's just it—

And the evil choice is the Dragon!

But I needn't explain it to you, sir; *you've* made up your mind,

You're like your father—one of the dedicated

Whose life is a quest, whose death is a victory.

Yes! God bless you! *You've* made up your mind!

ROLAND (*slowly and contemplatively*).

But have I, Peter? Have I?

(*Verbal transition.*)

993

SYLVIE.

Have you, Roland dearest? Really made up your mind?

ROLAND (*without expression*).

I go away today.

SYLVIE.

That's no answer.

You go away because they tell you to.

Because your mother's brought you up on nothing

But out of date beliefs and mock heroics.

It's easy enough for her—

ROLAND (*indignantly*).

Easy for her?

Who's given her flesh and blood—and I'm the seventh son!

SYLVIE.

I've heard all that. They call it sacrifice

But each new death is a stone in a necklace to her.

Your mother, Roland, is mad.

ROLAND (*with quiet conviction*).

The world is mad.

SYLVIE.

Not all of it, my love. Those who have power

Are mad enough but there *are* people, Roland,

Who keep themselves to themselves or rather to each other,

Living a sane and gentle life in a forest nook or a hill pocket,

Perpetuating their kind and their kindness, keeping

Their hands clean and their eyes keen, at one with

Themselves, each other and nature. I had thought

That you and I perhaps—

ROLAND.

There is no perhaps

In my tradition, Sylvie.

SYLVIE.

You mean in your family's.

Isn't it time you saw that you were different?

You're no knight errant, Roland.

ROLAND.

No, I'm not.

But there is a word 'Necessity'—

SYLVIE.

Necessity? You mean your mother's orders.

ROLAND (*controlled*).

Not quite. But apart from that,

I saw a man today—they call him Blind Peter—

SYLVIE.

Leave the blind to mislead the blind. That Peter

Is where he is because of his own weakness;

You can't help him, Roland.

ROLAND.

Maybe not—

(*with sudden insight*).

But maybe I can do something to prevent

A recurrence of Blind Peters.

SYLVIE.

Imagination!

ROLAND.

Imagination? . . . That things can be bettered?

That action can be worth-while? That there are ends

Which, even if not reached, are worth approaching?

Imagination? Yes, I wish I had it—

I have a little—You should support that little

And not support my doubts.

(*A drum-roll is heard.*)

ROLAND.

Listen; there is the drum.

They are waiting for me at the gate.

Sylvie, I—

SYLVIE.

Kiss me at least.

(*Pause, while the drum changes rhythm.*)

ROLAND.

I shall never—

SYLVIE.

See me again?

You will, Roland, you will.

I know you. You will set out but you won't go on,

Your common sense will triumph, you'll come back.

994

And your love for me will triumph
and in the end—

ROLAND.

This is the end. Goodbye.

(*The drum swells and ends on a peak. This is
the Scene of Departure.*)

TUTOR.

To you, Roland, my last message:
For seven years I have been your tu-
tor.
You have worked hard on the whole
but whether really
You have grasped the point of it all
remains to be seen.
A man lives on a sliding staircase—
Sliding downwards, remember; to be
a man
He has to climb against it, keeping
level
Or even ascending slightly; he will
not reach
The top—if there is a top—and when
he dies
He will slump and go down regard-
less. All the same
While he lives he must climb. Re-
member that.
And I thank you for your attention.
Goodbye, Roland.

SERGEANT-TRUMPETER.

To you, Roland, my last message:
You are off now on the Quest like
your brothers before you
To take a slap at the Evil that never
dies.
Well, here's this trumpet; sling it
around your waist
And keep it bright and clean till the
time comes
When you have to sound the chal-
lenge—the first and the last time—
And I trust you will do your old in-
structor credit
And put the fear of God—or of Man
—into that Dragon.
That's all now. God bless you. But re-
member—
Hold that note at the end.

MOTHER.

To you, Roland, my last message:

Here is a ring with a blood-red stone.
So long as
This stone retains its color, it means
that I
Retain my purpose in sending you on
the Quest.
I put it now on your finger.

ROLAND.

Mother! It burns.

MOTHER.

That is the heat in the stone. So long
as the stone is red
The ring will burn and that small cir-
cle of fire
Around your little finger will be also
The circle of my will around your
mind.
I gave a ring like this to your father,
Roland,
And to John and Roger and Denis
and Henry and Michael
And to Gavin the last before you. My
will was around and behind them
Should ever you doubt or waver,
look at this ring—
And feel it burn—and go on.

ROLAND.

Mother! Before I go—

MOTHER.

No more words. Go!
Turn your face to the sea. (*Raising
her voice.*) Open the gates there!
(*aside*)
The March of Departure, Sergeant.
Let my son go out—my last. And
make the music gay!

(*The March begins at full volume, then gradually dwindles as Roland and the listener move
away. By the time the music has vanished Roland has reached the Port, where he addresses
a stranger.*)

ROLAND.

Forgive me stopping you, sir—

SOAK (*old, alcoholic, leering*).

Forgive you? Certainly not.
I'm on my way to the Tavern.

ROLAND.

I'm on my way to the quays. Is it
this turning or next?

SOAK.

Any turning you like. Look down these stinking streets—
There's sea at the end of each of 'em.
Yes, young man, but what's at the end of the sea?
Never believe what they said when you booked your passage.

ROLAND.

But I haven't booked it yet.

SOAK.

Not booked your passage yet! Why, then there's no need to hurry.
You come with me to the Tavern; it's only a step.

ROLAND.

I cannot spare a step.

SOAK.

All right, all right;
If you won't come to the Tavern, the Tavern must come to you.
Ho there, music!

(*The orchestra strikes up raggedly—continuing while he speaks.*)

SOAK.

That's the idea. Music does wonders, young man.
Music can build a palace, let alone a pub.
Come on, you masons of the Muses, swing it,
Fling me up four walls. Now, now, don't drop your tempo;
Easy with those hods. All right; four walls.
Now benches—tables—No! No doors or windows.
What drunk wants daylight? But you've left out the bar.
Come on—'Cellos! Percussion! All of you! A bar!
That's right. Dismiss!

(*The music ends.*)

SOAK.

Barmaid.

BARMAID.

Yes, sir?

SOAK.

Give us whatever you have and make it triple.

ROLAND.

Just a small one for me, please.

SOAK.

Oh, don't be so objective. One would think,
Looking at your long face, that there's a war on.

ROLAND.

But—

SOAK.

There is no war on—and you have no face.
Drink up. Don't be objective.

ROLAND.

What in the name of—

BARMAID.

Look, dearie; don't mind *him*.
He always talks like that. You take my tip;
You're new here and this town is a sea-port,
The tone is rather. . . . You go somewhere inland.

ROLAND.

But how can I?
I have to go to sea.

BARMAID (*seriously*).

The sea out there leads nowhere.

SOAK.

Come, sweetheart, the same again.

BARMAID.

Nowhere, I've warned you. (*In a whisper.*) As for our friend here,
Don't stay too long in his company.

SOAK.

What's that? Don't stay too long in my what?

BARMAID.

Company was the word.

SOAK.

Company? I have none. Why, how could I?
There's never anyone around where I am.
I exist for myself and all the rest is projection.
Come on, projection, drink! Dance on your strings and drink!

BARMAID.

Oblige him, dearie, oblige him.

SOAK.

There! My projection drinks.

I wrote this farce before I was born, you know—

This puppet play. In my mother's womb, dear boy—

I have never abdicated the life of the womb.

Watch, Mabel: my new puppet drinks again—

A pretty boy but I've given him no more lines.

Have I, young man?

(*pause*)

You see, he cannot speak.

All he can do henceforward is to drink—

Look! A pull on the wire—the elbow lifts.

Give him the same again.

BARMAID.

Well . . .

SOAK.

There is no well about it. Except the well

That has no bottom and that fills the world.

Triplets, I said. Where are those damned musicians?

Buck up, you puppets! Play!

(*The orchestra strikes up a lullaby, continued behind his speech.*)

SOAK (*sleepily*).

Good. Serenade me now till I fall asleep

And all the notes are one—and all the sounds are silence.

Unity, Mabel, unity is my motto,

The end of drink is a whole without any parts—

A great black sponge of night that fills the world.

And when you squeeze it, Mabel, it drips inwards.

D'you want me to squeeze it? Right. Piano there.

Piano—I must sleep. Didn't you hear me?

Piano, puppets. All right, pianissimo. Nissimo . . . nissimo . . . issimo . . .

(*The music ends and only his snoring is heard.*)

ROLAND.

A puppet? . . . A projection. . . . How he lies!

And yet I've sometimes thought the same, you know—

The same but the other way round.

There is no evidence for anything

Except my own existence—he says his.

But he's wrong anyway—look at him snoring there.

If I were something existing in his mind

How could I go on now that he's asleep.

SOAK (*muffled*).

Because I'm dreaming you.

ROLAND.

Dreaming?

BARMAID.

Yes, sir.

He does have curious dreams.

SOAK.

Yes, and the curious thing about my dreams

Is that they always have an unhappy ending

For all except the dreamer. Thus at the moment

You'd never guess, young man, what rôle I've cast you for—

ROLAND.

What the—

BARMAID.

Never mind, dear.

Tomorrow he'll wake up.

ROLAND.

Tomorrow *he'll* wake up?

And I—Shall I wake up? Perhaps to find

That this whole Quest is a dream. Perhaps I'm still at home

In my bed by the window looking across the valley

Between the yew-trees to where Sylvie lives

Not among yews but apples—

(*He is interrupted by a terrific voice crashing in on the 'Bar' from the outer world.*)

STENTOR.

All aboard!

ROLAND.

What's that?

STENTOR.

All aboard!

SOAK.

You'd never guess

What happens in my dream. . . .

STENTOR.

All aboard! All aboard!

Come along there, young man—unless you want to be left.

All aboard for the Further Side of the Sea,

10   For the Dead End of the World and the Bourne of No Return!

(*The noise of a crowd materializes, increasing.*)

STENTOR.

All Aboard, ladies and gents, knaves and fools, babes and sucklings,

Philistines,   pharisees,   parasites, pimps,

Nymphos and dipsos—All Aboard!

Lost souls and broken bodies; make it snappy.

20   That's right, folks. Mind your feet on the gangway.

(*Through the racket of gadarening passengers is heard the mechanical voice of the Ticket Collector.*)

TICKET COLLECTOR.

Ticket?   Thank   you. . . . Ticket? Thank you. . . . Ticket? Thank you. . . . Ticket? . . . Thank you. . . .

(*The crowd noises fade out; Roland is now below decks.*)

STEWARD (*with an 'off-straight' accent*).

30   This way, sir. Let me show you your stateroom.

Hot and cold and a blue light over the bed.

Ring once for a drink, twice for an aspirin.

Now if you want anything else—a manicure, for example.—

ROLAND.

No, steward. A sleeping draught.

STEWARD (*archly*).

Sir! In the morning?

ROLAND.

Morning be damned. My head aches. 40

STEWARD.

Drinking last night, sir?

ROLAND.

Thinking.

STEWARD (*rattling it off*).

Thinking? That's too bad, sir.

But you'll soon get over that, sir.

In this ship nobody thinks, sir.

Why should they? They're at sea, sir. . . .

And if your brain's at sea, sir—

ROLAND (*angrily*).

Listen! I want a sleeping draught,

How many times do I have to ring 50 for that?

STEWARD (*unperturbed*).

As many times as you like, sir.

If you can keep awake, sir.

(*pimpishly*).

But talking of sleeping draughts, sir,

Do you hear that lady playing the fiddle?

ROLAND.

Fiddle? No, I don't.

STEWARD.

Ah, that's because she plays it in her head. 60

But she's a very nice lady, sir.

Her name, sir, is Neaera.

ROLAND.

Why should I care what her name is?

I tell you, steward—

STEWARD.

Of course if you'd rather play tombola—

ROLAND.

Tombola?

STEWARD (*throwing it away*).

Game of chance, sir. They call out numbers.

Kills the time, sir. Rather like life, sir. 70

You can buy your tickets now in the lounge.

The ship's started, you know, sir.

ROLAND.

Oh, so the ship's started?

(*worried*)

But I can't hear the engines.

STEWARD.

Can't you, sir? I was right then.

ROLAND.

Right? What do you mean?

STEWARD.

I thought so the moment I saw you.
You don't, sir; of course you don't.

ROLAND.

Don't what, damn you? Don't what?

STEWARD.

You don't know where you're going,
sir.

(The ship's engines are heard on the orchestra; from them emerges the chatter of the lounge with the banal laughter of tombola players.)

OFFICER.

Clickety-click, sixty-six. . . .
Kelly's Eye; Number One. . . .
And we—

CROWD *(raggedly)*.

Shake the Bag!

(The orchestral engines give place to a solo violin.)

NEAERA *(to herself, velvety)*.

. . . Andantino . . . rallentando . . .
adagio—

(Her violin-playing breaks off.)

NEAERA *(foreign accent)*.

Mon Dieu! You startled me.

ROLAND.

I'm sorry, I—

NEAERA *(cooingly)*.

Do sit down. So you're going Nowhere too?

ROLAND.

On the contrary, Madam—

NEAERA.

Call me Neaera.

ROLAND.

But—

NEAERA.

And I'll call you Roland.

ROLAND.

How do you know my name?

NEAERA.

A little bird told me. A swan, if you
want to know;
He sang your name and he died.
That's right, sit down. I've seen your
dossier too.

ROLAND.

Seen my—

NEAERA.

Oh yes, chéri. In the Captain's cabin.

ROLAND.

But how can I have a dossier? I've
done nothing.

NEAERA.

That's just it. It's dull.
But the future part amuses me.
Oh yes, my dear, this dossier includes 40
the future—
And you don't come out of it well.

ROLAND.

What do you mean?

NEAERA.

You never believed in this Quest of
yours, you see—
The Dark Tower—the Dragon—all
this blague.
That's why you were so easy to seduce
In the idle days at sea—the days that 50
are just beginning.

(Her violin begins again, then gives way to the lounge chatter, covering a passage of time.)

OFFICER.

Key of the Door: Twenty-One!
Eleventh Hour: Eleven!
Ten Commandments: Nine!
Kelly's Eye: Number One!
And we—

CROWD.

Shake the Bag!

(The violin re-emerges.) 60

NEAERA.

. . . Lento . . . accelerando . . .
presto . . . calando . . . morendo . . .

(The violin fades away; it is meant to have established an affaire between Roland and Neaera.)

STEWARD *(slyly)*.

Well, sir? So the lady is still practis-
ing.
Golden days, sir, golden days.
At sea, sir, have you noticed
One doesn't notice time? 70
You probably feel you just came on
board yesterday

And yet you got your sea-legs weeks ago, sir.

ROLAND.

Sea-legs? Why, this trip has been so calm
I've never felt—

STEWARD.

That's right, sir; never feel.
There's nothing in life but profit and pleasure.
Allegro assai—some people plump for pleasure.
But I now fancy the profit—

(*Receiving a tip.*)

Ah thank you, sir, thank you.
The sea today in the sun, sir, looks like what shall I say, sir?

ROLAND.

The sea today? A dance of golden sovereigns.

NEAERA.

The sea today is adagios of doves.

ROLAND.

The sea today is gulls and dolphins.

NEAERA.

The sea today is noughts and crosses.

OFFICER (*cutting in rapidly*).

And we—

CROWD.

Shake the Bag!

NEAERA.

The sea today, Roland, is crystal.

ROLAND.

The sea today, Neaera, is timeless.

NEAERA.

The sea today is drums and fifes.

ROLAND.

The sea today is broken bottles.

NEAERA.

The sea today is snakes and ladders.

OFFICER (*as before*).

Especially snakes!

CROWD.

Especially snakes!

NEAERA (*wheedling*).

Roland, what's that ring? I've never seen one like it.

ROLAND.

There is no other ring like it.

NEAERA.

A strange ring for a man. . . .

My color, you know—that red. . . .
Why do you twitch your finger?

ROLAND.

Because it burns.

NEAERA.

It burns?
Like tingling ears perhaps? Someone is thinking of you.

ROLAND (*startled—and suddenly depressed*).

What? . . . I hope not.
(*changing the subject*)
Come, darling, let's have a drink.

OFFICER.

And we—

CROWD.

Shake the Bag!

ROLAND.

The sea today is drunken marble.

NEAERA.

The sea today is silver stallions.

ROLAND.

The sea today is—Tell me, steward;
Where's all this floating seaweed come from?

STEWARD.

I imagine, sir—forgive me mentioning it—
That we are approaching land.

ROLAND.

Land!

STEWARD.

Yes, sir—but you won't be landing, of course.
The best people never land, sir.

ROLAND.

No? . . . (*to himself, fatalistically*)
I suppose not.

(*Neaera's violin is heard again.*)

NEAERA (*to herself*).

. . . piu sonoro . . . con forza . . . accelerando . . . crescendo . . .

(*The orchestra is added for a final crashing chord and at once we hear the hubbub of a crowd.*)

STENTOR.

Anyone more for the shore? Anyone more for the shore?
Line up there on the forward deck
All what wants to chance their neck!
Anyone more for the shore?

TICKET COLLECTOR.

This way: thank you—This way: thank you—

This way: thank you—This way: thank you—

STENTOR.

Anyone more? Hurry up please!

But remember this: Once you're off You can't come back not ever on board.

We leave at once. At once!

TICKET COLLECTOR.

10   This way: thank you—This way: thank you—This way: thank you—This way: thank you.

1ST PASSENGER (*cockney*).

Here, here, who're you shoving? What's the blinkin' hurry?

HIS WIFE.

That's right.

1ST PASSENGER.

Some people seem very keen to land in the future.

Can't use their eyes—if you ask me!

HIS WIFE.

That's right. Look at them vicious

20   rocks.

1ST PASSENGER.

And that tumble-down shack what thinks it's a Customs House.

HIS WIFE.

And them horrible mountains behind it.

2ND PASSENGER (*northern*).

You'd think this country was uninhabited.

TICKET COLLECTOR.

This way: thank you—This way: thank you—(*with finality*) This way: thank you!

30   (*wearily*) O.K., sir. That's the lot.

STENTOR.

Gangway up! Gangway up!

Clear away there. Mind your heads!

NEAERA.

What are you staring at, Roland?

Come away, chéri; the show's over.

There goes the gangway; we're moving out now.

What *are* you staring at, darling?

ROLAND (*to himself*).

Was that . . . was that . . . I

couldn't see in the face of the sun but—

Steward, you've sharp eyes.   40

Did you see over there on the quay, sitting on a rusty bollard—

STEWARD.

Hsh, sir, Neaera will hear you.

Yes, sir; a very nice piece.

She was looking at you, sir, too—staring in fact, one might say.

Seems to be staring still—but what's she doing now?

Climbing up on the bollard?

Good Lord, sir, that's bad form; she's   50 making gestures.

SYLVIE (*distant cry*).

Roland! . . . Roland! . . .

ROLAND.

Sylvie!

I knew it. Out of my way there!

STENTOR.

Here, here, here! Stop him!

Man gone mad there! Don't let him jump!

(*General commotion.*)

NEAERA.

Roland! Come back!

(*A loud splash from the orchestra.*)   60

STENTOR.

Man overboard! Man overboard!

(*The crowd reacts excitedly.*)

STENTOR.

Lifebuoy! Where's the lifebuoy?

VOICE.

Garn! This here ship don't carry no lifebuoys.

Nor he won't need one. Look! He's climbing up on the quay.

(*The orchestral engines start up again.*)

OFFICER (*triumphantly*).

And we—

CROWD.

Shake the Bag!   70

NEAERA (*now revealing her hardness*).

Well, James. . . . That's that.

STEWARD.

Yes, madam.

NEAERA.

You can drop the madam now.

STEWARD.

Yes, Neaera—my sweetie-pie.

NEAERA (*matter-of-fact*).

That's more like it, James, my great big he-man.

Come to my cabin now; we'll count the takings.

(*The fading engines take the liner to sea; Roland is left on the Shore, with Sylvie sobbing.*)

ROLAND (*dead-pan*).

There she goes now.

SYLVIE (*echoing him*).

There she goes now. . . .

10 (*then bursting out*)

Roland, you are a hypocrite!

ROLAND (*quietly—but ashamed*).

No, Sylvie; merely a sleep-walker. Ugh! (*He shivers.*)

SYLVIE (*calm again*).

The sea must have been cold. Come, let's walk.

ROLAND.

How did you get here, Sylvie?

SYLVIE (*a shade bitter*).

I followed you—but not on a luxury liner.

Mine was a cargo boat, its limit was

20 seven knots.

ROLAND.

And yet you got here first.

And now I suppose you regret it.

Are you going to leave me, Sylvie?

SYLVIE.

How can I? We're marooned here.

This is a desolate land. (*With forced control*). I suggest we keep together.

ROLAND.

You have the gift of forgiveness.

SYLVIE.

I have the gift of common sense.

As you're bound to be seduced from

30 your so-called Quest,

In future, Roland, leave the seducing to me.

Or can't I, perhaps, compete with your ladies of pleasure?

ROLAND.

Pleasure? That was not pleasure.

SYLVIE.

It was. But it was not happiness.

ROLAND.

And *you* offer me happiness?

SYLVIE.

You doubt that I have it to offer?

ROLAND.

No, I don't doubt that. But my tutor

40 always said

Happiness cannot be taken as a present.

SYLVIE.

Forget your tutor. This is a foreign land

Where no one will interfere with us.

ROLAND.

No one? No *man* perhaps.

SYLVIE.

What do you mean by that?

ROLAND.

Look around you, Sylvie. See the deserted port,

The ruined shacks, the slag-heaps 50 covered with lichen

And behind it all the frown and fear of the forest.

This is the Dragon's demesne.

SYLVIE.

Roland, how childish you are.

ROLAND.

You think so? Look at this notice

That flaps here on the hoarding—

And this one and this one and this one.

SYLVIE (*reading*).

"Wanted for Murder". . . . "Wanted 60 for Murder". . . . "Wanted"—

ROLAND.

You're reading the words wrong. Not "for," Sylvie; "to!"

SYLVIE.

"Wanted to Murder." You're right. But what does it mean?

ROLAND.

It means we are on a soil where murder pays.

SYLVIE.

It pays in many places.

ROLAND.

Yes, but here

The paymaster is the government— 70 and pay-day

Is every day of the week.

The Dragon's doing, I tell you.

SYLVIE.

Well, if it is, *you* cannot cure it.
At the best you can cure yourself—
(*tentatively*)
And that only through love.

ROLAND.

Love?

SYLVIE (*stronger*)

Through me, Roland, through me.

(*pause*).

ROLAND (*quietly, as if solving a problem*).

Yes, I think you're right.

(*Then with sudden decisiveness*)

Sylvie, take this ring; I cannot wear
it now,
I have failed this ring—but this ring
will not fail you.

SYLVIE.

You mean . . . ?

ROLAND.

Yes. Let me put it on your finger.

SYLVIE.

Not yet, Roland. That must be done
in a church.

ROLAND.

And where can we find a church
round here?

SYLVIE (*half abstracted*).

What a strange color. Like the blood
of a child.

ROLAND.

I repeat! Where can we find a church
or a chapel here?

(*The Tout pops up. He speaks in broken English.*)

TOUT.

'Scusa. Lady and gentleman want
guide to chapel?

ROLAND.

God! Where did this come from?

TOUT.

Me? Me come from sewer.
Me accresited guide—very good, very
funny.
Lady and gentleman see chapel today?

ROLAND.

Where is this chapel of yours?

TOUT.

Chapel not mine, chapel belong to
God.
Me take you there up this road, see.
Me tell you history, very much his-
tory, cheap.

(*A distant bell is heard, which continues as
they speak.*)

TOUT.

That chapel-bell, tee-hee!
Ting-a-ling for the wedding!

ROLAND.

What wedding?

TOUT.

Me not know. No, sir, nobody know.
Happy pair not come yet.

SYLVIE.

Roland, this is a sign.
Tell him to show us the way.

TOUT.

Me show you the way sure.
Beautiful lady put best foot first.
Chapel up there in forest.

ROLAND.

In the forest?

TOUT.

Sure, boss. Chapel old.
Chapel in forest before forest grew.
But needs repairs now bad.
Haunted too—tee-hee!

ROLAND.

Haunted!

TOUT.

Sure, boss.
Plenty ghosts—tu-whit, tu-whoo.
Me need bonus for them ghosts.

ROLAND.

You'll have your bonus. Only get us
there quick.
Sylvie, we will exorcize these ghosts.
You know how, my dearest?

SYLVIE (*heart-felt*).

I know how.

(*The bell continues but is gradually submerged by orchestral chapel music. The latter
swells to a definite close, leaving Roland and
Sylvie in the Haunted Chapel. The voices echo
in the emptiness.*)

PRIEST (*old and tired but kindly*).

You have the ring? Good.

Before I complete this ceremony making you man and wife

I must deliver a warning.

The original sin is doubt.

And in these days of contempt for the individual

It is also the topical sin.

So if either of you has doubts of the holiness of marriage

Or if either of you has doubts of the other

And can conceive a time when he or she

Will think again and wish this thing undone,

Now is your time to speak.

(*pause*)

Good. So you have no doubts. There is one other formality.

Although there is no congregation present,

Although apart from ourselves and a few sparrows and field-mice

This chapel is now empty, I must still put the question:

If anyone here know just cause or impediment—

(*He is interrupted by voices with a strange acoustic.*)

BLIND PETER'S VOICE.

I do!

GAVIN'S VOICE.

I do!

FATHER'S VOICE.

I do!

BLIND PETER'S VOICE.

This young man who's come to you to get married

Promised me when he left, a week before I died,

As he would avenge my blindness and bring it about

How no one should go the way I went in future.

Well, has he done it? No, and he'll never do it—

Not if you splice him up to that poor simple girl

Who only dreams how he and she will be happy.

GAVIN'S VOICE.

No, Roland, my brother; Blind Peter is right.

Forget your dreams of a home. You can never be happy

If you forsake the Quest. And if you could—

Happiness is not all. You must go on—

Turn your back on this chapel, go on through the forest,

Alone, always alone, and then across the desert,

And at the other end of the desert—

FATHER'S VOICE (*very deep*).

You will find what I found, Roland.

ROLAND.

You?

FATHER'S VOICE.

You should know my voice though you never heard it.

Though you had not seen me, you knew my portrait.

ROLAND.

My father?

FATHER'S VOICE.

I am still waiting to be your father.

While you malinger, you are no son of mine.

ROLAND (*shattered*).

Sylvie. . . .

SYLVIE.

I know what you want. . . . Your ring.

(*She tries to retain self-control in making her renunciation.*)

There. . . . Back on your finger.

Look how it glows in this darkness.

ROLAND (*bitterly*).

Glows? It will burn me up.

SYLVIE.

Roland, before we part—

PRIEST.

This chapel is now closed. I am sorry.

Goodbye, my daughter; your way lies back,

Back by the road you came over the hopeless sea,

Back to your little house and your apple orchard
And there must you marry one of your own kind
And spray the trees in spring and raise the ladders in autumn
And spread the shining crop on the spare-room floor and—

ROLAND.

Sylvie, before we part—

PRIEST.

10 This chapel is now closed. I am sorry.
Goodbye, my son; your way lies forward,
Forward through the gibbering guile of the forest,
Forward through the silent doubt of the desert.
And let me warn you: if in the forest
You hear any voices call from the trees,
20 Pay no attention, Roland, pay no attention. . . .

(*His voice fades as forest music grows up; out of its tangle come the voices of the Birds, harsh and mechanical, speaking to a heavily stressed sing-song rhythm.*)

PARROT.

Pretty Polly! Pretty Polly!
Who's this coming now?

RAVEN.

Caw-caw! Caw-caw!
Who's a-walkin' in *my* forest?

PARROT.

30 Pretty Polly! The leaves have fallen.

RAVEN.

Caw-caw! He's walking late.

PARROT.

Pretty Polly! He's looking pale.

RAVEN.

Caw-caw! His bones will be paler.

PARROT.

Pretty Polly! Here he comes.

RAVEN.

Caw-caw! Greet him!

PARROT (*sneeringly*).

Where are you going, Roland, so fast?

RAVEN.

Roland, running away from your past?

BOTH.

You can't do *that!* You can't do *that!* 40

PARROT.

Still on the road? Still on the Quest?

RAVEN.

None achieve it but the best.

BOTH.

You're not the sort. You're not the sort.

PARROT.

Why not stop, my dear young man?

RAVEN.

Let heroes die as heroes can.

BOTH.

You must *live! You* must *live!*

(*The forest music swells up as Roland passes.*)

PARROT.

Pretty Polly! He's passed us by.

RAVEN.

Caw-caw! The devil take him. 50

PARROT.

Pretty Polly! The devil will.

(*The forest music gives place to desert music and Roland is heard soliloquizing.*)

ROLAND (*very tired.*)

Oh, this desert!
The forest was bad enough but this beats all.
When my tutor described it to me, it sounded strange
But now I am here, with the grit of it filling my shoes, 60
I find that the worst thing about it is this:
The desert is something familiar.
And with no end—no end.

(*The music ends. A mechanical voice creeps in.*)

CLOCK VOICE.

Tick Tock, Tick Tock,
Sand and grit, bones and waste,
A million hours—all the same,
A million minutes—each an hour, 70
And nothing stops for nothing starts

But the hands move, the dead hands
move,
 The desert is the only clock—
 Tick Tock, Tick Tock,
 Tick Tock, Tick Tock. . . .

(The Clock Voice recedes but can just be heard ticking as Roland speaks, with the Desert registering again musically.)

ROLAND.
 Flat—No shape—No color—Only here
10 and there
 A mirage of the past—something I've met before—
 Figures arising from dust, repeating themselves,
 Telling me things that I have no wish to remember.
 Mirage . . . mirage . . . mirage . . .

(The music ends and the Clock comes near again.)

CLOCK VOICE.
20 Tick Tock, Tick Tock,
 Tick Tock, Tick Tock. . . .

(continuing in the background as the first mirage is heard.)

SOAK.
 A pretty boy—but I've given him no more lines.
 He'd never guess what happens in my dream.
 Look—a pull on the wire, his feet move forward.
30 Left Right, Left Right. . . .

(He synchronizes with the Clock Voice as it comes again into the foreground.)

CLOCK VOICE. ⎱ Tick Tock etc.
SOAK.   ⎰ Left Right etc.

(They withdraw to the background as the second mirage appears.)

STEWARD.
 Golden days, sir, golden days.
 In the desert, sir, have you noticed
 One doesn't notice time?
40 But I thought so the moment I saw you:
 You don't know where you're going.
 Golden days, golden days. . . .

(He synchronizes with the Clock Voice and Soak—the same procedure.)

CLOCK VOICE. ⎱ Tick Tock, etc.
SOAK.   ⎱ Left Right, etc.
STEWARD. ⎰ Golden days, etc.
NEAERA.
 . . . adagio . . . rallentando . . .
 This dossier includes your future— 50
 You don't come out of it well.
 But kiss me, Roland, kiss me.
 Kiss me, kiss me. . . .
 (synchronizes).

CLOCK VOICE. ⎱ Tick Tock, etc.
SOAK.   ⎱ Left Right, etc.
STEWARD. ⎰ Golden days, etc.
NEAERA.   Kiss me, etc.
SYLVIE.
 But why must you go so quickly?
 Now that the sun's come out. 60
 You, Roland—you're no knight errant.
 Your love for me will triumph, you'll come back,
 Then you and I, you and I. . . .
 (synchronizes).

CLOCK VOICE. ⎱ Tick Tock, etc.
SOAK.   ⎱ Left Right, etc.
STEWARD. ⎰ Golden days, etc.
NEAERA.   Kiss me, etc.
SYLVIE.   You and I, etc. 70

(The five voices in the foreground, driving as it were at the camera, till Roland can bear it no longer.)

ROLAND *(screaming).*
 NO!

(The voices break off as if cut with a knife.)

ROLAND.
 Shapes of dust and fancy! Unreal voices!
 But where is the voice that launched me on my road?
 Where is the shape the first that I re- 80 member?
 Why doesn't *she* appear—even in fancy?
 It is the least she could—Mother, where are you?
 Yes, you; I'm calling you—my mother who sent me forth—

It was all your doing. But for you
I who had no beliefs of my own,
I who had no will of my own,
Should not be here today pursuing
A dark tower that is only dark
Because it does not exist. And Mother!
It is only your will that drives me still
As signified in the blood-red stone
I wear on my finger under my glove
That burns me like a living weal.
(*suddenly puzzled*).
. . . Burns me? . . . Burns me?
. . . It always has—
But have I gone numb? I can feel
nothing.
Off with this glove! I *can't* believe
that—

(*A chord from the orchestra.*)

ROLAND.

The ring! The ring!
The color is gone; the blood has gone
out of it.
But that must mean . . . that means
. . .

MOTHER'S VOICE (*in a different acoustic, whispering*).

It means, my son, that I want you
back.

ROLAND.

And the Quest then?

MOTHER.

Lapses.
On my deathbed I have changed my
mind;
I am bearing now a child of stone.
He can go on the Quest. But you, Roland—come back!

(*A pause while Roland takes in the implications.*)

ROLAND.

The ring . . . is always right.
Recall! Reprieve! A thousand years of
sunshine!
And the apples will be in bloom
round Sylvie's house.
Was that my mother's voice? Look at
the ring.

It is as pale as death, there is no
more breach of duty,
Her will is not behind me. Breach of
duty?
If she is dying, *there* is the breach of
duty—
Not to be there. Mother, you sent me
out
And I went out. Now that you call
me back
I will come back! The desert take this
ring—
It serves no further purpose!

(*An orchestral clink as he throws away the ring.*)

ROLAND (*startled*).

What was that?
It must have struck something hard.
That's the first
Sound I've heard in the desert.
Where did I throw that ring?
A stone? But a carved stone! Looks
like a
milestone,
As if the desert had any use for milestones!
(*with a hysterical half-laugh*)
How many miles to Babylon? Let's
see now;
These letters are choked with sand,
"To Those. . . . To Those. . . ."

(*He deciphers the inscription, reading it aloud slowly.*)

"To Those Who Did Not Go Back—
Whose Bones being Nowhere, their
signature is for All Men—
Who went to their Death of their
Own Free Will
Bequeathing Free Will to Others."

(*The Bird Voices cut in, in a different acoustic, jeering.*)

PARROT.

Pretty Polly! A tall story!

RAVEN.

Caw-caw! And not so new!

PARROT.

Pretty Polly! Unknown warriors!

RAVEN.

Caw-caw! Nobody cares!

PARROT.

"Who went to their death!"—Pretty Polly!

RAVEN.

"Of their own free will!"—Caw-caw!

ROLAND.

Of their own free will? It wasn't like that with me.

It was my mother pushed me to this point

And now she pulls me back. Let's see this ring—

10 Where's it fallen? Hm. Yes, there's no mistake,

Red no longer: my mother wants me back

And indeed it is high time; this desert has no end

Nor even any contour, the blank horizon

Retreats and yet retreats; without either rise or fall

20 Repeats, retreats, defeats; there is no sign of a tower—

You could see a tower for miles; there is not even a knoll,

Flatness is all—and nothing. Own free will?

(*He has been speaking quietly but now bursts out.*)

As if I, Roland, had ever. . . . Tutors, trumpeters, women,

30 Old soaks and crooked stewards, everyone I have met

Has played his music on me. Own free will!

Three words, not one of which I understand!

All right, Mother dear, I'm coming.

(*Pause.*)

Now. . . . Where are my footsteps? Better follow them back.

40 Back to the forest and through it and so to the shore of the sea.

Are these my footsteps? But how small they look!

Well, you're a small man, Roland— Better admit it—

You'll be still smaller now. . . . But are these my footsteps?

They are so near together—and I thought

I was walking with great strides! O 50 Roland, Roland,

You thought yourself a hero—and you walked

With little steps like that! Now you must watch

These niggling foot-prints all your return journey

To underline your shame. What's shame to me

Who never had free will? . . . "their 6 own free will

Bequeathing free will to others." Others indeed!

I begin to think my drunken friend was right

In his subjective tavern; there are no others

Apart from the projections of my mind

And, once that mind is empty, man's 7 a desert.

(*losing his temper*)

Others! Who are these others? Where can I find 'em?

CHILD'S VOICE (*out of the blue*).

Nowhere, Roland. Nowhere.

ROLAND.

There! What did I say? There *are* no—

CHILD'S VOICE.

You will never find us if you go forward—

For you will be dead before we are 8 born.

You will never find us if you go back—

For you will have killed us in the womb.

ROLAND.

What! So I am an infanticide now?

CHILD'S VOICE.

Not yet. But if you go back. . . .

ROLAND.

Who said I was going back?

CHILD'S VOICE.

I thought you had made up your mind. 9

ROLAND.

I never make up my mind!

Didn't I say that my mother—Look, I'll leave it to chance;

Chance is as good an arbiter as any.

Watch me, you unborn children. See this tiny cactus?

I will strip it leaf by leaf—let that decide—

This Year, Next Year, Eena—Meena —*you* know the game, you unborn children.

Now.

(*He counts in regular time, but with growing tension, as he picks off the leaves.*)

Forward—back; forward—back; forward—back—forward;

Back—forward; back—forward; back —forward—back;

Forward—back; forward—back; forward—back—forward;

Back—forward; back—forward; back forward—BACK.

There! The voice of chance. The oracle of the cactus.

Back! Back! That's what the cactus says.

But *I'm* . . .

(*He holds the suspense, then with decision.*)

. . . going forward, children!

Did you think that I'd let a cactus dictate to me?

Mother, don't pull on the string; you must die alone.

Forgive me, dear, but—I tell you I'm going forward.

Forward, Roland . . . into the empty desert,

Where all is flat and colorless and silent.

(*He pauses; the orchestra creeps in with a heart-beat rhythm.*)

Silent? . . . Then what's this?

Something new! A *sound!* But a sound of what?

Don't say that it's my heart! Why, Roland, you poor fool,

Who would think you had one? You must be afraid;

It is fear reveals the heart.

(*Heart-beat louder.*)

ROLAND.

Aha, you piece of clockwork— 50

Trying to have your little say while you can!

Before your wheels run down here in the empty desert.

(*Sudden chord; the heart-beat continues.*)

Empty? . . . Where have those mountains come from?

Closing round in a ring. Humpbacked horrors

That want to be in at the death. And 60 where's the horizon?

A moment ago this was level. What's the game?

A confidence trick? A trap! I am cooped in.

A circle of ugly cliffs—a lobster-pot of rock!

Silence, my stupid heart! This looks like . . . looks like what?

This looks like the great circus in 70 Ancient Rome,

Only there is no audience—and no lions.

(*suddenly noticing*)

No audience?

(*Chord; heart-beat behind—and steadily increasing.*)

No audience! Why, that's Gavin on top of that peak!

And Michael and Denis and Henry 80 and Roger and John!

And men that I've never seen—in outlandish clothes,

Some of them even in armor. And there's Blind Peter—

With sight in his eyes, for he's pointing—

And my father too—I remember him from the album—

And my tutor—he must be dead— 90 looking graver than ever

And—well to the front of course—my dear old Sergeant-Trumpeter.

(*Figure in the music; the succeeding voices, other than Roland's own, sound as if coming from somewhere far-off and above.*)

SERGEANT-TRUMPETER.

Roland! Hold the note at the end.

GAVIN.

Be ready, old boy. This is it!

BLIND PETER.

Strike a good blow to avenge Blind
Peter.

FATHER.

Your heritage, my son. You were born
to fight and—

ROLAND.

Fight? Fight whom? This circus has
no lions.

TUTOR.

No lions, Roland? Have you forgotten your lessons?

10 I never mentioned lions; it was a
dragon—
And only that for lack of a better
name.

ROLAND.

Yes, yes, dragon of course—but you
told me, my good tutor,
The Dragon would not appear until
I came to the Tower
And until I had blown my blast—
Well, there is no tower!

GAVIN.

20 That fooled *me*, Roland my brother.

FATHER.

Look over there, Roland my son.

ROLAND.

Where? . . . Oh, *that* little thing?
Like a wart coming out of the
ground!

FATHER.

It's growing, Roland, it's growing.

TUTOR.

You should recognize it from my lectures.

BLIND PETER.

That's the joker all right.
(*Figure in the music.*)

GAVIN.

30 The tower! The Dark Tower!

SERGEANT-TRUMPETER.

Quick now, my lad. Unsling your
trumpet.

ROLAND.

But—

FATHER.

It's growing, my son; waste no time.

ROLAND.

It's growing; yes, it's growing.

CHILD'S VOICE.

Growing! Ooh! Look at it.
Strike a good blow for us unborn children.

MOTHER (*closer than the rest*).

And strike a blow for all dead mothers.

GAVIN.

Jump to it, Roland.

FATHER.

Waste no time.

SERGEANT-TRUMPETER.

Remember that challenge call.
Blow it the way I taught you.

ROLAND (*beginning quiet but resolute and building.*)

Yes, dear friends, I will blow it the
way you taught me.
I, Roland, the black sheep, the unbeliever—
Who never did anything of his own
free will—
Will do this now to bequeath free
will to others.
(*full out*)
Ahoy there, tower, Dark Tower, you're
getting big.
Your shadow is cold upon me. What
of that?
And you, you Dragon or whatever
you are
Who make men beasts, come out—
here is a man;
Come out and do your worst.

(*The heart-beat, having reached its crescendo,
ends clean.*)

ROLAND (*restrained, in the sudden silence*).

Wrist be steady
As I raise the trumpet so—now fill my
lungs—

(*The Challenge Call rings out; the Sergeant-
Trumpeter speaks as the last long note is
reached.*)

SERGEANT-TRUMPETER.

Good lad, Roland. Hold that note at
the end.

(*The trumpet holds it, enriched and endorsed
by the orchestra. They come to a full close and
that is THE END.*)

DAVID SCHUBERT

David Schubert was born in New York in 1913. After a lonely and ingrown childhood, he studied at Amherst and at the College of the City of New York. He married Judith Ehre when both were very young. Trying to find work that would give him time for writing, he waited on tables, did library and editorial work, and spent some months in arranging exhibits in the Brooklyn Museum. Slowly his poetry began to be known and was published in *Poetry, The Nation, The Forum, The Virginia Quarterly Review, The Saturday Review of Literature, Smoke,* and *New Letters in America,* an anthology. Schubert published a group of poems, "The Single Scale," in the 1941 volume of *Five Young American Poets.*

The strain of World War II taxed his sensitive spirit and he suffered a complete breakdown. Just before this illness he had been working intensely preparing his poems for publication in book form; a volume is now being edited by his wife and friends. Not until his death in April 1945 did the critics place him as one of ". . . our likeliest of inadequately appreciated artists." A group of his poems appeared posthumously in *The Quarterly Review of Literature,* Vol. II, No. I, and in the accompanying editorial it was observed that Schubert's later poems "remark the widening abyss" and that ". . . what is astonishing is this poet's outspoken fearlessness before his grief."

Schubert belongs with the younger poets who are critical of the society in which they live and who in general indicate by an emphasis on the dearth of beauty and faith in our present society that some social changes are necessary. Always Schubert's poetry uniquely pictures the metropolis in all its horror and its pity.

He has been to some extent influenced by Federico García Lorca, the Spanish Loyalist poet who was killed by Rebel soldiers in 1936. Although Schubert did not read the poems of García Lorca until later, his first book revealed a similarity of spirit in these two poets, for Schubert, like García Lorca, takes the completely homely image and makes it the image of the world, and of a personal anguish which shines like a sword.

Intersection

Mr. Riscica in his undershirt
Sits on a kitchen chair and puffs a corn
    cob. He
Swings his feet on the curb. No place to
Go. Nothing to do. Behind the water tank on
    stilts
The whistle blew, ages ago. Out of the butter
    tub   5
The ailanthus tree turns with the turning sun.
Out of pine out of loam out of air
The wild geese flying! Look. See there?
Open the surface opening your eyes. Take
    care.
Giddyap, Rosinante, giddyap old scarecrow,
Poor nag—his bones sticking through.   11

Voices in the air. Autos wheel by with
People dancing there. She is looking for her
    husband
Who is sleeping on the subway or a park
    bench. As
You look, a man with a basket, old man   15
Wrinkled as a prune. In the basket at his feet
Are gladiolas, anthers veined. If you give him
    ten dollars
The rags and bones laid out for awakening,
    —new leg
Struts down the street at the corner of
Little Street and United States Street.

"Intersection" is reprinted by permission of the author.
10. **Rosinante,** the name of Don Quixote's horse. Both Don Quixote and his horse were bedraggled in appearance. Cervantes (1547–1616), the great Spanish novelist, wrote *Don Quixote* as a gentle but penetrating satire on the contrast between the actual world and the idealism of chivalry. Schubert here is contrasting the imaginary world of romance and the real world of the dirty street. 17. **If you . . . dollars, etc.** The construction here is curious. The poet means simply that if the old man were given ten dollars his death-like appearance would change to that of a man willing to live. 20. **Little Street . . . Street.** The names of the streets are used to suggest the idea that this unimportant and poor man lives in the United States.

The Christmas Tree and the Terror

I

S EA THAT used to come to the gates of the
    school"
And never crashed the gate,
I wonder, do you remember
The carollers crying with bitter cold,
Red apples for cheeks and candles?   5
O sea, we looked at you as exiles,
With Ditte chained in the house.
And poverty burrowed as a louse
In the hair of the poor; and sweat   9
Was crystalline and harps that holy evening.

II

Imagine the snow dropping on frame houses
Beside a river. A fat peasant woman
Carrying logs, her skirts blown awry.
Three curs with tails up in a raincoat sky.
She can see below the three smoke shafts   15
Of the power house, the abandoned summer
    porches.
She hurries home to eight glad eyes, four souls
To provide for. But the coals
Are flickering, are guttering as she walks.
There will be stockings waiting, oranges   20
And promises. Somewhere the nightingale.

III

At the foot of the holy Jesus
Holy Jesus, Holy child, she lay
An offering of tears and gray
Withered mountain laurel. This spring   25
Songs will be sung and lovers
Will thank the good god in catholic countries.
She prays for a half articulate thing;
Snow is blowing bitterly, the fox
Barked all night. Even the people   30
In the brick house looked at their clocks,
And smiled reassured, thinking of Christmas.

IV

Bring a wreath of ice skaters for the tree
Without roots in Washington Park.
Incandescent was the sea,   35
Incandescent was the dark.
The road curled about his head.
The rose was red.
Beggars and tramps thought perhaps
Of homes in Flint or Wilkes Barre.   40
The fox was caught in the trap
That night.

A snowman with pastel, child globs, warm
    globes
Of flower color; sleigh and bells   44
Along the Alps Road. Road that leads me back
To misery, broken and maculate road.
The silo half empty, the farm angles cut.
Along the bitter night you will return
By a celestial train you never discerned
Even in moments of utter sadness   50
When school began or the hired laborer
Dropped his heavy boots on the ground:
They stood like soldiers waiting for Taps to
    sound.
We stood about the tree thinking of heaven
Of earth and of all possible greenery: 55
A strange lamb from a strange scenery,
And the trams running on as usual,
And children playing in the streets,
And the rich people drinking coffee.

VI

Sea that used to come up to the gates of the
    school,   60
We were jealous of your freedom.
Now you will come again with the sound of
    muffled
Tiny drums, again, again. Now
Imagine, imagine, America, from the poet Al-
    berti
The veritable roots of Christmas Tree: 65
Gladness and singing and the warm South
In your mouth; hand in hand, land to
Land—singing the old year out with our blood.

"The Christmas Tree and the Terror," from *New Letters in America* (1937), edited by Horace Gregory and Eleanor Clark, reprinted by permission of the author and W. W. Norton & Company, Inc.
The Christmas . . . Terror. The poem uses the childhood image, the Christmas tree, and festival as a symbol of rebirth, projecting it forward into adult life in the last stanza, where Alberti, the Spanish Loyalist poet, is a symbol of the rebirth and renewal of faith of a people. **7. Ditte,** the name of a dog, named after the heroine of *Ditte,* by the modern Danish novelist Nexø, who wrote of the working-class problems.

33. tree . . . Park, a city image of Christmas festivities. Each year in Washington Square Park, New York, a large Christmas tree is set up. **43. A snowman, etc.,** imaginatively recalled childhood images of snow scenes like the Alps, followed by images of the return to work. **64. Alberti.** See note in column 1.

The Visitor

HE CAME from the mountains into this
Garden. Welcome, sir, all that I have is
  yours.

He came from the mountains, he spied
The kind shade. He sate with me under the oak
  tree.

What have you done in the mountain, sir,   5
Beside hunting the white deer all day?

In the mountains I hunted and I plotted
Your garden's destruction and ruin.

In the mountains I hunted a similitude
To obtain your trusting mood.   10

Therefore I slay you as
You dream of the friendship I bear.

Said the man from the mountains the mountains
Who came to visit me here.

The "Visitor" and "No Finis" are reprinted by permission of
Mrs. David Schubert.

But I shall, as I look only upward   15
My star being set in the mountains,

Said the man, the man from the mountains,
See only the fair garden that I murdered here

Said the man the man from the mountains.

No Finis

WHEN YOU cannot go further
It is time to go back and rest
Out of failure some
Thing shining.

As when a child I sat   5
On the stoop and spoke
The state licenses, the makes
Of autos going somewhere,—

To others I leave the fleeting
Memory of myself.

No Finis. This was one of Schubert's last poems before his
death.

JOHN BETJEMAN

As a writer of light verse, deft, witty, and sentimental, John Betjeman is almost an English institution. He was born in London in 1906 and was educated at Marlborough and Oxford. Before World War II, he worked in the publicity department of Shell-Mex, the British oil company, and edited the Shell Series of County Guides, two of which he himself wrote. His poems show not only a familiarity with the varieties of English architecture but a particularly sentimental love for its curiosities. For the English, therefore, he expresses their good-humored though sometimes traditional delight in the historical eccentricities to be seen along English streets. Betjeman's hobbies are church architecture, country towns, miniature railways, forgotten novelists, and topographical verse.

During the war, Betjeman was one of the heads of the film department of the British Ministry of Information. He was also Press Attaché at the British Legation in Dublin. He is now on the staff of the *Architectural Review*.

John Betjeman's popularity has begun to spread to America, where recently his books *New Bats in Old Belfries* and *Slick, But Not Streamlined* have been widely circulated. In his delightful introduction to the latter volume, W. H. Auden names Betjeman as the one poet of whom he is really jealous. This is understandable, since the two are curiously akin in spirit; Betjeman is in a way a lesser, more sentimental Auden. He took the war seriously and he takes his religion seriously, but he is still able to treat of them in light verse.

Some of Betjeman's books are *Ghastly Good Taste* (1933), *An Oxford University Chest* (1938), *English Cities and Small Towns* (1943), *Mount Zion* (1931), *Continual Dew* (1937), *Old Lights for New Chancels* (1940), *New Bats in Old Belfries* (1945), *Slick, But Not Streamlined* (1947), and *Selected Poems* (1948).

In Westminster Abbey

LET ME take this other glove off
  As the *vox humana* swells,
And the beauteous fields of Eden
  Bask beneath the Abbey bells.
Here, where England's statesmen lie,   5
Listen to a lady's cry.

Gracious Lord, oh bomb the Germans.
  Spare their women for Thy Sake,
And if that is not too easy
  We will pardon Thy Mistake.   10
But, gracious Lord, whate'er shall be,
Don't let anyone bomb me.

Keep our Empire undismembered
  Guide our Forces by Thy Hand,
Gallant blacks from far Jamaica,   15
  Honduras and Togoland;
Protect them Lord in all their fights,
And, even more, protect the whites.

Think of what our Nation stands for,
  Books from Boots' and country lanes,   20
Free speech, free passes, class distinction,
  Democracy and proper drains.
Lord, put beneath Thy special care
One-eighty-nine Cadogan Square.

Although dear Lord I am a sinner,   25
  I have done no major crime;
Now I'll come to Evening Service
  Whensoever I have time.
So, Lord, reserve for me a crown,
And do not let my shares go down.   30

I will labour for Thy Kingdom,
  Help our lads to win the war,
Send white feathers to the cowards
  Join the Women's Army Corps,
Then wash the Steps around Thy Throne
In the Eternal Safety Zone.   36

Now I feel a little better,
  What a treat to hear Thy Word,

Where the bones of leading statesmen,
  Have so often been interr'd.   40
And now, dear Lord, I cannot wait
Because I have a luncheon date.

Margate

FROM out the Queen's Highcliffe for weeks
    at a stretch
I watched how the mower evaded the vetch,
So that over the putting course rashes were
    seen
Of pink and of yellow among the burnt green.

How restful to putt, when the strains of a band
Announced a *thé dansant* was on at the Grand,
While over the privet, comminglingly clear,   7
I heard lesser "Co-Optimists" down by the
    pier.

Then east-facing terraces rested in shade
And fluttered with bathing things gaily dis-
    played,   10
As though loth to admit that a sun or a planet
Could ever forsake any corner of Thanet.

How lightly municipal, meltingly tarr'd
Were the walks through the Lawns by the
    Queen's Promenade   14
As soft over Cliftonville languished the light
Down Harold Road, Norfolk Road into the
    night.

Oh! then what a pleasure to see the ground
    floor
With tables for two laid as tables for four,
And bottles of sauce and Kia-Ora and squash
Awaiting their owners who'd gone up to
    wash,—   20

Who had gone up to wash the ozone from their
    skins
The sand from their legs and the Rock from
    their chins
To prepare for an evening of dancing and cards
And forget the sea-breeze on the dry prome-
    nades.

From third floor and fourth floor the children
    looked down   25
Upon ribbons of light in the salt-scented town;

The poems of John Betjeman are from *Slick, But Not Stream-lined* by John Betjeman. Copyright 1947 by John Betjeman. Reprinted by permission of Doubleday & Company, Inc.
In Westminster Abbey. This poem, published under a pseudonym in *The New Statesman and Nation*, called down many protests from Church newspapers, which were unaware that the author, John Betjeman, is a churchwarden and an Anglo-Catholic.   2. *vox humana*, a stop on an organ.   3. **Eden.** In the eighteenth century, certain Englishmen believed that England had actually been the site of the Garden of Eden.   20. **Boots'**, British chain drug store, with a lending library.   24. **Cadogan Square**, square in Kensington, London, of large middle-class houses.

Margate, popular seaside resort on the Isle of Thanet, Kent. 1. **Queen's Highcliffe**, a hotel.   6. *thé dansant*, an afternoon dance.   8. **"Co-Optimists,"** a group of traveling entertainers, well known throughout England in the 1920's. 15. **Cliftonville**, the residential section of Margate.   19. **Kia-Ora**, trade name for an English brand of orange and lemon essence or concentrate, known in England as "squash."

And more loud than the trams was the roar of
    the sea
As it washed in the shingle the scraps of their
    tea.

Beside the Queen's Highcliffe now rank grows
    the vetch,
Now dark is the terrace, a storm-battered
    stretch;   30
And I think, as the fairy-lit sights I recall,
It is these we are fighting for, foremost of all.

In Memory of Basil, Marquess of Dufferin and Ava

ON such a morning as this
    with the birds ricocheting their music
Out of the whelming elms
    to a copper beech's embrace
And a sifting sound of leaves   5
    from multitudinous branches
Running across the park
    to a chequer of light on the lake,
On such a morning as this
    with *The Times* for June the eleventh   10
Left with coffee and toast
    you opened the breakfast-room window
And, sprawled on the southward terrace, said:
    "That means war in September."

In Memory . . . Ava. Basil, Marquess of Dufferin and Ava,
born in 1909 and killed in action in Burma in 1945.

Friend of my youth, you are dead!   15
    and the long peal pours from the steeple
Over this sunlit quad
    in our University city
And soaks in Headington stone.
    Motionless stand the pinnacles.   20
Under a flying sky
    as though they too listened and waited
Like me for your dear return
    with a Bullingdon noise of an evening
In Sports-Bugatti from Thame   25
    that belonged to a man in Magdalen.
Friend of my youth, you are dead!
    and the quads are empty without you.

Then there were people about.
    Each hour, like an Oxford archway,   30
Opened on long green lawns
    and distant unvisited buildings
And you my friend were explorer
    and so you remained to me always
Humourous, reckless, loyal—   35
    my kind, heavy-lidded companion.
Stop, oh many bells, stop
    pouring on roses and creeper
Your unremembering peal
    this hollow, unhallowed V. E. day,—   40
I am deaf to your notes and dead
    by a soldier's body in Burma.

19. **Headington stone,** the quarries, north of Oxford, where
the stone for the buildings was cut.   24. **Bullingdon,** the
name of a drinking club at Oxford, whose members are all
either rich or athletic.   25. **Bugatti,** Italian racing car.
26. **Magdalen,** Oxford college.

❦ Impressions and Prophecies

WILLIAM SANSOM

It was a single, sharply realistic short piece,
"The Wall," published in the British magazine
Horizon in 1943, which more or less made an
overnight name for its author, William Sansom.
Since then he has become known as a novelist
as well as a writer of realistic short stories.

Sansom was born in England in 1912. After
attending school he spent some months studying German in Bonn, and then traveled in
France and Spain. Intended for a commercial
career, he then entered a bank in the City of
London. But an interest in writing (he had been

writing stories from the age of seven) and in drawing and composing light music prompted him to seek some way of earning money at least a little more in the creative spheres. As a result he went into advertising. He eventually graduated onto the radio side, and by 1939 was directing many programs every week. With the coming of the war, however, he dropped this work and entered the London Fire Service in the ranks, continuing as an active fireman throughout the war.

It was in his leisure hours in the fire stations that Sansom began to write more seriously, without view of publication or profit—and instantly, as he says, he became published. He has since contributed to numerous London literary periodicals and now has a number of published books to his credit. His first collection of short stories, *Fireman Flower*—not, for the most part, stories about fire-fighting—appeared in 1945, and a second collection, *Three,* in 1946. In 1946 Sansom published *Westminster in War*, a history of the bombing in the west end and Westminster areas of London. In both 1946 and 1947 he received literary scholarship awards from the Society of Authors, a London group.

A large selection of Sansom's shorter works was published under the title *Something Terrible, Something Lovely* in 1947. The following year he produced *South: Aspects and Images from Corsica, Italy and Southern France,* which he describes as a series of "landscapes with fictional figures" resulting from travels in those countries. A novella, *The Equilibriad,* and a novel, *The Body,* were scheduled for 1949.

The Wall

IT WAS our third job that night.

Until this thing happened, work had been without incident. There had been shrapnel, a few inquiring bombs, and some huge fires; but these were unremarkable and have since merged without identity into the neutral maze of fire and noise and water and night, without date and without hour, with neither time nor

"The Wall" reprinted from *Fireman Flower and Other Stories* by William Sansom by permission of Vanguard Press, Inc.

form, that lowers mistily at the back of my mind as a picture of the air-raid season. 10

I suppose we were worn down and shivering. Three A.M. is a meanspirited hour. I suppose we were drenched, with the cold hose water trickling in at our collars and settling down at the tails of our shirts. Without doubt the heavy brass couplings felt molded from metal-ice. Probably the open roar of the pumps drowned the petulant buzz of the raiders above, and certainly the ubiquitous fire glow made an orange stage-set of the streets. Black 20 water would have puddled the City alleys and I suppose our hands and our faces were black as the water. Black with hacking about among the burnt-up rafters. These things were an every-night nonentity. They happened and they were not forgotten because they were never even remembered.

But I do remember it was our third job. And there we were—Len, Lofty, Verno and myself, playing a fifty-foot jet up the face of a tall city 30 warehouse and thinking of nothing at all. You don't think of anything after the first few hours. You just watch the white pole of water lose itself in the fire and you think of nothing. Sometimes you move the jet over to another window. Sometimes the orange dims to black—but you only ease your grip on the ice-cold nozzle and continue pouring careless gallons through the window. You know the fire will fester for hours yet. However, that night the blank, indefinite 40 hours of waiting were sharply interrupted—by an unusual sound. Very suddenly a long rattling crack of bursting brick and mortar perforated the moment. And then the upper half of that five-story building heaved over towards us. It hung there, poised for a timeless second before rumbling down at us. I was thinking of nothing at all and then I was thinking of everything in the world.

In that simple second my brain digested eve- 50 ry detail of the scene. New eyes opened at the sides of my head so that, from within, I photographed a hemispherical panorama bounded by the huge length of the building in front of me and the narrow lane on either side.

Blocking us on the left was the squat trailer pump, roaring and quivering with effort. Water throbbed from its overflow valves and from leakages in the hose and couplings. A ceaseless stream spewed down its gray sides into the gut- 60 ter. But nevertheless a fat iron exhaust pipe glowed red-hot in the middle of the wet engine. I had to look past Lofty's face. Lofty was staring at the controls, hands tucked into his armpits for warmth. Lofty was thinking of nothing. He had a black diamond of soot over one eye, like the White-eyed Kaffir in negative.

To the other side of me was a free run up the alley. Overhead swung a sign—"Catto and Henley." I wondered what in hell they sold. Old stamps? The alley was quite free. A couple of lengths of dead, deflated hose wound over the darkly glistening pavement. Charred flotsam dammed up one of the gutters. A needle of water fountained from a hole in a live hose length. Beneath a blue shelter light lay a shattered coping stone. The next shop along was a tobacconist's, windowless, with fake display cartons torn open for anybody to see. The alley was quite free.

Behind me, Len and Verno shared the weight of the hose. They heaved up against the strong backward drag of water pressure. All I had to do was yell "Drop it"—and then run. We could risk the live hose snaking up at us. We could run to the right down the free alley —Len, Verno, and me. But I never moved. I never said "Drop it" or anything else. That long second held me hypnotized, rubber boots cemented to the pavement. Ton upon ton of red-hot brick hovering in the air above us numbed all initiative. I could only think. I couldn't move.

Six yards in front stood the blazing building. A minute before I would never have distinguished it from any other drab Victorian atrocity happily on fire. Now I was immediately certain of every minute detail. The building was five stories high. The top four stories were fiercely alight. The rooms inside were alive with red fire. The black outside walls remain untouched. And thus, like the lighted carriages of a night express, there appeared alternating rectangles of black and red that emphasized vividly the extreme symmetry of the window spacing; each oblong window shape posed as a vermilion panel set in perfect order upon the dark face of the wall. There were ten windows to each floor, making forty windows in all. In rigid rows of ten, one row placed precisely above the other, with strong contrasts of black and red, the blazing windows stood to atten-

tion in strict formation. The oblong building, the oblong windows, the oblong spacing. Orange-red color seemed to *bulge* from the black framework, assumed tactile values, like boiling jelly that expanded inside a thick black squared grill.

Three of the stories, thirty blazing windows and their huge frame of black brick, a hundred solid tons of hard, deep Victorian wall, pivoted over towards us and hung flatly over the alley. Whether the descending wall actually paused in its fall I can never know. Probably it never did. Probably it only seemed to hang there. Probably my eyes digested its action at an early period of momentum, so that I saw it "off true" but before it had gathered speed.

The night grew darker as the great mass hung over us. Through smoke-fogged fire glow the moonlight had hitherto penetrated to the pit of our alley through declivities in the skyline. Now some of the moonlight was being shut out as the wall hung ever farther over us. The wall shaded the moonlight like an inverted awning. Now the pathway of light above had been squeezed to a thin line. That was the only silver lining I ever believed in. It shone out—a ray of hope. But it was a declining hope, for although at this time the entire hemispherical scene appeared static, an imminence of movement could be sensed throughout—presumably because the scene was actually moving. Even the speed of the shutter which closed the photograph on my mind was powerless to exclude this motion from a deeper consciousness. The picture appeared static to the limited surface senses, the eyes and the material brain, but beyond that there was hidden movement.

The second was timeless. I had leisure to remark many things. For instance, that an iron derrick, slightly to the left, would not hit me. This derrick stuck out from the building and I could feel its sharpness and hardness as clearly as if I had run my body intimately over its contour. I had time to notice that it carried a foot-long hook, a chain with three-inch rings, two girder supports, and a wheel more than twice as large as my head.

A wall will fall in many ways. It may sway over to the one side or the other. It may crumble at the very beginning of its fall. It may remain intact and fall flat. This wall fell as flat as a pancake. It clung to its shape through ninety degrees to the horizontal. Then it detached itself from the pivot and slammed down on top of us.

The last resistance of bricks and mortar at the pivot point cracked off like automatic gunfire. The violent sound both deafened us and brought us to our senses. We dropped the hose and crouched. Afterwards Verno said that I knelt slowly on one knee with bowed head, like
10 a man about to be knighted. Well, I got my

knighting. There was an incredible noise—a thunderclap condensed into the space of an eardrum—and then the bricks and the mortar came tearing and burning into the flesh of my face.

Lofty, away by the pump, was killed. Len, Verno, and myself they dug out. There was very little brick on top of us. We had been lucky. We had been framed by one of those symmetrical, oblong window spaces. 20

IRWIN SHAW

Irwin Shaw has to his credit one novel, and two noteworthy plays, to counterbalance two or three others that have not been so successful; but he has written a large number of short stories, many of them distinguished, and it is likely that his future reputation will rest most securely upon his achievements in this type of fiction. He was born in Brooklyn in 1913 and spent most of his boyhood either there or in the neighboring borough of Manhattan. He made something of a name for himself as a semi-professional football player; but his main passion was for writing in the journalistic manner. An early connection with a nation-wide broadcasting company gave him his first real opportunity, and he poured millions of words into radio scripts.

In 1935 Shaw was attracted by a contest sponsored by the New Theatre League of New York for a play with liberal tendencies; the immediate result of this stimulus to his dramatic instincts was *Bury the Dead* (1936), originally a re-write of a play by the Austrian Hans Chlumberg, *Miracle at Verdun* (1931), which had been produced by the Theatre Guild some years before. But *Bury the Dead,* a brief and savage one-act indictment of war, made a sensation when it finally came to Broadway. Shaw improved on Chlumberg in many ways, partly by condensing the play, partly by changes in the cast of characters, and chiefly by the addition of a triumphant note at the end.

The author was then inveigled into going to Hollywood, where he prepared moving-picture scenarios. In the meantime he began to write miscellaneous sketches for various magazines, all of which showed keen powers of observation, a strong sense of humor, and excellent realism wedded to powerful liberal ideals. In 1939 he had another play produced on Broadway. This one, *The Gentle People,* is an ironic story of the failure of a young gangster to have his way with a group of supposedly mild folk; it is amusing in a mordant way and shows that Shaw had definitely established himself as a master of the "slice-of-life" brand of literature. Other plays, such as *Retreat to Pleasure* (1940) and *The Assassin* (1946), were unsuccessful. Shaw's first novel, *The Young Lions* (1948), is an ambitious tracing of several human lives as they meet and diverge on the tremendous framework of the war. But his many short stories, some of which have been collected in *Sailor off the Bremen* (1939), *Welcome to the City* (1942), and *Act of Faith, and Other Stories* (1946), exhibit best his amazingly sure and authentic dialogue, particularly in the American vernacular; and his choices of subject have been always extremely timely. In these stories, too, the broadening and deepening experiences he underwent, as a soldier during the Second World War, have given him a power to move his reader which he had not previously possessed. His future as a significant writer seems bright.

1018

Act of Faith

PRESENT it to him in a pitiful light," Olson was saying as they picked their way through the almost frozen mud toward the orderly-room tent. "Three combat-scarred veterans, who fought their way from Omaha Beach to . . . What was the name of the town we fought our way to?"

"Königstein," Seeger said.

"Königstein." Olson lifted his right foot heavily out of a puddle and stared admiringly at the three pounds of mud clinging to his overshoe. "The backbone of the Army. The noncommissioned officer. We deserve better of our country. Mention our decorations, in passing."

"What decorations should I mention?" Seeger asked. "The Marksman's Medal?"

"Never quite made it," Olson said. "I had a cross-eyed scorer at the butts. Mention the Bronze Star, the Silver Star, the Croix de Guerre with palms, the Unit Citation, the Congressional Medal of Honor."

"I'll mention them all." Seeger grinned. "You don't think the C.O.'ll notice that we haven't won most of them, do you?"

"Gad, sir," Olson said with dignity, "do you think that one Southern military gentleman will dare doubt the word of another Southern military gentleman in the hour of victory?"

"I come from Ohio," Seeger said.

"Welch comes from Kansas," Olson said, coolly staring down a second lieutenant who was passing. The lieutenant made a nervous little jerk with his hand, as though he expected a salute, then kept it rigid, as a slight, superior smile of scorn twisted at the corner of Olson's mouth. The lieutenant dropped his eyes and splashed on through the mud. "You've heard of Kansas," Olson said. "Magnolia-scented Kansas."

"Of course," said Seeger. "I'm no fool."

"Do your duty by your men, Sergeant." Olson stopped to wipe the cold rain off his face and lectured him. "Highest-ranking noncom present took the initiative and saved his comrades, at great personal risk, above and be-

yond the call of you-know-what, in the best traditions of the American Army."

"I will throw myself in the breach," Seeger said.

"Welch and I can't ask more," said Olson.

They walked heavily through the mud on the streets between the rows of tents. The camp stretched drearily over the Reims plain, with the rain beating on the sagging tents. The division had been there over three weeks, waiting to be shipped home, and all the meagre diversions of the neighborhood had been sampled and exhausted, and there was an air of watchful suspicion and impatience with the military life hanging over the camp now, and there was even reputed to be a staff sergeant in C Company who was laying odds they would not get back to America before July 4th.

"I'm redeployable," Olson sang. "It's so enjoyable." It was a jingle he had composed, to no recognizable melody, in the early days after the victory in Europe, when he had added up his points and found they came to only sixty-three, but he persisted in singing it. He was a short, round boy who had been flunked out of air cadets' school and transferred to the infantry but whose spirits had not been damaged in the process. He had a high, childish voice and a pretty, baby face. He was very good-natured, and had a girl waiting for him at the University of California, where he intended to finish his course at government expense when he got out of the Army, and he was just the type who is killed off early and predictably and sadly in moving pictures about the war, but he had gone through four campaigns and six major battles without a scratch.

Seeger was a large, lanky boy, with a big nose, who had been wounded at St.-Lô but had come back to his outfit in the Siegfried Line quite unchanged. He was cheerful and dependable and he knew his business. He had broken in five or six second lieutenants, who had later been killed or wounded, and the C.O. had tried to get him commissioned in the field, but the war had ended while the paperwork was being fumbled over at headquarters.

They reached the door of the orderly tent and stopped. "Be brave, Sergeant," Olson said. "Welch and I are depending on you."

"O.K.," Seeger said, and went in.

The tent had the dank, Army-canvas smell that had been so much a part of Seeger's life in the past three years. The company clerk was reading an October, 1945, issue of the Buffalo *Courier-Express,* which had just reached him, and Captain Taney, the company C.O., was seated at a sawbuck table which he used as a desk, writing a letter to his wife, his lips pursed with effort. He was a small, fussy man, with sandy hair that was falling out. While the fighting had been going on, he had been lean and tense and his small voice had been cold and full of authority. But now he had relaxed, and a little pot belly was creeping up under his belt and he kept the top button of his trousers open when he could do it without too public loss of dignity. During the war Seeger had thought of him as a natural soldier—tireless, fanatic about detail, aggressive, severely anxious to kill Germans. But in the last few months, Seeger had seen him relapsing gradually and pleasantly into the small-town hardware merchant he had been before the war, sedentary and a little shy, and, as he had once told Seeger, worried, here in the bleak champagne fields of France, about his daughter, who had just turned twelve and had a tendency to go after the boys and had been caught by her mother kissing a fifteen-year-old neighbor in the hammock after school.

"Hello, Seeger," he said, returning the salute with a mild, offhand gesture. "What's on your mind?"

"Am I disturbing you, sir?"

"Oh, no. Just writing a letter to my wife. You married, Seeger?" He peered at the tall boy standing before him.

"No, sir."

"It's very difficult." Taney sighed, pushing dissatisfiedly at the letter before him. "My wife complains I don't tell her I love her often enough. Been married fifteen years. You'd think she'd know by now." He smiled at Seeger. "I thought you were going to Paris," he said. "I signed the passes yesterday."

"That's what I came to see you about, sir."

"I suppose something's wrong with the passes." Taney spoke resignedly, like a man who has never quite got the hang of Army regulations and has had requisitions, furloughs, and requests for courts-martial returned for correction in a baffling flood.

"No, sir," Seeger said. "The passes're fine. They start tomorrow. Well, it's just—" He looked around at the company clerk, who was on the sports page.

"This confidential?" Taney asked.

"If you don't mind, sir."

"Johnny," Taney said to the clerk, "go stand in the rain someplace."

"Yes, sir," the clerk said, and slowly got up and walked out.

Taney looked shrewdly at Seeger and spoke in a secret whisper. "You pick up anything?" he asked.

Seeger grinned. "No, sir, haven't had my hands on a girl since Strasbourg."

"Ah, that's good." Taney leaned back, relieved, happy that he didn't have to cope with the disapproval of the Medical Corps.

"It's—well," said Seeger, embarrassed, "it's hard to say—but it's money."

Taney shook his head sadly. "I know."

"We haven't been paid for three months, sir, and—"

"Damn it!" Taney stood up and shouted furiously. "I would like to take every bloody, chair-warming old lady in the Finance Department and wring their necks."

The clerk stuck his head into the tent. "Anything wrong? You call for me, sir?"

"No!" Taney shouted. "Get out of here!"

The clerk ducked out.

Taney sat down again. "I suppose," he said, in a more normal voice, "they have their problems. Outfits being broken up, being moved all over the place. But it's rugged."

"It wouldn't be so bad," Seeger said, "but we're going to Paris tomorrow. Olson, Welch, and myself. And you need money in Paris."

"Don't I know it?" Taney wagged his head. "Do you know what I paid for a bottle of champagne on the Place Pigalle in September?" He paused significantly. "I won't tell you. You wouldn't have any respect for me the rest of your life."

Seeger laughed. "Hanging is too good for the guy who thought up the rate of exchange," he said.

"I don't care if I never see another franc as long as I live." Taney waved his letter in the air, although it had been dry for a long time.

There was silence in the tent, and Seeger swallowed a little embarrassedly. "Sir," he said, "the truth is, I've come to borrow some money for Welch, Olson, and myself. We'll pay it back out of the first pay we get, and that can't be too long from now. If you don't want to give it to us, just tell me and I'll understand and get the hell out of here. We don't like to ask, but you might just as well be dead as be in Paris broke."

Taney stopped waving his letter and put it down thoughtfully. He peered at it, wrinkling his brow, looking like an aged bookkeeper in the single, gloomy light that hung in the middle of the tent.

"Just say the word, Captain," Seeger said, "and I'll blow."

"Stay where you are, son," said Taney. He dug in his shirt pocket and took out a worn, sweat-stained wallet. He looked at it for a moment. "Alligator," he said, with automatic, absent pride. "My wife sent it to me when we were in England. Pounds don't fit in it. However . . ." He opened it and took out all the contents. There was a small pile of francs on the table in front of him when he finished. He counted them. "Four hundred francs," he said. "Eight bucks."

"Excuse me," Seeger said humbly. "I shouldn't've asked."

"Delighted," Taney said vigorously. "Absolutely delighted." He started dividing the francs into two piles. "Truth is, Seeger, most of my money goes home in allotments. And the truth is, I lost eleven hundred francs in a poker game three nights ago, and I ought to be ashamed of myself. Here." He shoved one pile toward Seeger. "Two hundred francs."

Seeger looked down at the frayed, meretricious paper, which always seemed to him like stage money anyway. "No, sir," he said. "I can't take it."

"Take it," Taney said. "That's a direct order."

Seeger slowly picked up the money, not looking at Taney. "Sometime, sir," he said, "after we get out, you have to come over to my house, and you and my father and my brother and I'll go on a real drunk."

"I regard that," Taney said gravely, "as a solemn commitment."

They smiled at each other, and Seeger started out.

"Have a drink for me," said Taney, "at the Café de la Paix. A small drink." He was sitting down to tell his wife he loved her when Seeger went out of the tent.

Olson fell into step with Seeger and they walked silently through the mud between the tents.

"Well, *mon vieux?*" Olson said finally.

"Two hundred francs," said Seeger.

Olson groaned. "Two hundred francs! We won't be able to pinch a whore's behind on the Boulevard des Capucines for two hundred francs. That miserable, penny-loving Yankee!"

"He only had four hundred," Seeger said.

"I revise my opinion," said Olson.

They walked disconsolately and heavily back toward their tent.

Olson spoke only once before they got there. "These raincoats," he said, patting his. "Most ingenious invention of the war. Highest saturation point of any modern fabric. Collect more water per square inch, and hold it, than any material known to man. All hail the quartermaster!"

Welch was waiting at the entrance of their tent. He was standing there peering excitedly and shortsightedly out at the rain through his glasses, looking angry and tough, like a big-city hack driver, individual and incorruptible even in the ten-million colored uniform. Every time Seeger came upon Welch unexpectedly, he couldn't help smiling at the belligerent stance, the harsh stare through the steel-rimmed G.I. glasses, which had nothing at all to do with the way Welch really was. "It's a family inheritance," Welch had once explained. "My whole family stands as though we were getting ready to rap a drunk with a beer glass. Even my old lady." Welch had six brothers, all devout, according to Welch, and Seeger from time to time idly pictured them standing in a row, on Sunday mornings in church, seemingly on the verge of general violence, amid the hushed Latin and the Sabbath millinery.

"How much?" Welch asked loudly.

"Don't make us laugh," Olson said, pushing past him into the tent.

"What do you think I could get from the French for my combat jacket?" Seeger said. He went into the tent and lay down on his cot.

Welch followed them in and stood between

1021

the two of them. "Boys," he said, "on a man's errand."

"I can just see us now," Olson murmured, lying on his cot with his hands clasped behind his head, "painting Montmartre red. Please bring on the naked dancing girls. Four bucks' worth."

"I am not worried," Welch announced.

"Get out of here." Olson turned over on his stomach.

"I know where we can put our hands on sixty-five bucks." Welch looked triumphantly first at Olson, then at Seeger.

Olson turned over slowly and sat up. "I'll kill you," he said, "if you're kidding."

"While you guys are wasting your time fooling around with the infantry," Welch said, "I used my head. I went into Reems and used my head."

"Rance," Olson said automatically. He had had two years of French in college and he felt, now that the war was over, that he had to introduce his friends to some of his culture.

"I got to talking to a captain in the Air Force," Welch said eagerly. "A little, fat old paddle-footed captain that never got higher off the ground than the second floor of Com Z headquarters, and he told me that what he would admire to do more than anything else is take home a nice shiny German Luger pistol with him to show to the boys back in Pacific Grove, California."

Silence fell on the tent, and Welch and Olson looked at Seeger.

"Sixty-five bucks for a Luger, these days," Olson said, "is a very good figure."

"They've been sellin' for as low as thirty-five," said Welch hesitantly. "I'll bet," he said to Seeger, "you could sell yours now and buy another one back when you got some dough, and make a clear twenty-five on the deal."

Seeger didn't say anything. He had killed the owner of the Luger, an enormous S.S. major, in Coblenz, behind some bales of paper in a warehouse, and the major had fired at Seeger three times with it, once nicking his helmet, before Seeger hit him in the face at twenty feet. Seeger had kept the Luger, a heavy, well-balanced gun, lugging it with him, hiding it at the bottom of his bedroll, oiling it three times a week, avoiding all opportunities of selling it, although he had once been offered a hundred dollars for it and several times eighty and ninety, while the war was still on, before German weapons became a glut on the market.

"Well," said Welch, "there's no hurry. I told the captain I'd see him tonight around eight o'clock in front of the Lion d'Or Hotel. You got five hours to make up your mind. Plenty of time."

"Me," said Olson, after a pause, "I won't say anything."

Seeger looked reflectively at his feet, and the two other men avoided looking at him.

Welch dug in his pocket. "I forgot," he said. "I picked up a letter for you." He handed it to Seeger.

"Thanks," Seeger said. He opened it absently, thinking about the Luger.

"Me," said Olson, "I won't say a bloody word. I'm just going to lie here and think about that nice, fat Air Force captain."

Seeger grinned a little at him and went to the tent opening to read the letter in the light. The letter was from his father, and even from one glance at the handwriting, scrawly and hurried and spotted, so different from his father's usual steady, handsome, professorial script, he knew that something was wrong.

"Dear Norman," it read, "sometime in the future, you must forgive me for writing this letter. But I have been holding this in so long, and there is no one here I can talk to, and because of your brother's condition I must pretend to be cheerful and optimistic all the time at home, both with him and your mother, who has never been the same since Leonard was killed. You're the oldest now, and although I know we've never talked very seriously about anything before, you have been through a great deal by now, and I imagine you must have matured considerably, and you've seen so many different places and people. Norman, I need help. While the war was on and you were fighting, I kept this to myself. It wouldn't have been fair to burden you with this. But now the war is over, and I no longer feel I can stand up under this alone. And you will have to face it sometime when you get home, if you haven't faced it already, and perhaps we can help each other by facing it together."

"I'm redeployable. It's so enjoyable," Olson was singing softly, on his cot. He fell silent after his burst of song.

Seeger blinked his eyes in the gray, wintry, rainy light, and went on reading his father's letter, on the stiff white stationery with the university letterhead in polite engraving at the top of each page.

"I've been feeling this coming on for a long time," the letter continued, "but it wasn't until last Sunday morning that something happened to make me feel it in its full force. I don't know how much you've guessed about the reason for Jacob's discharge from the Army. It's true he was pretty badly wounded in the leg at Metz, but I've asked around, and I know that men with worse wounds were returned to duty after hospitalization. Jacob got a medical discharge, but I don't think it was for the shrapnel wound in his thigh. He is suffering now from what I suppose you call combat fatigue, and he is subject to fits of depression and hallucinations. Your mother and I thought that as time went by and the war and the Army receded, he would grow better. Instead, he is growing worse. Last Sunday morning when I came down into the living room from upstairs he was crouched in his old uniform, next to the window, peering out."

"What the hell," Olson was saying. "If we don't get the sixty-five bucks we can always go to the Louvre. I understand the Mona Lisa is back."

"I asked Jacob what he was doing," the letter went on. "He didn't turn around. 'I'm observing,' he said. 'V-1s and V-2s. Buzz bombs and rockets. They're coming in by the hundred.' I tried to reason with him and he told me to crouch and save myself from flying glass. To humor him I got down on the floor beside him and tried to tell him the war was over, that we were in Ohio, 4,000 miles away from the nearest spot where bombs had fallen, that America had never been touched. He wouldn't listen. 'These're the new rocket bombs,' he said, 'for the Jews.'"

"Did you ever hear of the Panthéon?" Olson asked loudly.

"No," said Welch.

"It's free."

"I'll go," said Welch.

Seeger shook his head a little and blinked his eyes before he went back to the letter.

"After that," his father went on, "Jacob seemed to forget about the bombs from time to time, but he kept saying that the mobs were coming up the street armed with bazookas and Browning automatic rifles. He mumbled incoherently a good deal of the time and kept walking back and forth saying, 'What's the situation? Do you know what the situation is?' And once he told me he wasn't worried about himself, he was a soldier and he expected to be killed, but he was worried about Mother and myself and Leonard and you. He seemed to forget that Leonard was dead. I tried to calm him and get him back to bed before your mother came down, but he refused and wanted to set out immediately to rejoin his division. It was all terribly disjointed, and at one time he took the ribbon he got for winning the Bronze Star and threw it in the fireplace, then he got down on his hands and knees and picked it out of the ashes and made me pin it on him again, and he kept repeating, 'This is when they are coming for the Jews.'"

"The next war I'm in," said Olson, "they don't get me under the rank of colonel."

It had stopped raining by now, and Seeger folded the unfinished letter and went outside. He walked slowly down to the end of the company street, and, facing out across the empty, soaked French fields, scarred and neglected by various armies, he stopped and opened the letter again,

"I don't know what Jacob went through in the Army," his father wrote, "that has done this to him. He never talks to me about the war and he refused to go to a psychoanalyst, and from time to time he is his own bouncing, cheerful self, playing handball in the afternoons and going around with a large group of girls. But he has devoured all the concentration-camp reports, and I found him weeping when the newspapers reported that a hundred Jews were killed in Tripoli some time ago.

"The terrible thing is, Norman, that I find myself coming to believe that it is not neurotic for a Jew to behave like this today. Perhaps Jacob is the normal one, and I, going about my business, teaching economics in a quiet classroom, pretending to understand that the world is comprehensible and orderly, am really the mad one. I ask you once more to forgive me for writing you a letter like this, so different from any letter or any conversation I've ever had with you. But it is crowding me, too. I do not see rockets and bombs, but I see other things.

"Wherever you go these days—restaurants, hotels, clubs, trains—you seem to hear talk about the Jews, mean, hateful, murderous talk. Whatever page you turn to in the newspapers, you seem to find an article about Jews being killed somewhere on the face of the globe. And there are large, influential newspapers and well-known columnists who each day are growing more and more outspoken and more popular. The day that Roosevelt died I heard a drunken man yelling outside a bar, 'Finally they got the Jew out of the White House.' And some of the people who heard him merely laughed, and nobody stopped him. And on V-J Day, in celebration, hoodlums in Los Angeles savagely beat a Jewish writer. It's difficult to know what to do, whom to fight, where to look for allies.

"Three months ago, for example, I stopped my Thursday-night poker game, after playing with the same men for over ten years. John Reilly happened to say that the Jews got rich out of the war, and when I demanded an apology, he refused, and when I looked around at the faces of the men who had been my friends for so long, I could see they were not with me. And when I left the house, no one said good night to me. I know the poison was spreading from Germany before the war and during it, but I had not realized it had come so close.

"And in my economics class, I find myself idiotically hedging in my lectures. I discover that I am loath to praise any liberal writer or any liberal act, and find myself somehow annoyed and frightened to see an article of criticism of existing abuses signed by a Jewish name. And I hate to see Jewish names on important committees, and hate to read of Jews fighting for the poor, the oppressed, the cheated and hungry. Somehow, even in a country where my family has lived for a hundred years, the enemy has won this subtle victory over me—he has made me disfranchise myself from honest causes by calling them foreign, Communist, us-ing Jewish names connected with them as ammunition against them.

"Most hateful of all, I found myself looking for Jewish names in the casualty lists and secretly being glad when I saw them there, to prove that there, at least, among the dead and wounded, we belonged. Three times, thanks to you and your brothers, I found our name there, and, may God forgive me, at the expense of your blood and your brother's life, through my tears, I felt that same twitch of satisfaction.

"When I read the newspapers and see another story that Jews are still being killed in Poland, or Jews are requesting that they be given back their homes in France or that they be allowed to enter some country where they will not be murdered, I am annoyed with them. I feel that they are boring the rest of the world with their problems, that they are making demands upon the rest of the world by being killed, that they are disturbing everyone by being hungry and asking for the return of their property. If we could all fall in through the crust of the earth and vanish in one hour, with our heroes and poets and prophets and martyrs, perhaps we would be doing the memory of the Jewish race a service.

"This is how I feel today, son. I need some help. You've been to the war, you've fought and killed men, you've seen the people of other countries. Maybe you understand things that I don't understand. Maybe you see some hope somewhere. Help me. Your loving Father."

Seeger folded the letter slowly, not seeing what he was doing, because the tears were burning his eyes. He walked slowly and aimlessly across the dead, sodden grass of the empty field, away from the camp. He tried to wipe away his tears, because, with his eyes full and dark, he kept seeing his father and brother crouched in the old-fashioned living room in Ohio, and hearing his brother, dressed in the old, discarded uniform, saying, "These're the new rocket bombs. For the Jews."

He sighed, looking out over the bleak, wasted land. Now, he thought, now I have to think about it. He felt a slight, unreasonable twinge of anger at his father for presenting him with the necessity of thinking about it. The Army was good about serious problems. While you were fighting, you were too busy and frightened and weary to think about anything, and at other times you were relaxing, putting your brain on a shelf, postponing everything to that impossible time of clarity and beauty after the war. Well, now, here was the impossible, clear, beautiful time, and here was his father, demanding that he think. There are all sorts of Jews, he thought: there are the sort whose every waking moment is ridden by the knowledge of Jewishness; who see signs against the Jew in every smile on a streetcar, every whisper; who see pogroms in every newspaper article, threats in every change of the weather, scorn in every handshake, death behind each closed door. He had not been like that. He was young, he was big and healthy and easygoing, and people of all kinds had liked him all his life, in the Army and out. In America, especially, what was going on in Europe had been remote, unreal, unrelated to him. The chanting, bearded old men burning in the Nazi furnaces, and the dark-eyed women screaming prayers in Polish and Russian and German as they were pushed naked into the gas chambers, had seemed as shadowy and almost as unrelated to him, as he trotted out onto the stadium field for a football game, as they must have been to the men named O'Dwyer and Wickersham and Poole who played in the line beside him.

These tortured people had seemed more related to him in Europe. Again and again, in the towns that had been taken back from the Germans, gaunt, gray-faced men had stopped him humbly, looking searchingly at him, and had asked, peering at his long, lined, grimy face under the anonymous helmet, "Are you a Jew?" Sometimes they asked it in English, sometimes French, sometimes Yiddish. He didn't know French or Yiddish, but he learned to recognize that question. He had never understood exactly why they asked the question, since they never demanded anything of him, rarely even could speak to him. Then, one day in Strasbourg, a little, bent old man and a small, shapeless woman had stopped him and asked, in English, if he was Jewish. "Yes," he'd said, smiling at them. The two old people had smiled widely, like children. "Look," the old man had said to his wife. "A young American soldier. A Jew. And so large and strong." He

had touched Seeger's arm reverently with the tips of his fingers, then had touched the Garand Seeger was carrying. "And such a beautiful rifle."

And there, for a moment, although he was not particularly sensitive, Seeger had got an inkling of why he had been stopped and questioned by so many before. Here, to these bent, exhausted old people, ravaged of their families, familiar with flight and death for so many years, was a symbol of continuing life. A large young man in the uniform of the liberator, blood, as they thought, of their blood, but not in hiding, not quivering in fear and helplessness, but striding secure and victorious down the street, armed and capable of inflicting terrible destruction on his enemies.

Seeger had kissed the old lady on the cheek and she had wept, and the old man had scolded her for it while shaking Seeger's hand fervently and thankfully before saying goodbye.

Thinking back on it, he knew that it was silly to pretend that, even before his father's letter, he had been like any other American soldier going through the war. When he had stood over the huge, dead S.S. major with the face blown in by his bullets in the warehouse in Coblenz, and taken the pistol from the dead hand, he had tasted a strange little extra flavor of triumph. How many Jews, he'd thought, has this man killed? How fitting it is that I've killed him. Neither Olson nor Welch, who were like his brothers, would have felt that in picking up the Luger, its barrel still hot from the last shots its owner had fired before dying. And he had resolved that he was going to make sure to take this gun back with him to America, and plug it and keep it on his desk at home, as a kind of vague, half-understood sign to himself that justice had once been done and he had been its instrument.

Maybe, he thought, maybe I'd better take it back with me, but not as a memento. Not plugged, but loaded. America by now was a strange country for him. He had been away a long time and he wasn't sure what was waiting for him when he got home. If the mobs were coming down the street toward his house, he was not going to die singing and praying.

When he had been taking basic training, he'd heard a scrawny, clerkish soldier from Boston talking at the other end of the PX bar, over the watered beer. "The boys at the office," the scratchy voice was saying, "gave me a party before I left. And they told me one thing. 'Charlie,' they said, 'hold onto your bayonet. We're going to be able to use it when you get back. On the Yids.'"

He hadn't said anything then, because he'd felt it was neither possible nor desirable to fight against every random overheard voice raised against the Jews from one end of the world to the other. But again and again, at odd moments, lying on a barracks cot, or stretched out trying to sleep on the floor of a ruined French farmhouse, he had heard that voice, harsh, satisfied, heavy with hate and ignorance, saying above the beery grumble of apprentice soldiers at the bar, "Hold onto your bayonet."

And the other stories. Jews collected stories of hatred and injustice and inklings of doom like a special, lunatic kind of miser. The story of the Navy officer, commander of a small vessel off the Aleutians, who in the officers' wardroom had complained that he hated the Jews because it was the Jews who had demanded that the Germans be beaten first, and the forces in the Pacific had been starved in consequence. And when one of his junior officers, who had just come aboard, had objected and told the commander that he was a Jew, the commander had risen from the table and said, "Mister, the Constitution of the United States says I have to serve in the same Navy with Jews, but it doesn't say I have to eat at the same table with them." In the fogs and the cold, swelling Arctic seas off the Aleutians, in a small boat, subject to sudden, mortal attack at any moment. . . . And the million other stories. Jews, even the most normal and best adjusted, became living treasuries of them, scraps of malice and bloodthirstiness, clever and confusing and cunningly twisted so that every act by every Jew became suspect and blameworthy and hateful. Seeger had heard the stories and had made an almost conscious effort to forget them. Now, holding his father's letter in his hand, he remembered them all.

He stared unseeingly out in front of him. Maybe, he thought, maybe it would've been better to have been killed in the war, like Leonard. Simpler. Leonard would never have to face a crowd coming for his mother and father.

Leonard would not have to listen and collect these hideous, fascinating little stories that made of every Jew a stranger in any town, on any field, on the face of the earth. He had come so close to being killed so many times; it would have been so easy, so neat and final. Seeger shook his head. It was ridiculous to feel like that, and he was ashamed of himself for the weak moment. At the age of twenty-one, death was not an answer.

"Seeger!" It was Olson's voice. He and Welch had sloshed silently up behind Seeger, standing in the open field. "Seeger, *mon vieux*, what're you doing—grazing?"

Seeger turned slowly to them. "I wanted to read my letter," he said.

Olson looked closely at him. They had been together so long, through so many things, that flickers and hints of expression on each other's faces were recognized and acted upon. "Anything wrong?" Olson asked.

"No," said Seeger. "Nothing much."

"Norman," Welch said, his voice young and solemn. "Norman, we've been talking, Olson and me. We decided—you're pretty attached to that Luger, and maybe, if you—well—"

"What he's trying to say," said Olson, "is we withdraw the request. If you want to sell it, O.K. If you don't, don't do it for our sake. Honest."

Seeger looked at them standing there, disreputable and tough and familiar. "I haven't made up my mind yet," he said.

"Anything you decide," Welch said oratorically, "is perfectly all right with us. Perfectly."

The three of them walked aimlessly and silently across the field, away from camp. As they walked, their shoes making a wet, sliding sound in the damp, dead grass, Seeger thought of the time Olson had covered him in the little town outside Cherbourg, when Seeger had been caught, going down the side of a street, by four Germans with a machine gun in the second story of a house on the corner and Olson had had to stand out in the middle of the street with no cover at all for more than a minute, firing continuously, so that Seeger could get away alive. And he thought of the time outside St.-Lô when he had been wounded and had lain in a minefield for three hours and Welch and Captain Taney had come looking for him in the darkness and had found him and picked him up and run for it, all of them expecting to get blown up any second. And he thought of all the drinks they'd had together, and the long marches and the cold winter together, and all the girls they'd gone out with together, and he thought of his father and brother crouching behind the window in Ohio waiting for the rockets and the crowds armed with Browning automatic rifles.

"Say." He stopped and stood facing them. "Say, what do you guys think of the Jews?"

Welch and Olson looked at each other, and Olson glanced down at the letter in Seeger's hand.

"Jews?" Olson said finally. "What're they? Welch, you ever hear of the Jews?"

Welch looked thoughtfully at the gray sky. "No," he said. "But remember, I'm an uneducated fellow."

"Sorry, bud," Olson said, turning to Seeger.

"We can't help you. Ask us another question. Maybe we'll do better."

Seeger peered at the faces of his friends. He would have to rely upon them, later on, out of uniform, on their native streets, more than he had ever relied on them on the bullet-swept street and in the dark minefield in France. Welsh and Olson stared back at him, troubled, their faces candid and tough and dependable.

"What time," Seeger asked, "did you tell that captain you'd meet him?"

"Eight o'clock," Welch said. "But we don't have to go. If you have any feeling about that gun—"

"We'll meet him," Seeger said. "We can use that sixty-five bucks."

"Listen," Olson said, "I know how much you like that gun, and I'll feel like a heel if you sell it."

"Forget it," Seeger said, starting to walk again. "What could I use it for in America?"

STEPHEN VINCENT BENÉT

The brother of the poet William Rose Benét and brother-in-law of Elinor Wylie (p. 170), Stephen Vincent Benét came from a family whose absorbing passion was the writing and appreciation of literature. He was born at Bethlehem, Pennsylvania, on July 22, 1898. His paternal line had been traditionally military men, and his boyhood was spent at various army posts. Benét graduated from Yale University in 1919, took a master's degree in 1920, and studied for a time at the Sorbonne in Paris. From college days on, he had written verse, prose, and dramatic compositions; but not until 1926 did he find the opportunity to develop what had been in his mind for a long time: the creation of an American national epic poem. In that year he received a Guggenheim Fellowship to bring his dream to reality; the fruit of his fellowship was *John Brown's Body* (1928), a stirring narrative poem of the American Civil War, enormously successful and fully deserving of the Pulitzer Prize for Poetry which it won in 1929.

Although he continued to write verse, Benét's reputation as a poet never rose above the prestige he attained with *John Brown's Body;* indeed, it was as a writer of short stories that he grew in stature during the 1930's, and it seems likely now that he will be best remembered not as a sheer poet but as a writer of poetic narrative, whether in verse or prose. In other words, his poetic feeling, to say nothing of his poetic achievement, was incapable of extensive flights; but there are always warmth, color, and emotional drive in Benét's writings which render the epithet "poetic" most appropriate to his work as a whole. Notable in general are his simplicity and straightforwardness of presentation, his excellent sense of history and fact, his patriotism, and his emotional suggestiveness and suggestibility. *John Brown's Body* illustrates all these qualities; yet it is a significant commentary on Benét's poetic abilities that in retrospect, after twenty years, the most gripping passage in the work is the prose death-speech of John Brown himself, which the poet transcribed verbatim from the contemporary account of Brown's execution. On the other hand, earthy and folkloristic but profoundly moving to the romantic and patriotic reader is *The Devil and Daniel Webster* (1937), probably the best known of the author's short stories.

With the advent of radio drama and the darkening shadows of the imminent Second World War, Benét threw himself into the cause of American liberties; he became an ardent, even super-heated propagandist, and a warning prophet (too often, unfortunately, a Cassandra) of the dangers which were bearing down not only upon America but upon the whole civilized world. He became alarmed not only at the international situation but also at the threatening encroachment of soulless science and man's inability to control it properly. At the same time he developed a strong tendency toward the fantastically imaginative. In one poem he visualized a New York consumed by mysterious termites; in another there was a disastrous revolt of machines against their masters. He capped all this, however, with the extremely impressive "By the Waters of Babylon" (1937), which takes the reader to a day in the future when the atomic bomb, or its equivalent, has done its worst with our present-day civilization. As a tribute to the inevitable rôle of the poet as prophet, it should be recorded that this story was published eight years before the first atomic bomb burst over Hiroshima.

No doubt the strain of the years before the calamity proved too much for Benét's constitution; never strong, he died suddenly on March 13, 1943, long before his full capacities had been realized. But the author of *John Brown's Body* (1928), *Thirteen O'Clock* (1937), *Tales Before Midnight* (1938), and *Zero Hour* (1940) does not deserve to be soon forgotten.

By the Waters of Babylon

THE NORTH and the west and the south are good hunting ground, but it is forbidden to go east. It is forbidden to go to any of the Dead Places except to search for metal and then he who touches the metal must be a priest

or the son of a priest. Afterwards, both the man and the metal must be purified. These are the rules and the laws; they are well made. It is forbidden to cross the great river and look upon the place that was the Place of the Gods 10 —this is most strictly forbidden. We do not even say its name though we know its name. It is there that spirits live, and demons—it is there that there are the ashes of the Great Burning. These things are forbidden—they have been forbidden since the beginning of time.

My father is a priest; I am the son of a priest. I have been in the Dead Places near us, with my father—at first, I was afraid. When my father went into the house to search for the 20 metal, I stood by the door and my heart felt small and weak. It was a dead man's house, a spirit house. It did not have the smell of man, though there were old bones in a corner. But it is not fitting that a priest's son should show fear. I looked at the bones in the shadow and kept my voice still.

Then my father came out with the metal— a good, strong piece. He looked at me with both eyes but I had not run away. He gave me 30 the metal to hold—I took it and did not die. So he knew that I was truly his son and would be a priest in my time. That was when I was very young—nevertheless, my brothers would not have done it, though they are good hunters. After that, they gave me the good piece of meat and the warm corner by the fire. My father watched over me—he was glad that I should be a priest. But when I boasted or wept without a reason, he punished me more strictly 40 than my brothers. That was right.

After a time, I myself was allowed to go into the dead houses and search for metal. So I learned the ways of those houses—and if I saw bones, I was no longer afraid. The bones are light and old—sometimes they will fall into dust if you touch them. But that is a great sin.

I was taught the chants and the spells—I was taught how to stop the running of blood from a wound and many secrets. A priest must know 50 many secrets—that was what my father said. If the hunters think we do all things by chants and spells, they may believe so—it does not hurt them. I was taught how to read in the old books and how to make the old writings—that was hard and took a long time. My knowledge made me happy—it was like a fire in my heart.

Most of all, I liked to hear of the Old Days and the stories of the gods. I asked myself many questions that I could not answer, but it was good to ask them. At night, I would lie awake and listen to the wind—it seemed to me that it was the voice of the gods as they flew through the air.

We are not ignorant like the Forest People —our women spin wool on the wheel, our priests wear a white robe. We do not eat grubs from the tree, we have not forgotten the old writings, although they are hard to understand. Nevertheless, my knowledge and my lack of knowledge burned in me—I wished to know more. When I was a man at last, I came to my father and said, "It is time for me to go on my journey. Give me your leave."

He looked at me for a long time, stroking his beard, then he said at last, "Yes. It is time." That night, in the house of the priesthood, I asked for and received purification. My body hurt but my spirit was a cool stone. It was my father himself who questioned me about my dreams.

He bade me look into the smoke of the fire and see—I saw and told what I saw. It was what I have always seen—a river, and, beyond it, a great Dead Place and in it the gods walking. I have always thought about that. His eyes were stern when I told him—he was no longer my father but a priest. He said, "This is a strong dream."

"It is mine," I said, while the smoke waved and my head felt light. They were singing the Star song in the outer chamber and it was like the buzzing of bees in my head.

He asked me how the gods were dressed and I told him how they were dressed. We know how they were dressed from the book, but I saw them as if they were before me. When I had finished, he threw the sticks three times and studied them as they fell.

"This is a very strong dream," he said. "It may eat you up."

"I am not afraid," I said and looked at him with both eyes. My voice sounded thin in my ears but that was because of the smoke.

He touched me on the breast and the forehead. He gave me the bow and the three arrows.

"Take them," he said. "It is forbidden to travel east. It is forbidden to cross the river. It is forbidden to go to the Place of the Gods. All these things are forbidden."

"All these things are forbidden," I said, but it was my voice that spoke and not my spirit. He looked at me again.

"My son," he said. "Once I had young dreams. If your dreams do not eat you up, you may be a great priest. If they eat you, you are still my son. Now go on your journey."

I went fasting, as is the law. My body hurt but not my heart. When the dawn came, I was out of sight of the village. I prayed and purified myself, waiting for a sign. The sign was an eagle. It flew east.

Sometimes signs are sent by bad spirits. I waited again on the flat rock, fasting, taking no food. I was very still—I could feel the sky above me and the earth beneath. I waited till the sun was beginning to sink. Then three deer passed in the valley, going east—they did not wind me or see me. There was a white fawn with them —a very great sign.

I followed them, at a distance, waiting for what would happen. My heart was troubled about going east, yet I knew that I must go. My head hummed with my fasting—I did not even see the panther spring upon the white fawn. But, before I knew it, the bow was in my hand. I shouted and the panther lifted his head from the fawn. It is not easy to kill a panther with one arrow but the arrow went through his eye and into his brain. He died as he tried to spring—he rolled over, tearing at the ground. Then I knew I was meant to go east—I knew that was my journey. When the night came, I made my fire and roasted meat.

It is eight suns journey to the east and a man passes by many Dead Places. The Forest People are afraid of them but I am not. Once I made my fire on the edge of a Dead Place at night and, next morning, in the dead house, I found a good knife, little rusted. That was small to what came afterward but it made my heart feel big. Always when I looked for game, it was in front of my arrow, and twice I passed hunting parties of the Forest People without their knowing. So I knew my magic was strong and my journey clean, in spite of the law.

Toward the setting of the eighth sun, I came to the banks of the great river. It was half-a-day's journey after I had left the god-road—we do not use the god-roads now for they are falling apart into great blocks of stone, and the forest is safer going. A long way off, I had seen the water through trees but the trees were thick. At last, I came out upon an open place at the top of a cliff. There was the great river below, like a giant in the sun. It was very long, very wide. It could eat all the streams we know and still be thirsty. Its name is Ou-dis-sun, the Sacred, the Long. No man of my tribe had seen it, not even my father, the priest. It was magic and I prayed.

Then I raised my eyes and looked south. It was there, the Place of the Gods.

How can I tell what it was like—you do not know. It was there, in the red light, and they were too big to be houses. It was there with the red light upon it, mighty and ruined. I knew that in another moment the gods would see me. I covered my eyes with my hands and crept back into the forest.

Surely, that was enough to do, and live. Surely it was enough to spend the night upon the cliff. The Forest People themselves do not come near. Yet, all through the night, I knew that I should have to cross the river and walk in the places of the gods, although the gods ate me up. My magic did not help me at all and yet there was a fire in my bowels, a fire in my mind. When the sun rose, I thought, "My journey has been clean. Now I will go home from my journey." But, even as I thought so, I knew I could not. If I went to the place of the gods, I would surely die, but, if I did not go, I could never be at peace with my spirit again. It is better to lose one's life than one's spirit, if one is a priest and the son of a priest.

Nevertheless, as I made the raft, the tears ran out of my eyes. The Forest People could have killed me without fight, if they had come upon me then, but they did not come. When the raft was made, I said the sayings for the dead and painted myself for death. My heart was cold as a frog and my knees like water, but the burning in my mind would not let me have peace. As I pushed the raft from the shore, I began my death song—I had the right. It was a fine song.

"I am John, son of John," I sang. "My people are the Hill People. They are the men.

I go into the Dead Places but I am not slain.

I take the metal from the Dead Places but I am not blasted.

I travel upon the god-roads and am not afraid. E-yah! I have killed the panther, I have killed the fawn!

E-yah! I have come to the great river. No man has come there before.

It is forbidden to go east, but I have gone, forbidden to go on the great river, but I am there.

Open your hearts, you spirits, and hear my song.

Now I go to the place of the gods, I shall not return.

My body is painted for death and my limbs weak, but my heart is big as I go to the place of the gods!"

All the same, when I came to the Place of the Gods, I was afraid, afraid. The current of the great river is very strong—it gripped my raft with its hands. That was magic, for the river itself is wide and calm. I could feel evil spirits about me, in the bright morning: I could feel their breath on my neck as I was swept down the stream. Never have I been so much alone—I tried to think of my knowledge, but it was a squirrel's heap of winter nuts. There was no strength in my knowledge any more and I felt small and naked as a new-hatched bird—alone upon the great river, the servant of the gods.

Yet, after a while, my eyes were opened and I saw. I saw both banks of the river—I saw that once there had been god-roads across it, though now they were broken and fallen like broken vines. Very great they were, and wonderful and broken—broken in the time of the Great Burning when the fire fell out of the sky. And always the current took me nearer to the Place of the Gods, and the huge ruins rose before my eyes.

I do not know the customs of rivers—we are the People of the Hills. I tried to guide my raft with the pole but it spun around. I thought the river meant to take me past the Place of the Gods and out into the Bitter Water of the legends. I grew angry then—my heart felt strong. I said aloud, "I am a priest and the son of a priest!" The gods heard me—they showed me how to paddle with the pole on one side of the raft. The current changed itself—I drew near to the Place of the Gods.

When I was very near, my raft struck and turned over. I can swim in our lakes—I swam to the shore. There was a great spike of rusted metal sticking out into the river—I hauled myself up upon it and sat there, panting. I had saved my bow and two arrows and the knife I found in the Dead Place but that was all. My raft went whirling downstream toward the Bitter Water. I looked after it, and thought if it had trod me under, at least I would be safely dead. Nevertheless, when I had dried my bowstring and re-strung it, I walked forward to the Place of the Gods.

It felt like ground underfoot; it did not burn me. It is not true what some of the tales say, that the ground there burns forever, for I have been there. Here and there were the marks and stains of the Great Burning, on the ruins, that is true. But they were old marks and old stains. It is not true either, what some of our priests say, that it is an island covered with fogs and enchantments. It is not. It is a great Dead Place—greater than any Dead Place we know. Everywhere in it there are god-roads, though most are cracked and broken. Everywhere there are the ruins of the high towers of the gods.

How shall I tell what I saw? I went carefully, my strung bow in my hand, my skin ready for danger. There should have been the wailings of spirits and the shrieks of demons, but there were not. It was very silent and sunny where I had landed—the wind and the rain and the birds that drop seeds had done their work—the grass grew in the cracks of the broken stone. It is a fair island—no wonder the gods built there. If I had come there, a god, I also would have built.

How shall I tell what I saw? The towers are not all broken—here and there one still stands, like a great tree in a forest, and the birds nest high. But the towers themselves look blind, for the gods are gone. I saw a fish-hawk, catching fish in the river. I saw a little dance of white butterflies over a great heap of broken stones and columns. I went there and looked about me—there was a carved stone with cut-letters, broken in half. I can read letters but I could not understand these. They said UBTREAS. There was also the shattered image of a man or a god. It had been made of white stone and he wore his hair tied back like a woman's. His name was ASHING, as I read on the cracked half of a stone. I thought it wise to pray to ASHING, though I do not know that god.

How shall I tell what I saw? There was no smell of man left, on stone or metal. Nor were there many trees in that wilderness of stone. There are many pigeons, nesting and dropping in the towers—the gods must have loved them, or, perhaps, they used them for sacrifices. There are wild cats that roam the god-roads, green-eyed, unafraid of man. At night they wail like demons but they are not demons. The wild dogs are more dangerous, for they hunt in a pack, but them I did not meet till later. Everywhere there are the carved stones, carved with magical numbers or words.

I went North—I did not try to hide myself. When a god or a demon saw me, then I would die, but meanwhile I was no longer afraid. My hunger for knowledge burned in me—there was so much that I could not understand. After awhile, I knew that my belly was hungry. I could have hunted for my meat, but I did not hunt. It is known that the gods did not hunt as we do—they got their food from enchanted boxes and jars. Sometimes these are still found in the Dead Places—once, when I was a child and foolish, I opened such a jar and tasted it and found the food sweet. But my father found out and punished me for it strictly, for, often, that food is death. Now, though, I had long gone past what was forbidden, and I entered the likeliest towers, looking for the food of the gods.

I found it at last in the ruins of a great temple in the mid-city. A mighty temple it must have been, for the roof was painted like the sky at night with its stars—that much I could see, though the colors were faint and dim. It went down into great caves and tunnels—perhaps they kept their slaves there. But when I started to climb down, I heard the squeaking of rats, so I did not go—rats are unclean, and there must have been many tribes of them, from the squeaking. But near there, I found food, in the heart of a ruin, behind a door that still opened. I ate only the fruits from the jars—they had a very sweet taste. There was drink, too, in bottles of glass—the drink of the gods was strong and made my head swim. After I had eaten and drunk, I slept on the top of a stone, my bow at my side.

When I woke, the sun was low. Looking down from where I lay, I saw a dog sitting on his haunches. His tongue was hanging out of his mouth: he looked as if he were laughing. He was a big dog, with a grey-brown coat, as big as a wolf. I sprang up and shouted at him but he did not move—he just sat there as if he were laughing. I did not like that. When I reached for a stone to throw, he moved swiftly out of the way of the stone. He was not afraid of me; he looked at me as if I were meat. No doubt I could have killed him with an arrow, but I did not know if there were others. Moreover, night was falling.

I looked about me—not far away there was a great, broken god-road, leading North. The towers were high enough, but not so high, and while many of the dead-houses were wrecked, there were some that stood. I went toward this god-road, keeping to the heights of the ruins, while the dog followed. When I had reached the god-road, I saw that there were others behind him. If I had slept later, they would have come upon me asleep and torn out my throat. As it was, they were sure enough of me; they did not hurry. When I went into the dead-house, they kept watch at the entrance—doubtless they thought they would have a fine hunt. But a dog cannot open a door and I knew, from the books, that the gods did not like to live on the ground but on high.

I had just found a door I could open when the dogs decided to rush. Ha! They were surprised when I shut the door in their faces—it was a good door, of strong metal. I could hear their foolish baying beyond it but I did not stop to answer them. I was in darkness—I found stairs and climbed. There were many stairs, turning around till my head was dizzy. At the top was another door—I found the knob and opened it. I was in a long small chamber—on one side of it was a bronze door that could not be opened, for it had no handle. Perhaps there was a magic word to open it but I did not have the word. I turned to the door in the opposite side of the wall. The lock of it was broken and I opened it and went in.

Within, there was a place of great riches. The god who lived there must have been a powerful god. The first room was a small ante-room—I waited there for some time, telling the spirits of the place that I came in peace and not as a robber. When it seemed to me that they had had time to hear me, I went on. Ah, what riches! Few, even, of the windows had been broken—it was all as it had been. The great windows that looked over the city had not been broken at all though they were dusty and streaked with many years. There were coverings on the floors, the colors not greatly faded, and the chairs were soft and deep. There were pictures upon the walls, very strange, very wonderful—I remember one of a bunch of flowers in a jar—if you came close to it, you could see nothing but bits of color, but if you stood away from it, the flowers might have been picked yesterday. It made my heart feel strange to look at this picture—and to look at the figure of a bird, in some hard clay, on a table and see it so like our birds. Everywhere there were books and writings, many in tongues that I could not read. The god who lived there must have been a wise god and full of knowledge. I felt I had a right there, as I sought knowledge also.

Nevertheless, it was strange. There was a washing-place but no water—perhaps the gods washed in air. There was a cooking-place but no wood, and though there was a machine to cook food, there was no place to put fire in it. Nor were there candles or lamps—there were things that looked like lamps but they had neither oil nor wick. All these things were magic, but I touched them and lived—the magic had gone out of them. Let me tell one thing to show. In the washing-place, a thing said "Hot" but it was not hot to the touch—another thing said "Cold" but it was not cold. This must have been a strong magic but the magic was gone. I do not understand—they had ways—I wish that I knew.

It was close and dry and dusty in their house of the gods. I have said the magic was gone but that is not true—it had gone from the magic things but it had not gone from the place. I felt the spirits about me, weighing upon me. Nor had I ever slept in a Dead Place before—and yet, tonight, I must sleep there. When I thought of it, my tongue felt dry in my throat, in spite of my wish for knowledge. Almost I would have gone down again and faced the dogs, but I did not.

I had not gone through all the rooms when the darkness fell. When it fell, I went back to the big room looking over the city and made fire. There was a place to make fire and a box with wood in it, though I do not think they cooked there. I wrapped myself in a floor-covering and slept in front of the fire—I was very tired.

Now I tell what is very strong magic. I woke in the midst of the night. When I woke, the fire had gone out and I was cold. It seemed to me that all around me there were whisperings and voices. I closed my eyes to shut them out. Some will say that I slept again, but I do not think that I slept. I could feel the spirits drawing my spirit out of my body as a fish is drawn on a line.

Why should I lie about it? I am a priest and the son of a priest. If there are spirits, as they say, in the small Dead Places near us, what spirits must there not be in that great Place of the Gods? And would not they wish to speak? After such long years? I know that I felt myself drawn as a fish is drawn on a line. I had stepped out of my body—I could see my body asleep in front of the cold fire, but it was not I. I was drawn to look out upon the city of the gods.

It should have been dark, for it was night, but it was not dark. Everywhere there were lights—lines of light—circles and blurs of light —ten thousand torches would not have been the same. The sky itself was alight—you could barely see the stars for the glow in the sky. I thought to myself "This is strong magic" and trembled. There was a roaring in my ears like the rushing of rivers. Then my eyes grew used to the light and my ears to the sound. I knew that I was seeing the city as it had been when the gods were alive.

That was a sight indeed—yes, that was a sight: I could not have seen it in the body— my body would have died. Everywhere went the gods, on foot and in chariots—there were gods beyond number and counting and their chariots blocked the streets. They had turned night to day for their pleasure—they did not sleep with the sun. The noise of their coming and going was the noise of many waters. It was magic what they could do—it was magic what they did.

I looked out of another window—the great vines of their bridges were mended and the god-roads went East and West. Restless, restless, were the gods and always in motion! They burrowed tunnels under rivers—they flew in the air. With unbelievable tools they did giant works—no part of the earth was safe from them, for, if they wished for a thing, they summoned it from the other side of the world. And always, as they labored and rested, as they feasted and made love, there was a drum in their ears—the pulse of the giant city, beating and beating like a man's heart.

Were they happy? What is happiness to the gods? They were great, they were mighty, they were wonderful and terrible. As I looked upon them and their magic, I felt like a child—but a little more, it seemed to me, and they would pull down the moon from the sky. I saw them with wisdom beyond wisdom and knowledge beyond knowledge. And yet not all they did was well done—even I could see that—and yet their wisdom could not but grow until all was peace.

Then I saw their fate come upon them and that was terrible past speech. It came upon them as they walked the streets of their city. I have been in the fights with the Forest People —I have seen men die. But this was not like that. When gods war with gods, they use weapons we do not know. It was fire falling out of the sky and a mist that poisoned. It was the time of the Great Burning and the Destruction. They ran about like ants in the streets of their city—poor gods, poor gods! Then the towers began to fall. A few escaped—yes, a few. The legends tell it. But, even after the city had become a Dead Place, for many years the poison was still in the ground. I saw it happen, I saw the last of them die. It was darkness over the broken city and I wept.

All this, I saw. I saw it as I have told it, though not in the body. When I woke in the morning, I was hungry, but I did not think first of my hunger for my heart was perplexed and confused. I knew the reason for the Dead Places but I did not see why it had happened. It seemed to me it should not have happened, with all the magic they had. I went through the house looking for an answer. There was so much in the house I could not understand—

and yet I am a priest and the son of a priest. It was like being on one side of the great river, at night, with no light to show the way.

Then I saw the dead god. He was sitting in his chair, by the window, in a room I had not entered before, and, for the first moment, I thought that he was alive. Then I saw the skin on the back of his hand—it was like dry leather. The room was shut, hot and dry—no doubt 10 that had kept him as he was. At first I was afraid to approach him—then the fear left me. He was sitting looking out over the city—he was dressed in the clothes of the gods. His age was neither young nor old—I could not tell his age. But there was wisdom in his face and great sadness. You could see that he would have not run away. He had sat at his window, watching his city die—then he himself had died. But it is better to lose one's life than 20 one's spirit—and you could see from the face that his spirit had not been lost. I knew, that, if I touched him, he would fall into dust—and yet, there was something unconquered in his face.

That is all of my story, for then I knew he was a man—I knew then that they had been men, neither gods nor demons. It is a great knowledge, hard to tell and believe. They were men—they went a dark road, but they were 30 men. I had no fear after that—I had no fear going home, though twice I fought off the dogs and once I was hunted for two days by the Forest People. When I saw my father again, I prayed and was purified. He touched my lips and my breast, he said, "You went away a boy.

You come back a man and a priest." I said, "Father, they were men! I have been in the Place of the Gods and seen it! Now slay me, if it is the law—but still I know they were men."

He looked at me out of both eyes. He said, 40 "The law is not always the same shape—you have done what you have done. I could not have done it my time, but you come after me. Tell!"

I told and he listened. After that, I wished to tell all the people but he showed me otherwise. He said, "Truth is a hard deer to hunt. If you eat too much truth at once, you may die of the truth. It was not idly that our fathers forbade the Dead Places." He was right 50 —it is better the truth should come little by little. I have learned that, being a priest. Perhaps, in the old days, they ate knowledge too fast.

Nevertheless, we make a beginning. It is not for the metal alone we go to the Dead Places now—there are the books and the writings. They are hard to learn. And the magic tools are broken—but we can look at them and wonder. At least, we make a beginning. And, 60 when I am chief priest we shall go beyond the great river. We shall go to the Place of the Gods—the place new-york—not one man but a company. We shall look for the images of the gods and find the god ASHING and the others —the gods LICOLN and BILTMORE and MOSES. But they were men who built the city, not gods or demons. They were men. I remember the dead man's face. They were men who were here before us. We must build again.

GENERAL INDEX
AND
INDEX OF FIRST LINES

GENERAL INDEX

Names of authors represented by selections appear in boldface; the number in boldface after the name of the author refers to the page on which his biographical sketch appears.

Selections that are reprinted in this book are listed in boldface italics; the number in boldface after the title refers to the page on which the piece begins, the other numbers to pages on which there is a reference to the selection.

INDEX OF FIRST LINES

6 7 8 9 10 11 12 13 14 15 16 17 18 19 20 21 22 23 24 25   65 64 63 62 61

(5007)